CompTIA A+ Guide to IT Technical Support

NINTH EDITION

Jean Andrews, Joy Dark, Jill West

CENGAGE Learning

Australia • Canada • Mexico • Singapore • Spain • United Kingdom • United States

CENGAGE Learning

CompTIA A+ Guide to IT Technical Support, Ninth Edition, Jean Andrews, Jill West, Joy Dark

SVP, GM Skills & Global Product Management: Dawn Gerrain

Product Director: Kathleen McMahon

Product Team Manager: Kristin McNary

Senior Director, Development: Marah Bellegarde

Product Development Manager: Leigh Hefferon

Senior Content Developer: Michelle Ruelos Cannistraci

Product Assistant: Abigail Pufpaff

Vice President, Marketing Services: Jennifer Ann Baker

Marketing Director: Michele McTighe

Senior Production Director: Wendy Troeger

Production Director: Patty Stephan

Senior Content Project Manager: Brooke Greenhouse

Managing Art Director: Jack Pendleton

Cover image(s):

©iStockphoto/saicle

©iStockphoto/traffic_analyzer

©iStockphoto/simon2579

©iStockphoto/Kotkoa

For product information and technology assistance, contact us at
Cengage Learning Customer & Sales Support, 1-800-354-9706

For permission to use material from this text or product, submit all requests online at **www.cengage.com/permissions**
Further permissions questions can be e-mailed to
permissionrequest@cengage.com

Library of Congress Control Number: 2015957525

ISBN: 978-1-305-26643-8

Cengage Learning
20 Channel Center Street
Boston, MA 02210
USA

Cengage Learning is a leading provider of customized learning solutions with employees residing in nearly 40 different countries and sales in more than 125 countries around the world. Find your local representative at **www.cengage.com.**

Cengage Learning products are represented in Canada by Nelson Education, Ltd.

To learn more about Cengage Learning, visit **www.cengage.com**
Purchase any of our products at your local college store or at our preferred online store **www.cengagebrain.com**

Notice to the Reader

Publisher does not warrant or guarantee any of the products described herein or perform any independent analysis in connection with any of the product information contained herein. Publisher does not assume, and expressly disclaims, any obligation to obtain and include information other than that provided to it by the manufacturer. The reader is expressly warned to consider and adopt all safety precautions that might be indicated by the activities described herein and to avoid all potential hazards. By following the instructions contained herein, the reader willingly assumes all risks in connection with such instructions. The publisher makes no representations or warranties of any kind, including but not limited to, the warranties of fitness for particular purpose or merchantability, nor are any such representations implied with respect to the material set forth herein, and the publisher takes no responsibility with respect to such material. The publisher shall not be liable for any special, consequential, or exemplary damages resulting, in whole or part, from the readers' use of, or reliance upon, this material.

Printed in the United States of America
Print Number: 01 Print Year: 2015

Table of Contents

CompTIA A+ 220-901 and 220-902 Exams Mapped to Chapters . . . xi

CHAPTER 1

First Look at Computer Parts and Tools . . 1

What's Inside a Desktop Case . . . 2
- Form Factors Used By Desktop Cases, Power Supplies, and Motherboards . . . 8
- Drives, Their Cables, and Connectors . . . 15

First Look at Laptop Components . . . 17
- Special Keys, Buttons, and Input Devices On a Laptop . . . 21
- ExpressCard Slots . . . 22
- Docking Stations . . . 24
- Laptop Internal Components . . . 25
- What's Inside an All-in-One Computer . . . 26
- Maintaining Laptops and Mobile Devices . . . 27

First Look at Mobile Device Hardware . . . 29
- Connection Types . . . 30
- Storage Devices . . . 33
- Mobile Device Accessories . . . 33
- Field-Replaceable Parts for Mobile Devices . . . 34

Tools Used by a Computer Hardware Technician . . . 34
- Post Diagnostic Cards . . . 37
- Power Supply Tester . . . 38
- Multimeter . . . 39
- Loopback Plugs . . . 40

CHAPTER 2

Working Inside Desktop Computers and Laptops . . . 45

How to Work Inside a Desktop Computer Case . . . 46
- Step 1: Plan and Organize Your Work . . . 46
- Step 2: Open the Computer Case and Examine the System . . . 46
- Step 3: Remove Expansion Cards . . . 51
- Step 4: Remove the Motherboard, Power Supply, and Drives . . . 54
- Steps to Put a Computer Back Together . . . 59

Special Considerations When Supporting Laptops . . . 66
- Warranty Concerns . . . 66
- Service Manuals and Other Sources of Information . . . 68
- Diagnostic Tools Provided by Manufacturers . . . 69

How to Work Inside a Laptop Computer . . . 71

CHAPTER 3

All About Motherboards . . . 79

Motherboard Types and Features . . . 80
- Motherboard Form Factors . . . 80
- Processor Sockets . . . 82
- The Chipset . . . 87
- Buses and Expansion Slots . . . 92
- Onboard Ports and Connectors . . . 99

Configuring a Motherboard . . . 103
- Using BIOS Setup to Configure a Motherboard . . . 103
- Using UEFI Setup to Configure a Motherboard . . . 112

Maintaining a Motherboard . . . 115
- Updating Motherboard Drivers . . . 115
- Flashing BIOS . . . 117
- Flashing UEFI . . . 118
- Using Jumpers to Clear BIOS Settings . . . 118
- Replacing the CMOS Battery . . . 120

Installing or Replacing a Motherboard . . . 121
- How to Select a Desktop Motherboard . . . 121
- How to Install or Replace a Motherboard . . . 122

Replacing a Laptop System Board . . . 125

CHAPTER 4

Supporting Processors and Upgrading Memory . . . 133

Types and Characteristics of Processors . . . 134
- How a Processor Works . . . 137
- Intel Processors . . . 138
- AMD Processors . . . 141

Selecting and Installing a Processor 142
Select a Processor to Match System Needs 142
Install a Processor 144
Replacing the Processor in a Laptop 155
Memory Technologies 158
DIMM Technologies 160
How to Upgrade Memory 167
How Much Memory Do I Need and How Much Is Currently Installed? 167
How Many and What Kind of Memory Modules Are Currently Installed? 169
How Many and What Kind of Modules Can Fit on My Motherboard? 171
How Do I Select and Purchase the Right Memory Modules? 173
How Do I Install the New Modules? 175
How to Upgrade Memory on a Laptop 177

CHAPTER 5

Supporting the Power System and Troubleshooting Computers 185

Cooling Methods and Devices 186
Processor Coolers, Fans, and Heat Sinks 186
Case Fans and Other Fans and Heat Sinks 187
Liquid Cooling Systems 188
Selecting a Power Supply 189
Types and Characteristics of Power Supplies 190
How to Calculate Wattage Capacity 191
How to Approach a Hardware Problem 193
Step 1: Interview the User 195
Step 2: Back Up Data as Needed 195
Step 3: Examine the System and Establish a Theory 197
Steps 4, 5, and 6: Fix the Problem, Verify the Fix, and Document the Outcome 201
Special Concerns When Troubleshooting Mobile Device Hardware 202
Troubleshooting the Electrical System 203
Problems That Come and Go 204
Power Problems with the Motherboard 205
Problems with Overheating 206
Problems with Laptop Power Systems 211
Troubleshooting the Motherboard, Processor, and RAM 214
Troubleshooting Mobile Devices 222

CHAPTER 6

Supporting Hard Drives and Other Storage Devices 231

Hard Drive Technologies and Interface Standards 232
Technologies Used inside a Hard Drive 232
SATA Interface Standards Used by a Hard Drive 235
How to Select and Install Hard Drives 238
Selecting a Hard Drive 238
Steps to Install a SATA Drive 239
Installing a Drive in a Removable Bay 245
Installing a Small Drive in a Wide Bay 246
Installing a Hard Drive in a Laptop 247
Setting Up Hardware RAID 249
External Enclosures 254
Identifying Tape Drives 256
Supporting Other Types of Storage Devices 258
File Systems Used by Storage Devices 258
Standards Used by Optical Drives and Discs 259
Installing an Optical Drive 262
Replacing an Optical Drive on a Laptop 263
Solid-State Storage 264
Troubleshooting Hard Drives 267
Slow Performance 267
Hard Drive Problems During the Boot 268

CHAPTER 7

Survey of Windows Features and Support Tools 277

Windows Interfaces 278
Windows 8 Modern Interface 279
Windows 8 Desktop 283
Windows Tools for Users and Technicians 287
Windows 8 File Explorer and Windows 7 Windows Explorer 287
Control Panel 294
Folder Options 296
Power Options 297
System Window 299
System Information Window 301
Action Center 302

Windows Network Connections. 304
Windows Workgroup and Homegroup 304
Windows Domain 305
Public and Private Networks 306
Make a Windows 8 Network Connection. 307
Domain Setup 310
Windows User Accounts 311
Using a Microsoft Account with Windows 8 314
User Account Control Dialog Box 317

CHAPTER 8

Installing Windows. 325

How to Plan a Windows Installation 326
Choose the Edition, License, and Version of Windows 326
Verify Your System Qualifies for Windows . . . 327
Installations with Special Considerations. . . . 333
Choose the Type of Installation: In-Place Upgrade, Clean Install, or Dual Boot 338
Understand the Choices You'll Make During the Installation. 339
Final Checklist Before Beginning the Installation. 340
Installing Windows 8.1 and Windows 7 342
Steps to Perform a Windows 8.1 In-Place Upgrade 342
Windows 8.1 Upgrade from Microsoft Website 347
Windows 7 In-Place Upgrade 348
Steps to Perform a Windows 8.1 Clean Install 350
Steps to Perform a Windows 7 Clean Install 352
Steps to Set Up a Windows Multiboot 354
Using an Upgrade Product Key on a New Hard Drive 356
What to Do After a Windows Installation 360
Verify You Have Network Access. 361
Activate Windows 362
Install Windows Updates and Service Packs . . 362
Install Hardware. 364
Install Applications 371
Set Up User Accounts and Transfer User Data 371
Turn Windows Features On or Off 372
Special Concerns When Working in a Large Enterprise 372
Deployment Strategies for Windows 373
Using the USMT Software. 375

CHAPTER 9

Supporting I/O Devices. 383

Basic Principles for Supporting Devices. 384
Ports and Wireless Connections Used by Peripheral Devices 384
Installing I/O Peripheral Devices 389
Mouse or Keyboard 390
Barcode Readers 393
Biometric Devices 393
Digital Cameras and Camcorders 394
Webcams 396
Graphics Tablets 396
Motion Controllers 397
MIDI Devices 397
Touch Screens 399
KVM Switches. 399
Installing and Configuring Adapter Cards 400
Sound Cards and Onboard Sound 404
TV Tuner and Video Capture Cards 404
Replacing Expansion Cards in a Laptop 405
Supporting the Video Subsystem 408
Monitor Technologies and Features 408
Video Cards and Connectors 412
Changing Monitor Settings 417
Video Memory and Windows. 419
Troubleshooting I/O Devices 422
NumLock Indicator Light. 422
Device Manager 422
Troubleshooting Monitors and Video 424
Video System in a Laptop 431
Speakers in a Laptop. 435

CHAPTER 10

Maintaining Windows. 443

Schedule Preventive Maintenance. 444
Verify Critical Windows Settings. 444
Update Drivers and Firmware 444
Patch Management 445
Clean Up the Hard Drive 446

Backup Procedures 453
Planning for Disaster Recovery 454
Back Up User Data with Windows 8 File History 455
Back Up Windows System Files 460
Windows 8 Custom Refresh Image 462
Managing Files, Folders, and Storage Devices 465
How Partitions and File Systems Work 465
Commands to Manage Files and Folders 469
Use Disk Management to Manage Hard Drives 480
Windows Storage Spaces 487

CHAPTER 11

Optimizing Windows 495

Windows Utilities and Tools to Support the OS 496
What Are the Shell and the Kernel? 496
How Windows Manages Applications 497
Task Manager 498
Administrative Tools 505
System Configuration 506
Services Console 510
Computer Management 511
Microsoft Management Console (MMC) 511
Event Viewer 513
Print Management 517
Task Scheduler 518
Performance Monitor 520
Registry Editor 522
Display Settings and Graphics Software 527
Improving Windows Performance 529
Step 1: Perform Routine Maintenance 530
Step 2: Clean Windows Startup 530
Step 3: Check If the Hardware Can Support the OS 532
Step 4: Check for a History of Problems 533
Step 5: Consider Using ReadyBoost 533
Manually Removing Software 535
Step 1: First Try the Uninstall Routine 536
Step 2: Delete Program Files 536
Step 3: Delete Registry Entries 537
Step 4: Remove Program Shortcuts 538
Step 5: Remove Startup Processes 539

CHAPTER 12

Supporting Customers and Troubleshooting Windows 545

What Customers Want: Beyond Technical Know-How 546
Becoming a Competent and Helpful Support Technician 546
Planning for Good Service 550
Strategies to Troubleshoot Any Computer Problem 561
Step 1: Interview the User and Back Up Data 563
Step 2: Examine the System and Make Your Best Guess 565
Step 3: Test Your Theory 567
Step 4: Plan Your Solution and Then Fix the Problem 568
Step 5: Verify the Fix and Take Preventive Action 569
Step 6: Document What Happened 569
Troubleshooting Applications 571
General Steps for Solving Application Errors 571
Memory Diagnostics 574
System File Checker 576
Responding to Specific Error Messages 577

CHAPTER 13

Troubleshooting Windows Startup. . . . 587

Understanding the Boot Process 588
Different Ways to Boot 588
Startup UEFI/BIOS Controls the Beginning of the Boot 589
Steps to Boot the Computer and Start Windows 590
Tools for Troubleshooting Windows Startup Problems 597
What to Do Before a Problem Occurs 598
Tools for Least Invasive Solutions 602
Tools That Can Affect Windows System Files and Settings 612
Tools for Reinstalling Windows 616
Troubleshooting Windows Startup 622
Important Data on the Hard Drive 622
Error Messages and Problems 623

CHAPTER 14

Connecting To and Setting Up a Network 633

Understanding TCP/IP and Windows Networking. 634
Layers of Network Communication 634
How IP Addresses Get Assigned 638
How IPv4 Addresses Are Used 638
How IPv6 Addresses Are Used 642
View IP Address Settings. 645
Character-Based Names Identify Computers and Networks 646
TCP/IP Protocol Layers 648
Connecting a Computer to a Network 653
Connect to an Ethernet Wired or Wireless Wi-Fi Local Network. 653
Connect to a Wireless WAN (Cellular) Network 656
Create a Dial-Up Connection 659
Create a VPN Connection 661
Dynamic and Static IP Configurations 664
Alternate IP Address Configuration. 665
Manage Network Adapters 666
Setting Up a Multifunction Router for a SOHO Network. 670
Functions of a SOHO Router. 670
Install and Configure a Router on the Local Network 672
Limit Internet Traffic on Your Network 678
Set Up a Wireless Network. 683

CHAPTER 15

Supporting Network Hardware 695

Types of Networks and the Internet Connections They Use 696
Network Technologies Used for Internet Connections 696
Hardware Used by Local Networks 701
Dial-Up Modems 701
Switches and Hubs 701
Wireless Access Points and Bridges 703
Ethernet Cables and Connectors 704
Powerline Networking or Ethernet over Power (EoP) 708
Power over Ethernet (PoE) 710
Setting Up and Troubleshooting Network Wiring 711
Tools Used by Network Technicians. 712
How Twisted-Pair Cables and Connectors Are Wired 717
TCP/IP Utilities Used for Troubleshooting . . . 727
Strategies for Troubleshooting Network Connections 733

CHAPTER 16

Supporting Mobile Operating Systems. 747

Operating Systems Used on Mobile Devices 748
Android by the Open Handset Alliance and Google 748
iOS by Apple 751
Windows Phone by Microsoft 755
Comparing Open Source and Closed Source Operating Systems. 759
Configure, Sync, and Troubleshoot iOS Devices 759
Configure iOS Network Connections 760
Configure iOS Email 763
Sync, Back Up, and Restore from Backup in iOS 768
Troubleshoot iOS Devices. 776
Configure, Sync, and Troubleshoot Android Devices 781
Configure Android Network Connections 781
Configure Android Email 786
Sync, Update, Back Up, and Restore from Backup with Android 787
Troubleshoot Android Devices 790
Configure, Sync, and Troubleshoot Windows Mobile Devices. 794
Configure Windows Phone Network Connections 795
Configure Windows Phone Email, Sync, and Backup. 795
Update and Restore Windows Phone from Backup 798
Troubleshoot Windows Mobile Devices. 798

CHAPTER 17

Windows Resources on a Network. . . . 805

Supporting Client/Server Applications 806
Network Servers 806
Internet Explorer 807
Remote Desktop Connection (RDC) 815
Remote Assistance 820
Use Group Policy to Improve QoS for Applications 822
ODBC Data Sources 823
Controlling Access to Folders and Files 825
Classify User Accounts and User Groups 825
Methods to Assign Permissions to Folders and Files 828
How to Share Folders and Files. 830
How to Map a Network Drive or Network Printer. 842
Hidden Network Resources and Administrative Shares 844
Cloud Computing 846
Cloud Computing Categories. 847
Deployment Models for Cloud Computing. . . . 849

CHAPTER 18

Security Strategies 855

Securing a Windows Personal Computer 856
Use Windows to Authenticate Users 856
File and Folder Encryption. 861
Windows Firewall Settings 862
Local Security Policies Using Group Policy . . . 865
Use BitLocker Encryption 869
Use UEFI/BIOS Features to Protect the System . 870
Securing a Mobile Device. 871
Device Access Controls 871
Software Security 874
Mobile Security in Corporate Environments . . 876
Additional Methods to Protect Resources 877
Authenticate Users for Large Networks 877
Physical Security Methods and Devices 880
Digital Security Methods and Resources 881
Unified Threat Management (UTM) Appliance 881
Data Destruction and Disposal 882
Educate Users. 883
Dealing with Malicious Software on Personal Computers 885
What Are We Up Against? 885
Step-by-Step Attack Plan 887
Dealing with Malicious Software on Mobile Devices 898
Common Mobile Device Malware Symptoms . . 898
Mobile Device Tools and Malware Removal . . . 900
Software Licensing and Prohibited Content or Activity 903
Software Licensing 903
Corporate Policies for Dealing with Prohibited Content or Activity 904

CHAPTER 19

Supporting Printers and Customizing a System 911

Printer Types and Features 912
Laser Printers. 912
Inkjet Printers 914
Impact Printers 917
Thermal Printers. 917
Using Windows to Install, Share, and Manage Printers 919
Local or Network Printer 919
Wired or Wireless Printer Connections. 920
Install a Local or Network Printer. 921
Share a Printer on a Network. 924
Virtual Printing 928
Cloud Printing 928
Configure Printer Features and Add-On Devices 929
Printer Maintenance and Upgrades. 931
Online Support for Printers 931
Clean a Printer. 932
Calibrate a Printer 933
Printer Maintenance Kits. 934
Upgrade the Printer Memory or Hard Drive . . 938
Printer Firmware. 939
Troubleshooting Printers. 940
Printer Does Not Print. 940
Poor Print Quality. 948
Customizing Computer Systems 950
Graphics or CAD/CAM Design Workstation . . . 951
Audio and Video Editing Workstation 953
Virtualization Workstation. 954
Gaming PC. 954
Home Theater PC 955
Home Server PC 957
Thick Client and Thin Client 958

CHAPTER 20

Virtualization, Linux, and Mac OS X. . . 965

Virtualization Basics. 966
Server-Side Virtualization 966
Client-Side Virtualization 967
Virtual Machines and Hypervisors. 967
Linux Operating System 972
Directory and File Layout 975
Root Account and User Accounts 977
Linux Commands 978
The vi Editor 981
Assigning Permissions to Files or Directories . 984
Dual-Boot Systems and a Live CD 986
Backups and Updates 988
Mac OS X Operating System. 990
Use the Mac. 990
Maintain and Support a Mac 1003
Troubleshoot OS X Startup. 1012
Boot Camp. 1014

APPENDIX A

Safety Procedures and Environmental Concerns 1021

APPENDIX B

Entry Points for Startup Processes . . 1037

APPENDIX C

CompTIA A+ Acronyms 1041

Glossary. 1049

Index. 1093

CompTIA A+ 220-901 and 220-902 Exams Mapped to Chapters

CompTIA A+ Guide to IT Technical Support, Ninth Edition fully meets all of CompTIA's A+ 220-901 and 220-902 Exam Objectives.

CompTIA A+ 220-901

DOMAIN 1.0 HARDWARE

1.1 Given a scenario, configure settings and use BIOS/UEFI tools on a PC.

OBJECTIVES	CHAPTER	SECTION
◢ Firmware upgrades – flash BIOS	3	Flashing BIOS
◢ BIOS component information	3	Using BIOS Setup to Configure a Motherboard
• RAM	3	Using BIOS Setup to Configure a Motherboard
• Hard drive	3	Using BIOS Setup to Configure a Motherboard
• Optical drive	3	Using BIOS Setup to Configure a Motherboard
• CPU	3	Using BIOS Setup to Configure a Motherboard
◢ BIOS configurations	3	Using BIOS Setup to Configure a Motherboard
• Boot sequence	3	Using BIOS Setup to Configure a Motherboard
• Enabling and disabling devices	3	Using BIOS Setup to Configure a Motherboard
• Date/time	3	Using BIOS Setup to Configure a Motherboard
• Clock speeds	3	Using BIOS Setup to Configure a Motherboard
• Virtualization support	3	Using BIOS Setup to Configure a Motherboard
• BIOS security (passwords, drive encryption: TPM, lo-jack, secure boot)	3	Using BIOS Setup to Configure a Motherboard
◢ Built-in diagnostics	3	Configuring a Motherboard
◢ Monitoring	3	Using BIOS Setup to Configure a Motherboard
• Temperature monitoring	3	Using BIOS Setup to Configure a Motherboard
• Fan speeds	3	Using BIOS Setup to Configure a Motherboard
• Intrusion detection/notification	3	Using BIOS Setup to Configure a Motherboard
• Voltage	3	Using BIOS Setup to Configure a Motherboard
• Clock	3	Using BIOS Setup to Configure a Motherboard
• Bus speed	3	Using BIOS Setup to Configure a Motherboard

1.2 Explain the importance of motherboard components, their purpose, and properties.

OBJECTIVES	CHAPTER	SECTION
◢ Sizes	3	Motherboard Form Factors
• ATX	3	Motherboard Form Factors
• Micro-ATX	3	Motherboard Form Factors
• Mini-ITX	3	Motherboard Form Factors
• ITX	3	Motherboard Form Factors
◢ Expansion slots	3	Motherboard Form Factors
• PCI	3	Buses and Expansion Slots
• PCI-X	3	Buses and Expansion Slots
• PCIe	3	Buses and Expansion Slots
• miniPCI	3	Buses and Expansion Slots
◢ RAM slots	4	Memory Technologies
◢ CPU sockets	3	Processor Sockets
◢ Chipsets	3	The Chipset
• North Bridge	3	The Chipset
• South Bridge	3	The Chipset
◢ CMOS battery	3	Configuring a Motherboard
◢ Power connections and types	5	Types and Characteristics of Power Supplies

◢ Fan connectors	3	Configuring a Motherboard
◢ Front/Top panel connectors	2	How to Work Inside a Desktop Computer Case
• USB	2	How to Work Inside a Desktop Computer Case
• Audio	2	How to Work Inside a Desktop Computer Case
• Power button	2	How to Work Inside a Desktop Computer Case
• Power light	2	How to Work Inside a Desktop Computer Case
• Drive activity lights	2	How to Work Inside a Desktop Computer Case
• Reset button	2	How to Work Inside a Desktop Computer Case
◢ Bus speeds	3	Buses and Expansion Slots

1.3 Compare and contrast various RAM types and their features.

OBJECTIVES	CHAPTER	SECTION
◢ Types	4	Memory Technologies
• DDR	4	Memory Technologies
• DDR2	4	Memory Technologies
• DDR3	4	Memory Technologies
• SODIMM	4	Memory Technologies
• DIMM	4	Memory Technologies
• Parity vs. non-parity	4	Memory Technologies
• ECC vs. non-ECC	4	Memory Technologies
• RAM configurations	4	Memory Technologies
▯ Single channel vs. dual channel vs. triple channel	4	Memory Technologies
• Single sided vs. double sided	4	Memory Technologies
• Buffered vs. unbuffered	4	Memory Technologies
◢ RAM compatibility	4	How to Upgrade Memory

1.4 Install and configure PC expansion cards.

OBJECTIVES	CHAPTER	SECTION
◢ Sound cards	9	Installing and Configuring Adapter Cards
◢ Video cards	9	Installing and Configuring Adapter Cards
◢ Network cards	14	Connect to an Ethernet Wired or Wireless Wi-Fi Local Network
◢ USB cards	9	Installing and Configuring Adapter Cards
◢ Firewire cards	9	Installing and Configuring Adapter Cards
◢ Thunderbolt cards	9	Installing and Configuring Adapter Cards
◢ Storage cards	6	Setting Up Hardware RAID
◢ Modem cards	15	Dial-Up Modems
◢ Wireless/cellular cards	14	Connect to a Wireless WAN (Cellular) Network
◢ TV tuner cards	9	Installing and Configuring Adapter Cards
◢ Video capture cards	9	Installing and Configuring Adapter Cards
◢ Riser cards	3	Motherboard Types and Features

1.5 Install and configure storage devices and use appropriate media.

OBJECTIVES	CHAPTER	SECTION
◢ Optical drives	6	Standards Used by Optical Drives and Discs
• CD-ROM / CD-RW	6	Standards Used by Optical Drives and Discs
• DVD-ROM / DVD-RW / DVD-RW DL	6	Standards Used by Optical Drives and Discs
• Blu-Ray	6	Standards Used by Optical Drives and Discs
• BD-R	6	Standards Used by Optical Drives and Discs
• BD-RE	6	Standards Used by Optical Drives and Discs

◢ Magnetic hard disk drives	6	Hard Drive Technologies and Interface Standards
• 5400 rpm	6	Hard Drive Technologies and Interface Standards
• 7200 rpm	6	Hard Drive Technologies and Interface Standards
• 10,000 rpm	6	Hard Drive Technologies and Interface Standards
◢ Hot swappable drives	6	Hard Drive Technologies and Interface Standards
◢ Solid state/flash drives	6	Solid-State Storage
• Compact flash	6	Solid-State Storage
• SD	6	Solid-State Storage
• Micro-SD	6	Solid-State Storage
• Mini-SD	6	Solid-State Storage
• xD	6	Solid-State Storage
• SSD	6	Hard Drive Technologies and Interface Standards
• Hybrid	6	Hard Drive Technologies and Interface Standards
• eMMC	6	Solid-State Storage
◢ RAID types	6	Setting Up Hardware RAID
• 0	6	Setting Up Hardware RAID
• 1	6	Setting Up Hardware RAID
• 5	6	Setting Up Hardware RAID
• 10	6	Setting Up Hardware RAID
◢ Tape drive	6	About Tape Drives
◢ Media capacity	6	Standards Used by Optical Drives and Discs
• CD	6	Standards Used by Optical Drives and Discs
• CD-RW	6	Standards Used by Optical Drives and Discs
• DVD-RW	6	Standards Used by Optical Drives and Discs
• DVD	6	Standards Used by Optical Drives and Discs
• Blu-Ray	6	Standards Used by Optical Drives and Discs
• Tape	6	About Tape Drives
• DVD DL	6	Standards Used by Optical Drives and Discs

1.6 Install various types of CPUs and apply the appropriate cooling methods.

OBJECTIVES	CHAPTER	SECTION
◢ Socket types	3	Processor Sockets
• Intel: 775, 1155, 1156, 1366, 1150, 2011	4	Types and Characteristics of Processors
• AMD: AM3, AM3+, FM1, FM2, FM2+	4	Types and Characteristics of Processors
◢ Characteristics	4	Types and Characteristics of Processors
• Speeds	4	Types and Characteristics of Processors
• Cores	4	Types and Characteristics of Processors
• Cache size/type	4	Types and Characteristics of Processors
• Hyperthreading	4	Types and Characteristics of Processors
• Virtualization support	4	Types and Characteristics of Processors
• Architecture (32-bit vs. 64-bit)	4	Types and Characteristics of Processors
• Integrated GPU	4	Types and Characteristics of Processors
• Disable execute bit	4	Types and Characteristics of Processors
◢ Cooling	5	Cooling Methods and Devices
• Heat sink	5	Cooling Methods and Devices
• Fans	5	Cooling Methods and Devices
• Thermal paste	5	Cooling Methods and Devices
• Liquid-based	5	Cooling Methods and Devices
• Fanless/passive	5	Cooling Methods and Devices

1.7 Compare and contrast various PC connection interfaces, their characteristics and purpose.

OBJECTIVES	CHAPTER	SECTION
◢ Physical connections		
• USB 1.1 vs. 2.0 vs. 3.0	9	Ports and Wireless Connections Used by Peripheral Devices
○ Connector types: A, B, mini, micro	9	Ports and Wireless Connections Used by Peripheral Devices
• Firewire 400 vs. Firewire 800	9	Ports and Wireless Connections Used by Peripheral Devices
• SATA1 vs. SATA2 vs. SATA3, eSATA	6	Hard Drive Technologies and Interface Standards
• Other connector types	9	Ports and Wireless Connections Used by Peripheral Devices
○ VGA	9	Video Cards and Connectors
○ HDMI	9	Video Cards and Connectors
○ DVI	9	Video Cards and Connectors
○ Audio	9	Ports and Wireless Connections Used by Peripheral Devices
○ Analog	1	What's Inside a Desktop Case
○ Digital (Optical connector)	1	What's Inside a Desktop Case
○ RJ-45	1	What's Inside a Desktop Case
○ RJ-11	1	What's Inside a Desktop Case
○ Thunderbolt	1	First Look at Laptop Components
◢ Wireless connections	9	Ports and Wireless Connections Used by Peripheral Devices
• Bluetooth	9	Ports and Wireless Connections Used by Peripheral Devices
• RF	9	Ports and Wireless Connections Used by Peripheral Devices
• IR	9	Ports and Wireless Connections Used by Peripheral Devices
• NFC	9	Ports and Wireless Connections Used by Peripheral Devices
◢ Characteristics	9	Ports and Wireless Connections Used by Peripheral Devices
• Analog	9	Ports and Wireless Connections Used by Peripheral Devices
• Digital	9	Ports and Wireless Connections Used by Peripheral Devices
• Distance limitations	9	Ports and Wireless Connections Used by Peripheral Devices
• Data transfer speeds	9	Ports and Wireless Connections Used by Peripheral Devices
• Quality	9	Ports and Wireless Connections Used by Peripheral Devices
• DRM	9	Ports and Wireless Connections Used by Peripheral Devices
• Frequencies	9	Ports and Wireless Connections Used by Peripheral Devices

1.8 Install a power supply based on given specifications.

OBJECTIVES	CHAPTER	SECTION
◢ Connector types and their voltages	1	Form Factors Used by Desktop Cases, Power Supplies, and Motherboards
	5	Types and Characteristics of Power Supplies
• SATA	1	Form Factors Used by Desktop Cases, Power Supplies, and Motherboards
	5	Types and Characteristics of Power Supplies
• Molex	1	Form Factors Used by Desktop Cases, Power Supplies, and Motherboards
	5	Types and Characteristics of Power Supplies
• 4/8-pin 12v	1	Form Factors Used by Desktop Cases, Power Supplies, and Motherboards
	5	Types and Characteristics of Power Supplies
• PCIe 6/8-pin	1	Form Factors Used by Desktop Cases, Power Supplies, and Motherboards
	5	Types and Characteristics of Power Supplies
• 20-pin	1	Form Factors Used by Desktop Cases, Power Supplies, and Motherboards
	5	Types and Characteristics of Power Supplies

• 24-pin	1	Form Factors Used by Desktop Cases, Power Supplies, and Motherboards
	5	Types and Characteristics of Power Supplies
◢ Specifications	5	Types and Characteristics of Power Supplies
• Wattage	5	Types and Characteristics of Power Supplies
• Dual rail	5	Types and Characteristics of Power Supplies
• Size	5	Types and Characteristics of Power Supplies
• Number of connectors	5	Types and Characteristics of Power Supplies
• ATX	5	Types and Characteristics of Power Supplies
• Micro-ATX	5	Types and Characteristics of Power Supplies
• Dual voltage options	1	Form Factors Used by Desktop Cases, Power Supplies, and Motherboards

1.9 **Given a scenario, select the appropriate components for a custom PC configuration, to meet customer specifications or needs.**

OBJECTIVES	CHAPTER	SECTION
◢ Graphic / CAD / CAM design workstation	19	Graphics or CAD/CAM Design Workstation
• Multicore processor	19	Graphics or CAD/CAM Design Workstation
• High-end video	19	Graphics or CAD/CAM Design Workstation
• Maximum RAM	19	Graphics or CAD/CAM Design Workstation
◢ Audio/Video editing workstation	19	Audio and Video Editing Workstation
• Specialized audio and video card	19	Audio and Video Editing Workstation
• Large fast hard drive	19	Audio and Video Editing Workstation
• Dual monitors	19	Audio and Video Editing Workstation
◢ Virtualization workstation	19	Virtualization Workstation
• Maximum RAM and CPU cores	19	Virtualization Workstation
◢ Gaming PC	19	Gaming PC
• Multicore processor	19	Gaming PC
• High-end video/specialized GPU	19	Gaming PC
• High definition sound card	19	Gaming PC
• High-end cooling	19	Gaming PC
◢ Home Theater PC	19	Home Theater PC
• Surround sound audio	19	Home Theater PC
• HDMI output	19	Home Theater PC
• HTPC compact form factor	19	Home Theater PC
• TV tuner	19	Home Theater PC
◢ Standard thick client	19	Thick Client and Thin Client
• Desktop applications	19	Thick Client and Thin Client
• Meets recommended requirements for selected OS	19	Thick Client and Thin Client
◢ Thin client	19	Thick Client and Thin Client
• Basic applications	19	Thick Client and Thin Client
• Meets minimum requirements for selected OS	19	Thick Client and Thin Client
• Network connectivity	19	Thick Client and Thin Client
◢ Home Server PC	19	Home Server PC
• Media streaming	19	Home Server PC
• File sharing	19	Home Server PC
• Print sharing	19	Home Server PC
• Gigabit NIC	19	Home Server PC
• RAID array	19	Home Server PC

1.10 Compare and contrast types of display devices and their features.

OBJECTIVES	CHAPTER	SECTION
◢ Types	9	Monitor Technologies and Features
• LCD	9	Monitor Technologies and Features
○ TN vs. IPS	9	Monitor Technologies and Features
○ Flourescent vs. LED backlighting	9	Monitor Technologies and Features
• Plasma	9	Monitor Technologies and Features
• Projector	9	Monitor Technologies and Features
• OLED	9	Monitor Technologies and Features
◢ Refresh / frame rates	9	Monitor Technologies and Features
◢ Resolution	9	Monitor Technologies and Features
◢ Native resolution	9	Monitor Technologies and Features
◢ Brightness/lumens	9	Monitor Technologies and Features
◢ Analog vs. digital	9	Monitor Technologies and Features
◢ Privacy/antiglare filters	9	Monitor Technologies and Features
◢ Multiple displays	9	Monitor Technologies and Features
◢ Aspect ratios	9	Monitor Technologies and Features
• 16:9	9	Monitor Technologies and Features
• 16:10	9	Monitor Technologies and Features
• 4:3	9	Monitor Technologies and Features

1.11 Identify common PC connector types and associated cables.

OBJECTIVES	CHAPTER	SECTION
◢ Display connector types		
• DVI-D	9	Video Cards and Connectors
• DVI-I	9	Video Cards and Connectors
• DVI-A	9	Video Cards and Connectors
• DisplayPort	1	What's Inside a Desktop Case
• RCA	9	Video Cards and Connectors
• HD15 (i.e. DE15 or DB15)	1	What's Inside a Desktop Case
• BNC	15	Ethernet Cables and Connectors
• miniHDMI	9	Video Cards and Connectors
• miniDin-6	9	Video Cards and Connectors
◢ Display cable types	1	What's Inside a Desktop Case
• HDMI	9	Video Cards and Connectors
• DVI	9	Video Cards and Connectors
• VGA	9	Video Cards and Connectors
• Component	9	Video Cards and Connectors
• Composite	9	Video Cards and Connectors
• Coaxial	15	Ethernet Cables and Connectors
◢ Device cables and connectors		
• SATA	6	Hard Drive Technologies and Interface Standards
• eSATA	6	Hard Drive Technologies and Interface Standards
• USB	6	Hard Drive Technologies and Interface Standards
• Firewire (IEEE1394)	1	What's Inside a Desktop Case
• PS/2	1	What's Inside a Desktop Case
• Audio	1	What's Inside a Desktop Case

◢ Adapters and convertors		
• DVI to HDMI	9	Video Cards and Connectors
• USB A to USB B	9	Basic Principles for Supporting Devices
• USB to Ethernet	15	Ethernet Cables and Connectors
• DVI to VGA	9	Video Cards and Connectors
• Thunderbolt to DVI	9	Video Cards and Connectors
• PS/2 to USB	9	Mouse or Keyboard
• HDMI to VGA	9	Video Cards and Connectors

1.12 Install and configure common peripheral devices.

OBJECTIVES	CHAPTER	SECTION
◢ Input devices	9	Installing I/O Peripheral Devices
• Mouse	9	Mouse or Keyboard
• Keyboard	9	Mouse or Keyboard
• Scanner	9	Installing I/O Peripheral Devices
• Barcode reader	9	Barcode Readers
• Biometric devices	9	Biometric Devices
• Game pads	9	Installing I/O Peripheral Devices
• Joysticks	9	Installing I/O Peripheral Devices
• Digitizer	9	Graphics Tablets
• Motion sensor	9	Motion Controller
• Touch pads	9	Installing I/O Peripheral Devices
• Smart card readers	9	Installing I/O Peripheral Devices
• Digital cameras	9	Digital Cameras and Camcorders
• Microphone	9	Installing I/O Peripheral Devices
• Webcam	9	Webcams
• Camcorder	9	Digital Cameras and Camcorders
◢ Output devices		
• Printers	19	Using Windows to Install, Share, and Manage Printers
• Speakers	9	Installing I/O Peripheral Devices
• Display devices	9	Supporting the Video Subsystem
◢ Input & Output devices	9	Installing I/O Peripheral Devices
• Touch screen	9	Touch Screens
• KVM	9	KVM Switches
• Smart TV	9	Installing I/O Peripheral Devices
• Set-Top Box	9	Installing I/O Peripheral Devices
• MIDI enabled devices	9	MIDI Devices

1.13 Install SOHO multifunction device / printers and configure appropriate settings.

OBJECTIVES	CHAPTER	SECTION
◢ Use appropriate drivers for a given operating system	19	Using Windows to Install, Share, and Manage Printers
• Configuration settings	19	Configure Printer Features and Add-On Devices
○ Duplex	19	Configure Printer Features and Add-On Devices
○ Collate	19	Configure Printer Features and Add-On Devices
○ Orientation	19	Configure Printer Features and Add-On Devices
○ Quality	19	Configure Printer Features and Add-On Devices

◢ Device sharing	19	Share a Printer on a Network
• Wired	19	Using Windows to Install, Share, and Manage Printers
○ USB	19	Using Windows to Install, Share, and Manage Printers
○ Serial	19	Using Windows to Install, Share, and Manage Printers
○ Ethernet	19	Using Windows to Install, Share, and Manage Printers
• Wireless	19	Using Windows to Install, Share, and Manage Printers
○ Bluetooth	19	Using Windows to Install, Share, and Manage Printers
○ 802.11(a,b,g,n,ac)	19	Using Windows to Install, Share, and Manage Printers
○ Infrastructure vs. adhoc	19	Using Windows to Install, Share, and Manage Printers
• Integrated print server (hardware)	19	Share a Printer on a Network
• Cloud printing/remote printing	19	Cloud Printing
◢ Public/shared devices	19	Using Windows to Install, Share, and Manage Printers
• Sharing local/networked device via Operating System settings	19	Using Windows to Install, Share, and Manage Printers
○ TCP/Bonjour/AirPrint	19	Using Windows to Install, Share, and Manage Printers
• Data privacy	19	Using Windows to Install, Share, and Manage Printers
○ User authentication on the device	19	Using Windows to Install, Share, and Manage Printers
○ Hard drive caching	19	Using Windows to Install, Share, and Manage Printers

1.14 Compare and contrast differences between the various print technologies and the associated imaging process.

OBJECTIVES	CHAPTER	SECTION
◢ Laser	19	Laser Printers
• Imaging drum, fuser assembly, transfer belt, transfer roller, pickup rollers, separate pads, duplexing assembly	19	Laser Printers
• Imaging process: processing, charging, exposing, developing, transferring, fusing and cleaning	19	Laser Printers
◢ Inkjet	19	Inkjet Printers
• Ink cartridge, print head, roller, feeder, duplexing assembly, carriage and belt	19	Inkjet Printers
• Calibration	19	Calibrate a Printer
◢ Thermal	19	Thermal Printers
• Feed assembly, heating element	19	Thermal Printers
• Special thermal paper	19	Thermal Printers
◢ Impact	19	Impact Printers
• Print head, ribbon, tractor feed	19	Impact Printers
• Impact paper	19	Impact Printers
◢ Virtual	19	Virtual Printing
• Print to file	19	Virtual Printing
• Print to PDF	19	Virtual Printing
• Print to XPS	19	Virtual Printing
• Print to image	19	Virtual Printing

1.15 Given a scenario, perform appropriate printer maintenance.

OBJECTIVES	CHAPTER	SECTION
◢ Laser	19	Printer Maintenance and Upgrades
• Replacing toner, applying maintenance kit, calibration, cleaning	19	Printer Maintenance and Upgrades
◢ Thermal	19	Printer Maintenance and Upgrades
• Replace paper, clean heating element, remove debris	19	Printer Maintenance and Upgrades
◢ Impact	19	Printer Maintenance and Upgrades
• Replace ribbon, replace print head, replace paper	19	Printer Maintenance and Upgrades
◢ Inkjet	19	Printer Maintenance and Upgrades
• Clean heads, replace cartridges, calibration, clear jams	19	Printer Maintenance and Upgrades

DOMAIN 2.0 NETWORKING

2.1 Identify the various types of network cables and connectors.

OBJECTIVES	CHAPTER	SECTION
◢ Fiber	15	Ethernet Cables and Connectors
• Connectors: SC, ST and LC	15	Ethernet Cables and Connectors
◢ Twisted Pair	15	Ethernet Cables and Connectors
• Connectors: RJ-11, RJ-45	15	Ethernet Cables and Connectors
• Wiring standards: T568A, T568B	15	How Twisted-Pair Cables and Connectors Are Wired
◢ Coaxial	15	Ethernet Cables and Connectors
• Connectors: BNC, F-connector	15	Ethernet Cables and Connectors

2.2 Compare and contrast the characteristics of connectors and cabling.

OBJECTIVES	CHAPTER	SECTION
◢ Fiber	15	Ethernet Cables and Connectors
• Types (single-mode vs. multi-mode)	15	Ethernet Cables and Connectors
• Speed and transmission limitations	15	Ethernet Cables and Connectors
◢ Twisted pair	15	Ethernet Cables and Connectors
• Types: STP, UTP, CAT3, CAT5, CAT5e, CAT6, CAT6e, CAT7, plenum, PVC	15	Ethernet Cables and Connectors
• Speed and transmission limitations	15	Ethernet Cables and Connectors
• Splitters and effects on signal quality	15	Ethernet Cables and Connectors
◢ Coaxial	15	Ethernet Cables and Connectors
• Types: RG-6, RG-59	15	Ethernet Cables and Connectors
• Speed and transmission limitations	15	Ethernet Cables and Connectors
• Splitters and effects on signal quality	15	Ethernet Cables and Connectors

2.3 Explain the properties and characteristics of TCP/IP.

OBJECTIVES	CHAPTER	SECTION
◢ IPv4 vs. IPv6	14	Understanding TCP/IP and Windows Networking
◢ Public vs. private vs. APIPA/link local	14	Understanding TCP/IP and Windows Networking
◢ Static vs. dynamic	14	Understanding TCP/IP and Windows Networking
◢ Client-side DNS settings	14	Understanding TCP/IP and Windows Networking
◢ Client-side DHCP	14	Understanding TCP/IP and Windows Networking
◢ Subnet mask vs. CIDR	14	Understanding TCP/IP and Windows Networking
◢ Gateway	14	Understanding TCP/IP and Windows Networking

2.4 Explain common TCP and UDP ports, protocols, and their purpose.

OBJECTIVES	CHAPTER	SECTION
◢ Ports	14	TCP/IP Protocol Layers
• 21 – FTP	14	TCP/IP Protocol Layers
• 22 – SSH	14	TCP/IP Protocol Layers
• 23 – TELNET	14	TCP/IP Protocol Layers
• 25 – SMTP	14	TCP/IP Protocol Layers
• 53 – DNS	14	TCP/IP Protocol Layers
• 80 – HTTP	14	TCP/IP Protocol Layers
• 110 – POP3	14	TCP/IP Protocol Layers
• 143 – IMAP	14	TCP/IP Protocol Layers
• 443 – HTTPS	14	TCP/IP Protocol Layers
• 3389 – RDP	14	TCP/IP Protocol Layers
• 137-139, 445 - SMB	14	TCP/IP Protocol Layers
• 548 or 427 - AFP	14	TCP/IP Protocol Layers
◢ Protocols	14	TCP/IP Protocol Layers
• DHCP	14	TCP/IP Protocol Layers
• DNS	14	TCP/IP Protocol Layers
• LDAP	14	TCP/IP Protocol Layers
• SNMP	14	TCP/IP Protocol Layers
• SMB	14	TCP/IP Protocol Layers
• CIFS	14	TCP/IP Protocol Layers
• SSH	14	TCP/IP Protocol Layers
• AFP	14	TCP/IP Protocol Layers
◢ TCP vs. UDP	14	TCP/IP Protocol Layers

2.5 Compare and contrast various WiFi networking standards and encryption types.

OBJECTIVES	CHAPTER	SECTION
◢ Standards	14	Set Up a Wireless Network
• 802.11 a/b/g/n/ac	14	Set Up a Wireless Network
• Speeds, distances and frequencies	14	Set Up a Wireless Network
◢ Encryption types	14	Set Up a Wireless Network
• WEP, WPA, WPA2, TKIP, AES	14	Set Up a Wireless Network

2.6 Given a scenario, install and configure SOHO wireless/wired router and apply appropriate settings.

OBJECTIVES	CHAPTER	SECTION
◢ Channels	14	Set Up a Wireless Network
◢ Port forwarding, port triggering	14	Limit Internet Traffic on Your Network
◢ DHCP (on/off)	14	Install and Configure a Router on the Local Network
◢ DMZ	14	Limit Internet Traffic on Your Network

◢ NAT / DNAT	14	Functions of a SOHO Router
◢ Basic QoS	14	Install and Configure a Router on the Local Network
◢ Firmware	14	Install and Configure a Router on the Local Network
◢ UPnP	14	Install and Configure a Router on the Local Network

2.7 Compare and contrast Internet connection types, network types, and their features.

OBJECTIVES	CHAPTER	SECTION
◢ Internet Connection Types	15	Network Technologies Used for Internet Connections
• Cable	15	Network Technologies Used for Internet Connections
• DSL	15	Network Technologies Used for Internet Connections
• Dial-up	15	Network Technologies Used for Internet Connections
• Fiber	15	Network Technologies Used for Internet Connections
• Satellite	15	Network Technologies Used for Internet Connections
• ISDN	15	Network Technologies Used for Internet Connections
• Cellular	15	Network Technologies Used for Internet Connections
○ Tethering	15	Network Technologies Used for Internet Connections
○ Mobile hotspot	15	Network Technologies Used for Internet Connections
• Line of sight wireless internet service	15	Network Technologies Used for Internet Connections
◢ Network Types	15	Types of Networks and the Internet Connections They Use
• LAN	15	Types of Networks and the Internet Connections They Use
• WAN	15	Types of Networks and the Internet Connections They Use
• PAN	15	Types of Networks and the Internet Connections They Use
• MAN	15	Types of Networks and the Internet Connections They Use

2.8 Compare and contrast network architecture devices, their functions, and features.

OBJECTIVES	CHAPTER	SECTION
◢ Hub	15	Hardware Used by Local Networks
◢ Switch	15	Hardware Used by Local Networks
◢ Router	15	Hardware Used by Local Networks
◢ Access point	15	Hardware Used by Local Networks
◢ Bridge	15	Hardware Used by Local Networks
◢ Modem	15	Hardware Used by Local Networks
◢ Firewall	15	Hardware Used by Local Networks
◢ Patch panel	15	Setting Up and Troubleshooting Network Wiring
◢ Repeaters/extenders	15	Hardware Used by Local Networks
◢ Ethernet over Power	15	Powerline Networking or Ethernet over Power (EoP)
◢ Power over Ethernet injector	15	Power over Ethernet (PoE)

2.9 Given a scenario, use appropriate networking tools.

OBJECTIVES	CHAPTER	SECTION
◢ Crimper	15	Tools Used by Network Technicians
◢ Cable stripper	15	Tools Used by Network Technicians
◢ Multimeter	15	Tools Used by Network Technicians
◢ Tone generator & probe	15	Tools Used by Network Technicians
◢ Cable tester	15	Tools Used by Network Technicians
◢ Loopback plug	15	Tools Used by Network Technicians
◢ Punchdown tool	15	Tools Used by Network Technicians
◢ WiFi analyzer	15	Tools Used by Network Technicians

DOMAIN 3.0 MOBILE DEVICES

3.1 Install and configure laptop hardware and components.

OBJECTIVES	CHAPTER	SECTION
◢ Expansion options		
• Express card /34	1	First Look at Laptop Components
• Express card /54	1	First Look at Laptop Components
• SODIMM	4	Types of Memory Used in Laptops
• Flash	1	First Look at Laptop Components
• Ports/Adapters	1	First Look at Laptop Components
○ Thunderbolt	1	First Look at Laptop Components
○ DisplayPort	1	First Look at Laptop Components
○ USB to RJ-45 dongle	1	First Look at Laptop Components
○ USB to WiFi dongle	1	First Look at Laptop Components
○ USB to Bluetooth	1	First Look at Laptop Components
○ USB Optical Drive	1	First Look at Laptop Components
◢ Hardware/device replacement		
• Keyboard	1	How to Work Inside a Laptop Computer
• Hard Drive	1	First Look at Laptop Components
	6	Hard Drive Technologies and Interface Standards
○ SSD vs. Hybrid vs. Magnetic disk	6	Hard Drive Technologies and Interface Standards
○ 1.8in vs. 2.5in	6	Hard Drive Technologies and Interface Standards
• Memory	1	First Look at Laptop Components
	4	How to Upgrade Memory on a Laptop
• Smart card reader	1	First Look at Laptop Components
	6	Solid-State Storage
• Optical drive	1	First Look at Laptop Components
	6	Supporting Other Types of Storage Devices
• Wireless card	1	First Look at Laptop Components
	9	Replacing Expansion Cards in a Laptop
• Mini-PCIe	9	Replacing Expansion Cards in a Laptop
• Screen	9	Video System in a Laptop
• DC jack	1	First Look at Laptop Components
	5	Problems with Laptop Power Systems
• Battery	1	First Look at Laptop Components
	5	Problems with Laptop Power Systems
• Touchpad	9	How to Work Inside a Laptop Computer
• Plastics/frames	1	First Look at Laptop Components
	5	Problems with Laptop Power Systems
• Speaker	9	How to Work Inside a Laptop Computer
• System board	1	First Look at Laptop Components
	3	Replacing a Laptop System Board
• CPU	1	First Look at Laptop Components
	4	Replacing the Processor in a Laptop

3.2 Explain the function of components within the display of a laptop.

OBJECTIVES	CHAPTER	SECTION
◢ Types	9	Video System in a Laptop
• LCD	9	Video System in a Laptop
○ TN vs. IPS	9	Video System in a Laptop
○ Flourescent vs. LED backlighting	9	Video System in a Laptop
• OLED	9	Video System in a Laptop

◢ Wi-Fi antenna connector/placement	9	Replacing Expansion Cards in a Laptop
◢ Webcam	9	Replacing Expansion Cards in a Laptop
◢ Microphone	9	Replacing Expansion Cards in a Laptop
◢ Inverter	9	Video System in a Laptop
◢ Digitizer	9	Replacing Expansion Cards in a Laptop

3.3 **Given a scenario, use appropriate laptop features.**

OBJECTIVES	CHAPTER	SECTION
◢ Special function keys	1	First Look at Laptop Components
• Dual displays	1	First Look at Laptop Components
• Wireless (on/off)	1	First Look at Laptop Components
• Cellular (on/off)	1	First Look at Laptop Components
• Volume settings	1	First Look at Laptop Components
• Screen brightness	1	First Look at Laptop Components
• Bluetooth (on/off)	1	First Look at Laptop Components
• Keyboard backlight	1	First Look at Laptop Components
• Touch pad (on/off)	1	First Look at Laptop Components
• Screen orientation	1	First Look at Laptop Components
• Media options (fast forward/rewind)	1	First Look at Laptop Components
• GPS (on/off)	1	First Look at Laptop Components
• Airplane mode	1	First Look at Laptop Components
◢ Docking station	1	First Look at Laptop Components
◢ Physical laptop lock and cable lock	1	First Look at Laptop Components
◢ Rotating / removable screens	1	First Look at Laptop Components

3.4 **Explain the characteristics of various types of other mobile devices.**

OBJECTIVES	CHAPTER	SECTION
◢ Tablets	1	First Look at Mobile Device Hardware
◢ Smart phones	1	First Look at Mobile Device Hardware
◢ Wearable technology devices	1	First Look at Mobile Device Hardware
• Smart watches	1	First Look at Mobile Device Hardware
• Fitness monitors	1	First Look at Mobile Device Hardware
• Glasses and headsets	1	First Look at Mobile Device Hardware
◢ Phablets	1	First Look at Mobile Device Hardware
◢ e-Readers	1	First Look at Mobile Device Hardware
◢ Smart camera	1	First Look at Mobile Device Hardware
◢ GPS	1	First Look at Mobile Device Hardware

3.5 **Compare and contrast accessories & ports of other mobile devices.**

OBJECTIVES	CHAPTER	SECTION
◢ Connection types	1	First Look at Mobile Device Hardware
• NFC	1	First Look at Mobile Device Hardware
• Proprietary vendor specific ports (communication/power)	1	First Look at Mobile Device Hardware
• microUSB/miniUSB	1	First Look at Mobile Device Hardware
• Lightning	1	First Look at Mobile Device Hardware
• Bluetooth	1	First Look at Mobile Device Hardware
• IR	1	First Look at Mobile Device Hardware
• Hotspot / tethering	1	First Look at Mobile Device Hardware

◢ Accessories	1	First Look at Mobile Device Hardware
• Headsets	1	First Look at Mobile Device Hardware
• Speakers	1	First Look at Mobile Device Hardware
• Game pads	1	First Look at Mobile Device Hardware
• Docking stations	1	First Look at Mobile Device Hardware
• Extra battery packs/battery chargers	1	First Look at Mobile Device Hardware
• Protective covers / water proofing	1	First Look at Mobile Device Hardware
• Credit card readers	1	First Look at Mobile Device Hardware
• Memory/MicroSD	1	First Look at Mobile Device Hardware

DOMAIN 4.0 HARDWARE AND NETWORK TROUBLESHOOTING

4.1 Given a scenario, troubleshoot common problems related to motherboards, RAM, CPU and power with appropriate tools.

OBJECTIVES	CHAPTER	SECTION
◢ Common symptoms	5	Troubleshooting the Motherboard, Processor, and RAM
• Unexpected shutdowns	5	Troubleshooting the Motherboard, Processor, and RAM
• System lockups	5	Troubleshooting the Motherboard, Processor, and RAM
• POST code beeps	5	Troubleshooting the Motherboard, Processor, and RAM
• Blank screen on bootup	5	Troubleshooting the Motherboard, Processor, and RAM
• BIOS time and settings resets	5	Troubleshooting the Motherboard, Processor, and RAM
• Attempts to boot to incorrect device	5	Troubleshooting the Motherboard, Processor, and RAM
• Continuous reboots	5	Troubleshooting the Motherboard, Processor, and RAM
• No power	5	Troubleshooting the Motherboard, Processor, and RAM
• Overheating	5	Troubleshooting the Motherboard, Processor, and RAM
• Loud noise	5	Troubleshooting the Motherboard, Processor, and RAM
• Intermittent device failure	5	Troubleshooting the Motherboard, Processor, and RAM
• Fans spin – no power to other devices	5	Troubleshooting the Motherboard, Processor, and RAM
• Indicator lights	5	Troubleshooting the Motherboard, Processor, and RAM
• Smoke	5	Troubleshooting the Motherboard, Processor, and RAM
• Burning smell	5	Troubleshooting the Motherboard, Processor, and RAM
• Proprietary crash screens (BSOD/pin wheel)	5	Troubleshooting the Motherboard, Processor, and RAM
• Distended capacitors	5	Troubleshooting the Motherboard, Processor, and RAM
◢ Tools	1	Tools Used by a Computer Hardware Technician
• Multimeter	1	Tools Used by a Computer Hardware Technician
• Power supply tester	1	Tools Used by a Computer Hardware Technician
• Loopback plugs	1	Tools Used by a Computer Hardware Technician
• POST card / USB	1	Tools Used by a Computer Hardware Technician

4.2 Given a scenario, troubleshoot hard drives and RAID arrays with appropriate tools.

OBJECTIVES	CHAPTER	SECTION
◢ Common symptoms	6	Troubleshooting Hard Drives
• Read/write failure	6	Troubleshooting Hard Drives
• Slow performance	6	Troubleshooting Hard Drives
• Loud clicking noise	5	Troubleshooting the Motherboard, Processor, and RAM
• Failure to boot	6	Troubleshooting Hard Drives
• Drive not recognized	6	Troubleshooting Hard Drives
• OS not found	6	Troubleshooting Hard Drives
• RAID not found	6	Troubleshooting Hard Drives
• RAID stops working	6	Troubleshooting Hard Drives

• Proprietary crash screens (BSOD/pin wheel)	5	Troubleshooting the Motherboard, Processor, and RAM
• S.M.A.R.T. errors	6	Troubleshooting Hard Drives
◢ Tools	6	Troubleshooting Hard Drives
• Screwdriver	6	Troubleshooting Hard Drives
• External enclosures	6	Troubleshooting Hard Drives
• CHKDSK	6	Troubleshooting Hard Drives
• FORMAT	6	Troubleshooting Hard Drives
• File recovery software	5	Troubleshooting the Motherboard, Processor, and RAM
• Bootrec	6	Troubleshooting Hard Drives
• Diskpart	6	Troubleshooting Hard Drives
• Defragmentation tool	6	Troubleshooting Hard Drives

4.3 Given a scenario, troubleshoot common video, projector and display issues.

OBJECTIVES	CHAPTER	SECTION
◢ Common symptoms	9	Troubleshooting Monitors and Video
• VGA mode	9	Troubleshooting Monitors and Video
• No image on screen	9	Troubleshooting Monitors and Video
• Overheat shutdown	9	Troubleshooting Monitors and Video
• Dead pixels	9	Troubleshooting Monitors and Video
• Artifacts	9	Troubleshooting Monitors and Video
• Color patterns incorrect	9	Troubleshooting Monitors and Video
• Dim image	9	Troubleshooting Monitors and Video
• Flickering image	9	Troubleshooting Monitors and Video
• Distorted image	9	Troubleshooting Monitors and Video
• Distorted geometry	9	Troubleshooting Monitors and Video
• Burn-in	9	Troubleshooting Monitors and Video
• Oversized images and icons	9	Troubleshooting Monitors and Video

4.4 Given a scenario, troubleshoot wired and wireless networks with appropriate tools.

OBJECTIVES	CHAPTER	SECTION
◢ Common symptoms	15	Strategies for Troubleshooting Network Connections
• No connectivity	15	Strategies for Troubleshooting Network Connections
• APIPA/link local address	15	Strategies for Troubleshooting Network Connections
• Limited connectivity	15	Strategies for Troubleshooting Network Connections
• Local connectivity	15	Strategies for Troubleshooting Network Connections
• Intermittent connectivity	15	Strategies for Troubleshooting Network Connections
• IP conflict	15	Strategies for Troubleshooting Network Connections
• Slow transfer speeds	15	Strategies for Troubleshooting Network Connections
• Low RF signal	15	Strategies for Troubleshooting Network Connections
• SSID not found	15	Strategies for Troubleshooting Network Connections
◢ Hardware tools	15	
• Cable tester	15	Setting Up and Troubleshooting Network Wiring
• Loopback plug	15	Setting Up and Troubleshooting Network Wiring
• Punch down tools	15	Setting Up and Troubleshooting Network Wiring
• Tone generator and probe	15	Setting Up and Troubleshooting Network Wiring
• Wire strippers	15	Setting Up and Troubleshooting Network Wiring
• Crimper	15	Setting Up and Troubleshooting Network Wiring
• Wireless locator	15	Strategies for Troubleshooting Network Connections

◢ Command line tools	15	TCP/IP Utilities Used for Troubleshooting
• PING	15	TCP/IP Utilities Used for Troubleshooting
• IPCONFIG/IFCONFIG	15	TCP/IP Utilities Used for Troubleshooting
• TRACERT	15	TCP/IP Utilities Used for Troubleshooting
• NETSTAT	15	TCP/IP Utilities Used for Troubleshooting
• NBTSTAT	15	TCP/IP Utilities Used for Troubleshooting
• NET	15	TCP/IP Utilities Used for Troubleshooting
• NETDOM	15	TCP/IP Utilities Used for Troubleshooting
• NSLOOKUP	15	TCP/IP Utilities Used for Troubleshooting

4.5 **Given a scenario, troubleshoot and repair common mobile device issues while adhering to the appropriate procedures.**

OBJECTIVES	CHAPTER	SECTION
◢ Common symptoms		
• No display	9	Video System in a Laptop
• Dim display	9	Video System in a Laptop
• Flickering display	9	Video System in a Laptop
• Sticking keys	1	Maintaining Laptops and Mobile Devices
• Intermittent wireless	15	Strategies for Troubleshooting Network Connections
• Battery not charging	5	Troubleshooting Mobile Devices
• Ghost cursor/pointer drift	9	Video System in a Laptop
• No power	5	Troubleshooting Mobile Devices
• Num lock indicator lights	9	NumLock Indicator Light
• No wireless connectivity	15	Strategies for Troubleshooting Network Connections
• No Bluetooth connectivity	15	Strategies for Troubleshooting Network Connections
• Cannot display to external monitor	9	Changing Monitor Settings
• Touchscreen non-responsive	9	Video System in a Laptop
• Apps not loading	5	Troubleshooting Mobile Devices
• Slow performance	5	Troubleshooting Mobile Devices
• Unable to decrypt email	5	Troubleshooting Mobile Devices
• Extremely short battery life	5	Troubleshooting Mobile Devices
• Overheating	5	Troubleshooting Mobile Devices
• Frozen system	5	Troubleshooting Mobile Devices
• No sound from speakers	9	Speakers in a Laptop
• GPS not functioning	15	Strategies for Troubleshooting Network Connections
• Swollen battery	5	Troubleshooting Mobile Devices
◢ Disassembling processes for proper re-assembly	2	How to Work Inside a Laptop Computer
• Document and label cable and screw locations	2	How to Work Inside a Laptop Computer
• Organize parts	2	How to Work Inside a Laptop Computer
• Refer to manufacturer resources	2	How to Work Inside a Laptop Computer
• Use appropriate hand tools	2	How to Work Inside a Laptop Computer

4.6 Given a scenario, troubleshoot printers with appropriate tools.

OBJECTIVES	CHAPTER	SECTION
◢ Common symptoms	19	Troubleshooting Printers
• Streaks	19	Troubleshooting Printers
• Faded prints	19	Troubleshooting Printers
• Ghost images	19	Troubleshooting Printers
• Toner not fused to the paper	19	Troubleshooting Printers
• Creased paper	19	Troubleshooting Printers
• Paper not feeding	19	Troubleshooting Printers
• Paper jam	19	Troubleshooting Printers
• No connectivity	19	Troubleshooting Printers
• Garbled characters on paper	19	Troubleshooting Printers
• Vertical lines on page	19	Troubleshooting Printers
• Backed up print queue	19	Troubleshooting Printers
• Low memory errors	19	Troubleshooting Printers
• Access denied	19	Troubleshooting Printers
• Printer will not print	19	Troubleshooting Printers
• Color prints in wrong print color	19	Troubleshooting Printers
• Unable to install printer	19	Troubleshooting Printers
• Error codes	19	Troubleshooting Printers
• Printing blank pages	19	Troubleshooting Printers
• No image on printer display	19	Troubleshooting Printers
◢ Tools	19	
• Maintenance kit	19	Printer Maintenance Kits
• Toner vacuum	19	Clean a Printer
• Compressed air	19	Clean a Printer
• Printer spooler	19	Printer Does Not Print

CompTIA A+ 220-902

DOMAIN 1.0 WINDOWS OPERATING SYSTEMS

1.1 Compare and contrast various features and requirements of Microsoft Operating Systems (Windows Vista, Windows 7, Windows 8, Windows 8.1).

OBJECTIVES	CHAPTER	SECTION
◢ Features:		
• 32-bit vs. 64-bit	7	System Window
• Aero, gadgets, user account control, bit-locker, shadow copy, system restore, ready boost, sidebar, compatibility mode, virtual XP mode, easy transfer, administrative tools, defender, Windows firewall, security center, event viewer, file structure and paths, category view vs. classic view.	7	Windows Interfaces
	8	Windows Tools for Users and Technicians
	8	Verify Your System Qualifies for Windows
	8	Installations with Special Considerations
	8	Set Up User Accounts and Transfer User Data
	10	Backup Proceures
	10	Clean Up the Hard Drive
	10	Back Up Windows System Files
	11	Step 5: Consider Using ReadyBoost
	11	Administrative Tools
	11	Event Viewer
	18	Use BitLocker Encryption
	18	Step-by-Step Attack Plan
	18	Windows Firewall Settings
	18	Dealing with Malicious Software on Personal Computers
• Side by side apps, Metro UI, Pinning, One Drive, Windows store, Multimonitor task bars, Charms, Start Screen, Power Shell, Live sign in, Action Center.	7	Windows Interface
	7	Windows Tools for Users and Technicians
	7	Windows User Accounts
	10	Display Settings and Graphics Software
	11	Commands to Manage Files and Folders
◢ Upgrade paths – differences between in place upgrades, compatibility tools, Windows upgrade OS advisor	8	Choose the Type of Installation: In-Place Upgrade, Clean Install, or Dual Boot

1.2 Given a scenario, install Windows PC operating systems using appropriate methods.

OBJECTIVES	CHAPTER	SECTION
◢ Boot methods	8	How to Plan a Windows Installation
• USB	8	How to Plan a Windows Installation
• CD-ROM	8	How to Plan a Windows Installation
• DVD	8	How to Plan a Windows Installation
• PXE	8	Deployment Strategies for Windows
• Solid state/flash drives	8	How to Plan a Windows Installation
• Netboot	20	Troubleshoot OS X Startup
• External/hot swappable drive	8	How to Plan a Windows Installation
• Internal hard drive (partition)	8	How to Plan a Windows Installation
◢ Type of installations	8	How to Plan a Windows Installation
• Unattended installation	8	Deployment Strategies for Windows
• Upgrade	8	How to Plan a Windows Installation
• Clean install	8	How to Plan a Windows Installation
• Repair installation	8	How to Plan a Windows Installation
• Multiboot	8	How to Plan a Windows Installation
• Remote network installation	8	Deployment Strategies for Windows
• Image deployment	8	Deployment Strategies for Windows
• Recovery partition	8	Installations with Special Considerations
	13	Tools for Reinstalling Windows

• Refresh/restore	13	Tools for Reinstalling Windows
◢ Partitioning	10	Managing Files, Folders, and Storage Devices
• Dynamic	10	Managing Files, Folders, and Storage Devices
• Basic	10	Managing Files, Folders, and Storage Devices
• Primary	10	Managing Files, Folders, and Storage Devices
• Extended	10	Managing Files, Folders, and Storage Devices
• Logical	10	Managing Files, Folders, and Storage Devices
• GPT	10	Managing Files, Folders, and Storage Devices
◢ File system types/formatting		
• ExFAT	10	Managing Files, Folders, and Storage Devices
• FAT32	10	Managing Files, Folders, and Storage Devices
• NTFS	10	Managing Files, Folders, and Storage Devices
• CDFS	10	Managing Files, Folders, and Storage Devices
• NFS	17	How to Map a Network Drive or Network Printer
• ext3, ext4	20	Linux Commands
• Quick format vs. full format	10	Managing Files, Folders, and Storage Devices
◢ Load alternate third party drivers when necessary	8	Installations with Special Considerations
◢ Workgroup vs. Domain setup	7	Windows Network Connections
◢ Time/date/region/language settings	7	Control Panel
	8	Installing Windows 8.1 and Windows 7
◢ Driver installation, software and windows updates	8	What to Do After a Windows Installation
◢ Factory recovery partition	8	Installations with Special Considerations
◢ Properly formatted boot drive with the correct partitions/format	8	Installing Windows 8.1 and Windows 7

1.3 **Given a scenario, apply appropriate Microsoft command line tools.**

OBJECTIVES	CHAPTER	SECTION
◢ TASKKILL	12	Responding to Specific Error Messages
◢ BOOTREC	13	Error Messages and Problems
◢ SHUTDOWN	10	Commands to Manage Files and Folders
◢ TASKLIST	12	Responding to Specific Error Messages
◢ MD	10	Commands to Manage Files and Folders
◢ RD	10	Commands to Manage Files and Folders
◢ CD	10	Commands to Manage Files and Folders
◢ DEL	10	Commands to Manage Files and Folders
◢ FORMAT	10	Commands to Manage Files and Folders
◢ COPY	10	Commands to Manage Files and Folders
◢ XCOPY	10	Commands to Manage Files and Folders
◢ ROBOCOPY	10	Commands to Manage Files and Folders
◢ DISKPART	13	Tools That Can Affect Windows System Files and Settings
◢ SFC	12	System File Checker
◢ CHKDSK	10	Commands to Manage Files and Folders
◢ GPUPDATE	17	Use Group Policy to Improve QoS for Applications
◢ GPRESULT	17	How to Share Folders and Files
◢ DIR	10	Commands to Manage Files and Folders
◢ EXIT	10	Commands to Manage Files and Folders
◢ HELP	10	Commands to Manage Files and Folders
◢ EXPAND	10	Commands to Manage Files and Folders
◢ [command name] /?	10	Commands to Manage Files and Folders
◢ Commands available with standard privileges vs. administrative privileges.	10	Commands to Manage Files and Folders

1.4 Given a scenario, use appropriate Microsoft operating system features and tools.

OBJECTIVES	CHAPTER	SECTION
◢ Administrative	11	Administrative Tools
• Computer management	11	Computer Management
• Device manager	8	Install Hardware
• Local Users and Groups	17	Classify User Accounts and User Groups
• Local security policy	18	Local Security Policies Using Group Policy
• Performance monitor	11	Performance Monitor
• Services	11	Services Console
• System configuration	11	System Configuration
• Task scheduler	11	Task Scheduler
• Component services	12	Responding to Specific Error Messages
• Data sources	17	ODBC Data Sources
• Print management	11	Print Management
• Windows memory diagnostics	12	Memory Diagnostics
• Windows firewall	18	Windows Firewall Settings
• Advanced security	18	Windows Firewall Settings
◢ MSCONFIG	11	System Configuration
• General	11	System Configuration
• Boot	11	System Configuration
• Services	11	System Configuration
• Startup	11	System Configuration
• Tools	11	System Configuration
◢ Task Manager	11	Task Manager
• Applications	11	Task Manager
• Processes	11	Task Manager
• Performance	11	Task Manager
• Networking	11	Task Manager
• Users	11	Task Manager
◢ Disk management	10	Use Disk Management to Manage Hard Drives
• Drive status	10	Use Disk Management to Manage Hard Drives
• Mounting	10	Use Disk Management to Manage Hard Drives
• Initializing	10	Use Disk Management to Manage Hard Drives
• Extending partitions	10	Use Disk Management to Manage Hard Drives
• Splitting partitions	10	Use Disk Management to Manage Hard Drives
• Shrink partitions	10	Use Disk Management to Manage Hard Drives
• Assigning/changing drive letters	10	Use Disk Management to Manage Hard Drives
• Adding drives	10	Use Disk Management to Manage Hard Drives
• Adding arrays	10	Use Disk Management to Manage Hard Drives
• Storage spaces	10	Windows Storage Spaces
◢ Other	8	
• User State Migration tool (USMT)	8	Using the USMT Software
• Windows Easy Transfer	8	Set Up User Accounts and Transfer User Data
• Windows Upgrade Advisor	8	Verify Your System Qualifies for Windows
◢ System utilities		
• REGEDIT	11	The Registry Editor
• COMMAND	10	Commands to Manage Files and Folders
• SERVICES.MSC	11	Services Console

• MMC	11	Microsoft Management Console (MMC)
• MSTSC	17	Remote Desktop Connection (RDC)
• NOTEPAD	7	Windows Tools for Users and Technicians
• EXPLORER	7	Windows 8 File Explorer and Windows 7 Windows Explorer
• MSINFO32	7	System Information Window
• DXDIAG	11	Display Settings and Graphics Software
• DEFRAG	10	Schedule Preventive Maintenance
• System restore	10	Back Up Windows System Files
• Windows Update	10	Schedule Preventive Maintenance

1.5 **Given a scenario, use Windows Control Panel utilities.**

OBJECTIVES	CHAPTER	SECTION
◢ Internet options	17	Internet Explorer
• Connections	17	Internet Explorer
• Security	17	Internet Explorer
• General	17	Internet Explorer
• Privacy	17	Internet Explorer
• Programs	17	Internet Explorer
• Advanced	17	Internet Explorer
◢ Display/Display Settings	11	Display Settings and Graphics Software
• Resolution	11	Display Settings and Graphics Software
• Color depth	11	Display Settings and Graphics Software
• Refresh rate	11	Display Settings and Graphics Software
◢ User accounts	7	Windows User Accounts
◢ Folder options	7	Folder Options
• View hidden files	7	Folder Options
• Hide extensions	7	Folder Options
• General options	7	Folder Options
• View options	7	Folder Options
◢ System		
• Performance (virtual memory)	10	Schedule Preventive Maintenance
• Remote settings	17	Remote Desktop Connection (RDC)
• System protection	10	Back Up Windows System Files
◢ Windows firewall	18	Windows Firewall Settings
◢ Power options	7	Power Options
• Hibernate	7	Power Options
• Power plans	7	Power Options
• Sleep/suspend	7	Power Options
• Standby	7	Power Options
◢ Programs and features	8	Install Applications
◢ HomeGroup	7	Windows Network Connections
◢ Devices and Printers	8	Install Hardware
◢ Sound	7	Control Panel
◢ Troubleshooting	17	How to Share Folders and Files
◢ Network and Sharing Center	7	Windows Network Connections
◢ Device Manager	8	Install Hardware

1.6 Given a scenario, install and configure Windows networking on a client/desktop.

OBJECTIVES	CHAPTER	SECTION
◢ HomeGroup vs. WorkGroup	7	Windows Network Connections
◢ Domain setup	7	Windows Network Connections
◢ Network shares/administrative shares/ mapping drives	17	Controlling Access to Folders and Files
◢ Printer sharing vs. network printer mapping	17	How to Map a Network Drive or Network Printer
◢ Establish networking connections	14	Connecting a Computer to a Network
• VPN	14	Create a VPN Connection
• Dialups	14	Create a Dial-Up Connection
• Wireless	14	Connect to an Ethernet Wired or Wireless Wi-Fi Local Network
• Wired	14	Connect to an Ethernet Wired or Wireless Wi-Fi Local Network
• WWAN (Cellular)	14	Connect to a Wireless WAN (Cellular) Network
◢ Proxy settings	17	Internet Explorer
◢ Remote Desktop Connection	17	Remote Desktop Connection (RDC)
◢ Remote Assistance	17	Remote Assistance
◢ Home vs. Work vs. Public network settings	7	Windows Network Connections
◢ Firewall settings	18	Windows Firewall Settings
• Exceptions	18	Windows Firewall Settings
• Configuration	18	Windows Firewall Settings
• Enabling/disabling Windows firewall	18	Windows Firewall Settings
◢ Configuring an alternative IP address in Windows	14	Alternate IP Address Configuration
• IP addressing	14	Dynamic and Static Configuration
• Subnet mask	14	How IPv4 IP Addresses Are Used
• DNS	14	Dynamic and Static Configuration
• Gateway	14	Dynamic and Static Configuration
◢ Network card properties		
• Half duplex/full duplex/auto	14	Manage Network Adapters
• Speed	14	Manage Network Adapters
• Wake-on-LAN	14	Manage Network Adapters
• QoS	14	Manage Network Adapters
	17	Use Group Policy to Improve QoS for Applications
• BIOS (on-board NIC)	14	Manage Network Adapters

1.7 Perform common preventive maintenance procedures using the appropriate Windows OS tools.

OBJECTIVES	CHAPTER	SECTION
◢ Best practices	10	
• Scheduled backups	10	Backup Procedures
• Scheduled disk maintenance	10	Schedule Preventive Maintenance
• Windows updates	10	Schedule Preventive Maintenance
• Patch management	10	Schedule Preventive Maintenance
• Driver/firmware updates	10	Schedule Preventive Maintenance
• Antivirus/ Antimalware updates	10	Schedule Preventive Maintenance
◢ Tools		
• Backup	10	Backup Procedures
• System restore	10	Backup Procedures
• Recovery image	13	Tools for Troubleshooting Windows Startup Problems
• Disk maintenance utilities	10	Schedule Preventive Maintenance

DOMAIN 2.0 OTHER OPERATING SYSTEMS AND TECHNOLOGIES

2.1 **Identify common features and functionality of the Mac OS and Linux operating systems.**

OBJECTIVES	CHAPTER	SECTION
◢ Best practices	20	
• Scheduled backups	20	Backups and Updates Maintain and Support a Mac
• Scheduled disk maintenance	20	Backups and Updates Maintain and Support a Mac
• System updates/App store	20	Backups and Updates Maintain and Support a Mac
• Patch management	20	Backups and Updates Maintain and Support a Mac
• Driver/firmware updates	20	Backups and Updates Maintain and Support a Mac
• Antivirus/ Antimalware updates	20	Backups and Updates Maintain and Support a Mac
◢ Tools	20	
• Backup/Time Machine	20	Maintain and Support a Mac
• Restore/snapshot	20	Maintain and Support a Mac
• Image recovery	20	Troubleshoot OS X Startup
• Disk maintenance utilities	20	Maintain and Support a Mac
• Shell/Terminal	20	Linux Commands Use the Mac
• Screen sharing	20	Use the Mac
• Force Quit	20	Use the Mac
◢ Features	20	
• Multiple desktops/Mission Control	20	Use the Mac
• Key Chain	20	Use the Mac
• Spot Light	20	Use the Mac
• iCloud	20	Use the Mac
• Gestures	20	Use the Mac
• Finder	20	Use the Mac
• Remote Disc	20	Use the Mac
• Dock	20	Use the Mac
• Boot Camp	20	Boot Camp
◢ Basic Linux commands		
• ls	20	Linux Commands Use the Mac
• grep	20	Linux Commands Hands-On Project 20-4: Install FTP Server in Ubuntu
• cd	20	Linux Commands Use the Mac
• shutdown	20	Linux Commands
• pwd vs. passwd	20	Linux Commands Use the Mac
• mv	20	Linux Commands
• cp	20	Linux Commands
• rm	20	Linux Commands
• chmod	20	Linux Commands
• mkdir	20	Linux Commands Use the Mac
• chown	20	Linux Commands

• iwconfig/ifconfig	20	Linux Commands Use the Mac
• ps	20	Linux Commands
• q	20	Linux Commands
• su/sudo	20	Linux Commands
• apt-get	20	Linux Commands Backups and Updates
• vi	20	Linux Commands
• dd	20	Linux Commands

2.2 **Given a scenario, setup and use client-side virtualization.**

OBJECTIVES	CHAPTER	SECTION
◢ Purpose of virtual machines	20	Virtualization Basics
◢ Resource requirements	20	Virtual Machines and Hypervisors
◢ Emulator requirements	20	Virtual Machines and Hypervisors
◢ Security requirements	20	Virtual Machines and Hypervisors
◢ Network requirements	20	Virtual Machines and Hypervisors
◢ Hypervisor	20	Virtual Machines and Hypervisors

2.3 **Identify basic cloud concepts.**

OBJECTIVES	CHAPTER	SECTION
◢ SaaS	17	Cloud Computing
◢ IaaS	17	Cloud Computing
◢ Paas	17	Cloud Computing
◢ Public vs. Private vs. Hybrid vs. Community	17	Cloud Computing
◢ Rapid Elasticity	17	Cloud Computing
◢ On-demand	17	Cloud Computing
◢ Resource pooling	17	Cloud Computing
◢ Measured service	17	Cloud Computing

2.4 **Summarize the properties and purpose of services provided by networked hosts.**

OBJECTIVES	CHAPTER	SECTION
◢ Server roles	17	Network Servers
• Web server	17	Network Servers
• File server	17	Network Servers
• Print server	17	Network Servers
• DHCP server	17	Network Servers
• DNS server	17	Network Servers
• Proxy server	17	Network Servers
• Mail server	17	Network Servers
• Authentication server	17	Network Servers
◢ Internet appliance	18	Unified Threat Management (UTM) Appliance
• UTM	18	Unified Threat Management (UTM) Appliance
• IDS	18	Unified Threat Management (UTM) Appliance
• IPS	18	Unified Threat Management (UTM) Appliance
◢ Legacy / embedded systems	17	Network Servers

2.5 **Identify basic features of mobile operating systems.**

OBJECTIVES	CHAPTER	SECTION
◢ Android vs. iOS vs. Windows	16	Operating Systems Used on Mobile Devices
• Open source vs. closed source/ vendor specific	16	Comparing Open Source and Closed Source Operating Systems

• App source (play store, app store and store)	16	Operating Systems Used on Mobile Devices
• Screen orientation (accelerometer/gyroscope)	16	Operating Systems Used on Mobile Devices
• Screen calibration	16	Operating Systems Used on Mobile Devices
• GPS and geotracking	16	Operating Systems Used on Mobile Devices
• WiFi calling	16	Operating Systems Used on Mobile Devices
• Launcher/GUI	16	Operating Systems Used on Mobile Devices
• Virtual assistant	16	Operating Systems Used on Mobile Devices
• SDK/APK	16	Operating Systems Used on Mobile Devices
• Emergency notification	16	Operating Systems Used on Mobile Devices
• Mobile payment service	16	Operating Systems Used on Mobile Devices

2.6 **Install and configure basic mobile device network connectivity and email.**

OBJECTIVES	CHAPTER	SECTION
◢ Wireless / cellular data network (enable/disable)	16	Configure iOS Network Connections Configure Android Network Connections Configure Windows Phone Network Connections
• Hotspot	16	Configure iOS Network Connections Configure Android Network Connections Configure Windows Phone Network Connections
• Tethering	16	Configure iOS Network Connections Configure Android Network Connections Configure Windows Phone Network Connections
• Airplane mode	16	Configure iOS Network Connections Configure Android Network Connections Configure Windows Phone Network Connections
◢ Bluetooth	16	Configure iOS Network Connections Configure Android Network Connections Configure Windows Phone Network Connections
• Enable Bluetooth	16	Configure iOS Network Connections Configure Android Network Connections Configure Windows Phone Network Connections
• Enable pairing	16	Configure iOS Network Connections Configure Android Network Connections Configure Windows Phone Network Connections
• Find device for pairing	16	Configure iOS Network Connections Configure Android Network Connections Configure Windows Phone Network Connections
• Enter appropriate pin code	16	Configure iOS Network Connections Configure Android Network Connections Configure Windows Phone Network Connections
• Test connectivity	16	Configure iOS Network Connections Configure Android Network Connections Configure Windows Phone Network Connections
◢ Corporate and ISP email configuration	16	Configure iOS Email Configure Android Email Configure Windows Phone Email, Sync, and Backup
• POP3	16	Configure iOS Email Configure Android Email Configure Windows Phone Email, Sync, and Backup
• IMAP	16	Configure iOS Email Configure Android Email Configure Windows Phone Email, Sync, and Backup

• Port and SSL settings	16	Configure iOS Email Configure Android Email Configure Windows Phone Email, Sync, and Backup
• Exchange, S/MIME	16	Configure iOS Email Configure Android Email Configure Windows Phone Email, Sync, and Backup
◢ Integrated commercial provider email configuration	16	Configure iOS Email Configure Android Email Configure Windows Phone Email, Sync, and Backup
• Google/Inbox	16	Configure iOS Email Configure Android Email Configure Windows Phone Email, Sync, and Backup
• Yahoo	16	Configure iOS Email Configure Android Email Configure Windows Phone Email, Sync, and Backup
• Outlook.com	16	Configure iOS Email Configure Android Email Configure Windows Phone Email, Sync, and Backup
• iCloud	16	Configure iOS Email Configure Android Email Configure Windows Phone Email, Sync, and Backup
◢ PRI updates/PRL updates/ Baseband updates	16	Sync, Update, Back Up, and Restore from Backup with Android
◢ Radio firmware	16	Troubleshooting Android Devices
◢ IMEI vs. IMSI	16	Configure iOS Network Connections
◢ VPN	16	Configure iOS Network Connections Configure Android Network Connections Configure Windows Phone Network Connections

2.7 Summarize methods and data related to mobile device synchronization.

OBJECTIVES	CHAPTER	SECTION
◢ Types of data to synchronize	16	Sync, Back Up, and Restore from Backup in iOS Sync, Update, Back Up, and Restore from Backup with Android Configure Windows Phone Email, Sync, and Backup
• Contacts	16	Sync, Back Up, and Restore from Backup in iOS Sync, Update, Back Up, and Restore from Backup with Android Configure Windows Phone Email, Sync, and Backup
• Programs	16	Sync, Back Up, and Restore from Backup in iOS Sync, Update, Back Up, and Restore from Backup with Android Configure Windows Phone Email, Sync, and Backup
• Email	16	Sync, Back Up, and Restore from Backup in iOS Sync, Update, Back Up, and Restore from Backup with Android Configure Windows Phone Email, Sync, and Backup
• Pictures	16	Sync, Back Up, and Restore from Backup in iOS Sync, Update, Back Up, and Restore from Backup with Android Configure Windows Phone Email, Sync, and Backup
• Music	16	Sync, Back Up, and Restore from Backup in iOS Sync, Update, Back Up, and Restore from Backup with Android Configure Windows Phone Email, Sync, and Backup
• Videos	16	Sync, Back Up, and Restore from Backup in iOS Sync, Update, Back Up, and Restore from Backup with Android Configure Windows Phone Email, Sync, and Backup
• Calendar	16	Sync, Back Up, and Restore from Backup in iOS Sync, Update, Back Up, and Restore from Backup with Android Configure Windows Phone Email, Sync, and Backup
• Bookmarks	16	Sync, Back Up, and Restore from Backup in iOS Sync, Update, Back Up, and Restore from Backup with Android Configure Windows Phone Email, Sync, and Backup

• Documents	16	Sync, Back Up, and Restore from Backup in iOS Sync, Update, Back Up, and Restore from Backup with Android Configure Windows Phone Email, Sync, and Backup
• Location data	16	Sync, Back Up, and Restore from Backup in iOS Sync, Update, Back Up, and Restore from Backup with Android Configure Windows Phone Email, Sync, and Backup
• Social media data	16	Sync, Back Up, and Restore from Backup in iOS Sync, Update, Back Up, and Restore from Backup with Android Configure Windows Phone Email, Sync, and Backup
• eBooks	16	Sync, Back Up, and Restore from Backup in iOS Sync, Update, Back Up, and Restore from Backup with Android Configure Windows Phone Email, Sync, and Backup
◢ Synchronization methods		
• Synchronize to the Cloud	16	Sync, Back Up, and Restore from Backup in iOS Sync, Update, Back Up, and Restore from Backup with Android Configure Windows Phone Email, Sync, and Backup
• Synchronize to the Desktop	16	Sync, Back Up, and Restore from Backup in iOS Sync, Update, Back Up, and Restore from Backup with Android Configure Windows Phone Email, Sync, and Backup
◢ Mutual authentication for multiple services	18	Authenticate Users for Large Networks
◢ Software requirements to install the application on the PC	16	Sync, Back Up, and Restore from Backup in iOS
◢ Connection types to enable synchronization	16	Sync, Back Up, and Restore from Backup in iOS Sync, Update, Back Up, and Restore from Backup with Android Configure Windows Phone Email, Sync, and Backup

DOMAIN 3.0 SECURITY

3.1 Identify common security threats and vulnerabilities.

OBJECTIVES	CHAPTER	SECTION
◢ Malware	18	Dealing with Malicious Software on Personal Computers Dealing with Malicious Software on Mobile Devices
• Spyware	18	Dealing with Malicious Software on Personal Computers Dealing with Malicious Software on Mobile Devices
• Viruses	18	Dealing with Malicious Software on Personal Computers Dealing with Malicious Software on Mobile Devices
• Worms	18	Dealing with Malicious Software on Personal Computers Dealing with Malicious Software on Mobile Devices
• Trojans	18	Dealing with Malicious Software on Personal Computers Dealing with Malicious Software on Mobile Devices
• Rootkits	18	Dealing with Malicious Software on Personal Computers
• Ransomware	18	Dealing with Malicious Software on Personal Computers
◢ Phishing	18	Dealing with Malicious Software on Personal Computers Dealing with Malicious Software on Mobile Devices
◢ Spear phishing	18	Dealing with Malicious Software on Personal Computers Dealing with Malicious Software on Mobile Devices
◢ Spoofing	18	Dealing with Malicious Software on Personal Computers Dealing with Malicious Software on Mobile Devices
◢ Social engineering	18	Dealing with Malicious Software on Personal Computers Dealing with Malicious Software on Mobile Devices
◢ Shoulder surfing	18	Dealing with Malicious Software on Personal Computers Dealing with Malicious Software on Mobile Devices

◢ Zero day attack	18	Dealing with Malicious Software on Personal Computers Dealing with Malicious Software on Mobile Devices
◢ Zombie/botnet	18	Dealing with Malicious Software on Personal Computers Dealing with Malicious Software on Mobile Devices
◢ Brute forcing	18	Dealing with Malicious Software on Personal Computers Dealing with Malicious Software on Mobile Devices
◢ Dictionary attacks	18	Dealing with Malicious Software on Personal Computers Dealing with Malicious Software on Mobile Devices
◢ Non-compliant systems	18	Dealing with Malicious Software on Personal Computers Dealing with Malicious Software on Mobile Devices
◢ Violations of security best practices	18	Dealing with Malicious Software on Personal Computers Dealing with Malicious Software on Mobile Devices
◢ Tailgating	18	Physical Security Methods and Devices
◢ Man-in-the-middle	18	Dealing with Malicious Software on Personal Computers Dealing with Malicious Software on Mobile Devices

3.2 Compare and contrast common prevention methods.

OBJECTIVES	CHAPTER	SECTION
◢ Physical security	18	Physical Security Methods and Devices
• Lock doors	18	Physical Security Methods and Devices
• Mantrap	18	Physical Security Methods and Devices
• Cable locks	18	Physical Security Methods and Devices
• Securing physical documents/passwords/shredding	18	Physical Security Methods and Devices
• Biometrics	18	Authenticate Users for Large Networks
• ID badges	18	Authenticate Users for Large Networks
• Key fobs	18	Authenticate Users for Large Networks
• RFID badge	18	Authenticate Users for Large Networks
• Smart card	18	Authenticate Users for Large Networks
• Tokens	18	Authenticate Users for Large Networks
• Privacy filters	18	Physical Security Methods and Devices
• Entry control roster	18	Physical Security Methods and Devices
◢ Digital security	18	Digital Security Methods and Resources
• Antivirus/Antimalware	18	Dealing with Malicious Software on Personal Computers Dealing with Malicious Software on Mobile Devices
• Firewalls	18	Windows Firewall Settings
• User authentication/strong passwords	18	Use Windows to Authenticate Users
• Multifactor authentication	18	Use BitLocker Encryption
• Directory permissions	17	How to Share Folders and Files
• VPN	18	Securing a Mobile Device
• DLP	18	Securing a Mobile Device
• Disabling ports	14	Limit Internet Traffic on Your Network
• Access control lists	18	Digital Security Methods and Resources
• Smart card	18	Digital Security Methods and Resources
• Email filtering	18	Digital Security Methods and Resources
• Trusted/untrusted software sources	18	Digital Security Methods and Resources
◢ User education/AUP	18	Educate Users
◢ Principle of least privilege	17	Controlling Access to Folders and Files

3.3 Compare and contrast differences of basic Windows OS security settings.

OBJECTIVES	CHAPTER	SECTION
◢ User and groups	17	Classify User Accounts and User Groups
• Administrator	17	Classify User Accounts and User Groups
• Power user	17	Classify User Accounts and User Groups
• Guest	17	Classify User Accounts and User Groups
• Standard user	17	Classify User Accounts and User Groups
◢ NTFS vs. Share permissions	17	Controlling Access to Folders and Files
• Allow vs. deny	17	Controlling Access to Folders and Files
• Moving vs. copying folders and files	17	Controlling Access to Folders and Files
• File attributes	17	Controlling Access to Folders and Files
◢ Shared files and folders	17	Controlling Access to Folders and Files
• Administrative shares vs. local shares	17	Hidden Network Resources and Administrative Shares
• Permission propagation	17	Controlling Access to Folders and Files
• Inheritance	17	Controlling Access to Folders and Files
◢ System files and folders	10	Backup Procedures
◢ User authentication	18	Securing a Windows Personal Computer
• Single sign-on	7	Windows User Accounts
◢ Run as administrator vs. standard user	7	Windows User Accounts
◢ Bitlocker	18	Use BitLocker Encryption
◢ Bitlocker-To-Go	18	Use BitLocker Encryption
◢ EFS	18	File and Folder Encryption

3.4 **Given a scenario, deploy and enforce security best practices to secure a workstation.**

OBJECTIVES	CHAPTER	SECTION
◢ Password best practices	18	
• Setting strong passwords	18	Securing a Windows Personal Computer
• Password expiration	18	Local Security Policies Using Group Policy
• Changing default user names/passwords	18	Securing a Windows Personal Computer
• Screensaver required password	18	Securing a Windows Personal Computer
• BIOS/UEFI passwords	18	Use UEFI/BIOS Features to Protect the System
• Requiring passwords	18	Local Security Policies Using Group Policy
◢ Account management		
• Restricting user permissions	17	Controlling Access to Folders and Files
• Login time restrictions	18	Local Security Policies Using Group Policy
• Disabling guest account	18	Use Windows to Authenticate Users
• Failed attempts lockout	18	Local Security Policies Using Group Policy
• Timeout/screen lock	18	Use Windows to Authenticate Users
◢ Disable autorun	18	Local Security Policies Using Group Policy
◢ Data encryption	18	File and Folder Encryption
◢ Patch/update management	10	Schedule Preventive Maintenance

3.5 **Compare and contrast various methods for securing mobile devices.**

OBJECTIVES	CHAPTER	SECTION
◢ Screen locks	18	Securing a Mobile Device
• Fingerprint lock	18	Securing a Mobile Device
• Face lock	18	Securing a Mobile Device
• Swipe lock	18	Securing a Mobile Device
• Passcode lock	18	Securing a Mobile Device

◢ Remote wipes	18	Securing a Mobile Device
◢ Locator applications	18	Securing a Mobile Device
◢ Remote backup applications	18	Securing a Mobile Device
◢ Failed login attempts restrictions	18	Securing a Mobile Device
◢ Antivirus/Antimalware	18	Software Security
◢ Patching/OS updates	18	Securing a Mobile Device
◢ Biometric authentication	18	Securing a Mobile Device
◢ Full device encryption	18	Securing a Mobile Device
◢ Multifactor authentication	18	Securing a Mobile Device
◢ Authenticator applications	18	Securing a Mobile Device
◢ Trusted sources vs. untrusted sources	18	Securing a Mobile Device
◢ Firewalls	18	Securing a Mobile Device
◢ Policies and procedures	18	Mobile Security in Corporate Environments
• BYOD vs. corporate owned	18	Mobile Security in Corporate Environments
• Profile security requirements	18	Mobile Security in Corporate Environments

3.6 **Given a scenario, use appropriate data destruction and disposal methods.**

OBJECTIVES	CHAPTER	SECTION
◢ Physical destruction	18	Data Destruction and Disposal
• Shredder	18	Data Destruction and Disposal
• Drill / Hammer	18	Data Destruction and Disposal
• Electromagnetic (Degaussing)	18	Data Destruction and Disposal
• Incineration	18	Data Destruction and Disposal
• Certificate of destruction	18	Data Destruction and Disposal
◢ Recycling or repurposing best practices	18	Data Destruction and Disposal
• Low level format vs. standard format	18	Data Destruction and Disposal
• Overwrite	18	Data Destruction and Disposal
• Drive wipe	18	Data Destruction and Disposal

3.7 **Given a scenario, secure SOHO wireless and wired networks.**

OBJECTIVES	CHAPTER	SECTION
◢ Wireless specific	14	Set Up a Wireless Network
• Changing default SSID	14	Set Up a Wireless Network
• Setting encryption	14	Set Up a Wireless Network
• Disabling SSID broadcast	14	Set Up a Wireless Network
• Antenna and access point placement	14	Set Up a Wireless Network
• Radio power levels	14	Set Up a Wireless Network
• WPS	14	Set Up a Wireless Network
◢ Change default user-names and passwords	14	Install and Configure a Router on the Local Network
◢ Enable MAC filtering	14	Install and Configure a Router on the Local Network
◢ Assign static IP addresses	14	Install and Configure a Router on the Local Network
◢ Firewall settings	14	Limit Internet Traffic on Your Network
◢ Port forwarding/mapping	14	Limit Internet Traffic on Your Network
◢ Disabling ports	14	Limit Internet Traffic on Your Network
◢ Content filtering / parental controls	14	Limit Internet Traffic on Your Network
◢ Update firmware	14	Install and Configure a Router on the Local Network
◢ Physical security	14	Install and Configure a Router on the Local Network

DOMAIN 4.0 SOFTWARE TROUBLESHOOTING

4.1 Given a scenario, troubleshoot PC operating system problems with appropriate tools.

OBJECTIVES	CHAPTER	SECTION
◢ Common symptoms		
• Proprietary crash screens (BSOD/pin wheel)	13	Troubleshooting Windows Startup
• Failure to boot	13	Troubleshooting Windows Startup
• Improper shutdown	13	Troubleshooting Windows Startup
• Spontaneous shutdown/restart	13	Troubleshooting Windows Startup
• Device fails to start/detected	13	Troubleshooting Windows Startup
• Missing dll message	12	Responding to Specific Error Messages
• Services fails to start	12	Responding to Specific Error Messages
• Compatibility error	12	Responding to Specific Error Messages
• Slow system performance	11	Improving Windows Performance
• Boots to safe mode	13	Troubleshooting Windows Startup
• File fails to open	12	Responding to Specific Error Messages
• Missing NTLDR	13	Error Messages and Problems
• Missing Boot Configuration Data	13	Troubleshooting Windows Startup
• Missing operating system	13	Troubleshooting Windows Startup
• Missing Graphical Interface	13	Troubleshooting Windows Startup
• Missing GRUB/LILO	20	Hands-On Project 20-2: Install Ubuntu Server in a VM
• Kernel panic	20	Backups and Updates
• Graphical Interface fails to load	13	Troubleshooting Windows Startup
• Multiple monitor misalignment/orientation	11	Display Settings and Graphics Software
◢ Tools		
• BIOS/UEFI	10	How Partitions and File Systems Work
• SFC	12	System File Checker
• Logs	11	Event Viewer
• System Recovery Options	13	Tools for Troubleshooting Windows Startup Problems
• Repair disks	13	Tools for Troubleshooting Windows Startup Problems
• Pre-installation environments	13	Tools for Troubleshooting Windows Startup Problems
• MSCONFIG	11	Manually Removing Software
• DEFRAG	10	Schedule Preventive Maintenance
• REGSRV32	12	Responding to Specific Error Messages
• REGEDIT	11	Manually Removing Software
• Event viewer	11	Event Viewer
• Safe mode	13	Tools for Troubleshooting Windows Startup Problems
• Command prompt	10	Commands to Manage Files and Folders
	13	Tools for Troubleshooting Windows Startup Problems
• Uninstall/reinstall/repair	13	Tools for Troubleshooting Windows Startup Problems

4.2 **Given a scenario, troubleshoot common PC security issues with appropriate tools and best practices.**

OBJECTIVES	CHAPTER	SECTION
◢ Common symptoms	18	What Are We Up Against?
• Pop-ups	18	What Are We Up Against?
• Browser redirection	18	What Are We Up Against?
• Security alerts	18	What Are We Up Against?
• Slow performance	18	What Are We Up Against?
• Internet connectivity issues	18	What Are We Up Against?
• PC/OS lock up	18	What Are We Up Against?
• Application crash	18	What Are We Up Against?
• OS updates failures	18	What Are We Up Against?
• Rogue antivirus	18	What Are We Up Against?
• Spam	18	What Are We Up Against?
• Renamed system files	18	What Are We Up Against?
• Files disappearing	18	What Are We Up Against?
• File permission changes	18	What Are We Up Against?
• Hijacked email	18	What Are We Up Against?
○ Responses from users regarding email	18	What Are We Up Against?
○ Automated replies from unknown sent email	18	What Are We Up Against?
• Access denied	18	What Are We Up Against?
• Invalid certificate (trusted root CA)	18	Step-by-Step Attack Plan
◢ Tools		
• Antivirus software	18	Step-by-Step Attack Plan
• Antimalware software	18	Step-by-Step Attack Plan
• Recovery console	13	Error Messages and Problems
• Terminal	20	Linux Operating System Drive Maintenance Tools
• System restore/Snapshot	18	Step-by-Step Attack Plan
• Pre-installation environments	18	Step-by-Step Attack Plan
• Event viewer	18	Step-by-Step Attack Plan
• Refresh/restore	18	Step-by-Step Attack Plan
• MSCONFIG/Safe boot	18	Step-by-Step Attack Plan
◢ Best practice procedure for malware removal	18	Step-by-Step Attack Plan
1. Identify malware symptoms	18	Step-by-Step Attack Plan
2. Quarantine infected system	18	Step-by-Step Attack Plan
3. Disable system restore (in Windows)	18	Step-by-Step Attack Plan
4. Remediate infected systems	18	Step-by-Step Attack Plan
a. Update antimalware software	18	Step-by-Step Attack Plan
b. Scan and removal techniques (safe mode, pre-installation environment)	18	Step-by-Step Attack Plan
5. Schedule scans and run updates	18	Step-by-Step Attack Plan
6. Enable system restore and create restore point (in Windows)	18	Step-by-Step Attack Plan
7. Educate end user	18	Step-by-Step Attack Plan

4.3 **Given a scenario, troubleshoot common mobile OS and application issues with appropriate tools.**

OBJECTIVES	CHAPTER	SECTION
Common symptoms		
• Dim display	16	Troubleshoot iOS Devices Troubleshoot Android Devices Troubleshoot Windows Mobile Devices
• Intermittent wireless	16	Troubleshoot iOS Devices Troubleshoot Android Devices Troubleshoot Windows Mobile Devices
• No wireless connectivity	16	Troubleshoot iOS Devices Troubleshoot Android Devices Troubleshoot Windows Mobile Devices
• No bluetooth connectivity	16	Troubleshoot iOS Devices Troubleshoot Android Devices Troubleshoot Windows Mobile Devices
• Cannot broadcast to external monitor	16	Troubleshoot iOS Devices Troubleshoot Android Devices Troubleshoot Windows Mobile Devices
• Touchscreen non-responsive	16	Troubleshoot iOS Devices Troubleshoot Android Devices Troubleshoot Windows Mobile Devices
• Apps not loading	16	Troubleshoot iOS Devices Troubleshoot Android Devices Troubleshoot Windows Mobile Devices
• Slow performance	16	Troubleshoot iOS Devices Troubleshoot Android Devices Troubleshoot Windows Mobile Devices
• Unable to decrypt email	18	Common Mobile Device Malware Symptoms
• Extremely short battery life	16	Troubleshoot iOS Devices Troubleshoot Android Devices Troubleshoot Windows Mobile Devices
• Overheating	16	Troubleshoot iOS Devices Troubleshoot Android Devices Troubleshoot Windows Mobile Devices
• Frozen system	16	Troubleshoot iOS Devices Troubleshoot Android Devices Troubleshoot Windows Mobile Devices
• No sound from speakers	16	Troubleshoot iOS Devices Troubleshoot Android Devices Troubleshoot Windows Mobile Devices
• Inaccurate touch screen response	16	Troubleshoot iOS Devices Troubleshoot Android Devices Troubleshoot Windows Mobile Devices
• System lockout	18	Device Access Controls
Tools	16	Troubleshoot iOS Devices Troubleshoot Android Devices Troubleshoot Windows Mobile Devices
• Hard reset	16	Troubleshoot iOS Devices Troubleshoot Android Devices Troubleshoot Windows Mobile Devices
• Soft reset	16	Troubleshoot iOS Devices Troubleshoot Android Devices Troubleshoot Windows Mobile Devices

• Close running applications	16	Troubleshoot iOS Devices Troubleshoot Android Devices Troubleshoot Windows Mobile Devices
• Reset to factory default	16	Troubleshoot iOS Devices Troubleshoot Android Devices Troubleshoot Windows Mobile Devices
• Adjust configurations/settings	16	Troubleshoot iOS Devices Troubleshoot Android Devices Troubleshoot Windows Mobile Devices
• Uninstall/reinstall apps	16	Troubleshoot iOS Devices Troubleshoot Android Devices Troubleshoot Windows Mobile Devices
• Force stop	16	Troubleshoot iOS Devices Troubleshoot Android Devices Troubleshoot Windows Mobile Devices

4.4 **Given a scenario, troubleshoot common mobile OS and application security issues with appropriate tools.**

OBJECTIVES	CHAPTER	SECTION
◢ Common symptoms	18	
• Signal drop/weak signal	18	Common Mobile Device Malware Symptoms
• Power drain	18	Common Mobile Device Malware Symptoms
• Slow data speeds	18	Common Mobile Device Malware Symptoms
• Unintended WiFi connection	18	Common Mobile Device Malware Symptoms
• Unintended Bluetooth pairing	18	Common Mobile Device Malware Symptoms
• Leaked personal files/data	18	Common Mobile Device Malware Symptoms
• Data transmission overlimit	18	Common Mobile Device Malware Symptoms
• Unauthorized account access	18	Common Mobile Device Malware Symptoms
• Unauthorized root access	18	Common Mobile Device Malware Symptoms
• Unauthorized location tracking	18	Common Mobile Device Malware Symptoms
• Unauthorized camera/ microphone activation	18	Common Mobile Device Malware Symptoms
• High resource utilization	18	Common Mobile Device Malware Symptoms
◢ Tools		
• Antimalware	18	Mobile Device Tools and Malware Removal
• App scanner	18	Mobile Device Tools and Malware Removal
• Factory reset/Clean install	18	Mobile Device Tools and Malware Removal
• Uninstall/reinstall apps	18	Mobile Device Tools and Malware Removal
• WiFi analyzer	18	Mobile Device Tools and Malware Removal
• Force stop	18	Mobile Device Tools and Malware Removal
• Cell tower analyzer	18	Mobile Device Tools and Malware Removal
• Backup/restore	18	Mobile Device Tools and Malware Removal
○ iTunes/iCloud/Apple Configurator	16	Sync, Back Up, and Restore from Backup in iOS
○ Google sync	16	Sync, Update, Back Up, and Restore from Backup with Android
○ One Drive	16	Update and Restore Windows Phone from Backup

DOMAIN 5.0 OPERATIONAL PROCEDURES

5.1 Given a scenario, use appropriate safety procedures.

OBJECTIVES	CHAPTER	SECTION
◢ Equipment grounding	A	Protecting the Equipment
◢ Proper component handling and storage	A	Protecting the Equipment
• Antistatic bags	A	Protecting the Equipment
• ESD straps	A	Protecting the Equipment
• ESD mats	A	Protecting the Equipment
• Self-grounding	A	Protecting the Equipment
◢ Toxic waste handling	A	Protecting the Environment
• Batteries	A	Protecting the Environment
• Toner	A	Protecting the Environment
• CRT	A	Protecting the Environment
◢ Personal safety	A	Protecting Yourself
• Disconnect power before repairing PC	A	Protecting Yourself
• Remove jewelry	A	Protecting Yourself
• Lifting techniques	A	Protecting Yourself
• Weight limitations	A	Protecting Yourself
• Electrical fire safety	A	Protecting Yourself
• Cable management	A	Protecting Yourself
• Safety goggles	A	Protecting Yourself
• Air filter mask	A	Protecting Yourself
◢ Compliance with local government regulations	A	Protecting the Environment

5.2 Given a scenario with potential environmental impacts, apply the appropriate controls.

OBJECTIVES	CHAPTER	SECTION
◢ MSDS documentation for handling and disposal	A	Protecting the Environment
◢ Temperature, humidity level awareness and proper ventilation	A	Protecting the Equipment
◢ Power surges, brownouts, blackouts	A	Protecting the Equipment
• Battery backup	A	Protecting the Equipment
• Surge suppressor	A	Protecting the Equipment
◢ Protection from airborne particles	A	Protecting the Equipment
• Enclosures	A	Protecting the Equipment
• Air filters/Mask	A	Protecting Yourself
◢ Dust and debris	A	Protecting the Equipment
• Compressed air	A	Protecting the Equipment
• Vacuums	A	Protecting the Equipment
◢ Compliance to local government regulations	A	Protecting the Equipment

5.3 Summarize the process of addressing prohibited content/activity, and explain privacy, licensing, and policy concepts.

OBJECTIVES	CHAPTER	SECTION
◢ Incident Response	18	
• First response	18	Corporate Policies for Dealing with Prohibited Content or Activity
○ Identify	18	Corporate Policies for Dealing with Prohibited Content or Activity
○ Report through proper channels	18	Corporate Policies for Dealing with Prohibited Content or Activity
○ Data/device preservation	18	Corporate Policies for Dealing with Prohibited Content or Activity

• Use of documentation/ documentation changes	18	Corporate Policies for Dealing with Prohibited Content or Activity
• Chain of custody	18	Corporate Policies for Dealing with Prohibited Content or Activity
○ Tracking of evidence/ documenting process	18	Corporate Policies for Dealing with Prohibited Content or Activity
◢ Licensing / DRM / EULA	18	Software Licensing
• Open source vs. commercial license	18	Software Licensing
• Personal license vs. enterprise licenses	18	Software Licensing
◢ Personally Identifiable Information	18	Corporate Policies for Dealing with Prohibited Content or Activity
◢ Follow corporate end-user policies and security best practices	18	Educate Users

5.4 **Demonstrate proper communication techniques and professionalism.**

OBJECTIVES	CHAPTER	SECTION
◢ Use proper language – avoid jargon, acronyms, slang when applicable	12	What Customers Want: Beyond Technical Know-How
◢ Maintain a positive attitude / Project confidence	12	What Customers Want: Beyond Technical Know-How
◢ Actively listen (taking notes) and avoid interrupting the customer	12	What Customers Want: Beyond Technical Know-How
◢ Be culturally sensitive	12	What Customers Want: Beyond Technical Know-How
• Use appropriate professional titles, when applicable	12	What Customers Want: Beyond Technical Know-How
◢ Be on time (if late contact the customer)	12	What Customers Want: Beyond Technical Know-How
◢ Avoid distractions	12	What Customers Want: Beyond Technical Know-How
• Personal calls	12	What Customers Want: Beyond Technical Know-How
• Texting / Social media sites	12	What Customers Want: Beyond Technical Know-How
• Talking to co-workers while interacting with customers	12	What Customers Want: Beyond Technical Know-How
• Personal interruptions	12	What Customers Want: Beyond Technical Know-How
◢ Dealing with difficult customer or situation	12	What Customers Want: Beyond Technical Know-How
• Do not argue with customers and/ or be defensive	12	What Customers Want: Beyond Technical Know-How
• Avoid dismissing customer problems	12	What Customers Want: Beyond Technical Know-How
• Avoid being judgmental	12	What Customers Want: Beyond Technical Know-How
• Clarify customer statements (ask open ended questions to narrow the scope of the problem, restate the issue or question to verify understanding)	12	What Customers Want: Beyond Technical Know-How
• Do not disclose experiences via social media outlets	12	What Customers Want: Beyond Technical Know-How
◢ Set and meet expectations/timeline and communicate status with the customer	12	What Customers Want: Beyond Technical Know-How
• Offer different repair/replacement options if applicable	12	What Customers Want: Beyond Technical Know-How
• Provide proper documentation on the services provided	12	What Customers Want: Beyond Technical Know-How
• Follow up with customer/user at a later date to verify satisfaction	12	What Customers Want: Beyond Technical Know-How
◢ Deal appropriately with customers confidential and private materials	12	What Customers Want: Beyond Technical Know-How
• Located on a computer, desktop, printer, etc	12	What Customers Want: Beyond Technical Know-How

5.5 **Given a scenario, explain the troubleshooting theory.**

OBJECTIVES	CHAPTER	SECTION
◢ Always consider corporate policies, procedures and impacts before implementing changes.	12	
1. Identify the problem	12	Strategies to Troubleshoot Any Computer Problem
○ Question the user and identify user changes to computer and perform backups before making changes	12	Strategies to Troubleshoot Any Computer Problem
2. Establish a theory of probable cause (question the obvious)	12	Strategies to Troubleshoot Any Computer Problem
○ If necessary, conduct external or internal research based on symptoms	12	Strategies to Troubleshoot Any Computer Problem
3. Test the theory to determine cause	12	Strategies to Troubleshoot Any Computer Problem
○ Once theory is confirmed determine next steps to resolve problem	12	Strategies to Troubleshoot Any Computer Problem
○ If theory is not confirmed re-establish new theory or escalate	12	Strategies to Troubleshoot Any Computer Problem
4. Establish a plan of action to resolve the problem and implement the solution	12	Strategies to Troubleshoot Any Computer Problem
5. Verify full system functionality and if applicable implement preventive measures	12	Strategies to Troubleshoot Any Computer Problem
6. Document findings, actions and outcomes	12	Strategies to Troubleshoot Any Computer Problem

Introduction: CompTIA A+ Guide to IT Technical Support

CompTIA A+ Guide to IT Technical Support, Ninth Edition was written to be the very best tool on the market today to prepare you to support desktop and laptop computers as well as mobile devices. Previously titled, *A+ Guide to Mangaging and Maintaining Your PC* for eight editions, the text has been updated to include the most current hardware and software technologies, this book takes you from the just-a-user level to the I-can-fix-this level for hardware and software matters. It achieves its goals with an unusually effective combination of tools that powerfully reinforce both concepts and hands-on, real-world experiences. It also provides thorough preparation for the content on the new CompTIA A+ 220-901 and 220-902 Certification exams. Competency in using a computer is a prerequisite to using this book. No background knowledge of electronics is assumed. An appropriate prerequisite course for this book would be a general course in computer applications.

This book includes:

- ***Several in-depth, hands-on projects*** are spaced throughout each chapter that invite you to immediately apply and reinforce critical thinking and troubleshooting skills and are designed to make certain that you not only understand the material, but also execute procedures and make decisions on your own.
- ***Comprehensive review and practice end-of-chapter material***, including a chapter summary, key terms, review questions that focus on A+ content, critical thinking questions, and real-world problems to solve.
- ***Step-by-step instructions*** on installation, maintenance, optimization of system performance, and troubleshooting.
- ***A wide array of photos, drawings, and screen shots*** support the text, displaying in detail the exact software and hardware features you will need to understand to set up, maintain, and troubleshoot personal computers and small networks.

In addition, the carefully structured, clearly written text is accompanied by graphics that provide the visual input essential to learning and to help students master difficult subject matter. For instructors using the book in a classroom, instructor resources are available online.

Coverage is balanced—while focusing on new hardware and software, the text also covers the real work of an IT support technician, where some older technology remains in widespread use and still needs support. For example, the book covers how to use a 64-bit operating system to support the latest processors, but also addresses how to get the most out of a 32-bit OS with limited hardware resources. At the time of writing this text, Windows 8 and Windows 7 are the most popular Microsoft operating systems used on desktop and laptop computers. The text focuses on supporting Windows 8/7 systems, while also including light coverage of Windows Vista where knowledge of Vista is necessary for the CompTIA A+ 900 series exams. The text also has light coverage of Linux and Mac OS X operating systems for desktops and laptops and Android, iOS, and Windows Phone operating systems for mobile devices. Other new technologies covered include virtualization, cloud computing, UEFI firmware, GPT partitioning systems, and support for mobile device hardware.

This book provides thorough preparation for CompTIA's A+ 220-901 and 220-902 Certification examinations. This certification credential's popularity among employers is growing exponentially, and obtaining certification increases your ability to gain employment and improve your salary. To get more information on CompTIA's A+ certification and its sponsoring organization, the Computing Technology Industry Association, see their website at *www.comptia.org*.

FEATURES

To ensure a successful learning experience, this book includes the following pedagogical features:

- *Learning Objectives.* Every chapter opens with a list of learning objectives that sets the stage for you to absorb the lessons of the text.
- *Comprehensive Step-by-Step Troubleshooting Guidance.* Troubleshooting guidelines are included in almost every chapter. In addition, the chapter, "Supporting the Power System and Troubleshooting Computers," gives insights into general approaches to troubleshooting that help apply the specifics detailed in each chapter for different hardware and software problems. The chapters, "Supporting Customers and Troubleshooting Windows" and "Troubleshooting Windows Startup," also focus on troubleshooting applications and Windows.
- *Step-by-Step Procedures.* The book is chock-full of step-by-step procedures covering subjects from hardware and operating system installations and maintenance to troubleshooting the boot process or a failed network connection and optimizing system performance.
- *Art Program.* Numerous visually detailed photographs, three-dimensional art, and screen shots support the text, displaying hardware and software features exactly as you will see them in your work.
- *CompTIA A+ Table of Contents.* This table of contents gives the chapter and section that provides the primary content for each certification objective on the A+ exams. This is a valuable tool for quick reference.
- *Hands-On Projects.* These sections give you practice using the skills you have just studied so that you can learn by doing and know you have mastered a skill.
- *Applying Concepts.* These sections offer real-life, practical applications for the material being discussed. Whether outlining a task, developing a scenario, or providing pointers, the Applying Concepts sections give you a chance to apply what you've learned to a typical computer or network problem, so you can understand how you will use the material in your professional life.

A+ 220-901 A+ 220-902

A+ Icons. All of the content that relates to CompTIA's A+ 220-901 and A+ 220-902 Certification exams is highlighted with an A+ icon. The icon notes the exam name and the objective number. This unique feature highlights the relevant content at a glance, so that you can pay extra attention to the material.

Notes

Notes. Note icons highlight additional helpful information related to the subject being discussed.

A+ Exam Tip

A+ Exam Tip Boxes. These boxes highlight additional insights and tips to remember if you are planning to take the CompTIA A+ exams.

Caution

Caution Icons. These icons highlight critical safety information. Follow these instructions carefully to protect the computer and its data and to ensure your own safety.

OS Differences

OS Differences. These boxes point you to the differences among Windows 8, Windows 7, and Vista.

- *End-of-Chapter Material*. Each chapter closes with the following features, which reinforce the material covered in the chapter and provide real-world, hands-on testing:
  - *Chapter Summary*: This bulleted list of concise statements summarizes all major points of the chapter.
  - *Key Terms*: The content of each chapter is further reinforced by an end-of-chapter key term list. The definitions of all terms are included with this text in a full-length glossary.
  - *Review Questions*: You can test your understanding of each chapter with a comprehensive set of review questions. The "Reviewing the Basics" questions check your understanding of fundamental concepts focused on A+ content, while the "Thinking Critically" questions help you synthesize and apply what you've learned and also focus on A+ content.
  - *Real Problems, Real Solutions*: Each comprehensive problem allows you to find out if you can apply what you've learned in the chapter to a real-life situation.
- *Student Companion Site*. The companion website includes older content and additional resources that still might be important in some repair situations. The content includes the following historical and older content that might still be important in some computer repair situations. The content: The Hexademical Number System and Memory Addressing, Supporting Windows XP, Electricity and Multimeters, Facts About Legacy Motherboards, How an OS Uses System Resources, Facts About Legacy Processors, All About SCSI, Behind the Scenes with DEBUG, FAT Details, and Selecting and Installing Hard Drives Using Legacy Motherboards. Other helpful online references include Frequently Asked Questions, Sample Reports, Computer Inventory and Maintenance form, and Troubleshooting Flowcharts. A video archive of clips that feature Jean Andrews illustrating concepts and providing advice on the real world of computer repair is also included.

WHAT'S NEW IN THE NINTH EDITION

Here's a summary of what's new in the *Ninth Edition*:

- Content maps to all of CompTIA's A+ 220-901 and 220-902 exams.
- There is now more focus on A+, with non-A+ content moved online to the companion website or eliminated.
- The chapters focus on Windows 8 and Windows 7 with slight content about Windows Vista.
- New content is added (all new content was also new to the A+ 220-901 and 220-902 exams).
  - Windows 8 is added. Operating systems covered are now Windows 8, Windows 7, and Vista. New content on Linux, Mac OS X, and mobile operating systems (Android, iOS, and Windows Phone) is added.
  - Fifth Generation (Broadwell) and Fourth Generation (Haswell) processor and chipset architectures by Intel are covered in the chapter, "Supporting Processors and Upgrading Memory."
  - Enhanced content on supporting UEFI firmware is now included.

- Enhanced content on supporting mobile devices (including the Android OS, iOS, and Windows Phone) is covered in the chapter, "Supporting Mobile Operating Systems."
- New content on virtual printing and cloud printing is added to the chapter, "Supporting Printers and Customizing a System."
- Hands-On Projects in several chapters use virtual machines so that you get plenty of practice using this up-and-coming technology.
- New content on virtualization and supporting the Linux and Mac OS X operating systems is covered in the chapter, "Virtualization, Linux, and Mac OS X."
- New content on networking hardware devices, including patch panels, repeaters, extenders, EoP, PoE injectors, and Wi-Fi analyzers, is covered in the chapter, "Supporting Network Hardware."
- Enhanced content on mobile device hardware is covered in the chapter, "First Look at Computer Parts and Tools."
- Supporting GPT hard drives and Storage Spaces is covered in the chapter, "Maintaining Windows."
- Supporting and troubleshooting laptops is integrated throughout the text.

FEATURES OF THE NEW EDITION

Chapter **objectives** appear at the beginning of each chapter, so you know exactly what topics and skills are covered.

A+ Exam Tips include key points pertinent to the A+ exams. The icons identify the sections that cover information you will need to know for the A+ certification exams.

CHAPTER 14

Connecting To and Setting Up a Network

After completing this chapter, you will be able to:

- Explain the TCP/IP protocols and standards Windows uses for networking
- Connect a computer to a wired or wireless network
- Configure and secure a multifunction router on a local network

In this chapter, you learn how Windows uses TCP/IP protocols and standards to create and manage network connections, including how computers are identified and addressed on a network. You also learn to connect a computer to a network and how to set up and secure a small wired or wireless network.

This chapter prepares you to assume total responsibility for supporting both wired and wireless networks in a small-office/home-office (SOHO) environment. In the chapter, "Supporting Network Hardware," you learn more about the hardware used in networking, including network devices, connectors, cabling, networking tools, and the types of networks used for Internet connections. So let's get started by looking at how TCP/IP works in the world of Windows networking.

A+ Exam Tip Much of the content in this chapter applies to both the A+ 220-901 exam and the A+ 220-902 exam.

Caution You can damage a computer component with static electricity if you touch the component when you are not grounded. Before you touch a sensitive computer component, you first need to dissipate any static electricity on your body. You learn how to do that in the appendix, "Safety Procedures and Environmental Concerns." For now, to protect a working component your instructor has on display, don't touch; just look.

Hands-On Project 1-2 Examine the Power Supply, Motherboard, and Expansion Cards Inside a Desktop Case

A+ 220-901 1.7, 1.8, 1.11

If you have access to a desktop computer with the case cover removed, examine its components and answer the following questions. As you look, remember to not touch anything inside the case unless you are properly grounded.

1. Identify the power supply, motherboard, and any expansion cards that might be installed on the motherboard. Remember: Don't touch a component unless you are properly grounded. If the case is plugged into a power source, don't touch inside the case even if you are grounded.
2. Identify the cooler that is installed on top of the processor. This cooler is likely to have a fan on top and a heat sink that you can't see. The processor is hidden under the cooler.
3. Identify the memory modules and memory slots. How many memory slots are there? How many of these slots are populated?
4. If an expansion card is installed, what type of ports does the card provide at the rear of the case? Find the one screw that is used to attach the expansion card to the case.
5. Locate the screws that are attaching the motherboard to the case. How many screws are used? Do you see screw holes in the motherboard that are not being used? As a general rule of thumb, up to nine screws can be used to attach a motherboard to a case.
6. How many power cables are coming from the power supply? How many of these cables are connected to the motherboard? To other devices inside the computer? Identify each type of power cable the system is using.
7. Find the screws or clips that are attaching the power supply to the case. Is the power supply attached using screws, clips, or both screws and clips?

Cautions identify critical safety information.

Hands-On Projects provide practical exercises throughout each chapter so that you can practice the skills as they are learned.

Notes indicate additional content that might be of student interest or information about how best to study.

Notes Be aware that a laptop might show the Bluetooth icon in the taskbar even when the laptop does not support Bluetooth.

APPLYING | CONCEPTS MAKE A STRAIGHT-THROUGH CABLE USING T568B WIRING

A+ 220-901 2.1, 2.2, 2.9, 4.4

It takes a little practice to make a good network straight-through cable, but you'll get the hang of it after doing only a couple of cables. Figure 15-34 shows the materials and tools you'll need to make a network cable.

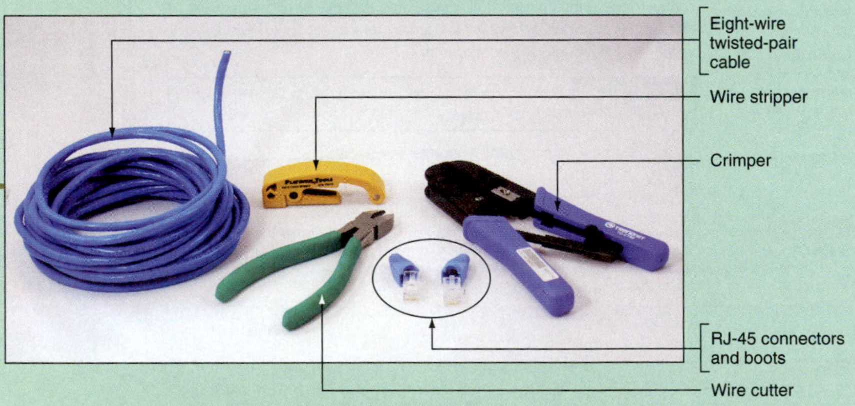

Figure 15-34 Tools and materials to make a network cable

Here are the steps to make a straight-through cable using the T568B standard:

1. Use wire cutters to cut the twisted-pair cable the correct length plus a few extra inches.
2. If your RJ-45 connectors include boots, slide two boots onto the cable.
3. Use wire strippers to strip off about two inches of the plastic jacket from the end of the wire. To do that, put the wire in the stripper and rotate the stripper around the wire to score the jacket (see Figure 15-35). You can then pull off the jacket.

Visual full-color graphics, photos, and screen shots accurately depict computer hardware and software components.

Applying Concepts sections provide practical advice or pointers by illustrating basic principles, identifying common problems, providing steps to practice skills, and encouraging creating solutions.

Chapter Summary bulleted lists of concise statements summarize all major points of the chapter, organized by primary headings.

>> CHAPTER SUMMARY

How to Work Inside a Desktop Computer Case

- When a hardware support technician is disassembling or reassembling a computer, it is important to stay organized, keep careful notes, and follow all the safety procedures to protect the computer equipment.
- Before opening a computer case, shut down the system, unplug it, disconnect all cables, and press the power button to drain residual power.
- An expansion card fits in a slot on the motherboard and is anchored to the case by a single screw or clip.

>> KEY TERMS

For explanations of key terms, see the Glossary for this text.

front panel connector
front panel header
spacer
standoff
ZIF connector

>> REVIEWING THE BASICS

1. When taking a computer apart, why is it important to not stack boards on top of each other?
2. Why is it important to remove loose jewelry before working inside a computer case?
3. When assembling a desktop computer, which do you install first, the drives or the motherboard?
4. What is the purpose of raised screw holes or standoffs installed between the motherboard and desktop case?
5. When installing the front panel wires to the motherboard front panel header, how do you know which pins to use for each wire if the pins on the header are not labeled?
6. How many pins does the CPU auxiliary power connector on a motherboard have?
7. Why are laptops usually more expensive than desktop computers with comparable power and features?
8. Why is the service manual so important to have when you disassemble a laptop?
9. When a laptop internal device fails, what three options can you use to deal with the problem?
10. After you have removed the AC adapter and all peripherals, what is the next component you should always remove before servicing any internal laptop components?

Key Terms are defined as they are introduced and listed at the end of each chapter. Definitions can be found in the Glossary.

Reviewing the Basics sections check understanding of fundamental concepts.

Thinking Critically sections require you to analyze and apply what you've learned.

>> THINKING CRITICALLY

1. You disassemble and reassemble a desktop computer. When you first turn it on, you see no lights and hear no sounds. Nothing appears on the monitor screen. What is the most likely cause of the problem? Explain your answer.
   a. A memory module is not seated properly in a memory slot.
   b. You forgot to plug up the monitor's external power cord.
   c. A wire in the case is obstructing a fan.
   d. Power cords to the motherboard are not connected.

>> REAL PROBLEMS, REAL SOLUTIONS

REAL PROBLEM 2-1 Taking a Lab Computer Apart and Putting It Back Together

A PC technician needs to be comfortable with taking apart a computer and putting it back together. In most situations, the essential tools you'll need for the job are an ESD strap, a Phillips-head screwdriver, a flathead screwdriver, paper, and pen.

Working with a partner and using a lab computer designated to be disassembled, take a computer apart. It is not necessary to remove the processor or memory modules from the motherboard, but be very careful to properly support the motherboard and processor as you remove them from the case. Then reassemble the system. Don't replace the computer case panel until your instructor has inspected all cable connections. Then turn on the computer and verify that all is working.

REAL PROBLEM 2-2 Setting Up a Service Center for Laptops

If you intend to set up your own computer repair shop, you might want to consider becoming a service center for a few brands of the more popular laptops. Reasons to become an authorized service center are that you have access to service manuals, parts lists, and wholesale parts for laptops. Do the following to research becoming an authorized service center:

1. Select a brand of laptops that you think you would like to service.
2. Research the website of this manufacturer and answer these questions:
   a. Where is the closest authorized service center for this brand of laptops?
   b. What are the requirements to become an authorized service center? Print the webpage showing the requirements.
   c. Is A+ certification one of those requirements?

Real Problems, Real Solutions allow you to apply what you've learned in the chapter to a real-life situation.

WHAT'S NEW WITH CompTIA® A+ CERTIFICATION

The CompTIA A+ exams include two exams, and you must pass both to become CompTIA A+ certified. The two exams are 220-901 and 220-902.

Here is a breakdown of the domain content covered on the two A+ exams.

CompTIA A+ 220-901 Exam	
Domain	**Percentage of Examination**
1.0 Hardware	34%
2.0 Networking	21%
3.0 Mobile Devices	17%
4.0 Hardware & Network Troubleshooting	28%
Total	100%

CompTIA A+ 220-902 Exam	
Domain	**Percentage of Examination**
1.0 Windows Operating Systems	29%
2.0 Other Operating Systems & Technologies	12%
3.0 Security	22%
4.0 Software Troubleshooting	24%
5.0 Operational Procedures	13%
Total	100%

CompTIA AUTHORIZED QUALITY CONTENT

CompTIA A+ Guide to IT Technical Support, Ninth Edition has earned CompTIA's Authorized Quality Content approval. The text has been reviewed and approved by ProCert Labs, a CompTIA appointed third party. CAQC approval indicates the textbook material meets CompTIA's comprehensive coverage of the exam objectives, instructional design standards and high quality criteria.

DISCOUNTED CompTIA CERTIFICATION EXAM VOUCHERS

As a CompTIA Authorized Partner, Cengage Learning is able to provide you with a promo code that saves you 10% off the non-member price of a CompTIA Exam voucher when purchased through the CompTIA Marketplace.

Save 10% when you use coupon code **CL10Percent** during checkout. Redeeming the coupon code is easy:

1. Go to **www.comptiastore.com.**
2. Select the CompTIA Certification you want.
3. Add the voucher to the cart (note that for A+ you will need a separate voucher for each exam).
4. Enter the code **CL10Percent** on the purchase screen and click **Apply**.

INSTRUCTOR'S MATERIALS

Please visit *login.cengage.com* and log in to access instructor-specific resources on the Instructor Companion Site, which includes the Instructor's Manual, Solutions Manual, Test creation tools, PowerPoint Presentation, Syllabus, and figure files.

Instructor's Manual: The Instructor's Manual that accompanies this textbook includes additional instructional material to assist in class preparation, including suggestions for classroom activities, discussion topics, and additional projects.

Solutions: Answers to the end-of-chapter material are provided. These include the answers to the Review Questions, Thinking Critically, and to the Hands-On Projects (when applicable), as well as Lab Manual Solutions.

Cengage Learning Testing Powered by Cognero: This flexible, online system allows you to do the following:

- Author, edit, and manage test bank content from multiple Cengage Learning solutions.
- Create multiple test versions in an instant.
- Deliver tests from your LMS, your classroom, or wherever you want.

PowerPoint Presentations: This book comes with Microsoft PowerPoint slides for each chapter. These are included as a teaching aid for classroom presentation, to make available to students on the network for chapter review, or to be printed for classroom distribution. Instructors, please feel at liberty to add your own slides for additional topics you introduce to the class.

Figure Files: All of the figures in the book are reproduced on the Instructor Companion Site. Similar to the PowerPoint presentations, these are included as a teaching aid for classroom presentation, to make available to students for review, or to be printed for classroom distribution.

TOTAL SOLUTIONS FOR CompTIA A+

MINDTAP FOR A+ GUIDE TO IT TECHNICAL SUPPORT, NINTH EDITION

MindTap is an online learning solution designed to help students master the skills they need in today's workforce. Research shows employers need critical thinkers, troubleshooters and creative problem-solvers to stay relevant in our fast paced technology-driven world. MindTap helps you achieve this with assignments and activities that provides hands-practice, real life relevance and certification test prep. Students are guided through assignments that help them master basic knowledge and understanding before moving on to more challenging problems.

MindTap activities and assignments are tied to CompTIA A+ certification exam objectives. The hands-on labs provide real-life application and practice. The IQ certification test prep engine allows students to quiz themselves on specific exam domains, and the pre- and post- course assessments are mock exams that measure exactly how much they have learned. Readings and "whiteboard shorts" support the lecture, while "In The News" assignments encourage students to stay current. MindTap is designed around learning objectives and provides the analytics and reporting to easily see where the class stands in terms of progress, engagement and completion rates. Use the content and learning path as-is or pick-and-choose how our materials will wrap around yours. You control what the students see and when they see it. Learn more at *http://www.cengage.com/mindtap/*.

- Instant Access Code: (ISBN: 9781305944558)
- Printed Access Code: (ISBN: 9781305944565)

LAB MANUAL FOR A+ GUIDE TO IT TECHNICAL SUPPORT, NINTH EDITION

This Lab Manual contains over 130 labs to provide students with additional hands-on experience and to help prepare for the A+ exam. The *Lab Manual* includes lab activities, objectives, materials lists, step-by-step procedures, illustrations, and review questions.

- Lab Manual (ISBN: 9781305266544)

COURSENOTES

This laminated quick reference card reinforces critical knowledge for CompTIA's A+ exam in a visual and user-friendly format. CourseNotes will serve as a useful study aid, supplement to the textbook, or as a quick reference tool during the course and afterward.

- A+ Exam #220-901 CourseNotes (ISBN: 9781305269248)
- A+ Exam #220-902 CourseNotes (ISBN: 9781305269255)

PC TROUBLESHOOTING POCKET GUIDE, NINTH EDITION

This compact and portable volume is designed to help students and technicians diagnose any computer problem quickly and efficiently. This guide is up to date and current for today's technologies (ISBN: 9781305266537).

ACKNOWLEDGMENTS

Thank you to the wonderful people at Cengage who continue to give their best and to go the extra mile to make the books what they are: Kristin McNary, Amy Savino, Michelle Ruelos Cannistraci, and Brooke Greenhouse. I'm grateful for all you've done. Thank you, Deb Kaufmann, our Developmental Editor extraordinaire, for your careful attention to detail and your awesome commitment to excellence, and to Karen Annett, our excellent copyeditor/proofreader. Thank you, Serge Palladino, for your careful attention to the technical accuracy of the book.

Thank you to all the people who took the time to voluntarily send encouragement and suggestions for improvements to the previous editions. Your input and help is very much appreciated. The reviewers of this edition all provided invaluable insights and showed a genuine interest in the book's success. Thank you to:

Susan Booth – Cape Fear Community College
Ron Cannon – Wichita Technical Institute
Steve Ebben – Fox Valley Technical College, Appleton
Glenn Goe – Stark State College
Abigale Trimble – Wichita Technical Institute

To the instructors and learners who use this book, we invite and encourage you to send suggestions or corrections for future editions. Please write to the author team at *jean.andrews@cengage.com*. We never ignore a good idea! And to instructors, if you have ideas for how to make a class in A+ Preparation a success, please share your ideas with other instructors! You can find us on Facebook at *http://www.facebook.com/JeanKnows*, where you can interact with the authors and other instructors.

This book is dedicated to the covenant of God with man on earth.

Jean Andrews, Ph.D.
Joy Dark
Jill West

ABOUT THE AUTHORS

Jean Andrews has more than 30 years of experience in the computer industry, including more than 13 years in the college classroom. She has worked in a variety of businesses and corporations designing, writing, and supporting application software; managing a PC repair help desk; and troubleshooting wide area networks. She has written numerous books on software, hardware, and the Internet, including the best-selling *A+ Guide to Hardware, Ninth Edition* and *A+ Guide to Software: Managing, Maintaining and Troubleshooting, Ninth Edition*. She lives in northern Georgia.

Joy Dark has worked in the IT field as a help-desk technician providing first-level support for a company with presence in 29 states, a second-tier technician in healthcare IT, and an operations specialist designing support protocols and structures finding her CompTIA A+ and HIT certifications useful. As a teacher, Joy has taught online courses in IT with the Stride Center in California and has taught English as a Second Language in the United States and South America. She has helped write several technical textbooks with Jean Andrews, her mother, and Jill West, her sister. Joy lives in Dalton, Georgia, with her two daughters and Doberman dog.

Jill West brings a unique variety of experience in writing, business, and education to the development of her innovative educational materials. She has taught multiple ages and content areas using a flipped classroom approach, distance learning, and educational counseling. Jill's résumé includes service with a nonprofit agency to inner-city disadvantaged populations, on-the-job training with a law firm, ten years working with Jean Andrews in textbook development, multiple entrepreneurial ventures, and CompTIA A+ and Network+ certifications. Her insights into the art of self-teaching provide students with effective tools for taking ownership of their own learning. Jill and her husband Mike live in the hills of northwest Georgia where they homeschool their four children.

READ THIS BEFORE YOU BEGIN

The following hardware, software, and other equipment are needed to do the Hands-On Projects in each chapter:

- You need a working desktop computer and laptop that can be taken apart and reassembled. You also need a working computer on which you can install an operating system. These computers can be the same or different computers. Use a Pentium or higher computer.
- Troubleshooting skills can better be practiced with an assortment of nonworking expansion cards that can be used to simulate problems.
- Windows 8 Professional and Windows 7 Professional are needed for most chapters. In addition, the Mac OS X is used in the chapter, "Virtualization, Linux, and Mac OS X."
- Internet access is needed for most chapters.
- Equipment required to work on hardware includes an ESD strap and flathead and Phillips-head screwdrivers. In addition, a power supply tester, cable tester, and can of compressed air are useful. Network wiring tools needed for the chapter, "Supporting Network Hardware," include a wire cutter, wire stripper, and crimper.
- An iOS or Android smart phone or tablet is needed for the chapter, "Supporting Mobile Operating Systems."
- A SOHO router that includes a wireless access point is needed for the chapter, "Connecting To and Setting Up a Network."

Caution Before undertaking any of the lab exercises, starting with the chapter, "First Look at Computer Parts and Tools," please review the safety guidelines in the appendix, "Safety Procedures and Environmental Concerns."

CHAPTER 1

First Look at Computer Parts and Tools

After completing this chapter, you will be able to:

- Identify the various parts inside a desktop computer case and describe how they connect together and are compatible
- Identify the various ports, slots, and internal components of a laptop computer and explain special concerns when supporting and maintaining laptops
- Describe various hardware components in mobile devices and types of wired and wireless connections mobile devices can make
- Describe the purpose of various tools you will need as a computer hardware technician

Like many other computer users, you have probably used your personal computer to play games, update your Facebook profile, write papers, or build Excel worksheets. This text takes you from being an end user of your computer to becoming an information technology (IT) support technician able to support all types of personal computers. The only assumption made here is that you are a computer user—that is, you can turn on your machine, load a software package, and use that software to accomplish a task. No experience in electronics is assumed.

As an IT support technician, you'll want to become A+ certified, which is the industry standard certification for IT support technicians. This text prepares you to pass the A+ 220-901 and 220-902 exams by CompTIA (*www.comptia.org*). The exams are required by CompTIA for A+ Certification.

In this chapter, you learn to recognize various hardware components you'll find inside desktop computer and laptop cases and about the tools you'll need to work inside the case. Later in the text, you learn to take a desktop and laptop apart and reassemble them.

★ A+ Exam Tip As you work your way through a chapter, notice the green and blue A+ mapping icons underneath headings. These page elements help you know to which objectives on which exam the content applies. After studying each chapter, take a look at the grid at the beginning of this text and make sure you understand each objective listed in the grid that is covered in the chapter.

WHAT'S INSIDE A DESKTOP CASE

A+ 220-901 1.7, 1.8, 1.11

Before we discuss the parts inside a desktop case, let's take a quick look at the case and the ports and switches on it. A computer case for any type of computer is sometimes called the chassis and houses the power supply, motherboard, processor, memory modules, expansion cards, hard drive, optical drive, and other drives. A computer case can be a tower case, a desktop case that lies flat on a desk, an all-in-one case used with an all-in-one computer, or a mobile case used with laptops and tablets. A tower case (see Figure 1-1) sits upright and can be as high as two feet and has room for several drives. Often used for servers, this type of case is also good for desktop computer users who anticipate upgrading, because tower cases provide maximum space for working inside a computer and moving components around. A desktop case lies flat and sometimes serves double-duty as a monitor stand. In the chapter, "Working Inside Desktop Computers and Laptops," you learn how to work inside a tower case, desktop case, laptop case, and all-in-one case.

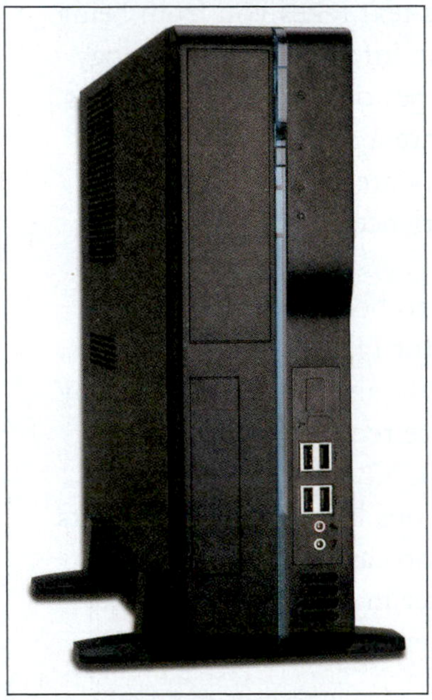

© Courtesy of IN WIN Development, Inc.

Figure 1-1 This slimline tower case supports a microATX motherboard

Notes Don't lay a tower case on its side when the computer is in use because the CD or DVD drive might not work properly. For the same reason, if a desktop case is designed to lie flat, don't set it on its end when the computer is in use.

Table 1-1 lists ports you might find on a desktop or mobile computer. Consider this table your introduction to these ports so that you can recognize them when you see them. Later in the text, you learn more about the details of each port.

A+ Exam Tip The A+ 220-901 exam expects you to know how to identify the ports shown in Table 1-1.

Port	Description
	A VGA (Video Graphics Array) port, also called a DB-15 port, DB15 port, HD15 port, or DE15 port, is a 15-pin, D-shaped, female port that transmits analog video. (Analog means a continuous signal with infinite variations as compared with digital, which is a series of binary values—1s and 0s.) All older monitors use VGA ports. (By the way, the HD15 [high-definition 15-pin] name for the port is an older name that distinguishes it from the early 9-pin VGA ports.)
	An S-Video port is a 4-pin or 7-pin round video port sometimes used to connect to a television. The 7-pin port is shown on the left. The 4-pin port is missing the extra pins in the middle and is the more common type.

Table 1-1 Ports used with desktop and mobile computers (continues)

Port	Description
	A DVI (Digital Video Interface) port transmits digital or analog video. Three types of DVI ports exist, which you learn about in the chapter, "Supporting I/O Devices."
	An HDMI (High-Definition Multimedia Interface) port transmits digital video and audio (not analog transmissions) and is often used to connect to home theater equipment.
	A DisplayPort transmits digital video and audio (not analog transmissions) and is slowly replacing VGA and DVI ports on personal computers.
 Courtesy of Creative Commons Attribution 3.0, Macfan97	A Thunderbolt port transmits video, data, and power on the same port and cable and is popular with Apple computers. The port is shaped the same as the DisplayPort and is compatible with DisplayPort devices. Up to six peripherals (for example, monitors and external hard drives daisy-chained together) can use the same Thunderbolt port.
	A network port, also called an Ethernet port, or an RJ-45 port, is used by a network cable to connect to the wired network. Fast Ethernet ports run at 100 Mbps (megabits per second), and Gigabit Ethernet runs at 1000 Mbps or 1 Gbps (gigabits per second). A megabit is one million bits and a gigabit is one billion bits. A bit is a binary value of 1 or 0.
	A system usually has three or more round audio ports, also called sound ports, for a microphone, audio in, audio out, and stereo audio out. These types of audio ports can transmit analog or digital data. If you have one audio cable to connect to a speaker or earbuds, plug it into the lime green sound port in the middle of the three ports. The microphone uses the pink port.
	An S/PDIF (Sony/Philips Digital Interface) sound port connects to an external home theater audio system, providing digital audio output and the best signal quality. S/PDIF ports always carry digital audio and can work with electrical or optical cable. When connected to a fiber-optic cable, the port is called an optical connector.
	A USB (Universal Serial Bus) port is a multipurpose I/O port that comes in several sizes and is used by many different devices, including printers, mice, keyboards, scanners, external hard drives, and flash drives. Some USB ports are faster than others. Hi-Speed USB 2.0 is faster than regular USB, and Super-Speed USB 3.0 is faster than USB 2.0.
	A FireWire port (also called an IEEE 1394 port, pronounced "I-triple-E 1394 port") is used for high-speed multimedia devices such as digital camcorders.

Table 1-1 Ports used with desktop and mobile computers (continues)

Port	Description
	An external SATA (eSATA) port is used by an external hard drive or other device using the eSATA interface. eSATA is faster than FireWire.
	A PS/2 port, also called a mini-DIN port, is a round 6-pin port used by a keyboard or mouse. The ports look alike but are not interchangeable. On a desktop, the purple port is for the keyboard, and the green port is for the mouse. Many newer computers use USB ports for the keyboard and mouse rather than the older PS/2 ports.
	An older serial port, sometimes called a DB9 port, is a 9-pin male port used on older computers. It has been mostly replaced by USB ports. Occasionally, you see a serial port on a router where the port is used to connect the router to a device a technician can use to monitor and manage the router.
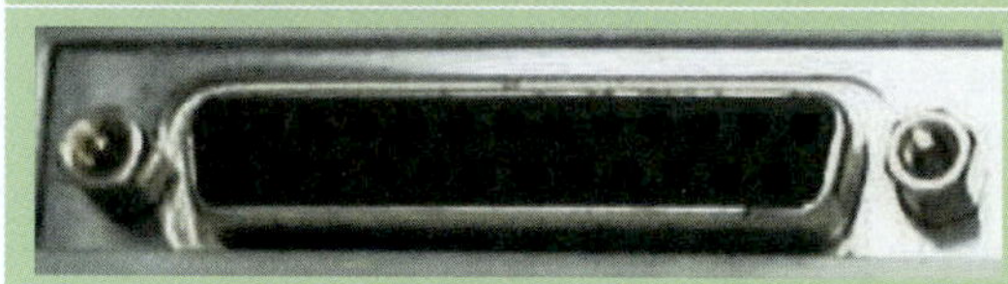	A parallel port, also called an LPT port, is a 25-pin female port used by older printers. This older port has been replaced by USB ports.
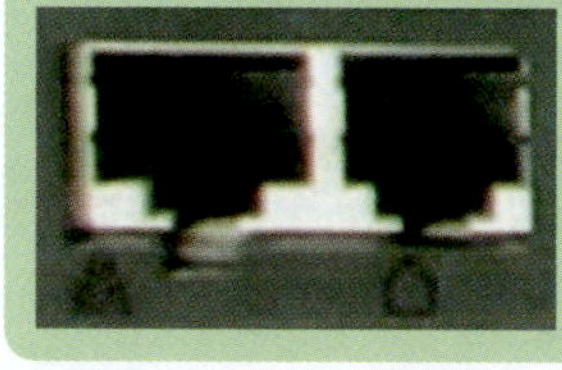	A modem port, also called an RJ-11 port, is used to connect dial-up phone lines to computers. A modem port looks like a network port, but is not as wide. In the photo, the right port is a modem port and the left port is a network port, shown for comparison.

Table 1-1 Ports used with desktop and mobile computers (continued)

I know you're eager to open a case and work inside it, but first let's get familiar with the major components in the case and how to work with them safely so you don't fry a motherboard or bend delicate connectors. Figure 1-2 shows the inside of a computer case.

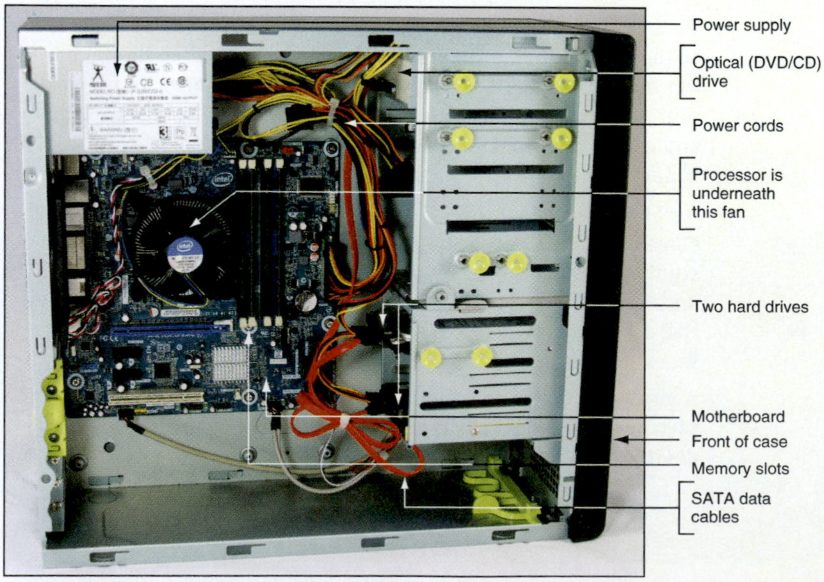

Figure 1-2 Inside the computer case

Here is a quick explanation of the main components installed in the case, which are called internal components:

- ***The motherboard, processor, and cooler.*** The motherboard, also called the main board, the system board, or the techie jargon term, the mobo, is the largest and most important circuit board in the computer. The motherboard contains a socket to hold the processor or CPU. The central processing unit (CPU), also called the processor or microprocessor, does most of the processing of data and instructions for the entire system. Because the CPU generates heat, a fan and heat sink might be installed on top to keep it cool. A heat sink consists of metal fins that draw heat away from a component. The fan and heat sink together are called the processor cooler. Figure 1-3 shows the top view of a motherboard, and Figure 1-4 shows the ports on the side of a motherboard.

Figure 1-3 All hardware components are either located on the motherboard or directly or indirectly connected to it because they must all communicate with the CPU

Figure 1-4 Ports provided by a motherboard

- *Expansion cards.* A motherboard has expansion slots to be used by expansion cards. An expansion card, also called an adapter card, is a circuit board that provides more ports than those provided by the motherboard. Figure 1-5 shows a video card that provides three video ports. Notice the cooling fan and heat sink on the card, which help to keep the card from overheating. The trend today is for most ports in a system to be provided by the motherboard (called onboard ports) and less use of expansion cards.

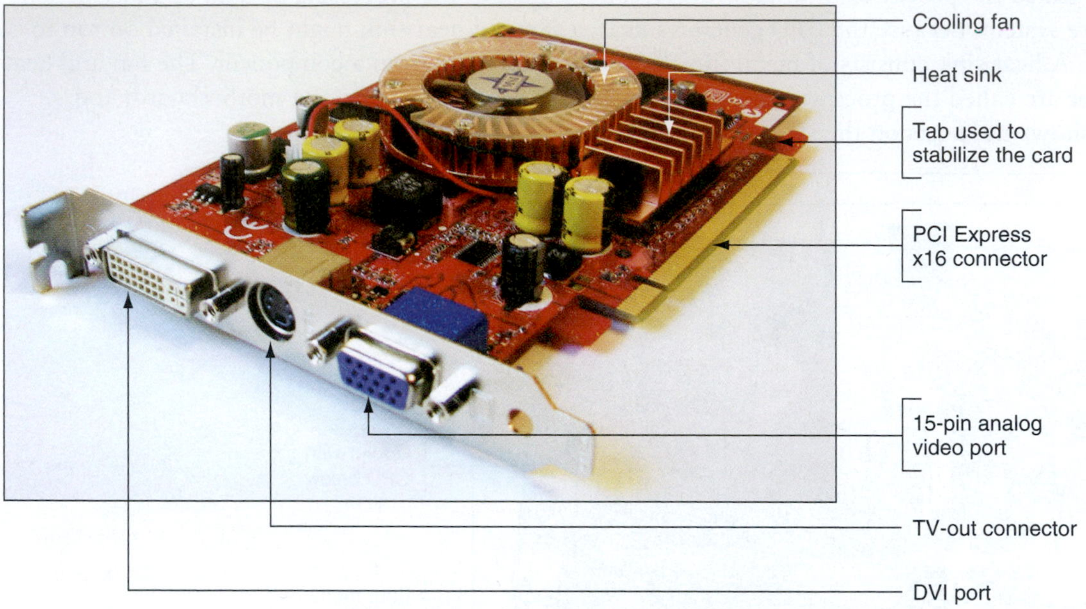

Figure 1-5 The easiest way to identify this video card is to look at the ports on the end of the card

- *Memory modules.* A desktop motherboard has memory slots, called DIMM (dual inline memory module) slots, to hold memory modules. Figure 1-6 shows a memory module installed in one DIMM slot and three empty DIMM slots. Memory, also called RAM (random access memory), is temporary storage for data and instructions as they are being processed by the CPU. The memory module shown in Figure 1-6 contains several RAM chips. Video cards also contain some embedded RAM chips for video memory.

Figure 1-6 A DIMM holds RAM and is mounted directly on a motherboard

- *Hard drives and other drives.* A system might have one or more hard drives, an optical drive, a tape drive, or, for really old systems, a floppy drive. A hard drive, also called a hard disk drive (HDD), is permanent storage used to hold data and programs. For example, the Windows 8 operating system and applications are installed on the hard drive. All drives in a system are installed in a stack of drive bays at the front of the case. The system shown in Figure 1-2 has two hard drives and one optical drive installed. These three drives are also shown in Figure 1-7. The larger hard drive is a magnetic drive, and the smaller hard drive is a solid-state drive. Each drive has two connections for cables: The power cable connects to the power supply, and another cable, used for data and instructions, connects to the motherboard.

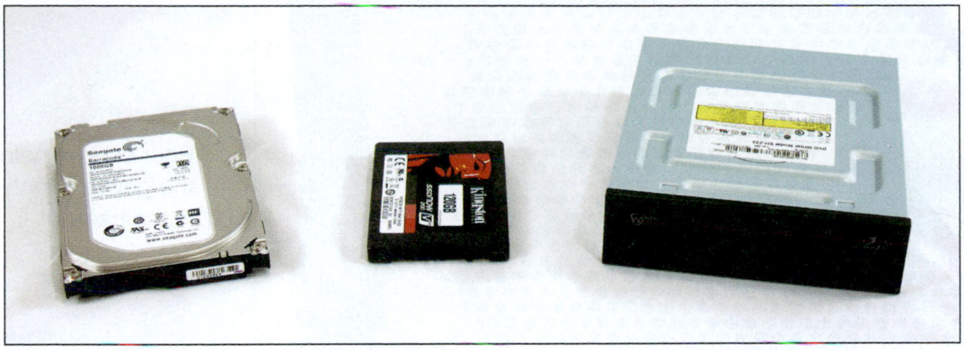

Figure 1-7 Two types of hard drives (larger magnetic drive and smaller solid-state drive) and a DVD drive

- ***A power supply.*** A computer power supply, also known as a power supply unit (PSU), is a box installed in a corner of the computer case (see Figure 1-8) that receives and converts the house current so that components inside the case can use it. Most power supplies have a dual-voltage selector switch on the back of the computer case where you can switch the input voltage to the power supply to 115 V used in the United States or 220 V used in other countries. See Figure 1-9. The power cables can connect to and supply power to the motherboard, expansion cards, and drives.

Notes If you ever need to change the dual-voltage selector switch, be sure you first turn off the computer and unplug the power supply.

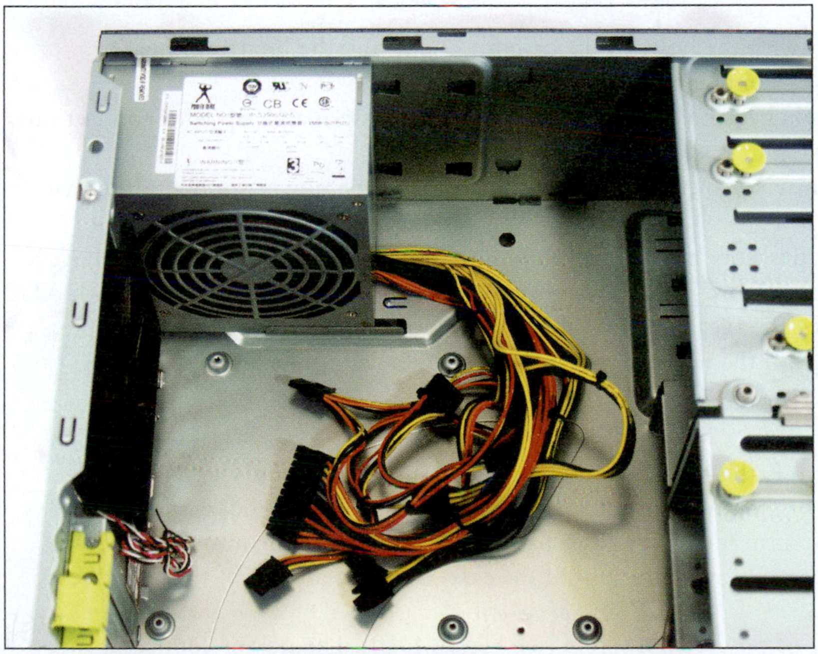

Figure 1-8 Power supply with attached power cables

Figure 1-9 The dual-voltage selector switch sets the input voltage to the power supply

FORM FACTORS USED BY DESKTOP CASES, POWER SUPPLIES, AND MOTHERBOARDS

A+
220-901
1.7, 1.8,
1.11

The desktop computer case, power supply, and motherboard must all be compatible and fit together as an interconnecting system. The standards that describe the size, shape, screw hole positions, and major features of these interconnected components are called form factors. Using a matching form factor for the motherboard, power supply, and case assures you that:

- The motherboard fits in the case.
- The power supply cords to the motherboard provide the correct voltage, and the connectors match the connections on the board.
- The holes in the motherboard align with the holes in the case for anchoring the board to the case.
- The holes in the case align with ports coming off the motherboard.
- For some form factors, wires for switches and lights on the front of the case match up with connections on the motherboard.
- The holes in the power supply align with holes in the case for anchoring the power supply to the case.

The two form factors used by most desktop and tower computer cases and power supplies are the ATX and microATX form factors. Motherboards use these and other form factors that are compatible with ATX or microATX power supplies and cases. You learn about other motherboard form factors in the chapter, "All About Motherboards." Following are the important details about ATX and microATX.

ATX FORM FACTOR

ATX (Advanced Technology Extended) is the most commonly used form factor today. It is an open, nonproprietary industry specification originally developed by Intel in 1995, and has undergone several revisions since then. The original ATX form factor for cases had case fans blowing air into the case, but early revisions to the form factor had fans blowing air out of the case. Blowing air out of the case does a better job of keeping the system cool.

An ATX power supply has a variety of power connectors (see Figure 1-10). The power connectors are listed in Table 1-2 and several of them are described next.

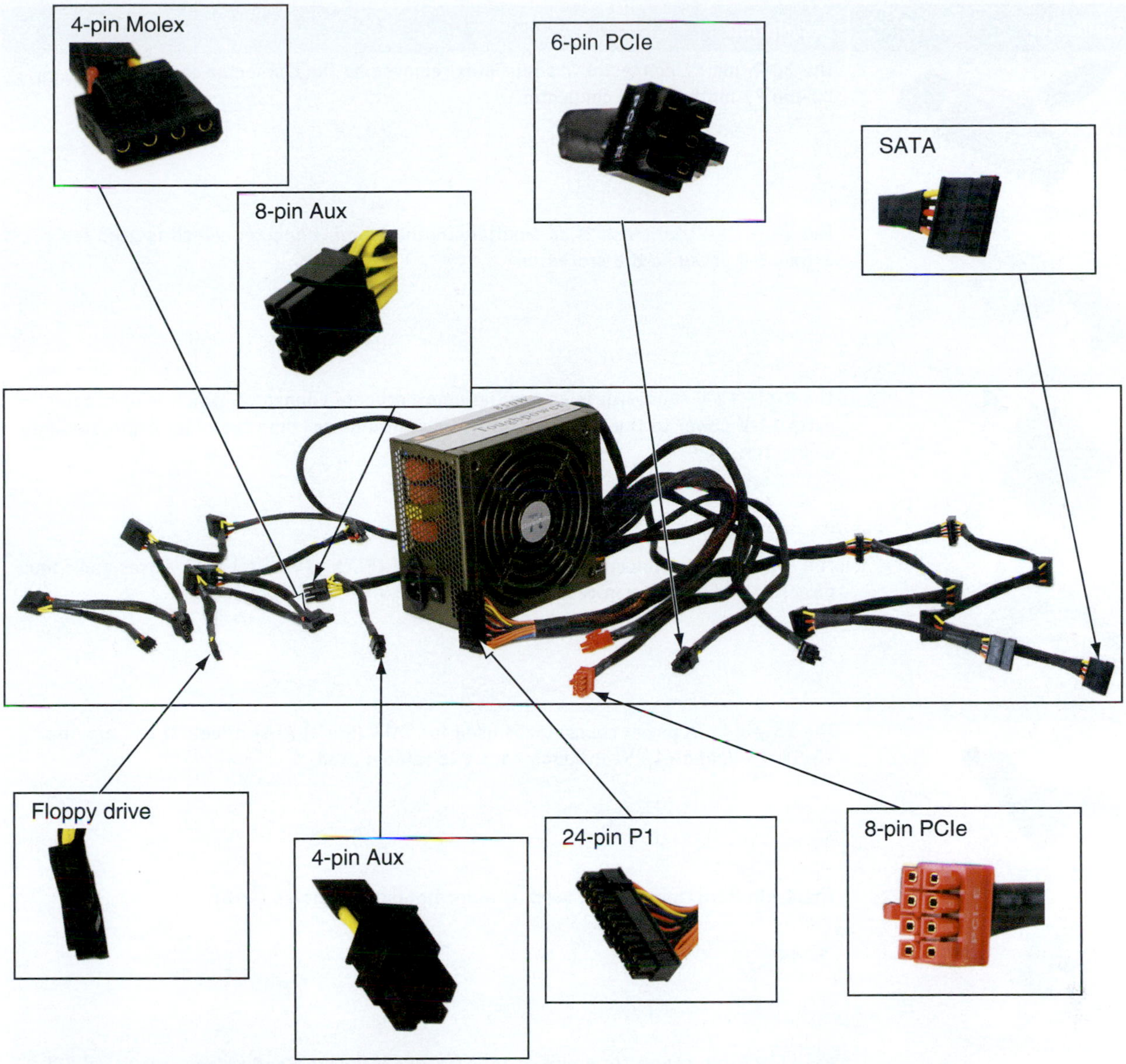

Figure 1-10 ATX power supply with connectors

Connector	Description
	**The 20-pin P1 connector is the main motherboard power connector used in the early ATX systems.**
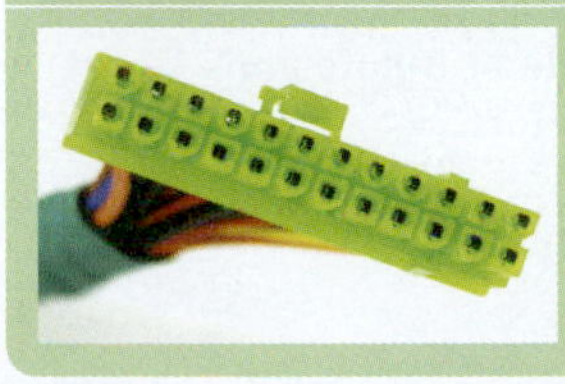	**The 24-pin P1 connector, also called the 20+4 pin connector, is the main motherboard power connector used today.**

Table 1-2 Power supply connectors (continues)

Connector	Description
	The 20+4 pin P1 connector has four pins removed so the connector can fit into a 20-pin P1 motherboard connector.
	The 4-pin 12-V connector is an auxiliary motherboard connector, which is used for extra 12-V power to the processor.
	The 8-pin 12-V connector is an auxiliary motherboard connector, which is used for extra 12-V power to the processor, providing more power than the older 4-pin auxiliary connector.
	The 4-pin Molex connector is used for older IDE (PATA or Parallel ATA) drives and some newer SATA drives. It can provide +5 V and +12 V to the drive.
	The 15-pin SATA power connector is used for SATA (Serial ATA) drives. It can provide +3.3V, +5 V, and +12 V, although +3.3 V is seldom used.
	The 4-pin Berg connector is used by older floppy disk drives (FDD).
	The PCIe 6-pin connector provides an extra +12 V for high-end video cards using PCI Express, Version 1 standard.
	The PCIe 8-pin connector provides an extra +12 V for high-end video cards using PCI Express, Version 2.
	The PCIe 6/8-pin connector is used by high-end video cards using PCIe x16 slots to provide extra voltage to the card and can accommodate a 6-hole or 8-hole port. To get the 8-pin connector, combine both the 6-pin and 2-pin connectors.

Table 1-2 Power supply connectors (continued)

★ A+ Exam Tip The A+ 220-901 exam expects you to know about each connector listed in Table 1-2.

Power connectors have evolved because components using new technologies require more power. As you read about the following types of power connectors and why each came to be, you'll also learn about the evolving expansion slots and expansion cards that drove the need for more power:

- ***20-pin P1 connector.*** The first ATX power supplies and motherboards used a single 20-pin P1 power connector that provided +3.3 volts, +5 volts, +12 volts, –12 volts, and an optional and rarely used –5 volts. See Figure 1-11. This 20-pin power connector was sufficient for powering expansion cards installed in PCI (Peripheral Component Interconnect) expansion slots on the motherboard (see Figure 1-12). Several versions of PCI slots evolved over time, which you learn about in the chapter, "All About Motherboards."

Figure 1-11 The first ATX P1 power connector used 20 pins

Figure 1-12 A PCI expansion card about to be installed in a PCI slot

Figure 1-13 The 4-pin 12-volt auxiliary power connector on a motherboard with power cord connected

- ***4-pin and 8-pin auxiliary connectors.*** When processors began to require more power, the ATX Version 2.1 specifications added a 4-pin auxiliary connector near the processor socket to provide an additional 12 V of power (see Figure 1-13). A power supply that provides this 4-pin 12-volt power cord is called an ATX12V power supply. Later boards replaced the 4-pin 12-volt power connector with an 8-pin motherboard auxiliary connector that provided more amps for the processor.

- ***24-pin or 20+4-pin P1 connector.*** Later, when faster PCI Express (PCIe) slots were added to motherboards, more power was required and a new ATX specification (ATX Version 2.2) allowed for a 24-pin P1 connector, also called the 20+4 power connector. The 20-pin power cable will still work in the new 24-pin connector. Looking back at Figure 1-3, you can see one long blue PCIe ×16 slot (16 lanes for 16-bit transfers on this slot) that can be used by a video card and two short black PCIe ×1 slots (for 1-bit transfers) that can be used for other expansion cards that fit this type slot.

  The extra 4 pins on the 24-pin P1 connector provide +12 volts, +5 volts, and +3.3 volts pins. Motherboards that support PCI Express and have the 24-pin P1 connector are sometimes called Enhanced ATX boards. Figure 1-14 shows a 20-pin P1 power cord from the power supply and a 24-pin P1 connector on a motherboard. Figure 1-15 shows the pinouts for the 24-pin power cord connector, which is color-coded to wires from the power supply. The 20-pin connector is missing the lower four pins, which are listed in the photo and diagram.

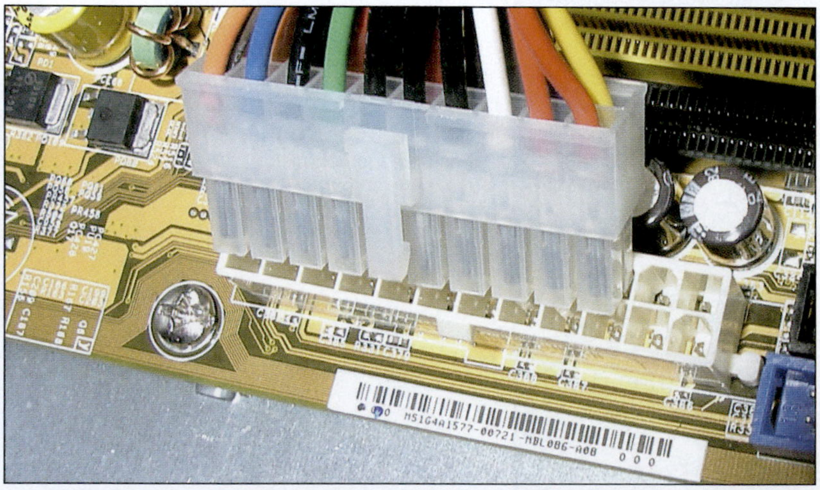

Figure 1-14 A 20-pin power cord ready to be plugged into a 24-pin P1 connector on an ATX motherboard

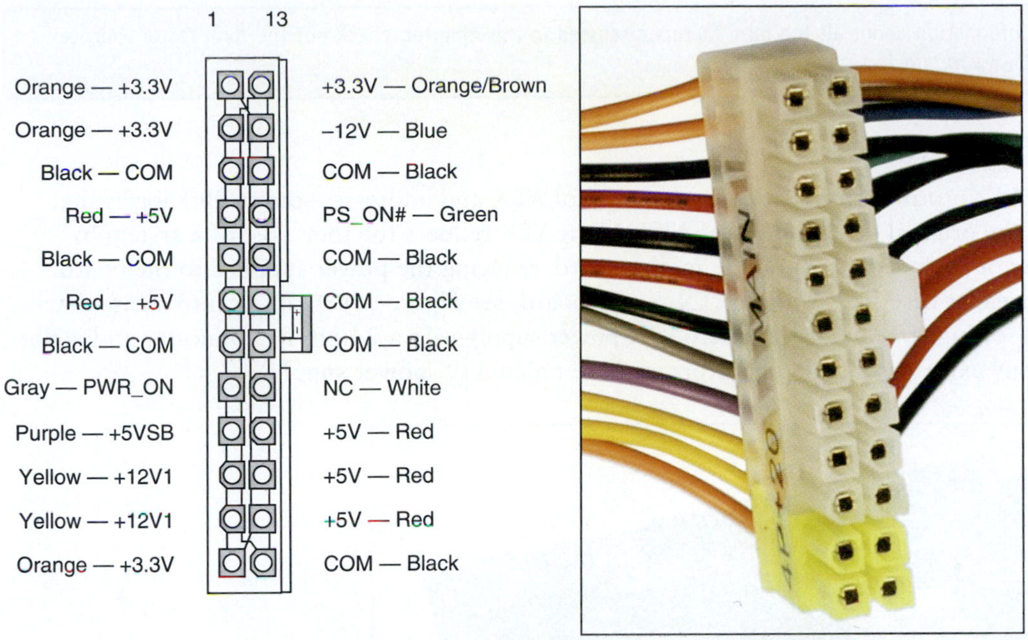

Figure 1-15 P1 24-pin power connector follows ATX Version 2.2 and higher standards

Figure 1-16 shows a PCIe ×16 video card. The edge connector has a break that fits the break in the slot. The tab at the end of the edge connector fits into a retention mechanism at the end of the slot, which helps to stabilize a heavy video card.

Figure 1-16 This PCIe ×16 video card has a 6-pin PCIe power connector to receive extra power from the power supply

- ***6-pin and 8-pin PCIe connectors.*** Video cards draw the most power in a system, and ATX Version 2.2 provides for power cables to connect directly to a video card to provide it additional power than comes through the PCIe slot on the motherboard. The PCIe power connector might have 6 or 8 pins. PCI Express, Version 1, defined the 6-pin connector, and PCI Express, Version 2, defined the 8-pin connector. The video card shown in Figure 1-16 has a 6-pin connector on the end of the card. A PCIe 6/8-pin connector can also be located on the motherboard to supply extra power for the video card.

Notes For more information about all the form factors discussed in this chapter, check out the form factor website sponsored by Intel at *www.formfactors.org*.

MICROATX FORM FACTOR

The microATX (MATX) form factor is a major variation of ATX and addresses some technologies that have emerged since the original development of ATX. MicroATX reduces the total cost of a system by reducing the number of expansion slots on the motherboard, reducing the power supplied to the board, and allowing for a smaller case size. A microATX motherboard (see Figure 1-17) will fit into a case that follows the ATX 2.1 or higher standard. A microATX power supply uses a 24-pin P1 connector and is not likely to have as many extra wires and connectors as those on an ATX power supply.

Figure 1-17 This microATX motherboard by Biostar is designed to support an AMD processor

A+ Exam Tip The A+ 220-901 exam expects you to recognize and know the more important features of the ATX and microATX form factors used by power supplies.

Hands-On Project 1-1 Identify Ports and Parts

A+ 220-901 1.7, 1.8, 1.11

Do the following to identify computer ports and parts that your instructor might have on display:

1. Look on the front and back of your computer case and list the type of ports the computer offers.
2. For a power supply, list the number and type of power connectors.
3. For a motherboard, list the number and type of expansion slots on the board. Does the board have a 20-pin or 24-pin P1 connector? What other power connectors are on the board? How many memory slots does the board have?
4. For expansion cards, examine the ports on the back of the card. Can you tell by the ports the purpose of the card? What type of slot does the card use?

Caution You can damage a computer component with static electricity if you touch the component when you are not grounded. Before you touch a sensitive computer component, you first need to dissipate any static electricity on your body. You learn how to do that in the appendix, "Safety Procedures and Environmental Concerns." For now, to protect a working component your instructor has on display, don't touch; just look.

Hands-On | Project 1-2 Examine the Power Supply, Motherboard, and Expansion Cards Inside a Desktop Case

A+ 220-901 1.7, 1.8, 1.11

If you have access to a desktop computer with the case cover removed, examine its components and answer the following questions. As you look, remember to not touch anything inside the case unless you are properly grounded.

1. Identify the power supply, motherboard, and any expansion cards that might be installed on the motherboard. Remember: Don't touch a component unless you are properly grounded. If the case is plugged into a power source, don't touch inside the case even if you are grounded.
2. Identify the cooler that is installed on top of the processor. This cooler is likely to have a fan on top and a heat sink that you can't see. The processor is hidden under the cooler.
3. Identify the memory modules and memory slots. How many memory slots are there? How many of these slots are populated?
4. If an expansion card is installed, what type of ports does the card provide at the rear of the case? Find the one screw that is used to attach the expansion card to the case.
5. Locate the screws that are attaching the motherboard to the case. How many screws are used? Do you see screw holes in the motherboard that are not being used? As a general rule of thumb, up to nine screws can be used to attach a motherboard to a case.
6. How many power cables are coming from the power supply? How many of these cables are connected to the motherboard? To other devices inside the computer? Identify each type of power cable the system is using.
7. Find the screws or clips that are attaching the power supply to the case. Is the power supply attached using screws, clips, or both screws and clips?

Now let's learn about the drives you might find installed inside a system.

DRIVES, THEIR CABLES, AND CONNECTORS

A+ 220-901 1.7, 1.8, 1.11

A computer might have one or more hard drives, an optical drive (CD, DVD, or Blu-ray), tape drive, or some other type of drive. A drive receives power by a power cable from the power supply, and communicates instructions and data through a cable attached to the motherboard. Most hard drives, optical drives, and tape drives today use the **serial ATA (SATA)** standard.

Notes If you support older desktop computers, you might see some drives using the slower and older PATA (parallel ATA) standard, also called the IDE (Integrated Drive Electronics) or EIDE (Enhanced IDE) standard, for drive connections. PATA used a 40-pin connector on the motherboard and a wide ribbon cable that could accommodate one or two drives on the cable. Figure 1-18 shows two PATA ribbon cables, each connecting a drive to the motherboard.

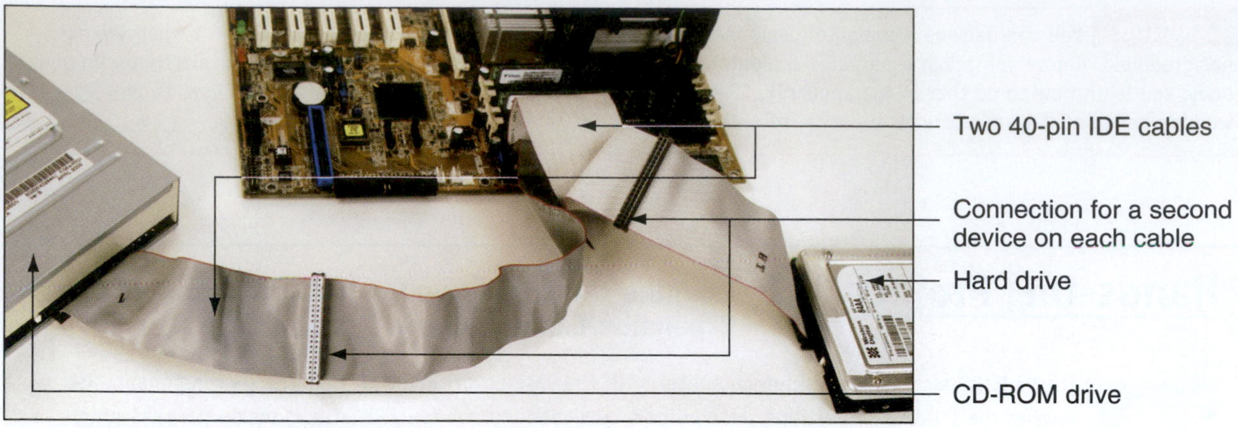

Figure 1-18 Two PATA devices connected to a motherboard using both PATA or IDE connections and two cables

SATA and PATA standards are published by the American National Standards Institute (ANSI, see *www.ansi.org*). Figure 1-19 shows a SATA cable connecting a hard drive and motherboard. SATA cables can only connect to a SATA connector on the motherboard in one direction (see Figure 1-20). SATA drives get their power from a power cable that connects to the drive using a SATA power connector (refer back to the photo in Table 1-2).

Figure 1-19 A hard drive subsystem using the SATA data cable

Figure 1-20 A SATA cable connects to a SATA connector in only one direction; use red connectors on the motherboard first

Hands-On | Project 1-3 Identify Drives and Their Connectors

A+
220-901
1.7, 1.8,
1.11

If your instructor has provided a display of drives, for each drive identify the purpose of the drive (for example, a hard drive or optical drive) and the type of power connector the drive uses (for example, SATA or Molex). If you have access to a computer with the case cover removed, answer the following questions:

1. List the drives installed, the purpose of each drive, and the type of interface and power connector it uses.
2. How many connectors does the motherboard have for drives? Identify each type of connector (SATA or PATA).

Now that you know about what's inside a desktop computer case, let's take a look at laptop computers.

FIRST LOOK AT LAPTOP COMPONENTS

A+
220-901
3.1, 3.3,
3.4, 3.5

A laptop, also called a notebook, is designed for portability (see Figure 1-21a and 1-21b) and can be just as powerful as a desktop computer. More than half of personal computers purchased today are laptops, and almost 30 percent of personal computers currently in use are laptops. Laptops use the same technology as desktops, but with modifications to use less power, take up less space, and operate on the move.

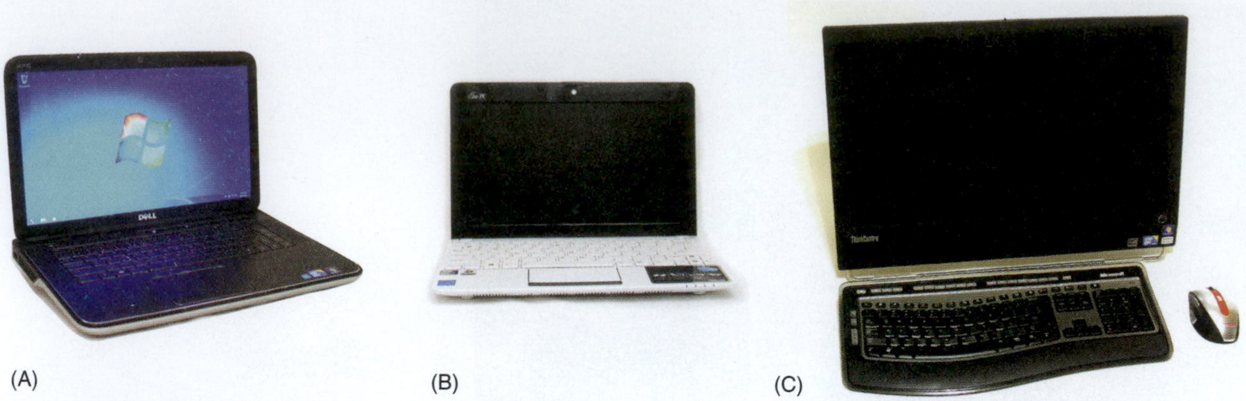

(A) (B) (C)

Figure 1-21 A laptop, netbook, and all-in-one computer

iStockphoto.com/Rasslava

Figure 1-22 A laptop with a rotating display can do double-duty as a tablet computer

Laptops come in several varieties, including some with a touch screen that also allows you to handwrite on it with a stylus and some with a rotating screen or removable screen that allows you to use the laptop as a tablet (see Figure 1-22). Another variation of a laptop is a netbook (Figure 1-21b) that is smaller and less expensive than a laptop and has fewer features. An all-in-one computer (Figure 1-21c) has the monitor and computer case built together and uses components that are common to both a laptop and desktop. Because all-in-one computers use many laptop components and are serviced in similar ways, we include them in this chapter.

A laptop provides ports on its sides, back, or front for connecting peripherals (see Figure 1-23). Ports common to laptops as well as desktop systems include USB, FireWire, network, dial-up modem (seldom seen on newer laptops), and audio ports (for a microphone, headset, or external speakers). Video ports might include one or more VGA, DisplayPort, Thunderbolt (on Apple laptops), or HDMI ports to connect to a projector, second monitor, or television. On the side or back of the laptop, you'll see a lock connector that's used to physically secure the laptop with a cable lock (see Figure 1-24) and a DC jack to receive power from the AC adapter. Also, a laptop may have an optical drive, but netbooks usually don't have optical drives.

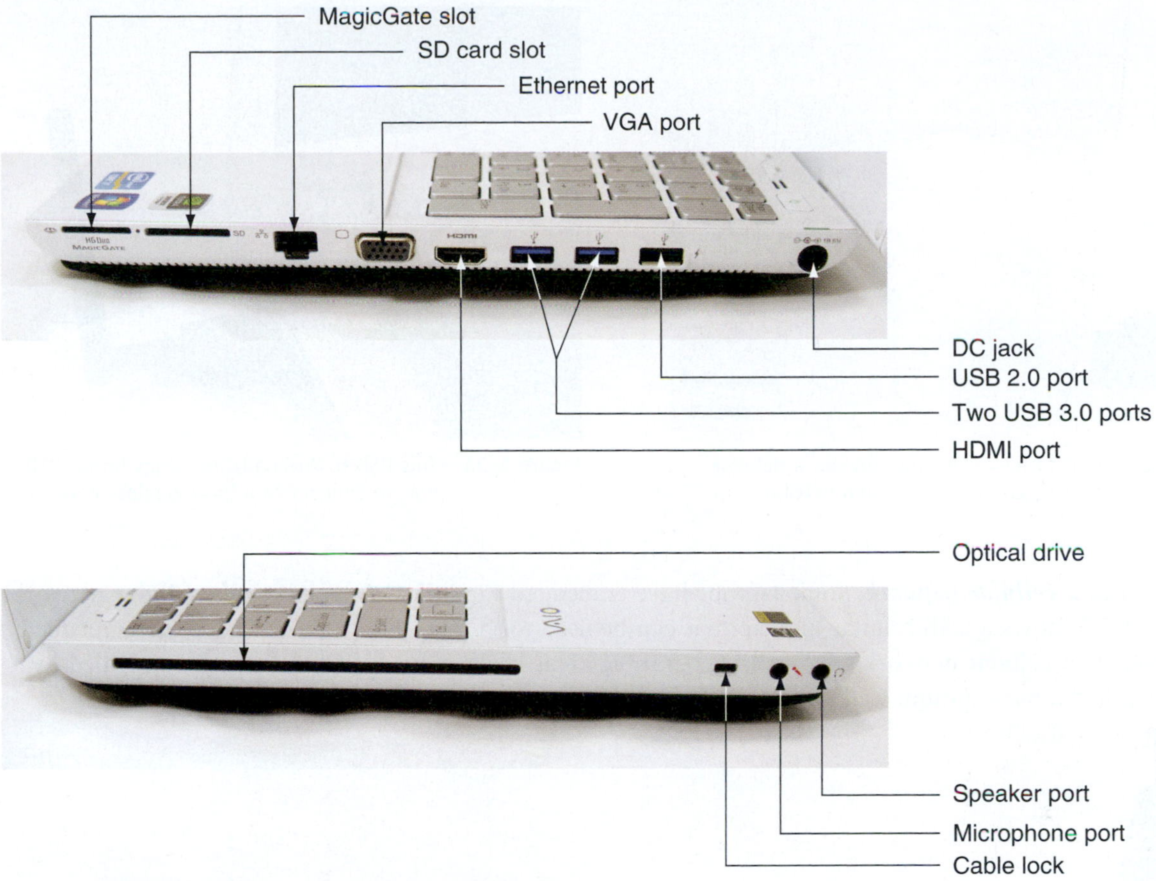

Figure 1-23 Ports and slots on a laptop computer

Source: Kensington Technology Group

Figure 1-24 Use a cable lock system to secure a notebook computer to a desk to help prevent it from being stolen

Notice the two slots in Figure 1-23 used for flash memory cards: a MagicGate slot and an SD card slot. Each can support several types of flash memory cards that you learn about later in the text.

When a laptop is missing a port or slot you need, you can usually find a USB dongle to provide the port or slot. Here are some options:

- ***Connect to a local wired network.*** Figure 1-25 shows a USB to RJ-45 dongle. Plug the dongle into a USB port and plug a network cable into the RJ-45 port the dongle provides to connect the laptop to a wired network.
- ***Connect to a local wireless network.*** Figure 1-26 shows a USB to Wi-Fi dongle, which allows you to connect a laptop that doesn't have wireless capability to a wireless network. Wi-Fi (Wireless Fidelity) is the common name for standards for a local wireless network.

Figure 1-25 USB to RJ-45 dongle provides a network port to connect to a wired network

Figure 1-26 This USB to Wi-Fi adapter plugs into a USB port to connect to a local wireless network

- ***Connect to a cellular network.*** Some laptops have embedded capability to connect to a cellular network. Figure 1-27 shows a USB cellular modem that can be used for a laptop that doesn't have the embedded technology. A cellular network consists of geographic areas of coverage called cells, each controlled by a tower, called a base station. Cell phones are called that because they use a cellular network.

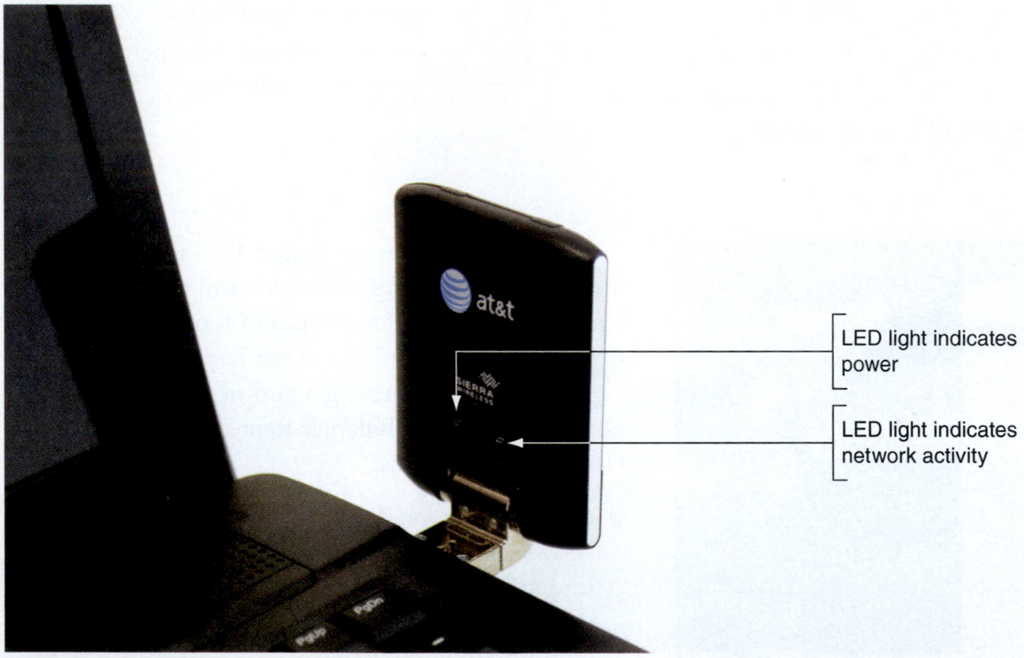

Figure 1-27 This USB device by Sierra Wireless provides a wireless connection to a cellular network

- ***Connect to a Bluetooth device.*** When a laptop doesn't have Bluetooth capability, you can use a USB to Bluetooth adapter to connect to a Bluetooth wireless device such as a Bluetooth printer or smart phone. Bluetooth is a short-range wireless technology to connect two devices in a small personal network.
- ***Use an external optical drive.*** When a laptop or netbook doesn't have an optical drive, you can use a USB optical drive. Plug the USB optical drive into a USB port so that you can use CDs and DVDs with the laptop or netbook.

SPECIAL KEYS, BUTTONS, AND INPUT DEVICES ON A LAPTOP

A+
220-901
3.1, 3.3,
3.4, 3.5

Buttons or switches might be found above the keyboard, and the top row of keys contains the function keys. To use a function key, hold down the Fn key as you press the function key. Here are the purposes of a few keys and buttons. Some of them change Windows settings. Know that these same settings can also be changed using Windows tools:

- ***Volume setting.*** You can set the volume using the volume icon in the Windows taskbar. In addition, some laptops offer buttons or function keys to control the volume (see Figure 1-28).

Figure 1-28 On this laptop, use the Fn and the F2, F3, or F4 key to control volume; use the Fn key and the F5 or F6 key to control screen brightness; and use the Fn key and the F7 key to manage dual displays

Figure 1-29 The touch pad is the most common pointing device on a notebook

- ***Keyboard backlight.*** Function keys can be used to control the keyboard backlight to light up the keyboard.
- ***Touch pad on or off.*** Other function keys can turn on or off the touch pad, which is the most common pointing device on a laptop (see Figure 1-29). Some people prefer to use a USB wired or wireless mouse instead of a touch pad.
- ***Screen brightness and screen orientation.*** Function keys can control the screen brightness on many laptops. Screen brightness can also be controlled in Windows display settings. Some laptops allow you to use a function key to change the screen orientation to landscape or portrait so you can use the laptop turned on its end.
- ***Dual displays.*** Most laptops use a function key to control dual displays. For example, for one laptop, the combination of the Fn key and the F7 key (refer back to Figure 1-28) displays the box shown in Figure 1-30. Use arrow keys to use only the LCD panel, duplicate or extend output to the external monitor, or use only the external monitor. Dual displays can also be managed using Windows display settings.

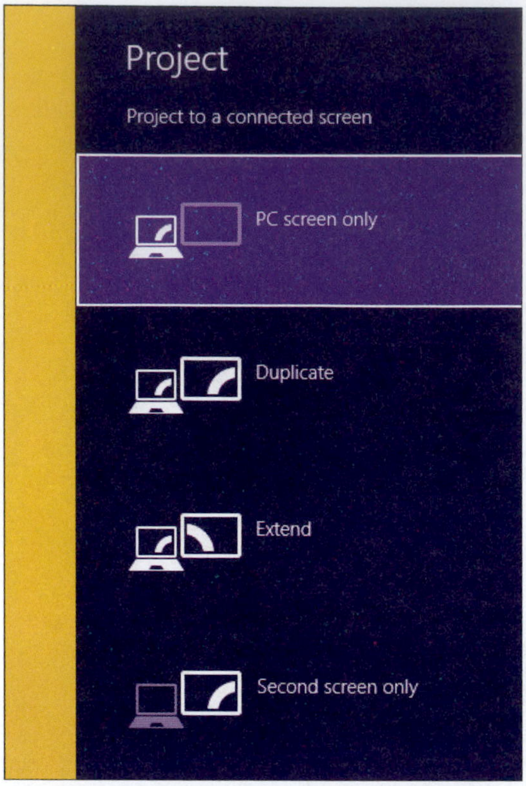

Figure 1-30 Control dual monitors on a Windows 8 laptop

- ***Bluetooth, Wi-Fi, or cellular on or off.*** Some laptops use function keys such as Fn with F5 or F6 to toggle Bluetooth, Wi-Fi, or cellular on or off, or a laptop might have a switch for this purpose. You can also control these wireless technologies using Windows settings or software utilities provided by the manufacturer. When you turn off all wireless technologies, the computer is said to be in airplane mode.
- ***Media options.*** Some laptops provide buttons or allow you to use function keys to fast forward, stop, pause, or rewind audio or video media playing in an optical drive.
- ***GPS on or off.*** If a laptop has a GPS (Global Positioning System) receiver to calculate its position on the Earth, the laptop might provide a button or function key to turn the GPS on or off. The Global Positioning System is a system of 24 or more satellites orbiting the Earth, and a GPS receiver can locate three or more of these satellites at any time and from these three locations, calculate its own position in a process called trilateration.

Notes If the keyboard fails and you're not able to immediately exchange it, know that you can plug in an external keyboard to a USB port to use in the meantime.

And now onward to ExpressCard slots and docking stations.

EXPRESSCARD SLOTS

A+ 220-901 3.1, 3.3, 3.4, 3.5

Most peripheral devices on today's laptops use a USB port to connect to the laptop. Before USB devices became so popular, a laptop offered ExpressCard slots to connect peripheral devices. See Figure 1-31. These slot and card standards were designed and supported by the PCMCIA (Personal Computer Memory Card International Association) and are sometimes called PCMCIA cards. The cards were used by many devices, including modems, network cards for wired or wireless networks, sound cards, FireWire (IEEE 1394) controllers, USB controllers, flash memory adapters, TV tuners, and hard disks. Most new laptops don't have these slots, but you still need to know how to support them because you'll see them on older laptops.

Figure 1-31 ExpressCard/54 slot has an eject button on the left side of the slot

> **★ A+ Exam Tip** The A+ 220-901 exam expects you to know how to install and configure ExpressCard/34 and ExpressCard/54 cards and slots.

ExpressCard uses the PCI Express bus standard or the USB 2.0 standard. Two sizes of ExpressCards exist: **ExpressCard/34** is 34mm wide and **ExpressCard/54** is 54mm wide, as shown in Figure 1-32. Notice the offset in the ExpressCard/54 card. An ExpressCard/34 card can fit into an ExpressCard/54 slot, but not vice versa. An ExpressCard slot is fully hot-pluggable (you can add a card while the system is on), hot-swappable (exchange or add a card while the system is on), and supports autoconfiguration. An ExpressCard/54 card that provides two eSATA ports for external SATA drives is shown in Figure 1-33.

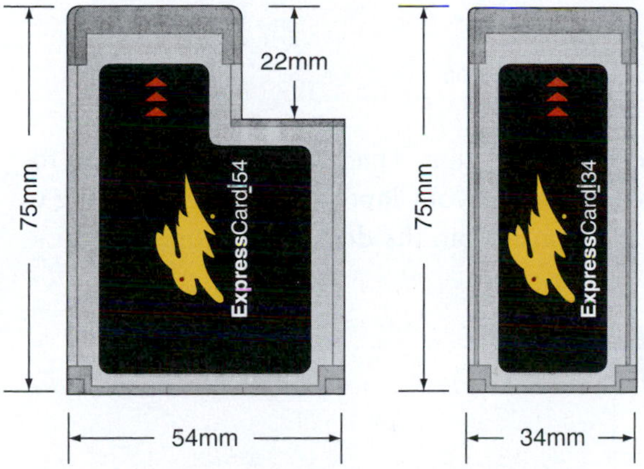

Figure 1-32 Dimensions of ExpressCard cards

Source: SIIG, Inc.

Figure 1-33 This ExpressCard/54 card supports two eSATA drives

Windows must provide two services for an ExpressCard: a socket service and a card service. The socket service establishes communication between the card and the laptop when the card is first inserted. The card service provides the device driver to interface with the card after the socket is created.

The first time you insert an ExpressCard in a laptop, Windows automatically guides you through the installation steps in which you can use the drivers provided by the hardware manufacturer or use Windows drivers. The next time you insert the card in the laptop, the card is detected and starts without help.

ExpressCards can be hot-swapped (inserted or removed while the system is on), but you must stop one card before inserting another. To stop the card, use the Safely Remove Hardware icon in the notification area of the Windows taskbar.

After you have stopped the card, push on the card, which causes it to pop out of the slot. Some ExpressCard slots have an eject button to pop out the card. Then you can remove the card.

Caution Inserting an ExpressCard while the laptop is shutting down or booting up can cause damage to the card and/or to the laptop. Also, a card might give problems when you insert or remove the card while the laptop is in hibernation or sleep mode.

DOCKING STATIONS

A+ 220-901 3.1, 3.3, 3.4, 3.5

Some notebooks have a connector, called a **docking port**, on the bottom or sides of the laptop (see Figure 1-34) to connect to a docking station. A **docking station** provides ports to allow a laptop to easily connect to a full-sized monitor, keyboard, AC power adapter, and other peripheral devices. See Figure 1-35. Laptop manufacturers usually offer a docking station as an additional option.

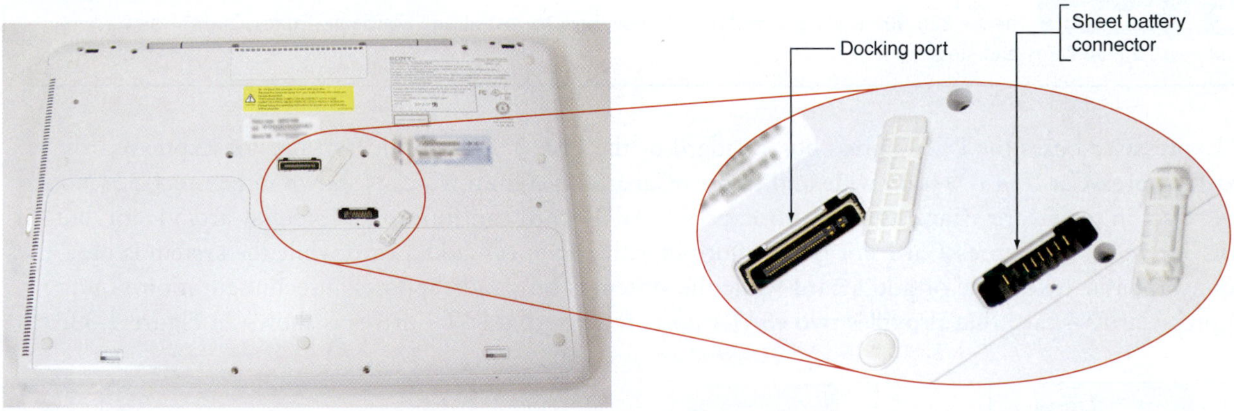

Figure 1-34 The docking port and sheet battery connector on the bottom of a laptop

To use a docking station, plug all the peripherals into the docking station. Then connect your laptop to the station. No software needs installing. When you need to travel with your laptop, rather than having to unplug all the peripherals, all you have to do is disconnect the laptop from the docking station.

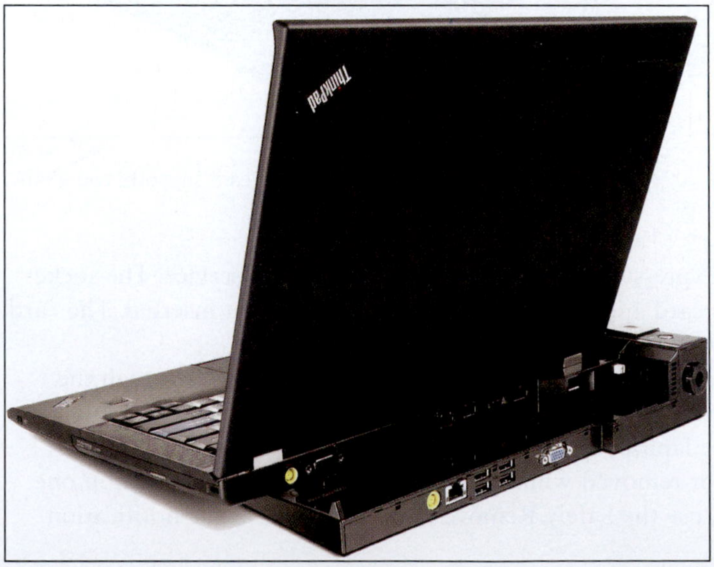

Courtesy of Lenovo

Figure 1-35 Docking station for a Lenovo ThinkPad

1

LAPTOP INTERNAL COMPONENTS

A+
220-901
3.1, 3.3,
3.4, 3.5

Figure 1-36 shows the inside of a laptop case after the cover on the bottom of the laptop has been removed. Here is a list of important components, most of which you can see in the photo:

Figure 1-36 Bottom of a laptop with cover removed

- ***Battery pack.*** The battery pack is not shown because you always remove the battery first before opening a laptop case.
- ***Hard drive.*** The 2.5-inch hard drive is secured in its bay with two screws. When you remove the screws, you can use the plastic tab to lift the drive from its bay.

Figure 1-37 A DIMM used in desktops compared with a SO-DIMM used in laptop computers

- ***CPU, heat sink, and fan.*** The CPU is hidden under the heat sink, which is labeled in the figure. The heat sink draws heat from the CPU and pipes it to the fan, also labeled in the figure. The fan blows the heat out of the laptop case.
- ***Memory.*** Laptops use smaller memory modules than the DIMMs used in desktop computers. In the figure, you can see two SO-DIMMs (small outline DIMMs) installed. Figure 1-37 shows a DIMM and a SO-DIMM for size comparison.

- *Wireless card.* The wireless card is installed to the left of the hard drive in Figure 1-36. You can see two wires leading to the wireless antennas, which are installed in the laptop lid.
- *System board.* Look for the blue system board (in laptop documentation, the motherboard is usually called the system board) under the heat sink, memory, and fan. If you look carefully, you can see microchips and other components on the board.
- *Optical drive.* The optical drive is not visible in the photo. To replace it, you first remove a single screw holding the drive in place and then slide the drive to the left and out of the case. This one screw is labeled in Figure 1-36.

Other hardware components you are likely to find in a laptop case include a small speaker and smart card reader and writer. In the chapter, "Working Inside Desktop Computers and Laptops," you learn how to disassemble and reassemble a laptop.

WHAT'S INSIDE AN ALL-IN-ONE COMPUTER

A+
220-901
3.1, 3.3,
3.4, 3.5

An all-in-one computer uses a mix of components sized for a desktop computer and a laptop. Let's get the general idea of what's inside the case of an all-in-one by looking at the inside of the Lenovo ThinkCentre all-in-one shown earlier in Figure 1-21. Figure 1-38 shows the computer with the case cover removed. Notice in the figure the hard drive is a 3.5-inch drive appropriate for a desktop system, and the memory modules are SO-DIMMs appropriate for a laptop. So goes the hybrid nature of an all-in-one. The fan and heat sink look more like that of a laptop computer, but the processor socket on the motherboard is a desktop processor socket, another hybrid design.

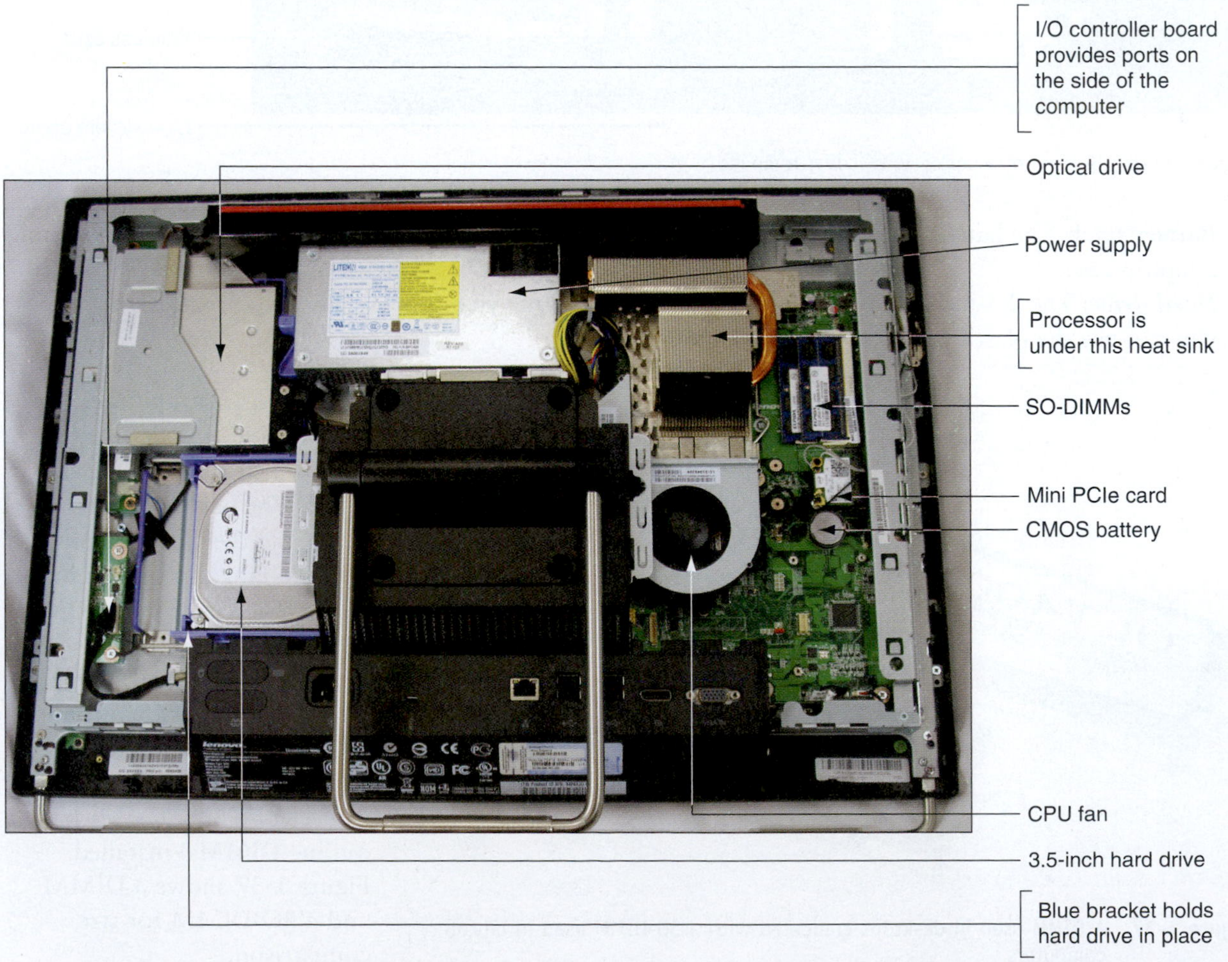

Figure 1-38 Components inside an all-in-one computer

Several components are easy to exchange in this all-in-one without further disassembly. For example, the Mini PCIe card for wireless connectivity, shown in Figure 1-39, is easy to get to, as are the SO-DIMMs you can partly see on the right side of the photo.

Figure 1-39 CMOS battery and Mini PCIe wireless card

To work inside an all-in-one, you'll need the service manual to know how to open the case and replace internal components. Also, for some components, such as the motherboard and power supply, you'll need to buy the replacement component from the all-in-one manufacturer because these components are likely to be proprietary as with many laptop components. For specific directions about replacing parts in an all-in-one, see the service manual.

MAINTAINING LAPTOPS AND MOBILE DEVICES

A+
220-901
3.1, 3.3,
3.4, 3.5

Laptops and mobile devices tend to not last as long as desktop computers because they are portable and, therefore, subject to more wear and tear. A device's user manual gives specific instructions on how to care for the device. Those instructions follow these general guidelines:

- LCD panels on devices are fragile and can be damaged fairly easily. Take precautions against damaging a laptop or other device's LCD panel. Don't touch it with sharp objects like ballpoint pens.
- Don't pick up or hold a laptop by the lid. Pick it up and hold it by the bottom. Keep the lid closed when the laptop is not in use.
- Only use battery packs and AC adapters recommended by the laptop manufacturer. Keep the battery pack away from moisture or heat, and don't attempt to take the pack apart. When it no longer works, dispose of it correctly. For laptops, you might consider buying an extra battery pack to use when the first one discharges. You can also buy battery chargers so that you can charge one while the other is in use.
- Don't tightly pack a laptop or tablet in a suitcase because the LCD panel might get damaged. Use a good-quality carrying case and make a habit of always transporting the laptop in the carrying case. Don't place heavy objects on top of the laptop case.
- Don't move the laptop while the hard drive is being accessed (when the drive indicator light is on). Wait until the light goes off.

- Don't put the laptop close to an appliance such as a TV, large audio speakers, or refrigerator that generates a strong magnetic field, and don't place your cell phone on a laptop while the phone is in use.
- Always use passwords to protect access to your laptop or mobile device so you are better protected when connected to a public network or the device is stolen or used by an unauthorized person.
- Keep your laptop or device at room temperature. For example, never leave it in a car overnight when it is cold, and don't leave it in a car during the day when it's hot. Don't expose your laptop or device to direct sunlight for an extended time.
- Don't leave the laptop or device in a dusty or smoke-filled area. Don't use it in a wet area such as near a swimming pool or in the bathtub. Don't use it at the beach where sand can get in it.
- Don't power it up and down unnecessarily.
- Protect the laptop from overheating by not running it when it's still inside the case, resting on a pillow, or partially covered with a blanket or anything else that would prevent proper air circulation around it.
- If a laptop has just come indoors from the cold, don't turn it on until it reaches room temperature. In some cases, condensation can cause problems. Some manufacturers recommend that when you receive a new laptop shipped to you during the winter, you should leave it in its shipping carton for several hours before you open the carton to prevent subjecting the laptop to a temperature shock.
- Protect a laptop against static electricity. If you have just come in from the cold on a low-humidity day when there is the possibility that you are carrying static electricity, don't touch the laptop until you have grounded yourself.
- Before placing a laptop in a carrying case for travel, remove any CDs, DVDs, or USB flash drives, and put them in protective covers. Verify that the system is powered down and not in sleep mode, which will drain the battery.
- If a laptop gets wet, you can partially disassemble it to allow internal components to dry. Give the laptop several days to dry before attempting to turn it on. Don't use heat to speed up the drying time.
- Keep current backups of important data on a laptop or device in case it fails or is stolen.

A well-used laptop, especially one that is used in dusty or dirty areas, needs cleaning occasionally. Here are some cleaning tips:

1. Clean the LCD panel with a soft dry cloth. If the panel is very dirty, you can use monitor wipes to clean it or dampen the cloth with water. Some manufacturers recommend using a mixture of isopropyl alcohol and water to clean an LCD panel. Be sure the LCD panel is dry before you close the lid.
2. Use a can of compressed air meant to be used on computer equipment to blow dust and small particles out of the keyboard, trackball, and touch pad. Turn the laptop at an angle and direct the air into the sides of the keyboard. Then use a soft, damp cloth to clean the key caps and touch pad.
3. Use compressed air to blow out all air vents on the laptop to make sure they are clean and unobstructed.
4. If keys are sticking, remove the keyboard so you can better spray under the keys with compressed air. If you can remove the key cap, remove it and clean the key contact area with contact cleaner. One example of a contact cleaner you can use for this purpose is Stabilant 22 (*www.stabilant.com*). Reinstall the keyboard and test it. If the key still sticks, replace the keyboard.
5. Remove the battery and clean the battery connections with a contact cleaner.

Hands-On | Project 1-4 Observe Laptop Features

Examine a laptop, its documentation, and the manufacturer's website, and then answer these questions:

1. What ports are on the laptop?
2. Does the laptop have an ExpressCard slot? If so, which type of ExpressCard slot does the laptop have?
3. What type of memory slots does the laptop have?
4. List the purpose of each function key on the keyboard.
5. List the purpose of each button on the top or bottom of the keyboard.
6. What is the cost of a new battery pack?

Now that you know about some of the parts and components in desktops, laptops, and all-in-ones, let's turn our attention to the components found in a few other mobile devices, including tablets, smart phones, phablets, and wearable technology devices.

FIRST LOOK AT MOBILE DEVICE HARDWARE

A+ 220-901 3.1, 3.3, 3.4, 3.5

Here's a list of the mobile devices that you, as an IT support technician, might be called on to support:

- *Smart phone.* A smart phone is primarily a cell phone that also includes abilities to send text messages with photos, videos, or other multimedia content attached; surf the web; manage email; play games; take photos and videos; and download and use small apps. Most smart phones use touch screens for input (see Figure 1-40) and a few have a physical keyboard and a touch screen. Some smart phones allow for voice input.

Stockphoto.com/Hocus-focus

Figure 1-40 Most smart phones don't have a keyboard and use a touch screen for input

- *Tablets and phablets.* A tablet is a computing device with a touch screen that is larger than a smart phone and has functions similar to a smart phone. Most tablets can connect to Wi-Fi networks and use Bluetooth or NFC (Near Field Communication) to wirelessly connect to nearby devices. Some tablets have the ability to use a cellular network for data transmissions and phone calls. Installed apps, such as Skype, can make voice phone calls, send text, and make video calls. When you can use your tablet to make a phone call, the distinction between a smart phone and a tablet is almost nonexistent, except for size.

  A phablet bridges this size exception. A phablet (pronounced "*fab*-let") has the same capabilities of a smart phone or tablet, but is smaller than a tablet and larger than a smart phone.
- *E-readers.* An e-reader is a mobile device that holds digital versions of books, newspapers,

magazines, and other printed documents, which are usually downloaded to the device from the web. An e-reader can connect to the Internet using a Wi-Fi wireless connection or a wired connection to a computer that is connected to the Internet. In addition, content can be stored on a flash memory card, which is inserted in the e-reader.

- *Smart cameras.* A smart camera is a digital camera that has embedded computing power to make decisions about the content of the photos or videos it records, including transmitting alerts over a wired or wireless network when it records certain content. Smart cameras, sometimes called vision sensors, can be used to initiate alerts for surveillance of a protected area or to monitor manufacturer automated assembly lines for potential problems.
- *Wearable technology devices.* Wearable technology devices, including smart watches (see Figure 1-41), wristbands, arm bands, eyeglasses, headsets, and clothing, can be used as computing devices to make phone calls, send text messages, transmit data, and check email; wearable technology fitness monitors can measure heart rate, count pool laps or miles jogged or biked, and a host of other activities. These devices can sync up with a computer for power and communication, similar to how other mobile devices work. Many people believe smart watches will eventually replace smart phones as the personal communication device of choice.

iStockphoto.com/Mutlu Kurtbas

Figure 1-41 The app screen on a smart watch by Apple, Inc.

CONNECTION TYPES

A+
220-901
3.1, 3.3,
3.4, 3.5

Here are some ways a mobile device can connect to the outside world:

- *Wi-Fi local wireless network and cellular network.* Most mobile devices have Wi-Fi capability and can connect to a Wi-Fi local wireless network. In addition, smart phones and some laptops, tablets, phablets, and wearable mobile devices can connect to a cellular network. To connect to a cellular network, the device must have cellular capability and a subscription to the cellular network carrier, for example, AT&T or Verizon. Two types of technologies are used to connect to cellular networks: GSM (Global System for Mobile Communication) and CDMA (Code Division Multiple Access). With GSM networks, information about your subscription is kept on a small SIM (Subscriber Identity Module) card inserted in the device. Figure 1-42 shows the slot on the side of an Apple iPad where you can insert a SIM card so that the iPad can connect to the cellular network.

Figure 1-42 A SIM card is required for a mobile device to use most cellular networks

- ***Bluetooth and Infrared.*** Mobile devices might have the capability to connect to other nearby wireless devices using a Bluetooth, IR, or NFC connection. Figure 1-43 shows an iPad connected to a keyboard using Bluetooth. **Infrared (IR)** is a wireless connection that requires an unobstructed "line of sight" between transmitter and receiver. Smart phones and other mobile devices sometimes offer an IR interface that can be used with an app to control a television in place of its remote control.
- ***NFC.*** **Near Field Communication (NFC)** is a wireless technology that establishes a communication link between two NFC devices that are within 4 inches of each other. For example, when you tap your smart phone with that of your friend, the two phones can use NFC to exchange contact information. NFC can also be used to read an NFC tag, which is a small microchip that can be embedded in just about anything, including a key chain tag, printed flyer, or billboard (see Figure 1-44). The NFC tag dispenses information to any NFC-enabled smart phone or other device that comes within 4 inches of the tag.

Figure 1-43 An iPad and a wireless keyboard can connect using Bluetooth

Figure 1-44 These programmable NFC tags have sticky backs for attaching to a flat surface like a wall, desk, or car dashboard

- ***Wired connection.*** Smart phones, tablets, phablets, and wearable devices can make a wired connection to a computer. This connection can be used to charge the device, download software updates, upload data to the computer, back up data, and restore software or data. The device's port used for power and communication may be a type of USB port or a proprietary vendor-specific port. Some USB connectors used for this purpose include **microUSB** (see Figure 1-45a) or the smaller **miniUSB** (see Figure 1-45b). Newer Apple iPhones, iPods, and iPads use the proprietary **Lightning port** and connector for power and communication (see Figure 1-46).

(A) (B)

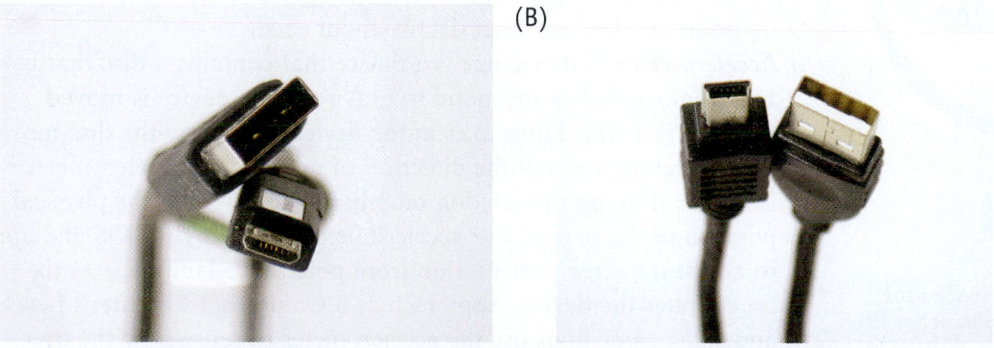

Figure 1-45 Some mobile devices may connect using a (a) microUSB or (b) miniUSB port

Figure 1-46 A Lightning cable by Apple, Inc., has a USB connector for the computer end and a Lightning connector for an iPhone or iPad

- ***Tethering and mobile hotspots.*** When a mobile device is connected to the Internet by way of its cellular network, you can allow other computers and devices to use this same connection. For example, in Figure 1-47, the smart phone is tethered by USB to a laptop so that the laptop can use the cellular

Figure 1-47 Tether your smart phone to your laptop using a USB cable

network to connect to the Internet. If the smart phone has Wi-Fi capabilities, the smart phone can create its own Wi-Fi hotspot for other computers and devices to connect to wirelessly. An app on the smart phone controls these connections, and your carrier subscription must allow for tethering and for providing mobile hotspots.

Figure 1-48 A gyroscope uses gravity to sense its relative position to the Earth

A mobile device can use an accelerometer and GPS receiver to sense its position. Here are brief details about each:

- ***Accelerometer.*** A gyroscope is a device that contains a disc that is free to move and can respond to gravity as the device is moved (see Figure 1-48). Three axes in the device sense how the disc moves and, therefore, can tell the direction of motion. An accelerometer is a type of gyroscope used in mobile devices to sense the physical position of the device. The accelerometer is used by the OS and apps to adjust the screen orientation from portrait to landscape as the user rotates the device. Apps such as a Compass, Carpenter's Leveler, and some game apps use the accelerometer to sense how the user is moving the device.

- ***GPS receiver.*** Mobile devices might contain a GPS receiver to determine its position by using the GPS satellite data or data from the position of nearby cellular towers. A cellular-enabled device with a GPS receiver is likely to use both types of data to find its position. A mobile device routinely reports its position to the owner of its operating system. For example, a device may report its position to Apple (for devices that use the iOS operating system by Apple, Inc.), Google (for devices that use the Android operating system by Google), or Microsoft (for devices that use the Windows Phone operating system by Microsoft) at least twice a day, and usually more often, which makes it possible for these companies to track your device's whereabouts, which is called geotracking. Law enforcement agencies sometimes use this data to reconstruct a person's travels.

STORAGE DEVICES

A+
220-901
3.1, 3.3,
3.4, 3.5

Mobile devices store their apps and data on a solid-state device (SSD), a type of flash memory. In addition, a device might have an external slot where you can plug in a smart card such as an SD card or MicroSD card to provide extra storage. Figure 1-49 shows a memory card slot on an Android tablet, and Figure 1-50 shows a MicroSD card. The iPhone, iPad, and iPod don't have these external slots for a smart card.

Figure 1-49 An Android device might provide a memory card slot to allow for extra storage

Figure 1-50 A mobile device might use a MicroSD card to add extra flash memory storage to the device

An Android or Microsoft device might also have a USB port that you can use to plug in a USB flash drive to provide extra storage or transfer files and folders to other devices. Apple mobile devices don't have USB ports.

MOBILE DEVICE ACCESSORIES

A+
220-901
3.1, 3.3,
3.4, 3.5

You can buy all kinds of accessories for mobile devices, such as wireless keyboards, speakers, earbuds, headsets, game pads, docking stations, printers, extra batteries, USB adapters, chargers, credit card readers for accepting payments by credit card, and protective covers for waterproofing. For example, Figure 1-51 shows a car docking station for a smart phone. Using this car dock, the smart phone is a GPS device giving driving directions.

Figure 1-51 A smart phone and a car docking station

FIELD-REPLACEABLE PARTS FOR MOBILE DEVICES

A+
220-901
3.1, 3.3,
3.4, 3.5

For the purposes of IT support technicians supporting mobile devices, know there are few field-replaceable units (FRU) in mobile devices because the cost of replacement, including parts and labor, generally exceeds the value of fixing rather than replacing the device. Although it is possible to replace the screens in some mobile devices, a support technician is not generally expected to take the time to do so. SIM cards and batteries can be replaced, and accessories such as a battery charger or earbuds can be attached.

Hands-On | Project 1-5 Explore www.ifixit.com

Replacing the battery in a smart phone or tablet is a handy skill for an IT support technician to have. If you have a smart phone or tablet or know a friend who has one, find out the brand and model of the device. Search the *www.ifixit.com* website, which is a wiki-based site with tons of guides for tearing down, repairing, and reassembling all kinds of products, including smart phones, tablets, and laptops. Does the site offer a guide for replacing the battery in your device or your friend's device? If so, list the high-level steps for the repair. What tools would you need to actually make the repair?

TOOLS USED BY A COMPUTER HARDWARE TECHNICIAN

A+
220-901
4.1

Every IT support technician who plans to repair desktop or laptop computers or mobile devices needs a handy toolbox with a few essential tools. Several hardware and software tools can help you maintain a computer and diagnose and repair computer problems. The tools you choose depend on the amount of money you can spend and the level of hardware support you expect to provide.

Essential tools for computer hardware troubleshooting are listed here, and several of them are shown in Figure 1-52. You can purchase some of these tools in a computer toolkit, although most toolkits contain items you really can do without.

Figure 1-52 Tools used by IT support technicians when maintaining, repairing, or upgrading computers

One of the more important tools is an ESD strap (also called a ground bracelet), which protects against ESD when working inside the computer case. Electrostatic discharge (ESD) is another name for static electricity, which can damage chips and destroy motherboards, even though it might not be felt or seen with the naked eye. Use the strap to connect or ground your hand to the case, as shown in Figure 1-53, and any static electricity between you and the case is dissipated.

Figure 1-53 An ESD strap, which protects computer components from ESD, can clip to the side of the computer case and eliminate ESD between you and the case

Here is a list of essential tools:

- An ESD strap (also called a ground bracelet)
- Flathead screwdriver
- Phillips-head or crosshead screwdriver
- Torx screwdriver set, particularly size T15
- Tweezers, preferably insulated ones, for picking pieces of paper out of printers or dropped screws out of tight places
- Extractor, a spring-loaded device that looks like a hypodermic needle (When you push down on the top, three wire prongs come out that can be used to pick up a screw that has fallen into a place where hands and fingers can't reach.)
- Software, including recovery CD or DVD for any OS you might work on (you might need several, depending on the OSs you support), antivirus software on bootable CDs or USB flash drives, and diagnostic software

The following tools might not be essential, but they are very convenient:

- Cans of compressed air (see Figure 1-54), small portable compressor, or antistatic vacuum cleaner to clean dust from inside a computer case
- Cleaning solutions and pads such as contact cleaner, monitor wipes, and cleaning solutions for CDs, DVDs, tapes, and drives

Figure 1-54 A can of compressed air is handy to blow dust from a computer case

- Multimeter to check cables and the power supply output
- Power supply tester
- Needle-nose pliers for removing jumpers and for holding objects (especially those pesky nuts on cable connectors) in place while you screw them in
- Cable ties to tie cables up and out of the way inside a computer case
- Flashlight to see inside the computer case
- AC outlet ground tester
- Network cable tester
- Loopback plugs to test ports
- Small cups or bags to help keep screws organized as you work
- Antistatic bags (a type of Faraday cage) to store unused parts

- Chip extractor to remove chips (To pry up the chip, a simple screwdriver is usually more effective, however.)
- Pen and paper for taking notes
- POST diagnostic cards

Notes It's important to know how to stay safe when working inside computers. Before opening a computer case and using the tools described in this section, be sure to read the appendix, "Safety Procedures and Environmental Concerns." As you work inside a computer, follow all the safety guidelines discussed in this appendix.

Keep your tools in a toolbox designated for hardware troubleshooting. If you put discs and hardware tools in the same box, be sure to keep the discs inside a hard plastic case to protect them from scratches and dents. In addition, make sure the diagnostic and utility software you use is recommended for the hardware and software you are troubleshooting.

Now let's turn our attention to the details of several IT support technician tools, including diagnostic cards, power supply testers, multimeters, and loopback plugs.

POST DIAGNOSTIC CARDS

A+ 220-901 4.1

Although not an essential tool, a POST diagnostic card, also called a POST card, or motherboard test card, can be of great help to discover and report computer errors and conflicts that occur when you first turn on a computer and before the operating system (such as Windows 8) is launched. To understand what a POST card does, you need to know about the firmware, which is programs and data stored on the motherboard. Two types of firmware may be used on motherboards:

- The older BIOS (basic input/output system) contains system BIOS to manage essential devices (such as the keyboard, mouse, hard drive, and monitor) before the OS is launched, startup BIOS to start the computer, and BIOS setup to change the motherboard configuration or settings. Figure 1-55 shows an embedded firmware chip on a motherboard that contains the BIOS programs.

Figure 1-55 This firmware chip contains flash ROM and CMOS RAM; CMOS RAM is powered by the coin battery located near the chip

- Newer motherboards use Unified Extensible Firmware Interface (UEFI) firmware that is more robust and secure than BIOS. Just as with BIOS, UEFI is responsible for managing essential devices before the OS is launched, starting the computer, and managing motherboard settings. UEFI can also assure that the boot is secure and no rogue operating system hijacks the system.

So now back to the usefulness of a POST card. The POST (power-on self test) is a series of tests performed by the startup UEFI/BIOS when you first turn on a computer. These tests determine if startup UEFI/BIOS can communicate correctly with essential hardware components required for a successful boot. If you have a problem that prevents the computer from booting that you suspect is related to hardware, you can install the POST card in an expansion slot on the motherboard. For laptops, some cards install in a USB port. Then attempt to boot. The card monitors the boot process and reports errors, usually as coded numbers on a small LED panel on the card. You then look up the number online or in the documentation that accompanies the card to get more information about the error and its source. Figure 1-56 shows a POST diagnostic card, the Post Code Master card by Microsystems Developments, Inc. (*www.postcodemaster.com*).

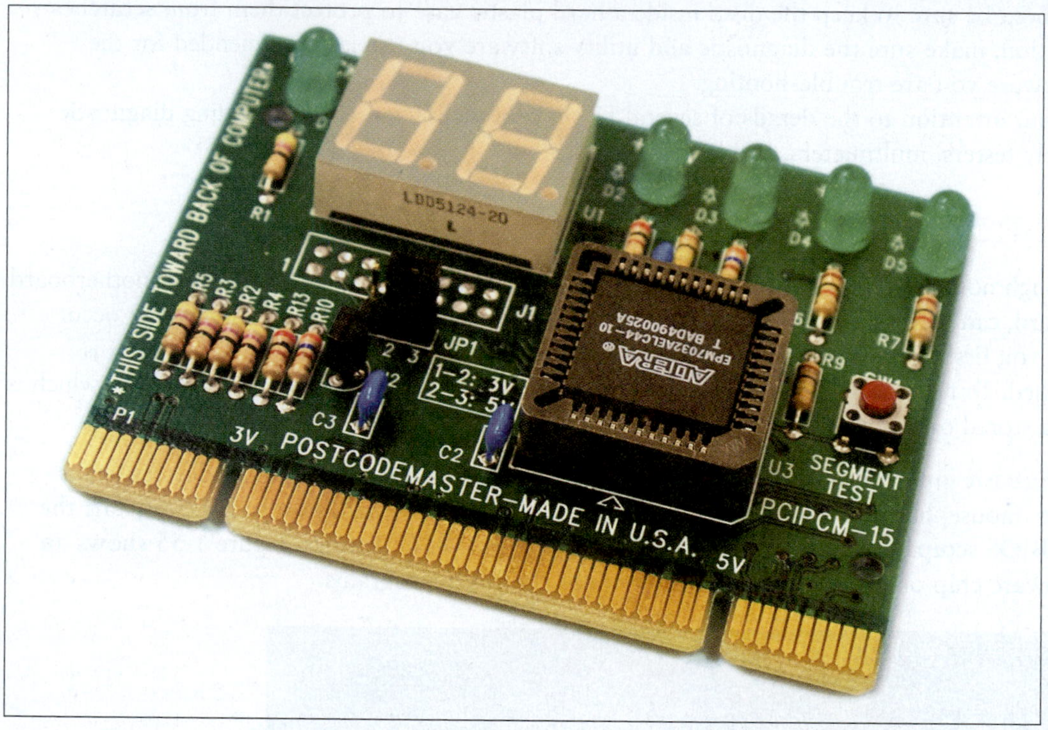

Figure 1-56 Post Code Master diagnostic card by Microsystems Developments, Inc., installs in a PCI slot

Before purchasing these or any other diagnostic tools or software, read the documentation about what they can and cannot do, and read some online product reviews. Try using Google.com and searching on "computer diagnostic card reviews."

> **Notes** Some Dell computers have lights on the case that blink in patterns to indicate a problem early in the boot before the OS loads. These blinking lights give information similar to that given by POST cards.

POWER SUPPLY TESTER

A+ 220-901 4.1

A power supply tester is used to measure the output of each connector coming from the power supply. You can test the power supply when it is outside or inside the case. As you saw earlier in Figure 1-8, the power supply provides several cables and connectors that power various components inside the computer case. A power supply tester has plugs for each type of cable. Connect a power cable to the tester, plug up the power supply, and turn on the tester. An LCD panel reports the output of each lead (see Figure 1-57).

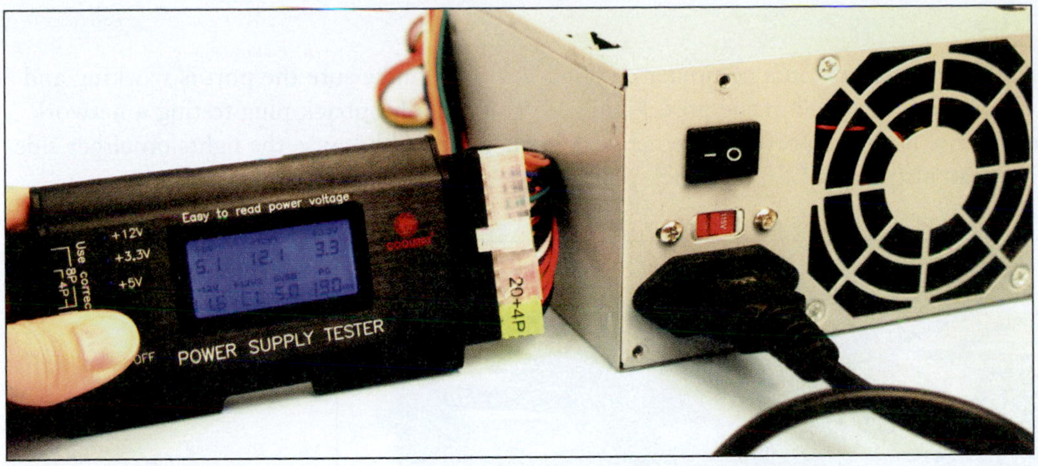

Figure 1-57 Use a power supply tester to test the output of each power connector on a power supply

MULTIMETER

A+ 220-901 4.1

A **multimeter** (see Figure 1-58) is a more general-purpose tool that can measure several characteristics of electricity in a variety of devices. Some multimeters can measure voltage, current, resistance, or continuity. (Continuity determines that two ends of a cable or fuse are connected without interruption.) When set to measure voltage, you can use it to measure output of each pin on a power supply connector. Set to measure continuity, a multimeter is useful to test fuses, to determine if a cable is good, or to match pins on one end of a cable to pins on the other end.

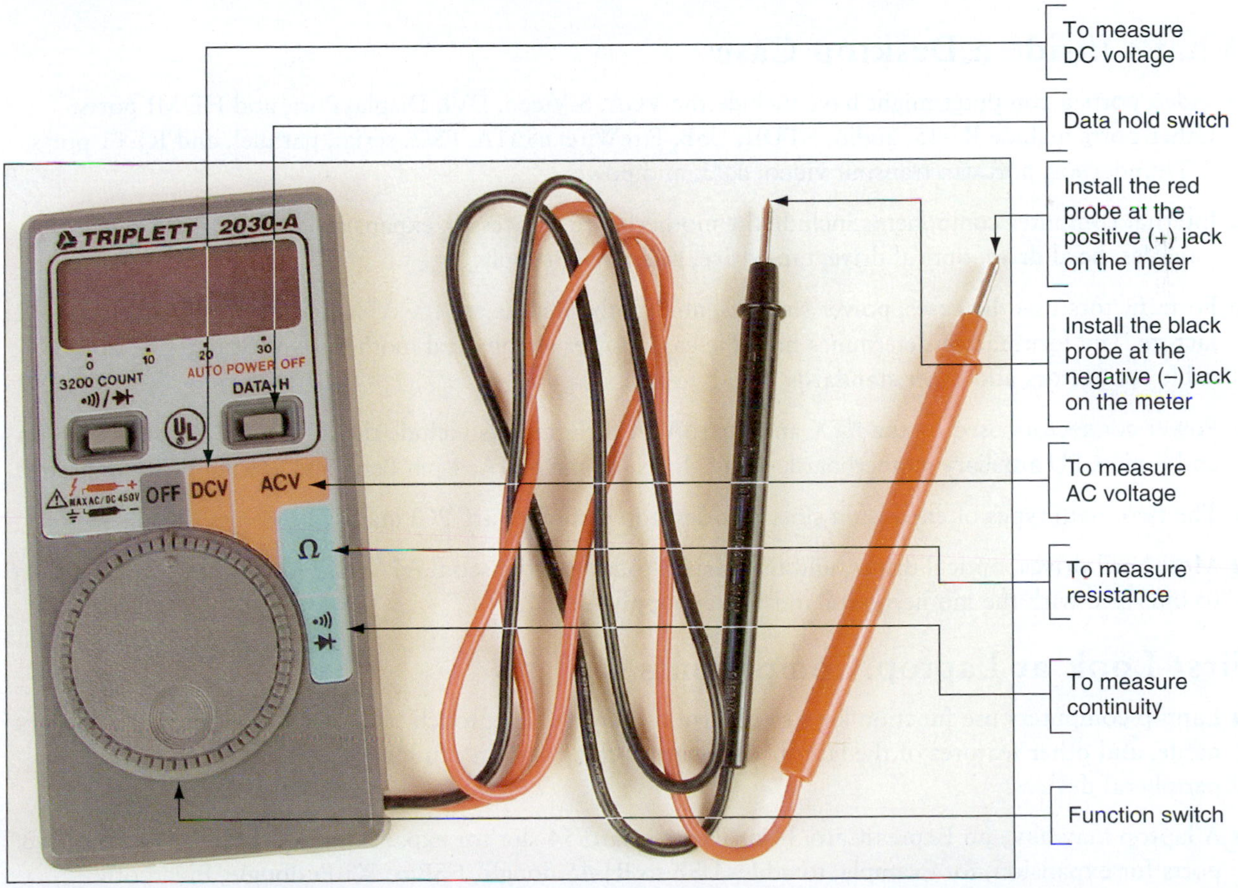

Figure 1-58 This digital multimeter can be set to measure voltage, resistance, or continuity

LOOPBACK PLUGS

A loopback plug is used to test a port in a computer or other device to make sure the port is working and might also test the throughput or speed of the port. Figure 1-59 shows a loopback plug testing a network port on a laptop. You know both the port and the network cable are good because the lights on either side of the port are lit. You can also buy a USB loopback plug to test USB ports.

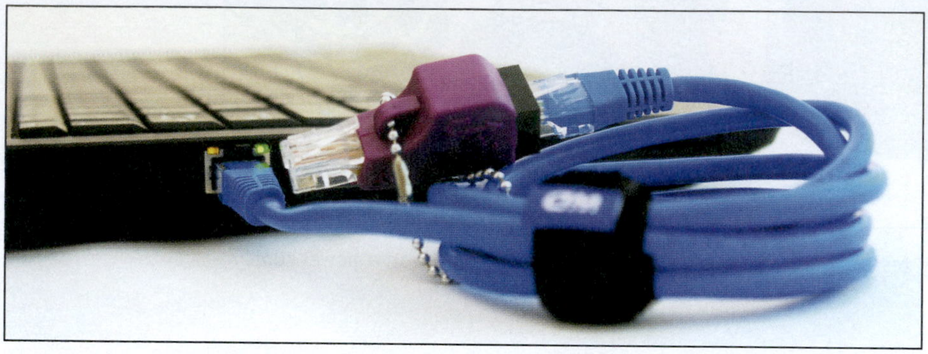

Figure 1-59 A loopback plug testing a network port and network cable

Now that you know about computer parts and their connections and the tools you need, you're ready to learn how to work inside a desktop or laptop case.

>> CHAPTER SUMMARY

What's Inside a Desktop Case

- Video ports a computer might have include the VGA, S-Video, DVI, DisplayPort, and HDMI ports. Other ports include RJ-45, audio, S/PDIF, USB, FireWire, eSATA, PS/2, serial, parallel, and RJ-11 ports. A Thunderbolt port can transmit video, data, and power.
- Internal computer components include the motherboard, processor, expansion cards, DIMM memory modules, hard drive, optical drive, tape drive, and power supply.
- Form factors used by cases, power supplies, and motherboards are the ATX and microATX form factors. The form factor determines how the case, power supply, and motherboard fit together and the cable connectors and other standards used by each.
- Power connectors used by the ATX and microATX form factors include the 20-pin P1, 24-pin P1, 4-pin and 8-pin CPU auxiliary motherboard, 4-pin Molex, 15-pin SATA, 4-pin Berg, and 6/8-pin PCIe connectors.
- The two main types of expansion slots in a desktop computer are PCI and PCI Express (PCIe).
- Most hard drives, optical drives, and tape drives today use the serial ATA (SATA) standards for the drive to interface with the motherboard and power supply.

First Look at Laptop Components

- Laptop computers use function keys to control display, volume, touch pad, media options, GPS, airplane mode, and other features of the laptop. A laptop docking station can make it easy to disconnect peripheral devices.
- A laptop may have an ExpressCard/34 or ExpressCard/54 slot for expansion. You can also use the USB ports for expansion, for example, to add a USB to RJ-45 dongle, USB to Wi-Fi dongle, Bluetooth capability, or a USB optical drive.

- Internal laptop components include the keyboard, hard drive, memory, smart card reader, optical drive, wireless card, screen, DC jack, battery pack, touch pad, speaker, system board, CPU, heat sink, and fan.
- An all-in-one computer uses a combination of components designed for desktop computers and laptops.

First Look at Mobile Device Hardware

- Mobile devices an IT support technician may be called on to service include smart phones, tablets, phablets, e-readers, smart cameras, GPS devices, and wearable technology devices such as smart watches, fitness monitors, glasses, and headsets.
- A mobile device might make a connection to the outside world using a cellular network, Wi-Fi network, Bluetooth, IR, NFC, tethering, creating its own hotspot, or wired connection. A wired connection may use a microUSB, miniUSB, or proprietary port, such as the Lightning port by Apple.
- A mobile device most likely will have an accelerometer to sense how the user is moving the device and a GPS receiver to sense the device's location and for geotracking.

Tools Used by a Computer Hardware Technician

- Common tools for a computer hardware technician include an ESD strap, screwdrivers, tweezers, flashlight, compressed air, and cleaning solutions and pads.
- Special tools a hardware technician might need include a POST diagnostic card, power supply tester, multimeter, and loopback plugs.

>> KEY TERMS

For explanations of key terms, see the Glossary for this text.

★ A+ Exam Tip To help you prepare for the A+ exams, the key terms in each chapter focus on the terms you need to know for the exams. Before you sit for the exams, be sure to review all the key terms in the Glossary.

4-pin 12-V connector
8-pin 12-V connector
20-pin P1 connector
24-pin P1 connector
accelerometer
airplane mode
all-in-one computer
analog
ATX (Advanced Technology Extended)
ATX12V power supply
audio port
base station
BIOS (basic input/output system)
BIOS setup
Bluetooth
cellular network
central processing unit (CPU)
chassis
DB15 port
DB9 port
DE15 port
desktop case
digital
DIMM (dual inline memory module)
DisplayPort
docking port
docking station
dual-voltage selector switch
DVI (Digital Video Interface) port
electrostatic discharge (ESD)
e-reader
Ethernet port
expansion card
ExpressCard
ExpressCard/34
ExpressCard/54
external SATA (eSATA) port
field replaceable unit (FRU)
FireWire port
firmware
fitness monitor
form factor
geotracking
GPS (Global Positioning System)
gyroscope
hard disk drive (HDD)
hard drive
HD15 port
HDMI (High-Definition Multimedia Interface) port
heat sink
hotspot
IEEE 1394 port
infrared (IR)
internal components
keyboard backlight
laptop
Lightning port
loopback plug
LPT port
main board
microATX (MATX)
microprocessor
microUSB
miniUSB
modem port
Molex connector
motherboard
multimeter
Near Field Communication (NFC)
netbook
network port
notebook
optical connector
parallel port
PCI (Peripheral Component Interconnect)
PCI Express (PCIe)
PCIe 6/8-pin connector

PCMCIA card
phablet
POST (power-on self test)
POST card
POST diagnostic card
power supply
power supply tester
power supply unit (PSU)
processor
PS/2 port
RAM (random access memory)
RJ-11 port
RJ-45 port
SATA power connector
screen orientation
serial ATA (SATA)
serial port
SIM (Subscriber Identity Module) card
smart camera
smart phone
S/PDIF (Sony/Philips Digital Interface) sound port
SO-DIMM (small outline DIMM)
startup BIOS
S-Video port
system BIOS
system board
tablet
tethered
Thunderbolt port
touch pad
tower case
Unified Extensible Firmware Interface (UEFI)
USB (Universal Serial Bus) port
USB optical drive
USB to Bluetooth adapter
USB to RJ-45 dongle
USB to Wi-Fi dongle
VGA (Video Graphics Array) port
video memory
vision sensor
wearable technology device
Wi-Fi (Wireless Fidelity)

>> REVIEWING THE BASICS

1. List six types of video ports.
2. Which is faster, a Hi-Speed USB port or a SuperSpeed USB port?
3. What type of output does an S/PDIF port provide?
4. What is the purpose of an expansion slot on a motherboard?
5. What should be the setting for a dual-voltage selector switch on a power supply when using a computer in the United States?
6. How is the best way to determine if a cable inside a computer is a data and instruction cable or a power cable?
7. What technology standard is commonly used today for hard drives to interface with the motherboard in a system?
8. How many pins did the first P1 power connector to the motherboard have that was used with the original ATX?
9. What type of expansion slot requires extra power so that 4 more pins had to be added to the older 20-pin P1 power connector on the motherboard?
10. What device might require extra power so that it uses the 12V 6-pin power connector? In what two locations might you find the connector?
11. What is the purpose of the 4-pin auxiliary connector on a motherboard?
12. What is the purpose of the 4-pin Molex connector?
13. Why are laptops usually more expensive than desktop computers with comparable power and features?
14. Which two types of buses may be used by ExpressCard slots?
15. Which port do you use to connect a docking station to a laptop?
16. Which type of memory module is used in a desktop computer? Which type is used in a laptop computer?
17. What wireless technology is used when two smart phones in close proximity exchange contact information?

18. Which tool can a computer hardware technician use when taking apart a computer to best protect computer components against ESD?
19. What is the purpose of a POST diagnostic card?
20. What are the three purposes accomplished by the motherboard BIOS?

>> THINKING CRITICALLY

1. You purchase a new desktop computer that does not have wireless capability, and then you decide that you want to use a wireless connection to the Internet. What are the least expensive ways (choose two) to upgrade your system to wireless?
   a. Trade in the computer for another computer that has wireless installed.
   b. Purchase a second computer that has wireless capability.
   c. Purchase a wireless expansion card and install it in your system.
   d. Purchase a USB wireless adapter and connect it to the computer by way of a USB port.
2. What type of computer is likely to use SO-DIMMs, have an internal power supply, and use a desktop processor socket?
3. A friend asks you for help in determining the best product to buy: a laptop, tablet, or smart phone. She is a paralegal and spends a lot of time at the courthouse researching real estate titles. She wants a device to take notes with as she works. List three questions you would ask her to help her make her decision.
4. When troubleshooting a computer hardware problem, which tool might help with each of the following problems?
   a. You suspect the network port on a computer is not functioning.
   b. The system fails at the beginning of the boot and nothing appears on the screen.
   c. A hard drive is not working and you suspect the Molex power connector from the power supply might be the source of the problem.

>> REAL PROBLEMS, REAL SOLUTIONS

REAL PROBLEM 1-1 Planning Your Computer Repair Toolkit

Research on the web to find the following tools for sale: ESD strap, set of flathead and Phillips-head screwdrivers, can of compressed air, monitor cleaning wipes, multimeter, power supply tester, cable ties, flashlight, loopback plug to test an Ethernet port, POST diagnostic card, and toolbox.

Print or save the webpage showing each tool and its price. What is the total cost of this set of tools? If you were building your own computer repair toolkit, which tools would you purchase first if you could not afford the entire set of tools? Which tools not listed would you add to your toolbox?

CHAPTER 2

Working Inside Desktop Computers and Laptops

After completing this chapter, you will be able to:

- Take apart a desktop computer and put it back together
- Explain the special considerations when supporting laptop computers that are different than supporting desktop computers
- Take apart a laptop computer and put it back together

Taking apart and servicing a computer are tasks that every A+ certified technician needs to know how to do. As part of your preparation to become A+ certified, try to find old desktop and laptop computers you can take apart. If you can locate the service manual for a laptop, you should be able to take it apart, repair it (assuming the parts are still available and don't cost more than the computer is worth), and get it up and running again. Have fun with this chapter and enjoy tinkering with these computers!

HOW TO WORK INSIDE A DESKTOP COMPUTER CASE

A+
220-901
1.2, 1.4,
1.5, 1.8

In this part of the chapter, you learn how to take apart a desktop computer and put it back together. This skill is needed in this and other chapters as you learn to add or replace computer parts inside the case and perhaps even build a system from scratch. As you read the following steps, you might want to perform the Hands-On Projects, which allow you to follow along by taking a computer apart. As you do so, be sure to follow all the safety precautions found in Appendix A "Safety Procedures and Environmental Concerns." In the steps that follow, each major computer component is identified and described. You learn much more about each component later in the text. Take your time—*don't rush*—as you take apart a computer for the first time. It can be a great learning experience or an expensive disaster! As you work, pay attention to the details, and work with care.

STEP 1: PLAN AND ORGANIZE YOUR WORK

A+
220-901
1.2, 1.4,
1.5, 1.8

When you first begin to learn how to work inside a computer case, make it a point to practice good organization skills. If you keep your notes, tools, screws, and computer parts well organized, your work goes smoother and is more fun. Here are some tips to keep in mind:

- Make notes as you work so that you can backtrack later if necessary. (When you're first learning to take a computer apart, it's really easy to forget where everything fits when it's time to put it back together. Also, in troubleshooting, you want to avoid repeating or overlooking things to try.)
- Remove loose jewelry that might get caught in cables and components as you work.
- To stay organized and not lose small parts, keep screws and spacers orderly and in one place, such as a cup or tray.
- Don't stack boards on top of each other: You could accidentally dislodge a chip this way. When you remove a circuit board or drive from a computer, carefully lay it on an antistatic mat or in an antistatic bag in a place where it won't get bumped.
- When handling motherboards, cards, or drives, don't touch the chips on the device. Hold expansion cards by the edges. Don't touch any soldered components on a card, and don't touch the edge connectors unless it's absolutely necessary. All this helps prevent damage from static electricity. Also, your fingerprints on the edge connectors can cause later corrosion.
- To protect a microchip, don't touch it with a magnetized screwdriver.
- Never ever touch the inside of a computer that is turned on. The one exception to this rule is when you're using a multimeter to measure voltage output.
- Consider the monitor and the power supply to be "black boxes." Never remove the cover or put your hands inside this equipment unless you know about the hazards of charged capacitors and have been trained to deal with them. The power supply and monitor contain enough power to kill you, even when they are unplugged.
- As you work, remember to watch out for sharp edges on computer cases that can cut you.
- In a classroom environment, after you have reassembled everything, have your instructor check your work before you put the cover back on and power up.

Now that you've prepared your work area and tools, put on your ESD strap and let's get started with opening the computer case.

STEP 2: OPEN THE COMPUTER CASE AND EXAMINE THE SYSTEM

A+
220-901
1.2, 1.4,
1.5, 1.8

Here are the steps to open a computer case:

1. ***Back up important data.*** If you are starting with a working computer, make sure important data is first backed up. Copy the data to an external storage device such as a flash drive or external hard drive. If something goes wrong while you're working inside the computer, at least your data will be safe.

2. ***Power down the system and unplug it.*** Remove discs from the optical drive. Then power down the system and unplug the power, monitor, mouse, and keyboard cables, and any other peripherals or cables attached and move them out of your way.

> **Caution** When you power down a computer and even turn off the power switch on the rear of the computer case, know that residual power is still on. Some motherboards even have a small light inside the case to remind you of this fact and to warn you that power is still getting to the system. Therefore, be sure to always unplug the power cord before opening a case.

3. ***Press and hold down the power button for a moment.*** After you unplug the computer, press the power button for about three seconds to completely drain the power supply (see Figure 2-1). Sometimes when you do so, you'll hear the fans quickly start and go off as residual power is drained. Only then is it safe to work inside the case.

Figure 2-1 Press the power button after the computer is unplugged

4. ***Have a plastic bag or cup handy to hold screws.*** When you reassemble the computer, you will need to insert the same screws in the same holes. This is especially important with the hard drive because screws that are too long can puncture the hard drive housing so be careful to label those screws clearly.

5. ***Open the case cover.*** Sometimes I think figuring out how to open a computer case is the most difficult part of disassembling. If you need help figuring it out, check the user manual or website of the case manufacturer. To remove the computer case cover, do the following:

   - Some cases require you to start by laying the case on its side and removing the faceplate on the front of the case first. Other cases require you to remove a side panel first, and really older cases require you to first remove the entire sides and top as a single unit. Study your case for the correct approach.
   - Most cases have panels on each side of the case that can be removed. It is usually necessary to only remove the one panel to expose the top of the motherboard. To know which panel to remove, look at where the ports are on the rear of the case. For example, in Figure 2-2, the ports on this motherboard are on the left side of the case, indicating the bottom of the motherboard is on the left. Therefore, you will want to remove the right panel to expose the top of this motherboard. Lay the case down to its

left so that the ports and the motherboard are sitting on the bottom. Later, depending on how drives are installed, it might become necessary to remove the bottom panel in order to remove the screws that hold the drives in place.

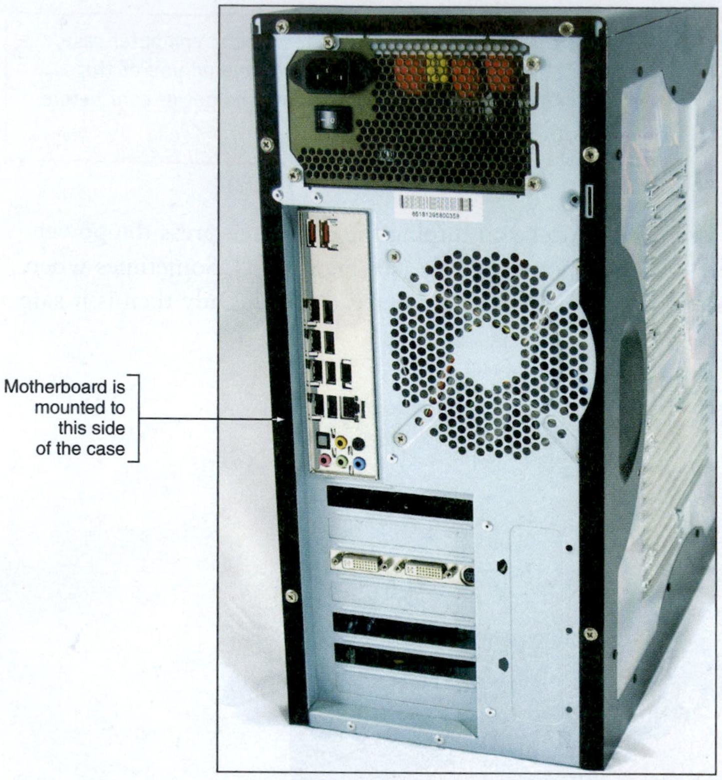

Figure 2-2 Decide which side panel to remove

- Locate the screws or clips that hold the side panel in place. Be careful not to unscrew any screws besides these. The other screws probably are holding the power supply, fan, and other components in place (see Figure 2-3). Place the screws in the cup or bag used for that purpose. Some cases use clips on a side panel in addition to or instead of screws (see Figure 2-4).

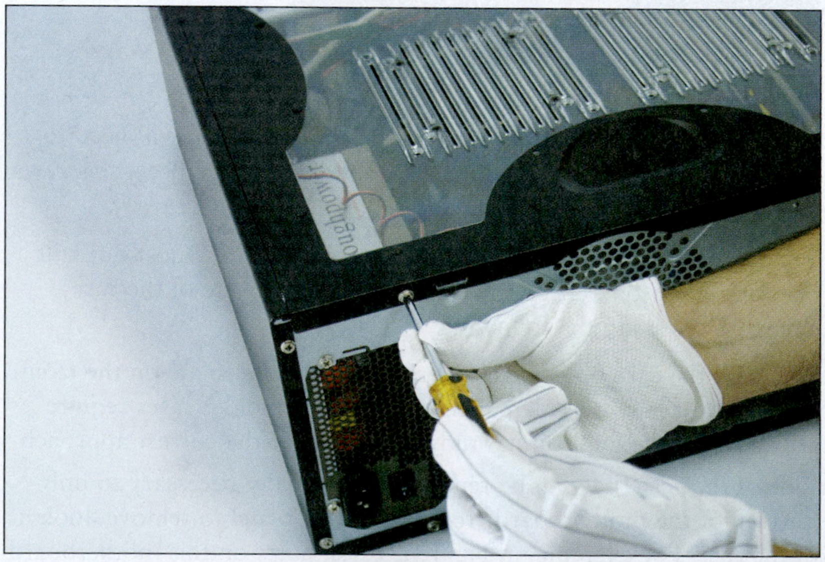

Figure 2-3 Locate the screws that hold the side panel in place

Figure 2-4 On this system, clips hold the side panel in place

- After the screws are removed, slide the panel toward the rear, and then lift it off the case (see Figure 2-5).

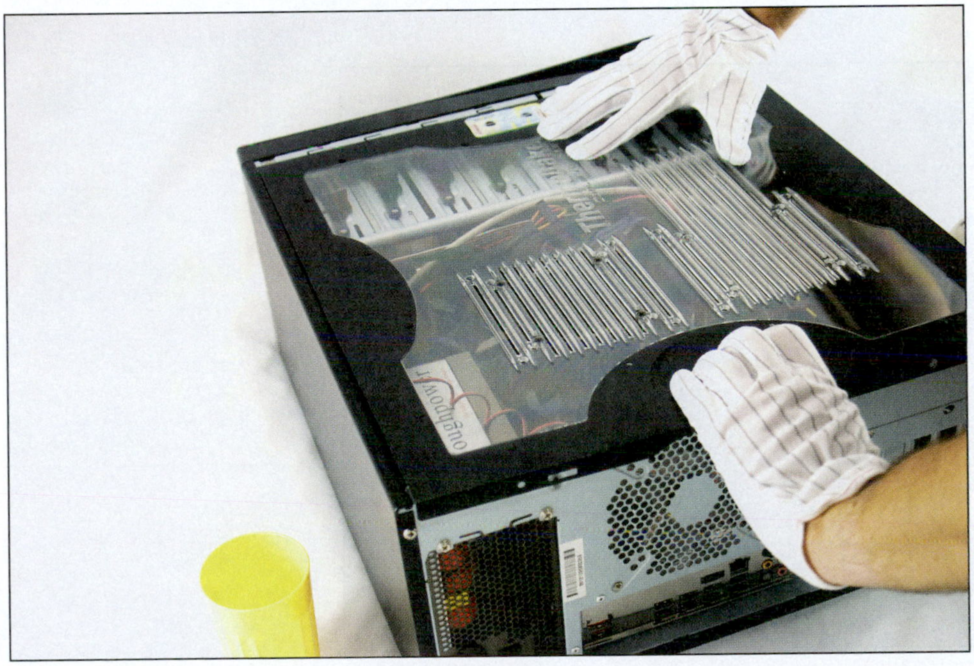

Figure 2-5 Slide the panel to the rear of the case

- Some cases require you to pop the front panel off the case before removing the side panels. Look for a lever on the bottom of the panel and hinges at the top. Squeeze the lever to release the front panel and lift it off the case (see Figure 2-6).

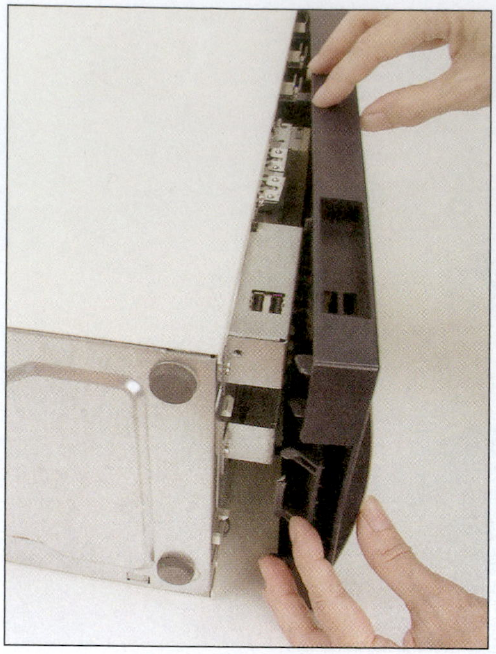

Figure 2-6 Some cases require you to remove the front panel before removing the side panel of a computer case

- Then remove a single screw (see Figure 2-7) and slide the side panel to the front and then off the case.

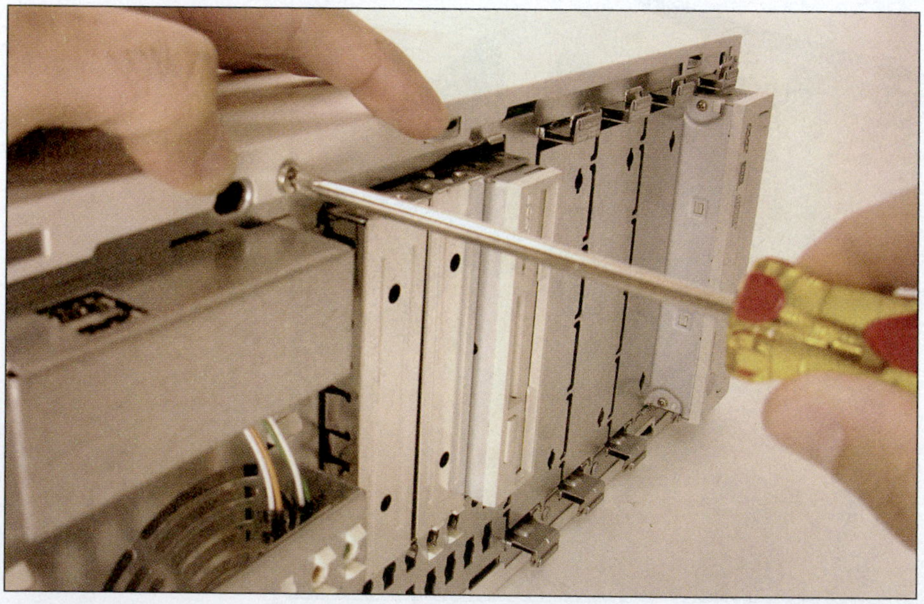

Figure 2-7 One screw holds the side panel in place

6. ***Clip your ESD strap to the side of the computer case.*** To dissipate any charge between you and the computer, put on your ESD strap if you have not already done so. Then clip the alligator clip on the strap cable to the side of the computer case (see Figure 2-8).

Figure 2-8 Attach the alligator clip of your ground bracelet to the side of the computer case

After you open a computer case, the main components you see inside are the power supply, motherboard, and drives installed in drive bays. You also see a lot of cables and wires connecting various components. These cables are power cables from the power supply to various components, or cables carrying data and instructions between components. The best way to know the purpose of a cable is to follow the cable from its source to its destination.

Hands-On | Project 2-1 Open a Computer Case

Using a desktop or tower computer, identify all the ports on the front or rear of the case. If you need help, see Table 1 in the chapter, "First Look at Computer Parts and Tools." Look at the rear of the case. On which side is the motherboard? Examine the case and determine how to open it. Shut down the system, and unplug the power cable. Disconnect all other cables. Press the power button on the front of the case to discharge residual power. Carefully open the case. Remember to not touch anything inside the case unless you are using an ESD strap or antistatic gloves to protect components against ESD.

Draw a diagram of the inside of the case and label all drives, the motherboard, the cooler, DIMM memory modules, the power supply, and any expansion cards installed. Leave the case open so you'll be ready for Hands-On Project 2-2 coming up later.

STEP 3: REMOVE EXPANSION CARDS

A+
220-901
1.2, 1.4,
1.5, 1.8

If you plan to remove several components, draw a diagram of all cable connections to the motherboard, expansion cards, and drives. You might need this cable connection diagram to help you reassemble. Note where each cable begins and ends, and pay particular attention to the small wires and connectors that connect the lights, switches, and ports on the front of the case to the motherboard front panel connectors. It's important to be careful about diagramming these because it is so easy to connect them in the wrong position later when you reassemble. If you want, use a felt-tip marker to make a mark across components, to indicate a cable connection, board placement, motherboard orientation, speaker connection, brackets, and so on, so that you can simply line up the marks when you reassemble. This method, however, probably won't work for the front case wires because they are so small. For these, consider writing down the color of the wires and their position on the pins or taking a photo of the wires in their positions with a digital camera (see Figure 2-9).

Figure 2-9 Diagram the pin locations of the color-coded wires that connect to the front of the case

> **Notes** A connector on a motherboard that consists of pins that stick up from the board is called a header. For example, the group of pins shown in Figure 2-9 is called the **front panel header**.

Computer systems vary in so many ways, it's impossible to list the exact order to disassemble one. Most likely, however, you need to remove the expansion cards first. Do the following to remove the expansion cards:

1. Remove any wire or cable connected to the card.
2. Remove the screw holding the card to the case (see Figure 2-10).

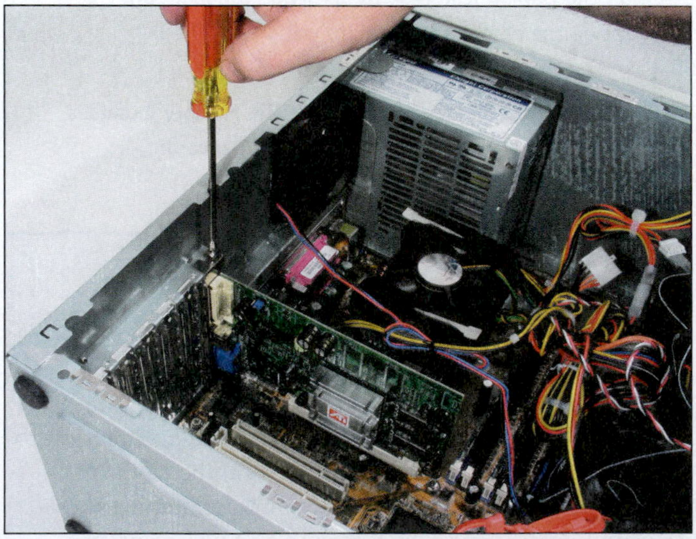

Figure 2-10 Remove the screw holding an expansion card to the case

3. Grasp the card with both hands and remove it by lifting straight up. If you have trouble removing it from the expansion slot, you can *very slightly* rock the card from end to end (*not* side to side). Rocking the card from side to side might spread the slot opening and weaken the connection.
4. As you remove the card, don't put your fingers on the edge connectors or touch a chip, and don't stack the cards on top of one another. Lay each card aside on a flat surface, preferably in an antistatic bag.

Notes Cards installed in PCI Express × 16 slots use a latch that helps to hold the card securely in the slot. To remove these cards, use one finger to hold the latch back from the slot, as shown in Figure 2-11, as you pull the card up and out of the slot.

Figure 2-11 Hold the retention mechanism back as you remove a video card from its expansion slot

Hands-On Project 2-2 Identify Connectors Used on an Installed Motherboard

If necessary, remove the case cover to your desktop computer. Next, remove the expansion cards from your system. With the expansion cards out of the way, you can more clearly see the power cables and other cables and cords connected to the motherboard. Diagrams and notes are extremely useful when disassembling and reassembling a system. To practice this skill, draw a large rectangle that represents the motherboard. On the rectangle, label every header or connector that is used on the board. Include on the label the type of cable that is used and where the other end of the cable connects.

STEP 4: REMOVE THE MOTHERBOARD, POWER SUPPLY, AND DRIVES

A+
220-901
1.2, 1.4,
1.5, 1.8

Depending on the system, you might need to remove the motherboard next or remove the drives next. My choice is to first remove the motherboard. It and the processor are the most expensive and easily damaged parts in the system. I like to get them out of harm's way before working with the drives. However, in some cases, you must remove the drives or the power supply before you can get to the motherboard. Study your situation and decide which to do first. To remove the motherboard, do the following:

1. Unplug the power supply lines to the motherboard.
2. Unplug SATA cables connected to the motherboard.
3. The next step is to disconnect wires leading from the front or top of the computer case to the motherboard, which are called the front panel connectors. If you don't have the motherboard manual handy, be very careful to diagram how these wires connect because they are rarely labeled well on a motherboard. Make a careful diagram and then disconnect the wires. Figure 2-12 shows five leads and the pins on the motherboard front panel header that receive these leads. The pins are color-coded and cryptically labeled on the board.

Figure 2-12 Five leads from the front panel connect to two rows of pins on the motherboard front panel header

4. Disconnect any other cables or wires connected to the motherboard. A case fan might be getting power by a small wire connected to the motherboard. In addition, USB ports on the front of the computer case might be connected by a cable to the motherboard.
5. You're now ready to remove the screws that hold the motherboard to the case. A motherboard is installed so that the bottom of the board does not touch the case. If the fine traces or lines on the bottom of the board were to touch the case, a short would result when the system is running. To keep the board from touching the case, screw holes are elevated, or you'll see spacers, also called standoffs, which are round plastic or metal pegs that separate the board from the case. Carefully pop off these spacers and/or remove the screws (up to nine) that hold the board to the case (see Figure 2-13) and then remove the board. Set it aside in a safe place. Figure 2-14 shows a motherboard sitting to the side of these spacers. One spacer is in place and the other is lying beside its case holes. Also notice in the photo the two holes in the motherboard where screws are used to connect the board to the spacers.

Figure 2-13 Remove up to nine screws that hold the motherboard to the case

Figure 2-14 This motherboard connects to a case using screws and spacers that keep the board from touching the case

Notes When you're replacing a motherboard in a case that is not the same size as the original board, you can use needle-nose pliers to unplug a standoff so you can move it to a new hole.

6. The motherboard should now be free and you can carefully remove it from the case, as shown in Figure 2-15. Lift the board by its edges, as shown in the figure.

Caution Never lift a motherboard by the cooler because doing so might create an air gap between the cooler and the processor, which can cause the processor to later overheat.

Figure 2-15 Remove the motherboard from the case

Caution Some processors have heavy cooling assemblies installed on top of them. For these systems, it is best to remove the cooler before you take the motherboard out of the case because the motherboard is not designed to support this heavy cooler when the motherboard is not securely seated in the case. How to remove the cooler is covered in the chapter, "Supporting Processors and Upgrading Memory."

7. To remove the power supply from the case, look for screws that attach the power supply to the computer case, as shown in Figure 2-16. Be careful not to remove any screws that hold the power supply housing together. You do not want to take the housing apart. After you have removed the screws, the power supply still might not be free. Sometimes, it is attached to the case on the underside by recessed slots. Turn the case over and look on the bottom for these slots. If they are present, determine in which direction you need to slide the power supply to free it from the case.

Figure 2-16 Removing the power supply mounting screws

8. Remove each drive next, handling the drives with care. Here are some tips:

- Some drives have one or two screws on each side of the drive attaching the drive to the drive bay. After you remove the screws, the drive slides to the front or to the rear and then out of the case.
- Sometimes, there is a catch underneath the drive that you must lift up as you slide the drive forward.
- Some drive bays have a clipping mechanism to hold the drive in the bay. First release the clip and then pull the drive forward and out of the bay (see Figure 2-17). Handle the drives with care. Some drives have an exposed circuit board on the bottom of the drive. Don't touch this board.

Figure 2-17 To remove this CD drive, first pull the clip forward to release the drive from the bay

- Some cases have a removable bay for small drives (see Figure 2-18). These bays can hold narrow drives such as hard drives and tape drives. The bay is removed first and then the drives are removed from the bay. To remove the bay, first remove the screws or release the clip holding the bay in place and then slide the bay out of the case. The drives are usually installed in the bay with two screws on each side of each drive. Remove the screws and then the drives (see Figure 2-19).

Figure 2-18 Push down on the clip and then slide the removable bay forward and out of the case

Figure 2-19 Drives in this removable bay are held in place with screws on each side of the bay

STEPS TO PUT A COMPUTER BACK TOGETHER

A+
220-901
1.2, 1.4,
1.5, 1.8

To reassemble a computer, reverse the process of disassembling. Here is where your diagrams will be really useful and having the screws and cables organized will also help. In the directions that follow, we're also considering the possibility that you are installing a replacement part as you reassemble the system. Do the following:

1. Install components in the case in this order: power supply, drives, motherboard, and cards. When installing drives, know that for some systems, it's easier to connect data cables to the drives and then slide the drives into the bay. If the drive is anchored to the bay with screws or latches, be careful to align the front of the drive flush with the front of the case before installing screws or pushing in the latches (see Figure 2-20).

Figure 2-20 Align the front of the drive flush with the case front and then anchor with a screw

2. Place the motherboard inside the case. Make sure the ports stick out of the I/O shield at the rear of the case and the screw holes line up with screw holes on the bottom of the case. Figure 2-21 shows how you must align the screw holes on the motherboard with those in the case. There should be at least six screw sets, and there might be as many as nine. Use as many screws as there are holes in the motherboard. Figure 2-22 shows one screw being put in place.

Figure 2-21 Align screw holes in the case with those on the motherboard

Figure 2-22 Use one screw in each screw hole on the motherboard

3. Connect the power cords from the power supply to the motherboard. A system will always need the main P1 power connector and most likely will need the 4-pin auxiliary connector for the processor. Other power connectors might be needed depending on the devices you later install in the system. Here are the details:

   - Connect the P1 power connector from the power supply to the motherboard (see Figure 2-23).

Figure 2-23 The 24-pin connector supplies power to the motherboard

- Connect the 4-pin auxiliary power cord coming from the power supply to the motherboard, as shown in Figure 2-24. This cord supplies the supplemental power required for the processor.

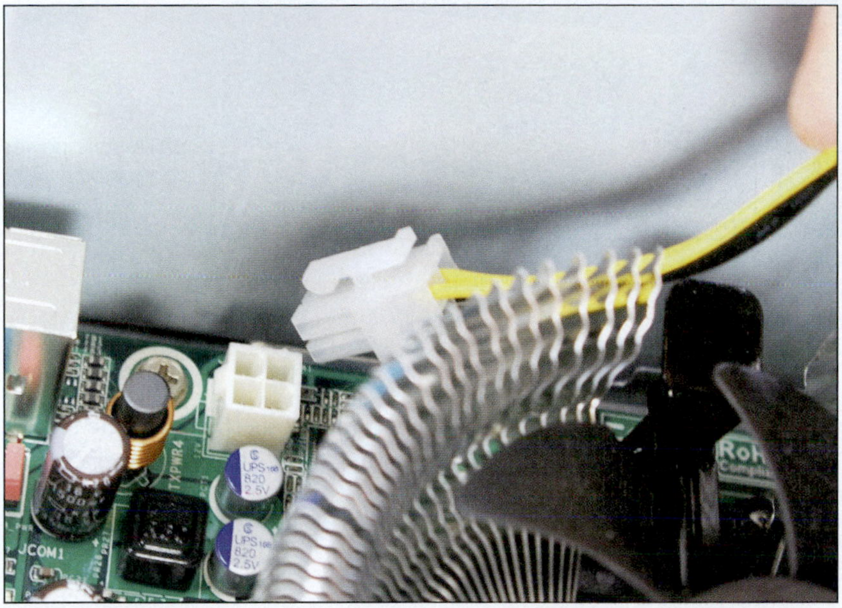

Figure 2-24 The auxiliary 4-pin power cord provides power to the processor

- A board might have a 6-pin or 8-pin PCIe power connector (see Figure 2-25). If the board has either connector, connect the 6-pin or 8-pin cord from the power supply to the connector. If a power supply doesn't have this connector, you can use an adapter to convert two Molex connectors to a PCIe connector.

Figure 2-25 8-pin PCIe Version 2.0 power connector

- Some boards designed to support multiple PCIe video cards will have additional power connectors on the board to power these wattage-hungry cards. For example, Figure 2-26(a) shows a Molex-style connector on one board that provides auxiliary power to PCIe graphics cards. This same board offers a SATA-style connector, shown in Figure 2-26(b). The motherboard documentation says to use just one of these auxiliary power connectors to provide additional wattage for PCIe video cards.

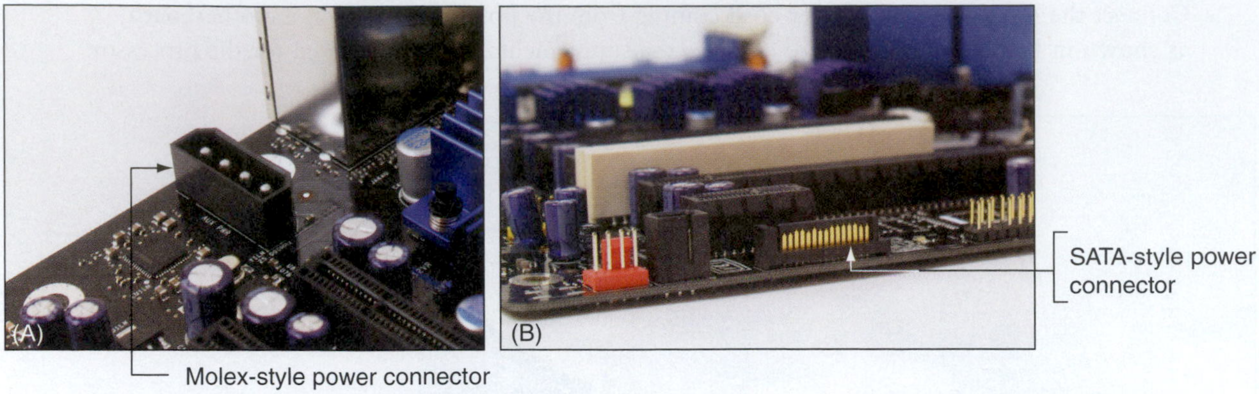

Figure 2-26 Auxiliary power connectors to support PCIe

- To power the case fan, connect the power cord from the fan to pins on the motherboard labeled Fan Header. Alternately, some case fans use a 4-pin Molex connector that connects to a power cable coming directly from the power supply.
- If a CPU and cooler are already installed on the motherboard, connect the power cord from the CPU fan to the pins on the motherboard labeled CPU Fan Header.

4. Connect the wire leads from the front panel of the case to the front panel header on the motherboard. These are the wires for the switches, lights, and ports on the front or top of the computer. Because your case and your motherboard might not have been made by the same manufacturer, you need to pay close attention to the source of the wires to determine where they connect on the motherboard. For example, Figure 2-27 shows a computer case that has seven connectors from the front panel that connect to the motherboard. Figure 2-28 shows the front panel header on the motherboard for these lights and switches. If you look closely at the board in Figure 2-28, you can see labels identifying the pins.

Figure 2-27 Seven connectors from the front panel connect to the motherboard

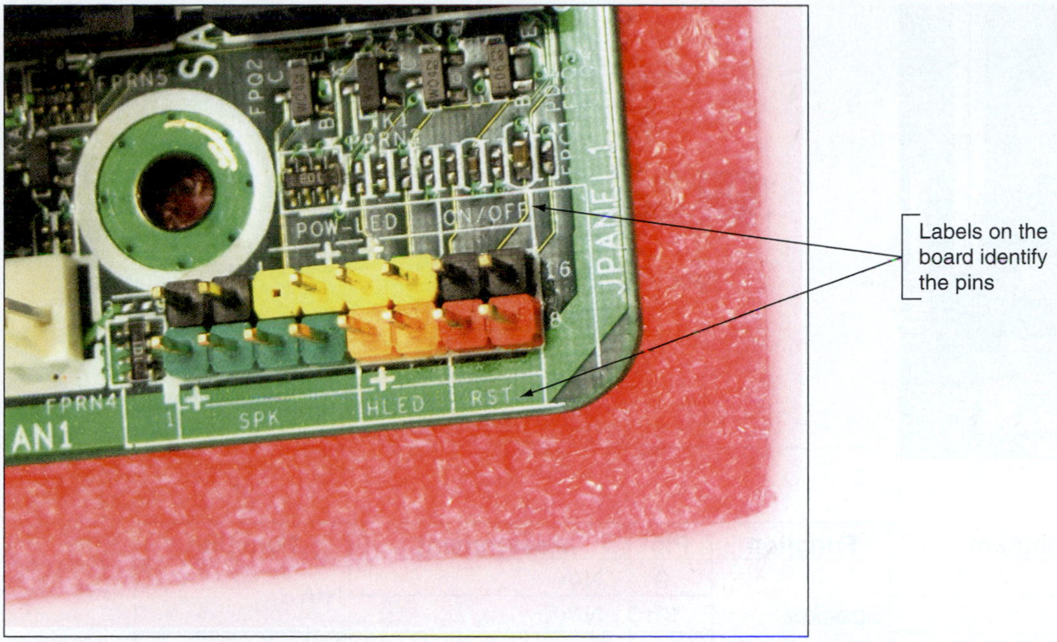

Figure 2-28 Front panel header uses color-coded pins and labels

The five smaller connectors on the right side of Figure 2-27 from right to left are labeled as follows:

- *Power SW*. Controls power to the motherboard; must be connected for the PC to power up
- *HDD LED*. Controls the drive activity light on the front panel that lights up when any SATA or IDE device is in use (HDD stands for hard disk drive; LED stands for light-emitting diode; and an LED is a light on the front panel.)
- *Power LED+*. Positive LED controls the power light and indicates that power is on
- *Power LED−*. Negative LED controls the power light; the two positive and negative leads indicate that power is on
- *Reset SW*. Switch used to reboot the computer

Notes Positive wires connecting the front panel to the motherboard are usually a solid color, and negative wires are usually white or striped.

To help orient the larger connectors on the motherboard pins, look for a small triangle embedded on the connector that marks one of the outside wires as pin 1 (see Figure 2-27). Look for pin 1 to be labeled on the motherboard as a small 1 embedded to either the right or the left of the group of pins. If the labels on the board are not clear, turn to the motherboard user guide for help. The diagram in Figure 2-29 shows what you can expect from one motherboard user guide. Notice pin 1 is identified as a square pin in the diagram, rather than round like the other pins.

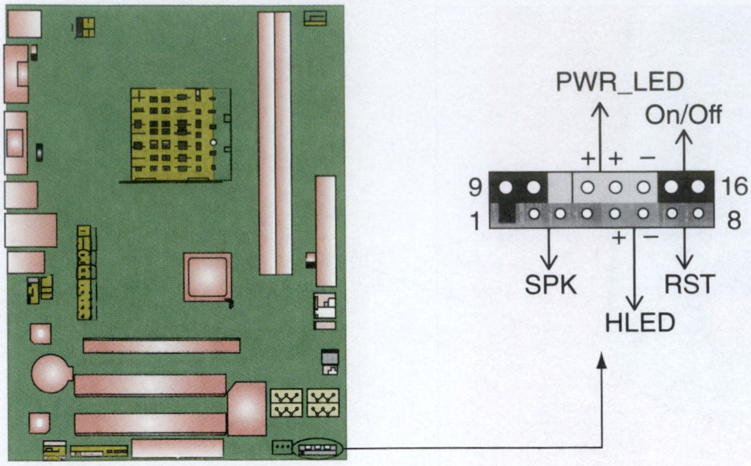

Pin	Assignment	Function	Pin	Assignment	Function
1	+5 V	Speaker connector	9	N/A	N/A
2	N/A		10	N/A	
3	N/A		11	N/A	N/A
4	Speaker		12	Power LED (+)	Power LED
5	HDD LED (+)	Hard drive LED	13	Power LED (+)	
6	HDD LED (–)		14	Power LED (–)	
7	Ground	Reset button	15	Power button	Power-on button
8	Reset control		16	Ground	

Figure 2-29 Documentation for front panel header connections

> **Notes** If the user guide is not handy, you can download it from the motherboard manufacturer's website. Search on the brand and model number of the board, which is imprinted somewhere on the board.

Sometimes the motherboard documentation is not clear, but guessing is okay when connecting a wire to a front panel header connection. If it doesn't work, no harm is done. Figure 2-30 shows all front panel wires in place and the little speaker also connected to the front panel header pins.

Figure 2-30 Front panel header with all connectors in place

5. Connect wires to ports on the front panel of the case. Depending on your motherboard and case, there might be cables to connect audio ports or USB ports on the front of the case to headers on the motherboard. Audio and USB connectors are the two left connectors shown in Figure 2-27. You can see these ports for audio and USB on the front of the case in Figure 2-31. Look in the motherboard documentation for the location of these connectors. The audio and USB connectors are labeled for one board in Figures 2-32(a) and (b).

Figure 2-31 Ports on the front of the computer case

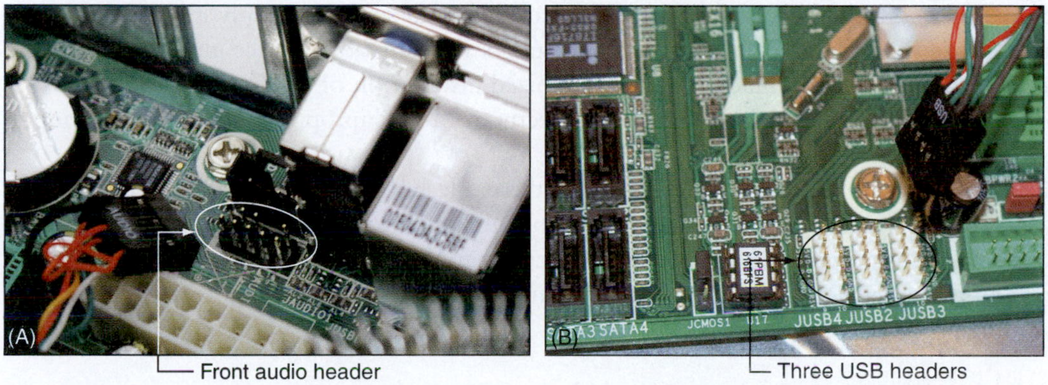

Figure 2-32 Connectors for front panel ports

6. Install the video card and any other expansion cards. Push the card straight down into the slot, being careful to not rock side to side, and install the screw to secure the card to the case.
7. Take a few minutes to double-check each connection to make sure it is correct and snug. Verify all required power cords are connected correctly and the video card is seated solidly in its slot. Also verify that no wires or cables are obstructing fans. You can use cable ties to tie wires up and out of the way.
8. Plug in the keyboard, monitor, and mouse.
9. In a classroom environment, have the instructor check your work before you close the case and power up.

10. Turn on the power and check that the PC is working properly. If the PC does not work, most likely the problem is a loose connection. Just turn off the power and go back and check each cable connection and each expansion card. You probably have not solidly seated a card in the slot. After you have double-checked, try again.

Now step back and congratulate yourself on a job well done! By taking a computer apart and putting it back together, you've learned much about how computer parts interconnect and work.

Hands-On Project 2-3 Close the Case

The case cover to your desktop computer is off from doing the previous exercises. Before you close your case, it's always a good idea to quickly clean it first. Using a can of compressed air, blow the dust away from fans and other components inside the case. Be careful to not touch components unless you are properly grounded. When you're done, close the case cover.

Now we turn our attention to laptops.

SPECIAL CONSIDERATIONS WHEN SUPPORTING LAPTOPS

A+
220-901
3.1, 4.5

Laptops and their replacement parts cost more than desktop computers with similar features because their components are designed to be more compact and stand up to travel. They use compact hard drives, small memory modules, and CPUs that require less power than regular components. Whereas a desktop computer is often assembled from parts made by a variety of manufacturers, laptop computers are almost always sold by a vendor that either manufactured the laptop or had it manufactured as a consolidated system. Factors to consider that generally apply more to laptop than desktop computers are the original equipment manufacturer's warranty, the service manuals and diagnostic software provided by the manufacturer, the customized installation of the OS that is unique to laptops, and the advantage of ordering replacement parts directly from the laptop manufacturer or other source authorized by the manufacturer.

In many situations, the tasks of maintaining, upgrading, and troubleshooting a laptop require the same skills, knowledge, and procedures as when servicing a desktop computer. However, you should take some special considerations into account when caring for, supporting, upgrading, and troubleshooting laptops. These same concerns apply to netbooks and all-in-one computers. Let's begin with warranty concerns.

WARRANTY CONCERNS

A+
220-901
3.1, 4.5

Most manufacturers or retailers of laptops offer at least a one-year warranty and the option to purchase an extended warranty. Therefore, when problems arise while the laptop is under warranty, you are dealing with a single manufacturer or retailer to get support or parts. After the laptop is out of warranty, this manufacturer or retailer can still be your one-stop shop for support and parts.

Caution The warranty often applies to all components in the system, but it can be voided if someone other than an authorized service center services the laptop. Therefore, you, as a service technician, must be very careful not to void a warranty that the customer has purchased. Warranties can be voided by opening the case, removing part labels, installing other-vendor parts, upgrading the OS, or disassembling the system unless directly instructed to do so by the authorized service center help desk personnel.

Before you begin servicing a laptop, to avoid problems with a warranty, always ask the customer, "Is the laptop under warranty?" If the laptop is under warranty, look at the documentation to find out how to get technical support. Options are chat sessions on the web, phone numbers, and email. Use the most appropriate option. Before you contact technical support, have the laptop model and serial number ready (see Figure 2-33). You'll also need the name, phone number, and address of the person or company that made the purchase. Consider asking the customer for a copy of the receipt and warranty so that you'll have the information you need to talk with support personnel.

Figure 2-33 The model and serial number stamped on the bottom of a laptop are used to identify the laptop to service desk personnel

Based on the type of warranty purchased by the laptop's owner, the manufacturer might send an on-site service technician, ask you to ship or take the laptop to an authorized service center, or help you solve the problem by an online chat session or over the phone. Table 2-1 lists some popular manufacturers of laptops, netbooks, and all-in-ones. Manufacturers of laptops typically also produce all-in-ones because of the features they have in common.

Manufacturer	Website
Acer	*us.acer.com* and *us.acer.com/ac/en/US/content/support*
Apple Computer	*www.apple.com* and *www.apple.com/support*
ASUS	*usa.asus.com* and *www.asus.com/us/support/*
Dell Computer	*www.dell.com* and *support.dell.com*
Fujitsu/Fuji	*www.fujitsu.com* and *www.fujitsu.com/support*
Gateway	*www.gateway.com* and *support.gateway.com*
Hewlett Packard (HP)	*www.hp.com* and *www8.hp.com/us/en/support.html*
Lenovo (formerly IBM ThinkPad)	*www.lenovo.com* and *support.lenovo.com*
Microsoft	*www.microsoft.com*
Samsung	*www.samsung.com* and *www.samsung.com/support*
Sony (VAIO)	*store.sony.com* and *esupport.sony.com*
Toshiba America	*www.toshiba.com/tai/* and *www.toshiba.com/tai/support.jsp*

Table 2-1 Laptop, netbook, and all-in-one manufacturers

SERVICE MANUALS AND OTHER SOURCES OF INFORMATION

A+
220-901
3.1, 4.5

Desktop computer cases tend to be similar to one another, and components in desktop systems are usually interchangeable among manufacturers. Not so with laptops. Laptop manufacturers typically take great liberty in creating their own unique computer cases, buses, cables, connectors, drives, circuit boards, fans, and even screws, all of which are likely to be proprietary in design.

Every laptop model has a unique case. Components are installed in unique ways and opening the case for each laptop model is done differently. Because of these differences, servicing laptops can be very complicated and time consuming. For example, a hard drive on one laptop is accessed by popping open a side panel and sliding the drive out of its bay. However, to access the hard drive on another model laptop, you must remove the keyboard. If you are not familiar with a particular laptop model, you can damage the case frame or plastics as you pry and push trying to open it. Trial and error is likely to damage a case. Even though you might successfully replace a broken component, the damaged case will result in an unhappy customer.

Fortunately, a laptop service manual can save you much time and effort—if you can locate one (see Figure 2-34). Most laptop manufacturers closely guard these service manuals and release them only to authorized service centers. Two laptop manufacturers, Lenovo (formerly IBM ThinkPad) and Dell, provide their service manuals online free of charge. HP also does an excellent job of offering online support. For example, in Figure 2-35, you can see a video in progress showing you the steps to replace the optical drive in an HP laptop. I applaud Lenovo, Dell, and HP for the generous documentation about how their laptops are disassembled and the options to purchase proprietary parts without first being an authorized service center.

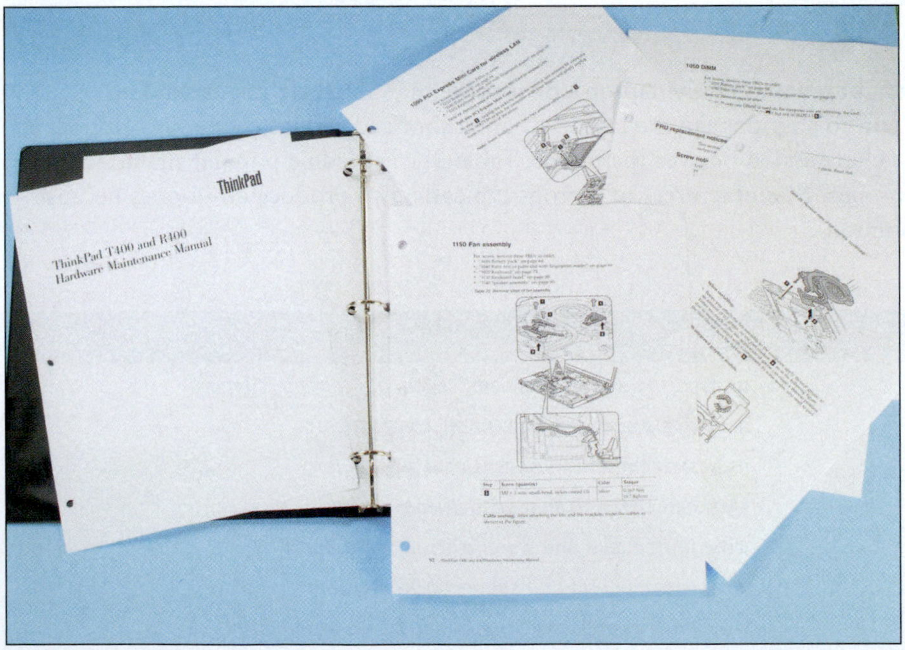

Figure 2-34 A laptop service manual tells you how to use diagnostic tools, troubleshoot a laptop, and replace components

2

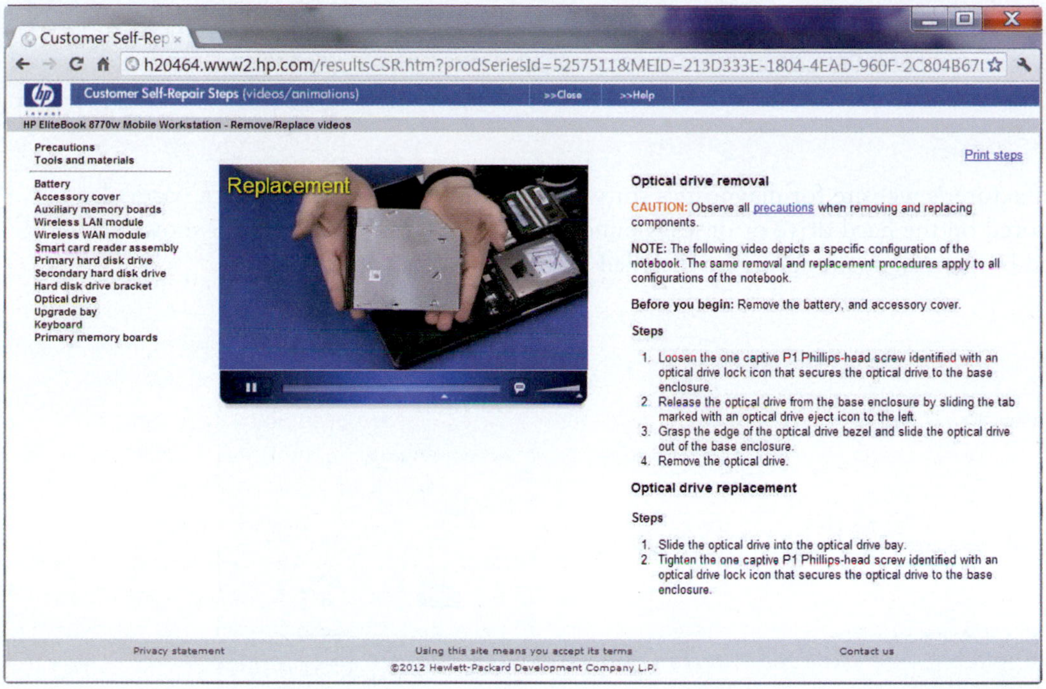

Source: hp.com

Figure 2-35 The HP website (*www.hp.com*) provides detailed instructions and videos for troubleshooting and replacing components

> **Notes** The wiki-type website *ifixit.com* does an excellent job of providing its own teardown and reassemble instructions for many brands and models of laptops.

For all laptop manufacturers, check the Support or FAQ pages of their websites for help in tasks such as opening a case without damaging it and locating and replacing a component. Be aware that some manufacturers offer almost no help at all. Sometimes, you can find service manuals on the web. To find your manual, search on the model of laptop, for example, search on "Sony VGN-CR120E laptop service manual".

Don't forget about the user manuals. They might contain directions for upgrading and replacing components that do not require disassembling the case, such as how to upgrade memory or install a new hard drive. User manuals also include troubleshooting tips and procedures and possibly descriptions of UEFI/BIOS settings. In addition, you can use a web search engine to search on the computer model, component, or error message, which might give you information about the problem and solution.

DIAGNOSTIC TOOLS PROVIDED BY MANUFACTURERS

A+
220-901
3.1, 4.5

Most laptop manufacturers provide diagnostic software that can help you test components to determine which component needs replacing. As one of the first steps when servicing a laptop, check the user manual, service manual, or manufacturer's website to determine if diagnostic software exists and how to use it. Use the software to pinpoint the problem component, which can then be replaced.

Notes When you purchase a replacement part for a laptop from the laptop's manufacturer, most often the manufacturer also sends you detailed instructions for exchanging the part.

Check the manufacturer's website for diagnostics software that can be downloaded for a particular model laptop or stored on the hard drive or on CDs bundled with the laptop. Figure 2-36 shows a window provided by the diagnostics program installed on the hard drive of one laptop.

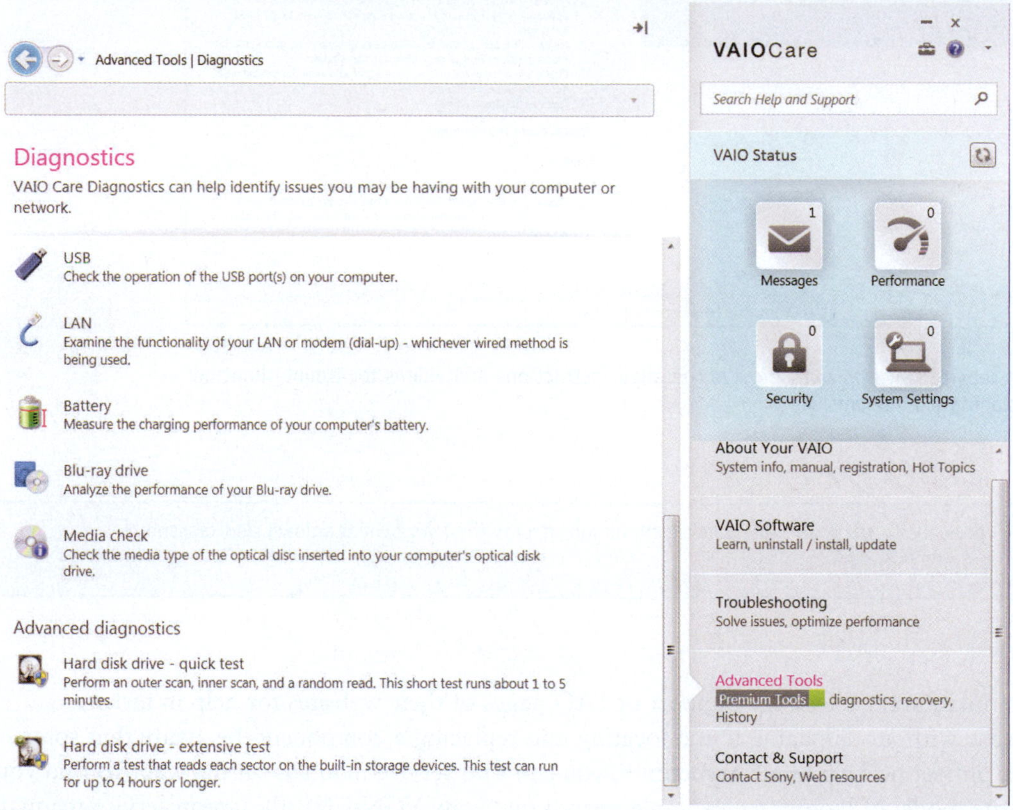

Source: Sony

Figure 2-36 Use diagnostics software provided by a laptop manufacturer to troubleshoot hardware problems

One example of diagnostic software is PC-Doctor, which is used by several manufacturers, including Lenovo, Fujitsu, and HP laptops. The diagnostic software is stored on the hard drive or on CD. If stored on CD, you can boot from the CD to run the tests. If the software is stored on the hard drive, you can run it from the Windows Start menu or by pressing a function key at startup before Windows loads. Either way, PC-Doctor can run tests on the keyboard, video, speakers, touch pad, optical drive, wireless LAN, motherboard, processor, ports, hard drive, and memory. To learn how to use the software, see the laptop's service manual or user manual.

Lenovo offers PC-Doctor for DOS that you can download from their website at *www.lenovo.com/support* and burn to a CD. Boot from the CD and use the command-line interface of the older DOS operating system to run the tests. You can also find a stand-alone version of PC-Doctor for DOS and PC-Doctor for Windows at *www.pc-doctor.com*. You can purchase it at this site; it's expensive but might be worth it if you plan to service many laptops.

Hands-On | Project 2-4 Research Laptop Service Manuals

Do the following to find a service manual for a laptop that you have access to, such as one belonging to you or a friend:

1. What are the brand, model, and serial number of the laptop?
2. What is the website of the laptop manufacturer? Print a webpage on that site that shows the documentation and/or drivers available for this laptop.
3. If the website provides a service manual for disassembling the laptop, download the manual. Print two or three pages from the manual showing the title page and table of contents for the manual.
4. If the website does not provide a service manual, search the Internet for the manual. If you find it, download it and print the title page and table of contents.

Now let's turn our attention to how to disassemble and reassemble a laptop.

HOW TO WORK INSIDE A LAPTOP COMPUTER

A+
220-901
3.1, 4.5

Sometimes it is necessary to open a laptop case so you can upgrade memory, exchange a hard drive, or replace a failed component such as the LCD panel, video inverter, keyboard, touch pad, processor, optical drive, DC jack, fan, motherboard, CMOS battery, Mini-PCIe card, wireless card, or speaker. Most laptops sold today are designed so that you can easily purchase and exchange memory modules or hard drives. However, replacing a broken LCD panel or motherboard can be a complex process, taking several hours. Most likely, you will choose to replace the entire laptop rather than doing these labor-intensive and costly repairs.

Screws and nuts on a laptop are smaller than a desktop system and therefore require smaller tools. Figure 2-37 shows a display of several tools used to disassemble a laptop, although you can get by without several of them. Here's the list:

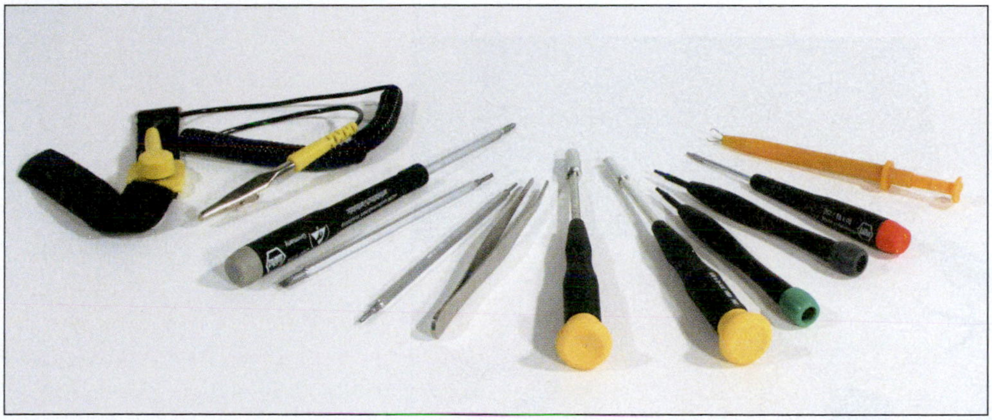

Figure 2-37 Tools for disassembling a laptop

- ESD strap
- Small flathead screwdriver
- Number 1 Phillips-head screwdriver
- Dental pick (useful for prying without damaging plastic cases, connectors, and screw covers such as the one in Figure 2-38)

Figure 2-38 Use a small screwdriver or dental pick to pry up the plastic cover hiding a screw

- Torx screwdriver set, particularly size T5
- Something such as a pillbox to keep screws and small parts organized
- Notepad for note taking or digital camera (optional)
- Flashlight (optional)
- Three-prong extractor to pick up tiny screws (optional)

Working on laptops requires extra patience. Just as when you are working with desktop systems, before opening the case of a laptop or touching sensitive components, you should always wear an ESD strap to protect the system against ESD. You can attach the alligator clip end of the strap to an unpainted metallic surface on the laptop. This surface could be, for instance, a port on the back of the laptop (see Figure 2-39). If a ground strap is not available, first dissipate any ESD between you and the laptop by touching a metallic unpainted part of the laptop, such as a port on the back, before you touch a component inside the case.

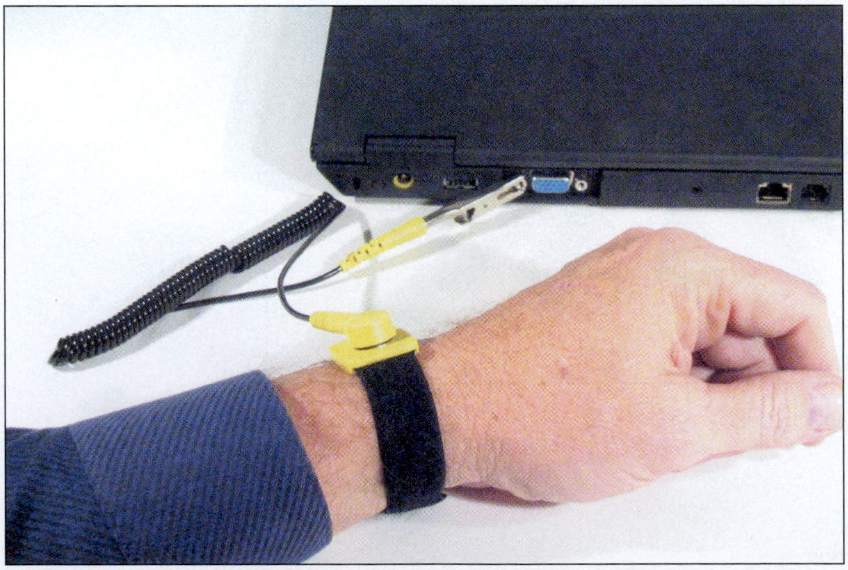

Figure 2-39 To protect the system against ESD, attach the alligator clip of a ground strap to an I/O port on the back of the laptop

Laptops contain many small screws of various sizes and lengths. When reassembling, put screws back where they came from so that when you reassemble the system, you won't use screws that are too long and that can protrude into a sensitive component and damage it. As you remove a screw, store or label it so you know where it goes when reassembling. One way to do that is to place screws in a pillbox with each compartment labeled. Another way is to place screws on a soft padded work surface and use white labeling tape to label each set of screws. A third way to organize screws is to put them on notebook paper and write beside them where the screw belongs (see Figure 2-40). My favorite method of keeping up with all those screws is to tape the screw beside the manufacturer documentation that I'm following to disassemble the laptop (see Figure 2-41). Whatever method you use, work methodically to keep screws and components organized so you know what goes where when reassembling.

Figure 2-40 Using a notepad can help you organize screws so you know which screw goes where when reassembling

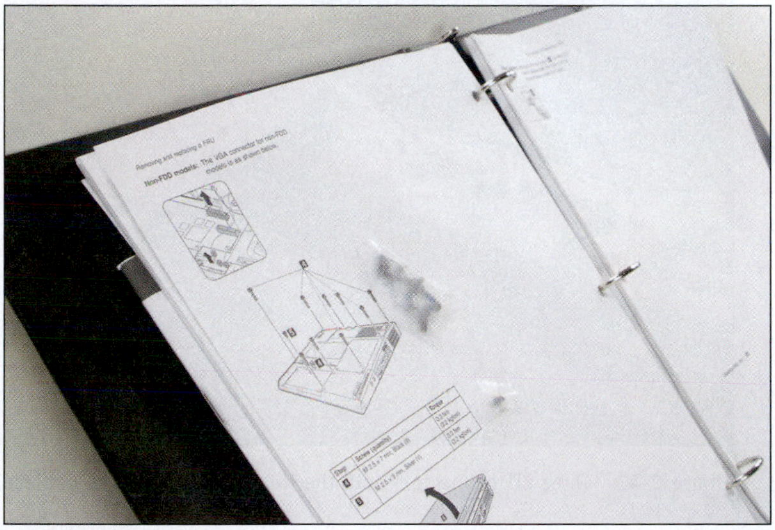

Figure 2-41 Tape screws beside the step in the manufacturer documentation that told you to remove the screw

★ A+ Exam Tip The A+ 220-901 exam expects you to know the importance of keeping parts organized when disassembling a laptop as well as the importance of having manufacturer documentation to know the steps to disassembly.

As you disassemble the computer, if you are not following directions from a service manual, keep notes as you work to help you reassemble later. Draw diagrams and label things carefully. Include in your drawings cable orientations and screw locations. You might consider using a digital camera. Photos that you take at each step in the disassembly process will be a great help when it's time to put the laptop back together.

When disassembling a laptop, consider the following tips:

- Make your best effort to find the hardware service manual for the particular laptop model you are servicing. The manual should include all the detailed steps to disassemble the laptop and a parts list of components that can be ordered from the laptop manufacturer. If you don't have this manual, your chances of successfully replacing an internal component are greatly reduced! And, if you don't have much experience disassembling a laptop, it is not wise to attempt to do so without this manual.
- Consider the warranty that might still apply to the laptop. Remember that opening the case of a laptop under warranty most likely will void the warranty. Make certain that any component you have purchased to replace an internal component will work in the model of laptop you are servicing.
- Take your time. Patience is needed to keep from scratching or marring plastic screw covers, hinges, and the case.
- As you work, don't force anything. If you find yourself forcing something, you're likely to break it.
- Always wear an ESD strap or use other protection against ESD.
- When removing cables, know that sometimes cable connectors are **ZIF connectors**. To disconnect a cable from a ZIF connector, first pull up on the connector and then remove the cable, as shown in Figure 2-42. Figure 2-43 shows a laptop using three ZIF connectors that hold the three keyboard cables in place.

Figure 2-42 To disconnect a ZIF connector, first push up on the connector to release the latch, and then remove the cable

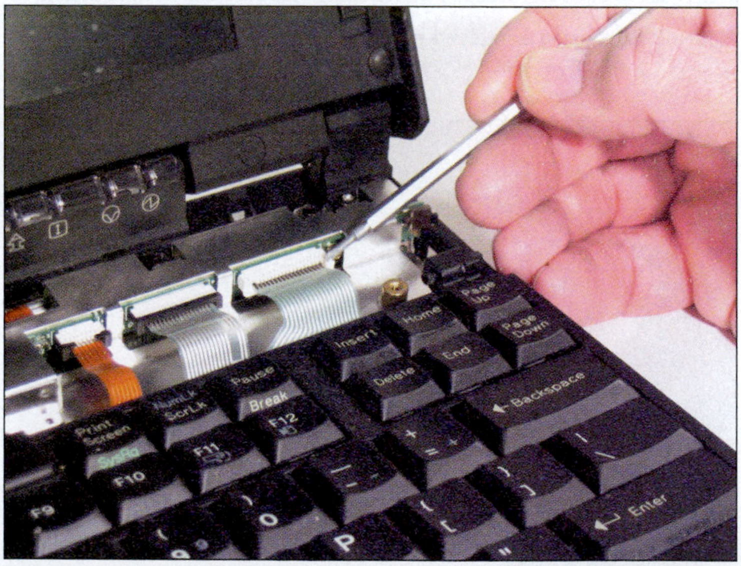

Figure 2-43 Three ZIF connectors hold the three keyboard cables in place

- Again, use a dental pick or very small screwdriver to pry up the plastic cover hiding a screw.
- Some laptops use plastic screws that are intended to be used only once. The service manual will tell you to be careful to not overtighten these screws and to always use new screws when reassembling a laptop.

- Disassemble the laptop by removing each field replaceable unit (FRU) in the order given by the service manual for your laptop. For example, one manufacturer says that to replace the motherboard for a laptop, remove components in this order: battery pack, RAM door, keyboard, middle cover, hinge cover, DVD drive and bracket, mini PCIe adapter, keyboard bezel assembly, fan assembly, CPU, CPU fixture, and DVD drive bracket. After all these components are removed, you can then remove the motherboard. Follow the steps to remove each component in the right order.

When reassembling a laptop, consider these general tips:

- Reassemble the laptop in the reverse order of the way you disassembled it. Follow each step carefully.
- Be sure to tighten, but not overtighten, all screws. Loose screws or metal fragments in a laptop can be dangerous; they might cause a short as they shift about inside the laptop.
- Before you install the battery or AC adapter, verify that there are no loose parts inside the laptop. Pick it up and gently shake it. If you hear anything loose, open the case and find the loose component, screw, spring, or metal flake, and fix the problem.

>> CHAPTER SUMMARY

How to Work Inside a Desktop Computer Case

- When a hardware support technician is disassembling or reassembling a computer, it is important to stay organized, keep careful notes, and follow all the safety procedures to protect the computer equipment.
- Before opening a computer case, shut down the system, unplug it, disconnect all cables, and press the power button to drain residual power.
- An expansion card fits in a slot on the motherboard and is anchored to the case by a single screw or clip.

Special Considerations When Supporting Laptops

- Laptop computers are designed for travel. They use the same technology as desktop computers, with modifications for space, portability, and power conservation. A laptop generally costs more than a desktop with comparable power and features. Special concerns when supporting a laptop also apply to supporting a netbook or all-in-one computer.
- When supporting laptops, pay careful attention to what the warranty allows you to change on the computer.
- The laptop manufacturer documentation, including the service manual, diagnostic software, and recovery media, is useful when disassembling, troubleshooting, and repairing a laptop.

How to Work Inside a Laptop Computer

- Field replaceable units in a laptop can include the memory modules, hard drive, LCD panel, video inverter, keyboard, touch pad, processor, optical drive, DC jack, fan, motherboard, CMOS battery, Mini-PCIe card, wireless card, or speakers.
- When an internal component needs replacing, consider the possibility of disabling the component and using an external peripheral device in its place. Don't jeopardize the warranty on a laptop by opening the case or using components not authorized by the manufacturer.
- Replacing the laptop might be more cost effective than performing labor-intensive repairs, such as replacing the motherboard.

- When disassembling a laptop, the manufacturer's service manual is essential.
- When upgrading components on a laptop, including memory, use components that are the same brand as the laptop, or use only components recommended by the laptop's manufacturer.
- Follow the directions in a service manual to disassemble a laptop. Keep small screws organized as you disassemble a laptop because the laptop will have a variety of sizes and lengths of screws. Some manufacturers use plastic screws and recommend you use new screws rather than reuse the old ones.

>> KEY TERMS

For explanations of key terms, see the Glossary for this text.

front panel connector
front panel header
spacer
standoff
ZIF connector

>> REVIEWING THE BASICS

1. When taking a computer apart, why is it important to not stack boards on top of each other?
2. Why is it important to remove loose jewelry before working inside a computer case?
3. When assembling a desktop computer, which do you install first, the drives or the motherboard?
4. What is the purpose of raised screw holes or standoffs installed between the motherboard and desktop case?
5. When installing the front panel wires to the motherboard front panel header, how do you know which pins to use for each wire if the pins on the header are not labeled?
6. How many pins does the CPU auxiliary power connector on a motherboard have?
7. Why are laptops usually more expensive than desktop computers with comparable power and features?
8. Why is the service manual so important to have when you disassemble a laptop?
9. When a laptop internal device fails, what three options can you use to deal with the problem?
10. After you have removed the AC adapter and all peripherals, what is the next component you should always remove before servicing any internal laptop components?

>> THINKING CRITICALLY

1. You disassemble and reassemble a desktop computer. When you first turn it on, you see no lights and hear no sounds. Nothing appears on the monitor screen. What is the most likely cause of the problem? Explain your answer.
    a. A memory module is not seated properly in a memory slot.
    b. You forgot to plug up the monitor's external power cord.
    c. A wire in the case is obstructing a fan.
    d. Power cords to the motherboard are not connected.

2. You are looking to buy a laptop on a budget and want to save money by not purchasing an extended service agreement with the manufacturer beyond the first year. What should you consider when choosing manufacturers to limit your search? Which manufacturers would you choose and why?
3. A four-year-old laptop will not boot and presents error messages on screen. You have verified with the laptop technical support that these error messages indicate the motherboard has failed and needs replacing. What is the first question you should ask yourself before performing the repair?
   a. Will replacing the motherboard be more costly than purchasing a new laptop?
   b. Can you find a replacement motherboard?
   c. Can you find the service manual to show you how to replace the motherboard?
   d. Is the laptop still under warranty?

>> REAL PROBLEMS, REAL SOLUTIONS

REAL PROBLEM 2-1 Taking a Lab Computer Apart and Putting It Back Together

A PC technician needs to be comfortable with taking apart a computer and putting it back together. In most situations, the essential tools you'll need for the job are an ESD strap, a Phillips-head screwdriver, a flathead screwdriver, paper, and pen.

Working with a partner and using a lab computer designated to be disassembled, take a computer apart. It is not necessary to remove the processor or memory modules from the motherboard, but be very careful to properly support the motherboard and processor as you remove them from the case. Then reassemble the system. Don't replace the computer case panel until your instructor has inspected all cable connections. Then turn on the computer and verify that all is working.

REAL PROBLEM 2-2 Setting Up a Service Center for Laptops

If you intend to set up your own computer repair shop, you might want to consider becoming a service center for a few brands of the more popular laptops. Reasons to become an authorized service center are that you have access to service manuals, parts lists, and wholesale parts for laptops. Do the following to research becoming an authorized service center:

1. Select a brand of laptops that you think you would like to service.
2. Research the website of this manufacturer and answer these questions:
   a. Where is the closest authorized service center for this brand of laptops?
   b. What are the requirements to become an authorized service center? Print the webpage showing the requirements.
   c. Is A+ certification one of those requirements?
   d. Some laptop manufacturers offer a program that falls short of becoming an authorized service center but does provide support for IT professionals so that repair technicians can order laptop parts. Does the manufacturer offer this service? If so, what must you do to qualify?

If you try one brand of laptop and can't find the information you need, try another brand. Sometimes this information can only be obtained by contacting the manufacturer directly. And one more hint: To use *www.google.com* to search a particular site, begin the search string with *site:hostname.com*.

REAL PROBLEM 2-3 Taking Apart a Laptop

If you enjoy putting together a thousand-piece jigsaw puzzle, you'll probably enjoy working on laptop computers. With desktop systems, replacing a component is not a time-consuming task, but with laptops, the job could take half a day. If you take the time to carefully examine the laptop's case before attempting to open it, you will probably find markings provided by the manufacturer to assist you in locating components that are commonly upgraded. If you have a service manual, your work will be much easier than without one.

The best way to learn to disassemble a laptop is to practice on an old one that you can afford to break. Find an old Dell or Lenovo or IBM ThinkPad for which you can download the service manual from the Dell or Lenovo website. Carefully and patiently follow the disassembly instructions and then reassemble it. When done, you can congratulate yourself and move on to newer laptops.

CHAPTER 3

All About Motherboards

After completing this chapter, you will be able to:

- Describe and contrast various types and features of motherboards
- Configure a motherboard using BIOS or UEFI firmware
- Maintain a motherboard, including updating drivers, flashing UEFI/BIOS, and replacing the CMOS battery
- Select, install, and replace a motherboard
- Replace a laptop system board

In previous chapters, you learned how to work inside a computer and began the process of learning about each major component or subsystem in a computer case. In this chapter, we build on all that knowledge to learn about motherboards, which techies sometimes call the mobo. You'll learn about the many different features of a motherboard, including motherboard sockets, chipsets, buses, expansion slots, and onboard ports and connectors. Then you'll learn how to support a motherboard, and that includes configuring, maintaining, installing, and replacing it. A motherboard is considered a field replaceable unit, so it's important to know how to replace one, but the good news is you don't need to know how to repair one that is broken. Troubleshooting a motherboard works hand in hand with troubleshooting the processor and other components that must work to boot up a computer, so we'll leave troubleshooting the motherboard until later chapters.

MOTHERBOARD TYPES AND FEATURES

A+
220-901
1.2, 1.4,
1.6

A motherboard is the most complicated component in a computer. When you put together a computer from parts, generally you start with deciding which processor and motherboard you will use. Everything else follows these two decisions. Take a look at the details of Figure 3-1, which shows a microATX motherboard by Intel that can hold an Intel Core i7, Core i5, or Core i3 processor in the LGA1155 processor socket. When selecting a motherboard, generally you'd need to pay attention to the form factor, processor socket, chipset, buses and number of bus slots, and other connectors, slots, and ports. In this part of the chapter, we'll look at the details of each of these features so that you can read a technical motherboard ad with the knowledge of a pro and know how to select the right motherboard when replacing an existing one or when building a new system.

Figure 3-1 The Intel desktop motherboard DH67GD uses the microATX form factor and has the processor, cooler, and memory modules installed

MOTHERBOARD FORM FACTORS

A+
220-901
1.2

Recall from the chapter, "First Look at Computer Parts and Tools," that a motherboard form factor determines the size of the board and its features that make it compatible with power supplies and cases. The most popular motherboard form factors are ATX, microATX (a smaller version of ATX), and Mini-ITX (a smaller version of microATX). You saw a microATX motherboard in Figure 3-1. Figure 3-2 shows an ATX board, and a Mini-ITX board is shown in Figure 3-3. The Mini-ITX board is also commonly referred to as an ITX board.

Figure 3-2 The Intel DX58SO motherboard uses the ATX form factor and is designed with the gamer in mind

Courtesy of ASUSTeK Computer, Inc.

Figure 3-3 A Mini-ITX motherboard

Table 3-1 lists the popular and not-so-popular form factors used by motherboards, and Figure 3-4 shows a comparison of the sizes and hole positions of the ATX, microATX, and Mini-ITX boards. Each of these three boards can fit into an ATX computer case and use an ATX power supply.

Form Factor	Motherboard Size	Description
ATX, full size	Up to 12" × 9.6" (305mm × 244mm)	A popular form factor that has had many revisions and variations.
MicroATX	Up to 9.6" × 9.6" (244mm × 244mm)	A smaller version of ATX.
Mini-ITX (aka ITX)	Up to 6.7" × 6.7" (170mm × 170mm)	A small form factor (SFF) board used in low-end computers and home theater systems. The boards are often used with an Intel Atom processor and are sometimes purchased as a motherboard-processor combo unit.
NLX	Up to 9" × 13.6" (229mm × 345mm)	A low profile form factor used in low-end systems with a riser card.

Table 3-1 Motherboard form factors

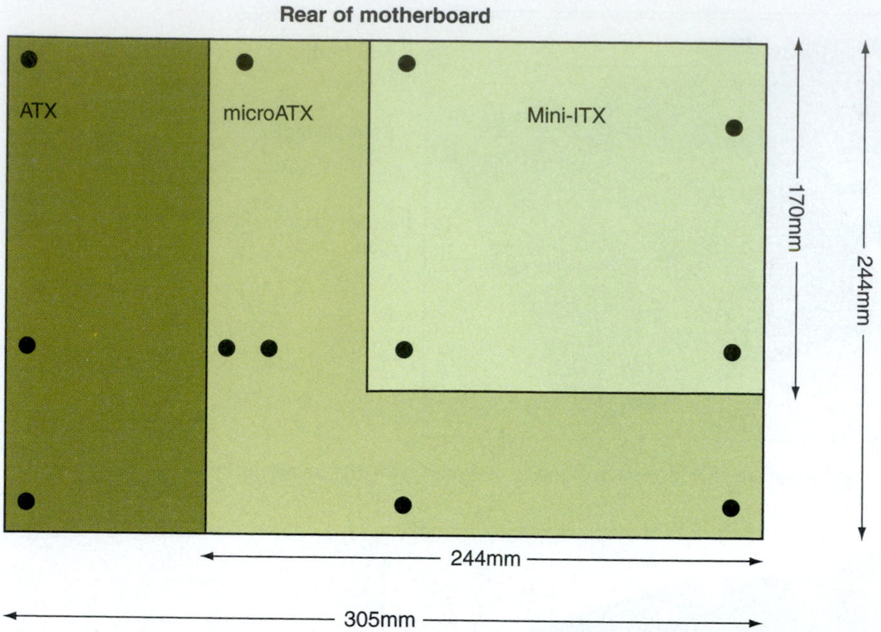

Figure 3-4 Sizes and hole positions for the ATX, microATX, and Mini-ITX motherboards

★ A+ Exam Tip The A+ 220-901 exam expects you to know about the ATX, microATX, Mini-ITX, and ITX motherboard form factors.

PROCESSOR SOCKETS

A+ 220-901 1.6

Another important feature of a motherboard is the processor socket. This socket and the chipset determine which processors a board can support. A socket for a desktop or laptop computer is designed to hold either an Intel processor or an AMD processor. Some older processors were installed on the motherboard in a long narrow slot, but all processors sold today use sockets. Now let's look at sockets for Intel and AMD processors.

SOCKETS FOR INTEL PROCESSORS

Table 3-2 lists the sockets used by Intel processors for desktop systems. The first two sockets are currently used by new Intel processors. The last six sockets in the table have been discontinued by Intel, but you still need to be able to support them because you might be called on to replace a processor or motherboard that uses one of these legacy sockets. The types of memory listed in the table that are used with these sockets are explained in detail in the chapter, "Supporting the Power System and Troubleshooting Computers." Intel also makes several Itanium and Xeon processors designed for servers. These server processors might use different sockets than those listed in the table. Mobile processor sockets are also not included in the table.

Intel Socket Name	Used by Processor Family	Description
LGA1150 (aka Socket H3)	Fourth Generation (Haswell) Core i7, Core i5, Core i3, Pentium, and Celeron	◢ 1150 pins in the socket touch 1150 lands on the processor. ◢ LGA1150 (see Figure 3-5) supports DDR3 memory.

Table 3-2 Sockets for Intel processors used for desktop computers (continues)

Intel Socket Name	Used by Processor Family	Description
LGA1155 and FCLGA1155 (aka Socket H2)	Third Generation (Ivy Bridge) Core i7 Extreme, Core i7, Core i5, Core i3, Pentium, and Celeron	◢ 1155 pins in the socket touch 1155 lands on the processor. ◢ The LGA1155 (see Figure 3-6) works with DDR3 memory and was designed to replace the LGA1156 socket.
LGA2011 (aka Socket R)	Second Generation (Sandy Bridge) Core i7 Extreme, Core i7, Core i5, Core i3, Pentium, and Celeron	◢ 2011 pins in the socket touch 2011 lands on the processor, which uses a flip-chip land grid array (FCLGA). ◢ Supports DDR3 and DDR4 memory. ◢ Designed to replace LGA1366, used in high-end gaming and server computers and may require a liquid cooling system.
LGA1156 (aka Socket H or H1)	Core i7, Core i5, Core i3, Pentium, and Celeron	◢ 1156 pins in the socket touch 1156 lands on the processor, which uses a flip-chip land grid array (FCLGA). ◢ Works with DDR3 memory.
LGA1366 (aka Socket B)	Core i7, Core i7 Extreme	◢ 1366 pins in the socket touch 1366 lands on the processor. ◢ Works with DDR3 memory.
LGA771 (aka Socket J)	Core 2 Extreme	◢ 771 pins in the socket touch 771 lands on the processor. ◢ Used on high-end workstations and low-end servers. ◢ Works with DDR2 memory on boards that have two processor sockets.
LGA775 (aka Socket T)	Core 2 Extreme, Core 2 Quad, Core 2 Duo, Pentium Dual-Core, Pentium Extreme Edition, Pentium D, Pentium Pentium 4, Pentium 4 Extreme Edition, and Celeron	◢ 775 pins in the socket touch 775 lands on the processor. ◢ Works with DDR3 and DDR2 memory.

Table 3-2 Sockets for Intel processors used for desktop computers (continued)

> ★ **A+ Exam Tip** The A+ 220-901 exam expects you to know about Intel LGA sockets, including the 775, 1155, 1156, 1366, 1150, and 2011 LGA sockets.

Figure 3-5 Socket LGA1150 with protective cover installed

Figure 3-6 The LGA1155 socket is used by a variety of Intel processors

Sockets and processors use different methods to make the contacts between them. Here is a list of the more important methods:

- A pin grid array (PGA) socket has holes aligned in uniform rows around the socket to receive the pins on the bottom of the processor. Early Intel processors used PGA sockets, but they caused problems because the small delicate pins on the processor were easily bent as the processor was installed in the socket. Some newer Intel mobile processors, including the Second Generation Core i3, Core i5, and Core i7 processors, use the PGA988 socket or the FCPGA988 socket in laptops.
- A land grid array (LGA) socket has blunt protruding pins on the socket that connect with lands or pads on the bottom of the processor. The first LGA socket was the LGA775 socket. It has 775 pins and is shown with the socket lever and top open in Figure 3-7. Another LGA socket is the LGA1366 shown in Figure 3-8. LGA sockets generally give better contacts than PGA sockets, and the processor doesn't have the delicate pins so easily damaged during an installation. You learn how to use both sockets in the chapter, "Supporting the Power System and Troubleshooting Computers."

Figure 3-7 Socket LGA775 is the first Intel socket to use lands rather than pins

Figure 3-8 The LGA1366 socket with socket cover removed and load level lifted ready to receive a processor

Notes Figure 3-9 shows a close-up photo of the LGA775 socket and the bottom of a Pentium processor. Can you make out the pads or lands on the processor and the pins in the socket?

Figure 3-9 Socket LGA775 and the bottom of a Pentium processor

- Some sockets can handle a processor using a flip-chip land grid array (FCLGA) processor package or a flip-chip pin grid array (FCPGA) package. The chip is flipped over so that the top of the chip is on the bottom and makes contact with the socket. The LGA1155 socket has a flip-chip version, which is called the FCLGA1155 socket. The two sockets are not compatible.
- A staggered pin grid array (SPGA) socket has pins staggered over the socket to squeeze more pins into a small space.
- A ball grid array (BGA) connection is not really a socket. The processor is soldered to the motherboard, and the two are always purchased as a unit. For example, the little Atom processors often use this technology with a Mini-ITX motherboard in low-end computers or home theater systems.

Caution When a processor is installed in a socket, extreme care must be taken to protect the socket and the processor against ESD and from damage caused by bending the pins or scratching the socket holes during the installation. Take care to not touch the bottom of the processor or the pins or holes of the socket, which can leave finger oil on the gold plating of the contact surfaces. This oil can later cause tarnishing and lead to a poor contact.

So that even force is applied when inserting the processor in the socket, all current processor sockets have one or two levers on the sides of the socket. These sockets are called zero insertion force (ZIF) sockets, and this lever is used to lift the processor up and out of the socket. Push the levers down and the processor moves into its pin or hole connectors with equal force over the entire housing. Because the socket and processor are so delicate, processors generally should not be removed or replaced repeatedly.

SOCKETS FOR AMD PROCESSORS

Table 3-3 lists the AMD sockets for desktop systems. AMD has chosen to use the PGA socket architecture for its desktop processors. (Some of AMD's server processors use Socket F, which is an LGA socket.) Figure 3-10 shows the AM2+ socket. The lever on the side of the socket is lifted, and an Athlon 64 processor is about to be inserted. If you look closely near the lower edge of the processor, you can see the small delicate pins that will seat into the holes of the socket.

AMD Socket	Used by Processor Family	Description
FM2+	Used with the A10-, A8-, and A6-Series of processors	◢ 906 holes for pins (PGA) ◢ Uses AMD Steamroller architecture with integrated graphics controller in the processor ◢ Works with DDR3 memory
FM2	Used with the Trinity line of processors	◢ 904 holes for pins (PGA) ◢ Uses AMD Piledriver architecture with integrated graphics controller in the processor ◢ Works with DDR3 memory
FM1	AMD A4, A6, A8, E2, Athlon II	◢ 905 holes for pins (PGA) ◢ Works with DDR3 memory
AM3+	AMD FX	◢ 942 holes for pins (PGA) ◢ Uses Bulldozer architecture and is compatible with AM3 processors ◢ Works with DDR3 memory
AM3 or AMD3	Phenom II	◢ 941 holes for pins (PGA) ◢ Works with DDR3 or DDR2 memory

Table 3-3 Sockets for AMD processors used for desktop computers

Figure 3-10 AMD Athlon 64 processor to be inserted into an AM2+ socket

> ★ **A+ Exam Tip** The A+ 220-901 exam expects you to know about these AMD sockets: AM3, AM3+, FM1, FM2, and FM2+.

MATCH A PROCESSOR TO THE SOCKET AND MOTHERBOARD

As you glance over Tables 3-2 and 3-3, you'll notice the same processor family listed under several different sockets. For example, the AMD Athlon family of processors offers many versions of the Athlon. Among these are the Athlon X2 Dual-Core, the Athlon Neo, and the Athlon 64 X2 Dual-Core. Because these various processors within the same processor family use different sockets, you must be careful when matching a processor to a motherboard. To be certain you have a good match, search the Intel (*www.intel.com*) or AMD (*www.amd.com*) website for the exact processor you are buying and make sure the socket it uses is the same as the socket on the motherboard you plan to use.

Also, look at the motherboard manufacturer's website or user guide for a list of processors that the motherboard supports. It's not likely to support every processor that uses its socket because the motherboard chipset is designed to work only with certain processors.

> ★ **A+ Exam Tip** The A+ 220-901 exam does not expect you to be familiar with the processor sockets used by laptop computers. For laptops, generally, it is more cost effective to replace a laptop that has a damaged processor than to replace the processor. If you are called on to replace a laptop processor, however, always use a processor the laptop manufacturer recommends for the particular laptop model and system board CPU socket.

THE CHIPSET

A+ 220-901 1.2

A **chipset** is a set of chips on the motherboard that works closely with the processor to collectively control the memory, buses on the motherboard, and some peripherals. The chipset must be compatible with the processor it serves. The two major chipset manufacturers are Intel (*www.intel.com*) and AMD (*www.amd.com*).

Intel dominates the chipset market for several reasons: It knows more about its own Intel processors than other manufacturers do, and it produces the chipsets most compatible with the Intel family of processors.

INTEL CHIPSETS

Intel has produced far too many chipsets to list them here. To see a complete comparison chart of all Intel chipsets, start at the Intel link *ark.intel.com*.

Here is a list of the more significant chipset families by Intel:

- ***North Bridge and South Bridge use a hub architecture.*** Beginning with the release in 2006 of the Intel i800 series of chipsets, a hub using the Accelerated Hub Architecture is used to connect buses (see Figure 3-11). This hub has a fast and slow end, and each end is a separate chip on the motherboard. The fast end of the hub, called the **North Bridge**, contains the graphics and memory controller, and connects directly to the processor by way of a 64-bit bus, called the **Front Side Bus (FSB)**, **system bus**, or host bus. The slower end of the hub, called the **South Bridge**, contains the I/O controller hub (ICH). All I/O (input/output) devices, except video, connect to the hub by using the slower South Bridge. Notice that in Figure 3-11, the primary PCI Express slot, the slot designated for the video card, has direct access to the North Bridge, but other PCI Express slots must access the processor by way of the slower South Bridge. On a motherboard, when you see two major chip housings for the chipset, one is controlling the North Bridge and the other is controlling the South Bridge (refer to Figure 3-2). Other chipset manufacturers besides Intel also use the North Bridge and South Bridge architecture for their chipsets.

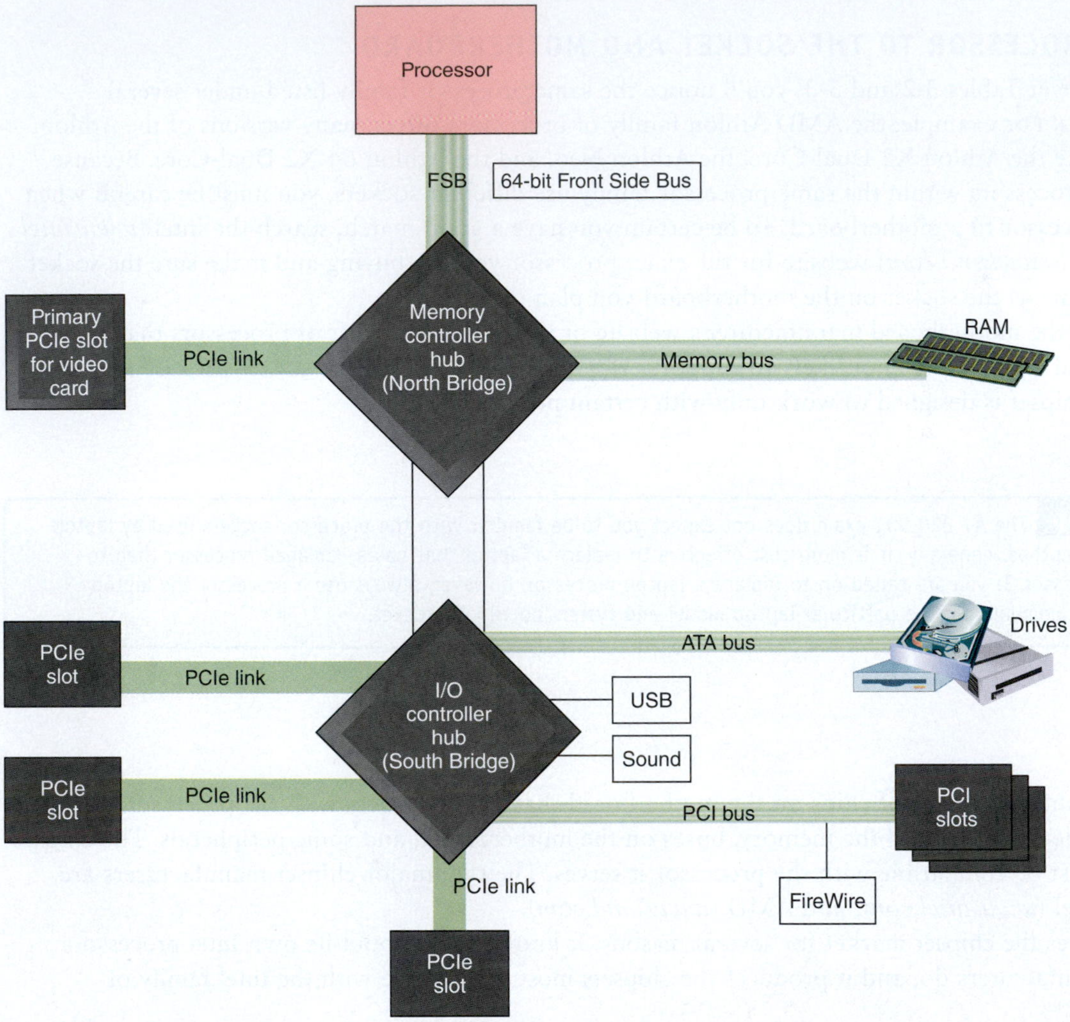

Figure 3-11 The chipset's North Bridge and South Bridge control access to the processor for all components

- ***Nehalem chipsets with the memory controller in the processor.*** The release of the X58 chipset in 2008 was significant because, with previous chipsets, the memory controller was part of the North Bridge. But beginning with the X58, the memory controller was contained in the processor housing. For example, in Figure 3-12, the Core i7 processor contains the memory controller. Notice that memory connects directly to the processor rather than to the North Bridge. Another significant change is the 64-bit Front Side Bus was replaced with a technology called the QuickPath Interconnect (QPI). The QPI has 16 lanes for data packets and works similar to how PCI Express works. All Intel chipsets since the X58 use QuickPath Interconnects. A motherboard using the X58 chipset is shown in Figure 3-13. The board comes with a fan that can be clipped to the top of the North Bridge to help keep the chipset cool.

  Nehalem chipsets, which Intel has begun to call the previous generation of chipsets, support the Intel LGA1366 socket, the Core i7 processors, and PCI Express Version 2. They can also support either SLI or CrossFire technologies. (SLI and CrossFire are two competing technologies that allow for multiple video cards installed in one system.)

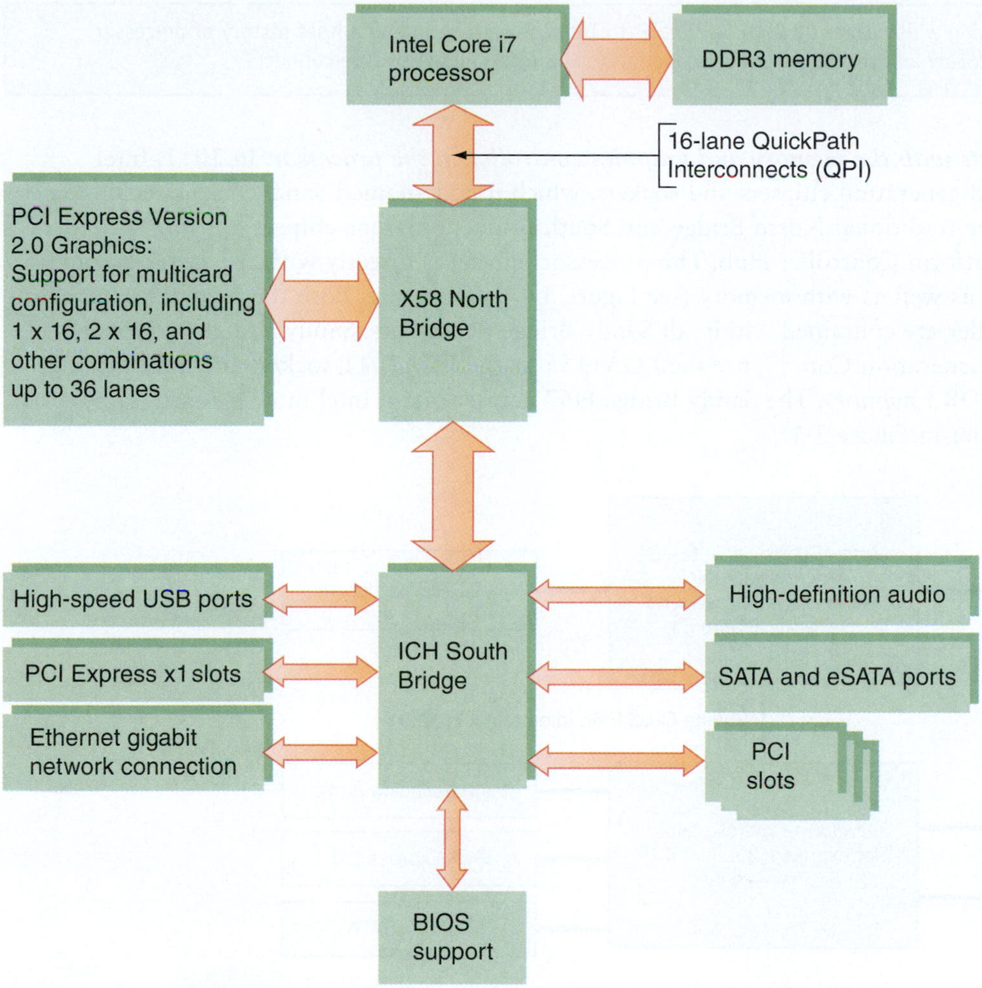

Figure 3-12 X58 chipset architecture

Figure 3-13 The X58 chipset uses heat sinks to stay cool

Notes For an interesting white paper by Intel on QuickPath Interconnect, including a brief history of processor interfaces, go to *www.intel.com* and search on "An Introduction to the Intel QuickPath Interconnect."

- ***Sandy Bridge chipsets with the memory and graphics controller in the processor.*** In 2011, Intel introduced its second-generation chipsets and sockets, which it code-named Sandy Bridge technologies. Rather than using the traditional North Bridge and South Bridge, only one chipset housing is needed, which houses the Platform Controller Hub. The processor interfaces directly with the faster graphics PCI Express 2.0 bus as well as with memory (see Figure 3-14). Therefore, both the memory controller and graphics controller are contained within all Sandy Bridge processors. Sandy Bridge processors, such as the Second Generation Core i7, use the LGA1155 or the LGA2011 socket, and Sandy Bridge motherboards use DDR3 memory. The Sandy Bridge H67 chipset on an Intel motherboard is shown in Figure 3-15 and earlier in Figure 3-1.

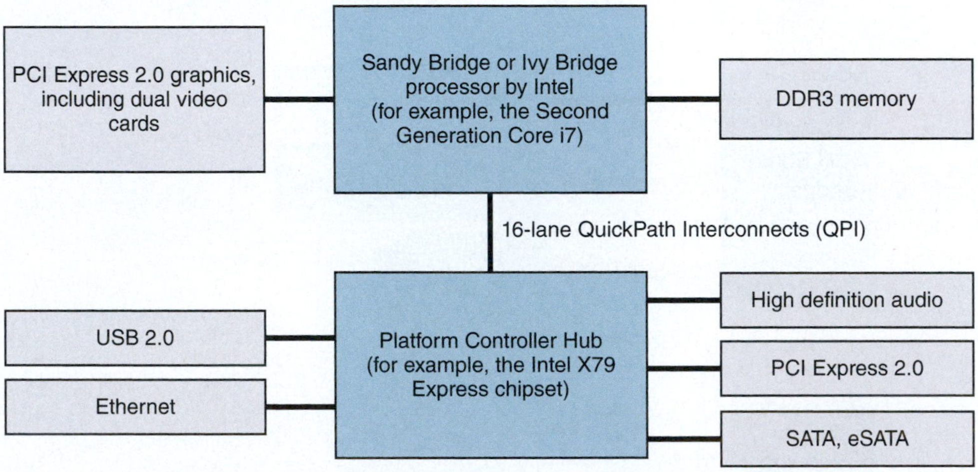

Figure 3-14 The Sandy Bridge architecture uses a single chipset hub, called the Platform Controller Hub

Figure 3-15 The Sandy Bridge H67 chipset on the Intel DH67GD motherboard sits under a heat sink to keep it cool

- ***Ivy Bridge chipsets.*** Third-generation processors and chipsets by Intel, released in 2012 and code-named Ivy Bridge, use less power, squeeze more transistors into a smaller space, and perform better than earlier products. Ivy Bridge chipsets include B75, Q75, Q77, H77, Z75, and Z77. Several Ivy Bridge processors use the LGA1155 socket for backward compatibility with earlier motherboards. The Ivy Bridge chipset uses a single Platform Controller Hub.

- *Haswell and Broadwell chipsets.* In 2013, Intel introduced the Haswell chipsets, which work with the LGA1150 and LGA2011 sockets in desktops and servers and also work with low-power processors in laptops and ultrabooks (very thin laptops). The chipsets work with DDR3 and DDR4 memory and use less power than previous chipset architectures. Broadwell chipsets, released in 2015, are a little faster than the Haswell chipsets and can also use the LGA1150 socket.

Notes The Skylake chipset architecture is expected to be released by the time this text is published. The chipset will use the new LGA1151 socket and will support DDR3 and DDR4 memory.

AMD CHIPSETS

AMD specializes in chipsets and graphics processors (called a graphics processor unit or GPU) that target the gaming and hobbyist markets. The two current chipset families by AMD are:

- *A-Series chipsets.* These chipsets are designed to support the AMD Accelerated Processing Unit (APU). An APU is a combination of a CPU and a graphics processor unit (GPU) in the same processor housing. In traditional desktops with high graphics needs, the CPU is installed on the motherboard and a GPU is embedded on a video card, also called a graphics adapter, installed in the system. The A-Series chipsets also support AMD CrossFire technology, which uses dual video cards in the same system.
- *9-Series chipsets.* These chipsets are designed to support AMD processors that can have up to eight cores. You'll learn more about processor cores in the chapter, "Supporting Processors and Upgrading Memory."

Hands-On | Project 3-1 Identify the Intel Chipset and Processor on Your Computer

A+ 220-901 1.4

Intel offers two utilities you can download and run to identify an installed Intel processor or chipset. Do the following to use the utilities:

- If you are using a computer with an Intel processor, download and run the Processor Identification Utility available at: *www.intel.com/p/en_US/support/highlights/processors/toolspiu*
- If you are using a computer with an Intel processor and your operating system is a 32-bit OS, download and run the Chipset Identification Utility available at: *www.intel.com/support/chipsets/sb/CS-009266.htm*

Websites change often, so if these links don't work, try searching the Intel website for each utility. What information does each utility provide about your processor and chipset?

Hands-On | Project 3-2 Research the Intel ARK Database

A+ 220-901 1.4

Intel provides an extensive database of all its processors, chipsets, motherboards, and other products at *ark.intel.com*. Research the database and answer these questions:

1. List three Fourth Generation Core i7 processors. For each processor, list the Processor Number (model), the maximum memory it supports, the PCI Express version it supports (version 1.1, 2.0, 3.0, or 4.0), and the socket it uses.
2. List three Intel motherboards for desktops: An ATX board, a microATX board, and a Mini-ITX board. For each motherboard, list the processor socket it provides, the chipset it uses, the maximum memory it supports, and the number of PCIe slots it has.

(continues)

3. The X99 chipset is designed for gaming computers using the Core i7 processor. What is the launch date for theX99 chipsets?

Find the block diagram for the X99 chipset and answer the following:

4. Which processor socket does the X99 chipset support?

5. Do PCI Express 3.0 graphics adapters connect directly to the processor or to the X99 chipset?

6. Do High-Speed USB ports connect directly to the processor or to the X99 chipset?

BUSES AND EXPANSION SLOTS

A+ 220-901 1.2

When you look carefully at a motherboard, you see many fine lines on both the top and the bottom of the board's surface (see Figure 3-16). These lines, sometimes called **traces**, are circuits or paths that enable data, instructions, and power to move from component to component on the board. This system of pathways used for communication and the protocol and methods used for transmission are collectively called the **bus**. (A **protocol** is a set of rules and standards that any two entities use for communication.) The parts of the bus that we are most familiar with are the lines of the bus that are used for data; these lines are called the **data bus**. A bus can also carry electrical power (to power components on the motherboard), control signals (to coordinate activity), and memory addresses (for one program to tell another program where to find data or instructions).

Figure 3-16 On the bottom of the motherboard, you can see bus lines terminating at the CPU socket

All data and instructions inside a computer exist in binary, which means there are only two states: on and off. Binary data is put on a line of a bus by placing voltage on that line. We can visualize that bits are "traveling" down the bus in parallel, but in reality, the voltage placed on each line is not "traveling"; rather, it is all over the line. When one component at one end of the line wants to write data to another component, the two components get in sync for the write operation. Then, the first component places voltage on several lines of the bus, and the other component immediately reads the voltage on these lines. The CPU or other devices interpret the voltage, or lack of voltage, on each line on the bus as binary digits (0s or 1s).

The width of a data bus is called the data path size. Some buses have data paths that are 8, 16, 32, 64, 128, or more bits wide. For example, a bus that has eight wires, or lines, to transmit data is called an 8-bit bus. Figure 3-17 shows an 8-bit bus between the CPU and memory that is transmitting the letter A (binary 0100 0001). All bits of a byte are placed on their lines of the bus at the same time: no voltage for binary zero and voltage for binary one. For every eight bits of a bus, a bus might use a ninth bit for error checking. Adding a check bit for each byte allows the component reading the data to verify that it is the same data written to the bus.

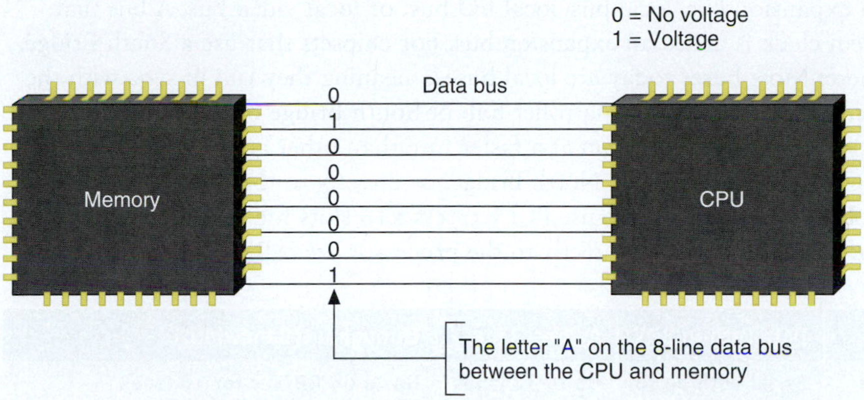

Figure 3-17 A data bus has traces or lines that carry voltage interpreted by the CPU and other devices as bits

One of the most interesting lines, or circuits, on a bus is the system clock or system timer, which is dedicated to timing the activities on the motherboard much like a metronome helps a musician with timing. The chipset sends out a continuous pulsating electrical signal on one line of the system bus. This one system clock line, dedicated to carrying the pulse, is read by other components on the motherboard (including the processor, bus slots, memory slots, and so forth) and ensures that all activities are synchronized. Remember that everything in a computer is binary, and this includes the activities themselves. Instead of continuously working to perform commands or move data, the CPU, bus, and other devices work in a binary fashion—do something, stop, do something, stop, and so forth. Each device works on a clock cycle or beat of the clock. Some devices, such as the CPU, do two or more operations on one beat of the clock, and others do one operation for each beat. Some devices might even do something on every other beat, but most components inside the system work according to these beats or cycles.

You can think of this as similar to children jumping rope. The system clock (child turning the rope) provides the beats or cycles, while devices (children jumping) work in a binary fashion (jump, don't jump). In the analogy, some children jump two or more times for each rope pass.

Notes If the processor requests something from a slow device and the device is not ready, the device issues a wait state, which is a command to the processor to wait for slower devices to catch up.

The speed of memory, Front Side Bus, processor, or other component is measured in hertz (Hz), which is one cycle per second; megahertz (MHz), which is one million cycles per second; and gigahertz (GHz), which is one billion cycles per second. Common ratings for memory are 1333 MHz and 1866 MHz. Common ratings for Front Side Buses are 2600 MHz, 2000 MHz, 1600 MHz, 1333 MHz, 1066 MHz, 800 MHz, 533 MHz, or 400 MHz. A CPU operates from 166 MHz to almost 4 GHz. The CPU can put data or instructions on its internal bus at a much higher rate than does the motherboard. Although we often refer to the speed of the CPU and memory, talking about the frequency of these devices is more accurate, because the term *speed* implies a continuous flow, while the term *frequency* implies a digital or binary flow: on and off, on and off.

Notes Rather than measuring the frequency of a system bus, sometimes you see a system bus measured in performance such as the GA-990FXA-UD3 motherboard by GIGABYTE (see *www.gigabyte.us*). This system bus is rated at 5.2 GT/s or 5200 MT/s. One GT/s is one billion transfers per second, and one MT/s is one million transfers per second.

A motherboard can have more than one bus, each using a different protocol, speed, data path size, and so on. Table 3-4 lists the various buses used on motherboards today, in order of throughput speed from fastest to slowest. (Throughput is sometimes called bandwidth.) Looking at the second column of Table 3-4, you can see that a bus is called an expansion bus, local bus, local I/O bus, or local video bus. A bus that does not run in sync with the system clock is called an expansion bus. For chipsets that use a South Bridge, expansion buses always connect here. Most buses today are local buses, meaning they run in sync with the system clock. If a local bus connects to the slower I/O controller hub or South Bridge of the chipset, it is called a local I/O bus. Because the video card needs to run at a faster rate than other adapter cards, this one slot always connects to the faster end of the chipset, the North Bridge, or directly to the processor when using Sandy Bridge or later technologies. Today's boards use PCI Express x16 slots for video cards. These video buses that connect to the older North Bridge or directly to the processor are called local video buses.

Bus	Bus Type	Data Path in Bits	Address Lines	Throughput(Bandwidth)
PCI Express Version 4.0 (not yet released)	Local video and local I/O	Serial with up to 32 lanes	Up to 32 lanes	Up to 64 GB/sec for 16 lanes
PCI Express Version 3.0	Local video and local I/O	Serial with up to 32 lanes	Up to 32 lanes	Up to 32 GB/sec for 16 lanes
PCI Express Version 2.0	Local video and local I/O	Serial with up to 32 lanes	Up to 32 lanes	Up to 16 GB/sec for 16 lanes
PCI Express Version 1.1	Local video and local I/O	Serial with up to 16 lanes	Up to 16 lanes	Up to 8 GB/sec for 16 lanes
PCI-X	Local I/O	64	32	Up to 8.5 GB/sec
PCI	Local I/O	32 or 64	32 or 64	133, 266, or 532 MB/sec
FireWire 400 and 800	Local I/O or expansion	1	Serial	Up to 3.2 Gbps (gigabits per second)
USB 1.1, 2.0, and 3.0	Expansion	1	Serial	12 or 480 Mbps (megabits per second) or 5.0 Gbps (gigabits per second)

Table 3-4 Buses listed by throughput

A+ Exam Tip The 220-901 exam expects you to know about the PCI, PCI-X, PCIe, and MiniPCI expansion slots.

So now let's look at the details of the PCI, PCI-X, and PCIe expansion slots used in desktops. We'll also discuss the MiniPCI expansion slots used in laptops. The FireWire and USB buses are discussed in the chapter, "Supporting I/O Devices."

CONVENTIONAL PCI

The first PCI bus had a 32-bit data path, supplied 5 V of power to an adapter card, and operated at 33 MHz. It was the first bus that allowed adapter cards to run in sync with the CPU. PCI Version 2.x introduced the 64-bit, 3.3-V PCI slot, doubling data throughput of the bus. Because a card can be damaged if installed in the wrong voltage slot, a notch in a PCI slot distinguishes between a 5-V slot and a 3.3-V slot. A Universal PCI card can use either a 3.3-V or 5-V slot and contains both notches (see Figure 3-18). Conventional PCI is no longer evolving and ended up with four types of slots and six possible PCI card configurations to use these slots. These slots and cards include 32-bit PCI and 64-bit PCI-X, all shown in Figure 3-19.

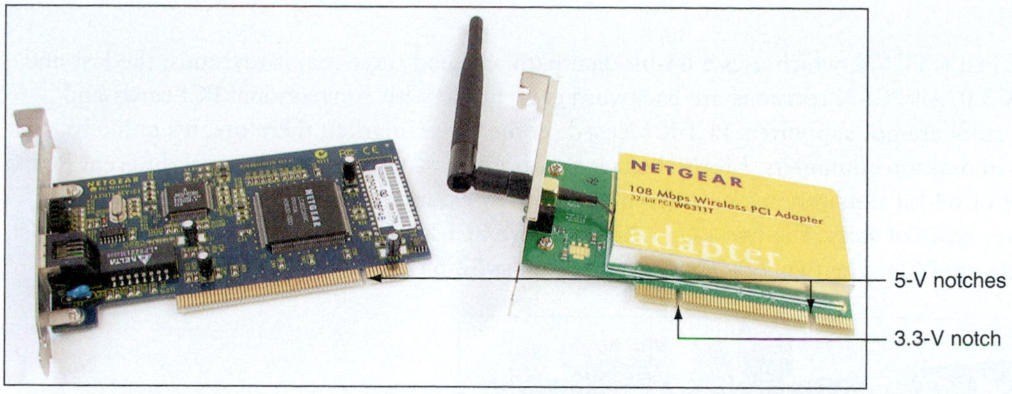

Figure 3-18 A 32-bit, 5-V PCI network card and a 32-bit, universal PCI wireless card show the difference in PCI notches set to distinguish voltages in a PCI slot

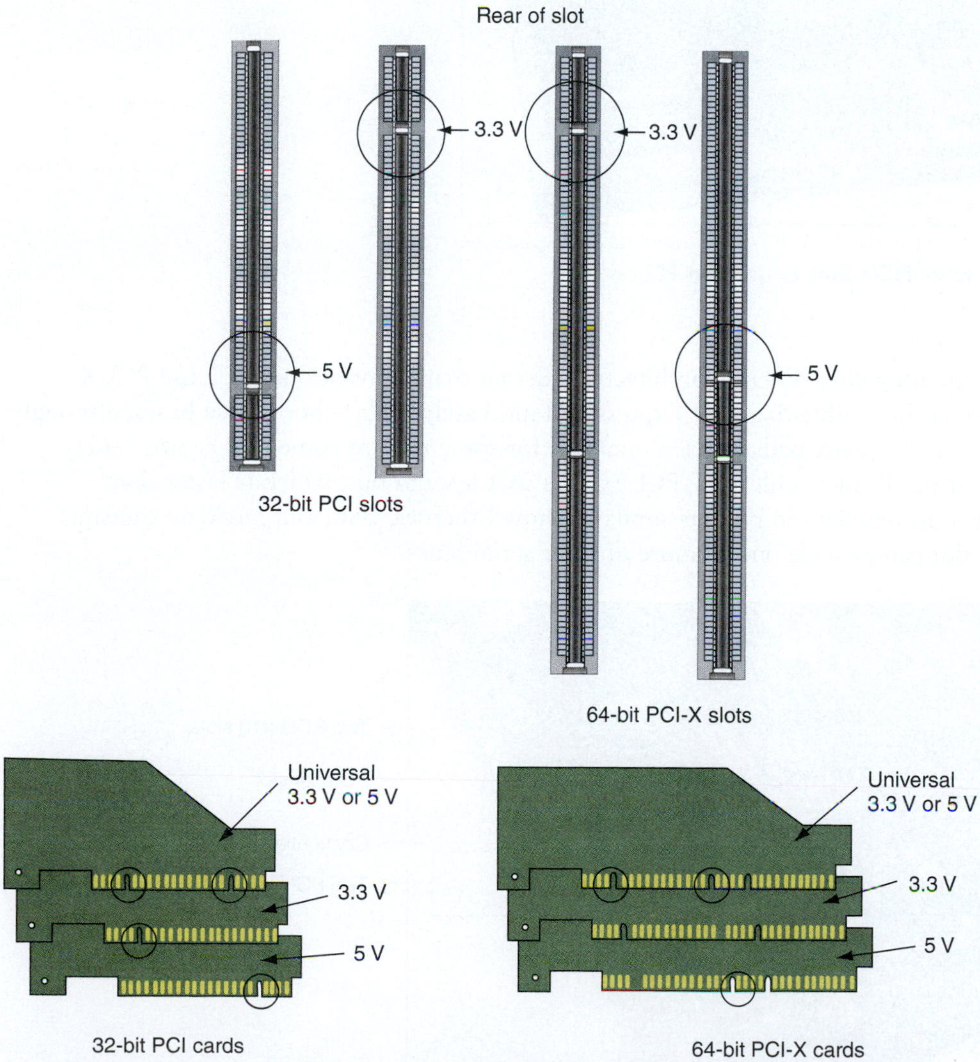

Figure 3-19 With PCI Version 2.x, there are four possible types of expansion slots and six differently configured PCI expansion cards to use these slots

PCI-X

The next evolution of PCI is PCI-X, which uses a 64-bit data path and had three major revisions; the last and final revision is PCI-X 3.0. All PCI-X revisions are backward compatible with conventional PCI cards and slots, except 5-V PCI cards are not supported. PCI-X focused on the server market; therefore, it's unlikely you'll see PCI-X slots in desktop computers. Motherboards that use PCI-X tend to have several different PCI slots with some 32-bit or 64-bit slots running at different speeds. For example, Figure 3-20 shows a server motherboard with three types of slots. The two long white slots are PCI-X; the two shorter white slots are PCI, and the two black slots are PCIe. The two PCI-X slots can use most 32-bit and 64-bit PCI or PCI-X cards.

Courtesy of Super Micro Computer, Inc.

Figure 3-20 The two long white PCI-X slots can support PCI cards

PCI EXPRESS

PCI Express (PCIe) uses an altogether different architectural design than conventional PCI and PCI-X and is not backward compatible with either. PCI Express will ultimately replace both these buses, although it is expected PCI Express will coexist with conventional PCI for some time to come (see Figure 3-21). Whereas PCI uses a 32-bit or 64-bit parallel bus, PCI Express uses a serial bus, which is faster than a parallel bus because it transmits data in packets similar to how Ethernet, USB, and FireWire transmit data. A PCIe expansion slot can provide one or more of these serial lanes.

Figure 3-21 Three types of PCIe slots and one conventional PCI slot

Another difference in PCI Express is how it connects to the processor. One or more PCI Express slots used for video cards have a direct link to the North Bridge or to the processor (using Sandy Bridge or later architecture). Refer back to Figures 3-10, 3-11, and 3-13.

PCI Express currently comes in four different slot sizes called PCI Express ×1 (pronounced "by one"), ×4, ×8, and ×16. Figure 3-21 shows three of these slots. Notice in the photo how the PCIe slots are not as tall and the pins are closer together than the conventional PCI slot. A PCI Express ×1 slot contains a single lane for data; this lane is actually four wires. One pair of wires is used to send data and the other pair receives data, one bit at a time. The ×16 slot contains 16 lanes, with each lane timed independently of other lanes. The more lanes you have, the more data gets transmitted in a given time. Therefore, a ×16 slot is faster than a ×4 slot, which is faster than a ×1 slot. A shorter PCI Express card (such as a ×1 card) can be installed in a longer PCI Express slot (such as a ×4 slot).

Revisions of PCIe include PCIe version 1.1, PCIe version 2.0 and 2.1, PCIe version 3.0, and PCIe version 4.0. Here are important facts about each PCIe version:

- ***PCIe version 1.0.*** The original PCIe version 1.0 allowed for 150 W to PCIe cards. Pins on the expansion card provide 75 W, and a new 6-pin PCIe connector from the power supply provides an additional 75 W.
- ***PCIe version 1.1.*** PCIe version 1.1 allowed for more wattage to PCIe cards, up to 225 W. The standard allows for two 6-pin PCIe connectors from the power supply to the card. Therefore, the total 225 W comes as 75 W from the slot and 150 W from the two connectors.
- ***PCIe version 2.0.*** PCIe version 2.0 doubled the frequency of the PCIe bus and allows for up to 32 lanes on one slot (though few motherboards or cards actually use 32 lane slots). The allowed wattage to one PCIe 2.0 card was increased to a total of 300 W by using a new 8-pin PCIe power connector that provides 150 W (see Figure 3-22). The 300 W to the card come from the slot (75 W), from the 8-pin connector (150 W), and an additional 75 W come from a second auxiliary connector on the motherboard. This second connector can be a 6-pin PCIe connector, a Molex-style connector, or a SATA-style connector. You'll see an example of these connectors later in this chapter.

Figure 3-22 8-pin PCIe Version 2.0 power connector

- ***PCIe versions 3.0 and 4.0.*** PCIe version 3.0 roughly doubles the speed of PCIe version 2.0 and is backward compatible with PCIe version 2.0 components. PCIe version 4.0 doubles the speed of PCIe version 3.0 and is also backward compatible with earlier PCIe standards; PCIe version 4.0 devices are not yet available on the market.

MINI PCI AND MINI PCIe IN LAPTOP COMPUTERS

Smaller versions of the PCI and PCIe slots are used in laptops, all-in-one computers, and with small form factor motherboards such as the Mini-ITX board. The Mini PCI slot follows the PCI standards and the Mini PCI Express slot follows the PCI Express standards. To save space, the slots lay flat on the motherboard and hold an expansion card parallel to the board.

Mini PCIe slots have 52 or 54 pins on the edge connector and have one notch offset from the center of the slot (see Figure 3-23). One screw holds the card securely in the slot. The Mini PCI slot is wider and has 100 or 124 pins and a notch slightly offset from the end of the slot (see Figure 3-24).

Figure 3-23 Mini PCIe slot with a Wireless Mini PCIe card installed

Figure 3-24 A Mini PCI card has a notch near the side of the edge connector

PCI RISER CARDS USED TO EXTEND THE SLOTS

A+ 220-901 1.4

Suppose you are installing a Mini-ITX or microATX motherboard into a low-profile or slimline case that does not give you enough room to install a PCI card standing up in an expansion slot. In this situation, a PCI riser card can solve the problem. The riser card installs in the slot and provides another slot at a right angle (see Figure 3-25). When you install an expansion card in this riser card slot, the card sits parallel to the motherboard, taking up less space. These riser cards come for all types of PCI slots, including PCIe, PCI-X, and conventional PCI.

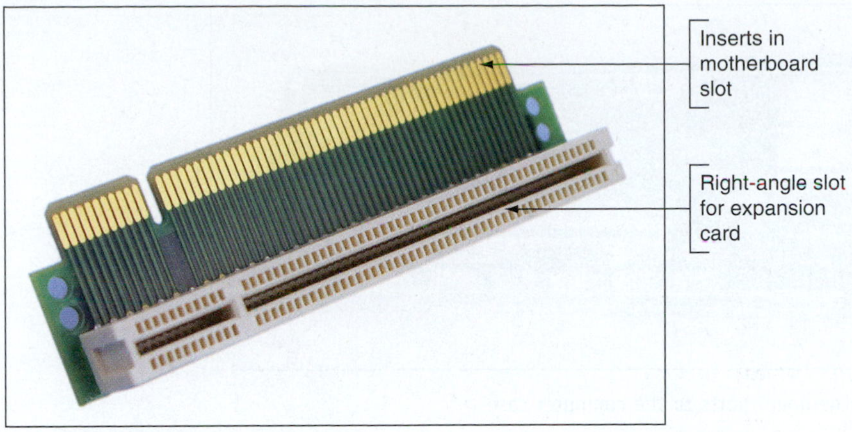

Figure 3-25 PCI riser card provides a 3.3-V slot or 5-V slot depending on which direction the card is inserted in the PCI slot

ONBOARD PORTS AND CONNECTORS

A+ 220-901 1.2

In addition to expansion slots, a motherboard might also have several ports and internal connectors. Ports coming directly off the motherboard are called onboard ports or integrated components. Almost all motherboards have two or more USB ports and sound ports. Boards might also offer a network port, FireWire (IEEE 1394) port, one or more video ports, one or more eSATA ports (for external SATA hard drives), parallel port, serial port, a port for a wireless antenna, and PS/2 ports for a mouse and keyboard. Older motherboards might have a modem port. Figure 3-26 shows ports on an entry-level desktop motherboard.

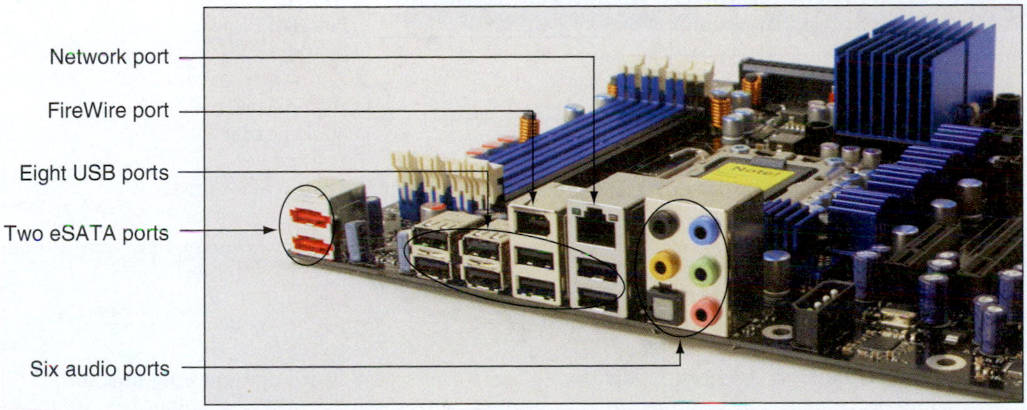

Figure 3-26 A motherboard provides ports for common I/O devices

When you purchase a motherboard, the package includes an I/O shield, which is the plate that you install in the computer case that provides holes for these I/O ports. The I/O shield is the size designed for the case's form factor, and the holes in the shield are positioned for the motherboard ports (see Figure 3-27). When you first install a motherboard, you might need to install the drivers that come on the DVD or CD bundled with the board before some of the motherboard ports will work. How to install the motherboard drivers is covered later in this chapter.

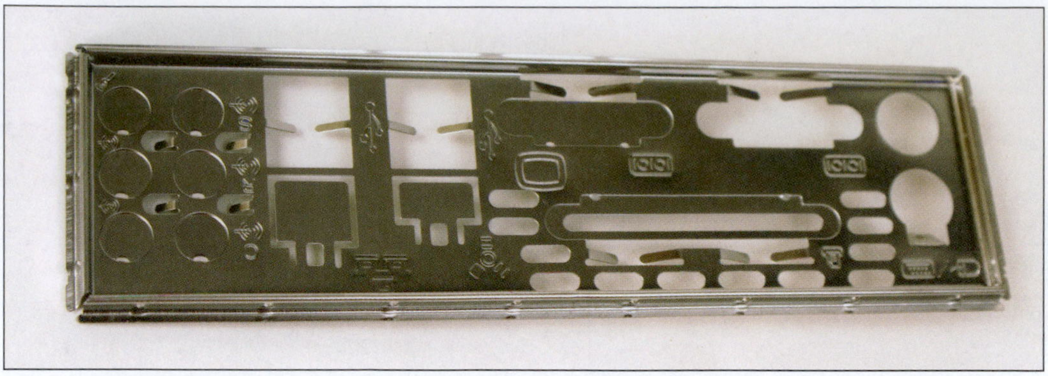

Figure 3-27 The I/O shield fits the motherboard ports to the computer case

A motherboard might have several internal connectors, including SATA, USB, and FireWire (IEEE 1394) connectors. When you purchase a motherboard, look in the package for the motherboard manual either printed or on DVD or CD. It will show a diagram of the board with a description of each connector. For example, the connectors for the motherboard in Figure 3-28 are labeled as the manual describes them. If a connector is a group of pins sticking up on the board, the connector is called a header. You will learn to use most of these connectors in later chapters.

Figure 3-28 Internal connectors on a motherboard for drives and ports on the front of the case

APPLYING | CONCEPTS FIND THE MOTHERBOARD DOCUMENTATION

A+ 220-901 1.4

The motherboard user guide is essential to identifying components on a board and knowing how to support the board. This guide can be a PDF file stored on the CD or DVD that came bundled with the motherboard. If you don't have the CD, you can download the user guide from the motherboard manufacturer's website.

To find the correct user guide online, you need to know the board manufacturer and model. If a motherboard is already installed in a computer, you can use the Windows System Information utility (msinfo32.exe) to report the brand and model of the board. To access the utility, for Windows 8.x, from the desktop, right-click **Start**, click **Run**, and type **msinfo32.exe** in the Run box. (For Windows 7/Vista, click **Start**, type **msinfo32.exe** in the Search box, and press **Enter**.) In the System Information window, click **System Summary**. In the System Summary information in the right pane, look for the motherboard information labeled as the System Manufacturer and System Model (see Figure 3-29).

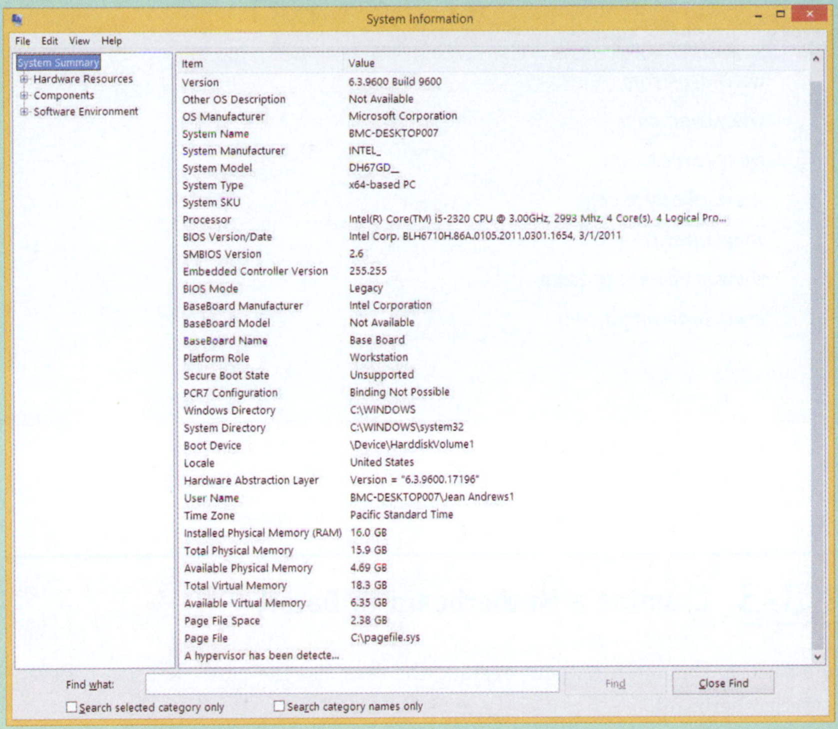

Figure 3-29 Use the System Information window to identify the motherboard brand and model

If the motherboard is not installed or the system is not working, look for the brand and model imprinted somewhere on the motherboard (see Figure 3-30). Next, go to the website of the motherboard manufacturer and download the user guide. Websites for several motherboard manufacturers are listed in Table 3-5. The diagrams, pictures, charts, and explanations of settings and components in the user guide will be invaluable to you when supporting this board.

Figure 3-30 The motherboard brand and model are imprinted somewhere on the board

(continues)

Manufacturer	Web Address
ASUS	*www.asus.com*
Evga	*www.evga.com*
ASRock	*www.asrock.com*
Gigabyte Technology Co., Ltd.	*www.gigabyte.com*
Intel Corporation	*www.intel.com*
Micro-Star International (MSI)	*www.msicomputer.com*
Super Micro Computer, Inc.	*www.supermicro.com*

Table 3-5 Major manufacturers of motherboards

Hands-On Project 3-3 Examine a Motherboard in Detail

A+
220-901
1.4

1. Look at the back of a desktop computer. Without opening the case, list the ports that you believe come directly from the motherboard.
2. Remove the cover of the case, which you learned to do in the chapter, "Working Inside Desktop Computers and Laptops." List the different expansion cards in the expansion slots. Was your guess correct about which ports come from the motherboard?
3. To expose the motherboard so you can identify its parts, remove all the expansion cards.
4. Draw a diagram of the motherboard and label these parts:
   - Processor socket
   - Chipset
   - RAM (each DIMM slot)
   - CMOS battery
   - Expansion slots (Identify the slots as PCI, PCIe x1, PCIe x4, or PCIe x16.)
   - Each port coming directly from the motherboard
   - Power supply connections
   - SATA drive connectors
5. What is the brand and model of the motherboard?
6. Locate the manufacturer's website. If you can find the motherboard manual on the site, download it. Find the diagram of the motherboard in the manual and compare it with your diagram. Did you label components correctly?
7. Reassemble the computer, as you learned to do in the chapter, "Working Inside Desktop Computers and Laptops."

Hands-On | Project 3-4 Examine Motherboard Documentation

A+
220-901
1.4

Using the motherboard brand and model installed in your computer, or another motherboard brand and model assigned by your instructor, download the user guide from the motherboard manufacturer and answer these questions:

1. What processors does the board support?
2. What type of RAM does the board support?
3. What is the maximum RAM the board can hold?
4. If the board has a PCIe slot, what version of PCIe does the board use?
5. What chipset does the board use?

Now that you know what to expect when examining or selecting a motherboard, let's see how to configure a board.

CONFIGURING A MOTHERBOARD

A+
220-901
1.1

Firmware on the motherboard is used to enable or disable a connector, port, or component; control the frequency of the CPU, security features, and what happens when the PC first boots; and monitor various activities of the board. Today's motherboards may use these types of firmware:

- *BIOS*. BIOS is used on older motherboards.
- *UEFI*. Unified Extensible Firmware Interface (UEFI) is replacing BIOS and is used on most motherboards made after 2012. Microsoft requires UEFI in order for the system to be certified for Windows 8 and later. UEFI is also required for hard drives larger than 2 TB. (One terabyte or TB equals 1000 gigabytes or GB.)
- *UEFI with BIOS*. Most personal computer motherboards contain UEFI firmware with BIOS also provided for backward compatibility with older devices.

As an IT support technician, you need to know how to configure the BIOS or UEFI firmware settings. We first look at how to configure BIOS settings and then we'll see how to configure UEFI settings.

USING BIOS SETUP TO CONFIGURE A MOTHERBOARD

A+
220-901
1.1

The motherboard settings don't normally need to be changed except, for example, when there is a problem with hardware, or a power-saving feature or security feature (such as a power-on password) needs to be disabled or enabled.

A+ Exam Tip The A+ 220-901 exam expects you to know about BIOS settings regarding RAM, the hard drive, optical drive, CPU, boot sequence, enabling and disabling devices, system date and time, virtualization support, passwords, drive encryption, and monitoring temperature, fan speeds, intrusion detection, voltage, and clock and bus speeds. All these settings are covered in this part of the chapter.

ACCESS THE BIOS SETUP PROGRAM

You access the BIOS setup program by pressing a key or combination of keys during the boot process. For most motherboards, you press F2 or Del during the boot. For a few older motherboards, you press Ctrl+Alt+Esc. See the motherboard documentation to know for sure which keys to press. A message such as the following usually appears on the screen near the beginning of the boot:

```
Press DEL to change Setup
```

or

```
Press F2 for Setup
```

When you press the appropriate key or keys, a setup screen appears with menus and Help features that are often very user-friendly. Although the exact menus depend on the BIOS maker, the sample screens that follow will help you become familiar with the general contents of BIOS setup screens. Figure 3-31 shows a main menu for setup. On this menu, you can view information about the BIOS version, processor model and speed, memory speed, total memory, and the amount of memory in each memory slot. You can also change the system date and time.

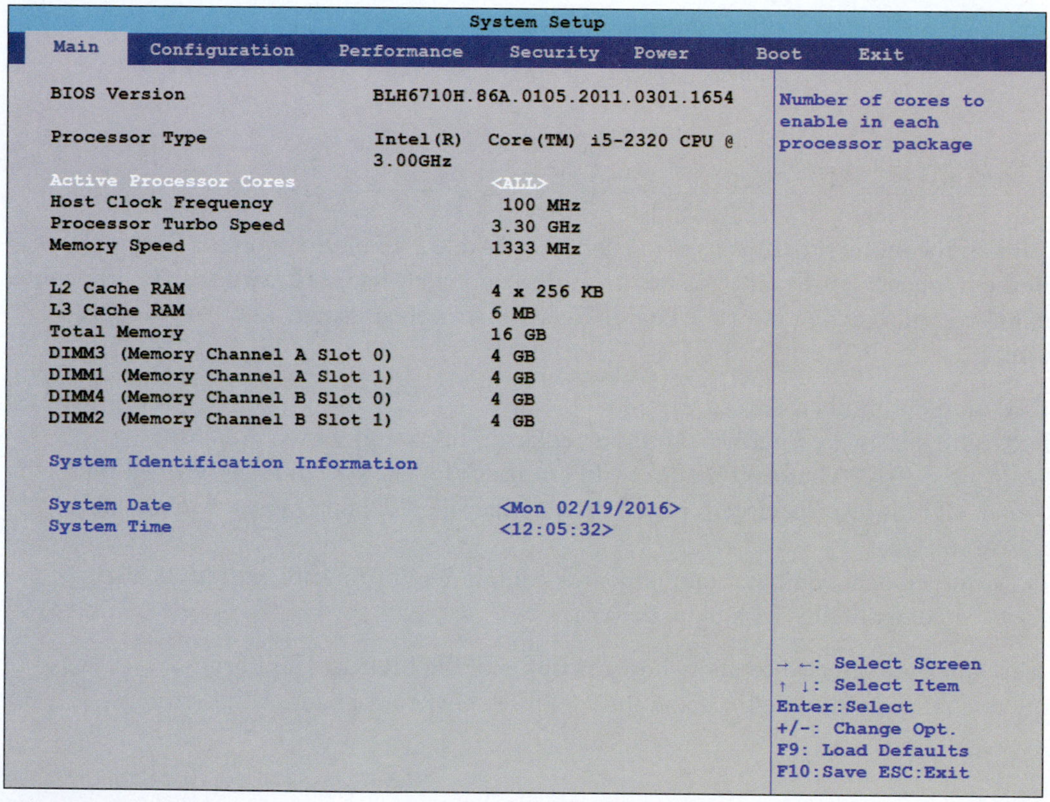

Source: Intel

Figure 3-31 BIOS setup main menu

Notes For a comprehensive list of BIOS manufacturers and links to their websites, visit *support.microsoft.com/en-us/kb/243909*.

Now let's examine setup screens that apply to the boot sequence, virtualization, built-in diagnostics, monitoring the system, and security.

CHANGE THE BOOT SEQUENCE

Figure 3-32 shows an example of a boot menu in BIOS setup. Here, you can set the order in which the system tries to boot from certain devices (called the boot sequence or boot priority). Most likely when you first install a hard drive or an operating system, you will want to have the BIOS attempt to first boot from a DVD so that you can install Windows from the setup DVD. After the OS is installed, to prevent accidental boots from a DVD or other media, change setup BIOS to boot first from the hard drive. Notice in Figure 3-32 the option to perform a UEFI Boot. This particular motherboard holds both BIOS and UEFI firmware.

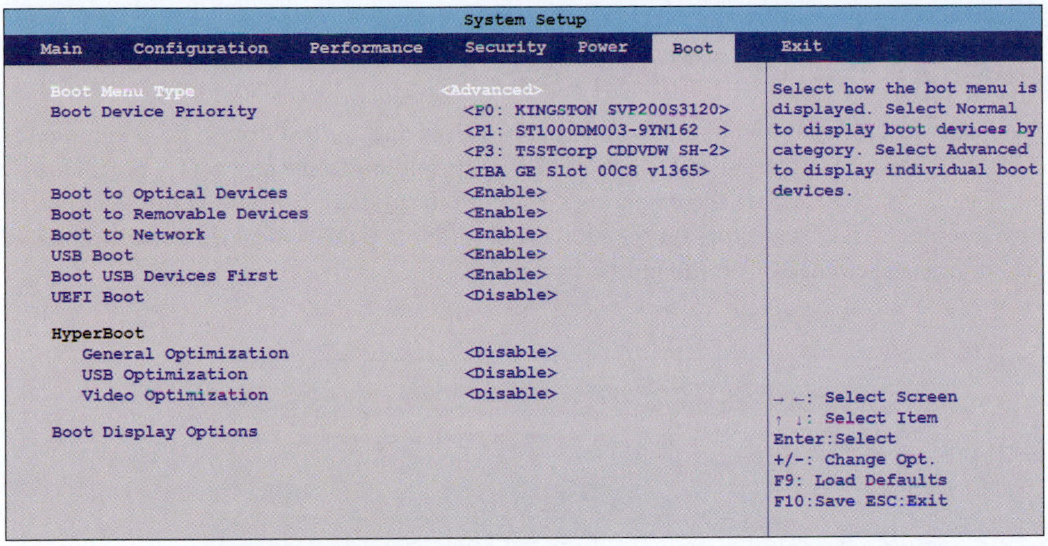

Source: Intel

Figure 3-32 Set the boot priority order in BIOS setup

Also, the BIOS setup boot screens might give you options regarding built-in diagnostics that occur at the boot. Recall from the chapter, "First Look at Computer Parts and Tools," that these tests are called the POST (power-on self test). You can configure some motherboards to perform a quick boot and bypass the extensive POST. For these systems, if you are troubleshooting a boot problem, be sure to set BIOS to perform the full POST.

CONFIGURE ONBOARD DEVICES

You can enable or disable some onboard devices (for example, a network port, FireWire port, USB ports, or video ports) using setup BIOS. For one system, the Configuration screen shown in Figure 3-33 does the job. On this screen, you can enable or disable a port or group of ports, and you can configure the Front Panel Audio ports for Auto, High Definition audio, and Legacy audio, or you can disable these audio ports. What you can configure on your system depends on the onboard devices the motherboard offers.

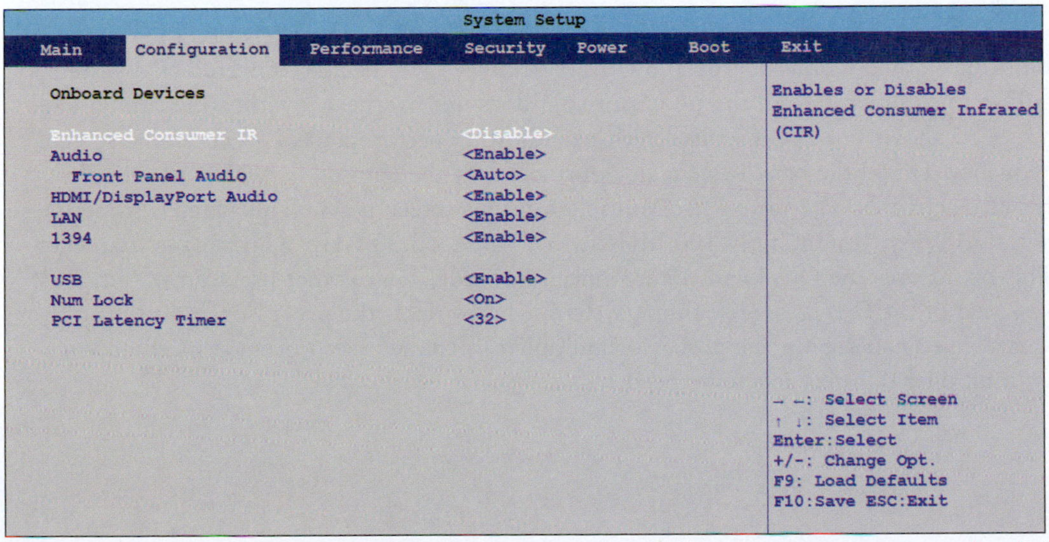

Source: Intel

Figure 3-33 Enable and disable onboard devices

Notes You don't have to replace an entire motherboard if one port fails. For example, if the network port fails, use BIOS setup to disable the port. Then use an expansion card for the port instead.

VIEW HARD DRIVE AND OPTICAL DRIVE INFORMATION

Using setup BIOS, you can view information about installed hard drives and optical drives. For example, in Figure 3-34, one system shows five internal SATA and eSATA ports and one external eSATA port. One 120-GB hard drive is installed on SATA port 0, and another 1000-GB hard drive is installed on SATA port 1. Both ports are internal SATA connectors on the motherboard. Notice the optical drive is installed on SATA port 3, also an internal connector on the motherboard.

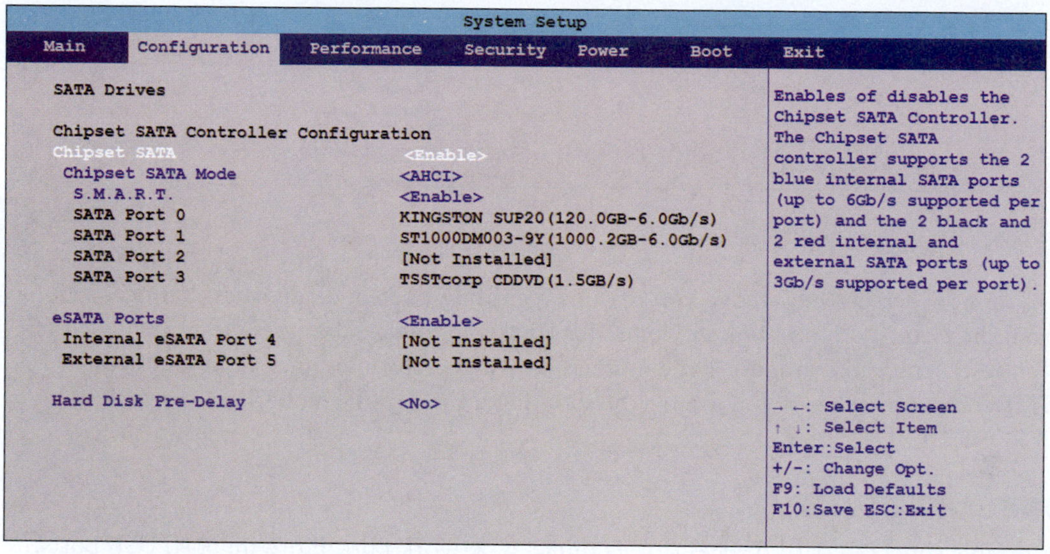

Source: Intel

Figure 3-34 A BIOS setup screen showing a list of drives installed on the system

PROCESSOR AND CLOCK SPEEDS

Overclocking is running a processor, memory, motherboard, or video card at a higher speed than the manufacturer recommends. Some motherboards allow overclocking. If you decide to overclock a system, pay careful attention to the temperature of the processor so it does not overheat; overheating can damage the processor. Figure 3-35 shows one BIOS setup screen for adjusting performance. Notice on the screen the Host Clock Frequency. This is the basic system clock provided by the chipset, by which all other components synchronize activities. The Core Max Multiplier on this screen is 33. (This value is sometimes called the bus/core ratio.) When you multiply 100 MHz by 33, you get 3.30 GHz, which is the frequency of the processor. This board uses the QuickPath Interconnect. For older boards that use a Front Side Bus, you can change the speed of the FSB to overclock the system, which affects the processor and memory speeds. On some boards, you can change the processor multiplier to change the processor speed and/or change the memory multiplier to affect memory speed.

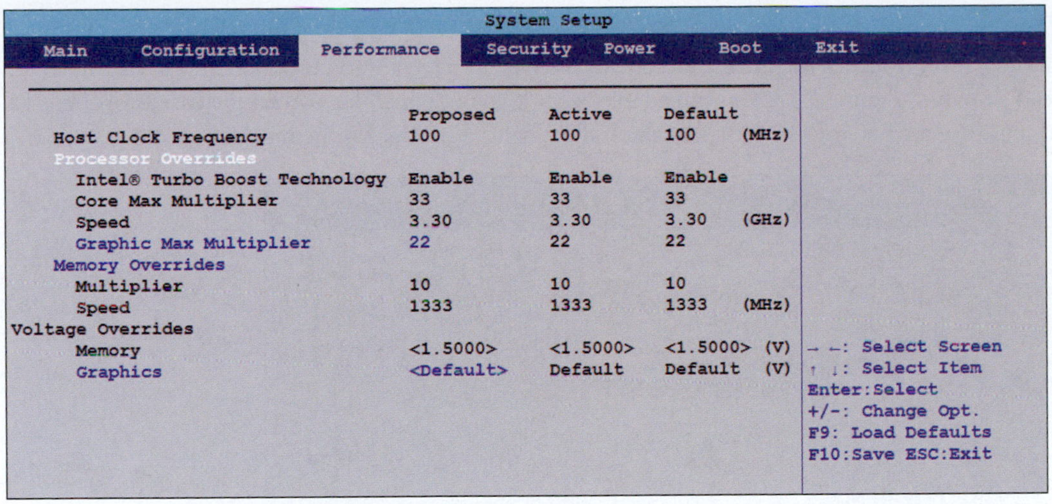

Source: Intel

Figure 3-35 A motherboard might give options for changing the clock speed or multipliers for the processor and memory

MONITOR TEMPERATURES, FAN SPEEDS, AND VOLTAGES

Using BIOS setup screens, you can monitor temperatures inside the case, fan speeds, and voltages. One BIOS screen that allows you to monitor these values and also control fan speeds is shown in Figure 3-36. Case and CPU fans on modern computers adjust their speeds based on the temperatures of the CPU, memory, and motherboard. You can also install software (for example, SpeedFan by Alfredo Comparetti at *www.almico.com/speedfan.php*) in Windows to monitor temperatures and control fan speeds. To use the software, you might need to change a BIOS setting to allow software to control the speeds. For this system, when you select Processor Temperature, you can set the threshold temperatures that software uses to create an alert.

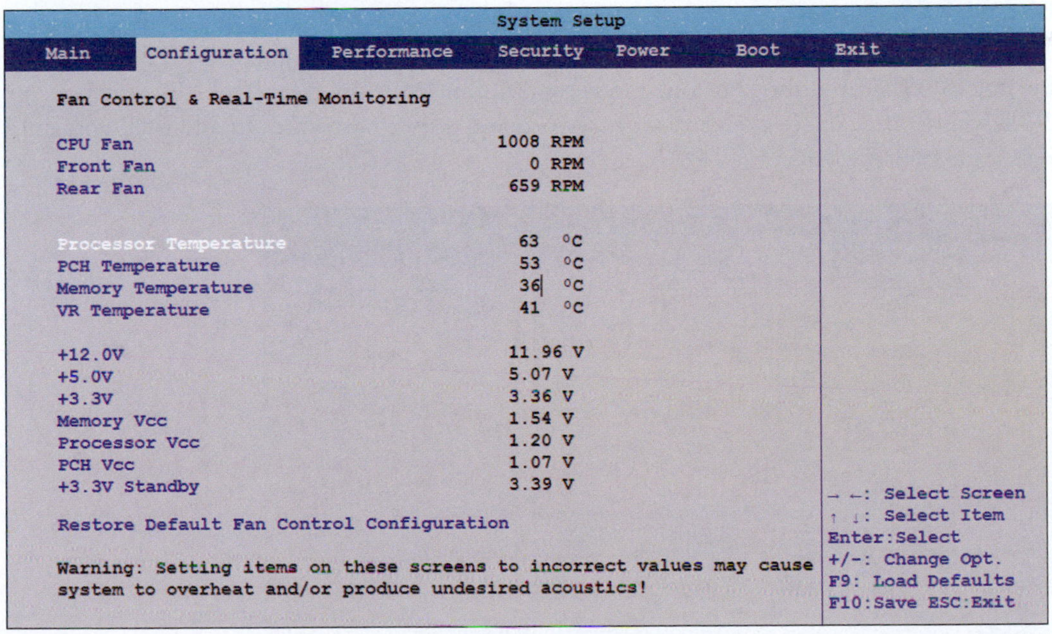

Source: Intel

Figure 3-36 Monitor temperatures, fan speeds, and voltages in a system

INTRUSION DETECTION

BIOS settings might offer several security features, and one of these is an intrusion-detection alert. For example, for the BIOS setup screen shown in Figure 3-37, you can enable event logging, which logs when the case is opened. To use the feature, you must use a cable to connect a switch on the case to a header on the motherboard.

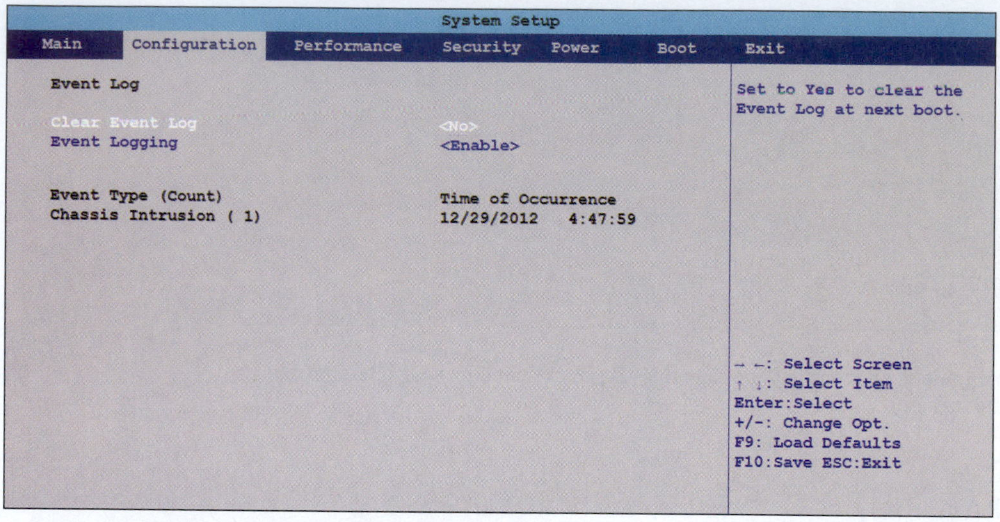

Source: Intel

Figure 3-37 BIOS is enabled to log a chassis intrusion

When the security measure is in place and the case is opened, BIOS displays an alert the next time the system is powered up. For example, the alert message at startup might be "Chassis Intruded! System has halted." If you see this message, know that the case has been opened. Reboot the system and the system should start up as usual. To make sure the alert was not tripped by accident, verify that the case cover is securely in place. Also, sometimes a failed CMOS battery can trip the alert. Intrusion-detection devices are not a recommended best practice for security. False alerts are annoying, and criminals generally know how to get inside a case without tripping the alert.

POWER-ON PASSWORDS

Another security feature is power-on passwords assigned in BIOS setup to prevent unauthorized access to the computer and/or the BIOS setup utility. For one motherboard, this security screen looks like the one shown in Figure 3-38, where you can set a supervisor password and a user password. In addition, you can configure how the user password works.

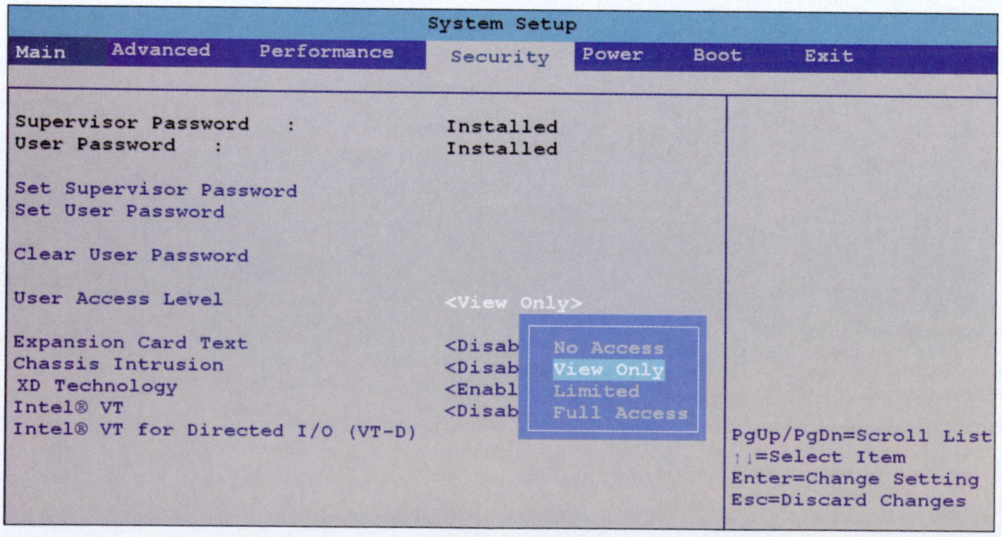

Source: Intel

Figure 3-38 Set supervisor and user passwords in BIOS setup to lock down a computer

The choices under User Access Level are **No Access** (the user cannot access the BIOS setup utility), **View Only** (the user can access BIOS setup, but cannot make changes), **Limited** (the user can access BIOS setup and make a few changes such as date and time), and **Full Access** (the user can access the BIOS setup utility and make any changes). When supervisor and user passwords are both set and you boot the system, a box to enter a password is displayed. What access you have depends on which password you enter. Also, if both passwords are set, you must enter a valid password to boot the system. By setting both passwords, you can totally lock down the computer from unauthorized access.

A+ Exam Tip The A+ 220-901 exam expects you to know how to use BIOS setup to secure a workstation from unauthorized use.

Notes For added protection, configure the BIOS setup utility so that a user cannot boot from a removable device such as a CD, USB device, or floppy disk.

Caution In the event that passwords are forgotten, know that supervisor and user passwords to the computer can be reset by setting a jumper (group of pins) on the motherboard to clear all BIOS customized settings and return BIOS setup to its default settings. To keep someone from using this technique to access the computer, you can use a computer case with a lockable side panel and install a lock on the case. How to use jumpers is covered later in this chapter.

BIOS SUPPORT FOR VIRTUALIZATION

Virtualization is when one physical machine hosts multiple activities that are normally done on multiple machines. One type of virtualization is the use of virtual machines. A virtual computer or virtual machine (VM) is software that simulates the hardware of a physical computer. Each VM running on a computer works like a physical computer and is assigned virtual devices such as a virtual motherboard and virtual hard drive. Examples of VM software are Windows Virtual PC, Microsoft Hyper-V, and Oracle VirtualBox. For most VM software to work, virtualization must be enabled in BIOS setup. Looking back at Figure 3-38, you can see the option to enable Intel VT. Intel VT is the name that Intel gives to its virtualization technology.

LOJACK FOR LAPTOPS TECHNOLOGY

LoJack is a technology embedded in the BIOS of many laptops to protect a system against theft. When you subscribe to the LoJack for Laptops service by Absolute (*www.absolute.com*), the Computrace Agent software is installed. The software and BIOS work together to protect the system. The company can locate your laptop whenever it connects to the Internet, and you can give commands through the Internet to lock the laptop or delete all data on it.

DRIVE ENCRYPTION AND DRIVE PASSWORD PROTECTION

Some motherboards and hard drives allow you to set a password that must be entered before someone can access the hard drive. This password is kept on the drive and works even if the drive is moved to another computer. Some manufacturers of storage media offer similar products. For example, Seagate (*www.seagate.com*) offers Maxtor BlackArmor, a technology that encrypts an entire external storage device that is password protected.

Notes Drive lock password protection might be too secure at times. I know of a situation where a hard drive with password protection became corrupted. Normally, you might be able to move the drive to another computer and recover some data. However, this drive asked for the password, but then could not confirm it. Therefore, the entire drive, including all the data, was inaccessible.

THE TPM CHIP AND HARD DRIVE ENCRYPTION

Many high-end computers have a chip on the motherboard called the TPM (Trusted Platform Module) chip. The BitLocker Encryption tool in Windows 8/7/Vista is designed to work with this chip; the chip holds the BitLocker encryption key (also called the startup key). The TPM chip can also be used with other encryption software that may be installed on the hard drive other than BitLocker. If the hard drive is stolen from the computer and installed in another computer, the data would be safe because BitLocker has encrypted all contents on the drive and would not allow access without the startup key stored on the TPM chip. Therefore, this method assures that the drive cannot be used in another computer. However, if the motherboard fails and is replaced, you'll need a backup copy of the startup key to access data on the hard drive.

★ A+ Exam Tip The A+ 220-901 exam expects you to know about drive encryption and the TPM chip.

When you use Windows to install BitLocker Encryption, the initialization process also initializes the TPM chip. Initializing the TPM chip configures it and turns it on. After BitLocker is installed, you can temporarily turn off BitLocker, which also turns off the TPM chip. For example, you might want to turn off BitLocker to test the BitLocker recovery process. Normally, BitLocker will manage the TPM chip for you, and there is no need for you to manually change TPM chip settings. However, if you are having problems installing BitLocker, one thing you can do is clear the TPM chip. *Be careful!* If the TPM chip is being used to hold an encryption key to protect data on the hard drive and you clear the chip, the encryption key will be lost. That means all the data will be lost, too. Therefore, don't clear the TPM chip unless you are certain it is not being used to encrypt data.

APPLYING | CONCEPTS MANAGE THE TPM CHIP

A+
220-901
1.1

To manage the TPM chip, follow these steps:

1. Log on to Windows using an administrator account.
2. In the Windows 8 Run box or the Windows 7/Vista Search box, enter the **tpm.msc** command and respond to the User Account Control box. The TPM Management console opens.
3. If no TPM chip is present, the console reports that. If your system has a TPM chip that is not yet initialized, the console will have the option under the Actions pane to Initialize TPM. If the TPM chip is already initialized and ready for use, the console looks similar to the one shown in Figure 3-39.

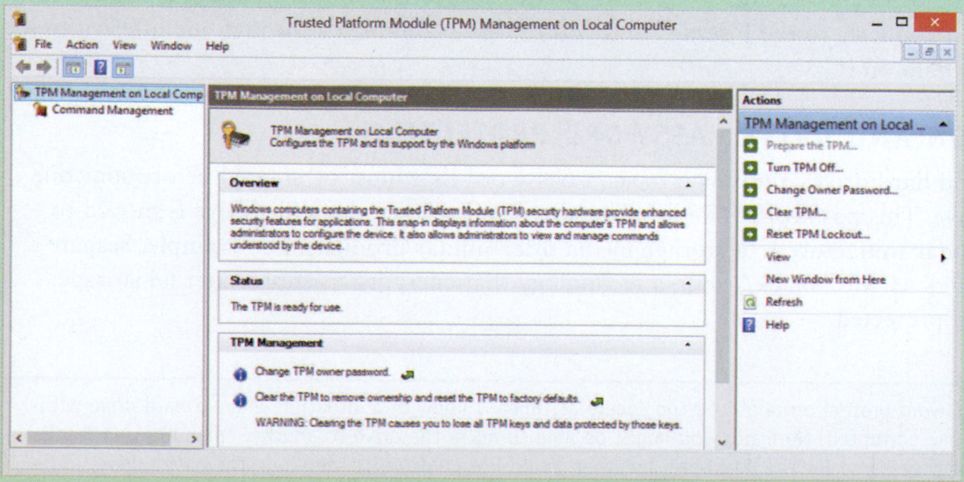

Figure 3-39 Use the TPM Management console to manage the TPM chip in Windows

4. Using the console, you can change the TPM owner password, turn TPM on or off, reset the TPM when it has locked access to the hard drive, and clear the TPM, which resets it to factory defaults. After you have made changes to the TPM chip, you will most likely be asked to restart the computer for the changes to take effect.

EXITING THE BIOS SETUP MENUS

When you finish with BIOS setup, an exit screen such as the one shown in Figure 3-40 gives you various options, such as exit and save your changes or exit and discard your changes. Notice in the figure that you also have the option to load BIOS default settings. This option can sometimes solve a problem when a user has made several inappropriate changes to the BIOS settings.

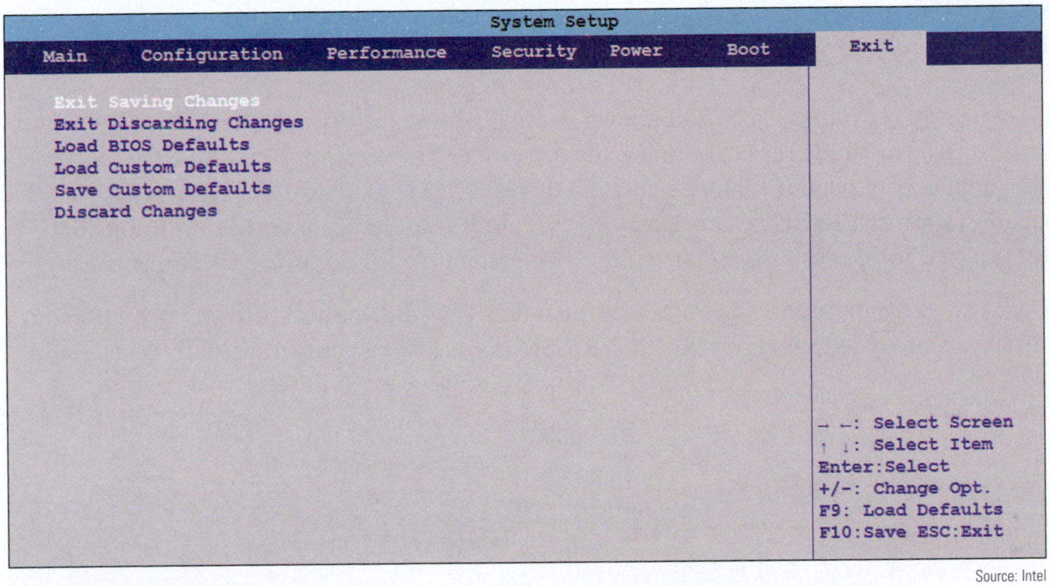

Source: Intel

Figure 3-40 BIOS setup Exit menu

Hands-On | Project 3-5 Examine BIOS Settings

A+ 220-901 1.1

Access the BIOS setup program on your computer and answer the following questions:

1. What key(s) did you press to access BIOS setup?
2. What brand and version of BIOS are you using?
3. What is the frequency of your processor?
4. What is the boot sequence order of devices?
5. Do you have an optical drive installed? What are the details of the installed drive?
6. What are the details of the installed hard drive(s)?
7. Does the BIOS offer the option to set a supervisor or power-on password? What is the name of the screen where these passwords are set?
8. Does the BIOS offer the option to overclock the processor? If so, list the settings that apply to overclocking.
9. Can you disable the onboard ports on the computer? If so, which ports can you disable, and what is the name of the screen(s) where this is done?
10. List three BIOS settings that control how power is managed on the computer.

USING UEFI SETUP TO CONFIGURE A MOTHERBOARD

A+
220-901
1.1

Extensible Firmware Interface (EFI), the original version of UEFI, was first developed by Intel. Today, Unified EFI (UEFI) is managed by several manufacturers and developers under the Unified EFI Forum (see *www.uefi.org*). UEFI firmware on the motherboard working with an operating system that supports UEFI improves on legacy BIOS in these ways:

- ***Faster and better booting.*** UEFI does a faster and better job of booting the system, handing over the boot to the OS, and loading device drivers and applications before the OS loads.
- ***Mouse-enabled interface.*** The mouse-enabled UEFI interface is more user friendly to get information about system components; configure the boot sequence, clock speed, virtualization, and power-on passwords; and monitor temperature, fan speeds, voltage, and bus speeds.
- ***Secure boot.*** UEFI version 2.3 and higher offers a secure boot, which prevents a system from booting up with drivers or an OS that are not digitally signed and trusted by the motherboard or computer manufacturer. For secure boot to work, the OS, such as Windows 8 or Linux Ubuntu version 14, must support UEFI.
- ***Support for hard drives larger than 2 TB.*** UEFI allows booting from hard drives larger than 2 TB. A hard drive uses one of two methods for partitioning the drive: The Master Boot Record (MBR) method is older, allows for four partitions and is limited to 2-TB drives. The GUID Partition Table (GPT) method is newer, allows for any size hard drive, and, for Windows, can have up to 128 partitions on the drive. GPT is required for drives larger than 2 TB or for systems that boot using UEFI firmware.

UEFI allows for backward compatibility. It can boot from a MBR hard drive and provides a BIOS boot through its Compatibility Support Module (CSM) feature. CSM is backward compatible with devices and drivers that use BIOS.

APPLYING | CONCEPTS EXPLORE UEFI SETUP

A+
220-901
1.1

Let's explore a few important UEFI setup screens that you need to be aware of. If you need help using UEFI setup, refer to the documentation for the motherboard manufacturer. Here are the steps for one system, but your UEFI screens might be different:

1. As with BIOS setup, to access the UEFI firmware, press a key, such as F12, F2, or Del, during the boot. A UEFI main screen appears. Figure 3-41 shows the main screen for one system, but yours might be different. On this screen, you can view information about the CPU and memory and change the language, date, or time. You can use your mouse or arrow keys to navigate through menus at the top of the screen to view and change information. Use the Ai Tweaker screen to overclock the CPU, the Advanced screen to configure the CPU, SATA, USB, onboard devices, power, and network settings, and the Monitor screen to monitor temperature, fans, and voltages. On the Boot screen, you can change the boot sequence and other boot settings. The Tool screen is used to flash UEFI and BIOS.

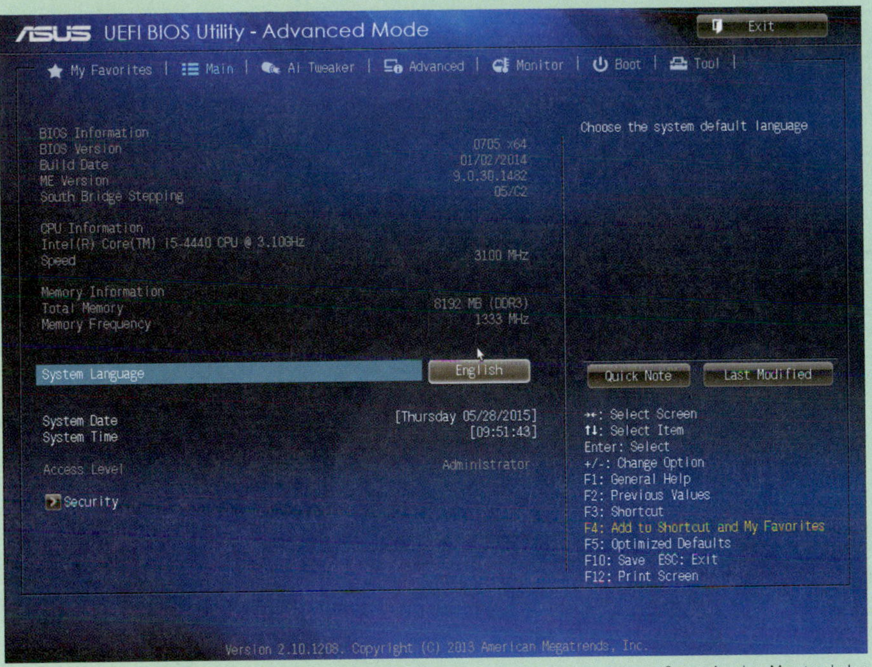

Source: American Megatrends, Inc.

Figure 3-41 UEFI main screen in Advanced Mode by Asus

2. To manage the CSM and Secure boot, click the **Boot** menu. On the Boot menu, first make sure Fast Boot is disabled (see Figure 3-42). Notice the two setup modes that are listed in the figure. Select CSM for backward compatibility with older BIOS devices and drivers and MBR hard drives. Select Secure Boot to boot using UEFI secure boot. For secure boot to work, CSM must be disabled, Windows 8 or another UEFI-aware OS must be installed, and the hard drive used for the boot must be partitioned using GPT.

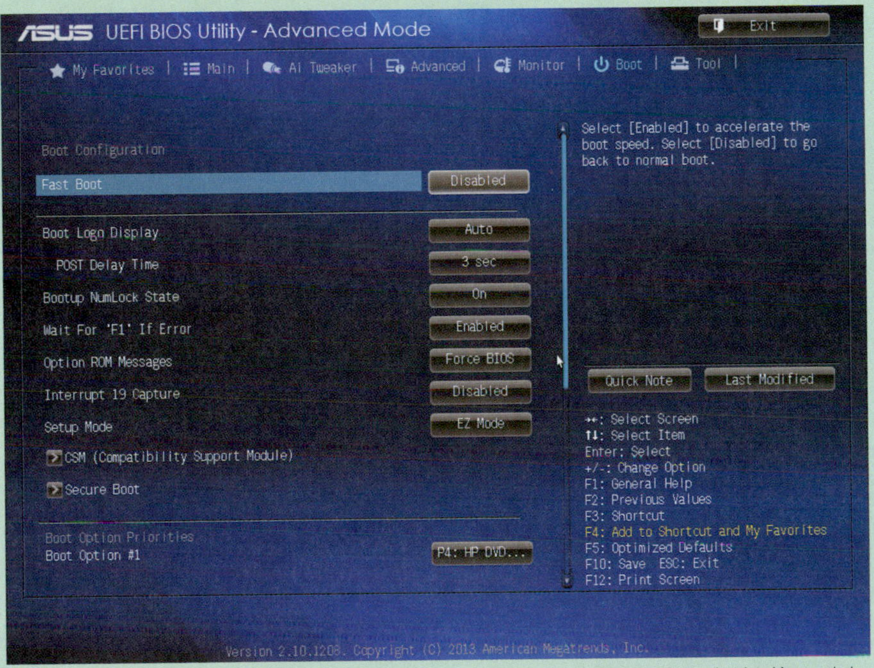

Source: American Megatrends, Inc.

Figure 3-42 Use CSM to boot a legacy BIOS system or disable it to implement UEFI secure boot

(continues)

3. To manage Secure boot, click **Secure Boot**. On the next screen, you can select the operating system that will be loaded when you have more than one OS installed on the system. To manage the keys used for a Secure boot, click **Key Management**. The screen in Figure 3-43 appears.

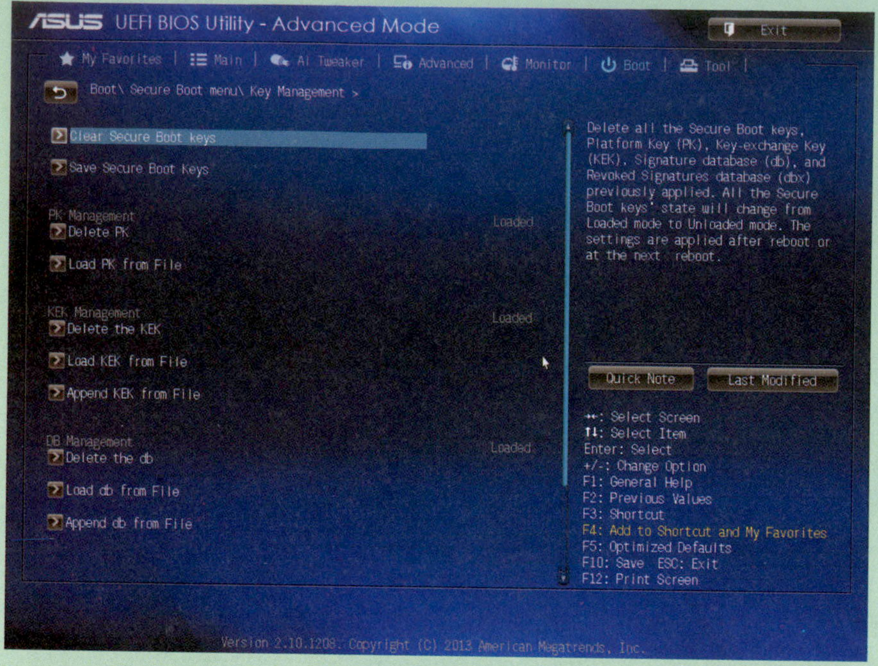

Source: American Megatrends, Inc.

Figure 3-43 Manage the UEFI secure boot keys and databases

4. A Secure boot uses the following keys, databases, and drivers, which are stored in flash memory on the motherboard and/or on the hard drive and can be managed using commands shown in Figure 3-43:

- The **signature database (db)** holds a list of digital signatures of approved operating systems, applications, and drivers that can be loaded by UEFI. Notice in Figure 3-43, the option to delete the db, load it from a file, or append to it.
- The **revoked signature database (dbx)** is a blacklist of signatures for software that has been revoked and is no longer trusted.
- The **Key-exchange Key (KEK)**, also called the **Key-enrollment Key (KEK)**, database is another database that holds digital signatures provided by OS manufacturers, such as Microsoft and Red Hat (a Linux manufacturer). The OS manufacturer or vendor that owns the keys can update them, which will in turn update the db or dbx. For example, an update may occur when a new OS is released or to revoke a bad release of an OS.
- The **Platform Key (PK)** is a digital signature belonging to the motherboard or computer manufacturer. The PK authorizes turning on or off Secure boot and updating the KEK database.
- **Option ROMs** are UEFI drivers, for example, video, keyboard, and mouse drivers required as the computer first boots, that are digitally signed and identified in the signature database.

Just as with BIOS, UEFI loads an OS and drivers at the beginning of the boot and then turns the control of the computer over to the OS. When UEFI secure boot is active, it checks the OS and each UEFI driver or application before it is loaded to verify it is signed and identified in the secure boot databases. The OS, drivers, and applications that are loaded by UEFI are stored in a system partition on the hard drive named efi. After the OS is launched, it can load additional drivers and applications that UEFI secure boot does not verify.

For normal operation, you would not be required to change secure boot settings unless you want to install hardware that is not certified by the OS or computer manufacturer. In this situation, you could disable secure boot, assuming the PK allows you to do so. When you disable secure boot, the system is no longer protected from rogue drivers or OS installing at the boot. Before you make any changes to the secure boot screen, be sure to use the option to Save Secure Boot Keys, which saves all the databases to a USB flash drive so that you can backtrack your changes later if need be.

Notes On laptops and other computers that carry the Windows 8 logo imprinted on the computer, the computer manufacturer is required to configure secure boot so that it cannot be disabled, which assures that only certified OS and drivers can be loaded by UEFI.

3

Now let's see what other tasks you might need to do when you are responsible for maintaining a motherboard.

MAINTAINING A MOTHERBOARD

A+ 220-901 1.1

To maintain a motherboard, you need to know how to update the motherboard drivers, flash BIOS or UEFI, and replace the CMOS battery. All these skills are covered in this part of the chapter.

A+ Exam Tip The A+ 220-901 exam expects you to know how to update drivers and firmware and replace the CMOS battery.

UPDATING MOTHERBOARD DRIVERS

A+ 220-901 1.1, 1.2

Device drivers are small programs stored on the hard drive that an operating system, such as Windows or Linux, uses to communicate with a specific hardware device, for example, a printer, network port on the motherboard, or scanner. The CD or DVD that comes bundled with the motherboard contains a user guide and drivers for its onboard components (for example, chipset, graphics, audio, network, and USB drivers), and these drivers need to be installed in the OS. For a motherboard, after installing the board, you can install the drivers from CD or DVD and later update drivers by downloading updates from the motherboard manufacturer's website. Updates are sometimes included in updates to Windows.

Notes The motherboard CD or DVD or the manufacturer's website might contain useful utilities, for example, a utility to monitor the CPU temperature and alert you if overheating occurs or a diagnostics utility for troubleshooting.

If a motherboard or one of its components is giving problems, try downloading and installing updated drivers from the motherboard manufacturer website. Figure 3-44 shows the download page for one Asus motherboard where you can download drivers and BIOS updates. When you download the drivers using the system with the motherboard installed, Asus selects the correct OS, as shown in the figure.

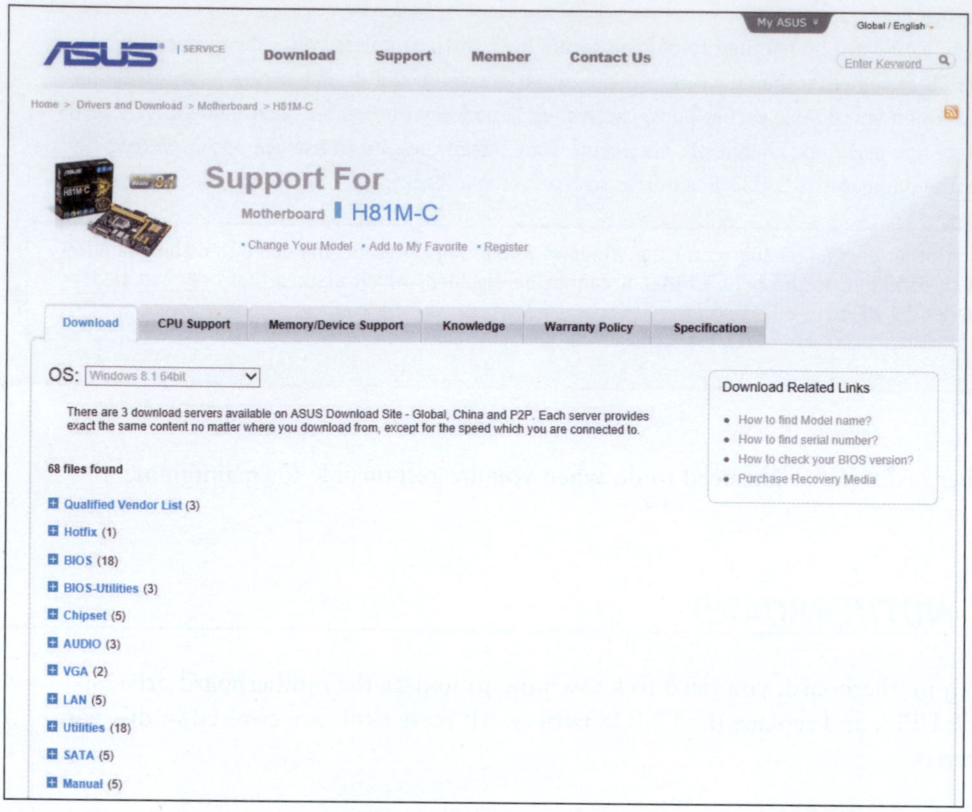

Source: ASUSTek Computer, Inc.

Figure 3-44 Download drivers, BIOS updates, documentation, utilities, and other help software from the motherboard manufacturer's website

If you must download the drivers from a computer that does not have the motherboard installed, be sure to select the correct OS (for example, Windows 7) and the correct type (32 bit or 64 bit). Always use 32-bit drivers with a 32-bit OS and 64-bit drivers with a 64-bit OS. The bit number is the number of bits the driver or OS can process at one time, and you want that to match up. To know what edition and type of Windows you are using, on the Windows 8 desktop, right-click **Start** and click **System**. For Windows 7/Vista, click **Start**, right-click **Computer**, and select **Properties**. The System window appears, giving you details about the Windows installation (see Figure 3-45).

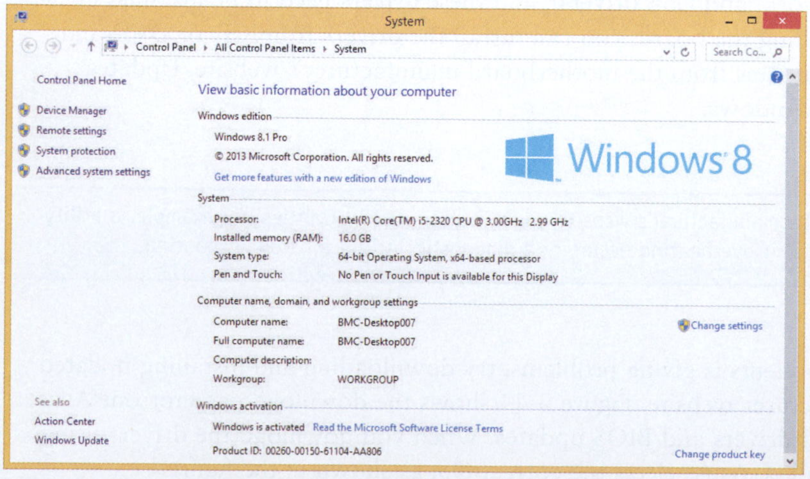

Figure 3-45 The System window reports the edition and type of OS installed

FLASHING BIOS

A+ 220-901 1.1

Recall that BIOS includes the BIOS setup program, the startup BIOS that manages the startup process, and the system BIOS that manages basic I/O functions of the system. All these programs are stored on a firmware chip. The process of upgrading or refreshing the programming stored on the firmware chip is called updating the BIOS or flashing BIOS. Here are some good reasons you might want to flash the BIOS:

- The system hangs at odd times or during the boot.
- Some motherboard functions have stopped working or are giving problems. For example, the onboard video port is not working.
- You want to incorporate some new features or component on the board. For example, a BIOS upgrade might be required before you upgrade the processor.

Caution Be sure you use the correct motherboard brand and model when selecting the BIOS update on the manufacturer's website. Trying to use the wrong update can cause problems.

The BIOS updates are downloaded from the motherboard manufacturer's website. To flash BIOS, always follow the directions that you can find in the user guide for your motherboard. Here are four methods that most motherboards can use:

- ***Express BIOS update.*** Some motherboards allow for an express BIOS update, which is done from Windows. Download the update file to your hard drive. Close all open applications. Double-click the file, which runs the update program, and follow the directions on screen. The system will reboot to apply the update.
- ***Update from a USB flash drive using BIOS setup.*** Copy the downloaded update file to a USB flash drive. Then restart the system and press a key at startup that launches the BIOS update process. (For some motherboard brands, you press F7.) A screen appears where you can select the USB flash drive. BIOS finds the update file on the flash drive, completes the update, and restarts the system.
- ***Update using a bootable CD.*** You can download an ISO file from the motherboard manufacturer's website that contains the BIOS update. An ISO file has an .iso file extension and contains an ISO image of a CD. You can use an ISO image to create a bootable CD with software and data on it. After you have created the bootable CD, boot from it and follow the directions on screen to flash the BIOS.

Notes To use Windows to burn a CD from an ISO file, first insert a blank CD in the optical drive. Then right-click the .iso file, select **Burn disc image**, and follow the directions on screen.

If the BIOS update is interrupted or the update gives errors, you are in an unfortunate situation. You might be able to revert to the earlier version. To do this, generally, you download the recovery file from the website and copy the file to a USB flash drive. Then set the jumper on the motherboard to recover from a failed BIOS update. Reboot the system and the BIOS automatically reads from the device and performs the recovery. Then reset the jumper to the normal setting and boot the system.

Notes To identify the BIOS version installed, look for the BIOS version number displayed on the main menu of BIOS setup. Alternately, you can use the System Information utility (msinfo32.exe) in Windows to display the BIOS version.

Makers of BIOS code are likely to change BIOS frequently because providing the upgrade on the Internet is so easy for them. Generally, however, follow the principle that "if it's not broke, don't fix it." Update your BIOS only if you're having a problem with your motherboard or there's a new BIOS feature you want to use. Also, don't update the BIOS unless the update is a later version than the one installed. One last word of caution: It's very important the update not be interrupted while it is in progress. A failed update can make your motherboard totally unusable. Be sure you don't interrupt the update, and make sure there are no power interruptions. For laptops, make sure the AC adapter is plugged in and powering the system.

Caution Be very careful that you upgrade BIOS with the correct upgrade and that you follow the manufacturer's instructions correctly. Upgrading with the wrong file could make your system BIOS useless. If you're not sure that you're using the correct upgrade, *don't guess*. Check with the technical support for your BIOS before moving forward. Before you call technical support, have the information that identifies your BIOS and motherboard available.

FLASHING UEFI

A+
220-901
1.1

UEFI updates are more secure than BIOS updates because they require digital signatures for the update to be verified. UEFI firmware, drivers, and databases can be updated by way of a USB flash drive or from within Windows. The process using a USB flash drive works like this:

1. Follow the motherboard manufacturer's directions to make the USB drive bootable and download the UEFI update files to the drive.
2. If secure boot is enabled, enter UEFI setup and disable secure boot. Also make sure the USB device is listed in the boot priority order before the hard drive.
3. For a laptop, plug the AC adapter into an external power source so that the power won't fail during the update.
4. Reboot the system, this time from the USB flash drive. Follow the manufacturer's directions to flash UEFI. For one manufacturer, you enter the **flash** command at a command prompt.
5. When prompted, reboot the system. For a secure boot system, go back to UEFI setup and enable secure boot.

Windows updates sometimes include UEFI updates that are handled similarly to driver updates published by hardware manufacturers. When Windows receives an update that it recognizes to be a UEFI update, it hands off the update to UEFI. On the next reboot, the Windows loader verifies the update against the UEFI signature database. If the signature is validated, the update passes to the UEFI firmware. The firmware is then responsible for applying the update and displays a screen letting the user know to not disturb the system while the update is in progress. After the update is completed, the Windows loader continues loading the OS.

Notes If a UEFI update fails to complete, UEFI may reboot and try again up to three times. After the third attempt, the update will be discarded and UEFI will roll back a partial update.

USING JUMPERS TO CLEAR BIOS SETTINGS

A+
220-901
1.1

A motherboard may have jumpers that you can use to clear BIOS/UEFI settings, which returns BIOS/UEFI setup to factory default settings. You might want to clear settings when flashing BIOS didn't work or failed to complete correctly or a power-on password is forgotten and you cannot boot the system.

A **jumper** is two small posts or metal pins that stick up on the motherboard, used to hold configuration information. An open jumper has no cover, and a closed jumper has a cover on the two pins (see Figure 3-46). Look at the jumper cover in Figure 3-46(b) that is "parked," meaning it is hanging on a single pin for safekeeping, but is not being used to turn a jumper setting on.

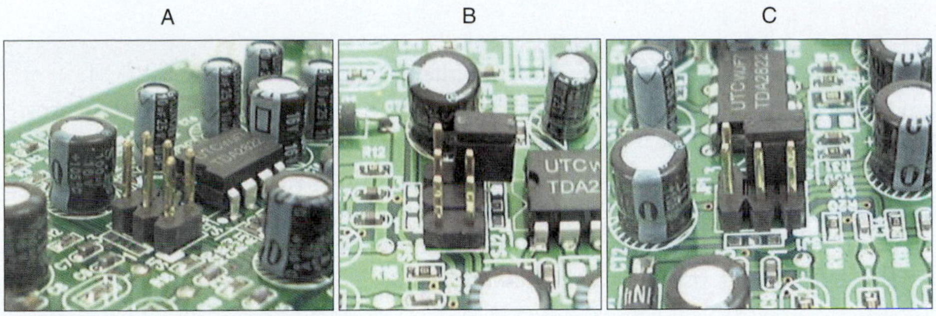

Figure 3-46 A 6-pin jumper group on a circuit board: (a) has no jumpers set to on, (b) has a cover parked on one pin, and (c) is configured with one jumper setting turned on

Most motherboards today allow you to set a supervisor password (to make changes in BIOS setup) or a power-on password (to get access to the system). Know that these passwords are not the same password that can be required by a Windows OS at startup. If both passwords are forgotten, you cannot use the computer. However, jumpers can be set to clear both passwords. Also, if flashing BIOS fails, a jumper can be set to undo the update.

For example, Figure 3-47 shows a group of three jumpers on one board. (The tan jumper cap is positioned on the first two jumper pins on the left side of the group.) Figure 3-48 shows the motherboard documentation on how to use these jumpers. When jumpers 1 and 2 are closed, which they are in the figure, normal booting happens. When jumpers 2 and 3 are closed, passwords to BIOS setup can be cleared on the next boot. When no jumpers are closed, on the next boot, the BIOS will recover itself from a failed update. Once set for normal booting, the jumpers should be changed only if you are trying to recover when a power-up password is lost or flashing BIOS has failed. To know how to set jumpers, see the motherboard documentation.

Figure 3-47 This group of three jumpers controls the BIOS configuration

Jumper Position	Mode	Description
1 3	Normal (default)	The current BIOS configuration is used for booting.
1 3	Configure	After POST, the BIOS displays a menu in CMOS setup that can be used to clear the user and supervisor power-on passwords.
1 3	Recovery	Recovery is used to recover from a failed BIOS update. Details can be found on the motherboard CD.

Figure 3-48 BIOS configuration jumper settings

REPLACING THE CMOS BATTERY

A+
220-901
1.2

Motherboard settings may be stored in flash memory in the firmware or in CMOS RAM. CMOS (complementary metal-oxide semiconductor) is a method of manufacturing microchips, and CMOS RAM is a small amount of memory stored on the motherboard that retains the data even when the computer is turned off because it is charged by a nearby lithium coin-cell battery (see Figure 3-49). If the CMOS battery is disconnected or fails, setup information is lost. An indication that the battery is getting weak is that the system date and time are incorrect after power has been disconnected to the PC. A message about a low battery can also appear at startup.

Figure 3-49 The coin-cell battery powers CMOS RAM when the system is turned off and unplugged

★ A+ Exam Tip The A+ 220-901 exam expects you to know about the CMOS battery.

The CMOS battery on the motherboard is considered a field replaceable unit. The battery is designed to last for years and recharges when the motherboard has power. However, on rare occasions, you might need to replace one if the system loses BIOS settings when it is unplugged. Make sure the replacement battery is an exact match to the original or is one the motherboard manufacturer recommends for the board. Power down the system, unplug it, press the power button to drain the power, and remove the case cover. Use your ESD strap to protect the system against ESD. The old battery can be removed with a little prying using a flathead screwdriver. The new battery pops into place. For more specific directions, see the motherboard documentation.

Hands-On | Project 3-6 Examine How to Clear BIOS Settings

A+
220-901
1.1

You can complete the following activity only if you have the documentation for a motherboard: Locate the jumper on the board that returns BIOS setup to default settings and label this jumper on your diagram. It is often found near the CMOS battery. Some boards might have more than one, and some have none.

Now let's turn our attention to installing or replacing a motherboard.

INSTALLING OR REPLACING A MOTHERBOARD

A+
220-901
4.1

A motherboard is considered a field replaceable unit, so you need to know how to replace one when it goes bad. In this part of the chapter, you learn how to select a motherboard and then how to install or replace one in a desktop or laptop computer.

HOW TO SELECT A DESKTOP MOTHERBOARD

A+
220-901
4.1

Because the motherboard determines so many of your computer's features, selecting the motherboard is, in most cases, your most important decision when you purchase a desktop computer or assemble one from parts. Depending on which applications and peripheral devices you plan to use with the computer, you can take one of three approaches to selecting a motherboard. The first approach is to select the board that provides the most room for expansion, so you can upgrade and exchange components and add devices easily. A second approach is to select the board that best suits the needs of the computer's current configuration, knowing that when you need to upgrade, you will likely switch to new technology and a new motherboard. The third approach is to select a motherboard that meets your present needs with moderate room for expansion.

Ask the following questions when selecting a motherboard:

1. What form factor does the motherboard use?
2. Which brand (Intel or AMD) and model processors does the board support? Which chipset does it use? How much memory can it hold? What memory speeds does the board support?
3. What type and how many expansion slots are on the board (for example, PCI Express 3.0 or PCI)?
4. How many and what hard drive controllers and connectors are on the board (for example, SATA or eSATA)?
5. What are the embedded devices on the board, and what internal slots or connections does the board have? (For example, the board might provide a network port, wireless antenna port, FireWire port, two or more USB ports, video port, and so forth.)
6. Does the board fit the case you plan to use?
7. What are the price and the warranty on the board? Does the board get good reviews?
8. How extensive and user friendly is the documentation?
9. How much support does the manufacturer supply for the board?

Sometimes a motherboard contains an onboard component more commonly offered as a separate device. One example is support for video. The video port might be on the motherboard or might require a video card. The cost of a motherboard with an embedded component is usually less than the combined cost of a motherboard with no embedded component and an expansion card. If you plan to expand, be cautious about choosing a proprietary board that has many embedded components. Often such boards do not easily accept add-on devices from other manufacturers. For example, if you plan to add a more powerful video card, you might not want to choose a motherboard that contains an onboard video port. Even though you can likely disable the video port in UEFI/BIOS setup, there is little advantage to paying the extra money for it.

Notes If you have an embedded component, make sure you can disable it so you can use another external component if needed. Components are disabled in UEFI/BIOS setup.

Table 3-5 shown earlier in the chapter lists some manufacturers of motherboards and their web addresses. For motherboard reviews, check out *www.motherboards.org* and *www.pcmag.com*, or do a general search of the web.

HOW TO INSTALL OR REPLACE A MOTHERBOARD

A+
220-901
4.1

When you purchase a motherboard, the package comes with the board, I/O shield, documentation, drivers, and various screws, cables, and connectors. When you replace a motherboard, you pretty much have to disassemble an entire computer, install the new motherboard, and reassemble the system, which you learned to do earlier. The following list is meant to be a general overview of the process and is not meant to include the details of all possible installation scenarios, which can vary according to the components and case you are using. The best place to go for detailed instructions on installing a motherboard is the motherboard user guide.

Caution As with any installation, remember the importance of using an ESD strap to ground yourself when working inside a computer case to protect components against ESD.

The general process for replacing a motherboard is as follows:

1. ***Verify that you have selected the right motherboard to install in the system.*** The new motherboard should have the same form factor as the case, support the RAM modules and processor you want to install on it, and have other internal and external connectors you need for your system.
2. ***Get familiar with the motherboard documentation, features, and settings.*** Especially important are any connectors and jumpers on the motherboard. It's a great idea to read the motherboard user guide from cover to cover. At the least, get familiar with what it has to offer and study the diagrams in it that label all the components on the board. Learn how each connector and jumper is used. You can also check the manufacturer's website for answers to any questions you might have.
3. ***Remove components so you can reach the old motherboard.*** Use an ESD strap. Turn off the system and disconnect all cables and cords. Press the power button to dissipate the power. Open the case cover and remove all expansion cards. Disconnect all internal cables and cords connected to the old motherboard. To safely remove the old motherboard, you might have to remove drives. If the processor cooler is heavy and bulky, you might remove it from the old motherboard before you remove the motherboard from the case.
4. ***Install the I/O shield.*** The I/O shield is a metal plate that comes with the motherboard and fits over the ports to create a well-fitting enclosure for them. A case might come with a standard I/O shield already in place. Hold the motherboard up to the shield and make sure the ports on the board will fit the holes in the shield (see Figure 3-50). If the holes in the shield don't match up with the ports on the board, punch out the shield and replace it with the one that came bundled with the motherboard.

Figure 3-50 Make sure the holes in the I/O shield match up with the ports on the motherboard

5. ***Install the motherboard.*** Place the motherboard into the case and, using spacers or screws, securely fasten the board to the case. Because coolers are heavy, most processor instructions say to install the motherboard before installing the processor and cooler to better protect the board or processor from being damaged. On the other hand, some motherboard manufacturers say to install the processor and cooler and then install the motherboard. Follow the order given in the motherboard user guide. The easiest approach is to install the processor, cooler, and memory modules on the board and then place the board in the case (see Figure 3-51).

Figure 3-51 Motherboard with processor, cooler, and memory modules installed is ready to go in the case

6. *Install the processor and processor cooler.* The processor comes already installed on some motherboards, in which case you just need to install the cooler. How to install a processor and cooler is covered in the chapter, "Supporting Processors and Upgrading Memory."
7. *Install RAM into the appropriate slots on the motherboard.* How to install RAM is covered in the chapter, "Supporting Processors and Upgrading Memory."
8. *Attach cabling that goes from the case switches to the motherboard, and from the power supply and drives to the motherboard.* Pay attention to how cables are labeled and to any information in the documentation about where to attach them. The chapter, "First Look at Computer Parts and Tools," can help you identify the types of power connectors. You'll need to connect the P1 connector, the fan connectors, and the processor auxiliary power connector. Position and tie cables neatly together to make sure they don't obstruct the fans and the airflow.
9. *Install the video card on the motherboard.* This card should go into the primary PCI Express ×16 slot. If you plan to install multiple video cards, install only one now and check out how the system functions before installing the second one.
10. *Plug the computer into a power source, and attach the monitor, keyboard, and mouse.* Initially install only the devices you absolutely need.
11. *Boot the system and enter UEFI/BIOS setup.* Make sure settings are set to the default. If the motherboard comes new from the manufacturer, it will already be at default settings. If you are salvaging a motherboard from another system, you might need to reset settings to the default. You will need to do the following while you are in UEFI/BIOS setup:
    - Check the time and date.
    - Make sure fast boot (also called abbreviated POST) is disabled. While you're installing a motherboard, you generally want it to do as many diagnostic tests as possible. After you know the system is working, you can choose fast boot.
    - Set the boot order to the hard drive, and then the optical drive, if you will be booting the OS from the hard drive.
    - Leave everything else at their defaults unless you know that particular settings should be otherwise.
    - Save and exit.
12. *Observe POST and verify that no errors occur.*
13. *Verify Windows starts with no errors.* If Windows is already installed on the hard drive, boot to the Windows desktop. Use Device Manager to verify that the OS recognizes all devices and that no conflicts are reported.
14. *Install the motherboard drivers.* If your motherboard comes with a CD that contains some motherboard drivers, install them now. You will probably need Internet access so that the setup process can download the latest drivers from the motherboard manufacturer's website. Reboot the system one more time, checking for errors.
15. *Install any other expansion cards and drivers.* Install each device and its drivers, one device at a time, rebooting and checking for conflicts after each installation.
16. *Verify that everything is operating properly, and make any final OS and UEFI/BIOS adjustments, such as setting power-on passwords.*

Notes Whenever you install or uninstall software or hardware, keep a notebook with details about the components you are working on, configuration settings, manufacturer specifications, and other relevant information. This helps if you need to backtrack later and can also help you document and troubleshoot your computer system. Keep all hardware documentation for this system together with the notebook in an envelope in a safe place.

3

Hands-On | Project 3-7 Insert and Remove Motherboards

A+
220-901
4.1

Using old or defective expansion cards and motherboards, practice inserting and removing expansion cards and motherboards. In a lab or classroom setting, the instructor can provide extra cards and motherboards for exchange.

REPLACING A LAPTOP SYSTEM BOARD

A+
220-901
3.1

Replacing the system board (motherboard) on a laptop probably means you'll need to fully disassemble the entire laptop except the LCD assembly in the lid. Therefore, before you tackle the job, consider alternatives. If available, use diagnostic software from the laptop manufacturer to verify that the problem is a failed system board. If a port or component on the system board has failed, consider installing an external device rather than replacing the entire board. Replacing the system board is a big deal, so consider that the cost of repair, including parts and labor, might be more than the laptop is worth. A new laptop might be your best solution.

If you do decide to replace a system board, use a replacement purchased from the laptop manufacturer. Here is the general procedure for replacing the system board in one laptop:

1. Remove the keyboard, optical drive, and mini PCIe card.
2. The next step is to remove the laptop lid and keyboard bezel assembly. To do this, first remove two screws on the back of the laptop (see Figure 3-52) and the screws on the bottom of the laptop. You can then crack the case by lifting the laptop lid and keyboard bezel from the case (see Figure 3-53).

Figure 3-52 Remove two screws on the back of the notebook

Figure 3-53 Cracking the notebook case

3. Lift up the assembly and look underneath to see two cables connecting the assembly to the motherboard (see Figure 3-54). Disconnect these two cables and set the assembly aside.

Figure 3-54 Lift the assembly to locate the two cable connections

4. To remove the CPU fan assembly, remove screws (see Figure 3-55) and then lift the fan assembly up. Then open the CPU socket and remove the CPU.

Figure 3-55 Remove the screws holding the CPU fan assembly in place

5. The DVD drive can now be removed, and the motherboard is fully exposed.
6. Remove a single screw that holds the motherboard in place (see Figure 3-56) and lift the board out of the case. Figure 3-57 shows the bottom of the board. Both top and bottom are packed with components. When reassembling the system, all steps are done in reverse.

Figure 3-56 Remove the single screw attaching the system board to the case

Figure 3-57 Bottom of the system board

>> CHAPTER SUMMARY

Motherboard Types and Features

- The motherboard is the most complicated of all components inside the computer. It contains the processor socket and accompanying chipset, firmware holding the UEFI/BIOS, memory slots, expansion slots, jumpers, ports, and power supply connections. The motherboard you select determines both the capabilities and limitations of your system.
- The most popular motherboard form factors are ATX, microATX, and Mini-ITX.

- A motherboard will have one or more Intel sockets for an Intel processor or one or more AMD sockets for an AMD processor.
- The chipset embedded on the motherboard determines what kind of processor and memory the board can support.
- Major advancements in past Intel chipsets included the Accelerated Hub Architecture (using the North Bridge and South Bridge), Nehalem chipsets (using the memory controller on the processor), and Sandy Bridge chipsets (using the memory and graphics controller on the processor). All later chipsets use the memory and graphics controller in the processor package.
- Buses used on motherboards include conventional PCI, PCI-X, and PCI Express. PCI Express is replacing all the other bus types.
- Some components can be built into the motherboard, in which case they are called onboard components. Other components can be attached to the system in some other way, such as on an expansion card.

Configuring a Motherboard

- The firmware that controls a motherboard and the boot is the older BIOS or the newer UEFI. Most UEFI firmware provides for backward compatibility with BIOS devices.
- Motherboard settings that can be configured using UEFI/BIOS setup include changing the boot priority order, enabling or disabling onboard devices, support for virtualization, and security settings (for example, power-on passwords and intrusion detection). You can also view information about the installed processor, memory, and storage devices and temperatures, fan speeds, and voltages.

Maintaining a Motherboard

- Motherboard drivers might need updating to fix a problem with a board component or to use a new feature provided by the motherboard manufacturer.
- To flash BIOS, use a utility program in Windows, a USB flash drive, or a bootable CD.
- To update UEFI, you can boot from a USB flash drive that holds the updates, or Windows can receive an update during the normal Windows update process and then pass it on to the UEFI firmware, which applies the update.
- Jumpers on the motherboard may be used to clear UEFI/BIOS settings, restoring them to factory default. The CMOS battery that powers CMOS RAM might need replacing.

Installing or Replacing a Motherboard

- When selecting a motherboard, pay attention to the form factor, chipset, expansion slots, and memory slots used and the processors supported. Also notice the internal and external connectors and ports the board provides.
- When installing a motherboard, first study the motherboard and its manual, and set jumpers on the board. Sometimes the processor and cooler are best installed before installing the motherboard in the case. When the cooling assembly is heavy and bulky, it is best to install it after the motherboard is securely seated in the case.

Replacing a Laptop System Board

- For laptops, it's usually more cost effective to replace the laptop than to replace a failed system board.

>> KEY TERMS

For explanations of key terms, see the Glossary for this text.

Accelerated Processing Unit (APU)
ball grid array (BGA)
BitLocker Encryption
bus
chipset
CMOS (complementary metal-oxide semiconductor)
CMOS battery
CMOS RAM
Compatibility Support Module (CSM)
data bus
data path size
device driver
EFI (Extensible Firmware Interface)
flashing BIOS
flip-chip land grid array (FCLGA)
flip-chip pin grid array (FCPGA)
Front Side Bus (FSB)
gigahertz (GHz)
GUID Partition Table (GPT)
hertz (Hz)
I/O shield
ISO image
ITX
jumper
Key-enrollment Key (KEK)
Key-exchange Key (KEK)
land grid array (LGA)
LoJack
Master Boot Record (MBR)
megahertz (MHz)
Mini-ITX
PCI
PCI Express
North Bridge
onboard port
option ROM
overclocking
PCI Express (PCIe)
PCI-X
pin grid array (PGA)
Platform Key (PK)
protocol
QuickPath Interconnect (QPI)
revoked signature database (dbx)
riser card
secure boot
signature database (db)
small form factor (SFF)
South Bridge
staggered pin grid array (SPGA)
system bus
system clock
TPM (Trusted Platform Module) chip
trace
Unified Extensible Firmware Interface (UEFI)
virtual machine (VM)
virtualization
wait state
zero insertion force (ZIF) socket

>> REVIEWING THE BASICS

1. What are the three most popular form factors used for motherboards?
2. Which type of Intel chipsets was the first to support the graphics controller to be part of the processor?
3. How many pins does the Intel Socket B have? What is another name for this socket?
4. What type of memory does the LGA1155 socket work with? Which socket was it designed to replace?
5. Does the Sandy Bridge chipset family use two chipset housings on the motherboard or a single chipset housing? The Nehalem chipset?
6. How many pins does the AMD socket AM3 have?
7. Which part of a Nehalem chipset connects directly to the processor, the North Bridge or the South Bridge?
8. How does the throughput of PCI Express Version 3.0 compare to PCIe Version 2.0?
9. What is the maximum wattage that a PCIe Version 2.0 expansion card can draw?
10. What type of power connector on the motherboard was introduced with PCIe Version 1.0? How much power does this connector provide?
11. What type of power connector was introduced with PCIe Version 2.0? How much power does this connector provide?
12. If you are installing an expansion card into a case that does not have enough clearance above the motherboard for the card, what device can you use to solve the problem?
13. Which chip on the motherboard does Windows BitLocker Encryption use to secure the hard drive?
14. How can you find out how many memory slots are populated on a motherboard without opening the computer case?

15. What are two reasons you might decide to flash BIOS?
16. What is the easiest way to obtain the latest software to upgrade BIOS?
17. What can you do if the power-on password and the supervisor password to a system have been forgotten?
18. How is CMOS RAM powered when the system is unplugged?
19. Describe how you can access the BIOS setup program.
20. Does Windows 7 support a secure boot in UEFI? Windows 8? Linux Ubuntu version 14?
21. Which partitioning method must be used for partitioning a 4-TB hard drive?
22. If a USB port on the motherboard is failing, what is one task you can do that might fix the problem?
23. What might the purpose be for a SATA-style power connector on a motherboard?
24. What is the purpose of installing standoffs or spacers between the motherboard and the case?
25. When installing a motherboard, suppose you forget to connect the wires from the case to the front panel header. Will you be able to power up the system? Why or why not?

>> THINKING CRITICALLY

1. Why don't all buses on a motherboard operate at the same speed?
2. When you turn off the power to a computer and unplug it at night, it loses the date, and you must reenter it each morning. What is the problem and how do you solve it?
3. Why do you think the trend is to put more control such as the graphics controller and the memory controller in the processor rather than in the chipset?
4. When troubleshooting a desktop motherboard, you discover the network port no longer works. What is the best and least expensive solution to this problem? If this solution does not work, which solution should you try next?
   a. Replace the motherboard.
   b. Disable the network port and install a network card in an expansion slot.
   c. Use a wireless network device in a USB port to connect to a wireless network.
   d. Return the motherboard to the factory for repair.
   e. Update the motherboard drivers.
5. A computer freezes at odd times. At first you suspect the power supply or overheating, but you have eliminated overheating and replaced the power supply without solving the problem. What do you do next?
   a. Replace the processor.
   b. Replace the motherboard.
   c. Reinstall Windows.
   d. Replace the memory modules.
   e. Flash BIOS.

3

>> REAL PROBLEMS, REAL SOLUTIONS

REAL PROBLEM 3-1 Labeling the Motherboard

Figure 3-58 shows a blank diagram of an ATX motherboard. Using what you learned in this chapter and in the chapter, "First Look at Computer Parts and Tools," label as many components as you can. If you would like to print the diagram, look for "Figure 3-58" in the online content that accompanies this text at *www.cengagebrain.com*. For more information on accessing this content, see the Preface.

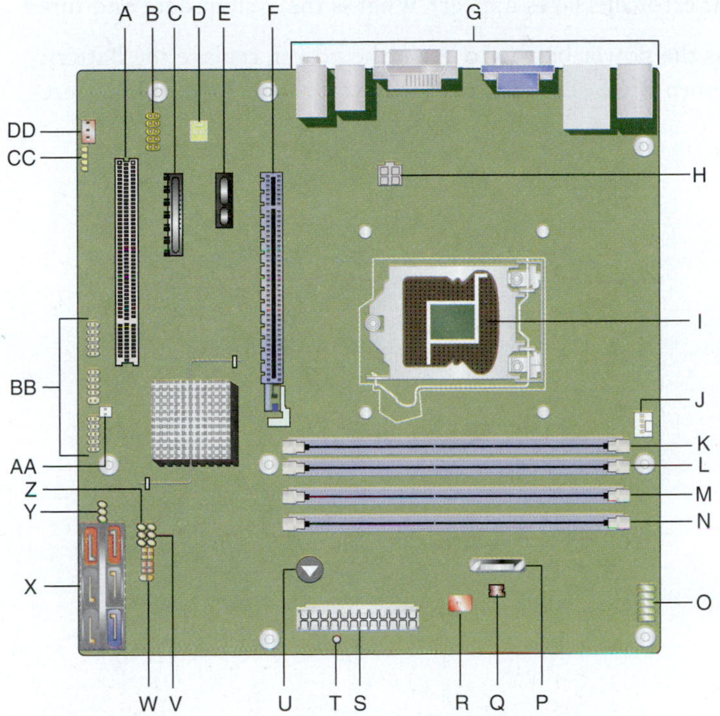

Figure 3-58 Label the motherboard

REAL PROBLEM 3-2 Selecting a Replacement Motherboard

When a motherboard fails, you can select and buy a new board to replace it. Suppose the motherboard in your computer has failed and you want to buy a replacement and keep your repair costs to a mum. Try to find a replacement motherboard on the web that can use the same case, power supply, processor, memory, and expansion cards as your current system. If you cannot find a good match, what other components might have to be replaced (for example, the processor or memory)? What is the total cost of the replacement parts? Save or print webpages showing what you need to purchase.

REAL PROBLEM 3-3 Researching Maintaining a Motherboard

Using the motherboard user guide that you downloaded in Hands-On Project 3-4, answer the following questions:

1. How many methods can be used to flash UEFI/BIOS on the motherboard? Describe each method. If your system uses BIOS rather than UEFI, what can you do to recover the system if flashing BIOS fails?
2. Locate the CMOS battery on the diagram of the motherboard. What are the steps to replace this battery?

Using a computer in your school lab, do the following to practice replacing the CMOS battery:

1. Locate the CMOS battery on your motherboard. What is written on top of the battery? Using the web, find a replacement for this battery. Print the webpage showing the battery. How much does the new battery cost?
2. Enter BIOS setup on your computer. Write down any BIOS settings that are not default settings. You'll need these settings later when you reinstall the battery.
3. Turn off and unplug the computer, press the power button to drain the system of power, open the case, remove the battery, and boot the PC. What error messages appear? What is the system date and time?
4. Power down the computer, unplug it, press the power button to drain the power, replace the battery, and boot the PC. Close up the case and return BIOS settings to the way you found them. Make sure the system is working normally.

CHAPTER 4

Supporting Processors and Upgrading Memory

After completing this chapter, you will be able to:

- Compare characteristics and purposes of Intel and AMD processors used for personal computers
- Install and upgrade a processor
- Compare the different kinds of physical memory and how they work
- Upgrade memory

Previously, you learned about motherboards. In this chapter, you learn about the two most important components on the motherboard, which are the processor and memory. You learn how a processor works, about the many different types and brands of processors, and how to match a processor to the motherboard.

Memory technologies have evolved over the years. When you support an assortment of desktop and laptop computers, you'll be amazed at all the different variations of memory modules used not only in newer computers, but also in older computers still in use. A simple problem of replacing a bad memory module can become a complex research project if you don't have a good grasp of current and past memory technologies.

The processor and memory modules are considered field replaceable units (FRUs), so you'll learn how to install and upgrade a processor and memory modules. Upgrading the processor or adding more memory to a system can sometimes greatly improve performance. How to troubleshoot problems with the processor or memory is covered in the chapter, "Supporting the Power System and Troubleshooting Computers."

TYPES AND CHARACTERISTICS OF PROCESSORS

A+ 220-901 1.1, 1.6

The processor installed on a motherboard is the primary component that determines the computing power of the system (see Figure 4-1). Recall that the two major manufacturers of processors are Intel (*www.intel.com*) and AMD (*www.amd.com*).

Figure 4-1 An AMD Athlon 64 X2 installed in socket AM2+ with cooler not yet installed

In this chapter, you learn a lot of details about processors. As you do, try to keep these nine features of processors at the forefront. These features affect performance and compatibility with motherboards:

- ***Feature 1: Processor speed.*** The processor frequency is the speed at which the processor operates internally and is measured in gigahertz, such as 3.3 GHz. Current Intel and AMD processors run at 1.8 GHz up to more than 4.4 GHz.
- ***Feature 2: Socket and chipset the processor can use.*** Recall that important Intel sockets for desktop systems are the LGA1150, LGA1155, LGA1156, LGA2011, LGA1366, and LGA775. AMD's important desktop sockets are AM3+, AM3, AM2+, AM2, FM1, FM2+, and FM2 sockets.
- ***Feature 3: Processor architecture (32 bits or 64 bits).*** All desktop and laptop processors sold today from either Intel or AMD are hybrid processors, which can process 64 bits or 32 bits at a time. A hybrid processor can use a 32-bit operating system (OS) or a 64-bit OS. Windows 8 and most editions of Windows 7 come in either type.
- ***Feature 4: Multiprocessing abilities.*** The ability of a system to do more than one thing at a time is accomplished by several means:
  - ***Multiprocessing.*** Two processing units (called arithmetic logic units or ALUs) installed within a single processor is called multiprocessing. The Pentium was the first processor that contained two ALUs, which means the processor can execute two instructions at the same time.
  - ***Multithreading.*** Each processor or core processes two threads at the same time. When Windows hands off a task to the CPU, it is called a thread and might involve several instructions. To handle two threads, the processor requires extra registers, or holding areas, within the processor

housing that it uses to switch between threads. In effect, you have two logical processors for each physical processor or core. Intel calls this technology Hyper-Threading and AMD calls it HyperTransport. The feature must be enabled in UEFI/BIOS setup and the operating system must support the technology.

- *Multicore processing*. Multiple processors can be installed in the same processor housing (called multicore processing). A processor package might contain up to eight cores (dual-core, triple-core, quad-core, and so forth). In Figure 4-2, this quad-core processor contains four cores or CPUs. Using multithreading, each core can handle two threads. Therefore, the processor appears to have up to eight logical processors as it can handle eight threads from the operating system.

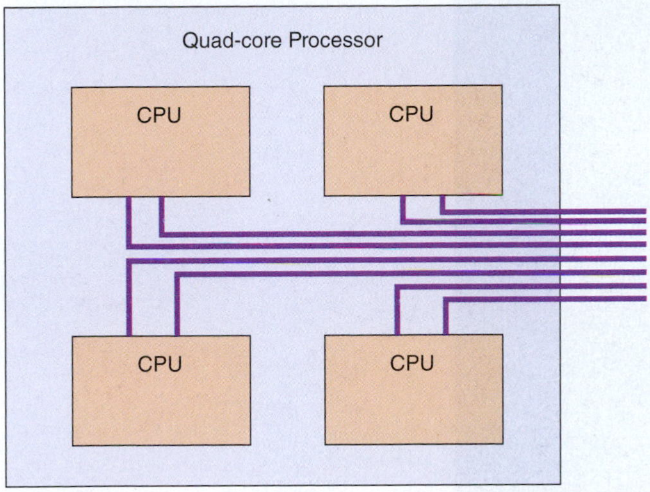

Figure 4-2 This quad-core processor has four cores and each core can handle two threads

- *Dual processors*. A server motherboard might have two processor sockets, called dual processors or a multiprocessor platform (see Figure 4-3). A processor (for example, the Xeon processor for servers) must support this feature.
- ***Feature 5: Memory cache, which is the amount of memory included within the processor package***. Today's processors all have some memory on the processor chip (called a die). Memory on the processor die is called Level 1 cache (L1 cache). Memory in the processor package, but not on the processor die, is called Level 2 cache (L2 cache). Some processors use a third cache farther from the processor core, but still in the processor package, which is called Level 3 cache (L3 cache). Memory used in a memory cache is static RAM (SRAM; pronounced "S-Ram"). Memory used on the motherboard loses data rapidly and must be refreshed often. It is, therefore, called volatile memory or dynamic RAM (DRAM; pronounced "D-Ram"). SRAM is faster than DRAM because it doesn't need refreshing; it can hold its data as long as power is available.

Courtesy of Intel Corporation

Figure 4-3 This motherboard for a server has two processor sockets, which allow for a multiprocessor platform

- *Feature 6: Security.* Execute Disable Bit (EDB) (also called eXecute Disable [XD] by Intel, Enhanced Virus Protection by AMD, and disable execute bit by CompTIA) is security built into a processor so that it can work with the operating system to designate an area of memory for holding data or instructions. When an area is designated for data, instructions stored in this area are not executed, thus preventing a buffer overflow attack by malicious software, which attempts to run its code from an area of memory assigned to another program for its data. EDB requires a compatible OS. You can enable EDB using the BIOS or UEFI setup screen (see Figure 4-4). It is important to remember that even though EDB can stop malware from executing, it cannot remove it. You still need to use anti-malware software to remove the malware.

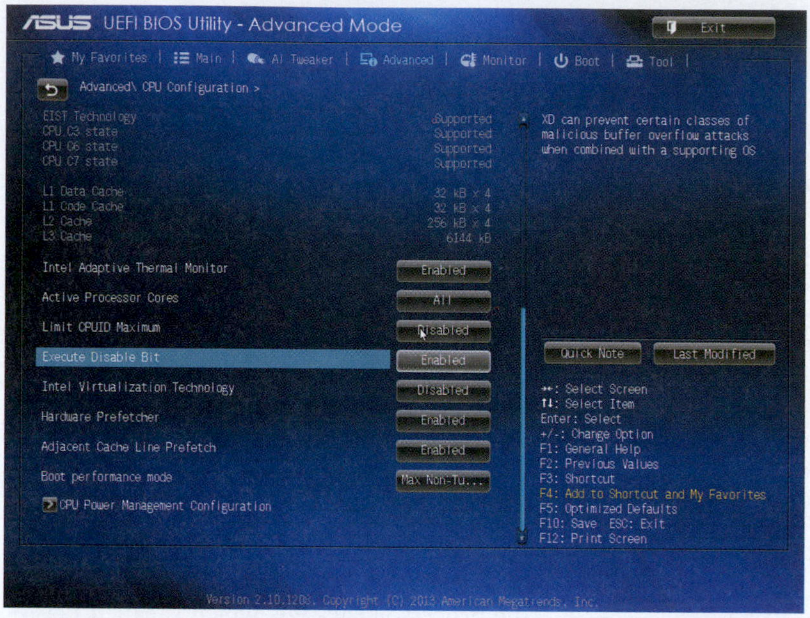

Source: American Megatrends, Inc.

Figure 4-4 The Execute Disable Bit is enabled using the UEFI setup screen

- ***Feature 7: The memory features on the motherboard that the processor can support.*** DRAM memory modules that might be used on a motherboard include DDR, DDR2, DDR3, or DDR4. Besides the type of memory, a processor can support certain amounts of memory, memory speeds, and number of memory channels (single, dual, triple, or quad channels). All these characteristics of memory are discussed later in the chapter.
- ***Feature 8: Support for virtualization.*** A computer can use software to create and manage multiple virtual machines and their virtual devices. Most processors sold today support virtualization, and the feature must be enabled in UEFI/BIOS setup.
- ***Feature 9: Integrated graphics.*** A processor might include an integrated GPU. A graphics processing unit (GPU) is a processor that manipulates graphic data to form the images on a monitor screen. The GPU might be on a video card, on the motherboard, or embedded in the CPU package. When inside the CPU package, it is called integrated graphics. Many AMD processors and all the Intel second generation and higher processors have integrated graphics.

> **★ A+ Exam Tip** The A+ 220-901 exam expects you to be familiar with the characteristics of processors. Know the purposes and characteristics of Hyper-Threading, core processing, types of cache, virtualization, integrated GPU, disable execute bit (CompTIA's name for EDB), and 32-bit versus 64-bit processing.

Let's now turn our attention to a discussion of how a processor works, including several of the processor features just listed. Then you'll learn about the families of Intel and AMD processors.

HOW A PROCESSOR WORKS

A+
220-901
1.1, 1.6

Although processors continue to evolve, they all have some common elements. These elements are diagrammed in Figure 4-5 for the Pentium processor. The Pentium made several major advances in processor technologies when it was first introduced. Because of its historical significance and the foundation it created for today's processors, it's a great place to start when learning how a processor works.

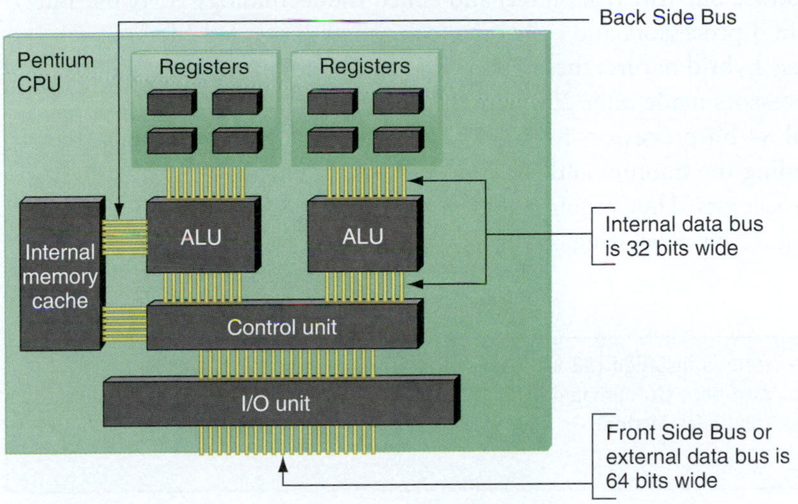

Figure 4-5 Since the Pentium processor was first released in 1993, the standard has been for a processor core to have two arithmetic logic units so that it can process two instructions at once

A processor contains these basic components diagrammed in Figure 4-5 for the Pentium processor:

- An input/output (I/O) unit manages data and instructions entering and leaving the processor.
- A control unit manages all activities inside the processor itself.
- One or more arithmetic logic units (ALUs) do all logical comparisons and calculations inside the processor. All desktop and laptop processors sold today contain two ALUs in each processor core within the processor package.
- Registers, which are small holding areas on the processor chip, work much like RAM does outside the processor to hold counters, data, instructions, and addresses that the ALU is currently processing.
- Internal memory caches (L1, L2, and possibly L3 or L4) hold data and instructions waiting to be processed by the ALU.
- Buses inside the processor connect components within the processor housing. These buses run at a much higher frequency than the motherboard buses that connect the processor to the chipset and memory on the motherboard.

If the processor operates at 3.2 GHz internally and the Front Side Bus is operating at 800 MHz, the processor operates at four times the FSB speed. This factor is called the **multiplier**. As you learned in the chapter, "All About Motherboards," you can view the actual processor frequency and the clock speed using the UEFI/BIOS setup screens. You can also change the multiplier or the clock speed in order to overclock or throttle the processor.

In Figure 4-5, you can see the internal data bus for the Pentium was only 32 bits wide. More important, however, than the width of the internal bus is the fact that each ALU and register in the early Pentiums could process only 32 bits at a time. All desktop and laptop processors sold today from either Intel or AMD contain ALUs and registers that can process 32 bits or 64 bits at a time. To know which type of operating system to install, you need to be aware of three categories of processors currently used on desktop and laptop computers:

- *32-bit processors.* These older processors are known as x86 processors because Intel used the number 86 in the model number of these processors. If you are ever called on to install Windows on one of these old Pentium computers, you must use a 32-bit version of Windows. These processors can handle only 32-bit instructions from the OS.
- *Processors that can process 32 bits or 64 bits.* These hybrid processors are known as x86-64 bit processors. AMD was the first to produce one (the Athlon 64) and called the technology AMD64. Intel followed with a version of its Pentium 4 processors and called the technology Extended Memory 64 Technology (EM64T). Because of their hybrid nature, these processors can handle a 32-bit OS or a 64-bit OS. All desktop or laptop processors made after 2007 are of this type.
- *64-bit processors.* Intel makes several 64-bit processors for workstations or servers that use fully implemented 64-bit processing, including the Itanium and Xeon processors. Intel calls the technology IA64, but they are also called x64 processors. They require a 64-bit operating system and can handle 32-bit applications only by simulating 32-bit processing.

Notes To know which type of operating system is installed (32-bit or 64-bit) and other information about the Windows installation, recall from the chapter, "All About Motherboards," that you can use the System window. To open the System window in Windows 8, press **Win+X** and click **System**. In Windows 7, click **Start**, right-click **Computer**, and select **Properties**.

Each core in a processor has its own cache and can also share a cache. Figure 4-6 shows how quad-core processing can work if the processor uses an L3 cache and an internal memory controller. Each core within a processor has its own independent internal L1 and L2 caches. The L1 cache is on the die and the L2 cache is off the die. In addition, all the cores might share an L3 cache within the processor package. Recall that prior to the memory controller being in the processor package, it was part of the North Bridge chipset. Putting the controller inside the processor package resulted in a significant increase in system performance.

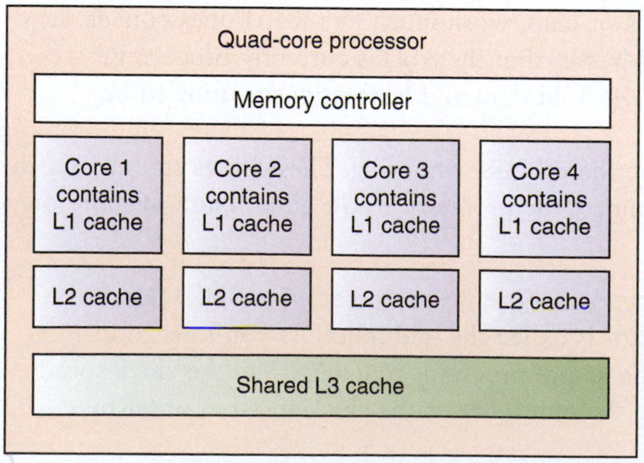

Figure 4-6 Quad-core processing with L1, L2, and L3 cache and the memory controller within the processor housing

INTEL PROCESSORS

A+ 220-901 1.1, 1.6

Intel's current families of processors for the desktop include the Core, Atom, Celeron, and Pentium families of processors. In addition, Intel groups its processors into Sixth Generation, Fifth Generation, Fourth Generation, Third Generation, Second Generation, and Previous Generation processors. Each generation improves on how the processor and chipset are integrated in the system. Processors in each family are listed in Table 4-1. Some significant retired processors are also listed. Later in the chapter, you'll learn about the memory technologies mentioned in the table.

Processor	Speed	Description
Fifth-Generation (Broadwell) Processors		
Core i7	Up to 3.8 GHz	6-MB cache, quad core 1333/1600/1866 MHz DDR3 memory Dual-channel memory
Core i5	Up to 3.6 GHz	4-MB cache, quad core 1333/1600/1866 MHz DDR3 memory Dual-channel memory
Fourth-Generation (Haswell) Processors		
Core i7	Up to 4.4 GHz	8-MB cache, quad core 1333/1600 MHz DDR3 memory Dual-channel memory
Core i5	Up to 3.6 GHz	4- to 6-MB cache, quad or dual core 1333/1600 MHz DDR3 memory Dual-channel memory
Core i3	Up to 3.8 GHz	3- to 4-MB cache, dual core 1333/1600 MHz DDR3 memory Dual-channel memory
Third-Generation (Ivy Bridge) Processors		
Core i7	Up to 3.9 GHz	8-MB cache, quad core 1333/1600 MHz DDR3 memory Dual-channel memory
Core i5	Up to 3.8 GHz	6-MB cache, quad core 1333/1600 MHz DDR3 memory Dual-channel memory
Core i3	Up to 3.5 GHz	3-MB cache, dual core 1333/1600 MHz DDR3 memory Dual-channel memory
Second-Generation (Sandy Bridge) Processors		
Core i7 Extreme	Up to 3.9 GHz	15-MB cache, six cores 1066/1333/1600 MHz DDR3 memory Quad-channel memory
Core i7	Up to 3.9 GHz	8- to 12-MB cache, four or six cores 1066/1333/1600 MHz DDR3 memory Dual- or quad-channel memory
Core i5	Up to 3.8 GHz	3- to 6-MB cache, dual or quad core 1066/1333 MHz DDR3 memory Dual-channel memory
Core i3	Up to 3.4 GHz	3-MB cache, dual core 1066/1333 MHz DDR3 memory Dual-channel memory
Pentium	Up to 3.0 GHz	3-MB cache 1066/1333 MHz DDR3 memory Dual-channel memory
Previous-Generation Processors		
Core i7 Extreme	Up to 3.4 GHz	8- or 12-MB cache 1066 MHz DDR3 memory Triple-channel memory
Core i7	Up to 3.3 GHz	8- or 12-MB cache, four or six cores 800/1066/1333 MHz DDR3 memory Dual- or triple-channel memory

Table 4-1 Current Intel processors (continues)

Processor	Speed	Description
Core i5	Up to 3.3 GHz	4- or 8-MB cache, dual or quad core 1066/1333 MHz DDR3 memory Dual-channel memory
Core i3	Up to 3.3 GHz	Dual core, 4-MB cache 1066/1333 MHz DDR3 memory Dual-channel memory
Atom	Up to 2.1 GHz	Up to 1-MB cache, some dual core 800/1066 MHz DDR3 memory 667/800 MHz DDR2 memory Single-channel memory
Celeron, Celeron Desktop, Celeron D	1.6 to 3.6 GHz 533/667/800 MHzFSB	128-KB to 1-MB cache
Core 2 Extreme, Core 2 Quad, Core 2 Duo	Up to 3.2 GHz 533 to 1600 MHz FSB	2- to 12-MB cache Dual or quad core
Pentium Extreme, Pentium, Pentium 4, Pentium D	Up to 3.7 GHz	Up to 4-MB cache, some dual core

Table 4-1 Current Intel processors (continued)

An Intel Sandy Bridge Core i5 processor is shown in Figure 4-7. You can purchase a processor with or without the cooler. When it's purchased with a cooler, it's called a boxed processor. The cooler is also shown in the photo. If you purchase the cooler separately, make sure it fits the socket you are using.

Figure 4-7 The Intel Core i5 processor (processor number i5-2320) with boxed cooler

Each processor listed in Table 4-1 represents several processors that vary in performance and functionality. To help identify a processor, Intel uses a processor number. For example, two Core i7 processors are identified as i7-940 and i7-920. To find details about an Intel processor, search the Intel ARK database at *ark.intel.com* (see Figure 4-8).

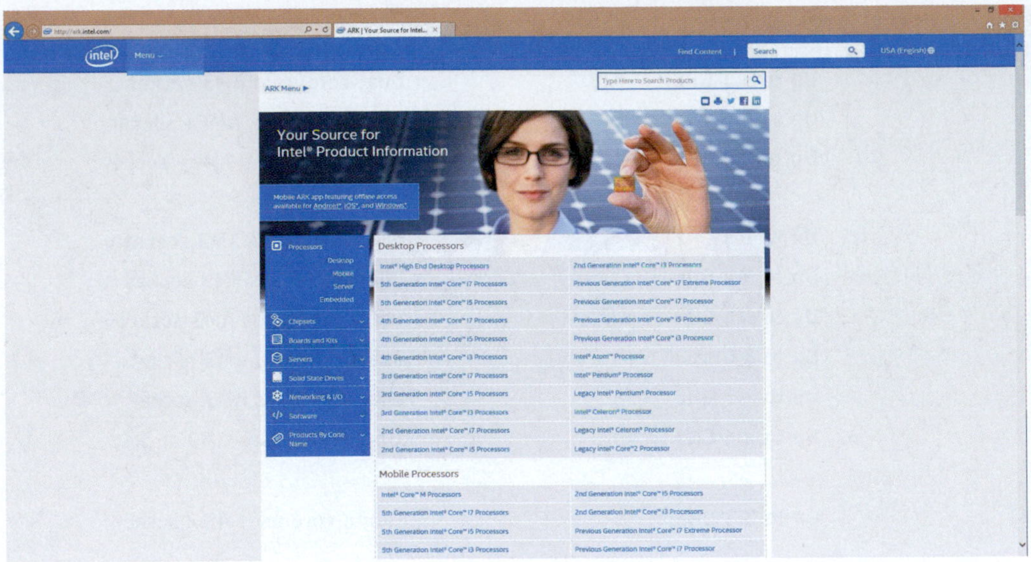

Source: Intel

Figure 4-8 The Intel ARK database at *ark.intel.com* lists details about all Intel products

Some of the Intel mobile processors are packaged in the Centrino processor technology. Using the Centrino technology, the Intel processor, chipset, and wireless network adapter are all interconnected as a unit, which improves laptop performance. Several Intel mobile processors have been packaged as a Centrino processor. You also need to be aware of the Intel Atom processor, which is Intel's low-powered processor and is used in low-cost desktops, laptops, and netbooks.

AMD PROCESSORS

A+
220-901
1.1, 1.6

Processors by Advanced Micro Devices, Inc., or AMD (*www.amd.com*) are popular in the game and hobbyist markets, and are generally less expensive than comparable Intel processors. Recall that AMD processors use different sockets than do Intel processors, so the motherboard must be designed for one manufacturer's processor or the other, but not both. Many motherboard manufacturers offer two comparable motherboards—one for an Intel processor and one for an AMD processor.

The current AMD processor families are the FX, Phenom, Athlon, Sempron, A Series, and E Series for desktops and the Athlon, Turion, V Series, Phenom, and Sempron for laptops. Table 4-2 lists the current AMD processors for desktops. Figure 4-9 shows an FX processor by AMD.

Processor	Core Speed	Description
FX Black Edition Family		
FX 4-Core Black Edition	Up to 3.6 GHz	Quad-core uses AM3+ socket
FX 6-Core Black Edition	Up to 3.3 GHz	Six-core uses AM3+ socket
FX 8-Core Black Edition	Up to 3.6 GHz	Eight-core uses AM3+ socket
Phenom Family		
Phenom II X6	Up to 3 GHz	Six-core uses AM3 socket
Phenom II X6 Black	Up to 3.2 GHz	Six-core uses AM3 socket
Phenom II X4	Up to 3.2 GHz	Quad-core uses AM3 socket
Phenom II X3	Up to 2.5 GHz	Triple-core uses AM3 socket

Table 4-2 Current AMD processors (continues)

Processor	Core Speed	Description
Phenom II X2	Up to 3.1 GHz	Dual-core uses AM3 socket
Phenom X4	Up to 2.6 GHz	Quad-core uses AM2+ socket
Phenom X3	Up to 2.4 GHz	Triple-core uses AM2+ socket
Athlon Family		
Athlon II X4	Up to 2.3 GHz	Quad-core uses AM3 socket
Athlon X4	Up to 3.2 GHz	Quad-core uses FM2 socket
Athlon II X3	Up to 3.4 GHz	Triple-core uses AM3 socket
Athlon II X2	Up to 3 GHz	Dual-core uses AM3 socket
Athlon X2	Up to 2.3 GHz	Dual-core uses AM3 socket
Athlon	Up to 2.4 GHz	Single-core uses AM2 socket
Sempron Family		
Sempron	Up to 2.3 GHz	Single-core uses AM2 socket

Table 4-2 Current AMD processors (continued)

Courtesy of Advanced Micro Devices, Inc.

Figure 4-9 The AMD FX processor can have up to eight cores

In the next part of the chapter, you learn the detailed steps to select and install a processor in several of the popular Intel and AMD sockets used by desktop computers.

SELECTING AND INSTALLING A PROCESSOR

A+ 220-901 1.6

A hardware technician is sometimes called on to assemble a desktop computer from parts, exchange a processor that is faulty, add a second processor to a dual-processor system, or upgrade an existing processor to improve performance. In each situation, it is necessary to know how to match a processor for the system in which it is installed. And then you need to know how to install the processor on the motherboard for each of the current Intel and AMD sockets used for desktop and laptop systems. In this part of the chapter, you learn about selecting and installing processors in desktops. Later in the chapter, you learn about selecting and installing processors in laptops.

SELECT A PROCESSOR TO MATCH SYSTEM NEEDS

A+ 220-901 1.6

When selecting a processor, the first requirement is to select one that the motherboard is designed to support. Among the processors the board supports, you need to select the best one that meets the general requirements of the system and the user's needs. To get the best performance, use the highest-performing processor the board supports. However, sometimes you need to sacrifice performance for cost.

APPLYING | CONCEPTS SELECT A PROCESSOR

Your friend, Alice, is working toward her A+ certification. She has decided the best way to get the experience she needs before she sits for the exam is to build a system from scratch. She has purchased an Asus motherboard and asked you for some help selecting the right processor. She tells you that the system will later be used for light business needs and she wants to install a processor that is moderate in price to fit her budget. She says she doesn't want to install the most expensive processor the motherboard can support, but neither does she want to sacrifice too much performance or power.

The documentation on the Asus website (*support.asus.com*) for the ASUS H81M-C motherboard gives this information:

- The microATX board contains the H81 chipset and socket LGA1150 and uses DDR3 memory.
- CPUs supported include a long list of Fourth-Generation Core i3, Core i5, and Core i7 processors and Celeron and Pentium processors. Here are five processors found in this list:
  - Intel Core i7-4790, 3.6 GHz, 8-MB cache
  - Intel Core i5-4590, 3.3 GHz, 6-MB cache
  - Intel Core i3-4350, 3.6 GHz, 4-MB cache
  - Intel Celeron G1850, 2.9 GHz, 2-MB cache
  - Intel Pentium G3260, 3.3 GHz, 3-MB cache

Based on what Alice has told you, you decide to eliminate the most expensive processors (the Core i7) and the least-performing processors (the Celerons and Pentiums). That decision narrows your choices down to the Core i3 and Core i5. Before you select one of these processors, you need to check the list on the Asus site to make sure the specific Core i3 or Core i5 processor is in the list. Look for the exact processor number, for example, the Core i3-4350. Also double-check and make sure the processor uses the correct socket and is a Fourth-Generation processor.

You will also need a cooler assembly. If your processor doesn't come boxed with a cooler, select a cooler that fits the processor socket and gets good reviews. You'll also need some thermal compound if it is not included with the cooler.

The cooler is bracketed to the motherboard using a wire or plastic clip. A creamlike **thermal compound** is placed between the bottom of the cooler heat sink and the top of the processor. This compound eliminates air pockets, helping to draw heat off the processor. The thermal compound transmits heat better than air and makes an airtight connection between the fan and the processor. When processors and coolers are boxed together, the cooler heat sink might have thermal compound already stuck to the bottom (see Figure 4-10).

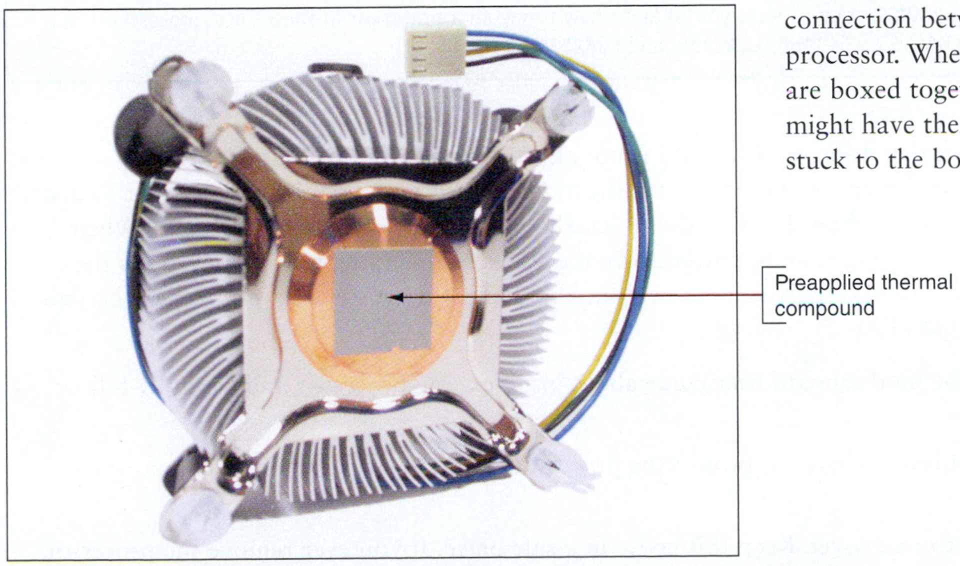

Figure 4-10 Thermal compound is already stuck to the bottom of this cooler that was purchased boxed with the processor

INSTALL A PROCESSOR

A+
220-901
1.6

Now let's look at the details of installing a processor in Intel LGA1150, LGA1155, LGA1366, LGA775, and AMD AM2+ sockets.

INSTALLING AN INTEL PROCESSOR IN SOCKET LGA1150

We're installing the Intel Core i5-4440 processor in Socket LGA1150 shown in Figure 4-11. In the photo, the socket has its protective cover in place.

Figure 4-11 Intel socket LGA1150 with protective cover in place

> **★ A+ Exam Tip** The A+ 220-901 exam expects you to know how to install a processor in these Intel processor sockets: LGA775, LGA1150, LGA1155, LGA1156, LGA1366, and LGA2011.

When building a new system, if the motherboard is not already installed in the case, follow the directions of the motherboard manufacturer to install the motherboard and then the processor or to install the processor and then the motherboard. The order of installation varies among manufacturers. When replacing a processor in an existing system, power down the system, unplug the power cord, press the power button to drain the system of power, and open the case. Follow these steps to install the processor and cooler using socket LGA1150:

1. Read all directions in the motherboard user guide about installing the processor and carefully follow them in order.
2. Use an ESD strap or antistatic gloves to protect the processor, motherboard, and other components against ESD.
3. Remove the socket protective cover. Keep this cover in a safe place. If you ever remove the processor, put the cover back on the socket to protect the socket. While the socket is exposed as in Figure 4-12, be *very careful* to not touch the pins in the socket.

Figure 4-12 The exposed socket is extremely delicate

4. Open the socket by pushing down on the socket lever and gently pushing it away from the socket to lift the lever. As you fully open the socket lever, the socket load plate opens, as shown in Figure 4-13.

Figure 4-13 The load plate is open, and ready for the processor

5. Remove the clear plastic protective cover from the processor. While the processor contacts are exposed, take extreme care to not touch the bottom of the processor. Hold it only at its edges. (It's best to use antistatic gloves as you work, but the gloves make it difficult to handle the processor.) Put the processor cover in a safe place and use it to protect the processor if you ever remove the processor from the socket.
6. Hold the processor with your index finger and thumb and orient the processor so that the two notches on the edge of the processor line up with the posts embedded on the socket. Gently lower the processor straight down into the socket. Don't allow the processor to tilt, slide, or shift as you put it in the socket. To protect the pads, it needs to go straight down into the socket.
7. Check carefully to make sure the processor is aligned correctly in the socket. Closing the socket without the processor fully seated can destroy the socket. Figure 4-14 shows the processor fully seated in the socket. Close the socket load plate so that it catches under the screw head at the front of the socket.

Figure 4-14 Orient the processor so the notches line up with the posts on the socket

8. Push down on the lever and gently return it to its locked position.

We are now ready to install the cooler. Before installing a cooler, read the directions carefully and make sure you understand them. Clips that hold the fan and heat sink to the processor frame or housing are sometimes difficult to install. The directions might give you important tips. Follow these general steps:

1. The motherboard has four holes to anchor the cooler. You can see them labeled in Figure 4-15. Examine the cooler posts that fit over these holes and the clips, screws, or wires that will hold the cooler firmly in place. Make sure you understand how this mechanism works.
2. If the cooler has thermal compound preapplied, remove the plastic from the compound. If the cooler does not have thermal compound applied, put a small dot of compound (about the size of a small pea) in the center of the processor (see Figure 4-15). When the cooler is attached and the processor

Figure 4-15 If the cooler does not have preapplied thermal compound, apply it on top of the processor

is running, the compound spreads over the surface. Don't use too much—just enough to later create a thin layer. If you use too much compound, it can slide off the housing and damage the processor or circuits on the motherboard. To get just the right amount, you can buy individual packets that each contain a single application of the thermal compound.

> **Notes** When removing and reinstalling a processor, use a soft dry cloth to carefully remove all the old thermal compound from both the processor and the cooler. Don't try to reuse the compound.

3. Verify the locking pins on the cooler are turned as far as they will go in a counterclockwise direction. (Make sure the pins don't protrude into the hollow plastic posts that go down into the motherboard holes.) Align the cooler over the processor so that all four posts fit into the four holes on the motherboard and the fan power cord can reach the fan header on the motherboard.
4. Push down on each locking pin until you hear it pop into the hole. To help keep the cooler balanced and in position, push down two opposite pins and then push the remaining two pins in place. Using a flathead screwdriver, turn the locking pin clockwise to secure it (see Figure 4-16). (Later, if you need to remove the cooler, turn each locking pin counterclockwise to release it from the hole.)

Figure 4-16 The pins are turned clockwise to secure the cooler to the motherboard

Notes If you later notice the CPU fan is running far too often, you might need to tighten the connection between the cooler and the processor.

5. Connect the power cord from the cooler fan to the 4-pin CPU fan header on the motherboard near the processor, as shown in Figure 4-17.

Figure 4-17 Connect the cooler fan power cord to the motherboard CPU fan header

After the processor and cooler are installed and the motherboard is installed in the case, make sure cables and cords don't obstruct fans or airflow, especially airflow around the processor and video card. Use cable ties to tie cords and cables up and out of the way.

Make one last check to verify that all power connectors are in place and other cords and cables connected to the motherboard are correctly done. You are now ready to plug back up the system, turn it on, and verify all is working. If the power comes on (you hear the fan spinning and see lights), but the system fails to work, most likely the processor is not seated solidly in the socket or some power cord has not yet been connected or is not solidly connected. Turn everything off, unplug the power cord, press the power button to drain power, open the case, and recheck your installation. If the system comes up and begins the boot process, but suddenly turns off before the boot is complete, most likely the processor is overheating because the cooler is not installed correctly. Turn everything off, unplug the power cord, press the power button to drain power, open the case, and verify that the cooler is securely seated and connected.

After the system is up and running, you can check UEFI/BIOS setup to verify that the system recognized the processor correctly. The setup screen for one processor is shown in Figure 4-18.

Also check in UEFI/BIOS setup the CPU and motherboard temperatures to verify the CPU is not overheating. For the UEFI setup in this system, this screen is under the Monitor menu, as shown in Figure 4-19.

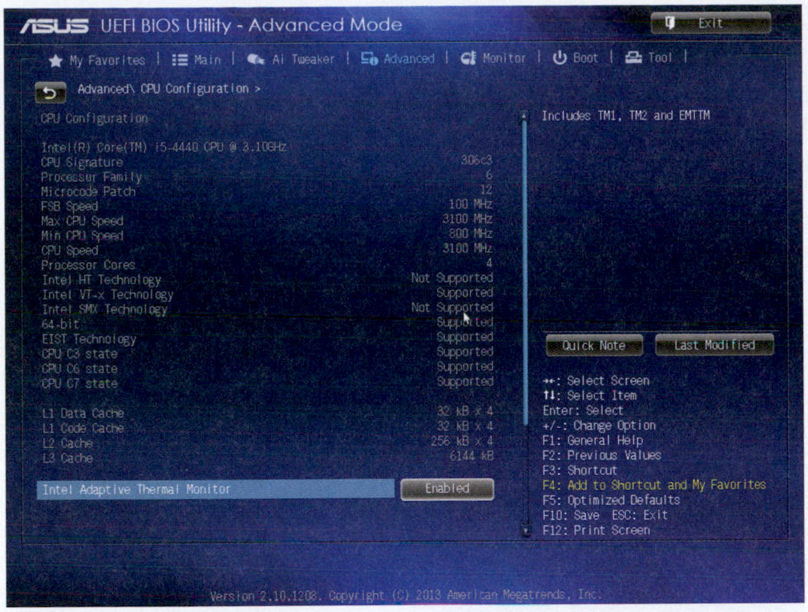

Source: American Megatrends, Inc.

Figure 4-18 Verify the CPU is recognized correctly by UEFI setup

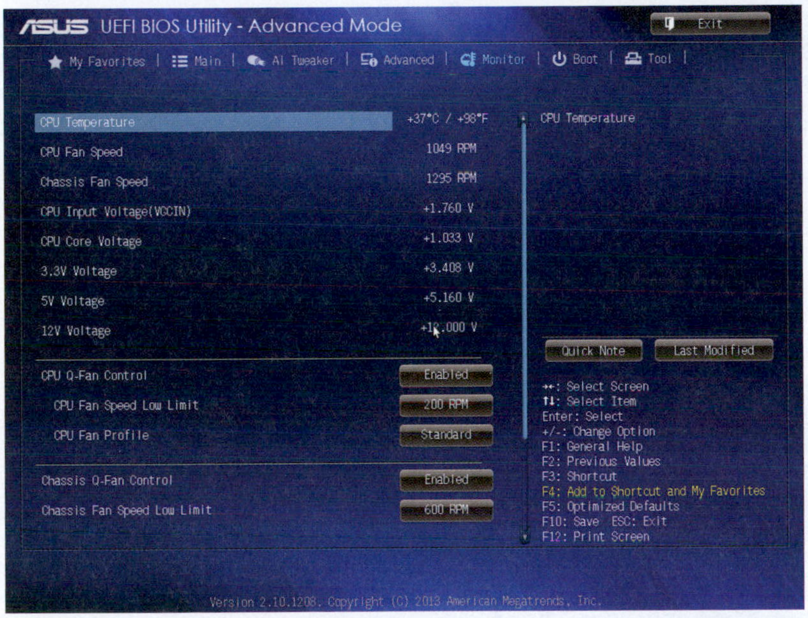

Source: American Megatrends, Inc.

Figure 4-19 Verify the processor temperature is within an acceptable range

The maximum processor temperature varies by processor; to know the maximum, download the datasheet specifications for the processor from the Intel website (*ark.intel.com*). For the Intel Core i5-4440, the processor will stop execution if the temperature rises above 130 degrees. If you see the temperature rising this high, open the case cover and verify that the processor fan is running. Perhaps a wire is in the way and preventing the fan from turning or the fan wire is not connected. Other troubleshooting tips for processors are covered in the chapter, "Supporting the Power System and Troubleshooting Computers."

INSTALLING AN INTEL PROCESSOR IN SOCKET LGA1155

The installations of all processors and sockets in this part of the chapter are similar to that of installing a processor in Socket LGA1150, so we will not repeat many of those steps. Listed next are the differences when installing a processor in the LGA1155 socket. These socket pins are delicate, so work slowly and take care. Here is how to work with this socket:

1. Open the socket by pushing down on the socket lever and gently pushing it away from the socket to lift the lever (see Figure 4-20). You can then lift the socket load plate, as shown in Figure 4-21. Next, remove the socket protective cover.

Figure 4-20 Release the lever from the socket

Figure 4-21 Lift the socket load plate to expose the processor socket

2. To install the processor, hold the processor with your index finger and thumb and orient the processor so that the gold triangle on the corner of the processor lines up with the right-angle mark embedded on the motherboard just outside a corner of the socket (see Figure 4-22). Gently lower the processor straight down into the socket. Don't allow the processor to tilt, slide, or shift as you put it in the socket. To protect the pads, it needs to go straight down into the socket.

Figure 4-22 Align the processor in the socket using the gold triangle and the right-angle mark

3. You can now lower the socket load plate and return the lever to its locked position (see Figure 4-23).

Figure 4-23 The socket screw head secures the socket load plate

Figure 4-24 Lift the socket load plate

INSTALLING AN INTEL PROCESSOR IN SOCKET LGA1366

Listed next are the differences when installing a processor in the LGA1366 socket:

1. To open the socket, press down on the socket lever and gently push it away from the socket to lift the lever. You can then lift the socket load plate, as shown in Figure 4-24. Next, remove the socket protective cover.

2. To install the processor, hold the processor with your index finger and thumb and orient the processor so that the notches on the two edges of the processor line up with the two posts on the socket. You can see the notch and post on the right side of the processor and socket in Figure 4-25. Gently lower the processor straight down into the socket. Don't allow the processor to tilt, slide, or shift as you put it in the socket. To protect the pins, it needs to go straight down into the socket.

Figure 4-25 Orient the processor over the socket so that the notches on each side of the processor match the posts on each side of the socket

3. You can now lower the socket load plate and return the lever to its locked position.

INSTALLING AN INTEL PROCESSOR IN SOCKET LGA775

Socket LGA775 is shown in Figure 4-26 along with a Pentium processor and cooler. In the photo, the socket is open and the protective cover removed. The processor is lying upside down in front of the cooler. When installing a processor in socket LGA775, do the following:

1. Push down on the lever and gently push it away from the socket to lift it. Lift the socket load plate. Remove the socket protective cover.

Figure 4-26 A Pentium, cooler, and open socket 775

2. Orient the processor so that the notches on the two edges of the processor line up with the two notches on the socket. Gently place the processor in the socket. Socket LGA775 doesn't have those delicate pins that Socket LGA1366 has, but you still need to be careful to not touch the top of the socket or the bottom of the processor as you work.
3. Close the socket cover. Push down on the lever and gently return it to its locked position.

INSTALLING AN AMD PROCESSOR IN SOCKET AM2+

When installing an AMD processor in AMD socket AM2, AM2+, or other AMD sockets, do the following:

1. Open the socket lever. If there's a protective cover over the socket, remove it.
2. Holding the processor very carefully so you don't touch the bottom, orient the four empty positions on the bottom with the four empty positions in the socket (see Figure 4-27). For some AMD sockets, a gold triangle on one corner of the processor matches up with a small triangle on a corner of the socket. Carefully lower the processor into the socket. Don't allow it to tilt or slide as it goes into the socket. The pins on the bottom of the processor are very delicate, so take care as you work.

Figure 4-27 Orient the four alignment positions on the bottom of the processor with those in the socket

3. Check carefully to make sure the pins in the processor are sitting slightly into the holes. Make sure the pins are not offset from the holes. If you try to use the lever to put pressure on these pins and they are not aligned correctly, you can destroy the processor. You can actually feel the pins settle into place when you're lowering the processor into the socket correctly.
4. Press the lever down and gently into position (see Figure 4-28).

Figure 4-28 Lower the lever into place, which puts pressure on the processor

5. You are now ready to apply the thermal compound and install the cooler assembly. For one system, the black retention mechanism for the cooler is already installed on the motherboard (see Figure 4-29). Set the cooler on top of the processor, aligning it inside the retention mechanism.

Figure 4-29 Align the cooler over the retention mechanism

6. Next, clip into place the clipping mechanism on one side of the cooler. Then push down firmly on the clip on the opposite side of the cooler assembly; the clip will snap into place. Figure 4-30 shows the clip on one side in place for a system that has a yellow retention mechanism and a black cooler clip. Later, if you need to remove the cooler, use a Phillips screwdriver to remove the screws holding the retention mechanism in place. Then remove the retention mechanism along with the entire cooler assembly.

Figure 4-30 The clips on the cooler attach the cooler to the retention mechanism on the motherboard

7. Connect the power cord from the fan to the 4-pin CPU fan header on the motherboard next to the processor.

Notes How to troubleshoot problems with the processor, motherboard, and RAM is covered in the chapter, "Supporting the Power System and Troubleshooting Computers."

Hands-On Project 4-1 Research a Processor Upgrade or Replacement

To identify your motherboard and find out the processor and processor socket a motherboard is currently using, you can use UEFI/BIOS setup, Windows utilities, or third-party software such as Speccy at *www.periform.com/speccy*. To research processors a board can support, you can use the motherboard user guide, the website of the motherboard manufacturer, and for Intel processors, the Intel site at *ark.intel.com*. Research the current processor and processor socket of your computer's motherboard and which processors your board can support, and answer the following questions:

1. What is the brand and model of your motherboard? What processor socket does it use? How did you find your information?
2. Identify the currently installed processor, including its brand, model, speed, and other important characteristics. How did you find your information?
3. List three or more processors the board supports according to the motherboard documentation or website.
4. Search the web for three or more processors that would match this board. Save or print three webpages showing the details and prices of a high-performing, moderately performing, and low-performing processor the board supports.
5. If your current processor fails, which processor would you recommend for this system? Explain your recommendation.

Now assume the Core i7 920 processor that you saw installed in Figure 4-25 has gone bad. The motherboard in which it is installed is the Intel DX58SO desktop board. The owner of the motherboard has requested that you keep the replacement cost as low as possible. What processor would you recommend for the replacement? Save or print a webpage showing the processor and its cost.

Hands-On Project 4-2 Insert and Remove a Processor

In this project, you remove and install a processor. As you work, be very careful to not bend pins on the processor or socket, and protect the processor and motherboard against ESD. Do the following:

1. Verify the computer is working. Turn off the system, unplug it, press the power button, and open the computer case. Put on your ESD strap. Remove the cooler assembly. Remove all the thermal compound from the cooler and processor.
2. Reinstall the processor and thermal compound. Have your instructor check the thermal compound. Install the cooler.
3. Replace the case cover, power up the system, and verify all is working.

REPLACING THE PROCESSOR IN A LAPTOP

A+
220-901
3.1

Before replacing the processor in a laptop, consider the laptop might still be under warranty. Also consider it might be more cost effective to replace the laptop rather than replacing the processor, including the cost of parts and labor. If you do decide to replace a processor in a laptop, be sure to select a processor supported by the laptop manufacturer for the particular model laptop. The range of processors supported by a laptop does not usually include as many options as those supported by a desktop motherboard.

For many laptops, removing the cover on the bottom of a laptop exposes the processor fan and heat sink assembly. When you remove this assembly, you can then open the socket and remove the processor. For example, looking at the laptop shown in Figure 4-31, you can see the processor heat sink and fan assembly exposed. To remove the assembly, remove the seven screws and the fan power connector (see Figure 4-32). Then lift the assembly straight up, being careful not to damage the processor underneath.

Figure 4-31 The cover is removed from the bottom of a laptop exposing several internal components

For another laptop, the heat sink and fan assembly is also exposed when you remove the cover on the bottom of the laptop (see Figure 4-33). Notice the heat sink on this laptop extends to the processor and chipset. You remove several screws and then lift the entire assembly out as a unit. For both laptops, the heat sink fits on top of the processor and the fan sits to the side of the processor. This design is typical of many laptops. However, some laptops require you to remove the keyboard and the keyboard bezel to reach the fan assembly and processor under the bezel.

Figure 4-32 Seven screws hold the processor heat sink and fan assembly in place

Figure 4-33 Remove the cover from the bottom of the laptop to expose the heat sink and fan assembly and to reach the processor

Figure 4-34 shows the heat sink and fan assembly removed in one laptop, exposing the processor. Notice the thermal compound on the processor. To remove the processor, turn the CPU socket screw 90 degrees to open the socket, as shown in the figure. Most Intel and AMD sockets have this socket screw on the side of the socket, as shown in Figure 4-34, although other sockets have the screw on the corner of the socket.

Figure 4-34 Open the CPU socket

Lift the CPU from the socket. Be careful to lift straight up without bending the CPU pins. Figure 4-35 shows the processor out of the socket. If you look carefully, you can see the missing pins on one corner of the processor and socket. This corner is used to correctly orient the processor in the socket, which is socket 478B.

Before you place the new processor into the socket, be sure the socket screw is in the open position. Then delicately place the processor into its socket. If it does not drop in completely, consider that the screw might not be in the full open position. Be sure to use thermal compound on top of the processor. Intel recommends

Figure 4-35 The processor removed from socket 478B

0.2 grams of compound, which is about the size of a small pea. To make sure you use just the right amount of compound, consider buying it in individual packets that are measured for a single application.

Now let's turn our attention to the various memory technologies used in personal computers, and how to upgrade memory.

MEMORY TECHNOLOGIES

A+
220-901
1.2, 1.3

Recall that random access memory (RAM) temporarily holds data and instructions as the CPU processes them and that the memory modules used on a motherboard are made of dynamic RAM or DRAM. DRAM loses its data rapidly, and the memory controller must refresh it several thousand times a second. RAM is stored on memory modules, which are installed in memory slots on the motherboard (see Figure 4-36).

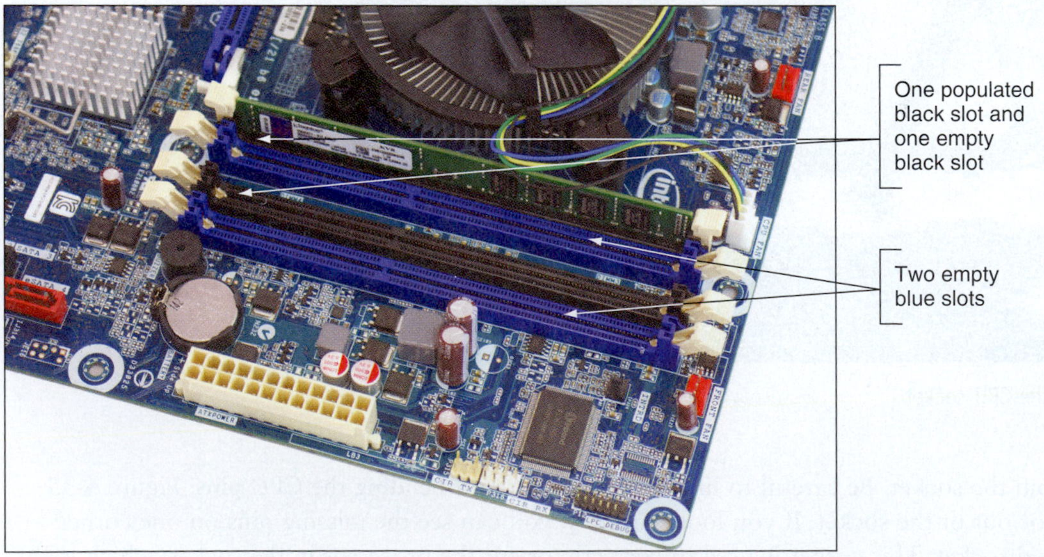

Figure 4-36 RAM on motherboards today is stored in DIMMs

A+ Exam Tip The A+ 220-901 exam expects you to know the purposes and characteristics of DDR, DDR2, and DDR3 memory technologies.

Several variations of DRAM have evolved over the years. Here are the four major categories of memory modules:

- All new motherboards for desktops sold today use a type of memory module called a DIMM (dual inline memory module).
- Laptops use a smaller version of a DIMM called a SO-DIMM (small outline DIMM and pronounced "sew-dim"). MicroDIMMs are used on subnotebook computers and are smaller than SO-DIMMs.
- An older type of module is a RIMM, which is designed by Rambus, Inc.
- Really old computers used SIMMs (single inline memory modules). You're unlikely to ever see these modules in working computers.

The major differences among these modules are the width of the data path that each type of module accommodates and the way data moves from the system bus to the module. DIMMs have seen several evolutions. Five versions of DIMMs, one RIMM, and two types of SIMMs are shown in Table 4-3. Notice the notches on the modules, which prevent the wrong type of module from being inserted into a memory slot on the motherboard. The table includes older and current memory technologies.

Description of Module	Example
288-pin DDR4 DIMM is currently the fastest memory with lower voltage requirements. It can support quad or dual channels or function as single DIMMs. It has one notch near the center of the edge connector.	 Source: kingston.com
240-pin DDR3 DIMM can support quad, triple, or dual channels or function as single DIMMs. It has an offset notch farther from the center than a DDR2 DIMM.	
240-pin DDR2 DIMM can support dual channels or function as single DIMMs. It has one notch near the center of the edge connector.	
184-pin DDR DIMM can support dual channels or function as a single DIMM. It has one offset notch.	
168-pin SDRAM DIMM has two notches on the module. The positions of these notches depend on the memory features the DIMM uses.	
RIMM has 184 pins and two notches near the center of the edge connector.	
72-pin SIMMs were installed in groups of two modules to each bank of memory.	
30-pin SIMMs were installed in groups of four modules to each bank of memory.	

Table 4-3 Types of memory modules

In this chapter, you see tons of different technologies used by RAM and so many can get a little overwhelming. You need to know about them because each motherboard you might support requires a specific type of RAM. Figure 4-37 is designed to help you keep all these technologies straight. You might find it a useful road map as you study each technology in the chapter. And who keeps up with all these technologies? JEDEC (*www.jedec.org*) is the organization responsible for standards used by solid-state devices, including RAM technologies. The goal of each new RAM technology approved by JEDEC is to increase speed and performance without greatly increasing the cost.

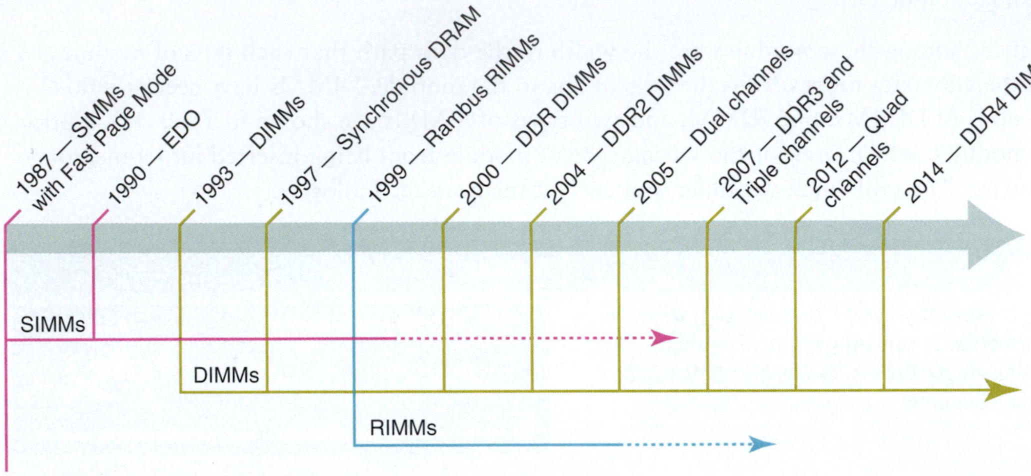

Figure 4-37 Timeline of memory technologies

Even though an older RAM technology is no longer used by new motherboards, RAM manufacturers continue to produce the older RAM because older motherboards require these replacement modules. In Figure 4-37, the dotted lines for SIMMs and RIMMs indicate these technologies are now obsolete. All new motherboards today use DIMMs. However, if you check some retail websites, you can see that RIMMs can still be purchased.

Notes For an interesting discussion on how RAM works, complete with animation, see the webpage by HowStuff Works, Inc., at *www.howstuffworks.com/ram.htm*.

We'll now look at each of the types of DIMM and SO-DIMM modules and the technologies they use.

DIMM TECHNOLOGIES

A+
220-901
1.2, 1.3

DIMMs use a 64-bit data path. (Some early DIMMs had a 128-bit data path, but they're now obsolete.) A DIMM (dual inline memory module) gets its name because it has independent pins on opposite sides of the module.

Early DIMMs did not run in sync with the system clock because they were too slow to keep up. Their speeds are measured in nanoseconds (ns), which is how long it takes for the module to read or write data. The first DIMM to run synchronized with the system clock was synchronous DRAM (SDRAM), which has two notches, and uses 168 pins. (Don't confuse SDRAM with SRAM. SRAM is static RAM used in processor memory caches, and SDRAM is dynamic RAM used on DIMMs.) Synchronized memory runs in step with the processor and system clock, and its speeds are measured just as processor and bus speeds are measured in MHz.

Double Data Rate SDRAM (DDR SDRAM, or SDRAM II, or simply DDR) is an improved version of SDRAM. DDR runs twice as fast as regular SDRAM, has one notch, and uses 184 pins. Instead of processing data for each beat of the system clock, as regular SDRAM does, it processes data when the beat rises and again when it falls, doubling the data rate of memory. If a motherboard runs at 200 MHz, DDR memory runs at 400 MHz. Three other improvements over DDR are DDR2, DDR3, and DDR4. DDR2 is faster and uses less power than DDR. DDR3 is faster and uses less power than DDR2. The trend continues with DDR4 being faster and using less power than DDR3. Both DDR2 and DDR3 use 240 pins. They are not compatible because their notches are not in the same position, and the different notch positions keep someone from installing a DDR2 or DDR3 DIMM in the wrong memory slot. DDR4 uses 288 pins.

Factors that affect the capacity, features, and performance of DIMMs include the number of channels they use, how much RAM is on one DIMM, the speed, error-checking abilities, and buffering. All these factors are discussed next.

SINGLE, DUAL, TRIPLE, AND QUAD CHANNELS

When you look at a motherboard, you might notice the DIMM slots are different colors. This color coding is used to identify the channel each slot uses. Channels have to do with how many DIMM slots the memory controller can address at a time. Early DIMMs only used a single channel, which means the memory controller can access only one DIMM at a time. To improve overall memory performance, dual channels allow the memory controller to communicate with two DIMMs at the same time, effectively doubling the speed of memory access. A motherboard that supports triple channels can access three DIMMs at the same time. Sandy Bridge technology introduced quad channels where the processor can access four DIMMs at the same time. DDR, DDR2, DDR3, and DDR4 DIMMs can use dual channels. DDR3 DIMMs can also use triple channels. DDR3 and DDR4 DIMMs can use quad channels. For dual, triple, or quad channels to work, the motherboard and the DIMM must support the technology.

Figure 4-38 shows how dual channeling works on a board with four DIMM slots. The board has two memory channels, Channel A and Channel B. With dual channeling, the two DIMMs installed in the two slots labeled Channel A can be addressed at the same time. If two more DIMMs are installed in the Channel B slots, they can be accessed at the same time.

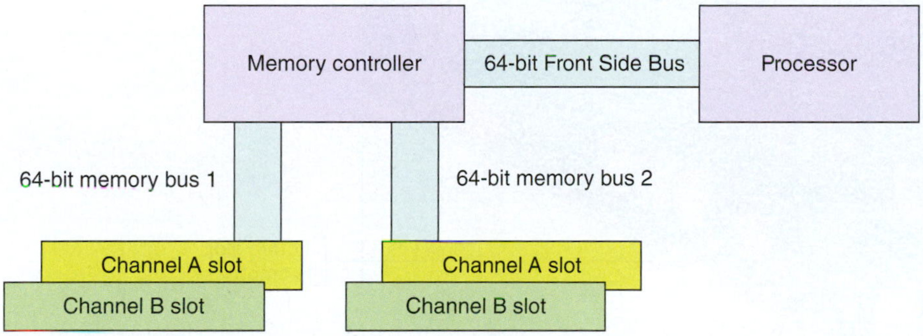

Figure 4-38 Using dual channels, the memory controller can read from two DIMMs at the same time

When setting up dual channeling, know that the pair of DIMMs in a channel must be equally matched in size, speed, and features, and it is recommended they come from the same manufacturer. A motherboard supporting dual channels was shown in Figure 4-36. The two black DIMM slots make up the first channel, and the two blue slots make up the second channel. To use dual channeling, matching DIMMs must be installed in the black slots and another matching pair in the blue slots, as shown in Figure 4-39. Know that the second pair of DIMMs does not have to match the first pair of DIMMs because the first channel runs independently of the second channel. If the two DIMM slots of a channel are not populated with matching pairs of DIMMs, the motherboard will revert to single channeling.

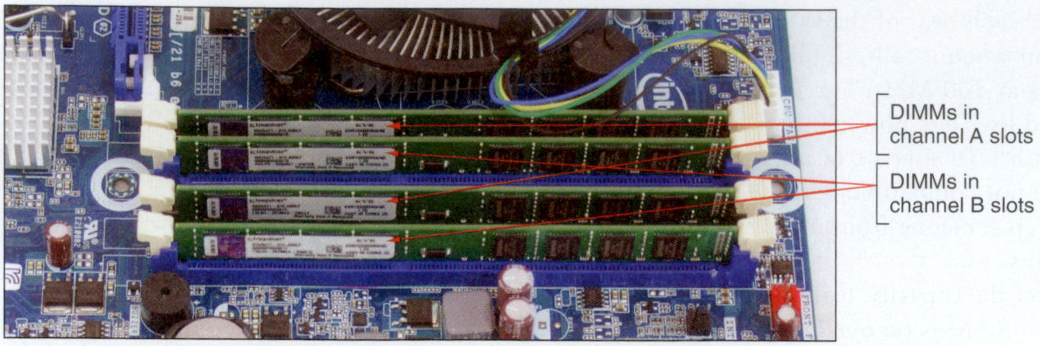

Figure 4-39 Matching pairs of DIMMs installed in four DIMM slots that support dual channeling

★ A+ Exam Tip The A+ 220-901 exam expects you to be able to distinguish between single-channel, dual-channel, and triple-channel memory installations.

For a triple-channel installation, three DIMM slots must be populated with three matching DDR3 DIMMs (see Figure 4-40). The three DIMMs are installed in the three blue slots on the board. This motherboard has a fourth black DIMM slot. You can barely see this black slot behind the three filled slots in the photo. If the fourth slot is used, then triple channeling is disabled, which can slow down performance. If a matching pair of DIMMs is installed in the first two slots and another matching pair of DIMMs is installed in the third and fourth slots, then the memory controller will use dual channels. Dual channels are not as fast as triple channels, but certainly better than single channels.

Figure 4-40 Three identical DDR3 DIMMs installed in a triple-channel configuration

The latest memory technology is quad channeling that was introduced with Intel Sandy Bridge chipsets and processors. Figure 4-41 shows an Intel motherboard that has the LGA2011 socket and eight memory slots. The processor can access four slots at the same time. The four black slots can be addressed by the processor on one memory channel and the four blue slots on another channel. Second Generation Sandy Bridge and later processors contain the memory controller within the processor package rather than on the chipset. To get the highest performance, memory slots are placed on either side of the processor in order to shorten the length of the memory bus. Because of the high performance of processors that use the LGA2011 socket, Intel recommends that systems using this socket use liquid cooling methods.

Courtesy of Intel Corporation

Figure 4-41 The Intel Desktop Board DX79TO has eight memory slots and supports two quad channels

DIMM SPEEDS

DIMM speeds are measured either in MHz (such as 1333 MHz or 800 MHz) or PC rating (such as PC6400). A PC rating is a measure of the total bandwidth in MB/second of data moving between the module and the CPU. To calculate the PC rating for a DDR DIMM, multiply the speed by 8 bytes because a DIMM has an 8-byte or 64-bit data path. For example, a DDR DIMM that runs at 800 MHz has a bandwidth or transfer rate of 800×8 or 6400 MB/second, which is expressed as a PC rating of PC6400. A DDR2 PC rating is usually labeled PC2, a DDR3 PC rating is labeled PC3, and a DDR4 PC rating is labeled PC4. In Figure 4-42, this memory ad shows the PC rating and lists speed as the DDR rate. Table 4-4 lists some current PC ratings.

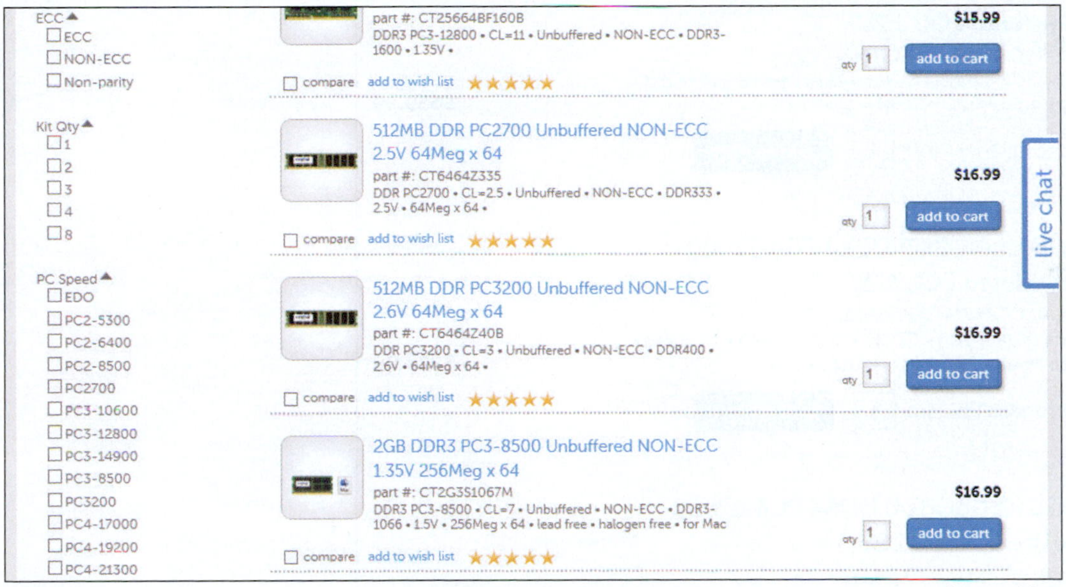

Source: crucial.com

Figure 4-42 Memory speed is expressed in PC rating and lists speed as DDR rating

★ A+ Exam Tip The A+ 220-901 exam expects you to be able to calculate PC ratings, given the transfers per second. To get the PC rating, multiply the transfers per second by eight. To get the speed, divide the PC rating by eight.

SINGLE-SIDED AND DOUBLE-SIDED DIMMs

A DIMM can have memory chips installed on one side of the module (called single-sided) or both sides of the module (called double-sided). Most desktop and laptop processors address memory 64 bits at a time. A memory bank is the memory a processor addresses at one time and is 64 bits wide, and a DIMM

Type of Memory	Speed	PC Rating
DDR4 DIMM	2666 MHz	PC4-21300
DDR4 DIMM	3000 MHz	PC4-24000
DDR4 DIMM	2133 MHz	PC4-17000
DDR3 DIMM	2000 MHz	PC3-16000
DDR3 DIMM	1800 MHz	PC3-14400
DDR3 DIMM	1333 MHz	PC3-10600
DDR2 DIMM	800 MHz	PC2-6400
DDR2 DIMM	667 MHz	PC2-5400
DDR DIMM	500 MHz	PC4000

Table 4-4 PC ratings for current memory modules

slot provides a 64-bit data path. However, some double-sided DIMMs provide more than one bank, which means the chips on the DIMM are grouped so that the memory controller addresses one group and then addresses another. These DIMMs are said to be dual ranked, and don't perform as well as DIMMs where all the memory is addressed at one time. Figure 4-43 shows some examples of DDR dual-ranked memory modules used in servers.

Source: crucial.com

Figure 4-43 Memory ad lists dual-ranked DDR4 memory

ERROR CHECKING AND PARITY

Because DIMMs intended to be used in servers must be extremely reliable, error-checking technology called ECC (error-correcting code) is sometimes used. The memory modules shown in Figure 4-43 are ECC memory. Some DDR, DDR2, DDR3, and DDR4 memory modules support ECC. A DIMM normally has an even number of chips on the module, but a DIMM that supports ECC has an odd number of chips on the module. The odd extra chip is the ECC chip. ECC compares bits written to the module to what is later read from the module, and it can detect and correct an error in a single bit of the byte. If there are errors in 2 bits of a byte, ECC can detect the error but cannot correct it. The data path width for DIMMs is normally 64 bits, but with ECC, the data path is 72 bits. The extra 8 bits are used for error checking. ECC memory costs more than non-ECC memory, but it is more reliable. For ECC to work, the motherboard and all installed modules must support it. Also, it's important to know that you cannot install a mix of ECC and non-ECC memory on the motherboard because such a mixture causes the system to not work.

As with most other memory technologies discussed in this chapter, when buying memory to add to a motherboard, match the type of memory to the type the board supports. To see if your motherboard supports ECC memory, look for the ability to enable or disable the feature in UEFI/BIOS setup, or check the motherboard documentation.

Older SIMMs used an error-checking technology called parity. Using parity checking, a ninth bit is stored with every 8 bits in a byte. If memory is using odd parity, it makes the ninth or parity bit either a 1 or a 0, to make the number of 1s in the nine bits odd. If it uses even parity, it makes the parity bit a 1 or a 0 to make the number of 1s in the 9 bits even.

A+ Exam Tip The A+ 220-901 exam expects you to know that parity memory uses 9 bits (8 bits for data and 1 bit for parity). You also need to be familiar with ECC and non-ECC memory technologies.

Later, when the byte is read back, the memory controller checks the odd or even state. If the number of bits is not an odd number for odd parity or an even number for even parity, a parity error occurs. A parity error always causes the system to halt. On the screen, you see the error message "Parity Error 1" or "Parity Error 2" or a similar error message about parity. Parity Error 1 is a parity error on the motherboard; Parity Error 2 is a parity error on an expansion card.

Figure 4-44 shows a SIMM for sale. It's pricy because this old technology is hardly ever used. Notice the module is non-parity memory. In the ad, the SIMM is called EDO memory. EDO (extended data out) is a technology used by SIMMs.

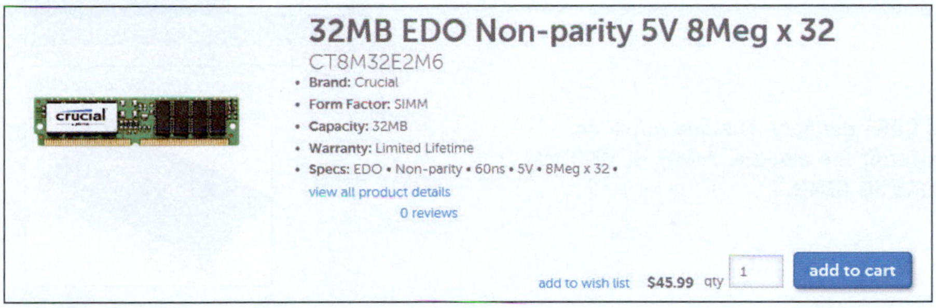

Source: crucial.com

Figure 4-44 A SIMM appears in a memory ad as EDO memory

Notes RAM chips that have become undependable and cannot hold data reliably can cause errors. Sometimes this happens when chips overheat or power falters.

BUFFERED AND REGISTERED DIMMs

Buffers and registers hold data and amplify a signal just before the data is written to the module. (Using buffers is an older technology than using registers.) Some DIMMs use buffers, some use registers, and some use neither. If a DIMM doesn't support registers or buffers, it's referred to as an unbuffered DIMM. Looking at the ad in Figure 4-42 for value memory used in desktops, you can see all the modules are unbuffered. However, in Figure 4-43, two of the kits of expensive server memory are registered DIMMs.

CAS LATENCY AND RAS LATENCY

Two other memory features are CAS Latency (CAS stands for "column access strobe") and RAS Latency (RAS stands for "row access strobe"), which are two ways of measuring access timing. Both features refer to the number of clock cycles it takes to write or read a column or row of data off a memory module. CAS Latency is used more than RAS Latency. Lower values are better than higher ones. For example, CL8 is a little faster than CL9.

Notes In memory ads, CAS Latency is sometimes written as CL, and RAS Latency might be written as RL.

Ads for memory modules might give the CAS Latency value within a series of timing numbers, such as 5-5-5-15. The first value is CAS Latency, which means the module is CL5. The second value is RAS Latency. Looking back at Figure 4-42, you can see CL ratings vary from 2.5 to 11.

Notes When selecting memory, use the memory type that the motherboard manufacturer recommends.

TYPES OF MEMORY USED IN LAPTOPS

Today's laptops use DDR4, DDR3L, DDR3, or DDR2 SO-DIMM (small outline DIMM) memory. Table 4-5 lists current SO-DIMMs. All of these memory modules are smaller than regular DIMMs.

A+ Exam Tip The A+ 220-901 exam expects you to know that DDR3, DDR2, and DDR memory can be found on SO-DIMMs.

Memory Module Description	Sample Memory Module
2.74" 260-pin SO-DIMM contains DDR4 memory. The one notch on the module is offset from the center of the module.	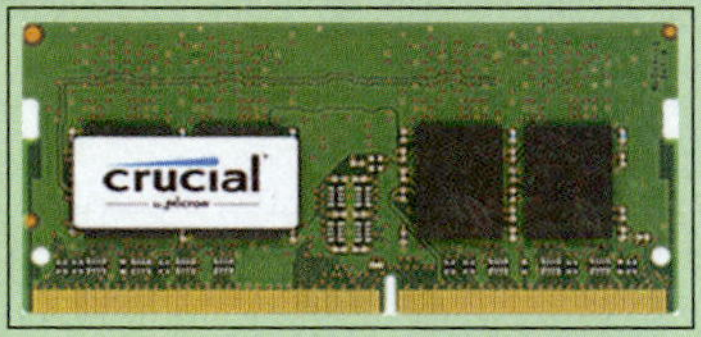 Source: crucial.com
2.66" 204-pin SO-DIMM contains DDR3 memory. The one notch on the module is offset from the center of the module. A DDR3L SO-DIMM uses less power than a regular DDR3 SO-DIMM.	 Courtesy of Kingston Technology Corporation
2.66" 200-pin SO-DIMM contains DDR2 SDRAM. One notch is near the side of the module.	 Courtesy of Kingston Technology Corporation
2.66" 200-pin SO-DIMM contains DDR SDRAM. One notch near the side of the module is slightly offset from the notch on a DDR2 SDRAM module.	 Courtesy of Micron Consumer Products

Table 4-5 Memory modules used in laptop computers (continues)

Memory Module Description	Sample Memory Module
2.66" 144-pin SO-DIMM contains SDRAM. One notch is slightly offset from the center of the module.	 Courtesy of Micron Consumer Products
2.35" 72-pin SO-DIMM has no notch on the edge connector.	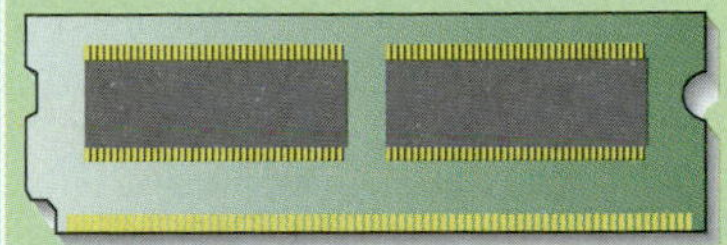
160-pin SO-RIMM contains Rambus memory and has two notches.	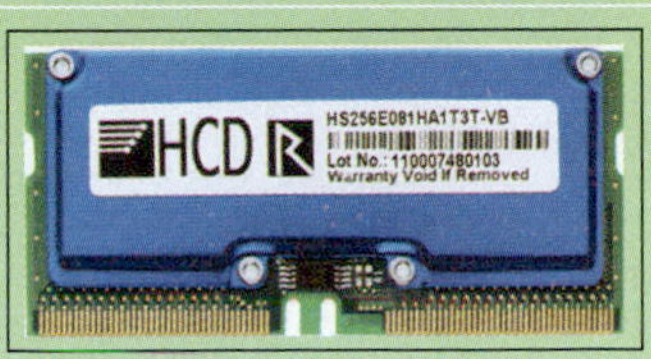 Courtesy of High Connection Density, Inc.

Table 4-5 Memory modules used in laptop computers (continued)

Just as with memory modules used in desktop computers, you can only use the type of memory the laptop is designed to support. The number of pins and the position of the notches on a SO-DIMM keep you from inserting the wrong module in a memory slot.

Now, onward to upgrading memory.

HOW TO UPGRADE MEMORY

A+
220-901
1.3, 3.1

To upgrade memory means to add more RAM to a computer. Adding more RAM might solve a problem with slow performance, applications refusing to load, or an unstable system. When Windows does not have adequate memory to perform an operation, it gives an "Insufficient memory" error or it slows down to a painful crawl.

When first purchased, many computers have empty slots on the motherboard, allowing you to add DIMMs or SO-DIMMs to increase the amount of RAM. Sometimes a memory module goes bad and must be replaced.

When you add more memory to your computer, you need answers to these questions:

- How much RAM do I need and how much is currently installed?
- How many and what kind of memory modules are currently installed on my motherboard?
- How many and what kind of modules can I fit on my motherboard?
- How do I select and purchase the right modules for my upgrade?
- How do I physically install the new modules?

All these questions are answered in the following sections.

HOW MUCH MEMORY DO I NEED AND HOW MUCH IS CURRENTLY INSTALLED?

A+
220-901
1.3, 3.1

With the demands today's software places on memory, the answer is probably, "All you can get." Windows 8 and Windows 7 need at least 2 GB, but more is better. The limit for a 32-bit OS is 4 GB installed RAM. A 64-bit Windows installation can handle more. For example, a 64-bit installation of Windows 8 can use up to 128 GB of RAM, and a 64-bit installation of Windows 7 Home Premium can use up to 16 GB of RAM.

APPLYING | CONCEPTS HOW MUCH MEMORY IS CURRENTLY INSTALLED?

In Windows, you can use the System Information window to report the amount of physical memory installed. From the Windows 8 desktop, right-click **Start**, click **Run**, and then type **msinfo32**. For Windows 7, click **Start** and type **msinfo32** in the Search box. The System Information window shown in Figure 4-45 reports the amount of installed physical memory. Notice on the window that 16 GB is installed.

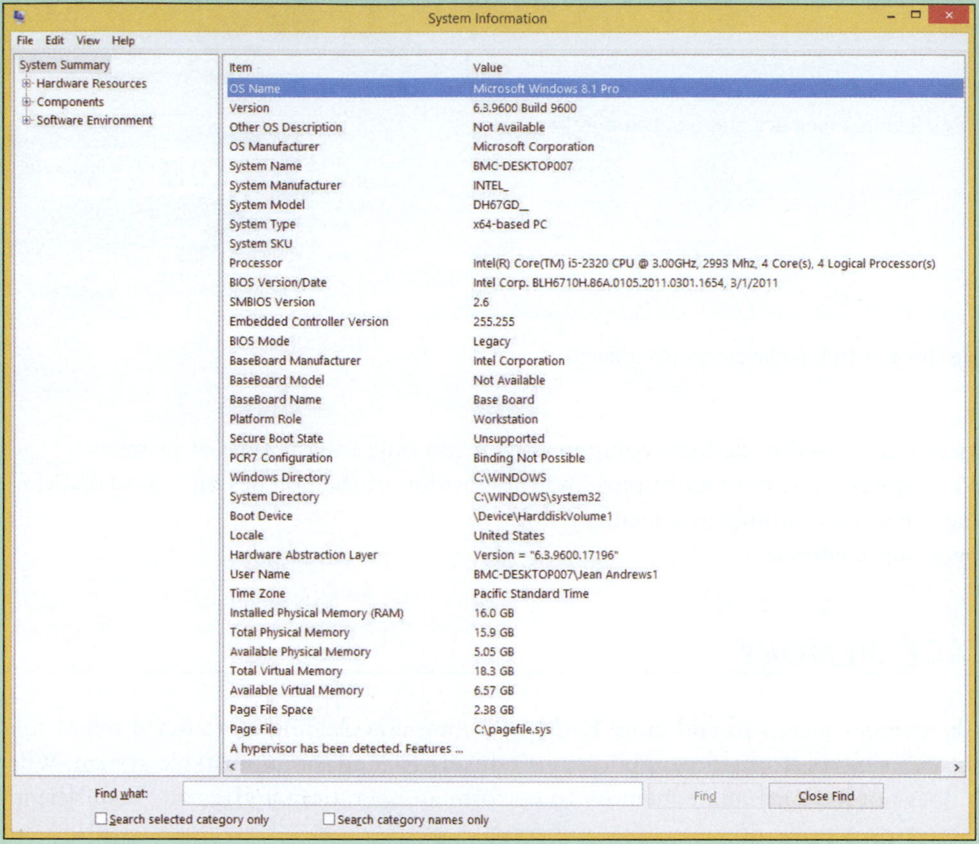

Figure 4-45 The System Information window reports installed physical memory

The BIOS setup screen shows more information about installed memory than does Windows. Reboot the computer and access BIOS setup (you learned how to do that in the chapter, "All About Motherboards"). The BIOS setup main menu for one system is shown in Figure 4-46. This screen shows the number of memory slots and how much RAM is installed in each slot. Notice the system has two memory channels of two slots each. You can, therefore, conclude this system is using dual channels.

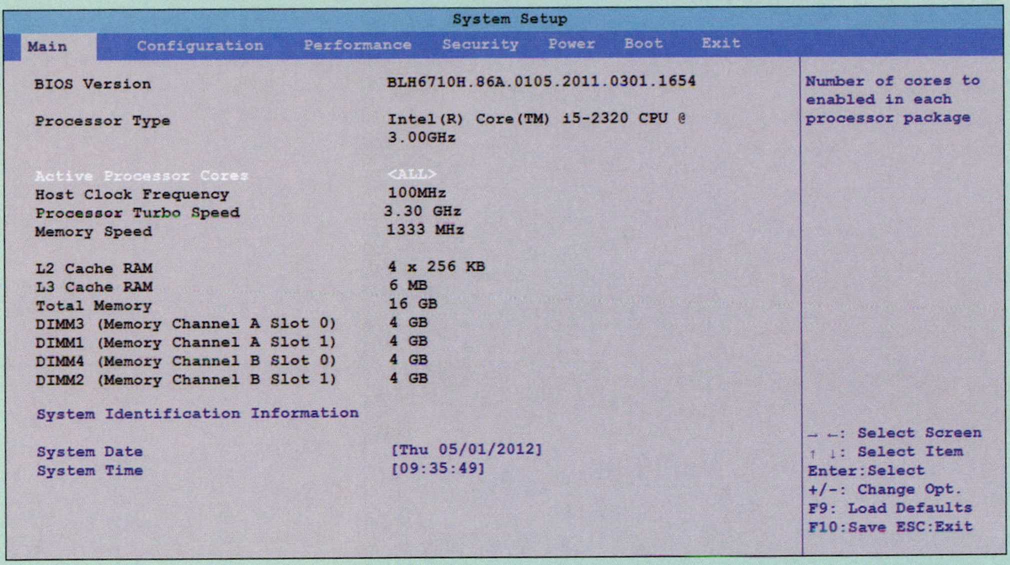

Source: Intel

Figure 4-46 BIOS setup reports memory configuration and amount

HOW MANY AND WHAT KIND OF MEMORY MODULES ARE CURRENTLY INSTALLED?

A+
220-901
1.3, 3.1

The next step to upgrading memory is to determine what type of memory modules the motherboard is currently using. If the board already has memory installed, you want to do your best to match the new modules with whatever is already installed. To learn what type of memory modules are already installed, do the following:

1. Open the case and look at the memory slots. How many slots do you have? How many are filled? Remove each module from its slot and look on it for imprinted type, size, and speed. For example, a module might say "PC2-4200/512MB." The PC2 tells you the memory is DDR2, the 4200 is the PC rating and tells you the speed, and the 512 MB is the size. This is not enough information to know exactly what modules to purchase, but it's a start.
2. Examine the module for the physical size and position of the notches. Compare the notch positions to those in Table 4-3.
3. Read your motherboard documentation. If the documentation is not clear (and some are not) or you don't have the documentation, look on the motherboard for the imprinted manufacturer and model (see Figure 4-47). With this information, you can search a good memory website such as Kingston (*www.kingston.com*) or Crucial (*www.crucial.com*), which can tell you what type of modules this board supports.

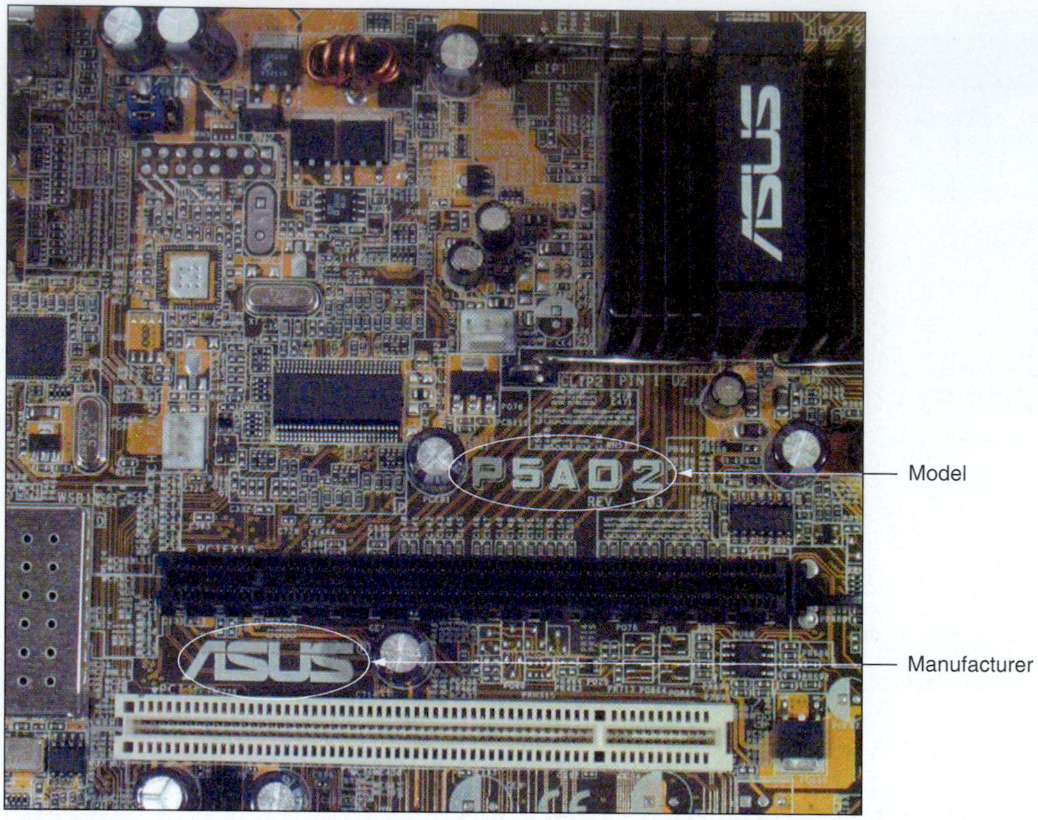

Figure 4-47 Look for the manufacturer and model of a motherboard imprinted somewhere on the board

4. Look in the documentation to see if the board supports dual channel, triple channel, or quad channels. If it does, most likely the memory slots on the board will be color-coded in pairs (for dual channels) or groups of three slots (for triple channels) or four slots (for quad channels). If the board supports multiple channels and modules are already installed, verify that matching DIMMs are installed in each channel.
5. If you still have not identified the module type, you can take the motherboard and the old memory modules to a good computer parts store and they should be able to match it for you.

Hands-On Project 4-3 Use an Online Memory Scanner

A great shortcut to research a memory upgrade is an online memory scanner. Go to *www.crucial.com/systemscanner* by Crucial. Download and run the Crucial System Scanner, which scans your system and reports what type of memory is installed and can be installed. Using the Crucial report, answer these questions:

1. Which motherboard do you have installed? How much memory is installed? How many memory slots does the board have? How many are populated?
2. What is the maximum memory the board supports? What type of memory does the board support? What would be the total cost of the memory upgrade if you were to max out the total memory on the board?

HOW MANY AND WHAT KIND OF MODULES CAN FIT ON MY MOTHERBOARD?

A+
220-901
1.3, 3.1

Now that you know what memory modules are already installed, you're ready to decide how much and what kind of modules you can add to the board. Keep in mind that if all memory slots are full, sometimes you can take out small-capacity modules and replace them with larger-capacity modules, but you can only use the type, size, and speed of modules that the board can support. Also, if you must discard existing modules, the price of the upgrade increases.

To know how much memory your motherboard can physically hold, read the documentation that comes with the board. You can always install DIMMs as single modules, but you might not get the best performance by doing so. For best performance, install matching DIMMs in all the slots (two, three, or four slots) on one channel. Now let's look at a few examples. The examples are ordered from a more recent motherboard to an older motherboard. As you study these examples, notice that the older the board, the more complicated the configuration can be and the harder it is to understand the documentation. Is life with computers getting simpler or what?

MOTHERBOARD USING DDR3 DUAL-CHANNEL DIMMs

The Intel Desktop Board DH67GD shown earlier in Figure 4-21 has four memory slots that use dual channeling. These slots are numbered in the user guide, as shown in Figure 4-48. The slots can hold Dual Channel DDR3 1333 MHz and 1066 MHz non-ECC, 1.35-V modules for up to 32 GB of RAM on this board. To use four DIMMs and dual channeling, install matching DIMMs in the two blue slots and matching DIMMs in the two black slots.

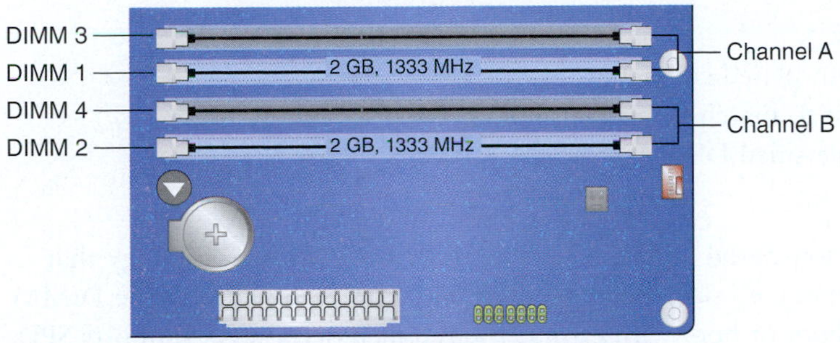

Figure 4-48 Documentation shows four DIMM slots that use dual channels

The motherboard user guide says it is possible to use only three DIMMs and dual channeling if you install matching DIMMs in the two blue slots and install a third DIMM in a black slot. This third DIMM must be equal in speed and total size of the DIMMs in the blue slots. For example, you can install two 4-GB DIMMs in the two blue slots and one 8-GB DIMM in a black slot for a total of 16-GB of RAM. If you install only a single DIMM on this board, it must go in the first blue slot, which is the blue slot closest to the processor.

MOTHERBOARD USING DDR3 TRIPLE-CHANNEL DIMMs

The Intel motherboard shown earlier in Figure 4-40 has four DDR3 memory slots that can be configured for single, dual, or triple channeling. The four empty slots are shown in Figure 4-49. If triple channeling is used, three matching DIMMs are used in the three blue slots. If the fourth slot is populated, the board reverts to single channeling. For dual channeling, install two matching DIMMs in the two blue slots farthest from the processor and leave the other two slots empty. If only one DIMM is installed, it goes in the blue slot in the farthest position from the processor.

Figure 4-49 Four DDR3 slots on a motherboard

The motherboard documentation says that these types of DIMMs can be used:

- The DIMM voltage rating no higher than 1.6 V
- Non-ECC DDR3 memory
- Serial Presence Detect (SPD) memory only
- Gold-plated contacts (some modules use tin-plated contacts)
- 1333 MHz, 1066 MHz, or 800 MHz (best to match the system bus speed)
- Unbuffered, nonregistered single- or double-sided DIMMs
- Up to 16 GB total installed RAM

The third item in the list needs an explanation. Serial Presence Detect (SPD) is a DIMM technology that declares to system UEFI/BIOS at startup the module's size, speed, voltage, and data path width. If the DIMM does not support SPD, the system might not boot or boot with errors. Today's memory always supports SPD.

MOTHERBOARD USING DDR DIMMs WITH DUAL CHANNELING

Let's look at another example of a DIMM installation. The Pentium motherboard allows you to use three different speeds of DDR DIMMs in one to four sockets on the board. The board supports dual channeling and has two blue slots for one channel and two black slots for the other channel. For dual channeling to work, matching DIMMs must be installed in the two blue sockets. If two DIMMs are installed in the two black sockets, they must match each other.

This board supports up to 4 GB of unbuffered, 184-pin, non-ECC memory running at PC3200, PC2700, or PC2100. The documentation says the system bus can run at 800 MHz, 533 MHz, or 400 MHz, depending on the speed of the processor installed. Therefore, the speed of the processor determines the system bus speed, which determines the speed of memory modules.

Figure 4-50 outlines the possible configurations of these DIMM modules, showing that you can install one, two, or four DIMMs and which sockets should hold these DIMMs. To take advantage of dual channeling on this motherboard, you must populate the sockets according to Figure 4-50, so that identical DIMM pairs are working together in DIMM_A1 and DIMM_B1 sockets (the blue sockets), and another pair can work together in DIMM_A2 and DIMM_B2 sockets (the black sockets).

The board has two installed DDR DIMMs. The label on one of these DIMMs is shown in Figure 4-51. The important items on this label are the size (256 MB), the speed (400 MHz or 3200 PC rating), and the CAS Latency (CL3). With this information and knowledge about what the board can support, we are now ready to select and buy the memory for the upgrade. For example, if you decide to upgrade the system to

Mode		Sockets			
		DIMM_A1	DIMM_A2	DIMM_B1	DIMM_B2
Single channel	(1)	Populated	—	—	—
	(2)	—	Populated	—	—
	(3)	—	—	Populated	—
	(4)	—	—	—	Populated
Dual channel*	(1)	Populated	—	Populated	—
	(2)	—	Populated	—	Populated
	(3)	Populated	Populated	Populated	Populated

**Use only identical DDR DIMM pairs*

Figure 4-50 Motherboard documentation shows that one, two, or four DIMMs can be installed

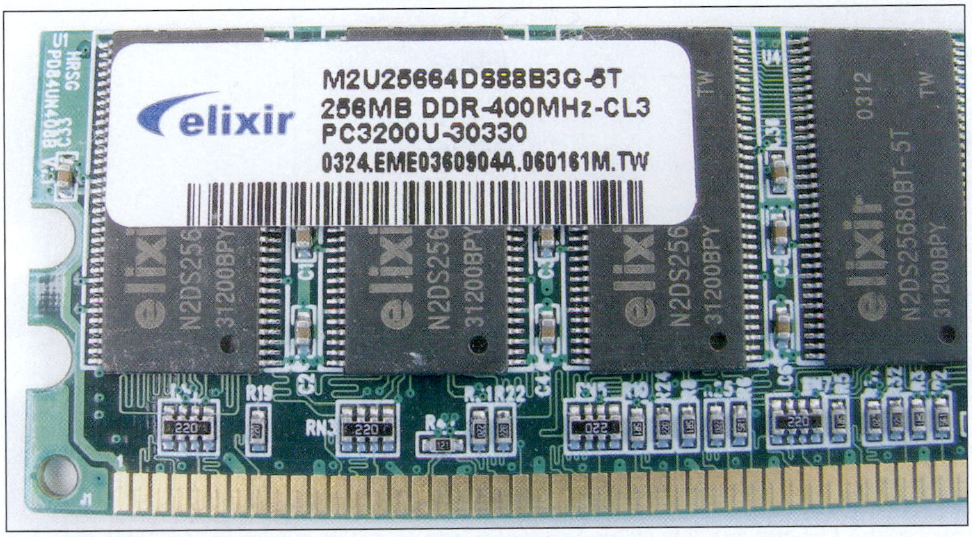

Figure 4-51 Use the label on this DIMM to identify its features

1 GB of memory, you would buy two DDR, 400 MHz, CL3 DIMMs that support dual channeling. For best results, you need to also match the manufacturer and buy Elixir memory.

HOW DO I SELECT AND PURCHASE THE RIGHT MEMORY MODULES?

A+
220-901
1.3, 3.1

You're now ready to make the purchase. As you select your memory, you might find it difficult to find an exact match to DIMMs already installed on the board. If necessary, here are some compromises you cannot or can make:

- Mixing unbuffered memory with buffered or registered memory won't work.
- When matching memory, for best results, also match the module manufacturer. But in a pinch, you can try using memory from two different manufacturers.
- If you mix memory speeds, know that all modules will perform at the slowest speed.

Now let's look at how to use a website or other computer ad to search for the right memory.

USING A WEBSITE TO RESEARCH YOUR PURCHASE

When purchasing memory from a website such as Crucial Technology's site (*www.crucial.com*) or Kingston Technology's site (*www.kingston.com*), look for a search utility that will match memory modules to your motherboard (see Figure 4-52). These utilities are easy to use and help you confirm you have made the right decisions about type, size, and speed to buy. They can also help if motherboard documentation is inadequate, and you're not exactly sure what memory to buy.

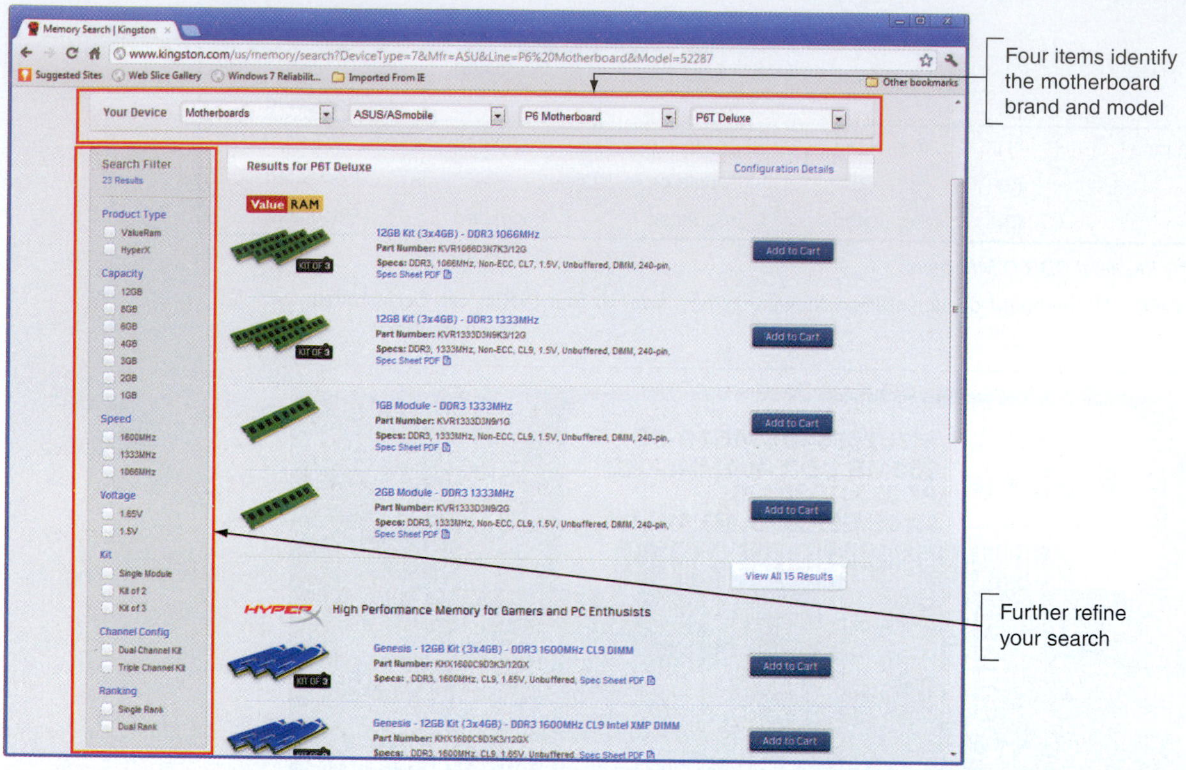

Source: kingston.com

Figure 4-52 The Kingston website DIMM recommendations for a particular motherboard

Let's look at one example on the Crucial site where we are looking to install memory in the Intel DH67GD motherboard discussed earlier in the chapter. The search results are shown in Figure 4-53.

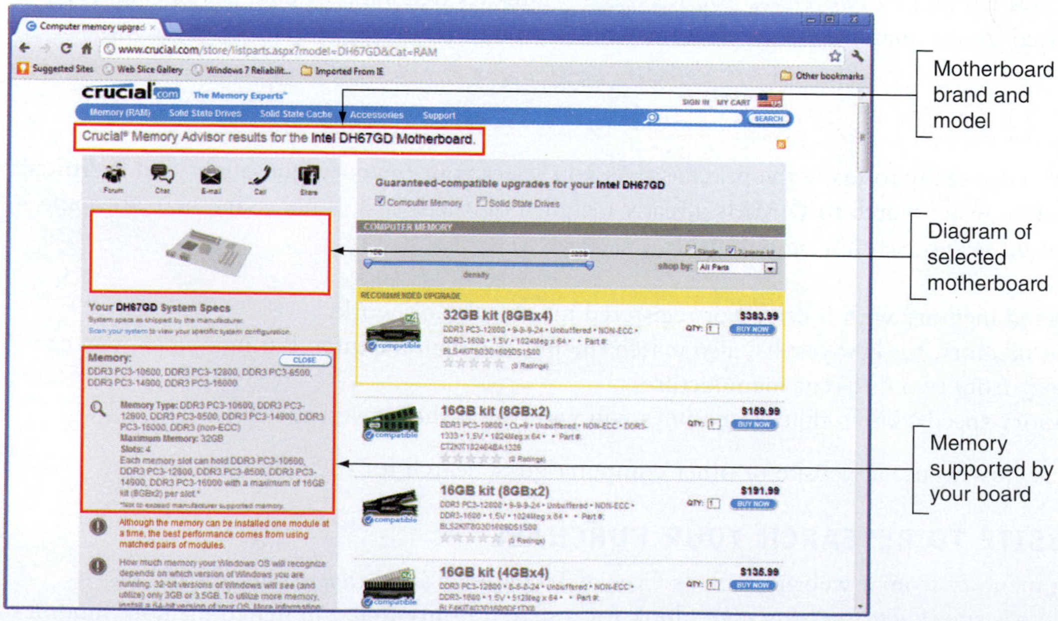

Source: crucial.com

Figure 4-53 Selecting memory off the Crucial website

Modules faster than the board supports are listed. They will work on the board, running at a slower speed, but it's not necessary to spend the money for speed you won't use. The best buy is the second item listed; these DIMMs are rated at 1333 MHz, which is the maximum speed the board supports.

Hands-On | Project 4-4 Plan and Price a Memory Upgrade

Using the information you gained about your computer in Hands-On Project 4-3, research the web to determine the total cost of the memory upgrade in order to max out the total memory on your computer. You can keep the cost down by using the modules you already have, but don't forget to match the speed of the modules already installed. Print two webpages from two sites other than the Crucial site that show the modules you would purchase. How much will the upgrade cost?

HOW DO I INSTALL THE NEW MODULES?

A+
220-901
1.3, 3.1

When installing RAM modules, be careful to protect the chips against static electricity, as you learned to do in the "Working Inside Desktop Computers and Laptops" chapter. Follow these precautions:

- Always use an ESD strap as you work.
- Turn off the power, unplug the power cord, press the power button, and remove the case cover.
- Handle memory modules with care.
- Don't touch the edge connectors on the memory module or on the memory slot.
- Don't stack cards or modules because you can loosen a chip.
- Usually modules pop into place easily and are secured by spring catches on both ends. Make sure that you look for the notches on one side or in the middle of the module that orient the module in the slot.

Let's now look at the details of installing a DIMM.

INSTALLING DIMMs

For DIMM modules, small clips latch into place on each side of the slot to hold the module in the slot, as shown in Figure 4-54. Some newer motherboards have only one latch on the slot. To install a DIMM, first pull the supporting arms on the sides of the slot outward. Look on the DIMM edge connector for the notches,

Figure 4-54 Clips on each side of a slot hold a DIMM in place

which help you orient the DIMM correctly over the slot, and insert the DIMM straight down into the slot. When the DIMM is fully inserted, the supporting clips should pop back into place. Figure 4-55 shows a DIMM being inserted into a slot on a motherboard. Apply pressure on both ends of the DIMM at the same time.

Figure 4-55 Insert the DIMM into the slot by pressing down until the support clips lock into position

Most often, placing memory on the motherboard is all that is necessary for installation. When the computer powers up, it counts the memory present without any further instruction and senses the features that the modules support, such as ECC or buffering. For some really old computers, you must tell BIOS setup the amount of memory present. Read the motherboard documentation to determine what yours requires. If the new memory is not recognized, power down the system and reseat the module. Most likely it's not installed solidly in the slot.

Hands-On Project 4-5 Examine UEFI/BIOS Settings

On your home or lab computer, use UEFI/BIOS setup to answer these questions:

1. Which processor is installed? What is the processor frequency?
2. What are the UEFI/BIOS settings that apply to the processor and how is the processor configured?
3. What information does UEFI/BIOS report about total memory installed and how each memory slot is populated? Does the board support dual, triple, or quad channeling? How do you know?

Hands-On Project 4-6 Upgrade Memory

To practice installing additional memory in a computer in a classroom environment, remove the DIMMs from one computer and place them in another computer. Boot the second computer and check that it counts the additional memory. When finished, return the borrowed modules to the original computer.

HOW TO UPGRADE MEMORY ON A LAPTOP

A+
220-901
3.1

Before upgrading memory, make sure you are not voiding the laptop's warranty. Search for the best buy, but make sure you use memory modules made by or authorized by your laptop's manufacturer and designed for the exact model of your laptop. Installing generic memory might save money but might also void the laptop's warranty.

Upgrading memory on a laptop works about the same way as with upgrading memory on a desktop: Decide how much memory you can upgrade and what type of memory you need, purchase the memory, and install it. As with a desktop computer, be sure to match the type of memory to the type the laptop supports.

Hands-On | Project 4-7 Upgrade Laptop Memory

A friend has a Lenovo ThinkPad X200 laptop and is looking for ways to improve its performance. He's cleaned up the hard drive and is now considering the possibility of upgrading memory. Windows reports the system has 2 GB of RAM. He opens the cover on the bottom of the case and discovers that both SO-DIMM slots are filled. How much will the upgrade cost to bring total RAM in the system to 4 GB? Print the webpage to support your answer. What type and speed of SO-DIMMs does this laptop use?

APPLYING | CONCEPTS UPGRADE MEMORY ON A LAPTOP

Most laptops are designed for easy access to memory. Follow these steps to exchange or upgrade memory for one laptop:

1. Back up data and shut down the system. Remove peripherals, including the AC adapter. Remove the battery. Be sure to use a ground bracelet as you work.
2. Many laptops have a RAM door on the bottom of the laptop. For some laptops, this door is in the battery cavity. Turn the laptop over and loosen the screws on the RAM door. (It is not necessary to remove the screws.)
3. Raise the door (see Figure 4-56) and remove the door from its hinges. The two memory slots are exposed.

Figure 4-56 Raise the DIMM door on the bottom of the notebook

(continues)

4. Notice in Figure 4-57 that one slot is filled and one is available for a memory upgrade. Also notice in the figure that when you remove the RAM door, the CMOS battery is exposed. This easy access to the battery makes exchanging it very easy. To remove a SO-DIMM, pull the clips on the side of the memory slot apart slightly (see Figure 4-58). The SO-DIMM will pop up out of the slot and can then be removed. If it does not pop up, you can hold the clips apart as you pull the module up and out of the slot.

Figure 4-57 SO-DIMM slots, one installed SO-DIMM, and the CMOS battery are exposed

Figure 4-58 Pull apart the clips on the memory slot to release the SO-DIMM

5. To install a new SO-DIMM, insert the module at an angle into the slot (see Figure 4-59) and gently push it down until it snaps into the clips (see Figure 4-60). Replace the RAM door.

Figure 4-59 Insert a new SO-DIMM into a memory slot

Figure 4-60 Push down on the SO-DIMM until it pops into the clips

6. Replace the battery, plug in the power adapter, and power up the laptop.

>> CHAPTER SUMMARY

Types and Characteristics of Processors

- The most important component on the motherboard is the processor, or central processing unit. The two major manufacturers of processors are Intel and AMD.
- Processors are rated by the processor speed, the socket and chipset the processor can use, processor architecture (32-bit or 64-bit), multicore rating, how much internal memory cache the processor has, amount and type of RAM the processor can support, and the computing technologies the processor can use.
- A processor's memory cache inside the processor housing can be an L1 cache (contained on the processor die), L2 cache (off the die), and L3 cache (farther from the core than L2 cache).
- The core of a processor has two arithmetic logic units (ALUs). Multicore processors have two, three, or more cores (called dual core, triple core, quad core, and so forth). Each core can process two threads at once if the feature is enabled in UEFI/BIOS setup.
- The current families of Intel processors for desktops include the Core, Atom, Celeron, and Pentium families of processors. Several different processors are within each family.
- The current AMD desktop processor families are the FX, Phenom, Athlon, and Sempron. Several processors exist within each family.

Selecting and Installing a Processor

- Select a processor that the motherboard supports. A board is likely to support several processors that vary in performance and price.
- When installing a processor, always follow the directions given in the motherboard user guide and be careful to protect the board and processor against ESD. Current Intel sockets LGA1150, LGA1155, LGA1366, and LGA775 use a socket lever and socket load plate. When opening these sockets, lift the socket lever and then the socket load plate, install the processor, and then close the socket. Many AMD sockets have a socket lever, but not a socket load plate.

Memory Technologies

- DRAM is stored on DIMMs for desktop computers and SO-DIMMs for laptops.
- Types of current DIMMs are DDR4 with 288 pins, DDR3 and DDR2 DIMMs that have 240 pins, and DDR DIMMs with 184 pins.
- DIMMs can be single-sided or double-sided. Some double-sided DIMMs provide more than one memory bank and are called dual ranked or quad ranked. A memory bank has a 64-bit data path and is accessed by the processor independently of other banks.
- DIMMs can work together in dual channels, triple channels, and quad channels so that the memory controller can access more than one DIMM at a time to improve performance. In a channel, all DIMMs must match in size, speed, and features. DDR3 DIMMs can use dual, triple, or quad channeling, but DDR and DDR2 DIMMs can only use dual channels. DDR4 DIMMs can use dual or quad channels.
- DIMM speeds are measured in MHz (for example, 1333 MHz) or PC rating (for example, PC3-10600).
- The memory controller can check memory for errors and possibly correct those errors using ECC (error-correcting code). Using parity, an older technology, the controller could only recognize an error had occurred, but not correct it.
- Buffers and registers are used to hold data and amplify a data signal. A DIMM is rated as a buffered, registered, or unbuffered DIMM.
- CAS Latency (CL) and RAS Latency (RL) measure access time to memory. The lower values are faster than the higher values.
- Today's laptops use DDR4, DDR3L, DDR3, or DDR2 SO-DIMMs.

How to Upgrade Memory

- When upgrading memory, use the type, size, and speed the motherboard supports and match new modules to those already installed. Features to match include DDR4, DDR3, DDR2, DDR, size in MB or GB, speed (MHz or PC rating), buffered, registered, unbuffered, single-sided, double-sided, CL rating, tin or gold connectors, support for dual, triple, or quad channeling, ECC, and non-ECC. Using memory made by the same manufacturer is recommended.
- When upgrading components on a laptop, including memory, use components that are the same brand as the laptop, or use only components recommended by the laptop's manufacturer.

>> KEY TERMS

For explanations of key terms, see the Glossary for this text.

buffer overflow attack
CAS Latency
Centrino
DDR
DDR2
DDR3
DDR3L
DDR4
DIMM (dual inline memory module)
Double Data Rate SDRAM (DDR SDRAM)
double-sided
dual channels
dual processors
dual ranked
dynamic RAM (DRAM)
ECC (error-correcting code)
Execute Disable Bit (EDB)
graphic processing unit (GPU)
Hyper-Threading
Hyper Transport
Level 1 cache (L1 cache)
Level 2 cache (L2 cache)
Level 3 cache (L3 cache)
memory bank
multicore processing
multiplier
multiprocessing
multiprocessor platform
parity
parity error
processor frequency
quad channels
RAS Latency
RIMM
SDRAM II
SIMM (single inline memory module)
single channel
single-sided
SO-DIMM (small outline DIMM)
static RAM (SRAM)
synchronous DRAM (SDRAM)
thermal compound
thread
triple channels
x86 processor
x86-64 bit processor

4

>> REVIEWING THE BASICS

1. Who are the two major manufacturers of processors?
2. What is the name of the memory cache that is on the same die as the processor?
3. What is the name of the memory cache that is closest to the processor die but is not housed on the die?
4. What is the name of the Intel technology that allows a processor to handle two threads at the same time?
5. How many threads can a quad-core processor handle at once?
6. Which two Intel processor sockets use a screw head to hold down the socket load plate?
7. What is the purpose of the Execute Disable Bit?
8. Which is faster, SRAM or DRAM? Why?
9. How many pins are on a DDR3 DIMM? DDR2 DIMM?
10. How many pins are on a DDR DIMM?
11. How many notches does a DDR3 DIMM have?
12. Which DIMM performs better, a double-sided dual-ranked DIMM or a double-sided single-ranked DIMM?
13. What prevents a DDR DIMM from being installed in a DDR2 DIMM slot on a motherboard?
14. Which module, a DDR3 or DDR2 DIMM, uses lower voltage?
15. In a memory ad for DIMMs, you notice 64Meg ×72 for one DIMM and 64Meg ×64 for another DIMM. What does the 72 tell you about the first DIMM?
16. What type of DIMM supports triple channeling?
17. If 2 bits of a byte are in error when the byte is read from ECC memory, can ECC detect the error? Can it fix the error?
18. A DIMM memory ad displays 5-5-5-15. What is the CAS Latency value of this DIMM?
19. What is the most amount of RAM that can be used by a 32-bit installation of Windows 7 Professional?
20. A motherboard uses dual channeling, but you have four DIMMs available that differ in size. The motherboard supports all four sizes. Can you install these DIMMs on the board? Will dual channeling be enabled?
21. How many pins does a DDR3 SO-DIMM have? A DDR2 SO-DIMM?
22. Which is faster, CL3 memory or CL5 memory?
23. You are looking to purchase two DIMMs running at 400 MHz. You find DIMMs advertised at PC4000 and PC3200. Which do you purchase?
24. You need to find out how much RAM is installed in a system. What command do you execute to launch the System Information utility?
25. Although ECC memory costs more than non-ECC memory, why would you choose to use it? Which type of computer typically requires ECC memory?

>> THINKING CRITICALLY

1. You need to upgrade memory in a system but you don't have the motherboard documentation available. You open the case and notice that the board has four DIMM slots; three slots are colored yellow and one slot is black. What type of DIMM does the board likely use? How can you be sure?
2. If your motherboard supports DIMM memory, will RIMM memory still work on the board?
3. If your motherboard supports ECC DDR3 memory, can you substitute non-ECC DDR3 memory?
4. You have just upgraded memory on a computer from 1 GB to 2 GB by adding one DIMM. When you first turn on the PC, the memory count shows only 1 GB. Which of the following is most likely the source of the problem? What can you do to fix it?
   a. Windows is giving an error because it likely became corrupted while the computer was disassembled.
   b. The new DIMM you installed is faulty.
   c. The new DIMM is not properly seated.
   d. The DIMM is installed in the wrong slot.
5. Your motherboard supports dual channeling and you currently have two slots used in Channel A on the board; each module holds 1 GB. You want to install an additional 1 GB of RAM. Will your system run faster if you install two 512-MB DIMMs or one 1-GB DIMM? Explain your answer.

>> REAL PROBLEMS, REAL SOLUTIONS

REAL PROBLEM 4-1 Understanding Dual-Processor Motherboards

Print the webpage of a picture of a motherboard that supports dual processors. Use one of these websites to find the picture:

- ASUS at *www.asus.com*
- Intel at *www.intel.com*

Answer these questions about the motherboard:

1. What is the manufacturer and model number of the motherboard?
2. What type of memory and how much memory does the board support?
3. What operating systems does the board support?
4. What processors does the board support?

REAL PROBLEM 4-2 Troubleshooting Memory

Follow the rules outlined earlier in the text to protect the computer against ESD as you work. Remove the memory module in the first memory slot on a motherboard, and boot the PC. Did you get an error? Why or why not?

REAL PROBLEM 4-3 Playing the Memory Research Game

In a group of four players with Internet access and a fifth person who is the scorekeeper, play the Memory Research Game. The scorekeeper asks a question and then gives players one minute to find the best answer. Five points are awarded to the player who has the best answer at the end of each one-minute play. The scorekeeper can use these questions or make up his or her own. If you use these questions, mix up the order:

1. What is the fastest DDR3 DIMM sold today?
2. What is the largest size DDR2 DIMM sold today?
3. What is the largest size fully buffered ECC 240-pin DDR2 DIMM sold today?
4. What is the lowest price for an 8-GB 240-pin ECC DDR3 DIMM?

CHAPTER 5

Supporting the Power System and Troubleshooting Computers

After completing this chapter, you will be able to:

- Describe the methods and devices for keeping a system cool
- Select a power supply to meet the power needs of a system
- Demonstrate an organized approach to solving any computer problem, especially hardware problems occurring during the boot
- Troubleshoot problems with the electrical system
- Troubleshoot problems with the motherboard, processor, and RAM
- Troubleshoot hardware problems with mobile devices

In the first chapters of this text, you learned much about the motherboard, processor, and RAM. This chapter focuses on how to keep these heat-producing components cool. You learn about the fans, heat sinks, and other devices needed to keep a system cool. You also learn about one more essential component of a computer system, the power supply, including how to select a power supply to meet the wattage needs of a system.

Then we focus on troubleshooting these various hardware subsystems and components. You study the troubleshooting techniques and procedures to get the full picture of what it's like to have the tools and knowledge in hand to solve any computer hardware-related problem. Then you learn to practically apply these skills to troubleshooting the electrical system, motherboard, processor, and memory. Finally, you learn about troubleshooting the hardware in mobile devices. By the end of this chapter, you should feel confident that you can face a problem with hardware and understand how to zero in on the source of the problem and its solution.

COOLING METHODS AND DEVICES

A+ 220-901 1.6

The processor, motherboard, memory modules, expansion cards, and other components in the case produce heat, and, if they get overheated, the system can get unstable and components can fail or be damaged. As a hardware technician, you need to know how to keep a system cool. Devices that are used to keep a system cool include CPU fans, case fans, coolers, heat sinks, and liquid cooling systems.

In this part of the chapter, you learn about these several methods to keep the system cool. We begin with keeping the processor cool.

PROCESSOR COOLERS, FANS, AND HEAT SINKS

A+ 220-901 1.6

Because a processor generates so much heat, computer systems use a cooling assembly designed for a specific processor to keep temperatures below the processor maximum temperature. If a processor reaches its maximum temperature, it automatically shuts down. Good processor coolers maintain a temperature of 90–110 degrees F (32–43 degrees C). The cooler (see Figure 5-1) sits on top of the processor and consists of a fan and a heat sink. A heat sink is made of metal that draws the heat away from the processor into the fins. The fan can then blow the heat away. You learned to install a cooler in the chapter, "Supporting Processors and Upgrading Memory."

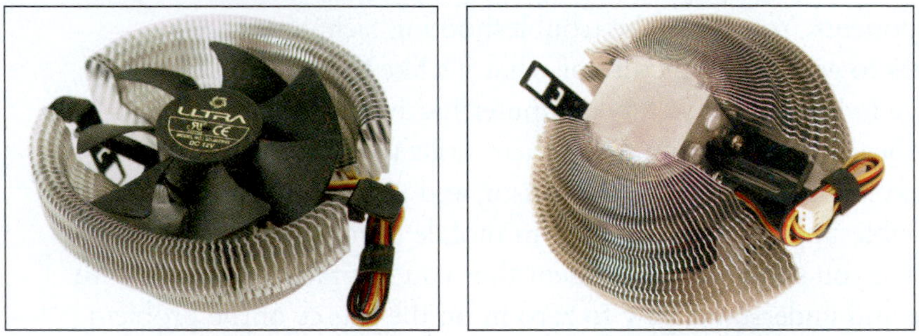

Figure 5-1 A cooler sits on top of a processor to help keep it cool

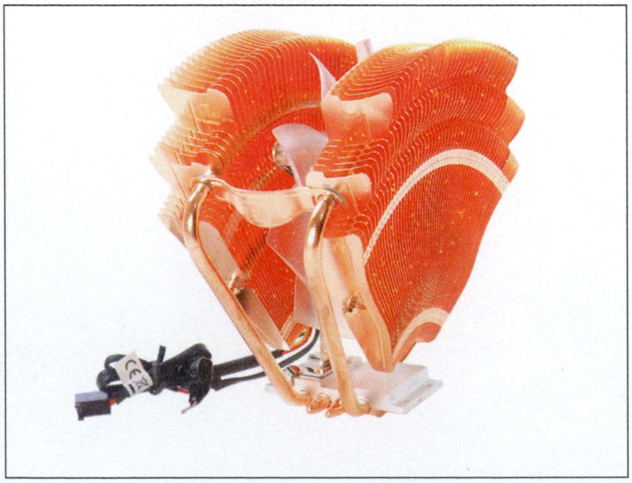

Figure 5-2 The Thermaltake V1 copper cooler fits Intel LGA1366 and LGA775 and AMD AM2 and AM2+ sockets

A cooler is made of aluminum, copper, or a combination of both. Copper is more expensive, but does a better job of conducting heat. For example, the Thermaltake (*www.thermaltake.com*) multisocket cooler shown in Figure 5-2 is made of copper and has an adjustable fan control.

Recall that the cooler is bracketed to the motherboard using a wire or plastic clip and thermal compound is placed between the bottom of the cooler heat sink and the top of the processor. To get its power, the cooler fan power cord connects to a 4-pin fan header on the motherboard (see Figure 5-3). The fan connector will have three or four holes. A three-hole connector can fit onto a 4-pin header; just ignore the last pin. A 4-pin header on the motherboard supports pulse width modulation (PWM) that controls fan speed in order to reduce the overall noise in a system. If you use a cooler fan power cord with three pins, know that the fan will always operate at the same speed.

Figure 5-3 A cooler fan gets its power from a 4-pin PWM header on the motherboard

Figure 5-4 A passive or fanless cooler uses heat pipes to dissipate heat from the CPU

For enthusiasts trying to run a desktop computer with less noise, a fanless CPU cooler, also called a passive CPU cooler, can help (see Figure 5-4). These coolers contain heat pipes, which contain a small amount of liquid that becomes a vapor when heated, and the vapor draws the heat away from the CPU toward the fins on the cooler. There the heat can be blown away by case fans. Most passive CPU coolers are very large, so before you buy one, be sure it will fit in your computer case with all other components installed. Also, most motherboards give a startup error if a cable is not attached to the CPU fan header. Because these coolers don't have a fan cable, you will need to attach another cable to the header. For some systems, you can connect a case fan to the header.

CASE FANS AND OTHER FANS AND HEAT SINKS

A+
220-901
1.6

To prevent overheating, you can also install additional case fans. Most cases have one or more positions on the case to hold a case fan to help draw air out of the case. Figure 5-5 shows holes on the rear of a case designed to hold a case fan.

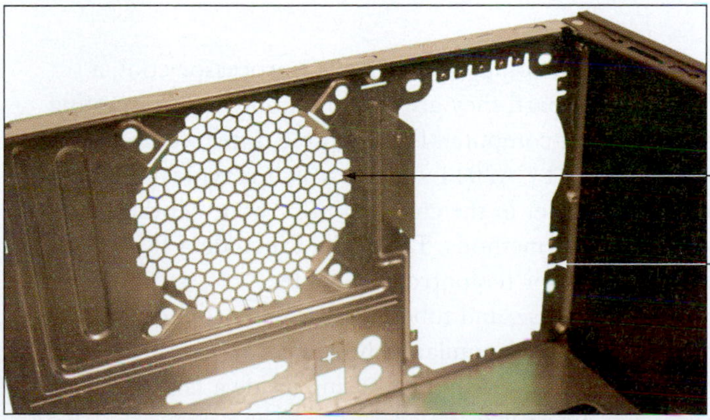

Figure 5-5 Install a case fan on the rear of this case to help keep the system cool

A computer case might need as many as seven or eight fans mounted inside the case; however, the trend is to use fewer and larger fans. Generally, large fans tend to perform better and run quieter than small fans.

Processors and video cards, also called graphics cards, are the two highest heat producers in a system. Some graphics cards come with a fan on the side of the card. You can also purchase heat sinks and fans to mount on a card to keep it cool. Another solution is to use a fan card mounted next to the graphics card. Figure 5-6 shows a PCI fan card. Be sure you select the fan card that fits the expansion slot you plan to use, and make sure there's enough clearance beside the graphics card for the fan card to fit.

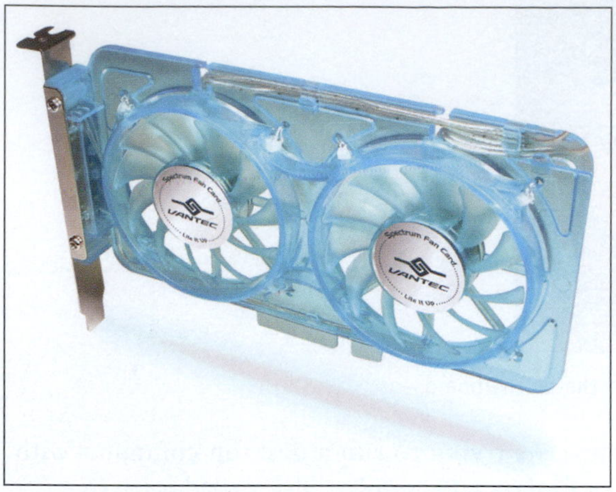

Courtesy of Vantec Thermal Technologies

Figure 5-6 A PCI fan card by Vantec can be used next to a high-end graphics card to help keep it cool

For additional cooling, consider a RAM cooler such as the one shown in Figure 5-7. It clips over a DIMM. A fan might be powered by a SATA power connector or 4-pin Molex power connector. The fan shown in Figure 5-7 uses a Molex connector. You can use an adapter to convert a SATA or Molex connector to whichever the power supply provides.

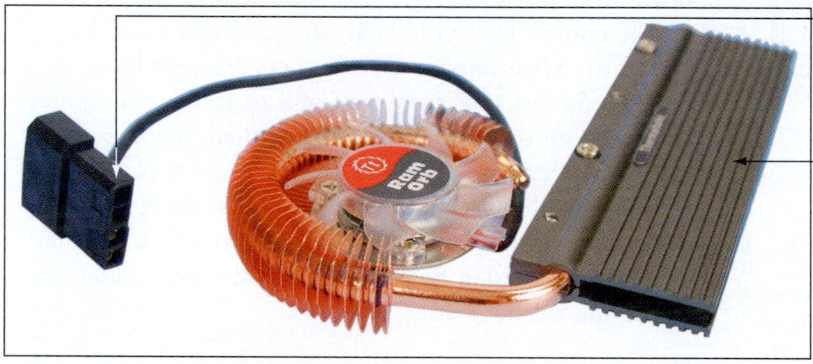

Figure 5-7 A RAM cooler keeps memory modules cool

When selecting any fan or cooler, take into consideration the added noise level and the ease of installation. Some coolers and fans can use a temperature sensor that controls the fan. Also consider the guarantee made by the cooler or fan manufacturer.

LIQUID COOLING SYSTEMS

A+ 220-901 1.6

In addition to using fans, heat sinks, and thermal compound to keep a processor cool, a liquid cooling system can be used. For the most part, they are used by hobbyists attempting to overclock to the max a processor in a gaming computer. For example, Intel recommends a liquid cooling system for processors that use the LGA2011 socket, which is typically used on hobbyist and gaming computers. (You learned about this socket in the chapter, "All About Motherboards.") Liquid cooling systems tend to run quieter than other cooling methods. They might include a PCIe or PCI card that has a power supply, temperature sensor, and processor to control the cooler.

Using liquid cooling, a small pump sits inside the computer case, and tubes move liquid around components and then away from them to a place where fans can cool the liquid, similar to how a car radiator works. Figure 5-8 shows one liquid cooling system where the liquid is cooled by fans sitting inside a large case. Sometimes, however, the liquid is pumped outside the case, where it is cooled.

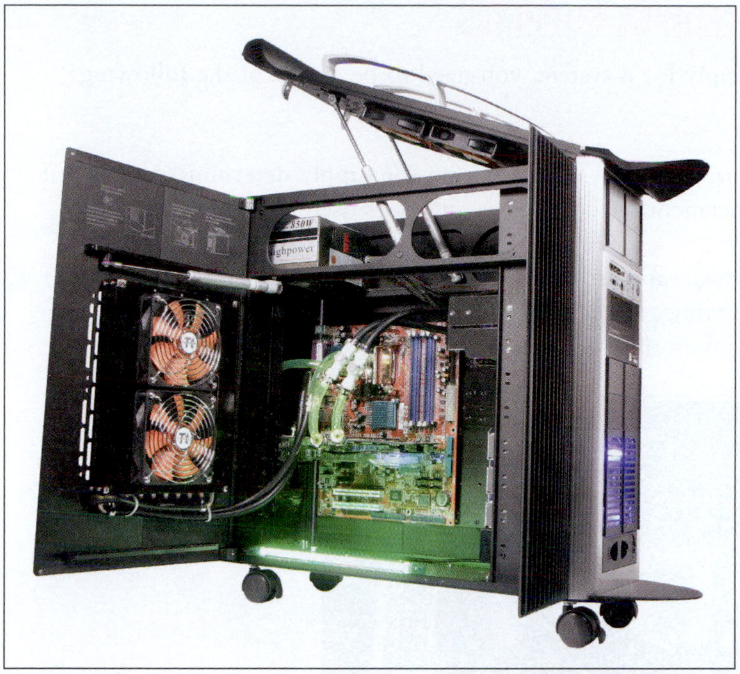

Courtesy of Thermaltake (USA) Inc.

Figure 5-8 A liquid cooling system pumps liquid outside and away from components where fans can then cool the liquid

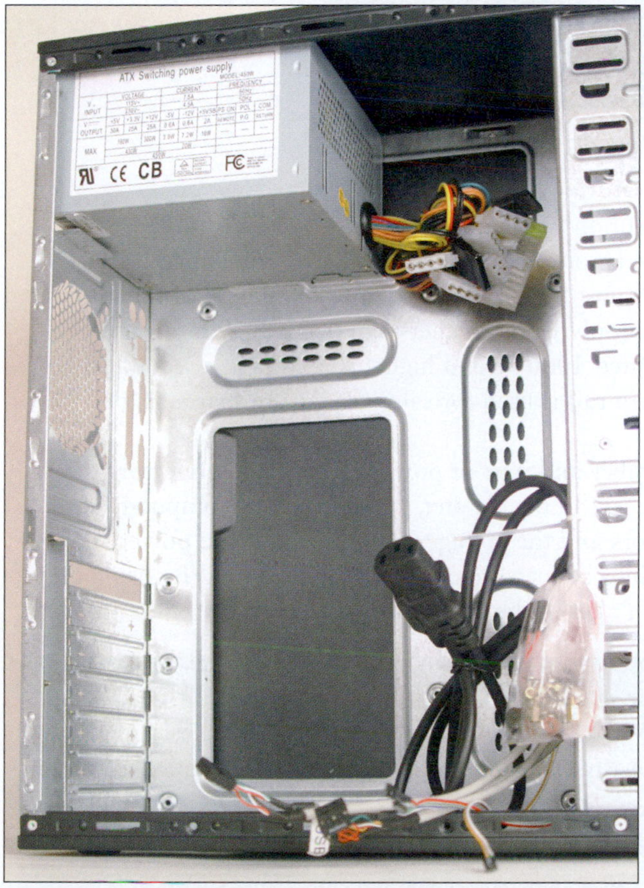

Figure 5-9 This case comes with a power supply, power cord, and bag of screws

Now let's turn our attention to the power supply.

SELECTING A POWER SUPPLY

A+
220-901
1.2, 1.8

In the chapter, "Working Inside Desktop Computers and Laptops," you learned how to uninstall and install a power supply unit (PSU). Reasons you might need to replace a power supply are when a power supply fails, or the power supply in an existing system is not adequate for the system. When building a new system, you can purchase a computer case with the power supply already installed (see Figure 5-9), or you can purchase a power supply separate from the case.

TYPES AND CHARACTERISTICS OF POWER SUPPLIES

A+
220-901
1.2, 1.8

As you select the right power supply for a system, you need to be aware of the following power supply features:

- *ATX or microATX form factor*. The form factor of a power supply determines the size of the power supply and the placement of screw holes and slots used to anchor the power supply to the case.
- *Wattage ratings*. A power supply has a wattage rating for total output maximum load (for example, 500 W, 850 W, or 1000 W) and individual wattage ratings for each of the voltage output circuits. These wattage capacities are listed in the documentation and on the side of a power supply, as shown in Figure 5-10.

Figure 5-10 Consider the number and type of power connectors and the wattage ratings of a power supply

When selecting a power supply, pay particular attention to the capacity for the +12 V rail. (A *rail* is the term used to describe each circuit provided by the power supply.) The +12 V rail is the most used, especially in high-end gaming systems. Notice in Figure 5-10, the +12 V rail gets 360 W of the maximum 525 W load. Sometimes you need to use a power supply with a higher-than-needed overall wattage to get enough wattage on this one rail. Also, a PSU rated 1000 W and higher might have a second +12 V rail and is called a dual rail power supply. The extra rail is used for safety to ensure that a single +12 V rail is not overloaded.

- *Number and type of connectors*. Consider the number and type of power cables and connectors the unit provides. Connector types are shown in Table 1-2 in the chapter, "First Look at Computer Parts and Tools." Table 5-1 lists some common connectors and the voltages they supply. Some power supplies include detached power cables that you can plug into connectors on the side of the unit. By using only the power cables you need, extra power cables don't get in the way of airflow inside the computer case.

Connector	Voltages	Description
SATA	+3.3 V, +5 V, +12 V	Power to SATA drives, 5 pin
Molex	+5 V, +12 V	Power to older IDE drives and used with some older SATA drives, 4 pin
4/8-pin 12 V	+12 V	Auxiliary power to CPU
PCIe 6/8 pin	+12 V	Auxiliary power to PCIe cards
20-pin P1	+3.3 V, ±5 V, ±12 V	Older main power connector to motherboard
24-pin P1	+3.3 V, ±5 V, ±12 V	Newer main power connector to motherboard

Table 5-1 Power supply connectors and voltages

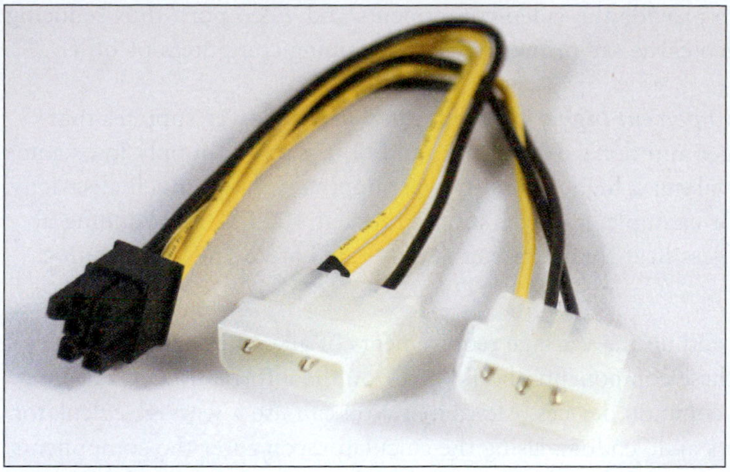

Figure 5-11 This adapter converts two Molex cables to a single 12 V 6-pin PCIe connector

★ A+ Exam Tip The A+ 220-901 exam expects you to know the voltage output of the power connectors listed in Table 5-1. Consider memorizing the table.

Notes If a power supply doesn't have the connector you need, it is likely you can buy an adapter to convert one connector to another. For example, Figure 5-11 shows an adapter that converts two Molex cables to one 12 V 6-pin PCIe connector.

5

- *Fans inside the PSU.* Every power supply has a fan inside its case; some have two fans. The fan can be mounted on the back or top of the PSU. Fans range in size from 80mm to 150mm wide. The larger the fan, the better job it does and the quieter it runs. Some PSUs can automatically adjust the fan speed based on the internal temperature of the system.

Notes Some power supplies are designed without fans so that they can be used in home theater systems or other areas where quiet operation is a requirement.

- *Dual voltage options.* Expect a power supply to have a dual-voltage selector switch on the back where you can switch input voltage to 115 V for the United States or 220 V for other countries.
- *Extra features.* Consider the warranty of the power supply and the overall quality. Some power supplies are designed to support two video cards used in a gaming computer. Two technologies used for dual video cards are SLI by NVIDIA and Crossfire by AMD. If you plan to use dual video cards, use a PSU that supports SLI or Crossfire used by the video cards. Know that more expensive power supplies are quieter, last longer, and don't put off as much heat as less expensive ones. Also, expect a good power supply to protect the system against overvoltage. A power supply rated with Active PFC runs more efficiently and uses less electricity than other power supplies.

HOW TO CALCULATE WATTAGE CAPACITY

A+
220-901
1.2, 1.8

When deciding what wattage capacity you need for the power supply, consider the total wattage requirements of all components inside the case as well as USB and FireWire devices that get their power from ports connected to the motherboard.

★ A+ Exam Tip The A+ 220-901 exam expects you to know how to select and install a power supply. You need to know how to decide on the wattage, connectors, and form factor of the power supply.

Keep these two points in mind when selecting the correct wattage capacity for a power supply:

- *Video cards draw the most power.* Video cards draw the most power in a system, and they draw from the +12 V output. If your system has a video card, pay particular attention to the +12 V rating.

The current trend is for the motherboard to provide the video components and video port, thus reducing the overall wattage needs for a system. Video cards are primarily used in gaming computers or other systems that require high-quality graphics.

- ***The power supply should be rated about 30 percent higher than expected needs.*** Power supplies that run at less than peak performance last longer and don't overheat. In addition, a power supply loses some of its capacity over time. Also, don't worry about a higher-rated power supply using too much electricity. Components only draw what they need. For example, a power supply rated at 1000 W and running at a 500 W draw will last longer and give off less heat than a power supply rated at 750 W and running at a 500 W draw.

To know what size power supply you need, add up the wattage requirements of all components, and add 30 percent. Technical documentation for these components should give you the information you need. Table 5-2 lists appropriate wattage ratings for common devices. Alternately, you can use a wattage calculator provided on the website of many manufacturers and vendors. Using the calculator, you enter the components in your system and then the calculator will recommend the wattage you need for your power supply.

Devices	Approximate Wattage
Motherboard, processor, memory, keyboard, and mouse	200–300 W
Fan	5 W
SATA hard drive	15–30 W
DVD/CD drive	20–30 W
PCI video card	50 W
PCI card (network card, FireWire card, or other PCI card)	20 W
PCIe ×16 video card	150–300 W
PCIe ×16 card other than a video card	100 W

Table 5-2 To calculate the power supply rating you need, add up total wattage

Caution Some older Dell motherboards and power supplies do not use the standard P1 pinouts for ATX, although the power connectors look the same. For this reason, never use a Dell power supply with a non-Dell motherboard, or a Dell motherboard with a non-Dell power supply, without first verifying that the power connector pinouts match; otherwise, you might destroy the power supply, the motherboard, or both.

Table 5-3 lists a few case and power supply manufacturers.

Manufacturer	Website
Antec	*www.antec.com*
Cooler Master	*www.coolermaster.com*
EVGA	*www.evga.com*
FirePower Technology	*www.firepower-technology.com*
Rosewill	*www.rosewill.com*
Sentey	*www.sentey.com*
Silverstone	*www.silverstonetek.com*
Thermaltake	*www.thermaltakeusa.com*
Zalman	*www.zalman.com*

Table 5-3 Manufacturers of cases and power supplies for personal computers

Hands-On Project 5-1 Calculate Wattage Capacity for Your System

A+
220-901
1.8

Do the following to compare the wattage capacity of the power supply installed in your computer with the recommended value:

1. Search the web for a power supply wattage calculator. Be sure the one you use is provided by a reliable website. For example, the ones at *newegg.com* and *extreme.outervision.com* are reliable. (At *newegg.com*, click **Computer Hardware** and then click **Power Supply Wattage Calculator**. At *extreme.outervision.com*, click **eXtreme Power Supply Calculator**.)
2. Enter the information about your computer system. Print or save the webpage showing the resulting calculations.
3. What is the recommended wattage capacity for a power supply for your system?
4. Look on the printed label on the power supply currently installed in your computer. What is its wattage capacity?
5. If you had to replace the power supply in your system, what wattage capacity would you select?

Hands-On Project 5-2 Shop for a Power Supply

A+
220-901
1.8

Shop online for a power supply to meet the needs of each of the following systems. Print or save the webpage showing the power supply, its features, and its price:

1. A regular desktop system for light computing has a moderately priced motherboard and processor, onboard video, two SATA hard drives, a DVD-RW drive, and two case fans. The system needs a microATX power supply rated at least 450 W.
2. A file server has a high-end motherboard and processor using the LGA2011 socket, 8 modules of DDR4 RAM, onboard video, one SSD SATA hard drive, five magnetic SATA hard drives, DVD-RW drive, tape drive, PCI RAID card, and four fans. The system needs an ATX power supply rated at about 550 W.
3. A gaming system has a high-end motherboard and processor, two high-end video cards using SLI technology, two SATA hard drives, a Blu-ray drive, and four fans. The system needs an ATX power supply rated at about 800 W. The two high-end video cards require about 275 W each.
4. Suppose the gaming system in Number 3 is generating extra heat because of overclocking and a liquid cooling system has been installed. To account for the needs of the liquid cooling system, the power supply needs to be upgraded to 1800 W.

So far in the text, you have learned about motherboards, processors, RAM, and the electrical system, which are the principal hardware components of a computer. With this hardware foundation in place, you're ready to learn about computer troubleshooting. Let's start with an overview of how to approach any hardware problem, and then we'll turn our attention to the details of troubleshooting the electrical system, motherboard, RAM, and CPU.

HOW TO APPROACH A HARDWARE PROBLEM

A+
220-901
3.0, 4.1

A good IT support technician over time builds a strong network of resources he or she can count on when solving computer problems. Here are some resources to help you get started with your own list of reliable and time-tested sources of help:

- *The web*. Do a web search on an error message, short description of the problem, or model and manufacturer of a device to get all sorts of help on the web. Check out the website of the product manufacturer or search a support forum. It's likely that others have encountered the same problem and posted the question and answer. If you search and cannot find your answer, you can post a new question. *Youtube.com* videos might help. Many technicians enjoy sharing what they know online, but be careful, however. Not all technical advice is correct or well intentioned.
- *Chat, forums, or email technical support*. Support from the hardware and software manufacturers can help you interpret an error message or provide general support in diagnosing a problem. Most technical support is available during working hours by way of an online chat session.
- *Manufacturer's diagnostic software*. Many hardware device manufacturers provide diagnostic software, which is available for download from their websites. For example, you can download Diagnostic Tools (can be used to copy all data from a drive that won't boot to another device), SeaTools for Windows (must be installed in Windows), or SeaTools for DOS (used to create a bootable CD that contains the software) and use the software to diagnose problems with Seagate and Maxtor drives. See Figure 5-12. Search the support section of a manufacturer's website to find diagnostic software and guidelines for using it.

Notes Always check compatibility between utility software and the operating system you plan to use.

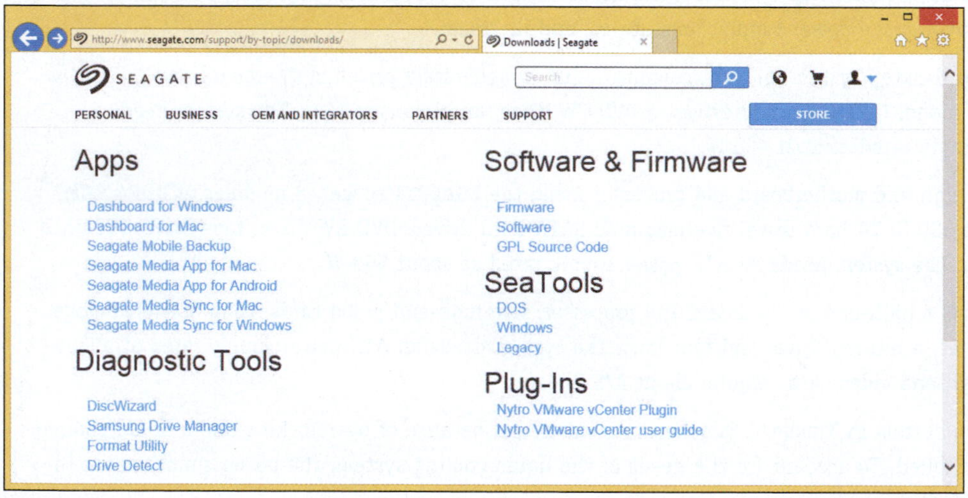

Source: www.seagate.com

Figure 5-12 Download diagnostic software tools from a manufacturer's website

- *User manuals*. Refer to your user manuals, which often list error messages and their meanings. They also might contain a troubleshooting section and list any diagnostic tools available.
- *Technical associates in your organization can help*. Be sure to ask for advice when you're stuck. Also, after making a reasonable and diligent effort to resolve a problem, getting the problem fixed could become more important than resolving it yourself. There comes a time when you might need to turn the problem over to a more experienced technician. (In an organization, this process is called escalating the problem.)

Next, let's examine the six-step model for computer troubleshooting. You'll learn much more about these steps in later chapters. Keep in mind, however, that these steps are only the beginning of computer troubleshooting. As an IT technician, expect that you will build your own style and steps for troubleshooting based on your own experiences over time.

STEP 1: INTERVIEW THE USER

A+ 220-901 4.1

When an end user brings any computer problem to you, begin the troubleshooting process by interviewing the user. When you interview the user, you might want to include these questions:

- Can you describe the problem and describe when the problem first started and when it occurs?
- Was the computer recently moved?
- Was any new hardware or software recently installed?
- Was any software recently reconfigured or upgraded?
- Did someone else use your computer recently?
- Does the computer have a history of similar problems?
- Is there important data on the drive that is not backed up?
- Can you show me how to reproduce the problem?

After you gather this basic information, you can prioritize what to do and begin diagnosing and addressing the problem. If the computer will not start or starts with errors so that you cannot reach the Windows desktop, setting priorities helps focus your work. For most users, data is the first priority unless they have a recent backup.

STEP 2: BACK UP DATA AS NEEDED

A+ 220-901 4.1

If the hard drive has important data on it that has not been backed up, your first priority is most likely to recover the data. Here are three options for doing that:

- ***Move the hard drive to another system.*** If a system won't boot from the hard drive, consider removing the drive and installing it as a second drive in a working system. If the file system on the problem drive is intact, you might be able to copy data from the drive to the primary drive in the working system.

  To move the hard drive to a working computer, you don't need to physically install the drive in the drive bay. Open the computer case. Carefully lay the drive on the case and connect a power cord and data cable (see Figure 5-13). Then turn on the computer. While you have the computer turned on, be *very careful* to not touch the drive or touch inside the case. Also, while a tower case is lying on its side like the one in Figure 5-13, don't use the optical drive.

Figure 5-13 Move a hard drive to a working computer to recover data on the drive

Start the computer and sign in to Windows using an Administrator account. (If you don't sign in with an Administrator account, you must provide the password to an Administrator account before you can access the files on the newly connected hard drive.) When Windows finds the new drive, it assigns it a drive letter. Use Explorer in Windows 8/7/Vista or third-party software to copy files from this drive to the primary hard drive in this system or to another storage media. Then return the drive to the original system and turn your attention to solving the original problem.

Notes An easier way to temporarily install a hard drive in a system is to use a USB port. Figure 5-14 shows a SATA-to-USB converter kit. The SATA connector can be used for desktop or laptop hard drives because a SATA connector is the same for both. A SATA-to-USB converter is really handy when recovering data and troubleshooting problems with hard drives that refuse to boot.

Figure 5-14 Use a USB-to-SATA converter to recover data from a drive using a SATA connector

- *Use file recovery software.* File recovery software is third-party software that can help recover deleted and corrupted files. On the Internet, do a search on "data recovery" for lots of examples. One good product is GetDataBack by Runtime Software (*www.runtime.org*), which can recover data and program files even when Windows cannot recognize the drive. Another example is Seagate Recovery Services (see Figure 5-15), which includes various tools and services, including file recovery software PC Trial.

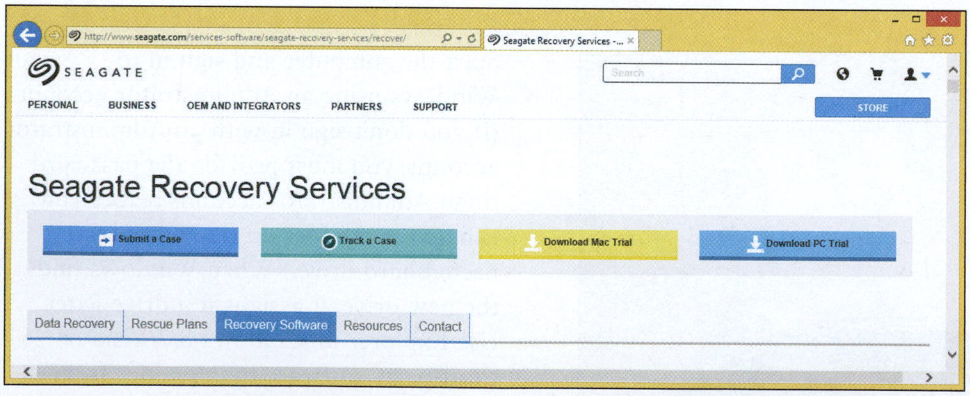

Source: www.seagate.com

Figure 5-15 File recovery software made available by Seagate, a hard drive manufacturer

- *Hire a professional file recovery service.* If your data is extremely valuable and other methods have failed, you might want to consider a professional data recovery service. They're expensive, but getting the data back might be worth it. To find a service, do a web search on "data recovery." Before selecting a service, be sure to read reviews, understand the warranty and guarantees, and perhaps get a recommendation from a satisfied customer. For example, in Figure 5-15, click **Data Recovery** to see a description of the service offered by Seagate.

STEP 3: EXAMINE THE SYSTEM AND ESTABLISH A THEORY

A+ 220-901 4.1

After data is secure, you're ready to tackle the problem and its solution. Most computer problems are simple and can be simply solved, but you do need a game plan. That's how Figure 5-16 can help. The flowchart focuses on problems that affect the boot. As you work your way through it, you're eliminating one major computer subsystem after another until you zero in on the problem. After you've discovered the problem, many times the solution is obvious.

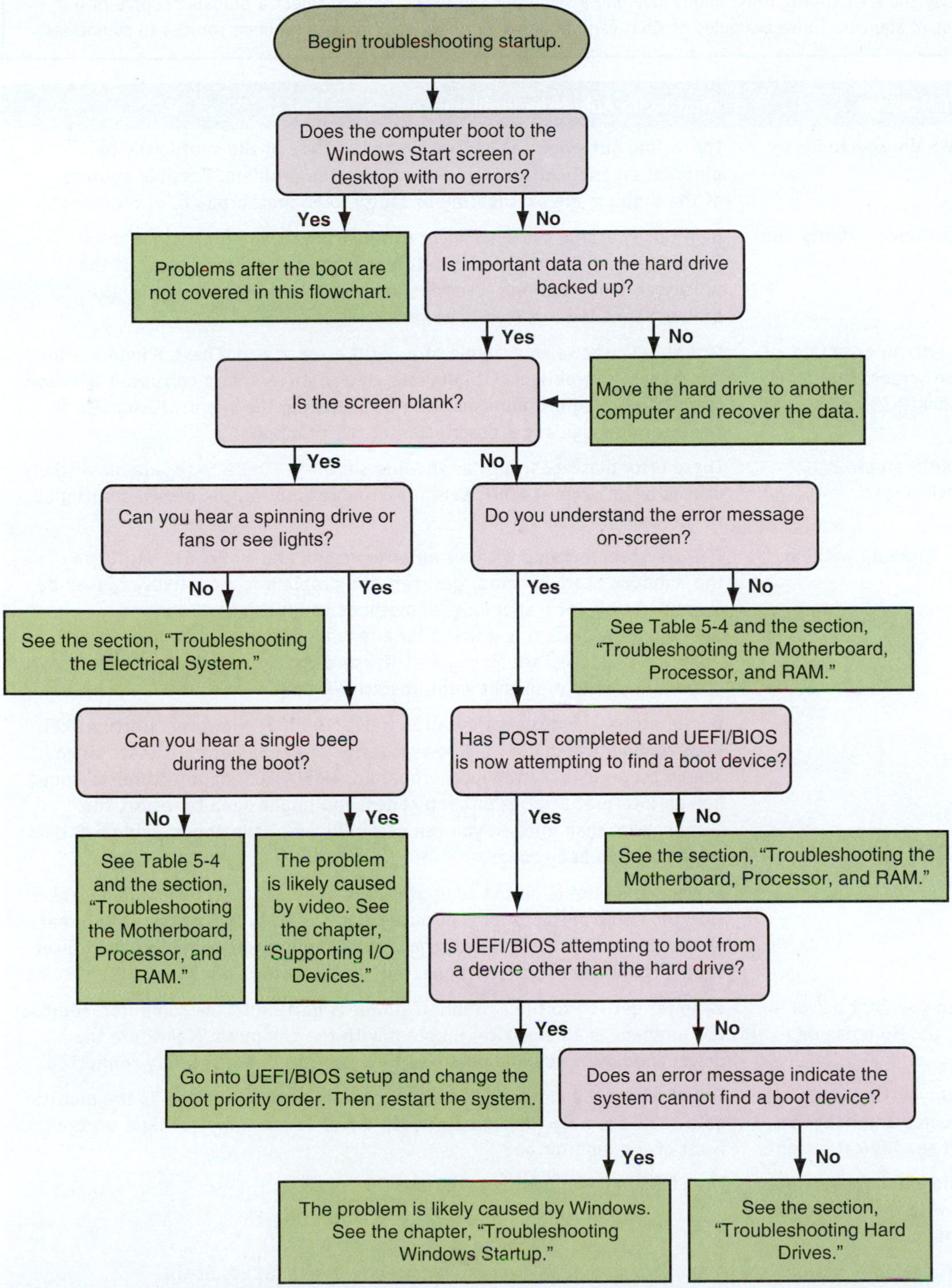

Figure 5-16 Use this flowchart when first facing a computer problem

As Figure 5-16 indicates, troubleshooting a computer problem is divided into problems that occur during the boot and those that occur after the Windows Start screen or desktop has successfully loaded. Problems that occur during the boot might happen before Windows starts to load or during Windows startup. Read the flowchart in Figure 5-16 very carefully to get an idea of the symptoms you might be faced with that would cause you to suspect each subsystem.

Also, Table 5-4 can help as a general guideline for the primary symptoms and what are likely to be the sources of a problem.

★ A+ Exam Tip The A+ 220-902 exam might give you a symptom and expect you to select a probable source of a problem from a list of sources. These examples of what can go wrong can help you connect problem sources to symptoms.

Symptom or Error Message	What to Do About the Problem
System shuts down unexpectedly	Try to find out what was happening at the time of the shutdowns to pinpoint an application or device causing the problem. Possible sources of the problem are overheating or faulty RAM, motherboard, or processor.
System shuts down unexpectedly and starts back up	Begin by checking the system for overheating. Is the processor cooler fan working? Go to UEFI/BIOS setup and check the temperature of the processor. When the processor overheats and the system restarts, the problem is called a processor thermal trip error.
System locks up with an error message on a blue screen, called a blue screen of death (BSOD)	Figure 5-17 shows an example of a BSOD error screen. These Windows errors are caused by problems with devices, device drivers, or a corrupted Windows installation. Begin troubleshooting by searching the Microsoft website for the error message and a description of the problem.
System locks up with an error message on a black screen	These error messages, such as the one shown in Figure 5-18, are most likely caused by an error at POST. Begin by troubleshooting the device mentioned in the error message.
System freezes or locks up without an error message	If the system locks up without an error screen and while still displaying the Windows Start screen or desktop, the problem is most likely caused by an application not responding. Sometimes you'll see the Windows pinwheel indicating the system is waiting for a response from a program or device. Open the Windows Task Manager utility and end any application that is not responding. If that doesn't work, restart Windows.
POST code beeps	One or no beep indicates that all is well after POST. However, startup UEFI/BIOS communicates POST errors as a series of beeps before it tests video. Search the website of the motherboard or UEFI/BIOS manufacturer to know how to interpret a series of beep codes. You might need to restart the system more than once so you can carefully count the beeps. Table 5-5 lists some common beep codes.
No power	If you see no lights on the computer case and hear no spinning fans, make sure the surge protector or wall outlet has power. Is the switch on the rear of the case on? Is the dual voltage selector switch set correctly? Are power supply connectors securely connected? Is the power supply bad?
Blank screen when you first power up the computer, and no noise or indicator lights	Is power getting to the system? If power is getting to the computer, address the problem as an electrical problem with the computer. Make sure the power supply is good and power supply connectors are securely connected.
Blank screen when you first power up the computer, and you can hear the fans spinning and see indicator lights	Troubleshoot the video subsystem. Is the monitor turned on? Is the monitor data cable securely connected at both ends? Is the indicator light on the front of the monitor on?
BIOS loses its time and date settings "CMOS battery low" error message appears during the boot	The CMOS battery is failing. Replace the battery.
System reports less memory than you know is installed	A memory module is not seated correctly or has failed. Begin troubleshooting memory.

Table 5-4 Symptoms or error messages caused by hardware problems and what to do about them (continues)

Symptom or Error Message	What to Do About the Problem
System attempts to boot to the wrong boot device	Go into UEFI/BIOS setup and change the boot device priority order.
Fans spin, but no power to other devices	Begin by checking the power supply. Are connectors securely connected? Use a power supply tester to check for correct voltage outputs.
Smoke or burning smell	Consider this a serious electrical problem. Immediately unplug the computer.
Loud whining noise	Most likely the noise is made by the power supply or a failing hard drive. There might be a short. The power supply might be going bad or is underrated for the system.
Clicking noise	A clicking noise likely indicates the hard drive is failing. Replace the drive as soon as possible.
Intermittent device failures	Failures that come and go might be caused by overheating or failing RAM, the motherboard, processor, or hard drive. Begin by checking the processor temperature for overheating. Then check RAM for errors and run diagnostics on the hard drive.
Distended capacitors	Failed capacitors on the motherboard or other circuit board are sometimes distended and discolored on the top of the capacitor. Replace the motherboard.
Error appears during boot: *Intruder detection error*	An intrusion detection device installed on the motherboard has detected that the computer case was opened. Suspect a security breach.
Error appears during boot: *Overclocking failed. Please enter setup to reconfigure your system*	Overclocking should be discontinued. However, this error might not be related to overclocking; it can occur when the power supply is failing.
Possible error messages: *No boot device available* *Hard drive not found* *Fixed disk error* *Invalid boot disk* *Inaccessible boot device or drive* *Invalid drive specification*	Startup BIOS did not find a device to use to load the operating system. Make sure the boot device priority order is correct in BIOS setup. Then begin troubleshooting the hard drive.
Possible error messages: *Missing operating system* *Error loading operating system*	Windows startup programs are missing or corrupted. How to troubleshoot Windows startup is covered in the chapter, "Troubleshooting Windows Startup."
Continuous reboots	See explanation later in this chapter.

Table 5-4 Symptoms or error messages caused by hardware problems and what to do about them (continued)

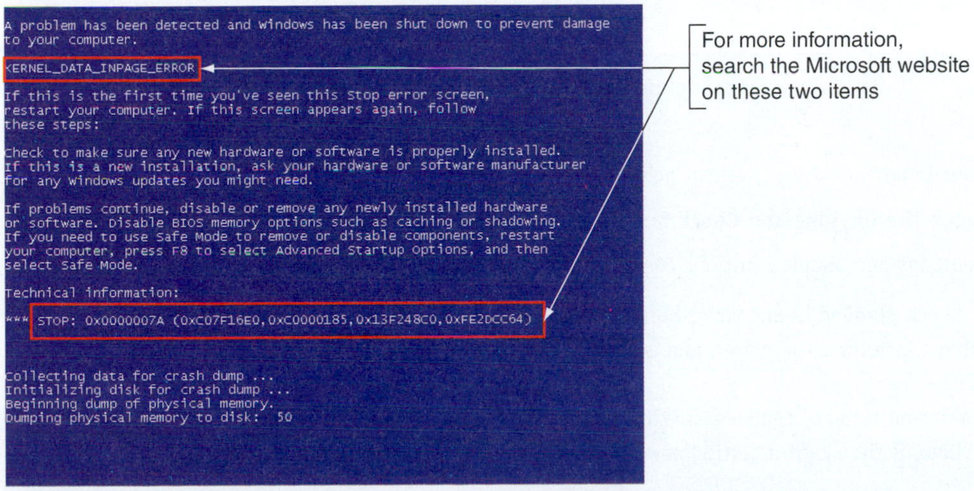

Figure 5-17 Search the Microsoft website for information about a BSOD error

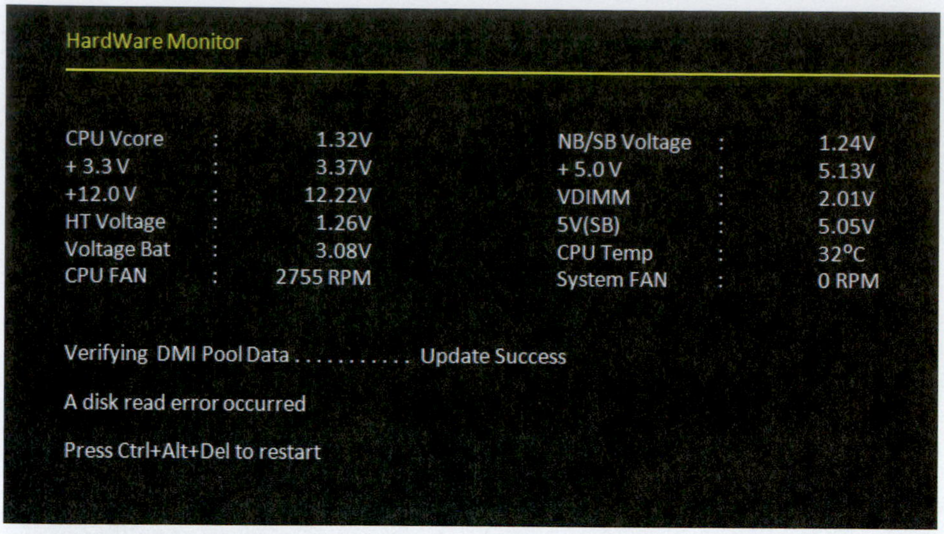

Source: Intel

Figure 5-18 A POST error message on a black screen shown early in the boot

Beeps During POST	Description
1 short beep or no beep	The computer passed all POST tests
1 long and 2 short beeps	Award BIOS: A video problem, no video card, bad video memory Intel BIOS: A video problem
Continuous short beeps	Award BIOS: A memory error Intel BIOS: A loose card or short
1 long and 1 short beep	Intel BIOS: Motherboard problem
1 long and 3 short beeps	Intel BIOS: A video problem
3 long beeps	Intel BIOS: A keyboard controller problem
Continuous 2 short beeps and then a pause	Intel BIOS: A video card problem
Continuous 3 short beeps and then a pause	Intel BIOS: A memory error
8 beeps followed by a system shutdown	Intel BIOS: The system has overheated
Continuous high and low beeps	Intel BIOS: CPU problem

Table 5-5 Common beep codes and their meanings for Intel and Award BIOS

APPLYING | CONCEPTS FOUR TROUBLESHOOTING RULES

A+ 220-901 4.1

Here are four important rules that can help you solve many hardware problems:

Rule 1: Check the Obvious and Check Simple Things First

Check for obvious and simple solutions first. Here are some tips:

- Is the external device plugged in and turned on? Are the data cable connections solid at both ends? Is there a wall light switch controlling the power, and is it turned on? Is the surge suppressor you're using plugged in and turned on?
- For expansion cards and memory modules, are they seated solidly in their slots? For sound, is the volume knob turned up? For video, is the monitor getting power, turned on, connected, and is the screen resolution correct?

- Consider the application using the device. For example, if you are having problems trying to use a USB scanner, try scanning using a different application.

Rule 2: Trade Known Good for Suspected Bad

When diagnosing hardware problems, this method works well if you can draw from a group of parts that you know work correctly. Suppose, for example, video does not work. The parts of the video subsystem are the video card, the power cord to the monitor, the cord from the monitor to the computer case, and the monitor itself. Also, don't forget that the video card is inserted into an expansion slot on the motherboard, and the monitor depends on electrical power. As you suspect each of these five components to be bad, you can try them one at a time beginning with the easiest one to replace: the monitor. Trade the monitor for one that you know works. If this theory fails, trade the power cord, trade the cord to the computer's video port, move the video card to a new slot, and trade the video card. When you're trading a good component for a suspected bad one, work methodically by eliminating one component at a time.

Rule 3: Trade Suspected Bad for Known Good

An alternate approach works well in certain situations. If you have a working computer that is configured similarly to the one you are troubleshooting (a common situation in many corporate or educational environments), rather than trading good for suspected bad, you can trade suspected bad for good. Take each component that you suspect is bad and install it in the working computer. If the component works on the good computer, then you have eliminated it as a suspect. If the working computer breaks down, then you have probably identified the bad component.

Rule 4: Divide and Conquer

Isolate the problem. In the overall system, remove one hardware or software component after another, until the problem is isolated to a small part of the whole system. As you divide a large problem into smaller components, you can analyze each component separately. You can use one or more of the following to help you divide and conquer on your own system:

- In Windows, stop all nonessential services running in the background to eliminate them as the problem.
- Boot from a bootable DVD to eliminate the OS and startup files on the hard drive as the problem.
- Remove any unnecessary hardware devices, such as a second video card, optical drive, and even the hard drive.

Once down to the essentials, start exchanging components you know are good for those you suspect are bad, until the problem goes away. You don't need to physically remove the optical drive or hard drive from the bays inside the case. Simply disconnect the data cable and the power cable.

STEPS 4, 5, AND 6: FIX THE PROBLEM, VERIFY THE FIX, AND DOCUMENT THE OUTCOME

A+
220-901
4.1

After you understand the problem, you're ready to plan steps to resolve the problem. After the fix, be sure to verify the system works. Perform one last hard boot and make sure everything works as expected. If you're working with a user, ask the user to also verify the problem is fixed. In addition, ask yourself if anything could have been done to prevent the problem from happening in the first place. If so, take preventive action. Finally, most organizations require troubleshooting a computer problem be documented in a call tracking or help desk application where you are expected to record your findings, actions, and outcomes. Throughout the rest of this text, you'll have many opportunities to practice the troubleshooting skills introduced here.

Hands-On | Project 5-3 Research Beep Codes

A+
220-901
4.1

Identify the motherboard and UEFI/BIOS version installed in your computer. Locate the motherboard user guide on the web and find the list of beep codes that the UEFI/BIOS might give at POST. If the manual doesn't give this information, search the support section on the website of the motherboard manufacturer or search the website of the UEFI/BIOS manufacturer. List the beep codes and their meanings for your motherboard.

SPECIAL CONCERNS WHEN TROUBLESHOOTING MOBILE DEVICE HARDWARE

A+
220-901
3.0

When a component on a laptop or other mobile device needs replacing or upgrading, first you need to consider the warranty and how much time the repair will take. Before you decide to upgrade or repair an internal component, take into consideration these three alternatives:

- ***Return the mobile device to the manufacturer or another service center for repair.*** If the mobile device is under warranty, you need to return it to the manufacturer to do any serious repair work such as fixing a broken LCD panel on a laptop. However, for simple repair and upgrade tasks, such as upgrading memory or exchanging a hard drive on a laptop, most likely you can do these simple jobs by yourself without concern for voiding a warranty. Manufacturers allow a user to exchange the hard drive or memory when these components are accessible by way of a door or cover on the bottom of the laptop and it's not necessary to open the case. If you're not sure about the possibility of voiding the warranty, check with the manufacturer before you begin working on the mobile device. If the device is not under warranty and you don't have the experience or time to fix a broken component, find out how much the manufacturer will charge to do the job. Also, consider taking the device to a mobile device repair shop. Know that some mobile device manufacturers refuse to sell internal components or service manuals that explain how to take the device apart except to authorized service centers. In this case, you have few options but to use the authorized service center for repairs.

Caution Before you send a laptop or other device for repairs, if possible, back up any important data on the device. It's possible the service center will format the hard drive or install a new drive on a laptop or do a factory reset for a mobile device.

- ***Substitute an external component for an internal component.*** Replacing components on mobile devices can be time consuming and require a lot of patience. For a laptop, consider using BIOS setup to disable an internal component and then use an external device in its place. For example, if a keyboard fails, you can use a wireless keyboard with an access point connected to the USB port. Also, if the Ethernet port fails, the simplest solution might be to disable the port and use a USB network adapter to provide the Ethernet port.
- ***Replace the internal device.*** Before deciding to replace an internal device that is not easy to get to, such as an LCD panel in a laptop, first find out if you can get the manufacturer documentation necessary to know how to open the laptop case and exchange the component. Also consider if the cost of parts and labor is worth more than the value of the device. Buying a new device might be the best solution for your customer.

Notes Check out *www.ifixit.com* for directions for device teardowns and repairs. You can also buy on the site the specific tools you might need for a teardown.

Now you're ready to look at how to troubleshoot each subsystem that is critical to booting up the computer. We begin with the electrical system.

TROUBLESHOOTING THE ELECTRICAL SYSTEM

APPLYING | CONCEPTS

A+
220-901
4.1

Your friend Sharon calls to ask for your help with a computer problem. Her system has been working fine for over a year, but now strange things are happening. Sometimes the system powers down for no apparent reason while she is working, and sometimes Windows locks up. As you read this section, look for clues as to what the problem might be. Also, as you read, think of questions to ask your friend that will help you diagnose the problem.

A+
220-901
4.1

Electrical problems can occur before or after the boot and can be consistent or intermittent. Many times repair technicians don't recognize the cause of a problem to be electrical because of the intermittent nature of some electrical problems. In these situations, the hard drive, memory, the OS, or even user error might be suspected as the source of the problem and then systematically eliminated before the electrical system is suspected. This section will help you to be aware of symptoms of electrical problems so that you can zero in on the source of an electrical problem as quickly as possible.

Possible symptoms of a problem with the electrical system are:

- The computer appears "dead"—no indicator lights and no spinning drive or fan.
- The computer sometimes locks up during booting. After several tries, it boots successfully.
- Error codes or beeps occur during booting, but they come and go.
- You smell burnt parts or odors. (Definitely not a good sign!)
- The computer powers down at unexpected times.
- The computer appears dead, but you hear a whine coming from the power supply.

Without opening the computer case, the following list contains some questions you can ask and things you can do to solve a problem with the electrical system. The rule of thumb is "try the simple things first." Most computer problems have simple solutions.

- If you smell any burnt parts or odors, don't try to turn the system on. Identify the component that is fried and replace it.
- When you first plug up power to a system and hear a whine coming from the power supply, the power supply might be inadequate for the system or there might be a short. Don't press the power button to start up the system. Unplug the power cord so that the power supply will not be damaged. The next step is to open the case and search for a short. If you don't find a short, consider upgrading the power supply.
- Is the power cord plugged in? If it is plugged into a power strip or surge suppressor, is the device turned on and also plugged in?
- Is the power outlet controlled by a wall switch? If so, is the switch turned on?
- Are any cable connections loose?
- Is the circuit breaker blown? Is the house circuit overloaded?
- Are all switches on the system turned on? Computer? Monitor? Surge suppressor or UPS (uninterruptible power supply)?
- Is there a possibility the system has overheated? If so, wait a while and try again. If the system comes on, but later turns itself off, you might need additional cooling fans inside the unit. How to solve problems with overheating is covered later in this chapter.
- Older computers might be affected by electromagnetic interference (EMI). Check for sources of electrical or magnetic interference such as fluorescent lighting or an electric fan or copier sitting near the computer case.

Caution Before opening the case of a brand name computer, such as a Gateway or Dell, consider the warranty. If the system is still under warranty, sometimes the warranty is voided if the case is opened. If the warranty prevents you from opening the case, you might need to return the system to a manufacturer's service center for repairs.

If the problem is still not solved, it's time to look inside the case. First, turn off the computer, unplug it, press the power button to drain residual power, and then open the case. Next, do the following:

- Check all power connections from the power supply to the motherboard and drives. Also, some cases require the case's front panel be in place before the power-on button will work. Are all cards securely seated?
- If you smell burnt parts, carefully search for shorts and frayed and burnt wires. Disassemble the parts until you find the one that is damaged.
- If you suspect the power supply is bad, test it with a power supply tester.

PROBLEMS THAT COME AND GO

A+
220-901
4.1

If a system boots successfully to the Windows Start screen or desktop, you still might have a power system problem. Some problems are intermittent; that is, they come and go. Generally, intermittent problems are more difficult to solve than a dead system. There can be many causes of intermittent problems, such as an inadequate power supply, overheating, and devices and components damaged by ESD. Here are some symptoms that might indicate an intermittent problem with the electrical system after the boot:

- The computer stops or hangs for no reason. Sometimes it might even reboot itself.
- Memory errors appear intermittently.
- Data is written incorrectly to the hard drive.
- The keyboard stops working at odd times.
- The motherboard fails or is damaged.
- The power supply overheats and becomes hot to the touch.
- The power supply fan whines and becomes very noisy or stops.

Here is what to do to eliminate the electrical system as the source of an intermittent problem:

1. *Consider the power supply is inadequate.* If the power supply is grossly inadequate, it will whine when you first plug up the power. If you have just installed new devices that are drawing additional power, verify the wattage rating of the power supply is adequate for the system.

   You can also test the system to make sure you don't have power problems by making all the devices in your system work at the same time. For instance, you can make two hard drives and the DVD drive work at the same time by copying files from one hard drive to the other while playing a movie on the DVD. If the new drive and the other drives each work independently, but data errors occur when all work at the same time, suspect a shortage of electrical power.

2. *Suspect the power supply is faulty.* You can test it using either a power supply tester (the easier method) or a multimeter (the more tedious method). However, know that a power supply that gives correct voltages when you measure it might still be the source of problems because power problems can be intermittent. Also be aware that an ATX power supply monitors the range of voltages provided to the motherboard and halts the motherboard if voltages are inadequate. Therefore, if the power supply appears "dead," your best action is to replace it.

3. *The power supply fan might not work.* Don't operate the computer if the fan does not work because computers without cooling fans can quickly overheat. Usually just before a fan stops working, it hums or whines, especially when the computer is first turned on. If this has just happened, replace the power supply. After you replace the power supply, if the new fan does not work, you have to dig deeper to find

the source of the problem. You can now assume the problem wasn't the original fan. A short somewhere else in the system drawing too much power might cause the problem. To troubleshoot a nonfunctional fan, which might be a symptom of another problem and not a problem of the fan itself, follow these steps:

a. Turn off the power and remove all power cord connections to all components except the motherboard. Turn the power back on. If the fan works, the problem is with one of the systems you disconnected, not with the power supply, the fan, or the motherboard.

b. Turn off the power and reconnect one card or drive at a time until you identify the device with the short.

c. If the fan does not work when all devices except the motherboard are disconnected, the problem is the motherboard or the power supply. Because you have already replaced the power supply, you can assume the problem is the motherboard and it's time to replace it.

POWER PROBLEMS WITH THE MOTHERBOARD

A+
220-901
4.1

A short might occur if some component on the motherboard makes improper contact with the chassis. This short can seriously damage the motherboard. For some cases, check for missing standoffs (small plastic or metal spacers that hold the motherboard a short distance away from the bottom of the case). A missing standoff most often causes these improper connections. Also check for loose standoffs or screws under the board that might be touching a wire on the bottom of the board and causing a short.

Shorts in the circuits on the motherboard might also cause problems. Look for damage on the bottom of the motherboard. These circuits are coated with plastic, and quite often damage is difficult to spot. Also look for burned-out capacitors that are spotted brown or corroded. You'll see examples of burned-out capacitors later in the chapter.

APPLYING | CONCEPTS

Back to Sharon's computer problem. Here are some questions that will help you identify the source of the problem:

A+
220-901
4.1

- Have you added new devices to your system? (These new devices might be drawing too much power from an overworked power supply.)
- Have you moved your computer recently? (It might be sitting beside a heat vent or electrical equipment.)
- Does the system power down or hang after you have been working for some time? (This symptom might have more than one cause, such as overheating or a power supply, processor, memory, or motherboard about to fail.)
- Has the computer case been opened recently? (Someone working inside the case might not have used a ground bracelet and components are now failing because of ESD damage.)
- Are case vents free so that air can flow? (The case might be close to a curtain covering the vents.)

Intermittent problems like the one Sharon described are often heat related. If the system only hangs but does not power off, the problem might be caused by faulty memory or bad software, but because it actually powers down, you can assume the problem is related to power or heat.

If Sharon tells you that the system powers down after she's been working for several hours, you can probably assume overheating. Check that first. If that's not the problem, the next thing to do is replace the power supply.

Caution Never replace a damaged motherboard with a good one without first testing or replacing the power supply. You don't want to subject another good board to possible damage.

PROBLEMS WITH OVERHEATING

A+
220-901
4.1

As a repair technician, you're sure to eventually face problems with computers overheating. Overheating can happen as soon as you turn on the computer or after the computer has been working a while. Overheating can cause intermittent errors, the system to hang, or components to fail or not last as long as they normally would. (Overheating can significantly shorten the life span of the CPU and memory.) Overheating happens for many reasons, including improper installation of the CPU cooler or fans, overclocking, poor airflow inside the case, an underrated power supply, a component going bad, or the computer's environment (for example, heat or dust).

Here are some symptoms that a system is overheating:

- The system hangs or freezes at odd times or freezes just a few moments after the boot starts.
- A Windows BSOD error occurs during the boot.
- You cannot hear a fan running or the fan makes a whining sound.
- You cannot feel air being pulled into or out of the case.

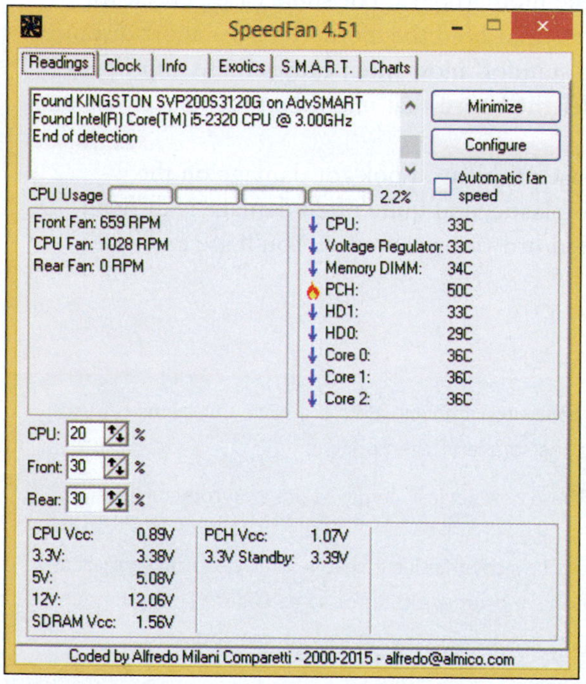

Source: SpeedFan by Alfredo Milani Comparetti

Figure 5-19 SpeedFan monitors fan speeds and system temperatures

If you suspect overheating, go into UEFI/BIOS screens and view the temperature monitors for the system. To protect the expensive processor and other components, you can also purchase a temperature sensor. The sensor plugs into a power connection coming from the power supply and mounts on the side of the case or in a drive bay. The sensor sounds an alarm when the inside of the case becomes too hot. To decide which temperature sensor to buy, use one recommended by the case manufacturer. You can also install utility software that can monitor system temperatures. For example, SpeedFan by Alfredo Comparetti is freeware that can monitor fan speeds and temperatures (see Figure 5-19). A good website to download the freeware is *www.filehippo.com/download_speedfan*. Be careful to not download other freeware available on the site.

Here are some simple things you can do to solve an overheating problem:

1. If the system refuses to boot or hangs after a period of activity, suspect overheating. Immediately after the system hangs, go into UEFI/BIOS setup and find the screen that reports the CPU temperature. The temperature should not exceed that recommended by the CPU manufacturer.
2. Excessive dust insulates components and causes them to overheat. Use compressed air, a blower, or an antistatic vacuum to remove dust from the power supply, the vents over the entire computer, and the processor cooler fan (see Figure 5-20). To protect the fan, don't allow it to spin as you blow air into it. Overspinning might damage a fan.

Figure 5-20 Dust in this cooler fan can cause the fan to fail and the processor to overheat

> **Notes** When working in a customer's office or home, be sure you clean up any mess you create from blowing dust out of a computer case.

3. Check airflow inside the case. Are all fans running? You might need to replace a fan. Is there an empty fan slot on the rear of the case? If so, install a case fan in the slot (see Figure 5-21). Orient the fan so that it blows air out of the case. The power cord to the fan can connect to a fan header on the motherboard or to a power connector coming directly from the power supply.

Figure 5-21 Install one exhaust fan on the rear of the case to help pull air through the case

4. If there are other fan slots on the side or front of the case, you can also install fans in these slots. However, don't install more fans than the case is designed to use.

5. Can the side of the case hold a chassis air guide that guides outside air to the processor? If it has a slot for the guide and the guide is missing, install one. However, don't install a guide that obstructs the CPU cooler. How to install an air guide is covered later in this section.

6. A case is generally designed for optimal airflow when slot openings on the front and rear of the case are covered and when the case cover is securely in place. To improve airflow, replace missing faceplates over empty drive bays and replace missing slot covers over empty expansion slots. See Figure 5-22.
7. Are cables in the way of airflow? Use tie wraps to secure cables and cords so that they don't block airflow across the processor or get in the way of fans turning. Figure 5-23 shows the inside of a case where cables are tied up and neatly out of the way of airflow from the front to the rear of the case.

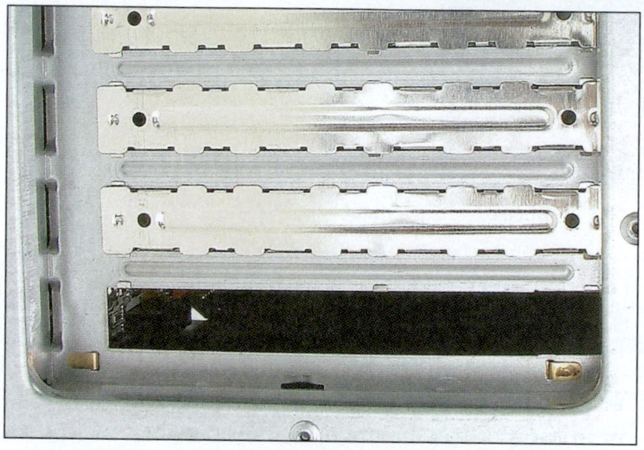

Figure 5-22 For optimum airflow, don't leave empty expansion slots and bays uncovered

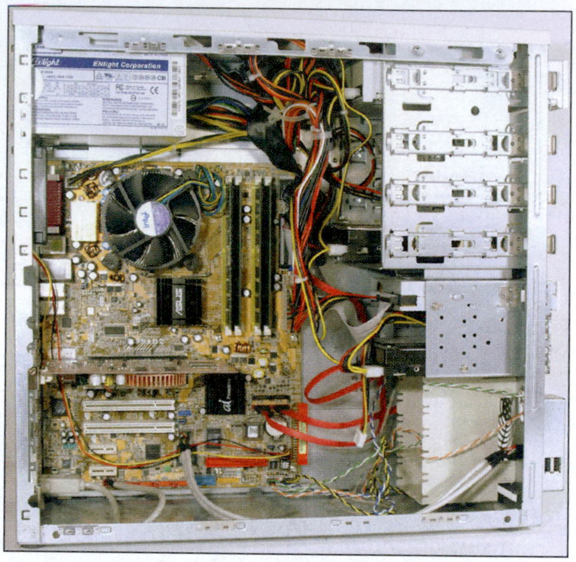

Figure 5-23 Use cable ties to hold cables out of the way of fans and airflow

8. A case needs some room to breathe. Place it so there are at least a few inches of space on both sides and the top of the case. If the case is sitting on carpet, put it on a computer stand so that air can circulate under the case and also to reduce carpet dust inside the case. Many cases have a vent on the bottom front of the case and carpet can obstruct airflow into this vent (see Figure 5-24). Make sure drapes are not hanging too close to fan openings.

Figure 5-24 Keep a tower case off carpet to allow air to flow into the bottom air vent

9. Verify the cooler is connected properly to the processor. If it doesn't fit well, the system might not boot and certainly the processor will overheat. If the cooler is not tightly connected to the motherboard and processor or the cooler fan is not working, the processor will quickly overheat as soon as the computer is turned on. Has thermal compound been installed between the cooler and processor?
10. After you close the case, leave your system off for at least 30 minutes. When you power up the computer again, let it run for 10 minutes, go into UEFI/BIOS setup, check the temperature readings, and reboot. Next, let your system run until it shuts down. Power it up again and check the temperature in UEFI/BIOS setup again. A significant difference in this reading and the first one you took after running the computer for 10 minutes indicates an overheating problem.
11. Check UEFI/BIOS setup to see if the processor is being overclocked. Overclocking can cause a system to overheat. Try restoring the processor and system bus frequencies to default values.
12. Have too many peripherals been installed inside the case? Is the case too small for all these peripherals? Larger tower cases are better designed for good airflow than smaller slimline cases. Also, when installing cards, try to leave an empty slot between each card for better airflow. The same goes for drives. Try not to install a group of drives in adjacent drive bays. For better airflow, leave empty bays between drives. Take a close look at Figure 5-23, where you can see space between each drive installed in the system.
13. Flash UEFI/BIOS to update the firmware on the motherboard. How to flash UEFI/BIOS is covered in the chapter, "All About Motherboards."
14. Thermal compound should last for years, but eventually it will harden and need replacing. If the system is several years old, replace the thermal compound.

★ A+ Exam Tip The A+ 220-902 exam expects you to recognize that a given symptom is possibly power or heat related.

If you try the preceding list of things to do and still have an overheating problem, it's time to move on to more drastic solutions. Consider whether the case design allows for good airflow; the problem might be caused by poor air circulation inside the case. The power supply fan in ATX cases blows air out of the case, pulling outside air from the vents in the front of the case across the processor to help keep it cool. Another exhaust fan is usually installed on the back of the case to help the power supply fan pull air through the case. In addition, most processors require a cooler with a fan installed on top of the processor. Figure 5-25 shows a good arrangement of vents and fans for proper airflow and a poor arrangement.

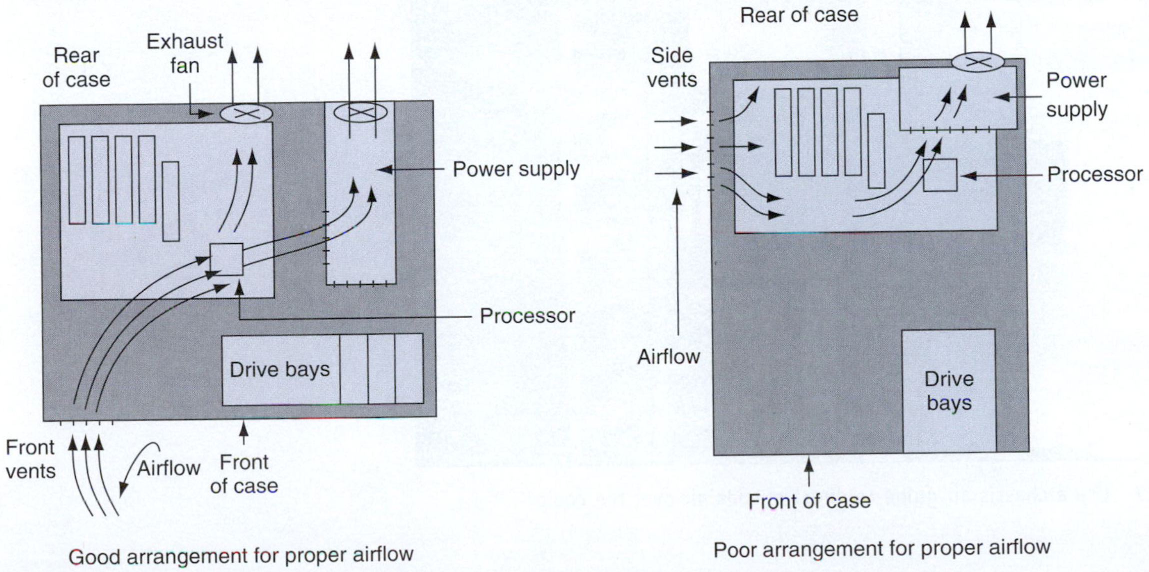

Figure 5-25 Vents and fans need to be arranged for best airflow

For better ventilation, use a power supply that has vents on the bottom and front of the power supply, as shown in Figure 5-26. Compare that with the power supply in Figure 5-21 that has vents only on the front and not on the bottom.

Figure 5-26 This power supply has vents on the bottom to provide better airflow inside the case

An intake fan on the front of the case might help pull air into the case. Intel recommends you use a front intake fan for high-end systems, but AMD says a front fan for ATX systems is not necessary. Check with the processor and case manufacturers for specific instructions as to the placement of fans and what type of fan and heat sink to use.

Intel and AMD both recommend a chassis air guide (CAG) as part of the case design. This air guide is a round air duct that helps to pull and direct fresh air from outside the case to the cooler and processor (see Figure 5-27). The guide should reach inside the case very close to the cooler, but not touch it. Intel recommends the clearance be no greater than 20mm and no less than 12mm. If the guide obstructs the cooler, you can remove the guide, but optimum airflow will not be achieved.

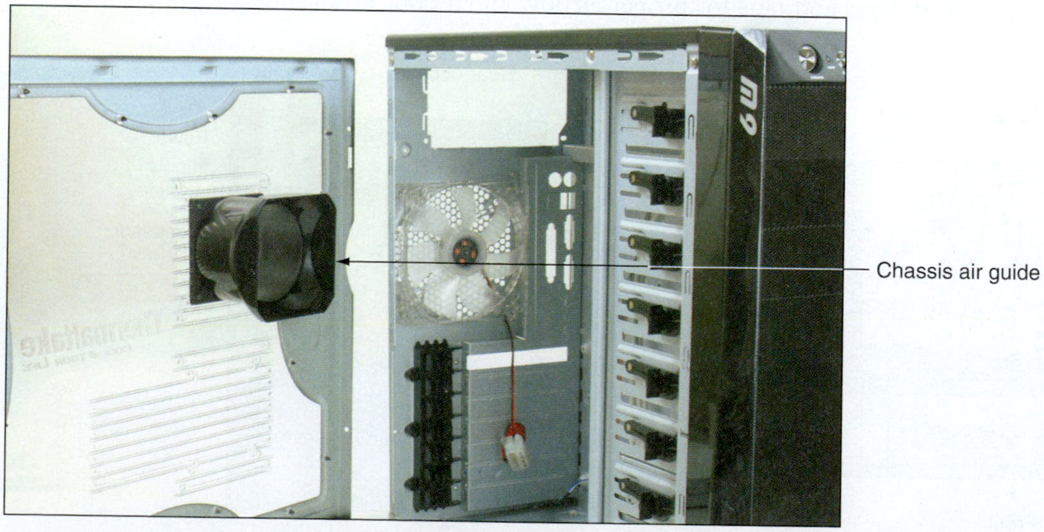

Figure 5-27 Use a chassis air guide to direct outside air over the cooler

Be careful when trying to solve an overheating problem. Excessive heat can damage the CPU and the motherboard. Never operate a system if the case fan, power-supply fan, or cooler fan is not working.

Hands-On | Project 5-4 Identify Airflow Through a Case

A+
220-901
4.1

Turn on a computer and feel the front and side vents to decide where air is flowing into and out of the case. Identify where you believe fans are working to produce the airflow. Power down the computer, unplug it, and press the power button to completely drain the power. Then open the computer case. Are fans located where you expected? Which fans were producing the strongest airflow through the case when the system was running? In which direction is each case fan drawing air, into the case or out of the case?

Hands-On | Project 5-5 Blow Dust Out of a Case

A+
220-901
4.1

If necessary, open the case cover to your desktop computer. Using a can of compressed air, blow the dust away from all fans and other components inside the case. Be careful to not touch components unless you are properly grounded. When you're done, close the case cover.

PROBLEMS WITH LAPTOP POWER SYSTEMS

A+
220-901
4.1

A laptop can be powered by an AC adapter (which uses regular house current to power the laptop) or an installed battery pack. Battery packs today use lithium ion technology. Most AC adapters today are capable of auto-switching from 110 V to 220 V AC power. Figure 5-28 shows an AC adapter that has a green light that indicates the adapter is receiving power.

Figure 5-28 This AC adapter for a laptop uses a green light to indicate power

Some mobile users like to keep an extra battery on hand in case the first one uses up its charge. When the laptop signals that power is low, shut down the system, remove the old battery, and replace it with a charged one. To remove a battery, generally, you release a latch and then remove the battery, as shown in Figure 5-29.

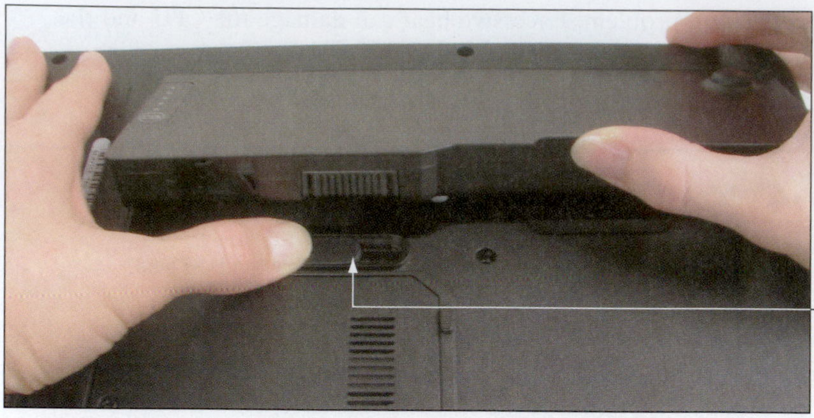

Figure 5-29 Release a latch to remove the battery from a laptop

For best battery charge times, some laptops can use two batteries. For example, the laptop in Figure 5-30 uses a second battery called a **sheet battery** that fits on the bottom of the laptop. The two batteries together give about 12 hours of use between charges. The sheet battery comes with an adapter so you can charge it when it's disconnected from the laptop.

Figure 5-30 The second battery for this laptop is a sheet battery that attaches to the bottom of the laptop and adds up to six hours to the battery charge

Notes If you're using the AC adapter to power your laptop when the power goes out, the installed battery serves as a built-in UPS. The battery immediately takes over as your uninterruptible power supply (UPS). Also, a laptop has an internal surge protector. However, for extra protection, you might want to use a power strip that provides surge protection.

Here are some problems you might encounter with laptop power systems and their solutions:

- If power is not getting to the system or the battery indicator light is lit when the AC adapter should be supplying power, verify the AC adapter is plugged into a live electrical outlet. Is the light on the AC adapter lit? Check if the AC adapter's plug is secure in the electrical outlet. Check the connections on both sides of the AC adapter transformer. Check the connection at the DC jack on the laptop. Try exchanging the AC adapter for one you know is good. The DC jack might need replacing. Most laptops allow you to replace the DC jack without replacing the entire system board. Check the service manual for the laptop to see how labor-intensive is the repair before you decide to proceed.
- If the battery is not charging when the AC adapter is plugged in, the problem might be with the battery or the motherboard. A hot battery might not charge until it cools down. If the battery is hot, remove it

from the computer and allow it to cool to room temperature. Check the battery for physical damage. If the battery is swollen or warped, replace it. If it shows no physical signs of damage, try to recharge it. If it does not recharge, replace the battery pack. If a known-good battery does not recharge, you have three options: (1) Replace the system board, (2) replace the laptop, or (3) use the laptop only when it's connected to power using the AC adapter.

APPLYING | CONCEPTS TEST AN AC ADAPTER

A+ 220-901 4.1

If the system fails only when the AC adapter is connected, it might be defective. Try a new AC adapter, or, if you have a multimeter, use it to verify the voltage output of the adapter. Do the following for an adapter with a single center pin connector:

1. Unplug the AC adapter from the computer, but leave it plugged into the electrical outlet.
2. Using a multimeter set to measure voltage in the 1 to 20 V DC range, place the red probe of the multimeter in the center of the DC connector that would normally plug into the DC outlet on the laptop. Place the black probe on the outside cylinder of the DC connector (see Figure 5-31).
3. The voltage range should be plus or minus 5 percent of the accepted voltage. For example, if a laptop is designed to use 16 V, the voltage should measure somewhere between 15.2 and 16.8 V DC.

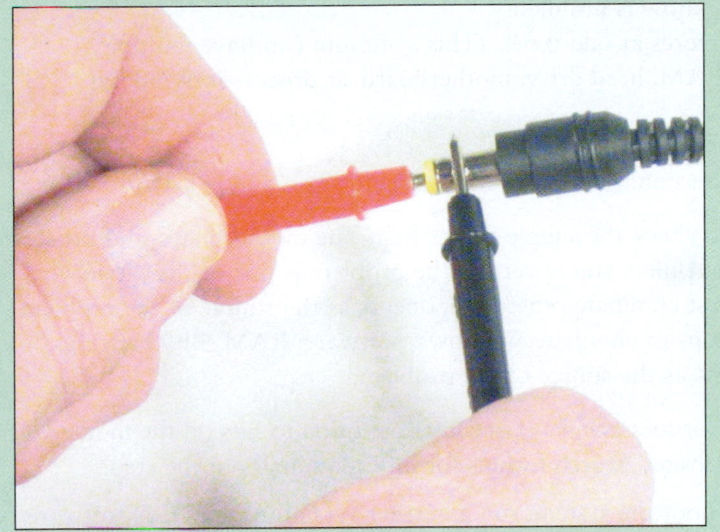

Figure 5-31 To use a multimeter to test this AC adapter, place the red probe (which, in the photo, is in the person's left hand) in the center connector and the black probe on the outside

Hands-On | Project 5-6 POST Diagnostics Cards for Laptops

A+ 220-901 4.1

Suppose you spend much of your day diagnosing problems with laptop computers. Laptops have a Mini PCI or Mini PCIe slot that works in a similar way to PCI and PCIe slots on desktop systems. Search the web for diagnostic cards that you can use in a mini PCI or mini PCIe slot that can help you diagnose hardware problems with laptops. Print the webpages showing your findings. Which diagnostic card would you choose to buy and why?

TROUBLESHOOTING THE MOTHERBOARD, PROCESSOR, AND RAM

A+
220-901
4.1

The field replaceable units (FRUs) on a motherboard are the processor, the processor cooler assembly, RAM, and the CMOS battery. Also, the motherboard itself is an FRU. As you troubleshoot the motherboard and discover that some component is not working, such as a network port, you might be able to disable that component in UEFI/BIOS setup and install a card to take its place.

A+ Exam Tip The A+ 220-901 exam expects you to know how to troubleshoot problems with motherboards, processors, and RAM.

When you suspect a bad component, a good troubleshooting technique is to substitute a known-good component for the one you suspect is bad. Be cautious here. A friend once had a computer that wouldn't boot. He replaced the hard drive, with no change. He replaced the motherboard next. The computer booted up with no problem; he was delighted, until it failed again. Later he discovered that a faulty power supply had damaged his original motherboard. When he traded the bad one for a good one, the new motherboard also got zapped! If you suspect problems with the power supply, check the voltage coming from the power supply before putting in a new motherboard.

Symptoms that a motherboard, processor, or memory module is failing can appear as:

- The system begins to boot but then powers down.
- An error message is displayed during the boot. Investigate this message.
- The system reports less memory than you know is installed.
- The system becomes unstable, hangs, or freezes at odd times. (This symptom can have multiple causes, including a failing power supply, RAM, hard drive, motherboard or processor, Windows errors, and overheating.)
- Intermittent Windows or hard drive errors occur.
- Components on the motherboard or devices connected to it don't work.

Remember the troubleshooting principle to check the simple things first. The motherboard and processor are expensive and time consuming to replace. Unless you're certain the problem is one of these two components, don't replace either until you first eliminate other components as the source of the problem.

If you can boot the system, follow these steps to eliminate Windows, software, RAM, BIOS settings, and other software and hardware components as the source of the problem:

1. If an error message appears, Google the error message. Pay particular attention to hits on the motherboard or processor manufacturer or Microsoft websites. Search forums for information about the error.
2. The problem might be a virus. If you can boot the system, run a current version of antivirus software to check for viruses.
3. A memory module might be failing. In Windows 8/7/Vista, use the **Memory Diagnostics** tool to test memory. Even if Windows is not installed, you can still run the tool by booting the system from the Windows setup DVD. How to use the Memory Diagnostics tool is coming up later in this chapter.

Notes Other than the Windows Memory Diagnostics tool, you can use the Memtest86 utility to test installed memory modules. Check the site *www.memtest86.com* to download this program.

4. Suspect the problem is caused by an application or by Windows. In Windows, the best tool to check for potential hardware problems is Device Manager.
5. In Windows, download and install any Windows updates or patches. These updates might solve a hardware or application problem.

Notes Another useful Windows tool for troubleshooting hardware problems is Event Viewer, which reports logs of hardware and application errors. A Real Problems, Real Solutions activity at the end of this chapter gives you experience using Event Viewer.

6. Ask yourself what has changed since the problem began. If the problem began immediately after installing a new device or application, uninstall the device or applications.
7. A system that does not have enough RAM can sometimes appear to be unstable. Using the System window, find out how much RAM is installed, and compare that with the recommended amounts. Consider upgrading RAM.
8. The UEFI/BIOS might be corrupted or have wrong settings. Check UEFI/BIOS setup. Have settings been tampered with? Is the CPU speed set incorrectly or is it overclocked? Reset UEFI/BIOS setup to restore default settings.
9. Disable any quick booting features in UEFI/BIOS so that you get a thorough report of POST. Then look for errors reported on the screen during the boot.
10. Flash BIOS to update the firmware on the board.
11. Check the motherboard manufacturer's website for diagnostic software that might identify a problem with the motherboard.
12. Update all drivers of motherboard components that are not working. For example, if the USB ports are not working, try updating the USB drivers with those downloaded from the motherboard manufacturer's website. This process can also update the chipset drivers.
13. If an onboard port or device isn't working, but the motherboard is stable, follow these steps:
    a. Verify the problem is not with the device using the port. Try moving the device to another port on the same computer or move the device to another computer. If it works there, return it to this port. The problem might have been a bad connection.
    b. Go into UEFI/BIOS setup and verify the port is enabled.
    c. Check Device Manager and verify Windows recognizes the device or port with no errors. For example, Device Manager shown in Figure 5-32 reports the onboard Wi-Fi adapter is disabled. Try to enable the device.

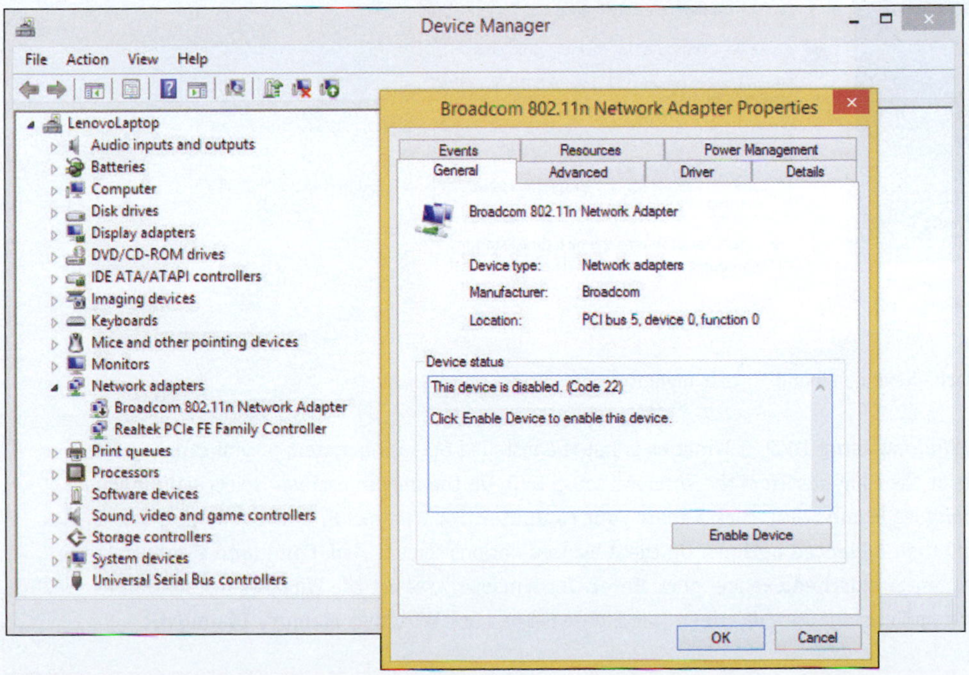

Figure 5-32 Device Manager reports a problem with an onboard port

d. Next try updating the motherboard drivers for this device from the motherboard manufacturer's website.
e. If you have a loopback plug, use it to test the port.
f. If the problem is still not solved, disable the port in BIOS setup and install an expansion card to provide the same type of port or connector.

14. Suspect the problem is caused by a failing hard drive. How to troubleshoot a failing drive is covered in the chapter, "Supporting Hard Drives and Other Storage Devices."
15. Suspect the problem is caused by overheating. How to check for overheating is covered earlier in this chapter.
16. Verify the installed processor is supported by the motherboard. Perhaps someone has installed the wrong processor.

APPLYING | CONCEPTS USE WINDOWS MEMORY DIAGNOSTICS

A+
220-901
4.1

Errors with memory are often difficult to diagnose because they can appear intermittently and might be mistaken as application errors, user errors, or other hardware component errors. Sometimes these errors cause the system to hang, a blue screen error might occur, or the system continues to function with applications giving errors or data getting corrupted. You can quickly identify a problem with memory or eliminate memory as the source of a problem by using the Windows 8/7/Vista Memory Diagnostics tool. Use one of these two methods to start the utility:

- ***Use the mdsched.exe command from within Windows.*** To open a command prompt window from the Windows 8 desktop, right-click **Start** and click **Command Prompt**. (In Windows 7, click **Start**, enter **command** or **cmd**, and press **Enter**.) In the command prompt window, enter **mdsched.exe** and press **Enter**. A dialog box appears (see Figure 5-33) asking if you want to run the test now or on the next restart.

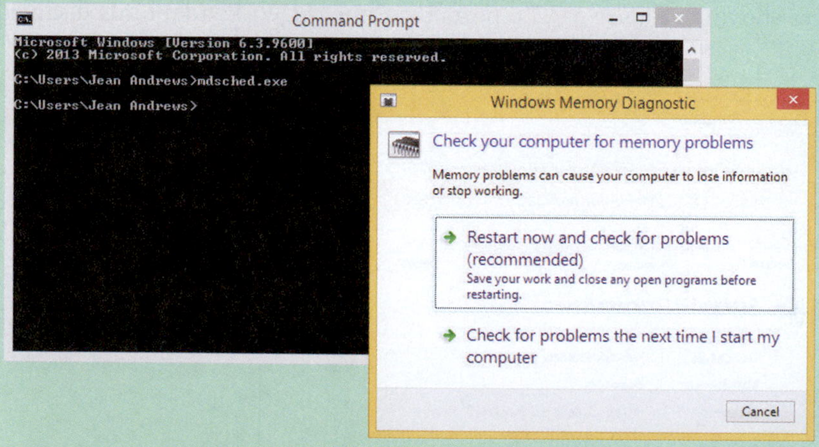

Figure 5-33 Use the mdsched.exe command to test memory

- ***Boot from the Windows setup DVD.*** If Windows is not the installed operating system or you cannot boot from the hard drive, boot the computer from the Windows setup DVD. On the opening screen, select your language. On the next screen (see Figure 5-34), click **Repair your computer**. For Windows 8, in the following boxes, click **Troubleshoot** and then **Advanced options**. On the Advanced options screen, click **Command Prompt**. At the command prompt, enter **mdsched.exe** and press **Enter**. For Windows 7, select the Windows installation to repair. On the System Recovery Options screen (see Figure 5-35), click **Windows Memory Diagnostic**.

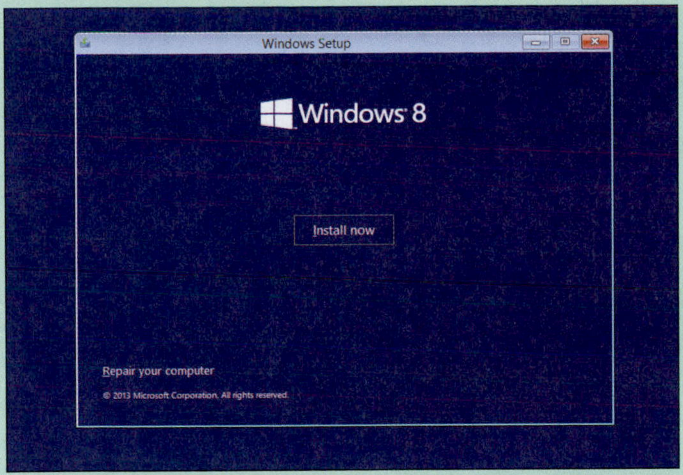

Figure 5-34 Opening menu when you boot from the Windows 8 setup DVD

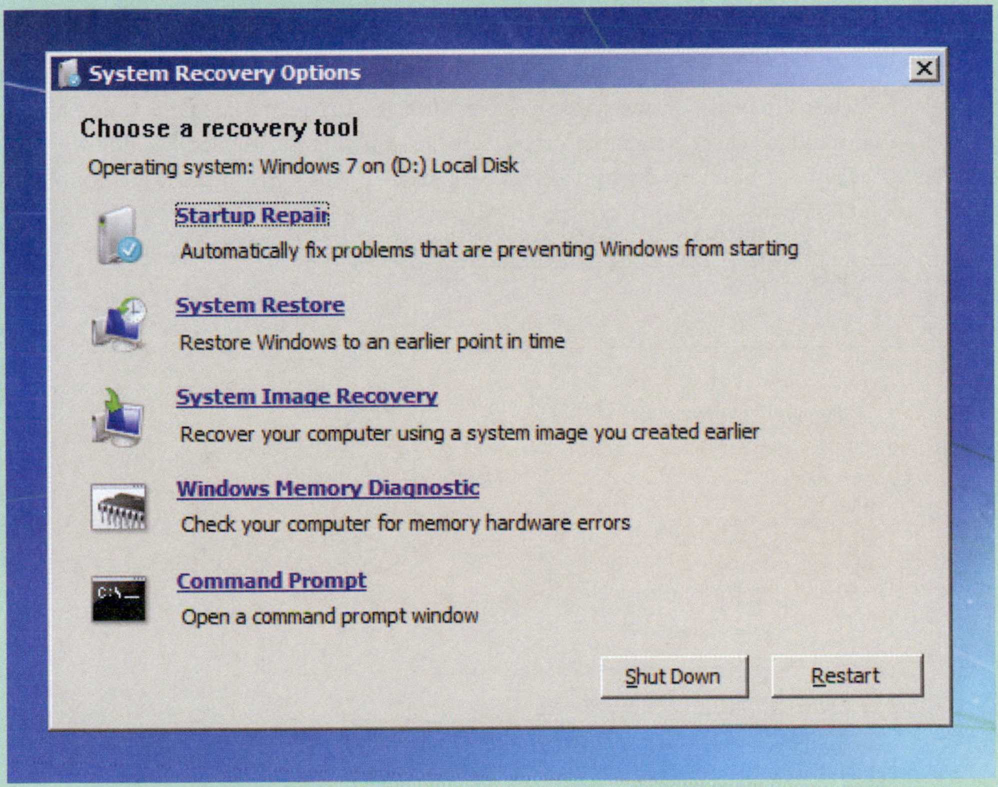

Figure 5-35 Test memory using the Windows 7 System Recovery Options menu

If the tool reports memory errors, replace all memory modules installed on the motherboard.

APPLYING | CONCEPTS USE DEVICE MANAGER TO DELETE THE DRIVER STORE

A+ 220-901 4.1

One thing you can do to solve a problem with a device is to uninstall and reinstall the device. When you first install a device, Windows stores a copy of the driver package in a **driver store**. When you uninstall the device, you can tell Windows to also delete the driver store. If you don't delete the driver store, Windows uses it when you install the device again. That's why the second time you install the same device Windows does not ask you for the location of the drivers. Windows might also use the driver store to automatically install the device on the next reboot without your involvement.

All this is convenient unless there is a problem with the driver store. To get a true fresh start with an installation, you need to delete the driver store. To do that, first sign in to Windows using an account with administrative privileges and then follow these steps:

1. To open Device Manager from the Windows 8 desktop, right-click **Start** and click **Device Manager**. (In Windows 7, click **Start** and click **Control Panel**. In Control Panel Classic icon view, click **Device Manager**.) Device Manager opens.

A+ Exam Tip The A+ 220-902 exam expects you to be familiar with Control Panel in Classic icon view. If Control Panel is showing Category view, click **Category**, and then click **Large icons** or **Small icons**.

2. Right-click the device and click **Properties** in the shortcut menu. Click the **Driver** tab and click **Uninstall**. In the Confirm Device Uninstall box, check **Delete the driver software for this device**, and click **OK**. See Figure 5-36. The installed drivers and the driver store are both deleted. When you reinstall the device, you'll need the drivers on CD or downloaded from the web.

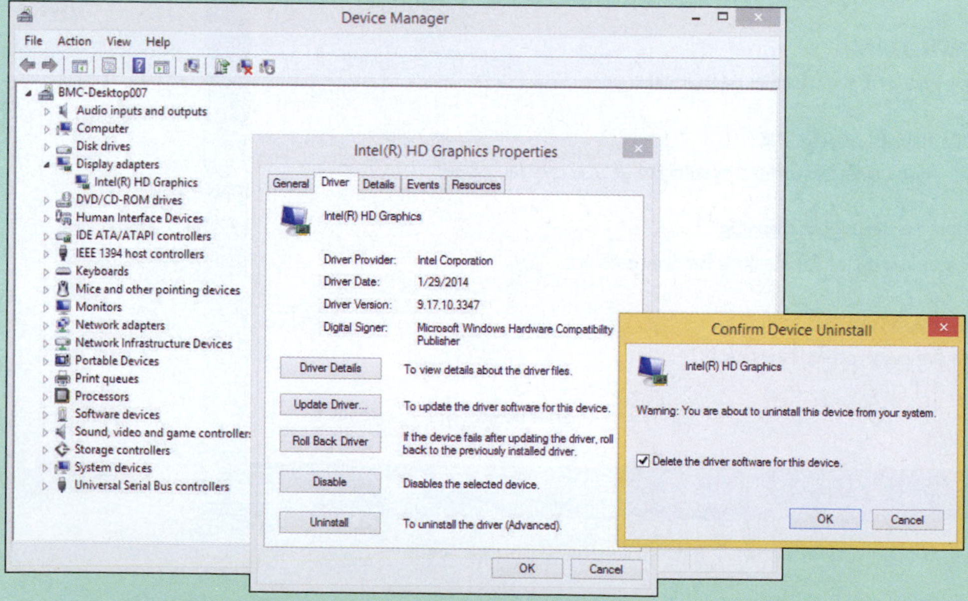

Figure 5-36 Use Device Manager to uninstall the drivers and delete the driver store for a device

Also know if the check box is missing on the Confirm Device Uninstall box, the drivers are embedded in Windows and you cannot delete the driver store for these devices. Examples of these devices are the optical drive, hard drive, and generic keyboard, which all have embedded Windows drivers.

We're working our way through what to do when the system locks up, gives errors, or generally appears unstable. Another problem that can occur at the boot is continuous reboots, which can be caused by overheating, a failing processor, motherboard, or RAM, or a corrupted Windows installation. For Windows 8, many continuous restart errors can be solved by performing a Startup Repair process. Follow these steps:

1. Boot from the Windows 8 setup DVD. (You might need to first change the boot priority order in UEFI/BIOS setup to boot first from the optical drive.)
2. On the opening screen, select your language. On the next screen (refer back to Figure 5-34), click **Repair your computer**. Next click **Troubleshoot** and then **Advanced options**. On the Advanced options screen (see Figure 5-37), click **Startup Repair** and follow directions on screen.

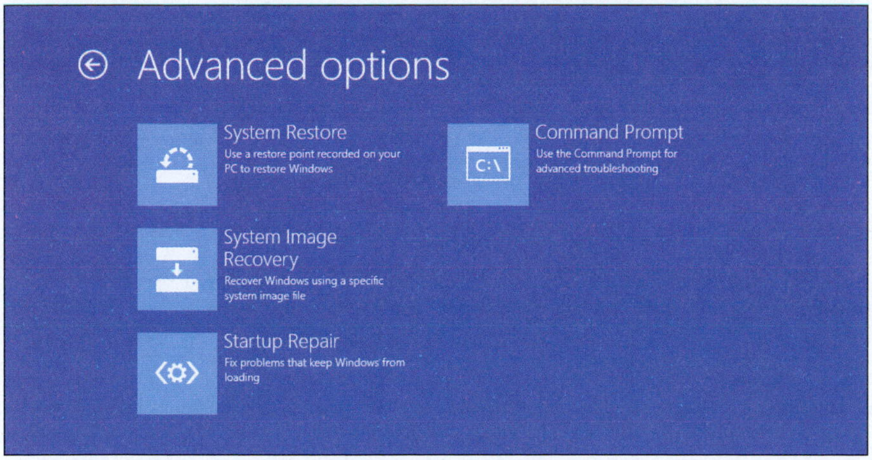

Figure 5-37 Startup Repair on the Advanced options menu can solve problems launching Windows 8

For Windows 7/Vista, error messages disappear before they can be read as the system reboots. To disable these automatic restarts, press F8 as Windows starts up. The Advanced Boot Options menu appears (see Figure 5-38). Select Disable automatic restart on system failure. When you restart Windows,

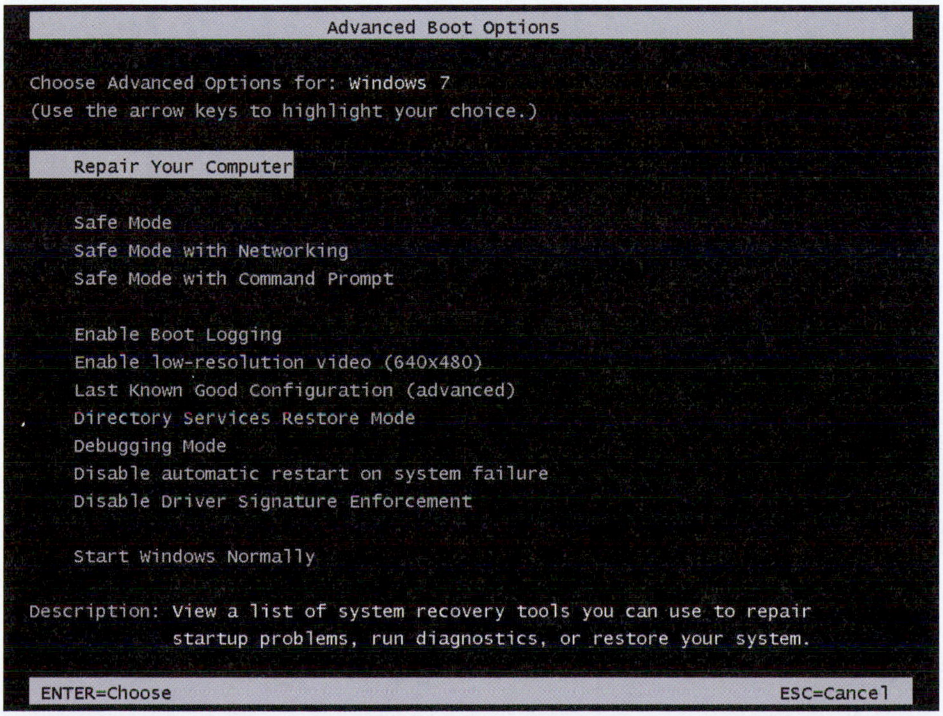

Figure 5-38 Press F8 during the boot to see the Windows 7 Advanced Boot Options menu

the error message stays on screen long enough for you to read it. Search the Microsoft websites (*support .microsoft.com* and *technet.microsoft.com*) for information about the hardware component causing the problem and what to do about it. BSOD errors might apply to the motherboard, video card, RAM, processor, hard drive, or some other device for which Windows is trying to load device drivers.

If you have checked Windows and UEFI/BIOS settings and searched the web for help and still have not identified the source of the problem, it's time to open the case and check inside. As you do so, be sure to use an ESD strap and follow other procedures to protect the system against ESD. With the case open, follow these steps:

1. Check that all the power and data cables the system is using are securely connected. Try reseating all expansion cards and DIMM modules.
2. Look for physical damage on the motherboard. Look for frayed traces on the bottom of the board or discolored, distended, or bulging capacitors on the board.
3. Reduce the system to essentials. Remove any unnecessary hardware, such as expansion cards, and then watch to see if the problem goes away. If the problem goes away, replace one component at a time until the problem returns and you have identified the component causing the trouble.
4. Try using a POST diagnostic card. It might offer you a clue as to which component is giving a problem.
5. Suspect the problem is caused by a failing power supply. It's less expensive and easier to replace than the motherboard or processor, so eliminate it as a cause before you move on to the motherboard or processor.
6. Exchange the processor.
7. Exchange the motherboard, but before you do, measure the voltage output of the power supply or simply replace it, in case it is producing too much power and has damaged the board.

APPLYING CONCEPTS DISCOLORED CAPACITORS

A+ 220-901 4.1

Jessica complained to Wally, her IT support technician, that Windows was occasionally giving errors, data would get corrupted, or an application would not work as it should. At first, Wally suspected Jessica might need a little more training on how to open and close an application or save a file, but he discovered user error was not the problem. He tried reinstalling the application software Jessica most often used, and even reinstalled Windows, but the problems persisted.

Notes Catastrophic errors (errors that cause the system to not boot or a device to not work) are much easier to resolve than intermittent errors (errors that come and go).

Wally began to suspect a hardware problem. Carefully examining the motherboard revealed the source of the problem: failing capacitors. Look carefully at Figure 5-39 and you can see five bad **discolored capacitors** with bulging heads. (Know that sometimes a leaking capacitor can also show crusty corrosion at the base of the capacitor.) When Wally replaced the motherboard, the problems went away.

Figure 5-39 These five bad capacitors have bulging and discolored heads

Hands-On | Project 5-7 Troubleshoot Memory

A+
220-901
4.1

Do the following to troubleshoot memory:

1. Open the Windows System window and record the amount of memory in your system.
2. Follow the rules to protect a computer against ESD as you work. Remove the memory module in the first memory slot on the motherboard, and boot the computer. Did you get an error? Why or why not? Replace the module and verify the system starts with no errors and that the full amount of memory is recognized by Windows.
3. Use the Windows 8/7/Vista Memory Diagnostics tool to test memory. About how long did the test take? Were any errors reported?

Hands-On | Project 5-8 Sabotage and Repair a Computer

A+
220-901
4.1

Open the computer case and create a hardware problem with your computer that prevents the system from booting without damaging a component. For example, you can disconnect a data cable or power cable or loosen a DIMM in a memory slot. Close the computer case and restart the system. Describe the problem as a user would describe it who does not know much about computer hardware. Power down the system and fix the problem. Boot up the system and verify all is well.

TROUBLESHOOTING MOBILE DEVICES

A+
220-901
4.5

Here is what to do for problems with a cell phone that is overheating:

- Check if the heat is coming from the bottom of the cell phone where the battery is located. If so, try these things:
  - Use a different AC adapter to charge the battery.
  - If the phone is not under warranty, open the case and examine the battery for damage. Is it swollen or warped? If so, replace the battery. If the phone is under warranty, lay the phone on a flat surface. If the phone appears warped, take it in for repair.

> **Notes** Some Android cell phones will provide information about the device when you enter ***#*#4636#*#*** in the phone keypad. In the screen that appears, select Battery Information. If the Battery Health screen reports "unknown," suspect a bad battery. The temperature of the battery is also reported on this screen, which should be less than 40°C.

- If heat is coming from other areas of the phone, try these things:
  - Too many apps might be open. Close all apps you're not currently using.
  - Follow troubleshooting steps for your phone's operating system to resolve the problem. These steps include updating the OS. For more information, see the chapter, "Supporting Mobile Operating Systems."
  - The phone processor might be overworked by streaming data (watching a movie online), playing a game, or texting. Allow the phone to rest and cool down.
  - Consider removing the phone from a case that doesn't allow heat to dissipate.

If you decide the battery is the problem, check if the phone is under warranty. If not, you are likely to find teardown directions to replace the battery online. For example, at *ifixit.com* the kit to replace the iPhone 5 battery includes the battery, tools, and directions (see Figure 5-40). You can also watch videos on the site to step you through the process.

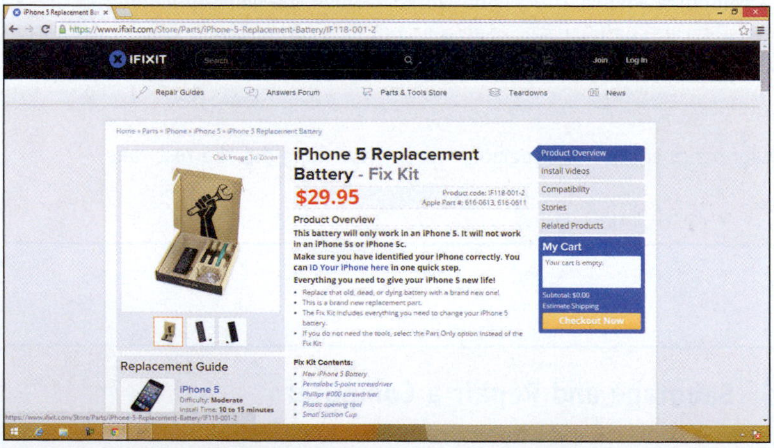

Source: IFIXIT

Figure 5-40 At *www.ifixit.com*, you can purchase tools, parts, and instructions to replace an iPhone battery

Here are some other problems and solutions for cell phones and phablets:

- For a frozen system, do the following:
  - For the iPhone or iPad, reset the device. To do so, hold down the Wake/sleep button and the Home button at the same time for at least 10 seconds until the Apple logo appears.

- For a frozen Android device, you can reboot the system by following manufacturer directions for a reboot for the specific device. As a last resort, you can open the back of the device and remove and reinstall the battery.
- For Windows Phone, first try holding down the Power button and then swipe Slide down to power off. Power back up your phone. If that doesn't work, press and hold the Volume Down and Power buttons at the same time for at least 10 seconds until you feel a vibration. If that doesn't work, open the back of the device and remove and reinstall the battery.
- When the battery charge lasts an extremely short time, first try exchanging the AC adapter (charger). If that doesn't work, exchange the battery unless the device is under warranty.
- When installing apps that don't load or load slowly, a hot or failing battery might be the problem. Other problems might be a failing network connection. Reset the Wi-Fi or Bluetooth connection. If your device is connected to your computer with a USB connection, check the USB connection.
- For slow performance, close apps you're not using, clean Android cached data, and disable live wallpapers. Consider performing a factory reset and start over by installing only the apps you actually use. For more information, see the chapter, "Supporting Mobile Operating Systems."
- Email encryption is done using a public key and private key. You distribute your public key to those who want to send you encrypted email and you keep the private key on your device. If your device is unable to decrypt email, most likely you'll need to generate a new public key and private key and distribute your new public key to those who send you encrypted email.

5

APPLYING | CONCEPTS LESSONS LEARNED

A+
220-901
4.1

Sophia is putting together a computer from parts for the first time. She has decided to keep costs low and is installing an AMD processor on a microATX motherboard, using all low-cost parts. She installed the hard drive, optical drive, and power supply in the computer case. Then she installed the motherboard in the case, followed by the processor, cooler, and memory. Before powering up the system, she checked all connections to make sure they were solid and read through the motherboard documentation to make sure she did not forget anything important. Next, she plugs in the monitor to the onboard video port and then plugs in the keyboard and power cord. She takes a deep breath and turns on the power switch on the back of the computer. Immediately, she hears a faint whine, but she's not sure what is making the noise. When she presses the power button on the front of the case, nothing happens. No fans, no lights. Here are the steps Sophia takes to troubleshoot the problem:

1. She turns off the power switch and unplugs the power cord. She remembers to put on her ground bracelet and carefully checks all power connections. Everything looks okay.
2. She plugs in the system and presses the power button again. Still all she hears is the faint whine.
3. She presses the power button a second and third time. Suddenly a loud pop followed by smoke comes from the power supply, and the strong smell of electronics fills the room! Sophia jumps back in dismay.
4. She removes a known-good power supply from another computer, disconnects the blown power supply, and connects the good one to the computer. When she turns on the power switch, she hears that same faint whine. Quickly she turns off the switch and unplugs the power cord. She does not want to lose another power supply!
5. Next, Sophia calls technical support of the company that sold her the computer parts. A very helpful technician listens carefully to the details and tells Sophia that the problem sounds like a short in the system. He explains that a power supply might whine if too much power is being drawn. As Sophia hangs up the phone, she begins to think that the problem might be with the motherboard installation.

(continues)

6. She removes the motherboard from the case, and the source of the problem is evident: She forgot to install spacers between the board and the case. The board was sitting directly on the bottom of the case, which had caused the short.
7. Sophia installs the spacers and reinstalls the motherboard. Using the good power supply, she turns on the system. The whine is gone, but the system is dead.
8. Sophia purchases a new power supply and motherboard, and this time, carefully uses spacers in every hole used by the motherboard screws. Figure 5-41 shows one installed spacer and one ready to be installed. The system comes up without a problem.

Figure 5-41 Spacers installed in case holes keep the motherboard from causing a short

In evaluating her experience with her first computer build, Sophia declares the project a success. She was grateful she had decided to use low-cost parts for her first build. She learned much from the experience and will never, ever forget to use spacers. She told a friend, "I made a serious mistake, but I learned from it. I feel confident I know how to put a system together now, and I'm ready to tackle another build. When you make mistakes and get past them, your confidence level actually grows because you learn you can face a serious problem and solve it."

>> CHAPTER SUMMARY

Cooling Methods and Devices

- Devices that are used to keep a processor and system cool include CPU coolers and fans, thermal compound, case fans, heat sinks, and liquid cooling.
- Liquid cooling systems use liquids pumped through the system to keep it cool and are sometimes used by hobbyists when overclocking a system.

Selecting a Power Supply

- Important features of a power supply to consider when purchasing it are its form factor, wattage capacity, number and type of connectors it provides, and warranty.
- To decide on the wattage capacity of a power supply, add up the wattage requirements for all components in a system and then increase that total by about 30 percent. The wattage provided by the +12 V rail is also important.

How to Approach a Hardware Problem

- If possible, always begin troubleshooting a computer problem by interviewing the user. Find out when the problem started and what happened about the time it started. You also need to know if important data on the computer is not backed up. When troubleshooting, set your priorities based on user needs.
- Sources that can help with hardware troubleshooting are the web, online technical support and forums, diagnostic software, user manuals, and your network of technical associates.
- When troubleshooting, check the simple things first. For example, you can scan for viruses, test RAM, and run diagnostic software before you begin the process of replacing expensive components.
- Decide if a computer problem occurs before or after a successful boot and if it is caused by hardware or software. After you have fixed the problem, verify the fix and document the outcome.
- When troubleshooting mobile devices, consider the warranty and that replacing a component might cost more than replacing the device. If possible, substitute an external component for an internal one.

Troubleshooting the Electrical System

- To determine if a system is getting power, listen for spinning fans or drives and look for indicator lights.
- Use a power supply tester to test the power supply.
- Intermittent problems that come and go are the most difficult to solve and can be caused by hardware or software. The power supply, motherboard, RAM, processor, hard drive, and overheating can cause intermittent problems.
- Removing dust from a system, providing for proper ventilation, and installing extra fans can help to keep a system from overheating.
- The battery and the DC jack are considered field replaceable units in a laptop that pertain to the power system.
- Use a multimeter to check the voltage output of an AC adapter.

Troubleshooting the Motherboard, Processor, and RAM

- UEFI/BIOS gives beep codes when a POST error occurs during the boot before it tests video.
- Error messages on a black screen during the boot are usually put there by startup UEFI/BIOS during POST.
- Error messages on a blue screen during or after the boot are put there by Windows and are called the blue screen of death (BSOD).
- The motherboard, processor, RAM, processor cooler assembly, and CMOS battery are field replaceable units.
- An unstable system that freezes or hangs at odd times can be caused by a faulty power supply, RAM, hard drive, motherboard, or processor, Windows error, or overheating.
- A POST diagnostic card can troubleshoot problems with the motherboard.

Troubleshooting Mobile Devices

- A mobile device battery that overheats or quickly loses its charge might need replacing, but first try replacing the AC adapter (charger).
- For a frozen system, try resetting an iPhone or iPad, rebooting an Android device, or resetting Windows Phone. You can also try removing the battery and reinstalling it.

>> KEY TERMS

For explanations of key terms, see the Glossary for this text.

AC adapter
auto-switching
blue screen of death (BSOD)
case fan
chassis air guide (CAG)
cooler
discolored capacitor
driver store
dual rail
fanless CPU cooler
file recovery software
heat sink
lithium ion
Memory Diagnostics
passive CPU cooler
processor thermal trip error
sheet battery
Windows pinwheel

>> REVIEWING THE BASICS

1. What are the two major components of a processor cooler assembly?
2. How many pins does the CPU fan header on a motherboard have?
3. If the power connector from the CPU fan has only three pins, it can still connect to the 4-pin header, but what functionality is lost?
4. How do you determine the wattage capacity needed by a power supply?
5. Which one component in a high-end gaming computer is likely to draw the most power?
6. When you first turn on a computer and you don't hear a spinning drive or fan or see indicator lights, is the problem hardware or software related?
7. What is a Windows error message called that appears on a blue screen?
8. How many beeps does startup UEFI/BIOS give to indicate a successful POST?
9. Which two components in a system might give out a loud whining noise?
10. What Windows utility can you use to test RAM?
11. Which Windows tool is best to use to verify that hardware components installed in Windows are working properly?
12. What is the purpose of standoffs installed between the bottom of the case and the motherboard?
13. If a system hangs after being used for several hours and you suspect overheating, what can you do to easily monitor the CPU and system temperature?
14. What are two reasons to tie cables up and out of the way inside a computer case?
15. Why should a tower case not sit on thick carpet?
16. For most computer cases, does air flow from front to rear or rear to front?
17. Which type of CPU cooler contains heat pipes?
18. What can you do if a port on the motherboard is faulty and a device requires this type of port?
19. What can you do to stop a computer from repeatedly restarting in a continuous loop?
20. When a cell phone overheats, why is it important to find out whether the heat is coming from the bottom of the phone or from other areas of the phone?

>> THINKING CRITICALLY

1. How much power is consumed by a load drawing 5 A with 120 V across it?
2. What is a reasonable wattage capacity for a power supply to be used with a system that contains a DVD drive, three hard drives, and a high-end video card?
   a. 250 W
   b. 1000 W
   c. 700 W
   d. 150 W
3. You upgrade a faulty PCIe video card to a recently released higher-performing card. Now the user complains that Windows 8 hangs a lot and gives errors. Which is the most likely source of the problem? Which is the least likely source?
   a. Overheating
   b. Windows does not support the new card
   c. The drivers for the card need updating
   d. Memory is faulty
4. What should you immediately do if you turn on a computer and smell smoke or a burning odor?
   a. Unplug the computer.
   b. Dial 911.
   c. Find a fire extinguisher.
   d. Press a key on the keyboard to enter BIOS setup.
5. When you boot up a computer and hear a single beep, but the screen is blank, what can you assume is the source of the problem?
   a. The video card or onboard video
   b. The monitor or monitor cable
   c. Windows startup
   d. The processor
6. You suspect that a power supply is faulty, but you use a power supply tester to measure its voltage output and find it to be acceptable. Why is it still possible that the power supply may be faulty?
7. Someone asks you for help with a computer that hangs at odd times. You turn it on and work for about 15 minutes, and then the computer freezes and powers down. What do you do first?
   a. Replace the surge protector.
   b. Replace the power supply.
   c. Wait about 30 minutes for the system to cool down and try again.
   d. Install an additional fan.

5

>> REAL PROBLEMS, REAL SOLUTIONS

REAL PROBLEM 5-1 Replacing a Power Supply

Suppose you turn on a system and everything is dead—no lights, nothing on the monitor screen, and no spinning fan or hard drive. You verify the power to the system works, all power connections and power cords are securely connected, and all pertinent switches are turned on. You can assume the power supply has gone bad. It's time to replace it. To prepare for this situation in a real work environment, exchange power supplies with another student in your lab who is using a computer that has a power supply rated at about the same wattage as yours. Then verify that your system starts up and works.

REAL PROBLEM 5-2 Using Event Viewer to Troubleshoot a Hardware Problem

Just about anything that happens in Windows is recorded in Event Viewer (Eventvwr.msc). You can find events such as a hardware or network failure, OS error messages, or a device that has failed to start. When you first encounter a Windows, hardware, application, or security problem, get in the habit of checking Event Viewer as one of your first steps toward investigating the problem. To save time, first check the Administrative Events log because it filters out all events except Warning and Error events, which are the most useful for troubleshooting. Do the following to practice using Event Viewer:

1. For Windows 8, press **Win+X**, click **Run**, and enter **eventvwr.msc**. For Windows 7, enter **eventvwr.msc** in the Search box. Event Viewer opens. Drill down into the **Custom Views** list in the left pane and click **Administrative Events**. Scroll through the list of Error or Warning events and list any that indicate a possible hardware problem. Make note of the first event in the list.
2. Disconnect the network cable.
3. In the Event Viewer menu bar, click **Action** and **Refresh** to refresh the list of events. How many new events do you see? Click each new event to see its details below the list of events until you find the event that tells you the network cable was unplugged. Figure 5-42 shows Event Viewer for Windows 7. Describe the details of the event about the network cable.
4. Tinker around with other hardware on your computer. What actions did you take that triggered a Warning or Error event in Event Viewer?

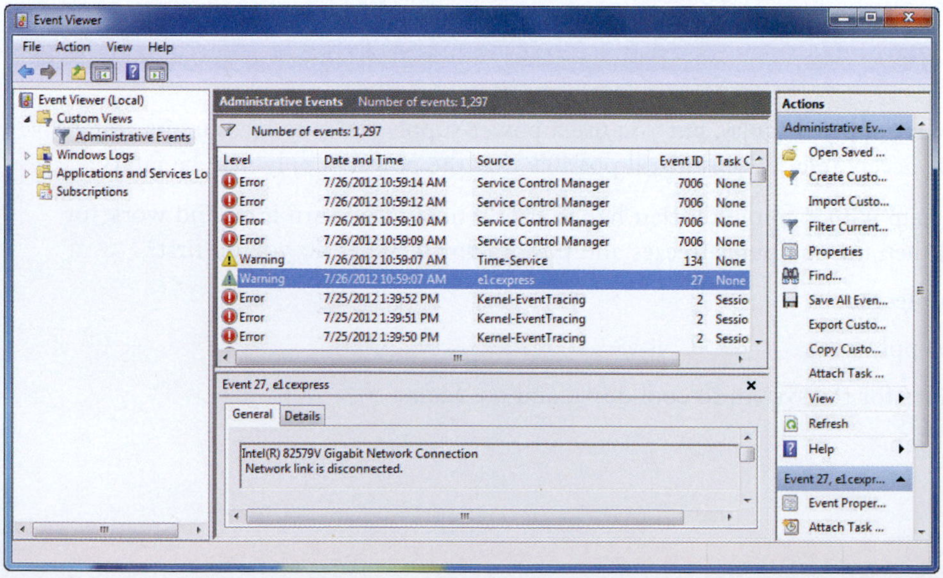

Figure 5-42 Use Event Viewer to find logs that can help with troubleshooting hardware problems

REAL PROBLEM 5-3 Troubleshooting a Hung System

A user complains to you that her system hangs for no known reason. After asking her a few questions, you identify these symptoms:

- The system hangs after about 15–20 minutes of operation.
- When the system hangs, it doesn't matter what application is open or how many applications are open.
- When the system hangs, it appears as though power is turned off: There are no lights, spinning drives, or other evidence of power.

You suspect overheating might be the problem. To test your theory, you decide to do the following:

1. You want to verify that the user has not overclocked the system. How do you do that?
2. You decide to check for overheating by examining the temperature of the system immediately after the system is powered up and then again immediately after the system hangs. Describe the steps you take to do this.
3. After doing the first two steps, you decide overheating is the cause of the problem. What are four things you can do to fix the problem?

CHAPTER

6

Supporting Hard Drives and Other Storage Devices

After completing this chapter, you will be able to:

- Discuss technologies used inside a hard drive and how a computer communicates with a hard drive
- Install and support a hard drive
- Identify tape drives and tape cartridges
- Support optical drives and flash memory devices
- Troubleshoot hard drives

The hard drive is the most important permanent storage device in a computer, and supporting hard drives is one of the more important tasks of a computer support technician. This chapter introduces the different kinds of hard drive technologies and the ways a computer interfaces with a hard drive. You learn how to select and install the different types of hard drives and how to troubleshoot hard drive problems. You also learn about tape drives and how to select and install optical drives in desktops and laptops. The chapter also covers flash memory cards, including which type of card to buy for a particular need.

HARD DRIVE TECHNOLOGIES AND INTERFACE STANDARDS

A+
220-901
1.5, 1.7,
1.11

A hard disk drive (HDD), most often called a hard drive, comes in two sizes for personal computers: the 2.5" size is used for laptop computers and the 3.5" size is used for desktops. See Figure 6-1. In addition, a smaller 1.8" size hard drive (about the size of a credit card) is used in some low-end laptops and other equipment such as MP3 players.

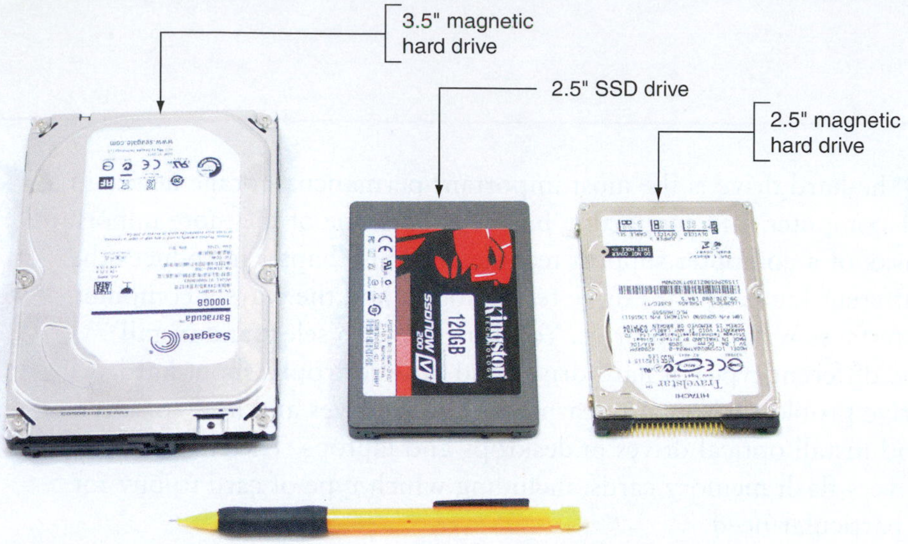

Figure 6-1 A hard drive for a desktop is larger than those used in laptops

> **Notes** In technical documentation, you might see a hard drive abbreviated as HDD (hard disk drive). However, this chapter uses the term *hard drive*.

Now let's look at the technologies used inside a hard drive and then we'll turn to how the drive interfaces with the computer.

TECHNOLOGIES USED INSIDE A HARD DRIVE

A+
220-901
1.5, 1.7,
1.11

The two types of hardware technologies used inside the drive are solid-state and magnetic. In addition, some drives use a combination of both technologies. Here are important details about each:

- ***Solid-state drive.*** A solid-state drive (SSD), also called a solid-state device (SSD), is called solid-state because it has no moving parts. The drives are built using nonvolatile memory, which is similar to that used for USB flash drives. Recall that this type of memory does not lose its data even after the power is turned off.

  In an SSD drive, flash memory is stored on EEPROM (Electronically Erasable Programmable Read-Only Memory) chips inside the drive housing. The chips contain grids of rows and columns with two transistors at each intersection that hold a 0 or 1 bit. One of these transistors is called a floating gate and accepts the 0 or 1 state according to a logic test called NAND (stands for "Not AND"). Therefore, the memory in an SSD is called NAND flash memory. EEPROM chips are limited as to the number of times transistors can be reprogrammed. Therefore, the life span of an SSD drive is based on the number of write operations to the drive. (The number of read operations does not affect the life span.) For example, one SSD manufacturer guarantees its SSD drives for 20 GB of write operations per day for three years. For normal use, a drive would not be used that much and would last much longer.

> **Notes** Many solid-state drive manufacturers reserve blocks on the drive that are used when blocks begin to prove they are no longer reliable. Also, a technique called **wear leveling** assures that the logical block addressing does not always address the same physical blocks in order to distribute write operations more evenly across the device.

Because flash memory is expensive, solid-state drives are much more expensive than magnetic hard drives, but they are faster, more reliable, last longer, and use less power than magnetic drives. Figure 6-2 shows two sizes of solid-state drives (2.5" and 1.8") and what the inside of an SSD hard drive looks like. The 1.8" drives are used in some laptops and other small mobile devices.

Courtesy of Toshiba America Electronic Components

Figure 6-2 Solid-state drives by Toshiba

- *Magnetic hard drive.* A **magnetic hard drive** has one, two, or more platters, or disks, that stack together and spin in unison inside a sealed metal housing that contains firmware to control reading and writing data to the drive and to communicate with the motherboard. The top and bottom of each disk have a **read/write head** that moves across the disk surface as all the disks rotate on a spindle (see Figure 6-3). All the read/write heads are controlled by an actuator, which moves the read/write heads across the disk surfaces in unison. The disk surfaces are covered with a magnetic medium that can hold data as magnetized spots. The spindle rotates at 5400, 7200, or 10,000 RPM (revolutions per minute). The faster the spindle, the better performing the drive.

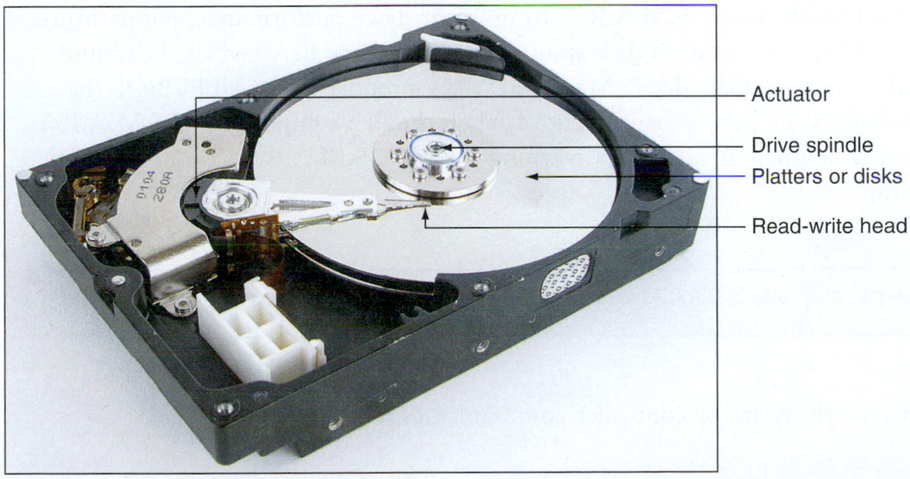

Figure 6-3 Inside a magnetic hard drive

Data is organized on a magnetic hard drive in concentric circles called tracks (see Figure 6-4). Each track is divided into segments called sectors (also called records). Older hard drives used sectors that contained 512 bytes. Most current hard drives use 4096-byte sectors.

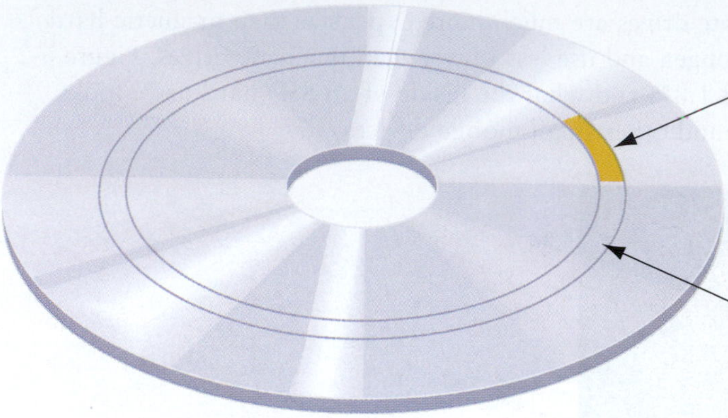

Figure 6-4 A hard drive is divided into tracks and sectors; several sectors make one cluster

- ***Hybrid hard drives.*** A hybrid hard drive (H-HDD), sometimes called a solid-state hybrid drive (SSHD), uses both technologies. The flash component serves as a buffer to improve drive performance. Some hybrid drives perform just as well as an SSD drive. For a hybrid drive to function, the operating system must support it.

Before a magnetic drive leaves the factory, sector markings are written to it in a process called low-level formatting. (This formatting is different from the high-level formatting that Windows does after a drive is installed in a computer.) The hard drive firmware, UEFI/BIOS on the motherboard, and the OS use a simple sequential numbering system called logical block addressing (LBA) to address all the sectors on the drive. SSD drives are marked into blocks, which are communicated to the motherboard and OS, which read/write to the drive in blocks just as with magnetic drives.

The size of each block and the total number of blocks on the drive determine the drive capacity. Today's drive capacities are usually measured in GB (gigabytes) or TB (terabytes, each of which is 1024 gigabytes). Magnetic drives are generally much larger in capacity than SSD drives.

You need to be aware of one more technology supported by both SSD and magnetic hard drives called S.M.A.R.T. (Self-Monitoring Analysis and Reporting Technology), which is used to predict when a drive is likely to fail. System UEFI/BIOS uses S.M.A.R.T. to monitor drive performance, temperature, and other factors. For magnetic drives, it monitors disk spin-up time, distance between the head and the disk, and other mechanical activities of the drive. Many SSD drives report to the UEFI/BIOS the number of write operations, which is the best measurement of when the drive might fail. If S.M.A.R.T. suspects a drive failure is about to happen, it displays a warning message. S.M.A.R.T. can be enabled and disabled in UEFI/BIOS setup.

Notes Malware has been known to give false S.M.A.R.T. alerts.

Now let's look at how the drive's firmware or controller communicates with the motherboard.

SATA INTERFACE STANDARDS USED BY A HARD DRIVE

A+
220-901
1.5, 1.7,
1.11

All hard drives in today's personal computers use the SATA interface standards to connect to the motherboard. The serial ATA or SATA (pronounced "*say*-ta") standard uses a serial data path, and a SATA data cable can accommodate a single SATA drive (see Figure 6-5).

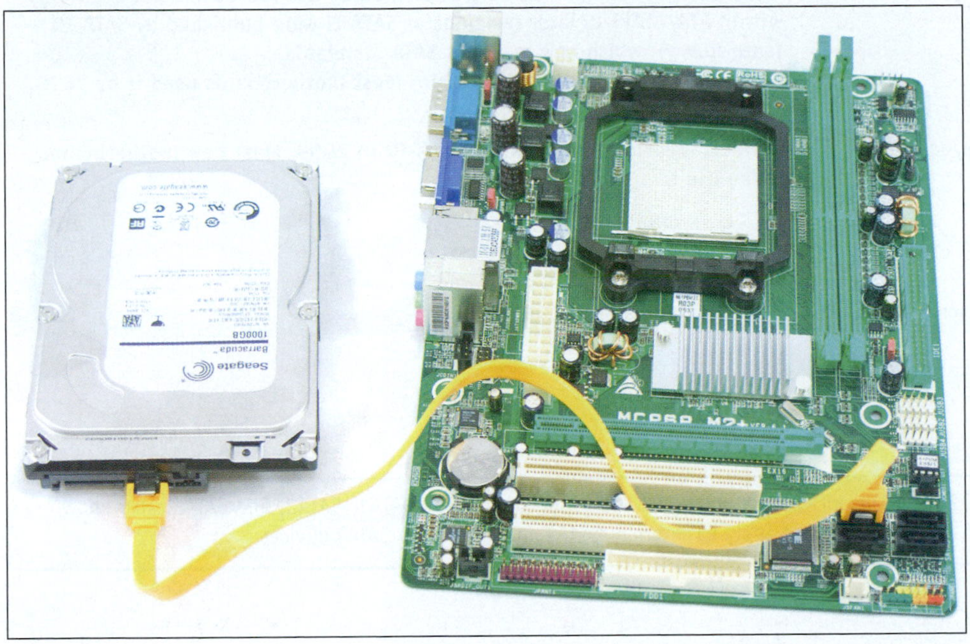

Figure 6-5 A SATA cable connects a single SATA drive to a motherboard SATA connector

6

Notes Years ago, hard drives used the Parallel ATA (PATA) standards, also called the IDE (Integrated Drive Electronics) standards, to connect to a motherboard. PATA allowed for one or two IDE connectors on a motherboard, each using a 40-pin data cable. Two drives could connect to one cable. In addition, a few personal computer hard drives used the SCSI (pronounced "scuzzy") interface standard.

External hard drives can connect to a computer by way of external SATA (eSATA), FireWire, or USB. Be sure the port provided by the computer uses the same standard that the external drive uses, for example, SuperSpeed USB 3.0 or eSATA III. If the port is not fast enough, you can install an expansion card to provide faster ports.

A consortium of manufacturers, called the Serial ATA International Organization (SATA-IO; see *sata-io.org*) and led by Intel, developed the SATA standards, and the standards also have the oversight of the T13 Committee (*t13.org*). SATA has had three major revisions, which are summarized in Table 6-1.

Notes Interface standards for drives define data speeds and transfer methods between the drive controller, the UEFI/BIOS, the chipset on the motherboard, and the OS. The standards also define the type of cables and connectors used by the drive and the motherboard or expansion cards.

SATA Standard	Data Transfer Rate	Comments
SATA Revision 1.x* SATA I or SATA1 Serial ATA-150 SATA/150 SATA-150	1.5 Gb/sec	SATA, first introduced as an ATA/ATAPI-7 standard, was published as part of a revision to the older PATA standards managed by the T13 Committee (*t13.org*) that governed the PATA standards.
SATA Revision 2.x* SATA II or SATA2 Serial ATA-300 SATA/300 SATA-300	3 Gb/sec	The first SATA II standards were published by the T13 Committee (*t13.org*) within ATA/ATAPI-8; later revisions of SATA II were published by SATA-IO (*sata-io.org*), which now manages SATA standards. The standard first came out in 2006. Most motherboards used it by 2010.
SATA Revision 3.x* SATA III or SATA3 Serial ATA-600 SATA/600 SATA-600	6 Gb/sec	SATA III was first published by SATA-IO in 2009. Most new motherboards today use this standard.

*Name assigned by the SATA-IO organization

Table 6-1 SATA standards

★ A+ Exam Tip The A+ 220-901 exam expects you to know the speeds used by SATA1, SATA2, and SATA3, also known as SATA I, SATA II, and SATA III. These speeds apply to internal (SATA) and external (eSATA) devices.

SATA interfaces are used by all types of drives, including hard drives, CD, DVD, Blu-ray, and tape drives. SATA supports hot-swapping, also called hot-plugging. With **hot-swapping**, you can connect and disconnect a drive while the system is running. Hard drives that can be hot-swapped cost significantly more than regular hard drives.

A SATA drive connects to one internal SATA connector on the motherboard by way of a 7-pin SATA data cable and uses a 15-pin SATA power connector (see Figure 6-6). An internal SATA data cable can be up to 1 meter in length. A motherboard might have two or more SATA connectors; use the connectors in the order recommended in the motherboard user guide. For example, for the four connectors shown in Figure 6-7, you are told to use the red ones before the black ones.

Figure 6-6 A SATA data cable and SATA power cable

Figure 6-7 This motherboard has two black and two red SATA II ports

Figure 6-8 Two eSATA ports on a motherboard

In addition to internal SATA connectors, the motherboard or an expansion card can provide **external SATA (eSATA)** ports for external drives (see Figure 6-8). External SATA drives use a special external shielded SATA cable up to 2 meters long. Seven-pin eSATA ports run at the same speed as the internal ports using SATA I, II, or III standards. The eSATA port is shaped differently from an internal SATA connector so as to prevent people from using the unshielded internal SATA data cables with the eSATA port.

When purchasing a SATA hard drive, keep in mind that the SATA standards for the drive and the motherboard need to match. If either the drive or the motherboard uses a slower SATA standard than the other device, the system will run at the slower speed. Other hard drive characteristics to consider when selecting a drive are covered later in the chapter.

Hands-On | Project 6-1 Examine UEFI/BIOS Settings for a Hard Drive

A+
220-901
1.5

Following the directions given in the chapter, "All About Motherboards," view the UEFI/BIOS setup information on your computer, and write down all the UEFI/BIOS settings that apply to your hard drive. Explain each setting that you can. What is the size of the installed drive? Does your system support S.M.A.R.T.? If so, is it enabled?

Now that you know about the various hard drive technologies and interfaces, let's see how to select and install a hard drive.

HOW TO SELECT AND INSTALL HARD DRIVES

A+
220-901
1.4, 1.5,
1.11, 3.1,
4.2

In this part of the chapter, you learn how to select a hard drive for your system. Then, you learn the details of installing a SATA drive. Next, you learn how to deal with using removable bays, the problem of installing a hard drive in a bay that is too wide for it, and special considerations to install a hard drive in a laptop. You also learn how to set up a RAID system.

SELECTING A HARD DRIVE

A+
220-901
1.4, 1.5,
1.11

When selecting a hard drive, keep in mind that to get the best performance from the system, the system UEFI/BIOS and the hard drive must support the same standard. If they don't support the same standard, they revert to the slower standard that both can use, or the drive will not work at all. There's no point in buying an expensive hard drive with features that your system cannot support.

Therefore, when making purchasing decisions, you need to know what standards the motherboard or controller card providing the drive interface can use. To find out, see the documentation for the board or the card. For the motherboard, you can look at UEFI/BIOS setup screens to see which standards are mentioned. However, know that when installing a drive, you don't need to know which SATA standard a hard drive supports because the startup UEFI/BIOS uses autodetection. With autodetection, the UEFI/BIOS detects the new drive and automatically selects the correct drive capacity and configuration, including the best possible standard supported by both the hard drive and the motherboard.

Notes To learn how to match up and install really old motherboards or drives, see the content "Selecting and Installing Hard Drives using Legacy Motherboards" in the online content that accompanies this text. For more information, see the Preface.

When purchasing a hard drive, consider the following factors that affect performance, use, and price:

- ***The capacity of the drive.*** Today's hard drives for desktop systems are in the range of 1 TB for SSD drives to more than 6 TB for magnetic drives. The more gigabytes or terabytes, the higher the price. Magnetic drives have larger capacity for the money than solid-state drives.
- ***The spindle speed.*** Magnetic hard drives for desktop systems run at 5400, 7200, or 10,000 RPM (revolutions per minute). The most common is 7200 RPM. The higher the RPMs, the faster the drive.
- ***The interface standard.*** Use the standards your motherboard supports. For SATA, most likely that will be SATA II or SATA III. For external drives, common standards are eSATA, FireWire 800 or 400, and SuperSpeed or Hi-Speed USB.
- ***The cache or buffer size.*** For magnetic hard drives, buffer memory improves hard drive performance and can range in size from 2 MB to 128 MB. The more the better, though the cost goes up as the size increases. A buffer helps because the hard drive reads ahead of the requested data and stores the extra data in the buffer. If the next read is already in the buffer, the controller does not need to return to the spinning platters for the data. Buffering especially improves performance when managing large files, such as when working with videos or movies.

A hard drive manufacturer might produce both magnetic drives and solid-state drives. Some hard drive manufacturers are listed in Table 6-2. Most manufacturers of memory also make solid-state drives.

Manufacturer	Website
Crucial	*www.crucial.com*
Kingston Technology	*www.kingston.com*
Samsung	*www.samsung.com*
Seagate Technology and Maxtor	*www.seagate.com* or *www.maxtor.com*
Western Digital	*www.wdc.com*

Table 6-2 Hard drive manufacturers

Now let's turn our attention to the step-by-step process of installing a SATA drive.

STEPS TO INSTALL A SATA DRIVE

A+ 220-901 1.4, 1.5, 1.11

In Figure 6-9, you can see the back of a SATA hard drive. A SATA drive might have jumpers used to set features such as the ability to power up from standby mode. Most likely, if jumpers are present on a SATA drive, the factory has set them as they should be and advises you not to change them.

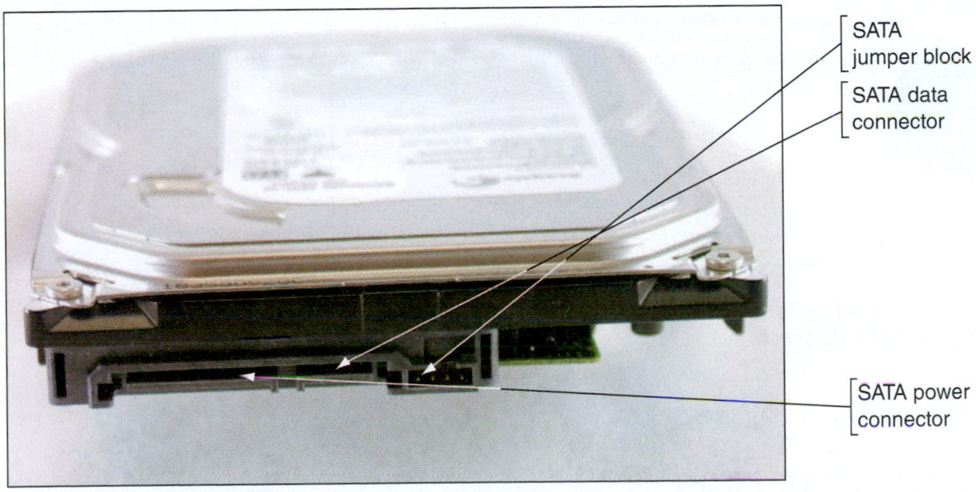

Figure 6-9 Rear of a SATA drive

★ A+ Exam Tip The A+ 220-901 exam expects you to know how to configure SATA devices in a system. What you learn in this chapter about installing a SATA hard drive in a system also applies to installing a SATA optical drive or tape drive. Hard drives, optical drives, and tape drives use a SATA data connector and a power connector.

Some SATA drives have two power connectors, as does the one in Figure 6-10. Choose between the SATA power connector (which is the preferred connector) or the legacy 4-pin Molex connector, but never install two power cords to the drive at the same time because this could damage the drive.

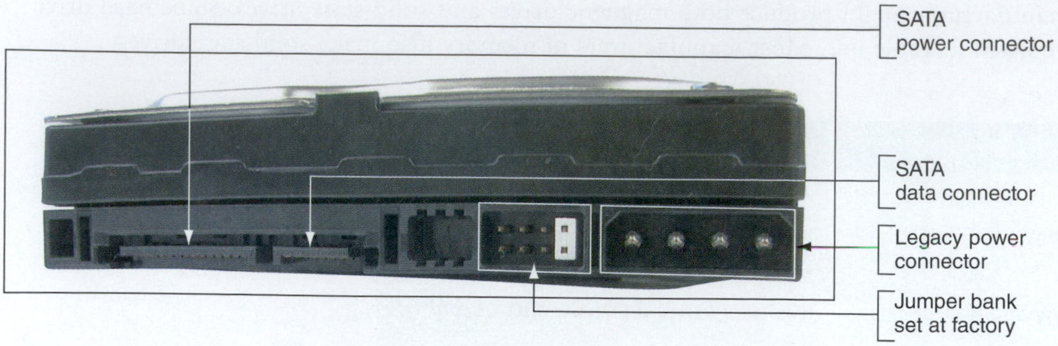

Figure 6-10 Rear of a SATA drive with two power connectors

You can also purchase a SATA controller card that can provide internal SATA connectors and external eSATA connectors. You might want to use a controller card when (1) the motherboard drive connectors are not functioning, or (2) the motherboard does not support a fast SATA standard that your hard drives use. Figure 6-11 shows a PCIe storage controller card that offers two internal SATA III connections and two eSATA III ports.

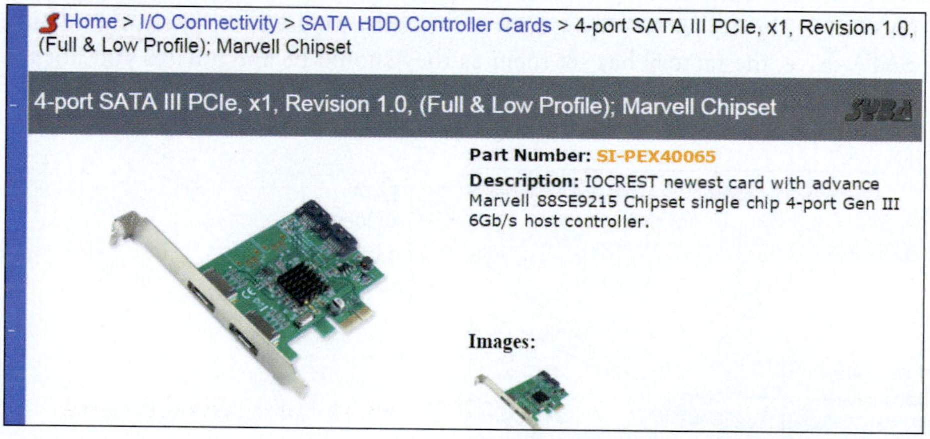

Source: SYBA at *www.sybausa.com*

Figure 6-11 SATA storage controller card by SYBA has two external and two internal ports and supports 6 Gbps SATA III speeds

Here is the step-by-step process of installing a SATA drive in a desktop system.

STEP 1: KNOW YOUR STARTING POINT

As with installing any other devices, before you begin installing a hard drive, make sure you know where your starting point is. Do this by answering these questions: How is your system configured? Is everything working properly? Verify which of your system's devices are working before installing a new one. Later, if a device does not work, the information will help you isolate the problem. Keeping notes is a good idea whenever you install new hardware or software or make any other changes to your computer system. Write down what you know about the system that might be important later.

Notes When installing hardware and software, don't install too many things at once. If something goes wrong, you won't know what's causing the problem. Install one device, start the system, and confirm that the new device is working before installing another.

STEP 2:READ THE DOCUMENTATION AND PREPARE YOUR WORK AREA

Before you take anything apart, carefully read all the documentation for the drive and controller card, as well as the part of your motherboard documentation that covers hard drive installation. Make sure that you can visualize all the steps in the installation. If you have any questions, keep researching until you locate the answer. You can also call technical support, or ask a knowledgeable friend for help. As you get your questions answered, you might discover that what you are installing will not work on your computer, but that is better than coping with hours of frustration and a disabled computer. You cannot always anticipate every problem, but at least you can know that you made your best effort to understand everything in advance. What you learn with thorough preparation pays off every time!

You're now ready to set out your tools, documentation, new hardware, and notebook. Remember the basic rules concerning static electricity. Be sure to protect against electrostatic discharge (ESD) by wearing an ESD strap during the installation. You need to also avoid working on carpet in the winter when there's a lot of static electricity.

Some added precautions for working with a hard drive are as follows:

- Handle the drive carefully.
- Do not touch any exposed circuitry or chips.
- Prevent other people from touching exposed microchips on the drive.
- When you first take the drive out of the static-protective package, touch the package containing the drive to a screw holding an expansion card or cover, or to a metal part of the computer case, for at least two seconds. This drains the static electricity from the package and from your body.
- If you must set down the drive outside the static-protective package, place it component-side-up on a flat surface.
- Do not place the drive on the computer case cover or on a metal table.

If you're assembling a new system, in most situations, it's best to install drives before you install the motherboard so that you will not accidentally bump sensitive motherboard components with the drives.

STEP 3: INSTALL THE DRIVE

So now you're ready to get started. Follow these steps to install the drive in the case:

1. Shut down the computer and unplug it. Then press the power button for three seconds to drain residual power. Remove the computer case cover. Check that you have an available power cord from the power supply for the drive.

> **Notes** If there are not enough power cords from a power supply, you can purchase a Y connector that can add an additional power cord.

2. Decide which bay will hold the drive. To do that, examine the locations of the drive bays and the length of the data cables and power cords. Bays designed for hard drives do not have access to the outside of the case, unlike bays for optical drives and other drives in which discs are inserted. Also, some bays are wider than others to accommodate wide drives such as a DVD drive. Will the data cable reach the drives and the motherboard connector? If not, rearrange your plan for locating the drive in a bay, or purchase a custom-length data cable. Some bays are stationary, meaning the drive is installed inside the bay because it stays in the case. Other bays are removable; you remove the bay and install the drive in the bay, and then return the bay to the case.
3. For a stationary bay, slide the drive in the bay, and using a screwdriver, secure one side of the drive with one or two short screws (see Figure 6-12). It's best to use two screws so the drive will not move in the bay, but sometimes a bay only provides a place for a single screw on each side. Some drive bays provide one or two tabs that you can pull out before you slide the drive in the bay and then push the

tabs in to secure the drive. Another option is a sliding tab (see Figure 6-13) that is used to secure the drive. Pull the tab back, slide in the drive, and push the tab forward to secure the drive.

Figure 6-12 Secure one side of the drive with one or two screws

> **Caution** Be sure the screws are not too long. If they are, you can screw too far into the drive housing, which will damage the drive itself.

Figure 6-13 This drive bay uses tabs to secure the drive

4. When using screws to secure the drive, carefully, without disturbing the drive, turn the case over and put one or two screws on the other side of the drive (see Figure 6-14). To best secure the drive in the case, use two screws on each side of the drive.

Figure 6-14 Secure the other side of the drive with one or two screws

Notes Do not allow torque to stress the drive. In other words, don't force a drive into a space that is too small for it. Also, placing two screws in diagonal positions across the drive can place pressure diagonally on the drive.

5. Check the motherboard documentation to find out which SATA connectors on the board to use first. For example, five SATA connectors are shown in Figure 6-15. The documentation says the two blue SATA connectors support 6.0 Gb/s and slower speeds, and the two black and one red SATA connectors support 3.0 Gb/s and slower speeds. On this board, be sure to connect your fastest hard drive to a blue connector. For some boards, the hard drive that has the bootable OS installed must be connected to the first SATA connector, which is usually labeled SATA 0. For both the drive and the motherboard, you can only plug the cable into the connector in one direction. A SATA cable might provide a clip on the connector to secure it (see Figure 6-16).

Figure 6-15 Five SATA connectors support different SATA standards

Figure 6-16 A clip on a SATA connector secures the connection

6. Connect a 15-pin SATA power connector or 4-pin Molex power connector from the power supply to the drive (see Figure 6-17).

Figure 6-17 Connect the SATA power cord to the drive

7. Check all your connections and power up the system.
8. To verify the drive was recognized correctly, enter UEFI/BIOS setup and look for the drive. Figure 6-18 shows a UEFI setup screen on one system that has four SATA connectors. A hard drive is installed on one of the faster yellow SATA connectors and a DVD drive is installed on one of the slower brown SATA connectors.

Notes If the drive light on the front panel of the computer case does not work after you install a new drive, try reversing the LED wire on the front panel header on the motherboard.

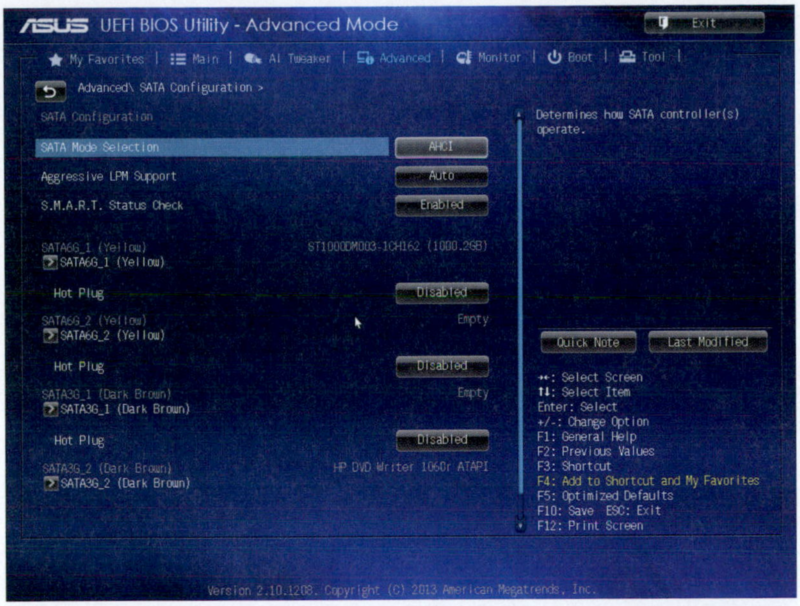

Source: American Megatrends, Inc.

Figure 6-18 UEFI setup screen showing a SATA hard drive and DVD drive installed

You are now ready to prepare the hard drive for first use. If you are installing a new hard drive in a system that is to be used for a new Windows installation, boot from the Windows setup DVD, and follow the directions on the screen to install Windows on the new drive. If you are installing a second hard drive in a system that already has Windows installed on the first hard drive, you use the Disk Management utility in Windows to prepare the drive for first use (called partitioning and formatting the drive). How to install Windows is covered in the "Installing Windows" chapter, and how to use Disk Management is covered in the chapter, "Maintaining Windows."

INSTALLING A DRIVE IN A REMOVABLE BAY

A+ 220-901 1.4, 1.5, 1.11

Now let's see how a drive installation goes when you are dealing with a removable bay. Figure 6-19 shows a computer case with a removable bay that has a fan at the front of the bay to help keep the drives cool. (The case manufacturer calls the bay a fan cage.) The bay is anchored to the case with three black locking pins. The third locking pin from the bottom of the case is disconnected in the photo.

Figure 6-19 The removable bay has a fan in front and is anchored to the case with locking pins

Unplug the cage fan from its power source. Turn the handle on each locking pin counterclockwise to remove it. Then slide the bay to the front and out of the case. Insert the hard drive in the bay, and use two screws on each side to anchor the drive in the bay (see Figure 6-20). Slide the bay back into the case, and reinstall the locking pins. Plug in the cage fan power cord.

Figure 6-20 Install the hard drive in the bay using two screws on each side of the drive

INSTALLING A SMALL DRIVE IN A WIDE BAY

A+ 220-901 1.4, 1.5, 1.11

If you are mounting a hard drive into a bay that is too large, a universal bay kit can help you securely fit the drive into the bay. These inexpensive kits should create a tailor-made fit. In Figure 6-21, you can see how the universal bay kit adapter works. The adapter spans the distance between the sides of the drive and the bay. Figure 6-22 shows a SATA SSD drive with the brackets connected. Because SSD drives are usually smaller than magnetic drives, you're likely to need a bay kit to fit these drives into most desktop computer cases.

Figure 6-21 Use the universal bay kit to make the drive fit the bay

Figure 6-22 SSD drive with bay kit connected

INSTALLING A HARD DRIVE IN A LAPTOP

A+
220-901
3.1

When purchasing and installing an internal hard drive or optical drive in a laptop, see the laptop manufacturer's documentation about specific sizes and connectors that will fit the laptop. Also be aware of voiding a warranty if you don't follow the laptop manufacturer's directions. Here is what you need to know when shopping for a laptop hard drive:

- A desktop hard drive is 3.5 inches wide and a laptop drive is 2.5 inches or 1.8 inches wide. Because the form factor of a laptop drive is more compact, it costs more than a desktop drive holding the same amount of data. Some laptop hard drives use SSD (solid-state device) technology.
- Today's laptop hard drives use a SATA interface, and older laptops used a PATA interface. Check your laptop manual to know which type of hard drive to buy, or remove the old drive and see which interface it uses. SATA data and power connectors on a laptop hard drive look the same as those in a desktop installation.

Before deciding to replace a hard drive, consider these issues:

- If the old drive has crashed, you'll need the recovery media to reinstall Windows and the drivers. Make sure you have the recovery media before you start.
- If you are upgrading from a low-capacity drive to a higher-capacity drive, you need to consider how you will transfer data from the old drive to the new one. One way to do that is to use a USB-to-SATA converter. Using this converter, both drives can be up and working on the laptop at the same time, so you can copy files.

To replace a hard drive, older laptop computers required that you disassemble the laptop. With newer laptops, you should be able to easily replace a drive. For example, for one laptop, first power down the system, remove peripherals, including the AC adapter, and remove the battery pack. Then remove a screw that holds the drive in place (see Figure 6-23).

Caution To protect sensitive components, never open a laptop case without first unplugging the AC adapter and removing the battery pack.

Figure 6-23 This one screw holds the hard drive in position

Open the lid of the laptop slightly so that the lid doesn't obstruct your removing the drive. Turn the laptop on its side and push the drive out of its bay (see Figure 6-24). Then remove the plastic cover from the drive. Move the cover to the new drive, and insert the new drive in the bay. Next, replace the screw and power up the system.

Figure 6-24 Push the drive out of its bay

When the system boots up, if UEFI/BIOS setup is set to autodetect hard drives, UEFI/BIOS recognizes the new drive and searches for an operating system. If the drive is new, boot from the Windows recovery DVD and install the OS.

> **Notes** It is possible to give general directions on desktop computer repair that apply to all kinds of brands, models, and systems. Not so with laptops. Learning to repair laptops involves learning unique ways to assemble, disassemble, and repair laptop components for specific brands and models of laptops.

For some laptops, such as the one shown in Figure 6-25, you remove a cover on the bottom of the computer to expose the hard drive. Then remove one screw that anchors the drive. You can then remove the drive.

Figure 6-25 Remove a cover on the bottom of the laptop to exchange the hard drive, which is attached to a proprietary bracket

SETTING UP HARDWARE RAID

A+ 220-901 1.5, 1.11

For most personal computers, a single hard drive works independently of any other installed drives. A technology that configures two or more hard drives to work together as an array of drives is called RAID (redundant array of inexpensive disks or redundant array of independent disks). Two reasons you might consider using RAID are:

- To improve fault tolerance, which is a computer's ability to respond to a fault or catastrophe, such as a hardware failure or power outage, so that data is not lost. If data is important enough to justify the cost, you can protect the data by continuously writing two copies of it, each to a different hard drive. This method is most often used on high-end, expensive file servers, but it is occasionally appropriate for a single-user workstation.
- To improve performance by writing data to two or more hard drives so that a single drive is not excessively used.

TYPES OF RAID

Several types of RAID exist; the four most commonly used are RAID 0, RAID 1, RAID 5, and RAID 10. Following is a brief description of each, including another method of two disks working together, called spanning. The first four methods are diagrammed in Figure 6-26:

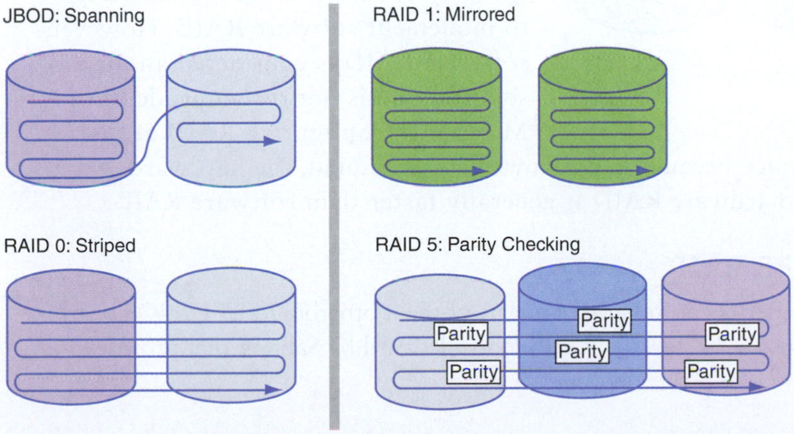

Figure 6-26 Ways that hard drives can work together

- **Spanning**, sometimes called JBOD (just a bunch of disks), uses two hard drives to hold a single Windows volume, such as drive E:. Data is written to the first drive, and, when it is full, the data continues to be written to the second.
- **RAID 0** also uses two or more physical disks to increase the disk space available for a single volume. RAID 0 writes to the physical disks evenly across all disks so that no one disk receives all the activity and therefore improves performance. Windows calls RAID 0 a **striped volume**. To understand that term, think of data striped—or written across—several hard drives. RAID 0 is preferred to spanning.
- **RAID 1** is a type of mirroring that duplicates data on one drive to another drive and is used for fault tolerance. Each drive has its own volume, and the two volumes are called mirrors. If one drive fails, the other continues to operate and data is not lost. Windows calls RAID 1 a **mirrored volume**.
- **RAID 5** stripes data across three or more drives and uses parity checking, so that if one drive fails, the other drives can re-create the data stored on the failed drive by using the parity information. Data is not duplicated, and, therefore, RAID 5 makes better use of volume capacity. RAID-5 drives increase performance and provide fault tolerance. Windows calls these drives **RAID-5 volumes**.
- **RAID 10**, also called **RAID 1+0** and pronounced "RAID one zero" (*not* "RAID ten"), is a combination of RAID 1 and RAID 0. It takes at least four disks for RAID 10. Data is mirrored across pairs of disks, as shown at the top of Figure 6-27. In addition, the two pairs of disks are striped, as shown at the bottom of Figure 6-27. To help you better understand RAID 10, in the figure notice the data labeled as A, A, B, B across the first stripe. RAID 10 is the most expensive solution that provides the best redundancy and performance.

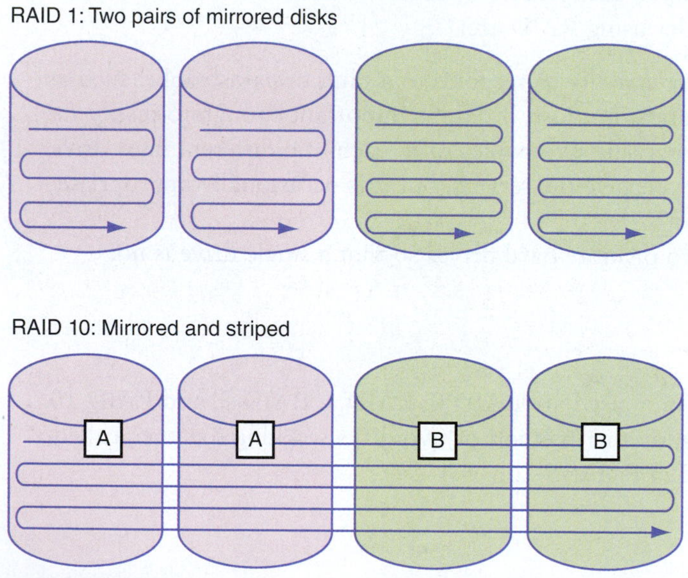

Figure 6-27 RAID 1 and RAID 10

> **A+ Exam Tip** The A+ 220-901 exam expects you to be able to contrast RAID 0, RAID 1, RAID 5, and RAID 10.

All RAID configurations can be accomplished at the hardware level (called hardware RAID) or at the operating system level (called software RAID). Using Windows 7 to implement software RAID, the Disk Management utility is used to configure a group of hard drives in a RAID array. In Windows 8, you can use the Disk Management utility or the new Windows 8 Storage Spaces utility to implement software RAID. However, software RAID is considered an unstable solution and is not recommended by Microsoft. Configuring RAID at the hardware level is considered best practice because if Windows gets corrupted, the hardware might still be able to protect the data. Also, hardware RAID is generally faster than software RAID.

HOW TO IMPLEMENT HARDWARE RAID

Hardware RAID can be set up by using a RAID controller that is part of the motherboard UEFI/BIOS or by using a RAID controller **storage card**. Figure 6-28 shows a RAID controller card by Sabrent that provides four SATA ports.

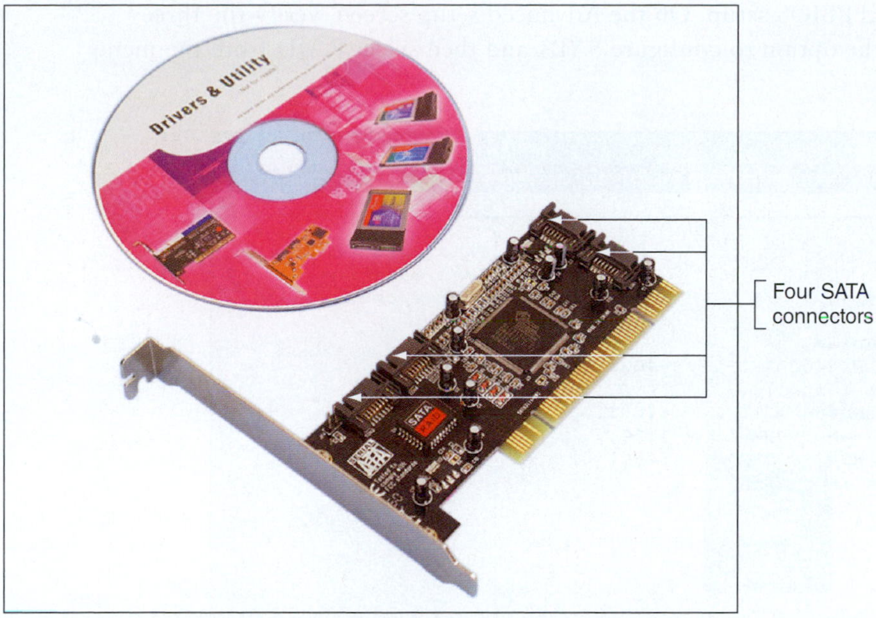

Figure 6-28 RAID controller card provides four SATA internal connectors

A+ Exam Tip The A+ 220-901 exam expects you to be able to set up hardware RAID.

When installing a hardware RAID system, for best performance, all hard drives in an array should be identical in brand, size, speed, and other features. Also, if Windows is to be installed on a hard drive that is part of a RAID array, RAID must be implemented before Windows is installed. As with installing any hardware, first read the documentation that comes with the motherboard or RAID controller and follow those specific directions rather than the general guidelines given here. Make sure you understand which RAID configurations the board supports.

For one motherboard that has six SATA connectors that support RAID 0, 1, 5, and 10, here are the general directions to install the RAID array using three matching hard drives in a RAID-5 array:

1. Install the three SATA drives in the computer case and connect each drive to a SATA connector on the motherboard (see Figure 6-29). To help keep the drives cool, the drives are installed with an empty bay between each drive.

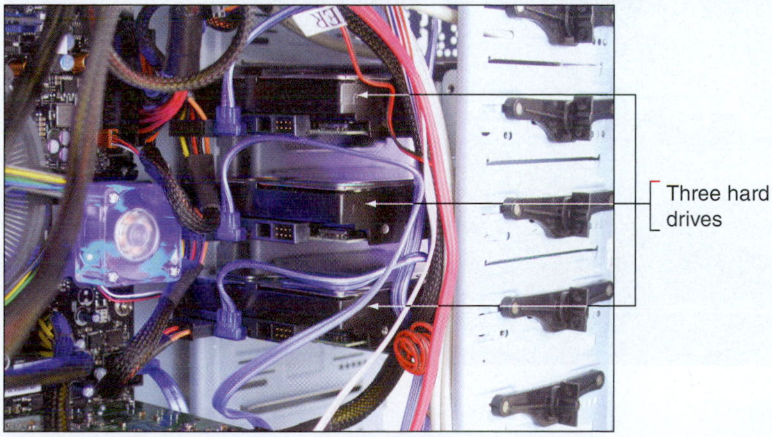

Figure 6-29 Install three matching hard drives in a system

2. Boot the system and enter UEFI/BIOS setup. On the Advanced setup screen, verify the three drives are recognized. Select the option to configure SATA and then select RAID from the menu (see Figure 6-30).

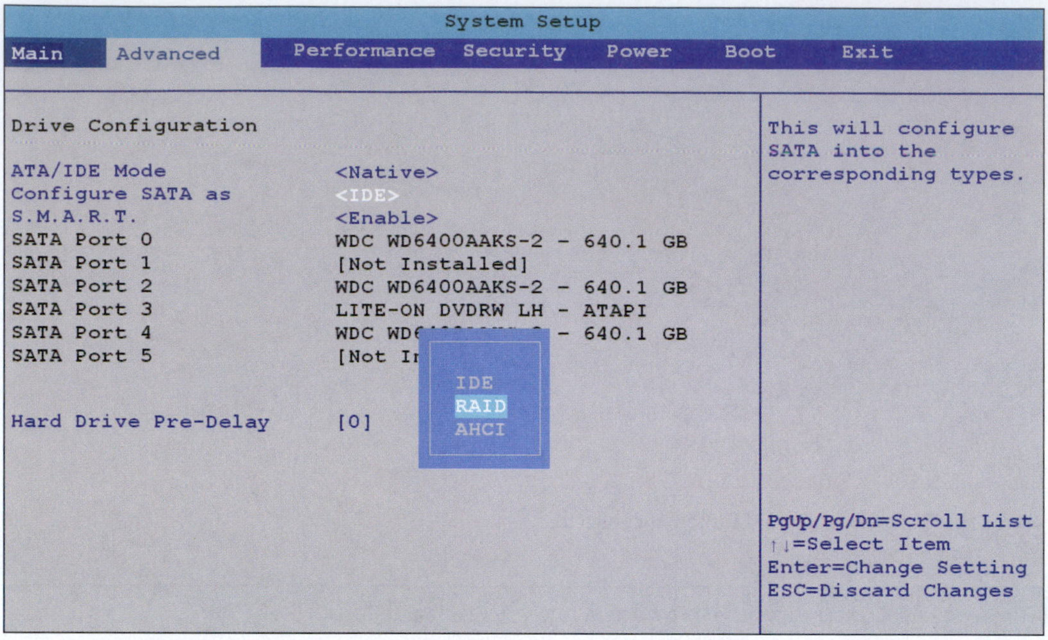

Source: Intel

Figure 6-30 Configure SATA ports on the motherboard to enable RAID

3. Reboot the system and a message is displayed on screen: "Press <Ctrl+I> to enter the RAID Configuration Utility." Press **Ctrl** and **I** to enter the utility (see Figure 6-31). Notice in the information area that the three drives are recognized and their current status is Non-RAID Disk.

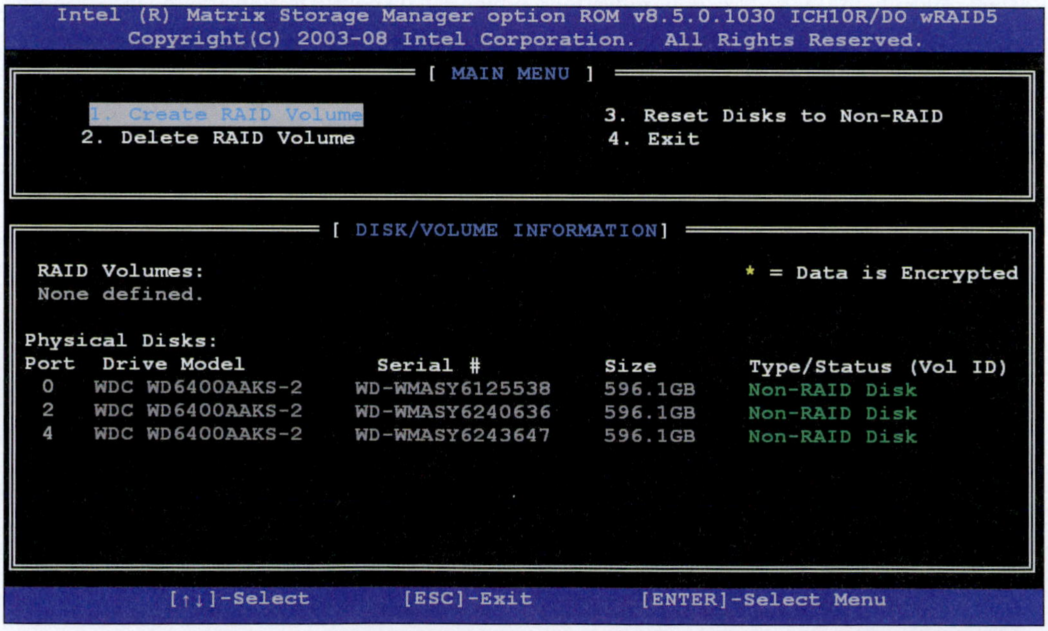

Source: Intel

Figure 6-31 BIOS utility to configure a RAID array

4. Select option 1 to **Create RAID Volume.** On the next screen shown in Figure 6-32, enter a volume name (FileServer in our example).

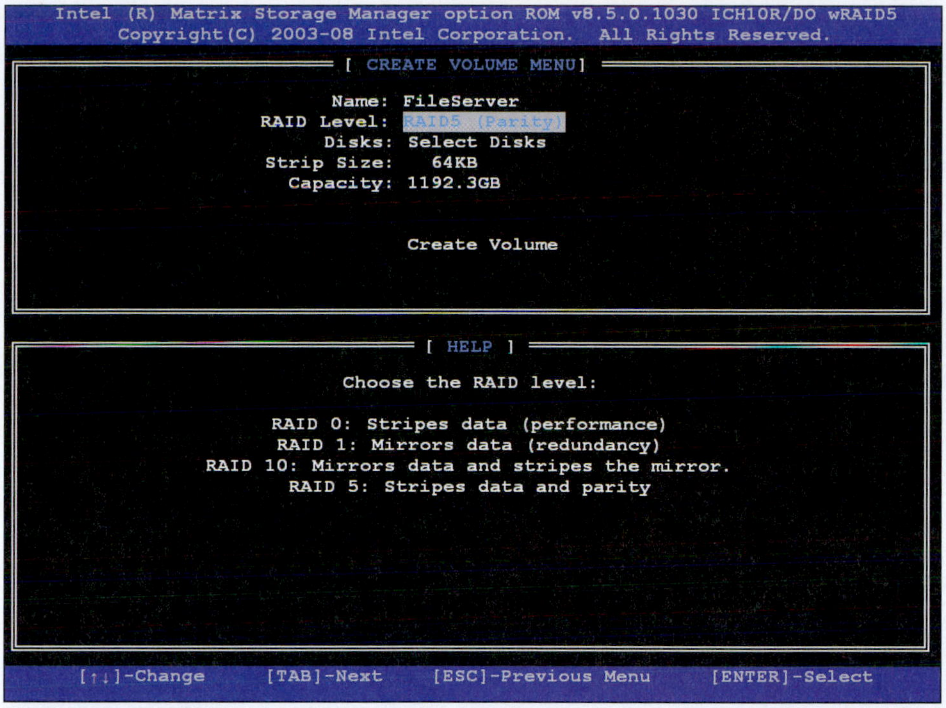

Source: Intel

Figure 6-32 Make your choices for the RAID array

5. Under RAID Level, select **RAID5 (Parity)**. Because we are using RAID 5, which requires three hard drives, the option to select the disks for the array is not available. All three disks will be used in the array.
6. Select the value for the Strip Size. (This is the amount of space devoted to one strip across the striped array. Choices are 32 KB, 64 KB, or 128 KB.)
7. Enter the size of the volume. The available size is shown in Figure 6-32 as 1192 GB, but you don't have to use all the available space. The space you don't use can later be configured as another array. (In this example, I entered 500 GB.)
8. Select **Create Volume** to complete the RAID configuration. A message appears warning you that if you proceed, all data on all three hard drives will be lost. Type **Y** to continue. The array is created and the system reboots.

You are now ready to install Windows. Windows 8/7/Vista have built-in hardware RAID drivers and, therefore, automatically "see" the RAID array as a single 500-GB hard drive. After Windows is installed on the drive, Windows will call it drive C:.

APPLYING | CONCEPTS TROUBLESHOOT HARD DRIVE INSTALLATIONS

A+
220-901
4.2

Sometimes, trouble crops up during an installation. Keeping a cool head; thinking things through carefully a second, third, and fourth time; and using all available resources will most likely get you out of any mess.

Installing a hard drive is not difficult, unless you have an unusually complex situation. For example, your first hard drive installation should not involve the extra complexity of installing a RAID array. If a complicated installation is necessary and you have never installed a hard drive, ask for expert help.

(continues)

The following list describes errors that cropped up during a few hard drive installations; the list also includes the causes of the errors and what was done about them. Everyone learns something new when making mistakes, and you probably will, too. You can then add your own experiences to this list:

- Shawn physically installed a SATA hard drive. He turned on the machine and accessed UEFI/BIOS setup. The hard drive was not listed as an installed device. He checked and discovered that autodetection was not enabled. He enabled it and rebooted. Setup recognized the drive.
- When first turning on a previously working computer, Susan received the following error message: "Hard drive not found." She turned off the machine, checked all cables, and discovered that the data cable from the motherboard to the drive was loose. She reseated the cable and rebooted. POST found the drive.
- Lucia physically installed a new hard drive, replaced the cover on the computer case, and booted the computer with a Windows setup DVD in the drive. POST beeped three times and stopped. Recall that diagnostics during POST are often communicated by beeps if the tests take place before POST has checked video and made it available to display the messages. Three beeps on some computers signal a memory error. Lucia turned off the computer and checked the memory modules on the motherboard. A module positioned at the edge of the motherboard next to the cover had been bumped as she replaced the cover. She reseated the module and booted again, this time with the cover still off. The error disappeared.
- Jason physically installed a new hard drive and turned on the computer. He received the following error: "No boot device available." He forgot to insert a Windows setup DVD. He put the disc in the drive and rebooted the machine successfully.
- The hard drive did not physically fit into the bay. The screw holes did not line up. Juan got a bay kit, but it just didn't seem to work. He took a break, went to lunch, and came back to make a fresh start. Juan asked others to help view the brackets, holes, and screws from a fresh perspective. It didn't take long to discover that he had overlooked the correct position for the brackets in the bay.

Caution When things are not going well, you can tense up and make mistakes more easily. Be certain to turn off the machine before doing anything inside! Not doing so can be a costly error. For example, a friend had been trying and retrying to boot for some time and got frustrated and careless. She plugged the power cord into the drive without turning the computer off. The machine began to smoke and everything went dead. The next thing she learned was how to replace a power supply!

EXTERNAL ENCLOSURES

A+
220-901
1.5, 1.11

Hard drives are sometimes stored in external enclosures such as the one shown in Figure 6-33. These enclosures make it easy to expand the storage capacity of a single computer or to make available hard drive storage to an entire network. For network attached storage (NAS), the enclosure connects to the network using an Ethernet port. When the storage is used by a single computer, the connection is made using a USB or eSATA port. Regardless of how the enclosure connects to a computer or network, the hard drives inside the enclosure might use a SATA connection.

Courtesy of D-Link Corporation

Figure 6-33 The NAS ShareCenter Pro 1100 by D-Link can hold four hot-swappable SATA hard drives totaling 12 TB of storage, has a dual-core processor and 512 MB of RAM, and supports RAID

Here is what you need to know about supporting these external enclosures:

- An enclosure might contain firmware that supports RAID. For example, a switch on the rear of one enclosure for two hard drives can be set for RAID 0, RAID 1, or stand-alone drives. Read the documentation for the enclosure to find out how to manage the RAID volumes.
- To replace a hard drive in an enclosure, see the documentation for the enclosure to find out how to open the enclosure and replace the drive.
- If a computer case is overheating, one way to solve this problem is to remove the hard drives from the case and install them in an external enclosure. However, it's better to leave the hard drive that contains the Windows installation in the case.

Hands-On | Project 6-2 Select a Replacement Hard Drive

A+
220-901
1.5

Suppose one of the 640-GB Western Digital hard drives installed in the RAID array and shown in Figure 6-29 has failed. Search the Internet and find a replacement drive as close to this drive as possible. Print three webpages showing the sizes, features, and prices of three possible replacements. Which drive would you recommend as the replacement drive and why?

Hands-On | Project 6-3 Prepare for Hard Drive Hardware Problems

A+
220-901
4.2

1. Boot your PC and make certain that it works properly. Turn off your computer, remove the computer case, and disconnect the data cable to your hard drive. Turn on the computer again. Write down the message that appears.
2. Turn off the computer and reconnect the data cable. Reboot and make sure the system is working again.
3. Turn off the computer and disconnect the power supply cord to the hard drive. Turn on the computer. Write down the error message that appears.
4. Turn off the computer, reconnect the power supply, and reboot the system. Verify the system is working again.

Hands-On | Project 6-4 Install a Hard Drive

A+
220-901
1.5

In a lab that has one hard drive per computer, you can practice installing a hard drive by removing a drive from one computer and installing it as a second drive in another computer. When you boot up the computer with two drives, verify that both drives are accessible in Windows 8 File Explorer or Windows 7/Vista Windows Explorer. Then remove the second hard drive, and return it to its original computer. Verify that both computers and drives are working.

Now let's move on to other types of storage devices, including tape drives, optical drives, and flash cards.

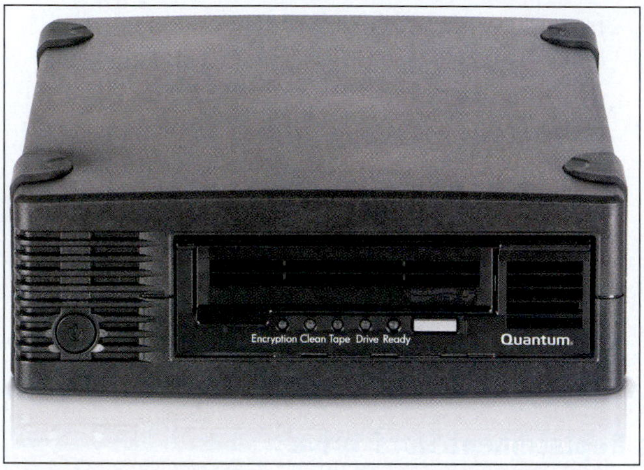

Courtesy of Quantum Corporation

Figure 6-34 The LTO-5 HH tape drive by Quantum writes to LTO Ultrium 5 and LTO Ultrium 4 tapes and reads from LTO Ultrium 5, LTO Ultrium 4, and LTO Ultrium 3 tapes. It provides AES 256-bit data encryption security, WORM functionality, and partitioning capability.

IDENTIFYING TAPE DRIVES

A+
220-901
1.5, 1.11

Tape drives (see Figure 6-34) are an inexpensive way of backing up an entire hard drive or portions of it. Because tape drives are less expensive for backups than external hard drives, CDs, DVDs, or USB flash drives, they are still used for backups even though other methods are more convenient. Tapes currently have up to 185 TB true tape capacity and come in several types and formats. Some tape drives and tape cartridges support WORM (write once and read many). WORM drives and cartridges assure that data written on the tape will not be deleted or overwritten. Most tape drives come bundled with backup software to use them.

★ A+ Exam Tip The A+ 220-901 exam expects you to know how to install a tape drive and how to select the right tapes for the drive.

The biggest disadvantage of using tape drives is that data is stored on tape by sequential access; to read data from anywhere on the tape, you must start at the beginning of the tape and read until you come to the sought-after data. Sequential access makes recovering files slow and inconvenient, which is why tapes are not used for general-purpose data storage.

Notes Two basic ways computers access data is random access and sequential access. As an analogy, "pick a card, any card" is random access and "take the first card in the stack" is sequential access.

Tape drives accommodate one of two kinds of tapes: full-sized data cartridges are $4 \times 6 \times \frac{5}{8}$ inches, and the smaller minicartridges, like the one shown in Figure 6-35, are $3\frac{1}{4} \times 2\frac{1}{2} \times \frac{3}{5}$ inches. Minicartridges are more popular because their drives can fit into a standard 3-inch drive bay of a computer case.

Figure 6-35 Minicartridge for a tape drive has a write-protect switch

Here is a list of some of the more common types of tape cartridges:

- ***DDS (Digital Data Storage).*** DDS-1, DDS-2, DDS-3, DDS-4, and DDS-5 are popular types. DDS-5 holds up to 36 GB of native or 72 GB of compressed data. DDS-5 is also called DAT72.
- ***LTO (Linear Tape-Open).*** LTO Ultrium 2, LTO Ultrium 3, LTO Ultrium 4, and LTO Ultrium 5 are sometimes referred to as LTO cartridges. LTO Ultrium 5 holds up to 1.5 TB of native or 3.0 TB of compressed data. Figure 6-36 shows an LTO Ultrium 3 tape.

Figure 6-36 This Maxel LTO Ultrium 3 data tape cartridge can hold up to 800 GB of compressed data

- ***DLT (Digital Linear Tape).*** DLT IV or DLT-4 holds up to 40 GB of native or 80 GB of compressed data.
- ***SDLT (Super Digital Linear Tape).*** Super DLT II holds up to 300 GB of native or 600 GB of compressed data.
- ***Travan.*** Travan cartridges vary from TR-1 through TR-7. The TR-7 holds 20 GB of native and 40 GB of compressed data.
- ***AIT (Advanced Intelligent Tape).*** AIT types have been around a long time and include AIT Turbo, AIT-1 through AIT-5, and S-AIT. S-AIT holds up to 1.3 TB of compressed data.
- ***SLR (Scalable Linear Recording).*** SLR types include SLR1 through SLR140. SLR140 holds 70 GB of native or 140 GB of compressed data.

When selecting a tape drive, consider how many and what type of cartridges the drive can use and how it interfaces with the computer. The drive might be able to read from more types of cartridges than it can write to. A tape drive can be external or internal. An external tape drive costs more but can be used by more than one computer. An internal tape drive can interface with a computer using a SATA, PATA, or SCSI connection. An external tape drive can connect to a computer using a USB, FireWire, SCSI, SAS, or eSATA port.

Notes For an interesting photo gallery of tape media, see *backupworks.com*.

SUPPORTING OTHER TYPES OF STORAGE DEVICES

A+
220-901
1.5, 1.11

Before we explore the details of several other types of storage devices, including optical discs, USB flash drives, and memory cards, let's start with the file systems they might use.

FILE SYSTEMS USED BY STORAGE DEVICES

A+
220-901
1.5, 1.11

A storage device, such as a hard drive, CD, DVD, USB flash drive, or memory card, uses a file system to manage the data stored on the device. A file system is the overall structure the OS uses to name, store, and organize files on a drive. In Windows, each storage device is assigned a drive letter. In Windows 8 File Explorer or Windows 7/Vista Windows Explorer, to see what file system a device is using, right-click the device and select **Properties** from the shortcut menu. The device Properties box appears, which shows the file system and storage capacity of the device (see Figure 6-37).

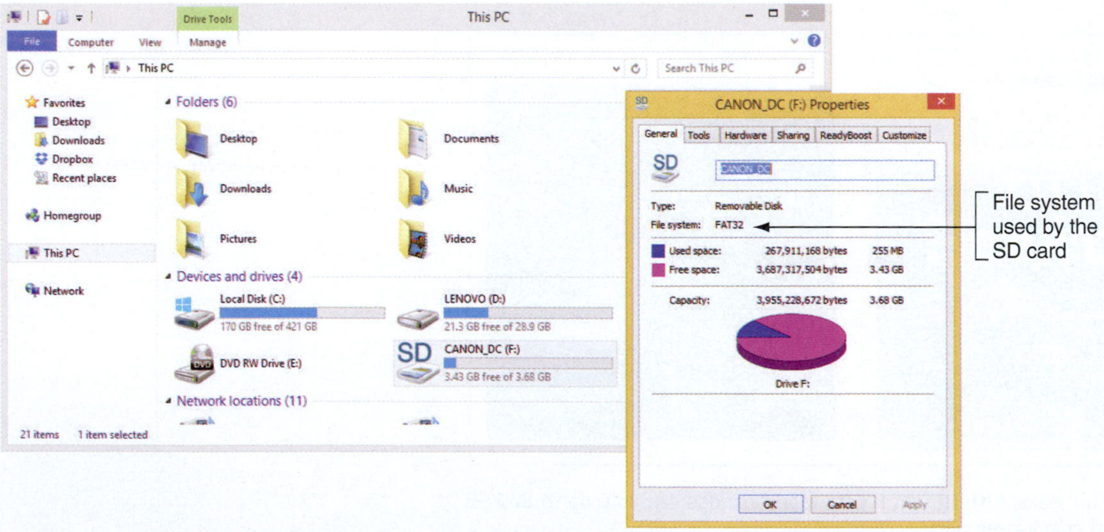

Figure 6-37 This 4-GB SD card is using the FAT32 file system

Installing a new file system on a device is called formatting the device, and the process erases all data on the device. One way to format a device is to right-click the device and select **Format** from the shortcut menu. In the box that appears, you can select the file system to use (see Figure 6-38). The New Technology file system (NTFS) is primarily used by hard drives. The exFAT file system is used by large-capacity removable storage devices such as large-capacity USB flash drives, memory cards, and some external hard drives. In addition, the older FAT32 and FAT file systems are used by smaller-capacity devices. If you have problems with a device, make sure it's using a file system appropriate for your situation.

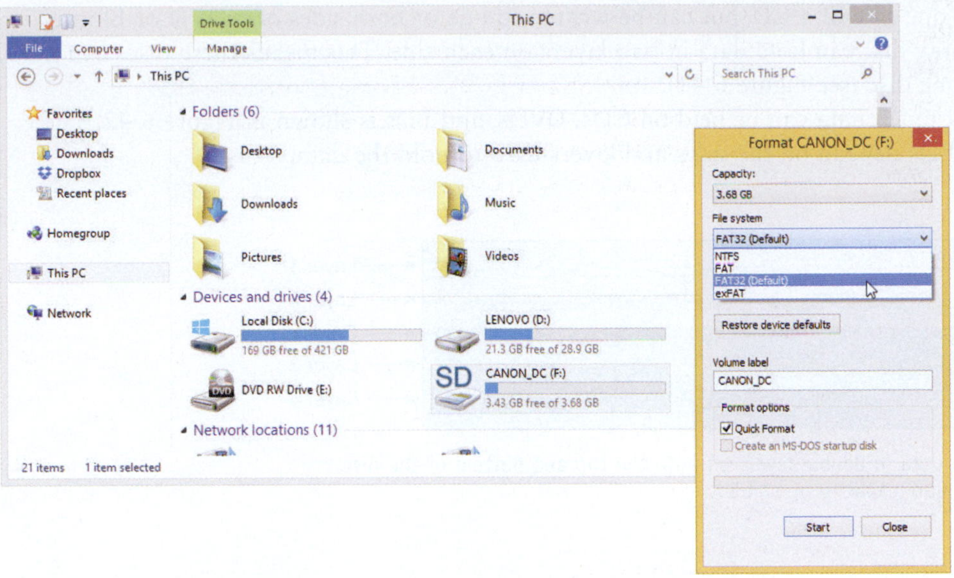

Figure 6-38 A storage device can be formatted using Windows Explorer

Now let's look at the types of optical drives you might be called on to support.

STANDARDS USED BY OPTICAL DRIVES AND DISCS

A+ 220-901 1.5, 1.11

CDs, DVDs, and Blu-ray discs use similar laser technologies. Tiny lands and pits on the surface of a disc represent bits, which a laser beam can read. This is why they are called optical storage technologies. CD (compact disc) drives use the CDFS (Compact Disc File System) or the UDF (Universal Disk Format) file system, while DVD (digital versatile disc or digital video disc) drives and Blu-ray Disc (BD) drives use the newer UDF file system.

Blu-ray drives are backward compatible with DVD and CD technologies, and DVD drives are backward compatible with CD technologies. Depending on the drive features, an optical drive might be able to read and write to BDs, DVDs, and CDs. An internal optical drive can interface with the motherboard by way of a SATA connection. An external drive might use an eSATA, FireWire, or USB port. Figure 6-39 shows an internal DVD drive, and Figure 6-40 shows an external DVD drive.

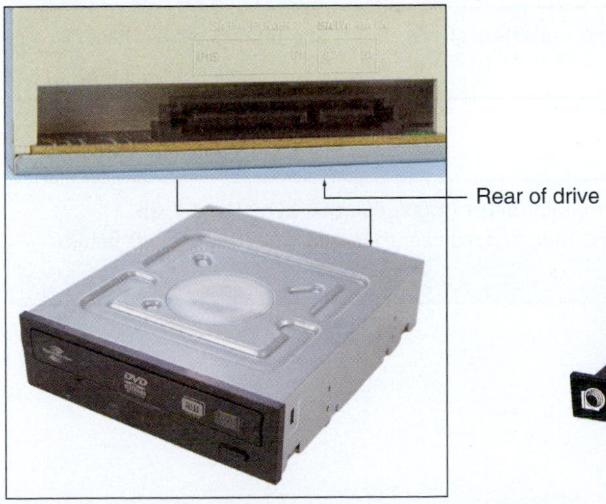

Figure 6-39 This internal DVD drive uses a SATA connection

Courtesy of Plextor

Figure 6-40 The PX-610U external DVD±RW drive by Plextor uses a USB 2.0 port

Data is written to only one side of a CD, but can be written to one or both sides of a DVD or Blu-ray disc. Also, a DVD or Blu-ray disc can hold data in two layers on each side. This means these discs can hold a total of four layers on one disc (see Figure 6-41).

The breakdown of how much data can be held on CDs, DVDs, and BDs is shown in Figure 6-42. The capacities for DVDs and BDs depend on the sides and layers used to hold the data.

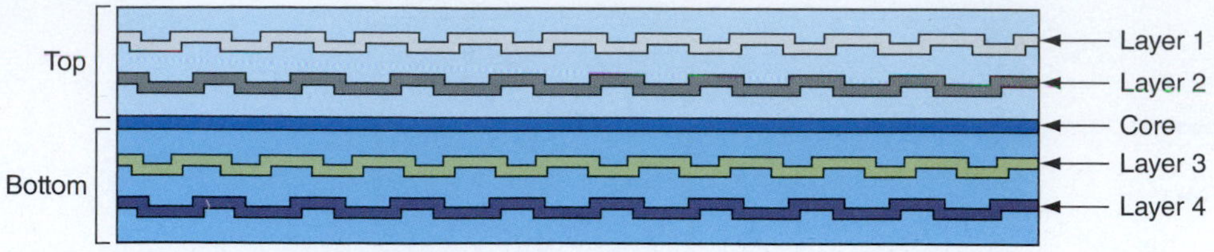

Figure 6-41 A DVD can hold data in double layers on both the top and bottom of the disc, yielding a maximum capacity of 17 GB

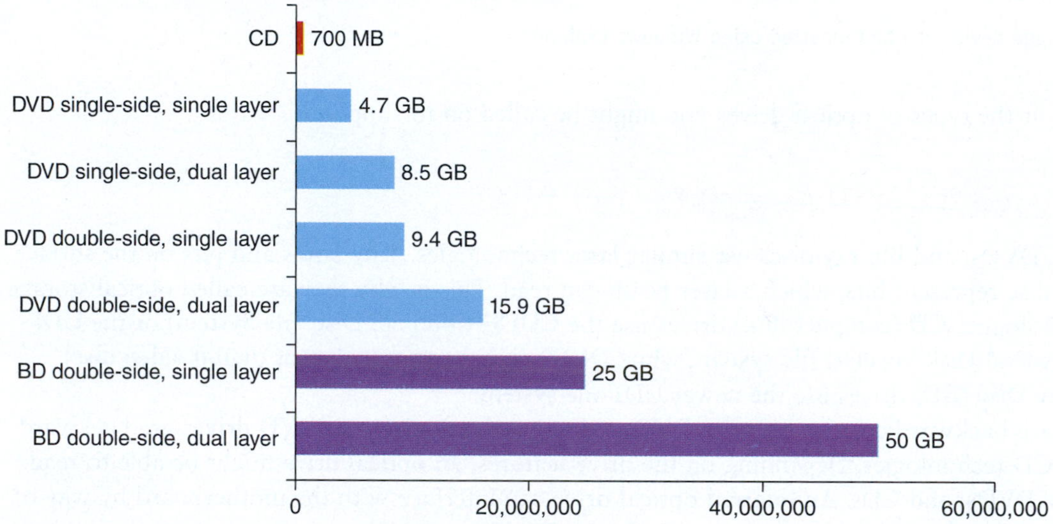

Figure 6-42 Storage capacities for CDs, DVDs, and BD discs

> **A+ Exam Tip** The A+ 220-901 exam expects you to know the capacities of CDs, DVDs, and Blu-ray discs. These capacities are all listed in Figure 6-42.

> **Notes** The discrepancy in the computer industry between one billion bytes (1,000,000,000 bytes) and 1 GB (1,073,741,824 bytes) exists because 1 KB equals 1024 bytes. Even though documentation might say that a DVD holds 17 GB, in fact, it holds 17 billion bytes, which is only 15.90 GB.

When shopping for an optical drive, suppose you see a couple of ads like those shown in Figure 6-43. To sort out the mix of disc standards, Table 6-3 can help. The table lists the popular CD, DVD, and Blu-ray disc standards.

Source: *tigerdirect.com*

Figure 6-43 Ads for internal and external DVD burners

Disc Standard	Description
CD-ROM disc or drive	*CD-read-only memory.* A CD-ROM disc burned at the factory can hold music, software, or other data. The bottom of a CD-ROM disc is silver. A CD-ROM drive can read CDs.
CD-R disc	*CD recordable.* A CD-R disc is a write-once CD.
CD-RW disc or drive	*CD rewriteable.* A CD-RW disc can be written to many times. A CD-RW drive can write to a CD-RW or CD-R disc and also overwrite a CD-RW disc.
DVD-ROM drive	*DVD read-only memory.* A DVD-ROM drive can also read CDs or DVDs.
DVD-R disc	*DVD recordable, single layer.* A DVD-R disc can hold up to 4.7 GB of data and is a write-once disc.
DVD-R DL disc	*DVD recordable in dual layers.* Doubles storage to 8.5 GB of data on one disc surface.
DVD-RW disc or drive	*DVD rewriteable.* A DVD-RW disc is also known as an erasable, recordable drive or a write-many disc. The speeds in an ad for an optical drive indicate the maximum speed supported when burning this type of disc, for example, DVD-RW 6X.
DVD-RW DL disc or drive, aka DL DVD drive	*DVD rewriteable, dual layers.* A DVD-RW DL disc doubles storage capacity to 8.5 GB.
DVD+R disc or drive	*DVD recordable.* Similar to but faster than DVD-R. Discs hold about 4.7 GB of data.
DVD+R DL disc or drive	*DVD recordable, dual layers.* Doubles disc storage to 8.5 GB on one surface.
DVD+RW disc or drive	*DVD rewriteable.* Faster than DVD-RW.
DVD-RAM disc or drive	*DVD Random Access Memory.* Rewriteable and erasable. You can erase or rewrite certain sections of a DVD-RAM disc without disturbing other sections of the disc, and the discs can handle many times over the number of rewrites (around 100,000 rewrites), compared with about a thousand rewrites for DVD-RW and DVD+RW discs. DVD-RAM discs are popular media used in camcorders and set-top boxes.
BD-ROM drive	*BD read-only memory.* A Blu-ray BD-ROM drive can also read DVDs, and some can read CDs.
BD-R disc or drive	*BD recordable.* A BD-R drive might also write to DVDs or CDs.
BD-RE disc or drive	*BD rewriteable.* A BD-RE drive might also write to DVDs or CDs.

Table 6-3 Optical discs and drive standards

A+ Exam Tip The A+ 220-901 exam expects you to know about the combo optical drives and burners, including CD, CD-RW, DVD, DVD-RW, DVD DL, Blu-ray, BD-R, and BD-RE combo drives.

Notes CDs, DVDs, and BDs are expected to hold their data for many years; however, you can prolong the life of a disc by protecting it from exposure to light.

Hands-On | Project 6-5 Learn How Optical Drives Work

A+ 220-901 1.5

Optical drives and other removable storage technologies are interesting to study. Check out the animated explanation at the website *howstuffworks.com*. Search on "How Removable Storage Works." List 10 facts you learned about optical drives.

INSTALLING AN OPTICAL DRIVE

A+ 220-901 1.5, 1.11

Internal optical drives on today's computers use a SATA interface. Figure 6-44 shows the rear of a SATA optical drive. An optical drive is usually installed in the drive bay at the top of a desktop case (see Figure 6-45). After the drive is installed in the bay, connect the data and power cables.

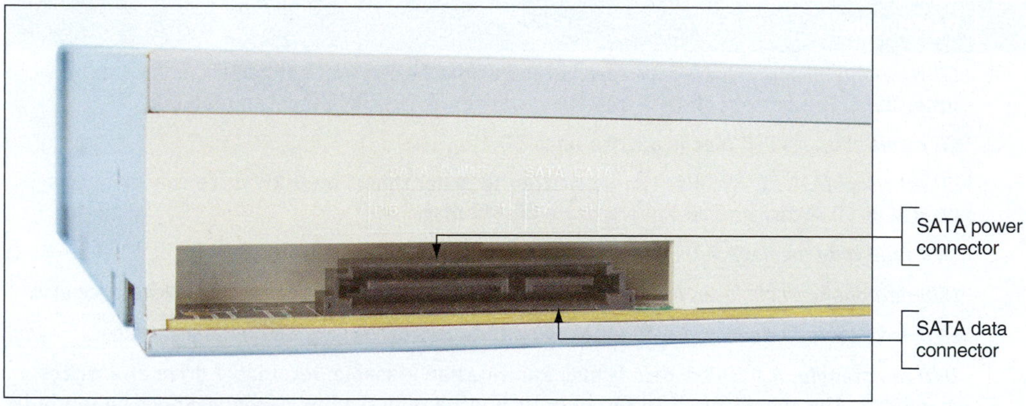

Figure 6-44 Rear of a SATA optical drive

Figure 6-45 Slide the drive into the bay flush with the front panel

★ **A+ Exam Tip** The A+ 220-901 exam expects you to know how to install a CD, DVD, or Blu-ray drive.

Windows 8/7/Vista supports optical drives using its own embedded drivers without add-on drivers. Therefore, when Windows first starts up after the drive is installed, it recognizes the drive and installs drivers. Use Device Manager to verify the drive installed with no errors and is ready to use.

REPLACING AN OPTICAL DRIVE ON A LAPTOP

A+ 220-901 1.5, 1.11

Some of the newest laptops do not have an optical drive in order to save on the size and weight of a laptop, but instead use an external optical drive. However, several new laptops still include the optical drive, and if it goes bad on a laptop, it is likely cheaper to replace the optical drive than to replace the laptop. For some systems, you'll need to first remove the keyboard to expose an optical drive. Follow along as we remove the DVD drive from one laptop system:

1. *Very important:* Unplug the AC adapter and remove the battery pack.
2. For this laptop, to remove the keyboard, you first remove one screen on the bottom of the case and then turn the case over and pry up the keyboard. You can then move the keyboard to one side. You can leave the ribbon cable from the motherboard to the keyboard connected. When you move the keyboard out of the way, the DVD drive is exposed, as shown in Figure 6-46.

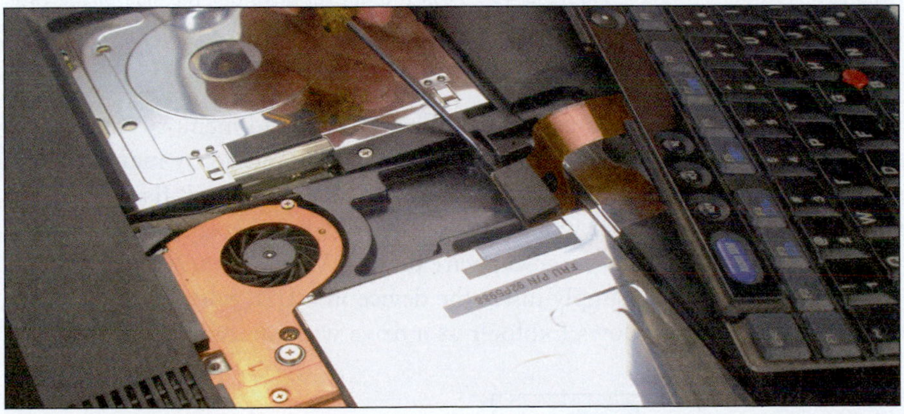

Figure 6-46 Remove the keyboard to expose the optical drive

3. Remove the screw that holds the DVD drive to the laptop (see Figure 6-47).

Figure 6-47 Remove the screw that holds the DVD drive

4. Slide the drive out of the bay (see Figure 6-48).
5. When you slide the new drive into the bay, make sure you push it far enough into the bay so that it solidly connects with the drive connector at the back of the bay. Replace the screw.

For other systems, the optical drive can be removed by first removing a cover from the bottom of the laptop. Then you remove one screw that secures the drive. Next, push the optical drive out of the case (see Figure 6-49).

Figure 6-48 Slide the drive out of the bay

Figure 6-49 Push the optical drive out the side of the case

SOLID-STATE STORAGE

A+
220-901
1.5, 1.11

Types of solid-state storage include SSD hard drives, USB flash drives, and memory cards. USB flash drives currently for sale range in size from 128 MB to 1 TB and go by many names, including a flash pen drive, jump drive, thumb drive, and key drive. Several USB flash drives are shown in Figure 6-50. Flash drives might work at USB 2.0 or USB 3.0 speed and use the FAT (for small-capacity drives) or exFAT file system (for large-capacity drives). Windows 8/7/Vista has embedded drivers to support flash drives. To use one, simply insert the device in a USB port. It then shows in Windows 8 File Explorer or Windows 7/Vista Windows Explorer as a drive with an assigned letter.

Figure 6-50 USB flash drives come in a variety of styles and sizes

To make sure that data written to a flash drive is properly saved before you remove the flash drive from the computer, double-click the **Safely Remove Hardware** icon in the notification area of the Windows taskbar (see Figure 6-51). The Safely Remove Hardware box opens, also shown in Figure 6-51. After you click the device listed, it is then safe to remove it.

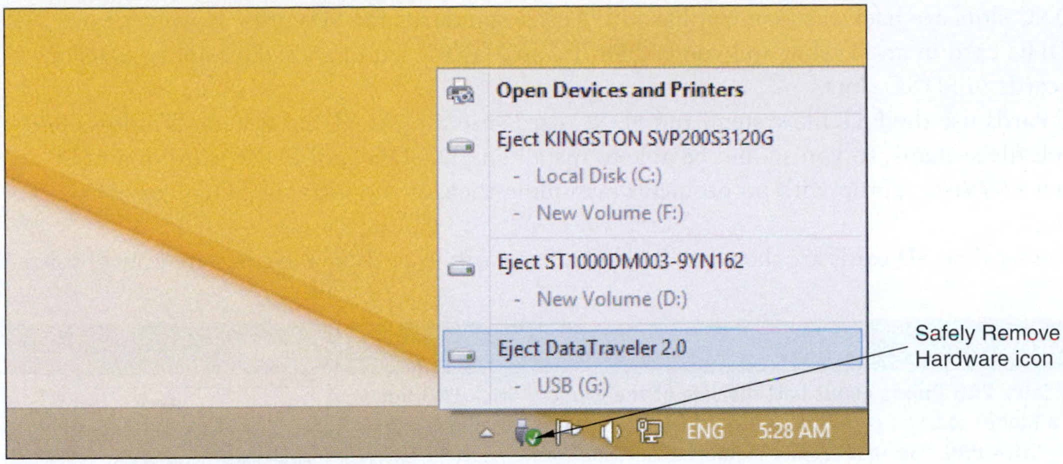

Figure 6-51 Safely Remove Hardware icon and dialog box

Memory cards might be used in digital cameras, tablets, cell phones, MP3 players, digital camcorders, and other portable devices, and most laptops have memory card slots provided by a built-in **smart card reader**. If there is not a memory card slot included in the device, you can add an external smart card reader that uses a USB connection. The most popular memory cards are **Secure Digital (SD) cards**, which follow the standards of the SD Association (*sdcard.org*), and are listed in Table 6-4. The three standards used by SD cards are 1.x (regular SD), 2.x (SD High Capacity or SDHC), and 3.x (SD eXtended Capacity or SDXC). In addition, these cards come in three physical sizes.

	Full-size SD	MiniSD	MicroSD
SD SD 1.x Holds up to 2 GB	SD card 	MiniSD card 	MicroSD card 
SD High Capacity SD 2.x Holds 2 GB to 32 GB	SDHC card 	MiniSDHC 	MicroSDHC card 
SD eXtended Capacity SD 3.x Holds 32 GB to 2 TB	SDXC card 	N/A	MicroSDXC card 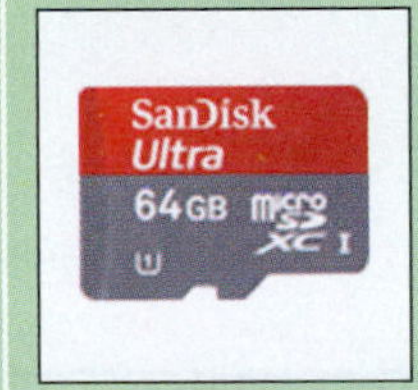 Courtesy of SanDisk

Table 6-4 Flash memory cards that follow the SD Association standards

SDHC and SDXC slots are backward compatible with earlier standards for SD cards. However, you cannot use an SDHC card in an SD slot, and you cannot use an SDXC card in an SDHC slot or SD slot. Only use SDXC cards in SDXC slots.

SD and SDHC cards use the FAT file system, and SDXC cards use the exFAT file system. Windows 8/7/Vista support both file systems, so you should be able to install an SD, SDHC, or SDXC card in an SD slot on a Windows 8/7/Vista laptop with no problems (assuming the slot supports the SDHC or SDXC card you are using).

Memory cards other than SD cards are shown in Table 6-5. Some of the cards in Table 6-5 are now obsolete.

Flash Memory Device	Example
The Sony Memory Stick PRO Duo is about half the size of the Memory Stick PRO but is faster and has a higher storage capacity (up to 2 GB). You can use an adapter to insert the Memory Stick PRO Duo in a regular Memory Stick slot.	
Compact Flash (CF) cards come in two types, Type I (CFI) and Type II (CFII). Type II cards are slightly thicker. CFI cards will fit a Type II slot, but CFII cards will not fit a Type I slot. The CF standard allows for sizes up to 137 GB, although current sizes range up to 32 GB. UDMA CompactFlash cards are faster than other CompactFlash cards. UDMA (Ultra Direct Memory Access) transfers data from the device to memory without involving the CPU.	
MultiMediaCard (MMC) looks like an SD card, but the technology is different and they are not interchangeable. Generally, SD cards are faster than MMC cards.	
Embedded MMC (eMMC) is internal storage used instead of using an SSD drive in inexpensive mobile devices such as cell phones, tablets, and laptops.	 Courtesy of SanDisk
The Memory Stick is used in Sony cameras and camcorders. A later version, the Memory Stick PRO, improved on the slower transfer rate of the original Memory Stick.	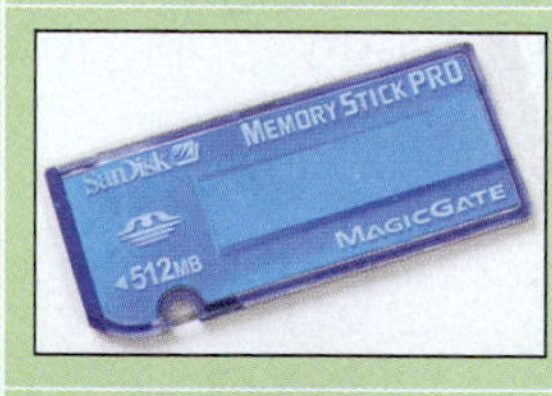
The xD-Picture Card has a compact design (about the size of a postage stamp), and currently holds up to 2 GB of data. You can use an adapter to insert this card into a PC Card slot on a laptop computer or a CF slot on a digital camera.	

Table 6-5 Flash memory cards

★ A+ Exam Tip The A+ 220-901 exam expects you to know about SD, MicroSD, MiniSD, Compact Flash, eMMC, and xD memory cards.

Figure 6-52 shows several flash memory cards together so you can get an idea of their relative sizes. Sometimes a memory card is bundled with one or more adapters so that a smaller card will fit a larger card slot.

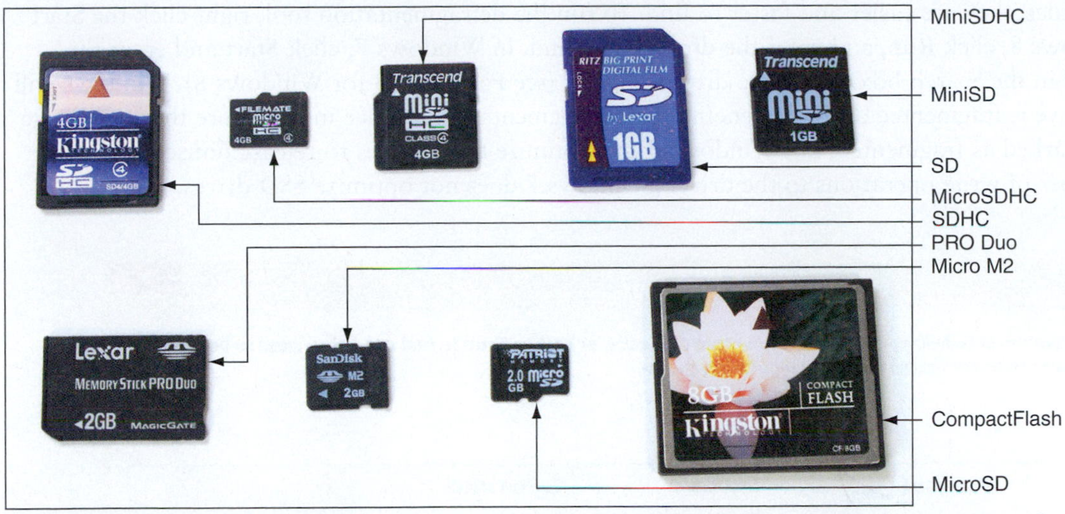

Figure 6-52 Flash memory cards

Hands-On | Project 6-6 Shop for Storage Media

A+
220-901
1.5

Shop online and print or save webpages showing the following devices. Two online sites you can use are Micro Center (*microcenter.com*) and TigerDirect (*tigerdirect.com*):

1. DVD+R DL discs, which are usually sold in packs. What is the storage capacity of each disc? How many discs are in the pack? What is the price per disc?
2. DVD+RW disc, which is usually sold as a single. What is the price per disc? How many more times expensive is a DVD+RW disc than a DVD+R disc?
3. The largest-capacity USB flash drive you can find. What is its capacity and price?
4. The eight types of SD memory cards in Table 6-4. What is the storage capacity and price of each card? Which type of SD card gives you the most storage per dollar?

TROUBLESHOOTING HARD DRIVES

A+
220-901
4.2

In this part of the chapter, you learn how to troubleshoot problems with hard drives. Problems caused by the hard drive during the boot can be caused by the hard drive subsystem, by the file system on the drive, or by files required by Windows when it begins to load. When trying to solve a problem with the boot, you need to decide if the problem is caused by hardware or software. All the problems discussed in this section are caused by hardware.

SLOW PERFORMANCE

A+
220-901
4.2

One of the most common complaints about a computer is that it is running slowly. When files are physically written over a magnetic hard drive in disconnected fragments on the drive, slow performance can result. (SSD drives don't suffer from slow performance when files are fragmented on the drive.) A quick fix for fragmented files is to run the defragmentation tool on the hard drive. Windows 8/7/Vista automatically defragments a magnetic hard drive once a week, but you can run the defragmentation tool independently of the scheduled maintenance. The Windows defragmentation tool rearranges fragments or parts of files in contiguous clusters so that, when the computer is searching for files, they are easier and faster to find. To run the defragmentation tool, right-click the **Start** button in Windows 8, click **Run**, and enter the **dfrgui** command. In Windows 7, click **Start** and enter the **dfrgui** command in the Search box. Select the drive to defrag (see Figure 6-53 for Windows 8). Windows will tell you if the drive is fragmented and will benefit from defragmentation. Notice in the figure that solid-state drives are not marked as fragmented, but Windows 8 can optimize these drives to release unused space to reduce the number of write operations to the drive. (Windows 7 does not optimize SSD drives.)

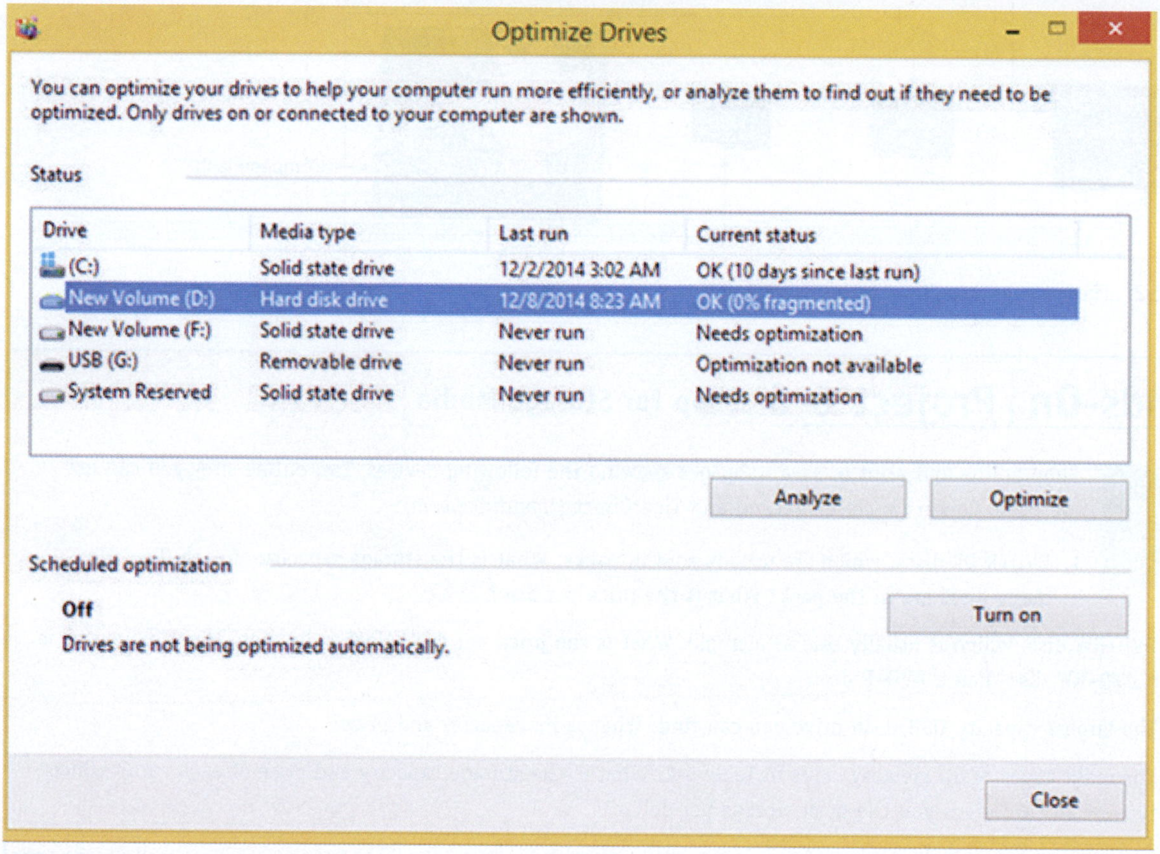

Figure 6-53 Windows reports the selected volume D: is not fragmented

HARD DRIVE PROBLEMS DURING THE BOOT

A+
220-901
4.2

Hardware problems usually show up at POST, unless there is physical damage to an area of the hard drive that is not accessed during POST. Hardware problems often make the hard drive totally inaccessible. If UEFI/BIOS cannot find a hard drive at POST, it displays an error message similar to these:

```
No boot device available
Hard drive not found
OS not found
Read/write failure
Fixed disk error
Invalid boot disk
Inaccessible boot device
```

```
Drive not recognized
RAID not found
RAID stops working
Numeric error codes in the 1700s or 10400s
S.M.A.R.T. errors during the boot
```

The reasons UEFI/BIOS cannot access the drive can be caused by the drive, the data cable, the electrical system, the motherboard, or a loose connection. Here is a list of things to do and check before you open the case:

1. If UEFI/BIOS displays numeric error codes or cryptic messages during POST, check the website of the UEFI/BIOS manufacturer for explanations of these codes or messages.
2. Check UEFI/BIOS setup for errors in the hard drive configuration. If you suspect an error, set UEFI/BIOS to default settings, make sure autodetection is turned on, and reboot the system.
3. Try booting from another bootable media such as the Windows setup DVD or a USB flash drive or CD with the Linux OS and diagnostics software installed (for example, Hiren's BootCD software at *hirensbootcd.org*). If you can boot using another media, you have proven that the problem is isolated to the hard drive subsystem. You can also use the bootable media to access the hard drive, run diagnostics on the drive, and possibly recover its data.
4. For a RAID array, use the firmware utility to check the status of each disk in the array and to check for errors. Press a key at startup to access the RAID UEFI/BIOS utility. This utility lists each disk in the array and its status. You can search the website of the motherboard or RAID controller manufacturer for an interpretation of the messages on this screen and what to do about them. If one of the disks in the array has gone bad, it might take some time for the array to rebuild using data on the other disks. In this situation, the status for the array is likely to show as Caution.

   After the array has rebuilt, your data should be available. However, if one of the hard drives in the array has gone bad, you need to replace the hard drive. After you have replaced the failed drive, you must add it back to the RAID array. This process is called rebuilding a RAID volume. How to do this depends on the RAID hardware you are using. For some motherboards or RAID controller cards, you use the RAID firmware. For others, you use the RAID management software that came bundled with the motherboard or controller. You install this software in Windows and use the software to rebuild the RAID volume using the new hard drive.

If the problem is still not solved, open the case and check these things. Be sure to protect the system against ESD as you work:

1. Remove and reattach all drive cables.
2. If you're using a RAID or SATA controller card, remove and reseat it or place it in a different slot. Check the documentation for the card, looking for directions for troubleshooting.
3. Inspect the drive for damage, such as bent pins on the connection for the cable.
4. Determine if a magnetic hard drive is spinning by listening to it or lightly touching the metal drive (with the power on).
5. Check the cable for frayed edges or other damage.
6. Check the installation manual for things you might have overlooked. Look for a section about system setup, and carefully follow all directions that apply.
7. S.M.A.R.T. errors that display during the boot result from UEFI/BIOS reporting that the drive has met a threshold point of failure. Back up the data and replace the drive as soon as possible.
8. When Windows installed on a hard drive cannot launch, it might present a BSOD (blue screen of death) screen with error messages or it might hang and you see a never-ending spinning Windows pinwheel or wait icon. Windows includes several tools for checking a hard drive for errors and repairing a corrupted

Windows installation that are covered in the chapter,"Troubleshooting Windows Startup." Without getting into these details of supporting Windows, here are a few simple things you can try:

a. *Use Windows 8/7/Vista Startup Repair.* The Startup Repair utility restores many of the Windows files needed for a successful boot. Following directions given in the chapter,"Supporting the Power System and Troubleshooting Computers," boot from the Windows setup DVD. For Windows 8, on the opening screen, select your language, and click **Repair your computer**. Next choose **Troubleshoot**, then choose **Advanced options**. On Advanced options (see Figure 6-54), click **Startup Repair** and follow the on-screen instructions. In Windows 7, boot from the Windows setup DVD, click **Repair your computer**, and sign in to the Windows system installed on the hard drive. Next, on the System Recovery Options menu (see Figure 6-55), select **Startup Repair**.

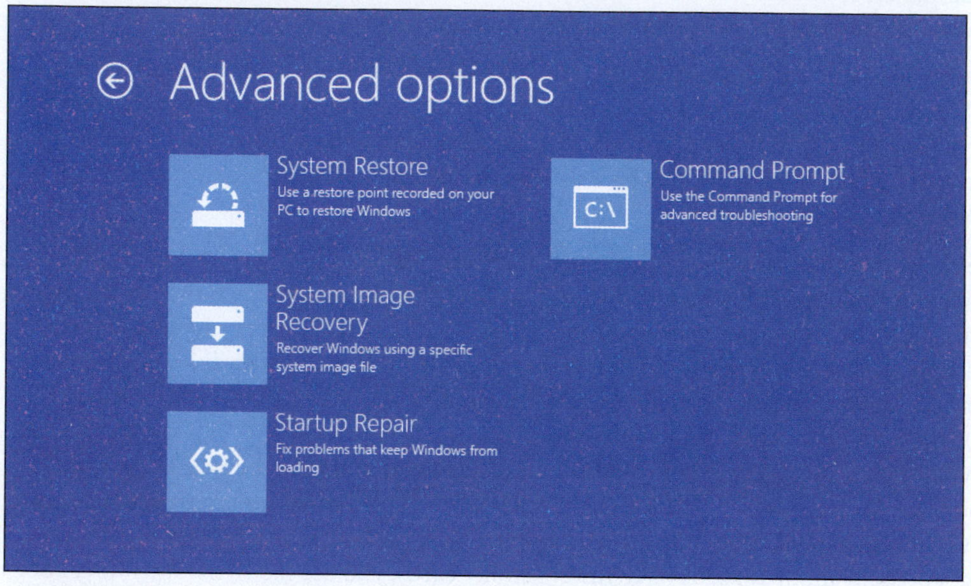

Figure 6-54 Select Startup Repair to fix problems with Windows startup

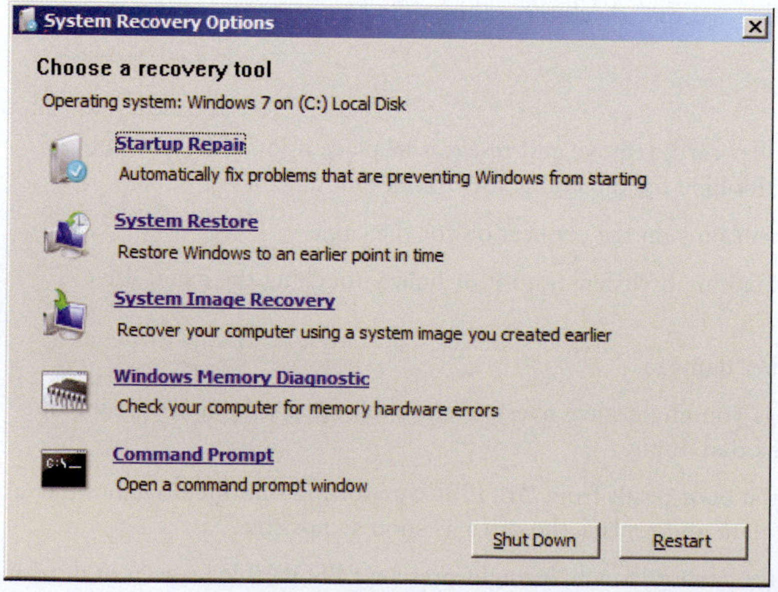

Figure 6-55 Recovery tools in Windows Recovery Environment (Windows RE) for a Windows 7 installation

b. *Use the chkdsk command.* To make sure the hard drive does not have bad sectors that can corrupt the file system, you can use the chkdsk command. To use the command in Windows 8, select Command Prompt from the Advanced options menu (refer back to Figure 6-54). In Windows 7, select Command Prompt from the System Recovery Options menu (refer back to Figure 6-55). At the command prompt that appears, use this chkdsk command to search for bad sectors on drive C: and recover data:

```
chkdsk C: /r
```

c. *Repair the BCD.* The BCD (Boot Configuration Data) is a small database that holds parameters Windows needs for a successful boot. At a command prompt, use this bootrec command to rebuild the BCD:

```
bootrec /RebuildBCD
```

d. *Repair the MBR.* When a hard drive is using the MBR method to manage partitions on the drive, the bootrec command can be used to fix problems with the MBR program that is needed to start Windows. Use this command:

```
bootrec /FixMBR
```

e. *Repair the boot sector.* The boot sector holds the MBR partition table. To repair a corrupted boot sector, use this command:

```
bootrec /FixBoot
```

9. Check the drive manufacturer's website for diagnostic software. Sometimes this software can be run from a bootable CD. Run the software to test the drive for errors.
10. If it is not convenient to create a bootable CD with hard drive diagnostic software installed, you can move the drive to a working computer and install it as a second drive in the system. Then you can use the diagnostic software installed on the primary hard drive to test the problem drive. While you have the drive installed in a working computer, be sure to find out if you can copy data from it to the good drive, so that you can recover any data not backed up. Remember that you set the drive on the open computer case (see Figure 6-56) or use a SATA-to-USB converter to connect the drive to a USB port. If you have the case open with the computer turned on, be *very careful* to not touch the drive or touch inside the case.

Figure 6-56 Temporarily connect a faulty hard drive to another system to diagnose the problem and try to recover data

11. After you have tried to recover the file system on the drive and before you decide to replace the hard drive, try these things to clean the drive and get a fresh start:

    a. ***Format a hard drive volume.*** If you decide the hard drive volume is corrupted and you want to start over, open a Windows command prompt and use the format command to erase everything on the volume. In this example, D: is the drive letter for the volume:

    ```
    format D:
    ```

    b. ***Use diskpart to start over with a fresh file system.*** If formatting the volume doesn't work, you can erase the hard drive partitions using the diskpart command. When you enter diskpart at a command prompt, the DISKPART> prompt appears. Then use these commands to wipe everything off the hard drive. In the example, you are erasing partition 1 on disk 0.

    ```
    list disk
    select disk 0
    list partition
    select partition 1
    clean
    ```

    Use the **exit** command to exit the diskpart utility. You can then reinstall Windows, which partitions the hard drive again. If Windows cannot recognize the drive, it's probably time to replace hardware in the hard drive subsystem.

12. If the drive still does not boot, exchange the three field replaceable units—the data cable, the storage card (if the drive is connected to one), and the hard drive itself—for a hard drive subsystem. Do the following, in order, and test the hard drive after each step:

    a. Reconnect or swap the drive data cable.

    b. Reseat or exchange the drive controller card, if one is present.

    c. Exchange the hard drive for a known good drive.

13. Sometimes older drives refuse to spin at POST or a failing drive can make a loud clicking noise. Drives that have trouble spinning often whine at startup for several months before they finally refuse to spin altogether. If your drive whines loudly when you first turn on the computer, never turn off the computer and replace the drive as soon as possible. One of the worst things you can do for a drive that is having difficulty starting up is to leave the computer turned off for an extended period of time. Some drives, like old cars, refuse to start if they are unused for a long time. A drive making a loud clicking noise most likely is not accessible and must be replaced.

14. A bad power supply or a bad motherboard also might cause a disk boot failure.

If the problem is solved by exchanging the hard drive, take the extra time to reinstall the old hard drive to verify that the problem was not caused by a bad connection.

>> CHAPTER SUMMARY

Hard Drive Technologies and Interface Standards

- A hard disk drive (HDD) comes in three sizes: 3.5" for desktop computers and 2.5" and 1.8" for laptops.
- A hard drive can be a magnetic drive, a solid-state drive, or a hybrid drive. A solid-state drive contains flash memory and is more expensive, faster, more reliable, and uses less power than a magnetic drive.
- Most hard drives, tape drives, and optical drives use the SATA interface standards. External SATA ports are called eSATA ports.

- Three SATA standards provide data transfer rates of 1.5 Gb/sec (using SATA I), 3.0 Gb/sec (using SATA II), and 16.0 Gb/sec (using SATA III).
- S.M.A.R.T. is a self-monitoring technology whereby the UEFI/BIOS monitors the health of the hard drive and warns of an impending failure.

How to Select and Install Hard Drives

- When selecting a hard drive, consider the storage capacity, technology (solid-state or magnetic), spindle speed, interface standard, and buffer size (for hybrid drives).
- SATA drives require no configuration and are installed using a power cord and a single SATA data cable.
- Laptop hard drives plug directly into a SATA connection on the system board.
- RAID technology uses an array of hard drives to provide fault tolerance and/or improvement in performance. Choices for RAID are RAID 0 (striping using two drives), RAID 1 (mirroring using two drives), RAID 5 (parity checking using three drives), and RAID 10 (striping and mirroring combined using four drives).
- Hardware RAID is implemented using the motherboard UEFI/BIOS or a RAID controller card. Software RAID is implemented in Windows. Best practice is to use hardware RAID rather than software RAID.
- Multiple hard drives can be installed in a single external enclosure to expand the storage capacity of a single computer or to make hard drive storage available on a network.

Identifying Tape Drives

- Tape drives are an inexpensive way to back up an entire hard drive or portions of it. Tape drives are more convenient for backups than drives. The disadvantage of tape drives is that data can only be accessed sequentially.

Supporting Other Types of Storage Devices

- File systems a storage device might use in Windows include NTFS, exFAT, FAT32, and FAT.
- CDs, DVDs, and BDs are optical discs with data physically embedded into the surface of the disc. Laser beams are used to read data off the disc by measuring light reflection.
- Optical discs can be recordable (such as a CD-R disc) or rewriteable (such as a DVD-RW disc).
- Flash memory cards are a type of solid-state storage. Types of flash memory card standards by the SD Association include SD, MiniSD, MicroSD, SDHC, MiniSDHC, MicroSDHC, SDXC, and MicroSDXC. Other memory cards include Memory Stick PRO Duo, Memory Stick PRO, Sony Memory Stick Micro M2, CompactFlash I and II, eMMC, and xD-Picture Card.

Troubleshooting Hard Drives

- Defragmenting a magnetic hard drive can sometimes improve slow performance of the drive.
- Problems caused by the hard drive during the boot can be caused by the hard drive subsystem, by the file system on the drive, or by files required by Windows when it begins to load. After the boot, bad sectors on a drive can cause problems with corrupted files.
- To determine if the hard drive is the problem when booting, try to boot from another media, such as the Windows setup DVD.
- For problems with a RAID volume, use the RAID controller firmware (on the motherboard or on the RAID controller card) or RAID management software installed in Windows to report the status of the array and to rebuild the RAID volume.

- To determine if a drive has bad sectors, use the chkdsk command. You can run the command after booting to the System Recovery Options menu using the Windows setup DVD.
- The bootrec command can be used to rebuild the BCD, repair the MBR, or repair the boot sector of a hard drive.
- Use the format command to erase everything on a Windows volume.
- Use commands within the diskpart utility to completely erase a partition on a hard drive.
- Field replaceable units in the hard drive subsystem are the data cable, optional storage card, and hard drive.

>> KEY TERMS

For explanations of key terms, see the Glossary for this text.

autodetection
BCD (Boot Configuration Data)
BD-R
BD-RE
Blu-Ray Disc (BD)
bootrec
CD (compact disc)
CDFS (Compact Disc File System)
CD-ROM
CD-RW
chkdsk
CompactFlash (CF) card
data cartridge
defragmentation tool
diskpart
DVD (digital versatile disc or digital video disc)
DVD-ROM
DVD-RW
DVD-RW DL
embedded MMC (eMMC)
external enclosure
external SATA (eSATA)
fault tolerance
file system
format
formatting
hard disk drive (HDD)
hard drive
hot-swapping
hybrid hard drive (H-HDD)
low-level formatting
magnetic hard drive
minicartridge
mirrored volume
MultiMediaCard (MMC)
NAND flash memory
RAID (redundant array of inexpensive disks or redundant array of independent disks)
RAID 0
RAID 1
RAID 1+0
RAID 10
RAID 5
RAID-5 volume
read/write head
Secure Digital (SD) card
sequential access
serial ATA (SATA)
S.M.A.R.T. (Self-Monitoring Analysis and Reporting Technology)
smart card reader
solid-state device (SSD)
solid-state drive (SSD)
spanning
Startup Repair
storage card
striped volume
UDF (Universal Disk Format) file system
wear leveling
xD-Picture Card

>> REVIEWING THE BASICS

1. What three types of technologies are used inside hard drives?
2. At what three speeds in revolutions per minute might the spindle inside a hard drive rotate?
3. When the OS addresses the sectors on a hard drive as one long list of sequential sectors, what is this technology called?
4. What is the transfer speed for SATA I? SATA II? SATA III?
5. How many pins does a SATA internal data cable have? How many pins does a SATA power cable have?
6. What term describes the technology that allows you to exchange a hard drive without powering down the system?
7. Which RAID level mirrors one hard drive with a second drive so that the same data is written to both drives?
8. Which RAID level stripes data across multiple drives to improve performance and also provides fault tolerance?

9. How many hard drives are necessary to implement RAID 10?
10. When implementing RAID on a motherboard, where do you enable the feature?
11. What type of file system is used by Blu-ray discs?
12. What type of file system is used by SDXC memory cards?
13. How much data can a CD hold?
14. How much data can a double-sided, dual-layer DVD hold?
15. How much data can a double-sided, single-layer BD hold?
16. Which costs more, a CD-R or a CD-RW disc?
17. Which type of flash memory card is currently the smallest type of card?
18. What command-prompt command do you use to determine if a drive has bad sectors?
19. What command can you use to rebuild the BCD?
20. What physical sizes of hard drives are installed in laptops?

>> THINKING CRITICALLY

1. You install a SATA hard drive and then turn on the computer for the first time. You access UEFI/BIOS setup and see that the drive is not recognized. Which of the following do you do next?
   a. Turn off the computer, open the case, and verify that memory modules on the motherboard have not become loose.
   b. Turn off the computer, open the case, and verify that the data cable and power cable are connected correctly and jumpers on the drive are set correctly.
   c. Verify that UEFI/BIOS autodetection is enabled.
   d. Reboot the computer and enter UEFI/BIOS setup again to see if it now recognizes the drive.
2. You want to install an SSD drive in your desktop computer, but the drive is far too narrow to fit snugly into the bays of your computer case. Which of the following do you do?
   a. Install the SSD in a laptop computer.
   b. Buy a bay adapter that will allow you to install the narrow drive in a desktop case bay.
   c. This SSD is designed for a laptop. Flash UEFI/BIOS so that your system will support a laptop hard drive.
   d. Use a special SATA controller card that will support the narrow hard drive.
3. Mark each statement as true or false:
   a. PATA hard drives are older and slower than SATA hard drives.
   b. SATA 1 is about 10 times faster than SATA 3.
   c. RAID 0 can be implemented using only a single hard drive.
   d. RAID 5 requires five hard drives working together at the same speed and capacity.
   e. You can use an internal SATA data cable with an eSATA port.
   f. A SATA internal data cable has 7 pins.

>> REAL PROBLEMS, REAL SOLUTIONS

REAL PROBLEM 6-1 Recovering Data

Your friend has a Windows 8 desktop system that contains important data. He frantically calls you to say that when he turns on the computer, the lights on the front panel light up and he can hear the fan spin for a moment and then all goes dead. His most urgent problem is the data on his hard drive, which is not backed up. The data is located in several folders on the drive. What is the quickest and easiest way to solve the most urgent problem, recovering the data? List the major steps in that process.

REAL PROBLEM 6-2 Using Hardware RAID

You work as an IT support technician for a boss who believes you are really bright and can solve just about any problem he throws at you. Folks in the company have complained one time too many that the file server downtime is just killing them, so he asks you to solve this problem. He wants you to figure out what hardware is needed to implement hardware RAID for fault tolerance.

You check the file server's configuration and discover it has a single hard drive using a SATA connection with Windows Server 2012 installed. There are four empty bays in the computer case and four extra SATA power cords. You also discover an empty PCIe x4 slot on the motherboard. UEFI/BIOS setup does not offer the option to configure RAID, but you think the slot might accommodate a RAID controller.

Complete the investigation and do the following:

1. Decide what hardware you must purchase and print webpages showing the products and their cost.
2. What levels of RAID does the RAID controller card support? Which RAID level is best to use? Print any important information in the RAID controller documentation that supports your decisions.
3. What is the total hardware cost of implementing RAID? Estimate how much time you think it will take for you to install the devices and test the setup.

CHAPTER 7

Survey of Windows Features and Support Tools

After completing this chapter, you will be able to:

- Use Windows to interface with users, files and folders, applications, and hardware
- Use Windows tools to explore, examine, and support the system
- Make network connections using Windows
- Manage local user accounts and Microsoft accounts in Windows

In this chapter, you learn about Microsoft Windows and how this operating system provides the interface between users and applications and between applications and hardware devices. You learn to use several Windows tools and utilities that are useful to view and manage storage devices, examine a system, and troubleshoot simple problems with hardware and applications. You also learn how Windows connects to a network and accesses resources on a network. Finally, you learn about user accounts, including how to create and manage them.

A+ Exam Tip In this text, you learn about Windows 8.1, Windows 8.0, Windows 7, and a little about Windows Vista. All these operating systems are covered on the A+ 220-902 exam. (Windows 10 is not on the exam.) In the text, we use Windows 8 to refer to Windows 8.0 and Windows 8.1.

WINDOWS INTERFACES

A+
220-902
1.1

An operating system (OS) is software that controls a computer. In general, you can think of an operating system as the middleman between applications and hardware, between the user and hardware, and between the user and applications (see Figure 7-1).

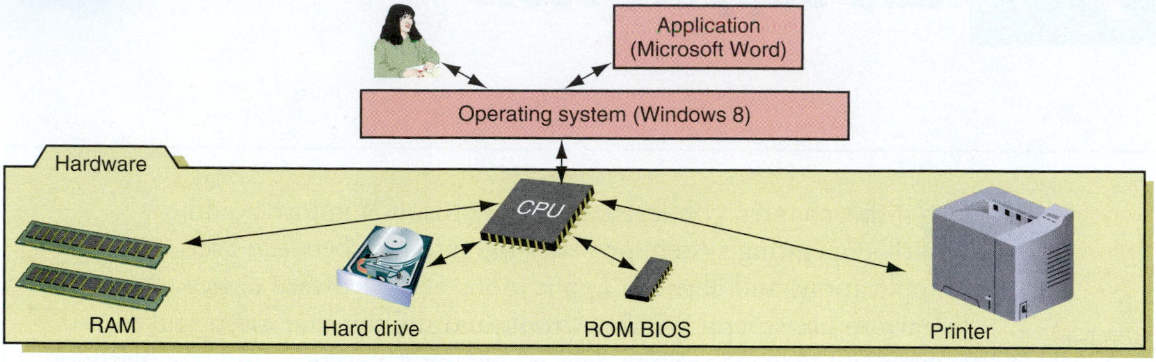

Figure 7-1 Users and applications depend on the OS to relate to all applications and hardware components

Several applications might be installed on a computer to meet various user needs, but a computer really needs only one operating system. Although there are important differences among them, all operating systems share the following four main functions:

- *Function 1*: Provide a user interface
    - Performing housekeeping procedures requested by the user, often concerning storage devices, such as reorganizing a hard drive, deleting files, copying files, and changing the system date
    - Providing a way for the user to manage the desktop, hardware, applications, and data
- *Function 2*: Manage files
    - Managing files on hard drives, DVD drives, CD drives, USB flash drives, and other drives
    - Creating, storing, retrieving, deleting, and moving files
- *Function 3*: Manage hardware
    - Managing the UEFI/BIOS (programs permanently stored on hardware devices)
    - Managing memory, which is a temporary place to store data and instructions as they are being processed
    - Diagnosing problems with software and hardware
    - Interfacing between hardware and software (that is, interpreting application software needs to the hardware and interpreting hardware needs to application software)
- *Function 4*: Manage applications
    - Installing and uninstalling applications
    - Running applications and managing the interface to the hardware on behalf of an application

By the time this text is published, Microsoft will have released Windows 10; currently, however, Windows 8 is the latest Microsoft operating system and is an upgrade to Windows 7, which was preceded by Windows Vista. Every IT support technician needs to be a power user of Windows 8 and also be familiar with Windows 7.

Notes This chapter assumes Windows 8 or Windows 7 is already installed on your computer, and it would be great if you have access to both operating systems as you work your way through this chapter. If Windows is not yet installed, read the chapter, "Installing Windows," and install Windows 8 or 7. Then you can return to this chapter to learn how to use the OS.

The editions of Windows 8 include Windows 8, Windows 8 Professional, Windows 8 Enterprise, and Windows RT. Windows 8.1 is a free update or release of the original Windows 8. Editions of Windows 7 include Windows 7 Ultimate, Windows 7 Enterprise, Windows 7 Professional, Windows 7 Home Premium, Windows 7 Home Basic, and Windows 7 Starter.

> **A+ Exam Tip** The A+ 220-902 exam covers Windows 8.1, Windows 8, Windows 7, and Windows Vista. For the most part, Windows 7 and Vista work alike. Important information about Vista where it differs from Windows 7 is presented in OS Differences boxes.

Every Windows OS offers a graphical user interface (GUI; pronounced "GOO-ee") that uses graphics instead of with a command-driven interface. Windows 8 has two graphical user interfaces, the modern interface and the desktop. Windows 7 offers one graphical user interface, the desktop. We next examine all three interfaces.

WINDOWS 8 MODERN INTERFACE

A+ 220-902 1.1

The Windows 8 modern interface, also called the Windows 8 interface and formerly called the Metro User Interface or Metro UI, presents the Start screen to the user. The Start screen contains tiles that represent lean apps, which use few system resources and are designed for social media, social networking, and the novice end user (see Figure 7-2). Click a tile to open its app. Some apps use live tiles, which offer continuous real-time updates. For example, the People app has a live tile to make it easy to keep up with updates on Facebook, LinkedIn, and Twitter.

> **Notes** In this text, we use Windows 8 as an umbrella term to cover Windows 8.0 (the first release of Windows 8) and Windows 8.1 (the free update to Windows 8.0).

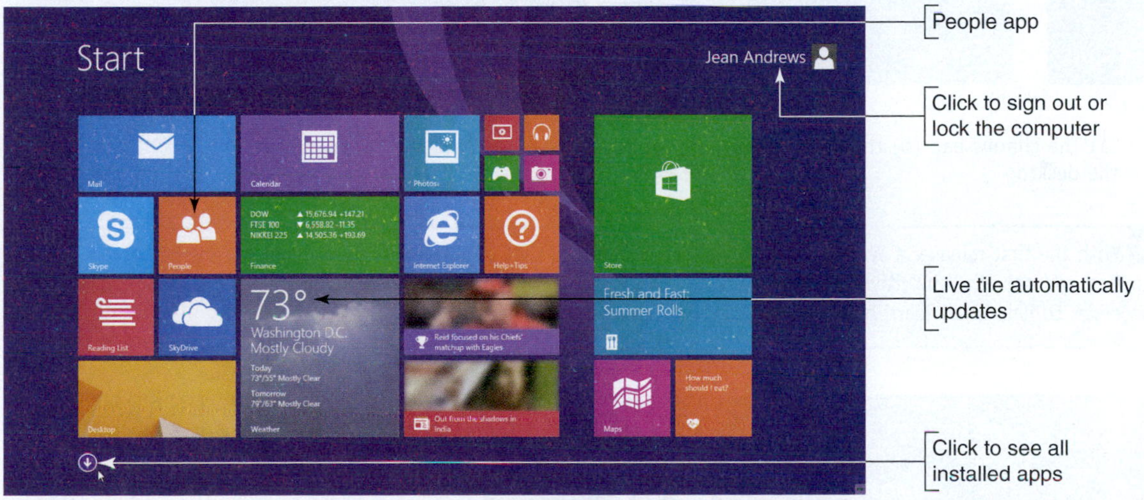

Figure 7-2 The Windows 8 Start screen is used to view app tiles and to open apps

The modern interface uses pages in comparison to the windows used on the desktop. The interface is specifically designed for touch screens.

> **Notes** To conserve system resources, you can turn off a live tile. To do so, right-click the tile on the Start screen and then click **Turn live tile off** in the shortcut menu that appears. You can also use Task Manager to find out how the app is affecting overall system performance. You learn to use Task Manager in a later chapter.

> **Notes** The figures and steps in this text use Windows 8.1 Professional and Windows 7 Professional. If you are using a different edition of Windows 8 or 7, your screens and steps may differ slightly from those presented here.

THE CHARMS BAR AND THE SETTINGS CHARM

The charms bar appears on the right side of any Windows 8 screen when you move your pointer to a right corner (see Figure 7-3a). It gives handy access to common tasks such as returning to the Start screen, searching for content, connecting to a wireless network, personalizing the Start screen, or changing other Windows settings. In the charms bar, click a charm to select it. The Settings charm can be particularly useful, and items at the top of the Settings pane can change depending on the situation. Figure 7-3b shows the Settings pane from the Start screen, and Figure 7-3c shows the Settings pane from the desktop.

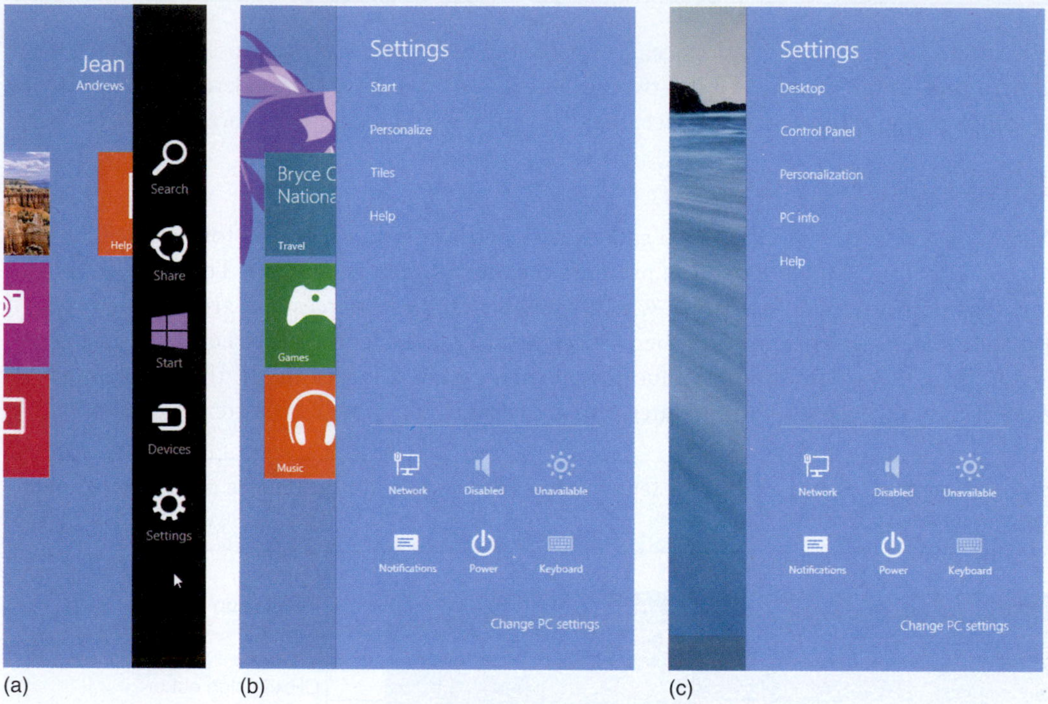

Figure 7-3 (a) The charms bar, (b) the Settings pane on the Start screen, and (c) the Settings pane on the desktop

> **Notes** With the first release of Windows 8, many users complained that important items like the charms bar were difficult to find and not at all intuitive to use. As a result, beginning with Windows 8.1, Microsoft added tips that randomly appear on screen to help users learn how to use the new interface.

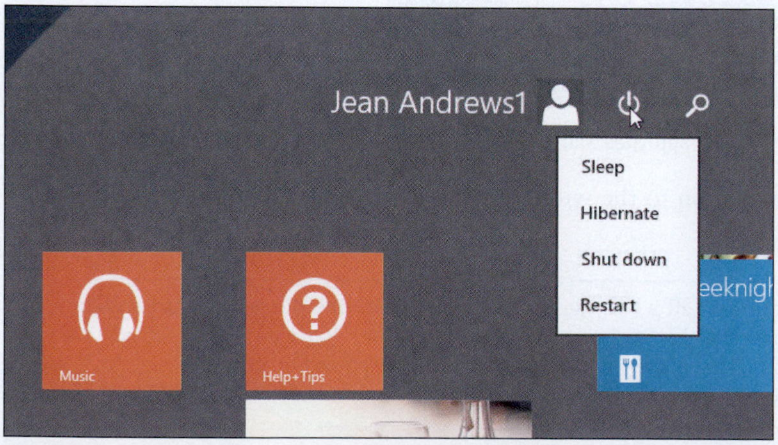

Figure 7-4 Use the Power icon at the top of the Start screen to shut down or restart the system

THE SETTINGS CHARM AND THE POWER ICON

The Power icon in the upper-right corner of the Start screen can be used to shut down or restart the computer. Click the **Power** icon, and then click an item in the menu that appears (see Figure 7-4). The items on this menu always include Shut down and Restart, and, depending on the configuration, might also include Sleep and Hibernate.

APPLYING | CONCEPTS SIGN IN TO WINDOWS 8 AND USE THE WINDOWS 8 INTERFACE

A+ 220-902 1.1

Although the Windows 8 interface is designed to work best with a touch screen, you can also use a mouse and keyboard. Follow these steps to learn how to sign in to Windows 8 and manage apps using the Windows 8 interface:

1. When you first start up a Windows 8 computer, you see the lock screen shown in Figure 7-5a. Click anywhere on the screen and the sign-in screen appears (see Figure 7-5b). To sign in, select a user account and enter the account password. The Start screen appears.

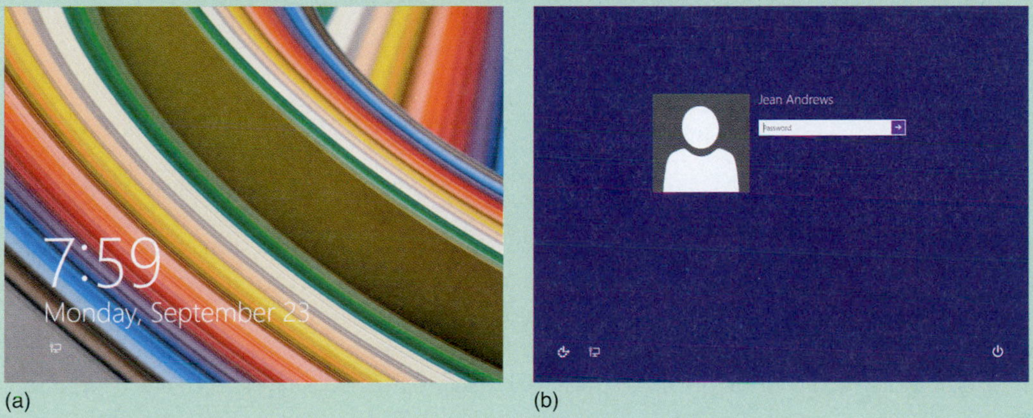

Figure 7-5 (a) The Windows lock screen, and (b) the Windows sign-in screen

> **Notes** These instructions assume you are using a mouse and keyboard. If you're using a touch screen, simply tap instead of click; press and hold instead of right-click; double-tap instead of double-click; and swipe to scroll the screen to the right or left.

2. To open an app, click the app tile on the Start screen. If the app works in the Windows 8 modern interface, the app page opens. (If the app works on the Windows desktop, the desktop appears and the application window opens.)
3. To return to the Start screen, press the **Win** key. Open a second app, which fills the entire screen.

> **Notes** In Windows, there are multiple ways to do the same thing. For example, to return to the Start screen (a) press the **Win** key, (b) move your pointer to the lower left of the screen and click the **Start** (Windows logo) button that appears, or (c) move your pointer to a right corner of the screen and click the **Start** (Windows logo) charm in the charms bar that appears.

4. You can snap a page to the left or right side of the screen so a second page can share the screen, which is called **side-by-side apps**. To snap a page, first move your pointer to the top of the screen—the pointer changes to a hand. Then press and drag the page down and to the left or right side of the screen. The page snaps to the side, and the second app takes up the other side of the screen. You can press and drag the vertical bar between the two pages to adjust the page sizes (see Figure 7-6).

> **Notes** To snap pages, your screen resolution must be at least 1366 × 768.

(continues)

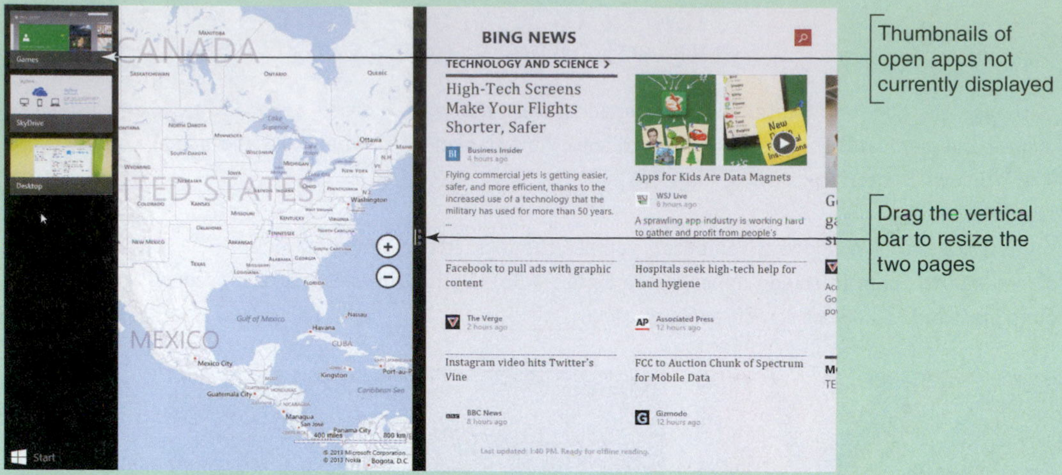

Figure 7-6 Two app pages show on the screen with other open apps shown as thumbnails in the left pane

5. Open three other apps using each of these three methods:

- If the app tile isn't showing, move your pointer to the bottom of the screen. You can then use the scroll bar that appears to scroll the screen to the right or left to see more apps on the Start screen. (You can also move your pointer to the far left or right side of the screen to scroll the screen.)
- Some apps are not on the Start screen. Move your pointer to the bottom of the Start screen and a down arrow appears. Click the **arrow** to see the Apps screen, which shows all installed apps. Click one to open it.

Notes Right-click a tile on the Start screen or Apps screen to select it and view its shortcut menu (see Figure 7-7). To uninstall the app, click **Uninstall** in the menu.

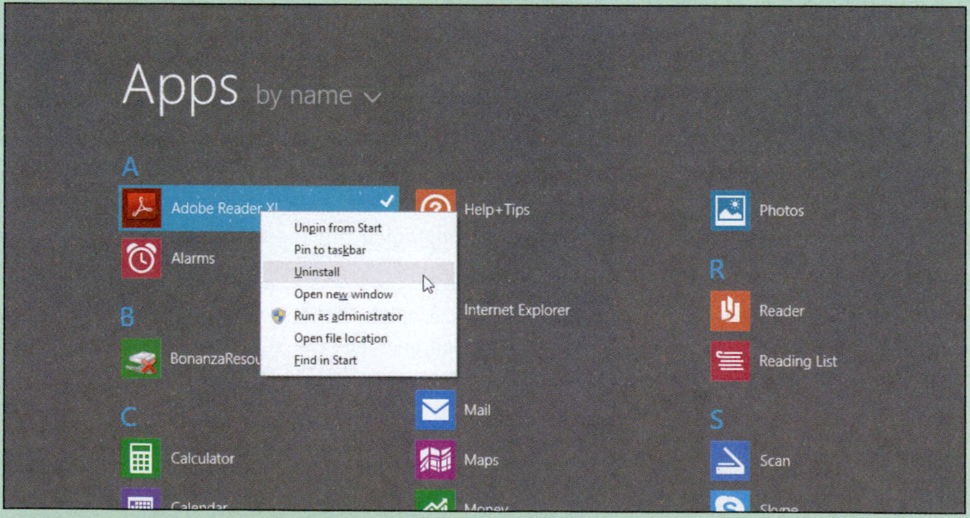

Figure 7-7 Apps screen lists all installed apps

- You can also use the Search feature to open an app. On the Start screen, start typing the name of the app. As you type, the Search pane appears. For example, in Figure 7-8, you can see the top of the pane when *no* is typed. The remaining letters in *notepad* automatically appear in the Search box, and other possibilities are listed in the pane. If you want to open the Notepad app, click it. By default, the Search app searches for apps, Windows settings, files, web images, and web videos. If you click an item at the bottom of the pane, Internet Explorer opens to find it on the web.

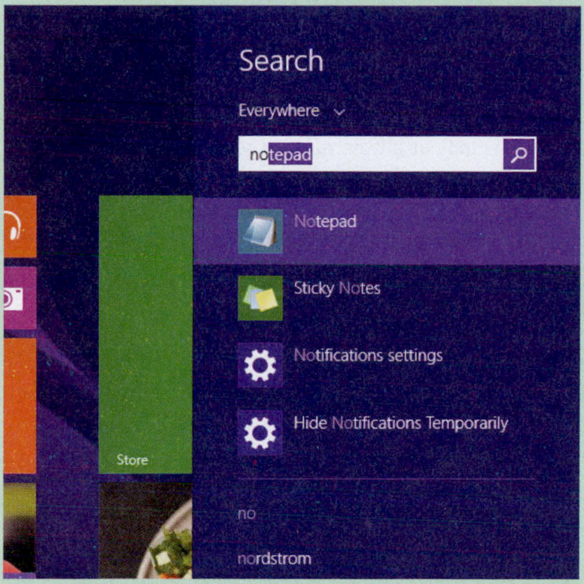

Figure 7-8 Use Search to search for apps, settings, files, and content within other apps and on the web

6. Only two apps can use the screen at one time. To see thumbnails of open apps that are not on the screen, move your pointer to the upper-left corner of the screen (refer to Figure 7-6).
7. To close a selected app, move your pointer to the top of the screen. A menu bar appears. Click the red **X** on the far right of the menu bar. Close all open apps.

7

WINDOWS 8 DESKTOP

A+ 220-902 1.1, 1.5

Tools used by technicians to support, secure, and troubleshoot Windows, as well as productivity software, such as Microsoft Office, QuickBooks, and Dreamweaver, are primarily accessed from the desktop. To access the desktop, click the Desktop tile on the Start screen. When you move your pointer to a right corner of the desktop screen, the charms bar appears, as shown in Figure 7-9. Click the **Start** charm in the charms bar to return to the Start screen. Alternately, you can click the Start button in the taskbar to return to the Start screen.

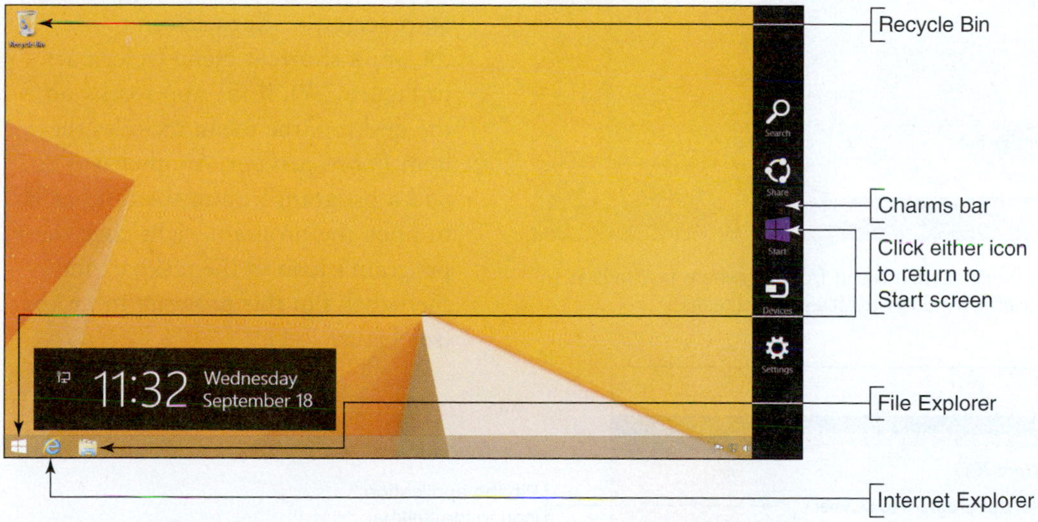

Figure 7-9 Windows 8 desktop with charms bar in view

The taskbar is normally located at the bottom of the Windows desktop, displaying information about open programs and providing quick access to others. By default, Windows 8 places the Internet Explorer and File Explorer icons in the Quick Launch toolbar, which is on the left side of the taskbar. Click an icon to open the program. An open application displays a program icon in the taskbar to the right of the toolbar.

The notification area, also called the system tray or systray, is usually on the right side of the taskbar and displays open services. A service is a program that runs in the background to support or serve Windows or an application. The services in the notification area include the volume or sound control and network connectivity.

Notes If you have a sluggish Windows system, one thing you can do is look at all the running services in the notification area and try to disable the services that are taking up system resources. How to do that is covered in the chapter, "Optimizing Windows."

To launch a program from the desktop, use one of these methods:

- *Start screen*. Click the **Start** button to return to the Start screen and use the Start screen to open a program. For example, on the Start screen, start typing the name of an application, and then click it when it appears in the search list. If it's a desktop application, the program window launches on the desktop.
- *Quick Launch menu*. To launch most Windows support tools, right-click the **Start** button and select an item from the Quick Launch menu that appears (see Figure 7-10). Click an item to open it. You can also press **Win+X** to launch the menu from anywhere in Windows 8, including the Start screen.
  Notice the *Shut down or sign out* item near the bottom of the menu. When you point to it, you see submenu items that always include Shut down, Sign out, and Restart. Depending on your system configuration, you might also see Sleep or Hibernate.
- *Pin to taskbar*. For a desktop program you use often, you can add its icon to the taskbar on the desktop, which is called pinning to the taskbar. To do that, right-click an app on the Start screen or Apps screen to see the app's shortcut menu (refer back to Figure 7-7). If the app works on the desktop, the menu includes the item *Pin to taskbar*. Another way to add a program icon to the taskbar is to open the program, right-click the program's icon in the taskbar, and then click **Pin this program to taskbar** (see Figure 7-11).

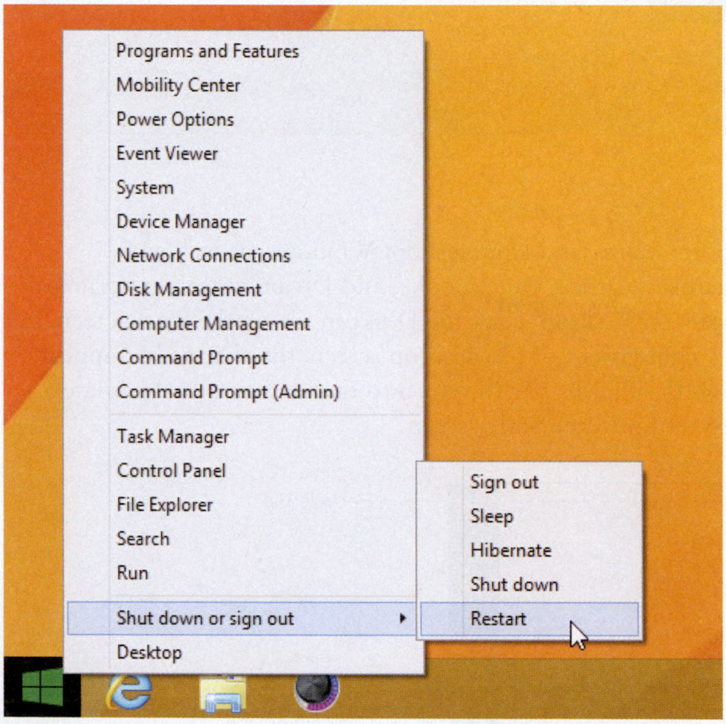

Figure 7-10 Use the Quick Launch menu from anywhere in Windows to access useful Windows utilities and screens

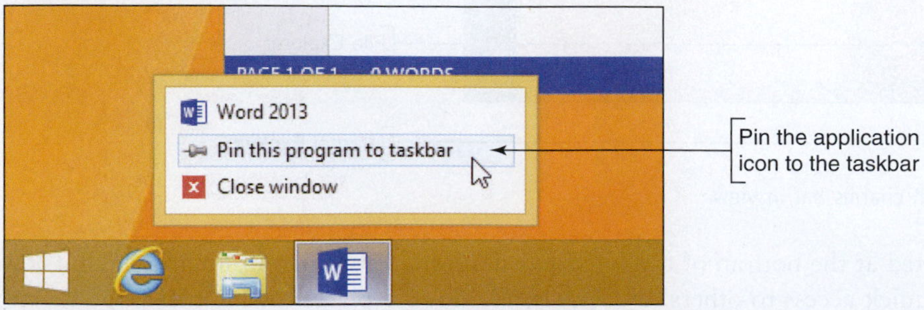

Figure 7-11 Pin an open program to the taskbar on the Windows desktop

- ***Double-click the program file name in File Explorer.*** File Explorer allows you to view and manage files and folders on your computer or the network. To open File Explorer, click the **File Explorer icon** in the taskbar. You can launch a program by double-clicking the program file name in File Explorer. You learn to use File Explorer later in this chapter.
- ***Shortcut on desktop.*** You can place a shortcut to a program on the desktop. How to do that is coming up later in this chapter.
- ***Run box.*** If you know the name of the program file, you can open the Quick Launch menu and click **Run**. The Run box appears. Type the name of the program file and press **Enter**. For example, the program file name of the Notepad text editor is notepad.exe. When you type **notepad** in the Run box and press **Enter**, the Notepad window appears. See Figure 7-12. (Windows assumes the file extension for a program is .exe, so it's not necessary to type the extension.)

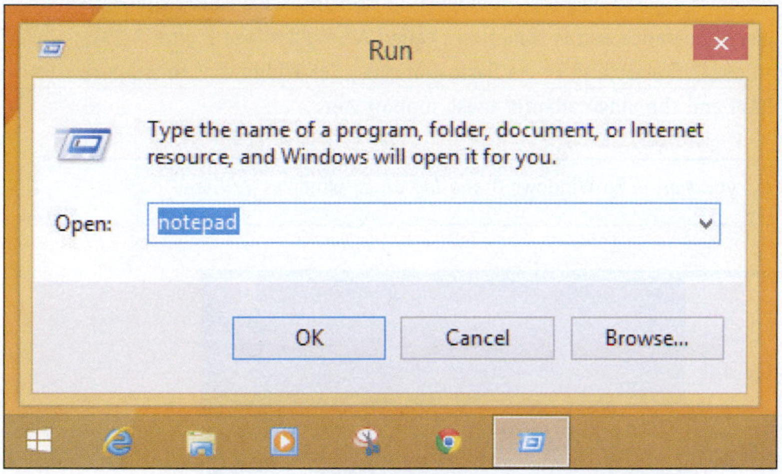

Figure 7-12 Use the Run box to launch a program

7

Here are a few tips about managing windows on the desktop:

- Drag the title bar of a window to move the window. Use the buttons in the upper-right corner to resize, maximize, minimize, and close a window.
- Drag a window to the top of the screen to maximize it. Drag the window downward on the screen to return it to its original size. Drag a window to the right or left of the screen so that it snaps to the side of the screen to fill half the screen.
- Press and shake (drag back and forth quickly) the title bar of a window to minimize all other windows except the one you shake. Shake again to restore the size of the other windows.

Hands-On Project 7-1 Practice Using the Charms Bar and Quick Launch Menu

A+ 220-902 1.1, 1.5

Do the following to practice using the charms bar and Quick Launch menu:

1. Click the **Power** icon on the Start screen. What are the options on the Power icon menu?
2. Open the **Quick Launch** menu, and practice using several options on the menu. What are the submenu items that appear when you point to *Shut down or sign out*?
3. Click **Power Options** on the Quick Launch menu. Find the settings in the Power Options window that allow you to change the options available in the *Shut down or sign out* menu.
4. Go to the **Start** screen. Click your user name in the upper-right corner of the Start screen. What options appear in the dropdown menu? Use the Lock and Sign out options, and describe what each option does.

Now, onward to the Windows 7 desktop.

WINDOWS 7 THE WINDOWS 7 DESKTOP

A+ 220-902 1.1

In Windows 7 (and Vista), the desktop is the initial screen that is displayed after the user logs on and Windows is loaded. Just as with Windows 8, you can move, maximize, resize, minimize, shake, and close windows on the desktop. The Windows 7/Vista desktop provides a 3D user interface called the **Aero user interface** that gives a glassy appearance and is sometimes called Aero glass (see Figure 7-13). (TheAero interface is not available for the Windows 7 Starter and Home Basic editions.) For Windows 7 to support Aero, the system must have at least 1 GB of RAM and the video adapter must support Aero.

Notes According to Microsoft terminology, you *sign in* to Windows 8 and *log on* to Windows 7/Vista.

Figure 7-13 The Windows 7 desktop using the Aero interface has a glassy transparent look

Notes If you are using the Aero interface, you can get a flip 3D view of applications by pressing **Win+Tab** (the Windows key and the Tab key). Then use the Tab key to move from one open application to another.

The Windows 7/Vista desktop can have gadgets on it, such as the clock gadget shown in Figure 7-13. A **gadget** is a mini-app that provides information such as the time, date, news headlines, or weather. To control Windows 7 gadgets, right-click the desktop and select **Gadgets** from the shortcut menu that appears.

OS Differences Windows 7 gadgets can appear anywhere on the desktop, but Vista gadgets appear in the Vista **sidebar** on the right side of the Vista desktop.

To start a program, click the **Start** button to access the Start menu, click an icon pinned to the taskbar, double-click a shortcut on the desktop, click the **Start** button and enter the program file name in the Search box, or double-click the program file name in Windows Explorer. **Windows Explorer** is the Windows 7/Vista utility used to view and manage files and folders.

Figure 7-14 The Windows 7 Start menu

Click the Start button to see the Windows 7 Start menu, which is shown in Figure 7-14. Notice in the figure that the username for the person currently logged on is shown at the upper right of the Start menu.

User-oriented applications that are used often are listed in the white left column (as shown in the figure) and can change from time to time. Items in the darker right column give access to user libraries and files and to OS utilities. A Windows 7 **library** is a collection of folders.

Now that you're familiar with the Windows interfaces, let's learn to use several tools that are helpful to both users and technicians.

WINDOWS TOOLS FOR USERS AND TECHNICIANS

A+
220-902
1.1, 1.2,
1.4, 1.5

All users need to know how to use File Explorer or Windows Explorer. In addition, a technician needs to know how to use the Control Panel, Power Options, System window, System Information window, and Action Center. All these tools are covered in this part of the chapter.

WINDOWS 8 FILE EXPLORER AND WINDOWS 7 WINDOWS EXPLORER

A+
220-902
1.4

Windows 8 File Explorer or Windows 7 Windows Explorer is opened in these ways:

- Click the yellow File Explorer or Windows Explorer icon in the taskbar. If an Explorer window is already open, it becomes the active window.
- From the Windows 8 desktop, open the Quick Launch menu (press **Win+X**) and click **File Explorer** in the menu. For Windows 7, right-click **Start** and select **Open Windows Explorer** from the menu that appears. If an Explorer instance is already open, a new instance of Explorer is created. Having two instances of Explorer open makes it easy to drag and drop files and folders from one location to another.
- Open the Windows 8 Quick Launch menu, click **Run**, type **explorer** in the Run box, and press **Enter**. For Windows 7, click **Start**, type **explorer** in the Search box, and press **Enter**. You can use this method to open multiple instances of Explorer.

The Windows 8 File Explorer window has tabs near the top of the window (see Figure 7-15). These tabs can change depending on the situation. You click a tab to see its ribbon or a dropdown menu that appears with more tools. The Computer ribbon is shown in the figure. The Windows 7 Windows Explorer window doesn't use ribbons (see Figure 7-16).

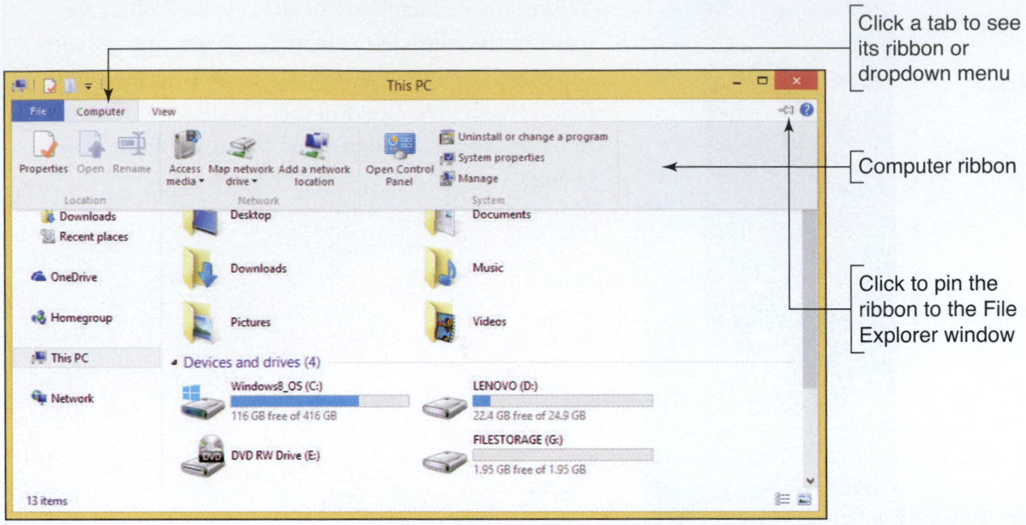

Figure 7-15 Windows 8 File Explorer window with the Computer ribbon shown

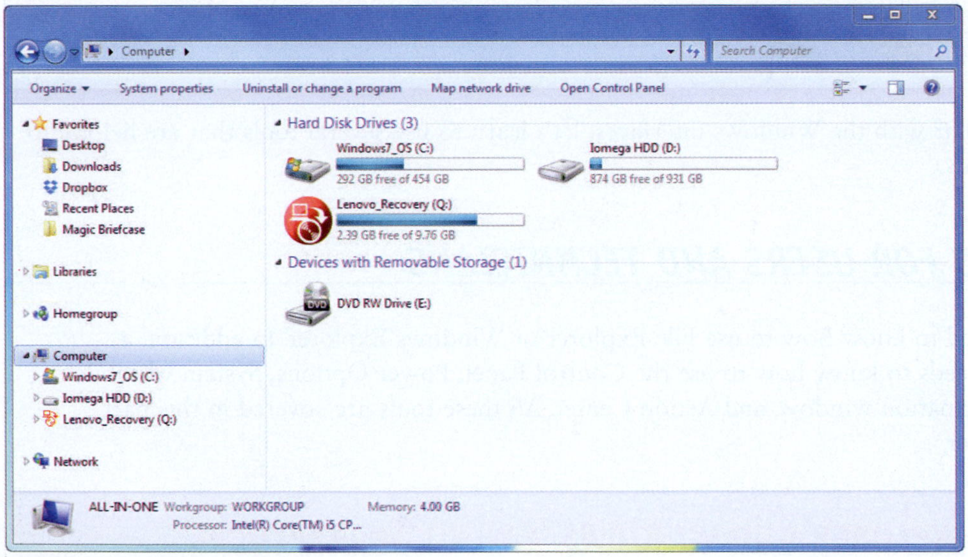

Figure 7-16 Windows 7 Windows Explorer window with the Computer item in the left pane selected

Let's see how to use the Explorer windows to manage files and folders and other system resources.

FILES AND DIRECTORIES

Every OS manages a hard drive, optical drive, USB drive, or other type of drive by using directories (also called folders), subdirectories, and files. The drive is organized with a single **root directory** at the top of the top-down hierarchical structure of subdirectories, as shown in Figure 7-17. The exception to this rule is a hard drive because it can be divided into partitions that can have more than one **volume** such as drive C: and drive D: on the same physical hard drive (see Figure 7-18). For a volume, such as drive C:, the root directory is written as C:. Each volume has its own root directory and hierarchical structure of subdirectories. You can think of volumes as logical drives within the one physical drive.

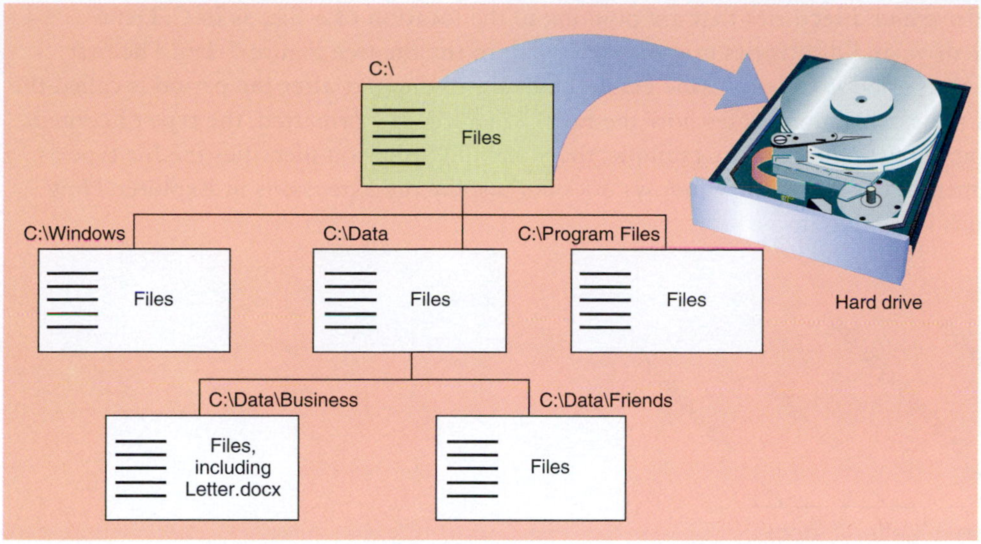

Figure 7-17 Storage devices such as a USB drive, DVD, or hard drive are organized into directories and subdirectories that contain files

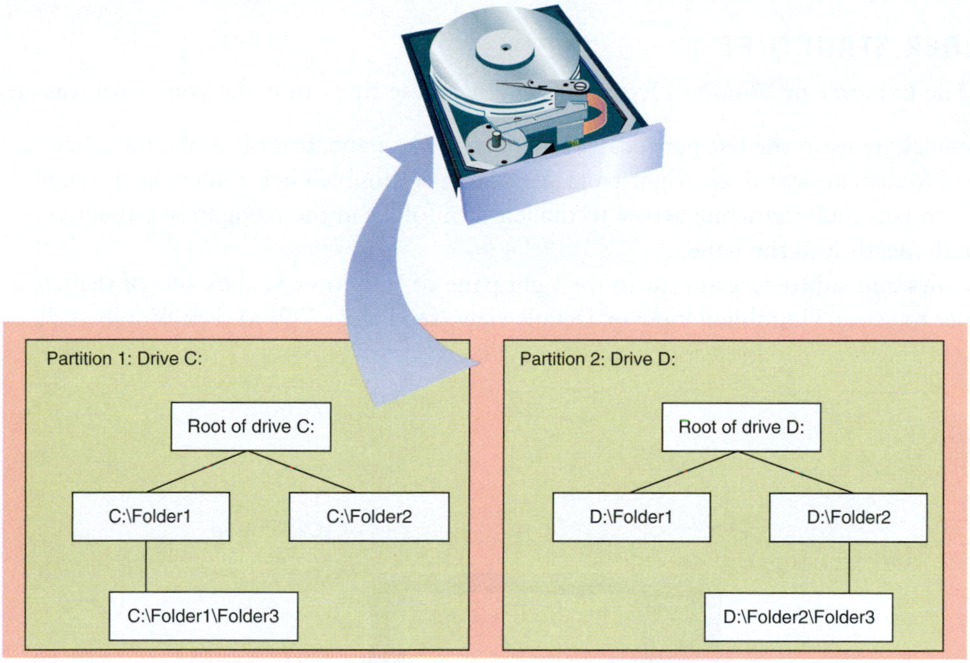

Figure 7-18 A hard drive can be divided into one or more partitions that can each contain a volume such as drive C: or drive D:

As shown in Figure 7-17, the root directory can hold files or other directories, which can have names such as C:\Data. These directories, called subdirectories, child directories, folders, or subfolders can, in turn, have other directories listed in them. Any directory can have files and other subdirectories listed in it; for example, Figure 7-17 shows that one file on drive C: is C:\Data\Business\Letter.docx. In this path to the file, the C: identifies the volume and is called the drive letter. Drive letters used for a hard drive, CD, USB drive, or DVD are C:, D:, E:, and so forth.

Notes Technicians tend to call a directory a folder when working in File Explorer or Windows Explorer, but when working with a command-line interface, they call a directory a directory.

When you refer to a drive and directories that are pointing to the location of a file, as in C:\Data\Business\Letter.docx, the drive and directories are called the path to the file (see Figure 7-19). The first part of the name before the period is called the file name (Letter), and the part after the period is called the file extension (.docx). A file extension indicates how the file is organized or formatted, the type of content in the file, and what program uses the file. For example, the .docx file extension identifies the file type as a Microsoft Word document file. By default, Windows does not display file extensions in Explorer. How to display these extensions is coming up.

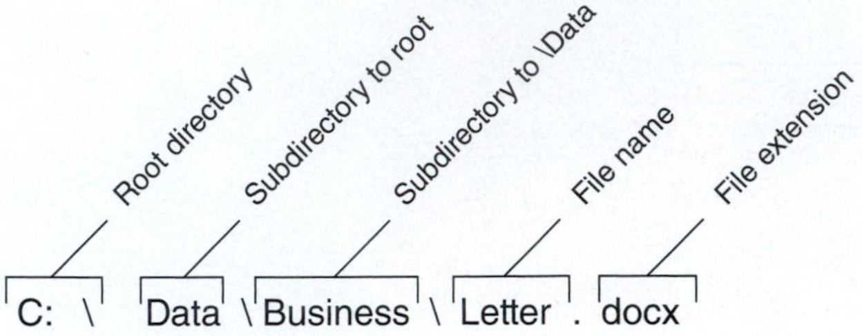

Figure 7-19 The complete path to a file includes the volume letter, directories, file name, and file extension; the colon, backslashes, and period are required to separate items in the path

NAVIGATE THE FOLDER STRUCTURE

When working with the File Explorer or Windows Explorer window, these tips can make your work easier:

- *Tip 1*: Click or double-click items in the left pane, called the navigation pane, to drill down into these items. The folders or subfolders appear in the right pane. You can also double-click folders in the right pane to drill down. When you click the white arrow to the left of a folder in the navigation pane, its subfolders are listed underneath it in the pane.
- *Tip 2*: To control how files and subfolders appear in the right pane of Windows 8, click one of the icons in the lower-right corner to select Thumbnail view or Details view (see Figure 7-20a). For Windows 7, click the View icon in the menu bar and select your view (see Figure 7-20b).

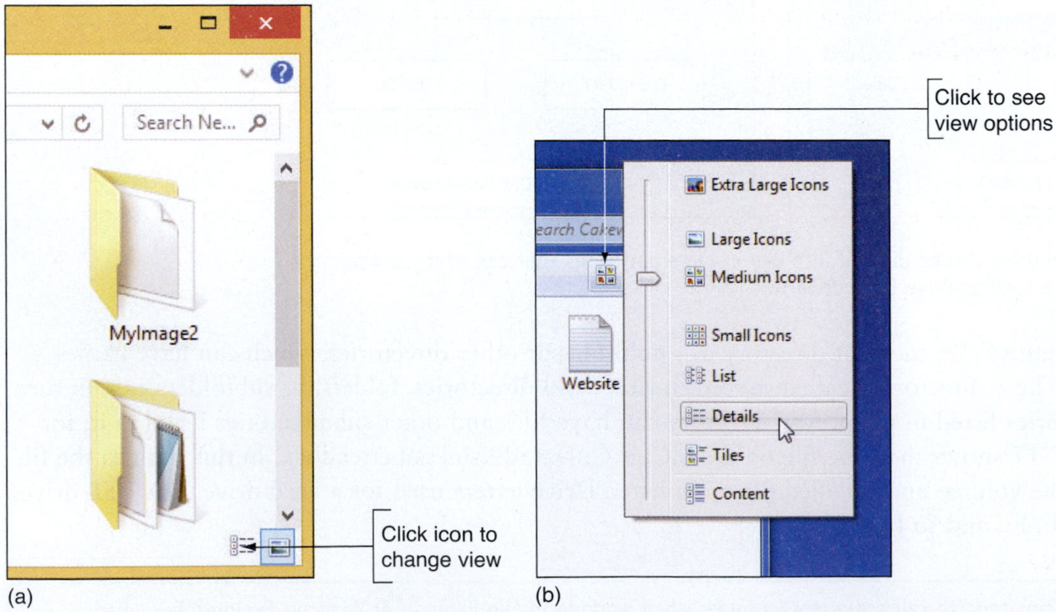

Figure 7-20 Click the View icon to change how files and folders display in the right pane of (a) Windows 8 File Explorer or (b) Windows 7 Windows Explorer

- *Tip 3*: To control the column headings that appear in Details view, right-click a column heading and select the headings that you want to appear (see Figure 7-21). To control which column is used to sort items in Details view, click a column heading.

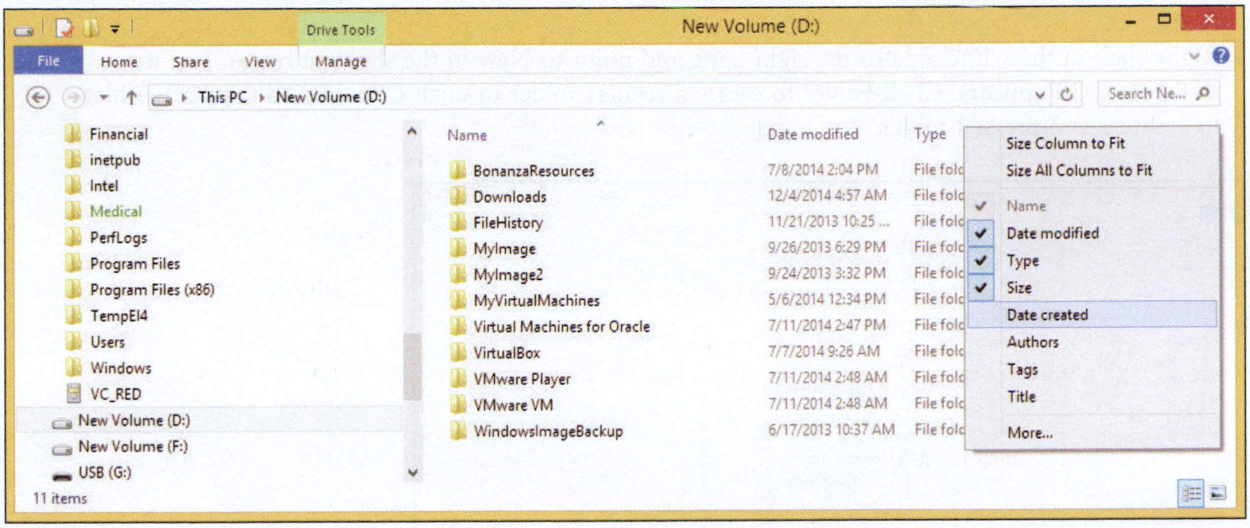

Figure 7-21 Right-click a column heading to select columns to display in Details view

- *Tip 4*: To search for a folder or file, use the Search box in the upper-right corner of the window.
- *Tip 5*: Use the forward and back arrows in the upper-left corner to move forward and backward to previous views.
- *Tip 6*: Click a right arrow in the path displayed in the address bar at the top of the Explorer window to see a drop-down list of subfolders (see Figure 7-22). Click one to move to this subfolder.

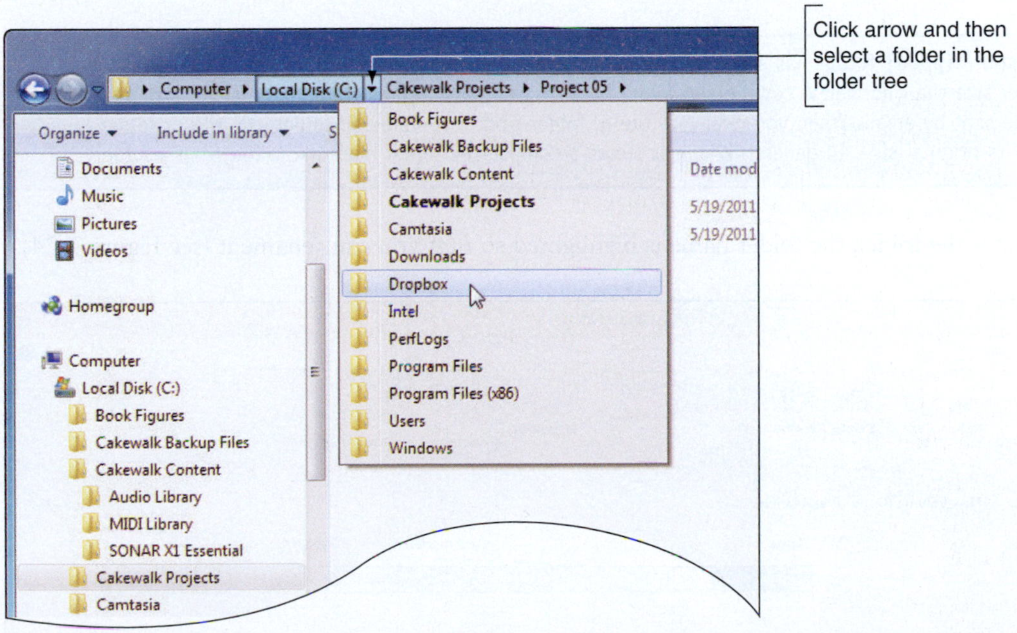

Figure 7-22 Click a right arrow in the address bar to move up the folder tree and down to a new folder

CREATE A FOLDER

To create a folder, first select the folder you want to be the parent folder. (Remember that a parent folder is the folder that contains the child folder.) Next, use one of these methods to create the new folder:

- In Windows 8, select the **Home** ribbon and click **New folder**. In Windows 7, click **New folder** on the menu bar.
- Right-click in the white area of the right pane and point to **New** in the shortcut menu. The menu in Figure 7-23 appears. Click **Folder** to create a regular folder or click **Compressed (zipped) Folder** to create a compressed folder.

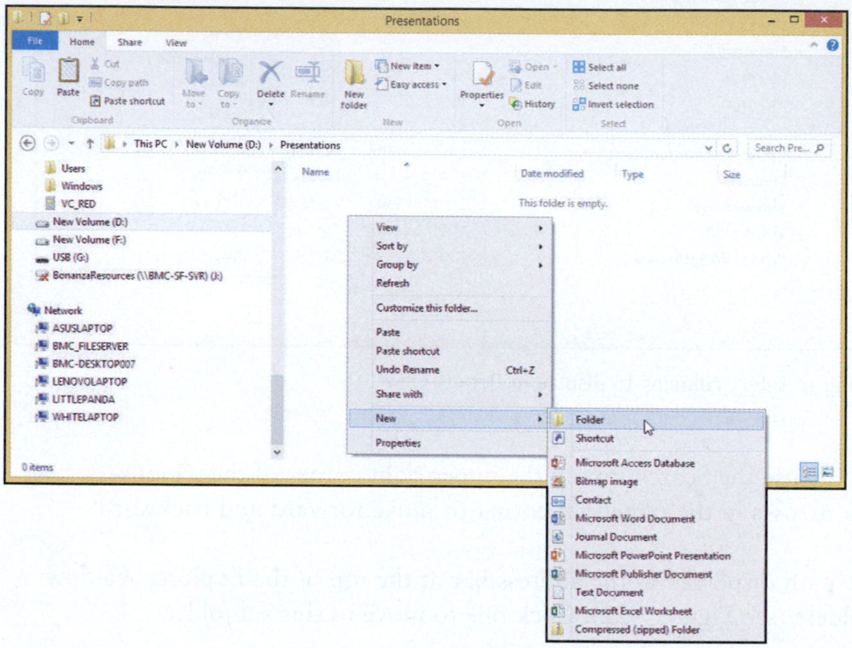

Figure 7-23 Create a new file, folder, or compressed folder

> **Notes** A **compressed (zipped) folder** has a .zip extension. Any file or folder that you put in this folder will be compressed to a smaller size than normal. A compressed folder is often used to compress files to a smaller size so they can more easily be sent by email. When you remove a file or folder from a compressed folder, the file or folder is uncompressed back to its original size. In general, Windows treats a compressed folder more like a file than a folder.

After Windows creates the folder, the folder name is highlighted so that you can rename it (see Figure 7-24).

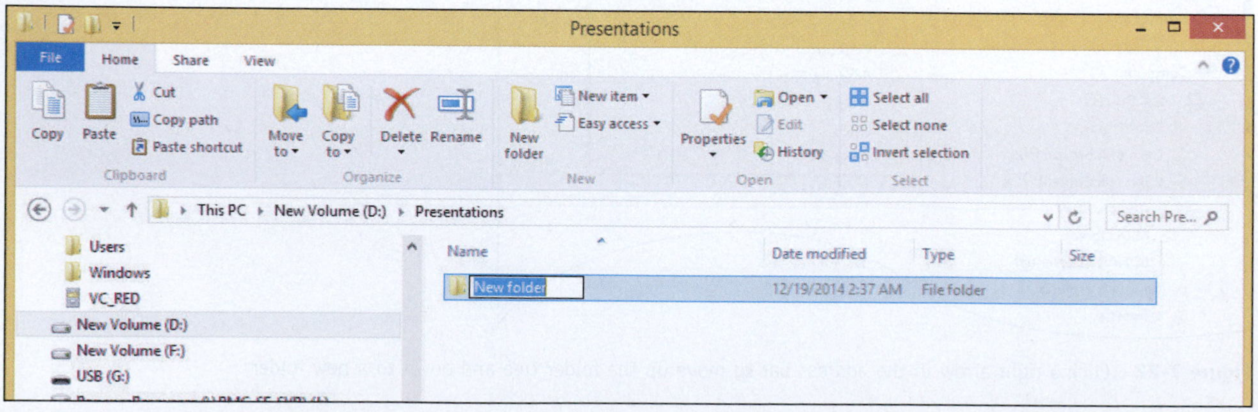

Figure 7-24 Edit the new folder's name

> **Notes** The Windows desktop is itself a folder and is located at C:\Users*username*\Desktop. For example, if the user, Anne, creates a folder on her desktop named Downloads, this folder is located at C:\Users\Anne\Desktop\Downloads.

CREATE A FILE

You can create a file using a particular application, or you can create a file using File Explorer or Windows Explorer. In Explorer, right-click in the unused white area in the right pane of the window and point to **New** in the shortcut menu. The menu lists applications you can use to create a file in the current folder (see Figure 7-23). Click the application and the file is created. You can then rename the file. However, to keep the proper file association, don't change the file extension.

COPY, MOVE, RENAME, OR DELETE FILES OR FOLDERS

Use these handy tips to copy, move, rename, and delete files or folders using File Explorer or Windows Explorer:

- To copy a file or folder, right-click it and select **Copy** from the shortcut menu. Then right-click in the white area of the folder where the copied item is to go and select **Paste** from the shortcut menu. You can also use the Cut and Paste commands to move an item to a new location.
- Drag and drop an item to move or copy it to a new location. If the location is on the same drive as the original location, the file or folder will be automatically deleted from its original location. If you don't want it deleted, hold down the **Ctrl** key while you drag and drop the item.
- To rename a file or folder, right-click it and select **Rename** from the shortcut menu. Change the name and click off the file or folder to deselect it. You cannot rename a data file when an application has the file open; first close the data file and then rename it.
- To delete a file or folder, select the item and press the **Delete** key. Or you can right-click the item and select **Delete** from the shortcut menu. Either way, a confirmation dialog box asks if you are sure you want to delete the item. If you click **Yes**, you send the file or folder and all its contents, including subfolders, to the Recycle Bin.

> **Notes** In Windows, the difference between a window and a dialog box is that a window can be resized, but a dialog box cannot be resized.

- To select multiple items to delete, copy, or move at the same time, hold down the **Shift** or **Ctrl** key as you click. To select several adjacent items in a list, click the first item and **Shift-click** the last item. To select nonadjacent items in a list, hold down the **Ctrl** key as you click each item.

Files deleted from the hard drive are stored in the Recycle Bin on the desktop. Emptying the Recycle Bin will free up your disk space. To empty the Recycle Bin, right-click the bin and select **Empty Recycle Bin** from the shortcut menu.

> **Notes** In this chapter, you learn how to use File Explorer or Windows Explorer to create, copy, move, delete, and rename files and folders. In the chapter, "Maintaining Windows," you will learn that you can do these same tasks using commands from a command prompt.

CREATE A SHORTCUT

To create a shortcut on the Windows desktop to a data file or program, use File Explorer or Windows Explorer to locate the data file or program file, right-click it, and click **Create shortcut** in the menu that appears. For example, in Figure 7-25, you can see a shortcut to the C:\Windows\System32\notepad.exe program is about to be placed on the Windows desktop.

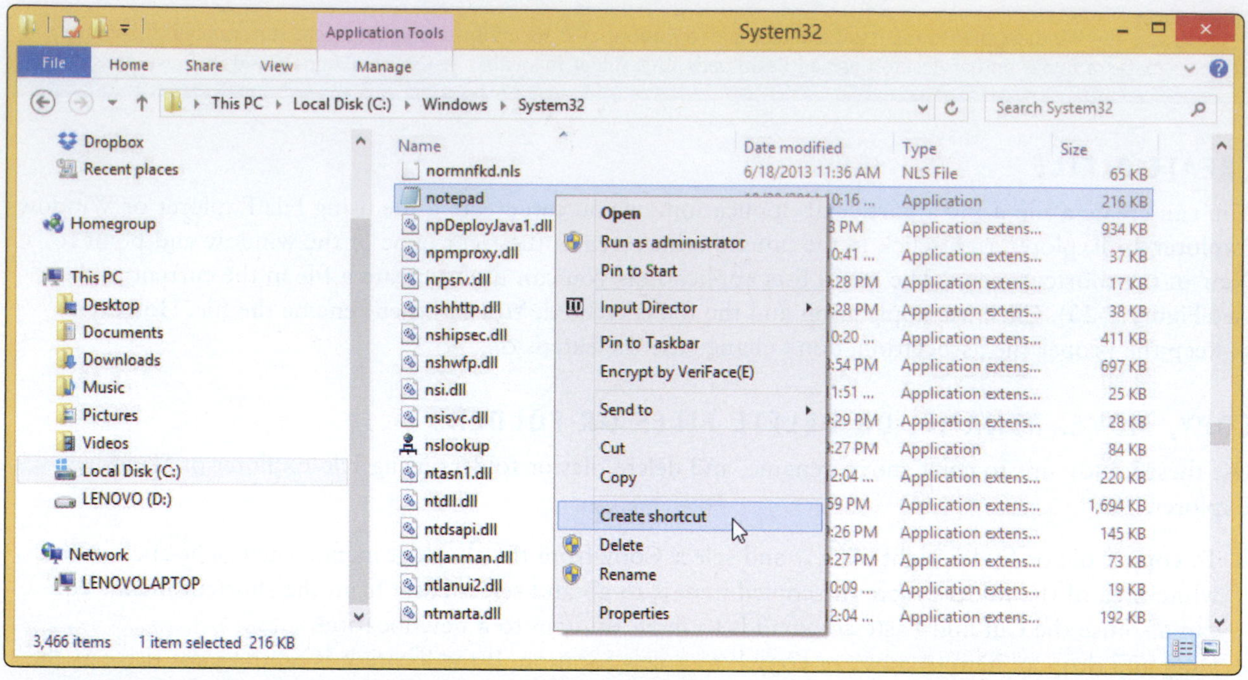

Figure 7-25 Place a shortcut to a program file on the Windows desktop

Hands-On | Project 7-2 Create Shortcuts

A+
220-902
1.4

Do the following to practice creating shortcuts on the Windows desktop:

1. Open Windows 8 File Explorer or Windows 7 Windows Explorer and create a folder under the root directory of the hard drive called **\Temp**. List the steps you took.
2. Add a subfolder to \Temp called **\MyFiles**. List the steps you took.
3. Create a text file in the MyFiles folder named **Text1.txt**. List the steps you took.
4. Create a shortcut to the MyFiles folder on the Windows desktop. List the steps you took.
5. Rename the file **Text2.txt**.
6. Double-click the shortcut on the desktop. What error did you get?
7. The program file for Microsoft Paint is mspaint.exe. Use Windows Explorer to locate the program file and launch the Microsoft Paint program.
8. Create a shortcut to Microsoft Paint on the Windows desktop. Launch Microsoft Paint using the shortcut.
9. To clean up after yourself, delete the \Temp folder and the shortcuts. Close the two Paint windows.

CONTROL PANEL

A+
220-902
1.1, 1.2

Control Panel is a window containing several small utility programs called applets that are used to manage hardware, software, users, and the system. (In general, a utility program is a program used to maintain a system or fix a computer problem.) To access Control Panel in Windows 8, right-click **Start** and click **Control Panel.** In Windows 7, click **Start** and click **Control Panel.**

By default, Control Panel appears in Category view where utilities are grouped by category. To switch to Classic view, click **Category** and select either Large icons or Small icons. Figure 7-26 shows the Windows 8 Control Panel in Small icons view. Use the Search box in the title bar to help find information and utilities in Control Panel.

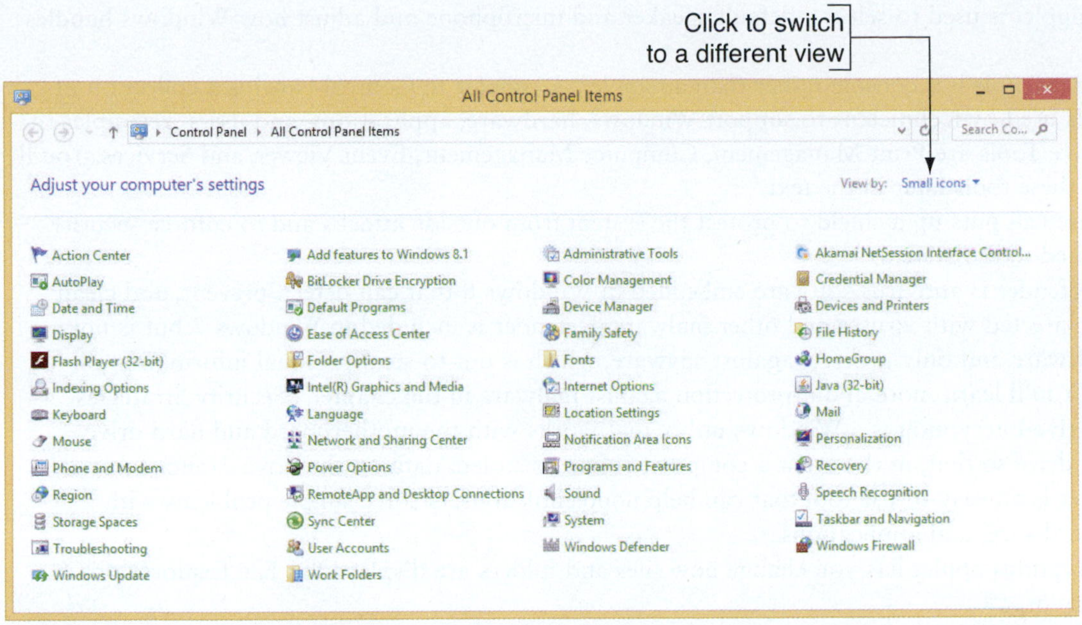

Figure 7-26 Many technicians prefer to use Control Panel in Classic view to more easily access utilities

> **★ A+ Exam Tip** The A+ 220-902 exam expects you to contrast Control Panel Category view and Classic view and to know how to use Classic view, which generally presents more options to a technician than does Category view.

Here is a short list of some of the applets in Control Panel. Later in the text, you learn to use these and other Control Panel applets:

- The **Date and Time applet** is used to set the date and time in Windows. The Date and Time tab is shown in Figure 7-27a where you can change the date, time, and time zone. Windows can pick up the date and time from UEFI/BIOS firmware on the motherboard. Alternately, on the Internet Time tab (see Figure 7-27b), you can allow Windows to automatically synchronize the date and time with the *time.windows.com* website.

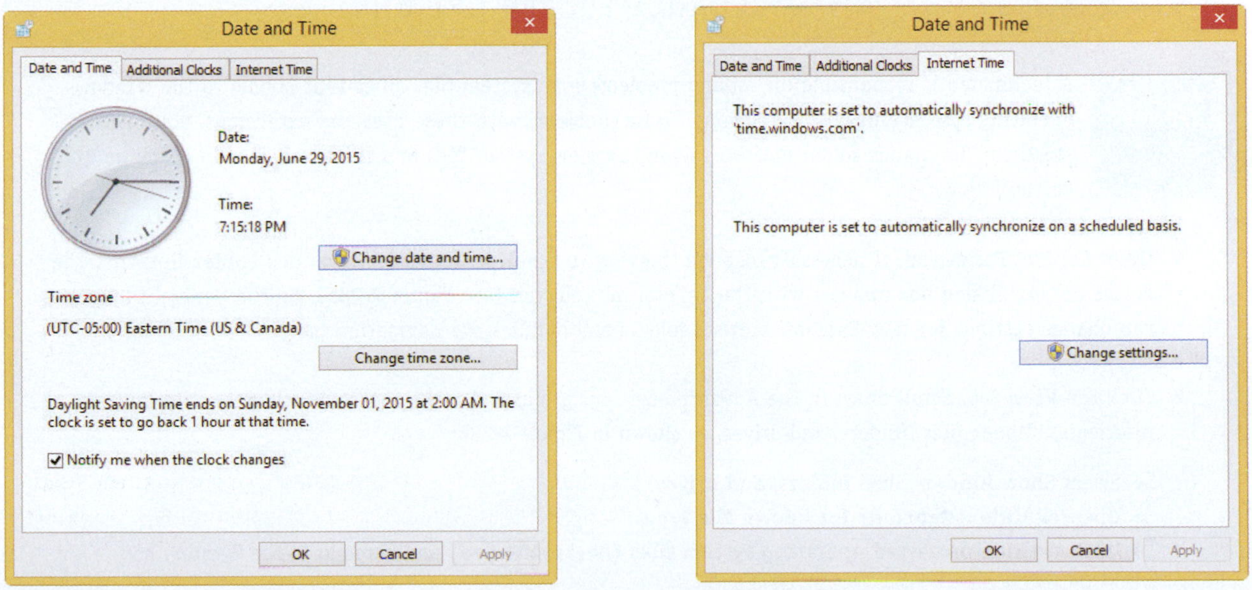

(a) (b)

Figure 7-27 Use the Date and Time applet (a) to manually adjust the date and time, or (b) to automatically synchronize Windows date and time to *time.windows.com* or to a different Internet time server

- The Sound applet is used to select a default speaker and microphone and adjust how Windows handles sounds.
- Administrative Tools is a console rather than an applet. A console in Control Panel is a collection of support tools used by technicians to support Windows, hardware, applications, and users. Examples of Administrative Tools are Print Management, Computer Management, Event Viewer, and Services. You'll learn to use these tools later in the text.
- Windows Firewall puts up a shield to protect the system from outside attacks and to enforce security policies applied to the system.
- Windows Defender is antivirus software embedded in Windows 8 that can detect, prevent, and clean up a system infected with viruses and other malware. Defender is included in Windows 7 but is not antivirus software and only protects against spyware, which is out to steal personal information on a computer. You'll learn more about protection against malware in the chapter, "Security Strategies."
- BitLocker Drive Encryption is a Windows utility that works with the motherboard and hard drive to encrypt a drive so that, in the event a computer is lost or stolen, data on the drive cannot be read.
- Action Center is an easy-to-use tool that can help nontechnical users solve simple problems with Windows, hardware, and applications.
- The Folder Options applet lets you change how files and folders are displayed in File Explorer or Windows Explorer.

FOLDER OPTIONS

A+
220-902
1.5

The Folder Options applet in Control Panel can be used to view and change options assigned to folders. These options control how users view the files in the folder and what they can do with these files. In File Explorer or Windows Explorer, Windows has an annoying habit of hiding file extensions if it knows which application is associated with a file extension. For example, just after installation, it hides .exe, .com, .sys, and .txt file extensions, but does not hide .docx, .pptx, or .xlsx file extensions until the software to open these files has been installed. Also, Windows really doesn't want you to see its own system files, and it hides these files from view until you force it to show them.

APPLYING CONCEPTS CHANGE FOLDER OPTIONS

A+
220-902
1.5

A technician is responsible for solving problems with system files (files that belong to the Windows operating system) and file extensions. To fix problems with these files and extensions, you need to see them. To change folder options so you can view system files and file extensions in Windows 8/7, do the following:

1. **Open Control Panel** and, if necessary, change the view to **Small icons** view. Then click **Folder Options**. The Folder Options dialog box appears with the General tab selected (see Figure 7-28a). On the General tab, you can change settings for how Explorer browses folders and handles the navigation pane.

2. Click the **View** tab. Scroll down in the Advanced settings group and make these selections to show hidden information about files, folders, and drives, as shown in Figure 7-28b:

   - Select **Show hidden files, folders, and drives.**
   - Uncheck **Hide extensions for known file types.**
   - Uncheck **Hide protected operating system files (Recommended)** and respond to the Warning box.

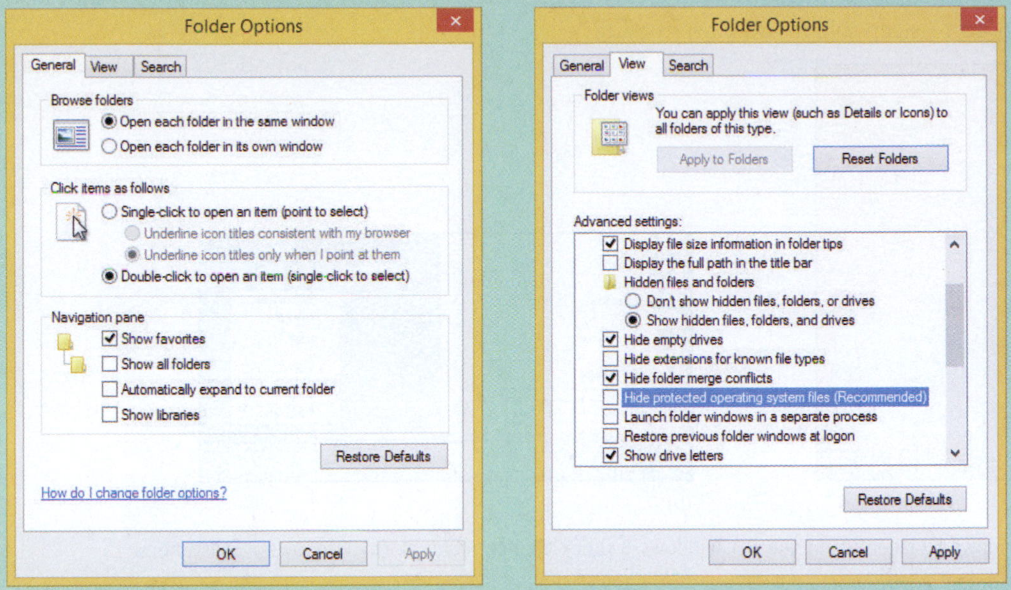

(a) (b)

Figure 7-28 Use the Folder Options box to control how Windows Explorer works and displays files and folders

3. To save your changes and close the Folder Options box, click **OK**.

★ A+ Exam Tip The A+ 220-902 exam expects you to know how to view hidden files and file extensions in File Explorer and Windows Explorer.

POWER OPTIONS

A+ 220-902 1.5

The Power Options applet of Control Panel can help you conserve power and increase the time before a battery pack on a laptop needs recharging. Power is managed by putting the computer into varying degrees of suspend or sleep modes.

★ A+ Exam Tip The A+ 220-902 exam expects you to know how to manage power, including using power plans, sleep (suspend), hibernate, and standby modes.

Here are the different power-saving states:

- *Sleep mode.* Using Windows 8/7/Vista, you can put the computer into sleep mode, also called suspend mode, to save power when you're not using the computer. If applications are open or other work is in progress, Windows first saves the current state, including open files, to memory and saves some of the work to the hard drive. Then everything is shut down except memory and enough of the system to respond to a wake-up. In sleep mode, the power light on the laptop might blink from time to time. (A laptop generally uses about 1 to 2 percent of battery power for each hour in sleep mode.) To wake up the computer, press the power button or, for some computers, press a key or touch the touch pad. Windows wakes up in about two seconds. When Windows is in sleep mode, it can still perform Windows updates and scheduled tasks. Windows can be configured to go to sleep after a period of inactivity, or you can manually put it to sleep. To put the system to sleep manually in Windows 8, you can use the charms bar as you learned to do earlier in the chapter. You can also open the **Quick Launch** menu, point to **Shut down or sign out**, and click **Sleep** (see Figure 7-29a). For Windows 7, click **Start**, click the arrow to the right of Shut down, and then click **Sleep** (see Figure 7-29b). A laptop might also be configured to go to sleep when you close the lid.

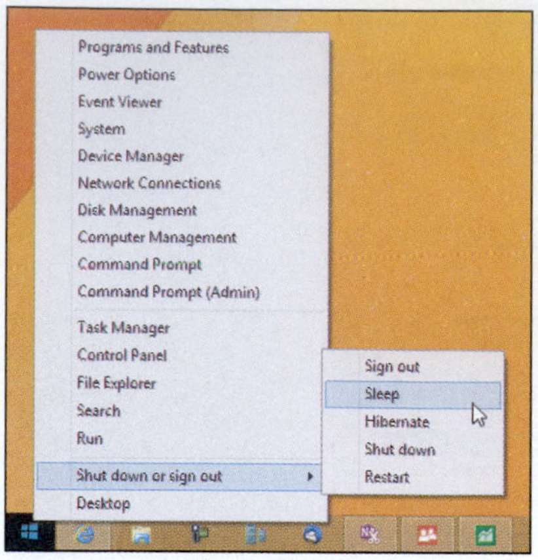

(a)

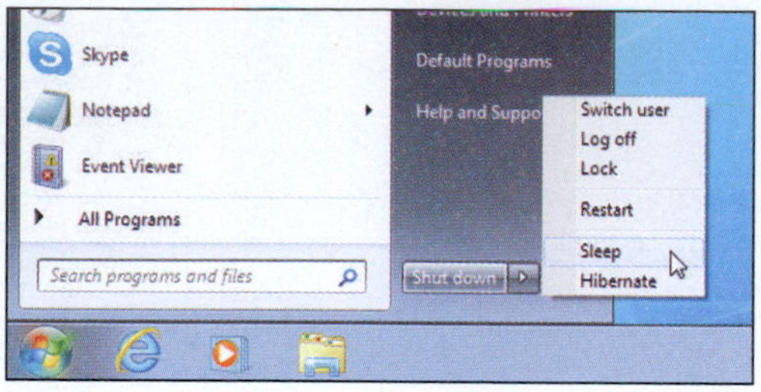

(b)

Figure 7-29 Put Windows to sleep using the (a) Windows 8 Quick Launch menu or (b) Windows 7 Start menu

- ***Hibernation.*** Hibernation saves all work to the hard drive and powers down the system. When you press the power button, Windows reloads its state, including all open applications and documents. When Windows is in sleep mode on a laptop and senses the battery is critically low, it will put the system into hibernation.

Notes Recall that hard drives are permanent or nonvolatile storage and memory is temporary or volatile storage. A hard drive does not require power to hold its contents, but memory, on the other hand, is volatile and loses its contents when it has no power. In hibernation, the computer has no power and everything must, therefore, be stored on the hard drive.

APPLYING | CONCEPTS — CONFIGURE WINDOWS POWER-MANAGEMENT SETTINGS

A+ 220-902 1.5

Follow these steps to configure power in Windows 8/7:

1. In Control Panel in Classic view, click **Power Options**. The Power Options window opens. Figure 7-30 shows the window for one laptop. The plans might be different for other laptops.

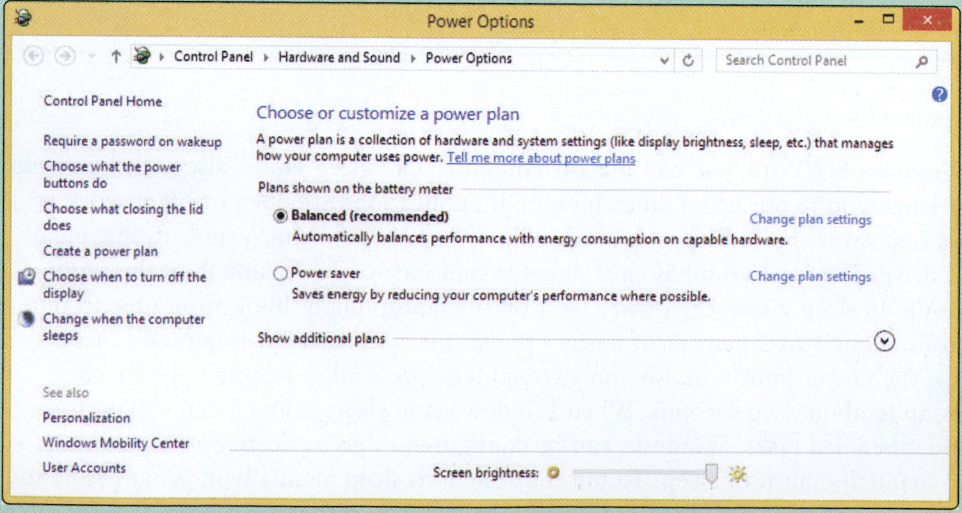

Figure 7-30 Power plans in Windows 8

2. You can customize each plan. For example, under Balanced (recommended), click **Change plan settings**. The Edit Plan Settings window appears (see the left side of Figure 7-31). Notice in the figure the various times of inactivity before the computer goes into sleep mode, which are called sleep timers.

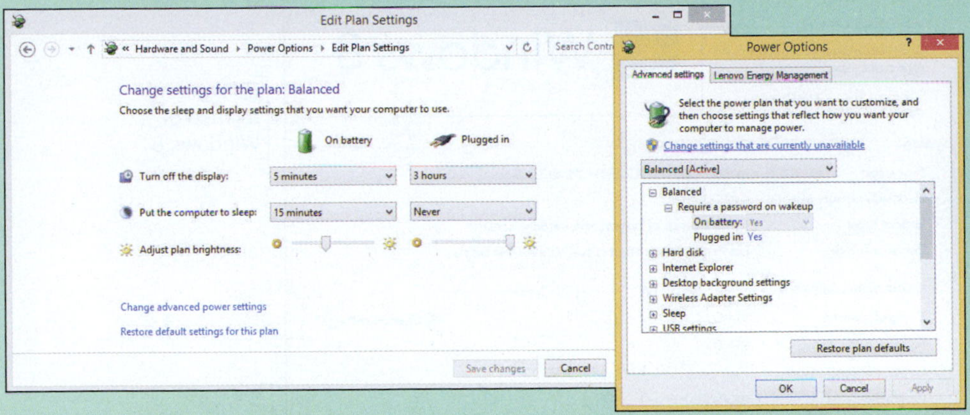

Figure 7-31 Customize a power plan

3. To see other changes you can make, click **Change advanced power settings**. Using this Power Options box (see the right side of Figure 7-31), you can do such things as control the minutes before the hard drive turns off; control what happens when you close the lid, press the sleep button, or press the power button; or set the brightness level of the LCD panel to conserve power. You can also use this box to set what happens when the battery gets low or critically low. Make your changes and click **OK** to close the box.

4. If you made changes, click **Save changes** in the Edit Plan Settings window. Close the Power Options window.

7

As an IT support technician, you need to be able to sit down at a working computer and within 5 or 10 minutes find the details about what software and hardware is installed on the system and the general health of the system. Within 20 minutes, you should be able to solve any minor problems the computer might have such as a broken network connection. Some quick-and-easy support tools that can help you are the System window, System Information window, and Action Center. All these tools are discussed next.

A+ Exam Tip The A+ 220-902 exam expects you to know how to use File Explorer, Windows Explorer, the System window, the System Information window, and the Action Center. If the utility can be accessed by more than one method, you are expected to know all of the methods.

SYSTEM WINDOW

A+ 220-902 1.1

The System window is your friend. It can give you a quick look at what hardware and software are installed and can get you to other useful Windows tools. To open the System window in Windows 8, open the Quick Launch menu (press **Win+X**) and click **System**. In Windows 7, click **Start**, right-click **Computer**, and select **Properties** from the shortcut menu. (Alternately, you can open **Control Panel** and click **System**.) Figure 7-32 shows the resulting System window for one Windows 8 laptop.

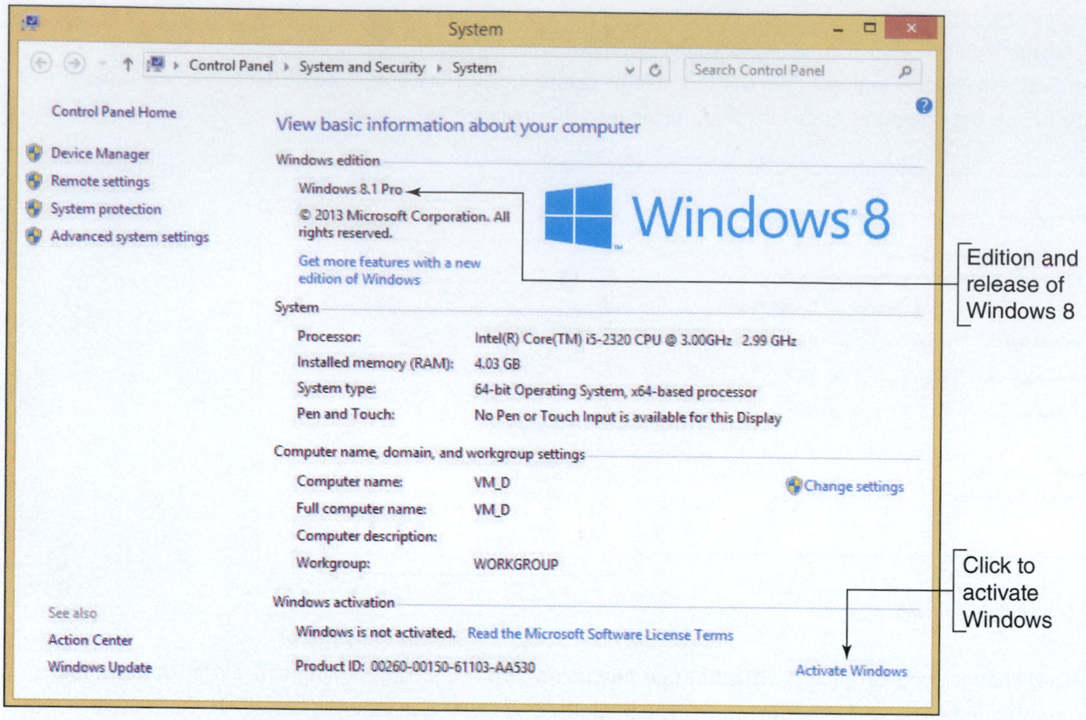

Figure 7-32 System window reports Windows 8.1 Pro is installed but not yet activated

So what technical information are you looking at? Here is the rundown:

- Windows 8/7 comes in several editions and you can see this system has the Windows 8.1 Professional edition installed.
- The type of OS installed is a 64-bit OS. A **32-bit operating system** processes 32 bits at a time, and a **64-bit operating system** processes 64 bits at a time. Most editions of Windows 8/7 come in either 32-bit or 64-bit versions. A 64-bit OS performs better than a 32-bit OS, but requires more memory. A 32-bit OS can support up to 4 GB of memory, and a 64-bit OS can support much more. The details of how much memory each edition of Windows can support are covered in the chapter, "Installing Windows."
- The processor installed is the Intel Core i5-2320 and about 4 GB of RAM is installed.
- You can also see that Windows 8.1 is not activated. To activate Windows, make sure you're connected to the Internet and click **Activate Windows**. The product key used during the installation will be verified during activation.

OS Differences Recall that Windows 8 offers free major updates and the only one Microsoft has published to date is Windows 8.1. However, Windows 7 handles major updates differently. A major update to Windows 7 is called a **service pack**, and the Windows 7 System window reports which service packs, if any, have been installed. See Figure 7-33. Minor updates or fixes that are released more frequently for Windows 8 or 7 are called **patches** and are not reported on the System window.

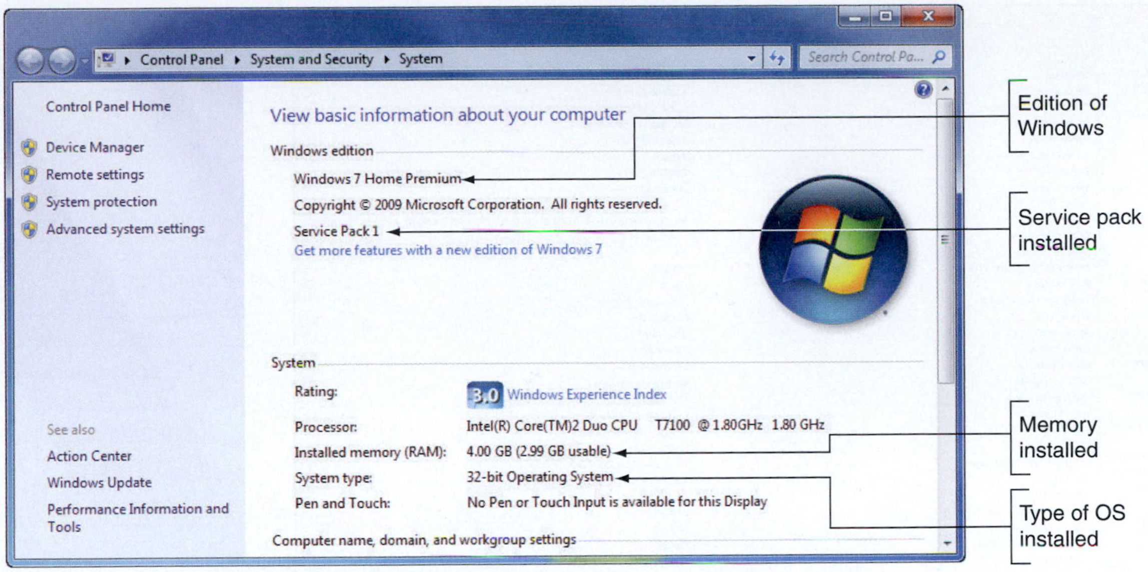

Figure 7-33 A 32-bit version of Windows 7 Home Premium with Service Pack 1 installed

That's a lot of useful information for a first look at a computer.

SYSTEM INFORMATION WINDOW

A+ 220-902 1.1, 1.4

Turn to the System Information (msinfo32.exe) window for more details about a system, including installed hardware and software, the current system configuration, and currently running programs. For example, you can use it to find out what BIOS version is installed on the motherboard, how much RAM is installed, the directory where the OS is installed, the size of the hard drive, the names of currently running drivers, a list of startup programs, print jobs in progress, currently running tasks, and much more. Because the System Information window gives so much useful information, help desk technicians often ask a user on the phone to open it and read to the technician information about the computer.

When strange error messages appear during startup, use the System Information window to get a list of drivers that loaded successfully. Device drivers are small programs stored on the hard drive that tell the computer how to communicate with a specific hardware device such as a printer, network card, or scanner. If you have saved the System Information report when the system was starting successfully, comparing the two reports can help identify the problem device.

To run System Information in Windows 8, open the **Quick Launch** menu, click **Run**, enter **msinfo32.exe** in the Run box, and press **Enter**. In Windows 7, click **Start**, and enter **msinfo32.exe** in the Search box and press **Enter**. The System Information window for one computer is shown in Figure 7-34. To drill down to more information in the window, click items in the left pane.

7

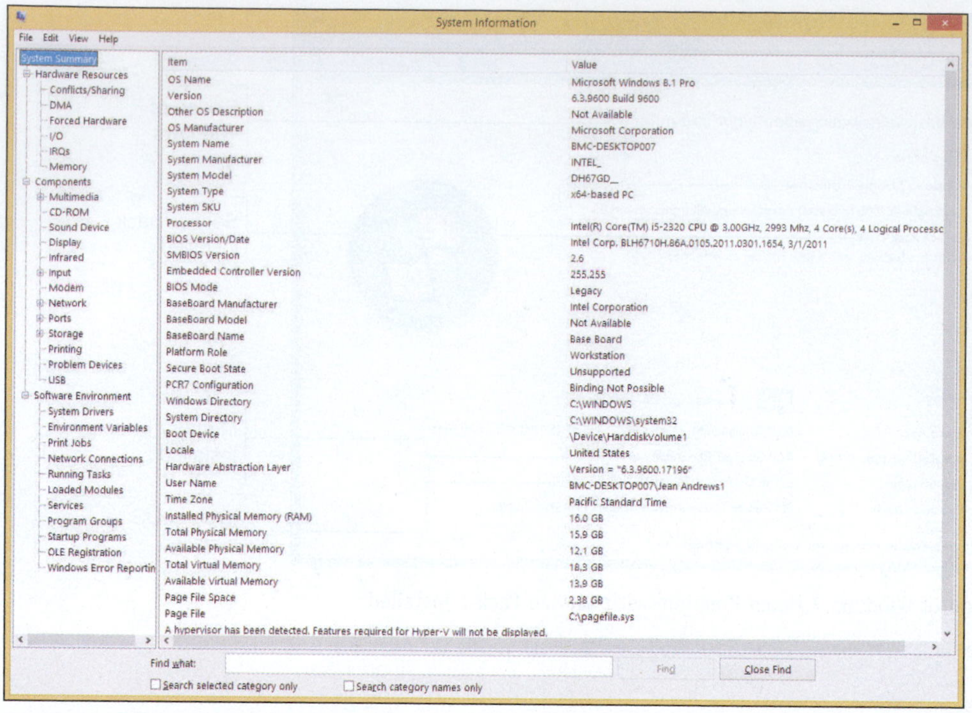

Figure 7-34 Use the System Information utility to examine details about a system

Hands-On | Project 7-3 Use the System Information Utility

A+ 220-902 1.1, 1.4

Do the following to run the System Information utility and gather information about your system:

1. Use the **msinfo32.exe** command to launch the System Information window.
2. Browse through the different levels of information in this window and answer the following questions:
   a. What OS and OS version are you using?
   b. What is your CPU speed?
   c. What is your BIOS manufacturer and version?
   d. How much video RAM is available to your video adapter card? Explain how you got this information.
   e. What is the name of the driver file that manages your network adapter? Your optical drive?

ACTION CENTER

A+ 220-902 1.1

The Action Center is the tool to use when you want to make a quick jab at solving a computer problem. If a hardware or application problem is easy to solve, the Action Center can probably do it in a matter of minutes because it lists errors and issues that need attention and proposed solutions. The Action Center flag appears in the notification area of the taskbar. If the flag has a red X beside it, as shown in Figure 7-35, Windows considers the system has an important issue that needs resolving immediately. When you click the flag, you can see a brief report of issues, as shown in the figure.

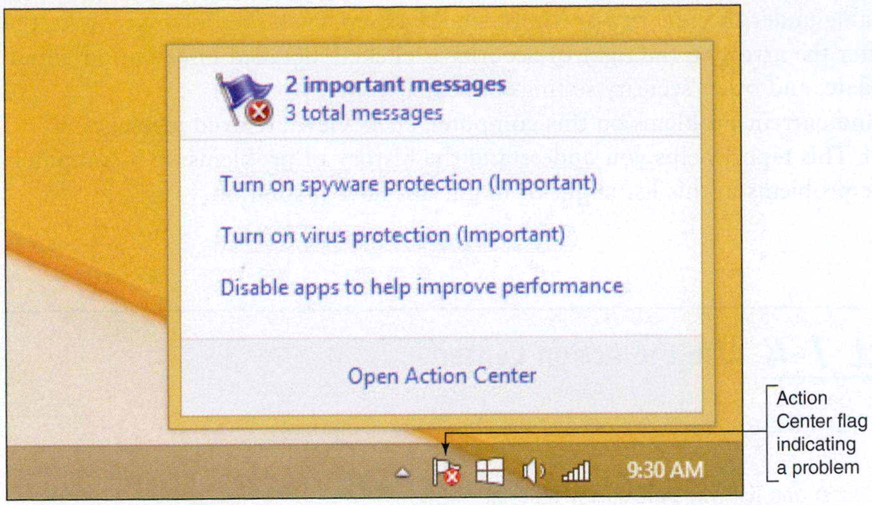

Figure 7-35 A red X on the Action Center flag in the taskbar indicates a critical issue needs resolving

> **★ A+ Exam Tip** The A+ 220-902 exam expects you to know about the Windows Vista **Security Center**. It was the predecessor to the Windows 8/7 Action Center and gave quick-and-easy access to several Windows tools, including Windows Firewall, Windows Update, anti-malware settings, including that of Windows Defender, and other security settings.

To open the Action Center, you can click the red flag in the taskbar and then click **Open Action Center**. Alternately, you can open **Control Panel** and click **Action Center**. The Action Center window for one Windows 8 computer is shown in Figure 7-36. (The Windows 7 Action Center is similar.) Notice the colored bar to the left of a problem. The red color indicates a critical problem that needs immediate attention. In this example, antivirus software is not running on the system. The orange color indicates a less critical problem, such as apps running in the background that might be slowing down the system or no backups are scheduled. Click the button to the right of a problem to find a recommended solution.

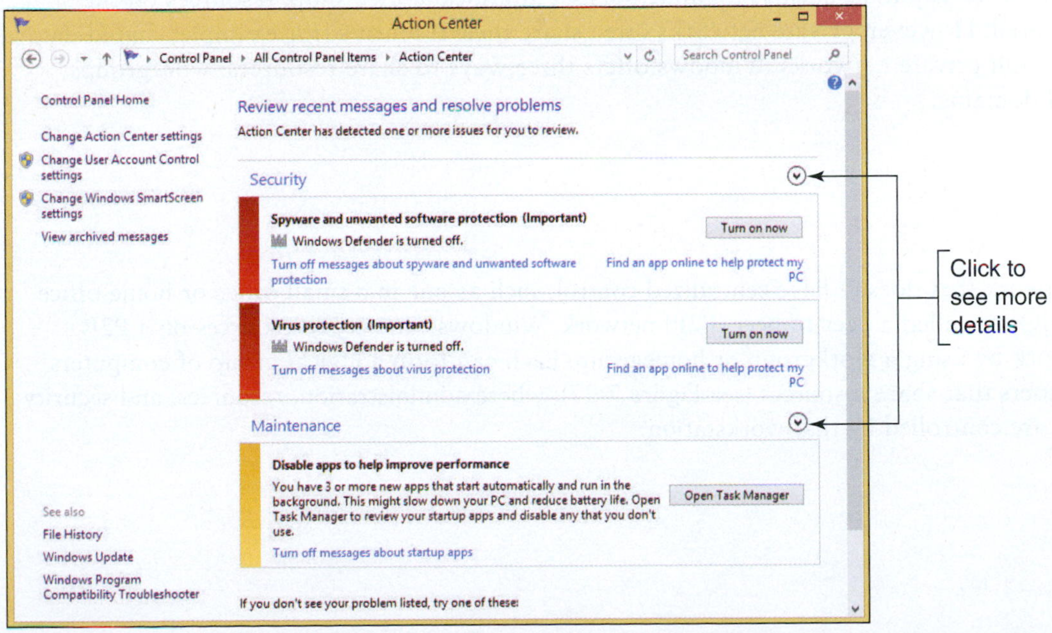

Figure 7-36 The Action Center shows a critical problem that needs a resolution

To see other information available under the Security or Maintenance group, click the down arrow to the right of a group. For example, after the arrow to the right of Security is clicked, detailed information about Windows Firewall, Windows Update, and other security settings appears.

To see a complete list of past and current problems on this computer, click **View archived messages** in the left pane of the Action Center. This report helps you understand the history of problems on a computer that you are troubleshooting. The problems in this list might or might not have a solution.

Hands-On | Project 7-4 Use the Action Center

A+
220-902
1.1

Using Windows 8/7, follow these steps to explore and use the Action Center:

1. Open the Action Center and list any problems it reports.
2. If a problem is listed, follow the links in Action Center to investigate possible solutions to the problem. If appropriate for your system, apply any solutions not yet applied. Make notes regarding the solutions you applied and the results of applying these solutions.
3. In the left pane of the Action Center, click **View archived messages.** Do you find a previous problem with this computer that already has a solution applied? If so, double-click the problem to read about the solution. Describe the problem and the solution that was applied.

WINDOWS NETWORK CONNECTIONS

A+
220-902
1.5, 1.6

An essential task of IT technicians is to connect computers to a wired or wireless network and support these connections. Before we get into the Windows networking tools to help you, let's start by looking at the ways Windows accesses resources on a network.

If a network is public, such as a public hotspot at a local coffee shop, resources on the network aren't shared. However, private networks often share their resources (for example, shared data files and printers). On private networks, Windows offers three ways to share resources: workgroups, homegroups, and domains.

WINDOWS WORKGROUP AND HOMEGROUP

A+
220-902
1.5, 1.6

A network that doesn't have centralized control, such as one in a small office or home office (SOHO), is called a peer-to-peer (P2P) network. Windows can access resources on a P2P network by using a workgroup or homegroup. Each can form a logical group of computers and users that share resources (see Figure 7-37), where administration, resources, and security on a workstation are controlled by that workstation.

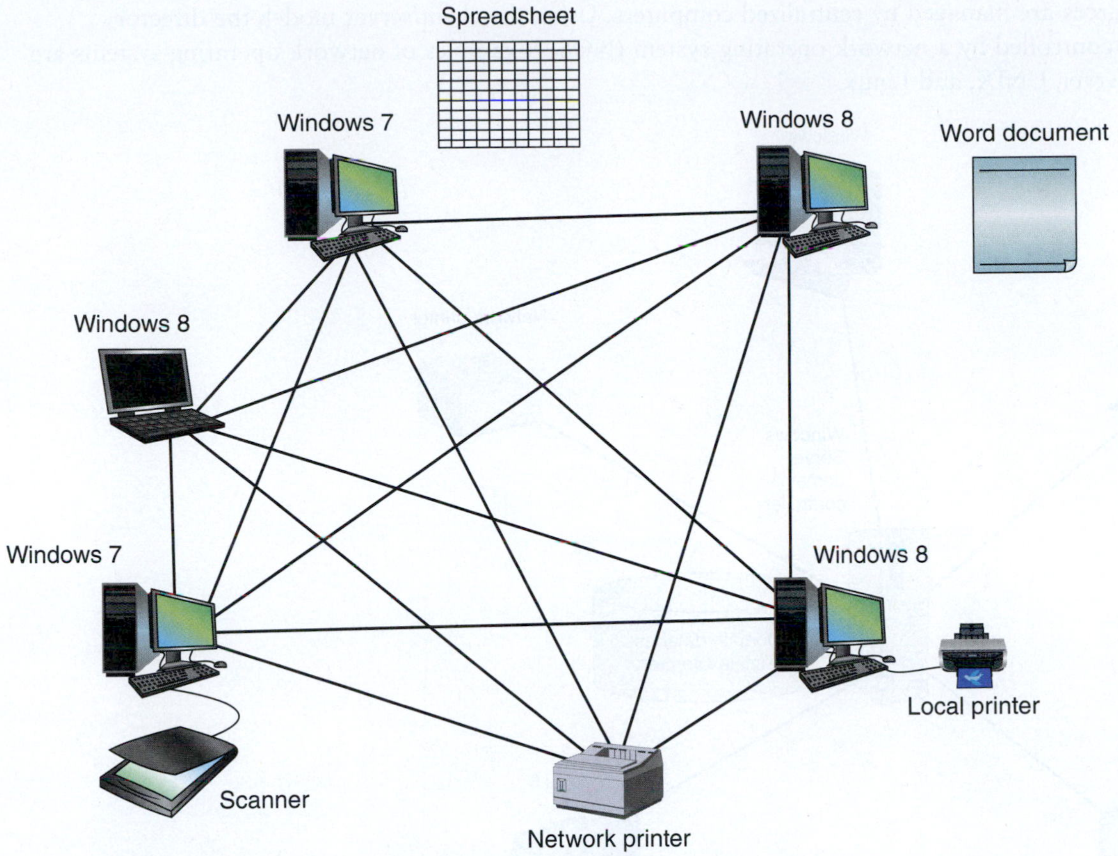

Figure 7-37 A Windows workgroup or homegroup is a type of peer-to-peer network where no single computer controls the network and each computer controls its own resources

> **Notes** When looking at the diagrams in Figure 7-37 and later in Figure 7-38, know that the connecting lines describe the logical connections between computers and not the physical connections. Both networks might be physically connected the same way, but logically, resources are controlled by each computer on the network or by using a centralized database. In network terminology, the arrangement of physical connections between computers is called the **physical topology**. The logical way the computers connect on a network is called the **logical topology**.

In a Windows **workgroup**, each computer maintains a list of users and their rights on that particular computer. The computer allows a user on the network to access local resources based on the rights she has been given. In a **homegroup**, each computer shares files, folders, libraries, and printers with other computers in the homegroup. A homegroup provides less security than a workgroup because any user of any computer in the homegroup can access homegroup resources.

> **A+ Exam Tip** The A+ 220-902 exam expects you to contrast a workgroup, homegroup, and domain. You also need to know that homegroups only apply to Windows 8/7, but not to Windows Vista, which does not support homegroups.

WINDOWS DOMAIN

A+ 220-902 1.5, 1.6

A Windows **domain** is implemented on a larger, private network, such as a corporate or college network. The domain forms a logical group of networked computers that share a centralized directory database of user account information and security for the entire group of computers (see Figure 7-38). A Windows domain is a type of **client/server** network, which is a network where resources are managed by centralized computers. Using the client/server model, the directory database is controlled by a network operating system (NOS). Examples of network operating systems are Windows Server, UNIX, and Linux.

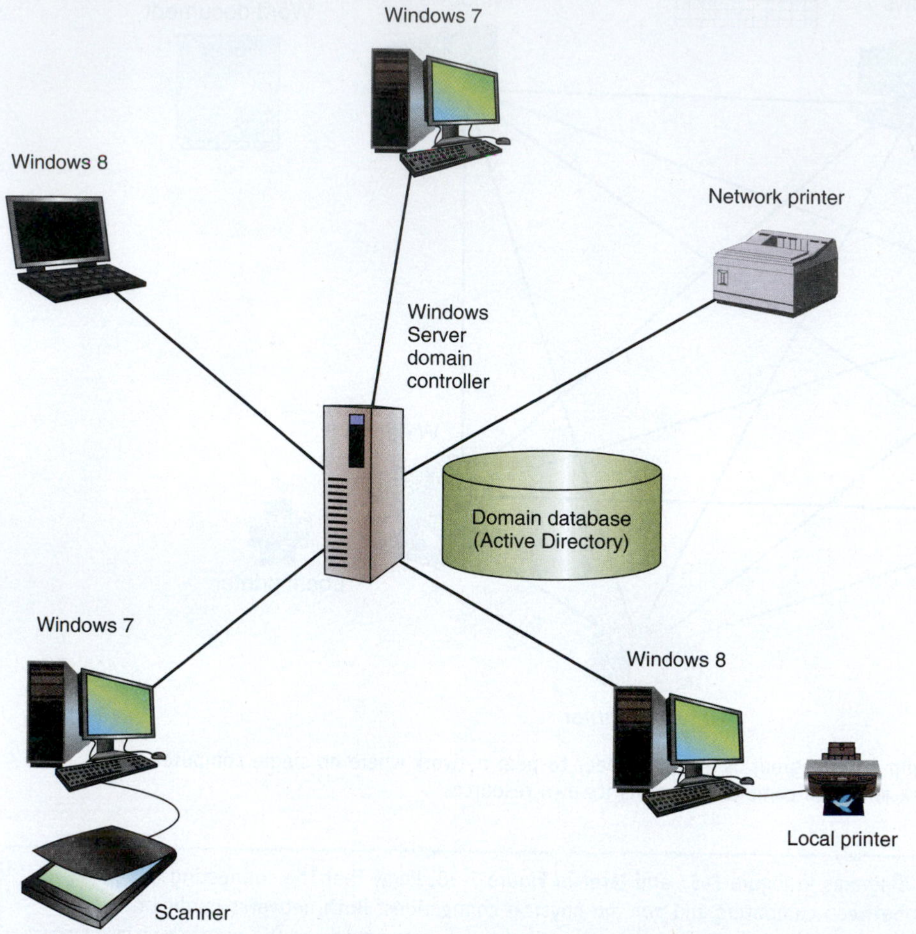

Figure 7-38 A Windows domain is a type of client/server network where security on each computer or other device is controlled by a centralized database on a domain controller

> **Notes** Windows Home Editions do not support joining a domain. If you plan to join a domain on your network, install Windows 8.1 Professional or Enterprise, or Windows 7 Professional, Enterprise, or Ultimate editions.

Windows Server controls a network using the directory database called Active Directory. Each user on the network must have his own domain-level account called a global account, network ID, domain account, or global username, which is kept in Active Directory and assigned by the network or system administrator. If you are connecting a computer to a domain, the administrator will tell you the network ID and password to the domain that you can use to sign in to the network.

> **Notes** If your computer is part of a domain, when Windows starts up, press **Ctrl+Alt+Del** to display a sign-in screen, and then enter your network ID and password.

PUBLIC AND PRIVATE NETWORKS

A+ 220-902 1.5, 1.6

When you connect to a public network, such as when you connect your laptop to a public wireless network at a local airport, you always want to ensure that your computer is protected from outside hackers and malware. Windows 8 offers two types of network security:

- ***Public network.*** When using Public network security, Windows configures strong firewall settings and you cannot join a homegroup or domain.
- ***Private network.*** When using Private network security, you can join a homegroup or domain and share files and printers.

Windows 7 offers three network security options, which are managed by Network Discovery settings that allow this computer to see other computers on the network and other computers can see this computer:

- ***Public network.*** Network Discovery is turned off and you cannot join a homegroup or domain. This option is the most secure.
- ***Home network.*** Network Discovery is turned on and you can join a homegroup.
- ***Work network.*** Network Discovery is turned on, you can join a domain, but you cannot join a homegroup.

MAKE A WINDOWS 8 NETWORK CONNECTION

A+
220-902
1.5, 1.6

To make a wired connection to a network, unless you have an unusual network setup, simply plug in the network cable and Windows does the rest.

To create a wireless connection in Windows 8, you can use the charms bar or the Network icon in the taskbar on the Windows 8 desktop. Here are directions when using the charms bar:

1. On the charms bar, click the **Settings** charm, and then click the Network icon. A list of available wireless networks appears (see Figure 7-39a). Click one to select it, and then click **Connect** (see Figure 7-39b).

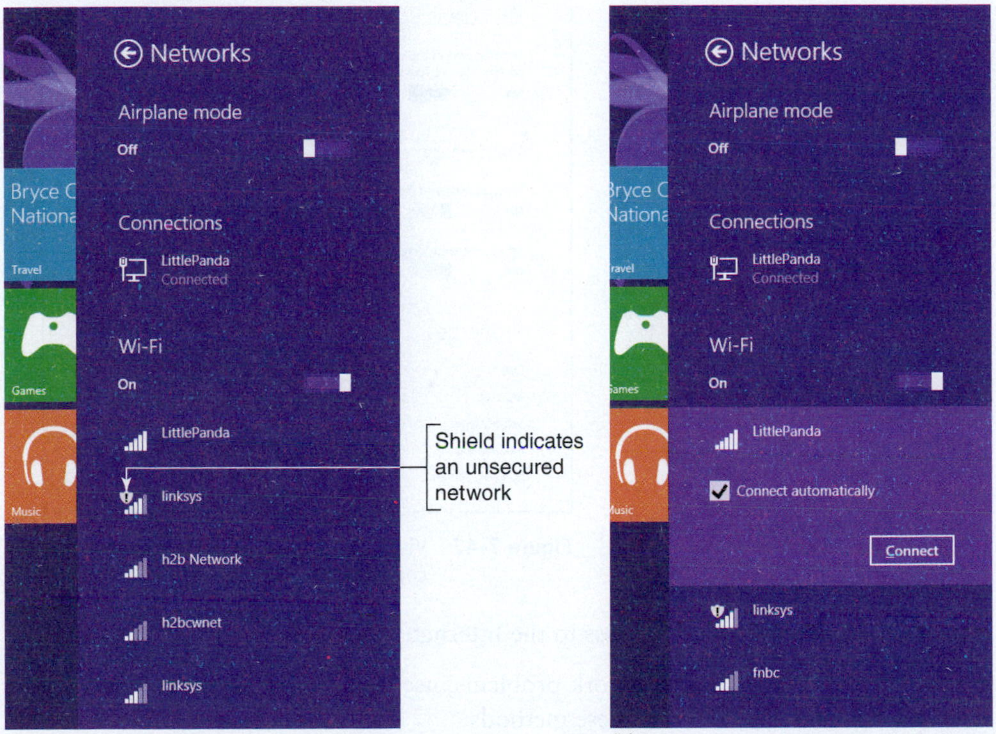

(a) (b)

Figure 7-39 (a) View a list of available wireless networks, and (b) select a wireless network to connect

2. If the network is secured, you must enter the security key to the wireless network to connect.

   To view and change network security settings, click the **Settings** charm and click **Change PC settings.** On the PC settings screen, click **Network.** On the Network screen, if necessary, click **Connections** (see Figure 7-40).

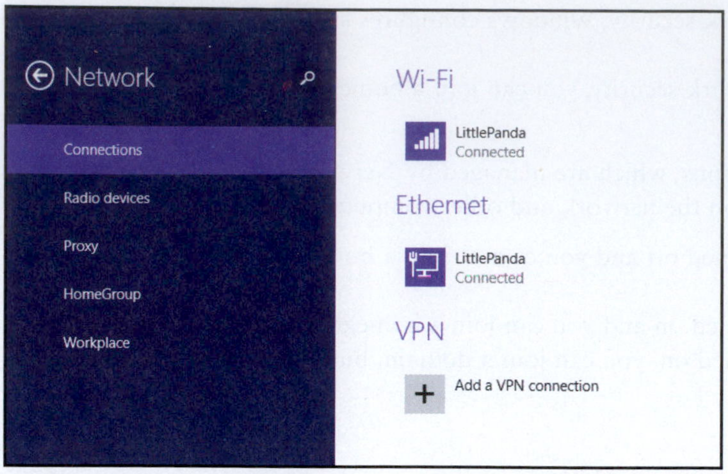

Figure 7-40 Use the Network screen to manage the security of network connections

> **Notes** When you click **HomeGroup** on the Network screen shown in Figure 7-40, you can use the HomeGroup page that appears to join or leave a homegroup, view the homegroup password, and decide whether libraries and printers are shared with the homegroup. These homegroup settings can also be managed from the Network and Sharing Center.

When you click a connection in the right pane, you can view and change some of the properties for the connection. For example, Figure 7-41 shows a wired connection and Figure 7-42 shows a wireless connection. To set the network security to Private, turn on **Find devices and content.** To set the network security to Public, turn this setting off.

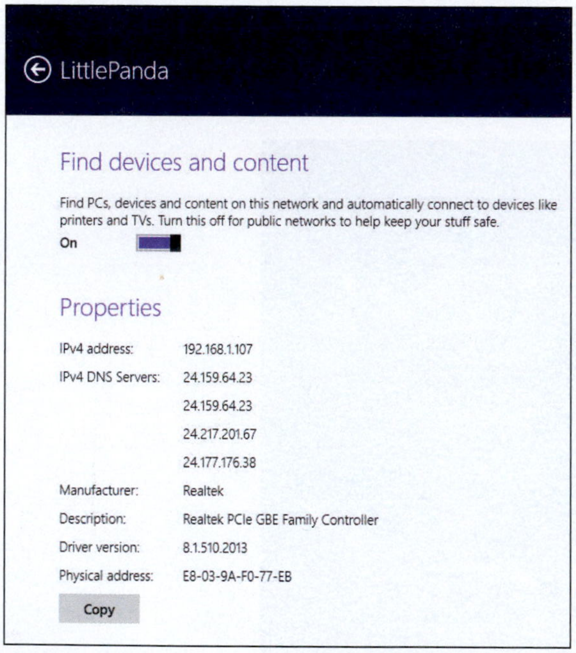

Figure 7-41 View and manage a wired network connection

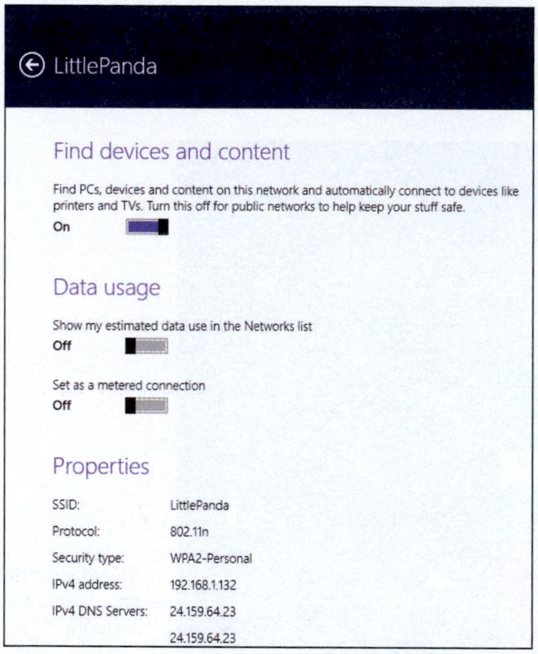

Figure 7-42 View and manage a wireless network connection

3. Open your browser window and verify you have access to the Internet.

To view network information and to troubleshoot network problems, use the Network and Sharing Center. To open the Network and Sharing Center, use one of these methods:

- On the desktop, right-click the **Network** icon in the taskbar, and click **Open Network and Sharing Center** in the shortcut menu that appears.
- Open **Control Panel** in Classic view and click **Network and Sharing Center.**

The Network and Sharing Center is shown in Figure 7-43. Notice you can see the active connections and network security setting. In later chapters, you'll learn to use the Network and Sharing Center to troubleshoot network problems.

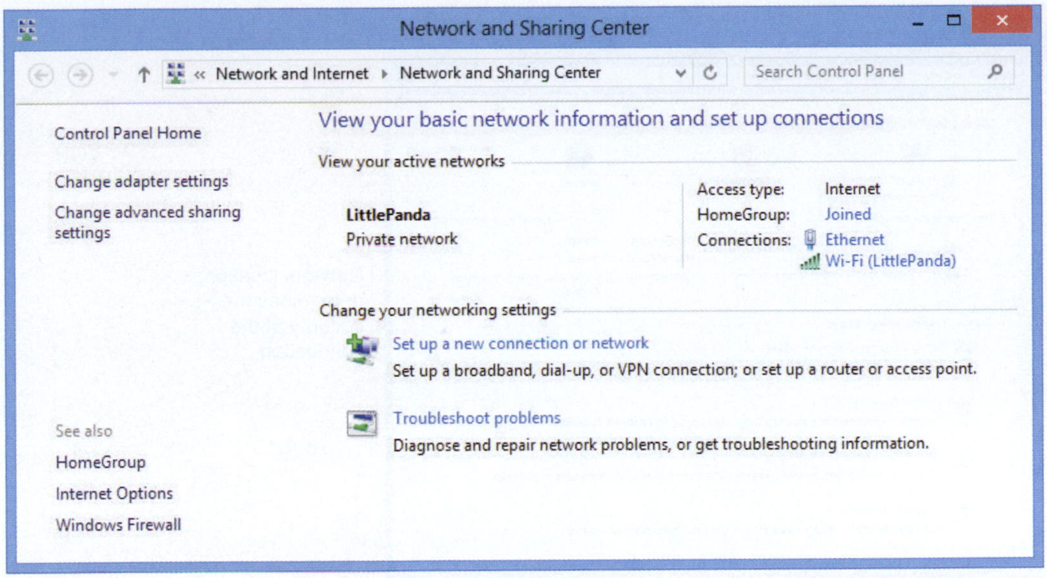

Figure 7-43 Windows 8 Network and Sharing Center reports network information and gives access to network troubleshooting tools

WINDOWS 7 MAKE A WINDOWS 7 NETWORK CONNECTION

A+
220-902
1.5, 1.6

In Windows 7, to connect to a wireless network and secure the connection, do the following:

1. Click the Network icon in the taskbar. A list of available networks appears. Click a network and click **Connect** (see Figure 7-44). If the network is secured, enter the security key the first time you connect and click **OK**.

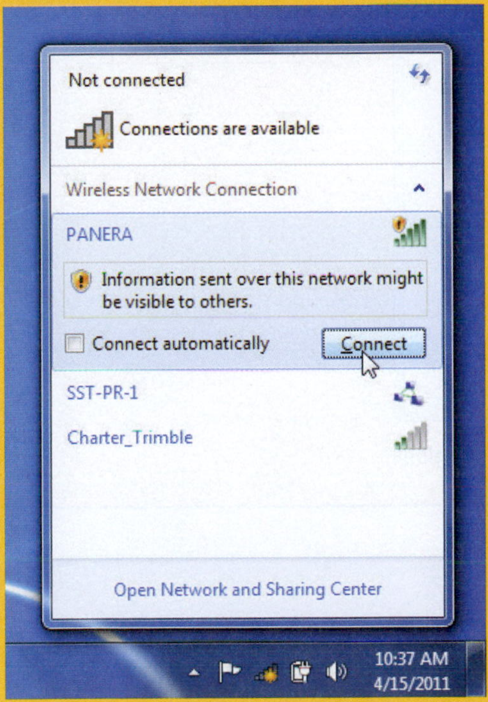

Figure 7-44 Windows orders the list of wireless networks in the area from strongest to weakest signals

2. To verify or change the security setting, open the **Network and Sharing Center** window (see Figure 7-45). For example, to change the security to Public network (the highest level of security), if the network location says Home network or Work network, click it. The Set Network Location box appears (see Figure 7-46). Click **Public network** and click **Close**.

(continues)

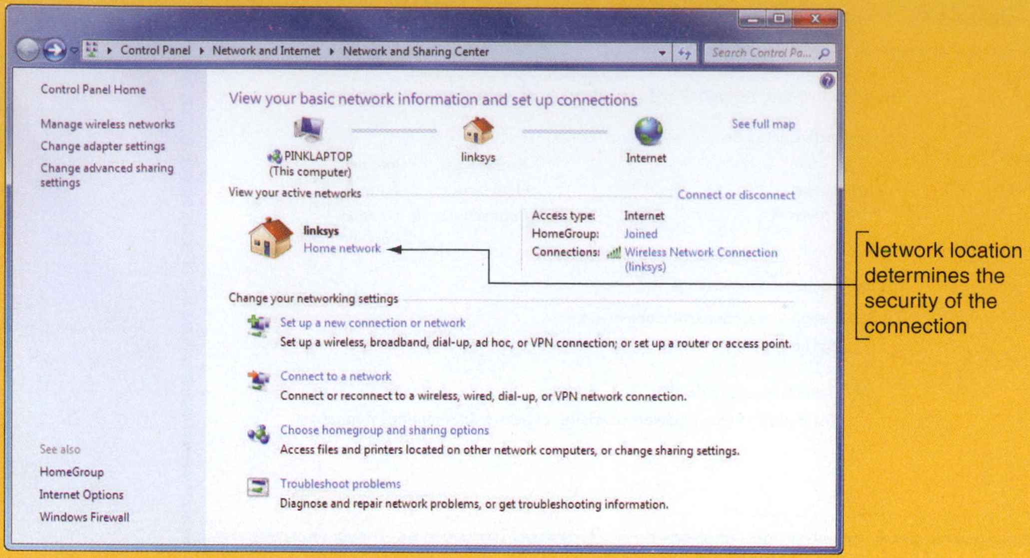

Figure 7-45 Verify that your connection is secure

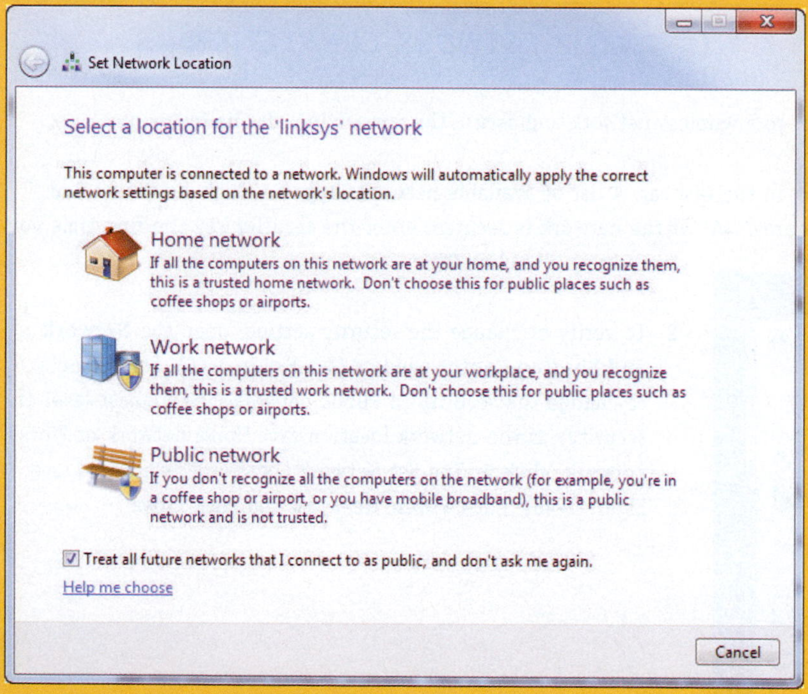

Figure 7-46 For best protection on a network, use the Public network location

DOMAIN SETUP

A+ 220-902 1.5, 1.6

If a computer is already connected to a network and you want to access resources controlled by a Windows domain on the network, you'll need the network ID and password to the domain provided by the network administrator. Then open the System window (see Figure 7-47). Under *Computer name, domain, and workgroup settings*, click **Change settings.** In the System Properties box that appears, click **Network ID** and follow directions on screen. The next time you restart the computer, you can sign in with your network ID and password and authenticate to the domain.

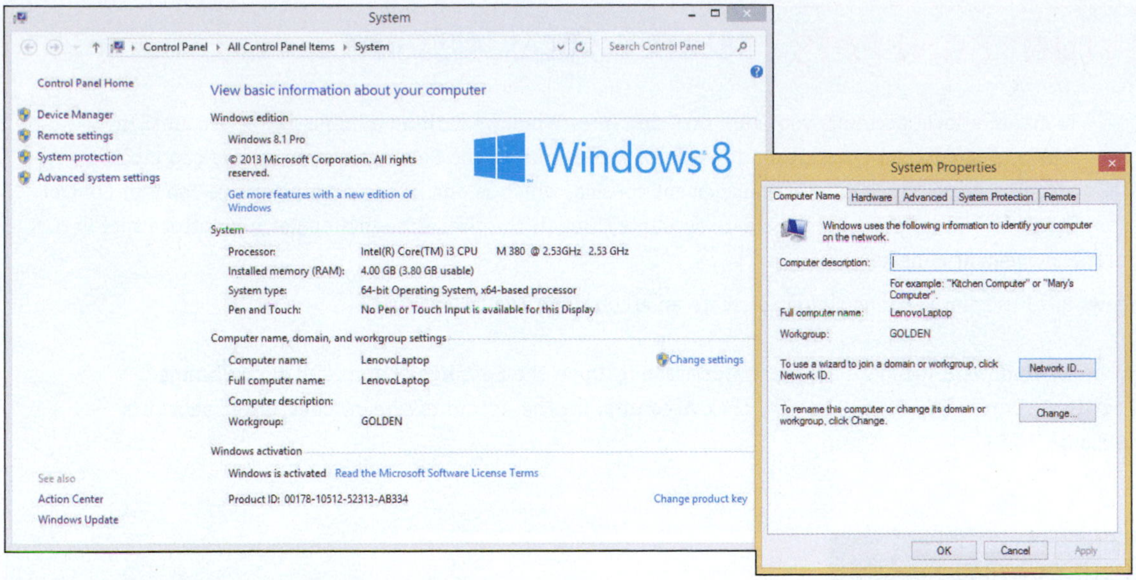

Figure 7-47 Set up Windows to join a domain

The details of securing and managing shared resources on a network and troubleshooting network connections are covered later in the text.

We now turn our attention to the various types of user accounts supported by Windows.

WINDOWS USER ACCOUNTS

A+ 220-902 1.1, 1.5, 3.3

A user must sign in to Windows with a valid user account to gain access to the OS. Windows supports various types and privileges for user accounts. Here's a brief overview:

- ***The scope of the account.*** A local account is created on the local computer and is recognized only on the local computer. As you have already learned, a network ID is created by a network administrator in a centralized database that manages an entire corporate network. When you sign in to Windows using a network ID, you are authenticated to the local computer and also to the Windows domain or network.
- ***Privileges for the account.*** In Windows, there are two types of privileges assigned to a user account: an administrator account and a standard account. An administrator account has more privileges than a standard account and is used by those responsible for maintaining and securing the system. In addition, Windows 8 offers a third type of privilege: a child account that parents can set up for their children, which has very limited privileges.
- ***A Microsoft account.*** For Windows 8, a Microsoft account is an email address, which allows you to access several types of online accounts, including Microsoft OneDrive, Facebook, LinkedIn, Twitter, Skype, *Outlook.com*, and others. A Microsoft account is an example of a single sign-on (SSO) account, which accesses multiple, independent resources, systems, or applications after signing in one time to one account. To set up a Microsoft account, go to the *live.com* website and link an email address to the Microsoft account. The account is assigned a OneDrive, which is 15 GB of free storage space in the cloud. You can pay for additional storage, and you can also use Microsoft's free cloud apps to manage data files stored on your OneDrive. A Microsoft account can be linked to a local account or a network ID and can be assigned the privileges of a standard account or an administrative account.

APPLYING | CONCEPTS CREATE A LOCAL ACCOUNT

A+
220-902
1.5

To create a local account, you must first sign in to Windows with an administrative account. In Windows 8, you can then create a new local account using the Settings charm, or you can create accounts using the Computer Management console, which is one of the Administrative Tools in Control Panel. In Windows 7, you can create accounts through the User Accounts applet in Control Panel or the Computer Management console.

In Windows 8, to use the Settings charm to create an account, do the following:

1. Sign in to Windows 8 using an administrator account. Open the **Settings** charm, and click **Change PC settings**. On the PC settings screen, click **Accounts**. On the Accounts screen, click **Other accounts** (see Figure 7-48).

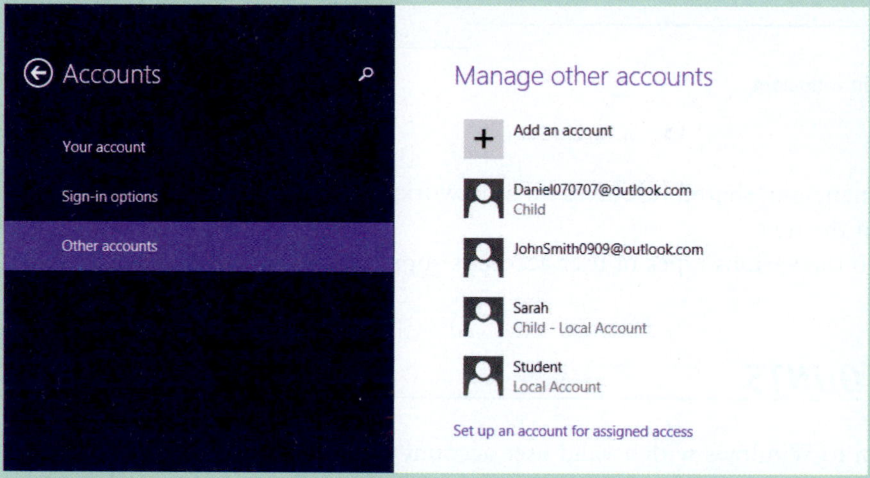

Figure 7-48 Set up a new user account

2. Click **Add an account**. The *How will this person sign in?* screen appears (see Figure 7-49) where you have four options:

   - To set up an existing Microsoft account on this computer, enter the email address for the account, and click **Next**.
   - To sign up for a new email address that will also be a Microsoft account, click **Sign up for a new email address**.
   - To set up a child account, click **Add a child's account**.
   - To set up a regular local account (not a Microsoft account), click **Sign in without a Microsoft account (not recommended)**, and click **Next**. Follow directions on screen to set up the account.

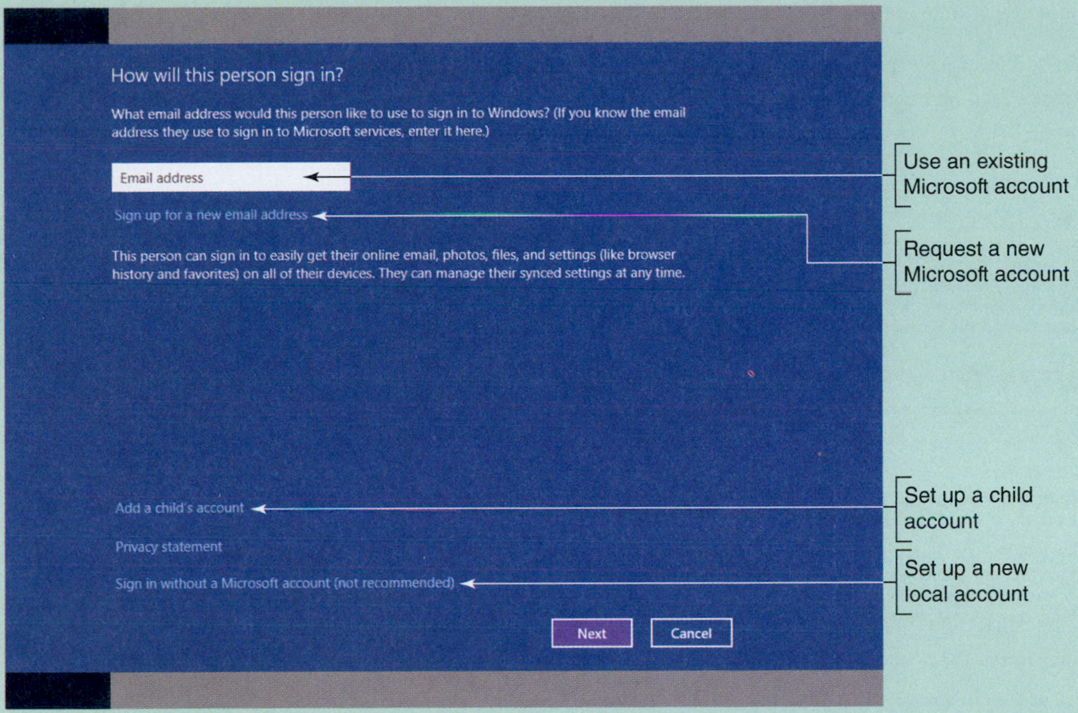

Figure 7-49 Four ways to set up a new user account

The first time a user signs in to Windows with the account, user files and folders (called the user profile) are created in the C:\Users folder.

By default, a new account is a Standard user account. Later, if you want to remove an account or change the account type (for example, to make a standard user account an administrator account), return to the Accounts screen, and click **Other accounts.**

To remove an account, click the account, and click **Remove.** To edit the account type, select the account, and click **Edit.** In the Edit account pane, you can change the account type to an Administrator, Standard User, or Child account (see Figure 7-50).

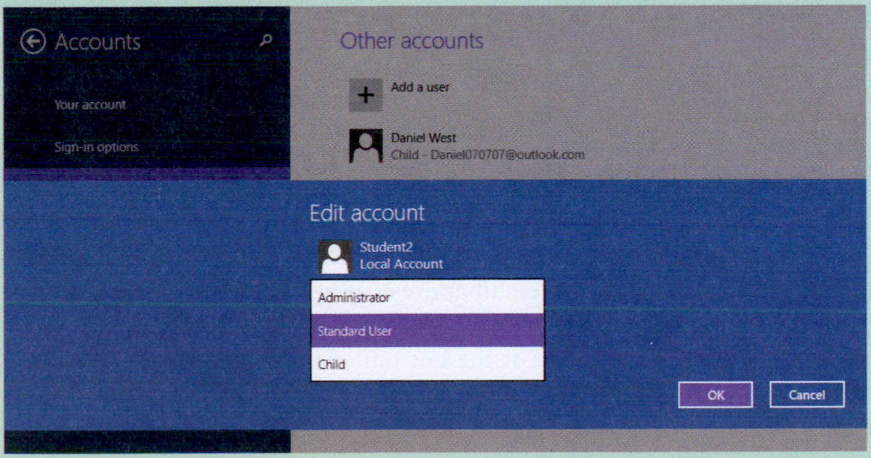

Figure 7-50 Use the Settings charm to change an account type

(continues)

Follow these steps to create a local user account in Windows 7:

1. Sign in to Windows 7 using an administrator account. Open Control Panel in Classic view and click **User Accounts**. Click **Manage another account**. Click **Create a new account**.
2. In the next window, enter the username (see Figure 7-51). Select Standard user or Administrator. Click **Create Account**.

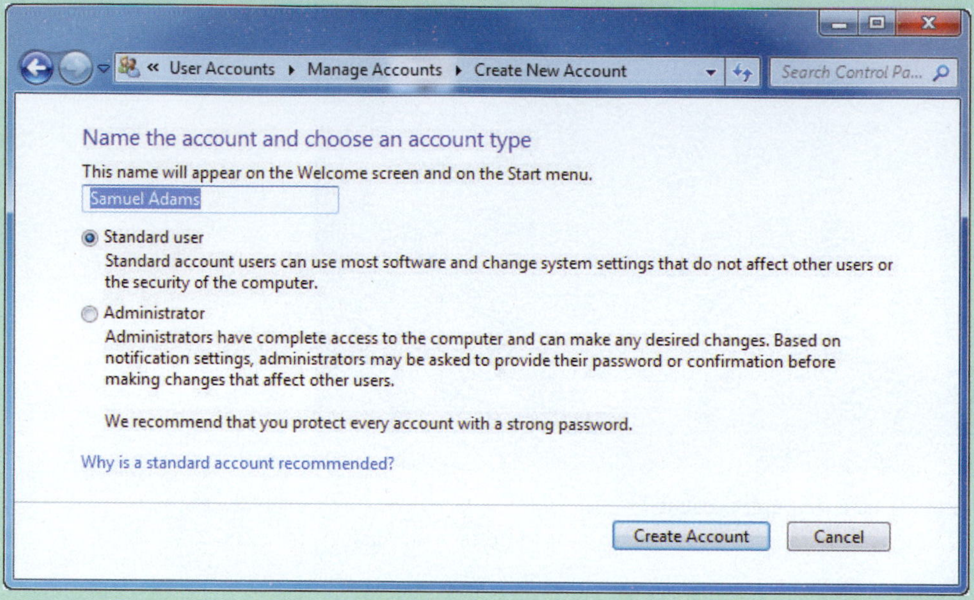

Figure 7-51 Enter the username and decide the privilege level for the new account

You can also use the User Accounts applet in Windows 7 Control Panel to create a password for an account and remove an account.

USING A MICROSOFT ACCOUNT WITH WINDOWS 8

A+ 220-902 1.1, 1.5, 3.3

There are advantages and disadvantages of signing in to Windows using a Microsoft account, including:

- ***Personal settings across several devices.*** When you use the same Microsoft account to sign in to multiple computers connected to the Internet, your personal settings follow you to each computer, including your themes, Internet Explorer favorites, and language preferences.
- ***OneDrive storage in the cloud.*** When you sign in to Windows 8 using your Microsoft account, which is called a live sign in, Windows automatically signs you in to your OneDrive, Facebook, LinkedIn, Mail, or other online accounts that are set up with this email address. When you open the OneDrive app on the Start screen, you see the folders at the root level of your OneDrive (see Figure 7-52). Right-click white space on the page to see the status bar at the bottom of the screen where you can create new folders. Click a folder to see its contents, and right-click a folder or file to see options to manage the item, such as delete, copy, cut, or rename a folder or file or add files to a folder. OneDrive is embedded in many features of Windows 8. For example, you can see it listed in the left pane of File Explorer (refer back to Figure 7-15).

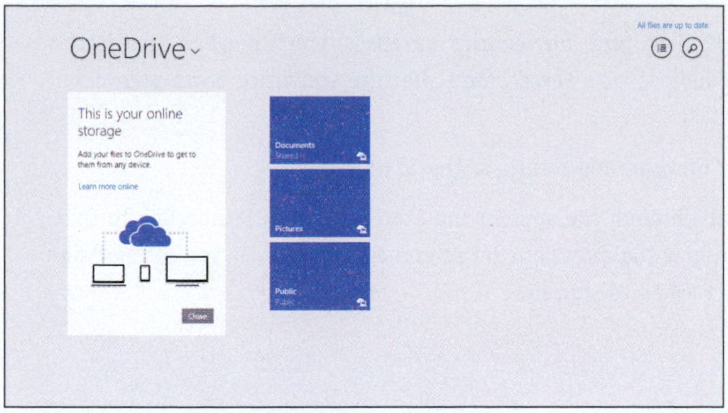

Figure 7-52 OneDrive app page shows folders stored on a OneDrive

- *Windows Store*. When you are signed in to Windows with a Microsoft account, you can access the online Windows Store where you can purchase and download apps that use the Windows 8 interface, similar to the way apps on smart phones and tablets are purchased. Apps purchased from the Windows Store can be synced with up to five computers that use your Microsoft account.
- *Private settings stored on the local computer.* A disadvantage of using your Microsoft account to sign in to Windows is that your private settings and access to your apps and online accounts are stored on the local computer. Therefore, you would only want to set up your Microsoft account on a computer where you trust those with administrative access to the computer. For many, this means using a Microsoft account only on your own personal computers that are under your complete control. When you are not signed in to Windows with your Microsoft account, you can still use a browser to access online accounts, including your OneDrive. See Figure 7-53.

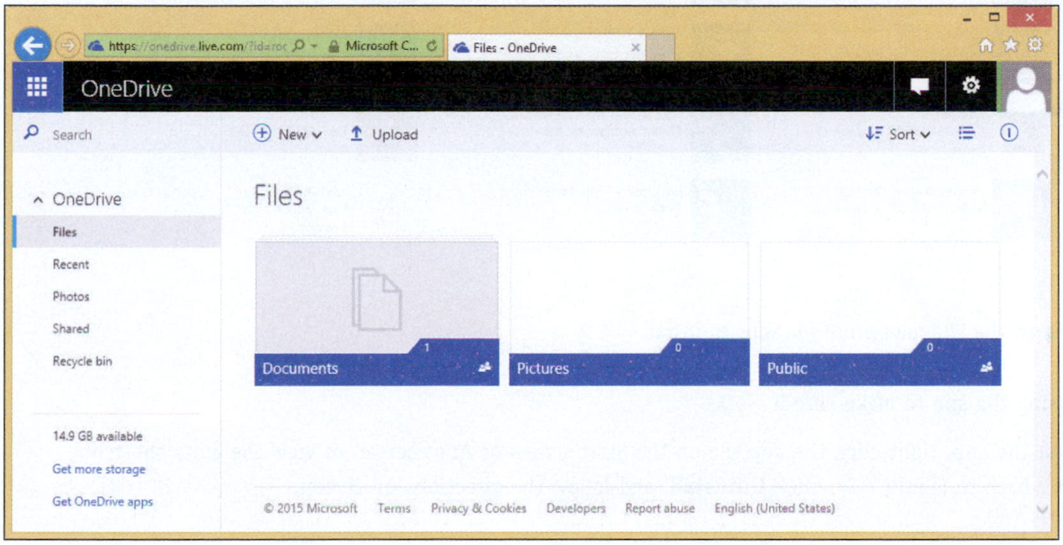

Figure 7-53 Use a browser to access your OneDrive storage area at *live.com* without signing in to Windows with your Microsoft account

Hands-On | Project 7-5 Install and Uninstall Windows 8 Apps

A+ 220-902 1.1

Windows 8 apps are installed from the Windows Store, and you must have a Microsoft account to do so. If you don't already have an account, you can get one free at *live.com*. Follow these steps to use a Microsoft account to install an app and then uninstall it:

1. If you don't already have a Microsoft account, go to the Windows desktop, open Internet Explorer, and go to **signup.live.com**. To create the account, you can use an existing email address (for example, someone@sample.edu) or request a new email address, which will be an *outlook.com*, *hotmail.com*, or *live.com* address.

(continues)

You'll need to enter your name, gender, and birth date, and, for security purposes, you'll need to associate a cell phone number and/or an alternate email address with the account. Be sure you write down your email address and password for your Microsoft account.

2. After you have created your account, close your browser, and return to the Start screen.
3. To install an app, click the **Store** tile. Next, scroll through the apps in the Store or use its Search box to find an app (see Figure 7-54). Click a free one, and follow the directions on screen to install it. If you did not sign in to Windows using a Microsoft account, you are asked to sign in.

Figure 7-54 Search the Windows Store for apps to install

4. Practice using the app to make sure it works.
5. To uninstall the app, right-click the app tile on the Start screen or Apps screen to view the app's shortcut menu (refer back to Figure 7-7). Click **Uninstall**, and follow the directions on screen.

CONNECTING A MICROSOFT ACCOUNT TO A LOCAL ACCOUNT OR NETWORK ID

You can connect an existing local account or network ID to a Microsoft account. To do so, open the **charms** bar, select the **Settings** charm, select **Change PC settings**, and click **Accounts**. Select **Your account** and then click **Connect to a Microsoft account**. Follow directions on screen.

Notes To connect a network ID on a domain to a Microsoft account, Group Policies controlling the Windows domain must allow it. After the connection, the Microsoft account is used to authenticate to the domain.

If you want to switch the user account on a Windows 8 computer from a Microsoft account back to a local account or network ID, open the **charms** bar and go to the **PC settings** screen, click **Accounts**, and then click **Disconnect** (see Figure 7-55).

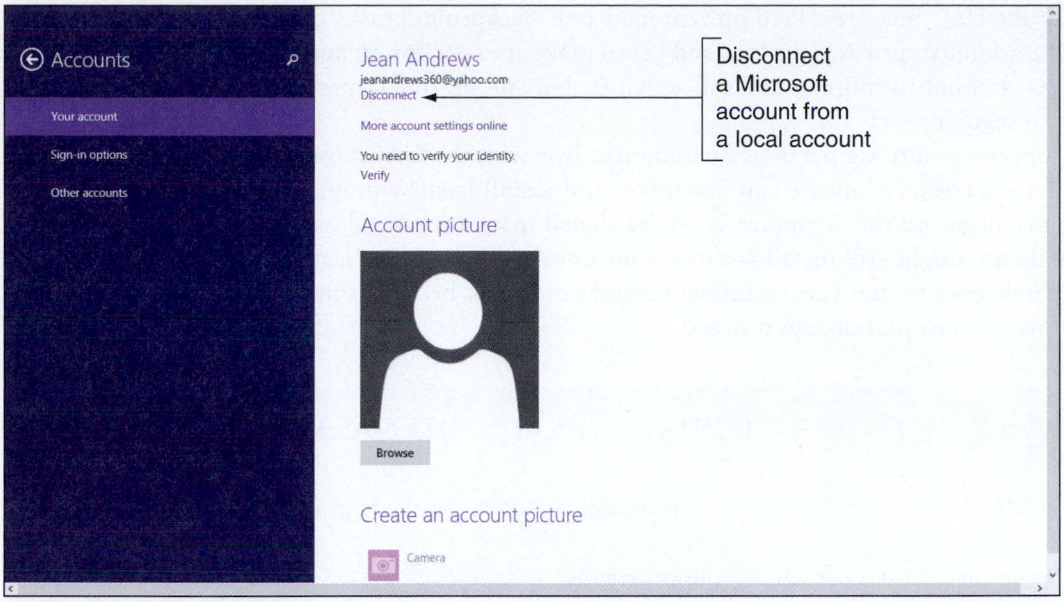

Figure 7-55 The Windows user account can be converted from a Microsoft account to a local user account

Recall that you can sign in to Windows using a local account, network ID, or Microsoft account. As you ponder the differences among these accounts, consider where the account is authenticated:

- A local account is authenticated on the local computer and gives access to the local computer. An administrator local account has more access than a standard local account.
- A network ID is authenticated by a computer on the network, which gives you access to the local computer and other resources on the network.
- A Microsoft account is authenticated on the *live.com* website, which gives access to the local computer and online resources, such as OneDrive and Facebook.com. A Microsoft account can also be associated with a network ID so that you can sign in with the Microsoft account and be authenticated to the network as well as to *live.com*.

USER ACCOUNT CONTROL DIALOG BOX

A+
220-902
1.1

At some point while working with a computer to maintain or troubleshoot it, the User Account Control (UAC) dialog box, shown in Figure 7-56, will pop up. When the UAC box appears, if you are signed in as an administrator, all you have to do is click Yes to close the box and move on, as shown in Figure 7-56a. If the user account does not have administrative privileges, you'll have the opportunity to enter the password of an administrative account to continue, as shown in Figure 7-56b.

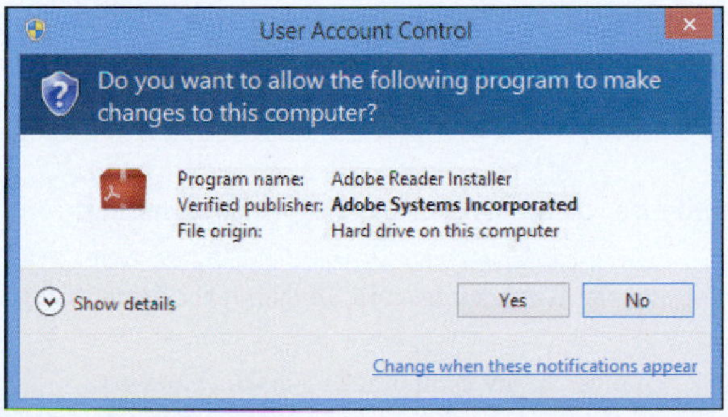

(a)

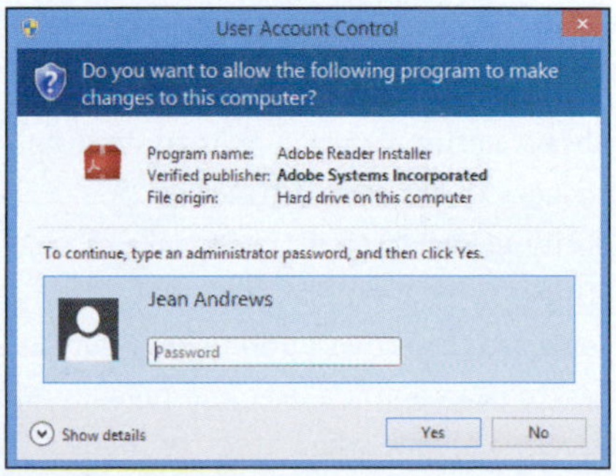

(b)

Figure 7-56 (a) The User Account Control box of an administrator does not require an administrative password; (b) the UAC box of a standard user requires an administrative password

The purposes of the UAC box are: (1) to prevent malicious background tasks from gaining administrative privileges when the administrator is signed in, and (2) to make it easier for an administrator to sign in using a less powerful user account for normal desktop activities, but still be able to perform administrative tasks while signed in as a regular user.

For example, suppose you're signed in as an administrator with the UAC box turned off and click a malicious link on a website. Malware can download and install itself without your knowledge and might get admin privileges on the computer. If you're signed in as a standard user and the UAC box is turned off, the malware might still install without your knowledge but with lesser privileges. The UAC box stands as a gatekeeper to malware installing behind your back because someone has to click the UAC box before the installation can proceed.

APPLYING CONCEPTS CONTROL THE UAC DIALOG BOX

A+ 220-902 1.1

Using Windows 8/7, you can control how the UAC box works. Do the following:

1. Open the Control Panel and click **User Accounts**.
2. In the User Accounts window, click **Change User Account Control settings**. The User Account Control Settings window appears (see Figure 7-57).

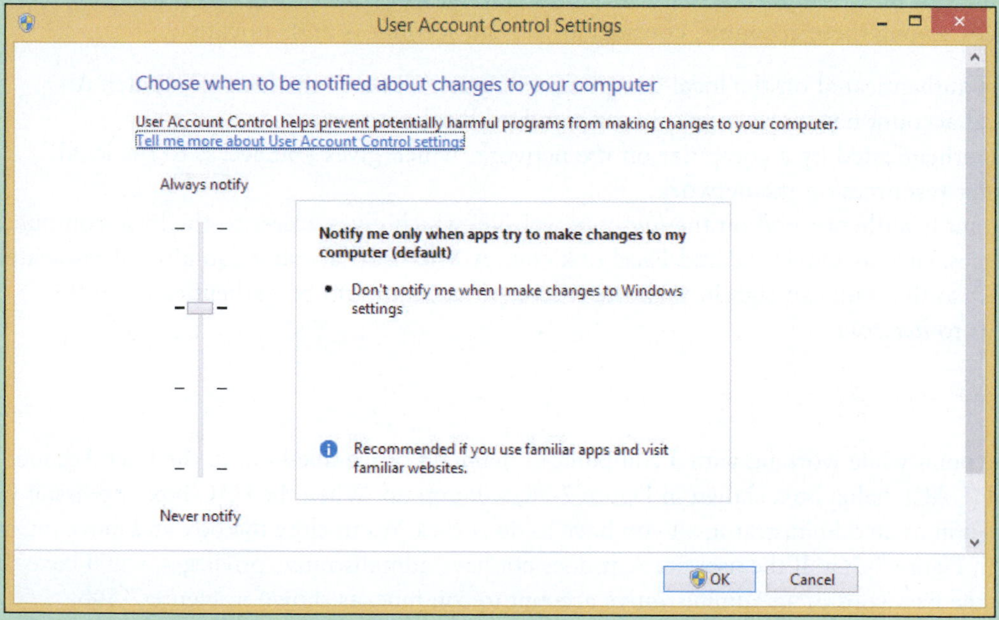

Figure 7-57 Windows provides options to control the UAC box

3. Change when the UAC box appears. Here is a description of the four options shown in Figure 7-57:
   - Always notify me when apps try to install software or make other changes to the computer and when I make changes to Windows settings.
   - Notify me when apps try to make changes, but don't notify me when I make changes to Windows settings. (This is the default setting.)
   - Same as the second option above but, in addition, do not dim the Windows desktop. Dimming the Windows desktop can alarm a user and take up resources.
   - Never notify me when apps try to install software or make changes to my computer or I make changes to Windows settings.
4. Click **OK** and respond to the UAC box.

★ A+ Exam Tip The A+ 220-902 exam expects you to know how to change the settings that control when the UAC box appears.

>> CHAPTER SUMMARY

Windows Interfaces

- An operating system manages hardware; runs applications; provides an interface for users; and stores, retrieves, and manipulates files.
- Windows 8 offers two GUIs: the modern interface and the Windows 8 desktop. The Windows 7/Vista desktop offers the Aero user interface.
- Ways to launch a program from the Windows 8 desktop include using the Start screen, the Quick Launch menu, an icon pinned to the taskbar, File Explorer, a shortcut on the desktop, and the Run option on the Quick Launch menu.
- Ways to launch a program from the Windows 7 desktop include using the Start menu, the Search box, an icon pinned to the taskbar, Windows Explorer, or a shortcut on the desktop.

Windows Tools for Users and Technicians

- Windows 8 File Explorer and Windows 7 Windows Explorer are used to manage files and folders on storage devices. Folders are organized in a top-down hierarchical structure of subfolders.
- The file extension indicates how the file contents are organized and formatted and what program uses the file.
- Control Panel gives access to a group of utility programs used to manage the system. Technicians generally prefer the Classic view for Control Panel.
- The Folder Options applet in Control Panel changes the way files and folders are displayed in Explorer.
- The Power Options applet in Control Panel manages power settings on a computer.
- The System window gives a quick overview of the system, including which edition and version of Windows is installed and the amount of installed memory.
- The System Information window gives much information about the computer, including hardware, device drivers, the OS, and applications.
- The Action Center is a centralized location used to solve problems with security and computer maintenance.

Windows Network Connections

- Windows 8/7 supports workgroups, homegroups, and domains to manage resources on a private network. Vista supports workgroups and domains.
- A network ID and password are used to authenticate to a Windows domain, which gives access to resources on the network.
- Windows 8 supports public and private settings for network security, and Windows 7 supports public, home, and work settings for network security.
- To connect to a wireless network in Windows 8, use the Settings charm or the Network icon in the taskbar on the desktop. Windows 7 uses the Network icon in the taskbar to connect to a wireless network.

7

- Use the Network and Sharing Center to view information about network connections and solve network problems.
- Use the System window to set up a computer to connect to a Windows domain.

Windows User Accounts

- Windows supports local accounts that are recognized only on the local computer and network IDs that are recognized on a Windows domain.
- Two main types of privileges can be assigned to a Windows account: An administrator account has more privileges than a standard account and is required when maintaining and securing a system.
- Windows 8 offers a Microsoft account that is authenticated online at the *live.com* website. The account is assigned a OneDrive, which is storage in the cloud.
- Use the Settings charm to manage Windows 8 user accounts. In Windows 7, use the User Accounts applet in Control Panel. For Windows 8/7, the Computer Management console in the Administrative Tools group in Control Panel can be used for advanced management of user accounts.
- You can associate a Microsoft account with a local account or network ID on a domain.
- The User Account Control box helps prevent malware from installing itself on a system. The UAC box settings are controlled in the User Accounts applet in Control Panel.

>> KEY TERMS

For explanations of key terms, see the Glossary for this text.

32-bit operating system
64-bit operating system
Action Center
Active Directory
Administrative Tools
administrator account
Aero user interface
BitLocker Drive Encryption
Category view
charm
charms bar
child directory
Classic view
client/server
compressed (zipped) folder
console
Control Panel
Date and Time applet
device driver
domain
domain account
File Explorer
file extension
file name
folder
Folder Options applet
gadget
global account
graphical user interface (GUI)
hibernation
homegroup
library
live sign in
live tiles
local account
logical topology
Metro User Interface (Metro UI)
Microsoft account
modern interface
navigation pane
Network and Sharing Center
network ID
Notepad
notification area
OneDrive
operating system (OS)
patch
path
peer-to-peer (P2P)
physical topology
pinning
Power Options applet
Quick Launch menu
Recycle Bin
root directory
Security Center
service
service pack
sidebar
side-by-side apps
single sign-on (SSO)
sleep mode
sleep timer
Sound applet
standard account
Start screen
subdirectory
suspend mode
System Information
system tray
System window
systray
taskbar
User Account Control (UAC) dialog box
volume
Windows 8.1
Windows Defender
Windows Explorer
Windows Firewall
Windows Store
workgroup

>> REVIEWING THE BASICS

1. List four major functions of an OS.
2. Which app do you use on the Windows 8 Start screen to install new apps?
3. What might happen to the Windows system if too many services are running as indicated by multiple icons in the notification area of the taskbar?
4. What part of a file name does Windows use to know which application to open to manage the file?
5. What is the program file name and extension of File Explorer?
6. When you use File Explorer or Windows Explorer to delete a file from the hard drive, where does Windows put the file?
7. Which keys do you press to open the Windows 8 Quick Launch menu?
8. What file extension is used to name a compressed folder?
9. What is the program name for the System Information utility?
10. By default, when does Windows hide file extensions in File Explorer?
11. Which Windows 7 window can be used to get a report of the history of problems on a computer?
12. What are the two basic Windows 8 settings for network security?
13. List three types of user accounts available in Windows 8.
14. Which Windows 8 charm can you use to set up a new user account?
15. When does a user need to enter a password into the UAC box in order to continue?

>> THINKING CRITICALLY

1. Suppose you have purchased and installed apps from the Windows Store on your Windows 8 home computer using your Microsoft account. At work, you connect your Microsoft account to your network ID to sign in to your work computer. Will the apps installed on your home computer now be installed on your work computer? Select the best answer.
   a. No, because apps from the Windows Store are only installed on the device where they were originally purchased.
   b. Yes, because apps purchased with your Microsoft account are installed on up to five computers you sign in to using this account.
   c. No, because syncing apps to all computers that use your Microsoft account is disabled by default.
   d. Yes, because when you purchase an app from the Windows Store, you can designate that app be synced with all computers that use your Microsoft account.
   e. No, because apps can never be synced on work computers that belong to a Windows domain.
2. A user clicks the OneDrive app on the Windows 8 Start screen and Windows requests her Microsoft account and password. Which of the following statements are true?
   a. Another user has used the OneDrive app on this computer.
   b. This is the first time the user has opened the OneDrive app.

c. The user doesn't have a Microsoft account.

d. The user did not sign in to Windows using a Microsoft account.

3. What two Windows tools can you use to know how much RAM is installed on your system?

4. Mary wants her 32-bit installation of Windows 7 Professional to run faster. She has 4 GB of memory installed on the motherboard. She decides more memory will help. She installs an additional 2 GB of memory for a total of 6 GB, but does not see any performance improvement. What is the problem and what should you tell Mary?

   a. She should use Control Panel to install the memory in Windows 7. After it is installed, performance should improve. Tell Mary how to open the Control Panel.

   b. A 32-bit OS cannot use more than 4 GB of memory. Tell Mary she has wasted her money.

   c. A 32-bit OS cannot use more than 4 GB of memory. Tell Mary to upgrade her system to the 64-bit version of Windows 7 Professional.

   d. A 32-bit OS cannot use more than 4 GB of memory. Explain to Mary the problem and discuss with her the possible solutions.

5. Jack needs to email two documents to a friend but the files are so large his email server bounced them back as undeliverable. What is your advice?

   a. Tell Jack to open the documents and break each of them into two documents and then email the four documents separately.

   b. Tell Jack to put the two documents in a compressed folder and email the folder.

   c. Tell Jack to put each document in a different compressed folder and email each folder separately.

   d. Tell Jack to put the documents on a USB drive and snail mail the drive to his friend.

>> REAL PROBLEMS, REAL SOLUTIONS

REAL PROBLEM 7-1 Using Windows Help and Support

The best IT support technicians are the ones continually teaching themselves new skills. You can teach yourself to use and support Windows by using the web and the Windows Help and Support utility. To start the utility in Windows 8, type Help and Support on the Start screen. In Windows 7, click Start and click Help and Support. If you are connected to the Internet, clicking links can take you to the Microsoft website where you can find information and watch videos about Windows.

Do the following to learn to research a topic so you can become an independent learner about Windows:

1. The Windows 8/7 Snipping Tool can help you take screen shots of the Windows desktop. These screen shots are useful when documenting computer problems and solutions. Use Windows Help and Support to find out how to use the Snipping Tool. Use it to take a screen shot of your Windows desktop. Save the screen shot into a file on a USB flash drive or on the hard drive. Print the file contents.

2. Windows 7 Home Premium, Professional, Enterprise, and Ultimate editions all support the Aero interface. If you are using one of these editions, find out how to turn the Aero interface off and on. Describe the difference in the appearance of Windows when using Aero and not using it.

3. Access the *support.microsoft.com* website for Windows 8/7 support. Save or print one article from the Knowledge Base that addresses a problem when installing Windows 8/7.

4. Search the web for the purpose of the Pagefile.sys file. What website did you use to find your answer? Why is the Microsoft.com website considered the best source for information about the Pagefile.sys file?

REAL PROBLEM 7-2 Documenting How to Use Windows 8

This real problem requires a microphone, and a webcam would also be useful. Make a screen recording with voice-over to teach end users how to use Windows 8. Do the following:

1. Screencast-O-Matic offers free software to make a screen recording with voice and video. Go to **screencast-o-matic.com** and launch the online video recording software. You might be required to download and install the software.
2. Select a Windows 8 feature to explain. For example, you can explain how to open and close an app, install or uninstall an app, create a new user account, empty the Recycle Bin, or use the charms bar or search feature. You or your instructor might have other ideas.
3. Use the Screencast-O-Matic software to make a screen recording to show how to use the Windows 8 feature you selected. The recording should be no longer than three minutes. Explain the steps as you go. The software records your screen movements, your voice (if a microphone is detected), and video (if a webcam is detected).
4. View the video. If you see a problem, record it again. When you're satisfied with your video, save it as an MP4 file.

REAL PROBLEM 7-3 Launching the Windows 8 Desktop at Startup

Some users prefer to go directly to the Windows 8 desktop rather than to the Start screen at Windows startup. To make this change, you'll need Windows 8.1 installed. Go to the Windows desktop, right-click the taskbar, and click Properties. In the Taskbar and Navigation properties box, click the Navigation tab. Then check When I sign in or close all apps on a screen, go to the desktop instead of Start. See Figure 7-58. Apply your changes. When you next sign in to Windows, you are taken directly to the desktop.

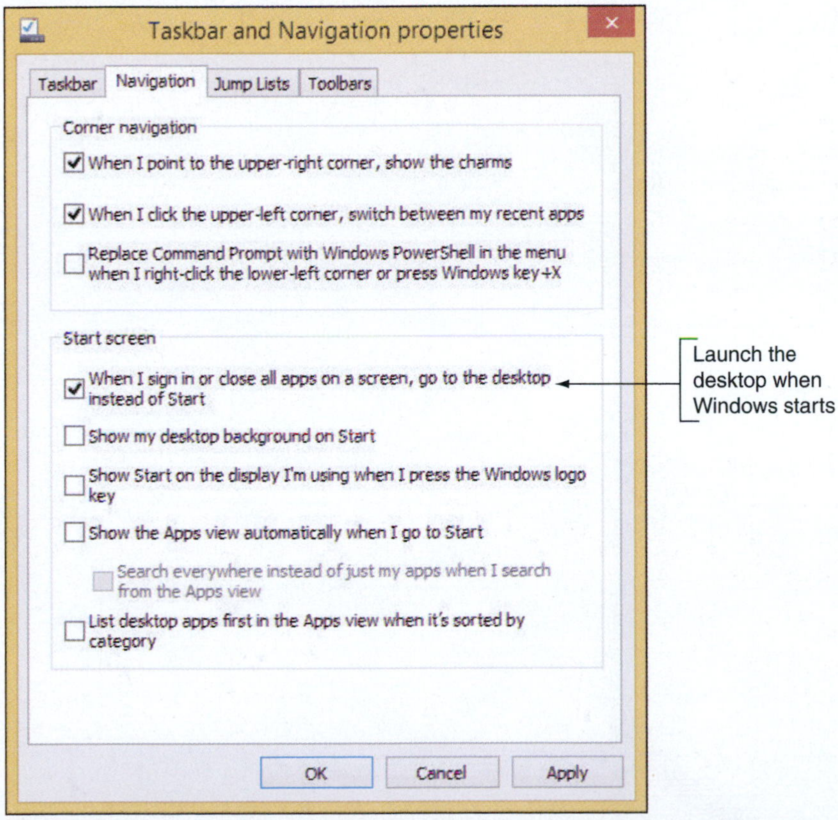

Figure 7-58 Control what happens when you navigate Windows 8

CHAPTER 8

Installing Windows

After completing this chapter, you will be able to:

- Plan a Windows installation
- Install Windows 8.1 and Windows 7
- Configure Windows settings after the installation
- Discuss special concerns when installing Windows in a large enterprise

Windows 8, 7, and Vista all share the same basic Windows architecture, and all have similar characteristics. Windows 8 includes a free upgrade to Windows 8.1 via the Windows Store. Windows 8.1 and Windows 7 are available for purchase directly from Microsoft, but you can no longer purchase Windows 8.0 or Vista. (However, Windows 8.0 and Vista can be purchased from other vendors.) Mainstream support of Windows Vista by Microsoft ended in 2012, and extended support is slated to end in 2017. Because many individual users and corporations still rely on Vista, you still need to know how to support it.

By the time this text is published, Windows 10 should be available. How to install and support Windows 10 is not covered in this text.

This chapter discusses how to plan a Windows installation and the steps to perform a Windows 8.1 or Windows 7 installation in various scenarios, including what to do after the OS is installed. You also learn about what to expect when installing Windows on computers in a large enterprise.

Notes In the text, we use Windows 8 to refer to Windows 8.0 and Windows 8.1.

HOW TO PLAN A WINDOWS INSTALLATION

A+ 220-902 1.1, 1.2, 1.6

As an IT support technician, you can expect to be called on to install Windows in a variety of situations. You might need to install Windows on a new hard drive, after an existing Windows installation has become corrupted, or to upgrade from one OS to another. Many decisions need to be made before the installation, and most of these decisions apply to any Windows operating system.

CHOOSE THE EDITION, LICENSE, AND VERSION OF WINDOWS

A+ 220-902 1.1, 1.2

When buying a Windows operating system, know that the price is affected by the Windows edition and type of license you purchase. You also need to decide between 32-bit and 64-bit architecture. In this part of the chapter, you learn about your options when purchasing Windows and how to make sure your computer qualifies for the version and edition you've selected.

EDITIONS OF WINDOWS

Windows 8 provides a choice of these editions designed to satisfy a variety of consumer needs:

- **Windows 8.1** is the edition of choice for a laptop or desktop computer used in a home or small office. This edition supports homegroups, but it doesn't support joining a domain or BitLocker Encryption.
- **Windows 8.1 Professional (Windows 8.1 Pro)** includes additional features at a higher price, while **Windows 8.1 Pro for Students** is available for a lower price to students, faculty, and staff at eligible institutions. **Windows Pro Pack** can be installed on a Windows 8.1 machine to add the functionality of Windows 8.1 Pro to the more basic edition. Windows 8.1 Pro supports homegroups, joining a domain, BitLocker, Client Hyper-V, Remote Desktop, and Group Policy. (You'll learn about these tools later in the text.)
- **Windows 8.1 Enterprise** allows for volume licensing in a large, corporate environment.
- **Windows RT**, a lighter edition, is available for tablets, netbooks, and other mobile devices.

Windows 7 editions include Windows 7 Starter, Windows 7 Home Basic, Windows 7 Home Premium, Windows 7 Professional, Windows 7 Enterprise, and Windows 7 Ultimate. Each edition comes at a different price with different features and capabilities.

Editions of **Windows Vista** are Windows Vista Starter, Windows Vista Home Basic, Windows Vista Home Premium, Windows Vista Business, Windows Vista Enterprise, and Windows Vista Ultimate.

Notes An antitrust ruling (a ruling to break up monopolies) in Europe requires that Microsoft must offer editions of Windows that do not include multimedia utilities. Windows 8.1 and 7, therefore, come in N, K, and KN editions that do not include Windows Media Player and other media technologies or, in Windows 8.1, some media apps such as Sound Recorder and Skype. If you have an N or KN edition of Windows, you can, however, legally download the utilities from the Microsoft website.

OEM, FULL RETAIL, OR UPGRADE RETAIL LICENSE

When buying Windows, you can purchase a retail license or an **Original Equipment Manufacturer (OEM) license**. The OEM license costs less but can be installed only on a new computer. The boxed retail package contains the 32-bit DVD and 64-bit DVD (see Figure 8-1). You can also purchase and download Windows 8.1 from the Microsoft online store at *microsoftstore.com*. The retail license costs less if you purchase a license to upgrade from Windows 7 to Windows 8.1 using Microsoft's Windows 8.1 Upgrade Assistant, as explained below. You are required to purchase the Windows 8.1 full license for a new computer or any computer that has an OS other than Windows 8 or Windows 7 installed.

Figure 8-1 A Windows 8.1 package comes with two DVDs and one product key

Notes The Windows 8.1 setup DVD is the same whether you're upgrading from Windows 7 or performing a clean installation. However, you cannot use an OEM disk for an upgrade installation.

32-BIT OR 64-BIT ARCHITECTURE

Recall that an operating system can process 32 bits or 64 bits at a time. A 64-bit installation of Windows generally performs better than a 32-bit installation if you have enough RAM. Table 8-1 shows how much RAM popular editions of Windows can support. Another advantage of 64-bit installations of Windows is they can support 64-bit applications, which run faster than 32-bit applications. Even though you can install 32-bit applications in a 64-bit OS, for best performance, always choose 64-bit applications. Keep in mind that 64-bit installations of Windows require 64-bit device drivers.

8

Notes All processors (CPUs) used in personal computers today are hybrid processors and can handle a 32-bit or 64-bit OS. However, the Intel Itanium and Xeon processors used in high-end workstations and servers are true 64-bit processors and require a 64-bit OS.

Operating System	32-Bit Architecture	64-Bit Architecture
Windows 8.1	4 GB	128 GB
Windows 8.1 Pro Windows 8.1 Enterprise	4 GB	512 GB
Windows 7 Home Premium	4 GB	16 GB
Windows 7 Professional Windows 7 Enterprise Windows 7 Ultimate	4 GB	192 GB

Table 8-1 Maximum memory supported by Windows 8.1 and 7 editions and versions

Notes How much memory or RAM you can install in a computer depends not only on the OS installed, but also on how much memory the motherboard can hold. To know how much RAM a motherboard can support, see the motherboard documentation.

VERIFY YOUR SYSTEM QUALIFIES FOR WINDOWS

A+
220-902
1.1, 1.2

The minimum hardware requirements for Windows 8/7/Vista are listed in Table 8-2. (These minimum requirements are also the Microsoft recommended requirements.) In addition to the requirements listed, Microsoft added to Windows 8 requirements three technologies used by the processor (NX, PAE, and SSE2). All processors built in the last 10 years use these technologies, so the move was intended to not allow Windows 8 to be installed on a system that was older than 10 years. Know, however, that Microsoft occasionally changes the minimum and recommended requirements for an OS.

Hardware	For 32-Bit Windows	For 64-Bit Windows
Processor	1 GHz or faster; for Windows 8, support for NX, PAE, and SSE2	
Memory (RAM)	1 GB	2 GB
Free hard drive space	16 GB	20 GB
Video device and driver	DirectX 9 device with WDDM 1.0 or higher driver	

Table 8-2 Minimum and recommended hardware requirements for Windows 8/7/Vista

Notes The three processor technologies are NX (Never Execute or No Execute), which prevents malware from hiding in the data storage area of another program; PAE (Physical Address Extension), which was originally intended to allow 32-bit processors to use more than 4 GB of RAM but is no longer used for that purpose because it gave device drivers a big headache; and SSE2 (Streaming SIMD Extensions 2), which allows a processor to execute a single instruction multiple times.

WINDOWS 8 UPGRADE ASSISTANT

The simplest way to find out if a system can be upgraded to Windows 8.1 is to download, install, and run the Windows 8.1 Upgrade Assistant (called the Upgrade Advisor in Windows 7). You can find the software and instructions on how to use it at *windows.microsoft.com/en-US/windows-8/upgrade-from-windows-7-tutorial*. Microsoft also offers the Windows Compatibility Center at *microsoft.com/windows/compatibility* (see Figure 8-2). You can search under both software and hardware to find out if they are compatible with Windows 8.1. The site sometimes offers links to patches or fixes for a program or device so that it will work with Windows 8.1. Before you upgrade to Windows 8.1, research each item that's not compatible, install an update if available, or uninstall the software or device. You can deal with most problems after Windows 8.1 is installed unless it's a critical device such as your network adapter. (You don't want to install Windows 8.1 only to find out later you can't access the network or Internet.)

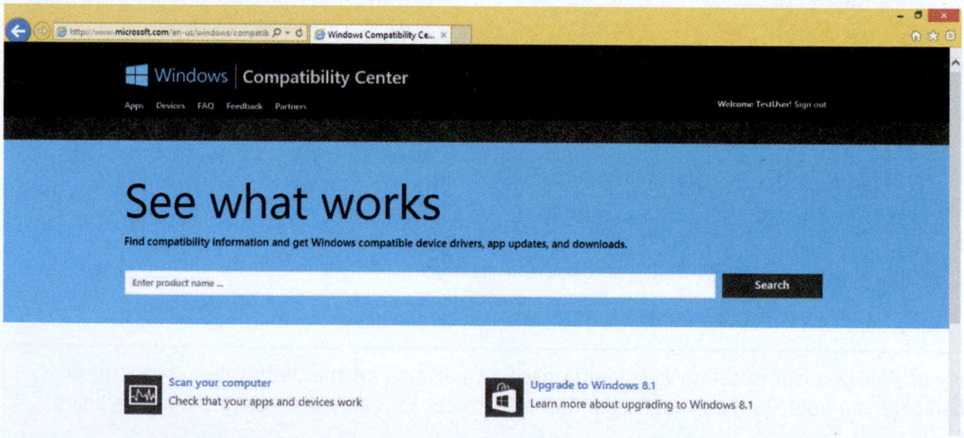

Figure 8-2 Use the Windows 8.1 Compatibility Center to find out if your hardware and software qualify for Windows 8.1

Notes Websites change often. If you can't find the Upgrade Assistant at the link given, try this search string using *google.com*: **windows 8.1 upgrade assistant site: microsoft.com.**

To find out if a Vista system qualifies for an upgrade to Windows 7, download and run the Windows 7 Upgrade Advisor. To find it, type this search string at *google.com*: **windows 7 upgrade advisor site:microsoft.com** and click the top link in the search results.

MBR OR GPT PARTITIONING SYSTEM

You need to be aware of the partitioning method you will use on the hard drive. A hard drive is divided into one or more partitions. Windows can use one of two methods to partition a hard drive: The Master Boot Record (MBR) method is older, allows for four partitions, and is limited to 2-TB drives. The GUID Partition Table (GPT) method is newer, allows for any size hard drive, and, for Windows, can have up to 128 partitions on the drive. GPT is required for drives larger than 2 TB.

When an MBR or GPT partition is formatted with a file system and assigned a drive letter (such as drive C:), it is called a volume. A file system is the overall structure an OS uses to name, store, and organize files on a volume, and Windows is always installed on a volume that uses the NTFS file system. For most installations, you install Windows on the only hard drive in the computer and allocate all the space on the drive to one partition that Windows setup calls drive C:. Windows is installed in the C:\Windows folder.

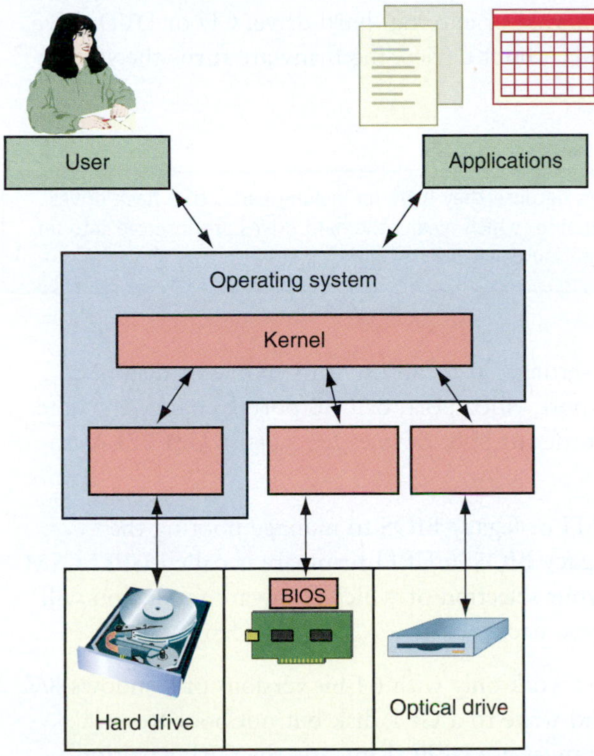

Figure 8-3 Windows relates to hardware by way of device drivers or system UEFI/BIOS

8

UEFI OR LEGACY BIOS FIRMWARE

To understand if your system qualifies for Windows 8/7, it helps to understand how Windows relates to hardware by using device drivers and system UEFI/BIOS, as shown in Figure 8-3. (In the figure, the kernel is that part of Windows responsible for relating to hardware.)

When a computer is first turned on, it uses some devices such as the keyboard, monitor, and hard drive before the OS starts up. The motherboard UEFI/BIOS is contained on a chip on the motherboard (see Figure 8-4) and manages these essential devices. This chip is called a firmware chip because it holds programs.

Figure 8-4 A chip on a motherboard contains UEFI or BIOS used to start the computer, hold motherboard settings, and run essential devices. The chip retains power from a nearby coin battery when the computer is turned off.

Older motherboards use firmware called **BIOS (basic input/output system)**. A much-improved replacement for BIOS is **UEFI (Unified Extensible Firmware Interface)**, which stores its setup information and some drivers on the motherboard and also on the hard drive. Most motherboards today support a combination of the two types of firmware, commonly called UEFI/BIOS. The motherboard UEFI/BIOS provides three main functions:

- The **system UEFI/BIOS** contains instructions for running essential hardware devices before an operating system is started. After the OS is started, it might continue to use system UEFI/BIOS or use device drivers to communicate with these devices.
- The **startup UEFI/BIOS** starts the computer and finds a boot device that contains an operating system. Boot devices that a system might support include an internal or external hard drive, CD or DVD drive, bootable USB flash drive, and the network. After it finds a boot device, the firmware turns the startup process over to the OS.

> **Notes** **Solid-state drives** are faster than magnetic hard drives because they have no moving parts. USB flash drives are also solid-state devices. Some hard drives might be **hot-swappable**, which means the hard drives are inserted into an easily accessible hot-swap bay and can be exchanged without powering down the system.

- The **setup UEFI/BIOS** is used to change motherboard settings. You can use it to enable or disable a device on the motherboard (for example, the network port, video port, or USB ports), change the date and time that is later passed to the OS, and select the order of boot devices for startup UEFI/BIOS to search when looking for an operating system to load.

Most computers today give you the option of using UEFI or legacy BIOS to manage booting the computer and turning it over to the operating system. Legacy BIOS in UEFI firmware is called **UEFI CSM (Compatibility Support Module) mode**. You must make your selection of which firmware mode you will use *before* you install Windows. Here are points to help you decide:

- UEFI and the GPT partitioning system for the hard drive work only with 64-bit versions of Windows 8/7. However, a 32-bit version of Windows 8/7 can read and write to a GPT disk but not boot from it.
- If the computer has a hard drive larger than 2 TB, you must use UEFI firmware, the GPT partition system, and a 64-bit version of Windows.
- UEFI has a security system called **Secure Boot**, which helps to prevent malware from hijacking a system during or before the operating system load. UEFI and Windows work together to ensure that no unsecured device driver, application, or OS component is loaded. If you want to use Secure Boot, you must use UEFI, GPT, and a 64-bit edition of Windows.
- To install Windows on an MBR hard drive, you must run UEFI in CSM mode. To install Windows on a GPT drive, you must use UEFI and disable CSM mode.

APPLYING | CONCEPTS SELECT THE FIRMWARE MODE

A+ 220-902 1.2

So how do you select your firmware mode before you start the Windows installation? Follow these steps:

1. To access UEFI/BIOS setup, press a key, such as **Del** or **F2**, early in the boot process before Windows starts to load. When the UEFI/BIOS setup screen appears, look for a screen to manage the boot. For example, the Boot screen for one motherboard's firmware is shown in Figure 8-5.

Source: American Megatrends, Inc.

Figure 8-5 The Boot screen for one UEFI/BIOS setup

2. To use legacy BIOS, which requires the MBR partitioning system:
   a. Click **CSM (Compatibility Support Module)** and make sure that CSM is enabled (see Figure 8-6).

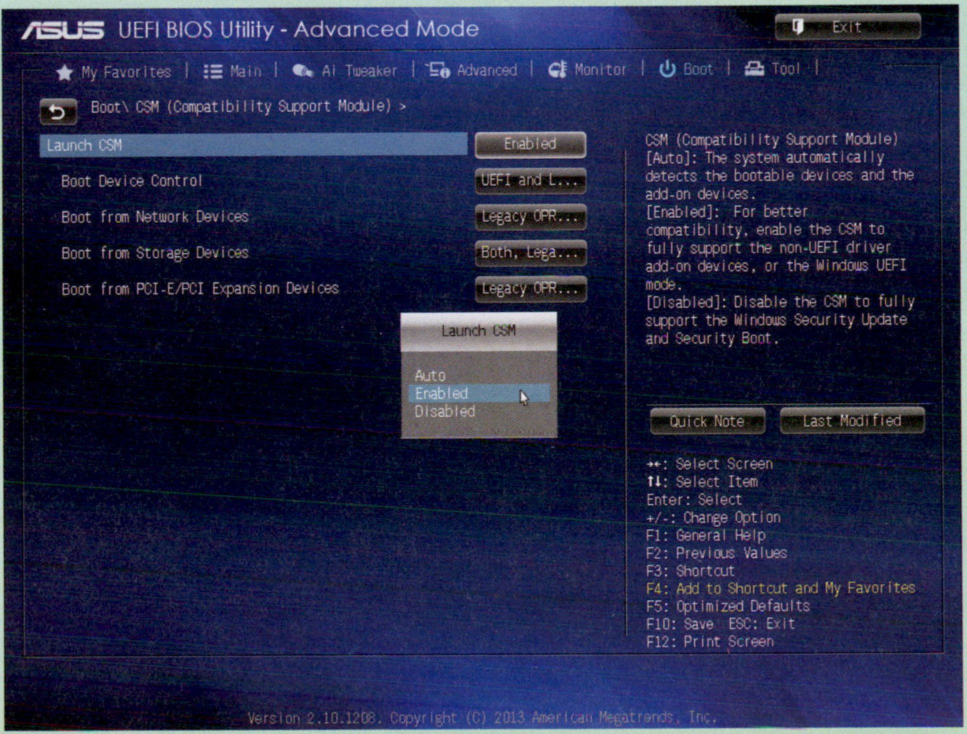

Source: American Megatrends, Inc.

Figure 8-6 Enable or disable CSM mode

8

(continues)

b. On the Boot screen (Figure 8-5), click **Secure Boot**. In the Secure Boot menu, select **Other OS** for the OS Type (see Figure 8-7).

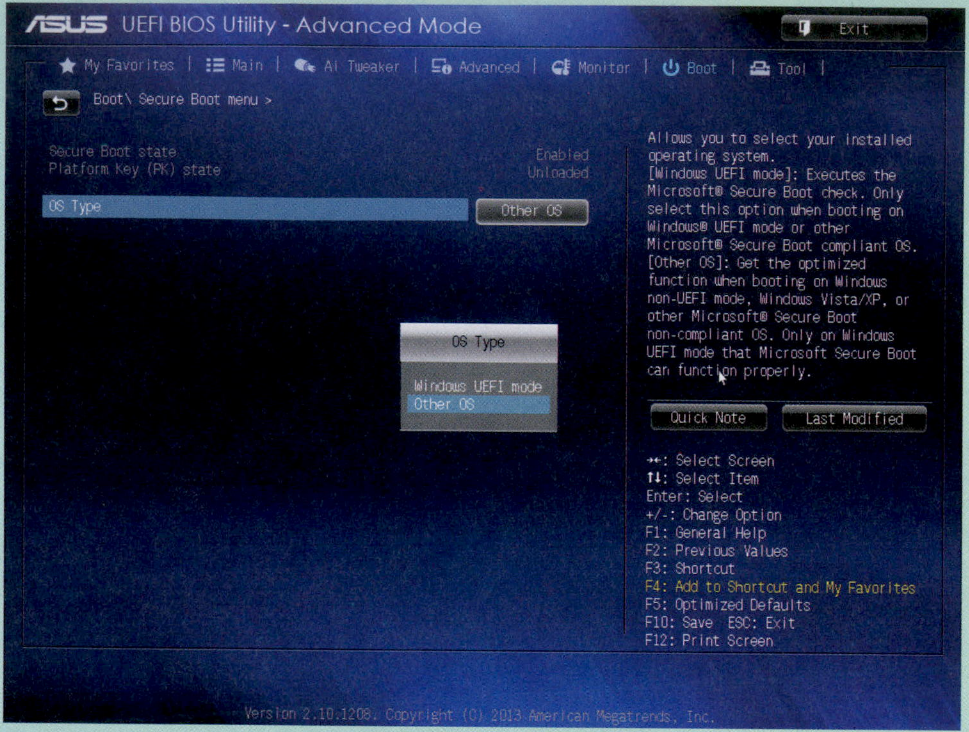

Source: American Megatrends, Inc.

Figure 8-7 Select Other OS to allow Windows to install on an MBR hard drive

To use UEFI firmware and the GPT partitioning system, use these same screens to disable **CSM** (see Figure 8-6) and set the OS Type to **Windows UEFI mode** (see Figure 8-7).

DEVICE DRIVERS

Device drivers are small programs stored on the hard drive that tell the computer how to communicate with a specific hardware device such as a printer, network card, or scanner. These drivers are installed on the hard drive when the OS is first installed, or when new hardware is added to the system. A device driver is written to work for a specific OS, such as Windows 8.1 or 7. In addition, a 32-bit OS requires 32-bit drivers, and a 64-bit OS requires 64-bit drivers.

Windows provides some device drivers, and the manufacturer of the hardware device provides others. When you purchase a printer, video card, digital camera, scanner, or other hardware device, a CD that contains the device drivers is usually bundled with the device along with a user manual (see Figure 8-8). You can also download the drivers for a device from the manufacturer's website.

Figure 8-8 A device such as this video card comes packaged with its device drivers stored on a CD

Be sure you have the correct Windows device drivers for all your critical devices such as your network card or motherboard. To find the drivers, look on the CD that came bundled with the device or check the website of the device manufacturer. Remember that a 64-bit OS requires all 64-bit drivers.

If you are not sure if your devices will work with Windows 8/7, one solution is to set up a dual boot. A dual boot, also called a multiboot, allows you to install the new OS without disturbing the old one so you can boot to either OS. After the installation, you can test your software or hardware. If they work under the new OS, you can delete the old one. If they don't work, you can still boot to the old OS and use it. How to set up a dual boot is covered later in this chapter.

If you have applications written for Windows 7 or Vista that are not compatible with Windows 8, you can use compatibility mode to solve the problem. Compatibility mode is a group of settings that can be applied to older drivers or applications that might cause them to work in Windows 8. You learn more about compatibility mode later in this chapter.

Hands-On | Project 8-1 Prepare for an Upgrade

A+
220-902
1.1, 1.2

On a computer with Windows 7 installed, access the Microsoft website *windows.microsoft.com/en-US/windows-8/upgrade-from-windows-7-tutorial* and locate, download, and run the Windows 8.1 Upgrade Assistant to find out if the computer is ready for a Windows 8.1 installation. Make a list of any hardware or software components found to be incompatible with Windows 8.1, and draw up a plan for getting the system ready for a Windows 8.1 upgrade.

INSTALLATIONS WITH SPECIAL CONSIDERATIONS

A+
220-902
1.1, 1.2

Depending on the circumstances and the available hardware, you might be faced with an installation on a computer that does not have a DVD drive, a computer that needs a factory recovery, or an installation in a virtual computer. All of these special considerations are discussed next.

WHEN THE COMPUTER DOES NOT HAVE A DVD DRIVE

You can buy Windows 8.1 on DVD or download it from the Internet. If the computer does not have a DVD drive, consider these options:

- ***Download Windows 8.1 from the Microsoft website.*** Purchase Windows 8.1 on the Microsoft website (*microsoftstore.com*), download it to your computer's hard drive, and install it from there. This option assumes the computer already has a working OS installed. You can also follow directions on the website to create a bootable USB flash drive with the files you downloaded and install Windows using this USB flash drive.
- ***Use an external DVD drive.*** Use an external DVD drive, which will most likely connect to the computer by way of a USB port. If the computer does not already have an OS installed, you must boot from this USB port. To do so, access UEFI/BIOS setup and set the boot order for the USB as the first boot device. The boot order is the order of devices that startup UEFI/BIOS looks to for an OS. Recall you can enter UEFI/BIOS setup by pressing a key at startup. Then locate the appropriate UEFI/BIOS setup screen. For example, the BIOS setup screen shown in Figure 8-9 shows a removable device as the first boot device. You can then boot from the external DVD drive and install Windows.

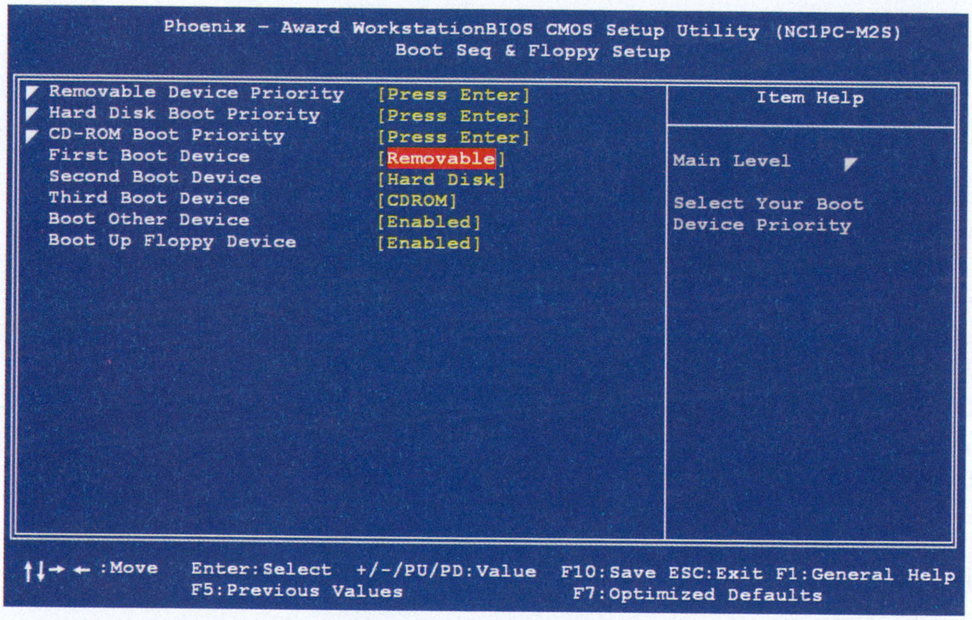

Source: Phoenix Technologies

Figure 8-9 Set the boot order in BIOS setup

- ***Use a DVD drive on another computer on the network.*** Share the DVD drive on another computer onto the network. Then go to the computer that is to receive the Windows installation and locate the DVD drive on the network. Double-click the setup.exe program to run the installation across the network. Alternately, you can copy the files on the DVD from the other computer to your hard drive. Again, this option assumes the computer already has a working OS installed. How to share folders and drives on a network is covered later in this text.

FACTORY RECOVERY PARTITION

If you have a laptop computer or a brand-name computer, such as a Dell, IBM, or Gateway, and you need to reinstall Windows, follow the recovery procedures given by the computer manufacturer. A hard drive is divided into one or more partitions, and the hard drive on a brand-name computer is likely to have a hidden recovery partition that contains a recovery utility and installation files.

To access the utilities on the hidden partition so that you can perform a repair installation, press a key during startup. The key to press is displayed on the screen early in the boot before the OS is loaded. If you don't see the message, search the website of the computer manufacturer to find the key combination. For one Dell laptop, you press Ctrl + F11 to start the recovery. One Gateway computer displays the message *Press F11 to start recovery*. When you press these keys, a menu displays, giving you the opportunity to reinstall Windows from setup files kept in the hidden partition.

Sometimes a manufacturer puts a utility in this hidden partition that can be used to create recovery discs (see Figure 8-10). However, the discs must have already been created if they are to be there to help you in the event the entire hard drive fails. You might also be able to purchase these CDs or DVDs on the computer manufacturer's website.

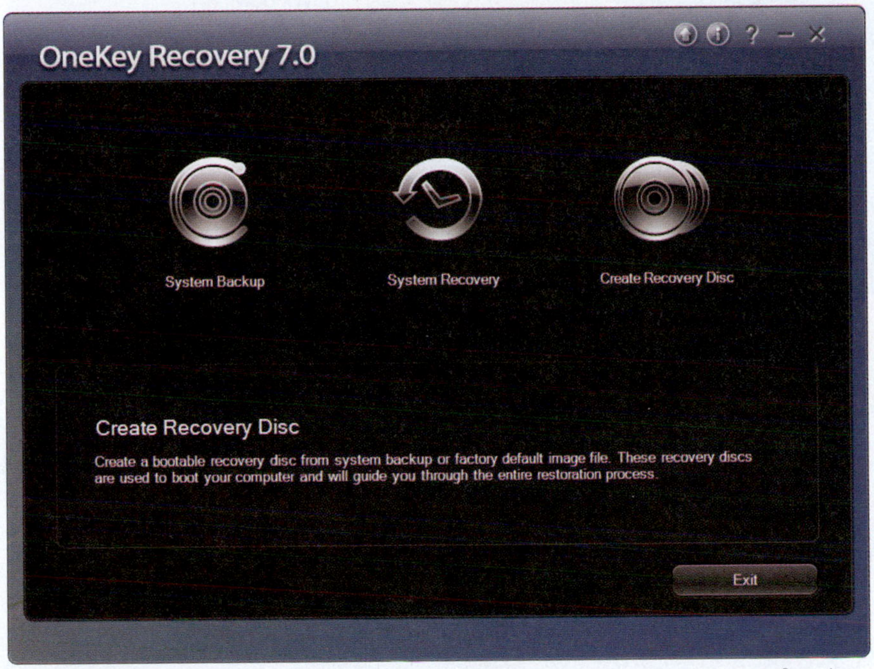

Source: Lenovo

Figure 8-10 Use the recovery utility on this laptop to create DVDs that can be used to recover the system in the event the hard drive fails

Notes In general, it's best not to upgrade an OS on a laptop unless you want to use some feature the new OS offers. For laptops, follow the general rule, "If it ain't broke, don't fix it." Many hardware components in a laptop are proprietary, and the laptop manufacturer is the only source for these drivers. If you are considering upgrading a laptop to Windows 8.1, check the laptop manufacturer's website for advice and to download Windows 8.1 drivers, which are called **third-party drivers** because they are not included in UEFI/BIOS or Windows. It's very important you have available a Windows 8.1 driver for your network port without having to depend on the network or Internet to get one after Windows 8.1 is installed. Also know that many Windows 7 drivers work with Windows 8.1.

INSTALLATION IN A VIRTUAL COMPUTER

Another type of Windows installation is when you install Windows in a virtual computer. A virtual computer or virtual machine (VM) is software that simulates the hardware of a physical computer. Using this software, you can install and run multiple operating systems at the same time on a single computer, which is called the host machine. These multiple instances of operating systems can be used to train users, run legacy software, and support multiple operating systems. For example, help-desk technicians can run a virtual machine for each OS they support on a single computer and quickly and easily switch from one OS to another by clicking a window. Another reason to use a virtual machine is that you can capture screen shots of the boot process in a virtual machine, which is the way the screen shots during the boot were made for this text.

Software used to manage VMs installed on a workstation is called a **hypervisor**. Some popular hypervisors for Windows are Client Hyper-V and Virtual PC by Microsoft (*www.microsoft.com*), VirtualBox by Oracle (*www.virtualbox.org*), and VMware Player by VMware, Inc. (*www.vmware.com*). Client Hyper-V is embedded in Windows 8 Pro or Enterprise, but is not available for other Windows releases. Virtual PC is free for download in all other editions of Windows 7 or 8 except Windows 7 Starter. VirtualBox and VMware Player are freeware. Be aware that virtual machine programs require a lot of memory and might slow down your system. Figure 8-11 shows two virtual machines running under VirtualBox.

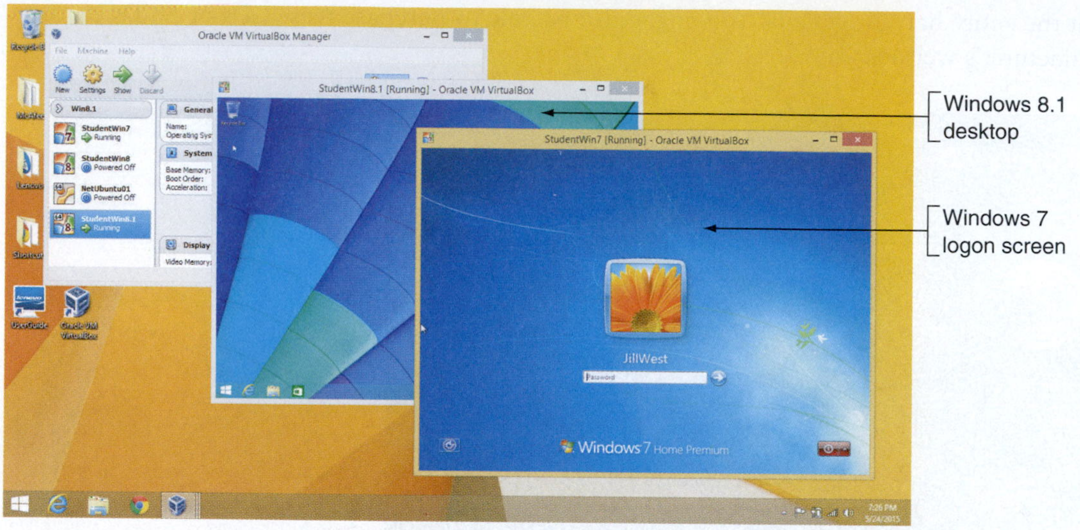

Source: VirtualBox (Oracle)

Figure 8-11 Two virtual machines running under VirtualBox

> **Notes** **Windows XP Mode**, which CompTIA calls **virtual XP mode**, is a Windows XP installation that runs under Virtual PC, and can be installed on a Windows 7 Professional, Enterprise, or Ultimate computer. When you install an OS in Virtual PC, normally you must have a valid product key for the installation, but an XP product key is not required for XP Mode. Windows XP Mode is not supported in Windows 8, although it is still possible to install Windows XP in a virtual machine in Windows 8.

If you are upgrading many computers to Windows 8.1 in a large enterprise, more automated methods are used for installations. Installation files are made available over the network or on bootable USB flash drives or DVDs. These automated methods are discussed later in this chapter.

Hands-On Project 8-2 Install and Run VirtualBox

> **Notes** If you don't want to use VirtualBox as your hypervisor, you can substitute another client hypervisor, such as VMware Player or Client Hyper-V. Note that Client Hyper-V does not play well on the same computer with other hypervisors, and can cause problems such as failed network connectivity. For that reason, don't enable Hyper-V on a Windows 8 computer that has another hypervisor installed.

On a Windows 8/7 computer, go to the Oracle VirtualBox website (*www.virtualbox.com*) and download and install VirtualBox on your computer. To set up a new virtual machine, open VirtualBox and click **New** at the top of the VirtualBox window. The *Create Virtual Machine* box shown in Figure 8-12 appears. Assign the VM a name and select **Windows 8.1 (32 bit)** from the Version drop-down menu. Click **Next**. Leave the default memory size selection of **1024 MB** and click **Next**. Be sure that **Create a virtual hard drive now** is checked and click **Create**.

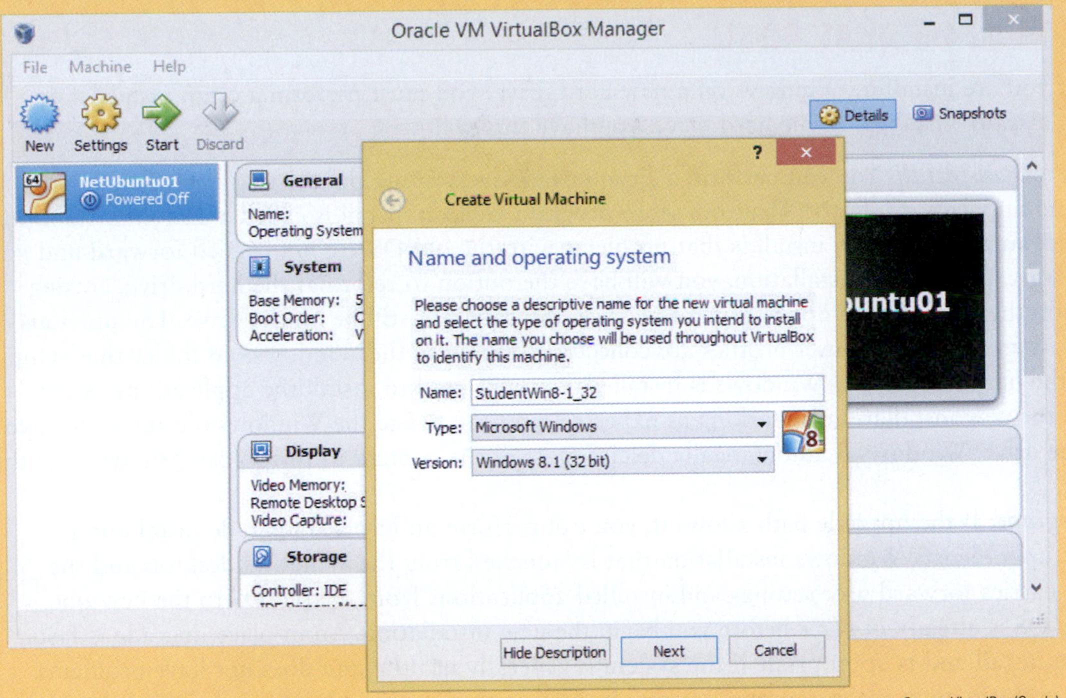

Source: VirtualBox (Oracle)

Figure 8-12 Using VirtualBox to set up a new virtual machine

A wizard launches and steps you through the process of creating a new machine. During the process, you can select the virtual machine file type, the type of space allocation for the VM's hard drive, and the hard drive size. For the hard drive file type, make sure the default selection **VDI (VirtualBox Disk Image)** is checked (unless directed otherwise by your instructor), and click **Next**.

Be sure the default selection **Dynamically allocated** is checked so that space on the physical computer's hard drive is used only when it's needed by the VM. Click **Next**. Change the size of the virtual hard drive to **16 GB**, as shown at the bottom of Figure 8-13, and click **Create**. When you complete the wizard, the new virtual machine is listed in the VirtualBox window.

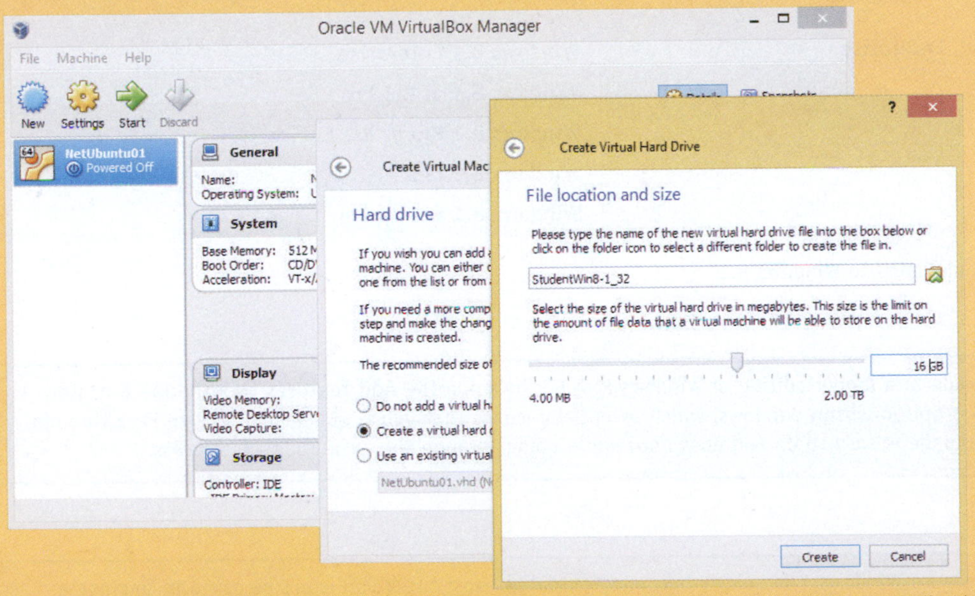

Source: VirtualBox (Oracle)

Figure 8-13 A 32-bit Windows installation requires at least 16 GB of hard drive space

In a project later in this chapter, you install Windows 8.1 in this VM.

CHOOSE THE TYPE OF INSTALLATION: IN-PLACE UPGRADE, CLEAN INSTALL, OR DUAL BOOT

A+
220-902
1.1, 1.2

If you are installing Windows on a new hard drive, you must perform a clean install. If an OS is already installed on the hard drive, you have three choices:

- ***Clean install.*** You can perform a clean install, overwriting the existing operating system and applications. In the Windows setup program, a clean install is called a custom installation. The main advantage of a clean install is that problems with the old OS are not carried forward and you get a fresh start. During the installation, you will have the option to reformat the hard drive, erasing everything on the drive. If you don't format the drive, the data will still be on the drive. The previous operating system settings and user profiles are collectively stored in the Windows.old folder that setup creates on the hard drive. After Windows is installed, you will need to install the applications. After you're sure the new installation is working as expected, you can delete the Windows.old folder to save space on the drive. Windows 8 automatically deletes most of the content of this folder 28 days after the installation.
- ***In-place upgrade.*** If the upgrade path allows it, you can perform an in-place upgrade installation. An in-place upgrade is a Windows installation that is launched from the Windows desktop and the installation carries forward user settings and installed applications from the old OS to the new one. A Windows OS is already *in place* before you begin the new installation. An in-place upgrade is faster than a clean install and is appropriate if the system is generally healthy and does not have problems. In order to perform an in-place upgrade, Microsoft requires that certain editions and versions of Windows be installed already. These qualifying OSs are called upgrade paths. Table 8-3 outlines the acceptable upgrade paths for Windows 8.1. There is no upgrade path from Windows Vista or XP to Windows 8.1. Even though you can purchase an upgrade license to install Windows 8.1 on these systems, you must perform a clean install.

From OS	To OS
Windows 7 Starter, Home Basic, Home Premium	Windows 8.1
Windows 7 Starter, Home Basic, Home Premium, Professional, Ultimate	Windows 8.1 Pro
Windows 7 Professional, Enterprise	Windows 8.1 Enterprise
Windows 8	Windows 8.1 or 8.1 Pro
Windows 8 Pro	Windows 8.1 Pro or 8.1 Enterprise
Windows 8.1	Windows 8.1 Pro
Windows 8.1 Pro	Windows 8.1 Enterprise

Table 8-3 In-place upgrade paths to Windows 8.1

Notes You can upgrade to a higher edition of Windows 8 or 8.1 by using the **Add features to Windows 8** or **Add features to Windows 8.1** option within Windows, which essentially means that you're purchasing the Pro Pack through Windows directly. The upgrade is easy to do and does not require going through the entire upgrade process.

OS Differences Because Windows 7 is quickly becoming outdated, most likely you won't be asked to upgrade a computer to Windows 7. However, if you need to see the upgrade paths to Windows 7, do a *google.com* web search on **windows 7 upgrade paths site:technet.microsoft.com**.

- ***Multiboot.*** You can install Windows in a second partition on the hard drive and create a dual-boot situation with the other OS, or even install three OSs, each in its own partition in a multiboot environment. Don't create a dual boot unless you need two operating systems, such as when you need to verify that applications and hardware work under Windows 8.1 before you delete the old OS. Windows 8/7/Vista all require that they be the only operating system installed on a partition. So to set up a dual boot, you'll need at least two partitions on the hard drive or a second hard drive.

In addition to the information given in Table 8-3, keep in mind these tips:

- A 64-bit version of Windows can only be upgraded to a 64-bit OS. A 32-bit OS can only be upgraded to a 32-bit OS.
- If you want to install a 64-bit version of Windows on a computer that already has a 32-bit OS installed, you must perform a clean install.
- You cannot upgrade from Windows XP or Vista to Windows 8, and you cannot upgrade from XP to Windows 7. You must perform a clean install.

UNDERSTAND THE CHOICES YOU'LL MAKE DURING THE INSTALLATION

A+ 220-902 1.1, 1.2, 1.6

While Windows is installing, you must choose which drive and partition to install Windows, the size of a new partition, and how Windows will connect to the network. Next you learn about what might affect your decisions regarding the size of the Windows partition and how Windows will connect to the network.

THE SIZE OF THE WINDOWS PARTITION

For a clean install or dual boot, you can decide to not use all the available space on the drive for the Windows partition. Here are reasons to not use all the available space:

- ***You plan to install more than one OS on the hard drive, creating a dual-boot system.*** For example, you might want to install Windows 7 on one partition and leave room for another partition where you intend to install Windows 8.1, so you can test software under both operating systems. (When setting up a dual boot, always install the older OS first.)
- ***Some people prefer to use more than one partition or volume to organize data on their hard drives.*** For example, you might want to install Windows and all your applications on one partition and your data on another. Having your data on a separate partition makes backing up easier. In another situation, you might want to set up a volume on the drive that is used exclusively to hold backups of data on another computer on the network. The size of the partition that will hold Windows 8/7 and its applications should be at least 16 GB for a 32-bit install and 20 GB for the 64-bit install, but a larger volume is nearly always preferred.

Caution It's convenient to back up one volume to another volume on a different hard drive. However, don't back up one volume to another volume on the same hard drive, because when a hard drive fails, quite often all volumes on the drive are damaged and you will lose both your data and your backup.

Later in this text, you learn to use the Disk Management utility after Windows is installed to create partitions from unallocated space and to resize, delete, and split existing partitions.

NETWORK CONFIGURATION

Recall from the chapter, "Survey of Windows Features and Support Tools," that all editions of Windows 8/7/Vista can join a workgroup, Windows 8/7 can join a homegroup, and business editions of Windows 8/7 can join a homegroup or Windows domain. (Vista does not support homegroups.) To join a domain, you'll need the network ID and password assigned to you by the network administrator of the private network. To join a homegroup, you'll need the password to the homegroup, and to join a workgroup, you'll need the name of the workgroup. You can connect to a workgroup, homegroup, or domain during the installation, or you can wait and make the connection after the installation is complete.

You also need to know that the Windows installation process usually has no problems connecting to the network and the Internet without your help. However, you might need to know how the IP address is assigned. An IP address uniquely identifies a computer on the network. It might be assigned dynamically (IP address is assigned by a server each time the workstation connects to the network) or statically (IP address is permanently assigned to the workstation). If the network is using static IP addressing, you need the IP address for the workstation.

FINAL CHECKLIST BEFORE BEGINNING THE INSTALLATION

A+
220-902
1.1, 1.2

Before you begin the installation, complete the final checklist shown in Table 8-4 to verify that you are ready.

Notes For new installations, look for the product key written on the cover of the Windows setup DVD, on a card inside the DVD case, or affixed to the back of the Windows documentation booklet, as shown in Figure 8-14. If you are reinstalling Windows on an existing system and you can't find the product key documentation, you can download and run freeware to tell you the key. For example, try Magical Jelly Bean freeware at *magicaljellybean.com/keyfinder*.

Questions to Answer	Further Information
Does the computer meet the minimum or recommended hardware requirement?	CPU: RAM: Hard drive partition size: Free space on the partition:
Do you have in hand the Windows device drivers for your hardware devices and application setup CDs?	List hardware and software that need to be upgraded:
Do you have the product key available?	Product key:
How will users be recognized on the network?	Homegroup password: Workgroup name: Domain name: Computer name: Network ID: Network password:
How will the computer be recognized on the network?	Static or dynamic IP addressing: IP address (for static addressing):
Will you do an upgrade or clean install?	Current operating system: Does the old OS qualify for an upgrade?
For a clean install, will you set up a dual boot?	List reasons for a dual boot: Size of the second partition: Free space on the second partition:
Have you backed up important data on your hard drive?	Location of backup:

Table 8-4 Checklist to complete before installing Windows

Figure 8-14 The Windows product key found on the inside of a retail package or on the outside of an OEM package

Before getting into the step-by-step instructions of installing an OS, here are some general tips about installing Windows:

- Verify you have all application software CDs or DVDs available and all device drivers.
- Back up all important data on the drive. How to perform backups is covered in the chapter, "Maintaining Windows."
- For upgrade installations and clean installs in which you do not plan to reformat the hard drive, run antivirus/anti-malware software to make sure the drive is free from malware. If Windows will not start and you suspect malware might be a problem, plan to reformat the hard drive during the installation so you know the hard drive is clean of malware.
- If you want to begin the installation by booting from the Windows setup DVD or other media such as a USB device, use UEFI/BIOS setup to verify that the boot sequence is first the optical drive or USB device, and then the hard drive.
- In UEFI/BIOS setup, disable any virus protection setting that prevents the boot area of the hard drive from being altered.
- For a system that uses UEFI firmware, set the firmware to use UEFI mode (to use GPT and possibly Secure Boot) or UEFI CSM mode (to use MBR partitions on the hard drive). Know that Windows will install on a GPT drive only when UEFI CSM mode is disabled and will install on an MBR drive only when UEFI CSM mode is enabled.
- For a laptop computer, connect the AC adapter and use this power source for the complete OS installation, updates, and installation of hardware and applications. You don't want the battery to fail in the middle of the installation process.

Notes If your current installation of Windows is corrupted, you might be able to repair the installation rather than reinstalling Windows. The chapter, "Troubleshooting Windows Startup," covers what to do to fix a corrupted Windows installation.

INSTALLING WINDOWS 8.1 AND WINDOWS 7

A+
220-902
1.2, 1.6,
4.1

In this part of the chapter, you learn the steps to install Windows 8.1 and Windows 7 as an in-place upgrade, clean install, and dual boot, and how to handle the special situation of using a Windows upgrade product key to install Windows on a new hard drive. As you install and configure software, be sure to document what you did. This documentation will be helpful for future maintenance and troubleshooting. In a project at the end of this chapter, you will develop a documentation template.

Let's begin with how to perform an in-place upgrade of Windows 8.1.

STEPS TO PERFORM A WINDOWS 8.1 IN-PLACE UPGRADE

A+
220-902
1.2, 1.6

The Windows 8.1 upgrade package comes with a 32-bit DVD and a 64-bit DVD. The product key is on a card found in a slip pocket inside the box. Here are the steps to perform an in-place upgrade from Windows 7 to Windows 8.1 when you're working with a Windows 8.1 setup DVD:

1. As with any upgrade installation, before you start the upgrade, do the following:
   a. Scan the system for malware using an updated version of anti-malware software. When you're done, be sure to close the anti-malware application so it's not running in the background.
   b. Uninstall any applications or device drivers you don't intend to use in the new installation.
   c. Make sure your backups of important data are up to date and then close any backup software running in the background.
2. Insert the Windows 8.1 setup DVD. If the setup program doesn't start automatically and the AutoPlay dialog box doesn't open, open Windows Explorer and double-click the **setup.exe** program in the root of the DVD. Respond to the UAC box. The setup program loads files, examines the system, and reports any problems it finds. If it finds the system meets minimum hardware requirements, setup asks permission to go online for updates (see Figure 8-15). Make your selection and click **Next**.

OS Differences The steps and screen shots for an in-place upgrade in this section are for Windows 8.1. The steps for Windows 8.0 work about the same way.

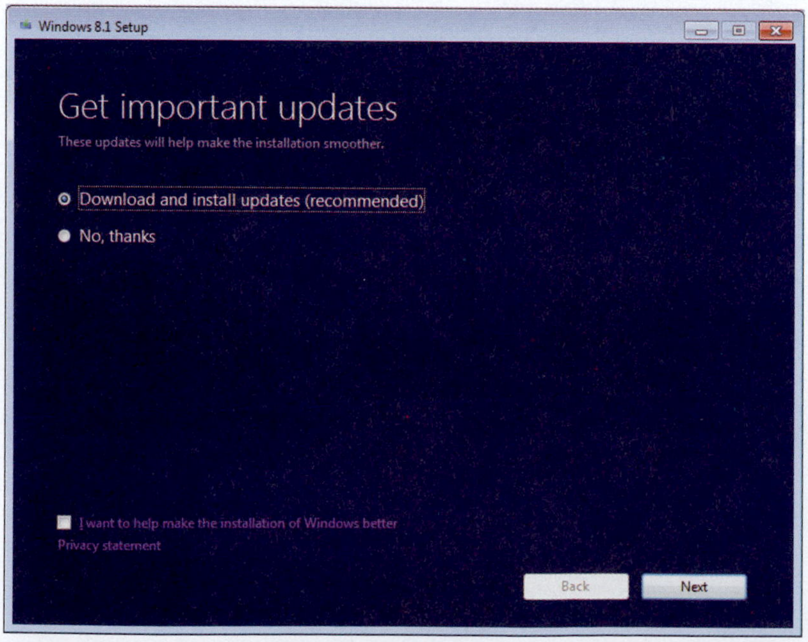

Figure 8-15 Decide how you will handle updates to the setup process

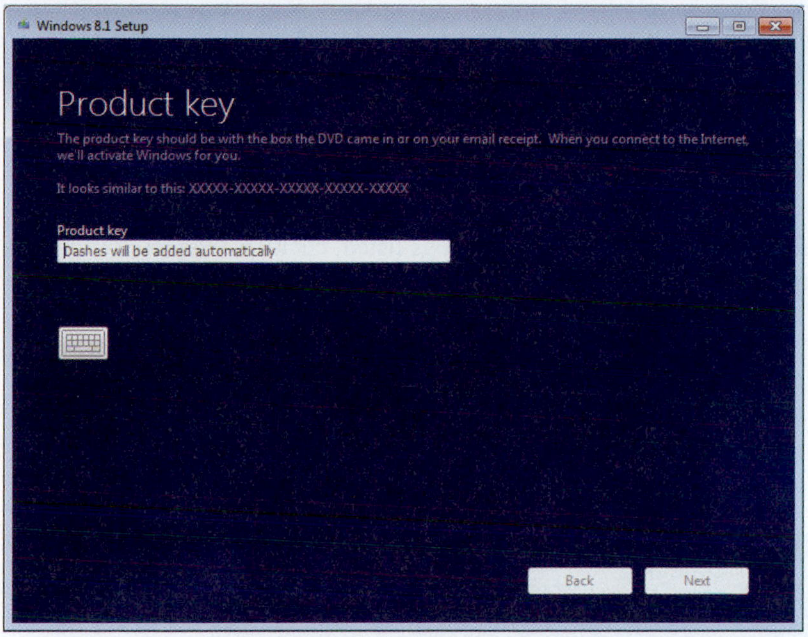

Figure 8-16 The product key is verified as a valid key before you can continue with the installation

3. The next window requests the product key (see Figure 8-16). Enter the product key and Windows verifies the key is a valid key. If the computer is connected to the Internet, setup will automatically activate Windows during the installation. Click **Next**.
4. The License terms window appears. Check **I accept the license terms** and click **Accept**.
5. On the Choose what to keep window (see Figure 8-17), decide what you want to do with Windows settings, personal files, and apps:
   - The first two options perform upgrades to Windows 8.1.
   - The Nothing option performs a clean install of Windows 8.1. Everything on drive C: is deleted and the Windows.old folder is created, which holds files from the old installation. Other volumes on the hard drive are not disturbed.

For an upgrade installation, choose the first option and click **Next.** On the next screen, verify the choices listed and click **Install** to begin the installation.

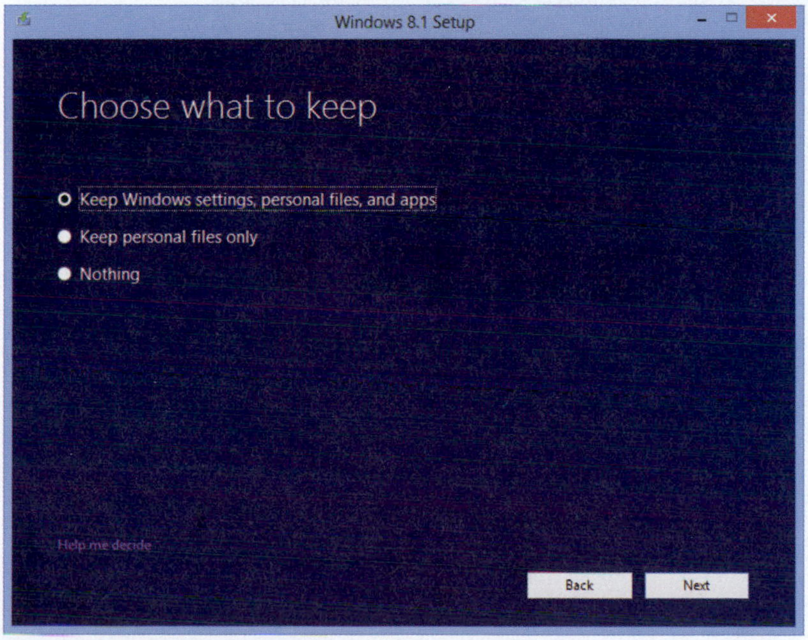

Figure 8-17 Decide what to keep of the old installation

Notes When setup recognizes that it cannot perform an upgrade, but must perform a clean install, the first option on the window in Figure 8-17 is missing.

6. During the installation, setup might restart the system several times. Near the end of the installation, you are asked to select a screen color.
7. Next, the Settings screen appears (see Figure 8-18). To use the settings listed, click **Use express settings**. To customize the settings, click **Customize** and make your selections for these settings:
   - Settings for sharing and connecting to devices
   - Automatic Windows updates
   - Privacy settings for apps and Internet Explorer
   - Information sent to Microsoft

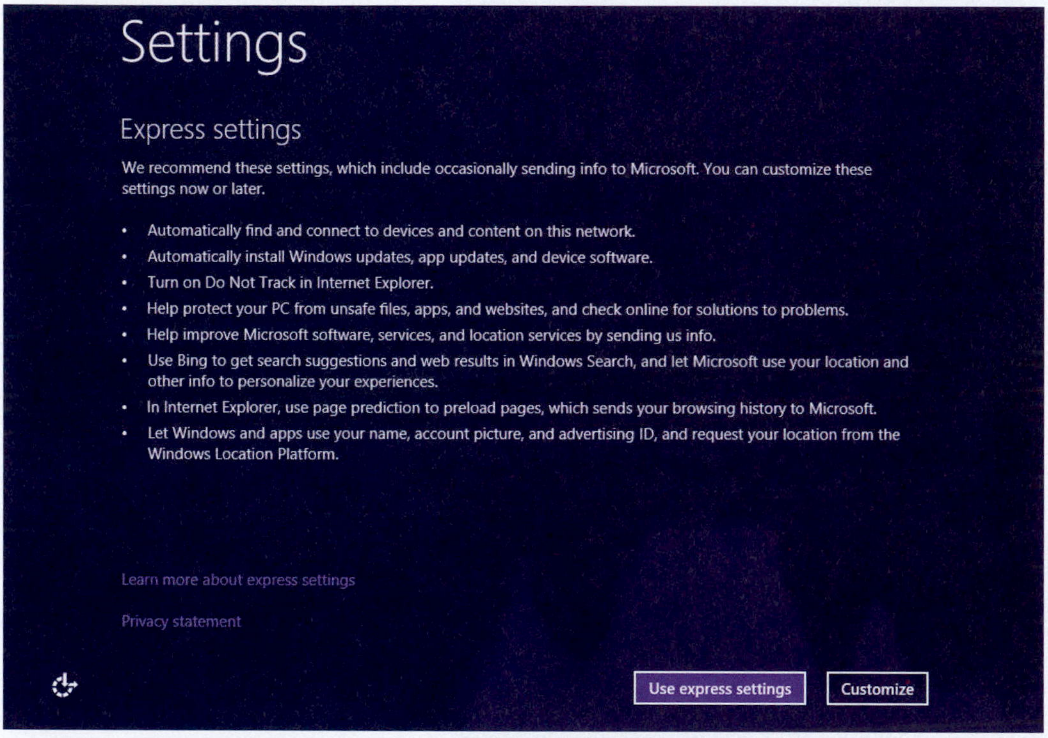

Figure 8-18 Decide which settings to accept

Notes An in-place upgrade uses the existing selections for network connections and hard drive volumes; therefore, you're not asked to make these decisions during the upgrade process.

8. If the computer is connected to the Internet, on the next screen, you are given the opportunity to enter a Microsoft account that you can use to sign in to Windows (see Figure 8-19). Recall that a Microsoft account is associated with an email address registered at *live.com*. You also have the option to continue using a local account or domain account, although setup makes the option a little difficult to find.

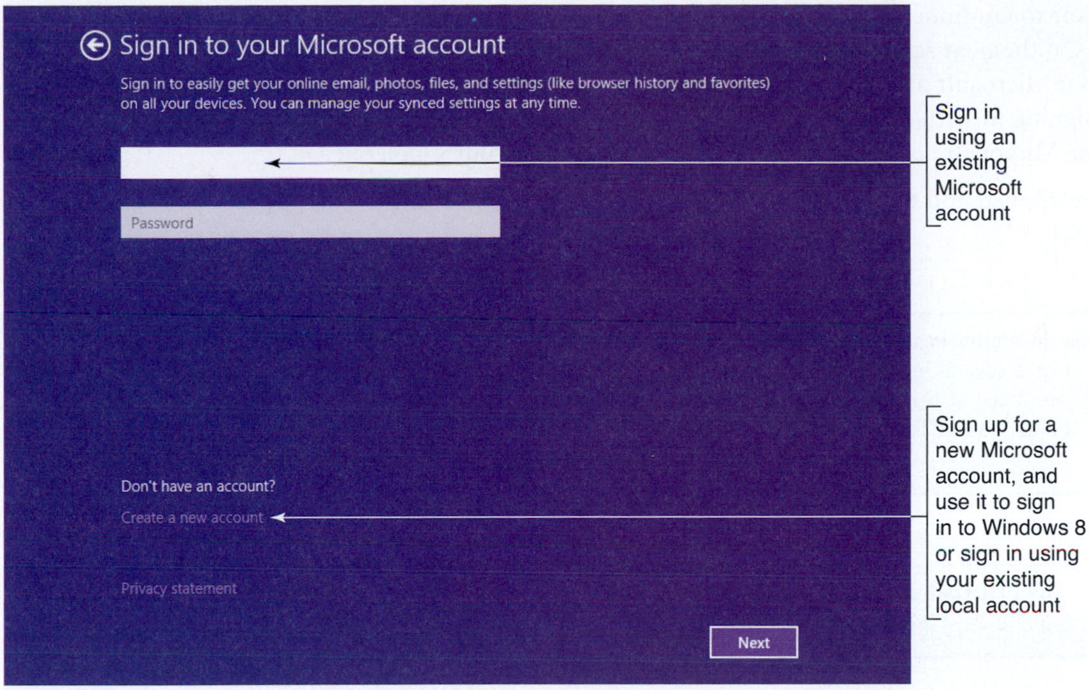

Figure 8-19 Decide which account you will use to sign in to Windows 8.1

You have three options for setting up Windows 8.1 sign in:

- To use an existing Microsoft account, enter the email address and password and click **Next**.
- If you want to create a new Microsoft account, click **Create a new account**. On the next screen that appears (see Figure 8-20), enter the information for the new account and click **Next**. Notice on the screen you can get a new Microsoft email address (outlook.com, hotmail.com, or live.com address) or you can use an existing email address (one that is not managed by Microsoft).

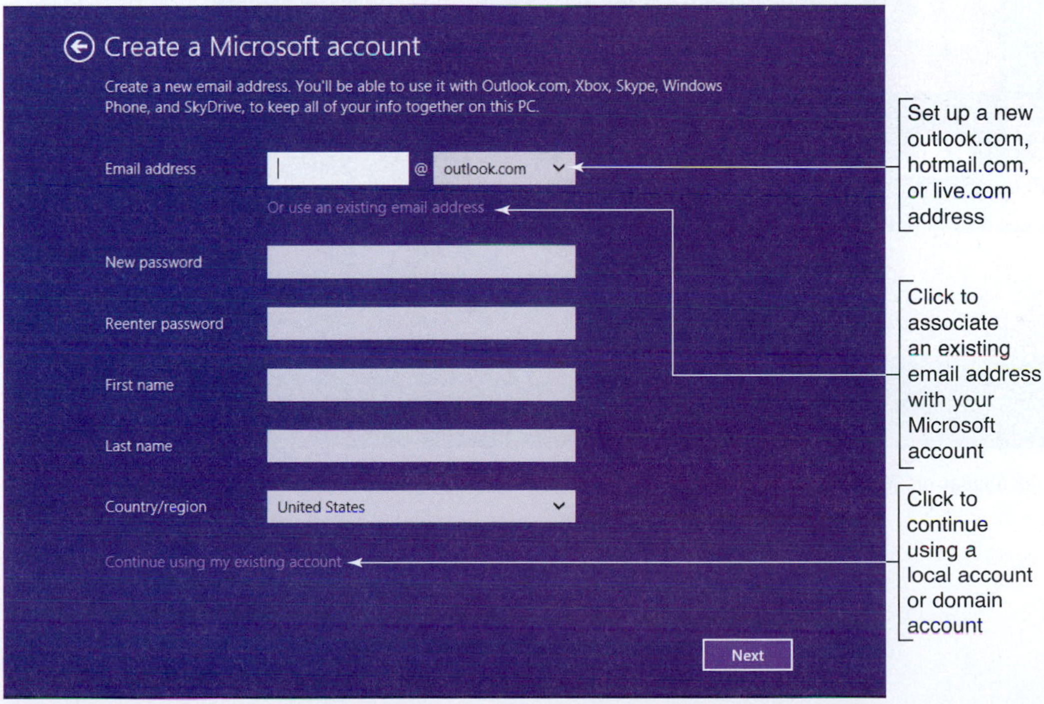

Figure 8-20 Create a new Microsoft account and use it to sign in to Windows 8.1 or continue using a local or domain account

8

- If you want to continue using a local account, on the screen shown in Figure 8-19, click **Create a new account**. On the next screen (see Figure 8-20), click **Continue using my existing account**. (You can switch to a Microsoft account later, after Windows 8.1 is installed.)

9. If you're signing in with a Microsoft account, follow directions on screen to set up how you want to secure your Microsoft account on this computer and set up your OneDrive.
10. Settings are applied and the Windows Start screen appears. You can now use the new installation of Windows 8.1.

Notes If you have problems installing Windows, search the Microsoft website (*support.microsoft.com*) for solutions. Windows setup creates several log files during the installation that can help you solve a problem. Locations of Windows 8 setup log files are listed at this link: *technet.microsoft.com/en-us/library/hh824819.aspx*.
For Windows 7, the list can be found in the Microsoft Knowledge Base Article 927521 at this link: *support.microsoft.com/kb/927521*.

Notes When you first start using Windows 8.1 after an installation, it provides tips on screen to help you learn to use the OS (see Figure 8-21). The only way to get rid of a tip on screen is to follow its directions.

Figure 8-21 Tip boxes appear on Windows 8.1 screens to help you learn to use the OS

WINDOWS 8.1 UPGRADE FROM MICROSOFT WEBSITE

A+
220-902
1.2, 1.6

You just saw how to perform an upgrade using the Windows setup DVD. You can also download from the Microsoft website the files you need to perform the upgrade. To do that, Microsoft requires you first run the Upgrade Assistant. Here's how to get started:

1. After you have your Windows computer ready to upgrade, go to **windows.microsoft.com/en-gb/windows-8/upgrade-assistant-download-online-faq.** Download and run the Windows 8.1 Upgrade Assistant. Make sure you have Windows 8.1 device drivers already downloaded for critical devices such as your network adapter.
2. If you're ready to proceed with the upgrade, click **Next** to continue.
3. The *Choose what to keep* window appears (refer back to Figure 8-17). Choose **Keep Windows settings, personal files, and apps,** and then click **Next**.
4. On the next screen, Microsoft recommends the right edition of Windows (see Figure 8-22). To buy the edition, click **Order**. On the next screen, click **Checkout**.

8

Source: Upgrade Assistant

Figure 8-22 Microsoft offers editions of Windows 8.1 for purchase

5. Follow directions on screen to enter your name, phone number, email address, and billing address, and pay for and start the download.
6. After the download completes, the Install Windows 8 screen appears. You can click *Install now* to continue with the installation. If you click *Install by creating media*, you are given the opportunity to create a bootable USB flash drive or DVD that contains the Windows setup files. Later, you can use the USB flash drive or DVD to perform the upgrade or a clean install of Windows 8.1. You're also given the opportunity to save the setup files to an ISO file. An ISO file, also called an ISO image or disc image, is an International Organization for Standardization image of an optical disc and includes the file system used. An ISO file has an .iso file extension. As you'll see later in the chapter, the ISO file is a handy tool when you want to install Windows in a virtual machine.

Notes Best practice is to save the Windows setup files to a storage device or ISO image. You never know when you'll need the files to repair a corrupted Windows installation.

Notes If you have an optical drive that can write to DVDs and you want to burn a DVD from an ISO file, insert a blank DVD in your optical drive and double-click the ISO file. Follow directions on screen and Windows does the rest.

WINDOWS 7 IN-PLACE UPGRADE

A+ 220-902 1.2, 1.6, 4.1

When would you ever be called on to upgrade a Vista system to Windows 7? Suppose a Vista computer has several applications and device drivers installed that will not work in Windows 8.1, but will work in Windows 7. An in-place upgrade to Windows 7 will improve performance and security without having to deal with the hassle and expense of incompatible apps and drivers in Windows 8.1.

An in-place upgrade to Windows 7 is similar to that of Windows 8.1, with these exceptions:

- *Check for compatibility*. After inserting the Windows 7 DVD in the DVD drive, you then launch Windows 7 **setup.exe** just as you learned to do for Windows 8.1 setup. Respond to the Vista UAC box. If you have not yet performed the Windows 7 Upgrade Advisor process, do so by clicking **Check compatibility online** in the opening menu shown in Figure 8-23. To proceed with the installation, click **Install now**.

Figure 8-23 Opening menu when you launch Windows 7 setup from within Windows

OS Differences A Vista installation works the same as a Windows 7 installation.

- ***Product key.*** Windows 8 setup asks for and requires you enter a product key early in the installation, but Windows 7 asks for the product key near the end of the installation (see Figure 8-24). You're not required to enter the product key in this window and you can uncheck **Automatically activate Windows when I'm online.** You can enter the product key and activate Windows after the installation is finished. You have 30 days before you must activate Windows 7.

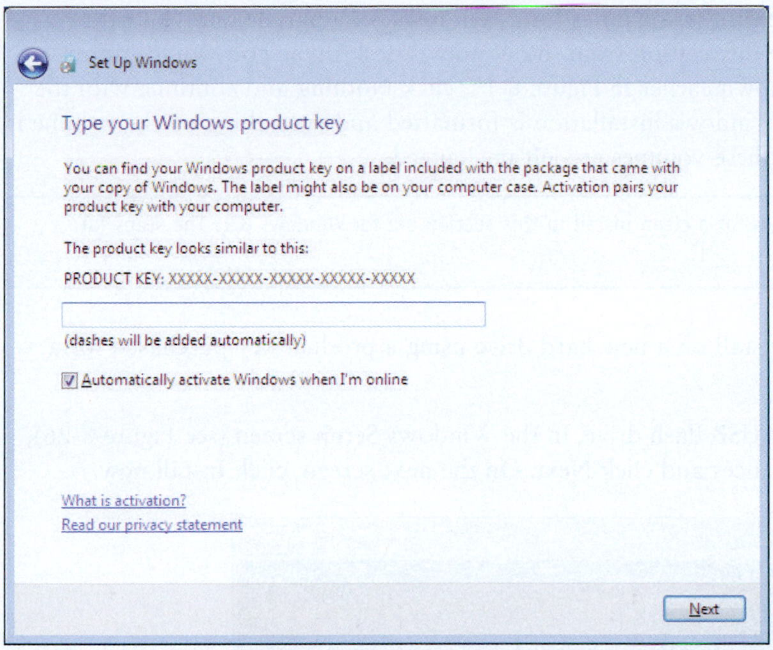

Figure 8-24 Enter the product key

- ***Network location.*** Windows 7 setup requires you select a network location (see Figure 8-25). Click the option that is appropriate to your network connection. You learned about these network locations in the chapter, "Survey of Windows Features and Support Tools." If you choose Home network, you are given the opportunity to create a homegroup or enter the homegroup password to join an existing homegroup. Recall you can change these settings later using the Network and Sharing Center.

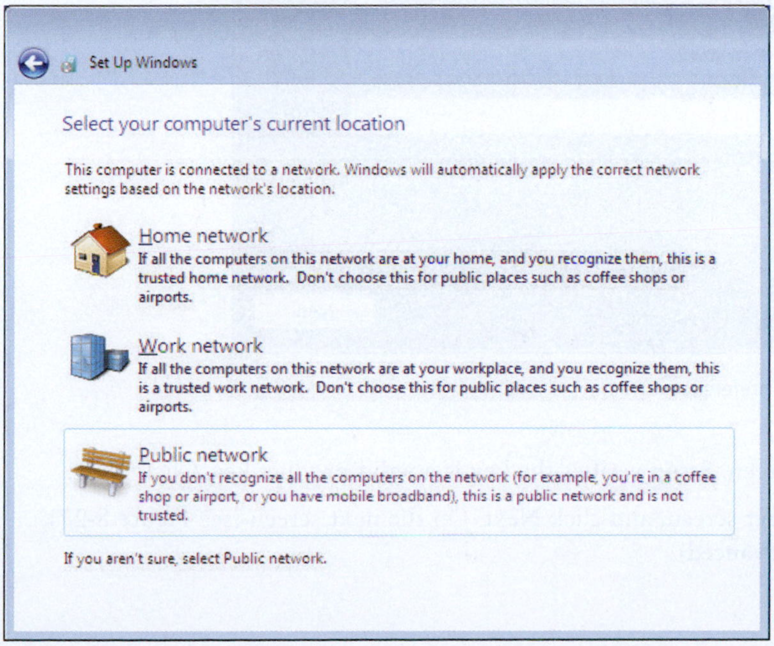

Figure 8-25 Select network settings

STEPS TO PERFORM A WINDOWS 8.1 CLEAN INSTALL

A+
220-902
1.2, 1.6

Recall that a clean install is the best option to use if the current installation is sluggish or giving problems, the currently installed OS does not allow for an in-place upgrade, or you're installing Windows 8.1 on a new desktop computer you're building.

If you have a Windows 7/Vista installation that qualifies for a Windows 8.1 upgrade and you need to do a clean install, begin by starting the installation from the Windows desktop as you would for an upgrade. When you get to the window shown earlier in Figure 8-17, click **Nothing** and continue with the installation. The volume holding the old Windows installation is formatted and everything on the volume is lost. If the hard drive has other volumes, these volumes are left unchanged.

OS Differences The steps and screen shots for a clean install in this section are for Windows 8.1. The steps for Windows 8.0 work about the same way.

Here are the steps to perform a clean install on a new hard drive using a product key purchased for a new installation of Windows 8.1:

1. Boot from the Windows setup DVD or USB flash drive. In the Windows Setup screen (see Figure 8-26), select the language and regional preferences and click **Next**. On the next screen, click **Install now**.

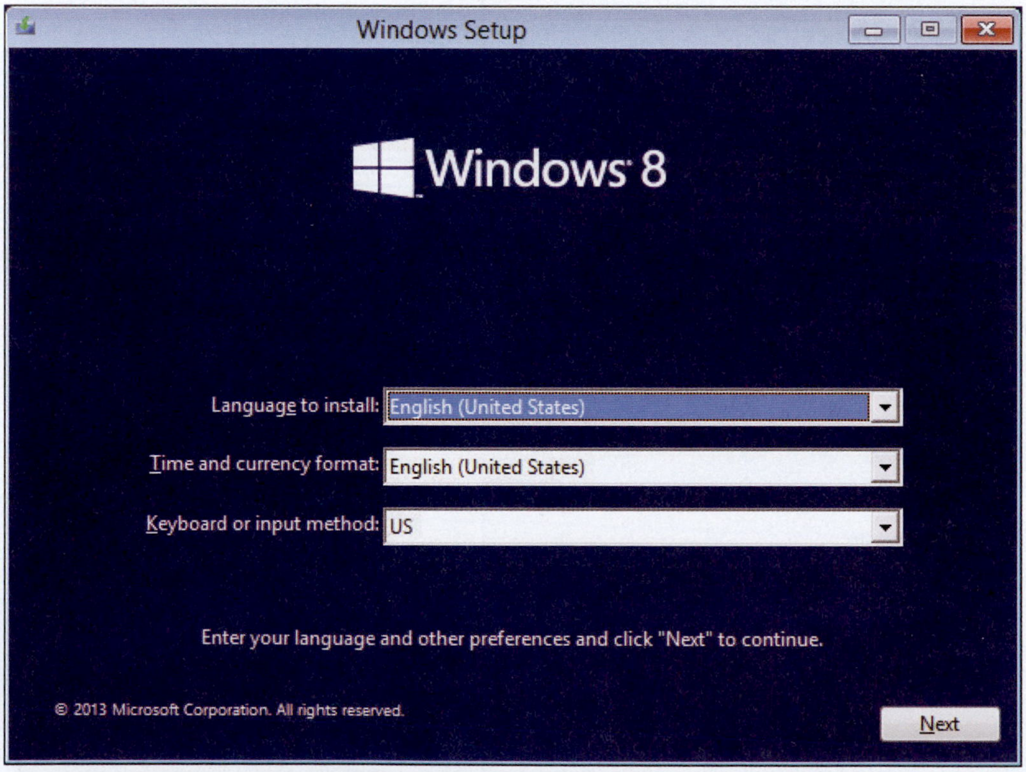

Figure 8-26 Decide on language and keyboard preferences

2. Enter your product key on the next screen. Setup verifies the key is a valid product key. Click **Next**.
3. Accept the license agreement on the next screen, and click **Next**. On the next screen (see Figure 8-27), click **Custom: Install Windows only (advanced)**.

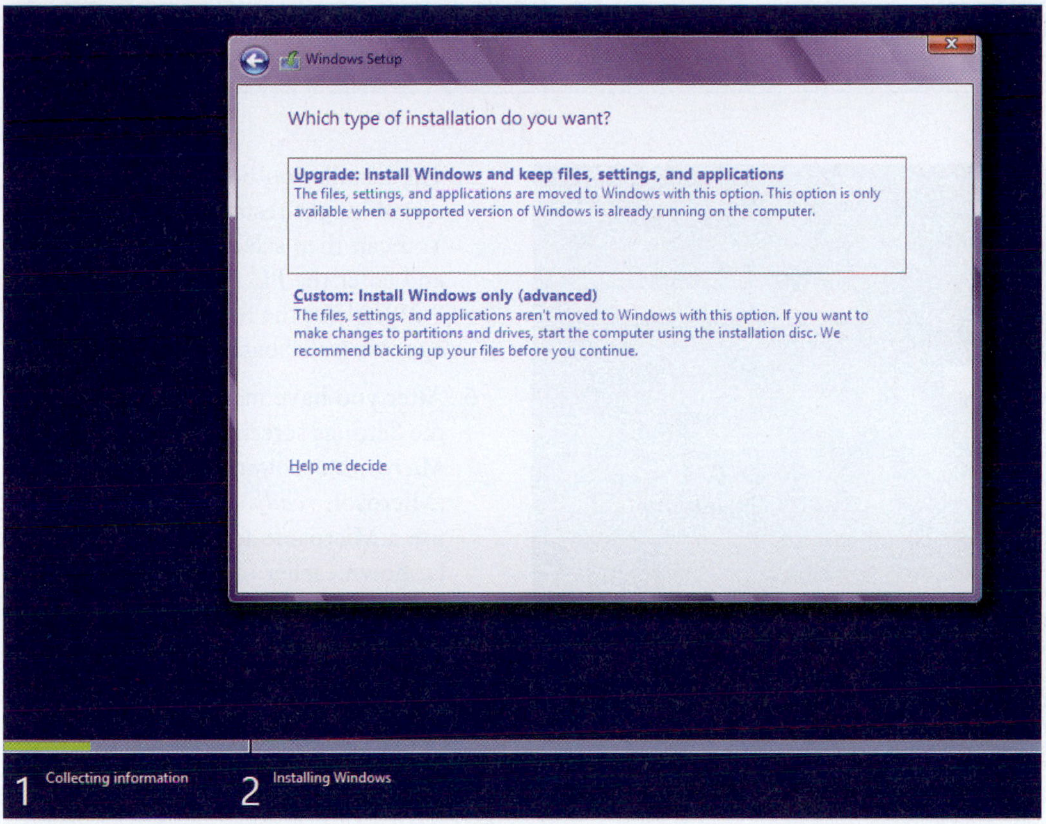

Figure 8-27 Decide between an upgrade and a clean install

4. The *Where do you want to install Windows?* screen appears. Select the drive and volume where you want to install Windows. Figure 8-28 shows the screen that appears for a new hard drive that has not been partitioned. By default, setup will use the entire unallocated space for the Windows volume. If you want to use only a portion of the space, click **New** and enter the size of the volume. (Setup will also create a small reserved partition that it later uses for system files and the startup process.) Click **Next** to continue.

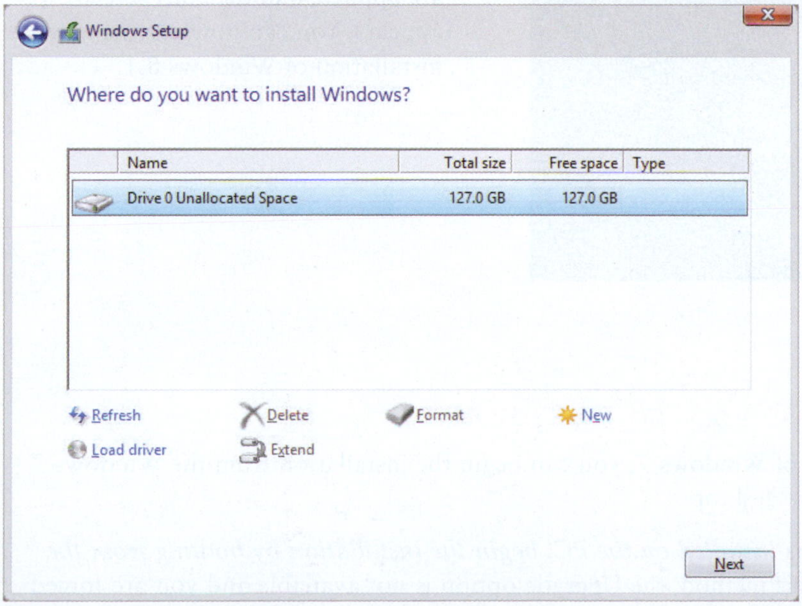

Figure 8-28 This hard drive has not yet been partitioned

Notes If you don't see the *New* link on the *Where do you want to install Windows?* screen, click **Drive options (advanced)** to see this and other links you can use to manage the space on the hard drive.

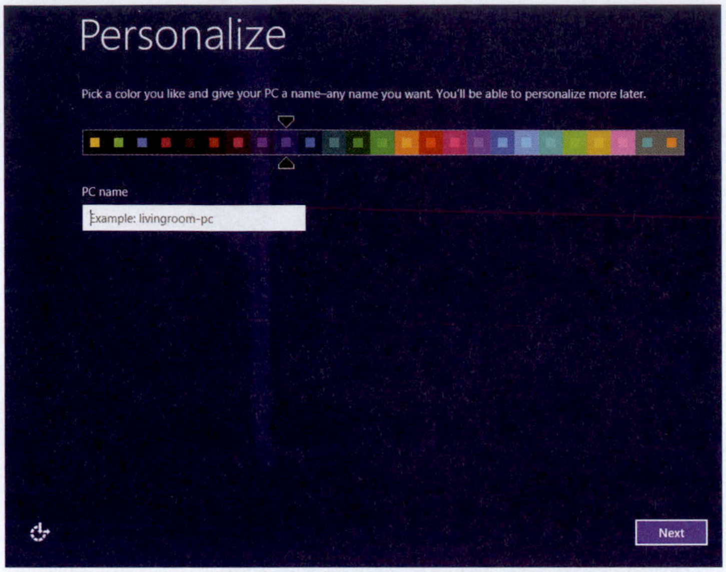

Figure 8-29 Decide on screen color, and enter a computer name

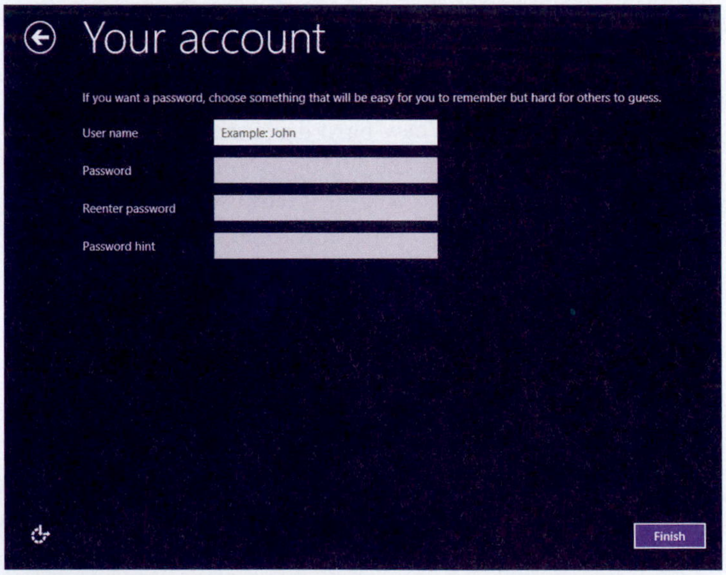

Figure 8-30 Set up a local account

5. The installation begins, and the system might restart several times. You can then select a screen color and enter the PC name (see Figure 8-29). Next, the Settings screen appears (refer back to Figure 8-18).

6. After you have made your choices on the Settings screen, the *Sign in to your Microsoft account* screen appears (Microsoft *really* encourages you to use a Microsoft account). The screen is shown earlier in Figure 8-19. Just as with an in-place upgrade, you can sign in using an existing Microsoft account or create a new Microsoft account. In addition, you can create a new local account.

   If you want to create a new local account, click **Create a new account**. On the next screen, click **Sign in without a Microsoft account**. The screen shown in Figure 8-30 appears. Enter the local account name, password, and password hint, and then click **Finish**.

7. The installation continues, settings are applied, and the Start screen appears. You can now use the new installation of Windows 8.1.

STEPS TO PERFORM A WINDOWS 7 CLEAN INSTALL

A+ 220-902 1.2, 1.6

To perform a clean install of Windows 7, you can begin the installation from the Windows 7 DVD or from the Windows desktop:

- ***If no operating system is installed on the PC, begin the installation by booting from the Windows 7 DVD.*** Using this method, the Upgrade option is not available and you are forced to do a Custom installation, also called a clean install.

- ***If an operating system is already installed on the PC, you can begin the installation from the Windows desktop or by booting from the Windows 7 DVD.*** Either way, you can perform a Custom installation. If you are using an upgrade license of Windows 7, setup will verify that a Windows OS is present, which qualifies you to use the upgrade license. This is the method to use when upgrading from Windows XP to Windows 7; you are required to perform a clean install even though setup verifies that Windows XP is present.
- ***If you are installing a 64-bit OS when a 32-bit OS is already installed or vice versa, you must begin the installation by booting from the DVD.*** Setup still allows you to use the less-expensive upgrade license even though you are performing a clean install because it is able to verify a Windows installation is present.

Follow these steps to begin the installation by booting from the Windows 7 DVD:

1. Insert the Windows 7 DVD in the DVD drive and start the system, booting directly from the DVD. If you have trouble booting from the disk, go into UEFI/BIOS setup and verify that your first boot device is the optical drive. On the first screen (see Figure 8-31), select your language and regional preferences and click **Next**.

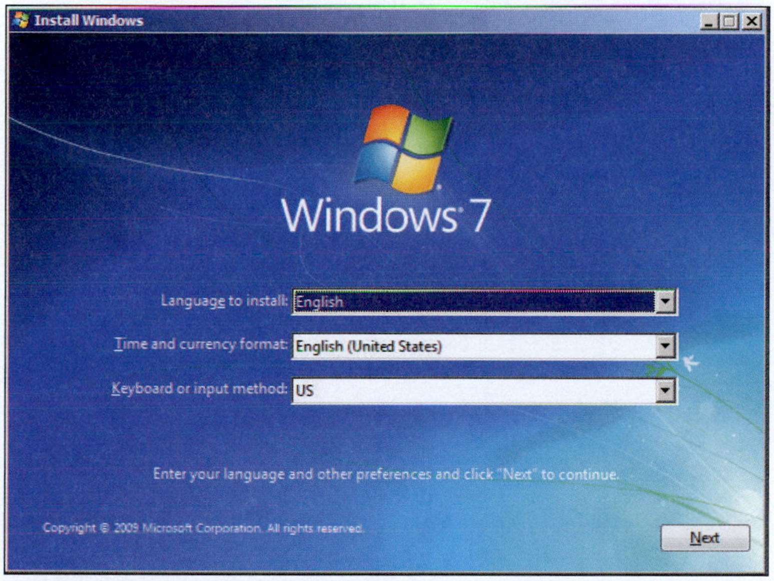

Figure 8-31 Select language, time, and keyboard options

2. The opening menu shown in Figure 8-32 appears. Click **Install now**.

Figure 8-32 Screen to begin the Windows 7 installation

3. On the next screen, accept the license agreement. On the next screen, select the type of installation you want. Choose **Custom (advanced)**.
4. On the next screen, select an existing partition on the hard drive to hold the installation or select unallocated space for setup to use to create a partition.
5. The installation is now free to move forward. At the end of this process, the window in Figure 8-33 appears asking for a local account username and computer name. The next screen asks for a password for the local account.

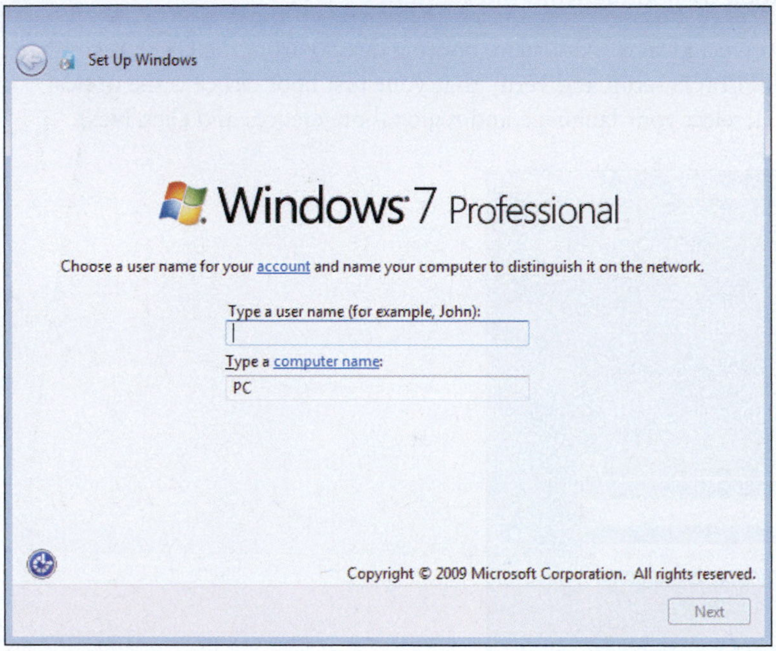

Figure 8-33 Choose a username and computer name

6. The installation now continues the same way as an upgrade installation. You are asked to enter the product key, Windows update settings, time and date settings, and network settings. Windows Update downloads and installs updates and you are asked to restart the system. After the restart, the logon screen appears. After you log in, the Windows 7 desktop loads and the installation is complete.

STEPS TO SET UP A WINDOWS MULTIBOOT

A+ 220-902 1.2, 1.6

You can install two or more operating systems on the same computer in a multiboot situation, for example, Windows 8.1, Windows 7, and Ubuntu Desktop. Each OS must have its own hard drive partition and each partition must have enough free space to hold the OS. Recall that Windows 8/7 needs *at least* 16 GB (32-bit) or 20 GB (64-bit) free space. Also know you cannot boot more than one OS at a time. To create a multiboot environment, always install Windows operating systems in order from older to newer.

Notes If an OS is already installed, you might need to shrink a partition to make room for a second partition to hold the next OS. For Windows, use Disk Management to shrink a partition, create a new partition, or format a partition. Windows requires the NTFS file system. How to use Disk Management is covered in the chapter, "Maintaining Windows."

Here are the steps to set up a dual-boot system with two operating systems (using Windows 7 and 8.1 as examples):

1. Install Windows 7. If you plan to install Windows 8.1 on the same hard drive as Windows 7, leave some unallocated space for the Windows 8.1 partition. To do that, refer back to Figure 8-28. (This Windows setup screen works the same in Windows 7 as in Windows 8.1.) On this screen, click **New**. You can then specify how much of the total unallocated space you want to use for the Windows 7 installation.
2. To install Windows 8.1, first make sure you have (a) a second partition with enough free space to hold the Windows 8.1 installation, (b) enough unallocated space on the drive to create a new partition while installing Windows 8.1, or (c) a second hard drive to hold the Windows 8.1 installation.
3. Start the Windows 8.1 installation by booting from the Windows 8.1 setup DVD or USB flash drive. The Windows Setup screen shown earlier in Figure 8-26 appears. Follow steps given earlier in this chapter to perform a clean install.
4. When you're asked where to install Windows, select the partition or unallocated space to hold the installation. For example, select **Unallocated Space** to hold the Windows 8.1 installation, as shown in Figure 8-34. Don't select the partition where the older operating system is already installed; doing so causes setup to install Windows 8.1 in place of the older OS. Continue on to complete the clean install.

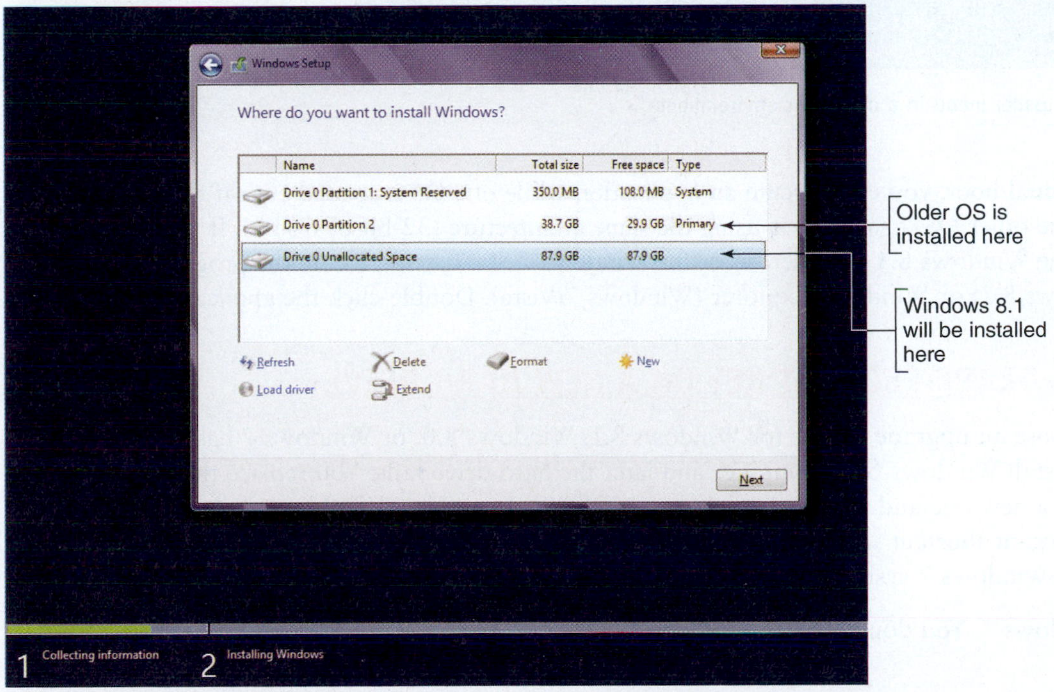

Figure 8-34 Select unallocated space or a partition other than the one used by the first OS installation

After the installation, when you boot with a dual boot, the boot loader menu automatically appears and asks you to select an operating system, as shown in Figure 8-35.

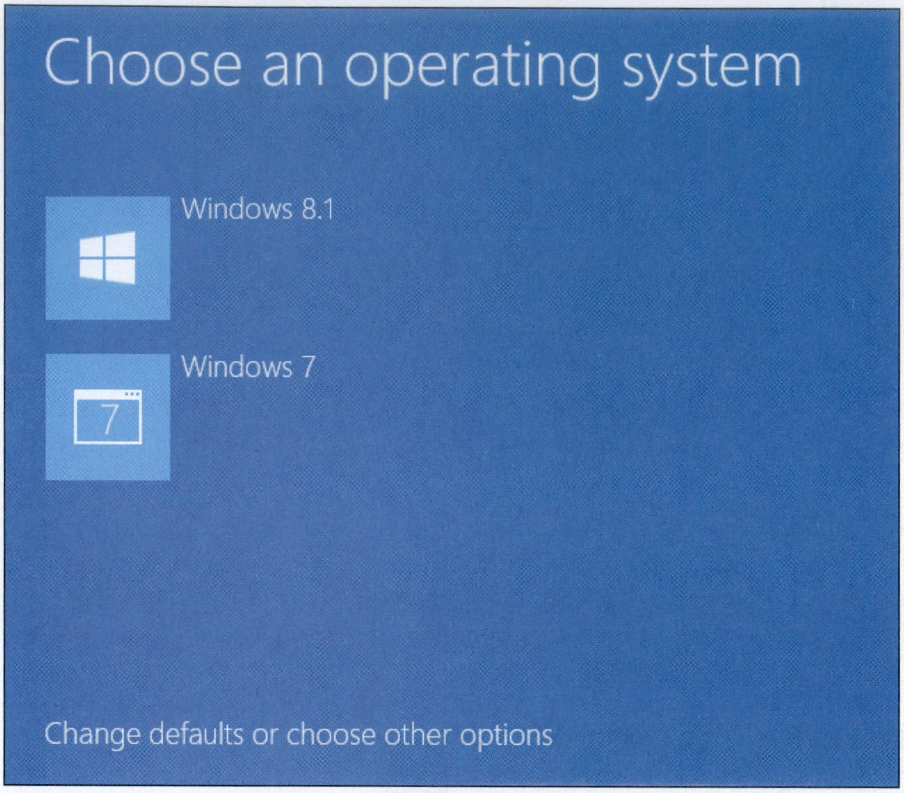

Figure 8-35 Boot loader menu in a dual-boot environment

When using a dual boot, you can execute an application while one OS is loaded even if the application is installed under the other OS if each OS is using the same architecture (32-bit or 64-bit). If the application is not listed on the Windows 8.1 Start screen or the Windows 7 Start menu, locate the program file in File Explorer (Windows 8.1) or Windows Explorer (Windows 7/Vista). Double-click the application to run it.

USING AN UPGRADE PRODUCT KEY ON A NEW HARD DRIVE

A+
220-902
1.2, 1.6

Suppose an upgrade license for Windows 8.1, Windows 8.0, or Windows 7 has been used to install Windows on a computer and later the hard drive fails. You replace the hard drive with a new one and now you need to reinstall Windows. You'll find lots of elegant and not so elegant shortcut solutions on the web, but here's the official Microsoft answer, using the example where a Windows 7 system was upgraded to Windows 8.0 and then updated to Windows 8.1:

1. Reinstall Windows 7. You don't need to enter the product key during the installation or activate Windows 7.
2. Reinstall Windows 8.0 using the upgrade product key and make sure Windows 8 is activated after the installation.
3. Download and install the free Windows 8.1 upgrade from the Windows Store.

In a situation where a Windows Vista system was upgraded to Windows 7, you can do the following so that you don't have to install Vista:

1. Install Windows 7 using your upgrade media. Don't enter the product key during the installation.
2. Reinstall Windows 7 as an upgrade. Windows setup should accept the upgrade product key during the installation and Windows should automatically activate.

APPLYING | CONCEPTS CONVERT AN MBR DRIVE TO GPT

Suppose you want to use a 64-bit version of Windows and UEFI firmware mode, thus requiring you to use the GPT partitioning system. However, your hard drive has already been partitioned with the MBR system. The error won't show up until you get to the step in the installation where you select the partition or unallocated space on the hard drive to hold the Windows installation (see Figure 8-36).

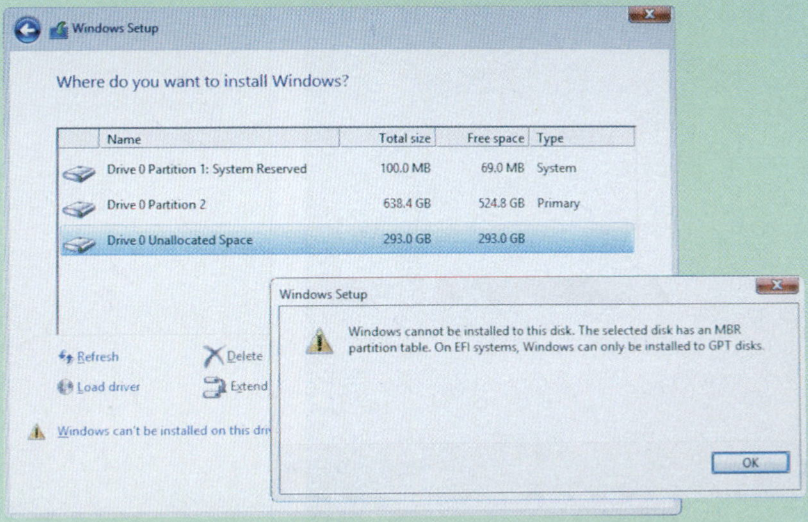

Figure 8-36 Error appears when Windows in UEFI mode requires the GPT partitioning system

Follow these steps to use the **diskpart** command to wipe the partition system off the hard drive. All data on the drive will be destroyed and then you can convert the drive to GPT:

1. Restart the computer from the Windows setup DVD and select your language and regional preferences. Click **Next**. On the next screen, select **Repair your computer** (see Figure 8-37).

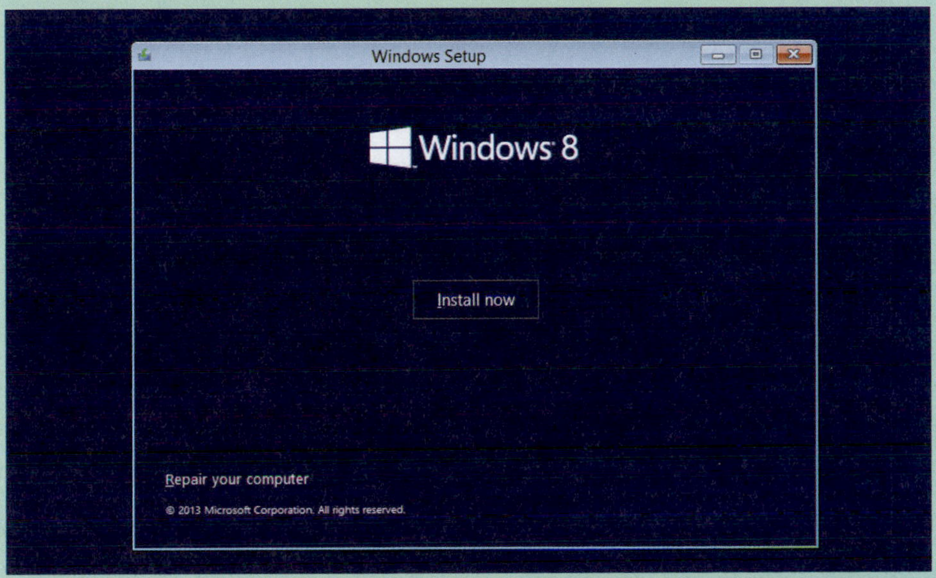

Figure 8-37 Use the Windows setup DVD to repair your computer and launch a command prompt

(continues)

2. On the next screen, click **Troubleshoot**. On the Troubleshoot screen, click **Advanced options**. On the Advanced options screen, click **Command Prompt**. A command prompt window appears. Type **diskpart** and press **Enter**. The DISKPART> prompt appears, as shown in Figure 8-38.

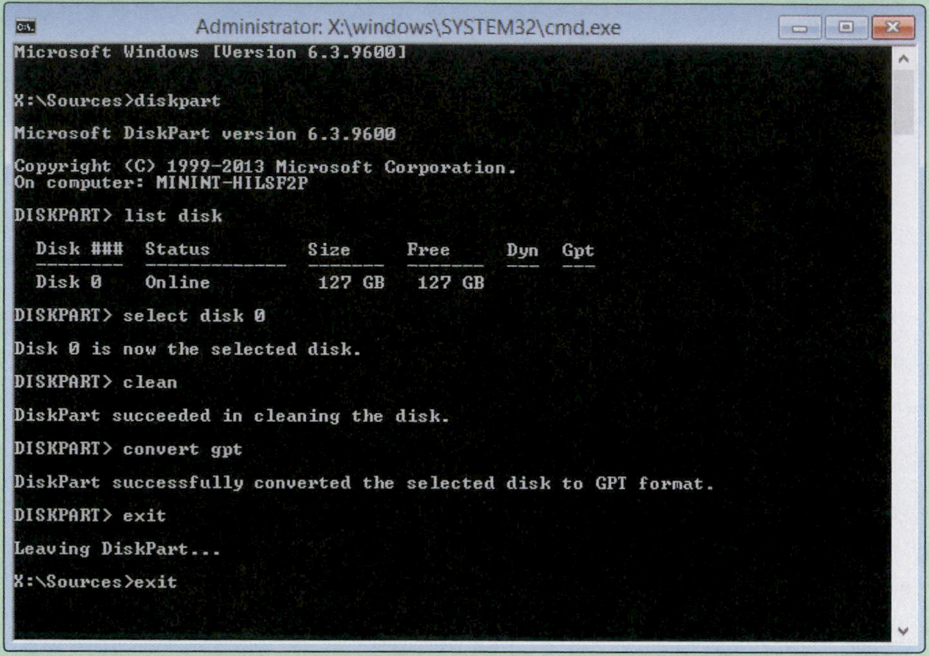

Figure 8-38 The command prompt window with diskpart running

3. At the DISKPART> prompt, use these commands to select the hard drive, clean it, and convert it to a GPT drive:

Command	Description
`list disk`	List the hard drives installed. If you have more than one hard drive, use the size of the drive to determine which one you want to clean. Most likely, you will have one hard drive identified as Disk 0.
`select disk 0`	Make Disk 0 the selected hard drive.
`clean`	Clean the partition table and all partitions from the drive.
`convert gpt`	Convert the partitioning system to GPT.
`exit`	Exit the diskpart utility.

4. Enter one more **exit** command to close the command prompt window. On the setup screen that appears, click **Turn off your PC**.

5. You can now restart the system and install Windows in UEFI mode, which uses the GPT partitioning system.

Hands-On Project 8-3 Use the Internet for Problem Solving

Access the **support.microsoft.com** website for Windows 8.1 or Windows 7 support. Print one article from the Knowledge Base that addresses a problem when installing Windows 8.1 or Windows 7. In your own words, write a paragraph describing the problem and a paragraph explaining the solution. If you don't understand the problem or the solution from this article, do a search online for additional information so that you can give a well-rounded description of both the problem and the solution.

Hands-On Project 8-4 Install Windows

Follow the instructions in the chapter to install Windows 8.1 or Windows 7 as either an upgrade or clean install. Write down each decision you had to make as you performed the installation. If you get any error messages during the installation, write them down and list the steps you took to recover from the error. How long did the installation take? If you have a hypervisor (virtual machine software) installed on your computer, you can do this project in a VM.

Hands-On Project 8-5 Install Windows 8.1 in a VM

Earlier in the chapter, in Hands-On Project 8-2, you installed VirtualBox on your computer and created a VM. Use this VM to install a 32-bit version of Windows 8.1. You can use this VM installation of Windows 8.1 in projects later in the text.

To start this virtual machine and install an OS in it, first make sure you have the correct ISO file available to the host computer. Windows is best installed in a VM by using an ISO image.

Click on the VM you created earlier, then click **Start**. VirtualBox asks for the location of the startup disk (see Figure 8-39). Select the correct location then click **Start**. The VM boots up, finds the ISO file, and starts the OS installation, as shown in Figure 8-40.

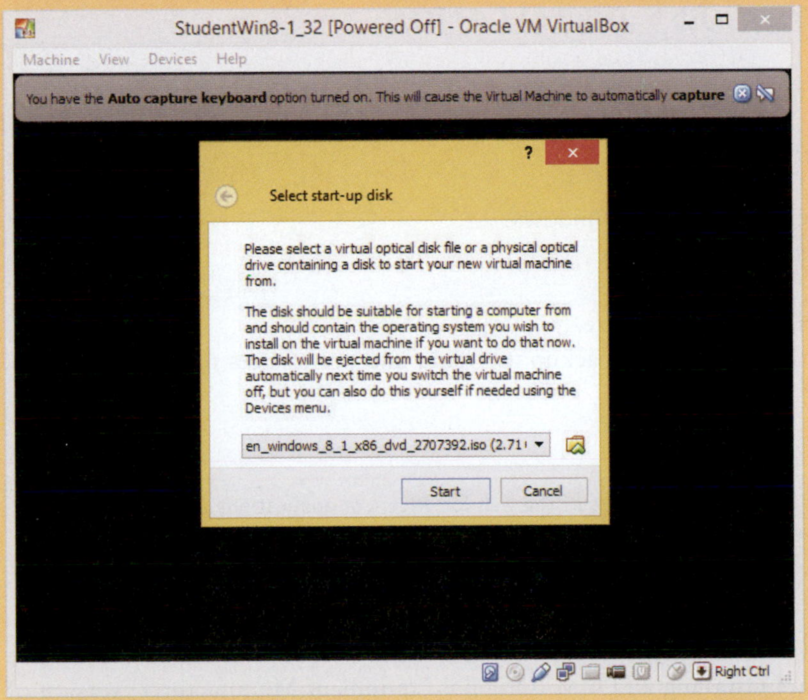

Source: VirtualBox (Oracle)

Figure 8-39 Locate the correct ISO file

(continues)

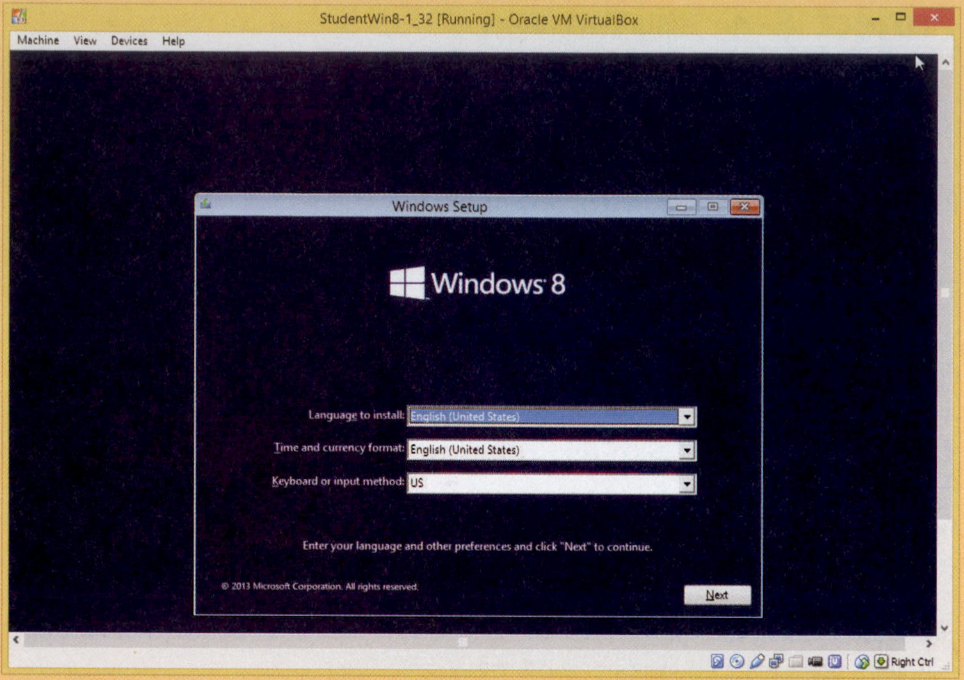

Source: VirtualBox (Oracle)

Figure 8-40 A new VM is installing Windows 8.1

WHAT TO DO AFTER A WINDOWS INSTALLATION

A+ 220-902 1.1, 1.2, 1.4, 1.5, 4.1

After you have installed Windows, you need to do the following:

- Verify you have network access.
- Activate Windows.
- Install updates and service packs for Windows.
- Verify automatic updates are set as you want them.
- Install hardware.
- Install applications, including anti-malware software.
- Set up user accounts and transfer or restore from backup user data and preferences to the new system.
- Turn Windows features on or off.

Caution To protect your computer from malware, don't surf the web for drivers or applications until you have installed Windows updates and service packs and also installed and configured anti-malware software.

In addition, if you are installing Windows on a laptop, you will want to use Control Panel to configure power-management settings. If you are installing an OEM (Original Equipment Manufacturer) version of Windows 7, look for a sticker on the outside of the DVD case. This sticker contains the product key and is called the Certificate of Authenticity. Put the sticker on the bottom of a laptop or the side or rear of a desktop computer (see Figure 8-41). Windows 8 doesn't provide the sticker.

Figure 8-41 Paste the Windows 7 Certificate of Authenticity sticker on a new desktop

Now let's look at the details of the items in the preceding list.

VERIFY YOU HAVE NETWORK ACCESS

A+
220-902
1.2, 1.5

To make a wired connection to a network when using Windows, simply plug in the network cable and Windows does the rest. To create a wireless connection, follow the steps you learned in the chapter, "Survey of Windows Features and Support Tools."

To verify you have access to the local network and to the Internet, do the following:

1. Open File Explorer or Windows Explorer and verify you can see other computers on the network (see Figure 8-42). Try to drill down to see shared resources on these computers.

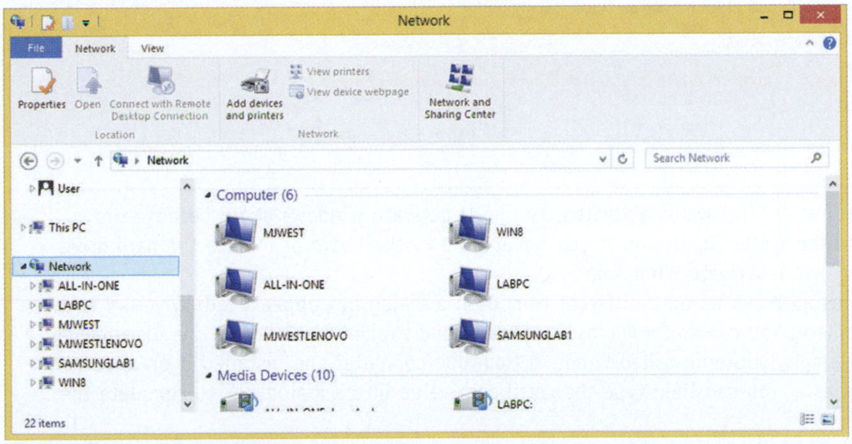

Figure 8-42 Use File Explorer to access resources on your network

2. To verify you have Internet access, open Internet Explorer and try to navigate to a couple of websites.

If a problem arises, consider that the problem might be that you need to install the drivers for the motherboard, including the drivers for the onboard network port. Also, the IP address, wireless network, or network security settings might be wrong. How to configure network settings and troubleshoot network connections are covered later in the chapter, "Connecting To and Setting Up a Network."

ACTIVATE WINDOWS

A+
220-902
1.2, 1.5

In order to make sure a valid Windows license has been purchased for each installation of Windows, Microsoft requires product activation. Windows 8.1 setup requires you enter a product key during the installation and, if the computer is connected to the Internet, Windows will automatically activate on the next restart after the installation completes. Recall from earlier in the chapter, you have more control over when to activate Windows 7. For Windows 7, you're not required to enter the product key during installation, and you can activate Windows 7 any time within the 30-day grace period.

To view the activation status, go to the System window. Figure 8-43 shows the window for one system that is not activated. To activate, make sure you're connected to the Internet and click **Activate Windows**. On the next screen, if necessary, you can enter a new product key and then activate Windows.

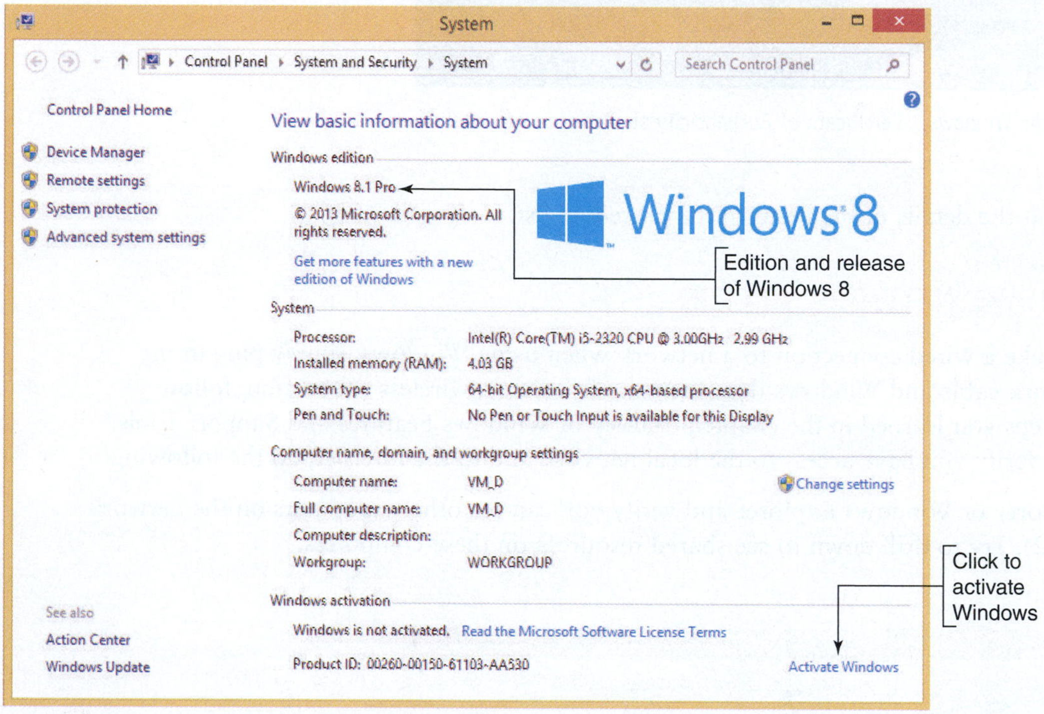

Figure 8-43 System window

Notes If you change the product key after Windows is activated, you must activate Windows again because the activation is tied to the product key and the system hardware. If you replace the motherboard or replace the hard drive and memory at the same time, you must also reactivate Windows.

If you use the same product key to install Windows on a different computer, a dialog box appears telling you of the suspected violation of the license agreement. You can call a Microsoft operator and explain what caused the discrepancy. If your explanation is reasonable (for example, you uninstalled Windows from one computer and installed it on another), the operator can issue you a valid certificate. You can then type the certificate value into a dialog box to complete the boot process.

INSTALL WINDOWS UPDATES AND SERVICE PACKS

A+
220-902
1.1, 1.2,
1.5

The Microsoft website offers patches, fixes, and updates for known problems and has an extensive knowledge base documenting problems and their solutions. It's important to keep these updates current on your system to fix known problems and plug up security holes that might allow malware in. Be sure to install updates before you attempt to install software or hardware.

To view and manage Windows update settings, open the **System** window and click **Windows Update** in the left pane (refer back to Figure 8-43). In the Windows Update window (see Figure 8-44), you can view updates and install them. Before you move on, make sure all important updates are installed. To check for new updates, click **Check for updates** in the left pane. Windows selects the updates in the order the system can receive them, and will not necessarily list all the updates you need on the first pass. Keep installing important updates and checking for more updates until no more updates are available. You might need to restart the system after certain updates are installed.

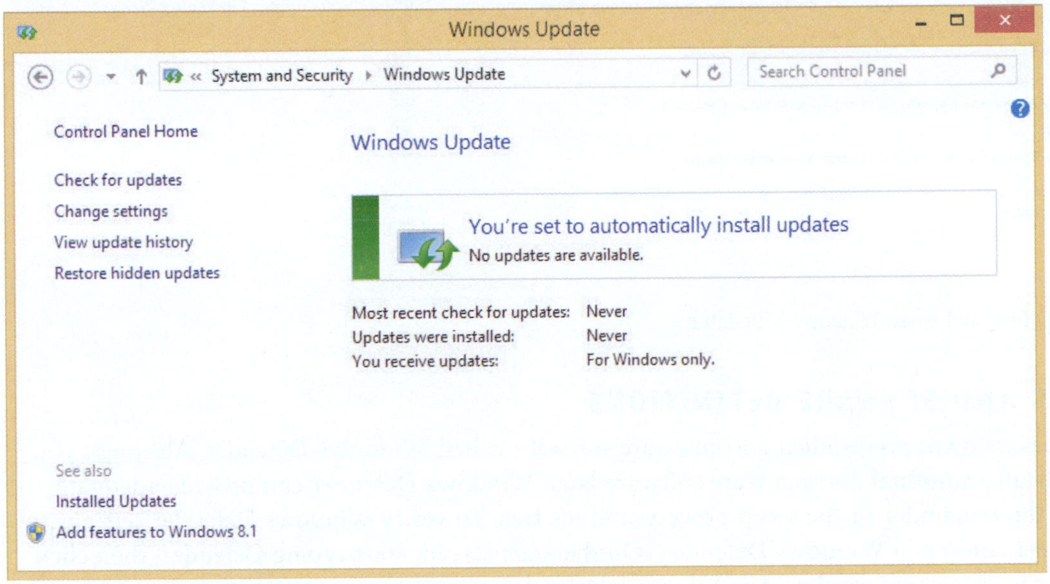

Figure 8-44 View and manage Windows updates

If Windows 8.0 is installed, you can update it to Windows 8.1 for free. Open the Windows Store app on the Start screen, select the Windows 8.1 update, and follow directions on screen to download and install it.

OS Differences Recall that Windows 7 releases major updates as a **service pack**. On a Windows 7 system, if you see a service pack listed in the updates, install all the updates listed above it. Then install the service pack as the only update to install. It takes about 30 minutes and a reboot to download and install a service pack. Only the latest service pack for an OS will install because the latest service pack includes all the content from previous service packs.

Hands-On Project 8-6 Update Windows

On a Windows 8.1 system connected to the Internet, open the System window and click **Windows Update**. Windows Update searches the Microsoft website and recommends Windows updates. Print the webpage showing a list of recommended updates. For a lab computer, don't perform the updates unless you have your instructor's permission.

CONFIGURE AUTOMATIC UPDATES

Next, you need to make sure the update settings are as you want them. In the Windows Update window, click **Change settings**. In the Change settings window (see Figure 8-45), you can decide when and how updates are installed. The recommended setting is to allow Windows to automatically download and install updates daily. However, if you are not always connected to the Internet, your connection is very slow, or you want more control over which updates are installed, you might want to manage the updates differently. To change how and when updates are installed or to decide whether Windows can wake up your computer to perform updates, click **Updates will be automatically installed during the maintenance window**.

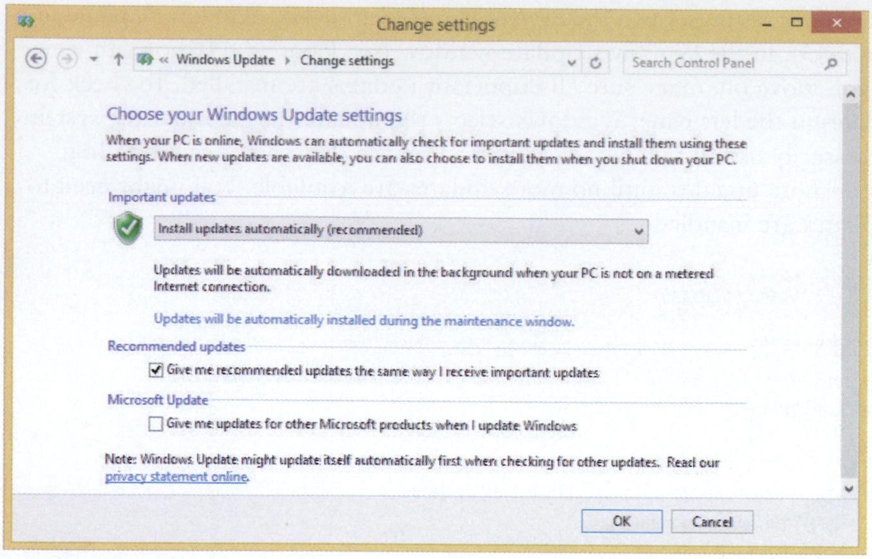

Figure 8-45 Manage how and when Windows is updated

UPDATE VIRUS AND SPYWARE DEFINITIONS

Windows 8 includes its own, preinstalled anti-malware software called Windows Defender. Although you might decide to install additional anti-malware software later, Windows Defender can provide adequate protection during the remainder of the setup process, and it's free. To verify Windows Defender settings, go to the Start screen and open Windows Defender. (On the Start screen, start typing **Defender**, then click **Windows Defender** in the search results.) The Windows Defender window appears on the desktop. Click the **Update** tab, then click **Update**.

After Defender has updated, click the **Settings** tab, and if necessary click **Real-time protection** in the menu on the left. Make sure the **Turn on real-time protection (recommended)** check box is checked. If not, check the box and click **Save changes**.

OS Differences Windows 7 comes with Windows Defender installed, but Defender only protects against spyware and not other types of malware. To install anti-malware software in Windows 7, you can go to the Microsoft website and download and install Microsoft Security Essentials The link is *windows.microsoft.com/en-us/windows/security-essentials-download*.

INSTALL HARDWARE

A+ 220-902 1.2, 1.4, 1.5, 4.1

You're now ready to install the hardware devices that were not automatically installed during the Windows installation. As you install each device, reboot and verify the software or device is working before you move on to the next item. Most likely, you will need to do the following:

- *Install the drivers for the motherboard.* If you were not able to connect to the network earlier in the installation process, it might be because the drivers for the network port on the motherboard are not installed. Installing the motherboard drivers can solve the problem. These drivers might come on a CD bundled with the motherboard, or you can use another computer to download them from the motherboard manufacturer's website. To start the installation, double-click a setup program on the CD or a program that was previously downloaded from the web.
- *Even though Windows has embedded video drivers, install the drivers that came with the video card so that you can use all the features the card offers.* These drivers are on disc or downloaded from the video card manufacturer's website.

- ***Install the printer.*** For a network printer, run the setup program that came with the printer and this program will find and install the printer on the network. Alternately, open Control Panel in Classic view and open the Devices and Printers window. Then click **Add a printer** and follow the directions on screen. To install a local USB printer, all you have to do is plug in the USB printer, and Windows will install the printer automatically.
- ***For other hardware devices, always read and follow the manufacturer's directions for the installation.*** Sometimes you are directed to install the drivers before you connect the device, and sometimes you will first need to connect the device.

If a problem occurs while Windows is installing a device, it automatically launches the Action Center to help find a solution. For example, Figure 8-46 shows the error message window that appeared when a USB keyboard and USB printer were connected to a computer following a Windows 7 installation.

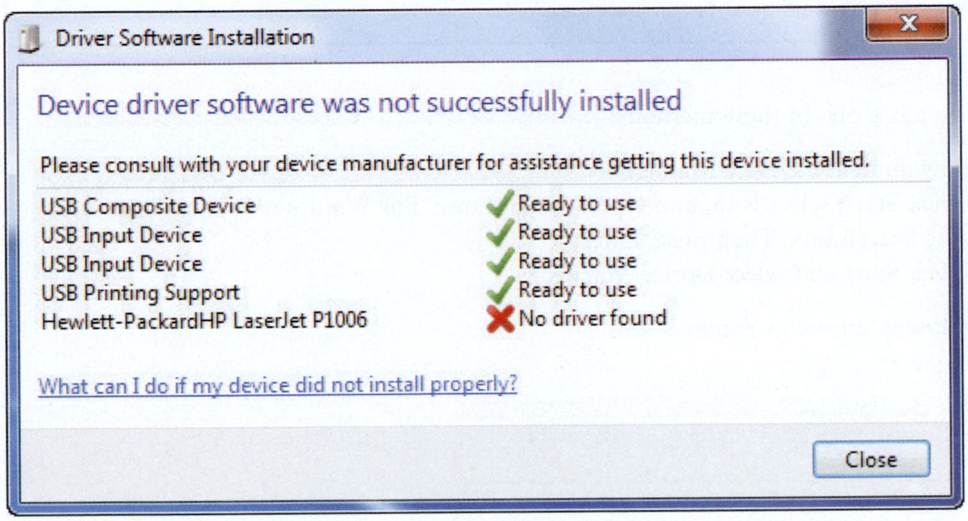

Figure 8-46 Windows 7 reports a problem with a driver for a USB printer

Immediately after this first window appeared, the window in Figure 8-47 appeared, which is provided by the Action Center. When the user clicked *Click to download and install the new driver from the Hewlett-Packard Company website*, the driver was immediately downloaded and installed with no errors.

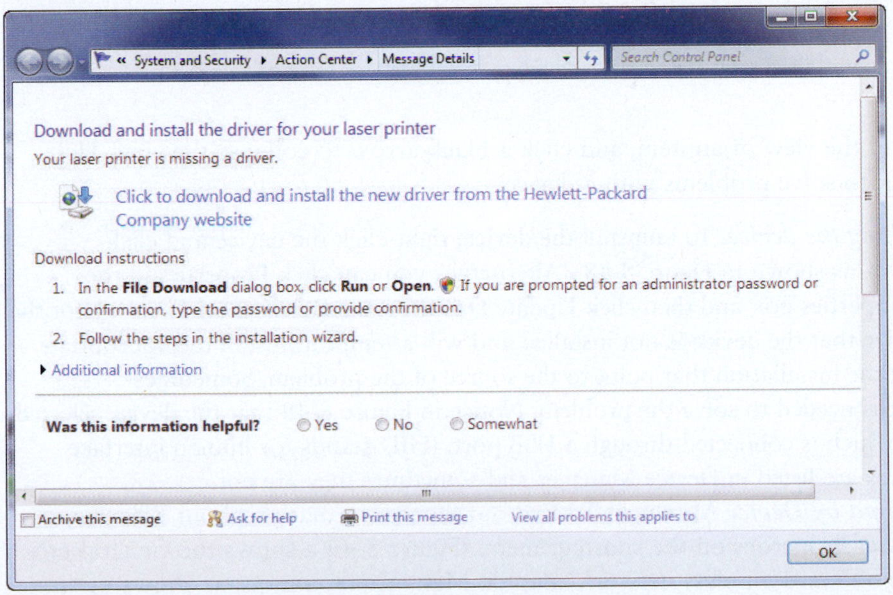

Figure 8-47 Windows offers to find the missing USB printer driver

Recall that you can also open the Action Center at any time to see a list of problems and solutions. If the problem is still not resolved after following the solutions offered by the Action Center, turn to Device Manager.

USE DEVICE MANAGER

Device Manager (its program file is named devmgmt.msc) is your primary Windows tool for managing hardware. It lists all installed hardware devices and the drivers they use. Using Device Manager, you can disable or enable a device, update its drivers, uninstall a device, and undo a driver update (called a driver rollback).

> ★ **A+ Exam Tip** The A+ 220-902 exam expects you to know in what scenarios it is appropriate to use Device Manager. You also need to know how to use the utility and how to evaluate its results.

To access Device Manager, use one of these methods:

- Open the System window and click **Device Manager**.
- For Windows 8, right-click **Start**, select **Run**, and type **devmgmt.msc**. For Windows 7, click **Start** and type **Devmgmt.msc** in the Search box. Then press **Enter**.
- For Windows 8, right-click **Start** and select **Device Manager**.

A Device Manager window is shown in Figure 8-48.

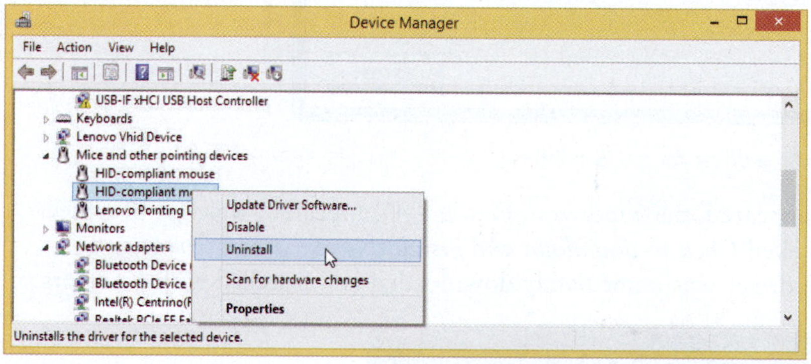

Figure 8-48 Use Device Manager to uninstall, disable, or enable a device

Click a white arrow to expand the view of an item, and click a black arrow to collapse the view. Here are ways to use Device Manager to solve problems with a device:

- ***Try uninstalling and reinstalling the device.*** To uninstall the device, right-click the device and click **Uninstall** on the shortcut menu, as shown in Figure 8-48. (Alternately, you can click **Properties** in the shortcut menu to open the Properties box and then click **Update Driver** on the Driver tab.) Then reboot the system. Windows will recognize that the device is not installed and will attempt to install the appropriate driver. Look for issues during the installation that point to the source of the problem. Sometimes reinstalling a device is all that is needed to solve the problem. Notice in Figure 8-48 that the device selected is an HID-compliant mouse, which is connected through a USB port. (HID stands for human interface device.) Sometimes USB devices are listed in Device Manager and sometimes they are not.
- ***Look for error messages offered by Device Manager.*** To find out more information about a device, right-click the device and select **Properties** on the shortcut menu. Figure 8-49 a shows the General tab of the Properties box for the onboard wireless network adapter. Many times, a message shows up in this box reporting the source of the problem and suggesting a solution.

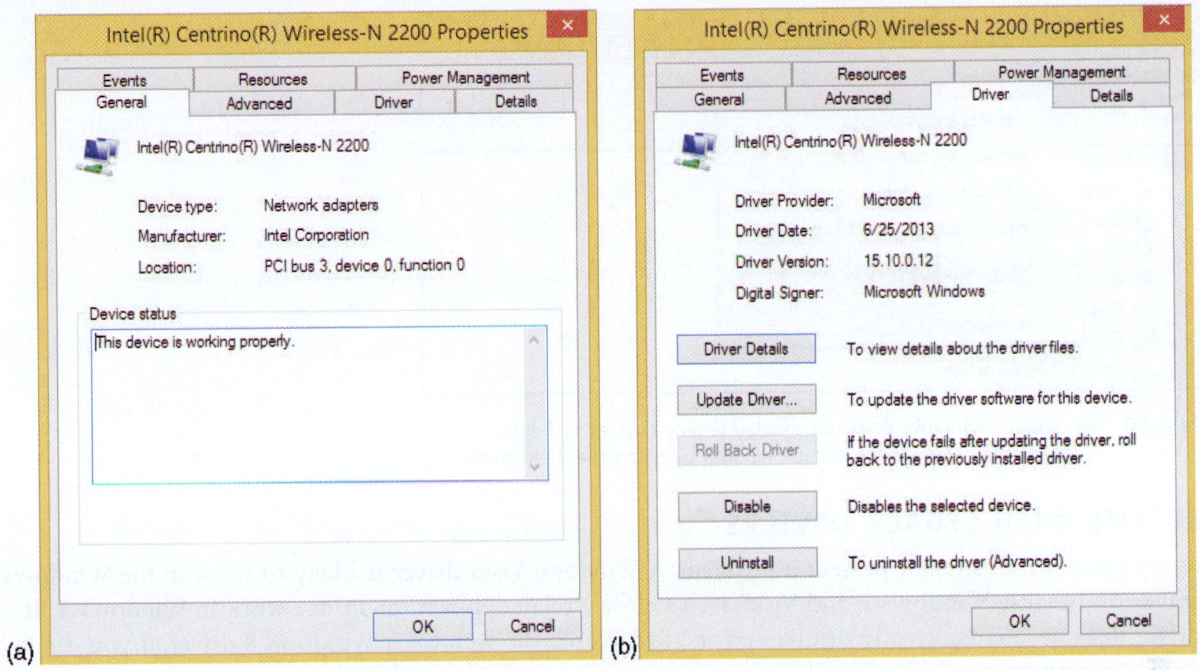

Figure 8-49 (a) Use the device Properties box to solve problems with device drivers, and (b) update device drivers.

- ***Update the drivers.*** Click the **Driver** tab (see Figure 8-49b) to update the drivers and roll back (undo) a driver update.

APPLYING CONCEPTS UPDATE DEVICE DRIVERS

Follow these steps to use Device Manager to update device drivers:

1. For best results, locate and download the latest driver files from the manufacturer's website to your hard drive. Be sure to use 64-bit drivers for a 64-bit OS and 32-bit drivers for a 32-bit OS. If possible, use Windows 8.1 drivers for Windows 8.1 and Windows 7 drivers for Windows 7.
2. Using Device Manager, right-click the device and select **Properties** from the shortcut menu. The Properties window for that device appears. Select the **Driver** tab and click **Update Driver**. The Update Driver Software box opens.
3. To search the Internet for drivers, click **Search automatically for updated driver software**. If you have already downloaded drivers to your PC, click **Browse my computer for driver software**, and point to the downloaded files. Note that Windows is looking for an .inf file to identify the drivers. Continue to follow the directions on screen to complete the installation.

Notes By default, Device Manager hides legacy devices that are not Plug and Play. To view installed legacy devices, click the **View** menu of Device Manager, and check **Show hidden devices** (see Figure 8-50).

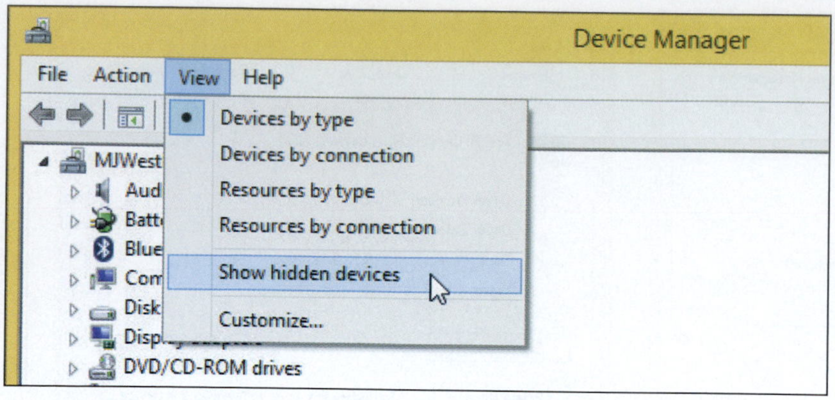

Figure 8-50 By default, Windows does not display legacy devices in Device Manager; you show these hidden devices by using the View menu

PROBLEMS WITH LEGACY DEVICES

Older hardware devices might present a problem. A Windows Vista driver is likely to work in the Windows 7 installation because Windows 7 and Vista are so closely related, but it might not work in Windows 8. If the driver does not load correctly or gives errors, first search the web for a Windows 8 driver. If you don't find one, try running the driver installation program in compatibility mode, which is explained next.

APPLYING | CONCEPTS TROUBLESHOOT DEVICE DRIVERS

In the example that follows, the installation program for an older network printer worked under Windows 7 but did not load correctly on Windows 8.1. Follow these steps to use compatibility mode with the driver installation program:

1. Using File Explorer, locate the program file with an .exe file extension for the driver installation program. Right-click the program file and select **Troubleshoot compatibility** from the shortcut menu (see Figure 8-51). The Program Compatibility utility launches.

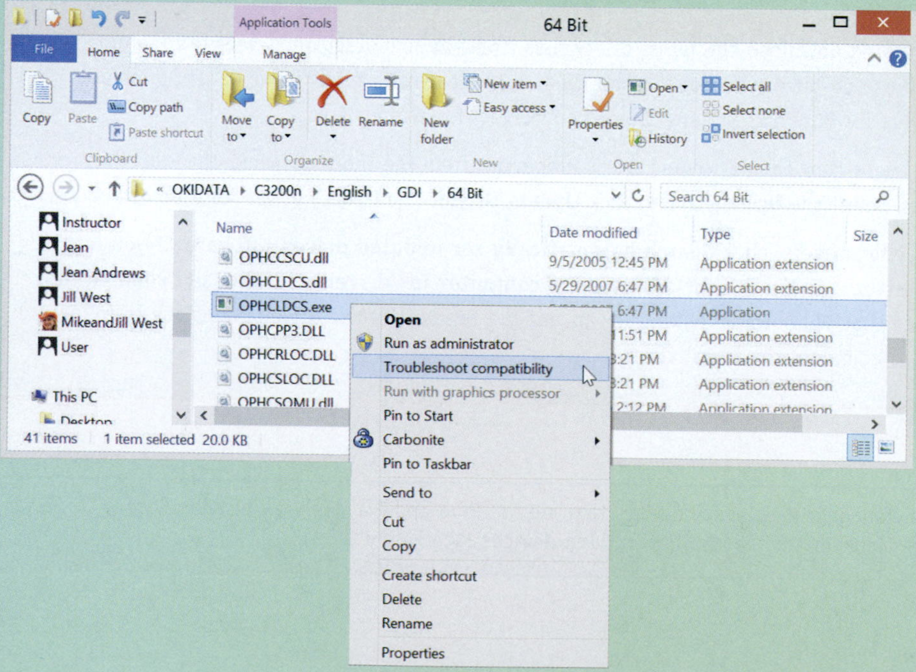

Figure 8-51 Run the Program Compatibility utility from the shortcut menu of the program that is giving a problem

2. On the first screen of the troubleshooter utility, select **Troubleshoot program** (see Figure 8-52).

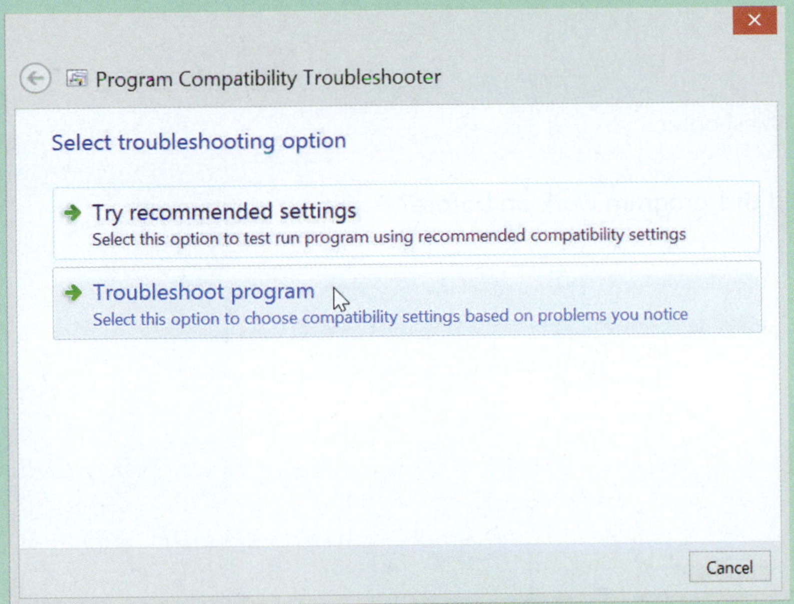

Figure 8-52 Troubleshoot the problem with the legacy installation program

3. On the next screen, check the problems that apply (see Figure 8-53). In the example, the driver worked fine in Windows 7, so select **The program worked in earlier versions of Windows but won't install or run now**. Click **Next**.

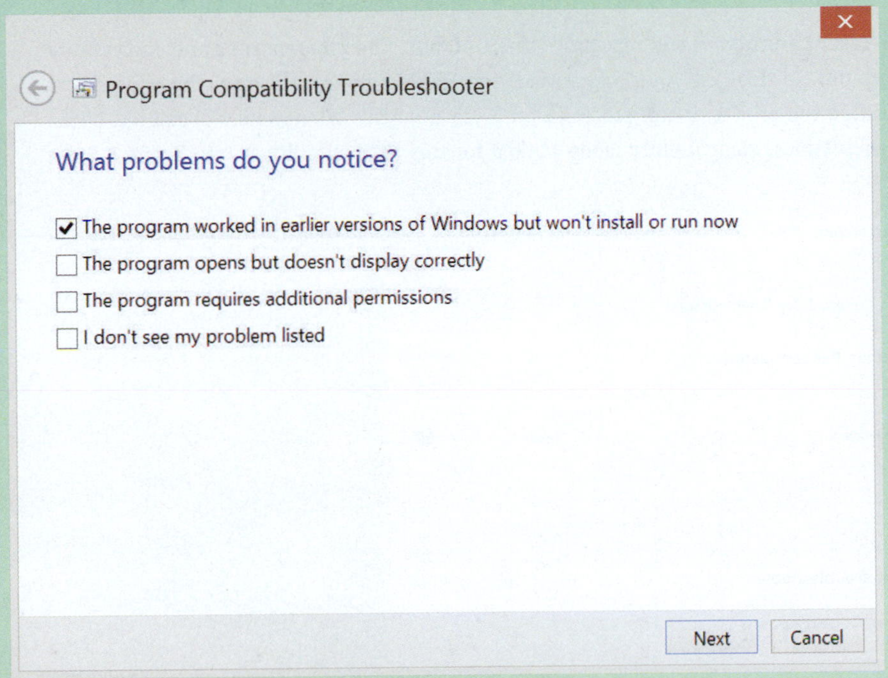

Figure 8-53 Select all the problems that apply

(continues)

4. On the next screen, the troubleshooter asks for the OS with which the program worked (see Figure 8-54). For this example, you would select **Windows 7** and click **Next**.

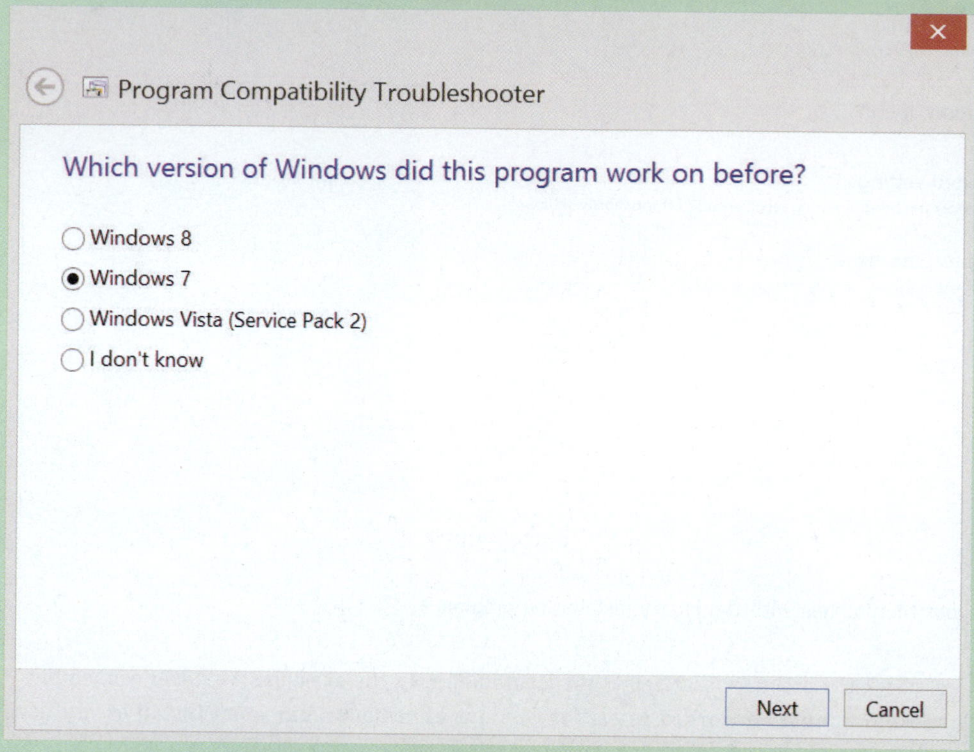

Figure 8-54 Select the operating system with which the program worked

5. On the next screen, click **Test the program** and respond to the UAC box. The program runs and successfully fixes the drivers for the printer. In this case, checking Devices and Printers in Control Panel shows no errors with the printer. Upon testing the printer, it can process a print job from this Windows 8.1 computer. Click **Next** and save the program settings. Compatibility mode worked for this particular driver (see Figure 8-55).

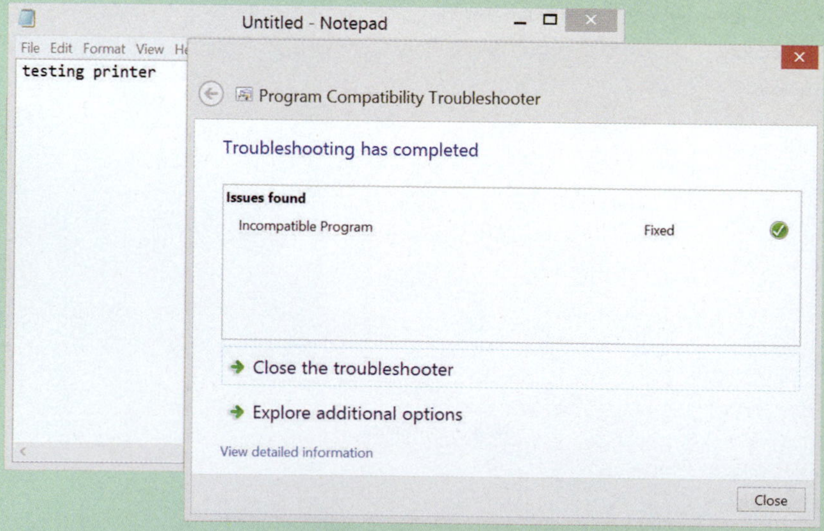

Figure 8-55 Windows successfully fixed the incompatible printer program

INSTALL APPLICATIONS

A+
220-902
1.2, 1.5

Applications can be installed in Windows 8/7 from CD or DVD, from a downloaded application file, directly from the web, or, for Windows 8, from the Windows Store.

To install applications from a disc, insert the setup CD or DVD, and follow the directions on screen to launch the installation routine. For software downloaded from the Internet, open File Explorer or Windows Explorer and double-click the program filename to begin the installation. When installing a program directly from the web, click the link on the website to install the software and follow directions on screen. To install apps in the Windows 8 interface, use the Store app on the Start screen. (Later in the text, you'll learn what to do when an installation fails.) After an application is installed, you might also need to install any updates available for the application on the manufacturer's website.

If you need to uninstall an application, open **Control Panel** and click **Programs and Features**. (For Windows 8, you can press **Win+X** and click **Programs and Features**.) The Programs and Features window appears, listing the programs installed on this computer where you can uninstall, change, or repair these programs. Select a program from the list. Based on the software, the buttons at the top of the list will change. For example, in Figure 8-56, the Camtasia Studio 8 software offers the option to Uninstall, Change, or Repair the software.

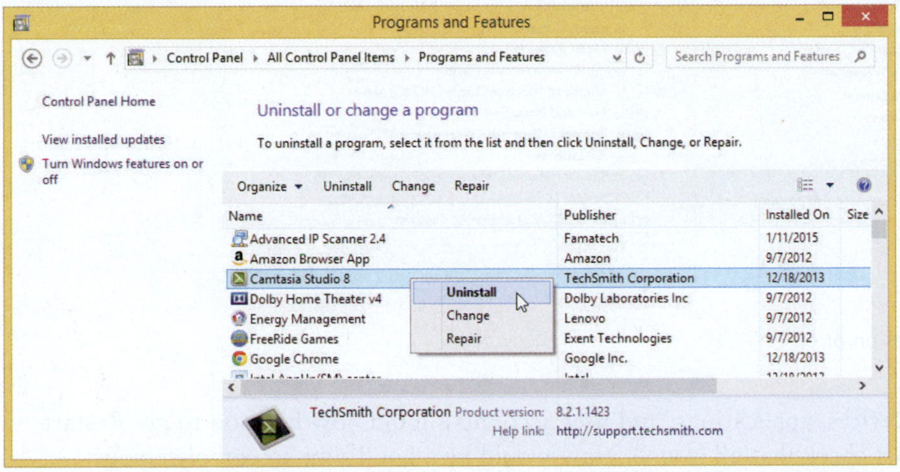

Figure 8-56 Select a program from the list to view your options to manage the software

Recall that you can also uninstall a Windows 8 app by using the Start screen or Apps screen. Right-click the app tile and then click **Uninstall** in the status bar that appears at the bottom of the screen.

SET UP USER ACCOUNTS AND TRANSFER USER DATA

A+
220-902
1.1, 1.2,
1.5

Remember that you can use the Windows 8 Settings charm or the Windows 7 User Accounts applet in Control Panel to create user accounts. In addition, you can use the Computer Management console in Windows 8/7 to create accounts. After you have created user accounts in a new installation of Windows, you might want to transfer user data and settings from another computer to this one.

For individuals or small organizations, use Windows Easy Transfer in Windows 8/7/Vista to copy user data and settings from one computer to another. The utility is easy to use and you can find directions in Windows Help and Support. For large corporations that use a Windows domain, a more advanced tool is required, the User State Migration Tool (USMT). This tool is discussed later in this chapter.

Notes After moving user data and settings from one computer to another, the best practice is to leave the user data and settings on the original computer untouched for at least two months. This practice gives the user plenty of time to make sure everything has been moved over.

TURN WINDOWS FEATURES ON OR OFF

A+
220-902
1.2, 1.5

You can save on system resources by turning off Windows 8/7 features you will not use, and you might need to turn on some features that are, by default, turned off. To control Windows features, in the left pane of the Programs and Features window, click **Turn Windows features on or off** (refer to Figure 8-56). The Windows Features box opens (see Figure 8-57). Check or uncheck the features you want or don't want and then click **OK**. Sometimes a restart is necessary for the changes to take effect.

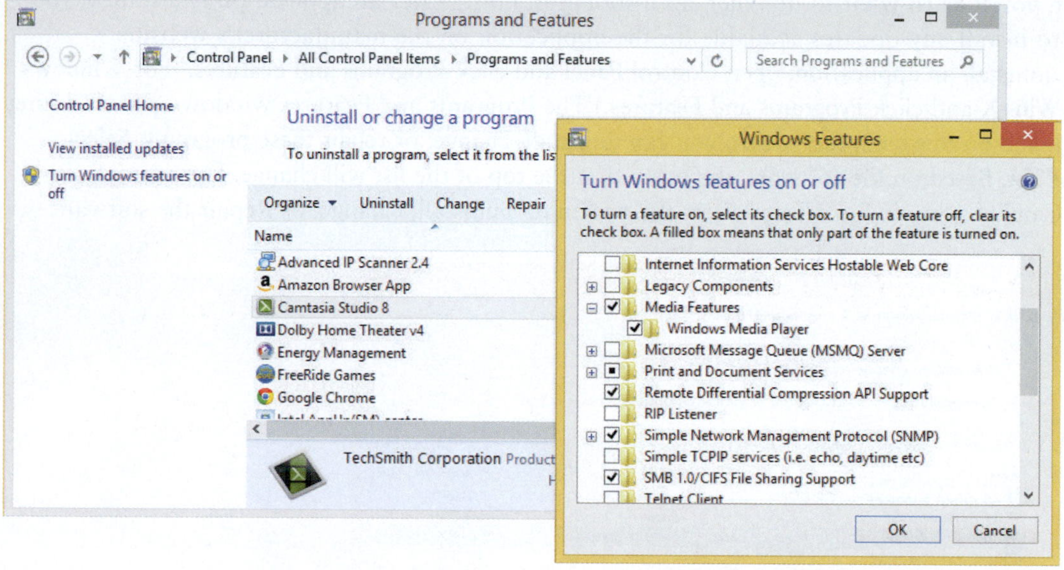

Figure 8-57 Turn Windows features on or off

The Windows installation, devices, applications, and user accounts should now be good to go. Restart the computer and make one last check that all is well. Now would be a good time to complete your documentation and make a backup of the entire Windows volume in the event of a hard drive failure or corrupted installation. How to make backups is covered in the chapter, "Maintaining Windows."

Hands-On | Project 8-7 Create a Documentation Form

Create a document that technicians can use when installing Windows and performing all the chores mentioned in the chapter that need doing before and after the installation. The document needs a checklist of what to do before the installation and a checklist of what to do after the installation. It also needs a place to record decisions made during the installation, the applications and hardware devices installed, user accounts created, and any other important information that might be useful for future maintenance or troubleshooting. Don't forget to include a way to identify the computer, the name of the technician doing the work, and when the work was done.

SPECIAL CONCERNS WHEN WORKING IN A LARGE ENTERPRISE

A+
220-902
1.1, 1.2,
1.4

Working as an IT support technician in a large corporate environment is different from working as an IT support technician for a small company or with individuals. In this part of the chapter, you learn how Windows is installed on computers in an enterprise and a little about providing ongoing technical support for Windows in these organizations.

DEPLOYMENT STRATEGIES FOR WINDOWS

A+
220-902
1.1, 1.2,
1.4

Earlier in the chapter, you learned how to install Windows using a setup DVD, USB flash drive, or files downloaded from the Microsoft website. You perform the installation while sitting at the computer, responding to each query made by the setup program. Then you must configure Windows and install device drivers and applications. If, however, you were responsible for installing Windows on several hundred computers in a large corporation, you might want a less time-consuming method to perform the installations. These methods are called deployment strategies. A deployment strategy is a procedure to install Windows, device drivers, and applications on a computer and can include the process to transfer user settings, application settings, and user data files from an old installation to the new installation.

Microsoft suggests four deployment strategies; the one chosen depends on the number of computers to be deployed and determines the amount of time you must sit in front of an individual computer as Windows is installed (this time is called the touch time). As an IT support technician in a large corporation, most likely you would not be involved in choosing or setting up the deployment strategy. But you need to be aware of the different strategies so that you have a general idea of what will be expected of you when you are asked to provide desk-side or help-desk support as Windows is being deployed in your organization.

The four deployment strategies are discussed next.

8

HIGH-TOUCH WITH RETAIL MEDIA (RECOMMENDED FOR FEWER THAN 100 COMPUTERS)

The high-touch with retail media strategy is the strategy used in the installations described earlier in the chapter. All the work is done by a technician sitting at the computer. To save time doing multiple installations, you can copy the Windows setup files to a file server on the network and share the folder. Then at each computer, you can execute the setup program on the server to perform a clean install or upgrade of the OS. A server used in this way is called a distribution server. Except for upgrade installations, applications must be manually installed after the OS is installed.

To transfer user settings, application settings, and user data files to a new installation (a process called migrating), you can use Windows Easy Transfer (a manual process that is easy to use) or the User State Migration Tool (more automated and more difficult to set up and use). Windows Easy Transfer is part of Windows 8/7/Vista. The User State Migration Tool (USMT) is a command-line tool that works only when the computer is a member of a Windows domain. USMT is included in the Windows Assessment and Deployment Kit (ADK) for Windows 8, and in the Windows Automated Installation Kit (AIK) for Windows 7. Both can be downloaded from the Microsoft website, and both contain a group of tools used to deploy Windows in a large organization.

HIGH-TOUCH WITH STANDARD IMAGE (RECOMMENDED FOR 100 TO 200 COMPUTERS)

To use the high-touch using a standard image strategy, a system administrator prepares an image called a standard image that includes the Windows OS, drivers, and applications that are standard to all the computers that might use the image. A standard image is hardware independent, meaning it can be installed on any computer. (In the chapter "Maintaining Windows," you learn to create other types of images that can only be used on the computer that created them.)

Drive-imaging software is used to copy the entire hard drive to another bootable media in the process called drive imaging. Tools included in the Windows ADK or AIK or third-party software can be used. Examples of third-party drive-imaging software are True Image by Acronis (*www.acronis.com*), Ghost by Symantec (*www.symantec.com*), and Todo Backup Free, a freeware version of the Todo Backup software by EaseUS (*www.easeus.com*). A standard image is usually stored on an 8-GB or larger bootable USB flash drive (UFD) or on a bootable DVD along with Windows setup files.

Notes To see a video introducing how to create a standard image, check out this video at the Microsoft Technet site: *technet.microsoft.com/en-us/windows/ee530017.aspx*.

Installing a standard image on another computer is called image deployment, which always results in a clean install rather than an upgrade. To begin, boot the computer from the bootable flash drive or DVD that contains the image. A menu appears to begin the Windows installation. When you finish this Windows installation, the standard image is installed. USMT can then be used to transfer user settings, user data files, and application settings to the new installation.

The high-touch using a standard image strategy takes longer to set up than the previous strategy because a system administrator must prepare the image and must set up USMT, but it takes less time to install on each computer and also assures the administrator that each computer has a standard set of drivers and applications that are configured correctly.

LITE-TOUCH, HIGH-VOLUME DEPLOYMENT (RECOMMENDED FOR 200 TO 500 COMPUTERS)

The lite-touch, high-volume deployment strategy uses a deployment server on the network to serve up the installation after a technician starts the process. The files in the installation include Windows, device drivers, and applications, and collectively are called the distribution share.

The technician starts the installation by booting the computer to Windows PE. Windows Preinstallation Environment (Windows PE) is a minimum operating system used to start the installation. It is included in the Windows ADK for Windows 8 or in the Windows AIK for Windows 7, and it can be installed on a USB flash drive, CD, or DVD to make the device bootable. The technician boots from the device, which might be configured to display a menu to choose from multiple distribution shares available on the deployment server.

The technician can also boot the computer directly to the network to receive Windows PE from the deployment server. For a legacy BIOS system, set the first item in the boot device priority to be Ethernet (see Figure 8-58). For a UEFI system, look for an advanced setup screen in UEFI setup to enable PXE Support. Then reboot the system. The computer boots to the Preboot eXecution Environment or Pre-Execution Environment (PXE) that is contained in the UEFI or BIOS code on the motherboard. PXE searches for a server on the network to provide a bootable operating system (Windows PE on the deployment server).

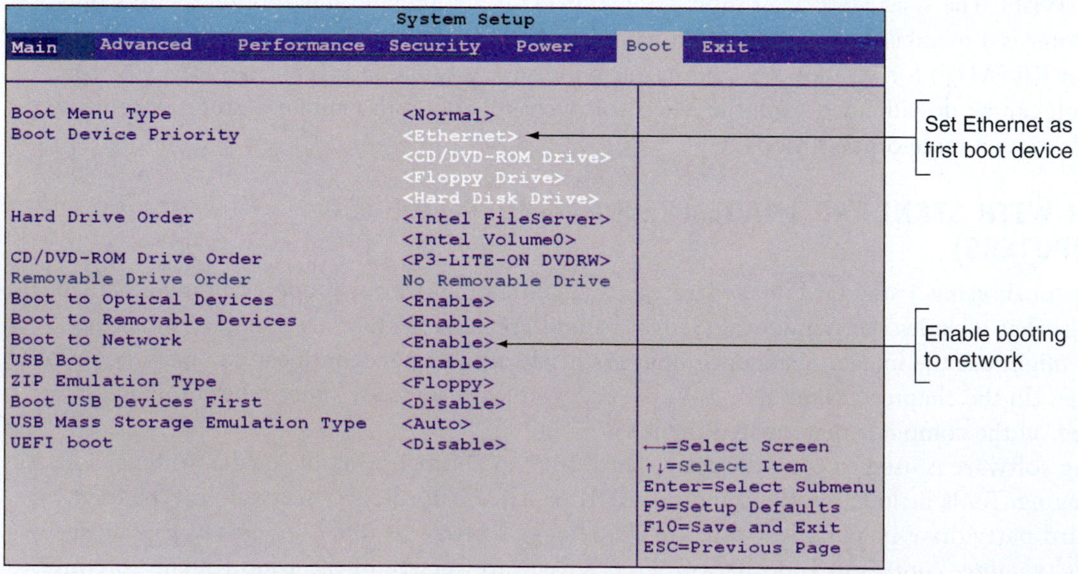

Source: Intel

Figure 8-58 Configure BIOS setup to boot to the network

After the installation begins, the technician is not required to respond to prompts by the setup program, which is called an unattended installation. These responses, such as the administrator password or domain name, are stored in an answer file. The User State Migration Tool is then used to transfer user settings, user data files, and application settings to the new installation.

For high-touch strategies, a technician would normally sit at a computer and use the Windows 8 Upgrade Assistant or the Windows 7 Upgrade Advisor to determine if the system qualifies for the upgrade before performing the installation. Using lite-touch deployments, a more automated method of qualifying a computer is preferred. The Microsoft Assessment and Planning (MAP) Toolkit can be used by a system administrator from a network location to query hundreds of computers in a single scan. The software automatically examines hardware and applications on each computer to verify compatibility with Windows 7 or 8. The MAP software might also be used by the system administrator before deciding to deploy a new OS to determine what computer hardware upgrades or application software upgrades are required that must be included in the overall deployment budget.

ZERO-TOUCH, HIGH-VOLUME DEPLOYMENT (RECOMMENDED FOR MORE THAN 500 COMPUTERS)

8

The zero-touch, high-volume deployment strategy is the most difficult to set up and requires complex tools. The installation does not require a technician to start the process (called pull automation). Rather, the installation uses push automation, meaning that a server automatically pushes the installation to a computer when a user is not likely to be sitting at it. The entire remote network installation is automated and no user intervention is required. The process can turn on a computer that is turned off and even works when no OS is installed on the computer or the current OS is corrupted.

Notes IT support technicians find that large enterprises appreciate quick-and-easy solutions to desktop or laptop computer problems. Technicians quickly learn their marching orders are almost always "replace or reimage." Little time is given to trying to solve the underlying problem when hardware can quickly be replaced or a Windows installation can quickly be reimaged.

USING THE USMT SOFTWARE

A+
220-902
1.2, 1.4

Let's look briefly at what to expect when using the USMT software, which is included in the Windows 8 ADK software and the Windows 7 AIK software. To prepare to use USMT, a system administrator must first install the ADK or AIK software on his or her computer. In Microsoft documentation, this computer is called the technician computer. The source computer is the computer from which the user settings, application settings, and user data files are taken. The destination computer is the computer that is to receive this data. Sometimes the source computer and the destination computer are the same computer. An example is when you perform a clean installation of Windows 8/7 on a computer that has an earlier version of Windows installed and you want to transfer user files and settings from the older installation to the new installation.

Notes USMT uses hard-link migration of user files and settings when the source computer and the destination computer are the same computer. Hard-link migration does not actually copy files and settings, but leaves them on the hard drive without copying. This method makes USMT extremely fast when the hard drive is not formatted during the Windows installation.

The USMT software uses three commands:

- scanstate copies settings and files from the source computer to a safe location.
- loadstate applies these settings and files to the destination computer.
- usmtutils provides encryption options and hard-link management.

Here are the general steps to use USMT:

1. Download and install the ADK or AIK software on the technician computer.
2. Copy the USMT program files from the technician computer to the source computer.
3. Run the scanstate command on the source computer to copy user files and settings to a file server or other safe location.
4. Install Windows, device drivers, and applications on the destination computer.
5. Run the loadstate command to apply user files and settings from the file server to the destination computer.

A+ Exam Tip The A+ 220-902 exam expects you to know about the User State Migration Tool (USMT).

The scanstate, loadstate, and usmtutils command lines can be lengthy and include references to .xml files in the command line along with other parameters. The details of these command lines are not covered in this text. Most likely, the commands are stored in batch files provided by the system administrator. A batch file has a .bat file extension and contains a list or batch of OS commands that are executed as a group. These batch files might be automatically executed as part of a zero-touch installation or manually executed in a lite-touch or high-touch installation. To manually execute a batch file, you type the name of the batch file at a command prompt.

Notes For detailed instructions on using USMT that a system administrator might use, go to *technet.microsoft.com* and search on *using USMT for IT professionals*.

>> CHAPTER SUMMARY

How to Plan a Windows Installation

- Editions of Windows 8 are Windows 8, Windows 8 Professional, Windows 8 Enterprise, and Windows RT. All editions come in 32- or 64-bit versions.
- The Windows 7 editions are Windows 7 Starter, Windows 7 Home Basic, Windows 7 Home Premium, Windows 7 Professional, Windows 7 Enterprise, and Windows 7 Ultimate.
- Windows can be purchased as the less-expensive OEM version or the more-expensive retail version. The OEM version can only be installed on a new computer.
- Each edition of Windows 8 and Windows 7 (except Windows 7 Starter) is available in either 32- or 64-bit versions. A 32-bit OS cannot address as much memory as a 64-bit OS. A 64-bit OS performs better and requires more memory than a 32-bit OS.
- Before purchasing Windows, make sure your system meets the minimum hardware requirements and all the hardware and applications will work under the OS. A 64-bit OS requires 64-bit drivers.

- A computer might have legacy BIOS installed on the motherboard or have the newer UEFI firmware installed. Most UEFI firmware offers the option to support legacy BIOS when in UEFI CSM mode.
- A hard drive contains one or more partitions or volumes and can use the MBR or GPT partitioning system. To use UEFI Secure Boot, the partitioning system must be GPT and the Windows installation must be 64 bit.
- Normally, Windows is installed on the C: volume in the C:\Windows folder. The volume in which Windows is installed must use the NTFS file system.
- Windows can be installed from the setup DVD, USB flash drive, files downloaded from the Internet, hidden partition on the hard drive (called a factory recovery partition), or in a virtual machine.
- Virtual machine software can provide multiple instances of operating systems for training users, running legacy software, and supporting multiple operating systems.
- Windows can be installed as an in-place upgrade, a clean installation, or in a multiboot environment with another OS.

Installing Windows 8.1 and Windows 7

8

- A technician needs to know how to perform an in-place upgrade, a clean install, or a multiboot with Windows.
- The steps for installing or upgrading Windows 8.0 are about the same as those for Windows 8.1.
- A clean install is the best option to use if the current installation is sluggish or giving problems, or if you're installing Windows on a new desktop computer that you're building.
- In a multiboot, each OS must be installed on its own partition. Make sure you have enough free space on a partition before installing Windows onto it, and make sure it doesn't currently hold an OS.

What to Do After a Windows Installation

- After a Windows installation, verify you have network access, activate Windows, install any Windows updates or Windows 7 service packs, verify automatic updates are configured correctly, install hardware and applications, create user accounts and transfer or restore from backup user data and preferences, and turn Windows features on or off.

Special Concerns When Working in a Large Enterprise

- Four deployment strategies for installing Windows in a large enterprise are high-touch with retail media, high-touch with a standard image, lite-touch with high volume, and zero-touch with high volume. Which strategy to use depends on the number of computers to deploy. Zero-touch deployments require the most time to set up, but do not require a technician to be at the computer when the installation happens.

>> KEY TERMS

For explanations of key terms, see the Glossary for this text.

answer file
batch file
BIOS (basic input/output system)
boot loader menu
Certificate of Authenticity
clean install
compatibility mode
custom installation
deployment strategy
device driver
Device Manager
disc image
diskpart
distribution server
distribution share
drive imaging
dual boot
file system
GUID Partition Table (GPT)
hard-link migration
high-touch using a standard image
high-touch with retail media
hot-swappable
hypervisor

image deployment
in-place upgrade
ISO file
ISO image
lite-touch, high-volume deployment
loadstate
Master Boot Record (MBR)
Microsoft Assessment and Planning (MAP) Toolkit
multiboot
Original Equipment Manufacturer (OEM) license
Preboot eXecution Environment or Pre-Execution Environment (PXE)
product activation
Programs and Features
pull automation
push automation
recovery partition
remote network installation
repair installation
scanstate
Secure Boot
service pack
setup UEFI/BIOS
solid-state drive
standard image
startup UEFI/BIOS
system UEFI/BIOS
third-party driver
UEFI CSM (Compatibility Support Module) mode
unattended installation
Unified Extensible Firmware Interface (UEFI)
Upgrade Advisor
Upgrade Assistant
upgrade path
User State Migration Tool (USMT)
usmtutils
virtual machine (VM)
virtual XP mode
volume
Windows 7
Windows 8.1
Windows 8.1 Enterprise
Windows 8.1 Pro for Students
Windows 8.1 Professional (Windows 8.1 Pro)
Windows Assessment and Deployment Kit (ADK)
Windows Automated Installation Kit (AIK)
Windows Defender
Windows Easy Transfer
Windows Preinstallation Environment (Windows PE)
Windows Pro Pack
Windows RT
Windows Vista
Windows XP Mode
Windows.old folder
zero-touch, high-volume deployment

>> REVIEWING THE BASICS

1. How much free space on the hard drive is required to install a 64-bit version of Windows 8.1?
2. How do you start the process to reinstall an OS on a laptop computer using the backup files stored on a recovery partition?
3. What are three free applications mentioned in the chapter that can be used to create virtual machines?
4. When upgrading from Windows Vista to Windows 8.1, can you perform an in-place upgrade?
5. Which Windows architecture is required to enable the UEFI Secure Boot? Which partitioning system?
6. Which file system is used on the volume where Windows is installed?
7. When trying to install Windows in UEFI mode on a hard drive that is using the MBR partitioning system, which command can you use to get a special prompt in a command prompt window where you can then remove the partitioning system and convert the drive to GPT?
8. What is the minimum number of partitions that the MBR partitioning system can support?
9. Which partitioning method must you use for a 4-TB hard drive?
10. If you suspect a computer is infected with a virus, why is it not a good idea to perform an upgrade installation of Windows rather than a clean install?
11. After setting up a dual-boot installation with Windows 7 and Windows 8.1, how do you boot the system into Windows 7?
12. After a Windows installation, what is the easiest way to determine that you have Internet access?
13. What Windows 8 tool can you use to migrate user data and settings from a Windows 7 installation on one computer to the new Windows 8 installation on a different computer?
14. What is the primary Windows tool for managing hardware devices?
15. What window is used to uninstall a program in Windows 8? What Windows 8 screen is used to uninstall an app?

16. What three processor technologies are required to install Windows 8?
17. Why does Microsoft require these three processor technologies, even though they are currently available on all processors sold today?
18. How can you find out if a system qualifies for a Windows 8.1 upgrade?
19. Which window on the Windows 8 desktop can you use to find out if the Windows installation has been activated?
20. What is an advantage of using a dynamic hard drive in a VM?
21. Are you required to enter the product key during the Windows 7 installation?
22. Using an unattended installation of Windows, what is the name of the file that holds the responses a technician would normally give during the installation?
23. What are the three commands used by the User State Migration Tool?
24. To use the User State Migration Tool, how must a computer connect to the network?
25. Where is the PXE programming code stored that is used to boot a computer when it is searching for an OS on the network?

>> THINKING CRITICALLY

1. You are planning an upgrade from Windows 7 to Windows 8.1. Your system uses a network card that you don't find listed on the Microsoft Windows 8.1 list of compatible devices. What do you do next?
   a. Abandon the upgrade and continue to use Windows 7.
   b. Check the website of the network card manufacturer for a Windows 8.1 driver.
   c. Buy a new network card.
   d. Install a dual boot for Windows 7 and Windows 8.1 and only use the network when you have Windows 7 loaded.
2. You have just installed Windows 8.1 and now attempt to install your favorite game that worked fine under Windows 7. When you attempt the installation, you get an error. What is your best next step?
   a. Purchase a new version of your game, one that is compatible with Windows 8.1.
   b. Download any updates to Windows 8.1.
   c. Reinstall Windows 7.
   d. Install a VM running Windows 7.
3. You have 32-bit Windows 7 Home Premium installed on your computer, and you purchase the upgrade license of Windows 8.1 Professional. You want to install Windows 8.1 using the 64-bit architecture. Which way(s) can you install Windows 8.1?
   a. You can perform an upgrade, but not a clean install.
   b. You can perform an upgrade or a clean install.
   c. You can perform a clean install, but not an upgrade.
   d. In this situation, you cannot install Windows 8.1 using the upgrade license. You must go back and purchase the full license of Windows 8.1.

4. A laptop reports that it has made a wireless network connection, but it cannot access the network or the Internet. Arrange the following steps in the best order to troubleshoot the problem:
   a. Use Device Manager to uninstall the wireless adapter and install it again.
   b. Disable and enable the wireless network adapter.
   c. Disconnect the connection, and connect again to the wireless network.
   d. Use Device Manager to update the wireless adapter drivers.

>> REAL PROBLEMS, REAL SOLUTIONS

REAL PROBLEM 8-1 Recovering Data from a Corrupted Windows Installation

As an IT support technician for a small organization, it's your job to support the computers, the small network, and the users. One of your coworkers, Jason, comes to you in a panic. His Windows 8.1 system won't boot, and he has lots of important data files in several locations on the drive. He has no idea in which folder some of the files are located. Besides the application data he's currently working on, he's especially concerned about losing email addresses, email, and his Internet Explorer Favorites links.

After trying everything you know about recovering Windows 8.1, you conclude the OS is corrupted beyond repair. You decide there might be a way to remove the hard drive from Jason's computer and connect it to another computer so that you can recover the data. Search the Internet and find a device that you can use to connect Jason's hard drive to another computer using a USB port on that computer. The hard drive uses a SATA hard drive interface. Print the webpage showing the device and its price.

REAL PROBLEM 8-2 Troubleshooting an Upgrade

Your friend, Thomas, has upgraded his Windows 7 desktop to Windows 8.1. After the installation, he discovers his media card reader does not work. He calls you on the phone asking you what to do. Do the following to plan your troubleshooting approach:

1. List the questions you should ask Thomas to help diagnose the problem.
2. List the steps you would take if you were sitting at the computer solving the problem.
3. What do you think is the source of the problem? Explain your answer.

REAL PROBLEM 8-3 Creating Windows 8.1 Setup on a USB Flash Drive or DVD

Microsoft offers a solution to those who installed Windows 8.1 from the web but failed to save the Windows setup files to a DVD or USB flash drive and later need these files to reinstall Windows 8.1. Follow these steps to create Windows setup on a DVD or USB flash drive:

1. Go to the Microsoft webpage **windows.microsoft.com/en-us/windows-8/create-reset-refresh-media.** Download and run the Windows Installation Media Creation Tool. On the first window, select your language, edition of Windows 8.1, and architecture (see Figure 8-59).

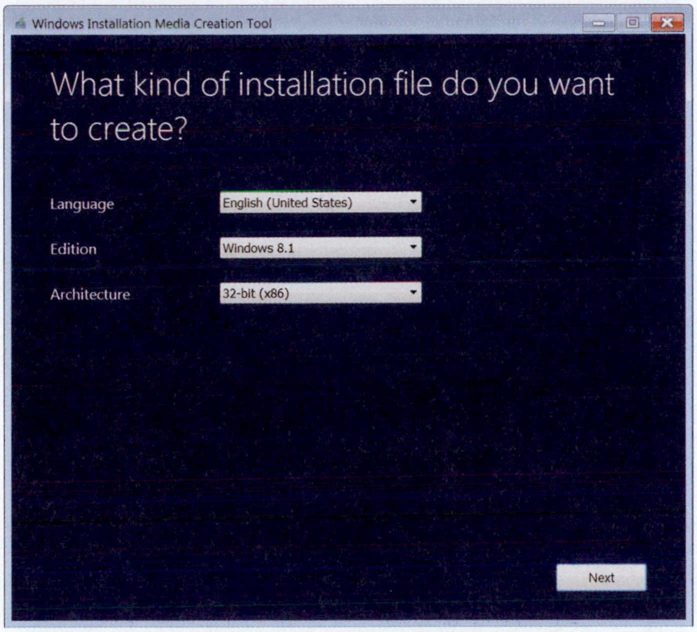

Figure 8-59 Select options to download Windows 8.1 setup files

2. On the next screen (see Figure 8-60), do one of the following:

- To create a bootable USB flash drive, select **USB flash drive.** When you click **Next,** the download begins and files are created on the drive.

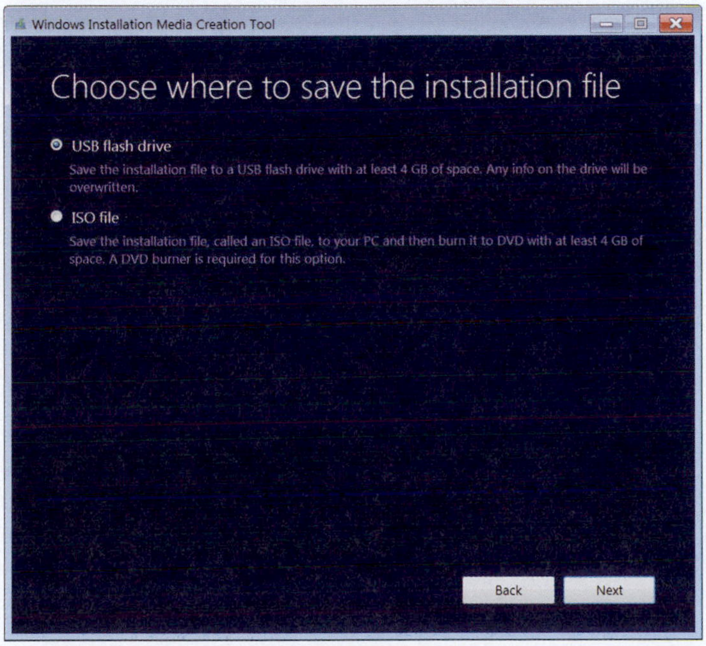

Figure 8-60 Select USB flash drive to hold Windows 8.1 setup files and folders

- If you want to burn a DVD, select **ISO file.** The file is created in the same folder where you saved the Windows Installation Media Creation Tool program that you downloaded in Step 1. (This ISO file is handy for installing Windows in a VM.) On the next screen, click **Open DVD burner** and follow directions on screen to burn the DVD.

CHAPTER 9

Supporting I/O Devices

After completing this chapter, you will be able to:

- Describe the general approach technicians use to install and support I/O devices
- Install and configure several I/O devices, such as barcode readers, biometric devices, digital cameras, webcams, graphic tablets, and touch screens
- Install and configure adapter cards
- Support the video subsystem, including selecting a monitor and video card and supporting dual monitors and video memory
- Troubleshoot common problems with I/O devices

This chapter is packed full of details about the many I/O (input/output) devices an IT support technician must be familiar with and must know how to install and support. Most of us learn about new technologies as we need to use a device or when a client or customer requests our help with purchasing decisions or solving a problem with a device. Good technicians soon develop the skills of searching the web for explanations, reviews, and ads about a device and can quickly turn to support websites for how to install, configure, or troubleshoot a device. This chapter can serve as your jump start toward learning about many computer parts and devices used to enhance a system. It contains enough information to get you started toward becoming an expert at computer devices.

We begin with the basic skills common to supporting any device, including how to use Device Manager and how to select the right port for a new peripheral device. Then you learn to install I/O devices and adapter cards and to support the video subsystem. Finally, you learn how to troubleshoot problems with I/O devices.

BASIC PRINCIPLES FOR SUPPORTING DEVICES

A+
220-901
1.4, 1.7

An I/O or storage device can be either internal (installed inside the computer case) or external (installed outside the case and called a peripheral device). These basic principles apply to supporting both internal and external devices:

- ***Every device is controlled by software.*** When you install a new device, such as a barcode reader or scanner, you must install both the device and the device drivers to control the device. These device drivers must be written for the OS you are using. Recall from earlier chapters that the exceptions to this principle are some simple devices, such as the keyboard, which are controlled by the system UEFI/BIOS. Also, Windows has embedded device drivers for many devices. For example, when you install a video card, Windows can use its embedded drivers to communicate with the card, but to use all the features of the card, you can install the drivers that came bundled with the card.
- ***When it comes to installing or supporting a device, the manufacturer knows best.*** In this chapter, you learn a lot of principles and procedures for installing and supporting a device, but when you're on the job installing a device or fixing a broken one, read the manufacturer's documentation and follow those guidelines first. For example, for most installations, you install the device before you install the device driver. However, for some devices, such as a digital camera and a wireless keyboard, you might need to install the device driver first. Check the device documentation to know which to do first.
- ***Some devices need application software to use the device.*** For example, after you install a scanner and its device drivers, you might also need to install Adobe Photoshop to use the scanner.
- ***A device is no faster than the port or slot it is designed to use.*** When buying a new external device, pay attention to the type of port for which it is rated. For example, an external hard drive designed to use a USB 2.0 port will work using a USB 3.0 port, but will work at the USB 2.0 speed even when it's connected to a faster USB 3.0 port. For another example, a TV tuner card in a PCI slot will not work as fast as a TV tuner card in a PCI Express slot because of the different speeds of the slots.
- ***Use an administrator account in Windows.*** When installing hardware devices under Windows, you need to be signed in to the system with a user account that has the highest level of privileges to change the system. This type of account is called an administrator account.
- ***Problems with a device can sometimes be solved by updating the device drivers.*** Device manufacturers often release updates to device drivers. Update the drivers to solve problems with the device or to add new features. You can use Device Manager in Windows to manage devices and their drivers.
- ***Install only one device at a time.*** If you have several devices to install, install one and restart the system. Make sure that device is working and all is well with the system before you move on to install another device.

Recall that Device Manager (its program file is named devmgmt.msc) is your primary Windows tool for managing hardware. It lists almost all installed hardware devices and the drivers they use. (Printers and many USB devices are not listed in Device Manager.) Using Device Manager, you can disable or enable a device, update its drivers, uninstall a device, and undo a driver update (called a driver rollback).

Before we move on to installing devices, you need to be familiar with the ports on a computer. When selecting a new device, to get the best performance, select one that uses the fastest port available on your computer.

PORTS AND WIRELESS CONNECTIONS USED BY PERIPHERAL DEVICES

A+
220-901
1.7

Many ports used by peripheral or external devices are pictured in Table 1 in the chapter, "First Look at Computer Parts and Tools." When deciding what type of port a new device should use, the speed of the port is often a tiebreaker. Table 9-1 shows the speeds of various ports, from fastest to slowest. Because wireless connections are sometimes an option, they are also included in the table for comparison. For example, you might need to decide between a USB 2.0 printer connection and a Bluetooth wireless connection. This table can help you decide if speed should be a consideration.

★ A+ Exam Tip The A+ 220-901 exam expects you to be able to compare the speeds and distances among USB (1.1, 2.0, and 3.0), FireWire 400 and 800 ports, and Bluetooth, Infrared, and NFC wireless connections. The facts you need to know are found in Table 9-1.

Port or Wireless Type	Maximum Speed	Maximum Cable Length or Wireless Range
eSATA Version 3 (eSATA-600)	6.0 Gbps (gigabits per second)	Cable lengths up to 2 meters
SuperSpeed USB (USB 3.0)	5.0 Gbps	Cable lengths up to 3 meters
eSATA Version 2 (eSATA-300)	3.0 Gbps	Cable lengths up to 2 meters
eSATA Version 1 (eSATA-150)	1.5 Gbps or 1500 Mbps (megabits per second)	Cable lengths up to 2 meters
FireWire 800 (also called 1394b)	1.2 Gbps or 800 Mbps	Cable lengths up to 100 meters
Wi-Fi 802.11n RF (radio frequency) of 2.4 GHz or 5.0 GHz	Up to 500 Mbps	Range up to 70 meters
Hi-Speed USB (USB 2.0)	480 Mbps	Cable lengths up to 5 meters
FireWire 400 (also called 1394a)	400 Mbps	Cable lengths up to 4.5 meters
Original USB (USB 1.1)	12 Mbps or 1.5 Mbps	Cable lengths up to 3 meters
Wi-Fi 802.11g RF of 2.4 GHz	Up to 54 Mbps	Range up to 100 meters
Wi-Fi 802.11a RF of 5.0 GHz	Up to 54 Mbps	Range up to 50 meters
Wi-Fi 802.11b RF of 2.4 GHz	Up to 11 Mbps	Range up to 100 meters
Bluetooth wireless RF of 2.4 GHz	Up to 3 Mbps	Range up to 10 meters
Infrared (IR) wireless Invisible light; frequency range of 100 to 400 THz (terahertz or 1 trillion hertz), just above red light	Up to 4 Mbps for fast speed IR; up to 1.15 Mbps for medium speed IR, and up to 115 Kbps (kilobits per second) for slow speed IR	Range up to 5 meters
Near Field Communication (NFC) RF of 13.56 MHz	Up to 424 kbps	Range up to 10 centimeters

Table 9-1 Data transmission speeds for various port types and wireless connections

USB CONNECTIONS

Here is a summary of important facts you need to know about USB connections:

1. The USB Implementers Forum, Inc. (*www.usb.org*), the organization responsible for developing USB, uses the symbols shown in Figure 9-1 to indicate SuperSpeed USB (USB 3.0), Hi-Speed USB (USB 2.0), or Original USB (USB 1.1).

Source: USB Forum

Figure 9-1 SuperSpeed, Hi-Speed, and Original USB logos appear on products certified by the USB Forum

2. As many as 127 USB devices can be daisy-chained together using USB cables. In a daisy chain, one device provides a USB port for the next device.
3. USB uses serial transmissions, and USB devices are hot-swappable, meaning that you can plug or unplug one without first powering down the system.
4. A USB cable has four wires, two for power and two for communication. The two power wires (one is hot and the other is ground) allow the host controller to provide power to a device. Table 9-2 shows the different USB connectors on USB cables.

Notes Sometimes a mouse that uses USB 2.0 gives problems when plugged into a USB 3.0 port. If a mouse refuses to work or is unstable, try moving it to a USB 2.0 port.

Cable and Connectors	Description
A-Male to B-Male cable 	**The A-Male connector on the left is flat and wide and connects to an A-Male USB port on a computer or USB hub.** **The B-Male connector on the right is square and connects to a USB 1.x or 2.0 device such as a printer.**
Mini-B to A-Male cable 	**The Mini-B connector has five pins and is often used to connect small electronic devices, such as a digital camera, to a computer.**
A-Male to Micro-B cable 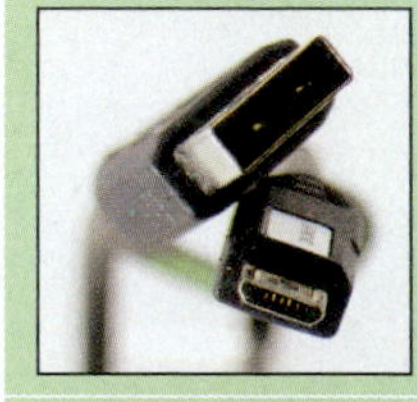	**The Micro-B connector has five pins and has a smaller height than the Mini-B connector. It's used on digital cameras, cell phones, and other small electronic devices.**
A-Male to Micro-A cable 	**The Micro-A connector has five pins and is smaller than the Mini-B connector. It's used on digital cameras, cell phones, and other small electronic devices.**
USB 3.0 A-Male to USB 3.0 B-Male cable 	**This USB 3.0 B-Male connector is used by SuperSpeed USB 3.0 devices such as printers or scanners. Devices that have this connection can also use regular B-Male connectors, but this USB 3.0 B-Male connector will not fit the connection on a USB 1.1 or 2.0 device. USB 3.0 A-Male and B-Male connectors and ports are blue.**
USB 3.0 A-Male to USB 3.0 Micro-B cable 	**The USB 3.0 Micro-B connector is used by SuperSpeed USB 3.0 devices. The connectors are not compatible with regular Micro-B connectors.**

Table 9-2 USB connectors

Notes A USB 3.0 A-Male connector or port has additional pins compared with USB 1.1 or 2.0 ports and connectors but still is backward compatible with USB 1.1 and 2.0 devices. A USB 3.0 A-Male or B-Male connector or port is usually blue. Take a close look at the blue and black USB ports shown in Figure 4 in the chapter "First Look at Computer Parts and Tools."

FIREWIRE (IEEE 1394) CONNECTIONS

USB and FireWire competed as a solution for fast I/O connections for a few years, but USB clearly won that contest, and now FireWire is hardly used in new devices. FireWire standards are managed by the 1394 Trade Association (*www.1394ta.org*). The official name of these standards is IEEE 1394, and other names used are FireWire (first used by Apple) and i.LINK (first used by Sony). The most common name used today is FireWire. Here are the key facts you need to know about FireWire:

- FireWire uses serial transmissions, and FireWire devices are hot-swappable.
- FireWire 800 (1394b) allows for up to 63 FireWire devices to be daisy-chained together. FireWire 400 (1394a) allows for up to 16 daisy-chained devices.
- FireWire 400 (1394a) supports two types of connectors and cables: a 4-pin connector that does not provide voltage to a device and a 6-pin connector that does. Figure 9-2 shows a cable that plugs into a 6-pin FireWire port to provide a 4-pin connector for a FireWire device.

9

Notes IEEE 1394a ports with six pins are the most common FireWire ports on motherboards.

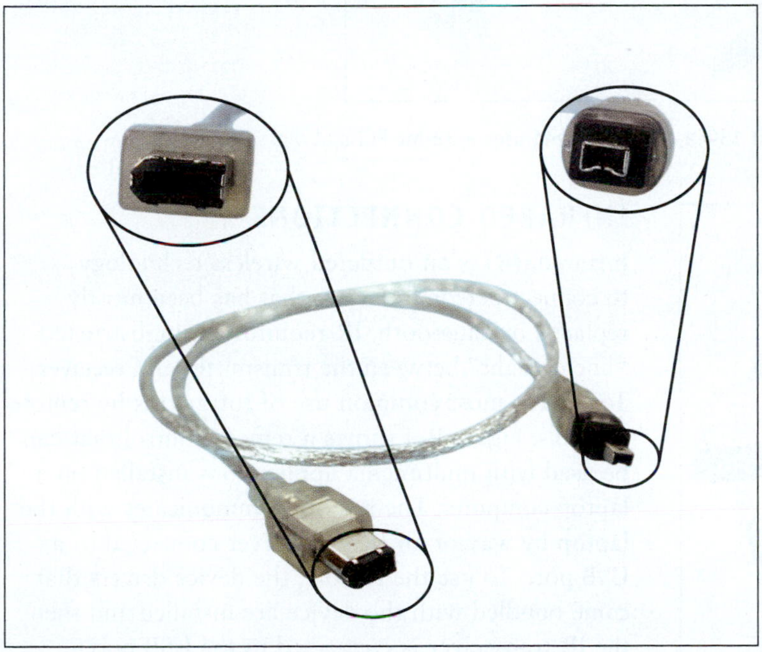

Figure 9-2 IEEE 1394a cable provides a smaller 4-pin and larger 6-pin connectors

- FireWire 800 (1394b) uses a 9-pin rectangular connector. Figure 9-3 shows a FireWire 800 adapter card that provides three 1394 ports: two 1394b 9-pin ports and one 1394a 6-pin port. The power cable connected to the card plugs into a 4-pin Molex power cable from the power supply to provide extra power to the card. The latest 1394 standard is 1394c, which allows FireWire 800 to use a standard network port and network cable.

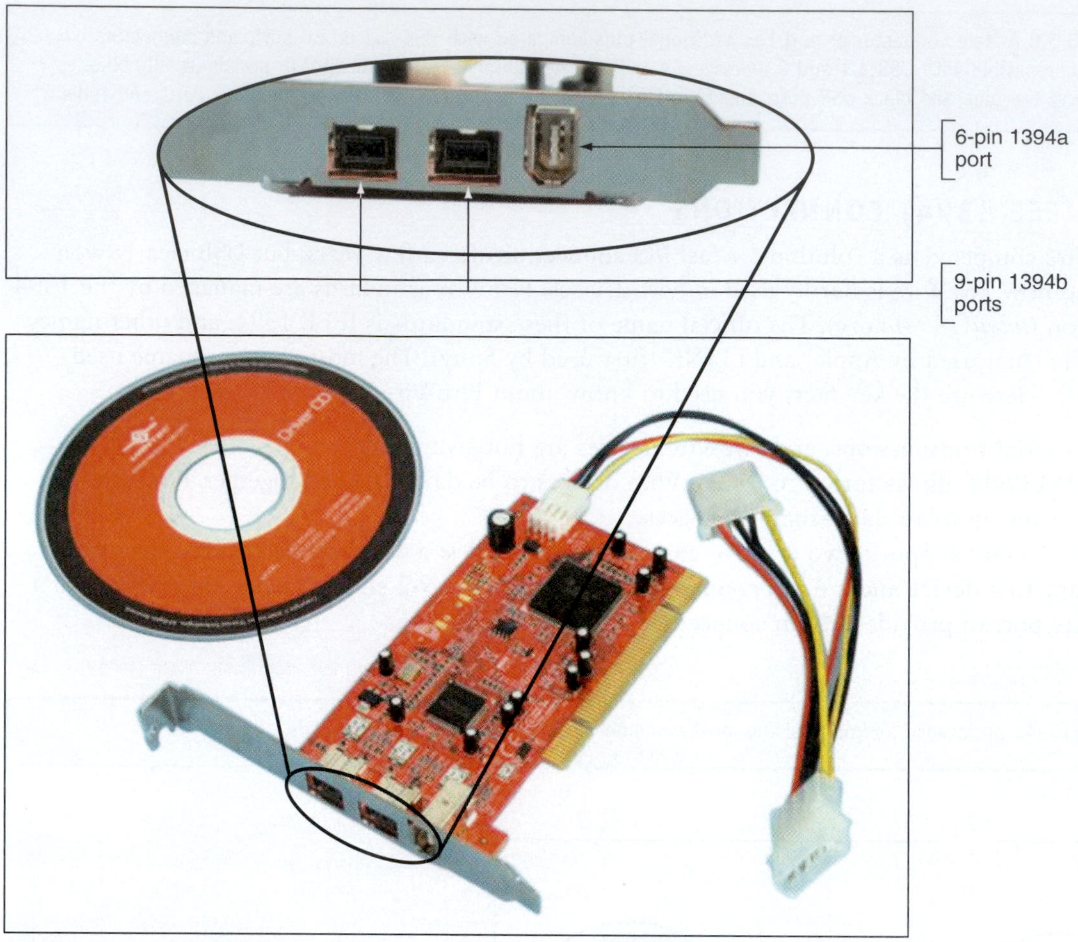

Figure 9-3 This 1394 adapter card supports both 1394a and 1394b and uses a 32-bit PCI slot

Figure 9-4 This remote control is an Infrared device that uses an IR transceiver connected to a laptop by way of a USB port

INFRARED CONNECTIONS

Infrared (IR) is an outdated wireless technology to connect personal devices that has been mostly replaced by Bluetooth. IR requires an unobstructed "line of sight" between the transmitter and receiver. Today, the most common use of Infrared is by remote controls. Figure 9-4 shows a remote control that can be used with multimedia applications installed on a laptop computer. The remote communicates with the laptop by way of an IR transceiver connected to a USB port. To use the remote, the device drivers that came bundled with the device are installed and then the IR transceiver is connected to the USB port.

Notes Infrared standards are defined by the Infrared Data Association (IrDA). Its website is *www.irda.org*.

Now that you know about the ports and wireless connections used for external devices, let's see how to install them.

INSTALLING I/O PERIPHERAL DEVICES

A+
220-901
1.12

Installing peripheral or external devices is easy to do and usually goes without a hitch. All devices need device drivers or UEFI/BIOS to control them and to interface with the operating system. Simple input devices, such as the mouse and keyboard, can be controlled by the UEFI/BIOS or have embedded device drivers built in to the OS. For these devices, you usually don't have to install additional device drivers.

Peripheral devices you might be called on to install include a keyboard, mouse, touch pad, barcode reader, biometric device (for example, a fingerprint reader), touch screen, motion controller, scanner, microphone, game pad, joystick, digitizer, digital camera, smart card reader, webcam, camcorder, MIDI-enabled devices, speakers, and display devices. These installations are similar, so learning to do one will help you do another. Here are the general procedures to install any peripheral device:

1. ***Read the manufacturer's directions.*** I know you don't want to hear that again, but when you follow these directions, the installation goes better. If you later have a problem with the installation and you ask the manufacturer for help, being able to say you followed the directions exactly as stated goes a long way toward getting more enthusiastic help and cooperation.

2. ***Make sure the drivers provided with the device are written for the operating system (OS) you are using.*** Recall that 64-bit drivers are required for a 64-bit operating system, and 32-bit drivers are required for a 32-bit OS. You can sometimes use drivers written for older Windows versions in newer Windows versions, but for best results, use drivers written for the OS installed. You can download the drivers you need from the manufacturer's website.

3. ***Make sure the motherboard port you are using is enabled.*** Most likely it is enabled, but if the device is not recognized when you plug it in, go into UEFI/BIOS setup and make sure the port is enabled. In addition, UEFI/BIOS setup might offer the option to configure a USB port to use SuperSpeed (USB 3.0), Hi-Speed USB (USB 2.0), or original USB (USB 1.1). Figure 9-5 shows the BIOS setup screen for one system where you can enable or disable onboard devices. In addition, if you are having problems with a motherboard port, don't forget to update the motherboard drivers that control the port.

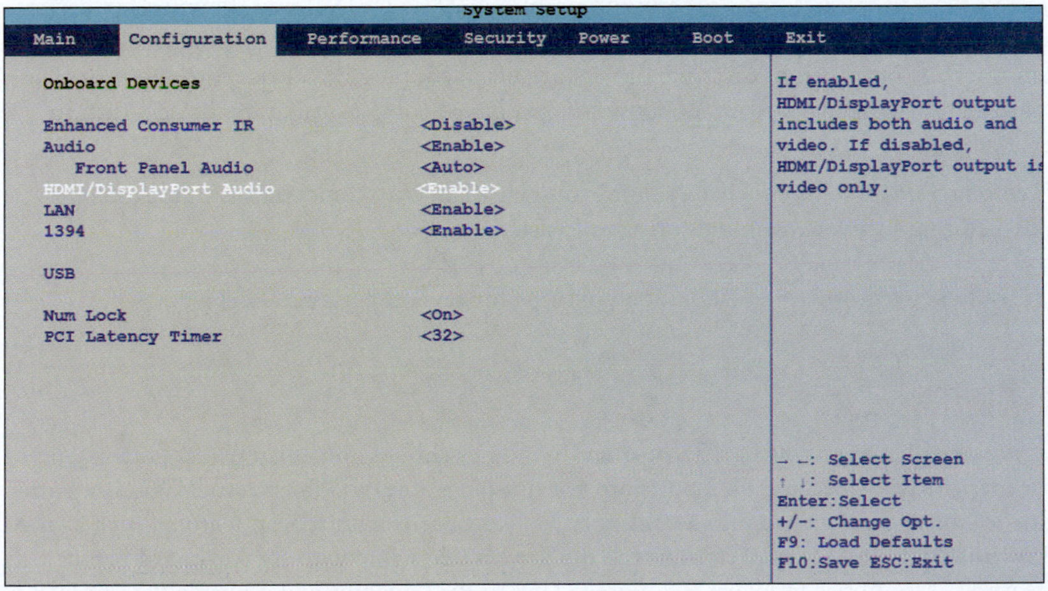

Source: Intel

Figure 9-5 Use BIOS setup to enable or disable onboard ports

4. ***Install drivers or plug in the device.*** Some devices, such as a USB printer, require that you plug in the device before installing the drivers, and some devices require you to install the drivers before plugging in the device. For some devices, it doesn't matter which is installed first. Carefully read and follow the device documentation. For example, the documentation for one digital camera says that if you install the camera before installing the driver, the drivers will not install properly.

   If you plug in the device first, Device Setup launches and steps you through the installation of drivers (see Figure 9-6). As Device Setup works, an icon appears in the taskbar. To see the Device Setup box, as shown in the figure, click the icon.

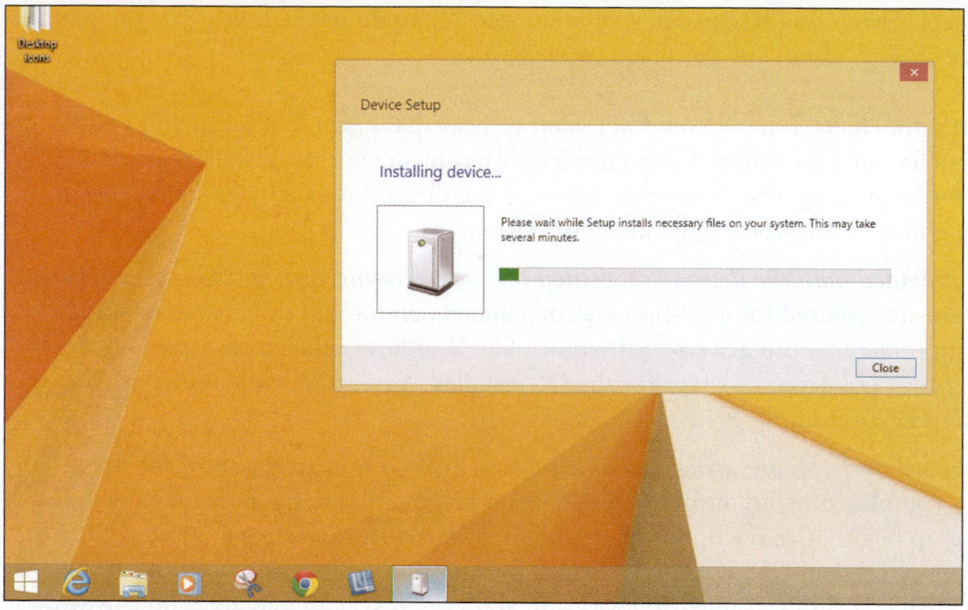

Figure 9-6 Device Setup begins installing a new device

   If you need to install the drivers first, run the setup program on CD or DVD. If you downloaded drivers from the web, double-click the driver file and follow the directions on screen. It might be necessary to restart the system after the installation. After the drivers are installed, plug the device into the port. The device should immediately be recognized by Windows. If you have problems using the device, turn to Device Manager for help.

5. ***Install the application software to use the device.*** For example, a FireWire camcorder is likely to come bundled with video-editing software. Run the software to use the device.

Now let's look at some key features and installation concerns for several peripheral devices.

MOUSE OR KEYBOARD

A+
220-901
1.12

Plug a mouse or keyboard into a USB port and Windows should immediately recognize it and install generic drivers. Because PS/2 ports are not hot-pluggable, you must restart Windows after plugging a mouse or keyboard into a PS/2 port. For keyboards with special features such as the one shown in Figure 9-7, you need to install the drivers that came with the keyboard before you can use these features. Also notice in Figure 9-7 a green USB to PS/2 adapter and a purple PS/2 to USB adapter, which can solve the problem when a case has PS/2 ports and doesn't have enough USB ports.

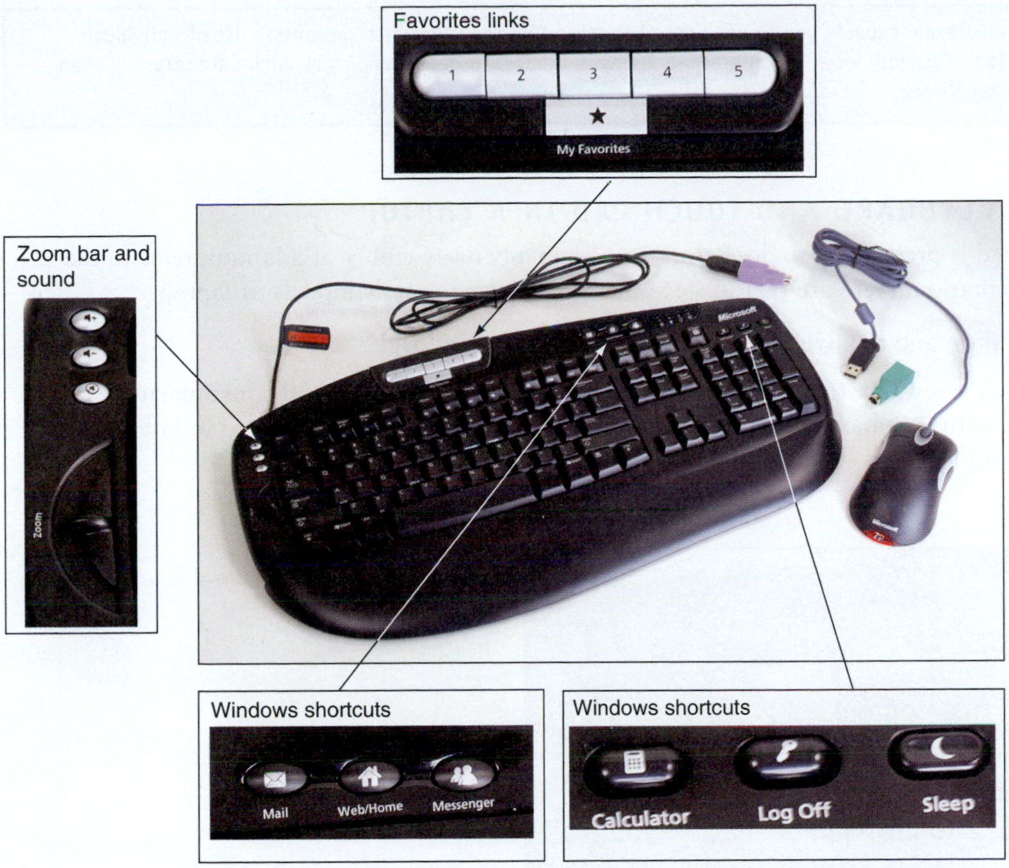

Figure 9-7 The mouse and keyboard require drivers to use the extra buttons and zoom bar

You can later use Device Manager to uninstall, disable, or enable most devices. However, USB devices are managed differently. To uninstall a USB device such as the USB keyboard shown in Figure 9-7, use the Programs and Features window. To open the window in Windows 8, press **Win+X** and click **Programs and Features.** For Windows 7, click **Start**, click **Control Panel**, and click **Programs and Features.** In the Programs and Features window (see Figure 9-8), select the device and click **Uninstall.** Follow the directions on screen to uninstall the device.

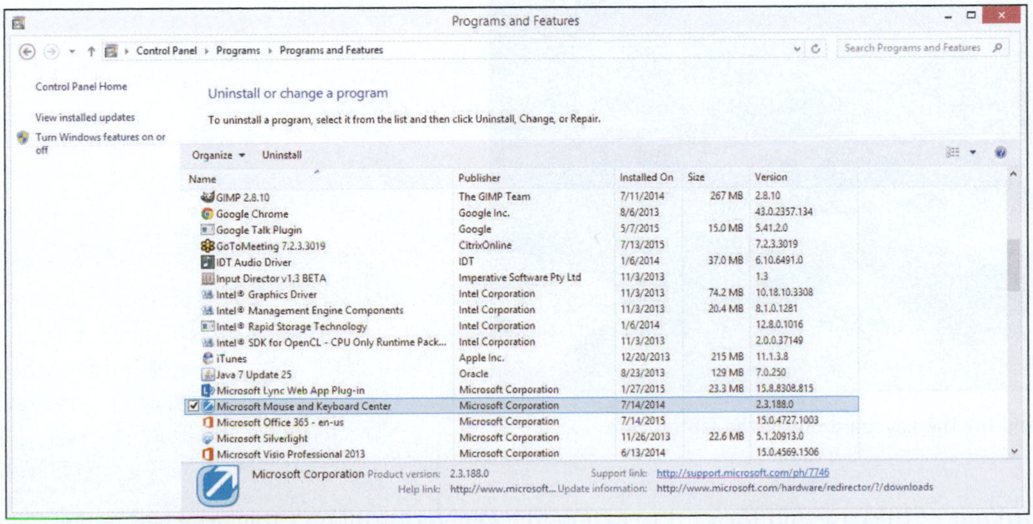

Figure 9-8 USB devices are listed as installed programs

Notes The A+ 220-901 exam expects you to use Control Panel in Classic view, which presents a list of individual items. If Control Panel is in Category view, which presents items in groups, to get Classic view, click **Category** and then click **Small icons** or **Large icons**.

REPLACING THE KEYBOARD AND TOUCH PAD IN A LAPTOP

Replacing the keyboard is pretty easy to do. Before you begin any disassembly of a laptop, refer to the manufacturer documentation. Here are typical steps that are similar to many models of laptops:

1. Power down the laptop and remove the AC adapter and the battery pack.
2. Remove two or more screws on the bottom of the laptop (see Figure 9-9). (Only the manufacturer documentation can tell you which ones because there are probably several of them used to hold various components in place.)

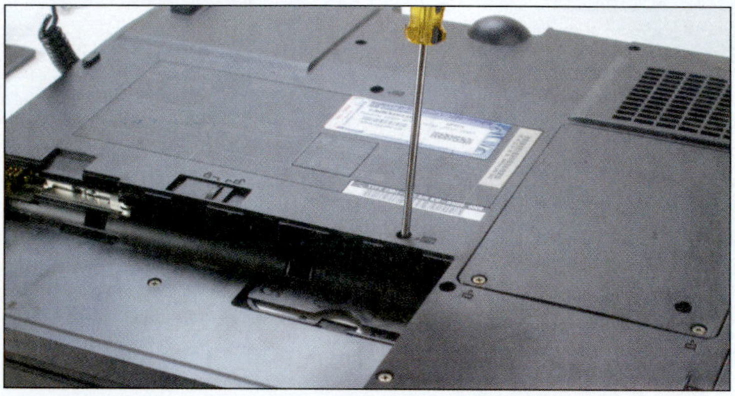

Figure 9-9 Remove screws on the bottom of the laptop

3. Turn the laptop over and open the lid. Gently push the keyboard toward the lid while pulling it up to release it from the case (see Figure 9-10).

Figure 9-10 Pry up and lift the keyboard out of the laptop case

4. Bring the keyboard out of the case and forward to expose the keyboard ribbon cable attached underneath the board. Use a screwdriver to lift the cable connector up and out of its socket (see Figure 9-11).

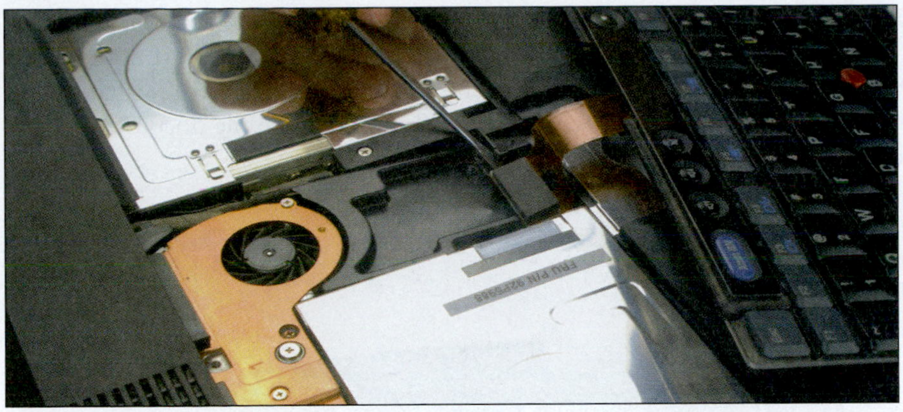

Figure 9-11 Disconnect the keyboard cable from the motherboard

5. Replace the keyboard following the steps in reverse order.

Sometimes the touch pad and keyboard are one complete field replaceable unit (FRU). If the touch pad is a separate component, it might be part of the keyboard bezel, also called the palm rest. This bezel is the flat cover that surrounds the keyboard. Most likely you have to remove the keyboard before you can remove the keyboard bezel.

9

BARCODE READERS

A+
220-901
1.12

A barcode reader is used to scan barcodes on products at the point of sale (POS) or when taking inventory. The reader might use a wireless connection, a serial port, a USB port, or a keyboard port. If the reader uses a keyboard port, most likely it has a splitter (called a keyboard wedge) on it for the keyboard to use, and data read by the barcode reader is input into the system as though it were typed using the keyboard. Figure 9-12 shows a barcode reader by Intermec that is a laser scanner and uses Bluetooth to connect wirelessly to the computer.

Courtesy of Intermec Technologies

Figure 9-12 Handheld or hands-free barcode scanner by Intermec Technologies

BIOMETRIC DEVICES

A+
220-901
1.12

A biometric device is an input device that inputs biological data about a person, used to identify a person's fingerprint, handprint, face, voice, eye, or handwritten signature. For example, you can use a fingerprint reader to sign in to Windows or to access an iPhone using Touch ID technology. These fingerprint readers should not be considered the only authentication to control access to sensitive data: for that, use a strong password, which is a password that is not easy to guess.

Fingerprint readers can look like a mouse and use a wireless or USB connection, such as the one shown in Figure 9-13, or they can be embedded on a keyboard, flash drive, or laptop case. For mobile devices, the fingerprint reader can be activated by pressing a button or touch screen. Most fingerprint readers that are not embedded in other devices use a USB connection. As with other USB devices, read the documentation to know if you should install the drivers first or the device first.

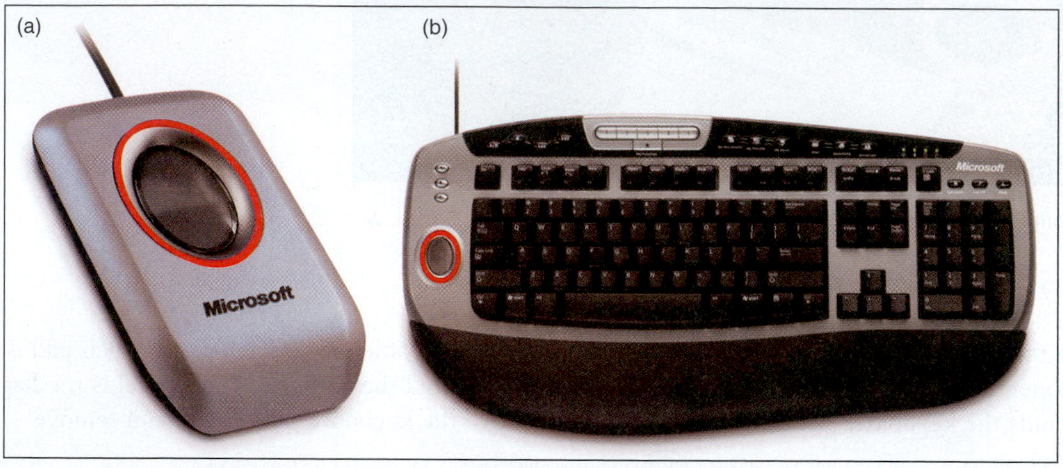

Figure 9-13 Fingerprint readers can (a) look like a mouse, but smaller, or (b) be embedded on a keyboard

DIGITAL CAMERAS AND CAMCORDERS

A+
220-901
1.12

A digital camera or camcorder can hold images and videos both in embedded memory that cannot be removed or exchanged and in removable flash memory cards. Both of these types of memory retain data without a battery. Here are two ways to transfer images from your camera or camcorder to a computer:

- ***Connect the camera or camcorder to the computer using a cable.*** Using embedded memory or flash memory cards, you can connect the device to your computer using a USB or FireWire port and cable. To connect the device to the computer, you might need to first install the software and then connect the device, or you might need to connect the device and then install the software. Read the camera or camcorder documentation to find out which order to use. After the device and software are installed, the software displays a menu to download images or video to your computer.
- ***Install the memory card in the computer.*** If images or video are stored on a flash memory card installed in your device, you can remove the card and then insert it in a flash memory card slot on your computer. Most laptop computers have one or more of these slots (see Figure 9-14).

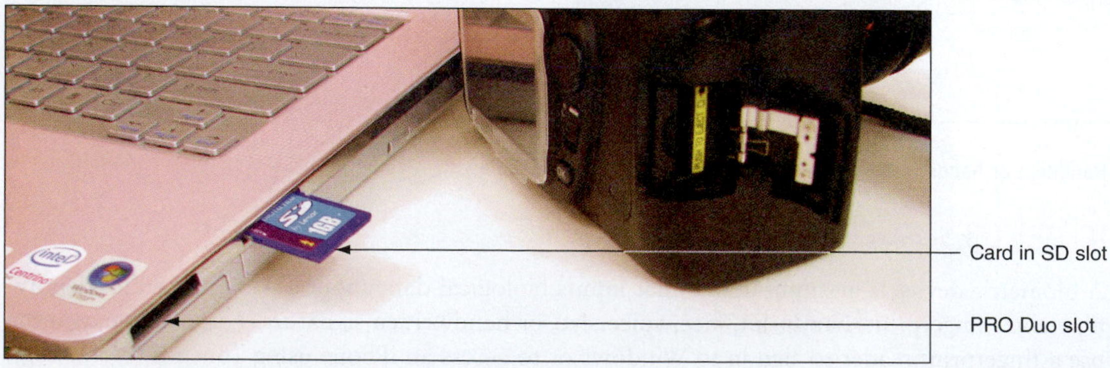

Figure 9-14 This laptop has two flash memory card slots

If your computer doesn't have this slot, or the slot is not compatible with the type of card you are using, you have two choices:

- Perhaps you can purchase an adapter so that your smaller memory card will fit into a larger card slot. Figure 9-15 shows examples of these adapters.

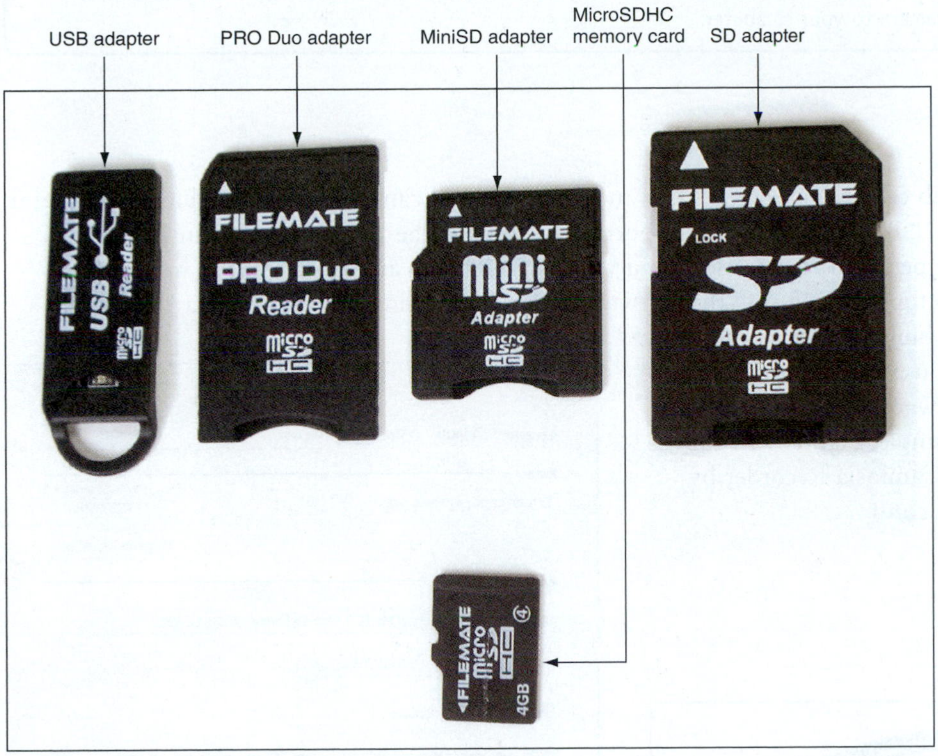

Figure 9-15 MicroSDHC card with four adapters

- You can install a USB smart card reader that provides a memory card slot to fit your card. Figure 9-16 shows one reader that connects to a computer using a USB port.

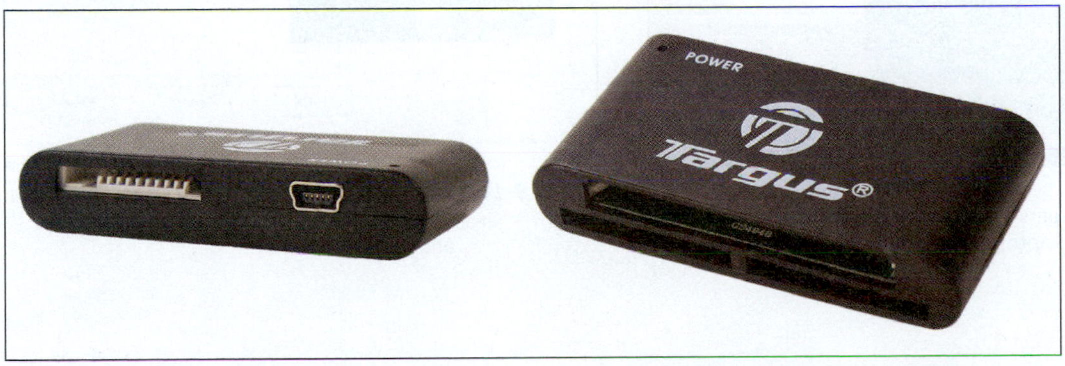

Figure 9-16 This Hi-Speed USB card reader/writer by Targus can read CompactFlash I and II, MicroDrive, SDHC, SD, MMC, xD, Memory Stick, PRO Duo, and Mini SD cards

When the memory card is recognized by Windows, it is assigned a drive letter and you can see it listed in Windows 8 File Explorer or Windows 7 Windows Explorer. Use Explorer to copy, move, and delete files from the card.

9

Notes It's interesting to know that TWAIN (Technology Without An Interesting Name) is a standard format used by scanners and digital cameras and other devices for transferring images.

A+ Exam Tip The A+ 220-901 exam expects you to know how to install the software bundled with your digital camera before attaching the camera to your computer.

WEBCAMS

A+
220-901
1.12

A webcam (web camera) is embedded in most laptops and can also be installed as a peripheral device using a USB port or some other port. For example, the webcam shown in Figure 9-17 works well for personal chat sessions and videoconferencing and has a built-in microphone. First, use the setup CD to install the software and then plug in the webcam to a USB port.

A webcam comes with a built-in microphone. You can use this microphone or use the microphone port on the computer. Most software allows you to select these input devices. For example, Figure 9-18 shows the Tools Options box for Camtasia Recorder by TechSmith (*www.techsmith.com*).

© iStockphoto/Eric Ferfuson

Figure 9-17 This personal web camera clips to the top of your laptop and has a built-in microphone

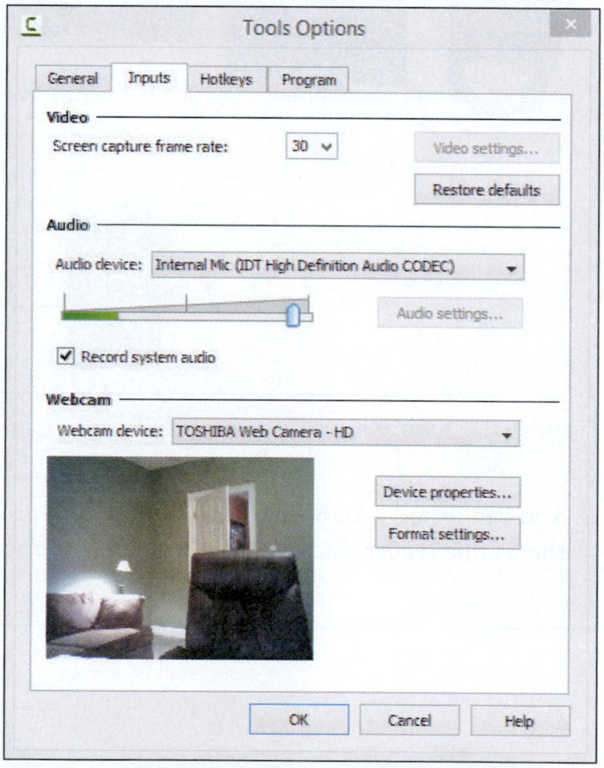

Source: Camtasia Recorder by TechSmith

Figure 9-18 The Camtasia Recorder application allows you to change the input devices used for video and sound

GRAPHICS TABLETS

A+
220-901
1.12

Another input device is a graphics tablet, also called a digitizing tablet or digitizer, that is used to hand draw and is likely to connect by a USB port (see Figure 9-19). It comes with a stylus that works like a pencil on the tablet. The graphics tablet and stylus can be a replacement to a mouse or touch pad on a laptop, and some graphics tablets come with a mouse. Graphics tablets are popular with graphic artists and others who use desktop publishing applications.

Figure 9-19 A graphics tablet and stylus are used to digitize a hand drawing

Install the graphics tablet the same way you do other USB devices. Additional software might be bundled with the device to enhance its functions, such as inputting handwritten signatures into Microsoft Word documents.

MOTION CONTROLLERS

A+ 220-901 1.12

A motion controller, sometimes called a motion sensor, provides input to the computer by sensing the motion of your fingers and hands. Figure 9-20 shows an example of a motion controller that uses a USB connection. It senses the space just above the controller where motions by your hands and fingers are used to control the computer. Motion controllers are commonly used with gaming consoles such as Xbox One or the Wii. Graphic designers or engineers who work with 3D images might also use a motion controller to manipulate designs, and motion controllers are also used in hospitals to allow surgeons access to vital data while maintaining a sterile environment. As with other USB devices, read the documentation to know if you should install the drivers first or the device first.

9

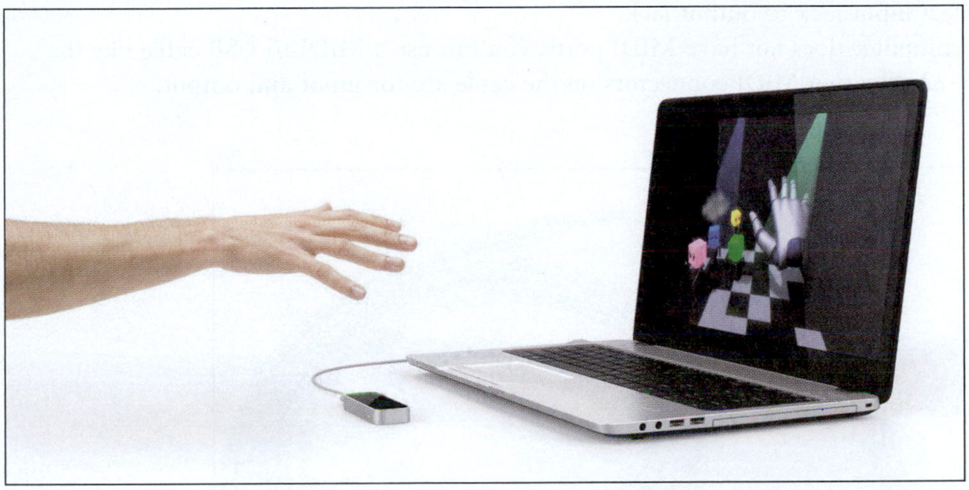

Site: https://www.leapmotion.com/

Figure 9-20 Leap Motion offers an affordable motion controller

MIDI DEVICES

A+ 220-901 1.12

MIDI (musical instrument digital interface), pronounced "middy," is a set of standards that are used to represent music in digital form. Using the MIDI format, each individual note played by each individual instrument is digitally stored. MIDI standards are used to connect electronic music equipment, such as musical keyboards and mixers, or to connect this equipment to a computer for input, output, and editing. Most sound cards can play MIDI files, and most electronic instruments have MIDI ports.

A MIDI port is a 5-pin DIN port that looks like a PS/2 keyboard port, only larger. Figure 9-21 shows MIDI ports on electronic drums. A MIDI port is either an input port or an output port, but not both. Normally, you would connect the MIDI output port to a mixer, but you can also use it to connect to a computer.

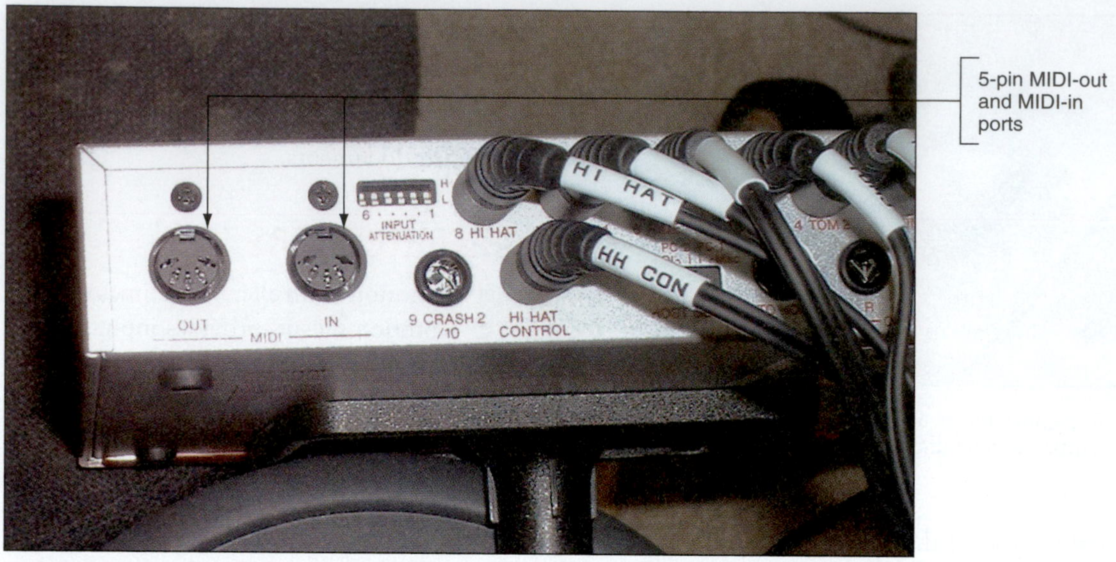

Figure 9-21 MIDI ports on an electronic drum set

Here are ways to connect a musical instrument to a computer using the MIDI standards:

- ***MIDI to MIDI.*** A few sound cards provide MIDI ports. Use two MIDI cables to connect output jack to input jack and to connect input jack to output jack.
- ***MIDI to USB.*** If your computer does not have MIDI ports, you can use a MIDI-to-USB cable like the one shown in Figure 9-22. The two MIDI connectors on the cable are for input and output.

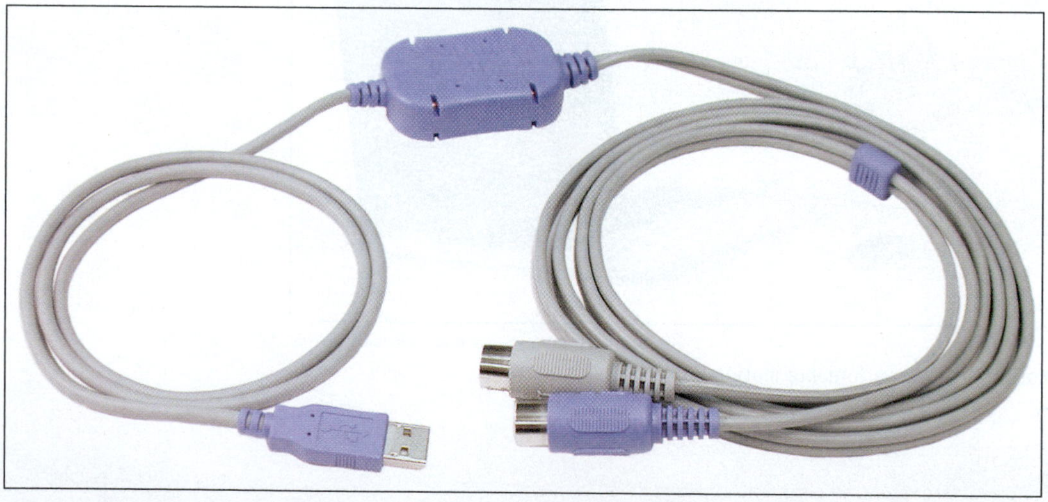

Figure 9-22 MIDI-to-USB cable lets you connect an electronic musical instrument to your computer

- ***USB to USB.*** Newer instruments have a USB port to interface with a computer using MIDI data transmissions.
- ***USB to MIDI.*** A USB port on an instrument can also connect to MIDI ports on a computer sound card.

★ A+ Exam Tip The A+ 220-901 exam expects you to know how to install and configure MIDI devices.

To mix and edit music using MIDI on your computer, you'll need MIDI editing software such as JAMMER Pro by SoundTrek (*www.soundtrek.com*). Before connecting the instrument to your computer, install the software that you intend to use to manage the music. Then, connect the instrument.

TOUCH SCREENS

A+
220-901
1.12

A **touch screen** is an input device that uses a monitor or LCD panel as the backdrop for input options. In other words, the touch screen is a grid that senses taps, finger pinches, and slides and sends these events to the computer by way of a USB port or other type of connection. Some laptops have built-in touch screens, and you can also install a touch screen on top of a monitor screen as an add-on device. As an add-on device, the touch screen has its own AC adapter to power it. Some monitors for desktop systems have built-in touch screen capability.

For add-on desktop monitors, clamp the touch screen over the monitor. For most installations, you install the drivers before you connect the touch screen to the computer by way of a USB port. After you install the drivers and the touch screen, you must use management software that came bundled with the device to decide how much of the monitor screen is taken up by the touch screen and to calibrate the touch screen. Later, if the monitor resolution is changed, the touch screen must be recalibrated.

KVM SWITCHES

A+
220-901
1.12

A **KVM (Keyboard, Video, and Mouse) switch** allows you to use one keyboard, monitor, and mouse for multiple computers. A KVM switch can be useful in a server room or testing lab where you use more than one computer and want to keep desk space clear of multiple keyboards, mice, and monitors or you simply want to lower the cost of peripherals. Figure 9-23 shows a KVM switch that can connect a keyboard, monitor, mouse, microphone, and speakers to two computers. The device uses USB ports for the keyboard and mouse.

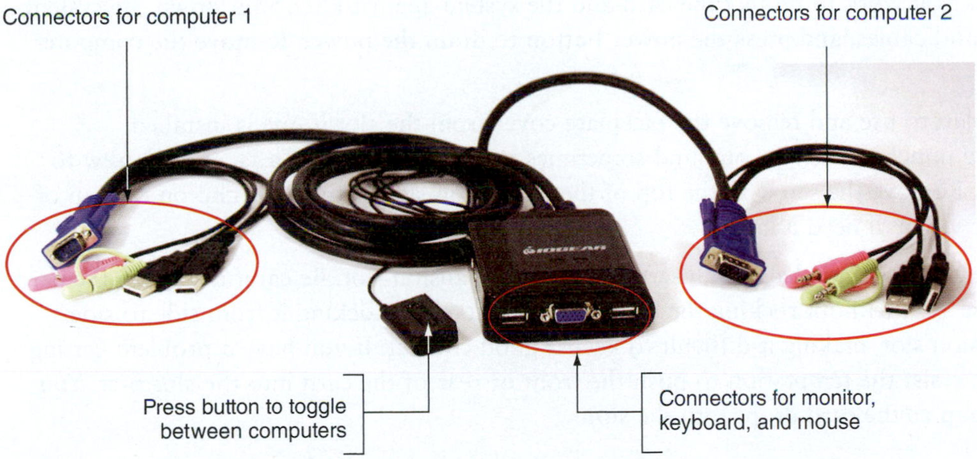

Figure 9-23 This KVM switch connects two computers to a keyboard, mouse, monitor, microphone, and speakers and uses USB for the keyboard and mouse

A KVM switch does not require that you install device drivers to use it. Just plug in the cables from each computer to the device. Also plug in one set of a monitor, mouse, keyboard, and possibly a microphone and speakers to the device. Switch between computers by using a hot key on the keyboard, buttons on the top of the KVM switch, or a wired remote such as the one shown in Figure 9-23.

INSTALLING AND CONFIGURING ADAPTER CARDS

A+
220-901
1.4, 3.1

In this part of the chapter, you learn to install and configure adapter cards. These cards include a video card, sound card, storage controller card, serial and parallel port card, Thunderbolt card, FireWire card, USB card, storage card, TV tuner card, and video capture card. The purpose of adding an adapter card to a system is to have available the external ports or internal connectors the card provides.

Regardless of the type of card you are installing, when preparing to install an adapter card, be sure to verify and do the following:

- ***Verify the card fits an empty expansion slot.*** Recall that there are several PCI and PCI Express standards; therefore, make sure the card will fit the slot. To help with airflow, try to leave an empty slot between cards. Especially try to leave an empty slot beside the video card, which puts off a lot of heat.
- ***Verify the device drivers for your OS are available.*** Check the card documentation and make sure you have the drivers for your OS. For example, you need to install 64-bit Windows 8 device drivers in a 64-bit installation of Windows 8. It might be possible to download drivers for your OS from the website of the card manufacturer.
- ***Back up important data that is not already backed up.*** Before you open the computer case, be sure to back up important data on the hard drive.
- ***Know your starting point.*** Know what works and doesn't work on the system. Can you connect to the network and the Internet, print, and use other installed adapter cards without errors?

Here are the general directions to install an adapter card. They apply to any type of card.

1. Read the documentation that came with the card. For most cards, you install the card first and then the drivers, but some adapter card installations might not work this way.
2. If you are installing a card to replace an onboard port, access UEFI/BIOS setup and disable the port.
3. Wear an ESD strap as you work to protect the card and the system against ESD. Shut down the system, unplug power cords and cables, and press the power button to drain the power. Remove the computer case cover.
4. Locate the slot you plan to use and remove the faceplate cover from the slot if one is installed. Sometimes a faceplate punches or snaps out, and sometimes you have to remove a faceplate screw to remove the faceplate. Remove the screw in the top of the expansion slot or raise the clip on the top of the slot. Save the screw; you'll need it later.
5. Remove the card from its antistatic bag and insert it into the expansion slot. Be careful to push the card straight down into the slot, without rocking the card from side to side. Rocking it from side to side can widen the expansion slot, making it difficult to keep a good contact. If you have a problem getting the card into the slot, resist the temptation to push the front or rear of the card into the slot first. You should feel a slight snap as the card drops into the slot.

Recall that PCIe x16 slots use a retention mechanism in the slot to help stabilize a heavy card (see Figure 9-24). For these slots, you might have to use one finger to push the stabilizer to the side as you push the card into the slot. Alternately, the card might snap into the slot and then the retention mechanism snaps into position. Figure 9-25 shows a PCIe video card installed in a PCIe x16 slot.

Figure 9-24 A white retention mechanism on a PCIe x16 slot pops into place to help stabilize a heavy video card

Figure 9-25 A PCIe video card installed in a PCIe x16 slot

6. Insert the screw that anchors the card to the top of the slot (see Figure 9-26). Be sure to use this screw. If it's not present, the card can creep out of the slot over time.

Figure 9-26 Secure the card to the case with a single screw

9

7. Connect any power cords or data cables the card might use. For example, a video card might have a 6-pin or 8-pin PCIe power connector for a power cord from the power supply to the card (see Figure 9-27). (If the power supply does not have the right connector, you can buy an inexpensive adapter to convert a 4-pin Molex connector to a PCIe connector.) In another example, look at Figure 9-3 shown earlier in the chapter. This FireWire card requires a power connection using a 4-pin Molex power cable from the power supply.

Figure 9-27 Connect a power cord to the PCIe power connector on the card

8. Make a quick check of all connections and cables, and then replace the case cover. (If you want, you can leave the case cover off until you've tested the card, in case it doesn't work and you need to reseat it.) Plug up the external power cable and essential peripherals.
9. Start the system. When Windows starts, it should detect a new hardware device is present and attempt to automatically install the drivers. As the drivers are installed, a message might appear above the taskbar. When you click the message, the Device Setup window appears (refer back to Figure 9-6). You can cancel the wizard and manually install the drivers.
10. Insert the CD that came bundled with the card and launch the setup program on the CD. The card documentation will tell you the name of the program (examples are Setup.exe and Autorun.exe). Figure 9-28 shows the opening menu for one setup program for a video card. Click **Install Video Drivers** and follow the on screen instructions to install the drivers. If you are using downloaded driver files, double-click the file to begin the installation and follow the directions on screen.

Notes All 64-bit drivers must be certified by Microsoft to work in Windows. However, some 32-bit drivers might not be. During the driver installation, if you see a message that says 32-bit drivers have not been certified, go ahead and give permission to install the drivers if you obtained them from the manufacturer or another reliable source.

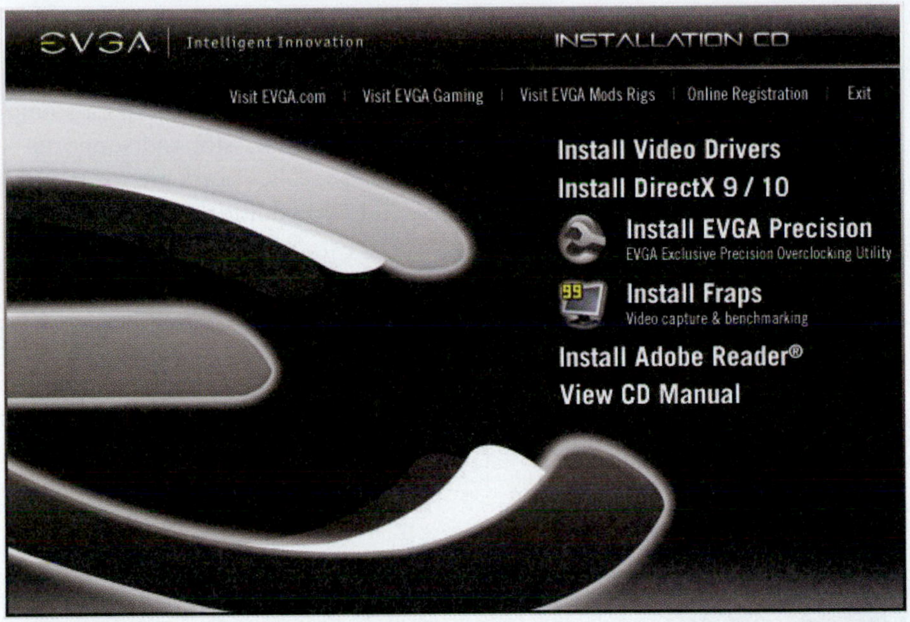

Source: EVGA

Figure 9-28 Opening menu to install video drivers

11. After the drivers are installed, you might be asked to restart the system. Then you can configure the card or use it with application software. If you have problems with the installation, turn to Device Manager and look for errors reported about the device. The card might not be properly seated in the slot.

Notes Some motherboards provide extra ports that can be installed in faceplate openings off the back of the case. For example, Figure 9-29 shows a module that has a game port and two USB ports. To install the module, remove a faceplate and install the module in its place. Then connect the cables from the module to the appropriate connectors on the motherboard.

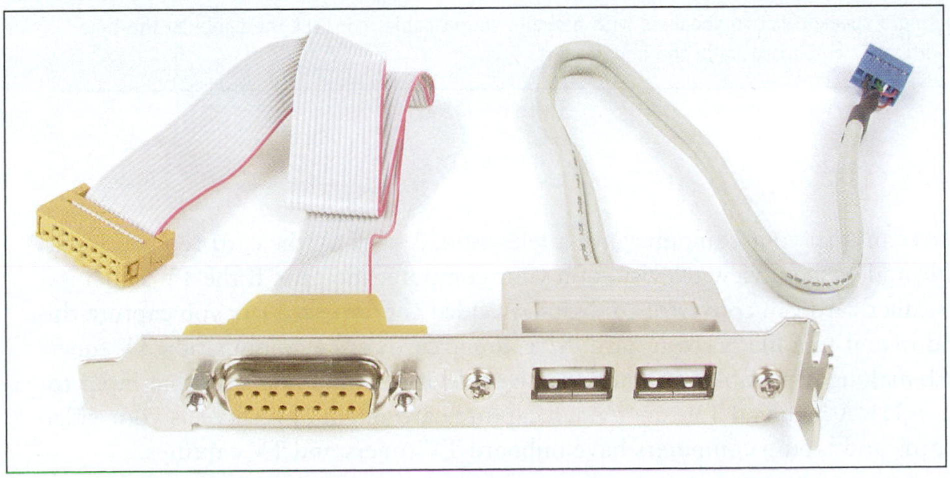

Figure 9-29 This I/O module provides two USB ports and one game port

Now let's turn our attention to a little information about three types of cards you might be called on to install. As with any adapter card you install, be sure to get familiar with the user guide before you start the installation so that you know the card's hardware and software requirements and what peripheral devices it supports.

SOUND CARDS AND ONBOARD SOUND

A+
220-901
1.4

A sound card (an expansion card with sound ports) or onboard sound (sound ports embedded on a motherboard) can play and record sound, and save it in a file. Figure 9-30 shows a sound card by Creative (*us.creative.com*). This Sound Blaster card uses a PCIe x1 slot and supports up to eight surround sound version 7.1 speakers. The color-coded speaker ports are for these speakers: front left and right, front center, rear left and right, subwoofer, and two additional rear speakers. The two S/PDIF (Sony/Philips Digital InterFace) ports are used to connect to external sound equipment such as a CD or DVD player.

Courtesy of Creative Technology Ltd.

Figure 9-30 Sound Blaster X-Fi Titanium sound card by Creative uses a PCIe x1 slot

Notes If you are using a single speaker or two speakers with a single sound cable, connect the cable to the lime-green sound port on the motherboard, which is usually the middle port.

TV TUNER AND VIDEO CAPTURE CARDS

A+
220-901
1.4

A TV tuner card can turn your computer into a television. A port on the card receives input from a TV cable and lets you view television on your computer monitor. If the TV signal is analog, the TV tuner card can convert it to digital. A video capture card lets you capture this video input and save it to a file on your hard drive. Some cards are a combination TV tuner card and video capture card, making it possible for you to receive television input and save that input to your hard drive (see Figure 9-31). A high-end TV tuner/video capture card might also serve as your video card. Also, some motherboards and laptop computers have onboard TV tuners and TV captures.

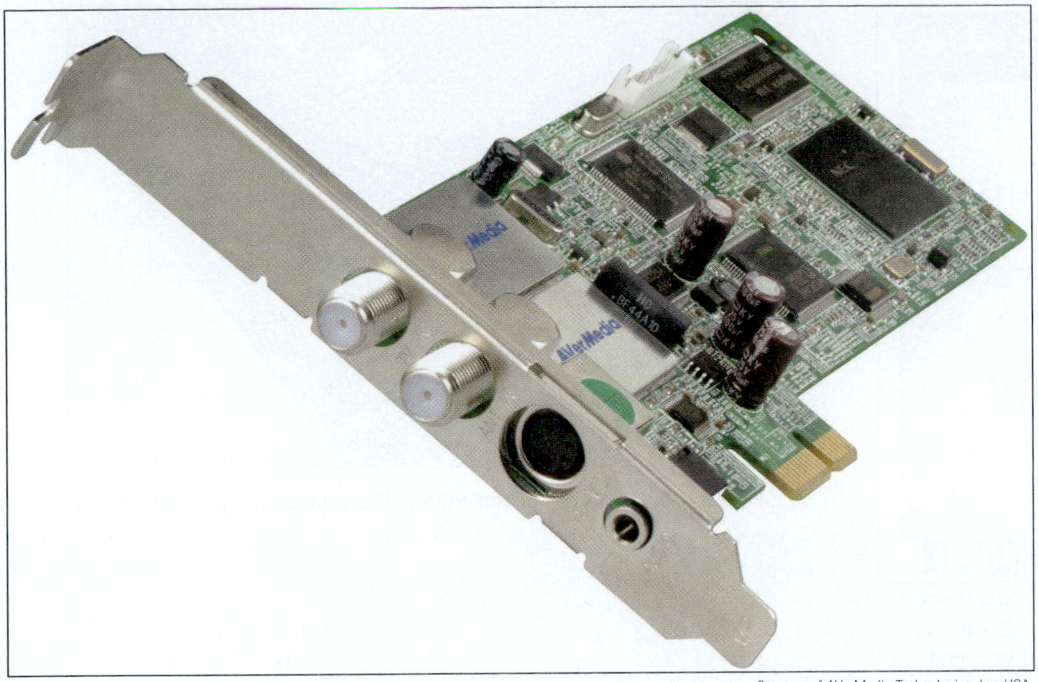

Courtesy of AVerMedia Technologies, Inc. USA.

Figure 9-31 The AVerMedia AVerTV PVR 150 Plus TV tuner and video capture card uses a PCIe x1 slot and works alongside a regular video card

When installing a TV tuner or capture card, most likely you will install the drivers, install the card, and then install the application software that comes bundled with the card. You can then configure and manage the card using the applications.

Hands-On | Project 9-1 Install a Device

A+
220-901
1.4

Install a device on a computer. If you are working in a classroom environment, you can simulate an installation by moving a device from one computer to another. Devices that you might consider installing are a video card, webcam, or fingerprint reader.

REPLACING EXPANSION CARDS IN A LAPTOP

A+
220-901
1.4, 3.1

A laptop does not contain the normal PCI Express or PCI slots found in desktop systems. Newer laptops are likely to use the **Mini PCI Express** slots (also called **Mini PCIe** slots) that use the PCI Express standards applied to laptops. Mini PCI Express slots use 52 pins on the edge connector. These slots can be used by many kinds of Mini PCIe cards. These cards are often used to enhance communications options for a laptop, including Wi-Fi wireless, cellular WAN, and Bluetooth Mini PCIe cards. Figure 9-32 shows a Mini PCI Express Sierra Wireless mobile broadband Internet card. Older laptops use a Mini PCI slot (see Figure 9-33), which uses PCI standards. Mini PCI cards are about twice the size of Mini PCI Express cards. Figure 9-34 shows a Wi-Fi Mini PCI card by MikroTik.

Source: Sierra Wireless

Figure 9-32 MC8775 PCI Express Mini card by Sierra Wireless used for voice and data transmissions on cellular networks

Figure 9-33 A Mini PCI slot follows PCI standards applied to laptops

Courtesy of MikroTik

Figure 9-34 Wireless IEEE 802.11a/b/g/n Mini PCI card by MikroTik

For many laptops, you can remove a cover on the bottom of the laptop to expose expansion cards so that you can exchange them without an extensive disassemble. For example, to remove the cover on the bottom of one Lenovo laptop, first remove several screws and then lift the laptop cover up and out. Several internal components are exposed, as shown in Figure 9-35.

Figure 9-35 Removing the cover from the bottom of a laptop exposes several internal components

The half-size Mini PCIe wireless Wi-Fi card shown in Figure 9-36 has two antennas. To remove the card, first remove the one screw shown in the photo and disconnect the two black and white antenna wires. Then slide the card forward and out of the slot. You can then install a new card.

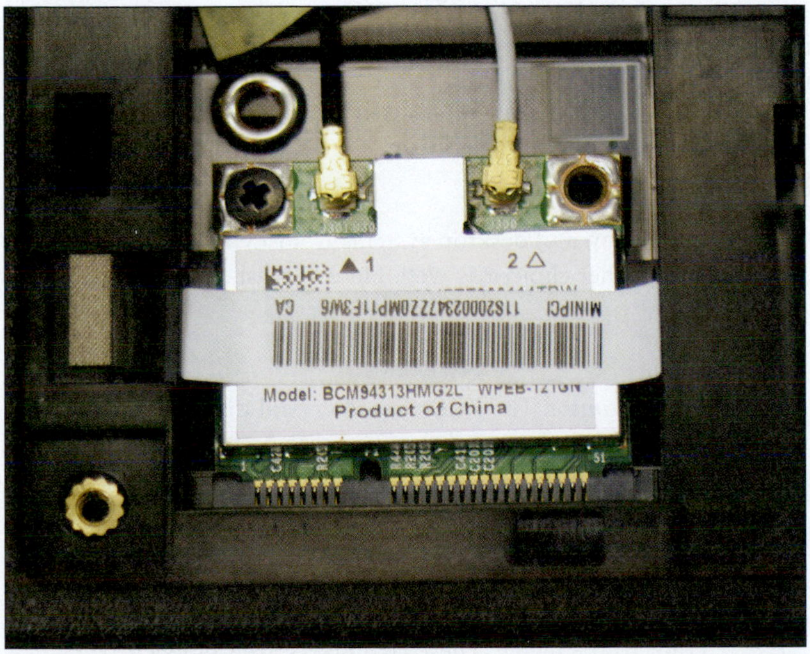

Figure 9-36 This half-size Mini PCIe wireless card is anchored in the expansion slot with one screw

Figure 9-37 shows a full-size Mini PCIe card installed in a different laptop. First disconnect the one antenna and remove the one screw at the top of the card, and then pull the card forward and out of the slot.

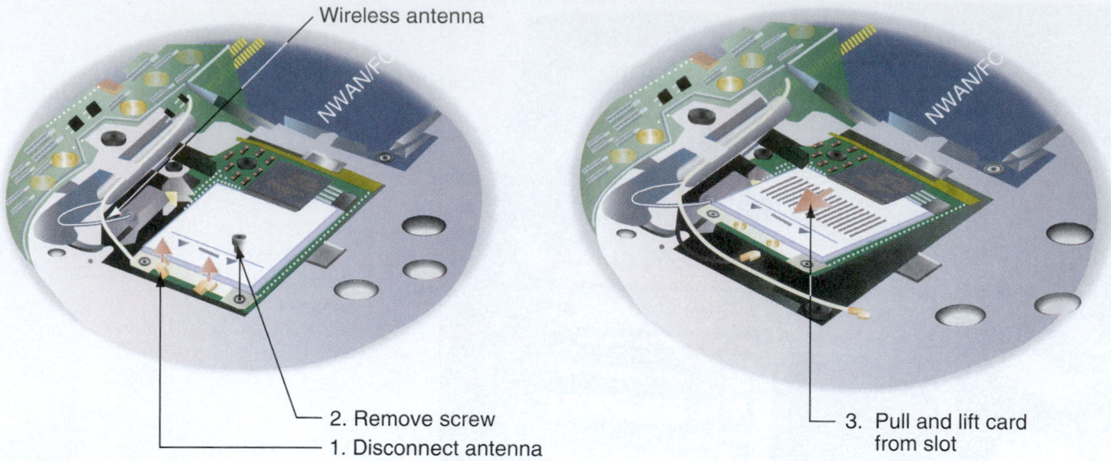

Figure 9-37 How to remove a Mini PCI Express card

A+ Exam Tip The A+ 220-901 exam expects you to be able to replace a Mini PCIe card in a laptop.

After you have installed a Mini PCIe card that is a Bluetooth, cellular WAN, or other wireless adapter, try to connect the laptop to the wireless network. If you have problems making a connection, verify that Device Manager reports the device is working properly and that Event Viewer has not reported error events about the device.

SUPPORTING THE VIDEO SUBSYSTEM

A+ 220-901 1.4, 1.7, 1.10, 1.11

The primary output device of a computer is the monitor. The two necessary components for video output are the monitor and the video card (also called the video adapter and graphics adapter) or a video port on the motherboard. In this part of the chapter, you learn about monitors, video cards, the video connectors they use, and how to support the video subsystem.

MONITOR TECHNOLOGIES AND FEATURES

A+ 220-901 1.10

The most popular type of monitor for laptop and desktop systems is an LCD flat-screen monitor (see Figure 9-38), but you have other choices as well. Here is a list and description of each type of monitor:

Figure 9-38 An LCD monitor

- *LCD monitor.* The LCD (liquid crystal display) monitor, also called a flat-panel monitor, was first used in laptops. The monitor produces an image using a liquid crystal material made of large, easily polarized molecules. Figure 9-39 shows the layers of the LCD panel that together create the image. At the center of the layers is the liquid crystal material. Next to it is the layer responsible for providing color to the image. These two layers are sandwiched between two grids of electrodes forming columns and rows. Each intersection of a row electrode and a column electrode forms one pixel on the LCD panel. Software can address each pixel to create an image.

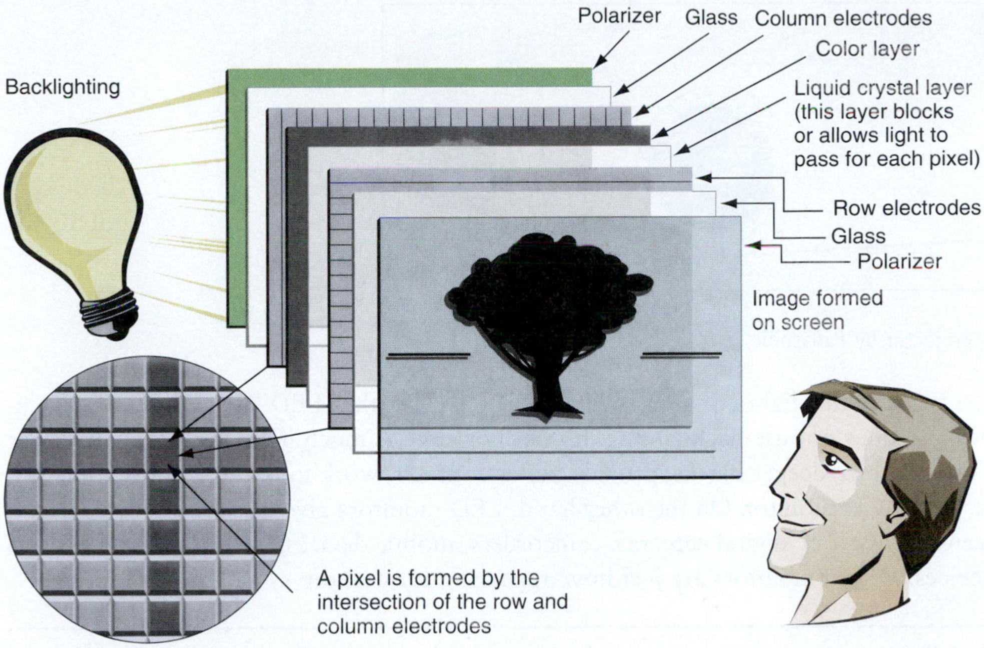

Figure 9-39 Layers of an LCD panel

Two common classes of LCD monitors are:

- Twisted Nematic (TN) LCD monitors are preferred by gamers because they have fast response times to keep fast-moving images crisp. However, TN monitors are brighter, consume more power, and have limited viewing angles.
- In-Plane Switching (IPS) monitors are a newer technology that offers truer color images and better viewing angles. However, IPS monitors are expensive and have slower response times.

The LCD panel does not produce any light so it needs a source of light, called backlighting. There are two common types of backlighting:

- Cold Cathode Fluorescent Lamp (CCFL) backlighting, also called fluorescent backlighting, is an older technology first used in laptop monitors. It uses one or two fluorescent tubes to light the panel. An inverter circuit board provides power to the fluorescent light. Two fluorescent tubes (CCFL-2) requires two inverter boards.
- LED (light-emitting diode) backlighting receives its DC power directly from the motherboard and doesn't use an inverter. The growing trend for most monitor manufacturers is to use LED backlighting, which provides a better range and accuracy of color and uses less power than fluorescent backlighting. LED technology also uses less mercury, and is, therefore, kinder to the environment when an LCD monitor is disposed of. When you see a monitor advertised as an LED monitor, know the monitor is an LCD monitor that uses LED backlighting.

- *Plasma monitor.* A plasma monitor provides high contrast with better color than LCD monitors. They work by discharging xenon and neon plasma on flat glass and don't contain mercury. Plasma monitors are expensive and heavy and are generally available only in large commercial sizes.
- *Projector.* A digital projector (see Figure 9-40) is used to shine a light that projects a transparent image onto a large screen and is often used in classrooms or with other large groups. Several types of technologies are used by projectors, including LCD. A projector is often installed on a computer as a dual monitor, which you learn how to do later in the chapter.

Courtesy of Panasonic Corporation of North America

Figure 9-40 Portable XGA projector by Panasonic

- ***OLED monitor.*** An OLED (organic light-emitting diode) monitor uses a thin LED layer or film between two grids of electrodes and does not use backlighting. It does not emit as much light as an LCD monitor does, and, therefore, can produce deeper blacks, provide better contrast, work in darker rooms, and use less power than can an LCD monitor. On the other hand, LED monitors give less glare than OLED monitors. OLED screens are used by digital cameras, camcorders, mobile devices, and other small portable electronic devices. OLED monitors are just now appearing for desktop systems.

> **A+ Exam Tip** The A+ 220-901 exam expects you to know about these monitor types and technologies: LCD, LED, plasma, projector, and OLED.

A laptop display almost always uses LCD technology, although laptops that use OLED display are available. It is expected that laptops will one day use plasma display because plasma is expected to use only about 20 percent as much power as LCD and gives better quality display than LCD. Some laptop LCD panels use LED backlighting to improve display quality and conserve power.

> **A+ Exam Tip** The A+ 220-901 exam expects you to know about the components within the display of a laptop, including LCD, LED, OLED, and plasma types. You also need to know about backlighting and the function of an inverter.

For desktops, by far the most popular monitor type is LCD. Figure 9-41 shows an ad for one high-end LCD monitor. Table 9-3 explains the features mentioned in the ad.

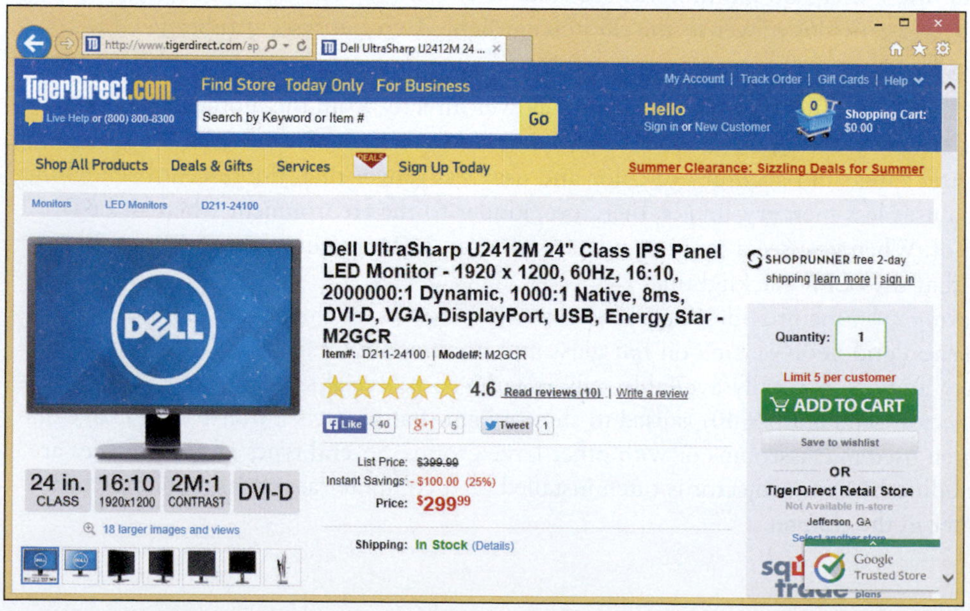

Source: tigerdirect.com

Figure 9-41 An ad for a monitor lists cryptic monitor features

★ A+ Exam Tip The A+ 220-901 exam expects you to know about these monitor features: refresh rate, resolution, native resolution, brightness in lumens, and analog and digital connectors used.

Monitor Characteristic	Description
Screen size	The screen size is the diagonal length of the screen surface in inches.
Aspect ratio	The aspect ratio is the proportional relationship between width and height. Common aspect ratios are 4:3, 16:9, and 16:10. Sometimes, an image must be converted from one aspect ratio to another. Three ways to convert a standard 4:3 image to a wide screen 16:9 is to add black bars to either side of the image to fill in the space; stretch the image horizontally, which creates distortion; or zoom without distorting the image until the image touches the sides, which will crop the top and bottom of the image.
Refresh rate	The refresh rate is the number of times a monitor screen is built or refreshed in one second, measured in Hz (cycles per second). The ad in Figure 9-41 shows the monitor refresh rate as 60 Hz (60 frames per second)—the higher, the better. Related to refresh rate, the response time is the time it takes to build one frame, measured in ms (milliseconds)—the lower, the better. The ad in Figure 9-41 shows a response time of 8 ms (time to build one frame).
Pixel pitch	A pixel is a spot or dot on the screen that can be addressed by software. The pixel pitch is the distance between adjacent pixels on the screen—the smaller the number, the better. An example of a pixel pitch is .283mm.
Resolution	The resolution is the number of spots or pixels on a screen that can be addressed by software. Values can range from 640 × 480 up to 4096 × 2160 for high-end monitors. Popular resolutions are 1920 × 1080 and 1366 × 768.
Native resolution	The native resolution is the number of pixels built into the LCD monitor. Using the native resolution usually gives the highest-quality image.
Contrast ratio	Contrast ratio is the contrast between true black and true white on the screen—the higher the contrast ratio, the better. 1000:1 is better than 700:1. An advertised dynamic contrast ratio is much higher than the contrast ratio, but is not a true measurement of contrast. Dynamic contrast adjusts the backlighting to give the effect of an overall brighter or darker image. For example, in Figure 9-41, the contrast ratio is 1000:1, and the dynamic ratio is 20,000,000:1. When comparing quality of monitors, pay attention to the contrast ratio, more so than the dynamic ratio.
Viewing angle	The viewing angle is the angle of view when a monitor becomes difficult to see. A viewing angle of 170 degrees is better than 140 degrees.
Backlighting or brightness	Brightness is measured in cd/m^2 (candela per square meter), which is the same as $lumens/m^2$ (lumens per square meter). In addition, the best LED backlighting for viewing photography is class IPS, which provides the most accurate color.
Connectors	Options for connectors are VGA, DVI-I, DVI-D, HDMI, DisplayPort, and Apple's Thunderbolt. Some monitors offer more than one connector (see Figure 9-42). These and other connectors used by video cards and monitors are discussed later in the chapter.
Other features	LCD monitors can also provide a privacy or antiglare surface, tilt screens, microphone input, speakers, USB ports, adjustable stands, and perhaps even a port for your iPod. Some monitors are also touch screens, so they can be used with a stylus or finger touch.

Table 9-3 Important features of a monitor

Caution If you spend many hours in front of a computer, you may strain your eyes. To protect your eyes from strain, look away from the monitor into the distance every few minutes. Use a good monitor with a high refresh rate or low response time. The lower refresh rates that cause monitor flicker can tire and damage your eyes. When you first install a monitor, set the refresh rate at the highest value the monitor can support.

9

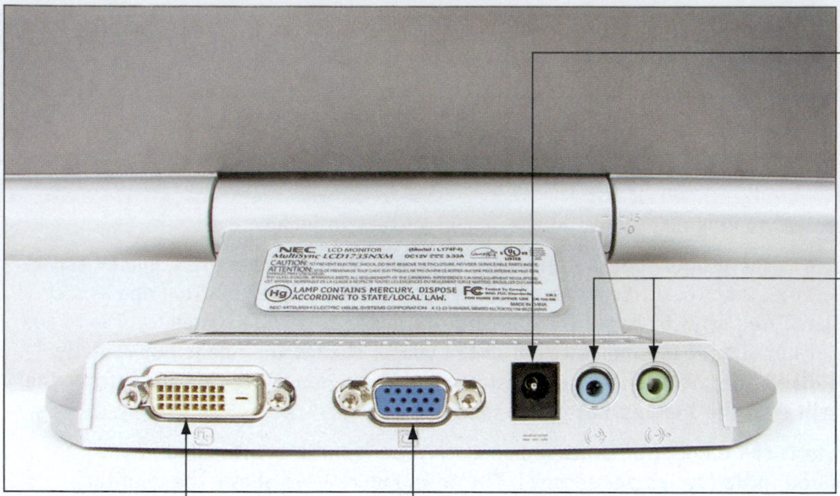

Figure 9-42 The rear of this LCD monitor shows digital and analog video ports to accommodate a video cable with either a 15-pin analog VGA connector or a digital DVI connector

VIDEO CARDS AND CONNECTORS

A+
220-901
1.4, 1.7,
1.10, 1.11

Video cards (see Figure 9-43) are sometimes called graphics adapters, graphics cards, or display cards. Most motherboards sold today have one or more video ports integrated into the motherboard. If you are buying a motherboard with a video port, make sure that you can disable the video port on the motherboard if it gives you trouble. You can then install a video card and use its video port rather than the port on the motherboard. Recall that a video card can use a PCI or PCI Express slot on the motherboard. The fastest slot to use is a PCIe x16 slot.

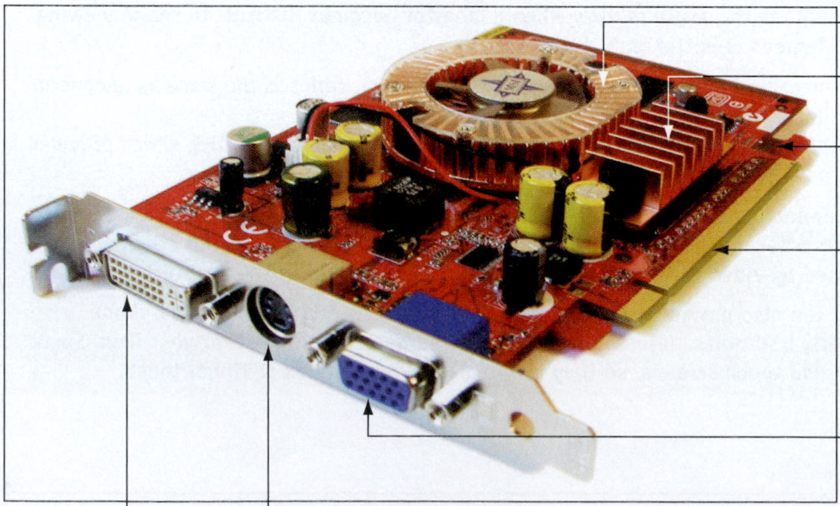

Figure 9-43 The PCX 5750 graphics card by MSI Computer Corporation uses the PCI Express x16 local bus

Recall that types of video ports include VGA, S-Video, DVI, DisplayPort, and HDMI connectors. In addition to these ports, you also need to know about a composite video, miniHDMI, Mini-DIN-6, DVI-I, DVI-D, and DVI-A ports. All these ports are described here:

- ***VGA.*** The 15-pin VGA port is the standard analog video port and transmits three signals of red, green, and blue (RGB). A VGA port is sometimes called a DB-15 port.
- ***DVI ports.*** DVI ports were designed to replace VGA, and variations of DVI can transmit analog and/or digital data. The five DVI standards for pinouts are shown in Figure 9-44. Three DVI connectors are shown in Figure 9-45. The DVI standards specify the maximum length for DVI cables is 5 meters, although some video cards produce a strong enough signal to allow for longer DVI cables.

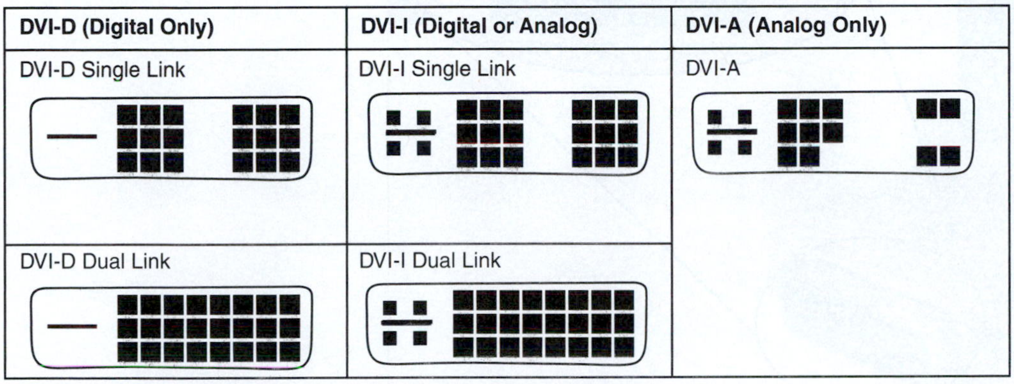

Figure 9-44 Five pinout arrangements for DVI ports and connectors

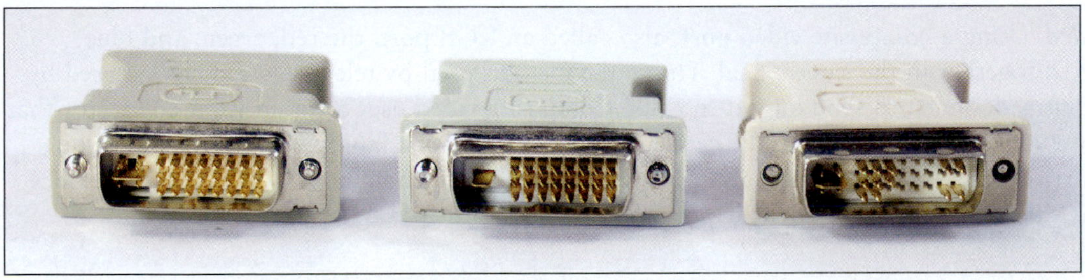

Figure 9-45 Three types of DVI connectors: (left) DVI-I, (middle) DVI-D, and (right) DVI-A

Here are the variations of DVI:

- ***DVI-D.*** The DVI-D port only transmits digital data. Using an adapter to convert a VGA cable to the port won't work. You can see a DVI-D port in Figure 9-46a.

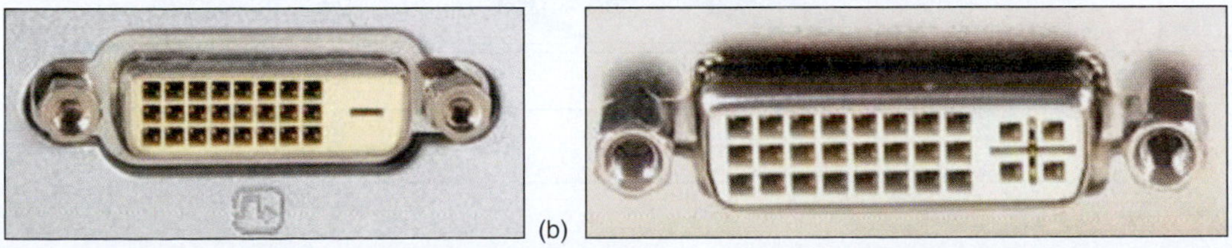

(a) (b)

Figure 9-46 Two types of DVI ports: (a) DVI-D, (b) DVI-I

- *DVI-I.* The DVI-I port (see Figure 9-46b) supports both analog and digital signals. If a computer has this type of port, you can use a digital-to-analog adapter to connect an older analog monitor to the port using a VGA cable (see Figure 9-47). If a video card has a DVI port, most likely it will be the DVI-I port (the one with the four extra holes) so that you can use an adapter to convert the port to a VGA port.
- *DVI-A.* The DVI-A port only transmits analog data. You don't see these very often.

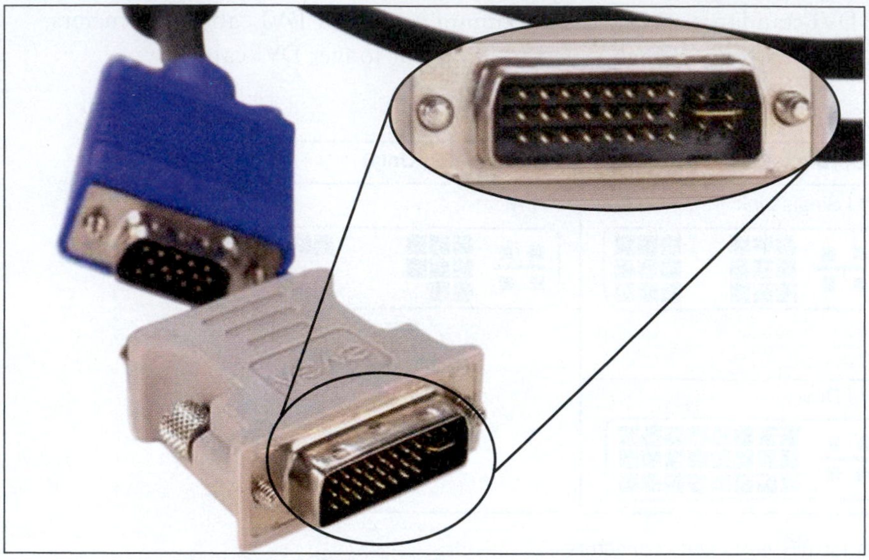

Figure 9-47 Digital-to-analog video port converter using DVI-I connector with extra four pins

- *Composite video.* Using a composite video port, also called an RGB port, the red, green, and blue (RGB) are mixed together in the same signal. This is the method used by television and can be used by a video card that is designed to send output to a TV. Composite video uses a round RCA connector that is usually yellow and has a single pin in the center. Figure 9-48 shows a laptop that has a composite video input port so that you can use the laptop as your display for a game box. Composite video does not produce as sharp an image as VGA video or S-Video.

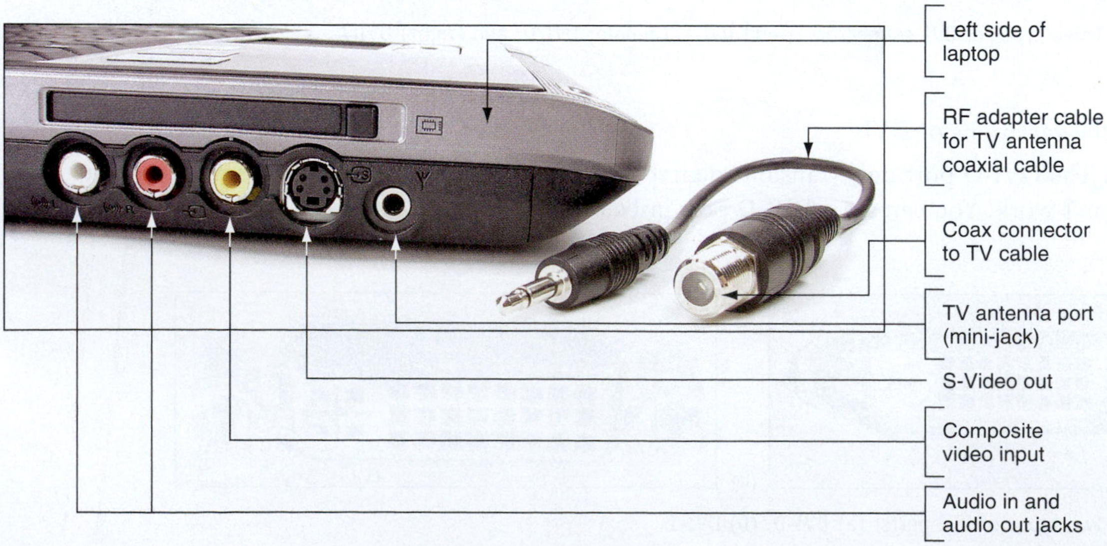

Figure 9-48 This laptop designed for multimedia applications has an embedded TV tuner and can also receive audio and video input from game boxes

- *S-Video (Super-Video) ports.* An S-Video port is a 4-pin or 7-pin round port used by some televisions and video equipment. An S-Video cable is shown in Figure 9-49. A few older video cameras use a 6-pin variation of S-Video. The connector is called a Mini-DIN -6 connector and looks like a PS/2 connector used by a keyboard or mouse. (In general, a DIN connector is always round with multiple pins in the connector.)

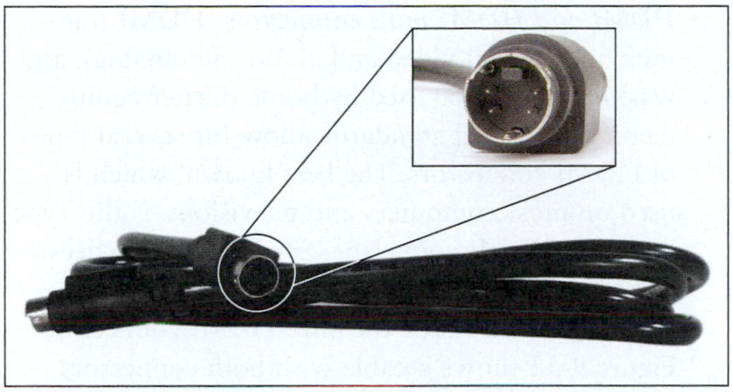

Figure 9-49 An S-Video cable used to connect a video card to an S-Video port on a television

- *Component video.* Whereas composite video has the red, green, and blue mixed in the same signal, component video has been split into different components and carried as separate signals. Figure 9-50 shows five RCA connectors on one component video and audio cable. Three lines carry video (red, blue, and green), and the red and white lines are used for audio (audio in and audio out).

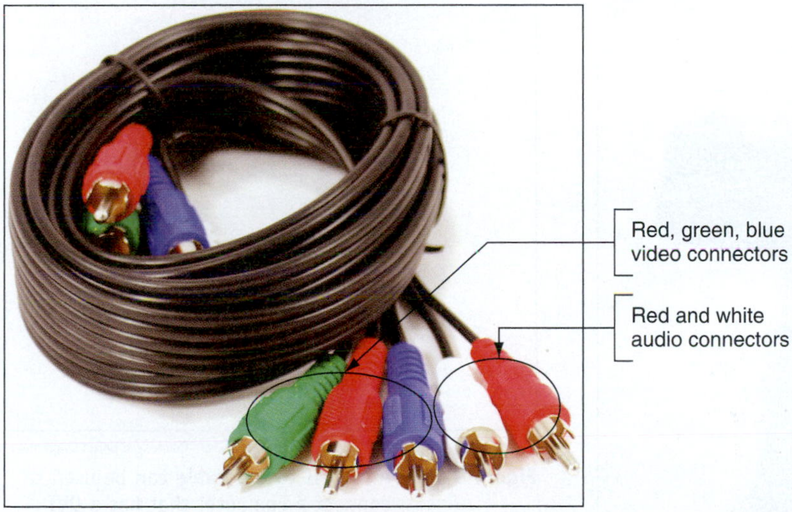

Figure 9-50 Component video and audio cable uses five RCA connectors

- *DisplayPort.* DisplayPort was designed to replace DVI and can transmit digital (not analog) video and audio data. It uses data packet transmissions similar to those of Ethernet, USB, and PCI Express, and is expected to ultimately replace VGA, DVI, and HDMI on desktop and laptop computers. Besides the regular DisplayPort used on video cards and desktop computers, laptops might use the smaller Mini DisplayPort. Figure 9-51 shows a DisplayPort to Mini DisplayPort cable. Some DisplayPort controllers allow you to use a DisplayPort-to-HDMI adapter so the port can be used with an HDMI connection. Maximum length for DisplayPort cables is 15 meters.

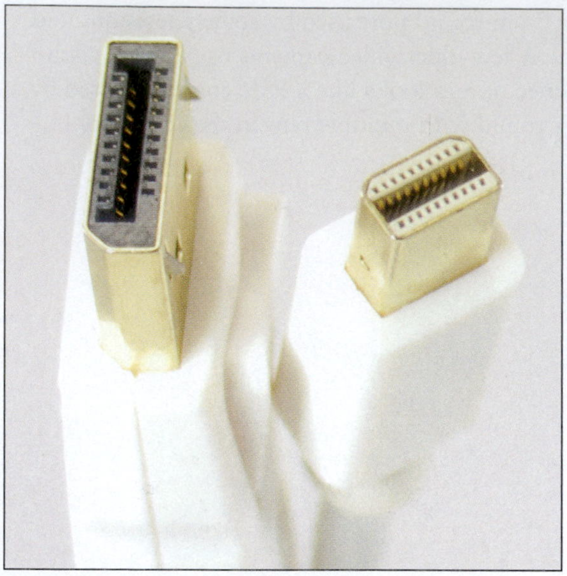

Figure 9-51 DisplayPort to Mini DisplayPort cable

UEFI/BIOS setup can be used to manage onboard DisplayPort and HDMI ports. For example, look at Figure 9-5 shown earlier in the chapter, where you can enable or disable the audio transmissions of DisplayPort and HDMI ports and still use these ports for video.

- ***HDMI and HDMI mini connectors.*** HDMI transmits both digital video and audio (not analog), and was designed to be used by home theater equipment. The HDMI standards allow for several types of HDMI connectors. The best known, which is used on most computers and televisions, is the Type A 19-pin HDMI connector. Small mobile devices can use the smaller Type C 19-pin HDMI mini connector, also called the mini-HDMI connector. Figure 9-52 shows a cable with both connectors that is useful when connecting some devices like a smart phone to a computer. Figure 9-53 shows an HDMI to DVI-D cable. Because HDMI does not transmit analog data, the connector works only on DVI-D and DVI-I ports, not DVI-A ports. To connect HDMI to VGA, you need an HDMI to VGA adapter with signal conversion because VGA is analog and HDMI is digital. The maximum length of an HDMI cable depends on the quality of the cable; no maximum length has been specified.

Figure 9-52 HDMI to miniHDMI cable

Courtesy of Belkin Corporation

Figure 9-53 An HDMI to DVI cable can be used to connect a computer that has a DVI port to home theater equipment that uses an HDMI port

Digital Rights Management (DRM) is meant to protect digital content and prevent piracy. DRM involves both software and hardware. HDMI and DVI allow for protected content to stay encrypted until it is on the presentation device. If you end up with a blank screen when playing a movie or no sound when listening to a CD, the problem may be that DRM is blocking the signal to prevent it from being pirated. In addition to protecting content from being pirated, DRM also limits quality of content based on its authorization. For example, a high-definition movie must be limited to DVD quality on video outputs that are not approved by DRM.

★ A+ Exam Tip The A+ 220-901 exam expects you to know about these video connector types: VGA (DB-15), HDMI, Mini HDMI, DisplayPort, S-Video, Mini-DIN-6, composite (RGB), component, RCA, DVI-D, DVI-I, and DVI-A.

Hands-On | Project 9-2 Research Video Port Adapters

Research the web and find devices that can be used as solutions to these problems. Print or save the webpage showing the device and price:

1. Find an adapter that allows you to connect a Thunderbolt port on a computer to a DVI monitor using a DVI cable.
2. Find an adapter that allows you to connect a Mini DisplayPort on your laptop to a DVI-D port on your monitor. Also find a cable that will work with the adapter.
3. Find an adapter that will allow you to connect a DVI-I port on your desktop to a VGA monitor, using a VGA cable.

Now let's see how to configure a monitor or dual monitors connected to a Windows computer.

CHANGING MONITOR SETTINGS

A+ 220-901 1.4, 1.7, 1.10, 1.11

Settings that apply to the monitor can be managed by using the monitor buttons and Windows utilities. Using the monitor buttons, you can adjust the horizontal and vertical position of the screen on the monitor surface and change the brightness and contrast settings. For laptops, the brightness and contrast settings can be changed using function keys on the laptop.

APPLYING | CONCEPTS INSTALL DUAL MONITORS

A+ 220-901 1.10

To increase the size of your Windows desktop, you can install more than one monitor for a single computer. To install dual monitors, you need two video ports on your system, which can come from motherboard video ports, a video card that provides two video ports, or two video cards.

To install a second monitor in a dual-monitor setup using two video cards, follow these steps:

1. Verify the original video card works properly and decide whether it is to be the primary monitor.
2. Boot the computer and enter UEFI/BIOS setup. If UEFI/BIOS setup has the option to select the order in which video cards are initialized, verify the currently installed card is configured to initialize first. For example, for the UEFI/BIOS system in Figure 9-54, the video adapter in the PCIe slot initializes first before other video adapters. If it does not initialize first, then, when you install the second card, video might not work at all when you first boot with two cards.

(continues)

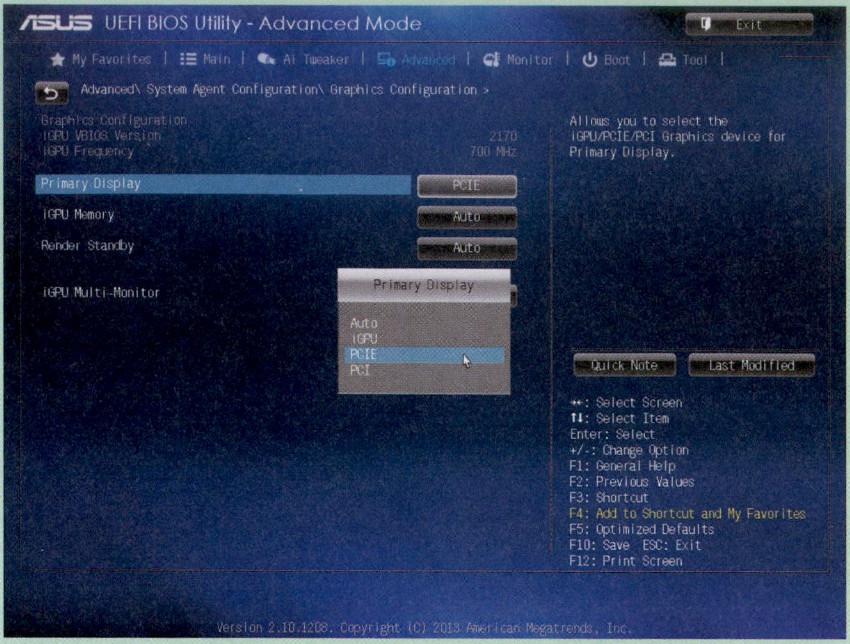

Source: American Megatrends, Inc.

Figure 9-54 In UEFI/BIOS setup, verify the currently installed video adapter is set to initialize first

3. Install a second video card in an empty slot. A computer might have a second PCIe slot or an unused PCI slot you can use. Attach the second monitor.
4. Boot the system. Windows recognizes the new hardware and launches Device Setup. You can use the utility to install the video card drivers or cancel the utility and install them manually as you learned to do earlier in the chapter.

Here are the steps to configure dual monitors:

1. Connect two monitors to your system. Open **Control Panel** in Classic view, click **Display**, and then click **Adjust resolution**. The Screen Resolution window appears (see Figure 9-55).

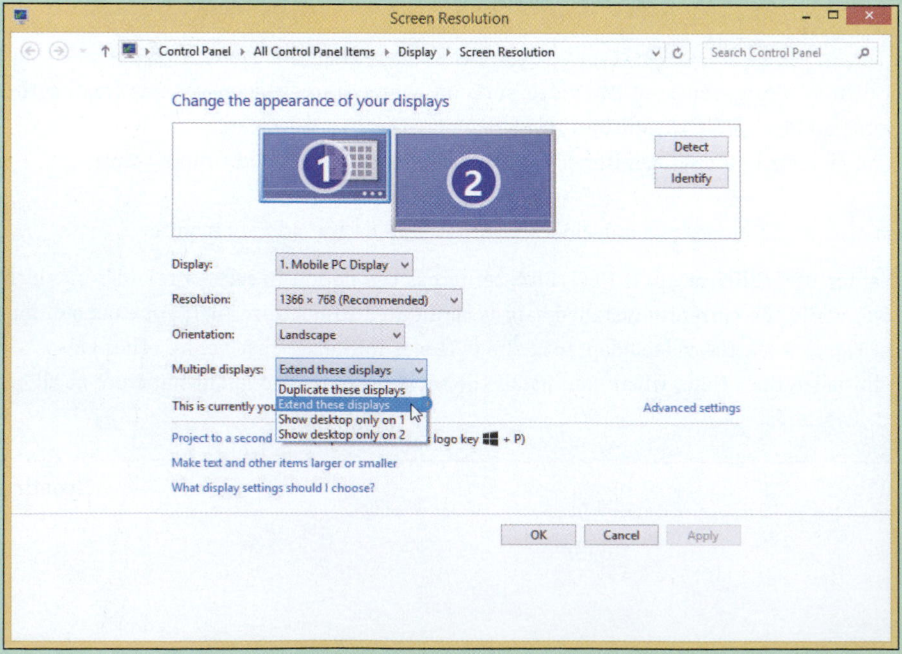

Figure 9-55 Configure each monitor in a dual-monitor configuration

2. Notice the two numbered boxes that represent your two monitors. When you click one of these boxes, the drop-down menu changes to show the selected monitor, and the screen resolution and orientation (Landscape, Portrait, Landscape flipped, or Portrait flipped) follow the selected monitor. This lets you customize the settings for each monitor. If necessary, use drag-and-drop to arrange the boxes so that they represent the physical arrangement of your monitors.

Notes In Figure 9-55, if you arrange the two boxes side by side, your extended desktop will extend left or right. If you arrange the two boxes one on top of the other, your extended desktop will extend up and down.

3. Adjust the screen resolution according to your preferences. For the sharpest images, use the native resolution for each monitor. Most often, the native resolution is the highest resolution listed, but this is not always the case. To know for certain the native resolution, see the documentation that came with the monitor.
4. The Screen Resolution window (refer back to Figure 9-55) allows you to select how to handle multiple displays. You can extend your desktop onto the second monitor, duplicate displays, or disable display on either monitor. To save the settings, click **Apply**. The second monitor should initialize and show the extended or duplicated desktop.
5. Close the **Screen Resolution** window. For an extended desktop, open an application and verify you can use the second monitor by dragging the application window over to the second monitor's desktop.

After you add a second monitor to your system, you can move from one monitor to another simply by moving your mouse over the extended desktop. Switching from one monitor to the other does not require any special keystroke or menu option.

Most laptop computers are designed to be used with projectors and provide a VGA, DisplayPort, or HDMI port for this purpose. To use a projector, plug in the projector to the extra port and then turn it on. For a laptop computer, use a function key to activate the video port and toggle between extending the desktop to the projector, using only the projector, duplicating the screen on the projector, or not using the projector. When giving a presentation, most presenters prefer that they see their presentation duplicated on the LCD screen and the projector.

Notes For group presentations that require a projector, the software used for the presentations is likely to be Microsoft PowerPoint. If you configure your projector as a dual monitor, you can use PowerPoint to display a presentation to your audience on the projector at the same time you are using your LCD display to manage your PowerPoint slides. To do so, for PowerPoint, select the **SLIDE SHOW** tab. In the Set Up group, click **Set Up Slide Show**. In the Set Up Show box under Multiple monitors, check **Show Presenter View** or **Use Presenter View** and click **OK**.

9

VIDEO MEMORY AND WINDOWS

A+
220-901
1.4, 1.7,
1.10, 1.11

Video cards have their own processor called a graphics processing unit (GPU) or visual processing unit (VPU). These processors use graphics RAM installed on the card so that RAM on the motherboard is not tied up with video data. (If a motherboard offers a video port rather than using a video card, the GPU is part of the onboard video controller and is called integrated video. For integrated video, RAM on the motherboard is used for video data, or some video RAM is embedded on the motherboard.)

The more RAM installed on the card, the better the performance. Most video cards used and sold today use DDR2, DDR3, Graphics DDR3 (GDDR3), GDDR4, or GDDR5 memory. Graphics DDR memory is faster than regular DDR memory and does a better job of storing 3D images. Some video cards have as much as 2 GB of graphics memory.

Most Windows 7/Vista editions offer the Aero user interface (also called Aero glass), which has a 3D appearance. Windows 8 removed Aero glass, but kept a few of the same features. The hardware must qualify for Aero glass before Windows can enable it. These requirements include onboard video or a video card that supports DirectX 9 or higher, has at least 128 MB of video memory, and uses the Windows Display Driver Model (WDDM). The Windows Display Driver Model is a Windows component that manages graphics. DirectX is a Microsoft software development tool that software developers can use to write multimedia applications such as games, video-editing software, and computer-aided design software. Components of DirectX include DirectDraw, DirectMusic, DirectPlay, and Direct3D. The video firmware on the video card or motherboard chipset can interpret DirectX commands to build 3D images as presented to them by the WDDM. In addition, Windows relies on DirectX and the WDDM to produce the Aero user interface.

If an application, such as a game or desktop publishing app, that relies heavily on graphics is not performing well or giving errors, the problem might be video memory or the version of DirectX the system is using. You can use the dxdiag.exe command to display information about hardware and diagnose problems with DirectX. To use the command in Windows 8, press **Win+X** and click **Run**. Then type **dxdiag.exe** in the Run box and press **Enter**. For Windows 7, click **Start**, type **dxdiag.exe** in the Search box, and press **Enter**. Respond to a message box that appears asking if you want to check if your drivers are digitally signed. Then the opening window shown in Figure 9-56 appears. Look for the version of DirectX installed (version 11 in the figure).

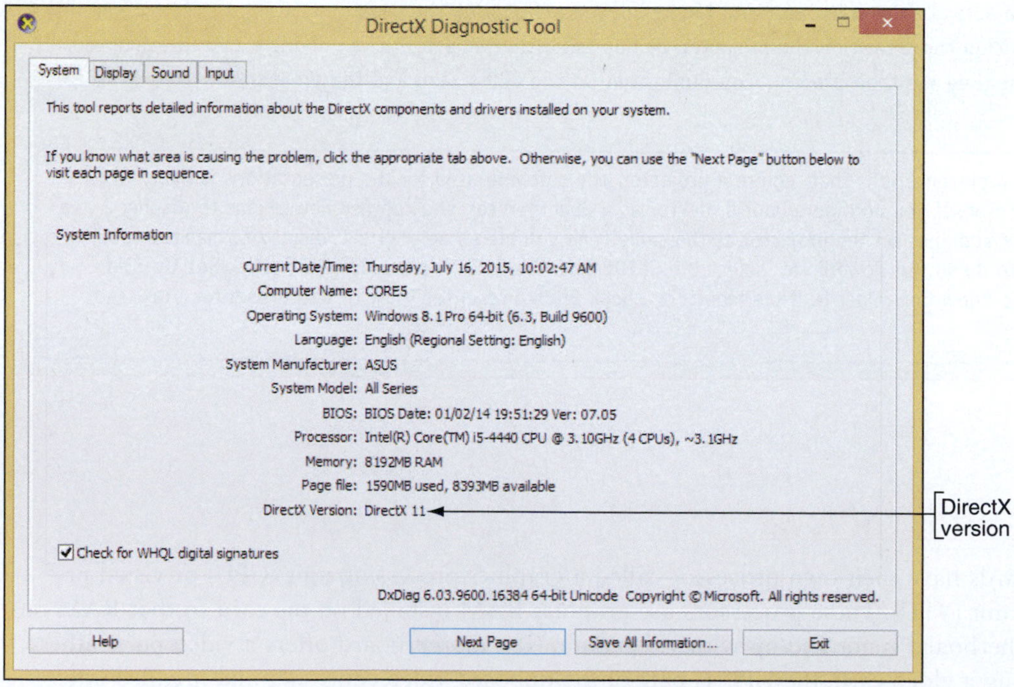

Figure 9-56 The DirectX Diagnostic tool reports information about DirectX components

To find out the latest version of DirectX published by Microsoft, go to *www.microsoft.com* and search on "DirectX End-User Runtime Web Installer." The download page similar to Figure 9-57 appears. If you want to install a new version of DirectX, click **Download** and follow the directions on screen.

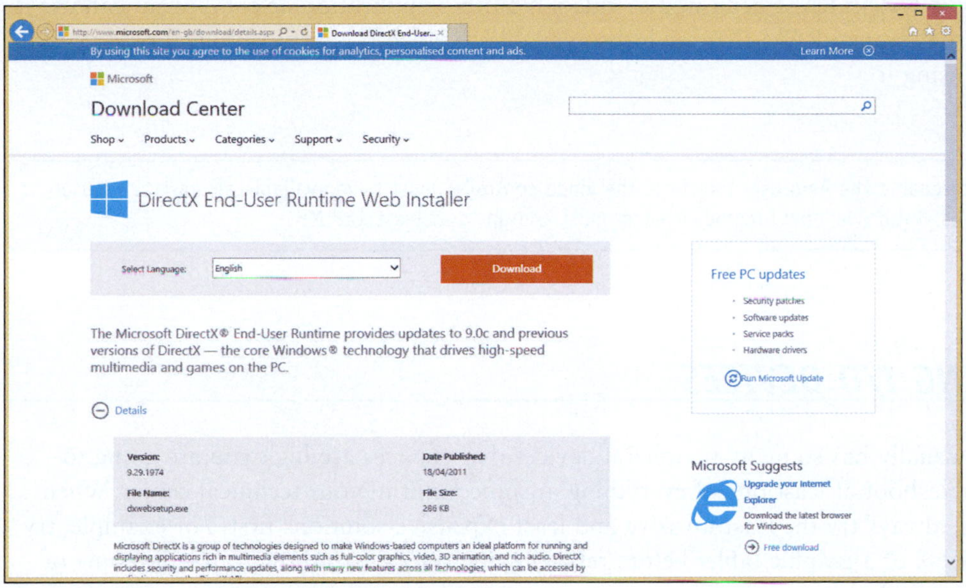

Figure 9-57 Download the latest version of DirectX

Video memory available to the graphics processor can be the graphics memory embedded on the video card or on the motherboard, system memory, or a combination of both. To see the video memory available to Windows, use Control Panel to open the **Screen Resolution** window (refer back to Figure 9-55). Click **Advanced settings**. The video properties box appears. Figure 9-58 shows two properties boxes for two systems. Figure 9-58a is for a laptop computer, and Figure 9-58b is for a desktop computer.

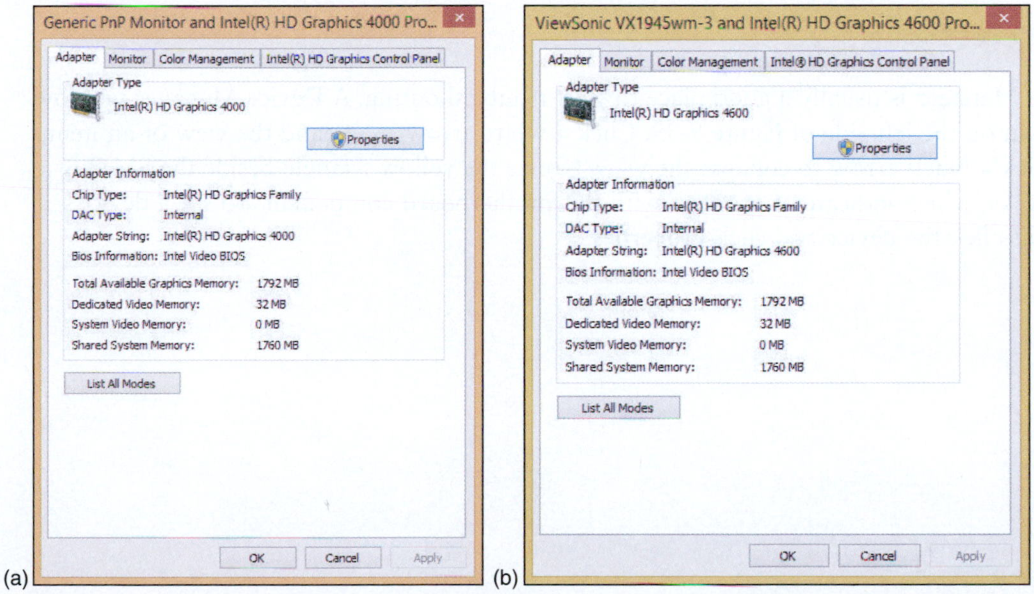

Figure 9-58 Memory allocated to video under Windows 8 (a) for a laptop computer, and (b) for a desktop computer

Here is an explanation of the four entries in the dialog box that concern video memory:

- Total Available Graphics Memory is total memory that may be available to the video subsystem.
- Dedicated Video Memory is found on a video card or embedded on the motherboard. The motherboard in both the laptop and desktop have 32 MB of graphics memory.
- System Video Memory is system RAM dedicated to video. No other application or component can use it.
- Shared System Memory is system RAM that might be available to video if another application or component is not already using it.

Notes For Windows 7 to enable the Aero user interface, the video controller must have available at least 128 MB of video memory. In other words, Total Available Graphics Memory must add up to at least 128 MB.

TROUBLESHOOTING I/O DEVICES

A+ 220-901 3.1, 3.2, 4.3, 4.5

A computer usually has so many peripheral devices that chances are high you are going to have to troubleshoot at least one of everything at some point in your technical career. When this happens, always try the least invasive and least expensive solutions first. For example, try updating drivers of a graphic tablet before replacing it. So let's learn how to handle some of the errors or problems you might encounter.

NUMLOCK INDICATOR LIGHT

A+ 220-901 4.3, 4.5

If a user complains she cannot sign in to Windows even when she's certain she is entering the correct password, ask her to make sure the NumLock key is set correctly. Laptops use this key to toggle between the keys interpreted as letters and numbers. Most laptops have a NumLock indicator light near the keyboard.

DEVICE MANAGER

A+ 220-901 4.3, 4.5

Device Manager is usually a good place to start troubleshooting. A Device Manager window is shown on the left side of Figure 9-59. Click a white arrow to expand the view of an item, and click a black arrow to collapse the view. Notice the yellow triangle beside the SM Bus Controller, which indicates a problem with this motherboard component. To see a device's properties box, right-click the device and click **Properties**.

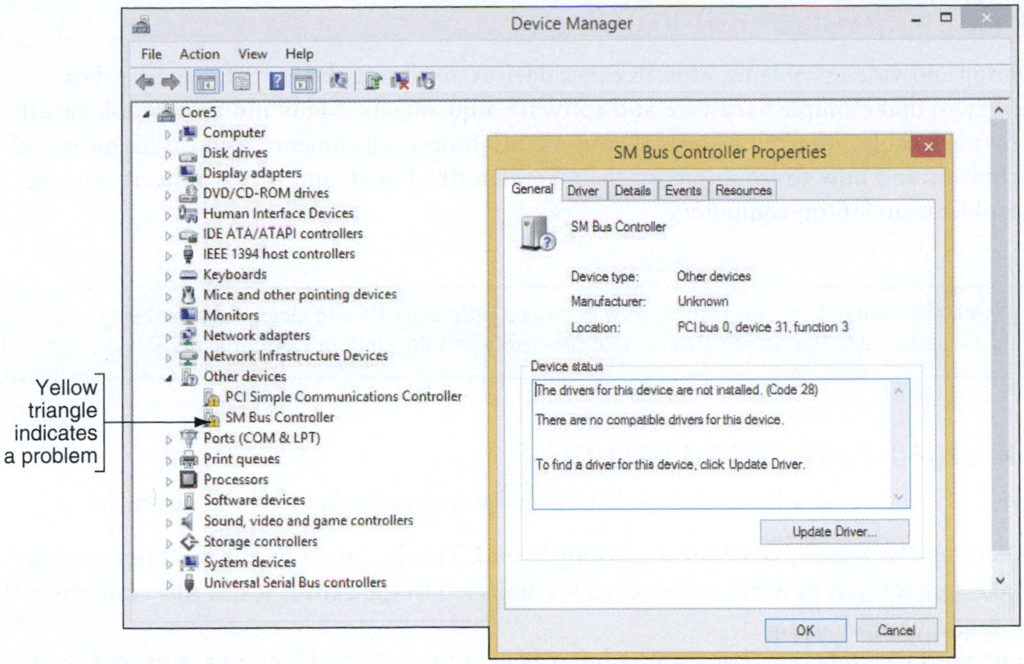

Figure 9-59 Use Device Manager to solve problems with hardware devices

First try updating the drivers. (Click **Update Driver** on the General tab or the Driver tab.) If a driver update creates a problem, you can roll back (undo) the driver update if the previous drivers were working. (Windows does not save drivers that were not working before the driver update.) If you are still having a problem with a device, try uninstalling it and installing it again. (To uninstall the device, click **Uninstall** on the Driver tab.) Then reboot and reinstall the device, looking for problems during the installation that point to the source of the problem. Sometimes reinstalling a device is all that is needed to solve the problem.

If Windows is not able to locate new drivers for a device, locate and download the latest driver files from the manufacturer's website to your hard drive. Be sure to use 64-bit drivers for a 64-bit OS and 32-bit drivers for a 32-bit OS. If possible, use Windows 8 drivers for Windows 8, Windows 7 drivers for Windows 7, and Vista drivers for Vista. You can double-click the downloaded driver files to launch the installation.

UPDATING PORT OR SLOT DRIVERS ON A LAPTOP

If you ever have a problem with a port or slot on a laptop, first turn to Device Manager to see if errors are reported and to update the drivers for the port or slot. The laptop manufacturer has probably stored backups of the drivers on the hard drive under support tools and on the recovery media if the recovery media is available. You can also download the latest drivers from the manufacturer's website. If the problem is still not solved after updating the drivers, try using Device Manager to uninstall the port or slot drivers and then use the support tools to reinstall the drivers.

Hands-On Project 9-3 Update Device Drivers

A+ 220-901 4.5

Using your home or lab computer connected to the Internet, go to Device Manager and attempt to update the drivers on all your installed devices. Which devices did Windows find newer drivers for?

TROUBLESHOOTING MONITORS AND VIDEO

A+
220-901
4.3, 4.5

For monitor and video problems, as with other devices, try doing the easy things first. For instance, try to make simple hardware and software adjustments. Many monitor problems are caused by poor cable connections or bad contrast/brightness adjustments. Typical monitor and video problems and how to troubleshoot them are described next, and then you learn how to troubleshoot video problems on laptop computers.

> **Notes** A user very much appreciates a support technician who takes a little extra time to clean a system being serviced. When servicing a monitor, take the time to clean the screen with a soft dry cloth or monitor wipe.

PROBLEMS WITH VIDEO CARD INSTALLATIONS

When you install a video card, here is a list of things that can go wrong and what to do about them:

- *When you first power up the system, you hear a whining sound.* This is caused by the card not getting enough power. Make sure a 6-pin or 8-pin power cord is connected to the card if it has this connector. The power supply might be inadequate.
- *When you first start up the system, you see nothing but a black screen.* Most likely this is caused by the onboard video port not being disabled in UEFI/BIOS setup. Disable the port.
- *When you first start up the system, you hear a series of beeps.* UEFI/BIOS cannot detect a video card. Make sure the card is securely seated. The video slot or video card might be bad.
- *Error messages about video appear when Windows starts.* This can be caused by a conflict in onboard video and the video card. Try disabling onboard video in Device Manager.
- *Games crash or lock up.* Try updating drivers for the motherboard, the video card, and the sound card. Also install the latest version of DirectX. (You learn about DirectX later in the chapter.) Then try uninstalling the game and installing it again. Then download all patches for the game.

MONITOR INDICATOR LIGHT IS NOT ON; NO IMAGE ON SCREEN

If you hear one or no beep during the boot and you see a blank screen, then UEFI/BIOS has successfully completed POST, which includes a test of the video card or onboard video. You can then assume the problem must be with the monitor or the monitor cable. Ask these questions and try these things:

1. Is the monitor power cable plugged in?
2. Is the monitor turned on? Try pushing the power button on the front of the monitor. An indicator light on the front of the monitor should turn on, indicating the monitor has power.
3. Is the monitor cable plugged into the video port at the back of the computer and the connector on the rear of the monitor?
4. Try a different monitor and a different monitor cable that you know are working.

> **Notes** When you turn on your computer, the first thing you see on the screen is the firmware on the video card identifying itself. You can use this information to search the web, especially the manufacturer's website, for troubleshooting information about the card.

MONITOR INDICATOR LIGHT IS ON; NO IMAGE ON SCREEN

For this problem, try the following:

1. Make sure the video cable is securely connected at the computer and the monitor. Most likely the problem is a bad cable connection.
2. If the monitor displays POST but goes blank when Windows starts to load, the problem is Windows and not the monitor or video. Boot from the Windows setup DVD and perform a Startup Repair, which you learned to do in the chapter, "Supporting the Power System and Troubleshooting Computers." If this works, change the driver and resolution. Other tools for troubleshooting Windows are covered later in the text.
3. The monitor might have a switch on the back for choosing between 110 volts and 220 volts. Check that the switch is in the correct position.
4. The problem might be with the video card. If you have just installed the card and the motherboard has onboard video, go into BIOS setup and disable the video port on the motherboard.
5. Verify the video cable is connected to the video port on the video card and not to a disabled onboard video port.
6. Using buttons on the front of the monitor, check the contrast adjustment. If there's no change, leave it at a middle setting.
7. Check the brightness or backlight adjustment. If there's no change, leave it at a middle setting.
8. If the monitor-to-computer cable detaches from the monitor, exchange it for a cable you know is good, or check the cable for continuity. If this solves the problem, reattach the old cable to verify that the problem was not simply a bad connection.
9. Test a monitor you know is good on the computer you suspect to be bad. If you think the monitor is bad, make sure that it also fails to work on a good computer.
10. Open the computer case and reseat the video card. If possible, move the card to a different expansion slot. Clean the card's edge connectors, using a contact cleaner purchased from a computer supply store.
11. If there are socketed chips on the video card, remove the card from the expansion slot and then use a screwdriver to press down firmly on each corner of each socketed chip on the card. Chips sometimes loosen because of temperature changes; this condition is called chip creep.
12. Trade a good video card for the video card you suspect is bad. Test the video card you think is bad on a computer that works. Test a video card you know is good on the computer that you suspect is bad. Whenever possible, do both.
13. Test the RAM on the motherboard with memory diagnostic software.
14. For a motherboard that is using a PCI-Express video card, try using a PCI video card in a PCI slot or a PCIe ×1 video card in a PCIe ×1 slot. A good repair technician keeps an extra PCI video card around for this purpose.
15. Trade the motherboard for one you know is good. Sometimes, though rarely, a peripheral chip on the motherboard can cause the problem.

SCREEN GOES BLANK 30 SECONDS OR ONE MINUTE AFTER THE KEYBOARD IS LEFT UNTOUCHED

A Green motherboard (one that follows energy-saving standards) used with an Energy Saver monitor can be configured to go into standby or sleep mode after a period of inactivity. Using this feature can also help prevent burn-in. Burn-in is when a static image stays on a monitor for many hours leaving a permanent impression of that image on the monitor. An alternate method to avoid burn-in is to use a screen saver that has a moving image or a rotation of varying images. To wake up the computer, press any key on the keyboard or press the power button. Use the Power Options applet in Control Panel to configure the sleep settings on a computer.

Notes Problems might occur if the motherboard power-saving features are turning off the monitor, and Windows screen saver is also turning off the monitor. If the system hangs when you try to get the monitor going again, try disabling one or the other. If this doesn't work, disable both.

POOR DISPLAY

In general, you can solve problems with poor display by using controls on the monitor and using Windows settings. Do the following:

- ***LCD monitor controls.*** Use buttons on the front of an LCD monitor to adjust color, brightness, contrast, focus, and horizontal and vertical positions.
- ***Windows display settings.*** Use Windows settings to adjust font size, screen resolution, brightness, color, and Clear Type text. Open Control Panel in Classic view and click **Display**. Use these settings to adjust the display:
  - To make sure Clear Type text is selected, click **Adjust ClearType text** and turn on ClearType (see Figure 9-60). Then follow the steps in the wizard to improve the quality of text displayed on the screen.

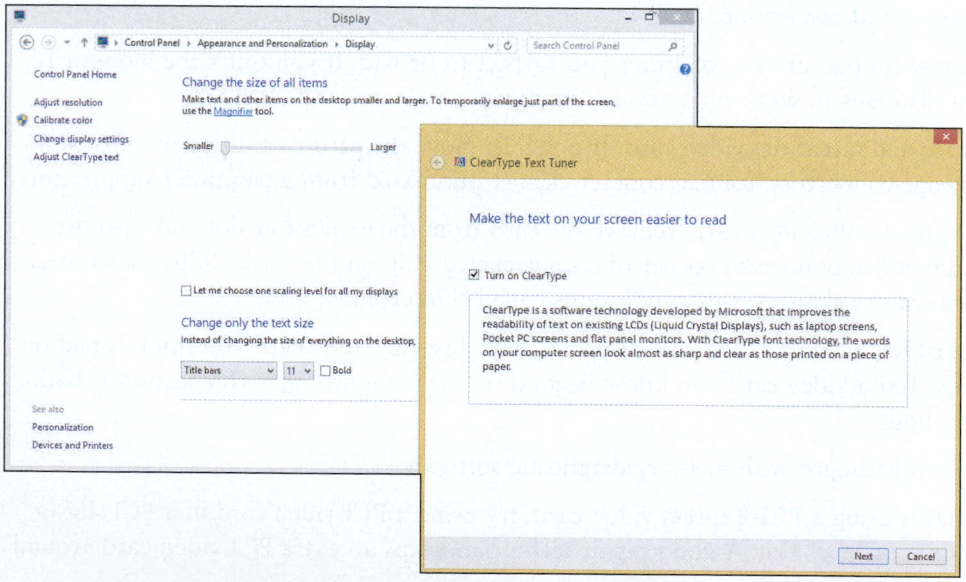

Figure 9-60 ClearType in Windows improves the display of text on the screen

  - LCD monitors will not experience distorted geometry if the resolution is set to the native resolution. So if monitor shows distorted geometry where images are stretched inappropriately, adjust the resolution. Also a low resolution can cause oversized images or icons. To adjust screen resolution, click **Change display settings** in the Display window.

Notes If adjusting the resolution doesn't correct oversized images or icons, try updating the video drivers.

- To calibrate colors, click **Calibrate color** in the Display window and follow the directions on screen. As you do so, color patterns appear (see Figure 9-61). Use these screens to adjust the gamma settings, which define the relationships among red, green, and blue as well as other settings that affect the display.

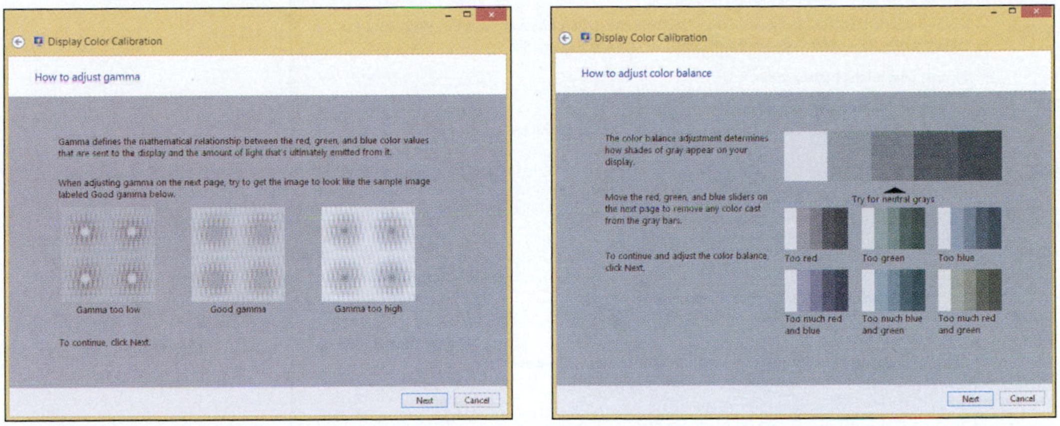

Figure 9-61 Two screens in the Windows 8 color calibration wizard

9

- ***Update the video drivers.*** The latest video drivers can solve various problems with the video subsystem, including poor display.

Here are a few other display problems and their solutions:

- ***Dead pixels.*** An LCD monitor might have pixels that are not working called dead pixels, which can appear as small white, black, or colored spots on your screen. A black or white pixel is likely to be a broken transistor, which cannot be fixed. Having a few dead pixels on an LCD monitor screen is considered acceptable and usually not covered under the manufacturer's warranty.

> **Notes** A pixel might not be a dead pixel (a hardware problem), but only a stuck pixel (a software problem). You might be able to use software to fix stuck pixels. For example, run the online software at *www.flexcode.org/lcd2.html* to fix stuck pixels. The software works by rapidly changing all the pixels on the screen. (Be aware the screen flashes rapidly during the fix.)

- ***Dim image.*** A laptop computer dims the LCD screen when the computer is running on battery to conserve the charge. You can brighten the screen using the Windows display settings. To do so, open **Control Panel** in Classic view, click **Display**, and then click **Adjust brightness** (see Figure 9-62). To check if settings to conserve power are affecting screen brightness, note the power plan that is selected. Click **Change plan settings** for this power plan. On the next screen, you can adjust when or if the screen will dim (see Figure 9-63). If the problem is still not resolved, it might be a hardware problem. How to troubleshoot hardware in laptops is covered later in this chapter.

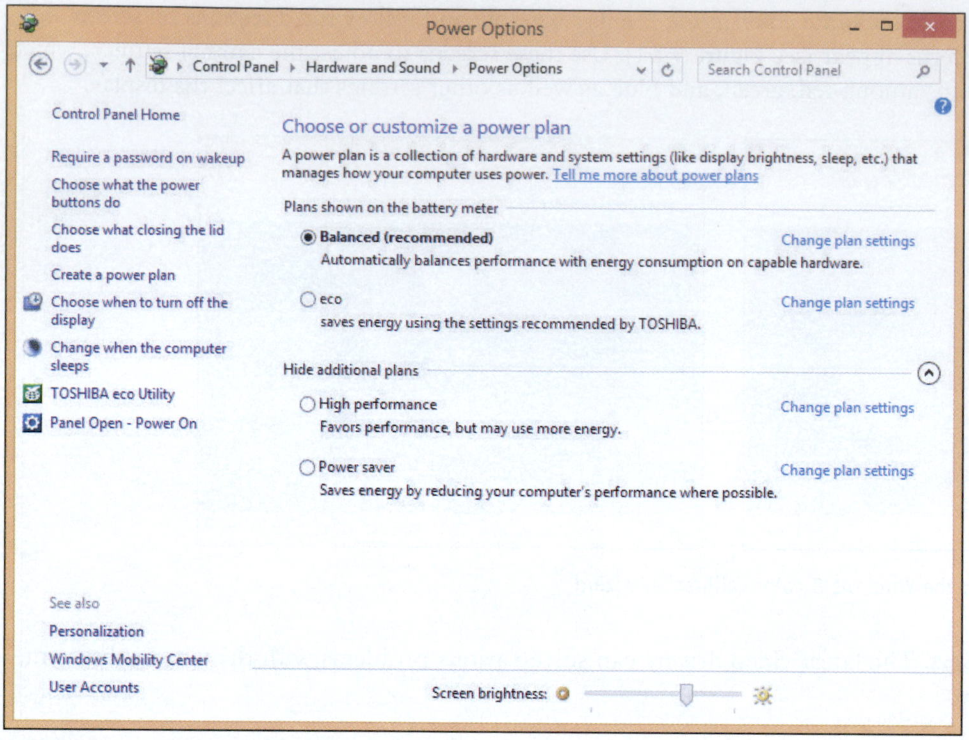

Figure 9-62 Adjust screen brightness at the bottom of this screen

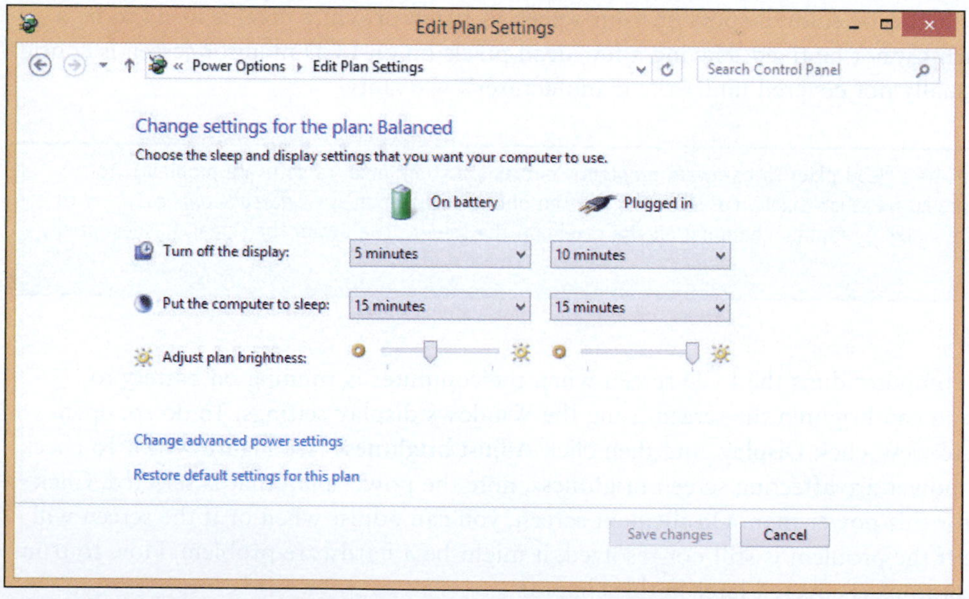

Figure 9-63 Change power plan options to affect how or if the screen dims

A dim image in a desktop monitor might be caused by a faulty video card or a faulty monitor. To find out which is the problem, connect a different monitor. If the monitor is the problem, most likely the backlighting in the LCD monitor is faulty and the monitor needs replacing.

- *Artifacts.* Horizontally torn images on screen are called artifacts (see Figure 9-64), and happen when the video feed from the video controller gets out of sync with the refresh of the monitor screen. The problem can be caused by hardware or software. A common cause is when the GPU on the video card overheats. You can test that possibility by downloading and running freeware to monitor the temperature of the CPU and the GPU while you're playing a video game. If you notice the problem occurs when the GPU

Figure 9-64 A simulation of horizontal tears on an image called artifacts

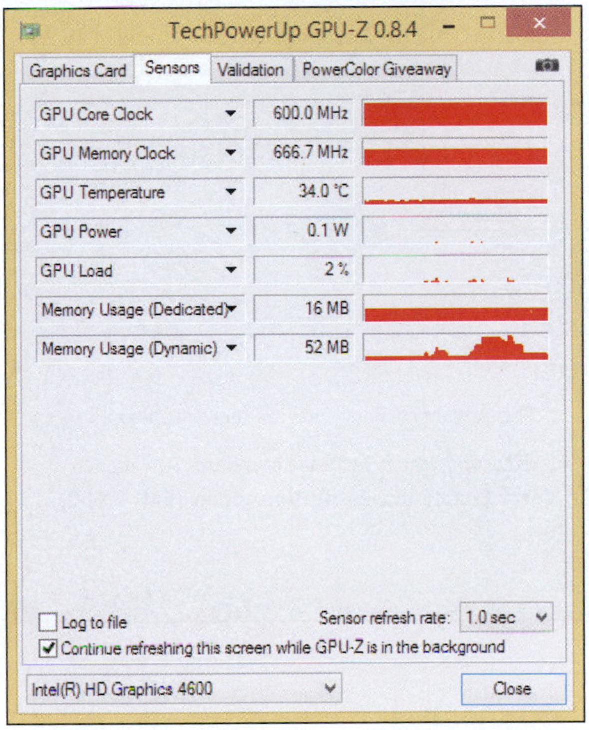

Source: GPU-Z by TechPowerUp

Figure 9-65 GPU-Z monitors the GPU temperature

temp is high, install extra fans around the video card to keep it cool. Two freeware programs to monitor temperatures are CPU-Z by CPUID (*www.cpuid.com/softwares/cpu-z.html*) and GPU-Z by TechPowerUp (*www.techpowerup.com/gpuz*). See Figure 9-65.

Notes In this text, we've given several options for various freeware utilities. It's a good idea to know about your options for several reasons. Each freeware utility has different options; owners of freeware might not update their utility in a timely manner, and websites might decide to include adware with their downloads.

Try updating the video drivers. However, if you see artifacts on the screen before Windows loads, then you know the problem is not caused by the drivers. The problem might be caused by the monitor. Try using a different monitor to see if the problem goes away. If so, replace the monitor.

Overclocking can cause artifacts. Other causes of artifacts are the motherboard or video card going bad, which can happen if the system has been overheating or video RAM on the card is faulty. Try replacing the video card. The power supply also might be the problem.

In general, to improve video quality, upgrade the video card and/or monitor. Poor display might be caused by inadequate video RAM. Your video card might allow you to install additional video RAM. See the card's documentation.

9

APPLYING | CONCEPTS CORRECT WINDOWS DISPLAY SETTINGS WHEN THE SCREEN IS UNREADABLE

A+ 220-901 4.3, 4.5

When the display settings don't work, you can easily return to standard VGA settings called **VGA mode**, which includes a resolution of 640 × 480 or 800 × 600 for some systems.

To use VGA mode when Windows 8 is able to boot and you can use at least one monitor, do the following:

1. Press **Win+X** and click **Run**. In the Run box, type **msconfig.exe** and press **Enter**. The System Configuration box appears. Click the **Boot** tab (see Figure 9-66).

(continues)

2. On the Boot tab, check **Base video** and click **OK**. In the box that appears, click **Restart**. The system will restart in VGA mode. You can now adjust display settings or reinstall video drivers.
3. After you fix any problems with video, open the System Configuration box and click **Normal startup** on the General tab. Then restart Windows.

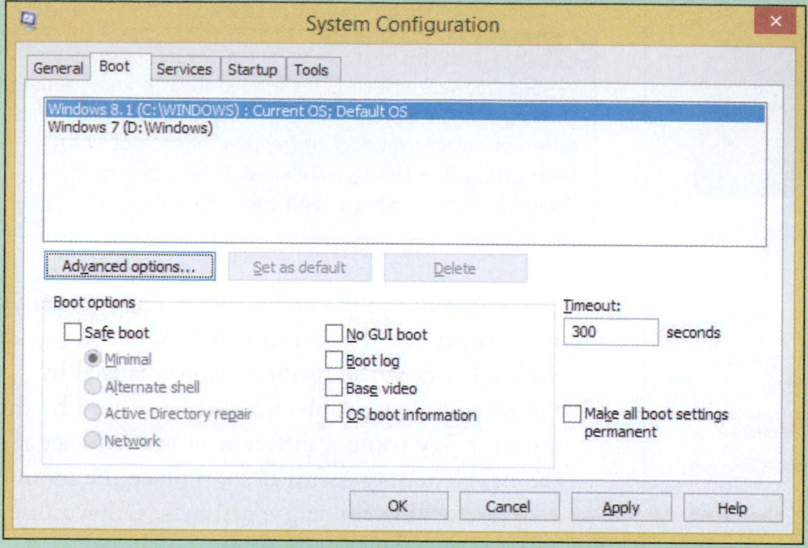

Figure 9-66 Control how Windows boots

To use VGA mode in Windows 7/Vista, do the following:

1. Reboot the system and press the **F8** key after the first beep. The Advanced Boot Options menu appears.
2. Select **Safe Mode** to boot up with minimal configurations of Windows, which includes standard VGA mode. Alternately, to boot Windows normally and use VGA mode, select **Enable low-resolution video (640 × 480)**.

Change the display settings and then restart Windows.

Hands-On Project 9-4 Adjust Windows Display Settings

A+ 220-901 4.3, 4.5

To practice changing display settings, do the following:

1. Using the Windows 8 Display window, calibrate the color displayed on your monitor screen. Verify ClearType text is enabled.
2. Try different screen resolutions supported by your monitor. Then verify the monitor is set to use the highest refresh rate it supports.
3. To view your Windows desktop in VGA mode, use the instructions given earlier to boot to Windows 8 Basic video or Windows 7 Enable low-resolution video (640 x 480). Then restart Windows and return your system to normal Windows display settings.

VIDEO SYSTEM IN A LAPTOP

A+ 220-901 3.1, 3.2, 4.3, 4.5

If the LCD panel shows a black screen, but the power light indicates that power is getting to the system, the video subsystem might be the source of the problem. Do the following:

1. Look for an LCD cutoff switch or button on the laptop (see Figure 9-67). The switch must be on for the LCD panel to work.

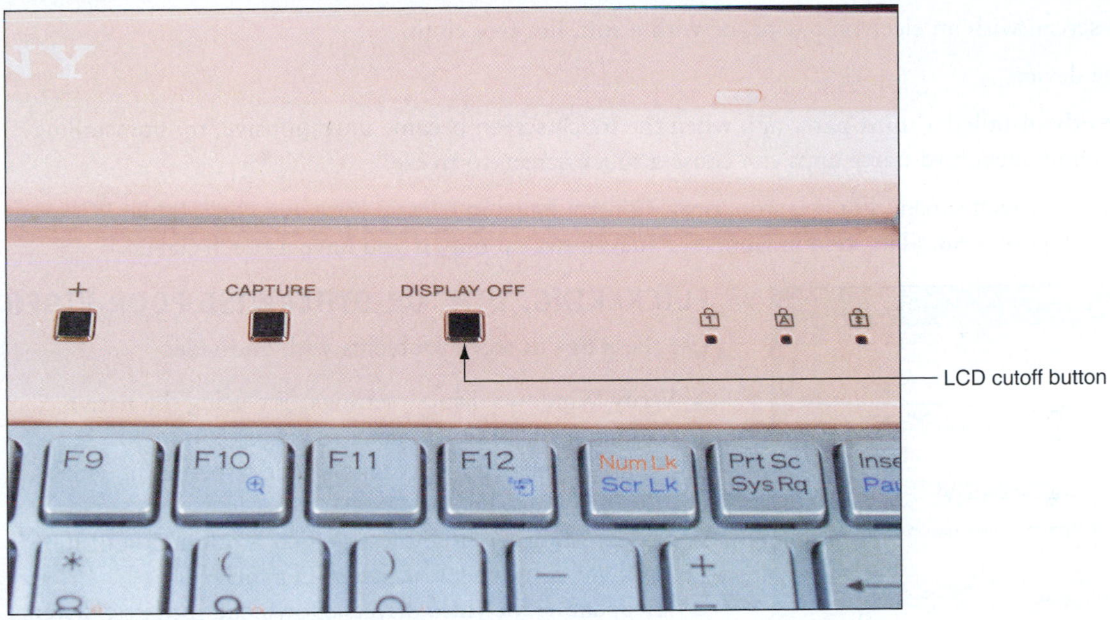

Figure 9-67 LCD cutoff button on a laptop

2. If using an onboard video port, try to use the video port to connect it to an external monitor. After you connect the monitor, use a function key to toggle between the LCD panel, the external monitor, and both the panel and monitor. If the external monitor works, but the LCD panel does not work, try these things using the external monitor:
   - Check Device Manager for warnings about the video controller and to update the video drivers.
   - Check Event Viewer for reported problems with the video subsystem. You learned about Event Viewer in the chapter, "Supporting the Power System and Troubleshooting Computers."
3. If you still can't get the LCD panel on a laptop to work, but the external monitor does work, you have proven the problem is with the LCD panel assembly. In a laptop, a dim screen or no display can be caused by a bad inverter. If replacing the inverter does not help, the next task is to replace the LCD panel. Be aware the replacement components might cost more than the laptop is worth. Steps to replace the LCD panel in a laptop are covered later in the chapter.

CANNOT CONNECT TO EXTERNAL MONITOR

When wanting to expand desktop space or possibly troubleshoot video problems, you need to be able to use an external monitor with a laptop. If the connection to the external monitor fails, try the following solutions:

1. Make sure the monitor is getting power.
2. Use the Function keys to toggle between the laptop display and the external monitor. (Alternately, you can press Win+P to toggle between displays.)
3. Try using a different cable.
4. Try using a different connection if the laptop and monitor have another option available.

9

TOUCH SCREEN IS NONRESPONSIVE

Smart phones, tablets, and some laptops offer a touch screen. If the touch screen becomes unresponsive, try the following solutions:

1. Wash and thoroughly dry your hands.
2. If there is a case or screen protector, remove it. Some screen protectors are too thick and interfere with the touch screen interface. Use a screen protector that is licensed for your device.
3. Clean the screen with an electronic wipe, or with a soft, lint-free cloth.
4. Restart the device.
5. If you recently installed a third-party app when the touch screen became unresponsive, try uninstalling that app. Sometimes third-party apps can cause a touch screen to freeze.
6. Recalibrate the touch screen. For a laptop, open Control Panel in Classic view and click **Tablet PC Settings**. See Figure 9-68. (The item in Control Panel shows up only if you have a touch screen.)

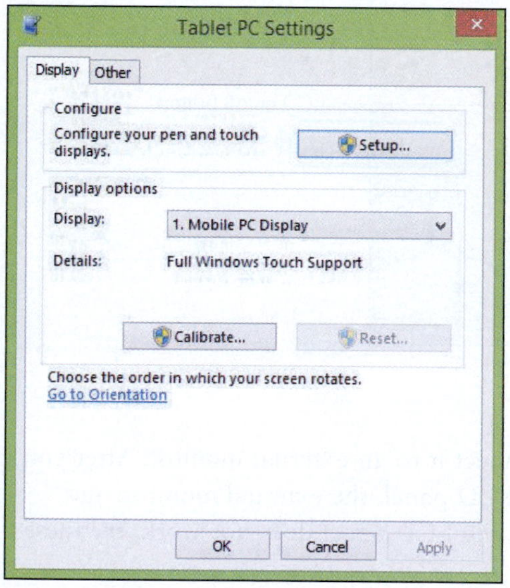

Figure 9-68 Calibrate the touch screen on a laptop

FLICKERING, DIM, OR OTHERWISE POOR VIDEO

Use these tips to solve problems with bad video:

- Verify Windows display settings. Try using the native resolution for the LCD panel. This resolution will be the highest resolution available unless the wrong video drivers are installed.
- Try adjusting the brightness, which is a function of the backlight component of the LCD panel.
- Try updating the video drivers. Download the latest drivers from the laptop's manufacturer's website. Bad drivers can cause an occasional ghost cursor on screen. A ghost cursor is a trail left behind when you move the mouse.
- A flickering screen can be caused by bad video drivers, a low refresh rate, a bad inverter, or loose connections inside the laptop. To adjust the refresh rate, use Control Panel to open the Display window. In the Display window, click **Change display settings.** In the Screen Resolution window, click **Advanced settings.** On the Monitor tab, select the highest refresh rate available (see Figure 9-69).

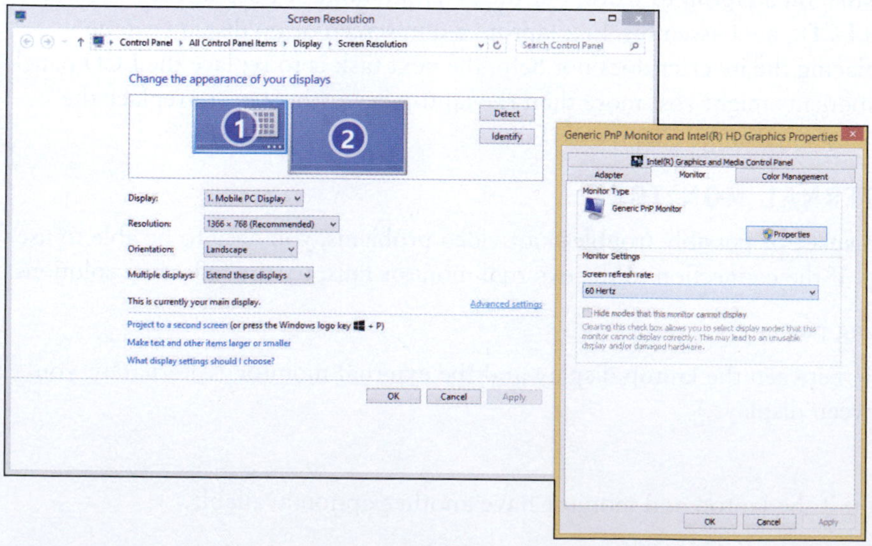

Figure 9-69 Use the highest refresh rate the system supports

REPLACING THE LCD PANEL IN A LAPTOP

Because the LCD panel is so fragile, it is one component that is likely to be broken when a laptop is not handled properly. If the LCD display is entirely black, most likely you'll have to replace the entire LCD assembly. However, for a laptop that uses fluorescent backlighting, if the screen is dim, but you can make out that some display is present, the problem might be the inverter. The inverter board converts DC to AC used to power the backlighting of the LCD panel (see Figure 9-70). Check with the laptop manufacturer to confirm that it makes sense to first try replacing just the relatively inexpensive inverter board before you replace the more expensive entire LCD panel assembly. If the entire assembly needs replacing, the cost of the assembly might exceed the value of the laptop.

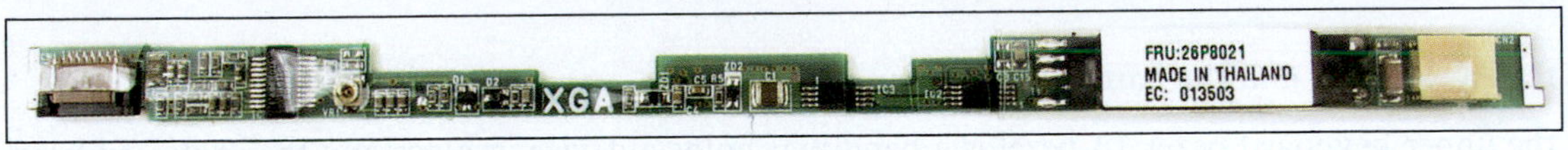

Figure 9-70 A ThinkPad inverter board

Sometimes, a laptop LCD panel, including the entire cover and hinges, is considered a single field replaceable unit, and sometimes components within the LCD assembly are considered FRUs. For example, the field replaceable units for the display panel in Figure 9-71 are the LCD front bezel, the hinges, the LCD

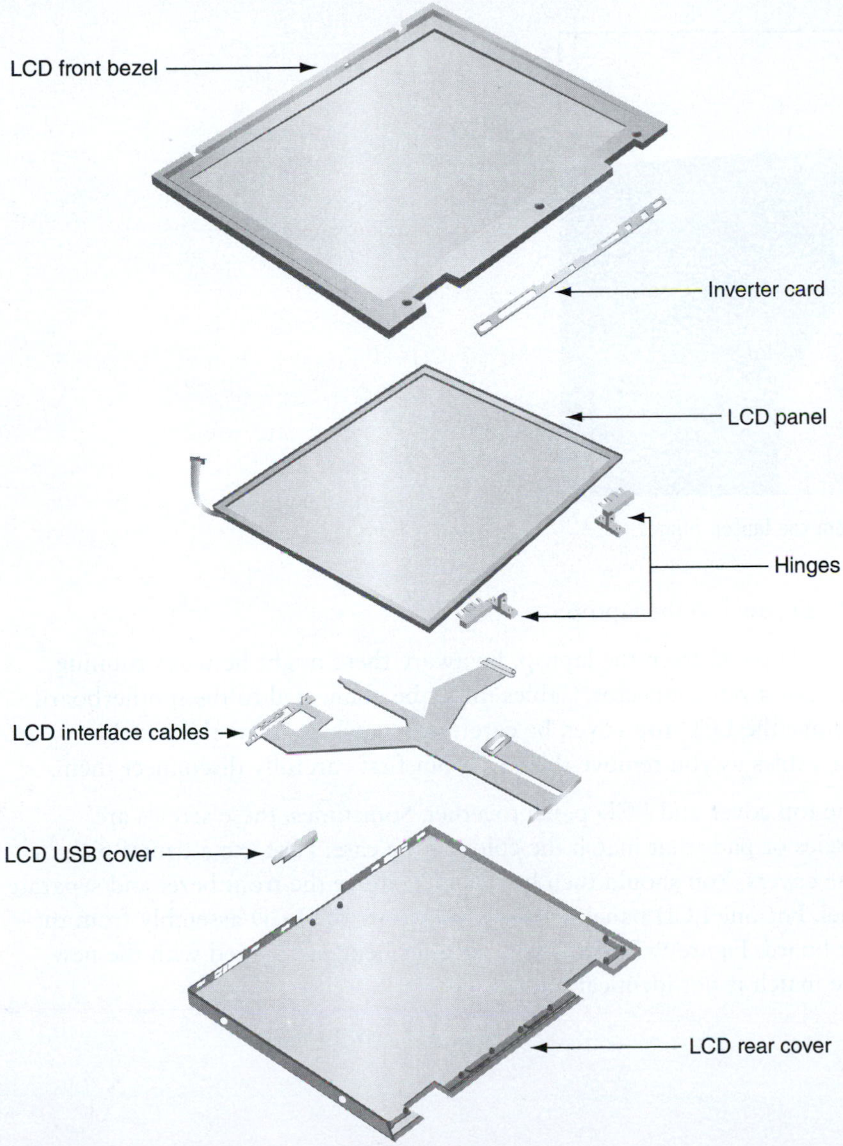

Figure 9-71 Components in an LCD assembly

panel, the inverter board, the LCD interface cables, the LCD USB cover, and the rear cover. Also know that an LCD assembly might include a microphone, webcam, or speakers that are embedded in the laptop lid. For other laptops, the microphone and speakers are inside the case. The speakers are considered a field replaceable unit. In addition, a Wi-Fi antenna might be in the lid of the laptop, which is why if you need a better Wi-Fi signal, you should raise the lid of the laptop. When you disassemble the lid, you must disconnect the antenna from the bottom part of the laptop.

Some high-end laptops contain a video card that has embedded video memory. This video card might also need replacing. In most cases, you would replace only the LCD panel and perhaps the inverter board.

Before you begin any disassembly of a laptop, refer to the manufacturer documentation. The following are some general directions to replace an LCD panel:

1. Remove the AC adapter and the battery pack.
2. Remove the upper keyboard bezel. (A bezel is a band that holds a device in place and the keyboard bezel is a band around the keyboard that holds it in place.) You might also need to remove the keyboard.
3. Remove the screws holding the hinge in place and remove the hinge cover. Figure 9-72 shows a laptop with a metal hinge cover, but some laptops use plastic covers that you can easily break as you remove them. Be careful with the plastic ones.

Figure 9-72 Remove the hinge cover from the laptop hinge

4. Remove the screws holding the LCD panel to the laptop.
5. You're now ready to remove the LCD panel from the laptop. Be aware there might be wires running through the hinge assembly, cables, or a pin connector. Cables might be connected to the motherboard using ZIF connectors. As you remove the LCD top cover, be careful to watch for how the panel is connected. Don't pull on wires or cables as you remove the cover, but first carefully disconnect them.
6. Next, remove screws that hold the top cover and LCD panel together. Sometimes, these screws are covered with plastic or rubber circles or pads that match the color of the case. First use a dental pick or small screwdriver to pick off these covers. You should then be able to remove the front bezel and separate the rear cover from the LCD panel. For one LCD panel, when you separate the LCD assembly from the lid cover, you can see the inverter board. Figure 9-73 shows the inverter being compared with the new one to make sure they match. The match is not identical but should work.

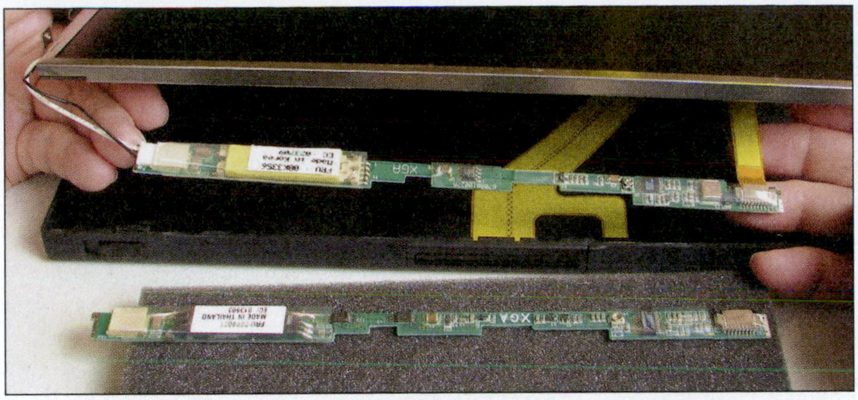

Figure 9-73 The inverter is exposed and is compared with the new one

7. Disconnect the old inverter and install the new one. When disconnecting the ribbon cable from the old inverter, notice you must first lift up on the lock holding the ZIF connector in place, as shown in Figure 9-74.
8. Install the new inverter. Reassemble the LCD panel assembly. Make sure the assembly is put together with a tight fit so that all screws line up well.
9. Reattach the LCD panel assembly to the laptop.

Figure 9-74 Lift up on the ZIF connector locking mechanism before removing the ribbon cable

SPEAKERS IN A LAPTOP

A+
220-901
3.1, 3.2,
4.3, 4.5

Laptops and other mobile devices have built-in speakers. If you're not getting any sound from the speakers, try the following solutions:

- Make sure the volume is turned up.
- Update the audio output drivers.
- Run the Playing Audio troubleshooting tool. Open Control Panel in Classic view and select **Troubleshooting.** In the Hardware and Sound group, select **Troubleshoot audio playback.** Follow the on-screen instructions for the Playing Audio troubleshooting wizard.

Sometimes speakers might get cracks or tears in the membrane that creates the sound, but also consider that laptop speakers are generally quieter than external speakers. When laptop speakers start sounding weak or unclear, first try updating the speaker drivers using Device Manager. You can also try plugging an external set of speakers to the audio port of the laptop. If using external speakers isn't convenient for the user, then you can replace the broken speakers.

Hands-On Project 9-5 Research Replacing Speakers in a Laptop

Your friend Andrea has an old laptop, an HP Pavilion zd8000, and it is still serving her well. The only complaint she has is the left speaker has a static sound to it. The other speaker sounds good. She asks you to help her out. You know that, because the other speaker is still good, you need to replace the one bad speaker. Research on the Internet to find the speaker replacement part, find an online tutorial on how to replace the speaker for Andrea's laptop, then answer the following questions:

1. What is the price for the replacement speaker? Cite your source.
2. Is the cost of replacement worth more than what the laptop is worth?
3. Provide your source for the online tutorial.
4. After reviewing an online tutorial explaining the steps to replace the speaker, how long would you guess it would take you to replace the speaker, assuming everything goes as planned?
5. List the tools needed to replace the speaker.

>> CHAPTER SUMMARY

Basic Principles for Supporting Devices

- Adding new devices to a computer requires installing hardware and software. Even if you know how to generally install an I/O device, always follow the specific instructions of the product manufacturer.
- Use Device Manager under Windows to manage hardware devices and to solve problems with them.
- Popular I/O ports on a motherboard include eSATA (Versions 1, 2, and 3), FireWire 800 and 400, and USB (Versions 1, 2, and 3). Older ports include parallel, serial, and PS/2 ports.
- Wireless connections can use Wi-Fi 802.11a/b/g/n, Bluetooth, and Infrared standards.
- USB connectors include the A-Male, B-Male, Mini-B, Micro-B, Micro-A, USB 3.0 B-Male, and USB 3.0 Micro-B connectors.

Installing I/O Peripheral Devices

- When installing devices, use 32-bit drivers for a 32-bit OS and 64-bit drivers for a 64-bit OS.
- A touch screen is likely to use a USB port. Software is installed to calibrate the touch screen to the monitor screen and receive data input.
- Biometric input devices, such as a fingerprint reader, collect biological data and compare it with that recorded about the person to authenticate the person's access to a system.
- A KVM switch lets you use one keyboard, monitor, and mouse with multiple computers.

Installing and Configuring Adapter Cards

- Generally, when an adapter card is physically installed in a system and Windows starts up, it detects the card and then you install the drivers using the Windows wizard. However, always follow specific instructions from the device manufacturer when installing an adapter card because the order of installing the card and drivers might be different.

- A TV tuner card turns your computer or laptop into a television. A video capture card allows you to capture input from a camcorder or directly from TV. Combo cards have both abilities. A sound card allows you to input audio and use multispeaker systems.

Supporting the Video Subsystem

- Types of monitors include LCD monitor, plasma monitor, projector, and OLED monitor. An LCD monitor can use two types of backlighting: fluorescent and LED.
- Technologies and features of LCD monitors include screen size, refresh rate, pixel pitch, resolution, native resolution, contrast ratio, viewing angle, backlighting, and connectors that a monitor uses.
- Video ports that a video card or motherboard might provide are VGA, DVI-I, DVI-D, DVI-A, composite video, S-Video, component video, DisplayPort, HDMI, and HDMI mini ports.
- Use the Screen Resolution window to configure a monitor resolution and configure dual monitors.
- To use the Aero user interface, Windows 7/Vista requires a video card or onboard video to have at least 128 MB of video RAM, support DirectX version 9 or higher, and use the Windows Display Driver Model (WDDM).
- The dxdiag.exe command is used to report information about hardware, including the video card and which version of DirectX it is using.

Troubleshooting I/O Devices

- Use Device Manager to update drivers on I/O devices giving trouble.
- Video problems can be caused by the monitor, video cable, video card, onboard video, video drivers, or Windows display settings.
- To bypass Windows display settings, boot the system to the Advanced Boot Options menu and select Safe Mode or Enable low-resolution video (640 × 480).
- A few dead pixels on an LCD monitor screen are considered acceptable by the manufacturer.
- Artifacts on the monitor screen can be caused by hardware, software, overheating, or overclocking. Try updating video drivers and checking for high temperatures.

>> KEY TERMS

For explanations of key terms, see the Glossary for this text.

1394a
1394b
A-Male connector
artifact
B-Male connector
barcode reader
biometric device
burn-in
Cold Cathode Fluorescent Lamp (CCFL)
composite video port
contrast ratio
DB-15
dead pixel
Device Manager
Digital Rights Management (DRM)
digitizer
digitizing tablet
DirectX
DisplayPort
distorted geometry
DVI-A
DVI-D
DVI-I
dxdiag.exe
FireWire 400
FireWire 800
flat-panel monitor
fluorescent backlighting
ghost cursor
graphics tablet
HDMI connector
HDMI mini connector
hot-swappable
Infrared (IR)
In-Plane Switching (IPS)
inverter circuit board
KVM (Keyboard, Video, and Mouse) switch
LCD (liquid crystal display)
LED (light-emitting diode)
Micro-A connector
Micro-B connector
MIDI (musical instrument digital interface)
Mini-B connector
Mini-DIN-6 connector
Mini DisplayPort
mini-HDMI connector
Mini PCI Express
Mini PCIe
motion controller
motion sensor

native resolution
OLED (organic light-emitting diode)
pixel
pixel pitch
plasma monitor
projector
RCA connector
refresh rate
resolution
response time
RGB port
sound card
stylus
touch screen
TV tuner card
Twisted Nematic (TN)
USB 3.0 Micro-B connector
VGA mode
video capture card

>> REVIEWING THE BASICS

1. Which is faster, an eSATA-600 port or a FireWire 800 port?
2. What is the speed for Hi-Speed USB?
3. How many times faster is a Hi-Speed USB port than an Original USB port running at 12 Mbps?
4. Which is faster, USB 3.0 or eSATA 600?
5. Which is faster, Wi-Fi 802.11n or Bluetooth?
6. How many pins does a FireWire 800 port have?
7. What type of wireless transmission requires a line-of-sight clearance?
8. Will a printer rated to use USB 3.0 work when you connect the printer's USB cable into a USB 2.0 port on your computer?
9. What is the easiest way to tell if a USB port on a laptop computer is using the USB 3.0 standard?
10. For an LCD monitor, what is the best resolution to use?
11. Which gives less glare, an LED monitor or an OLED monitor?
12. Which gives a better measurement for the quality of an LCD monitor, the contrast ratio or the dynamic contrast ratio?
13. What command do you use to find out which version of DirectX your video card is using?
14. Name two types of ports a keyboard might use.
15. Which Windows utility is most likely the one to use when uninstalling an expansion card?
16. Would you expect all the devices listed in UEFI/BIOS setup to also be listed in Device Manager? Would you expect all devices listed in Device Manager to also be listed in UEFI/BIOS setup?
17. Why is it best to leave a slot empty between two expansion cards?
18. Which speaker port should you use when connecting a single speaker to a PC?
19. What type of adapter card allows you to connect your computer to cable so that you can watch TV on your computer?
20. Which is faster, SuperSpeed USB or FireWire 800?
21. Why might a musical keyboard have two MIDI ports?
22. What can you do if a port on the motherboard is faulty and a device requires this type of port?
23. What are two screen resolutions that might be used by VGA mode?
24. What is another name for a VGA port?
25. Which type of drivers must always be certified in order to be installed in Windows?

>> THINKING CRITICALLY

1. If a PS/2 keyboard does not work on your system and yet you know the keyboard is good, what is the best solution?
   a. Disable the PS/2 port in UEFI/BIOS setup and use a PS/2 splitter to install a keyboard and mouse using the PS/2 mouse port.
   b. Install a USB keyboard on a USB port.
   c. Exchange the PS/2 port on your motherboard.
   d. Replace the motherboard.
2. You plug a new scanner into a USB port on your Windows 7 system. When you first turn on the scanner, what should you expect to see?
   a. A message displays by the scanner software telling you to reboot your system.
   b. Windows Device Setup launches to install drivers.
   c. Your system automatically reboots.
   d. An error message from the USB controller appears.
3. You turn on your Windows 7 computer and see the system display POST messages. Then the screen turns blue with no text. Which of the following items could be the source of the problem?
   a. The video card
   b. The monitor
   c. Windows
   d. Microsoft Word software installed on the system
4. You have just installed a new sound card in your system, and Windows says the card installed with no errors. When you plug up the speakers and try to play a music CD, you hear no sound. What is the first thing you should do? The second thing?
   a. Check Device Manager to see if the sound card is recognized and has no errors.
   b. Reinstall Windows 7.
   c. Use Device Manager to uninstall the sound card.
   d. Identify your sound card by opening the case and looking on the card for the manufacturer and model.
   e. Check the volume controls on the speaker amplifier and in Windows.
   f. Use Device Manager to update the sound card drivers.
5. You have just installed a new DVD drive and its drivers under Windows 8. The drive will read a CD but not a DVD. You decide to reinstall the device drivers. What is the first thing you do?
   a. Open Control Panel and click Add New Hardware.
   b. Open Device Manager and choose Update Driver.
   c. Remove the data cable from the DVD drive so Windows will no longer recognize the drive and allow you to reinstall the drivers.
   d. Open Device Manager and uninstall the drive.

6. Match the following ports to the diagrams in Figure 9-75. Note that some ports are not used: Dual Link DVI-I, Single Link DVI-D, parallel, USB Type A, USB Type B, FireWire 400, VGA, DisplayPort, Mini Display Port, 4-pin S-Video, HDMI, PS/2, and serial.

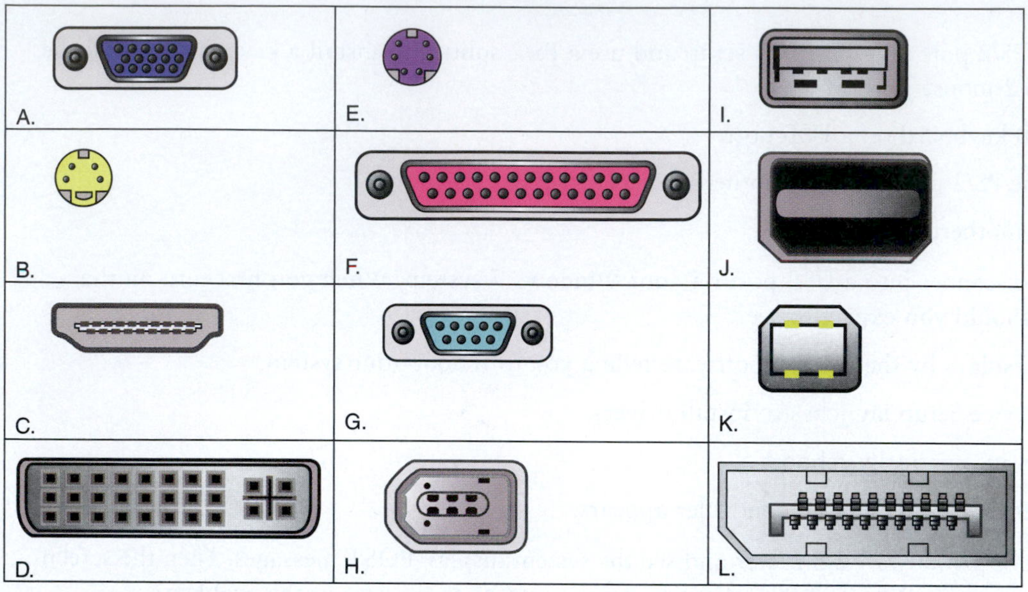

Figure 9-75 Identify ports

>> REAL PROBLEMS, REAL SOLUTIONS

REAL PROBLEM 9-1 Helping with Upgrade Decisions

Upgrading an existing system can sometimes be a wise thing to do, but sometimes the upgrade costs more than the system is worth. Also, if existing components are old, they might not be compatible with components you want to use for the upgrade. A friend, Renata, asks your advice about several upgrades she is considering. Answer these questions:

1. Renata has a four-year-old desktop computer that has a Core2 Duo processor and 2 GB of memory. It does not have a FireWire port. She wants to use a camcorder that has a FireWire 400 interface to a PC. How would she perform the upgrade, and what is the cost? Save or print webpages to support your answers.
2. Her computer has one USB port, but she wants to use her USB printer at the same time she uses her USB scanner. How can she do this, and how much will it cost? Save or print webpages to support your answers.
3. Renata also uses her Windows 8 computer for gaming and wants to get a better gaming experience. The computer is using onboard video and has an empty PCI Express video slot. What is the fastest and best graphics card she can buy? How much does it cost? Save or print webpages to support your answer.
4. What is the total cost of all the upgrades Renata wants? Do you think it is wise for her to make these upgrades or would it be wiser to purchase a new system? How would you explain your recommendation to her?

REAL PROBLEM 9-2 Using Input Director

Input Director is software that lets you use one keyboard and mouse to control two or more computers that are networked together. You can download the free software from *www.inputdirector.com*. To use the software, you need to know the host name of each computer that will share the keyboard and mouse. To find out the host name, in Windows 8, right-click **Start** and select **System**. In Windows 7 right-click **Computer** and select **Properties**. The host name is listed as the Computer name.

Working with a partner, download and install Input Director and configure it so that you and your partner are using the same keyboard and mouse for your computers.

REAL PROBLEM 9-3 Researching a Computer Ad

Pick a current website or magazine ad for a complete, working desktop computer system, including computer, monitor, keyboard, and software, together with extra devices such as a mouse or printer. Research the details of the ad and write a two- to four-page report describing and explaining these details. This project provides a good opportunity to learn about the latest offerings on the market as well as current pricing.

REAL PROBLEM 9-4 Working with a Monitor

Do the following to practice changing monitor settings and troubleshooting monitor problems:

1. Practice changing the display settings, including the wallpaper, screen saver, and appearance. If you are not using your own computer, be sure to restore each setting after making changes.
2. Pretend you have made a mistake and selected a combination of foreground and background colors that makes reading the screen impossible. Solve the problem by booting Windows into Safe Mode. Correct the problem and then reboot.
3. Change the monitor resolution. Try several resolutions. Make a change and then make the change permanent. You can go back and adjust it later if you want.
4. Work with a partner who is using a different computer. Unplug the monitor in the computer lab or classroom, loosen or disconnect the computer monitor cable, or turn the contrast and brightness all the way down while your partner does something similar to the other computer. Trade computers and troubleshoot the problems.
5. Wear an ESD strap. Turn off the computer, press the power button, remove the case cover, and loosen the video card. Turn on the computer and write down the problem as a user would describe it. Turn off the computer, reseat the card, and verify that everything works.
6. Turn off your system. Insert into the system a defective video card provided by your instructor. Turn on the system. Describe the resulting problem in writing, as a user would.

CHAPTER 10

Maintaining Windows

After completing this chapter, you will be able to:

- Set up and perform scheduled preventive maintenance tasks to keep Windows healthy
- Prepare for disaster by keeping good backups of user data and Windows system files
- Use commands to manage files and folders and use Disk Management to manage hard drives

Earlier in the text, you learned how to install Windows. This chapter takes you to the next step in learning how to support a Windows operating system: maintaining the OS after it is installed. Most Windows problems stem from poor maintenance. If you are an IT support technician responsible for the ongoing support of several computers, you can make your work easier and your users happier by setting up and executing a good maintenance plan for each computer you support. A well-maintained computer gives fewer problems and performs better than one that is not maintained. In this chapter, you learn how to schedule regular maintenance tasks, prepare for disaster by setting up backup routines for user data and system files, use commands to manage files and folders, and manage a hard drive.

This text covers Windows 8.1, 8.0, 7, and Vista. As you read, you might consider following the steps in the chapter first using a Windows 8.1 system, and then going through the chapter again using a Windows 7 system.

SCHEDULE PREVENTIVE MAINTENANCE

A+
220-902
1.4, 1.5,
1.7, 3.4,
4.1

Regular preventive maintenance can keep a Windows computer performing well for years. At least once a month, you need to verify critical Windows settings and clean up the hard drive. These skills are covered in this part of the chapter. If you notice the system is slow as you do this maintenance, you need to dig deeper to optimize Windows. How to optimize Windows is covered later in the chapter "Optimizing Windows."

Notes When you're responsible for a computer, be sure to keep good records of all that you do to maintain, upgrade, or fix the computer. When performing preventive maintenance, take notes and include those in your documentation. The Computer Inventory and Maintenance document available at *cengagebrain.com* can help you organize your notes.

VERIFY CRITICAL WINDOWS SETTINGS

A+
220-902
1.4, 1.7,
3.4

Three Windows settings discussed here are critical for keeping the system protected from malware and hackers. Users sometimes change these settings without realizing their importance. Check the three settings and, if you find settings that are incorrect, take time to explain to the primary user of the computer how important these settings are. Here are the critical Windows settings you need to verify:

- *Windows updates.* Install any important Windows updates or Windows 7 service packs that are waiting to be installed and verify that Windows Update is configured to automatically allow updating. These updates may include updates to Windows, applications, device drivers, and firmware. You learned how to configure Windows Update in the chapter "Installing Windows."
- *Antivirus/anti-malware software.* To protect a system against malicious attack, you also need to verify that anti-malware software is configured to scan the system regularly and that it is up to date. If you discover it is not scanning regularly, take the time to do a thorough scan for viruses.
- *Network security setting.* To secure the computer against attack from the network, check that the network security type (public or private in Windows 8; public, work, or home in Windows 7) is set correctly for the optimum firewall settings. How to verify the network type was covered in the chapter "Survey of Windows Features and Support Tools." Further details of configuring network security are discussed in the chapter "Security Strategies."

Notes Don't forget that what you learn about maintaining Windows also applies to Windows in a VM. When maintaining a VM, make sure Windows in a VM is updated, anti-malware software is installed and running, and network settings are secure.

UPDATE DRIVERS AND FIRMWARE

A+
220-902
1.4, 1.5, 1.7,
3.4, 4.1

As part of routine maintenance, you normally would not update device drivers unless a device is having a problem or you want to use a new feature available with a driver update. In the chapter, "Installing Windows," you learned to use Device Manager to update drivers. A few devices have firmware on the device that can be updated, which is called flashing firmware. For example, after a RAID controller had its drivers updated by Device Manager, new tabs appeared on the controller's properties box that are put there by the drivers (see Figure 10-1). To flash the firmware on this controller card, you first download the flash image file from the device manufacturer's website. Then click **Browse** and locate the file. Next, click **Program Flash** to begin the firmware update.

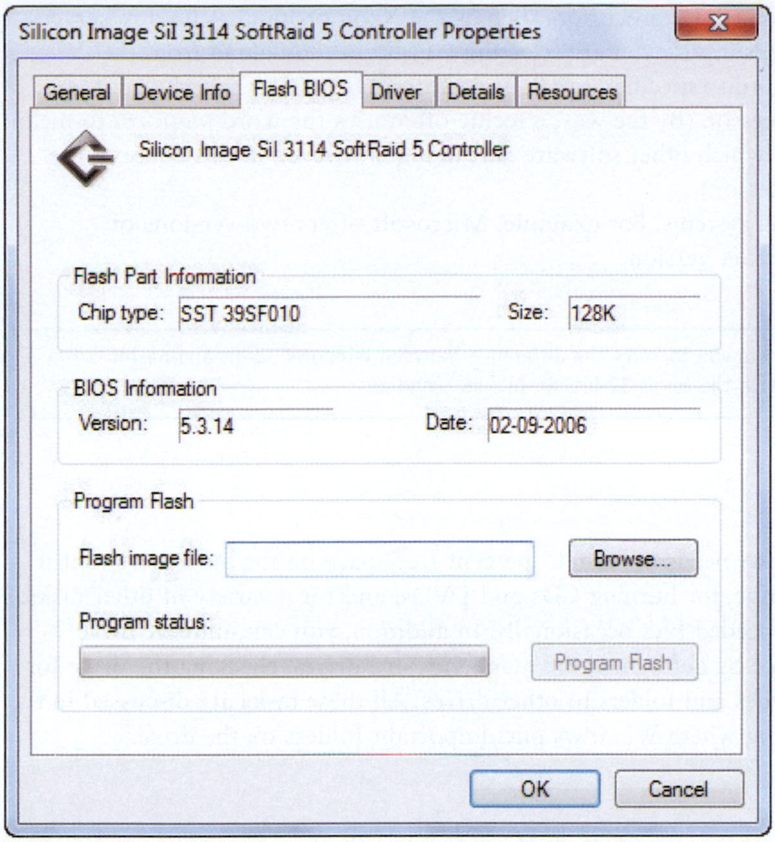

Figure 10-1 Use the device's properties box to flash the firmware on some devices

PATCH MANAGEMENT

A+ 220-902 1.7

When researching a problem, suppose you discover that Microsoft or a manufacturer's website offers a fix or patch for Windows, a device driver, or an application. To download and apply the right patch, you need to make sure you get a 32-bit patch for a 32-bit installation of Windows, a device driver, or an application. For a 64-bit installation of Windows, make sure you get a 64-bit device driver. An application installed in a 64-bit OS might be a 32-bit application or a 64-bit application.

The documentation on the Microsoft or other websites might be cryptic about the type of patch. Follow these guidelines when reading error messages or documentation:

- The term x86 refers to 32-bit CPUs or processors and to 32-bit operating systems. For example, suppose you need to download a patch from Microsoft to fix a Windows 8.1 problem you are having with USB devices. The article on the Microsoft website that applies to your problem says to download the patch if you are using a Windows 8.1, x86-based version. This means you can use this patch if you are using a 32-bit version of Windows 8.1.
- All CPUs installed in personal computers today are hybrid processors that can process either 32 bits or 64 bits. The term x86-64 refers to these processors, such as the Intel Core i5 or an AMD Phenom processor. (AMD64 refers specifically to these hybrid AMD processors.) The term x86-64 can also refer to a 64-bit OS. For example, a Windows message might say, "You are attempting to load an x86-64 operating system." Take that to mean you are attempting to load a 64-bit OS onto a computer that has a hybrid 32-bit/64-bit processor installed, such as the Phenom II X4 or Intel Core i5.

- The term IA64 refers specifically to 64-bit Intel processors such as the Xeon or Itanium used in servers or high-end workstations. For example, suppose you are selecting a utility to download from the Microsoft website. One choice for the utility specifies an IA64 platform. Only select this choice if you have installed an Itanium or Xeon processor. (By the way, a techie often uses the word *platform* to mean the processor and operating system on which other software is running. However, in this context, the operating system's platform is the processor.)
- The term x64 refers to 64-bit operating systems. For example, Microsoft offers two versions of Windows 8.1: the x86 version and the x64 version.

★ A+ Exam Tip The A+ 220-902 exam expects you to know the difference between Windows 32-bit and 64-bit versions. You are also expected to be familiar with the terms 32-bit, 64-bit, x86, and x64.

CLEAN UP THE HARD DRIVE

A+ 220-902 1.4, 1.5, 1.7, 3.4, 4.1

For best performance, Windows needs at least 15 percent free space on the hard drive that it uses for defragmenting the drive, for burning CDs and DVDs, and for a variety of other tasks, so it's important to delete unneeded files occasionally. In addition, you can improve drive performance and free up space by defragmenting magnetic hard drives, checking the drive for errors, compressing folders, and moving files and folders to other drives. All these tasks are discussed in the following subsections. We begin by learning where Windows puts important folders on the drive.

DIRECTORY STRUCTURES

Folder or directory locations you need to be aware of include those for user files, program files, and Windows data. In the folder locations given in this discussion, we assume Windows is installed on drive C:.

User Profile Namespace

When a user first signs in to Windows, a **user profile** is created, which is a collection of user data and settings, and consists of two general items:

- ***A user folder together with its subfolders.*** These items are created under the C:\Users folder, for example, C:\Users\Jean Andrews. This folder contains a group of subfolders collectively called the **user profile namespace**. (In general, a namespace is a container to hold data, for example, a folder.)
- ***NTUSER.DAT.*** NTUSER.DAT is a hidden file stored in the C:\Users*username* folder and contains user settings. Each time the user logs on, the contents of this file are copied to a location in the registry.

Program Files

Here is where Windows stores program files unless you select a different location when a program is installed:

- Program files are stored in C:\Program Files for 32-bit versions of Windows. Only 32-bit applications can be installed in a 32-bit installation of Windows.
- In 64-bit versions of Windows, 64-bit programs are stored in the C:\Program Files folder, and 32-bit programs are stored in the C:\Program Files (x86) folder. (For best performance, when you have the option, install 64-bit applications in a 64-bit installation of Windows.)

Here are folders that applications and some utilities use to launch programs at startup:

- A program file or shortcut to a program file stored in the C:\Users*username*\AppData\Roaming\Microsoft\Windows\Start Menu\Programs\Startup folder launches at startup for an individual user.
- A program file or shortcut to a program file stored in the C:\ProgramData\Microsoft\Windows\Start Menu\Programs\Startup folder launches at startup for all users.

Folders for Windows Data

An operating system needs a place to keep hardware and software configuration information, user preferences, and application settings. This information is used when the OS is first loaded and when needed by hardware, applications, and users. Windows uses a database called the registry for most of this information. In addition, Windows keeps some data in text files called initialization files, which often have an .ini or .inf file extension.

Here are some important folder locations used for the registry and other Windows data:

- ***Registry location.*** The Windows registry is stored in the C:\Windows\System32\config folder.
- ***Backup of the registry.*** A backup of the registry is stored in the C:\Windows\System32\config\RegBack folder.
- ***Fonts.*** Fonts are stored in the C:\Windows\Fonts folder.
- ***Temporary files.*** These files, which are used by Windows when it is installing software and performing other maintenance tasks, are stored in the C:\Windows\Temp folder.
- ***Offline files.*** Offline files are stored in the client-side caching (CSC) folder, which is C:\Windows\CSC. This folder is created and managed by the Offline Files utility, which allows users to work with files in the folder when the computer is not connected to the corporate network. Later, when a connection happens, Windows syncs up the offline files and folders stored in the C:\Windows\CSC folder with those on the network.

Notes Most often, Windows is installed on drive C:, although in a dual-boot environment, one OS might be installed on C: and another on a different drive. For example, Windows 7 can be installed on C: and Windows 8 installed on E:. Also, drive C: for one OS in a dual-boot system is likely to have a different drive letter in the other OS.

If the drive letter of the Windows volume is not known, it is written in Microsoft documentation as *%SystemDrive%*. For example, the location of the Program Files folder is written as *%SystemDrive%*\Program Files.

USE THE DISK CLEANUP UTILITY

Begin cleaning up the drive by finding out how much free space the drive has. Then use the Windows Disk Cleanup (cleanmgr.exe) utility to delete temporary files on the drive.

APPLYING CONCEPTS USE DISK CLEANUP

A+
220-902
1.7

Follow these steps to find out how much free space is on the drive, and use Disk Cleanup:

1. Open Windows 8 File Explorer or Windows 7 Windows Explorer and right-click the volume on which Windows is installed, most likely drive C:. Select **Properties** from the shortcut menu. The drive Properties box appears, as shown on the left side of Figure 10-2. You can see the free space on this drive C: is 155 GB, which is about 37 percent of the volume.

(continues)

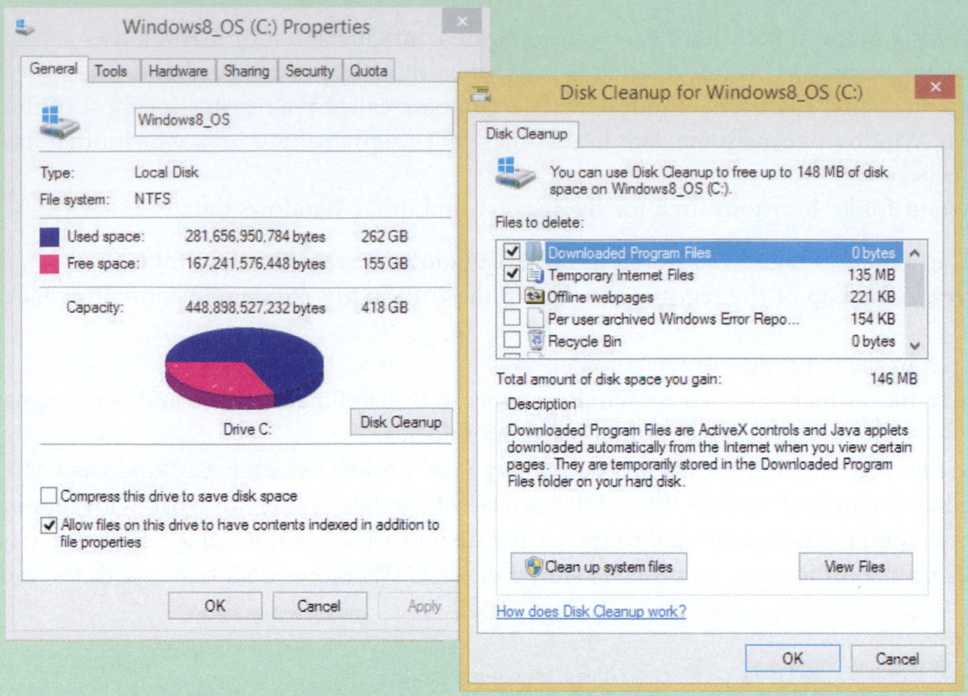

Figure 10-2 Use File Explorer to find out how much free space is on drive C:

2. On the General tab, click **Disk Cleanup**. (Alternatively, you can access the utility by executing the **cleanmgr.exe** program.) Disk Cleanup calculates how much space can be freed and then displays the Disk Cleanup box, shown on the right side of Figure 10-2. Select the files you want to delete.

3. Click **Clean up system files** to see temporary system files that you can also delete. The Disk Cleanup tab in Figure 10-3a shows the result for one computer. Notice in the figure the option to delete files from Previous Windows installation(s), which can free up additional hard drive space. This space is used by the Windows. old folder, which was created when Windows 8 was installed as an upgrade from Windows 7 and stored the old Windows, Program Files, and User folders in the Windows.old folder. If the user assures you that no information, data, or settings are needed from the old Windows installation, it's safe to delete these files to free up the space.

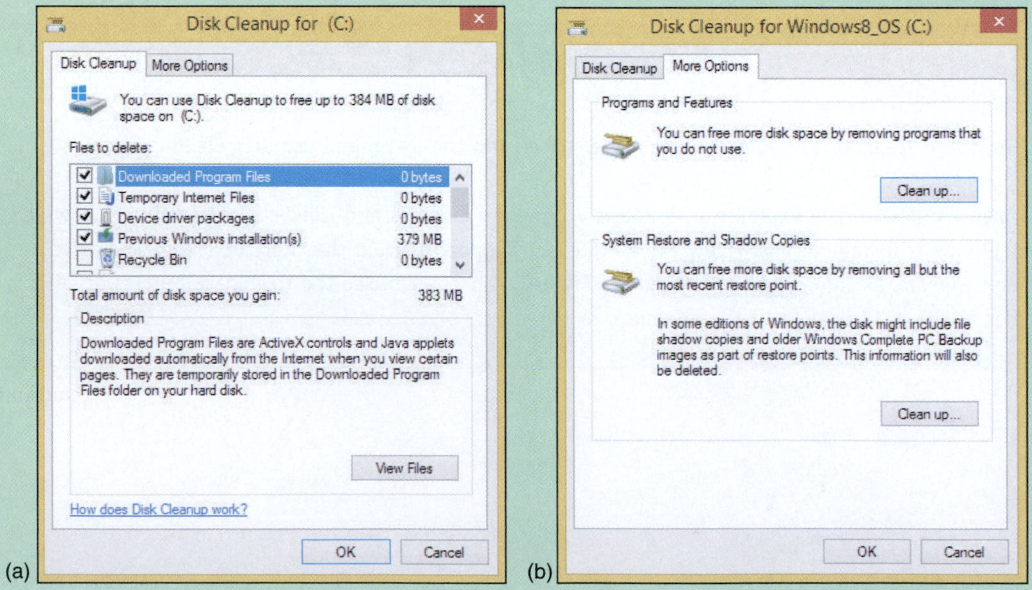

Figure 10-3 Clean up system files no longer needed in order to free up disk space

4. If you still need more free space, click the **More Options** tab (see Figure 10-3b) in the Disk Cleanup box. In the Programs and Features area, click **Clean up**. You are taken to the Programs and Features window where you can uninstall unneeded software to recover that space. Also on the More Options tab in the Disk Cleanup box, when you click **Clean up** under the System Restore and Shadow Copies area, Windows will delete all but the most recent restore points that are created by System Restore. (You will learn more about System Restore later in this chapter.)

DEFRAG THE HARD DRIVE

Two types of hard drives are magnetic hard disk drives (HDDs), which contain spinning platters, and solid-state drives (SSDs), which contain flash memory. For magnetic hard drives, Windows automatically defragments the drive once a week. To defragment is to rearrange fragments or parts of files on the drive so each file is stored on the drive in contiguous clusters.

In a file system, a cluster, also called a file allocation unit, is a group of whole sectors. The number of sectors in a cluster is fixed and is determined when the file system is first installed. A file is stored in whole clusters, and the unused space at the end of the last cluster, called slack, is wasted free space. As files are written and deleted from a drive, clusters are used, released, and used again. New files written on the drive can be put in available clusters spread over the drive. Over time, drive performance is affected when the moving read/write arm of a magnetic drive must move over many areas of the drive to collect all the fragments of a file. Defragmenting a drive rewrites files in contiguous clusters and improves drive performance.

Because a solid-state drive has no moving parts, defragmenting does not improve read/write time. In fact, defragmenting a solid-state drive can reduce the life of the drive and is not recommended. Windows disables defragmenting for solid-state drives.

Notes To find out what type of hard drive is installed, use Device Manager or the System Information window (msinfo32.exe). For example, Figure 10-4 shows the Windows 8 System Information window drilled down to the Storage Disks area, and you can see the model information for two hard drives installed in the system. A quick search on the web shows the first hard drive is a magnetic HDD and the second hard drive is SSD.

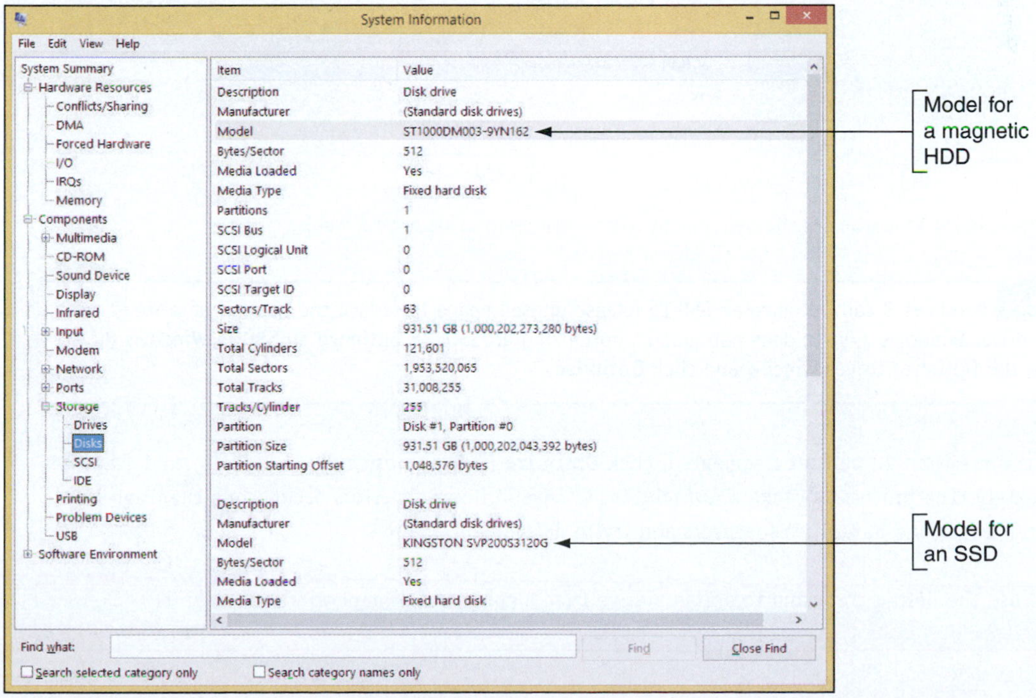

Figure 10-4 Use the System Information window to find the brand and model number for the hard drive

APPLYING | CONCEPTS VERIFY SCHEDULED DRIVE MAINTENANCE

A+
220-902
1.7

To verify that Windows 8/7/Vista is defragmenting a magnetic drive and not defragmenting a solid-state drive, do the following:

1. Use Explorer to open the Properties box for a drive and click the **Tools** tab (see the left side of Figure 10-5), and then click **Optimize** (or **Defragment now** in 7/Vista). In the Optimize Drives box (Disk Defragmenter in 7/Vista), as shown on the right side of Figure 10-5, verify the defrag settings. This system has two hard drives installed. Drive C: is an SSD and drive D: is a magnetic HDD. To have Windows tell you if a drive needs defragmenting, select a drive and click **Analyze** (**Analyze disk** in 7/Vista).
2. In Figure 10-5, you can see optimization is turned off. To turn it on for drive D:, select the drive and click **Turn on**. In the box that appears, which is showing in the bottom of the figure, check **Run on a schedule (recommended)** and select **Weekly** for the Frequency. Click **OK**.

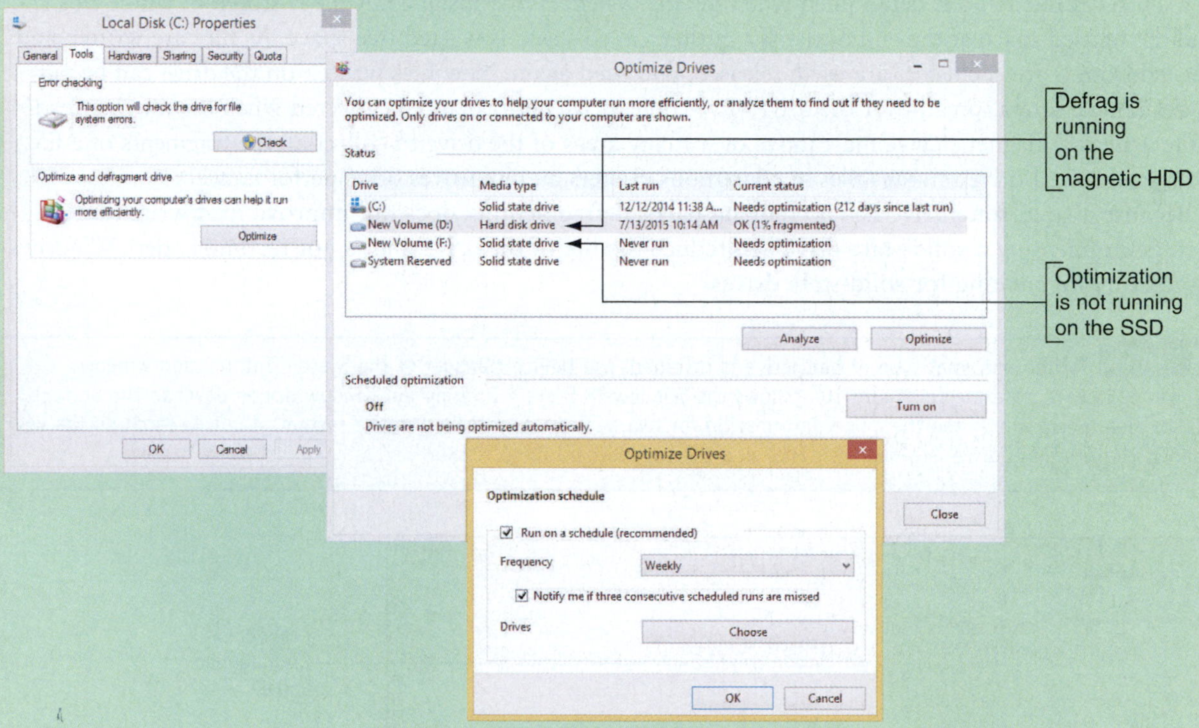

Figure 10-5 Windows is set to automatically defragment a magnetic hard drive once a week

OS Differences Windows 8 can optimize an SSD to release unused space to reduce the number of write operations to the drive. Windows 7/Vista does not support optimizing an SSD. To optimize an SSD in Windows 8, select the drive in the Optimize Drives window and click **Optimize**.

3. If the drive is more than 10 percent fragmented, click **Optimize** (**Defragment now** in 7/Vista) to defrag the drive immediately. The process can take a few minutes to several hours. If errors occur while the drive is defragmenting, check the hard drive for errors and try to defragment again.

You can also use the defrag command to defrag a drive from a command prompt window.

CHECK THE HARD DRIVE FOR ERRORS

Next, to make sure the drive is healthy, you need to search for and repair file system errors. The error-checking utility searches for bad sectors on a volume and recovers the data from them if possible. It then marks the sector as bad so that it will not be reused.

To use the error-checking utility in Explorer, right-click the drive, and select **Properties** from the shortcut menu. Click the **Tools** tab, and then click **Check** (**Check now** in 7/Vista). In the Error-checking dialog box, click **Scan drive**. (In 7/Vista, check **Automatically fix file system errors** and **Scan for and attempt recovery of bad sectors** in the Check Disk dialog box, and then click **Start**.) For the utility to correct errors on the drive, it needs exclusive use of all files on the drive. When Windows has exclusive use, the drive is called a locked drive. Therefore, a dialog box appears telling you about the problem and asking your permission to scan the drive the next time Windows starts. Reboot the system and let her rip.

You can also use the chkdsk command from the command prompt window to check a drive for errors.

FREE UP SPACE ON THE DRIVE

To free up some space on the hard drive, consider these tips:

- ***Uninstall software you no longer use.*** Doing so will free up some space on the hard drive, and, if the software loads a service or program during Windows startup, Windows startup might see performance improvement.
- ***Move data off the drive.*** Consider moving home videos, movies, photos, and other data to an external hard drive or burning them to DVDs or CDs, or transfer them to an online storage service such as Microsoft's OneDrive or Google's Drive.
- ***Move programs off the drive.*** If your Windows volume needs more free space, you can uninstall a program and reinstall it on a second hard drive installed in the system. An installation routine usually gives you the option to point to another location to install the program other than the default C:\Program Files or C:\Program Files (x86) folder.
- ***Use drive or folder compression.*** Windows offers drive and folder compression that can save on hard drive space. However, it is not recommended that you compress the volume on which Windows is stored. To compress a folder or file on an NTFS drive, open the file or folder **Properties** box, and click **Advanced** on the General tab. Then click **Compress contents to save disk space**, and click **OK**.

Notes Windows installs on an NTFS volume, but if a second volume on the drive is formatted using the FAT32 file system, you can convert the volume to NTFS. For large drives, NTFS is more efficient and converting might improve performance. NTFS also offers better security and file and folder compression. For two Microsoft Knowledge Base articles about converting from FAT to NTFS, go to *support.microsoft.com* and search for articles 156560 and 314097. The first article discusses the amount of free space you'll need to make the conversion, and the second article tells you how to convert.

MOVE THE VIRTUAL MEMORY PAGING FILE

Windows uses a file, Pagefile.sys, in the same way it uses memory. This file is called virtual memory and is used to enhance the amount of RAM in a system. Normally, the file, pagefile.sys, is a hidden file stored in the root directory of drive C:. To save space on drive C:, you can move Pagefile.sys to another volume on the same hard drive or to a different hard drive, but don't move it to a different hard drive unless you know the other hard drive is at least as fast as this drive. If the drive is at least as fast as the drive on which Windows is installed, performance should improve. Also, make sure the new volume has plenty of free space to hold the file—at least three times the amount of installed RAM.

A+ Exam Tip The A+ 220-902 exam expects you to know how to configure virtual memory for optimal performance.

APPLYING | CONCEPTS CHANGE THE LOCATION OF PAGEFILE.SYS

To change the location of Pagefile.sys in Windows 8/7/Vista, follow these steps:

1. Open the System window and click **Advanced system settings** in the left pane. The System Properties box appears with the Advanced tab selected (see Figure 10-6).

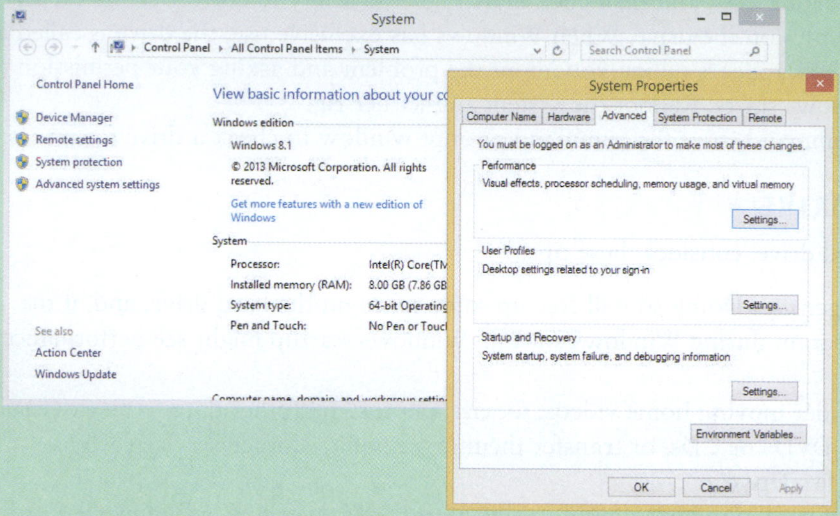

Figure 10-6 Manage virtual memory using the System Properties box

2. In the Performance section, click **Settings**. In the Performance Options box, select the **Advanced** tab and click **Change**. The Virtual Memory dialog box appears.
3. Uncheck **Automatically manage paging file size for all drives** (see Figure 10-7). Select the drive where you want to move the paging file. For best performance, allow Windows to manage the size of the paging file. If necessary, select **System managed size** and click **Set**.

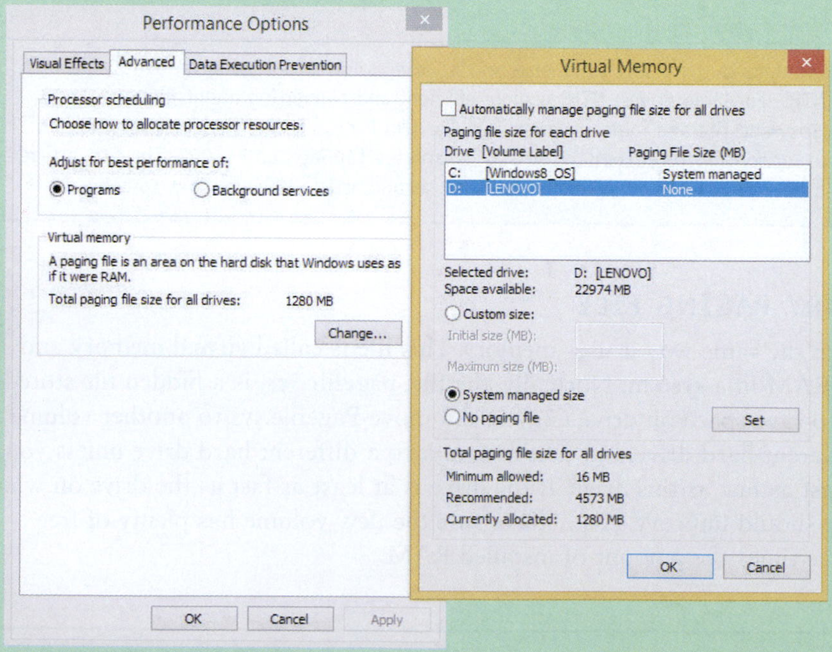

Figure 10-7 Move Pagefile.Sys to a different drive

4. Click **OK**. Windows informs you that you must restart the system for the change to take effect. Click **OK** to close the warning box.
5. Click **Apply** and close all boxes. Then restart the system.

If you still don't have enough free space on the Windows volume, consider adding a second hard drive to the system. In fact, if you install a second hard drive that is faster than the Windows hard drive, know that reinstalling Windows on the faster hard drive will improve performance. You can then use the slower and older hard drive for data.

Notes If the Windows system is still slow and sluggish, know that later in the course you'll learn more about how to optimize Windows so it performs better.

Hands-On | Project 10-1 Perform Routine Maintenance

A+ 220-902 1.7

Sign in to a Windows 8 or Windows 7 system using a Standard user account. Step through the process described in the chapter to do the following routine maintenance. As you work, note which chores you cannot perform unless you know the password to an administrator account. Do the following:

1. Verify critical Windows settings in Windows Update, anti-malware software, and the Network and Sharing Center.
2. Use the Disk Cleanup utility to clean up the hard drive.
3. Find out the brand and model of the hard drive that holds Windows. What is the brand and model? Is the drive a magnetic or solid-state drive? How do you know?
4. Check defrag settings and change them as necessary. Analyze the hard drive and determine if it needs defragmenting or optimizing. If so, optimize the drive.
5. Check the hard drive for errors.
6. Compress the My Documents folder.

Now let's look at how to perform on-demand backups and to schedule routine backups.

BACKUP PROCEDURES

A+ 220-902 1.1, 1.4, 1.5, 1.7, 3.3

A backup is an extra copy of a data or software file that you can use if the original file becomes damaged or destroyed. Losing data due to system failure, a virus, file corruption, or some other problem really makes you appreciate the importance of having backups.

Notes With data and software, here's a good rule of thumb: If you can't get along without it, back it up.

APPLYING | CONCEPTS **BACKUPS PAY OFF**

Dave was well on his way to building a successful career as an IT repair technician. His PC repair shop was doing well, and he was excited about his future. But one bad decision changed everything. He was called to repair a server at a small accounting firm. The call was on the weekend when he was normally off, so he was in a hurry to get the job done. He arrived at the accounting firm and saw that the problem was an easy one to fix, so he decided not to do a backup before working on the system. During his repairs, the hard drive crashed and all data on the drive was lost—four million dollars' worth! The firm sued, Dave's business license was stripped, and he was ordered to pay the money the company lost. A little extra time to back up the system would have saved his whole future. True story!

Because most of us routinely write data to the hard drive, in this section, we focus on backing up from the hard drive to another media. However, when you store important data on any media—such as a flash drive, external hard drive, or CD—always keep a copy of the data on another media. Never trust important data to only one media.

In this part of the chapter, you learn how to make a disaster recovery plan and then learn how to use Windows to back up user data, critical Windows system files, and entire volumes.

PLANNING FOR DISASTER RECOVERY

A+
220-902
1.1, 1.7

The time to prepare for disaster is before it occurs. If you have not prepared, the damage from a disaster will most likely be greater than if you had made and followed disaster recovery plans. Suppose the hard drive on your computer stopped working and you lost all its data. What would be the impact? Are you prepared for this to happen? Here are decisions you need to make for your backup and recovery plans:

- ***Decide on the backup destination.*** For example, options include online backup, network drive, CD, DVD, Blu-ray, SD card, USB flash drive, external hard drive, or other media. Here are points to keep in mind:
  - For individuals or small organizations, an online backup service such as Carbonite (*carbonite.com*) or Mozy (*mozy.com*) is the easiest, most reliable, and most expensive solution. You pay a yearly subscription for the service, and they guarantee your backups, which are automatically done when your computer is connected to the Internet. If you decide to use one of these services, be sure to restore files from backup occasionally to make sure your backups are happening as you expect and that you can recover a lost file.
  - Even though it's easy to do, don't make the mistake of backing up your data to another volume or folder on your same hard drive. When a hard drive crashes, most likely all volumes go down together and you will have lost your data and your backup. Back up to another media and, for extra safety, store it at an off-site location.
- ***Decide on the backup software.*** Windows offers a backup utility. However, you can purchase third-party backup software that might offer more features. An external hard drive often comes with backup software already installed on the drive. However, before you decide to use an all-in-one backup system, be certain you understand the risks of not keeping backups at an off-site location and keeping all your backups on a single media.
- ***Decide how simple or complex your backup strategy needs to be.*** A backup and recovery plan for individuals or small organizations might be very simple. But large organizations might require backups be documented each day, scheduled at certain times of the day or night, and recovery plans tested on a regular basis. Know the requirements of your organization when creating a backup and recovery plan. As a general rule of thumb, back up data for about every 4 to 6 hours of data entry. This might mean a backup needs to occur twice a day, daily, weekly, or monthly. Find out the data entry habits of workers before making your backup schedule and deciding on the folders or volumes to back up.

After you have a backup plan working, test the recovery plan. In addition, you need to occasionally retest the recovery plan to make sure all is still working as you expect. Do the following:

- ***Test the recovery process.*** Erase a file on the hard drive, and use the recovery procedures to verify that you can re-create the file from the backup. This verifies that the backup medium works, that the recovery software is effective, and that you know how to use it. After you are convinced that the recovery works, document how to perform it.
- ***Keep backups in a safe place and routinely test them.*** Don't leave a backup disk lying around for someone to steal. Backups of important and sensitive data should be kept under lock and key at an off-site location. In case of fire, keep enough backups off-site so that you can recover data even if the entire building is destroyed. Routinely verify that your backups are good by performing a test recovery of a backed-up file or folder. Backups are useless if the data on the backup is corrupted.

A+ Exam Tip The A+ 220-902 exam expects you to know how to create and use backups and best practices when scheduling backups.

Now let's see how to back up user data, important Windows system files, and the entire Windows volume. We begin with how to back up user data.

BACK UP USER DATA WITH WINDOWS 8 FILE HISTORY

A+ 220-902 1.1, 1.4, 1.5, 1.7, 3.3

Windows 8 File History backs up user data stored in several locations, including Windows 8 libraries, user desktop, Internet Explorer favorites, contact folders, and offline OneDrive files (for Microsoft accounts). When the backup is enabled, it first makes a full backup to another media. By default, it scans for file and folder changes every hour and keeps as many generations of backups as it has free space on the storage device.

The File History utility is available as a window on the Windows desktop or an app in the Windows 8 interface. For most control over the utility, use the window on the desktop. Follow these steps:

1. First connect your backup device. Open Control Panel in Classic view, and then click **File History**. Figure 10-8 shows a File History window that recognizes a drive to hold the backups. The drive in the figure is an external hard drive with plenty of free space. To turn on File History, click **Turn on**.

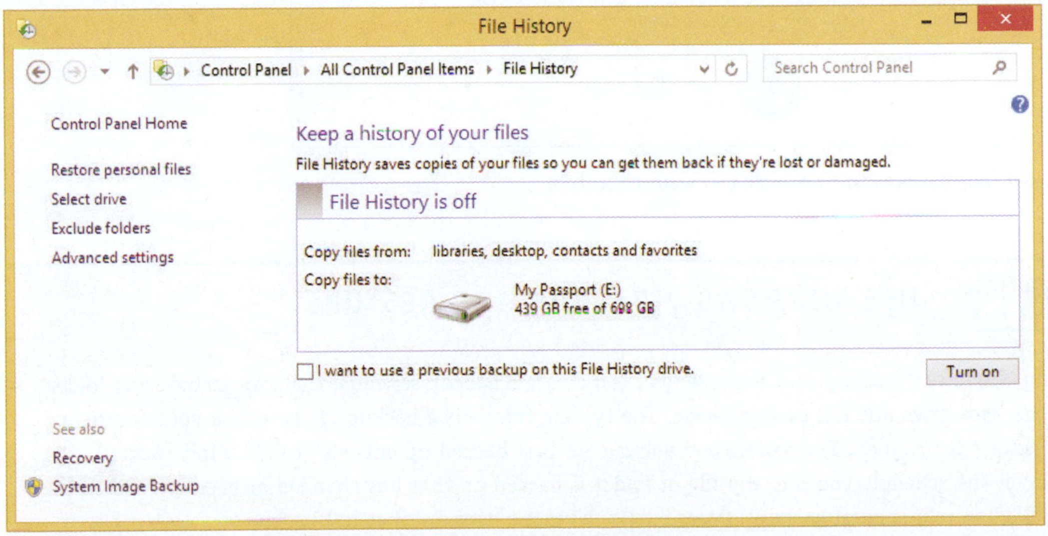

Figure 10-8 Turn on and off File History and control its settings

2. To manage these backups, click **Advanced settings**. On the Advanced Settings window, you can set how often backups are made (every 10 minutes up to daily) and how long old backups should be kept (forever, until space is needed, 1 month, 1 year, and so forth). You can also view a history of events and clean up old backups to free up space.

Notes To open File History in the Windows 8 interface, open the **Settings** charm and click **Change PC settings**. In the PC settings pane, click **Update and recovery** and then click **File History**.

USE FILE HISTORY TO RECOVER A CORRUPTED OR LOST FILE OR FOLDER

To recover items from File History backups, in the File History window, click **Restore personal files**. In the window that appears (see Figure 10-9), use the left and right arrow keys on either side of the green button at the bottom of the window to select a backup and drill down into a backup to find the file or folder you need. Select an item to see a preview, and then click the green **Restore** button at the bottom of the window to restore it. If you prefer to save the previous version in a different location so as not to lose the newest version of that file, right-click the **Restore** button, and click **Restore to**. Navigate to the location where you want to save the previous version, and then click **Select Folder**.

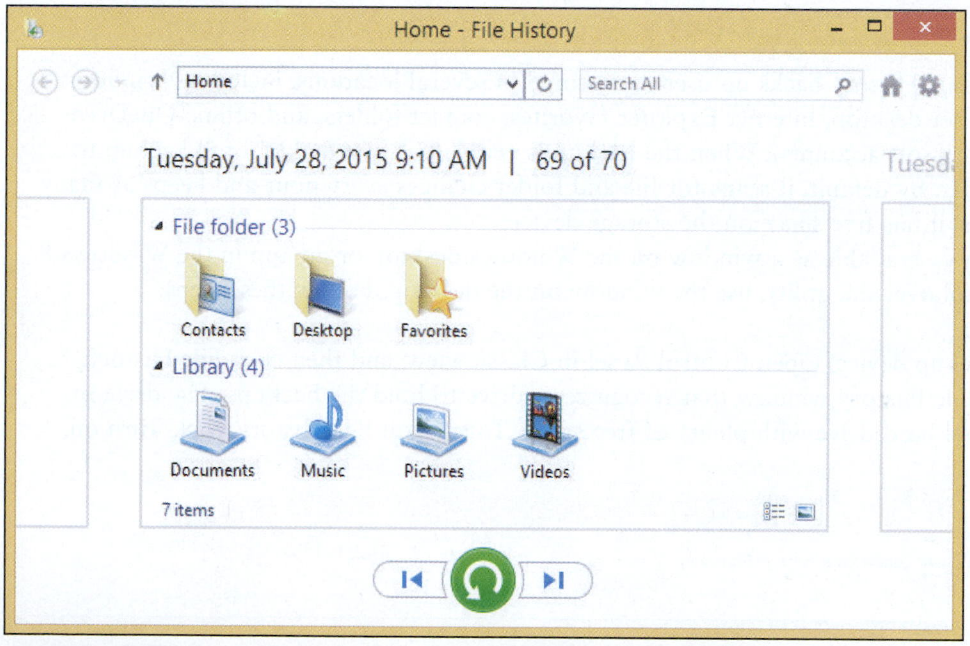

Figure 10-9 Drill down into backups to find what you want to restore

WINDOWS 7 USE WINDOWS 7 BACKUP AND RESTORE

A+ 220-902 1.1, 1.4, 1.5, 1.7, 3.3

Using Windows 7 **Backup and Restore**, you can create a backup schedule that can include any folder on the hard drive and the system image. The **system image** is a backup of the entire volume where Windows 7 is installed. The folders and volume are first backed up entirely (called a full backup). Then on the schedule you set, any file or folder is backed up that has changed or been created since the last backup (called an incremental backup). Occasionally, Windows does another full backup.

Follow these steps to learn how to set up a backup schedule using Windows 7 Backup and Restore:

1. Open Control Panel in Classic view, and click **Backup and Restore**. If no backup has ever been scheduled on the system, the window will look like the one shown in Figure 10-10. Click **Set up backup**.

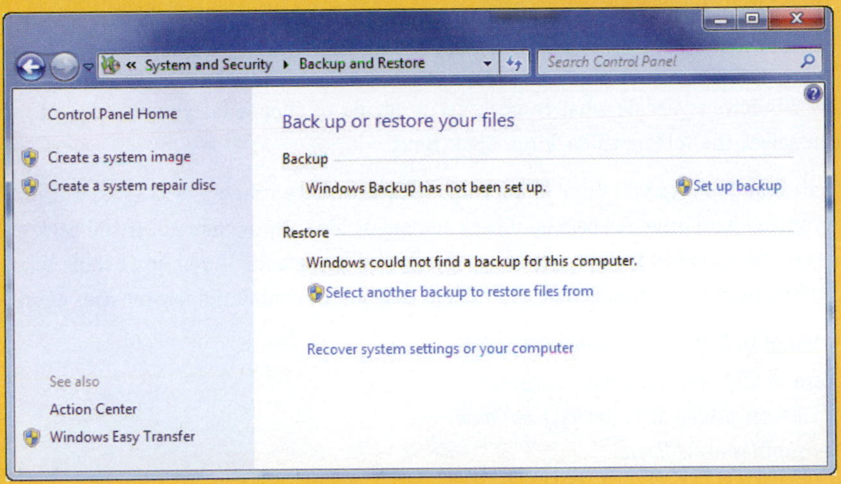

Figure 10-10 Use the Backup and Restore window in Windows 7 to create a system image

2. In the next dialog box (see Figure 10-11), select the media to hold the backup. In Figure 10-11, choices are volume E: (a second internal hard drive), the DVD drive, and OneTouch (an external hard drive). Make your selection and click **Next**.

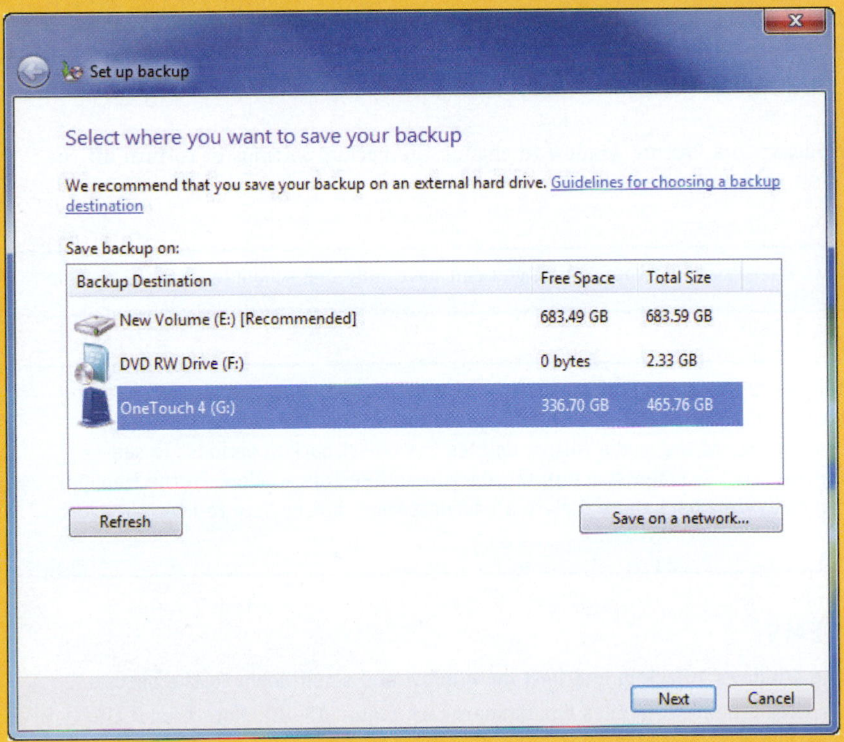

Figure 10-11 Select the destination media to hold the backup

(continues)

Notes Windows 7 Professional, Ultimate, and Enterprise editions allow you to save the backup to a network location. To use a shared folder on the network for the backup destination, click **Save on a network** (see Figure 10-11). In the resulting box, click **Browse** and point to the folder. Also enter the user name and password on the remote computer that the backup utility will use to authenticate to that computer when it makes the backup. You cannot save to a network location when using Windows 7 Home editions. For these editions, the button *Save on a network* is missing in the window where you select the backup destination.

3. In the next box, you can allow Windows to decide what to back up or decide to choose for yourself. Select **Let me choose** so that you can select the folders to back up. Click **Next**.
4. In the next box, select the libraries and folders you want to back up. Click the white triangle beside Local Disk (C:) to drill down to any folder on the hard drive for backup. Check folders or libraries to back up. If the backup media can hold the system image, the option to include the image is selected by default. If you don't want to include the image, uncheck it. Click **Next** to continue. Here are folders that might contain important user data:
   - Application data is usually found in C:\Users*username*\AppData.
   - Internet Explorer favorites are in C:\Users*username*\Favorites.
   - Better still, back up the entire user profile at C:\Users*username*.
   - Even better, back up all user profiles at C:\Users.
5. In the next box, verify the correct folders and libraries are selected. To change the default schedule, click **Change schedule**. In the next box, you can choose to run the backup daily, weekly, or monthly and select the time of day. Make your selections, and click **OK**.
6. Review your backup settings, and click **Save settings and run backup**. The backup proceeds. A **shadow copy** is made of any open files so that files that are currently open are included in the backup.

A+ Exam Tip The A+ 220-902 exam expects you to know what a shadow copy is.

Later, you can return to the Backup and Restore window to change the backup settings or to turn off the backup.

Notes One limitation of Windows Backup and Restore is that you can have only one scheduled backup routine.

Notes After Windows does a full backup, it only backs up files that have changed since the last full backup. Occasionally, it does another full backup. Each full backup is called a backup period. It keeps as many backup periods as it has space on the backup media. As the media fills, it deletes the oldest backup periods. To see how space is used on your backup media, click **Manage space** in the Backup and Restore window. In the Manage Windows Backup disk space, you can click **View backups** to delete a backup period, but be sure to keep the most recent backup periods.

RECOVER BACKED-UP ITEMS

To recover backed-up items, open the Windows 7 Backup and Restore window and scroll down to the bottom of the window and click **Restore my files**. The Restore Files box appears (see Figure 10-12). Note that if the *Restore my files* button is missing from the Backup and Restore window, your backup media might not be available to Windows. You might need to plug in the media and then use Windows Explorer to verify you can access the backup folder on the media.

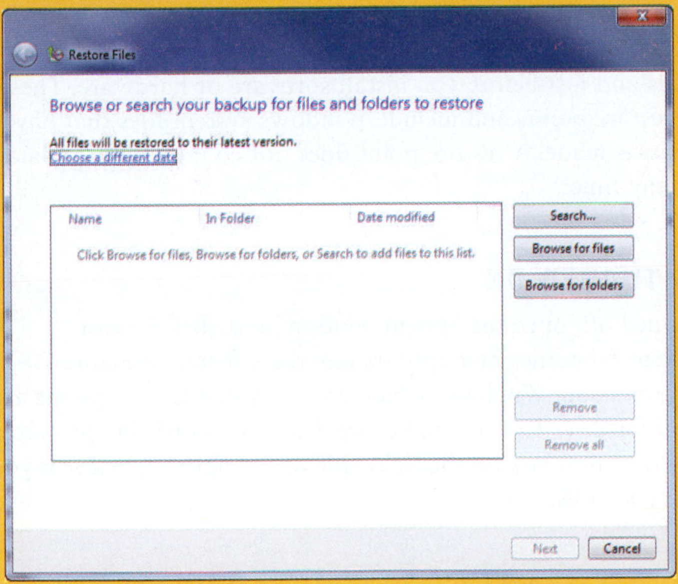

Figure 10-12 Locate the files and folders on the backup media to restore

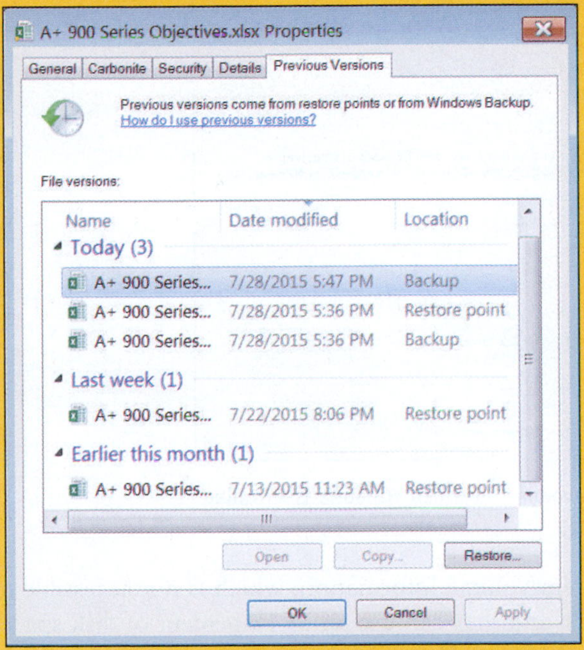

Figure 10-13 Restore a file or folder from a previous version

Use one of the three buttons on the window to locate the file or folder. *Search* allows you to search for a file or folder when you only know part of the file name or folder name. *Browse for files* allows you to drill down to the file to restore. *Browse for folders* allows you to search for the folder to restore. You can locate and select multiple files or folders to restore. Then follow the directions on screen to restore all the selected items.

To restore a folder or file to a previous version, follow these steps:

1. Use Windows Explorer to copy—not move—the corrupted folder or file to a new location. When you restore a file or folder to a previous version, the current file or folder can be overwritten by the previous version. By saving a copy of the current file or folder to a different location, you can revert to the copy if necessary.
2. Right-click the file or folder and select **Restore previous versions** from the shortcut menu. The Properties box for the file or folder appears with the Previous Versions tab selected. Windows displays a list of all previous versions of the file or folder it has kept (see Figure 10-13).
3. Select the version you want and click **Restore**. A message box asks if you are sure you want to continue. Click **Restore**, and then click **OK**.
4. Open the restored file or folder and verify it is the version you want. If you decide you need another version, delete the file or folder, and copy the file or folder you saved in Step 1 back into the original location. Then return to Step 2 and try again, this time selecting a different previous version.

BACK UP WINDOWS SYSTEM FILES

A+
220-902
1.1, 1.4, 1.5,
1.7, 3.3

The Windows **System Protection** utility automatically backs up system files and stores them on the hard drive at regular intervals and just before you install software or hardware. These snapshots of the system are called **restore points** and include Windows system files that have changed since the last restore point was made. A restore point does not contain all user data, and you can manually create a restore point at any time.

MAKE SURE SYSTEM PROTECTION IS TURNED ON

To make sure System Protection has not been turned off, open the System window, and click **System protection**. The System Protection tab of the System Properties box appears (see the left side of Figure 10-14). Make sure protection is turned on for the drive containing Windows, which indicates that restore points are created automatically. In Figure 10-14, protection for drive C: is on and other drives are not being protected. To make a change, click **Configure**. The System Protection box on the right side of the figure appears. If you make a change to this box, click **Apply**, and then click **OK**.

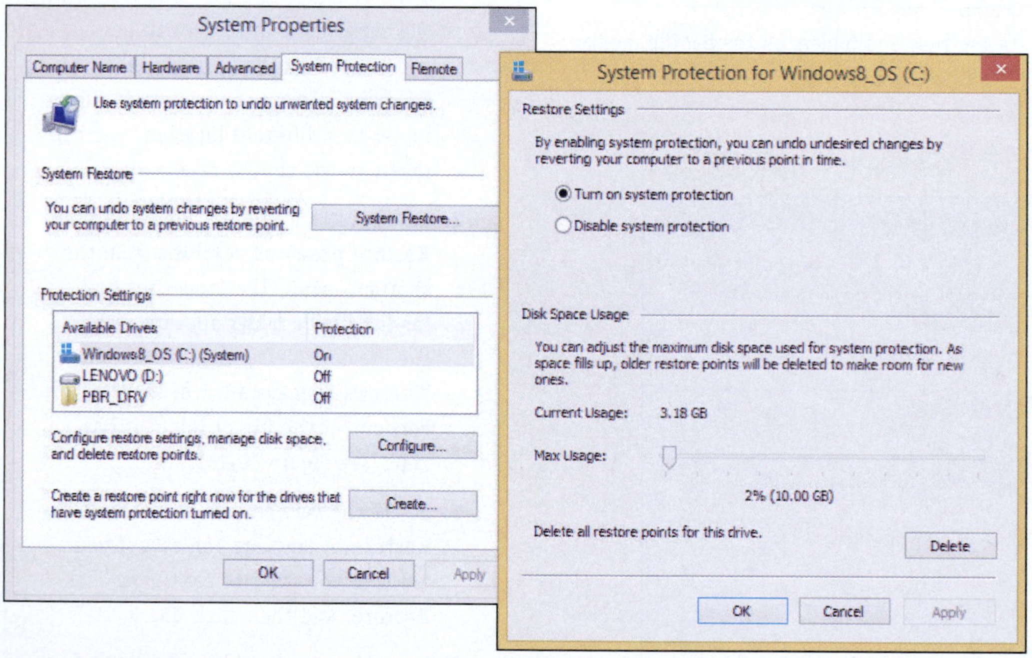

Figure 10-14 Make sure System Protection is turned on for the volume on which Windows is installed

Restore points are normally kept in the folder C:\System Volume Information, which is not accessible to the user. Restore points are taken at least every 24 hours, and they can use up to 15 percent of disk space. If disk space gets very low, restore points are no longer made, which is one more good reason to keep about 15 percent or more of the hard drive free.

MANUALLY CREATE A RESTORE POINT

To manually create a restore point, use the System Protection tab of the System Properties box, as shown on the left side of Figure 10-14. Click **Create**. In the System Protection box, enter a name for the restore point, such as "Before I tested software," and click **Create**. The restore point is created.

APPLY A RESTORE POINT

System Restore (rstrui.exe) restores the system to its condition at the time a restore point was made. If you restore the system to a previous restore point, user data on the hard drive will not be altered, but you can affect installed software and hardware, user settings, and OS configuration settings. When you use System Restore to roll back the system to a restore point, any changes made to these settings after the restore point was created are lost; therefore, always use the most recent restore point that can fix the problem so that you make the least intrusive changes to the system.

To return the system to a previous restore point and to practice opening a utility from the command prompt, do the following:

1. Click **Start**, type **rstrui.exe** in the Search box, and press **Enter**. The System Restore box opens. Click **Next**.
2. In the next box, the most recent restore points appear. For most situations, the most recent is the one to select so as to make the least possible changes to your system. Select a restore point (see Figure 10-15), and click **Next**.
3. Windows asks you to confirm your selection. Click **Finish** and respond to the warning box. The system restarts and the restore point is applied.

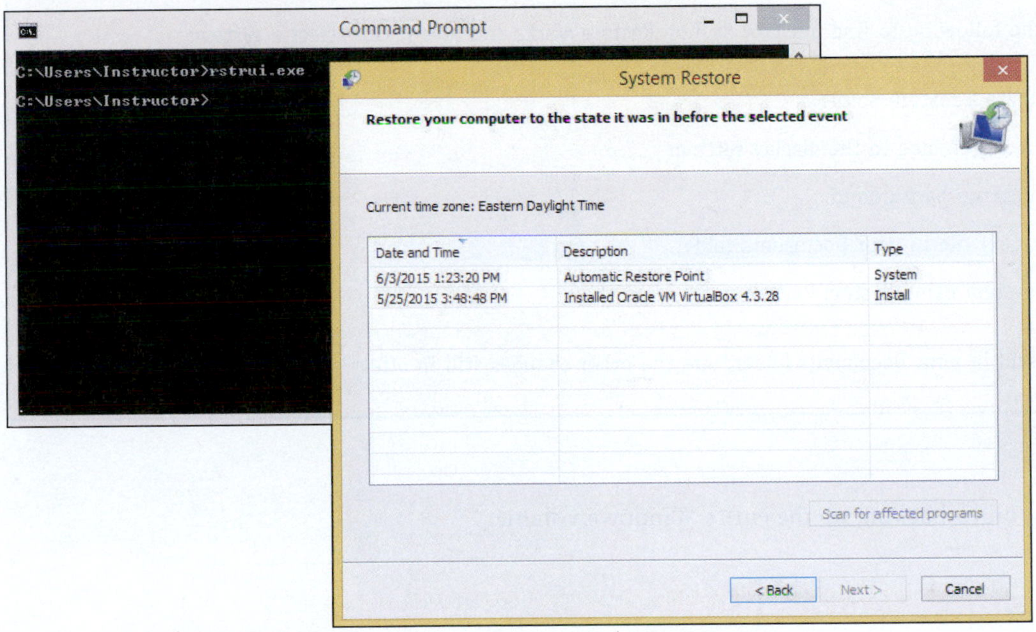

Figure 10-15 Select a restore point

POINTS TO REMEMBER ABOUT SYSTEM RESTORE

System Restore is a great tool to try to fix a device that is not working, restore Windows settings that are giving problems, or solve problems with applications. Although it's a great tool in some situations, it does have its limitations. Keep these points in mind:

- *Point 1:* System Restore won't help if you don't have restore points to use. System Protection must be turned on so that restore points are automatically created.
- *Point 2:* Restore points replace certain keys in the registry but cannot completely rebuild a totally corrupted registry. Therefore, System Restore can recover from errors only if the registry is somewhat intact.

- *Point 3:* The restore process cannot remove a virus or worm infection. However, it might help you start a system that is infected with a virus that launches at startup. After Windows has started, you can then use anti-malware software to remove the infection.
- *Point 4:* System Restore might create a new problem. Often when using a restore point, anti-malware software gets all out of whack and sometimes even needs reinstalling. Therefore, use restore points sparingly.
- *Point 5:* System Restore might make many changes to a system. If you know which change caused a problem, try to undo that particular change first. The idea is to use the least invasive solution first. For example, if updating a driver has caused a problem, first try Driver Rollback to undo that change. Driver Rollback is performed using Device Manager.
- *Point 6:* Restore points are kept in a hidden folder on the hard drive. If that area of the drive is corrupted, the restore points are lost. Also, if a user turns System Protection off, all restore points are lost.
- *Point 7:* Viruses and other malware sometimes hide in restore points. To completely clean an infected system, you need to delete all restore points by turning System Protection off and back on.
- *Point 8:* If Windows will not start, you can launch System Restore using startup recovery tools, which are covered in the chapter, "Troubleshooting Windows Startup."

Hands-On | Project 10-2 Use System Restore

A+
220-902
1.1

Do the following to find out how System Restore works and how it can affect a system:

1. Create a restore point.
2. Make a change to the display settings.
3. Change the desktop background.
4. Create a new text file in your Documents folder.
5. Restore the system using System Restore.

Is the text file still in your Documents folder? Are the other changes still in effect? Why or why not?

And now moving on to backing up the entire Windows volume.

WINDOWS 8 CUSTOM REFRESH IMAGE

A+
220-902
1.1, 1.4, 1.5, 1.7, 3.3

A custom refresh image is an image of the entire Windows volume, including the Windows installation, Windows 8 apps, desktop applications, and user settings and data. The best time to create the image is right after you've installed Windows, hardware, applications, and user accounts and customized Windows settings. The image is stored in a single file named CustomRefresh.wim in the folder you specify. The WIM file uses the Windows Imaging File (WIM) format, which is a compressed file that contains many related files.

Here are the steps to create a Windows 8 custom refresh image:

1. Open an elevated command prompt window. One way to do that is to press **Win+X** and click **Command Prompt (Admin)**. Respond to the UAC box. The Administrator: Command Prompt window opens.
2. Enter this command, substituting any drive and folder for that shown in the command line (see Figure 10-16):

```
recimg /createimage D:\MyImage
```

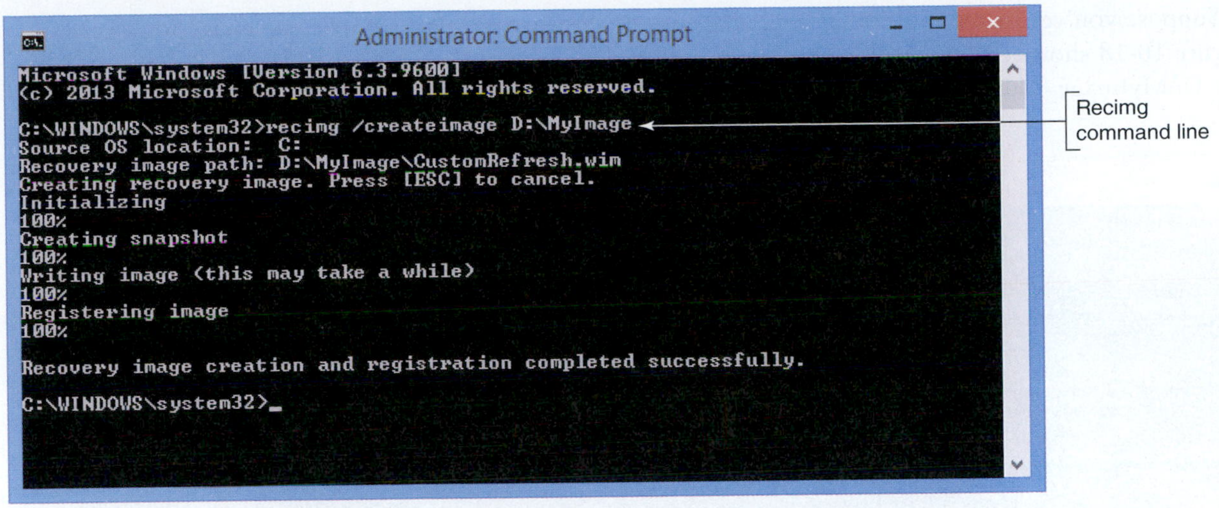

Figure 10-16 Use the recimg command to create a custom refresh image and register the image with the system

Creating the image takes some time and then the image and its location are registered as the **active recovery image**. The image is stored in a large file and you can view it using File Explorer (see Figure 10-17). You can create as many refresh images as you like, but only one is designated as the active recovery image, and it's the one that will be used when you refresh the Windows 8 installation. How to perform a Windows refresh is covered in the chapter, "Troubleshooting Windows Startup."

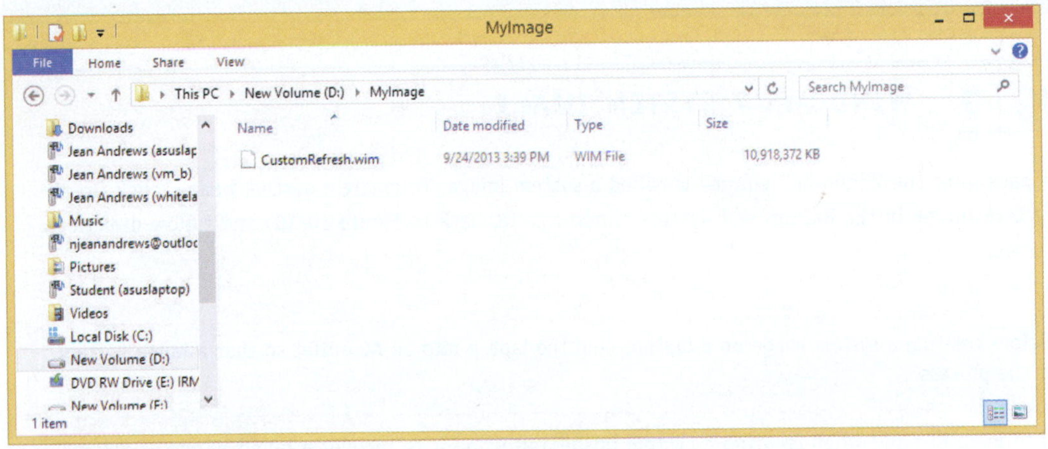

Figure 10-17 File Explorer shows the refresh image WIM file

The recimg command can also be used to manage refresh images. The parameters for the command are listed in Table 10-1.

Command	Description
`recimg /createimage <path>`	Creates the refresh image and registers its location as the active refresh image.
`recimg /showcurrent`	Displays the location of the active refresh image.
`bcdedit /set {default} bootmenupolicy legacy`	Deregisters the active recovery image. During the refresh process, Windows will not find an image and will revert to a hidden recovery partition on the hard drive or the Windows 8 setup files for the refresh.
`recimg /setcurrent <path>`	Registers a refresh image in the path given. The image at this location is now the active refresh image.

Table 10-1 The recimg command and parameters

Suppose you've created multiple refresh images and you want to select a particular image for a refresh. Figure 10-18 shows the commands you can use to change the active refresh image from the one stored in the D:\MyImage folder to one stored in the D:\MyImage2 folder.

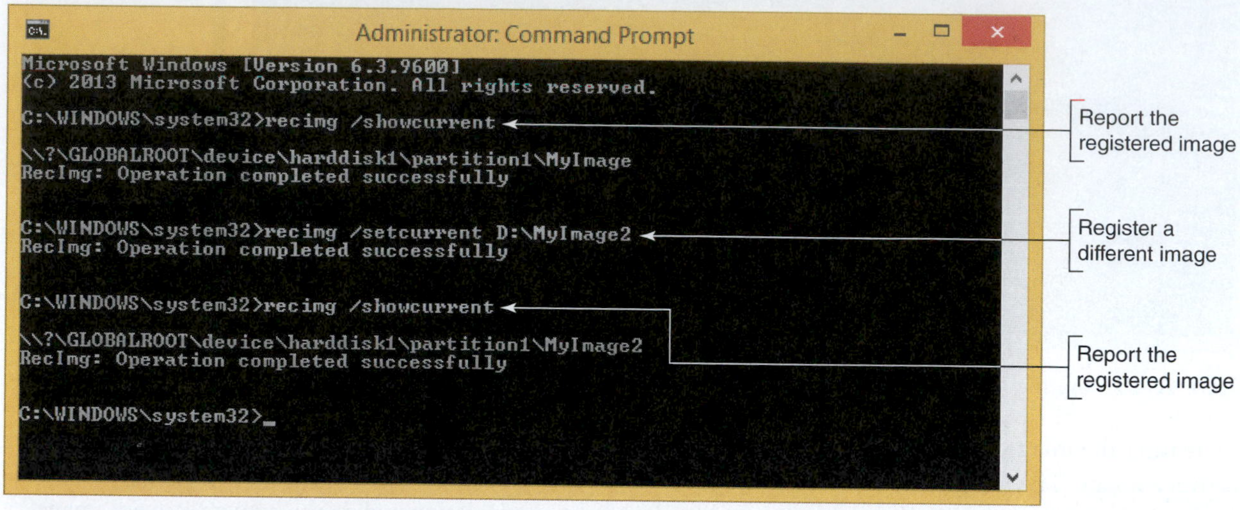

Figure 10-18 Use the recimg command with parameters to manage refresh images

Notes Because a refresh image must be named CustomRefresh.wim, you must store each image in a separate folder.

WINDOWS 7 — WINDOWS 7 SYSTEM IMAGE

A+ 220-902 1.1, 1.4, 1.5, 1.7, 3.3

The backup of the Windows 7 volume is called a system image. To create a system image, click **Create a system image** in the Backup and Restore window (refer back to Figure 10-10) and follow directions on screen.

Caution Before creating a system image on a laptop, plug the laptop into an AC outlet so that a failed battery will not interrupt the process.

Here are points to keep in mind when creating a system image and using it to recover a failed Windows volume:

- ***A system image includes the entire drive C: or other drive on which Windows is installed.*** When you restore a hard drive using the system image, everything on the volume is deleted and replaced with the system image.
- ***A system image must always be created on an internal or external hard drive.*** When scheduling the backup of your data folders, you can include the system image in the backup procedure. Even if the files and folders are being copied to a USB drive, CD, or DVD, the system image will always be copied to a hard drive.
- ***Don't depend just on the system image as your backup.*** You should also back up individual folders that contain user data. If individual data files or folders need to be recovered, you cannot rely on the system image because recovering data using the system image would totally replace the entire Windows volume with the system image.
- ***You can create a system image any time after Windows is installed, and then you can use this image to recover from a failed hard drive.*** Using the system image to recover a failed hard drive is called reimaging the drive. The details of how to reimage the drive are covered later in the chapter "Troubleshooting Windows Startup."

Notes The system image you create can be installed only on the computer that was used to create it. A hardware-independent image is called a standard image and was discussed in the chapter "Installing Windows."

Notes For backward compatibility, Windows 8 allows you to create a system image. To do so, click **System Image Backup** in the File History window. However, a custom refresh image is more flexible and easier to use than a system image.

OS Differences Windows Vista uses different backup methods than Windows 8 or 7 to back up user data, system files, and the Windows volume. The backup of the Vista volume is called the Complete PC Backup.

MANAGING FILES, FOLDERS, AND STORAGE DEVICES

A+ 220-902 1.1, 1.2, 1.3, 1.4, 4.1

In this part of the chapter, you learn to manage files and folders on the hard drive and other storage devices using commands in a command prompt window and to manage hard drive partitions and volumes using the Disk Management utility. Let's begin the discussion with how partitions and file systems work in Windows.

HOW PARTITIONS AND FILE SYSTEMS WORK

A+ 220-902 1.2

Recall that a hard drive is organized using sectors, blocks, partitions, volumes, and file systems. Let's see how it all works.

SECTORS AND BLOCKS

All data is stored on a magnetic hard drive in sectors, sometimes called records. Each sector on the drive is the same size, and for most hard drives, that size is 512 bytes. Sector markings used to organize the drive are done before it leaves the factory in a process called low-level formatting. The size of a sector and the total number of sectors on a drive determine the drive capacity. UEFI/BIOS and the OS can address groups of sectors on the drive in blocks, which is called Logical Block Addressing (LBA). SSD drives don't use sectors; space on an SSD drive is divided into blocks or LBAs that can be addressed by the UEFI/BIOS and OS. Today's drive capacities are measured in GB (gigabytes, roughly one million bytes) or TB (terabytes, roughly one trillion bytes).

Notes For magnetic hard drives, each platter is divided into concentric circles called tracks, and each track is divided into sectors (see Figure 10-19). Magnetic drive sectors are usually 512 bytes, but blocks on SSDs can be larger: 4 KB or 16 KB.

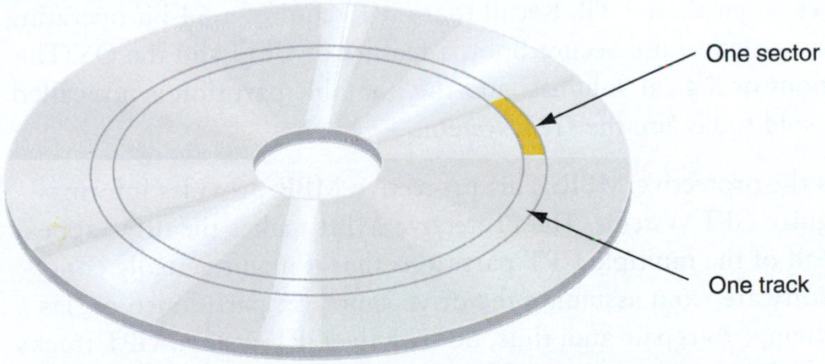

Figure 10-19 A magnetic hard drive is divided into concentric circles called tracks, and tracks are divided into sectors

PARTITIONS

A drive is further divided into one or more partitions using one of two partitioning systems:

- *MBR partitions*. The Master Boot Record (MBR) partitioning system keeps a map of these partitions in a partition table stored in the very first sector on the hard drive called the MBR. Recall that the MBR system is required when a computer is using a 32-bit operating system, legacy BIOS, or UEFI in CSM mode. The MBR partition table can track up to four partitions on a drive. A drive can have one, two, or three primary partitions, also called volumes. The fourth partition is called an extended partition and can hold one or more volumes called logical drives, which are tracked in their own partition table separately from the primary partitions. Figure 10-20 shows how an MBR hard drive is divided into three primary partitions and one extended partition.

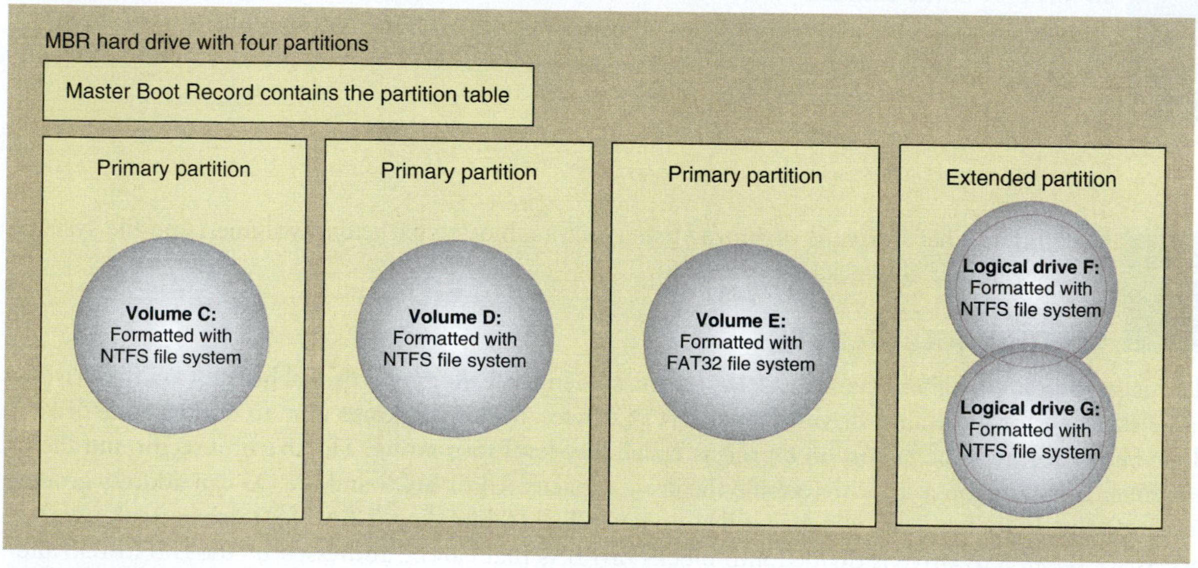

Figure 10-20 A hard drive with four partitions; the fourth partition is an extended partition

> **A+ Exam Tip** The A+ 220-902 exam expects you to know the difference between a primary and extended partition and between a volume and logical drive on an MBR hard drive.

- *GPT partitions*. The Globally Unique Identifier Partition Table (GUID or GPT) system can support up to 128 partitions and is required for drives larger than 2 TB. Recall that GPT requires a 64-bit operating system and UEFI firmware enabled and is needed to use Secure Boot, a feature of UEFI and the OS. The GPT system does not use extended partitions or logical volumes, and the bootable partition is not called an active partition. Most new computers sold today use the GPT system.

  The first sector in a GPT system contains the protective MBR. This protective MBR provides information to legacy software that doesn't recognize GPT systems. The protective MBR makes the drive appear to consist of a single MBR partition instead of the multiple GPT partitions that it might actually contain, but this is sufficient to keep legacy software from assuming the drive is not yet partitioned or has a corrupted MBR system, which it might attempt to repair and, thus, destroy the GPT system. GPT tracks all partitions in a single partition table, which it stores in the GPT header immediately following the protective MBR. GPT systems also back up the partition table at the end of the disk (see Figure 10-21). On Windows systems, there can be up to 128 partitions in between the two GPT headers.

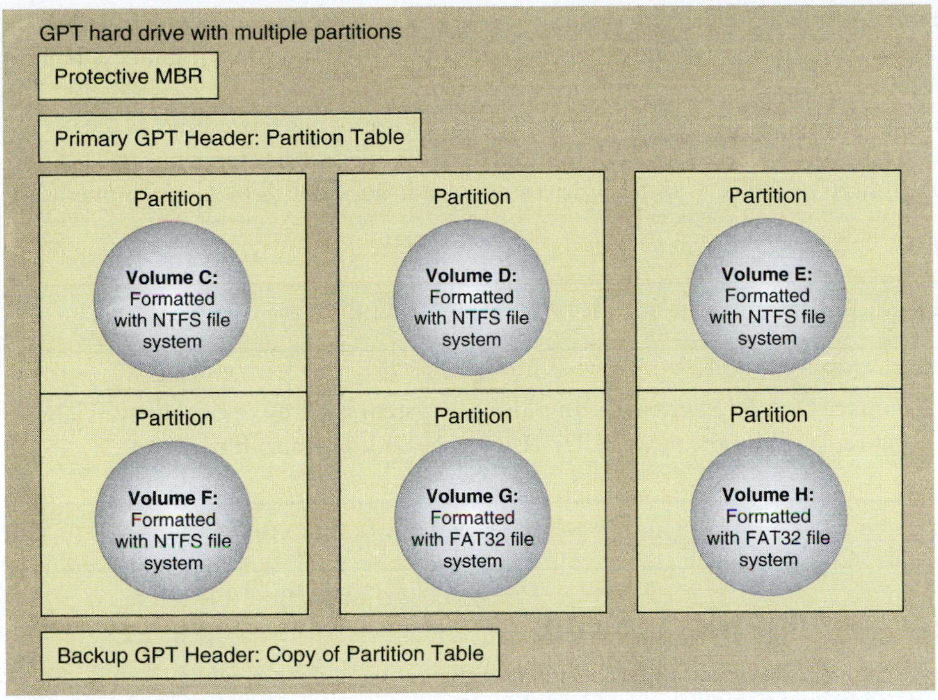

Figure 10-21 A hard drive using GPT

FILE SYSTEM

Before a partition or drive can be used, it must be assigned a drive letter such as C: or D: and formatted using a file system. Recall that the file system is the overall structure an OS uses to name, store, and organize files on a drive. Windows 8 and Windows 7 support three types of file systems for hard drives: NTFS, FAT32, and exFAT. NTFS is the most reliable and secure and is used for the volume on which Windows is installed. Installing a drive letter, file system, and root directory on a volume is called formatting the drive, also called high-level formatting, and can happen during the Windows installation.

> **Notes** In most Microsoft documentation, a partition is called a partition until it is formatted with a file system, and then it is called a volume.

Here is a list of file systems supported by Windows that you can choose for volumes and drives that don't hold the Windows installation:

- *NTFS.* Choose the NTFS file system for hard drives because it uses smaller allocation units or cluster sizes than FAT32, which means it makes more efficient use of disk space when storing many small files. NTFS is more reliable; gives fewer errors; supports encryption, disk quotas (limiting the hard drive space available to a user), file and folder compression; and offers better security. As an example of the better security with NTFS, if you boot the system from another boot media such as a CD, you can access a volume using a FAT file system. If the volume uses NTFS, an administrator password is required to gain access.
- *ReFS.* The latest file system by Microsoft is the Resilient File System (ReFS), designed to improve on the NTFS file system by offering better fault tolerance (eliminating the need for repairs using chkdsk) and allowing for better compatibility with virtualization and data redundancy in a RAID system. ReFS is not widely used on personal computers, but it is expected to eventually replace NTFS. The 64-bit version of Windows 8.1 supports ReFS.

- *exFAT*. Choose the exFAT file system for large external storage devices that you want to use with other operating systems. For example, you can use a smart card formatted with exFAT in a Mac or Linux computer or in a digital camcorder, camera, or smart phone. exFAT uses the same structure as the older FAT32 file system, but with a 64-bit-wide file allocation table (FAT). exFAT does not use as much overhead as the NTFS file system and is designed to handle very large files, such as those used for multimedia storage.
- *FAT32*. Use FAT32 for small hard drives or USB flash drives because it does not have as much overhead as NTFS.

A+ Exam Tip The A+ 220-902 exam expects you to know about the FAT32, exFAT, NTFS, and CDFS file systems.

- *CDFS and UDF*. CDFS (Compact Disk File System) is an older file system used by optical discs (CDs, DVDs, and BDs), and is being replaced by the newer UDF (Universal Disk Format) file system.

OS Differences For Windows Vista, the exFAT file system is available only if Service Pack 1 is installed.

HOW PARTITIONS ARE USED DURING THE BOOT

With MBR hard drives, one of the primary partitions is designated the active partition, which is the bootable partition that startup UEFI/BIOS turns to when searching for an operating system to start up. In GPT systems, this bootable partition is called the EFI System Partition (ESP), and UEFI turns to this partition to find and start the operating system. The OS program it looks for in this partition and starts is called the boot loader or boot manager.

In Windows, the MBR active partition or the ESP System Partition is called the system partition and, for Windows 8/7, the boot manager is named BootMgr (with no file extension). The boot manager turns to the volume that is designated the boot partition, where the Windows operating system is stored, and continues the process of starting Windows.

In Figure 10-22, you can see an example of an MBR hard drive in a two-drive system. In this computer, disk 0 is an SSD and disk 1 is a magnetic hard drive. The OS is stored on disk 0, which makes for a faster boot. On disk 0, the first partition is the System Reserved partition and is designated the active partition and the Windows system partition. The boot partition is drive C: where Windows is stored. Figure 10-23 shows a GPT system that contains a single hard drive. It contains a recovery partition, the EFI System Partition, and drive C:, which is designated the boot partition and holds the Windows 8 installation.

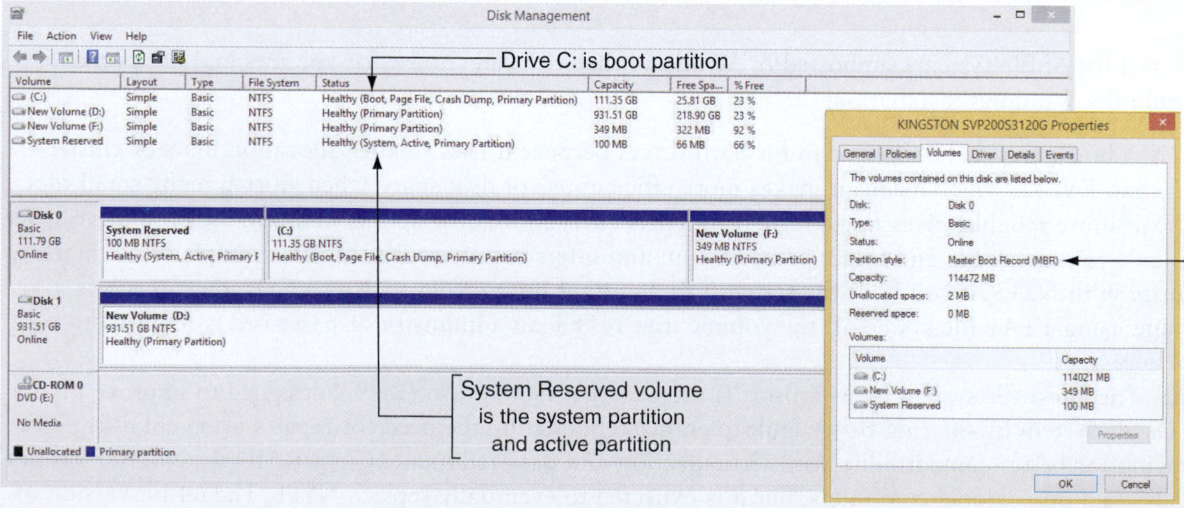

Figure 10-22 Two MBR disks with Windows 8 installed on disk 0

Notes In Figures 10-22 and 10-23, to view the Properties box for a hard drive, right-click the Disk box on the far-left side of the window and click **Properties** in the shortcut menu. Click the Volumes tab to see the type of disk, MBR or GPT.

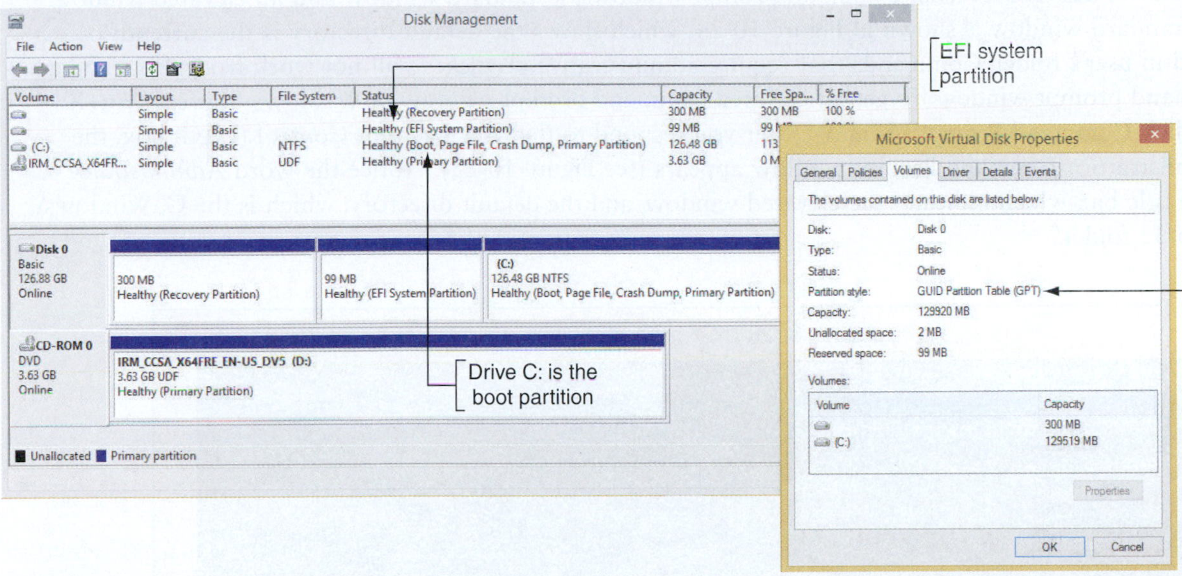

Figure 10-23 GPT disk with Windows 8 installed

Notes Don't be confused by the terminology here. It is really true that, according to Windows terminology, the Windows OS is on the boot partition, and the boot manager is on the system partition, although that might seem backward. The computer starts or boots from the system partition and loads the Windows operating system from the boot partition.

COMMANDS TO MANAGE FILES AND FOLDERS

A+ 220-902 1.1, 1.2, 1.3, 1.4, 4.1

IT support technicians find it is much faster to manipulate files and folders using commands in a command prompt window than when using File Explorer (or Windows Explorer in Windows 7). In addition, in some troubleshooting situations, you have no other option but to use a command prompt window. For Windows 8, to open the command prompt window, press **Win+X** and click **Command Prompt**. The command prompt window is shown in Figure 10-24.

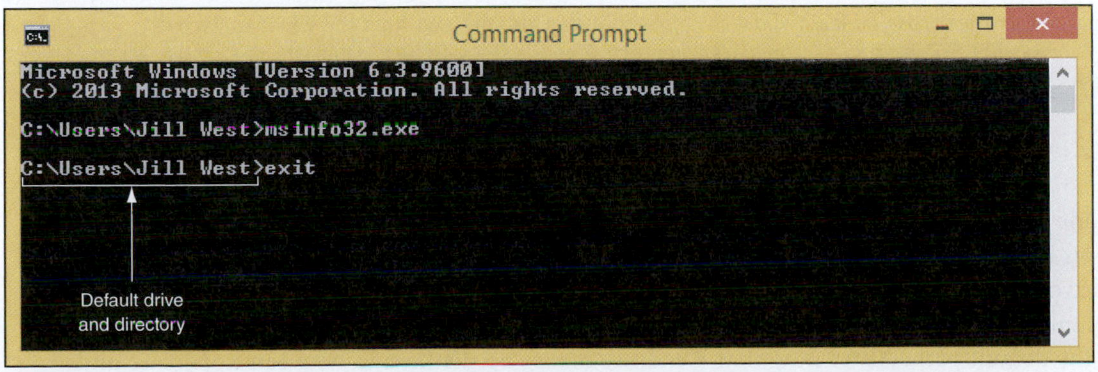

Figure 10-24 Use the exit command to close the command prompt window

OS Differences To open the command prompt window in Windows 7, enter **command** or **cmd** in the Search box and press **Enter**. Alternately, you can click **Start**, **All Programs**, **Accessories**, and **Command Prompt**.

Windows has two levels of command prompt windows: a standard window and an elevated window. The standard window is shown in Figure 10-24, which shows the default directory is the currently signed-in user's folder. Commands that require administrative privileges will not work from this standard command prompt window. To get an elevated command prompt window in Windows 8, press **Win+X** and click **Command Prompt (Admin)**. After you respond to the User Account Control (UAC) box, the Administrator: Command Prompt window appears (see Figure 10-25). Notice the word *Administrator* in the title bar, which indicates the elevated window, and the default directory, which is the C:\Windows\system32 folder.

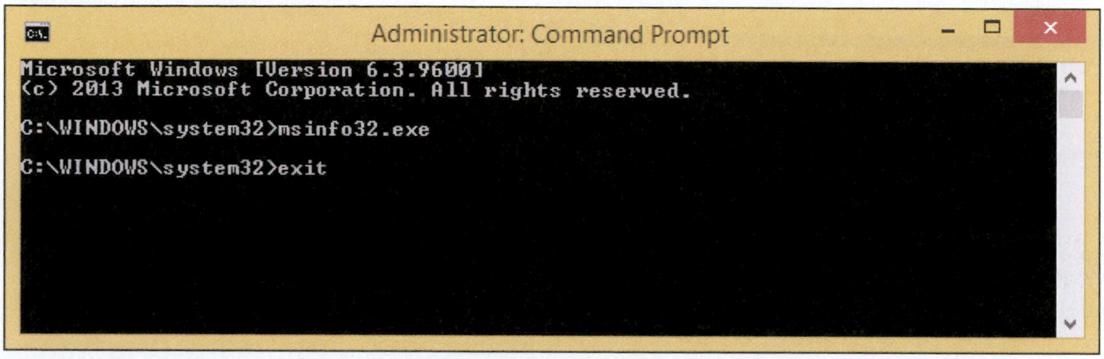

Figure 10-25 An elevated command prompt window has administrative privileges

OS Differences To get an elevated command prompt window in Windows 7, click **Start**, **All Programs**, **Accessories**, and right-click **Command Prompt**. Then select **Run as administrator** from the shortcut window and respond to the UAC box.

Here are some tips for working in a command prompt window:

- Type **cls** and press **Enter** to clear the window.
- To retrieve the last command you entered, press the up arrow. To retrieve the last command line one character at a time, press the right arrow.
- To terminate a command before it is finished, press **Ctrl+C**, **Ctrl+Break**, or **Ctrl+Pause**.
- To close the window, type **exit** (see Figure 10-25) and press **Enter**.

Notes Many of the commands you learn about in this section can also be used from the Windows Recovery Environment (Windows RE). Windows RE can be loaded from the Windows setup DVD to troubleshoot a system when Windows refuses to load. How to use the Recovery Environment is covered later in the text.

If the command you are using applies to files or folders, the path to these files or folders is assumed to be the default drive and directory. The default drive and directory, also called the current drive and directory, shows in the command prompt. It is the drive and directory that the command will use if you don't give a drive and directory in the command line. For example, in Figure 10-24, the default drive is C: and the default path is C:\Users\Jill West. If you use a different path in the command line, the path you use overrides the default path. Also know that Windows makes no distinction between uppercase and lowercase in command lines (however, Linux does).

Now let's look at the file-naming conventions you will need to follow when creating files, wildcard characters you can use in command lines, and several commands useful for managing files and folders.

FILE-NAMING CONVENTIONS

When using the command prompt window to create a file, keep in mind that file name and file extension characters can be the letters *a* through *z*, the numbers *0* through *9*, and the following characters:

```
_ ^ $ ~ ! # % & - { } ( ) @ ' `
```

In a command prompt window, if a path or file name has spaces in it, it is sometimes necessary to enclose the path or file name in double quotation marks.

WILDCARD CHARACTERS IN COMMAND LINES

As you work at the command prompt, you can use wildcard characters in a file name to say that the command applies to a group of files or to abbreviate a file name if you do not know the entire name. The question mark (?) is a wildcard for one character, and the asterisk (*) is a wildcard for one or more characters. For example, if you want to find all files in a directory that start with *A* and have a three-letter file extension, you would use the following command:

```
dir a*.???
```

A+ Exam Tip The A+ 220-902 exam expects you to know how to use the shutdown, md, rd, cd, del, format, copy, xcopy, robocopy, chkdsk, dir, exit, help, and expand commands, which are all covered in this section.

Notes Many commands can use parameters in the command line to affect how the command will work. Parameters (also called options, arguments, or switches) often begin with a slash followed by a single character. In this chapter, you learn about the basic parameters used by a command for the most common tasks. For a full listing of the parameters available for a command, use the help command. Another way to learn about commands is to follow this link on the Microsoft website: *technet.microsoft.com/en-us/library/cc772390(WS.10).aspx.*

HELP OR <*COMMAND NAME*> /?

Use the help command to get help about any command. You can enter help followed by the command name or enter the command name followed by /?. Table 10-2 lists some sample applications of this command.

Command	Result
help xcopy xcopy /?	Gets help about the xcopy command
help	Lists all commands
help xcopy | more	Lists information about the xcopy command one line at a time

Table 10-2 Sample help commands

DIR [<*FILENAME*>] [/P] [/S] [/W]

Use the dir command to list files and directories. In Microsoft documentation about a command (also called the command syntax), the brackets [ ] in a command line indicate the parameter is optional. In addition, the parameter included in < >, such as <filename>, indicates that you can substitute any file name in the command. This file name can include a path or file extension. Table 10-3 lists some examples of the dir command.

Command	Result
`dir /p`	Lists one screen at a time
`dir /w`	Presents information using wide format, where details are omitted and files and folders are listed in columns on the screen
`dir *.txt`	Lists all files with a .txt file extension in the default path
`dir d:\data\*.txt`	Lists all files with a .txt file extension in the D:\data folder
`dir myfile.txt`	Checks that a single file, such as myfile.txt, is present
`dir /s`	Includes subdirectory entries

Table 10-3 Sample dir commands

MD *[DRIVE:] PATH*

The md (make directory) command creates a subdirectory under a directory. Note that in the command lines in this section, the command prompt is not bolded, but the typed command is in bold. To create a directory named \game on drive C:, you can use this command:

C:\> **md C:\game**

The backslash indicates that the directory is under the root directory. If a path is not given, the default path is assumed. This command also creates the C:\game directory:

C:\> **md game**

To create a directory named chess under the \game directory, you can use this command:

C:\> **md C:\game\chess**

Figure 10-26 shows the result of the dir command on the directory game. Note the two initial entries in the directory table: . (dot) and . . (dot, dot). The md command creates these two entries when the OS initially sets up the directory. You cannot edit these entries with normal OS commands, and they must remain in the directory for the directory's lifetime. The . (dot) entry points to the subdirectory itself, and the .. (dot, dot) entry points to the parent directory, which, in this case, is the root directory.

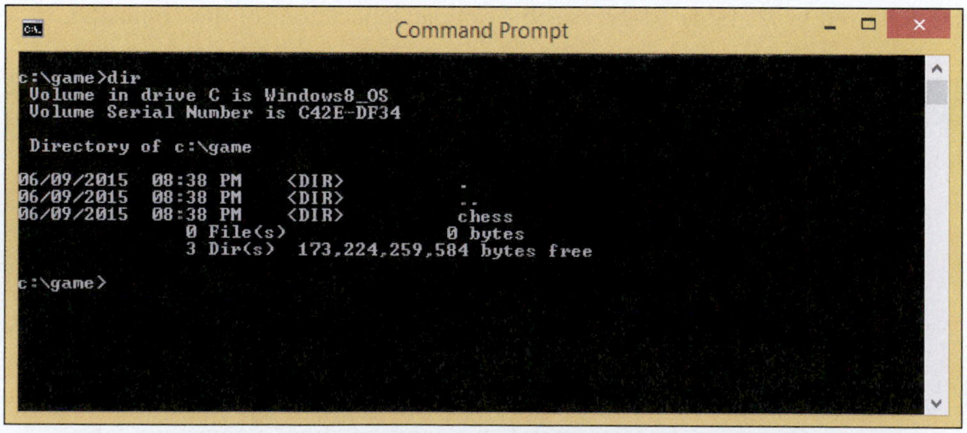

Figure 10-26 Results of the dir command on the game directory

CD [*DRIVE:*]*PATH* OR CD..

The cd (change directory) command changes the current default directory. You enter cd followed by the drive and the entire path that you want to be current, like so:

```
C:\> cd C:\game\chess
```

The command prompt now looks like this:

```
C:\game\chess>
```

To move from a child directory to its parent directory, use the .. (dot, dot) variation of the command:

```
C:\game\chess> cd..
```

The command prompt now looks like this:

```
C:\game>
```

Remember that .. (dot, dot) always means the parent directory. You can move from a parent directory to one of its child directories simply by stating the name of the child directory:

```
C:\game> cd chess
```

The command prompt now looks like this:

```
C:\game\chess>
```

Remember not to put a backslash in front of the child directory name; doing so tells the OS to go to a directory named chess that is directly under the root directory.

RD [*DRIVE:*]*PATH* [/S]

The rd (remove directory) command removes a directory. Unless you use the /s switch, three things must be true before you can use the rd command:

- The directory must contain no files.
- The directory must contain no subdirectories.
- The directory must not be the current directory.

A directory is ready for removal when only the . (dot) and .. (dot, dot) entries are present. For example, to remove the \game directory when it contains the chess directory, the chess directory must first be removed, like so:

```
C:\> rd C:\game\chess
```

Or, if the \game directory is the current directory, you can use this command:

```
C:\game> rd chess
```

After you remove the chess directory, you can remove the game directory. However, it's not good to attempt to saw off a branch while you're sitting on it; therefore, you must first leave the \game directory like so:

```
C:\game> cd..
C:\> cd \game
```

When you use the /s switch with the rd command, the entire directory tree is deleted, including all its subdirectories and files.

DEL OR ERASE *<FILENAME>*

The del or erase command erases files or groups of files. Note that in the command lines in this section, the command prompt is not bolded, but the typed command is in bold.

To erase the file named Myfile.txt, use the following command:

```
E:\> del myfile.txt
```

To erase all files in the current default directory, use the following command:

```
E:\Docs> del *.*
```

To erase all files in the E:\Docs directory, use the following command:

```
C:\> erase e:\docs\*.*
```

A few files don't have a file extension. To erase all files that are in the current directory and that have no file extensions, use the following command:

```
E:\Docs> del *.
```

REN *<FILENAME1> <FILENAME2>*

The ren (rename) command renames a file. *<filename1>* can include a path to the file, but *<filename2>* cannot. To rename Project.docx in the default directory to Project_Hold.docx:

```
E:\Docs> ren Project.docx Project_Hold.docx
```

To rename all .txt files to .doc files in the C:\Data folder:

```
ren C:\Data\*.txt *.doc
```

COPY *<SOURCE> [<DESTINATION>]* [/V] [/Y]

The copy command copies a single file or group of files. The original files are not altered. To copy a file from one drive to another, use a command similar to this one:

```
E:\> copy C:\Data\Myfile.txt E:\mydata\Newfile.txt
```

The drive, path, and file name of the source file immediately follow the copy command. The drive, path, and file name of the destination file follow the source file name. If you don't specify the file name of the destination file, the OS assigns the file's original name to this copy. If you omit the drive or path of the source or the destination, then the OS uses the current default drive and path.

To copy the file Myfile.txt from the root directory of drive C: to drive E:, use the following command:

```
C:\> copy myfile.txt E:
```

Because the command does not include a drive or path before the file name Myfile.txt, the OS assumes that the file is in the default drive and path. Also, because there is no destination file name specified, the file written to drive E: will be named Myfile.txt.

To copy all files in the C:\Docs directory to the USB flash drive designated drive E:, use the following command:

```
C:\> copy c:\docs\*.* E:
```

To make a backup file named System.bak of the System file in the \Windows\system32\config directory of the hard drive, use the following command:

```
C:\Windows\system32\config> copy system system.bak
```

If you use the copy command to duplicate multiple files, the files are assigned the names of the original files. When you duplicate multiple files, the destination portion of the command line cannot include a file name.

Here are two switches or parameters that are useful with the copy command:

- */v.* When the /v switch is used, the size of each new file is compared with the size of the original file. This slows down the copying, but verifies that the copy is done without errors.
- */y.* When the /y switch is used, a confirmation message does not appear asking you to confirm before overwriting a file.

> **Notes** When trying to recover a corrupted file, you can sometimes use the copy command to copy the file to new media, such as from the hard drive to a USB drive. During the copying process, if the copy command reports a bad or missing sector, choose the option to ignore that sector. The copying process then continues to the next sector. The corrupted sector will be lost, but others can likely be recovered. The recover command can be used to accomplish the same thing.

RECOVER *<FILENAME>*

Use the recover command to attempt to recover a file when parts of the file are corrupted. The command is best used from the Windows Recovery Environment. To use it, you must specify the name of a single file in the command line, like so:

```
C:\Data> recover Myfile.txt
```


EXPAND [/D] *<SOURCE>* [<DESTINATION>]

The expand command extracts files from compressed distribution files, which are often used to distribute files for software installations. Table 10-4 lists examples of the command.

Command	Result
`expand /d \installme`	Lists files contained in the \installme folder. Does not expand or extract the files.
`expand myprogram.cab`	Extracts the files in the myprogram.cab file. A .cab file is a cabinet file, which is a type of distribution file that contains compressed files.
`expand myprogram.cab -f:myfile.exe`	Extracts only the myfile.exe file from the myprogram.cab cabinet file.

Table 10-4 Sample expand commands

XCOPY *<SOURCE> [<DESTINATION>]* [/S] [/C] [/Y] *[/D:DATE]*

The xcopy command is more powerful than the copy command. It follows the same general command-source-destination format as the copy command, but it offers several more options. Table 10-5 shows some of these options.

Command	Result
`xcopy C:\docs\*.* E: /s`	Use the /s switch to include subdirectories in the copy; this command copies all files in the directory C:\docs, as well as all subdirectories under \docs and their files, to drive E, unless the subdirectory is empty
`xcopy C:\docs\*.* E: /e`	Same as /s but empty subdirectories are included in the copy
`xcopy C:\docs\*.* E: /d: 03-14-15`	The /d switch examines the date; this command copies all files from the directory C:\docs created or modified on or after March 14, 2015
`xcopy C:\docs\*.* E: /y`	Use the /y switch to overwrite existing files without prompting
`xcopy C:\docs\*.* E: /c`	Use the /c switch to keep copying even when an error occurs

Table 10-5 Sample xcopy commands

ROBOCOPY <*SOURCE*> <*DESTINATION*> [/S] [/E] [/LOG:*FILENAME*] [*/LOG+:FILENAME*] [/MOVE] [/PURGE]

The robocopy (robust file copy) command is similar to the xcopy command. It offers more options than xcopy and is intended to replace xcopy. A few options for robocopy are listed in Table 10-6.

Command	Result
`robocopy C:\docs\*.* E: /s`	The /s switch includes subdirectories in the copy but does not include empty directories
`robocopy C:\docs\*.* E: /e`	The /e switch includes subdirectories, even the empty ones
`robocopy C:\docs\*.* E: /log:Mylog.txt`	Records activity to a log file and overwrites the current log file
`robocopy C:\docs\*.* E: /log+:Mylog.txt`	Appends a record of all activity to an existing log file
`robocopy C:\docs\*.* E: /move`	Moves files and directories, deleting them from the source
`robocopy C:\docs\*.* E: /purge`	Deletes files and directories at the destination that no longer exist at the source

Table 10-6 Sample robocopy commands

CHKDSK [*DRIVE*:] [/F] [/R]

The chkdsk (check disk) command fixes file system errors and recovers data from bad sectors. Earlier in the chapter, you learned to check for errors using the drive properties box, which does so by launching the chkdsk command. Recall that a file is stored on the hard drive as a group of clusters. The FAT32 and exFAT file systems use a FAT (file allocation table) to keep a record of each cluster that belongs to a file. The NTFS file system uses a database to hold similar information called the master file table (MFT). In Figure 10-27, you can see that each cell in the FAT represents one cluster and contains a pointer to the next cluster in a file.

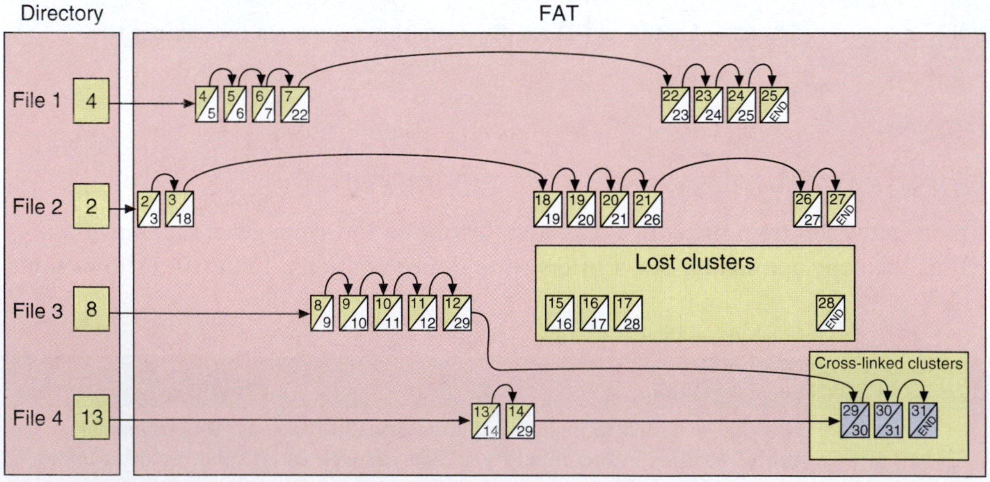

Figure 10-27 Lost and cross-linked clusters

Notes For an interesting discussion of how the FAT works, see the document FAT Details.pdf on the companion website for this text at *www.cengagebrain.com*. See the Preface for more information.

Used with the /f parameter, chkdsk searches for and fixes two types of file system errors made by the FAT or MFT:

- ***Lost clusters (also called lost allocation units).*** Lost clusters are clusters that are marked as used clusters in the FAT or MFT, but the cluster does not belong to any file. In effect, the data in these clusters is lost.
- ***Cross-linked clusters.*** Cross-linked clusters are clusters that are marked in the FAT or MFT as belonging to more than one file.

Used with the /r parameter, chkdsk checks for lost clusters and cross-linked clusters and also checks for bad sectors on the drive. The FAT and MFT keep a table of bad sectors that they normally do not use. However, over time, a sector might become unreliable. If chkdsk determines that a sector is unreliable, it attempts to recover the data from the sector and also marks the sector as bad so that the FAT or MFT will not use it again.

Used without any parameters, the chkdsk command only reports information about a drive and does not make any repairs.

In the following sample commands, the command prompt is not showing as the default drive and directory are not important. To check the hard drive for file system errors and repair them, use this command:

```
chkdsk C:/f
```

To redirect a report of the findings of the chkdsk command to a file that you can later print, use this command:

```
chkdsk C:>Myfile.txt
```

Use the /r parameter of the chkdsk command to fix file system errors and also examine each sector of the drive for bad sectors, like so:

```
chkdsk C:/r
```

If chkdsk finds data that it can recover, it asks you for permission to do so. If you give permission, it saves the recovered data in files that it stores in the root directory of the drive.

Notes Use either the /f or /r parameter with chkdsk, but not both. Using both parameters is redundant. For the most thorough check of a drive, use /r.

The chkdsk command will not fix anything unless the drive is locked, which means the drive has no open files. If you attempt to use chkdsk with the /f or /r parameter when files are open, chkdsk tells you of the problem and asks permission to schedule the run the next time Windows is restarted. Know that the process will take plenty of time. Keep in mind that you must use an elevated command prompt window to run chkdsk.

Notes The chkdsk command is also available from the Windows Recovery Environment.

DEFRAG [*DRIVE*:] [/C]

The defrag command examines a magnetic hard drive for fragmented files (files written to a disk in noncontiguous clusters) and rewrites these files to the drive in contiguous clusters. You use this command to optimize a magnetic hard drive's performance. Table 10-7 shows two examples of the command. Recall that it's not a good idea to defrag solid-state storage devices such as an SSD, flash drive, or smart card. Doing so can shorten the life of the drive.

Command	Result
`defrag C:`	**Defrag drive C:**
`defrag /c`	**Defrag all volumes on the computer, including drive C:**

Table 10-7 Sample defrag commands

The defrag command requires an elevated command prompt window in Windows. It is not available under the Windows Recovery Environment. Earlier in the chapter, you learned to defrag a drive using the Windows drive properties box.

FORMAT <*DRIVE:*> [/V:*LABEL*] [/Q] [FS:<*FILESYSTEM*>]

You can format a hard drive or other storage device using Disk Management. In addition, you can use the format command from a command prompt window and from the Windows Recovery Environment. This high-level format installs a file system on the device and *erases all data on the volume*. Table 10-8 lists various sample uses of the format command.

Command	Description
`format D:`	**Performs a full format of drive D: using the default file system for the volume type.**
`format D: /q`	**Performs a quick format of drive D: by re-creating an empty root directory. Use it to quickly format a previously formatted disk that is in good condition; /q does not read or write to any other part of the disk.**
`format D: /fs:NTFS`	**Formats drive D: using the NTFS file system.**
`format D: /fs:FAT32`	**Formats drive D: using the FAT32 file system.**
`format D: /fs:EXFAT`	**Formats drive D: using the extended FAT file system.**

Table 10-8 Sample format commands

SHUTDOWN [/M *COMPUTERNAME*] [/I] [/R] [/S] [/F] [/T *XX*]

Use the shutdown command to shut down the local computer or a remote computer. You must be signed in with an administrator account to use this command. By default, the command gives users a 30-second warning before shutdown. To shut down a remote computer on the network, you must have an administrator account on that computer and be signed on the local computer with that same account and password. Table 10-9 lists some shutdown commands.

Command	Description
`shutdown /r`	**Restart the local computer.**
`shutdown /s /m \\bluelight`	**Shut down the remote computer named \\bluelight.**
`shutdown /s /m \\bluelight /t 60`	**Shut down the \\bluelight computer after a 60-second delay.**
`shutdown /i`	**Displays the Remote Shutdown Dialog box so you can choose computers on the network to shut down.**
`shutdown /s /full /t 0`	**In Windows 8, immediately performs a full shutdown rather than hibernating the kernel, which is normally done to prepare for a Windows 8 QuickStart.**

Table 10-9 Sample shutdown commands

Hands-On | Project 10-3 Use a Batch File

A file with a .bat file extension is called a batch file. You can use a batch file to execute a group of commands, sometimes called a script, from a command prompt. Do the following to learn to use a batch file:

1. Using a command prompt window, copy the files in your Documents folder (My Documents in Windows 7) to a folder named \Save on a USB flash drive. Don't include subfolders in the copy.
2. Using Notepad, create a batch file named MyBatch.bat on the USB flash drive that contains the commands to do the following:
   a. Create the C:\Data folder and a subfolder named C:\Data\Documents.
   b. Copy all the files in your \Save folder to the C:\Data\Documents folder.
   c. List the contents of the C:\Data\Documents folder.
3. Using a command prompt window, execute the MyBatch.bat file and fix any problems you see. What happens when you execute the batch file and the C:\Data\Documents folder already exists?

WINDOWS POWERSHELL

Windows PowerShell is designed to replace the command prompt utility for providing a command-line interface. Like the command prompt utility, users enter commands to be executed. Unlike the command prompt, Windows PowerShell processes objects, called cmdlets (pronounced "command-lets"), that have been built with the .NET Framework programming tools instead of processing the text in a command line in order to perform tasks. This means that when entering a command into PowerShell, the utility is essentially running a prebuilt program, similar to the batch file you just created and ran in Hands-On Project 10-3. Windows PowerShell contains thousands of cmdlets so that users don't have to build their own. Technicians or programmers who program their own cmdlets can build customized objects using the pre-existing cmdlets as building blocks.

Let's see how a few cmdlets work in PowerShell. The get-help cmdlet gives help about a cmdlet and the get-process cmdlet lists all processes running on a computer. Do the following to practice using these and other cmdlets:

1. To open Windows 8 PowerShell, press **Win+X**, click **Run**, type **powershell** in the Run box, and press **Enter**.

> **OS Differences** In Windows 7, click **Start**, **All Programs**, **Accessories**, and **Windows PowerShell**. You might see other options in the Windows PowerShell folder, such as Windows PowerShell (x86), which is a 32-bit version of Windows PowerShell on 64-bit computers, or Windows PowerShell ISE, which is an administrator-level version of Windows PowerShell called the Integrated Scripting Environment (ISE). Click **Windows PowerShell** to open.

2. Enter the command **`get-help get-process`**, which requests information (get-help) on the get-process cmdlet.
3. View a more detailed description of the get-process cmdlet with the command **`get-help get-process -detailed`**.
4. Generate a list of all the processes running on your computer by entering the cmdlet **`get-process`**.
5. To list all cmdlets installed on a system, enter the cmdlet **`get-command`**.
6. As you can see, get cmdlets provide information on the item requested, but don't access the item itself. To start a program, use a start cmdlet instead. For example, to open Notepad, enter the cmdlet **`start-process notepad.exe`**.

USE DISK MANAGEMENT TO MANAGE HARD DRIVES

A+
220-902
1.2, 1.4

The primary tool for managing hard drives is Disk Management. In the "Installing Windows" chapter, you learned how to install Windows on a new hard drive. This installation process initializes, partitions, and formats the drive. After Windows is installed, you can use Disk Management to install and manage drives. In this part of the chapter, you learn to use Disk Management to manage partitions on a drive, prepare a new drive for first use, mount a drive, use Windows dynamic disks, and troubleshoot problems with the hard drive.

RESIZE, CREATE, AND DELETE PARTITIONS

Suppose you have installed Windows 8 on a hard drive and used all available space on the drive for the one partition. Now you want to split the partition into two partitions so you can install Windows 10 in a dual-boot installation with Windows 8. You can use Disk Management (diskmgmt.msc) to shrink the original partition, which frees up some space for the new Windows 10 partition. Follow these steps in Windows 8:

1. To open the Disk Management window, use one of these methods:
   - Press **Win+X** and click **Disk Management**.
   - Press **Win+X**, click **Run**, and enter **diskmgmt.msc** in the Run box.

OS Differences To open the Disk Management window in Windows 7, click **Start**, type **Disk Management** or **diskmgmt.msc** in the Search box, and press **Enter**.

2. The Disk Management window opens (see Figure 10-28). To shrink the existing partition, right-click in the partition space and select **Shrink Volume** from the shortcut menu (see Figure 10-28). The Shrink dialog box appears showing the amount of free space on the partition. Enter the amount in MB to shrink the partition, which cannot be more than the amount of free space so that no data on the partition will be lost. (For best performance, be sure to leave at least 15 percent free space on the disk.) Click **Shrink**. The disk now shows unallocated space.

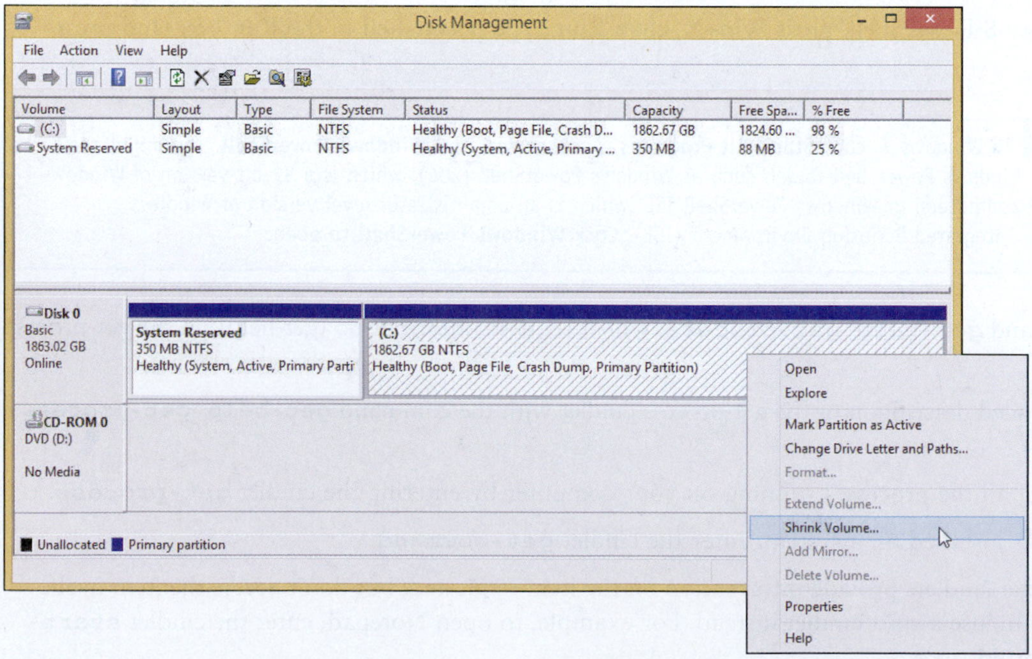

Figure 10-28 Shrink a volume to make room for a new partition

3. To create a new partition in the unallocated space, right-click in that space and select **New Simple Volume** from the shortcut menu (see Figure 10-29). The New Simple Volume Wizard opens.

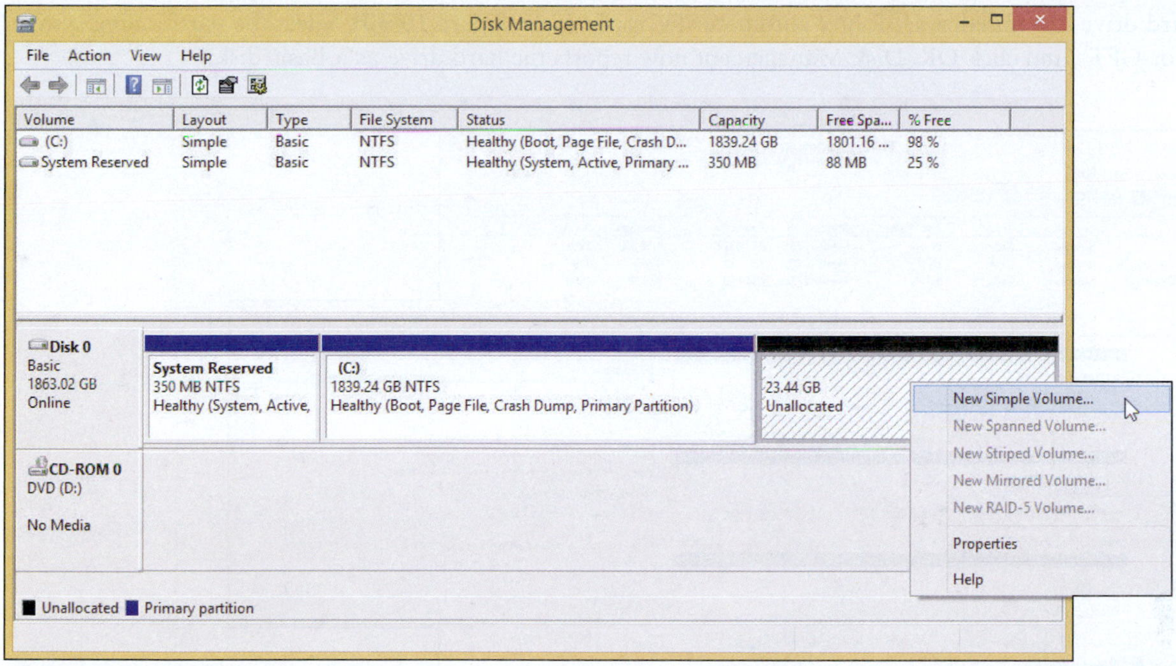

Figure 10-29 Use unallocated space to create a new partition

4. Follow the directions on screen to enter the size of the volume in MB and select a drive letter for the volume, a file system, and the size for each allocation unit (also called a cluster). It's best to leave the cluster size at the default value. You can also decide to do a quick format. The partition is then created and formatted with the file system you chose.

Notice in Figure 10-28 the options on the shortcut menu for this MBR system where you can make the partition the active partition (the one UEFI/BIOS looks to for an OS), change the drive letter for a volume, format the volume (erases all data on the volume), extend the volume (increase the size of the volume), and shrink or delete the volume. An option that is not available for the particular volume and situation is grayed.

★ **A+ Exam Tip** The A+ 220-902 exam expects you to know how to use Disk Management to extend and split partitions and configure a new hard drive in a system.

PREPARE A DRIVE FOR FIRST USE

When you install a new, second hard drive in a computer, use Disk Management to prepare the drive for use. This happens in a two-step process:

Step 1: Initialize the Disk

When the disk is initialized, Windows identifies the disk as a basic disk. A basic disk is a single hard drive that works independently of other hard drives. When you first open Disk Management after you have installed a new hard drive, the Initialize Disk box automatically appears (see Figure 10-30). Select the partitioning system (MBR or GPT), and click **OK**. Disk Management now reports the hard drive as a Basic disk.

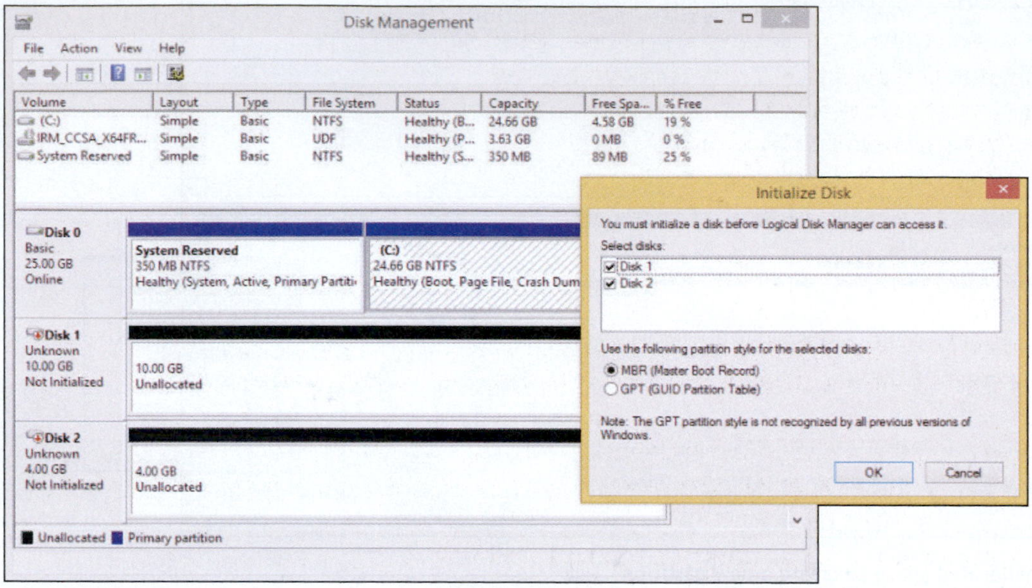

Figure 10-30 Use the Initialize Disk box to set up a partitioning system on new hard drives

> **Notes** After installing a new hard drive, if you don't see the Initialize Disk box when you first open Disk Management, right-click in the Disk area and select **Initialize Disk** from the shortcut menu. The box will appear.

Step 2: Create a Volume and Format It with a File System

To create a new volume on a disk, right-click in the unallocated space, select **New Simple Volume** from the shortcut menu, and follow the directions on screen to select the size of the volume, assign a drive letter and name to the volume, and select the file system. When the process is finished, the drive is formatted and ready for use. When you open Explorer, you should see the new volume listed.

> **Notes** Recall you can use the diskpart command to convert an MBR disk to a GPT disk. However, all data on the disk is lost when you do the conversion. In the chapter "Troubleshooting Windows Startup," you learn more about diskpart and other commands used to manage a hard drive.

HOW TO MOUNT A DRIVE

A mounted drive is a volume that can be accessed by way of a folder on another volume so that the folder has more available space. A mounted drive is useful when a folder is on a volume that is too small to hold all the data you want in the folder. In Figure 10-31, the mounted drive gives the C:\Projects folder a capacity of 20 GB. The C:\Projects folder is called the mount point for the mounted drive.

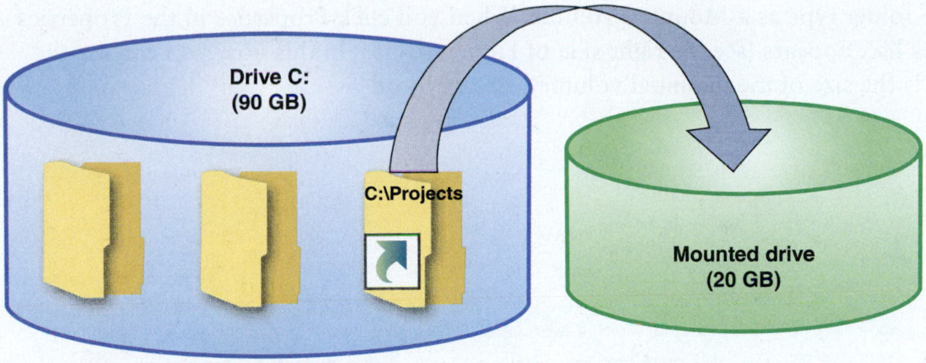

Figure 10-31 The C:\Projects folder is the mount point for the mounted drive

Follow these steps to mount a drive:

1. Make sure the volume that is to host the mounted drive uses the NTFS file system. The folder on this volume, called the mount point, must be empty. You can also create the folder during the mount process. In this example, we are mounting a drive to the C:\Projects folder.
2. Using Disk Management, right-click in the unallocated space of a disk. In our example, we're using Disk 1 (the second hard drive). Select **New Simple Volume** from the shortcut menu. The New Simple Volume Wizard launches. Using the wizard, specify the amount of unallocated space you want to devote to the volume. (In our example, we are using 20 GB, although the resulting size of the C:\Projects folder will only show about 19 GB because of overhead.)
3. As you follow the wizard, the box shown on the left side of Figure 10-32 appears. Select **Mount in the following empty NTFS folder**, and then click **Browse**. In the Browse for Drive Path box that appears (see the right side of Figure 10-32), you can drill down to an existing folder or click **New Folder** to create a new folder on drive C:.

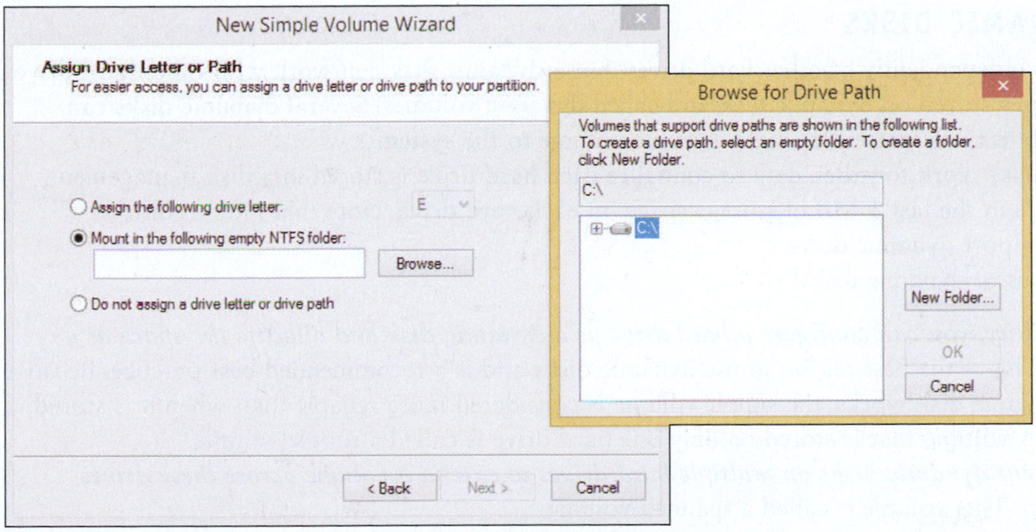

Figure 10-32 Select the folder that will be the mount point for the new volume

4. Complete the wizard by selecting a file system for the new volume and an Allocation unit size (the cluster size). The volume is created and formatted.
5. To verify the drive is mounted, open Explorer and then open the Properties box for the folder. In our example, the Properties box for the C:\Projects folder is shown in the middle of Figure 10-33. Notice the

Properties box reports the folder type as a Mounted Volume. When you click Properties in the Properties box, the volume Properties box appears (see the right side of Figure 10-33). In this box, you can see the size of the volume, which is the size of the mounted volume, less overhead.

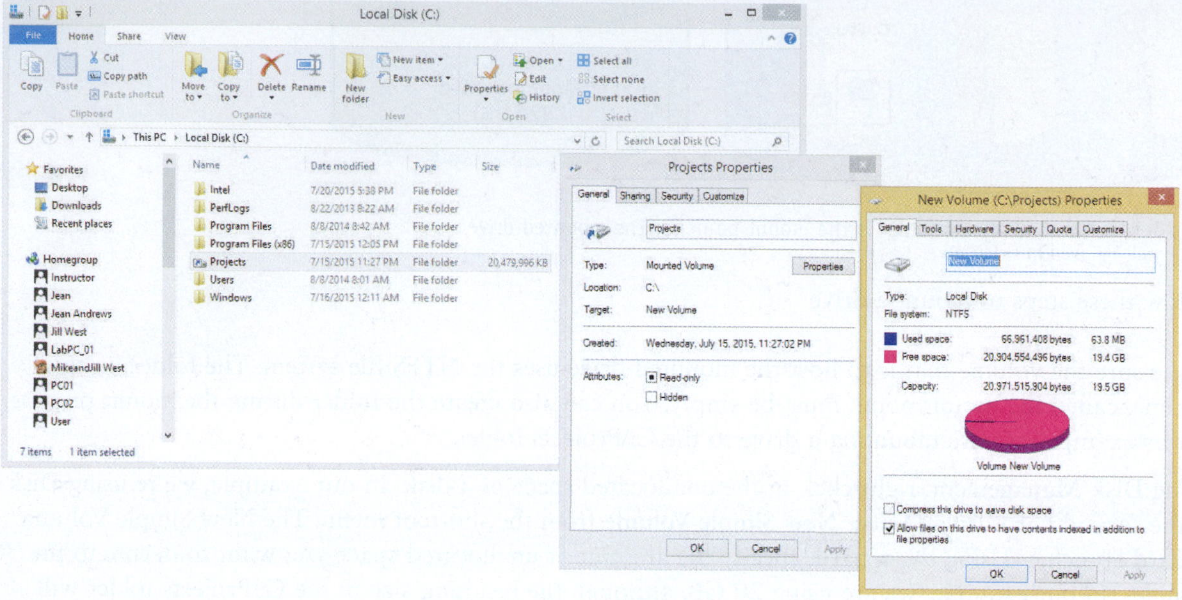

Figure 10-33 The mounted drive in Explorer appears as a very large folder

You can think of a mount point, such as C:\Projects, as a shortcut to a volume on a second hard drive. If you look closely at the left window in Figure 10-33, you can see the shortcut icon beside the Projects folder.

WINDOWS DYNAMIC DISKS

A basic disk works independently of other hard drives, but a dynamic disk can work with other hard drives to hold data. Volumes stored on dynamic disks are called dynamic volumes. Several dynamic disks can work together to collectively present a single dynamic volume to the system.

When dynamic disks work together, data to configure each hard drive is stored in a disk management database that resides in the last 1 MB of storage space on each hard drive. Note that Home editions of Windows do not support dynamic disks.

Here are three uses of dynamic disks:

- ***For better reliability, you can configure a hard drive as a dynamic disk and allocate the space as a simple volume.*** This is the best reason to use dynamic disks and is a recommended best practice. Because of the way a dynamic disk works, the simple volume is considered more reliable than when it is stored on a basic disk. A volume that is stored on only one hard drive is called a simple volume.
- ***You can implement dynamic disks on multiple hard drives to extend a volume across these drives (called spanning).*** This volume is called a spanned volume.
- ***Dynamic disks can be used to piece data across multiple hard drives to improve performance.*** The technology to configure two or more hard drives to work together as an array of drives is called RAID (redundant array of inexpensive disks or redundant array of independent disks). Joining hard drives together to improve performance is called striping or RAID 0. The volume is called a striped volume (see Figure 10-34). When RAID is implemented in this way using Disk Management, it is called software RAID. A more reliable way of configuring RAID is to use UEFI/BIOS setup on a motherboard that supports RAID, which is called hardware RAID.

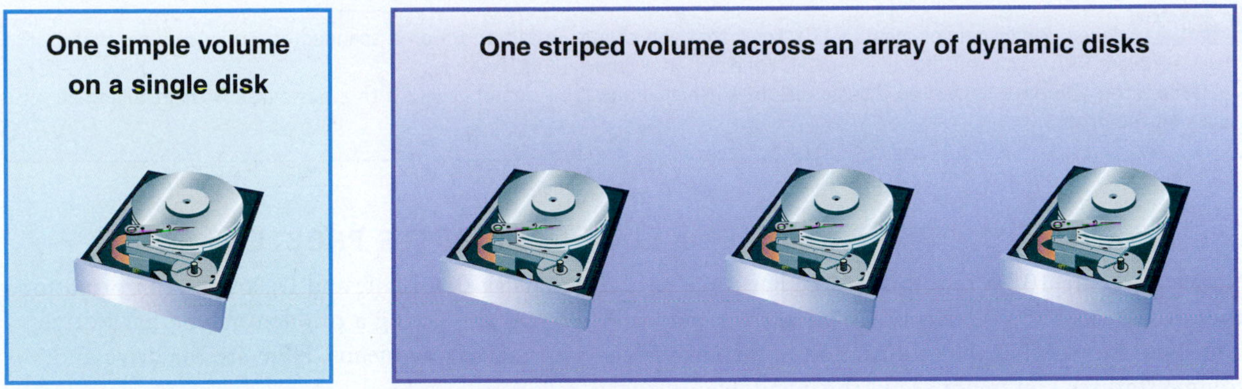

Figure 10-34 A simple volume is stored on a single disk, but a striped volume is stored on an array of dynamic disks

You can use Disk Management to convert two or more basic disks to dynamic disks. Then you can use unallocated space on these disks to create a simple, spanned, or striped volume. To convert a basic disk to dynamic, right-click the Disk area and select **Convert to Dynamic Disk** from the shortcut menu (see Figure 10-35), and then right-click free space on the disk and select **New Simple Volume, New Spanned Volume,** or **New Striped Volume** from the shortcut menu. If you were to use spanning or striping in Figure 10-35, you could make Disk 1 and Disk 2 dynamic disks that hold a single volume. The size of the volume would be the sum of the space on both hard drives.

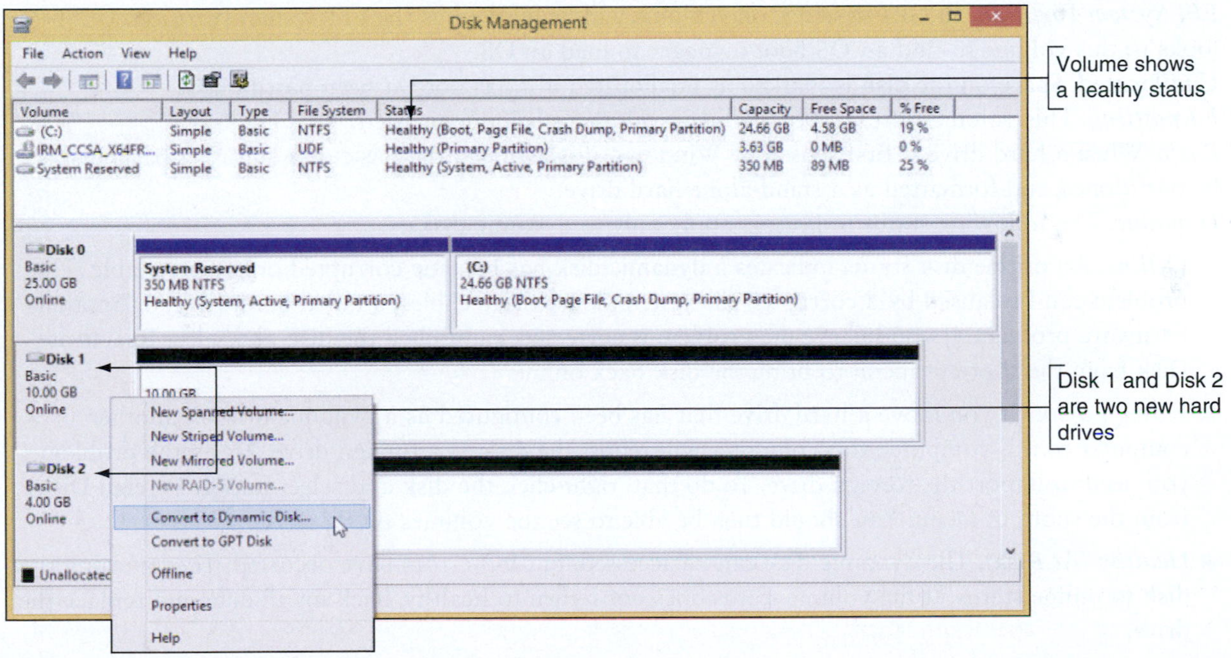

Figure 10-35 Convert a basic disk to a dynamic disk

Now for some serious cautions about software RAID where you use Windows for spanning and striping: Microsoft warns that when Windows is used for software RAID, the risk of catastrophic failure increases and can lead to data loss. Microsoft suggests you only use Windows spanning or striping when you have no other option. In other words, spanning and striping in Windows aren't very safe—to expand the size of a volume, use a mounted drive or use hardware RAID.

Notes When Windows implements RAID, know that you cannot install an OS on a spanned or striped volume that uses software RAID. You can, however, install Windows on a hardware RAID drive.

Also, after you have converted a basic disk to a dynamic disk, you cannot revert it to a basic disk without losing all data on the drive.

USE DISK MANAGEMENT TO TROUBLESHOOT HARD DRIVE PROBLEMS

Notice in Figure 10-35 that this system has three hard drives, Disk 0, Disk 1, and Disk 2, and information about the disks and volumes is shown in the window. When you are having a problem with a hard drive, it helps to know what the information in the Disk Management window means. Here are the drive and volume statuses you might see in this window:

- *Healthy.* The healthy volume status shown in Figure 10-35 indicates that the volume is formatted with a file system and that the file system is working without errors.
- *Failed.* A failed volume status indicates a problem with the hard drive or that the file system has become corrupted. To try to fix the problem, make sure the hard drive data cable and power cable are secure. Data on a failed volume is likely to be lost. For dynamic disks, if the disk status is Offline, try bringing the disk back online (how to do that is coming up later in this list).
- *Online.* An online disk status indicates the disk has been sensed by Windows and can be accessed by either reading or writing to the disk.
- *Active.* One volume on an MBR system will be marked as Active. This is the volume that startup BIOS looks to for an OS boot manager to load.
- *EFI System Partition.* In GPT systems, one volume will be marked as the EFI System Partition. UEFI looks to this volume to find an OS boot manager to load an OS.
- *Unallocated.* Space on the disk is marked as unallocated if it has not yet been partitioned.
- *Formatting.* This volume status appears while a volume is being formatted.
- *Basic.* When a hard drive is first sensed by Windows, it is assigned the Basic disk status. A basic disk can be partitioned and formatted as a stand-alone hard drive.
- *Dynamic.* The following status indicators apply only to dynamic disks:
  - *Offline.* An offline disk status indicates a dynamic disk has become corrupted or is unavailable. The problem can be caused by a corrupted file system, loose drive cables, a failed hard drive, or another hardware problem. If you believe the problem is corrected, right-click the disk and select **Reactivate Disk** from the shortcut menu to bring the disk back online.
  - *Foreign drive.* If you move a hard drive that has been configured as a dynamic disk on another computer to this computer, this computer will report the disk as a foreign drive. To fix the problem, you need to import the foreign drive. To do that, right-click the disk and select **Import Foreign Disks** from the shortcut menu. You should then be able to see the volumes on the disk.
  - *Healthy (At Risk).* The dynamic disk can be accessed, but I/O errors have occurred. Try returning the disk to online status. If the volume status does not return to healthy, back up all data and replace the drive.

If you are still having problems with a hard drive, volume, or mounted drive, check Event Viewer for events about the drive that might have been recorded there. These events might help you understand the nature of the problem and what to do about it. How to use Event Viewer is covered in the chapter, "Optimizing Windows."

Hands-On | Project 10-4 Use Disk Management on a Virtual Machine

A+ 220-902 1.2, 1.4

To complete the Hands-On Projects in the chapter "Installing Windows," you used VirtualBox software to install Windows in a virtual machine. Use this VM to practice using Disk Management. Dothe following:

1. Open Windows VirtualBox, but do not open the virtual machine.
2. With the virtual machine selected, click **Settings**. Use the Settings box to add a new hard drive to the VM, as shown in Figure 10-36: Click **Storage** in the left pane, click **Controller: SATA** in the center pane, and then click the **Add Hard Disk** icon. Click the **Create new disk** button.

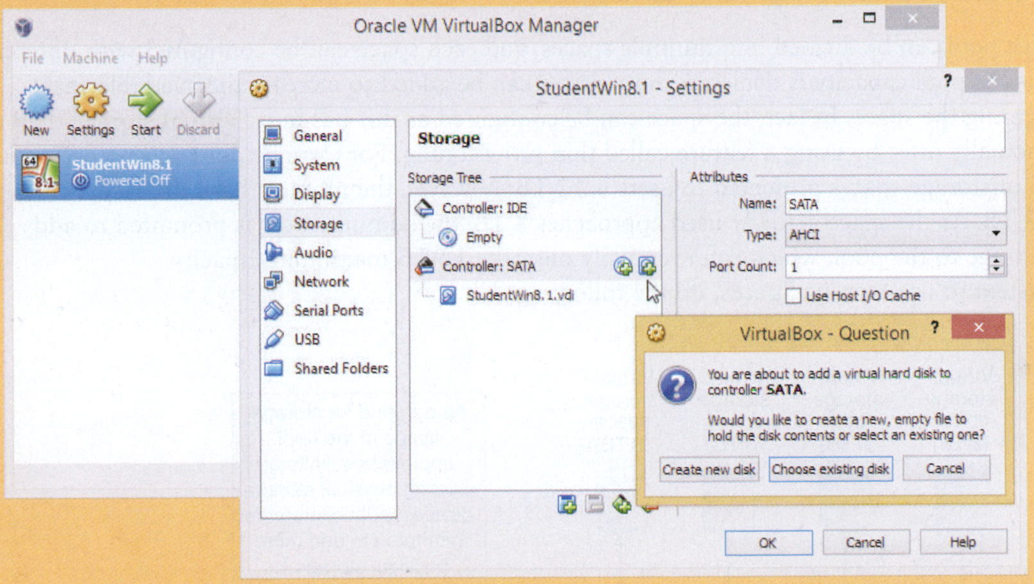

Source: VirtualBox

Figure 10-36 The Add Hard Disk icon is one option to the right of the SATA controller listing

3. In the Create Virtual Hard Drive dialog box, keep the default selection for **VDI (VirtualBox Disk Image)** unless directed otherwise by your instructor. Click **Next**. Keep the default **Dynamically allocated** option, and click **Next**. Keep the default drive name and location, change the size to **4 GB**, and then click **Create**. Click **OK**.
4. Start up the VM, sign in to Windows, and open Disk Management.
5. Use Disk Management to initialize the new disk and partition it. Create two partitions on the disk, one formatted using the NTFS file system and one using the FAT32 file system.
6. View the new volumes using File Explorer.
7. Create and save a snip of your screen showing the virtual machine with the new volumes created. Email the snip to your instructor.

WINDOWS STORAGE SPACES

A+ 220-902 1.4

Storage Spaces is new with Windows 8 and is a potential replacement for traditional Windows software RAID. With Storage Spaces, you can create a storage pool using any number of internal or external backup drives that use interfaces such as SATA (Serial ATA), SAS (Serial Attached SCSI), or even USB. Then you create one or more virtual drives, called spaces, from this pool, which appear as normal drives in File Explorer. Drives used for Storage Spaces can be formatted with the NTFS or ReFS file system.

Storage Spaces is designed for resiliency, which resists data loss in the event of drive failure. The following storage options offer varying degrees of resiliency in Storage Spaces:

- *Simple*. A simple storage space combines multiple physical drives into a single logical drive with no built-in data backup. This option offers no resiliency.
- *Two-way mirroring*. A logical drive can be mirrored, which means the data is duplicated across multiple physical drives used to create the space.
- *Three-way mirroring*. In three-way mirroring, data is stored in triplicate to provide additional resiliency against data loss, although this feature requires that at least five physical drives be used to create the storage pool.
- *Parity*. To provide even greater resiliency, parity spaces maintain multiple copies of data (depending upon the configuration) plus parity checking, which is a way to check backed-up data for any loss and re-create compromised data through parity calculations.

A single storage pool can be divided into multiple spaces, and each space can be configured with different resiliency settings. As pool capacity is depleted, more drives can be added to increase the available space without reconfiguring the space. In fact, the space can be configured as if it has more virtual storage than the physical drives actually offer by using a feature called thin provisioning. For example, in Figure 10-37, you can see the total of storage spaces presented to users is 12 TB; however, the physical hard drive capacities add up to only 8 TB. As the space actually used approaches 8 TB, the administrator is prompted to add more physical storage to the pool, which can eventually meet the 12-TB maximum capacity.

To set up a system to use Storage Spaces, do the following:

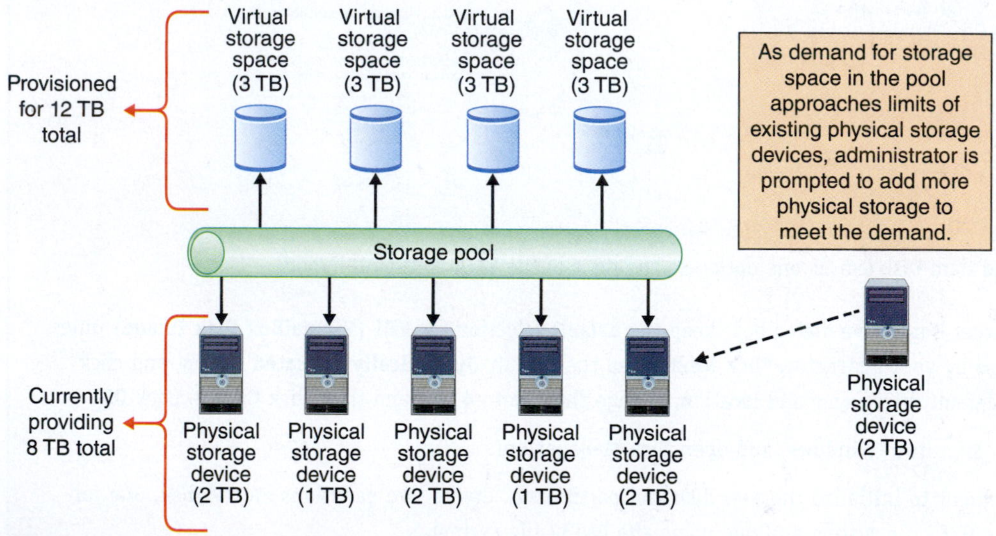

Figure 10-37 Thin provisioning allows for additional physical devices as needed without reconfiguring space available to users

1. Attach any drives to the computer that you intend to use for your storage pool. These can include SATA, SAS, or certain USB devices, and they do not have to match in capacity. All data on the storage drives will be lost during formatting, so be sure to back up anything important.
2. Open Control Panel and click **Storage Spaces**. Click **Create a new pool and storage space**. Respond to the UAC dialog box.
3. Any drives that are compatible with Storage Spaces will be listed. Select the drives to format. All data on the selected drives will be lost.

4. In the Create a storage space window (see Figure 10-38), assign a name and drive letter for the storage space, and select a file system. File system options include NTFS and ReFS.

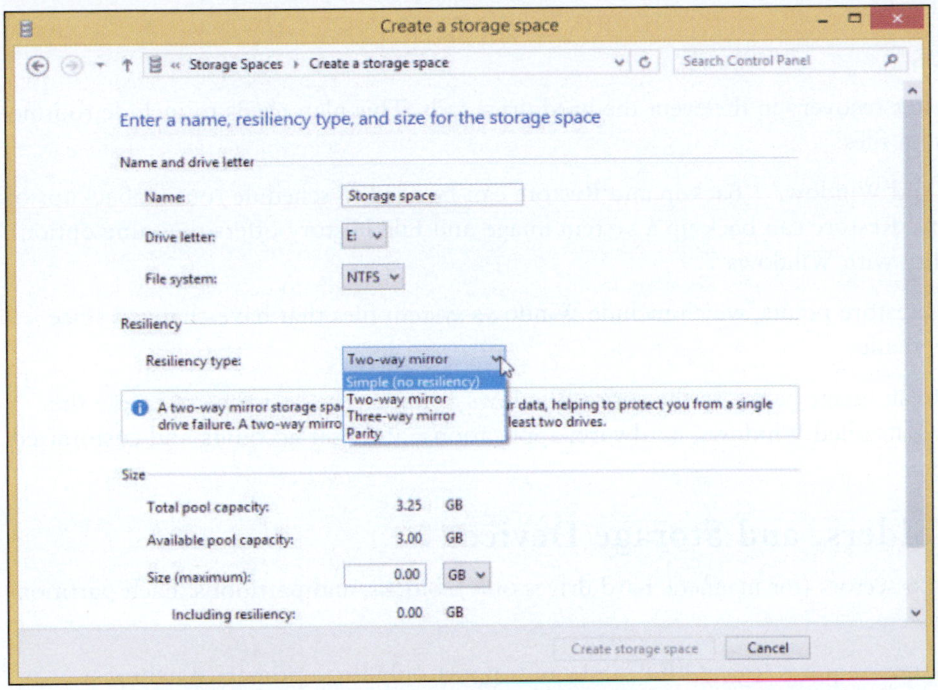

Figure 10-38 Select a resiliency type for a new storage space

5. Select a resiliency type. Options include simple (no resiliency), two-way mirror, three-way mirror, and parity. Then, if you plan to use thin provisioning, adjust the maximum size of the storage pool. Sizes can be set in GB or TB. Click **Create storage space**. The storage space is created and formatted.

6. After the storage space is created, you can return to the Storage Spaces window to change the name, drive letter, and size of an existing storage space.

>> CHAPTER SUMMARY

Schedule Preventive Maintenance

- Regular preventive maintenance includes verifying Windows settings, cleaning up the hard drive, defragmenting the hard drive, checking the drive for errors, uninstalling unwanted software, and doing whatever else is necessary to free up enough space on the hard drive for Windows to perform well.
- Windows stores user profiles in the C:\Users folder.
- For best performance, allow at least 15 percent of free space on the Windows volume. The easiest way to clean up temporary files is to use the Disk Cleanup utility in the drive properties box.
- You can defrag a magnetic hard drive by using the drive properties box or the defrag command. By default, Windows automatically defrags magnetic hard drives weekly.
- Use the chkdsk utility to check the drive for errors and recover data. The utility can be accessed from a command prompt or the drive properties box.
- Windows supports compressed (zipped) folders and NTFS folder and file compression. You can also compress an NTFS volume.

- Virtual memory uses hard drive space as memory to increase the total amount of memory available. Virtual memory is stored in a paging file named pagefile.sys. To save space on drive C:, you can move the file to another volume or hard drive.

Backup Procedures

- You need a plan for disaster recovery in the event the hard drive fails. This plan needs to include routine backups of data and system files.
- Windows 8 File History and Windows 7 Backup and Restore can be used to schedule routine backups of user data files. Backup and Restore can back up a system image and File History offers the same option for backward compatibility with Windows 7.
- System Protection creates restore points, which include Windows system files that have changed since the last restore point was made.
- A Windows 8 custom refresh image backs up the entire Windows volume. The best time to create the image is right after you've installed Windows, hardware, applications, and user accounts and customized Windows settings.

Managing Files, Folders, and Storage Devices

- A hard drive is divided into sectors (for magnetic hard drives only), blocks, and partitions. Each partition is formatted with a file system.
- The MBR partitioning system requires legacy BIOS and can support only three primary partitions and one extended partition.
- The GPT partitioning system requires UEFI and a 64-bit OS. It can support up to 128 partitions, Secure Boot, and hard drives larger than 2 TB.
- Commands useful to manage files, folders, and storage media include help, dir, del, ren, copy, recover, expand, xcopy, robocopy, md, cd, rd, chkdsk, defrag, and format.
- Use Disk Management to manage hard drives and partitions. Use it to create, delete, and resize partitions, mount a drive, manage dynamic disks, and solve problems with hard drives.
- Windows 8 Storage Spaces is expected to replace the Windows solution for software RAID and can support thin provisioning, which allows for physical hard drives to be added to the storage pool as need demands.

>> KEY TERMS

For explanations of key terms, see the Glossary for this text.

active partition
active recovery image
Backup and Restore
basic disk
boot partition
BootMgr
cd (change directory)
CDFS (Compact Disk File System)
chkdsk (check disk)
cluster
Complete PC Backup
copy
custom refresh image
defrag
defragment
del
dir
Disk Cleanup
dynamic disk
dynamic volume
EFI System Partition (ESP)
elevated command prompt window
erase
expand
extended partition
FAT (file allocation table)
file allocation unit
File History
formatting
fragmented file
Globally Unique Identifier Partition Table (GUID or GPT)
hardware RAID
help
high-level formatting
initialization files
logical drive
low-level formatting
Master Boot Record (MBR)
master file table (MFT)
md (make directory)
mount point
mounted drive
Offline Files
pagefile.sys
partition table

primary partition
quick format
RAID (redundant array of inexpensive disks or redundant array of independent disks)
RAID 0
rd (remove directory)
recover
registry
ren (rename)
resiliency
Resilient File System (ReFS)
restore point
robocopy (robust file copy)
sector
shadow copy
shutdown
simple volume
slack
software RAID
Storage Spaces
striping
system image
system partition
System Protection
System Restore
thin provisioning
track
UDF (Universal Disk Format)
user profile
user profile namespace
virtual memory
wildcard
Windows PowerShell
xcopy

>> REVIEWING THE BASICS

1. What are the three Windows settings critical to securing a computer that need to be verified as part of regular maintenance?
2. What folder holds the Windows registry? What folder holds a backup of the registry?
3. What folder holds 32-bit programs installed in a 64-bit installation of Windows?
4. What file in the user account folder stores user settings?
5. What is the purpose of the C:\Windows\CSC folder?
6. What is the purpose of the Windows.old folder?
7. How can you manually delete the Windows.old folder?
8. By default, how often does Windows automatically defrag a magnetic hard drive?
9. On what type of hard drive does Windows disable defragmenting?
10. What are two reasons to uninstall software you no longer use?
11. What is the file name and default path of the Windows paging file used for virtual memory?
12. What type of storage media must be used to create a Windows system image?
13. What Windows 8 utility is used to back up user data? What Windows 7 utility is used to back up user data?
14. Why is it important to not store a backup of drive C: on another partition on the same hard drive?
15. What is the *%SystemRoot%* folder as used in Microsoft documentation?
16. What Windows utility creates restore points?
17. How can you delete all restore points?
18. In what folder are restore points kept?
19. Which dialog box can you use to manually create a restore point?
20. To use the GPT partitioning system on a hard drive, what firmware is required? What operating system architecture?
21. In a command line, what is the purpose of the `?` in a file name?
22. What is the purpose of the `|more` parameter at the end of a command line?
23. What is the command to list all files and subdirectories in a directory?
24. What type of command prompt window is needed to run the chkdsk command?
25. When you want to use chkdsk to fix file system errors and the drive is not locked, when does Windows schedule the chkdsk command to run?

10

26. What command is intended to replace xcopy?
27. Which Windows utility can you use to split a partition into two partitions?
28. Which is more stable, RAID implemented by Windows or RAID implemented by hardware?
29. When you move a dynamic disk to a new computer, what status will Disk Management first assign the drive?
30. What is the feature of Windows 8 Storage Spaces that allows an administrator to add physical hard drives to the storage pool as available space fills up?

>> THINKING CRITICALLY

1. Write and test commands to do the following. (Answers can vary.)
   a. Create a folder named C:\data
   b. Create a folder named C:\data\test1 and a folder named C:\data\test2
   c. Copy Notepad.exe to the test1 folder
   d. Move Notepad.exe from the test1 folder to the test2 folder
   e. Make C:\ the default folder
   f. Without changing the default folder, list all files in the test2 folder
   g. Delete the test2 folder
   h. Delete the C:\data folder
2. You are trying to clean up a slow Windows 8 system that was recently installed in place of the old Windows 7 installation, and you discover that the 75-GB hard drive has only 5 GB of free space. The entire hard drive is taken up by drive C:. What is the best way to free up some space?
   a. Compress the entire hard drive.
   b. Move the /Program Files folder to an external hard drive.
   c. Delete the Windows.old folder.
   d. Reduce the size of the paging file.
3. Which is the best first step to protect important data on your hard drive?
   a. Use dynamic disks to set up a striped volume so that the data has redundancy.
   b. Back up the data to another media.
   c. Compress the folder that holds the data.
   d. Put password protection on the data folder.
4. The A+ exams expect you to be able to launch many Windows utilities by using the program file name of the utility. What is the program file name for each of the following utilities? (*Hint*: You might need to look online for some of these.)
   a. Command prompt
   b. System Information
   c. System Restore
   d. Device Manager
   e. Disk Cleanup
   f. Disk Management

>> REAL PROBLEMS, REAL SOLUTIONS

REAL PROBLEM 10-1 Researching the WinSxS Folder

While cleaning up a hard drive, you begin to look for folders that are excessively large and discover the C:\Windows\WinSxS folder is more than 7 GB. That's almost half the size of the entire C:\Windows folder on this drive. Use the web to research the purpose of the WinSxS folder. What goes in this folder and how does it get there? How can the size of the folder be reduced without causing major trouble with the OS? Write a brief one-page paper about this folder and cite at least three articles you find on the web about it.

REAL PROBLEM 10-2 Cleaning Up a Sluggish Windows System

Do you have a Windows system that is slow and needs optimizing? If not, talk with family and friends and try to find a slow system that can use your help. Using all the tools and techniques presented in this chapter, clean up this sluggish Windows system. Take detailed notes as you go, listing what you checked before you started to solve the problems, describing what you did to solve the problems, and describing the results of your efforts. What questions did you have along the way? Bring these questions to class for discussion.

REAL PROBLEM 10-3 Creating a Virtual Hard Drive

You can use the Disk Management tool or the diskpart command to create a Virtual Hard Drive (VHD) on a physical computer. The VHD is a file that takes up some free space on the physical hard drive, but to Windows it appears as a second hard drive. You can store data in folders and files on the VHD and even install Windows in the VHD. Follow these steps to create a VHD:

1. In Disk Management, click **Action** in the menu bar and click **Create VHD**. Follow directions on screen to create the VHD, specifying its location on the hard drive and its size. You can make the size dynamically expanding. The VHD is listed as a Disk in the Disk Management window.
2. Right-click the new disk and click **Initialize Disk**. Use the GPT partitioning system for the disk.
3. To format the disk, right-click the unallocated space on the disk and click **New Simple Volume**. The VHD is now ready for use and appears in File Explorer or Windows Explorer as a new volume.

Discuss in your class and research online how a VHD might be useful. What are two uses of a VHD, in which a VHD offers advantages over using a physical hard drive?

>> REAL PROBLEMS, REAL SOLUTIONS

REAL PROBLEM 10-1 Researching the WinSxS Folder

While cleaning up a hard drive, you begin to look for folders that are excessively large and discover the C:\Windows\WinSxS folder is more than 7 GB. That's almost half the size of the entire C:\Windows folder on this drive. Use the web to research the purpose of the WinSxS folder. What goes in this folder and how does it get there? How can the size of the folder be reduced without causing major trouble with the OS? Write a brief one-page paper about this folder and cite at least three articles you find on the web about it.

REAL PROBLEM 10-2 Cleaning Up a Sluggish Windows System

Do you have a Windows system that is slow and needs optimizing? If not, talk with family and friends and try to find a slow system that can use your help. Using all the tools and techniques presented in this chapter, clean up this sluggish Windows system. Take detailed notes as you go, listing what you checked before you started to solve the problems, describing what you did to solve the problems, and describing the results of your efforts. What questions did you have along the way? Bring these questions to class for discussion.

REAL PROBLEM 10-3 Creating a Virtual Hard Drive

You can use the Disk Management tool or the diskpart command to create a Virtual Hard Drive (VHD) on a physical computer. The VHD is a file that takes up some free space on the physical hard drive, but to Windows it appears as a second hard drive. You can store data in folders and files on the VHD and even install Windows in the VHD. Follow these steps to create a VHD:

1. In Disk Management, click **Action** in the menu bar and click **Create VHD**. Follow directions on screen to create the VHD, specifying its location on the hard drive and its size. You can make the size dynamically expanding. The VHD is listed as a Disk in the Disk Management window.
2. Right-click the new disk and click **Initialize Disk**. Use the GPT partitioning system for the disk.
3. To format the disk, right-click the unallocated space on the disk and click **New Simple Volume**. The VHD is now ready for use and appears in File Explorer or Windows Explorer as a new volume.

Discuss in your class and research online how a VHD might be useful. What are two uses of a VHD, in which a VHD offers advantages over using a physical hard drive?

CHAPTER 11

Optimizing Windows

After completing this chapter, you will be able to:

- Solve Windows problems using Windows utilities and tools
- Optimize Windows to improve performance
- Manually remove software

In the chapter, "Maintaining Windows," you learned about the tools and strategies to maintain Windows and about the importance of keeping good backups. This chapter takes you one step further as an IT support technician so that you can get the best performance out of Windows. We begin the chapter learning about the Windows tools you'll need to optimize Windows. Then we turn our attention to the steps you can follow to cause a sluggish Windows system to perform at its best and how to manually remove software that does not uninstall using normal methods. As you read the chapter, you might consider following along using a Windows 8 or Windows 7 system.

Notes Windows installed in a virtual machine is an excellent environment to use when practicing the skills in this chapter.

WINDOWS UTILITIES AND TOOLS TO SUPPORT THE OS

A+ 220-902 1.1, 1.4, 1.5, 4.1

Knowledge is power when it comes to supporting Windows. In this part of the chapter, you learn more about how Windows works and to use some Windows tools to poke around under the hood to see what is really happening that is slowing Windows down or giving other problems.

WHAT ARE THE SHELL AND THE KERNEL?

A+ 220-902 4.1

It might sound like we're talking about a grain of wheat, but Windows has a shell and a kernel and you need to understand what they are and how they work so you can solve problems with each. A **shell** is the portion of an OS that relates to the user and to applications. The **kernel** is responsible for interacting with hardware. Figure 11-1 shows how the shell and kernel relate to users, applications, and hardware. In addition, the figure shows a third component of an OS, the configuration data. For Windows, this data is primarily contained in the registry.

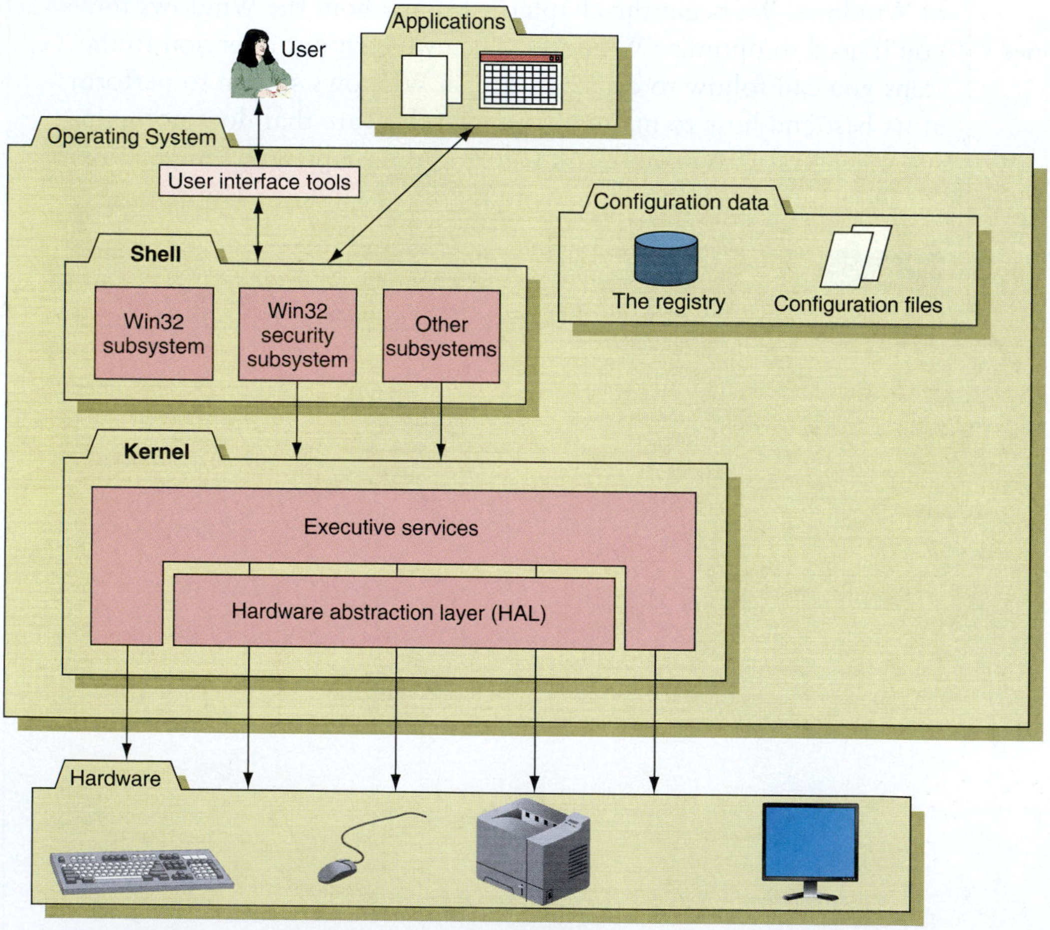

Figure 11-1 Inside an operating system, different components perform various functions

THE WINDOWS SHELL

The shell provides tools such as File Explorer or the Windows desktop as a way for the user to do such things as select music to burn to a CD or launch an application. For applications, the shell provides commands and procedures that applications can call on to do such things as print a document, read from a storage device, or display a photograph on screen.

The shell is made up of several subsystems that all operate in user mode, which means these subsystems have only limited access to system information and can access hardware only through other OS services. One of these subsystems, the Win32 security subsystem, provides sign-in to the system and other security functions, including privileges for file access. All applications relate to Windows by way of the Win32 subsystem.

THE WINDOWS KERNEL

The kernel, or core, of the OS is responsible for interacting with hardware. Because the kernel operates in kernel mode, it has more power to communicate with hardware devices than the shell has. Applications operating under the OS cannot get to hardware devices without the shell passing those requests to the kernel. This separation of tasks provides for a more stable system and helps to prevent a wayward application from destabilizing the system.

The kernel has two main components: (1) the HAL (hardware abstraction layer), which is the layer closest to the hardware, and (2) the executive services interface, which is a group of services that operate in kernel mode between the user mode subsystems and the HAL. Executive services contained in the ntoskrnl.exe program file manage memory, I/O devices, file systems, some security, and other key components directly or by way of device drivers.

When Windows is first installed, it builds the HAL based on the type of CPU installed. The HAL cannot be moved from one computer to another, which is one reason you cannot copy a Windows installation from one computer to another.

HOW WINDOWS MANAGES APPLICATIONS

A+
220-902
1.4

When an application is first installed, its program files are normally stored on the hard drive. When the application is launched, the program is copied from the hard drive into memory and there it is called a process. A process is a program that is running under the authority of the shell, together with the system resources assigned to it. System resources might include other programs it has started and memory addresses to hold its data. When the process makes a request for resources, this request is made to the Win32 subsystem and is called a thread. A thread is a single task, such as the task of printing a file that the process requests from the kernel. Figure 11-2 shows two threads in action, which is possible because the process and Windows support multithreading. Sometimes a process is called an instance, such as when you say to a user, "Open two instances of Internet Explorer." Technically, you are saying to open two Internet Explorer processes.

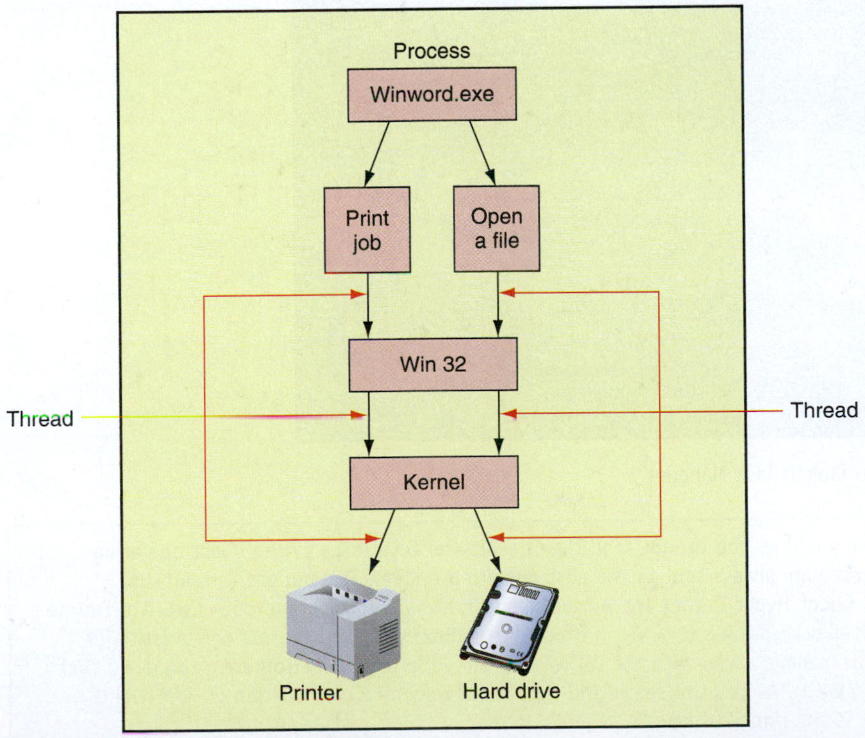

Figure 11-2 A process with more than one thread is called multithreading

11

★ A+ Exam Tip The A+ 220-902 exam expects you to know how to use Task Manager, System Configuration, Services console, Computer Management console, MMC, Event Viewer, Task Scheduler, Registry Editor, Performance Monitor, and Print Management. All these tools are covered in this part of the chapter.

Now that you are familiar with the concepts of how Windows works, let's see how to use some tools that can help us manage Windows components and processes.

TASK MANAGER

A+ 220-902 1.4

Task Manager (taskmgr.exe) lets you view the applications and processes running on your computer as well as information about process and memory performance, network activity, and user activity. Several ways to access Task Manager are:

- Press **Ctrl+Alt+Del**. Depending on your system, the security screen (see Figure 11-3) or Task Manager appears. If the security screen appears, click **Task Manager**. This method works well when the system has a problem and is frozen.
- Right-click a blank area in the taskbar on the desktop, and select **Task Manager** in Windows 8 or **Start Task Manager** in Windows 7 from the shortcut menu.
- Press **Ctrl+Shift+Esc**.
- For Windows 8, press **Win+X** and click **Task Manager** in the Quick Launch menu. For Windows 7, click **Start**, enter **taskmgr.exe** in the Search box, and press **Enter**.

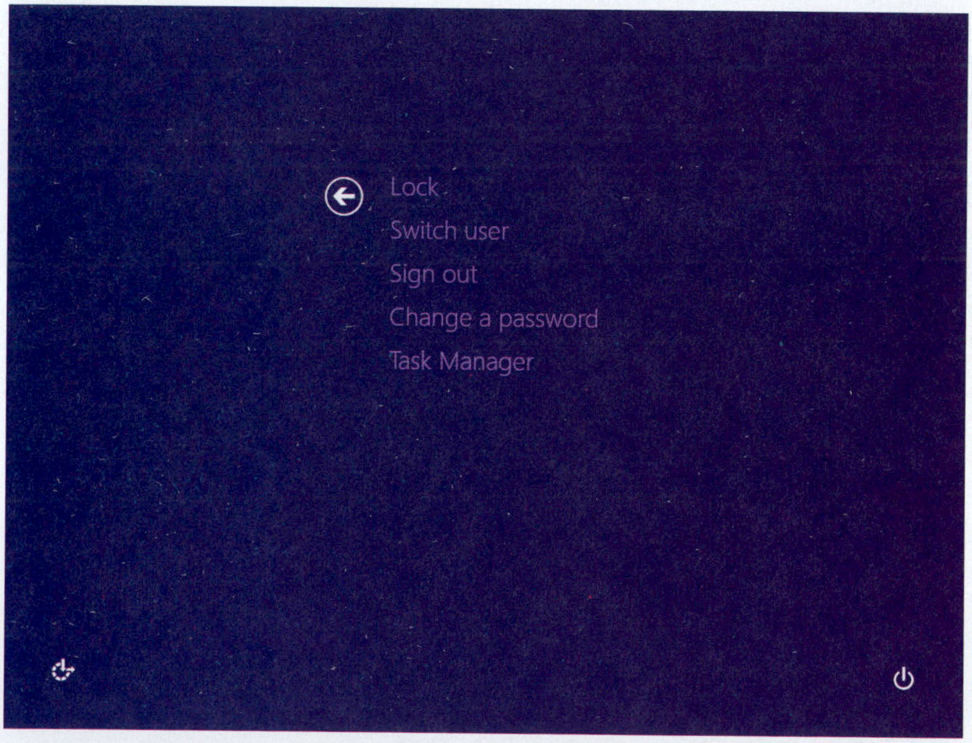

Figure 11-3 Use the security screen to launch Task Manager

Notes When working with a virtual machine, you cannot send the Ctrl+Alt+Del keystrokes to the guest operating system in the VM because these keystrokes are always sent to the host operating system. To send the Ctrl+Alt+Del keystrokes to a VM in Windows 8.1 Pro Client Hyper-V, click the **Action** menu in the VM window and click **Ctrl+Alt+Delete** (see Figure 11-4a). To send the Ctrl+Alt+Del keystrokes to a VM in Oracle VirtualBox, you must press a combination of keystrokes. To find out the keystrokes to manage a VM, with the VM window active, press **Host+Home**. In the menu that appears, point to **Machine** (see Figure 11-4b). As you can see in the figure, the keystroke combination is Host+Del. (By default, the Host key in VirtualBox is the right Ctrl key.)

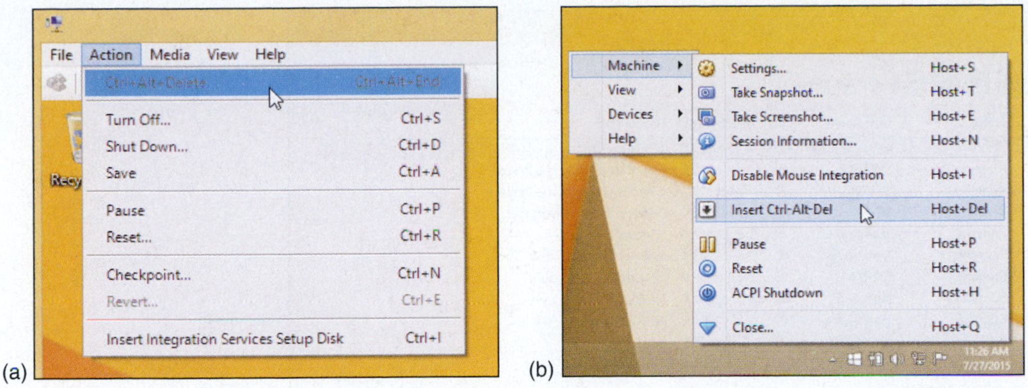

Source: Oracle VirtualBox

Figure 11-4 Send the Ctrl+Alt+Del keystrokes to a VM managed by (a) Windows 8.1 Pro Client Hyper-V or (b) Oracle VirtualBox

The Windows 8 Task Manager window is shown in Figure 11-5. If you see very limited information in the window, click **More details** to see the details shown in the figure.

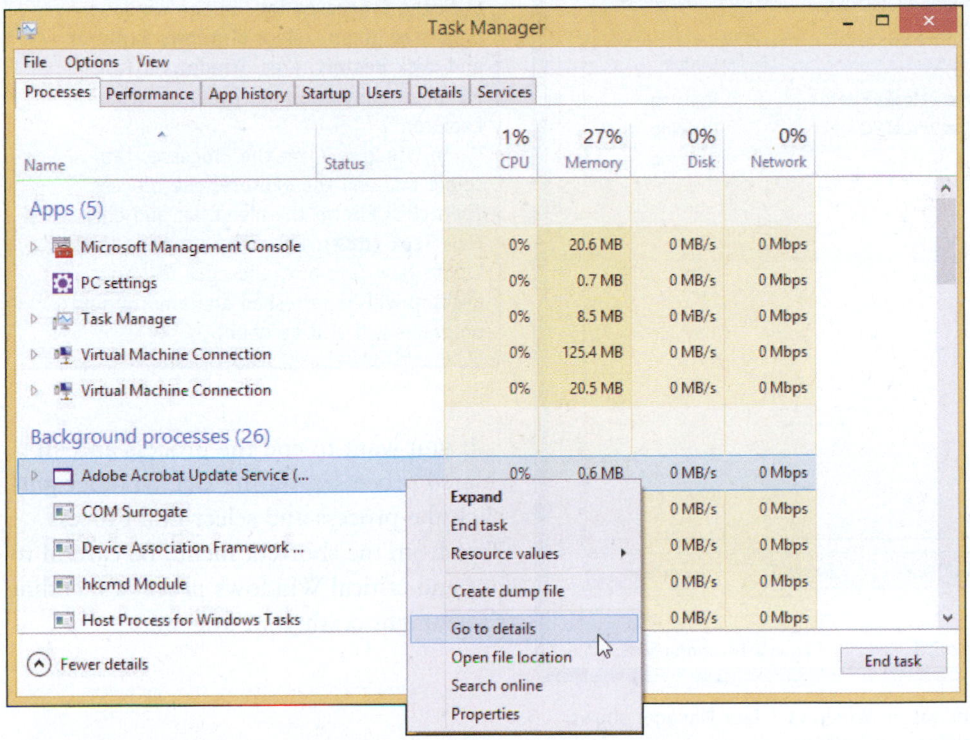

Figure 11-5 Windows 8 Task Manager window with Processes tab selected

Let's take a look at the Task Manager tabs.

PROCESSES TAB AND DETAILS TAB

The Processes tab shows running processes organized by Apps, Background processes, and Windows processes. Right-click a process, and click **Go to details** (see Figure 11-5) to jump to the Details tab where you see the name of the program file and other details about the running program. On the Details tab (see Figure 11-6), if a process is hung, it is reported as Not Responding. To end the task, select it and click **End task**. The application will attempt a normal shutdown; if data has not been saved, you are given the opportunity to save it.

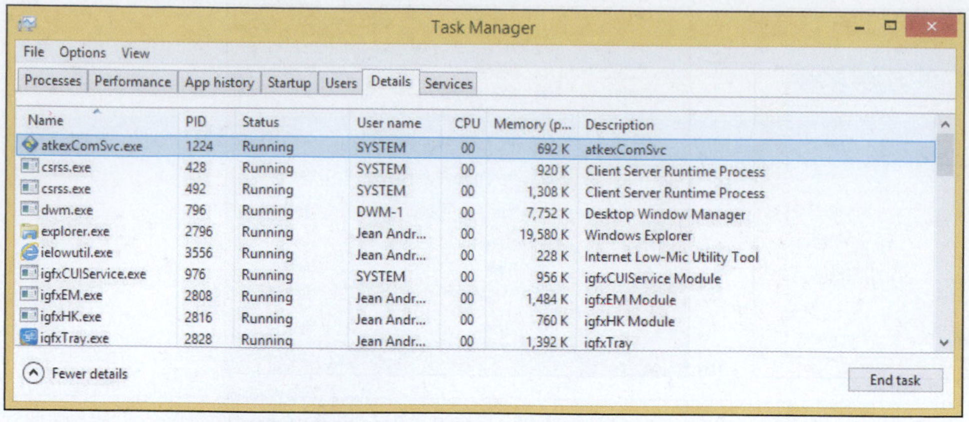

Figure 11-6 Use the Details tab to end a task that is not responding

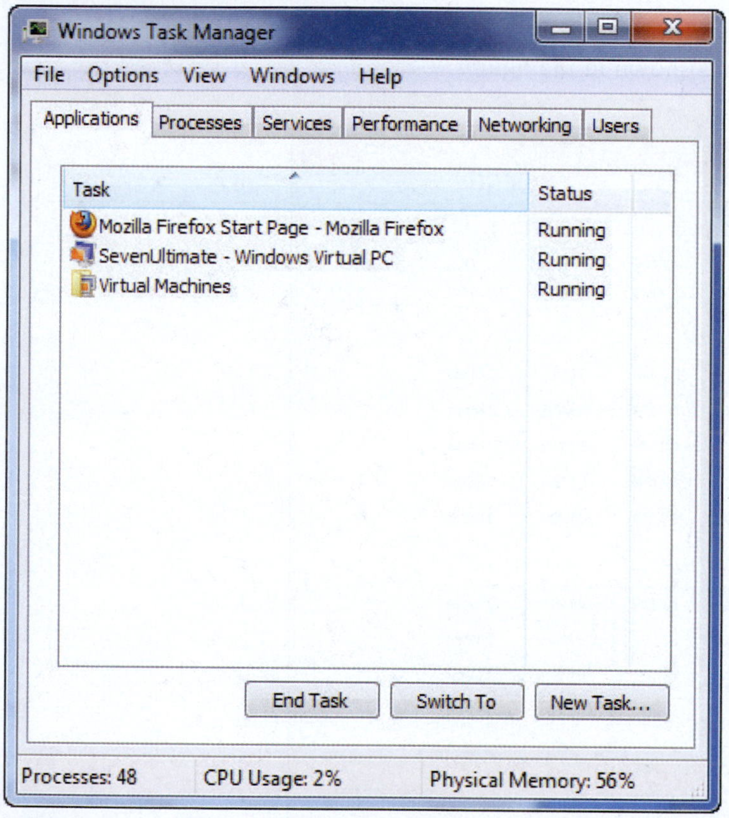

Figure 11-7 The Applications tab in Windows 7 Task Manager shows the status of active applications

> **Notes** If your desktop locks up, you can use Task Manager to refresh it. To do so, press **Ctrl+Alt+Del** and open **Task Manager**. Click the **Processes** tab. In the Windows processes group, select **Windows Explorer** and click **Restart**. (Yes, Windows 8 Task Manager really does call Explorer "Windows Explorer.")
>
> In Windows 7, on the Processes tab, select and end the **explorer.exe** process. Then click **File** in the menu bar and click **New Task (Run)**. Enter **Explorer.exe** in the Create New Task box, and click **OK**. Your desktop will be refreshed and any running programs will still be open.

If you want to end the process and all related processes, on the Details tab, right-click the process and select **End Process Tree** from the shortcut menu. Be careful to not end critical Windows processes; ending these might crash your system.

> **OS Differences** The Windows 7/Vista Task Manager window has six tabs: Applications, Processes, Services, Performance, Networking, and Users. The Applications tab of Task Manager (see Figure 11-7) is used to view a list of running processes. You can end a process that is not responding on this tab or end it on the Processes tab.

> **A+ Exam Tip** The A+ 220-902 exam expects you to understand the purposes of each tab in Task Manager for Windows 8 and Windows 7.

PERFORMANCE TAB

The Performance tab of Task Manager (see Figure 11-8) allows you to monitor performance of key devices in the system and network connections. For example, Figure 11-8 shows Memory selected where you can monitor how much RAM is currently used. When you select CPU, the Performance tab reports whether Hardware-assisted Virtualization is enabled.

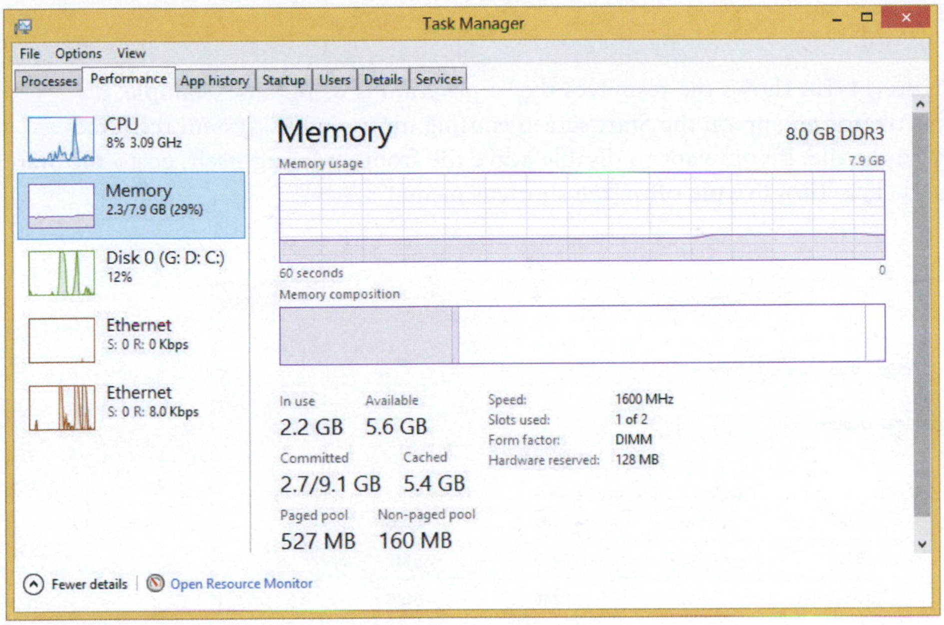

Figure 11-8 Use the Performance tab to view system resource usage

Click **Open Resource Monitor** on this tab to open the Resource Monitor, which monitors the CPU, hard drive, network, and memory in real time (see Figure 11-9). If you suspect CPU, memory, disk, or network resources are being used excessively by a process, you can use Resource Monitor to identify the process. Check for such a process if you suspect malware might be at work in a denial-of-service (DoS) attack.

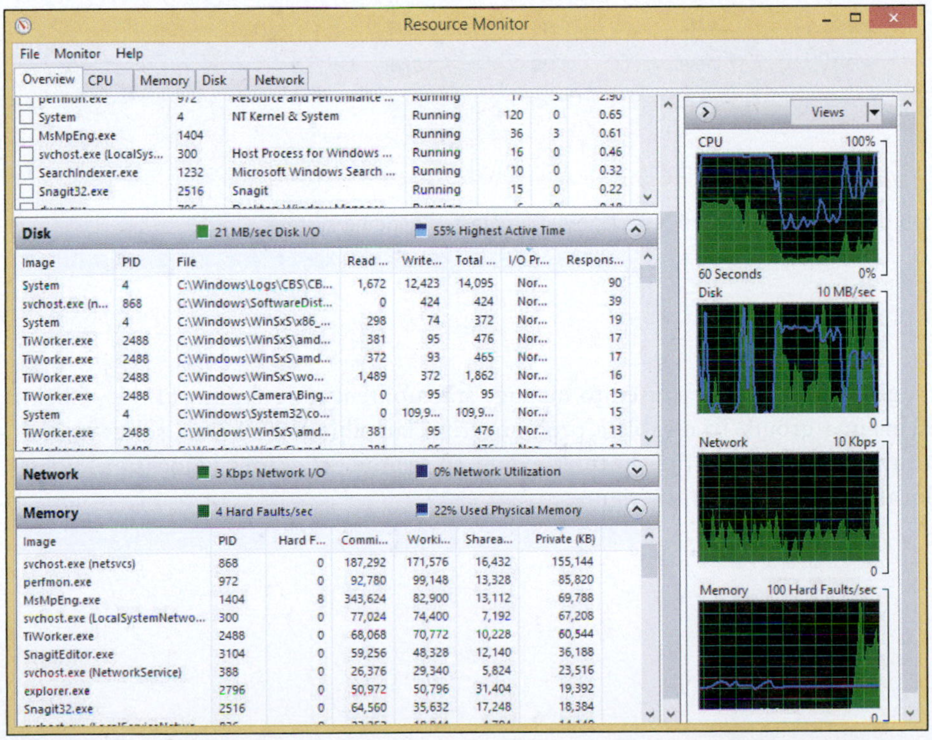

Figure 11-9 Resource Monitor monitors devices and the network in real time

> **OS Differences** In Windows 7/Vista, the Performance tab of Task Manager monitors performance of the CPU and memory and also gives you access to the Resource Monitor. To monitor the performance of network connections, see the Networking tab of Task Manager. Alternately, you can use the Windows 7 Resource Monitor to monitor the performance of the CPU, memory, hard drive, and network connections.

APP HISTORY TAB

The App history tab (see Figure 11-10) shows the resources that a program is using. For example, it's useful when deciding if a live tile for an app on the Start screen is using up too many system resources as it provides live information on the tile. If you want to disable a live tile from updating itself, go to the **Start** screen, right-click the tile, and click **Turn live tile off** in the shortcut menu.

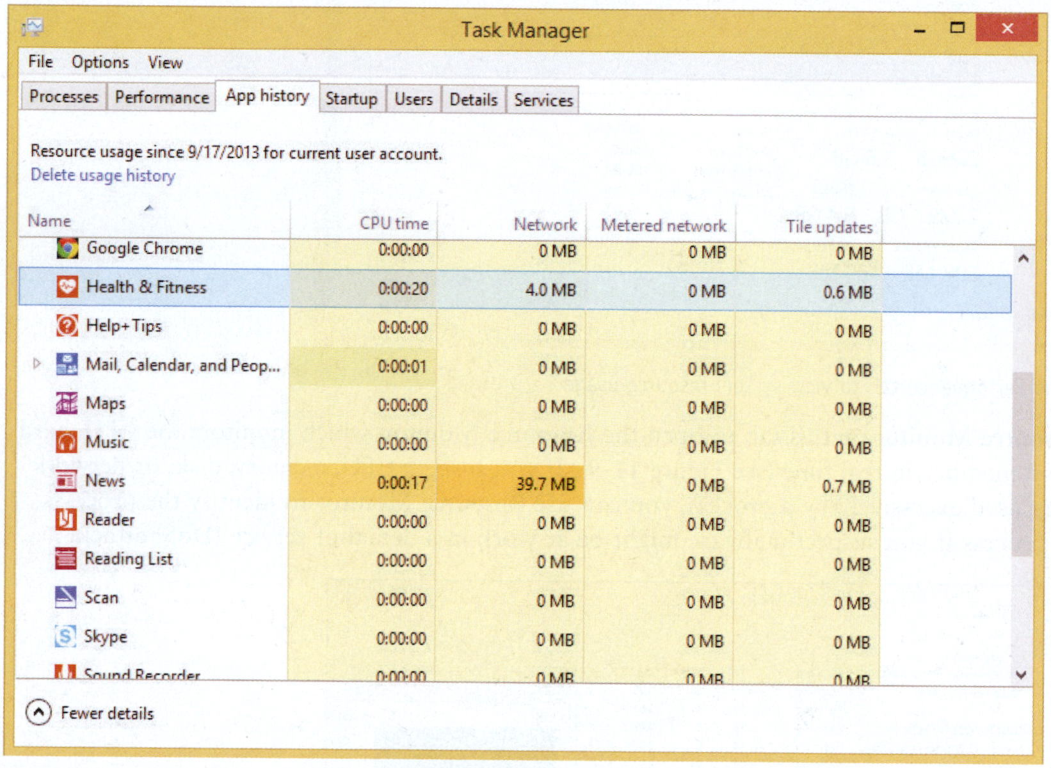

Figure 11-10 The App history tab can help you decide if a background program is hogging system resources

STARTUP TAB

The Startup tab of Task Manager in Windows 8 is used to manage startup items (see Figure 11-11). Click a white arrow to expand the items in a group. To disable a program from launching at startup, select it, and click **Disable** at the bottom of the window or in the shortcut menu. To see the program file location, right-click it, and click **Open file location**, as shown in the figure.

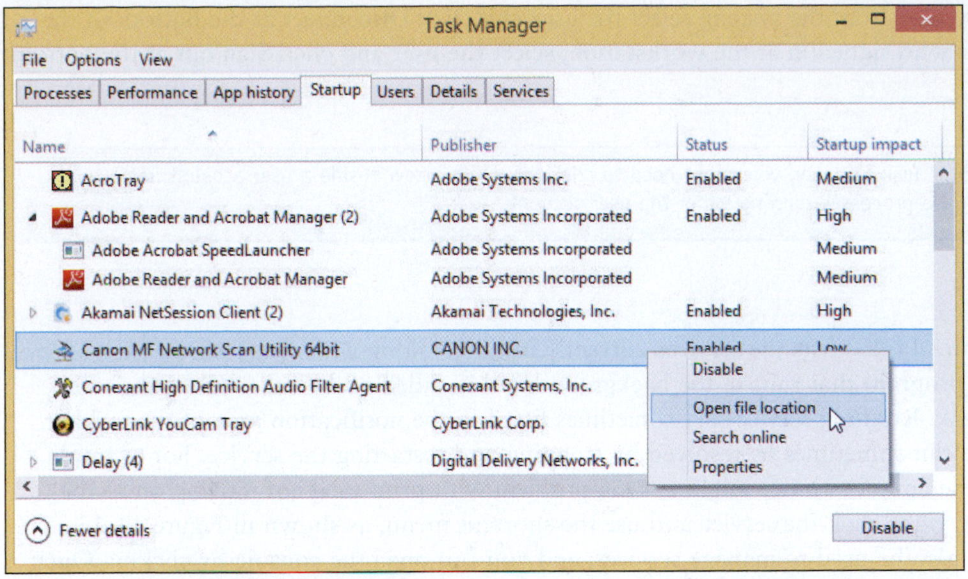

Figure 11-11 Startup processes are managed on the Startup tab of Task Manager

USERS TAB

The Users tab (see Figure 11-12) lists currently signed-in users and gives performance information that can help you identify processes started by a signed-in user that might be affecting overall system performance. Notice that the statuses of some programs on this tab are listed as Suspended. In Windows 8, if certain apps remain idle for a short time, they're suspended so they don't require the attention of the CPU. When the app is used again, it automatically comes out of suspension, and the CPU once again begins servicing it.

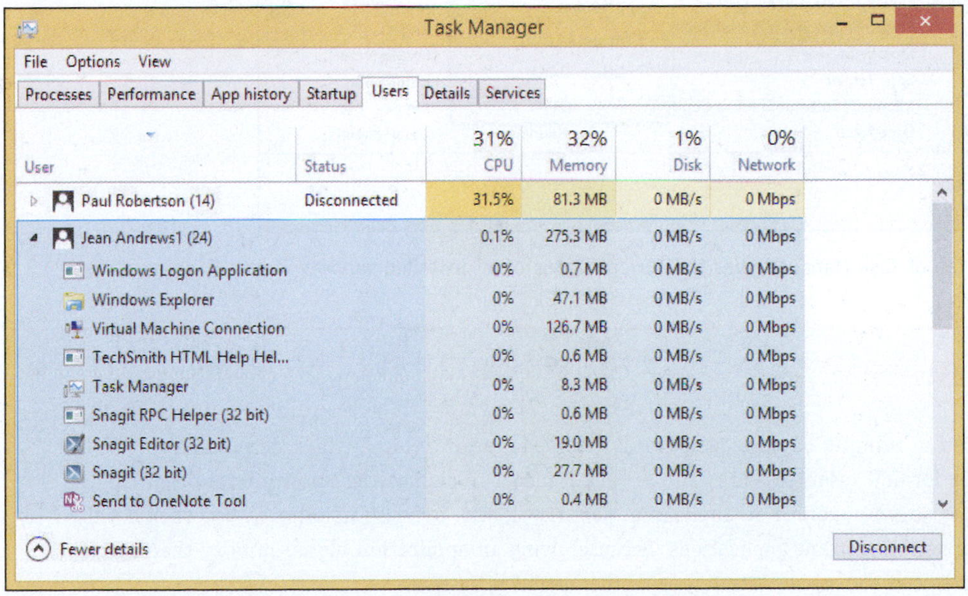

Figure 11-12 The Users tab shows system resources used by each signed-in user

11

To disconnect a remote user from the system, select the user and click **Disconnect** at the bottom of the screen. To sign out a user who signed in at the workstation, select the user and click **Sign out** at the bottom of the screen.

Notes On the Users tab of Task Manager, you might need to click the white arrow beside a user account name to expand the view so you can see processes running under the user account.

SERVICES TAB

The Services tab (see Figure 11-13) lists the services currently installed along with the status of each service. Recall that a service is a program that runs in the background and is called on by other programs to perform a background task. Running services are sometimes listed in the notification area of the taskbar. A problem with a service can sometimes be resolved by stopping and restarting the service. For example, stopping and restarting the Spooler service might solve a problem with print jobs not moving on to the printer. To stop or restart, right-click the service and use the shortcut menu, as shown in Figure 11-13. The Services console can also be used to manage services, and you can open the console by clicking **Open Services** at the bottom of the window. How to use this console is discussed later in the chapter.

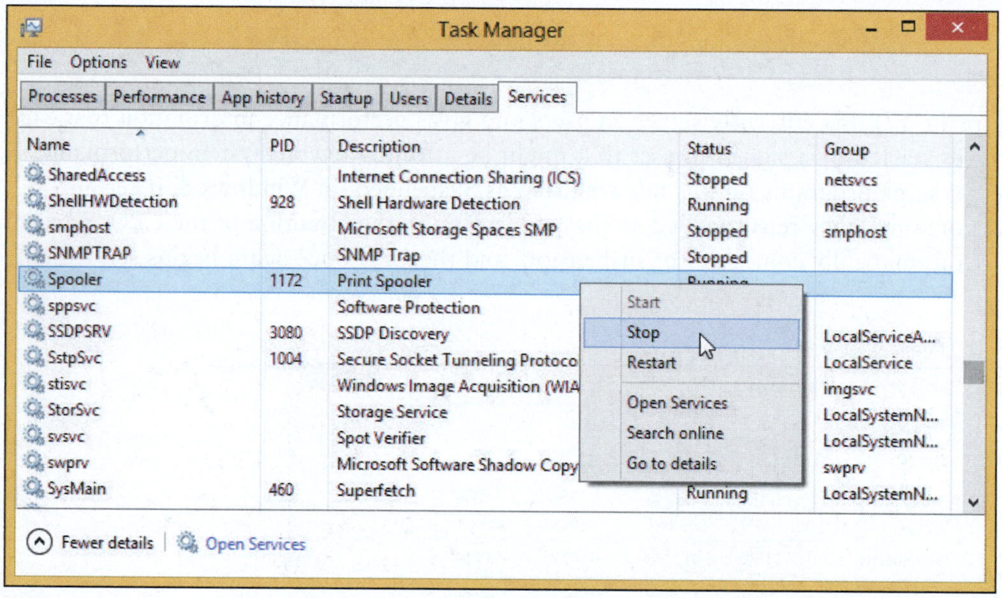

Figure 11-13 The Services tab of Task Manager gives the current status of all installed services

APPLYING | CONCEPTS ADJUST THE PRIORITY LEVEL OF AN APPLICATION

A+ 220-902 1.4

Each application running on your computer is assigned a priority level, which determines its position in the queue for CPU resources. You can use Task Manager to change the priority level for an application that is already open. If an application performs slowly, increase its priority. You should only do this with very important applications, because giving an application higher priority than certain background system processes can sometimes interfere with the operating system.

To use Task Manager to change the priority level of an open application, do the following:

1. In Task Manager, on the Processes tab, right-click the application and click **Go to details**.
2. On the Details tab, right-click the selected program and point to **Set priority**. Set the new priority to **Above normal** (see Figure 11-14). If that doesn't give satisfactory performance, then try **High**.

Remember that any changes you make to an application's priority level affect only the current session.

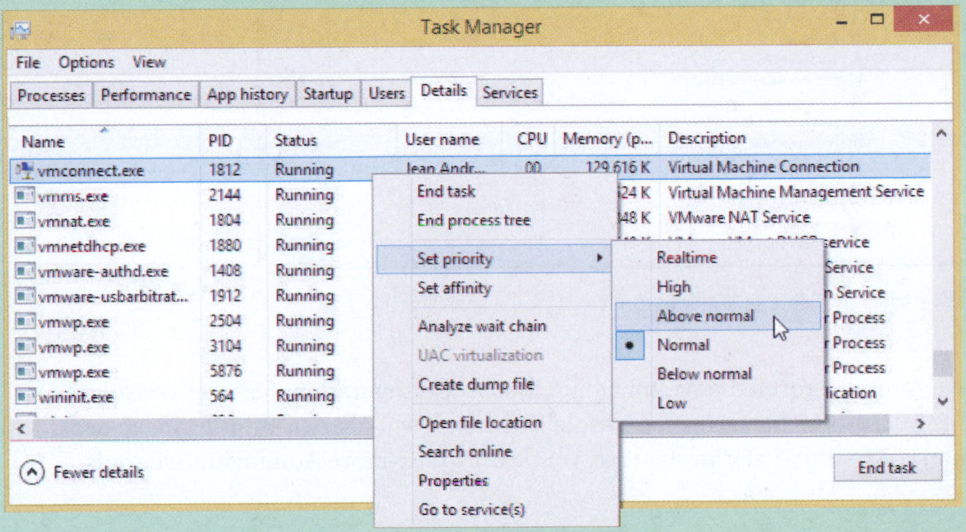

Figure 11-14 Change the priority level of a running application

OS Differences For Windows 7/Vista, to set the priority for a process, begin with the **Applications** tab. Right-click the application and select **Go To Process**. On the Processes tab, right-click the selected process and point to **Set Priority**. You can then set the new priority.

ADMINISTRATIVE TOOLS

A+
220-902
1.4

Windows offers a group of Administrative Tools in Control Panel that are used by technicians and developers to support Windows. To see the list of tools, open Control Panel in Classic view and then click **Administrative Tools**. Figure 11-15 shows the Administrative Tools window for Windows 8 Pro. The Home editions of Windows don't include the Local Security Policy (controls many security settings on the local computer) or Print Management (manages print servers on a network).

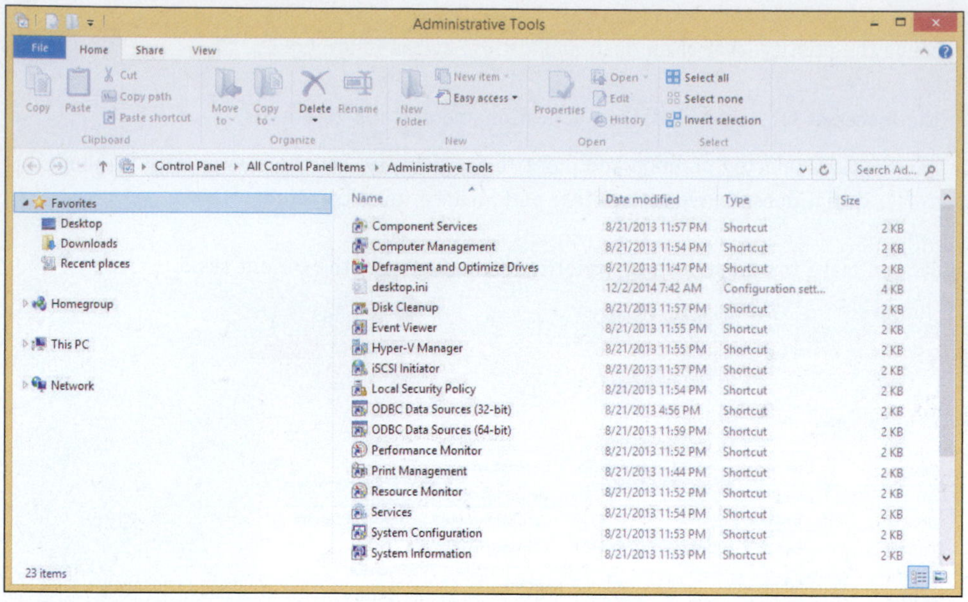

Figure 11-15 Administrative tools available in Windows 8 Pro

Several Administrative tools are covered next, including System Configuration, Services console, Computer Management, Microsoft Management Console (MMC), Event Viewer, Print Management, Task Scheduler, and Performance Monitor. Later in the text, you learn to use more Administrative tools.

SYSTEM CONFIGURATION

A+
220-902
1.4

You can use the System Configuration (msconfig.exe) utility, which is commonly pronounced "*M-S-config*," to temporarily disable programs from launching at startup in order to troubleshoot a startup problem. To open the System Configuration box, enter **msconfig.exe** in the Windows 8 Run box or in the Windows 7 Search box. The Windows 8 System Configuration box is shown in Figure 11-16 with the General tab selected.

Notes To open the Windows 8 Run box, press **Win+X** and click **Run** in the Quick Launch menu. To open the Windows 7 Search box, click **Start**.

Caution Don't depend on System Configuration to be a permanent fix to disable a startup program or service. Once you've decided you want to make the change permanent, use other methods to permanently remove that process from Windows startup. For example, you might uninstall a program, remove it from a startup folder, or use the Services console to disable a service.

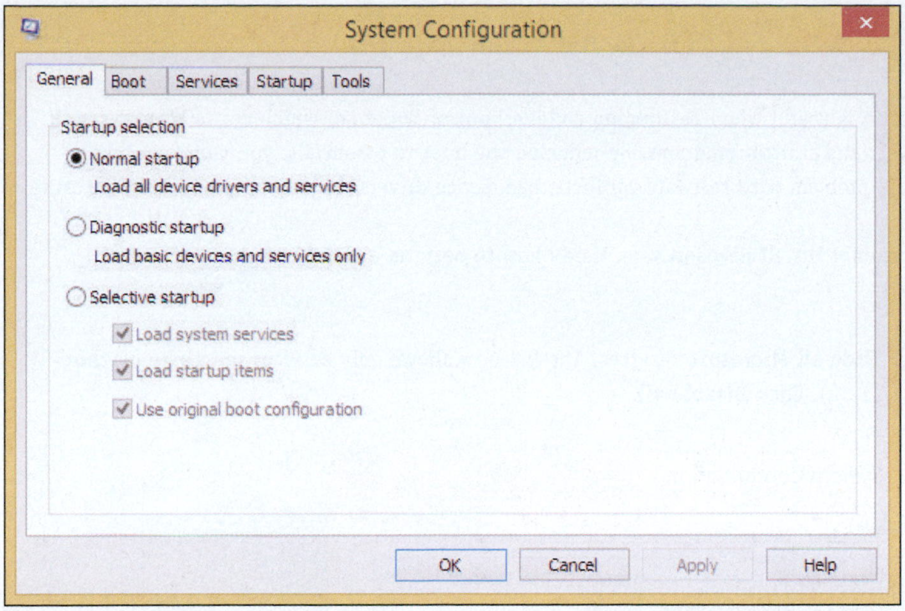

Figure 11-16 Use the General tab to control how Windows starts

Use the Boot tab (see Figure 11-17) to see information about the boot and control some boot settings. For example, in Figure 11-17, you can see this computer is set for a dual boot and, using this box, you can delete one of the choices for a dual boot from the boot loader menu. Also notice on the Boot tab the Boot options to apply when starting Windows. You learn more about these options in the chapter, "Troubleshooting Windows Startup."

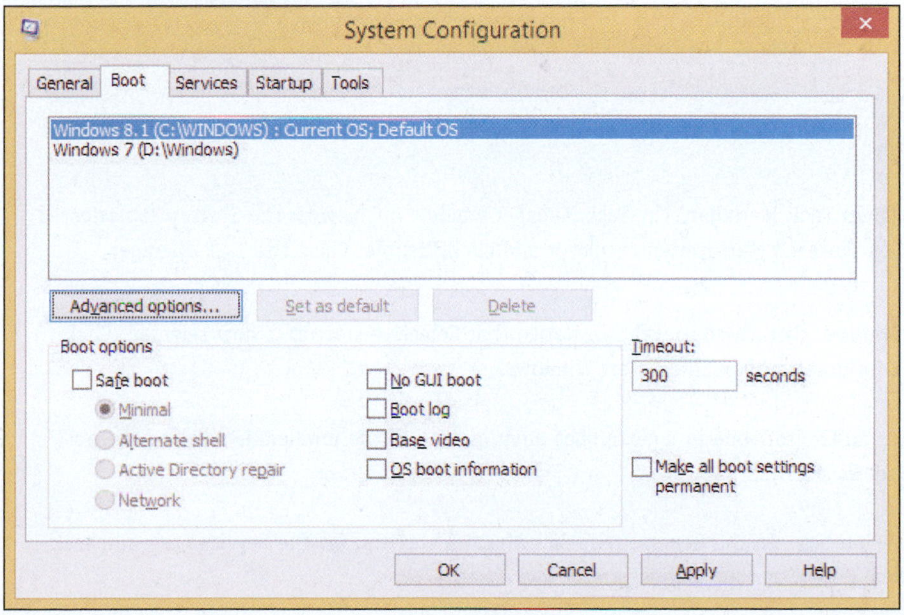

Figure 11-17 Use the Boot tab to control boot settings

11

APPLYING CONCEPTS PERFORM A CLEAN BOOT

A+
220-902
1.4

System Configuration is useful when performing a **clean boot** of Windows, which starts Windows with a basic set of drivers and startup programs. By reducing the boot to essentials, you can sometimes identify and solve a problem with software conflicts, bad device drivers, or startup processes that cause slow performance.

Suppose, for example, you cannot install new software. Here's how to perform a clean boot to verify other software is not in conflict:

1. On the Services tab, check **Hide all Microsoft services**. The list now shows only services put there by third-party software (see Figure 11-18). Click **Disable all**.

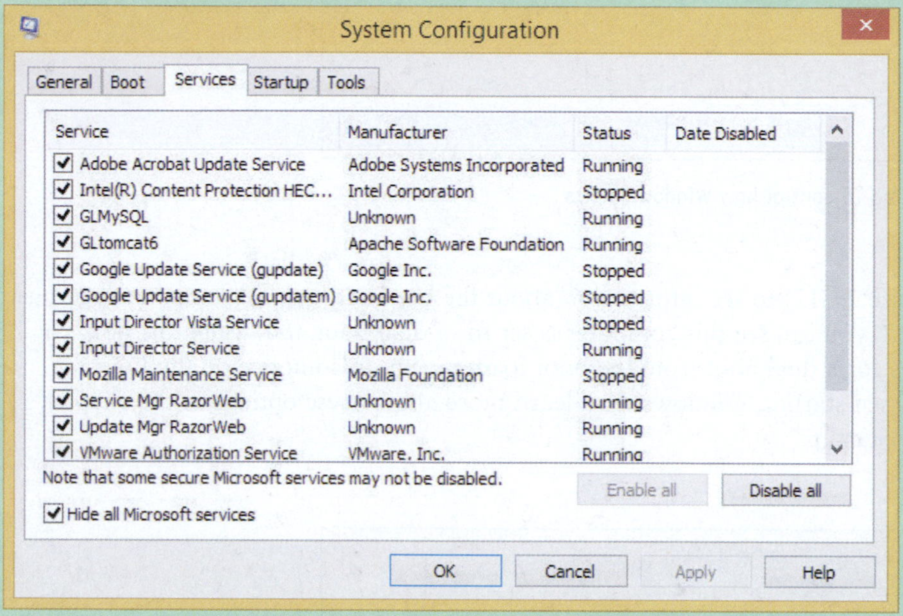

Figure 11-18 Use the Services tab of System Configuration to view and control services launched at startup

2. On the Startup tab, click **Open Task Manager**. The Task Manager window opens with the Startup tab selected (refer back to Figure 11-11). For each startup item, select it and click **Disable**. Close the Task Manager window.

3. In the System Configuration box, click the **General** tab. Notice that Selective startup is now selected. Click **Apply**. Close the System Configuration box and restart Windows.

Now you can try again to install the software in a clean boot environment. If the problem is resolved, here's how to return to a normal Windows startup:

1. Open the System Configuration box. On the General tab, click **Normal startup**. On the Services tab, uncheck **Hide all Microsoft services**. Verify that all services are now checked.

2. On the Startup tab, click **Open Task Manager**. In the Task Manager window, select each startup item and enable it. Close all windows.

The Tools tab in the System Configuration box gives you quick access to other Windows tools you might need during a troubleshooting session (see Figure 11-19).

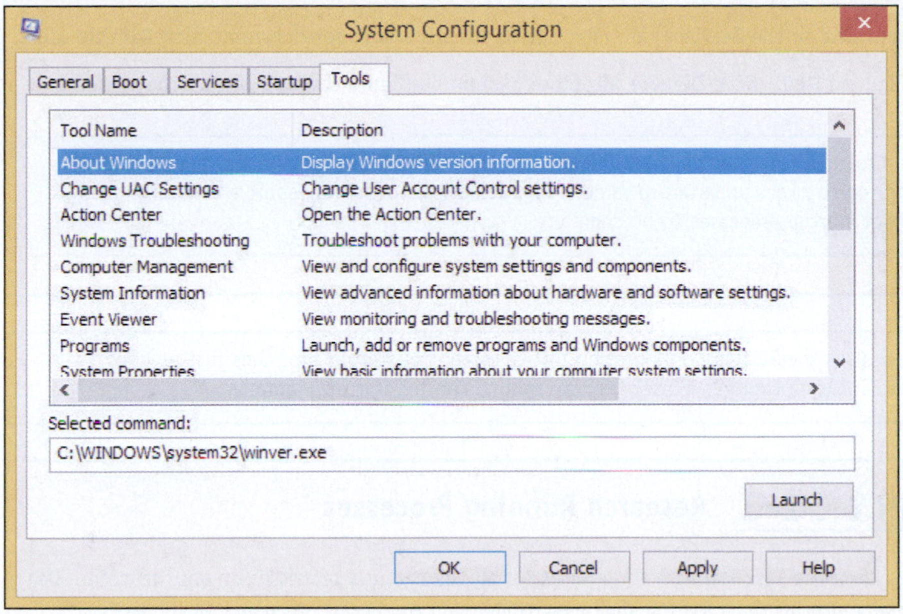

Figure 11-19 The Tools tab makes it easy to find troubleshooting tools

WINDOWS | 7 SYSTEM CONFIGURATION

A+ 220-902 1.4

Windows 8 allows you to disable and enable startup processes on the Startup tab of Task Manager. In Windows 7, the Startup tab in System Configuration is used for this same purpose (see Figure 11-20). The Startup tab can also be useful when trying to understand how a program is launched at startup because it offers the Location column. This column shows the registry key or startup folder where the startup entry is made.

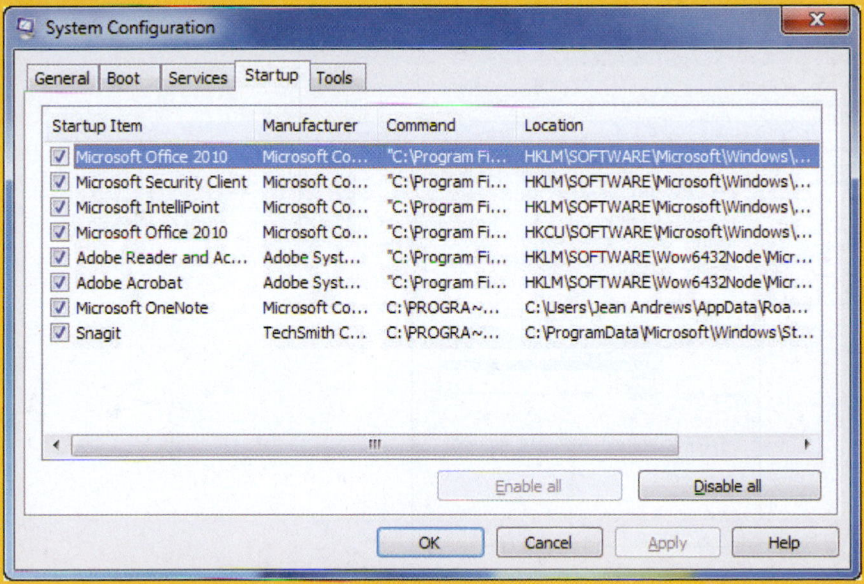

Figure 11-20 Use the Windows 7 Startup tab of System Configuration to select startup processes to enable or disable

(continues)

Here's how to use Windows 7 System Configuration to perform a clean boot:

1. Click **Start**, type **msconfig.exe** in the Search box, and then press **Enter**.
2. In the System Configuration box on the Services tab, check **Hide all Microsoft services** and click **Disable all**.
3. On the Startup tab (see Figure 11-20), click **Disable all**. Close System Configuration and restart the system.

Notes System Configuration reports only what it is programmed to look for when listing startup programs and services. It looks only in certain registry keys and startup folders, and sometimes does not report a startup process. Therefore, don't consider its list of startup processes to be complete.

OS Differences Windows Vista uses the System Configuration utility to control startup programs just as does Windows 7. In addition, Vista offers Software Explorer, a user-friendly tool to control startup programs.

Hands-On | Project 11-1 Research Running Processes

Boot to the Windows desktop and then use Task Manager to get a list of all the running processes on your machine. Use the Windows Snipping Tool to save and print the Task Manager screens showing the list of processes. Next, perform a clean boot. Which processes that were loaded normally are not loaded when the system is running after a clean boot?

SERVICES CONSOLE

A+ 220-902 1.4

The **Services console** (the program file is services.msc) is used to control the Windows and third-party services installed on a system. To launch the Services console, enter **services.msc** in the Windows 8 Run box or the Windows 7 Search box. If the Extended tab at the bottom of the window is not selected, click it (see Figure 11-21). This tab gives a description of a selected service.

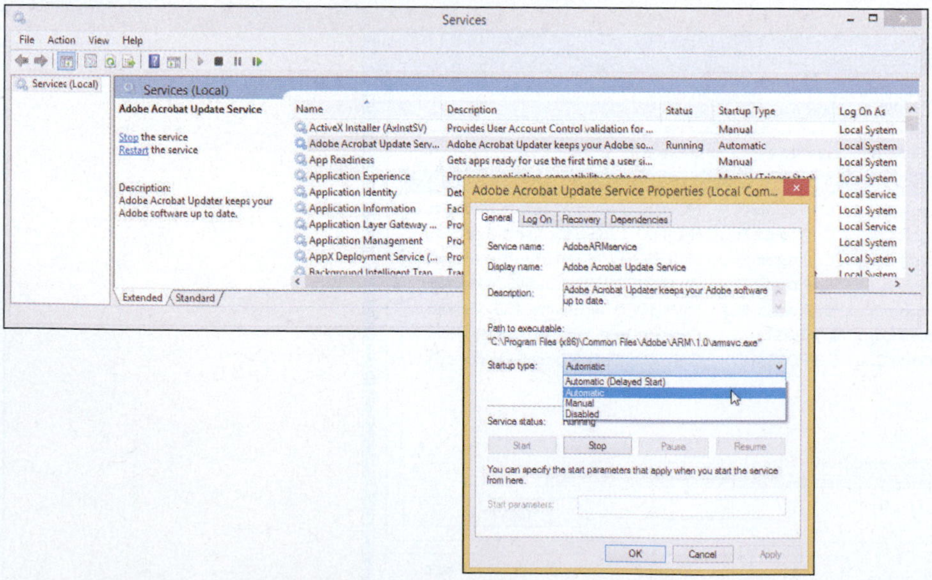

Figure 11-21 The Services console is used to manage Windows services

When you click a service to select it and the description is missing, most likely the service is a third-party service put there by an installed application and, in fact, it might be malware. To get more information about a service or to stop or start a service, right-click its name and select **Properties** from the shortcut menu. In the Properties box (see Figure 11-21), the startup types for a service are:

- *Automatic (Delayed Start).* Starts shortly after startup, after the user signs in, so as not to slow down the startup process
- *Automatic.* Starts when Windows loads
- *Manual.* Starts as needed
- *Disabled.* Cannot be started

Notes If you suspect a Windows system service is causing a problem, you can use System Configuration to disable the service. If this works, then try replacing the service file with a fresh copy from the Windows setup DVD.

COMPUTER MANAGEMENT

A+ 220-902 1.4

Computer Management (compmgmt.msc) contains several tools that can be used to manage the local computer or other computers on the network. The window is called a console because it consolidates several Windows Administrative tools. To use most of these tools, you must be signed in as an administrator, although you can view certain settings in Computer Management if you are signed in with lesser privileges.

As with most Windows tools, there are several ways to access Computer Management:

- Enter **compmgmt.msc** in the Windows 8 Run box or the Windows 7 Search box.
- For Windows 8, press **Win+X** and click **Computer Management** in the Quick Launch menu. For Windows 7, click **Start**, right-click **Computer**, and select **Manage** from the shortcut menu.
- In Control Panel, look in the **Administrative Tools** group.

11

The Computer Management window is shown in Figure 11-22. Using this window, you can access Task Scheduler, Event Viewer, Shared Folders, Local Users and Groups, Performance Monitor, Device Manager, Disk Management, and the Services console. Several tools available from the Computer Management window are covered in this chapter.

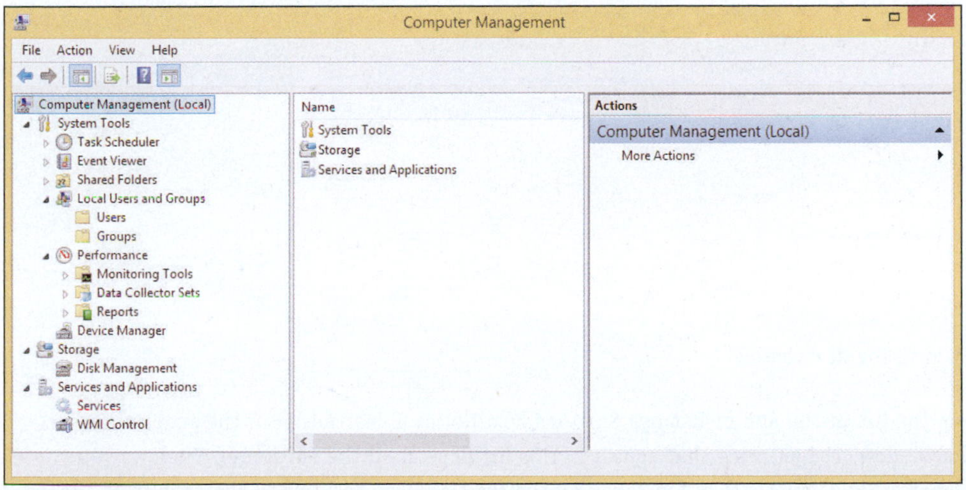

Figure 11-22 Windows Computer Management combines several Administrative tools into a single, easy-to-access window

MICROSOFT MANAGEMENT CONSOLE (MMC)

A+ 220-902 1.4

Microsoft Management Console (MMC; the program file is mmc.exe) is a Windows utility that can be used to build your own customized console windows. In a console, these individual tools are called snap-ins. A console is saved in a file with an .msc file extension, and a snap-in in a console can itself be a console. To use all the functions of MMC, you must be signed in with administrator privileges.

Notes A program that can work as a snap-in under the MMC has an .msc file extension.

APPLYING CONCEPTS CREATE A CONSOLE

A+ 220-902 1.4

If you find yourself often using a few Windows tools, consider putting them in a console stored on your desktop. Follow these steps to create a console:

1. Enter **mmc.exe** in the Windows 8 Run box or the Windows 7 Search box. Respond to the UAC box. An empty console window appears, as shown in Figure 11-23.

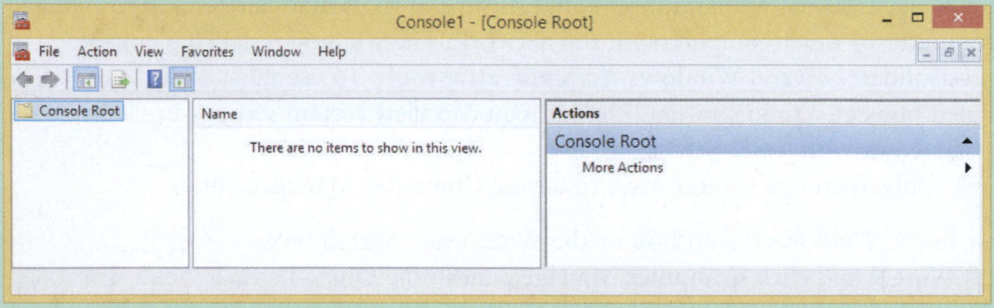

Figure 11-23 An empty console

2. Click **File** in the menu bar and then click **Add/Remove Snap-in**. The Add or Remove Snap-ins box opens, as shown on the left side of Figure 11-24.

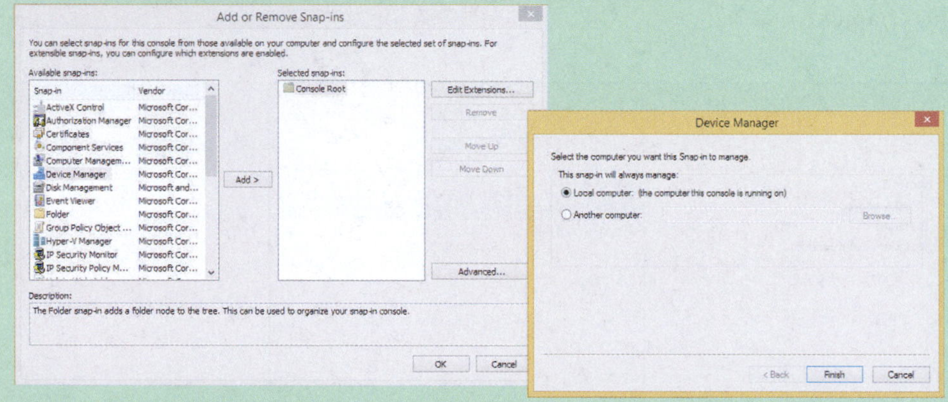

Figure 11-24 Add a snap-in to the new console

3. Select a snap-in from the list in the Add or Remove Snap-ins box. Notice a description of the snap-in appears at the bottom of the window. The snap-ins that appear in this list depend on the edition of Windows you have installed and what other components are installed on the system. Click **Add** to add the snap-in to the console.
4. If parameters for the snap-in need defining, a dialog box opens that allows you to set up these parameters. The dialog box offers different selections, depending on the snap-in being added. For example, when Device Manager is selected, a dialog box appears, asking you to select the computer that Device Manager will monitor (see the right side of Figure 11-24). Select **Local computer (the computer this console is running on)** and click **Finish**. The snap-in now appears in the list of snap-ins for this console.

5. Repeat Steps 3 and 4 to add all the snap-ins that you want to the console. When you finish, click **OK** in the Add or Remove Snap-ins box.
6. To save the console, click **File** in the menu bar and then click **Save As**. The Save As dialog box opens. A good place to save a console is the Windows desktop. Then close all windows.

Notes After you create a console, you can copy the .msc file to any computer.

Hands-On | Project 11-2 Use the Microsoft Management Console

A+
220-902
1.4

Using the Microsoft Management Console in Windows 8 or Windows 7, create a customized console. Put two snap-ins in the console: Device Manager and Event Viewer. Store your console on the Windows desktop. Copy the console to another computer and install it on the Windows desktop.

EVENT VIEWER

A+
220-902
1.1, 1.4,
4.1

11

Just about anything that happens in Windows is logged by Windows, and these logs can be viewed using Event Viewer (eventvwr.msc). You can find events such as a hardware or network failure, OS error messages, a device or service that has failed to start, or General Protection Faults, which can cause Windows to lock up or hang.

Event Viewer is a Computer Management console snap-in, and you can open it by using the Computer Management window, by entering **Event Viewer** or **Eventvwr.msc** in the Windows 8 Run box or the Windows 7 Search box, or by using the Administrative Tools group in Control Panel. The Event Viewer window is shown in Figure 11-25.

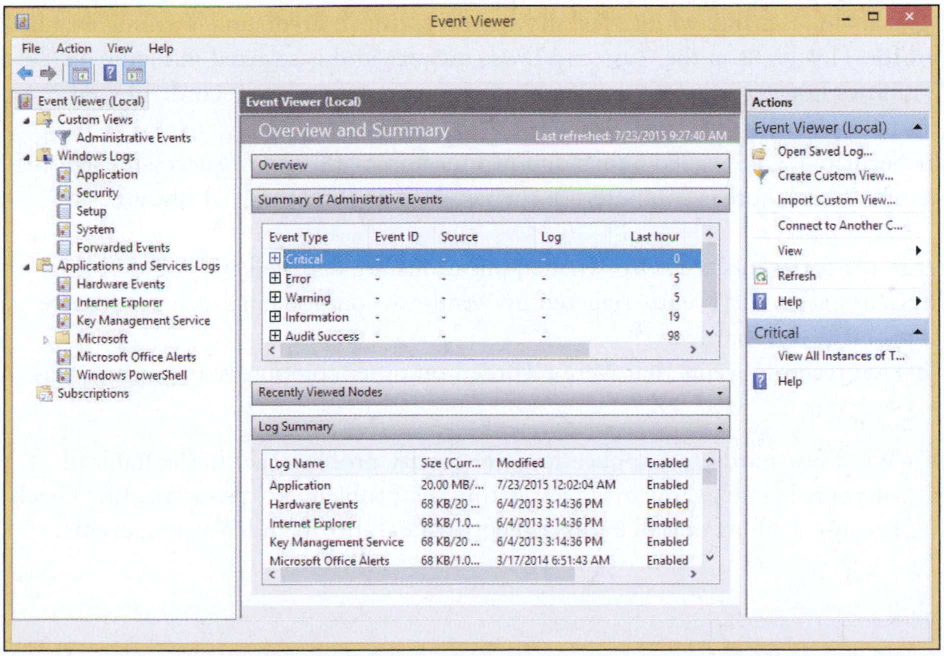

Figure 11-25 Use Event Viewer to see logs about hardware, Windows, security, and applications events

The different views of logs are listed in the left pane, and you can drill down into subcategories of these logs. First select a log in the left pane. To sort a list of events, click a column heading in the middle pane. Click an event in the middle pane to see details about the event. For example, in Figure 11-26, the Administrative Events log shows Windows had a problem loading a device driver.

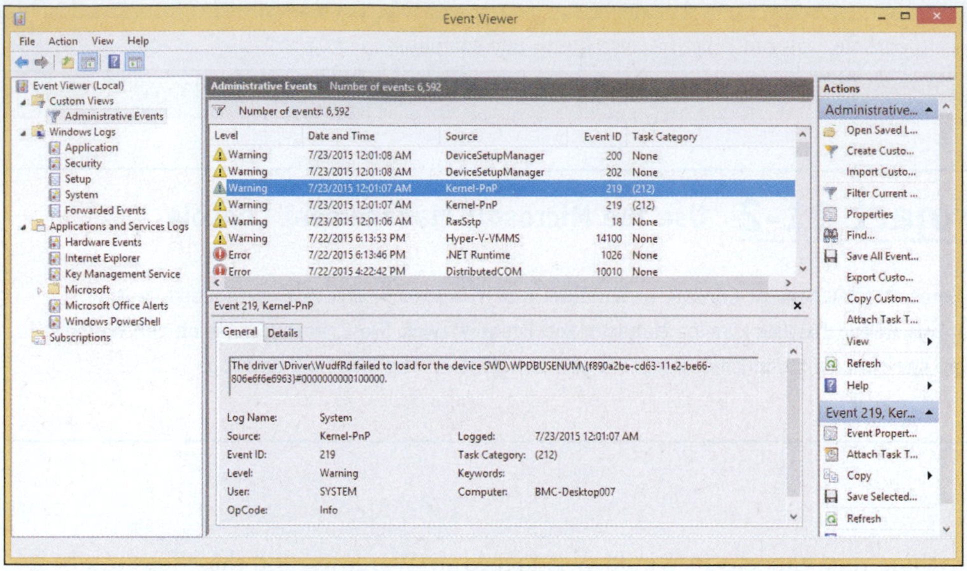

Figure 11-26 Click an event to see details about the event

The types of events are Critical, Error, Warning, Information, and Audit Success. Error events are the most important and indicate something went wrong with the system, such as a scheduled backup failed to work. Warning events indicate failure might occur in the future, and Critical events indicate a problem occurred with a critical Windows process.

Here are the views of logs that are the most useful:

- ***Administrative Events log.*** This log is a filtered log that shows only Critical, Error, and Warning events intended for the administrator. This log is in the Custom Views category and is selected in Figure 11-26.
- ***Application log.*** In the Windows Logs group, look in the Application log for events recorded by an application. This log might help you identify why an application is causing problems.
- ***Security log.*** Events in the Security log are called audits and include successful and unsuccessful sign-ins to a user account and attempts from another computer on the network to access shared resources on this computer.
- ***Setup log.*** Look in the Setup log for events recorded when applications are installed.
- ***System log.*** Look in the System log to find events triggered by Windows components, such as a device driver failing to load or a problem with hardware.
- ***Forwarded Events log.*** This log receives events that were recorded on other computers and sent to this computer.

When you first encounter a Windows, hardware, application, or security problem, get in the habit of checking Event Viewer as one of your first steps toward investigating the problem. To save time, first check the Administrative Events log because it filters out all events except Critical, Error, and Warning events.

CREATE CUSTOM LOG FILES

You can filter events and create a log of only your filtered events. Then you can save this custom view to an .evtx file, which you can use to document a problem or email to someone who is helping you troubleshoot a problem. To create a custom view, right-click any log in the left pane and select **Create Custom View** from the shortcut menu. The Create Custom View box appears (see Figure 11-27), which offers many ways to filter events.

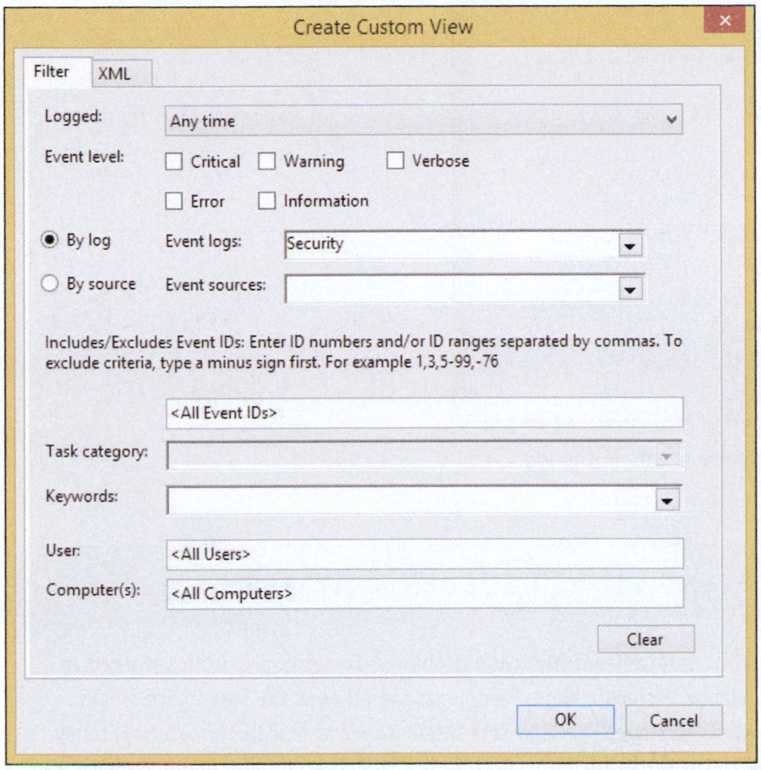

Figure 11-27 Criteria to filter events in Event Viewer for a custom view

After you select the filters, click **OK**. In the next box, name your custom view and click **OK**. Your custom view is now listed in the left pane. To save the view to an .evtx file, right-click it and click **Save All Events in Custom View As**. In the Save As box that appears, name the file and browse to where you want to save it. Then click **Save**. A good place to save an event log file is the desktop. Later, to view the log file, double-click the file name and it will open in Event Viewer.

LIMIT SIZE OF LOGS

To control the size of a log in Event Viewer, you can clear it. Right-click a log and click **Clear Log** in the shortcut menu. Before clearing the log, Event Viewer gives you a chance to save it. Be default, Event Viewer sets a maximum size for each log and overwrites older events with newer ones when the maximum size is reached. To change this setting so that you can control the maximum size of a log file and to cause the events to be archived before they are overwritten, right-click a log and select **Properties** from the log's shortcut menu. The properties box for the Application log is shown in Figure 11-28.

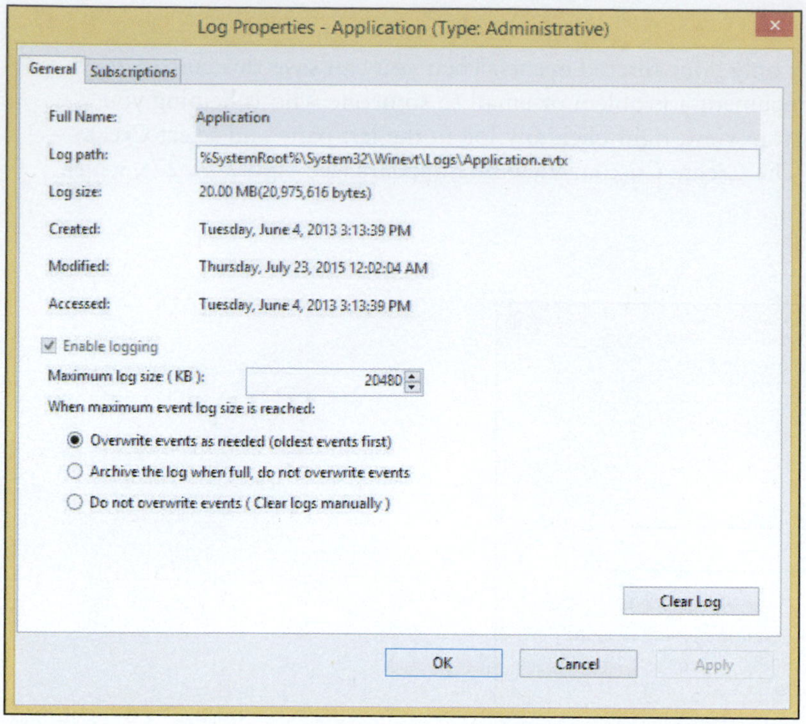

Figure 11-28 Control the size of a log file and archive events in the log

APPLYING | CONCEPTS EVENT VIEWER SOLVES A MYSTERY

A+
220-902
1.1, 1.4,
4.1

Event Viewer can be useful in solving intermittent hardware problems. For example, I once worked in an office where several people updated Microsoft Word documents stored on a file server. For weeks, people complained about these Word documents getting corrupted. We downloaded the latest patches for Windows and Microsoft Office and scanned for viruses, thinking that the problem might be with Windows or the application. Then we suspected a corrupted template file for building the Word documents. But nothing we did solved our problem of corrupted Word documents. Then one day someone thought to check Event Viewer on the file server. Event Viewer had faithfully been recording errors when writing to the hard drive. What we had suspected to be a software problem was, in fact, a failing hard drive, which was full of bad sectors. We replaced the drive and the problem went away. That day I learned the value of checking Event Viewer very early in the troubleshooting process.

Hands-On | Project 11-3 Use Event Viewer

A+
220-902
1.1, 1.4,
4.1

Event Viewer can be intimidating to use but is really nothing more than a bunch of logs to search and manipulate. If you have Microsoft Office installed, open a Word document, make some changes in it, and close it without saving your changes. Now look in **Applications and Services Logs** and **Microsoft Office Alerts**. What event is recorded about your actions?

PRINT MANAGEMENT

A+ 220-902 1.4

Windows professional and business editions offer the Print Management (printmanagement .msc) utility in the Administrative Tools group of Control Panel. (Home editions don't provide the Print Management tool.) You can use it to monitor and manage printer queues for all printers on the network. In Print Management, each computer on the network that shares a printer with other computers on the network is considered a print server.

APPLYING CONCEPTS LEARN TO USE PRINT MANAGEMENT

A+ 220-902 1.4

Follow these steps to learn to use Print Management:

1. Open **Control Panel** in Classic view, click **Administrative Tools**, and double-click **Print Management**. The Print Management window appears.
2. In the Print Servers group, drill down to your local computer and click **Printers**. The list of printers installed on your computer appears, as shown in Figure 11-29.

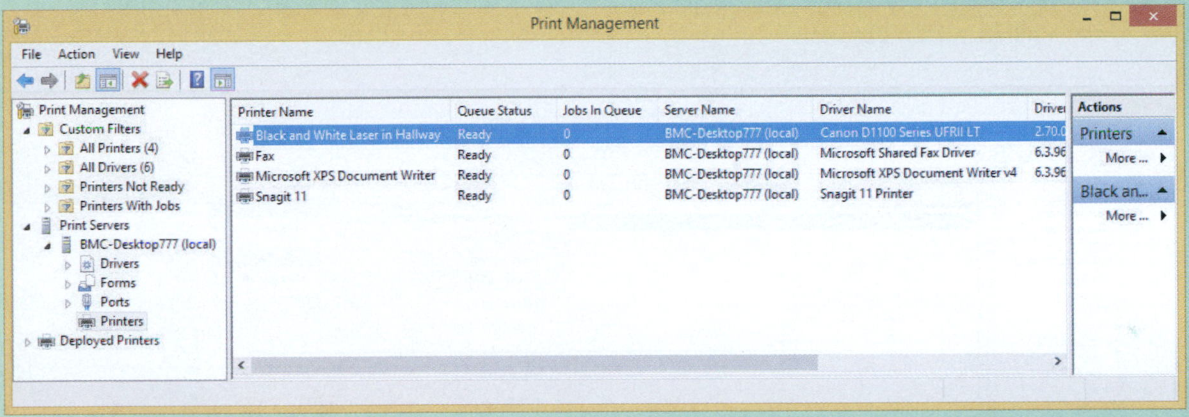

Figure 11-29 Use Print Management to monitor and manage printers on the network

3. To add other print servers to the list, right-click **Print Servers** in the left pane and click **Add/Remove Servers**. In the Add/Remove Servers box (see the left side of Figure 11-30), click **Browse**. Locate the computer (see the right side of Figure 11-30) and click **Select Server**. The computer is now listed under Add servers in the Add/Remove Servers box. Click **Add to List**. The computer is listed in the Print servers area. Click **OK** to close the Add/Remove Servers box.

(continues)

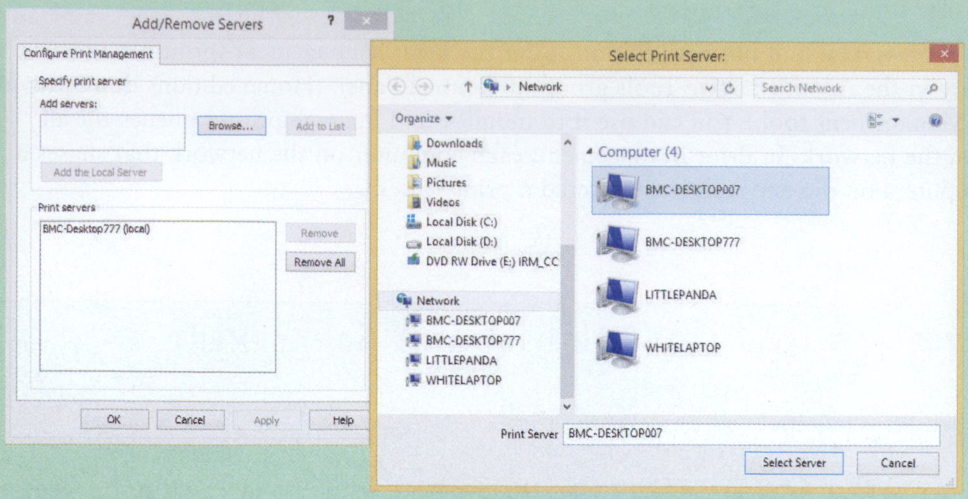

Figure 11-30 Select a print server to monitor and manage

4. The computer is now listed as a print server in the left pane of the Print Management window. Notice in Figure 11-31, you can view a computer on the network that has its printer offline and one job in the queue. Right-click this printer to see a menu with options shown in the figure that you can use to manage the printer and its printer queue.

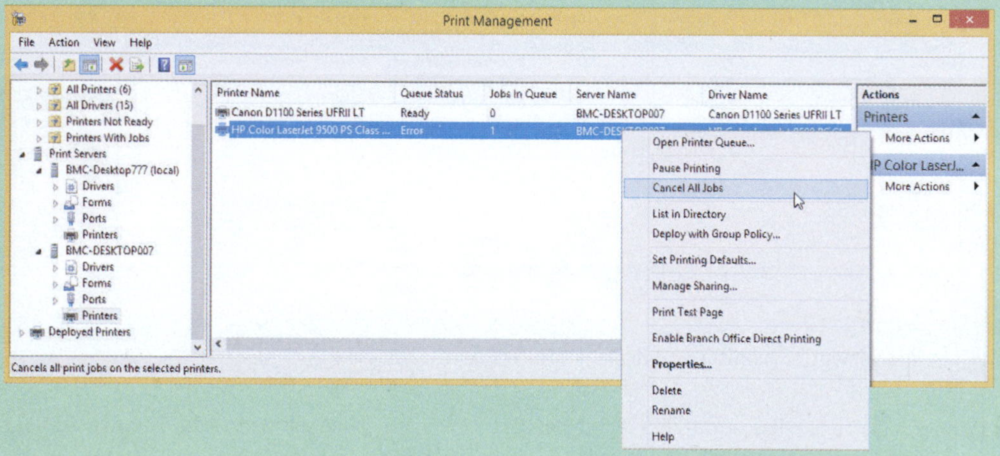

Figure 11-31 Manage print servers, printers, and printer queues on the network

TASK SCHEDULER

A+ 220-902 1.4

Windows **Task Scheduler** (taskschd.msc) is also among the Administrative Tools in Control Panel and is a Computer Management console that can be set to launch a task or program at a future time, including at startup. When applications install, they might schedule tasks to check for and download their program updates. Task Scheduler stores tasks in a file stored in the C:\Windows\System32\Tasks folder. For example, in Figure 11-32, File Explorer shows 10 scheduled tasks in the folder and other tasks are stored in two subfolders.

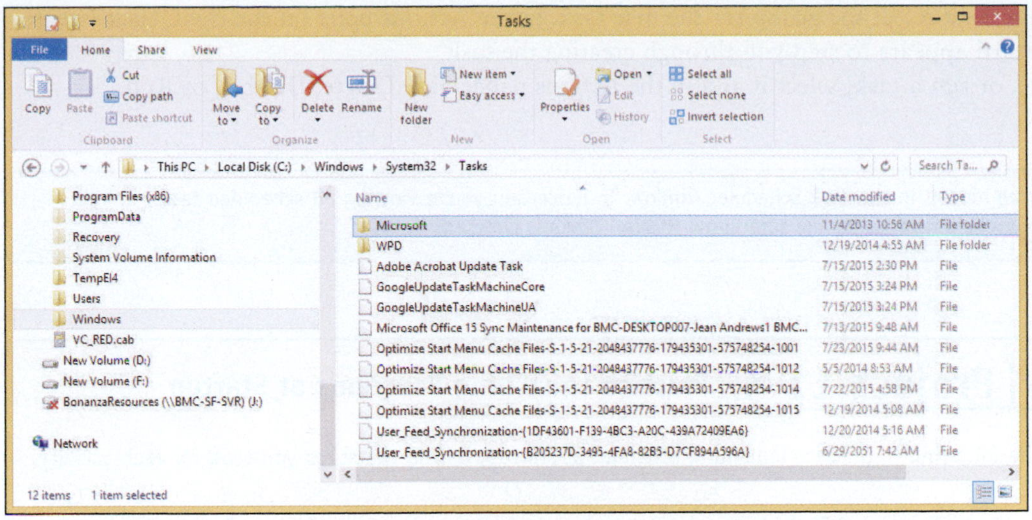

Figure 11-32 The Tasks folder contains tasks managed by Task Scheduler

To open Task Scheduler, enter **taskschd.msc** in the Windows 8 Run box or the Windows 7 Search box. Alternately, from Control Panel, double-click **Task Scheduler** in the Administrative Tools group. The Task Scheduler window is shown in Figure 11-33.

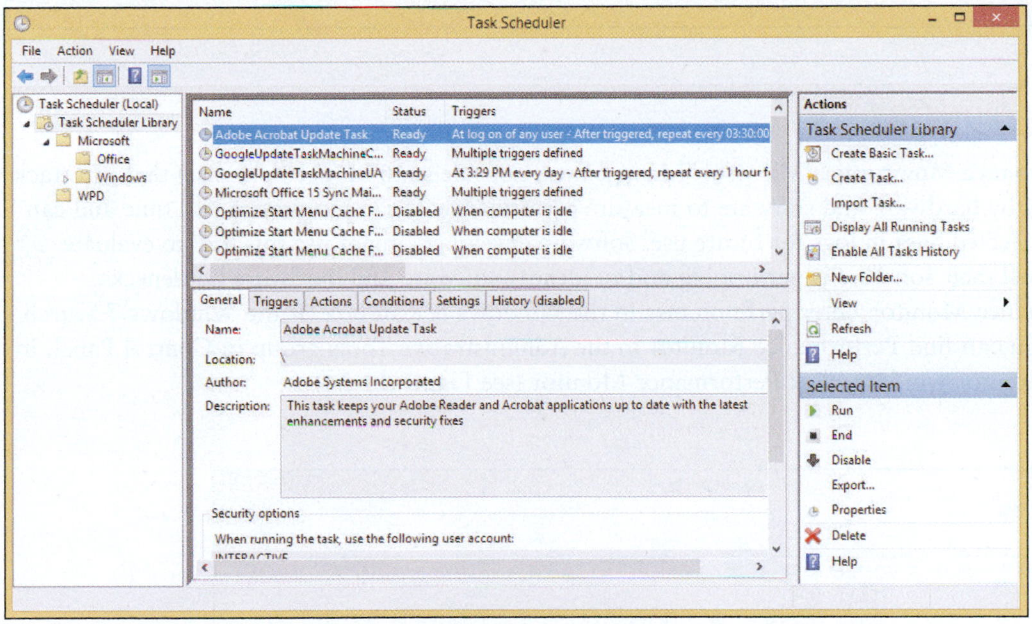

Figure 11-33 View and manage tasks from the Task Scheduler window

Here is what you need to know to use the Task Scheduler window:

- In the left pane, drill down into groups and subgroups. Notice in the left pane of Figure 11-33, the groups and subgroups match up with the folder structure in the Tasks folder of File Explorer, shown in Figure 11-32. Tasks in a group are listed in the middle pane.
- To see details about a task, including what triggers it, what actions it performs, the conditions and settings related to the task, and the history of past actions, select the task and then click the tabs in the lower-middle pane. For example, in the list of tasks shown in Figure 11-33, you can see that the Adobe Acrobat Update Task is scheduled to run when any user signs in.

- To add a new task, first select the group for the new task. In the Actions pane on the right, click **Create Basic Task**. A wizard appears to step you through creating the task.
- To delete, disable, or run a task, select it and in the Actions pane, click Delete, Disable, or Run.

> **Notes** Tasks can be hidden in the Task Scheduler window. To be certain you're viewing all scheduled tasks, unhide them. In the menu bar, click **View** and make sure **Show Hidden Tasks** is checked.

Hands-On | Project 11-4 Practice Launching Programs at Startup

A+ 220-902 1.4

Do the following to practice launching programs at startup, listing the steps you took for each activity:

1. Configure Scheduled Tasks to launch Notepad each time the computer starts and any user signs in. List the steps you took.
2. Put a shortcut in a startup folder so that any user launches a command prompt window at startup. See the appendix, "Entry Points for Windows Startup Programs," for a list of startup folders.
3. Restart the system and verify that both programs are launched. Did you receive any errors?
4. Remove the two programs from the startup process.

PERFORMANCE MONITOR

A+ 220-902 1.4, 4.1

Performance Monitor is a Microsoft Management Console snap-in (perfmon.msc) that can track activity by hardware and software to measure performance. It can monitor in real time and can save collected data in logs for future use. Software developers might use this tool to evaluate how well their software is performing and to identify software and hardware bottlenecks.

To open Performance Monitor, enter **perfmon.msc** in the Windows 8 Run box or the Windows 7 Search box. Alternately, you can find Performance Monitor in the Administrative Tools group in Control Panel. In the Performance Monitor window, click Performance Monitor (see Figure 11-34).

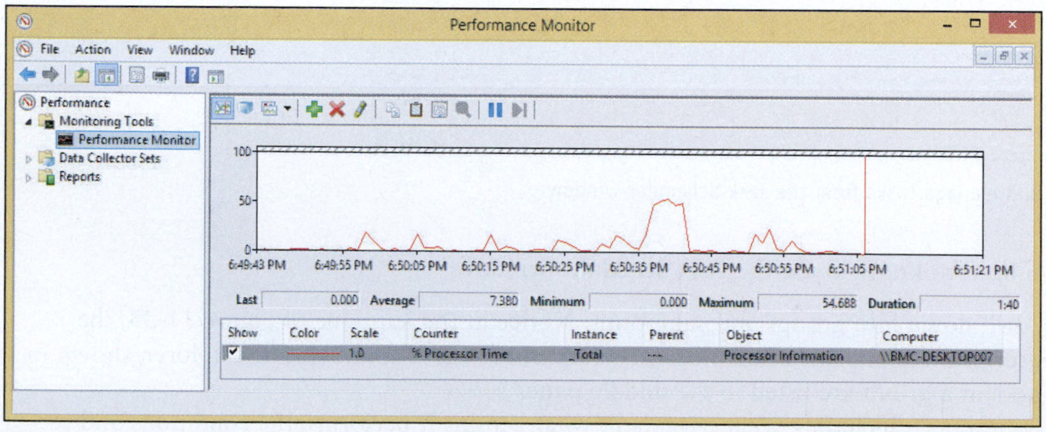

Figure 11-34 Performance Monitor uses counters to monitor various activities of hardware and software

Performance Monitor offers hundreds of counters used to examine many aspects of the system related to performance. The Windows default setting is to show the %Processor Time counter the first time you open the window (see Figure 11-34). This counter appears as a red line in the graph and tracks activity of the processor.

To keep from unnecessarily using system resources, only use the counters you really need. For example, suppose you want to track hard drive activity. You first remove the %Processor Time counter. To delete a counter, select the counter from the list so that it is highlighted and click the red **X** above the graph.

Next add two counters: the % Disk Time counter and Avg. Disk Queue Length counter in the PhysicalDisk group. The % Disk Time counter tracks the percentage of time the hard drive is in use, and the Avg. Disk Queue Length counter tracks the average number of processes waiting to use the hard drive. To add a counter, click the green **plus sign** above the graph. Then, in the Add Counters box, select a counter and click **Add**. Figure 11-35 shows the Add Counters box with two counters added. After all your counters are added, click **OK**.

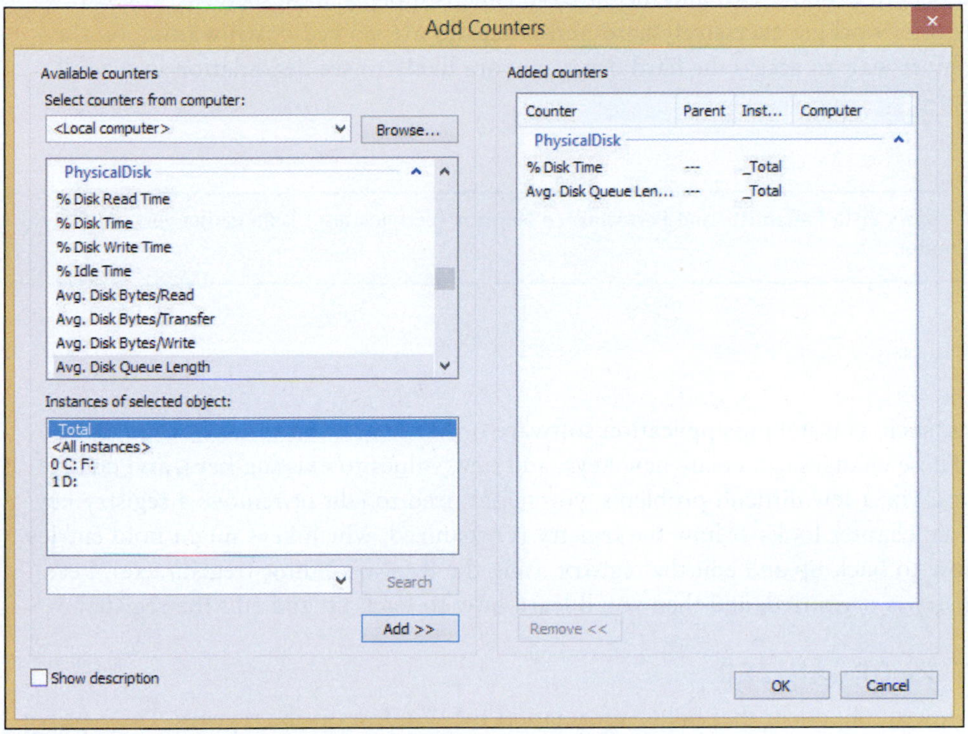

Figure 11-35 Add counters to set up what Performance Monitor tracks

Allow Performance Monitor to keep running while the system is in use, and then check the counters. The results for one system are shown in Figure 11-36. Select each counter and note the average, minimum, and maximum values for the counter.

Figure 11-36 Two counters can measure hard drive performance

If the Avg. Disk Queue Length is above two and the % Disk Time is more than 80 percent, you can conclude that the hard drive is working excessively hard and processes are slowed down waiting on the drive. Anytime a process must wait to access the hard drive, you are likely to see degradation in overall system performance.

OS Differences The Windows Vista **Reliability and Performance Monitor** (perfmon.msc) is an earlier version of Windows 8/7 Performance Monitor.

REGISTRY EDITOR

A+
220-902
1.4, 4.1

Many actions, such as installing application software or hardware, can result in changes to the registry. These changes can create new keys, add new values to existing keys, and change existing values. For a few difficult problems, you might need to edit or remove a registry key. This part of the chapter looks at how the registry is organized, which keys might hold entries causing problems, and how to back up and edit the registry using the **Registry Editor** (regedit.exe). Let's first look at how the registry is organized, and then you'll learn how to back up and edit the registry.

HOW THE REGISTRY IS ORGANIZED

The most important Windows component that holds information for Windows is the registry. The **registry** is a database designed with a treelike structure (called a hierarchical database) that contains configuration information for Windows, users, software applications, and installed hardware devices. During startup, Windows builds the registry in memory and keeps it there until Windows shuts down. During startup, after the registry is built, Windows reads from it to obtain information to complete the startup process. After Windows is loaded, it continually reads from many of the subkeys in the registry.

Windows builds the registry from the current hardware configuration and from information it takes from these files:

- Five files stored in the C:\Windows\System32\config folder; these files are called hives, and they are named the SAM (Security Accounts Manager), SECURITY, SOFTWARE, SYSTEM, and DEFAULT hives. (Each hive is backed up with a log file and a backup file, which are also stored in the C:\Windows\System32\config folder.)
- C:\Users*username*\Ntuser.dat file, which holds the preferences and settings of the currently signed-in user.

After the registry is built in memory, it is organized into five high-level keys (see Figure 11-37). Each key can have subkeys, and subkeys can have more subkeys and can be assigned one or more values. The way data is organized in the hive files is different from the way it is organized in registry keys. Figure 11-38 shows the relationship between registry keys and hives. For example, in the figure, notice that the HKEY_CLASSES_ROOT key contains data that comes from the SOFTWARE and DEFAULT hive, and some of this data is also stored in the larger HKEY_LOCAL_MACHINE key.

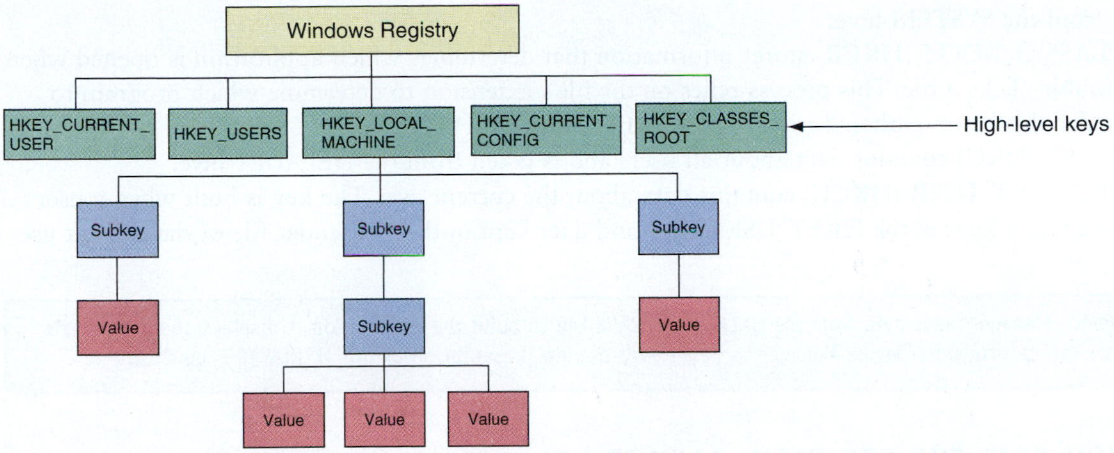

Figure 11-37 The Windows registry is logically organized in five keys with subkeys

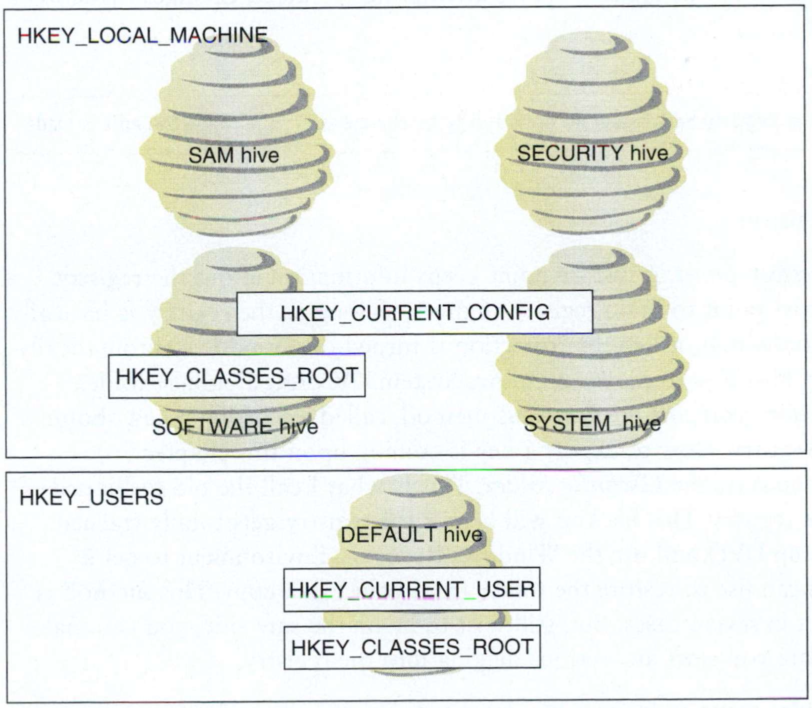

Figure 11-38 The relationship between registry keys and hives

Here are the five keys, including where they get their data and their purposes:

- HKEY_LOCAL_MACHINE (HKLM) is the most important key and contains hardware, software, and security data. The data is taken from four hives: the SAM hive, the SECURITY hive, the SOFTWARE hive, and the SYSTEM hive. In addition, the HARDWARE subkey of HKLM is built when the registry is first loaded, based on data collected about the current hardware configuration.
- HKEY_CURRENT_CONFIG (HKCC) contains information that identifies each hardware device installed on the computer. Some of the data is gathered from the current hardware configuration when the registry is first loaded into memory. Other data is taken from the HKLM key, which got its data primarily from the SYSTEM hive.
- HKEY_CLASSES_ROOT (HKCR) stores information that determines which application is opened when the user double-clicks a file. This process relies on the file's extension to determine which program to load. Data for this key is gathered from the HKLM key and the HKCU key.
- HKEY_USERS (HKU) contains data about all users and is taken from the DEFAULT hive.
- HKEY_CURRENT_USER (HKCU) contains data about the current user. The key is built when a user signs in using data kept in the HKEY_USERS key and data kept in the Ntuser.dat file of the current user.

Notes Device Manager reads data from the HKLM\HARDWARE key to build the information it displays about hardware configurations. You can consider Device Manager to be an easy-to-view presentation of this HARDWARE key data.

BEFORE YOU EDIT THE REGISTRY, BACK IT UP!

When you need to edit the registry, if possible, make the change from the Windows tool that is responsible for the key—for example, by using the Programs and Features applet in Control Panel. If that doesn't work and you must edit the registry, always back up the registry before attempting to edit it. Changes made to the registry are implemented immediately.

Caution There is no undo feature in the Registry Editor, and no opportunity to change your mind once the edit is made.

Here are the ways to back up the registry:

- *Use System Protection to create a restore point.* A restore point keeps information about the registry. You can restore the system to a restore point to undo registry changes, as long as the registry is basically intact and not too corrupted. Also know that, if System Protection is turned on, Windows automatically makes a daily backup of the registry hive files to the C:\Windows\System32\Config\RegBack folder.
- *Back up a single registry key just before you edit the key.* This method, called exporting a key, should always be used before you edit the registry. How to export a key is coming up in this chapter.
- *Make an extra copy of the C:\Windows\System32\config folder.* This is what I call the old-fashioned shotgun approach to backing up the registry. This backup will help if the registry gets totally trashed. You can boot from the Windows setup DVD and use the Windows Recovery Environment to get a command prompt window that you can use to restore the folder from your extra copy. This method is drastic and not recommended except in severe cases. But, still, just to be on the safe side, you can make an extra copy of this folder just before you start any serious digging into the registry.

In some situations, such as when you're going to make some drastic changes to the registry, you'll want to play it safe and use more than one backup method. Extra registry backups are always a good thing! Now let's look at how to back up an individual key in the registry, and then you'll learn how to edit the registry.

Backing Up and Restoring Individual Keys in the Registry

A less time-consuming method of backing up the registry is to back up a particular key that you plan to edit. However, know that if the registry gets corrupted, having a backup of only a particular key most likely will not help you much when trying a recovery. Also, although you could use this technique to back up the entire registry or an entire tree within the registry, it is not recommended.

To back up a key along with its subkeys in the registry, follow these steps:

1. Open the Registry Editor. To do that, enter **regedit** in the Windows 8 Run box or the Windows 7 Search box and respond to the UAC box. Figure 11-39 shows the Registry Editor with the five main keys and several subkeys listed. Click the triangles on the left to see subkeys. When you select a subkey, such as KeyboardClass in the figure, the names of the values in that subkey are displayed in the right pane along with the data assigned to each value.

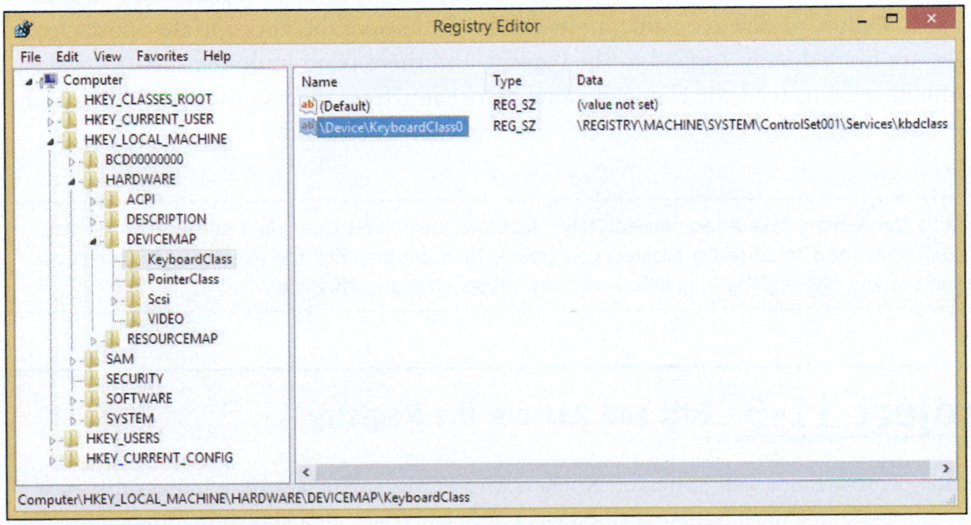

Figure 11-39 The Registry Editor showing the five main keys, subkeys, values, and data

> **Notes** The full path to a selected key displays in the status bar at the bottom of the editor window. If the status bar is missing, click **View** in the menu bar and make sure **Status Bar** is checked.

2. Suppose we want to back up the registry key that contains a list of installed software, which is HKLM\SOFTWARE\Microsoft\Windows\CurrentVersion\Uninstall. (HKLM stands for HKEY_LOCAL_MACHINE.) First click the appropriate triangles to navigate to the key. Next, right-click the key and select **Export** from the shortcut menu, as shown in Figure 11-40. The Export Registry File dialog box appears.

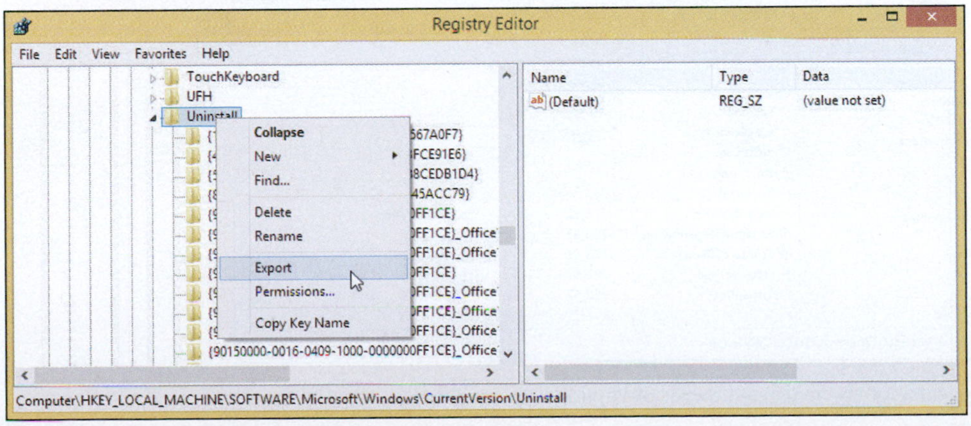

Figure 11-40 Using the Registry Editor, you can back up a key and its subkeys with the Export command

3. Select the location to save the export file and name the file. A convenient place to store an export file while you edit the registry is the desktop. Click **Save** when done. The file saved will have a .reg file extension.
4. You can now edit the key. Later, if you need to undo your changes, exit the Registry Editor and double-click the saved export file. The key and its subkeys saved in the export file will be restored. After you're done with an export file, delete it so that no one accidentally double-clicks it and reverts the registry to an earlier setting.

Editing the Registry

Before you edit the registry, you should use one or more of the four backup methods just discussed so that you can restore it if something goes wrong. To edit the registry, open the **Registry Editor** (**regedit.exe**), and locate and select the key in the left pane of the Registry Editor, which will display the values stored in this key in the right pane. To edit, rename, or delete a value, right-click it and select the appropriate option from the shortcut menu. Changes are immediately applied to the registry and there is no undo feature. (However, Windows or applications might need to read the changed value before it affects their operations.) To search the registry for keys, values, and data, click **Edit** in the menu bar and then click **Find**.

Caution Changes made to the registry take effect immediately. Therefore, take extra care when editing the registry. If you make a mistake and don't know how to correct a problem you create, then double-click the exported key to recover. When you double-click an exported key, the registry is updated with the values stored in this key.

Hands-On Project 11-5 Edit and Restore the Registry

A+ 220-902 1.4, 4.1

When you install Windows on a new computer, Windows setup gives you opportunity to enter the registered owner and registered organization of the computer. Practice editing and restoring the registry by doing the following to change the registered owner name:

1. In the Windows 8 Run box or the Windows 7 Search box, enter **winver.exe**, which displays the About Windows box. Who is the registered owner and registered organization of your computer?
2. Using the Registry Editor, export the registry key HKEY_LOCAL_MACHINE\SOFTWARE\Microsoft\Windows NT\CurrentVersion to an export file stored on the desktop.
3. With the HKEY_LOCAL_MACHINE\SOFTWARE\Microsoft\Windows NT\CurrentVersion key selected in the left pane, double-click **RegisteredOwner** value in the right pane. The Edit String box appears (see Figure 11-41). Change the Value data, which is highlighted in the box and click **OK**. Close the Registry Editor window.

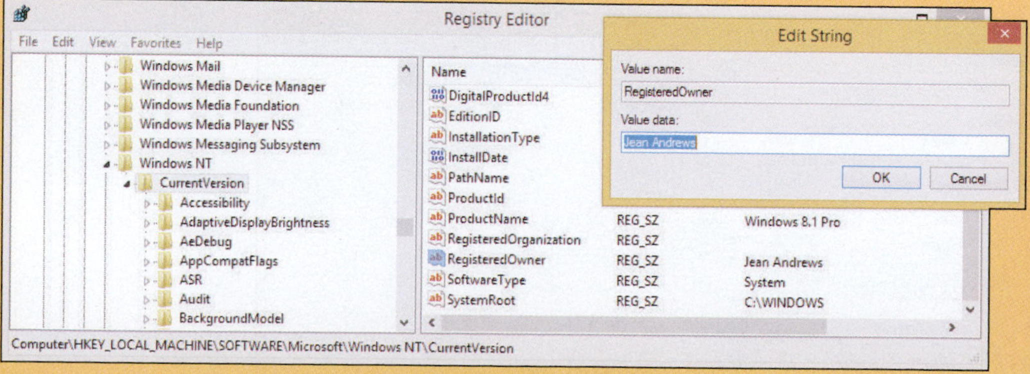

Figure 11-41 Change the name of the registered owner of Windows

4. Use the **winver** command again to display the About Windows box. Did the new name show as the registered owner? Close the box.
5. To restore the Value data to its original name, double-click the exported key on your desktop. Once again, use the **winver** command to display the About Windows box and verify the original name is restored. Close the box.
6. Delete the exported registry key stored on the desktop.

From these directions, you can see that changes made to the registry take effect immediately. Therefore, take extra care when editing the registry. If you make a mistake and don't know how to correct a problem you create, then you can restore the key that you exported by exiting the Registry Editor and double-clicking the exported key.

DISPLAY SETTINGS AND GRAPHICS SOFTWARE

A+
220-902
1.1, 1.5,
4.1

Use the Display applet in Control Panel to manage display settings. In Control Panel, open the Display applet and the Display window shown in Figure 11-42 appears.

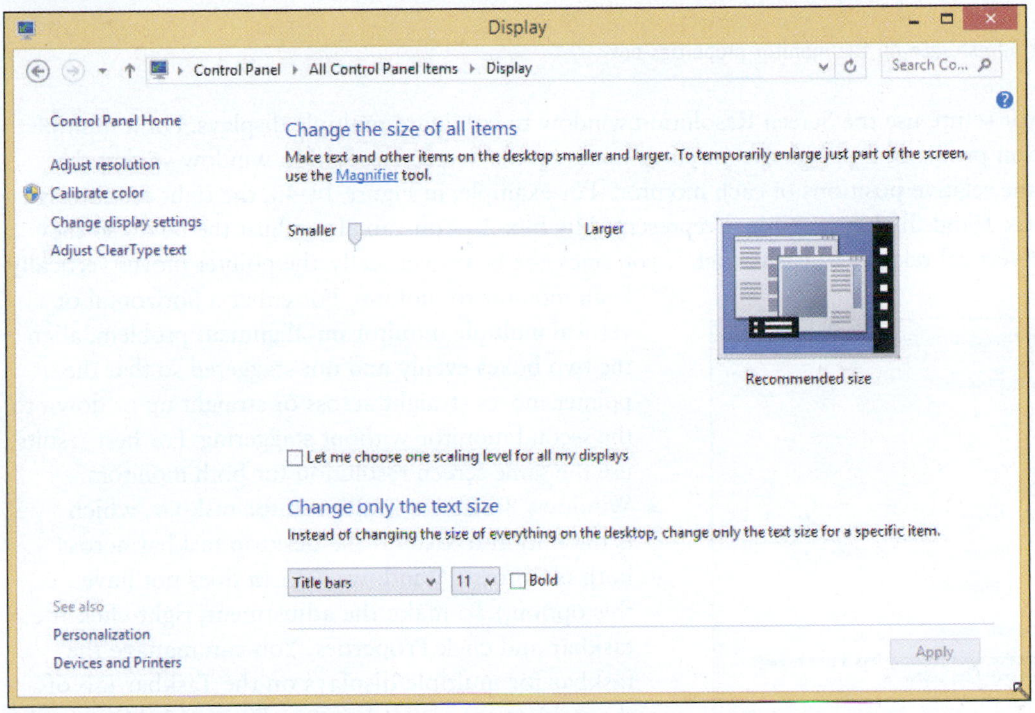

Figure 11-42 Adjust display settings

Here are a few basic display settings:

- To adjust color depth, click **Calibrate color** on the Display window and follow directions on screen.
- To adjust **resolution** (the number of horizontal and vertical pixels used to build one screen), click Adjust resolution. On the Screen Resolution window (see the right side of Figure 11-43), select the highest or recommended resolution. The recommended resolution is usually the **native resolution**, which is the optimal resolution the monitor was designed to support.

- The refresh rate is the number of times the monitor refreshes the screen in one second. To set the rate, click **Advanced settings** on the Screen Resolution window. The video adapter properties box appears. Click the **Monitor** tab and select the highest value available under Screen refresh rate (see Figure 11-43).

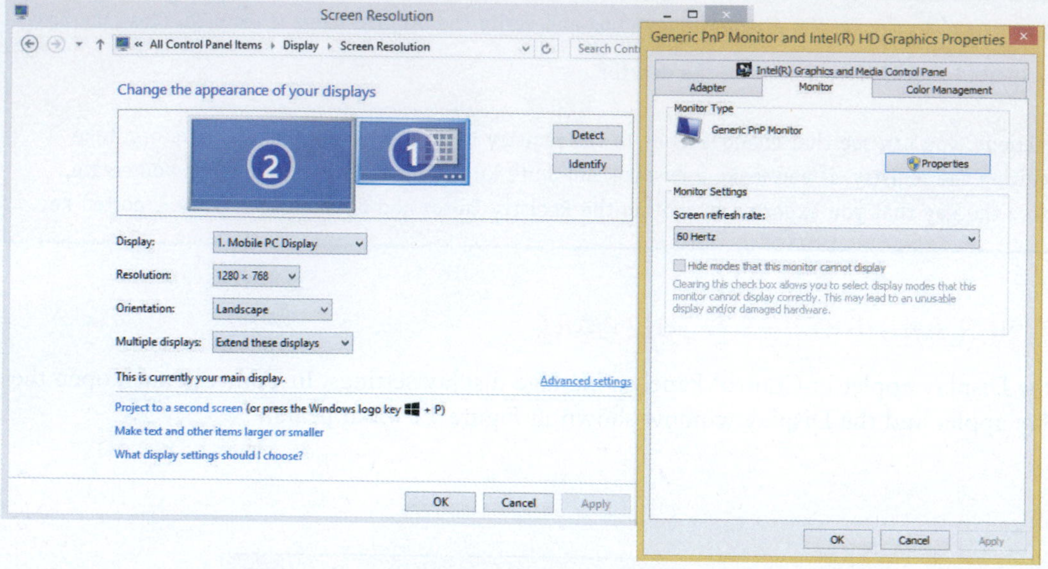

Figure 11-43 Adjust refresh rate on the monitor properties box

- For a dual-monitor setup, use the Screen Resolution window to configure multiple displays. For a multiple monitor orientation problem, drag the two monitor boxes on the Screen Resolution window so that the boxes represent the relative positions of each monitor. (For example, in Figure 11-43, the right monitor is represented by box 1 and the left monitor is represented by box 2.) You can also adjust the boxes so they are horizontal or vertical relative to each other. If you stack the boxes vertically, the pointer moves vertically from monitor to monitor. For either a horizontal or vertical multiple monitor misalignment problem, align the two boxes evenly and not staggered so that the pointer moves straight across or straight up or down to the second monitor without staggering. For best results, use the same screen resolution for both monitors.
- Windows 8 offers a multimonitor taskbar, which is the option to extend the desktop taskbar across both monitors. (Windows 7/Vista does not have this option.) To make the adjustment, right-click the taskbar and click **Properties**. You can manage the taskbar for multiple displays on the Taskbar tab of the taskbar properties box (see Figure 11-44).

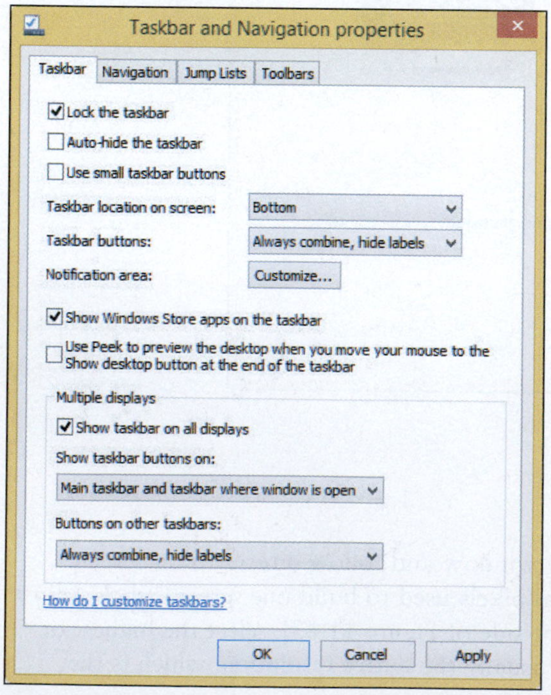

Figure 11-44 Use the taskbar properties box to manage the taskbar on multiple displays

Recall from the chapter, "Installing Windows," that Windows requires the video adapter and drivers support DirectX 9. DirectX is a Microsoft software development tool that software developers can use to write multimedia applications, such as games, video-editing software, and computer-aided design software. The video firmware on the video card or motherboard chipset can interpret DirectX commands to build 3D.

If an application, such as a game or desktop publishing app that relies heavily on graphics is not performing well or giving errors, the problem might be the version of DirectX the system is using. You can use the dxdiag.exe command to display information about hardware and diagnose problems with DirectX. To use the command, enter **dxdiag.exe** in the Windows 8 Run box or the Windows 7 Search box. The first time you use the command, a message box appears asking if you want to check if your drivers are digitally signed. Then the opening window shown in Figure 11-45 appears. Look for the version of DirectX installed (version 11 in the figure).

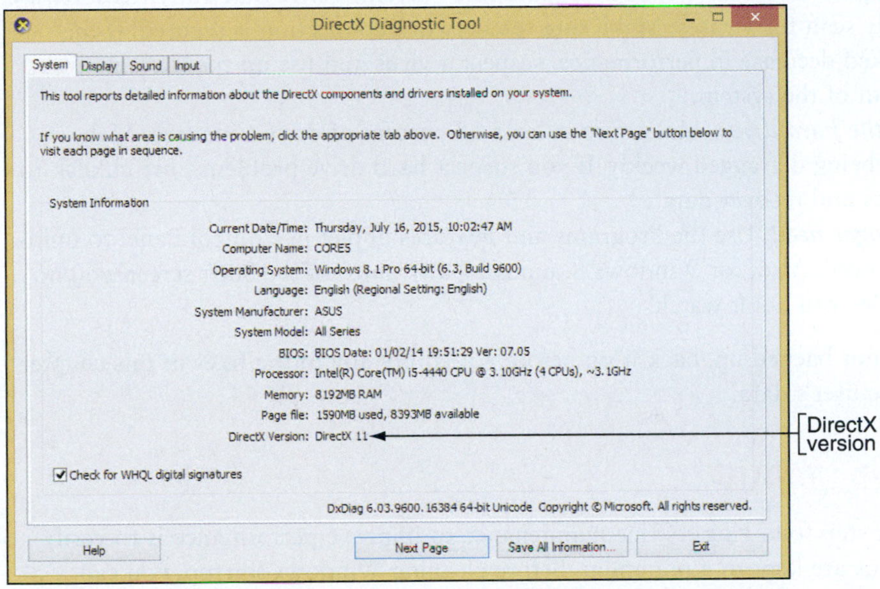

Figure 11-45 The DirectX Diagnostic tool reports information about DirectX components

To find out the latest version of DirectX published by Microsoft, go to *www.microsoft.com* and search on "DirectX End-User Runtime Web Installer." You can use a link on the page to download and install a new version of DirectX.

Now let's turn our attention to the step-by-step procedures using the tools you just learned about to improve Windows performance.

IMPROVING WINDOWS PERFORMANCE

A+ 220-902 1.1, 4.1

In this part of the chapter, you learn to search for problems affecting performance and to clean up the Windows startup process. These step-by-step procedures go beyond the routine maintenance tasks you learned about in the chapter, "Maintaining Windows." We're assuming Windows starts with no errors. If you are having trouble loading Windows, it's best to address the error first rather than to use the tools described here to improve performance. How to handle errors that keep Windows from starting is covered in the chapter, "Troubleshooting Windows Startup."

★ A+ Exam Tip The A+ 220-902 exam expects you to know how to troubleshoot and solve problems with slow system performance.

Now let's look at five steps you can take to improve Windows performance.

STEP 1: PERFORM ROUTINE MAINTENANCE

A+
220-902
4.1

It might seem pretty mundane, but the first things you need to do to improve performance of a sluggish Windows system are the routine maintenance tasks that you learned in the chapter, "Maintaining Windows." These tasks are summarized here:

- ***Verify critical Windows settings.*** Make sure Windows updates are current. Verify that antivirus software is updated and set to routinely scan for viruses. Make sure the network connection is secured. If the system is experiencing a marked decrease in performance, suspect a virus and use up-to-date antivirus software to perform a full scan of the system.
- ***Clean up, defrag, and check the hard drive.*** Make sure at least 15 percent of drive C: is free. Make sure a magnetic hard drive is being defragged weekly. If you suspect hard drive problems, use chkdsk to check the hard drive for errors and recover data.
- ***Uninstall software you no longer need.*** Use the Programs and Features applet in Control Panel to uninstall programs you no longer need. Also, for Windows 8, uninstall any apps on the Start screen you no longer use and turn off live tiles you don't watch.

As always, if valuable data is not backed up, back it up before you apply any of the fixes in this chapter. You don't want to risk losing the user's data.

STEP 2: CLEAN WINDOWS STARTUP

A+
220-902
4.1

The most important step following routine maintenance to improve performance is to verify that startup programs are kept to a minimum. Before cleaning Windows startup, you can perform a clean boot to set a benchmark for the time it takes to start Windows when only the bare minimum of programs are launched.

OBSERVE PERFORMANCE IN A CLEAN BOOT

To find out if programs and services are slowing down Windows startup, perform a clean boot, which was described earlier in the chapter, and watch to see if performance improves. Do the following:

1. Use a stopwatch or a watch with a second hand to time a normal startup from the moment you press the power button until the wait icon on the Windows desktop disappears.
2. Time the boot again, this time using a clean boot.

If the difference is significant, follow the steps in this part of the chapter to reduce Windows startup to essentials. If the performance problem still exists after a clean boot, you can assume that the problem is with hardware or Windows settings and you can proceed to *Step 3: Check If the Hardware Can Support the OS.*

INVESTIGATE AND ELIMINATE STARTUP PROGRAMS

To speed up startup, search for unnecessary startup programs you can eliminate. Tools that can help are System Configuration (msconfig.exe), startup folders, and Task Manager. Follow these steps to investigate startup:

1. Open the **Startup** tab in Windows 8 Task Manager or the **Startup** tab in Windows 7 System Configuration. In the list of startup items, look for a specific startup program you don't want. If you're not sure of the purpose of a program, for Windows 8, right-click the program and click **Search online** in the shortcut menu. (For Windows 7, scroll to the right in the Command column to see the location and name of the startup program file and use that information for a web search.) Then search the web for information on this program. Be careful to use only reliable sites for credible information.

Caution A word of caution is important here: Many websites will tell you a legitimate process is malicious so that you will download and use their software to get rid of the process. However, their software is likely to be adware or spyware that you don't want. Make sure you can trust a site before you download from it or take its advice.

2. If you want to find out if disabling a startup entry gives problems or improves performance, temporarily disable it using Windows 8 Task Manager or Windows 7 System Configuration. To permanently disable a startup item, it's best to uninstall the software or remove the entry from a startup folder. See the appendix, "Entry Points for Windows Startup Processes," for a list of startup folders.

Notes The startup folder for all users is hidden by default. In the chapter, "Survey of Windows Features and Support Tools," you learned how to unhide folders that are hidden.

3. As you research startup processes, Task Manager can tell you what processes are currently running. Open Task Manager and select the **Processes**. If you see a process and want to know its program file location, in Windows 8, right-click the process and click **Open file location**. File Explorer opens at the program file's location.

OS Differences For Windows 7, to find out the file location, click **View** and click **Select Columns**. In the Select Process Page Columns, check **Image Path Name** and click **OK**. The Image Path Name column is added to the Processes tab.

For extremely slow systems that need a more drastic fix, set Windows for a clean boot. Then restart the system and see what problems you get into with a program disabled that you really need. Then enable just the ones you decide you need.

Regardless of the method you use, be sure to restart the system after each change and note what happens. Do you get an error message? Does a device or application not work? If so, you have probably disabled a service or program you need.

Has performance improved? If performance does not improve by disabling services or startup programs, go back and enable them again. If no non-Microsoft service or startup program caused the problem, then you can assume the problem is caused by a Microsoft service or startup program. Start disabling them one at a time.

Caution You might be tempted to disable all Microsoft services. If you do so, you are disabling Networking, Event Logging, Error Reporting, Windows Firewall, Windows Installer, Windows Backup, Print Spooler, Windows Update, System Protection, and other important services. These services should be disabled only when testing for performance problems and then immediately enabled when the test is finished. Also, know that if you disable the Volume Shadow Copy service, all restore points kept on the system will be lost. If you intend to use System Restore to fix a problem with the system, don't disable this service. If you are not sure what a service does, read its description in the Services console before you change its status.

Remember that you don't want to permanently leave System Configuration or Task Manager in control of startup. After you have used these two tools to identify the problem, use other tools to permanently remove a service or program from startup that is causing a problem. Use the Services console to disable a service, use the Programs and Features window to uninstall software, and remove program files from startup folders. After the problem is fixed, return System Configuration and/or Task Manager to a normal startup.

Don't forget to restart the computer after making a change to verify that all is well.

CHECK FOR UNWANTED SCHEDULED TASKS

When applications install, they often schedule tasks to check for and download their program updates, and malware sometimes hides as a scheduled task. Scheduled tasks might be unnecessary and can slow a system down. The best way to uninstall a scheduled task is to uninstall the software that is responsible for the task. Open the Task Scheduler window and search through tasks looking for those you think are unnecessary or causing trouble. Research the software the task works with and then you might decide to uninstall the software or disable the task.

Don't forget to restart the system to make sure all is well before you move on.

MONITOR THE STARTUP PROCESS

Now that you have the startup process clean, you will want to keep it that way. You can use several third-party tools to monitor any changes to startup. A good one is WinPatrol by Ruiware (*www.winpatrol.com*). Download and install the free version of the program to run in the background to monitor all sorts of things, including changes to the registry, startup processes, Internet Explorer settings, and system files. In Figure 11-46, you can see how WinPatrol gave an alert when it detected malware about to register itself as a service to launch at startup. WinPatrol displays a little black Scotty dog in the notification area of the taskbar to indicate it's running in the background and guarding your system. Also, many antivirus programs monitor the startup process and inform you when changes are made.

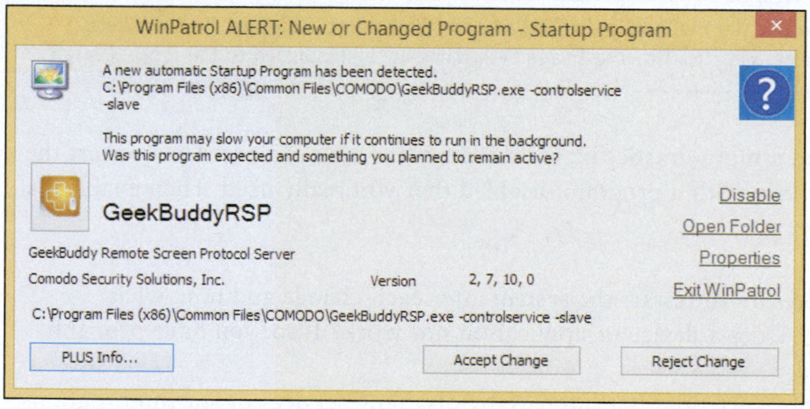

Source: Ruiware WinPatrol

Figure 11-46 WinPatrol by Ruiware alerts you when a program is making a system change

Hands-On | Project 11-6 Monitor Startup Items with WinPatrol

1. Using Task Manager and/or System Configuration, disable all the non-Windows startup items and services. Restart your computer.
2. Download and install WinPatrol from *www.winpatrol.com*.
3. Using Task Manager and/or System Configuration, enable all of the disabled startup items and services and restart the computer.
4. Are the startup programs and services able to start? What messages are displayed on the screen?

STEP 3: CHECK IF THE HARDWARE CAN SUPPORT THE OS

A+
220-902
4.1

The system might be slow because the OS does not have the hardware resources it needs. Use System Information (msinfo32.exe) to find the model and speed of the installed processor and hard drive and the amount of memory installed. Compare all these values with the minimum and recommended requirements for Windows listed in the chapter, "Installing Windows."

If you suspect that the processor, hard drive, or memory is a bottleneck, use Performance Monitor to get more information. If the bottleneck appears to be graphics, the problem might be solved by updating the graphics drivers or video adapter.

If you find that the system is slow because of a hardware component, discuss the situation with the user. You might be able to upgrade the hardware or install another OS that is compatible with the hardware that is present. Upgrading from Windows 7 to Windows 8.1 can often improve performance in a computer that has slow hardware components. Better still, perform a clean installation of Windows 8.1 so that you get a fresh start with installed applications, plug-ins, and background services that might be slowing down the system.

STEP 4: CHECK FOR A HISTORY OF PROBLEMS

A+
220-902
4.1

If you have the opportunity to interview the user, try to identify when the slow performance problem began. You can then use the Action Center and Reliability Monitor to find out what changes were made to the system around that time and what other problems occurred. Open Control Panel in Classic view and then open **Action Center**. In the Action Center, expand the **Maintenance** group and click **View reliability history**. The Reliability Monitor opens (see Figure 11-47).

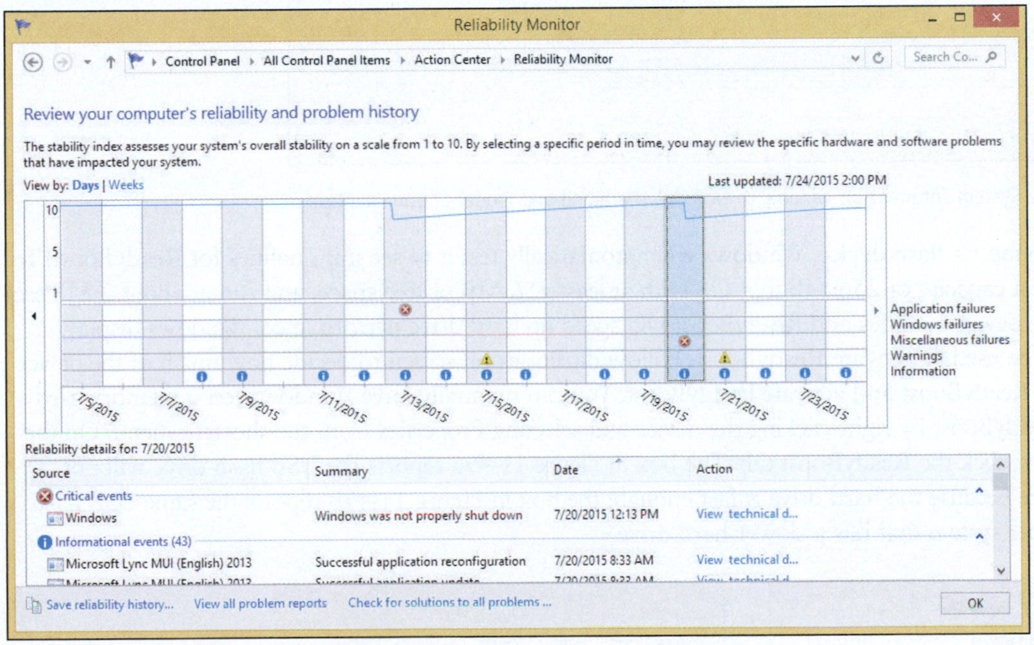

Figure 11-47 Use the Reliability Monitor to search for when a problem began and what else happened about that time

Click a date to see a list of activities on that day. If you don't know when the problem started, skim through the line graph at the top of the Reliability Monitor window and look for drops in the graph. Also look for critical events indicated by a red X (refer to Figure 11-47).

STEP 5: CONSIDER USING READYBOOST

A+
220-902
1.1, 4.1

Windows ReadyBoost uses a flash drive or secure digital (SD) memory card to boost hard drive performance. The faster flash memory is used as a buffer to speed up hard drive access time. You see the greatest performance increase using ReadyBoost when you have a slow magnetic hard drive (running at less than 7200 RPM). To find out what speed your hard drive is using, use System Information (msinfo32.exe) and drill down into the Components, Storage group, and select Disks (see Figure 11-48). The model of the hard drive appears in the right pane. Use Google to search on this brand and model; a quick search shows this drive runs at 5400 RPM. It's, therefore, a good candidate to benefit from ReadyBoost.

A+ Exam Tip The A+ 220-902 exam expects you to know how to use ReadyBoost to improve performance.

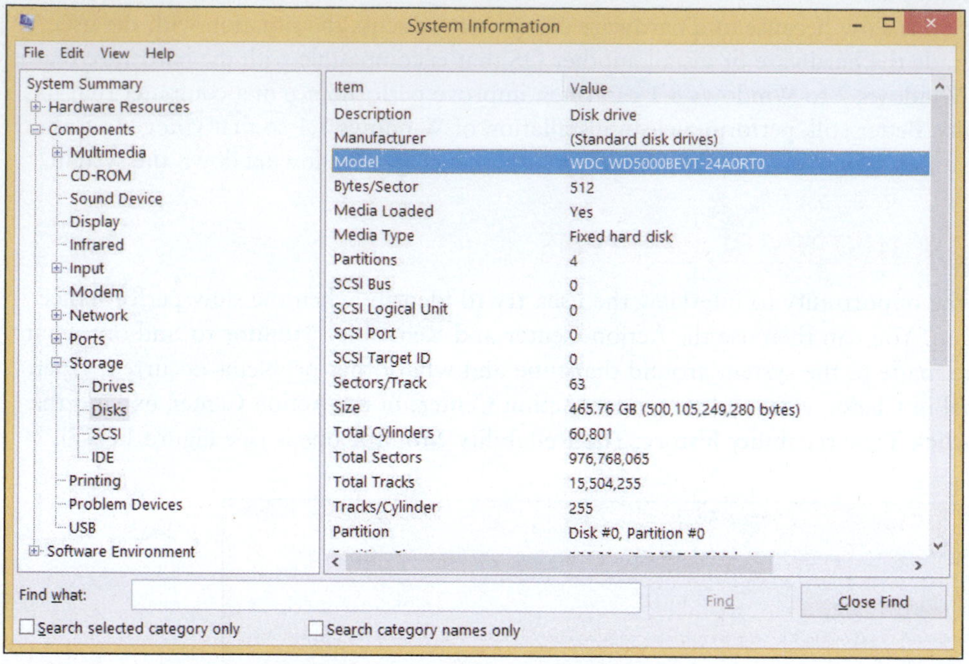

Figure 11-48 Use the System Information window to find out the brand and model of your hard drive

When you first connect a flash device, Windows will automatically test it to see if it qualifies for ReadyBoost. To qualify, it must have a capacity of 256 MB to 4 GB with at least 256 MB of free space, and run at about 2 MB/sec of throughput. If the device qualifies and ReadyBoost will speed up hard drive performance, Windows displays a dialog box that can be used to activate ReadyBoost. Follow directions on screen to decide how much of the device memory to allot for ReadyBoost and activate ReadyBoost. You can manually have Windows test a memory card or flash drive for ReadyBoost by right-clicking the device and selecting **Properties** from the shortcut menu. On the device properties box, click the **ReadyBoost** tab. The box in Figure 11-49a reports the USB flash drive will not improve performance because the hard drive is fast enough; the box in Figure 11-49b reports the same USB flash drive will help another system that has a slower hard drive.

(a)

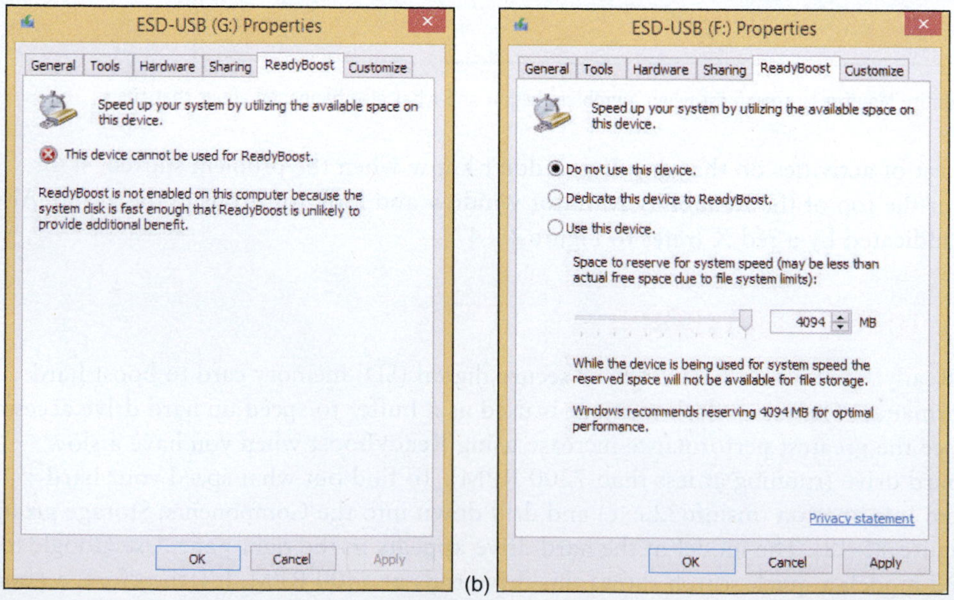

(b)

Figure 11-49 The ReadyBoost tab gives information about a device and system qualifying for ReadyBoost

The best flash devices to use for ReadyBoost are the ones that can take advantage of the faster ports. For example, a SuperSpeed USB (USB 3.0) device and port is about 10 times faster than a Hi-Speed USB (USB 2.0) device and port. Incidentally, when you remove the device, no data is lost because the device only holds a copy of the data.

WINDOWS 7 DISABLE THE AERO INTERFACE

A+
220-902
1.1, 4.1

The Windows 7/Vista Aero interface might be slowing down the system because it uses memory and computing power. Try disabling it. If performance improves, you can conclude that the hardware is not able to support the Aero interface. At that point, you might want to upgrade memory, upgrade the video card, or leave the Aero interface disabled.

To disable the Aero interface using Windows 7, do the following:

1. Right-click the desktop and select **Personalize** from the shortcut menu. The Personalization window opens (see Figure 11-50).
2. Scroll down to and click **Windows 7 Basic** and close the window.

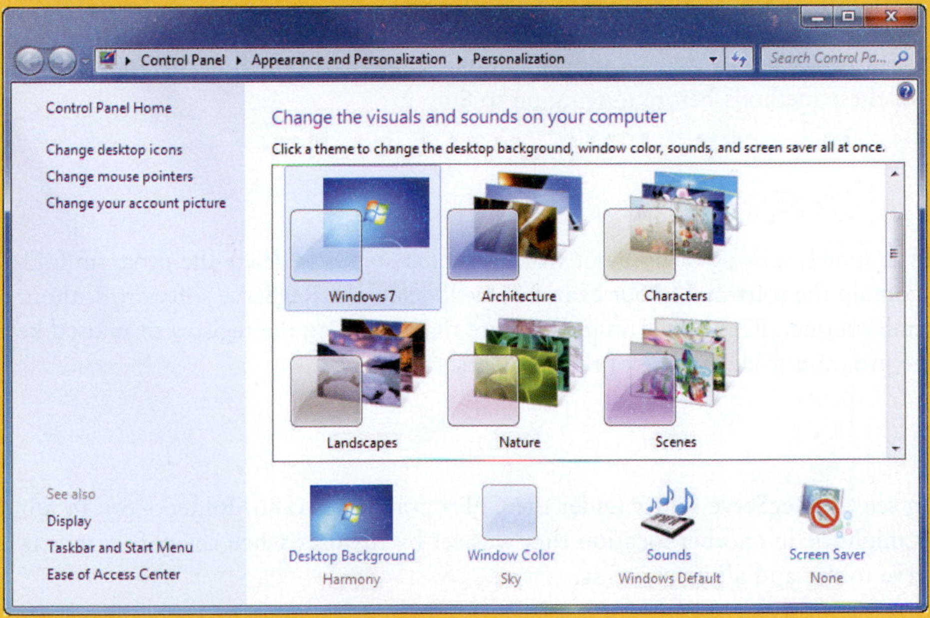

Figure 11-50 Disable the Windows 7 Aero interface to conserve system resources

OS Differences Recall that the Vista sidebar appears on the Windows desktop to hold apps called gadgets. The sidebar uses system resources and disabling it can improve performance. To do that, right-click the sidebar and select **Properties** from the shortcut menu. In the Sidebar Properties box, uncheck **Start Sidebar when Windows starts** and click **OK**.

MANUALLY REMOVING SOFTWARE

A+
220-902
1.1, 1.4,
4.1

In this part of the chapter, we focus on getting rid of programs that refuse to uninstall or give errors when uninstalling. In these cases, you can manually uninstall a program. Doing so often causes problems later, so use the methods discussed in this section only as a last resort after normal uninstall methods have failed.

This part of the chapter discusses the following steps to manually remove software:

1. First try to locate and use an uninstall routine provided by the software. If this works, you are done and can skip the next steps.
2. Delete the program folders and files that hold the software.
3. Delete the registry entries used by the software.
4. Remove the entries in the Start menu and delete any shortcuts on the desktop.
5. Remove any entries that launch processes at startup.

Notes Before uninstalling software, make sure it's not running in the background. For example, antivirus software cannot be uninstalled if it's still running. You can use Task Manager to end all processes related to the software, and you can use the Services console to stop services related to the software. Then remove the software.

Now let's step through the process of manually removing software.

STEP 1: FIRST TRY THE UNINSTALL ROUTINE

A+ 220-902 4.1

Most programs written for Windows have an uninstall routine that can be accessed from the Programs and Features window and Windows 8 apps can be uninstalled on the Start screen. First, try one of these methods before moving on to Step 2.

STEP 2: DELETE PROGRAM FILES

A+ 220-902 4.1

If the uninstall routine is missing or does not work, the next step is to delete the program folders and files that contain the software. In our example, we'll delete the RegServe software without using its uninstall routine. (RegServe is utility software that can clean the registry of unused keys.)

Look for the program folder in one of these folders:

- C:\Program Files
- C:\Program Files (x86)

In Figure 11-51, you can see the RegServe folder under the C:\Program Files (x86) folder. Keep in mind, however, the program files might be in another location that was set by the user when the software was installed. Delete the **RegServe** folder and all its contents.

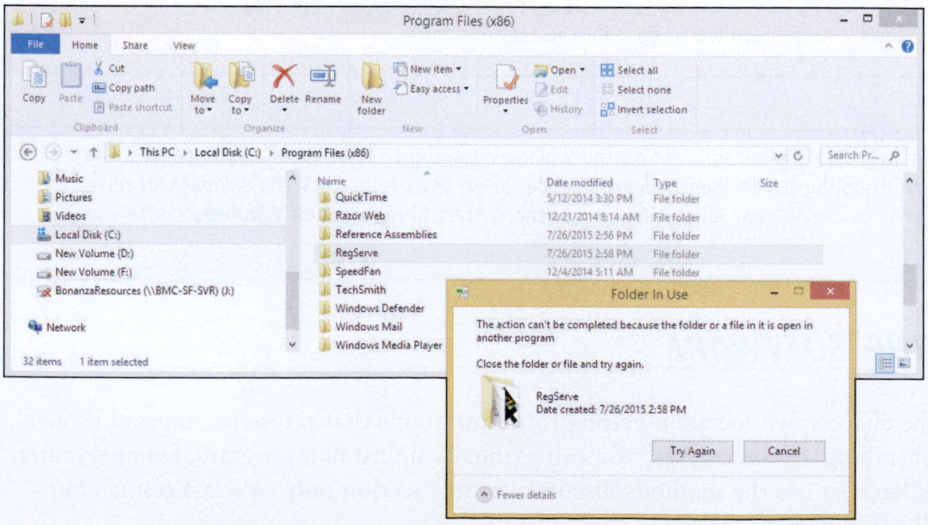

Figure 11-51 Program files are usually found in the Program Files or Program Files (x86) folder

As you do, you might see the Folder In Use box shown on the right side of Figure 11-51 saying the program is in use. In this situation, do the following:

1. Look for the program file reported on the Processes tab of Task Manager. If you see it listed, end the process. For Windows 8, be sure to look in the Windows Explorer group (see Figure 11-52). For Windows 7, the Command Line column can help you find the right program.

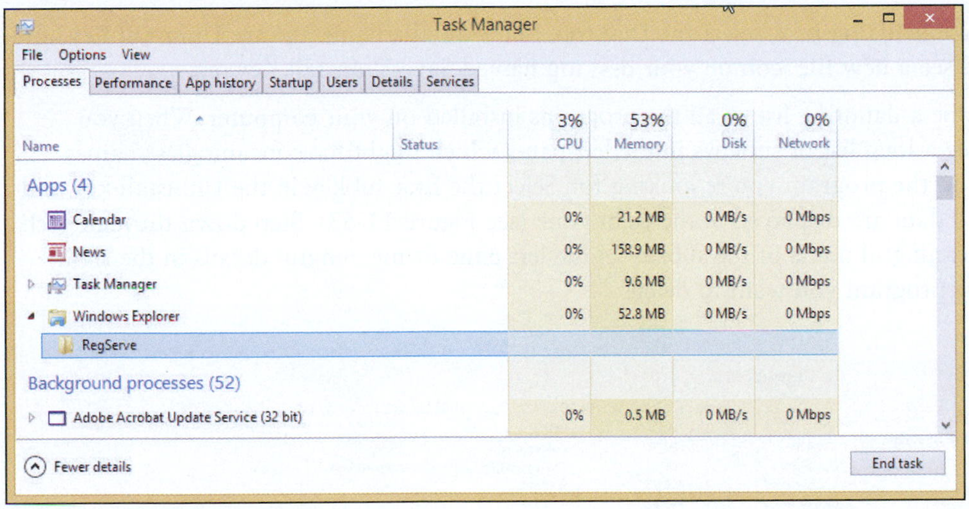

Figure 11-52 Task Manager shows a service is running and needs to be stopped before the program files can be deleted

2. If you don't find the program on the Processes tab, check the **Services** tab. If you find it there, select it and stop the service.
3. After the program or service is stopped, try to delete the program folder again. If you still cannot delete the folder, look for other running programs or services associated with the software. Look for a program or service that has a program file location in the RegServe folder or its subfolders.

STEP 3: DELETE REGISTRY ENTRIES

A+
220-902
1.4, 4.1

Editing the registry can be dangerous, so do this with caution and be sure to back up first! Do the following to delete registry entries that cause a program to be listed as installed software in the Programs and Features window of Control Panel:

1. To be on the safe side, back up the entire registry using one or more of the methods discussed earlier in the chapter.
2. Open the Registry Editor by using the **regedit** command in the Search box.
3. Locate a key that contains the entries that make up the list of installed software. Use this criteria to decide which key to locate:

- For a 32-bit program installed in a 32-bit OS or for a 64-bit program installed in a 64-bit OS, locate this key: HKEY_LOCAL_MACHINE\Software\Microsoft\Windows\CurrentVersion\Uninstall
- For a 32-bit program installed in a 64-bit OS, locate this key: HKEY_LOCAL_MACHINE\SOFTWARE\Wow6432Node\Microsoft\Windows\CurrentVersion\Uninstall

Notes Recall that 32-bit programs normally install in the \Program Files (x86) folder on a 64-bit system. These 32-bit programs normally use the Wow6432Node subkey in the registry of a 64-bit OS.

4. Back up the Uninstall key to the Windows desktop so that you can backtrack, if necessary. To do that, right-click the **Uninstall** key and select **Export** from the shortcut menu (see Figure 11-40 earlier in the chapter).
5. In the Export Registry File dialog box, select the **Desktop**. Enter the file name as **Save Uninstall Key**, and click **Save**. You should see a new file icon on your desktop named Save Uninstall Key.reg.
6. The Uninstall key can be a daunting list of all the programs installed on your computer. When you expand the key, you see a long list of subkeys in the left pane, which might have meaningless names that won't help you find the program you're looking for. Select the first subkey in the Uninstall key and watch as its values and data are displayed in the right pane (see Figure 11-53). Step down through each key, watching for a meaningful name of the subkey in the left pane or meaningful details in the right pane until you find the program you want to delete.

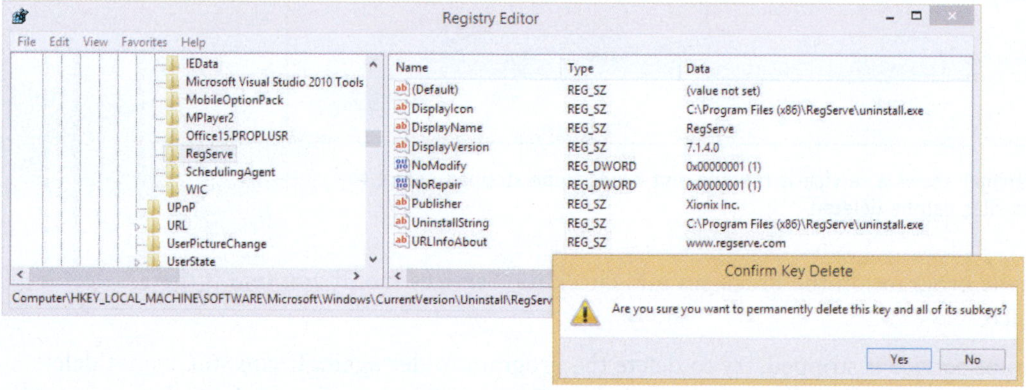

Figure 11-53 Select a subkey under the Uninstall key to display its values and data in the right pane

7. To delete the key, right-click the key and select **Delete** from the shortcut menu. Confirm the deletion, as shown in Figure 11-53. Be sure to search through all the keys in this list because the software might have more than one key. Delete them all and exit the Registry Editor.
8. Open the Programs and Features window and verify that the list of installed software is correct and the software you are uninstalling is no longer listed.
9. If the list of installed software is not correct, to restore the Uninstall registry key, double-click the **Save Uninstall Key.reg** icon on your desktop.
10. As a last step when editing the registry, clean up after yourself by deleting the Save Uninstall Key.reg file on your desktop. Right-click the icon and select **Delete** from the shortcut menu.

STEP 4: REMOVE PROGRAM SHORTCUTS

A+ 220-902 1.1, 4.1

For Windows 8, go to the Start screen and type the name of the program. The Problem with Shortcut box appears (see Figure 11-54). Click **Yes** and the program will no longer be listed on the Start screen or Apps screen. For Windows 7, to remove the program from the All Programs menu, right-click it and select **Delete** from the shortcut menu. If the program has shortcuts on the desktop, delete these.

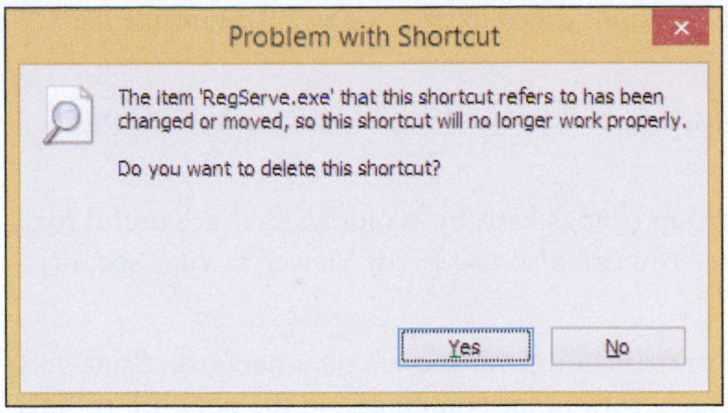

Figure 11-54 Delete the program shortcut from the Windows 8 Start screen or Apps screen

STEP 5: REMOVE STARTUP PROCESSES

A+ 220-902 1.1, 4.1

Restart the system and watch for any startup errors about a missing program file. The software might have stored startup entries in the registry, in startup folders, or as a service that is no longer present and causing an error. If you see an error, use System Configuration or Task Manager to find out how the program is set to start. This entry point is called an orphaned entry. You'll then need to delete this startup entry by editing the registry, deleting a shortcut in a startup folder, or disabling a service using the Services console.

It's unlikely you will be able to completely remove all keys in the registry that the software put there. A registry cleaner can help you find these orphaned keys, but if no errors appear at startup, you can just leave these keys untouched. Also, an installation might put program files in the C:\Program Files\Common Files or the C:\Program Files (x86)\Common Files folder. Most likely you can just leave these untouched as well. Address all error messages you encounter and stop there.

11

>> CHAPTER SUMMARY

Windows Utilities and Tools to Support the OS

- The Windows OS is made up of two main components, the shell and the kernel. The shell provides an interface for users and applications. The kernel is responsible for interacting with hardware.
- A process is a program running under the shell, together with all the resources assigned to it. A thread is a single task that a process requests from the kernel.
- Task Manager (taskmgr.exe) lets you view services and other running programs, CPU and memory performance, network activity, and user activity. It is useful to stop a process that is hung.
- Tools listed in the Administrative Tools group of Control Panel are used by technicians and developers to support Windows and applications.
- System Configuration (msconfig.exe) can be used to temporarily disable startup processes to test for performance improvement and find a startup program causing a problem.
- System Configuration and Task Manager can be used to perform a clean boot, which reduces the boot to essentials.
- The Services console (services.msc) is used to manage Windows and application services. When and if a service starts can be controlled from this console.

- The Computer Management console (compmgmt.msc) contains a group of Windows Administrative tools useful for managing a system.
- The Microsoft Management Console (MMC) can be used to build your own custom consoles from available snap-ins.
- The Event Viewer (eventvwr.msc) console displays a group of logs kept by Windows that are useful for troubleshooting problems with software and hardware. You can also use Event Viewer to view security audits made by Windows.
- The Print Management utility can be used to manage printers and print servers on a network. Print Management considers any computer that shares a printer with other computers on the network to be a print server.
- Task Scheduler (taskschd.msc) schedules and runs tasks, which are stored in C:\Windows\System32\Tasks folder.
- Performance Monitor (perfmon.msc) uses counters to track activity by hardware and software to evaluate performance.
- The Registry Editor (regedit.exe) is used to edit the registry in real time. There is no way to use the Registry Editor to undo changes you make to the registry. Therefore, you should always make a backup before editing it.
- The Display applet in Control Panel can be used to change the screen resolution and refresh rate and adjust color depth. The taskbar properties box can be used to extend the Windows 8 taskbar across both monitors in a dual-monitor setup.
- The dxdiag command can be used to verify the version of DirectX.

Improving Windows Performance

- The five high-level steps to improve Windows performance are (1) routine maintenance, (2) clean Windows startup, (3) check if hardware can support the OS, (4) check for a history of problems to find the source of a problem, and (5) consider using ReadyBoost to improve a slow hard drive's performance. For Windows 7/Vista, disable the Aero interface.

Manually Removing Software

- To manually delete software, delete the program files, registry keys, shortcuts to the program on the Start screen, Apps screen, or Windows 7 All Programs menu, and items in startup folders.

>> KEY TERMS

For explanations of key terms, see the Glossary for this text.

Administrative Tools
clean boot
Computer Management console
DirectX
dxdiag.exe
Event Viewer
executive services
HAL (hardware abstraction layer)
HKEY_CLASSES_ROOT (HKCR)
HKEY_CURRENT_CONFIG (HKCC)
HKEY_CURRENT_USER (HKCU)
HKEY_LOCAL_MACHINE (HKLM)
HKEY_USERS (HKU)
kernel
kernel mode
Microsoft Management Console (MMC)
multimonitor taskbar
multiple monitor misalignment
multiple monitor orientation
native resolution
Performance Monitor
Print Management
process
ReadyBoost
refresh rate
registry
Registry Editor
Reliability and Performance Monitor
Reliability Monitor
resolution
Services console
shell
snap-in
System Configuration
Task Manager
Task Scheduler
thread
user mode

>> REVIEWING THE BASICS

1. If a program is hung and not responding, how can you stop it?
2. If a necessary program is using too much of system resources and bogging down other applications, what can you do to fix the problem?
3. How can you view a list of users currently signed in to the computer?
4. What is the program file name and extension of System Configuration?
5. If a nonessential service is slowing down startup, how can you permanently disable it?
6. What should be the startup type of a service that should not load at startup but might be used later after startup? What tool can you use to set the startup type of a service?
7. List three snap-ins that can be found in the Computer Management console that are used to manage hardware and track problems with hardware.
8. What is the file extension of a console that is managed by Microsoft Management Console?
9. What is the program file name and extensions of the Microsoft Management Console?
10. Which log in Event Viewer would you use to find out about attempted sign-ins to a computer?
11. Which log in Event Viewer would you use if you suspect a problem with the hard drive?
12. Which log in Event Viewer lists only Critical, Error, and Warning events?
13. Which Administrative tool can you use to clear the print queue of another computer on the network that has a shared printer?
14. Does Windows 8 allow you to extend the desktop taskbar across both monitors in a dual-monitor setup? Windows 7?
15. What is the path to the Ntuser.dat file?
16. How is the Ntuser.dat file used?
17. What command do you use to find out what version of DirectX your video card is using?
18. Which Windows tool can you use to find out if the hard drive is slowing down Windows performance?
19. Which registry key contains information that Device Manager uses to display information about hardware?
20. If performance improves when Windows is loaded in a clean boot, what can you conclude?
21. If performance does not improve when Windows is loaded in a clean boot, what can you conclude?
22. When using System Configuration to stop startup services including Microsoft services, which service should you not stop so that restore points will not be lost?
23. In what folder does Task Scheduler keep scheduled task?
24. What is the purpose of the Wow6432Node subkey in the Windows registry?
25. What is the name of the window used to uninstall software?

>> THINKING CRITICALLY

1. You need to install a customized console on 10 computers. What is the best way to do that?
   a. When installing the console on the first computer, write down each step to make it easier to do the same chore on the other nine.
   b. Create the console on one computer and copy the .mmc file to the other nine.
   c. Create the console on one computer and copy the .msc file to the other nine.
2. What is the name of the program that you can enter in the Windows 8 Run box to execute Event Viewer? What is the process that is running when Event Viewer is displayed on the screen? Why do you think the running process is different from the program name?
3. When cleaning up the startup process, which of these should you do first?
   a. Use the Registry Editor to look for keys that hold startup processes.
   b. Run System Configuration to see what processes are started.
   c. After you have launched several applications, use Task Manager to view a list of running tasks.
   d. Run the Defrag utility to optimize the hard drive.
4. Using the Internet, investigate each of the following startup processes. Identify the process and write a one-sentence description:
   a. Acrotray.exe
   b. Ieuser.exe
5. Using Task Manager, you discover an unwanted program that is launched at startup. Of the items listed below, which ones might lead you to the permanent solution to the problem? Which ones would not be an appropriate solution to the problem? Explain why they are not appropriate.
   a. Look at the registry key that launched the program to help determine where in Windows the program was initiated.
   b. Use Task Manager to disable the program.
   c. Search Task Scheduler for the source of the program being launched.
   d. Use System Configuration to disable the program.
   e. Search the startup folders for the source of the program.
6. List the program file name and path for the following utilities. (*Hint:* You can use Explorer or a Windows search to locate files.)
   a. Task Manager
   b. System Configuration
   c. Services Console
   d. Microsoft Management Console
   e. Registry Editor

>> REAL PROBLEMS, REAL SOLUTIONS

REAL PROBLEM 11-1 Using RegServe

RegServe by Xionix can be downloaded free from the *regserve.com* website. Download, install, and run the software. How many orphaned registry keys did it find on your computer? Which software installed on your computer is responsible for these orphaned keys? Do you think your system would benefit from allowing RegServe to clean your registry? If you decide to use RegServe to clean the registry, be sure to create a restore point first so you can undo the changes to your registry, if necessary.

REAL PROBLEM 11-2 Cleaning Up Startup

Using a computer that has a problem with a sluggish startup, apply the tools and procedures you learned in this chapter to clean up the startup process. Take detailed notes of each step you take and its results. (If you are having a problem finding a computer with a sluggish startup, consider offering your help to a friend, a family member, or a nonprofit organization.)

REAL PROBLEM 11-3 Manually Removing Software

To practice your skills of manually removing software, install WinPatrol from *www.winpatrol.com*. (If you did Project 11-6, the software is already installed.) Then, following the directions in the chapter, manually remove the software, listing the steps you used. (Do not use the uninstall routine provided by WinPatrol.) After you have manually removed the software, reboot the system. Did you get any error messages?

CHAPTER 12 Supporting Customers and Troubleshooting Windows

After completing this chapter, you will be able to:

- Support customers in the nontechnical ways that they want and expect, beyond your technical skills
- Apply general strategies and steps to troubleshoot and solve any computer problem
- Troubleshoot application problems using appropriate Windows tools

When a computer gives you problems, a good plan for solving that problem can help you to not feel so helpless. This chapter is designed to give you just that—a plan with all the necessary details and tools so that you can determine just what has gone wrong and what to do about it.

Equally important when troubleshooting computers is handling customer concerns. Knowing how to effectively work with people in a technical world is one of the most sought-after skills in today's service-oriented work environments. Just before writing this chapter, an employer told me, "It's not hard to find technically proficient people these days. But it's next to impossible to find people who know how to get along with others and can be counted on when managers are not looking over their shoulders." I could sense his frustration, but I also felt encouraged to know that good social skills and good work ethics can take you far in today's world. My advice to you is to take this chapter seriously. It's important to be technically proficient, but the skills learned in this chapter just might be the ones that make you stand out above the crowd to land that new job or promotion.

In this chapter, we begin with interpersonal skills (people skills, sometimes called soft skills) needed by an IT support technician. Then we move on to how to troubleshoot any computer problem, and drill down into the specifics of troubleshooting applications.

Notes This chapter focuses on problems that occur after the Windows desktop has loaded. Recall that you learned how to solve hardware problems, including those that cause the system to not boot, in the chapter, "Supporting the Power System and Troubleshooting Computers." You'll learn how to solve software problems when Windows refuses to start in the chapter, "Troubleshooting Windows Startup."

WHAT CUSTOMERS WANT: BEYOND TECHNICAL KNOW-HOW

A+
220-902
5.4

Probably the most significant indication that an IT technician is doing a good job is that customers are consistently satisfied. In your career as an IT support technician, commit to providing excellent service and to treating customers as you would want to be treated in a similar situation. One of the most important ways to achieve customer satisfaction is to do your best by being prepared, both technically and personally. Being prepared includes knowing what customers want, what they don't like, and what they expect from an IT technician.

Notes People respond in kind to the position of facial muscles presented to them. Try smiling when you first greet someone and watch to see what happens.

BECOMING A COMPETENT AND HELPFUL SUPPORT TECHNICIAN

A+
220-902
5.4

The following traits distinguish a competent and helpful technician from a technician who is incompetent or unhelpful in the eyes of the customer:

- ***Trait 1. Be dependable and reliable.*** Customers appreciate and respect those who do as they say. If you promise to be back at 10:00 the next morning, be back at 10:00 the next morning. If you cannot keep your appointment, never ignore your promise. Call, apologize, let the customer know what happened, and reschedule your appointment. Also, do your best to return phone calls the same day and email within two days.

Notes Quote from R.C., an employer: "When I choose a person to work for me, in a lot of cases, I choose based on his or her past dependability or attendance. I am less concerned about a person's ability because I can train anyone to do a specific job. I cannot, however, train anyone to do anything if he or she is not present for me to train. Being dependable and reliable has a profound impact on customer relationships as well."

- ***Trait 2. Keep a positive and helpful attitude.*** This helps establish good customer relationships. You communicate your attitude in your tone of voice, the words you choose, how you use eye contact, your facial expressions, how you dress, and in many other subjective and subtle ways. Generally, your attitudes toward your customers stem from how you see people, how you see yourself, and how you see your job. Your attitude is a heart issue, not a head issue. To improve your attitude, you must do it from your heart. That's pretty subjective and cannot be defined with a set of rules, but it always begins with a decision to change. As you work with customers or users, make it a habit to not talk down to or patronize them. Don't make the customers or users feel inferior. People appreciate it when they feel your respect for them, even when they have made a mistake or are not knowledgeable. If a problem is simple to solve, don't make the other person feel he or she has wasted your time. Your customer or user should always be made to feel that the problem is important to you.

APPLYING | CONCEPTS CUSTOMER SERVICE

A+
220-902
5.4

Josie walked into a computer parts store and wandered over to the cleaning supplies looking for Ace monitor wipes. She saw another brand of wipes, but not the ones she wanted. Looking around for help, she noticed Mary stocking software on the shelves in the next aisle. She walked over to Mary and asked her if she could help her find Ace monitor wipes. Mary put down her box, walked over to the cleaning supply aisle without speaking, picked up a can of wipes and handed them to Josie, still without speaking a word. Josie explained she was looking for Ace wipes. Mary yells over three aisles to a coworker in the back room, "Hey,

Billy! This lady says she wants Ace monitor wipes. We got any?" Billy comes from the back room and says, "No, we only carry those," pointing to the wipes in Mary's hand, and returns to the back room. Mary turns to Josie and says, "We only carry these," and puts the wipes back on the shelf. She turns to walk back to her aisle when Josie says to Mary, "Well, those Ace wipes are great wipes. You might want to consider carrying them." Mary says, "I'm only responsible for software." Josie leaves the store.

Discuss this situation in a small group of students and answer the following questions:

1. If you were Josie, how would you feel about the service in this store?
2. What would you have expected to happen that did not happen?
3. If you were Mary, how could you have provided better service?
4. If you were Billy, is there anything more you could have done to help?
5. If you were the store manager, what principles of good customer service would you want Billy and Mary to know that would have helped them in this situation?

- ***Trait 3. Listen without interrupting your customer.*** When you're working with or talking to a customer, focus on him or her. Don't assume you know what your customer is about to say. Let her say it, listen carefully, and don't interrupt. Make it your job to satisfy this person, not just your organization, your boss, your bank account, or the customer's boss.

© iStockphoto.com/Sportstock

Figure 12-1 Learn to listen before you decide what a user needs or wants

- ***Trait 4. Use proper and polite language.*** Speak politely and use language that won't confuse your customer. Avoid using slang or jargon (technical language that only technical people can understand). Avoid acronyms (initial letters that stand for words). For example, don't say to a nontechnical customer, "I need to ditch your KVM switch," when you could explain yourself better by saying to the customer, "I need to replace that little switch box on your desk that controls your keyboard, monitor, and mouse."
- ***Trait 5. Show sensitivity to cultural differences.*** Cultural differences happen because we are from different countries and societies or because of physical disabilities. Culture can cause us to differ in how we define or judge good service. For example, culture can affect our degree of tolerance for uncertainty. Some cultures are willing to embrace uncertainty, and others strive to avoid it. Those who tend to avoid uncertainty can easily get upset when the unexpected happens. For these people, you need to make special efforts to communicate early and often when things are not going as expected. For the physically disabled, especially the hearing- or sight-impaired, communication can be more difficult. It's your responsibility in these situations to do

whatever is necessary to find a way to communicate. And it's especially important to have an attitude that expresses honor and patience, which you will unconsciously express in your tone of voice, your choice of words, and your actions.

- ***Trait 6. Take ownership of the problem.*** Taking ownership of the customer's problem means to accept the customer's problem as your own problem. Doing that builds trust and loyalty because the customer knows you can be counted on. Taking ownership of a problem also increases your value in the eyes of your coworkers and boss. People who don't take ownership of the problem at hand are likely to be viewed as lazy, uncommitted, and uncaring. One way to take ownership of a problem is to not engage your boss in unproductive discussions about a situation that he expects you to handle on your own.

APPLYING CONCEPTS SELF-CONTROL

A+
220-902
5.4

Jack had had a bad day on the phones at the networking help desk in Atlanta. An electrical outage coupled with a generator failure had caused servers in San Francisco to be down most of the day. The entire help-desk team had been fielding calls all day explaining to customers why they did not have service and about expected recovery times. The servers were finally online, but it was taking hours to get everything reset and functioning. No one had taken a break all afternoon, but the call queue was still running about 20 minutes behind. Todd, the boss, had asked the team to work late until the queue was empty. It was Jack's son's birthday and his family was expecting Jack home on time. Jack moaned as he realized he might be late for Tyler's party. Everyone pushed hard to empty the queue. As Jack watched the last call leave the queue, he logged off, stood up, and reached for his coat.

And then the call came. Jack was tempted to ignore it, but decided it had to be answered. It was Lacy. Lacy was the executive assistant to the CEO (chief executive officer over the entire company) and when Lacy calls, all priorities yield to Lacy, and Lacy knows it. The CEO was having problems printing to the laser printer in his office. Would Jack please walk down to his office and fix the problem? Jack asks Lacy to check the simple things like, "Is the printer turned on? Is it plugged in?" Lacy gets huffy and says, "Of course, I've checked that. Now come right now. I need to go." Jack walks down to the CEO's office, takes one look at the printer, and turns it on.

He turns to Lacy and says, "I suppose the on/off button was just too technical for you." Lacy glares at him in disbelief. Jack says, "I'll be leaving now." As he walks out, he begins to form a plan as to how he'll defend himself to his boss in the morning, knowing the inevitable call to Todd's office will come.

In a group of two or four students, role-play Jack and Todd and discuss these questions:

1. Todd is informed the next morning of Jack's behavior. Todd calls Jack into his office. He likes Jack and wants him to be successful in the company. Jack is resistant and feels justified in what he did. As Todd, what do you think is important that Jack understand? How can you explain this to Jack so he can accept it? What would you advise Jack to do? In role-play, one student plays the role of Jack, and another the role of Todd.
2. Switch roles or switch team members and replay the roles.
3. What are three principles of relating to people that would be helpful for Jack to keep in mind?

- ***Trait 7. Portray credibility.*** Convey confidence to your customers. Don't allow yourself to appear confused, afraid, or befuddled. Troubleshoot the problem in a systematic way that portrays confidence and credibility. Get the job done, and do it with excellence. Credible technicians also know when the job is beyond their expertise and when to ask for help.
- ***Trait 8. Work with integrity and honesty.*** Don't try to hide your mistakes from your customer or your boss. Everyone makes mistakes, but don't compound them by a lack of integrity. Accept responsibility and do what you can to correct the error.

- *Trait 9. Know the law with respect to your work.* For instance, observe the laws concerning the use of software. Don't use or install pirated software.
- *Trait 10. Look and behave professionally.* A professional at work knows to not allow his emotions to interfere with business relationships. If a customer is angry, allow the customer to vent, keeping your own professional distance. (You do, however, have the right to expect a customer not to talk to you in an abusive way.) Dress appropriately for the environment. Take a shower each day, and brush your teeth after each meal. Use mouthwash. Iron your shirt. If you're not in good health, try as best you can to take care of the problem. Your appearance matters. And finally—don't use rough language. It is *never* appropriate.

Notes Your customers might never remember what you said or what you did, but they will always remember how you made them feel.

Hands-On | Project 12-1 Evaluate Your Own Interpersonal Skills with Customers and Coworkers

Assume that you are working as an IT support technician for a corporation. Your job requires you to give desk-side support to users, answer the phone at the help desk, and make an occasional on-site call at corporate branches. Answer the following questions:

1. In the role of desk-side support to users, what do you think is your strongest social skill that would help you succeed in this role?
2. What is likely to be your greatest interpersonal weakness that might present a challenge to you in this role?
3. What is one change you might consider making that will help you to improve on this weakness?
4. In the role of phone support at the help desk, what part of that job would you enjoy the most? What part would give you the greatest challenge?
5. When making on-site calls to corporate branches, what part of this job would you enjoy the most? What interpersonal skills, if any, would you need to develop so that you could do your best in this role?

12

Hands-On | Project 12-2 The Johari Window Online Game

The Johari (pronounced "Joe-Harry" after the two men who created it) window reveals an interesting view of how we relate to others. Sometimes when we evaluate our own interpersonal skills, we overlook our greatest assets that others can see. This project is designed to help others reveal to you those assets. The house in Figure 12-2 represents who we are. Room 1 is what we know about ourselves that we allow others to see. Room 2 is what others see about us that we don't see ourselves (our blind spots). Room 3 is what we see about ourselves that we hide from others. And Room 4 contains traits in us that we don't know about and neither do others see—traits yet to be discovered.

As we move Bar A to the right, we are making a conscious decision to reveal more about ourselves to others, which is a technique successful salespeople often use to immediately connect with their customers. The theory is that if you move Bar A to the right, not only are you choosing to reveal what you normally would hide, but you are also moving the bar so that more of Room 4 can be seen in Room 2. This means that others can see more about you that you don't see. When we allow others to tell us something about ourselves, we are moving Bar B away from us, which, in effect,

(continues)

allows us to see more of who we really are. Therefore, to learn more about yourself, you can do two things: Reveal more of yourself to others and allow others to tell you more about yourself. Try playing the Interactive Johari Window game by Kevan Davis. You can find it at *www.kevan.org*.

Then answer the following questions:

1. What five or six descriptive words did you use to describe yourself at the beginning of the game?
2. What words did others use to describe you?

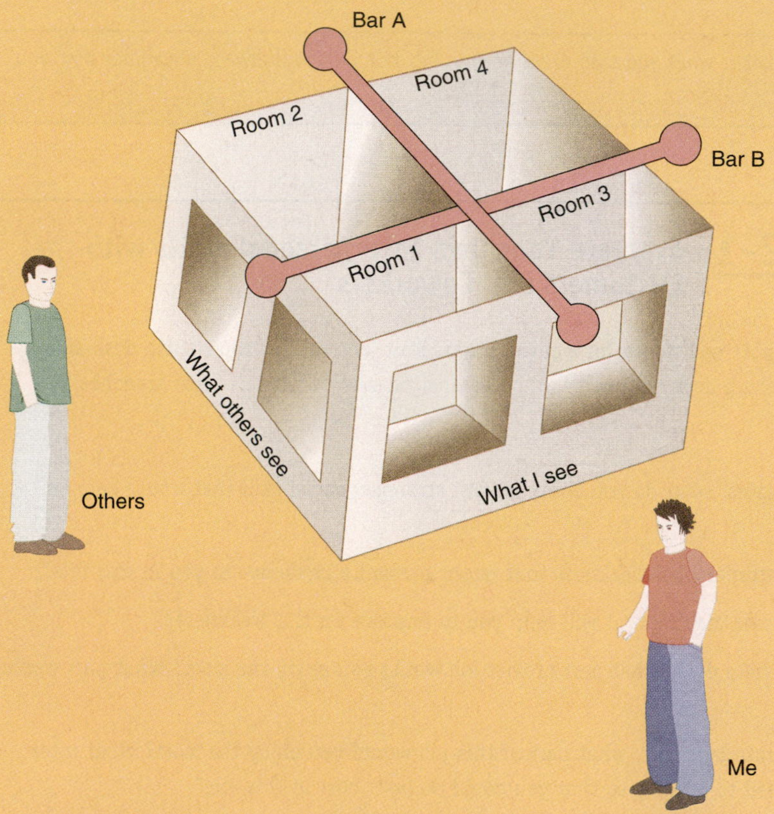

Figure 12-2 Johari Window demonstrates the complexity of how we see ourselves and how others see us

3. How has input from your friends adjusted how you see yourself?
4. How might this adjustment affect the way you will relate to customers and coworkers on the job?
5. If you were to play the Interactive Johari Window game a second time, would you still use the same five or six descriptive words you used the first time? If your answer is no, what new words would you use?

PLANNING FOR GOOD SERVICE

A+ 220-902 5.4

Your customers can be "internal" (you both work for the same company, in which case you might consider the customer your colleague) or "external" (your customers come to you or your company for service). Customers can be highly technical or technically naive, represent a large company or simply own a home computer, be prompt or slow at paying their bills, want only the best (and be willing to pay for it) or be searching for bargain service, be friendly and easy to work with or demanding and condescending. In each situation, the key to success is always the same: Don't allow circumstances or personalities to affect your commitment to excellence and to treat the customer as you would want to be treated.

★ A+ Exam Tip The A+ 220-902 exam expects you to know that when servicing a customer, you should be on time, avoid distractions, set and meet expectations and timelines, communicate the status of the solution with the customer, and deal appropriately with customers' confidential materials.

Most good service for customers of IT support begins with entries in call tracking software, so let's begin there.

CALL TRACKING SOFTWARE

Your organization is likely to use call tracking software to track support calls and give technicians a place to keep their call notes. Figure 12-3 shows a window in *everything HelpDesk* software, which is a popular call tracking application.

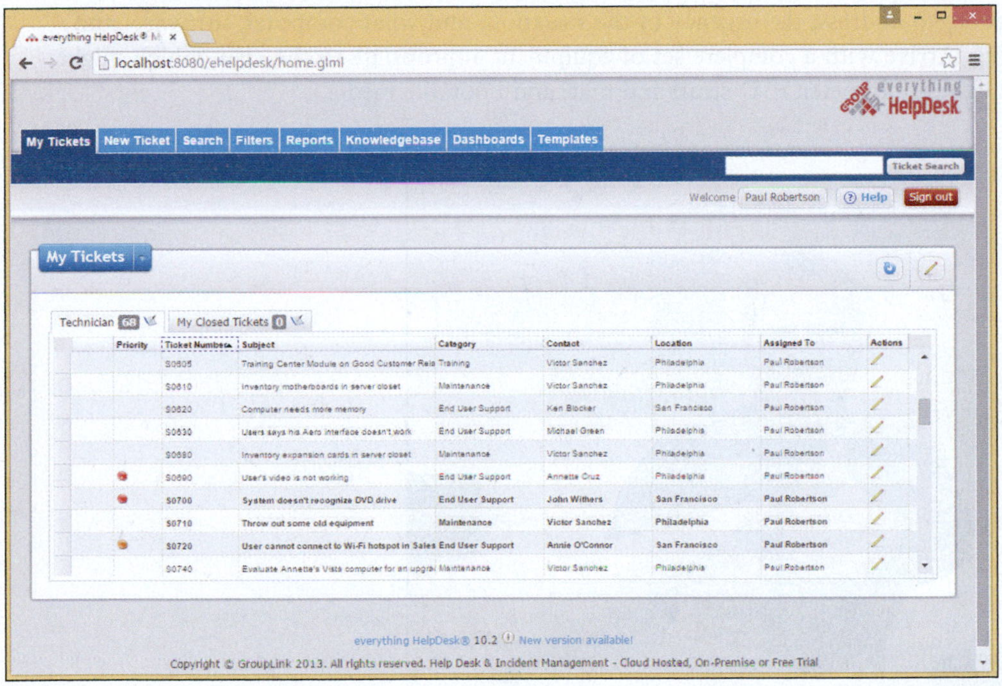

Source: everything HelpDesk

Figure 12-3 Call tracking software allows you to create, edit, and close tickets used by technicians

When someone initiates a call for help, whoever receives the call starts the process by creating a ticket, which is a record of the request and what is happening to resolve it. The call tracking software might track: (1) the date, time, and length of help-desk or on-site calls, (2) causes of and solutions to problems already addressed, (3) who is currently assigned to the ticket and who has already worked on it, (4) who did what and when, and (5) how each call was officially resolved. The ticket is entered into the call tracking system and stays open until the issue is resolved. Support staff assigned to the ticket document their progress under this ticket in the call tracking system. As an open ticket ages, more attention and resources are assigned to it, and the ticket might be escalated (passed on to someone more experienced or who has more resources available) until the problem is finally resolved and the ticket closed. Help-desk personnel and managers acknowledge and sometimes even celebrate those who consistently close the most tickets!

12

As you support customers and solve computer problems, it's very important to include detailed information in your call notes so that you have this information as you problem solve or later, when faced with a similar problem. Sometimes another person must pick up your open ticket and should not have to waste time finding out information you already knew. Also, tracking-system notes are sometimes audited.

INITIAL CONTACT WITH A CUSTOMER

Your initial contact with a customer might be when the customer comes to you, such as in a retail setting, when you go to the customer's site, when the customer calls you on the phone, when the customer reaches you by chat or email, or when you are assigned a ticket already entered in a call tracking system. In each situation, always follow the specific guidelines of your employer. Let's look at some general guidelines for handling first contact with customers.

When you answer the phone, identify yourself and your organization. (Follow the guidelines of your employer on what to say.) Follow company policies to obtain specific information you should take when answering an initial call, such as name (get the right spelling), phone number, and business name. For example, your company might require that you obtain a licensing or warranty number to determine whether the customer is entitled to receive your support. After you have obtained all the information you need in order to know that you are authorized to help the customer, open up the conversation for the caller to describe the problem.

Prepare for on-site visits by reviewing information given to you by whoever took the call. Know the problem you are going to address; the urgency of the situation; and what computer, software, and hardware need servicing. Arrive with a complete set of equipment appropriate to the visit, which might include a toolkit, flashlight, multimeter, ESD strap and mat, and bootable media.

Figure 12-4 If a customer permits it, begin each new relationship with a handshake

When you arrive at the customer's site, greet the customer in a friendly manner and shake his or her hand. Use Mr. or Ms. and last names or Sir or Ma'am rather than first names when addressing the customer, unless you are certain the customer expects you to use a first name. If the site is a residence, know that you should never stay at a site when only a minor is present. If a minor child answers the door, ask to speak with an adult and don't allow the adult to leave the house with only you and the child present.

After initial greetings, the first thing you should do is listen and ask questions. As you listen, it's fine to take notes, but don't start the visit by filling out your paperwork. Save the paperwork for later, or have the essentials already filled out before you reach the site.

INTERVIEW THE CUSTOMER

Troubleshooting begins by interviewing the user. As you ask the user questions, take notes and keep asking questions until you thoroughly understand the problem. Have the customer reproduce the problem, and carefully note each step taken and its results. This process gives you clues about the problem and about the customer's technical proficiency, which helps you know how to communicate with the customer.

> **★ A+ Exam Tip** The A+ 220-902 exam expects you to be able to clarify customer statements by asking open-ended questions to narrow the scope of the problem and by restating the issue or question.

Use diplomacy and good manners when you work with a user to solve a problem. For example, if you suspect that the user dropped the computer, don't ask, "Did you drop the laptop?" Put the question in a less accusatory manner: "Could the laptop have been dropped?"

SET AND MEET CUSTOMER EXPECTATIONS

A professional technician knows that it is her responsibility to set and meet expectations with a customer. It's important to create an expectation of certainty with customers so that they are not left hanging and don't know what will happen next.

Part of setting expectations is to establish a timeline with your customer for the completion of a project. If you cannot solve the problem immediately, explain to the customer what needs to happen and the timeline that he should expect for a solution. Then keep the customer informed about the progress of the solution. For example, you can say to a customer, "I need to return to the office and research the cost of parts that need replacing. I'll call you tomorrow before 10:00 a.m. with an estimate." If later you find out you need more time, call the customer before 10:00 a.m., explain your problem, and give him a new time to expect your call. This kind of service is very much appreciated by customers and, if you are consistent, you will quickly gain their confidence.

Another way to set expectations is to give the customer an opportunity to make decisions about repairs to the customer's equipment. When explaining to the customer what needs to be done to fix a problem, offer repair or replacement options if they apply. Don't make decisions for your customer. Explain the problem and what you must do to fix it, giving as many details as the customer wants. When a customer must make a choice, state the options in a way that does not unfairly favor the solution that makes the most money for you as the technician or for your company. For example, if you must replace a motherboard (a costly repair in parts and labor), explain to the customer the total cost of repairs and then help him decide if it is to his advantage to purchase a new system or repair this one.

© iStockphoto.com/Dean Mitchell

Figure 12-5 Advise and then allow a customer to make repair or purchasing decisions

12

WORKING WITH A CUSTOMER ON SITE

As you work with a customer on site, avoid distractions as you work. Don't accept personal calls or texts on your cell phone, and definitely don't check social media sites when you're on the job. Most organizations require that you answer calls from work, but keep the calls to a minimum. Be aware that the customer might be listening, so be careful to not discuss problems with coworkers, the boss, or other situations that might put the company, its employees, or products in a bad light with the customer. If you absolutely must excuse yourself from the on-site visit for personal reasons, explain to the customer the situation and return as soon as possible.

When working at a user's desk, follow these general guidelines:

1. As you work, be as unobtrusive as possible. Consider yourself a guest in the customer's office or residence. Don't make a big mess. Keep your tools and papers out of the customer's way. Don't pile your belongings and tools on top of the user's papers, books, and so forth.
2. Protect the customer's confidential and private materials. For example, if you are working on the printer and discover a budget report in the out tray, quickly turn it over so you can't read it, and hand it to the customer. If you notice a financial spreadsheet is displayed on the customer's computer screen, step away and ask the user if she wants to first close the spreadsheet before you work with the computer. If sensitive documents are lying on the customer's desk, you might let him know and ask if he would like to put them out of your view or in a safe place.
3. Don't take over the mouse or keyboard from the user without permission.
4. Ask permission again before you use the printer or other equipment.
5. Don't use the phone without permission.
6. Accept personal inconvenience to accommodate the user's urgent business needs. For example, if the user gets an important call while you are working, don't allow your work to interfere. You might need to stop work and perhaps leave the room.
7. Also, if the user is present, ask permission before you make a software or hardware change, even if the user has just given you permission to interact with the computer.
8. Don't disclose information about a customer on social media sites, and don't use those public outlets to complain about difficulties with a customer.

© iStockphoto.com/Sportstock

Figure 12-6 Teaching a user how to fix her problem can prevent it from reoccurring

In some IT support situations, it is appropriate to consider yourself a support to the user as well as to the computer. Your goals can include educating the user, as well as repairing the computer. If you want users to learn something from a problem they caused, explain how to fix the problem and walk them through the process if necessary. Don't fix the problem yourself unless they ask you to. It takes a little longer to train the user, but it is more productive in the end because the user learns more and is less likely to repeat the mistake.

WORKING WITH A CUSTOMER ON THE PHONE

Phone support requires more interaction with customers than any other type of IT support. To understand the problem and also give clear instructions, you must be able to visualize what the customer sees at his or her computer. Patience is required if the customer must be told each key to press or command button to click. Help-desk support requires excellent communication skills, good phone manners, and lots of patience. As your help-desk skills improve, you will learn to think through the process as though you were sitting in front of the computer yourself. Drawing diagrams and taking notes as you talk can be very helpful. In some cases, help-desk support personnel might have software that enables the remote control of customers' computers. Examples of this type of software are GoToAssist by Citrix at *www.netviewer.com* and LogMeIn Rescue by LogMeIn at *secure.logmeinrescue.com*. Always communicate clearly with customers when using this type of software, so that they understand what type of access they are allowing you to have on their computers.

If your call is accidentally disconnected, call back immediately. Don't eat or drink while on the phone. If you must put callers on hold, tell them how long it will be before you get back to them. Speak clearly and don't talk too fast. Don't complain about your job, your boss or coworkers, your company, or other companies or products to your customers. A little small talk is okay and is sometimes beneficial in easing a tense situation, but keep it upbeat and positive.

DEALING WITH DIFFICULT CUSTOMERS

Most customers are polite and appreciate your help. And, if you make it a habit to treat others as you want to be treated, you'll find that most of your customers will tend to treat you well, too. However, occasionally you'll have to deal with a difficult customer. In this part of the chapter, you learn how to work with customers who are not knowledgeable, who are overly confident, and who complain.

When the Customer Is Not Knowledgeable

When on site, you can put a computer in good repair without depending on a customer to help you. But when you are trying to solve a problem over the phone, with a customer as your only eyes, ears, and hands, a computer-illiterate user can present a challenge. Here are some tips for handling this situation:

- *Tip 1.* Be specific with your instructions. For example, instead of saying, "Open File Explorer," say, "Using your mouse, right-click the Start button, and click File Explorer from the menu."

Figure 12-7 Learn to be patient and friendly when helping users

- *Tip 2.* Don't ask the customer to do something that might destroy settings or files without first having the customer back them up carefully. If you think the customer can't handle your request, ask for some on-site help.

12

- *Tip 3.* Frequently ask the customer what is displayed on the screen to help you track the keystrokes and action.
- *Tip 4.* Follow along at your own computer. It's easier to direct the customer, keystroke by keystroke, if you are doing the same things.
- *Tip 5.* Give the customer plenty of opportunity to ask questions.
- *Tip 6.* Genuinely compliment the customer whenever you can to help the customer gain confidence.
- *Tip 7.* If you determine that the customer cannot help you solve the problem without a lot of coaching, you might need to tactfully request that the caller have someone with more experience call you. The customer will most likely breathe a sigh of relief and have someone take over the problem.

Notes When solving computer problems in an organization other than your own, check with technical support within that organization instead of working only with the user. The user might not be aware of policies that have been set on his computer to prevent changes to the OS, hardware, or applications.

When the Customer Is Overly Confident

Sometimes customers might want to give advice, take charge of a call, withhold information they think you don't need to know, or execute commands at the computer without letting you know, so you don't have enough information to follow along. A situation like this must be handled with tact and respect for the customer. Here are a few tips:

- *Tip 1.* When you can, compliment the customer's knowledge, experience, or insight.
- *Tip 2.* Slow the conversation down. You can say, "Please slow down. You're moving too fast for me to follow. Help me catch up."
- *Tip 3.* Don't back off from using problem-solving skills. You must still have the customer check the simple things, but direct the conversation with tact. For example, you can say, "I know you've probably already gone over these simple things, but could we just do them again together?"
- *Tip 4.* Be careful not to accuse the customer of making a mistake.
- *Tip 5.* Even though the customer might be using technical jargon, keep to your policy of not using jargon back to the customer unless you're convinced he truly understands you.

A+ Exam Tip The A+ 220-902 exam expects you to know that it is important to not minimize a customer's problem and to not be judgmental toward a customer.

When the Customer Complains

When you are on site or on the phone, a customer might complain to you about your organization, products, or service or the service and product of another company. Consider the complaint to be helpful feedback that can lead to a better product or service and better customer relationships. Here are a few suggestions that can help you handle complaints and defuse customer anger:

- *Suggestion 1.* Be an active listener, and let customers know they are not being ignored. Look for the underlying problem. Don't take the complaint or the anger personally.
- *Suggestion 2.* Give the customer a little time to vent, and apologize when you can. Then start the conversation from the beginning, asking questions, taking notes, and solving problems. Unless you must have the information for problem solving, don't spend a lot of time finding out exactly whom the customer dealt with and what happened to upset the customer.
- *Suggestion 3.* Don't be defensive. It's better to leave the customer with the impression that you and your company are listening and willing to admit mistakes. No matter how much anger is expressed, resist the temptation to argue or become defensive.

- *Suggestion 4.* Know how your employer wants you to handle a situation where you are verbally abused. If this type of language is happening, you might say something like this in a very calm tone of voice: "I'm sorry, but my employer does not require me to accept this kind of talk."
- *Suggestion 5.* If the customer is complaining about a product or service that is not from your company, don't start off by saying, "That's not our problem." Instead, listen to the customer complain. Don't appear as though you don't care.
- *Suggestion 6.* If the complaint is against you or your product, identify the underlying problem if you can. Ask questions and take notes. Then pass these notes on to people in your organization who need to know.
- *Suggestion 7.* Sometimes simply making progress or reducing the problem to a manageable state reduces the customer's anxiety. As you are talking to a customer, summarize what you have both agreed on or observed so far in the conversation.
- *Suggestion 8.* Point out ways that *you* think communication could be improved. For example, you might say, "I'm sorry, but I'm having trouble understanding what you want. Could you please slow down, and let's take this one step at a time."

Figure 12-8 When a customer is upset, try to find a place of agreement

12

APPLYING CONCEPTS CULTURE OF HONOR

A+ 220-902 5.4

Andy was one of the most intelligent and knowledgeable support technicians in his group working for CloudPool, Inc. He was about to be promoted to software engineer and today was his last day on the help desk. Sarah, a potential customer with little computer experience, calls asking for help accessing the company website. Andy says, "The URL is www dot cloud pool dot com." Sarah responds, "What's a URL?" Andy's patience grows thin. He's thinking to himself, "Oh, help! Just two more hours and I'm off these darn phones." He answers Sarah in a tone of voice that says, hey, I really think you're an idiot! He says to her, "You know, lady! That address box at the top of your browser. Now enter www dot cloud pool dot com!" Sarah gets all flustered and intimidated and doesn't know what to say next. She really wants to know what a browser is, but instead she says, "Wait. I'll just ask someone in the office to help me," and hangs up the phone.

Discuss the situation with others in a small group and answer these questions:

1. If you were Andy's manager and overheard this call, how would you handle the situation?
2. What principles of working with customers does Andy need to keep in mind?

Two students sit back-to-back, one playing the role of Andy and the other playing the role of Sarah. Play out the entire conversation. Others in the group can offer suggestions and constructive criticism.

THE CUSTOMER DECIDES WHEN THE WORK IS DONE

When you think you've solved the problem, allow the customer to decide when the service is finished to his or her satisfaction. For remote support, generally, the customer ends the call or chat session, not the technician. If you end the call too soon and the problem is not completely resolved, the customer can be frustrated, especially if it is difficult to contact you again.

For on-site work, after you have solved the problem, complete these tasks before you close the call:

1. If you changed anything on the computer after you booted it, reboot one more time to make sure you have not caused a problem with the boot.
2. Allow the customer enough time to be fully satisfied that all is working. Does the printer work? Print a test page. Does the network connection work? Can the customer sign in to the network and access data on it?
3. If you backed up data before working on the problem and then restored the data from backups, ask the user to verify that the data is fully restored.
4. Review the service call with the customer. Summarize the instructions and explanations you have given during the call. This is an appropriate time to fill out your paperwork and explain to the customer what you have written. Then ask if she has any questions.
5. Explain preventive maintenance to the customer (such as deleting temporary files from the hard drive or cleaning the mouse). Most customers don't have preventive maintenance contracts for their computers and appreciate the time you take to show them how they can take better care of their equipment. One technician keeps a pack of monitor wipes in his toolkit and ends each call by cleaning the customer's monitor screen.

To demonstrate a sincere concern for your customer's business and that you have owned their problem, it's extremely important to follow up later with the customer and ask if he is still satisfied with your work and if he has any more questions. For example, you can say to the customer, "I'll call you on Monday to make sure everything is working and you're still satisfied with the work." And then on Monday make that call. As you do, you're building customer loyalty.

> ★ **A+ Exam Tip** The A+ 220-902 exam expects you to know to follow up with the customer at a later date to verify his or her satisfaction.

SOMETIMES YOU MUST ESCALATE A PROBLEM

You are not going to solve every computer problem you encounter. Knowing how to escalate properly so the problem is assigned to those higher in the support chain is one of the first things you should learn on a new job. Know your company's policy for escalation. What documents or entries in the call-tracking software do you use? Who do you contact? How do you pass the problem on (email, phone call, or an online entry in a database)? Do you remain the responsible "support" party, or does the person now addressing the problem become the new contact? Are you expected to keep in touch with the customer and the problem, or are you totally out of the picture?

When you escalate, let the customer know. Tell the customer you are passing the problem on to someone who is more experienced or has access to more extensive resources. If you check back with the customer only to find out that the other support person has not called or followed through to the customer's satisfaction, don't lay blame or point fingers. Just do whatever you can to help within your company guidelines. Your call to the customer will go a long way toward helping the situation.

WORKING WITH COWORKERS

Learn to be a professional when working with coworkers. A professional at work is someone who puts business matters above personal matters. In big bold letters, I can say **the key to being professional is to learn to not be personally offended when someone lets you down or does not please you.** Remember, most people do the best they can considering the business and personal constraints they're up against. Getting offended leads to becoming bitter about others and about your job. Learn to keep negative opinions to yourself, and to expect the best of others. When a coworker starts to gossip, try to politely change the subject.

Know your limitations and be willing to admit when you can't do something. For example, Larry's boss stops by his desk and asks him to accept one more project. Larry already is working many hours overtime just to keep up. He needs to politely say to his boss, "I can accept this new project only if you relieve me of some of these tasks."

© iStockphoto.com/Chris Schmidt

Figure 12-9 Coworkers who act professionally are fun to work with

12

APPLYING | CONCEPTS ACTIVE LEARNING

A+ 220-902 5.4

Ray was new at the corporate help desk that supported hospitals across the nation. He had only had a couple of weeks of training before he was turned loose on the phones. He was a little nervous the first day he took calls without a mentor sitting beside him. His first call came from Fernanda, a radiology technician who was trying to sign in to the network to start the day. When Fernanda entered her network ID and passcode, an error message appeared saying her user account was not valid. She told Ray she had tried it several times on two different computers. Ray checked his database and found her account, which appeared to be in good order. He asked her to try it again. She did and got the same results. In his two weeks of training, this problem had never occurred. He told her, "I'm sorry, I don't know how to solve this problem." She said, "Okay, well, thank you

(continues)

anyway," and hung up. She immediately called the help-desk number back and the call was answered by Jackie, who sits across the room from Ray. Fernanda said, "The other guy couldn't fix my problem. Can you help me?"

"What other guy?" Jackie asks. "I think his name was Ray." "Oh, him! He's new and he doesn't know much, and besides that he should have asked for help. Tell me the problem." Jackie resets the account and the problem is solved.

In a group of three or more students, discuss and answer the following questions:

1. What mistake did Ray make? What should he have done or said?
2. What mistake did Jackie make? What should she have done or said?
3. What three principles of relating to customers and coworkers would be helpful for Ray and Jackie to keep in mind?

Hands-On | Project 12-3 Handle Conflict at Work

Jenny works with a team of seven other professionals. Linda, a team member, is a very close personal friend of the boss. With the boss's approval, Linda took a sudden and unexpected two-week vacation to go on a cruise during the team's most difficult month of the year. One team member, Jason, had to work 16 days nonstop, without a day off during Linda's vacation. Other team members soon began complaining and resenting Linda for the unbearable workload her vacation caused them. A few weeks back from vacation, Linda began to notice that she was being excluded from informal luncheons and after-work gatherings. She confided in Jenny that she could not understand why everyone seemed to be mad at her. Jenny, not wanting to cause trouble, said nothing to Linda. In a group of four or five classmates, discuss the answers to the following questions:

1. If you were Jenny, what would you do?
2. What would you do if you were Linda?
3. What would you do if you were Jason?
4. What would you do if you were another team member?
5. If you were the boss and got wind of the resentment against Linda, what would you do?

Hands-On | Project 12-4 Learn to Be a Good Communicator

Working with a partner, discuss ways to respond to the following statements made by a customer. Then decide on your best response.

1. My computer is all dark.
2. I got so mad at my laptop, I threw it on the floor. Now it won't start. I think it's still under warranty.
3. My dog chewed the mouse cord and now nothing works.
4. I heard you tell that other customer that your product stinks. I came here to buy one. Now what am I to do?
5. I don't see the "any" key. Where is it?

Hands-On | Project 12-5 Learn to Interact with the User

Rob, an IT service technician, has been called on site to repair a desktop computer. He has not spoken directly with the user, Lisa, but he knows the floor of the building where she works and can look for her name on her cubicle. The following is a description of his actions. Create a table with two columns. List in one column the mistakes he makes in the following description, and in the next column describe the correct actions he should have taken.

Rob's company promised that a service technician would come sometime during the next business day after the call was received. Rob was given the name and address of the user and the problem, which was stated as "PC will not boot." Rob arrived the following day at about 10:00 a.m. He found Lisa's cubicle, but she was not present. Because Lisa was not present, Rob decided not to disturb the papers all over her desk, so he laid his notebooks and tools on top of her work.

Rob tried to boot the computer, and it gave errors indicating a corrupted file system on the hard drive. He successfully booted from a DVD and was able to access a directory list of drive C:. The list was corrupted and jumbled and he realized most of the files were corrupted. Next, Rob used a recovery utility to try to recover the files and directories but was unable to do so. He began to suspect that a virus had caused the problem, so he ran a virus scan program that did not find the suspected virus.

He made a call to his technical support to ask for suggestions. Technical support suggested he try erasing everything on the hard drive to remove any possible viruses and then reinstall Windows. Rob cleaned everything off the hard drive and was on the phone with technical support, in the process of reloading Windows from the company's file server, when Lisa arrived.

Lisa took one look at her computer and gasped. She caught her breath and asked where her data was. Rob replied, "A virus destroyed your hard drive. I had to reformat."

Lisa tried to explain the importance of the destroyed data. Rob replied, "Guess you'll learn to make backups now." Lisa left to find her manager.

12

Hands-On | Project 12-6 Learn from the Best

Relate a firsthand experience when a technician, coworker, help-desk personnel, or salesperson followed best practices while helping a customer or coworker. What is a principle this person applied that could help you when working with your own customers or coworkers?

Now let's turn our attention to general strategies and tips that can help you troubleshoot any computer problem.

STRATEGIES TO TROUBLESHOOT ANY COMPUTER PROBLEM

A+
220-902
5.5

When a computer doesn't work and you're responsible for fixing it, you should generally approach the problem first as an investigator and discoverer, always being careful not to compound the problem through your own actions. If the problem seems difficult, see it as an opportunity to learn something new. Ask questions until you understand the source of the problem. Once you understand it, you're almost done because most likely the solution will be evident. If you take the attitude that you can understand the problem and solve it, no matter how deeply you have to dig, you probably *will* solve it.

One systematic method to solve a problem used by most expert troubleshooters is the six steps diagrammed in Figure 12-10, which can apply to both software and hardware problems.

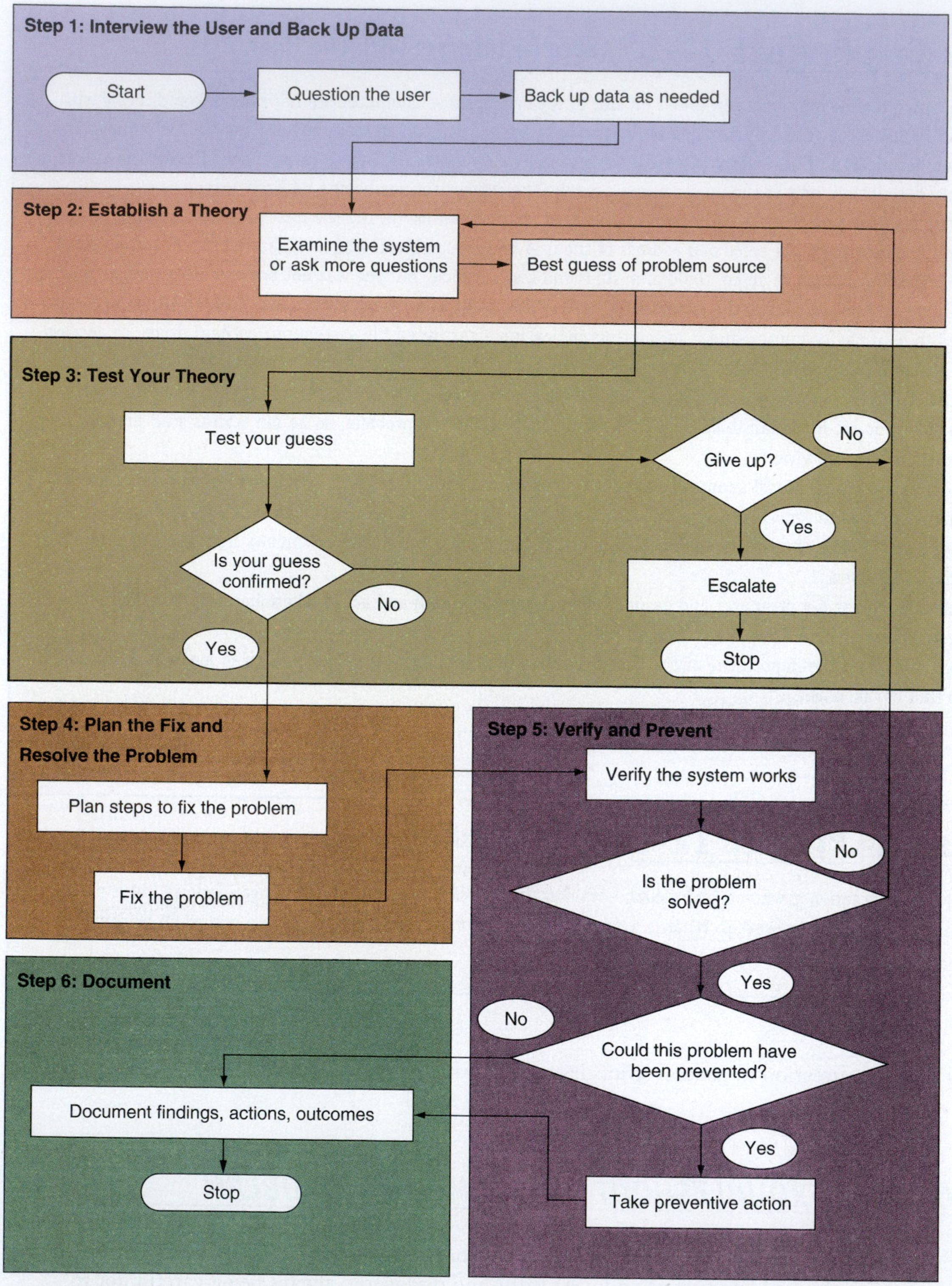

Figure 12-10 General approach to problem solving

★ A+ Exam Tip The A+ 220-902 exam expects you to know about all the aspects of troubleshooting theory and strategy and how to apply the troubleshooting procedures and techniques described in this section. Read over A+ 220-902 Objective 5.5 and compare it with Figure 12-10. You'll find the objectives with this text.

Here are the steps:

1. Interview the user and back up data before you make any changes to the system.
2. Examine the system, analyze the problem, and make an initial determination of what is the source of the problem.
3. Test your theory. If the theory is not confirmed, form another theory or escalate the problem to someone higher in your organization with more experience or resources.
4. After you know the source of the problem, plan what to do to fix the problem and then fix it.
5. Verify the problem is fixed and that the system works. Take any preventive measures to make sure the problem doesn't happen again.
6. Document activities, outcomes, and what you learned.

Now let's examine the process step-by-step. As you learn about these six steps, you'll also learn about 13 rules useful when troubleshooting. Here's the first rule.

Rule 1: Approach the Problem Systematically
When trying to solve the problem, start at the beginning and walk through the situation in a thorough, careful way. This one rule is invaluable. Remember it and apply it every time. If you don't find the explanation to the problem after one systematic walkthrough, then repeat the entire process. Check and double-check to find the step you overlooked the first time. Most problems with computers are simple, such as a loose cable or incorrect Windows setting. Computers are logical through and through. Whatever the problem is, it's also very logical. Also, if you are faced with more than one problem on the same computer, work on only one problem at a time. Trying to solve multiple problems at the same time can get too confusing.

STEP 1: INTERVIEW THE USER AND BACK UP DATA

A+
220-902
5.5

Every troubleshooting situation begins with interviewing the user if he or she is available. If you have the opportunity to speak with the user, ask questions to help you identify the problem, how to reproduce it, and possible sources of the problem. Also ask about any data on the hard drive that is not backed up.

A+ Exam Tip The A+ 220-902 exam expects you to know how to interact with a user and know what questions to ask, given a troubleshooting scenario.

Here are some questions that can help you learn as much as you can about the problem and its root cause:

1. Please describe the problem. What error messages, unusual displays, or failures did you see? (Possible answer: I see this blue screen with a funny-looking message on it that makes no sense to me.)
2. When did the problem start? (Possible answer: When I first booted after loading this neat little screen saver I downloaded from the web.)
3. What was the situation when the problem occurred? (Possible answers: I was trying to start up my laptop. I was opening a document in Microsoft Word. I was using the web to research a project.)
4. What programs or software were you using? (Possible answer: I was using Internet Explorer.)
5. What changes have recently been made to the system? For example, did you recently install new software or move your computer system? (Possible answer: Well, yes. Yesterday I moved the computer case across the room.)

6. Has there been a recent thunderstorm or electrical problem? (Possible answer: Yes, last night. Then when I tried to turn on my computer this morning, nothing happened.)
7. Have you made any hardware, software, or configuration changes? (Possible answer: No, but I think my sister might have.)
8. Has someone else used your computer recently? (Possible answer: Sure, my son uses it all the time.)
9. Is there some valuable data on your system that is not backed up that I should know about before I start working on the problem? (Possible answer: Yes! Yes! My term paper! It's not backed up! You gotta save that!)
10. Can you show me how to reproduce the problem? (Possible answers: Yes, let me show you what to do.)

Based on the answers you receive, ask more penetrating questions until you feel the user has given you all the information he or she knows that can help you solve the problem. As you talk with the user, keep in mind rules 2, 3, and 4.

Rule 2: Establish Your Priorities
This rule can help make for a satisfied customer. Decide what your first priority is. For example, it might be to recover lost data or to get the computer back up and running as soon as possible. When practical, ask the user or customer for help deciding on priorities.

Rule 3: Beware of User Error
Remember that many problems stem from user error. If you suspect this is the case, ask the user to show you the problem and carefully watch what the user is doing.

Rule 4: Keep Your Cool and Don't Rush
In some situations, you might be tempted to act too quickly and to be drawn into the user's sense of emergency. But keep your cool and don't rush. For example, when a computer stops working, if unsaved data is still in memory or if data on the hard drive has not been backed up, look and think carefully before you leap! A wrong move can be costly. The best advice is not to hurry. Carefully plan your moves. Research the problem using documentation or the web if you're not sure what to do, and don't hesitate to ask for help. Don't simply try something, hoping it will work, unless you've run out of more intelligent alternatives!

After you have talked with the user, be sure to back up any important data that is not currently backed up before you begin work on the computer. If the computer is working well enough to boot to the Windows desktop, you can use File Explorer or Windows Explorer to copy data to a flash drive, another computer on the network, or other storage media.

★ A+ Exam Tip The A+ 220-902 exam expects you to know the importance of making backups before you make changes to a system.

If the computer is not healthy enough to use Explorer, don't do anything to jeopardize the data. If you must take a risk with the data, let it be the user's decision to do so, not yours. Try to boot the system. If the system will not boot to the Windows desktop, know that you can remove the hard drive from the system and use a converter to connect the drive to a USB port on another computer. You can then copy the data to the other computer. Next, return the hard drive to the original computer so you can begin troubleshooting the problem.

If possible, have the user verify that all important data is safely backed up before you continue to the next troubleshooting step. If you're new to troubleshooting and don't want the user looking over your shoulder while you work, you might want to let him or her know you'd prefer to work alone. You can say something like, "Okay, I think I have everything I need to get started. I'll let you know if I have another question."

STEP 2: EXAMINE THE SYSTEM AND MAKE YOUR BEST GUESS

A+
220-902
5.5

You're now ready to start solving the problem. Rules 5 and 6 can help.

Rule 5: Make No Assumptions
This rule is the hardest to follow because there is a tendency to trust anything in writing and assume that people are telling you exactly what happened. But documentation is sometimes wrong, and people don't always describe events as they occurred, so do your own investigating. For example, if the user tells you that the system boots up with no error messages but that the software still doesn't work, boot for yourself. You never know what the user might have overlooked.

Rule 6: Try the Simple Things First
Most problems are so simple and obvious that we overlook them because we expect the problem to be difficult. Don't let the complexity of computers fool you. Most problems are easy to fix. Really, they are! To save time, check the simple things first, such as whether a power switch is not turned on or a cable is loose. Generally, it's easy to check for a hardware problem before you check for a software problem. For example, if a USB drive is not working, verify the drive works on another computer before verifying the drivers are installed correctly.

Follow this process to form your best guess (best theory) and test it:

1. ***Reproduce the problem and observe for yourself what the user has described.*** For example, if the user tells you the system is totally dead, find out for yourself. Plug in the power and turn on the system. Listen for fans and look for lights and error messages. Suppose the user tells you that Internet Explorer will not open. Try opening it yourself to see what error messages might appear. As you investigate the system, refrain from making changes until you've come up with your theory as to what the source of the problem is. Can you duplicate the problem? Intermittent problems are generally more difficult to solve than problems that occur consistently.
2. ***Decide if the problem is hardware or software related.*** Sometimes you might not be sure, but make your best guess. For example, if the system fails before Windows starts to load, chances are the problem is a hardware problem. If the user tells you the system has not worked since the lightning storm the night before, chances are the problem is electrical. If the problem is that Explorer will not open even though the Windows desktop loads, you can assume the problem is software related. In another example, suppose a user complains that his Word documents are getting corrupted. Possible sources of the problem might be that the user does not know how to save documents properly, the application or the OS might be corrupted, the computer might have a virus, or the hard drive might be intermittently failing. Investigate for yourself, and then decide if the problem is caused by software, hardware, or the user.
3. ***Make your best guess as to the source of the problem, and don't forget to question the obvious.*** Here are some practical examples of questioning the obvious and checking the simple things first:
   - The video doesn't work. Your best guess is the monitor cables are loose or the monitor is not turned on.
   - Excel worksheets are getting corrupted. Your best guess is the user is not saving the workbook files correctly.
   - The DVD drive is not reading a DVD. Your best guess is the DVD is scratched.

- The system refuses to boot and gives the error that the hard drive is not found. Your best guess is internal cables to the drive are loose.

Rule 7: Become a Researcher

Following this rule is the most fun. When a computer problem arises that you can't easily solve, be as tenacious as a bulldog. Search the web, ask questions, read more, make some phone calls, and ask more questions. Take advantage of every available resource, including online help, documentation, technical support, and books such as this one. Learn to perform advanced searches using a good search engine on the web, such as *www.google.com*. What you learn will be yours to take to the next problem. This is the real joy of computer troubleshooting. If you're good at it, you're always learning something new.

If you're having a problem deciding what might be the source of the problem, keep in mind Rule 7 and try searching these resources for ideas and tips:

- The specific application, operating system, or hardware you support must be available to you to test, observe, and study and to use to re-create a customer's problem whenever possible.
- In a corporate setting, hardware and software products generally have technical documentation available. If you don't find it on hand, know that you are likely to find user manuals and technical support manuals as .pdf files that can be downloaded from the product manufacturers' websites. These sites might offer troubleshooting and support pages, help forums, chat sessions, email support, and links to submit a troubleshooting ticket to the manufacturer (see Figure 12-11). For Windows problems, the best websites to search are *technet.microsoft.com* or *support.microsoft.com*.

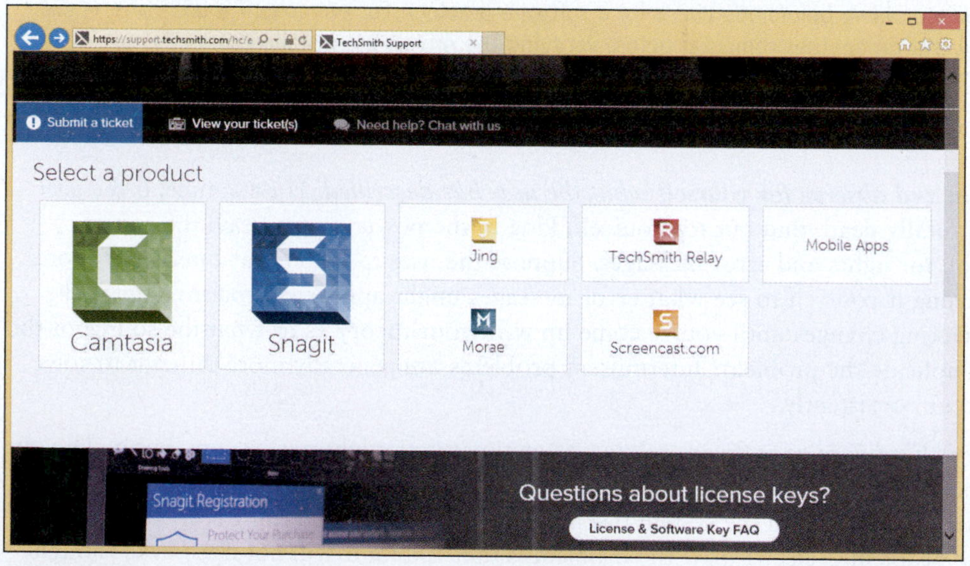

Source: Techsmith Corporation

Figure 12-11 Search manufacturer websites for help with a hardware or software product

- Use a search engine to search the web for help. In your search string, include an error message, symptom, hardware device, or description of the problem. The chances are always good that someone has had exactly the same problem, presented the problem online, and someone else has presented a step-by-step solution. All you have to do is find it! As you practice this type of web research, you'll get better and better at knowing how to form a search string and which websites are trustworthy and present the best information. If your first five minutes of searching doesn't turn up a solution, please don't give up! It might take patience and searching for 20 minutes or more to find the solution you need. As you search, most likely you'll learn more and more about the problem, and you'll slowly zero in on a solution.

- Some companies offer an expert system for troubleshooting. An expert system is software that is designed and written to help solve problems. It uses databases of known facts and rules to simulate human experts' reasoning and decision making. Expert systems for IT technicians work by posing questions about a problem to be answered by the technician or the customer. The response to each question triggers another question from the software until the expert system arrives at a possible solution or solutions. Many expert systems are "intelligent," meaning the system will record your input and use it in subsequent sessions to select more questions to ask and approaches to try. Therefore, future troubleshooting sessions on this same type of problem tend to zero in more quickly toward a solution.

Notes To limit your search to a particular site when using *www.google.com*, use the *site:* parameter in the Search box. For example, to search only the Microsoft site for information about the defrag command, enter this search string: **defrag site:*microsoft.com***

STEP 3: TEST YOUR THEORY

A+ 220-902 5.5

For simple problems, you can zip right through Steps 3, 4, and 5 in Figure 12-10. Here are two examples where Steps 3, 4, and 5 go very fast:

- The video does not work and you suspect loose cables or the monitor is not turned on. You check the video cable connection (Step 3) and discover it's loose. As you connect it (Step 4), the video display works. Problem solved. You now can take the time to screw the video cable to the connection (Step 5) so that the problem won't happen again.
- Excel worksheets are getting corrupted. As you watch the user save a file, you discover he is saving files in an incorrect format that other software in the office cannot read (Step 3). You step the user through saving the file correctly and then verify that others can open the file (Step 4). You explain to the user which format to use (Step 5). The problem is then solved, and it's not likely to happen again.

Here are two examples of Step 3 that include testing a guess that is not correct:

- The optical drive won't read a DVD and you suspect the DVD is scratched. When you check the disc, it looks fine. Your next guess is the optical drive is not recognized by Windows. You check Device Manager, and it reports errors with the drive. Your next guess is that drivers are corrupted.
- The system refuses to boot and gives the error message that the hard drive is not found. Internal cable connections are solid. Your next guess is the drive is not getting power.

Here are two examples of Step 3 where your guess is correct, and then you move on toward Step 4 to plan a solution:

- Word files are getting corrupted. After eliminating several simple causes, you guess that the hard drive is going bad. You check Event Viewer and discover Windows has recorded write errors to the drive multiple times (Step 3). Your theory is confirmed that the drive is bad and needs replacing (Step 4).
- The video display does not work. You check cables and power and verify monitor settings controlled by buttons on the front of the monitor are all okay, but still no video. You guess the video cable might be bad and exchange it with one you know is good, but still no video. Therefore, you guess that the monitor is bad. You move the monitor to a working computer and it still does not work. You try a good monitor on the first computer, and it works fine. Your guess that the monitor is bad has been confirmed (Step 3). Next, you plan how to purchase a new monitor (Step 4).

As you test your guesses, keep in mind rules 8 through 11.

Rule 8: Divide and Conquer
This rule is the most powerful. Isolate the problem. In the overall system, remove one hardware or software component after another until the problem is isolated to a small part of the whole system. As you divide a large problem into smaller components, you can analyze each component separately. You can use one or more of the following to help you divide and conquer:

- In Windows, perform a clean boot to eliminate all nonessential startup programs and services as a possible source of the problem.
- Boot from a bootable DVD or flash drive to eliminate the Windows installation and the hard drive as the problem.

Rule 9: Write Things Down
Keep good notes as you're working. They'll help you think more clearly. Draw diagrams. Make lists. Clearly and precisely write down what you're learning. If you need to leave the problem and return to it later, it's difficult to remember what you have observed and already tried. When the problem gets cold like this, your notes will be invaluable.

Rule 10: Don't Assume the Worst
When it's an emergency and your only copy of data is on a hard drive that is not working, don't assume that the data is lost. Much can be done to recover data. If you want to recover lost data on a hard drive, don't write anything to the drive; you might write on top of lost data, eliminating all chances of recovery.

Rule 11: Reboot and Start Over
This is an important rule. Fresh starts are good, and they uncover events or steps that might have been overlooked. Take a break! Get away from the problem. Begin again.

By the time you have finished Step 3, the problem might already be solved or you will know the source of the problem and will be ready to plan a solution.

STEP 4: PLAN YOUR SOLUTION AND THEN FIX THE PROBLEM

A+
220-902
5.5

Some solutions, such as replacing a hard drive or a motherboard, are expensive and time consuming. You need to carefully consider what you will do and the order in which you will do it. When planning and implementing your solution, keep rules 12 and 13 in mind.

Rule 12: Use the Least Invasive Solution First
As you solve computer problems, always keep in mind that you don't want to make things worse, so you should use the least invasive solution. Keep in mind that you want to fix the problem in such a way that the system is returned to normal working condition with the least amount of effort and least changes to the system. For example, don't format the hard drive until you've first tried to fix the problem without having to erase everything on the drive. In another example, don't reinstall Microsoft Office until you have tried applying patches to the existing installation.

Rule 13: Know Your Starting Point
Find out what works and doesn't work before you take anything apart or try some possible fix. Suppose you decide to install a new anti-malware program. After the installation, you discover Microsoft Office gives errors and you cannot print to the network printer. You don't know if the anti-malware program is causing problems or the problems existed before you began work. As much as possible, find out what works or what doesn't work before you attempt a fix.

Do the following to plan your solution and fix the problem:

1. Consider different solutions and select the least invasive one.
2. Before applying your solution, as best you can, determine what works and doesn't work about the system so you know your starting point.
3. Fix the problem. This might be as simple as plugging up a new monitor. Or it might be as difficult as reinstalling Windows and applications software and restoring data from backups.

STEP 5: VERIFY THE FIX AND TAKE PREVENTIVE ACTION

A+ 220-902 5.5

After you have fixed the problem, reboot the system and verify all is well. Can you reach the Internet, use the printer, or use Microsoft Office? If possible, have the user check everything and verify that the job is done satisfactorily. If either of you finds a problem, return to Step 2 in the troubleshooting process to examine the system and form a new theory as to the cause of the problem.

After you and the user have verified all is working, ask yourself the question, "Could this problem have been prevented?" If so, go the extra mile to instruct the user, set Windows to automatically install updates, or do whatever else is appropriate to prevent future problems.

STEP 6: DOCUMENT WHAT HAPPENED

A+ 220-902 5.5

Good documentation helps you take what you learned into the next troubleshooting situation, train others, develop effective preventive maintenance plans, and satisfy any audits or customer or employer queries about your work. Most companies use call tracking software for this purpose. Be sure to include initial symptoms, the source of the problem, and what you did to fix it. Make the notes detailed enough so that you can use them later when solving similar problems.

For on-site support, a customer expects documentation about your services. Include in the documentation sufficient details broken down by cost of individual parts, hours worked, and cost per hour. Give the documentation to the customer at the end of the service and keep a copy for yourself. For phone support, the documentation stays in-house.

12

APPLYING CONCEPTS TAKE GOOD NOTES

A+ 220-902 5.5

Daniel had not been a good note taker in school, and this lack of skill was affecting his work. His manager, Jonathan, had been watching Daniel's notes in the ticketing system at the help desk he worked on and was not happy with what he saw. Jonathan had pointed out to Daniel more than once that his cryptic notes with sketchy information would one day cause major problems. On Monday morning, calls were hammering the help desk because a server had gone down over the weekend and many internal customers were not able to get to their data. Daniel escalated one call from a customer named Matt to a tier-two help desk. Later that day, Sandra, a tier-two technician, received the escalated ticket, and to her dismay the phone number of the customer was missing. She called Daniel. "How am I to call this customer? You only have his first name, and these notes about the problem don't even make sense!" Daniel apologized to Sandra, but the damage was done.

Two days later, an angry Matt calls the manager of the help desk to complain that his problem is still not solved. Jonathan listens to Matt vent and apologizes for the problem his help desk has caused. It's a little embarrassing to Jonathan to have to ask Matt for his call-back information and to repeat the details of the problem. He gives the information to Sandra and the problem gets a quick resolution.

Discuss this situation in a small group and answer the following questions:

1. If you were Daniel, what could you do to improve note taking in the ticketing system?
2. After Sandra called, do you think Daniel should have told Jonathan about the problem? Why or why not?
3. If you were Jonathan, how would you handle the situation with Daniel?

Two students play the role of Daniel and Jonathan when Jonathan calls Daniel into his office to discuss the call he just received from Matt. The other students in the group can watch and make suggestions as to how to improve the conversation.

Hands-On | Project 12-7 Document an Intermittent Problem

Intermittent problems can make troubleshooting challenging. The trick in diagnosing problems that come and go is to look for patterns or clues as to when the problems occur. If you or the user can't reproduce the problem at will, ask the user to keep a log of when the problems occur and exactly what messages appear. Tell the user that intermittent problems are the hardest to solve and might take some time, but you won't give up. Show the user how to take a screen shot of the error messages when they appear. It might also be appropriate to ask him to email the screen shot to you. Do the following:

1. Use the Windows 8/7 Snipping Tool to take a snip of your Windows desktop showing the Task Manager window open. If you need help using the Snipping Tool, see Windows Help and Support.
2. Save the snip and email it to your instructor.

Hands-On | Project 12-8 Research IT Support Sites

The web is an excellent resource to use when problem solving, and it's helpful to know which websites are trustworthy and useful. Access each of the websites listed in Table 12-1, and print one webpage from each site that shows information that might be useful for a support technician. If the site offers a free email newsletter, consider subscribing to it. Answer the following questions about these sites:

1. Which site can help you find out what type of RAM you can use on your computer?
2. Which site explains Moore's Law? What is Moore's Law?
3. Which site offers a free download for data recovery software?
4. Which site gives a review about registry cleaning software?
5. Which two sites allow you to post a question about computer repair to a forum?
6. Which site offers a tutorial to learn C programming?
7. Which site offers free antivirus software published by the site owners?

Organization	Website
CNET, Inc.	*cnet.com*
Experts Exchange (subscription site)	*experts-exchange.com*
F-Secure Corp	*f-secure.com*
How Stuff Works	*howstuffworks.com*
How-To Geek	*howtogeek.com*
iFixit	*ifixit.com*
Kingston Technology (information about memory)	*kingston.com*
Microsoft Technical Resources	*support.microsoft.com* *technet.microsoft.com*
PC World	*pcworld.com*
TechRepublic	*techrepublic.com*
Tom's Hardware Guide	*tomshardware.com*

Table 12-1 Technical information websites

With tons of information in hand about serving customers and solving problems, let's dig into some actual troubleshooting.

TROUBLESHOOTING APPLICATIONS

A+
220-902
1.3, 1.4,
3.3, 4.1

A problem with an application might be caused by the application, the hardware, the operating system, the data, other applications in conflict with this one, or the user. We begin this part of the chapter by looking at some general steps to help you solve a problem with an application. We then look at some Windows tools to help you solve application problems, and some specific error messages and what to do about them.

Notes As you are troubleshooting a problem and make a change to the system, be sure to restart Windows and check to see if the problem is resolved before you move on to the next fix.

GENERAL STEPS FOR SOLVING APPLICATION ERRORS

A+
220-902
4.1

This section covers a variety of steps you can take to try to solve a problem with an application. As you work your way through these steps, keep in mind where each step fits in the overall strategy given earlier in the chapter for solving any computer problem.

STEP 1: INTERVIEW THE USER AND BACK UP DATA

Worth saying again: Start with interviewing the user:

1. ***Interview the user and back up data.*** Find out as much information as you can from the user about the problem, when it started, and what happened to the system around the time the problem started. Also ask if valuable data is on the system. If so, back it up.
2. ***Ask the user to reproduce the problem while you watch.*** Many problems with applications are caused by user error. Watch carefully as the user shows you the problem. If you see him making a mistake, be tactful as you explain the problem and its solution.
3. ***Try a reboot.*** Reboots solve a lot of application problems and one might be a shortcut to your solution. If that doesn't work, no harm is done and you're ready to begin investigating the system.

STEP 2: ERROR MESSAGES, THE WEB, COWORKERS, AND LOGS MIGHT HELP

Windows might display an error message and offer a solution. Logs kept by Windows can offer clues. Here are a few examples of how to get help from Windows, the web, and coworkers:

- ***View error messages in the Action Center.*** The Action Center tracks problems with applications, hardware, and Windows (see Figure 12-12). In the Action Center, click **View archived messages** to see a history of past problems and double-click a problem to read the details about it.

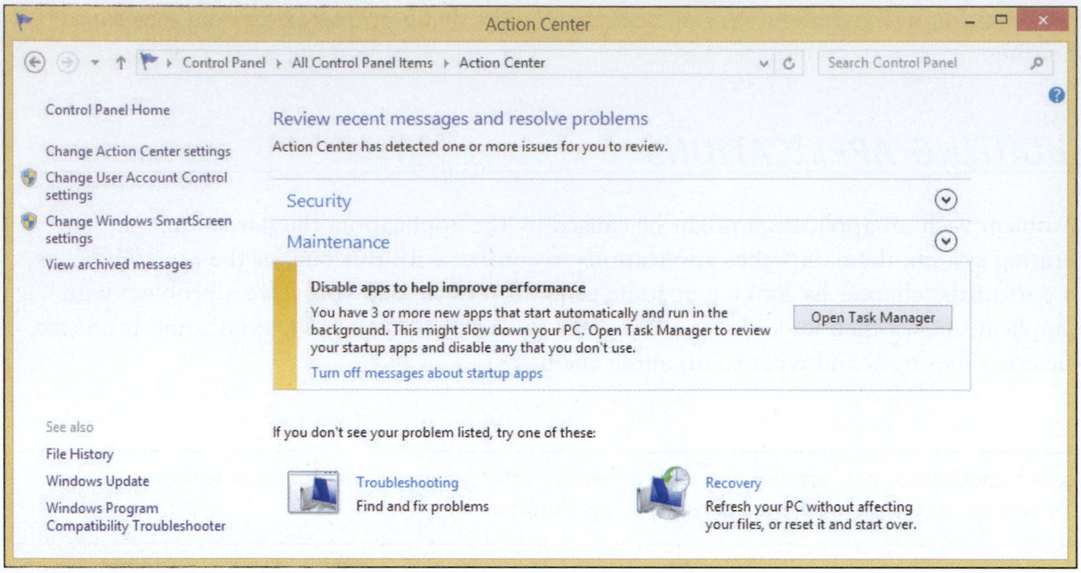

Figure 12-12 Windows 8 suggests disabling some startup applications to increase the system's performance

- ***Use Event Viewer and Reliability Monitor to look for clues.*** The Event Viewer logs might give clues about applications and the system. Hard drive errors often appear as application errors. Use Reliability Monitor to look for errors with other applications or with key hardware components such as the hard drive. You learned to use both tools in the chapter, "Optimizing Windows."
- ***Find and ask for help.*** You might find more information about a problem by searching the website of the application manufacturer for support and help. Also, search the web on the error message, application, or description of the problem. Look for forums where others have posted the same problem with the same app. Someone else has likely posted a solution. However, be careful and don't take the advice unless you trust the website. After you've made a reasonable effort to find help on your own, ask for help from coworkers who are more experienced.

> **Notes** Working while a customer looks over your shoulder can be awkward. A customer needs her IT support technician to appear confident and in charge. To maintain your customer's confidence in your technical abilities, you might want to find privacy when searching the web or talking with coworkers.

STEP 3: CONSIDER THE DATA OR THE APPLICATION IS CORRUPTED

Now that you've interviewed the user, backed up important data, examined the system, and investigated the problem, it's time to come up with a theory as to the cause of the problem. Consider and do these things:

- ***Consider data corruption.*** For applications that use data files such as Microsoft Office, it might appear that the application has a problem when the problem is really a corrupted data file. Try creating an entirely new data file. If that works, then suspect that previous errors might be caused by corrupted data. You might be able to recover part of a corrupted file by changing its file extension to .txt and importing it into the application as a text file.
- ***Check application settings for errors.*** Maybe a user has made one too many changes to the application settings, which can cause a problem with missing toolbars and other functions. Write down each setting the user has changed and then restore all settings back to their default values. If the problem

is solved, restore each setting to the way the user had it until you find the one causing the problem. The process will take some time, but users can get upset if you change their application settings without justification.

- ***Repair the application.*** The application setup might have the option to repair the installation. Look for it in the Programs and Features window, on the setup disc for the application, or on the manufacturer's website.
- ***Uninstall and reinstall the application.*** Do so with caution because you might lose any customized settings, macros, or scripts. Also know this still might not solve a problem with a corrupted application because registry entries might not be properly reset during the uninstall process.

STEP 4: CONSIDER OUTSIDE INTERFERENCE

The problem might be caused by a virus, Windows, other applications, or hardware. Check these things:

- ***A virus might be causing the problem.*** Scan for viruses and check Task Manager to make sure some strange process is not interfering with your applications.
- ***The computer might be low on system resources or another application might be interfering.*** Close all other applications.
- ***Maybe a service failed to start.*** Research the application documentation and find out if the app relies on a service to work. Use the Services console to make sure the service has started. If the service has failed to start, make sure it has an Automatic or Manual setting.
- ***The problem might be bad memory.*** Following the directions given later in this chapter, use the Memory Diagnostics tool (mdsched.exe) to test memory. If it finds errors, replace the memory modules.
- ***The problem might be a corrupted hard drive.*** To eliminate the hard drive as the source of an application error, use the chkdsk command with the /r parameter to check the drive and recover data in bad sectors.
- ***A background program or other software might be conflicting with the application.*** To eliminate compatibility issues with other software, run the application after a clean boot. You learned to perform a clean boot in the chapter, "Optimizing Windows." Recall a clean boot eliminates third-party software from starting during the boot. If a clean boot allows the application to run without errors, you need to methodically disable each third-party program one-by-one until you discover the one in conflict.

12

STEP 5: CONSIDER WINDOWS MIGHT BE THE PROBLEM

A problem with an application can sometimes be solved by updating or restoring Windows system files. Do the following:

- ***Download Windows updates.*** Make sure all critical and important Windows updates are installed. Microsoft Office updates are included in Windows updates.
- ***Use System File Checker.*** For essential hardware devices, use the System File Checker (SFC), which is covered later in this section, to verify and replace system files. Use the command **sfc /scannow**.
- ***Boot Windows in Safe Mode.*** Safe Mode loads Windows with a minimum configuration and can create a stable environment when Windows gets corrupted. It goes beyond a clean boot in that it eliminates third-party software from launching at the boot and also reduces Windows startup processes to only those essential to launch Windows. There are several ways to start Safe Mode, which you learn about in the chapter, "Troubleshooting Windows Startup." One way is to use System Configuration. Enter **msconfig.exe** in the Windows 8 Run box or the Windows 7 Search box to open the System Configuration window and click the **Boot** tab. Check **Safe boot** (see Figure 12-13). If the application needs the Internet to work, select **Network**. Click **OK** and restart the system.

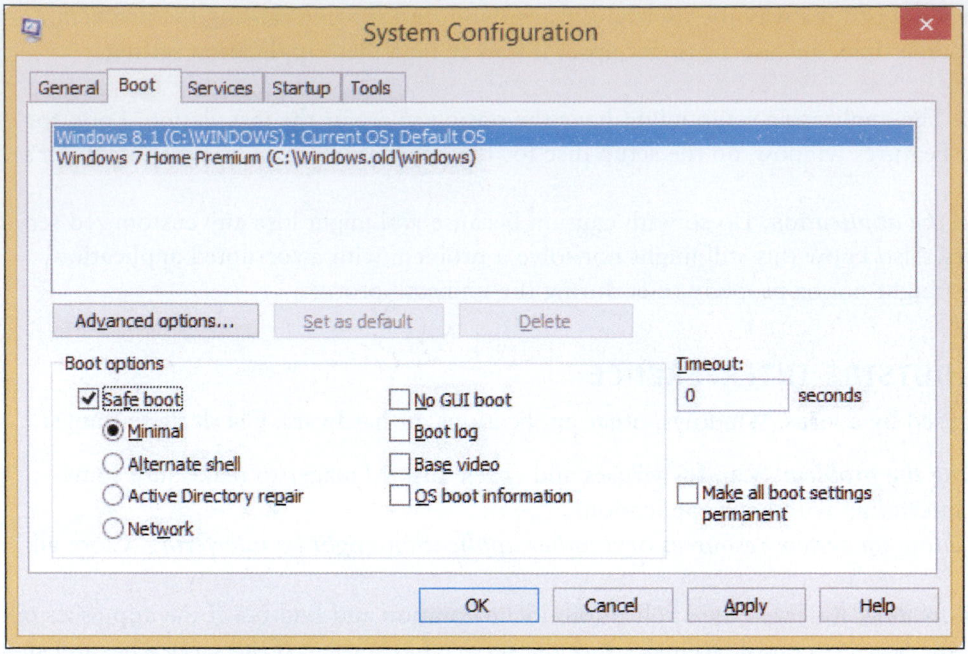

Figure 12-13 Restart Windows in a Safe boot with minimal Windows configuration

If the application works in Safe Mode, you can assume the problem is not with the application but with the operating system, device drivers, or other software that loads at startup. To return the system to a normal startup, open System Configuration again and click **Normal startup** on the General tab.

- *Use System Restore.* If you can identify the approximate date the error started and that date is in the recent past, use System Restore (rstrui.exe). Select a restore point just before the problem started. Reverting to a restore point can solve problems with registry entries the application uses that have become corrupted. However, System Restore can cause problems of its own, so use it with caution.

A+ Exam Tip The 220-902 exam expects you to know when and how to use System Restore to solve a Windows, hardware, or application problem.

A+ Exam Tip If an often-used Windows utility can be launched from a command prompt, the A+ 220-902 exam expects you to know the program name of that utility.

Caution When researching a problem, suppose you discover that Microsoft or a manufacturer's website offers a fix or patch you can download and apply. To get the right patch, recall you need to make sure you get a 32-bit patch for a 32-bit installation of Windows, a device driver, or an application. For a 64-bit installation of Windows, make sure you get a 64-bit device driver. An application installed in a 64-bit OS might be a 32-bit application or a 64-bit application.

Now let's learn to use the Memory Diagnostics and System File Checker tools, which can be useful when troubleshooting application problems.

MEMORY DIAGNOSTICS

A+
220-902
1.4, 4.1

Errors with memory are often difficult to diagnose because they can appear intermittently and might be mistaken as application errors, user errors, or other hardware component errors. Sometimes these errors cause the system to hang, a BSOD (blue screen of death) error might occur, or the system continues to function with applications giving errors or data getting corrupted. You can quickly identify a problem with memory or eliminate memory as the source of a problem by using the Windows Memory Diagnostics (mdsched.exe) tool. It works before Windows is loaded to test memory for errors, and can be used on computers that don't have Windows installed. Use one of these two methods to start the utility:

- *Method 1.* In a command prompt window on the Windows desktop, enter **mdsched.exe** and press **Enter**. A dialog box appears (see Figure 12-14) asking if you want to run the test now or on the next restart.

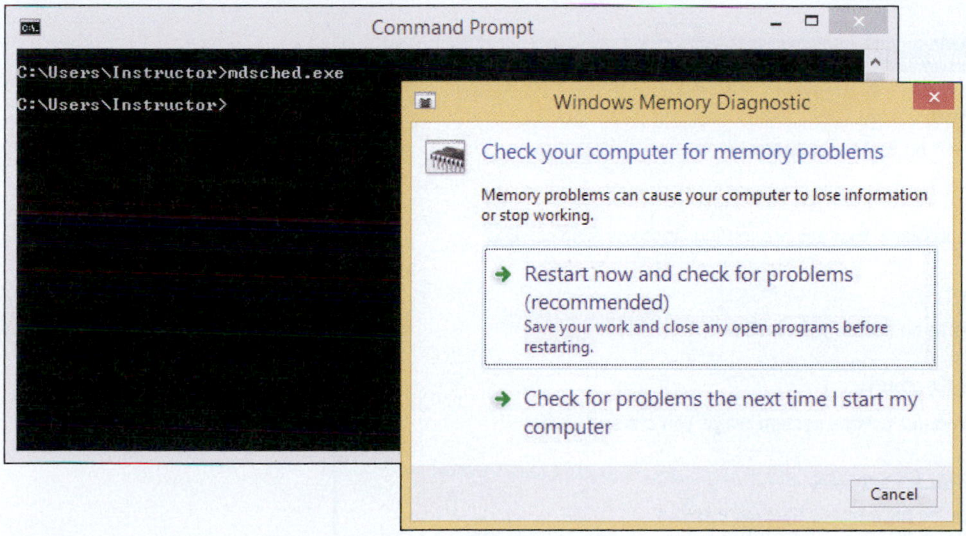

Figure 12-14 Use the mdsched.exe command to test memory

- *Method 2.* If you cannot boot from the hard drive, boot the computer from the Windows setup DVD or some other recovery media such as a Windows 8 recovery drive or a Windows 7 repair disc. (You learn more about these options in the chapter, "Troubleshooting Windows Startup.") On the opening screen, select your language. On the next screen (see Figure 12-15), click **Repair your computer**.

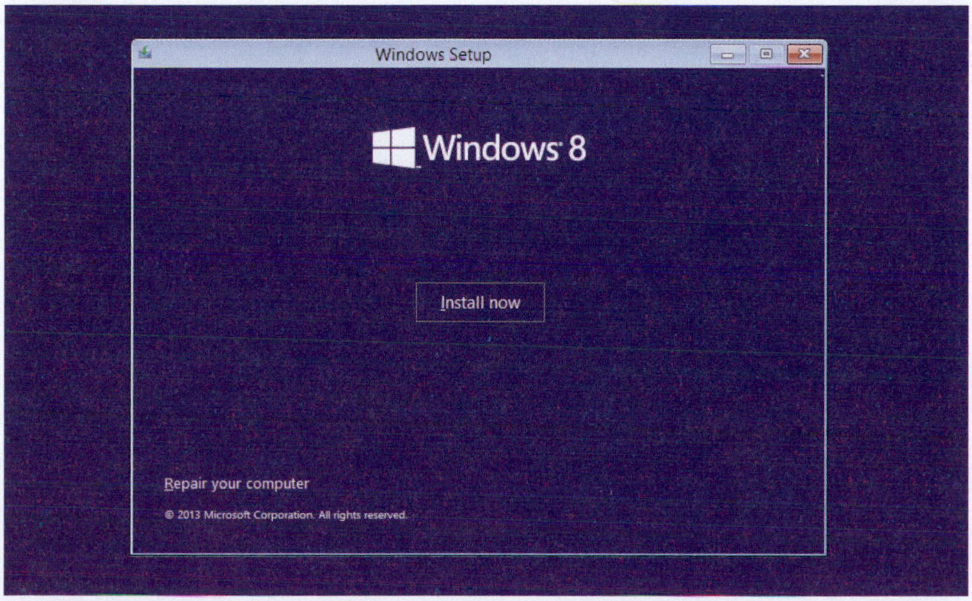

Figure 12-15 Opening menu when you boot from the Windows 8 setup DVD

On the next screen, do one of the following:

- For Windows 8, click **Troubleshoot** and then **Advanced options**. On the Advanced options screen, click **Command Prompt**. A command prompt window appears. At the command prompt, enter **mdsched.exe** and press **Enter**.
- For Windows 7, select the Windows installation to repair. On the System Recovery Options screen (see Figure 12-16), click **Windows Memory Diagnostic** and follow the directions on screen.

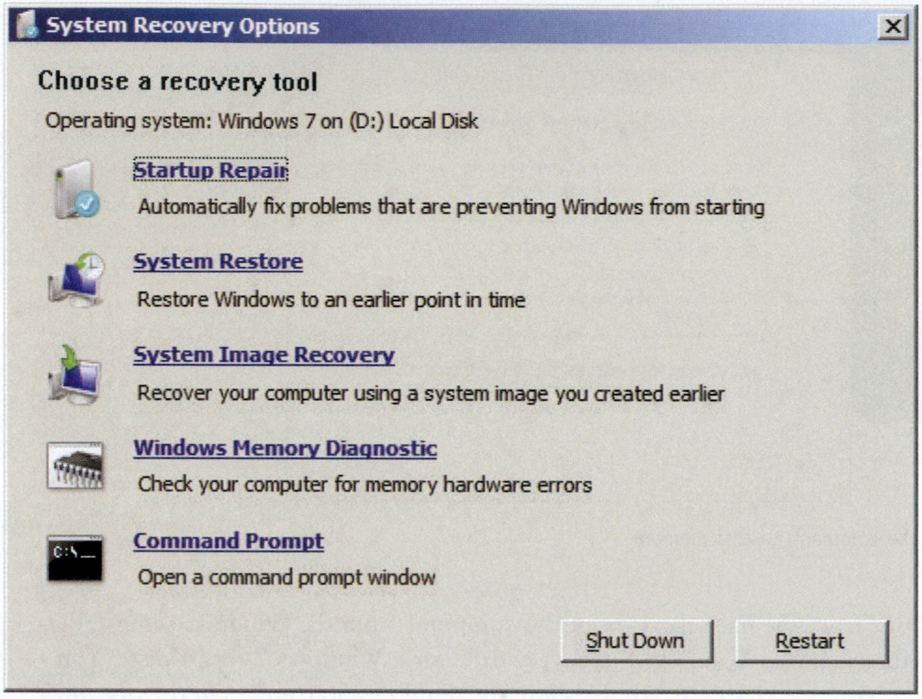

Figure 12-16 Test memory using the Windows 7 System Recovery Options menu

If the tool reports memory errors, replace all memory modules installed on the motherboard.

SYSTEM FILE CHECKER

A+
220-902
1.3, 4.1

A Windows application or hardware problem might be caused by a corrupted Windows system file. That's where System File Checker might help. System File Checker (SFC) protects system files and keeps a cache of current system files in case it needs to refresh a damaged file. To use the utility to scan all system files and verify them, first close all applications and then enter the command **sfc /scannow** in an elevated command prompt window (see Figure 12-17). If corrupted system files are found, you might need to provide the Windows setup DVD to restore the files. If you have problems running the SFC utility, boot the computer into Safe Mode and run the sfc /scannow command again in Safe Mode. If you still have problems, know that you will learn more about repairing system files in the chapter, "Troubleshooting Windows Startup."

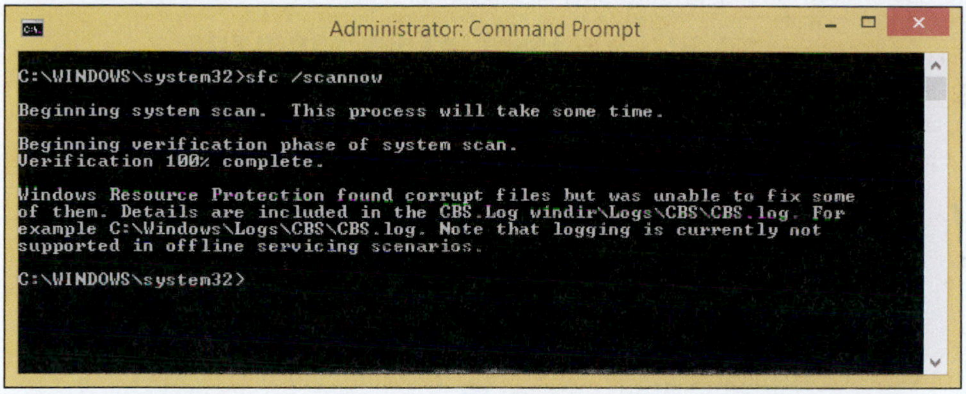

Figure 12-17 Use System File Checker to verify Windows system files

> **Notes** Recall from the chapter, "Maintaining Windows," that you can get an elevated command prompt window in Windows 8 by right-clicking **Start** and clicking **Command Prompt (Admin)**. In Windows 7, click **Start**, **All Programs**, and **Accessories**. Then right-click **Command Prompt** and select **Run as administrator** from the shortcut menu.

RESPONDING TO SPECIFIC ERROR MESSAGES

A+ 220-902 1.3, 1.4, 3.3, 4.1

In this part of the chapter, we look at some specific error messages that relate to problems with applications.

WHEN AN APPLICATION HANGS

If an application is locked up and not responding, use Task Manager to end it. If Task Manager can't end a process, use the tasklist and taskkill commands. The tasklist command returns the process identifier (PID), which is a number that identifies each running process. The taskkill command uses the process ID to kill the process. Using Notepad as a sample application, do the following:

1. Open a command prompt window and start Notepad with the command **`notepad.exe`**. Be sure the Notepad window and the command prompt window are positioned so both are visible on your screen. Use the **`tasklist | more`** command to get a list of processes currently running (press the Spacebar to scroll to the next page). Note the PID of the Notepad process, for example, 7132.
2. Enter the command **`taskkill /f /pid:7132`**, using the PID you noted in Step 1. The /f parameter forcefully kills the process. Be careful using this command; it is so powerful that you can end critical system processes that will cause the system to shut down.

WHEN A FILE FAILS TO OPEN

Windows depends on the file extension to associate a data file with an application used to open it, which it calls the file association. An application associated with a file extension is called its default program. When you double-click a data file and Windows examines the file extension and doesn't know which application to call on to open the file, it displays an error message. The solution to this problem is to change the file association for the data file's file extension.

APPLYING | CONCEPTS SOLVE FILE ASSOCIATION PROBLEMS

A+
220-902
4.1

In our example, the Transact.dbf file shown in Figure 12-18a is a legacy database file created by dBASE, and the error box in Figure 12-18a appeared when the user double-clicked the file.

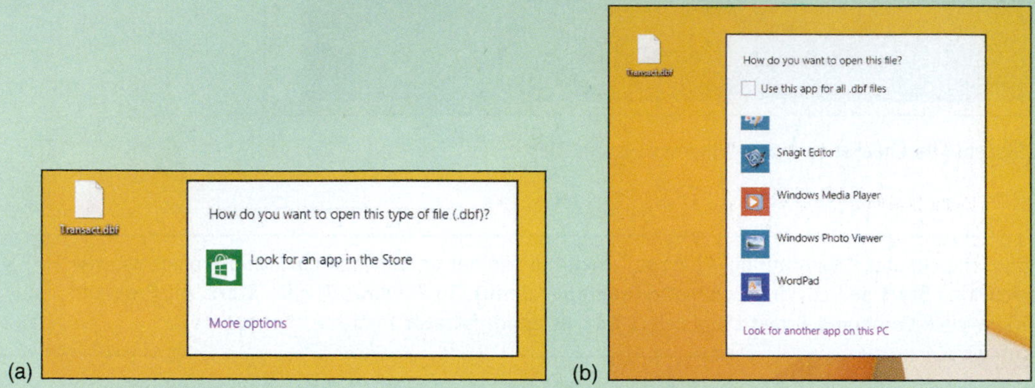

Figure 12-18 Windows does not know which application to use to open the data file

Follow these steps to instruct Windows 8 to use Microsoft Excel to open files with a .dbf file extension:

1. Click **More options** (see Figure 12-18a). At the bottom of the box (see Figure 12-18b), click **Look for another app on this PC**. (For Windows 7, click **Select a program from a list of installed programs**.)
2. The *Open with* window appears. Locate the program file for Microsoft Excel, as shown in Figure 12-19 and click **Open**. (If you don't know an application's program file and location, launch the application and then open Task Manager. On the Processes tab of Task Manager, right-click the application and click **Open file location**. File Explorer or Windows Explorer opens and highlights the program file. You can see the path to the program file at the top of the Explorer window.)

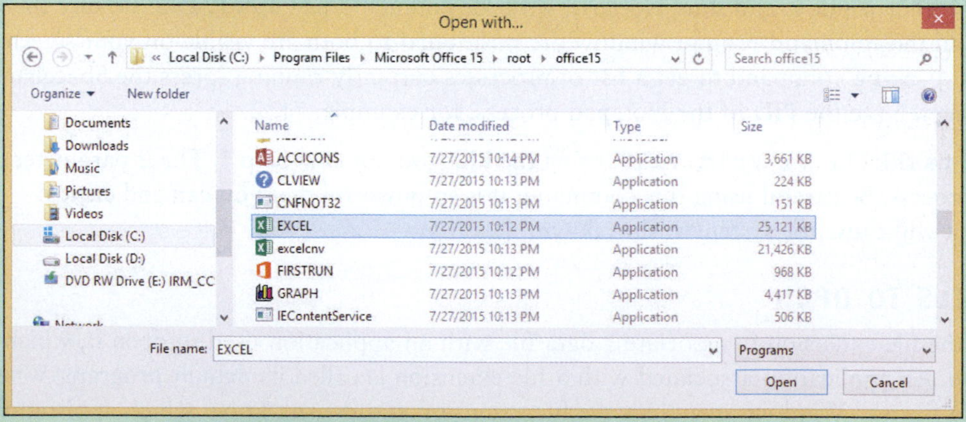

Figure 12-19 Locate and select the EXCEL.exe application program file

3. When you double-click the **Transact.dbf** file, the file opens in an Excel window. Also the icon used for the file on the desktop is now the Excel icon.

If you need to change the program associated with a file extension, use the Default Programs applet in Control Panel. For example, suppose you tried to associate the Transact.dbf file with Microsoft Access and when you opened the file, Access gave an error. Follow these steps to change the file association to Excel:

1. Open Control Panel in Classic view and click **Default Programs**. The Default Programs window opens. Click **Associate a file type or protocol with a program**. The list of current associations appears in the Set Associations window.
2. Select the file extension you want to change (see Figure 12-20) and click **Change program**. A dialog box appears asking how you want to open the file (as shown in the middle of Figure 12-20).

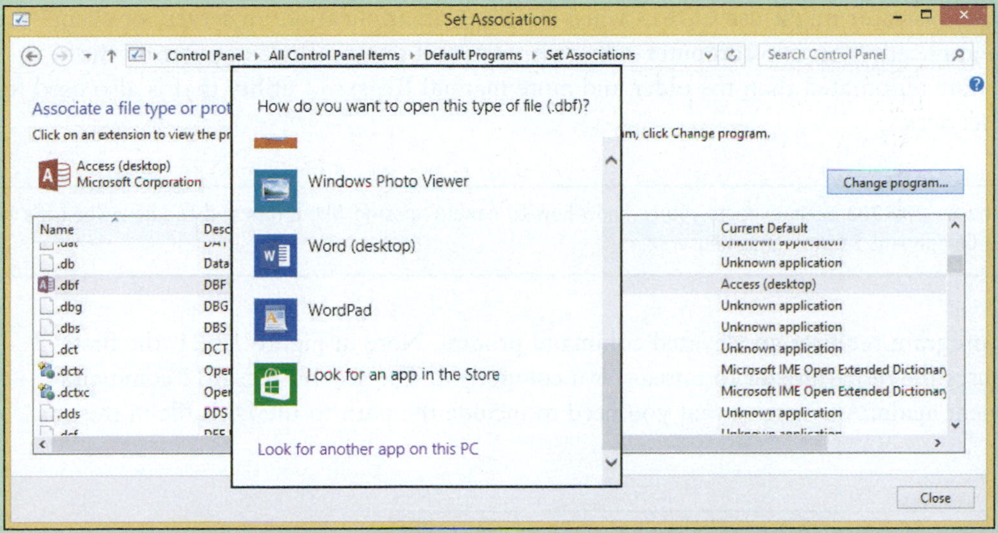

Figure 12-20 Select the default program to associate with a file extension

3. The box displays installed programs that can handle the selected file extension. If you don't see the program you want, click **More options** and scroll to the bottom of the list. Then click **Look for another app on this PC** (in Windows 7, click **Browse**) to find it in the Program Files or Program Files (x86) folder on your hard drive. Otherwise, make your selection (and in Windows 7, click **OK**). Then close all windows.

WHEN A SERVICE FAILS TO START

A message about a service failing to start can be caused by a corrupted or missing service program, or the service might not be configured to launch at startup. Recall from the "Optimizing Windows" chapter that you can use the Services console (services.msc) to enable, disable, start, or stop a service. A service can be disabled at startup using the System Configuration tool (msconfig.exe), and Task Manager (taskmgr.exe) can give you a list of all running services.

If you get an error message that a service has failed to start, check the Services console to make sure the service is set to start automatically. Make sure the Startup type is set to Automatic or Automatic (Delayed Start). Use the service's Properties box in the console to find the path and file name to the executable program. Then use Explorer to make sure the program file is not missing. You might need to reinstall the service or the application that uses the service.

WHEN A DLL IS MISSING OR A COMPONENT IS NOT REGISTERED

Most applications have a main program file that uses a collection of many small programs called components or objects that serve the main program. The main program for an application has an .exe file extension and relies on several component services that often have a .dll file extension. (DLL stands for

Dynamic Link Library.) Problems with applications can be caused by a missing DLL program or a broken association between the main program and a component.

If you get an error message about a missing DLL, the easiest way to solve this problem might be to reinstall the application. However, if that is not advisable, you can identify the path and name of the missing DLL file and recover it from backup or from the application installation files.

On the other hand, the file might be present and undamaged, but the application cannot find it because the relationship between the two is broken. Relationships between a main program and its components are normally established by entries in the registry when the application is installed. The process is called registering a component. In addition, the Component Services (also called COM+) tool, which is a Microsoft Management Console snap-in, can be used to register components. The tool is often used by application developers and system administrators when developing and deploying an application. For example, a system administrator might use COM+ when installing an application on servers or client computers where an application on one computer calls an application on another computer on the network. COM+ is more automated than the older and more manual Regsvr32 utility that is also used to register component services.

A+ Exam Tip The A+ 220-902 exam expects you to know how to handle missing DLL errors and to know when it's appropriate to use the Component Services and Regsvr32.

The regsvr32.exe program requires an elevated command prompt. Note in Figure 12-21, the first regsvr32 command uses the /u parameter to unregister a component. The second regsvr32 command registers the component again. Also notice that you need to include the path to the DLL file in the command line.

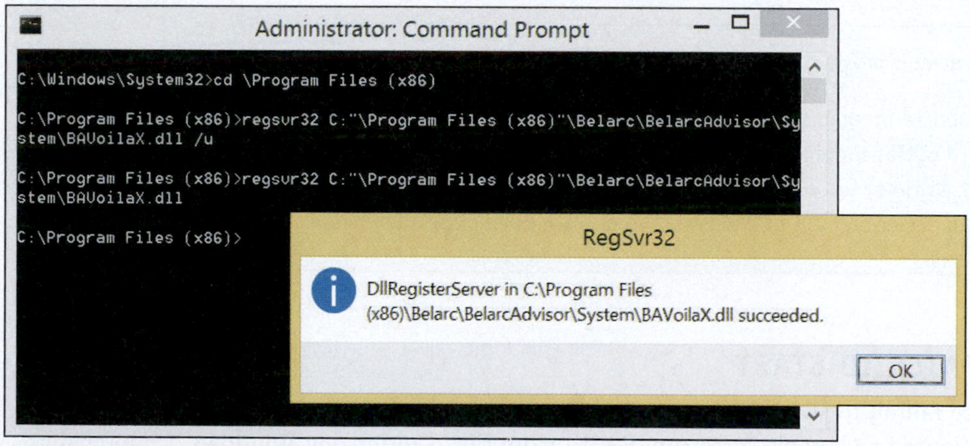

Figure 12-21 Use the regsvr32 command to register or unregister an application component

As an IT support technician, you might be asked by a system administrator or software provider to use the COM+ or Regsvr32 tool to help solve a problem with an application giving errors. Suppose you get this error when installing an application:

```
Error 1928 "Error registering COM+ application."
```

When you contact the help desk of the application provider, you might be instructed to use the COM+ tool to solve the problem. To open the tool, open Control Panel and click **Administrative Tools**, then double-click **Component Services**. The Component Services window is shown in Figure 12-22. To learn how to use the tool, click **Help** in the menu bar.

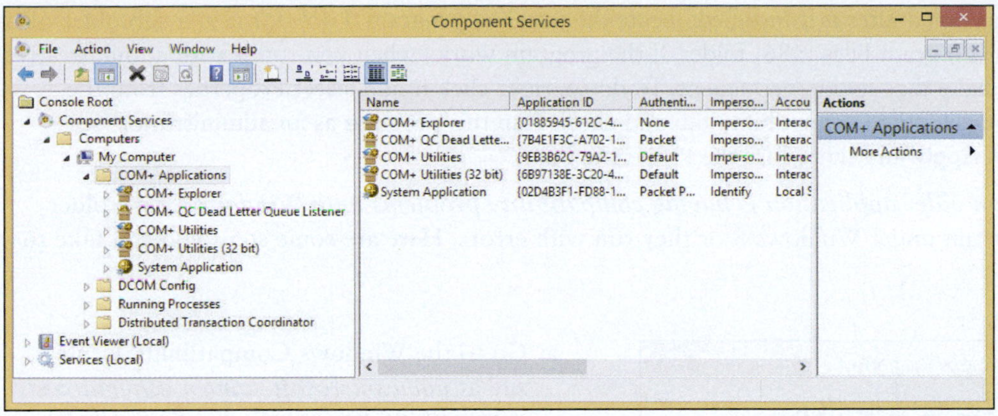

Figure 12-22 Use the Component Services window to register components used by an application

WHEN THE APPLICATION HAS NEVER WORKED

If the application has never worked, follow these steps:

1. ***Update Windows and search the web.*** Installing all important and critical Windows updates can sometimes solve a problem with an application that won't install. Also check the website of the software manufacturer and the Microsoft support site (*support.microsoft.com*) for solutions. Search on the application name or the error message you get when you try to run it.
2. ***Run the installation program or application as an administrator.*** The program might require that the user have privileges not assigned to the current user account. Try running the application with administrator privileges, which Windows calls a secondary logon. If the installation has failed, use Explorer to locate the installation executable file. Right-click it and select **Run as administrator** from the shortcut menu (see Figure 12-23).

> **Notes** To run a program using a user account other than administrator, hold down the Shift key and right-click the program file. Then select **Run as different user** from the shortcut menu. You must then enter the user name and password of another user account in the Windows Security box.

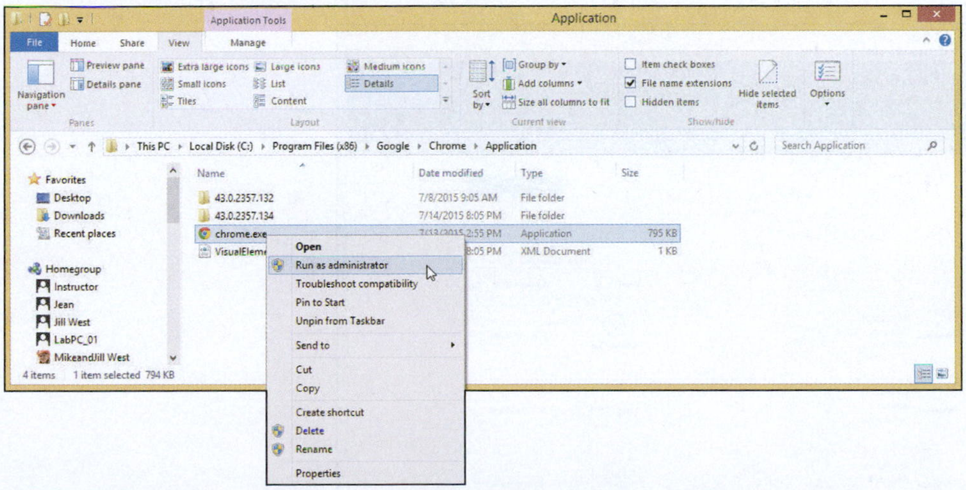

Figure 12-23 Execute a program using administrative privileges

If the application has failed after it is installed, locate the installed program. Look for it in a subfolder of the Program Files or Program Files (x86) folder. If the program works when you run it with administrative privileges, you can make that setting permanent. To do so, right-click it and select **Properties** from the shortcut menu. Then click the **Compatibility** tab and check **Run this program as an administrator** (see Figure 12-24). Click **Apply** and then close the Properties box.

3. ***Consider whether an older application is having compatibility problems with Windows.*** Some older applications cannot run under Windows 8 or they run with errors. Here are some steps you can take to fix the problem:

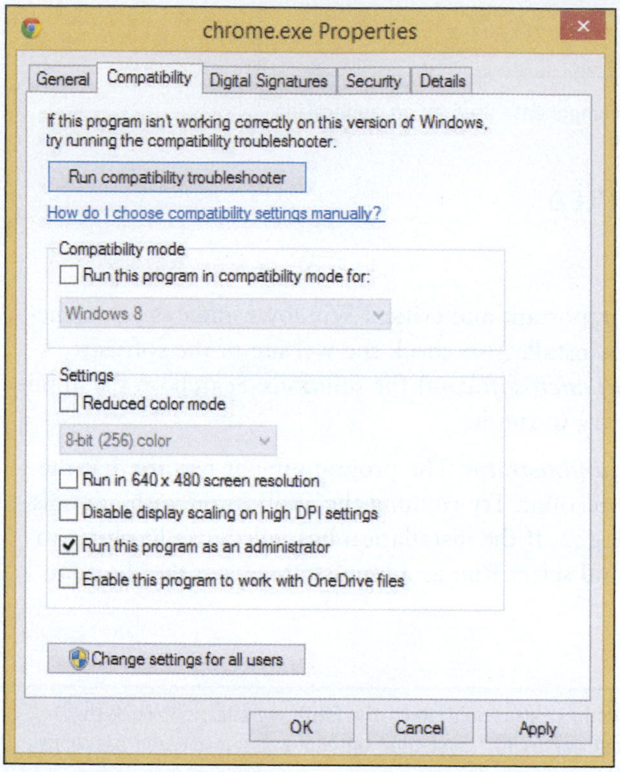

Figure 12-24 Permanently change the privilege level of an application

a. Go to the Windows Compatibility Center site at *www.microsoft.com/en-us/windows/compatibility/CompatCenter/Home* and search for the application. The site reports problems and solutions for known legacy software. For example, search on the application **WinPatrol**, then under the *Compatible with* menu, click **Windows 8.1.** You find that Microsoft recommends Version 25 or 28 for Windows 8.1 (see Figure 12-25). Use the 32-bit or 64-bit type appropriate for your system. If the version and type you are using are not compatible, try to replace or upgrade the software.

b. Try running the application in compatibility mode. To do that, on the Compatibility tab of the program file Properties box shown earlier in Figure 12-24, check **Run this program in compatibility mode for:**. Then, from the drop-down menu, select the operating system that the application was written to run under. Click **Apply** and close the Properties box.

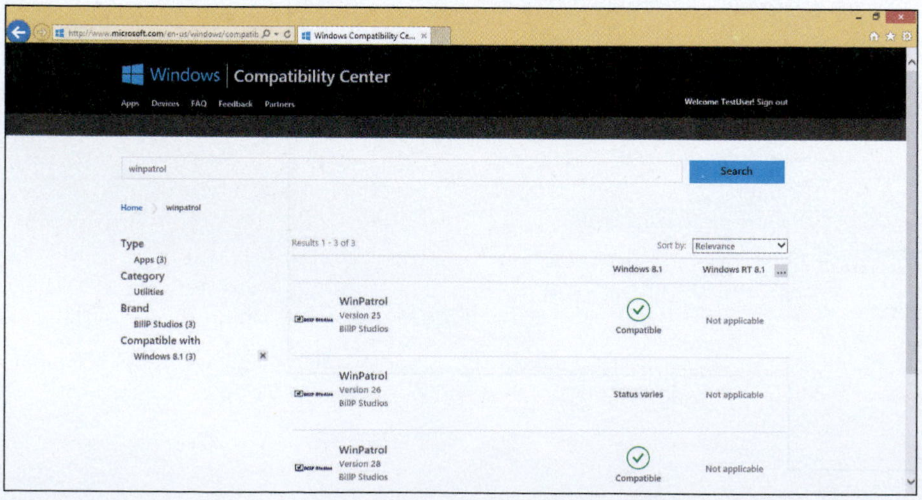

Figure 12-25 Microsoft tracks software and hardware compatible with Windows 8.1

> **OS Differences** For Windows 7 Professional, Ultimate, or Enterprise editions, try running the program in Windows XP Mode. Recall from the chapter, "Installing Windows," that Windows XP Mode can be used to install XP in a virtual machine under Windows 7. Applications installed in XP Mode work in the XP environment. Only use this option as a last resort because XP Mode takes up a lot of system resources.

4. ***Verify that the application is digitally signed.*** Although applications that are not digitally signed can still run on Windows, a digital signature does verify that the application is not a rogue application and that it is certified as Windows-compatible by Microsoft. To view the digital signature, select the **Digital Signatures** tab of the program file's Properties box. Select a signer in the list and click **Details** (see Figure 12-26). If the Digital Signatures tab is missing, the program is not digitally signed.

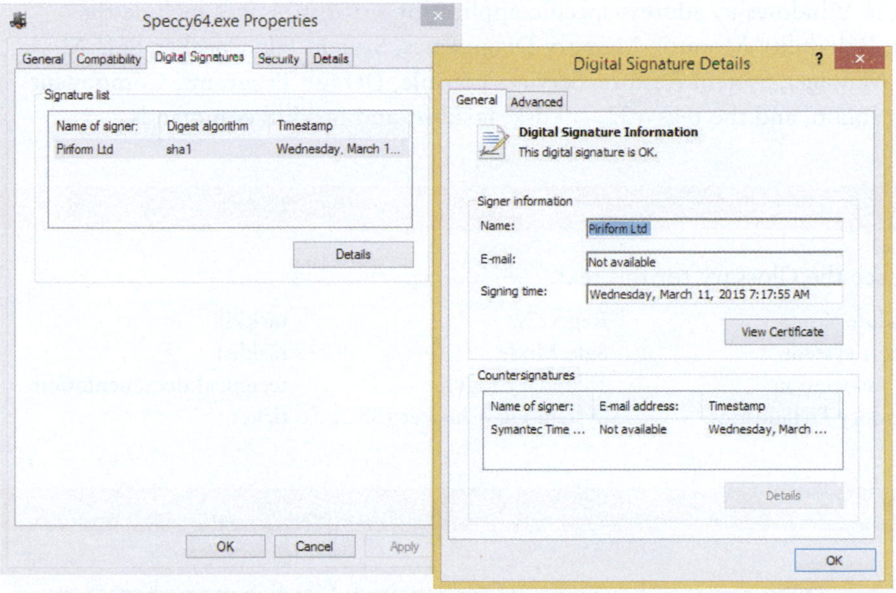

Figure 12-26 This program is digitally signed

>> CHAPTER SUMMARY

What Customers Want: Beyond Technical Know-How

- Customers want more than just technical know-how. They want a positive and helpful attitude, respect, good communication, sensitivity to their needs, ownership of their problem, dependability, credibility, integrity, honesty, and professionalism.
- Customers expect their first contact with you to be professional and friendly, and they want you to put listening to their problem or request as your first priority.
- Know how to ask penetrating questions when interviewing a customer about a problem or request.
- Set and meet customer expectations by using good communication about what you are doing or intending to do and allowing the customer to make decisions where appropriate.
- Deal confidently and gracefully with customers who are difficult, including those who are not knowledgeable, are overly confident, or complain.
- When you first start a new job, find out how to escalate a problem you cannot solve.

Strategies to Troubleshoot Any Computer Problem

- The six steps in the troubleshooting process are (1) interview the user and back up data, (2) examine the system and form a theory of probable cause (your best guess), (3) test your theory, (4) plan a solution and implement it, (5) verify that everything works and take appropriate preventive measures, and (6) document what you did and the final outcome.

Troubleshooting Applications

- A problem with an application might be caused by the application, the hardware, the operating system, the data, other applications in conflict with this one, or the user.
- Windows error messages and logs can help you examine a system looking for the source of an application problem.
- Tools and features available in Windows to address specific application error messages include the Action Center, Event Viewer, Reliability Monitor, Memory Diagnostics, System File Checker, Safe Mode, System Configuration, Task Manager, System Restore, Services console, Default Programs, Component Services (COM+), secondary logon, and the regsvr32, chkdsk, tasklist, and taskkill commands.

>> KEY TERMS

For explanations of key terms, see the Glossary for this text.

call tracking software
Component Services (COM+)
default program
escalate
expert system
file association
Memory Diagnostics
Regsvr32
Safe Mode
secondary logon
System File Checker (SFC)
taskkill
tasklist
technical documentation
ticket

>> REVIEWING THE BASICS

1. Assume that you are a customer who wants to have a computer repaired. List five main characteristics that you would want to see in your computer repair person.
2. What is one thing you should do when you receive a phone call requesting on-site support, before you make an appointment?
3. You make an appointment to do an on-site repair, but you are detained and find out that you will be late. What is the best thing to do?
4. When making an on-site service call, what should you do before making any changes to software or before taking the case cover off a computer?
5. What should you do after finishing your computer repair?
6. What is a good strategy to follow if a conflict arises between you and your customer?
7. You have exhausted your knowledge of a problem and it still is not solved. Before you escalate it, what else can you do?
8. If you need to make a phone call while on a customer's site and your cell phone is not working, what do you do?
9. What is one thing you can do to help a caller who needs phone support and is not a competent computer user?
10. Describe what you should do when a customer complains to you about a product or service that your company provides.

11. What are the six steps that you can use to solve any computer problem?
12. How many bits does an x86-based operating system process at one time?
13. What is the command to use the Memory Diagnostics tool?
14. What is the command to use the System File Checker to immediately verify system files?
15. What GUI tool can you use to stop a program that is hung?
16. What command-line tool can you use to stop a program that is hung?
17. How can you eliminate the possibility that an application error is caused by another application or service running in the background?
18. How does Windows know which application to use to open a file when you double-click the file in File Explorer or Windows Explorer?
19. Which two tools might a software developer or system administrator use to register a component of an application in the Windows registry?
20. If an application works when the system is loaded in Safe Mode, but does not work when Windows is loaded normally, what can you assume?

>> THINKING CRITICALLY

1. You own a small computer repair company and a customer comes to you with a laptop that will not boot. After investigating, you discover the hard drive has crashed. What should you do first?
   a. Install a hard drive the same size and speed as the original.
   b. Ask the customer's advice about the size drive to install, but select a drive the same speed as the original drive.
   c. Ask the customer's advice about the size and speed of the new drive to install.
   d. If the customer looks like he can afford it, install the largest and fastest drive the system can support.
2. You have repaired a broken LCD panel in a laptop computer. However, when you disassembled the laptop, you bent the hinge on the laptop lid so that it now does not latch solidly. When the customer receives the laptop, he notices the bent hinge and begins shouting at you. What do you do first? Second?
   a. Explain to the customer you are sorry but you did the best you could.
   b. Listen carefully to the customer and don't get defensive.
   c. Apologize and offer to replace the bent hinge.
   d. Tell the customer he is not allowed to speak to you like that.
3. As a help-desk technician, list four good detective questions to ask if a user calls to say, "My computer won't boot."
4. A user tells you that Microsoft Word gives errors when saving a file. What should you do first?
   a. Install Windows updates, which also include patches for Microsoft Word.
   b. Ask the user when the problem first started.
   c. Ask the user to save the error message as a screen shot the next time the error occurs and email it to you.
   d. Use Task Manager to end the Microsoft Word program.

>> REAL PROBLEMS, REAL SOLUTIONS

REAL PROBLEM 12-1 Summarizing Windows Troubleshooting Tools

When you're stuck on a problem, it's helpful to have a quick-and-easy reference of the tools available to you in Windows. In this project, you create a table to gather all of this information into one place. In the "Troubleshooting Windows Startup" chapter, you will add more tools to this table.

1. Using your choice of word-processing software (such as Microsoft Word) or spreadsheet software (such as Microsoft Excel), create a table with the following headings: **Tool, Steps to access,** and **Description.**
2. Under the *Tool* heading, list all of the Windows tools covered in this chapter and in earlier chapters, such as Event Viewer, Task Manager, Action Center, and Memory Diagnostics.
3. Complete the remainder of the table with the steps needed to access each tool and a brief, one- or two-sentence description of each. For Computer Management, for example, you might say, "Access from the Control Panel, or enter compmgmt.msc at a command prompt." Be sure to include the program name of the utility if it can be launched from the command prompt. The description for Disk Management might say, "Use it to view and modify partitions on hard drives and to format drives." Be sure to note whether a tool is available only for certain releases of Windows, such as "New with Windows 8."

Keep this table handy, as it can be very useful when troubleshooting problems in Windows.

REAL PROBLEM 12-2 Writing Your Own Scenario for Developing Interpersonal Social Skills

In the chapter, you read several scenarios where technical support people failed to serve their customers well or failed to relate professionally with coworkers. Recall a similar situation where you observed poor service from a technician or salesperson. Write the scenario using fictitious names. Then write three questions to help other students think through what went wrong, what should have happened, and some principles of relating to customers or coworkers that could have helped if they had been applied. Present your scenario in class or with a student group for discussion.

REAL PROBLEM 12-3 Installing and Using Help-Desk Software

Go to *www.spiceworks.com* and watch a few of the videos about Spiceworks Help Desk Software. Then download, install, and run the software. Practice using the software to add help-desk workers, open a ticket, assign a worker to a ticket, and resolve and close the ticket.

Consider setting up an IT help desk where your classmates can provide end-user support to other students and instructors at your school as they have problems with their personal computers. One computer in the class would be designated the help-desk computer that holds the Spiceworks Help Desk Software for the entire class. Classmates are entered in Spiceworks as help-desk workers and are assigned tickets as users request help. Spiceworks can be set up to receive requests for help through an email account, and you can advertise the email address as a way to offer support for students and instructors on campus. What other ways can you use to advertise your help desk and provide a way for your customers to contact the help desk? Some IT support classes have run extremely successful help desks and have received small donations for services.

CHAPTER 13

Troubleshooting Windows Startup

After completing this chapter, you will be able to:

- Describe the boot process from the time you press the power button until the Windows Start screen or desktop loads
- Apply appropriate Windows tools to solve Windows startup problems
- Troubleshoot Windows startup problems

You've already learned how to deal with Windows and application problems that occur after Windows has started. In this chapter, you take your troubleshooting skills one step further by learning to deal with startup problems caused by Windows. When Windows fails to start, it can be stressful if important data has not been backed up or the user has pressing work to do with the computer. What helps more than anything else is to have a good understanding of Windows startup and a good plan for approaching startup problems.

We begin the chapter with a discussion of what happens when you first turn on a computer and Windows starts. The more you understand about startup, the better your chances of fixing startup problems. Then you learn about Windows tools specifically designed to handle startup problems. Finally, you learn about strategies for solving startup problems.

UNDERSTANDING THE BOOT PROCESS

A+
220-902
4.1

Knowledge is power. The better you understand what happens when you first turn on a computer until Windows is loaded and the Windows Start screen or desktop appears, the more likely you will be able to solve a problem when Windows cannot start. Let's begin by noting the differences between a hard boot and a soft boot.

Notes Most techies use the terms *boot* and *startup* interchangeably. However, in general, the term *boot* refers to the hardware phase of starting up a computer. Microsoft consistently uses the term *startup* to refer to how its operating systems are booted, well, started, I mean.

DIFFERENT WAYS TO BOOT

A+
220-902
4.1

The term booting comes from the phrase "lifting yourself up by your bootstraps" and refers to the computer bringing itself up to a working state without the user having to do anything but press the on button. Two fundamental ways to boot a computer are:

- A hard boot, or cold boot, involves turning on the power with the on/off switch.
- A soft boot, or warm boot, involves using the operating system to reboot. In Windows, a soft boot is called a restart.

A hard boot takes more time than a soft boot because in a soft boot, the initial steps performed by UEFI/BIOS in a hard boot don't happen. To save time in most circumstances, you should use a soft boot (Windows restart). A hard boot initializes the processor and clears memory. So if a restart doesn't work or you want to make certain you get a fresh start, use a Windows shutdown followed by a hard boot.

WINDOWS SHUTDOWN AND RESTART

Windows shutdown orderly closes all open applications, user sessions, services, devices, and system processes and then powers down the computer. The Windows 8 Fast Startup feature speeds up startup by performing a partial hibernation at shutdown. At shutdown, Windows saves the drivers and kernel state in the Windows hibernate file, hiberfil.sys, and then reads from this file on the next cold boot. The feature is enabled by default and can be disabled in the Power Options applet in Control Panel. A shutdown from the Start screen (see Figure 13-1a) uses Fast Startup hibernation when the feature is enabled. Even when Fast Startup is enabled, a shutdown from the desktop always performs a full shutdown (see Figure 13-1b).

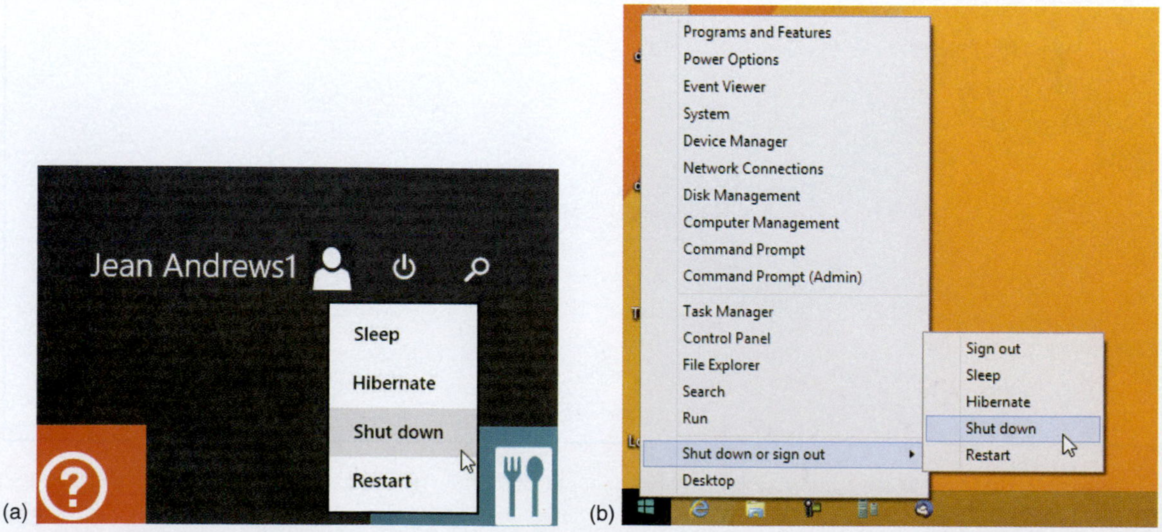

Figure 13-1 For a shutdown, Windows 8 uses Fast Startup on the Start screen, but not from the desktop

A restart in Windows 8 does not use Fast Startup hibernation, which means the kernel and drivers are completely reloaded at startup as is done with a full shutdown.

OS Differences Windows 7 doesn't have the Fast Startup feature. A Windows 7 shutdown always performs a full shutdown and a Windows 7 restart always reloads the kernel and drivers.

POWER BUTTONS AND SWITCHES ON A COMPUTER CASE

If Windows is hung and you can't use the OS to perform a restart or shutdown, look for power or reset buttons on the front or rear of the case. For example, one computer has three power switches: a power button and a reset button on the front of the case and a power switch on the rear of the case (see Figure 13-2).

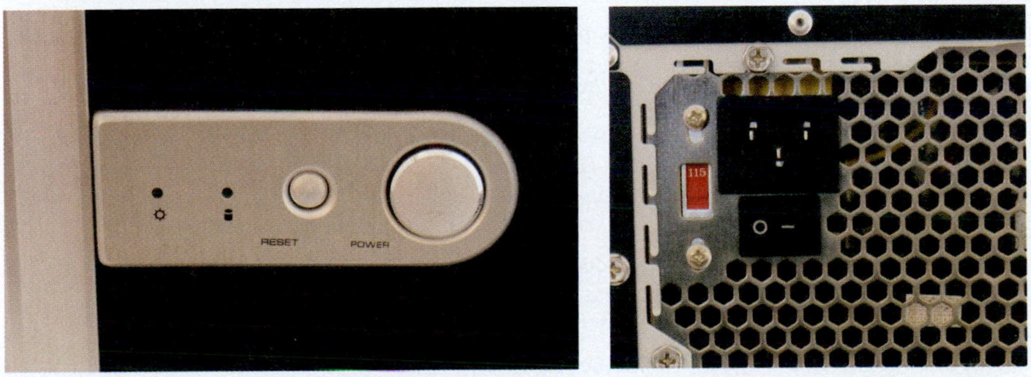

Figure 13-2 This computer case has two power buttons on the front and one power switch on the rear of the case

They work like this:

- The power button in front can be configured as a "soft" power button, causing a Windows restart.
- The reset button initializes the CPU so that it restarts at the beginning of the UEFI/BIOS startup program. The computer behaves as though the power were turned off and back on and then goes through the entire boot process.
- The switch on the rear of the case simply turns off the power abruptly and is a "hard" power button. If you use this switch, wait 30 seconds before you press the power button on the front of the case to boot the system. This method gives you the greatest assurance that memory will clear. However, if Windows is abruptly stopped, it might give an error message when you reboot.

How the front two buttons work can be controlled in UEFI/BIOS setup. Know, however, that different cases offer different options.

STARTUP UEFI/BIOS CONTROLS THE BEGINNING OF THE BOOT

A+ 220-902 4.1

The startup UEFI/BIOS is programming contained on the firmware chip on the motherboard that is responsible for getting a system up and going and finding an OS to load. Recall that UEFI is a mini-operating system that is gradually replacing the legacy BIOS standards. UEFI improves on processes for booting, securing the boot, loading device drivers and applications before the OS loads, and handing over the boot to the OS.

If Secure Boot in UEFI is enabled, UEFI systems run security checks to protect against malware designed to attack during the boot. UEFI stores device drivers and information about Secure Boot on a nonvolatile RAM (NVRAM) chip and in a hidden partition on the hard drive called the EFI System Partition (ESP). Recall UEFI/BIOS searches for and then turns to a boot device to find an operating system to launch. During startup, you can change the boot device priority order used for this search by accessing UEFI/BIOS setup.

13

Next let's see what happens during the boot, from the time power is turned on until Windows is started. In these steps, we assume the OS is loaded from the hard drive.

STEPS TO BOOT THE COMPUTER AND START WINDOWS

A+
220-902
4.1

Before we get into the steps, check out Table 13-1. It lists the components and files stored on the hard drive that are necessary to start Windows. The table can serve as a guide as you study the steps.

Component or File	Path*	Description
BIOS systems using MBR partitioning		
MBR	First sector of the hard drive is called the Master Boot Record (MBR)	BIOS looks to the partition table in the MBR to locate the active partition.
System partition	Also called the active partition or System Reserved partition	The system partition holds the Boot Manager, Boot Configuration Data (BCD) store, and other files and folders needed to begin Windows startup. For Windows, these files are stored in the root and \Boot directory of the hidden system partition.
Boot Manager	In the root of the system partition	Windows Boot Manager, bootmgr (with no file extension), accesses the BCD store and locates the Windows Boot Loader.
BCD store	\Boot directory on the system partition	The Boot Configuration Data (BCD) store is a database file named BCD (no file extension) and is organized the same as a registry hive. It contains boot settings that control the Boot Manager and can be viewed and edited with the bcdedit command.
UEFI systems using GPT partitioning		
GPT partition table	At the beginning of the hard drive and a backup copy at the end of the drive	UEFI looks to the GPT partition table to locate the EFI System Partition.
System partition	EFI System Partition (ESP) is normally 100 MB to 200 MB in size.	The system partition holds the Windows Boot Manager, BCD, and other supporting files. For Windows, the Boot Manager is bootmgfw.efi and is stored in \EFI\Microsoft\Boot. A backup copy of bootmgfw.efi is at \EFI\Boot\bootx64.efi.
Boot Manager	For Windows, \EFI\Microsoft\Boot on the ESP	Bootmgfw.efi loads EFI applications based on variables stored in NVRAM and reads the BCD store to find out other boot parameters (such as a dual boot).
BCD store	\EFI\Microsoft\Boot on the ESP	BCD store entries point the Windows Boot Manager to the location of the Windows Boot Loader program.
All Windows BIOS and UEFI systems		
Windows Boot Loader	C:\Windows\System32*	Windows Boot Manager turns control over to the Windows Boot Loader, which loads and starts essential Windows processes. Two versions of the program file are: winload.exe (BIOS) winload.efi (UEFI)
Resume from hibernation	C:\Windows\System32	This Windows Boot Loader is used when Windows resumes from hibernation: winresume.exe (BIOS) winresume.efi (UEFI)

Table 13-1 Software components and files needed to start Windows (continues)

Component or File	Path*	Description
Ntoskrnl.exe	C:\Windows\System32	Windows kernel
Hal.dll	C:\Windows\System32	Dynamic link library handles low-level hardware details
Smss.exe	C:\Windows\System32	Sessions Manager program responsible for starting user sessions
Csrss.exe	C:\Windows\System32	Win32 subsystem manages graphical components and threads
Winlogon.exe	C:\Windows\System32	Logon process
Services.exe	C:\Windows\System32	Service Control Manager starts and stops services
Lsass.exe	C:\Windows\System32	Authenticates users
System registry hive	C:\Windows\System32\Config	Holds data for the HKEY_LOCAL_MACHINE key of the registry
Device drivers	C:\Windows\System32\Drivers	Drivers for required hardware

* It is assumed that Windows is installed in C:\Windows.

Table 13-1 Software components and files needed to start Windows (continued)

A successful boot depends on essential hardware devices, UEFI/BIOS, and the operating system all performing without errors. Let's look at the steps to start a Windows computer. Several of these steps are diagrammed in Figures 13-3 and 13-4 to help you visually understand how the steps work.

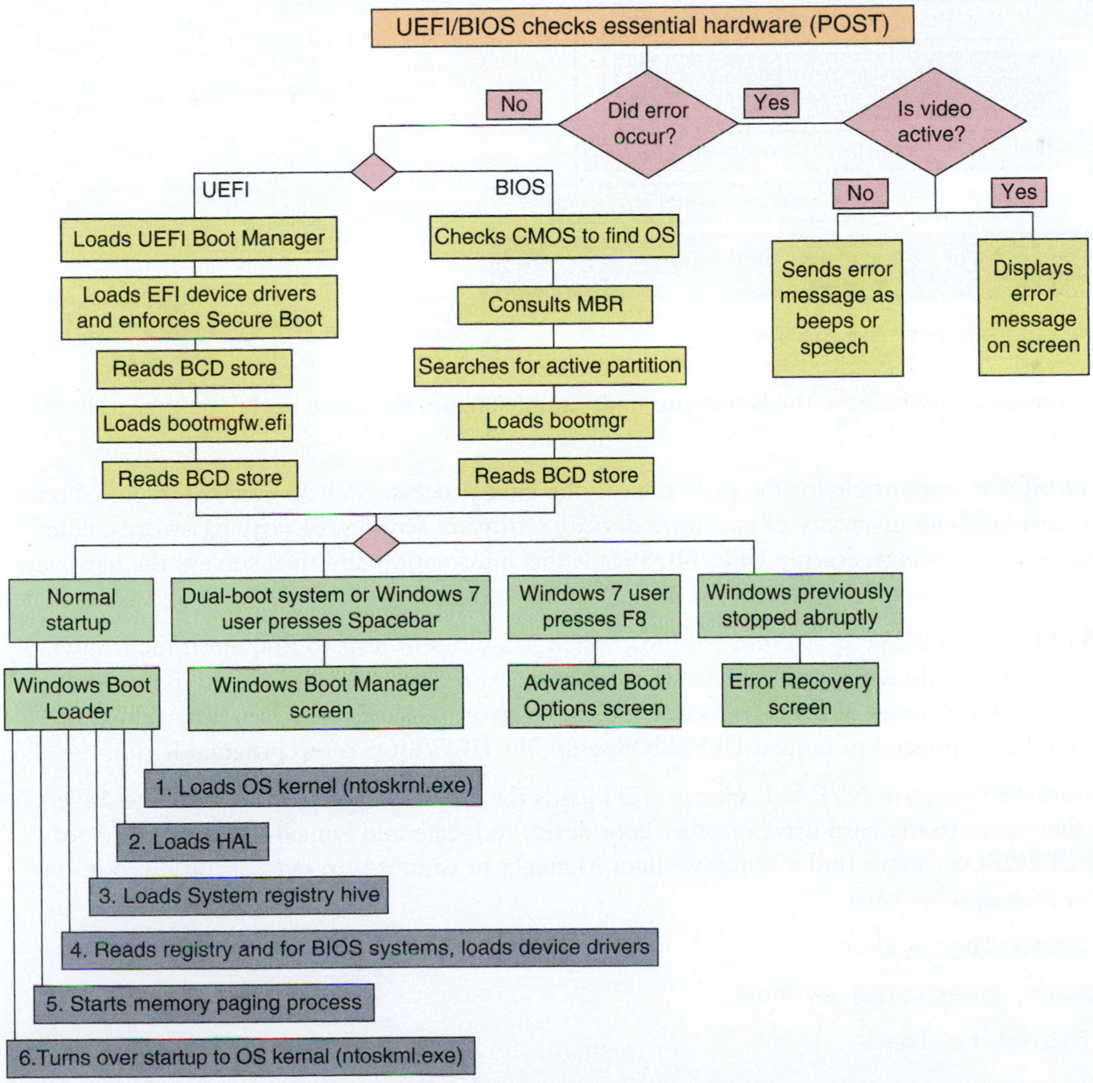

Figure 13-3 Steps to booting the computer and loading Windows

13

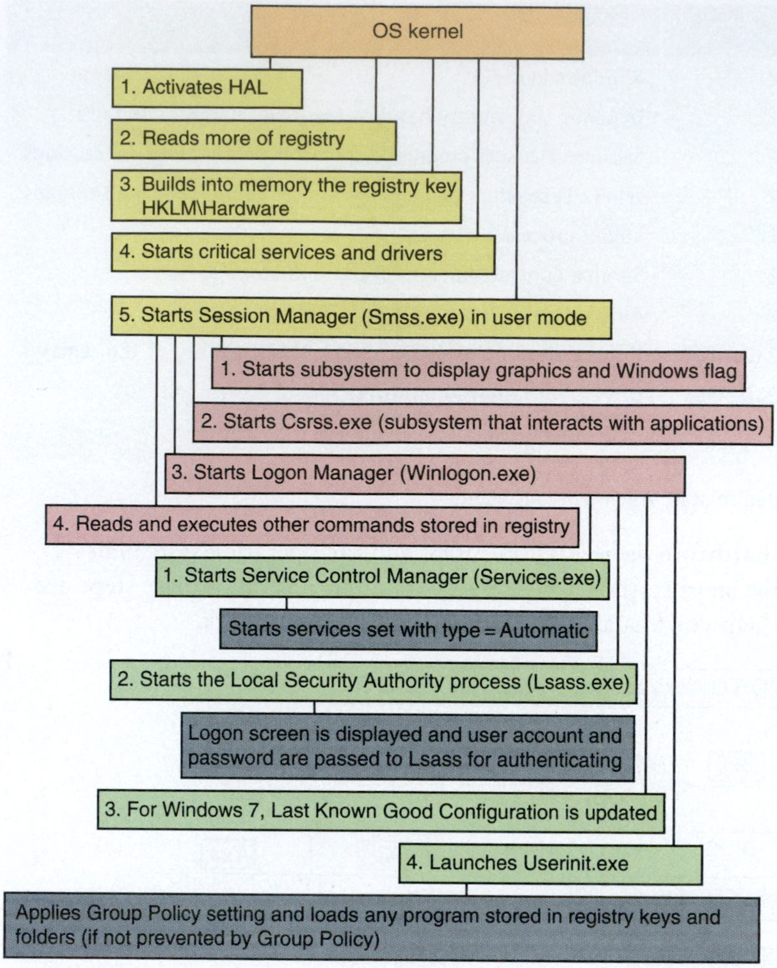

Figure 13-4 Steps to complete loading Windows

Study these steps carefully because the better you understand startup, the more likely you'll be able to solve startup problems:

1. Startup UEFI/BIOS is responsible for the early steps in the boot process. NVRAM or CMOS RAM on the motherboard holds an inventory of hardware devices, hardware settings, security passwords, date and time, and startup settings. Startup UEFI/BIOS reads this information and then surveys the hardware devices it finds present, comparing it with the list kept in its RAM.
2. Startup UEFI/BIOS runs POST (power-on self test), which is a series of tests to find out if the firmware can communicate correctly with essential hardware components required for a successful boot. Any errors are indicated as a series of beeps, recorded speech, or error messages on screen (after video is checked). If the key is pressed to request UEFI/BIOS setup, the UEFI/BIOS setup program is run.
3. Based on information kept in NVRAM, startup UEFI loads the UEFI boot manager and device drivers. UEFI/BIOS then turns to the hard drive or other boot device to locate and launch the Windows Boot Manager. If UEFI/BIOS cannot find a Windows Boot Manager or cannot turn over operation to it, one of these error messages appears:

```
Missing operating system
Error loading operating system
Windows failed to load
Invalid partition table
```

4. The Windows Boot Manager does the following:
   a. It reads the settings in the BCD.
   b. The next step, one of three, depends on entries in the BCD and these other factors:
      - *Option 1.* For normal startups that are not dual booting, no menu appears and Boot Manager finds and launches the Windows Boot Loader program.
      - *Option 2.* If the computer is set up for a dual-boot environment, Boot Manager displays the *Choose an operating system* screen, as shown in Figure 13-5.
      - *Option 3.* If Windows was previously stopped abruptly or another error occurs, the Windows 8 Startup Menu appears (see Figure 13-6) to give you the option to troubleshoot the problem.

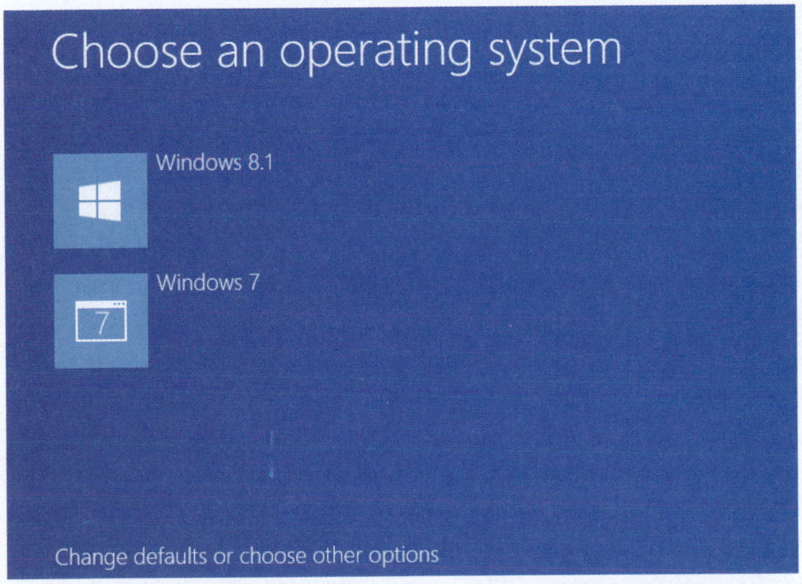

Figure 13-5 In a dual-boot setup, Windows Boot Manager provides a choice of operating systems

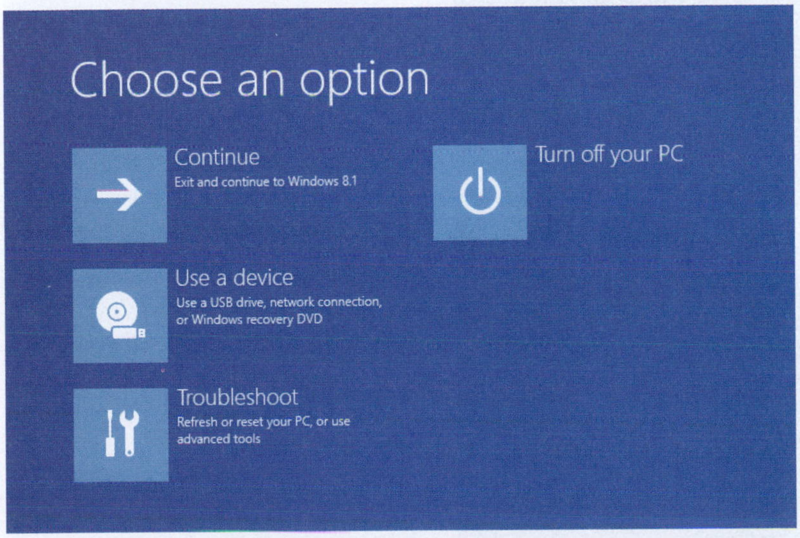

Figure 13-6 Windows 8 Startup Menu offers the opportunity to troubleshoot a problem with startup

13

5. Windows Boot Loader (winload.exe or winload.efi) is responsible for loading Windows components. It does the following:
   a. For normal startups, Boot Loader loads into memory the OS kernel, Ntoskrnl.exe, but does not yet start it. Boot Loader also loads into memory the Hardware Abstraction Layer (Hal.dll), which will later be used by the kernel.
   b. Boot Loader loads into memory the system registry hive (C:\Windows\System32\Config\System).
   c. Boot Loader then reads the registry key just created, HKEY_LOCAL_ MACHINE\SYSTEM\Services, looking for and loading into memory device drivers that must be launched at startup. The drivers are not yet started.
   d. Boot Loader starts up the memory paging process and then turns over startup to the OS kernel (Ntoskrnl.exe).
6. The kernel (Ntoskrnl.exe) does the following:
   a. It activates the HAL, reads more information from the registry, and builds into memory the registry key HKEY_LOCAL_ MACHINE\HARDWARE, using information that has been collected about the hardware.
   b. The kernel then starts critical services and drivers that are configured to be started by the kernel during the boot. Recall that drivers interact directly with hardware and run in kernel mode, while services interact with drivers. Most services and drivers are stored in C:\Windows\System32 or C:\Windows\System32\Drivers and have an .exe, .dll, or .sys file extension.
   c. After the kernel starts all services and drivers configured to load during the boot, it starts the Session Manager (Smss.exe), which runs in user mode.
7. The Session Manager (Smss.exe) loads the graphical interface and starts the client/server run-time subsystem (csrss.exe), which also runs in user mode. Csrss.exe is the Win32 subsystem component that interacts with applications.
8. Smss.exe starts the Logon Manager (winlogon.exe) and reads and executes other commands stored in the registry, such as a command to replace system files placed there by Windows Update.
9. Winlogon.exe does the following:
   a. It starts the Service Control Manager (services.exe). Services.exe starts all services listed with the startup type of Automatic in the Services console.

Figure 13-7 Windows 8 sign-in screen

   b. Winlogon.exe starts the Local Security Authority process (lsass.exe). The sign-in screen appears (see Figure 13-7), and the user account and password are passed to the lsass.exe process for authenticating.
   c. Winlogon.exe launches userinit.exe. For Windows 8, the Start screen or desktop (explorer.exe) is launched. For Windows 7, the desktop is launched.
10. Userinit.exe applies Group Policy settings and any programs not trumped by Group Policy that are stored

in startup folders and startup registry keys. See the appendix, "Entry Points for Windows Startup Processes," for a list of these folders and registry keys.

The Windows startup is officially completed when the Windows Start screen or desktop appears and the pinwheel wait icon disappears.

WINDOWS 7 STARTUP

A+ 220-902 4.1

Windows 8 and Windows 7 generally use the same startup processes, which are outlined in earlier in Figures 13-3 and 13-4. However, here are a few key differences:

- If Windows 7 was previously stopped abruptly or another error occurs, the Windows 7 Error Recovery screen (see Figure 13-8) appears.

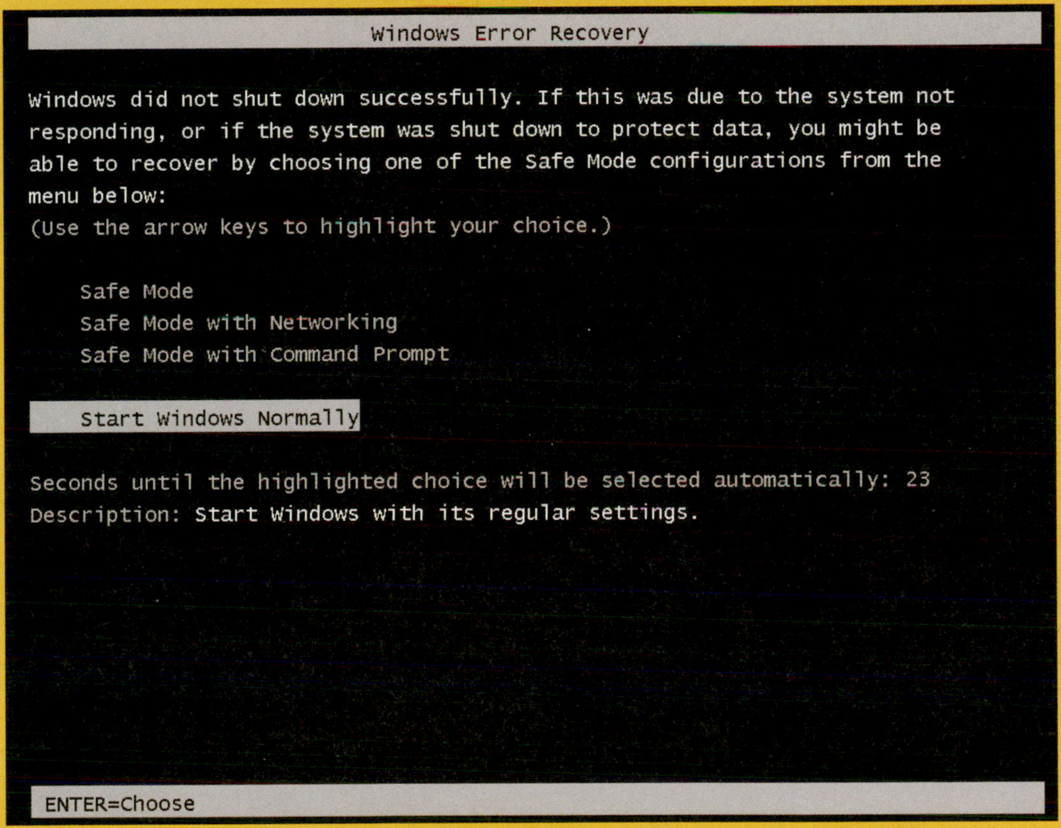

Figure 13-8 This window appears if Windows 7 has been abruptly stopped

- If the user presses the Spacebar near the beginning of Windows startup, the Windows 7 Boot Manager screen appears, which allows you to run Windows Memory Diagnostics.
- If the user presses F8 at startup, the Windows 7 Advanced Boot Options screen appears (see Figure 13-9).

(continues)

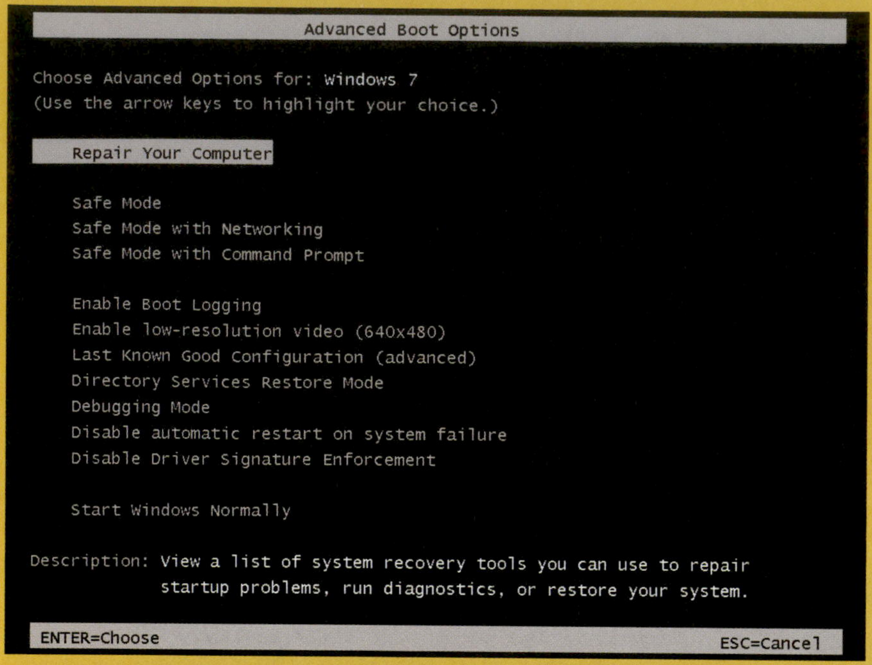

Figure 13-9 Press F8 during the boot to launch the Windows 7 Advanced Boot Options menu

Hands-On | Project 13-1 Examine the System Partition Contents

A+
220-902
4.1

Normally, you cannot see the contents of the system partition. However, if you first assign the partition a drive letter, you can view its contents. First, open the **Folder Options** applet in Control Panel and verify that system files and all file extensions are not hidden and can be viewed. Then open **Disk Management** and find out if the hard drive on which Windows is installed is using the MBR or GPT partitioning system.

Do the following if the hard drive is using the MBR system:

1. In **Disk Management**, right-click the **System Reserved** partition and click **Change Drive Letter and Paths**. Click **Add** and follow directions on screen to assign the partition a drive letter.
2. Open File Explorer or Windows Explorer and drill down into the new volume (see Figure 13-10). You should find bootmgr in the root and BCD in the \Boot folder on the volume.

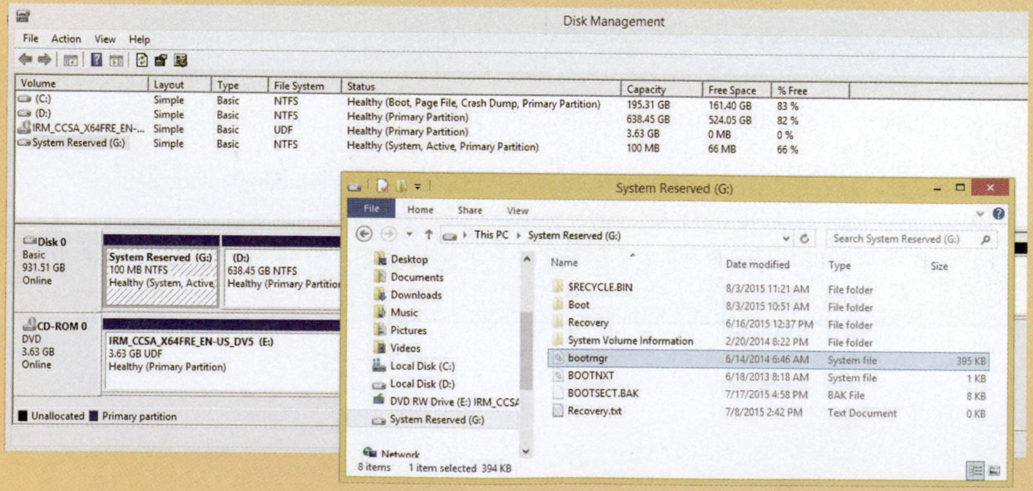

Figure 13-10 Assign a drive letter to the System Reserved partition so that you can view its contents

Do the following if the hard drive is using the GPT system:

1. Open an elevated command prompt window. Then enter the following commands:

`diskpart`	**Open the diskpart command prompt**
`list disk`	**List installed hard drives**
`select disk 0`	**Select the hard drive on which Windows is installed**
`list partition`	**List the partitions on the selected drive**
`select partition 2`	**Select the system partition (it's about 100 MB in size)**
`assign letter=z`	**Assign drive letter z to the partition**
`exit`	**Exit the diskpart utility**

2. At the command prompt, use the dir and cd commands to examine the folders and files on drive z:. Are you able to locate the BCD and bootmgfw.efi files?

When you are finished, remove the drive letter from the system partition so that users won't accidentally change its contents.

With this basic knowledge of the boot in hand, let's turn our attention to the Windows tools that can help you solve problems when Windows refuses to load.

TOOLS FOR TROUBLESHOOTING WINDOWS STARTUP PROBLEMS

A+ 220-902 1.2, 1.3, 1.7, 4.1

When troubleshooting startup, it helps to have a road map, which is the purpose of the diagram in Figure 13-11. It can help you organize in your mind the various ways to boot the system and the menus and procedures available to you depending on how you boot the system.

13

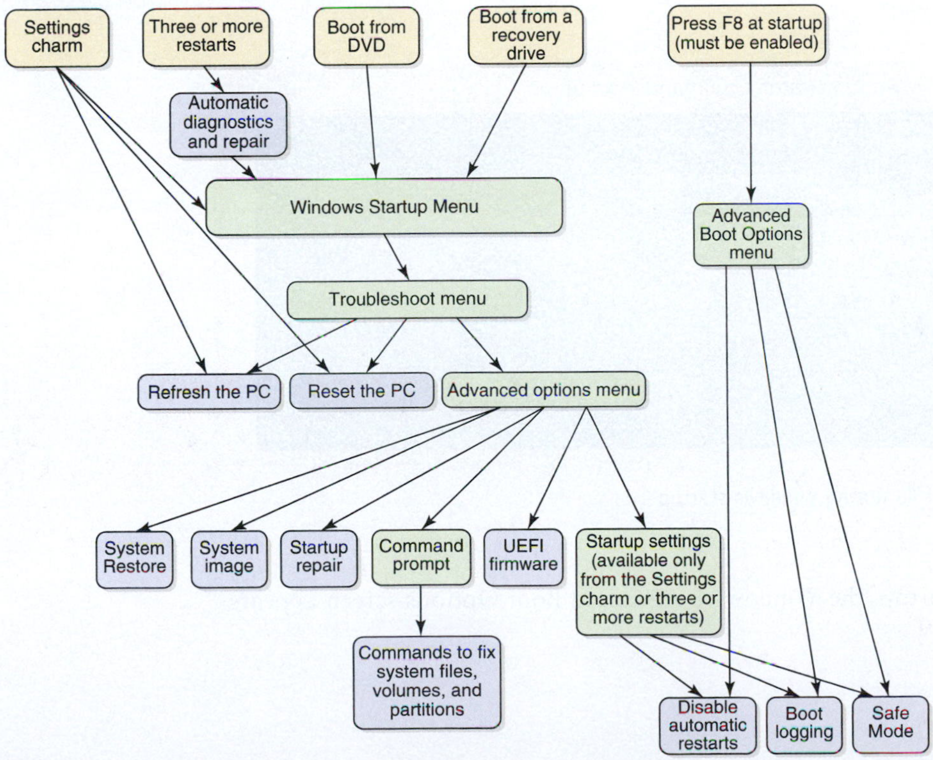

Figure 13-11 Methods to boot the system, menus that appear, and tools available on menus used to troubleshoot startup problems

As you learn to use each tool, keep in mind that you want to use the tool that makes as few changes to the system as possible to fix the problem. In this part of the chapter, the tools are divided into three groups: the least invasive and easy solutions, tools that can affect Windows system files and user settings, and tools to rebuild the Windows installation, even to the point of reinstalling Windows. Before we dig into these tools, let's look at what you can do before a problem occurs in order to make troubleshooting easier and more effective.

WHAT TO DO BEFORE A PROBLEM OCCURS

A+
220-902
4.1

Good preparation will make troubleshooting startup problems much simpler and more successful. When you are responsible for a computer and while the computer is still healthy, be sure to complete the following tasks:

- *Keep good backups.* The chapter "Maintaining Windows" covers methods to back up data, applications, and user settings.
- *Create a Windows 8 custom refresh image.* Windows 8 offers the option of creating a custom refresh image of the Windows 8 volume. As you learned in the chapter "Maintaining Windows," this image should be created right after you've installed Windows, hardware, applications, and user accounts, and customized Windows settings. You can store the image on the hard drive so it's easy for an end user to get to it when needed or copy it to a network drive, external drive, or some other safe location.
- *Configure Windows 8 to use the F8 key at startup.* The F8 key gives you access to the Advanced Boot Options menu in Windows, which you'll learn about later in this chapter. Windows 8 has the feature disabled by default, and Windows 7 has it enabled. In Windows 8, to enable the F8 key at startup, you'll need an elevated command prompt window. Press **Win+X**, click **Command Prompt (Admin)**, and respond to the UAC box. In the command prompt window, enter this command (see Figure 13-12):

```
bcdedit /set {default} bootmenupolicy legacy
```

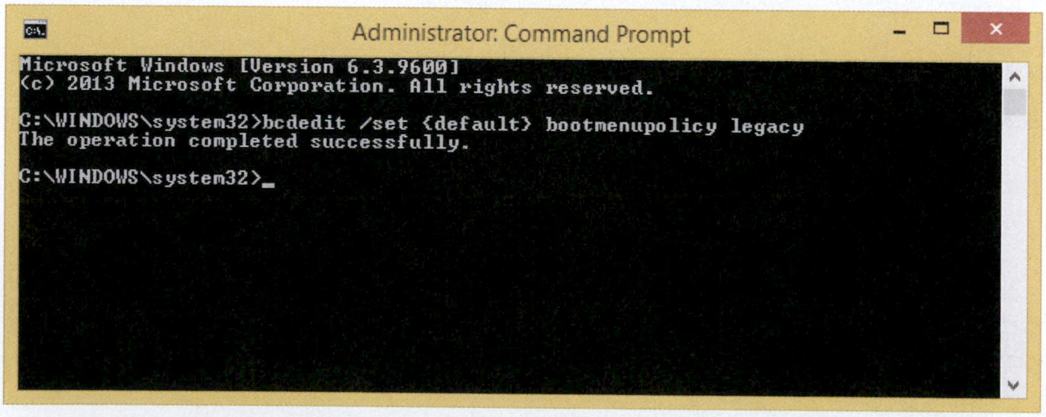

Figure 13-12 Enable the use of F8 during Windows startup

When you press **F8** at startup, the Windows 8 Advanced Boot Options screen appears (see Figure 13-13).

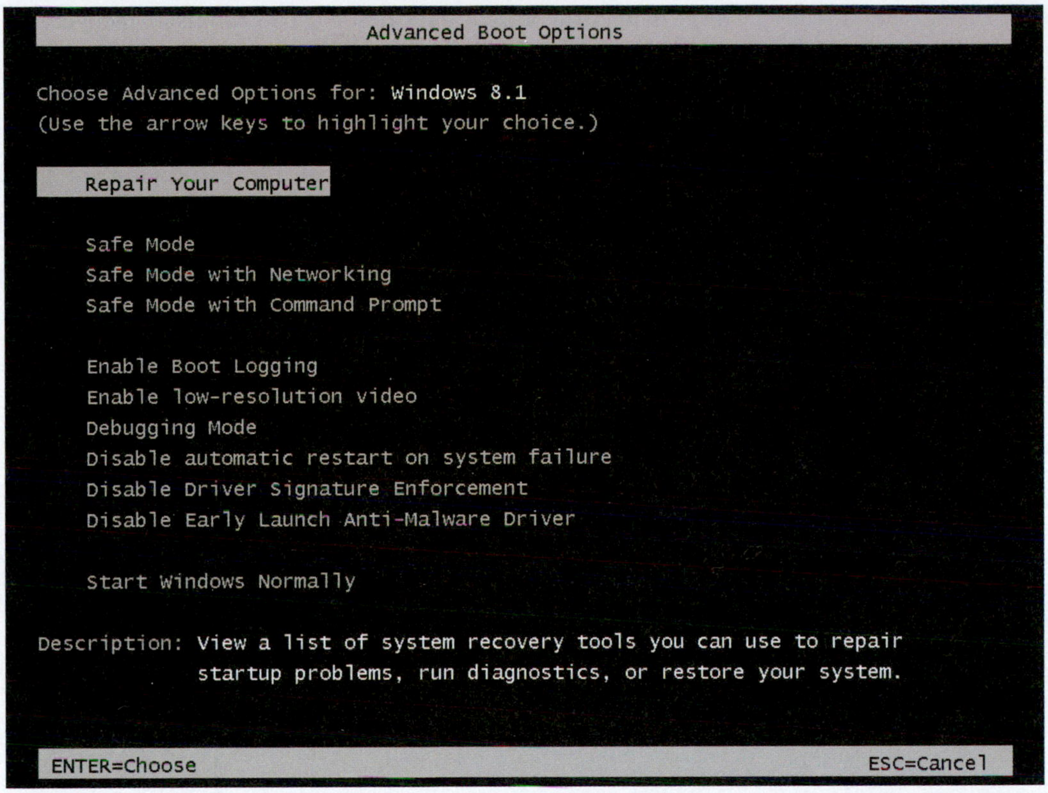

Figure 13-13 Use the Advanced Boot Options menu to troubleshoot difficult startup problems

Later, if you want to disable the use of F8 at startup, open an elevated command prompt window and enter this command:

```
bcdedit /set {default} bootmenupolicy standard
```


> **Caution** As you learn to troubleshoot Windows 8 startup, don't depend on the F8 key to work during the boot because you never know when you'll work on a computer that has it disabled.

- *Create a recovery drive.* Although it's possible to use recovery media created on a different computer than the one you are troubleshooting, the process is simplified if you already have these tools on hand. Let's learn how to do that now.

CREATE A RECOVERY DRIVE

If the computer won't start up, you'll need a bootable device with Windows repair tools on it to start the system and fix problems. Windows 8 provides two recovery device options, depending on the drive hardware available. Here are options for that device:

- If the computer has an optical drive, you can boot from the Windows setup DVD and use Windows RE to fix problems, which is discussed later in this section.
- You can use a tool new to Windows 8, called a recovery drive. A recovery drive is a bootable USB flash drive. Many mobile computers don't have an optical drive, which can make a recovery drive an essential troubleshooting tool.

> **Notes** A recovery drive is bit-specific: Use a 32-bit recovery drive to repair a 32-bit Windows installation and a 64-bit recovery drive to repair a 64-bit installation.

The key to optimal success with a recovery drive is to create it *before* it's needed. You can use a recovery drive on a broken computer that was created on a different computer. However, if a computer has an OEM recovery partition put there by the manufacturer of a laptop, all-in-one, or other brand-name computer, you have the option to copy this partition to the recovery drive in order to retain OEM resources. If the drive is to hold the OEM recovery partition, it should be about 16 GB. Otherwise, an 8-GB flash drive is large enough.

Here are the steps to create the recovery drive:

1. Plug in a USB flash drive. Know that the entire drive will be formatted and everything on the drive will be lost.
2. Open the **Control Panel** in Classic view and click **Recovery**. In the Recovery window that appears (see Figure 13-14), click **Create a recovery drive**. Respond to the UAC box.

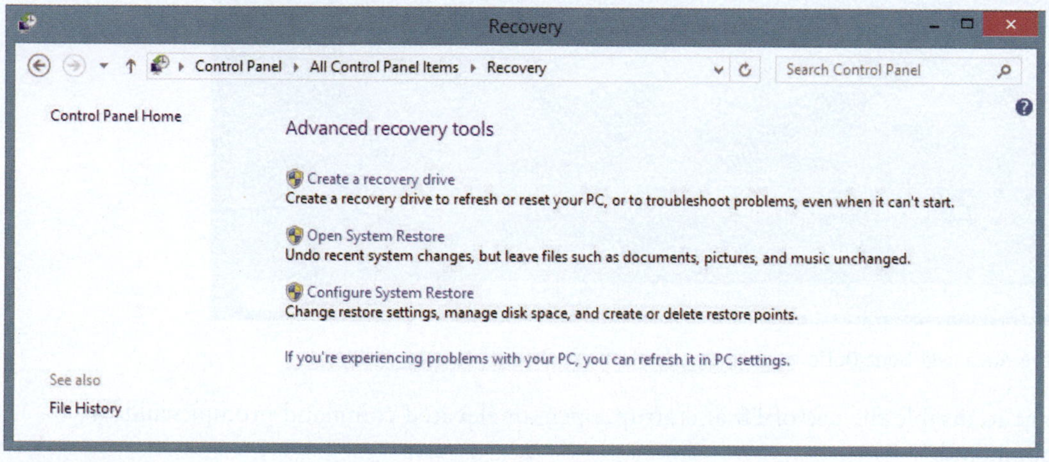

Figure 13-14 The Recovery window in Control Panel is used to create a recovery drive

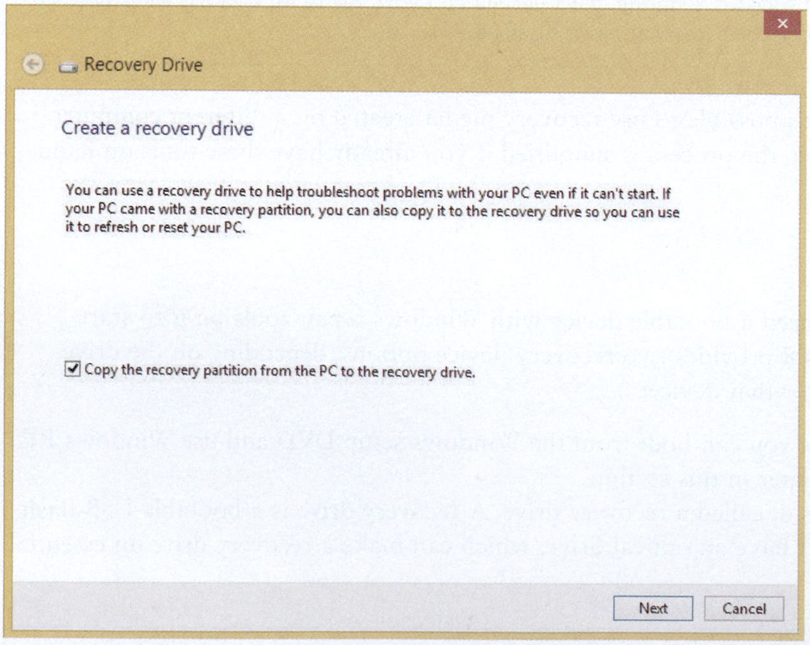

Figure 13-15 If the computer has a recovery partition, you have the option to copy it to the recovery drive

3. The Recovery Drive dialog box appears (see Figure 13-15). If the computer doesn't have an OEM recovery partition, the check box on this dialog box is gray and not available. If the computer has an OEM recovery partition, the check box is available and you can check it to copy the recovery partition to the recovery drive. Click **Next** to continue.
4. A list of installed drives appears (see Figure 13-16). Be careful to select the USB flash drive because everything on the drive will be lost. Click **Next**. A message on the next screen warns you that everything on the drive will be deleted. Click **Create**. The drive is created, which takes some time. Then click **Finish**.

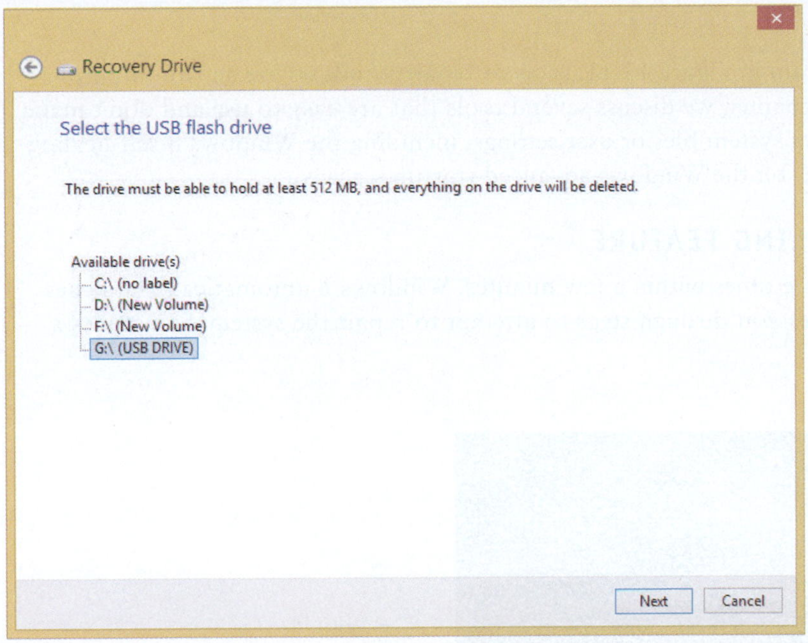

Figure 13-16 Select the USB flash drive that will become the recovery drive

Be sure to label the flash drive well and put it in a safe place. For example, you can put it in an envelope and label it "Recovery drive for John Hawkins 64-bit Windows 8 Sony laptop" and store it in the computer's documentation file.

Notes If you copied the OEM recovery partition to the USB flash drive and are short on hard drive space on the computer, you can use Disk Management to delete the recovery partition to free up some space and then expand the Windows volume.

WINDOWS 7 CREATE A SYSTEM REPAIR DISC

A+ 220-902 4.1

In Windows 7, you can create a Windows 7 system repair disc, which you can use to launch Windows RE. To create a Windows 7 system repair disc, click **Create a system repair disc** in the Windows 7 Backup and Restore window (see Figure 13-17). A 32-bit Windows 7 installation will create a 32-bit version of the repair disc, and a 64-bit Windows 7 installation will create a 64-bit version of the repair disc. A repair disc created on one computer can be used on a different computer even if they are using different editions of Windows 7, but be sure to use a 32-bit disc for a 32-bit installation and a 64-bit disc for a 64-bit Windows installation.

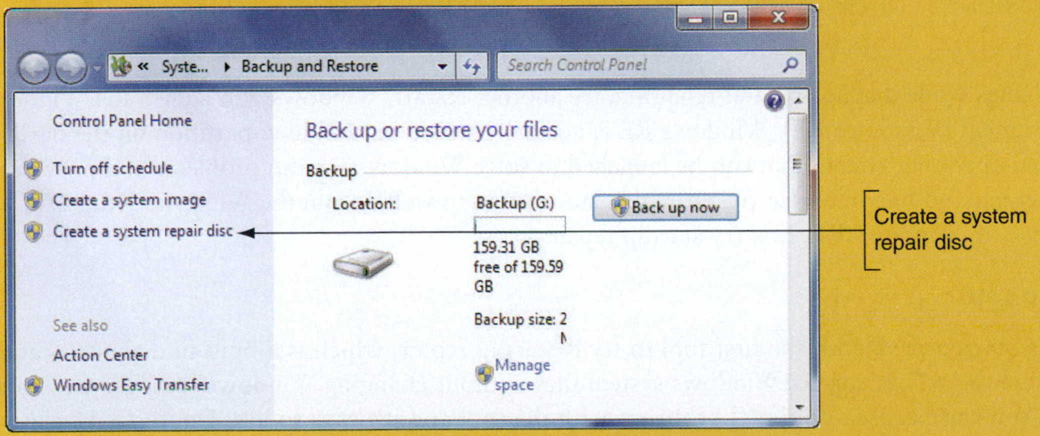

Figure 13-17 Use Windows 7 Backup and Restore to create a system repair disc to use instead of the Windows setup DVD

Notes To launch Windows RE from a Windows setup DVD or Windows 7 repair disc, be sure to use a 64-bit DVD for a 64-bit installation of Windows and a 32-bit DVD for a 32-bit installation of Windows. To boot from a DVD, you might have to change the boot sequence in UEFI/BIOS setup to put the optical drive first above the hard drive.

13

TOOLS FOR LEAST INVASIVE SOLUTIONS

A+
220-902
4.1

Looking back at the diagram in Figure 13-11, tools to repair Windows are shown in purple boxes. In this part of the chapter, we discuss several tools that are easy to use and don't make major changes to Windows system files or user settings, including the Windows 8 self-healing feature and several options on the Windows advanced startup screens.

USE WINDOWS 8'S SELF-HEALING FEATURE

If you restart the computer at least three times within a few minutes, Windows 8 automatically launches diagnostics (see Figure 13-18) and takes you through steps to attempt to repair the system. Sometimes a few restarts is all you need to do.

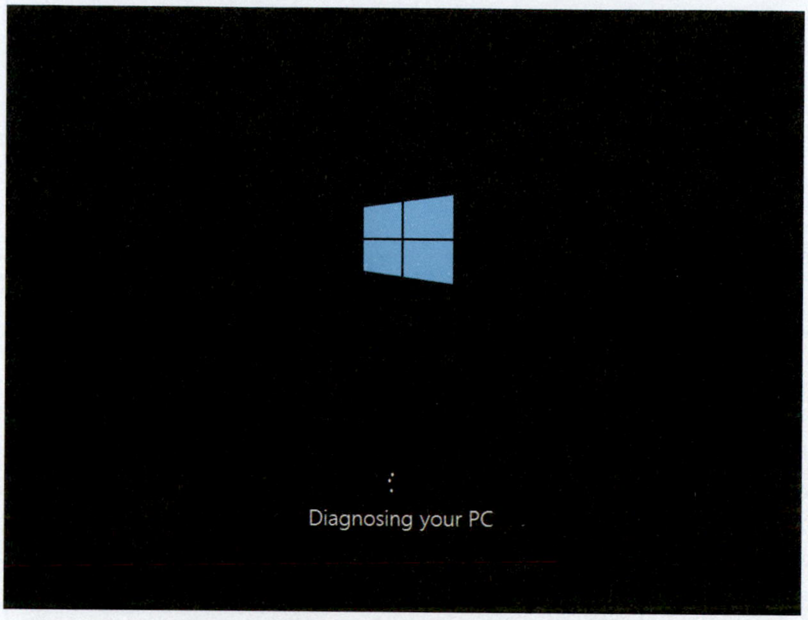

Figure 13-18 Windows automatically launches diagnostic procedures after the third restart within a few minutes

If the system hangs while diagnosing and repairing, try another restart. Windows will launch the Windows Recovery Environment (Windows RE). Windows RE is normally stored on a hidden partition on the hard drive and is a lean operating system that can be launched to solve Windows startup problems and provides a graphical and command-line interface. You can also launch Windows RE from the Windows setup DVD or a recovery drive. In Windows RE, first try startup repair.

STARTUP REPAIR

When addressing startup problems, the first tool to try is startup repair, which is a built-in diagnostic and repair tool in Windows 8/7. It can fix Windows system files without changing Windows settings, user data, or applications. You can't cause additional problems with the tool and it's easy to use. Figure 13-11 shows that startup repair can be launched from the Windows 8 Settings charm, by three or more restarts, or by booting from the Windows setup DVD or a recovery drive.

Follow these steps to use startup repair from the Settings charm:

1. On the Windows 8 charms bar, click **Settings.** In the Settings pane, click **Change PC settings.** In the left pane of the PC settings window, click **Update and recovery.** In the Update and recovery pane, click **Recovery** and click **Restart now** (see Figure 13-19).

Notes A shortcut method to launch Windows RE from within Windows is to go to the Windows sign-in screen. Click the **Power** icon and hold down the Shift key as you click **Restart**.

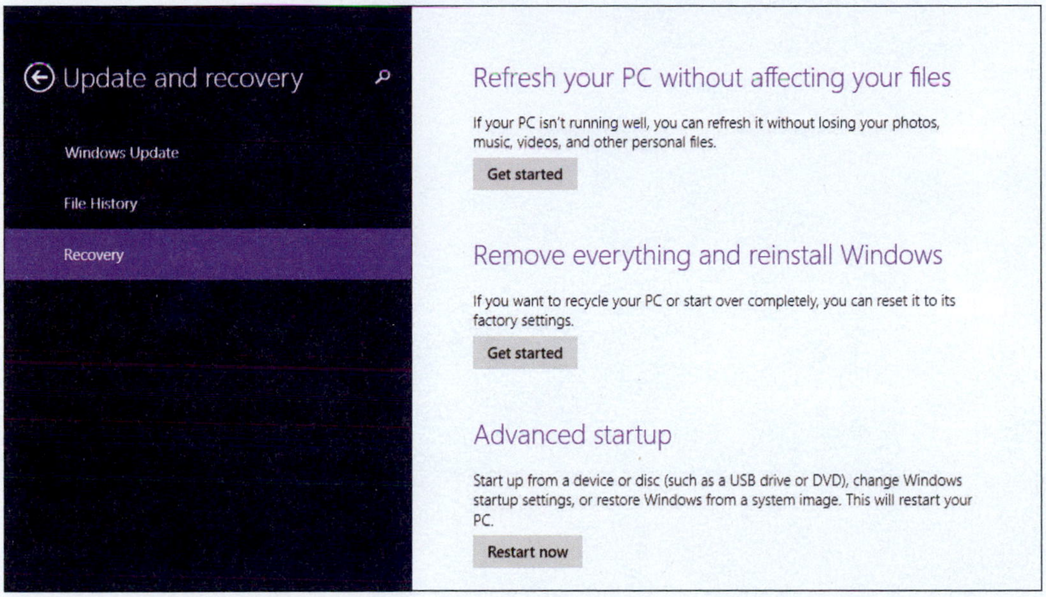

Figure 13-19 Refresh or reset a computer or restart the computer in advanced startup mode

Notes You must be signed in to Windows 8 with an administrator account to see all the options on the Recovery pane that are shown in Figure 13-19.

13

2. Windows restarts and launches Windows RE. The first screen provided by Windows RE is called the Windows Startup Menu and is shown in Figure 13-20. When you click **Troubleshoot**, the Troubleshoot screen in Figure 13-21 appears. Using this screen, notice you can refresh or reset the computer, which are more invasive solutions than startup repair. Click **Advanced options**.

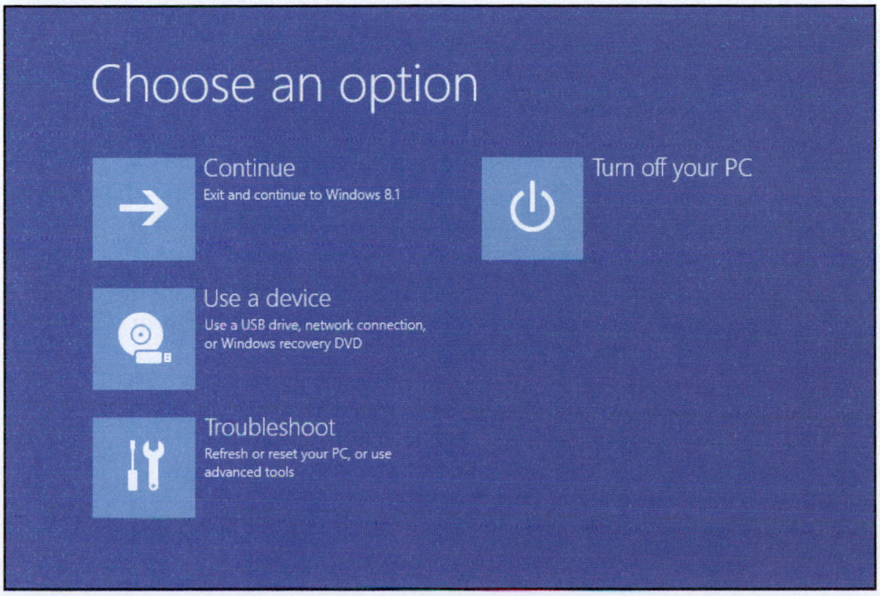

Figure 13-20 Windows Startup Menu indicates Windows RE is launched

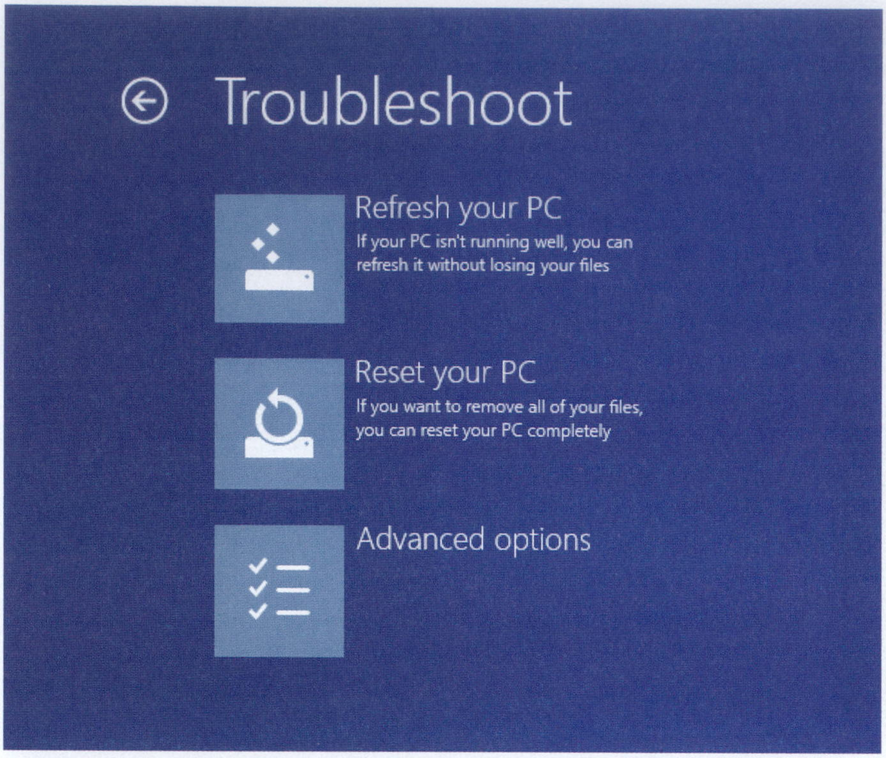

Figure 13-21 Windows RE offers refresh and reset options to solve a computer problem

3. From the Advanced options screen (see Figure 13-22), you can perform a System Restore (apply a restore point), use a system image to recover the Windows volume (for backward compatibility with the Windows 7 system image), perform a startup repair, get to a command prompt, and change startup settings. Click **Startup Repair**. Windows RE examines the system, fixes problems, reports what it did, and might offer suggestions for further fixes. A log file of the process can be found at C:\Windows\System32\LogFiles\SRT\SRTTrail.txt.

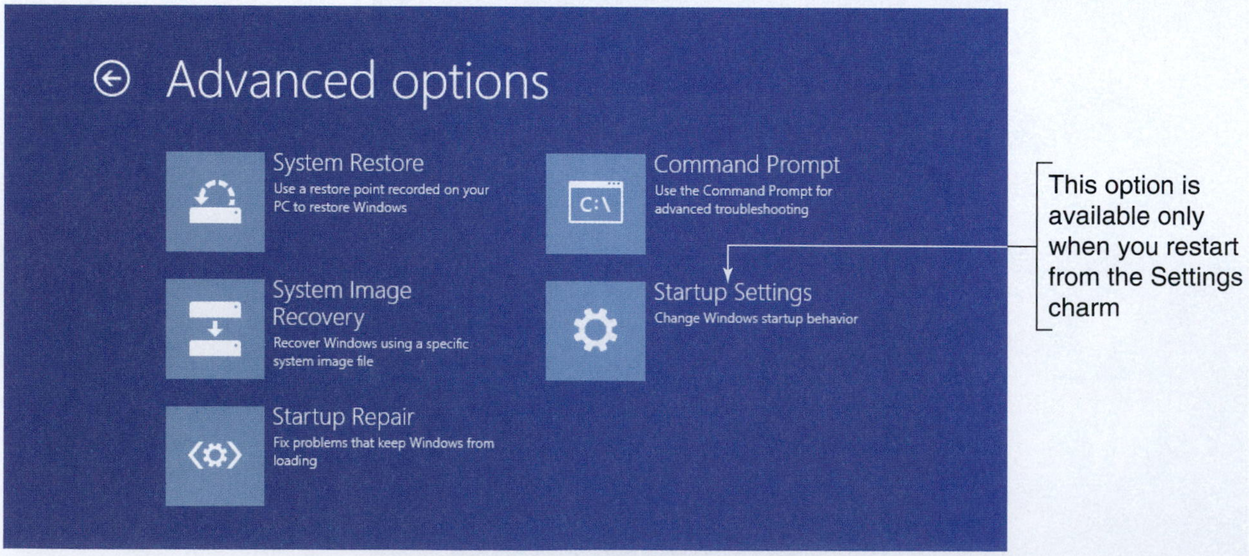

Figure 13-22 More advanced tools for solving startup problems

Notes Depending on the situation, you might see a sixth option on the Advanced options screen, which is UEFI Firmware Settings. Use this option to change settings in a computer's UEFI firmware.

WINDOWS 7 STARTUP REPAIR

A+
220-902
4.1

Windows RE in Windows 7 offers many of the same startup troubleshooting tools as does Windows 8. In Windows 7, to perform a startup repair, press **F8** at startup to launch the Advanced Boot Options screen (refer back to Figure 3-9). Click **Repair Your Computer**, which launches Windows RE. On the next screen, enter an administrator user account and password. Then the System Recovery Options box appears (see Figure 13-23). Click **Startup Repair** and follow directions on screen.

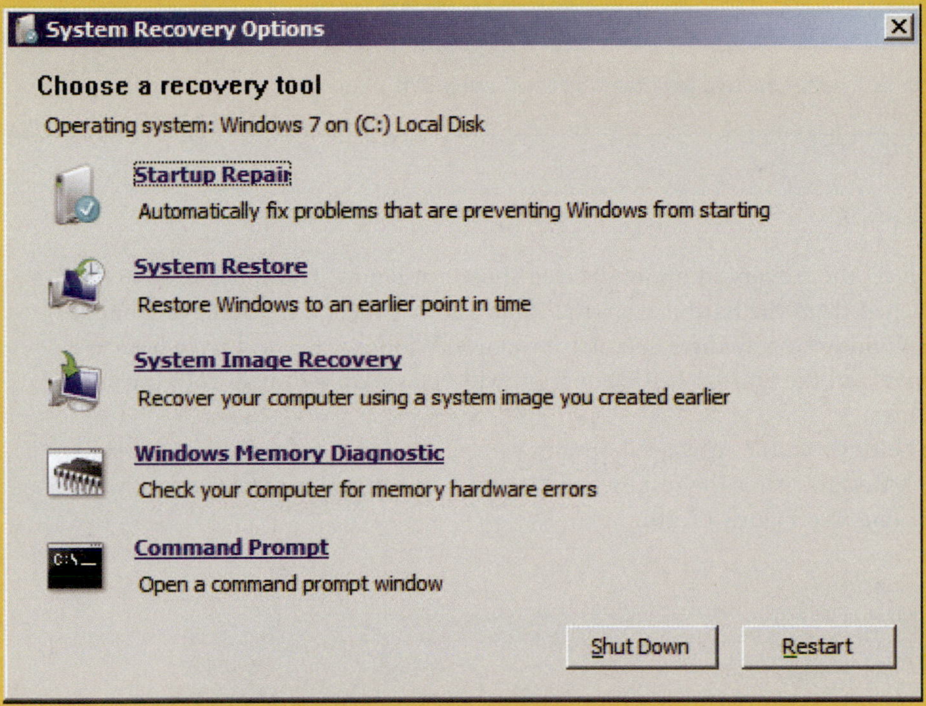

Figure 13-23 Recovery tools in Windows RE for a Windows 7 installation

If Windows is totally trashed, pressing F8 at startup won't work. In this situation, boot the computer from the Windows 7 setup DVD. On the Install Windows screen (see Figure 13-24), click **Repair your computer**. Windows RE launches. On the following screens, select your language and enter an administrator user account and password. The System Recovery Options window appears where you can select **Startup Repair**.

(continues)

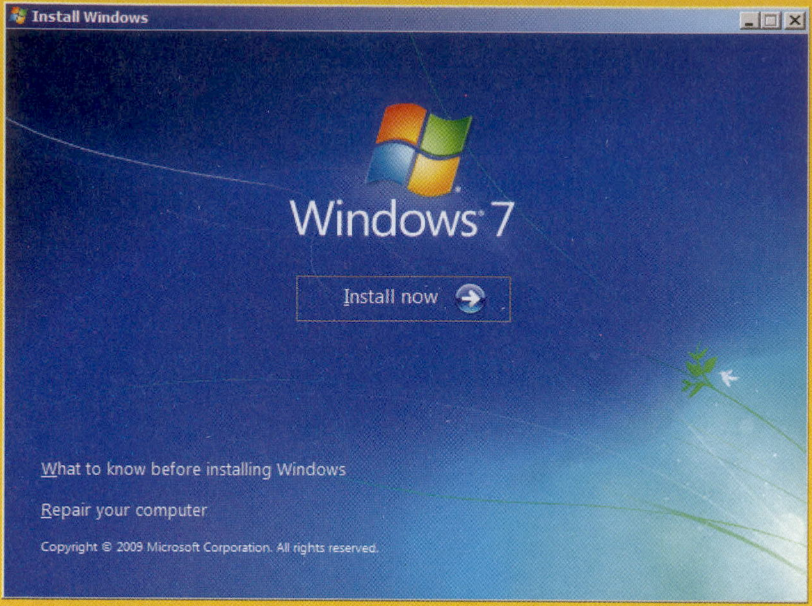

Figure 13-24 Launch Windows RE after booting from the Windows 7 setup DVD

CHANGE STARTUP SETTINGS

The Startup Settings option on the Advanced options screen shown in Figure 13-22 is available only when Windows RE is launched from the hard drive rather than another media. If you have launched Windows RE from within Windows or by three successive restarts, Windows RE will have been launched from the hard drive and the Startup Settings option will be available to help solve problems with critical Windows settings.

When you click **Startup Settings** on the Advanced options screen, the Startup Settings screen shown in Figure 13-25 appears. Click **Restart**. After the restart, another Startup Settings screen appears, which has more options than the first one (see Figure 13-26).

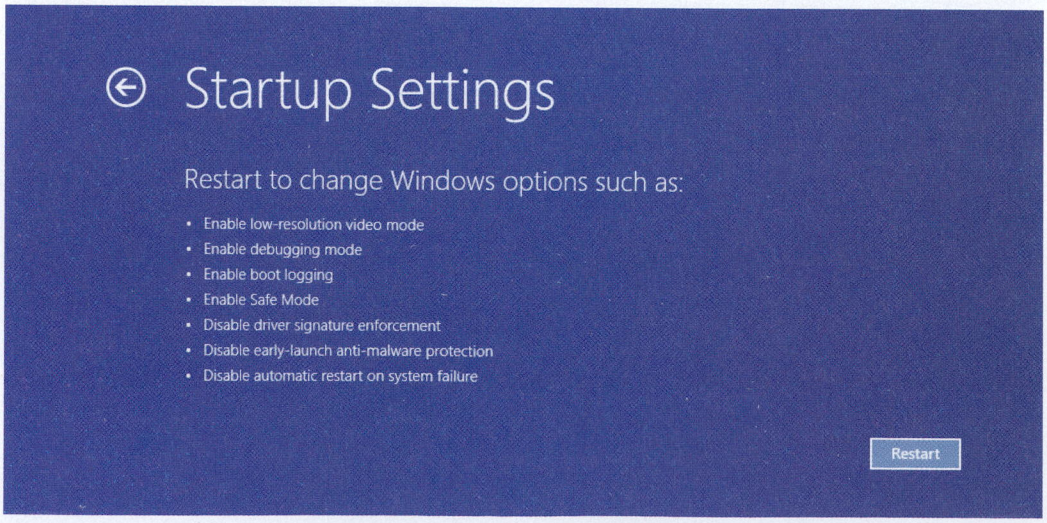

Figure 13-25 Restart the computer to get to more advanced troubleshooting tools

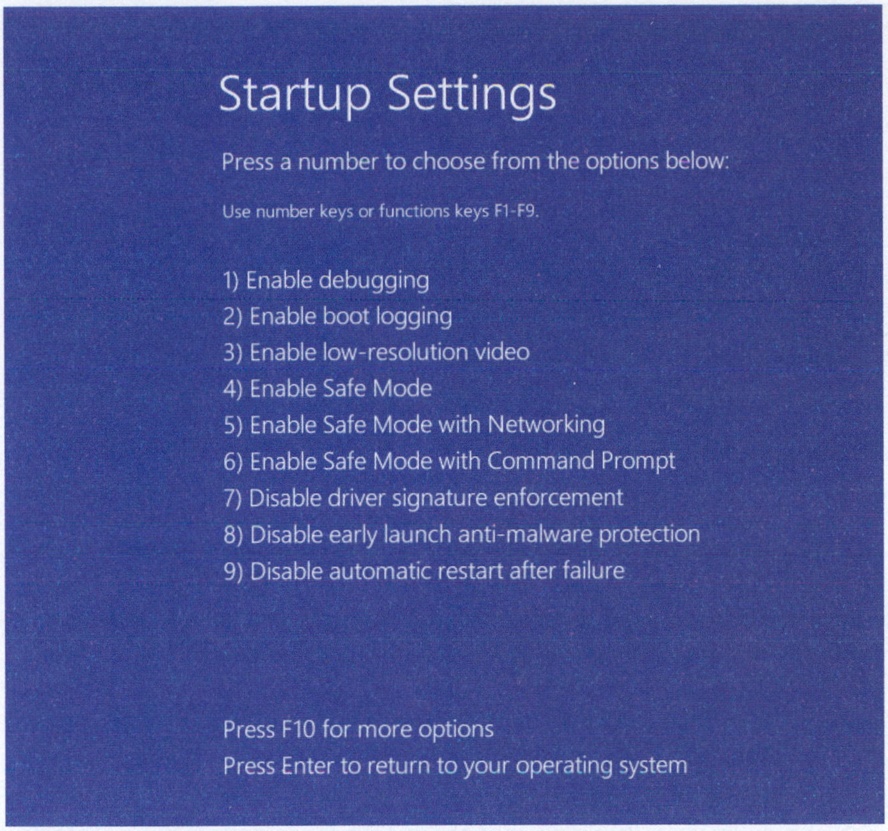

Figure 13-26 Press a function key or number to restart the system in a given mode

Press numbers or function keys F1 through F9 to launch the tools on this screen. Windows 7 offers similar tools on its Advanced Boot Options screen (refer back to Figure 13-9). Here's a quick rundown of what the Windows 8/7 tools do.

Press 1 or F1: Enable Debugging

This tool moves system boot logs from the failing computer to another computer for evaluation. The computers must be connected by way of a serial port.

Press 2 or F2: Enable Boot Logging

Windows loads normally and all files used during the load process are recorded in a log file, C:\Windows\Ntbtlog.txt (see Figure 13-27). Use this option to see what did and did not load during the boot. For instance, if you have a problem getting a device to work, check Ntbtlog.txt to see what driver files loaded. Boot logging is much more effective if you have a copy of Ntbtlog.txt that was made when everything worked as it should. Then you can compare the good load with the bad load, looking for differences.

Notes The Ntbtlog.txt file is also generated when you boot into Safe Mode.

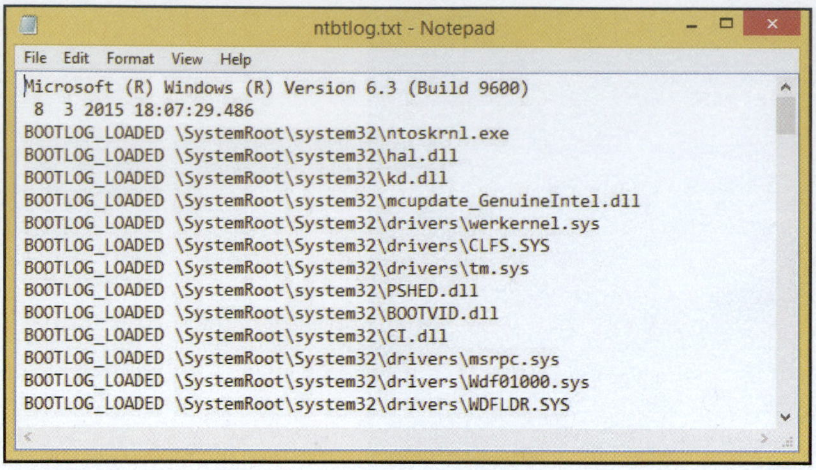

Figure 13-27 Sample Ntbtlog.txt file

> **Notes** If Windows hangs during the boot, try booting using the option Enable Boot Logging. Then look at the last entry in the Ntbtlog.txt file. This entry might be the name of a device driver causing the system to hang.

Press 3 or F3: Enable Low-Resolution Video (640 × 480)

Use this option when the video settings don't allow you to see the screen well enough to fix a bad setting (for example, black fonts on a black background). Booting in this mode gives you a very plain, standard VGA video. You can then go to the Display settings, correct the problem, and reboot normally. You can also use this option if your video drivers are corrupted and you need to update, roll back, or reinstall the video drivers.

Press 4 or F4: Enable Safe Mode

After you sign in to Windows, the Safe Mode desktop appears (see Figure 13-28). Launching Safe Mode and then restarting the system sometimes solve a startup problem. However, you can also go to the Start screen in Safe Mode to launch anti-malware software to scan the system for malware. You can open Event Viewer to find events helpful in troubleshooting the system, run the System File Checker command (**sfc /scannow**) to restore system files, use Device Manager to roll back a driver, use Memory Diagnostics to verify memory, use the **chkdsk /r** command to check for file system errors, configure Windows for a clean boot on the next restart, and perform other troubleshooting tasks.

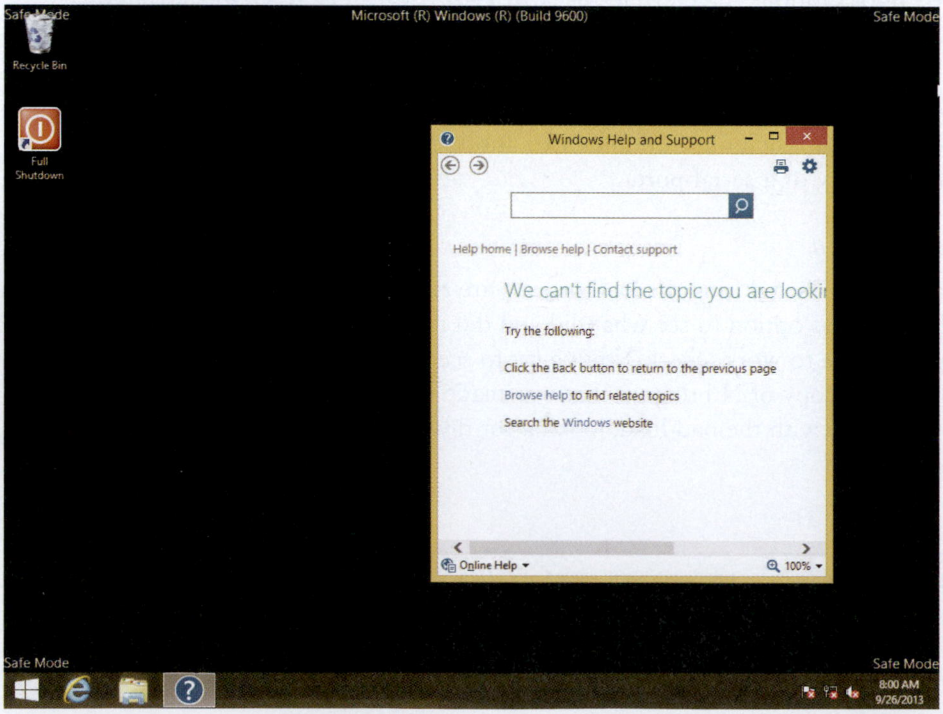

Figure 13-28 Safe Mode desktop

★ A+ Exam Tip The A+ 220-902 exam expects you to know how to use Safe Mode and chkdsk to help resolve a Windows startup problem.

Press 5 or F5: Enable Safe Mode with Networking

Use this option when you need access to the network to solve the problem. For example, you might need to download updates to your anti-malware software. Also use this mode when the Windows installation files are available on the network, rather than the Windows setup DVD, and you need to access those files.

Press 6 or F6: Enable Safe Mode with Command Prompt

If Safe Mode can't start, try Safe Mode with Command Prompt, which doesn't attempt to load the graphical interface. At the command prompt, use the **sfc /scannow** command to verify system files (see Figure 13-29). If the problem is still not solved, you can use this command to launch System Restore: **`C:\Windows\system32\rstrui.exe`.** Then follow the directions on screen to select a restore point (see Figure 13-30).

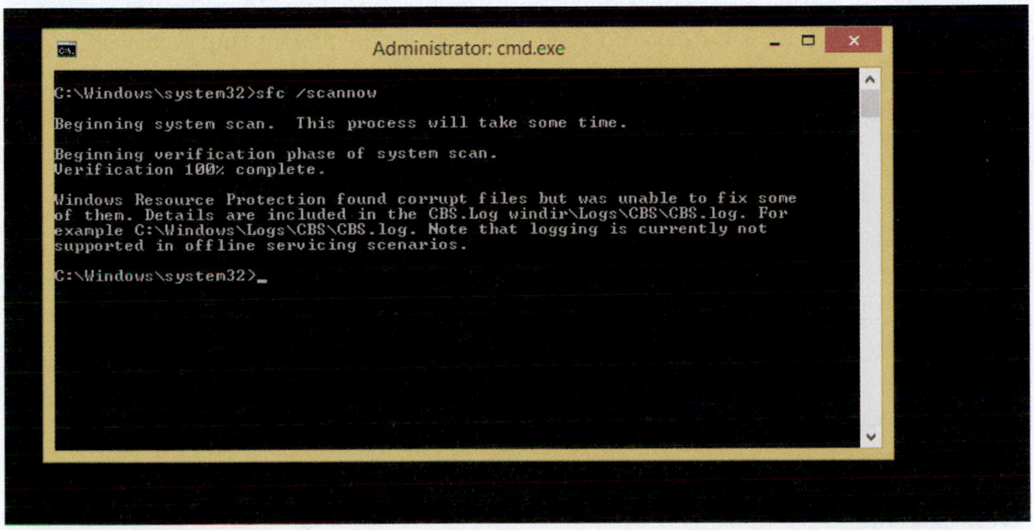

Figure 13-29 SFC finds and repairs corrupted system files

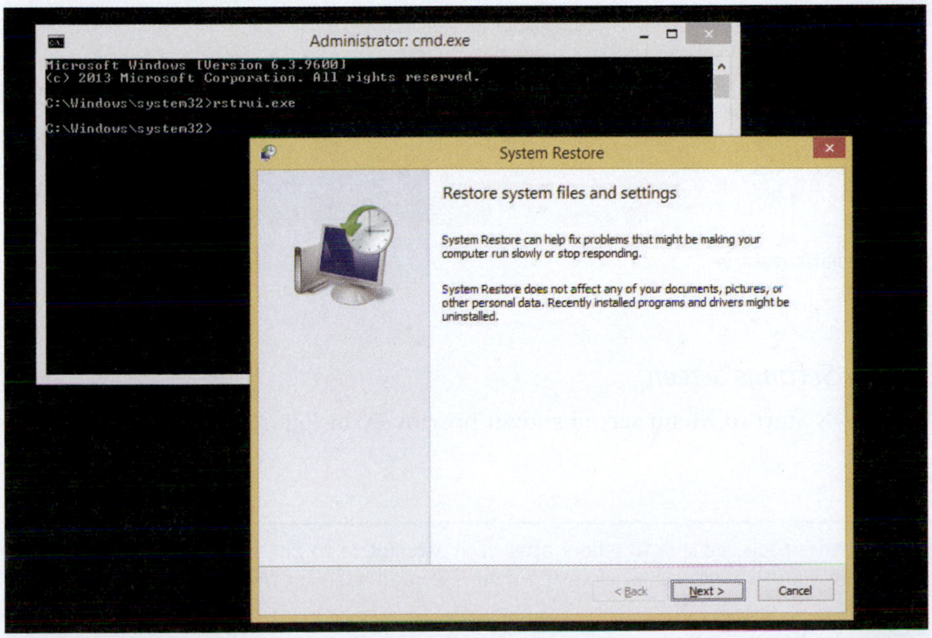

Figure 13-30 Use System Restore after booting to Safe Mode with Command Prompt

Press 7 or F7: Disable Driver Signature Enforcement

All 64-bit editions of Windows require that kernel-mode drivers be digitally signed. Disabling driver signature enforcement is used by developers who are testing kernel-mode device drivers that are not yet digitally signed. Don't use this option for troubleshooting Windows startup because doing so might allow malware drivers to load.

Press 8 or F8: Disable Early Launch Anti-Malware Driver

Windows 8 allows anti-malware software to launch a driver before any third-party drivers are launched so it can scan these drivers for malware. Unless you're sure a driver is the problem, don't disable this security feature. (Windows 7 doesn't offer this option on its Advanced Boot Options screen.)

Press 9 or F9: Disable Automatic Restart on System Failure

By default, Windows automatically restarts immediately after a blue screen of death (BSOD) stop error, which is described in more detail later in this chapter. The error can cause the system to continually reboot rather than shut down. Press **F9** to disable automatic restarts and stop the rebooting. To make this setting permanent, open the **System** window and click **Advanced system settings.** In the Startup and Recovery group of the System Properties box, click **Settings,** and on the Startup and Recovery box, uncheck **Automatically restart** (see Figure 13-31). Click **OK** twice and close the System window.

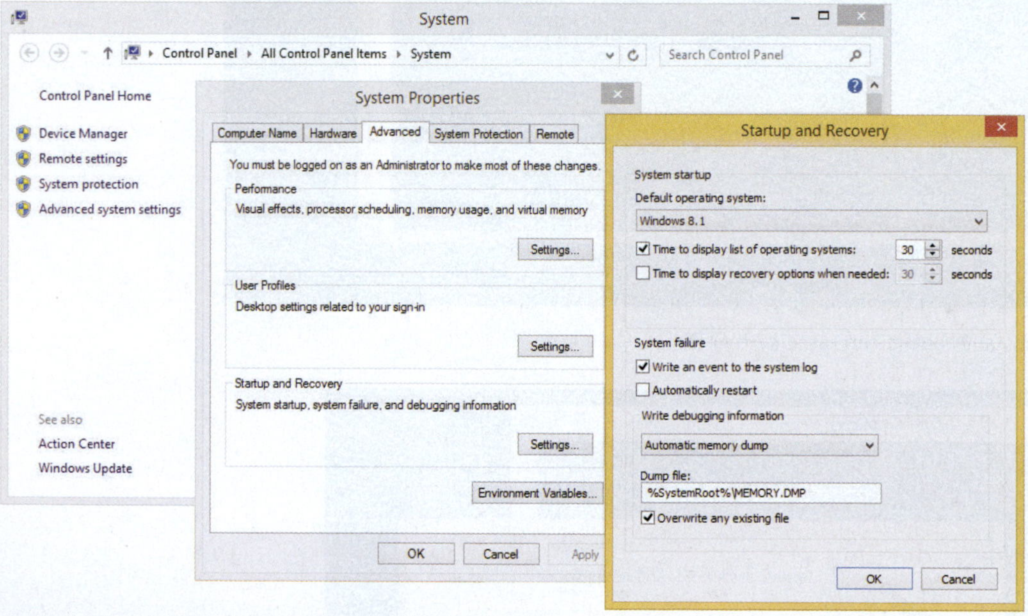

Figure 13-31 Permanently disable automatic restarts

Press F10: Return to the Startup Settings Screen

Press F10 to return to the Windows 8 Startup Menu screen shown previously in Figure 13-20.

> **Notes** As you use these startup settings tools, be sure to reboot after each attempt to fix the problem to make sure the problem has not been resolved before you try another tool. To exit Windows RE and relaunch Windows, press **Enter** on the Startup Settings screen.

WINDOWS | 7 LAST KNOWN GOOD CONFIGURATION

A+ 220-902 4.1

One option available in the Advanced Boot Options menu for Windows 7 (refer back to Figure 13-9) that is no longer available for Windows 8 is the Last Known Good Configuration, which has been replaced by System Restore and a computer refresh for Windows 8. For Windows 7, registry settings collectively called the **Last Known Good Configuration** are saved in the registry each time the user successfully logs on to the system. If your problem is caused by a bad hardware or software installation and you get an error message the first time you restart the system after the installation, using the Last Known Good can, in effect, undo your installation and solve your problem.

Remember, the Last Known Good registry settings are saved each time a user logs on to Windows 7. Therefore, it's important to try the Last Known Good early in the troubleshooting session before a good one is overwritten with a bad Last Known Good. (However, know that if you sign in to Safe Mode, the Last Known Good is not saved.)

Hands-On | Project 13-2 Use Boot Logs and System Information to Research Startup

A+ 220-902 4.1

Boot logs can be used to generate a list of drivers that were loaded during a normal startup and during the Safe Mode startup. Do the following to use boot logs to research startup:

1. Boot to the normal Windows desktop with boot logging enabled. Save the boot log just created to a different name or location so it will not be overwritten on the next boot.
2. Reboot the system in Safe Mode, which also creates a boot log. Compare the two logs, identifying differences in drivers loaded during the two boots. To compare the files, you can print both files and lay them side by side for comparison. An easier method is to compare the files using the Compare tool in Microsoft Word.
3. Use the System Information utility or other methods to identify the hardware devices loaded during normal startup but not loaded in Safe Mode. Which devices on your system did not load in Safe Mode?

As you identify the drivers not loaded during Safe Mode, these registry keys might help with your research:

- Lists drivers and services loaded during Safe Mode: HKLM\System\CurrentControlSet\Control\SafeBoot\Minimal
- Lists drivers and services loaded during Safe Mode with Networking: HKLM\System\CurrentControlSet\Control\SafeBoot\Network

13

Hands-On | Project 13-3 Take Ownership and Replace a Windows System File

A+ 220-902 4.1

The System File Checker (SFC) tool can be used to find and replace corrupted Windows system files. The tool keeps a log of its actions (refer back to Figure 13-29), and, if it cannot replace a corrupted file, you can find that information in the log file. Then you can manually replace the file. To do so, you can use the takeown command to take ownership of a system file and the icacls command to get full access to the file. The Microsoft Knowledge Base Article 929833 at *support.microsoft.com* explains how to use these two commands.

(continues)

Do the following to practice manually replacing a system file:

1. Boot the computer into Safe Mode with Command Prompt.
2. Take ownership and gain full access to the C:\Windows\System32\jscript.dll file. What commands did you use?
3. Rename the jscript.dll file to jscript.dll.hold. Run the **sfc /scannow** command. Did SFC restore the jscript.dll file? What is the path and file name of the log file listing repairs?
4. SFC restores a file using files stored on the Windows setup DVD or other folders on the hard drive. If SFC cannot restore a file, you might find a fresh copy in the C:\Windows\winsxs folder or its subfolders. Search these folders. Did you find a version of jscript.dll that is the same file size as the one in C:\Windows\System32? Other than the C:\Windows\winsxs folder, where else can you find a known good copy of a corrupted system file?

Notes To use a command prompt window to search for a file in a folder and its subfolders, use the **dir /s** command.

TOOLS THAT CAN AFFECT WINDOWS SYSTEM FILES AND SETTINGS

A+
220-902
4.1

Tools that affect Windows system files, Windows settings, user settings, and applications include System Restore and several commands that you can execute from a command prompt in Windows RE. These tools are discussed next.

SYSTEM RESTORE

Windows gives you several opportunities during the startup troubleshooting process to use System Restore to restore the system to an earlier point in time when a restore point was made. You can select System Restore from the Windows 8 Advanced options screen (refer back to Figure 13-22) or the Windows 7 Advanced Boot Options screen (refer back to Figure 13-9). You can also perform System Restore in Safe Mode or from a command prompt.

System Restore can cause problems of its own because Windows updates and updates to anti-malware software can be lost and hardware devices and applications might need to be reinstalled. System Restore won't help if the file system is corrupted or the registry is trashed. In these situations, the command prompt might help.

THE COMMAND PROMPT WINDOW IN WINDOWS RE

A+
220-902
1.3, 4.1

Use the command prompt window in Windows RE when the graphical interface is missing or corrupted or you want to use a specific command to fix a problem when Windows refuses to start. Using this command prompt, you have administrator privileges and full read and write access to all files on all drives. Many commands you learned about in the chapter, "Maintaining Windows," can be used at this command prompt. To access the Windows RE command prompt, follow these steps:

1. Depending on the health of your Windows system, do one of the following:
   - If you can start Windows, launch Windows RE from the Settings charm as you learned to do earlier in the chapter. The system restarts and the Windows Startup Menu (refer back to Figure 13-6) appears.
   - If you cannot launch Windows, boot from the Windows setup DVD or a recovery drive. (You might need to first change the boot device priority order in UEFI/BIOS to boot first from the optical drive or USB device.) On the Windows Setup screen (see Figure 13-32), click **Repair your computer**. On the next screen, choose your keyboard. The Windows Startup Menu appears.

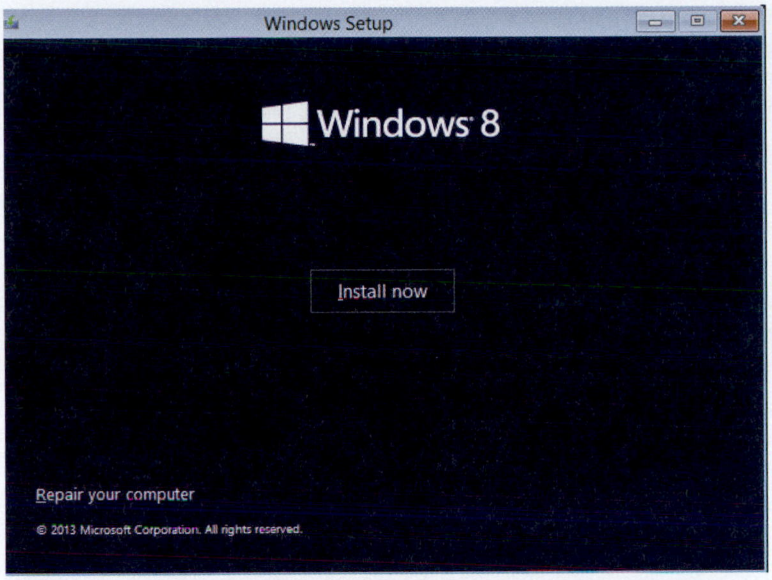

Figure 13-32 Use the Windows setup DVD to launch Windows RE

2. On the Windows Startup Menu, click **Troubleshoot.** On the Troubleshoot screen (refer back to Figure 13-21), click **Command Prompt** (refer back to Figure 13-22).
3. If Windows RE is able to read registry entries on the hard drive, it will ask you to sign in using an administrator account.

Next are some examples of how to use the Windows RE command prompt to repair a system.

MANAGE DATA FILES AND SYSTEM FILES

Use the **sfc /scannow** command to restore critical Windows system files. Use the cd, copy, rename, and delete commands to manage data and system files. For example, if key registry files are corrupted or deleted, the system will not start. You can restore registry files using those saved in the C:\Windows\System32\Config\RegBack folder. This RegBack folder contains partial backups of the registry files put there after a successful boot. Use the commands in Table 13-2 to restore the registry files. In the table, we assume Windows is installed on drive C:. However, know that Windows RE is likely to assign a different drive letter to the Windows volume.

Command Line	Description
1. `c:`	Makes drive C: the current drive. The default directory is root.
2. `dir`	Examines the contents of drive C:. If this is not your Windows volume, try a different drive letter.
3. `cd \windows\system32\config`	Makes the Windows registry folder the current folder.
4. `ren default default.save` 5. `ren sam sam.save` 6. `ren security security.save` 7. `ren software software.save` 8. `ren system system.save`	Renames the five registry files.
9. `cd regback`	Makes the registry backup folder the current folder.

Table 13-2 Steps to restore the registry files (continues)

13

Command Line	Description
10. `copy system c:\windows\system32\config`	For hardware problems, first try copying just the System hive from the backup folder to the registry folder and then reboot.
11. `copy software c:\windows\system32\config`	For software problems, first try copying just the Software hive to the registry folder, and then reboot.
12. `copy system c:\windows\system32\config` 13. `copy software c:\windows\system32\config` 14. `copy default c:\windows\system32\config` 15. `copy sam c:\windows\system32\config` 16. `copy security c:\windows\system32\config`	If the problem is still not solved, try copying all five hives to the registry folder and reboot.

Table 13-2 Steps to restore the registry files (continued)

After you try each fix, reboot the system to see if the problem is solved before you do the next fix.

REPAIR AND MANAGE A HARD DRIVE

A corrupted file system or partition can cause a failure to boot. Use the chkdsk /r command to repair the file system. Use the format command to reformat the volume (all files will be lost). Use the diskpart command to manage hard drives, partitions, and volumes. When you enter diskpart at a command prompt, the DISKPART> prompt appears where you can enter diskpart commands. Some important diskpart commands are listed in Table 13-3; you have already learned to use several. Diskpart can also be used in a normal command prompt window.

Diskpart Command	Description
`list disk`	Lists installed hard disk drives.
`select disk`	Selects a hard disk or other storage device. For example: `select disk 0`
`list partition`	Lists partitions on selected disk.
`select partition`	Selects a partition on the selected disk. For example: `select partition 1`
`clean`	Removes any partition or volume information from the selected disk. Can be useful to remove dynamic disk information or a corrupted partition table or if you just want a fresh start when partitioning a hard disk. All data and partition information on the disk are deleted.
`convert gpt`	Converts an empty disk from MBR to GPT.
`create partition primary`	Creates a primary partition on the currently selected hard disk.
`assign`	Assigns a drive letter to a partition. For example: `assign letter=z`
`remove`	Removes a drive letter from a volume. For example: `remove letter=z`

`format`	Formats the currently selected partition. For example:
	`format fs=ntfs quick`
	`format fs=fat32`

`active`	Makes the selected partition the active partition.

Table 13-3 Important diskpart commands used at the DISKPART> prompt (continues)

Diskpart Command	Description
`inactive`	**Makes the selected partition inactive.**

`detail`	**Shows details about the selected disk, partition, or volume:**
	`detail disk`
	`detail partition`
	`detail volume`

`exit`	**Exits the diskpart utility.**

Table 13-3 Important diskpart commands used at the DISKPART> prompt (continued)

Notes For a complete list of diskpart commands, go to the Microsoft support site (*technet.microsoft.com*) and search on "DiskPart Command-Line Options".

ENABLE NETWORKING

Networking is not normally available from the Windows RE command prompt. Use the **wpeinit** command to enable networking. The wpeinit command initializes Windows PE. Recall from the chapter, "Installing Windows," that Windows PE is the preinstallation-environment operating system that is launched prior to installing Windows in a clean install and includes networking components.

USE BOOTREC AND BCDEDIT TO REPAIR THE FILE SYSTEM AND KEY BOOT FILES

A failure to boot can be caused by a corrupted BCD. Use the bootrec command to repair the BCD and boot sectors. Use the bcdedit command to manually edit the BCD. (Be sure to make a copy of the BCD before you edit it.) Use the bootsect command to repair a dual-boot system. To get helpful information about these commands, enter the command followed by /?, such as **bcdedit /?**. Some examples of the bootrec and bcdedit commands are listed in Table 13-4.

13

Command Line	Description
`bootrec /scanOS`	**Scans the hard drive for Windows installations not stored in the BCD**
`bootrec /rebuildBCD`	**Scans for Windows installations and rebuilds the BCD**
`bootrec /fixboot`	**Repairs the boot sector of the system partition**
`bootrec /fixmbr`	**Repairs the MBR**
`bcdedit /enum`	**Displays the contents of the BCD**

Table 13-4 Bootrec and bcdedit commands to repair system files and the file system

Although a startup repair should solve the problem when you get an error message at startup that "Bootmgr is missing," rebuilding the BCD store should also be able to resolve the same problem on a BIOS and MBR system.

A+ Exam Tip The A+ 220-901 and 220-902 exams expect you to know how to use the bootrec and diskpart commands.

Hands-On | Project 13-4 View the BCD Store

A+
220-902
4.1

On two or more computers, open an elevated command prompt window and use the bcdedit /enum command to view the BCD store. One BCD store is shown in Figure 13-33.

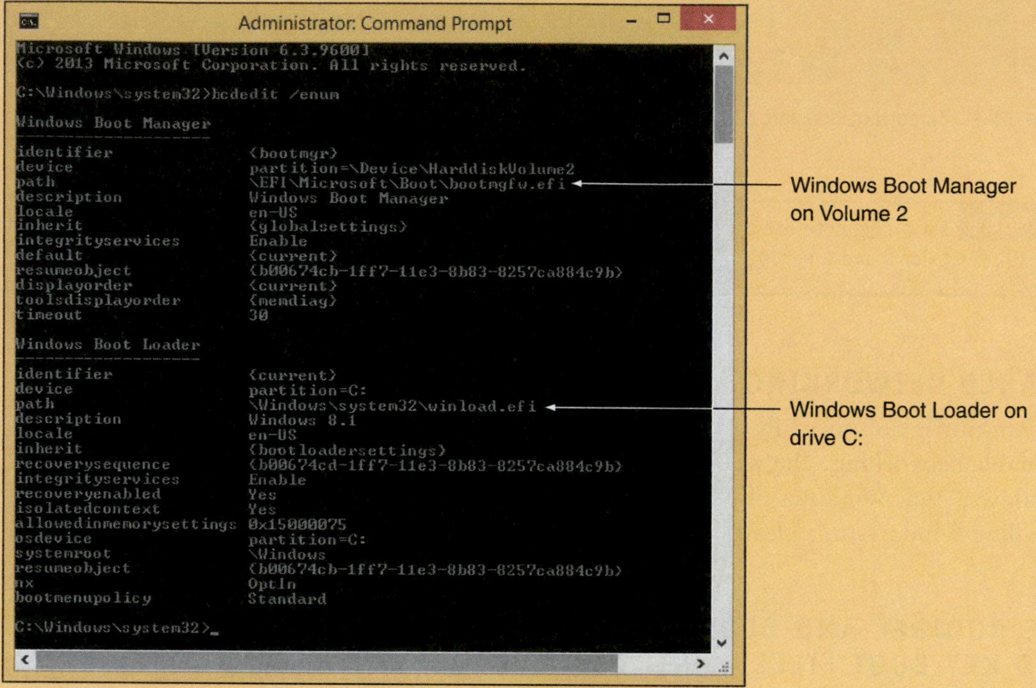

Figure 13-33 A BCD store on a computer that uses the GPT partitioning system

Answer the following questions:

1. Can you view the BCD store and determine if the system is using the MBR or GPT partitioning system? Why or why not?
2. Explain how you can look at the BCD store and tell if the system is a single boot or multiboot system.

TOOLS FOR REINSTALLING WINDOWS

A+
220-902
1.2, 1.7,
4.1

All of the startup troubleshooting tools so far in this chapter are designed to repair a Windows installation. However, sometimes Windows is beyond repair and you need to reinstall it. The following startup troubleshooting tools affect the entire Windows installation on a computer rather than a few files or settings. Let's discuss your options for a reinstall, including an OEM recovery partition, Windows 8 refresh and reset, and Windows 8/7 system image.

OEM RECOVERY PARTITION

Laptops, all-in-one computers, and brand-name desktops come with the OS preinstalled at the factory. This OEM (original equipment manufacturer) build of the OS is likely to be customized, and, for laptops, the drivers might be specific to proprietary devices installed in the laptop.

The laptop or brand-name computer is likely to have a recovery partition on the hard drive that contains a copy of the OS build, device drivers, diagnostics programs, and preinstalled applications needed to restore the system to its factory state. This partition might or might not be hidden. For example, Figure 13-34 shows the Disk Management information for a hard drive on one laptop that has a 14.75-GB recovery partition.

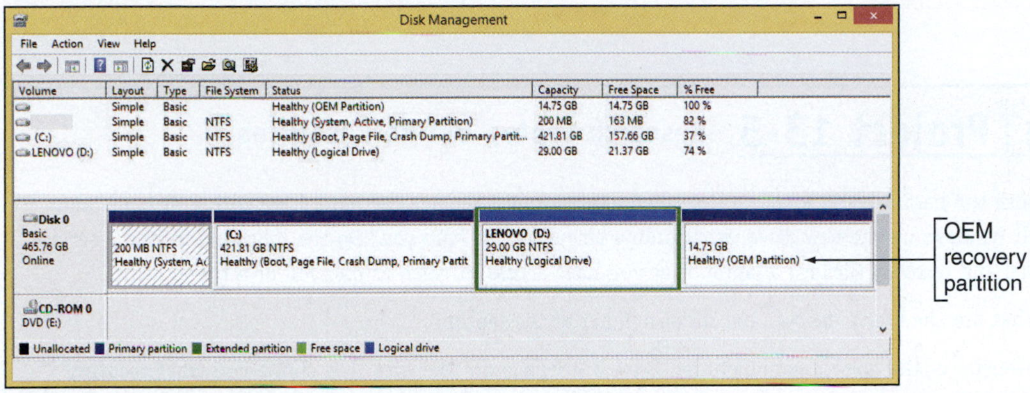

Figure 13-34 This laptop hard drive has a 14.75-GB recovery partition that can be used to recover the system

To know how to access the recovery tools stored on a recovery partition, see the manufacturer's website or look for a message at the beginning of the boot, such as "Press ESC for diagnostics" or "Press F12 to recover the system." For one Sony laptop, you press the red **Assist** button during the boot (see Figure 13-35). When you press the key or button, a menu appears giving you options to diagnose the problem, to repair the current OS installation, or to completely rebuild the entire hard drive to its factory state.

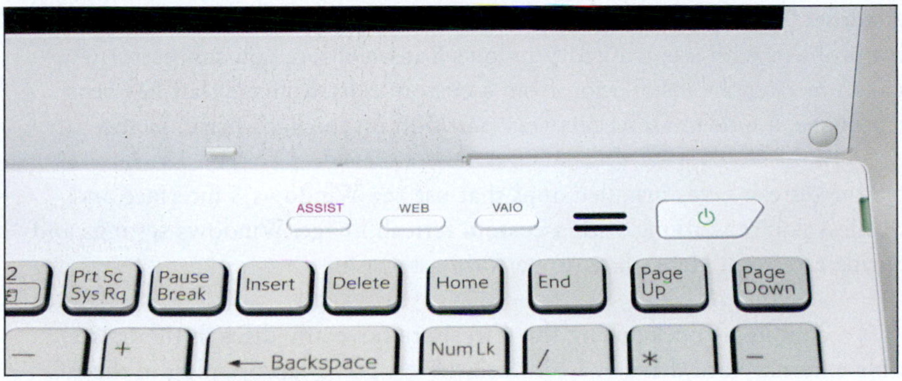

Figure 13-35 For this laptop, press the Assist button during the boot to launch programs on the recovery partition

Recall that an OEM recovery partition can be saved when you create a recovery drive for Windows 8. Unless the recovery partition has been saved, it won't be any help at all if the hard drive is broken or corrupted. In this situation, you're dependent on other recovery media. Older laptops came bundled with the full recovery on CDs. For today's laptops, you might have the option to use a working computer to download the recovery media from the manufacturer's website and use it to create a bootable USB flash drive or DVD. You can then use the media to install Windows to its factory state on a new hard drive installed in the laptop.

> **Notes** When you first become responsible for a laptop, make a Windows 8 recovery drive to a USB flash drive that includes the OEM recovery partition in case you must replace the laptop's hard drive. Know that, if the laptop is more than three years old, the manufacturer might no longer provide the recovery media.

13

Caution Upgrading Windows on a laptop is not a good idea unless you have a good reason to do so. If you do decide to upgrade, upgrade the OS using an OS build purchased from the laptop manufacturer, which should include the OS and device drivers specific to your laptop. If you decide to upgrade the OS using an off-the-shelf version of Windows, be careful to determine that all components in the system are compatible with the upgrade.

Hands-On | Project 13-5 Research Laptop Online Resources

A+ 220-902 4.1

Suppose the hard drive in a laptop has failed and you must replace the hard drive with a new one and install Windows on the new drive. What online resources can help you? Do the following to find a service manual and recovery files for a laptop that you have access to, such as one you or a friend owns:

1. What are the brand, model, and serial number of the laptop?
2. What is the website of the laptop manufacturer? Print a webpage on that site that shows you what recovery files are available for download to install Windows on a new hard drive for this laptop.
3. If the website provides a service manual, download the manual and print the pages that show how to replace the hard drive.
4. Based on what you have learned about online support for this laptop, what backups or recovery media do you think need to be created now before a hard drive crash occurs.

REFRESH A WINDOWS 8 COMPUTER

In the chapter, "Maintaining Windows," you learned to create a Windows 8 custom refresh image of the Windows volume. To solve a problem with a corrupted Windows 8 installation, you can perform a Windows 8 refresh. The refresh can recover the installation from a custom refresh image that has been designated as the active recovery image, a hidden OEM recovery partition on the hard drive, or the Windows 8 setup DVD.

When you refresh a computer, the refresh saves installed apps that use the Windows 8 interface and current user settings and data. Unless you're working with a custom refresh image, Windows settings and desktop applications are lost during a refresh. Here's how to perform a refresh:

1. Because the system will restart a couple of times during the refresh, remove any discs in the optical drive and unplug any bootable external hard drive or USB flash drives. For a laptop, plug in the AC adapter so you don't lose battery power during the refresh. If the computer doesn't have a recovery partition and you haven't made a custom refresh image, insert the Windows setup DVD in the optical drive, which the refresh will use to perform a partial in-place upgrade of Windows 8.
2. Do one of the following, depending on the health of the Windows installation:
   - If you can launch Windows, on the charms bar, click **Settings**, click **Change PC settings**, click **Update and recovery**, and click **Recovery**. Click **Get started** under *Refresh your PC without affecting your files* (refer back to Figure 13-19). A warning message appears (see Figure 13-36). Click **Next**. Click **Refresh**.

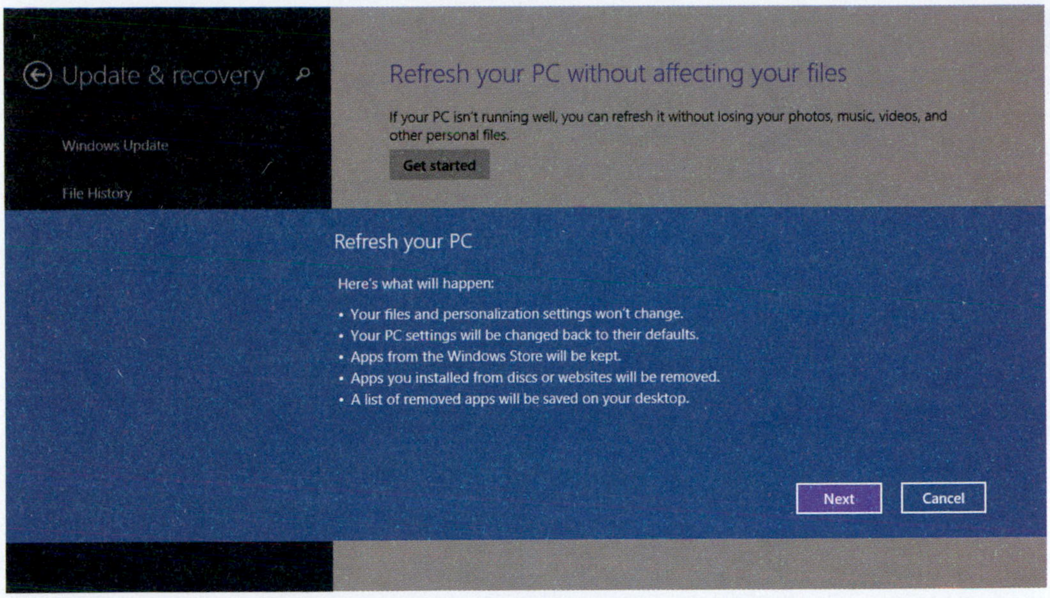

Figure 13-36 Windows lists what to expect from a refresh

- If you cannot launch Windows, boot from the Windows setup DVD or a recovery drive. When booting from the Windows setup DVD, the Windows Setup screen appears, as shown earlier in Figure 13-32. Click **Repair your computer.** (When booting from a recovery drive, the Setup screen doesn't show.) On the next screen, choose your keyboard. The Windows Startup Menu appears (refer back to Figure 13-20). Click **Troubleshoot.** On the Troubleshoot screen (refer back to Figure 13-21), click **Refresh your PC.**

3. Windows verifies there's enough free space on the hard drive to perform the refresh. A lot of space (as much as half the space on the Windows volume) is needed because Windows will store the old Windows installation in a Windows.old folder and will also need space to back up apps and data. If there's not enough space, an error occurs, and you'll need to delete files or folders or move them to a different location to free up enough space and start the refresh again.

4. Another warning message appears. Click **Refresh** to continue. Next, user settings and data and Windows 8 apps are backed up, and Windows searches for media or an image to use to reinstall Windows. It uses this order for the search:

   a. *It checks for a custom refresh image.* If a custom refresh image was previously made and registered with the system, this image is used to refresh the system. (If desktop applications were included in the image, they are included in the refresh. Any desktop applications that were installed after the refresh image was created are lost and must be manually reinstalled.)

   b. *If no custom refresh image is found, it checks for an OEM recovery partition.* If it finds an OEM recovery partition, the image on the partition is used to refresh the computer to its factory state.

   c. *If no image or recovery partition is found, it requests the Windows setup DVD if it's not already available.* The refresh process will use the Windows setup DVD to perform a partial in-place upgrade of Windows 8.

5. The system restarts and the refresh begins. Progress is reported on screen as a percentage of completion. The Windows volume is formatted, and Windows is reinstalled from an image or from the Windows setup files. User settings, data, and Windows 8 apps are restored from backup, and the system restarts.

6. The names of desktop applications lost during the refresh are stored in a file on the Windows desktop named Removed Apps.html (see Figure 13-37). Open the file to see the list of applications. You'll need to reinstall these applications.

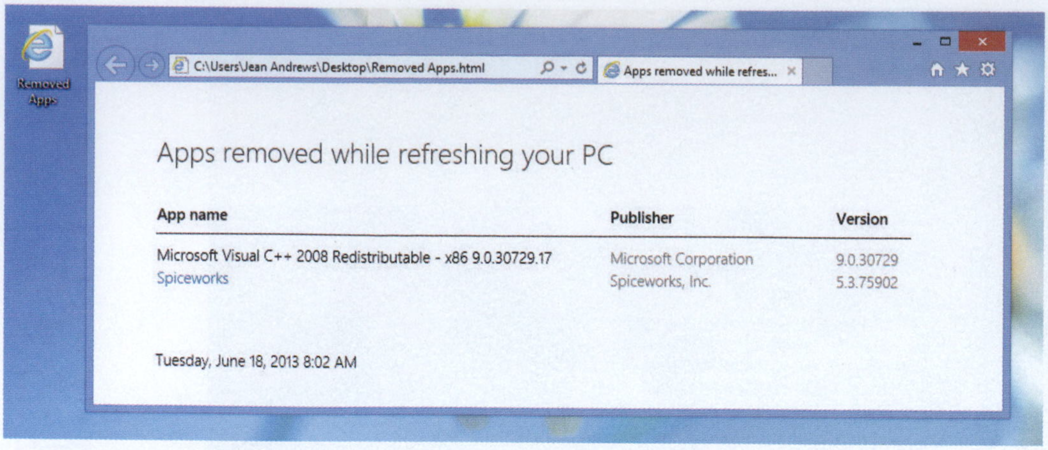

Figure 13-37 View a list of desktop applications lost during the refresh

7. The refresh created a Windows.old folder containing the old Windows installation. After you're sure you don't need anything in it, you can delete the folder to free up the disk space.

RESET A WINDOWS 8 COMPUTER

You might want to reset a computer when you're about to give it away or recycle it or totally want to start over. The Windows volume is formatted and Windows is reinstalled. If an OEM recovery partition is present, the system is reset to its factory state. If there's no recovery partition, the process requests the Windows setup DVD, which it uses to reinstall Windows. All user data and settings and installed apps are lost. You can use the recovery methods provided by the manufacturer (for example, press F12 or F10 at startup) or you can use Windows 8 to reset the system.

Here are the Windows 8 steps to reset a computer:

1. If a recovery partition is present, it will be used for the reset. If there's no recovery partition, insert the Windows setup DVD in the optical drive, which the reset process uses to perform a clean install of Windows.
2. Do one of the following:
   - If you can launch Windows, go to the **Update and recovery** screen and click **Get started** under *Remove everything and reinstall Windows* (refer back to Figure 13-19). A warning message appears. Click **Next.**
   - If you cannot launch Windows, boot from the Windows setup DVD or a recovery drive and make your way to the Troubleshoot screen shown earlier in Figure 13-21. Click **Reset your PC.**
3. If the system contains more than one volume or hard drive, Windows asks if you want to format all drives or just the Windows volume. Click a box to make your selection.
4. On the next screen (see Figure 13-38), you're asked to decide between a quick format and a thorough format. A thorough format makes it less likely someone can recover data on the drive. Make your selection by clicking a box.

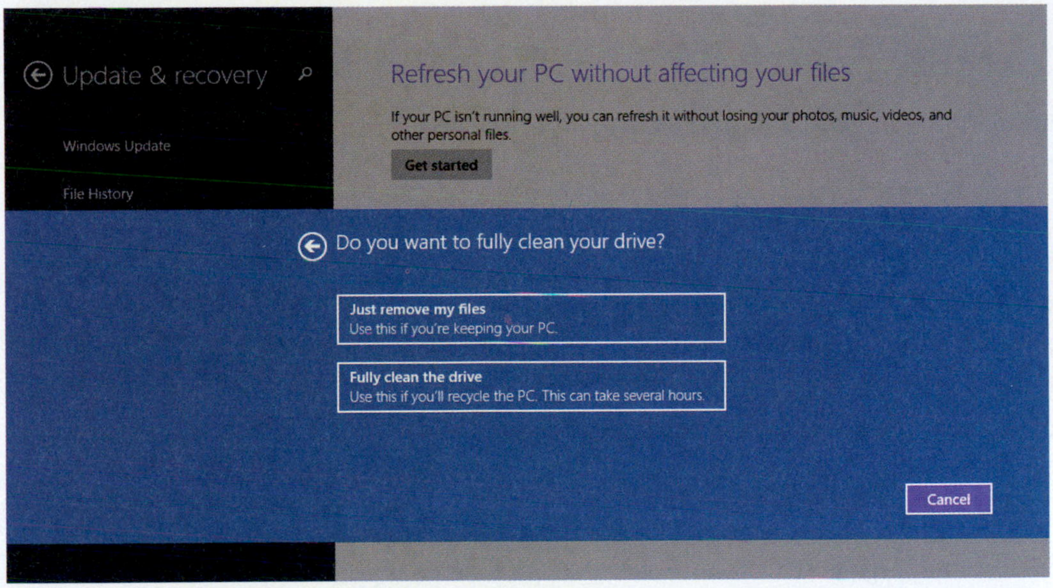

Figure 13-38 Decide the type of format the reset will use

5. On the next screen, another warning appears. Click **Reset** to start the process. The system restarts and resetting begins. After another restart, you can step through the process of preparing Windows for first use.

WINDOWS 7 SYSTEM IMAGE

A+ 220-902 4.1

Recall from the chapter, "Maintaining Windows," a Windows 7 system image is a backup of the entire Windows volume and Windows 8 allows you to create a system image for backward compatibility with Windows 7. For Windows 8, always use a custom refresh image over a system image because it's more flexible and easier to use than a system image.

In Windows 7, to recover the system using a system image, launch Windows 7 from the Windows setup DVD or a recovery drive. When booting from a Windows setup DVD, on the Install Windows screen (refer back to Figure 13-24), click **Repair your computer.** Windows RE launches. On the following screens, select your language and enter an administrator user account and password.

The System Recovery Options box appears, listing a menu of Windows RE recovery tools (refer back to Figure 13-23). Click **System Image Recovery** and follow directions on screen to point to the location of the system image. Everything on the Windows volume is erased and replaced with the system image.

INSTALL WINDOWS OVER THE NETWORK

Recall from the chapter "Installing Windows" that in an enterprise environment you can install Windows from a deployment image on the network. You must boot the computer to the network where it finds and loads Windows PE on the deployment server. For a legacy BIOS system, go into BIOS setup and set the first boot device to be Ethernet. For a UEFI system, look for an advanced setup screen in UEFI setup to enable PXE Support. The computer then boots to the Preboot eXecution Environment (PXE) and PXE then searches for a server on the network to provide Windows PE and the deployment image.

A+ Exam Tip The A+ 220-902 exam expects you to know how to use a preinstallation environment and a recovery image to help resolve a Windows startup problem.

Hands-On | Project 13-6 Practice Using System Recovery Options

A+
220-902
4.1

Using Windows 8 or 7, launch Windows RE and do the following:

1. Execute the startup repair process. What were the results?
2. Launch System Restore. What is the most recent restore point? (Do not apply the restore point.)
3. Using the command prompt window, open the Registry Editor. What command did you use? Close the editor.
4. Using the command prompt window, copy a file from your Documents folder to a flash drive. Were you able to copy the file successfully? If not, what error message(s) did you receive?

TROUBLESHOOTING WINDOWS STARTUP

A+
220-902
4.1

And now the fun begins! With your understanding of the boot process and Windows tools for troubleshooting startup in hand, let's work through a bunch of errors and problems that can affect Windows startup and see what can be done about them. When troubleshooting a startup problem, follow procedures to interview the user, back up important data or verify you have current backups, research and identify any error messages, and determine what has just changed that might be the source of the problem.

When you know the source of the problem, decide which tool will be the least invasive to use, yet still will fix the problem. If that doesn't work, move on to the next tool. Remember that tools are described earlier in the chapter from least to most invasive. Here's a recap of some of the more important tools discussed earlier:

- Multiple restarts of Windows 8
- Startup repair
- Boot logging to help you better understand the problem
- From a command prompt, chkdsk and SFC
- Memory Diagnostics
- Safe Mode and then a clean boot
- Use anti-malware software to scan for malware
- System Restore
- System Configuration and Task Manager to reduce startup programs and services
- Refresh the computer
- Reset the computer

IMPORTANT DATA ON THE HARD DRIVE

A+
220-902
4.1

Troubleshooting a computer problem should always start with the most important question: Is there important data on the hard drive not backed up? Even if data is lost or corrupted, you might be able to recover it using Windows tools, third-party file recovery software, or commercial data recovery services. One good product is GetDataBack by Runtime Software (*www.runtime.org*), which can recover data and program files even when Windows cannot recognize the drive.

For less than $30, you can purchase a SATA-to-USB converter kit (see Figure 13-39) that includes a data cable and power adapter. You can use one of these kits to temporarily connect a desktop or laptop hard drive to a USB port on a working computer. Set the drive beside your computer and plug one end of the data cable into the drive and the other into the USB port. The AC adapter supplies power to the drive. While power is getting to the drive, be careful to not touch the circuit board on the drive.

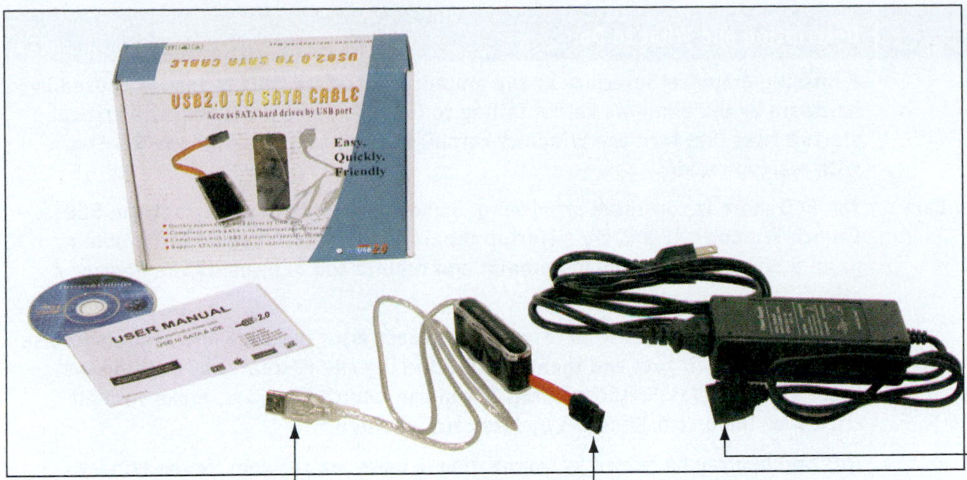

Figure 13-39 Use a SATA-to-USB converter to recover data from a drive using a SATA connector

Using File Explorer or Windows Explorer, you can browse the drive and copy data to other media. After you have saved the data, you can use diagnostic software from the hard drive manufacturer to examine the drive and possibly repair it or return the drive to its own computer and start troubleshooting there.

ERROR MESSAGES AND PROBLEMS

A+
220-902
4.1

Table 13-5 summarizes some symptoms and error messages caused by hardware, device drivers, or Windows that prevent Windows from booting. Hardware errors can present as errors messages on a black screen or a Windows blue screen of death (BSOD) stop error. A stop error can be caused by a corrupted registry, a system file that is missing or damaged, a device driver that is missing or damaged, bad memory, or a corrupted or failing hard drive. Also, sometimes Windows hangs with the pinwheel spinning, continuously restarts, or does an abrupt and improper shutdown.

Symptom or Error Message	Description and What to Do
A disk read error occurred Nonsystem disk or disk error Invalid boot disk Hard drive not found Disk boot failure No boot device found	Startup UEFI/BIOS cannot communicate with the hard drive. Check UEFI/BIOS setup for the boot sequence and try to boot from another device. This is likely a hardware problem. For Windows 8, try going into UEFI/BIOS setup and disabling any quick boot features. This causes UEFI/BIOS to do a more thorough job of POST and reports more information on the screen as it performs POST. The drive might be failing. To recover data from the drive, move it to another computer and install it as a second hard drive.
Invalid partition table Invalid drive specification Error loading operating system Missing operating system Drive not recognized	MBR sector is damaged or the active partition is corrupt or missing. Use the repair commands from the Windows RE command prompt window.
Operating system not found Missing operating system Missing bootmgr	Windows system files are missing or corrupted. Boot to Windows RE and use tools there. First try startup repair. Use chkdsk to fix hard drive errors. Use System File Checker (SFC) to restore Windows system files. Try System Restore.
Automatically boots into Safe Mode	This action can occur when Windows recognizes a problem with the registry or other startup files. Attempt to use System Restore to apply a restore point. For Windows 7, use the Last Known Good Configuration on the Advanced Boot Options menu.

Table 13-5 Error messages and what to do about them (continues)

13

Symptom or Error Message	Description and What to Do
No graphics appear when Windows is started	A missing graphical interface or the graphical interface fails to load is caused by hardware or the Windows kernel failing to load. To solve problems with critical startup files that load the Windows kernel, use the tools in Windows RE. Begin with startup repair.
Missing Boot Configuration Data	The BCD store is corrupted or missing. Sometimes a virus can corrupt the BCD. Launch Windows RE and try a startup repair. If this doesn't solve the problem, go to a Windows RE command prompt and rebuild the BCD, using the bootrec /rebuildBCD command.
Stop error, or BSOD occurs during startup	Use the Microsoft website to research the exact error message and error code. Use the startup repair tool and then examine the log file it creates at C:\Windows\System32\LogFiles\Srt\Srttrail.txt. If you can launch Windows, make sure all critical or important Windows updates are installed.
Improper shutdown	This problem can be caused by overheating, a hardware problem, or the Windows kernel. After a restart, check Event Viewer for clues, apply Windows updates, verify memory with Memory Diagnostics, and use chkdsk to check the hard drive for errors.
Spontaneous shutdowns and restarts	First, use the Startup Settings screen (refer back to Figure 13-26) to disable the automatic restarts so that you can view the error messages on screen and troubleshoot the underlying problem. Research the error messages on screen as you would a BSOD error. Use the startup repair tool and then examine the log file it creates at C:\Windows\System32\LogFiles\Srt\Srttrail.txt.
Device fails to start or is not detected	Address this issue first as a hardware problem. Check the device's cable connections. Try the device in a working computer. Check Device Manager for errors reported. Use Device Manager to uninstall the device and restart Windows. Search the device manufacturer's website for troubleshooting procedures and to download diagnostic software for the device. Restart the system and enable boot logging. Check the Ntbtlog.txt file to see if the correct driver files loaded.
Errors after the user has signed in to Windows	For application errors, use System Configuration (msconfig.exe) and Task Manager to perform a clean boot. If the error goes away, research each non-Microsoft program or service to find the problem. Try to repair the application. If the error persists, uninstall and reinstall the application. For Windows errors, boot into Safe Mode and run System File Checker, System Restore, chkdsk /r, and Memory Diagnostics. Install all critical and important Windows updates. Check the Ntbtlog.txt log file for clues. Compare it with one made during a normal boot with Enable Boot Logging selected.

Table 13-5 Error messages and what to do about them (continued)

★ A+ Exam Tip The A+ 220-902 exam expects you to know how to use System Information (msconfig.exe) to help you resolve a Windows startup problem.

★ A+ Exam Tip The A+ 220-902 exam expects you to know about the Windows XP Ntldr boot loader program, a repair disk, and the Recovery Console. When starting Windows XP, a "missing Ntldr" error message can be resolved by booting the system from a Windows XP repair disk. After booting from the floppy disk, you can launch the Windows XP Recovery Console and use commands in this console to copy the Ntldr program file on the floppy disk to the hard drive.

Next, we give a few more details about several of the errors listed in Table 13-5.

BSOD OR STOP ERRORS

A BSOD, or stop error, happens when processes running in kernel mode encounter a problem and Windows must stop the system. In such situations, a blue screen appears with a cryptic error message such as the one in Figure 13-40. Look on the blue screen for the stop error at the top and the specific number of the error near the bottom of the screen, as labeled in Figure 13-40.

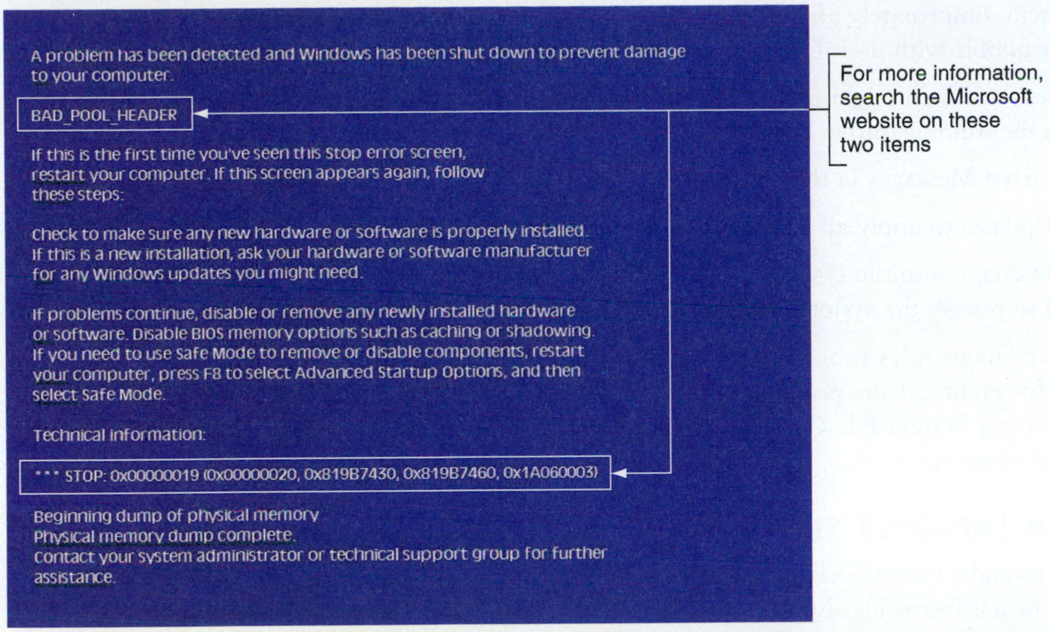

Figure 13-40 A blue screen of death (BSOD) is definitively not a good sign; time to start troubleshooting

Stop errors can occur during or after startup. Here's what to do when you get a stop error:

1. As for the tools useful in solving stop errors, put the web at the top of your list! (But don't forget that some sites are unreliable and others mean you harm.) Search the Microsoft website on the two items labeled in Figure 13-40.
2. If the blue screen names the device driver or service that caused the problem, use File Explorer or Windows Explorer on a working computer to locate the program file. Driver files are stored in the C:\Windows\System32\drivers folder. Right-click the file and select **Properties** from the shortcut menu. The Details tab of the Properties box tells you the purpose of the file (see Figure 13-41). You can then reinstall the device or program that caused the problem.

13

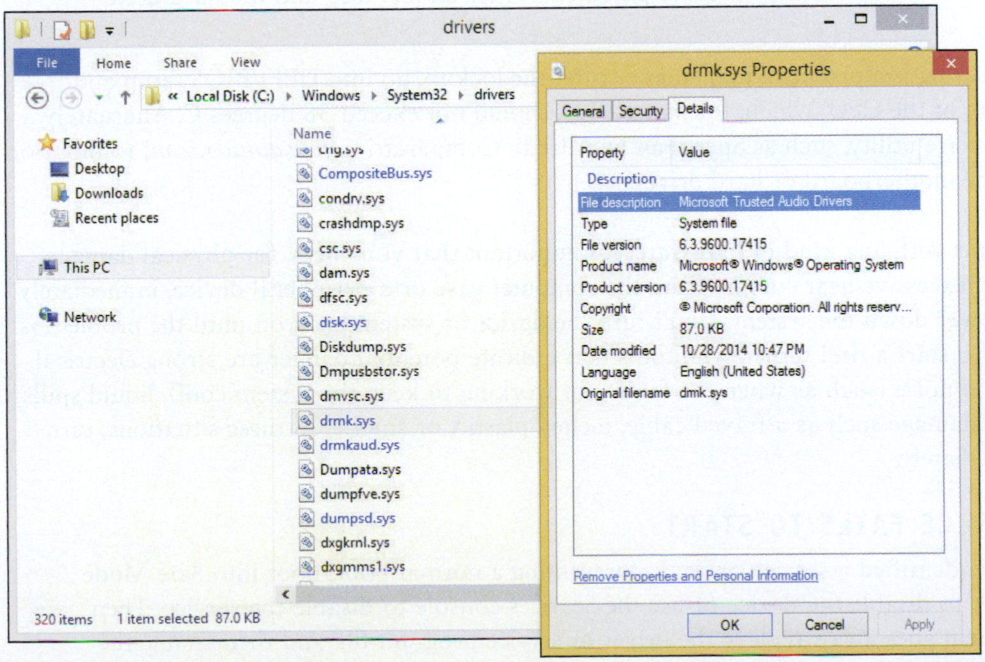

Figure 13-41 Use the Details tab of a driver's Properties box to identify the purpose of the driver

3. Reboot the system. Immediately after a reboot following a stop error, Windows displays an error message box or bubble with useful information. Follow the links in the box.
4. Check Event Viewer, which might provide events it has logged. Recall that critical errors and warnings are recorded in the Administrative Events log.
5. Also check Archived Messages in the Action Center for clues.
6. Use Windows Updates to apply all important and critical updates.
7. Undo any recent changes to the system. If you are not sure which changes to undo, consider using System Restore to restore the system to the point in time before the problem started.
8. Use the Memory Diagnostics tool to check memory and use chkdsk with the /r parameter to check the hard drive for errors. If the problem is still not resolved, you might need to repair Windows system files by using System File Checker, Safe Mode, or other Windows startup repair tools discussed in this chapter.

DEALING WITH IMPROPER SHUTDOWNS

Improper shutdowns and a system lockup that cause a computer to freeze and require that it be restarted are most likely caused by hardware. Hardware that can cause these errors include memory, the motherboard, CPU, video card, or the system overheating. I/O devices such as the keyboard, mouse, or monitor or application errors don't usually cause these types of catastrophic problems.

A+ Exam Tip The 220-902 exam expects you to know how to solve problems when the system shuts down improperly.

When these types of errors occur, try and check these things:

1. Check Event Viewer to see if it has reported a hardware failure.
2. Apply any important or critical Windows updates.
3. Use Memory Diagnostics and chkdsk with the /r parameter to check memory and the hard drive for errors.
4. If you suspect overheating is a problem, immediately after the lockup, go into UEFI/BIOS setup and check the temperature of the CPU, which, for most CPUs, should not exceed 38 degrees C. Alternately, you can install a freeware utility, such as SpeedFan by Alfredo Comparetti (*www.almico.com*) to monitor the temperature of the motherboard or hard drive.

When solving problems with any kind of hardware, it's important that you check for physical damage to the device. If you feel excessive heat coming from the computer case or a peripheral device, immediately unplug the device or power down the system. Don't turn the device or system back on until the problem is solved; you don't want to start a fire! Other symptoms that indicate potential danger are strong electrical odors, unusual noises, no noise (such as when the fan is not working to keep the system cool), liquid spills on a device, and visible damage such as a frayed cable, melted plastic, or smoke. In these situations, turn off the equipment immediately.

A DEVICE OR SERVICE FAILS TO START

After you believe you've identified a service or device preventing a normal boot, boot into Safe Mode and use Device Manager to disable the device or use the Services console to disable the service. Then reboot, and, if the problem goes away, replace the driver or service program file and then enable the driver or service.

If you cannot boot into Safe Mode, open the command prompt window in Windows RE. Then back up the registry and open the Registry Editor using the regedit command. Drill down to the service or device key. The key that loads services and drivers can be found in this location:

HKEY_LOCAL_MACHINE\System\CurrentControlSet\Services

Disable the service or driver by changing the Start value to 0x4. Close the Registry Editor and reboot. If the problem goes away, use the copy command to replace the service or driver program file, and restart the service or driver.

Hands-On | Project 13-7 Rebuild Pagefile.sys

A+
220-902
4.1

If a stop error indicates that Pagefile.sys is corrupted, you can rebuild the file. Search the *support.microsoft.com* website for the steps to rebuild Pagefile.sys and then practice these steps by rebuilding Pagefile.sys. List the steps you took to rebuild the file.

Hands-On | Project 13-8 Use Windows RE to Solve a Startup Problem

A+
220-902
4.1

On a system that uses the MBR partitioning method for the hard drive, use File Explorer or Windows Explorer to rename the bootmgr file in the root directory of the hidden System Reserved partition. Reboot the system. What error message do you see? Now use Windows RE to restore the bootmgr file. List the steps taken to complete the repair.

13

>> CHAPTER SUMMARY

Understanding the Boot Process

- When you first turn on a system, startup UEFI/BIOS on the motherboard takes control to examine hardware components and find an operating system to load.
- UEFI stores information, drivers, and applications used for the startup in NVRAM and the EFI System Partition (ESP).
- Windows startup is managed by the Windows Boot Manager. For a BIOS system, the program is bootmgr. For a UEFI system, the program is bootmgfw.efi. The Windows Boot Loader is winload.exe or winload.efi. The Boot Configuration Data (BCD) store contains Windows startup settings.

Tools for Troubleshooting Windows Startup Problems

- Before a problem occurs, make sure you have good backups of user data and a Windows 8 custom refresh image or a Windows 7 system image. You might also want to create a Windows 8 recovery drive and configure Windows 8 to use F8 at startup, which launches the Advanced Boot Options screen.
- The Windows Recovery Environment (Windows RE) can be started from within Windows, from the Windows setup DVD, or from a recovery drive. For Windows 7, press F8 at startup to launch Windows RE.
- Tools for startup troubleshooting include startup repair, Memory Diagnostics, System Restore, Safe Mode, enabling boot logging, refresh, reset, and applying a Windows 7 system image.
- Commands that might be useful when repairing Windows include bootrec, bcdedit, diskpart, chkdsk, and sfc.

Troubleshooting Windows Startup

- If a hard drive contains valuable data but will not boot, you might be able to recover the data by installing the drive in another system as the second, nonbooting hard drive in the system.
- Use the web to research stop errors on the error title and error number listed on the blue screen.
- Improper shutdowns are most likely hardware related. Event Viewer might record failures. Use Memory Diagnostics and chkdsk to check memory and the hard drive. Consider overheating and monitor the system temperature.
- When a device or service causes the system to hang during a normal boot, boot into Safe Mode and disable the device or service. Then you can replace the drivers or service program file.

>> KEY TERMS

For explanations of key terms, see the Glossary for this text.

bcdedit
blue screen of death (BSOD)
Boot Configuration Data (BCD) store
booting
bootrec
bootsect
chkdsk /r
cold boot
diskpart
EFI System Partition (ESP)
Fast Startup
format
hard boot
Last Known Good Configuration
nonvolatile RAM (NVRAM)
POST (power-on self test)
recovery drive
refresh
reset
soft boot
startup repair
system repair disc
warm boot
Windows Boot Loader
Windows Recovery Environment (Windows RE)

>> REVIEWING THE BASICS

1. What test does startup UEFI/BIOS perform when you first turn on a computer to verify it can communicate with essential hardware devices?
2. Where is the MBR partition table on a hard drive found?
3. Is the bootmgr file stored in the boot partition or the system partition?
4. What is the name of the Boot Manager program in a UEFI system? On which partition is the program stored?
5. What is the name of the Windows boot loader program for a BIOS system? For a UEFI system?
6. What is the name of the Windows kernel program?
7. What is the name of the program that manages Windows logon?
8. Which registry hive is loaded first during Windows startup?
9. Where does Windows store device driver files?
10. Stop errors happen when which type of processes encounter an error?
11. What is the command to use the System File Checker to immediately verify system files?
12. In Windows 7, which key do you press to launch the Advanced Boot Options window during Windows startup?

13. A stop error halts the system while it is booting, and the booting starts over in an endless loop of restarts. How can you solve this problem using the Windows 8 Startup Settings screen?
14. When is the Windows startup process completed?
15. What command in Windows RE can you use to rebuild the BCD file?
16. What command in Windows RE gives you opportunity to manage partitions and volumes installed on the system?
17. Which log in Event Viewer only tracks errors and warnings?
18. If you are having a problem with a driver, which of the following is the least invasive solution: update the driver or use System Restore?
19. What is the name of the log file and its location that is created when you enabled boot logging on the Windows 8 Startup Setting menu or the Windows 7 Advanced Boot Options menu?
20. What information is contained in the C:\Windows\System32\LogFiles\SRT\SRTTrail.txt file?

>> THINKING CRITICALLY

1. When the Windows registry is corrupted and you cannot boot from the hard drive, what tool or method is the best option to fix the problem?
   a. Boot into Safe Mode and use System Restore to repair the registry.
   b. Use the Last Known Good Configuration on the Advanced Boot Options menu.
   c. Use commands from the Windows Recovery Environment to recover the registry from backup.
   d. Refresh Windows using a custom refresh image.
2. Your Windows system boots to a blue screen stop error and no Start screen or desktop. What do you do first?
   a. Reinstall Windows.
   b. Use the web to research the stop error messages and numbers.
   c. Attempt to boot into Windows RE using the Windows setup DVD or a recovery drive.
   d. Verify the system is getting power.
3. You have important data on your hard drive that is not backed up and your Windows installation is so corrupted you know that you must refresh the entire installation. What do you do first?
   a. Use System Restore.
   b. Make every attempt to recover the data.
   c. Perform an in-place upgrade of Windows.
   d. Reformat the hard drive and reinstall Windows.
4. Your computer displays the error message "A disk read error occurred." You try to boot from the Windows setup DVD and you get the same error. What is most likely the problem?
   a. The Windows setup DVD is scratched or damaged in some way.
   b. The hard drive is so damaged the system cannot read from the DVD.
   c. Both the optical drive and the hard drive have failed.
   d. Boot device order is set to boot from the hard drive before the optical drive.

5. When a driver is giving problems in Windows 8, which tool offers the least intrusive solution?
   a. Device Manager
   b. Windows 8 reset
   c. System Restore
   d. Windows 8 refresh
6. An error message is displayed during Windows startup about a service that has failed to start and then the system locks up. You try to boot into Safe Mode, but get the same error message. What do you try next?
   a. Use the command prompt to edit the registry.
   b. Boot to Windows RE and enable boot logging.
   c. Perform an in-place upgrade of Windows 7.
   d. Boot to Windows RE and perform a startup repair.

>> REAL PROBLEMS, REAL SOLUTIONS

REAL PROBLEM 13-1 Summarizing Windows Troubleshooting Tools

In the chapter "Supporting Customers and Troubleshooting Windows," you started building a reference table of tools available in Windows for troubleshooting. In this project, you will expand your table to include new tools covered in this chapter.

1. Return to your tools reference table from the chapter "Supporting Customers and Troubleshooting Windows." Under the *Tool* heading, add to your list all of the Windows tools covered in this chapter, such as Safe Mode and startup repair.
2. Complete the remainder of the table with the steps needed to access each tool and a brief, one- or two-sentence description of each. Be sure to include the program name of the utility if it can be launched from the command prompt. Also be sure to note whether a tool is available only for certain releases of Windows, such as "New with Windows 8."

REAL PROBLEM 13-2 Sabotaging a Windows System

In a lab environment, follow these steps to find out if you can corrupt a Windows system so that it will not boot, and then repair the system. (This problem can be done using a Windows installation in a virtual machine.) Don't forget about the takeown and icacls commands discussed in this chapter.

1. Rename or move one of the program files listed in Table 13-1. Which program file did you select? In what folder did you find it?
2. Restart your system. Did an error occur? Check in Explorer. Is the file restored? What Windows feature repaired the problem?
3. Try other methods of sabotaging the Windows system, but carefully record exactly what you did to sabotage the boot. Can you make the boot fail?
4. Now recover the Windows system. List the steps you took to get the system back to good working order.

REAL PROBLEM 13-3 Creating a Stop Error

This project is more difficult than it might first appear. Using a VM with Windows 8 installed, create a BSOD or stop error. Take a screen shot of the BSOD. List the steps you took to make Windows 8 crash.

REAL PROBLEM 13-4 Recovering Data from a Hard Drive

To practice recovering data from a hard drive that won't boot, create a folder on a VM with Windows 8 installed. Put data files in the folder. What is the name of your folder? Move the hard drive to another working VM and install it as a second hard drive in the system. Copy the data folder to the primary hard drive in this second VM. Now return the hard drive to the original VM and verify the VM starts with no errors. List the steps you used in this project.

CHAPTER 14 Connecting To and Setting Up a Network

After completing this chapter, you will be able to:

- Explain the TCP/IP protocols and standards Windows uses for networking
- Connect a computer to a wired or wireless network
- Configure and secure a multifunction router on a local network

In this chapter, you learn how Windows uses TCP/IP protocols and standards to create and manage network connections, including how computers are identified and addressed on a network. You also learn to connect a computer to a network and how to set up and secure a small wired or wireless network.

This chapter prepares you to assume total responsibility for supporting both wired and wireless networks in a small-office/home-office (SOHO) environment. In the chapter, "Supporting Network Hardware," you learn more about the hardware used in networking, including network devices, connectors, cabling, networking tools, and the types of networks used for Internet connections. So let's get started by looking at how TCP/IP works in the world of Windows networking.

★ A+ Exam Tip Much of the content in this chapter applies to both the A+ 220-901 exam and the A+ 220-902 exam.

UNDERSTANDING TCP/IP AND WINDOWS NETWORKING

A+
220-901
2.3, 2.4

When two computers communicate using a local network or the Internet, communication happens at three levels (hardware, operating system, and application). The first step in communication is one computer must find the other computer. The second step is both computers must agree on the methods and rules for communication (called protocols). Then one computer takes on the role of making requests from the other computer. A computer making a request from another is called the client and the one answering the request is called the server. Most communication between computers on a network or the Internet uses this client/server model. For example, in Figure 14-1, someone uses a web browser on a client to request a webpage from a web server. To handle this request, the client computer must first find the web server, the protocols for communication are established, and then the request is made and answered. Hardware, the OS, and the applications on both computers are all involved in this process.

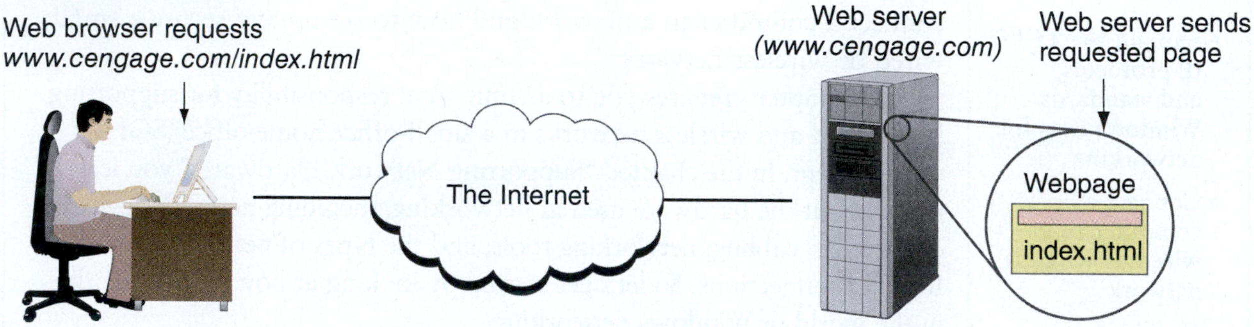

Figure 14-1 A web browser (client software) requests a webpage from a web server (server software); the web server returns the requested data to the client

Let's first look at the layers of communication that involve hardware, the OS, and applications and then see how computers are addressed and found on a network or the Internet. Then we'll see how a client/server request is made by the client and answered by the server.

LAYERS OF NETWORK COMMUNICATION

A+
220-901
2.3, 2.4

When your computer at home is connected to your Internet service provider (ISP) off somewhere in the distance, your computer and a computer on the Internet must be able to communicate. When two devices communicate, they must use the same protocols so that the communication makes sense. For almost all networks today, including the Internet, the group or suite of protocols used is called TCP/IP (Transmission Control Protocol/Internet Protocol).

Communication between two computers happens in layers. In Figure 14-2, you can see how communication starts with an application (browser) passing a request to the OS, which passes the request to the network card and then on to the network. When the request reaches the network card on the server, the network card passes it on to the OS and then the OS passes it on to the application (the web server).

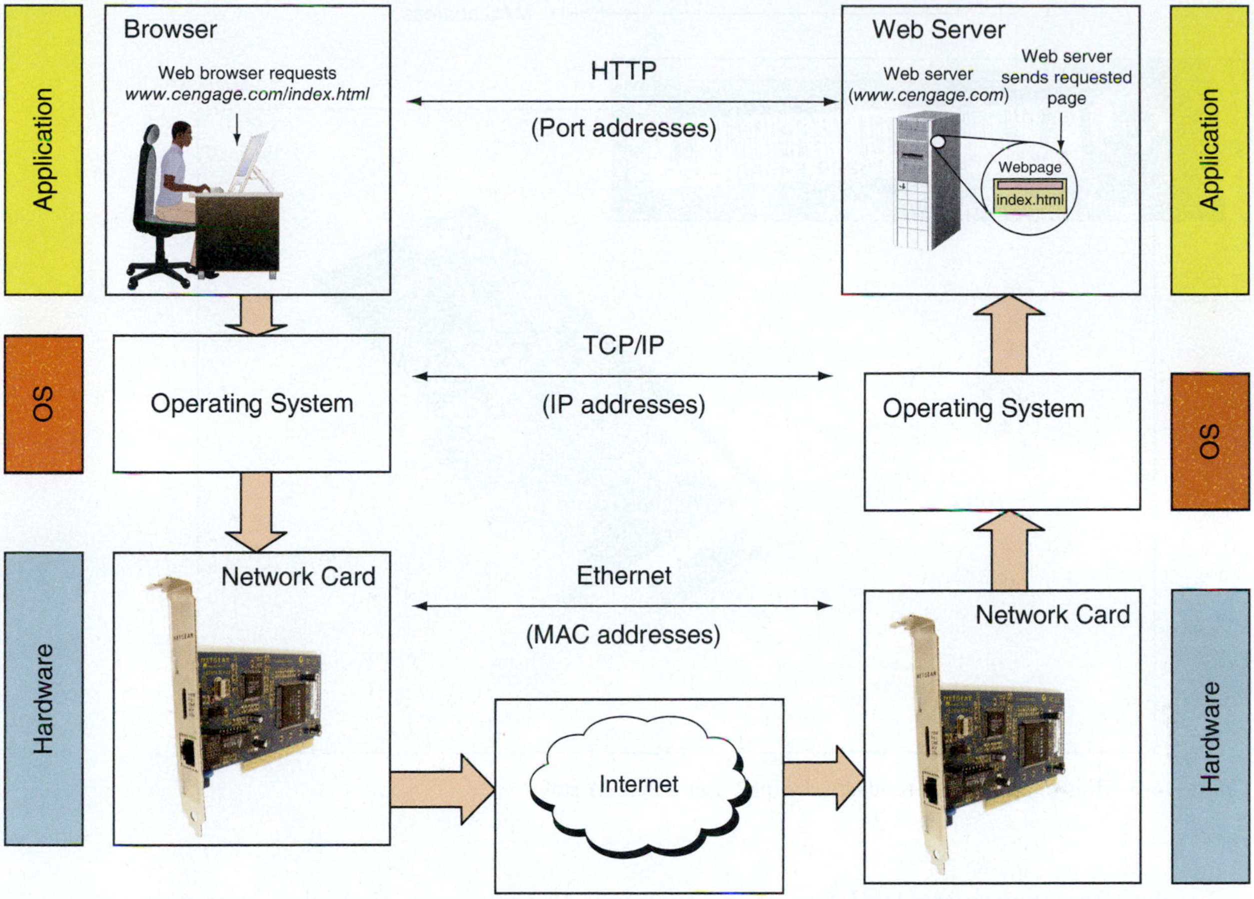

Figure 14-2 Network communication happens in layers

Listed next is a description of each level of communication:

- ***Level 1: Hardware level.*** At the root level of communication is hardware. The hardware or physical connection might be wireless or might use network cables, phone lines (for DSL or dial-up), or TV cable lines (for a cable modem). For local wired or wireless networks, a network adapter (also called a network card, a network interface card, or a NIC) inside your computer is part of this physical network. Every network adapter (including a network card, network port on a motherboard, onboard wireless, or wireless NIC) has a 48-bit (6-byte) number hard-coded on the card by its manufacturer that is unique for that device (see Figure 14-3). The number is written in hexadecimal, and is called the MAC (Media Access Control) address, hardware address, physical address, adapter address, or Ethernet address. Part of the MAC address identifies the manufacturer that is responsible for making sure that no two network adapters have the same MAC address. MAC addresses are used to locate a computer on a local area network (LAN). A local area network (LAN) is a network bound by routers or other gateway devices. A router is a device that manages traffic between two or more networks and can help find the best path for traffic to get from one network to another. A gateway is any device or computer that network traffic can use to leave one network and go to a different network.

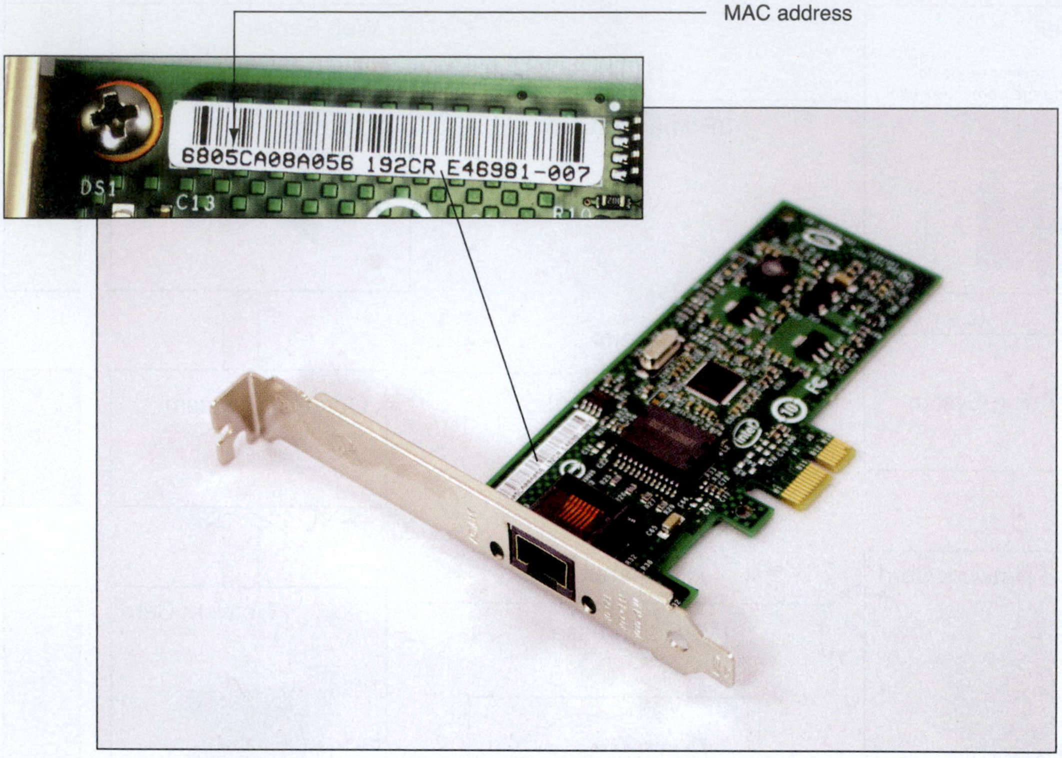

Figure 14-3 This Gigabit Ethernet adapter by Intel uses a PCIe x1 slot

- *Level 2: Operating system level.* Operating systems use IP addresses to find other computers on a network. An IP address is a 32-bit or 128-bit string that is assigned to a network connection when the connection is first made. Whereas a MAC address is only used to find a computer on a local network, an IP address can be used to find a computer anywhere on the Internet (see Figure 14-4) or on an intranet. An intranet is any private network that uses TCP/IP protocols. A large enterprise might support an intranet that is made up of several local networks. A local network can further be divided into smaller networks and each of these smaller networks is called a subnetwork or subnet. IP addresses are used to find computers on subnets, an intranet, or the Internet.

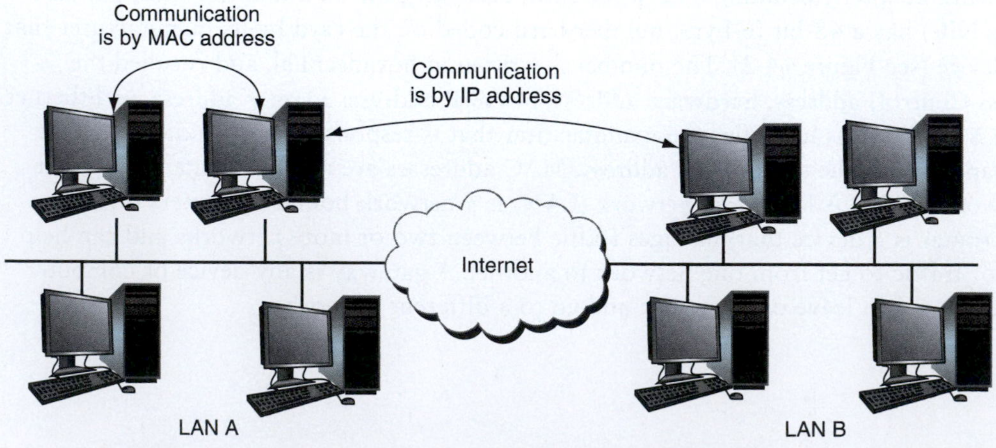

Figure 14-4 Computers on the same LAN use MAC addresses to communicate, but computers on different LANs use IP addresses to communicate over the Internet

- *Level 3: Application level.* Most applications used on the Internet or a local network are client/server applications. Client applications, such as Internet Explorer, Google Chrome, or Outlook, communicate with server applications such as a web server or email server. Each client and server application installed on a computer listens at a predetermined address that uniquely identifies the application on the computer. This address is a number and is called a port number, port, or port address. For example, you can address a web server by entering into a browser address box an IP address followed by a colon and then 80, which is the port number for a web server application. Suppose a computer with an IP address of 136.60.30.5 is running both an email server, which listens at port 25, and a web server application listening at port 80. If a client computer sends a request to 136.60.30.5:25, the email server that is listening at that port responds. On the other hand, if a request is sent to 136.60.30.5:80, the web server listening at port 80 responds (see Figure 14-5).

Figure 14-5 Each server running on a computer is addressed by a unique port number

Figure 14-6 shows how communication moves from a browser to the OS to the hardware on one computer and on to the hardware, OS, and web server on a remote computer. As you connect a computer to a network, keep in mind that the connection must work at all three levels. And when things don't work right, it helps to understand that you must solve the problem at one or more levels. In other words, the problem might be with the physical equipment, with the OS, or with the application.

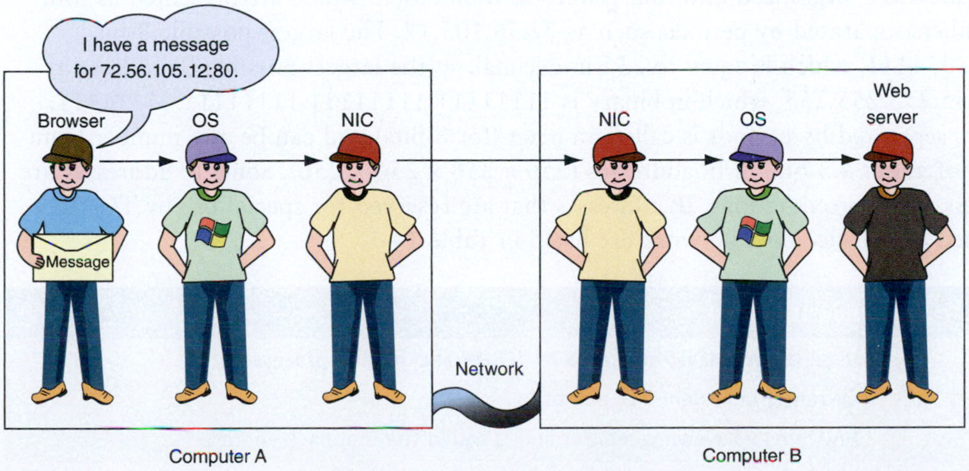

Figure 14-6 How a message gets from a browser to a web server using three levels of communication

Before a message is transmitted on a network, if it is too long, it's broken up into segments. Also, header and trailer information are added, including the IP addresses of the source computer and destination computer, the application's port number, and the protocols for communication the message uses on the network. When this information is added, the message is called a segment, datagram, packet, or frame depending on what information has been added to the header and trailer and which layer of communication added the information.

HOW IP ADDRESSES GET ASSIGNED

A+
220-901
2.3, 2.4

An IP address has 32 bits or 128 bits. When the Internet and TCP/IP were first invented, it seemed that 32 bits were more than enough to satisfy any needs we might have for IP addresses because this standard, called **Internet Protocol version 4 (IPv4)**, created about four billion potential IP addresses. Today we need many more than four billion IP addresses over the world. Partly because of a shortage of 32-bit IP addresses, **Internet Protocol version 6 (IPv6)**, which uses an IP address with 128 bits, was developed. Currently, the Internet uses a mix of 32-bit and 128-bit IP addresses. The Internet Assigned Numbers Authority (IANA at *iana.org*) is responsible for keeping track of assigned IP addresses and has already released all its available 32-bit IP addresses. IP addresses leased from IANA today are all 128-bit addresses.

A MAC address is embedded on a network adapter at the factory, but IP addresses are assigned manually or by software. Recall that an IP address can be a **dynamic IP address** (IP address is assigned by a server each time the computer or device connects to the network) or a **static IP address** (IP address is permanently assigned to the computer or device).

A+ Exam Tip The A+ 220-901 exam expects you to know what a DHCP server is and to understand how to use static and dynamic IP addressing.

For dynamic IP addresses, a **DHCP (Dynamic Host Configuration Protocol)** server gives an IP address to a computer when it first attempts to initiate a connection to the network and requests an IP address. A computer or other device (such as a network printer) that requests an address from a DHCP server is called a **DHCP client**. It is said that the client is leasing an IP address. A DHCP server that serves up IPv6 addresses is often called a **DHCPv6 server**. How to configure a Windows computer to use dynamic or static IP addressing is covered later in the chapter.

Next, let's see how IPv4 addresses are used, and then you'll learn about IPv6 addresses.

HOW IPv4 ADDRESSES ARE USED

A+
220-901
2.3, 2.4

A 32-bit IP address is organized into four groups of 8 bits each, which are presented as four decimal numbers separated by periods, such as 72.56.105.12. The largest possible 8-bit number is 11111111, which is equal to 255 in decimal, so the largest possible IP address in decimal is 255.255.255.255, which in binary is 11111111.11111111.11111111.11111111. Each of the four numbers separated by periods is called an **octet** (for 8 bits) and can be any number from 0 to 255, making a total of about 4.3 billion IP addresses (256 × 256 × 256 × 256). Some IP addresses are reserved, so these numbers are approximations. IP addresses that are reserved for special use by TCP/IP and should not be assigned to a device on a network are listed in Table 14-1.

IP Address	How It Is Used
255.255.255.255	Used for broadcast messages by TCP/IP background processes
0.0.0.0	Currently unassigned IP address
127.0.0.1	Indicates your own computer and is called the **loopback address**

Table 14-1 Reserved IP addresses

The first part of an IP address identifies the network, and the last part identifies the host. When messages are routed over the Internet, the network portion of the IP address is used to locate the right local network. After the message arrives at the local network, the host portion of the IP address is used to identify the one computer on the network that is to receive the message. How does a computer or other network device know what part of an IP address identifies the network and what part identifies the host? It relies on a subnet mask for this information.

SUBNET MASKS

The subnet mask identifies which part of an IP address is the network portion and which part is the host portion. A computer or other device can use its subnet mask to know if an IP address of another computer is on its network or another network (see Figure 14-7).

Figure 14-7 A host (router, in this case) can always determine if an IP address is on its network

A subnet mask has 32 bits and is a string of 1s followed by a string of 0s, for example, 11111111.11111111.11110000.00000000. The 1s in a subnet mask say, "On our network, this part of an IP address is the network part," and the group of 0s says, "On our network, this part of an IP address is the host part." On Windows screens, a subnet mask is displayed in decimal, for example the subnet mask of 11111111.11111111.00000000.00000000 is 255.255.0.0 in decimal.

Suppose the IP address of a computer on Network A is 201.18.20.160 and the subnet mask is 11111111.11111111.00000000.00000000. The subnet mask tells Windows that the first 16 bits or two octets of the IP address is the network ID. Therefore, when Windows is deciding how to communicate with a computer that has an IP address of 201.18.20.208, it knows the computer is on its own network, but a computer with an IP address of 201.19.23.160 is on another network.

Let's look at one more example. Suppose the IP address of a computer is 19.200.60.6 and its subnet mask is 255.255.240.0. Is a computer with the IP address 19.200.51.100 on its network? Here's the logic to find out:

Question	Answer
1. What is my IP address in binary?	19.200.60.6 in binary is: 00010011.11001000.00111100.00000110.
2. What is the other IP address in binary?	19.200.51.100 in binary is: 00010011.11001000.00110011.01100100.
3. Based on my subnet mask, how many bits in my IP address identify my network?	255.255.240.0 in binary is: 11111111.11111111.11110000.00000000. 20 bits identify the network.
4. Do the first 20 bits in my IP address match the first 20 bits in the other IP address?	Compare the 20 red bits in the two IP addresses: 00010011.11001000.00111100.00000110 00010011.11001000.00110011.01100100 Yes, they match.
5. Is the other IP address on my network?	Yes.

Sometimes an IP address and subnet mask are written using a shorthand notation like 15.50.212.59/20, where the /20 means that the first 20 bits in the IP address identify the network. This notation is sometimes called slash notation or **CIDR notation** (pronounced "*cider notation*"), named after the CIDR (Classless Interdomain Routing) standards that were written in 1993 about subnetting.

Hands-On Project 14-1 Practice Using Subnet Masks

A+
220-901
2.3, 2.4

To practice your skills using subnet masks, fill in Table 14-2. First, convert decimal values to binary and then record your decisions in the last column.

Local IP Address	Subnet Mask	Other IP Address	On the Same Network? (Yes or No)
15.50.212.59 Binary: ________	255.255.240.0 Binary: ________	15.50.235.80 Binary: ________	
192.168.24.1 Binary: ________	255.255.248.0 Binary: ________	192.168.31.198 Binary: ________	
192.168.0.1 Binary: ________	255.255.255.192 Binary: ________	192.168.0.63 Binary: ________	
192.168.0.10 Binary: ________	255.255.255.128 Binary: ________	192.168.0.120 Binary: ________	

Table 14-2 Practice using subnet masks

That brings us to a fun way of explaining subnet masks. Suppose all the tall sticks shown in Figure 14-8 belong to the same large network that has been subnetted. The short stick represents the subnet mask for all subnets. How many subnets are in the network? Which sticks belong in the same subnet as Stick 5? As Stick 6?

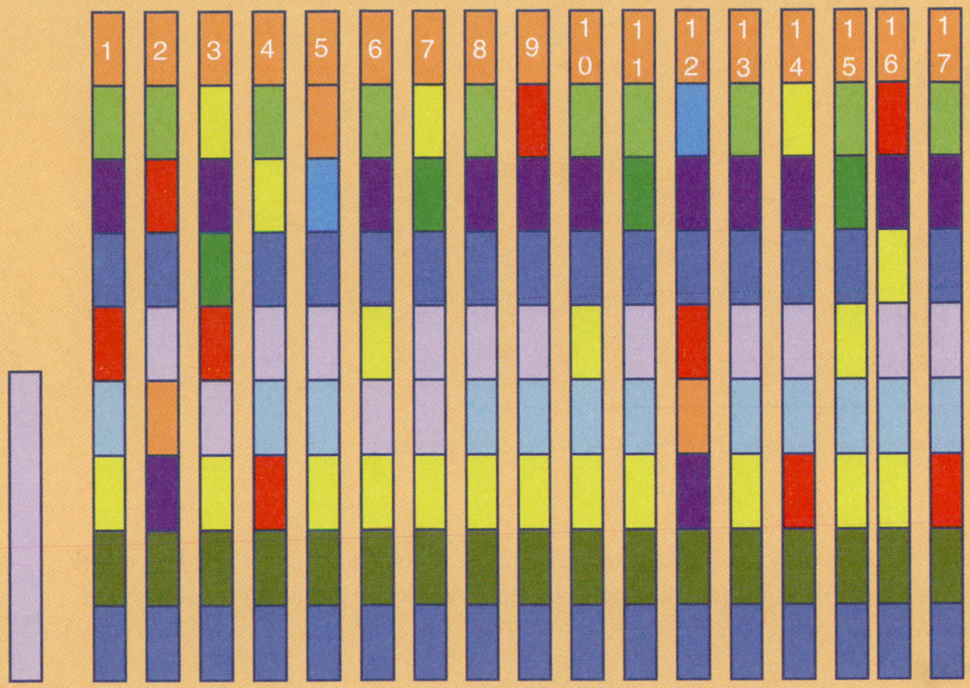

Figure 14-8 The short stick represents a subnet mask for several subnets of sticks

PUBLIC, PRIVATE, AND AUTOMATIC PRIVATE IP ADDRESSES

IP addresses available to the Internet are called public IP addresses. To conserve the number of public IP addresses, some blocks of IP addresses have been designated as private IP addresses that are not allowed on the Internet. Private IP addresses are used within a company's private network, and computers on this network can communicate with one another using these private IP addresses.

IEEE recommends that the following IP addresses be used for private networks:

- 10.0.0.0 through 10.255.255.255
- 172.16.0.0 through 172.31.255.255
- 192.168.0.0 through 192.168.255.255

If a computer first connects to the network that is using dynamic IP addressing and is unable to lease an IP address from the DHCP server, it generates its own Automatic Private IP Address (APIPA) in the address range 169.254.*x*.*y*.

Notes IEEE, a nonprofit organization, is responsible for many Internet standards. Standards are proposed to the networking community in the form of an RFC (Request for Comment). RFC 1918 outlines recommendations for private IP addresses. To view an RFC, visit the website *www.rfc-editor.org*.

NAT (Network Address Translation) is a technique designed to conserve the number of public IP addresses needed by a network. A router or other gateway device stands between a private network and the Internet and substitutes the private IP addresses used by computers on the private network with its own public IP address when these computers need access to the Internet. See Figure 14-9. Besides conserving public IP addresses, another advantage of NAT is security; the gateway hides the entire private network behind this one address.

14

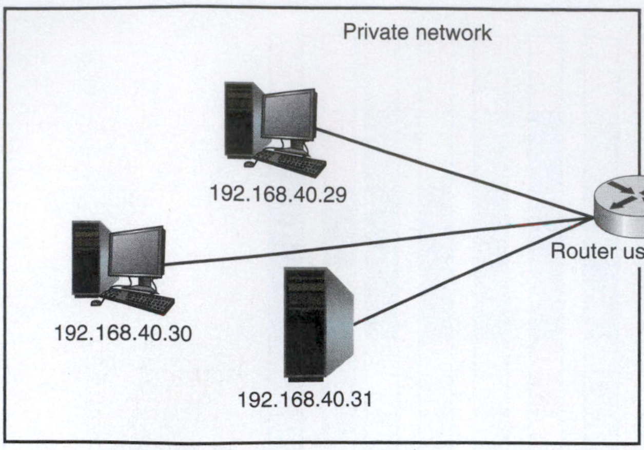

Figure 14-9 NAT allows computers with private IP addresses to access the Internet

In Windows, the ipconfig command can be used to show the IP addresses assigned to all network connections. Notice in Figure 14-10 that the computer has been assigned a private IPv4 address of 192.168.31.198 for the wireless connection.

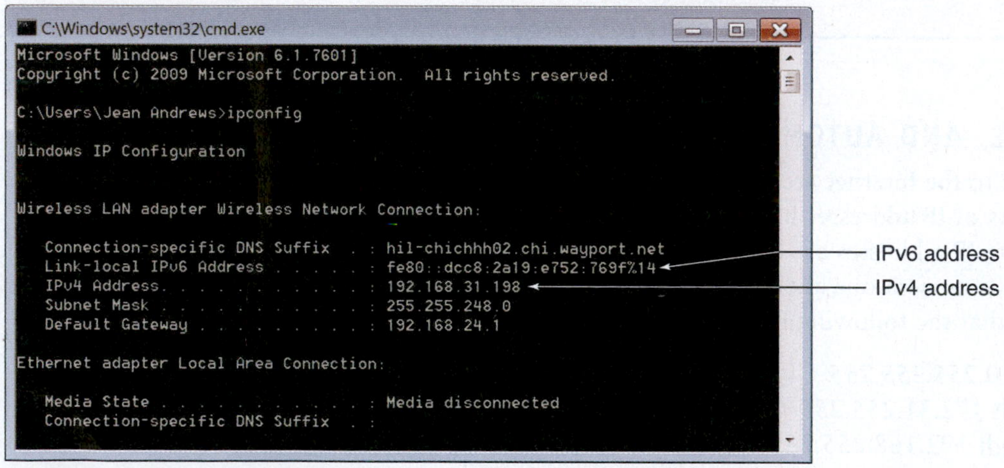

Figure 14-10 The wireless network connection has been assigned a private IPv4 address

HOW IPv6 ADDRESSES ARE USED

A+ 220-901 2.3, 2.4

Using the IPv6 standards, more has changed than just the number of bits in an IP address. To improve routing capabilities and speed of communication, IPv6 changed the way IP addresses are used to find computers on the Internet. Let's begin our discussion of IPv6 by looking at how IPv6 addresses are written and displayed:

- An IPv6 address has 128 bits that are written as eight blocks of hexadecimal numbers separated by colons, like this: 2001:0000:0B80:0000:0000:00D3:9C5A:00CC.
- Each block is 16 bits. For example, the first block in the address above is 2001 in hex, which can be written as 0010 0000 0000 0001 in binary.
- Leading zeros in a four-character hex block can be eliminated. For example, the IP address above can be written as 2001:0000:B80:0000:0000:D3:9C5A:CC.

- If blocks contain all zeros, they can be written as double colons (::). The IP address above can be written two ways:
  - 2001::B80:0000:0000:D3:9C5A:CC
  - 2001:0000:B80::D3:9C5A:CC

To avoid confusion, only one set of double colons is used in an IP address. In this example, the preferred method is the second one: 2001:0000:B80::D3:9C5A:CC because the address is written with the fewest zeros.

The way computers communicate using IPv6 has changed the terminology used to describe TCP/IP communication. Here are a few terms used in the IPv6 standards:

- A link, sometimes called the local link, or local network, is a local area network (LAN) or wide area network (WAN) bounded by routers.
- A node is any device that connects to the network, such as a computer, printer, or router. An interface is a node's attachment to a link. The attachment can be a logical attachment, such as when a virtual machine connects to the network, or a physical attachment, such as when a network adapter connects to the wired network.
- The last 64 bits or 4 blocks of an IP address identify the interface and are called the interface ID or interface identifier. These 64 bits uniquely identify an interface on the local network.
- Neighbors are nodes on the same local network.

So far, very few networks solely use IPv6. Most networks, including the Internet, rely on IPv4 protocols. On IPv4 networks, tunnels are used to allow IPv6 messages to travel on the network. A tunnel works by encapsulating an IPv6 message inside an IPv4 message. Two common tunneling protocols are ISATAP (pronounced "eye-sa-tap" and stands for Intra-Site Automatic Tunnel Addressing Protocol) and Teredo (pronounced "ter-EE-do"), which is named after the Teredo worm that bores holes in wood. Teredo IPv6 addresses begin with 2001.

IPv6 supports these three types of IP addresses:

- A unicast address is used to send messages to a single node on a network. Three types of unicast addresses are link-local addresses, unique local addresses, and global addresses.
- A multicast address is used to deliver messages to all nodes in a targeted, multicast group, such as when video is streaming from a server to multiple nodes on a network.
- An anycast address is used by routers and can identify multiple destinations and a message is delivered only to the closest destination.

Recall that with IPv4 broadcasting, messages are sent to every node on a local network. However, IPv6 doesn't use broadcasting, which reduces network traffic. The concepts of broadcasting, multicasting, anycasting, and unicasting are illustrated in Figure 14-11.

Table 14-3 lists the currently used address prefixes for these types of IP addresses. In the future, we can expect more prefixes to be assigned as they are needed.

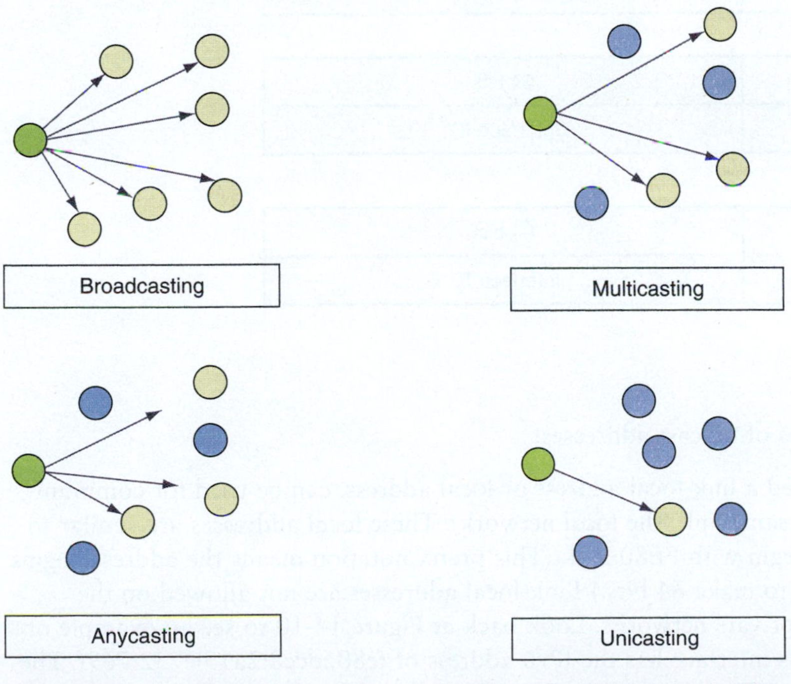

Figure 14-11 Concepts of broadcasting, multicasting, anycasting, and unicasting

14

IP Address Type	Address Prefix
Link-local address	FE80::/64 (First 64 bits are always 1111 1110 1000 0000...)
Unique local address	FC00::/7 (First 7 bits are always 1111 1100)
Global address	2000::/3 (First 3 bits are always 001)
Multicast	FF00::/8 (First 8 bits are always 1111 1111)
Unassigned address	0::0 (All zeroes)
Loopback address	0::1, also written as ::1 (127 zeroes followed by 1)

Table 14-3 Address prefixes for types of IPv6 addresses

> **★ A+ Exam Tip** The A+ 220-901 exam expects you to know the prefixes listed in Table 14-3 and to know the IPv6 loopback address.

Three types of unicast addresses are link-local, unique link-local, and global addresses, which are graphically shown in Figure 14-12.

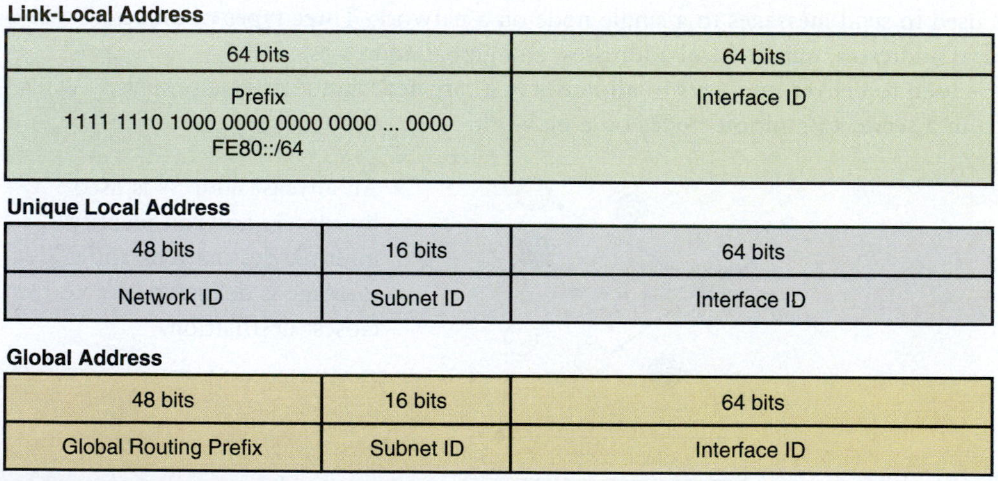

Figure 14-12 Three types of IPv6 addresses

Here is a description of the three types of unicast addresses:

- A link-local unicast address, also called a link-local address or local address, can be used for communicating with neighboring nodes in the same link (the local network). These local addresses are similar to IPv4 private IP addresses and most begin with FE80::/64. (This prefix notation means the address begins with FE80 followed by enough zeros to make 64 bits.) Link-local addresses are not allowed on the Internet or allowed to travel outside private networks. Look back at Figure 14-10 to see an example of a link-local address where the wireless interface has the IPv6 address of fe80::dcc8:2a19:e752:769f. The first 64 bits are fe80:: and the interface ID is dcc8:2a19:e752:769f.

- A unique local address is a private address that can travel across subnets within the private network. These addresses are used by network administrators when subnetting a large network.
- A global unicast address, also called a global address, can be routed on the Internet. These addresses are similar to IPv4 public IP addresses. The first 48 bits of the address is the Global Routing Prefix. When an ISP assigns a global address to a customer, it's these 48 bits that it assigns. An organization that leases one Global Routing Prefix from its ISP can use it to generate many IPv6 global addresses.

SUBNETS

IPv6 uses subnetting but doesn't need a subnet mask because the subnet ID that identifies a subnet is part of the IPv6 address. The subnet ID is the 16 bits following the first 48 bits of the address. When a large IPv6 network is subnetted, a DHCPv6 server assigns a node in a subnet a global address or unique local address that contains the correct subnet ID for the node's subnet.

> **Notes** An excellent resource for learning more about IPv6 and how it works is the e-book, *TCP/IP Fundamentals for Microsoft Windows*. To download the free PDF, search for it at *www.microsoft.com/download*.

VIEW IP ADDRESS SETTINGS

A+ 220-901 2.3, 2.4

In summary, let's use the ipconfig command to take a look at the IPv4 and IPv6 addresses assigned to all network connections on a computer (see Figure 14-13).

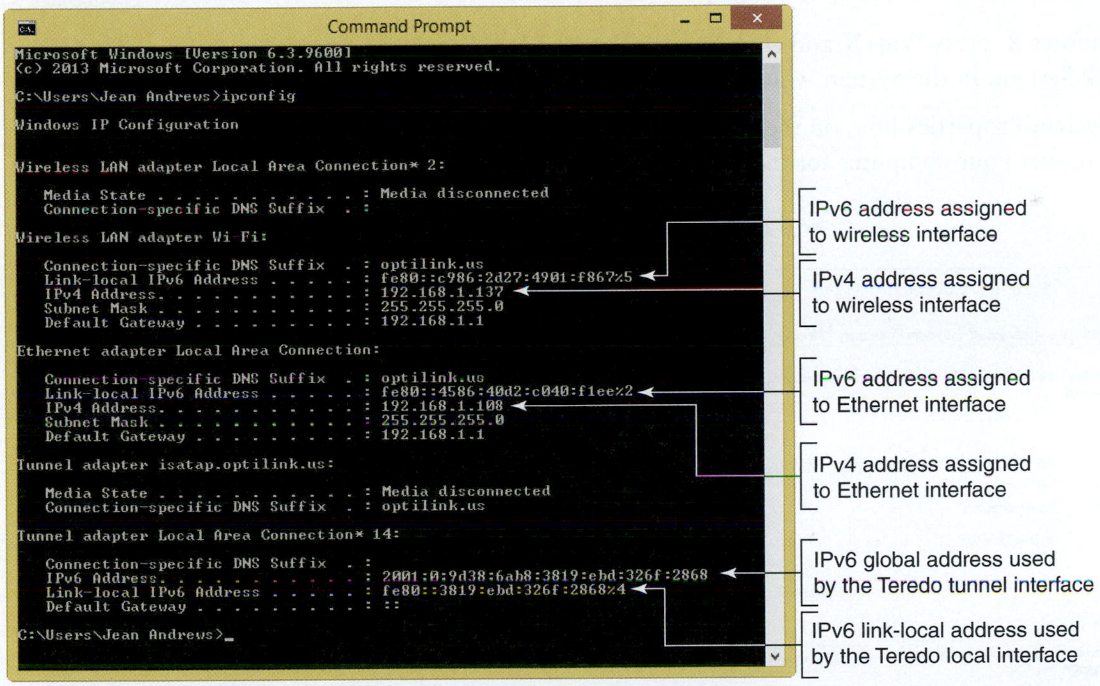

Figure 14-13 The ipconfig command showing IPv4 and IPv6 addresses assigned to this computer

Notice in the figure the four IP addresses that have been assigned to the physical connections:

- Windows has assigned the wireless connection two IP addresses, one IPv4 address and one IPv6 address.
- The Ethernet LAN connection has also been assigned an IPv4 address and an IPv6 address.

The IPv6 addresses are followed by a % sign and a number; for example, %5 follows the first IP address. This number is called the zone ID or scope ID and is used to identify the interface in a list of interfaces for this computer.

14

IPv6 addressing is designed so that a computer can self-configure its own link-local IP address, which is similar to how IPv4 uses an Automatic Private IP Address (APIPA). Here's what happens when a computer using IPv6 first makes a network connection:

1. The computer creates its IPv6 address by using the FE80::/64 prefix and uses its MAC address to generate an interface ID for the last 64 bits.
2. It then performs a duplicate address detection process to make sure its IP address is unique on the network.
3. Next, it asks if a DHCPv6 server is present on the network to provide configuration information. If a server responds with DHCP information, the computer uses whatever information this might be, such as the IP addresses of DNS servers or its own IP address. Because a computer can generate its own link-local IP address, a DHCPv6 server usually serves up only global or unique local addresses.

CHARACTER-BASED NAMES IDENTIFY COMPUTERS AND NETWORKS

A+ 220-901 2.3, 2.4

Remembering an IP address is not always easy, so character-based names are used to substitute for IP addresses. Here are the possibilities:

- A **host name**, also called a **computer name**, is the name of a computer and can be used in place of its IP address. The name can have up to 63 characters, including letters, numbers, and special characters. Examples of computer names are www, ftp, Jean's Computer, TestBox3, and PinkLaptop. Recall you can assign a computer name while installing Windows. In addition, you can change the computer name at any time using the System window:

1. For Windows 8, press **Win+X** and click **System**. For Windows 7, open Control Panel in Classic view and click **System**. In the System window, click **Advanced system settings**.
2. In the System Properties box, on the Computer Name tab (see Figure 14-14), click **Change**. You will need to restart your computer for the change to take effect.

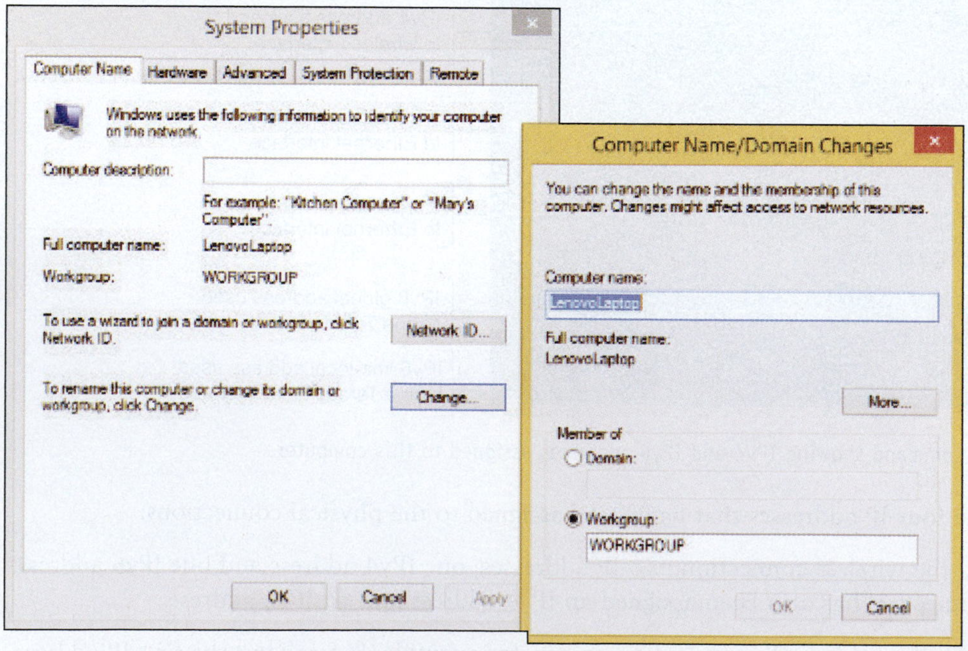

Figure 14-14 View and change the computer name

- Recall that a workgroup is a group of computers on a peer-to-peer network that are sharing resources. The workgroup name assigned to this group is only recognized within the local network.
- A domain name identifies a network. Examples of domain names are the names that appear before the period in *microsoft.com*, *course.com*, and *mycompany.com*. The letters after the period are called the top-level domain and tell you something about the domain. Examples are .com (commercial), .org (nonprofit), .gov (government), and .info (general use).
- A fully qualified domain name (FQDN) identifies a computer and the network to which it belongs. An example of an FQDN is *www.cengage.com*. The host name is *www* (a web server), *cengage* is the domain name, and *com* is the top-level domain name of the Cengage network. Another FQDN is *joesmith.mycompany.com*.

On the Internet, a fully qualified domain name must be associated with an IP address before this computer can be found. This process of associating a character-based name with an IP address is called name resolution. The DNS (Domain Name System or Domain Name Service) protocol is used by a DNS server to find an IP address for a computer when the fully qualified domain name is known. On home or small company networks, the ISP is responsible for providing access to one or more DNS servers as part of the service it provides for Internet access. Larger corporations have their own DNS servers to perform name resolution for the enterprise network. When an individual or organization, which has its own DNS servers, leases a public IP address and domain name and sets up a website, it is responsible for entering the name resolution information into its primary DNS server. This server can present the information to other DNS servers on the web and is called the authoritative name server for the website.

A+ Exam Tip The A+ 220-901 exam expects you to be familiar with client-side DNS and the A+ 220-902 exam expects you to be able to configure DNS on a client computer.

Notes When you enter a fully qualified domain name such as *www.cengage.com* in a browser address bar, that name is translated into an IP address followed by a port number. It's interesting to know that you can skip the translation step and enter the IP address and port number in the address box. See Figure 14-15.

14

Figure 14-15 A website can be accessed by its IP address and port number: http://69.32.208.74:80

When Windows is trying to resolve a computer name to an IP address, it first looks in the DNS cache it holds in memory. If the computer name is not found in the cache, Windows then turns to a DNS server if it has the IP address of the server. When Windows queries the DNS server for a name resolution, it is called the DNS client.

Hands-On | Project 14-2 View and Clear the DNS Cache

A+
220-901
2.3, 2.4

Open a command prompt window and use the **ipconfig /displaydns** command to view the DNS cache on your computer. Then use the **ipconfig /flushdns** command to clear the DNS cache.

TCP/IP PROTOCOL LAYERS

A+
220-901
2.3, 2.4

Recall that a protocol is an agreed-to set of rules for communication between two parties. Operating systems and client/server applications on the Internet all use protocols that are supported by TCP/IP. The left side of Figure 14-16 shows these different layers of protocols and how they relate to one another. As you read this section, this figure can serve as your road map to the different protocols.

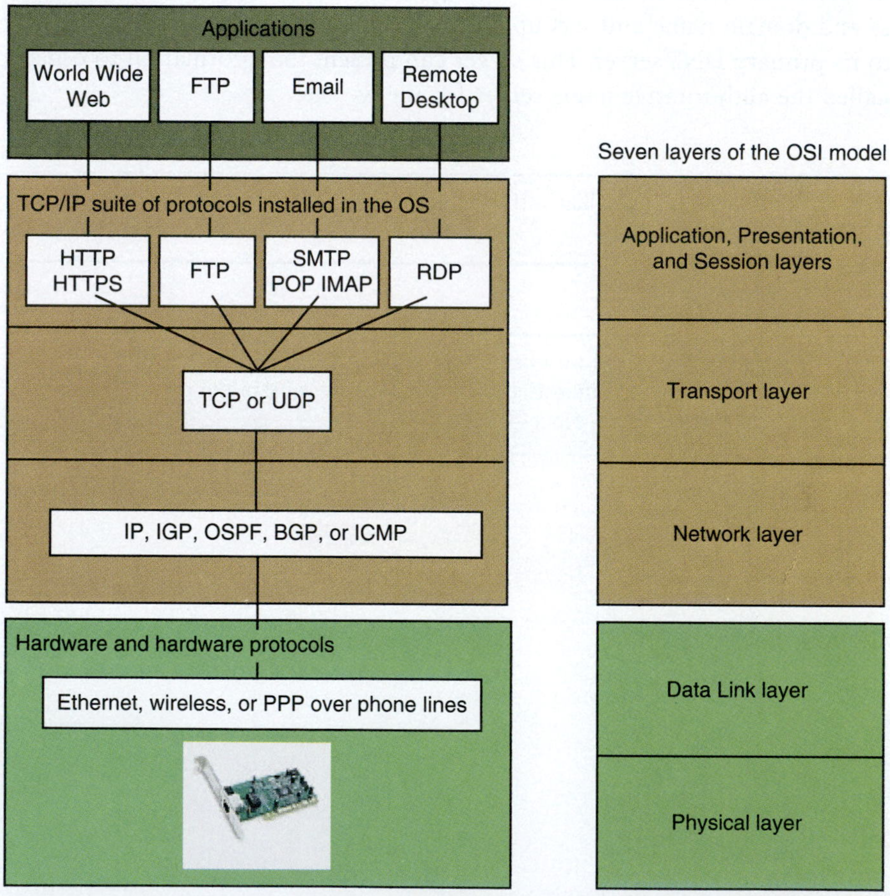

Figure 14-16 How software, protocols, and technology on a TCP/IP network relate to each other

Notes When studying networking theory, the **OSI model** is used, which divides network communication into seven layers. In the OSI model, protocols used by hardware are divided into two layers (Data Link and Physical layers), and TCP/IP protocols used by the OS are divided into five layers (Network, Transport, Session, Presentation, and Application layers). These seven layers are shown on the right side of Figure 14-16.

In the following sections, the more significant applications and operating system protocols are introduced. However, you should know that the TCP/IP protocol suite includes more protocols than just those mentioned in this chapter; only some of them are shown in Figure 14-16.

TCP/IP PROTOCOLS USED BY THE OS

Looking back at Figure 14-16, you can see three layers of protocols between the applications and the hardware protocols. These three layers make up the heart of TCP/IP communication. In the figure, TCP or UDP manages communication with the applications protocols above them as well as the protocols shown underneath TCP and UDP, which control communication on the network.

TCP Guarantees Delivery

Remember that all communication on a network happens by way of messages delivered from one location on the network to another. In TCP/IP, the protocol that guarantees message delivery is TCP (Transmission Control Protocol). TCP makes a connection, sends the data, checks whether the data is received, and resends it if it is not. TCP is, therefore, called a connection-oriented protocol. TCP is used by applications such as web browsers and email. Guaranteed delivery takes longer and is used when it is important to know that the data reached its destination.

For TCP to guarantee delivery, it uses protocols at the IP layer to establish a session between client and server to verify that communication has taken place. When a TCP message reaches its destination, an acknowledgment is sent back to the source (see Figure 14-17). If the source TCP does not receive the acknowledgment, it resends the data or passes an error message back to the higher-level application protocol.

Figure 14-17 TCP guarantees delivery by requesting an acknowledgment

> **A+ Exam Tip** The A+ 220-901 exam expects you to be able to contrast the TCP and UDP protocols.

UDP Provides Fast Transmissions

On the other hand, UDP (User Datagram Protocol) does not guarantee delivery by first connecting and checking whether data is received; thus, UDP is called a connectionless protocol or best-effort protocol. UDP is used for broadcasting, such as streaming video or sound over the web, where guaranteed delivery is not as important as fast transmission. UDP is also used to monitor network traffic.

TCP/IP PROTOCOLS USED BY APPLICATIONS

Some common applications that use the Internet are web browsers, email, chat, FTP, Telnet, Remote Desktop, and Remote Assistance. Here is a bit of information about several of the protocols used by these and other applications:

- *HTTP.* HTTP (Hypertext Transfer Protocol) is the protocol used for the World Wide Web and used by web browsers and web servers to communicate. You can see when a browser is using this protocol by looking for http at the beginning of a URL in the address bar of a browser, such as *http://www.microsoft.com.*
- *HTTPS.* HTTPS (HTTP secure) refers to the HTTP protocol working with a security protocol such as Secure Sockets Layer (SSL) or Transport Layer Security (TLS), which is better than SSL, to create

a secured socket. A socket is a connection between a browser and web server. HTTPS is used by web browsers and servers to secure the socket by encrypting the data before it is sent and then decrypting it before the data is processed. To know a secured protocol is being used, look for https in the URL, as in *https://www.wellsfargo.com*.

- ***SMTP.*** SMTP (Simple Mail Transfer Protocol) is used to send an email message to its destination (see Figure 14-18). The email server that takes care of sending email messages (using the SMTP protocol) is often referred to as the SMTP server.

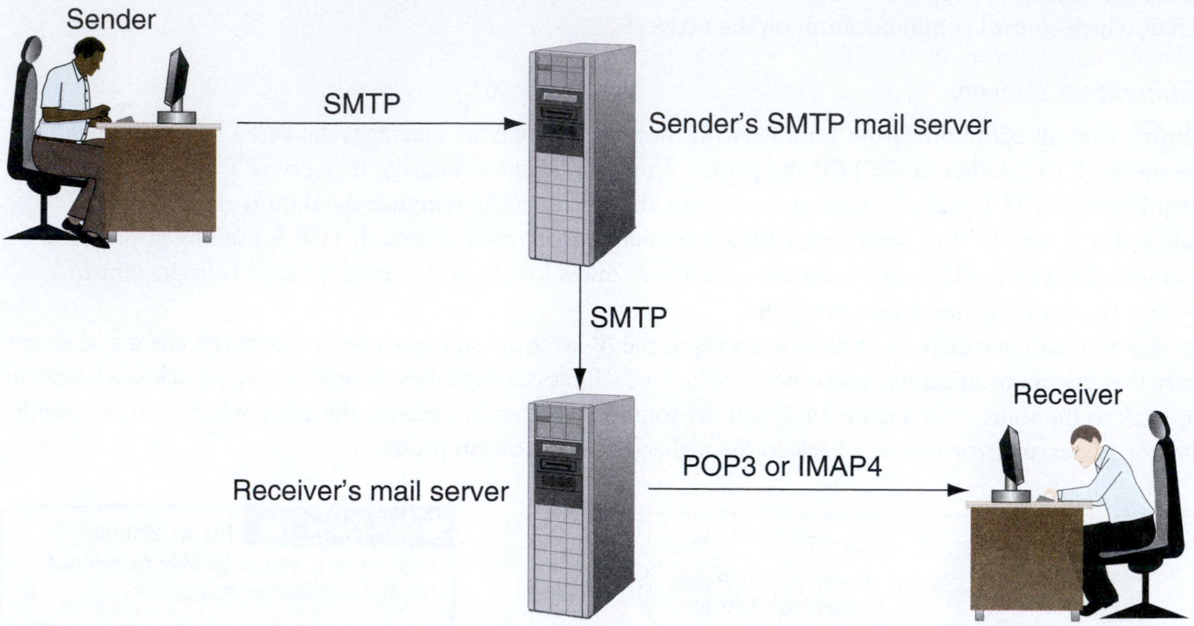

Figure 14-18 The SMTP protocol is used to send email to a recipient's mail server, and the POP3 or IMAP4 protocol is used by the client to receive email

- ***POP and IMAP.*** After an email message arrives at the destination email server, it remains there until the recipient requests delivery. The recipient's email server uses one of two protocols to deliver the message: POP3 (Post Office Protocol, version 3) or IMAP4 (Internet Message Access Protocol, version 4). Using POP3, email is downloaded to the client computer and, unless the default setting is changed, the email is then deleted from the email server. Using IMAP, the client application manages the email stored on the server.
- ***Telnet.*** The Telnet protocol is used by Telnet client/server applications to allow an administrator or other user to control a computer remotely. Telnet is not considered secure because transmissions in Telnet are not encrypted.
- ***LDAP.*** Lightweight Directory Access Protocol (LDAP) is used by various client applications when the application needs to query a database. For example, an email client on a corporate network might query a database that contains the email addresses for all employees or an application might query a database of printers looking for a printer on the corporate network or Internet. Data sent and received using the LDAP protocol is not encrypted; therefore, an encryption layer is sometimes added to LDAP transmissions.
- ***SMB.*** Server Message Block (SMB) is a file access protocol originally developed by IBM and used by Windows to share files and printers on a network. The current release of the SMB protocol is CIFS, also called SMB2.
- ***AFP.*** AFP (Apple Filing Protocol) is a file access protocol used by early editions of the Mac operating system by Apple and is one protocol in the suite of Apple networking protocols called AppleTalk. (TCP/IP has replaced AppleTalk for most networking protocols in the Mac OS.) Current Mac OS releases use SMB2 for file access, and support AFP for backward compatibility with earlier versions of the Mac OS.

- *CIFS.* CIFS (Common Internet File System), also called SMB2, is a file access protocol and the cross-platform version of SMB used between Windows, Linux, Mac OS, and other operating systems.
- *FTP.* FTP (File Transfer Protocol) is used to transfer files between two computers. Web browsers can use the protocol. Also, third-party FTP client software, such as CuteFTP by GlobalSCAPE (*www.cuteftp.com*) and others, offers more features for file transfer than does a browser. By default, FTP transmissions are not secure. Secure FTP (SFTP) uses SSH encryption.
- *SSH.* The Secure Shell (SSH) protocol encrypts transmission so they cannot be intercepted by a hacker. SSH is used in various situations for encryption, such as SFTP. SSH is commonly used in Linux to pass sign-in information to a remote computer and control that computer over a network. Because it's secure, SSH is preferred over Telnet on Linux systems.
- *SNMP.* Simple Network Management Protocol (SNMP) is used to monitor network traffic. It is used by the Microsoft SNMP Agent application that monitors traffic on a network and helps balance that traffic.
- *RDP.* Remote Desktop Protocol (RDP) is used by the Windows Remote Desktop and Remote Assistance utilities to connect to and control a remote computer.

★ A+ Exam Tip The A+ 220-901 exam expects you to know about the following application protocols: FTP, SSH, Telnet, SMTP, DNS, HTTP, POP3, IMAP, HTTPS, RDP, SMB, AFP, DHCP, LDAP, SNMP, and CIFS.

APPLYING | CONCEPTS INTERNET EXPLORER AND FTP

A+ 220-901 2.3, 2.4

To use FTP in Internet Explorer, enter the address of an FTP site in the address box, for example, *ftp.cengage.com*. A logon dialog box appears where you can enter a user name and password (see Figure 14-19). When you click **Log on**, you can see folders on the FTP site and the FTP protocol displays in the address bar, as in *ftp://ftp.cengage.com*. It's easier to use File Explorer or Windows Explorer to transfer files rather than Internet Explorer.

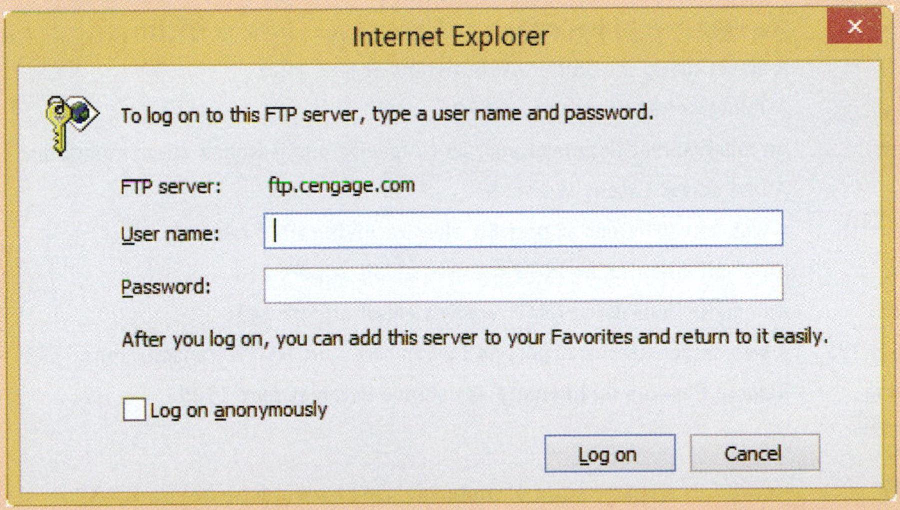

Figure 14-19 Log on to an FTP site

After you have located the FTP site, to use Explorer for file transfers, press **Alt**, which causes the menu bar to appear. In the menu bar, click **View**, **Open FTP site in File Explorer** (see Figure 14-20). Explorer opens, showing files and folders on the FTP site. You can copy and paste files and folders from your computer to the site.

(continues)

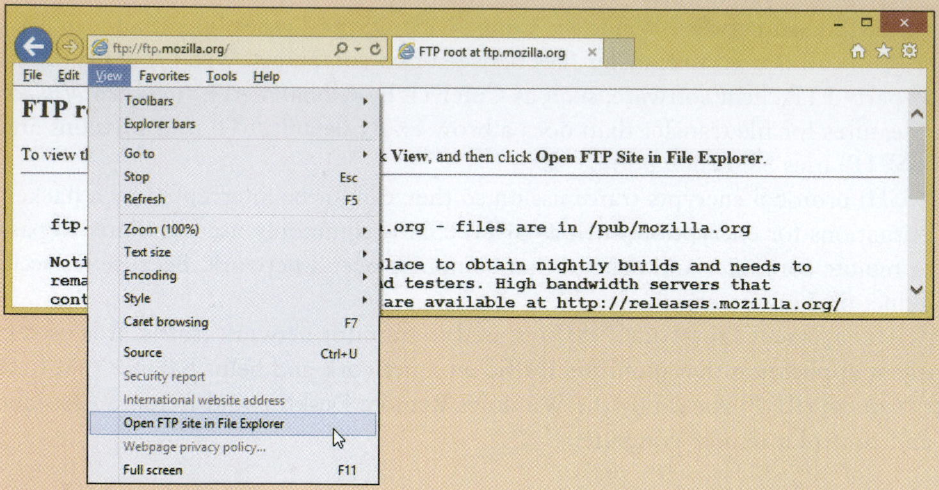

Figure 14-20 Use File Explorer to transfer files using the FTP protocol

Recall that client/server applications use ports to address each other. Table 14-4 lists the port assignments for common applications.

A+ Exam Tip The A+ 220-901 exam expects you to know the common port assignments of the FTP, SSH, Telnet, SMTP, DNS, HTTP, POP3, IMAP, HTTPS, RDP, SMB, and AFP protocols. Before sitting for this exam, be sure to memorize these ports listed in Table 14-4.

Port	Protocol and App	Description
20	FTP client	The FTP client receives data on port 20 from the FTP server.
21	FTP server	The FTP server listens on port 21 for commands from an FTP client.
22	SSH server	A server using the SSH protocol listens at port 22.
23	Telnet server	A Telnet server listens at port 23.
25	SMTP email server	An email server listens at port 25 to receive email from a client computer.
53	DNS server	A DNS server listens at port 53.
80	Web server using HTTP	A web server listens at port 80 when receiving HTTP requests.
110	POP3 email client	An email client using POP3 receives email at port 110.
143	IMAP email client	An email client using IMAP receives email at port 143.
443	Web server using HTTPS	A web server listens at port 443 when receiving HTTPS transmissions.
3389	RDP apps, including Remote Desktop and Remote Assistance	Remote Desktop and Remote Assistance listen at port 3389.
137, 138, and 139	SMB over NetBIOS	**NetBIOS** is a legacy suite of protocols used by Windows before TCP/IP. To support legacy NetBIOS applications on a TCP/IP network, TCP offers **NetBIOS over TCP/IP**. Earlier versions of SMB required NetBIOS over TCP/IP be enabled. Ports used on these networks are: ◢ SMB over UDP uses ports 137 and 138. ◢ SMB over TCP uses ports 137 and 139. Current versions of SMB don't require NetBIOS over TCP.

Table 14-4 Common TCP/IP port assignments for client/server applications (continues)

Port	Protocol and App	Description
445	SMB direct over TCP/IP	Current releases of SMB and SMB2 use port 445 for both TCP and UDP traffic.
427	SLP and AFP	Service Location Protocol (SLP) uses port 427 to find printers and file sharing devices on a network. AFP relies on SLP and port 427 to find resources on a local network.
548	AFP	AFP over TCP/IP is used for file sharing and file services.

Table 14-4 Common TCP/IP port assignments for client/server applications (continued)

Now that you have an understanding of TCP/IP and Windows networking, let's apply that knowledge to making network connections.

CONNECTING A COMPUTER TO A NETWORK

A+
220-902
1.6

Connecting a computer to a network is quick and easy in most situations. In the chapter, "Survey of Windows Features and Support Tools," you learned to connect to a wired and wireless network. We begin with a summary of that information and then you learn to connect to a WWAN (cellular network), how to make a dial-up connection, and how to connect to a VPN.

★ A+ Exam Tip The A+ 220-902 exam expects you to know how to connect to a wired, wireless, cellular, dial-up, or VPN network.

14

CONNECT TO AN ETHERNET WIRED OR WIRELESS WI-FI LOCAL NETWORK

A+
220-902
1.5, 1.6

To connect a computer to a network using an Ethernet wired or Wi-Fi wireless connection, follow these steps:

1. In general, before you connect to any network, the network adapter and its drivers must be installed and Device Manager should report no errors.
2. Do one of the following to connect to the network:
   - For a wired network, plug in the network cable to the Ethernet port. The port is also called an RJ-45 port (RJ stands for registered jack) and looks like a large phone jack. Indicator lights near the network port should light up to indicate connectivity and activity. For Ethernet, Windows should automatically configure the connection.
   - For a wireless network, in Windows 8, you can use the charms bar or the Network icon in the taskbar on the Windows 8/7 desktop. On the desktop, click the Network icon in the taskbar and select a wireless network. Click **Connect**. If the network is secured, you must enter the security key to the wireless network to connect.
3. Open your browser and make sure you can access the web. For wireless connections, some hotspots provide a home page where you must enter a code or agree to the terms of use before you can use the network. On a private network, open File Explorer or Windows Explorer and drill down into the Network group to verify network resources are available (see Figure 14-21).

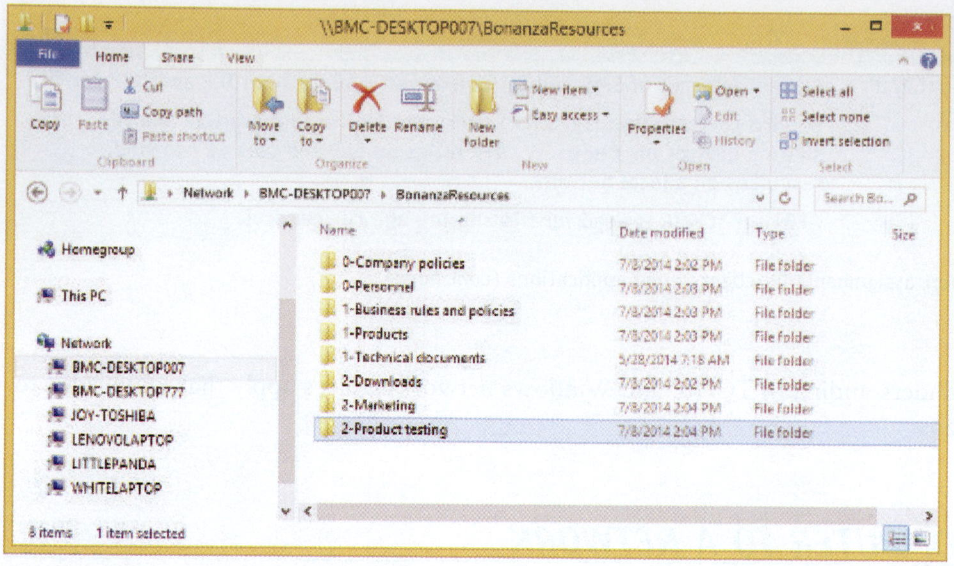

Figure 14-21 File Explorer shows resources on the network

For wireless connections, you can view the status of the connection, including the security key used to make the connection. Do the following:

1. For Windows 8/7, open **Control Panel** in Classic view and open the **Network and Sharing Center.** Alternately, you can right-click the Network icon in the desktop taskbar and click **Open Network and Sharing Center.** The Network and Sharing Center is shown in Figure 14-22. Click **Change adapter settings.** The Network Connections window appears (see Figure 14-23).

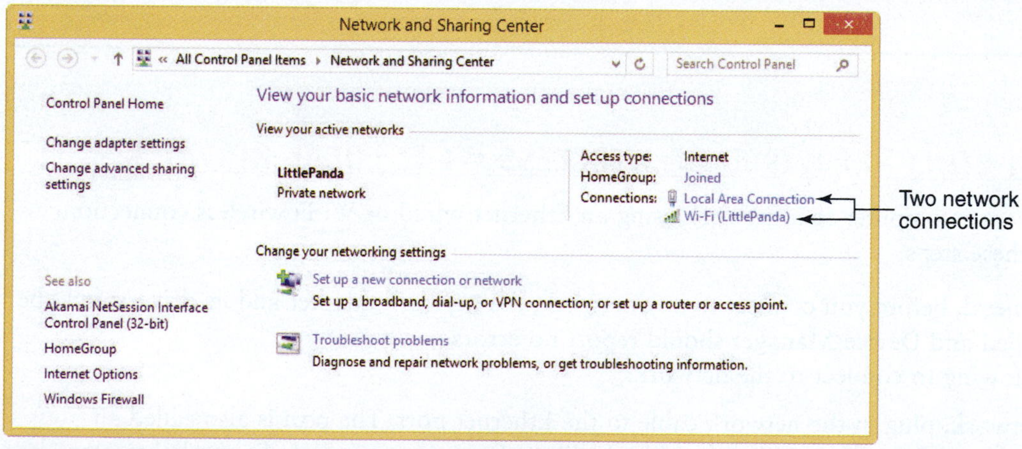

Figure 14-22 The Network and Sharing Center reports two healthy network connections

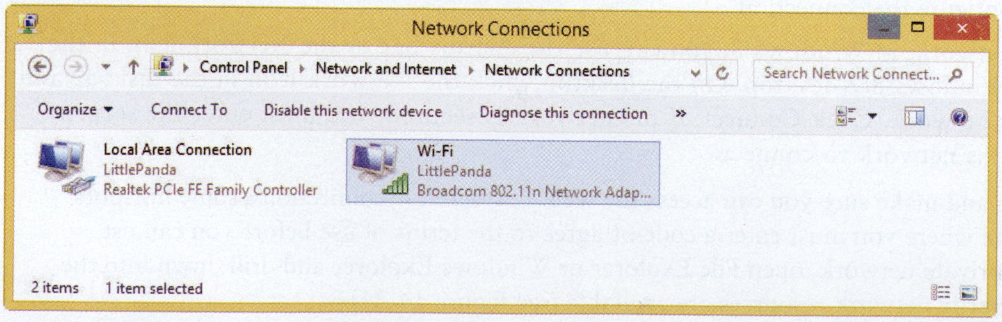

Figure 14-23 The Network Connections window can be used to repair broken connections

Notes For Windows 8, a shortcut to open the Network Connections window is to press **Win+X** and click **Network Connections**.

2. In the Network Connections window, right-click the **Wi-Fi** connection and click **Status**. In the Wi-Fi Status box (see Figure 14-24), click **Wireless Properties**. On the Wireless Properties box, select the **Security** tab. To view the security key, check **Show characters**. You can also see the security and encryption types that Windows automatically sensed and applied when it made the connection.

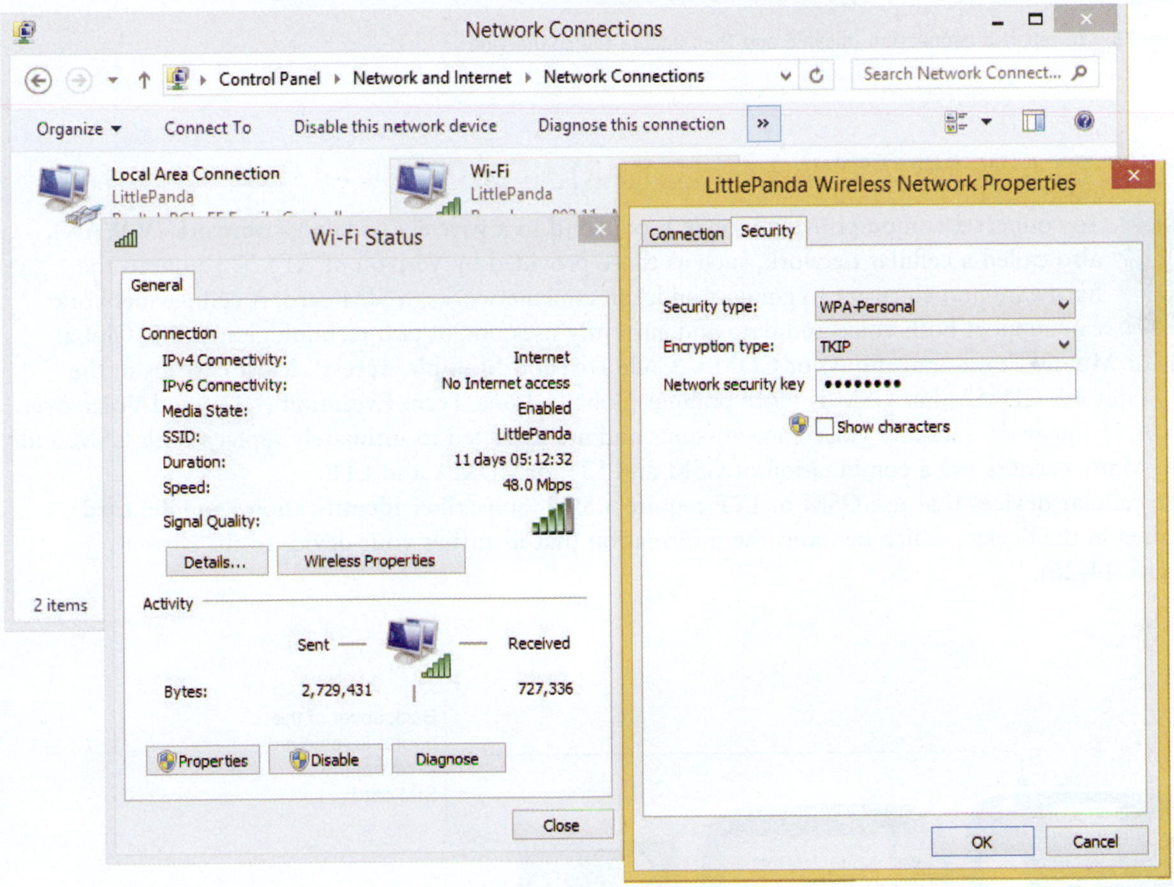

Figure 14-24 Verify the Network security key for the wireless network is correct

If you have a problem making a network connection, you can reset the connection. Open the Network Connections window and right-click the network connection. Select **Disable** from the shortcut menu as shown in Figure 14-25. Right-click the connection again and select **Enable**. The connection is reset. Try again to browse the web or access resources on the network. If you still don't have local or Internet access, it's time to dig a little deeper into the source of the problem. More networking troubleshooting tools and solutions are covered in the chapter, "Supporting Network Hardware."

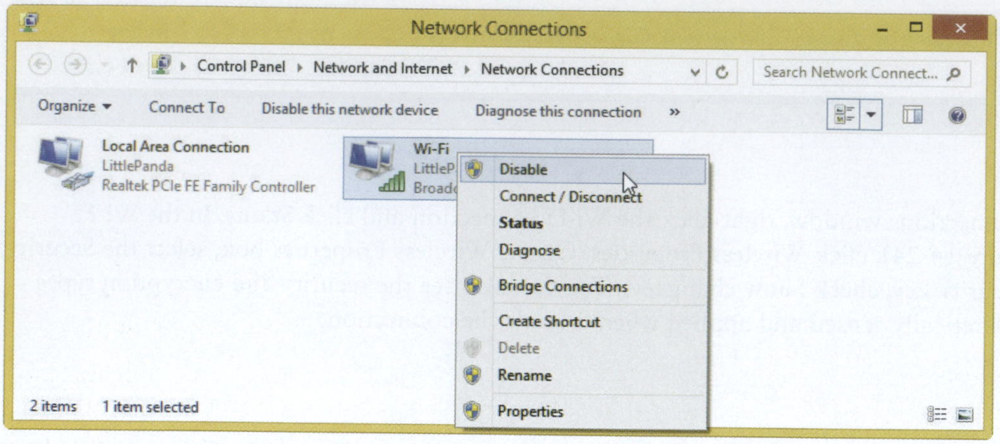

Figure 14-25 To repair a connection, disable and then enable the connection

CONNECT TO A WIRELESS WAN (CELLULAR) NETWORK

A+
220-902
1.6

To connect a computer using mobile broadband to a wireless wide area network (WWAN), also called a cellular network, such as those provided by Verizon or AT&T, you need the hardware and software to connect and, for some networks, a SIM card. A cellular network can support both voice and data and currently uses one of two technologies: GSM (Global System for Mobile Communications) or CDMA (Code Division Multiple Access). Most carriers in the United States use CDMA, but GSM is more popular globally. Long Term Evolution (LTE) and Voice over LTE (VoLTE) provide data and voice transmissions and are expected to ultimately replace both GSM and CDMA. Many carriers use a combination of GSM and LTE or CDMA and LTE.

Those cellular devices that use GSM or LTE require a SIM (Subscriber Identification Module) card be installed in the device, which contains the information that identifies your device to the carrier (see Figure 14-26).

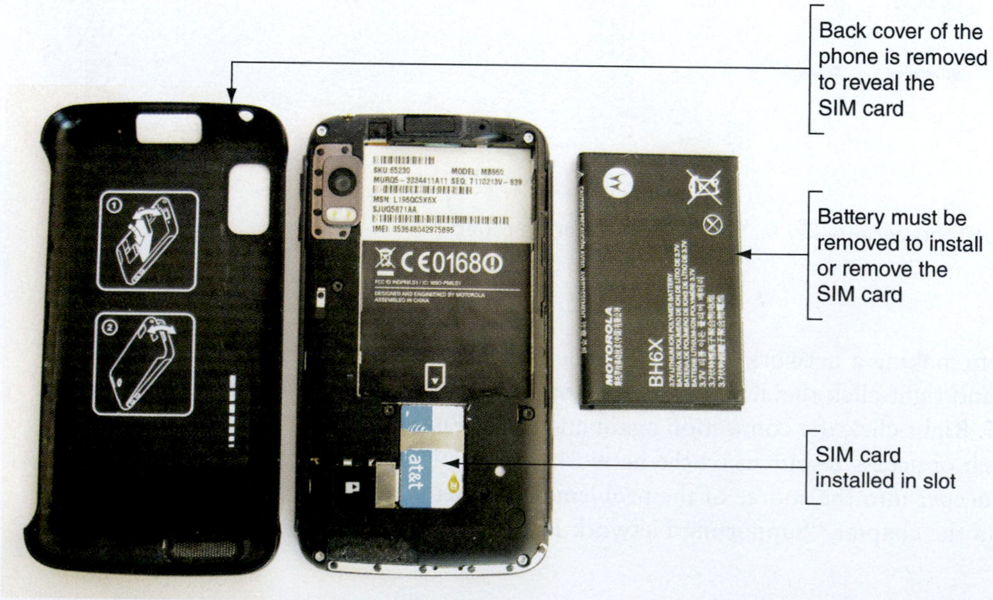

Figure 14-26 A SIM card contains proof that your device can use a cellular network

Here are your options for software and hardware devices that can connect to a cellular network:

- ***Use an embedded mobile broadband modem.*** A laptop or other mobile device might have an embedded broadband modem. In this situation, you still need to subscribe to a carrier.
- ***Tether your cell phone to your computer.*** You can tether your cell phone to your computer. The cell phone connects to the cellular network and provides communication to your computer. The phone and computer can connect by way of a USB cable (see Figure 14-27), a proprietary cable provided by your cell phone manufacturer, or a Bluetooth or Wi-Fi wireless connection. Your contract with the carrier must allow tethering.

Figure 14-27 Tether your cell phone to your laptop using a USB cable

- ***Use a USB broadband modem.*** For any computer, you can use a USB broadband modem (sometimes called an air card), such as the one shown in Figure 14-28. The device requires a contract with a cellular carrier.

When you purchase any of these devices from a carrier or manufacturer, most likely detailed instructions are included for connecting to the cellular network. Follow those instructions rather than the generic ones presented here. Generally, here's how you can connect to a cellular network:

- ***Use an embedded broadband modem.*** For laptops or other mobile devices that have an embedded modem, if a SIM card is required, insert the card in the device. For some laptops, the card slot might be in the battery bay, and you must remove the battery to find the slot. Then use

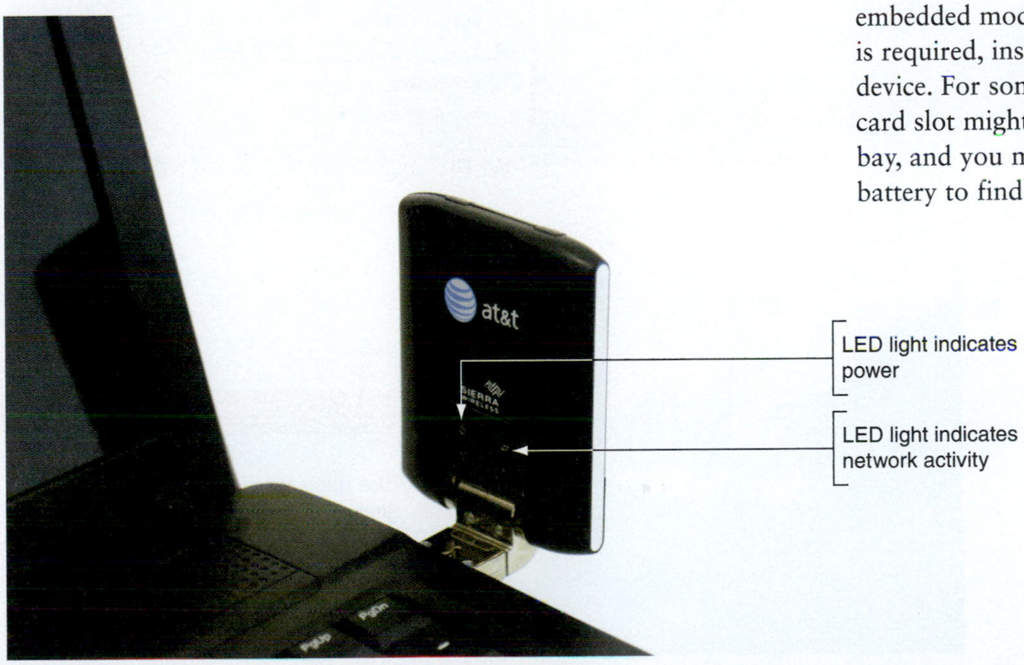

Figure 14-28 A USB broadband modem by Sierra Wireless

a program installed on the device to connect to the cellular network. In addition, the mobile operator might provide software for you to use.

- ***Tether your cell phone.*** To tether your cell phone to your computer, your carrier is likely to provide you software to make the connection. If software is provided, install the software first and then tether your cell phone to your computer. Use the software to make the connection.
- ***Use a USB broadband modem.*** When using a USB broadband modem, if needed, insert the SIM card in the modem (see Figure 14-29). When you insert the modem into a USB port, Windows finds the device, and the software stored on the device automatically installs and runs. A window then appears provided by the software that allows you to connect to the cellular network.

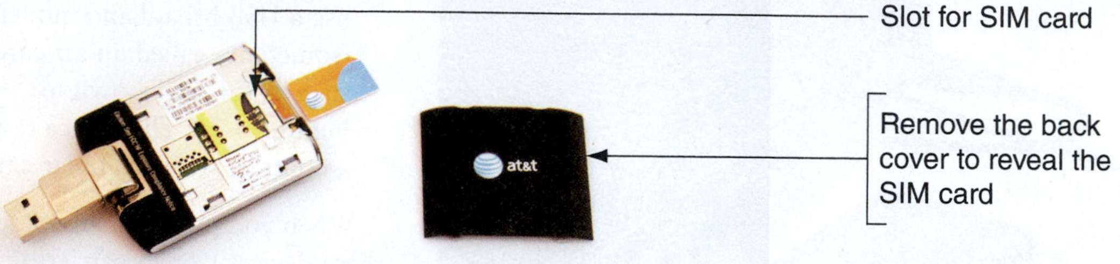

Figure 14-29 A SIM card with subscription information on it might be required to use a cellular network

The software might prompt you to go to the website of your carrier and activate the phone number used by the modem. Figure 14-30 shows the software provided by one modem. Notice you can connect to the mobile network or the Wi-Fi network, but not both at the same time.

Source: AT&T Communications Manager

Figure 14-30 Use the management software to connect and disconnect from the Mobile (cellular) or Wi-Fi network

CREATE A DIAL-UP CONNECTION

A+
220-902
1.6

You never know when you might be called on to support an older dial-up connection. Here are the bare-bones steps you need to set up and support this type of connection:

1. Install an internal or external dial-up modem. Make sure Device Manager recognizes the card without errors.
2. Plug the phone line into the modem port on your computer and into the wall jack.
3. Open the **Network and Sharing Center** window. In the Network and Sharing Center window (refer back to Figure 14-22), click **Set up a new connection or network**. In the dialog box that appears (see Figure 14-31), select **Connect to the Internet - Set up a broadband or dial-up connection to the Internet** and click **Next**.

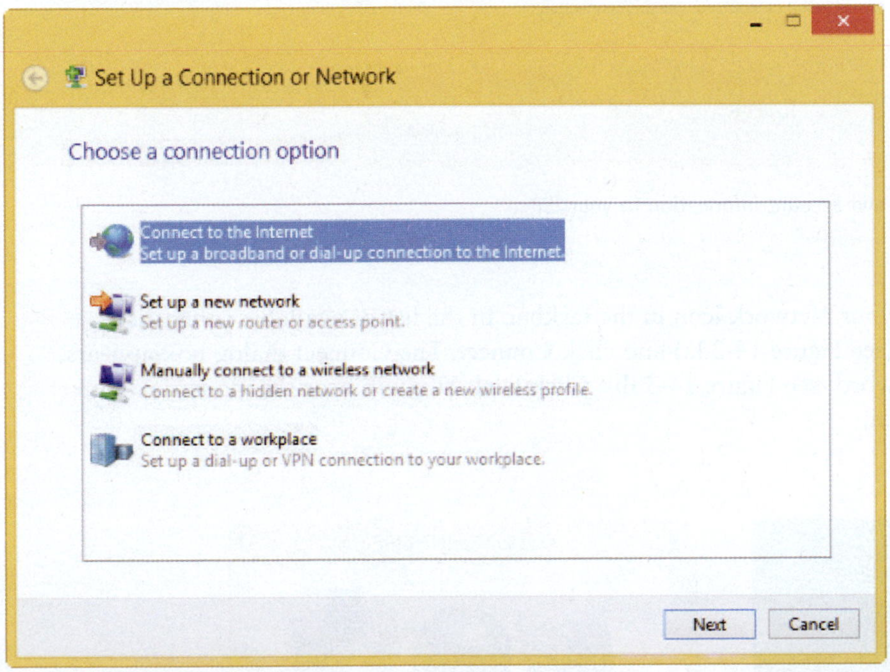

Figure 14-31 Create a dial-up connection to an ISP

4. In the next box, click **Dial-up**. In the next box (see Figure 14-32), enter the phone number to your ISP, your ISP user name and password, and the name you decide to give the dial-up connection, such as the name and city of your ISP. Then click **Create**.

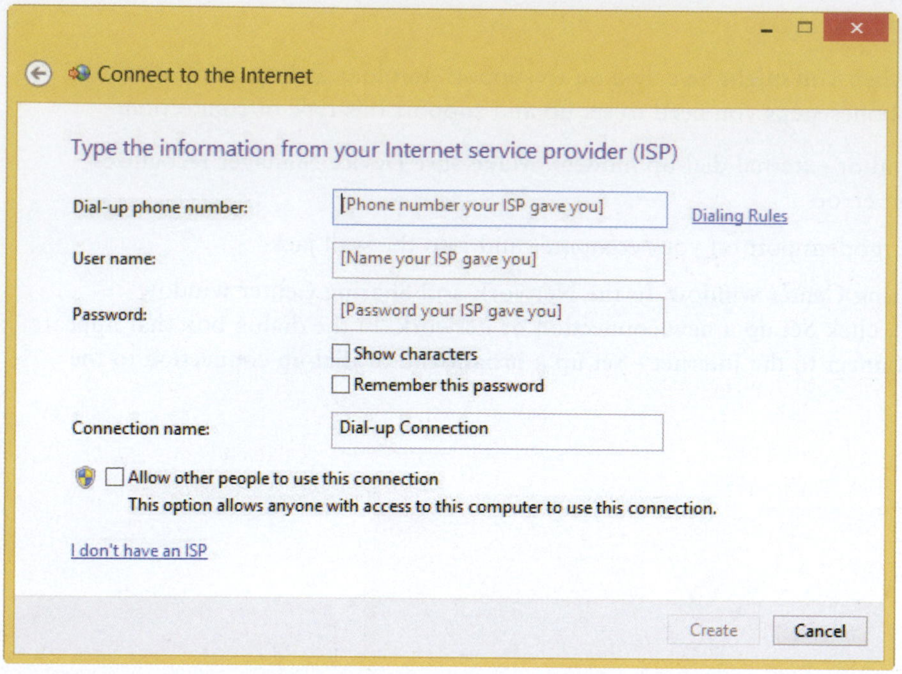

Figure 14-32 Enter phone number and account information to your ISP

To use the connection, click your Network icon in the taskbar. In the list of available connections, select your dial-up connection (see Figure 14-33a) and click **Connect**. The Connect dialog box appears, where you can enter your password (see Figure 14-33b). Click **Dial**. You will hear the modem dial up the ISP and make the connection.

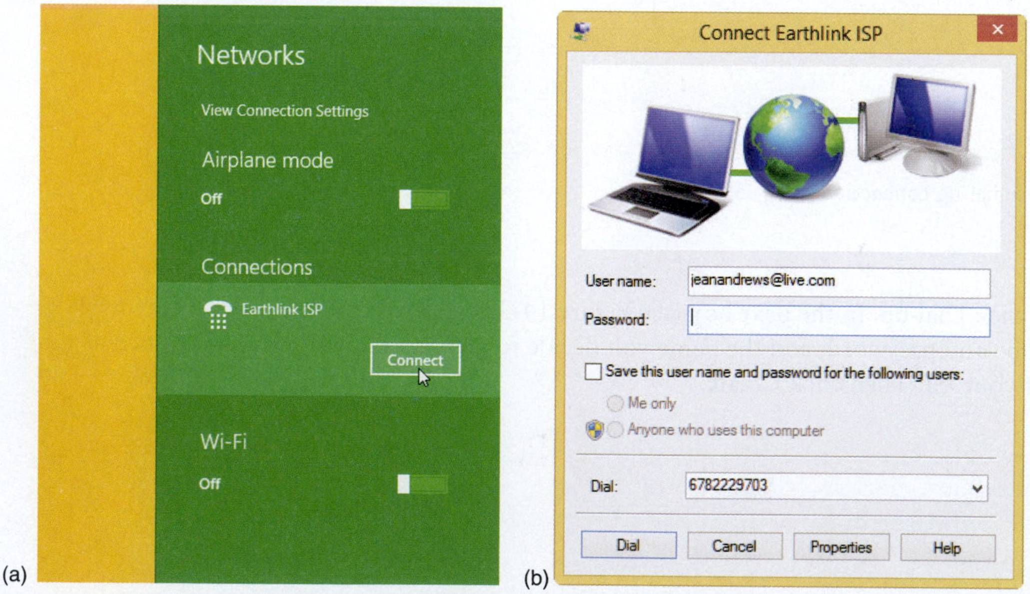

Figure 14-33 (a) Select your dial-up connection, and (b) enter the password to your ISP

If the dial-up connection won't work, here are some things you can try:

- Is the phone line working? Plug in a regular phone and check for a dial tone. Is the phone cord securely connected to the computer and the wall jack?
- Does the modem work? Check Device Manager for reported errors about the modem. Does the modem work when making a call to another phone number (not your ISP)?
- Check the Dial-up Connection Properties box for errors. To do so, click **Change adapter settings** in the Network and Sharing Center, and then right-click the dial-up connection and select **Properties** from the shortcut menu. Is the phone number correct? Does the number need to include a 9 to get an outside line? Has a 1 been added in front of the number by mistake? If you need to add a 9, you can put a comma in the field like this "9,4045661200", which causes a slight pause after the 9 is dialed.
- Try dialing the number manually from a phone. Do you hear beeps on the other end? Try another phone number.
- When you try to connect, do you hear the number being dialed? If so, the problem is most likely with the phone number, the phone line, or the user name and password.
- Try removing and reinstalling the dial-up connection.

CREATE A VPN CONNECTION

A+
220-902
1.6

A virtual private network (VPN) is often used by employees when they telecommute to connect to the corporate network by way of the Internet. A VPN protects data by encrypting it from the time it leaves the remote computer until it reaches a server on the corporate network. The encryption technique is called a tunnel or tunneling (see Figure 14-34).

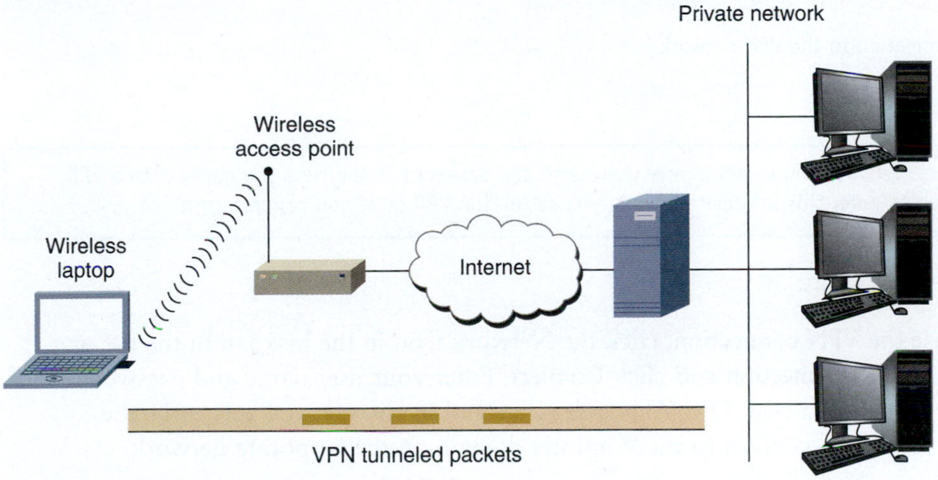

Figure 14-34 With a VPN, tunneling is used to send encrypted data over wired and wireless networks and the Internet

A VPN can be managed by operating systems, routers, or third-party software such as OpenVPN (*openvpn.net*). A VPN connection is a virtual connection, which means you are really setting up the tunnel over an existing connection to the Internet. When creating a VPN connection on a personal computer, always follow directions given by the network administrator who set up the VPN. The company website might provide VPN client software to download and install on your computer.

Here are the general steps to use Windows to connect to a VPN:

1. In the Network and Sharing Center (refer back to Figure 14-22), click **Set up a new connection or network.** Then select **Connect to a workplace - Set up a dial-up or VPN connection to your workplace** (refer back to Figure 14-31) and click **Next**.

2. In the Connect to a Workplace box, click **Use my Internet connection** (VPN). In the next box, enter the IP address or domain name of the network (see Figure 14-35). Your network administrator can provide this information. Name the VPN connection and click **Create**.

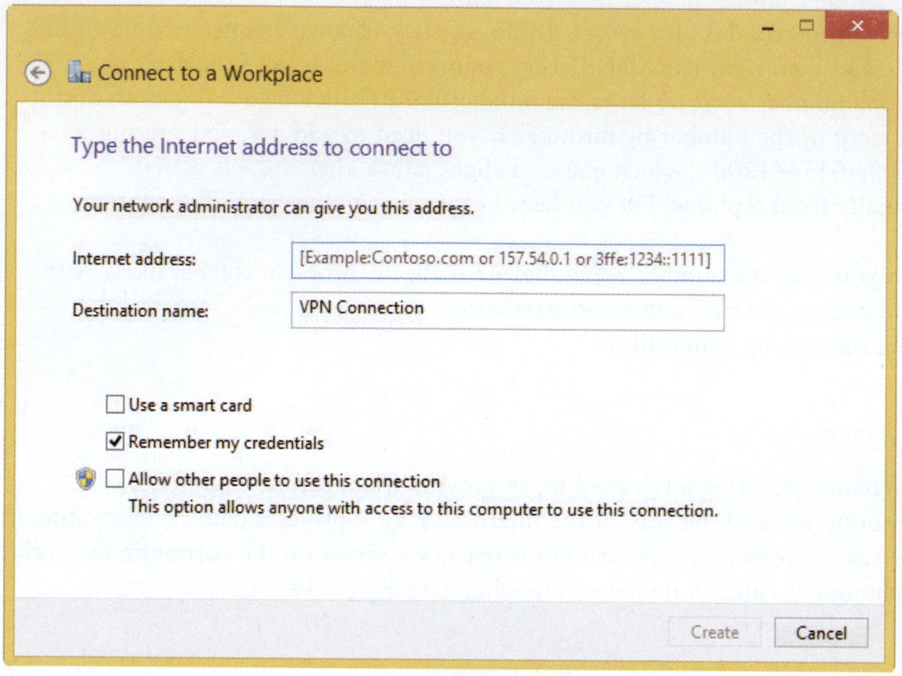

Figure 14-35 Enter logon information to the VPN network

OS Differences Windows 8 requires you to enter your user name and password at the time you connect to a VPN. Windows 7 gives you the option to enter this information when you set up the VPN or as you connect to it.

Whenever you want to use the VPN connection, click the Network icon in the taskbar. In the list of available networks, click the **VPN connection** and click **Connect**. Enter your user name and password (for Windows 8, see Figure 14-36) and click **OK**. Your user name and password are likely to be the network ID and password you use to connect to the Windows domain on the corporate network.

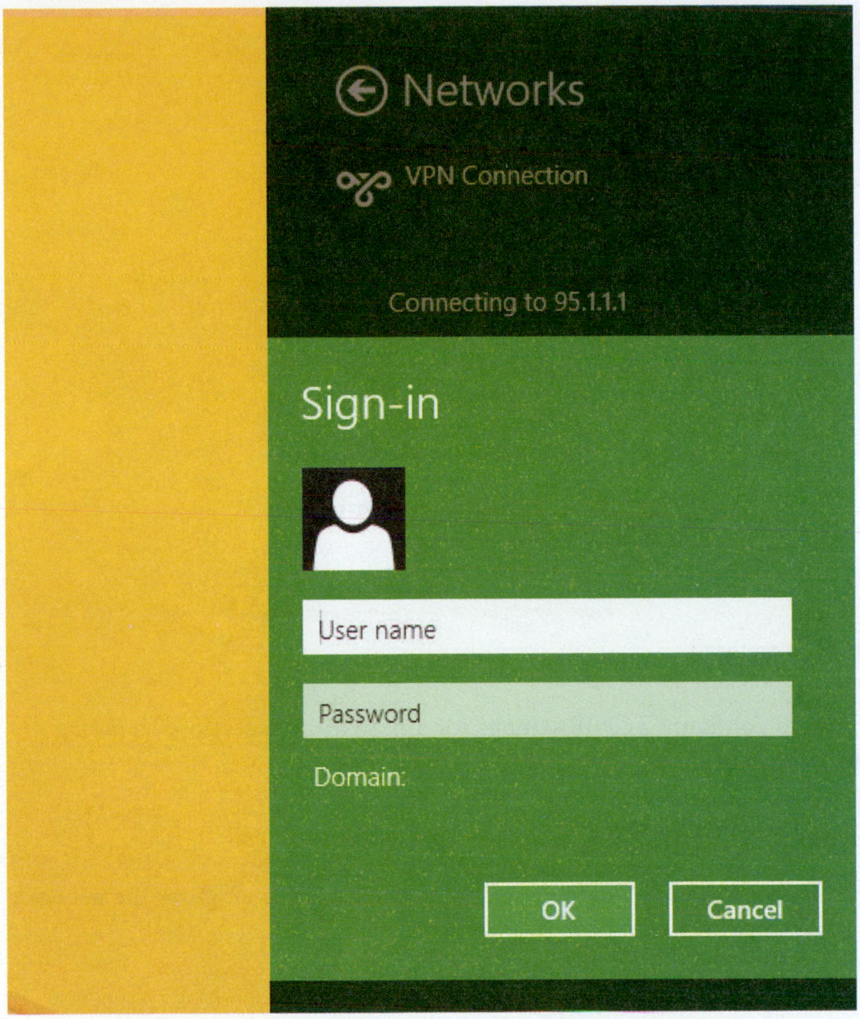

Figure 14-36 Enter your user name and password to connect to your VPN

After the connection is made, you can use your browser to access the corporate secured intranet websites or other resources. The resources you can access depend on the permissions assigned the user account.

Problems connecting to a VPN can be caused by the wrong authentication protocols used when passing the user name and password to the VPN. To configure these settings, in the Network and Sharing Center, click **Change adapter settings**. In the Network Connections window, right-click **VPN Connection** and click **Properties**. In the Properties box, select the **Security** tab (see Figure 14-37). Here you can select the authentication protocols given to you by the network administrator.

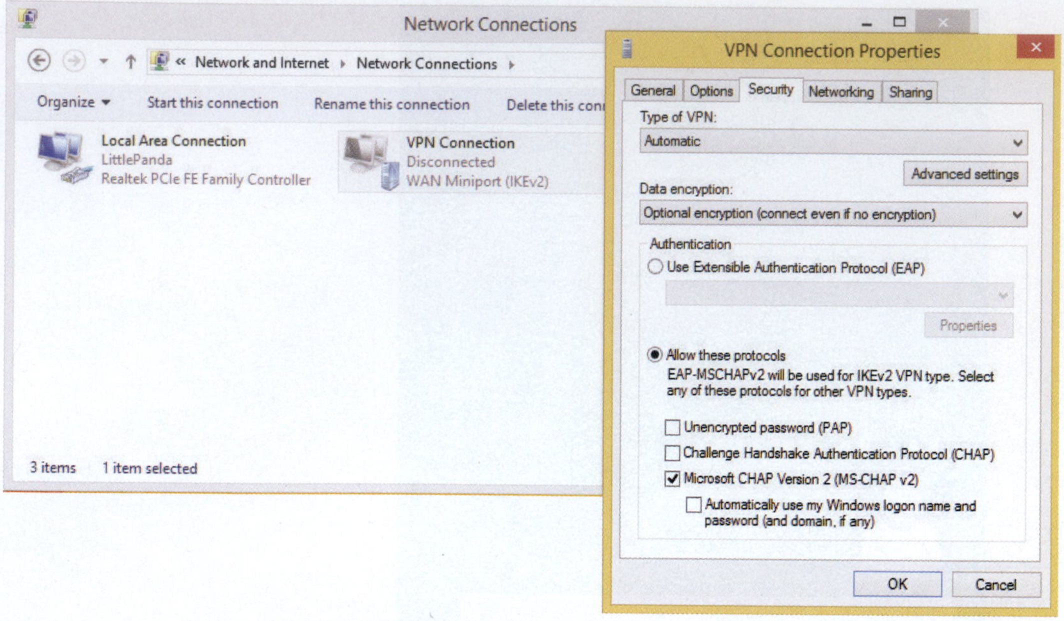

Figure 14-37 Select the VPN's authentication protocol

Now let's turn our attention to how to configure TCP/IP settings for a network connection, including dynamic, static, and alternate address configurations.

DYNAMIC AND STATIC IP CONFIGURATIONS

A+
220-902
1.6

By default, Windows assumes dynamic IP addressing and automatically configures the network connection. However, some networks use static IP addresses.

To configure dynamic and static IP addresses, follow these steps:

1. Open the **Network Connections** window. Right-click the network connection and click **Properties**. In the Properties box, click the **Networking** tab, which is the middle box shown in Figure 14-38 for the Local Area Connection (Ethernet). Select **Internet Protocol Version 4 (TCP/IPv4)** and click **Properties**. The TCP/IPv4 Properties box appears (see the right side of Figure 14-38).

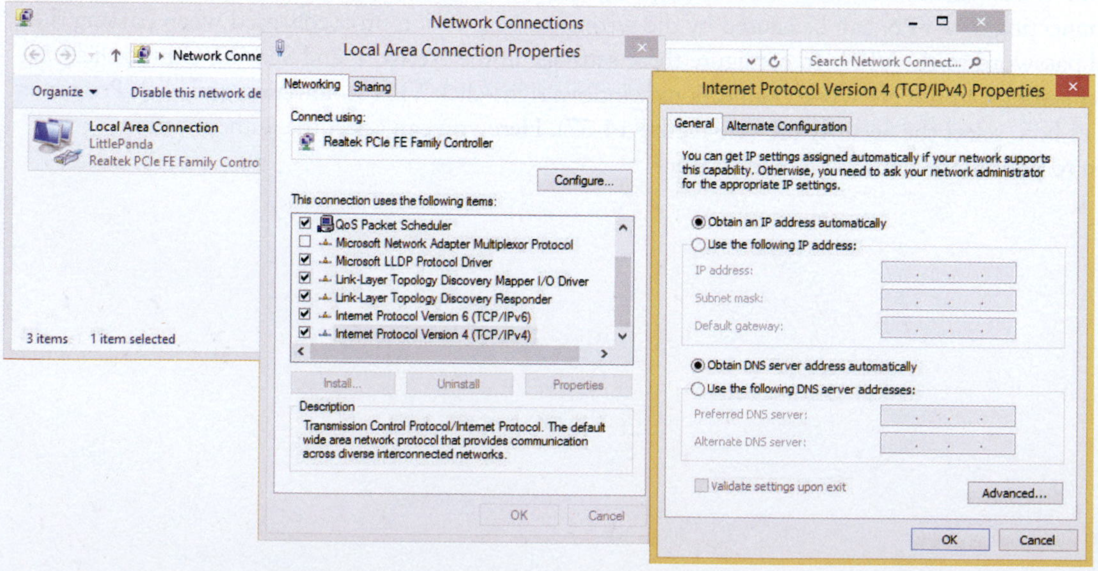

Figure 14-38 Configure TCP/IPv4 for static or dynamic addressing

2. By default, dynamic IP addressing is used, which selects *Obtain an IP address automatically* and *Obtain DNS server address automatically*. To change the settings to static IP addressing, select **Use the following IP address**. Then enter the IP address, subnet mask, and default gateway. (A default gateway is the gateway a computer uses to access another network if it does not have a better option.)
3. If you have been given the IP addresses of DNS servers, select **Use the following DNS server addresses** and enter up to two IP addresses. If you have other DNS IP addresses, click **Advanced** and enter them on the **DNS** tab of the Advanced TCP/IP Settings box.

Notes Notice in Figure 14-38 that you can select Internet Protocol Version 6 (TCP/IPv6) and click Properties to change IPv6 properties, including static and dynamic address configuration.

You can also uncheck Internet Protocol Version 6 (TCP/IPv6) to disable it. For most situations, you need to leave it enabled. A bug in Windows 7 might prevent you from joining a homegroup if IPv6 is disabled.

ALTERNATE IP ADDRESS CONFIGURATION

A+ 220-902 1.6

Suppose an employee with a laptop often travels, and her work network uses static IP addressing, and, as you know, most public networks use dynamic IP addressing. How do you configure her computer's TCP/IP settings? For travel, you would configure the computer to use dynamic IP addressing for public networks. However, when the computer attempts to connect to the corporate network, the computer won't be able to find a DHCP server to get an IP address, subnet mask, default gateway, and DNS server addresses, and it will default to an Automatic Private IP Address (APIPA) and won't have the information it needs to connect to the network or Internet. The solution is to create an alternate configuration that the computer will use if it cannot find a DHCP server.

To create an alternate configuration, on the TCP/IPv4 Properties box shown in Figure 14-38, click the **Alternate Configuration** tab. By default, the alternate configuration is Automatic private IP address. See Figure 14-39. Select **User configured**. Then enter a static IP address, subnet mask, default gateway, and DNS server addresses for the alternate configuration to be used on the company network. Click **OK** and close all boxes.

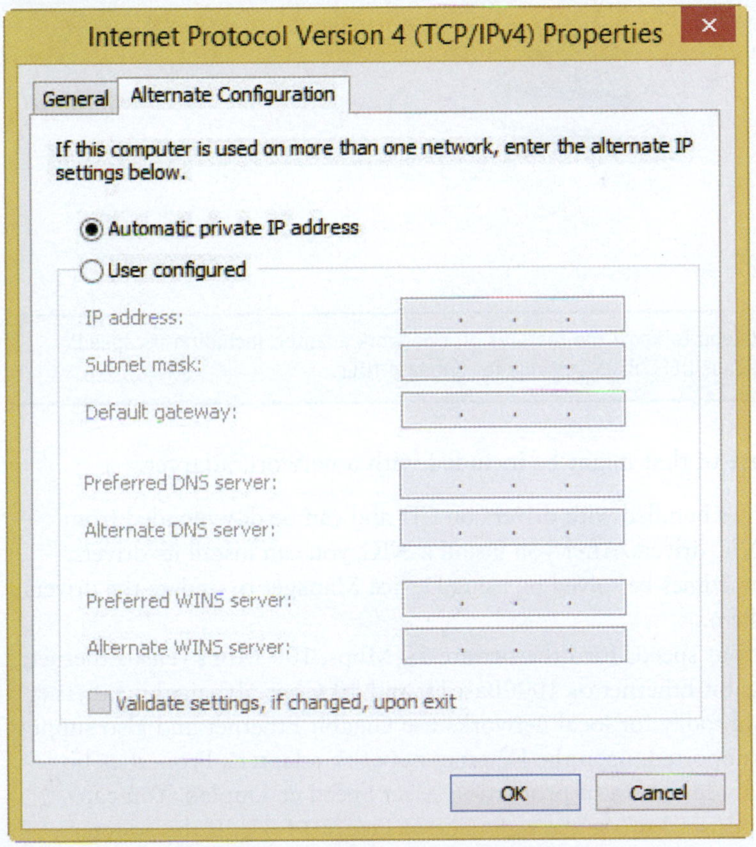

Figure 14-39 Create an alternate static IP address configuration

14

★ A+ Exam Tip The A+ 220-902 exam expects you to know how to configure an alternate IP address, including setting the static IP address, subnet mask, DNS addresses, and gateway address.

MANAGE NETWORK ADAPTERS

A+ 220-902 1.6

A computer makes a direct connection to a local wired network by way of a network adapter, which might be a network port embedded on the motherboard or a network interface card (NIC) designed for installation in an expansion slot on the motherboard (refer back to Figure 14-3). In addition, the adapter might also be an external device plugged into a USB port (see Figure 14-40). The wired network adapter provides a network port. A network adapter is often called a NIC, even when it's not really a card but a USB device or a network port embedded on the motherboard, which can be called an onboard NIC.

Figure 14-40 USB device provides an Ethernet port

★ A+ Exam Tip The A+ 220-902 exam expects you to know the features of a network adapter, including its speeds, half duplex, full duplex, Wake-on-LAN, QoS, and about UEFI/BIOS settings for onboard NICs.

Here are the features you need to be aware of that might be included with a network adapter:

- ***The drivers a NIC uses.*** A NIC usually comes bundled with drivers on CD and can be downloaded from the web. Windows has several embedded NIC drivers. After you install a NIC, you can install its drivers. Problems with the network adapter can sometimes be solved by using Device Manager to update the drivers or uninstall the drivers and then reinstall them.
- ***Ethernet speeds.*** For wired networks, the four speeds for Ethernet are 10 Mbps, 100 Mbps (Fast Ethernet; technical name is 100BaseT), 1 Gbps (Gigabit Ethernet or 1000BaseT), and 10 Gbps (10-gigabit Ethernet or 10GBaseT). Most network adapters sold today for local networks use Gigabit Ethernet and also support the two slower speeds. To see the speeds supported, open the Ethernet network adapter's Properties box in Device Manager. Select the Advanced tab. In the list of properties, select Speed & Duplex. You can then see available speeds in the Value dropdown list (see the right side of Figure 14-41). If the adapter connects with slower network devices on the network, the adapter works at the slower speed. Notice in the dropdown list choices for half duplex or full duplex. Full duplex sends and receives transmissions at the same time. Half duplex works in only one direction at a time. Select Auto Negotiation for Windows to use the best possible speed and duplex.

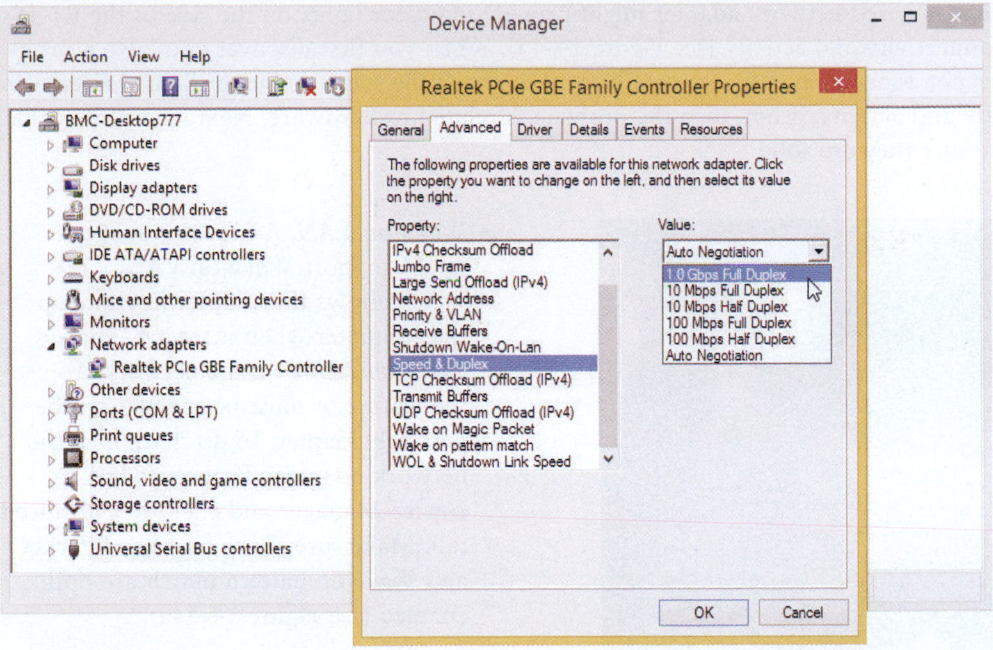

Figure 14-41 Set the speed and duplex for the network adapter

> **Notes** The speed of a network depends on the speed of each device on the network and how well a router manages that traffic. Routers, switches, and network adapters currently run at three speeds: Gigabit Ethernet (1000 Mbps or 1 Gbps), Fast Ethernet (100 Mbps), or Ethernet (10 Mbps). If you want your entire network to run at the fastest speed, make sure all your devices are rated for Gigabit Ethernet.

- ***MAC address.*** Every network adapter (wired or wireless) has a 48-bit (6-byte) identification number, called the MAC address or physical address, hard-coded on the card by its manufacturer that is unique for that adapter, and this number is used to identify the adapter on the network. An example of a MAC address is 00-0C-6E-4E-AB-A5. Most likely, the MAC address is printed on the device. You can also have Windows tell you the MAC address by entering the **ipconfig /all** command in a command prompt window (see Figure 14-42).

14

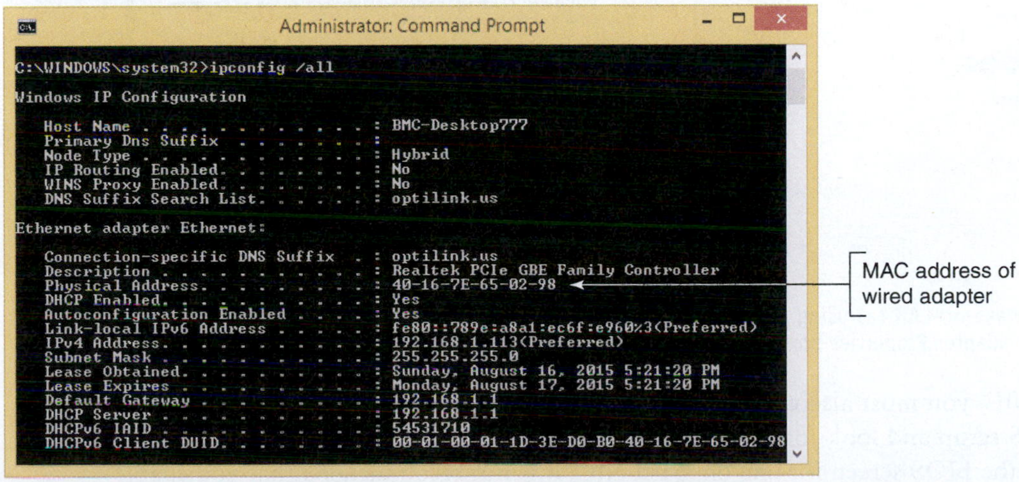

Figure 14-42 Use the ipconfig /all command to show the MAC address of a network adapter

- ***Status indicator lights.*** A wired network adapter might provide indicator lights on the side of the RJ-45 port that indicate connectivity and activity (see Figure 14-43). When you first discover you have a problem with a computer not connecting to a network, be sure to check the status indicator lights to verify you have connectivity and activity. If not, then the problem is related to hardware. Next, check the cable connections to make sure they are solid.

Figure 14-43 Status indicator lights for the onboard network port

- ***Wake-on-LAN.*** A network adapter might support Wake-on-LAN, which allows the adapter to wake up the computer when it receives certain communication on the network. To use the feature, it must be enabled on the network adapter. To do that, open the network adapter's Properties box in Device Manager and click the **Advanced** tab. Make sure **Wake on Magic Packet** and **Wake on pattern match** are both enabled (see Figure 14-44a).

> **Notes** Some network adapters provide a Power Management tab in the Properties box. To use the Power Management tab to enable Wake-on-LAN, check **Allow this device to wake the computer** (see Figure 14-44b).

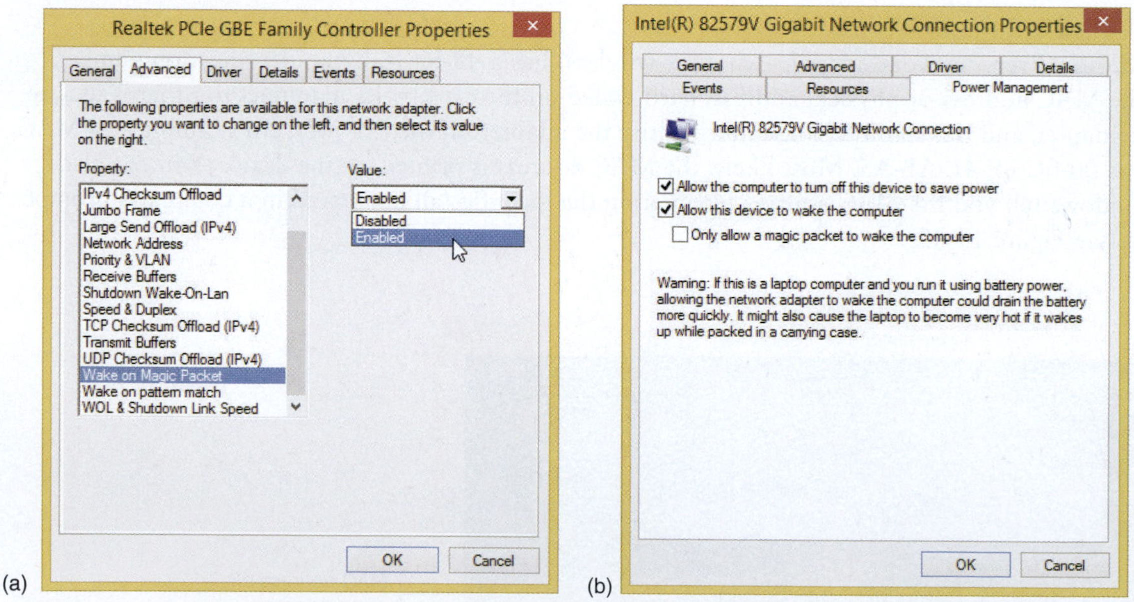

Figure 14-44 Enable Wake-on-LAN (a) using the Advanced tab, or (b) using the Power Management tab of the network adapter Properties box

For an onboard NIC, you must also enable Wake-on-LAN in UEFI/BIOS setup. Reboot the computer and enter UEFI/BIOS setup and look for the option on a power-management screen in UEFI/BIOS setup. Figure 14-45 shows the BIOS screen for one onboard NIC. It is not recommended that you enable Wake-on-LAN for a wireless network adapter.

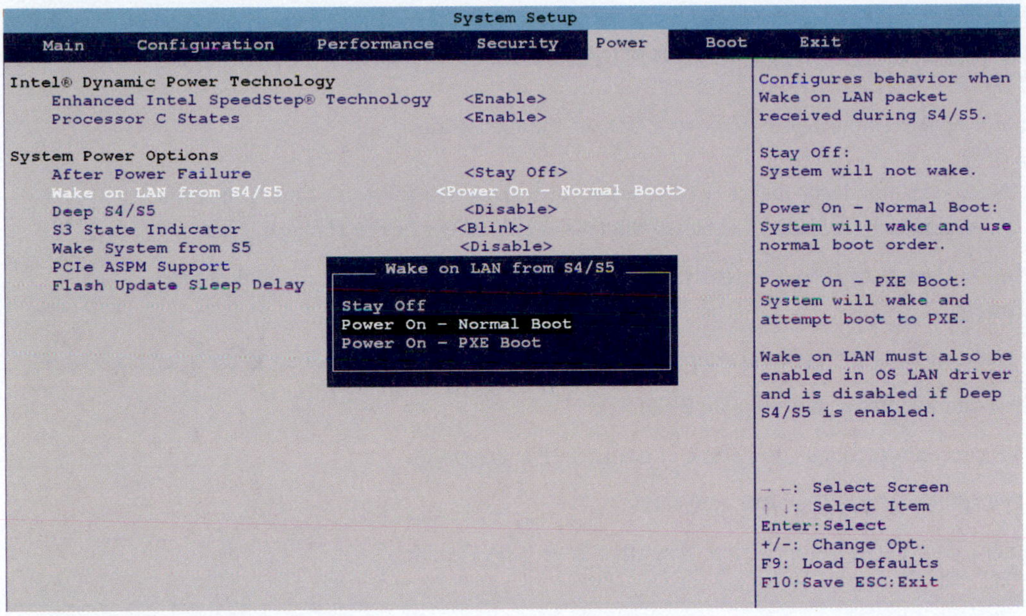

Source: Intel

Figure 14-45 Use the Power screen in the BIOS setup to enable Wake-on-LAN

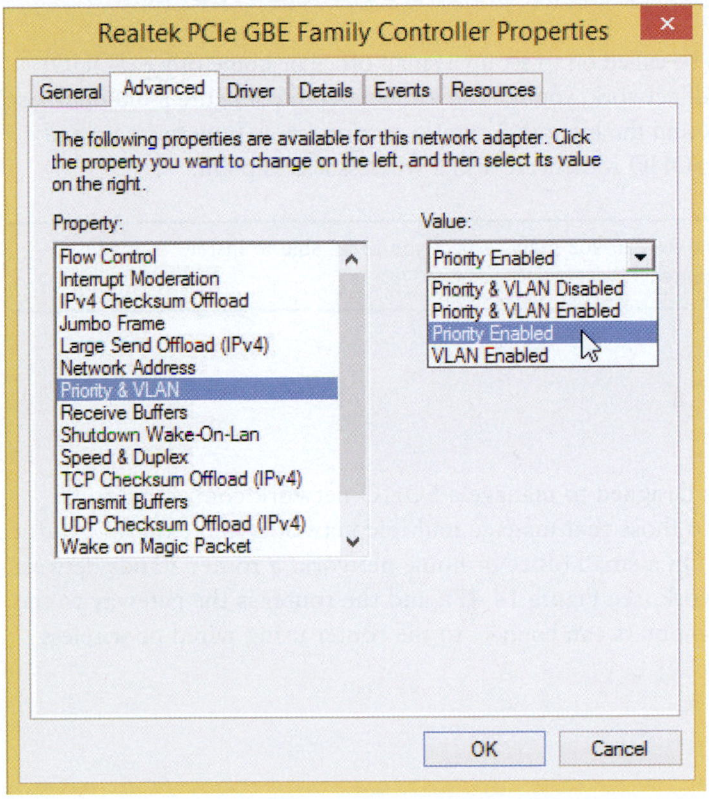

Figure 14-46 Select Priority Enabled to allow the network adapter to support QoS on the network

- ***Quality of Service (QoS).*** Another feature of a network adapter is the ability to control which applications have priority on the network. The feature must be enabled and configured on the router and also enabled on the network adapters and configured in Windows for every computer on the network using the high-priority applications. To enable Quality of Service (QoS) for a NIC, open the network adapter Properties box in Device Manager. On the Advanced tab, make sure **Priority Enabled** is selected, as shown in Figure 14-46. (If the option is not listed, the adapter does not support QoS.) Later in this chapter, you learn how to configure a router to use QoS. To configure an application to use QoS, you can use Group Policy in professional and business editions of Windows. How to use Group Policy is covered in the chapter, "Windows Resources on a Network."

Hands-On | Project 14-3 Investigate TCP/IP Settings

A+
220-902
1.6

Using a computer connected to a network, answer these questions:

1. What is the hardware device used to make this connection (network card, onboard port, wireless)? List the device's name as Windows sees it in the Device Manager window.
2. What is the MAC address of the wired or wireless network adapter? What command or window did you use to get your answer?
3. For a wireless connection, is the network secured? If so, what is the security type? What is the encryption type?
4. What is the IPv4 address of the network connection?
5. Are your TCP/IP version 4 settings using static or dynamic IP addressing?
6. What is the IPv6 address of your network connection?
7. Disable and enable your network connection. Now what is your IPv4 address?

SETTING UP A MULTIFUNCTION ROUTER FOR A SOHO NETWORK

A+
220-901
2.5, 2.6

A+
220-902
3.2, 3.7

An IT support technician is likely to be called on to set up a small office or home office (SOHO) network. As part of setting up a small network, you need to know how to configure a multipurpose router to stand between the network and the Internet. You also need to know how to set up and secure a wireless access point. Most SOHO routers are also a wireless access point.

★ A+ Exam Tip The A+ 220-901 and A+ 220-902 exams expect you to be able to install, configure, and secure a SOHO wired and wireless router.

FUNCTIONS OF A SOHO ROUTER

A+
220-901
2.5, 2.6

A+
220-902
3.2, 3.7

Routers can range from small ones designed to manage a SOHO network connecting to an ISP (costing around $75 to $200) to those that manage multiple networks and extensive traffic (costing several thousand dollars). On a small office or home network, a router stands between the ISP network and the local network (see Figure 14-47), and the router is the gateway to the Internet. Note in the figure that computers can connect to the router using wired or wireless connections.

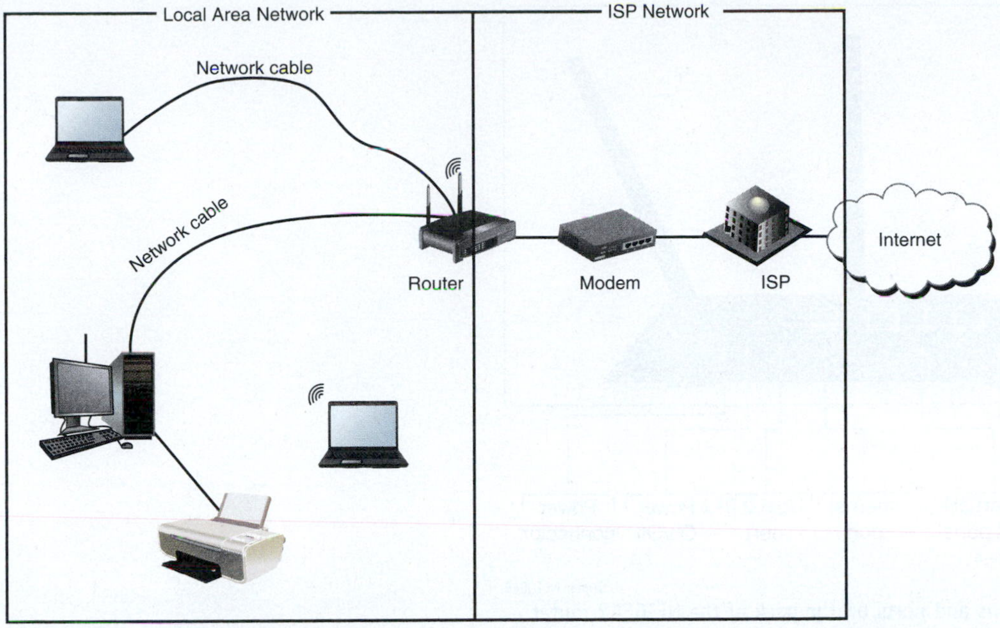

Figure 14-47 A router stands between a local network and the ISP network and manages traffic between them

A typical SOHO router is usually several devices in one:

- *Function 1:* As a router, it stands between two networks, the ISP network and the local network, and routes traffic between the two networks.
- *Function 2:* As a switch, it manages several network ports that can be connected to wired computers or to a switch that provides more ports for more computers.
- *Function 3:* As a DHCP server, it can provide IP addresses to networked computers.
- *Function 4:* As a wireless access point (WAP), it enables a wireless computer to connect to the network. This wireless connection can be secured using wireless security features.
- *Function 5:* As a firewall, it blocks unwanted traffic initiated from the Internet and can restrict Internet access for local computers behind the firewall. Restrictions on local computers can apply to days of the week, time of day, keywords used, or certain websites. It can limit network and Internet access to only specified computers, based on their MAC addresses. It also provides Network Address Translation (NAT) so that computers on the LAN can use private or link-local IP addresses.
- *Function 6:* As an FTP server, you can connect an external hard drive to the router, and the FTP firmware on the router can be used to share files with network users.

An example of a multifunction router is the Nighthawk AC1900 by NETGEAR shown in Figures 14-48 and 14-49. It has one Internet port for the broadband modem (cable modem or DSL modem) and four ports for computers on the network. The USB port can be used to plug in a USB external hard drive for use by any computer on the network. The router is also a wireless access point having multiple antennas to increase speed and range.

Source: Amazon.com

Figure 14-48 NETGEAR Nighthawk AC1900 Dual band Wi-Fi Gigabit router

14

Figure 14-49 Connections and ports on the back of the NETGEAR router

INSTALL AND CONFIGURE A ROUTER ON THE LOCAL NETWORK

A+ 220-901 2.5, 2.6

A+ 220-902 3.2, 3.7

When deciding where to physically place a router, consider the physical security of the router and, as a wireless access point, make sure the router is centrally located to create the best Wi-Fi hotspot for users. For physical security, don't place the router in a public location in a small business, such as the lobby. For best security, place the router behind a locked door accessible only to authorized personnel in a location with access to network cabling. The indoor range for a Wi-Fi hotspot is up to 70 meters; the range is affected by many factors, including interference from walls, furniture, electrical equipment, and other nearby hotspots. For the best Wi-Fi strength, position your router or a stand-alone wireless access point in the center of where you want your hotspot and know that a higher position (near the ceiling) works better than a lower position (on the floor).

Notes Some wireless access points are plenum rated, meaning that, according to fire codes, they can be installed in the plenum area between floors in a building or above a suspended ceiling. For these types of installation, network technicians are careful to follow local fire codes and must take into account how the device might affect airflow in the plenum.

For routers that have external antennas, raise the antennas to vertical positions. Plug in the router and connect network cables to the local network. Connect the network cable from the ISP modem or other device to the uplink port on the router.

To configure a router for the first time or change its configuration, always follow the directions of the manufacturer rather than the general directions given here. You can use any computer on the network that uses a wired connection (it doesn't matter which one) to configure the firmware on the router. You'll need the IP address of the router and the default user name and password to the router setup. To find this information, look in the router documentation or search online for your model and brand of router.

Here are the general steps for one router, the Nighthawk AC1900 by NETGEAR, although the setup screens for your router may be different:

1. Open your browser and enter the IP address of the router in the address box. In our example, the address is 192.168.1.1. The Windows Security box appears (see Figure 14-50). For our router, the default user name and password is **admin**, although yours might be different.

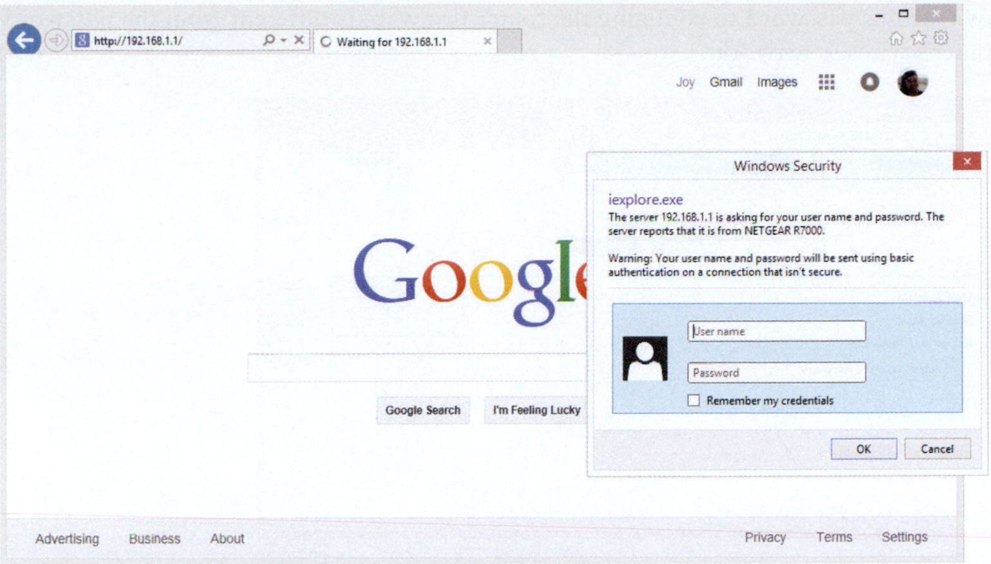

Figure 14-50 Enter the user name and password to the router firmware utility

2. The main setup page of the router firmware appears in your browser window. Figure 14-51 shows the main page for a router that has already been configured. Notice the BASIC tab is selected. Most of the settings you'll need are on the ADVANCED tab. Begin by poking around to see what's available and to find the setting you need. If you make changes, be sure to save your changes. When finished, click **Logout** and close the browser window.

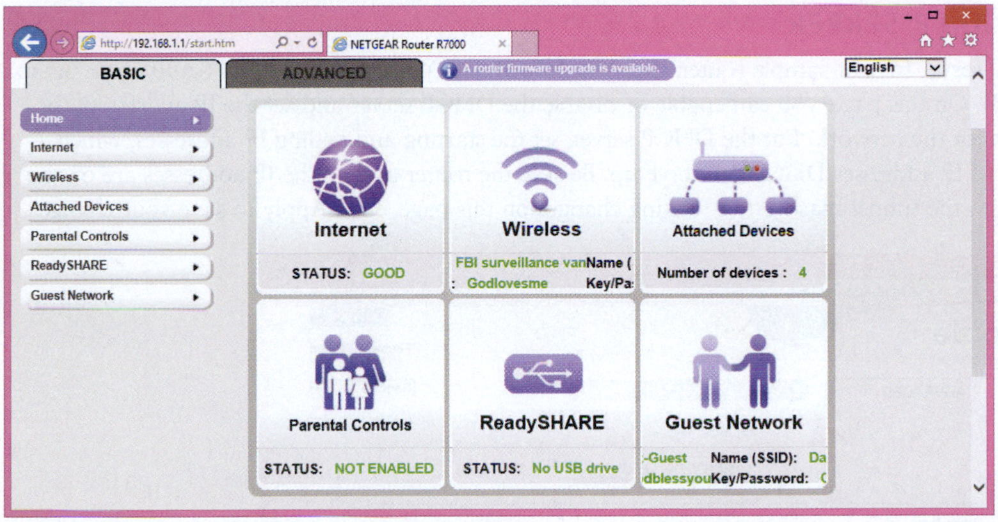

Source: NETGEAR

Figure 14-51 Main screen for router firmware setup

Following are some changes that you might need to make to the router's configuration. The first setting should always be done.

CHANGE THE ROUTER PASSWORD

It's extremely important to protect access to your network and prevent others from hijacking your router. If you have not already done so, change the default password to your router firmware. For our router, click the **ADVANCED** tab, click **Administration**, and click **Set Password** (see Figure 14-52). Change the password and click **Apply**. If the firmware offers the option, disable the ability to configure the router from over the wireless network. Know that this password to configure the router firmware is different from the password needed to access the router's wireless network.

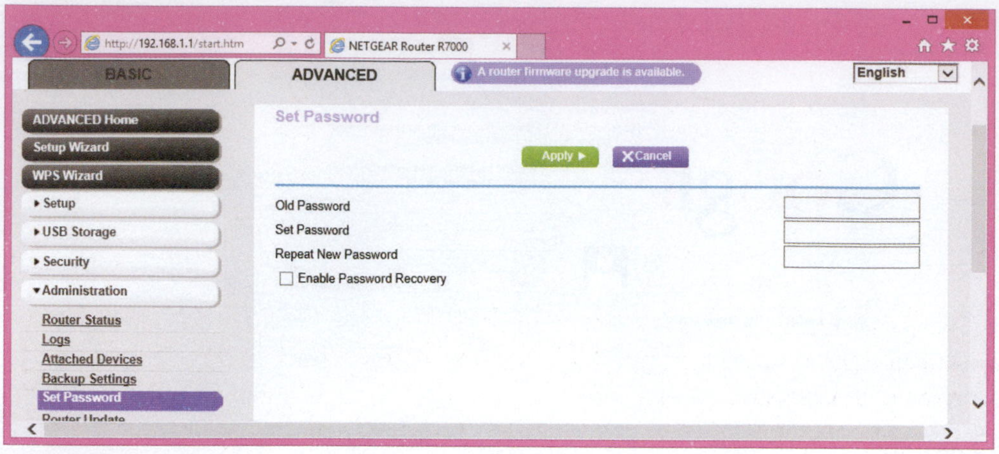

Source: NETGEAR

Figure 14-52 Change the router firmware password

> **Caution** Changing the router password is especially important if the router is a wireless router. Unless you have disabled or secured the wireless access point, anyone outside your building can use your wireless network. If they guess the default password to the router, they can change the password to hijack your router. Also, your wireless network can be used for criminal activity. When you first install a router, before you do anything else, change your router password and disable the wireless network until you have time to set up and test the wireless security. And, to give even more security, change the default user name to another user name if the router utility allows that option.

CONFIGURE THE DHCP SERVER

To configure the DHCP server for our sample router, click the **ADVANCED** tab and then **LAN Setup** in the Setup group (see Figure 14-53). On this page, you can enable or disable the DHCP server and set the IP address of the router and subnet mask for the network. For the DHCP server, set the starting and ending IP addresses, which determines the number of IP addresses DHCP can serve up. Be sure the router and all the IP addresses are on the same subnet, according to the subnet mask. After making changes on this page, click **Apply** to save your changes.

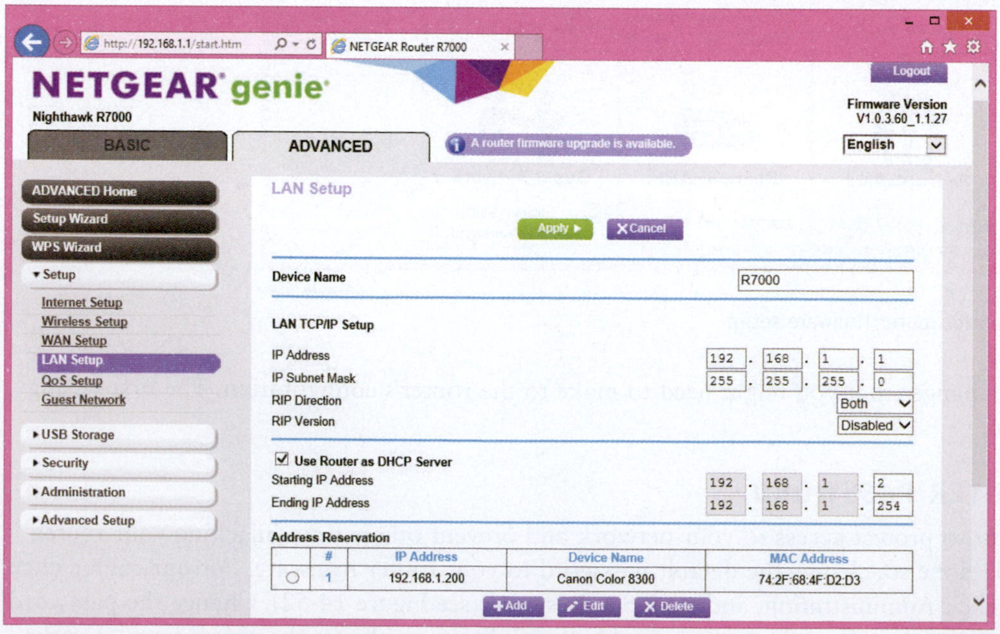

Source: NETGEAR

Figure 14-53 Configure the DHCP server in the router firmware

ASSIGN STATIC IP ADDRESSES

A computer or network printer might require a static IP address, which is called address reservation. For example, when a computer is running a web server on the local network, it needs a static IP address so that other computers on the network that need access to this intranet website can find the web server. A network printer also needs a static IP address so computers will always be able to find the printer. Do the following:

1. To identify the computer or printer, you'll need its MAC address. When the client is connected to the network, on the ADVANCED tab, click **Attached Devices** in the Administration group (see Figure 14-54). Copy the MAC address (select it and press **CTRL+C**) or write it down.

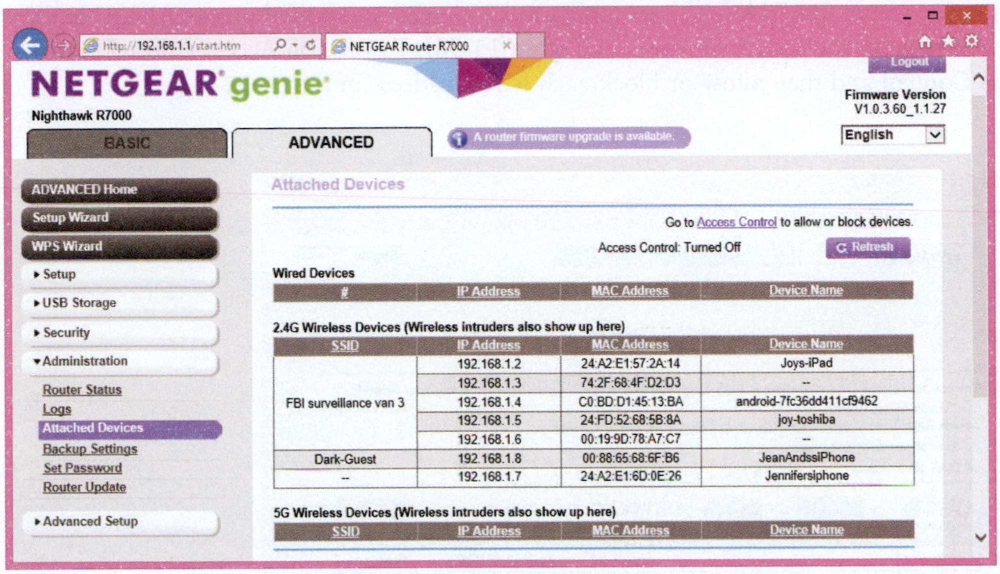

Source: NETGEAR

Figure 14-54 View the MAC addresses of devices connected to the network

2. To assign a static IP address to the client, on the LAN Setup page shown in Figure 14-53, click **Add** under **Address Reservation**. In the IP address field, enter the IP address to assign to the computer or printer. Be sure to use an IP address in the LAN's subnet, such as 192.168.1.200 in our example. Select the MAC address from the list of attached devices or copy or type the MAC address in the field. Click **Apply** to save your changes. In Figure 14-55, a Canon network printer is set to receive the IP address 192.168.1.200 each time it connects to the network.

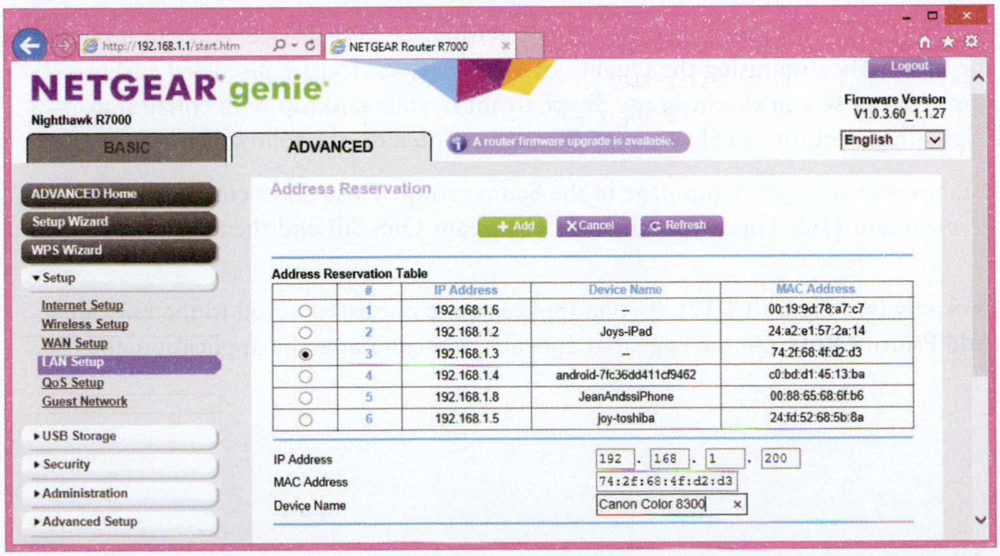

Source: NETGEAR

Figure 14-55 Use address reservation to assign a static IP address to a computer or other device

14

Notes If you are running a web server on the Internet, you will need a public IP address for your router and a static private IP address for the web server. For this situation, you can lease a public IP address from your ISP at an additional cost. You will also need to enable port forwarding to the server, which is discussed later in this chapter.

MAC ADDRESS FILTERING

MAC address filtering allows you to control access to your network to only certain computers or devices. If a MAC address is not entered in a table of MAC addresses, the computer is not allowed to connect to the network. For our sample router, the MAC address table can be viewed and edited on the ADVANCED tab on the Access Control page in the Security group (see Figure 14-56). To turn on Access Control, check the box **Turn on Access Control** and then allow or block each MAC address in the table.

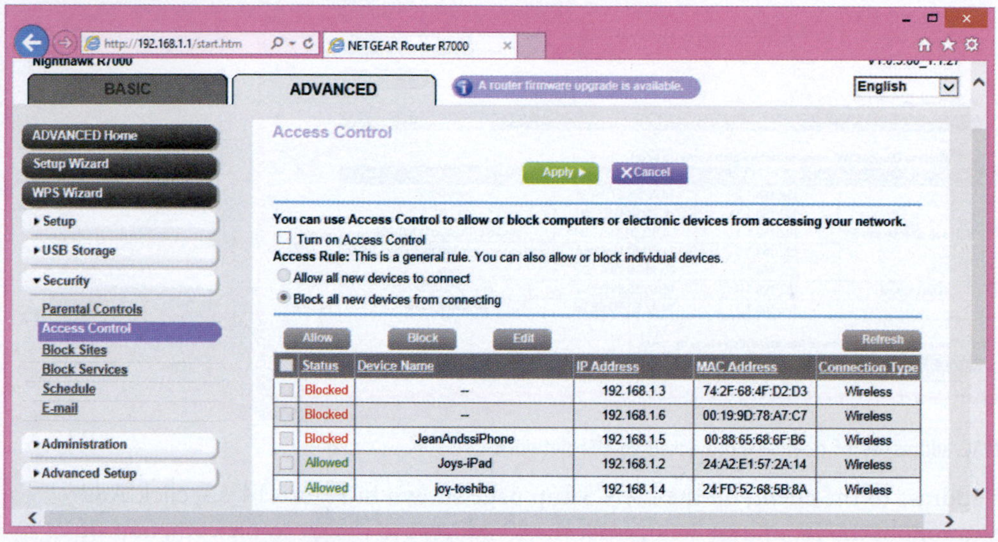

Source: NETGEAR

Figure 14-56 Use MAC address filtering to allow and block devices on the network

IMPROVE QoS FOR AN APPLICATION

As you use your network and notice that one application is not getting the best service, you can improve network performance for this application using the Quality of Service (QoS) feature discussed earlier in this chapter. For example, suppose you routinely use Skype to share your desktop with collaborators over the Internet. To assign a high priority to Skype for our sample router, do the following:

1. On the ADVANCED tab, select the **QoS Setup** page in the Setup group. This router configures both upstream QoS and downstream QoS. For Skype, click the **Upstream QoS** tab and then click **Setup QoS rule.**

2. Select **Skype** and click **Apply** (see Figure 14-57). If your application is not listed, scroll to the bottom of the list and click **Add Priority Rule.** On the page that appears, you can name the application and the port(s) it uses.

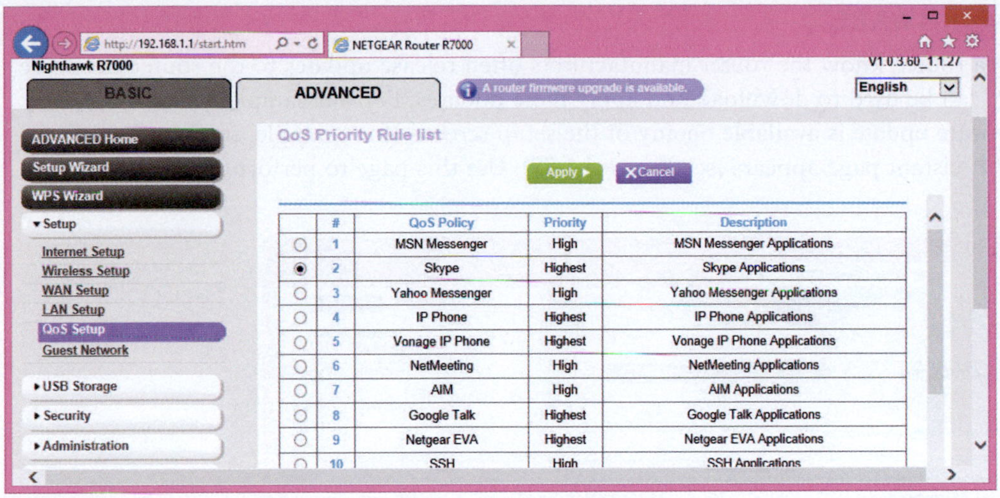

Source: NETGEAR

Figure 14-57 Apply a QoS rule to the selected app

UNIVERSAL PLUG AND PLAY

Universal Plug and Play (UPnP) helps computers on the local network automatically discover and communicate with services provided by other computers on the local network. Enable UPnP if computers on the network use applications, such as messaging, gaming, or Windows Remote Assistance, which run on other local computers and there is a problem establishing communication. Basically, a computer can use the router to advertise its service and automatically communicate with other computers on the network. UPnP is considered a security risk because shields between computers are dropped, which hackers might exploit. Therefore, use UPnP with caution.

For our sample router, UPnP is enabled on the UPnP page in the Advanced Setup group on the ADVANCED tab (see Figure 14-58). Any computers and their ports that are currently using UPnP are listed.

14

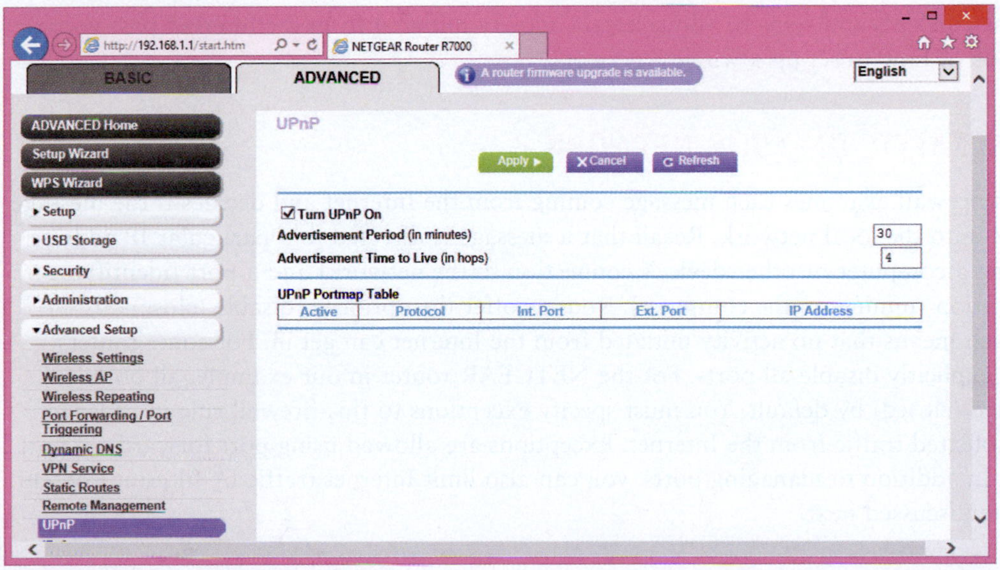

Source: NETGEAR

Figure 14-58 Turn on UPnP

UPDATE ROUTER FIRMWARE

As part of maintaining a router, know the router manufacturers often release updates to the router firmware. The router setup utility can be used to download and apply these updates. For our sample router, when you click **A router firmware update is available** on any of the setup screens (for example, see Figure 14-58), the Firmware Upgrade Assistant page appears (see Figure 14-59). Use this page to perform the upgrade.

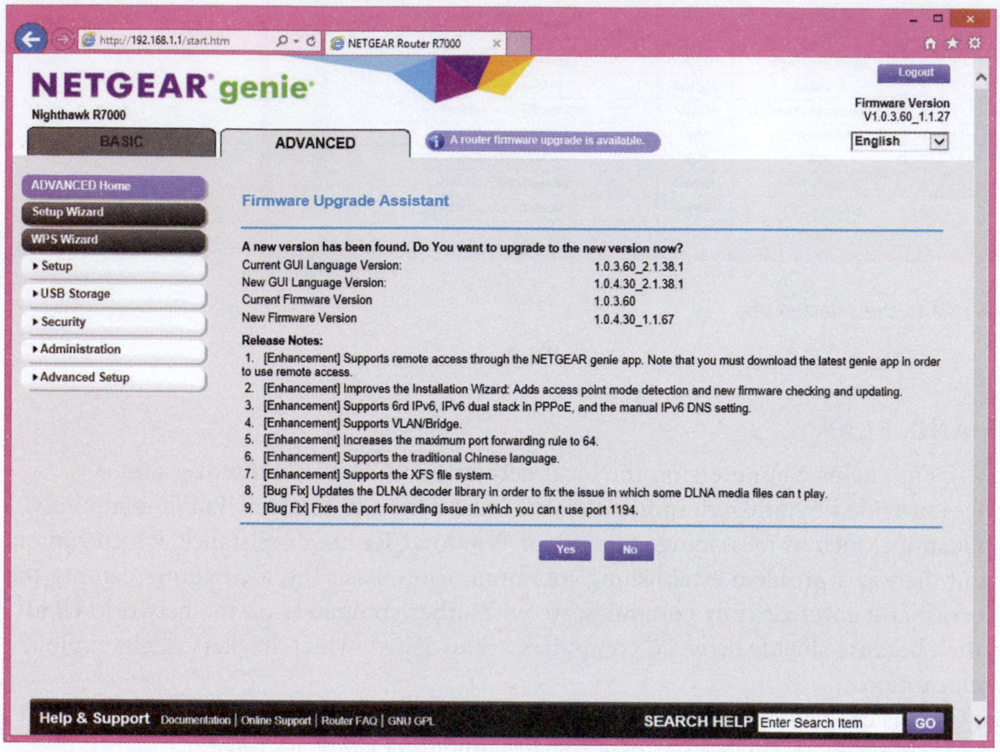

Source: NETGEAR

Figure 14-59 Update router firmware

Now let's look at the concepts and steps to allow certain activity initiated from the Internet past your firewall. Then we'll look at how to set up a wireless network.

LIMIT INTERNET TRAFFIC ON YOUR NETWORK

A+
220-901
2.5, 2.6

A+
220-902
3.2, 3.7

A router's firewall examines each message coming from the Internet and decides if the message is allowed onto the local network. Recall that a message is directed to a particular IP address (identifying a computer or other device's connection to the network) and a port (identifying the application running on the computer). Routers offer the option to disable (close) all ports, which means that no activity initiated from the Internet can get in. For some routers, you must explicitly disable all ports. For the NETGEAR router in our example, all ports are disabled (closed) by default. You must specify exceptions to this firewall rule in order to allow unsolicited traffic from the Internet. Exceptions are allowed using port forwarding, port triggering, or a DMZ. In addition to managing ports, you can also limit Internet traffic by filtering content. All these techniques are discussed next.

★ A+ Exam Tip The A+ 220-901 and 220-902 exams expect you to know how to implement port forwarding, port triggering, and a DMZ.

PORT FORWARDING

Suppose you're hosting an Internet game or website or want to use Remote Desktop to access your home computer from the Internet. In these situations, you need to enable (open) certain ports to certain computers so that activity initiated from the Internet can get past your firewall. This technique, called port forwarding or port mapping, means that when the firewall receives a request for communication from the Internet to the specific computer and port, the request will be allowed and forwarded to that computer on the network. The computer is defined to the router by its static IP address. For example, in Figure 14-60a, port 80 is open and requests to port 80 are forwarded to the web server that is listening at that port. This one computer on the network is the only one allowed to receive requests at port 80.

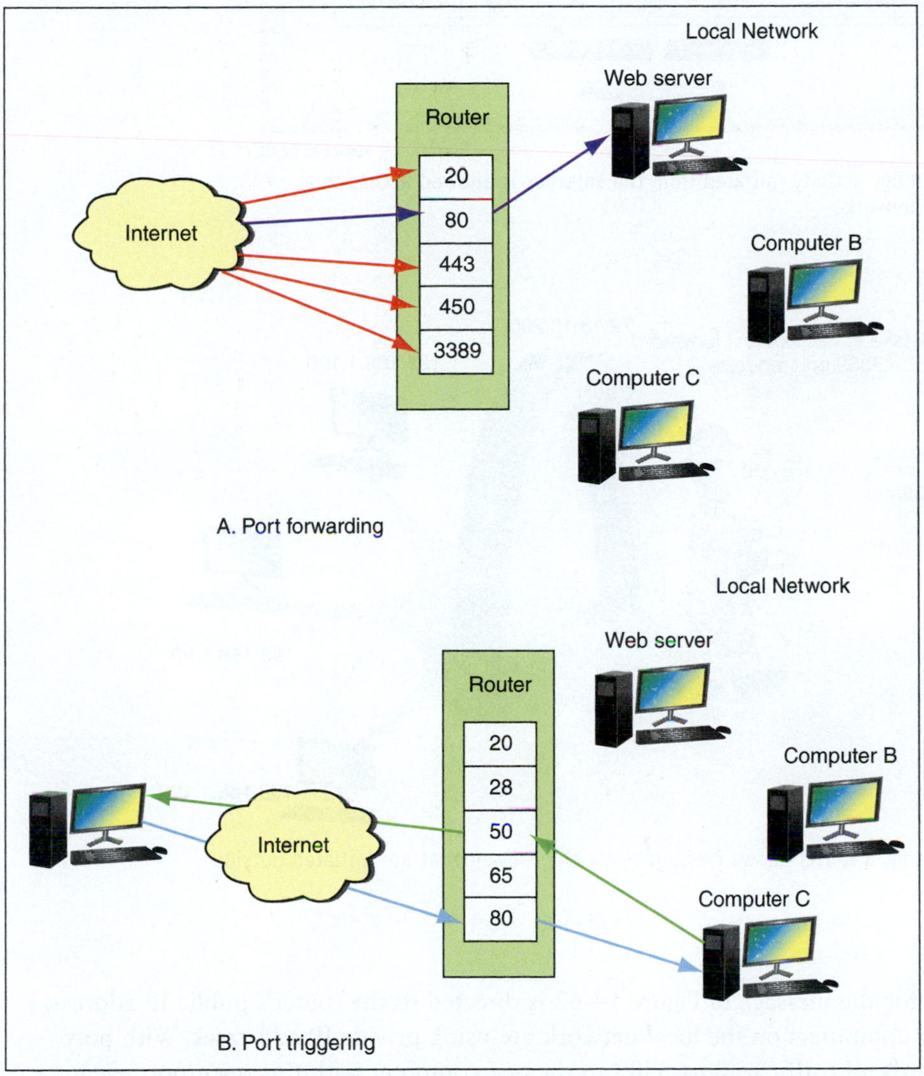

Figure 14-60 Port forwarding and port triggering

To configure port forwarding for our sample router, on the ADVANCED tab, click **Port Forwarding/Port Triggering** in the Advanced Setup group (see Figure 14-61) and verify **Port Forwarding** is selected. Select the **Service Name** and enter the static IP address of the computer providing the service in the Server IP Address field and click **Add.** Notice in the figure that the Remote Desktop application outside the network can use port forwarding to communicate with the computer whose IP address is 192.168.1.90 using port 3389. The situation is illustrated in Figure 14-62. This computer is set to support the Remote Desktop server application. You will learn to use Remote Desktop in the chapter, "Windows Resources on a Network."

14

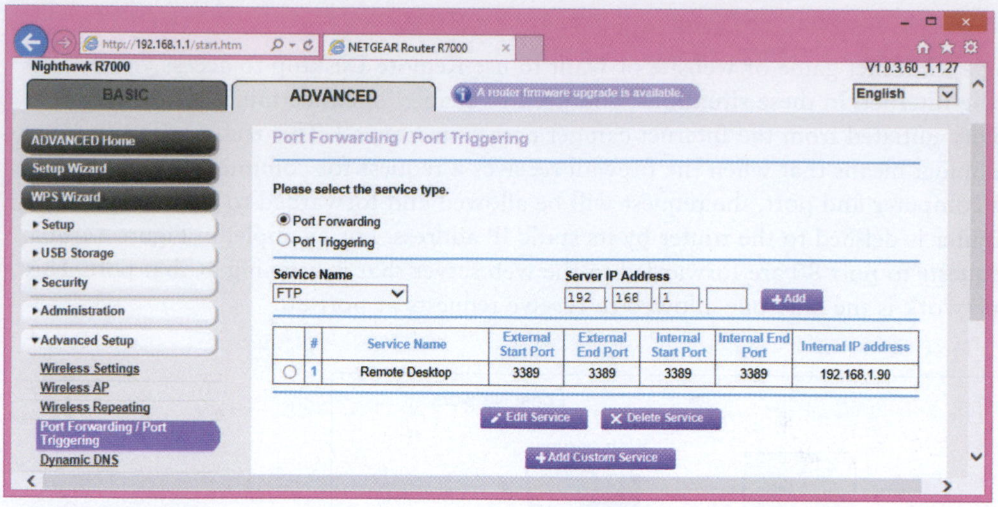

Source: NETGEAR

Figure 14-61 Using port forwarding, activity initiated from the Internet is allowed access to a computer on the network

Figure 14-62 With port forwarding, a router allows messages past the firewall that are initiated outside the network

Also notice the IP address for the message in Figure 14-62 is directed to the router's public IP address. The router is using NAT and computers on the local network are using private IP addresses. With port forwarding, the router forwards all traffic to port 3389 to the one computer with this open port even though traffic is directed to the router's public IP address. For this reason, port forwarding is sometimes called Destination Network Address Translation (DNAT).

Notes By the way, if you want to use a domain name rather than an IP address to access a computer on your network from the Internet, you'll need to purchase the domain name and register it in the Internet name space to associate it with your static IP address assigned by your ISP. Several websites on the Internet let you do both; one site is by Network Solutions at *networksolutions.com*.

PORT TRIGGERING

Port triggering opens a port when a computer on the network initiates communication through another port, and is often used with Internet gaming. For example, in Figure 14-60b, Computer C sends a message to port 50 to a computer on the Internet. The router is configured to open port 80 for communication from this remote computer. Port 80 is closed until this trigger occurs. Port triggering does not require a static IP address for the computer inside the network, and any computer can initiate port triggering. The router will leave port 80 open for a time. If no more data is received from port 50, then it closes port 80.

To configure port triggering on our sample router, select **Port Triggering** on the page shown in Figure 14-61. Click **Add Service**. In the Port Triggering page that appears (see Figure 14-63), type a descriptive name for the service. For Service User, selecting **Any** allows any computer to use the service or you can enter a specific IP address of a remote computer. Select the Service Type (TCP, UDP, or both) and enter the triggering port (the outbound traffic port that will open the inbound ports). Under Inbound Connection, select the Connection Type (TCP, UDP, or both) and the range of ports that will be open for inbound traffic. This information about types of service and ports should be available from the documentation for the application you are using.

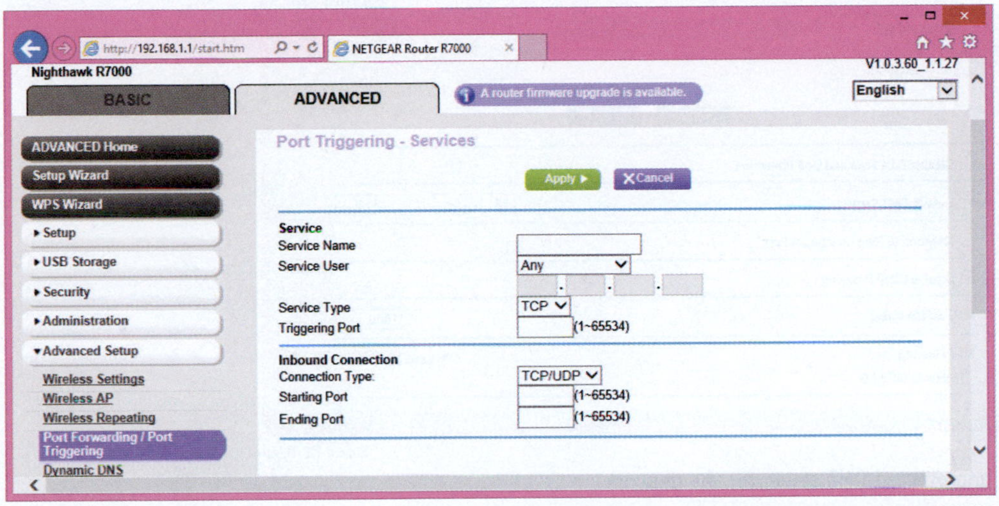

Source: NETGEAR

Figure 14-63 For port triggering, identify the service, the triggering port, and the ports to open

Here are some tips to keep in mind when using port forwarding or port triggering:

- You must lease a static IP address for your router from your ISP so that people on the Internet can find you. Most ISPs will provide you a static IP address for an additional monthly fee.
- For port forwarding to work, the computer on your network must have a static IP address so that the router knows where to send the communication.
- If the computer using port triggering stops sending data, the router might close the triggered port before communication is complete. Also, if two computers on the network attempt to trigger the same port, the router will not allow data to pass to either computer.
- Using port forwarding, your computer and network are more vulnerable because you are allowing external users directly into your private network. For better security, turn on port forwarding only when you know it's being used.

DMZ

A DMZ (demilitarized zone) in networking is a computer or network that is not protected by a firewall or has limited protection. You can drop all your shields protecting a computer by putting it in a DMZ and the firewall no longer protects it. If you are having problems getting port forwarding or port triggering to work, putting a computer in a DMZ can free it to receive any communication from the Internet. All unsolicited traffic from the Internet that the router would normally drop is forwarded to the computer designated as the DMZ server.

Caution If a DMZ computer is compromised, it can be used to attack other computers on the network. Use it only as a last resort when you cannot get port forwarding or port triggering to work. It goes without saying to not leave the DMZ enabled unless you are using it.

To set up a DMZ server for our sample router, on the ADVANCED tab, select **WAN Setup** in the Setup group (see Figure 14-64). Check **Default DMZ Server** and enter the static IP address of the computer.

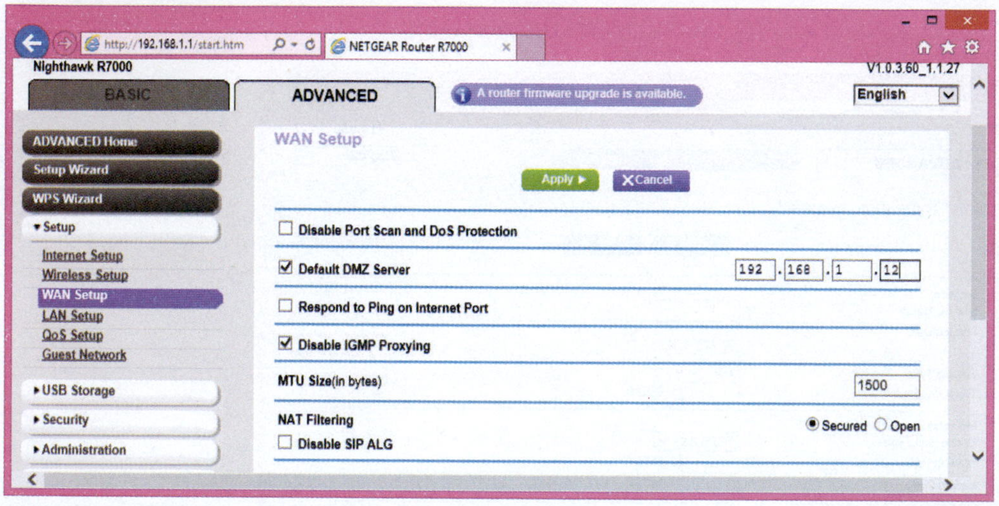

Source: NETGEAR

Figure 14-64 Set up an unprotected DMZ server for the network

CONTENT FILTERING AND PARENTAL CONTROLS

Routers normally provide a way for employers or parents to limit the content that computers on the local network can access on the Internet. Filtering can apply to specific computers, users, websites, categories of websites, keywords, services, time of day, and day of week. Filters can apply to black lists (lists what cannot be accessed) or white lists (lists what can be accessed).

For our sample router, content filtering and parental controls are managed in the Security group on the ADVANCED tab. Here are the options:

- The Parental Controls page provides access to the Live Parental Controls application and website at *www.netgear.com/lpc* where parents can manage content allowed from the Internet and monitor websites and content accessed.
- The Block Sites page (see Figure 14-65) allows you to enter keywords or websites to block. Notice you can also specify a trusted IP address of a computer on the network that is allowed access to this content.

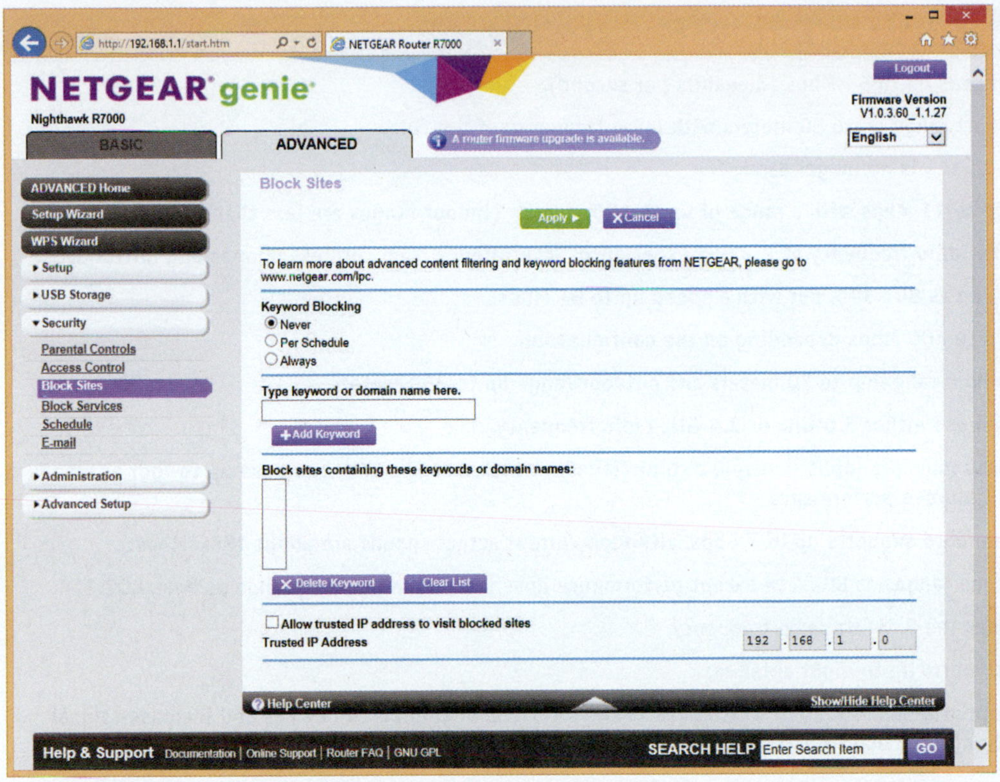

Source: NETGEAR

Figure 14-65 Block sites by keyword or domain names

- The Block Services page can block services on the Internet. For example, you can block Internet gaming services or email services or allow the service based on a schedule. You will need to know the ports these services use. You can also specify the IP addresses of computers to which the block applies.
- The Schedule page allows you to specify the schedule of time and day a blocked service can be used.
- The E-mail page gives you the option for the router to email to you a log of router activities.

Now let's turn our attention to configuring a wireless access point provided by a router.

SET UP A WIRELESS NETWORK

A+ 220-901 2.5, 2.6

A wireless network is created by a wireless access point (WAP). The standards for a local wireless network are called Wi-Fi (Wireless Fidelity), and their technical name is IEEE 802.11. The IEEE 802.11 standards, collectively known as the 802.11 a/b/g/n/ac standards, have evolved over the years and are summarized in Table 14-5.

A+ 220-902 3.2, 3.7

A+ Exam Tip The A+ 220-901 exam expects you to know about 802.11 a/b/g/n/ac standards, their speeds, distances, and frequencies.

Wi-Fi Standard	Speeds, Distances, and Frequencies
IEEE 802.11a	◢ Speeds up to 54 Mbps (megabits per second). ◢ Short range up to 50 meters with radio frequency of 5.0 GHz. ◢ 802.11a is no longer used.
IEEE 802.11b	◢ Up to 11 Mbps with a range of up to 100 meters. (Indoor ranges are less than outdoor ranges.) ◢ The radio frequency of 2.4 GHz experiences interference from cordless phones and microwaves.
IEEE 802.11g	◢ Same as 802.11b, but with a speed up to 54 Mbps.
IEEE 802.11n	◢ Up to 600 Mbps depending on the configuration. ◢ Indoor range up to 70 meters and outdoor range up to 250 meters. ◢ Can use either 5.0-GHz or 2.4-GHz radio frequency. ◢ Uses multiple input/multiple output (MIMO), which means a WAP can have up to four antennas to improve performance.
IEEE 802.11ac	◢ Standard supports up to 7 Gbps, although current actual speeds are about 1300 Mbps. ◢ Same ranges as 802.11n except performance does not weaken at long range as does 802.11n. ◢ Uses the 5.0-GHz radio frequency. ◢ Supports up to eight antennas. ◢ Supports beamforming, which detects the locations of connected devices and increases signal strength in that direction.

Table 14-5 Older and current Wi-Fi standards

Wireless computers and other devices on the wireless LAN (WLAN) must support the latest wireless standard for it to be used. If not, the connection uses the latest standard both the WAP and client support. Figure 14-66 shows a wireless adapter that has two antennas and supports the 802.11n standard. Most new adapters, wireless computers, and mobile devices support 802.11ac and are backward compatible with older standards.

Figure 14-66 Wireless network adapter with two antennas supports 802.11b/g/n Wi-Fi standards

Now let's look at the various features and settings of a wireless access point and how to configure them.

Notes When configuring your wireless access point, it's important you are connected to the router by way of a wired connection. If you change a wireless setting and you are connected wirelessly, your wireless connection will immediately be dropped and you cannot continue configuring the router until you connect again.

SECURITY KEY

The most common and effective method of securing a wireless network is to require a security key before a client can connect to the network. By default, a network that uses a security key encrypts data on the network. Use the router firmware to set the security key. For best security, enter a security key that is different from the password you use to the router utility.

Notes To make the strongest passphrase or security key, use a random group of numbers, uppercase and lowercase letters, and, if allowed, at least one symbol. Also use at least eight characters in the passphrase.

For our sample router, the security key can be set on the ADVANCED tab, Wireless Setup page in the Setup group (see Figure 14-67) and is called the Password or Network Key. Click **Apply** to save your changes.

Source: NETGEAR

Figure 14-67 Configure the router's wireless access point

SET ENCRYPTION

When you set a security key, routers by default encrypt wireless transmissions, and you can change the encryption protocols used or disable encryption. (Encrypting transmissions slows down the network; disabling encryption can improve performance and might be appropriate when you are not concerned about transmissions being hacked.) The three main protocols for encryption for 802.11 wireless networks are:

- *WEP.* WEP (Wired Equivalent Privacy) is no longer considered secure because the key used for encryption is static (it doesn't change).
- *WPA.* WPA (Wi-Fi Protected Access), also called TKIP (Temporal Key Integrity Protocol) encryption, is stronger than WEP and was designed to replace it. With WPA encryption, encryption keys are constantly changing.
- *WPA2.* WPA2 (Wi-Fi Protected Access 2), also called the 802.11i standard, is the latest and best wireless encryption standard. It is based on the AES (Advanced Encryption Standard), which improved on the way TKIP generated encryption keys. All wireless devices sold today support the WPA2 standard.

To configure encryption for our sample router, first, notice in Figure 14-67 that this router supports two wireless frequencies: 2.4 GHz used by 802.11 b/g/n standards and 5 GHz used by 802.11 a/n/ac. The security key applies to either band, but each band can have its own encryption type. For the best security, set both bands to **WPA-PSK [TKIP] + WPA2-PSK [AES]** encryption. This setting means a wireless connection will use WPA2 encryption unless an older device does not support it, in which case the connection reverts to WPA encryption. Click **Apply** to save your changes.

CHANGE THE DEFAULT SSID AND DISABLE SSID BROADCASTING

The Service Set Identifier (SSID) is the name of a wireless network. When you look at Figure 14-67, you can see that each frequency band has its own SSID and you can change that name. Each band is its own wireless network, which the access point (router) connects to the local wired network. When you give each band its own SSID and connect a wireless computer to your network, you can select the band by selecting the appropriate SSID. If your computer supports 802.11ac, you would want to select the SSID for the 5-GHz band in order to get the faster speeds of the 802.11ac standard. If you selected the SSID for the 2.4-GHz band, the connection would revert to the slower 802.11n standard.

Notes Notice in Figure 14-67 the option to select the mode a wireless network will use, which determines the speed of the wireless network. Recall the 802.11ac standard currently supports the speed of 1300 Mbps. If you select a slower mode for the 5-GHz band, such as 600 Mbps, in effect you are preventing the 802.11ac standard from being used on the network and connections will revert to the 802.11n standard that uses the 600-Mbps speed. For best results, use the fastest mode the band supports.

Also notice in Figure 14-67 the option to Enable SSID Broadcast. When you disable SSID broadcasting, the wireless network will appear as Unnamed or Unknown Network. When a client selects this network, you are given the opportunity to enter the SSID. If you don't enter the name correctly, you will not be able to connect. This security method is not considered strong security because software can be used to discover an SSID that is not broadcasted.

SELECT CHANNELS FOR THE WLAN

A channel is a specific radio frequency within a broader frequency. For example, two channels in the 5-GHz band are 5.180-GHz and 5.200-GHz channels. In the United States, eleven channels are available for wireless communication in the 5-GHz or 2.4-GHz bands. In North America, the 5-GHz band uses channels 36, 40, 44, and 48, and the 2.4-GHz band uses channels 1 through 14 (preferred nonoverlapping channels are 1, 6, and 11). For most networks, you can allow auto channel selection so that any channel in the frequency range (5-GHz or 2.4-GHz) will work. The device scans for the least-busy channel. However, if you are trying to solve a problem with interference from a nearby wireless network, you can set each network to a different channel and make the channels far apart to reduce interference. For example, for the 2.4-GHz band, set the network on one WAP to channel 1 and set the other WAP's network to channel 11.

RADIO POWER LEVELS

Some high-end access points allow you to adjust the radio power levels the wireless network can use. To reduce interference, limit the range of the network, or to save on electricity, reduce the power level.

WI-FI PROTECTED SETUP (WPS)

You also need to know about Wi-Fi Protected Setup (WPS), which is designed to make it easier for users to connect their computers to a wireless network when a hard-to-remember SSID and security key are used. WPS generates the SSID and security key using a random string of hard-to-guess letters and numbers. The SSID is not broadcasted, so both the SSID and security key must be entered to connect. Rather than having to enter these difficult strings, a user presses a button on a wireless computer or on the router or enters an eight-digit PIN assigned to the router (see Figure 14-68). All computers on the wireless network must support WPS for it to be used, and you must enable WPS on the router, as shown in the figure.

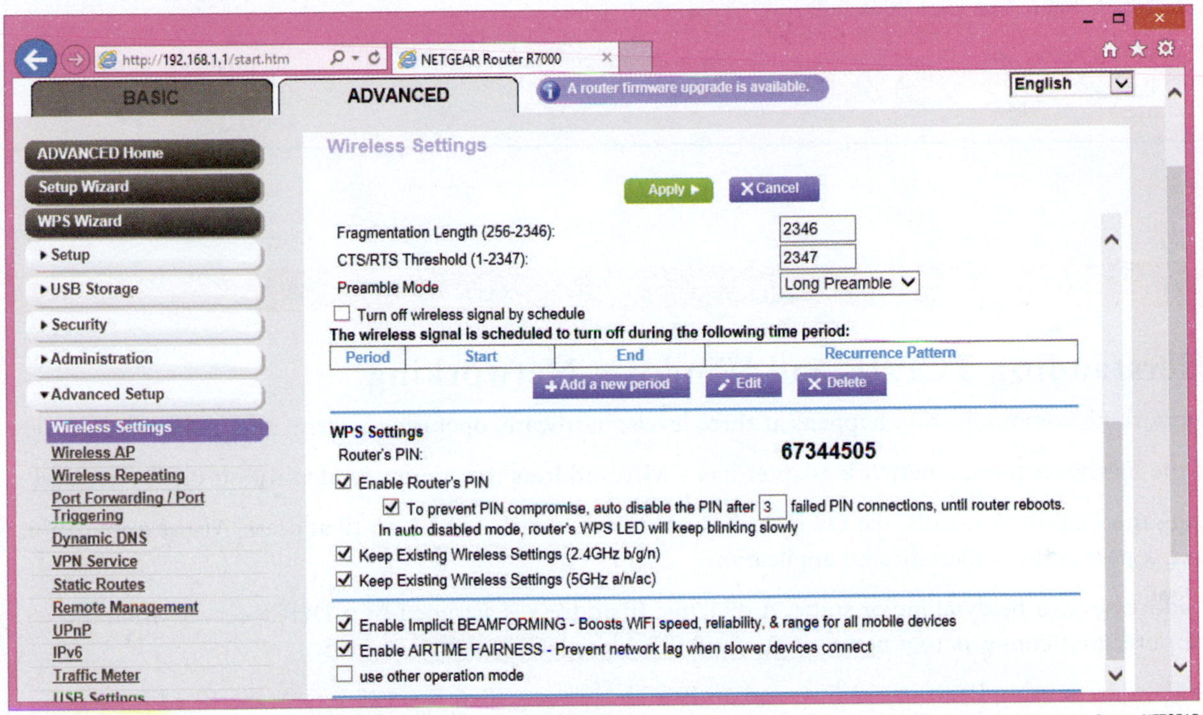

Source: NETGEAR

Figure 14-68 Enable WPS and decide how the router's PIN is used

WPS might be a security risk if it's not managed well. To improve WPS security, turn on auto disable so that WPS will disable after a few failed PIN entries. If routers don't have the auto disable feature, don't use WPS because an eight-digit PIN is easy to hack with repeated attempts. In addition, if the router has a WPS button to push, don't use WPS unless the router is in a secured physical location. For improved security, turn on WPS only when you are working with a user to connect to the wireless network and then turn it off.

> **★ A+ Exam Tip** The A+ 220-901 exam expects you to know about installing and configuring a wireless network, including Wi-Fi 802.11 standards, speeds, distances, and frequencies, Wi-Fi channels (1–11), and WEP, WPA, WPA2, TKIP, and AES encryption.

> **★ A+ Exam Tip** The A+ 220-902 exam expects you to know about installing and configuring a wireless network, including setting encryption, changing the default SSID and password, disabling SSID broadcasting, antenna and access point placements, radio power levels, and WPS.

Hands-On | Project 14-4 Research a Wireless LAN

A+
220-901
2.5, 2.6

A+
220-902
3.2, 3.7

Suppose you have a DSL connection to the Internet in your home and you want to connect two laptops and a desktop computer in a wireless network to the Internet. You need to purchase a multifunction wireless router like the one you learned to configure in this chapter. You also need a wireless adapter for the desktop computer. (The two laptops have built-in wireless networking.) Use the web to research the equipment needed to create the wireless LAN and answer the following:

1. Save or print two webpages showing two different multifunctional wireless routers. What are the brand, model, and price of each router?
2. Save or print two webpages showing two different wireless adapters a desktop computer can use to connect to the wireless network. Include one external device that uses a USB port and one internal device. What are the brand, model, and price of each device?
3. Which router and wireless adapter would you select for your home network? What is the total cost of both devices?

>> CHAPTER SUMMARY

Understanding TCP/IP and Windows Networking

- Networking communication happens at three levels: hardware, operating system, and application levels.
- At the hardware level, a network adapter has a MAC address that uniquely identifies it on the network.
- Using the TCP/IP protocols, the OS identifies a network connection by an IP address. At the application level, a port address identifies an application.
- IP addresses can be dynamic or static. A dynamic IP address is assigned by a DHCP server when the computer first connects to a network. A static IP address is manually assigned.
- An IP address using IPv4 has 32 bits, and an IP address using IPv6 has 128 bits. Some IP addresses are private IP addresses that can be used only on intranets.
- Using IPv4, a subnet mask determines the number of left most bits in an IP address that identify the local network. The remaining right most bits identify the host.
- Using IPv6, three types of IP addresses are a unicast address (used by a single node on a network), multicast address (used for one-to-many transmissions), and anycast address (used by routers).
- Types of unicast addresses are a global address (used on the Internet), a link-local address (used on a private network), and a unique local address (used on subnets in a large enterprise).
- A computer can be assigned a computer name (also called a host name), and a network can be assigned a domain name. A fully qualified domain name (FQDN) includes the computer name and the domain name. An FQDN can be used to find a computer on the Internet if this name is associated with an IP address kept by DNS servers.
- TCP/IP uses protocols at the application level (such as FTP, HTTP, and Telnet) and at the operating system level (such as TCP and UDP).

Connecting a Computer to a Network

- An IT support person needs to know how to configure TCP/IP settings and make a wired or wireless connection to an existing network.
- To connect to a wireless WAN or cellular network, you need a mobile broadband modem and a subscription to the cellular network. For some carriers, a SIM card is also required.
- A dial-up connection uses a telephone modem to make a connection to an ISP.

Setting Up a Multifunction Router for a SOHO Network

- A multifunction router for a small office/home office network might serve several functions, including a router, a switch, a DHCP server, a wireless access point, a firewall using NAT, and an FTP server.
- It's extremely important to change the password to configure your router as soon as you install it, especially if the router is also a wireless access point.
- To allow certain network traffic initiated on the Internet past your firewall, you can use port forwarding, port triggering, and a DMZ.
- To secure a wireless access point, you can require a security key, disable SSID broadcasting, and enable encryption (WPA2, WPA, or WEP). As with wired networks, you can also enable MAC address filtering.

>> KEY TERMS

For explanations of key terms, see the Glossary for this text.

802.11 a/b/g/n/ac
adapter address
address reservation
AES (Advanced Encryption Standard)
AFP (Apple Filing Protocol)
anycast address
AppleTalk
Automatic Private IP Address (APIPA)
beamforming
best-effort protocol
CDMA (Code Division Multiple Access)
channel
CIDR notation
CIFS (Common Internet File System)
client/server
computer name
connectionless protocol
connection-oriented protocol
default gateway
Destination Network Address Translation (DNAT)
DHCP (Dynamic Host Configuration Protocol)
DHCP client
DHCPv6 server
DMZ (demilitarized zone)
DNS (Domain Name System or Domain Name Service)
DNS client
DNS server
domain name
dynamic IP address
firewall
FTP (File Transfer Protocol)
FTP server
full duplex
fully qualified domain name (FQDN)
gateway
global address
global unicast address
GSM (Global System for Mobile Communications)
half duplex
hardware address
host name
HTTP (Hypertext Transfer Protocol)
HTTPS (HTTP secure)
IEEE 802.11ac
IEEE 802.11n
IMAP4 (Internet Message Access Protocol, version 4)
interface
interface ID
Internet Protocol version 4 (IPv4)
Internet Protocol version 6 (IPv6)
intranet
IP address
ipconfig
ISATAP
Lightweight Directory Access Protocol (LDAP)
link (local link)
link-local address
link-local unicast address
local area network (LAN)
Long Term Evolution (LTE)
loopback address
MAC (Media Access Control) address
MAC address filtering
multicast address
multiple input/multiple output (MIMO)
name resolution
NAT (Network Address Translation)
neighbors
NetBIOS
NetBIOS over TCP/IP
network adapter
network interface card (NIC)
node
octet
onboard NIC
OSI model
physical address
POP3 (Post Office Protocol, version 3)
port
port address
port forwarding
port mapping
port number
port triggering
private IP address
protocol
public IP address
Quality of Service (QoS)
Remote Desktop Protocol (RDP)
RJ-45
router

Secure FTP (SFTP)
Secure Shell (SSH)
Server Message Block (SMB)
Service Set Identifier (SSID)
SIM (Subscriber Identification Module) card
Simple Network Management Protocol (SNMP)
SMB2
SMTP (Simple Mail Transfer Protocol)
socket
static IP address
subnet
subnet ID
subnet mask
switch
TCP (Transmission Control Protocol)
TCP/IP (Transmission Control Protocol/Internet Protocol)
Telnet
Teredo
TKIP (Temporal Key Integrity Protocol)
UDP (User Datagram Protocol)
unicast address
unique local address
Universal Plug and Play (UPnP)
virtual private network (VPN)
Voice over LTE (VoLTE)
Wake-on-LAN
WEP (Wired Equivalent Privacy)
Wi-Fi (Wireless Fidelity)
Wi-Fi Protected Setup (WPS)
wireless access point (WAP)
wireless LAN (WLAN)
wireless wide area network (WWAN)
WPA (Wi-Fi Protected Access)
WPA2 (Wi-Fi Protected Access 2)

>> REVIEWING THE BASICS

1. How many bits are in a MAC address?
2. How many bits are in an IPv4 address? In an IPv6 address?
3. How does a client application identify a server application on another computer on the network?
4. What are IP addresses called that begin with 10, 172.16, or 192.168?
5. Describe the difference between public and private IPv4 addresses. If a network is using private IP addresses, how can the computers on that network access the Internet?
6. Why is it unlikely that you will find the IP address 192.168.250.10 on the Internet?
7. If no DHCP server is available when a computer configured for dynamic IP addressing connects to the network, what type of IPv4 address is assigned to the computer?
8. If a computer is found to have an IP address of 169.254.1.1, what can you assume about how it received that IP address?
9. What are the last 64 bits of an IPv6 address called? How are these bits used?
10. Name two tunneling protocols that are used for IPv6 packets to travel over an IPv4 network.
11. How is an IPv6 address used that begins with 2000::? That begins with FE80::?
12. How many bits are in the Subnet ID block? What are the values of these bits for a link-local IP address?
13. Which type of IPv6 address is used to create multiple subnets within a large organization?
14. What type of server serves up IP addresses to computers on a network?
15. Which TCP/IP protocol that manages packet delivery guarantees that delivery? Which protocol does not guarantee delivery, but is faster?
16. At what port does an SMTP email server listen to receive email from a client computer?
17. Which protocol(s) does a web server use when transmissions are encrypted for security?
18. What type of server resolves fully qualified domain names to IP addresses?

19. Which email protocol allows a client application to manage email stored on an email server?
20. What technology is used to present a public IP address to computers outside the LAN to handle requests to use the Internet from computers inside the LAN?
21. Which protocol is used when an application queries a database on a corporate network such as a database of printers?
22. What type of encryption protocol does Secure FTP (SFTP) use to secure FTP transmissions?
23. What two Windows applications use the RDP protocol and port 3389?
24. Which two versions of the 802.11 technologies can use multiple antennas at both the access point and the network adapter?
25. Which wireless encryption standard is stronger, WEP or WPA?
26. When securing a Wi-Fi wireless network, which is considered better security: to filter MAC addresses, use encryption, or not broadcast the SSID?
27. Would you expect WPS to be used when a wireless network is using strong security, weak security, or no security (as in a public hotspot)?

>> THINKING CRITICALLY

1. You have just installed a network adapter and have booted up the system, installing the drivers. You open File Explorer on a remote computer and don't see the computer on which you just installed the NIC. What is the first thing you check?
   a. Has TCP/IPv6 been enabled?
   b. Is the computer using dynamic or static IP addressing?
   c. Are the lights on the adapter functioning correctly?
   d. Has the computer been assigned a computer name?
2. Your boss asks you to transmit a small file that includes sensitive personnel data to a server on the network. The server is running a Telnet server and an FTP server. Why is it not a good idea to use Telnet to reach the remote computer?
   a. Telnet transmissions are not encrypted.
   b. Telnet is not reliable and the file might arrive corrupted.
   c. FTP is faster than Telnet.
   d. FTP running on the same computer as Telnet causes Telnet to not work.
3. You have just installed a SOHO router in a customer's home and the owner has called you saying his son is complaining that Internet gaming is too slow. His son is using a wireless connection to the network. Which possibilities should you consider in order to speed up the son's gaming experience? Select all that apply.
   a. Verify the wireless connection is using the fastest wireless standard the router supports.
   b. Disable encryption on the wireless network to speed up transmissions.
   c. Suggest the son use a wired Gigabit Ethernet connection to the network.
   d. Enable QoS for the gaming applications on the router and on the son's computer.

>> REAL PROBLEMS, REAL SOLUTIONS

REAL PROBLEM 14-1 Setting Up a Small Network

The simplest possible wired network is two computers connected together using a crossover cable. In a crossover cable, the send and receive wires are crossed so that one computer can send and the other computer receive on the same wire. At first glance, a crossover cable looks just like a regular network cable (also called a patch cable) except for the labeling (see Figure 14-69). (In the chapter, "Supporting Network Hardware," you learn how to distinguish between the cables by examining their connectors.)

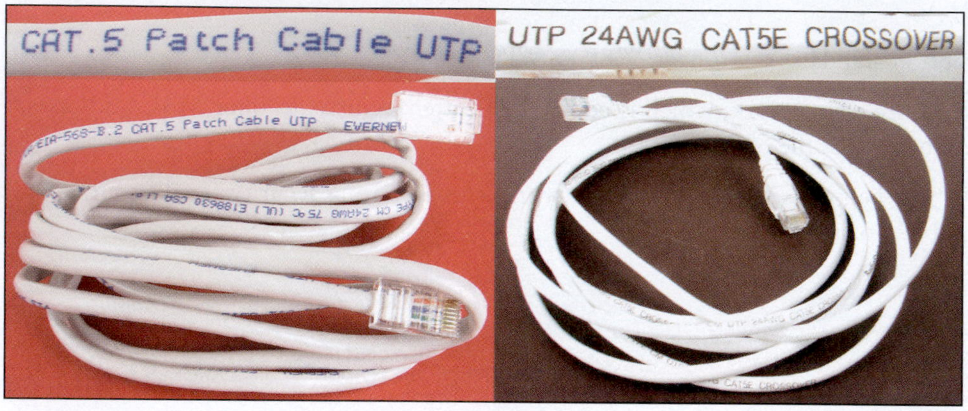

Figure 14-69 A patch cable and crossover cable look the same but are labeled differently

Do the following to set up and test the network:

1. Connect two computers using a crossover cable. Using the Network and Sharing Center, verify your network is up. What is the IPv4 address of Computer A? Of Computer B?
2. Join the two computers to the same homegroup. Then use File Explorer or Windows Explorer to view the files on the other computer shared with the homegroup.
3. Convert the TCP/IP configuration to static IP addressing. Assign a private IP address to each computer. Make sure the two computers are in the same subnet. What is the subnet mask? What is the IP address of Computer A? Of Computer B?
4. Verify you can still see files shared with the homegroup on each computer.
5. Assign a new IP address to each computer so they are not in the same subnet. What are the two IP addresses? Can you still see files shared with the homegroup on each computer?
6. Return the computers to the same subnet and verify each computer can find the other and its shared resources.

REAL PROBLEM 14-2 Using the Hosts File

The hosts file in the C:\Windows\System32\drivers\etc folder has no file extension and contains computer names and their associated IP addresses on the local network. An IT support technician can manually edit the hosts file when the association is needed for address resolution on the local network and a DNS server is not available on the local network.

> **Notes** For an entry in the hosts file to work, the remote computer must always use the same IP address. One way to accomplish this is to assign a static IP address to the computer. Alternately, if your DHCP server supports this feature, you can configure it to assign the same IP address to this computer each time it connects to the network.

Using your small network you set up in Real Problem 14-1, do the following to use the hosts file:

1. The ping command sends a request to a remote computer and the computer responds to verify communication. On Computer A, open a command prompt window and ping Computer B using its IP address. For example, if the IP address is 192.168.10.10, use this command: ping 192.168.10.10.
2. Try to ping Computer B, this time using its computer name. Did the ping work?
3. Use Notepad to edit the hosts file on Computer A and add the entry that associates the IP address of Computer B with its computer name.
4. Try to ping Computer B, this time using its computer name rather than IP address. Did the ping work?

CHAPTER 15

Supporting Network Hardware

After completing this chapter, you will be able to:

- Describe network types and the Internet connections they use
- Identify, compare, and contrast hardware used to build local networks
- Set up and troubleshoot the wiring in a small network

In the chapter, "Connecting To and Setting Up a Network," you learned how to connect a computer to a network and how to set up and secure a wired and wireless router for a small network. This chapter takes you one step further in supporting networks. You learn about the types of networks and the technologies used to build these networks. You also learn about the hardware devices, cables, and connectors used to construct a network. Finally, you learn about networking tools, how to terminate network cables, and how to troubleshoot problems with network hardware.

TYPES OF NETWORKS AND THE INTERNET CONNECTIONS THEY USE

A+
220-901
2.1, 2.2,
2.7

A computer network is created when two or more computers can communicate with each other. Networks can be categorized by several methods, including the technology used and the size of the network. When networks are categorized by size or physical area they cover, these are the categories used:

- *PAN.* A PAN (personal area network) consists of personal devices communicating at close range such as a cell phone and laptop computer. PANs can use wired connections (such as USB or FireWire) or wireless connections (such as Bluetooth or Infrared).
- *LAN.* A LAN (local area network) covers a small local area, such as a home, office, other building, or small group of buildings. LANs can use wired (most likely Ethernet) or wireless (most likely Wi-Fi, also called 802.11) technologies. A LAN is used for workstations, servers, printers, and other devices to communicate and share resources.
- *Wireless LAN.* A wireless LAN (WLAN) covers a limited geographical area, and is used in businesses, homes, restaurants, public parks, airports, schools, and many other places where network cabling is inconvenient to install or use.
- *MAN.* A MAN (metropolitan area network) covers a large campus or city. (A small MAN is sometimes called a CAN or campus area network.) Network technologies used can be wireless (most likely LTE) and/or wired (for example, Ethernet with fiber-optic cabling).
- *WAN.* A WAN (wide area network) covers a large geographical area and is made up of many smaller networks. The best-known WAN is the Internet. Some technologies used to connect a single computer or LAN to the Internet include DSL, cable Internet, satellite, cellular WAN, and fiber optic.

A+ Exam Tip The A+ 220-901 exam expects you to know about a LAN, WAN, PAN, and MAN.

Now let's look at network technologies used for Internet connections.

NETWORK TECHNOLOGIES USED FOR INTERNET CONNECTIONS

A+
220-901
2.1, 2.2,
2.7

To connect to the Internet, a network first connects to an Internet service provider (ISP), such as Earthlink or Comcast. The most common types of connections are DSL and cable Internet (commonly called cable or cable modem). See Figure 15-1. When connecting to an ISP, know that upload speeds are generally slower than download speeds. These rates differ because users generally download more data than they upload. Therefore, an ISP devotes more of the available bandwidth to downloading and less of it to uploading.

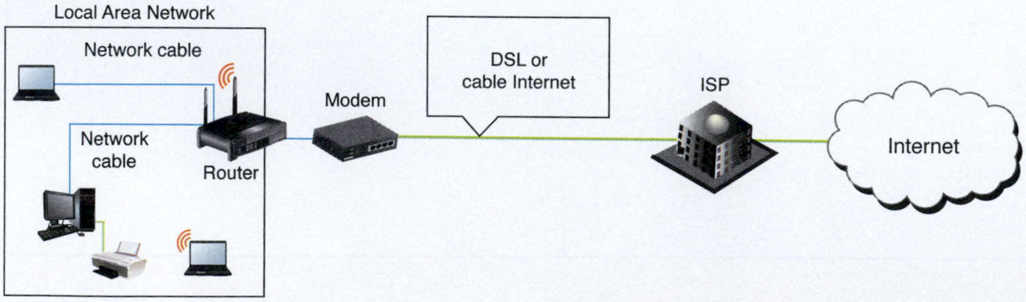

Figure 15-1 An ISP stands between a LAN and the Internet

Networks are built using one or more technologies that provide varying degrees of bandwidth. Bandwidth (the width of the band) is the theoretical number of bits that can be transmitted over a network at one time, similar to the number of lanes on a highway. In practice, however, the networking industry refers to bandwidth as a measure of the maximum rate of data transmission in bits per second (bps), thousands of bits per second (Kbps), millions of bits per second (Mbps), or billions of bits per second (Gbps). Bandwidth is the theoretical or potential speed of a network, whereas data throughput is the average of the actual speed. In practice, network transmissions experience delays, called latency, that result in slower network performance. For example, too many splitters can cause signal strength degradation, resulting in latency. Latency is measured by the round-trip time it takes for a data packet to travel from source to destination and back to source.

Table 15-1 lists network technologies used by local networks to connect to the Internet. The table is more or less ordered from slowest to fastest maximum bandwidth within each category, although latency can affect the actual bandwidth of a particular network.

Technology (Wireless or Wired)	Maximum Speed	Common Uses
Wireless Internet connection: Cellular		
2G cellular (second-generation cellular)	Up to 50 Kbps	Uses the mobile phone service on a cellular network for voice and data (digital) transmissions. Most 2G networks use an improved version of the GSM mobile phone service, although some use CDMA, which is a competing service.
2G EDGE or 2G E cellular	Up to 384 Kbps	Improved over 2G and uses the GSM mobile phone service. (EDGE stands for Enhanced Data for GSM Evolution.)
3G cellular (third-generation cellular)	At least 200 Kbps, but can be up to 4 Mbps	Improved over 2G EDGE and allows for transmitting data and video. Uses either CDMA or GSM mobile phone services. Speeds vary widely according to the revision standards used.
4G cellular (fourth-generation cellular)	100 Mbps to 1 Gbps	Higher speeds are achieved when the client stays in a fixed position. A 4G network uses either LTE (Long Term Evolution) or WiMAX technology. LTE is more popular and faster.
Wireless Internet connection: Satellite		
Satellite	Up to 15 Mbps	Requires a dish to send and receive from a satellite, which is in a relative fixed position with the Earth.
Wired Internet connection: Telephone		
Dial-up or regular telephone (POTS, for plain old telephone service)	Up to 56 Kbps	Slow access to an ISP using a modem and dial-up connection over phone lines.
ISDN	64 Kbps or 128 Kbps	ISDN (Integrated Services Digital Network) is an outdated business-use access to an ISP over dial-up phone lines.
SDSL (Symmetric Digital Subscriber Line)	Up to 22 Mbps	Equal bandwidth in both directions. SDSL is a type of broadband technology. (Broadband refers to a networking technology that carries more than one type of signal, such as DSL and telephone or cable Internet and TV.) DSL uses regular phone lines and is an always-up or always-on connection that does not require a dial-up.
ADSL (Asymmetric DSL)	640 Kbps upstream and up to 24 Mbps downstream	Most bandwidth is from ISP to user. Slower versions of ADSL are called ADSL Lite or DSL Lite. ISP customers pay according to a bandwidth scale.
VDSL (very-high-bit-rate DSL)	Up to 70 Mbps	A type of asymmetric DSL that works only a short distance.

Table 15-1 Networking technologies (continues)

15

Technology (Wireless or Wired)	Maximum Speed	Common Uses
Other wired Internet connections		
Cable Internet	Up to 160 Mbps, depends on the type of cable	Connects a home or small business to an ISP, and usually comes with a cable television subscription and shares cable TV lines. Fiber-optic cable gives highest speeds.
Dedicated line using fiber optic	Up to 43 Tbps	Dedicated fiber-optic line from ISP to business or home. Speeds widely vary with price.
Wired local network: Ethernet		
Fast Ethernet (100BaseT)	100 Mbps	Used for local networks.
Gigabit Ethernet (1000BaseT)	1000 Mbps or 1 Gbps	Fastest Ethernet standard for a local network.
Wireless local network: Wi-Fi		
Wi-Fi 802.11g wireless	Up to 54 Mbps	Compatible with and has replaced 802.11b.
802.11n wireless	Up to 600 Mbps	Compatible with and has replaced 802.11g.
802.11ac wireless	1.3 Gbps	Latest Wi-Fi technology.

Table 15-1 Networking technologies (continued)

Currently, cable Internet and DSL are the two most popular ways to make an Internet connection. Let's first compare these two technologies and then we'll look at satellite, fiber-optic dedicated lines, and cellular WANs.

★ A+ Exam Tip The A+ 220-901 exam expects you to be able to compare these network types used for Internet connections: cable, dial-up, DSL, fiber, satellite, ISDN, and cellular (mobile hotspot).

COMPARE CABLE INTERNET AND DSL

Here are the important facts about cable Internet and DSL:

- Cable Internet is a broadband technology that uses cable TV lines and is always connected (always up). With cable Internet, the TV signal to your television and the data signals to your computer or LAN share the same coaxial (coax) cable. The cable modem converts a computer's digital signals to analog when sending them and converts incoming analog data to digital.
- DSL (Digital Subscriber Line) is a group of broadband technologies that covers a wide range of speeds. DSL uses ordinary copper phone lines and a range of frequencies on the copper wire that are not used by voice, making it possible for you to use the same phone line for voice and DSL at the same time. When you make a regular phone call, you dial in as usual. However, the DSL part of the line is always connected (always up) for most DSL services.

When deciding between cable Internet and DSL, consider these points:

- Both cable Internet and DSL can sometimes be purchased on a sliding scale, depending on the bandwidth you want to buy. Subscriptions offer residential and the more-expensive business plans. Business plans are likely to have increased bandwidth and better support when problems arise.
- With cable Internet, you share the TV cable infrastructure with your neighbors, which can result in service becoming degraded if many people in your neighborhood are using cable Internet at the same time. I once used cable Internet in a neighborhood where I found I needed to avoid web surfing between 5:00 and 7:00 P.M. when folks were just coming in from work and using the Internet. With DSL, you're using a dedicated phone line, so your neighbors' surfing habits are not important.

- With DSL, static over phone lines in your house can be a problem. The DSL company provides filters to install at each phone jack (see Figure 15-2), but still the problem might not be fully solved. Also, your phone line must qualify for DSL; some lines are too dirty (too much static or noise) to support DSL. Figure 15-3 shows a DSL modem that can connect directly to a computer or to a router.

Figure 15-2 When DSL is used in your home, filters are needed on every phone jack except the one used by the DSL modem

Figure 15-3 This DSL modem connects to a phone jack and a computer or router to provide a broadband connection to an ISP

SATELLITE

People who live in remote areas and want high-speed Internet connections often are limited in their choices. DSL and cable options might not be available where they live, but satellite access is available from pretty much anywhere. Internet access by satellite is available even on airplanes. Passengers can connect to the Internet using a wireless hotspot and satellite dish on the plane. A satellite dish mounted on top of your house or office building communicates with a satellite used by an ISP offering the satellite service (see Figure 15-4). One disadvantage of satellite is that it requires line-of-sight connectivity without obstruction from mountains, trees, and tall buildings. Another disadvantage is that it experiences delays in transmission (called latency), especially when uploading, and is, therefore, not a good solution for an Internet connection that is to be used for videoconferencing or voice over Internet.

15

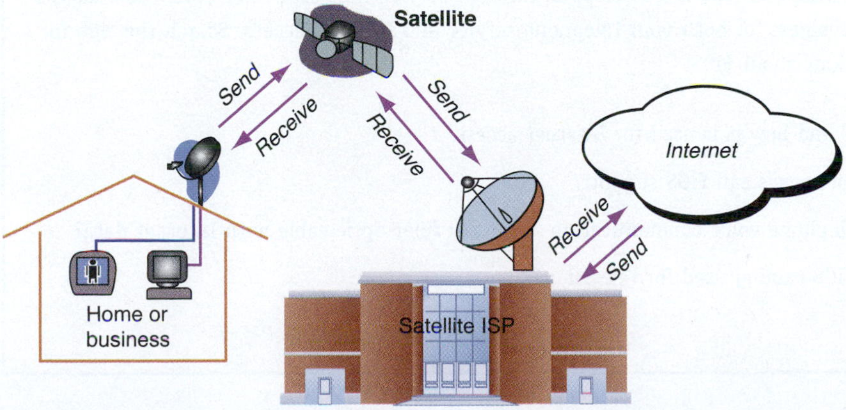

Figure 15-4 Communication by satellite can include television and Internet access

DEDICATED LINE USING FIBER OPTIC

Another broadband technology used for Internet access is fiber optic. The technology uses a dedicated line from your ISP to your place of business or residence. This dedicated line is called a point-to-point (PTP) connection because no other business or residence shares the line with you. Television, Internet data, and voice communication all share the broadband fiber-optic cable. Verizon calls the technology FiOS (Fiber Optic Service), and the fiber-optic cabling is used all the way from the ISP to your home. A provider might provide fiber-optic cabling up to your neighborhood and then use coaxial cable (similar to that used in cable Internet connections) for the last leg of the connection to your business or residence. Upstream and downstream speeds and prices vary.

CELLULAR WAN

A cellular network or cellular WAN consists of cells, and each cell is controlled by a base station (see Figure 15-5). The base station might include more than one transceiver and antenna on the same tower to support multiple technologies (such as LTE and GSM). Cell phones are called that because they use a cellular network.

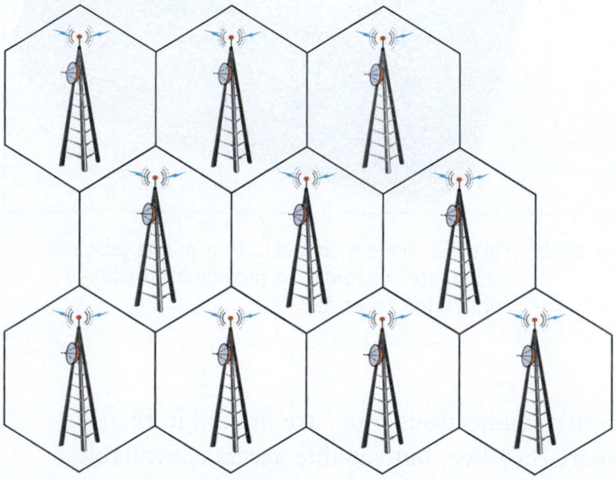

Figure 15-5 A cellular WAN is made up of many cells that provide coverage over a wide area

A laptop or tablet might have an embedded cellular adapter to connect to a cellular network. If not, you can use a USB broadband modem to make the connection, which is sometimes called an air card. Recall from the chapter, "Connecting To and Setting Up a Network," that you can also tether (by cable or Bluetooth) your smart phone or other mobile device to your computer so that the computer can connect to the ISP. Some mobile devices can create a mobile hotspot that computers and other mobile devices can connect by Wi-Fi to your device and on to the Internet.

Hands-On Project 15-1 Investigate Verizon FiOS

A+
220-901
2.1, 2.2, 2.7

Verizon (*verizon.com*) offers FiOS, an alternative to DSL and cable for wired broadband Internet access to a residence or small business. FiOS is a fiber-optic Internet service that uses fiber-optic cable all the way to your house or business for both your telephone service and Internet access. Search the web for answers to these questions about FiOS:

1. Give a brief description of FiOS and how it is used for Internet access.
2. What downstream and upstream speeds can FiOS support?
3. When using FiOS, does your telephone voice communication share the fiber-optic cable with Internet data?
4. What does Verizon say about FiOS cabling used for television?
5. Is FiOS available in your area?

HARDWARE USED BY LOCAL NETWORKS

A+
220-901
1.4, 1.11,
2.1, 2.2,
2.8

In this part of the chapter, you learn about the hardware devices that create and connect to networks. We discuss desktop and laptop devices, hubs, switches, bridges, and other network devices, and the cables and connectors these devices use.

DIAL-UP MODEMS

A+
220-901
1.4, 1.11,
2.1, 2.2

Of all the types of networking connections, dial-up or POTS (plain old telephone service) is the least expensive and slowest connection to the Internet. Dial-up connections are painfully slow, but you might still need them when traveling, and they're good at home when your broadband connection is down or when you just plain want to save money.

Modem cards in desktop computers provide two phone jacks, called RJ-11 jacks, so that one can be used for dial-up networking and the other jack can be used to plug in an extension telephone. Figure 15-6 shows a modem card that comes bundled with drivers on CD and a phone cord. Phone cords are a type of twisted-pair cable and use an RJ-11 connector. Twisted-pair cabling uses pairs of wires twisted together to reduce crosstalk. The RJ-11 jack has four connectors, and a phone cord can have one or two twisted pairs for a total of two or four wires in the cord. The cord carries power on the lines that can be used to power a simple telephone. Laptop computers that have embedded dial-up modem capability generally have only a single phone jack. Dial-up standards are no longer being revised, and the last dial-up modem standard is the V.92 standard.

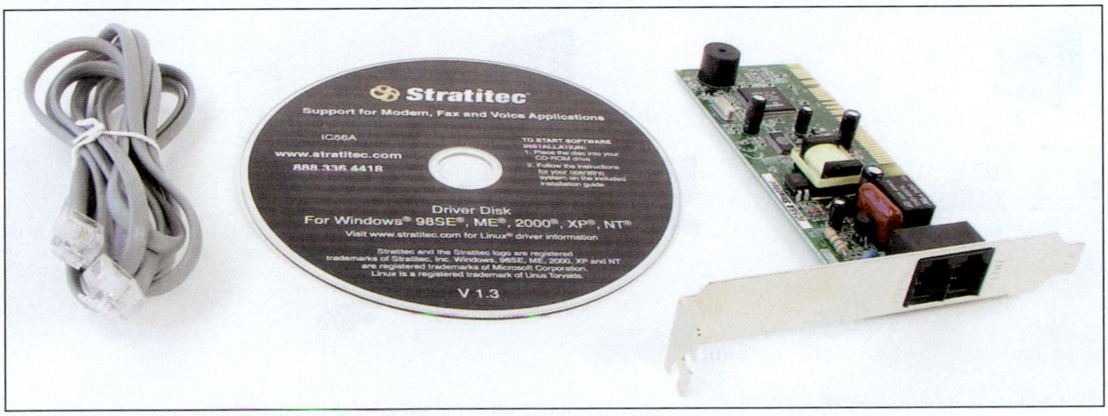

Figure 15-6 This 56K V.92 PCI modem card comes bundled with a phone cord and setup CD

When installing a modem card, be sure to follow manufacturer directions. Most directions say to install the drivers on CD before you physically install the modem. How to configure a modem card and set up a dial-up connection are covered in the chapter, "Connecting To and Setting Up a Network."

SWITCHES AND HUBS

A+
220-901
1.4, 1.11,
2.1, 2.2,
2.8

Today's Ethernet networks use a design called a star bus topology, which means that nodes are connected to one or more centralized devices, which are connected to each other (see Figure 15-7). A centralized device can be a switch or a hub. Each device handles a network message differently.

15

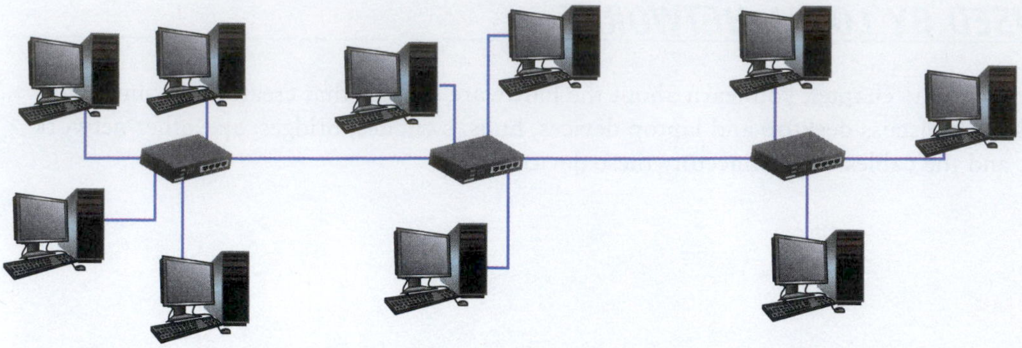

Figure 15-7 A star bus network formed by nodes connected to multiple switches

Notes In the chapter, "Connecting To and Setting Up a Network," you learned about packets, which are messages sent over a TCP/IP network with IP address header information added. Just before a packet is put on the network, the network adapter adds additional information to the beginning and end of the packet, and this information includes the source and destination MAC addresses. The packet, with this additional information, is now called a frame.

Here are the differences between a hub and a switch:

- An Ethernet **hub** transmits the data frame to every device, except the device that sent the frame, as shown in Figure 15-8a. A hub is just a pass-through and distribution point for every device connected to it, without regard for what kind of data is passing through and where the data might be going. Hubs are outdated technology, having been replaced by switches. Figure 15-9 shows a hub that supports 10 Mbps and 100 Mbps Ethernet speeds.

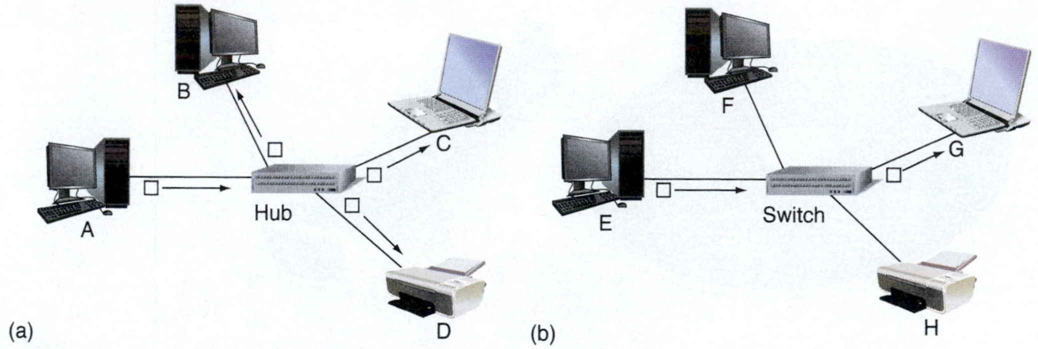

Figure 15-8 (a) A hub is a simple pass-through device to connect nodes on a network, and (b) a switch sends a frame to the destination node based on its MAC address

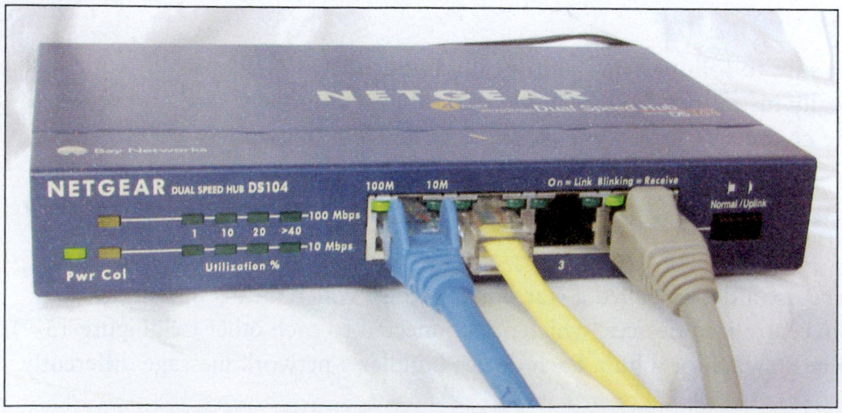

Figure 15-9 A hub is a pass-through device to connect nodes on a network

- A switch (see Figure 15-10) is smarter and more efficient than a hub because it keeps a table of all the MAC addresses for devices connected to it. When the switch receives a frame, it searches its MAC address table for the destination MAC address of the frame and sends the frame only to the device or interface using this MAC address (see Figure 15-8b). At first, a switch does not know the MAC addresses of every device connected to it. It learns this information as it receives frames and records the source MAC addresses in its MAC address table. When it receives a frame destined to a MAC address not in its table, the switch acts like a hub and broadcasts the frame to all devices except the one that sent it.

Figure 15-7, shown earlier in the chapter, uses three switches in sequence. Physically, the network cables that run between two switches or a switch and a computer might be inside a building's walls with a network jack on the wall providing an RJ-45 connector. You plug a network cable into the jack to make the connection. In practice, a small network might begin as one switch and three or four computers. As the need for more computers grows, new switches are added to provide these extra connections.

Another reason to add a switch to a network is to regenerate the network signal. An Ethernet cable should not exceed 100 meters (about 328 feet) in length. If you need to reach distances greater than that, you can add a switch in the line, which regenerates the signal.

Figure 15-10 A five-port Gigabit Ethernet switch by Linksys

WIRELESS ACCESS POINTS AND BRIDGES

A+
220-901
1.4, 1.11,
2.1, 2.2,
2.8

In the chapter, "Connecting To and Setting Up a Network," you learned that a router can also be a wireless access point. In addition, a wireless access point can be a dedicated device. The wireless access point, such as the one shown in Figure 15-11, can also be a bridge. A bridge is a device that stands between two segments of a network and manages network traffic between them. For example, one network segment might be a wireless network and the other segment might be a wired network; the wireless access point (AP) connects these two segments. Functioning as a

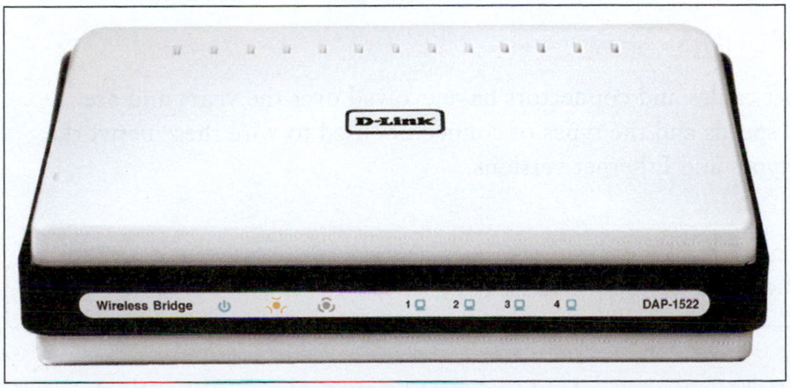

Courtesy of D-Link Corporation

Figure 15-11 Xtreme N Duo Wireless Bridge/Access Point by D-Link bridge, the AP helps to reduce the overall volume of network traffic by not allowing data frames across the bridge if it knows that the frame is addressed to a destination on its own segment. Figure 15-12 demonstrates the concept of a network bridge. (Logically, you can think of a switch as a multiport bridge.)

Figure 15-12 A bridge is an intelligent device making decisions concerning network traffic

Similar to a switch, a bridge at first doesn't know which nodes are on each network segment. It learns that information by maintaining a table of MAC addresses from information it collects from each frame that arrives at the bridge. Eventually, it learns which nodes are on which network segment and becomes more efficient at preventing frames from getting on the wrong segment, which can bog down network traffic.

Notes If your wireless access point does not reach the entire area you need to cover, you can add a repeater or an extender, which amplifies and retransmits the signal to a wider coverage area. Repeaters and extenders capture the Wi-Fi signal, boost it, and retransmit it to the new area. The difference between a repeater and an extender is that a repeater rebroadcasts the signal using a new network name, whereas an extender keeps the original network name.

A+ Exam Tip The A+ 220-901 exam expects you to know the functions and features of a hub, switch, router, access point, bridge, and modem.

ETHERNET CABLES AND CONNECTORS

A+ 220-901 2.1, 2.2, 2.8

Several variations of Ethernet cables and connectors have evolved over the years and are primarily identified by their speeds and the types of connectors used to wire these networks. Table 15-2 compares cable types and Ethernet versions.

A+ Exam Tip The A+ 220-901 exam expects you to know the details listed in Table 15-2.

As you can see from Table 15-2, the three main types of cabling used by Ethernet are twisted-pair, coaxial, and fiber optic. Coaxial cable is older and almost never used for current networking cable. Within each category, there are several variations discussed next.

Cable System	Speed	Cables and Connectors	Example of Connectors	Maximum Cable Length
10Base2 (ThinNet)	10 Mbps	Coaxial cable uses a BNC connector.	 Courtesy of Cables4Computer.com	185 meters or 607 feet
10Base5 (ThickNet)	10 Mbps	Coaxial uses an AUI 15-pin D-shaped connector.	 Courtesy of Black Box Corporation	500 meters or 1640 feet
10BaseT, 100BaseT (Fast Ethernet), 1000BaseT (Gigabit Ethernet), and 10GBaseT (10-Gigabit Ethernet)	10 Mbps, 100 Mbps, 1 Gbps, or 10 Gbps	Twisted pair (UTP or STP) uses an RJ-45 connector.	 Courtesy of Tyco Electronics	100 meters or 328 feet
10BaseF, 10BaseFL, 100BaseFL, 100BaseFX, 1000BaseFX, or 1000BaseX (fiber optic)	10 Mbps, 100 Mbps, 1 Gbps, or 10 Gbps	Fiber-optic cable uses ST or SC connectors (shown to the right) or LC and MT-RJ connectors (not shown).	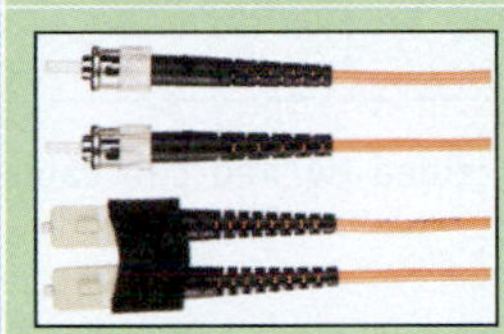 Courtesy of Black Box Corporation	Up to 2 kilometers (6562 feet)

Table 15-2 Variations of Ethernet and Ethernet cabling

TWISTED-PAIR CABLE

Twisted-pair cable is the most popular cabling method for local networks and uses an RJ-45 connector. The cable comes in two varieties: unshielded twisted-pair (UTP) cable and shielded twisted-pair (STP) cable. UTP cable is the least expensive and is commonly used on LANs. UTP is rated by twisted-pair category as listed in Table 15-3.

Twisted-Pair Category	Cable System	Frequency	Shielded or Unshielded	Comment
CAT-3	10BaseT	Up to 16 MHz	Unshielded	Currently used for phone lines.
CAT-5	10/100BaseT	Up to 100 MHz	Both	Has two cable pairs and seldom used today.
CAT-5e (Enhanced)	10/100BaseT, Gigabit Ethernet	Up to 100 MHz	Both	Has four twisted pairs and heavy duty sheath to help reduce crosstalk.
CAT-6	10/100BaseT, Gigabit Ethernet	Up to 250 MHz	Both	Less crosstalk because it has a plastic core that keeps the twisted pairs separated. CAT-6 and its variations are the most popular category used today.
CAT-6a	10/100BaseT, Gigabit Ethernet, 10Gig Ethernet	Up to 500 MHz	Both	Doubles the frequency of CAT-6. CAT-6a is sometimes unofficially called CAT-6e.
CAT-7	10/100BaseT, Gigabit Ethernet, 10Gig Ethernet	Up to 600 MHz	Individual pair shield and overall cable shield	Shielding almost completely eliminates crosstalk and improves noise reduction. Expected to have a longer life expectancy than previous twisted-pair categories.

Table 15-3 Twisted-pair categories

Figure 15-13 shows unshielded twisted-pair cables and the RJ-45 connector. Twisted-pair cable has four pairs of twisted wires for a total of eight wires. You learn more about how the eight wires are arranged later in the chapter.

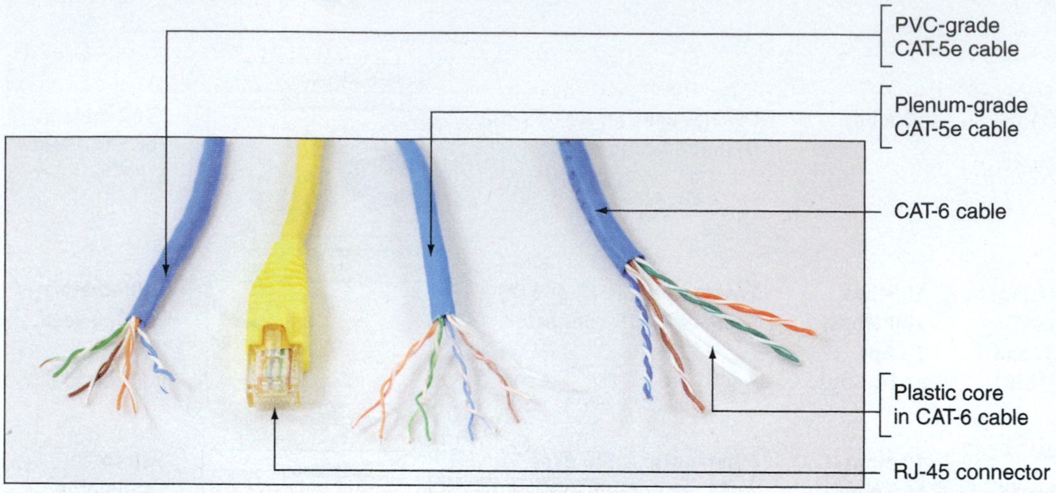

Figure 15-13 Unshielded twisted-pair cables and RJ-45 connector used for local wired networks

STP cable uses a covering or shield around each pair of wires inside the cable that protects it from electromagnetic interference caused by electrical motors, transmitters, or high-tension lines. It costs more than unshielded cable, so it's used only when the situation demands it.

> **Notes** Normally, the plastic covering of a cable is made of **PVC (polyvinyl chloride)**, which is not safe when used inside **plenums** (areas between the floors of buildings). In these situations, plenum cable covered with Teflon is used because it does not give off toxic fumes when burned. Plenum cable is two or three times more expensive than PVC cable. Figure 15-13 shows plenum cable and PVC cable, which are unshielded twisted-pair cables.

COAXIAL CABLE

Coaxial cable has a single copper wire down the middle and a braided shield around it (see Figure 15-14). The cable is stiff and difficult to manage, and is no longer used for networking. **RG-6 coaxial cable** is used for cable TV, having replaced the older and thinner **RG-59 coaxial cable** once used for cable TV. RG-6 cables use an **F connector** shown in Figure 15-15.

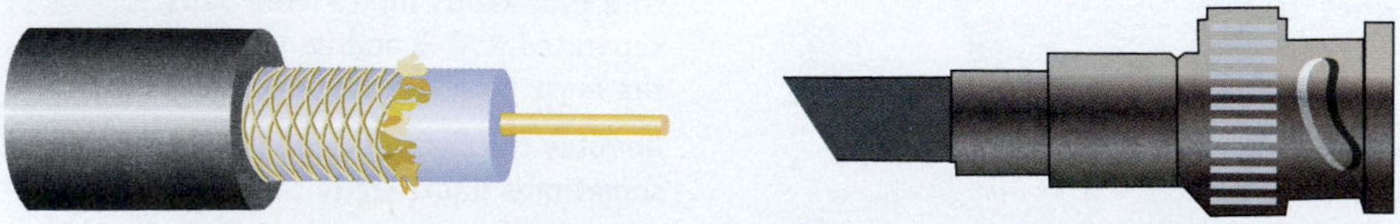

Figure 15-14 Coaxial cable and a BNC connector are used with ThinNet Ethernet

Figure 15-15 An RG-6 coaxial cable with an F connector used for connections to TV has a single copper wire

★ A+ Exam Tip The A+ 220-901 exam expects you to know about these cables and connectors: BNC, RJ-45, coaxial, SC, ST, LC, RJ-11, F connector, STP, UTP, CAT-3, CAT-5, CAT-5e, CAT-6, CAT-6e, plenum, PVC, RG-6, and RG-59.

FIBER OPTIC

Fiber-optic cables transmit signals as pulses of light over glass or plastic strands inside protected tubing, as illustrated in Figure 15-16. Fiber-optic cable comes in two types: single-mode (thin, difficult to connect, expensive, and best performing) and multimode (most popular). A single-mode cable uses a single path for light to travel in the cable and multimode cable uses multiple paths for light. Both single-mode and multimode fiber-optic cables can be constructed as loose-tube cables for outdoor use or tight-buffered cables for indoor or outdoor use. Loose-tube cables are filled with gel to prevent water from soaking into the cable, and tight-buffered cables are filled with synthetic or glass yarn, called strength wires, to protect the fiber-optic strands, as shown in Figure 15-16.

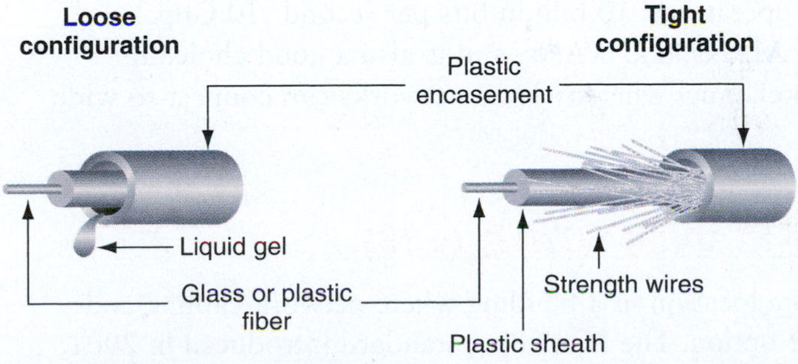

Figure 15-16 Fiber-optic cables contain a glass or plastic core for transmitting light

Fiber-optic cables can use one of four connectors, all shown in Figure 15-17. The two older types are ST (straight tip) connectors and SC (subscriber connector or standard connector) connectors. Two newer types are LC (local connector) connectors and MT-RJ (mechanical transfer registered jack) connectors. Any one of the four connectors can be used with either single-mode or multimode fiber-optic cable.

15

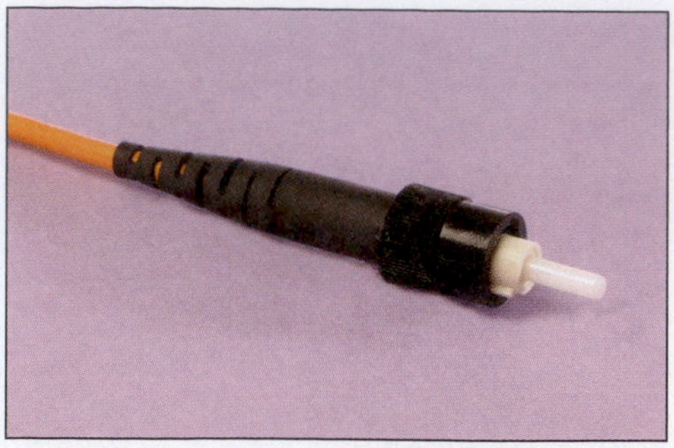

(a) ST (straight tip)

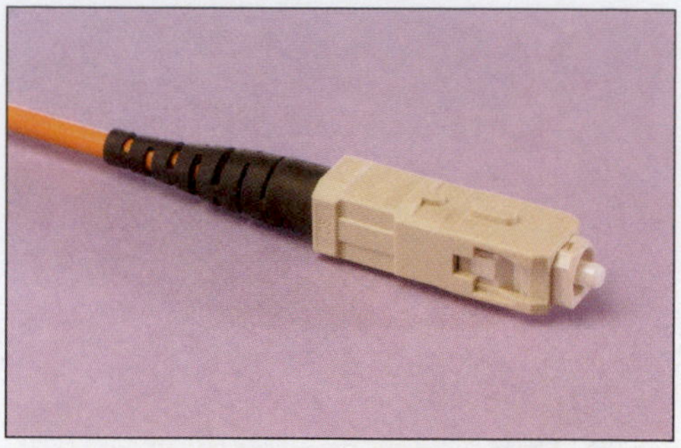

(b) SC (standard connector)

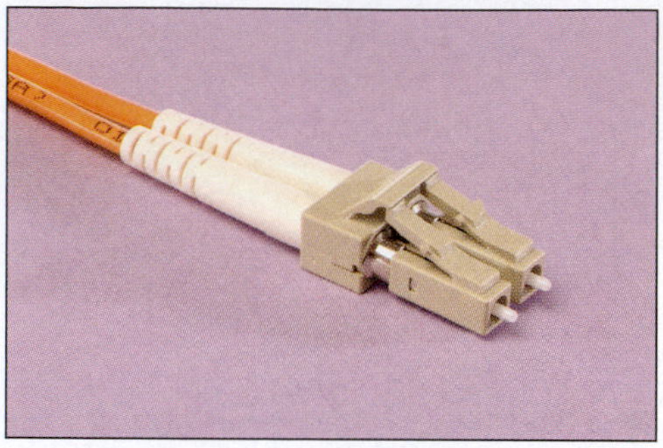

(c) LC (local connector)

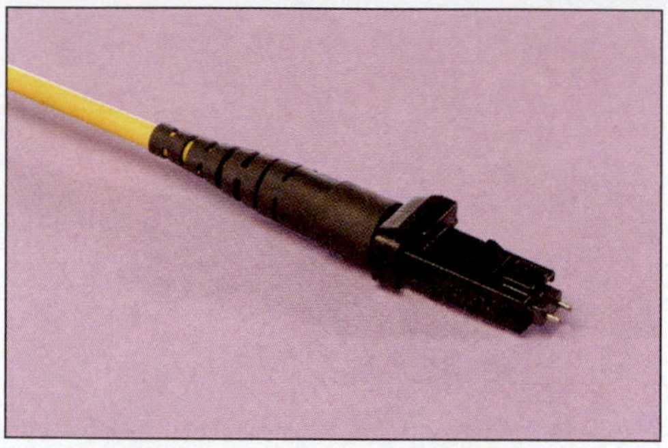

(d) MT-RJ (mechanical transfer RJ)

Courtesy Fiber Communications, Inc.

Figure 15-17 Four types of fiber-optic connectors: (a) ST, (b) SC, (c) LC, and (d) MT-RJ

ETHERNET STANDARDS AND CABLES

Recall that Ethernet can run at four speeds. Each version of Ethernet can use more than one cabling method. Here is a brief description of the transmission speeds and the cabling methods they use:

- *10-Mbps Ethernet.* This first Ethernet specification was invented by Xerox Corporation in the 1970s, and later became known as Ethernet.
- *100-Mbps Ethernet or Fast Ethernet.* This improved version of Ethernet (sometimes called 100BaseT or Fast Ethernet) operates at 100 Mbps and uses STP or UTP cabling rated CAT-5 or higher. 100BaseT networks can support slower speeds of 10 Mbps so that devices that run at either 10 Mbps or 100 Mbps can coexist on the same LAN. Two variations of 100BaseT are 100BaseTX and 100BaseFX. The most popular variation is 100BaseTX. 100BaseFX uses fiber-optic cable.
- *1000-Mbps Ethernet or Gigabit Ethernet.* This version of Ethernet operates at 1000 Mbps and uses twisted-pair cable and fiber-optic cable. Gigabit Ethernet is becoming the most popular choice for LAN technology. Because it can use the same cabling and connectors as Fast Ethernet, a company can upgrade from Fast Ethernet to Gigabit without rewiring the network.
- *10-Gigabit Ethernet.* This version of Ethernet operates at 10 billion bits per second (10 Gbps) and uses fiber-optic cable. It can be used on LANs, MANs, and WANs, and is also a good choice for backbone networks. (A backbone network is a channel whereby local networks can connect to wide area networks or to each other.)

POWERLINE NETWORKING OR ETHERNET OVER POWER (EOP)

A+
220-901
2.8

If you need network access to a remote location in a building where network cabling and Wi-Fi cannot reach, you have another option. The HomePlug standard introduced in 2001, powerline networking or Ethernet over Power (EoP), uses the power lines in a building to transmit data. Powerline networking is simple to set up, inexpensive, and can run at Gigabit speeds. Like Wi-Fi, the data is sent out on a network that you cannot necessarily contain because power lines are not confined to a single building. If a building or apartment is sharing a phase (electrical signal) with another building or apartment, the data might leak and be intercepted by a neighbor. For this reason, powerline adapters offer encryption (128-bit AES encryption) that is activated by pairing the adapters to each other. Alternately, you can install the manufacturer's utility on your computer to create a network key.

To use powerline networking, you need at least two powerline adapters (see Figure 15-18), which can be bought in pairs called a kit.

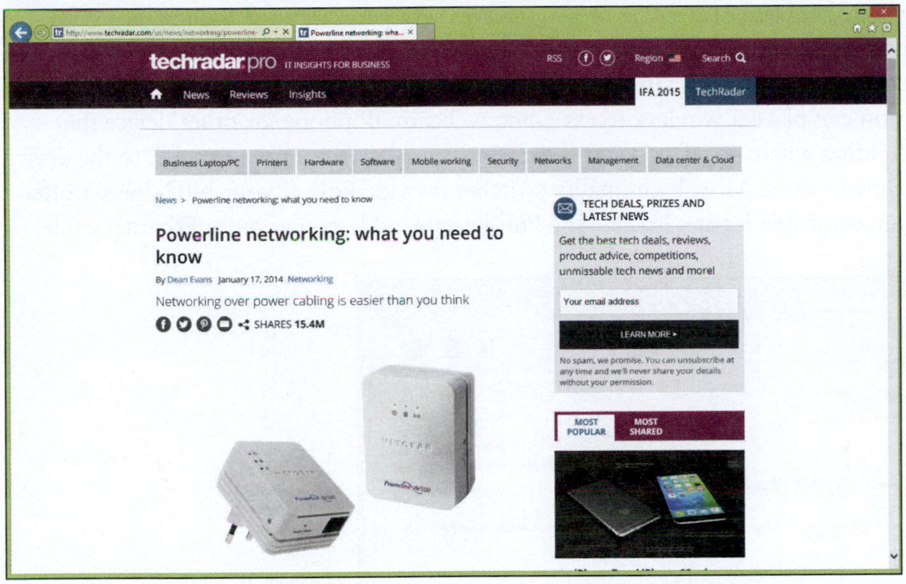

Source: www.techradar.com

Figure 15-18 A starter kit for powerline networking includes two adapters

To install powerline networking, follow these steps:

1. Connect a powerline adapter to your router using an Ethernet cable, then plug it directly into a wall outlet.
2. In the same room, connect a second adapter to your computer using an Ethernet cable and then plug it directly into a wall outlet.
3. To pair the two devices, press and hold the security button on the first adapter for a couple seconds. When the LED lights flash, you have less than two minutes to press and hold the security button on the second adapter until the LED lights flash. The two adapters are now paired using security encryption. For additional adapters, simply repeat this step with a new adapter one at a time.
4. You can now move the second adapter to its final destination in the building knowing that you have a secured connection.

Powerline networks are not without problems. Consider the following issues powerline networking presents:

- Powerline adapters must be plugged directly into a wall outlet. Plugging a powerline adapter into a power strip or surge protector or sharing an outlet with an energy hog like a space heater hinders the function of the device.
- Powerline adapters might be large and cover both outlets on a single wall plate. A few powerline adapters offer a pass-through outlet, but most do not.
- Sometimes people forget to use the encryption options and end up with an unsecured network.
- Distance degrades quality. If you have a map of the building's circuits, try to keep the two adapters as close on the same circuit as possible. Jumping circuits decreases signal strength.

When shopping for powerline adapters, consider these things:

- Most powerline manufacturers belong to the Homeplug Alliance group (*www.homeplug.org*). Make sure the adapter you are considering is Homeplug certified.
- Make sure the adapter is rated for the latest Homeplug AV2 speed standard for Gigabit-class data transfers.
- If you have limited wall outlets, you might need a powerline adapter that offers a pass-through outlet.

POWER OVER ETHERNET (POE)

A+
220-901
2.8

If you have the opposite problem of needing to get power where your network cabling has gone, you can use Power over Ethernet (PoE). **Power over Ethernet (PoE)** is a feature that might be available on high-end wired network adapters to allow power to be transmitted over Ethernet cable. Using this feature, you can place a wireless access point, webcam, IP phone, or other device that needs power in a position in a building where you don't have an electrical outlet. The Ethernet cable to the device provides both power and data transmissions. Most high-quality switches provide PoE. If your NIC doesn't offer PoE, you can add it using a PoE injector (see Figure 15-19). The **PoE injector** adds power to an Ethernet cable.

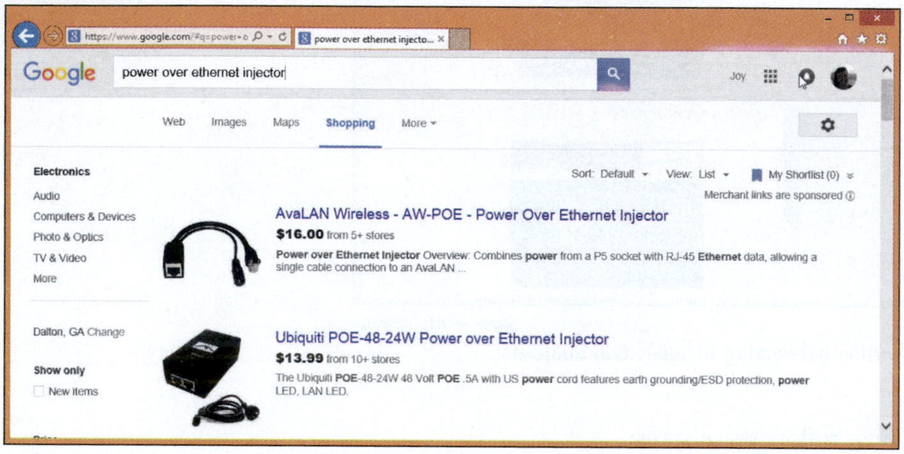

Source: https://www.google.com/webhp?hl=en#q=power+over+ethernet+injector&hl=en&tbm=shop

Figure 15-19 A PoE injector introduces power to an Ethernet cable

Some devices, such as a webcam, are designed to receive both power and data from the Ethernet cable. For other devices, you must use a splitter that splits the data and power transmissions before connecting to the device. PoE can provide up to 25.5 W from a single Ethernet port. The amount of power that reaches a device degrades with the length of the cable. Figure 15-20 shows a PoE switch and a splitter used to provide power to a non-PoE access point. When setting up a device to receive power by PoE, make sure the device sending the power, the splitter, and the device receiving the power are all compatible. Pay special attention to the voltage and wattage requirements and the type of power connector of the receiving device.

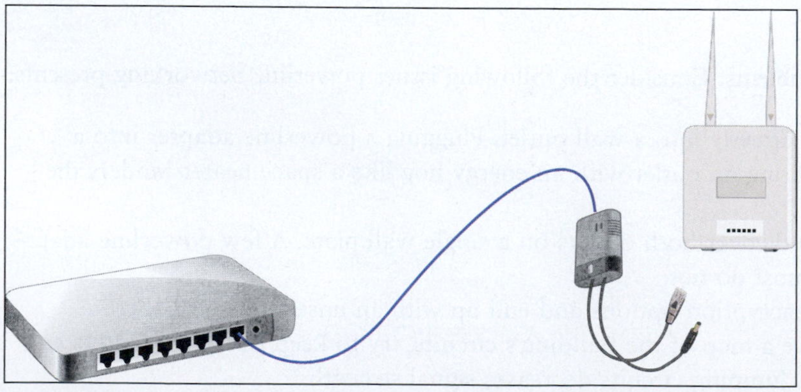

Figure 15-20 Use a PoE splitter if the receiving device is not PoE compatible

Hands-On | Project 15-2 Research a Network Upgrade

A+
220-901
1.4, 2.8

An IT support technician is often called on to research equipment to maintain or improve a computer or network and make recommendations for purchase. Suppose you are asked to upgrade a small network that consists of one switch and four computers from 100BaseT to Gigabit Ethernet. The switch connects to a router that already supports Gigabit Ethernet. Do the following to price the hardware needed for this upgrade:

1. Find three switches by different manufacturers that support Gigabit Ethernet and have at least five ports. Save or print the webpages describing each switch.
2. Compare the features and prices of the three switches. What additional information might you want to know before you make your recommendation for a small business network?
3. Find three network adapters by different manufacturers to install in the desktop computers to support Gigabit Ethernet. Save or print webpages for each NIC.
4. Compare features of the three network adapters. What additional information do you need to know before you make your recommendation?
5. Make your recommendations based on the moderate (middle-of-the-road) choices. What is the total price of the upgrade, including one switch and four network adapters?
6. What is one more question you need to have answered about other equipment before you can complete the price of the upgrade? Explain how you would find the answer to your question.

SETTING UP AND TROUBLESHOOTING NETWORK WIRING

A+
220-901
1.4, 2.1,
2.2, 2.9,
4.4, 4.5

To set up a small network, you'll need computers, switches, network cables, a router, and whatever device (for example, a DSL or cable modem) that provides Internet access. Some network cables might be wired inside walls of your building with wall jacks that use RJ-45 ports. These cables might converge in an electrical closet or server room. If network cables are lying on the floor, be sure to install them against the wall so they won't be a trip hazard. Take care that cables don't exceed the recommended length (100 meters for twisted pair). For best results, always use twisted-pair cables rated at CAT-5e or higher. (CAT-6 gives better performance than CAT-5e for Gigabit Ethernet, but it is a lot harder to wire and also more expensive.) To connect multiple computers, use switches rated at the same speed as your router and network adapters. For Gigabit speed on the entire network, you need to use all Gigabit switches and network adapters and a Gigabit router. However, if some devices run at slower speeds, most likely a switch or router can still support the higher speeds for other devices on the network.

If your router is also your wireless access point, take care in planning where to place it. Place the wireless access point near the center of the area where you want your wireless hotspot. The router also needs to have access to your cable modem or DSL modem. The modem needs access to the cable TV or phone jack where it receives service. Figure 15-21 shows a possible inexpensive wiring job where two switches and a router are used to wire two rooms for five workstations and a network printer. The only inside-wall wiring that is required is two back-to-back RJ-45 wall jacks on either side of the wall between the two rooms. The plan allows for all five desktop computers and a network printer to be wired with cabling neatly attached to the baseboards of the office without being a trip hazard.

15

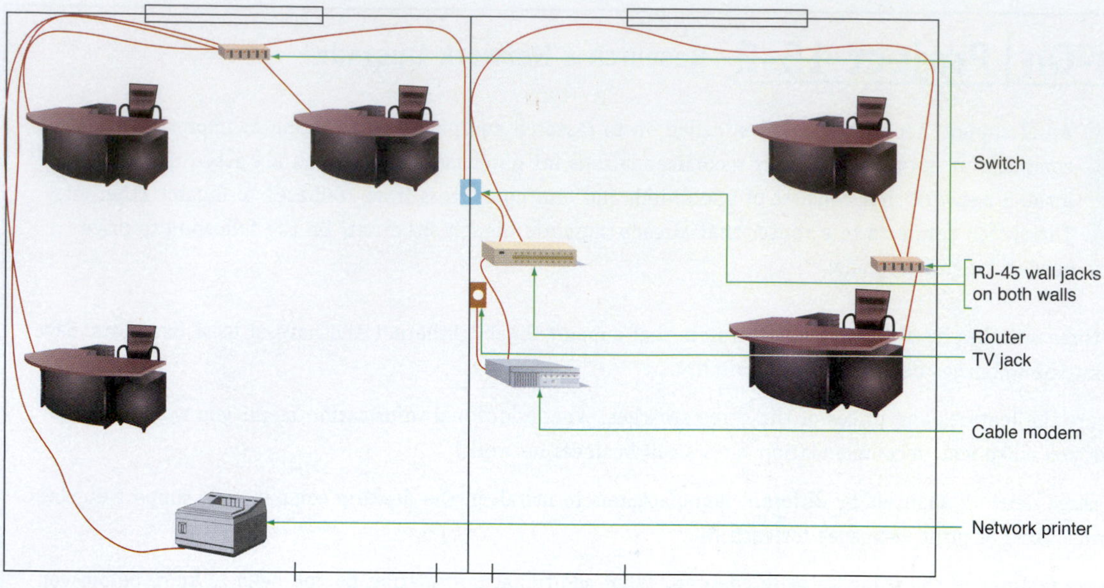

Figure 15-21 Plan the physical configuration of a small network

Now let's look at the tools you need to solve problems with network cabling, the details of how a network cable is wired, and how you can create your own network cables by installing RJ-45 connectors on twisted-pair cables.

TOOLS USED BY NETWORK TECHNICIANS

A+
220-901
2.9, 4.4

Here's a list of tools a network technician might want in his or her toolbox:

- ***Loopback plug.*** A loopback plug can be used to test a network cable or port. To test a port or cable, connect one end of the cable to a network port on a computer or other device, and connect the loopback plug to the other end of the cable (see Figure 15-22). If the LED light on the loopback plug lights up, the cable and port are good. Another way to use a loopback plug is to find out which port on a switch in an electrical closet matches up with a wall jack. Plug the loopback plug into the wall jack. The connecting port on the switch in the closet lights up. When buying a loopback plug, pay attention to the Ethernet speeds it supports. Some only support 100 Mbps; others support 100 Mbps and 1000 Mbps.

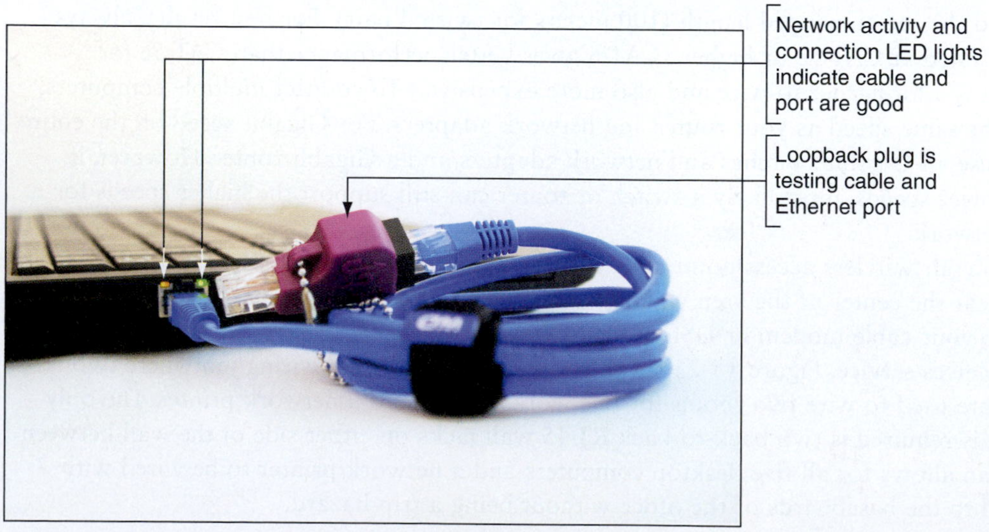

Figure 15-22 A loopback plug verifies the cable and network port are good

- *Cable tester.* A cable tester is used to test a cable to find out if it is good or to find out what type of cable it is if the cable is not labeled. You can also use a cable tester to locate the ends of a network cable in a building. A cable tester has two components, the remote and the base (see Figure 15-23).

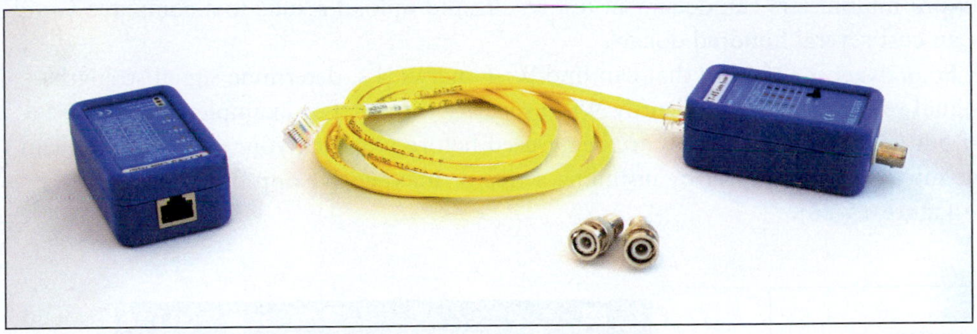

Figure 15-23 Use a cable tester pair to determine the type of cable and/or if the cable is good

To test a cable, connect each component to the ends of the cable and turn on the tester. Lights on the tester will show you if the cable is good and what type of cable you have. You'll need to read the user manual that comes with the cable tester to know how to interpret the lights.

You can also use the cable tester to find the two ends of a network cable installed in a building. Suppose you see several network jacks on walls in a building, but you don't know which jacks connect. Install a short cable in each of the two jacks or a jack and a port in a patch panel. Then use the cable tester base and remote to test the continuity, as shown in Figure 15-24. Whereas a loopback plug works with live cables and ports, a cable tester works on cables that are not live. You might damage a cable tester if you connect it to a live circuit, so before you start connecting the cable tester to wall jacks, be sure that you turn off all devices on the network.

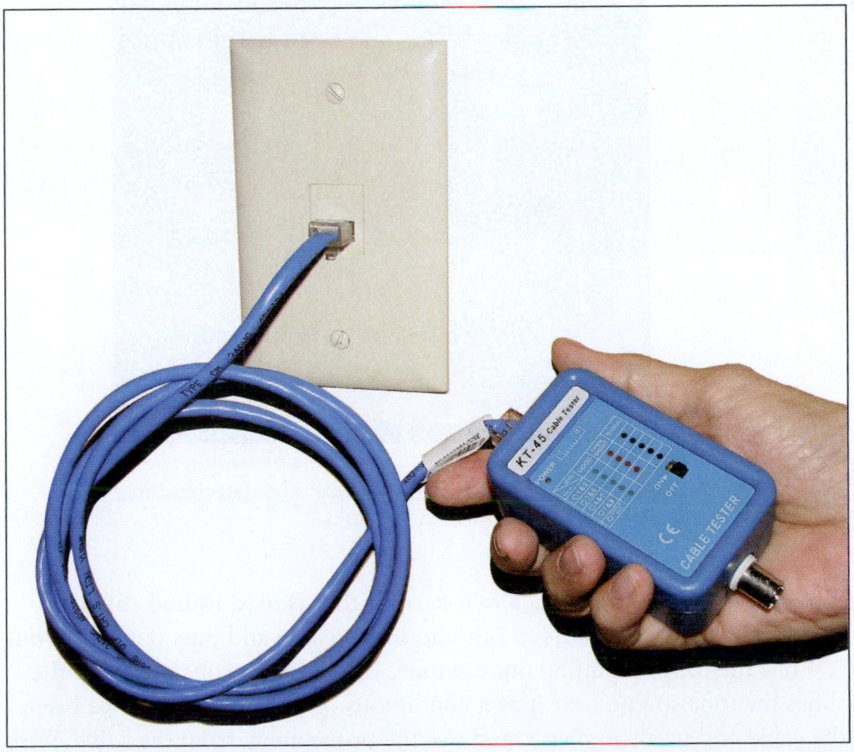

Figure 15-24 Use cable testers to find the two ends of a network cable in a building

15

- ***Network multimeter.*** You learned about multimeters in the chapter, "First Look at Computer Parts and Tools." A network multimeter (see Figure 15-25) is a multifunctional tool that can test cables, ports, and network adapters. When you connect it to your network, it can also detect the Ethernet speed, duplex status, default router on the network, length of a cable, voltage levels of PoE, and other network statistics and details. Many network multimeters can document test results and upload results to a computer. Good network multimeters can cost several hundred dollars.
- ***Wi-Fi analyzer.*** A Wi-Fi analyzer is software that can find Wi-Fi networks, determine signal strengths, help optimize Wi-Fi signal settings, and help identify Wi-Fi security threats. For example, you can use a Wi-Fi analyzer to find out which Wi-Fi channels are being used before you pick your channels. You can turn your smart phone into a Wi-Fi analyzer by installing a free or inexpensive app through your phone's app store (see Figure 15-26).

Courtesy of Fluke Corporation

Figure 15-25 The LinkRunner Pro network multimeter by Fluke Corporation works on Gigabit Ethernet networks using twisted-pair copper cabling

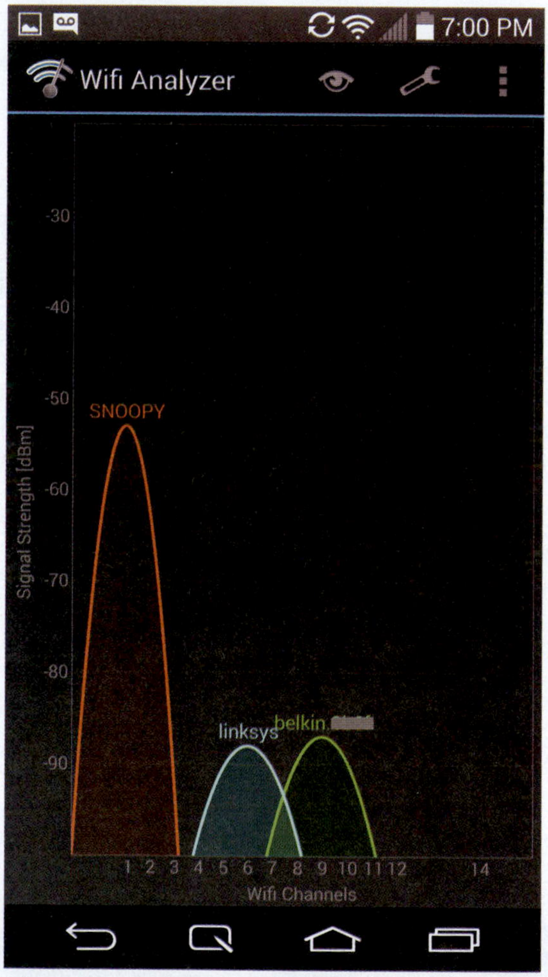

Source: Wifi Analyzer app for Android

Figure 15-26 This Wi-Fi Analyzer app detected three wireless networks

- ***Toner probe.*** A toner probe, sometimes called a tone probe, is a two-part kit that is used to find cables in the walls of a building. See Figure 15-27. The toner connects to one end of the cable and puts out a continuous or pulsating tone on the cable. While the toner is putting out the tone, you use the probe to search the walls for the tone. The probe amplifies the tone so you hear it as a continuous or pulsating beep. The beeps get louder when you are close to the cable and weaker when you move the probe away from the cable. With a little patience, you can trace the cable through the walls. Some toners can put out tones up to 10 miles on a cable and offer a variety of ways to connect to the cable, such as clips and RJ-45 and RJ-11 connectors.

Figure 15-27 A toner probe kit by Fluke Corporation

- *Wire stripper.* A wire stripper is used to build your own network cable or repair a cable. Use the wire stripper to cut away the plastic jacket or coating around the wires inside a twisted-pair cable so that you can install a connector on the end of the cable. How to use wire strippers is covered later in the chapter.
- *Crimper.* A crimper is used to attach a terminator or connector to the end of a cable. It applies force to pinch the connector to the wires in the cable to securely make a solid connection. Figure 15-28 shows a multifunctional crimper that can crimp a RJ-45 or RJ-11 connector. It also serves double-duty as a wire cutter and wire stripper.

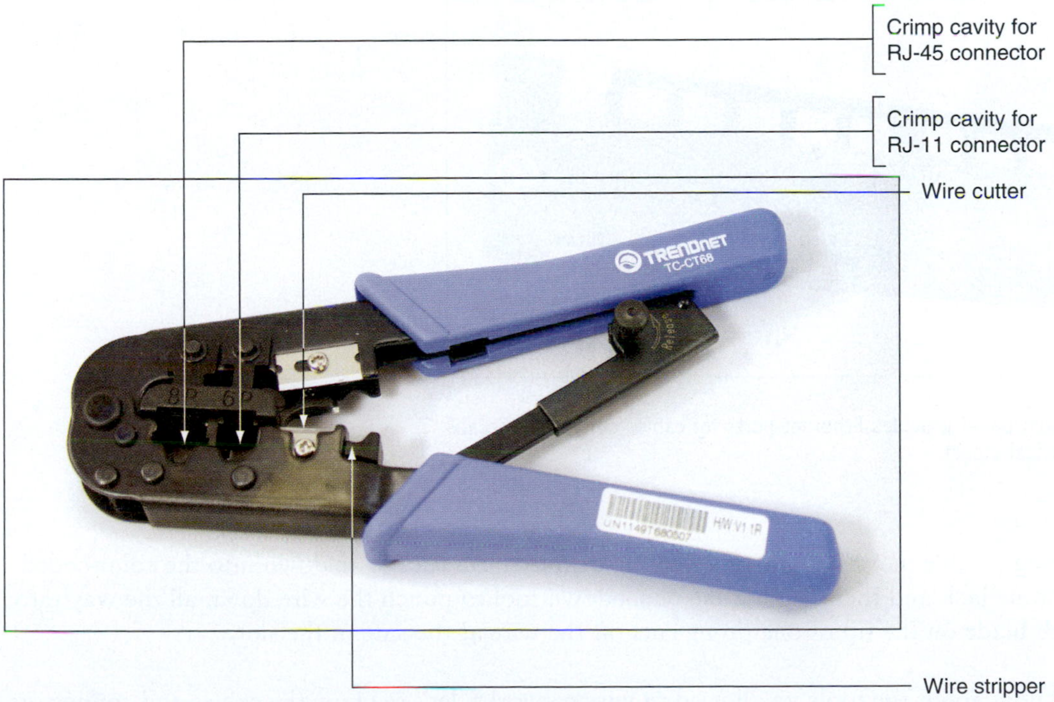

Figure 15-28 This crimper can crimp RJ-45 and RJ-11 connectors

- *Punchdown tool.* A punchdown tool, also called an impact tool (see Figure 15-29), is used to punch individual wires in a network cable into their slots in a keystone RJ-45 jack that is used in an RJ-45 wall jack. Later in the chapter, you learn how to use the tool with a keystone jack.

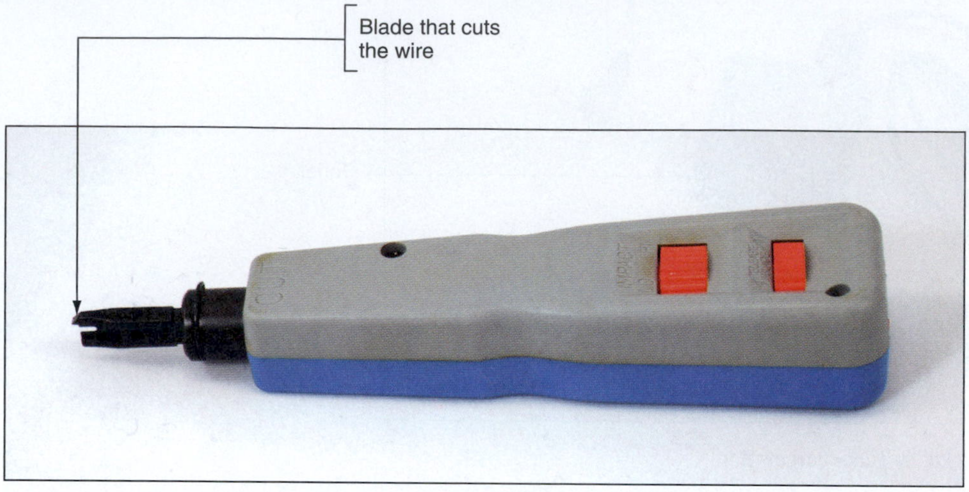

Figure 15-29 A punchdown tool forces a wire into a slot and cuts off the wire

Another use of a punchdown tool is to terminate network cables in a patch panel. A patch panel (see Figure 15-30) provides multiple network ports for cables that converge in one location such as an electrical closet or server room. Each port is numbered on the front of the panel. On the back side, keystone jacks are color-coded for the wires to be inserted.

Courtesy of Tripp Lite

Figure 15-30 A patch panel provides Ethernet ports for cables converging in an electrical closet

When terminating a cable in a keystone jack, you first gently push each wire down into the color-coded slot of the keystone jack and then you use the punchdown tool to punch the wire down all the way into the slot. A small blade on the tip of one prong cuts off the wire at the side of the slot.

Now that you know about the tools you'll need to wire networks, let's see how the cables and connectors are wired.

HOW TWISTED-PAIR CABLES AND CONNECTORS ARE WIRED

A+
220-901
2.1, 2.2

Recall from the chapter, "Connecting To and Setting Up a Network," that two types of network cables can be used when building a network: a straight-through cable and a crossover cable. A straight-through cable (also called a patch cable) is used to connect a computer to a switch or other network device. A crossover cable is used to connect two like devices such as a hub to a hub or a computer to a computer (to make the simplest network of all).

The difference between a straight-through cable and a crossover cable is the way the transmit and receive lines are wired in the connectors at each end of the cables. A crossover cable has the transmit and receive lines reversed so that one device receives off the line to which the other device transmits. Before the introduction of Gigabit Ethernet, 10BaseT and 100BaseT required that a crossover cable be used to connect two like devices such as a switch to a switch. Today's devices that support Gigabit Ethernet use auto-uplinking, which means you can connect a switch to a switch using a straight-through cable. Crossover cables are seldom used today except to connect a computer to a computer to create this simple two-node network.

Twisted-pair copper wire cabling uses an RJ-45 connector that has eight pins, as shown in Figure 15-31. 10BaseT and 100BaseT Ethernet use only four of these pins: pins 1 and 2 for transmitting data and pins 3 and 6 for receiving data. The other pins can be used for phone lines or for power (using PoE). Gigabit Ethernet uses all eight pins to transmit and receive data and can also transmit power on these same lines.

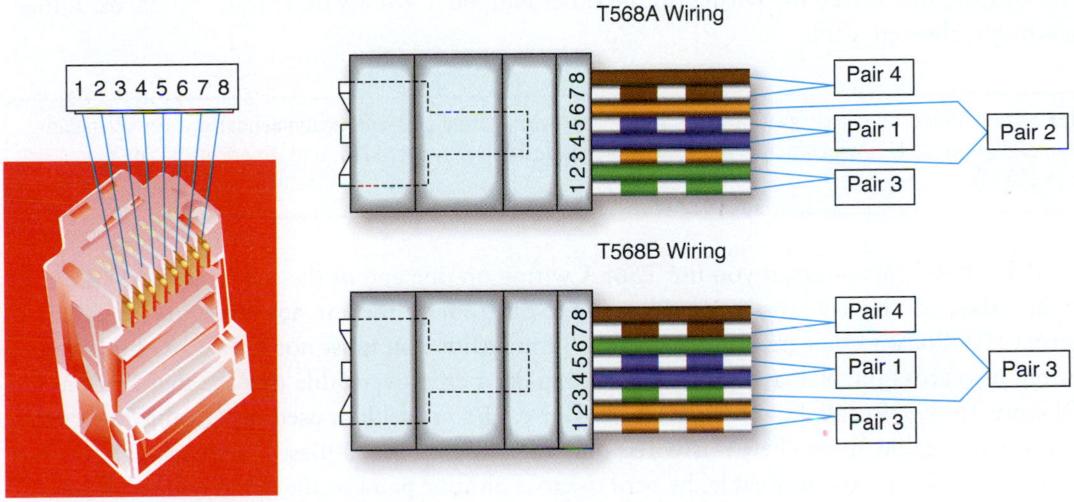

Figure 15-31 Pinouts for an RJ-45 connector

Twisted-pair cabling used with RJ-45 connectors is color-coded in four pairs, as shown in Figure 15-31. Pair 1 is blue, pair 2 is orange, pair 3 is green, and pair 4 is brown. Each pair has one solid wire and one striped wire. Two standards have been established in the industry for wiring twisted-pair cabling and RJ-45 connectors: T568A and T568B standards. Both are diagrammed in Figure 15-31 and listed in Table 15-4. The T568A standard has the green pair connected to pins 1 and 2 and the orange pair connected to pins 3 and 6. The T568B standard has the orange pair using pins 1 and 2 and the green pair using pins 3 and 6, as shown in the diagram and the table. For both standards, the blue pair uses pins 4 and 5, and the brown pair uses pins 7 and 8.

15

Pin	100BaseT Purpose	T568A Wiring	T568B Wiring
1	Transmit+	Pair 3: White/green	Pair 2: White/orange
2	Transmit-	Pair 3: Green	Pair 2: Orange
3	Receive+	Pair 2: White/orange	Pair 3: White/green
4	(Used only on Gigabit Ethernet)	Pair 1: Blue	Pair 1: Blue
5	(Used only on Gigabit Ethernet)	Pair 1: White/blue	Pair 1: White/blue
6	Receive-	Pair 2: Orange	Pair 3: Green
7	(Used only on Gigabit Ethernet)	Pair 4: White/brown	Pair 4: White/brown
8	(Used only on Gigabit Ethernet)	Pair 4: Brown	Pair 4: Brown

Table 15-4 The T568A and T568B Ethernet standards for wiring RJ-45 connectors

It doesn't matter which standard you use so long as you're *consistent*. The important thing is that the wiring on one end of the cable match the wiring on the other end, be it T568A or T568B standards. Either way, you have a straight-through cable.

Notes The T568A and T568B standards as well as other network wiring standards and recommendations are overseen by the Telecommunications Industry Association (TIA), Electronics Industries Alliance (EIA), and American National Standards Institute (ANSI).

For 10BaseT and 100BaseT networks, if you use T568A wiring on one end of the cable and T568B on the other end of the cable, you have a crossover cable (see the diagram on the left side of Figure 15-32). For Gigabit Ethernet (1000BaseT) that transmits data on all four pairs, you must not only cross the green and orange pairs but also cross the blue and brown pairs to make a crossover cable (see the diagram on the right side of Figure 15-32). Recall, however, that crossover cables are seldom used on Gigabit Ethernet. When you buy a crossover cable, most likely it is wired only for 10BaseT or 100BaseT networks. If you ever find yourself needing to make a crossover cable, be sure to cross all four pairs so the cable will work on 10BaseT, 100BaseT, and 1000BaseT networks. You can also buy an adapter to convert a straight-through cable to a crossover cable. But most likely the adapter only crosses two pairs and works only for 10BaseT or 100BaseT networks, such as the adapter shown in Figure 15-33.

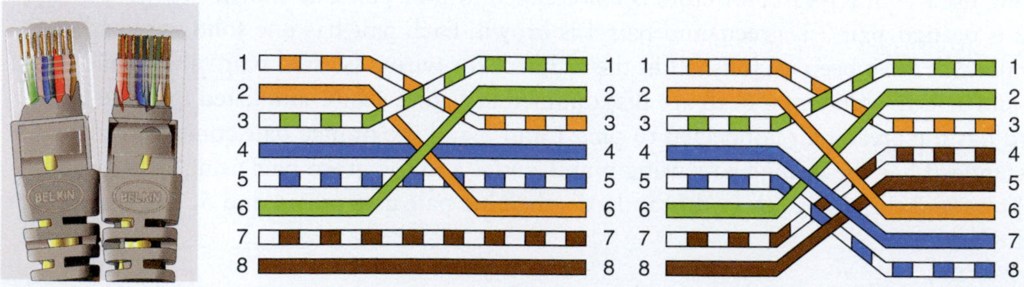

Figure 15-32 Two crossed pairs in a crossover cable is compatible with 10BaseT or 100BaseT Ethernet; four crossed pairs in a crossover cable is compatible with Gigabit Ethernet

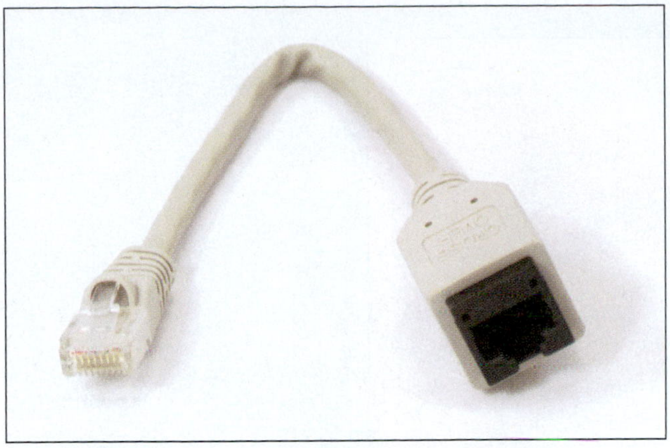

Figure 15-33 A crossover adapter converts a patch cable to a crossover cable for a 10BaseT or 100BaseT network

When you are wiring a network in a building that already has network wiring, be sure to find out if the wiring is using T568A or T568B. And then be sure you always use that standard. If you don't know which to use, use T568B because it's the most common, unless, however, you are working for the U.S. government, which requires T568A for all its networking needs.

APPLYING | CONCEPTS MAKE A STRAIGHT-THROUGH CABLE USING T568B WIRING

A+ 220-901 2.1, 2.2, 2.9, 4.4

It takes a little practice to make a good network straight-through cable, but you'll get the hang of it after doing only a couple of cables. Figure 15-34 shows the materials and tools you'll need to make a network cable.

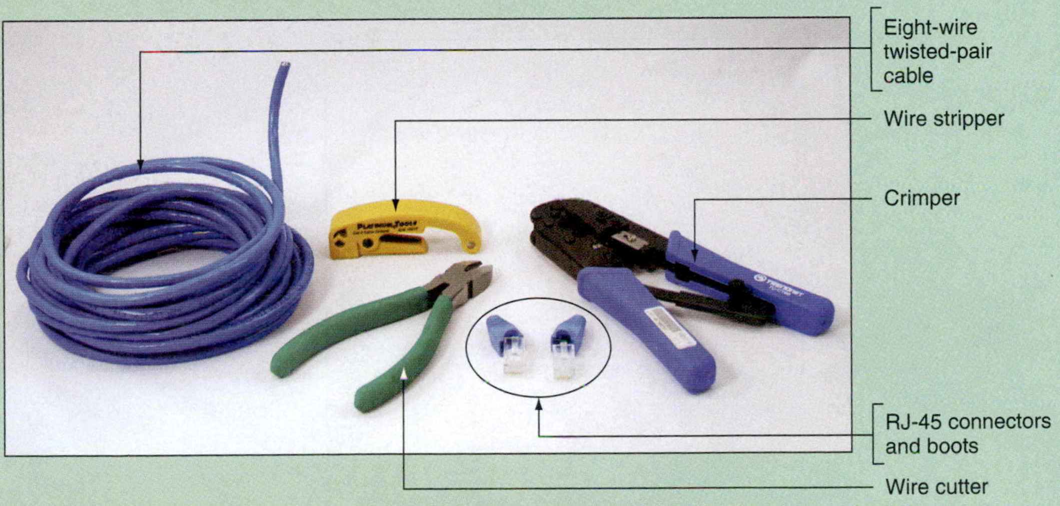

Figure 15-34 Tools and materials to make a network cable

Here are the steps to make a straight-through cable using the T568B standard:

1. Use wire cutters to cut the twisted-pair cable the correct length plus a few extra inches.
2. If your RJ-45 connectors include boots, slide two boots onto the cable.
3. Use wire strippers to strip off about two inches of the plastic jacket from the end of the wire. To do that, put the wire in the stripper and rotate the stripper around the wire to score the jacket (see Figure 15-35). You can then pull off the jacket.

(continues)

15

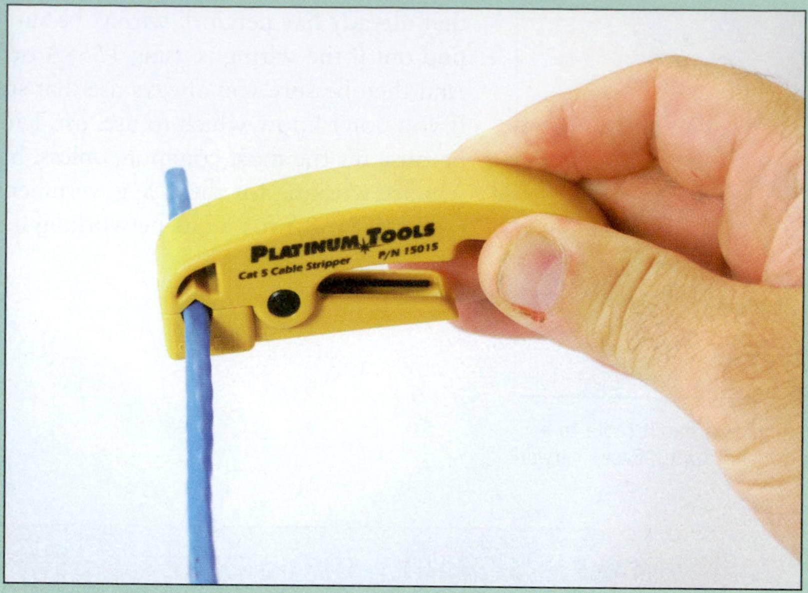

Figure 15-35 Rotate a wire stripper around the jacket to score it so you can slide it off the wire

4. Use wire cutters to start a cut into the jacket, and then use the rip cord to pull the jacket back a couple of inches (see Figure 15-36). Next, cut off the rip cord and the jacket. You take this extra precaution of removing the jacket because you might have nicked the wires with the wire strippers.

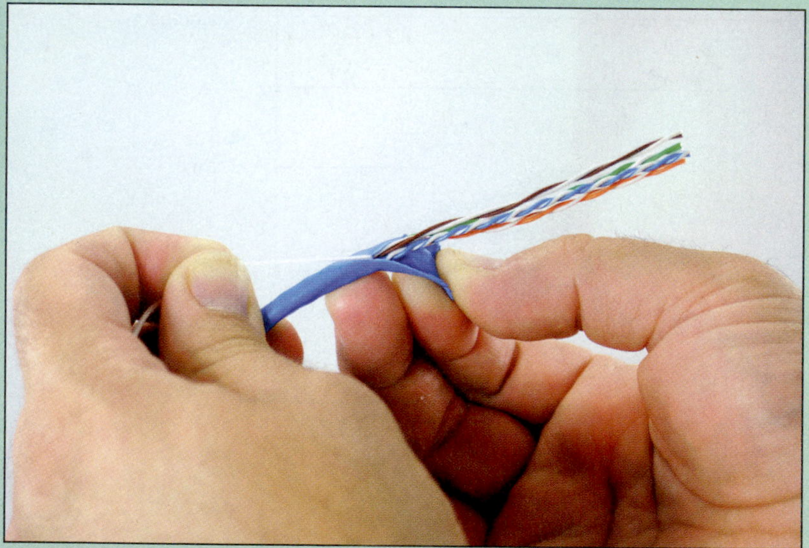

Figure 15-36 Rip back the jacket, and then cut off the extra jacket and rip cord

5. Untwist each pair of wires so you have the eight separate wires. Smooth each wire out, straightening out the kinks. Line up the wires in the T568B configuration (refer to Table 15-4).
6. Holding the tightly lined-up wires between your fingers, use wire cutters to cut the wires off evenly, leaving a little over an inch of wire. See Figure 15-37. To know how short to cut the wires, hold the RJ-45 connector up to the wires. The wires must go all the way to the front of the connector. The jacket must go far enough into the connector so that the crimp at the back of the connector will be able to solidly pinch the jacket.

Figure 15-37 Evenly cut off wires measured to fit in the RJ-45 connector with the jacket protruding into the connector

7. Be sure you have pin 1 of the connector lined up with the orange and white wire. Then insert the eight wires in the RJ-45 connector. Guide the wires into the connector, making sure they reach all the way to the front. (It helps to push up a bit as you push the wires into the connector.) You can jam the jacket firmly into the connector. Look through the clear plastic connector to make sure the wires are lined up correctly and they all reach the front and that the jacket goes past the crimp.

8. Insert the connector into the crimper tool. Use one hand to push the connector firmly into the crimper as you use the other hand to crimp the connector. See Figure 15-38. Use plenty of force to crimp. The eight blades at the front of the connector must pierce through to each copper wire to complete each of the eight connections, and the crimp at the back of the connector must solidly crimp the cable jacket to secure the cable to the connector (see Figure 15-39). Remove the connector from the crimper and make sure you can't pull the connector off the wire.

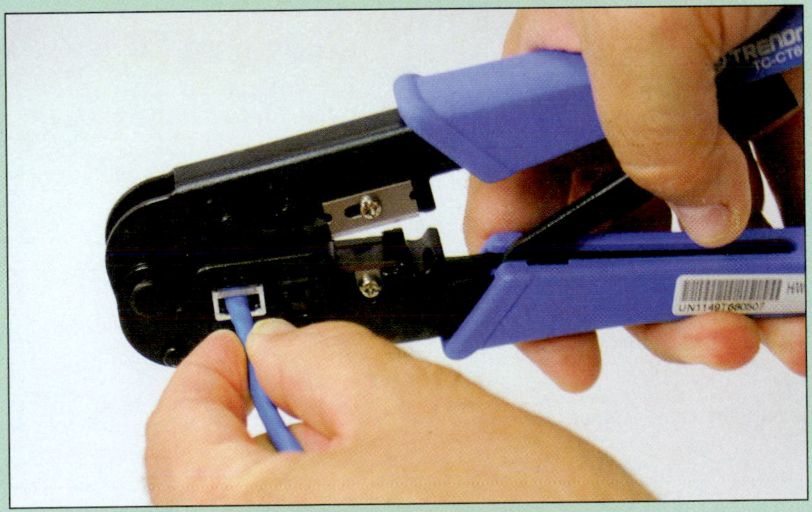

Figure 15-38 Use the crimper to crimp the connector to the cable

(continues)

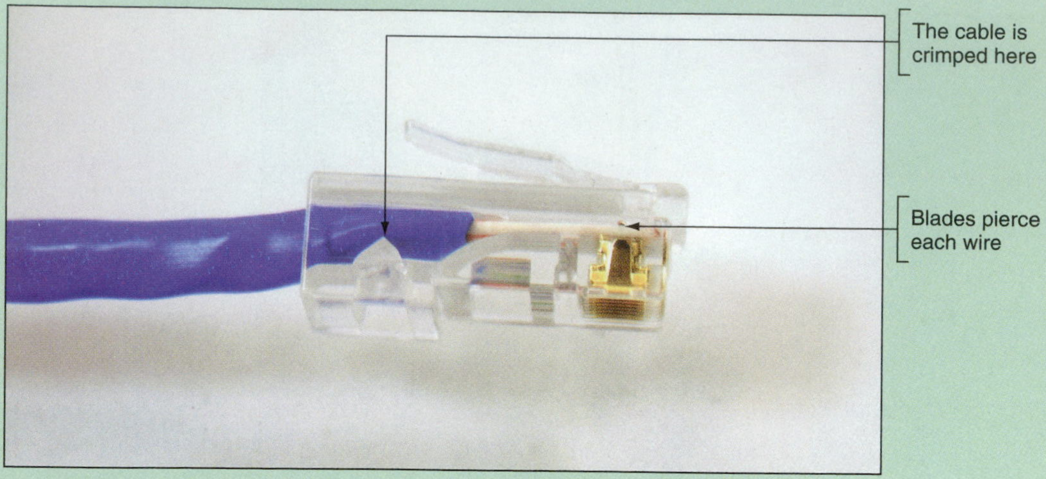

Figure 15-39 The crimper crimps the cable and cable jacket, and eight blades pierce the jacket of each individual copper wire

9. Slide the boot into place over the connector. Now you're ready to terminate the other end of the cable. Configure it to also use the T568B wiring arrangement. Figure 15-40 shows the straight-through cable with only one boot in place.

Figure 15-40 Finished patch cable with one boot in place

10. Use a cable tester to make sure the cable is good.

Notes You'll find several YouTube videos on network wiring. An excellent one of making a straight-through cable by CableSupply.com is posted at *www.youtube.com/watch?v=h7TjqnRl3QQ*.

Notes Networking standards that apply to wiring a keystone RJ-45 jack and a straight-through panel say that, to avoid crosstalk, the cable jacket should be removed to expose no more than three inches of twisted-pair wires, and that exposed twisted-pair wires should be untwisted no more than a half inch.

APPLYING | CONCEPTS WIRE A KEYSTONE JACK

A+ 220-901 2.1, 2.2, 2.9, 4.4

A keystone RJ-45 jack is used in a network wall jack. Here are the instructions to wire one:

1. Using a wire stripper and wire cutter, strip and trim back the jacket from the twisted-pair wire, leaving about two inches of wire exposed. Untwist the wires only so far as necessary so each wire can be inserted in the color-coded slot in the jack. The twists are needed to prevent crosstalk, and the untwisted wire should be no longer than a half inch. Figure 15-41 shows the wires in position for T568B wiring. Notice how the cable jacket goes into the keystone jack.

Figure 15-41 Eight wires are in position in a keystone jack for T568B wiring

2. Using the punchdown tool, make sure the blade side of the tool is on the outside of the jack. (The punchdown tool has Cut embedded on the blade side of the tool.) Push down with force to punch each wire into its slot and cut off the wire on the outside edge of the slot. It might take a couple of punches to do the job. See the left side of Figure 15-42. Place the jack cover over the jack, as shown in the right side of Figure 15-42.
3. The jack can now be inserted into the back side of a wall faceplate (see Figure 15-43). Make sure the wires in the jack are at the top of the jack. If you look closely at the faceplate, you can see the arrow pointing up. It's important the wires in the jack be at the top so that over the years dust doesn't settle on these wires. Use screws to secure the faceplate to the wall receptacle. Be sure to use a cable tester to check the network cable from its jack to the other end to make sure the wiring is good. When wiring a building, testing the cable and its two connections is called certifying the cable.

(continues)

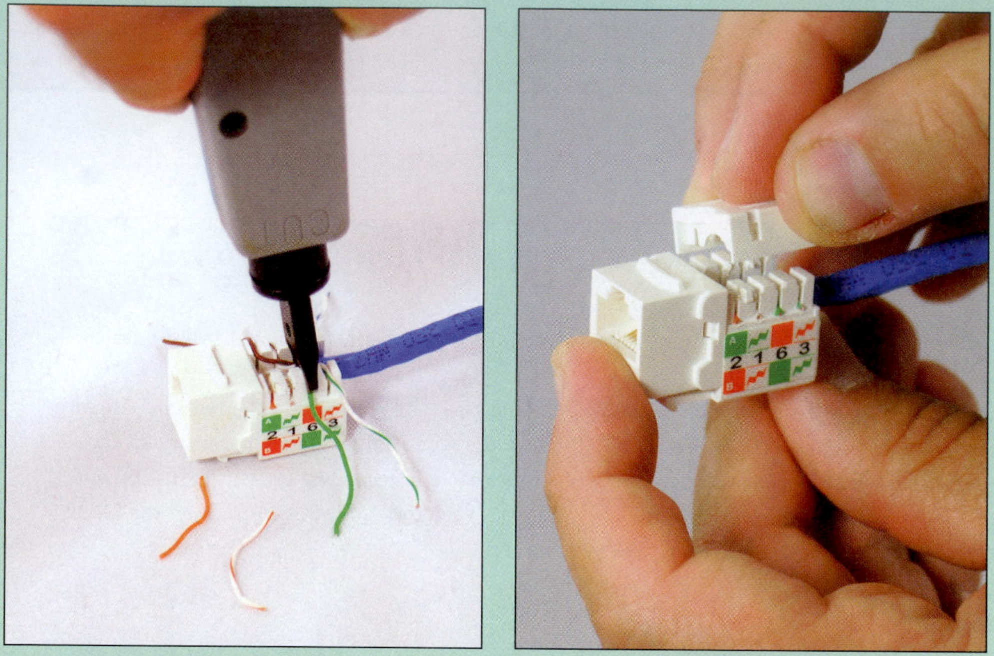

Figure 15-42 Use a punchdown tool to punch the wires into the keystone jack, and then place the cover in position

Figure 15-43 Insert the jack in the faceplate, making sure the wire connectors are at the top of the jack

Notes To see a video by CableSupply.com of using a punchdown tool to make an RJ-45 keystone jack, see *www.youtube.com/watch?v=sHy8mtW9eak*.

Some guidelines to follow when troubleshooting a network problem related to hardware are outlined in Figure 15-44 and listed here:

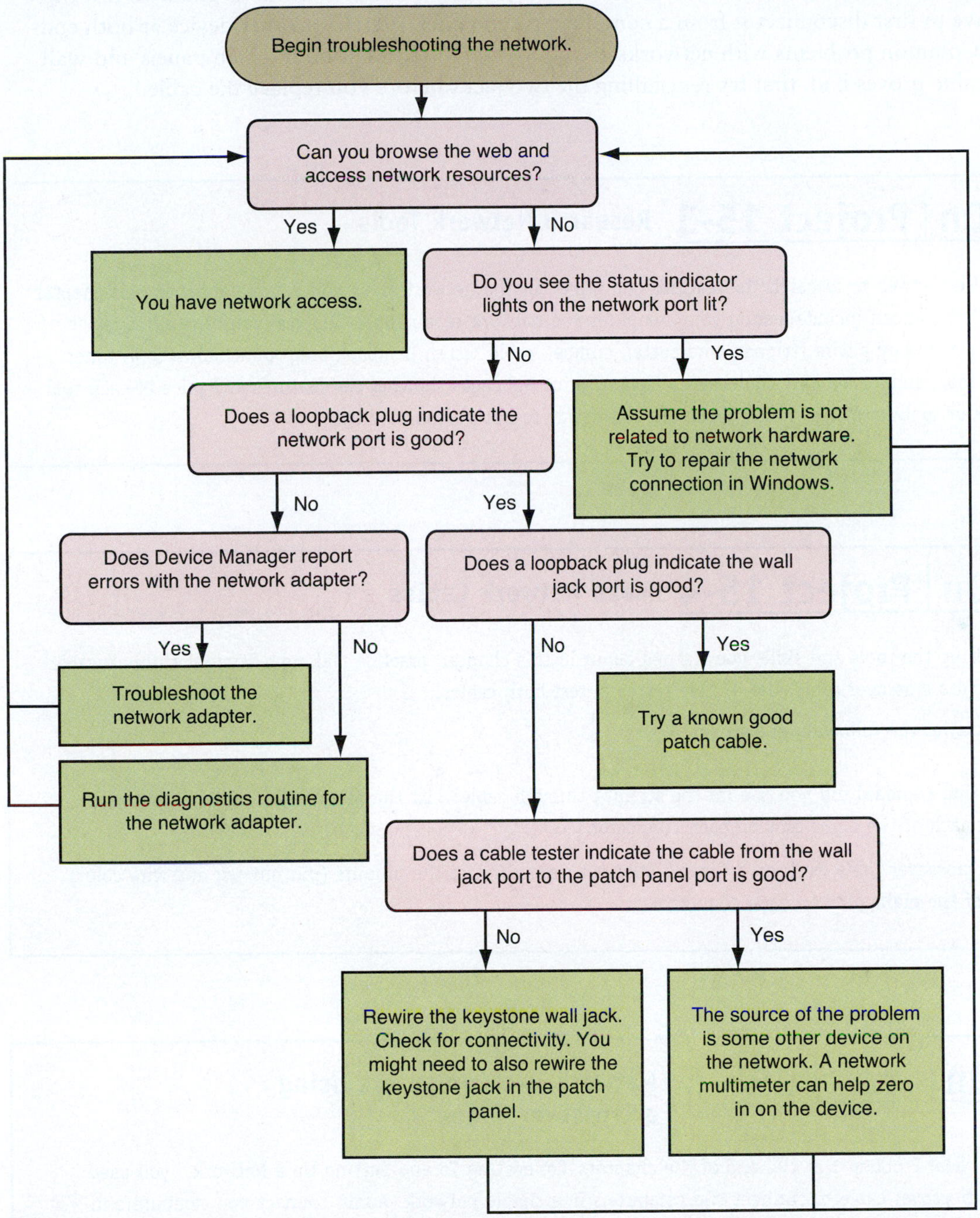

Figure 15-44 Flowchart to troubleshoot networking problems related to hardware

1. First check the status indicator lights on the network ports for connectivity and activity.
2. Use a loopback plug to verify each port. The loopback plug can work on ports provided by a computer, wall jack, patch panel, switch, router, or other device that is turned on. If you find a bad port, try a different port on a switch, router, or patch panel. You might need to replace the device.

3. For short straight-through cables connecting a computer to a wall jack or other nearby device, exchanging the straight-through cable for a known good one is easier and quicker than using a cable tester to test the cable.

4. Use a cable tester to verify a cable permanently installed alongside or inside a wall is good. To test the cable, you have to first disconnect it from a computer, patch panel, switch, or other device at both ends of the cable. Common problems with networks are poorly wired termination in patch panels and wall jacks. If the cable proves bad, first try reinstalling the two jacks before you replace the cable.

Hands-On Project 15-3 Research Network Tools

A+
220-901
2.9, 4.4

Use the web to research the features and prices for the network tools you learned about in this chapter that you can include among your computer and network repair tools. Suppose you have a budget of $200 to buy a wire stripper, wire cutter, crimper, cable tester, loopback plug, punchdown tool, toner probe, and/or network multimeter. Save or print webpages showing the features and price of each tool you select for your toolkit. Which, if any tools, did you decide to not purchase? Why?

Hands-On Project 15-4 Make Network Cables

A+
220-901
2.1, 2.2,
2.9, 4.4

Using the tools and skills you learned about in this chapter, practice making a straight-through cable and a crossover cable. Use a cable tester to test both cables.

Answer the following questions:

1. Which wiring standard did you use for the straight-through cable? List the pinouts (pin number and wire color) for each of the eight pins on each connector.
2. Will your crossover cable work on a Gigabit Ethernet network? List the pinouts (pin number and wire color) for each of the eight pins on each connector.

Hands-On Project 15-5 Network Two Computers Using a Crossover Cable

A+
220-901
2.1, 2.2

In Real Problem 1 at the end of the chapter, "Connecting To and Setting Up a Network," you used a crossover cable to connect two computers in a simple network. Again connect two computers in a simple network, but this time use the crossover cable you just made. What are the Ethernet speeds that each computer supports? Which speed is the network using? Verify the network connectivity by copying a file from one computer to the other.

To wrap up the chapter, we turn our attention to software tools you can use for troubleshooting network problems and the strategies for solving these problems.

TCP/IP UTILITIES USED FOR TROUBLESHOOTING

A+
220-901
4.4

Windows includes several TCP/IP utilities you can use to troubleshoot networking problems. In this part of the chapter, you learn to use ping, ipconfig, ifconfig, nslookup, tracert, the net commands, nbtstat, netstat, and netcom. Most of these program files are found in the \Windows\System32 folder.

A+ Exam Tip The A+ 220-901 exam expects you to know about these TCP/IP utilities: ping, ipconfig, ifconfig, tracert, netstat, nbtstat, net, netdom, and nslookup. You need to know when and how to use each utility and how to interpret results.

Notes Only the more commonly used parameters or switches for each command are discussed. For several of these commands, you can use the /? or /help parameter to get more help with the command. And for even more information about each command, search the *technet.microsoft.com* site.

Now let's see how to use each utility.

PING [-A] [-T] [*TARGETNAME*]

The ping (Packet InterNet Groper) command tests connectivity by sending an echo request to a remote computer. If the remote computer is online, detects the signal, and is configured to respond to a ping, it responds. (Responding to a ping is the default Windows setting.) Use ping to test for connectivity or to verify name resolution is working. A few examples of ping are shown in Table 15-5. Two examples are shown in Figure 15-45.

Ping Command	Description
`ping 69.32.142.109`	To test for connectivity using an IP address. If the remote computer responds, the round-trip times are displayed.
`ping -a 69.32.142.109`	The -a parameter tests for name resolution. Use it to display the host name and verify DNS is working.
`ping -t 69.32.142.109`	The -t parameter causes pinging to continue until interrupted. To display statistics, press Ctrl+Break. To stop pinging, press Ctrl+C.
`ping 127.0.0.1`	A loopback address test. The IP address 127.0.0.1 always refers to the local computer. If the local computer does not respond, you can assume there is a problem with the TCP/IP configuration.
`ping www.cengage.com`	Use a host name to find out the IP address of a remote computer. If the computer does not respond, assume there is a problem with DNS. On the other hand, some computers are not configured to respond to pings.

Table 15-5 Examples of the ping command

15

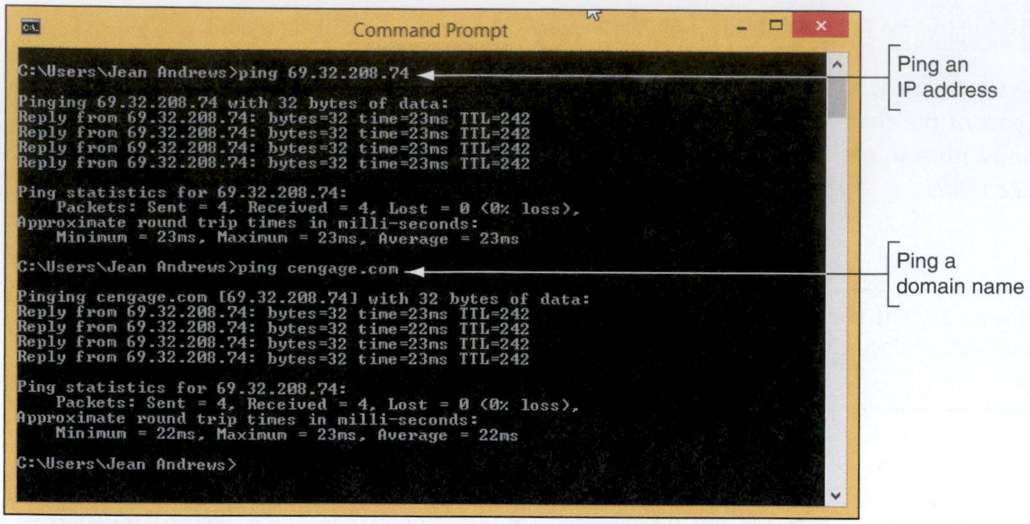

Figure 15-45 Use ping to test for connectivity and name resolution

IPCONFIG [/ALL] [/RELEASE] [/RENEW] [/DISPLAYDNS] [/FLUSHDNS]

The ipconfig (IP configuration) command can display TCP/IP configuration information and refresh the TCP/IP assignments to a connection, including its IP address. Some examples of the command are listed in Table 15-6.

Ipconfig Command	Description
`ipconfig /all`	Displays TCP/IP information.
`ipconfig /release`	Releases the IP address when dynamic IP addressing is being used.
`ipconfig /release6`	Releases an IPv6 address.
`ipconfig /renew`	Leases a new IP address from a DHCP server. Make sure you release the IP address before you renew it.
`ipconfig /renew6`	Leases a new IPv6 address from a DHCP IPv6 server. Make sure you release the IPv6 address before you renew it.
`ipconfig /displaydns`	Displays information about name resolutions that Windows currently holds in the DNS resolver cache.
`ipconfig /flushdns`	Flushes the name resolver cache, which might solve a problem when the browser cannot find a host on the Internet.

Table 15-6 Examples of the ipconfig command

IFCONFIG [-A] [INTERFACE] [UP] [DOWN]

The ifconfig (interface configuration) command is similar to ipconfig, and is used on UNIX, Linux, and Mac OS X operating systems. Some examples of the command are listed in Table 15-7.

Notes Commands entered in Linux, UNIX, and OS X are case sensitive: Upper- and lowercase matter.

Ifconfig Command	Description
`ifconfig`	Displays details of active interfaces and their assigned IP addresses. If a computer has only a single NIC, its interface name is most likely eth0.
`ifconfig -a`	Displays a list of active and inactive network interfaces.
`ifconfig <interface name>`	Displays details of a specific network interface. For example: `ifconfig eth0`
`ifconfig <interface name> up`	Enables a network interface. For example: `ifconfig eth0 up`
`ifconfig <interface name> down`	Disables a network interface. Disabling and enabling the network interface can sometimes solve a problem with network connectivity in Linux, UNIX, or OS X.

Table 15-7 Examples of the ifconfig command

> **Notes** You cannot use the ifconfig command to disable or enable the network interface without root access to the OS. In the chapter, "Virtualization, Linux, and Mac OS X," you learn how to use the sudo command to run a command that requires root access.

NSLOOKUP [COMPUTERNAME]

The nslookup (namespace lookup) command lets you read information from the Internet namespace by requesting information about domain name resolutions from the DNS server's zone data. Zone data is information about domain names and their corresponding IP addresses kept by a DNS server. For example, to find out what your DNS server knows about the domain name *www.microsoft.com*, use this command:

```
nslookup www.microsoft.com
```

Figure 15-46 shows the results. Notice in the figure that the DNS server reports one IPv4 address and two IPv6 addresses assigned to *www.microsoft.com*. It also reports that this information is nonauthoritative, meaning that it is not the authoritative, or final, name server for the *www.microsoft.com* computer name.

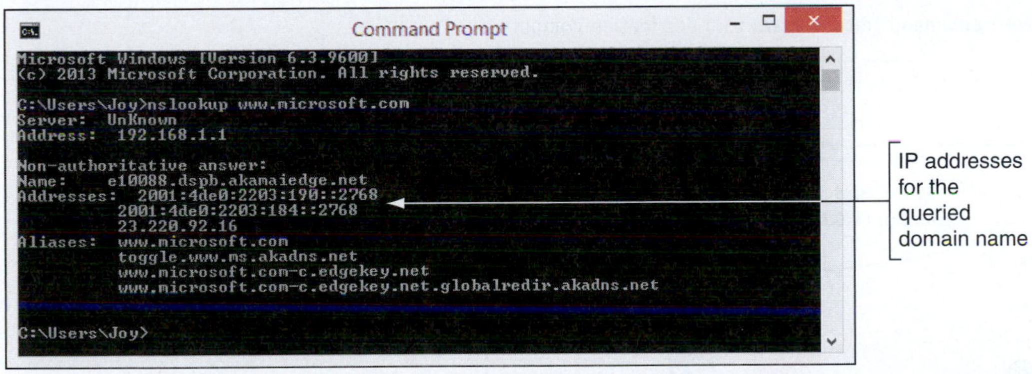

Figure 15-46 The nslookup command reports information about the Internet namespace

A reverse lookup is when you use the nslookup command to find the host name when you know a computer's IP address, such as:

```
nslookup 192.168.1.102
```

To find out the default DNS server for a network, enter the nslookup command with no parameters.

TRACERT [TARGETNAME]

The tracert (trace route) command can be useful when you're trying to resolve a problem reaching a destination host such as an FTP site or website. The command sends a series of requests to the destination computer and displays each hop to the destination. (A hop happens when a packet moves from one router to another.) For example, to trace the route to the *www.cengage.com* site, enter this command in a command prompt window:

`tracert www.cengage.com`

The results of this command are shown in Figure 15-47. A packet is assigned a Time to Live (TTL), which is the number of hop counts it can make before a router drops the packet and sends an ICMP message back to the host that sent the packet (see Figure 15-48). Internet Control Message Protocol (ICMP) messages are used by routers and hosts to communicate error messages and updates, and some routers don't send this information. The tracert command creates its report from these messages. If a router doesn't respond, the *Request timed out* message appears.

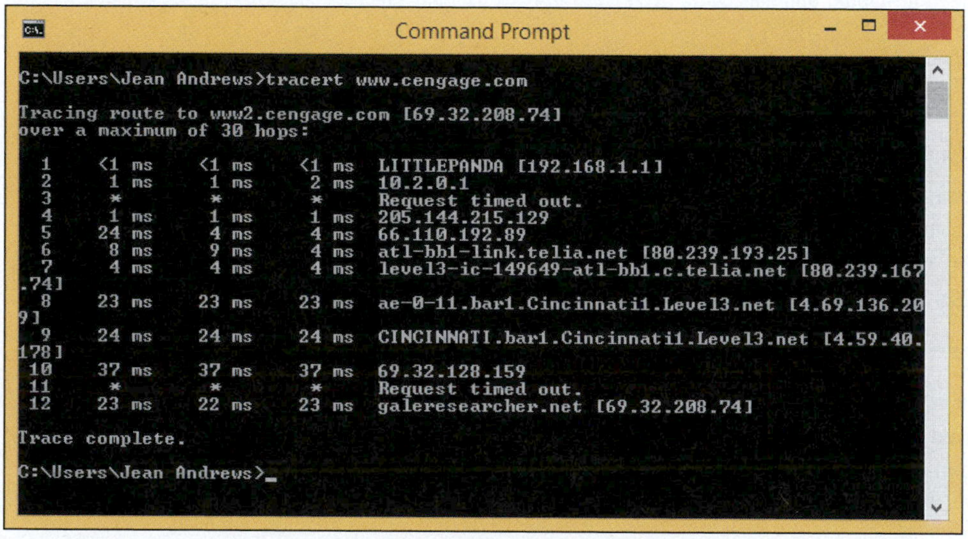

Figure 15-47 The tracert command traces a path to a destination computer

Figure 15-48 A router eliminates a packet that has exceeded its TTL

THE NET COMMANDS

The net command is several commands in one, and most of the net commands require an elevated command prompt window. In this section, you learn about the net use, net user, and net localgroup commands. The net use command connects or disconnects a computer from a shared resource or can display information about connections. For example, the following command makes a new connection to a remote computer and to a shared folder on that computer:

```
net use \\bluelight\Medical
```

Notes Other important net commands are net accounts, net config, net print, net share, and net view. You might want to do a Google search on these commands to find out how they work.

Use the following command to pass a user name and password to the \\bluelight remote computer and then map a network drive to the \Medical folder on that computer:

```
net use \\bluelight\Medical /user:"Jean Andrews" mypassword
net use z: \\bluelight\Medical
```

The double quotation marks are needed in the first command above because the user name has a space in it.

A persistent network connection is one that happens at each logon. To make the two commands persistent, add the /persistent parameter like this:

```
net use \\bluelight\Medical /user:"Jean Andrews" mypassword /persistent:yes
net use z: \\bluelight\Medical /persistent:yes
```

The net user command manages user accounts. For example, recall that the built-in administrator account is disabled by default. To activate the account, use this net user command:

```
net user administrator /active:yes
```

The net localgroup command adds, displays, or modifies local user groups. To display available local groups, use the following command:

```
net localgroup
```

To change a standard user account, Tom Jones, to an administrator account, use the following command:

```
net localgroup administrators "Tom Jones" /add
```

To change an administrator account, Tom Jones, to a standard account, use the following command:

```
net localgroup administrators "Tom Jones" /delete
```

15

NBTSTAT [-N] [-R] [-RR]

The nbtstat (NetBIOS over TCP/IP statistics) command is used to display statistics about the NetBT (NetBIOS over TCP/IP) protocol. NetBIOS is an older network protocol suite used before TCP/IP. Occasionally, you find a legacy application still in use that relies on NetBIOS and NetBIOS computer names. The NetBT protocol was developed to allow NetBIOS to work over a TCP/IP network.

Whereas TCP/IP uses a Hosts file on the local computer and a DNS server to resolve computer names, NetBIOS uses an Lmhosts file on the local computer and a WINS (Windows Internet Name Service) server to resolve NetBIOS computer names. Table 15-8 lists some nbtstat commands that you might use when a legacy application cannot access resources on the network.

Command	Description
`nbtstat -n`	Displays the NetBIOS name table on the local computer
`nbtstat -r`	Purges and rebuilds the NetBIOS name cache on the local computer using entries in the Lmhosts file
`nbtstat -RR`	Releases and renews the NetBIOS names kept by the WINS server

Table 15-8 Nbtstat commands

NETSTAT [-a] [-b] [-o]

The netstat (network statistics) command gives statistics about TCP/IP and network activity and includes several parameters. Table 15-9 lists a few netstat commands.

Command	Description
`netstat`	Lists statistics about the network connection, including the IP addresses of active connections.
`netstat >>netlog.txt`	Directs output to a text file.
`netstat -b`	Lists programs that are using the connection (see Figure 15-49) and is useful for finding malware that might be using the network. The –b switch requires an elevated command prompt.
`netstat -b -o`	Includes the process ID of each program listed. When you know the process ID, you can use the taskkill command to kill the process.
`netstat -a`	Lists statistics about all active connections and the ports the computer is listening on.

Table 15-9 Netstat commands

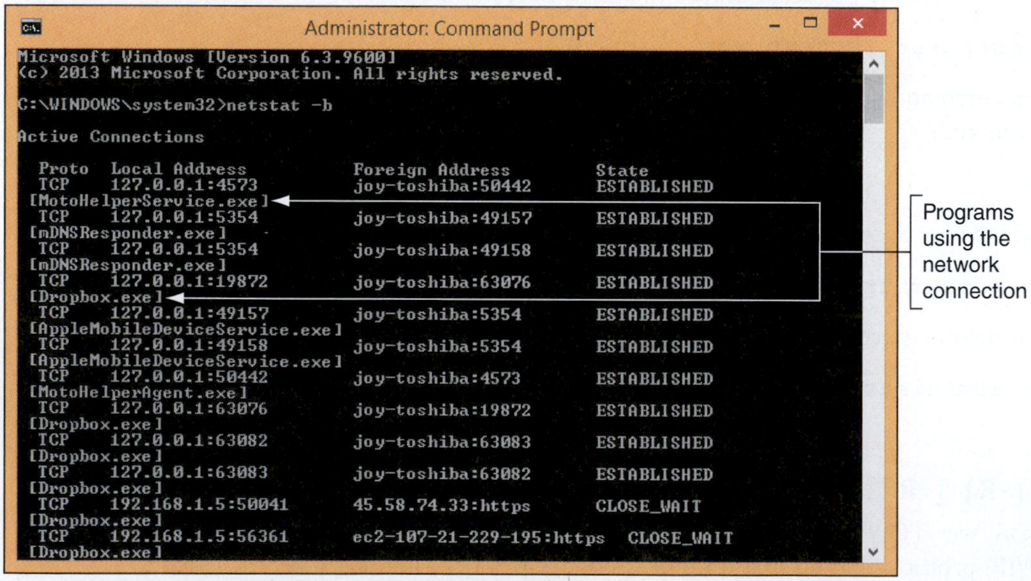

Figure 15-49 Netstat -b lists programs that are using a network connection

Notes Many commands other than netstat can use the >> parameter to redirect output to a text file. For example, try the ping or tracert command with this parameter.

NETDOM [ADD] [MOVE] [RESETPWD] [VERIFY]

The netdom (network domain) command allows administrators to manage Active Directory domains and trust relationships for Windows Server from the command prompt on the server or remotely from a Windows 8/7 workstation. The netdom command must be run using an elevated command prompt. Table 15-10 lists a few netdom commands.

Command	Description
`netdom add`	Adds a workstation to the domain
`netdom move`	Moves a workstation to a new domain
`netdom resetpwd`	Resets the password of the computer account for a domain controller
`netdom verify`	Verifies the connection is secure between a workstation and a domain controller

Table 15-10 Netdom commands

★ **A+ Exam Tip** Normally, the A+ exams don't require you to know about commands that are used only in Windows Server. This one netdom command is an exception and the A+ 220-901 exam expects you to be familiar with the command.

STRATEGIES FOR TROUBLESHOOTING NETWORK CONNECTIONS

A+ 220-901 1.4, 4.4, 4.5

With tools in hand, you're now ready to tackle network troubleshooting, including problem solving when there is no connectivity and limited or intermittent connectivity. Here is how to find out the extent of the problem:

1. To check for local connectivity, use File Explorer in Windows 8 or Windows Explorer in Windows 7 to try to access shared folders on the network. No connectivity might be caused by the network cable or its connection, a wireless switch not turned on, a bad network adapter, or TCP/IP settings in Windows.
2. Determine whether other computers on the network are having trouble with their connections. If the entire network is down, the problem is not isolated to the computer you are working on.
3. If you can access some, but not all, shared resources on the network, this limited connectivity problem might be caused by cables or a switch on the network or a problem at the computer sharing the resources you're trying to reach.
4. To test for Internet access, use a browser to surf the web. Problems with no Internet access can be caused by cables, a SOHO router, a broadband modem, or problems at the ISP.
5. To find out if a computer with limited or no connectivity was able to initially connect to a DHCP server on the network, check for an Automatic Private IP Address (APIPA). Recall from the chapter, "Connecting To and Setting Up a Network," that a computer assigns itself an APIPA if it is unable to find a DHCP server at the time it first connects to the network. Use the ipconfig command to find out the IP address (see Figure 15-50). In the results, an APIPA presents itself as the Autoconfiguration IPv4 Address, and the address begins with 169.254.

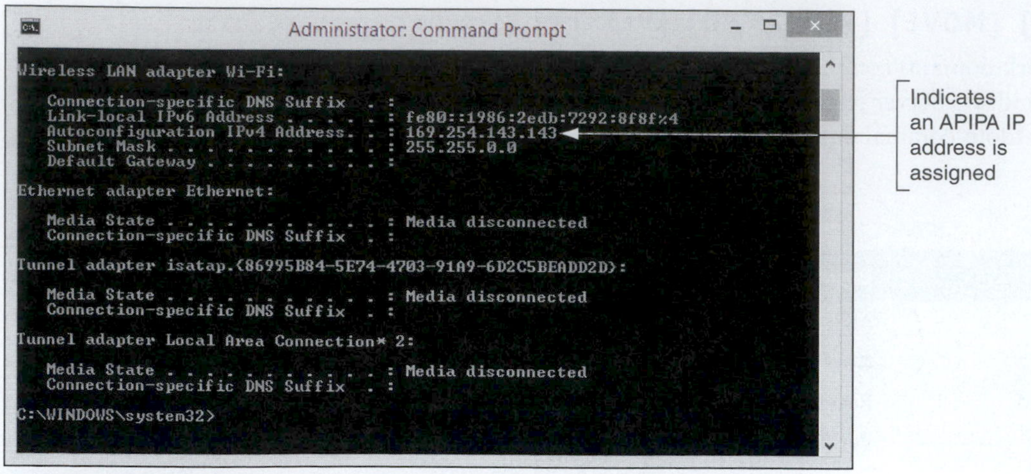

Figure 15-50 The network connection was not able to lease an IP address

Now let's see how to handle problems with no or intermittent connectivity and then we'll look at problems with Internet access.

PROBLEMS WITH NO CONNECTIVITY OR INTERMITTENT CONNECTIVITY

When a computer has no network connectivity or intermittent connectivity, begin by checking hardware and then move on to checking Windows network settings.

Follow these steps to solve problems with hardware:

1. Check the status indicator lights on the NIC or the motherboard Ethernet port. A steady light indicates connectivity and a blinking light indicates activity (see Figure 15-51). Check the indicator lights on the router or switch at the other end. Try a different port on the device. If the router or switch is in a server closet and the ports are not well labeled, you can use a loopback plug to find out which port the computer is using. If you don't see either light, this problem must be resolved before you consider OS or application problems.

Figure 15-51 Status indicator lights verify connectivity for a network port

2. Check the network cable connection at both ends. Is the cable connected to a port on the motherboard that is disabled? It might need to be connected to the network port provided by a network card. A cable tester can verify the cable is good or if it is the correct cable (patch cable or crossover cable). Try a different network cable.

3. For wireless networking, make sure the wireless switch on a laptop is turned on. If you have no connectivity, limited connectivity, or intermittent connectivity, move the laptop to a new position in the hotspot. Use a wireless locator to find the best position. Rebooting a laptop might solve the problem of not receiving a signal. Problems with a low RF signal can sometimes be solved by moving the laptop or connecting to a different wireless access point with a stronger RF signal.

4. After you've checked cable connections and the wireless switch and the problem still persists, turn to Windows to repair the network connection. Use one of these methods:
   - In an elevated command prompt window, use these two commands: **ipconfig /release** followed by **ipconfig /renew**.
   - In the Network and Sharing Center, click **Troubleshoot problems** to access a Windows network connectivity diagnostic tool (see Figure 15-52).
   - If that doesn't work, return to the Network and Sharing Center, click **Change adapter settings**, right-click the connection, and click **Disable**. Then right-click the connection again and click **Enable**.

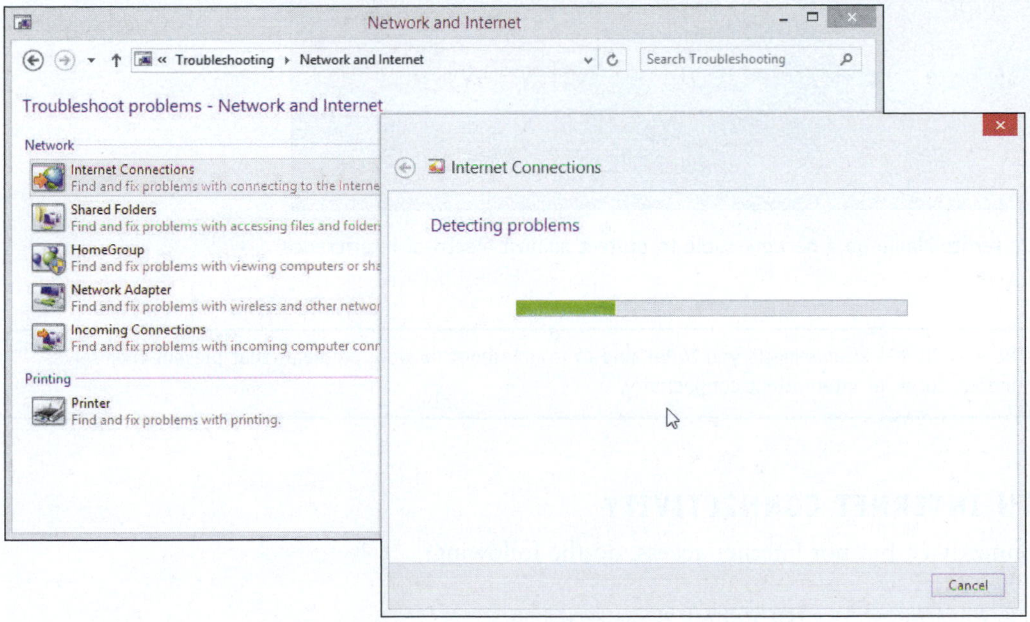

Figure 15-52 Windows indicates a network connectivity problem

If the problem is still not resolved, you need to dig deeper. Perhaps the problem is with the network adapter drivers. To solve problems with device drivers, which might also be related to a problem with the NIC, follow these steps:

1. Make sure the network adapter and its drivers are installed by checking for the adapter in Device Manager. Device Manager should report the device is working with no problems.

2. If errors are reported, try updating the device drivers. (Use another computer to download new drivers to a USB flash drive and then move the flash drive to this computer.) If the drivers still install with errors, look on the manufacturer's website or installation CD that came bundled with the adapter for diagnostic software that might help diagnose the problem.

3. If Device Manager still reports errors, try running anti-malware software and updating Windows. Then try replacing your network adapter. If that does not work, the problem might be a corrupted Windows installation.

Intermittent connectivity on a wired network might happen when a network device such as a VoIP phone is sensitive to electrical interference. You can solve this problem by attaching a ferrite clamp (see Figure 15-53) on the network cable near the port. This clamp helps to eliminate electromagnetic interference (EMI). Some cables come with preinstalled clamps, and you can also buy ferrite clamps to attach to other cables.

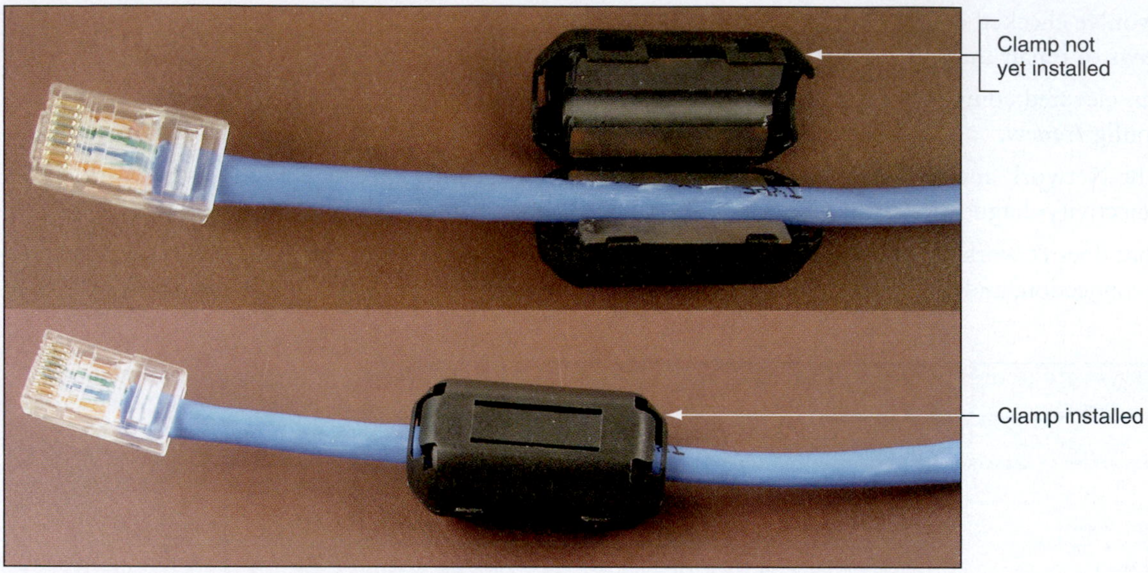

Figure 15-53 Install a ferrite clamp on a network cable to protect against electrical interference

> **★ A+ Exam Tip** The A+ 220-901 exam expects you to be able to troubleshoot network problems that present themselves as no connectivity or limited, local, or intermittent connectivity.

PROBLEMS WITH INTERNET CONNECTIVITY

If you have local connectivity, but not Internet access, do the following:

1. Try recycling the connection to the ISP. Follow these steps:
   - Unplug from the power source the cable modem, DSL modem, or other device that you use to connect to your ISP. Unplug the router. Wait about five minutes for the connection to break at the ISP.
   - Plug in the cable modem, DSL modem, or other ISP device. Wait until the lights settle. Then plug in your router.
   - On any computer on your network, use the Network and Sharing Center to repair the network connection. Open your browser and try to browse some websites.
2. For a cable modem, check to make sure your television works. The service might be down. For a DSL connection, check to make sure your phone gives a dial tone. The phone lines might be down.
3. To eliminate the router as the source of the problem, connect one computer directly to the broadband modem. If you can access the Internet, you have proven the problem is with the router or cables going to it. Connect the router back into the network and check all the router settings. The problem might be

with DHCP, the firewall settings, or port forwarding. Try updating the firmware on the router. If you are convinced all settings on the router are correct, but the connection to your ISP works without the router and does not work with the router, it's time to replace the router.

4. To eliminate DNS as the problem, follow these steps:
   - Try substituting a domain name for the IP address in a ping command:

     ```
     ping www.cengage.com
     ```

     If this ping works, then you can conclude that DNS works. If an IP address works, but the domain name does not work, the problem lies with DNS.
   - Try pinging your DNS server. To find out the IP address of your DNS server, use the nslookup command with no parameters or open the firmware utility of your router and look on a status screen.
5. If you're having a problem accessing a particular computer on the Internet, try using the tracert command, for example:

   ```
   tracert www.cengage.com
   ```

   The results show computers along the route that might be giving delays.
6. If one computer on the network cannot access the Internet but other computers can, make sure MAC address filtering on the router is disabled or this computer is allowed access.
7. Perhaps the problem is with your router firewall or Windows Firewall. How to verify router firewall settings is covered in the chapter, "Connecting To and Setting Up a Network." Windows Firewall is covered in the chapter, "Security Strategies."
8. If you still cannot access the Internet, contact your ISP.

If some computers on the network have both local and Internet connectivity, but one computer does not, move on to checking problems on that computer, which can include TCP/IP settings and problems with applications.

USE TCP/IP UTILITIES TO SOLVE CONNECTIVITY PROBLEMS

No connectivity or no Internet access can be caused by Windows TCP/IP configuration and connectivity. Follow these steps to verify that the local computer is communicating over the network:

15

1. Using the Network and Sharing Center or the ipconfig command, try to release the current IP address and lease a new address. This process solves the problem of an IP conflict with other computers on the network or your computer's failure to connect to the network.
2. To find out if you have local connectivity, try to ping another computer on the network. To find out if you have Internet connectivity and DNS is working, try to ping a computer on the Internet using its host address. Try **ping www.cengage.com**. If this last command does not work, try the tracert command to find out if the problem is outside or inside your local network. Try **tracert www.cengage.com**.
3. In a command prompt window, enter **ipconfig /all**. Verify the IP address, subnet mask, and default gateway. For dynamic IP addressing, if the computer cannot reach the DHCP server, it assigns itself an APIPA, which is listed as an Autoconfiguration IPv4 Address that begins with 169.254 (refer back to Figure 15-50). In this case, suspect that the computer is not able to reach the network or the DHCP server is down.
4. Next, try the loopback address test. Enter the command **ping 127.0.0.1** (with no period after the final 1). Your computer should respond. If you get an error, assume the problem is TCP/IP settings on your computer. Compare the configuration with that of a working computer on the same network.
5. If you're having a problem with slow transfer speeds, suspect a process is hogging network resources. Use the **netstat –b** command to find out if the program you want to use to access the network is actually running.

6. Firewall settings might be wrong. Are port forwarding settings on the router and in Windows Firewall set correctly? You learn to configure Windows Firewall in the chapter, "Security Strategies."
7. Two computers on the network might have the same computer name. This command reports the error:

```
net view \\computername
```

8. If the net view command using a computer name does not work, try the command using the remote computer's IP address, as in:

```
net view 192.168.1.102
```

   If this command works, the problem is likely with name resolution. Make sure the computer name you are using is correct.
9. If you're having problems getting a network drive map to work, try making the connection with the net use command like this:

```
net use z: \\computername\folder
```

   To disconnect a mapped network drive, use this command:

```
net use z: /delete
```

Now we move on to problems with wireless connectivity.

NO WIRELESS CONNECTIVITY

In a laptop, an internal wireless adapter uses an internal antenna, and the laptop might have a switch to turn on the internal wireless adapter or might use a key combination for that purpose. Look for the switch near the keyboard or on the side of the laptop (see Figure 15-54). Make sure the switch is set to the on position when you want to use wireless. The internal antenna might be embedded in the lid of the laptop. Raising the lid to a vertical position can sometimes improve the signal and solve a problem with intermittent connectivity.

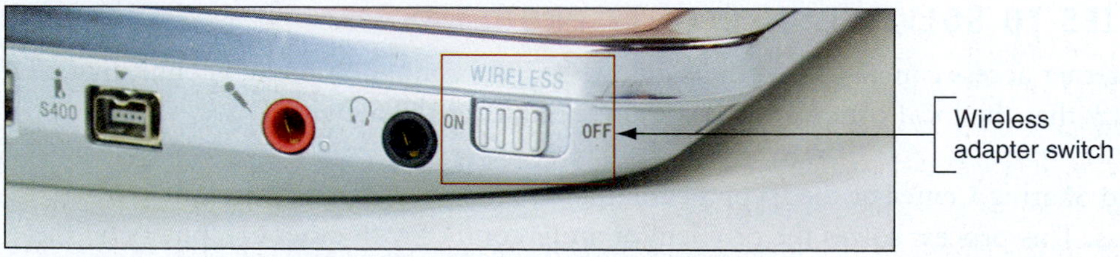

Figure 15-54 This switch controls an internal wireless adapter

Following is a list of more things you can try. After each step, see if you can connect to the wireless network; if not, continue on to the next step.

1. Make sure you are within range of the wireless access point.
2. Click your wireless icon in the system tray. Turn the wireless connection off, wait a few seconds, then turn it back on.
3. Using the Network and Sharing Center, disable and then enable the wireless network adapter.
4. Reboot the computer.
5. Update the device drivers for the wireless card.
6. Replace the wireless card (see Figure 15-55). For instructions on how to replace the Mini PCIe wireless card, refer to the chapter, "Supporting I/O Devices."

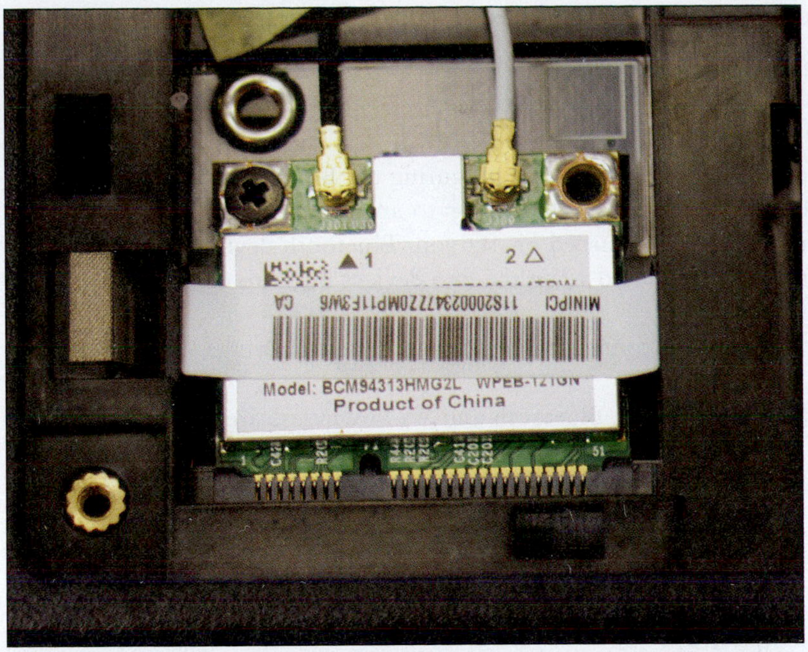

Figure 15-55 This half-size Mini PCIe wireless card is anchored in the expansion slot with one screw

WI-FI NETWORK NOT FOUND

Recall that a wireless access point broadcasts an SSID. Your computer typically will easily find the SSID of a Wi-Fi network and connect after entering the security key, if one is needed. If your computer does not detect an SSID that you know should be available, it might be because the SSID is hidden. If you know the SSID name and the security key, you can still connect to the network by following these steps:

1. Open the Network and Sharing Center.
2. Click **Set up a new connection or network.**
3. Select **Manually connect to a wireless network** (see Figure 15-56), and click **Next.**

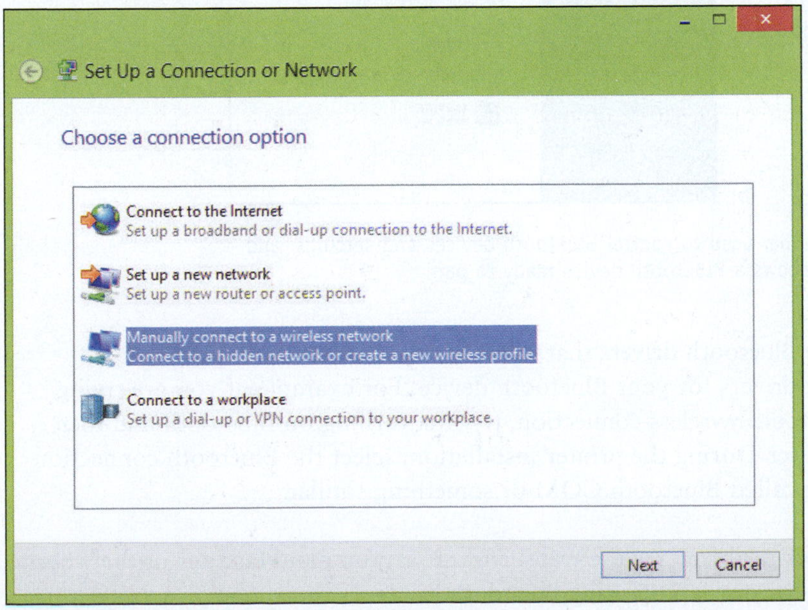

Figure 15-56 Set up a manual connection to a hidden SSID

4. Enter the network name, choose the security type, and enter the security key. Click **Next**.
5. Your wireless network is set up and you should be connected. Click **Close**.

NO BLUETOOTH CONNECTIVITY

If your laptop supports Bluetooth, read the documentation for configuring the Bluetooth connection that came with the laptop because Bluetooth setups differ from one laptop to another. Following the directions for your laptop, turn on Bluetooth. After Bluetooth is turned on, set your Bluetooth device near the laptop and it should pair up with it. Pairing up is the term used when the two devices begin to communicate and a passcode is requested to complete the connection.

If you are having problems getting the Bluetooth connection to work, try the following:

- Make sure Bluetooth is turned on (for some laptops, Bluetooth and Wi-Fi wireless are controlled by a function key or a wireless switch).
- Verify that Windows sees Bluetooth enabled. You might do this by using an applet in Control Panel, by using a program on the Windows 8 Start screen or Windows 7 Start menu, or by using the Bluetooth icon in the notification area of the desktop taskbar.

Notes Be aware that a laptop might show the Bluetooth icon in the taskbar even when the laptop does not support Bluetooth.

- Be sure you have downloaded and installed all Windows updates.
- Look in Device Manager to make sure the Bluetooth component is recognized with no errors. For some laptops, even though the component is an internal device, it is seen in Device Manager as a USB device.
- Make sure the other device has Bluetooth turned on. For example, when trying to communicate with a smart phone, you must use the menu on the phone to activate Bluetooth connections. Windows should see the Bluetooth device when you click the Bluetooth icon in the taskbar and then click **Add a Bluetooth Device**, as shown in Figure 15-57a. You can also manage Bluetooth devices from the *PC and devices* page in Windows 8, as shown in Figure 15-57b.

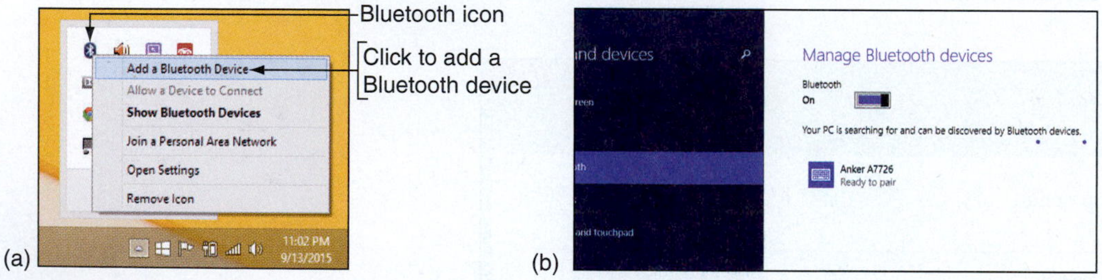

Figure 15-57 (a) Bluetooth icon on the taskbar used to control Bluetooth devices and settings, and (b) the PC and devices page shows a Bluetooth device ready to pair

- Try uninstalling and reinstalling the Bluetooth drivers that come bundled with your laptop.
- Try uninstalling and reinstalling the drivers for your Bluetooth device. For example, if you are trying to connect to a printer using a Bluetooth wireless connection, try first turning on Bluetooth and then uninstalling and reinstalling the printer. During the printer installation, select the Bluetooth connection for the printer port, which might be called Bluetooth COM or something similar.

For more ideas for solving a Bluetooth problem, try the website of the laptop manufacturer or the website of the device you are trying to connect to your laptop using Bluetooth.

GPS NOT FUNCTIONING

A Global Positioning System (GPS) allows your laptop to be used as a navigation device with mapping software. The advantages to using your laptop as a GPS device instead of a compact GPS device, like Garmin or TomTom, is a larger screen, more detailed routing, and better routing analysis. A GPS receiver connects to your laptop using a USB port. If your GPS is not working, try the following:

- Sometimes the GPS receiver does not work well when plugged directly in to the USB port on a laptop. Instead, try using a short USB extension cable that is usually included with the GPS receiver. This gives the GPS receiver some distance from your laptop so there is less interference caused by the laptop.
- Because a GPS uses satellites, a clear view of the sky is necessary for the GPS receiver to lock signal with the satellite. Make sure you are positioned so that the receiver is able to "see" a clear sky. Buildings, mountains, and trees can all be blocks.

Hands-On | Project 15-6 Use a Port Scanner

A+ 220-901 4.4, 4.5

Port scanning software can be used to find out how vulnerable a computer is with open ports. This project requires the use of two computers on the same network to practice using port scanning software. Do the following:

1. On Computer 1, download and install Advanced Port Scanner by Famatech at **http://www.advanced-port-scanner.com**. (Be careful to not accept other software offered while downloading.)
2. On Computer 2, set the network location to **Public network**. (For Windows 8, open the **Settings** charms, click the **Network** icon, click **View Connection Settings**, click **Connections**, select the network connection, and turn off **Find devices and content**. For Windows 7, open the **Network and Sharing Center** and click the network location to change it.)
3. On Computer 1, start Advanced Port Scanner and make sure that the range of IP addresses includes the IP address of Computer 2. Change the default port list to 0 through 6000. Then click **Scan**.
4. Browse the list and find Computer 2. List the number and purpose of all open ports found on Computer 2.
5. On Computer 2, set the network location to Private for Windows 8 and Home for Windows 7. Open the **System** window, click **Remote settings**, and allow Remote Assistance connections to this computer. Close all windows.
6. On Computer 1, rescan and list the number and purpose of each port now open on Computer 2. Figure 15-58 shows the results for one computer, but yours might be different.

(continues)

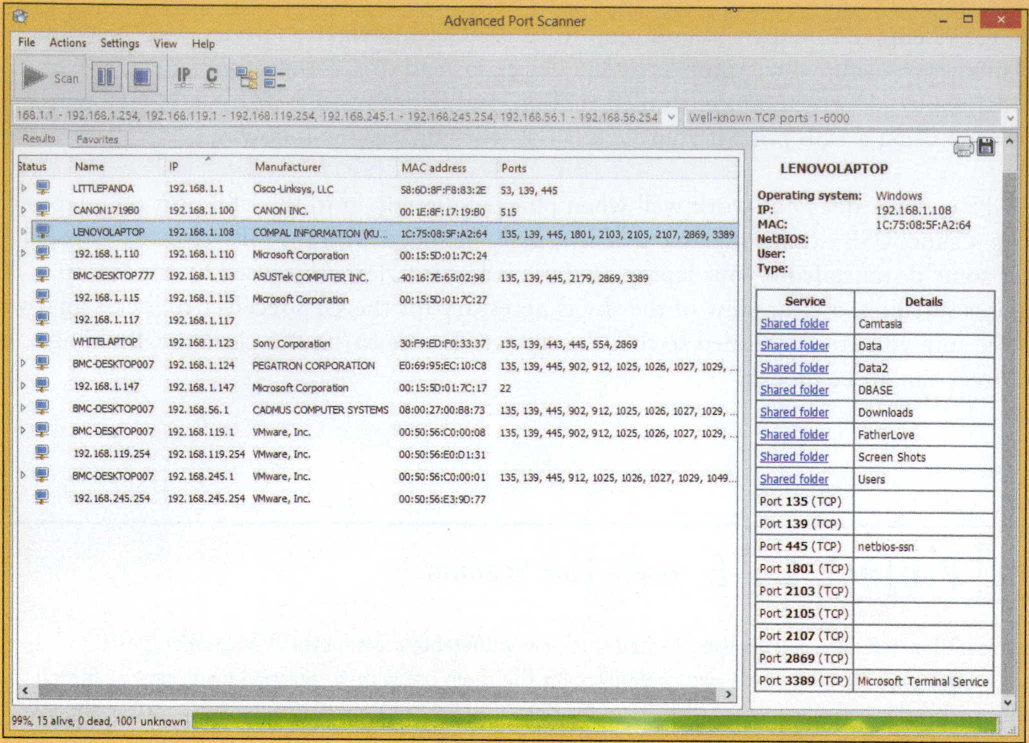

Source: Advanced Port Scanner by Famatech

Figure 15-58 Advanced Port Scanner shows open ports on networked computers

>> CHAPTER SUMMARY

Types of Networks and the Internet Connections They Use

- Networks are categorized by size as a PAN, LAN, Wireless LAN, MAN, or WAN.
- Performance of a network technology is measured in bandwidth and latency.
- The two most popular ways to connect to the Internet are cable Internet and DSL. Other methods used include satellite, dedicated fiber optic, dial-up, and cellular wireless technologies (2G, 3G, 4G, and/or LTE).

Hardware Used by Local Networks

- Networking hardware used on local networks can include dial-up modems, hubs, switches, routers, wireless access points, bridges, cables, and connectors.
- The most popular Ethernet cable is twisted pair using an RJ-45 connector. Phone lines use an RJ-11 connector.
- Switches and older hubs are used as a centralized connection for devices on a wired network. A bridge stands between two network segments and controls traffic between them.
- Most wired local networks use twisted-pair cabling that can be unshielded twisted-pair (UTP) cable or shielded twisted-pair (STP) cable. UTP is rated by category: CAT-3, CAT-5, CAT-5e, CAT-6, CAT-6a, and CAT-7. CAT-6e is an unofficial name for CAT-6a.

- Fiber-optic cables can use one of four connectors: ST, SC, LC, or MT-RJ. Any one of the four connectors can be used with single-mode or multimode fiber-optic cable.
- Powerline networking, also called Ethernet over Power (EoP), sends Ethernet transmissions over the power lines of a building or house. Power over Ethernet (PoE) sends power over Ethernet cables.

Setting Up and Troubleshooting Network Wiring

- Tools used to manage and troubleshoot network wiring and connectors are a loopback plug, cable tester, multimeter, toner probe, wire stripper, crimper, and punchdown tool.
- The RJ-45 connector has eight pins. Four pins (pins 1, 2, 3, and 6) are used to transmit and send data using the 10BaseT and 100BaseT speeds. Using 1000BaseT speed, all eight pins are used for transmissions.
- Two standards used to wire network cables are T568A and T568B. The difference between the T568A and T568B standards is the orange twisted-pair wires are reversed in the RJ-45 connector from the green twisted-pair wires.
- A straight-through cable uses the T568A or T568B standard on both connectors. A crossover cable for 10BaseT or 100BaseT uses T568A for one connector and T568B for the other connector. Crossover cables are generally not used on Gigabit Ethernet networks.
- Either T568A or T568B can be used to wire a network. To avoid confusion, don't mix the two standards in a building.
- Use wire strippers, wire cutters, and a crimper to make network cables. A punchdown tool is used to terminate cables in a patch panel or keystone RJ-45 jack. Be sure to use a cable tester to test or certify a cable you have just made.
- When troubleshooting network wiring, tools that can help are status indicator lights, loopback plugs, cable testers, Wi-Fi analyzers, toner probes, and network multimeters.
- Useful Windows TCP/IP utilities for network troubleshooting are ping, ipconfig, nslookup, tracert, net use, net user, net localgroup, nbtstat, netstat, and netdom. The Linux ifconfig command is similar to the Windows ipconfig command.
- When troubleshooting network problems, check hardware, device drivers, Windows, and the client or server application, in that order.

>> KEY TERMS

For explanations of key terms, see the Glossary for this text.

100BaseT
bandwidth
base station
BNC connector
bridge
broadband
cable Internet
cable tester
CAT-3
CAT-5
CAT-5e
CAT-6
CAT-6a
CAT-6e
CAT-7
cellular network
cellular WAN
coaxial cable
crimper
crossover cable
data throughput
DSL (Digital Subscriber Line)
Ethernet over Power (EoP)
extender
F connector
Fast Ethernet
ferrite clamp
fiber optic
fiber-optic cable
Gigabit Ethernet
hub
ifconfig (interface configuration)
Internet service provider (ISP)
ipconfig (IP configuration)
ISDN (Integrated Services Digital Network)
keystone RJ-45 jack
LAN (local area network)
latency
LC (local connector) connector
line-of-sight connectivity
loopback plug
MAN (metropolitan area network)
mobile hotspot
MT-RJ (mechanical transfer registered jack) connector
nbtstat (NetBIOS over TCP/IP statistics)
net localgroup
net use

net user
netdom (network domain)
netstat (network statistics)
network multimeter
nslookup (namespace lookup)
PAN (personal area network)
patch cable
patch panel
ping (Packet InterNet Groper)
plenum
PoE injector
Power over Ethernet (PoE)
powerline networking
punchdown tool
PVC (polyvinyl chloride)
repeater
reverse lookup
RG-59 coaxial cable
RG-6 coaxial cable
RJ-11 jack
SC (subscriber connector or standard connector) connector
shielded twisted-pair (STP) cable
ST (straight tip) connector
straight-through cable
switch
T568A
T568B
tether
tone probe
toner probe
tracert (trace route)
twisted-pair cabling
unshielded twisted-pair (UTP) cable
WAN (wide area network)
Wi-Fi analyzer
wire stripper
wireless LAN (WLAN)

>> REVIEWING THE BASICS

1. Place the following networking technologies in the order of their highest speed, from slowest to fastest: dial-up networking, cable Internet, Fast Ethernet, and 3G.
2. What is the difference between ADSL and SDSL?
3. Among satellite, cable Internet, and DSL, which technology experiences more latency?
4. When using DSL to connect to the Internet, the data transmission shares the cabling with what other technology?
5. When using cable Internet, the data transmission shares the cabling with what other technology?
6. What is the name of the port used by an Ethernet cable? What is the name of the port used by a dial-up modem?
7. If you want to upgrade your 100BaseT Ethernet network so that it will run about 10 times the current speed, what technology would you use?
8. What is the maximum length of a cable on a 100BaseT network?
9. What does the 100 in the name 100BaseT indicate?
10. Which type of networking cable is more reliable, STP or UTP? Which is normally used on LANs?
11. Which is more expensive, UTP CAT-6 cabling or STP CAT-6 cabling?
12. When looking at a network cable that is not labeled, describe how you can tell if the cable is a straight-through cable or a crossover cable.
13. What technology is used when power is transmitted on a network cable?
14. Describe the difference between a hub and a switch.
15. How is a wireless access point that is also a bridge more efficient in handling network traffic than a wireless access point that is not a bridge?
16. What type of cable uses an F connector?
17. Why does a CAT-6 cable have a plastic core? Which types of cabling are recommended for Gigabit Ethernet?
18. How many wires does a CAT-6 cable have? A CAT-6e cable? A coaxial cable?
19. Which tool can you use to verify that a network port on a computer is good?
20. After making a straight-through cable, which tool can you use to certify the cable?

21. Which tool can help you find a network cable in the walls of a building?
22. Which tool is used to firmly attach an RJ-45 connector to a network cable?
23. Which tool can help you find out which wall jack connects to which port on a switch in an electrical closet?
24. Name two types of devices or equipment where you might find a keystone RJ-45 jack.
25. List the number assigned to each pair and the color of each pair used in twisted-pair networking cables.
26. What two standards are used to wire networking cables?
27. Of the two standards in the previous question, which standard is the most common? Which is required for all U.S. government installations?
28. Using either of the two wiring standards, what are the colors of the two pairs used to send and/or receive data on a 100BaseT network?
29. How many pairs of wires are crossed in a crossover cable that will work on a 100BaseT network? On a 1000BaseT network?
30. To prevent crosstalk in a keystone RJ-45 jack, what is the maximum length of wire that should be untwisted?

>> THINKING CRITICALLY

1. Linda has been assigned the job of connecting five computers to a network. The room holding the five computers has three network jacks that connect to a switch in an electrical closet down the hallway. Linda decides to install a second switch in the room. The new switch has four network ports. She uses one port to connect the switch to a wall jack. Now she has five ports available (two wall jacks and three switch ports). While installing and configuring the NICs in the five computers, she discovers that the PCs connected to the two wall jacks work fine, but the three connected to the switch refuse to communicate with the network. What could be wrong and what should she try next?
2. If a Gigabit Ethernet NIC is having a problem communicating with a 100BaseT switch that only supports half duplex, what steps can you take to manually set the NIC to the speed and duplex used by the switch? Which speed and duplex should you choose?
3. You connect a computer to an RJ-45 wall jack using a straight-through cable. When you first open the browser on the computer, you discover it does not have Internet access. Put the following steps in the correct order to troubleshoot the problem:
   a. Use a loopback plug to verify the network port on the computer.
   b. Rewire the keystone RJ-45 wall jack.
   c. Use a loopback plug to verify the network port in the wall jack.
   d. Exchange the straight-through cable for a known good one.
   e. Verify the status indicator lights on the NIC.
   f. Use a cable tester to test the network cable and termination from the switch in the electrical closet to the wall jack.

>> REAL PROBLEMS, REAL SOLUTIONS

REAL PROBLEM 15-1 Setting Up a Wireless Access Point

As a computer and networking consultant to small businesses, you are frequently asked to find solutions to increasing demands for network and Internet access at a business. One business rents offices in a historical building that has strict rules for wiring. They have come to you asking for a solution for providing Wi-Fi access to their guests in the lobby of the building. Research options for a solution and answer the following questions:

1. Print or save webpages showing two options for a Wi-Fi wireless access point that can mount on the wall or ceiling. For one option, select a device that can receive its power by PoE from the network cable run to the device. For the other option, select a device that requires an electrical cable to the device as well as a network cable.
2. Print or save two webpages for a splitter that can be mounted near the second wireless access point that splits the power from data on the network cable. Make sure the power connectors for the splitter and the access point can work together.
3. To provide PoE from the electrical closet on the network cable to the wireless access point, print or save the webpage for an injector that injects power into a network cable. Make sure the voltage and wattage output for the injector are compatible with the needs of both wireless access points.
4. You estimate the distance for network cabling from the switch to the wireless access point is about 200 feet (61 meters). What is the cost of 200 feet of PVC CAT-6a cabling? For 200 feet of plenum CAT-6a cabling? For 200 feet of plenum CAT-7 cabling?
5. Of the options you researched, which option do you recommend? Using this option, what is the total cost of the Wi-Fi hotspot?

CHAPTER

16

Supporting Mobile Operating Systems

After completing this chapter, you will be able to:

- Identify and use significant features of Android, iOS, and Windows mobile operating systems
- Configure, synchronize, and troubleshoot mobile devices that use iOS
- Configure, synchronize, and troubleshoot mobile devices that use Android
- Configure, synchronize, and troubleshoot Windows mobile devices

Previous chapters have focused on supporting personal computers. This chapter deviates from this topic as we discuss operating systems on mobile devices such as smart phones and tablets. As mobile devices become more common, many people use them to surf the web, access email, and manage apps and data. As an IT support technician, you need to know about the operating systems and hardware used with mobile devices and how to help a user configure and troubleshoot these devices.

Because many employees expect to be able to use their mobile devices to access, synchronize, and edit data on the corporate network, data, settings, and apps stored on mobile devices need to be secured and synchronized to other storage locations. In this chapter, you learn how you can synchronize content on mobile devices to a personal computer or to storage in the cloud (on the Internet). Finally, in this chapter, you learn about tools and resources available for troubleshooting mobile operating systems.

OPERATING SYSTEMS USED ON MOBILE DEVICES

A+
220-902
2.5

The operating system for a mobile device is installed at the factory. Here are the three most popular ones in the United States:

- Android OS by Google (*android.com*) is based on Linux and is used on various smart phones and tablets. Currently, Android is the most popular OS for smart phones. Nearly 80 percent of the smart phones sold today use Android. Combining both smart phones and tablets, Android holds about 50 percent of the market.
- iOS by Apple (*apple.com*) is based on Mac OS X and is currently used on the iPhone, iPad, and iPod touch by Apple. Almost 20 percent of smart phones sold today are made by Apple and use iOS. About 40 percent of smart phones and tablets combined use iOS.
- Windows Phone (WP) by Microsoft (*microsoft.com*) is based on Windows and is used on various smart phones (not on tablets). Less than 3 percent of smart phones sold today use Windows Phone. (Windows tablets use the 32-bit version of the same Windows operating system used on desktop and laptop systems.)

The remaining market share for smart phones and tablets in the United States is shared by these mobile OSs:

- Java Micro Edition (ME) by Oracle (*oracle.com*) provides a basic platform for everything from smart phones to TV set-top boxes to printers. Most of these devices have limited computing power, and Java ME enables Java applications to run on these devices.
- The Symbian OS from the Symbian Foundation (*symbian.org*) is popular outside the United States and is used on devices made by multiple manufacturers, including Nokia, Samsung, Sony, and others.
- BlackBerry OS by BlackBerry Limited (*blackberry.com*) is a proprietary OS used on devices built by BlackBerry.
- Kindle Fire by Amazon (*amazon.com*) runs the Fire OS, which is based on Android and is deeply customized to meet the needs of Amazon's e-reader audience.

This chapter focuses on the Android, iOS, and Windows Phone operating systems used on smart phones and/or tablets.

A+ Exam Tip The A+ 220-902 exam expects you to know how to support the Android, iOS, and Windows Phone operating systems used with mobile devices.

ANDROID BY THE OPEN HANDSET ALLIANCE AND GOOGLE

A+
220-902
2.5

The Android operating system is based on the Linux OS and uses a Linux kernel. Linux and Android are open source, which means the source code for the operating system is available for free and anyone can modify and redistribute the source code. Open source software is typically developed as a community effort by many contributors. Android was originally developed by the Open Handset Alliance (*www.openhandsetalliance.com*), which is made up of many technology and mobile phone companies and led by Google, Inc.

In 2005, Google acquired this source code. Google does not own Android, but it has assumed a leadership role in development, quality control, and distributions of the Android OS and Android apps. Ongoing development of the Android OS code by Google and other contributors is released to the public as open source code.

GETTING TO KNOW AN ANDROID DEVICE

Releases of Android are named after desserts and include Froyo (frozen yogurt; version 2.2.x), Gingerbread (version 2.3.x), Honeycomb (version 3.x), Ice Cream Sandwich (version 4.0.x), Jelly Bean (version 4.1-4.3.x), KitKat (version 4.4+), and Lollipop (version 5.0-5.1.1). (Future releases of Android will follow in alphabetic order: M, N, O, and P.) At the time of this writing, most new phones and tablets ship with KitKat or Lollipop installed.

> **Notes** Google has announced that Marshmallow is the next release of Android and will be released by the time this text is in print.

Android's launcher, or graphical user interface (GUI), starts with multiple home screens and supports windows, panes, and 3D graphics. The Android OS can use an embedded browser, manage a database using SQLite, and connect to Wi-Fi, Bluetooth, and cellular networks. Most current Android mobile devices have no physical buttons on the front of the device. However, the user can configure up to five custom software buttons, called Home touch buttons, on the Action bar at the bottom of the screen, with the three default buttons typically being back, home, and overview (see Figure 16-1).

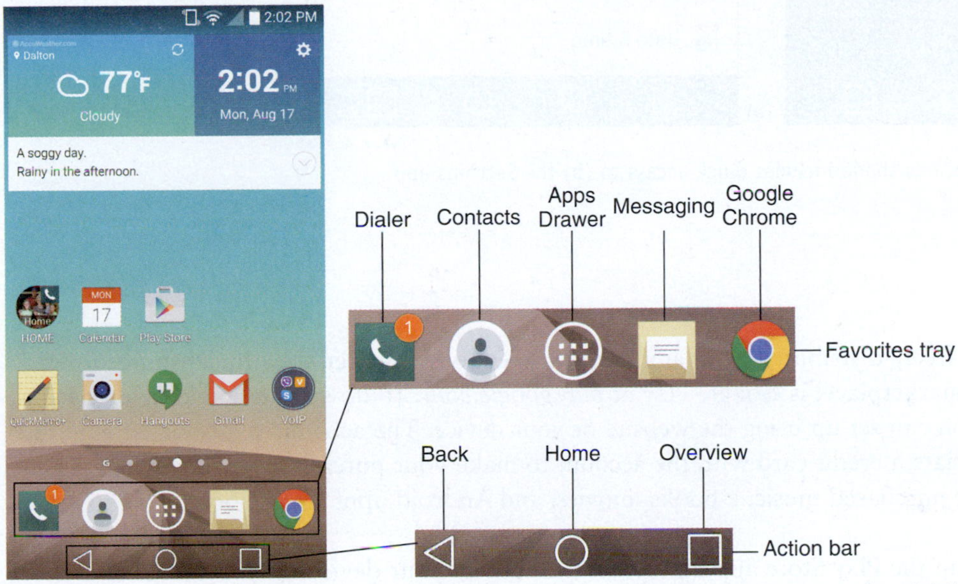

Source: Android

Figure 16-1 This LG smart phone has the Android Lollipop OS installed

On Android phones, up to seven apps or groups of apps can be pinned to the Favorites tray just above the Action bar. The pinned apps shown in Figure 16-1 are the Dialer (for making phone calls), Contacts, the Apps Drawer (lists and manages all your apps), Android's native Messaging app, and Google Chrome (web browser). Apps in the Favorites tray stay put as you move from home screen to home screen by swiping left or right. All but the Apps Drawer can be replaced by third-party apps.

Notifications provide alerts and related information about apps and social media. Notifications are accessed by swiping down from the top of the screen, as shown in Figure 16-2a. The Notifications shade provides access to the Quick Settings menu, such as Wi-Fi, Bluetooth, Volume, and Brightness. Tap the **Settings** (cog) icon in the upper-right corner to open the Settings app (see Figure 16-2b), or tap the back button in the Action bar to return to the home screen.

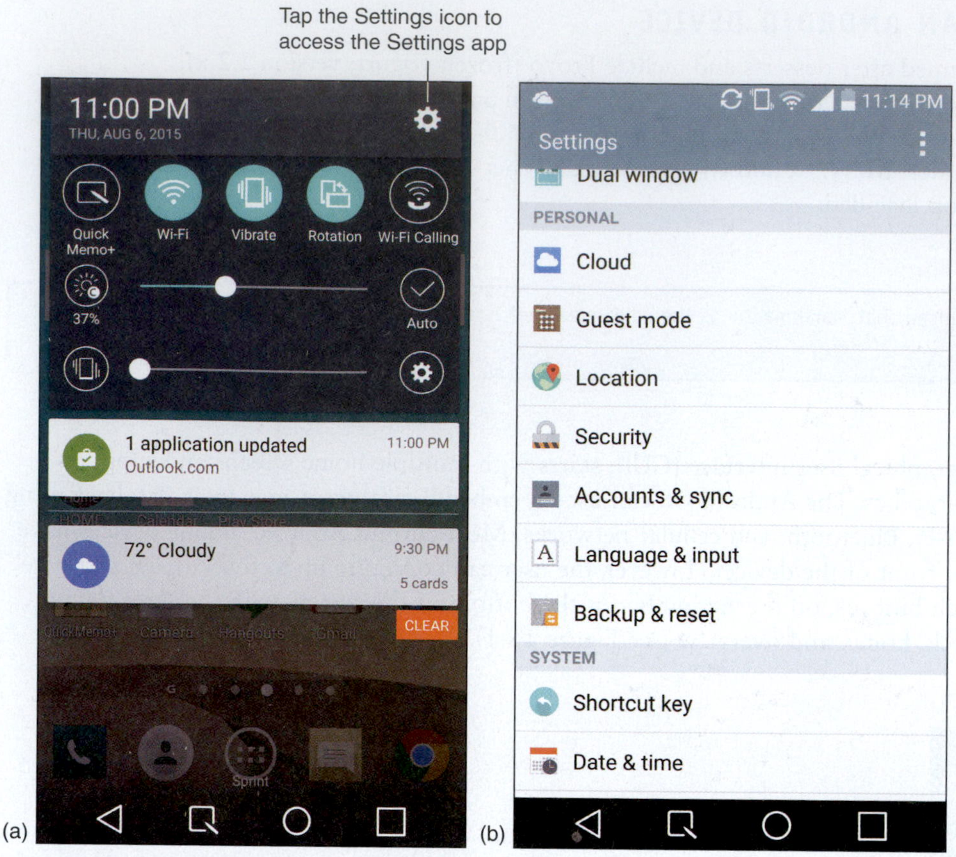

Source: Android

Figure 16-2 (a) The Notifications shade includes quick access to (b) the Settings app

ANDROID APPS

Android apps are sold or freely distributed from any source or vendor. However, the official source for apps, called the Android marketplace, is Google Play at *play.google.com*. To download content, you need a Google account, which you can set up using the website or your device. The account is associated with any valid email address. Associate a credit card with the account to make your purchases at Google Play. Then you can download free or purchased music, e-books, movies, and Android apps from Google Play to your mobile device.

To download an app, tap the **Play Store** app on the home screen of your device. (If you don't see the app icon on your home screen, tap the **Apps Drawer** and then tap **Play Store**.) The app takes you to Google Play, where you can search for apps, games, movies, music, e-books, and magazines (see Figure 16-3a). In addition, you can get apps and data from other sources, such as the Amazon Appstore for Android at *amazon.com* or directly from a developer. You can also use the Play Store app to manage updates to installed apps, as shown in Figure 16-3b.

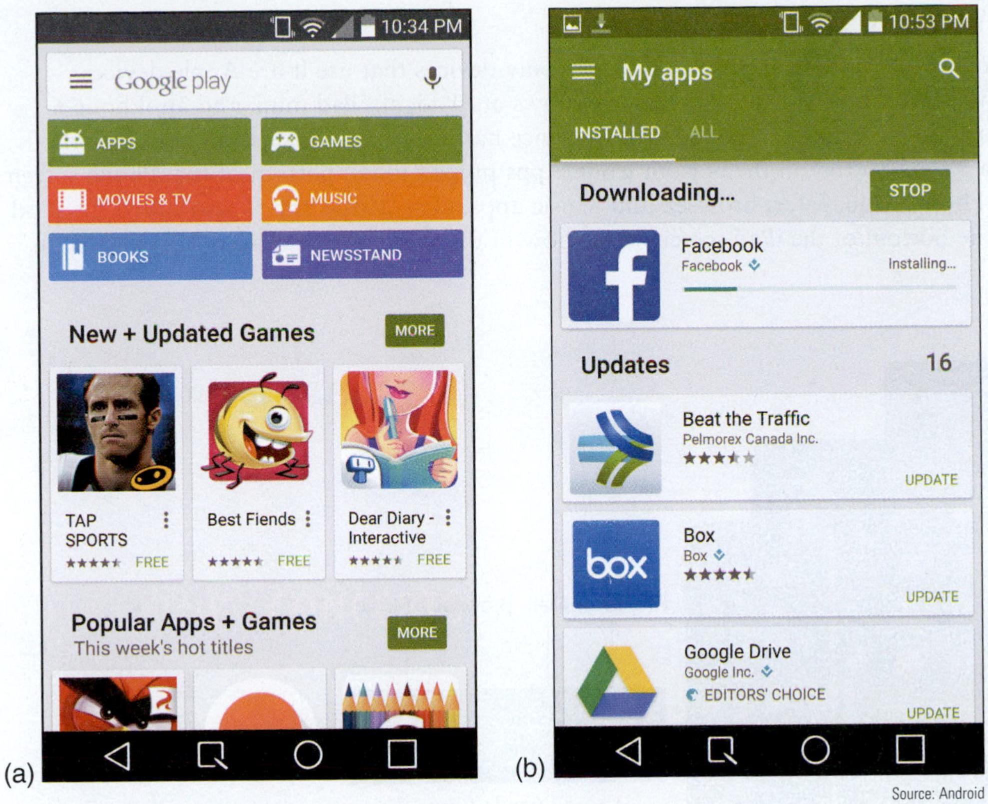

Source: Android

Figure 16-3 Use the Play Store app to (a) search Google Play for apps, music, e-books, movies, and more that you can download, as well as (b) updates to apps you already have

Google maintains the Android website at *android.com* where an app developer can download Android Studio, which includes Android SDK tools and an Android emulator, from *developer.android.com*. An SDK (Software Development Kit) is a group of tools that developers use to write apps. Android Studio is free and is released as open source. Most Android apps are written using the Java programming language. All the parts of an app are published as a package of files wrapped into one file with an .apk file extension using the APK (Android Application Package) package file format.

Now let's see how Apple's iOS differs from Android.

16

iOS BY APPLE

A+
220-902
2.5

Apple, Inc. (*www.apple.com*) owns, manufactures, and sells the Apple iPhone (a smart phone), iPad (a handheld tablet), and iPod touch (a multimedia recorder and player *and* a game player). These devices all use the iOS operating system, also developed and owned by Apple. iOS is based on Mac OS X, the operating system used by Apple desktop and laptop computers. There have been eight major releases of the iOS with a ninth released in beta at the time of this writing; the latest full version is iOS version 8.

GETTING TO KNOW AN iOS DEVICE

Because Apple is the sole owner and distributor of iOS, the only devices that use it are Apple devices (currently the iPhone, iPad, and iPod touch). Figure 16-4 shows an iPad, an iPad mini, and an iPhone 6 Plus (the iPhone 6 Plus is larger than the iPhone 6). Each device has a physical Wake/sleep button at the top of the device and a Home button on the bottom front. Apps pinned to the bottom of the iPhone screen in Figure 16-4 are the Phone, Mail, Safari browser, and Music apps. (The Music app is also called the iPod app.) Apps pinned to the bottom of the iPad screens that show in the figure are the Safari browser, Mail, and Videos apps.

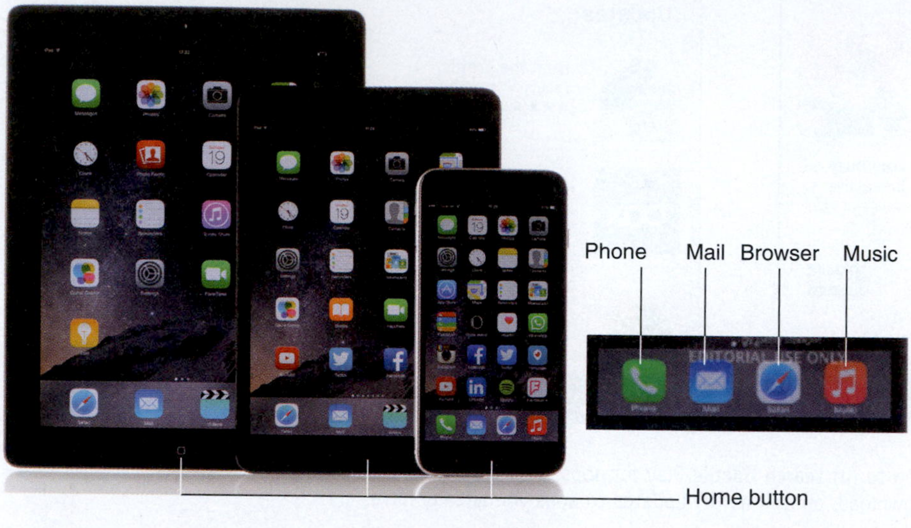

Figure 16-4 An iPad, an iPad mini, and an iPhone 6 Plus iPhone by Apple have iOS version 5.1 installed

Also, because Apple is the sole developer and manufacturer, it can maintain strict standards on its products, which means iOS is extremely stable and bug free. Apple's iOS is also a very easy and intuitive operating system to use. As with Mac OS X, iOS makes heavy use of icons.

Knowing a few simple navigation tips on an iOS device can help you get around a little more easily:

- Swipe down from the top of the screen to see the Notifications screen. Slide a notification, such as an iMessage, up to remove it and slide it down to access options for responding to it, such as replying to an iMessage. The types of notifications shown and other notification settings can be customized in the Settings app. For example, on an iPhone you can turn on or off government alerts such as AMBER alerts and other emergency notifications.

OS Differences You can adjust settings for emergency notifications in Android, too, but the steps to accomplish this task vary by device. Many Android devices offer these options in the Settings menu of the default Messaging app. Look for an option such as Emergency alerts. On other devices, on the Settings app tap **More**, then tap **Cell broadcasts**.

- To delete or move an app icon on the screen, press and hold the icon until all icons start to jiggle. As the icons jiggle, to delete an icon, press the X beside it. To move an icon, press and drag it to a new location. You can add new home screens by dragging an app icon off the screen to the right. To stop the jiggling, tap the Home button.
- Double-click the Home button to show the app switcher. Tap an app to switch to that screen, or swipe an app to the top of the screen to close it. Closing apps you're not using can save battery life.
- Press and hold the Home button to open Siri, iOS's virtual assistant service. A **virtual assistant** service or app, also called a personal assistant, responds to a user's voice commands with a personable, conversational interaction to perform tasks and retrieve information. iOS's Siri, as shown in Figure 16-5a, was the first of these virtual assistant services (Siri is more of a service than an app because of how deeply embedded it is within iOS), and has been around long enough to have become quite sophisticated. Siri uses information within the device to provide a customized experience.

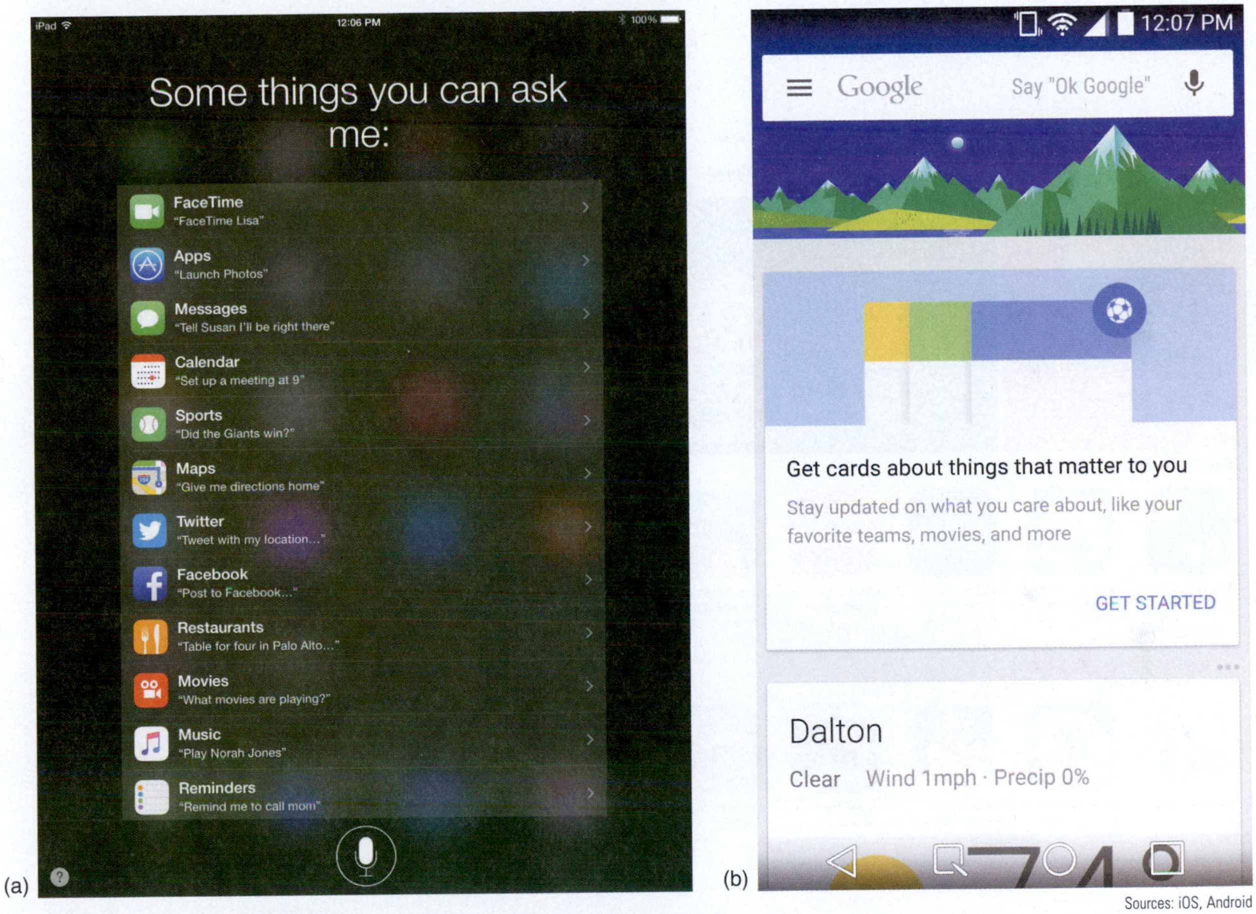

Sources: iOS, Android

Figure 16-5 (a) Siri settings are changed in the Settings app; (b) Google Now gives helpful information on cards

> **OS Differences** Android offers Google Now virtual assistant (see Figure 16-5b), which can be accessed through a web interface in addition to the installed app on the mobile device, and uses search histories and information collected during setup or later to customize a user's experience. Windows Phone 8.1 has a virtual assistant called Cortana that also customizes the user's experience.

iOS APPS

You can get Android apps from many sources, but the only place to go for an iOS app is Apple. Apple is the sole distributer of iOS apps at its **App Store**. Other developers can write apps for the iPhone, iPad, or iPod, but these apps must be sent to Apple for their close scrutiny. If they pass muster, they are distributed by Apple on its website. One requirement is that an app be written in the Objective-C, C, or C++ programming language. Apple offers app development tools, including the iOS SDK (Software Development Kit) at *developer.apple.com*.

When you first purchase an iPad or an iPod touch, you activate it by signing into the device with an **Apple ID**, or user account, using a valid email address and password, and associate this account with a credit card number. You can then go to the Settings app to download the latest updates to the iOS. Here are options for obtaining apps and other content:

- Use the App Store app on your mobile device (see Figure 16-6 for an iPad example) to search, purchase, and download (or download for free) apps, games, e-books, periodical content such as newspapers and magazines, and iTunes U content. (**iTunes U** contains lectures and even complete courses from many schools, colleges, and universities.)

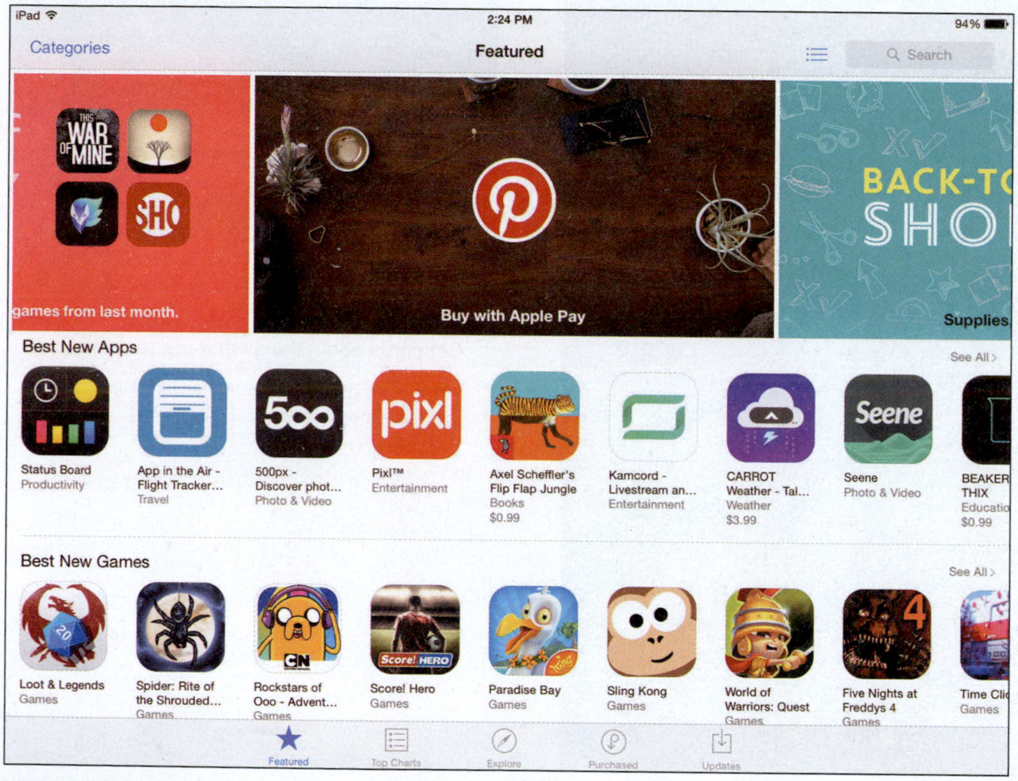

Source: Apple iOS

Figure 16-6 Use the App Store app to download content from the iTunes Store

- Use the **iTunes Store** app to search, purchase, and download (or download for free) content, including music, movies, TV shows, podcasts, and iTunes U content. Download and install the iTunes software on a Mac or Windows personal computer. Then connect your mobile device to the computer by way of a USB port. iTunes can then sync the device to iOS updates downloaded from *iTunes.com* and to content on your computer, which can be a helpful troubleshooting option, as you'll see later. You can also purchase content that is downloaded to your device by way of iTunes on your computer. Figure 16-7 shows the iTunes window when an iPhone is connected to the computer. How to use iTunes to sync data and apps on your device is covered later in the chapter.

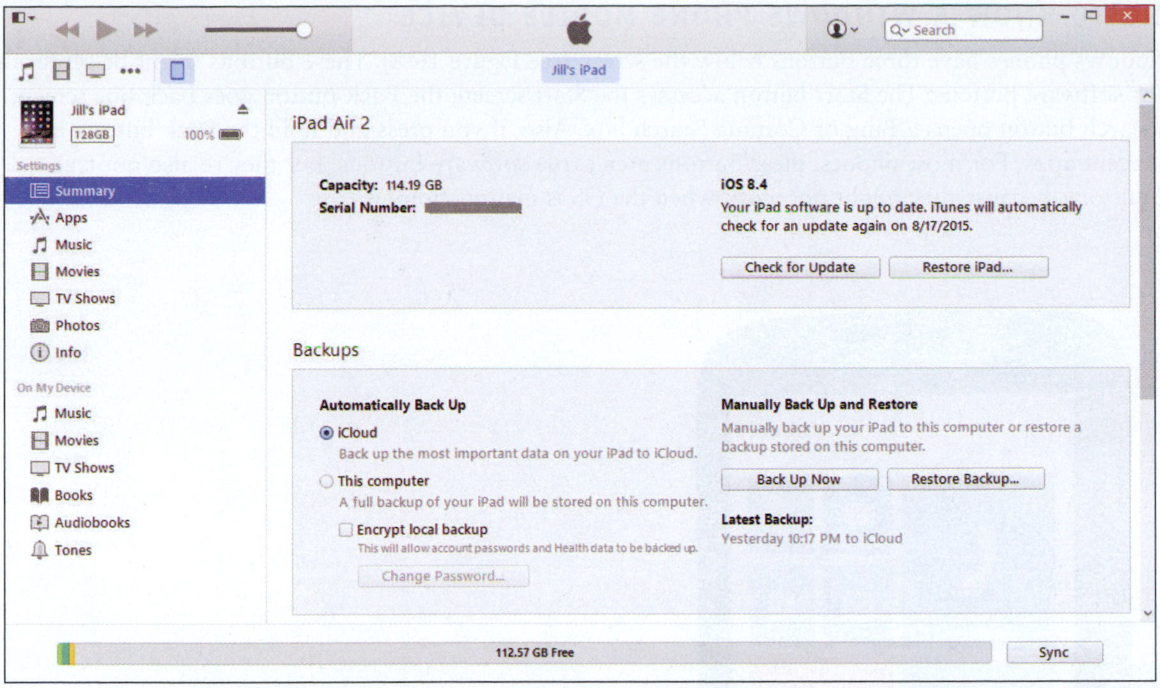

Source: iTunes

Figure 16-7 iTunes window shows summary information for an attached iPhone

Recall that apps can be downloaded to an iOS device only from Apple. People have discovered that it is possible to break through this restriction in a process called jailbreaking. **Jailbreaking** gives you root or administrative privileges to the operating system and the entire file system (all files and folders) and complete access to all commands and features. Jailbreaking was once illegal, but in 2010, the U.S. Copyright Office and the Library of Congress made a copyright ruling that a user has the right to download and use software that will jailbreak his or her iPhone. Note, however, that this ruling applies only to iPhones (and other smart phones), not iPads (or other tablets), due to some ambiguity in the definition of the word *tablet*. Also, jailbreaking voids any manufacturer warranty on the device, violates the End User License Agreement (EULA) with Apple, and might violate BYOD (Bring Your Own Device) policies in an enterprise environment. This jailingbreaking ruling applies only in the United States; other countries have addressed this issue differently.

Android and iOS hold the lion's share of the mobile operating system market. However, Microsoft offers some valid competition with its latest Windows mobile OS developments.

16

WINDOWS PHONE BY MICROSOFT

A+
220-902
2.5

The Windows Phone operating system by Microsoft is more or less a simplified version of the Windows operating system designed for desktop computers, laptops, and tablets. Windows Phone and Windows version numbers correspond: Windows Phone 8.1 corresponds to Windows 8.1. One of the biggest differences between Windows and Windows Phone is that Windows Phone does not have a desktop screen. Everything is accessed initially from the Start screen. As of the writing of this text, Microsoft has released its preview version of Windows 10 Mobile.

★ A+ Exam Tip The A+ 220-902 exam expects you to be able to use and support Windows 8.1/8/7 and Windows Phone 8.1. It does not cover Windows 10 or Windows 10 Mobile.

GETTING TO KNOW A WINDOWS PHONE MOBILE DEVICE

Most Windows phones have three buttons below the screen (see Figure 16-8). These buttons might be physical buttons or software buttons. The Start button accesses the Start screen; the Back button goes back one screen, and the Search button opens a Bing or Cortana Search box. Also, if you press and hold the Back button, it displays recent apps. For most phones, these buttons aren't true software buttons, but they're also not true physical buttons, because they might not work when the OS is malfunctioning.

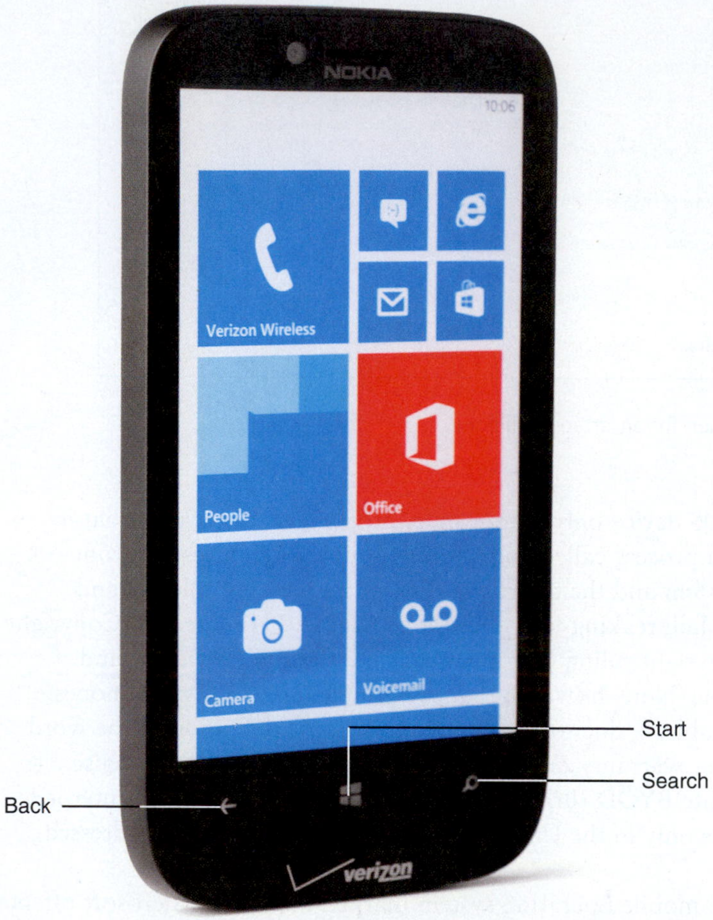

© iStockphoto.com/Mphillips007

Figure 16-8 Press and hold the Start button to activate Cortana, the Windows virtual assistant

Windows phones rely primarily on the Start screen for accessing apps. Just as with Windows 8, a tile icon on the Start screen represents an app. Here are some tips for getting around Windows Phone:

- Tap a tile on the Start screen to open its app. Scroll up or down to see more tiles. Press and hold to resize or reposition tiles. On many smart phones, pressing and holding a link functions like right-clicking with a mouse on a Windows desktop computer.

- Swipe down from the very top of the screen to see notifications in the Action Center (Figure 16-9a), similar to both Android and iOS. Like Android, there is also a Settings icon here to open the Settings app (Figure 16-9b). Settings can also be accessed via the Settings tile.

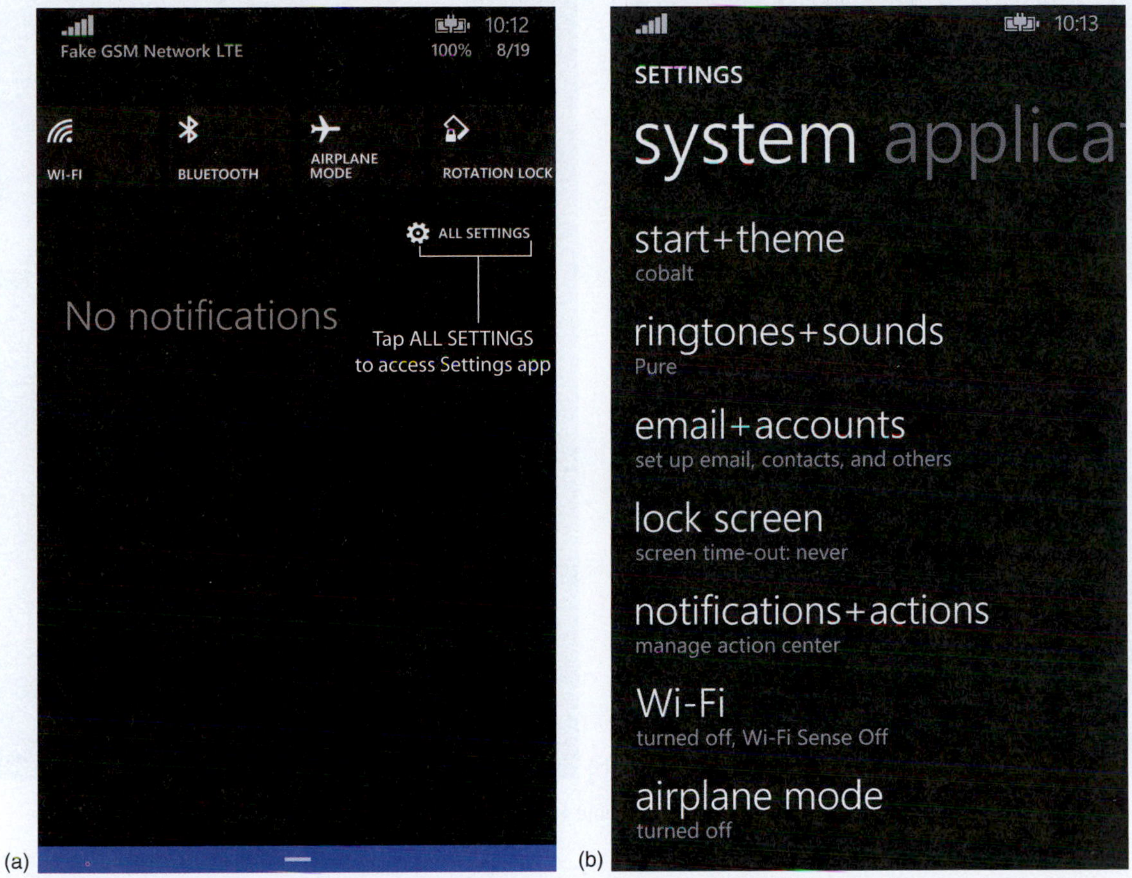

Figure 16-9 (a) Notifications appear in the Action Center; (b) the Settings app provides an extensive toolkit for customizing a Windows smart phone

- Swipe from the right to see the apps list (similar to clicking the down arrow on a Windows Start screen). Press and hold an app on the list to pin the app to the Start screen (see Figure 16-10a). On the Start screen, press and hold the app tile and then you can change its size and other characteristics. Tap the Store tile on the Start screen to find more apps (Figure 16-10b).

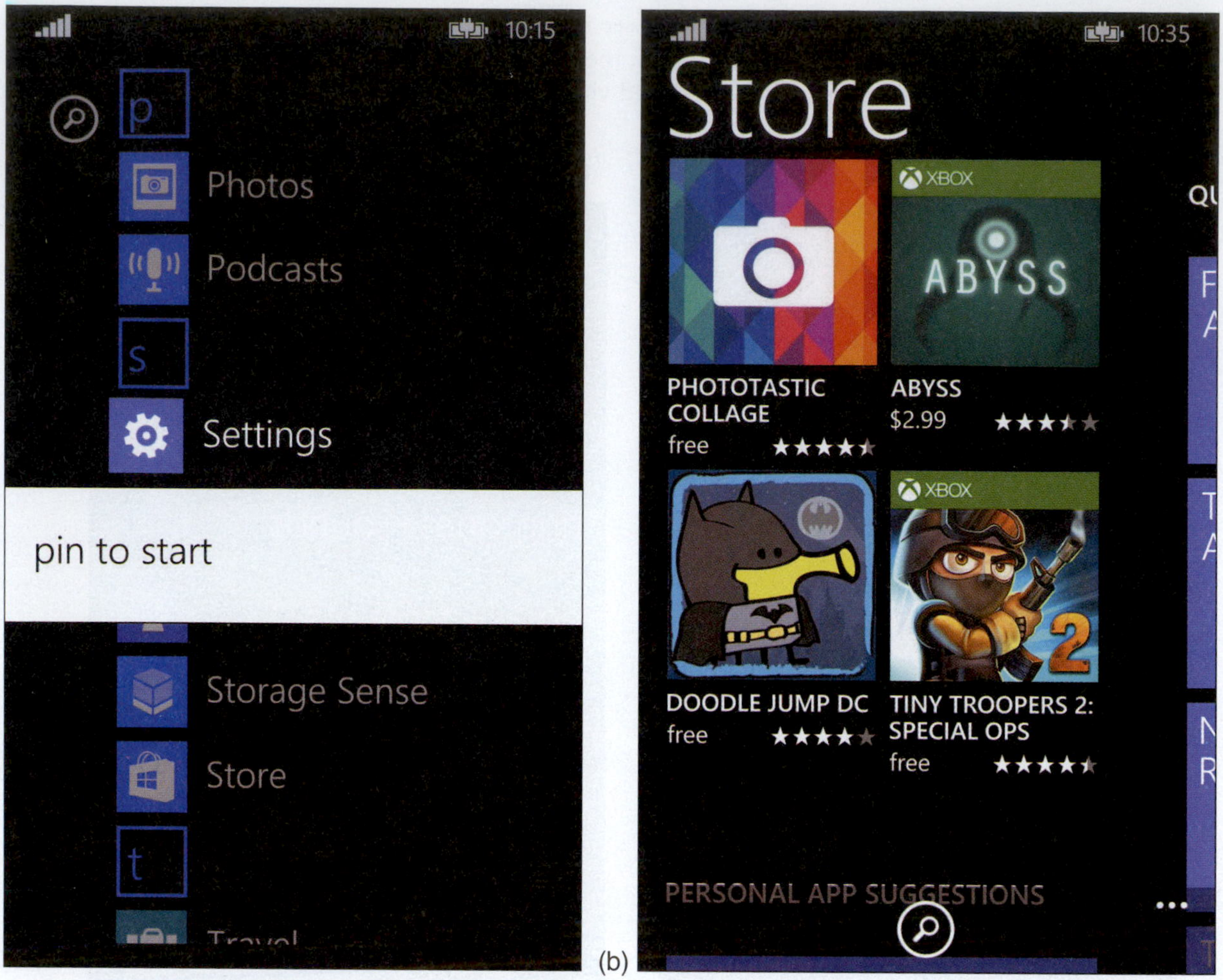

(a) (b)

Figure 16-10 (a) To pin an app to the Start screen, press and hold the app's icon and then tap **pin to start**; (b) get more apps from the Store

- While a menu is displayed in the Settings app, you can sometimes swipe from the right to see a submenu. Windows Phone is rich with settings options, making it easier to integrate Windows phones in an enterprise environment.

WINDOWS PHONE APPS

The availability of apps for Windows mobile devices is much more limited than what can be found for Android or iOS. Windows apps are obtained through the Microsoft Store (*microsoftstore.com*). The number of apps for Windows smart phones should increase soon, as Microsoft has announced that Windows 10 Mobile will be more compatible with both Android and iOS apps. This means app developers will more easily be able to adapt their existing apps for posting in the Microsoft Store. Additionally, like Android apps, Windows Phone apps can be obtained from third-party websites.

COMPARING OPEN SOURCE AND CLOSED SOURCE OPERATING SYSTEMS

A+
220-902
2.5

Open source operating systems (such as Android) and closed source, also called vendor-specific or commercial license, operating systems (such as iOS) have their advantages and disadvantages. Here are some key points to consider about releasing or not releasing source code:

- Apple carefully guards its iOS source code and internal functions of the OS. Third-party developers of apps have access only to APIs, which are calls to the OS. An app must be tested and approved by Apple before it can be sold in its online App Store. These policies assure users that apps are high quality. It also assures developers they have a central point of contact for users to buy their apps.
- The Android source code and the development and sale of apps are not closely guarded. Apps can be purchased or downloaded from Google Play, but they can also be obtained from other sources such as *Amazon.com* or directly from a developer. This freedom comes with a cost because users are not always assured of high-quality, bug-free apps, and developers are not always assured of a convenient market for their apps.
- Because any smart phone or tablet manufacturer can modify the Android source code, many variations of Android exist. These variations can make it difficult for developers to write apps that port to any Android platform. It can also make it difficult for users to learn to use new Android devices because of these inconsistencies.

★ A+ Exam Tip The A+ 220-902 exam expects you to understand the advantages and disadvantages of open source and closed source operating systems on mobile devices.

CONFIGURE, SYNC, AND TROUBLESHOOT iOS DEVICES

A+
220-902
2.5, 2.6,
2.7, 4.3

In this part of the chapter, you learn to configure network connections, and to update, secure, and back up data, content, and settings on an iOS device. Later in the chapter, you learn similar skills using Android and Windows devices. We begin with iOS because it's so easy to use and understand.

This chapter is intended to show you how to support a device that you might not own or normally use. Technicians are often expected to do such things! If you don't have an iPhone or iPad to use as you read through these sections, you can still follow along, paying careful attention to the screen shots taken on each device. Learning to use an iOS device is fun, and supporting one is equally easy.

Most of the settings you need to know to support an iOS device are contained in the Settings app, which you can find on the home screen (see Figure 16-11a). Basically, you can tap the Settings app and search through its menus and submenus until you find what you need. So let's get started.

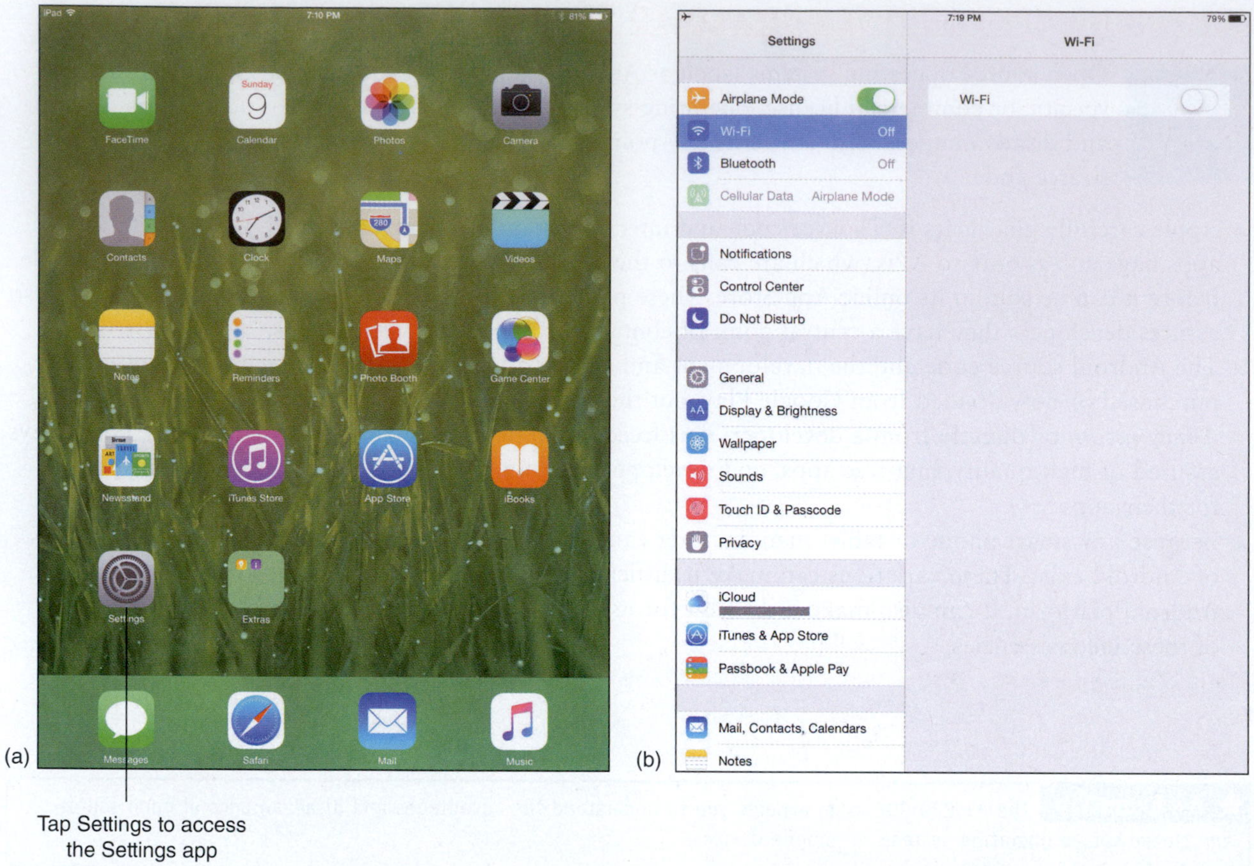

Source: iOS

Figure 16-11 (a) Tap the Settings app to configure iOS and apps; (b) in the Settings app, Airplane Mode turns off all three antennas that connect the iPhone or iPad to networks

CONFIGURE iOS NETWORK CONNECTIONS

A+ 220-902 2.5, 2.6, 2.7

An iOS mobile device can contain up to four antennas (Wi-Fi, GPS, Bluetooth, and cellular). The device uses a Wi-Fi, Bluetooth, or cellular antenna to connect to each type of network, and settings on the device allow you to enable or disable each antenna. Let's look at each type of connection.

Notes You can disable the three antennas in a mobile device that can transmit signals by enabling **Airplane mode** so that the device can neither transmit nor receive signals. To use Airplane mode, tap the **Settings** app and turn **Airplane Mode** on or off (see Figure 16-11b). It's not necessary to disable the GPS antenna because it only receives and never transmits.

A+ Exam Tip The A+ 220-902 exam expects you to know how to configure Wi-Fi, cellular data, Bluetooth, and VPN connections using the iOS, Android, and Windows mobile operating systems.

CELLULAR CONNECTION

Recall that a cellular network provided by a carrier (for example, AT&T or Verizon) is used for voice, text, and data communication. A cellular network uses GSM or CDMA for voice and another layer of technology for data transmissions. Options are 2G, EDGE (an earlier version of 3G), 3G, 4G, and 4G LTE. GSM and LTE require a SIM card installed in the device, and CDMA does not use a SIM card. (Although a CDMA and LTE carrier does require the SIM card for the LTE technology to work.) To make a cellular data connection, you must have a subscription with your carrier that includes a cellular data plan and then connect your device.

Here is information that might be used when a connection is first made to the network:

- The **IMEI (International Mobile Equipment Identity)** is a unique number that identifies each mobile phone or tablet device worldwide. It's usually reported within the *About* menu in the OS, and it might also be printed on a sticker on the device, such as behind the battery.
- The **IMSI (International Mobile Subscriber Identity)** is a unique number that identifies a cellular subscription for a device or subscriber, along with its home country and mobile network. This number is stored on the SIM card for networks that use SIM cards. For networks that don't use SIM cards, the number is kept in a database maintained by the carrier and is associated with the IMEI.
- The ICCID (Integrated Circuit Card ID) identifies the SIM card if the card is used. To know if a device is using a SIM card, look in the Settings app on the *About* menu in the General group. An ICCID entry indicates a SIM card is present.

When a carrier uses a SIM card, you can move the card from one device to another and the new device can connect to the carrier's network. When a carrier does not use a SIM card, you must contact the carrier and request permission to switch devices. If the carrier accepts the new device, the new IMEI will be entered in the carrier's database.

> **A+ Exam Tip** The A+ 220-902 exam expects you to know how to identify and distinguish between the IMEI and the IMSI.

> **Notes** The advantage of disabling cellular data and using Wi-Fi for data transmissions is that data transmissions over Wi-Fi are not charged against your cellular data subscription plan. Also, Wi-Fi is generally faster than most cellular connections.

To connect an iOS device to a cellular data network, tap **Settings**, **Cellular Data**, then **Set Up Cellular Data**. Select a carrier (see Figure 16-12a) and follow the on screen instructions. Also you can enable or disable Data Roaming and Cellular Data. Using data roaming might mean additional charges if you are in a different country, and disabling cellular data might save on carrier charges in certain situations.

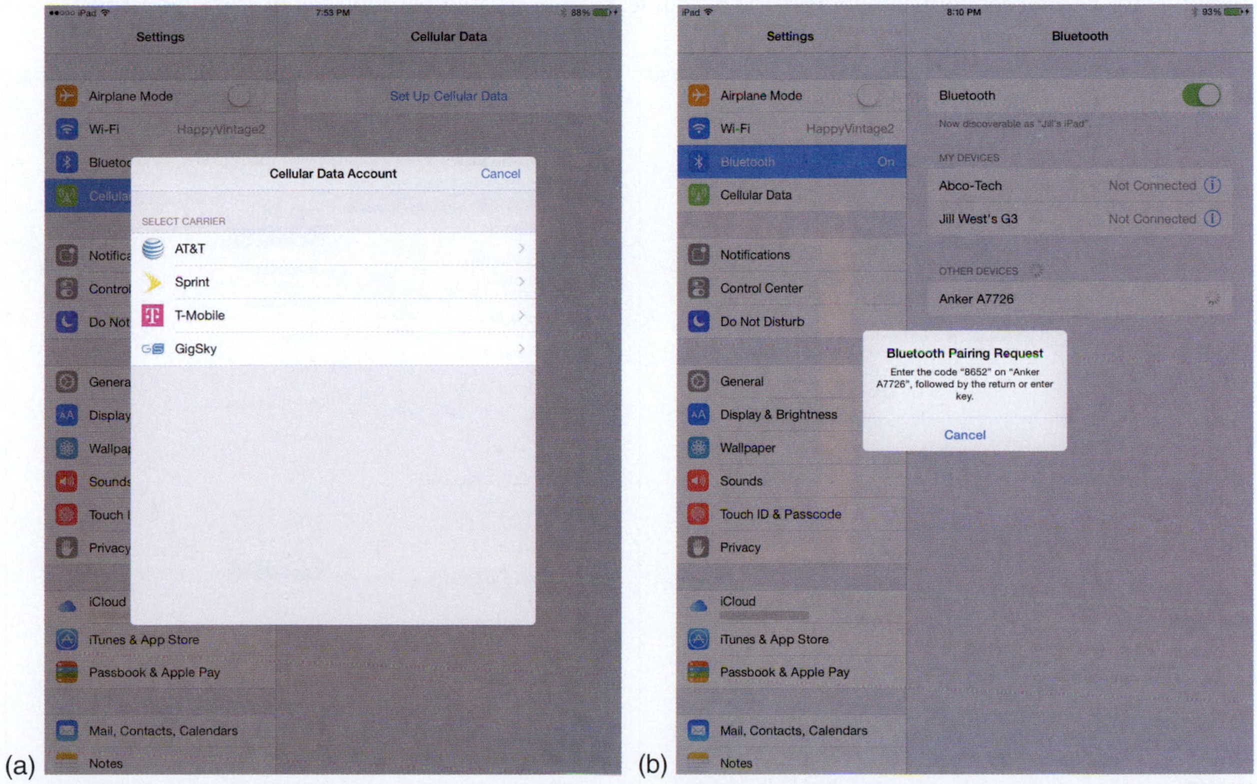

Source: iOS

Figure 16-12 (a) Connect to a cellular data network; (b) a PIN code is required to pair these two Bluetooth devices

CDMA carriers are likely to require that a cellular device have a Removable User Identity Module (R-UIM), which is a small card similar to a SIM card. The card contains a database file called the PRL (Preferred Roaming List), which lists the preferred service providers or radio frequencies your carrier wants the device to use. You can reset or update the list in the Settings app. For example, for an iPad, tap **Settings**, **General**, then scroll down and tap **Reset**. Tap **Subscriber Services**, then tap **Reprovision Account** and tap **OK**. Tap **OK** again when the update is complete.

> **OS Differences** Android devices on CDMA networks also require updated PRLs. To see the current PRL version, open the **Settings** app, scroll down and tap **About phone** or **About tablet**, then tap **Status.** To update the PRL, go back to the Settings app, then tap **System updates.** Tap **Update PRL**, and tap **OK** when the update is complete.

BLUETOOTH CONNECTION

To configure an iOS Bluetooth connection, first turn on the other Bluetooth device you want to connect to. Then on your mobile device, tap **Settings** and turn on Bluetooth. The device searches for other Bluetooth devices. If it discovers a Bluetooth device, tap it to connect. The two Bluetooth devices now begin the pairing process. The devices might require a Bluetooth PIN code to complete the Bluetooth connection. For example, in Figure 16-12b, an iPad and Bluetooth keyboard are pairing. To complete the connection, enter the four-digit PIN on the keyboard. To test the connection, enter text on the keyboard and make sure the text appears on the iPad screen in the active app.

If you have a problem connecting to a Bluetooth device, try turning that device off and back on. The device might also offer a pairing button or combination of buttons to enable pairing. When you press this button, a pairing light blinks, indicating the device is ready to receive a Bluetooth connection.

WI-FI CONNECTION

To configure an iOS Wi-Fi connection, tap **Settings, Wi-Fi.** On the Wi-Fi screen (Figure 16-13a), you can view available Wi-Fi hotspots, see which Wi-Fi network you are connected to, turn Wi-Fi off and on, and decide whether the device needs to ask before joining a Wi-Fi network. A Wi-Fi hotspot is an area where access to Wi-Fi Internet connectivity is made available, such as at a coffee shop, retail store, or airport.

(a) (b)

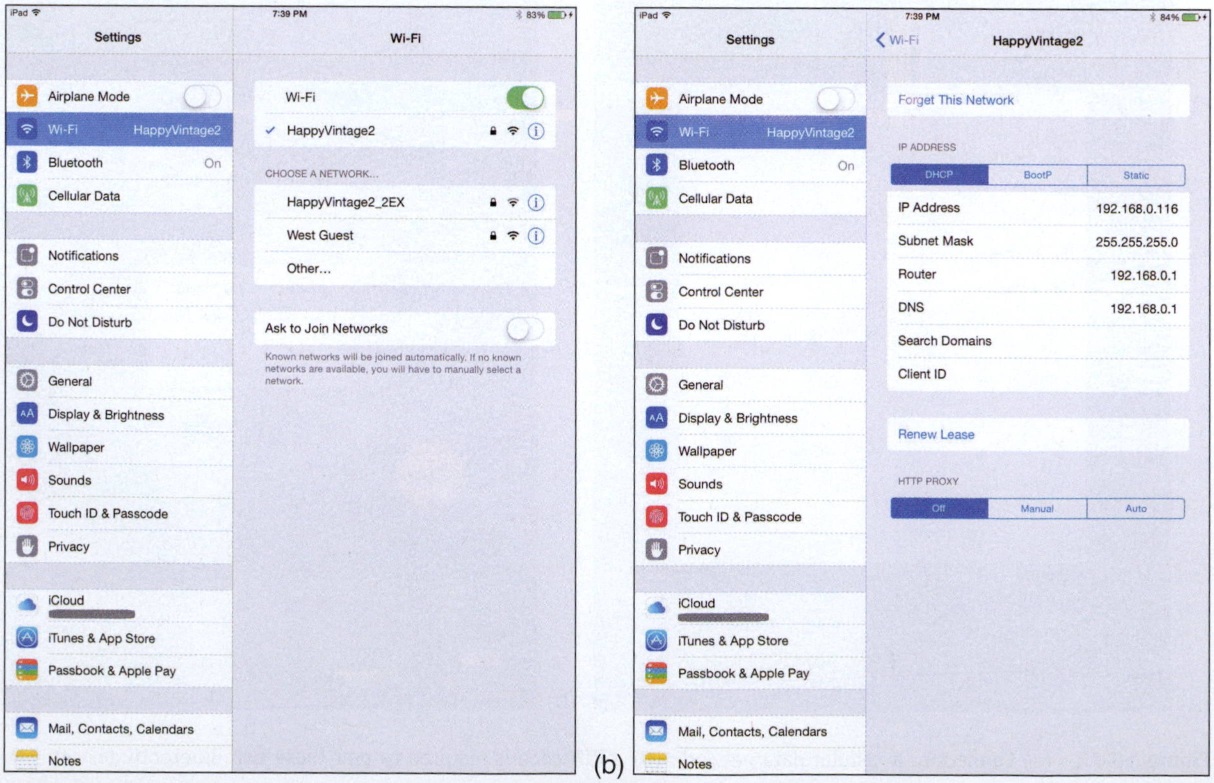

Source: iOS

Figure 16-13 (a) Turn on Wi-Fi and choose a Wi-Fi network; (b) configure Wi-Fi connection settings

When the device is within range of a Wi-Fi network, it displays the list of networks. Select one to connect. If the Wi-Fi network is secured, enter the security key to complete the connection. To change a network's settings, tap the name of the network (see Figure 16-13b).

VPN CONNECTION

Like desktop computers, a mobile device can be configured to communicate information securely over a virtual private network (VPN) connection. To create a VPN connection in iOS, tap **Settings**, **General**, then scroll down and tap **VPN**. Tap **Add VPN Configuration**. Follow directions to complete the connection, which will require you know the type of encryption protocol used (L2TP, PPTP, or IPsec), the IP address or domain name of the VPN server, and the user name and password to the corporate network.

CONFIGURE iOS EMAIL

A+
220-902
2.6, 2.7

Using a personal computer or mobile device, email can be managed in one of two ways:

- ***Use a browser.*** Using a browser, go to the website of your email provider and manage your email on the website. In this situation, your email is never downloaded to your computer or mobile device, and your messages remain on the email server until you delete them.
- ***Use an email client.*** An email client, such as Microsoft Outlook, can be installed on your personal computer, and/or you can use an email app on your mobile device. The client or app can either download email messages to your device (using the POP3 protocol) or can manage email on the server (using the IMAP protocol). When the client or app downloads the email, you can configure the server to continue to store the email on the server for later use or delete the email from the server. The built-in Mail app for managing email is available on iPhones and iPads.

Here is the information you'll need to configure the Mail app on an iOS device:

- ***Your email address and password.*** If your email account is with iCloud, Microsoft Exchange, Google, Yahoo!, AOL, or Outlook, your email address and password are all you need because the iOS can automatically set up these accounts.
- ***The names of your incoming and outgoing email servers.*** To find this information, check the support page of your email provider's website. For example, the server you use for incoming mail might be *pop.mycompany.com*, and the server you use for outgoing mail might be *smtp.mycompany.com*. The two servers might have the same name.
- ***The type of protocol your incoming server uses.*** The incoming server will use POP3 or IMAP. Using IMAP, you are managing your email on the server. For example, you can move a message from one folder to another and that change happens on the remote server. Using POP3, the messages are downloaded to your device where you manage them locally. Using POP3, the Mail app leaves the messages on the server (does not delete them), but you can change this setting if you want. 16
- ***Security used.*** Most likely, if email is encrypted during transmission using the SSL protocol, the configuration will happen automatically without your involvement. However, if you have problems, you need to be aware of these possible settings:
  - An IMAP server uses port 143 unless it is secured and using SSL. IMAP over SSL (IMAPS) uses port 993.
  - A POP3 server uses port 110 unless it is secured and using SSL. POP3 over SSL uses port 995.
  - Outgoing email is normally sent using the protocol SMTP. A more secure alternative called S/MIME (Secure/Multipurpose Internet Mail Extensions) is now available, however. S/MIME encrypts the email message and includes a digital signature, which validates the identity of the sender of the email message. This feature is enabled after the email account is set up on the device. The activation process is automated for accounts through Microsoft Exchange, and can be set up manually for other types of accounts. Look for this option on the Advanced settings screen, which you'll soon see how to access.

★ A+ Exam Tip The A+ 220-902 exam expects you to know about POP3, IMAP, SSL, and the ports they use. Before you sit for the exam, memorize the ports discussed in this section.

APPLYING | CONCEPTS CONFIGURE iOS EMAIL

A+ 220-902 2.6, 2.7

Follow these steps to configure the email client on an iOS device:

1. Tap **Settings** and then tap **Mail, Contacts, Calendars**. On the Mail, Contacts, Calendars screen, you can add a new email account and decide how email is handled. To add a new email account, tap **Add Account**. On the next screen, select the type of account (see Figure 16-14a) and enter your email address and password. If your email account type is not in the list, tap **Other** at the bottom of the list.

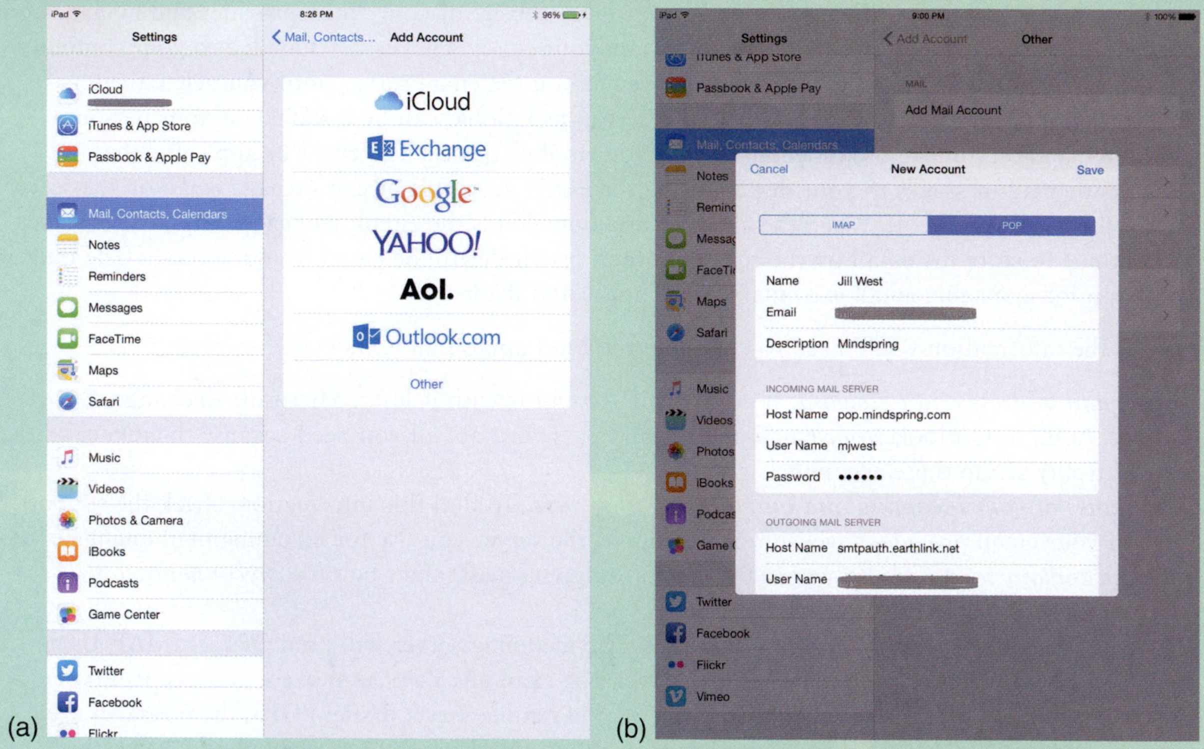

Source: iOS

Figure 16-14 (a) iOS can automatically set up several types of email accounts; (b) an email account is set up to use IMAP or POP3 for incoming mail

2. On the Other screen, tap **Add Mail Account**. On the New Account screen, enter your name, email address, password, and description (optional). Tap **Next**.

3. The device might be able to successfully establish your email account based on this information alone. When prompted, select the account elements you want to sync to this device, such as Mail, Notes, and Calendar. However, sometimes the Mail app chooses the wrong default settings (such as assuming POP3 when you want IMAP). To force the Mail app to allow manual selection of these settings, first enter a bogus email address or password. The account connection will fail, and the screen in Figure 16-14b will appear. Tap IMAP or POP and enter the correct settings. This includes the Host Name, User Name, and Password for both the incoming and outgoing mail servers. Then tap **Save**.

4. The Mail app assumes it is using SSL (to secure email in transit using encryption) and attempts to make the connection. If it cannot, it asks if you want it to try to make the connection without using SSL. Click **OK** to make that attempt.
5. To use the account, tap the **Mail** app on your home screen.

If you later need to verify the email account settings or delete the account, follow these steps:

1. Tap **Settings**, and then tap **Mail, Contacts, Calendars**. In the list of Accounts, tap the account. On the account screen, you can enable and disable the account and change the account settings.
2. To delete the account, tap **Delete Account** at the bottom of the screen (see Figure 16-15a).

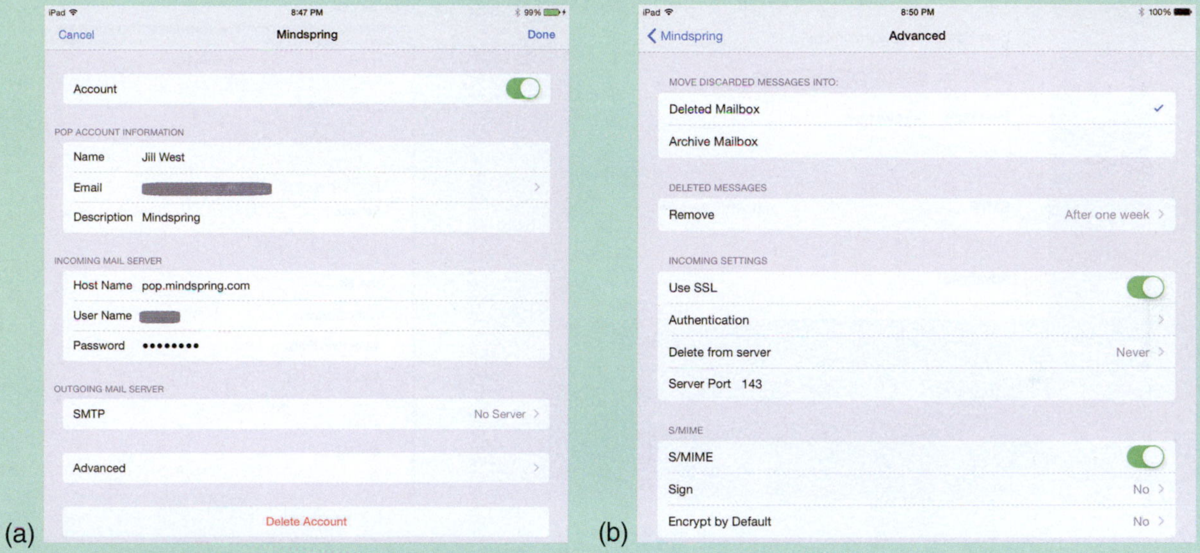

Source: iOS

Figure 16-15 (a) Delete an email account or use Advanced settings; (b) decide how messages are handled on the server after you receive them

3. To see advanced settings, tap **Advanced**. On the Advanced screen (see Figure 16-15b), tap **Delete from server** to decide how to handle mail you have downloaded using the POP3 protocol. Choices are *Never*, *Seven Days*, or *When removed from Inbox*.
4. Notice on the Advanced screen that you can enable and disable SSL. The server port that the app addresses might also need to be changed. You can also enable S/MIME to encrypt outgoing email messages. When this feature is enabled, you'll see a blue lock icon when creating new email messages, which you can click to activate S/MIME for that message.

Notes For IMAP accounts, tapping the account on the **Mail, Contacts, Calendars** screen shows a list of IMAP accounts, options for syncing Mail and Notes, and the option to delete the account. Tap the account again for configuration options, as shown in Figure 16-16a. Tap **Advanced** to see additional options, as shown in Figure 16-16b.

16

(continues)

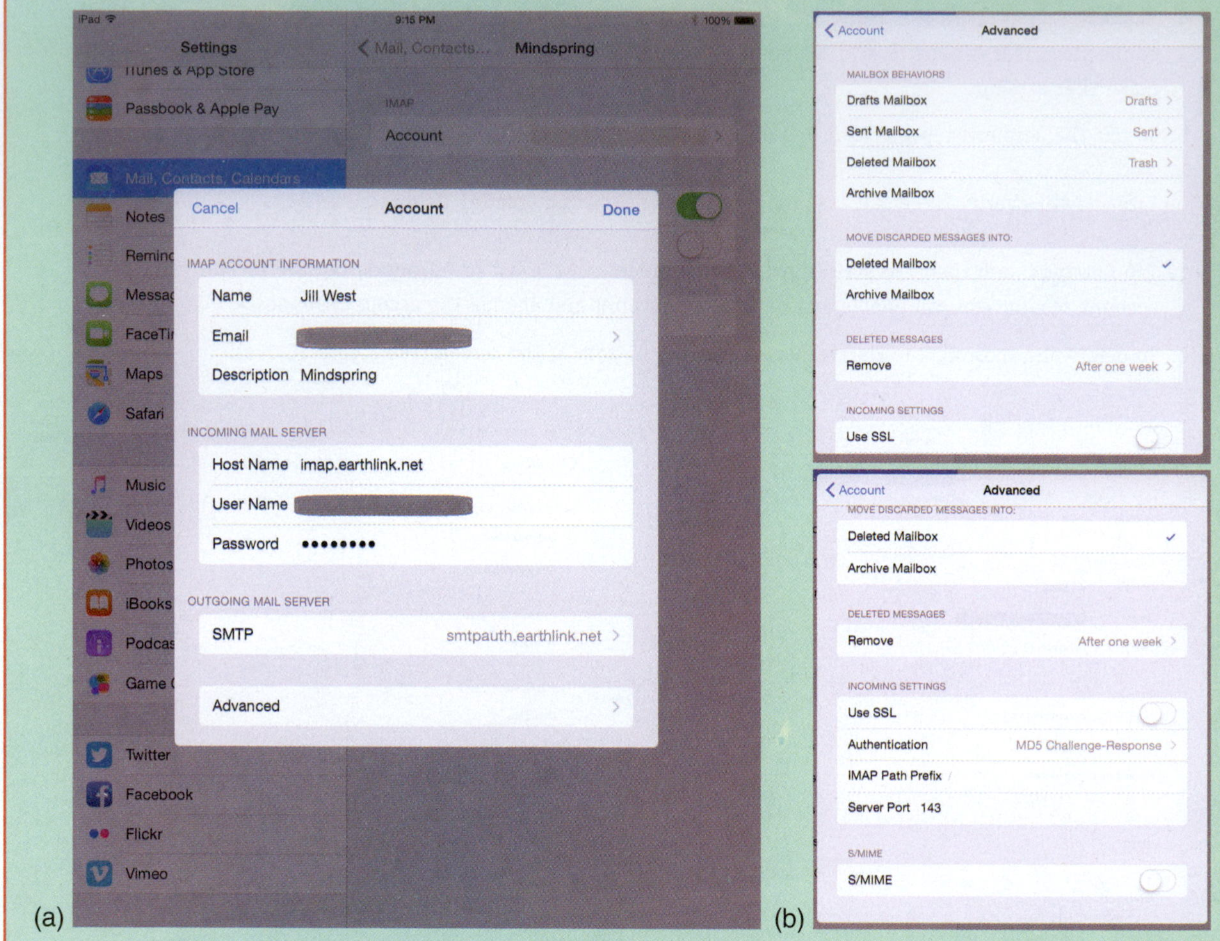

Source: iOS

Figure 16-16 (a) IMAP account settings; (b) the top and bottom portions of the Advanced menu for an IMAP account

You need to know about an exception in how email is managed when using a Gmail account. Gmail is an email service provided by Google at *mail.google.com*. Normally, when you use the Mail app, you can delete a message by selecting it and tapping **Delete** (see Figure 16-17a). However, using Gmail, by default, you archive a message rather than delete it (see Figure 16-17b).

Using most email services, a message arrives in your Inbox, which is a folder on the email server. You organize these messages by moving them to other folders or deleting them. Deleted messages are placed in the Trash folder and permanently deleted after a period of time. Using Gmail, a message remains in the Inbox, and you organize these messages by assigning each message one or more labels. When you archive a message, you move the message from the Inbox to the All Mail folder out of sight but still accessible. Therefore, when using the Mail app on an Apple device with a Gmail account, the Delete button is replaced with the Archive button.

To change the Gmail account so that you can delete messages, go to the home screen and tap **Settings** and then tap **Mail, Contacts, Calendars**. Tap the Gmail account and go into **Advanced** settings. On the Advanced screen (refer to Figure 16-16b) under *Move discarded messages into*, tap to select **Deleted Mailbox**. Return to the Account screen and tap **Done**. The Mail app will now have a Delete button for Gmail, as shown in Figure 16-17a.

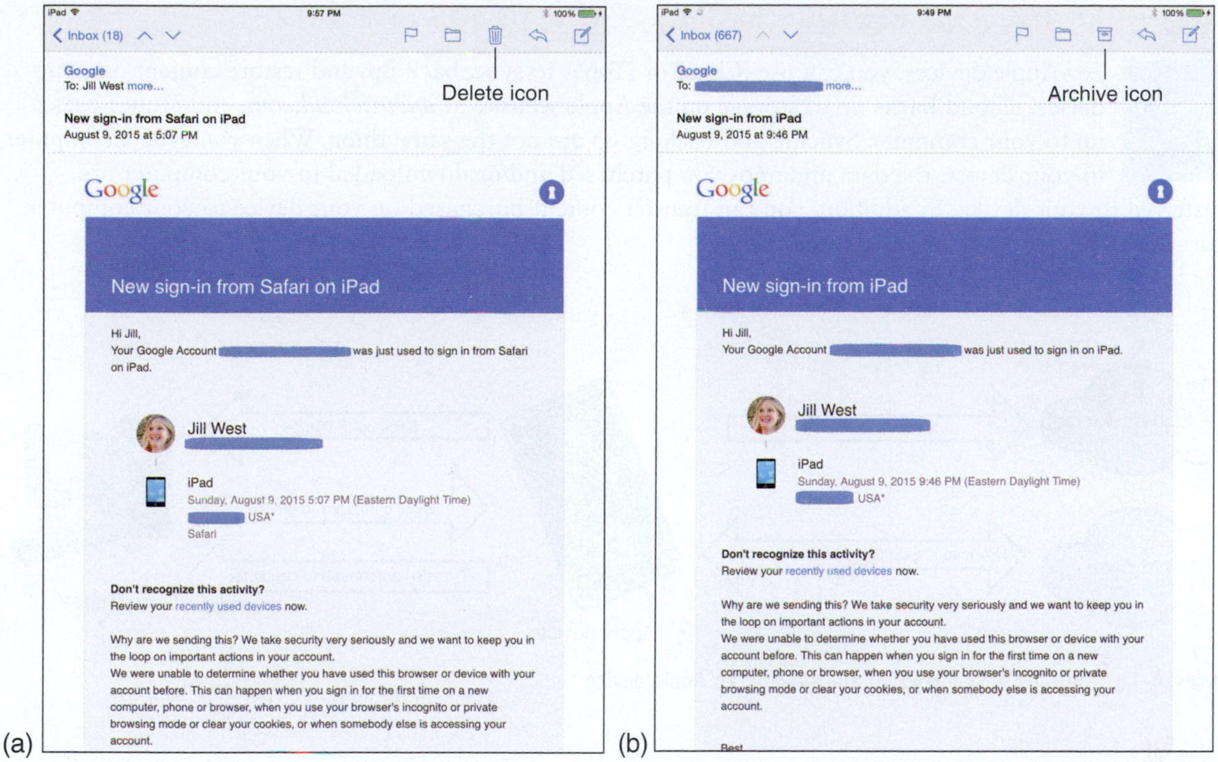

Sources: iOS, Google

Figure 16-17 Two methods for dealing with messages you no longer need: a) Using most email clients, delete a message, or b) using Gmail, archive a message

Microsoft Exchange is a server application that is popular with large corporations for handling employee email, contacts, and calendars. When you set up a Microsoft Exchange email account, the Mail app automatically enables ActiveSync, which causes all email, contacts, and calendar updates made on the Exchange server or on your mobile device to stay in sync. Any changes at either location are automatically and immediately transmitted to the other. You can change the ActiveSync settings by doing the following:

1. On the home screen, tap **Settings**, and tap **Mail, Contacts, Calendars.**
2. Select your Exchange email account. On the account screen, you can turn on or off the Mail, Contacts, Calendars, Reminders, and Notes settings. You can set the number of days, weeks, or months of email you want to stay in sync. You can also set up automatic out-of-office replies, and decide whether you want folders in addition to the Inbox folder to be pushed to you from the Exchange server.

A+ Exam Tip The A+ 220-902 exam expects you to know about special considerations when configuring Gmail and Exchange email accounts.

16

SYNC, BACK UP, AND RESTORE FROM BACKUP IN iOS

A+
220-902
2.6, 2.7

For Apple devices, you can use iCloud or iTunes to sync, back up, and restore content on your device. iCloud backs up to storage on the Apple website at *www.icloud.com*, and iTunes backs up to your computer. Syncing and backing up are not the same thing. When you sync a computer to your device, the data and apps you purchased and/or downloaded to your computer are transferred to your device. In addition, you can transfer content purchased on your device to your computer. Figure 16-18 helps sort out all these options.

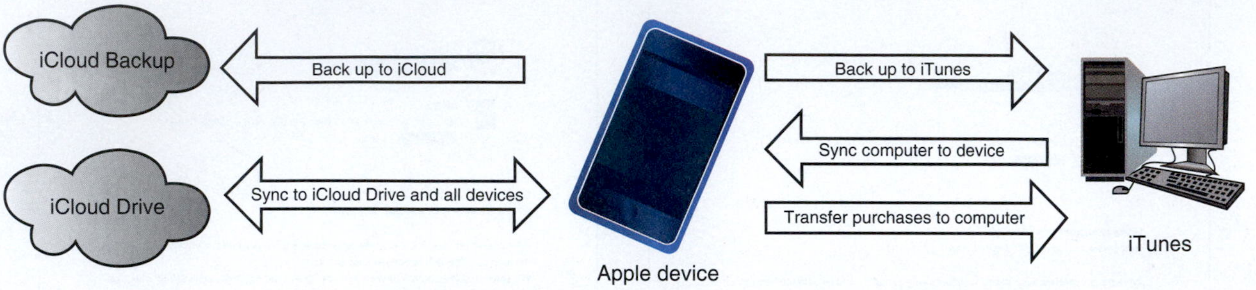

Figure 16-18 Options for backing up and syncing an Apple device

The advantages of backing up to iCloud are your devices automatically back up to iCloud whenever your device is connected to Wi-Fi and Apple is responsible for protecting your backups. The advantages of backing up to iTunes are you have more control over your backups and the cost for storage is less; however, you are responsible for maintaining your backups on your computer. Next, let's see how to sync and back up your content using iCloud and iTunes.

USE iCLOUD DRIVE TO SYNC CONTENT

Your Apple ID gives you a free iCloud account at *icloud.com* that can hold your iCloud Backup, iCloud Drive, iCloud Photo Library, iCloud Mail (using your *@icloud.com* email addresss), and data from apps that can interface with iCloud. The first 5 GB of storage is free. Music, apps, books, TV shows, and My Photo Stream you purchase from the Apple Store don't count against your 5 GB of storage.

You can sync files stored on iCloud Drive with any Apple mobile device or personal computer, and, when the iCloud Drive software is installed, you can sync content with a Windows computer. When you turn on iCloud Drive on an Apple device, content stored on your iCloud Drive is automatically synced with your device. To turn on iCloud Drive, open the **Settings** app, tap **iCloud**, and verify **iCloud Drive** is turned on. Now, any app on your device that can interact with iCloud Drive can use content at iCloud Drive.

APPLYING | CONCEPTS USE AN APP TO EXPORT A DOCUMENT TO iCLOUD DRIVE

A+
220-902
2.6, 2.7

The Documents Free app on an iPad can interface with iCloud Drive. Follow these steps to create a document in the app and save it to iCloud Drive:

1. To use the app to create a new document file, open the app, tap **iCloud** in the left pane to select the location where the file will be saved, then tap the "+" sign at the bottom of the screen. Select the type of document to create, as shown in Figure 16-19a.

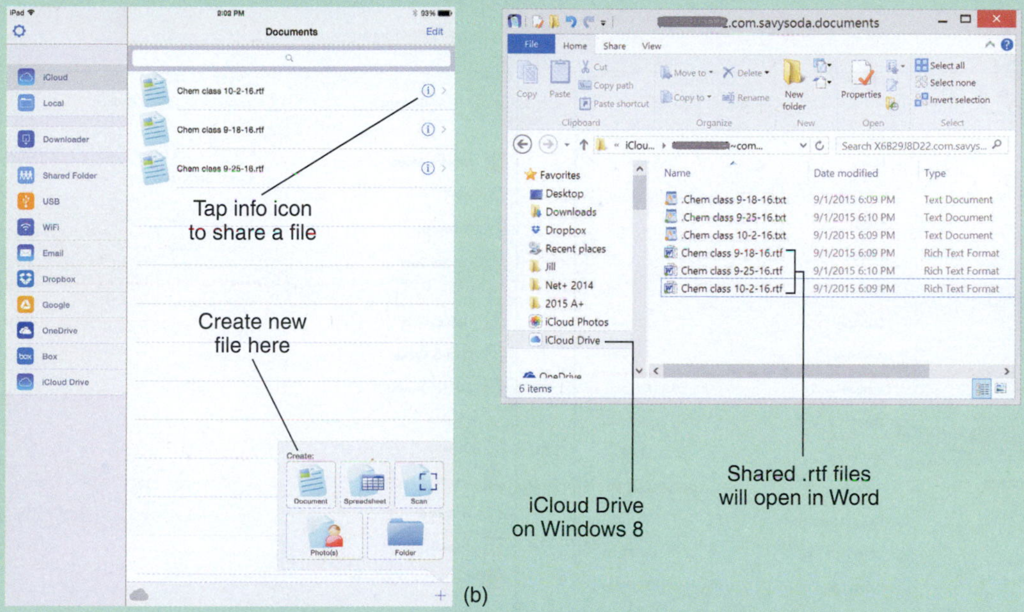

(a) (b)

Source: (a) Apple iOS and Documents Free by SavySoda Pty Ltd (savysoda.com)

Figure 16-19 (a) Access iCloud Drive through compatible apps on your device; (b) iCloud Drive files are automatically synced to all devices where it is installed, including Windows computers

2. After you're finished creating the document, to save it, tap **File** in the upper-left corner of the app and tap **Save** (to use the app's default name for the file) or **Save As** (to rename the file). To return to your Documents list, tap **File** and tap **Don't Save**. The file is now available inside the app's own folder in iCloud Drive at *icloud.com* and also on any device or computer that syncs with your iCloud Drive account.

   In Windows 8 on a personal computer, iCloud Drive is listed under Favorites in File Explorer, and there you can find the document file uploaded from your iPad, as shown in Figure 16-19b. (The app saves two copies of each file, one is an .rtf, or rich text format, file associated by default with Word, and one is a .txt, or text, file associated by default with WordPad.)

3. To download a document from iCloud Drive to the Documents Free app, on the Documents list screen, tap the **menu icon** in the upper-left corner. In the menu list that appears on the left side of the screen (see Figure 16-19a), tap **iCloud Drive**. You can then drill down into folders on your iCloud Drive and tap a file you want to download. The file can then be viewed and edited in the app.

16

> **Notes** Using any computer, open a browser and go to *icloud.com*. When you sign in with your Apple ID account, you can upload or download any file stored on your iCloud Drive to your computer.

USE iCLOUD BACKUP TO BACK UP CONTENT

To use iCloud Backup to back up your content to the cloud, follow these steps:

1. iCloud Backup requires iOS 5 or higher. To verify your Apple device is updated to iOS 5 or higher, tap **Settings, General, About** (see Figure 16-20a for an iPad screen).

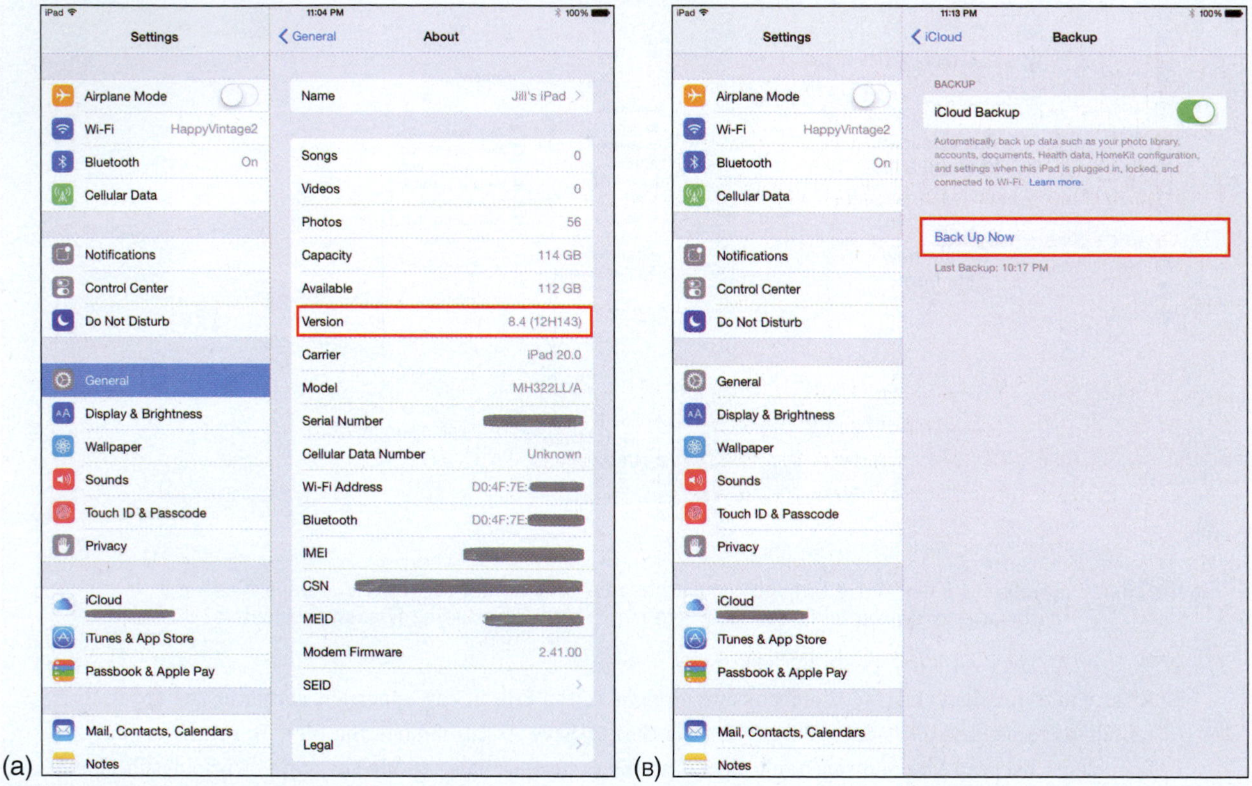

Source: iOS

Figure 16-20 (a) Verify your iOS is using version 5 or higher; (b) perform an iCloud backup at any time by tapping Back Up Now

2. To turn on iCloud Backup, tap **Settings**, then **iCloud**. Tap **Backup** and make sure iCloud Backup is turned on (see Figure 16-20b).

3. Select the items you want to back up (see Figure 16-21a), such as Mail, Contacts, Calendars, Reminders, Safari bookmarks, and so forth. Note that iCloud does not back up content already stored in the cloud, including apps, movies, podcasts, audio books, or data stored on your iCloud Drive. It also does not back up content you did not obtain from the iTunes Store, such as imported MP3s, videos, or CDs. To monitor your storage, tap **Storage**. The Storage pane is shown in Figure 16-21b.

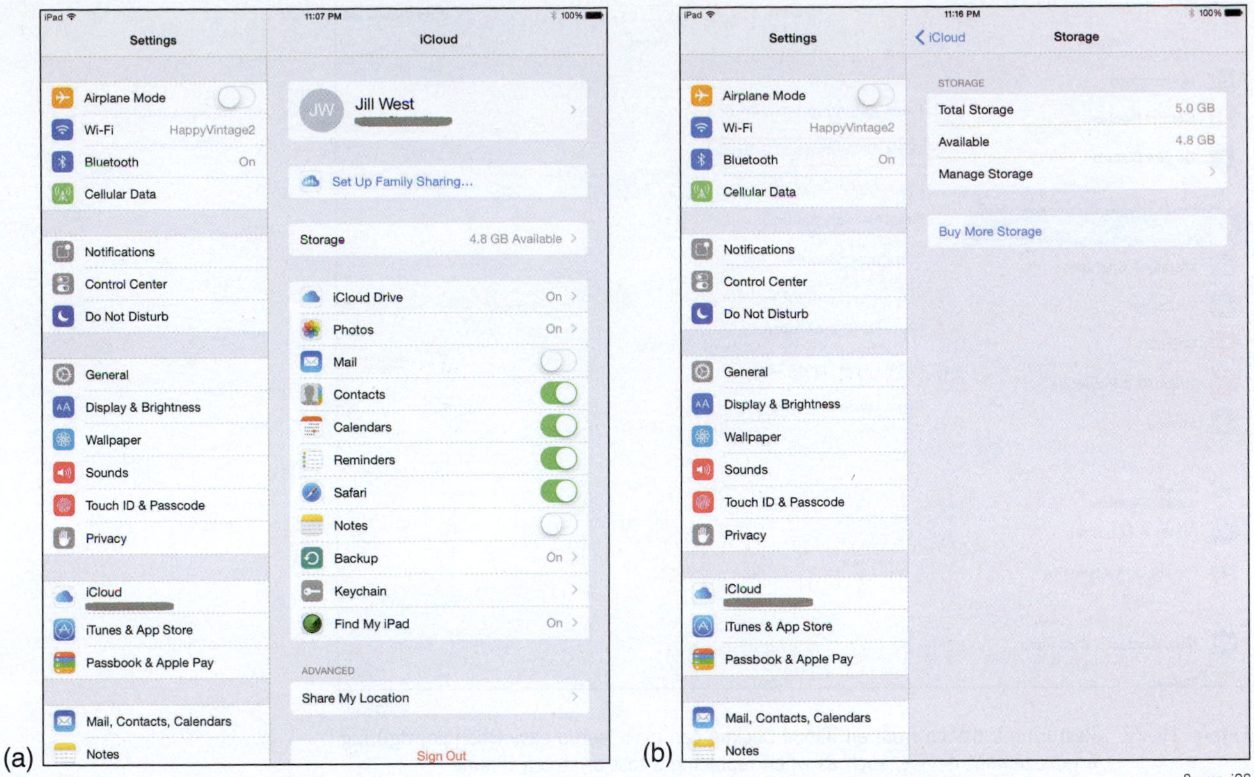

Source: iOS

Figure 16-21 (a) Decide what type of content to back up to iCloud; (b) view available storage on iCloud

4. iCloud Backup normally backs up whenever your device is connected to Wi-Fi. To back up manually to iCloud at any time, on the Backup screen shown in Figure 16-20b, you can tap **Back Up Now**.

> **Notes** To have your device report its location to iCloud, turn on **Find My iPad** or **Find My iPhone** (see Figure 16-21a). Later, if you lose your device, sign in to iCloud and this **location data** can be used to find your device on a map.

16

If you need to restore your data from iCloud Backup to your current device or to a new Apple device, here are your options:

- When you are setting up a new iOS device, the Setup process provides a screen asking if you want to restore from backup. Tap **Restore from iCloud Backup.** If you don't restore from backup during setup, the only way you can do it later is to erase everything on the new device and set up the device again.
- If you lose the content and settings on a device, to restore from backup, tap **Settings**, then **General.** Scroll to the bottom and tap **Reset**, then tap **Erase All Content and Settings** (refer to Figure 16-22). You will be given the opportunity to select a backup from iCloud through the Setup Assistant.

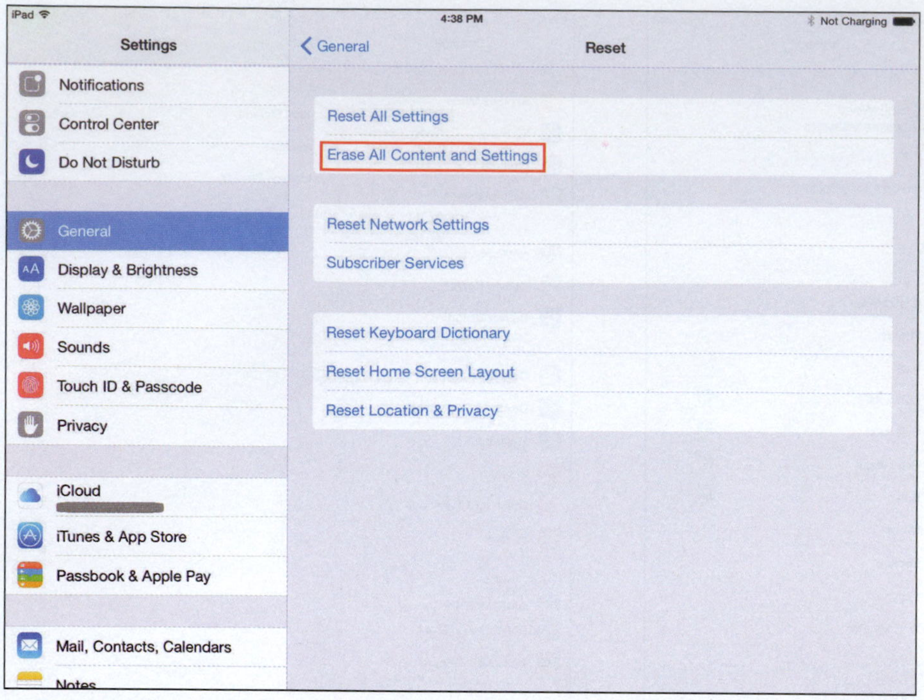

Source: iOS

Figure 16-22 Restoring a device from an iCloud backup can make setup easy when configuring a replacement device, such as when replacing a lost or stolen iPhone

Apps, music, and e-books you have previously downloaded from the iTunes Store can be downloaded again to this and other devices tied to your Apple ID. To automatically sync this content, tap **Settings** on the home screen and tap **iTunes & App Store**. On the iTunes & App Store screen (see Figure 16-23 for an iPad), turn on and configure Automatic Downloads for each type of content. Here you can also decide whether to use cellular data for automatic downloads.

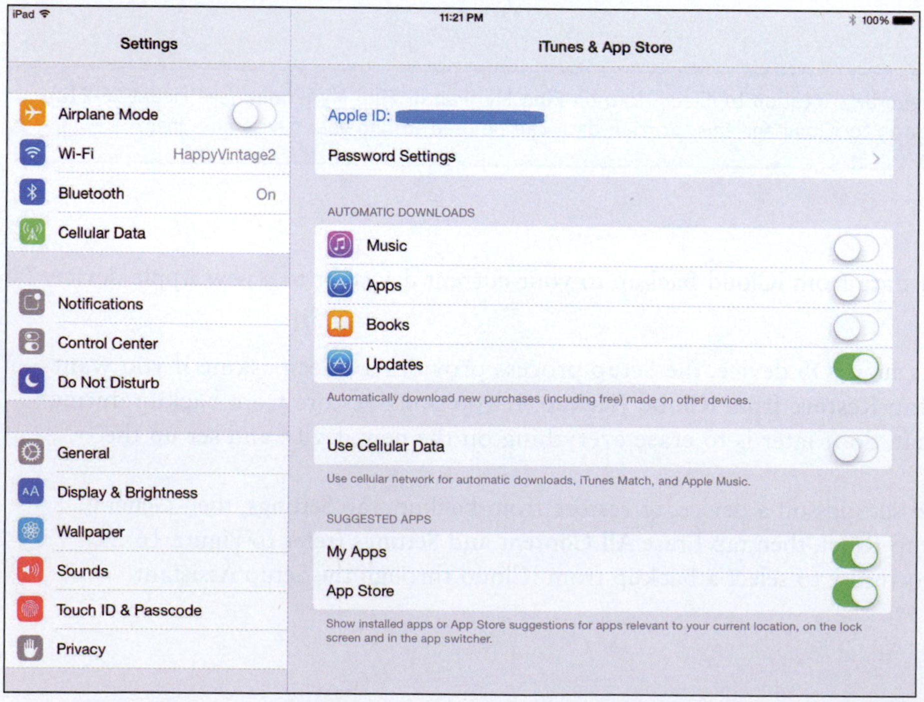

Source: iOS

Figure 16-23 Decide how to handle Automatic Downloads

USE iTUNES TO BACK UP AND SYNC CONTENT

After you have installed iTunes software on your computer, you can use it to back up and sync content, transfer purchased content from your device to your computer, and update iOS on your device. Follow these steps:

1. Make sure your computer qualifies for iTunes. For a Windows computer, iTunes can install under Windows 8/7 and needs 400 MB of free hard drive space. Install a 64-bit version of iTunes on a 64-bit OS and a 32-bit version of iTunes on a 32-bit OS.
2. Go to **apple.com/itunes/download** and download and install the software. After the software is installed, restart your computer.
3. Connect your device to your computer by way of a USB port. iTunes automatically launches and displays the window shown in Figure 16-24.

Source: iTunes

Figure 16-24 Opening window when you first connect a new device to iTunes

To see your options for backups, syncing, and transferring, in the iTunes window, click **File** and click **Devices**. Notice the four options shown in Figure 16-25 are Sync (transfers apps and data from the computer to the device), Transfer Purchases (transfers apps and data purchased on the device to the computer), Back Up (backs up content from the device to the computer), and Restore from Backup (restores backups to the device). To back up the device to the computer, click **Back Up**.

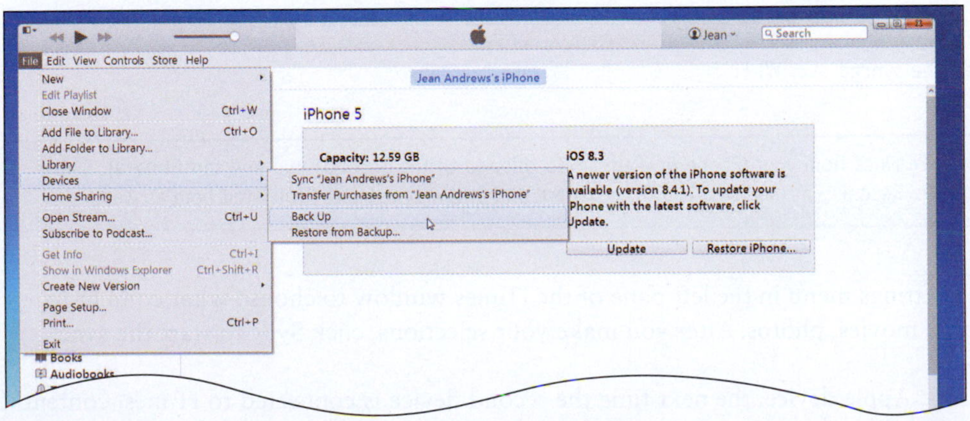

Source: iTunes

Figure 16-25 Four options for syncing, backing up, and restoring an Apple device

16

You can also perform a backup by clicking **Back Up Now** on the Summary screen in the Backups group (refer back to Figure 16-7).

When you back up content with iTunes, the backup is stored on your computer at this location when using Windows 8/7:

C:\Users*username*\AppData\Roaming\Apple Computer\MobileSync\Backup\

> **Notes** For best protection, be sure you make routine backups of the user profile folder on your computer. The user profile folder contains user settings and data, and part of this data is your iOS device backups.

iTunes automatically syncs the contacts, app data and app settings, documents, calendar, call history, photos and videos taken by the device, Wi-Fi and email passwords, Microsoft Exchange information, bookmarks, text messages and pictures, and voice messages.

To verify and customize exactly what iTunes is syncing, do the following:

1. With your device connected to your computer, select your device in the upper-left corner of the iTunes window. The Summary page was shown in Figure 16-7.
2. Scroll down to see the lower part of the Summary page, where you can choose how to sync, including allowing to sync when the iPad is in the same Wi-Fi network as the computer, as shown in Figure 16-26. You can also control what to sync.

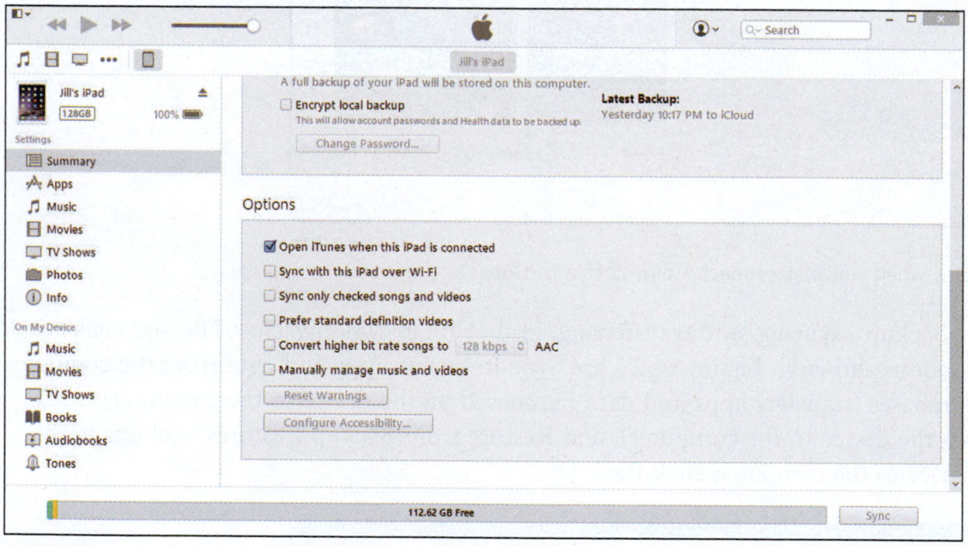

Source: iTunes

Figure 16-26 iOS devices can be synced over Wi-Fi

> **Notes** You can manage Wi-Fi syncs from your iPhone or iPad. To do this, go to the Settings app and tap **General.** Scroll down and tap **iTunes Wi-Fi Sync.** Recent syncs are shown on the screen, and a new sync can be initiated here as well.

3. Select options from the Settings menu in the left pane of the iTunes window to choose what content to sync, such as apps, music, movies, photos. After you make your selections, click **Sync** to start the sync.

If you have more than one Apple device, the next time the second device is connected to iTunes, content is synced to it (unless it's already set to sync over Wi-Fi). Using iTunes, any content on any device makes its way to the other devices and to your computer for backup.

RESTORE FROM AN iTUNES BACKUP

To restore from backup, connect the device to iTunes, select the device to show the Summary page, and in the Backups section, click **Restore Backup** in the shortcut menu (refer back to Figure 16-7). Also, when you are setting up a new device and you first connect it to iTunes on your computer, it will ask if you want to restore from backup or set up the device as a new device. You can also see in Figure 16-7 where you can update an iOS device through iTunes. From iOS version 5 and later, this is not necessary, as the device can receive updates automatically through a cellular or Wi-Fi connection.

> **Notes** To check for and install updates on the device itself, open the **Settings** app, then tap **General** in the left pane. On the right side, tap **Software Update.** Any available updates will be reported here and can be installed.

USE AIRDROP AND HANDOFF TO SYNC CONTENT

Beginning with iOS 7, iPhones and iPads can easily transfer files, such as photos, videos, and documents, between devices that belong to you or to someone else using a feature called AirDrop. Embedded in iOS, AirDrop uses Bluetooth to detect nearby compatible devices, then creates a peer-to-peer network using a Wi-Fi signal between the devices. The connections are protected by a firewall at each device, and transmissions are encrypted. AirDrop can be enabled for contacts only, or it can detect any compatible devices nearby regardless of who owns them, or it can be disabled completely. AirDrop settings are accessed through the Control Center, as shown in Figure 16-27a. To open the Control Center, swipe up from the bottom of the screen. To share files from within an app, open the app and tap **Share**. For example, Figure 16-27b shows the Maps app and the option to share the map location by AirDrop to a nearby MacBook.

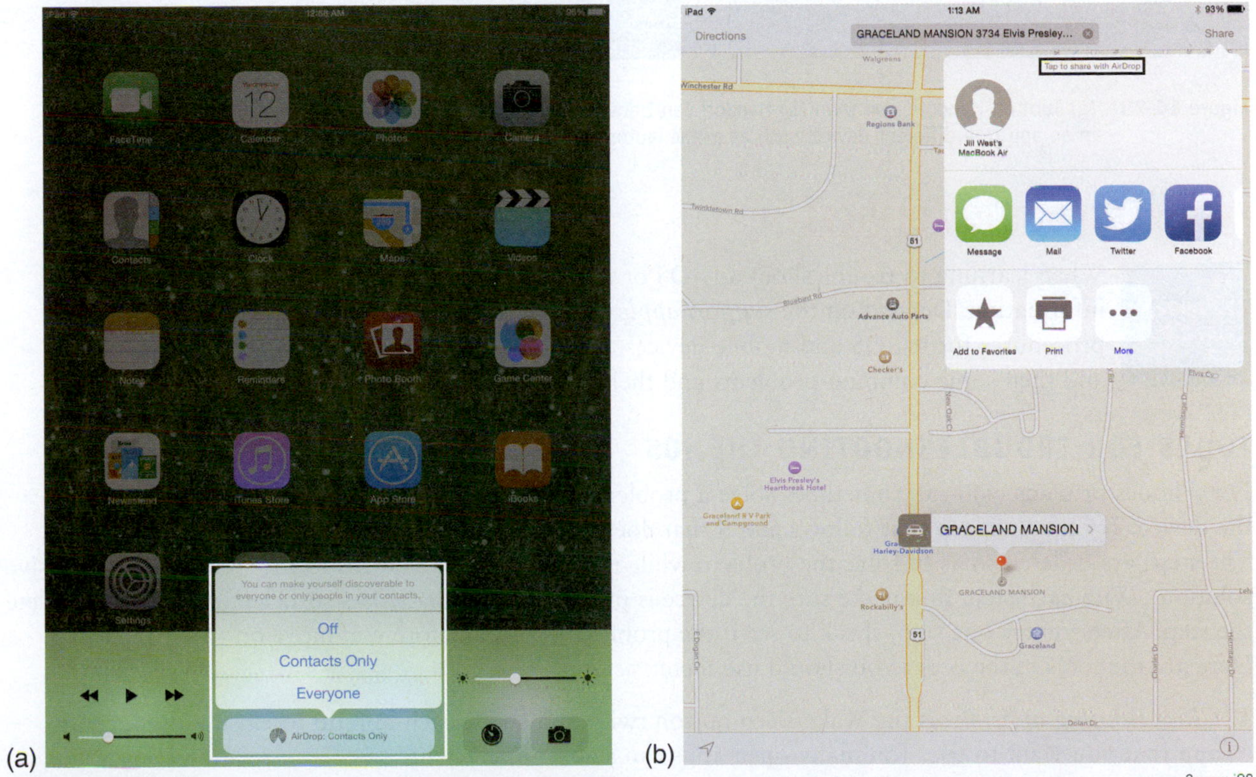

Source: iOS

Figure 16-27 (a) Turn on AirDrop in the Control Center; (b) many iOS apps, such as this Maps app, include the AirDrop sharing feature

Another synchronization tool designed to connect devices that all use the same Apple ID is Handoff. **Handoff** lets you start a task on one device, such as an iPad, then pick up that task on another device, such as a Mac desktop or laptop. To use Handoff, make sure that both devices are signed into iCloud with the same Apple ID, and that both devices have Bluetooth activated. To turn on Handoff on the iOS device, tap **Settings, General, Handoff & Suggested Apps**, and turn on **Handoff** (see Figure 16-28a). Now you're ready to use Handoff. For example, open a supported app on the iOS device, such as Safari, and then look for that app's icon on a Mac laptop. On the Mac computer, you'll see a small mobile device icon appended to the app's icon, as shown in Figure 16-28b. Click to open the app, and the app will pick up where you left off with the other device.

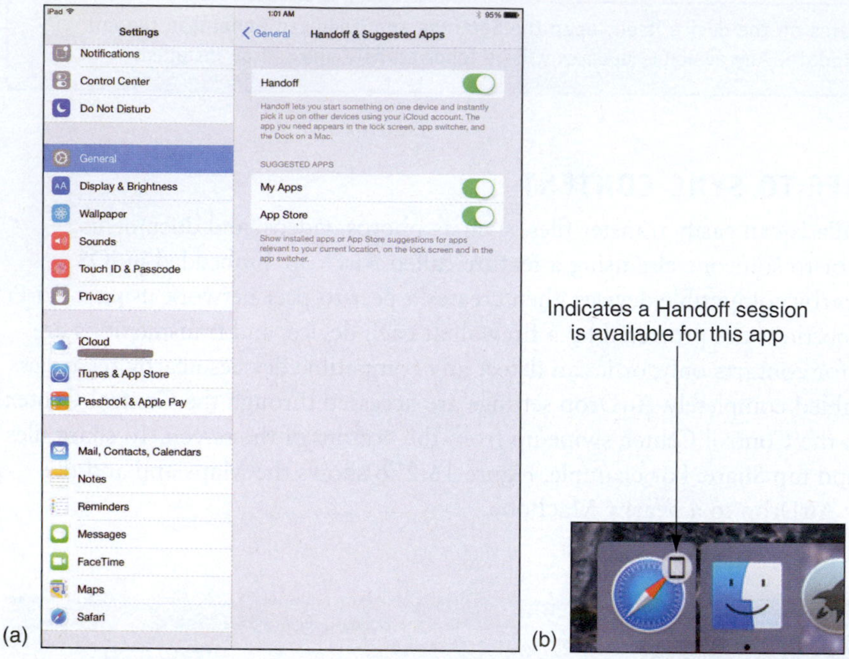

Source: iOS, OS X

Figure 16-28 (a) Turn on Handoff, and then (b) Handoff can transfer your current work in an app to a different device, such as a Mac laptop

TROUBLESHOOT iOS DEVICES

A+ 220-902 2.5, 2.6, 4.3

When learning to troubleshoot any OS or device, remember the web is a great source of information. Depend on the *support.apple.com* website to give you troubleshooting tips and procedures for its iOS and mobile devices. Let's first look at some troubleshooting tools and then some common problems and their solutions.

TOOLS FOR TROUBLESHOOTING THE iOS

For iPhones or iPads, you can sometimes solve a problem by restarting, resetting, updating, or restoring the device. Try the first step that follows and if that does not solve the problem, move on to the next step. The steps are ordered so as to solve the problem while making the least changes to the system (least intrusive solution). With each step, first make sure the device is plugged in or already has sufficient charge to complete the step. After you try one step, check to see if the problem is solved before you move on to the next step. Here are the tools in the order you should use them:

1. *Close running apps.* Press the Wake/sleep button twice and swipe each app up to close it. Reopen an app that you want to use. Too many open apps can shorten battery life.
2. *Uninstall and reinstall an app.* If an app is giving problems, uninstall it. (Press the app icon until it jiggles and then press the X beside the app icon.) Use the iTunes Store to download and reinstall the app.

3. *Restart the device.* To restart the device (perform a soft reset), press and hold the Wake/sleep button until the red slider bar appears and then drag the slider. Then press and hold the Wake/sleep button until the Apple logo appears. A soft reset puts the device in hibernation and does not clear memory.

OS Differences Each mobile OS defines a soft reset and hard reset differently. For iOS, a soft reset puts the device in hibernation and then restarts the device, and a hard reset is a hard boot, which involves a full shutdown of the device. For Android devices, a soft reset is a hard boot, and a hard reset, also called a factory reset, erases all data and restores the device to factory default state.

4. *Reset the device.* To reset the device (called a forced restart or hard reset), press and hold the Wake/sleep button and the Home button at the same time for at least 10 seconds until the Apple logo appears. A hard reset is like a full shutdown in Windows and performs a full clean boot.
5. *Update iOS.* To update iOS with the latest patches, first back up content and settings if possible. Then tap **Settings** and **Software Update**.
6. *Update from Recovery mode using iTunes.* This process attempts to update iOS without losing data or settings. Follow these steps:
   a. Make sure the latest version of iTunes is installed on your computer (you can also use someone else's computer and iTunes installation so long as iTunes is up to date).
   b. Connect the device to the computer and force it to restart by pressing and holding the Wake/sleep and Home buttons at the same time. Keep holding both buttons until the Recovery mode screen appears.
   c. Tap **Update** to reinstall iOS without erasing personal data.
   d. Don't unplug or interrupt the device during the update. If the device exits Recovery mode before the update is complete, force a restart again, and tap Update again.
7. *Reset all settings.* If you have not already done so, back up the data and settings. Then to erase settings, tap **Settings, General** and **Reset.** On the Reset screen (refer back to Figure 16-22), tap **Reset All Settings.**
8. *Erase all data and settings.* First, make every attempt to back up data and settings. Then to erase all data and settings, tap **Settings, General** and **Reset.** On the Reset screen (see Figure 16-22), tap **Erase All Content and Settings.**
9. *Restore the device.* This process reinstalls iOS and you will lose all your data on the device. The device is restored to its factory default condition, but you can then apply a backup if you have one. Before you perform a restore, try to back up all your data and settings. Then follow these steps:
   a. Make sure the latest version of iTunes is installed on your computer (you can also use someone else's computer and iTunes installation so long as iTunes is up to date). Also, if possible, make sure *Find My iPhone* or *Find My iPad* is turned off in the iCloud settings menu on the device.
   b. Connect the device to your computer and select it in iTunes. Click the **Summary** panel and click **Restore.** Click **Restore** again to confirm that you know all data and content will be deleted.
   c. Don't unplug or interrupt the device during the restore. iOS is reinstalled and all data and settings are lost.
   d. Next, restore your data and settings from backup. How to do that was covered earlier in the chapter.
10. *Restore the device from Recovery mode using iTunes.* This process might work to restore the device to its factory state when the restore process fails or when you cannot start the restore process, such as when the device restarts repeatedly, gets stuck during the startup process, or is frozen and not responding at all. The process does a firmware upgrade. All content and data are lost and the OS is refreshed. Follow these steps:
    a. Turn off the device and leave it off for a few minutes. If you have trouble turning off the device, press and hold the Wake/sleep button and the Home button at the same time.

b. While holding down the Home button, connect the device to your computer. If you see the device charging, wait a few minutes while it charges. Do not release the Home button while it is charging. When you see the Connect to iTunes screen, release the Home button.
c. iTunes should recognize the device and display a message saying the device is in Recovery mode and ask if you want to restore the device. Tap Restore and follow the directions on screen to restore the device to factory state.
d. Restore data and settings using the most recent backup.

If the device is still not working properly, search for more troubleshooting tips on the Apple website at *support.apple.com*, review the list of common problems below, or take the device to an Apple store for repair.

COMMON PROBLEMS AND SOLUTIONS

Some common problems with iOS devices can be addressed by checking specific settings or identifying particular malfunctions. If the suggestions listed here don't work, then move on to perform a soft reset, hard reset, and more invasive tools discussed earlier. Here are some problems and their solutions:

- ***Touch screen not responsive.*** Recall that Apple devices use a capacitive touch screen that does not get out of alignment unless there is a hardware problem. Here are some tips to try when a touch screen is giving you problems:
  - Clean the screen with a soft, damp cloth.
  - Don't use the touch screen when your hands are wet or you are wearing gloves.
  - Remove any plastic sheet or film protecting the touch screen.
- ***Dim display.*** When the display is dim, open the Control Center and adjust the screen brightness. To open the Control Center, swipe up from the bottom of the screen.
- ***Weak cellular signal.*** If you have a weak cellular signal or just want to save your cellular minutes, you can use Wi-Fi to connect to the Internet for VoIP voice communication. In the United States, Sprint and T-Mobile offer a feature called Wi-Fi calling, which uses VoIP over a Wi-Fi connection to the Internet. To enable Wi-Fi calling on an iPhone that uses one of these two carriers, tap **Settings** and **Phone**, then turn on **Wi-Fi Calling**. You can also install an app, such as Skype or LINE, on your iPhone and use it to make VoIP phone calls on a Wi-Fi network, regardless of the carrier you are using.

Caution When using Wi-Fi calling on your iPhone, confirm your Emergency Address from the link on the Wi-Fi Calling screen so that 911 services can respond to an emergency call from your phone if needed. Federal law requires that your carrier have a validated home address on file before activating Wi-Fi calling on your account. Your actual location can be updated on your phone each time you switch to a different wireless network.

- ***No sound or distorted sound from speakers.*** First, make sure the volume is turned up by pressing the device's physical **Up** volume button, or by checking Control Center, which you can access by swiping up from the bottom of the screen. Also, the problem could be that the sound output for the device is being misdirected. Check to see if Bluetooth is on, and if so, turn it off in order to make sure the device is not inadvertently connected to a Bluetooth headset or car stereo system. Also check Accessibility settings by tapping **Settings**, **General**, **Accessibility**. Some of the Accessibility audio settings can interfere with normal operation of the device's built-in speaker system. On iPhones, check that **Phone Noise Cancellation** is disabled.
- ***Screen won't rotate.*** A gyroscope is a device that contains a disc that is free to move and respond to gravity as the device is moved. An accelerometer is a type of gyroscope used in mobile devices to sense the physical position of the device, which helps the OS know when to adjust the screen orientation

from portrait to landscape. In iPhones and iPads, the accelerometer also enables features such as shake, where the user literally shakes the device to perform actions such as undoing the deletion of an email. If the screen won't rotate between portrait and landscape orientations, check to ensure the orientation isn't locked. Swipe up from the bottom of the screen to reveal the Control Center. The Orientation Lock icon is a padlock symbol with an arrow circling around it. Tap it to turn it on and off.

- ***Bluetooth connectivity issues.*** Sometimes an iOS update will cause issues with Wi-Fi network connectivity or Bluetooth pairings. For Bluetooth issues, first delete all known devices by tapping **Settings, Bluetooth,** then tap the info icon for each device and tap **Forget This Device**. Then, in the left panel, tap **General,** and scroll down and tap **Reset.** Tap **Reset Network Settings** and tap **Reset** on the warning box. This restores network settings to factory defaults, then you can attempt to re-pair a Bluetooth device with the iPad or iPhone.
- ***Wi-Fi connectivity issues.*** Lack of wireless connectivity or intermittent connectivity is often caused by problems with the signal that is being broadcast from the router or access point. First make sure the access point and router are working correctly, that the Wi-Fi network you want to connect to is visible to the device (not hidden), and that you're using the correct security key. For Wi-Fi issues on the device side, first start with Wi-Fi settings (in the Settings app, tap **Wi-Fi**) for the network you're trying to connect to. Tap the info icon, and try renewing the IP address (tap **Renew Lease** then tap **Renew**). If that doesn't work, tap **Forget This Network,** then retry connecting to the network. Finally, try resetting the network settings, as described above for Bluetooth connectivity issues.
- ***Overheating.*** For a true overheating problem, where the device is too hot to touch safely, power off and replace the device. However, all devices can get fairly warm if the display is left on for too long, if the surrounding environment is particularly hot, if the device is sitting on a soft surface, if the battery is going bad, or if the device remains plugged in to a power source for a long period of time. Don't use a mobile device in direct sunlight for long periods of time, try to turn off the display when you're not using it, and close apps that you're not using. This will also help conserve battery power.

> **Notes** If you know where the battery is located inside a mobile device, check for heat originating from that area of the device. If so, replacing the battery might be your solution. For most mobile devices, you can find tear-down instructions, videos, tools, and replacement parts for purchase at *ifixit.com*. Be aware you might void the warranty when you open the case.

16

- ***Location services not working in apps.*** A mobile device provides location-specific information by using Bluetooth and GPS information as well as crowd-sourced Wi-Fi and cellular databases built from anonymous, encrypted geo-tagged locations of Wi-Fi hotspots and cell towers. A GPS (Global Positioning System) receiver determines its position by using the GPS satellite data or data from the position of nearby cellular towers. Geotracking, which is the identification of a device's location in order to track the device's movements, relies heavily on location information. Many apps can only access this information if Location Services is enabled on the device (emergency calls can use location information even if Locations Services is not enabled). For example, Siri checks the device's current location before recommending Italian restaurants in the area.

  If an app is having trouble accessing location-specific information, check the Location Services settings by tapping **Settings, Privacy,** and then **Location Services,** which shows the screen in Figure 16-29. Tap **Share My Location** to determine whether apps like Messages and Find My Friends can share your location information with contacts. On the Location Services screen, tap the **About Location Services & Privacy** link to read more information about how your privacy is affected by sharing your location information.

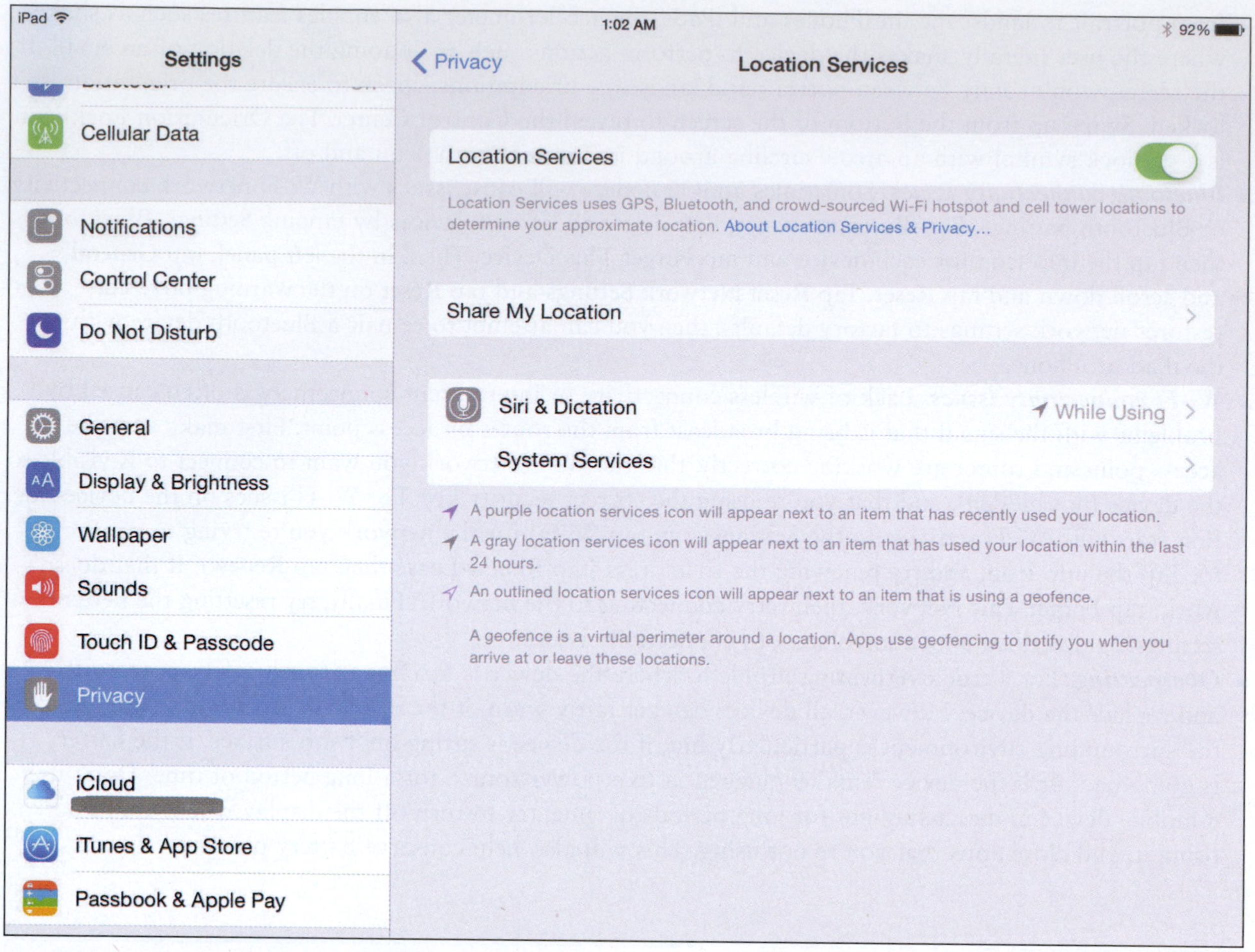

Source: iOS

Figure 16-29 The Location Services screen shows which apps have recently used your device's location information

- *System lockout.* If your iOS device is locked because of too many failed attempts at entering your passcode to sign in to the device, you can wait until the timer counts down on the screen and then attempt to enter the passcode again. If you have forgotten the passcode, Apple advises your only solution is to reset the device, which erases all data and settings, and then you can restore the device from backup. You have a few options for resetting the device:
  - If you set up Find My iPhone or Find My iPad, you can go to *icloud.com/find*, sign in with your Apple ID, select your device, and then erase it. The erase process resets the device to its factory state.
  - If you have previously synced the device with iTunes, connect the device to iTunes and allow it to sync. After the sync is completed, use iTunes to restore your device. When you reach the setup screen, tap **Restore from iTunes backup.**
  - If you have not set up Find My iPhone or Find My iPad and you've never synced with iTunes, install iTunes on your computer and connect your device. Then force restart the device: Press and hold the Wake/sleep button and Home button at the same time until you see the Apple logo appear and then the recovery mode screen appear. Tap **Restore.** iTunes will reset the device to factory state.

Hands-On | Project 16-1 Research iOS Browser Apps

A+
220-902
2.5

A smart phone or tablet comes with a built-in browser, but you can replace it with a third-party browser. Research browser apps and answer the following questions:

1. List three browser apps that are popular with Apple devices using iOS. List one feature for each app that makes it stand out.
2. The iPhone and iPad don't use Adobe Flash, and many websites depend on Flash. What workaround app can be used with iOS so that the iPhone and iPad can view content on these websites?

CONFIGURE, SYNC, AND TROUBLESHOOT ANDROID DEVICES

A+
220-902
2.5, 2.6,
2.7, 4.3

Because the Android operating system is open source, manufacturers can customize the OS and how it works in many variations. Therefore, it is not always possible to give specific step-by-step directions similar to those given for iOS. In this part of the chapter, you learn about general procedures you can follow to support an Android device. We also give a few examples for specific Android devices so that you can see how the step-by-step directions might work on an Android device.

Most of the settings you need to support an Android device are found in the Settings app; however, settings options might not be in the Settings app and some settings options might rely on third-party apps.

On the other hand, Android is usually fun to use and support because it offers so much flexibility and the potential to customize. Once you get comfortable with Android, you can do amazing things with it. Technicians who love to tinker with devices tend to gravitate to Android, and those who just want a quick and easy tool to use without a hassle choose iOS.

When you are assigned responsibility for supporting an Android device, begin with the user guide for the device, which you can download from the device manufacturer's website. The user guide is likely to tell you the detailed steps of how to connect to a network, configure email, update the OS, sync and back up settings and data, secure the device, and what to do when things go wrong.

16

Notes Most of us rarely follow step-by-step directions when learning to use a new device until when "all else fails, read the directions." This part of the chapter can give you an idea of what to look for on an Android device, and you can likely figure out the specific steps for yourself.

Now let's look at what to expect when supporting an Android device.

CONFIGURE ANDROID NETWORK CONNECTIONS

A+
220-902
2.5, 2.6,
2.7, 4.3

To configure settings on an Android device, use the Settings app, which can be found in the Apps Drawer or on the Notifications shade, as shown earlier in Figure 16-2. Figure 16-30 shows the Settings screen in list view on the left and in tab view on the right. Switch from list view to tab view by tapping the ellipsis icon in the upper-right corner, then tap **Switch to tab view** and tap **OK**.

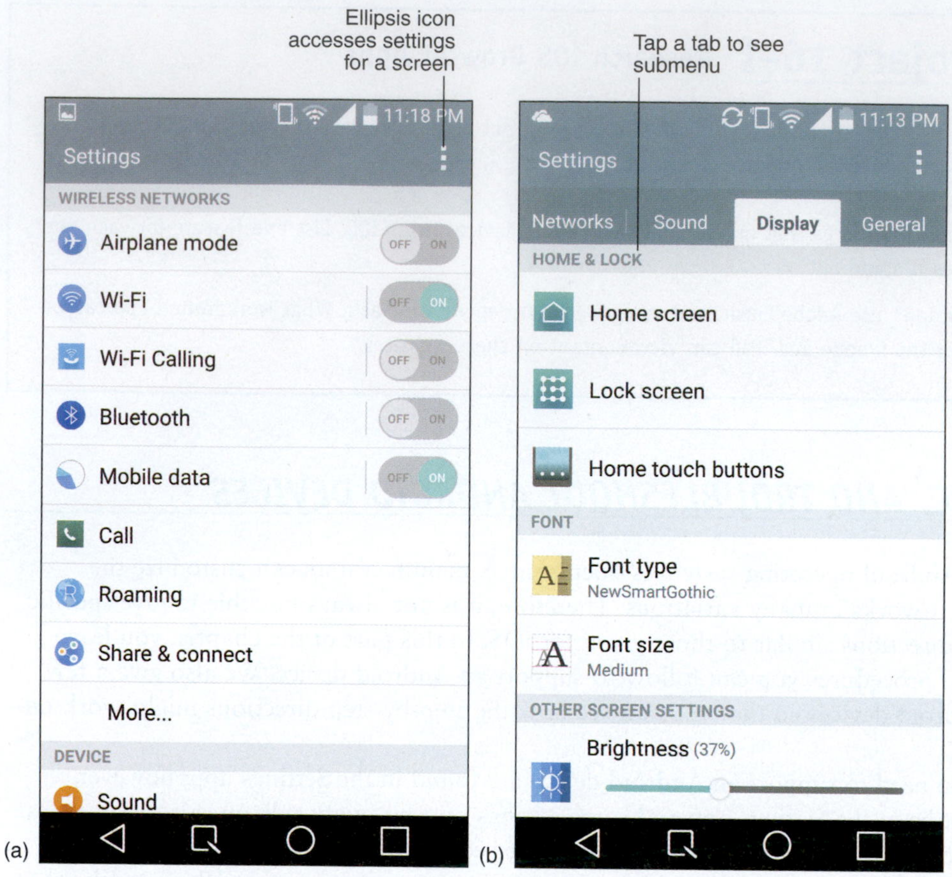

Source: Android

Figure 16-30 The Settings menu can be organized (a) by one long list or (b) by tabs and submenus

Network connections are configured using the Settings screen. Available settings can include:

- ***Turn Airplane mode on or off.*** Recall that Airplane mode disables all wireless network antennas and can help conserve data usage or battery power when your battery is low.
- ***Turn Wi-Fi on or off and configure Wi-Fi access points.*** Tap **Wi-Fi**. On the Wi-Fi settings screen, as shown in Figure 16-31a, you can add a Wi-Fi connection, manage existing networks, access the Advanced Wi-Fi settings screen (see Figure 16-31b), or explore the tutorial. When you first attempt to connect to a secured Wi-Fi network, you need its security key.

> **Notes** Searching for a Wi-Fi network can drain battery power. To make a battery charge last longer, disable Wi-Fi when you're not using it.

- ***Turn Wi-Fi calling on or off.*** Wi-Fi calling, available through certain carriers, allows you to make phone calls over a Wi-Fi network rather than needing a cellular network. Turn on Wi-Fi calling, then input 911 information, as shown in Figure 16-32a. You can also enable address notification (Figure 16-32b) so that you're prompted to update your location each time you connect with a new Wi-Fi network. These addresses are saved so the information won't have to be reentered the next time you visit that location.

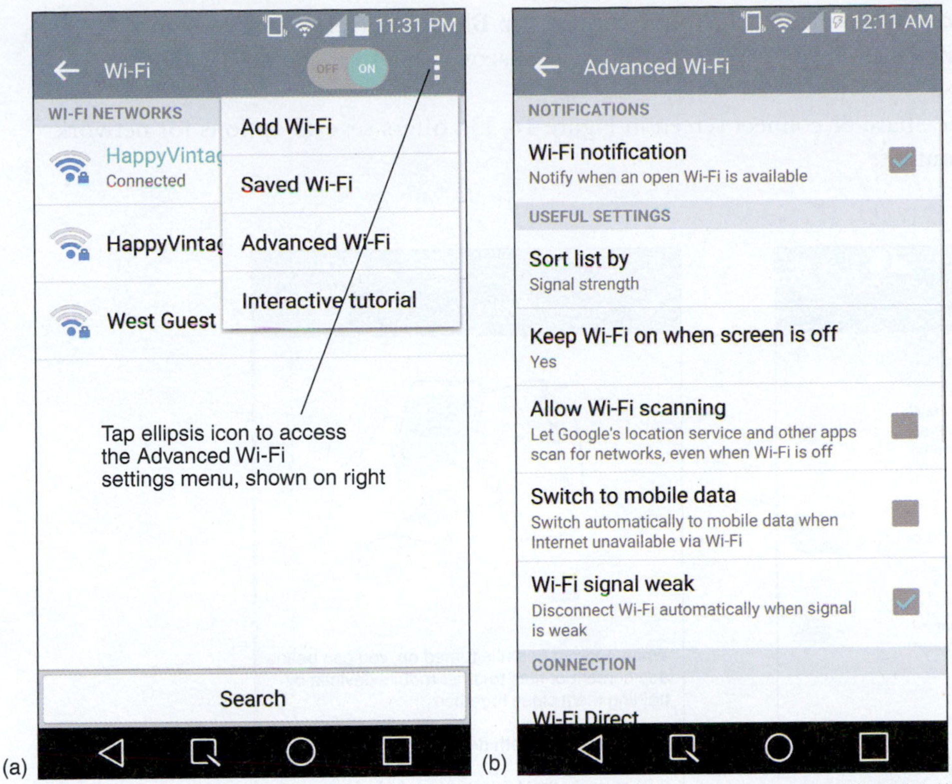

Source: Android

Figure 16-31 Configure Wi-Fi settings

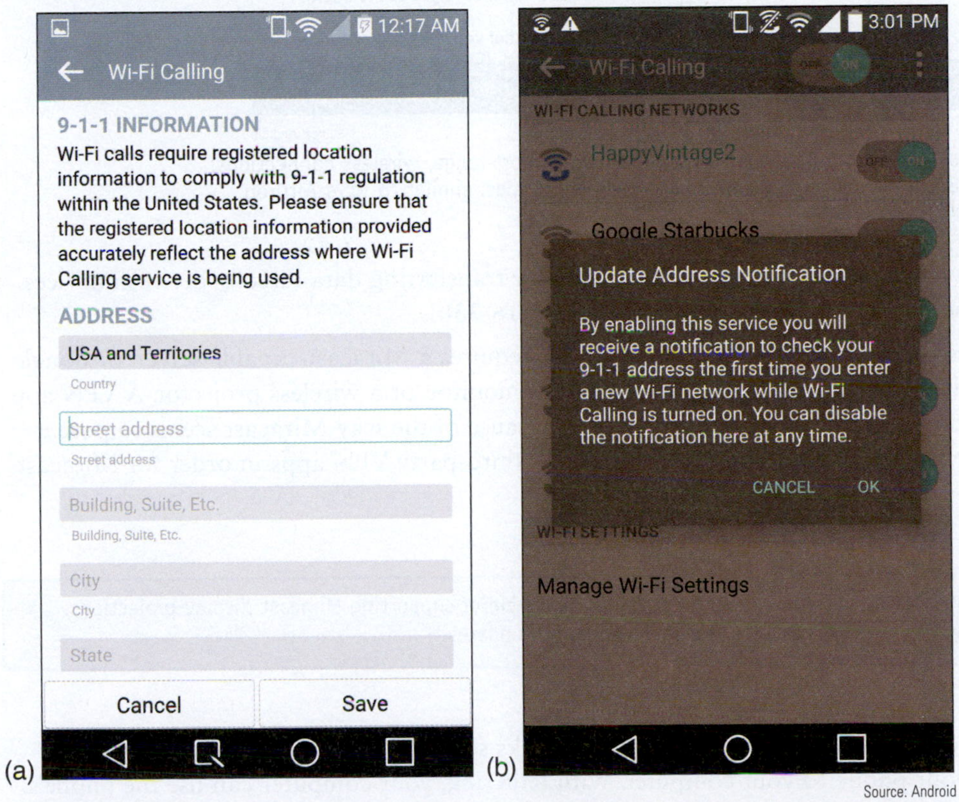

Source: Android

Figure 16-32 (a) 911 address information is required in order to use Wi-Fi calling service; (b) your phone can remind you to update your current location information when joining a new wireless network

16

- ***Turn Bluetooth on or off.*** To configure Bluetooth settings, tap **Bluetooth** (refer back to Figure 16-30a). On the Bluetooth settings screen, you can make the device discoverable so it can pair with other Bluetooth devices.
- ***Share and connect.*** The Share & connect screen in Figure 16-33a offers several options for network connections to share content:

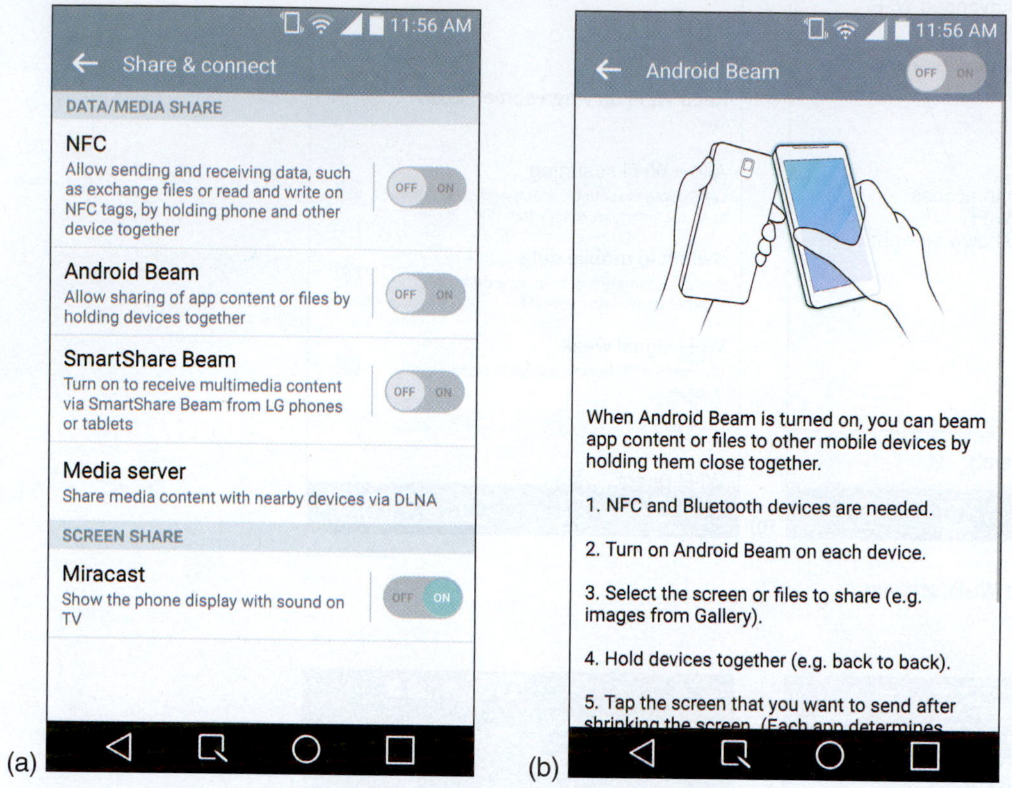

Source: Android

Figure 16-33 (a) This version of Android provides several options for short-range, wireless connections; (b) Android Beam uses both NFC and Bluetooth technologies, similar to iOS's AirDrop

  - NFC and Bluetooth technologies both provide options for transferring data directly between devices that are held in close proximity to each other (see Figure 16-33b).
  - Miracast is a wireless display-mirroring technology that requires a Miracast-capable screen or dongle in order to mirror the phone's display to a TV, a wireless monitor, or a wireless projector. A VPN app on the device sometimes disables the Miracast feature because of the way Miracast seems to pose a threat to VPN security. It might be necessary to uninstall third-party VPN apps in order for Miracast to work properly.

> **OS Differences** Windows 8.1 and Windows Phone 8.1 are also capable of supporting Miracast display projections. If it's not working in Windows, be sure to check for driver and firmware updates.

- ***Set up tethering.*** Figure 16-34 shows the Wireless & networks screen on an Android phone, which you can use to tether your phone to your computer. With tethering, your computer can use the phone's cellular network connection to access the Internet. This feature must be enabled on your cellular plan

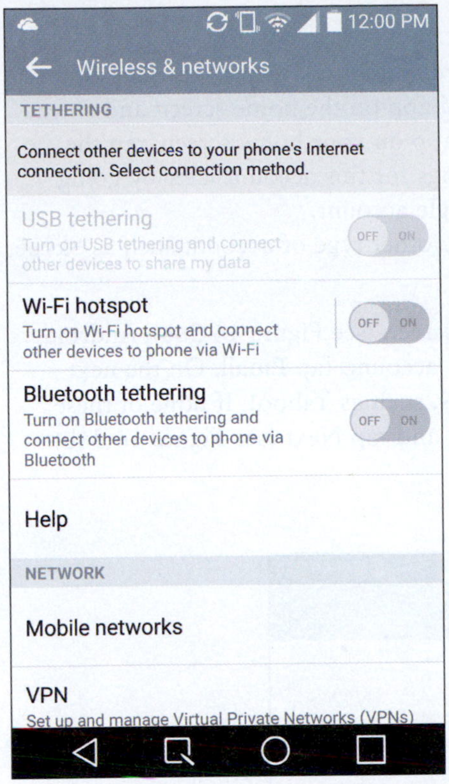

Source: Android

Figure 16-34 The Wireless & network settings screen on an Android phone

in order to use it; some carriers include the tethering feature as a standard service in their plans, whereas others charge extra. To set up tethering, tap one of the tethering options. (A tablet that does not have cellular capability will not have tethering options.)

- *Set up a VPN.* To set up a VPN in Android, tap **VPN** on the Wireless & network settings screen (see Figure 16-34). Figure 16-35a shows the configuration options, including the Type (which refers to the VPN protocol used, such as PPTP, L2TP/IPsec, and IPsec Xauth), Server address, and any encryption options. The advanced options shown in Figure 16-35b allow configuration of the DNS search domain, DNS server (Google's public DNS server is at IP address 8.8.8.8), and any forwarding routes. In addition to the built-in Android VPN client just shown, some Android devices also provide proprietary VPN configuration options.

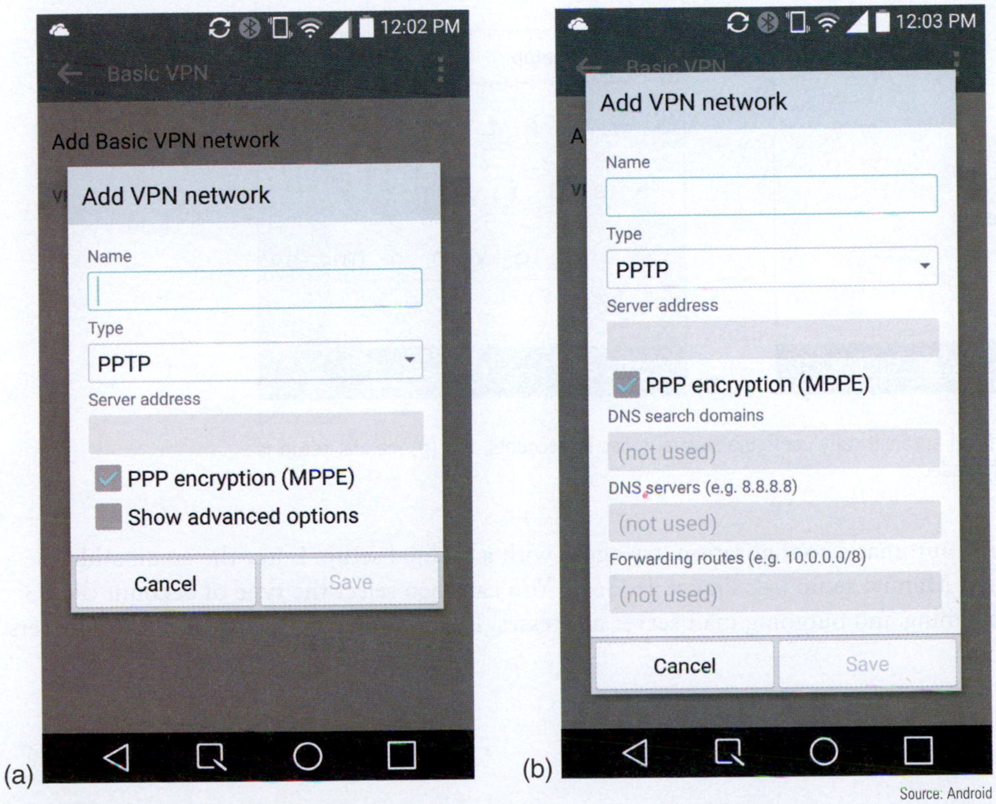

Source: Android

Figure 16-35 (a) Basic configuration for a VPN connection and (b) advanced VPN configuration options

CONFIGURE ANDROID EMAIL

A+ 220-902 2.6, 2.7

Because Google owns Gmail, Google makes it very easy to configure a Gmail account on an Android device. To set up a Gmail account, tap the **Gmail** app on the home screen and enter your Gmail account and password. (If you don't see the app on your home screen, tap the Apps Drawer, and then tap Gmail.) You can change settings for this account later by going to the Settings app, tapping **Accounts & sync**, and selecting your **Google** account.

Here are the steps to set up email accounts other than Gmail or any other type of account such as Skype, YouTube, Photobucket, Dropbox, or Facebook accounts:

1. Tap **Settings, Accounts & sync, Add account.** On the Add account screen (see Figure 16-36a), Android can automatically configure several types of accounts. For an email account, tap **Email.** On the next screen, you might be given options for different email account types, such as Yahoo!. If none of these is correct, tap **Other.** Next, enter your email account and password and tap **Next** (see Figure 16-36b). The account is automatically set up.

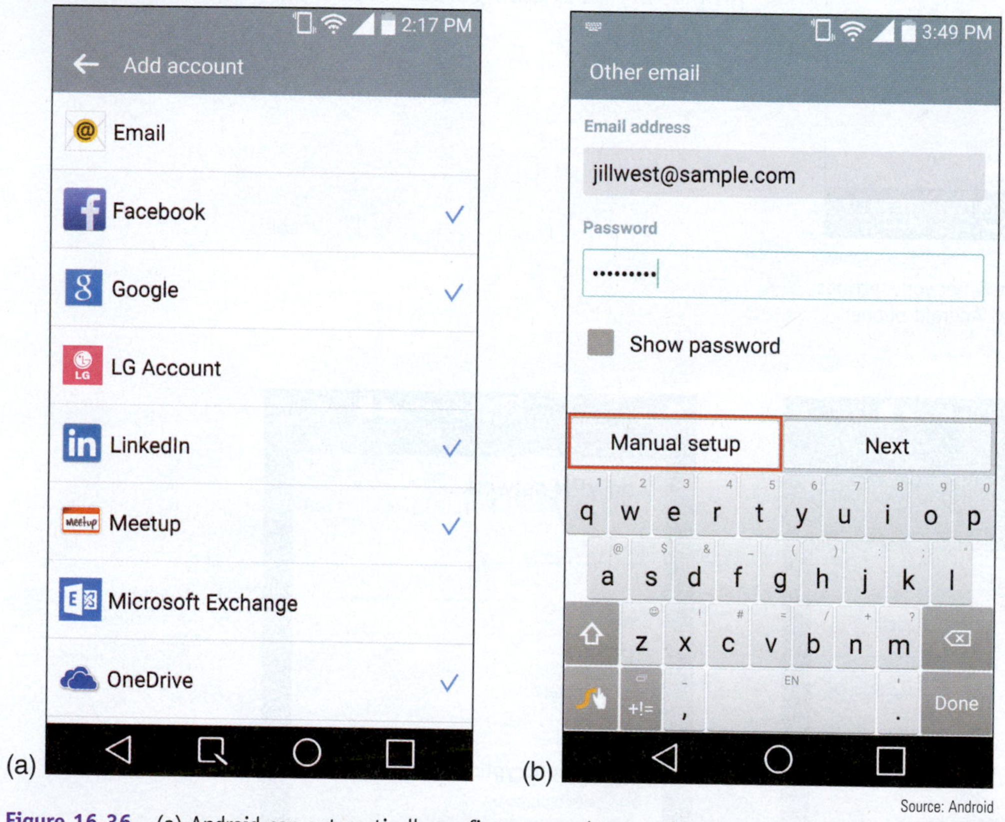

Figure 16-36 (a) Android can automatically configure several types of accounts, but (b) manual setup is available if needed

2. If you get errors using automatic configuration, try again with a manual setup. Enter the email address and password and tap **Manual setup** (see Figure 16-36b). You can then select the type of account (POP3 or IMAP4), enter incoming and outgoing mail server addresses, POP3 or IMAP4 protocols, port numbers, and email encryption.

SYNC, UPDATE, BACK UP, AND RESTORE FROM BACKUP WITH ANDROID

A+
220-902
2.5, 2.6,
2.7

Syncing, backing up, and restoring from backup with Android is much simpler now than it has been in the past. Additionally, Android offers more methods and options for these chores, and third-party apps can often be used. In this part of the chapter, you learn to sync with online accounts, sync all your apps to an app store, and back up any content to your personal computer.

SYNC USING ONLINE ACCOUNTS

Each Google product automatically syncs across devices when you're signed in to your account on that device. For example, the Gmail app on your phone will show the same information and configuration settings as the Gmail interface in your Chrome browser on your computer. Google Drive makes documents available to all of your Google-connected devices, and Google Calendar syncs appointments and reminders across devices. All data is web-based, so everything is accessible through a web browser (Google products work best in Chrome, of course). You can also sync contacts, calendars, photos, newsfeeds, messages, games, and other data with social media accounts such as Facebook, Twitter, Dropbox, LinkedIn, and others. If you notice an account is not syncing correctly, re-sync information for the account through the same *Accounts & sync* menu used to create the account. On the **Settings** app, tap **Accounts & sync**. Select an existing account to turn on sync, force a re-sync, or adjust other account settings.

USE THIRD-PARTY SYNCING APPS

For other content, such as pictures, music, and videos, third-party apps might better suit your needs. Some Android devices come preinstalled with sync apps. Some apps like OneDrive will sync entire folders in the background with no user intervention required, while others like Dropbox only sync files placed in the app's own folder. Some apps sync between a mobile device and computer, while others maintain those files in the cloud and the service is linked to the user's account.

SYNC APPS WITH YOUR APP SOURCE

Google Play maintains records of all apps for a particular Google account. A Google account is associated with an email address (Gmail or some other email address). To tie a Google account to your device, tap **Settings, Accounts & sync, Add account, Google Accounts**, and follow the directions on screen. The process allows you to create a Google account if you don't already have one.

You can sometimes solve a problem with an app by uninstalling it and then installing it again. To uninstall an app, open the Settings app and tap **Apps**. Press and hold the app you want to uninstall and then tap **Uninstall**.

To update an app or restore an app you uninstalled, follow these steps:

1. On the home screen, tap **Play Store**. The Google Play screen appears (see Figure 16-37a for an Android phone). Apps are tied to the Google account you used when you downloaded the app. Tap the menu icon, then tap **My apps** (see Figure 16-37b) to manage settings for your existing apps, including updates.

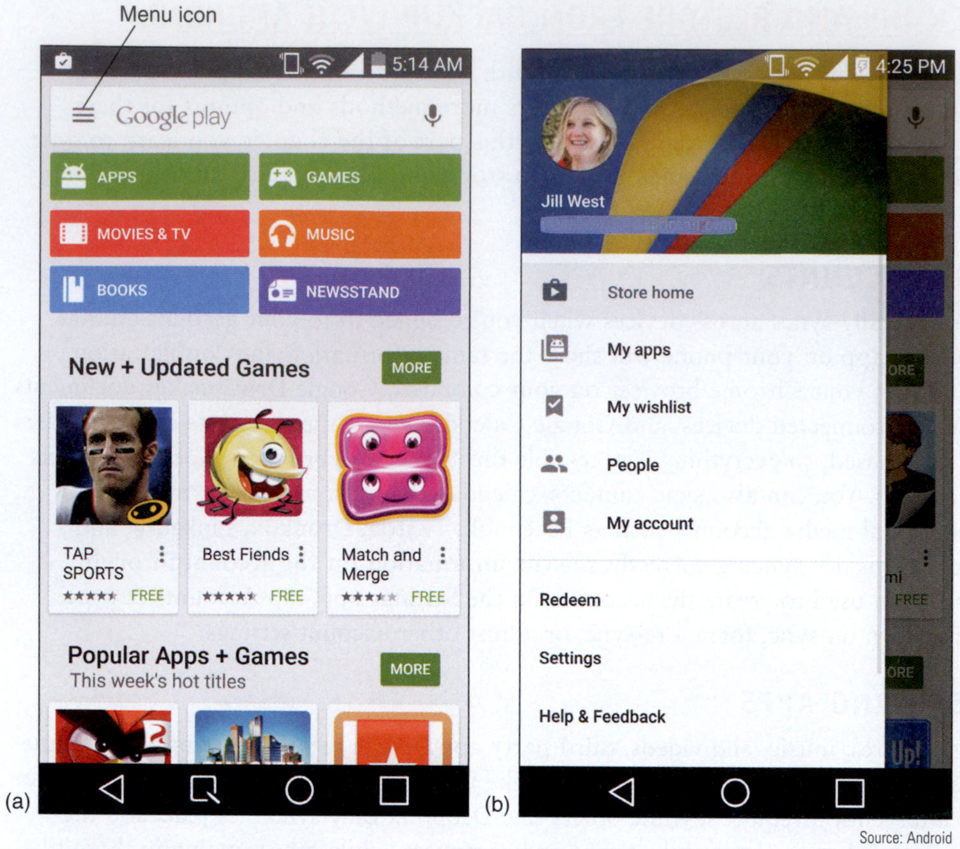

Figure 16-37 (a) Search for new apps in the Play Store and (b) manage your existing apps

2. On the My apps screen, the INSTALLED tab shows a list of apps already installed on the device. To update an app, tap **Update**, then tap **UPDATE** again on the app's screen and accept any access permission changes. To reinstall an app that has been uninstalled, tap **ALL** at the top of the screen. In the list of apps that you have previously downloaded or purchased from the Play Store, select the app and tap **INSTALL**. The app installs again. Notice on these screens that you're given information on permissions assigned to each app, including how it can use storage, the network, GPS locator service, and other hardware controls.

You can control how an app is updated. To do so, return to the Google Play screen and tap the menu icon (refer back to Figure 16-37a). Then tap **Settings**. On the Settings screen, tap **Auto-update apps** and choose to not auto-update apps, which gives you manual control over updates, or **Auto-update apps over Wi-Fi only** to conserve battery charge and use of the cellular data network.

In addition to the Play Store, you can purchase apps from other sites like *Amazon.com*. When you purchase an app from a source other than the Play Store, make sure the site provides the opportunity to restore the app if that becomes necessary.

UPDATE THE ANDROID OS

Updates to the Android OS are automatically pushed to the device from the manufacturer. Because each manufacturer maintains its own versions of Android, these updates might not come at the same time Google announces a major update. When the device receives notice of an update, it might display a message asking permission to install the update. With some devices, you can also manually check for updates at any time, although not all devices provide the option to perform a manual update of the Android OS. To see if manual updates can be performed on your device, go to the **Settings** app and tap

About. On the About screen, tap **System updates** or **Software update** or a similar item. The device turns to the manufacturer's website for information and reports updates available.

Before installing an OS update, you might want to read on the website the release instructions about the update, called Product Release Instructions (PRI), such as new features or patches the update provides and how long the update will take. Later, if a device is giving problems after an OS update or after the device has been rooted, which is similar to the concept of jailbreaking an iOS phone, check the PRI for information that might help you understand the nature of the problem.

BACK UP AND RESTORE ANDROID

Syncing your emails, contacts, calendar, photos, and other data through online accounts serves as a useful backup for that data should something happen to your phone. On the other hand, your app data, Wi-Fi passwords, and other settings can be backed up directly through the Android OS. To do this, go to the **Settings** app, then tap **Backup & reset**. Make sure that **Back up my data** is checked and change the backup account if needed. Your backup data is stored on Google's servers and is connected with your Google account. You can access much of this information directly through your account on the Google website, including recent browser searches, contacts, calendars, location history, alarms, and network connection settings like Wi-Fi passwords. On your mobile device, you can also choose to restore backed-up settings and data to an app that you reinstall after removing it.

You can back up the layout of your home screen and the wallpaper as well. In the **Settings** app, tap **Home screen**. Tap **Home backup & restore**, then **Backup**. Tap **Yes** to save the current home screen settings as a new backup file. To restore these settings later, return to the Home screen menu, tap **Home backup & restore**, and this time tap **Restore**. Tap **Yes** to confirm the restore request.

Hands-On | Project 16-2 Research Apps for Mobile Payment Services

A+ 220-902 2.5

iPhone and Android phones both offer some kind of **mobile payment service**, which allows you to use your smart phone to pay for merchandise or services at a retail checkout counter. iPhone has Apple Pay. Android can use the Google Wallet app and Android Pay will soon be embedded in the newest Android phones. Microsoft has announced that Windows 10 phones will also have a similar service. Mobile payment services use NFC (near field communication) technology, a short-range, low-power wireless technology, to exchange financial information between your phone and the reader at the checkout counter. You might want to pay with a credit card stored on your phone or get discounts with a store rewards account reported by your phone as you check out. But how secure is your sensitive financial information?

Research the following topics, then answer the following questions:

1. Research how mobile payment systems use NFC technology. How does NFC work? How can you activate NFC on an Android phone? An iPhone? A Windows phone?
2. Find and read some articles online or watch videos that describe the details of storing financial information for mobile payment systems, accessing the information when needed, and transmitting the information securely. What security measures are in place? Where is the data actually stored? What information is actually transmitted at the point of transaction?
3. List three third-party mobile payment apps available either in Apple's App Store, in Android's Play Store, or in Microsoft's Store. On which mobile OS versions will the apps work? What are advantages and disadvantages of each app? How much do the apps cost? What security measures do the apps use?
4. If you were to purchase one of these apps, which one would it be? Why?

TROUBLESHOOT ANDROID DEVICES

A+ 220-902 2.5, 2.6, 4.3

Follow these general tips to solve problems with Android devices. For more specific instructions, search the website of the device manufacturer:

1. *Force reboot or soft reset.* You can forcefully reboot the device, which, for Android devices is called a soft reset, by pressing and holding the power button. Power cycling a smart phone every few days is a good idea anyway to keep the phone functioning at peak efficiency. If this doesn't work, you can open the back cover of the device, remove the battery, and then reinstall the battery. Not all Android devices allow removal of the battery. In those cases, some devices offer a simulated battery pull. Research online to find out if this is an option.
2. *Uninstall and reinstall an app.* If you suspect an app is giving a problem, uninstall it and use the app store to reinstall it. How to do this was covered earlier in the chapter.
3. *Update Android.* Try installing Android updates, if available.
4. *Use Safe Mode.* Similar to Windows computers, Android offers a Safe Mode for troubleshooting OS and device issues. Be aware, however, that booting to Safe Mode might result in loss of some settings such as synchronization accounts. The combination of buttons to access Safe Mode varies by device, so consult the manufacturer's website for specific instructions. For one LG smart phone, to access Safe Mode you hold down the power button until the power menu appears. Tap and hold the **Power Off** option until the pop-up shown in Figure 16-38a appears. Tap **OK**, and the phone restarts into Safe Mode, as shown in Figure 16-38b. Notice the *Safe mode* flag at the bottom of the screen, and the default appearance of the home screen. In Safe Mode, only apps native to the Android installation can run, and troubleshooting tools can be accessed through the Settings app to back up data, test configuration issues, or reset the device. To exit Safe Mode, on the Notifications shade, tap the shield icon to restart the device and restore third-party apps.

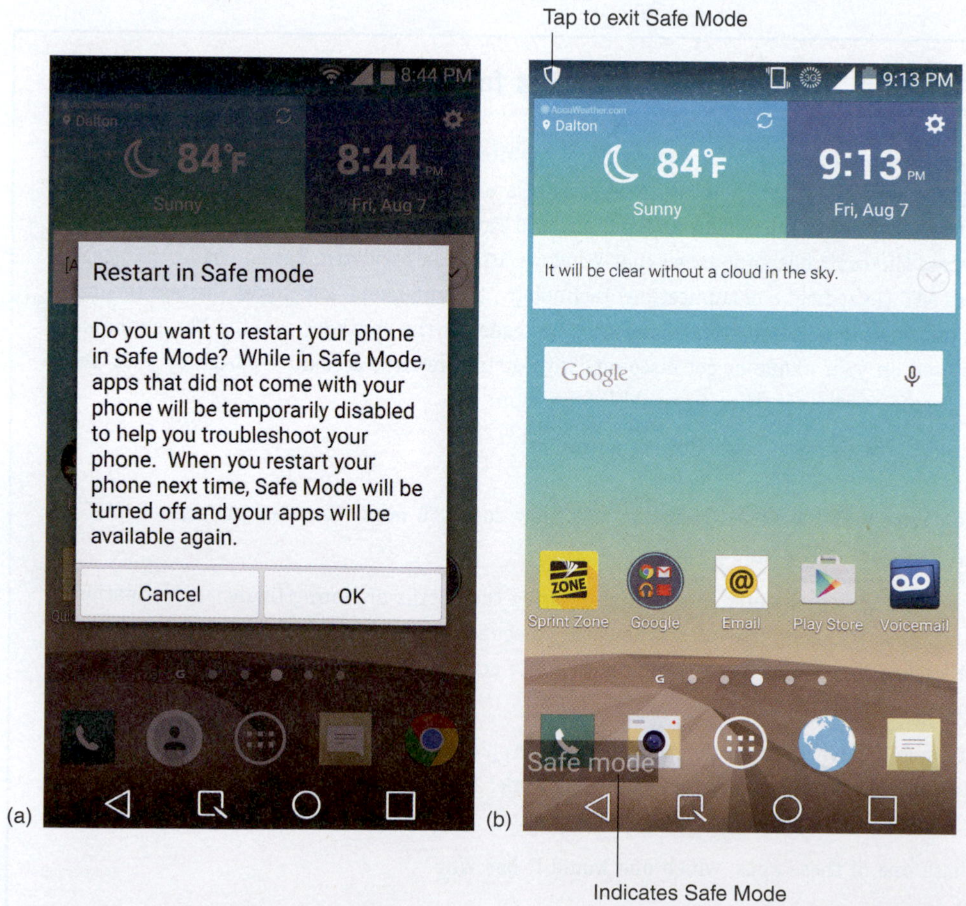

Figure 16-38 (a) Restart in Safe Mode, and (b) in Safe Mode, third-party apps don't load and default configuration settings are used

5. ***Update firmware.*** Updating the device's firmware can solve problems with network connections and other issues where the Android OS must interact with hardware. A firmware update, also called a baseband update, is distributed by the manufacturer of the device. Usually the firmware update is pushed out from the carrier along with an OS update, but not always. To determine the current baseband version of an Android device, on the **Settings** app, tap **About**, then **Software info**. You can take a screen shot to save the baseband version information before checking for an update. To update the firmware, on the **Settings** app, tap **System updates**, then **Update Firmware** (this menu might vary slightly between manufacturers). When the update is complete or it's reported that no update is available, tap **OK**.
6. ***Use Recovery mode.*** Take the device into Recovery mode, which is somewhat similar in concept to UEFI/BIOS setup in Windows. To do so, look for instructions on the manufacturer's website. Most likely, you need to hold down a combination of buttons. Once there, Android presents a menu where you can reboot the system, restore the system to factory state, and possibly other options. Try the reboot before you try the factory state, because this last option causes all your apps and data to be lost.
7. ***Factory reset or hard reset.*** As a last resort, you can perform a factory reset, which, for Android devices is also called a hard reset. The reset erases all data and settings and resets the device to its original factory default state. To do this, from the **Settings** app, tap **Backup & reset**, then tap **Factory data reset**.

Several issues commonly faced with Android devices can be addressed with a little understanding of what has gone wrong behind the scenes. Here's a description of how to handle some common problems:

- ***Dropped calls.*** Sometimes updating the device's firmware can solve problems with dropped calls because the update might apply to the radio firmware, which manages the cellular, Wi-Fi, and Bluetooth radios.
- ***Wireless connectivity problems.*** Intermittent connectivity problems might be caused by a weak Wi-Fi signal. By default, Android stops attempting to reconnect to a weak Wi-Fi signal in order to conserve battery power, but you can change this setting. On the Wi-Fi screen, tap the menu icon and then tap **Advanced Wi-Fi**. Uncheck **Wi-Fi signal weak** (see Figure 16-39a) so that the device will attempt to

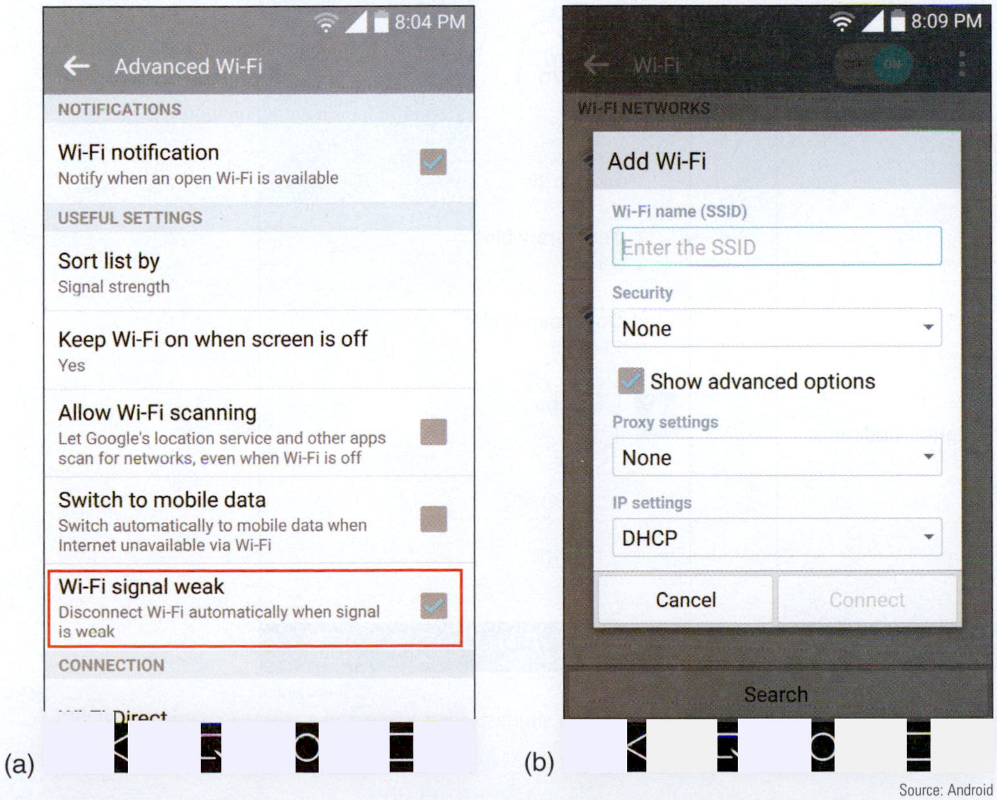

Figure 16-39 (a) Uncheck this setting to cause Wi-Fi to work even with a weak signal, and (b) connect to a hidden wireless network that is not broadcasting its SSID

maintain a connection even with a weak signal. Also check to make sure *Keep Wi-Fi on when screen is off* is set to **Yes** so the device won't have to reconnect to Wi-Fi every time the screen is turned back on. Some wireless networks are hidden and must be added manually. On the **Settings** app, tap **Wi-Fi**. Tap the menu icon in the upper-right corner of the screen (the three-dot ellipsis icon, as shown earlier in Figure 16-31a), then tap **Add Wi-Fi**. On the screen shown in Figure 16-39b, enter the SSID and security key for the hidden wireless network.

- ***Bluetooth not connecting.*** Make sure that Bluetooth is turned on by tapping the Bluetooth icon on the Notifications shade or on the Settings app. Also check Bluetooth settings. To do this, on the **Settings** app, tap **Bluetooth**, then tap the menu icon in the upper-right corner. From this menu, you can edit the phone's name, and most importantly, you can adjust the visibility time. Tap **Visibility timeout** and increase the visibility time so that the device you're attempting to pair with will have more time to identify the Android device for pairing.
- ***Apps not loading.*** You might find that there is insufficient space available on the device, especially if one app is taking up all of its allocated space, or memory is not available for the app you want to load. Uninstalling unused apps and deleting files no longer needed might solve the storage problem. You can download an app from the Play Store that can help clean up storage space, and other apps that report on how apps are using memory. You can also install a file manager app, such as ES File Explorer, to navigate through the directory and delete files or folders one at a time.

To view used and available storage space, go to the **Settings** app and tap **Storage**. You can see in Figure 16-40a where nearly 17 GB is still available on this device, apps are taking up almost 6 GB of the used space, and multimedia files (pictures, videos, and audio files) are taking up less than 100 MB total. From the **Settings** app, tap **Smart cleaning** for suggestions on files to delete and clear up space (see Figure 16-40b).

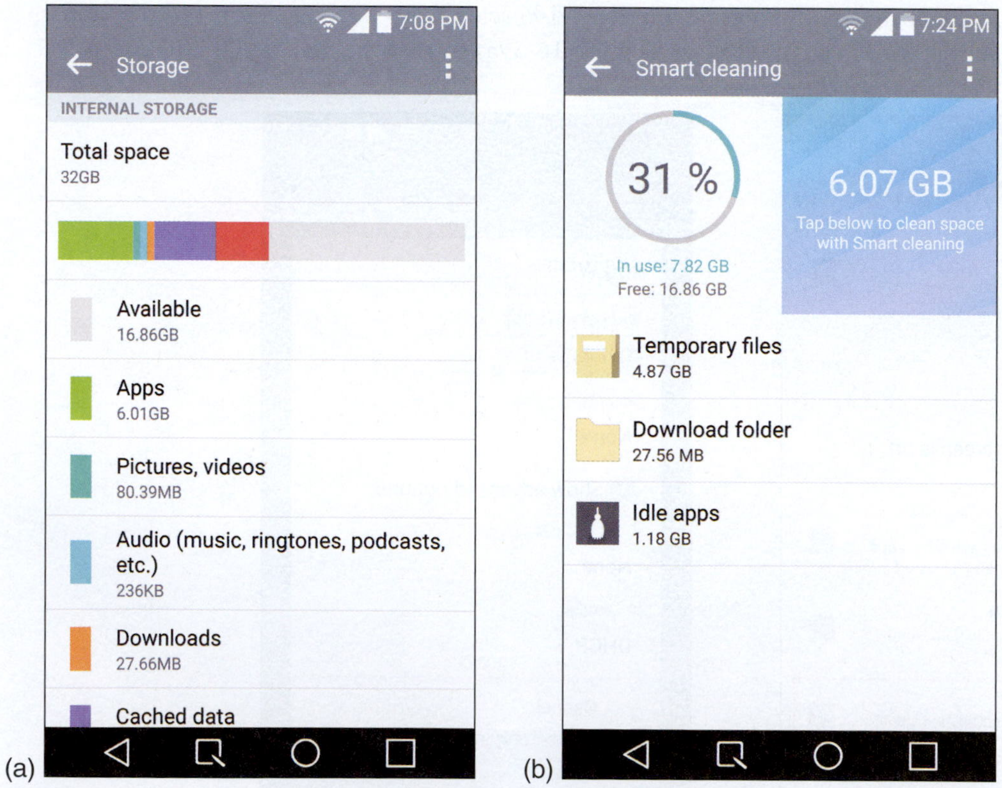

Source: Android

Figure 16-40 (a) Android reports how storage is used and (b) makes suggestions to free some storage space

- ***Slow performance.*** Having too many apps open at once will slow down overall performance (see Figure-16-41a). Tap the overview button on the Action bar, and swipe off to the side as many apps as possible to close them. You can also force stop an app. To see all installed apps, go to the **Settings** app and tap **Apps**. Swipe to the left to see the *Running* tab, which shows all running apps (see Figure 16-41b). Tap an app to force stop the app.

(a)

(b)

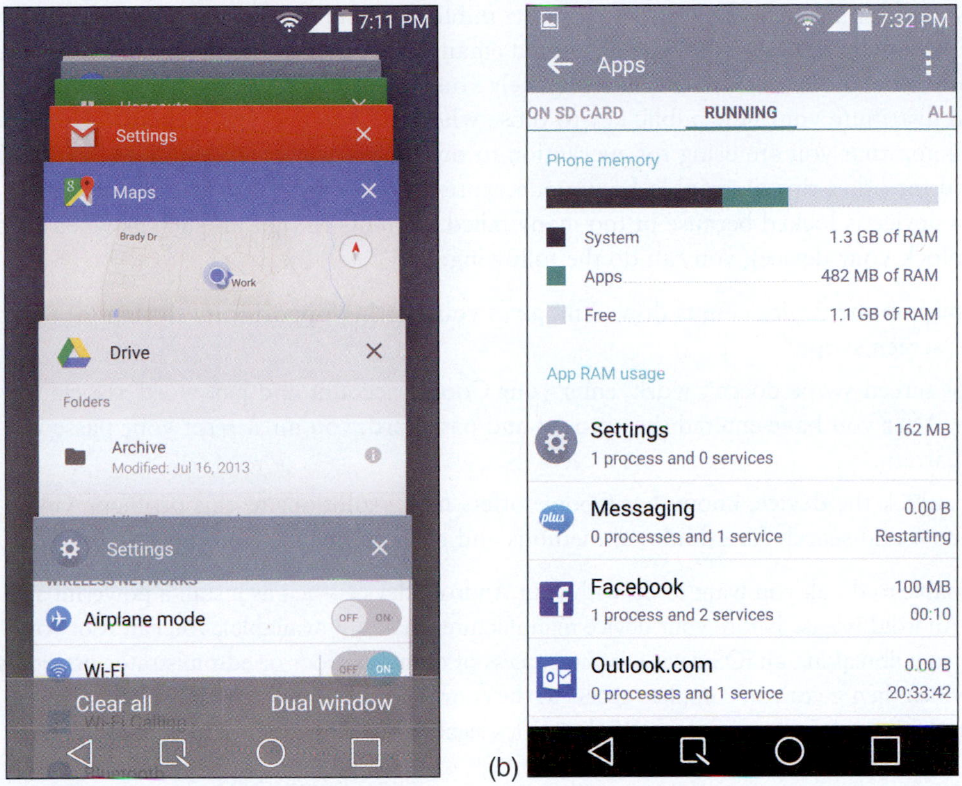

Source: Android

Figure 16-41 (a) View open apps and close the ones you're not using to conserve memory; (b) tap an app in the running apps list to force stop the app

16

- ***Short battery life.*** Too many apps running in the background will drain the battery quickly, as will Wi-Fi, Bluetooth, or other wireless technologies. Disable wireless connections and close apps when you're not using them to save battery juice. Many Android devices have replaceable batteries, so if a battery is performing poorly, consider replacing it.
- ***Dim display.*** Swipe down from the top of any screen to open the Notifications shade, then slide the Brightness slider to the right to brighten the screen. Make sure the **Auto** option is not selected so that you have more control over the screen's brightness level. This is especially helpful when trying to view the screen in bright daylight, but increasing the brightness level will also drain the battery more quickly.
- ***Inaccurate touch screen response.*** A cover on the screen can result in inaccurate touch screen responses. Also, accessibility settings can alter a touch screen's performance. Check accessibility settings in the Settings app. Scroll down and tap **Accessibility**. Touch feedback time is a particular suspect, as is Touch

control areas and Auto-rotate screen. You can also perform a motion sensor calibration. In the Settings app, tap **Gestures**, then tap **Motion sensor calibration**. Tap **Calibrate sensor** and follow on screen instructions.

- *Overheating.* Running several apps or keeping a smart phone's screen on for more than just a few minutes can heat up the device. Try turning the screen off for a while, and close unneeded apps. If this doesn't work, there might be something wrong with the device's battery, which would need to be checked by a technician at a service center.
- *Unable to decrypt email.* Email encryption is done using a public key and private key. You distribute your public key to those who want to send you encrypted email and you keep the private key on your device. If your device is unable to decrypt email, most likely you'll need to generate a new public key and private key and distribute your new public key to those who send you encrypted email. Search the website of the email app that you are using for encryption to find instructions for setting up new public and private keys and for other tips on troubleshooting decrypting problems.
- *System lockout.* If a device is locked because of too many failed attempts to sign in (such as when a child has attempted to unlock your device), you can do the following:

  1. Wait until the timer on the device counts down and gives you another opportunity to sign in. Enter your passcode or screen swipe.
  2. If the passcode or screen swipe doesn't work, enter your Google account and password associated with your device. After you have entered the account and password, you must reset your passcode or screen swipe pattern.
  3. If you still can't unlock the device, know that Google offers many solutions to this problem. Go to *accounts.google.com* and search for additional methods and tools to unlock your device.

If you find you are unable to do all you want to do with your Android device (such as install a powerful app or download the latest Android release before your device manufacturer makes it available), you can root your device. Rooting, similar to jailbreaking an iOS device, is the process of obtaining root or administrator privileges to an Android device, which then gives you complete access to the entire file system (all folders and files) and all commands and features. As with jailbreaking an iOS device, it's legal in the United States to root only smart phones, not tablets.

To root a device, you download and use third-party software. The process takes some time and might even involve restoring the device to its factory state. The process of rooting might corrupt the OS, and after the device is rooted, installed apps that require root access can corrupt the OS. For some manufacturers, rooting will void your warranty, and some carriers refuse to provide technical support for a rooted device. In addition, BYOD (Bring Your Own Device) policies in enterprise environments might not allow rooting. Avoid rooting if you can; if you decide to root a device, do so with caution!

CONFIGURE, SYNC, AND TROUBLESHOOT WINDOWS MOBILE DEVICES

A+
220-902
2.5, 2.6,
2.7, 4.3

Windows Phone tiles and menus are remarkably different from Android and iOS icon-based launchers. But the settings, options, and troubleshooting tools will feel familiar to you because they closely resemble those of Windows 8. Here's a quick overview of settings and troubleshooting tools on a Windows Phone device.

CONFIGURE WINDOWS PHONE NETWORK CONNECTIONS

A+
220-902
2.5, 2.6,
2.7

The Action Center, by default, provides direct links to Wi-Fi and Bluetooth connection apps, as well as the Airplane mode app. You can access the Action Center by swiping down from the top of the Start screen. Note that buttons in the Action Center are links to their respective apps, not toggle switches. Tapping Wi-Fi, for example, opens the Wi-Fi app, as shown in Figure 16-42a. The list of shortcuts in the Action Center can be customized by tapping **notifications+actions** in the Settings app, as shown in Figure 16-42b. Also use the Settings app to access cellular+SIM, NFC, Internet sharing (which is the same as tethering), and VPN connections.

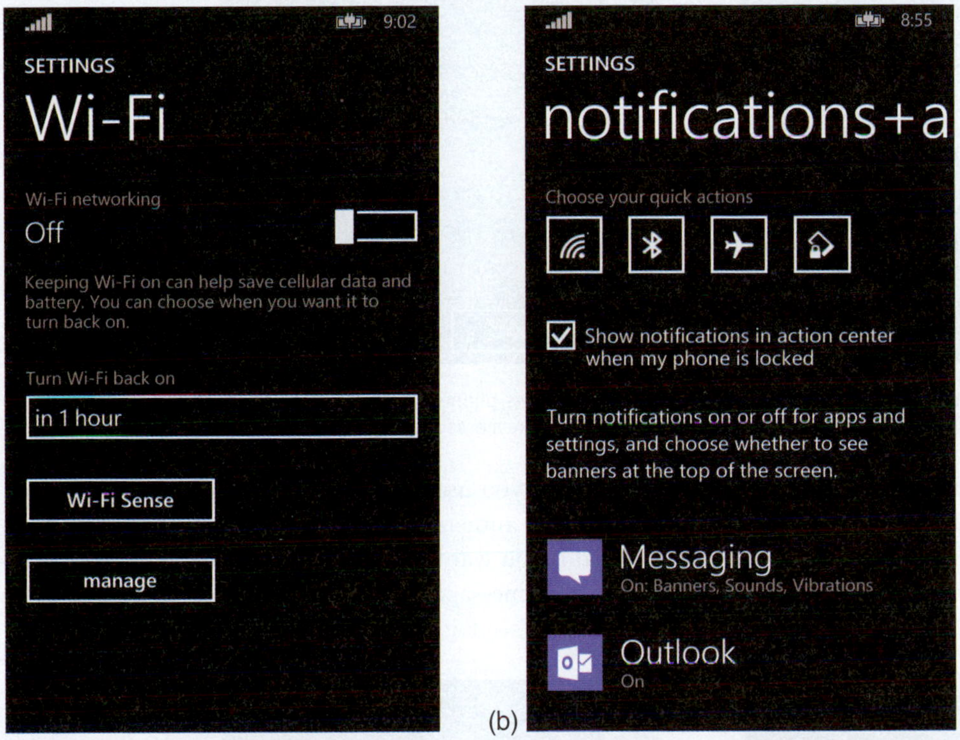

(a) (b)

Figure 16-42 (a) Use the Wi-Fi app to toggle Wi-Fi off and on; (b) several different apps can be added to the Action Center

16

CONFIGURE WINDOWS PHONE EMAIL, SYNC, AND BACKUP

A+
220-902
2.5, 2.6,
2.7

Windows Phone automatically syncs contacts, calendars, and email with an online email account such as a Microsoft account, and, similar to Windows on a desktop computer, documents can be automatically synced through OneDrive. The first Microsoft account used to set up the phone determines the apps and other benefits that will be available to that device, and is the account that will be associated with the device's backup data. Other Microsoft accounts such as Outlook.com or Live.com can be added later, but photos in those accounts will not be synced with the phone, and certain Xbox features will not be available through those accounts.

To add a Microsoft account to a Windows Phone, open the **Settings** app, then tap **email+accounts.** Tap **add an account**, then **Microsoft account**. An information screen, as shown in Figure 16-43a, describes the importance of this first Microsoft account configured on the device. Tap **sign in.**

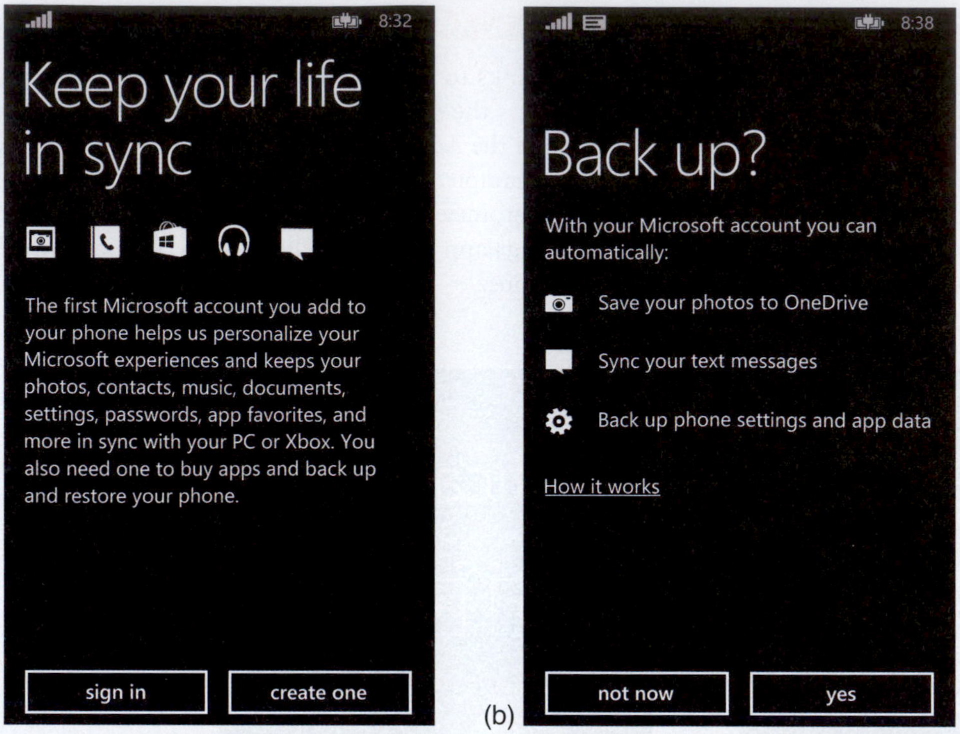

(a) (b)

Figure 16-43 (a) The first Microsoft account configured on a Windows phone will hold the phone's backups; (b) Windows Phone automatically backs up photos, text messages, phone settings, and app data

Enter your email address and password, then tap **next**. If you use two-factor authentication, you'll be required to verify your identity using the second form of authentication, such as a code sent by text message. After authentication is complete, you're asked if you want to back up content online from the phone (see Figure 16-43b). Tap **yes** to back up photos, text messages, phone settings, and app data. These options can be changed later in the backup app in Settings (see Figure 16-44a).

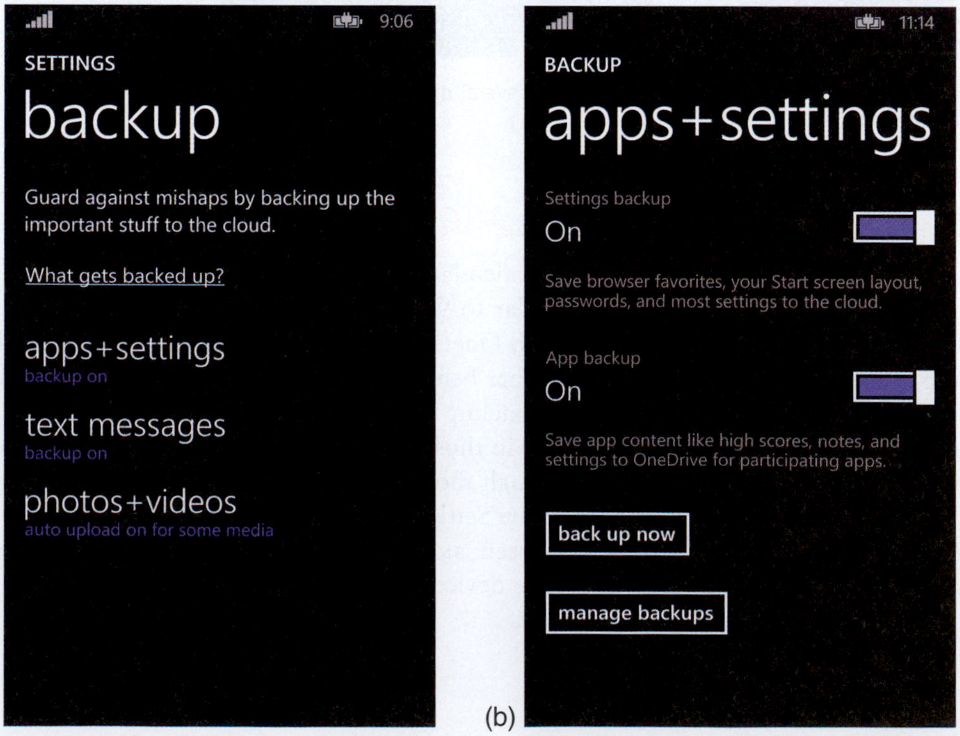

(a) (b)

Figure 16-44 (a) Tap each item to change its settings; (b) turn backup on to perform a manual backup

Notes Windows Phone performs automatic backups only when the device is connected to a Wi-Fi network and plugged in to a power source. To perform a manual backup, go to the **Settings** app, tap **backup**, then **apps+settings**. As shown in Figure 16-44b, tap the toggle switch to turn on **Settings backup** if it's not already on, then tap **back up now**.

The email tile on the Start screen gives direct access to this primary email account; Figure 16-45a shows an email notification on the Outlook tile. Other types of email accounts, as shown in Figure 16-45b, can also be configured automatically (meaning you won't have to provide server information or port numbers).

Figure 16-45 (a) The Outlook tile shows one new email; (b) Exchange, Yahoo!, Google, and iCloud email accounts can all be configured automatically

Microsoft account settings, such as theme and password, can be synced across devices using the **sync my settings** app in Settings. Location data can be synced through the **location** app. See Figure 16-46 to take a look at both of these menus.

16

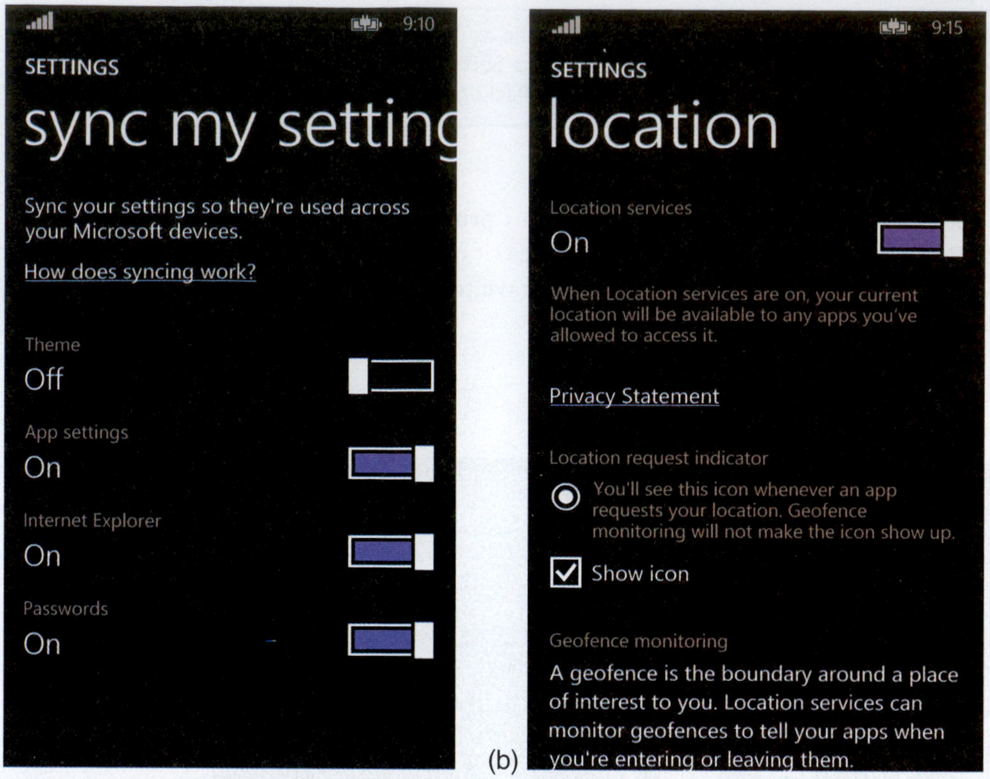

(a) (b)

Figure 16-46 (a) Sync your Microsoft account settings or (b) your location across devices

UPDATE AND RESTORE WINDOWS PHONE FROM BACKUP

A+
220-902
2.5, 2.7

Check for Windows Phone updates by opening the **Settings** app, then tap **phone update**. If no updates are currently pending, tap **check for updates**. On the phone update screen, you can also set the phone to automatically download updates.

Microsoft occasionally issues a critical update for Windows Phone, which generates an update notification; the update should be installed right away. Prompts remind users to install the update if the phone is not configured to install updates automatically. Even when configured for manual updates, Windows Phone will automatically install a required update in three days if the user does not manually install the update sooner.

Restoring a Windows phone from backup, or installing a backup on a new device, requires that you use the same Microsoft account that was used to create the backup. First connect the phone to a Wi-Fi network so you don't risk incurring charges for cellular data. When you first sign in with your Microsoft account, you're given the opportunity to restore from backup. Select the correct backup, then tap **next**. Complete the two-factor authentication process if required, then tap **next**. After the restore process is complete, tap **next**. You can enter passwords for accounts that were restored to the phone, or you can tap **skip** to wait until later. Tap **done** to complete the process.

TROUBLESHOOT WINDOWS MOBILE DEVICES

A+
220-902
2.5, 4.3

The following lists options for troubleshooting Windows mobile devices. Before you start troubleshooting, back up your phone's data, and then attempt the following options, which are listed in order from least invasive to most invasive:

1. *Power down and power up.* As with troubleshooting other mobile devices, begin with restarting the phone. Press and hold the **power** button for about three seconds until **slide down to power off** appears

on the screen. Swipe down, wait several seconds, and then press the **power** button again to turn the phone back on.

2. ***Force a restart.*** You can force the phone to restart by pressing and holding the **volume down** button and the **power** button together for 10–15 seconds until the phone restarts. This option is not available on all Windows Phone devices. Check the manufacturer's documentation for specific directions for these devices.
3. ***Remove the battery.*** If the battery can be removed, pull it out then put it back in. Press the **power** button to turn the phone back on. If removing power causes issues with signing in to your Microsoft account, go to **Settings** and tap **Date+time** to reset the time.
4. ***Update Windows Phone.*** Go to **Settings** and tap **update**. Check for updates and install any updates that are available.
5. ***Reset.*** Reset the phone to factory defaults. This wipes all user data and settings off the phone, so make sure you back up your data and settings first, if possible. On the **Settings** app, tap **about**, then tap **reset your phone**. A warning screen indicates that user content is about to be removed from the device. Tap **yes** to continue, and then tap **yes** on the second warning screen as well. Wait until the reset process is complete.
6. ***Force reset.*** Some Windows phones offer the ability to force a reset using the phone's physical buttons. This is helpful if the phone is completely unresponsive and you can't get to the Settings app. Check the manufacturer's documentation for specific steps. For some phones, the following procedure forces a reset: Press and hold the **volume down** and **power** buttons until the phone vibrates. Immediately release the volume down and power buttons, then press and hold the **volume down** button again until a large exclamation mark appears on the screen. Finally, press these four buttons in this order: **volume up, volume down, power, volume down**. The phone resets.
7. ***Software Recovery Tool.*** Some Windows phones can be reset and recovered using the Software Recovery Tool on your computer. Check the manufacturer's documentation for specific information on a particular model. The Software Recovery Tool erases all user content and settings on the phone. If you have a backup of this content, you can restore from backup after the reset. Complete the following steps to use your Windows computer to reset your Windows phone:
   a. First make sure the phone is fully charged.
   b. On a Windows 8/7 computer, download the Software Recovery Tool (search for article FA142987 on *microsoft.com*) that is designed for your device and install it.
   c. Open the application. Then connect the phone to the computer via a USB cable. Once the phone is detected, follow the on screen instructions.

16

Hands-On | Project 16-3 Select a Mobile Device

A+
220-902
2.5

Shop for a new smart phone or tablet that uses iOS, Android, or Windows Phone. Be sure to read some reviews about a device you are considering. Select two devices that you might consider buying and answer the following questions:

1. What is the device brand, model, and price?
2. What is the OS and version? Amount of storage space? Screen size? Types of network connections? Battery life? Camera pixels?
3. What do you like about each device? Which would you choose and why?

>> CHAPTER SUMMARY

Operating Systems Used on Mobile Devices

- The most popular operating systems used on mobile devices include Android by Google, iOS by Apple, and Windows and Windows Phone by Microsoft.
- Android is an open source OS, and anyone can develop and sell Android apps or variations in the Android OS. Google is the major distributor of Android and Android apps from its Google Play website.
- The iOS by Apple is used only on Apple devices, including the iPhone, iPad, and iPod touch. Apps for the iOS are distributed solely by Apple.
- Windows Phone by Microsoft works on smart phones and tracks version numbers alongside Windows for desktops, laptops, and tablets.

Configure, Sync, and Troubleshoot iOS Devices

- A cellular network provided by a carrier is used by cell phones for voice communication and text messaging. A smart phone or tablet might also contain the technology to connect to a cellular network for data transmission.
- iCloud Backup can be used to back up your device's content to the cloud and iCloud Drive can sync content to all of your iOS devices associated with an Apple ID.
- iTunes installed on a personal computer can be used to back up iOS content, sync content from the computer to the device, update iOS, and restore iOS from backup or to its factory state.
- To troubleshoot an iOS device, you can restart, reset, update, erase, restore, and recover iOS on the device.

Configure, Sync, and Troubleshoot Android Devices

- The Settings app on an Android device can be used to manage network connections, email, online accounts, updates to Android, and security.
- Each Google product, such as Gmail, Calendars, and Hangouts, syncs across devices when you're signed in to your account on that device. All data is web-based, so everything is also accessible through a web browser.
- Tools and techniques used to solve problems with Android devices include a forced reboot, uninstall and reinstall apps, update the Android OS, use Safe Mode, update firmware, use Recovery mode, and perform a factory reset.

Configure, Sync, and Troubleshoot Windows Mobile Devices

- The buttons in the Windows Phone Action Center provide direct links to their respective apps, not toggle switches for features.
- The first Microsoft account used to set up a phone determines the apps and other benefits that will be available to that device, and is the account that will be associated with the device's backup data.
- Even when configured for manual updates, Windows Phone will automatically install a required update in three days if the user does not manually install the update sooner.
- Some Windows phones offer the ability to force a reset using the phone's physical buttons. This is helpful if the phone is completely unresponsive and the Settings app is inaccessible.

>> KEY TERMS

For explanations of key terms, see the Glossary for this text.

accelerometer
Action bar
AirDrop
Airplane mode
Android
APK (Android Application Package)
App Store
Apple ID
Apps Drawer
Bluetooth PIN code
closed source
emergency notifications
factory default
Favorites tray
force stop
geotracking
Gmail
Google account
Google Play
GPS (Global Positioning System)
gyroscope
Handoff
hard reset
hotspot
iCloud Backup
iCloud Drive
IMEI (International Mobile Equipment Identity)
IMSI (International Mobile Subscriber Identity)
iOS
iPad
iPhone
iPod touch
iTunes Store
iTunes U
jailbreaking
launcher
location data
Microsoft Exchange
Microsoft Store
Miracast
mobile payment service
notifications
open source
pairing
PRL (Preferred Roaming List)
Product Release Instructions (PRI)
rooting
screen orientation
SDK (Software Development Kit)
S/MIME (Secure/Multipurpose Internet Mail Extensions)
soft reset
tethering
virtual assistant
Wi-Fi calling
Windows Phone (WP)

>> REVIEWING THE BASICS

1. List four types of antennas a smart phone might contain. Which three antennas are disabled in Airplane mode?
2. What company provides and oversees the Android Play Store? What is the website of this store?
3. List three Apple devices that use iOS.
4. Who is the sole distributor of apps for iOS?
5. What is one disadvantage to users when using an open source operating system on a mobile device?
6. Which programming language is used to write most Android apps? Apple requires that iOS apps be written in one of which three programming languages?
7. How can you configure a mobile device so it cannot connect to any network?
8. Which type of network connection requires that two devices pair before the connection is completed?
9. Which email protocol downloads email to be managed on the client machine? Which email protocol manages email on the server?
10. Which database needs to be updated so a smart phone knows which cell towers to connect with inside and outside the carrier's network?
11. Which email protocol uses port 110? 143? 993? 995?
12. Which security protocol is used to encrypt email?
13. Which protocol is a more secure alternative to using SMTP for outgoing email?

14. Which email server uses ActiveSync to sync all emails, contacts, and calendar updates on the server and client machines, including mobile devices?
15. Which procedure is the least intrusive solution to a problem with iOS, to reset an iOS device or to restore an iOS device?
16. What is the location of an iOS backup stored on a local Windows computer via iTunes?
17. What technology is available on both Windows Phone and Android to mirror the phone's display through a wireless connection with a TV?
18. What is the difference between tethering and hotspots?
19. What Google product provides free storage for photos, documents, and other content?
20. What type of item does an IMEI identify?

>> THINKING CRITICALLY

1. Suppose you find an app that cost you $4.99 is missing from your Android. What is the best way to restore the missing app?
   a. Go to backup storage and perform a restore to recover the lost app.
   b. Purchase the app again.
   c. Go to the Play Store where you bought the app and install it again.
   d. Go to the Settings app and perform an application restore.
2. Suppose you and your friend want to exchange lecture notes taken during class. She has an iPhone and you have an iPad. What is the easiest way to do the exchange?
   a. Cope the files to an SD card and move the SD card to each device.
   b. Drop the files in OneDrive and share notebooks with each other.
   c. Send a text to each other with the files attached.
   d. Transfer the files through an AirDrop connection.
3. You have set up your Android phone using one Google account and your Android tablet using a second Google account. Now you would like to download the apps you purchased on your phone to your tablet. What is the best way to do this?
   a. Set up the Google account on your tablet that you used to buy apps on your phone and then download the apps.
   b. Buy the apps a second time from your tablet.
   c. Back up the apps on your phone to your SD card and then move the SD card to your tablet and transfer the apps.
   d. Call Google support and ask them to merge the two Google accounts into one.

>> REAL PROBLEMS, REAL SOLUTIONS

REAL PROBLEM 16-1 Using the Microsoft Windows Phone Emulator

Microsoft offers a Windows Phone emulator embedded in its Visual Studio software, which can be used by developers of mobile apps for Windows Phone. You will need a Microsoft account to do this project. Follow these general directions to download, install, and run the emulator:

1. On a Windows 8.1 computer, go into UEFI/BIOS setup and verify that hardware-assisted virtualization is turned on. This UEFI/BIOS feature supports VMs running on the system and is required for the Windows emulator to work. You learned to use UEFI/BIOS setup earlier in the text.
2. Go to **visualstudio.com** and click the link **Download Community 2015** to download Visual Studio Community 2015. The downloaded file is vs_community.exe. Double-click the file to install the software. Under *Choose the type of installation*, select **Custom**. On the next screen, check **Windows 8.1 and Windows Phone 8.0/8.1 Tools** and continue with the installation, which can take some time.
3. After installation is complete, open **Visual Studio 2015** and create a new project. You will be asked to sign in to your Microsoft account and the account will be given a free developer license.
4. For the project template, in the left pane, click **Visual C#**, click **Windows**, click **Windows 8**, and click **Windows Phone**. In the middle pane, click **Blank App (Windows Phone)**. Click **OK** and the project is created.
5. To select the emulator for your project, click **Device** and select any of the emulator devices, as shown in Figure 16-47.

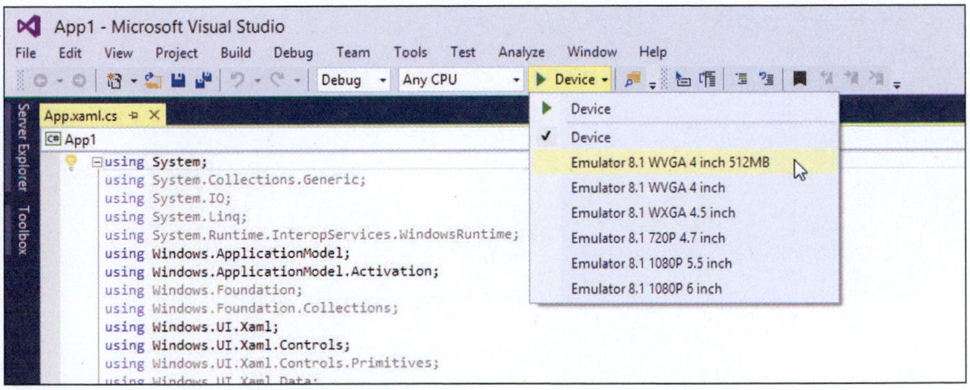

Figure 16-47 Select the emulator to use with your Visual Studio project

6. To start the emulator, click the **Emulator** button that replaces the Device button. The emulator tool opens (see Figure 16-48). Click the **Start** button at the bottom of the emulator to show the Start screen in the emulator. Explore the menus in the Windows Phone emulator.

Figure 16-48 Windows Phone 8.1 emulator

7. Take a screen shot of your emulator and email it to your instructor.

REAL PROBLEM 16-2 Using the Android SDK to Run an Android Emulator

This Real Problem is a challenging project and you might want to work with a partner so that you will have someone with whom to discuss solutions and share the work. Go to *Youtube.com* and watch some videos on downloading and installing the Android SDK and using it to install a virtual Android device using the Android Emulator. Then do the work to use the Android SDK and the Android Emulator to emulate an Android device. To prove you have accomplished this feat, take a screen shot of your virtual Android device running on your computer and email it to your instructor. Write a one-page report of your experience and include in it five or six tips that you think would help a student through this project.

CHAPTER

17

Windows Resources on a Network

After completing this chapter, you will be able to:

- Support some client/server applications
- Share and secure files and folders on a network
- Support cloud computing services on a network

In the chapter, "Connecting To and Setting Up a Network," you learned how to create and manage a network connection, and in the chapter, "Supporting Network Hardware," you learned about networking hardware. This chapter focuses on using a network for client/server applications, for sharing files and folders with network users, and for providing cloud computing services.

Security is always a huge concern when dealing with networks. In this chapter, you learn how to share resources on the network and still protect these resources from those who should not have access. In the chapter, "Security Strategies," we take security to a higher level and discuss many tools and techniques you can use to protect a computer or a SOHO network.

SUPPORTING CLIENT/SERVER APPLICATIONS

A+
220-902
1.3, 1.4,
1.5, 1.6,
2.4

Resources available on a network might include network services, such as email or file storage, or applications hosted by a server and used by a client. Client/server applications you will likely be expected to support include Internet Explorer, Remote Desktop, and other remote applications. You also need to know how to use Group Policy to configure Quality of Service (QoS) for client/server applications and how to link a data source through a network to database applications. All of these skills are covered in this part of the chapter.

NETWORK SERVERS

A+
220-902
2.4

Recall from the chapter, "Connecting To and Setting Up a Network," that a client computer contacts a server in order to request information or perform a task, such as when a web browser connects with a web server and requests a webpage. Many other types of server resources exist on a typical network. Some of these servers are standalone devices, but often multiple network services are provided by a single server computer, or servers might be embedded in other devices. For example, servers are sometimes embedded in router firmware (such as a SOHO router providing FTP services) or in an operating system (such as web server capabilities embedded in Windows Server 2012). Each time any of these components is updated, any legacy technology present on the network must be taken into consideration, which can result in a complex web of network server resources. Here's a brief list of several popular client/server resources used on networks and the Internet:

- *Mail server.* Email is a client/server application that involves two mail servers. Recall that SMTP is used to send email messages, and either POP3 or IMAP4 is used to deliver an email message to a client. An example of a popular email server application is Microsoft Exchange Server. Outlook, an application in the Microsoft Office suite of applications, is a popular email client application.
- *File server.* A file server stores files and makes them available to other computers. A network administrator can make sure this data is backed up regularly and kept secure.
- *Print server.* A print server manages network printers and makes them available to computers throughout the network. Expensive network printers can handle high-capacity print jobs from many sources, eliminating the need for a desktop printer at each workstation. If a network printer fails, a technician can sometimes diagnose and solve the problem from her workstation.
- *DHCP server.* Recall from the chapter, "Connecting To and Setting Up a Network," that a DHCP server leases an IP address to a computer when it first attempts to initiate a connection to the network and requests an IP address. The DHCP server is configured to pull from a range of IP addresses, which is called the DHCP scope.
- *DNS server.* DNS servers, as you learned in the chapter, "Connecting To and Setting Up a Network," store domain names and their associated IP addresses for computers on the Internet or a large enterprise network. DNS servers are responsible for name resolution, which happens when a client computer sends an FQDN (fully qualified domain name) to a DNS server and requests the IP address associated with this character-based name.

Notes A telltale sign that the network's DNS server is malfunctioning is when you can reach a website by its IP address, but not by its FQDN (fully qualified domain name).

- *Proxy server.* A proxy server is a computer that intercepts requests that a client, such as a browser, makes of another server, such as a web server. The proxy server substitutes its own IP address for the request using NAT protocols. An example of using a proxy server is when an ISP caches webpages to speed up requests for the same pages. After it caches a page, if another browser requests the same content, the proxy server can provide the content that it has cached. In addition, a proxy server sometimes acts as a gateway to the Internet, a firewall to protect the network, a filter for email, and to restrict Internet access by employees in order to force those employees to follow company policies.

- *Authentication server.* An authentication server authenticates users or computers to the network so that they can access network resources. Active Directory, which is a directory service included in Windows Server, is often used for this purpose on a Windows domain. The authentication server stores user or device credentials, such as user names and passwords, validates an authentication request, and determines the permissions assigned to each user, device, or group.
- *Web server.* A web server serves up webpages to clients. Many corporations have their own web servers, which are available privately on the corporate network. Other web servers are public, accessible from anywhere on the Internet. The most popular web server application is Apache (see *apache.org*), which primarily runs on UNIX or Linux systems and can also run on Windows. The second most popular web server is Internet Information Services (IIS), which is embedded in the Windows Server operating system.

INTERNET EXPLORER

A+
220-902
1.5, 1.6

By far, the most popular client/server applications on the Internet are a browser and web server. The latest release of Internet Explorer (IE) is version 11, although Windows 10 features a new browser called Microsoft Edge to replace Internet Explorer going forward. Windows 8.1 comes with IE version 11 installed, and earlier versions of Windows can upgrade to IE version 11 using Windows Update. To upgrade, open Windows Update and find and install the Internet Explorer 11 update. You can also go to the *microsoft.com* website and follow links to download and install IE11.

Here are some tips about using IE11:

- *Menu bar.* Internet Explorer has a menu bar, which you can see by pressing the **Alt** key. The menu appears for a long enough time for you to make one selection from the menu. If you want the menu bar to be permanently visible, right-click a blank area in the title bar and check **Menu bar** in the shortcut menu (see Figure 17-1). Notice in Figure 17-1, you can also add the command bar to the IE window.

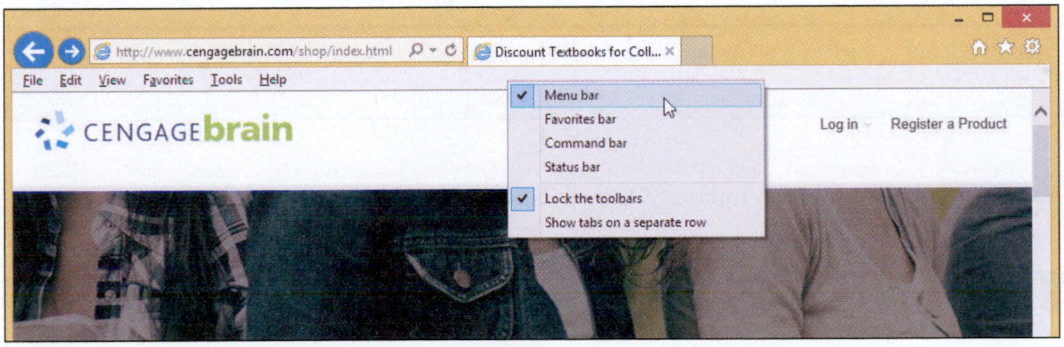

Figure 17-1 Access the shortcut menu from the title bar to control the Internet Explorer window

- *HTTP Secure.* Some web servers use HTTP with the SSL or TLS protocols to secure transmissions to and from the web server. To find out if HTTP Secure (HTTPS) is being used in IE11, look for https and a padlock icon in the browser address box. Click the padlock to get information about the site security (see Figure 17-2).

17

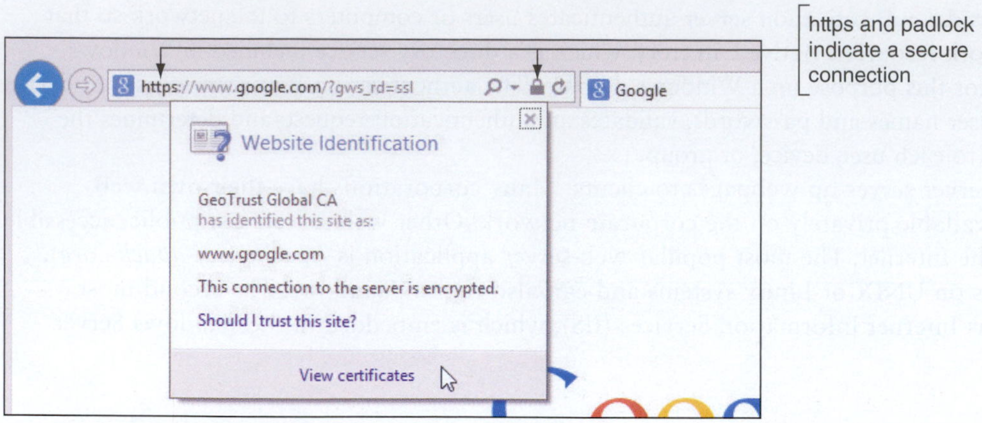

Website source: Google.com

Figure 17-2 A secure connection from browser to web server ensures all transmissions are encrypted

- ***Repair or disable.*** If you have a problem with IE11, use the same tools as you would for any Windows component to fix the problem, such as installing Windows updates, applying a restore point, or refreshing Windows 8. If you want to use a different browser, you can disable IE11. Open the **Programs and Features** window in Control Panel and click **Turn Windows features on or off.** In the Windows Features box, uncheck **Internet Explorer 11** and click **OK.**
- ***Internet Options box.*** Use the Internet Options box to manage Internet Explorer settings. To open the box, click the **Tools** icon on the right side of the IE title bar and click **Internet options.** Another method is to press **Alt**, which causes the menu bar to appear; then click **Tools, Internet options.** A third method is to click **Internet Options** in the Classic view of Control Panel. The Internet Options box appears. Whenever you make changes in the box, click **Apply** to apply these changes without closing the box. Alternately, you can click **OK** to save your changes and close the box.

Notes If you open the Internet Options box through Control Panel, the box is titled *Internet Properties* and the menus and options vary slightly.

Now let's see how to use each tab in the Internet Options box.

A+ Exam Tip The A+ 220-902 exam expects you to know how to use the General, Security, Privacy, Connections, Programs, and Advanced tabs on the Internet Options box.

GENERAL TAB

The General tab on the Internet Options box is shown on the left side of Figure 17-3.

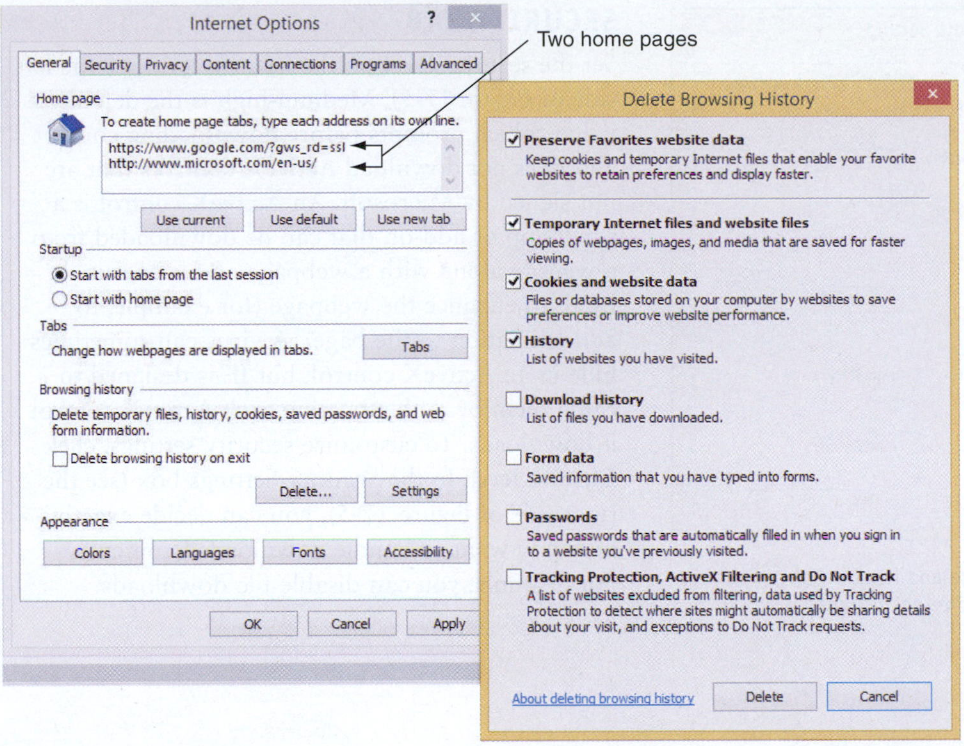

Figure 17-3 Use the General tab of the Internet Options box to delete your browsing history

Here's what you can do using the General tab:

- Change the home page or add a second home page tab. To add a second home page tab, insert the URL on a second line in the Home page area, as shown on the left side of Figure 17-3.
- To protect your identity and surfing records, it's a good idea to delete all your browsing history each time you use IE on a computer that is not your own. To delete this history, click **Delete**. In the Delete Browsing History box (see the right side of Figure 17-3), notice the item at the top. When you leave this item checked, any cookies used by websites in your Favorites list are *not* deleted. Select the items to delete and click **Delete**.
- If you want to delete your browsing history each time you close Internet Explorer, check **Delete browsing history on exit** on the General tab.
- Internet Explorer holds a cache containing previously downloaded content in case it is requested again. The cache is stored in several folders named Temporary Internet Files. To manage the IE cache, click **Settings** under Browsing history. The Website Data Settings box (called the Temporary Internet Files and History Settings box in Windows 7) appears, as shown in Figure 17-4. Use this box to change the maximum allowed space used for temporary Internet files and to control the location of these files.

17

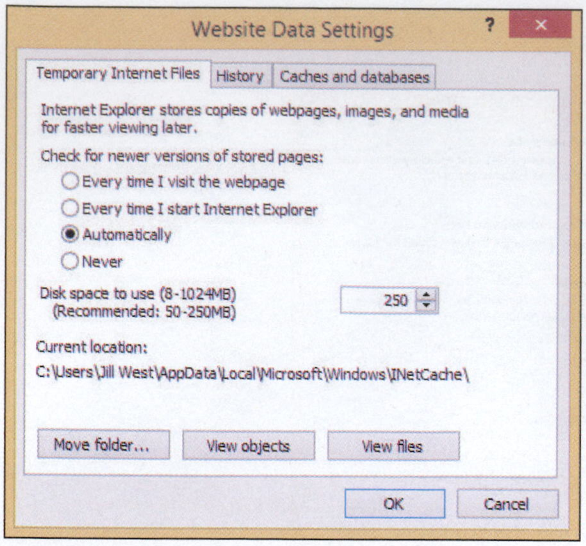

Figure 17-4 Control the size and location of temporary files used by Internet Explorer

SECURITY TAB

Set the security level on the Security tab (see the left side of Figure 17-5). Medium-high is the default value, which prompts before downloading content and does not download ActiveX controls that are not signed by Microsoft. An ActiveX control is a small app or add-on that can be downloaded from a website along with a webpage and is executed by IE to enhance the webpage (for example, to add animation to the page). A virus can sometimes hide in an ActiveX control, but IE is designed to catch them by authenticating each ActiveX control it downloads. To customize security settings, click **Custom level**. In the Security Settings box (see the right side of Figure 17-5), you can decide exactly how you want to handle downloaded content. For example, you can disable file downloads.

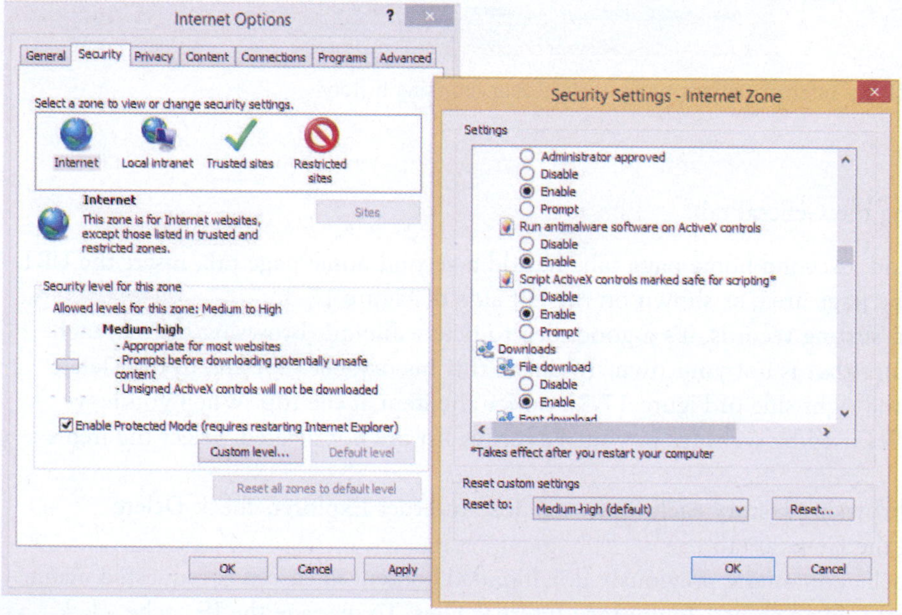

Figure 17-5 Use the Security tab to control what type of content is downloaded and how it is managed

PRIVACY TAB AND CONTENT TAB

Use the Privacy tab (see the left side of Figure 17-6) to block cookies that might invade your privacy or steal your identity. You can also use this tab to control the Pop-up Blocker, which prevents annoying pop-ups as you surf the web. To allow a pop-up from a particular website, click **Settings** and enter the URL of the website in the Pop-up Blocker Settings box (see the right side of Figure 17-6). Some pop-ups are useful, such as when you're trying to download a file from a website and the site asks permission to complete the download.

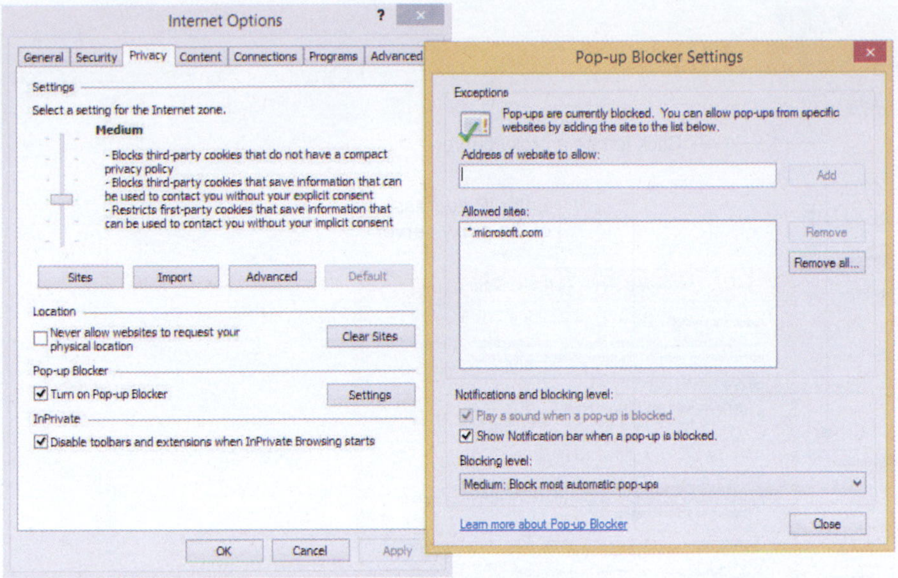

Figure 17-6 Use the Privacy tab to control pop-ups and cookies

The Content tab contains settings for Family Safety, certificates used by websites, and how AutoComplete and Feeds are handled.

CONNECTIONS TAB AND PROXY SETTINGS

The Connections tab allows you to configure proxy server settings and create a VPN connection. Many large corporations and ISPs use proxy servers to speed up Internet access. A web browser does not have to be aware that a proxy server is in use. However, one reason you might need to configure Internet Explorer to be aware of and use a proxy server is when you are on a corporate network and are having a problem connecting to a secured website (one using HTTP over SSL or another encryption protocol). The problem might be caused by Windows trying to connect using the wrong proxy server on the network. Check with your network administrator to find out if a specific proxy server should be used to manage secure website connections.

A+ Exam Tip The A+ 220-902 exam expects you to know how to configure proxy settings on a client desktop.

17

If you need to configure Internet Explorer to use a specific proxy server, on the Connections tab, click **LAN settings**. In the settings box, check **Use a proxy server for your LAN** and enter the IP address of the proxy server (see Figure 17-7). If your organization uses more than one proxy server, click **Advanced** and enter IP addresses for each type of proxy server on your network (see Figure 17-8). You can also enter a port address for each server. If you are trying to solve a problem of connecting to a server using HTTP over SSL or another secured protocol, enter the IP address of the proxy server that is used to manage secure connections in the Secure field of this box.

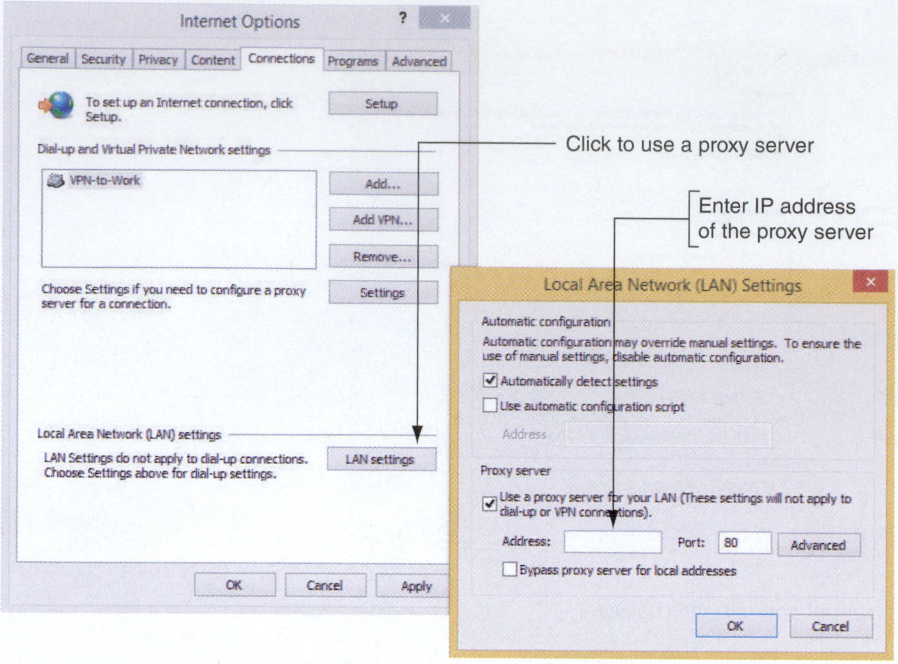

Figure 17-7 Configure Internet Explorer to use one or more proxy servers

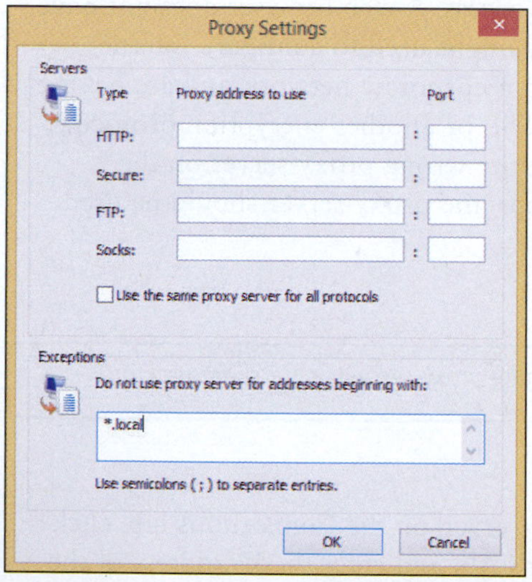

Figure 17-8 Enter the IP addresses of all proxy servers on your corporate network

Also notice on the Connections tab of the Internet Options box that you can create a VPN connection. To do so, click **Add VPN** (refer back to the left side of Figure 17-7) and follow the steps of the connection wizard. Recall from the chapter, "Connecting To and Setting Up a Network," that you can also create a VPN connection using the Network and Sharing Center.

PROGRAMS TAB

Add-ons, also called plug-ins, are small apps that help Internet Explorer to display multimedia content, manage email, translate text, or other actions. The Programs tab (see Figure 17-9) is used to manage add-ons.

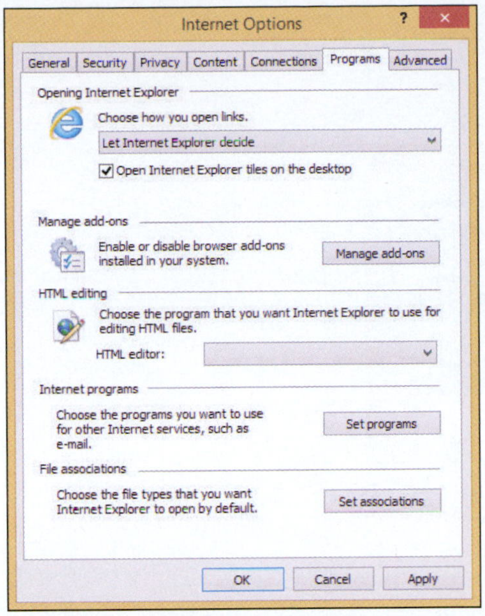

Figure 17-9 Use the Programs tab to manage add-ons and default applications used for Internet services

Click **Manage add-ons** to open the Manage Add-ons box (see Figure 17-10a). In the left pane under Show, you can display All add-ons, Currently loaded add-ons (default view), Run without permission, and Downloaded controls. Click an add-on to select it and see information about it in the lower pane. To disable an add-on, click **Disable**. To enable a disabled one, click **Enable**.

Downloaded ActiveX controls can be uninstalled using this window. To delete a selected ActiveX control, click **More information**. In the More Information box (see Figure 17-10b), click **Remove**. To see only the add-ons you can delete, select **Downloaded controls** in the Show dropdown list of the Manage Add-ons window. You can delete other add-ons using the Programs and Features window in Control Panel.

> **Notes** If you use Control Panel to open the Internet Properties box and open the Manage Add-ons box from there, the *Currently loaded add-ons* option is missing in the dropdown list under Show.

(a) (b)

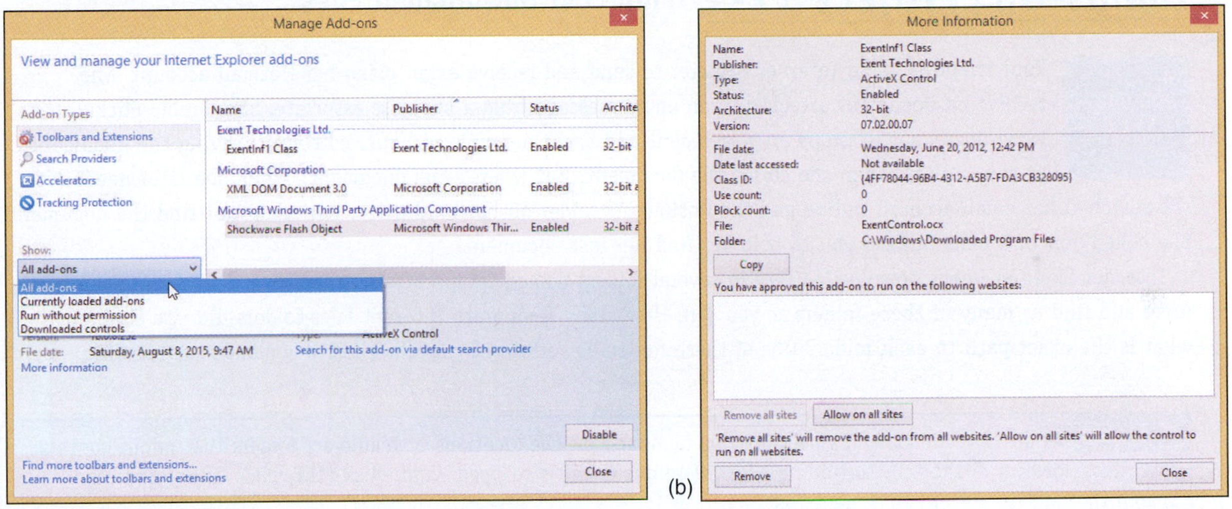

Figure 17-10 (a) Manage Internet Explorer add-ons, and (b) delete downloaded ActiveX controls

ADVANCED TAB

The Advanced tab (see the left side of Figure 17-11) contains several miscellaneous settings used to control Internet Explorer. If you suspect problems are caused by wrong settings, click **Reset** to return IE to all default settings. In the Reset Internet Explorer Settings box shown on the right side of Figure 17-11, make your decision about how to handle personal settings and then click **Reset**.

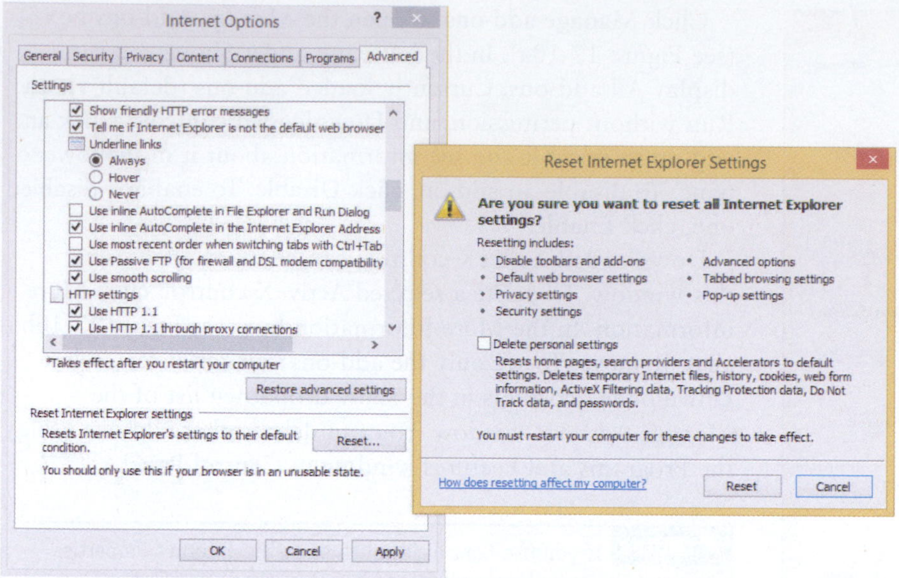

Figure 17-11 Solve problems with Internet Explorer by resetting it to default settings

Hands-On | Project 17-1 Find Lost Downloaded Files

A+ 220-902 1.5, 1.6

Your friend is using Internet Explorer to send and receive email using her Hotmail account. She received a document attached to an email message from a business associate. She double-clicked the Word document listed as an attachment and spent a couple of hours editing it, saving the document as she worked. Then she closed the document. But where's the document? When she later needed it, she searched her email account online and the Documents folder on her hard drive, but could not find the document. She called you in a panic asking you to help her find her lost document.

Internet Explorer keeps downloaded files in several folders named Temporary Internet Files. Search your hard drive and find as many of these folders as you can. How many Temporary Internet Files folders did you find and what is the exact path to each folder? One of these folders is certain to contain a lost downloaded document.

Notes As an IT technician, it's helpful to be familiar with the locations of temporary folders that might contain lost files. However, a shortcut to finding a lost Word document is to open Word, click **FILE,** click **Open**, and then search through the Recent Documents list.

Hands-On | Project 17-2 Use Google Chrome

Internet Explorer is not the only browser available, and many users prefer others such as Mozilla Firefox (*mozilla.org*) or Google Chrome (*google.com*). Go to the Google website and download and install Google Chrome. Use it to browse the web. How does it compare with Internet Explorer? What do you like better about it? What do you not like as well? When might you recommend that someone use Chrome rather than Internet Explorer? What security features does Google Chrome offer? What are the steps to import your favorites list from IE into Chrome?

REMOTE DESKTOP CONNECTION (RDC)

A+ 220-902 1.4, 1.5, 1.6

Remote Desktop Connection (RDC), commonly called Remote Desktop, gives a user access to a Windows desktop from anywhere on the Internet. As a software developer, I find Remote Desktop extremely useful when I work from a remote location (my home office) and need to access a corporate network to support software on that network. Using the Internet, I can access a file server on these secured networks to make my software changes. Remote Desktop is easy to use and relatively safe for the corporate network. To use Remote Desktop, the computer you want to remotely access (the server) must be running business or professional editions of Windows 8/7/Vista, but the computer you're using to access it (the client) can be running any version of Windows.

★ A+ Exam Tip The A+ 220-902 exam expects you to know how to use Remote Desktop.

APPLYING | CONCEPTS — CONFIGURE REMOTE DESKTOP ON TWO COMPUTERS

A+ 220-902 1.4, 1.5, 1.6

In this section, you see how to set up Remote Desktop for first use, and then you learn how to use it.

How to Set Up Remote Desktop for First Use

The host or server computer is the computer that is serving up Remote Desktop to client computers that can remote in to the server. To prepare your host computer, you need to configure the computer for static IP addressing and also configure the Remote Desktop service. Here are the steps needed:

1. Configure the computer for static IP addressing. How to assign a static IP address is covered in the chapter, "Connecting To and Setting Up a Network."
2. If your computer is behind a firewall, configure the router for port forwarding and allow incoming traffic on port 3389. Forward that traffic to the IP address of your desktop computer. You learned how to set up port forwarding in the chapter, "Connecting To and Setting Up a Network."
3. To turn on the Remote Desktop service, open the System window and click **Remote settings** in the left pane. The System Properties box appears with the Remote tab selected (see the middle of Figure 17-12). In this window, you can control settings for Remote Assistance and Remote Desktop. In the Remote Desktop area,

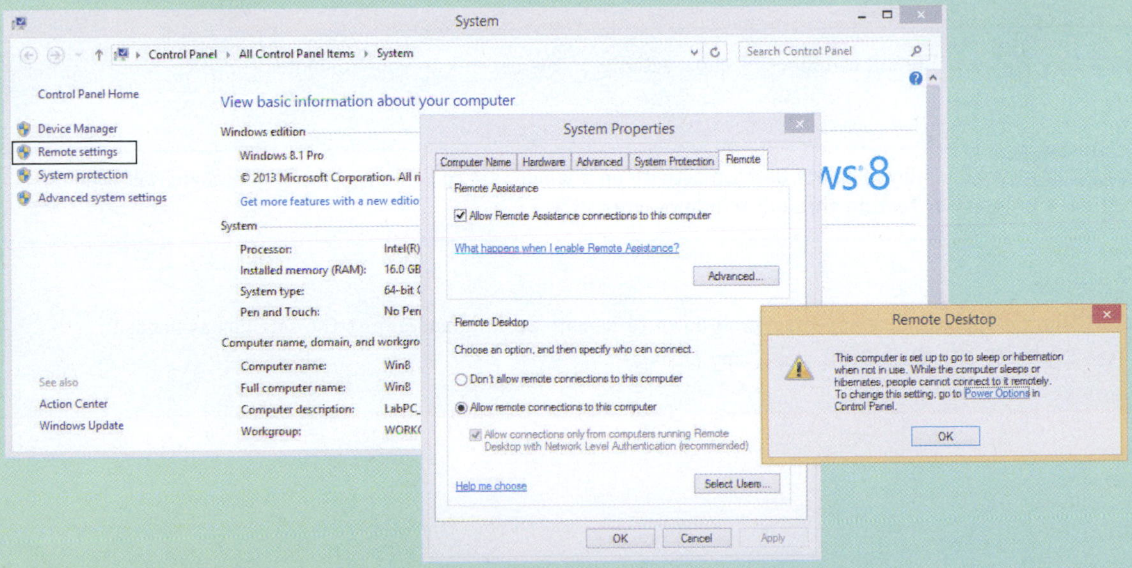

Figure 17-12 Configure a computer to run the Remote Desktop service

(continues)

check **Allow remote connections to this computer**. If a warning box appears about changing the power options in Control Panel (see the right side of Figure 17-12), click **OK** to close the box. Leave the box checked that says *Allow connections only from computers running Remote Desktop with Network Level Authentication (recommended)*.

OS Differences To enable Remote Desktop on a Windows 7 computer, in the Remote Desktop area of the Remote tab in the System Properties box, check **Allow connections from computers running any version of Remote Desktop (less secure).**

4. Users who have administrative privileges are allowed to use Remote Desktop by default, but other users need to be added. If you need to add a user, click **Select Users** and follow the directions on screen. Then close all windows.

5. Verify that Windows Firewall is set to allow Remote Desktop activity to this computer. To do that, open **Control Panel** in Classic view and click **Windows Firewall**. The Windows Firewall window appears (see Figure 17-13). In the left pane, click **Allow an app or feature through Windows Firewall.**

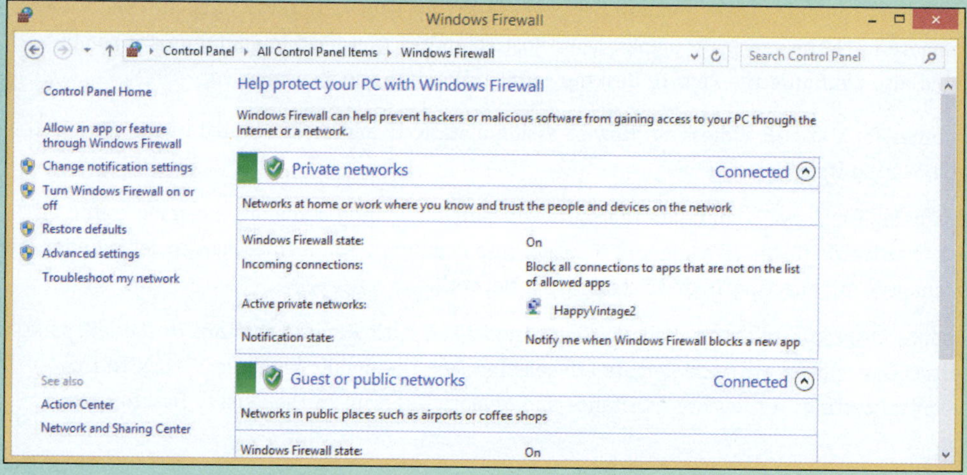

Figure 17-13 Windows Firewall can block or allow activity on the network to your computer

OS Differences To allow Remote Desktop activity on a Windows 7 computer, in the Windows Firewall window, click **Allow a program or feature through Windows Firewall.**

6. The Allowed apps window appears. Scroll down to Remote Desktop and adjust the settings as needed (see Figure 17-14). Click **OK** to apply any changes.

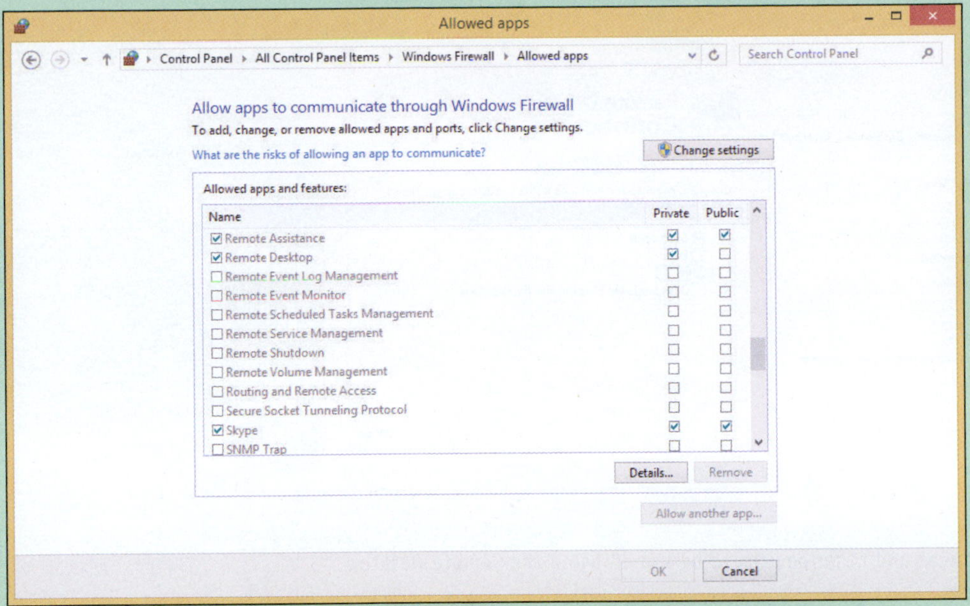

Figure 17-14 Allow Remote Desktop communication through Windows Firewall on your local computer

You are now ready to test Remote Desktop.

How to Use Remote Desktop

Try to use Remote Desktop from another computer somewhere on your local network and make sure that works before testing the Remote Desktop connection from the Internet. On the client computer, you can start Remote Desktop to remote in to your host computer by using the command **mstsc** (which stands for **Microsoft Terminal Services Client**). Follow these steps to use Remote Desktop:

1. Enter the **mstsc** command in the Windows 8 Run box or the Windows 7 Search box. The Remote Desktop Connection box opens (see Figure 17-15).
2. Enter the IP address or the host name of the computer to which you want to connect. If you decide to use a host name, begin the host name with two backslashes, as in *CompanyFileServer*.

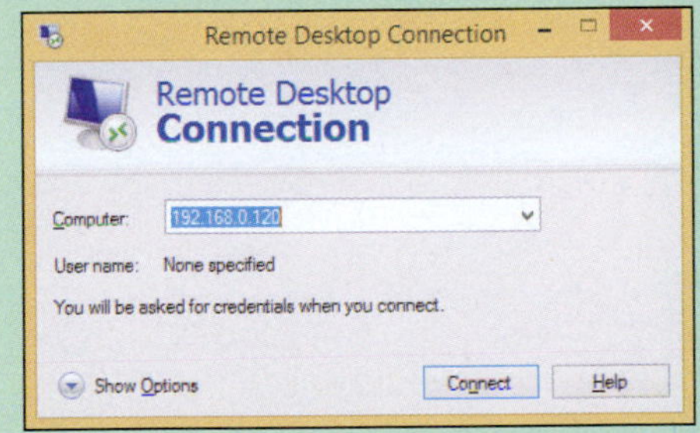

Figure 17-15 The IP address of the remote computer can be used to connect to it

Notes If you have trouble using the host name to make a Remote Desktop connection on a local network, try entering the host name and IP address of the remote computer in the hosts file in the C:\Windows\System32\drivers\etc folder of the client computer.

3. If you plan to transfer files from one computer to the other, click **Show Options** for Windows 8 or **Options** for Windows 7, and then click the **Local Resources** tab, as shown on the left side of Figure 17-16. Click **More**. The box on the right side of Figure 17-16 appears. Check **Drives**. Click **OK**. Click **Connect** to make the connection. If a warning box appears, click **Connect** again. If another warning box appears, click **Yes**.

(continues)

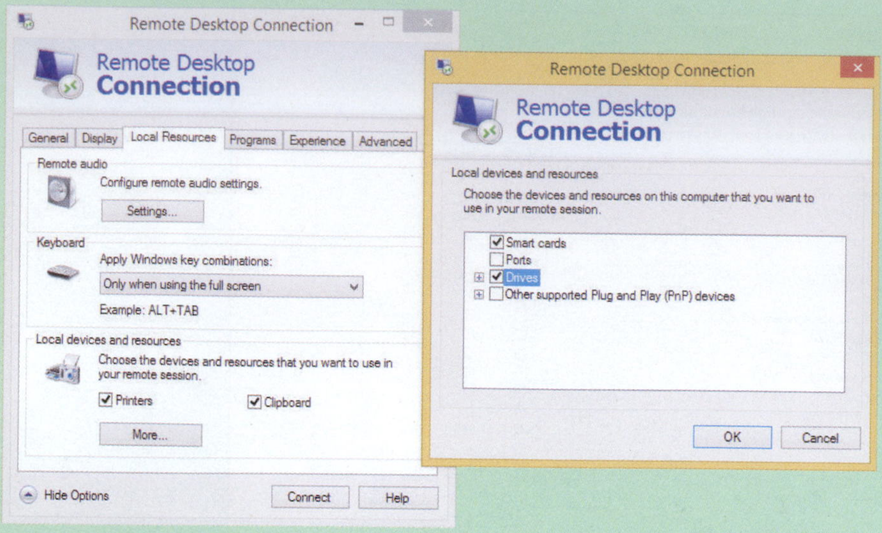

Figure 17-16 Allow drives and other devices to be shared using the Remote Desktop Connection

> **Notes** Server applications such as Remote Desktop listen for network activity from clients. If you want these server applications to be available at all times, you can set your network adapter properties to Wake-on-LAN, which you learned about in the chapter, "Connecting To and Setting Up a Network."

4. A Windows security box appears, which is displayed by the remote computer (see Figure 17-17). Sign in with a user name and password for the remote computer. If a warning box appears saying the remote computer might not be secure, click **Yes** to continue the connection.

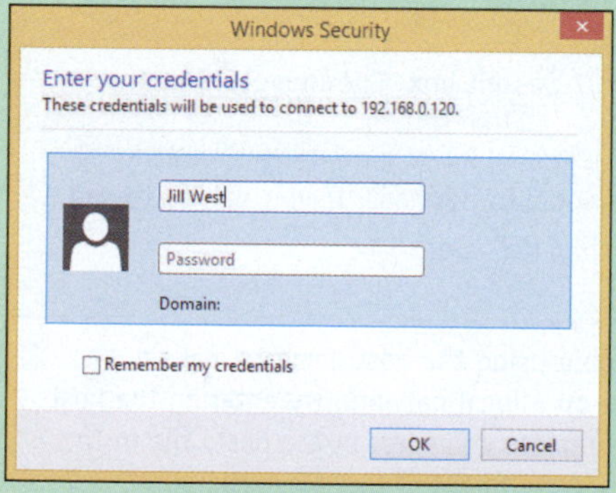

Figure 17-17 Enter your user name and password on the remote computer

5. The desktop of the remote computer appears with a toolbar at the top of the screen, as shown in Figure 17-18. Click **Restore Down** to show both the remote desktop and the local desktop on the same screen, as shown in Figure 17-19.

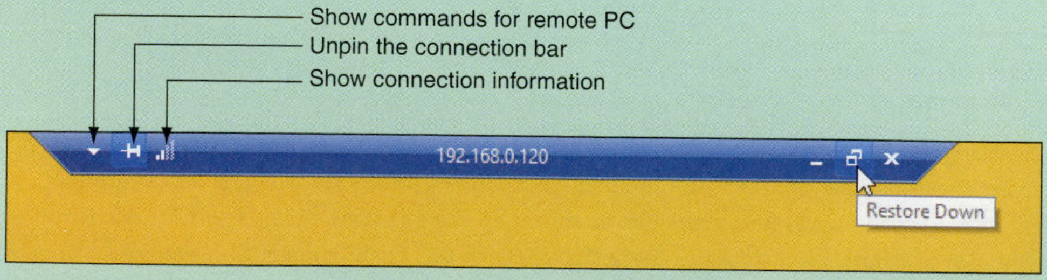

Figure 17-18 The RDC connection bar is pinned to the top of the window showing the remote computer's screen

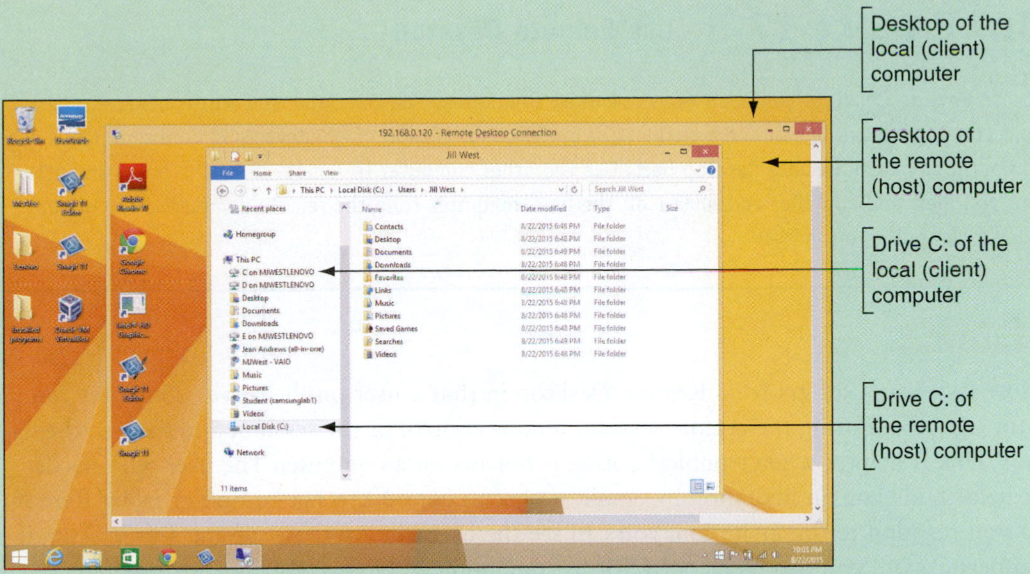

Figure 17-19 The desktop of the remote computer is available on your local computer

6. When you click in the remote desktop's window, you can work with the remote computer just as if you were sitting in front of it, except response time is slower. To move files back and forth between computers, use File Explorer or Windows Explorer on the remote computer. Files on your local computer and on the remote computer will appear in the Explorer window on the remote computer in the Windows 8 This PC group or the Windows 7 Computer group. For example, in Figure 17-19, you can see drive C: on each computer labeled in the figure. To close the connection to the remote computer, sign out from the remote computer or close the desktop window.

Notes Even though Windows normally allows more than one user to be signed in at the same time, this is not the case with Remote Desktop. When a Remote Desktop session is opened, all local users on the remote computer must sign out after receiving a warning, as shown in Figure 17-20.

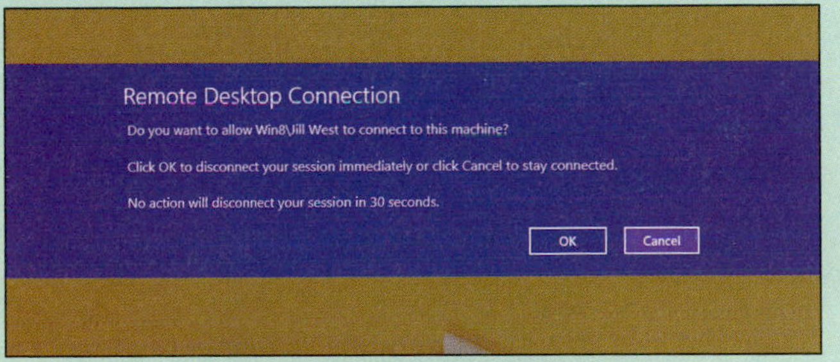

Figure 17-20 Local users must sign out before a Remote Desktop Connection can happen

Is your host computer as safe as it was before you set it to serve up Remote Desktop and enabled port forwarding to it? Actually, no, because a port has been opened, so take this into account when you decide to use Remote Desktop. In a project at the end of this chapter, you learn how you can take further steps to protect the security of your computer when using Remote Desktop. Alternately, you can consider using software that does not require you to open ports. Examples of this type of software, some of which are free, are TeamViewer (*teamviewer.com*), GoToMyPC by Citrix (*gotomypc.com*), and LogMeIn (*logmein.com*).

17

Hands-On | Project 17-3 Use Remote Desktop

A+
220-902
1.4, 1.5,
1.6

To use Remote Desktop, you need two networked computers. The computer you will configure as the host computer must be running a business or professional edition of Windows 8/7. Configure one computer to be the Remote Desktop host. Use the other computer to remote in to the host computer. Can you view and edit files and folders on the host computer from the remote computer? Try to copy a file from your local computer to the host.

REMOTE ASSISTANCE

A+
220-902
1.5, 1.6

Remote Assistance differs from Remote Desktop in that a user on the server computer can remain signed in during the remote session, retains control of the session, and can see the screen. This is helpful when troubleshooting problems on a computer. The user who needs your help sends you an invitation by email or chat to connect to her computer using Remote Assistance. When you respond to the invitation, you can see the user's desktop just as she sees it. And, if the user gives you permission, you can take control of her computer to change settings or do whatever else is needed to fix her problem or show her how to perform a task. Think of Remote Assistance as a way to provide virtual desk-side support.

There are several ways to initiate a Remote Assistance session:

- The user saves an invitation file and then sends that file to the technician. The file can be sent by any method, including email, chat, or posting to a shared folder on the network.
- The user can send an automated email through the Remote Assistance app. This option only works if the system is configured with a compatible email program.
- The user can use Easy Connect, which is the easiest method to start a Remote Assistance connection but only works if both computers used for the connection support the Easy Connect feature. Easy Connect requires Windows 8/7. Also know that some routers don't support the Peer Name Resolution Protocol (PNRP), which is the protocol Easy Connect uses to establish a Remote Assistance connection.
- The technician can initiate a session. This method is the most difficult to use, requiring that Group Policies be applied on the technician's computer.

To initiate a Remote Assistance connection from the host computer using Easy Connect, complete the following steps:

1. Open the **System** window and click **Remote settings** in the left pane. The System Properties box appears with the Remote tab selected (refer back to Figure 17-12).

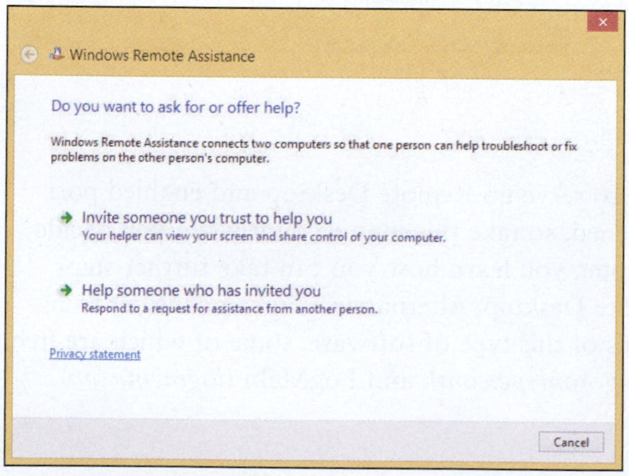

Figure 17-21 Create or respond to an invitation to connect

2. In the Remote Assistance area, check **Allow Remote Assistance connections to this computer**, and then click **OK**.
3. Open **Control Panel** in Category view. Click **System and Security**. Under System, click **Launch remote assistance**. (Alternately, you can press **Win+S** to open search and type **Invite**, then click **Invite someone to connect to your PC and help you.**) The Windows Remote Assistance box in Figure 17-21 appears.

OS Differences To launch Remote Assistance in Windows 7, click **Start**, type **Remote Assistance** in the Search box, and then click **Windows Remote Assistance**.

4. Click **Invite someone you trust to help you**, then click **Use Easy Connect**. Remote Assistance provides a password for the user to give the technician in order to create the connection, as shown in Figure 17-22. If needed, the user can also create an invitation file using this window.

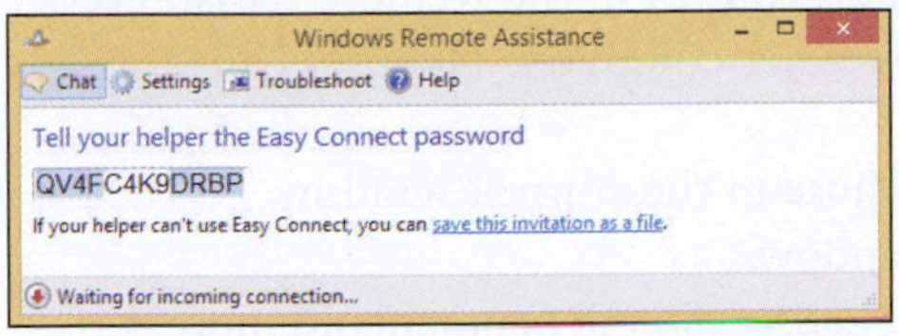

Figure 17-22 The Easy Connect password validates the connection

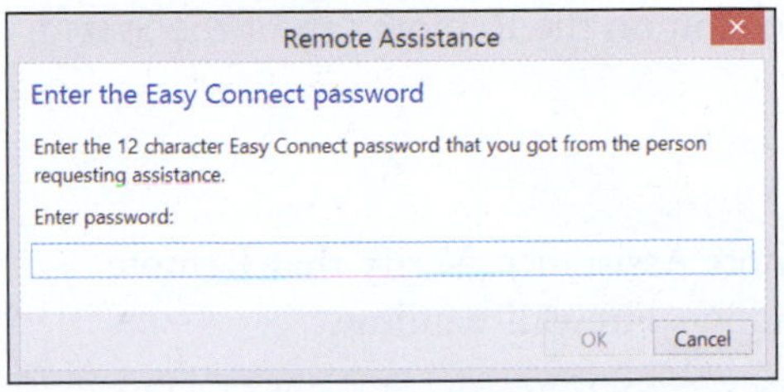

Figure 17-23 Enter the 12-character password created by Easy Connect on the other computer

The technician can respond to the Easy Connect invitation by entering the password into Remote Assistance, as follows:

1. Launch Remote Assistance, as described in Step 3 above.
2. In the Windows Remote Assistance window (shown in Figure 17-21), click **Help someone who has invited you**, then click **Use Easy Connect**.
3. Enter the 12-character password (see Figure 17-23), which is not case sensitive, and click **OK**.
4. The user's computer generates a warning box requesting permission for the technician's computer to connect. The user clicks **Yes** to allow the connection. The user's desktop turns black and the Remote Assistance management window appears. The technician's computer opens the Windows Remote Assistance window, as shown in Figure 17-24, with a live feed from the user's computer.

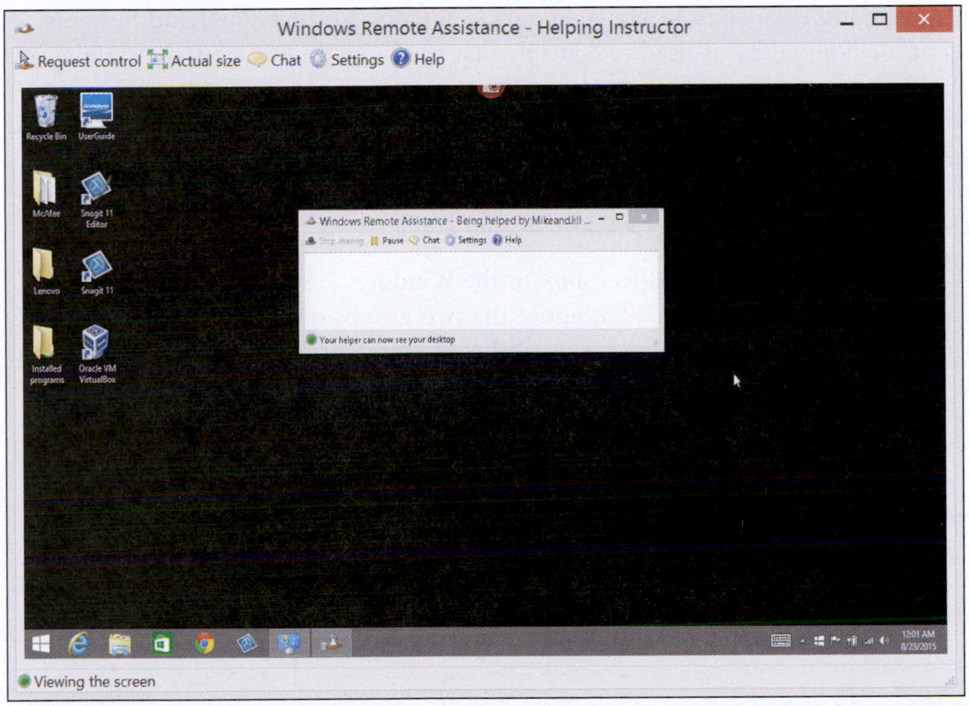

Figure 17-24 The size of the screen can be adjusted by using the toolbar options at the top

17

Here are some things you can do during a Remote Assistance session:

- To open a chat session with the user, click the **Chat** icon. A chat pane appears in the Remote Assistance window on both desktops.
- To ask the user if you can take control of her desktop, click **Request control** in the Remote Assistance control window. When the user accepts the request, you can control her computer. The user can stop sharing control by clicking **Stop sharing**.
- The user can hide her desktop from you at any time by clicking **Pause** in the control window.
- Either of you can disconnect the session by closing the control window.
- A log file is kept of every Remote Assistance session in the C:\Users*username*\Documents\Remote Assistance Logs folder. The file includes the chat session. If you type instructions during the chat session that will later help the user, she can use the log file to remind her of what was said and done.
- If an invitation created by a user is not used within six hours, the invitation expires. This time frame can be changed by clicking **Advanced** in the Remote Assistance section on the Remote tab of the System Properties dialog box.

If you have problems making the connection, do the following:

1. Windows Firewall on the user's computer might be blocking Remote Assistance. Verify that Remote Assistance is checked as an exception to blocked apps in the Windows Firewall window.
2. If you are outside the user's local network, the hardware firewall protecting her network might be blocking Remote Assistance. Verify that port forwarding on that hardware firewall is enabled for Remote Assistance. Remote Assistance uses port 3389, the same port used by Remote Desktop.

USE GROUP POLICY TO IMPROVE QoS FOR APPLICATIONS

A+
220-902
1.3, 1.6

Group Policy (gpedit.msc) is a console available only in Windows professional and business editions (not home editions) that is used to control what users can do and how the system can be used. Group Policy works by making entries in the registry; applying scripts to Windows startup, shutdown, and sign-in processes; and affecting security settings. Policies can be applied to the computer or to a user. Computer-based policies are applied just before the sign-in screen appears, and user-based policies are applied after sign in.

Follow these steps to use Group Policy to set the QoS level for an application:

1. Enter the **gpedit.msc** command in the Windows 8 Run box or the Windows 7 Search box. The Group Policy console opens. On the left side of Figure 17-25, notice the two groups of policies are Computer Configuration and User Configuration. To apply a policy to all users, create it under Computer

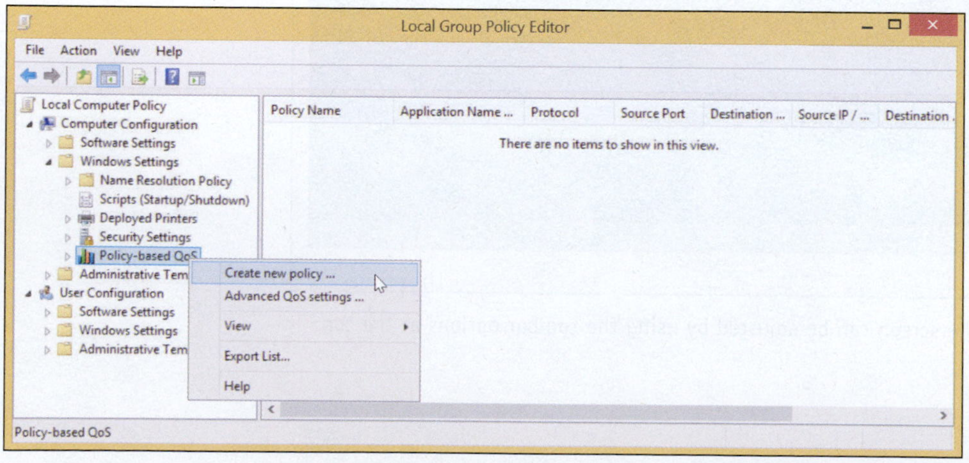

Figure 17-25 Use Group Policy to create a new QoS policy

Configuration. Also notice at the top of the list is Local Computer Policy, which means all policies apply only to the local computer.

2. In the Computer Configuration group, expand the Windows Settings group. Right-click **Policy-based QoS** and click **Create new policy,** as shown in Figure 17-25. A wizard opens to step you through the options for the policy (see Figure 17-26).

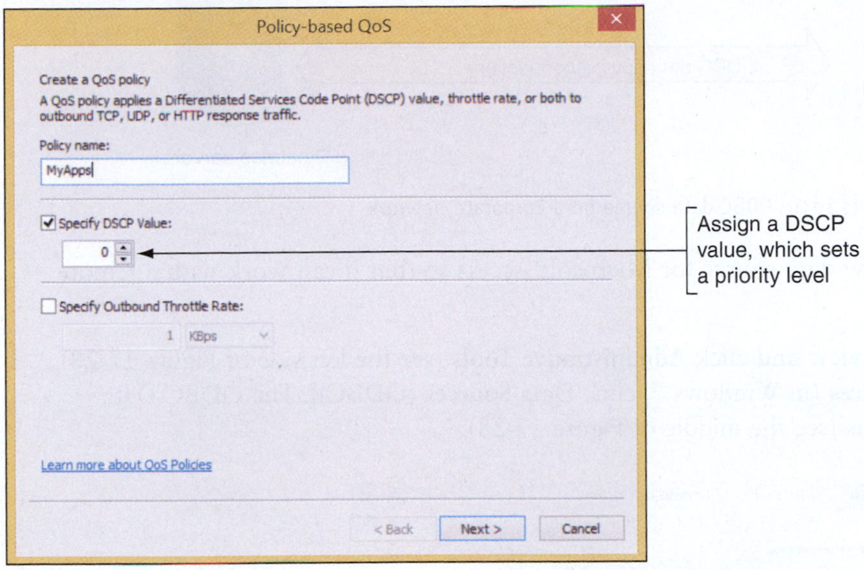

Figure 17-26 Name the QoS policy and enter a DSCP value that determines the priority level of the program(s) to which the policy applies

When creating a policy, here are important options that appear on different screens as you step through the wizard, but know you only need to use the ones that apply to your situation:

- The priority level is determined by a DSCP (Differentiated Services Code Point) value, which is a number from 0 to 63. The higher the number, the higher the priority.
- Outbound traffic can be throttled to limit the bandwidth assigned to an application.
- The policy can apply to all applications or a specific program. (The program name must have an .exe file extension.)
- You can specify the source IP address and/or destination IP address.
- You can select the protocol (TCP or UDP) and port numbers for the policy.
- When the wizard is finished, you are returned to the Group Policy console. Close the console. To apply the new policy, you can restart the computer or enter **gpupdate.exe** at a command prompt.

To get the most out of QoS, configure each router and computer on the network to use QoS.

17

ODBC DATA SOURCES

A+ 220-902 1.4

As an IT technician, you might be called on to help set up a local computer on a corporate network to connect to a remote database stored on a company database server. For example, suppose Microsoft Access is installed on the local computer and you want to configure it to connect to a Microsoft SQL Server database on the server. Open Database Connectivity (ODBC) is the technology used to create the data source, which provides access to the database and includes the drivers required to interface between Access and the data (see Figure 17-27). Drivers for Microsoft SQL Server must be installed on the local computer (Windows has SQL drivers installed by default). Then you can use the ODBC Data Sources tool in the Administrative Tools group of Control Panel to configure the data source.

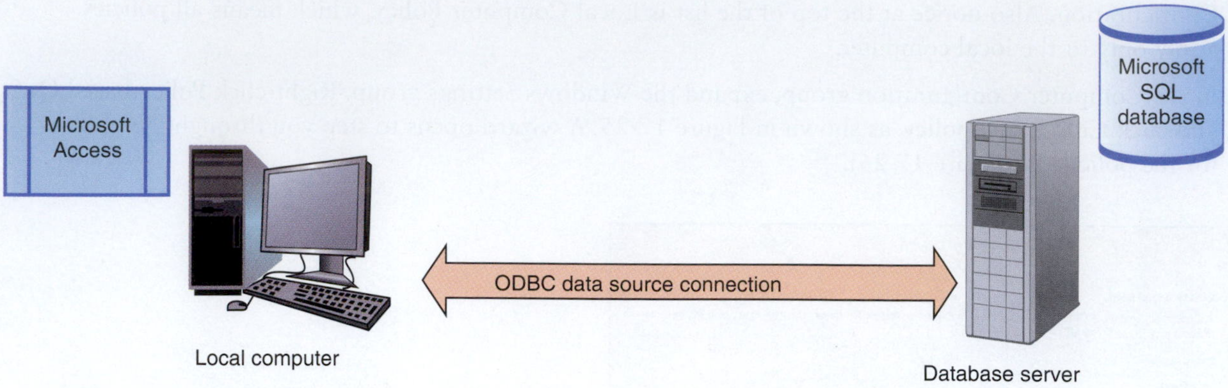

Figure 17-27 Microsoft Access connects to an ODBC data source on a corporate network

Do the following to create a new data source for Microsoft Access so that it can work with a remote Microsoft SQL Server database:

1. Open Control Panel in Classic view and click **Administrative Tools** (see the left side of Figure 17-28). Double-click **ODBC Data Sources** (in Windows 7, click **Data Sources (ODBC)**). The ODBC Data Source Administrator box opens (see the middle of Figure 17-28).

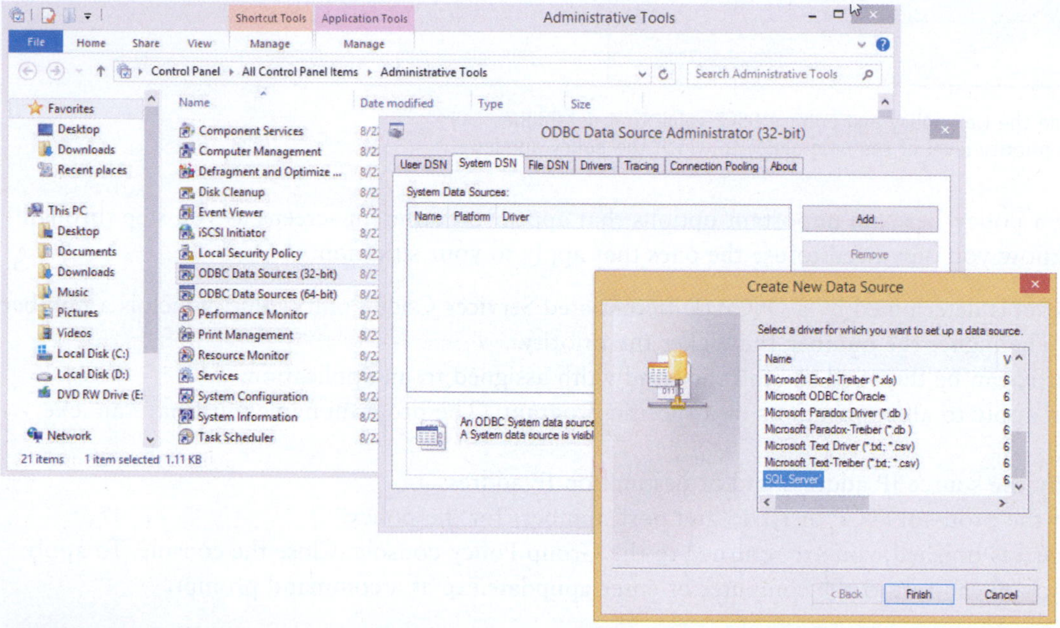

Figure 17-28 Use the Data Sources tool to create a connection between a foreign data source and an application

Notes On 64-bit Windows 8 systems, you're given the option of clicking ODBC for 32-bit applications or ODBC for 64-bit applications. Make your selection based upon the application. In this example, Microsoft Access is a 32-bit application. Therefore, you click **ODBC Data Sources (32-bit)**.

2. To make the data source apply to all users of the system, click the **System DSN** tab. (DSN stands for Data Source Name, and the **User DSN** tab applies only to the current user.) Click **Add**. The Create New Data Source box appears (see the right side of Figure 17-28). Scroll down to and select **SQL Server** and click **Finish**. Follow directions on screen to enter the name of the SQL Server computer on the network and the sign-in ID and password to SQL Server. The database administrator in your organization can supply this information.

Notes If you don't see the driver you need in the Create New Data Source box, close all windows and use Explorer to locate the C:\Windows\SysWOW64\Odbcad32.exe program file. When you double-click this file, the ODBC Data Source Administrator box appears and you can then access all ODBC drivers installed on the local computer.

Now let's turn our attention to managing another resource on the network: folders and files.

CONTROLLING ACCESS TO FOLDERS AND FILES

A+ 220-902 1.2, 1.3, 1.4, 1.5, 1.6, 3.2, 3.3, 3.4

Responsibility for a small network can include controlling access to folders and files for users of a local computer and for remote users accessing shared resources over the network. Managing shared resources is accomplished by (1) assigning rights to user accounts and (2) assigning permissions to folders and files.

Notes In Windows, the two terms, rights and permissions, have different meanings. Rights (also called privileges) refer to the tasks an account is allowed to do in the system (for example, installing software or changing the system date and time). **Permissions** refer to which user accounts or user groups are allowed access to data files and folders. *Rights are assigned to an account, and permissions are assigned to data files and folders.*

Let's first look at the strategies used for controlling rights to user accounts and controlling permissions to folders and files. Then you learn the procedures in Windows for assigning these rights and permissions.

CLASSIFY USER ACCOUNTS AND USER GROUPS

A+ 220-902 1.3, 1.4, 3.2, 3.3, 3.4

Computer users should be classified to determine the rights they need to do their jobs. For example, some users need the right to sign in to a system remotely and others do not. Other rights granted to users might include the right to install software or hardware, change the system date and time, change Windows Firewall settings, and so forth. Generally, when a new employee begins work, that employee's supervisor determines what rights the employee needs to perform his job. You, as the support technician, will be responsible to make sure the user account assigned to the employee has these rights and no more. This approach is called the **principle of least privilege**.

In Windows, the rights or privileges assigned to an account are established when you first create a user account, which is when you decide the account type. You can later change these rights by changing the user groups to which the account belongs. User accounts can be created from Control Panel (using any edition of Windows) or by using the Computer Management console (using business and professional editions of Windows). User accounts can be assigned to different user groups using the Computer Management console (using business and professional editions of Windows). (Home editions of Windows, therefore, cannot be used to manage user groups.)

17

TYPE OF USER ACCOUNT

Recall from the chapter, "Survey of Windows Features and Support Tools," that when you use Control Panel to manage user accounts, you can choose between two account types: Administrator or Standard. When you use Computer Management to create an account, the account type is automatically a standard user account. To create a user account using Computer Management, first open the Computer Management console (compmgmt.msc). Then right-click **Users** under **Local Users and Groups** and select

New User in the shortcut menu. (Windows Home editions don't include the Local Users and Groups option in the Computer Management console.) Enter information for the new user a nd click **Create** (see Figure 17-29).

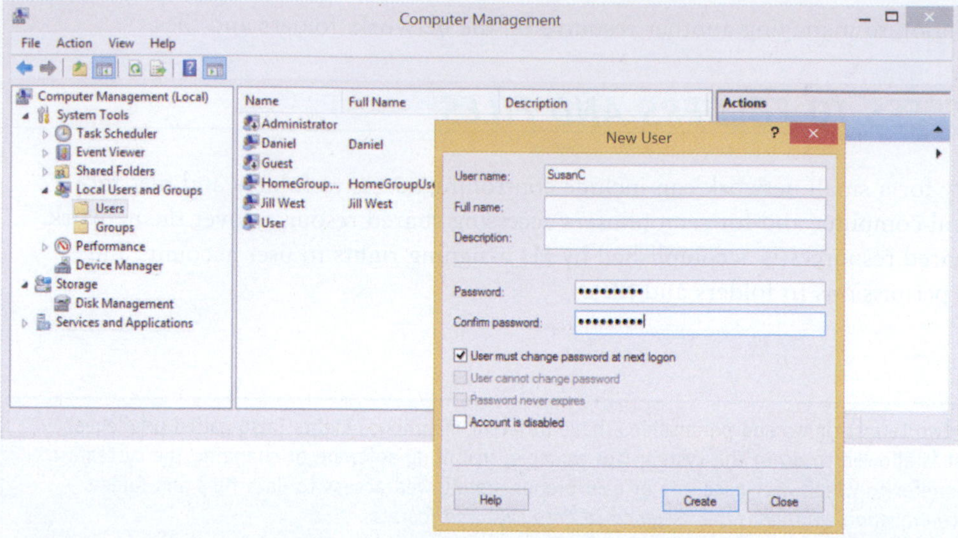

Figure 17-29 Create a new user

★ A+ Exam Tip The A+ 220-902 exam expects you to know about groups and the administrator, standard user, power user, and guest accounts.

BUILT-IN USER GROUPS

A user account can belong to one or more user groups. Windows offers several built-in user groups and you can create your own. Here are important built-in user groups:

- ***Administrators and Users groups.*** By default, administrator accounts belong to the Administrators group, and standard user accounts belong to the Users group. If you want to give administrator rights to a standard user account, use the Computer Management console to add the account to the Administrators group.
- ***Guests group.*** The Guests group has limited rights on the system and is given a temporary profile that is deleted when the user signs out. Windows automatically creates one account in the Guests group named the Guest account, which is disabled by default.
- ***Backup Operators group.*** An account in the Backup Operators group can back up and restore any files on the system regardless of its access permissions to these files.
- ***Power Users group.*** Windows XP has a Power Users group that can read from and write to parts of the system other than its own user profile folders, install applications, and perform limited administrative tasks. Windows 8/7/Vista offers a Power Users group only for backward compatibility with XP to be used with legacy applications that were designed to work in XP.

To view user groups installed on a system, open the Computer Management console and click **Groups** under Local Users and Groups (see Figure 17-30).

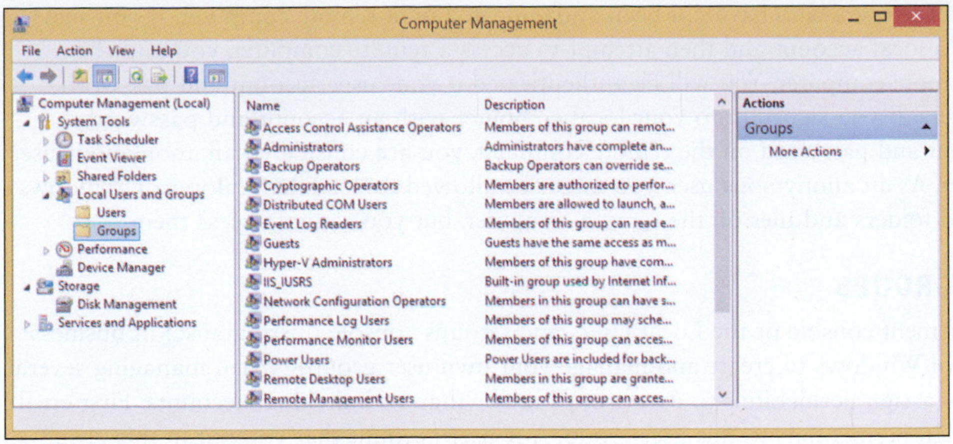

Figure 17-30 Users groups installed on a system

To change the groups a user account is in, click **Users**. The list of user accounts appears in the right pane of the console window (see the left side of Figure 17-31). Right-click the user account and select **Properties** in the shortcut menu. On the user account Properties box, click the **Member Of** tab (see the middle of Figure 17-31). Click **Add** and enter the user group name. You must type the user group name exactly as it appears in the list of user groups that you saw earlier in the list of groups (see Figure 17-30). (Alternately, you can click **Advanced**, click **Find Now**, and select the group name from the list of groups that appears.) Click **OK** twice to close both boxes.

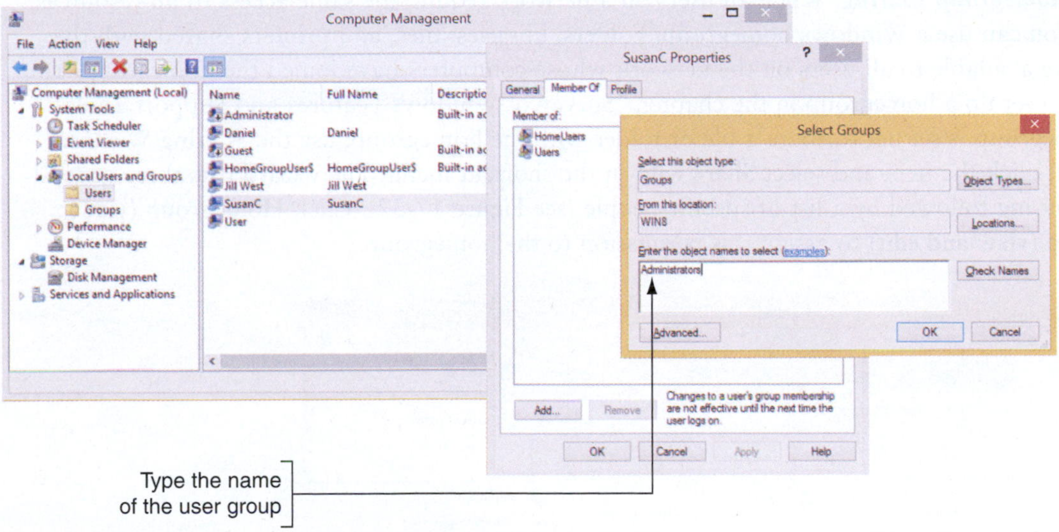

Figure 17-31 Add a user account to a user group

In addition to the groups you can assign to an account, Windows might automatically assign one of these built-in user groups to an account when it is determining permissions assigned to a file or folder:

- The **Authenticated Users group** includes all user accounts that can access the system except the Guest account. These accounts include domain accounts (used to sign in to the domain) and local accounts (used to sign in to the local computer). The accounts might or might not require a password. When you create a folder or file that is not part of your user profile, by default, Windows gives access to all Authenticated Users.
- The **Everyone group** includes the Authenticated Users group as well as the Guest account. When you share a file or folder on the network or to a homegroup, by default, Windows gives access to the Everyone group.

- **Anonymous users** are those users who have not been authenticated on a remote computer. If you sign in to a computer using a local account and then attempt to access a remote computer, you must be authenticated on the remote computer. You will be authenticated if your user account and password match on both computers. If you signed in to your local computer with an account and password that do not match an account and password on the remote computer, you are considered an anonymous user on the remote computer. As an anonymous user, you might be allowed to use File Explorer or Windows Explorer to view shared folders and files on the remote computer, but you cannot access them.

CUSTOMIZED USER GROUPS

Use the Computer Management console or the **Local Users and Groups** console (lusrmgr.msc) in business and professional editions of Windows to create and manage your own user groups. When managing several user accounts, it's easier to assign permissions to user groups rather than to individual accounts. First create a user group and then assign permissions to this user group. Any user account that you put in this group then acquires these permissions.

User groups work especially well when several users need the same permissions. For example, you can set up an Accounting group and a Medical Records group for a small office. Users in the Accounting department and users in the Medical Records department go into their respective user groups. Then you only need to manage the permissions for two groups rather than multiple user accounts.

METHODS TO ASSIGN PERMISSIONS TO FOLDERS AND FILES

A+
220-902
3.2, 3.3

There are three general strategies for managing shared files and folders, also called directories, in Windows:

- ***Homegroup sharing.*** When all users on a network require the same access to all resources, you can use a Windows homegroup. Folders, libraries, files, and printers shared with the homegroup are available to all users on the network whose computers have joined the homegroup. You learned how to set up a homegroup in the chapter, "Survey of Windows Features and Support Tools." After the homegroup is set up, to share a file or folder with the homegroup, use the Sharing Wizard. To do so, right-click the item and select **Share with** in the shortcut menu. The wizard lists three general options for sharing followed by a list of specific people (see Figure 17-32). Click **Homegroup (view)** or **Homegroup (view and edit)** to assign this permission to the homegroup.

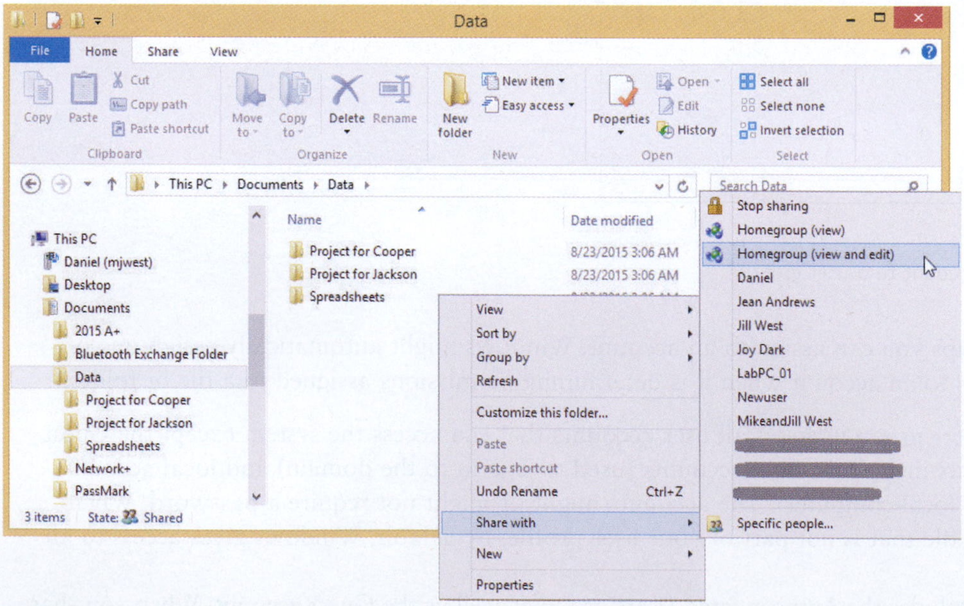

Figure 17-32 Share a folder with the homegroup

To verify the item is shared, select the folder or file in Explorer and look for the two-person shared icon in the status bar (see Figure 17-33). Notice in the status bar the item is assigned to the Homegroup group.

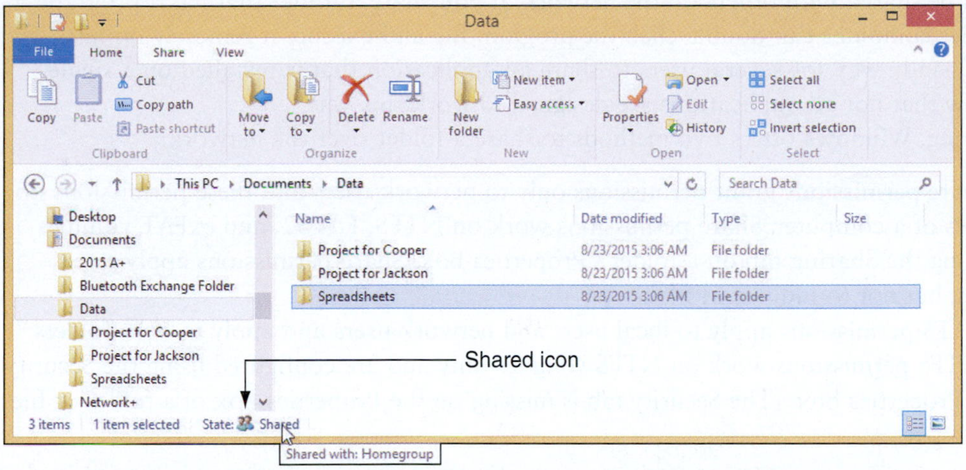

Figure 17-33 A folder shared with the homegroup shows the two-person Shared icon in the status bar of File Explorer

Notes If the Sharing Wizard is disabled, the four sharing options shown in Figure 17-32 will not appear when you click *Share with*. To enable the Sharing Wizard, using Control Panel, open the Folder Options box and, on the View tab, select Use Sharing Wizard (Recommended). See Figure 17-34. If the Sharing Wizard is not used, you must use advanced sharing methods covered later in the chapter.

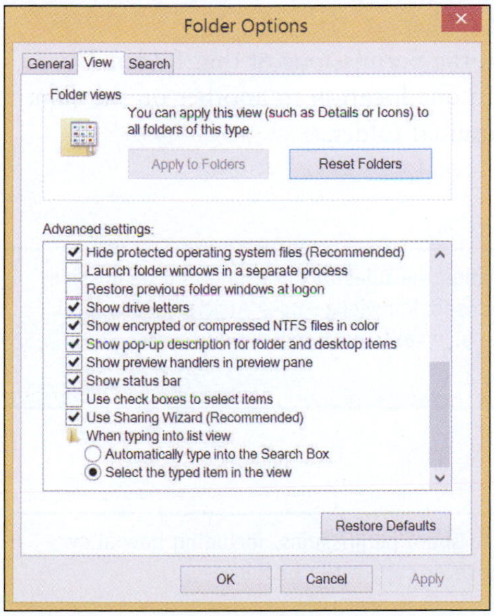

Figure 17-34 The Folder Options box shows the Sharing Wizard is enabled

A+ Exam Tip The A+ 220-902 exam expects you to know how to use the Folder Options box to enable or disable the Sharing Wizard.

- ***Workgroup sharing.*** For better security than a homegroup, use workgroup sharing. With this method, you decide which users on the network have access to which shared folder and the type of access they have. All rights and permissions are set up on each local computer so that each computer manages access to its files, folders, and printers shared on this peer-to-peer network.
- ***Domain controlling.*** If a Windows computer belongs to a domain instead of a workgroup or homegroup, all security is managed by the network administrator for the entire network.

In this chapter, we focus on workgroup sharing, which might use a file server. Here are some tips on which folders to use to hold shared data on a file server or personal computer:

- Private data for individual users is best kept in the C:\Users folder for that user. User accounts with limited or standard privileges cannot normally access these folders belonging to another user account. However, accounts with administrative rights do have access.
- The C:\Users\Public folder is intended to be used for folders and files that all users share. It is not recommended you use this folder for controlled access to data.

- For best security, create a folder not in the C:\Users folder and assign permissions to that folder and its subfolders. You can allow all users access or only certain users or user groups.

Some applications can be shared with others on the network. If you share a folder that has a program file in it, a user on another computer can double-click the program file and execute it remotely on his or her desktop. This is a handy way for several users to share an application that is installed on a single computer. However, know that not all applications are designed to work this way.

Using workgroup sharing, Windows offers two methods to share a folder over the network:

- ***Share permissions.*** **Share permissions** grant permissions only to network users and these permissions do not apply to local users of a computer. Share permissions work on NTFS, FAT32, and exFAT volumes and are configured using the Sharing tab on a folder's Properties box. Share permissions apply to a folder and its contents, but not to individual files.
- ***NTFS permissions.*** **NTFS permissions** apply to local users and network users and apply to both folders and individual files. NTFS permissions work on NTFS volumes only and are configured using the Security tab on a file or folder Properties box. (The Security tab is missing on the Properties box of a folder or file on a FAT volume.)

Here are some tips when implementing share permissions and NTFS permissions:

- If you use both share permissions and NTFS permissions on a folder, the most restrictive permission applies. For NTFS volumes, use only NTFS permissions because they can be customized better. For FAT volumes, your only option is share permissions.
- If NTFS permissions are conflicting, for example, when a user account has been given one permission and the user group to which this user belongs has been given a different permission, the more liberal permission applies.
- **Permission propagation** is when permissions are passed from parent to child. **Inherited permissions** are permissions that are attained from a parent object. For example, when you create a file or folder in a folder, the new object takes on the permissions of the parent folder.
- When you move or copy an object to a folder, the object takes on the permissions of that folder. The exception to this rule is when you move (not copy) an object from one location to another on the same volume. In this case, the object retains its permissions from the original folder.

Notes You can use the xcopy or robocopy command with parameters to change the rules for how inherited permissions are managed when copying and moving files. For more information, see the Microsoft Knowledge Base Article cc733145 at *https://technet.microsoft.com/en-us/library/cc733145*. Also check out the article at *http://social.technet.microsoft.com/wiki/contents/articles/1073.robocopy-and-a-few-examples.aspx*.

A+ Exam Tip The A+ 220-902 exam expects you to know about NTFS and share permissions, including how allow and deny conflicts are resolved and what happens to permissions when you move or copy a file or folder.

HOW TO SHARE FOLDERS AND FILES

A+ 220-902 1.5, 1.6, 3.2, 3.3

Now that you know about the concepts and strategies for sharing folders and files, let's look at the details of how to use Windows to manage user rights and file and folder permissions.

APPLYING | CONCEPTS CREATE USER ACCOUNTS WITH DATA ACCESS

A+ 220-902 1.5, 1.6, 3.2, 3.3

Nicole is responsible for a peer-to-peer network for a medical doctor's office. Four computers are connected to the small company network; one of these computers acts as the file server for the network. Nicole has created two classifications of data, Financial and Medical. Two workers (Nancy and Adam) require access to the Medical data, and two workers (Linda and Carlos) require access to the Financial folder. In addition, the doctor, Lucas, requires access to both categories of data. Here is what Nicole must do to set up the users and data:

1. Create folders named Financial and Medical on the file server. Create five user accounts, one each for Lucas, Nancy, Adam, Linda, and Carlos. All the accounts belong to the Windows standard user group. Create two user groups, Financial and Medical.
2. Using NTFS permissions, set the permissions on the Financial and Medical folders so that only the members of the appropriate group can access each folder.
3. Test access to both folders using test data and then copy all real data into the two folders and subfolders. Set up a backup plan for the two folders as you learned to do in the chapter, "Maintaining Windows."

Let's look at how each of these three steps is done.

Step 1: Create Folders, User Accounts, and User Groups

Follow these steps to create the folders, user accounts, and user groups on the file server computer that is using Windows 8/7 Professional:

1. Sign in to the system as an administrator.
2. Using an NTFS volume, create these two folders: **C:\Medical** and **C:\Financial**.
3. Open the Computer Management console or the Local Users and Groups console and create user accounts for **Lucas**, **Nancy**, **Adam**, **Linda**, and **Carlos**. The account types are automatically standard user accounts.
4. To create the Medical user group, right-click **Groups** under Local Users and Groups and select **New Group** in the shortcut menu. The New Group box appears. Enter the name of the group (**Medical**) and its description (**Users have access to the Medical folder**), as shown in Figure 17-35.

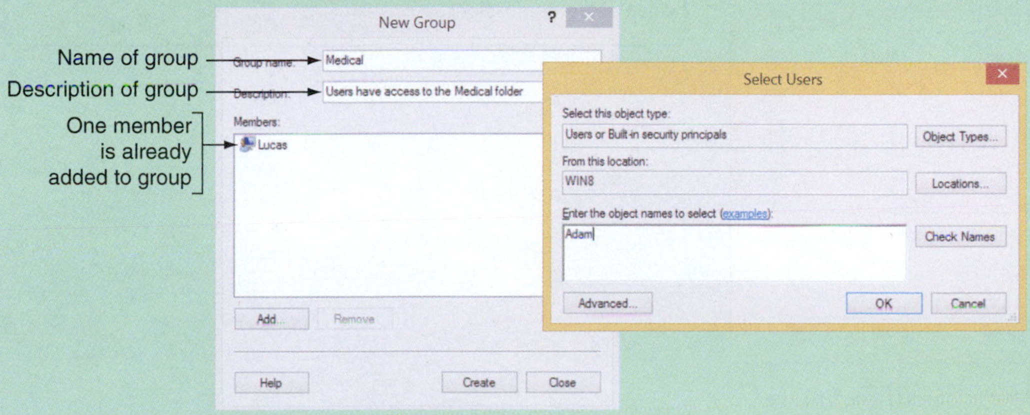

Figure 17-35 Setting up a new user group

5. Add all the users that need access to medical data (Lucas, Adam, and Nancy). To add members to the Medical group, click **Add**. The Select Users box opens, as shown on the right side of Figure 17-35. Under *Enter the object names to select*, enter the name of a user and click **OK**. As each user is added, his or her name appears

(continues)

17

under Members in the New Group box, as shown in Figure 17-35. To create the group, click **Create** in the New Group box.

6. In the same way, create the Financial group and add Lucas, Linda, and Carlos to the group. Later, you can use the Computer Management console to add or remove users from either group.
7. Close the Computer Management console.

A+ Exam Tip The A+ 220-902 exam expects you to be able to set up a user account or group and know how to change the group to which an account is assigned.

Step 2: Set NTFS Folder Permissions for User Groups

Follow these steps to set the NTFS permissions for the two folders:

1. Open File Explorer or Windows Explorer, right-click the **Medical** folder, and select **Properties** in the shortcut menu. The Properties box for the folder appears.
2. Click the **Security** tab (see Figure 17-36). Notice in the box that Authenticated Users, SYSTEM, Administrators, and Users all have access to the C:\Medical folder. When you select a user group, the type of permissions assigned to that group appears in the *Permissions* area. Table 17-1 gives an explanation of the more significant types of permission. Note that the Administrators group has full control of the folder. Also notice the checks under Allow are dimmed. These permissions are dimmed because they have been inherited from the parent object. In this case, the parent object is Windows default settings.

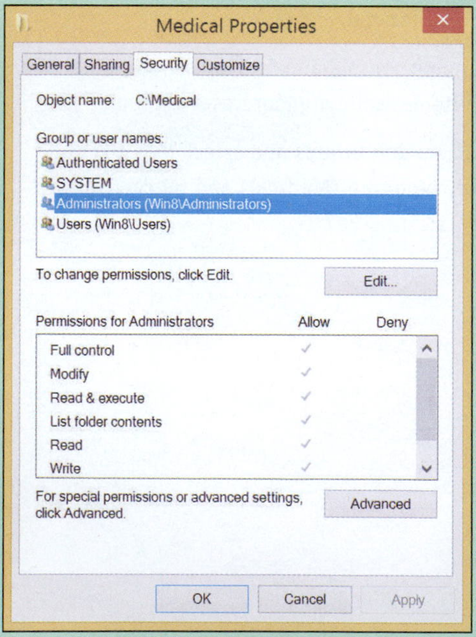

Figure 17-36 Permissions assigned to the Medical folder

Notes For a thorough discussion of how permissions work, see the Microsoft Knowledge Base article cc783530 at *https://technet.microsoft.com/en-us/library/Cc783530(v=WS.10).aspx*.

A+ Exam Tip The A+ 220-902 exam expects you to know that NTFS permissions can customize permissions better than share permissions.

Permission Level	Description
Full control	Can read, change, delete, and create files and subfolders, read file and folder attributes, read and change permissions, and take ownership of a file or folder.
Modify	Can read, change, and create existing files and subfolders. Can delete the folder or file, but cannot delete subfolders and their files. Can read and change attributes. Can view permissions but not change them. Cannot take ownership.
Read & execute	Can read folders and contents and run programs in a folder. (Applies to both files and folders.)
List folder contents	Can read folders and contents and run programs in a folder. (Applies only to folders.)
Read	Can read folders and contents.
Write	Can create a folder or file and change attributes, but cannot read data. This permission is used for a drop folder where users can drop confidential files that can only be read by a manager. For example, an instructor can receive student homework in a drop folder.

Table 17-1 Permission levels for files and folders

3. To remove the inherited status from these permissions so you can change them, click **Advanced**. The Advanced Security Settings box appears (see the left side of Figure 17-37). Click **Disable inheritance**. The Block Inheritance box appears (see the right side of Figure 17-37). To keep the current permissions, but remove the inherited status placed on them, click **Convert inherited permissions into explicit permissions on this object**. Click **Apply**.

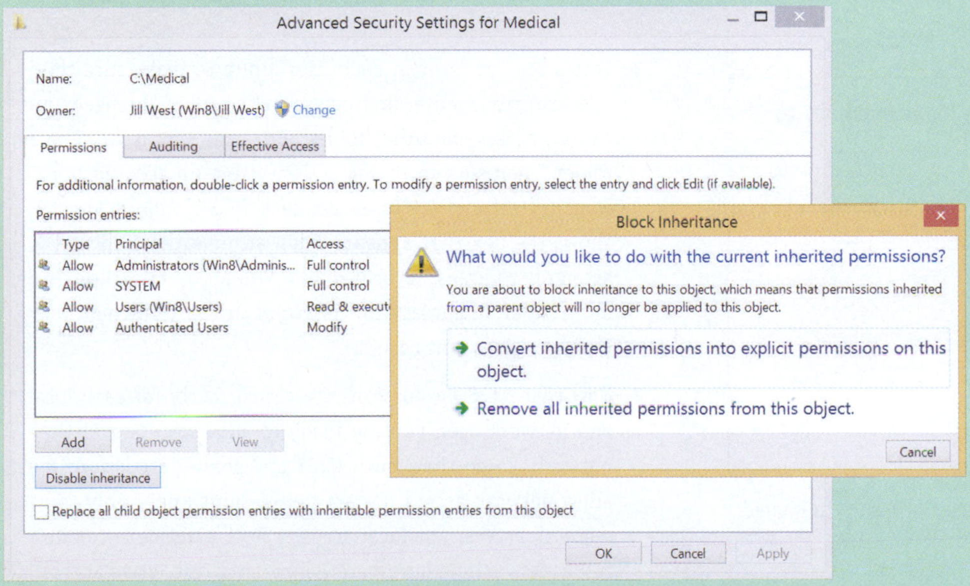

Figure 17-37 Remove the inherited status from the current permissions

OS Differences To remove the inherited status of folder permissions in Windows 7, in the Advanced Security Settings box, click **Change Permissions**. In the new Advanced Security Settings box, you can now uncheck **Include inheritable permissions from this object's parent**. A Windows Security warning box appears. To keep the current permissions, but remove the inherited status placed on them, click **Add**.

(continues)

4. Close the Advanced Security Settings box.
5. In the Medical Properties box, notice the permissions are now checked in black, indicating they are no longer inherited permissions and can be changed. Click **Edit** to change these permissions.
6. The Permissions box opens (see Figure 17-38). Select the **Authenticated Users** group and click **Remove.** Also remove the **Users** group. Don't remove the SYSTEM group, which gives Windows the access it needs. Also, don't remove the Administrators group. You need to leave that group as is so that administrators can access the data.

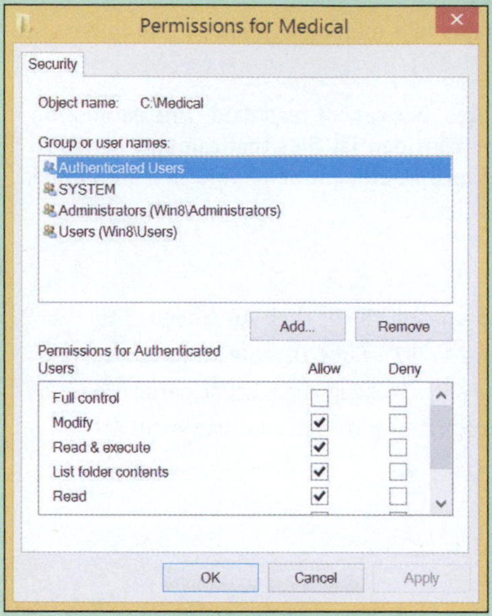

Figure 17-38 Change the permissions to a folder

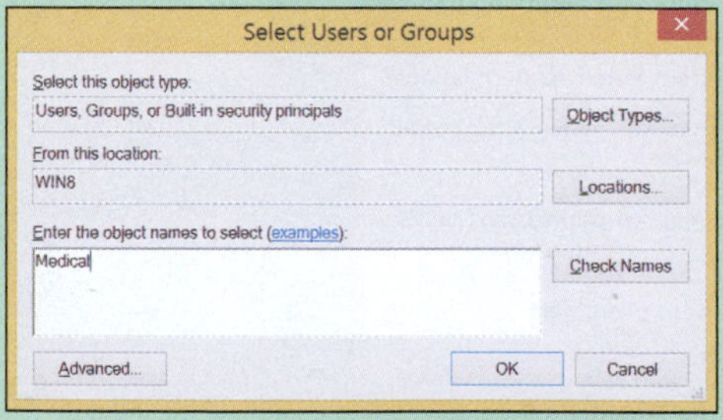

Figure 17-39 Add a user or group to shared permissions

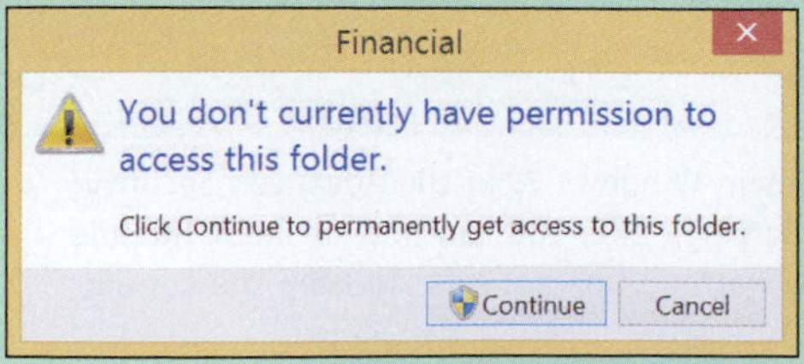

Figure 17-40 Access to a folder is controlled

7. To add a new group, click **Add**. The Select Users or Groups box opens. Under *Enter the object names to select*, type **Medical**, as shown in Figure 17-39, and click **OK**. The Medical group is added to the list of groups and users for this folder.
8. Using the check box under Permissions for Medical, check **Allow** under *Full control* to give that permission to this user group. Click **OK** twice to close the Properties box.
9. Change the permissions of the C:\Financial folder so that Authenticated Users and Users are not allowed access and the Financial group is allowed full control.

Step 3: Test, Set Share Permissions, and Go Live

It's now time to test your security measures. Do the following to test the NTFS permissions and implement your shared folders:

1. Test a user account in each user group to make sure the user can read, write, and delete in the folder he needs but cannot access the other folder. Put some test data in each folder. Then sign in to the system using an account you want to test and try to access each folder. Figure 17-40 shows the box that appears when an unauthorized user attempts to access a local folder. When you click **Continue**, entering an administrator password in the resulting UAC box gives you access.
2. Now that NTFS permissions are set correctly for each local and network user, you are ready to allow access over the network. To do that, both NTFS and share permissions must allow network access. (Share permissions apply only to network access, not local access.) Best practice is to allow full access using share permissions and restrictive access using NTFS permissions. The most restrictive permissions apply. To allow full access using share permissions, click the **Sharing** tab of each folder's properties box, and click **Advanced Sharing**.
3. In the Advanced Sharing box, if it is not already checked, check **Share this folder**. Then click **Permissions**. To add a new group, click **Add**. The Select Users or Groups box

opens. Under *Enter the object names to select*, type **Everyone** and click **OK**. The Everyone group is added to the list of groups and users for this folder.

4. With **Everyone** selected, check **Allow** under *Full control* to give that permission to the Everyone user group. Click **OK** twice and then close the Properties box.
5. Now that you have the security settings in place for one computer, go to each computer on the network and create the user accounts that will be using this computer. Then test the security and make sure each user can access or cannot access the \Financial and \Medical folders as you intend. Figure 17-41 shows the error message that appears when an unauthorized user attempts to access a network resource.

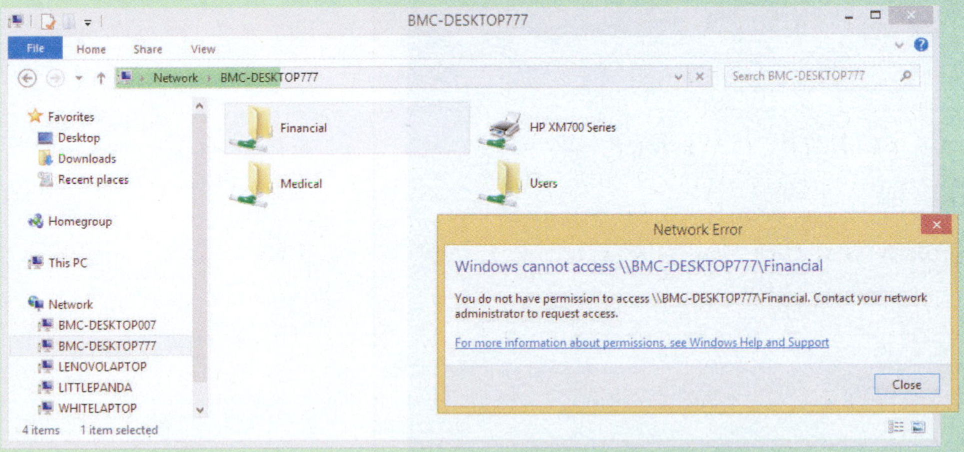

Figure 17-41 When a user is denied access to a network resource, there is no opportunity to provide access from this screen

6. To access shared folders, you can drill down into the Network group in File Explorer or Windows Explorer. Another method is to type the computer name—as in \\Win8—in the address bar of the Explorer window (see Figure 17-42).

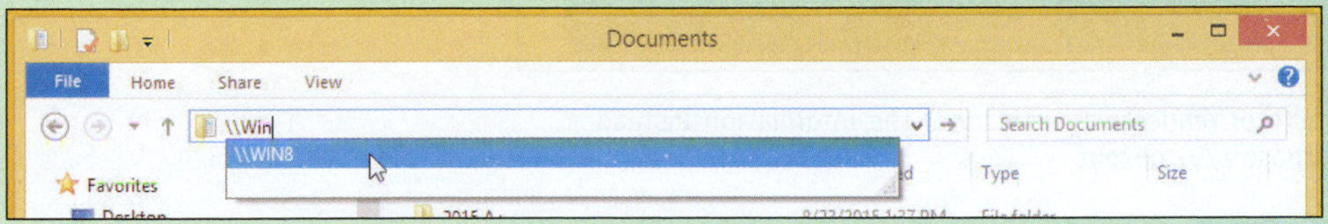

Figure 17-42 Use the computer name to access shared folders on that computer

7. After you are convinced the security works as you want it to, copy all the company data to subfolders in these folders. Check a few subfolders and files to verify that each has the permissions that you expect. And don't forget to put in place on the file server the backup procedures you learned about in the chapter, "Maintaining Windows."

17

USER AND GROUP INFORMATION WITH THE GPRESULT COMMAND

You can pull a list of all the groups a user belongs to with the gpresult command. This information can be helpful when troubleshooting user group issues or Group Policy problems. To retrieve information on a user other than the one signed in, open an elevated command prompt window and enter the command **gpresult /scope user /user** ***username*** **/r**. Figure 17-43 shows output for the user Adam and you can verify he belongs to the Medical group.

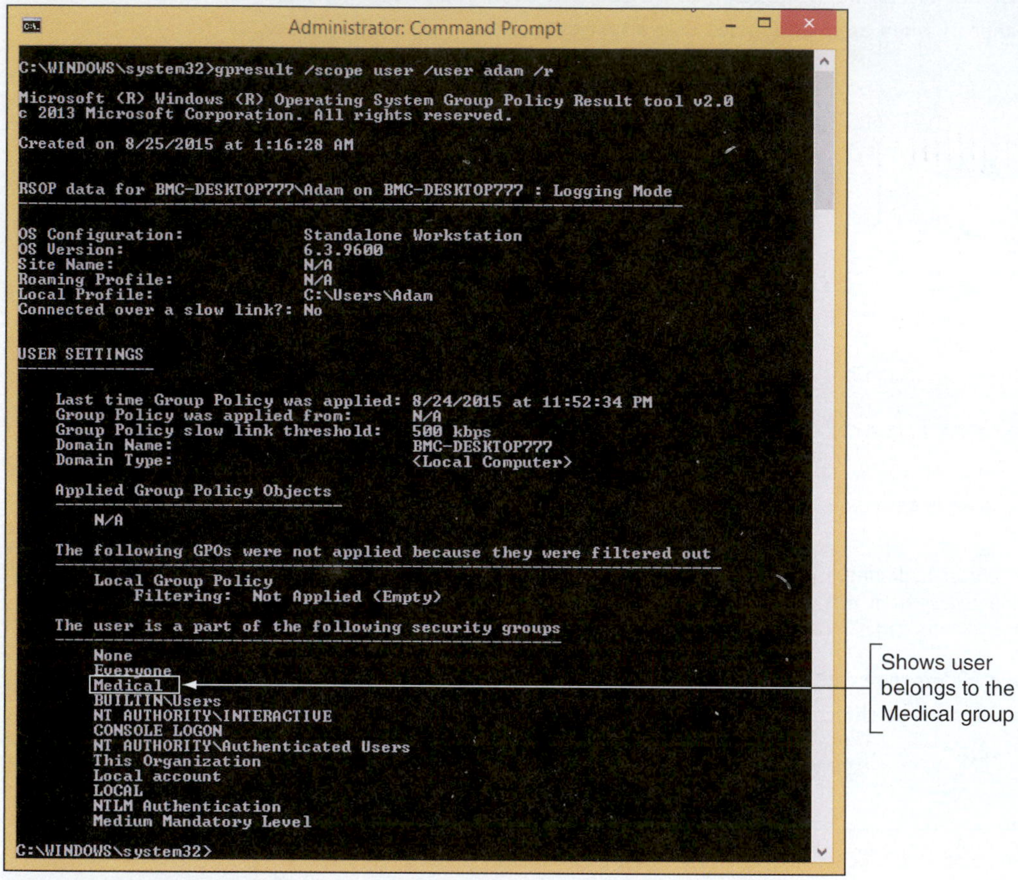

Figure 17-43 The /r parameter requests a summary of the information instead of more verbose (/v) output

To retrieve a summary of information for the computer rather than for a user, enter the command **gpresult /scope computer /r**, as shown in Figure 17-44. To learn more about gpresult, see the Microsoft Knowledge Base Article Bb490915 at *technet.microsoft.com*.

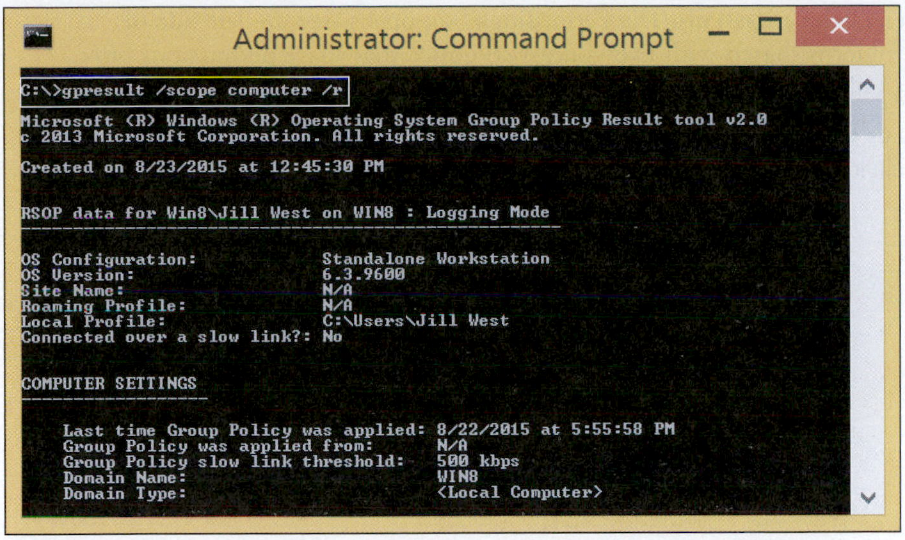

Figure 17-44 Setting the scope as *computer* requests information on computer-wide policies

HOW TO USE SHARE PERMISSIONS

Although you can mix NTFS permissions and share permissions on the same system, life is simpler if you use one or the other. For NTFS volumes, NTFS permissions are the way to go because they can be customized better than share permissions. However, you must use share permissions on FAT volumes. To do so, follow these steps:

1. Open the Properties box for the folder (*Personnel* in this case). Notice in Figure 17-45 the Security tab is missing because the folder is on a FAT volume. Select the **Sharing** tab and click **Advanced Sharing**. The Advanced Sharing box opens (see the right side of Figure 17-45).

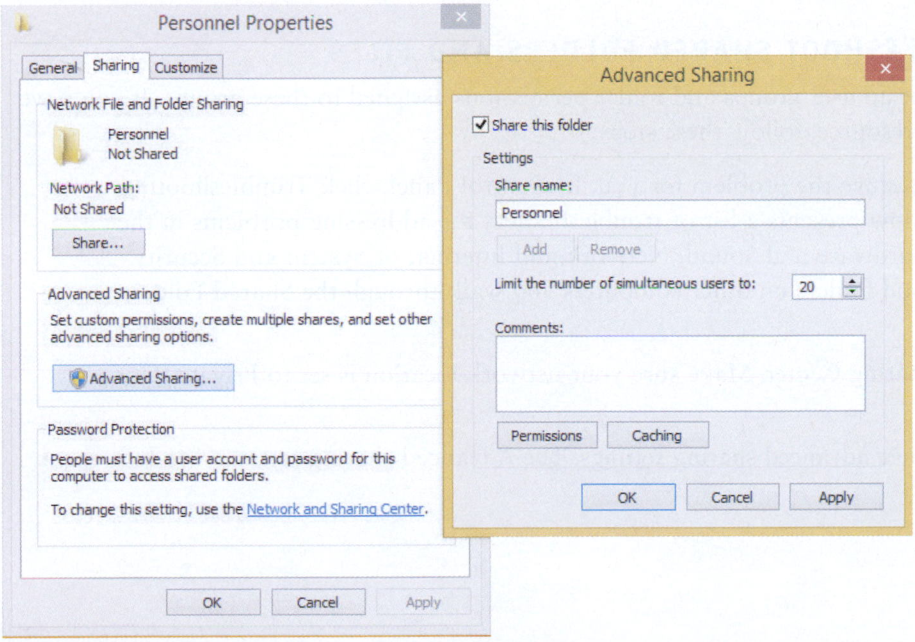

Figure 17-45 Use the Sharing tab of a folder Properties box to set up share permissions on a FAT volume

2. Check **Share this folder**. Then click **Permissions**. The Permissions box opens (see the left side of Figure 17-46). Initially, the folder is shared with Everyone. Also notice that share permissions offer only three permission levels, Full Control, Change, and Read.
3. Click **Add**. The Select Users or Groups box appears (see the right side of Figure 17-46). Enter a user account or user group and click **OK**.

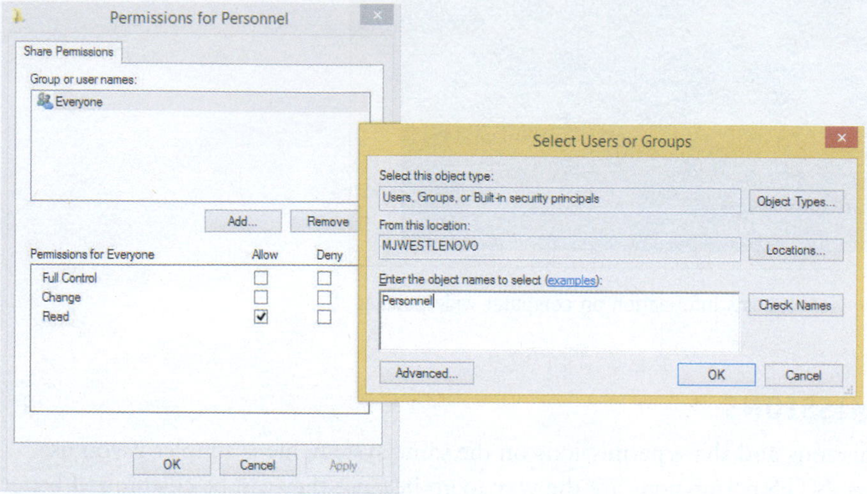

Figure 17-46 Add a user or user group to assign share permissions

4. To delete the Everyone group, select it in the Permissions box and click **Remove**. Click **OK** to close each open box in turn.

SUPPORT AND TROUBLESHOOT SHARED FOLDERS AND FILES

You have just seen how to set up user groups and folder permissions assigned to these groups. If you have problems accessing a shared resource, follow these steps:

1. Windows might be able to solve the problem for you. In Control Panel, click **Troubleshooting**. The Troubleshooting window presents a list of troubleshooters for addressing problems in the categories of Programs, Hardware and Sound, Network and Internet, or System and Security. Click **Access shared files and folders on other computers** and walk through the Shared Folders troubleshooter.
2. Open the Network and Sharing Center. Make sure your network location is set to Private (Home or Work for Windows 7).
3. In the left pane, click **Change advanced sharing settings**. The Advanced sharing settings window opens (see Figure 17-47).

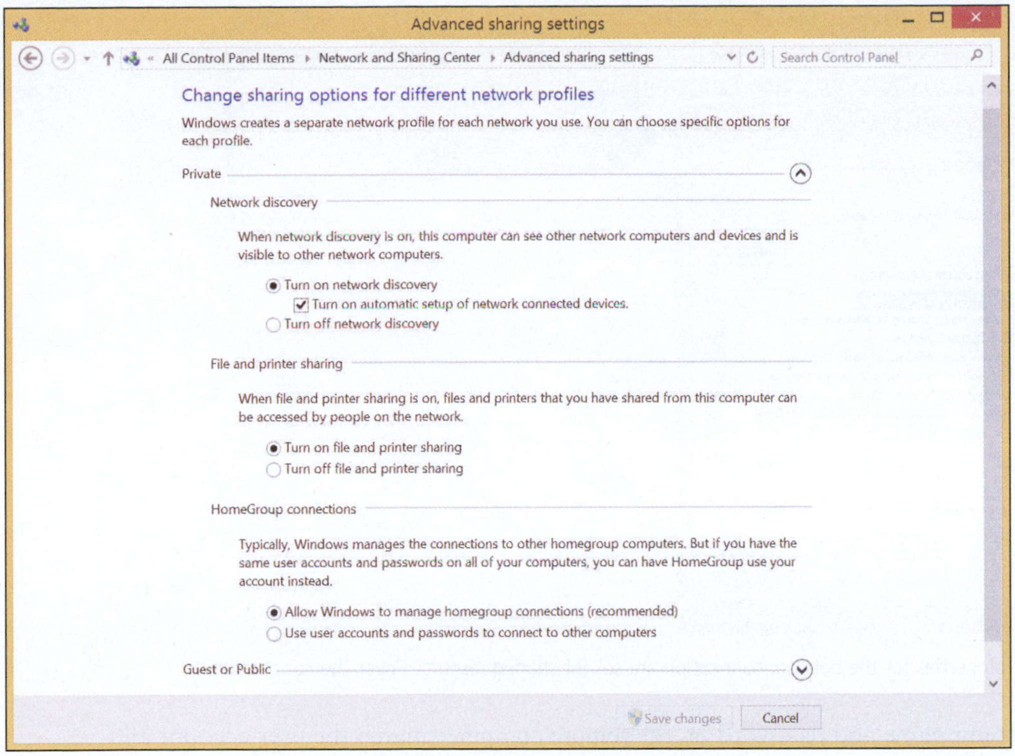

Figure 17-47 Use the Advanced sharing settings window to verify Windows is set to share resources

4. Verify the settings here are the default settings for a Private network profile:

- Select **Turn on network discovery** with **Turn on automatic setup of network connected devices** also checked.
- Select **Turn on file and printer sharing**.

> **★ A+ Exam Tip** The A+ 220-902 exam expects you to know the difference between a shared printer and a network printer. A printer installed locally on a computer can be shared with other computers. This is different than a network printer, which is accessed by each networked computer directly through the network.

- If you want Windows to handle access to Homegroup resources, under HomeGroup connections, select **Allow Windows to manage homegroup connections (recommended)**.

> **Notes** If you are using NTFS permissions along with less restrictive share permissions to share resources on a network, disable homegroup sharing, which can cause conflicts.

- If you want to share the Public folder to the network, under All Networks, in the Public folder sharing section, select **Turn on sharing so anyone with network access can read and write files in the Public folders.**
- If you want the added protection of requiring that all users on the network must have a valid user account and password on this computer, select **Turn on password protected sharing.**

After you have made your changes, click **Save changes** at the bottom of the window.

5. In the Network and Sharing Center, click **Change adapter settings**. Right-click the network connection icon, and select **Properties** in the shortcut menu. In the Properties box, verify that **File and Printer Sharing for Microsoft Networks** is checked (see Figure 17-48).

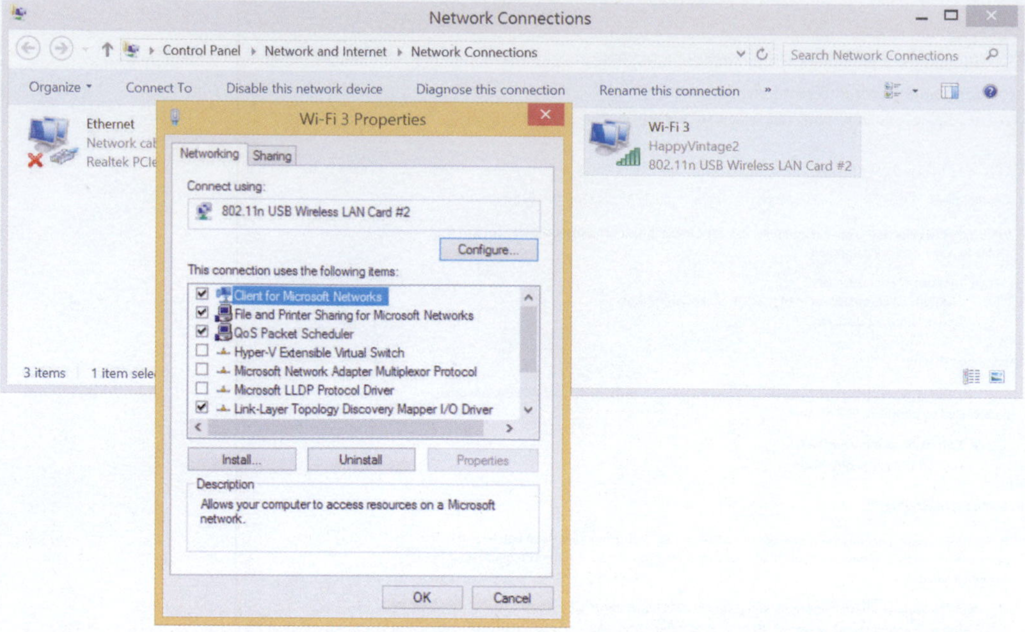

Figure 17-48 Verify the properties for the network connection are set for sharing resources over the connection

6. Verify the user account name and password on the remote computer match the user account and password on the host computer. If these accounts and passwords don't match, the user is considered an anonymous user and is denied access to resources shared on the remote computer.

Here are a few tips about managing shared folders and files:

- *Use advanced permissions settings.* If you need further control of the permissions assigned a user or group, click **Advanced** on the Security tab of a folder's Properties box. The Advanced Security Settings box appears (see Figure 17-49a). You can see that the Medical user group was given full control. To change these permission details, double-click the user group. In this example, the Medical group is being edited. The Permission Entry box opens. On Windows 8 systems only, click **Show advanced permissions** (see Figure 17-49b).

(a)

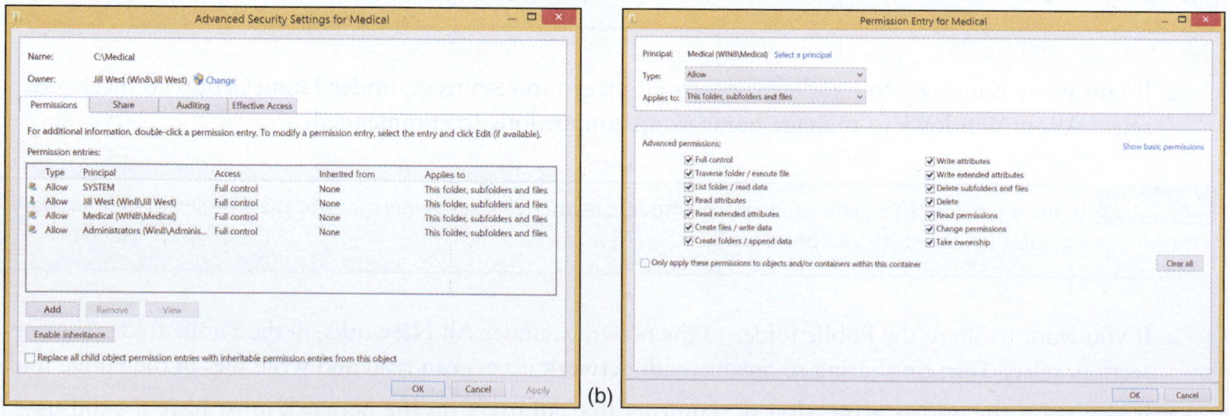

Figure 17-49 Advanced permissions settings

Detailed permissions can now be changed. Notice that the right to delete subfolders and files has been set to Deny, and the right to delete the folder itself has been set to Deny. Click **OK** to close each box. The resulting change means that users of the Medical group cannot delete or move a file or folder. (They can, however, copy the file or folder.)

★ A+ Exam Tip The A+ 220-902 exam expects you to be able to implement permissions so that a user can copy but not move a file or folder and understand how to apply Allow and Deny permissions.

- ***Manage permissions using the parent folder.*** When a subfolder is created, it is assigned the permissions of the parent folder. Recall that these inherited permissions appear dimmed, indicating they are inherited permissions. The best way to change inherited permissions is to change the permissions of the parent object. In other words, to change the permissions of the C:\Financial\QuickBooks folder, change the permission of the C:\Financial folder. Changing permissions of a parent folder affects all subfolders in that folder.
- ***Check the effective permissions.*** Permissions manually set for a subfolder or file can override inherited permissions. Permissions that are manually set are called explicit permissions. When a folder or file has inherited an explicit permission set, it might be confusing as to exactly which permissions are in effect. To know exactly which permissions for a file or folder are in effect, see the Advanced Security Settings box. (Look back at Figure 17-49a.) NTFS permissions are reported on the Permissions tab and share permissions are reported on the Share tab. Use the Effective Access tab (for Windows 7, the tab is called Effective Permissions) to get a detailed report of resources available to a particular user.
- ***Take ownership of a folder.*** The owner of a folder always has full permissions for the folder. If you are having a problem changing permissions and you are not the folder owner, try taking ownership of the folder. To do that, click **Advanced** on the Security tab of the folder's Properties box. The Advanced Security Settings box appears. Next to the name of the owner, click **Change**. The name of the new owner can then be entered (see Figure 17-50). Click **Check Names** to confirm the name is entered correctly and click **OK** twice.

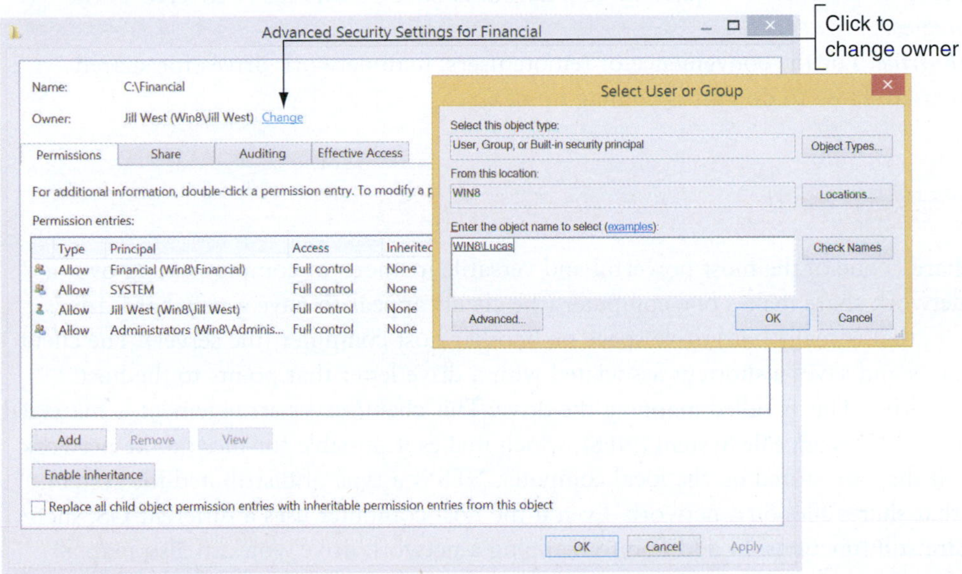

Figure 17-50 Change the owner of a folder

OS Differences For Windows 7, in the Advanced Security Settings box, click the **Owner** tab, then click **Edit.** The owner can then be edited. Select a user from the *Change owner to* list (see Figure 17-51) and click **Apply** to make that user the new owner. If a user is not listed, click **Other users or groups** and add the user. Close the Advanced Security Settings box and the Properties box, and reopen the Properties box for the change to take effect.

17

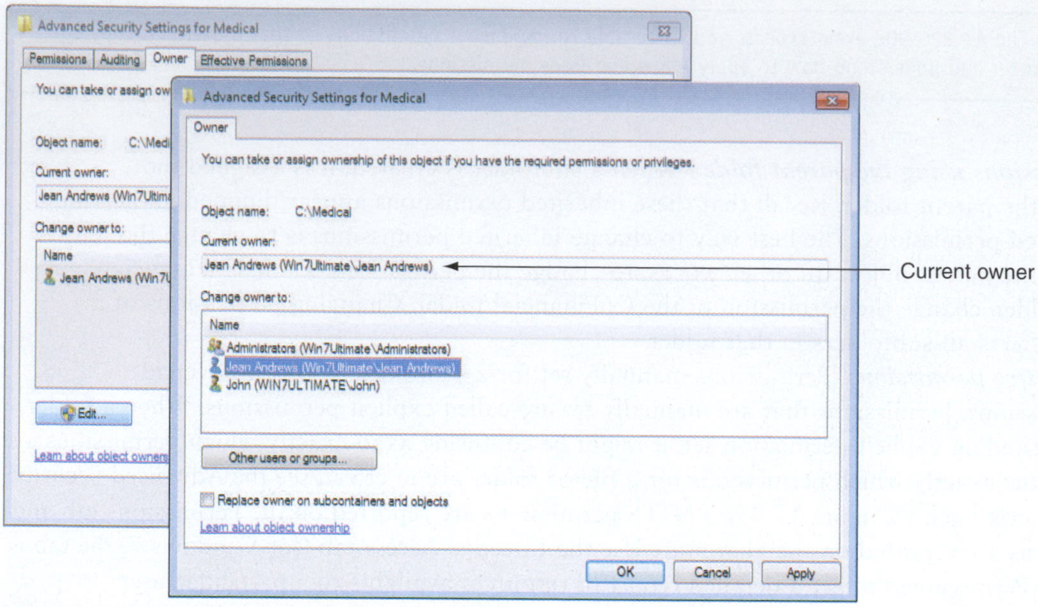

Figure 17-51 Change the owner of a folder in Windows 7

- ***Use only one workgroup.*** It is not necessary that all computers belong to the same workgroup in order to share resources. However, performance improves when they are all in the same workgroup.
- ***Require passwords for all user accounts.*** Don't forget that for best security, each user account needs a password. How to use Group Policy to require that all accounts have passwords is covered in the chapter, "Security Strategies."
- ***Use a mapped network drive.*** For the convenience of remote users, map network drives for shared folders that are heavily used. How to do that is coming up next.

HOW TO MAP A NETWORK DRIVE OR NETWORK PRINTER

A+
220-902
1.2, 1.6

A network share is one of the most powerful and versatile methods of communicating over a network. A network share makes one computer (the client) appear to have a new hard drive, such as drive E, that is really hard drive space on another host computer (the server). The client computer creates and saves a shortcut associated with a drive letter that points to the host computer's shared folder or drive. This is called mapping the drive. This client/server arrangement is managed by a Windows component, the Network File System (NFS), which makes it possible for files on the network to be accessed as easily as if they are stored on the local computer. NFS is a type of distributed file system (DFS), which is a system that shares files on a network. Even if the host computer uses a different OS, such as UNIX, the network share still functions. In addition to mapping a network drive, you can also map a network printer to a computer.

Notes A network-attached storage (NAS) device provides hard drive storage for computers on a network. Computers on the network can access this storage using a mapped network drive.

APPLYING | CONCEPTS MAP A NETWORK DRIVE AND NETWORK PRINTER

A+
220-902
1.6

To set up a network drive, follow these steps:

1. On the host computer, share the folder or entire volume to which you want others to have access.
2. On the remote computer that will use the network drive, open File Explorer. In the left pane, click **This PC**. At the top of the window, click the **Computer** tab and click **Map network drive**.

OS Differences On a remote computer running Windows 7, open Windows Explorer and press **Alt** to display the menu bar. Click the **Tools** menu and select **Map network drive**.

3. The Map Network Drive dialog box opens, as shown on the left side of Figure 17-52. Select a drive letter from the dropdown list.

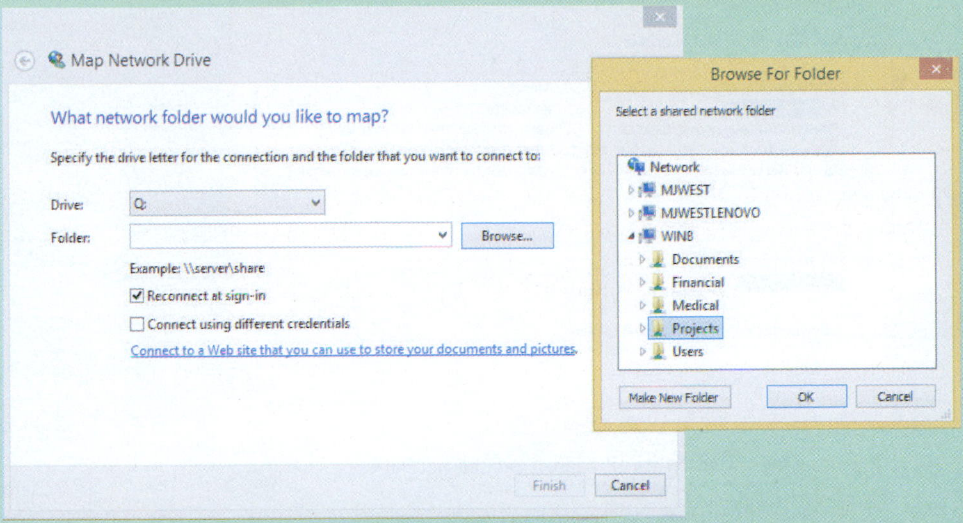

Figure 17-52 Mapping a network drive to a host computer

4. Click the **Browse** button and locate the shared folder or drive on the host computer (see the right side of Figure 17-52). Click **OK** to close the Browse For Folder dialog box, and click **Finish** to map the drive. The folder on the host computer now appears as one more drive in Explorer on your computer.

Notes When mapping a network drive, you can type the path to the host computer rather than clicking the Browse button to navigate to the host. To enter the path, in the Map Network Drive dialog box, use two backslashes, followed by the name of the host computer, followed by a backslash and the drive or folder to access on the host computer. For example, to access the Projects folder on the computer named Win8, enter **\\Win8\Projects** and then click **Finish**.

If a network drive does not work, go to the Network and Sharing Center, and verify that the network connection is good. You can also use the net use command to solve problems with mapped network drives. You learned about the net use command in the chapter, "Supporting Network Hardware."

Notes A host computer might be in sleep mode or powered down when a remote computer attempts to make a mapped drive connection at startup. To solve this problem, configure the host computer for Wake-on-LAN.

(continues)

Recall from the chapter, "Optimizing Windows," that you can connect a network printer to a server and the server can share the printer on the network. The Print Management console can be used to manage all shared printers on the network from a single workstation. You can also map a network printer directly to your computer, eliminating a print server or printer sharing from the process. Here's how:

1. Open **Control Panel** in Classic view and click **Devices and Printers**. Click **Add a printer** and select the printer available on the network (see Figure 17-53). Make sure you select a printer that shows its IP address; otherwise, you are connecting to a computer that has shared the printer to the network. If the printer doesn't show in the list, click **The printer that I want isn't listed**, and enter the name of the printer or its IP address, and click **Next**.

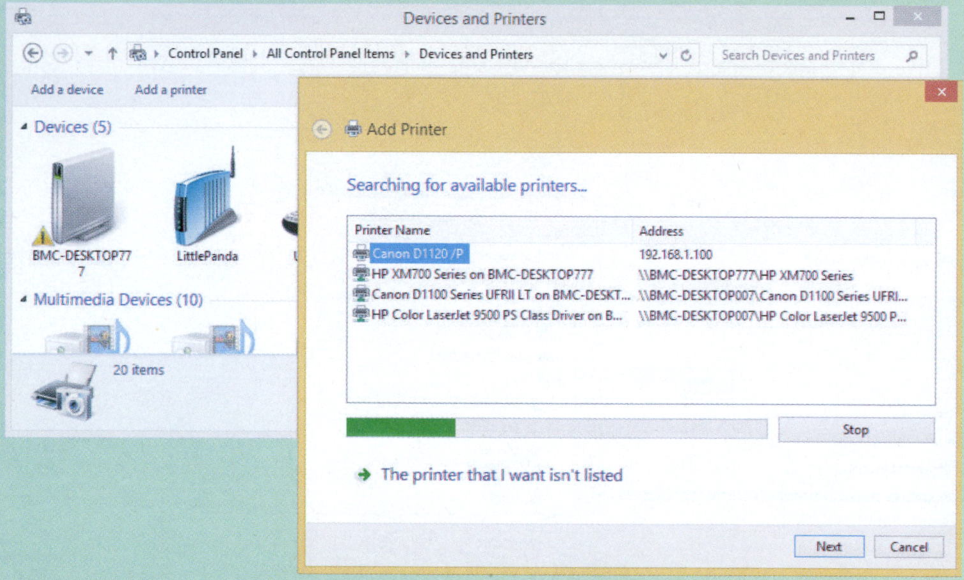

Figure 17-53 Select a network printer identified by its IP address on the network

2. Select and download the printer drivers if necessary. Click **Next**. You can choose whether to make this your default printer, then click **Finish**.

If you have problems mapping to a network printer, download the printer drivers from the website of the printer manufacturer and follow the manufacturer's directions to install the printer.

HIDDEN NETWORK RESOURCES AND ADMINISTRATIVE SHARES

A+ 220-902 1.6, 3.3

Sometimes your goal is to ensure that a folder or file is not accessible from the network or by other users, or is secretly shared on the network. When you need to protect confidential data from users on the network, you can do the following:

- *Disable File and Printer Sharing.* If no resources on the computer are shared, use the Network and Sharing Center to disable File and Printer Sharing for Microsoft Networks.
- *Hide a shared folder.* If you want to share a folder, but don't want others to see the shared folder in File Explorer or Windows Explorer, add a $ to the end of the share name in the Advanced Sharing box, as shown in Figure 17-54a. This shared and hidden folder is called a hidden share. Others on the network can access the folder only when they know its name. For example, if a folder's share name is Projects$ on the computer named Fileserver, in order to access the folder, a user must enter *Fileserver*\Projects$

in the Search box (see Figure 17-54b) on the remote computer and press **Enter**. The user on the remote computer can also search for the hidden share's location through the File Explorer or Windows Explorer Search box.

(a)
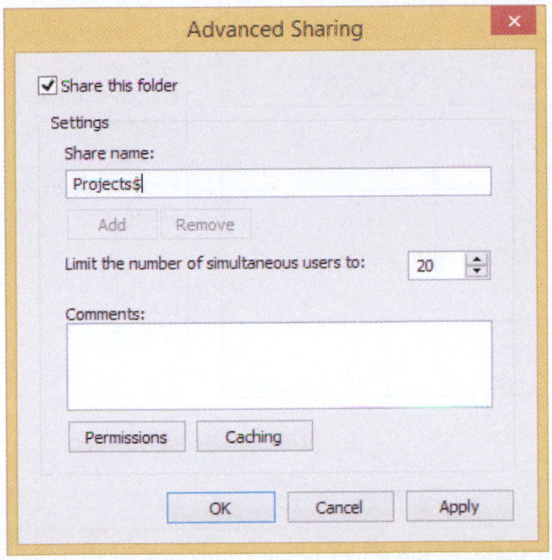

(b)
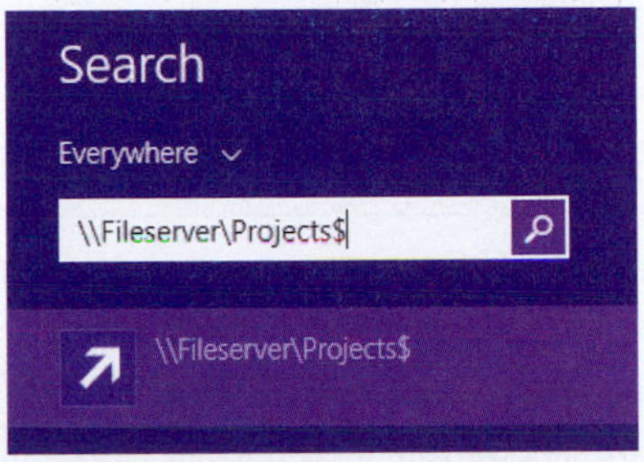

Figure 17-54 (a) A $ on the share name hides the share unless the exact name is used to locate it; (b) access a hidden, shared folder on the network by searching for its exact name

So far in this chapter, you have learned about folders and files on a computer that are shared with others on the network using local user accounts. These shares are called local shares. For computers that belong to a domain, you need to be aware of another way folders are shared, called administrative shares. Administrative shares are the folders that are shared by default that administrator accounts at the domain level can access. You don't need to manually share these folders because Windows automatically does so by default. Two types of administrative shares are:

- ***The %systemroot% folder.*** Enter the path ***computername*\admin$** to access the *%systemroot%* folder (most likely the C:\Windows folder) on a remote computer in order to work with that computer's system folders and files. For example, in Figure 17-55, the entry in the Explorer address bar is *\\MJWestLenovo\admin$*. Windows requests that the user authenticate with an administrator account to access this administrative share. The admin$ administrative share is called the Remote Admin share.

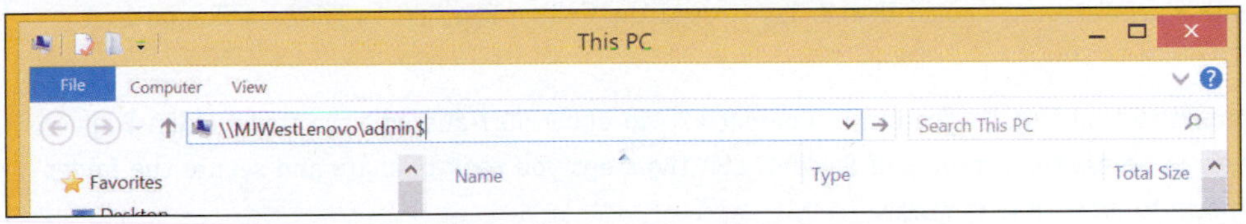

Figure 17-55 Access an administrative share on a domain

- ***Any volume or drive.*** To access the root level of any volume or drive on the network, enter the computer name and drive letter followed by a $, for example, \\MJWestLenovo\C$.

A+ Exam Tip The A+ 220-902 exam expects you to understand the difference between administrative shares and local shares.

Notes To see a list of all shares on a computer, open the **Computer Management** console and drill down to **System Tools**, **Shared Folders**, **Shares** (see Figure 17-56).

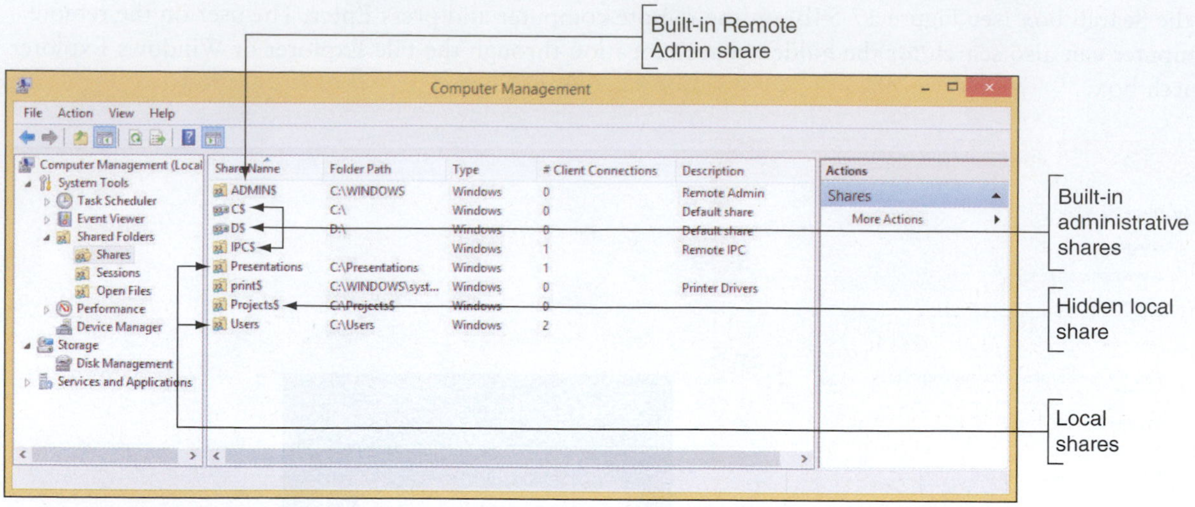

Figure 17-56 Use the Computer Management console to view all shares

> **Caution** When supporting a workgroup, you might be tempted to share all the drives on all computers so that you can have easy access remotely. However, to use local shares in this way is not a good security practice. Don't share the \Windows folder or an entire drive or volume on the network. These local shares appear in everyone's Explorer window. You don't want your system files and folders exposed like this.

Hands-On Project 17-4 Share and Secure a Folder

A+ 220-902 3.2, 3.3, 3.4

Using two computers networked together, do the following to practice sharing and securing folders using Windows:

1. Create a user account on Computer 1 named **User1**. In the My Documents folder for that account, create a folder named **Folder1**. Create a text file in the folder named **File1**. Edit the file and add the text **Golden Egg**.
2. On Computer 2, create a user account named **User2**. Try to read the Golden Egg text in File1 on Computer 1. What is the result?
3. Configure the computers so that User1 signed in to Computer2 can open File1 and edit the text Golden Egg, but User2 cannot view or access the contents of Folder1. List the steps you took to share and secure the folder and to test this scenario to make sure it works.
4. Now make the folder private so that it cannot be seen from Computer2 in File Explorer or Windows Explorer but it can be accessed if User1 knows the folder name. Describe how you did that.

CLOUD COMPUTING

A+ 220-902 2.3

At the beginning of this chapter, you learned about server resources available on a network, and throughout this chapter, you learned some ways of managing those resources. Not all of a network's resources reside on the local network. Cloud computing is when a third-party service or vendor makes computer resources available to its customers over the Internet. You've already learned about cloud storage services such as Dropbox, OneDrive, iCloud Drive, and Google Drive. Cloud computing can also provide many other types of resources, including applications, network services, websites, database servers, specialized developer applications, or even entire operating systems.

Regardless of the service provided, all cloud computing service models incorporate the following elements:

- *Service at any time.* On-demand service is available to users at any time. Cloud computing vendors often advertise uptime of their services, which is the percentage of time in any given year when their services were available online without disruption.
- *Elastic services and storage.* Rapid elasticity refers to the service's ability to be scaled up or down as the need level changes for a particular customer without requiring hardware changes that could be costly for the customer. Layers of services, such as applications, storage space, or number of users, can be added or removed upon request or automatically, depending upon the options made available by the service vendor.
- *Support for multiple client platforms.* Platform refers to the operating system, the runtime libraries or modules the OS provides to applications, and the hardware on which the OS runs. Cloud resources are made available to clients through standardized access methods that can be used with a variety of platforms, such as Windows, Linux, or Mac OS X, on any number of devices, such as desktops, laptops, tablets, and smart phones from various manufacturers.
- *Resource pooling and consolidation.* With resource pooling, services to multiple customers are hosted on shared physical resources, which are dynamically allocated to meet customer demand. Customers generally are not aware of where the physical devices providing cloud services are located geographically, which is called location independence.
- *Measured service.* Resources offered by a cloud computing vendor, such as storage, applications, bandwidth, and other services, are measured, or metered, for billing purposes and/or for the purpose of limiting any particular customer's use of that resource according to the service agreement. These measured services have reporting policies in place to ensure transparency between vendors and customers.

CLOUD COMPUTING CATEGORIES

A+
220-902
2.3

Cloud computing service models are categorized by the types of services they provide. The National Institute of Standards and Technology (NIST) has developed a standard definition for each category, which varies by the division of labor implemented. For example, as shown on the left side of Figure 17-57, an organization is traditionally responsible for their entire network, top to bottom. In this arrangement, the organization has its own network infrastructure devices, manages its own network services and data storage, and purchases licenses for its own operating systems and applications. The other three cloud computing service models illustrated in Figure 17-57 incrementally increase the amount of management responsibilities outsourced to cloud computing vendors. The following list describes these service models:

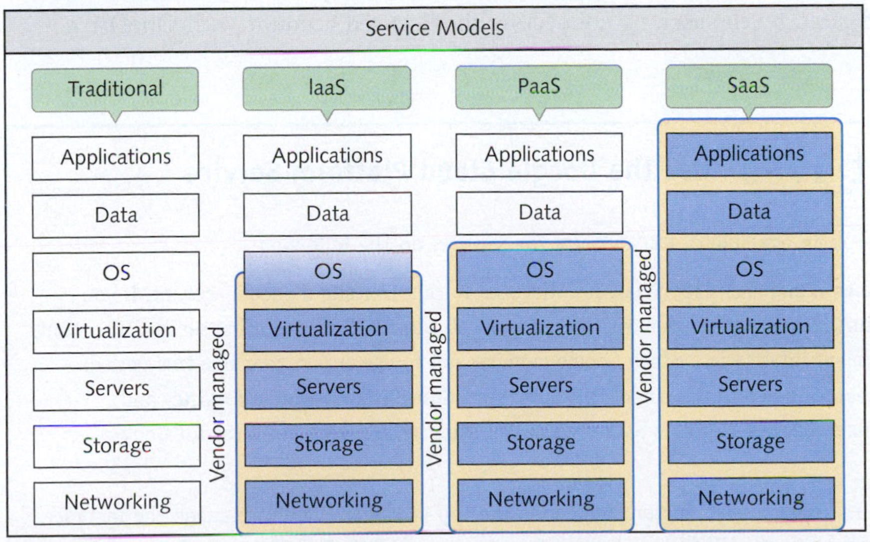

Figure 17-57 At each progressive level, the vendor takes over more computing responsibility for the customer

- *IaaS (Infrastructure as a Service).* With IaaS (Infrastructure as a Service), the customer rents hardware, including servers, storage, and networking, and can use these hardware services virtually. Customers are responsible for their own application installations, data management, and backup. In most situations, customers are also responsible for their own operating systems. For example, customers might install an OS on each virtual server provided by the vendor and use these servers to store data and host websites, email, DNS, or DHCP services, or install productivity software such as Microsoft Office for its employees. IaaS is ideal for fast-changing applications or to test software, or for startup businesses looking to save money by not having to invest in hardware. Examples of IaaS providers are Amazon Web Services (*aws.amazon.com*), Windows Azure (*azure.windows.com*), and Google Compute Engine (*cloud.google.com*).
- *PaaS (Platform as a Service).* With PaaS (Platform as a Service), a customer rents hardware, operating systems, and some applications that might support other applications the customer may install. PaaS is popular with software developers who require access to multiple platforms during the development process. A developer can build and test an application on a PaaS virtual machine made available over the web and then throw out the machine and start over with a new one with a few clicks in his browser window. Applications a PaaS vendor might provide to a developer are tailored to the specific needs of the project, such as an application to manage a database of test data. Examples of PaaS services include Google Cloud Platform and Microsoft Azure.
- *SaaS (Software as a Service).* With SaaS (Software as a Service), customers rent hardware, operating systems, and applications specific to the customer's needs. Applications are provided through an online user interface and are compatible with a multitude of devices and operating systems. Online email services, such as Gmail and Yahoo!, are good examples of SaaS. Google offers an entire suite of virtual software applications through Google Drive and their other embedded products. Except for the interface itself (the device and whatever browser software is required to access the website), the vendor provides every level of support from network infrastructure through data storage and application implementation.
- *XaaS (Anything as a Service or Everything as a Service).* In the XaaS (Anything as a Service or Everything as a Service) model, the "X" represents an unknown, just as it does in algebra. Here, the cloud can provide any combination of functions depending on a customer's exact needs.

Another SaaS implementation that doesn't quite fit the official definition of SaaS is rentable software, or software by subscription. Many companies are moving toward this subscription model, such as Adobe and Microsoft. When you buy an annual subscription to Office 365, for example, you must still install the software on your own computer, which means you must provide your own hardware, including a functioning OS. However, the downloadable software is available in formats that are compatible with multiple OSs, and the license provides for installation on multiple devices. This particular SaaS also includes built-in data storage, if desired by the user, by connecting the licensed account with OneDrive, a virtual data storage service.

Hands-On | Project 17-5 Use the Google Cloud Platform Service

A+
220-902
2.3

Google Cloud Platform is an example of PaaS. To use the service, do the following:

1. Go to **cloud.google.com** and click **Free Trial**. You will need to sign in using a Google account. If you don't have an account, you can create one with any valid email address. When you first set up an account, you must enter payment information, which Google promises not to use during your free trial period.
2. In the Developers Console, create a new project. Then drill down into **Compute**, **Compute Engine**, and **VM instances**. Create a VM instance of a Windows Server 2012 VM. Then wait several minutes for Google to create the instance.
3. Click the VM instances listed in your project. Buttons appear at the top of the window to manage the instance. Also note the External IP assigned to the VM instance. Click **Create or reset Windows password** and assign a

user name to your VM instance. Google Cloud assigns a password, which displays on screen (grayed out at the top of Figure 17-58).

4. Use the **mstsc** command to open Remote Desktop and remote in to your VM using its IP address, user name, and password. The lower window in Figure 17-58 shows the VM in a Remote Desktop Connection window. This Windows Server setup screen is the first screen that appears immediately after the first restart after installing Windows Server 2012.

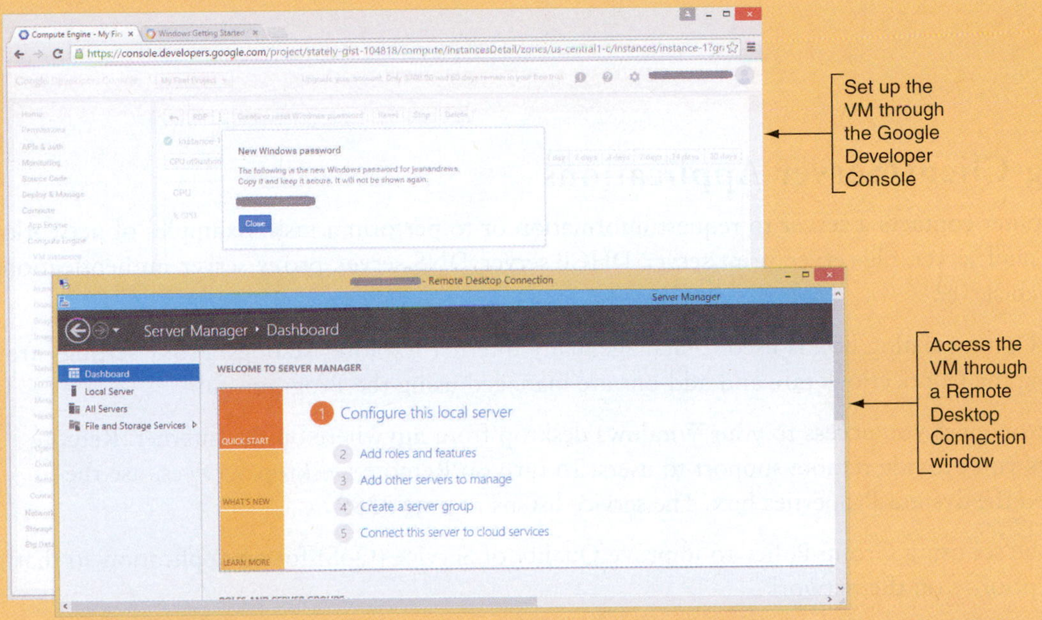

Source: Google, Inc.

Figure 17-58 Google Cloud Platform serves up a VM that has Windows Server 2012 installed

Notes You will use the Google Cloud Platform Service for another project in the chapter, "Virtualization, Linux, and Mac OS X." Do not disable your Google Cloud Platform account until after you have completed that project.

DEPLOYMENT MODELS FOR CLOUD COMPUTING

A+
220-902
2.3

Cloud computing services are delivered by a variety of deployment models, depending on who manages the cloud and who has access to it. The main deployment models you are likely to encounter are:

- *Public cloud.* In a public cloud, services are provided over the Internet to the general public. Google or Yahoo! email services are examples of public cloud deployment.
- *Private cloud.* In a private cloud, services are established on an organization's own servers, or established virtually for a single organization's private use. For example, an insurance company might have a centralized data center that provides cloud services in a private cloud to branch offices throughout the United States.
- *Community cloud.* In a community cloud, services are shared between multiple organizations, but not available publicly. Organizations with common interests, such as government regulatory requirements, might share resources in this way. For example, a medical database might be made accessible to all hospitals in a geographic area. In that case, the community cloud could be hosted internally by one or more of the organizations involved, or hosted by a third-party provider.

- *Hybrid cloud.* A hybrid cloud is a combination of public, private, and community clouds used by the same organization. For example, a company might store data in a private cloud, but use a public cloud email service.

In today's world, cloud computing is deeply integrated into nearly every user's experience of productivity or entertainment technology. With all its strengths and flexibility, privacy and security continue to be high-priority concerns when using cloud computing resources. You'll learn more about how to address security concerns in the chapter "Security Strategies."

>> CHAPTER SUMMARY

Supporting Client/Server Applications

- A client computer contacts a server to request information or to perform a task. Examples of network servers are a mail server, file server, print server, DHCP server, DNS server, proxy server, authentication server, and web server.
- The Internet Options dialog box is used to manage many Internet Explorer settings. Proxy settings are managed using the Connections tab, and add-ons are managed using the Programs tab.
- Remote Desktop gives you access to your Windows desktop from anywhere on the Internet. Remote Assistance lets you provide remote support to users. To turn on Remote Desktop Services, use the Remote tab on the System Properties box. The service listens at port 3389.
- A policy can be set using Group Policy to improve Quality of Service (QoS) for an application so that it gets a higher priority on the network.
- Open Database Connectivity (ODBC) can create a data source, which provides a remote database and its drivers to a client computer.

Controlling Access to Folders and Files

- Controlling access to folders and files on a network is done by assigning rights to user accounts and assigning permission to folders and files.
- Apply the principle of least privilege when assigning rights to users. You can change the rights an account has by adding it to or removing it from a user group.
- Customized user groups that you create make it easier to manage rights to multiple user accounts.
- Three ways to share files and folders on the network are to use homegroup sharing, workgroup sharing, and domain controllers. With workgroup sharing, you can use share permissions and/or NTFS permissions.
- A mapped network drive makes it easier for users to access drives and folders on the network.
- Peer-to-peer networks use local shares, and a Windows domain supports administrative shares. You can also hide network resources so that a user must know the name of the resource to access it.

Cloud Computing

- Cloud computing is providing computing resources over the Internet to customers.
- Cloud computing service models, including IaaS, PaaS, SaaS, and XaaS, are categorized by the types of services they provide and the degree that a third-party service or vendor is responsible for the resources.

- A public cloud service is available to the public, and a private cloud service is kept on an organization's own servers or made available by a vendor only for a single organization's private use. A community cloud is shared between multiple organizations, and a hybrid cloud is any combination of these service models.

>> KEY TERMS

For explanations of key terms, see the Glossary for this text.

ActiveX control
administrative share
Administrators group
anonymous users
Authenticated Users group
authentication server
Backup Operators group
cloud computing
community cloud
data source
Everyone group
file server
gpresult
Group Policy
Guests group
hidden share
hybrid cloud
IaaS (Infrastructure as a Service)
inherited permissions
Internet Options
local share
Local Users and Groups
location independence
mapping
measured service
mstsc (Microsoft Terminal Services Client)
name resolution
Network File System (NFS)
network share
NTFS permissions
on-demand
Open Database Connectivity (ODBC)
PaaS (Platform as a Service)
permission propagation
permissions
platform
Power Users group
principle of least privilege
print server
private cloud
proxy server
public cloud
rapid elasticity
Remote Admin share
Remote Assistance
Remote Desktop Connection (RDC)
resource pooling
SaaS (Software as a Service)
share permissions
subscription model
Users group
XaaS (Anything as a Service or Everything as a Service)

>> REVIEWING THE BASICS

1. If a computer is having trouble navigating to a website when you enter the URL into the browser's address box, but is able to access the site when you enter the web server's IP address, which server available to your network should you make sure is functioning correctly?
2. Which type of server can function as a firewall?
3. Which editions of Windows can be used to serve up Remote Desktop?
4. What is the listening port for Remote Desktop?
5. What type of file can a user send a technician in order to get help remotely, when using Remote Assistance?
6. What is the command to open the Group Policy console?
7. What folder in Windows is intended to be used for folders and files that all users of a computer share?
8. When using Control Panel to manage user accounts, what two types of user accounts can be configured?
9. What is the command to launch the Local Users and Groups Manager console?
10. Which type of user group provides backward compatibility with Windows XP?
11. Why doesn't the Properties box for a file have a Sharing tab?
12. When you view the Properties box for a folder, why might the Security tab be missing?

17

13. What type of permissions does a folder receive from its parent folder?

14. What type of permissions must be used on a FAT volume?

15. If a folder has 10 subfolders, what is the easiest way to change the permissions for all 10 folders?

16. If you are having a problem changing the permissions of a folder that was created by another user, what can you do to help solve the problem?

17. A shared folder whose share name ends with a $ is called a(n)____________________.

18. What command do you enter in the Explorer Search box to access the Remote Admin share on the computer named Fin?

19. What five elements define cloud computing services?

20. Gmail is an example of what type of cloud computing service model?

>> THINKING CRITICALLY

1. Your organization has set up three levels of data classification accessed by users on a small network:

- Low security: Data in the C:\Public folder.
- Medium security: Data in a shared folder that some, but not all, user groups can access.
- High security: Data in a shared and encrypted folder that requires a password to access. The folder is shared only to one user group.

Classify each of the sets of data:

a. Directions to the company Fourth of July party

b. Details of an invention made by the company president that has not yet been patented

c. Résumés presented by several people applying for a job with the company

d. Payroll spreadsheets

e. Job openings at the company

2. You work in the Accounting Department and have been using a network drive to post Excel workbook files to your file server as you complete them. When you attempt to save a workbook file to the drive, you see the error message: "You do not have access to the folder 'J:\'. See your administrator for access to this folder." What should you do first? Second? Explain the reasoning behind your choices.

a. Ask your network administrator to give you permission to access the folder.

b. Check File Explorer to verify that you can connect to the network.

c. Save the workbook file to your hard drive.

d. Using File Explorer, remap the network drive.

e. Reboot your computer.

>> REAL PROBLEMS, REAL SOLUTIONS

REAL PROBLEM 17-1 Implementing More Security for Remote Desktop

When Jacob travels on company business, he finds it's a great help to be able to access his office computer from anywhere on the road using Remote Desktop. However, he wants to make sure his office computer as well as the entire corporate network are as safe as possible. One way you can help Jacob add more security is to change the port that Remote Desktop uses. Knowledgeable hackers know that Remote Desktop uses port 3389, but if you change this port to a secret port, hackers are less likely to find the open port. Search the Microsoft Knowledge Base articles (*support.microsoft.com* and *technet.microsoft.com*) for a way to change the port that Remote Desktop uses. Practice implementing this change by doing the following:

1. Set up Remote Desktop on a computer using Windows 8 Professional or Windows 7 Professional or Ultimate. This computer is your host computer. Use another computer (the client computer) to create a Remote Desktop session to the host computer. Verify the session works by transferring files in both directions.
2. Next, change the port that Remote Desktop uses on the host computer to a secret port. Print a screen shot showing how you made the change. Use the client computer to create a Remote Desktop session to the host computer using the secret port. Print a screen shot showing how you made the connection using the secret port. Verify the session works by transferring files in both directions.
3. What secret port did you use? What two or more Microsoft Knowledge Base Articles gave you the information you needed?

REAL PROBLEM 17-2 Using Chrome Remote Desktop

Chrome Remote Desktop by Google lets users sign in to remote computers through a Chrome browser. This blend of cloud computing technology and remote desktop access can be handy when you need to support computers that use operating systems other than Windows. Complete the following steps to install and use Chrome Remote Desktop:

1. On Computer 1, download and install Google Chrome, and sign in. Then add the Chrome Remote Desktop add-in.
2. Configure Chrome Remote Desktop to allow access to your computer over the Internet. Run the Chrome Remote Desktop Host Installer after it is downloaded. Be sure to record your PIN in a safe place.
3. On Computer 2, download and install Google Chrome, and sign in. Then add the Chrome Remote Desktop add-in.
4. Configure Chrome Remote Desktop to allow access to your computer over the Internet. Run the Chrome Remote Desktop Host Installer after it is downloaded. Be sure to record your PIN in a safe place.
5. Use Chrome Remote Desktop to create a remote connection to Computer 2. Can you use the utility to view the desktop of Computer 2? Can you control Computer 2 from Computer 1? Can you control Computer 2 directly from its own desktop? What options are available from the Remote Desktop menu on Computer 1?
6. What other operating systems will Chrome Remote Desktop work with?
7. List three reasons why a user might find Chrome Remote Desktop useful. Be sure to consider the advantages of using it with Google Cloud Platform.

CHAPTER

18

Security Strategies

After completing this chapter, you will be able to:

- Secure a Windows personal computer
- Secure a mobile device
- Implement additional security techniques to protect a computer or SOHO network and its resources
- Recognize, remove, and protect personal computers against malicious software
- Recognize, remove, and protect mobile devices against malicious software
- Follow company policies to address issues of software copyright infringement and violations of prohibited content or activities

In the chapter, "Windows Resources on a Network," you learned the concepts and principles of classifying users and data and protecting that data by applying appropriate permissions to the data so that only the authorized users can access it. In this chapter, you learn about additional tools and techniques to secure the resources on a personal computer, mobile device, and small network. You also learn how to recognize that a personal computer or mobile device is infected with malware and how to clean an infected system and keep it clean. Finally, you learn about how your employer might expect you to deal with issues of software copyright infringement and when company policies are violated regarding prohibited content and activities.

This chapter gives you the basics of securing a personal computer, mobile device, or small network. Later in your career as a support technician, you can build on the skills of this chapter to implement even more security such as controlling how Windows stores its passwords. However, keep in mind that even the best security will eventually fail. As a thief once said, "Locks are for honest people," and a thief will eventually find a way to break through. Security experts tell us that security measures basically make it more difficult and time consuming for a thief to break through so that she gets discouraged and moves on to easier targets.

SECURING A WINDOWS PERSONAL COMPUTER

A+
220-902
1.1, 1.4,
1.5, 1.6,
3.2, 3.3,
3.4

When you have a choice in the security measures that you use, keep in mind two goals, which are sometimes in conflict. One goal is to protect resources, and the other goal is to not interfere with the functions of the system. A computer or network can be so protected that no one can use it, or so accessible that anyone can do whatever they want with it. The trick is to provide enough security to protect resources while still allowing users to work unhindered (Figure 18-1). Also, too much security can sometimes force workers to find insecure alternatives. For example, if you require users to change their passwords weekly, more of them might start writing their passwords down to help remember them.

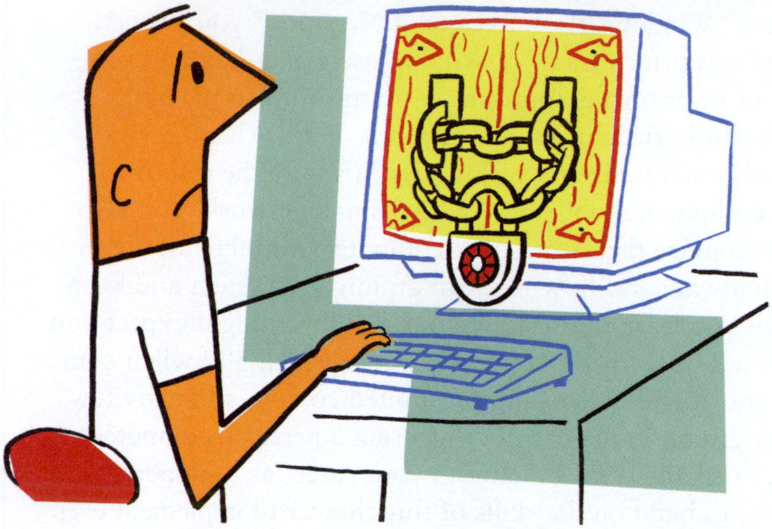

© Phil Marden/Getty Images

Figure 18-1 Security measures should protect resources without hindering how users work

Notes The best protection against attacks is layered protection. If one security method fails, the next might stop an attacker. When securing a workstation, use as many layers of protection as is reasonable for the situation and are justified by the value of the resources you are protecting.

USE WINDOWS TO AUTHENTICATE USERS

A+
220-902
3.4

Recall from the chapter, "Windows Resources on a Network," that controlling access to computer resources is done by authenticating and authorizing a user or process. A user is authenticated when he proves he is who he says he is. Recall that when a computer is on a Windows domain, the domain is responsible for authentication. For a peer-to-peer network, authentication must happen at the local computer. Normally, Windows authenticates a user with a Windows password.

As an administrator, when you first create an account, be sure to assign a password to that account. It's best to give the user the ability to change the password at any time. As an administrator, you can control how a user signs in, require a workstation be locked when the user steps away, disable the guest account, and reset a password if a user forgets it. Now let's see how to do all these chores to bring added security to a Windows computer.

REQUIRE SECURE SIGN-IN

Normally, when a computer is first booted or comes back from a sleep state, Windows displays a lock screen that can be dismissed by pressing a key on the keyboard or clicking anywhere on the screen, which then takes the user to the sign-in screen showing all active user accounts (see Figure 18-2). From here, a user clicks his account name and enters his password. Malware can sometimes display a false sign-in screen to trick users into providing user account passwords. A more secure method of sign in, called secure sign in or secure logon, requires the user to press **Ctrl+Alt+Delete** to get to a sign-in screen.

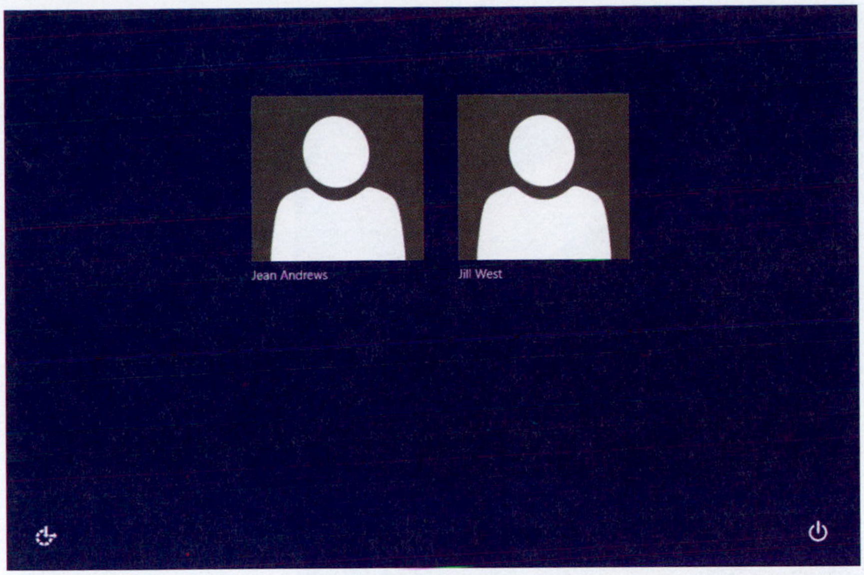

Figure 18-2 Windows 8 sign-in screen

The User Accounts utility (netplwiz.exe), also called the Network Places Wizard, can be used to change the way Windows sign-in works:

1. Enter the **netplwiz** command in the Windows 8 Run box or the Windows 7 Search box and respond to the UAC box. On the Users tab (see Figure 18-3a), you can add and remove users, change the user groups a user is in, and reset a password.
2. Click the **Advanced** tab (see Figure 18-3b). Check **Require users to press Ctrl+Alt+Delete**. Click **Apply** and close the box.

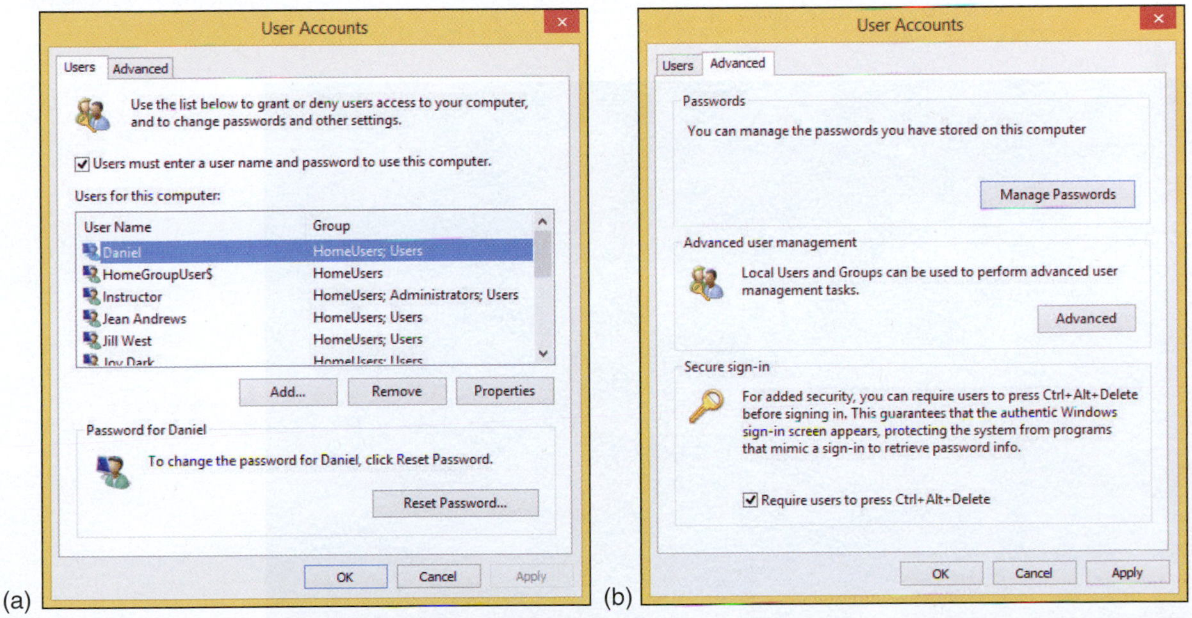

Figure 18-3 Change the way users sign in to Windows

When Ctrl+Alt+Delete is required, the lock screen looks like that shown in Figure 18-4. When a user presses Ctrl+Alt+Delete, the Windows sign-in screen that appears has not been known to be intercepted by malware.

18

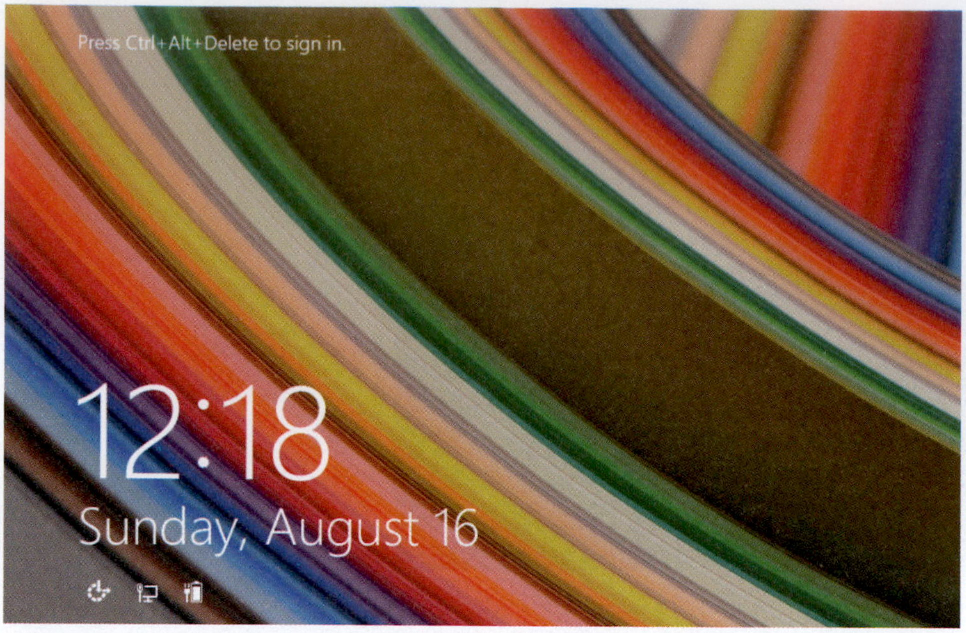

Figure 18-4 Windows 8 lock screen after the boot or returning from sleep state

LOCK A WORKSTATION

To keep a system secure, users need to practice the habit of locking down their workstation each time they step away from their desks. The quickest way to do this is to press **Win+L**. Another method is to press **Ctrl+Alt+Delete**. If the user is already signed in when she presses these keys, the security screen in Figure 18-5 appears. When the user clicks **Lock** (*Lock this computer* in Windows 7), Windows locks down. To unlock Windows, the user must enter her password. For this method to be effective, all user accounts need a password. Later in the chapter, you learn to use Group Policy to make passwords a requirement.

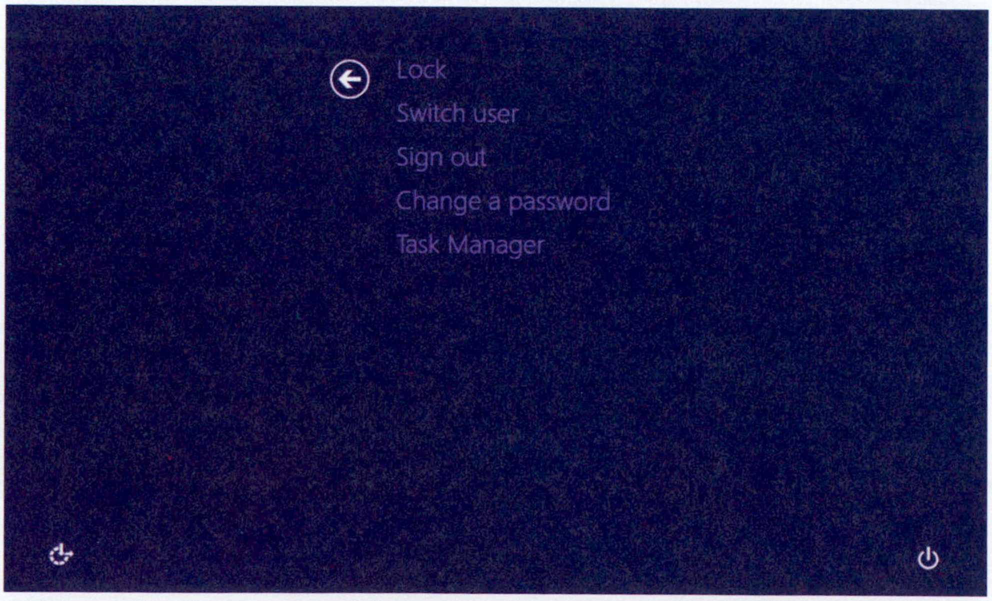

Figure 18-5 Screen that appears when a signed-in user presses Ctrl+Alt+Delete

APPLYING | CONCEPTS REQUIRE A PASSWORD TO WAKE A COMPUTER

A+
220-902
3.4

An unauthorized user might get access to a system when you step away from your workstation and forget to lock it. To better secure the workstation, you can activate the screen saver (turn off the display) after a short period of inactivity and require a password be used to turn on the display and wake up the computer. Follow these steps:

1. In Control Panel, click **Power Options**.
2. In the Power Options window (see Figure 18-6), set the power options so that the computer goes to sleep after a short period of inactivity. Also, in the Power Options window, click **Require a password on wakeup**.

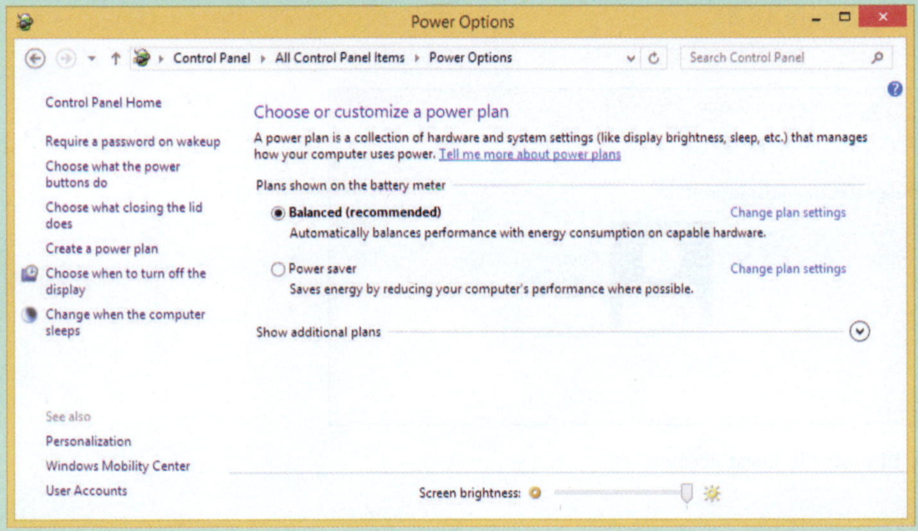

Figure 18-6 Windows power options available on the Power Options window to help lock down a workstation

3. In the System Settings window that appears, make sure **Require a password (recommended)** is selected (see Figure 18-7). If you need to change this setting, first click **Change settings that are currently unavailable.** Save your changes and close all windows.

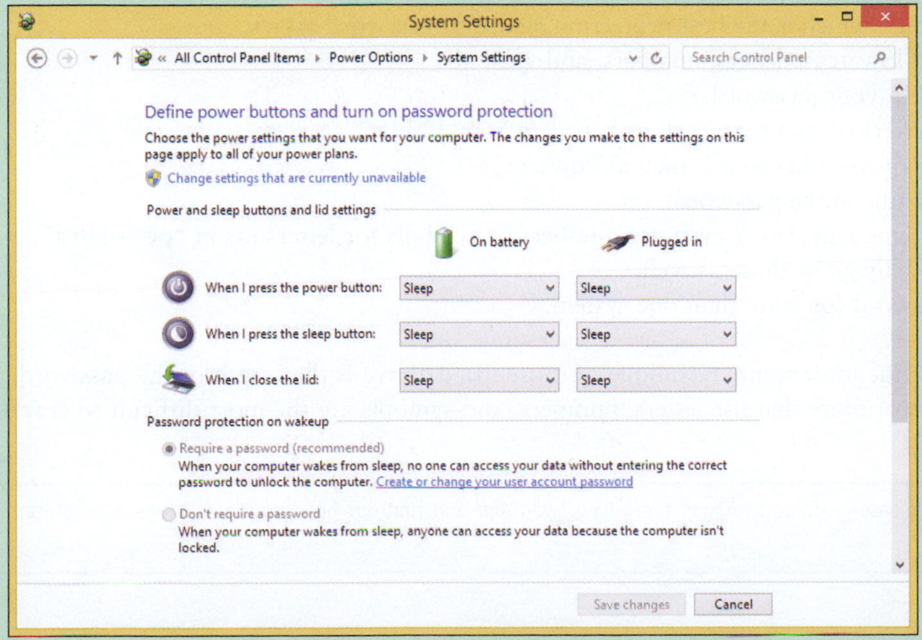

Figure 18-7 Require a password when the computer wakes up

18

Notes A user might forget a password and, as an administrator, you can reset the password. However, know that resetting a password locks the user out from encrypted files, email, or personal certificates saved on the computer and from using Internet or network passwords stored on the computer. For business editions of Windows, use the **Local Users and Groups** (lusrmgr.msc) utility to reset a password. For all editions of Windows, use the **netplwiz** command or Control Panel.

DISABLE THE GUEST ACCOUNT

The Guest account is disabled by default and should remain disabled. If you want to set up an account for visitors, create a standard account and name it Visitor. To make sure the Guest account is disabled, open **Control Panel** in Classic view, click **User Accounts**, and then click **Manage another account**. Respond to the UAC if necessary. In the list of accounts, verify the Guest account is turned off. If it is not, click it and click **Turn off the guest account** (see Figure 18-8).

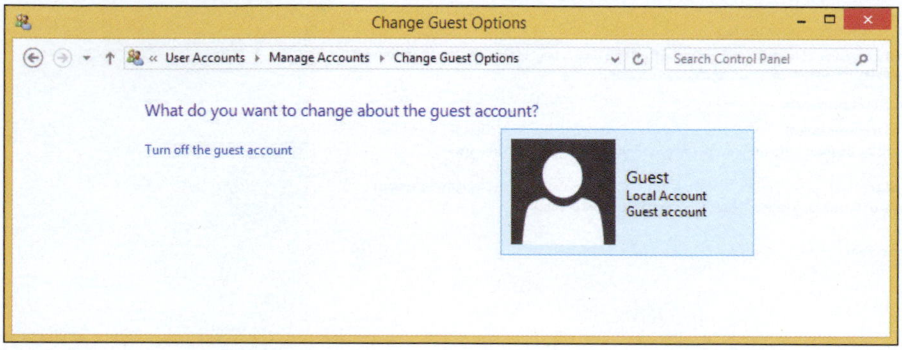

Figure 18-8 For best security, turn off the Guest account

CREATE STRONG PASSWORDS

A password needs to be a **strong password**, which means it should not be easy to guess either by humans or by computer programs using various methods, including a simple **brute force attack**, which tries every single combination of characters until it discovers your password.

A strong password, such as *y*3Q1693pEWJaTz1!*, meets all of the following criteria:

- Use 16 or more characters, which is the best protection against a password attack.
- Combine uppercase and lowercase letters, numbers, and symbols.
- Use at least one symbol in your password.
- Don't use consecutive letters or numbers, such as "abcdefg" or "12345."
- Don't use adjacent keys on your keyboard, such as "qwerty."
- Don't use your sign-in name in the password.
- Don't use words in any language. Don't even use numbers or symbols for letters (as in "p@ssw0rd") because programs can easily guess those as well.
- Don't use the same password for more than one system.

Studies have proven that the most secure technique of those listed above is the length of the password. Passwords of 16 characters or more that use letters, numbers, and symbols are the most difficult to crack.

Notes How secure is your password? Go to *howsecureismypassword.net* and find out how long it will take a computer to crack your password.

In some situations, a blank Windows password might be more secure than an easy-to-guess password such as "1234." That's because you cannot authenticate to a Windows computer from a remote computer unless the user account has a password. A criminal might be able to guess an easy password and authenticate remotely. For this reason, if your computer is always sitting in a protected room such as your home office and you don't intend to access it remotely, you might choose to use no password. However, if you travel with a laptop, always use a strong password.

Although it's not recommended you write your password down, if you do write it down, keep it in as safe a place as you would the data you are protecting. Don't send your passwords over email or chat. Change your passwords regularly, and don't type your passwords on a public computer. For example, computers in hotel lobbies or Internet cafés should only be used for web browsing—not for signing in to your email account or online banking account. These computers might be running keystroke-logging software put there by criminals to record each keystroke. Several years ago, while on vacation, I entered credit card information on a computer in a hotel lobby in a foreign country. Months later, I was still protesting $2 or $3 charges to my credit card from that country. Trust me. Don't do it—I speak from experience.

Hands-On | Project 18-1 Explore Password Management Software

Password management software, also called password vault software, such as KeePass (*keepass.info*), LastPass (*lastpass.com*), and Dashlane (*dashlane.com*), can hold your passwords safely so that you don't forget them or have to write them down. Choose two of these programs and a third of your own selection that interests you, then answer the following questions about each one:

1. Which platforms are supported?
2. Which web browsers are supported?
3. From how many competitors can the program import passwords?
4. What types of authentication are supported (e.g., master password, fingerprint, etc.)?
5. Where are the passwords stored? Are they synced across devices? How is the information protected?
6. What are some of the differences between the free edition of each program and the paid versions?
7. What happens to the user's account if the user dies or is otherwise incapacitated?

FILE AND FOLDER ENCRYPTION

18

A+
220-902
3.3

In Windows, files and folders can be encrypted using the Windows Encrypted File System (EFS). This encryption works only with the NTFS file system and business and professional editions of Windows. If a folder is marked for encryption, every file created in the folder or copied to the folder will be encrypted. An encrypted file remains encrypted if you move it from an encrypted folder to an unencrypted folder on the same or another NTFS volume. To encrypt a folder or file, right-click it and open its Properties box (see Figure 18-9). On the General tab, click **Advanced.** In the Advanced Attributes box, check **Encrypt contents to secure data** and click **OK.** In File Explorer or Windows Explorer, encrypted file and folder names are displayed in green.

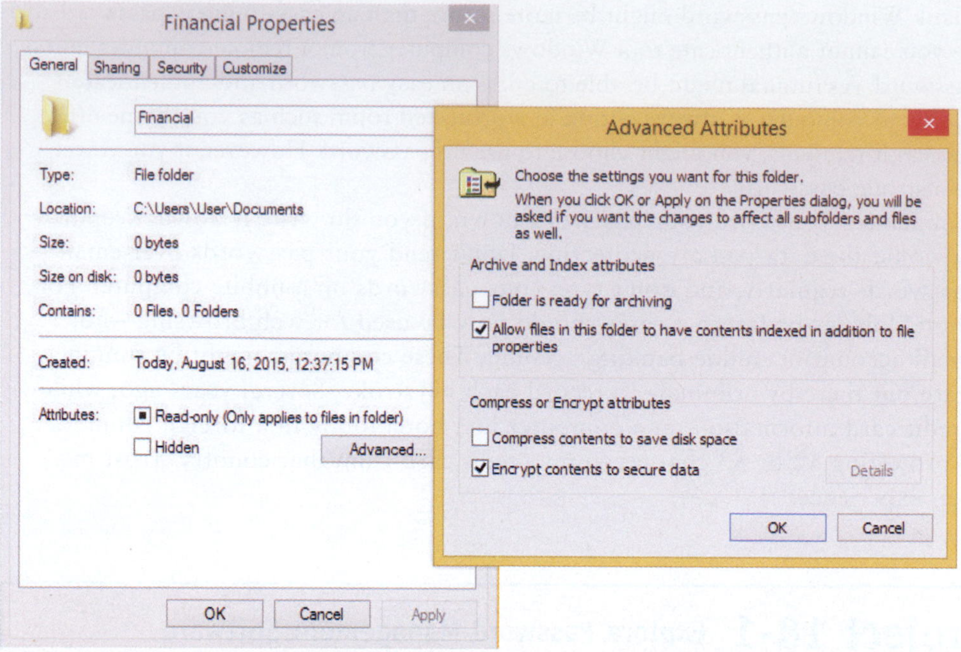

Figure 18-9 Encrypt a folder and all its contents

WINDOWS FIREWALL SETTINGS

A+ 220-902 1.1, 1.5, 1.6, 3.2, 3.4

Recall from the chapter, "Connecting To and Setting Up a Network," that a SOHO router can serve as a hardware firewall to protect its network from attack over the Internet. Recall that the best protection from attack is layered protection (see Figure 18-10). In addition to a network hardware firewall, a large corporation might use a software firewall, also called a corporate firewall, installed on a computer that stands between the Internet and the network to protect the network. This computer has two network cards installed, and the installed software firewall filters the traffic between the two cards.

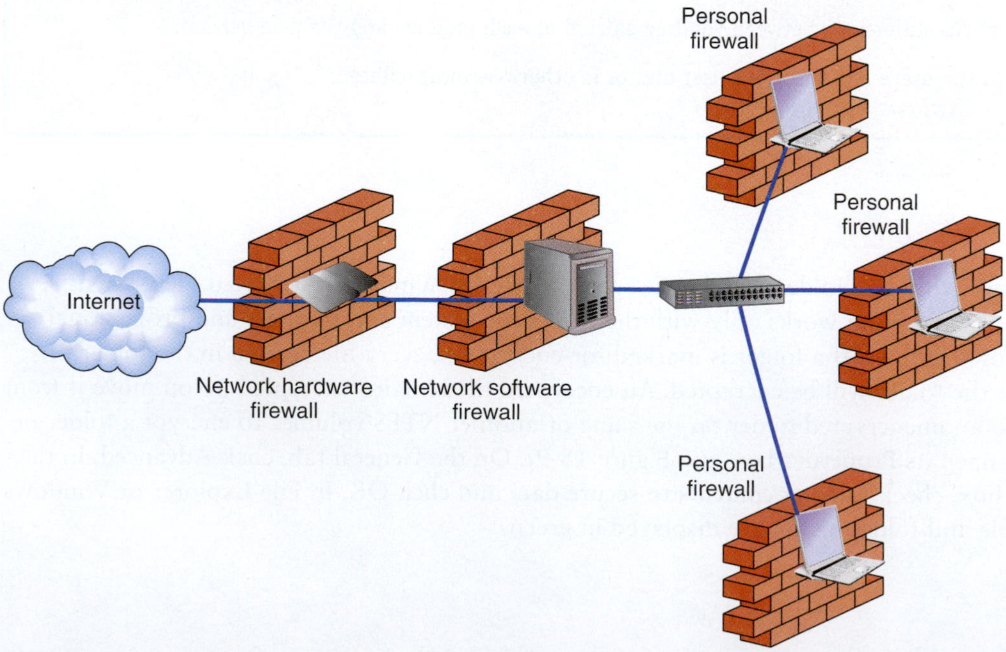

Figure 18-10 Three types of firewalls used to protect a network and individual computers on the network

A personal firewall, also called a host firewall or application firewall, is software installed on a personal computer to protect this computer. A personal firewall provides redundant protection from attacks over the Internet and also filters inbound traffic to protect a computer from attack from other computers on the same network and filters outbound traffic to prevent attacks on other computers on the same network. When setting up a SOHO network or a personal computer, configure a personal firewall on each computer.

Windows Firewall is a personal firewall that protects a computer from intrusion and from attacking other computers, and is automatically configured when you set up your security level for a new network connection. (Recall that, for Windows 8, the options are private and public security, and for Windows 7, the options are home, work, and public security.) However, you might want to customize these settings. For example, recall from the chapter, "Windows Resources on a Network," that you customized Windows Firewall to allow access through Remote Desktop connections.

APPLYING | CONCEPTS CONFIGURE WINDOWS FIREWALL

A+
220-902
1.1, 1.5,
1.6, 3.2,
3.4

Follow these steps to find out how to configure Windows Firewall:

1. Use one of these methods to open Windows Firewall:
   - Open the **Network and Sharing Center** and in the lower part of the left pane, click **Windows Firewall**.
   - In Control Panel in Classic view, click **Windows Firewall**.

   The Windows Firewall window is shown in Figure 18-11.

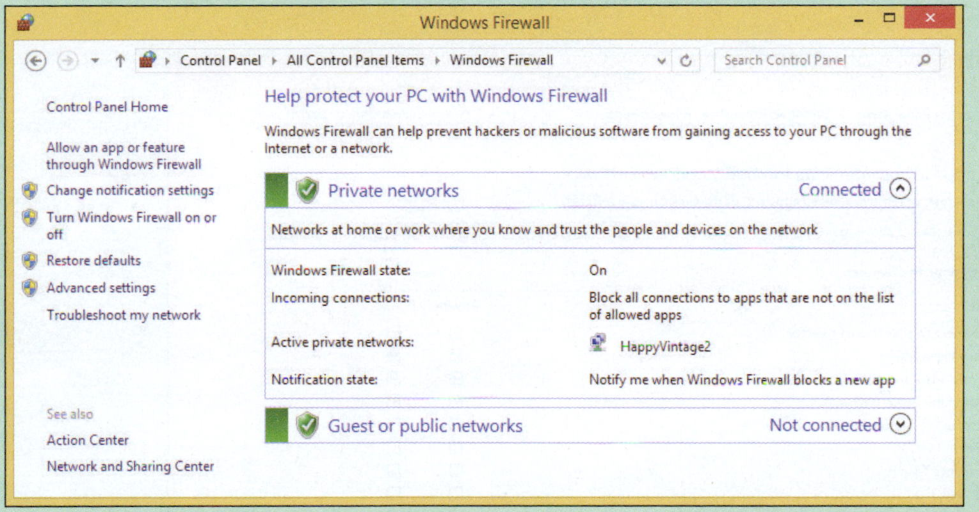

Figure 18-11 Windows Firewall shows the computer currently connected to a private network

2. To control firewall settings for each type of network location, click **Turn Windows Firewall on or off** in the left pane. Windows Firewall's Customize Settings window appears (see Figure 18-12). Notice in the figure Windows Firewall is turned on for each type of network location.

(continues)

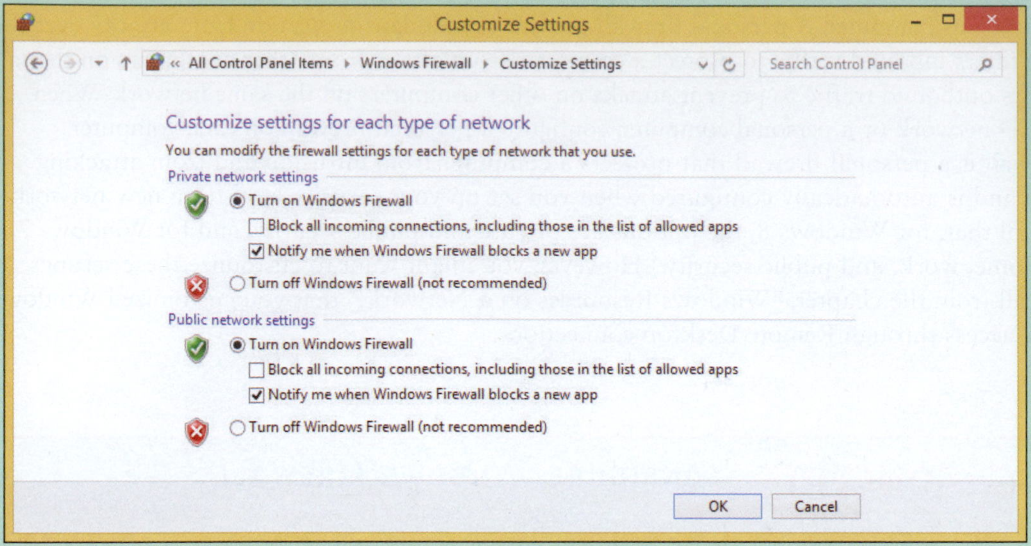

Figure 18-12 Customize settings for a private or public network

3. To allow no exceptions through the firewall on a private network (such as a home or work network) or public network, check **Block all incoming connections, including those in the list of allowed apps.** After you have made your changes, click **OK.**

4. You can allow an exception to your firewall rules. To change the programs allowed through the firewall, in the Windows Firewall window shown in Figure 18-11, click **Allow an app or feature through Windows Firewall.** The Allowed apps window appears (see Figure 18-13).

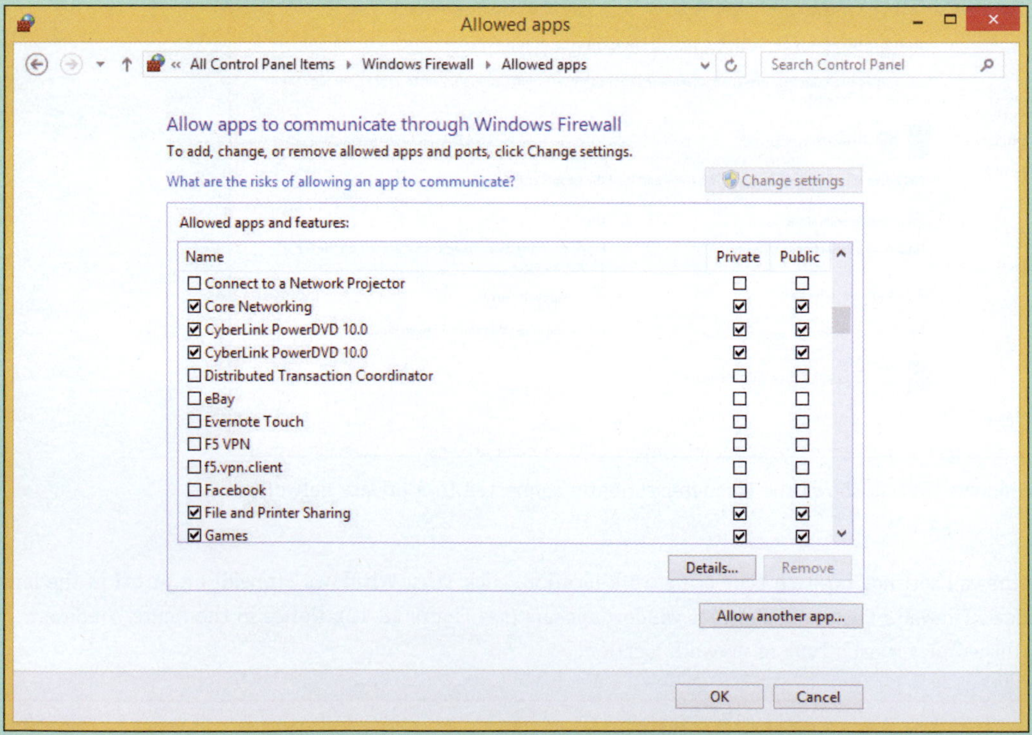

Figure 18-13 Allow programs to communicate through Windows Firewall

5. Find the program you want to allow to initiate a connection from a remote computer to this computer. In the right side of the window, click either **Private** or **Public** to indicate which type of network location the program is allowed to use. If you don't see your program in the list, click **Allow another app** to see more programs or to add your own. (If the option is gray, click **Change settings** to enable it.) When you are finished making changes, click **OK** to return to the Windows Firewall window.

6. For even more control over firewall settings, in the Windows Firewall window (refer back to Figure 18-11), click **Advanced settings**. The Windows Firewall with Advanced Security window opens. In the left pane, select Inbound Rules or Outbound Rules. A list of programs appears. Right-click a program and select **Properties** from the shortcut menu. Using the Properties box, you have full control of how exceptions work to get through the firewall, including which users, protocols, ports, and remote computers can use it (see Figure 18-14).

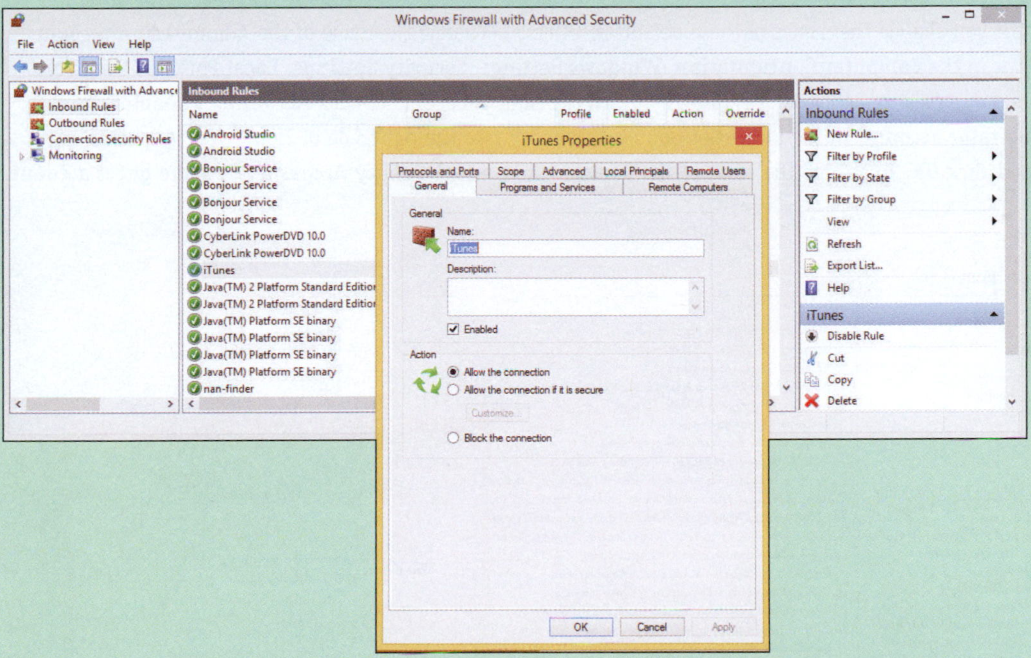

Figure 18-14 Use advanced settings to control exactly how a program can get through Windows Firewall

OS Differences In Vista, you can allow exceptions to Windows Firewall only by program name or port number.

LOCAL SECURITY POLICIES USING GROUP POLICY

A+ 220-902 1.4, 3.4

Recall from the chapter, "Windows Resources on a Network," that the Group Policy utility controls what users can do with a system and how the system is used and is available with business and professional editions of Windows. Using Group Policy, you can set security policies to help secure a workstation. For example, you can set policies to require all users to have passwords and to rename default user accounts.

APPLYING | CONCEPTS APPLY LOCAL SECURITY POLICIES

A+
220-902
1.4, 3.4

Follow these steps to set a few important security policies on the local computer:

1. Sign in to Windows using an administrator account on a system using Windows 8/8.1 Professional or Enterprise, or Windows 7 Professional, Ultimate, or Enterprise.
2. To start Group Policy, use the **gpedit.msc** command in the Windows 8 Run box or in the Windows 7 Search box. The Local Group Policy Editor console opens.
3. To change a policy, first use the left pane to drill down into the appropriate policy group and then use the right pane to view and edit a policy. Here are important security policies you might want to change:

   - ***Change default user names.*** A hacker is less likely to hack into the built-in Administrator account or Guest account if you change the names of these default accounts. To change the name of the Administrator account, drill down in the **Computer Configuration**, **Windows Settings**, **Security Settings**, **Local Policies, Security Options** group (see the left side of Figure 18-15). In the right pane, double-click **Accounts: Rename administrator account.** In the Properties box for this policy (see the right side of Figure 18-15), change the name and click **OK.** To change the name of the Guest account, use the policy **Accounts: Rename guest account.**

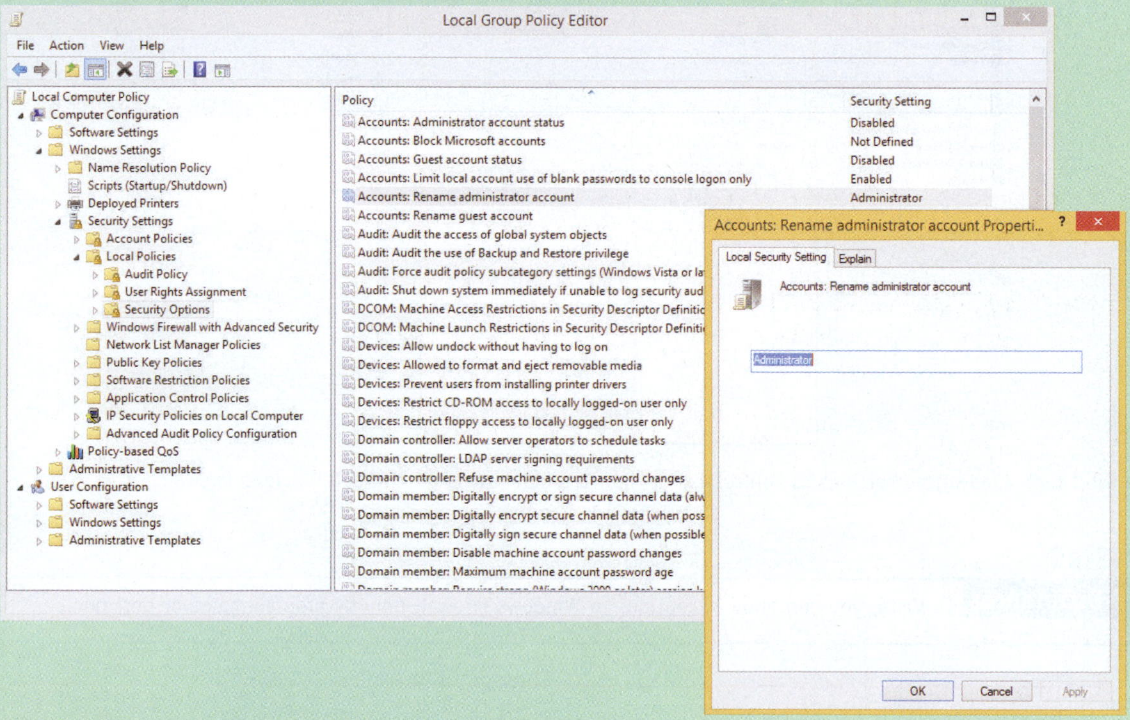

Figure 18-15 Use Group Policy to rename a default user account

> **Notes** The Properties box for many policies offers the Explain tab. Use this tab to read more about a policy and how it works.

   - ***Require user passwords.*** To require that all user accounts have passwords, drill down to the **Computer Configuration**, **Windows Settings**, **Security Settings**, **Account Policies**, **Password Policy** group (see the left side of Figure 18-16). Use the **Minimum password length** policy and set the minimum length to six or eight characters (see the right side of Figure 18-16). Additionally, reduce the password expiration time frame so users must create new passwords frequently. Use the **Maximum password age** policy to require users to reset their password every 60 days. (Best practice is to set the Maximum password age in the range of 30 to 90 days.)

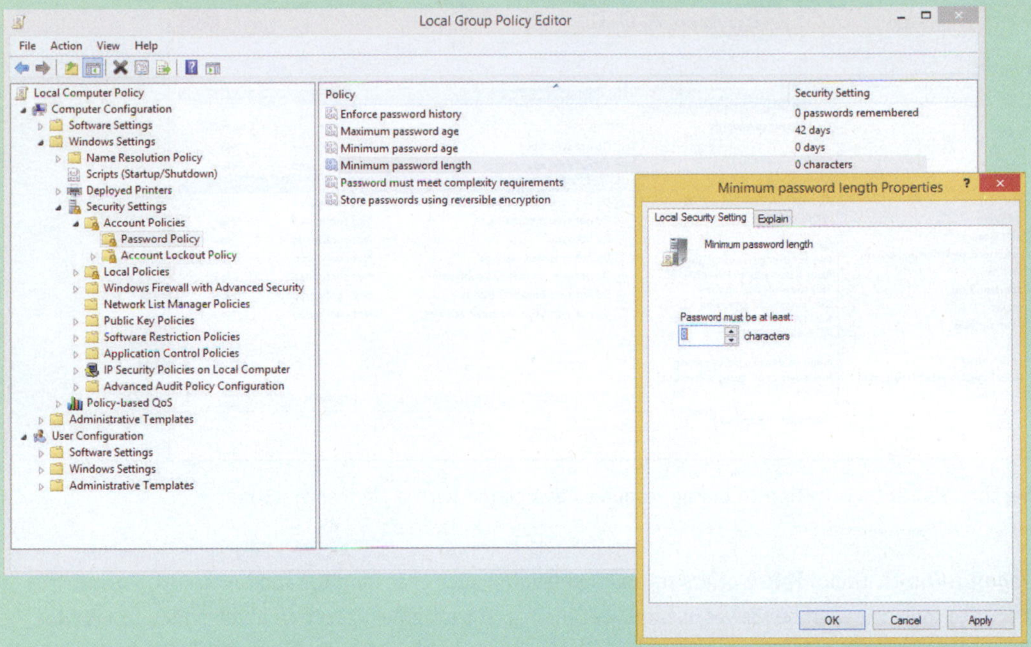

Figure 18-16 Require that each user account have a password by setting the minimum password length policy

- ***Set failed logon restrictions.*** Windows can be configured to lock a user account if too many incorrect logons are attempted. Drill down to the **Computer Configuration**, **Windows Settings**, **Security Settings**, **Account Policies**, **Account Lockout Policy** group. Use the **Account lockout threshold** to set the number of invalid logon attempts. When the number is exceeded, the account will be locked.
- ***Restrict logon hours.*** In many cases, users should only be allowed access to a workstation during specific hours, such as during office hours. Preventing access at other times of the day and throughout the weekend can increase a workstation's security. The schedule for a user's or group's logon hours is set through Active Directory, but individual workstations can be configured to respond differently once a user's logon hours have expired. To configure a workstation's response to the expiration of a user's logon hours, drill down to the **User Configuration**, **Administrative Templates**, **Windows Components**, **Windows Logon Options** group. Use the **Set action to take when logon hours expire** policy to choose Lock, Disconnect, or Logoff. If this policy is not enabled, the user's session will continue, but the user will not be able to log on outside of the assigned logon hours once the current session has been terminated.
- ***Disable Microsoft account resources.*** Recall that a Microsoft account is a single sign-on (SSO) account, which means it provides authentication to multiple services and resources. When a user signs in to a Windows 8 computer with a Microsoft account, she has access to online resources such as OneDrive and OneNote and can sync settings on this computer with other computers that use this same Microsoft account. Settings include Start screen tiles, desktop personalization, installed apps and app settings, web browser favorites, and passwords to apps, websites, and networks. (To see the settings you can sync when using a Microsoft account, in the charms bar, click **Settings**, click **Change PC settings**, click **OneDrive**, and click **Sync settings**.) Depending on your company's policy, you might need to restrict access to online resources and syncing settings that are linked to a user's Microsoft account. To disable OneDrive, for example, drill down to **Computer Configuration**, **Administrative Templates**, **Windows Components**, **OneDrive** group. Use the **Prevent the usage of OneDrive for file storage** policy. Enable this policy to prevent users and programs from accessing OneDrive. Additionally, in the **Windows Components** submenu, click the **Sync your settings** group and use these policies to disable syncing apps, app settings, passwords, and other Windows settings (see Figure 18-17).

(continues)

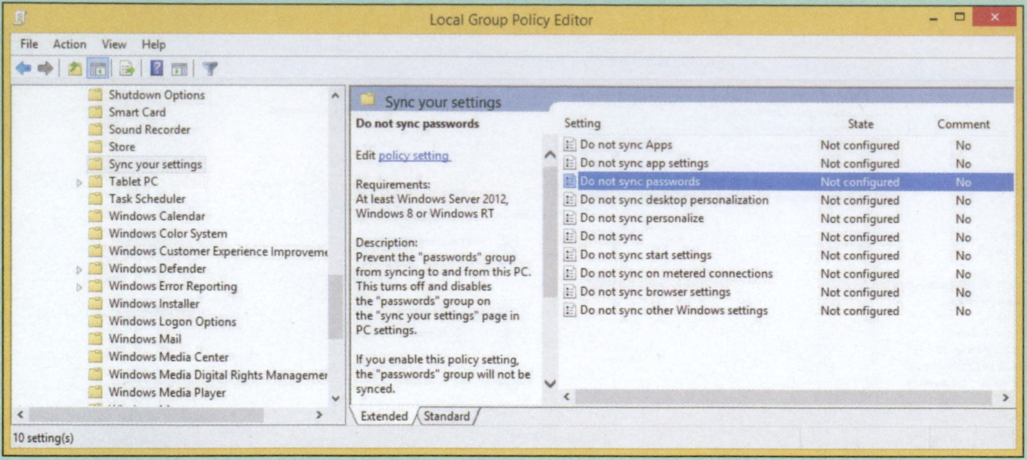

Figure 18-17 Restrict SSO authentication to online resources associated with a Microsoft account

- ***Audit logon failures.*** Group Policy offers several auditing policies that monitor and log security events. These Security logs can then be viewed using Event Viewer. For example, to set an audit policy to monitor a failed logon event, drill down to the **Computer Configuration**, **Windows Settings**, **Security Settings**, **Local Policies**, **Audit Policy** group. Use the **Audit logon events** policy. You can audit logon successes and failures. To keep the log from getting too big, you can select **Failure** to only log these events.
- ***Disable logon and shutdown scripts.*** Policies can run scripts for the computer or user during logon or shutdown. These scripts can contain programs, which might contain malware. To manage logon scripts, in the Computer Configuration or User Configuration group, drill down to the **Administrative Templates**, **System**, **Logon** group. Use the **Run these programs at user logon** policy. To manage shutdown scripts, drill down to the **Administrative Templates**, **System**, **Scripts** group. For a list of folders where Group Policy stores these scripts, see the appendix, "Entry Points for Windows Startup Processes."
- ***Disable AutoRun and AutoPlay.*** When attaching a USB flash drive or external hard drive, or inserting a disc in the optical drive, Windows automatically accesses the storage media and then requests instructions on what to do next. Media files can be played automatically, which is called AutoPlay. Executable files can be run automatically, which is called AutoRun. You can disable both of these features to add yet another layer of security protection. To disable AutoPlay, drill down to **Computer Configuration**, **Administrative Templates**, **Windows Components**, **AutoPlay Policies** group. Enable the **Turn off Autoplay** policy. To disable AutoRun, enable the **Set the default behavior for AutoRun** and use the **Disabled** option.

4. When you finish setting your local security policies, close the Local Group Policy Editor console. To put into effect the changes you have made, reboot the system or enter the command **gpupdate.exe** in a command prompt window. The **gpupdate** command refreshes local group policies as well as group policies set in Active Directory on a Windows domain.

Notes Sometimes policies overlap or conflict. To find out the resulting policies for the computer or user that are currently applied to the system, you can use the **gpresult** command in a command prompt window with parameters. To find out more about this command, search the *technet.microsoft.com* website.

★ A+ Exam Tip The A+ 220-902 exam expects you to know about the **Local Security Policy** snap-in, which is one of the Administrative Tools snap-ins in Control Panel. In Group Policy, the group of policies in the Local Computer Policy, Computer Configuration, Windows Settings, Security Settings group can also be edited from Control Panel. In Control Panel, open **Administrative Tools** and double-click **Local Security Policy**.

Hands-On | Project 18-2 Use Group Policy to Secure a Workstation

A+
220-902
1.4

Using Windows 8.1/8 Professional or Enterprise, or Windows 7 Professional, Ultimate, or Enterprise, set local security policies to require a password for each account, to audit failed logon events, and to create a logon script that displays the message, "The Golden Pineapple Was Here!" when anyone signs in to the system. Test your policies by verifying a password is required, your script executes when you sign in, and a failed sign-in event using an invalid password is logged and can be viewed in Event Viewer. Answer the following questions:

1. Which policies did you set and what setting was applied to each policy?
2. What software did you use to create your script? What is the exact path and file name (including the file extension) to your script?
3. Which log in Event Viewer shows the logon failure event?
4. List three more policies you find in Group Policy not discussed in this chapter that can make a workstation more secure.

USE BITLOCKER ENCRYPTION

A+
220-902
1.1, 3.3

BitLocker Drive Encryption in Windows professional and business editions locks down a hard drive by encrypting the entire Windows volume and any other volume on the drive. A similar feature, BitLocker To Go, encrypts data on a USB flash drive and restricts access by requiring a password. You need to be aware of the restrictions and possible risks before you decide to use BitLocker. It's intended to work in partnership with file and folder encryption to provide data security.

★ A+ Exam Tip The A+ 220-902 exam expects you to know about the features, benefits, and drawbacks of BitLocker Drive Encryption and BitLocker To Go.

The three ways you can use BitLocker Drive Encryption depend on the type of protection you need and the computer hardware available:

- *Computer authentication.* Many laptop computers have a chip on the motherboard called the TPM (Trusted Platform Module) chip. The TPM chip holds the BitLocker encryption key (also called the startup key). If the hard drive is stolen from the laptop and installed in another computer, the data would be safe because BitLocker would not allow access without the startup key stored on the TPM chip. Therefore, this method authenticates the computer. However, if the motherboard fails and is replaced, you'll need a backup copy of the startup key to access data on the hard drive. (You cannot move the TPM chip from one motherboard to another.)
- *User authentication.* For computers that don't have TPM, the startup key can be stored on a USB flash drive (or other storage device the computer reads before the OS is loaded), and the flash drive must be installed before the computer boots. This method authenticates the user. For this method to be the most secure, the user must never leave the flash drive stored with the computer. (Instead, the user might keep the USB startup key on his key ring.)
- *Computer and user authentication.* For *best* security, a password can be required at every startup in addition to TPM. Using this method, both the computer and the user are authenticated. This practice is an example of multifactor authentication (MFA), which uses more than one method to authenticate.

BitLocker Drive Encryption provides great security, but security comes with a price. For instance, you risk the chance your TPM will fail or you will lose all copies of the startup key. In these events, recovering the data can be messy. Therefore, use BitLocker only if the risks of BitLocker giving problems outweigh the risks of stolen data. And, if you decide to use BitLocker, be sure to make extra copies of the startup key and/or password and keep them in a safe location.

For detailed instructions on how to set up BitLocker Drive Encryption, see the Microsoft Knowledge Base "BitLocker Overview" article hh831713 at *technet.microsoft.com*.

USE UEFI/BIOS FEATURES TO PROTECT THE SYSTEM

A+ 220-902 3.4

Many motherboards for desktop and laptop computers offer several UEFI/BIOS security features, including UEFI secure boot, power-on passwords, support for intrusion-detection devices, and support for a TPM chip. Power-on passwords include a supervisor password (required to change UEFI/BIOS setup), user password (required to use the system or view UEFI/BIOS setup), and a drive lock password (required to access the hard drive). The drive lock password does not require a TPM chip and is stored on the hard drive so that it will still control access to the drive in the event the drive is removed from the computer and installed on another system. Figure 18-18 shows one BIOS setup Security screen where you can set the hard drive password. This screen can also be used to set the supervisor and user passwords to the system.

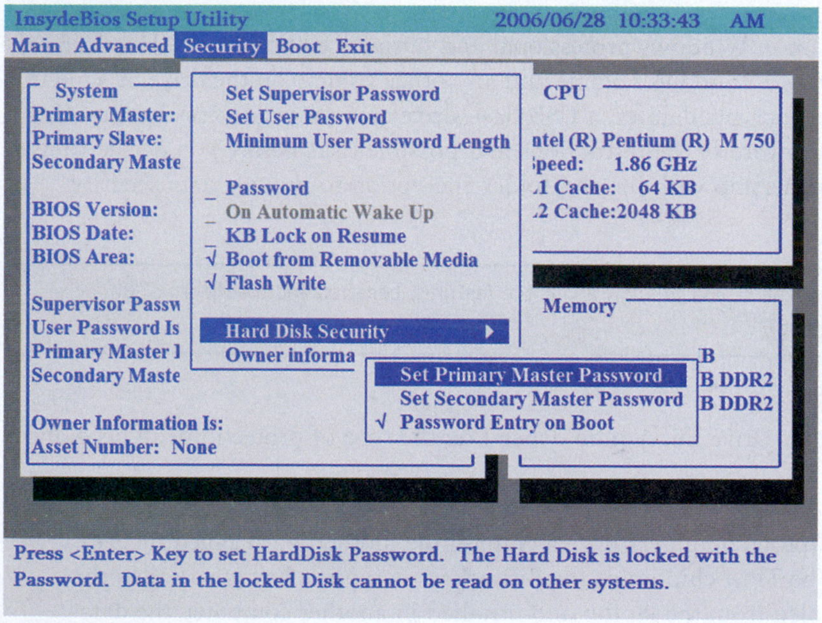

Source: Insyde Software

Figure 18-18 Submenu shows how to set a hard drive password that will be written on the drive

Some laptops contain the LoJack technology on the motherboard to support the laptop-tracking software Absolute LoJack® by Absolute Software (*absolute.com*). If you install the software on your laptop and the laptop is stolen, Absolute can lock down your hard drive and track down the laptop.

Now that you know about securing personal computers, let's turn our attention to securing mobile devices.

SECURING A MOBILE DEVICE

A+
220-902
3.5

Smart phones and tablets are with us everywhere, and most of us keep much personal and professional information on our smart phones. In the chapter, "Supporting Mobile Operating Systems," you learned about a lot of the features on smart phones and tablets that make the data on them more accessible. In this chapter, you learn how to make that information more secure. Here's a list of what might be stored on a smart phone or tablet that would be at risk if the device is lost, stolen, or damaged:

- Data kept by apps can reveal much about our lives. Consider data kept on these iPhone and Android apps: Email, calendar, call logs, voice mail, text messages, Dropbox, iCloud Drive, Google Maps, Hangouts, Gmail, QuickMemo, YouTube, Amazon, Facebook, Videos, Photos, Notes, Contacts, and web browsers (bookmarks and browsing history).
- Videos and photos we have taken might reveal private information and be tagged with date and time stamps and GPS locations.
- Network connection settings, including Wi-Fi security keys, email configuration settings, user names, and email addresses.
- Purchasing patterns and history as well as credit card information might be stored—or at least accessible for use—in mobile payment apps, apps developed by our favorite retailers, or through membership card databases.

To keep your data safe, consider controlling access to your devices and consider what apps you can use to protect the data. These methods are discussed in this part of the chapter along with BYOD (Bring Your Own Device) policies that might be used in an enterprise environment to secure corporate data stored on a device.

DEVICE ACCESS CONTROLS

A+
220-902
3.5

Because smart phones and tablets are so mobile, they get stolen more often than other types of computers. Therefore, protecting data on a mobile device is especially important. Consider the following lock methods to control access to the device:

- *Android screen lock.* A screen lock requires the correct input to unlock the device. Android devices provide a variety of options, as shown in Figure 18-19a. As the complexity of a lock code increases, so does the security of the device:
  - *Swipe.* Swipe your finger across the screen to unlock the device (not very secure but will prevent a pocket dial).
  - *Knock code.* Requires a pattern of taps on the screen.
  - *Pattern.* Requires a pattern to be drawn along dots on the screen (see Figure 18-19b).
  - *PIN.* Requires a numerical code, which is similar to iOS's passcode.
  - *Password.* Requires an alphanumeric code with letters and/or numbers.
  - *Face lock.* Uses the device's camera to perform facial recognition (this option is not available on the device shown in Figure 18-19a).

Some devices have different features that can still be accessed from the lock screen, such as emergency calls, weather information, a virtual assistant, or the camera app. A device might even let you post contact info, such as a friend's phone number, on the lock screen in case the device is lost and someone tries to return it. Thankfully, not everyone is a bad guy. Don't include the person's name with their phone number. Make sure they're informed and you have their permission to use their phone number for this purpose.

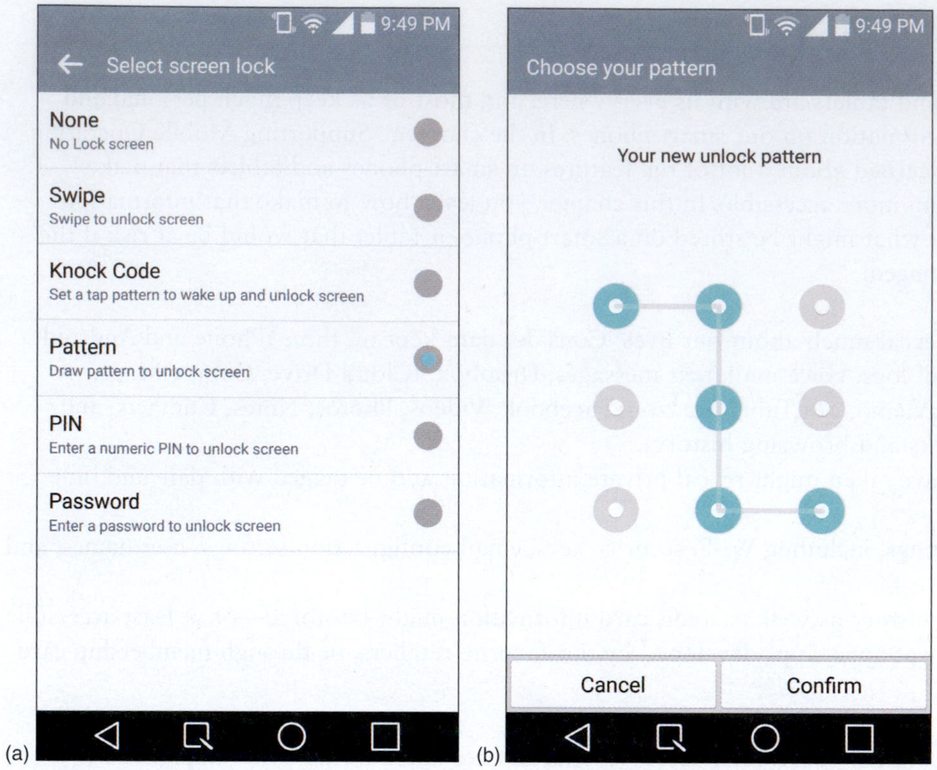

Source: Android

Figure 18-19 (a) Screen lock options, and (b) an unlock pattern follows dots on the screen

◢ *iOS screen lock.* Both iPhones and iPads offer a numerical passcode lock, and later models offer Touch ID, a fingerprint lock. The Home button on the iPhone and iPad acts as a fingerprint reader for this feature. Figure 18-20a shows the Touch ID & Passcode menu in the Settings app where these features can be enabled and configured.

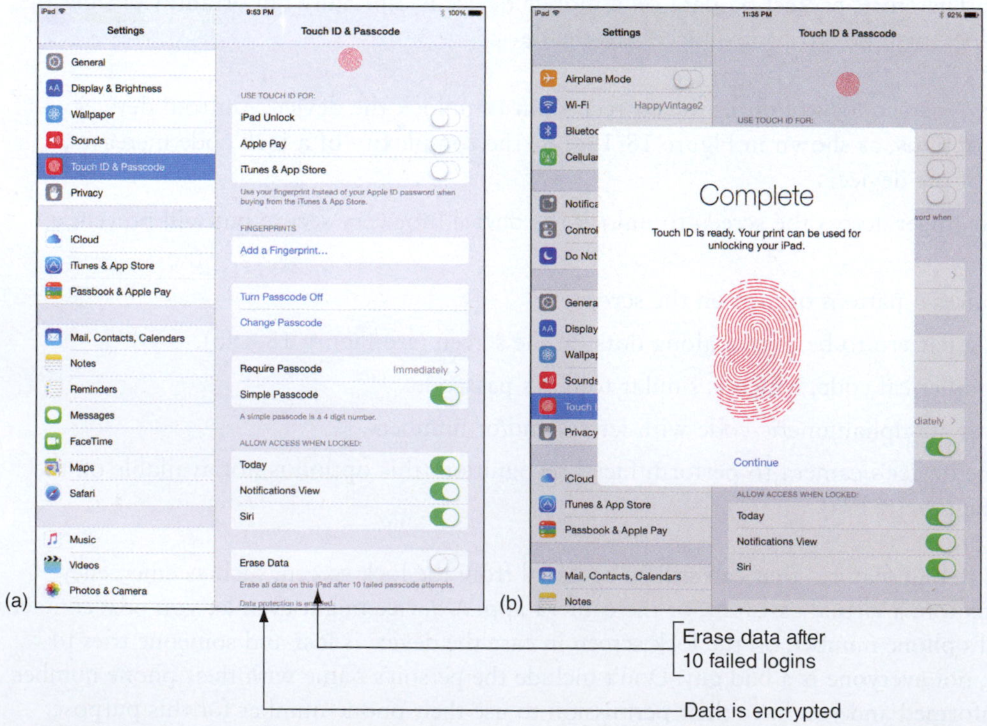

Source: Apple

Figure 18-20 (a) Use a numerical passcode to unlock an iPad, or (b) use your fingerprint to unlock

For best security, on the Touch ID & Passcode screen, turn off **Simple Passcode** so you can enter a strong password for your device and set **Require Passcode** to **Immediately**. Yes, both these features are annoying, but necessary for best security.

Notes In the chapter, "Supporting Mobile Operating Systems," you learned how to recover from a system lockout when the screen lock prevents access to your device.

- ***Biometric authentication.*** A biometric device is an input device that collects biological data about a person, which can identify a person's fingerprints, handprints, face, voice, retinal, iris, and handwritten signatures. Touch ID on an iPhone is one example of biometric authentication (see Figure 18-20b), as is the face lock on an Android phone. Iris scanners and voice recognition are other options for some devices.

Notes In some states, you cannot legally be forced to give your phone's password to investigators. But you are required to give your fingerprint.

- ***Full device encryption.*** Encrypting a device's data makes the data essentially useless to a thief. However, encryption might slow down device performance and the data is only as safe as the strength of the password keeping the data encrypted. Both Android and iOS devices offer full device encryption. With iOS, data is automatically encrypted when you set a screen lock password. To verify encryption, open the **Settings** app, tap **Passcode**, and then enter your passcode. At the bottom of the screen, verify *Data protection is enabled*, as shown in Figure 18-20a.
- ***Restrict iOS failed login attempts.*** When you set a screen lock, you can specify that data be erased after so many failed login attempts. For example, look back at Figure 18-20a to see near the bottom of the screen that if Erase Data is turned on, 10 failed login attempts causes all data on the device to be erased.

Caution If you have Erase Data turned on, be sure to keep backups of your data and other content. A small child can pick up your smart phone and with a little finger tapping accidentally erase all your data.

After five failed logins, the system locks down temporarily, and 10 failed logins results in the system locking down completely. The only way to access the system is to connect the device to iTunes where the device has already been synced to that installation of iTunes. You'll need to restore the device through iTunes using the latest backup, which you learned how to do in the chapter, "Supporting Mobile Operating Systems."

- ***Restrict Android failed login attempts.*** For Android, five failed logins causes the system to temporarily lock down. To restore functionality, some Android devices offer the option to sign in with the device owner's Google account credentials. For other devices, you can use Android Device Manager (*google.com/android/devicemanager*) to access a locked system, such as when the password has been forgotten.
- ***Multifactor authentication.*** Smart phones themselves can be used to authenticate to services and networks (for example, email, cloud services, corporate network accounts, VPNs, or even Facebook), as one of the two or more authentication techniques required for multifactor authentication. For example, you might first enter a password on a computer as the first authentication and then a code is sent as a text message to your smart phone and you must then enter the code in the computer as the second authentication. In another example, you enter a code in a computer that is at a certain location and the system you're signing in to checks the GPS location of your smart phone to make sure it is near the computer. In addition, authenticator apps, such as Google Authenticator for Android or iOS, Microsoft Authenticator for Windows Phone, or an independent competitor like Authy, can be installed on your smart phone and configured to provide multifactor authentication support for a huge variety of account types.

SOFTWARE SECURITY

A+ 220-902 3.5

In addition to controlling access to a device, you can use software to secure the data. Most of the methods discussed here require the user understand the importance of the security measure and how to use it:

- *OS updates and patches.* Android automatically pushes updates to many of its devices, but iOS devices and other mobile devices require manual updates. You learned how to update mobile device operating systems in the chapter, "Supporting Mobile Operating Systems."
- *Antivirus/anti-malware.* Because Apple closely protects iOS and iOS apps, it's unlikely an Apple device will need anti-malware software unless the device has been jailbroken. The Android OS and apps are not so closely guarded because apps can be downloaded from sources other than Google Play. Before installing an Android anti-malware app, be sure to read reviews about it. Most of the major anti-malware software companies provide Android anti-malware apps.
- *Trusted sources.* iOS devices are limited to installing apps only from Apple's App Store. Android and Windows devices can download and install apps from other sources, only some of which are trustworthy. Trusted sources generally include well-known app stores, such as Amazon Appstore for Android (*amazon.com*) or Slide ME (*slideme.org*). Look for lots of reviewer feedback as one measure of safety. Other trusted sources might include your bank's website, your employer, or your school, although often these apps are posted in Google Play (*play.google.com*) as well.

  Android allows you to limit app sources to only the Google Play Store, which can help reduce the threat of untrusted sources for apps. In the **Settings** app, tap **Security** and make sure that **Unknown sources** is unchecked, as shown in Figure 18-21a. If you do decide to use third-party app sources, be sure you already have a good anti-malware program and a firewall running on your device.

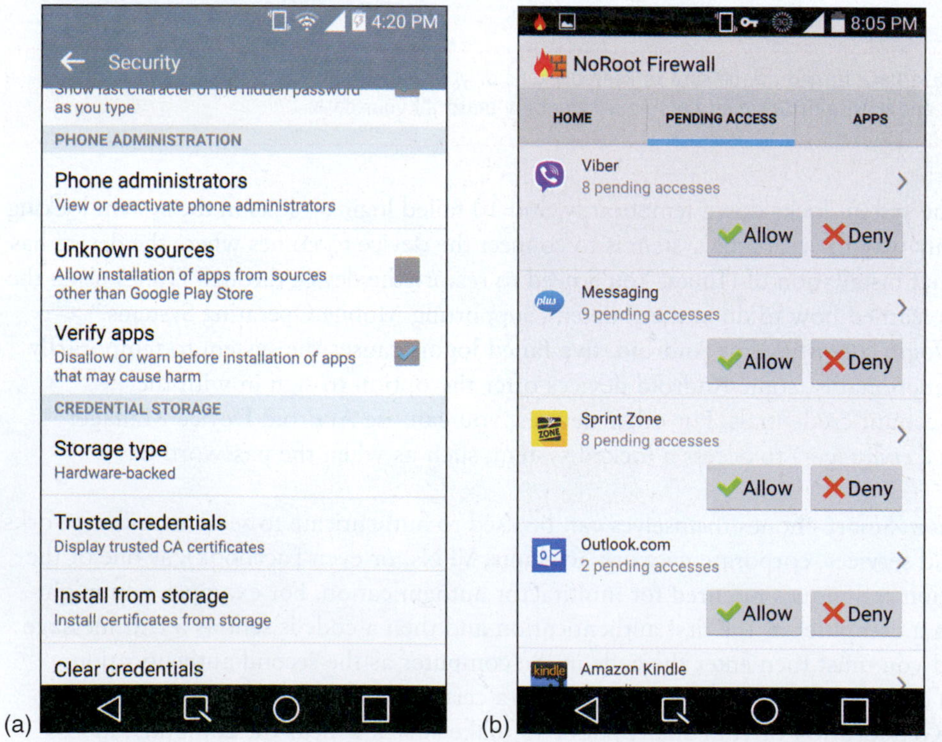

Source: Android

Figure 18-21 (a) Android security settings, and (b) a firewall app on an Android smart phone

- *Firewalls.* As with Windows computers, a firewall on a mobile device helps control what connections can be made by which programs or services. When you install an app, you're required to agree to the permissions it requests in order to get the app. A firewall gives you more control over what network access an app can have. For example, a firewall can prevent the Facebook app from sending SMS messages. Facebook's app might legitimately use SMS for two-factor authentication, but a firewall lets you decide if you're comfortable with the app having that level of access in exchange for being able to use that feature. Most firewall apps for mobile devices use VPN technology to mimic a VPN connection, which forces all network communication to be routed through that connection so the app can emulate firewall-type protection on the device. Figure 18-21b shows an example of one firewall app on an Android smart phone.
- *Android locator application and remote wipe.* You can use Android Device Manager (ADM at *google.com/android/devicemanager*) to locate your phone on a map, force it to ring at its highest volume, change the device password, or remotely erase all data from the device to protect your privacy, which is called a remote wipe. All of these features are built in to Android and are available if location access services are turned on. Third-party locator applications are also available in the Play Store.

  To turn on location access services on an Android smart phone, do the following:

  1. On the home screen, tap the **Apps Launcher**. Find and tap **Google Settings**. Note that this is not the same thing as the **Settings** app. The Google Settings app opens, as shown in Figure 18-22a.

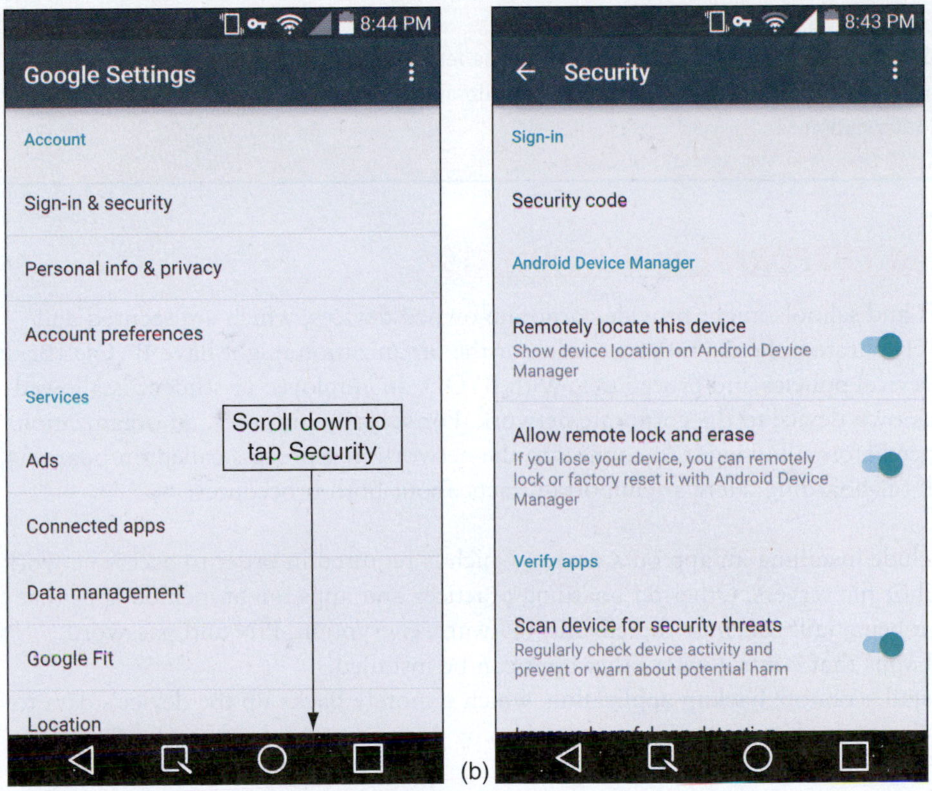

Source: Android

Figure 18-22 To enable Android Device Manager services that can be used in an emergency, (a) tap Security in Google Settings, and (b) turn on Android Device Manager features

  2. Scroll down and tap **Security**. On the Security screen, under Android Device Manager, make sure *Remotely locate this device* and *Allow remote lock and erase* sliders are turned **on**, as shown in Figure 18-22b.

- *iOS locator application and remote wipe.* Similar to Android Device Manager, iCloud offers the ability to locate a lost iOS device if the feature is already enabled on the device. On an iPad or iPhone, turn on Find My iPhone or Find My iPad in the Settings app. How to do that is covered in the chapter, "Supporting

Mobile Operating Systems." Besides using a browser on a computer to find your device, you can also download the free app, Find My iPhone or Find My iPad, to another Apple device and use it to locate your lost device. If you have given up on finding your device, you can use iCloud to perform a remote wipe.

Hands-On | Project 18-3 Practice Locating Your iOS or Android Device

A+ 220-902 3.5

Whether you have an Android device or an iOS device, knowing how to locate it when it gets lost or stolen or how to perform a remote wipe can be crucial skills in an emergency. Do the following to find out how these tasks work:

1. If you have an iOS device, go to **iCloud.com/#find**. If you have an Android device, go to **google.com/android/devicemanager**.
2. Sign in, and make sure the correct device is selected. Was the website able to locate your device? If not, check your device settings and make any adjustments necessary until the website successfully locates the device.
3. Explore the site to see how to make the device ring, how to lock the device by changing the passcode, and how to erase the device. What are the names of the three buttons that perform these tasks?

One potential snag in finding or remotely wiping your device would be relying on passwords stored in your device to access your Google or iCloud account. Be sure to store your sign-in information for these accounts in password vault software or memorize the information.

MOBILE SECURITY IN CORPORATE ENVIRONMENTS

A+ 220-902 3.5

Corporations and schools might provide corporate-owned devices, which are secured and managed by corporate policies and procedures, or the organization might have BYOD (Bring Your Own Device) policies and procedures. With BYOD, an employee or student is allowed to connect his own device to the corporate network. For security purposes, an organization configures a person's device before allowing it to connect to the network in a process called on-boarding. The reverse process is call off-boarding. Here are important facts about both procedures:

- On-boarding might include installing an app on a device, which is required in order to access network resources such as email or file servers. Other on-boarding practices and apps might include apps that prevent the device from being jailbroken or rooted, anti-malware, encryption, PIN and password enforcement apps, and apps that control what other apps can be installed.
- On-boarding might install a remote backup application, which remotely backs up the device's data to a company file server. For example, Canopy Remote Backup by Atos (*canopy-cloud.com*) provides cloud-based backups for laptops, tablets, and smart phones.
- Off-boarding might include the ability to perform a remote wipe on a device that is lost or stolen or when an employee is abruptly dismissed. The process might even include the ability to completely disable the device and make it unusable for any network access at all.
- Two examples of software that support on-boarding and off-boarding, including remote locks and wipes, are Microsoft Exchange Server and Google Apps Mobile Management software.

Regardless of who owns a device, any device allowed to connect to a secured corporate network must meet certain security configuration requirements, including encryption, firewalls, anti-malware measures, or use of VPN connections. These profile security requirements must be clearly outlined, and users must be educated on how to ensure their devices continue to meet the baseline requirements.

Hands-On | Project 18-4 Learn About Google Apps Mobile Management

Google has posted several videos to *Youtube.com* that you can use to learn about its products and services. Search *Youtube.com* for videos about Google Apps Mobile Management by Google. (To know if a video is by Google, look for *Uploaded by GoogleApps* on the *Youtube.com* webpage below the video.) Answer the following questions:

1. What app should a user install on his device to use some of the features of Google Apps Mobile Management? What is the price of the software?
2. Can an administrator use the software to require that mobile devices must use a passcode? To lock a device remotely? To find a device when it is lost?
3. Which of the following mobile operating systems other than Android can work with Google Apps Mobile Management: iOS, Blackberry, Windows Phone?
4. Is it possible for a user to perform a remote wipe, or must it always be performed by an administrator?

ADDITIONAL METHODS TO PROTECT RESOURCES

A+ 220-902 2.4, 3.1, 3.2, 3.4, 3.6

Securing data and other computer resources might seem like a never-ending task. Come to think of it, that's probably true. In this part of the chapter, you learn even more ways to securely authenticate users on a large network, physically protect computer resources, destroy data before you toss out a storage device, and educate users to not unintentionally compromise the security measures you've put in place.

AUTHENTICATE USERS FOR LARGE NETWORKS

A+ 220-902 3.2

Normally, Windows authenticates a user with a Windows password. However, the best authentication happens when a user (1) knows something (such as a Windows password) and (2) possesses something, which is called a security token (such as a smart card or a fingerprint scan). In this part of the chapter, you learn about smart cards and biometric data used with multifactor authentication. One warning to keep in mind is a smart card or biometric data should be used in addition to, and not as a replacement for, a Windows password.

SECURITY TOKENS AND SMART CARDS

18

A security token provides an additional method of authentication in multifactor authentication scenarios or can serve as a replacement for a password. The most popular type of token used to authenticate a user is a smart card, which is typically a business-card sized card with embedded circuitry and contact points, although smart card technology can also be integrated into other security token form factors. (You also need to know that some people don't consider a card to be a smart card unless it has an embedded microprocessor.)

The information on the smart card can be typed on a sign-in window by a user, read by a smart card reader (when the device is inserted into the reader), or transmitted wirelessly. See Figure 18-23. At the same time, some smart cards can receive information from the reader to confirm that the reader is authentic. This is called mutual authentication, which occurs any time authentication goes in both directions at the same time as both entities confirm the identity of the other.

© antos777/Shutterstock.com

Figure 18-23 Smart card is read by a smart card reader

Notes A common use of mutual authentication is sending a confirmation code by text to your smart phone using a phone number the server already has on file, which gives you reassurance that the server you're authenticating to is who it says it is.

A+ Exam Tip The A+ 220-902 exam expects you to know about biometric data, badges, smart cards, tokens, key fobs, and RFID badges used to authenticate to a computer system or network.

Here are some variations of security tokens:

- *Key fob*. A key fob is a security token that fits conveniently on a keychain, such as the one shown in Figure 18-24. The number on the key fob changes every 60 seconds. When a user signs in to the network, she must enter the number on the key fob, which is synchronized with the network authentication service. Entering the number proves that the user has the key fob in hand. Because the device doesn't actually make physical contact with the system, it is called a contactless token or disconnected token.

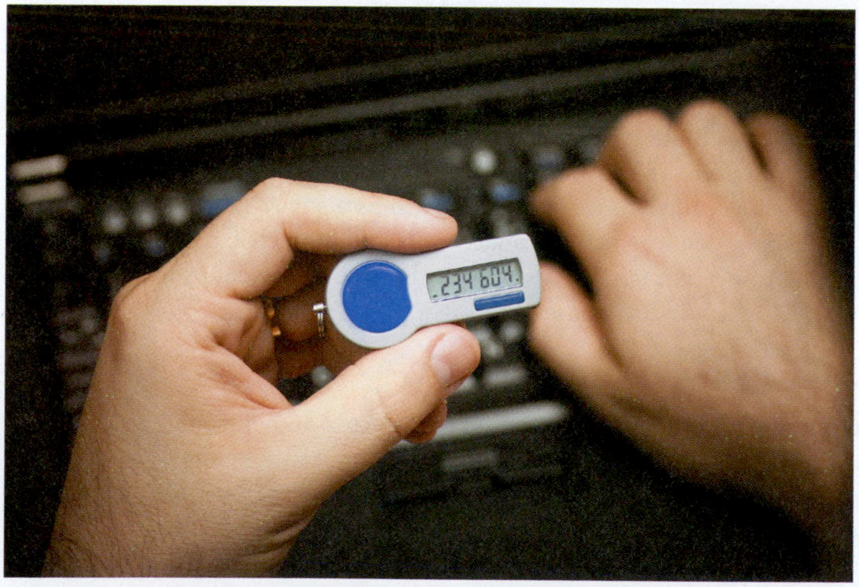

iStockphoto.com/David Clark

Figure 18-24 A security token such as this key fob is used to authenticate a user gaining access to a secured network

- ***Wireless token.*** Another type of contactless token uses wireless technology to transmit information kept by the token to the computer system. A Radio Frequency Identification (RFID) token transmits authentication to the system when the token gets in range of a query device. For example, an RFID badge worn by an employee can allow the employee entrance into a locked area of a building.

- ***Memory stripe card.*** An example of a contact token is an employee ID badge or other smart card with a magnetic stripe that can be read by a smart card reader (see Figure 18-25a). Because these cards don't contain a microchip, they are sometimes called memory cards. Some keyboards have an embedded smart card reader, and Figure 18-25b shows a reader that connects to a computer via a USB port. Used in this way, a memory stripe card is part of the authentication process into a network. The magnetic stripe can contain information about the user to indicate her rights on the system. The major disadvantage of this type of smart card is that each computer used for authentication must have one of these smart card reader machines installed. Also, in the industry, because a card with a magnetic stripe does not contain a microchip, some in the industry don't consider it to fit into the category of a smart card, but rather simply call it a magnetic stripe card.

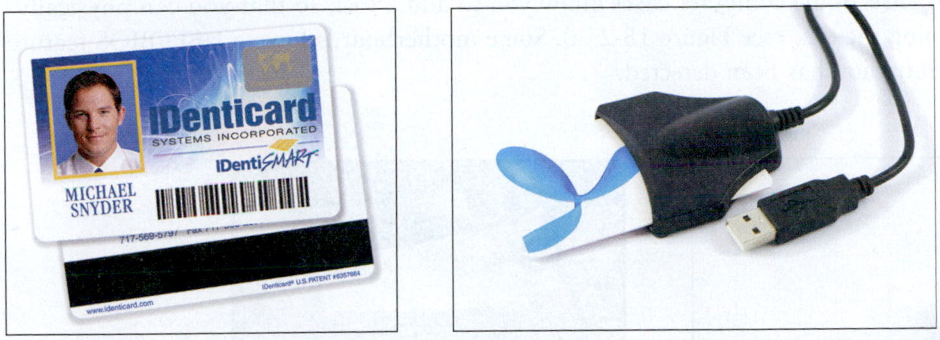

Courtesy of IDenticard Systems/ © Cousin_Avi/Shutterstock.com

Figure 18-25 (a) A smart card with a magnetic stripe can be used inside or outside a computer network, and (b) a USB reader for a magnetic stripe card

iStockphoto.com/viiwee

Figure 18-26 This access control device accepts typed code, fingerprint, or smart card input

- ***Cell phone with token.*** An app installed on a cell phone can hold the user's token, which includes a digital signature or digital certificate. A digital certificate is assigned by a Certification Authority (CA) (for example, VeriSign—*www.verisign.com*) and is used to prove you are who you say you are. The authentication can be sent to the network via a USB connection, text message, phone call, or Bluetooth connection. This method is sometimes used when an employee authenticates to a VPN connection to the corporate network.

BIOMETRIC DATA

As part of the authentication process, some systems use biometric data to validate the person's physical body, which, in effect, becomes the token. Figure 18-26 shows a biometric input device, a fingerprint scanner. Many mobile devices, such as iPads and some laptops, have fingerprint scanners built in. Other forms of biometric data include retinal scans (scans parts of the eye), handprints, face recognition, and voice recognition.

18

PHYSICAL SECURITY METHODS AND DEVICES

A+
220-902
2.4, 3.2,
3.6

Physically protecting a computer's resources is often seen by security experts as more important than digital security. Here are some best practices for physical security:

- ***If the data is really private, keep it behind a locked door or under lock and key.*** You can use all kinds of security methods to encrypt, password protect, and hide data, but if it really is that important, one obvious thing you can do is to keep the computer behind a locked door. You can also store the data on a removable storage device such as an external hard drive and, when you're not using the data, put the drive in a fireproof safe. And, of course, keep two copies. Sounds simple, but it works. Don't forget that printouts of sensitive documents should also be kept under lock and key as well as any passwords you might have written down.
- ***Lock down the computer case.*** Some computer cases allow you to add a lock so that you can physically prevent others from opening the case (see Figure 18-27a). Some motherboards have a UEFI/BIOS feature that alerts you when an intrusion has been detected.

(a)

(b)

Figure 18-27 To physically secure a computer, (a) use a computer case lock and key for a desktop to prevent intrusion, or (b) use a cable lock system for a laptop to prevent theft

- ***Use a lock and chain.*** You can also use a lock and chain to physically tie a computer to a desk or other permanent fixture so someone can't walk away with it. Figure 18-27b shows a cable lock system for a laptop. Most laptops have a security slot on the case to connect the cable lock.
- ***Use privacy filters.*** To keep other people from viewing a monitor screen, you can install a privacy filter that fits over the screen to prevent it from being read from a wide angle.
- ***Install a theft-prevention plate.*** As an added precaution, physically mark a computer case or laptop so it can be identified if it is later stolen. You embed a theft-prevention plate into the case or engrave your ID information into it. The numbers or bar code identify you, the owner, and can also clearly establish to police that the laptop has been stolen. Two sources of theft-prevention plates and cable locks are Computer Security Products, Inc., (*computersecurity.com*) and Flexguard Security System (*flexguard .com*). To further help you identify stolen equipment, record serial numbers and model numbers in a safe place separate from the equipment.
- ***Use a mantrap and security guard.*** The ultimate in physical security is a mantrap, which consists of two doors on either end of a small entryway where the first door must close before the second door can open. A separate form of identification might be required for each door, such as a badge for the first door and a fingerprint scan for the second door. A security guard might also maintain an entry control roster, which is a list of people allowed into the restricted area and a log of any approved visitors.

DIGITAL SECURITY METHODS AND RESOURCES

A+ 220-902 3.2

Windows Firewall is one example of digital-based security. Software can make up a significant portion of your defense resources. Following are some additional software security measures:

- *VPN (virtual private network)*. Recall from the chapter, "Connecting To and Setting Up a Network," that a VPN protects data by encrypting it over a remote connection to a private network.
- *Email filtering*. Email providers often offer email filtering to filter out suspicious email messages based on databases of known scams and spammers. Corporations might route incoming and outgoing email through a proxy server for filtering. Incoming email is inspected for scams or spam to protect against social engineering that might trick an employee into introducing malware into the corporate network.

  Outgoing email from employees might be filtered for inappropriate content. This lawful interception is intended to verify that an employee is complying with privacy laws (for example, laws that apply to confidential medical records) and is not accidentally or intentionally leaking corporate data and secrets. Email filtering software used in this way is an example of data loss prevention (DLP) software, which helps protect against leaking corporate data.
- *Trusted software sources*. It's important to download software only from trusted publishers *and* providers. Even software from a trusted publisher can be filled with destructive extras if the software is obtained from an untrusted provider. Be careful which sites you use for software downloads even when you know the software is trusted.
- *Access control lists*. An access control list (ACL) determines what user, device, or program has access to a particular resource, whether that's a printer, folder, file, or other resource on a corporate network, server, or workstation. Corporate networks manage ACLs through Active Directory on a Windows domain, but a single workstation can also be protected with properly configured permissions. In the chapter, "Windows Resources on a Network," you learned to assign NTFS permissions and share permissions to user accounts in order to secure a workstation on a peer-to-peer network.

UNIFIED THREAT MANAGEMENT (UTM) APPLIANCE

A+ 220-902 2.4

In the chapter, "Connecting To and Setting Up a Network," you learned that a router stands between the Internet and a private network to route traffic between the two networks and can also serve as a firewall to protect the network. A next-generation firewall (NGFW) combines firewall software with antivirus/anti-malware software. In addition, a NGFW device can offer comprehensive Unified Threat Management (UTM) services. A UTM appliance, also called a security appliance, network appliance, or Internet appliance, stands between the Internet and a private network, as does a router, and protects the network (see Figure 18-28).

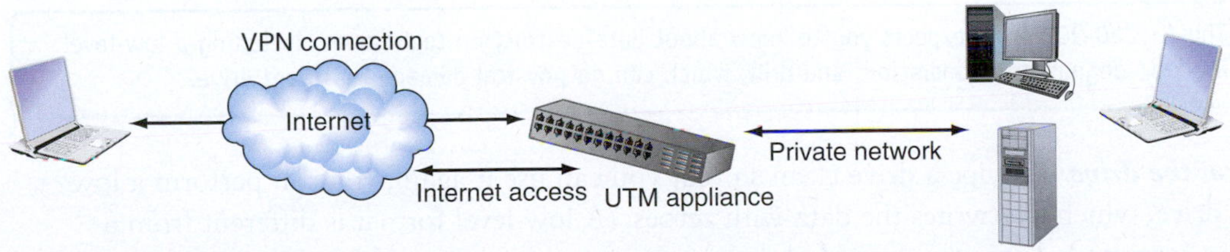

Figure 18-28 A UTM appliance is considered a next-generation firewall that can protect a private network

★ A+ Exam Tip The A+ 220-902 exam expects you to be able to summarize the purposes of services provided by a UTM Internet appliance, including an IDS and IPS.

A UTM appliance might offer these types of protections and services:

- *Firewall.* The firewall software filters incoming and outgoing network traffic according to IP addresses, ports, the type of messages the traffic contains, and how the message was initiated.
- *Antivirus and anti-malware software.* This software is usually much more advanced than what might be installed on a server or workstation.
- *Identity-based access control lists.* These lists control access of users or user groups and can log and report activity of these users and groups to reveal misuse, data leaks, or unauthorized access to resources. The company can use this feature to satisfy legal auditing requirements to detect and control data leaks.
- *Intrusion detection system.* An intrusion detection system (IDS) monitors all network traffic and creates alerts when suspicious activity happens. IDS software can run on a UTM appliance, router, server, or workstation.
- *Intrusion prevention system.* An intrusion prevention system (IPS) not only monitors and logs suspicious activity, but it can also prevent the threatening traffic from burrowing into the system.
- *VPN.* The appliance can provide a VPN to remote users of the network.

Figure 18-29 shows a UTM appliance by NETGEAR.

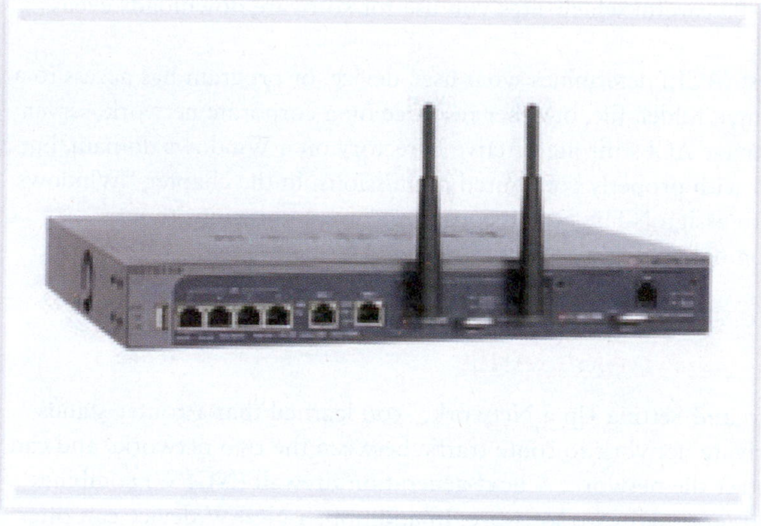

Source: netgear.com

Figure 18-29 ProSECURE UTM appliance by NETGEAR

DATA DESTRUCTION AND DISPOSAL

A+ 220-902 3.6

On the flip side of protecting valuable data is safely destroying data that is no longer needed. Don't throw out a hard drive, CD, DVD, tape, or other media that might have personal or corporate data on it unless you know the data can't be stolen off the device. Trying to wipe a drive clean by deleting files or even by using Windows to format the drive does not completely destroy the data. Here are some ways to destroy printed documents and sanitize storage devices:

- *Use a paper shredder.* Use a paper shredder to destroy all documents that contain sensitive data.

> **A+ Exam Tip** The A+ 220-902 exam expects you to know about data-destruction techniques, including a low-level format, drive wipe, shredder, degausser, incineration, and drill, which can do physical damage to a hard drive.

- *Overwrite data on the drive.* To wipe a drive clean so that you can use it again, you can perform a low-level format of a drive, which overwrites the data with zeroes. (A low-level format is different from a standard Windows format. A device receives a low-level format at the factory, which writes sector markings on the drive.) You can also use a zero-fill utility that also overwrites all data on the drive with zeroes. You can download a low-level format utility or zero-fill utility from many hard drive manufacturers.

  Either method works for most low-security situations, but professional thieves know how to break through this type of destruction. If you use one of these utilities, run it multiple times to write zeroes on top of zeroes. Data recovery has been known to reach 14 levels of overwrites because each bit is slightly offset from the one under it.

- ***Physically destroy the storage media.*** Use a drill to drill many holes through the drive housing all the way through to the other side of the housing. Break CDs and DVDs in half and do similar physical damage with a hammer to flash drives or tapes, even to the point of setting them on fire to incinerate them. Again, expert thieves can still recover some of the data.
- ***For magnetic devices, use a degausser.*** A degausser exposes a storage device to a strong electromagnetic field to completely erase the data on a magnetic hard drive or tape drive (see Figure 18-30). A degaussed drive can't be reused, but for the best destruction, use the degausser and also physically destroy the drive. Degaussing does not erase data on a solid-state hard drive or other flash media because these devices don't use a magnetic surface to hold data.

Figure 18-30 Use a degausser to sanitize a magnetic hard drive or tape

- ***For solid-state devices, use a Secure Erase utility.*** As required by government regulations for personal data privacy, the American National Standards Institute (ANSI) developed the ATA Secure Erase standards to wipe clean a solid-state device such as a USB flash drive or SSD drive. You can download a Secure Erase utility from the manufacturer of the device and run it to securely erase all data on the device and then reuse the drive.
- ***Use a secure data-destruction service.*** For the very best data destruction, consider a secure data-destruction service. To find a service, search the web for "secure data destruction." However, don't use a service unless you have thoroughly checked its references and guarantees of legal compliance that your organization is required to meet. The service should provide you with a digital certificate of destruction, which verifies that the data has been destroyed beyond recovery. Paper certificates can be forged, but digital certificates produced by the software performing the destruction will provide auditable results of the destruction process.

EDUCATE USERS

A+
220-902
3.1, 3.2,
3.4

Generally speaking, the weakest link in setting up security in a computer environment is people. That's because people can often be tricked into giving out private information. Even with all the news and hype about identity theft and criminal websites, it's amazing how well these techniques still work. Many users naively download a funny screen saver, open an email attachment, or enter credit card information on a website without regard to security. In the computer arena, social engineering is the practice of tricking people into giving out private information or allowing unsafe programs into the network or computer.

A good support technician is aware of the criminal practices used, and is able to teach users how to recognize and avoid this mischief. A document that can help educate users is an **acceptable use policy (AUP)**, which explains what users can and cannot do on the corporate network or with company data, and the penalties for violations. The AUP might also describe how these measures help protect the network's security. Here is a list of important security measures that users need to follow to protect passwords and the computer system:

- Never give out your passwords to anyone, not even a supervisor or tech support person who calls and asks for it.
- Don't store your passwords on a computer unless you use company-approved password vault software (for example, KeePass). Some organizations even forbid employees from writing down their passwords.
- Don't use the same password on more than one system (computer, network, application, or website).
- Be aware of **shoulder surfing**, when other people secretly peek at your monitor screen as you work. A privacy filter can help.
- Lock down your workstation each time you step away from your desk.
- Users need to be on the alert for **tailgating**, which is when someone who is unauthorized follows the employee through a secured entrance to a room or building. Another form of tailgating is when a user steps away from her computer and another person continues to use the Windows session when the system is not properly locked.

Beware of online social engineering techniques. For example, don't be fooled by scam email or an **email hoax** such as the one shown in Figure 18-31. When the user who received this email scanned the attached file using antivirus software, the software reported the file contained malware.

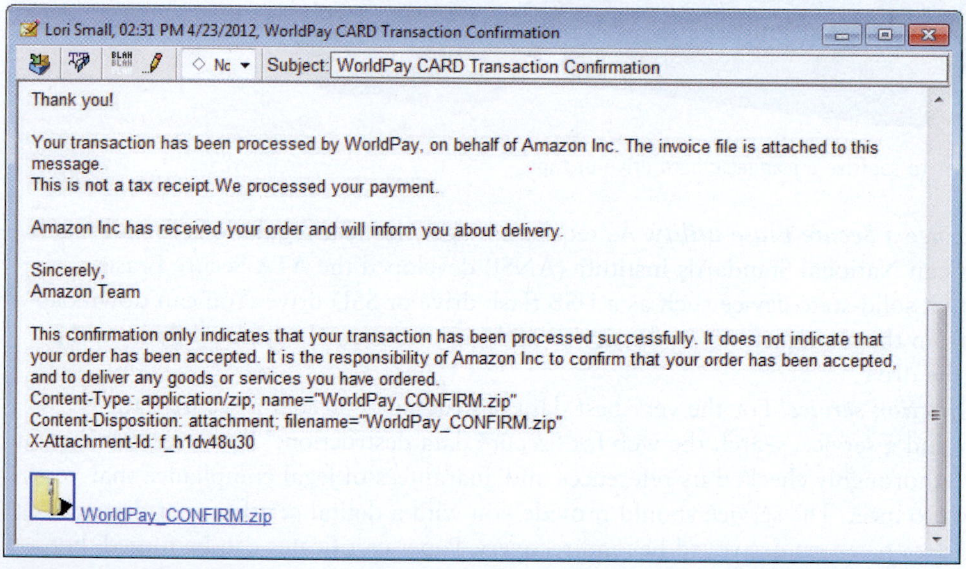

Figure 18-31 This phishing technique using an email message with an attached file is an example of social engineering

> ★ **A+ Exam Tip** The A+ 220-902 exam expects you to be aware of social engineering situations such as tailgating, phishing, and shoulder surfing that might compromise security.

Here are some good sites to help you debunk a virus hoax or email hoax:

- *snopes.com* by Barbara and David Mikkelson
- *securelist.com* by Kaspersky Lab
- *virusbtn.com* by Virus Bulletin, Ltd

Don't forward an email hoax. When you get a hoax, if you know the person who sent it to you, do us all a favor and send that person some of these links!

Here are some other types of online social engineering situations:

- Phishing (pronounced "fishing") is a type of identity theft in which the sender of an email message scams you into responding with personal data about yourself. Even more plausible is spear phishing, where the email appears to come from companies you already do business with. The scam artist baits you by asking you to verify personal data on your bank account, ISP account, credit card account, or something of that nature. Often you are tricked into clicking a link in the email message, which takes you to an official-looking site complete with corporate or bank logos, where you are asked to enter your user ID and password to enter the site. This tactic is called spoofing, which means the scam artist makes both the email and website look like the real thing.
- An email message might contain a link that leads to a malicious script. If you think an email is legitimate, to be on the safe side, still don't click the link. To keep a script from running, type the website's home page into your browser address bar and navigate to the relevant page on the website.

A study by Dell showed that 65 percent of business travelers have not secured the corporate data on their hard drives, and 42 percent don't back up that data. Here are some commonsense rules to help protect a laptop when traveling:

- When traveling, always know where your laptop is. If you're standing at an airport counter, tuck your laptop case securely between your ankles. At security checkpoints, pay attention to your belongings; tell yourself to stay focused. When flying, never check your laptop as baggage, and don't store it in airplane overhead bins; keep it at your feet.
- Never leave a laptop in an unlocked car. If you leave your laptop in a hotel room, use a laptop cable lock to secure it to a table.
- When at work, lock your laptop in a secure place or use a laptop cable lock to secure it to your desk.

An IT support technician will most certainly be called on to help a user rid a system of malware. Let's turn our attention to how to deal with that problem.

DEALING WITH MALICIOUS SOFTWARE ON PERSONAL COMPUTERS

A+
220-902
1.1, 1.5,
3.1, 3.2,
4.2

Malicious software, also called malware, or a computer infestation, is any unwanted program that means you harm and is transmitted to your computer without your knowledge. Grayware is any annoying and unwanted program that might or might not mean you harm, for example adware that produces all those unwanted pop-up ads. In this part of the chapter, you learn about the different types of malware and grayware, what to do to clean up an infected system, and how to protect a system from infection.

18

WHAT ARE WE UP AGAINST?

A+
220-902
3.1, 4.2

You need to know your enemy! Different categories of malicious software and scamming techniques are listed next:

- *Viruses.* A virus is a program that replicates by attaching itself to other programs. The infected program must be executed for a virus to run. The program might be an application, a macro in a document, a Windows system file, or a boot loader program.
- *Spyware.* Spyware spies on you to collect personal information about you that it transmits over the Internet to web-hosting sites. An example of spyware is a keylogger that tracks all your keystrokes and

can be used to steal a person's identity, credit card numbers, Social Security number, bank information, passwords, email addresses, and so forth.

- ***Worms.*** A worm is a program that copies itself throughout a network or the Internet without a host program. A worm creates problems by overloading the network as it replicates and can even hijack or install a server program such as a web server.
- ***Trojans.*** A Trojan does not need a host program to work; rather, it substitutes itself for a legitimate program. In most cases, a user launches it thinking she is launching a legitimate program. A Trojan is often embedded in the files of legitimate software that is downloaded from an untrustworthy website, or a user is tricked into opening an email attachment (refer back to Figure 18-31).
- ***Rootkits.*** A rootkit loads itself before the OS boot is complete. It can hide in boot managers, boot loader programs, or kernel mode device drivers. UEFI secure boot is especially designed to catch rootkits that launch during the boot. Because it is already loaded when most anti-malware software loads, it is sometimes overlooked by the software. A rootkit can hide folders that contain software it has installed, cause Task Manager to display a different name for its process, hide registry keys, and can operate in user mode or kernel mode. This last trick helps it remain undetected (see Figure 18-32).

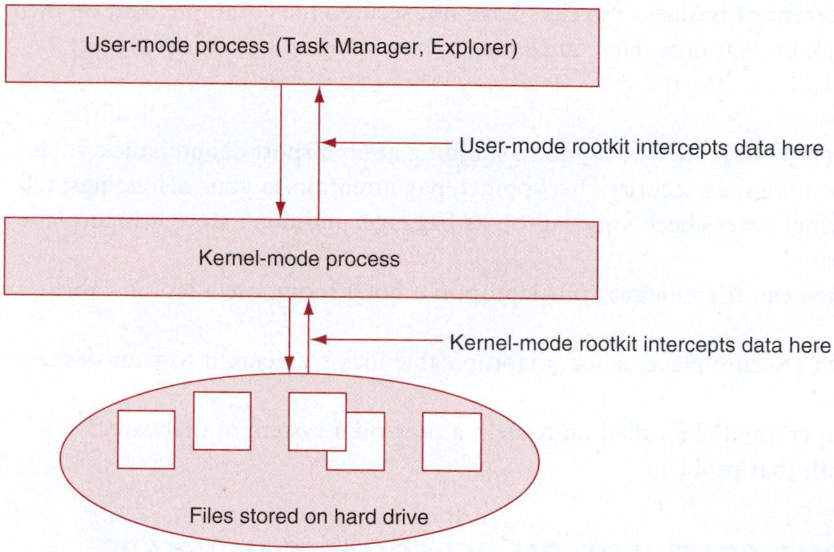

Figure 18-32 A rootkit can run in user mode or kernel mode

A rootkit running in user mode intercepts the API calls between the time when the API retrieves the data and when it is displayed in a window. A rootkit running in kernel mode actually interferes with the Windows kernel and substitutes its own information in place of the raw data read by the Windows kernel. Because most anti-malware software to one degree or another relies on Windows tools and components to work, the rootkit is not detected or cannot be deleted if the Windows tools themselves are infected.

> **Caution** If anti-malware software reports a rootkit is present, but cannot delete it, the best solution is to immediately disconnect the computer from the network (if you have not already done so), back up your important data, format your hard drive, and reinstall Windows.

- ***Ransomware.*** Ransomware holds your computer system hostage until you pay money. For example, the CryptoLocker Trojan program that did damage in 2014 was embedded in email attachments and was known to work on Windows, Android, and even some iOS systems. When the user clicked the attachment, the program encrypted the computer's personal files. If the user didn't pay within a 24-hour period, all the files were lost. Many users who did not have backups of their data chose to pay the ransom.

- *Zero-day attack.* A zero-day attack can happen when a hacker discovers a security hole in software that is unknown to the developer of the software. The race is on for the vendor to provide a patch to the software before hackers have even one day to use the hole to infect systems and steal user data. Microsoft normally publishes security patches on the second and fourth Tuesday of each month (known as patch Tuesday), but sometimes releases patches off schedule so that hackers have zero days to attack customers.
- *Man-in-the-middle attack.* In a man-in-the-middle attack, the attacker intercepts communication between two parties and reads and/or alters the content of messages. The attacker can pretend to be a legitimate website, network, FTP site, or person in a chat session. For example, a user might connect to an "evil twin" Wi-Fi hotspot, thinking it's a legitimate hotspot, and attempt to start a chat session with a business associate. The attacker pretends to be the business associate and continues the chat with the intention of obtaining private information. The best protection against man-in-the-middle attacks is to use digital certificates to identify a person or service before transmitting sensitive information.
- *Zombies and botnets.* A zombie is a computer that has been hacked, and the hacker is using the computer to run repetitive software in the background without the knowledge of its user. For example, the zombie might be email spamming or performing denial-of-service attacks (attacks from multiple computers that overwhelm a server with requests until new connections can no longer be accepted). A hacker might build an entire network of zombies, which is called a botnet (a network of robots). The CryptoLocker Trojan program was distributed by a botnet and ultimately isolated when the botnet was taken down.
- *Dictionary attack.* A dictionary attack can be used to crack a password by trying words in a dictionary. Password cracker software might combine a brute force attack with a dictionary attack to use smarter guessing to guess the password.

★ A+ Exam Tip The A+ 220-902 exam expects you to be able to compare and contrast viruses, Trojans, worms, spyware, ransomware, and rootkits. You also need to know about zero-day attacks, man-in-the-middle attacks, zombies, botnets, dictionary attacks, brute force attacks, and noncompliant systems.

- *Non compliant systems and violations of security best practices.* Administrators who remotely manage many servers or workstations on a large network might use configuration management software, such as Microsoft System Center, to remotely configure computers and monitor these configurations. Agents are installed on each computer to be monitored that routinely report the configuration back to the management software. The administrator routinely receives and reviews these reports, comparing the reported configurations with the established configuration baseline. For security purposes, she specifically looks for non compliant systems that violate security best practices, such as out-of-date anti-malware software or no anti-malware software installed.

18

STEP-BY-STEP ATTACK PLAN

A+ 220-902 4.2

This section is a step-by-step attack plan to clean up an infected system. We use anti-malware software, also called antivirus software, to remove all types of general malware, including viruses, spyware, worms, and rootkits. Then we'll use some Windows tools to check out the system to make sure all remnants of malware have been removed and the system is in tip-top order.

Caution If a system is highly infected and will later hold sensitive data, a fresh start might be in order. In fact, Microsoft recommends reinstalling Windows as the safest way to deal with highly infected systems.

For Windows 8, a refresh can be an excellent option if you have a custom refresh image and current backups of user data. For Windows 7, consider using a system image to reinstall Windows and then restore data from recent backups.

STEP 1: IDENTIFY MALWARE SYMPTOMS

An IT support technician needs to know how to recognize that a system is infected with malware and how to clean an infected system. Here are some warnings that suggest malicious software is at work:

- *Pop-up ads and browser redirection.* Basically, a user is losing control of his system. For example, Figure 18-33 shows the desktop immediately after a user signed in. Pop-up ads are randomly appearing and the browser home page has changed. A browser might also have an uninvited toolbar.

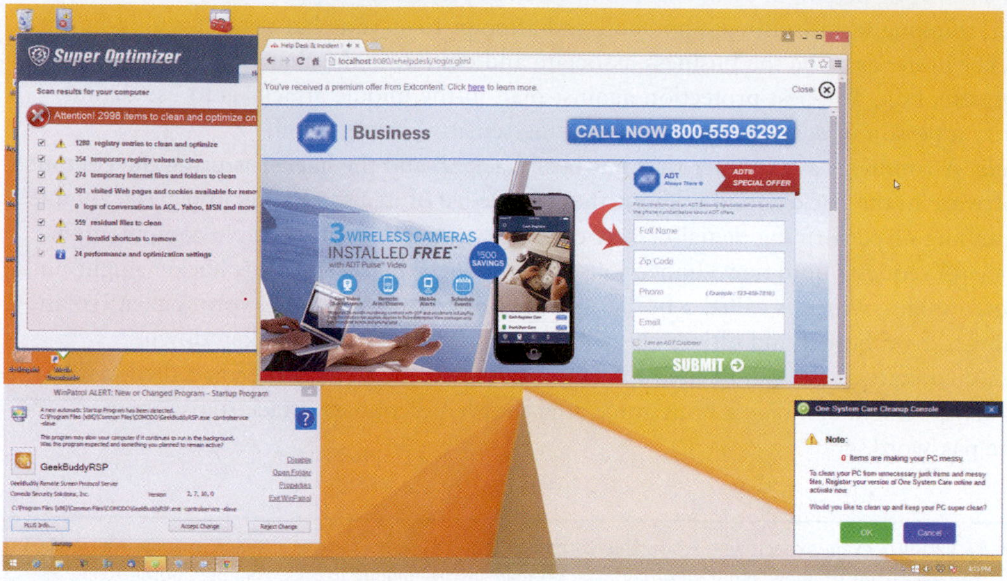

Source: Ruiware, LLC

Figure 18-33 A hijacked home page, security alerts, and pop-up ads indicate an infected system

- *Rogue antivirus software.* When the user above tried to run Windows Defender (anti-malware software embedded in Windows 8), it refused to run. She opened the Action Center to find that Defender had been disabled because other antivirus software she did not install was running. See Figure 18-34.

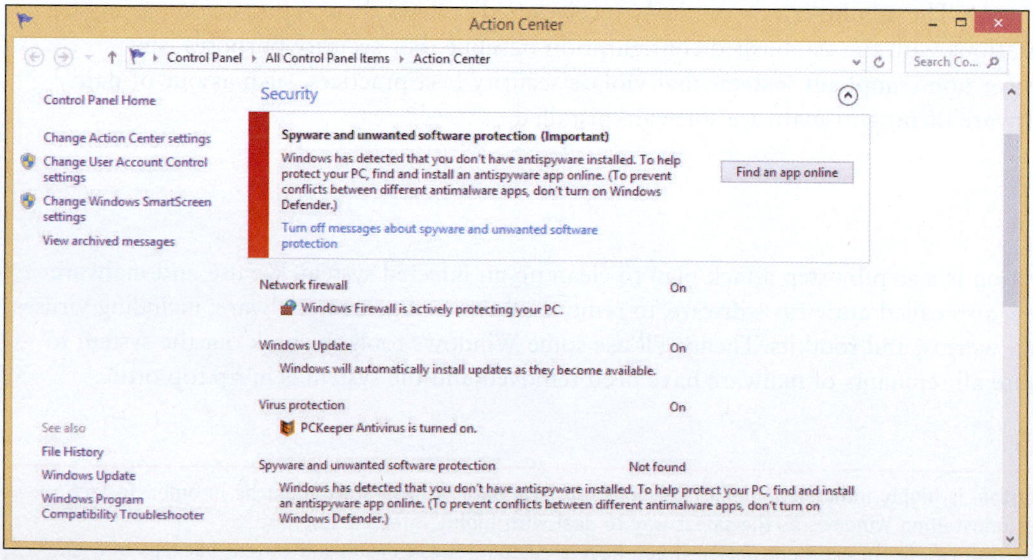

Figure 18-34 Action Center reports Windows Defender has been disabled and rogue antivirus software is running

Windows allows only one anti-malware product to run at a time. You can use Task Manager to stop the rogue antivirus software and then start Windows Defender.

- ***Slow performance or lockups.*** Generally, the system works much slower than it used to. Programs take longer than normal to load. Strange or bizarre error messages appear. Programs that once worked now give errors. Task Manager shows unfamiliar processes running. The system might even lock up.
- ***Internet connectivity issues, application crashes, and OS updates fail.*** These types of problems seem to plague the system with no reasonable explanation that is specific to the network, application, or Windows update. Remember that Event Viewer can be used to view logs of system crashes, application crashes, and failed OS updates.
- ***Problems with files.*** File names now have weird characters or their file sizes seem excessively large. Executable files have changed size or file extensions change without reason. Files mysteriously disappear or appear. Windows system files are renamed. Files constantly become corrupted. Files you could once access now give access denied messages, and file permissions change.
- ***Email problems.*** You receive email messages telling you that you have sent someone spam or an infected message, or you receive automated replies indicating you sent email you didn't know about. This type of attack indicates your email address or email client software on your computer has been hijacked.
- ***Problems updating your anti-malware software.*** Even though you can browse to other websites, you cannot access anti-malware software sites such as *www.symantec.com* or *www.mcafee.com*, and you cannot update your anti-malware software.
- ***Invalid digital certificates.*** An OS is responsible for validating certificates used to secure communication. For Windows, Microsoft maintains a database of trusted root certificates issued by Certification Authorities (CAs). (A root certificate is the original certificate issued by the CA.) When a Windows system opens a secure email or visits a secure website and encounters a new digital certificate, it requests the trusted root certificate from Microsoft, which is downloaded to the computer. The download happens seamlessly without the user's knowledge unless there's a problem. If Windows cannot obtain the root certificate to validate the email or website, it displays an error (see Figure 18-35). Don't trust websites or email whose certificates have expired or been revoked.

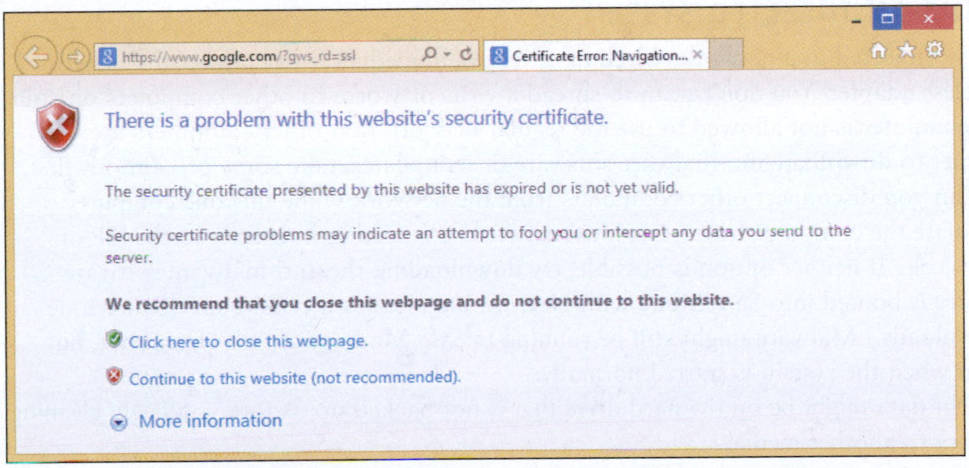

Figure 18-35 Windows reports a problem with a digital certificate

> **Notes** If a computer gives invalid certificate errors, check that the Windows date is correct. A wrong Windows date before the certificate was issued can cause the problem.

You can use the Certificate Manager (certmgr.msc) to view and delete root certificates (see Figure 18-36). For example, the Superfish virus injects a rogue root certificate into the Microsoft store of trusted certificates on the local computer so that it can perform a man-in-the-middle attack to display adware on secure websites a user visits. If you see a Superfish certificate listed among trusted root certificates, be sure to delete it.

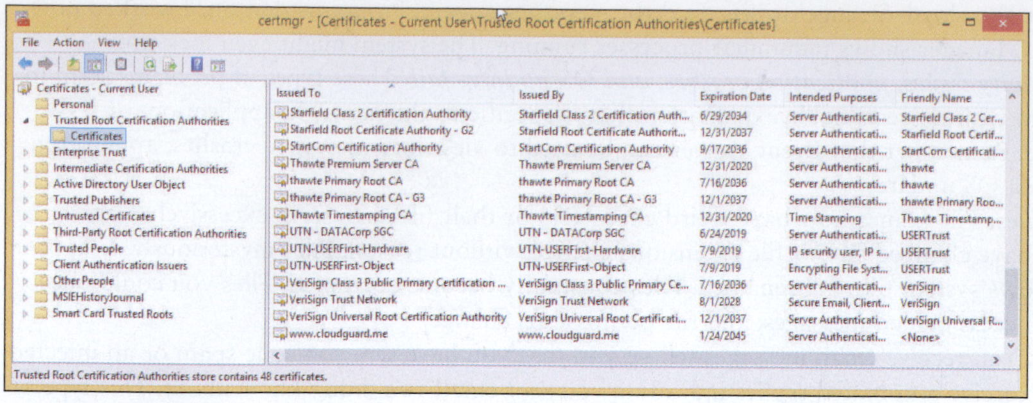

Figure 18-36 Windows Certificate Manager can be used to view and delete root certificates kept in the store of trusted certificates

> **A+ Exam Tip** The A+ 220-902 exam expects you to know about the common symptoms of malware listed previously and how to quarantine and remediate an infected system.

> **Notes** Malicious software is designed to do varying degrees of damage to data and software, although it does not damage computer hardware. However, when partition table information is destroyed on a hard drive, the hard drive can appear to be physically damaged.

STEP 2: QUARANTINE AN INFECTED SYSTEM

If an infected computer is connected to a network (wired or wireless), immediately disconnect the network cable or turn off the wireless adapter. You don't want to spread a virus or worm to other computers on your network. A quarantined computer is not allowed to use the regular network that other computers use. If you need to use the Internet to download anti-malware software or its updates, take some precautions first. Consider your options. Can you disconnect other computers from the network while this one computer is connected? Can you isolate the computer from your local network, connecting it directly to the ISP or a special quarantined network? If neither option is possible, try downloading the anti-malware software updates while the computer is booted into Safe Mode with Networking or after a clean boot. (Safe Mode doesn't always allow downloads.) Malware might still be running in Safe Mode or after a clean boot, but is less likely to do so than when the system is started normally.

Always keep in mind that data might be on the hard drive that is not backed up. Before you begin cleaning up the system, back up data to another media.

STEP 3: DISABLE SYSTEM RESTORE

In Windows, some malware hides its program files in restore points stored in the System Volume Information folder maintained by System Protection. If System Protection is on, anti-malware software can't clean this protected folder. To get rid of that malware, turn off System Protection so that anti-malware can clean the System Volume Information folder (see Figure 18-37). Realize that when you turn off System Protection, all your restore points are lost. To turn off System Protection, open the System window and click **System protection**. Later, when you are sure the system is clean, turn System Protection back on and create a new restore point that you can use in the future if problems arise.

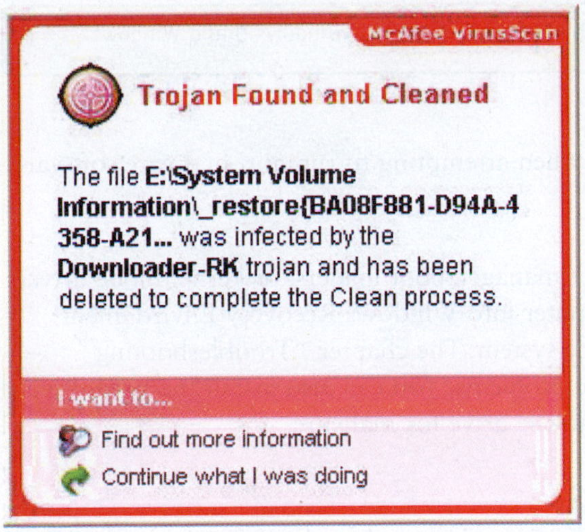

Source: McAfee VirusScan

Figure 18-37 Malware found in a restore point

> **Caution** Some highly infected systems will not allow anti-malware software to run. In this situation, you can boot the computer into Safe Mode and use System Restore to apply a restore point that was taken before the infection. Applying a restore point cannot be counted on to completely remove an infection, but it might remove startup entries the malware is using, making it possible to run the anti-malware software from the normal Windows desktop or run the software in Safe Mode. Consider that you might need to apply a restore point before you disable System Protection, which deletes all your restore points.

STEP 4: REMEDIATE THE INFECTED SYSTEM

Table 18-1 lists popular anti-malware software for personal computers and websites that also provide information about malware. Before selecting a product, be sure to read some reviews about it and check out some reliable websites that rate anti-malware software.

> **Caution** Beware of websites that appear as sponsored links at the top of search results for anti-malware software. These sites might make you think they are the home site for the software, but are really trying to lure you into downloading adware or spyware.

Anti-Malware Software	Website
Security Software by Trend Micro (for home use)	*trendmicro.com*
Intelligent Antivirus and Anti-malware by AVAST Software (home edition is free)	*avast.com*
AVG Antivirus Protection by AVG Technologies	*avg.com*
Bitdefender Antivirus	*bitdefender.com*
CLAMWIN Free Antivirus by ClamWin (open source and free)	*clamwin.com*
F-Secure Anti-Virus by F-Secure Corp	*f-secure.com*
Kaspersky Antivirus and Internet Security	*kaspersky.com*
Malwarebytes Anti-Malware (free version available)	*malwarebytes.org*
McAfee Total Protection	*mcafee.com*
Symantec Endpoint Protection	*symantec.com*
Panda Internet Security	*pandasecurity.com*
SUPERAntiSpyware	*superantispyware.com*
Microsoft Security Essentials (free)	*windows.microsoft.com*

Table 18-1 Anti-malware software and websites

> **OS Differences** **Windows Defender** anti-malware software is embedded in Windows 8 and can be accessed through Control Panel. Windows 7 includes Windows Defender, but the Windows 7 version finds only spyware, not viruses and other malware. For Windows 7, you can download and install Microsoft Security Essentials, which is free anti-malware software.

A+ Exam Tip The A+ 220-902 exam expects you to know about Windows Defender in Windows 8 and Windows 7.

Now let's look at different situations you might encounter when attempting to run anti-malware software.

When an Infected Computer Will Not Boot

If an infected computer will not boot, it might be that the boot manager, boot loaders, or kernel mode drivers launched at startup are infected or damaged. Launch the computer into Windows Recovery Environment (Windows RE) and use the Startup Repair process to repair the system. The chapter, "Troubleshooting Windows Startup," gives more information about solving boot problems. You can also install the hard drive as a second drive in another system and use that system to scan the drive for malware.

Update and Run Anti-Malware Software Already Installed

If anti-malware software is already installed and you suspect an infection, update the software and perform a full scan on the system. Do the following:

1. Make sure the anti-malware software is up to date. These updates download the latest malware definitions, also called malware signatures, which the software uses to define or detect new malware as it gets into the wild.
2. Use the anti-malware software to perform a full scan of the system. As it scans, the software might ask you what to do with an infected program or it might log this event in an event viewer or history log it keeps. For example, Windows Defender reports a threat, as shown in Figure 18-38. When you click **Clean PC**, you can decide what to do with the threat. In most situations, select **Remove** to delete the program.

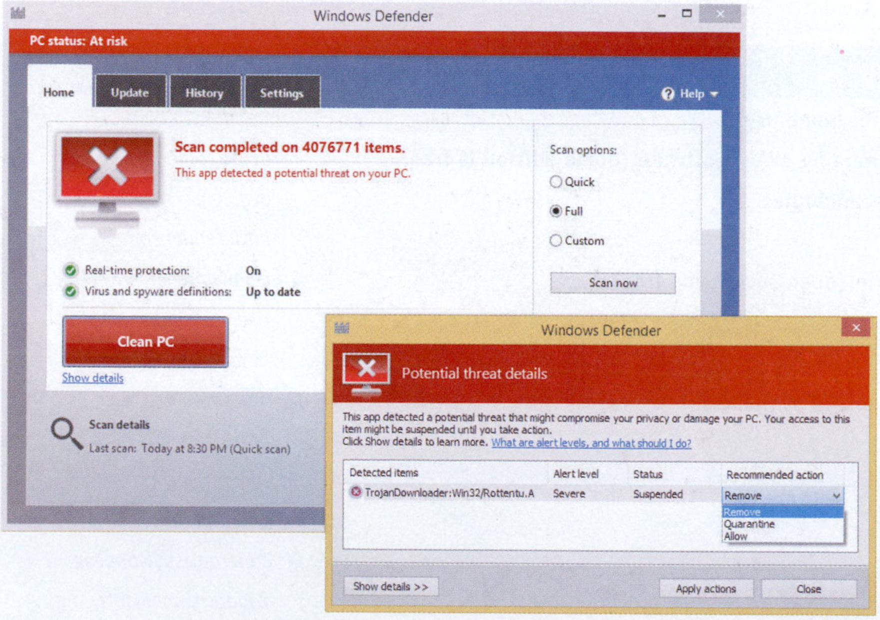

Figure 18-38 Decide what to do with a program that Windows Defender has identified as a severe threat to the system

3. After the scan is complete and you have decided what to do with each suspicious file, reboot the system and allow the software to update itself again and then scan the system again. Most likely, some new malware will be discovered. Keep rebooting and rescanning until a scan comes up clean.

> **Notes** If you ever encounter a virus that your updated anti-malware software did not find, be sure to let the manufacturer of the software know so they can research the problem.

Run Anti-Malware Software from a Networked Computer

If anti-malware software is not already installed, the most effective way to clean the computer is to run the software from another computer. Follow these steps:

1. Make sure the remote computer has its software firewall set for maximum protection and its installed anti-malware software is up to date and running.
2. Network the two computers and share drive C: on the infected computer. (Don't connect the infected computer to the entire network. If necessary, you can connect the two computers using a crossover cable or using a small switch and network cables.)
3. To make your work easier, you can map a network drive from the remote computer to drive C: on the infected computer.
4. Perform an anti-malware scan on the remote computer, pointing the scan to drive C: on the infected computer.

Install and Run Anti-Malware Software on the Infected Computer

If you don't have another computer available on the network to scan the infected computer, you can use another computer to purchase and download the anti-malware software and copy the downloaded files to a CD or flash drive that you can insert in the infected computer. Don't make the mistake of using the infected computer to purchase and download anti-malware software because keyloggers might be spying and collecting credit card information. During the installation process, the anti-malware software updates itself and performs a scan. You can also run free online anti-malware software without downloading and installing it, but be careful to use only reputable websites.

Install and Run Anti-Malware Software in Safe Mode

Some malware prevents anti-malware software from installing or running. In this situation, try booting the system in Safe Mode or performing a clean boot and installing the anti-malware software. Some viruses still load in Safe Mode or after a clean boot, and some anti-malware programs will not install in Safe Mode.

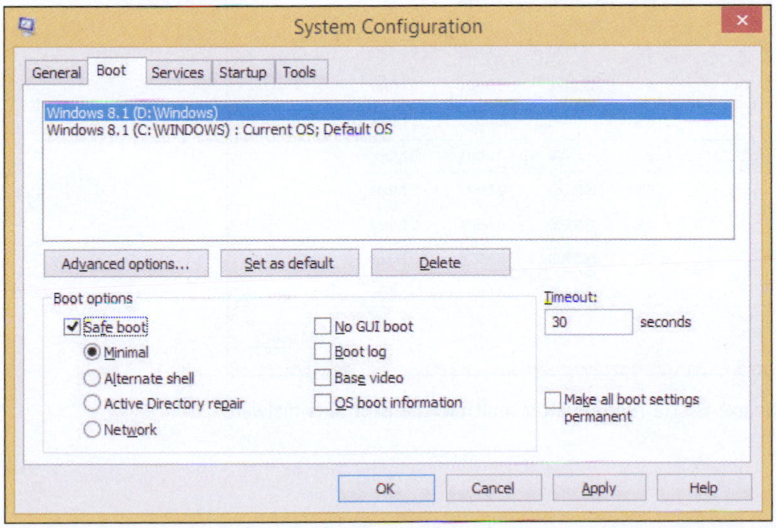

Figure 18-39 Use the Safe boot option to boot the system in Safe Mode to prevent malware from launching at startup

Recall that to launch Windows in Safe Mode, enter the **msconfig** command in the Windows 8 Run box or Windows 7 Search box. In the System Configuration box, on the Boot tab, check **Safe boot** (see Figure 18-39). To launch Safe Mode with Networking so that you can update your anti-malware software, select **Network** in the list of options. Then restart the system.

Notes If viruses are launched even after you boot in Safe Mode and you cannot get the anti-malware software to work, try searching for suspicious entries in the Windows registry subkeys under HKLM\System\CurrentControlSet\Control\SafeBoot. Subkeys under this key control what is launched when you boot into Safe Mode. How to edit the registry is covered in the chapter, "Optimizing Windows."

RUN THE ANTI-MALWARE SOFTWARE FROM A BOOTABLE RESCUE CD OR FLASH DRIVE

Some anti-malware products, such as the AVG Rescue CD software, offer the option to create a bootable USB flash drive or CD. You can then use this device to boot the system and run the anti-malware software from the device in this preinstallation environment. Most of the products listed earlier in Table 18-1 offer the option on their website to download software to create a bootable CD or flash drive. Be sure to use a healthy computer to create the rescue CD or flash drive. In addition, you might need to create a 32-bit version to scan a 32-bit Windows system or a 64-bit version to scan a 64-bit system. When selecting a product to create a bootable device, find one that can store the latest updates on the CD or flash drive so you don't need Internet access when you scan the infected system.

RUN MORE THAN ONE SCAN OF ANTI-MALWARE

After you've scanned the system using one of the methods just discussed, reboot and install anti-malware software on the hard drive. Update the software, and then keep scanning and rebooting until the scan report is clean.

If a second or third scan doesn't remove all symptoms of malware, consider installing and running a second anti-malware program. What one anti-malware program cannot detect or remove, another one might. For example, Windows Defender on one system removed malware it detected, but did not detect or remove the downloader dnsatlantic.exe, which hijacks a browser and is still running in the background (see Figure 18-40).

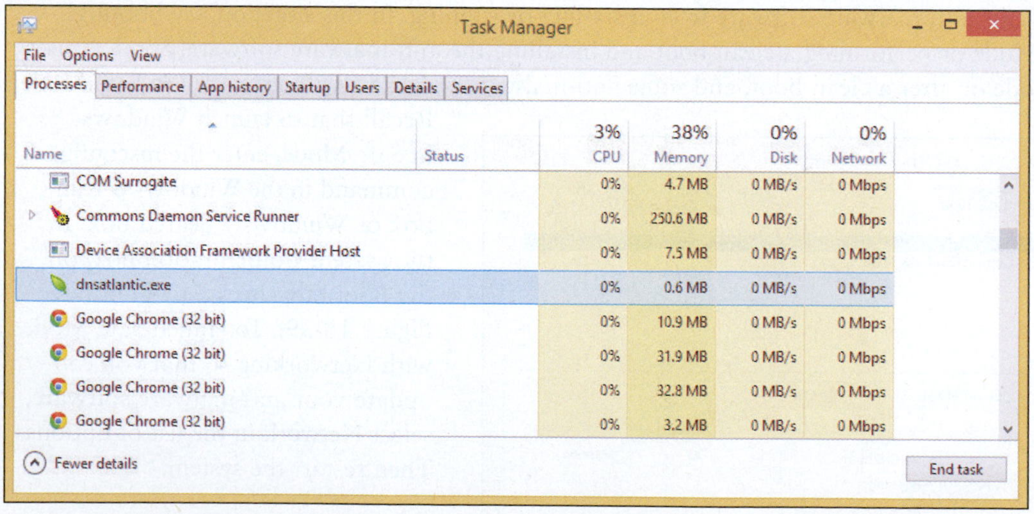

Figure 18-40 The malware downloader dnsatlantic.exe is still running after multiple scans of anti-malware software

In this situation, try another anti-malware program. For example, Microsoft Safety Scanner (*microsoft.com/security/scanner*) is not designed for on going malware prevention but can sometimes remove malware that Windows Defender did not find.

CLEAN UP WHAT'S LEFT OVER

Next, you'll need to clean up anything the anti-malware software left behind. Sometimes anti-malware software tells you it is not able to delete a file, or it deletes an infected file but leaves behind an orphaned entry in the registry or startup folders. If the anti-malware software tells you it was not able to delete or clean a file, first check the anti-malware software website for any instructions you might find to manually clean things up. Here are some general actions you can take to clean up what the software left behind:

1. ***Respond to any startup errors.*** On the first boot after anti-malware software has declared a system clean, you might still find some startup errors caused by incomplete removal of the malware. Use System Configuration and/or Task Manager to find out how a startup program is launched. If the program is launched from the registry, you can back up and delete the registry key. If the program is launched from a startup folder, you can move or delete the shortcut or program in the folder. See the chapter, "Optimizing Windows," for the details of how to remove unwanted startup programs.
2. ***Research malware types and program files.*** Your anti-malware software might alert you to a suspicious program file that it quarantines, and then ask you to decide if you want to delete it. Also, Task Manager and other tools might find processes you suspect are malware. The web is your best tool to use when making your decision about a program. Here are some websites that offer malware encyclopedias that are reliable and give you symptoms and solutions for malware:
   - Process Library by Uniblue Systems Limited at *www.processlibrary.com*
   - DLL Library by Uniblue Systems Limited at *www.liutilities.com*
   - All the anti-malware software sites listed earlier in the chapter in Table 18-1

   Beware of using other sites! Much information on the web is written by people who are just guessing, and some of the information is put there to purposefully deceive. Check things out carefully, and learn which sites you can rely on.
3. ***Delete files.*** For each program file the anti-malware software told you it could not delete, delete the program file yourself following these steps:

   a. First try File Explorer or Windows Explorer to locate a file and delete it. For peace of mind, don't forget to empty the Recycle Bin when you're done.

   b. If the file is hidden or access is denied, open an elevated command prompt window and use the commands listed in Table 18-2 to take control of a file so you can delete it. If the commands don't work using an elevated command prompt window, use the commands in a command prompt window in Windows RE.

Command	Description
`attrib -r -s filename.ext`	Remove the read-only and system attributes to a file.
`tasklist |more` `taskkill /f /pid:9999`	To stop a running process, first use the tasklist command to find out the process ID for the process. Then use the taskkill command to forcefully kill the process with the given process ID.
`takeown /f filename.ext`	Take ownership of a file.
`icacls filename.ext /GRANT ADMINISTRATORS:F`	Take full access of a file.

Table 18-2 Commands used to take control of a malware file so you can delete it

   c. To get rid of other malware files, delete all Internet Explorer temporary Internet files. To do so, use the Disk Cleanup process in the Drive C: properties box, or delete the browsing history using the Internet Options box.

   d. Delete all subfolders and files in the C:\Windows\Temp folder. Figure 18-41 shows where Windows Defender lists potentially unwanted programs (PuPs) that a Trojan downloader put in this folder.

18

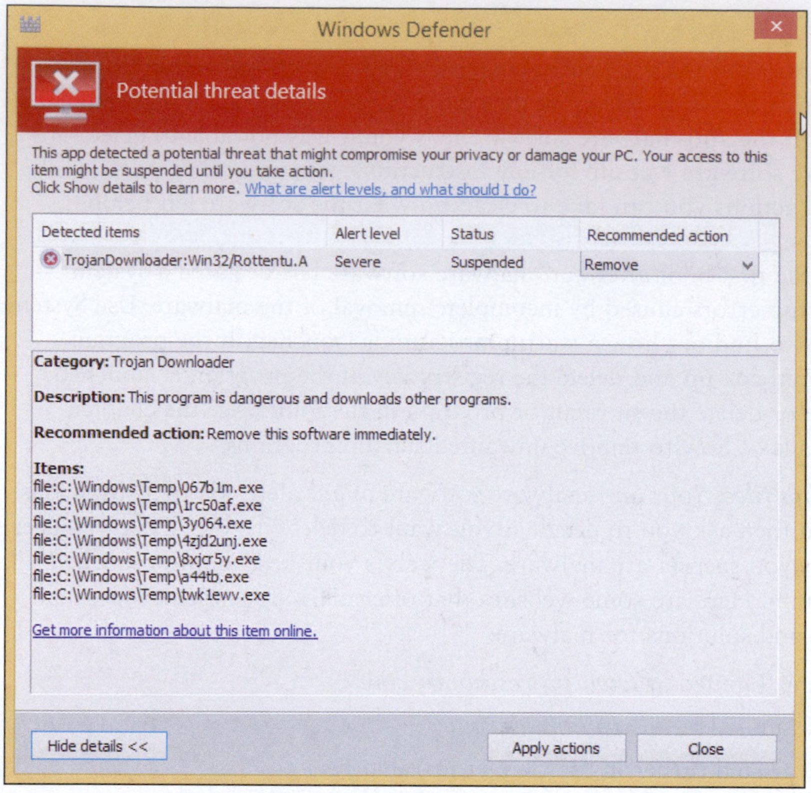

Figure 18-41 A Trojan downloader put programs in the C:/Windows/Temp folder, which must be manually deleted

4. *Clean the registry.* The appendix, "Entry Points for Windows Startup Processes," lists registry keys that can affect startup. You can search these keys and delete entries you don't want. After you have finished cleaning the registry, don't forget to restart the system to make sure all is well before you move on.

5. ***Clean up Internet Explorer and uninstall unwanted programs.*** Adware and spyware might install add-ons to Internet Explorer (including toolbars you didn't ask for), install cookie trackers, and change your Internet Explorer security settings. Anti-malware software might have found all these items, but as a good defense, take a few minutes to find out for yourself. The chapter, "Windows Resources on a Network," covers how to use the Internet Options box to search for unwanted add-ons and delete ActiveX controls. You can uninstall unwanted toolbars, plug-ins, and other software using the Programs and Features window (see Figure 18-42).

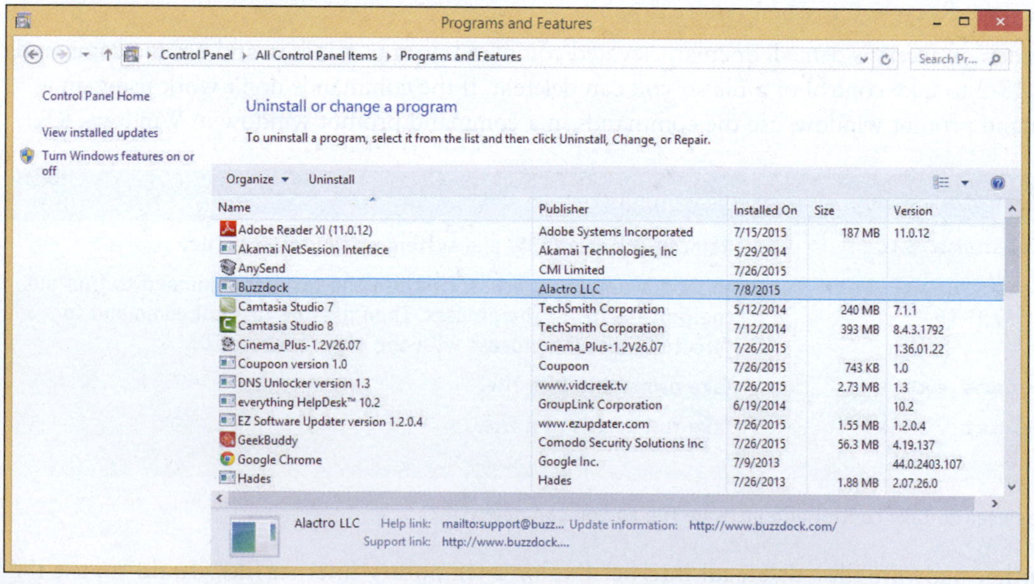

Figure 18-42 A Trojan downloader on this computer installed several unwanted programs, which must be uninstalled

STEP 5: PROTECT THE SYSTEM WITH SCHEDULED SCANS AND UPDATES

Once your system is clean, you'll certainly want to keep it that way. The three best practices you need to follow to protect a system against malware are:

- *Use anti-malware software.* Install and run anti-malware software and keep it current. Configure the software so that it (1) runs in the background in real time to alert users of malware that attempts to run or install, (2) automatically scans incoming email attachments, and (3) performs scheduled scans of the system and automatically downloads updates to the software. To find out what anti-malware software is installed and turned on, open the Action Center.
- *Always use a software firewall.* Never, ever connect your computer to an unprotected network without using a firewall. Windows Firewall is turned on by default. Recall that you can configure Windows Firewall to allow no uninvited communication in or to allow in the exceptions that you specify.
- *Keep Windows updates current.* Windows updates are continually being released to plug up vulnerable entrances in Windows where malware might attack and to update Windows Defender and Microsoft Security Essentials. Recall you can verify Windows Update settings by clicking **Windows Update** in the System window.

STEP 6: ENABLE SYSTEM PROTECTION AND CREATE A RESTORE POINT

Now that the system is clean, if System Protection is still turned off, turn it back on and create a restore point.

STEP 7: EDUCATE THE END USER

Now would be a good time to go over with the user some tips presented earlier in the chapter to keep the system free from malware. Sometimes the most overlooked step in preventing malware infections is to educate the user. Even with all your security measures in place, a user can still download and execute a Trojan, which can install more malware in the system.

★ A+ Exam Tip The A+ 220-902 exam expects you to know about the seven steps to remove malware. Memorize these seven steps and know how to use them.

Hands-On Project 18-5 Create and Use an Anti-Malware Software Rescue Disc

A+ 220-902 4.2

When an infected computer does not have anti-malware software installed, one method to clean the infection is to create and use an anti-malware rescue disc. Select anti-malware software that offers a free download to create a bootable USB flash drive or CD. For example, Windows Defender Offline or F-Secure Rescue CD can be used. Create a bootable USB flash drive or CD and use it to scan a computer. Answer the following questions:

1. What is the URL where you found the download to create a rescue disc or drive?
2. List the files in the root directory of the USB flash drive or CD that the software created.
3. Describe the menu or screen that appears when you booted from the rescue media.

Hands-On | Project 18-6 Download and Use Anti-Malware Software

A+
220-902
4.2

A free trial of AVG Protection software is available on the AVG site at *www.avg.com*. Do the following to download, install, and run the software:

1. Download the free trial version of AVG Protection software from the *www.avg.com* site and install the software.
2. Update the software with the latest malware signatures.
3. Perform a complete scan of the system. Were any suspicious programs found?
4. Set the software to scan the system daily.
5. Set the software to scan incoming email.

Hands-On | Project 18-7 Use the Web to Learn About Malware

One source of information about malware on the web is F-Secure Corporation. Go to the website *www.f-secure.com*, and find information about the latest malware threats. Answer the following questions:

1. Name and describe a recent Trojan downloader. How does the Trojan install and what is its payload (the harm it does)?
2. Name and describe a recent rootkit. How does the rootkit install and what is its payload?
3. Name a recent worm. How does it get into the network and what is its payload?

DEALING WITH MALICIOUS SOFTWARE ON MOBILE DEVICES

A+
220-902
4.4

In this part of the chapter, you learn how to deal with malicious software on mobile devices. We begin with how to recognize a device might be infected.

COMMON MOBILE DEVICE MALWARE SYMPTOMS

A+
220-902
4.4

Android and Windows Phone devices are more susceptible to malware than iOS devices because apps can be downloaded from other sites than Google or Microsoft. With iOS devices, apps can be obtained only from the Apple App Store and, therefore, are more strictly vetted. However, for any mobile device, malware can be introduced by a Trojan that a user accepts as an email attachment or by some other means or by macros embedded in shared documents.

Here are some symptoms that malware might be at work on an Android, iOS, or Windows Phone device:

- ***Battery drain, slow speeds, leaked data, strange text messages, and data transmission over limits.*** Battery power draining faster than normal or slow data upload or download speeds can indicate that apps are running in the background. For example, when the XAgent malware app installs on an Apple device with iOS version 7 or below, the app icon is hidden, and the app runs in the background. When you close the app, it restarts. The malware not only uses resources, it steals personal data and makes screen shots and sends them to a remote command-and-control (C&C) server. A C&C server might send coded text messages to your phone. If you receive strange text messages, suspect malware. Another indication of malware at work is a spike in your data usage charges on your phone bill.

- ***Dropped phone calls or weak signal.*** Dropped phone calls can happen when malware is interfering and trying to eavesdrop on your conversations or is performing other background activities.
- ***Unintended Wi-Fi and Bluetooth connections.*** Malicious Wi-Fi hotspots and Bluetooth devices can hijack a device or inject it with malware. When your mobile device connects to a malicious Wi-Fi hotspot, the device can receive a malicious script that repeatedly reboots your device, which prevents you from using the device. To prevent this type of attack, avoid the free Wi-Fi hotspots. To prevent your device from pairing with a malicious Bluetooth device, turn off Bluetooth when you're not using it.
- ***Unauthorized account access.*** A malicious app can steal passwords and data from other apps and can pretend to be a different app to get access to online accounts. If you suspect an online account has been hacked, consider malware might be on your mobile device that uses this account.
- ***Unauthorized location tracking.*** Spyware apps installed on a mobile device can report its location to a C&C server.
- ***Unauthorized use of camera or microphone.*** Unauthorized surveillance is a sure sign of malware. Stalker spyware apps have been known to take photos and send them to a C&C server; send a text alert to a hacker and then add the hacker to a live call; use the microphone to record live conversations and then send the recording to a C&C server; report Facebook, Skype, Viber, and iMessage activity, including passwords and location data; and upload all photos, videos, and text messages to a C&C server.
- ***Unauthorized root access.*** Malware is more likely to install on a jailbroken iOS device or rooted Android or Windows Phone device. Here's what you need to know:
  - ***Jailbroken iOS device.*** To find out if an iOS device has been jailbroken, look for an unusual app icon on the home screen, for example, the Installer app, Cydia app, or Icy app. If any of these apps is present, the device has been jailbroken. If you have any app icon on your home screen that is not available in the App Store, the app is most likely a jailbreak app or other malware. A jailbroken device can download apps from sources other than the Apple App Store. When you update iOS using iTunes, the jailbreak will be removed.
  - ***Rooted Android device.*** One way to find out if an Android device has been rooted is to download and run the Root Checker Basic free app. Figure 18-43 shows the report you get when Root Checker Basic reports a device is not rooted.

    Another way to tell if a device is rooted is to download a terminal window app. (A terminal window in Linux is similar to a command prompt window in Windows.) When you open the app, look at the command prompt. If the prompt is a #, the device is rooted. If the prompt is a $, the device is likely not rooted. With the $ prompt showing, try the sudo su root command, which in Linux allows you root access. If the prompt changes to #, the device is rooted.

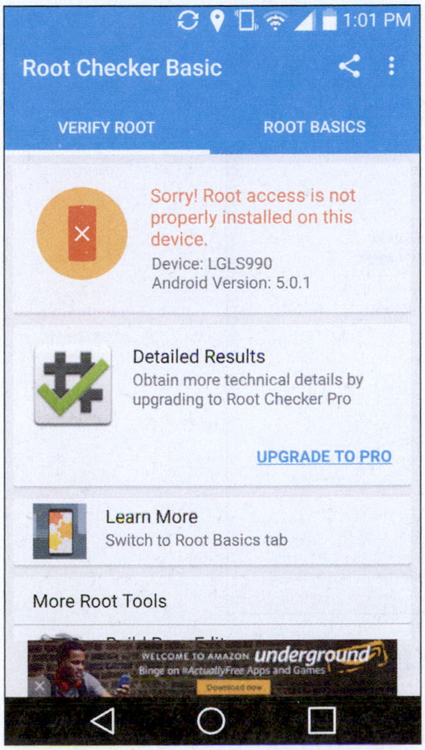

Source: Android

Figure 18-43 Root Checker Basic reports an Android device is not rooted

> **Notes** In Linux, the # command prompt displays when a user has root access and the $ command prompt displays when a user does not have root access.

  - ***Rooted Windows Phone.*** Although it was possible to root Windows Phone 7, as of this writing, there is currently no way to root Windows Phone 8.1.

18

MOBILE DEVICE TOOLS AND MALWARE REMOVAL

A+ 220-902 4.4

Here are general steps for removing malware from a mobile device, listed from least to most invasive:

- ***Uninstall the offending app.*** If you can identify the malware app, uninstall it. If the app won't uninstall, force stop it and try to uninstall again. Recall you can force stop Android apps using the Settings app. Tap **Apps**, swipe to the left to see running apps, and tap a running app to force stop it.
- ***Update the OS.*** For an iOS device, use iTunes on your computer to perform the update rather than updating the iOS directly from the device. For other devices, use the methods you learned about in the chapter, "Supporting Mobile Operating Systems."
- ***Remove root access to the device.*** An Android device that has been rooted cannot receive an Android OS update. To unroot the device so you can update it, use one of these methods:
  - ***Unroot with the app that was used to root the device.*** For example, if you find the SuperSU app installed on the device, most likely it was used to root the device. Open the app and tap **Full unroot** to unroot the device.
  - ***Download a root removal app.*** Search online for reviews about root removal apps before you select one. One example is the Universal Unroot app–download and install it to remove root access from the device.
- ***Perform a factory reset.*** The most sure fire way to remove malware is to back up your data and other content, reset your device to its factory default state, which is also called a clean install, and then restore your content from backup. Here are the steps for an iPhone:

1. Using iTunes on your computer, make sure iTunes is using the latest updates. Then connect your iPhone to your computer.
2. Use iTunes to back up your iPhone to the computer. In the Backups group, select **This computer** and click **Back Up Now** (see Figure 18-44). To verify the backup is made, click **Edit, Preferences, Device** and look for the backup listed.

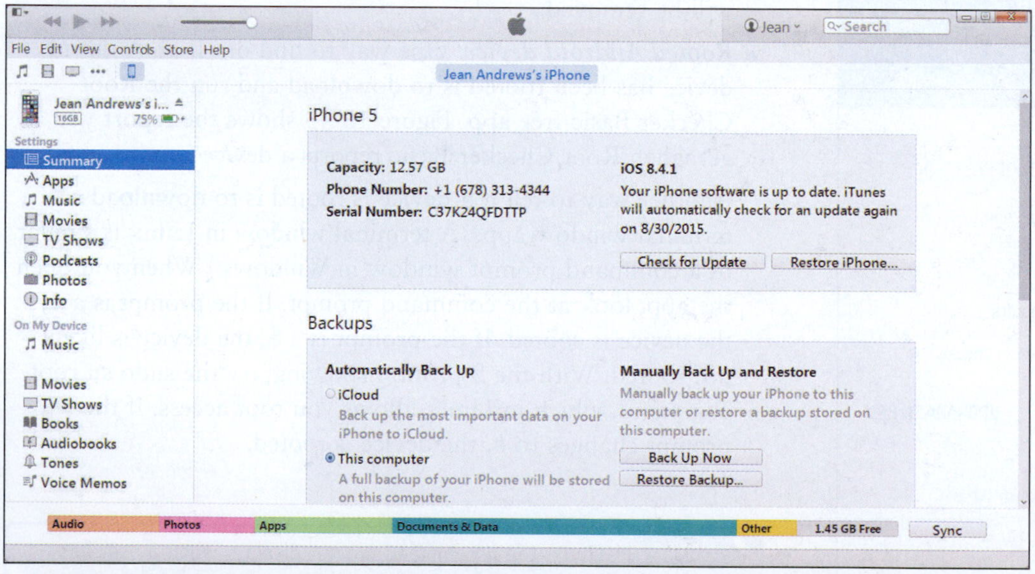

Source: Apple iOS

Figure 18-44 Use the Backups section in the iTunes window to manage backups to this computer

3. If you have made purchases on the iPhone that have not yet been backed up to the computer, you can click **File, Devices,** and **Transfer Purchased from "iPhone"**.
4. Click **Restore iPhone** to restore the device, which deletes all data and content and restores the device firmware to factory settings. After the restore, the device restarts and you are given the opportunity to select a previous backup to restore data and content. Select the backup you just made.

After you have removed malware on a mobile device, you will want to keep it clean. Here are a few tips:

- Don't jailbreak or root a device and keep OS updates current.
- Educate users about the importance of privacy settings (for example, disable cookies and turn off Bluetooth when it's not in use) and of not opening email attachments or downloading shared files from untrusted sources.
- Consider installing an anti-malware app. Apple claims that an iOS device cannot be infected with malware and does not make anti-malware apps available in the App Store. However, you can get an app from the App Store that monitors your device and scans for malware that might be in stored files, but not installed. For Android and Windows Phone devices, search online reviews and consider the features offered before deciding on an anti-malware app. An anti-malware app can scan apps and files for malware, scan for unauthorized surveillance, monitor security and privacy settings, find the device when it's lost and lock and remote wipe it, and maintain automatic updates.

In an enterprise environment, Wi-Fi analyzers and cellular network analyzers might be used to protect the network against intrusion. Next is a brief introduction to these tools.

WI-FI ANALYZERS

When you're responsible for a Wi-Fi network, you might want to consider monitoring it for rogue devices that could be attempting to hack transmissions. Wi-Fi analyzer software and hardware can be used to detect devices not authorized to use the network, identify attempts made by connected devices to hack transmissions, and even identify their physical location. Wi-Fi analyzers can also detect performance vulnerabilities and identify bottlenecks. They can detect security vulnerabilities, which allow a device to connect to the wireless network using a configuration the network is not set up to use (for example, an authorized channel or nonencrypted transmissions). An example of a Wi-Fi analyzer device is the OptiView tablet by Fluke Networks (*flukenetworks.com*), shown in Figure 18-45. This tablet computer comes preinstalled with AirMagnet WiFi Analyzer software, also by Fluke Networks. Figure 18-46 shows a demo window of the software.

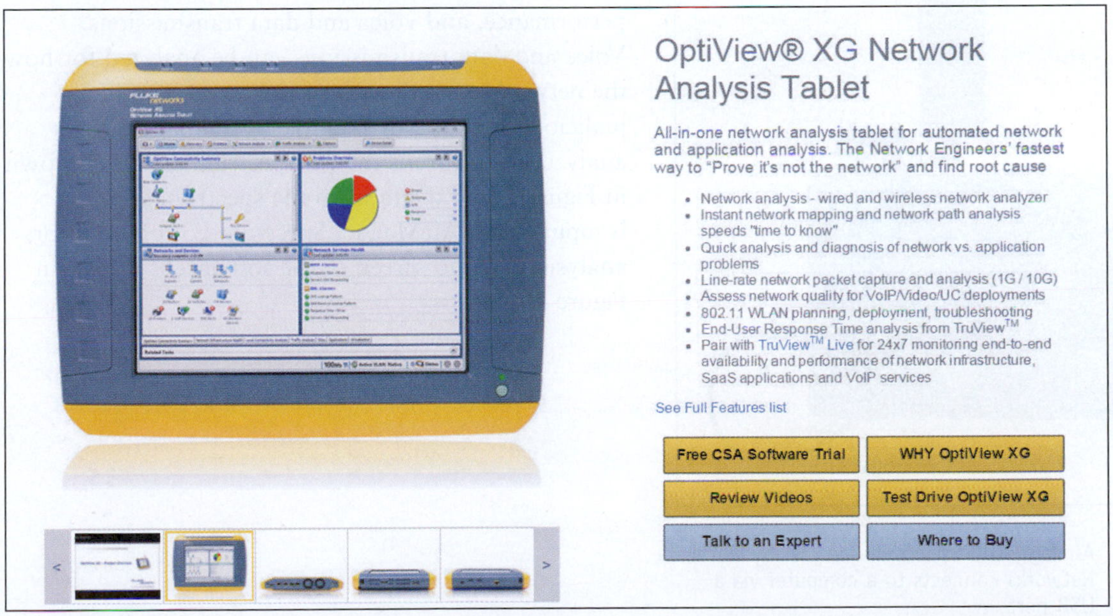

Source: flukenetworks.com

Figure 18-45 Wi-Fi analyzer tablet by Fluke Networks designed for monitoring enterprise-level wireless networks

18

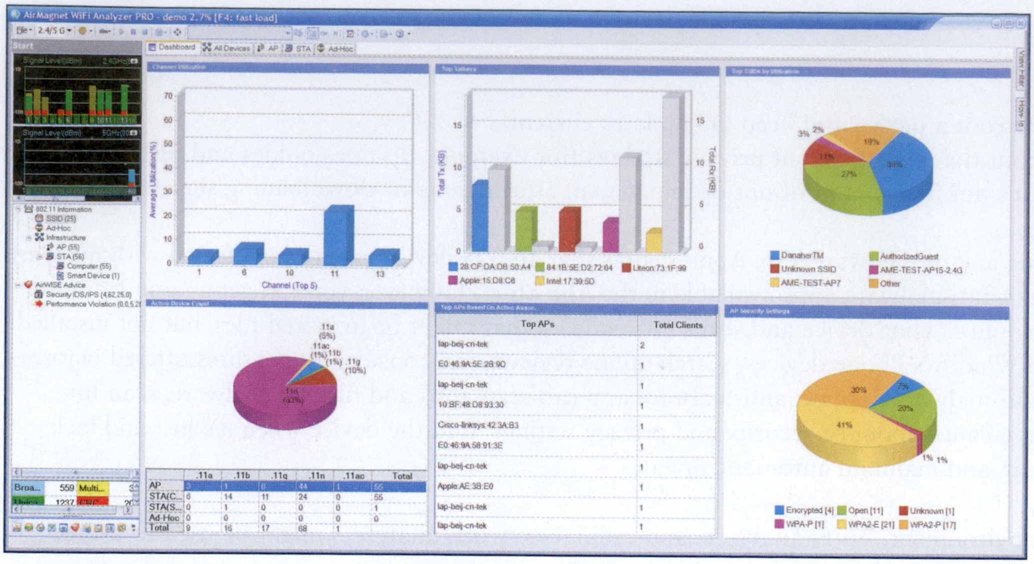

Source: flukenetworks.com

Figure 18-46 AirMagnet WiFi Analyzer PRO demo screen by Fluke Networks

CELLULAR NETWORK ANALYZERS

Large organizations that require cellular and Wi-Fi coverage over a large area (for example, a shopping mall or large hospital) might implement a distributed antenna system (DAS). Small antennas are installed over the facility to act as repeaters for cell tower and Wi-Fi access point (AP) coverage. In addition, with the trend toward BYOD (bring your own device), some organizations have found it necessary to closely monitor cellular connections to private networks to identify hackers performing tasks that appear malicious.

Cellular network analyzer software and hardware can be used to monitor cellular networks for signal strength of cell towers, WAPs, and repeaters, which can help technicians better position antennas in a DAS. The software can also monitor for interference, performance, and voice and data transmissions. Voice and data transmissions can be analyzed for how the network is used, with the intent of identifying malicious activity. An example of cellular network analyzer hardware is the RF spectrum analyzer shown in Figure 18-47. Data from the spectrum analyzer is input to the AirMagnet Spectrum ES software for analysis. A demo screen of the software is shown in Figure 18-48.

Source: Fluke Networks

Figure 18-47 AirMagnet RF spectrum analyzer by Fluke Networks connects to a computer via a USB port

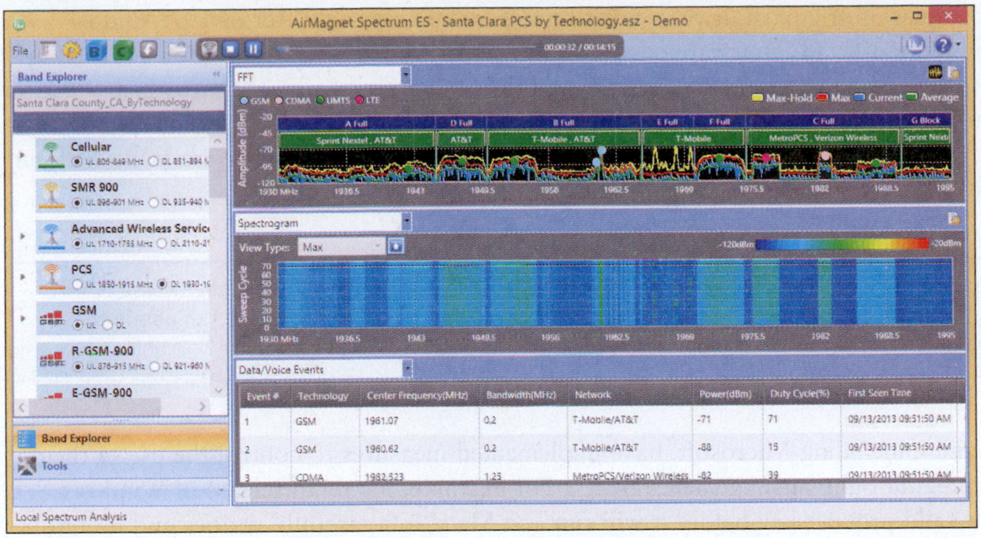

Source: Fluke Networks

Figure 18-48 AirMagnet Spectrum software analyzes cellular networks

SOFTWARE LICENSING AND PROHIBITED CONTENT OR ACTIVITY

A+
220-902
5.3

Many organizations have documented a code of conduct in policies that apply to their employees and/or customers. As an employee, you need to be aware of these codes of conduct and the procedures to follow when you believe these company policies have been broken. Examples of prohibited content or activity might be when an employee saves pornographic photos to company computers, uses company computers and time for personal shopping, or installs pirated software on these computers.

SOFTWARE LICENSING

A+
220-902
5.3

As an IT support technician, you need to be especially aware of the issues surrounding software licensing. As you have learned, open source software can be freely distributed and installed, but closed source software is owned by a vendor and a license is required to use the software. When someone purchases software from a software vendor, that person or organization has only purchased a commercial license for the software, which is the right to use it. The buyer does not legally *own* the software and, therefore, does not have the right to distribute it. The right to copy the work, called a copyright, belongs to the creator of the work or others to whom the creator transfers this right. Copyrights are intended to legally protect the intellectual property rights of organizations or individuals to creative works, which include books, images, and software. Your rights to use or copy the software are clearly stated in the End User License Agreement (EULA) that you agree to when you install the software (see Figure 18-49).

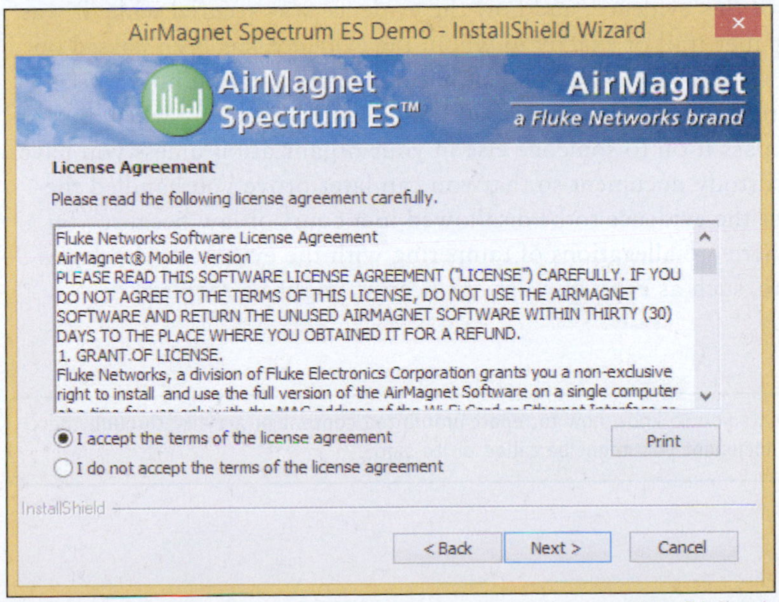

Source: Fluke Networks

Figure 18-49 Agreeing to the EULA is required before software installs

18

Making unauthorized copies of original software violates the Federal Copyright Act of 1976 and is called software piracy or, more officially, software copyright infringement. (This act allows for one backup copy of software to be made.) Making a copy of software and then selling it or giving it away is a violation of the law. Normally, only the employee who violated the copyright law is liable for infringement; however, in some cases, an employer or supervisor is also held responsible, even when the copies were made without the employer's knowledge.

Notes When an individual or organization purchases the right to install one instance of software, the license is called a **personal license**. By purchasing a **site license**, also called an **enterprise license**, a company can obtain the right to multiple installations of software.

Many software companies, including Microsoft, have implemented measures to control the use of their software, which is called digital rights management (DRM). For example, the retail release of Windows 8.1 must be activated with a valid product key before it will run and Microsoft carefully verifies and monitors that this product key is used only in one installation.

CORPORATE POLICIES FOR DEALING WITH PROHIBITED CONTENT OR ACTIVITY

A+ 220-902 5.3

When you start a new job, find out from your employer how to deal with prohibited content or activity so that you can follow corporate policies and security best practices. Here are some things you need to know:

- When you identify what you believe to be an infringement of the law or the company's code of conduct, where do you turn to report the issue? Make sure you go only through proper channels; don't spread rumors or accusations with those who are not in these channels.
- What data or device should you immediately preserve as evidence for what you believe has happened? For example, if you believe you have witnessed a customer or employee using a company computer for a crime, should you remove and secure the hard drive from the computer, or should you remove and secure the entire computer?
- Proper documentation surrounding the evidence of a crime is crucial to a criminal investigation. What documentation are you expected to submit and to whom is it submitted? This documentation might track the chain of custody for the evidence, which includes exactly what, when, and from whom evidence was collected; the condition of this evidence; and how the evidence was secured while it was in your possession. It also includes a paper trail of exactly to whom the evidence has been passed on and when. For example, suppose you suspect that a criminal act has happened and you hold a CD that you believe contains evidence of this crime. You need to carefully document exactly when and how you received the CD. Also, don't pass it on to someone else in your organization unless you have this person's signature on a chain-of-custody document so that you can later prove you handled the evidence appropriately. You don't want the evidence to be disallowed in a court of law because you have been accused of misconduct or there are allegations of tampering with the evidence. Also know that more information than a signature, such as copy of a driver's license, might be required to identify persons in the chain of custody.

A+ Exam Tip The A+ 220-902 exam expects you to know how to report prohibited content or activity through the proper channels and about a chain-of-custody document you might be called on to sign.

>> CHAPTER SUMMARY

Securing a Windows Personal Computer

- The netplwiz command can be used to require the user to press Ctrl+Alt+Delete to sign in to Windows.
- Windows power settings can be used to lock down a computer after a short period of inactivity and to require a password to unlock the computer.
- A strong password is not easy to guess and contains uppercase and lowercase letters, numbers, and symbols. Using long passwords is the best protection against attack.
- The Encrypted File System (EFS) is used with an NTFS volume for Windows business and professional editions.
- Windows Firewall can block all communication initiated outside the computer and can allow exceptions for certain programs, protocols, ports, and remote computers.
- Local Security Policies in Group Policy are used in Windows professional and business editions to set policies that can secure the local computer.
- BitLocker Encryption with Windows professional or business editions can lock down the entire hard drive. It can be set to authenticate the computer, authenticate the user, or authenticate both the computer and the user.
- UEFI/BIOS security features include passwords, drive lock passwords, UEFI secure boot, and support for a TPM chip and an intrusion-detection device.

Securing a Mobile Device

- Controlling access to a mobile device can be accomplished by a screen lock, biometric authentication (for example, fingerprint or voice recognition), full device encryption, system lock after failed login attempts, and multifactor authentication.
- Software used to secure a mobile device includes OS updates and patches, anti-malware, downloading software from only trusted sources, firewalls, and locator and remote wipe apps.
- In a corporate environment, on-boarding and off-boarding company policies for BYOD might include remote backup apps, remote wipes, encryption, firewalls, VPN connections, anti-malware, and apps that prevent jailbreaking and rooting.

Additional Methods to Protect Resources

- Large networks might use a security token or smart card in addition to a Windows password to authenticate a user in multifactor and/or mutual authentication.
- Security tokens include a smart card (key fob, wireless token, RFID badge, or cell phone with token) and biometric data (iris scan, retinal scan, or fingerprint scan).
- Physical security can include a locked door, lock and chain, privacy filter, theft-prevention plate, and mantrap.
- A UTM appliance might include a firewall, anti-malware, access control lists, intrusion detection and prevention systems, and a VPN.
- Data can be partly or completely destroyed using a paper shredder, low-level format, zero-fill utility, drill, degausser, or Secure Erase utility.
- Security methods include educating users against social engineering and how to best protect a laptop when traveling.

Dealing with Malicious Software on Personal Computers

- Malware includes a virus, spyware, keylogger, worm, Trojan, rootkit, ransomware, zero-day attack, man-in-the-middle attack, zombies, botnets, and dictionary attacks.
- Symptoms that malware is present include pop-up ads, slow performance, error messages, file errors, spam, and strange processes running.
- To protect against malware, (1) know how to identify common malware symptoms, (2) quarantine the infected system, (3) disable System Restore, (4) remediate the system, (5) protect the system with scheduled scans and updates, (6) enable System Protection and create a restore point, and (7) educate the end user. Some systems become so highly infected that the only solution is to reinstall Windows.

Dealing with Malicious Software on Mobile Devices

- Symptoms of malware on mobile devices include battery drain, slow speeds, leaked data, dropped calls, unintended Wi-Fi and Bluetooth connections, location tracking, unauthorized use of camera or microphone, and root access.
- To remediate an infected device, uninstall the offending app, update the OS, factory reset the device, and/or restore data from backup.
- Wi-Fi and cellular network analyzers can help an organization monitor and protect Wi-Fi and cellular networks.

Software Licensing and Prohibited Content or Activity

- Commercial licensing of software can be a personal license or enterprise license. Terms of the licensing agreement are found in the EULA.
- A chain-of-custody document provides a paper trail of the evidence in a criminal case and includes how, when, where, and by whom evidence was preserved and secured.

>> KEY TERMS

For explanations of key terms, see the Glossary for this text.

acceptable use policy (AUP)
access control list (ACL)
anti-malware software
antivirus software
ATA Secure Erase
biometric authentication
biometric device
BitLocker Drive Encryption
BitLocker To Go
botnet
brute force attack
BYOD (Bring Your Own Device)
cellular network analyzer
certificate of destruction
Certification Authority (CA)
chain of custody
commercial license
computer infestation
copyright
data loss prevention (DLP)
degausser
dictionary attack
digital certificate
digital rights management (DRM)
email filtering
email hoax
Encrypted File System (EFS)
End User License Agreement (EULA)
enterprise license
entry control roster
gpresult
gpupdate
grayware
intrusion detection system (IDS)
intrusion prevention system (IPS)
key fob
keylogger
Local Security Policy
Local Users and Groups
LoJack
malicious software
malware
malware definition
malware encyclopedia
malware signature
man-in-the-middle attack
mantrap
multifactor authentication (MFA)
mutual authentication
Network Places Wizard
next-generation firewall (NGFW)
noncompliant system
personal license
phishing
privacy filter
quarantined computer
ransomware
remote backup application
remote wipe
RFID badge
root certificate
rootkit
security token
shoulder surfing
site license

smart card
smart card reader
social engineering
software piracy
spear phishing
spoofing
spyware
strong password
tailgating
TPM (Trusted Platform Module)
Trojan
Unified Threat Management (UTM)
User Accounts
virus
Wi-Fi analyzer
Windows Defender
Windows Firewall
worm
zero-day attack
zombie

>> REVIEWING THE BASICS

1. Why is it more secure to require a user press Ctrl+Alt+Delete to sign in rather than displaying the Windows sign-in screen?
2. Which window available from Control Panel is used to require a Windows password to wake up a sleeping computer?
3. What command launches the User Accounts or Network Places Wizard, which can be used to manage users and their passwords?
4. Why is PINE963$&apple not a strong password?
5. What is the policy in Group Policy that can be set to audit failed logon events? Give the full path to the policy.
6. What hardware component is needed to set up BitLocker Encryption so that you can authenticate the computer?
7. What command can you use to refresh local group policies without having to reboot the system?
8. What type of employee badge does not have to be swiped by a card reader in order to allow the employee through a door?
9. What technique can be used so that sensitive company data on an employee's personal mobile device is not stolen when the device is stolen?
10. How can an Apple iOS device install an app that is downloaded from a source other than the Apple App Store?
11. What tool is best to use when destroying data on an SSD drive? Where can you get this tool?
12. What device can be installed on a laptop to prevent shoulder surfing?
13. Define and explain the differences between a virus, worm, and Trojan.
14. What is the best way to determine if an email message warning about a virus is a hoax?
15. What is the first thing you should do when you discover a computer is infected with malware?
16. What does anti-malware software look for to determine that a program or a process is a virus?
17. Which anti-malware software is embedded in Windows 8?
18. What registry key keeps information about services that run when a computer is booted into Safe Mode?
19. What folder is used by Windows to hold restore points?
20. What must you do to allow anti-malware software to scan and delete malware it might find in the data storage area where restore points are kept?

>> THINKING CRITICALLY

1. In which policy group of Group Policy is the policy that requires a smart card be used to authenticate a user to Windows?
   a. Computer Configuration, Windows Settings, Security Settings, Local Policies, Biometrics
   b. Computer Configuration, Administrative Templates, System, Logon
   c. Computer Configuration, Windows Settings, Security Settings, Local Policies, Security Options
   d. User Configuration, Administrative Templates, System, Logon
2. You open a folder Properties box to encrypt the folder, click Advanced, and discover *Encrypt contents to secure data* is dimmed. What is the most likely problem?
   a. Encryption has not been enabled. Use the Computer Management console to enable it.
   b. You are not using an edition of Windows that supports encryption.
   c. Most likely a virus has attacked the system and is disabling encryption.
   d. Encryption applies only to files, not folders.
3. A virus has attacked your hard drive and now when you start up Windows, instead of seeing the Windows Start screen, the system freezes and you see a blue screen of death. You have extremely important document files on the drive that you cannot afford to lose. What do you do first? Explain why this is your first choice.
   a. Try a data-recovery service even though it is very expensive.
   b. Remove the hard drive from the computer case and install it in another computer.
   c. Try GetDataBack by Runtime Software (*www.runtime.org*) to recover the data.
   d. Use Windows utilities to attempt to fix the Windows boot problem.
   e. Run antivirus software to remove the virus.
4. You sign in to your personal computer with your Microsoft account and then you want to verify your computer is a trusted device to make changes to the account settings. Microsoft sends a code to your cell phone in a text message. You enter the code on a Windows screen. This type of authentication is called:
   a. Multifactor authentication
   b. Mutual authentication
   c. Biometric authentication
   d. None of the above

>> REAL PROBLEMS, REAL SOLUTIONS

REAL PROBLEM 18-1 Recovering a Windows Password

You can use freeware to discover a forgotten Windows password, and hackers can use the software to steal a password. The stronger the password, the more difficult it is to discover. Follow these steps to learn more:

1. Create three user accounts on a system and assign the accounts an easy password (use only lowercase letters), a moderately easy password (use lowercase letters and numbers, but no symbols), and a strong password (see the rules given earlier in the chapter for strong passwords).

2. Go to **ophcrack.sourceforge.net** by Geeknet, Inc., and download the free ISO file that contains ophcrack Vista/7 LiveCD. (The software works in Windows 8/7/Vista.) Use the ISO file to burn the ISO image to a CD-R. Label the CD.
3. Boot from the CD. As it boots, it automatically searches for and lists the user accounts and passwords on the system. Answer the following questions:
    a. What is the name of the operating system the ophcrack software uses on the CD?
    b. Which user account passwords did ophcrack discover?
    c. If ophcrack did not discover a password, perhaps another freeware utility can. List three other password-cracking products that receive positive online reviews.

Keep the ophcrack LiveCD in your computer repair toolkit in case a client in the field asks you to help recover a forgotten Windows password.

REAL PROBLEM 18-2 Researching a Laptop with a TPM Chip

Many laptops sold today have a TPM chip, and some have encryption-enabled hard drives that don't require encryption software such as BitLocker. Research the web for a laptop that offers a TPM chip and answer these questions:

1. What is the brand and model laptop that has the TPM chip? Print the webpage listing the laptop specifications showing the chip.
2. Is the chip optional? If so, what is the cost of including the chip?
3. Does the laptop have an encryption-enabled hard drive?
4. Does the laptop come bundled with encryption software? If so, what is the name of the software?
5. Does the laptop offer a drive lock password?
6. What is the cost of the laptop, including the TPM chip?

2. Go to ophcrack.sourceforge.net by Objectif Sécurité, and download the free ISO file that contains ophcrack Vista/7 LiveCD. (The software works for Windows 8/7/Vista.) Use the ISO file to burn the ISO image to a CD-R. Label the CD.

3. Boot from the CD. As it boots, it automatically searches for and lists the user accounts and passwords on the system. Answer the following questions:

   a. What is the name of the operating system the ophcrack software uses on the CD?

   b. Which user account passwords did ophcrack discover?

   c. If ophcrack did not discover a password, perhaps another freeware utility can. List three other password cracking products that receive positive online reviews.

Keep the ophcrack Live CD in your computer repair toolkit in case a client in the field asks you to help recover a forgotten Windows password.

REAL PROBLEM 18-2 Researching a Laptop with a TPM Chip

Many laptops sold today have a TPM chip, and some have encryption-enabled hard drives that don't require encryption software such as BitLocker. Research the web for a laptop that offers a TPM chip and answer these questions:

1. What is the brand and model of a laptop that has the TPM chip? Print the webpage listing the laptop's specifications showing the chip.

2. Is the chip optional? If so, what is the cost of including the chip?

3. Does the laptop have an encryption-enabled hard drive?

4. Does the laptop come bundled with encryption software? If so, what is the name of the software?

5. Does the laptop offer a drive lock password?

6. What is the cost of the laptop, including the TPM chip?

CHAPTER 19

Supporting Printers and Customizing a System

After completing this chapter, you will be able to:

- Discuss printer types and features
- Install and share printers and manage printer features, add-on devices, and the printer queue
- Perform routine maintenance tasks necessary to support printers
- Troubleshoot printer problems
- Customize a computer system to meet customer needs

This chapter discusses the most popular types of printers and how to support them. As you work through the chapter, you learn about printer types and features, how to install a local or network printer, and how to share a printer with others on a network. You learn how to manage printer features, add-on devices, shared printers, and print jobs. Then, you learn about maintaining and troubleshooting printers. Finally, we wrap up the chapter with a discussion of how to select appropriate parts for a customized computer system to satisfy the specifications given by your customer.

PRINTER TYPES AND FEATURES

A+ 220-901 1.14, 1.15

The major categories of printer types include laser, inkjet (ink dispersion), impact, and thermal printers. In the following sections, we look at the different types of printers for desktop computing.

Notes For heavy business use, sometimes it's best to purchase one machine for one purpose, instead of bundling many functions into a single machine. For example, if you need a scanner and a printer, purchase a good printer and a good scanner rather than a combo machine. Routine maintenance and troubleshooting are easier and less expensive on single-purpose machines, although the initial cost is higher. On the other hand, for home or small office use, a combo device can save money and counter space.

LASER PRINTERS

A+ 220-901 1.14, 1.15

A laser printer is a type of electro-photographic printer that can range from a small, personal desktop model to a large, network printer capable of handling and printing large volumes continuously. Figure 19-1 shows an example of a typical laser printer for a small office.

Figure 19-1 Oki Data C3200n color laser printer

A+ Exam Tip The A+ 220-901 exam expects you to be familiar with these types of printers: laser, inkjet, thermal, and impact. You also need to know about virtual printers.

Laser printers require the interaction of mechanical, electrical, and optical technologies. Laser printers work by placing toner on an electrically charged rotating drum (sometimes called the imaging drum) and then depositing the toner on paper as the paper moves through the system at the same speed the drum is turning. Figure 19-2 shows the seven steps of laser printing.

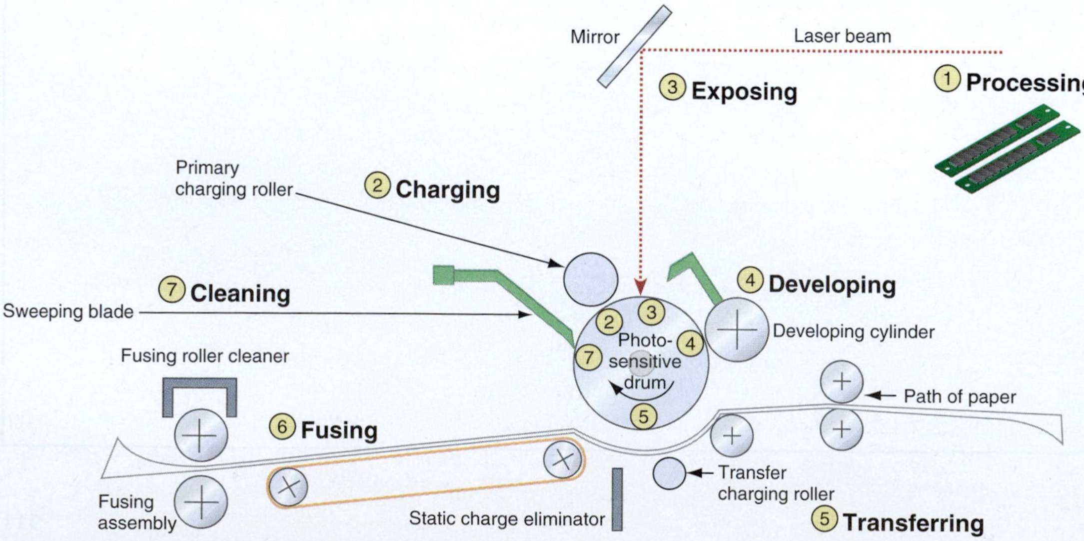

Figure 19-2 The seven progressive steps of laser printing

Note that Figure 19-2 shows only a cross-section of the drum, mechanisms, and paper. Remember that the drum is as wide as a sheet of paper. The mirror, blades, and rollers in the drawing are also as wide as paper. Also know that toner responds to a charge and moves from one surface to another if the second surface has a more positive charge than the first.

A+ Exam Tip The A+ 220-901 exam expects you to know the seven steps of laser printing.

The seven steps of laser printing are listed next:

1. ***Processing the image.*** A laser printer processes and prints an entire page at one time. The page comes to the printer encoded in a language the printer understands and the firmware inside the printer processes the incoming data to produce a bitmap (a bunch of bits in rows and columns) of the final page, which is stored in the printer's memory. One bitmap image is produced for monochrome images. For color images, one bitmap is produced for each of four colors. (The colors are blue, red, yellow, and black, better known as cyan, magenta, yellow, and black, and sometimes written as CMYK.)
2. ***Charging or conditioning.*** During charging, the drum is conditioned by a roller that places a high uniform electrical charge of -600 V on the surface of the drum. The roller is called the primary charging roller or primary corona, which is charged by a high-voltage power supply assembly. For some printers, a corona wire is used instead of the charging roller to charge the drum.
3. ***Exposing or writing.*** A laser beam controlled by motors and a mirror scans across the drum until it completes the correct number of passes. The laser beam is turned on and off continually as it makes a single pass down the length of the drum, once for each raster line, so that dots are exposed only where toner should go to print the image. For example, for a 1200 dots per inch (dpi) printer, the beam makes 1200 passes for every one inch of the drum circumference. For a 1200-dpi printer, 1200 dots are exposed or not exposed along the drum for every inch of linear pass. The 1200 dots per inch down this single pass, combined with 1200 passes per inch of drum circumference, accomplish the resolution of 1200 × 1200 dots per square inch of many laser printers. The laser beam writes an image to the drum surface as a -100 V charge. The -100 V charge on this image area will be used in the developing stage to transmit toner to the drum surface.

Notes A laser printer can produce better quality printouts than a dot matrix printer, even when printing at the same dpi, because it can vary the size of the dots it prints, creating a sharp, clear image. Hewlett-Packard (HP) calls this technology of varying the size of dots **REt (Resolution Enhancement technology)**.

4. ***Developing.*** The developing cylinder applies toner to the surface of the drum. The toner is charged and sticks to the developing cylinder because of a magnet inside the cylinder. A control blade prevents too much toner from sticking to the cylinder surface. As the cylinder rotates very close to the drum, the toner is attracted to the part of the surface of the drum that has a -100 V charge and repelled from the -600 V part of the drum surface. The result is that toner sticks to the drum where the laser beam has hit and is repelled from the area where the laser beam has not hit.
5. ***Transferring.*** In the transferring step (shown in Figure 19-2), a strong electrical charge draws the toner off the drum onto the paper. This is the first step that takes place outside the cartridge and the first step that involves the paper. The soft, black transfer roller puts a positive charge on the paper to pull the toner from the drum onto the paper. Then the static charge eliminator (refer again to Figure 19-2) weakens the charges on both the paper and the drum so that the paper does not stick to the drum. The stiffness of the paper and the small radius of the drum also help the paper move away from the drum and toward the fusing assembly. Very thin paper can wrap around the drum, which is why printer manuals usually instruct you to use only paper designated for laser printers.

6. *Fusing.* The fuser assembly uses heat and pressure to fuse the toner to the paper. Up to this point, the toner is merely sitting on the paper. The fusing rollers apply heat to the paper, which causes the toner to melt, and the rollers apply pressure to bond the melted toner into the paper. The temperature of the rollers is monitored by the printer. If the temperature exceeds an allowed maximum value (410 degrees F for some printers), the printer shuts down.
7. *Cleaning.* A sweeper strip cleans the drum of any residual toner, which is swept away by a sweeping blade. The charge left on the drum is then neutralized. Some printers use erase lamps in the top cover of the printer for this purpose. The lamps use red light so as not to damage the photosensitive drum.

For color laser printers, the writing process repeats four times, one for each toner color of cyan, magenta, yellow, and black. Each color requires a separate image drum. Then, the paper passes to the fusing stage, when the fuser bonds all toner to the paper and aids in blending the four tones to form specific colors.

★ A+ Exam Tip The A+ 220-901 exam expects you to be familiar with these laser printer terms: imaging drum, fuser assembly, transfer belt, transfer roller, pickup roller, separate pads, and duplexing assembly.

CARTRIDGES AND OTHER REPLACEABLE PARTS

The charging, exposing, developing, and cleaning steps use the printer components that undergo the most wear. To make the printer last longer, these steps are done inside a removable cartridge that can be replaced. For older printers, all four steps were done inside one cartridge. For newer printers, the cleaning, charging, and exposing steps are done inside the image drum cartridge. The developing cylinder is located inside the toner cartridge. The transferring is done using a transfer belt that can be replaced, and the fusing is done inside a fuser cartridge.

By using these multiple cartridges inside laser printers, the cost of maintaining a printer is reduced. You can replace one cartridge without having to replace them all. The toner cartridge needs replacing the most often, followed by the image drum, the fuser cartridge, and the transfer assembly, in that order.

Other printer parts that might need replacing include the pickup roller that pushes forward a sheet of paper from the paper tray and the separation pad (also called separate pad) that keeps more than one sheet of paper from moving forward. If the pickup roller is worn, paper misfeeds into the printer. If the separation pad is worn, multiple sheets of paper will be drawn into the printer. Sometimes you can clean a pickup roller or separation pad to prolong its life before it needs replacing.

Notes Before replacing expensive parts in a printer, consider whether a new printer might be more cost effective than repairing the old one.

DUPLEXING ASSEMBLY

A printer that is able to print on both sides of the paper is called a duplex printer or a double-sided printer. Many laser printers and a few inkjet printers offer this feature. After the front of the paper is printed, a duplexing assembly, which contains several rollers, turns the paper around and draws it back through the print process to print on the back of the paper. Alternately, some high-end printers have two print engines so that both sides of the paper are printed at the same time.

INKJET PRINTERS

A+ 220-901 1.14, 1.15

An inkjet printer (see Figure 19-3) uses a type of ink-dispersion printing and doesn't normally provide the high-quality resolution of laser printers. Inkjet printers are popular because they are small and can print color inexpensively. Most inkjet printers today can print high-quality photos, especially when used with photo-quality paper.

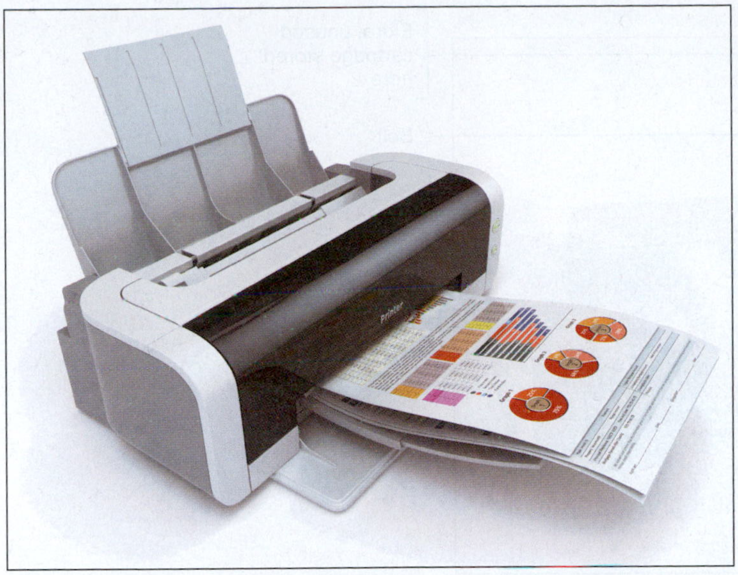

iStockphoto.com/Bet_Noire

Figure 19-3 An example of an inkjet printer

An inkjet printer uses a **print head** that moves across the paper, creating one line of the image with each pass. The printer puts ink on the paper using a matrix of small dots. Different types of inkjet printers form their droplets of ink in different ways. Printer manufacturers use several technologies, but the most popular is the bubble-jet. Bubble-jet printers use tubes of ink that have tiny resistors near the end of each tube. These resistors heat up and cause the ink to boil. Then, a tiny air bubble of ionized ink (ink with an electrical charge) is ejected onto the paper. A typical bubble-jet print head has 64 or 128 tiny nozzles, all of which can fire a droplet simultaneously. (High-end printers can have as many as 3,000 nozzles.) Plates carrying a magnetic charge direct the path of ink onto the paper to form shapes.

Inkjet printers include one or more **ink cartridges** to hold the different colors of ink for the printer. Figure 19-4 shows two ink cartridges. A black cartridge is on the left and a three-color cartridge is on the right. For this printer, a print head is built into each ink cartridge.

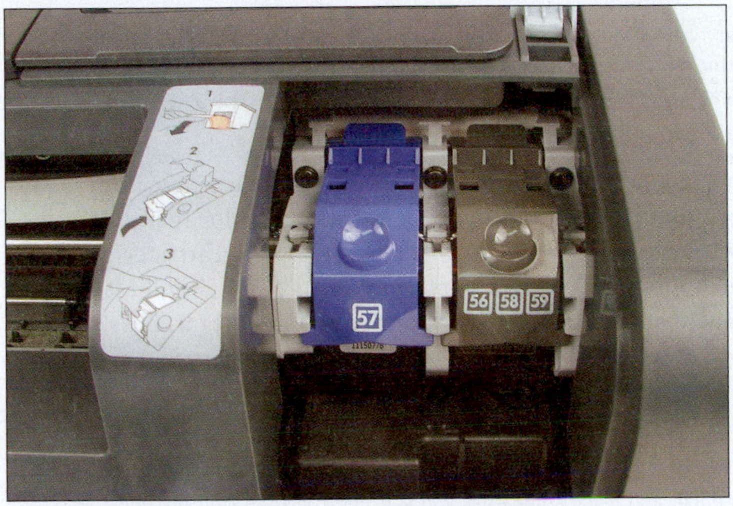

Figure 19-4 The ink cartridges of an inkjet printer

A stepper motor moves the print head and ink cartridges across the paper using a carriage and belt to move the assembly and a stabilizing bar to control the movement (see Figure 19-5). A paper tray can hold a stack of paper, or a paper feeder on the back of the printer can hold a few sheets of paper. The sheets stand up in the feeder and are dispensed one at a time. Rollers pull a single sheet into the printer from the paper tray or paper feeder. A motor powers these rollers and times the sheet going through the printer in the increments needed to print the image. When the printer is not in use, the assemblage sits in the far-right position shown in Figure 19-4, which is called the home position or parked position. This position helps protect the ink in the cartridges from drying out.

Some inkjet printers offer duplex printing. These printers are larger than normal inkjet printers because of the added space required for the duplexing assembly. For duplex printing, be sure to use heavy paper (rated at 24-pound paper or higher) so the ink doesn't bleed through.

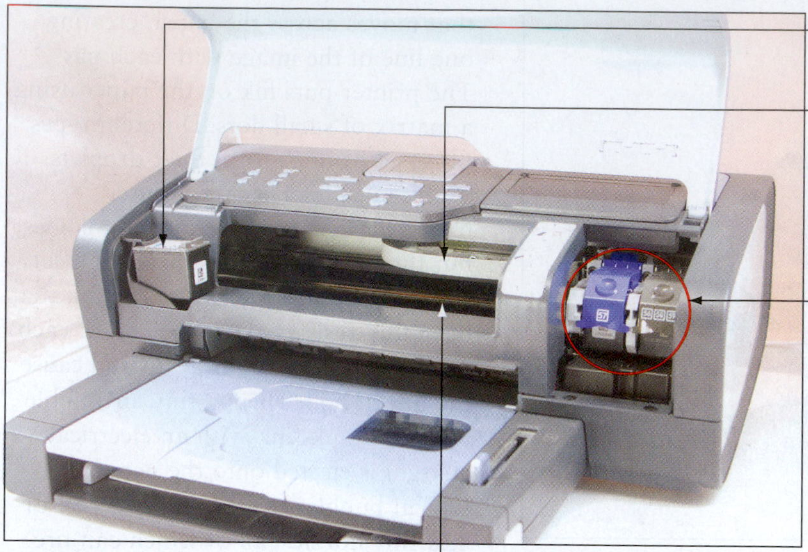

Figure 19-5 The belt and stabilizing bar used to move the print head across the page

Notes Weight and brightness are the two primary ways of measuring paper quality. The rated weight of paper (for example, 20 pounds to 32 pounds) determines the thickness of the paper. Brightness is measured on a scale of 92 to 100.

When purchasing an inkjet printer, look for the kind that uses two or four separate cartridges. One cartridge is used for black ink. Three cartridges, one for each color, give better quality color than one cartridge that holds all three colors. Some low-end inkjet printers use a single three-color cartridge and don't have a black ink cartridge. These printers must combine all colors of ink to produce a dull black. Having a separate cartridge for black ink means that it prints true black and, more important, does not use the more expensive colored ink. To save money, you should be able to replace an empty cartridge without having to replace all cartridges.

Notes To save money, you can refill an ink cartridge, and many companies will sell you the tools and ink you need as well as show you how to do it. You can also purchase refilled cartridges at reduced prices. When you purchase ink cartridges, make sure you know if they are new or refilled. Also, for best results, don't refill a cartridge more than three times.

Inkjet printers tend to smudge on inexpensive paper, and they are slower than laser printers. If a printed page later gets damp, the ink can run and get quite messy. The quality of the paper used with inkjet printers significantly affects the quality of printed output. You should use only paper that is designed for an inkjet printer, and you should use a high-grade paper to get the best results.

Notes Photos printed on an inkjet printer tend to fade over time, more so than photos produced professionally. To make your photos last longer, use high-quality paper (rated at high gloss or studio gloss) and use fade-resistant ink (such as Vivera ink by HP). Then protect these photos from exposure to light, heat, humidity, and polluted air. To best protect photos made by an inkjet printer, keep them in a photo album rather than displayed and exposed to light.

IMPACT PRINTERS

A+ 220-901 1.14, 1.15

An impact printer creates a printed page by using some mechanism that touches or hits the paper. The best-known impact printer is a dot matrix printer, which prints only text that it receives as raw data. It has a print head that moves across the width of the paper, using pins to print a matrix of dots on the page. The pins shoot against a cloth ribbon, which hits the paper, depositing the ink. The ribbon provides both the ink for printing and the lubrication for the pinheads. The quality of the print is poor compared with other printer types. However, three reasons you see impact printers still in use are: (1) They use continuous tractor feeds and fanfold paper (also called computer paper) rather than individual sheets of paper, making them useful for logging ongoing events or data, (2) they can use carbon paper to print multiple copies at the same time, and (3) they are extremely durable, give little trouble, and seem to last forever.

A+ Exam Tip The A+ 220-901 exam expects you to know about the print head, ribbon, and tractor feed in an impact printer and about impact paper used in the printer.

Maintaining a dot matrix impact printer is easy to do. The impact paper used by impact printers comes as a box of fanfold paper or in rolls (used with receipt printers). When the paper is nearing the end of the stack or roll, a color on the edge alerts you to replace the paper. Occasionally, you should replace the ribbon of a dot matrix printer. If the print head fails, check on the cost of replacing the head versus the cost of buying a new printer. Sometimes, the cost of the head is so high it's best to just buy a new printer. Overheating can damage a print head (see Figure 19-6), so keep it as cool as possible to make it last longer. Keep the printer in a cool, well-ventilated area, and don't use it to print more than 50 to 75 pages without allowing the head to cool down.

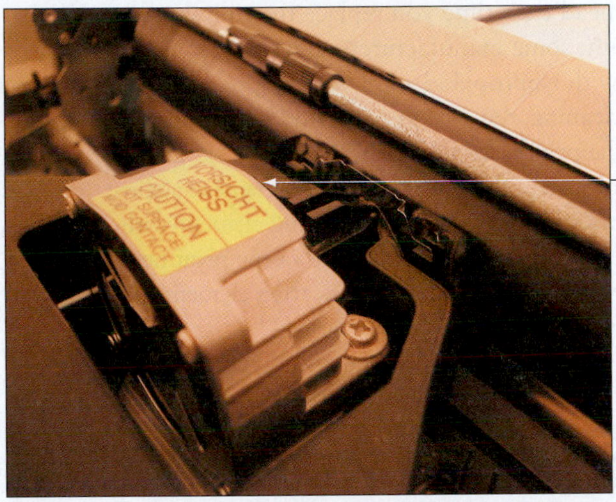

Figure 19-6 Keep the print head of a dot matrix printer as cool as possible so that it will last longer

THERMAL PRINTERS

A+ 220-901 1.14, 1.15

Thermal printers use heat to create an image. Two types of thermal printers are a direct thermal printer and a thermal transfer printer. The older direct thermal printer burns dots onto special coated paper, called thermal paper, as was done by older fax machines. The process requires no ink and does not use a ribbon. Direct thermal printers are often used as receipt printers that use rolls of thermal paper (see Figure 19-7). The printed image can fade over time.

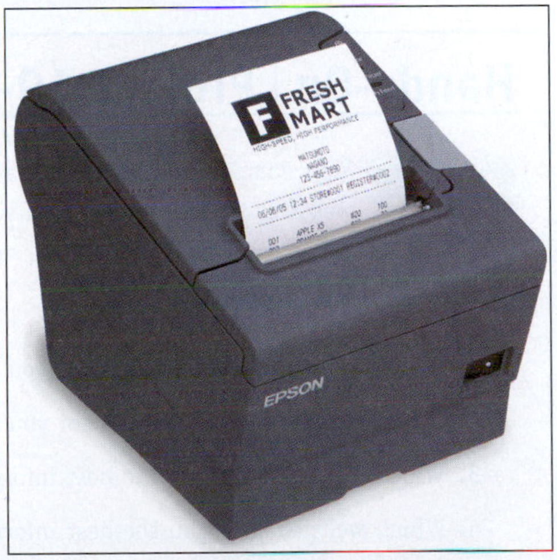

Courtesy of EPSON America, Inc.

Figure 19-7 The TM-T88V direct thermal printer by EPSON

A thermal transfer printer uses a ribbon that contains wax-based ink. The heating element melts the ribbon (also called foil) onto special thermal paper so that it stays glued to the paper as the feed assembly moves the paper through the printer. Thermal transfer printers are used to print receipts, barcode labels, clothing labels, or container labels. Figure 19-8 shows a thermal transfer printer used to make barcodes and other labels.

Thermal printers are reliable and easy to maintain. When you are responsible for a thermal printer, you know it's time to replace the paper roll when the roll shows the color down one edge. It's important to regularly clean the print head because build up can harden over time and permanently damage the head. Follow the printer manufacturer's directions to clean the print head. Some thermal printer ribbons have a print head cleaning stripe at the end of the ribbon, and it's a good idea to clean the head each time you replace the ribbon. Additionally, some manufacturers suggest cleaning the head with isopropyl alcohol wipes.

When cleaning, remove any dust and debris that gets down in the print head assembly. As you work, ground yourself to protect the sensitive heating element against static electricity. Don't touch the heating element with your fingers. Also, to prolong the life of the print head, use the lowest heat setting for the heating element that still gives good printing results.

Table 19-1 lists some printer manufacturers.

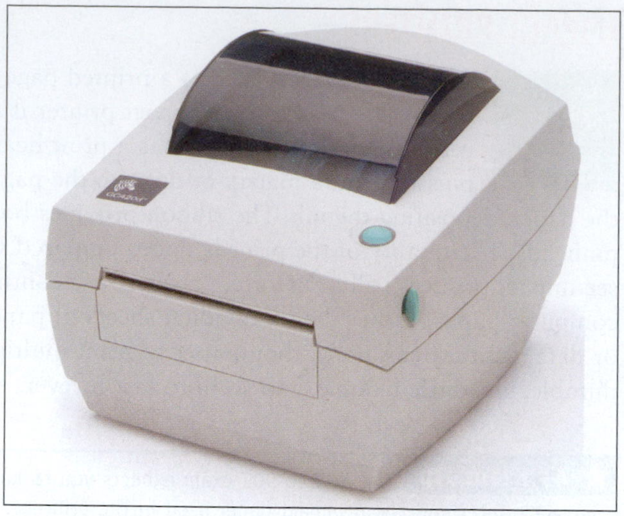

Courtesy of Zebra Technologies

Figure 19-8 The GC420 printer by Zebra is both a thermal transfer printer and a direct thermal printer

★ A+ Exam Tip The A+ 220-901 exam expects you to know about the feed assembly and heating element used in thermal printers and about the need for special thermal paper used in the older direct thermal printers.

Printer Manufacturer	Website
Brother	*brother-usa.com*
Canon	*usa.canon.com*
Hewlett-Packard	*hp.com*
Konica Minolta	*kmbs.konicaminolta.us*
Lexmark	*lexmark.com*
Oki Data	*okidata.com*
Samsung	*samsung.com*
Seiko Epson	*epson.com*
Xerox	*xerox.com*
Zebra Technologies	*zebra.com*

Table 19-1 Printer manufacturers

Hands-On Project 19-1 Research Printer Websites

A+ 220-901 1.14

Your company plans to purchase a new printer, and you want to evaluate the printer manufacturers' websites to determine which site offers the best support. Research three websites listed in Table 19-1 and answer these questions, supporting your answers with pages that you have saved or printed from the website:

1. Which website made it easiest for you to select a new printer, based on your criteria for its use?
2. Which website made it easiest for you to find help for troubleshooting printer problems?
3. Which website gave you the best information about routine maintenance for its printers?
4. Which website gave you the best information about how to clean its printers?

Now let's turn our attention to using Windows to install, share, and manage printers.

USING WINDOWS TO INSTALL, SHARE, AND MANAGE PRINTERS

A+ 220-901 1.12, 1.13

In this part of the chapter, you learn to install local and network printers, share an installed printer, and remotely use a shared printer. You also learn about virtual printing and how to configure printer add-ons and features. We begin with learning about a local printer and network printer.

LOCAL OR NETWORK PRINTER

A+ 220-901 1.12, 1.13

A printer connects to a single computer or to the network. A local printer connects directly to a computer by way of a USB port, serial port, or wireless connection (Bluetooth or Wi-Fi). Some printers support more than one method. A network printer has an Ethernet port to connect directly to the network or uses Wi-Fi to connect to a wireless access point. Some printers have both an Ethernet port and a USB port (see Figure 19-9). These printers can be installed as either a network printer (connecting directly to the network) or a local printer (connecting directly to a computer).

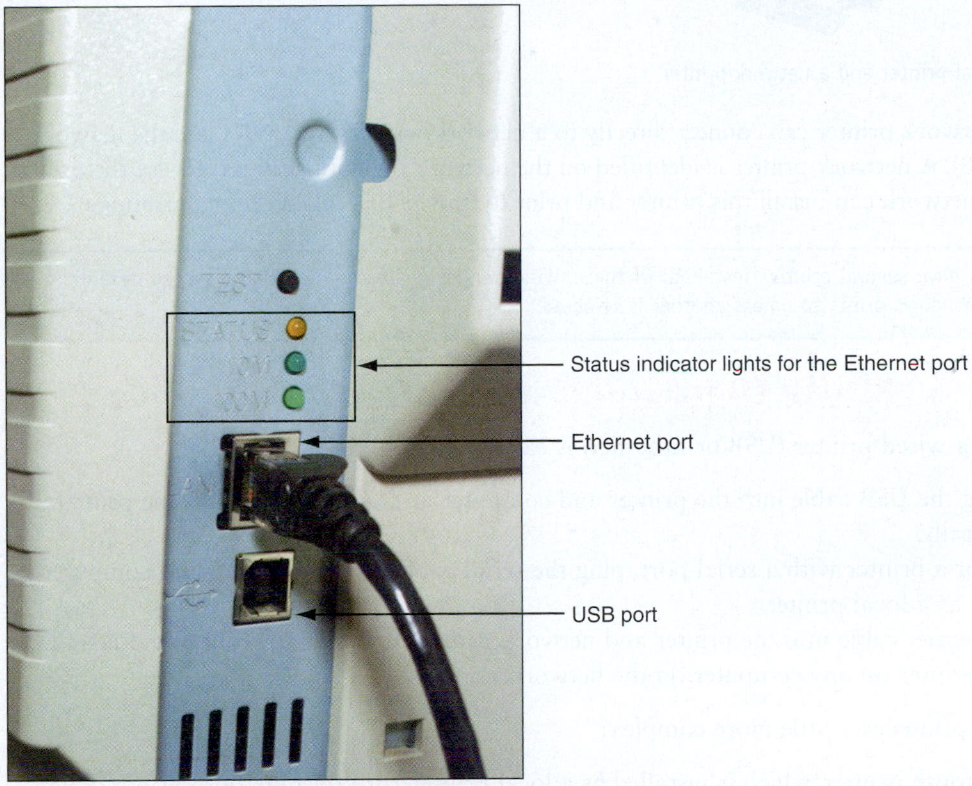

Figure 19-9 This printer has an Ethernet and USB port

19

The two ways to install a printer and make it available on a network are:

- *Local printer.* A local printer can be attached to a computer using a port (for example, USB, serial, or wireless) on the computer (see Computer A in Figure 19-10). For some network printers, it is possible to set up a local printer by using an Ethernet cable connected to the Ethernet port on the network printer and the Ethernet port on the computer. The printer can be dedicated to only this one computer, or you can share the printer for network users. For a shared local printer to be available to other computers on the network, the host computer must be turned on and not in sleep or standby mode. For another computer on the network to use the shared printer, the printer drivers must be installed on the remote computer.

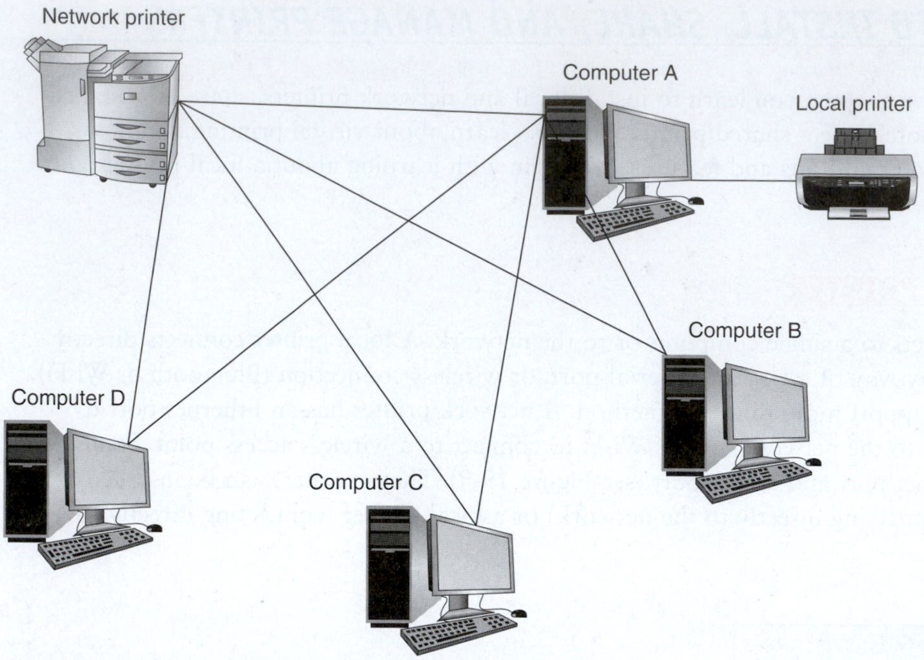

Figure 19-10 A shared local printer and a network printer

- *Network printer.* A network printer can connect directly to a network with its own NIC (see the network printer in Figure 19-10). A network printer is identified on the network by its IP address. To use the printer, any computer on the network can install this printer and print to it, which is called remote printing.

Notes A computer can have several printers installed. Of these, Windows designates one printer to be the **default printer**, which is the one Windows prints to unless another is selected.

WIRED OR WIRELESS PRINTER CONNECTIONS

A+ 220-901 1.12, 1.13

Connecting a wired printer (USB or Ethernet) is easy:

- *USB.* Plug the USB cable into the printer and computer and Windows installs the printer automatically.
- *Serial.* For a printer with a serial port, plug the serial cable into the printer and computer and install the printer as a local printer.
- *Ethernet.* Plug the Ethernet cable into the printer and network wall jack, switch, or router and install the printer as a network printer on any computer on the network.

Connecting a wireless printer is a little more complex:

- *Bluetooth.* For a Bluetooth printer, which is installed as a local printer, turn on Bluetooth in Windows, move the printer within range of the computer, and watch as the two Bluetooth devices pair up.
- *Wi-Fi ad hoc network.* For a Wi-Fi printer, you can connect the printer and computer directly to each other in a Wi-Fi ad hoc mode network. Put the printer within 30 feet of the computer. Then, in Windows 7, open the **Network and Sharing Center**, click **Set up a new connection or network**, click **Set up a wireless ad hoc (computer-to-computer) network**, and follow directions on screen. Windows 8 does not support ad hoc Wi-Fi; however, you can use third-party software to do the job. When using an ad hoc network, next, install the printer as a local printer. Some printers can handle up to four computers connected in an ad hoc Wi-Fi network.
- *Wi-Fi infrastructure network.* In infrastructure mode, Wi-Fi devices connect to a Wi-Fi access point, such as a SOHO router. Put the Wi-Fi printer within range of the access point and use controls on the printer to select the Wi-Fi network and enter the security key to the network if one is required. All Wi-Fi printers support infrastructure connections and some Wi-Fi printers can handle ad hoc connections.

> **Notes** Apple computers and mobile devices can print to **AirPrint** printers without having to first install the printer. For a Mac or iOS device to use an AirPrint printer, simply open the Print menu in any app. If an AirPrint printer is on the network, it will appear in the list of printers. An AirPrint printer is always capable of Wi-Fi connections to a wireless network and some have a USB or Ethernet port for wired connections. AirPrint printers are also capable of cloud printing, discussed later in this chapter.

INSTALL A LOCAL OR NETWORK PRINTER

A+ 220-901 1.12, 1.13

When you install a printer, printer drivers are required that are compatible with the installed operating system. Be sure to use 32-bit drivers for a 32-bit OS and 64-bit drivers for a 64-bit OS. Windows has many printer drivers built in. The drivers also come on a CD bundled with the printer or you can download them from the printer manufacturer's website.

Also, for some types of printers, you can launch the installation program that came bundled on CD with the printer or downloaded from the printer manufacturer's website. On the other hand, you can use the Windows 8/7 **Devices and Printers window** to install a printer. These windows are also used to manage and uninstall printers.

APPLYING CONCEPTS INSTALL A PRINTER

A+ 220-901 1.12, 1.13

Installing a network printer is sometimes called mapping a printer. Follow these steps to install a wired or Wi-Fi network printer, serial-port printer, or Bluetooth printer in Windows:

1. Make sure the printer is connected to the network or the computer. In Control Panel in Classic view, click **Devices and Printers**. In the Devices and Printers window, click **Add a printer**. Windows searches for available printers and lists them (see Figure 19-11).

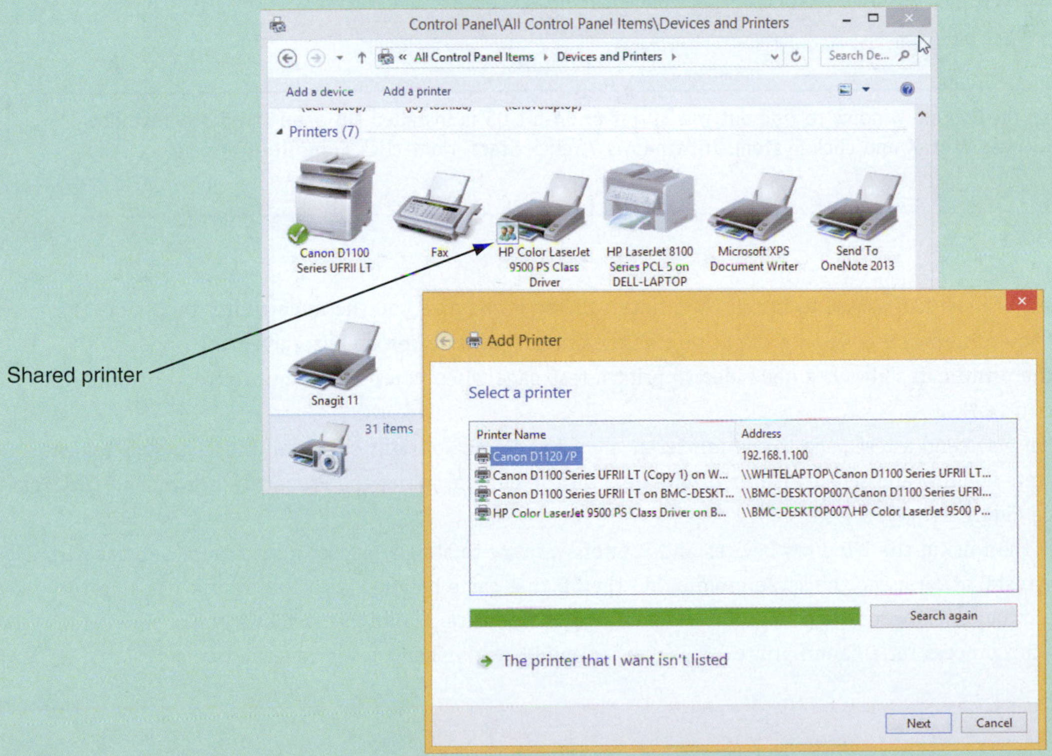

Figure 19-11 Use the Devices and Printers window to install a printer

(continues)

2. Select the printer and click **Next**. If your printer isn't listed, click **The printer that I want isn't listed** and select the printer from a list of printers for which Windows has drivers.
3. In the next box (see the left side of Figure 19-12), select the brand and model printer to use the drivers kept by Windows. To use drivers stored on CD or previously downloaded from the web, click **Have Disk**. The Install From Disk box appears (see the right side of Figure 19-12). Click **Browse** to locate the drivers; Windows is looking for an .inf file. Be sure to select 32-bit or 64-bit drivers, depending on which type of OS you are using.

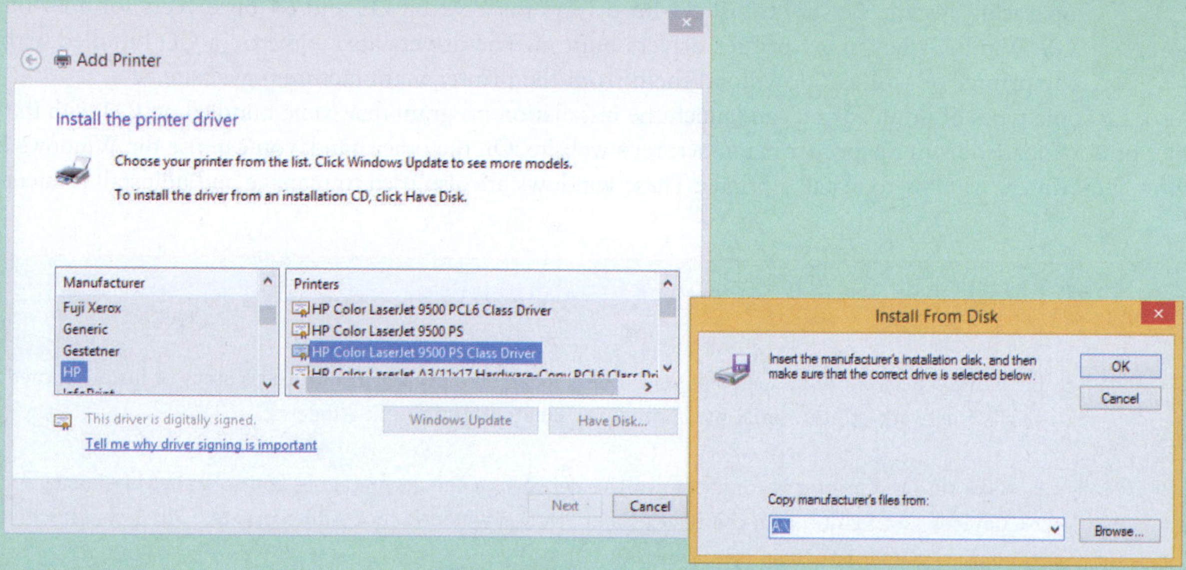

Figure 19-12 Locate printer drivers on CD or downloaded from the web

Notes Use the System window to find out if a 32-bit or 64-bit OS is installed. To open the System window in Windows 8, press **Win+X** and click **System**. In Windows 7, click **Start**, right-click **Computer**, and select **Properties**.

4. Continue to follow the wizard to install the printer. Dialog boxes give you the opportunity to change the name of the printer and designate the printer as the default printer. You are also given the opportunity to test the printer. It's always a good idea to print a test page when you install a printer to verify the installation works.

   You can also send a test page to the printer at any time. To do so, right-click the printer in the Devices and Printers window and select **Printer properties**. On the General tab of the Properties box, click **Print Test Page** (see Figure 19-13).

   Rather than using the Windows Devices and Printers window to start a printer installation, you can also start the installation using the setup program on the CD that came bundled with the printer or using the setup program downloaded from the printer manufacturer's website. Figure 19-14 shows one such window in the setup process for a Canon printer. This method might work when the first method fails.

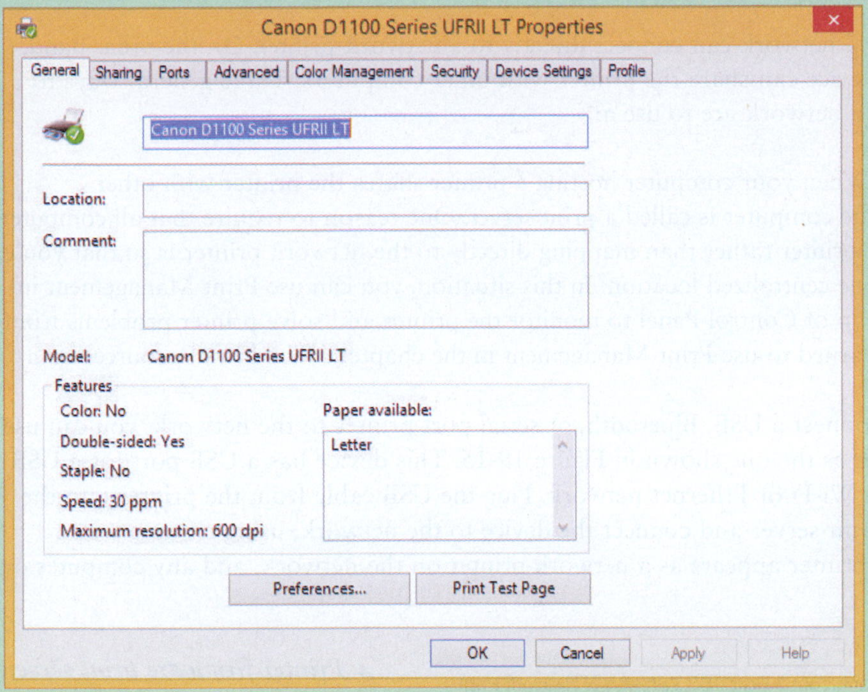

Figure 19-13 Send a test page to the printer to test connectivity to the printer, the printer, and the printer installation

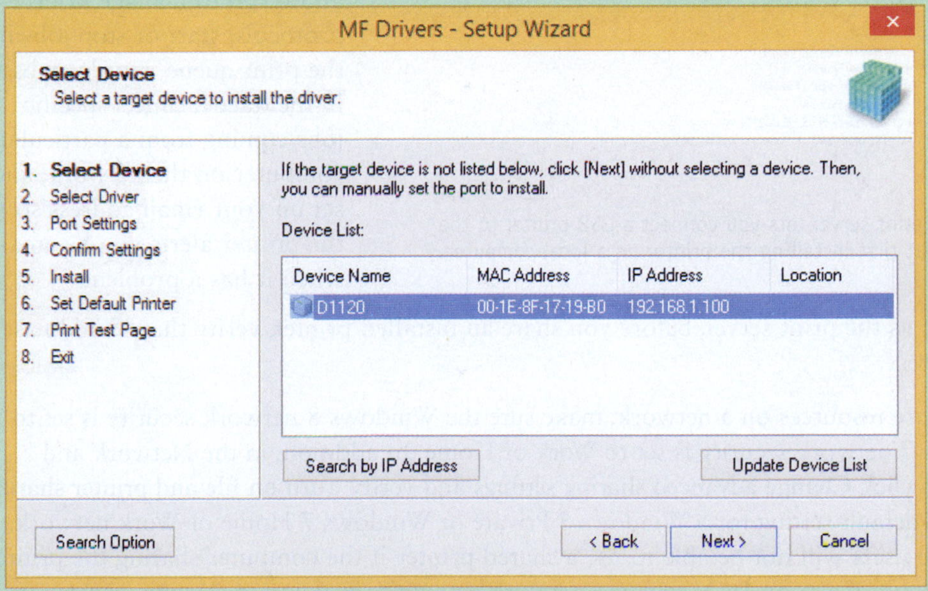

Source: Canon

Figure 19-14 Menu provided by a setup program that came bundled with a printer

★ **A+ Exam Tip** The A+ 220-901 exam expects you to know how to install a local and network printer in Windows.

19

SHARE A PRINTER ON A NETWORK

A+
220-901
1.12,
1.13

Each computer on a network can connect directly to a network printer. On the other hand, one computer or device can share the printer with other computers. Three general ways to share a printer on a network are to use a:

- *Computer as a print server.* When your computer hosting a printer shares the printer with other computers on the network, the computer is called a print server. One reason to require that all computers connect to a shared network printer rather than mapping directly to the network printer is so that you can manage all print jobs from one centralized location. In this situation, you can use Print Management in the Administrative Tools group of Control Panel to monitor the printer and solve printer problems from a centralized location. You learned to use Print Management in the chapter, "Windows Resources on a Network."
- *Hardware print server.* To connect a USB, Bluetooth, or serial-port printer to the network, you can use a hardware print server, such as the one shown in Figure 19-15. This device has a USB port for a USB printer and can connect to a Wi-Fi or Ethernet network. Plug the USB cable from the printer into the USB port of the hardware print server and connect the device to the network, using either a wired or wireless connection. The printer appears as a network printer on the network, and any computer on the network can connect to it.

Source: newegg.com

Figure 19-15 This hardware print server lets you connect a USB printer to the network without first installing the printer on a local computer

- *Printer firmware print server.* Some advanced printers have print server programs included in the printer firmware that allow you to manage print protocols, start or stop jobs in the print queue, reorder jobs in the queue, cancel specific jobs coming from a particular computer on the network, and set up your email address so the printer alerts you by email when it has a problem.

When using a computer as the print server, before you share an installed printer, verify these Windows settings for shared resources:

- *Security settings.* To share resources on a network, make sure the Windows 8 network security is set to Private or the Windows 7 network security is set to Work or Home. In addition, in the Network and Sharing Center, you can click **Change advanced sharing settings** and verify **Turn on file and printer sharing** is selected, which is the default setting for a Windows 8 Private or Windows 7 Home or Work network.
- *Wake-on-LAN.* Remote users will not be able to use a shared printer if the computer sharing the printer is asleep. You can configure Wake-on-LAN to cause network activity to wake up a sleeping computer. How to do that is covered in the chapter, "Connecting To and Setting Up a Network."

APPLYING | CONCEPTS CONFIGURE AND USE A SHARED PRINTER

A+
220-901
1.12,
1.13

To share an installed local or network printer with others on the network, follow these steps:

1. In the printer Properties box, click the **Sharing** tab. Check **Share this printer** (see the left side of Figure 19-16).

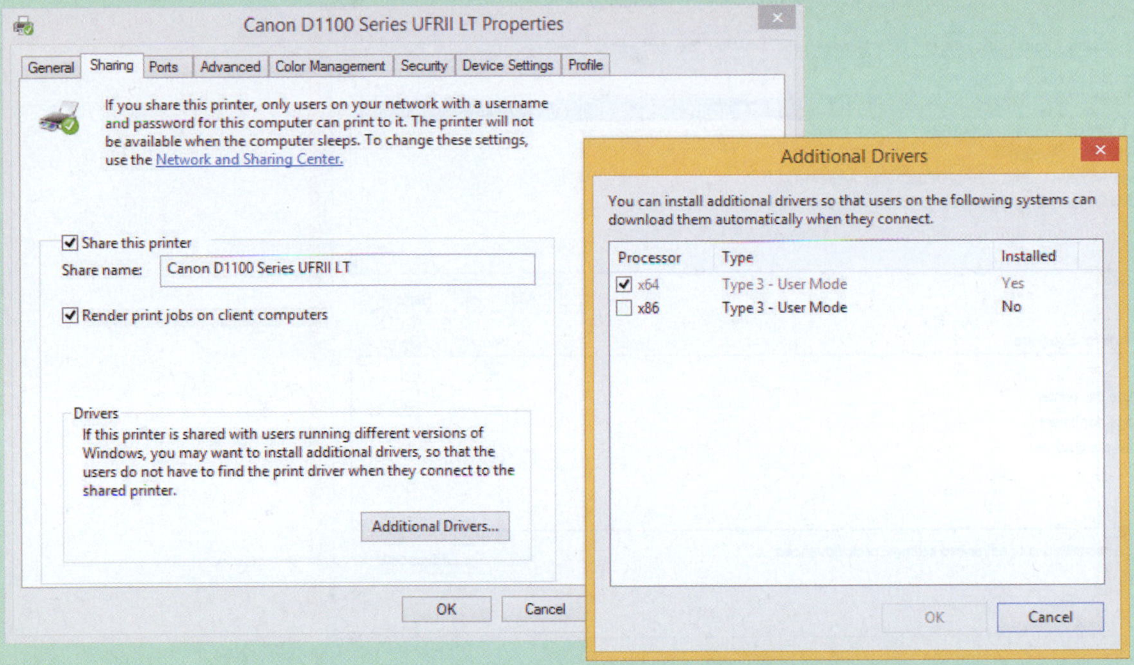

Figure 19-16 Share the printer and make decisions as to how printer sharing is handled

2. You can then change the share name of the printer. Notice in Figure 19-16 the option to control where print jobs are rendered. A print job can be prepared (rendered) on the remote computer (client computer) or this computer (print server). Your choice depends on which computer you think should carry this burden. You can test several print jobs on remote computers with rendering done at either location and see which method best uses computing resources on the network.

Notes Group Policy under Windows 7/Vista can be used to limit and control all kinds of printer-related tasks, including the number of printers that can be installed, how print jobs are sent to print servers (rendered or not rendered), which print servers the computer can use, and which printers on a network the computer can use.

3. If you want to make drivers for the printer available to remote users who are using an operating system other than the OS on this computer, click **Additional Drivers**.
4. The Additional Drivers box opens (see the right side of Figure 19-16). For 32-bit operating systems, select **x86**. For 64-bit operating systems, select **x64**. Click **OK** to close the box. You might be asked for the Windows setup DVD or other access to the installation files.
5. Click **OK** to close the Properties box. A shared printer shows a two-friends icon under it or in the status bar in the Devices and Printers window, and the printer is listed in the Network group in File Explorer or Windows Explorer of other computers on the network.

SECURE A SHARED PRINTER

Consider the security of your shared printer and the security of documents printed:

- *Secure the printer.* On the printer's Properties box (refer back to Figure 19-16), click the **Security** tab to manage who has access to the printer and permissions allowed. Notice in Figure 19-17 that the Everyone group can print but is not allowed to manage the printer or documents sent to it. Just as with shared files and folders, you can share the printer with specific users and/or set up a customized user group that is allowed to use a printer.

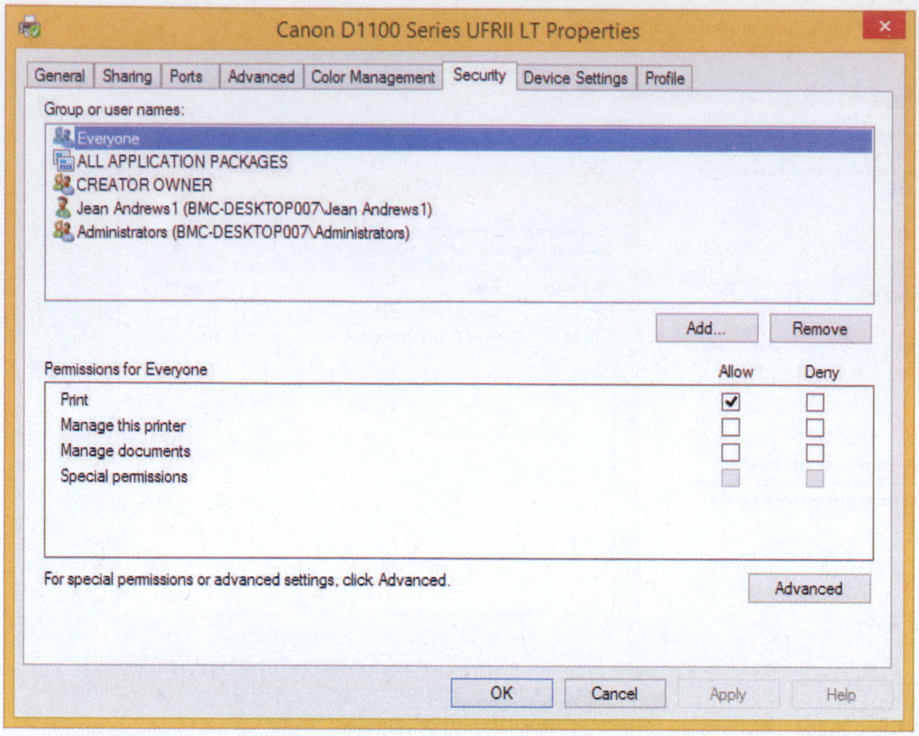

Figure 19-17 Security settings for a printer

◢ ***Secure the data.*** By default, documents sent to the printer are cached (spooled) to the hard drive of the print server and also cached on a hard drive that might be installed in a high-end printer. To prevent these print jobs from being hacked, don't allow caching to either hard drive. In Windows, to change the default setting for spooling, click the **Advanced** tab of the printer's Properties box (see Figure 19-18). Select **Print directly to the printer**. Not spooling to the hard drive slows down the printing process.

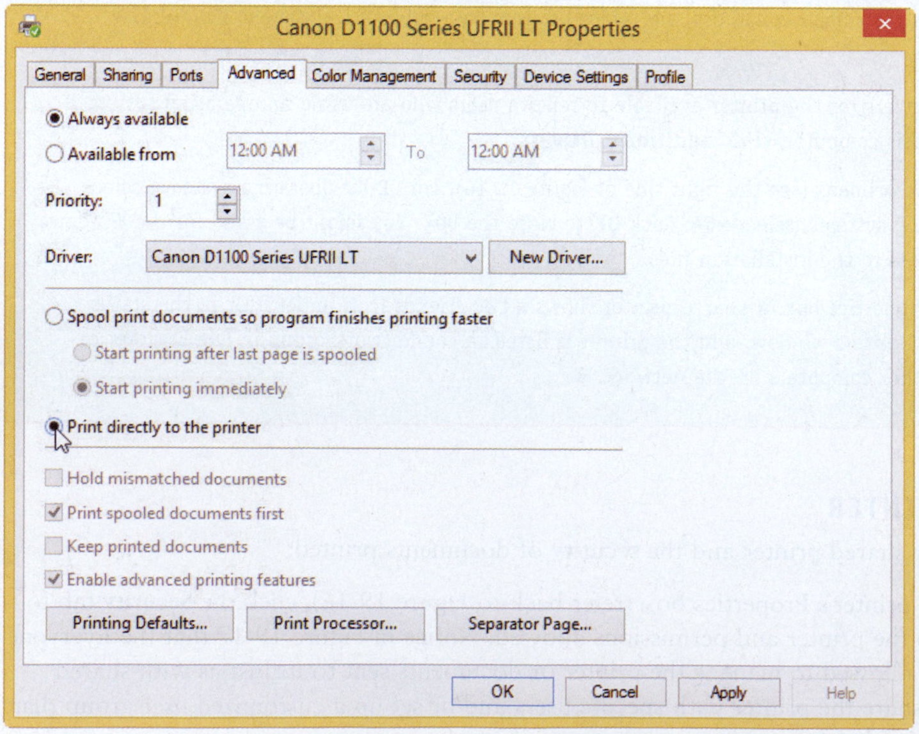

Figure 19-18 For best security, bypass caching print jobs to the hard drive

Notes When print jobs are spooled and the printer is not working or is turned off, the documents can back up in the printer queue. To manage the printer queue, double-click the printer in the Devices and Printers window. Click the queue link and use the menu bar in the queue window to manage the printer's queue.

USE A SHARED PRINTER

To install a shared printer on a remote computer, you can (1) Use the Devices and Printers window or (2) use File Explorer or Windows Explorer. Here are the general steps for both methods:

- *Devices and Printers window.* On a remote computer, in the Devices and Printers window, click **Add a printer** and follow the directions on screen to add a network printer. Select the shared printer, which has a host name in the printer address column (refer back to Figure 19-11). Windows attempts to use printer drivers found on the host computer. If it doesn't find the drivers, you will be given the opportunity to provide them on CD or another media.

  If you don't see a shared printer in the list of printers to add, the user account might not be authorized to access resources on the remote computer. In this situation, use the File Explorer or Windows Explorer method discussed next, which allows the user to authenticate to the remote computer.

Notes If you don't see a shared printer in the list of printers, consider if the printer is shared by a Mac computer on the network and Bonjour is not running on your Windows computer. **Bonjour** is an Apple program that is used to interface between computers and devices and share content and services between them, and is used by Windows to discover a printer shared by a Mac computer. If you suspect a Mac is sharing a printer, open the Services tab of Task Manager in Windows and verify Bonjour is running. You can download the Bonjour Print Services for Windows from the Apple website at *https://support.apple.com/downloads/bonjour%20for%20windows*.

- *File Explorer or Windows Explorer.* In the Explorer window, drill down into the computer that is sharing the printer. If the Windows Security box appears, you need to authenticate to the remote computer with a valid user account and password on the remote computer, as shown in Figure 19-19a. (For the user name to work, the printer must be shared with this specific user or user group and the password much match the password of this user on the remote computer.) After authentication, you can see the shared printer. Right-click the printer and select **Connect**. A warning box appears (see Figure 19-19b). Click **Install driver** and follow directions on screen.

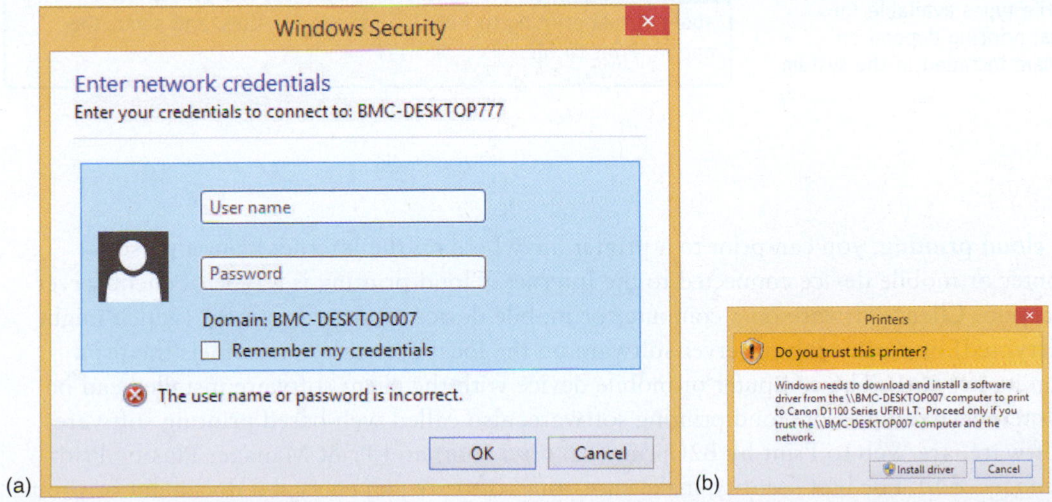

Figure 19-19 (a) Authenticate to the remote computer sharing the printer; (b) allow Windows to install drivers stored on the remote computer

After the printer is installed, be sure to send a test page to the printer to verify the installation is successful.

VIRTUAL PRINTING

A+
220-901
1.12,
1.13

Printing to a file instead of producing a hard copy at a printer is called virtual printing. The types of files you can virtually print depends on the software installed on your system. To see your options for virtual printing, open the Print menu or dialog box for an application. For example, Figure 19-20 shows the results for one system.

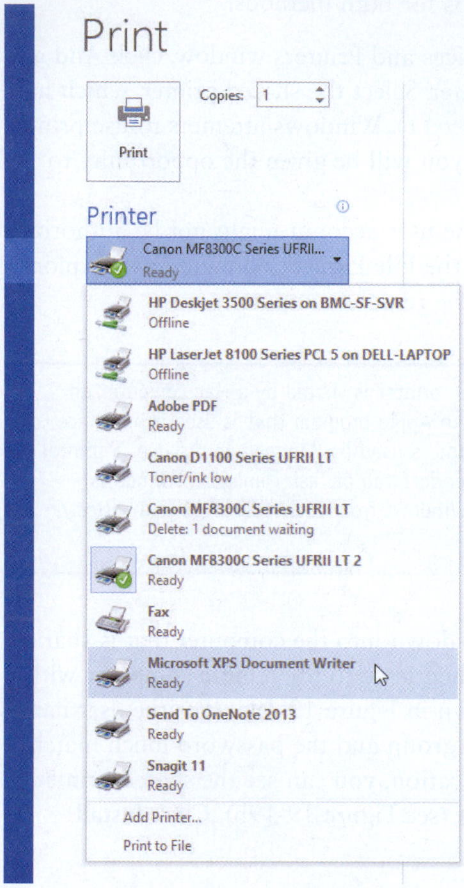

Figure 19-20 The file types available for virtual printing depend on software installed in the system

The items of interest listed in the figure are these types of files:

- ***PDF file.*** Because Adobe Acrobat is installed on this system, it is possible to virtually print to a PDF file.
- ***Image file, also called a bitmap file.*** Snagit is imaging software normally used to take screen shots. When you print to Snagit, you create an image that appears in the Snagit window. Then, you can use Snagit to save the image as a PNG, GIF, JPG, BMP, TIF, or another image file format.
- ***XPS file.*** Windows includes the Microsoft XPS Document Writer, which creates an XPS file. The file is similar to a PDF and can be viewed, edited, printed, faxed, emailed, or posted on websites. In Windows, the file is viewed in a browser window.
- ***Print to file.*** When you check **Print to file** on a Print menu, the print job is created for the currently selected printer and saved to a PRN file. The file contains the information a printer needs to print the document. Saving a print job to a PRN file and later printing it worked with older printers, but doesn't work with modern printers. Today, it's better to create a PDF or XPS document.

> **★ A+ Exam Tip** The A+ 220-901 exam expects you to know about virtual printing to PDF, XPS, and image files, and about the option, Print to file.

CLOUD PRINTING

A+
220-901
1.12,
1.13

With cloud printing, you can print to a printer anywhere on the Internet from a personal computer or mobile device connected to the Internet. Cloud printing is a type of client/server application. Client software on a computer or mobile device sends a document (which might be encrypted) or a print job to server software on the local network that funnels the print jobs to a printer on its network. The computer or mobile device with the client software installed can be anywhere on the Internet. Examples of cloud printing software, also called web-based printing software or web-to-print software, are Web to Print by B2Cprint (*b2cprint.com*) and Print Manager Plus by Print Manager (*printmanager.com*). For best security, make sure your software can encrypt a document or print job sent over the Internet.

Hands-On | Project 19-2 Print in the Cloud

A+
220-901
1.12,
1.13

To practice cloud printing using Google Cloud Print, you'll need a computer with an installed printer and another computer somewhere on the Internet. For the easiest solution to using Google Cloud Print, both computers need Google Chrome installed. You'll also need a Google account.

On the computer with an installed printer, do the following:

1. If you don't already have Google Chrome, go to **google.com/chrome/browser/desktop**, download, and install it.
2. Open Google Chrome and enter **chrome://devices** in the address box. Click **Add printers**. Sign in to Google with your Google account. If you don't already have an account, you can click **Create account** to create one.
3. The list of installed printers appears. Uncheck all printers except the one you want to use for cloud printing. Click **Add Printer(s)**.

On a computer anywhere on the Internet, do the following:

4. If necessary, install Google Chrome.
5. Open Google Chrome and sign in with your Google account. Navigate to a webpage you want to print. Click the menu icon in the upper-right corner of the Chrome window and click **Print**.
6. On the Print page, click **Change** and select the printer, which is listed in the Google Cloud Print group. Click **Print**. The page prints over the web to your printer.

Notes You can share your cloud printer with others who have a Google account. To do so, sign in to your Google account and go to **google.com/cloudprint**. There you'll see a list of print jobs sent to your printer. Click **Printers**. Select the printer you want to share and click **Share**. Enter the email address of your friend and click **Share**. Click **Close**. When your friend is signed in to Google, he can print to your printer from anywhere on the web.

CONFIGURE PRINTER FEATURES AND ADD-ON DEVICES

A+
220-901
1.12,
1.13

After the printer is installed, use the printer Properties box to manage printer features and hardware devices installed on the printer. To open the box, right-click the printer and choose **Printer properties**. On the Properties box, click the **Device Settings** tab. The options on this tab depend on the installed printer. Figure 19-21 shows the box for an HP printer. As you can see in the figure, duplex printing (2-sided printing) is available. You can also control the size of the paper installed in each input tray bin and various add-on devices for this printer, such as a printer hard drive, stapler, or stacker unit.

After you have installed new printer add-on equipment or a feature, the equipment or feature is listed as an option in the printer Properties box for the application used for printing a document. Options can include page orientation (landscape or portrait), collated or uncollated, 1-sided or 2-sided, and quality of printing (for example, general, graphics, or photo quality). For example, Figure 19-22 shows the printer Properties box for a laser printer when printing from Microsoft Word.

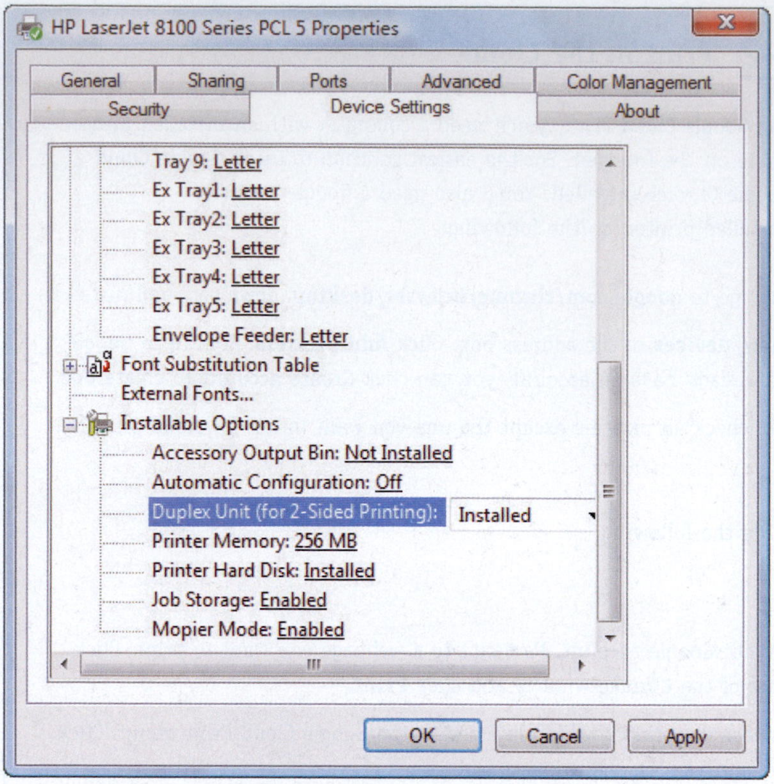

Figure 19-21 The Device Settings for an HP printer

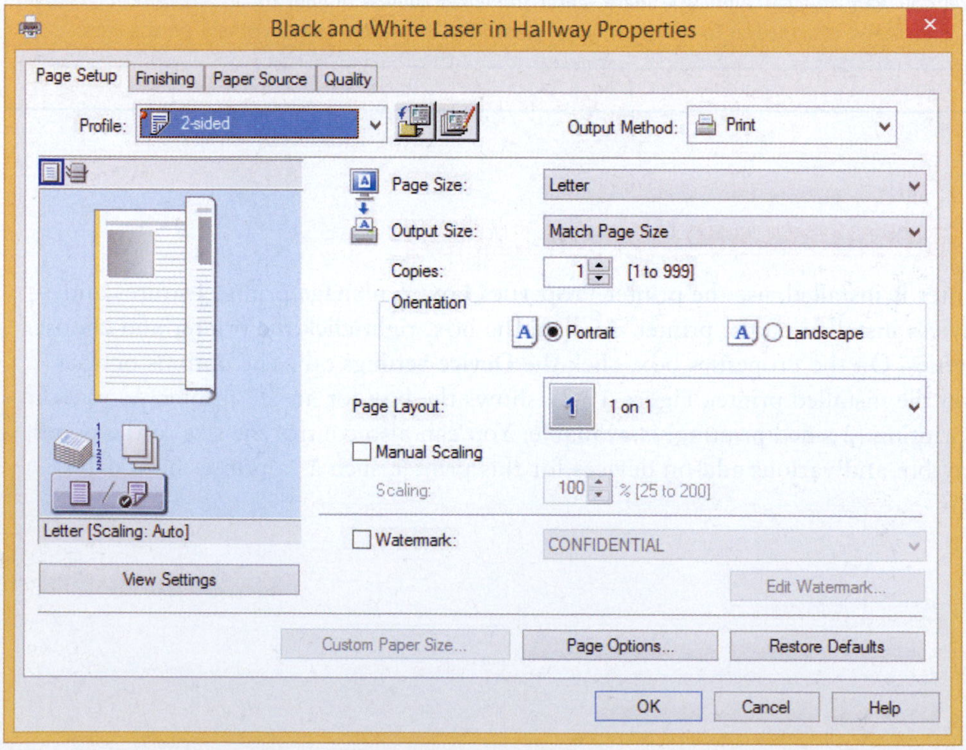

Figure 19-22 Choose options in a printer Properties dialog box

Hands-On Project 19-3 Share a Local Printer

A+
220-901
1.12,
1.13

Practice printer-sharing skills using Windows and a printer:

1. Install and share a local printer with others on the network.
2. Install a shared printer on a remote computer. Verify you can print to the printer from the remote computer.
3. Turn off the shared printer. Print again from the remote computer. On which computer is the print job queued? Cancel this print job.

Now let's turn our attention to tasks you might be called on to do when maintaining and upgrading a printer.

PRINTER MAINTENANCE AND UPGRADES

A+
220-901
1.15, 4.6

Printers generally last for years if they are properly used and maintained. To get the most out of a printer, it's important to follow the manufacturer's directions when using the device and to perform the necessary routine maintenance. For example, the life of a printer can be shortened if you allow the printer to overheat, don't use approved paper, or don't install consumable maintenance kits when they are required.

ONLINE SUPPORT FOR PRINTERS

A+
220-901
1.15, 4.6

The printer manufacturer's website is an important resource when supporting printers. Here are some things to look for:

- *Online documentation.* Expect the printer manufacturer's website to include documentation on installing, configuring, troubleshooting, using, upgrading, and maintaining the printer. Also look for information on printer parts and warranty, compatibility information, specifications and features of your printer, and how to recycle or dispose of a printer.
- *A knowledge base of common problems and what to do about them.* Some websites offer a forum where you can communicate with others responsible for supporting a particular printer. Also look for an online chat link or email address for technical support.
- *Updated device drivers.* Sometimes you can solve printer problems by downloading and installing the latest drivers. Also, a manufacturer makes new features and options available through these drivers. Be sure you download files for the correct printer and OS.
- *Replacement parts.* When a printer part breaks, buy only parts made by or approved by the printer manufacturer. Manufacturers also sell consumable supplies such as toner and ink cartridges.
- *Printer maintenance kits.* The best practice is to buy everything you need for routine maintenance either from the printer manufacturer or an approved vendor. If you buy from a nonapproved vendor, you risk damaging the printer, voiding its warranty, or shortening its life span.
- *Firmware updates.* Some high-end printers have firmware that can be flashed to solve problems and add features. Be careful to download the correct update for your printer.

Here are a few safety tips when working with printers:

- *Hot to touch.* Some laser printer parts can get hot enough to burn you while in operation. Before you work inside a laser printer, turn it off, unplug it, and wait about 30 minutes for it to cool down.

- ***Dangerous electricity.*** A printer might still keep power even when the printer on/off switch is turned off. To ensure that the printer has no power, unplug it. Even when a laser printer is unplugged, internal components might still hold a dangerous electrical charge for some time.
- ***Laser beam.*** For your protection, laser printers use a laser beam that is always enclosed inside a protective case inside the printer. Therefore, when servicing a laser printer, you should never have to look at the laser beam, which can damage your eyes.
- ***Static electricity.*** To protect memory modules and hard drives inside printers, be sure to use an ESD strap to protect these sensitive components when installing them. You don't need to wear an ESD strap when exchanging consumables such as toner cartridges, fuser assembles, or image drums.
- ***When no one is around.*** Here's one more tip to stay safe, but I don't want it to frighten you: When you work inside high-voltage equipment such as a laser printer, don't do it when no one else is around. If you have an emergency, someone needs to be close by to help you.

Notes When working with laser printer toner cartridges, if you get toner dust on your clothes or hands while exchanging the cartridge, don't use hot water to clean it up. Remember that heat sets the toner. Go outdoors and use a can of compressed air to blow off the toner. Then use cold water to clean your hands and clothes. It's a good idea to wear a smock or apron when working on printers.

Figure 19-23 shows an ink cartridge being installed in an inkjet printer. To replace a cartridge, turn on the printer and open the front cover. The printer releases the cartridges. You can then open the latch on top of the cartridge and remove it. Install the new cartridge as shown in the figure.

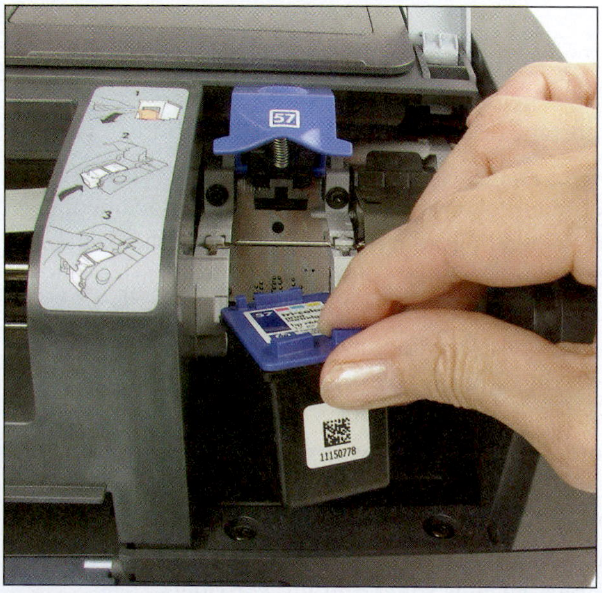

Figure 19-23 Installing an ink cartridge in an inkjet printer

CLEAN A PRINTER

A+
220-901
1.15, 4.6

A printer gets dirty inside and outside as stray toner, ink, dust, and bits of paper accumulate. As part of routine printer maintenance, you need to regularly clean the printer. How often depends on how much the printer is used and the work environment. Some manufacturers suggest a heavily used printer be cleaned weekly, and others suggest you clean it whenever you exchange the toner, ink cartridges, or ribbon.

Clean the outside of the printer with a damp cloth. Don't use ammonia-based cleaners. Clean the inside of the printer with a dry cloth and remove dust, bits of paper, and stray toner. Picking up stray toner can be a problem. Don't try to blow it out with compressed air because you don't want the toner in the air. Also, don't use an antistatic vacuum cleaner. You can, however, use a vacuum cleaner designed to pick up toner, called a **toner vacuum**. This type of vacuum does not allow the toner that it picks up to touch any conductive surface.

Some printer manufacturers also suggest you use an **extension magnet brush**. The long-handled brush is made of nylon fibers that are charged with static electricity and easily attract the toner like a magnet. For a laser printer, wipe the rollers from side to side with a dry cloth to remove loose dirt and toner. Don't touch the soft black roller (the transfer roller), or you might affect the print quality. You can find specific instructions for cleaning a printer on the printer manufacturer's website.

CALIBRATE A PRINTER

A+
220-901
1.15, 4.6

An inkjet printer might require calibration to align and/or clean the inkjet nozzles, which can solve a problem when colors appear streaked or out of alignment. To calibrate the printer, you might use the menu on the control panel of the printer or use software that came bundled with the printer. How to access these tools differs from one printer to another. See the printer manual to learn how to perform the calibration. For some printers, a Services tab is added to the printer Properties window. Other printer installations might put utility programs in the Start menu. The first time you turn on a printer after installing ink cartridges, it's a good idea to calibrate the printer.

If an inkjet printer still does not print after calibrating it, you can try to manually clean the cartridge nozzles. Check the printer manufacturer's website for directions. For most inkjet printers, you are directed to use clean, distilled water and cotton swabs to clean the face of the ink cartridge, being careful not to touch the nozzle plate. To prevent the inkjet nozzles from drying out, don't leave the ink cartridges out of their cradle for longer than 30 minutes. Here are some general directions:

1. Following the manufacturer's directions, remove the inkjet cartridges from the printer and lay them on their sides on a paper towel.
2. Dip a cotton swab in distilled water (not tap water) and squeeze out any excess water.
3. Hold an ink cartridge so that the nozzle plate faces up and use the swab to wipe clean the area around the nozzle plate, as shown in Figure 19-24. Do not clean the plate itself.

Figure 19-24 Clean the area around the nozzle plate with a damp cotton swab

4. Hold the cartridge up to the light and make sure that no dust, dirt, ink, or cotton fibers are left around the face of the nozzle plate. Make sure the area is clean.
5. Clean all the ink cartridges the same way and replace the cartridges in the printer.
6. Print a test page. If print quality is still poor, try calibrating the printer again.
7. If you still have problems, you need to replace the ink cartridges.

Laser printers automatically calibrate themselves periodically. You can instruct a laser printer to calibrate at any time by using the controls on the front of the printer or the browser-based utility program that is included in the firmware of a network printer. To access the utility, enter the IP address of the printer in the browser address box.

PRINTER MAINTENANCE KITS

A+
220-901
1.15, 4.6

Manufacturers of high-end printers provide **printer maintenance kits**, which include specific printer components, step-by-step instructions for performing maintenance, how often maintenance should be done, and any special tools or equipment you need to do maintenance. For example, the maintenance plan for the HP Color LaserJet 4600 printer says to replace the transfer roller assembly after printing 120,000 pages and replace the fusing assembly after 150,000 pages. The plan also says the black ink cartridge should last for about 9,000 pages and the color ink cartridge for about 8,000 pages. HP sells the image transfer kit, the image fuser kit, and the ink cartridges designed for this printer.

To find out how many pages a printer has printed so that you know if you need to do the maintenance, you need to have the printer give you the page count since the last maintenance. You can tell the printer to display the information or print a status report by using buttons on the front of the printer (see Figure 19-25) or you can use utility software from a computer connected to the printer. See the printer documentation to know how to get this report. For network printers that offer a browser-based utility, enter the IP address of the printer in your browser and use the utility to find the counters (Figure 19-26 shows such a utility for a Canon network printer).

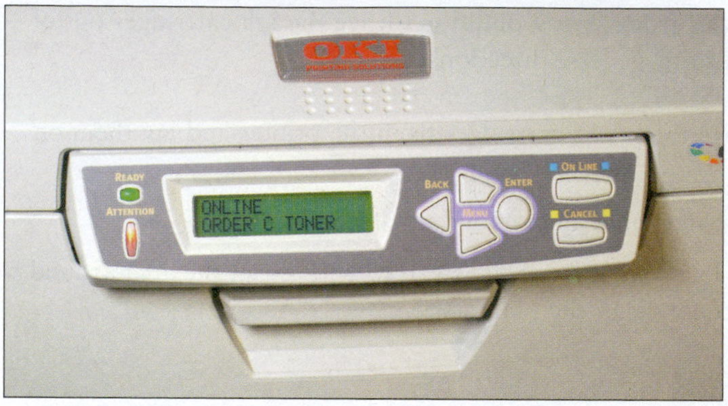

Figure 19-25 Use buttons on the front of the printer to display information, including the page count

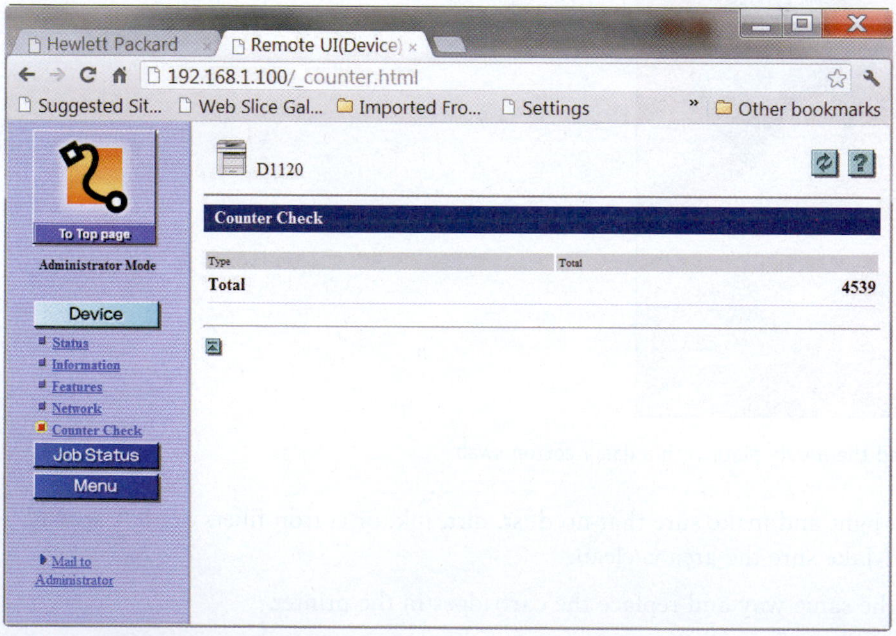

Source: Canon

Figure 19-26 Use the web-based printer utility to read the printer counters

After you have performed the maintenance, be sure to reset the page count so it will be accurate to tell you when you need to do the next routine maintenance. Keep a written record of the maintenance and other service done.

A+ Exam Tip The A+ 220-901 exam expects you to know about the importance of resetting the page count after installing a printer maintenance kit.

As examples of replacing printer consumables, let's look at how to replace a toner cartridge, image drum, and fuser for the Oki Data color laser printer shown earlier in Figure 19-1.

A+ Exam Tip The A+ 220-901 exam expects you to know how to replace a toner cartridge and apply a maintenance kit that can include an image drum or a fuser assembly.

A toner cartridge for this printer generally lasts for about 1,500 pages. Here are the steps to replace a color toner cartridge:

1. Turn off and unplug the printer. Press the cover release button on the upper-left corner of the printer and open the printer cover (see Figure 19-27).
2. Figure 19-28 shows the cover up. Notice the four erase lamps on the inside of the cover. Look inside the printer for the four toner cartridges and the fuser assembly labeled in Figure 19-29. Pull the blue toner cartridge release button forward to release the cartridge from the image drum below it and to which it is connected (see Figure 19-30).

Figure 19-27 Open the printer cover

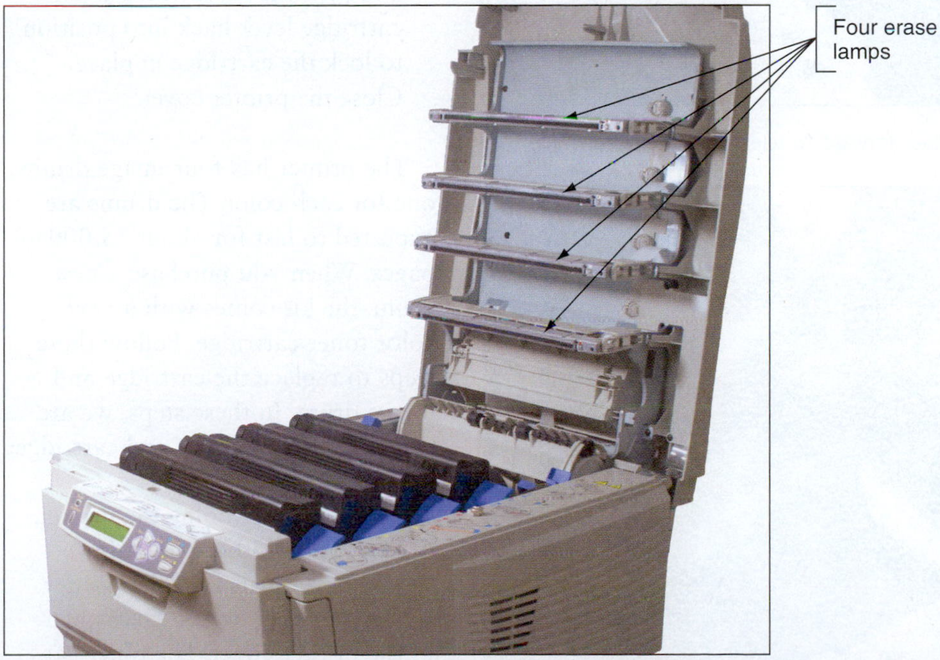

Figure 19-28 Cover lifted

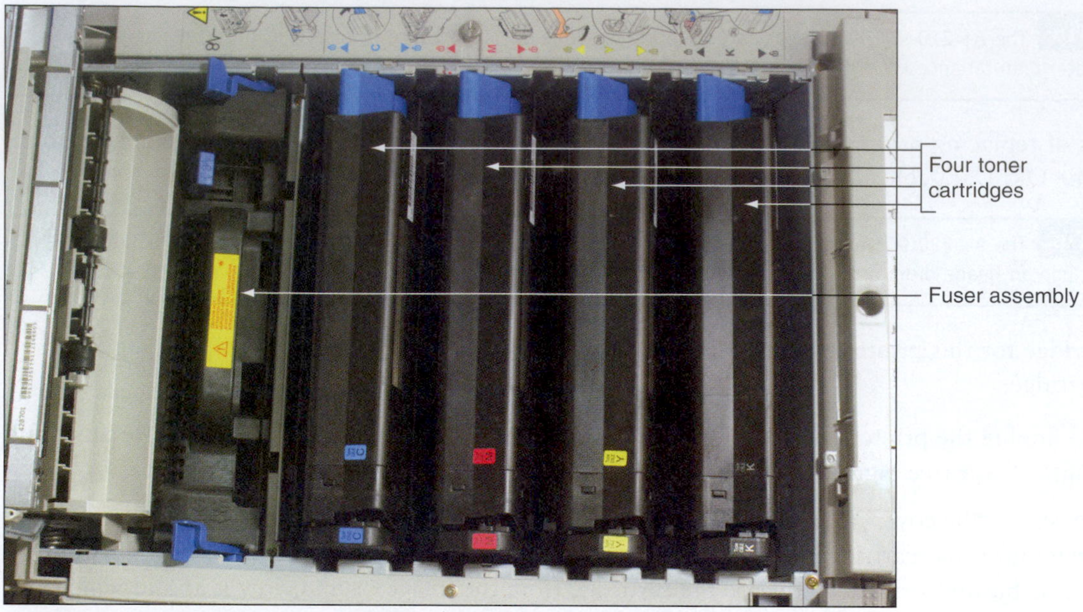

Figure 19-29 Inside the Oki Data printer

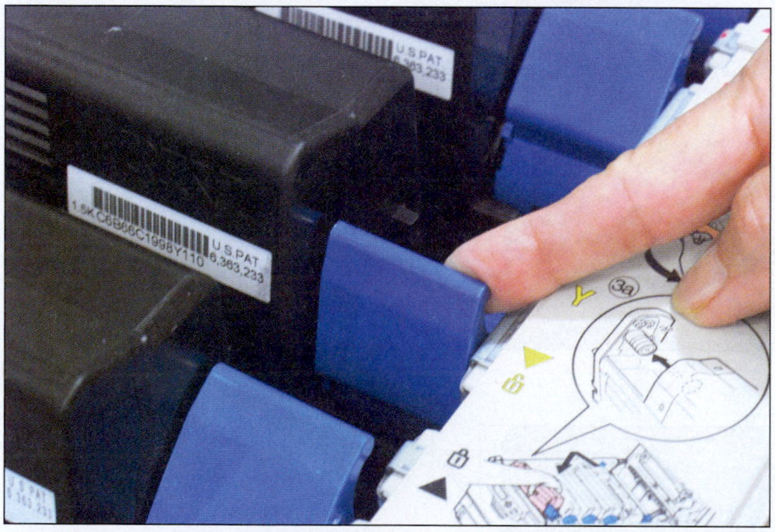

Figure 19-30 Push the blue lever forward to release the toner cartridge

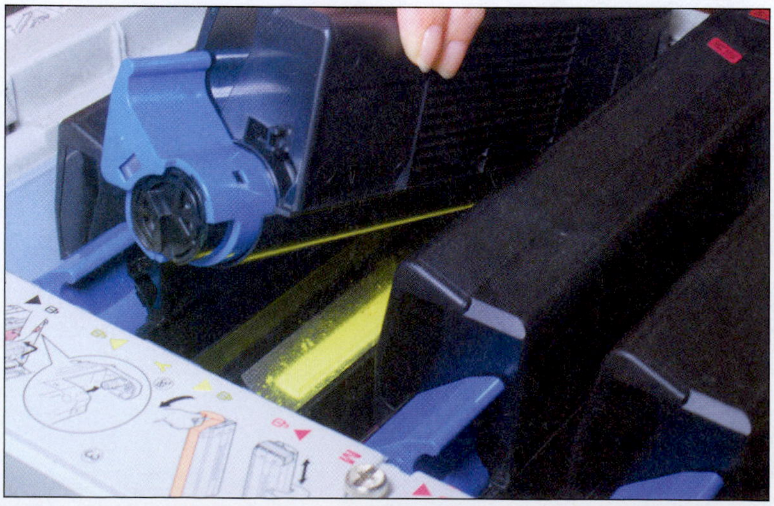

Figure 19-31 Remove the toner cartridge

3. Lift the cartridge out of the printer, lifting up on the right side first and then removing the left side (see Figure 19-31). Be careful not to spill loose toner.
4. Unpack the new cartridge. Gently shake it from side to side to loosen the toner. Remove the tape from underneath the cartridge, and place the cartridge in the printer by inserting the left side first and then the right side. Push the cartridge lever back into position to lock the cartridge in place. Close the printer cover.

The printer has four image drums, one for each color. The drums are expected to last for about 15,000 pages. When you purchase a new drum, the kit comes with a new color toner cartridge. Follow these steps to replace the cartridge and image drum. In these steps, we are using the yellow drum and cartridge:

1. Turn off and unplug the printer. Wait about 30 minutes after you have turned off the printer for it to cool down. Then open the printer cover. The toner car-

tridge is inserted into the image drum. Lift the drum together with the toner cartridge out of the printer (see Figure 19-32). Be sure to dispose of the drum and cartridge according to local regulations.

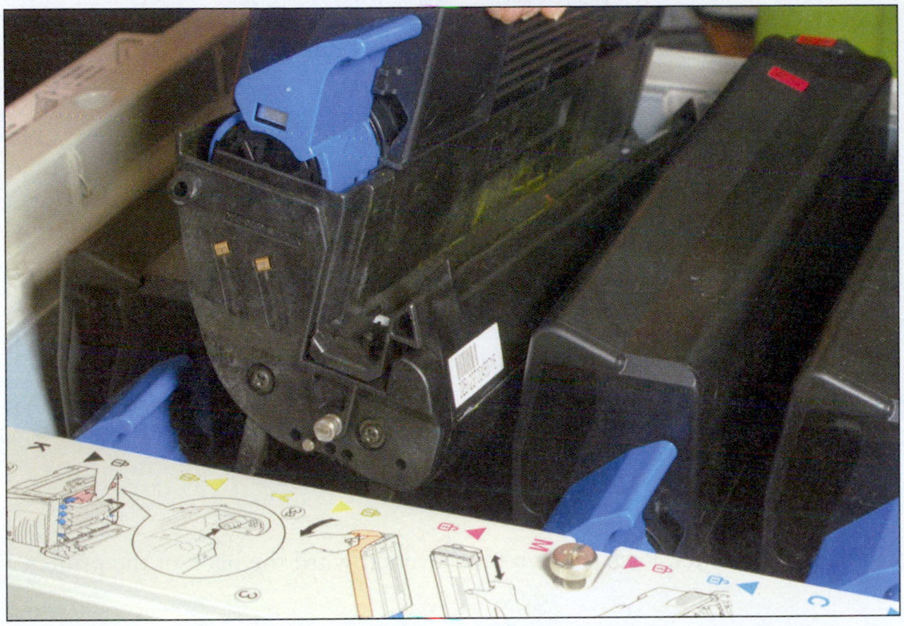

Figure 19-32 Remove the image drum and toner cartridge as one unit

2. Unpack the new image drum. Peel the tape off the drum and remove the plastic film around it. As you work, be careful to keep the drum upright so as not to spill the toner. Because the drum is sensitive to light, don't allow the drum to be exposed to bright light or direct sunlight. Don't expose it to normal room lighting for longer than five minutes.
3. Place the drum in the printer. Install the new toner cartridge in the printer. Close the printer cover.

The fuser should last for about 45,000 pages. To replace the fuser, follow these steps:

1. Turn off and unplug the printer. Allow the printer to cool and open the cover.
2. Pull the two blue fuser levers forward to unlock the fuser (see Figure 19-33).

Figure 19-33 Pull the two fuser levers forward to release the fuser

3. Lift the fuser out of the printer using the handle on the fuser, as shown in Figure 19-34.

Figure 19-34 Remove the fuser

4. Unpack the new fuser and place it in the printer. Push the two blue levers toward the back of the printer to lock the fuser in place.

Whenever you service the inside of this printer, as a last step always carefully clean the LED erase lamps on the inside of the top cover (see Figure 19-35). The printer maintenance kits you've just learned to use all include a wipe to clean these strips.

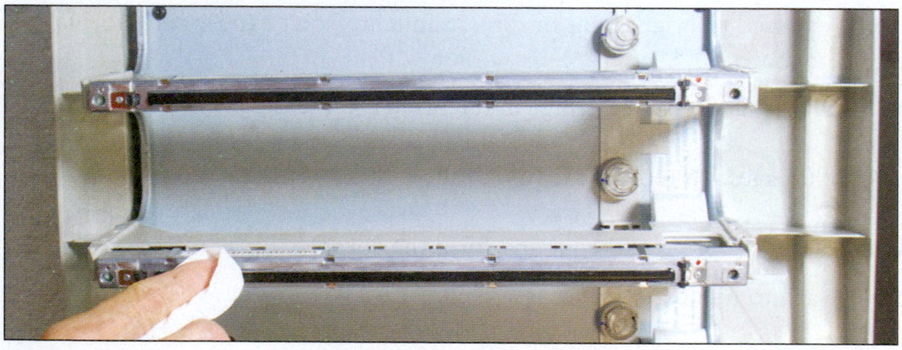

Figure 19-35 Clean the LED strips on the inside top cover

UPGRADE THE PRINTER MEMORY OR HARD DRIVE

A+ 220-901 1.15, 4.6

Some printers have internal hard drives to hold print jobs and fonts, and printers might also give you the option to install additional memory in the printer. Extra memory can speed up performance, reduce print errors, and prevent Out of Memory or Low Memory errors. Check the user guide to determine how much memory the printer can support and what kind of memory to buy or what kind of internal hard drive the printer might support.

As you work with printer hardware, be sure you turn off the printer and disconnect it from the power source. Also, use an antistatic ground bracelet to protect memory modules from static electricity. Most likely, you will use a screwdriver to remove a cover plate on the printer to expose a cavity where memory or a drive can be installed. To access memory on one printer, you remove thumbscrews on the back of the printer and then pull out the formatter board shown in Figure 19-36. Memory modules are installed on this board (see Figure 19-37). You can also install a hard drive in one of the two empty bays on the board. The hard drive comes embedded on a proprietary board that fits in the bay. After this equipment is installed, you must enable and configure it using the printer Properties window.

Figure 19-36 Remove the formatter board from the printer

PRINTER FIRMWARE

A+
220-901
1.15, 4.6

Most high-quality printers offer a utility embedded in the firmware that you can use to manage print jobs, view the status of the printer, see a job history, and check counters, such as the number of pages printed. These utilities are accessed through a browser. For one Canon printer, when you enter the IP address of the printer in a browser window and log on to the firmware utility, the window in Figure 19-38 appears.

Figure 19-37 Memory is installed on the formatter board

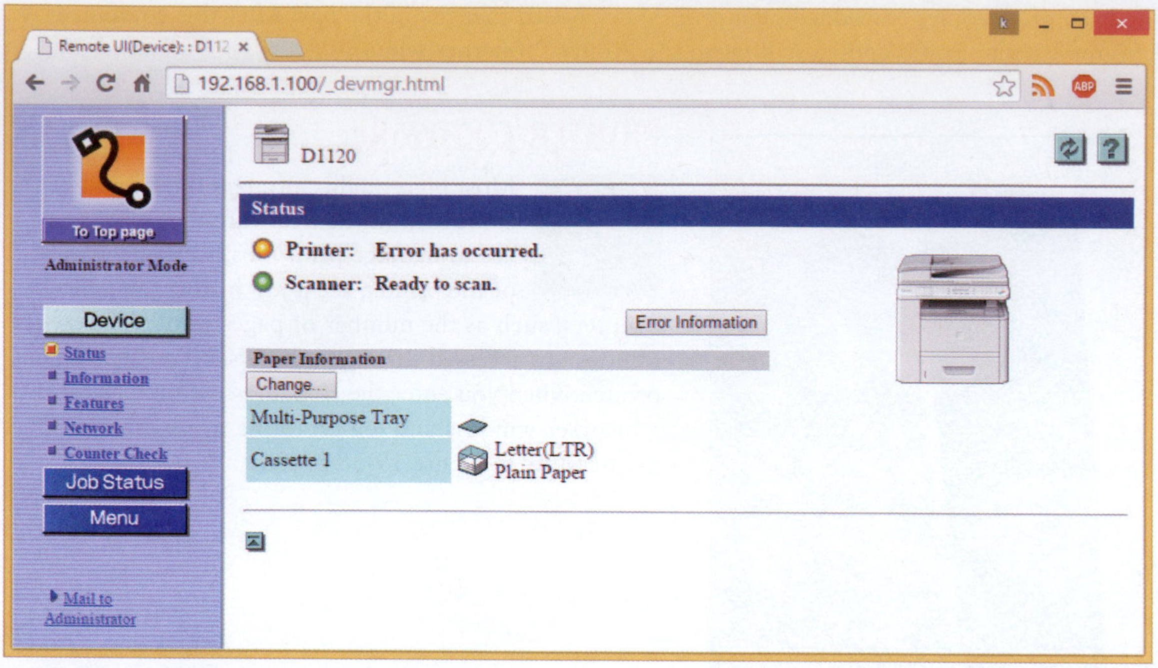

Source: Canon

Figure 19-38 Use the printer's web-based utility to view the printer status and manage print jobs

TROUBLESHOOTING PRINTERS

A+
220-901
1.15, 4.6

In this part of the chapter, you learn some general and specific printer troubleshooting tips. If you need more help with a printer problem, turn to the manufacturer's website for additional information and support.

APPLYING | CONCEPTS

A+
220-901
1.15, 4.6

Jill is the computer support technician responsible for supporting 10 users, their peer-to-peer network, printers, and computers. Everything was working fine when Jill left work one evening, but the next morning three users meet her at the door, complaining that they cannot print to the network printer and that important work must be printed by noon. What do you think are the first three things Jill should check?

As with all computer problems, begin troubleshooting by interviewing the user, finding out what works and doesn't work, and making an initial determination of the problem. When you think the problem is solved, ask the user to check things out to make sure he is satisfied with your work. And, after the problem is solved, be sure to document the symptoms of the problem and what you did to solve it.

PRINTER DOES NOT PRINT

A+
220-901
1.15, 4.6

When a printer does not print, the problem can be caused by the printer, the computer hardware or Windows, the application using the printer, the printer cable, or the network. Follow the steps in Figure 19-39 to isolate the problem.

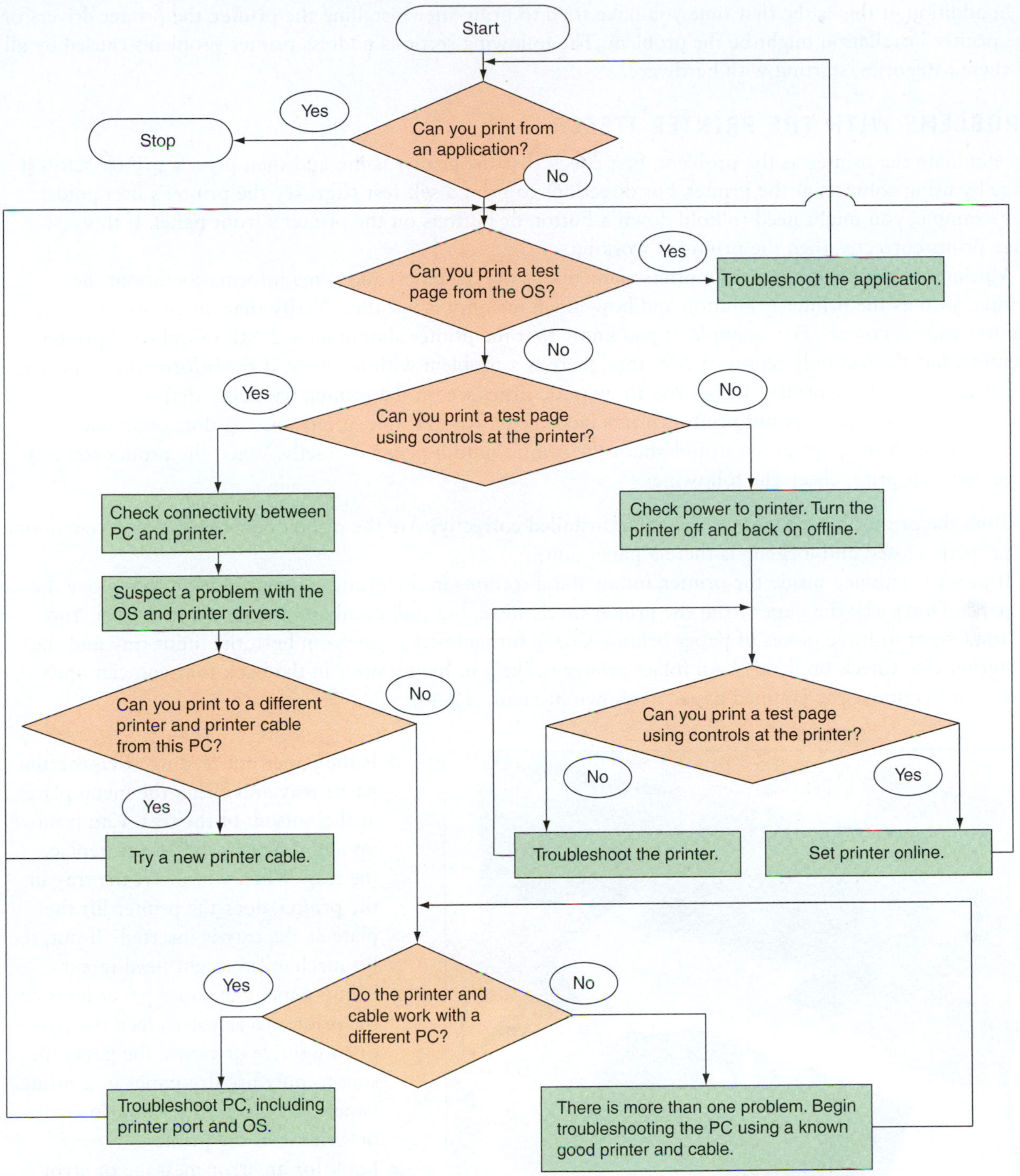

Figure 19-39 How to isolate a printer problem

As you can see in the figure, the problem can be isolated to one of the following areas:

- The printer itself
- Connectivity between the computer and its local printer
- Connectivity between the computer and a network printer
- The OS and printer drivers
- The application attempting to use the printer

In addition, if this is the first time you have tried to print after installing the printer, the printer drivers or the printer installation might be the problem. The following sections address printer problems caused by all of these categories, starting with hardware.

PROBLEMS WITH THE PRINTER ITSELF

To eliminate the printer as the problem, first check that the printer is on, and then print a printer self-test page by using controls at the printer. For directions to print a self-test page, see the printer's user guide. For example, you might need to hold down a button or buttons on the printer's front panel. If this test page prints correctly, then the printer is working.

A printer self-test page generally prints some text, some graphics, and some information about the printer, such as the printer resolution and how much memory is installed. Verify that the information on the test page is correct. For example, if you know that the printer should have 2 MB of onboard printer memory, but the test only reports 1 MB, then there is a problem with memory. If the information reported is not correct and the printer allows you to upgrade firmware on the printer, try doing that next.

If the self-test page does not print or prints incorrectly (for example, it has missing dots or smudged streaks through the page), then troubleshoot the printer until it prints correctly. When the printer self-test page does not print, check the following:

- Does the printer have paper? Is the paper installed correctly? Are the printer cover and rear access doors properly closed and locked? Is there a paper jam?
- If paper is jammed inside the printer, follow the directions in the printer documentation to remove the paper. Don't jerk the paper from the printer mechanism, but pull evenly on the paper, with care. You don't want to leave pieces of paper behind. Check for jammed paper from both the input tray and the output bin. Check both sides. An inkjet printer is likely to have a door in the back that you can open to gently remove the jammed paper, as shown in Figure 19-40.

Figure 19-40 Open the door on the back of an inkjet printer to remove jammed paper

- Is the paper not feeding? Remove the paper tray and check the metal plate at the bottom of the tray. Can it move up and down freely? If not, replace the tray. When you insert the tray in the printer, does the printer lift the plate as the tray is inserted? If not, the lift mechanism might need repair.
- Damp paper can cause paper jams or the printer to refuse to feed the paper or to wrinkle or crease the paper. Be sure to only use dry paper in a printer. Paper that is too thin can also crease or wrinkle in the printer.
- Look for an error message or error code in the control panel on the front of the printer. You might need to search the printer documentation or website to find out the meaning of a code. For example, error codes in the 79.xx range for HP printers can indicate a variety of problems from a print job with characters it does not understand to a failed memory module in the printer.
- For some error codes, the problem might be with a print job the printer cannot process. Cancel all print jobs and disconnect the printer from the network. If the control panel reports "Ready" or "Online," then you can assume the problem is with the network, computers, or print jobs, and not with the printer.

If the error code is still displayed, the problem is with the printer. Follow the directions on the printer manufacturer's website to address the error code.

- Try resetting the printer (for some printers, press the Reset button on the printer). Try powering down or unplugging the printer and starting it again. Check that power is getting to the printer. Try another power source.
- For an inkjet printer, check if nozzles are clogged. Sometimes, leaving the printer on for a while will heat up the ink nozzles and unclog them.
- For an impact printer, if the print head moves back and forth but nothing prints, check the ribbon. Is it installed correctly between the plate and print head? Is it jammed? If the ribbon is dried out, it needs to be replaced.
- Check the service documentation and printer page count to find out if routine maintenance is due or if the printer has a history of similar problems. Check the user guide for the printer and the printer manufacturer's website for other troubleshooting suggestions.

If you still cannot get a printer to work, you might need to take the printer to a certified repair shop. Before you do, though, try contacting the manufacturer. You might also be able to open a chat session on the printer manufacturer's website.

APPLYING | CONCEPTS

A+ 220-901 1.15, 4.6

Now back to Jill and her company's network printer problem. Generally, Jill should focus on finding out what works and what doesn't work, always remembering to check the simple things first. Jill should first go to the printer and check that the printer is online and has no error messages, such as a Paper Out message. Then, Jill should ask, "Can anyone print to this printer?" To find out, she should go to the closest computer and try to print a Windows test page. If the test page prints, she should next go to one of the three computers that do not print and begin troubleshooting that computer's connection to the network. If the test page did not print at the closest computer, the problem is still not necessarily the printer. To eliminate the printer as the problem, the next step is to print a self-test page at the printer. If that self-test page prints, then Jill should check other computers on the network. Is the entire network down? Can one computer see another computer on the network? Perhaps part of the network is down (maybe because of a switch serving one part of the network).

PROBLEMS WITH CONNECTIVITY FOR A NETWORK PRINTER OR SHARED PRINTER

If the self-test page prints but the Windows test page does not print and the printer is a network printer or shared printer, the problem might be with connectivity between the computer and the network printer or with the host computer that is sharing the printer.

★ A+ Exam Tip The A+ 220-901 exam expects you to know how to determine if connectivity between the printer and the computer is the problem when troubleshooting printer issues.

Follow these steps to solve problems with network printers:

19

- Is the printer online?
- Turn the printer off and back on. Try rebooting the computer.
- Verify that the correct default printer is selected.
- Consider the IP address of the printer might have changed, which can happen if the printer is receiving a dynamic IP address. Using Windows, delete the printer, and then install the printer again. If this solves the problem, assign a static IP address to the printer to keep the problem from reoccurring.
- Can you print to another network printer? If so, there might be a problem with the printer. Look at the printer's configuration.
- Try pinging the printer. To do that, open a command prompt window and enter **ping 192.168.1.100** (substitute the IP address of your printer). If the printer replies (see Figure 19-41), the problem is not network connectivity.

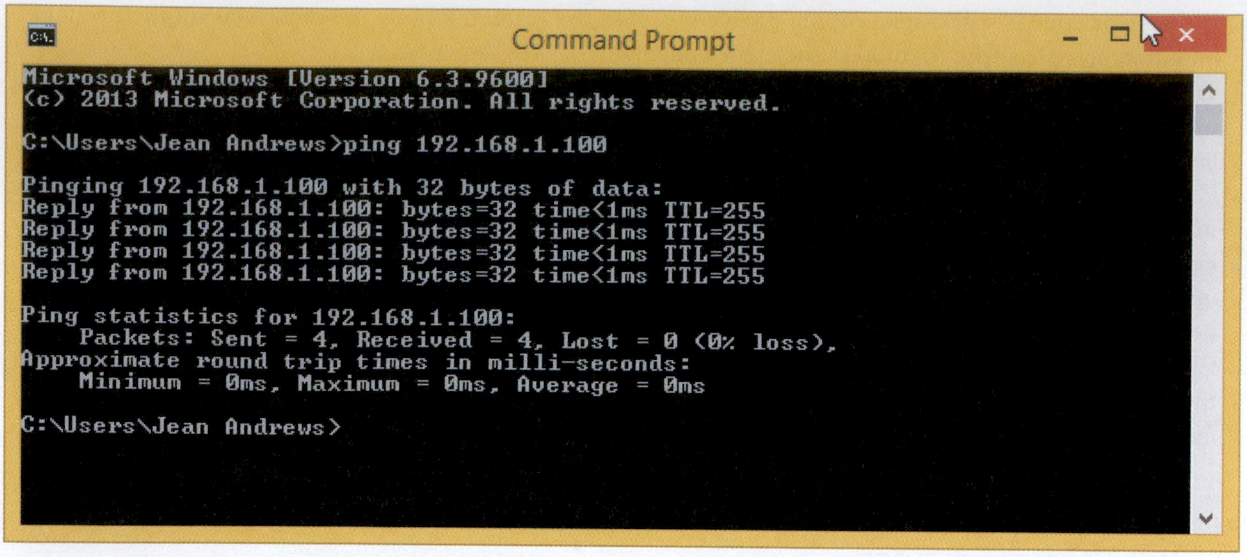

Figure 19-41 Use the ping command to determine if you have network connectivity with the printer

- If pinging doesn't work, try using another network cable for the printer. Check status indicator lights on the printer network port and on the switch or router to which the printer connects.
- Use the printer's browser-based utility and check for status reports and error messages. Run diagnostic software that might be available on the utility menu.
- Try flashing the network printer's firmware.

Even though you are using a network printer, the printer might have been installed as a printer that has been shared on the network. Let's look at an example of this situation. Figure 19-42 shows a Devices and Printers window with several installed printers. Notice the two installations of the Canon D1100 Series UFRII LT printer. The first installation was done installing the Canon D1100 as a network printer addressed by its IP address. The second installation was done by using a shared printer that was shared by another computer on the network named WHITELAPTOP. When you print using the first installation of the Canon D1100, you print directly over the network to the printer. But when you print to the second installation of the Canon D1100, you print by way of the WHITELAPTOP computer. If this computer is offline, the print jobs back up in the print queue until the computer is available.

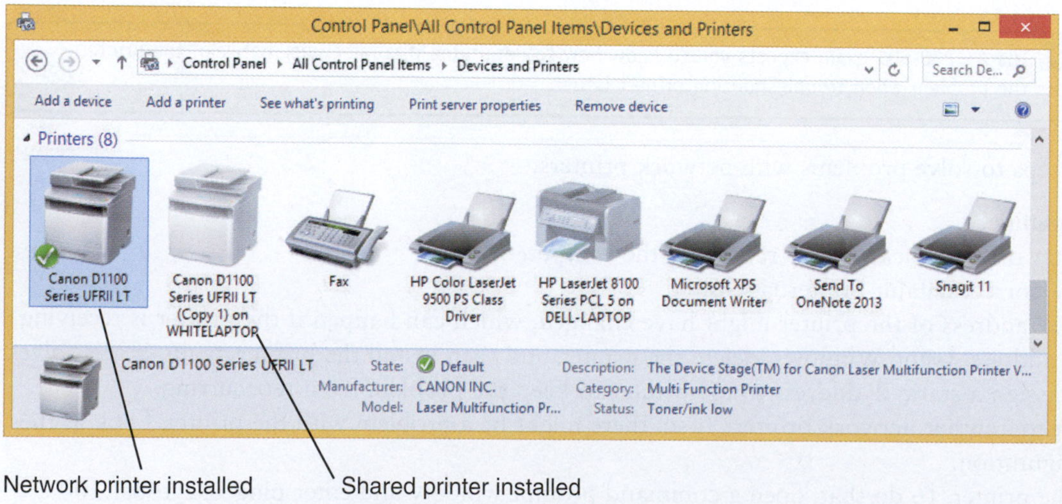

Figure 19-42 A network printer installed using two methods

When a computer has shared a local or network printer with others on the network, follow these steps to solve problems with these shared printers:

- Check that you can print a test page from the computer that has the printer attached to it locally or is sharing a network printer. If you cannot print from the host computer, solve the problem there before attempting to print from other computers on the network.
- Is enough hard drive space available on the client or host computer?
- Did you get an "Access denied" message when you tried to print from the remote computer? If so, you might not have access to the host computer. On the remote computer, go to File Explorer or Windows Explorer and attempt to drill down into resources on the printer's computer. Perhaps you have not entered a correct user account and password to access this computer; if so, you will be unable to use the computer's resources. Make sure you have a matching Windows user account and password on each computer.
- On the host computer, open the printer's Properties box and click the **Security** tab. Select **Everyone** and make sure Permissions for Everyone includes permission to print (refer back to Figure 19-17).
- Using Windows on the remote computer, delete the printer, and then install the printer again. Watch for and address any error messages that might appear.

PROBLEMS PRINTING FROM WINDOWS

If a self-test page works and you have already stepped through checking the printer connectivity, but you still cannot print a test page from Windows, try the following:

- The print spool might be stalled. Try deleting all print jobs in the printer's queue. In the Devices and Printers window, double-click the printer and click **document(s) in queue**. To cancel one document, right-click it and click **Cancel** in the shortcut menu (see Figure 19-43). To cancel all documents, click **Printer** and click **Cancel All Documents**. If the printer is still hung, try using buttons on the front of the printer to cancel print jobs. You can also power cycle the printer (turn it off and back on). Some printers have a Reset button for this purpose.

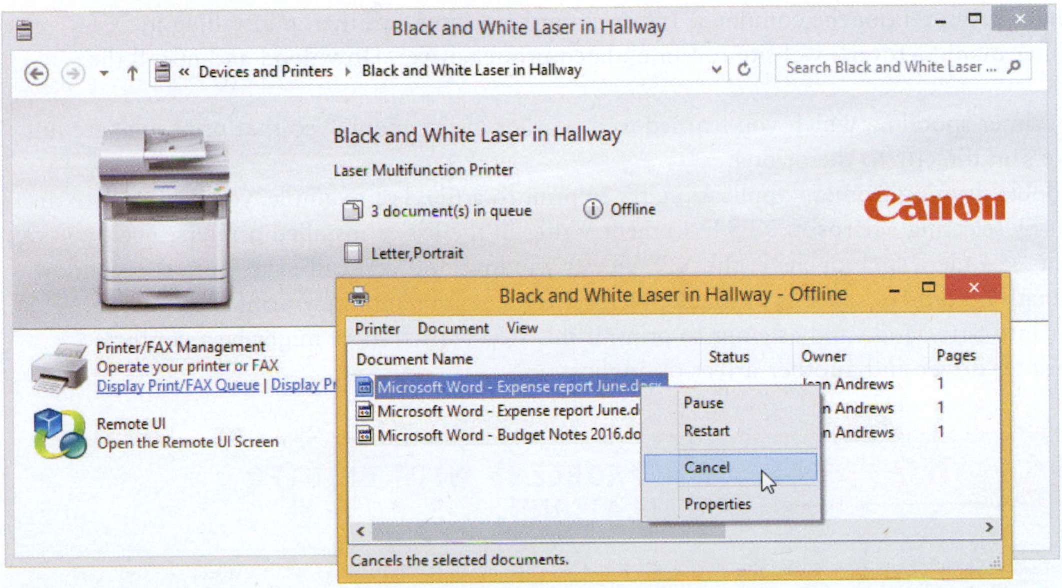

Source: Canon

Figure 19-43 Cancel the first print job in the printer queue

★ A+ Exam Tip The A+ 220-901 exam expects you to know how to solve problems with the print spool.

19

- Verify that the correct printer is used.
- Verify that the printer is online. See the printer documentation for information on how to determine the status from the control panel of the printer. For many printers, "Ready" appears in this control panel.
- Verify that the printer cable or cable connections are solid.
- Stop and restart the Windows Print Spooler service. Windows uses the Services console to stop, start, and manage background services used by Windows and applications. Do the following:
  1. To stop the service, enter **services.msc** in the Windows 8 Run box or the Windows 7 Search box. In the Services console, select **Print Spooler** (see Figure 19-44). Click **Stop** to stop the service.

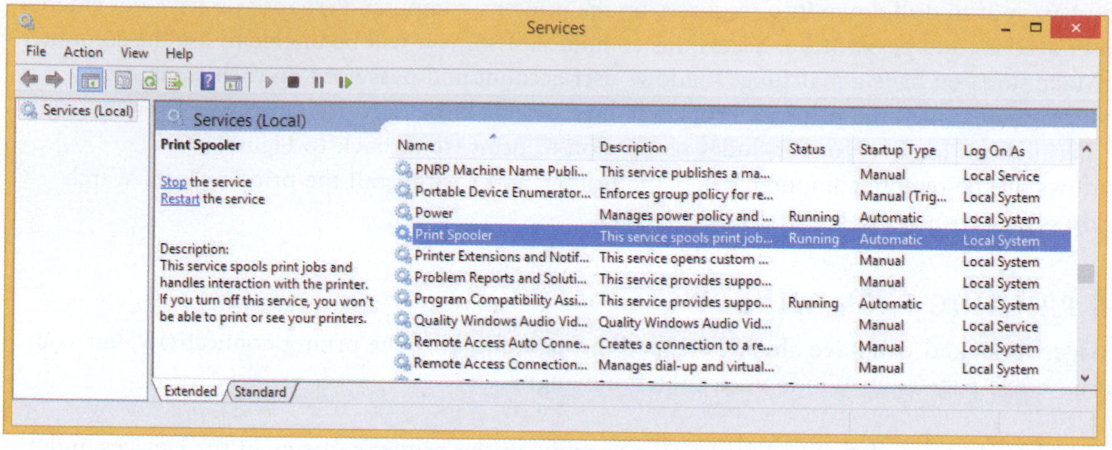

Figure 19-44 Use the Services console to stop and start the print spooler

  2. To delete any print jobs left in the queue, open File Explorer or Windows Explorer and delete all files in the C:\Windows\System32\spool\PRINTERS folder.
  3. Start the print spooler back up. To start up the print spooler, return to the Services console. With Print Spooler selected, click **Start**. Close the Services console window.

- If you still cannot print, reboot the computer. Try deleting the printer and then reinstalling it.
- Check the printer manufacturer's website for an updated printer driver. Download and install the correct driver.
- Try disabling printer spooling, which you learned to do earlier in the chapter, so that print jobs are not cached, but are sent directly to the printer.
- If you have trouble printing from an application, try to print to a file. For example, you can print to an XPS document by selecting Microsoft XPS Document Writer in the list of installed printers. Then you can double-click the .xps file, which opens in the XPS Viewer window, and you can print from this window.
- Verify that enough hard drive space is available for the OS to create temporary print files.
- Boot Windows into Safe Mode and attempt to print. If this step works, there might be a conflict between the printer driver and another driver or application.

APPLYING | CONCEPTS SOLVE PROBLEMS WITH PRINTER INSTALLATIONS

A+ 220-901 1.15, 4.6

Here are some steps you can take if the printer installation fails or installs with errors:

1. If you still have problems, consider that Windows might be using the wrong or corrupted printer drivers. Try removing the printer and then installing it again. To remove a printer, right-click the printer in the Devices and Printers window and click **Remove device**. Try to install the printer again.

2. If the problem is still not solved, completely remove the printer drivers by using the printui command. The Printer User Interface command, **printui**, is used by administrators to manage printers and printer drivers on remote computers. You can also use it to delete drivers on the local computer. Follow these steps:
   a. If the printer is listed in the Devices and Printers window, remove it. (Sometimes Windows automatically puts a printer there when it finds printer drivers are installed.)
   b. Before you can delete printer drivers, you must stop the print spooler service. Open the Services console and use it to stop the Print Spooler (refer to Figure 19-44). To delete any print jobs left in the queue, open Explorer and delete all files in the C:\Windows\System32\spool\PRINTERS folder.
   c. You can now start the print spooler back up. Because the printer is no longer listed in the Devices and Printers window, starting the spooler will not tie up these drivers.
   d. Open an **elevated command prompt window**, which is a window used to enter commands that have administrator privileges. To open the window, in Windows 8, press **Win+X** and click **Command Prompt (Admin)**. In Windows 7, click **Start**, **All Programs**, **Accessories**. Right-click **Command Prompt** and click **Run as administrator**. Respond to the UAC box.
   e. At the command prompt (see the left side of Figure 19-45), enter the command: `printui /s /t2` (In the command line, the /s causes the Print Server Properties box to open and the /t2 causes the Drivers tab to be the selected tab.)

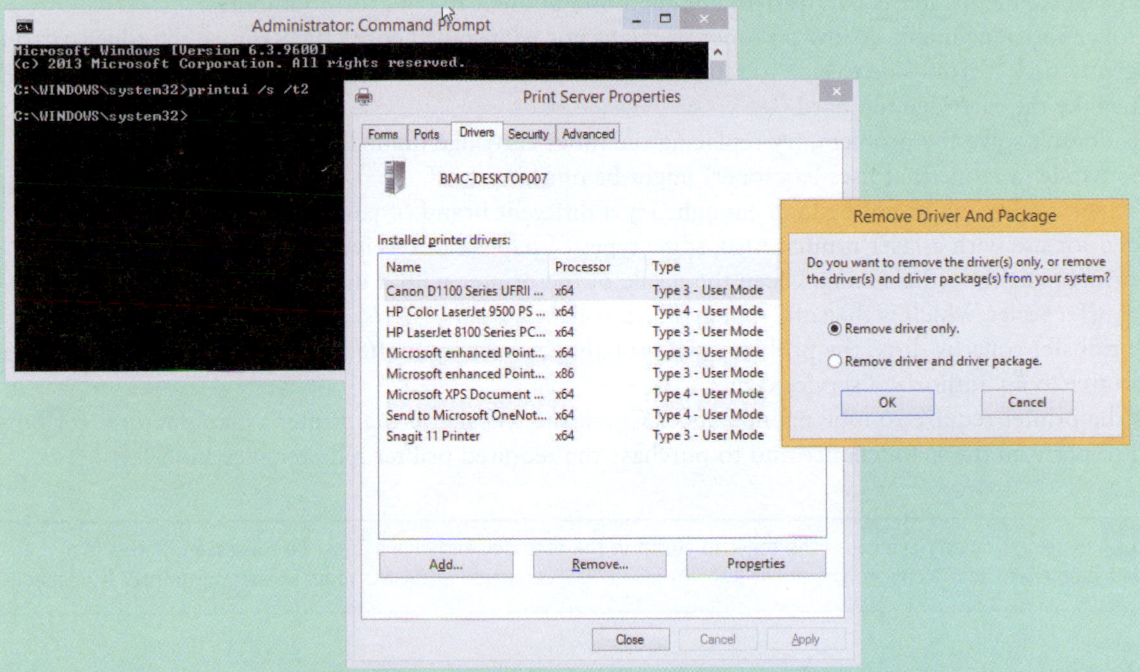

Figure 19-45 Use the printui command to delete printer drivers and possibly delete the driver package (driver store)

   f. The Print Server Properties box opens, as shown in the middle of Figure 19-45. Select the printer and click **Remove**. In the Remove Driver And Package box (see the right side of Figure 19-45), select **Remove driver only** and click **OK**. It is not necessary to remove the driver package. (This driver package, also called the driver store, can be installed on this computer or a remote computer and holds a backup of the printer drivers.)
   g. When a warning box appears, click **Yes**. Close all windows.

3. Try to install the printer again. Start the installation from the CD that came bundled with the printer or by using the printer setup program downloaded from the printer manufacturer's website.

POOR PRINT QUALITY

A+ 220-901 1.15, 4.6

Poor print quality can be caused by the printer drivers, the application, Windows, or the printer. Let's start by looking at what can cause poor print quality with laser printers and then move on to other problems that affect printouts.

A+ Exam Tip The A+ 220-901 exam expects you to know how to resolve problems with streaks, faded prints, ghost images, garbled characters on a page, vertical lines, low memory errors, and wrong print colors. All these problems are covered in this part of the chapter.

POOR PRINT QUALITY FOR LASER PRINTERS

For laser printers, poor print quality, including faded, smeared, wavy, speckled, or streaked printouts, often indicates that the toner is low. All major mechanical printer components that normally create problems are conveniently contained within the replaceable toner cartridge. In most cases, the solution to poor-quality printing is to replace this cartridge.

Follow these general guidelines to fix poor print quality with laser printers:

- If you suspect the printer is overheated, unplug it and allow it to cool for 30 minutes.
- The toner cartridge might be low on toner or might not be installed correctly. Remove the toner cartridge and gently rock it from side to side to redistribute the toner. Replace the cartridge. To avoid flying toner, don't shake the cartridge too hard.
- If this doesn't solve the problem, try replacing the toner cartridge immediately.
- Econo Mode (a mode that uses less toner) might be on; turn it off.
- The paper quality might not be high enough. Try a different brand of paper. Only use paper recommended for use with a laser printer. Also, some types of paper can receive print only on one side.
- The printer might need cleaning. Clean the inside of the printer with a dry, lint-free cloth. Don't touch the transfer roller, which is the soft, spongy black roller.
- If the transfer roller is dirty, the problem will probably correct itself after several sheets print. If not, take the printer to an authorized service center.
- Does the printer require routine maintenance? Check the website of the printer's manufacturer for how often to perform the maintenance and to purchase the required printer maintenance kit.

Notes Extreme humidity can cause the toner to clump in the cartridge and give a Toner Low message. If this is a consistent problem in your location, you might want to invest in a dehumidifier for the room where your printer is located.

- Streaking is usually caused by a dirty developer unit or corona wire. The developer unit is contained in the toner cartridge. Replace the cartridge or check the printer documentation for directions on how to remove and clean the developer unit. Allow the corona wire to cool and clean it with a lint-free swab.
- Speckled printouts can be caused by the laser drum. If cleaning the printer and replacing the toner cartridge don't solve the problem, replace the laser drum.

Notes If loose toner comes out with your printout, the fuser is not reaching the proper temperature and toner is not being fused to the paper. Professional service is required.

- Distorted images can be caused by foreign material inside the printer that might be interfering with the mechanical components. Check for debris that might be interfering with the printer operation.
- If the page has a gray background or gray print, the image drum is worn out and needs to be replaced.

- A ghosted image appears a few inches below the actual darker image on the page. Ghosted images are usually caused by a problem with the image drum or toner cartridge. The drum is not fully cleaned in the cleaning stage, and toner left on it causes the ghost image. If the printer utility installed with the printer offers the option to clean the drum, try that first. The next solution is to replace the less expensive toner cartridge. If the problem is still not solved, replace the image drum.

POOR PRINT QUALITY FOR INKJET PRINTERS

To troubleshoot poor print quality for an inkjet printer, check the following:

1. Is the correct paper for inkjet printers being used? The quality of paper determines the final print quality, especially with inkjet printers. In general, the better the quality of the paper used with an inkjet printer, the better the print quality. Don't use less than 20-pound paper in any type of printer, unless the printer documentation specifically says that a lower weight is satisfactory.
2. Is the ink supply low, or is there a partially clogged nozzle?
3. Remove and reinstall the cartridge(s).
4. Follow the printer's documentation to clean each nozzle. Is the print head too close to or too far from the paper?
5. There is a little sponge in some printers near the carriage rest that can become clogged with ink. It should be removed and cleaned.
6. If you are printing transparencies, try changing the fill pattern in your application.
7. Missing lines or dots on the printed page can be caused by the ink nozzles drying out, especially when the printer sits unused for a long time. Follow the directions given earlier in the chapter for cleaning inkjet nozzles.
8. Streaks or lines down the page can be caused by dust or dirt in the print head assemblage. Follow the manufacturer's directions to clean the inkjet nozzles.

GARBLED CHARACTERS ON PAPER

If scrambled or garbled characters print on all or part of a page, the problem can be caused by the document being printed, the application, connectivity between the computer and the printer, or the printer. Follow these steps to zero in on the problem:

1. First, cancel all print jobs in the print queue. Then try printing a different document from the same application. If the second document prints correctly, the problem is with the original document.
2. Try printing using a different application. If the problem is resolved, try repairing or reinstalling the application.
3. For a USB printer, the problem might be with a USB hub, port, or cable. Is the USB cable securely connected at both ends? If you are using a USB hub, remove the hub, connecting the printer directly to the computer. Try a different USB cable or USB port.
4. Recycle the printer by powering it down and back up or pressing a Reset button.
5. Update the printer drivers. To do that, go to the website of the printer manufacturer to find the latest drivers and follow their directions to install the drivers.
6. If the problem is still not solved, the printer might need servicing. Does the printer need maintenance? Search the website of the printer manufacturer for other solutions.

LOW MEMORY ERRORS

For some printers, an error occurs if the printer does not have enough memory to hold the entire page. For other printers, only a part of the page prints. Some might signal this problem by flashing a light or displaying an error message on their display panels, such as "20 Mem Overflow," "Out of memory," or "Low Memory." The solution is to install more memory or to print only simple pages with few graphics. Print a self-test page to verify how much memory is installed. Some printers give you the option to install a hard drive in the printer to give additional printer storage space.

WRONG PRINT COLORS

For a printer that is printing the wrong colors, do the following:

1. Some paper is designed to print on only one side. You might need to flip the paper in the printer.
2. Try adjusting the quality of print. How to do so varies by printer. For one color laser printer, open the **Printing Preferences** box and click the **Quality** tab (see the left side of Figure 19-46). You can try different selections on this box. To manually adjust the color, check **Manual Color Settings** and then click **Color Settings**. The box on the right side of Figure 19-46 appears.

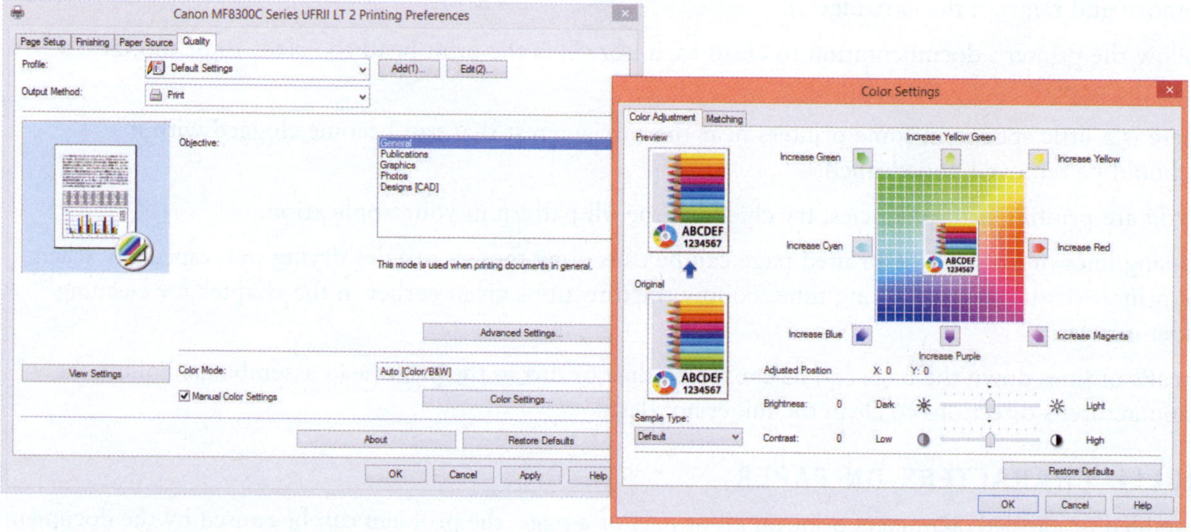

Source: Canon

Figure 19-46 Adjust printing quality and color

3. For an inkjet printer, try cleaning the ink cartridges and calibrating the printer. One step in doing that prints a self-test page. If the self-test page shows missing or wrong colors, the problem is with the ink cartridges. Try cleaning the ink nozzles. If that doesn't work, replace the ink cartridges.
4. For a laser printer, try calibrating the printer.

Now we wrap up the chapter with a discussion of customizing computer systems.

CUSTOMIZING COMPUTER SYSTEMS

A+
220-901
1.9, 1.12

Many computer vendors and manufacturers offer to build customized systems to meet specific needs of their customers. As a technical retail associate, you need to know how to recommend to a customer which computer components are needed for his or her specific needs. You also might be called on to select and purchase components for a customized system and perhaps even build this system from parts. In this part of the chapter, we focus on several types of customized systems you might be expected to know how to configure and what parts to consider when configuring these systems.

Here are important principles to keep in mind when customizing a system to meet customer needs:

- *Meet applications requirements.* Consider the applications the customer will use and make sure the hardware meets or exceeds the recommended requirements for these applications. Consider any special hardware the applications might require such as a joystick for gaming or a digital tablet for graphics applications.
- *Balance functionality and budget.* When working with a customer's budget, put the most money on the hardware components that are most needed for the primary intended purposes of the system. For example, if you are building a customized gaming PC, a RAID hard drive configuration is not nearly as important as the quality of the video subsystem.
- *Consider hardware compatibility.* When selecting hardware, start with the motherboard and processor. Then select other components that are compatible with this motherboard.

Now let's look at the components you need to consider when building these eight types of customized systems: graphics or CAD/CAM design workstation, audio and video editing workstation, virtualization workstation, gaming PC, home theater PC, home server PC, thick client, and thin client.

A+ Exam Tip The A+ 220-901 exam expects you to know how to customize each of the eight types of computers covered in this part of the chapter.

GRAPHICS OR CAD/CAM DESIGN WORKSTATION

A+ 220-901 1.9

You might be called on to configure a graphics or CAD/CAM (computer-aided design/computer-aided manufacturing) workstation. People who use these systems might be an engineer working with CAD software to design bridges, an architect who designs skyscrapers, a graphics designer who creates artistic pages for children's books, or a landscape designer who creates lawn and garden plans. Examples of the applications these people might use include AutoCAD Design Suite by Autodesk (*usa.autodesk.com*) or Adobe Illustrator by Adobe Systems (*www.adobe.com*).

These graphics-intensive, advanced applications perform complex calculations, use large and complex files, and can benefit from the most powerful of workstations. Because rendering 3D graphics is a requirement, a high-end or ultra-high-end video card is needed. Figure 19-47 shows one ultra-high-end customized CAD workstation by CAD Computers (*www.cadcomputers.com*).

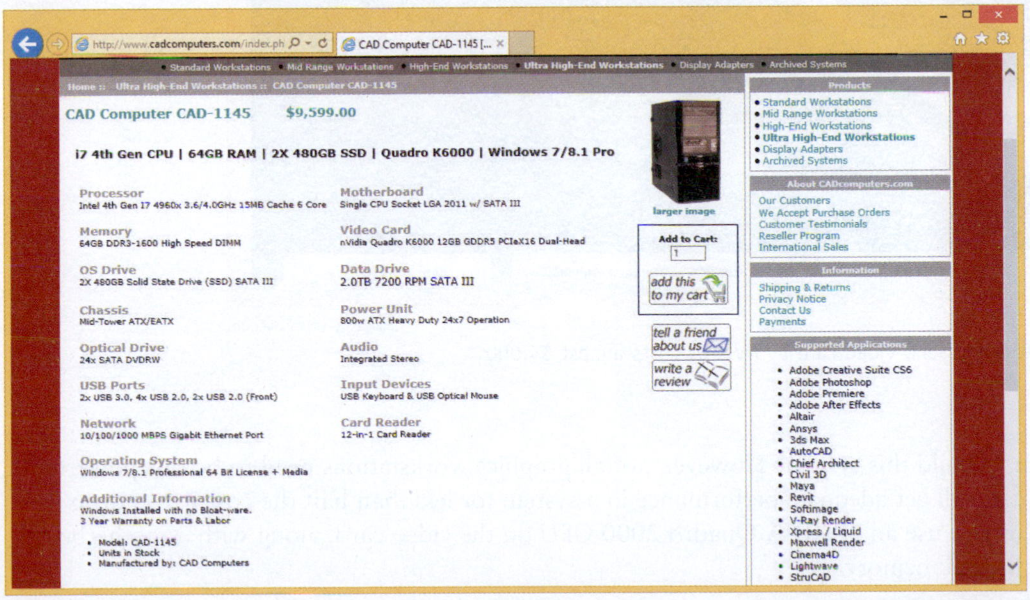

Source: cadcomputers.com

Figure 19-47 A high-end CAD workstation customized for maximum performance

19

Here is a breakdown of the requirements for these high-end workstations:

- ***Use a motherboard that provides quad channels for memory and plenty of memory slots and install a generous amount of RAM.*** In the ad shown in Figure 19-47, the system has 64 GB of installed RAM. For best performance, you can install the maximum amount of RAM the board supports.
- ***Use a powerful multicore processor with a large CPU cache.*** In the ad shown in Figure 19-47, the Intel Fourth Generation i7 processor, which is rated for high-end workstations and servers, has six cores and a 15-MB cache. This processor can handle the high demands of complex calculations performed by advanced software.
- ***Use fast hard drives with plenty of capacity.*** Notice the system in Figure 19-47 has two hard drives. The solid-state drive holds the Windows installation. The moderately fast second hard drive has a capacity of 2 TB to accommodate large amounts of data. For best hard drive performance in any system, be sure the motherboard and hard drives are all using SATA III.
- ***Use a high-end video card.*** To provide the best 3D graphics experience, use a high-end video card. Probably the best chipset manufacturer for high-end video cards is NVIDIA (*www.nvidia.com*). The ad in Figure 19-47 mentions the Quadro 6000. The Quadro family of graphics processors has the best-performing GPUs on the market, and the Quadro 6000 is the best Quadro currently sold (see Figure 19-48). It uses a PCIe ×16 slot and has 12 GB of GDDR5 video memory using a 384-bit video bus. The card has four HDMI ports and one DVI port. The card alone costs almost $4,000 and accounts for a major portion of the total system cost, which is almost $10,000.

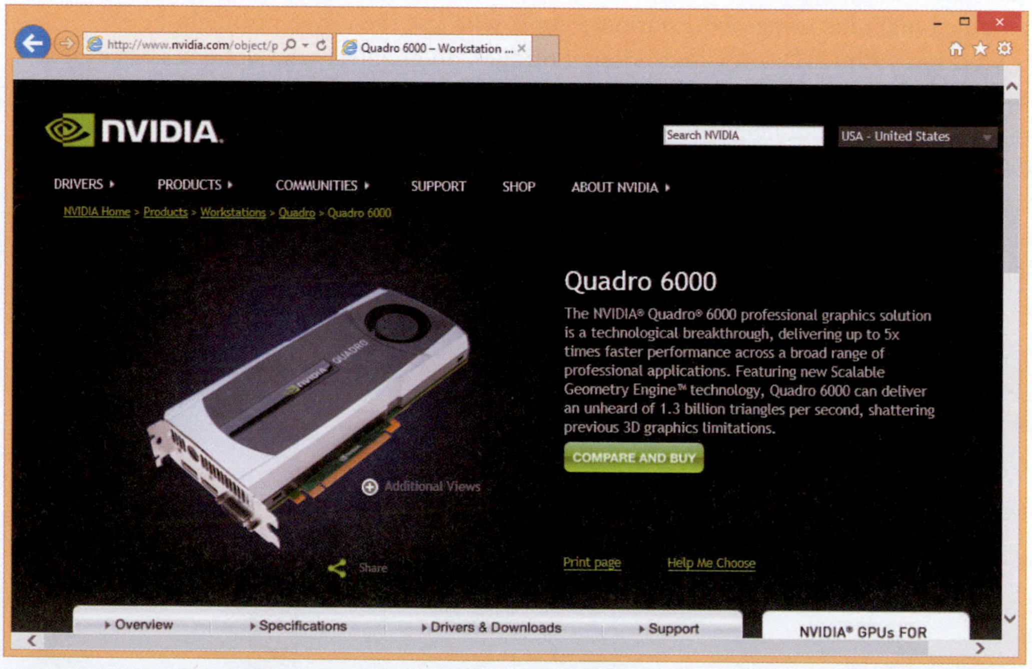

Source: www.nvidia.com

Figure 19-48 This ultra-high-end video card by NVIDIA costs almost $4,000

Wouldn't it be fun to build this system? However, not all graphics workstations need to be this powerful or this expensive. You can still get adequate performance in a system for less than half the cost if you drop the RAM down to 16 GB and use an NVIDIA Quadro 2000 GPU on the video card, along with a motherboard that supports dual-channel memory.

AUDIO AND VIDEO EDITING WORKSTATION

A+
220-901
1.9

Examples of professional applications software used to edit music, audio, video, and movies include Camtasia by TechSmith (*techsmith.com*), Adobe Production Premium by Adobe Systems (*adobe.com*), Media Composer by Avid (*avid.com*), and Final Cut Pro by Apple Computers (*apple.com*). (Final Cut Pro is used only on Macs, which are popular computers in the video-editing industry.) Audio- and video-editing applications are not usually as power-hungry as CAD/CAM and graphics applications. The major difference in requirements is that most audio and video editing does not require rendering 3D graphics; therefore, you can get by with a not-so-expensive graphics card and processor. Customers might require a Blu-ray drive and dual monitors. Recall that the best LCD monitors that provide the most accurate color are LED monitors with a class IPS rating. Figure 19-49 shows the specs for one customized video-editing workstation by ADK Media Group (*adkvideoediting.com*).

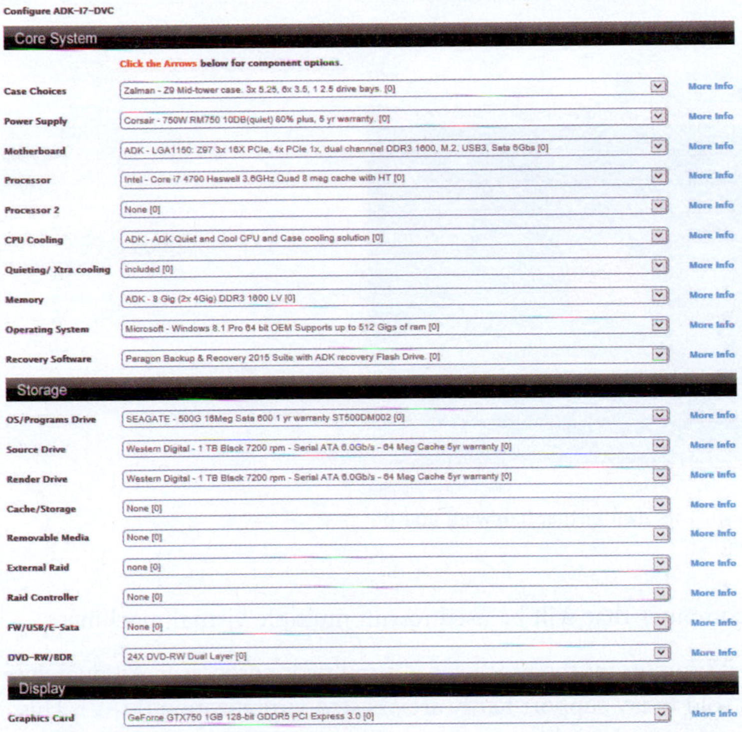

Source: www.adkvideoediting.com

Figure 19-49 This mid range video-editing workstation uses a Core i7 processor and GeForce graphics processor

Here is what you need for a mid range to high-end audio/video-editing workstation:

- Use a motherboard that supports dual, triple, or quad channel memory running at least at 1600-MHz RAM speed.
- Use a Core i7 or higher processor.
- Install at least 16 GB of RAM; more is better.
- Select a good video card that has a GeForce GTX graphics processor or better. GeForce is a family of graphics processors designed by NVIDIA that is not as high end as the Quadro graphics processors but still gives good video performance. Most users will require dual or triple monitors. You might need to consider dual video cards for optimum video performance or for more than two video ports.
- Use a good sound card, such as the Creative Sound Blaster Zx sound card. This sound card uses a PCIe slot. Before you purchase, research reviews online for a good sound card.
- Use a double-sided, dual-layer DVD burner and possibly a Blu-ray burner.
- Install one or more fast and large hard drives, running at least 7200 RPM.

19

VIRTUALIZATION WORKSTATION

A+
220-901
1.9

Virtualization is when one physical machine hosts multiple activities that are normally done on multiple machines. One way to implement virtualization is to use virtual machine management software, called a hypervisor, which creates and manages multiple virtual machines (VMs). Examples of hypervisors used on a desktop computer include VMware Workstation or Player, Windows Virtual PC by Microsoft, and Oracle VirtualBox. Each VM managed by a hypervisor has its own virtual hardware (virtual motherboard, processor, RAM, hard drive, and so forth) and can act like a physical computer. You can install an OS in each VM and then install applications in the VM. Figure 19-50 shows a Windows 8.1 Professional desktop with two virtual machines running that were created by Oracle VirtualBox. One VM is running Windows 8.1 Pro, and the other VM is running Windows 7 Home Premium. In the "Installing Windows" chapter, you learned how to set up a VM and install Windows in it.

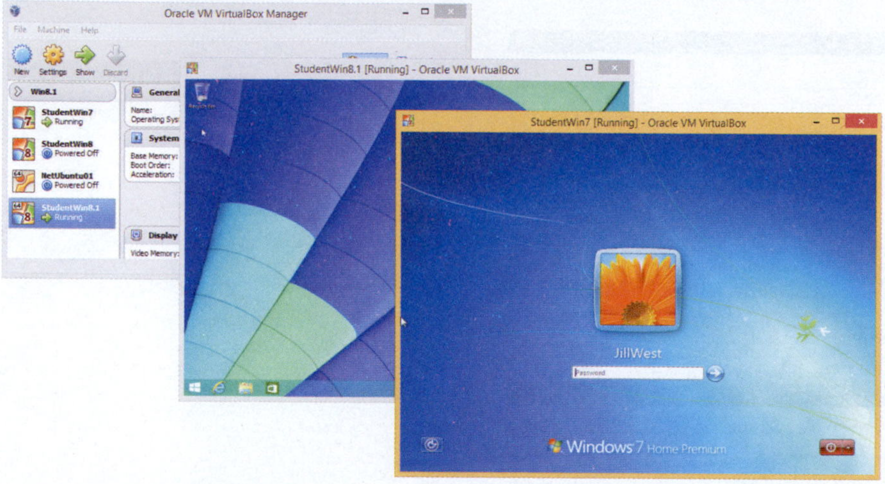

Source: Oracle VirtualBox

Figure 19-50 Two virtual machines running, each with its own virtual hardware and OS (Windows 8 and Windows 7) installed

Here are the requirements for a desktop computer that will be used to run multiple virtual machines:

- Each VM has its own virtual processor, so it's important the processor is a multicore processor. All dual-core or higher processors and all motherboards sold today support hardware-assisted virtualization (HAV). This technology enhances the processor support for virtual machines and is enabled in UEFI/BIOS setup.
- Some virtual machine management programs are designed so that each VM that is running ties up all the RAM assigned to it. Therefore, you need extra amounts of RAM when a computer is running several VMs.
- Each VM must have an operating system installed, and it takes about 20 GB for a Windows 8/7/Vista installation. In addition, you need hard drive space for each application installed in each VM. Make sure you have adequate hard drive space for each VM.

When deciding how to use the overall budget for a virtualization workstation, maximize the number of CPU cores and the amount of installed RAM.

GAMING PC

A+
220-901
1.9

Gaming computers benefit from a powerful multicore processor and a high-end video card and sound card. Gamers who are also computer hobbyists might want to overclock their CPUs or use dual video cards for extra video performance. Take extra care to make sure the cooling methods are adequate. Because of the heat generated by multiple video cards and overclocking, liquid cooling is sometimes preferred. Also recall that when using the LGA2011 socket, liquid cooling is a

Microsoft recommendation. Most gaming computers use onboard surround sound, or you can use a sound card to improve sound. A lighted case with a clear plastic side makes for a great look.

Figure 19-51 shows a group of gaming PCs built by iBUYPOWER (*ibuypower.com*). A couple of the PCs use liquid cooling, and all use a powerful processor with at least 8 GB of RAM. The video card uses a GeForce GTX or GT graphics processor or an AMD Radeon HD graphics processor. The Radeon line of graphics processors by AMD are comparable to the NVIDIA GeForce graphics processors.

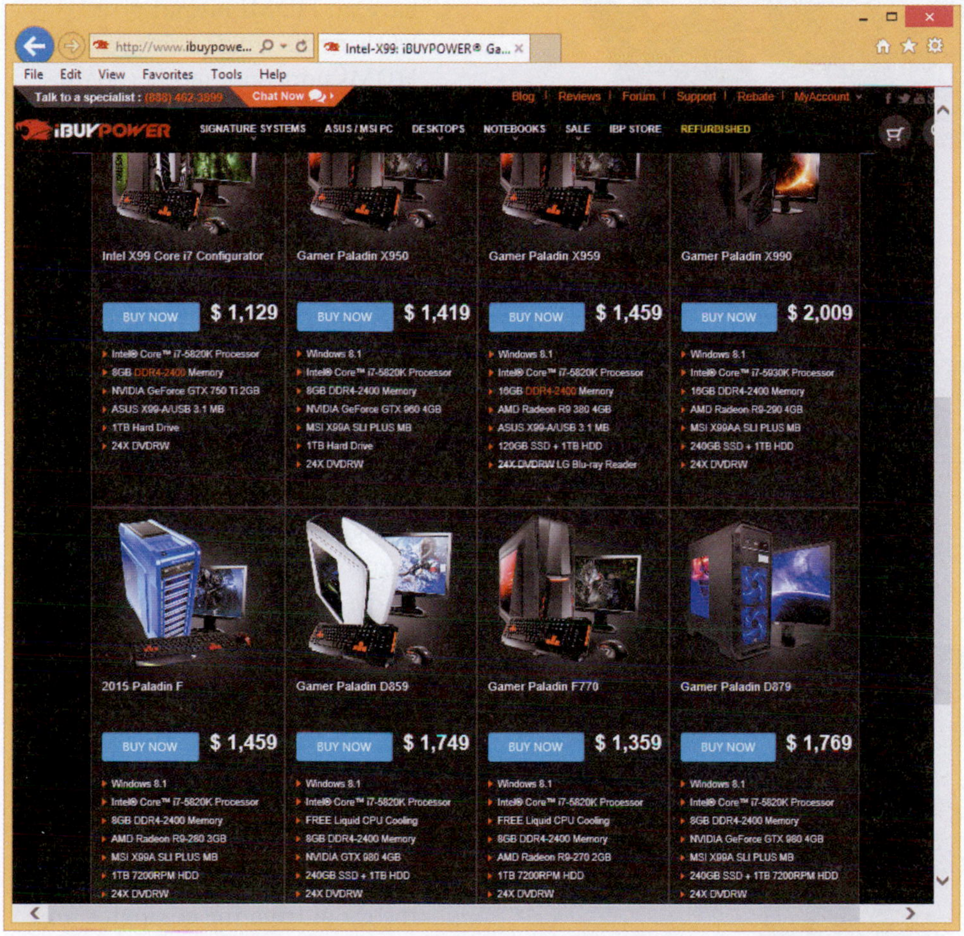

Source: www.ibuypower.com

Figure 19-51 A group of Intel Core i5 or Core i7 gaming PCs

HOME THEATER PC

A+ 220-901 1.9, 1.12

A Home Theater PC (HTPC) is designed to play and possibly record music, photos, movies, and video on a television or extra-large monitor screen. Because these large screens are usually viewed from across the room, application software is used to control output display menus and other clickable items in fonts large enough to read at a distance of 10 feet. This interface is called a 10-foot user interface. An HTPC is also known as a media center appliance.

A custom-built HTPC needs to include these features:

- *Application software.* The application controls the user interface and plays and records music and video. Examples of HTPC software include Windows Media Center, which is a free upgrade for Windows 8 Pro and integrated into Windows 7/Vista, Kodi (*kodi.tv*), and Plex (*plex.tv*).
- *HDMI port to connect video output to television.* And be sure to use a high-quality HDMI cable.
- *Cable TV input.* The best solution is to use a TV tuner card to connect the TV coax cable directly to the computer. Most TV tuner cards include a remote (see Figure 19-52). Some TV tuner cards are also

19

Courtesy of Hauppauge Computer Works, Inc.

Figure 19-52 Dual TV tuner card with IR remote lets you watch and record two TV programs at the same time

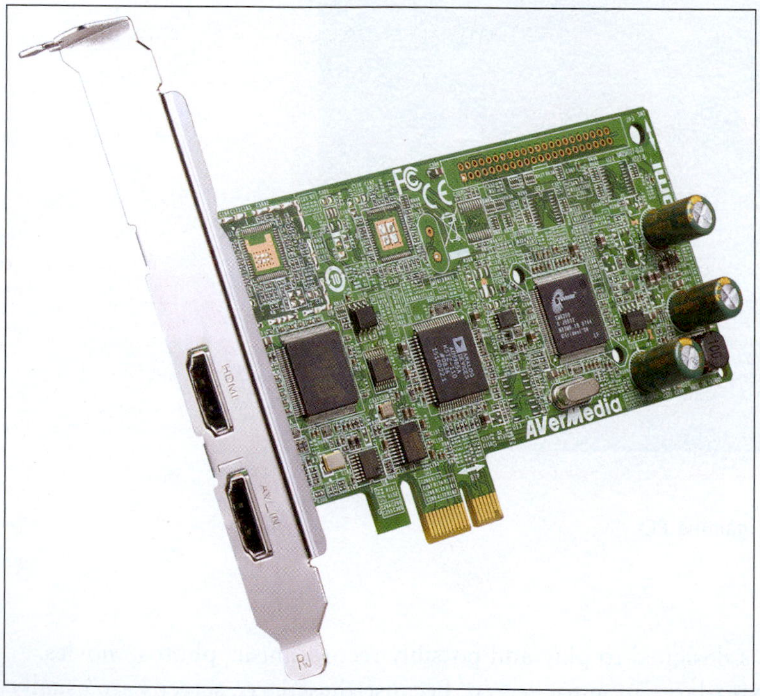

Courtesy of AVerMedia

Figure 19-53 The AVerMedia AVerTV HD DVR (C027) video capture card has two HDMI input ports and uses a PCIe × 1 expansion slot

video capture cards that offer the ability to record video and audio input. If the customer plans to use a TV cable box between the TV coax cable and the HTPC, you need to provide a way to make the connection. Most TV cable boxes have an HDMI output port. Realize this won't work with the HDMI port on a motherboard because these ports are output ports and you need an input port. To input to the computer using an HDMI port, you can use a video capture card that has an HDMI input port (see Figure 19-53).

- *Satellite TV input.* This setup requires a satellite set-top box supplied by the company providing the satellite TV service. The best solution is to use a TV tuner card to receive input from the satellite set-top box. Make sure the types of ports on the computer and the box match up.
- *Internet access.* A way to receive streaming video from the Internet. To connect to the Internet, use a Gigabit Ethernet port or Wi-Fi connection.
- *Remote control.* A way to remotely control the HTPC because most likely the user will be sitting across the room from the computer. You can use a wireless keyboard and mouse, although the range for these devices might be too short. Some TV tuner cards include a remote. Also consider an app you can download to a smart phone to make it work as the remote.
- *Low background noise.* Because these computers don't perform complex calculations, you don't need as much processor or RAM power as in other systems. For example, you can use the small Intel Atom processor with 4 GB of RAM. Therefore, you won't need an extensive cooling system. You do, however, want a system that runs quietly. You can reduce noise by using SSD hard drives and low-speed fans or no fans at all.

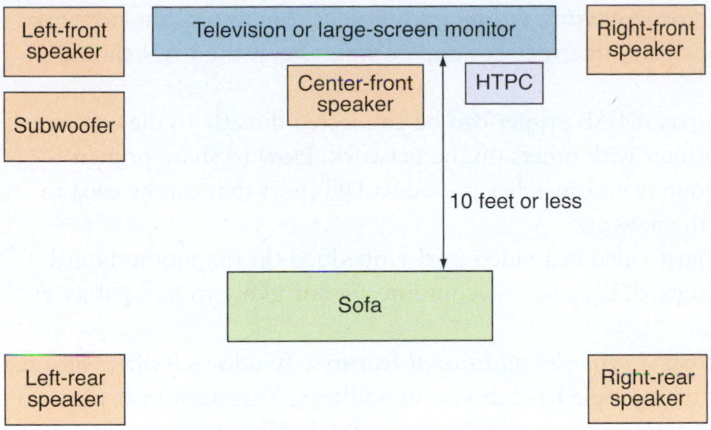

Figure 19-54 Speaker locations for surround sound

Courtesy of Silverstone Technology Co. Ltd.

Figure 19-55 The HTPC case by Silverstone is less than six inches high and has three silent fans

- ***Surround sound.*** The system should support surround sound using at least six speakers located around the room. In Figure 19-54, you can see the preferred location for six speakers. Three popular variations of surround sound are 5.1 (uses up to six channels and speakers), 7.1 (uses up to eight channels and speakers), and 9.1 (uses up to 10 channels and speakers). Most sound cards and motherboards support six channels or ports for sound.
- ***Case form factor.*** An HTPC should be small enough to fit on a shelf in an entertainment center, and several companies make **HTPC cases** specifically for this purpose. The HTPC case shown in Figure 19-55 accommodates a MicroATX, mini-ITX, or mini-DTX motherboard and power supply. (A mini-DTX motherboard is slightly wider than the mini-ITX board.) The case has drive bays for 3.5-inch and 2.5-inch drives.

Alternatives to the HTPC are to use a smart TV or a set-top box. A **smart TV** is a television that has the ability to run apps, store data, and connect to the Internet. A **set-top box** offers a regular television the ability to be "smart." Manufacturers such as Roku (*roku.com*), Amazon Fire TV (*amazon.com/fire-tv-stick*), and Google Chromecast (*google.com/chromecast*) sell set-top boxes complete with a remote control.

HOME SERVER PC

A+ 220-901 1.9

A home server PC is useful when you have several computers on a small home network and want to share files among them. You can use the computer to serve up these files and to stream video files and movies to client computers. One popular type of home server PC is Slingbox by Sling Media (*slingbox.com*). The device can serve up streaming media that you have stored on it not only to other computers in your home but also to a client computer anywhere on the Internet.

Here are the features and hardware you need to consider when customizing a home server computer:

- ***Use a processor with moderate power.*** The Intel Core i5 or Core i3 works well. A moderate amount of RAM is sufficient, for example, 6 to 8 GB.
- ***Storage speed and capacity need to be maximized.*** Use hardware RAID implemented on the motherboard to provide fault tolerance and high performance. Make sure the motherboard supports hardware RAID. Use fast hard drives (at least 7200 RPM) with plenty of storage capacity. Make sure the case has plenty of room for all the hard drives a customer might require.

- ***Network transfers need to be fast, especially for streaming videos and movies.*** Make sure the network port is rated for Gigabit Ethernet (1000 Mbps). All other devices and computers on the LAN should also use Gigabit Ethernet.
- ***Printer sharing needs to be an available resource.*** A USB printer can be connected directly to the computer and then you can use Windows to share the printer with others on the network. How to share printers is covered later in the text. Alternately, some routers and switches provide a USB port that can be used to connect a USB printer to other computers on the network.
- ***Onboard video works well.*** Recall that onboard video is a video port embedded on the motherboard and does not perform as well as a good video card. Because the computer is not likely to be used as a workstation, you don't need powerful video.
- ***Windows 7 can be used as the OS, but Windows 8 provides additional features.*** Windows 8 offers Storage Spaces, which can hold large multimedia files on multiple hard drives. In addition, if the customer plans to use the computer to back up files on client computers, know that Windows 8 File History is easier to implement and use than the Windows 7 Backup and Restore utility.

THICK CLIENT AND THIN CLIENT

A+
220-901
1.9

Recall that a desktop computer can use virtual machine management software (called a hypervisor) to provide one or more VMs, and in this situation the computer is called a virtualization workstation. In a corporate environment, the VM can also be provided by a virtualization server, which serves up a virtual machine to a client computer. The **virtualization server** provides a virtual desktop for users on multiple client machines. Most, if not all, processing is done on the server, which provides to the client the Virtual Desktop Infrastructure (VDI). See Figure 19-56.

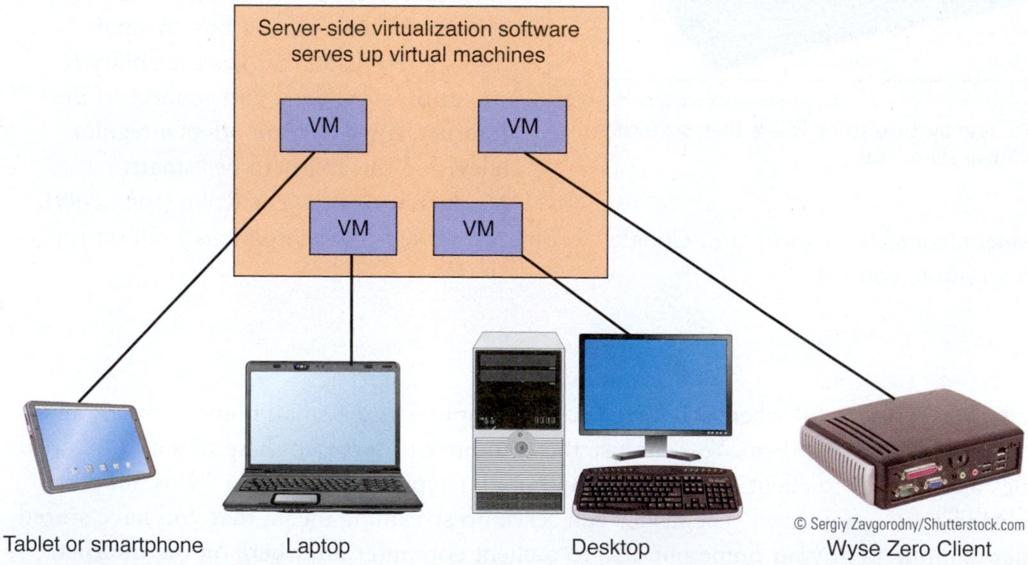

Figure 19-56 A virtualization server provides a desktop to each client computer or appliance

These VM clients that receive the virtual desktop from the server can be a thick client, thin client, or zero client. You might be called on to customize a thick client or thin client computer for a customer. (A zero client, also called a dumb terminal, is built by the manufacturer. It does not have an OS and is little more than an interface to the network with a keyboard, monitor, and mouse.) Here are the details for a thick client and thin client computer:

- A **thick client**, also called a fat client, is a regular desktop computer or laptop that is sometimes used as a client by a virtualization server. It can be a low-end or high-end desktop or laptop. It should meet the recommended requirements to run Windows 8/7 and any applications the user might require when it is being used as a stand-alone computer rather than a VM client.
- A **thin client** is a computer that has an operating system but has little computer power and might only need to support a browser used to communicate with the server. The server does most of the processing for the thin client. To reduce the cost of the computer, configure it to meet only the minimum requirements for Windows.

Hands-On Project 19-4 Research a Customized System

A+ 220-901 1.9

Working with a partner, design a gaming computer or a Home Theater PC by doing the following:

1. Search the web for a prebuilt system that you like. Print or save the webpage showing the detailed specifications for the system and its price. Which parts in the system do you plan to use for your system? Which parts would you not use or upgrade for your own system?
2. Search the web for the individual parts for your system. Save or print webpages showing all the parts you need to build this computer. Don't forget the case, power supply, motherboard, processor, RAM, hard drive, and other specialized components.
3. Make a list of each part with links to the webpage that shows the part for sale. What is the total cost of all parts?
4. Exchange your list and webpages with a partner and have your partner check your work to make sure each part is compatible with the entire system and nothing is missing. Do the same for your partner's list of parts.
5. After you are both convinced your list of parts is compatible and nothing is missing, submit your work to your instructor.

>> CHAPTER SUMMARY

Printer Types and Features

- The two most popular types of printers are laser and inkjet. Other types of printers are thermal printers and impact printers (dot matrix). Laser printers produce the highest quality, followed by inkjet printers. Dot matrix printers have the advantage of being able to print multicopy documents.
- The seven steps that a laser printer performs to print are processing, charging, exposing, developing, transferring, fusing, and cleaning. The charging, exposing, developing, and cleaning steps take place inside removable cartridges, which makes the printer easier to maintain.
- Inkjet printers print by shooting ionized ink at a sheet of paper. The quality of the printout largely depends on the quality of paper used with the printer.
- Dot matrix printers are a type of impact printer. They print by projecting pins from the print head against an inked ribbon that deposits ink on the paper.
- Direct thermal printers use heat to burn dots into special paper, and thermal transfer printers melt the ribbon or foil during printing.

Using Windows to Install, Share, and Manage Printers

- A printer is installed as a local printer connected directly to a computer or a network printer that works as a device on the network. Local printers can connect to a computer via a USB, serial, Bluetooth, or Wi-Fi connection. Network printers can connect to the network via an Ethernet or Wi-Fi connection. USB printers are installed automatically in Windows.
- Windows installs, manages, and removes a printer using the Devices and Printers windows. You can also install a printer using a setup program provided by the printer manufacturer. Always print a test page after installing a printer.
- A print server can be a computer on the network, a hardware device, or firmware embedded in a network printer.
- A printer can be shared in Windows so that others on the network can use it. To use a shared printer, the printer drivers must be installed on the remote computer.
- Network printers are identified on the network by their IP address.
- The Windows print queue is managed from the Devices and Printers window.
- Virtual printing prints to a file, and cloud printing prints to a printer via the Internet.
- Printer features, such as duplexing, collating, or page orientation, are managed in a printer properties box.

Printer Maintenance and Upgrades

- An inkjet or laser printer can be calibrated to align the color on the page. The nozzles of an inkjet printer tend to clog or dry out, especially when the printer remains unused. The nozzles can be cleaned automatically by means of printer software or buttons on the front panel of the printer.
- Check the page count of the printer to know when service is due and you need to order a printer maintenance kit. The page count can be reported on the printer panel or through a web-based utility in the printer firmware.
- Memory and a hard drive can be added to a printer to improve performance and prevent errors.

Troubleshooting Printers

- When troubleshooting printers, first isolate the problem. Narrow the source to the printer, connectivity between the computer and its local printer, the network, Windows, printer drivers, the application using the printer, or the printer installation. Test pages printed directly at the printer or within Windows can help narrow down the source of the problem.
- Poor print quality can be caused by the printer drivers, the application, Windows, or the printer. For a laser printer, consider that low toner can be the problem. For an inkjet printer, consider that the ink cartridges need cleaning or replacing. The quality of paper can also be a problem.
- A printer needs memory to render a print job. Low memory can cause part of the page not to print or a printer error.

Customizing Computer Systems

- As a technician, you might be called on to customize a system for a customer, including a graphics or CAD/CAM workstation, audio- and video-editing workstation, virtualization workstation, gaming PC, Home Theater PC (HTPC), home server PC, thick client, or thin client.
- A high-end video card is a requirement in a graphics, CAD/CAM, video-editing workstation, or a gaming PC. These systems also need powerful processors and ample RAM.

- A TV tuner card is needed in a Home Theater PC.
- A thick client needs to meet recommended requirements for Windows and applications, and a thin client is a low-end computer that only needs to meet the minimum requirements for Windows.

>> KEY TERMS

For explanations of key terms, see the Glossary for this text.

10-foot user interface
ad hoc mode
AirPrint
bitmap
Bonjour
calibration
charging
cloud printing
default printer
Devices and Printers window
direct thermal printer
duplex printer
duplexing assembly
elevated command prompt window
extension magnet brush
fuser assembly
hardware-assisted virtualization (HAV)
hardware print server
Home Theater PC (HTPC)
HTPC case
hypervisor
imaging drum
impact paper
impact printer
infrastructure mode
ink cartridge
inkjet printer
laser printer
local printer
network printer
pickup roller
print head
print server
printer maintenance kit
printer self-test page
printui
remote printing
REt (Resolution Enhancement technology)
separate pad
separation pad
Services console
set-top box
smart TV
thermal paper
thermal printer
thermal transfer printer
thick client
thin client
toner vacuum
tractor feed
transfer belt
transfer roller
virtual printing
virtualization server
XPS Document Writer

>> REVIEWING THE BASICS

1. List the seven steps used by a laser printer to print a page.
2. During the laser printing process, what determines when the toner sticks to the drum and when it does not stick to the drum?
3. What type of printer is most dependent on the quality of paper it uses to get the best printing results?
4. What should you do if an inkjet printer prints with missing dots or lines on the page?
5. What can you do to help a dot matrix printer last longer?
6. What feature on a printer must be enabled so that a printer can automatically print on both sides of the paper?
7. What is likely to be the problem when a laser printer consistently produces pages with gray print?
8. What kind of printer is assigned an IP address?
9. What two tools can you use to remove loose toner from inside a printer?
10. How can you prove a printer problem is not with the printer itself, but lies with the network, computer, OS, or application?
11. When you get a toner-low message, what can you do to extend the life of the toner cartridge before you replace the cartridge?
12. What causes a ghosted image on a printout?
13. What is likely the problem when a portion of a complicated page does not print?

14. What can you do to verify a printing problem is with an application or a document and not with Windows?
15. In a Home Theater PC, what is the purpose of an HDMI output port?
16. In a Home Theater PC, why might you need an HDMI input port? Which type of adapter card might provide this port?
17. Which system requires the best graphics card, a CAD workstation or a virtualization workstation?
18. Which is generally a better GPU, one in the NVIDIA Quadro family or one in the NVIDIA GeForce family?
19. Which socket mentioned in the chapter does Intel recommend you use with liquid cooling?
20. How many speakers or sound channels does surround sound version 5.1 use?

>> THINKING CRITICALLY

1. You are not able to print a Word document on a Windows 8 computer to a network printer. The network printer is connected directly to the network, but when you look at the Devices and Printers window, you see the name of the printer as \\SMITH\HP LaserJet 8100. In the following list, select the possible sources of the problem.
   - a. The SMITH computer is not turned on.
   - b. The HP LaserJet 8100 printer is not online.
   - c. The SMITH printer is not online.
   - d. The Windows 8 computer has a stalled print spool.
   - e. The HP LaserJet 8100 computer is not logged on to the workgroup.
2. You are not able to print a test page from your Windows 8 computer to your USB local HP DeskJet printer. Which of the following are possible causes of the problem?
   - a. The network is down.
   - b. The printer cable is not connected properly.
   - c. The Windows print spool is stalled.
   - d. You have the wrong printer drivers installed.
   - e. File and Printer Sharing is not enabled.

>> REAL PROBLEMS, REAL SOLUTIONS

REAL PROBLEM 19-1 Selecting a Color Printer for a Small Business

Jack owns a small real estate firm and has come to you asking for help with his printing needs. Currently, he has a color inkjet printer that he is using to print flyers, business cards, brochures, and other marketing materials. However, he is not satisfied with the print quality and wants to invest in a printer that produces more professional looking hard copy. He expects to print no more than 8,000 sheets per month and needs the ability to print envelopes, letter-size and legal-size pages, and business cards. He wants to be able to automatically print on both sides of a legal-size page to produce a three-column brochure. Research printer solutions and do the following:

1. Save or print webpages showing three printers to present to Jack that satisfy his needs. Include at least one laser printer and at least one printer technology other than laser in your selections.
2. Save or print webpages showing the routine maintenance requirements of these printers.
3. Save or print webpages showing all the consumable products (other than paper) that Jack should expect to have to purchase in the first year of use.
4. Calculate the initial cost of the equipment and the total cost of consumables for one year (other than paper) for each printer solution.
5. Prepare a list of advantages and disadvantages for each solution.
6. Based on your research, which of the three solutions do you recommend? Why?

CHAPTER 20

Virtualization, Linux, and Mac OS X

After completing this chapter, you will be able to:

- Implement and configure virtual machines and hypervisors
- Use various Linux commands to support applications and users
- Identify important features of Mac OS X

Throughout this course, you have practiced many of your new skills in virtual machines. In this chapter, you get a look behind the scenes at how virtualization works. Then you learn about two more operating systems for desktops and laptops other than Windows: Linux and OS X. As you will see in this chapter, understanding Windows gives you a solid foundation to approach learning and supporting other operating systems. IT technicians are expected to be familiar with a variety of operating systems and operating environments, and this chapter equips you for these skills.

VIRTUALIZATION BASICS

A+
220-902
2.2

Virtualization is when one physical machine hosts multiple activities that are normally done on multiple machines. Two general types of virtualization are server-side virtualization and client-side virtualization. The basic difference between the two is where the virtualizing takes place. Let's see how each can be implemented.

SERVER-SIDE VIRTUALIZATION

A+
220-902
2.2

Server-side virtualization provides a virtual desktop for users on multiple client machines. Most, if not all, processing is done on the server, which provides to the client the Virtual Desktop Infrastructure (VDI). See Figure 20-1.

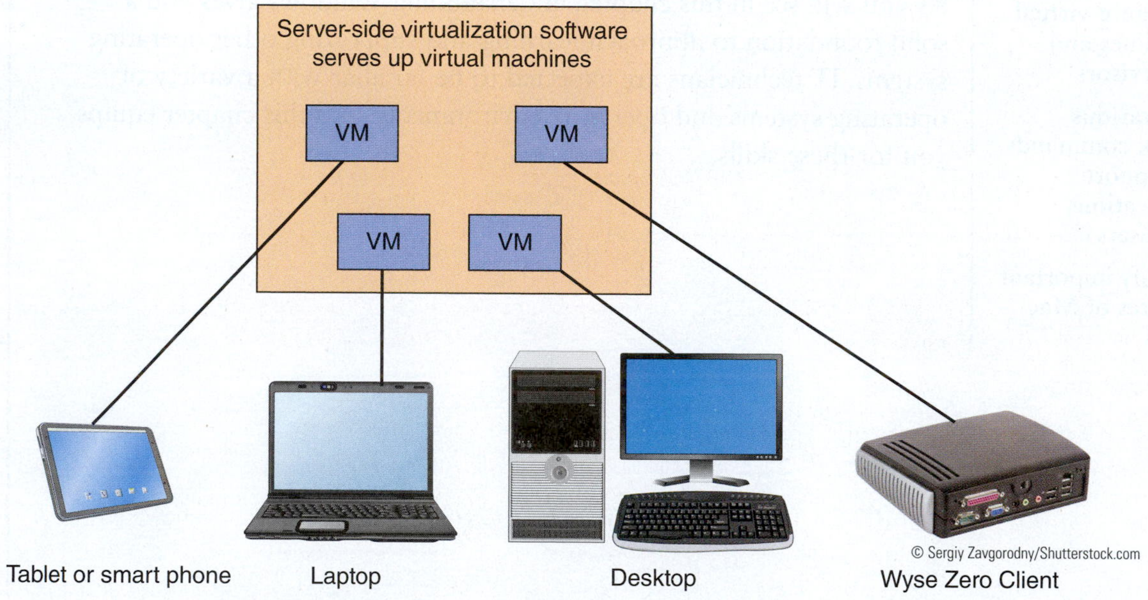

Figure 20-1 Server-side virtualization provides a virtual desktop to each user

With server-side virtualization, three categories of clients might be used, based on the computing power of the client:

- ***Thick client or fat client.*** The client computer can be a regular desktop computer or laptop. In this case, the client is called a thick client or fat client. The main advantage of using thick clients is the personal computer can be used for other purposes than server-side virtualization.
- ***Thin client.*** Because the client does little or no processing with server-side virtualization, a thin client can be used. A thin client is a computer that has an operating system, but has little computing power and might only need to support a browser used to communicate with the server. The main advantage of using thin clients is the reduced cost of the client machine. A decent tablet can serve as a thin client.
- ***Zero client.*** To even further reduce the cost of the client machine, a zero client, also called a dumb terminal or ultra-thin client, can be used. A zero client, such as a Wyse Zero Client, does not have an operating system and merely provides an interface between the user and the server. A zero client might contain little more than a keyboard, mouse, monitor, and network connection.

CLIENT-SIDE VIRTUALIZATION

A+
220-902
2.2

Using client-side virtualization, a personal computer provides multiple virtual environments for applications. Client-side virtualization can be implemented using several methods, including these three, which are presented from the least amount of computing done on the client machine to the most computing done on the client machine:

- *Presentation virtualization*. Using presentation virtualization, a remote application running on a server is controlled by a local computer. Presentation virtualization is a form of SaaS cloud computing. The user remotely controls the application running on the server and the application data is also stored on the server (see Figure 20-2).

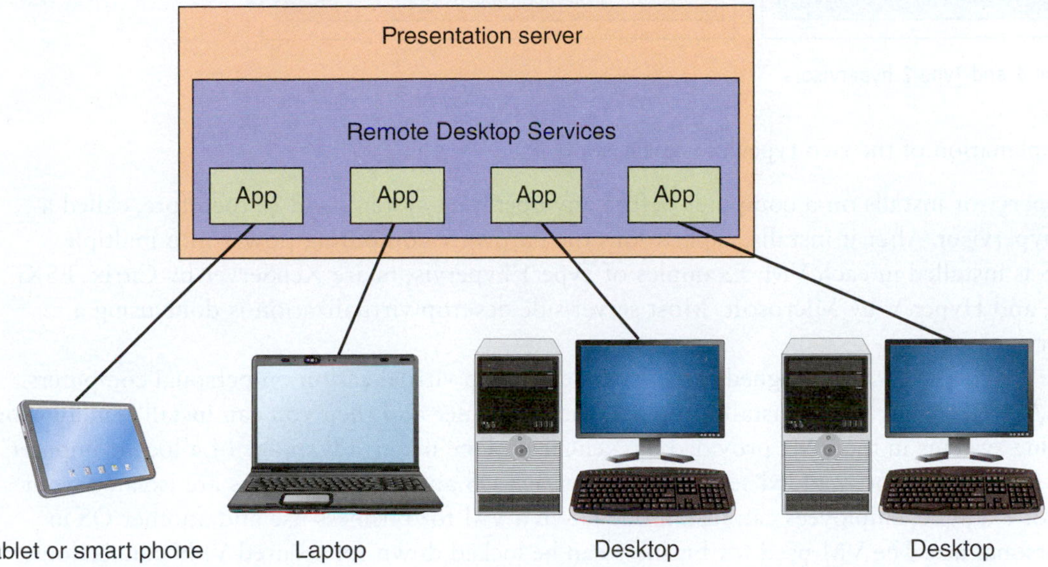

Figure 20-2 Microsoft Remote Desktop Services presents applications to the user at a local computer

- *Application virtualization*. Using application virtualization, an application can be made available to users without having to install the application on the user's computer. For example, Application Virtualization (App-V) by Microsoft manages applications so they don't install in Windows on the client computer. The App-V software is installed on the client computer. When a user selects an application from a list provided by App-V, App-V creates a virtual environment in memory for the application to install itself. The application doesn't make changes to the Windows registry or install components on the hard drive; the entire installation happens in memory. An application managed by App-V can be permanently stored on the local hard drive or on an application server.
- *Client-side desktop virtualization*. Using client-side desktop virtualization, software installed on a desktop or laptop manages virtual machines. Each VM has its own operating system installed. In the chapter, "Installing Windows," you learned that Oracle VirtualBox and VMware Player are two examples of freeware that can be installed on a computer and used to manage virtual machines. This type of software is called a hypervisor or virtual machine manager (VMM).

20

VIRTUAL MACHINES AND HYPERVISORS

A+
220-902
2.2

Let's look at the different types of hypervisors, the hardware requirements needed for client-side virtualization, and how to secure a virtual machine.

TYPE 1 AND TYPE 2 HYPERVISORS

Hypervisor software can be a Type 1 or Type 2 hypervisor. The differences are diagrammed in Figure 20-3.

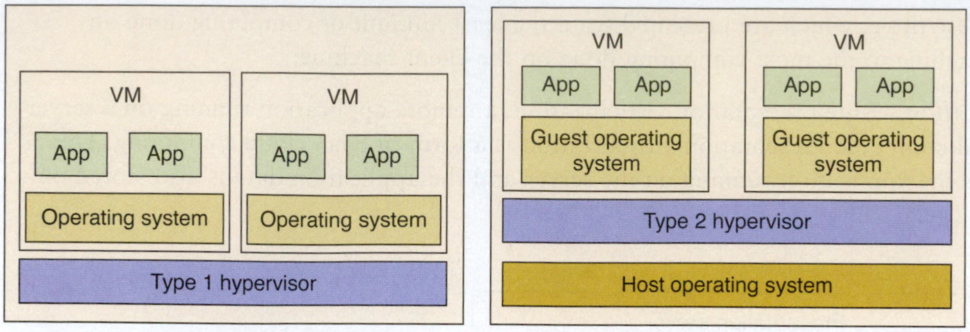

Figure 20-3 Type 1 and Type 2 hypervisors

Here is an explanation of the two types of hypervisors:

- A **Type 1 hypervisor** installs on a computer before any operating system, and is, therefore, called a bare-metal hypervisor. After it installs, it partitions the hardware computing power into multiple VMs. An OS is installed in each VM. Examples of Type 1 hypervisors are XenServer by Citrix, ESXi by VMware, and Hyper-V by Microsoft. Most server-side desktop virtualization is done using a Type 1 hypervisor.

  Some Type 1 hypervisors are designed for client-side desktop virtualization on personal computers. For example, XenClient by Citrix installs on a personal computer and then you can install Windows or other operating systems in the VMs provided by XenClient. One major advantage of a local computer running a Type 1 hypervisor is added security because each OS and its applications are isolated from the others. For example, employees can install one OS in a VM for business use and another OS in a VM for personal use. The VM used for business can be locked down for secured VPN connections, and the personal VM does not require so much security.

Notes To see some interesting videos of how XenClient by Citrix works and what it can do, go to *citrix.com/xenclient*.

- A **Type 2 hypervisor** installs in a host operating system as an application. Client Hyper-V, VirtualBox, and VMware Player are examples of Type 2 hypervisors. A Type 2 hypervisor is not as powerful as a Type 1 hypervisor because it is dependent on the host OS to allot its computing power. A VM in a Type 2 hypervisor is not as secure or as fast as a VM in a Type 1 hypervisor. Type 2 hypervisors are typically used on desktops and laptops when performance and security are not significant issues. Here are some ways that virtual machines provided by Type 2 hypervisors might be used:
  - Developers often use VMs to test applications. If you save a copy of a virtual hard drive (VHD) that has a fresh installation of Windows installed, you can easily build a new and fresh VM to test an application.
  - Help-desk technicians use VMs so they can easily switch from one OS to another when a user asks for help with a particular OS.
  - Honeypots are single computers or a network of computers that lure hackers to them so as to protect the real network. Virtual machines can be used to give the impression to a hacker that he has found a computer or entire network of computers. Administrators can monitor the honeypot for unauthorized activity.
  - Students use VMs to install and practice using and supporting different operating systems.

HARDWARE REQUIREMENTS

When preparing to install a hypervisor and virtual machines, you need to be aware of the hardware requirements:

- *The motherboard UEFI/BIOS.* The motherboard UEFI/BIOS and the processor should support hardware-assisted virtualization (HAV). For Intel processors, this feature is called IntelVT. For AMD processors, the technology is called AMD-V. Most of today's motherboards support the feature, and it must be enabled in UEFI/BIOS setup. Figure 20-4 shows the UEFI setup screen for one motherboard where the feature is called Intel® Virtualization Technology. When you enable the feature, also verify that all subcategories under the main category for hardware virtualization are enabled.

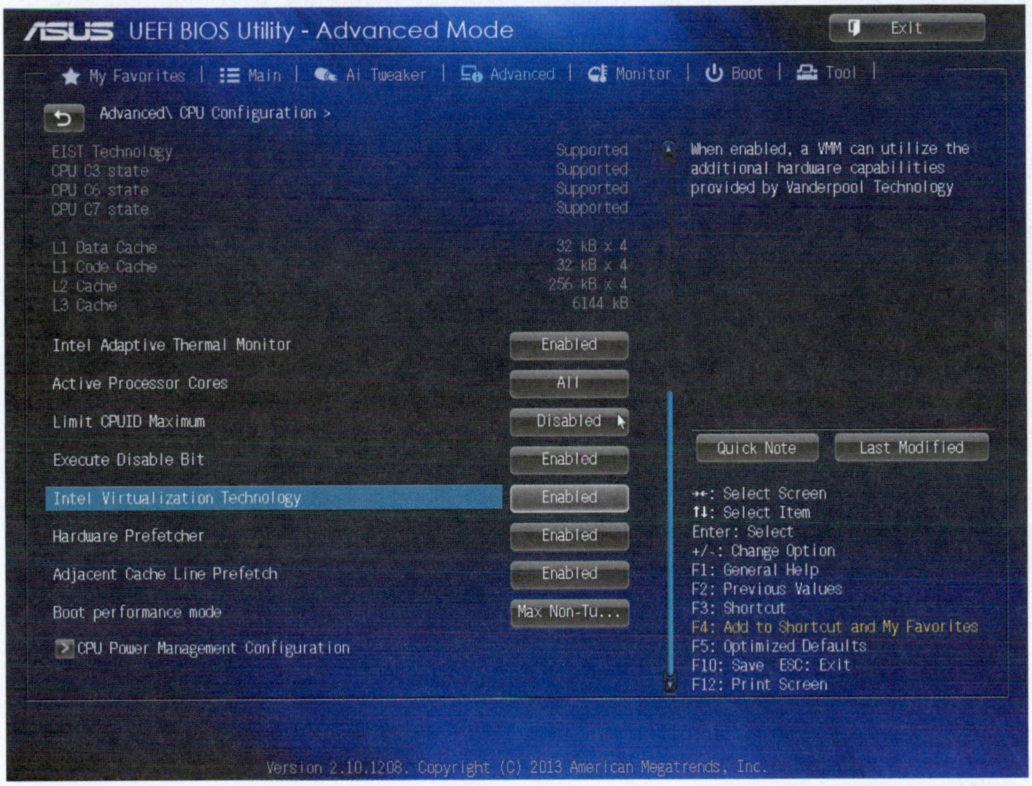

Source: Intel

Figure 20-4 UEFI/BIOS setup screen to enable hardware virtualization

- *Hard drive space.* See the requirements provided by the hypervisor manufacturer for hard drive space for the hypervisor. Each VM has its own virtual hard drive (VHD), which is a file stored on the physical hard drive and acts like a hard drive complete with its own boot sectors and file systems. You can configure this VHD to be a fixed size or dynamically expanding. The fixed size takes up hard drive space whether the VM uses the space or not. An expanding VHD increases in capacity as the VM uses the space. Remember that about 20 GB is required for a Windows installation. Therefore, you'll need at least 20 GB for each VM.
- *Processor and memory.* Most processors sold today support hardware-assisted virtualization. Plan on using at least a dual-core processor or better. A system needs lots of RAM when running multiple virtual machines. Some hypervisors tie up all the memory you have configured for a VM from the time the VM is opened until the VM is closed. Other hypervisors support dynamic memory, which ties up only the memory the VM is actually using.

Notes To see a list of Intel processors that support Intel VT, go to *ark.intel.com/Products/VirtualizationTechnology*.

When setting up a virtual machine, know that an emulator might be required. A hypervisor emulates hardware and presents this virtual hardware to each VM, which can include a virtual processor, memory, motherboard, hard drive, optical drive, keyboard, mouse, monitor, network adapter, SD card, USB device, smart phone, printer, and other components and peripherals. For example, recall from the chapter, "Supporting Mobile Operating Systems," you used Visual Studio and Client Hyper-V to create a Windows Phone emulator (see Figure 20-5). The emulator not only includes the Windows Phone OS, but also emulates the hardware of a smart phone.

Figure 20-5 Visual Studio and Client Hyper-V work together to emulate Windows Phone installed on a smart phone

A hypervisor offers a way to configure each VM, including which virtual hardware is installed. For example, when you launch VirtualBox, the VirtualBox Manager window shown on the left side of Figure 20-6 appears. To configure a VM, select the VM in the left pane and click **Settings**. The Settings box appears. Click the **Storage** menu, shown on the right side of Figure 20-6, to install and uninstall virtual hard drives in the VM.

Notice in the Settings box in Figure 20-6 that this VM has three hard drives installed. JumpWin8.1 is connected to SATA port 0 and contains the Windows 8.1 installation. NewDisk1 and NewDisk2 are smaller and are connected through SATA ports 1 and 2, respectively. The VM also has one optical drive with an .iso file mounted to it. Recall that an ISO file holds the image of a CD or DVD and can be used to hold Windows installation files. When you mount this file to the VM, you can install Windows in the VM from this virtual DVD, although many hypervisor programs will perform this step for you during setup of a new VM.

Click the **System** menu (see Figure 20-7) to configure motherboard settings, such as boot order and memory. Also consider network requirements for the VM. A VM can have one or more virtual network adapters. Click **Network** (see Figure 20-8) to change adapter settings. A VM connects to a local network the same as other computers and can share and use shared resources on the network. On the right side of the Settings box, you can control the number and type of installed network adapters up to four adapters.

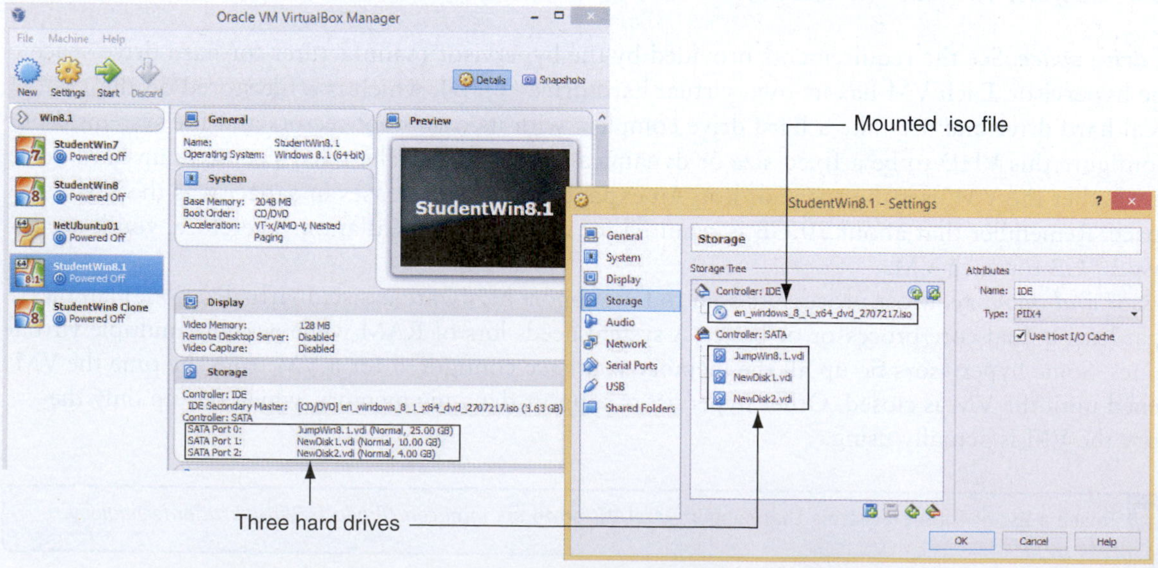

Source: Oracle VirtualBox

Figure 20-6 Emulated (virtual) hard drives are installed in a VM under VirtualBox

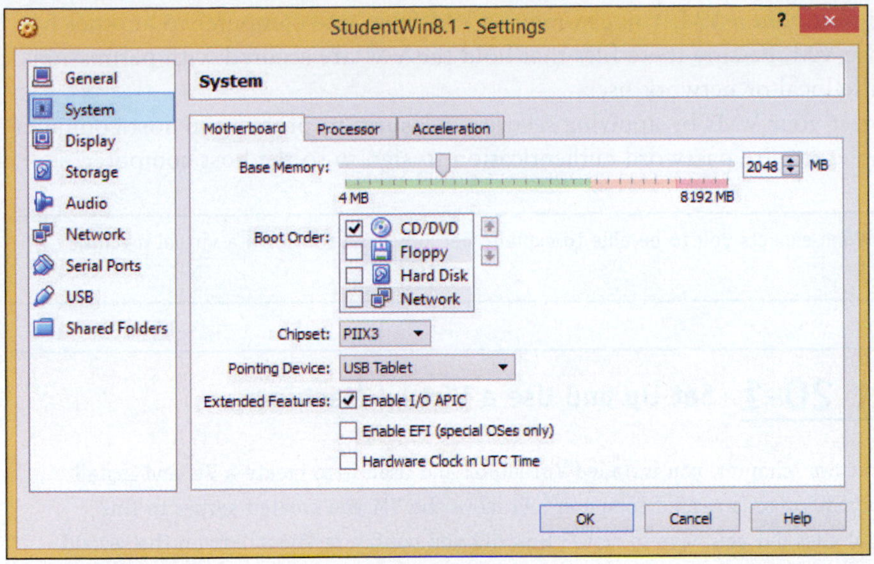

Source: Oracle VirtualBox

Figure 20-7 Configure motherboard settings in the VM to change the boot order

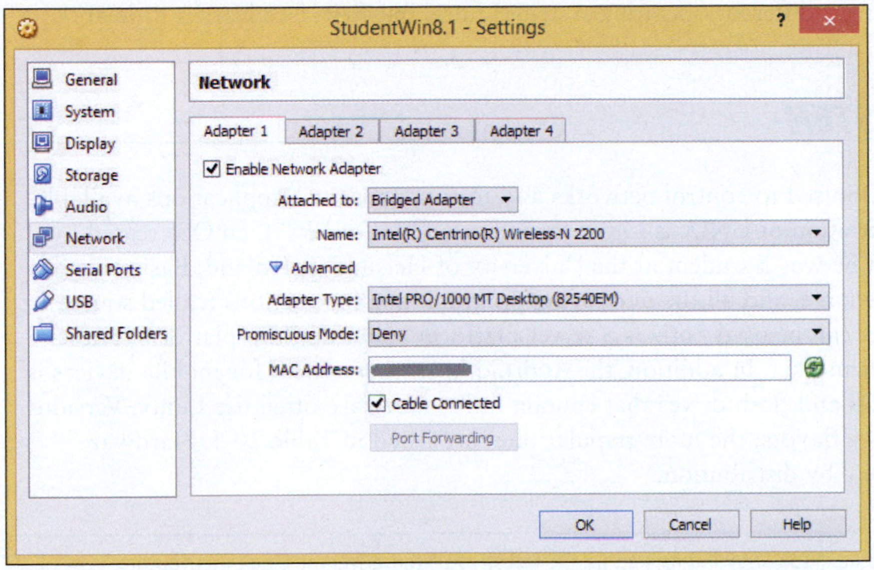

Source: Oracle VirtualBox

Figure 20-8 Configure up to four network adapters for a VM using Oracle VirtualBox

SECURE A VIRTUAL MACHINE

A virtual machine is susceptible to hackers and malware just as is a physical machine. When supporting a VM that holds sensitive data and has network and Internet connectivity or is located in a public area, keep these points in mind for securing the resources in the VM:

20

- *Secure the VM within the VM.* Using Windows installed in the VM, follow all the security measures you have learned throughout this text. For example, be sure to configure Windows Firewall in the VM, keep Windows updates current, install and run anti-malware software, require passwords for all user accounts in the VM, and encrypt data folders.
- *VMs should be isolated for best security.* One major advantage of using VMs on a desktop computer is that VMs running under a Type 1 hypervisor are isolated from each other. If one VM gets infected, the other VMs will not be affected.

- *Secure permissions to the files that hold a VM.* You can move a VM from one computer to another by moving the files that contain the VM. Be sure these files that hold the VM are secured with permissions that allow access only to specific local or network users.
- *Secure the host computer.* Protect your VMs by applying security measures to protect the host computer that holds the VMs. For example, require password authentication to sign in to the host computer.

A+ Exam Tip The A+ 220-902 exam expects you to be able to explain methods used to secure a virtual machine installed on a client computer.

Hands-On Project 20-1 Set Up and Use a Virtual Machine

A+ 220-902 2.2

In the "Installing Windows" chapter, you installed VirtualBox and used it to create a VM and install Windows 8. Install VirtualBox on a second computer and move the VM you created earlier to this second computer. What files did you have to move? How did you configure VirtualBox on the second computer to find and use the VM?

Next you'll create a VM running a different operating system: Linux. But first, let's learn a little about how Linux works.

LINUX OPERATING SYSTEM

A+ 220-902 1.2, 2.1, 4.1

UNIX is a popular OS used to control networks and to support server applications available on the Internet. A variation of UNIX is **Linux** (pronounced "Lih-nucks"), an OS created by Linus Torvalds when he was a student at the University of Helsinki in Finland. Basic versions of this OS are open source, and all the underlying programming instructions (called source code) are freely distributed. Linux can be used both as a server platform and a desktop platform, but its greatest popularity is in the server market. In addition, the Android operating system for mobile devices is based on Linux, and bootable CDs and flash drives that contain utility software often use Linux. Versions of Linux are called distributions or flavors; the more popular ones are listed in Table 20-1. Hardware requirements for Linux vary widely by distribution.

Notes For more information on Linux, see *linux.org* as well as the websites of the different Linux distributors.

Name	Comments	Website
Debian	This distribution specifically targets software enthusiasts. Debian is truly open source and maintained by developers of free software. It's slow to be updated with new features, which makes it a very stable OS.	*debian.org*
Fedora	Fedora is considered a cutting-edge distribution of Linux. If you're always wanting the latest and greatest of Linux, this distribution might be your first choice.	*getfedora.org*
Linux Mint	Linux Mint is based on Ubuntu with several features added.	*linuxmint.com*
Red Hat Enterprise Linux	Designed for enterprise use for servers and workstations, this commercial distribution is stable and comes with long-term support. The free version of Red Hat Enterprise is CentOS, which comes with no support.	*redhat.com*
Ubuntu	Ubuntu is probably the most popular distribution of Linux for desktops and servers with tons of online tutorials and help.	*ubuntu.com*

Table 20-1 Popular Linux distributions

Linux is popular because it's inexpensive, very stable (it seldom crashes), and is well suited to support various types of servers, such as a web server or email server. Linux itself is not a complete operating system, but is only the kernel for the OS. You also need a shell for user and application interfaces, and Linux shells vary widely by distributions. Many distributions of Linux include a GUI shell or desktop, which is called a windows manager. For example, Figure 20-9 shows the desktop or windows manager for Ubuntu Desktop.

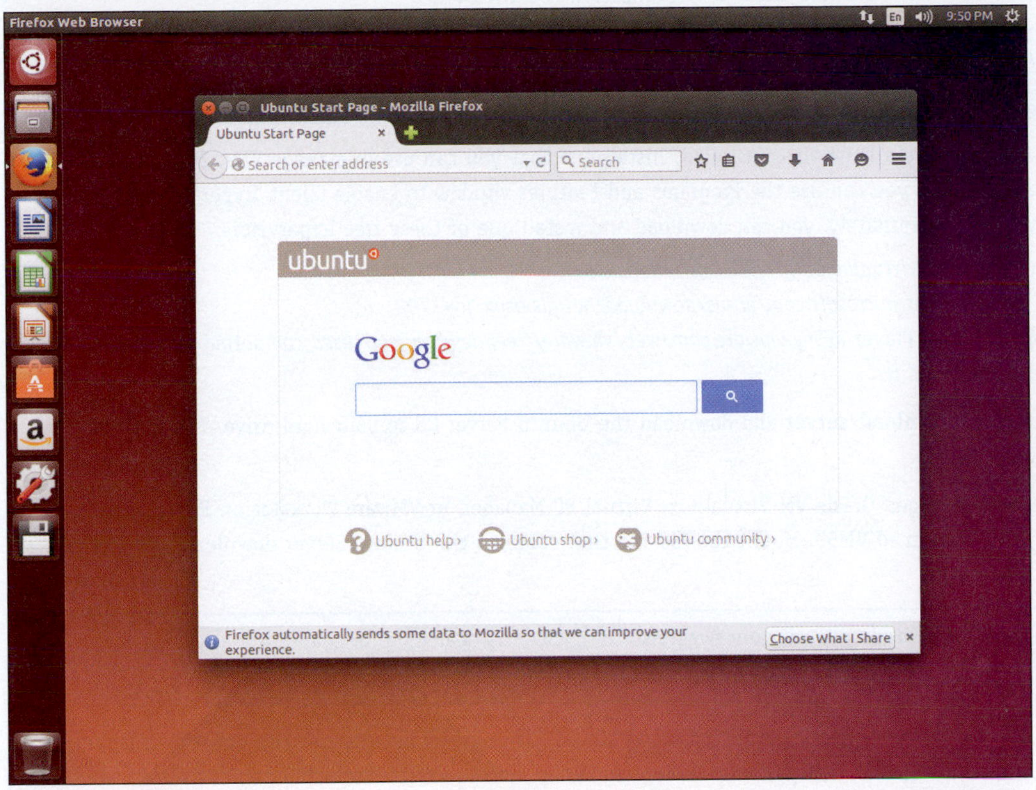

Source: Canonical Ltd.

Figure 20-9 Ubuntu Desktop with the Mozilla Firefox browser window open

Some distributions of Linux don't have a windows manager. For example, Ubuntu Server installs with only a command-line interface. In Linux, the **terminal** refers to the command-line interface for the OS and the default shell for the terminal is the **Bash shell**. The name stands for "Bourne Again Shell" and takes the best features from two previous shells, the Bourne and the Korn shells. In this chapter, we use Ubuntu Server and its default Bash shell. In Linux, a command prompt in the terminal is called a **shell prompt**.

Notes To find out what shell you're using, at a Linux shell prompt, enter the echo $SHELL command.

As an IT support technician, you should know a little about Linux, including a few basic commands, which are covered in this chapter. You will learn about root and user accounts, file structure, some common commands, and how to use the vi text editor. As you work, be aware that the organization of files and directories and the way each command works might be slightly different with the distribution and version of Linux you are using.

Hands-On | Project 20-2 Install Ubuntu Server in a VM

A+
220-902
2.1

To practice Linux skills covered in this chapter, you need an installation of Ubuntu Server. Follow these steps to install Ubuntu Server in a VM on a Windows computer:

1. On a Windows computer that has a 64-bit version of Windows installed, go into UEFI/BIOS setup and verify that hardware-assisted virtualization is turned on.

Notes Ubuntu Server is only available as a 64-bit OS. To install a 64-bit guest OS in a VM, the host OS must also be 64-bit.

2. If you don't already have a hypervisor installed, install one that you can use to manage VMs. For example, in 64-bit Windows 8.1 Pro, you can use the Programs and Features window to enable Client Hyper-V, which comes embedded in the OS. Alternately, you can download and install one of these free hypervisors:
   - Oracle VirtualBox at *virtualbox.org/wiki/Downloads*
   - Windows Virtual PC at *microsoft.com/en-us/download/details.aspx?id=3702*
   - VMware Workstation Player at *my.vmware.com/web/vmware/free#desktop_end_user_computing/vmware_workstation_player/12_0*
3. Go to **ubuntu.com/download/server** and download the Ubuntu Server OS to your hard drive. The file that downloads is an .iso file.
4. Open the Hyper-V Manager, Oracle VM VirtualBox, Virtual PC Manager, or VMware Workstation Player manager and create a new VM named VM50. Mount the ISO file that contains the Ubuntu Server download to a virtual DVD in your VM.

Notes If you need help learning to use your hypervisor of choice, try searching for some tutorial videos at *youtube.com* or on the hypervisor manufacturer's website.

5. Start up the VM and install Ubuntu Server, accepting all default settings. Be sure to write down your Ubuntu host name, Ubuntu user name, and password. When given the option, decline to install any extra software bundled with the OS. If needed, the software can be installed later.
6. During the installation, you might be asked whether you want to install the GRUB boot loader in the Master Boot Record on the hard drive (see Figure 20-10). **GRUB (GR and Unified Bootloader)** is a boot loader used

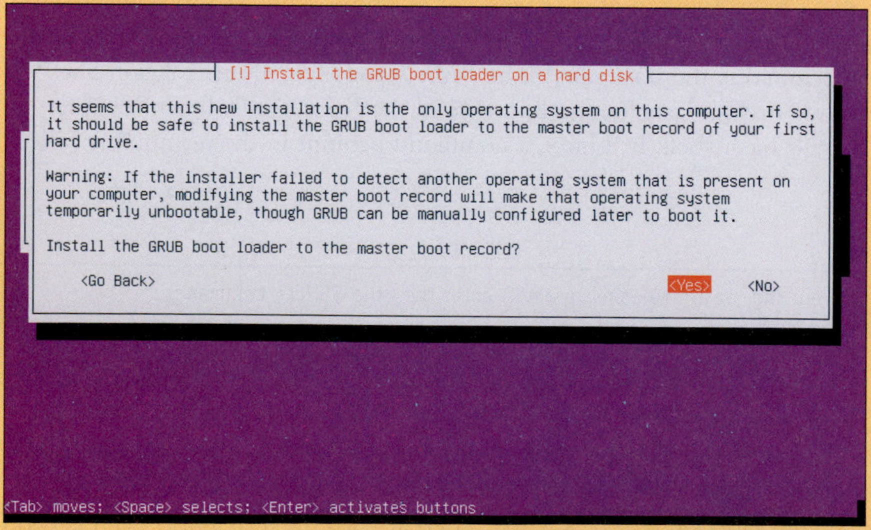

Source: Canonical Ltd.

Figure 20-10 Install GRUB to manage a dual boot with Ubuntu Server to manage dual-boot systems and should not be installed if another OS is managing the dual boot. You can, however, choose to install it because Ubuntu Server is the only OS in your VM.

7. After the VM restarts, Ubuntu Server launches, and you should see the terminal shell, as shown in Figure 20-11.

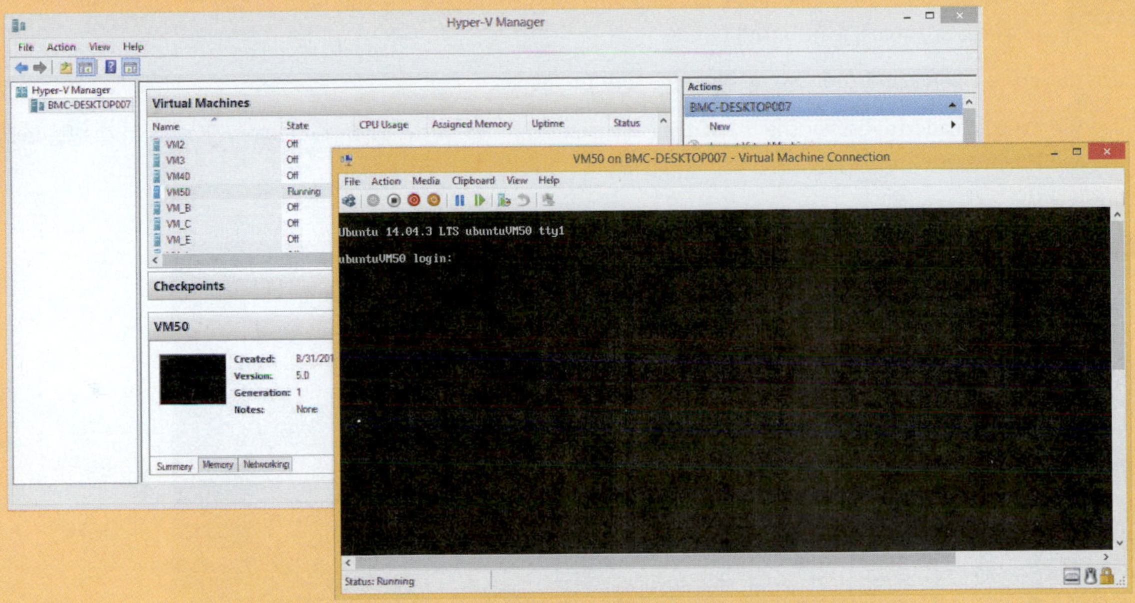

Source: Canonical Ltd.

Figure 20-11 Ubuntu Server is installed in a VM in Windows 8.1 Client Hyper-V

8. Enter your user name and password and you're logged in to Ubuntu Server. In the figure, the logged-in user is jean.

As you read along in the chapter learning about Linux commands, you can use your Ubuntu VM to practice these commands.

Notes As you learn to use Ubuntu, know that the *help.ubuntu.com* website contains a wealth of information about Ubuntu and links to even more help.

DIRECTORY AND FILE LAYOUT

A+ 220-902 2.1

Normally, the shell prompt includes the user name, host name, and the current directory, followed by a $. For example, in Figure 20-11, the first shell prompt shows the user name is jean, the host name is VM50, and the ~ character indicates the user's home directory, which for the jean account is /home/jean. When you first log in to Linux, the current directory is always the home directory of the logged-in user. (In Linux, directories in a path are separated with forward slashes, in contrast to the backward slashes used by Windows.)

APPLYING | CONCEPTS EXPLORE DIRECTORIES AND FILES

A+
220-902
2.1

Let's explore a few directories and files. As shown in Figure 20-12, use these commands:

1. Use the **pwd** command (print working directory) to display the full path to the current directory, which is /home/jean in the figure.
2. Use the **cd ..** command to move up one directory to /home.
3. Use the **ls** command to display the list of files and subdirectories in the /home directory. Notice in the figure, the one subdirectory in the /home directory is jean.

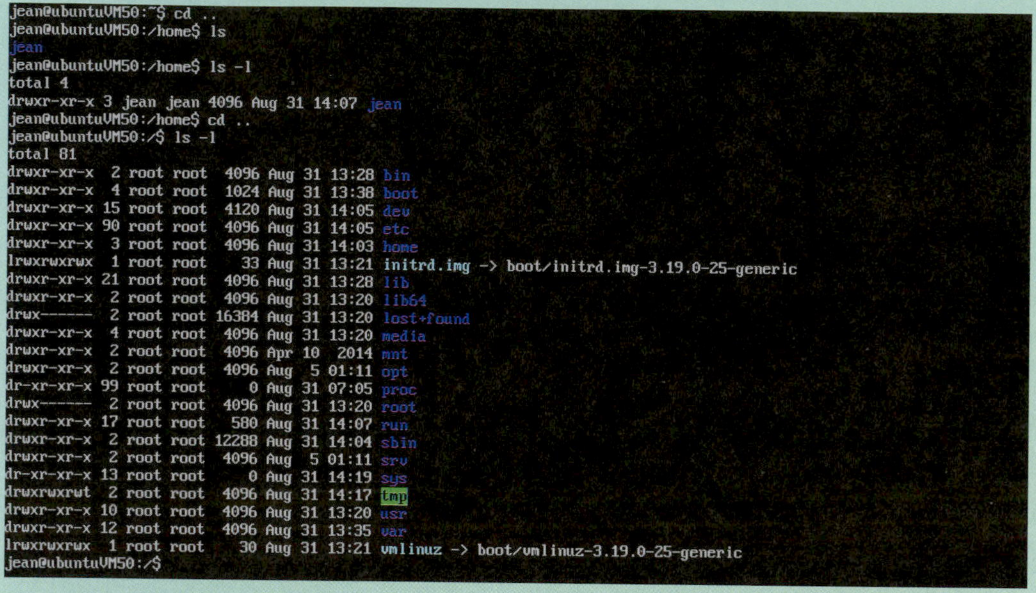

Source: Canonical Ltd.

Figure 20-12 Directories in the root

4. Use the **ls -l** command to display the results using the long format. (A space must precede the -l parameter.)

   Here is an explanation of the types of information in the list:

   - ***Attributes.*** The first 10 characters define the file or directory attributes. The first character identifies the type of item: A d is a directory; a – is a regular file, and an l indicates the item is a link to another location. The other nine characters define the read, write, and execute permissions assigned to the file or directory.
   - ***Links.*** The second column lists the number of links the item has. In Linux, a link is similar to a Windows shortcut to a file or directory.
   - ***Owners.*** The third column lists the user owner and the fourth column lists the group that owns the file or directory. In Figure 20-12, the owner is jean and the owner group is also jean.
   - ***Size, date, and name.*** The last columns list the size of the file or directory in bytes, the date the item was last modified, and the name of the file or directory.

5. When you use the **cd ..** command again, you move up to the main directory in Linux, called the root directory, which is indicated with a forward slash. The **ls -l** command lists the files and subdirectories in the root.

Table 20-2 lists some important directories that are created in the root during a typical Linux installation. (Some distributions of Linux modify the directory structure.) Not all directories in the root are listed in the table.

Directory	Description
/bin	Contains programs and commands necessary to boot the system and perform other system tasks not reserved for the administrator, such as shutdown and reboot.
/boot	Consists of components needed for the boot process, such as boot loaders.
/dev	Holds device names, which consist of the type of device and a number identifying the device. Actual device drivers are located in the /lib/modules /[kernel version]/ directory.
/etc	Contains system configuration data, including configuration files and settings and their subdirectories. These files are used for tasks such as configuring a user account, changing system settings, and configuring a domain name resolution service.
/home	Contains user data. Every user on the system has a directory in the /home directory, such as / home/jean or /home/scott, and when a user logs in, that directory becomes the current working directory.
/lib	Stores common libraries used by applications so that more than one application can use the same library at one time. An example is the library of C programming code, without which only the kernel of the Linux system could run.
/lost+found	Stores data that is lost when files are truncated or when an attempt to fix system errors is unsuccessful.
/opt	Contains installations of third-party applications such as web browsers that do not come with the Linux OS distribution.
/root	The home directory for the root user; contains only files specific to the root user. Don't confuse this directory with the root, which contains all the directories listed in this table.
/sbin	Stores commands required for system administration.
/tmp	Stores temporary files, such as the ones that applications use during installation and operation.
/usr	Constitutes the major section of the Linux file system and contains read-only data.
/var	Holds variable data such as logs, email, news, print spools, and administrative files.

Table 20-2 Important directories in a typical Linux root directory

ROOT ACCOUNT AND USER ACCOUNTS

A+ 220-902 2.1

For a Linux server, the system administrator is the person who installs updates to the OS (called patches), manages backup processes, supports the installation of software and hardware, sets up user accounts, resets passwords, and generally supports users. The system administrator has root privileges, which means that he or she can access all the functions of the OS; the principal user account is called the root account. Notice in Figure 20-12 that all the directories and files in the root directory belong to the root account.

When logged in to the root account, the administrator is called the superuser. By default, Ubuntu disables login to the root account. Later in the chapter, you learn how to use the sudo command to execute any command that requires root access when you are logged in to the system with a regular user account that has root privileges.

20

Notes The Linux command prompt for the root user is different from the command prompt for ordinary users. The root command prompt is #, and other users have the $ command prompt. See Figure 20-13. In the figure, the su command is used to change the currently logged-in user from root to jean.

Source: Canonical Ltd.

Figure 20-13 The user account, host name, and current directory appear in the shell prompt along with a # or $ to indicate root account or other account

LINUX COMMANDS

A+
220-902
2.1

Table 20-3 describes some basic Linux commands, together with simple examples of how some are used. As you read along, be aware that all commands entered in Linux are case sensitive, meaning that uppercase and lowercase matter.

Command	Description
adduser	Adds a user to a system: `adduser <username>`
apt-get	Used to install and remove packages in Linux. When you first install Linux, it installs with only a bare-bones set of commands and utilities and includes a library of packages that you can install as needed. For example, to install the SSH (Secure Shell) package so you can remote in to your Linux server, use this command: `sudo apt-get install ssh` The `apt-get` command requires root access, which means you must precede the command with `sudo`. See sudo later in this table.
cat	Lets you view the contents of a file. Many Linux commands can use the redirection symbol > to redirect the output of the command. For example, use the redirection symbol with the `cat` command to copy a file: `cat /etc/shells > newfile` The contents of the shells file are written to newfile.
cd	Changes the directory. For example: To change the directory to /etc: `cd /etc` To move up one level in the directory tree: `cd ..` To go to the root: `cd /`
chmod	Changes modes (or permissions) for a file or directory. You'll see several examples of this command later in the chapter.
chown	Changes the owner of a file or directory.
clear	Clears the screen. This command is useful when the screen has become cluttered with commands and data that you no longer need to view.
cp	Copies a file: `cp <source> <destination>`
dd	Copies and converts files, directories, partitions, and even entire DVDs or hard drives. It's a powerful command with many practical uses and parameters, and only a superuser can use it. The basic format of the command is: `dd if=<source> of=<destination>` For example, use this command to create an ISO file from the contents of a CD: `dd if=/dev/cdrom of=/tmp/cdimage.iso`

deluser	Removes a user from a system:
	`deluser <username>`
	Remove the user and his home directory:
	`deluser -remove-home <username>`

df	Stands for *disk filesystem* and displays the amount of free space on the hard drive. To see the file system the drive is using: `df -T`

Table 20-3 Some common Linux commands

Command	Description
echo	Displays information on the screen. For example, to display which shell is currently being used, enter this command: `echo $SHELL`
exit	Logs out; the login shell prompt appears, where you can log in again.
grep	Searches for a specific pattern in a file or in multiple files: `grep <pattern> <file>`

ifconfig	Used to troubleshoot problems with network connections under TCP/IP. This command can disable and enable network adapters and assign a static IP address to an adapter. For example, to show all configuration information:
	`ifconfig -a`
	To enable or disable an adapter, use the up or down parameter. For example, to enable eth0, the first Ethernet interface:
	`sudo ifconfig eth0 up`
	To assign a static IP address to the eth0 interface: `ifconfig eth0 192.168.1.90`

iwconfig	Works similarly to `ifconfig`, but applies only to wireless networks. Use it to display information about the wireless adapter's configuration or to change that configuration. Two examples: To set the wireless NIC to Ad-Hoc mode so that other devices within range can connect directly to it, use this command, where wlan0 identifies the wireless adapter: `iwconfig wlan0 mode Ad-Hoc` To force the NIC to use channel 3: `iwconfig wlan0 channel 3`
kill	Kills a process instead of waiting for the process to terminate. Use the `ps` command to list process IDs. To end a process, use the `kill` command followed by the PID. For example, to kill the process with PID of 984: `kill 984` The command sends a signal to the process to end itself orderly. If the process doesn't die peacefully, you can get the kernel involved to forcefully end the process: `kill -kill 984`
ls	Functions similarly to the DOS Dir command, which displays a list of directories and files. For example: To list files in the /etc directory, using the long parameter for a complete listing: `ls -l /etc` To include hidden files in the list: `ls -la /etc` (In Linux, hidden files begin with a . period.)
man	Displays the online help manual, called man pages. For example, to get information about the echo command: `man echo` The manual program displays information about the command. To exit the manual program, type `q`.
mkdir	Makes a new directory: `mkdir <directory>`
mv	Moves a file or renames it, if the source and destination are the same directory: `mv <source> <destination>`
parted	Manages partitions on a hard drive and works with MBR and GPT drives.
passwd	Changes your password. When a user enters the command, she is asked for the old password and then can change the password. The superuser can change the password for any account and does not need to enter the account's old password, making it possible to reset a forgotten password.
ping	Used to test network connections by sending a request packet to a host. If a connection is successful, the host will return a response packet. For example: `ping 192.168.1.100` The `ping` results continue until you manually stop the process. Press Ctrl+C to break out of the process. To specify the number of pings: `ping 192.168.1.100 -c 4`
ps	Stands for *process status* and displays the process table so that you can identify process IDs for currently running processes (once you know the process ID, you can use the `kill` command to terminate a process): To list processes of current user: `ps` To list processes owned by all users: `ps aux`

Table 20-3 Some common Linux commands (continues)

Command	Description
`pwd`	Shows the name of the current working directory: `pwd` When you first log in to Linux, the directory is `/home/`*`username`*.
`rm`	Removes or deletes the file or files that are specified: `rm <file>`
`rmdir`	Removes or deletes an empty directory: `rmdir <directory>`
`shutdown`	Automated shut down to the system. Here are options: To halt or shut down now: `sudo shutdown -h now` To warn users and then shut down: `sudo shutdown -h +10 "Everyone log out now. The system will shut down in 10 minutes for maintenance."` To reboot now: `sudo shutdown -r now`
su	Stands for *substitute user* and opens a new terminal shell for a different user account. When switching to superuser, add `sudo` to the command. To switch to the root account: `sudo su root` To switch back to the jean account: `su jean`
sudo	Stands for *substitute user to do the command* and is pronounced "sue-doe" or "sue-doo". When logged in as a normal user with an account that has the right to use root commands, you can start a command with sudo to run the command as the superuser. User password is required. For example: `sudo shutdown -h now`
`touch`	Creates a blank file in the current directory. For example: `touch myfile`
`vi`	Launches a full-screen editor that can be used to edit a file: `vi <file>`
`who`	Displays a list of users currently logged in: `who`

Table 20-3 Some common Linux commands (continued)

> **★ A+ Exam Tip** The A+ 220-902 exam expects you to be familiar with these Linux commands: ls, grep, cd, shutdown, pwd, passwd, mv, cp, rm, mkdir, chmod, iwconfig, ifconfig, ps, q, su, sudo, apt-get, vi, and dd.

Here are a few tips when using commands at a shell prompt:

- *Retrieve previous commands.* Press the arrow-up key to retrieve previously entered commands and then edit a command that appears.
- *Use wildcard characters.* Linux can use the `*` and `?` wildcard characters in command lines, similar to Windows. For example, the **`ls *.???`** command lists all items with any file name and the file extension must have three characters. In addition, Linux provides a third wildcard: Brackets can give a choice of characters. For example, the **`ls *.[abc]*`** command lists all files whose file extension begins with a, b, or c.
- *Redirect output.* Normally output from a command displays on the screen. To redirect that output to a file, use the redirection symbol >. For example, to redirect output of ifconfig to myfile, use this command: **`ifconfig >myfile`**
- *Page the output.* Append `|more` to the end of a command line to display the results of the command on the screen one page at a time. For example, to page the `ls` command: **`ls -l |more`**
- *Use Ctrl+C.* To break out of a command or process, press Ctrl+C. Use it to recover after entering a wrong command or to stop a command that requires a manual halt.

Hands-On Project 20-3 Practice Linux Commands

A+
220-902
2.1

Practice using Linux commands listed in Table 20-4 using the Ubuntu Server you created earlier. As you do so, you'll examine the directory structure, create a new directory, and put a blank file in it.

Task	Command	Description
1	`ls -l`	Lists files and directories in the current directory. In Linux, a directory is treated more like a file than a Windows directory.
2	`pwd`	Displays the full path to the current directory. When you first log in to a system, that directory is /home/*username*.
3	`mkdir mydir`	Creates a directory named mydir. The directory is created in the current directory.
4	`cd mydir`	Goes to the directory you just created in the /home/*username* directory.
5	`touch myfile`	Creates a blank file named myfile in the current directory.
6	`ls`	Lists current directory contents.
7	`cd ..`	Moves up one level in the directory tree.
8	`cd /etc`	Changes directory to the /etc directory, where text files are kept for configuring installed programs.
9	`ls`	Examines the contents of the /etc directory.
10	`cd /home`	Changes directory to the /home directory.
11	`ping 127.0.0.1`	Pings the loopback address. Pinging continues until you stop it by pressing Ctrl+C.
12	`ifconfig`	Displays TCP/IP configuration data.
13	`man ifconfig`	Displays the page from the Linux Manual about the `ifconfig` command. Press `q` to exit.
14	`df -T`	Displays free space on the hard drive and the file system used.
15	`exit`	Logs out; the login shell prompt appears, where you can log in again.

Table 20-4 Practice using Linux commands

Notes The current Linux file system is **ext4** (fourth extended file system), which replaced the ext3 file system. The **ext3** file system was the first file system to support journaling, which is a technique that tracks and stores changes to the hard drive and helps prevent file system corruption.

THE VI EDITOR

A+
220-902
2.1

20

The **vi editor** (visual editor) is a text editor that works in command mode (to enter commands) or in insert mode (to edit text). In this section, you learn how to create a text file in the vi editor, edit text, and save your changes. All vi commands are case sensitive.

Let's create and work with a file called mymemo:

1. If you are not already in your home directory, use the `cd` command to go there, for example: **`cd /home/jean`**
2. To open the vi editor and create the new file, enter the command **`vi mymemo`**. The vi editor screen appears and the file name is shown at the bottom of the screen.
3. When you first open the vi editor, you are in command mode. Type **`i`** to switch to Insert mode. When you are in Insert mode, the word INSERT is shown at the bottom of the screen.
4. Type the three sentences of Step 3 as the text for your memo (see Figure 20-14). Use your arrow keys to move over the text to edit it. You can also use the Insert key to switch between inserting text and overwriting text.

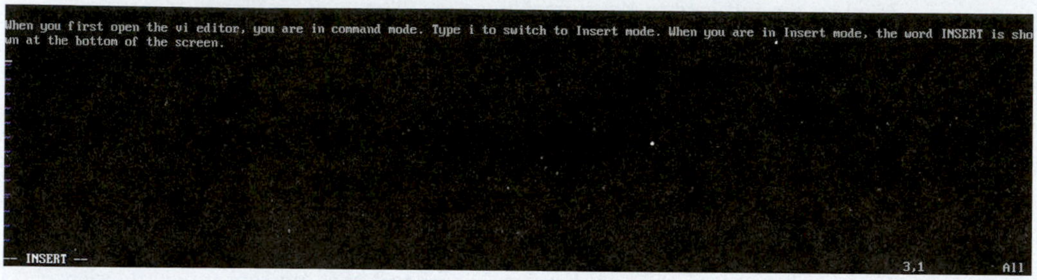

Source: Canonical Ltd.

Figure 20-14 The vi text editor in Insert mode

5. To switch back to command mode, first press the **Esc** key. Your pointer goes to the bottom of the screen. Type **:wq** to save the file and exit the editor.

Here is a list of enough vi commands to get you started with the editor. You can find other commands online:

`:w`	Save your changes and don't exit the editor
`:q`	Exit the editor after you have just saved your changes with the :w command
`:wq`	Save your changes and exit the editor
`:q!`	Quit without saving your changes

Hands-On Project 20-4 Install FTP Server in Ubuntu

A+
220-902
2.1

In this project, you set up an FTP server in Ubuntu. Follow these steps:

1. Using the same VM you created earlier, log in to Ubuntu Server with your user name and password.
2. To install the FTP program named vsftpd, enter this command:

```
sudo apt-get install vsftpd
```

3. Respond to the prompts and then wait for the package to install.
4. Now you need to configure the FTP program by editing the /etc/vsftpd.conf text file. But before you edit the file, go to the /etc directory and make a backup copy of the file just in case you need it later. The `sudo` command is needed because files in the /etc directory belong to root:

```
cd /etc
sudo cp vsftpd.conf vsftpd.backup
```

5. Use the vi editor to edit the FTP configuration file: **`sudo vi vsftpd.conf`**

6. Verify and/or change three lines in the file to create the settings listed. Part of the file, including the three lines, is shown in Figure 20-15.

`anonymous_enable=NO`	Disable anonymous logins.
`local_enable=YES`	If necessary, remove the # to uncomment the line and allow local users to log in.
`write_enable=YES`	If necessary, remove the # to uncomment the line and allow users to write to a directory.

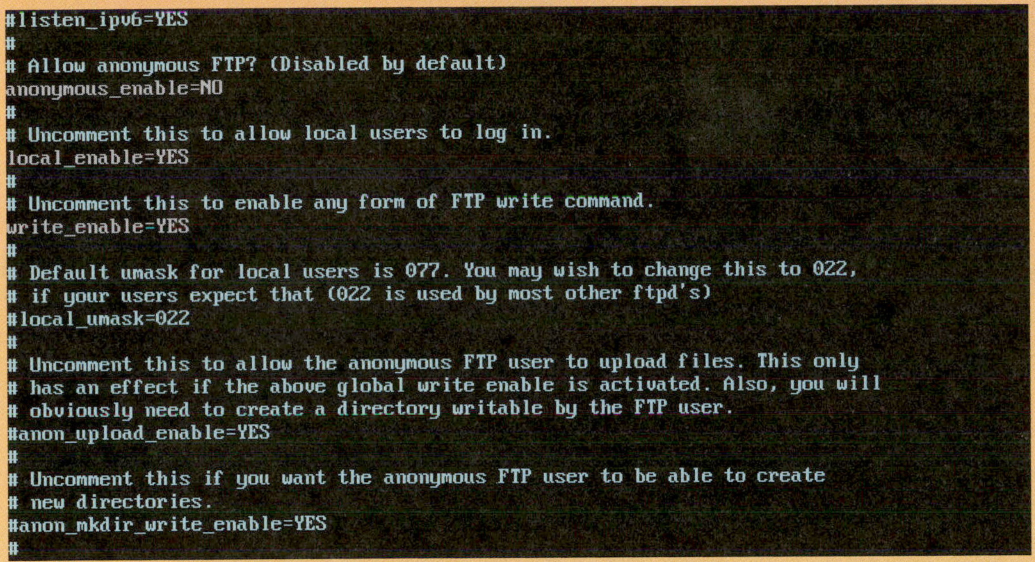

```
#listen_ipv6=YES
#
# Allow anonymous FTP? (Disabled by default)
anonymous_enable=NO
#
# Uncomment this to allow local users to log in.
local_enable=YES
#
# Uncomment this to enable any form of FTP write command.
write_enable=YES
#
# Default umask for local users is 077. You may wish to change this to 022,
# if your users expect that (022 is used by most other ftpd's)
#local_umask=022
#
# Uncomment this to allow the anonymous FTP user to upload files. This only
# has an effect if the above global write enable is activated. Also, you will
# obviously need to create a directory writable by the FTP user.
#anon_upload_enable=YES
#
# Uncomment this if you want the anonymous FTP user to be able to create
# new directories.
#anon_mkdir_write_enable=YES
#
```

Source: Canonical Ltd.

Figure 20-15 Part of the vsftpd.conf text file

7. Exit the vi editor, saving your changes. Restart the FTP service using this command: **`sudo restart vsftpd`**

8. To test your FTP server using the local machine, enter **`ftp 127.0.0.1`**. Then enter your user name and password. The ftp> prompt appears. Next use the **`dir`** command to see a list of directories and files. You should see the mydir directory and the mymemo file that you created in your /home/username directory earlier.

9. If you want to transfer files with FTP commands, use the **`get`** and **`put`** commands. To download the mymemo file, use the command **`get mymemo`**. Type **`bye`** to disconnect from the FTP server.

10. To find out the IP address of the server, type **`ifconfig`**.

11. Go to another computer on your local network, connect to your FTP server using the IP address of the server, and download the mymemo file to the local machine. See Figure 20-16. Your IP address might be different from the one shown in the figure.

12. Return to Ubuntu Server and examine the FTP log file /var/log/vsftpd.log. Because the file is short, you can use the `cat` command to display the entire log. The `sudo` command is required because /var files belong to root: **`sudo cat /var/log/vsftpd.log`**

(continues)

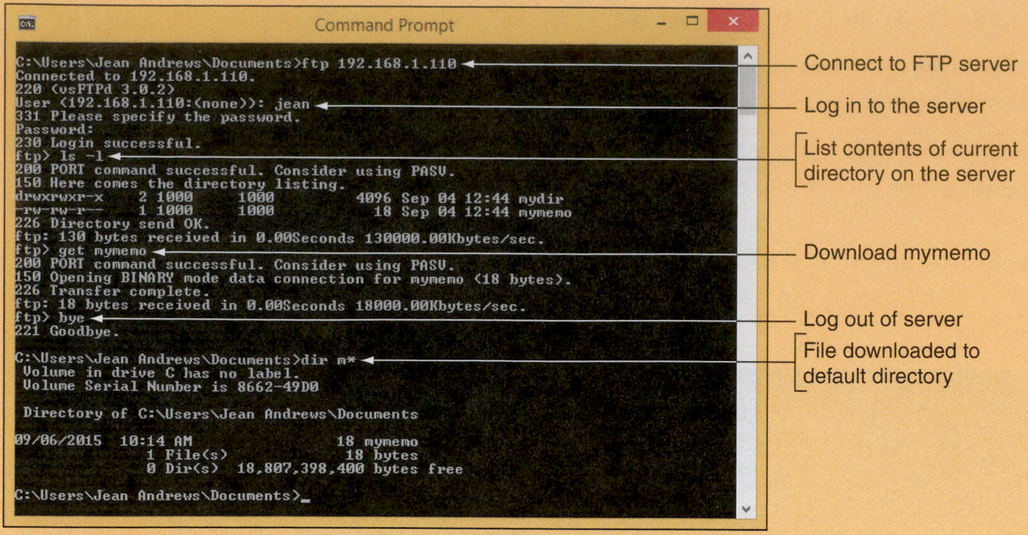

Figure 20-16 FTP in Windows can access an FTP server running under Linux

13. After much activity, log files can get quite long and the `grep` command can help you find a specific action, user, IP address, file name, or directory name. For example, to display lines in the log file that contain the text "LOGIN", use this `grep` command: **`sudo grep "LOGIN" /var/log/vsftpd.log`**

    The results of the `cat` and `grep` commands are shown in Figure 20-17.

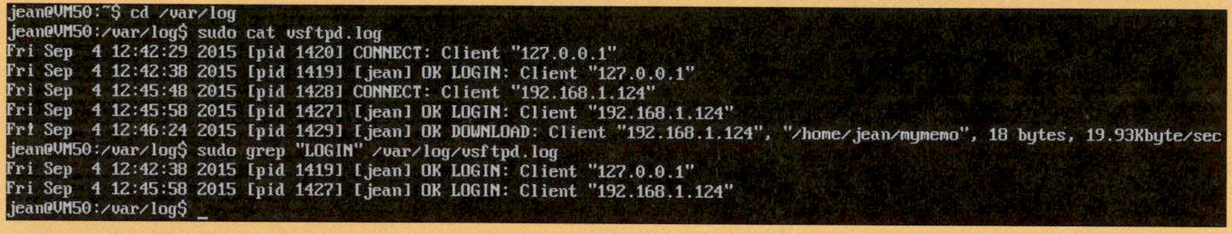

Source: Canonical Ltd.

Figure 20-17 The `grep` command can be used to search for specific text in log files

ASSIGNING PERMISSIONS TO FILES OR DIRECTORIES

A+ 220-902 2.1

A file or directory can have read, write, and/or execute permissions assigned to it. Permissions can be assigned to (a) the owner, (b) other users in the same group as the owner, and (c) all users. The chmod command is used to manage permissions for files and directories. To see current permissions, examine the 10 characters in the left column that display when you use the ls –l command. Here is the explanation of these characters:

- The first character identifies the type of item (d is a directory; - is a regular file).
- Characters 2–4 show the permissions assigned the owner (for example, rwx says the owner has read, write, and execute permissions).
- Characters 5–7 show the permissions assigned the group (for example, r-x says the group has read and execute permissions, but not write permission).
- Characters 8–10 show the permissions for others (for example, --- says others don't have read, write, or execute permission).

The chmod command changes these permissions. For example, suppose the output for the ls –l command on the /home/jean directory is that shown in Figure 20-18.

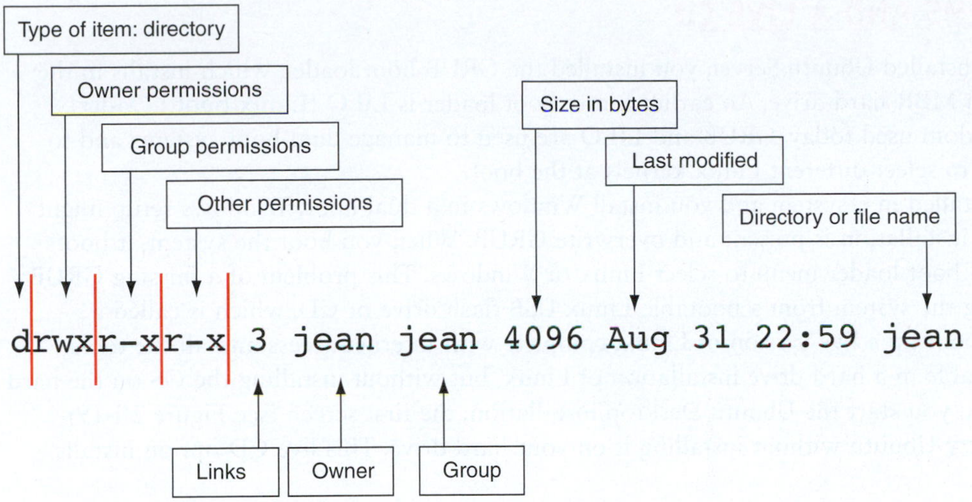

Figure 20-18 Information about the jean directory displayed by `ls-l`

As labeled in the figure, the permissions for jean as owner is rwx (read, write, and execute). The permissions for the jean group are r-x (read and execute, but not write), and the permissions for others are also r-x. If the user jean wants to give read, write, and execute permissions to everyone (group and other), she can use this command:

```
chmod go+rwx /home/jean
```

The **g** assigns permission to the group and the **o** assigns permissions to others. (**u** can assign permissions to the owner.) A plus (+) gives permissions and a minus (–) removes permissions.

Hands-On | Project 20-5 Change Permissions for a Directory

A+ 220-902 2.1

Follow these steps to change permissions for your home directory and then create a new user account to test these permissions:

1. Create a new user account named charlie. Log in to Ubuntu Server as charlie and try to copy a file to your own home directory. For example, you can use this command to make a new copy of the mymemo file you created earlier:

   ```
   cp mymemo mymemo.charlie
   ```

   When you do so, permission is denied.
2. Log back in to Ubuntu Server with your own account.
3. To install the chmod command, use this command:

   ```
   sudo apt-get install coreutils
   ```

4. Use the chmod command to give full read, write, and execute permissions to everyone for your home directory.
5. Log out and log back in to the system as charlie and verify that the user charlie can now copy a file to your home directory.

20

DUAL-BOOT SYSTEMS AND A LIVE CD

A+ 220-902 4.1

When you installed Ubuntu Server, you installed the GRUB boot loader, which installs in the MBR for an MBR hard drive. An earlier Linux boot loader is **LILO (LInux boot LOader)**, which is seldom used today. GRUB and LILO are used to manage dual-boot systems and to allow users to select different Linux kernels at the boot.

If Linux is already installed in a system and you install Windows in a dual boot, Windows setup might not recognize the Linux installation is present and overwrite GRUB. When you boot the system, it boots into Windows without a boot loader menu to select Linux or Windows. This problem of a missing GRUB can be solved by booting the system from a bootable Linux USB flash drive or CD, which is called a **live CD**. A live CD can boot up a live version of Linux, complete with Internet access and all the tools you normally have available in a hard drive installation of Linux, but without installing the OS on the hard drive. For example, when you start the Ubuntu Desktop installation, the first screen (see Figure 20-19) gives you the option to try Ubuntu without installing it on your hard drive. This live CD option installs Ubuntu only in memory.

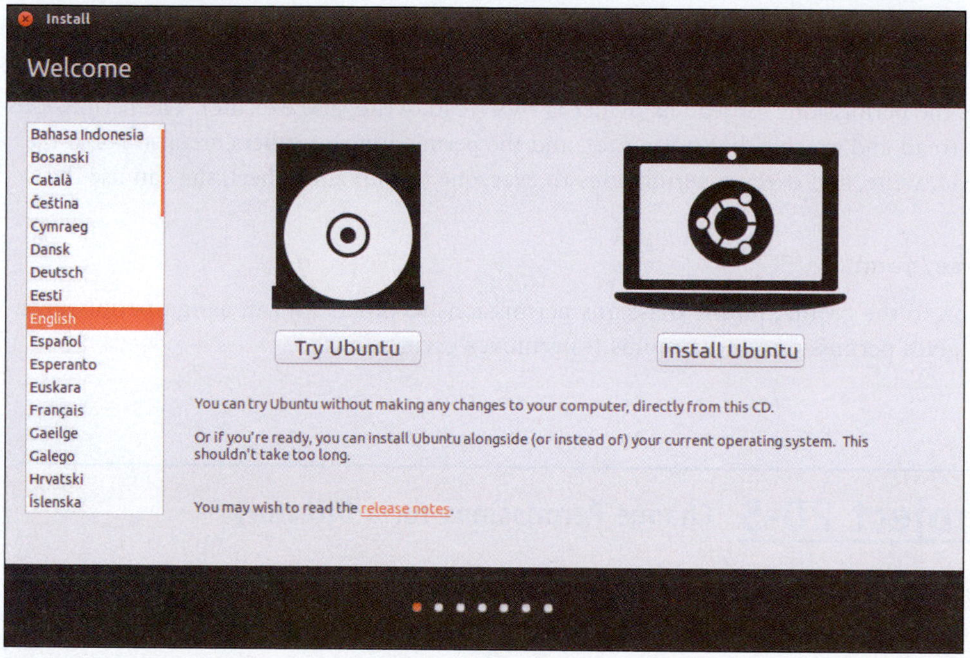

Source: Canonical Ltd.

Figure 20-19 Use a live CD to try Ubuntu Desktop without installing it on your hard drive

After booting from a live CD, you can reinstall GRUB and configure GRUB to manage the dual boot with Linux and Windows. The details of how to do that are beyond the scope of this chapter.

A+ Exam Tip The A+ 220-902 exam expects you to know about GRUB and LILO and the problem of a missing GRUB.

Notes In a dual boot with Windows and Linux, you might want to access files in either volume from either OS. Know that Linux can access the NTFS file system on the Windows volume, but Windows cannot access the ext4 file system on the Linux volume. You can, however, install in Windows third-party software, such as Paragon ExtFS for Windows (*paragon-software.com*), to access the ext4 volume.

Hands-On | Project 20-6 Install Ubuntu Desktop in a VM

A+
220-902
2.1, 2.2

Follow these steps to install Ubuntu Desktop in a VM:

1. Go to **ubuntu.com/download/desktop** and download the free Ubuntu Desktop OS to your hard drive. The file that downloads is an ISO file.
2. Open the Hyper-V Manager, Oracle VM VirtualBox, Virtual PC Manager, or VMware Workstation Player manager and create a new VM named VM60. Mount the ISO file that contains the Ubuntu Desktop download to a virtual DVD in your VM.
3. Start up the VM and install Ubuntu Desktop in the VM, accepting all default settings. Be sure to write down your Ubuntu host name, Ubuntu user name, and password. When given the option, decline to install any extra software bundled with the OS. If needed, the software can be installed later.
4. When asked to restart the VM, first dismount (remove) the ISO file from the optical drive so that the VM boots to the hard drive. After Ubuntu Desktop launches, log in with your user name and password. Figure 20-20 shows the desktop with the System Settings window open and the System menu displayed.

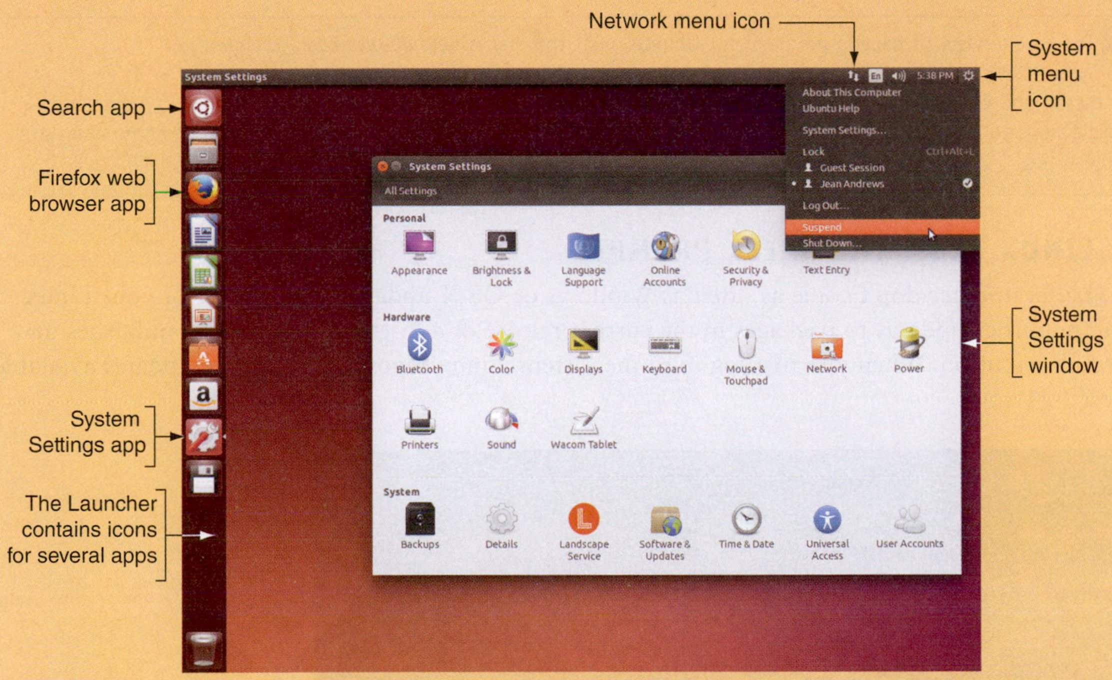

Sources: Canonical Ltd. and Mozilla Foundation

Figure 20-20 Ubuntu Desktop with the System Settings window and the Mozilla Firefox browser window open

5. Take a few minutes to poke around the desktop. For example, to open a Terminal window where you can enter Linux commands, click the **Search** icon to open the Search app and type **terminal**. Then click **Terminal** in the Applications group.
6. To shut down Ubuntu Desktop, click the **System** (cog) icon in the upper-right corner of the screen and click **Shut Down** in the System menu that appears.

To learn more about using Ubuntu Desktop, an excellent source of information is the Ubuntu Desktop Guide at *help.ubuntu.com/stable/ubuntu-help/*.

BACKUPS AND UPDATES

A+
220-902
2.1

When supporting a Linux system, an IT technician needs to know how to create and maintain scheduled backups and system updates. For Ubuntu, the tools you use depend on whether you plan to do these chores from the shell prompt in Ubuntu Server or the graphical user interface in Ubuntu Desktop.

Here is what you need to know to get you started with making backups:

- *What is a dump and clone?* In Linux, a dump is a collection of data that is copied to backup media. For example, when Linux encounters a kernel panic (an error from which it cannot recover), it dumps an image of memory to a disk file for later examination. The image is called a core dump. You can dump the entire Linux volume to an external hard drive or dump a data folder to a location on the network. The first dump is called the initial dump and subsequent incremental dumps are called appended dumps or incremental dumps. A clone is an image of the entire partition on which Linux is installed.
- *Which backup program should I use?* Before choosing a shell prompt command or graphical program for the desktop, research the program to find out what others are saying about it and how it works. Compare several programs to find the one right for you. Examples of backup programs include the dump and TAR commands used at a shell prompt and the graphical SimpleBackupSuite that works from the desktop.

Notes For an overview of backup programs for Ubuntu, visit this page: *help.ubuntu.com/community/BackupYourSystem%20*.

Also, the cron and crontab commands can be used to schedule any shell command in Linux, including cp commands for making backups to another media. The crontab (cron table) command is used to schedule jobs and the cron command executes these jobs.

UPDATE LINUX FROM THE SHELL PROMPT

In general, Linux updates don't come as often as Windows or OS X updates. The creator of your Linux distribution publishes updates to packages in the current release of a distribution and also publishes new releases of a distribution. When you first log in to the system, Linux reports the package updates available (see Figure 20-21).

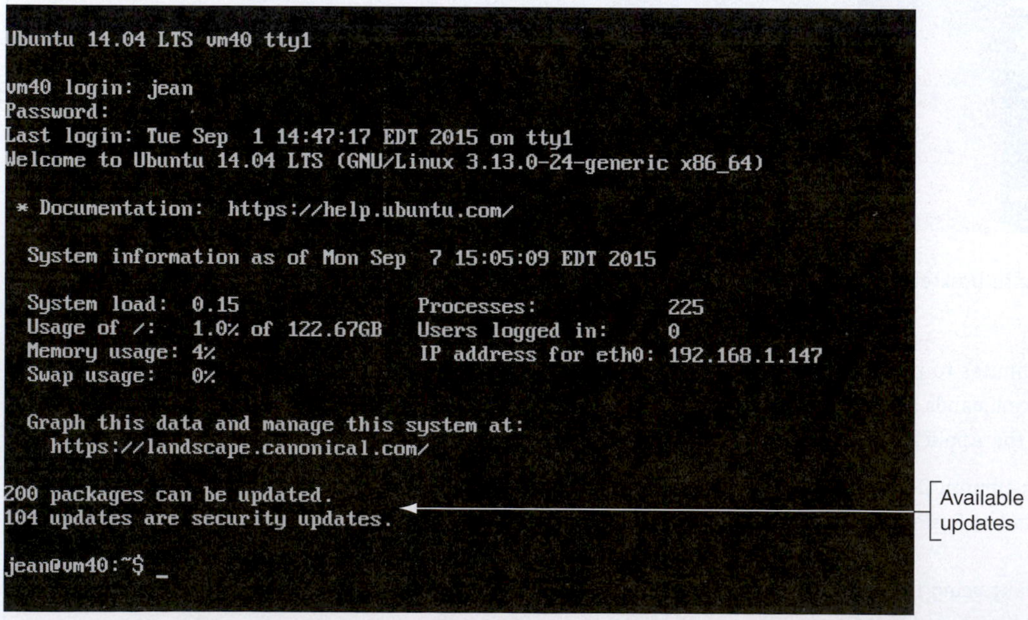

Source: Canonical Ltd.

Figure 20-21 Available Ubuntu package updates

At a shell prompt, use these commands to update the packages previously installed in your system:

1. To refresh the list of all available updates:

```
sudo apt-get update
```

2. To update only the installed packages:

```
sudo apt-get upgrade
```

A new release of a distribution contains all updates since the last release. As a Linux administrator, you need to stay aware of the latest release of the distribution you are using and decide when or if it's appropriate to upgrade to that release.

Before you upgrade to a new release, be sure you have backups of your data and a clone of the entire Linux partition. Here's how to upgrade to a new release for Ubuntu Server:

1. Follow the previous steps to update all packages installed in the system.
2. To make sure the latest update manager program is installed:

```
sudo apt-get install update-manager-core
```

3. To install the latest release of Ubuntu Server:

```
sudo do-release-upgrade
```

If a new release is **available**, the last command reports it and you can follow directions to install it.

UPDATE UBUNTU DESKTOP

In Ubuntu Desktop, the Software Updater app manages updates to packages and new releases of Ubuntu Desktop. To open the updater, click the **Search** app and type **updater** in the Search box. Then click **Software Updater** (see Figure 20-22).

Source: Canonical Ltd.

Figure 20-22 Find and launch Software Updater

The updater searches for updates. In the box that appears, click **Details of updates** to see a list of updates (see the left side of Figure 20-23). To install updates, select your updates and click **Install Now.** To change update settings, click **Settings.** In the Software & Updates box (see the right side of Figure 20-23), you can decide how updates are managed.

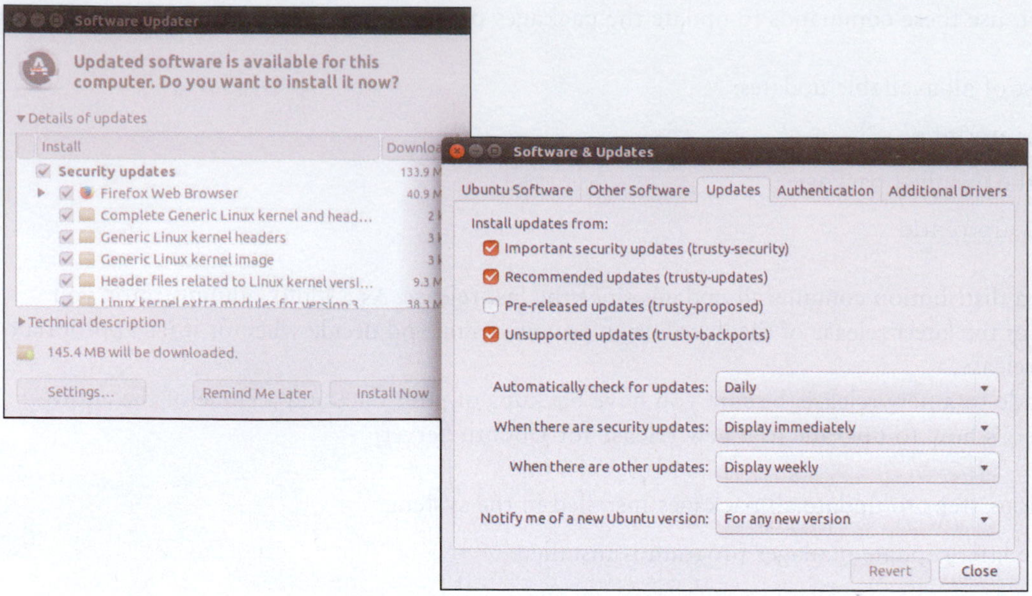

Source: Canonical Ltd.

Figure 20-23 Use the Software Updater to manage updates to Ubuntu Desktop

Now that you're familiar with Linux, let's move on to OS X.

MAC OS X OPERATING SYSTEM

A+
220-902
1.2, 2.1,
4.1, 4.2

OS X is the latest version of the proprietary operating system only available for Macintosh computers by Apple Inc. (*apple.com*). Like Linux, OS X is built on a UNIX foundation. The first Mac OS was released in 1984, and the final "classic" Mac OS, called Mac OS 9, was released in 1999. The first iteration of the desktop version of Mac OS X, dubbed "Cheetah," became available in 2001. From that point forward, the operating system continued to be called OS X (pronounced "O-S-ten") and received a version number to track its progress. The most recent release at the time of this writing, Yosemite, is version 10.10. Version 10.11, El Capitan, is already available in beta and is expected to be released as a free upgrade by the end of 2015.

USE THE MAC

A+
220-902
2.1, 4.2

Let's begin with a look at some major features of the Mac interface and how to use a Mac. In this section, you'll learn about the OS X desktop, Apple menu, multiple desktops, Finder, iCloud Drive, Keychain, System Preferences, Sharing, and Terminal.

GET TO KNOW THE OS X DESKTOP

The OS X desktop, with its major components labeled, is shown in Figure 20-24. The Finder application, which can help you find applications and data files, is open and active. Because Finder is the currently active application, the menu bar for the Finder window is displayed at the top of the screen. The menu bar provides drop-down menus that contain options for working with applications, files, and the interface.

By default, the dock appears at the bottom of the desktop. It contains shortcut icons to access frequently used applications. To open an application from its icon in the dock, click it once. The icons in the dock that represent open applications have a small, black dot underneath them. The OS X desktop can also include shortcuts that provide quick access to files, folders, and applications.

Source: Apple Inc.

Figure 20-24 The OS X desktop with a Finder window showing the Applications screen

When a window is open, three circles at the upper-left corner (see Figure 20-25a) let you manipulate the window. The red circle closes the window, the yellow circle minimizes the window to the dock in the lower-right corner of the screen (see Figure 20-25b), and the green circle maximizes the window to full-screen size. (To restore a maximized window, move your pointer to the top of the screen. The circle icons appear. Click the green circle.)

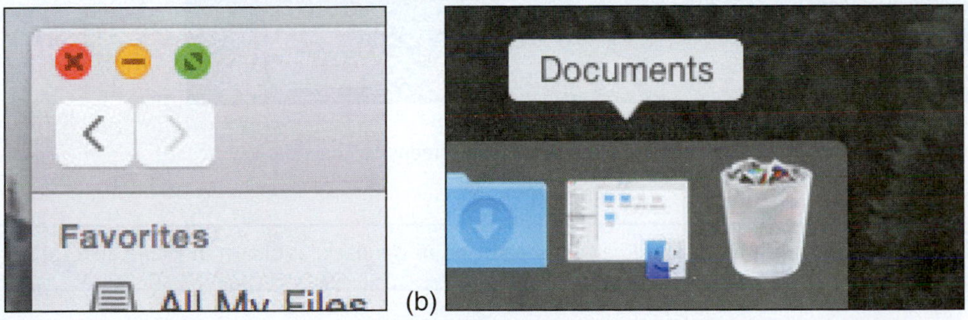

Source: Apple Inc.

Figure 20-25 (a) Close, minimize, or expand a window; (b) this Finder window has been minimized, but the app is still running and is easily accessible in the dock

Notes Closing an app's window does not close the app. To quit an app, secondary-click (tap two fingers on the trackpad or right-click the mouse) the app's icon in the dock and click **Quit** in the menu that appears above the dock. Alternately, when the app's window is active on the desktop, click the name of the app in the menu bar and click **Quit** at the bottom of the drop-down menu.

Navigating OS X is made easier with a few, simple gestures, or finger movements, on the trackpad. Later in this chapter, you learn how to change the trackpad settings. In the meantime, here are a few of the most important default gestures:

- *Secondary click.* A secondary click is similar in function to a right-click in Windows. To secondary click, tap the lower-right corner of the trackpad with one finger or right-click the mouse. (You can also configure a secondary click to tap the trackpad with two fingers.)

- *Scroll.* Scroll bars are typically hidden from view in OS X because the page can be scrolled by swiping two fingers up or down on the trackpad.
- *Zoom.* Similar to zoom on a mobile device, pinch two fingers together to zoom out and spread two fingers apart to zoom in.
- *Pinch.* Pinch with three fingers and your thumb to show the Launchpad (see Figure 20-26), which is somewhat similar to the Start screen in Windows and shows all apps installed on the computer. Spread apart with three fingers and your thumb to return to the desktop. If you're already on the desktop, spread apart three fingers and your thumb to push all open windows to the edges and clear the desktop.

Source: Apple Inc.

Figure 20-26 When more apps are installed, Launchpad creates additional screens to the side

> **Notes** You can also open the Launchpad by clicking the Launchpad icon in the dock, as shown in Figure 20-24.

- *Swipe.* The number of fingers, direction of the swipe, and location of the swipe can all cause different results. Some of the most useful are:
  - Swiping left or right with two fingers scrolls horizontally within an app (such as when scrolling through photos in the Photos app), and swiping left or right with three fingers switches between full-screen apps.
  - Swipe two fingers from the right edge of the trackpad to reveal the Notification Center, as shown in Figure 20-27.
  - Swipe up with three fingers to see Mission Control (see Figure 20-28), which gives an overview of all open windows and a thumbnail of Dashboard and the desktop. Dashboard (see Figure 20-29) contains widgets, such as a calendar, a calculator, a clock, and a weather report. Alternately, you can press F3 to access Mission Control.

Source: Apple Inc.

Figure 20-27 Click Edit at the bottom of the screen to customize the Notification Center

Source: Apple Inc.

Figure 20-28 Mission Control shows the open windows on the currently selected screen, which is the desktop

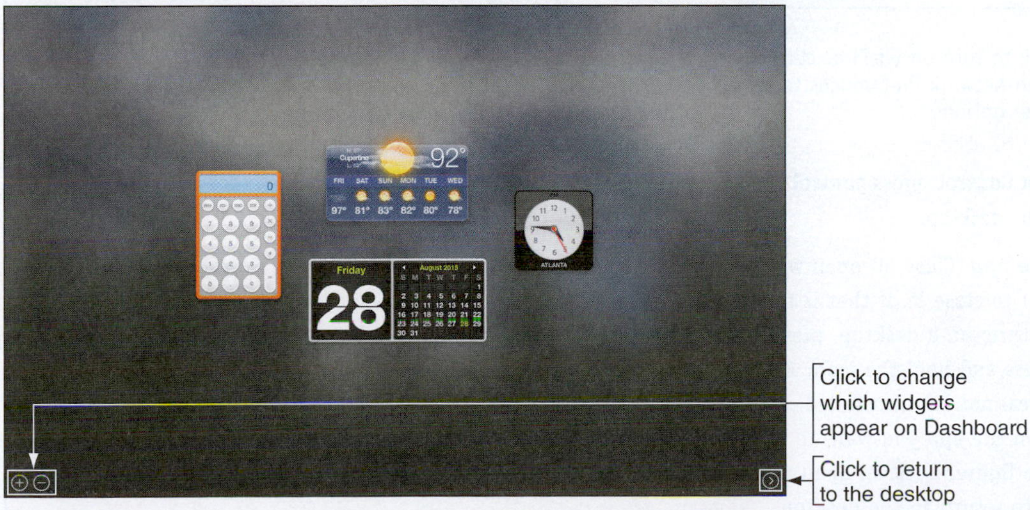

Source: Apple Inc.

Figure 20-29 Dashboard has four default widgets, and several apps include a widget view option

Spotlight is Mac's search app, and can be configured to search the local computer, Wikipedia, iTunes, the Maps app, the web, and more. Click the Spotlight icon at the upper right of the screen to open the Spotlight Search box (see Figure 20-30), or press the Apple Command key (⌘) + **spacebar**.

Source: Apple Inc.

Figure 20-30 Spotlight searches the local computer and online resources

Hands-On | Project 20-7 Practice Using the OS X Desktop

A+ 220-902 2.1

If you're not used to a Mac, the OS X desktop might feel strange compared with Windows. But with a little practice, you'll find all of the essential functions right at your fingertips. Complete the following steps to explore the OS X desktop:

1. ***Confirm that you have a Wi-Fi connection***. Look for the Wi-Fi icon in the upper-right corner of the screen. If there is no connection, the icon will look like an empty upside-down triangle (see Figure 20-31). Click the Wi-Fi icon, turn on Wi-Fi if necessary, and connect to the network.

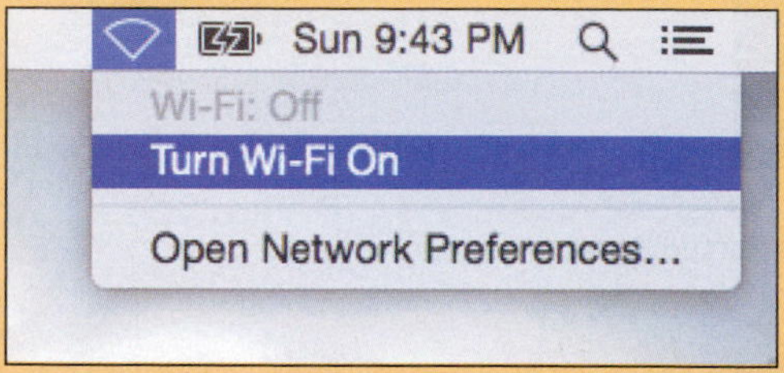

Source: Apple Inc.

Figure 20-31 Click to turn on Wi-Fi or click Open Network Preferences to set other options

2. ***Install an app from the App Store***. Click the App Store icon in the dock; sign in if necessary. Select a free app and install it. A good one to try is Evernote. After installation is complete, leave the App Store window open. Use Finder to open the app.
3. ***Switch between windows with Exposé***. Open two more windows, such as Safari and Maps. On a laptop, swipe down with three fingers to open Exposé. On a desktop, press **control + down arrow**. In Exposé, press **tab** to switch between windows. Press **esc** to return to the desktop.
4. ***See all open windows with Mission Control***. On a laptop, swipe up with three fingers to open Mission Control. On a desktop, to open **Mission Control**, press **control + up arrow** or the **F3 Mission Control** key. Click a window to go to that window on the desktop.
5. ***Uninstall the app***. Close all open windows on the desktop. You might need to use the Evernote menu on the menu bar to close it, if that is the app that you installed. Next, open Launchpad. On a laptop, use a trackpad gesture; on a desktop, press the **F4 Launchpad** key. In Launchpad, locate the icon for the app you installed. Press and hold the icon. All the icons jiggle. Some apps, such as Mission Control, are embedded in OS X and cannot be uninstalled; others that can be uninstalled have an x on the icon (see Figure 20-32). Click the **x** on the app you want to uninstall, then click **Delete** in the message bubble that appears, as shown in the figure. Click an open space on the screen to make the icons stop jiggling. Click the open space again to return to the desktop.

Source: Apple Inc.

Figure 20-32 Use the Launchpad to uninstall an app

APPLE MENU

The menu at the top of the OS X screen changes with each application that is active except for the Apple icon, which is always shown at the far left of the menu bar. The Apple menu (see Figure 20-33) opens when you click the Apple icon and is similar to the Microsoft Windows Start menu in that it is constantly accessible no matter what folder, window, or application you are using. Use the Apple menu to put the computer to sleep, log out, restart, or shut down the system.

The Apple menu also provides access to system information, system preferences settings, the App Store, recent items, and the Force Quit option. When you click Force Quit, the Force Quit Applications window opens (see Figure 20-34). Similar to ending a task from Task Manager in Windows, to force quit an app, select it and click **Force Quit**. The application closes. You can also access the Force Quit Applications window by pressing **⌘ + option + esc**.

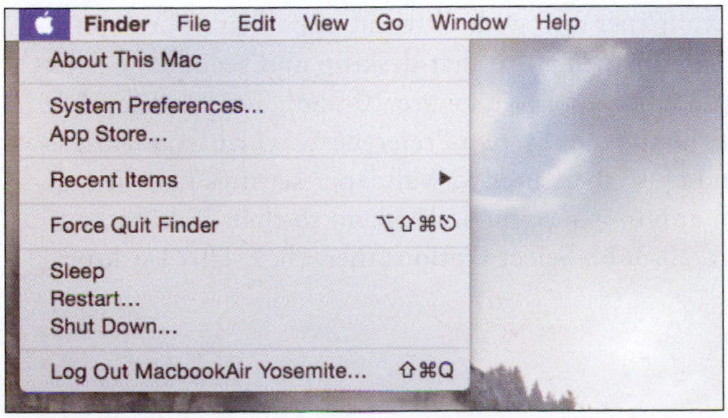

Source: Apple Inc.

Figure 20-33 The Apple menu is always available no matter which application is active

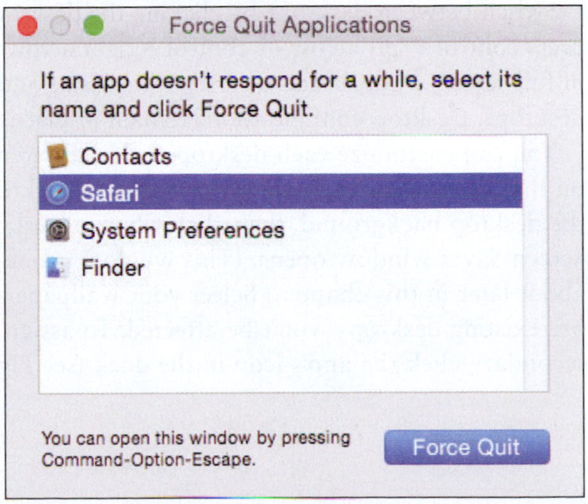

Source: Apple Inc.

Figure 20-34 Force Quit can be used to close an app that is not responding

MULTIPLE DESKTOPS

Mission Control includes a feature called multiple desktops, which, as its name says, is several desktop screens each with its own collection of open windows. Suppose you're working with several windows for a school project, and you have a few more windows open for a project at work. You can place the school project windows on one desktop, called a Space, and place the work project windows on a separate desktop or Space.

To accomplish this feat, first open Mission Control as described above. By default, a single desktop thumbnail shows at the top of the screen beside the Dashboard thumbnail (refer back to Figure 20-28), and all the open windows show in this one desktop. To create a second desktop, drag a window's thumbnail to the right side of the default desktop thumbnail, and drop the window. A second desktop appears to hold that window. Repeat with another window for a third and fourth desktops, as shown in Figure 20-35.

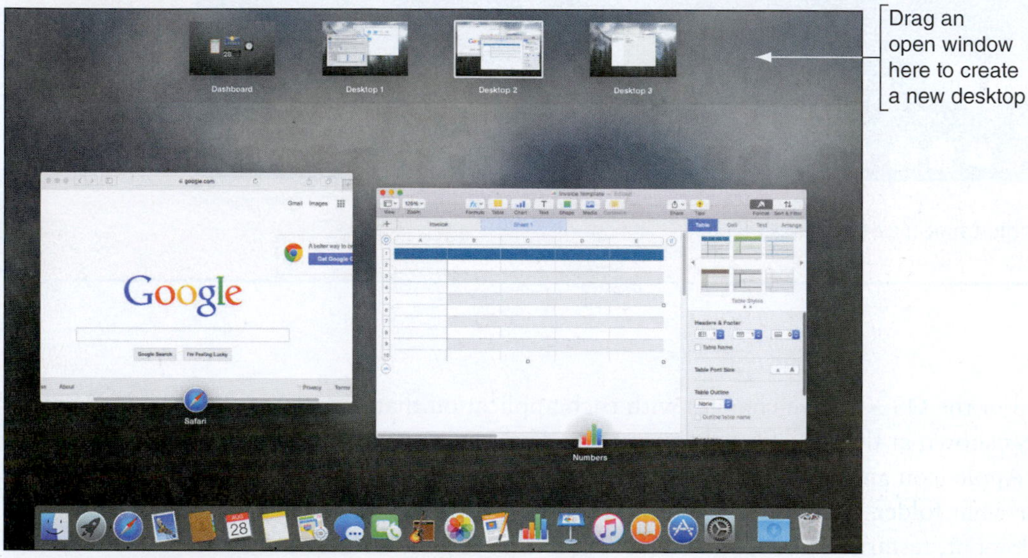

Source: Apple Inc.

Figure 20-35 Mission Control allows you to create multiple desktops to contain windows

Switch between desktops by clicking the desktop you want in Mission Control. Alternately, you can press **control + left arrow** or **control + right arrow** to switch between desktop screens. When an app is in full-screen mode, it acts as a separate Space and will show up in the list of Spaces as do the multiple desktops. Desktop configurations remain in place even when the computer is rebooted.

You can customize each desktop with a different wallpaper and with different apps that appear only on that desktop or in all desktops. To set a desktop's wallpaper, go to that desktop and secondary-click the desktop background, then click **Change Desktop Background** (see Figure 20-36a). The Desktop & Screen Saver window opens. (This window is one of the tools in System Preferences, which you learn about later in this chapter.) Select your wallpaper and close the window. Wallpaper settings in other, pre-existing desktops won't be affected. To assign an app to a specific desktop, go to that desktop and secondary-click the app's icon in the dock (see Figure 20-36b). Select **Options** then click **This Desktop**.

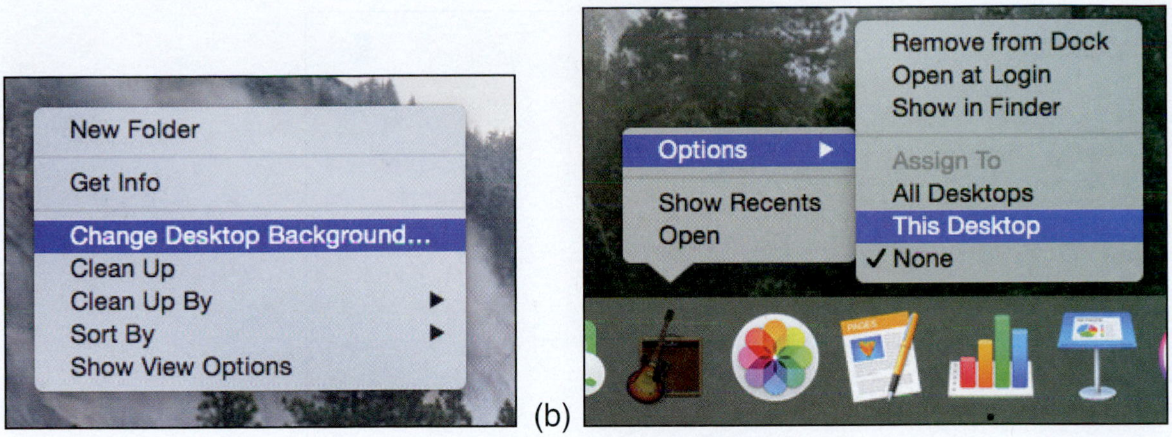

Source: Apple Inc.

Figure 20-36 (a) Set a different background for each desktop, and (b) assign different apps in the dock of each desktop

FINDER

The Mac's **Finder** window, shown earlier in Figure 20-24 and again here in Figure 20-37, functions something like File Explorer in Windows; use it to find and access Mac's files and applications. To open apps, click **Applications**, scroll to the app, and click it. To open files and folders, click **Documents** or some other location, such as iCloud Drive or Downloads. Double-click a folder to drill down into it, and double-click a document file to open it.

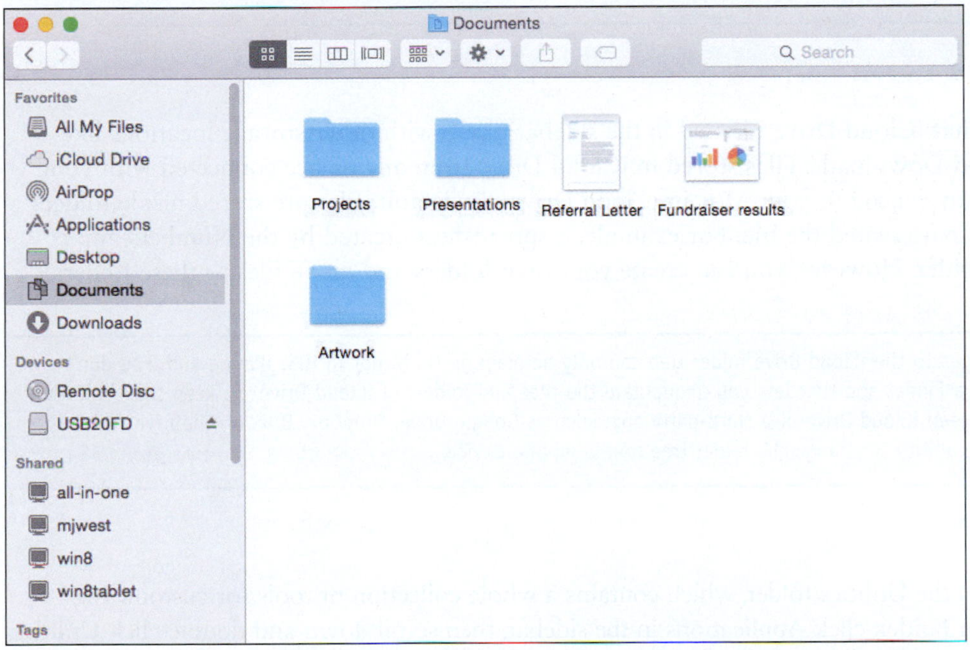

Source: Apple Inc.

Figure 20-37 The Finder window showing the Documents folder contents

Notes If you use an app frequently, such as GarageBand, you can add it to the dock. Click **Applications**, and then click and drag the app's icon to the dock.

SPOTLIGHT

If you're having a problem locating a file or folder, Spotlight can search for it. Open Spotlight and type the name of the file, folder, or text you want to find. For example, type **Projects** and Spotlight lists a folder named Projects as the Top Hit (see Figure 20-38).

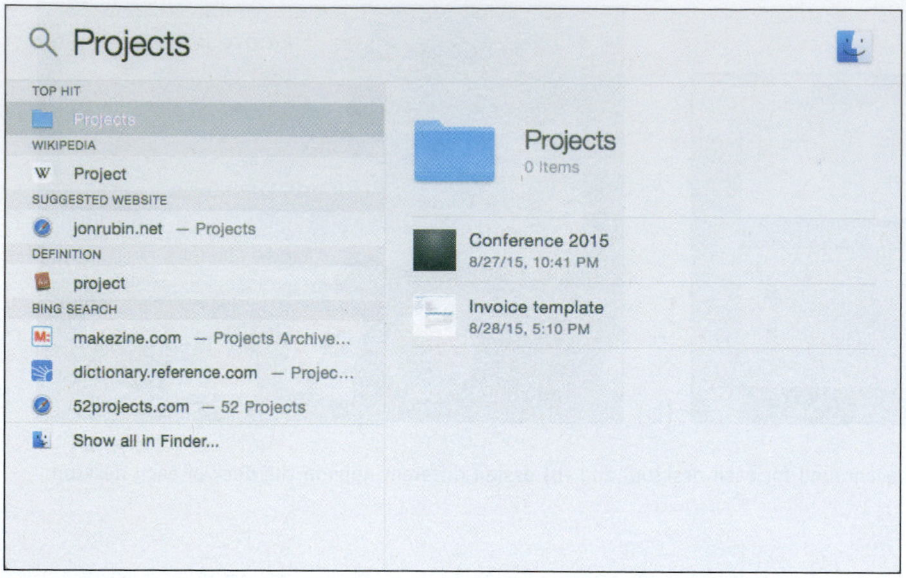

Source: Apple Inc.

Figure 20-38 Use Spotlight to search for files and folders

> **Notes** When you no longer need a file or folder, drag its icon to the Trash Can until the Trash Can is highlighted, and release. Note that this is the only way you can delete icons from the Finder window. When an item is in the Trash Can, you can recover it: Click **Trash Can** to open it and drag an item in the Trash Can to another location.

iCLOUD DRIVE

Notice in Figure 20-37 that iCloud Drive is listed in the sidebar along with other storage locations like Desktop, Documents, and Downloads. Files stored in iCloud Drive from any device connected with your Apple ID are automatically synced to your Mac in iCloud Drive. By default, files are stored inside folders titled by the application that created the file. For example, a spreadsheet created by the Numbers app is stored in the Numbers folder. However, you can create your own folders and move files to these folders.

> **OS Differences** Changes to the iCloud Drive folder tree can only be made in OS X, not in iOS. iPhone and iPad don't have an iCloud Drive app or a Finder app that lets you manipulate the files and folders of iCloud Drive. So keep this limitation in mind when choosing between iCloud Drive or a third-party app, such as Google Drive, Dropbox, Box, or OneDrive. These mobile apps all give you the ability to change the folder tree from a mobile device.

KEYCHAIN

Finder also gives access to the Utilities folder, which contains a whole collection of tools for customizing other features of OS X. In Finder, click **Applications** in the sidebar, then scroll down and double-click **Utilities**. Figure 20-39 shows the contents of the Utilities folder.

You'll learn about several of these utilities through the rest of this chapter. For now, let's look at Keychain, which is OS X's built-in password manager utility. To open Keychain, double-click **Keychain Access**. From the Keychain Access window (see the left side of Figure 20-40), you can view, edit, and remove accounts for applications, websites, servers, and other accounts that you've added, such as credit card numbers and bank accounts.

If you have problems with Keychain, verify or repair the Keychain configuration. In the **Keychain Access** menu, click **Keychain First Aid**. In the Keychain First Aid window (see the right side of Figure 20-40), make sure **Verify** is selected, then click **Start**. If the verification process reports a problem, select **Repair** and click **Start**.

Source: Apple Inc.

Figure 20-39 In Finder, use the Utilities folder to open useful tools to support the Mac

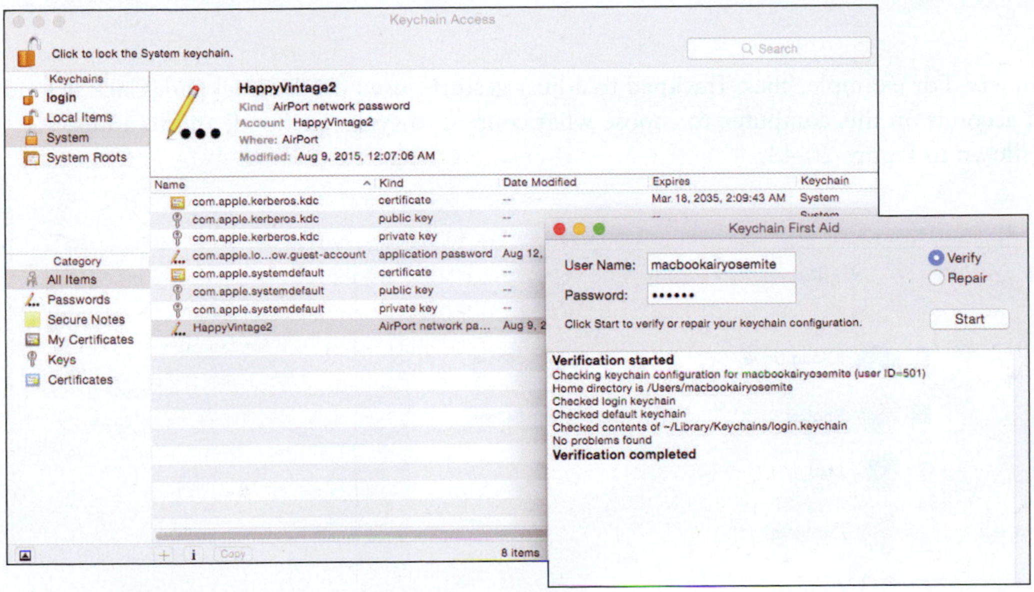

Source: Apple Inc.

Figure 20-40 The data stored in Keychain is encrypted

Source: Apple Inc.

Figure 20-41 System Preferences icon in the dock shows the app is open

SYSTEM PREFERENCES

System Preferences can be opened from the Apple menu (refer back to Figure 20-33), or from the System Preferences icon in the dock (see Figure 20-41). The System Preferences window is shown in Figure 20-42 and contains options for customizing the Mac interface.

System Preferences contains several useful tools, including the Desktop & Screen Saver window you saw earlier, Mission Control settings, Security & Privacy, Energy Saver, Time Machine, iCloud settings,

20

Source: Apple Inc.

Figure 20-42 The System Preferences window is used to customize the Mac interface

and Printers & Scanners. For example, click **Trackpad** to adjust gestures used on the trackpad. Click **iCloud** to set up an iCloud account on this computer, to choose what content to sync to iCloud, and to adjust account details, as shown in Figure 20-43.

Source: Apple Inc.

Figure 20-43 Choose what content to sync with iCloud

As an IT technician, the most important tools for you in System Preferences are accessed through Time Machine, Users & Groups, and Sharing. You'll learn more about Time Machine and Users & Groups later in this chapter. For now, let's see how Sharing works.

SHARING

In System Preferences, click **Sharing** to open the Sharing window where you can set up file and folder sharing on the network, printer sharing, remote access, and screen sharing. Screen Sharing (see Figure 20-44) works similarly to Remote Assistance in Windows. When you turn on Screen Sharing, you can then use the Messages app to remotely view and control another Mac computer.

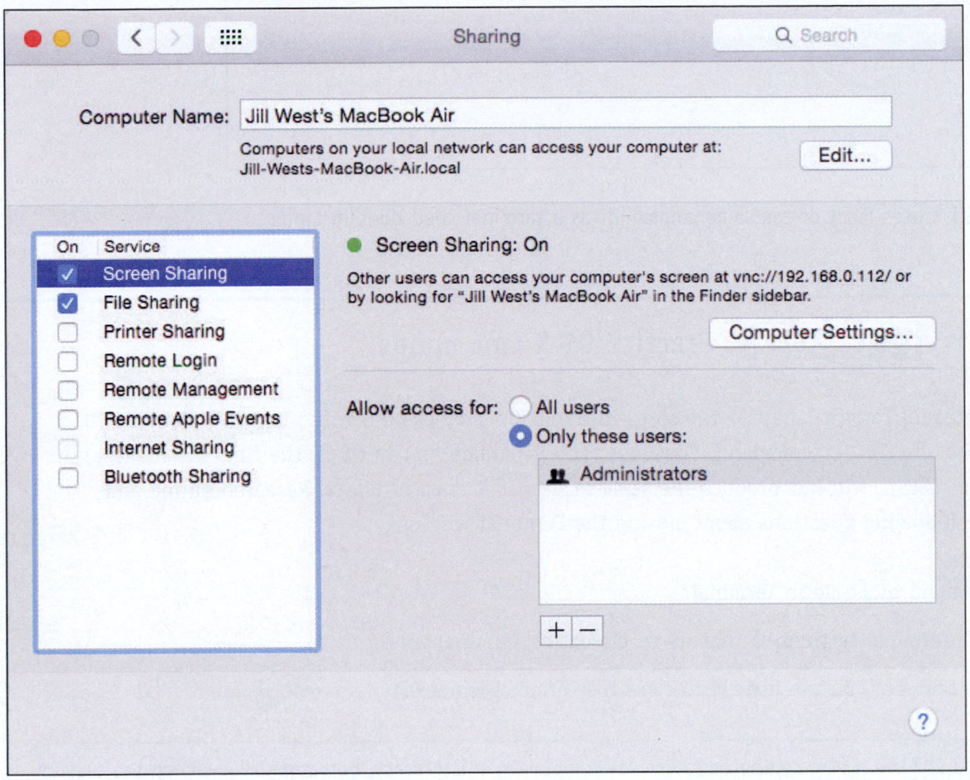

Source: Apple Inc.

Figure 20-44 Screen Sharing makes it easier to collaborate on projects or to help other users with their computers

If your Mac has an optical drive, the Sharing window includes the option *DVD or CD Sharing*. This feature, called Remote Disc, gives other Mac computers on the network access to this computer's optical drive. Remote Disc is especially useful when you need to install software or drivers from a disc on a Mac that doesn't have an optical drive. After you turn on *DVD or CD Sharing* on the Mac that has an optical drive, go to the Mac that doesn't have an optical drive and open Finder. In Finder, click **Remote Disc** in the sidebar under Devices (refer back to Figure 20-37).

OS Differences You can enable remote disc sharing on a Windows computer. To share a Windows computer's optical drive with Macs on your network, download and install **DVD or CD Sharing Update 1.0 for Windows**, available at the following website: *support.apple.com/kb/DL112?locale=en_US*.

20

TERMINAL

Terminal in OS X works much the same way as does a terminal shell in Linux. This is because both operating systems are based on UNIX. To open Terminal, first open **Finder**, click **Applications** in the sidebar, then scroll down and double-click the **Utilities** folder. Scroll down and double-click **Terminal**. (Alternately, press **⌘ + spacebar** to open Spotlight, type **Terminal**, and press **return**.) The Terminal window opens, as shown in Figure 20-45.

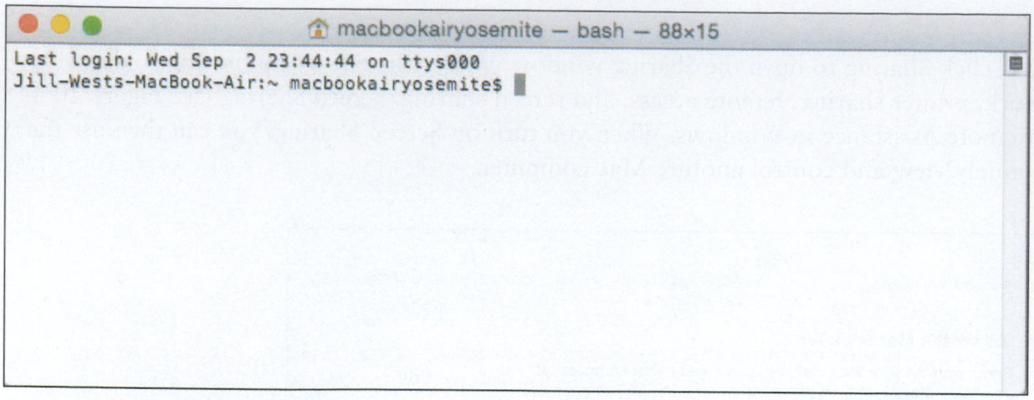

Source: Apple, Inc.

Figure 20-45 Terminal in OS X uses most of the same commands as a terminal shell does in Linux

Hands-On | Project 20-8 Practice OS X Commands

A+ 220-902 2.1

To practice using Terminal, repeat the steps in Hands-On Project 20-3 using the OS X Terminal window. (For the `df -T` command, don't use the `-T` parameter.) In OS X, the final command of that project, `exit`, will not produce the same results as it does in Linux. Research online and answer the following questions about closing the Terminal window:

1. What does the command `exit` do in Terminal?
2. How can you adjust Terminal settings so that `exit` closes the Terminal window?
3. What keyboard shortcut can you use instead to close the Terminal window?

Notes Even if you don't have a Mac computer to use for completing this project, you can still research the answers to the questions above. The information is readily available online.

Hands-On | Project 20-9 Kill a Process

A+ 220-902 2.1, 4.2

Terminal is a powerful tool and can be used to kill a hung process or to kill a process you suspect to be malware. First, try to use force quit to end the process. If that doesn't work, use Terminal to end the process. Follow these general directions to practice this skill:

1. Once again, install the Evernote app, but don't launch it.
2. Open **Terminal**. Use this command to list all running processes (the `x` option displays all processes, even those not started in this shell): **`ps x`**.
3. Leave Terminal open. Launch the Evernote app. Return to the Terminal window and list all running processes again. What are the Evernote app process IDs? Of the two process IDs, which one represents the application itself, and which one represents a login item?
4. The `pgrep` command combines the functionality of `ps` and `grep`. Research online to find the Apple man page for `pgrep`. What do the `-f` and `-l` options do?

5. Confirm the Evernote app's process IDs with the command **pgrep -f -l Evernote**. (Be sure to capitalize the *E* in Evernote.) Do the process IDs match the information you found earlier?
6. Use Terminal to kill the Evernote app (not the login item).
7. Return to the desktop and uninstall Evernote.

MAINTAIN AND SUPPORT A MAC

A+
220-902
2.1

In addition to working with files and applications, you will also need to know how to support and maintain OS X, including updates, backups, and hard drive maintenance. This section does not give you all you need to know to service Mac computers; it is simply intended to show you some important tools for working with the system. For more information specific to working with Macs, study books devoted specifically to the Mac, documentation and manuals that come with your system or its components, and the Apple website (*support.apple.com*).

Caution Many Apple computers are covered by an Apple Care warranty, which provides excellent coverage for Mac computers. Always be absolutely certain a Mac is not covered by Apple Care before opening the case or doing anything else that might void the warranty.

UPDATE OS X, DRIVERS, AND FIRMWARE

Just like Windows, OS X needs regular updates. Updates often address zero-day vulnerabilities, which makes these updates important to maintaining a healthy system. However, sometimes the updates themselves introduce bugs, which is why many Mac experts advise against setting OS X updates to install automatically. Instead, waiting a few days after an OS X update's release before manually installing the update gives you a chance to see if the update introduces any significant issues.

OS X updates come from the App Store. To manually update OS X, click the **App Store** icon in the dock, then click **Updates** in the toolbar. Any available updates will show near the top of the screen, as shown in Figure 20-46. Additional updates to apps might also be available in this window, depending on whether you've configured the computer to automatically install app updates.

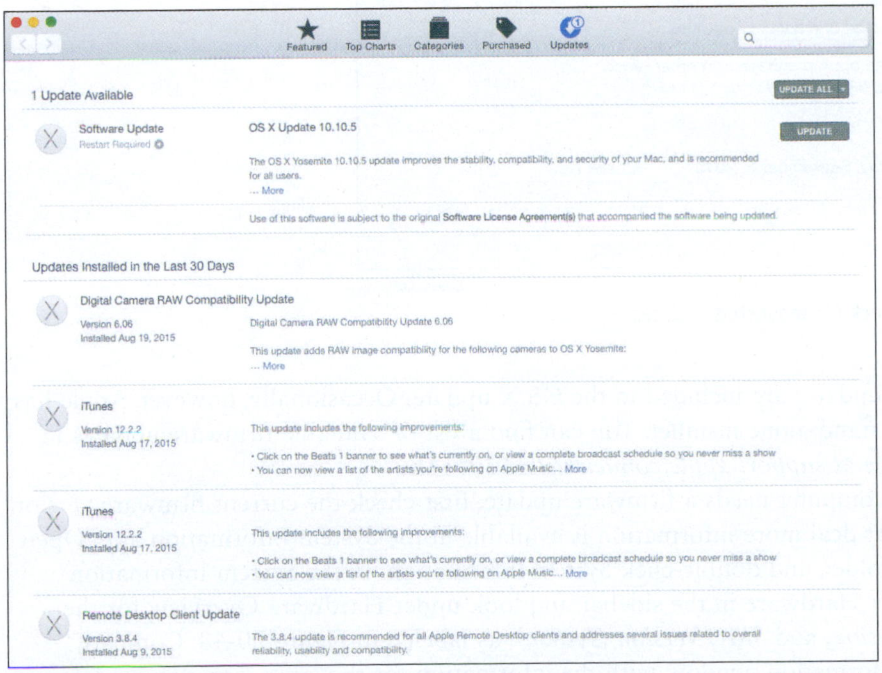

Source: Apple Inc.

Figure 20-46 The Updates window shows available updates and recently installed updates

20

Notes Printer, scanner, and graphics driver updates are usually included in the OS X updates. Other devices that require drivers, if not included in OS X, can be downloaded from the manufacturer's website and installed. These drivers will not be updated through OS X updates. If any problems are encountered with that device, you'll need to check the manufacturer's website for updates.

To change the settings for automatic updates, open **System Preferences** and click **App Store** (see Figure 20-47). Here is an explanation of each option presented:

- ***Automatically check for updates.*** This option must be checked for any of its sub options to be available.
- ***Download newly available updates in the background.*** This option downloads updates without installing them.
- ***Install app updates.*** This option installs all updates to App Store applications without first requiring user approval.
- ***Install OS X updates.*** This option installs all updates to the operating system without first requiring user approval.
- ***Install system data files and security updates.*** This option installs critical system patches that address known vulnerabilities.
- ***Automatically download apps purchased on other Macs.*** This option installs apps purchased through the App Store on other Mac computers using the same Apple ID.

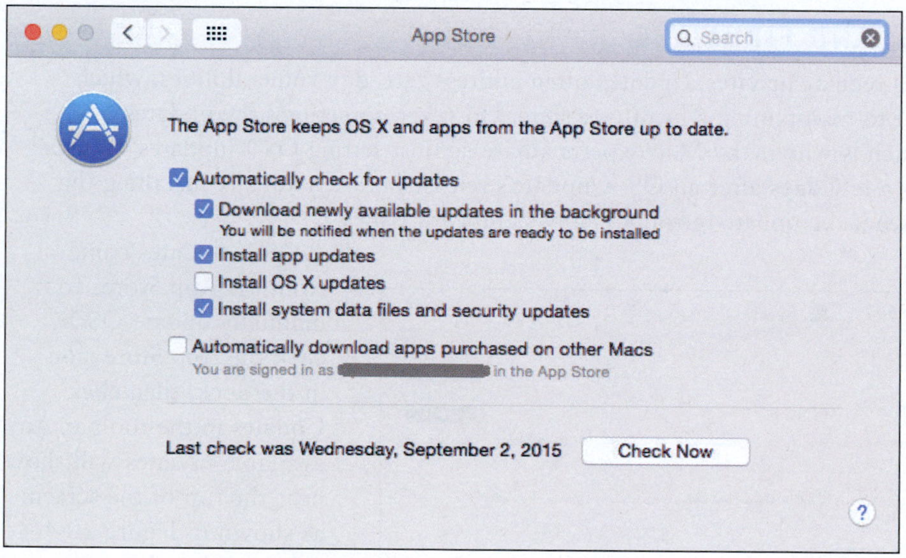

Source: Apple Inc.

Figure 20-47 Click Check Now to check for requested updates

Usually any needed firmware updates are included in the OS X update. Occasionally, however, Apple has released a firmware update as a stand-alone installer. You can find a list of available firmware updates in the Apple Knowledge Base Article at *support.apple.com/en-us/HT201518*.

To determine whether a Mac computer needs a firmware update, first check the current firmware version on the computer. This and a great deal more information is available in the System Information app. Open **Finder**, navigate to the **Utilities** folder, and double-click **System Information**. In the System Information window (see Figure 20-48), select Hardware in the sidebar and look under Hardware Overview for the *Model Identifier*, *Boot ROM Version*, and *SMC Version (system)*, as labeled in Figure 20-48. Compare the information in the System Information window with the information for the latest firmware update available on the *support.apple.com* website. Install a firmware update only if the version listed on Apple's website is newer than what is currently installed on the computer.

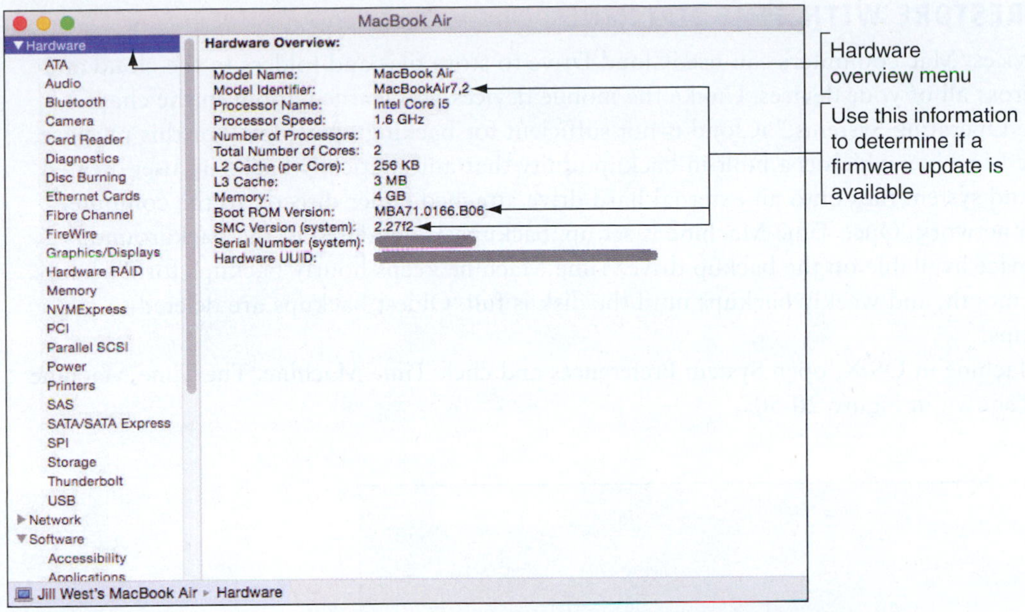

Source: Apple Inc.

Figure 20-48 The System Information window gives detailed information about the computer

> **Notes** The System Information app can also be opened from the Apple menu. Click the Apple icon, then click **About This Mac**, which gives an overview of the computer's system information, as shown in Figure 20-49. Then click **System Report** to open the System Information window that you saw in Figure 20-48.

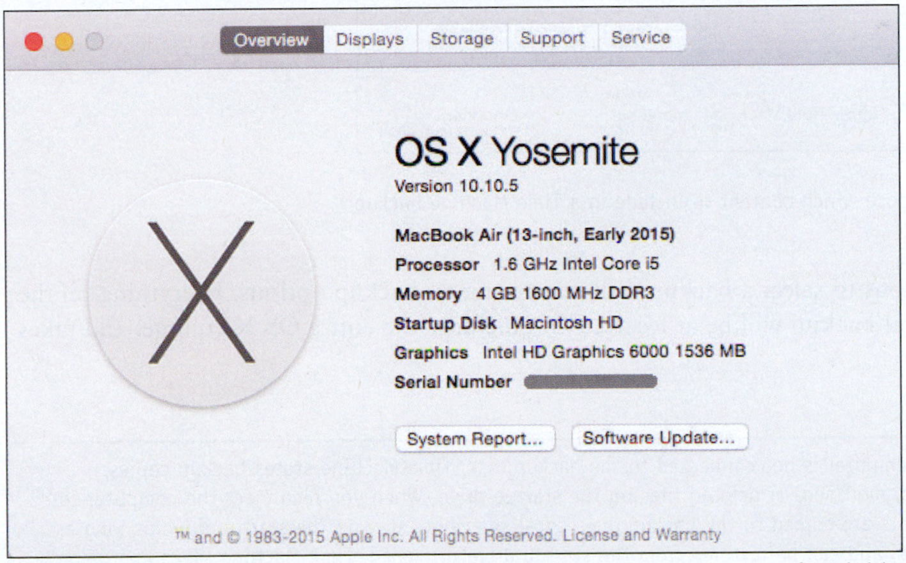

Source: Apple Inc.

Figure 20-49 Click System Report to go to the System Information window for more detailed information

> **Notes** Many experts believe that antivirus/anti-malware software is not required on a Mac computer. Whether this is true or not is still hotly debated. If you do choose to use anti-malware, however, be sure to keep it updated. One example of anti-malware for a Mac is AdwareMedic (*adwaremedic.com*) by Malwarebytes, which works well to remove adware that has infected a system.

20

BACK UP AND RESTORE WITH TIME MACHINE

Like iOS mobile devices, Mac computers can use iCloud Drive to store files and folders in the cloud and sync this content across all of your devices. Unlike the mobile devices you learned about in the chapter, "Supporting Mobile Operating Systems," iCloud is not sufficient for backing up a Mac. For this purpose, OS X includes Time Machine, which is a built-in backup utility that automatically backs up user-created data, applications, and system files onto an external hard drive attached either directly to the computer or through the local network. Once Time Machine is set up, backups are updated in the background. Depending on the space available on the backup drive, Time Machine keeps hourly backups for 24 hours, daily backups for a month, and weekly backups until the disk is full. Oldest backups are deleted to make space for new backups.

To set up Time Machine in OS X, open **System Preferences** and click **Time Machine**. The Time Machine window appears, as shown in Figure 20-50.

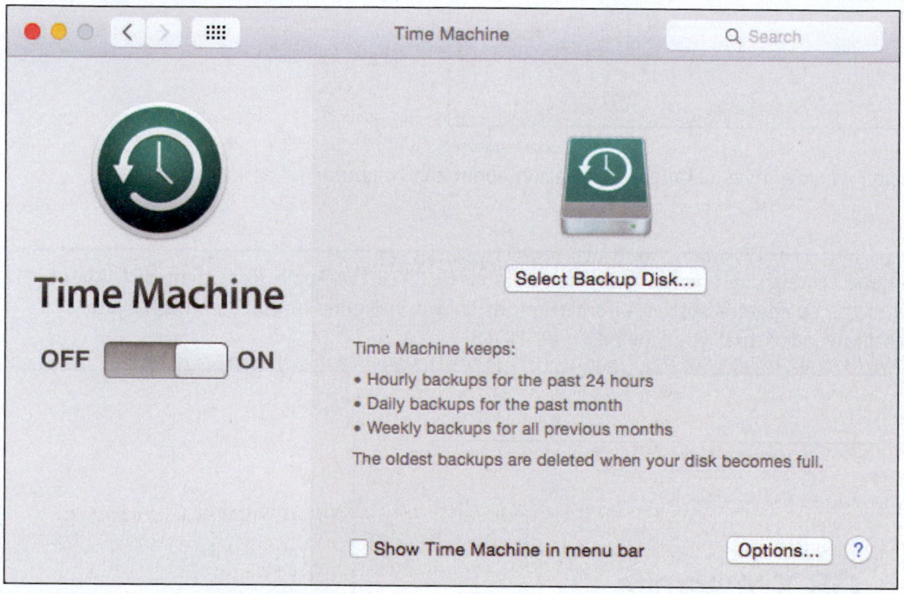

Source: Apple Inc.

Figure 20-50 Click Options to choose which content to include in a Time Machine backup

Follow the on-screen directions to select a backup disk and configure backup options. Everything on the disk will be erased. The original backup will be at least 20 GB, includes the entire OS X volume, and takes some time to complete.

Notes When your Mac OS X computer is not connected to the backup disk, Time Machine stores backup copies, called local snapshots, of created, modified, or deleted files on the startup drive. When you reconnect the computer to the backup disk, the local snapshots are copied to the backup disk. Local snapshots stay on the startup drive as long as they don't take up too much space, and can be restored from the startup drive if needed. Time Machine saves one daily snapshot each day and one weekly snapshot each week while the backup disk is disconnected.

To recover a file or folder from Time Machine, open **Finder**. In the **Applications** group, double-click **Time Machine**. The timeline and available backups in Finder appear (see Figure 20-51). Use the Finder window to locate the file or folder. Then go back though time to find the version of the file or folder you want to restore. To move through time, you can use the timeline on the right, the arrow buttons, or click a Finder window in the stack of available windows. Select the item and click **Restore**.

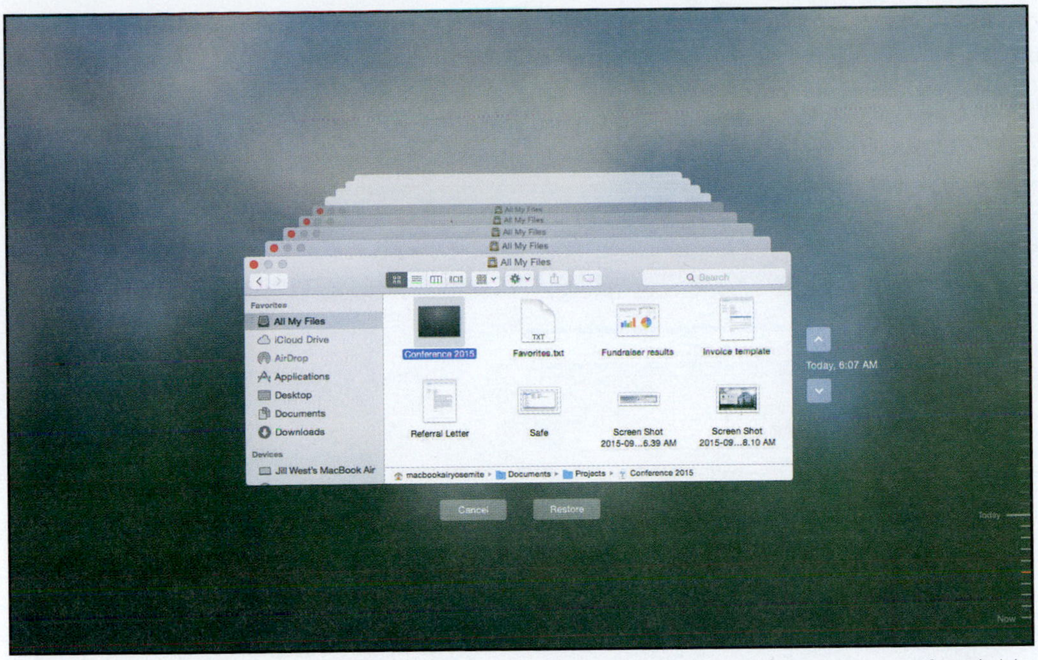

Source: Apple Inc.

Figure 20-51 Locate an item and then go back through time to find the version to restore

Later in this chapter, you learn how to use Time Machine to restore the entire OS X volume.

CLONE THE STARTUP DISK

The startup disk is the entire volume on which OS X is installed. In addition to a Time Machine backup of the entire startup disk, you can also clone the startup disk. The clone is a disk image and is stored in a DMG file.

> **Notes** A **DMG file** is a disk image file for a Mac and is similar to WIM or ISO files in Windows. In addition to storing clones, they're often used to hold app installers, as are EXE files in Windows.

To create a clone in OS X, follow these steps:

1. Boot into the Recovery System, which boots from a hidden volume on the startup disk. To do this, restart the computer and hold down **⌘ + r** until the Apple logo appears.
2. When the OS X Utilities window appears (see Figure 20-52), click **Disk Utility** and click **Continue**.

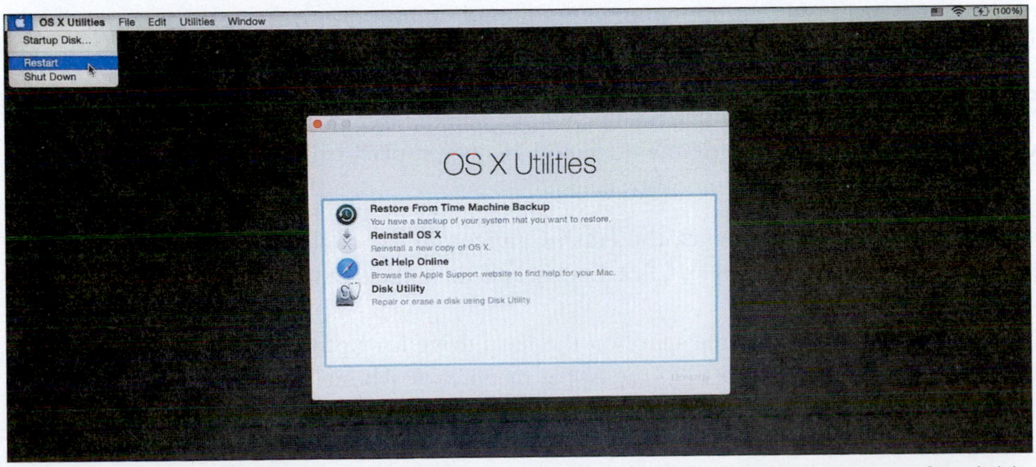

Source: Apple Inc.

Figure 20-52 Press **⌘ + r** during the boot to access the Recovery System and the OS X Utilities window

3. The Disk Utility window opens, as shown in Figure 20-53. In the sidebar, select the partition to be copied, and then click **New Image** at the top of the window. Give the image a name and select a location to save the DMG file, and then click **Save**.

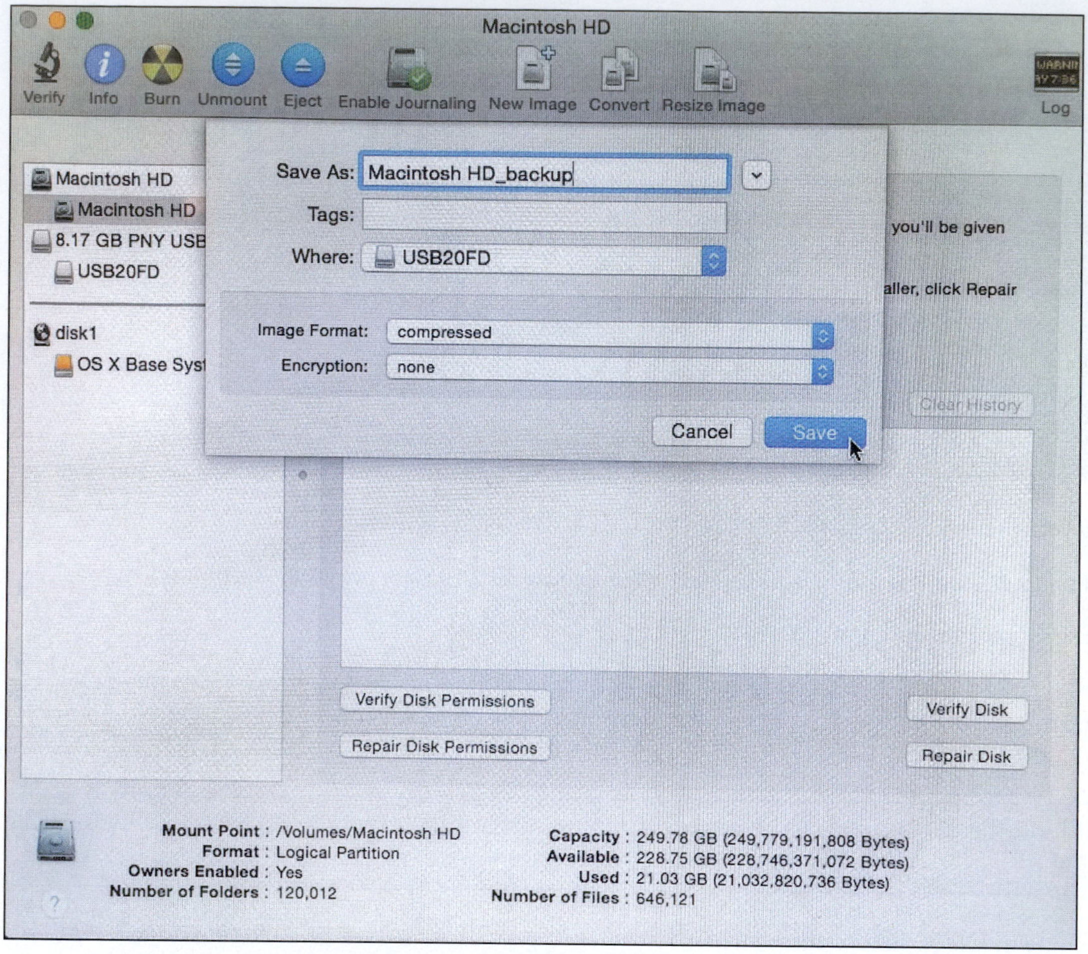

Source: Apple Inc.

Figure 20-53 When creating a clone, choose an encryption type to increase the security of the disk image

4. To exit the Recovery System and return to a normal boot, click **Restart** on the Apple menu.

Later in this chapter, you learn how to use a clone to restore the OS X volume.

DRIVE MAINTENANCE TOOLS

Hard drives in Mac computers require very little maintenance. However, performing a few simple tasks on a regular basis can help keep things running smoothly:

- *Empty the trash.* To empty the Trash Can, click the Trash Can icon in the dock. Trash Can contents appear in a Finder window (see Figure 20-54). Click **Empty** and then click **Empty Trash** in the warning box. Items are permanently deleted.
- *Free up space.* Maintain at least 15–20% free space on the hard drive for optimal performance. To see how much free space is available on the drive, in the Apple menu click **About This Mac**, and then click the **Storage** tab, as shown in Figure 20-55.

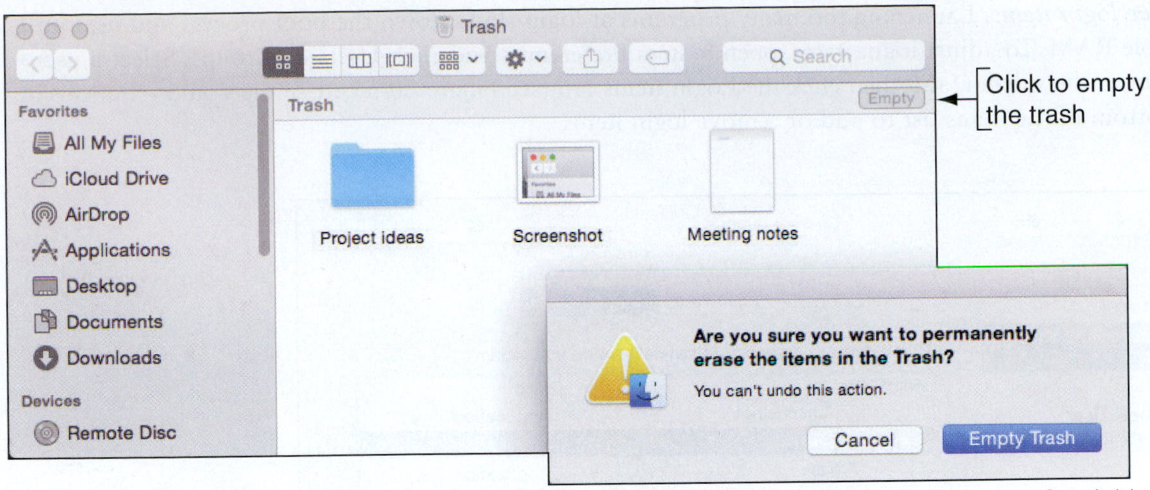

Source: Apple Inc.

Figure 20-54 Check the contents of the Trash Can before emptying it

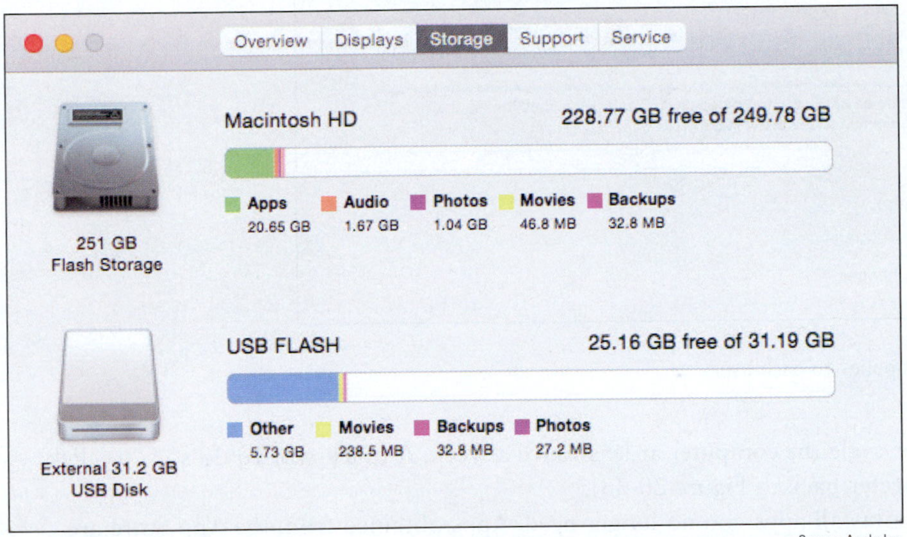

Source: Apple Inc.

Figure 20-55 Maintain at least 15% free space on the hard drive

- *Install updates.* Regularly check for and install OS X and app updates, which you learned how to do earlier in this chapter.
- *Verify no startup items.* Programs that automatically launch at startup are called **startup items** and programs that automatically launch after a user logs in are called **login items**. Apple discourages the use of startup items because they slow down the startup process and items in the startup folder might be malware. You can verify the system doesn't have startup items by looking in two directories that can contain startup items: /Library/StartupItems and /System/Library/StartupItems. Open Terminal and navigate to these directories, which you should find empty (see Figure 20-56).

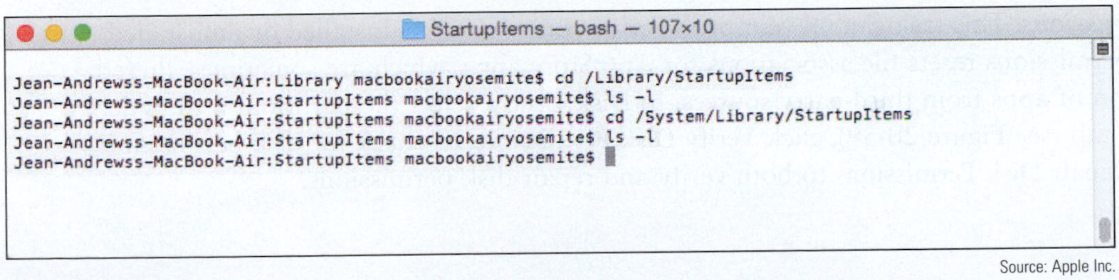

Source: Apple Inc.

Figure 20-56 Two directories can contain startup items and both directories are empty

- *Remove login items.* Launching too many programs at login slows down the boot process and uses up valuable RAM. To adjust login items, open **System Preferences** and click **Users & Groups**. Select a user account in the sidebar, and then click the **Login Items** tab (see Figure 20-57). Use the + and – buttons at the bottom of the items list to add or remove login items.

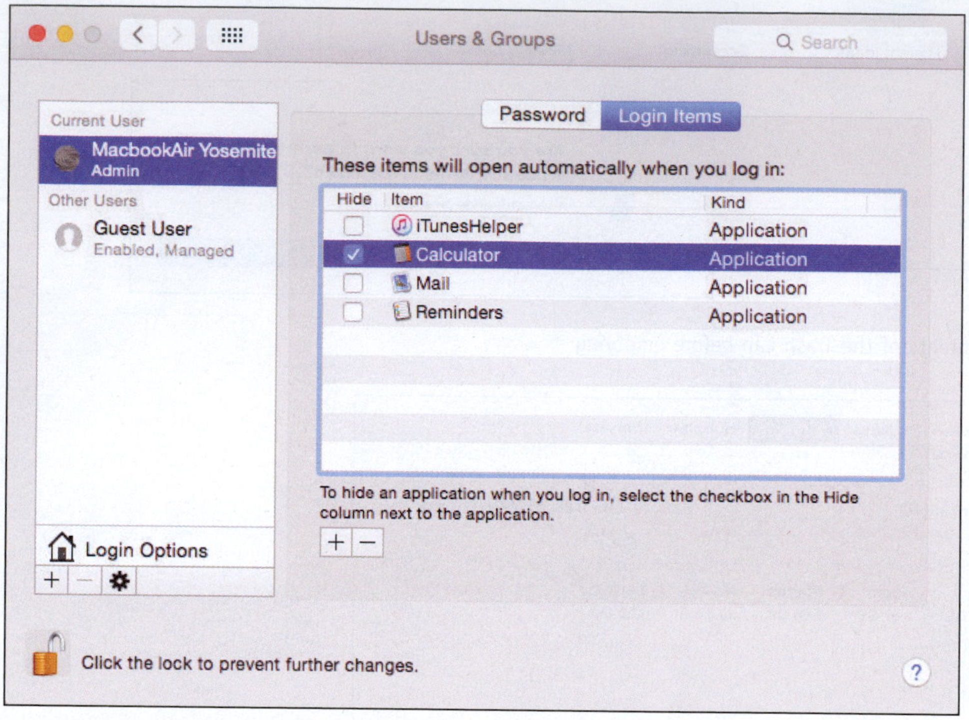

Source: Apple Inc.

Figure 20-57 List of login items applies to each user

- *Restart the computer.* Power cycle the computer at least once a week. A quick way to do so is to click **Restart** in the Apple menu (refer back to Figure 20-33).
- *Uninstall unneeded apps.* Uninstall apps you no longer need. Apps obtained from the App Store are uninstalled from Launchpad. For apps installed from other sources besides the App Store, locate the app in Finder and drag the app to the Trash Can. Empty the trash to complete the uninstallation.

REPAIRS USING THE DISK UTILITY APP

The Disk Utility app can be used to repair disk permissions and to repair hard drive corruptions. To open Disk Utility, open **Finder** and navigate to the **Utilities** folder. Double-click **Disk Utility**. The sidebar of the Disk Utility window (see Figure 20-58) shows attached drives with partitions listed below each drive. In Figure 20-58, the hard drive has a single partition, which can be changed on the Partition tab, and a USB flash drive is connected to the computer. Two disk maintenance tasks you can perform from Disk Utility include the following:

- *Repair disk permissions.* This task can prevent problems if you've recently installed or uninstalled apps. Repairing disk permissions resets file associations for App Store apps, which are sometimes altered during installation of apps from third-party sources. In Disk Utility, select the partition in the sidebar. On the **First Aid** tab (see Figure 20-59), click **Verify Disk Permissions** to check for disk permissions issues, or click **Repair Disk Permissions** to both verify and repair disk permissions.

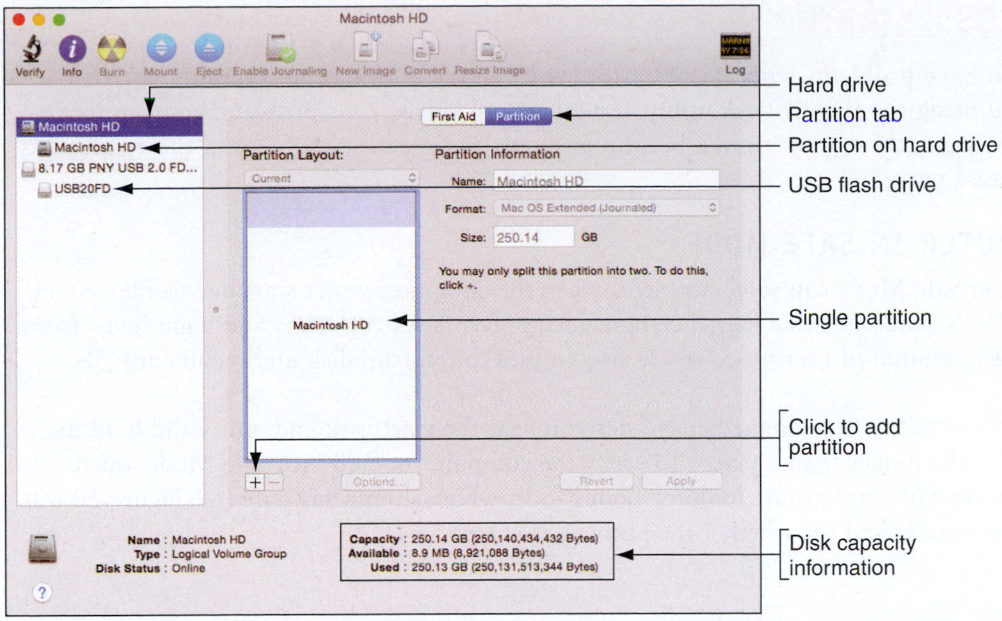

Source: Apple Inc.

Figure 20-58 Manage partitions from the Disk Utility app

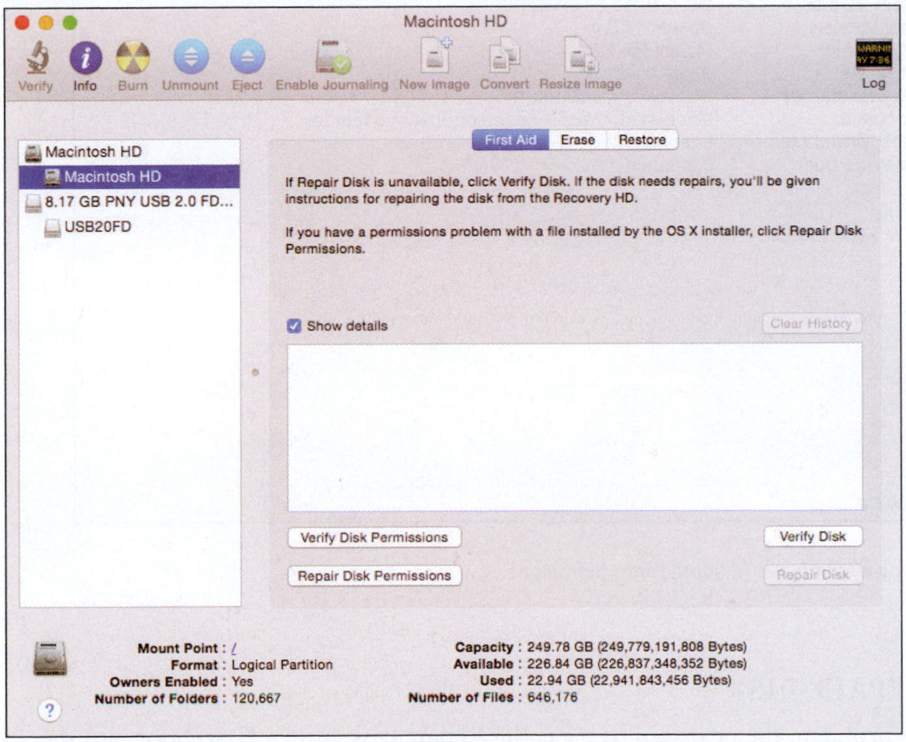

Source: Apple Inc.

Figure 20-59 The Erase and Restore tabs provide additional options for working with a disk

20

- ***Verify disk.*** Repair Disk checks the hard drive for minor problems, such as corrupted directory entries, and repairs them if necessary. This is especially important to perform if the system has recently frozen or experienced a sudden power loss. Notice in Figure 20-59 that Verify Disk is available, but Repair Disk is grayed out. This is because the disk cannot be repaired if the system is currently booted from that disk. Click **Verify Disk**. If the process finds errors, it will tell you to repair the disk using the Recovery System.

TROUBLESHOOT OS X STARTUP

A+
220-902
1.2, 2.1,
4.1

When you have problems with OS X startup, you can try booting the computer in Safe Mode and using the Repair Disk utility. If neither tool solves your problem, you can move on to recovering the system from a backup or clone or reinstalling OS X. All these solutions are discussed next.

START THE COMPUTER IN SAFE MODE

Starting the computer in Safe Mode can solve problems when the computer won't start due to file system errors. Safe Mode in OS X loads essential kernel components, prevents startup items and login items from launching, and loads a minimum of user processes. It also verifies the startup disk and repairs any file system errors it finds.

To boot the computer in Safe Mode, immediately after you hear the startup sound, press and hold the **shift** key. The boot will take longer than normal. To verify the computer booted into Safe Mode, open **System Information**. In the Software group, look for Boot Mode, which should say Safe (see Figure 20-60). Restart the computer normally and see whether the problem is solved.

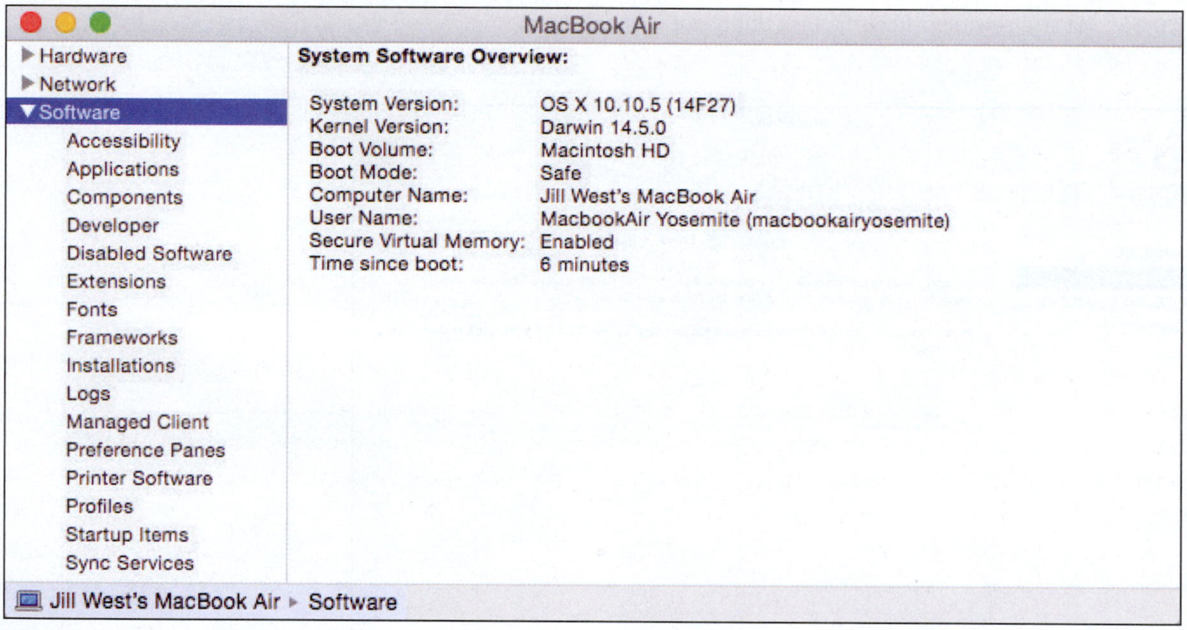

Source: Apple Inc.

Figure 20-60 Boot Mode indicates the computer is booted into Safe Mode

OS X RECOVERY AND REPAIR DISK

If Safe Mode didn't solve your problem, the next tool to try is the Repair Disk utility. First, boot into the Recovery System, then open **Disk Utility**. On the First Aid tab, click **Repair Disk** (see Figure 20-61), then restart into normal mode.

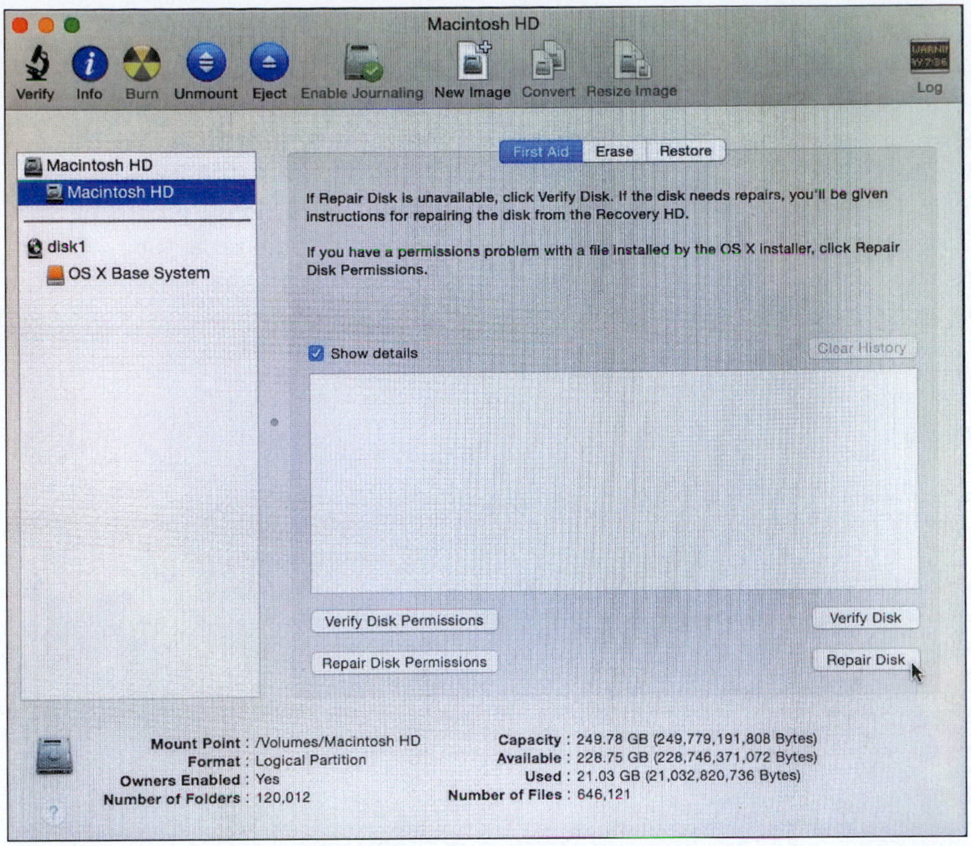

Source: Apple Inc.

Figure 20-61 Repair Disk repairs a corrupted OS X installation

RECOVERY FROM A TIME MACHINE BACKUP

If you have made a Time Machine backup of your system, you can use it to recover the startup disk. If the hard drive has failed, replace the hard drive and then connect your Time Machine backup device, for example, connect an external hard drive. Boot into the Recovery System. On the OS X Utilities window (refer back to Figure 20-52), select **Restore From a Time Machine Backup** and click **Continue**. Point to the backup device and follow directions on screen.

OS X RECOVERY WITH A CLONE OR THE INTERNET

You can also boot the system from a previously made clone. Any drive holding a clone DMG file can be used as a startup disk. Connect the drive to the computer, press and hold the **option** key during boot, and then select the drive that holds the clone DMG file to run the boot from that drive.

It's also possible to store the clone DMG file on a server on the network and, using a technology called NetBoot, the clone can be used to boot a Mac on the network or deploy OS X to multiple machines.

The image recovery process can also be performed over the Internet. If the Mac computer doesn't find a recovery image and is connected to the Internet, it will download and install OS X from the Apple website. However, obviously this will not be a customized image with your apps and settings already configured. You'll be starting from scratch. The version of OS X that came originally installed on your Mac will be installed.

20

Notes Many of these same steps can also help when troubleshooting kernel panics. A kernel panic is similar to a BSOD in Windows. It might be caused by something simple, like a crashed app or a network communication issue, or it might result from a corrupted OS X installation. OS X restarts automatically when experiencing a kernel panic. If the kernel panic continues to prompt restarts, OS X will stop trying after five attempts and shut down the computer.

BOOT CAMP

A+ 220-902 2.1

One more hard drive option you should be aware of is made possible by Boot Camp, a utility in OS X that allows you to install and run Windows on a Mac computer. You saw earlier in Figure 20-58 where the Macintosh HD in the figure held one partition. Boot Camp can split the partition and install Windows in the new partition for a dual boot. Access the Boot Camp Assistant through the Utilities folder; Figure 20-62 shows the first screen with options in the process of installing Windows on a Mac. After Windows is installed, you can choose which OS to use as your default for the computer, or press and hold the **option** key when starting the computer to reach the Startup Manager, which lets you choose from the installed operating systems.

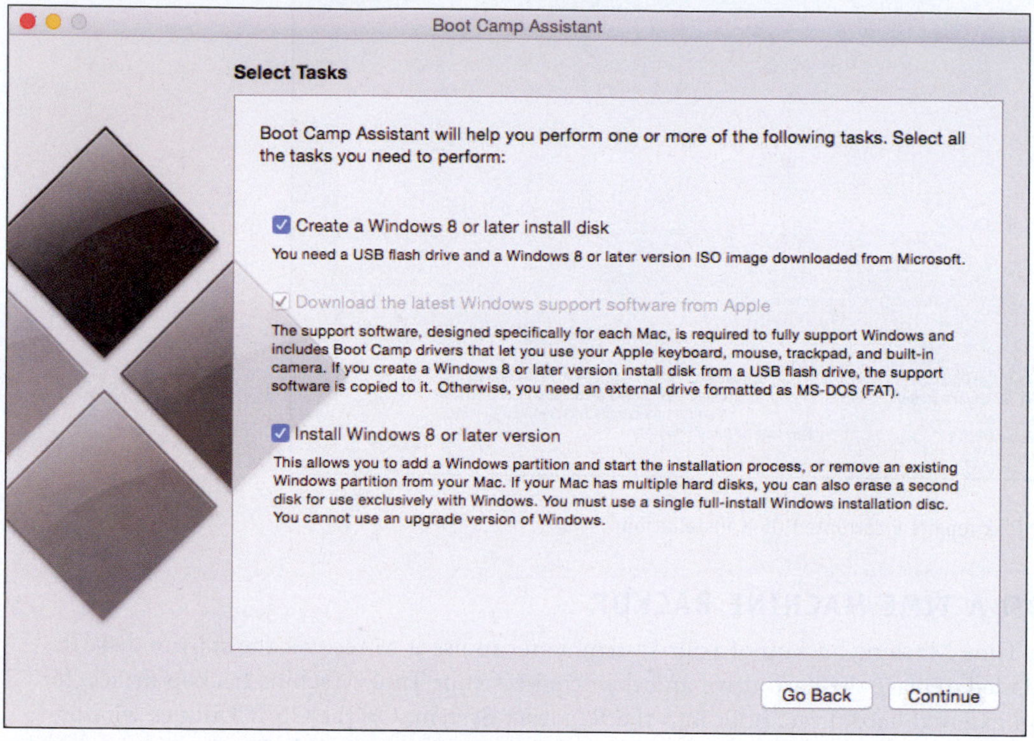

Source: Apple Inc.

Figure 20-62 Manage Windows installations from Boot Camp Assistant

>> CHAPTER SUMMARY

Virtualization Basics

- Server-side virtualization happens on the server, and client-side virtualization happens on the client machine.
- Three ways to implement client-side virtualization include presentation virtualization, application virtualization, and client-side desktop virtualization.
- Virtualization is done by creating multiple virtual machines on a physical machine using a hypervisor.
- A Type 1 hypervisor installs before any OS is installed and is called a bare-metal hypervisor. A Type 2 hypervisor is an application that installs in an OS. A Type 1 hypervisor is faster and more secure than a Type 2 hypervisor.

Linux Operating System

- Distributions of Linux provide a shell prompt in the Linux terminal and might also provide a desktop with a GUI. The default command-line shell for Linux is the Bash shell.

- The root account in Linux has access to all features of the OS. When logged in to the root account, the user is called the superuser.
- Important Linux commands include ls, grep, cd, shutdown, pwd, passwd, mv, cp, rm, mkdir, chmod, iwconfig, ifconfig, ps, q, su, sudo, apt-get, vi, and dd.
- A missing GRUB sometimes happens after installing Windows in a dual boot when Linux has been previously installed.
- Linux can access NTFS volumes created by Windows, but Windows cannot access ext4 volumes created by Linux unless third-party software is installed.

Mac OS X Operating System

- OS X is the latest version of the proprietary operating system available only for Macintosh computers by Apple Inc. Like Linux, OS X is built on a UNIX foundation.
- The dock appears at the bottom of the desktop. The icons in the dock that represent open applications have a small, black circle underneath them.
- Spotlight is Mac's search app, and can be configured to search the local computer, Wikipedia, iTunes, the Maps app, the web, and more.
- For IT technicians, the most important tools in System Preferences are accessed through Time Machine, Users & Groups, and Sharing. Screen Sharing, one of the Sharing tools, works similarly to Remote Assistance in Windows.
- OS X updates often address zero-day vulnerabilities, which makes these updates important to maintaining a healthy system.
- Time Machine is a built-in backup utility that automatically backs up user-created data, applications, and system files onto an external hard drive attached either directly to the computer or through the local network.
- Disk Utility can be used to repair disk permissions and to repair hard drive corruptions.
- A kernel panic is similar to a BSOD in Windows. It might be caused by something simple, like a crashed app or a network communication issue, or it might result from a corrupted OS X installation.
- Boot Camp is an OS X utility that allows you to install Windows on a Mac computer in a dual boot with OS X.

>> KEY TERMS

For explanations of key terms, see the Glossary for this text.

Apple menu
application virtualization
Application Virtualization (App-V)
apt-get
Bash shell
Boot Camp
chmod
chown
client-side desktop virtualization
client-side virtualization
clone
Dashboard
dd
DMG file
dock
dumb terminal
dump
emulator
ext3
ext4
fat client
Finder
force quit
gestures
grep
GRUB (GRand Unified Bootloader)
hardware-assisted virtualization (HAV)
hypervisor
ifconfig
iwconfig
kernel panic
Keychain
Launchpad
LILO (LInux boot LOader)
Linux
live CD
local snapshot
login item
Mission Control
multiple desktops
NetBoot
OS X
presentation virtualization
Recovery System
Remote Disc
root account
Screen Sharing
secondary click
server-side virtualization
shell prompt
Space
Spotlight
startup disk
startup item

su
sudo
superuser
System Preferences
terminal
thick client
thin client
Time Machine
Type 1 hypervisor
Type 2 hypervisor
ultra-thin client
vi editor
Virtual Desktop Infrastructure (VDI)
virtual machine manager (VMM)
virtualization
zero client

>> REVIEWING THE BASICS

1. Which type of client-side virtualization creates a virtual environment in memory for an application to run on a client machine?
2. In Question 1, what Microsoft software can be used to create this environment?
3. List two types of hypervisors and describe their fundamental differences.
4. What are the four main ways to secure a VM?
5. What is the Linux command to find out which shell you are using?
6. What is the name of the current Linux boot loader that is used to manage a dual boot?
7. What is the full path to the home directory of the user account lucio in Linux?
8. In which directory are you likely to find logs created by applications running in Linux?
9. In Linux, when logged in as a normal user with root privileges, which command must precede the apt-get command in the command line in order to install a program?
10. Which file system does Linux currently use for the volume on which Linux is installed?
11. Which Linux file system was the first to implement journaling?
12. What symbol displays in the shell prompt to indicate the logged-in user is root in Linux?
13. What is the Linux vi editor command to save your changes and exit the editor?
14. Why is the scroll bar typically hidden from view in OS X?
15. Which app manages multiple desktop screens in OS X?
16. Which app provides tools for customizing the Mac interface?
17. List the steps to open Terminal in OS X.
18. How can you install printer, scanner, and graphics driver updates in OS X?
19. How often does Time Machine create new backups, and how long are these backups kept?
20. What file format is used for OS X disk images?

>> THINKING CRITICALLY

1. You are managing an FTP server installed in Ubuntu Server. The server has created a very large log file, vsftpd.log. Which command is appropriate to search the log file for activity of the user charlie?
   a. `sudo cat /var/log/vsftpd.log`
   b. `grep "charlie" /var/log/vsftpd.log`
   c. `sudo grep "charlie" /var/log/vsftpd.log`
   d. `cat /var/log/vsftpd.log`

2. You need to use Repair Disk to repair the hard drive of a Mac computer. How should you reboot the computer?
   a. Open the Apple menu, then hold the shift key while clicking Restart.
   b. Reboot the computer. Press and hold the ? + r keys during boot.
   c. Reboot the computer. Immediately after you hear the startup sound, press and hold the shift key.
   d. Reboot the computer. Press and hold the option key during boot.
3. Explain why most Linux commands work about the same on a Mac computer as they do on a Linux system. Research online and find three examples of Linux commands other than the ones presented in this chapter that also work in OS X Yosemite.

>> REAL PROBLEMS, REAL SOLUTIONS

REAL PROBLEM 20-1 Using the Google Cloud Platform to Create a Ubuntu VM

Recall that Google Cloud Platform is an example of PaaS that you can use to learn a new operating system or develop apps. To use the service to create an Ubuntu VM, do the following:

1. Go to **cloud.google.com** and click **Free Trial**. You will need to sign in using a Google account. If you don't have an account, you can create one with any valid email address.
2. In the Developers Console, create a new project. Then drill down into **Compute**, **Compute Engine**, and **VM instances**. Create a VM instance with Ubuntu 15.04 installed as the OS. Then wait several minutes for Google to create the instance.
3. Click the VM instances listed in your project. Buttons appear at the top of the window to manage the instance. Also note the External IP assigned to the VM instance. Click **SSH** and remote in to your VM using the SSH utility. The VM opens in a separate window where you can use Ubuntu commands (see Figure 20-63).

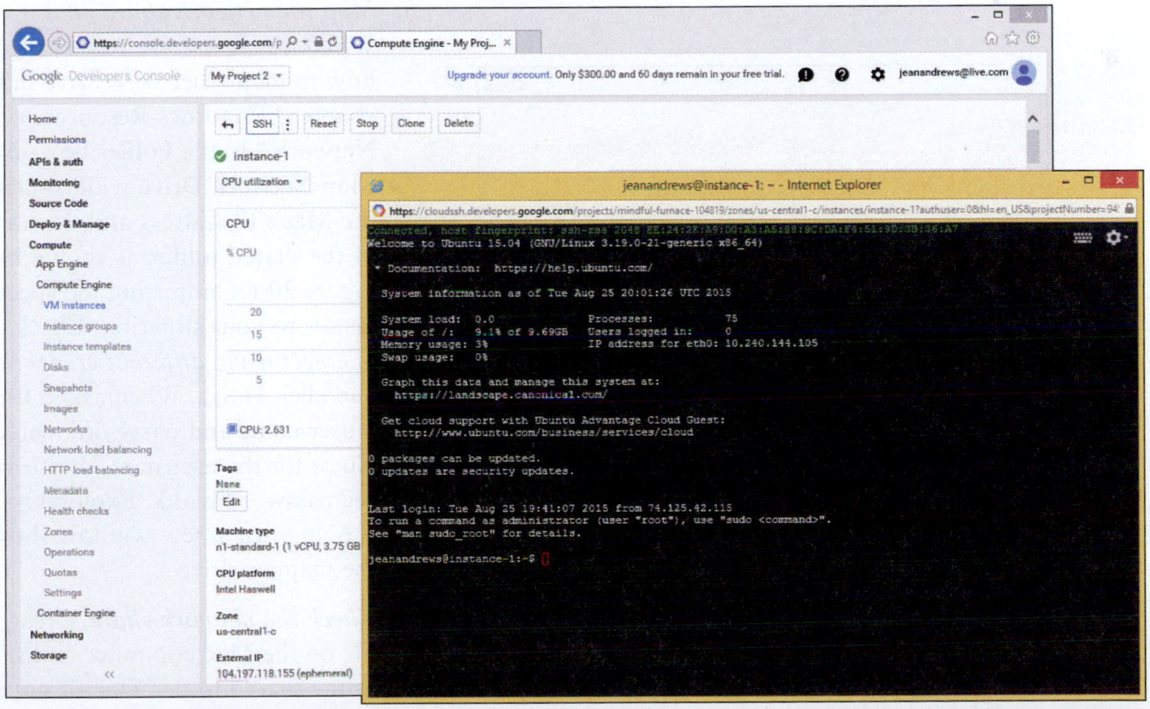

Source: Google and Canonical Ltd.

Figure 20-63 Google Cloud Platform serves up an instance of Ubuntu VM

20

Notes When you set up your Google Cloud account, your credit card information was required. If you're now done with your Google Cloud 60-day free trial, close your billing account so that your credit card will not be accidentally charged at the end of your free trial period. To do that, in the Developers Console, click the **Settings** cog icon and click **Billing**. Then click **Close billing account**.

REAL PROBLEM 20-2 Sharing a Folder on the Network from a Mac Computer and Mapping the Drive on a Windows Computer

In the chapter, "Windows Resources on a Network," you shared a folder on the network and mapped a network drive. These tasks can also be done in OS X, which makes it easier to share files between computers of various operating systems. Complete the following steps to set up a network share from a Mac computer:

1. *Create a folder to share.* Use Finder to create a subfolder in the Documents folder, and name the new folder **MeetingMinutes**.
2. *Set sharing options.* Open **System Preferences** and click **Sharing**. Select **File Sharing** in the sidebar and make sure it's turned on. Click the **Options** button and make sure that *Share files and folders using SMB* is checked. Under Windows File Sharing, check the box to turn on file sharing with Windows computers. Enter the Mac's user account password if necessary. Click **Done**.
3. *Share the folder.* Under Shared Folders, click the **+** button. Double-click the **MeetingMinutes** folder. Under Users, make sure the **Everyone** group is set to **Read Only**. Return to the System Preferences main window.
4. *Enable shared folders for the guest account.* Click **Users & Groups**. Click the lock icon in the lower-left corner of the window so you can make changes to user settings, and sign in. Click the **Guest User** account in the sidebar. Check *Allow guest users to connect to shared folders* and return to the main System Preferences window.
5. *Set a static IP address.* Click **Network**, and then click **Advanced**. Click the **TCP/IP** tab. Configure the IPv4 address with a manual address as directed by your instructor. Click **OK**.
6. *Map the network share on a Windows computer.* You learned how to map a network drive in the chapter, "Windows Resources on a Network." In the Folder box on the Map Network Drive window, enter the Mac's IP address and the name of the shared folder, as shown in Figure 20-64, adjusting the specific details to your situation. Check *Connect using different credentials*, and click **Finish**. When asked for a user name and password, enter **Guest** for the user name and leave the password blank. Explorer should open a new window showing the mapped drive.
7. *Check the network share.* Create a file on the Mac computer and save it to the shared folder. Does it appear in the mapped network drive on the

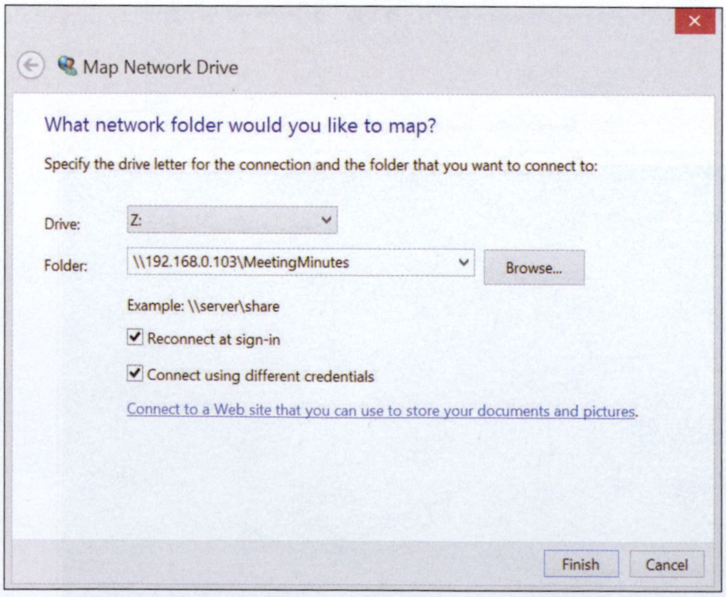

Figure 20-64 Folder information includes the IP address of the remote computer and folder name

Windows computer? If not, troubleshoot and fix the problem. Create a file on the Windows computer and save it to the shared folder. Does the file appear in the shared folder on the Mac computer? What do you think went wrong? What setting do you need to change so you can add files to the shared folder from the Windows computer? Did it work? If not, troubleshoot and fix the problem.

8. ***Change share permissions.*** Currently the folder is shared with anyone on the network. This is fine in certain situations, but it's not a best practice for most corporate networks. What changes can you make to restrict the shared folder to a single user? To a group of users?

9. ***Create a new user and a new group.*** List the steps to create a new user and a new user group on the Mac computer. What types of user accounts are available? What did you name the new user account and the new user group? Add both the new user and your own user account to the new group. Change the share settings on the MeetingMinutes folder so that the new user group has read and write privileges, and the Everyone group has Read Only privileges.

10. ***Take a screen shot and share it.*** With the Sharing window showing these new settings, take a screen shot. To do this, press **⌘ + shift + 4**, then press the **spacebar**. Click the **Sharing** window to capture a screen shot of the window. Drag the screen shot file from the desktop to the shared folder. Email this screen shot to your instructor.

APPENDIX A

Safety Procedures and Environmental Concerns

This appendix covers how to stay safe and protect the equipment and the environment as you perform the duties of an IT support technician. We begin by understanding the properties and dangers of electricity.

MEASURES AND PROPERTIES OF ELECTRICITY

A+
220-902
5.1, 5.2

In our modern world, we take electricity for granted, and we miss it terribly when it's cut off. Nearly everyone depends on it, but few really understand it. A successful hardware technician is not one who tends to encounter failed processors, fried motherboards, smoking monitors, or frizzed hair. To avoid these excitements, you need to understand how to measure electricity and how to protect computer equipment from its damaging power.

Let's start with the basics. To most people, volts, ohms, joules, watts, and amps are vague terms that simply mean electricity. All these terms can be used to measure some characteristic of electricity, as listed in Table A-1.

Unit	Definition	Computer Example
Volt (for example, 115 V)	A measure of electrical force measured in **volts**. The symbol for volts is V.	A power supply steps down the voltage from the 115 V house current to 3.3, 5, and 12 V that computer components can use.
Amp or ampere (for example, 1.5 A)	An **amp** is a measure of electrical current. The symbol for amps is A.	An LCD monitor requires about 5 A to operate. A small laser printer uses about 2 A. An optical drive uses about 1 A.
Ohm (for example, 20 Ω)	An **ohm** is a measure of resistance to electricity. The symbol for ohm is Ω.	Current can flow in typical computer cables and wires with a resistance of near zero Ω (ohm).
Joule (for example, 500 J)	A measure of work or energy. One **joule** (pronounced "jewel") is the work required to push an electrical current of 1 A through a resistance of 1 Ω. The symbol for joule is J.	A **surge suppressor** (see Figure A-1) is rated in joules—the higher the better. The rating determines how much work it can expend before it can no longer protect the circuit from a power surge.
Watt (for example, 20 W)	A measure of electrical power. One **watt** is one joule per second and measures the total electrical power needed to operate a device. Watts can be calculated by multiplying volts by amps. The symbol for watts is W.	The power consumption of an LCD computer monitor is rated at about 14 W. A DVD burner uses about 25 W when burning a DVD.

Table A-1 Measures of electricity

Figure A-1 A surge suppressor protects electrical equipment from power surges and is rated in joules

Notes To learn more about how volts, amps, ohms, joules, and watts measure the properties of electricity, see the content "Electricity and Multimeters" in the online content that accompanies this text at *cengagebrain.com*. To find out how to access this content, see the Preface to this text.

Now let's look at how electricity gets from one place to another and how it is used in house circuits and computers.

AC AND DC

A+ 220-902 5.1, 5.2

Electricity can be either AC, alternating current, or DC, direct current. Alternating current (AC) goes back and forth, or oscillates, rather than traveling in only one direction. House current in the United States is AC and oscillates 60 times in one second (60 hertz). Voltage in the system is constantly alternating from positive to negative, which causes the electricity to flow first in one direction and then in the other. Voltage alternates from +115 V to 115 V. AC is the most economical way to transmit electricity to our homes and workplaces. By decreasing current and increasing voltage, we can force alternating current to travel great distances. When alternating current reaches its destination, it is made more suitable for driving our electrical devices by decreasing voltage and increasing current.

Direct current (DC) travels in only one direction and is the type of current that most electronic devices require, including computers. A rectifier is a device that converts AC to DC, and an inverter is a device that converts DC to AC. A transformer is a device that changes the ratio of voltage to current. The power supply used in computers is both a rectifier and a transformer.

Large transformers reduce the high voltage on power lines coming to your neighborhood to a lower voltage before the current enters your home. The transformer does not change the amount of power in this closed system; if it decreases voltage, it increases current. The overall power stays constant, but the ratio of voltage to current changes, as illustrated in Figure A-2.

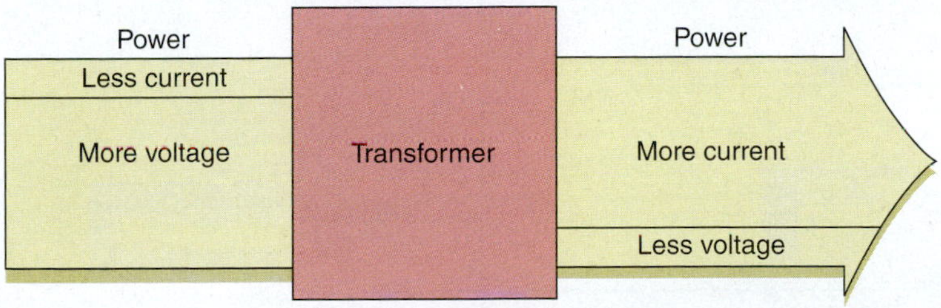

Figure A-2 A transformer keeps power constant but changes the ratio of current to voltage

Direct current flows in only one direction. Think of electrical current like a current of water that flows from a state of high pressure to a state of low pressure or rest. Electrical current flows from a high-pressure state (called hot) to a state of rest (called ground or neutral). For a power supply, a power line may be either +5 or -5 volts in one circuit, or +12 or -12 volts in another circuit. The positive or negative value is determined by how the circuit is oriented, either on one side of the power output or the other. Several circuits coming from the power supply accommodate different devices with different power requirements.

A

HOT, NEUTRAL, AND GROUND

A+ 220-902 5.1, 5.2

AC travels on a hot line from the power station to a building and returns to the power station on a neutral line. When the two lines reach the building and enter an electrical device, such as a lamp, the device controls the flow of electricity between the hot and neutral lines. If an easier path (one with less resistance) is available, the electricity follows that path. This can cause a short, a sudden increase in flow that can also create a sudden increase in temperature—enough to start a fire and injure both people and equipment. Never put yourself in a position where you are the path of least resistance between the hot line and ground!

Caution It's very important that PC components be properly grounded. Never connect a PC to an outlet or use an extension cord that doesn't have the third ground plug. The third line can prevent a short from causing extreme damage. In addition, the bond between the neutral and ground helps eliminate electrical noise (stray electrical signals) within the PC that is sometimes caused by other electrical equipment sitting very close to the computer.

To prevent uncontrolled electricity in a short, the neutral line is grounded. Grounding a line means that the line is connected directly to the earth, so that, in the event of a short, the electricity flows into the earth and not back to the power station. Grounding serves as an escape route for out-of-control electricity because the earth is always capable of accepting a flow of current. With computers, a surge suppressor can be used to protect a computer and its components against power surges.

Caution Beware of the different uses of black wire. In desktop computers and in DC circuits, black is used for ground, but in home wiring and in AC circuits, black is used for hot!

The neutral line to your house is grounded many times along its way (in fact, at each electrical pole) and is also grounded at the breaker box where the electricity enters your house. You can look at a three-prong plug and see the three lines: hot, neutral, and ground (see Figure A-3).

Figure A-3 A polarized plug showing hot and neutral, and a three-prong plug showing hot, neutral, and ground

Notes House AC voltage in the United States is about 110–120 V, but know that in other countries, this is not always the case. In many other countries, the standard is 220 V. Outlet styles also vary from one country to the next.

Now that you know about electricity, let's turn our attention to protecting yourself against the dangers of electricity and other factors that might harm you as you work around computers.

PROTECTING YOURSELF

A+
220-902
5.1, 5.2

To protect yourself against electrical shock, when working with any electrical device, including computers, printers, scanners, and network devices, disconnect the power if you notice a dangerous situation that might lead to electrical shock or fire. When you disconnect the power, do so by pulling on the plug at the AC outlet. To protect the power cord, don't pull on the cord itself. Also, don't just turn off the on/off switch on the device; you need to actually disconnect the power. Note that any of the following can indicate a potential danger:

- The power cord is frayed or otherwise damaged in any way.
- Water or other liquid is on the floor around the device or spilled on it.
- The device has been exposed to excess moisture.
- The device has been dropped or you notice physical damage.
- You smell a strong electronics odor.
- The power supply or fans are making a whining noise.
- You notice smoke coming from the computer case or the case feels unusually warm.

SAFELY WORK INSIDE COMPUTERS, PRINTERS, AND OTHER ELECTRICAL DEVICES

A+
220-902
5.1, 5.2

To personally stay safe, always do the following, before working inside computers, printers, and other electrical devices:

- ***Remove jewelry.*** Remove your jewelry that might come in contact with components. Jewelry is made of metal and might conduct electricity if it touches a component. It can also get caught in cables and cords inside computer cases.
- ***Power down the system and unplug it.*** For a computer, unplug the power, monitor, mouse, and keyboard cables, and any other peripherals or cables attached and move them out of your way.
- ***For a computer, press and hold down the power button for a moment.*** After you unplug the computer, press the power button for about three seconds to completely drain the power supply. Sometimes when you do so, you'll hear the fans quickly start and go off as residual power is drained. Only then is it safe to work inside the case.

ELECTRICAL FIRE SAFETY

A+
220-902
5.1

Never use water to put out a fire fueled by electricity because water is a conductor and you might get a severe electrical shock. A computer lab needs a fire extinguisher that is rated to put out electrical fires. Fire extinguishers are rated by the type of fires they put out:

- Class A extinguishers can use water to put out fires caused by wood, paper, and other combustibles.
- Class B extinguishers can put out fires caused by liquids such as gasoline, kerosene, and oil.
- Class C fire extinguishers use nonconductive chemicals to put out a fire caused by electricity. See Figure A-4.

A

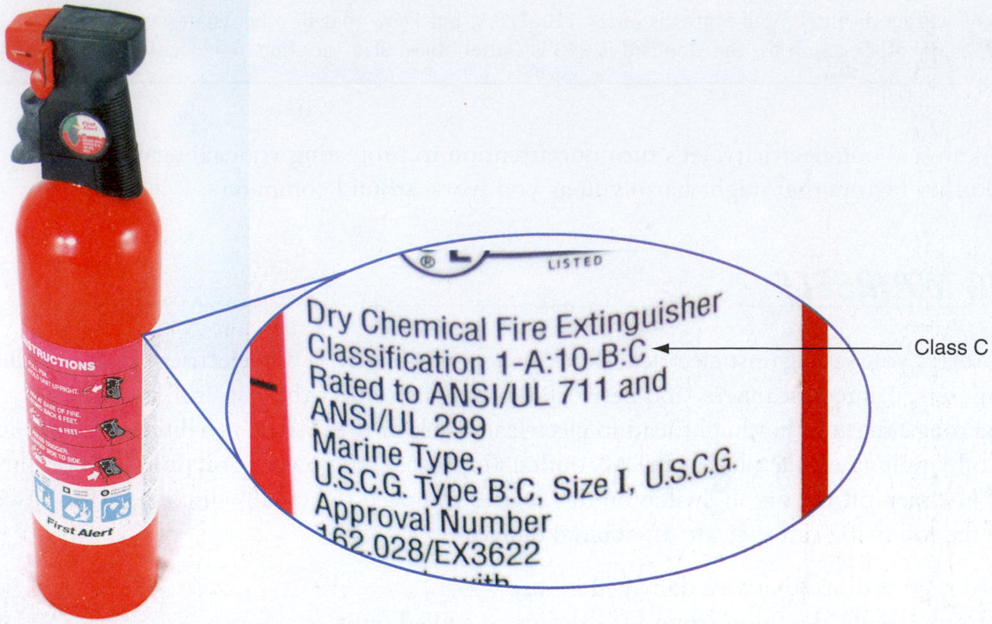

Figure A-4 A Class C fire extinguisher is rated to put out electrical fires

PROPER USE OF CLEANING PADS AND SOLUTIONS

A+ 220-902 5.1, 5.2

As a support technician, you'll find yourself collecting different cleaning solutions and cleaning pads to clean a variety of devices, including the mouse and keyboard, CDs, DVDs, Blu-ray discs and their drives, tapes and tape drives, and monitors. Figure A-5 shows a few of these products. For example, the contact cleaner in the figure is used to clean the contacts on the edge connectors of expansion cards; the cleaning can solve a problem with a faulty connection.

Figure A-5 Cleaning solutions and pads

Most of these cleaning solutions contain flammable and poisonous materials. Take care when using them so that they don't get on your skin or in your eyes. To find out what to do if you are accidentally exposed to a dangerous solution, look on the instructions printed on the can or check out the material safety data sheet (see Figure A-6). A **material safety data sheet (MSDS)** explains how to properly handle substances such as chemical solvents and how to dispose of them.

Figure A-6 Each chemical you use should have a material safety data sheet available

An MSDS includes information such as physical data, toxicity, health effects, first aid, storage, shipping, disposal, and spill procedures. It comes packaged with the chemical; you can order one from the manufacturer, or you can find one on the Internet (see *www.ilpi.com/msds*).

> **★ A+ Exam Tip** The A+ 220-901 exam expects you to know how to use MSDS documentation to find out how to dispose of chemicals so as to help protect the environment. You also need to know that you must follow all local government regulations when disposing of chemicals and other materials dangerous to the environment.

If you have an accident with these or other dangerous products, your company or organization might require you to report the accident to your company and/or fill out an incident report. Check with your organization to find out how to handle reporting these types of incidents.

MANAGING CABLES

A+ 220-902 5.1

People can trip over cables or cords left on the floor, so be careful that cables are in a safe place. If you must run a cable across a path or where someone sits, use a cable or cord cover that can be nailed or screwed to the floor. Don't leave loose cables or cords in a traffic area where people can trip over them (called a **trip hazard**).

LIFTING HEAVY OBJECTS

A+ 220-902 5.1

Back injury, caused by lifting heavy objects, is one of the most common injuries that happen at work. Whenever possible, put heavy objects, such as a large laser printer, on a cart to move them. If you do need to lift a heavy object, follow these guidelines to keep from injuring your back:

1. Looking at the object, decide which side of the object to face so that the load is the most balanced.
2. Stand close to the object with your feet apart.
3. Keeping your back straight, bend your knees and grip the load.
4. Lift with your legs, arms, and shoulders, and not with your back or stomach.
5. Keep the load close to your body and avoid twisting your body while you're holding it.
6. To put the object down, keep your back as straight as you can and lower the object by bending your knees.

Don't try to lift an object that is too heavy for you. Because there are no exact guidelines for when heavy is too heavy, use your best judgment as to when to ask for help.

SAFETY GOGGLES AND AIR FILTER MASK

A+
220-902
5.1

If you are required to work in an environment such as a factory where flying fragments, chips, or other particles are about, your employer might require you wear safety goggles to protect your eyes. In addition, if the air is filled with dust or other contaminants, your employer might require you to wear an air-purifying respirator, commonly called an air filter mask, which filters the dust and other contaminants from the air you breathe. If safety goggles or a mask is required, your employer is responsible for providing you one that is appropriate for the environment in which you are working.

PROTECTING THE EQUIPMENT

A+
220-902
5.1, 5.2

As you learn to troubleshoot and solve computer problems, you gradually begin to realize that many problems you face could have been avoided by good computer maintenance that includes protecting the computer against environmental factors such as humidity, dust, and out-of-control electricity.

PROTECT THE EQUIPMENT AGAINST STATIC ELECTRICITY OR ESD

A+
220-902
5.1

Suppose you come indoors on a cold day, pick up a comb, and touch your hair. Sparks fly! What happened? Static electricity caused the sparks. Electrostatic discharge (ESD), commonly known as static electricity, is an electrical charge at rest. When you came indoors, this charge built up on your hair and had no place to go. An ungrounded conductor (such as wire that is not touching another wire) or a nonconductive surface (such as your hair) holds a charge until the charge is released. When two objects with dissimilar electrical charges touch, electricity passes between them until the dissimilar charges become equal.

To see static charges equalizing, turn off the lights in a room, scuff your feet on the carpet, and touch another person. Occasionally, you can see and feel the charge in your fingers. If you can feel the charge, you discharged at least 1500 volts of static electricity. If you hear the discharge, you released at least 6000 volts. If you see the discharge, you released at least 8000 volts of ESD. A charge of only 10 volts can damage electronic components! *You can touch a chip on an expansion card or motherboard, damage the chip with ESD, and never feel, hear, or see the electrical discharge.*

ESD can cause two types of damage in an electronic component: catastrophic failure and upset failure. A catastrophic failure destroys the component beyond use. An upset failure damages the component so that it does not perform well, even though it may still function to some degree. Upset failures are more difficult to detect because they are not consistent and not easily observed. Both types of failures permanently affect the device. Components are easily damaged by ESD, but because the damage might not show up for weeks or months, a technician is likely to get careless and not realize the damage he or she is doing.

Caution Unless you are measuring power levels with a multimeter or power supply tester, never, ever touch a component or cable inside a computer case while the power is on. The electrical voltage is not enough to seriously hurt you but more than enough to permanently damage the component.

Before touching or handling a component (for example, a hard drive, motherboard, expansion card, processor, or memory modules), to protect it against ESD, always ground yourself first. You can ground yourself and the computer parts by using one or more of the following static control devices or methods:

- *ESD strap.* An ESD strap, also called a ground bracelet, antistatic wrist strap, or ESD bracelet, is a strap you wear around your wrist. The strap has a cord attached with an alligator clip on the end. Attach the clip to the computer case you're working on, as shown in Figure A-7. Any static electricity between you and the case is now discharged. Therefore, as you work inside the case, you will not damage the components with static electricity. The bracelet also contains a resistor that prevents electricity from harming you.

Figure A-7 A ground bracelet, which protects computer components from ESD, can clip to the side of the computer case and eliminate ESD between you and the case

Caution When working on a laser printer, *don't* wear the ESD strap because you don't want to be the ground for these high-voltage devices.

- ***Ground mats.*** A ground mat, also called an ESD mat, dissipates ESD and is commonly used by bench technicians (also called depot technicians) who repair and assemble computers at their workbenches or in an assembly line. Ground mats have a connector in one corner that you can use to connect the mat to the ground (see Figure A-8). If you lift a component off the mat, it is no longer grounded and is susceptible to ESD, so it's important to use an ESD strap with a ground mat.

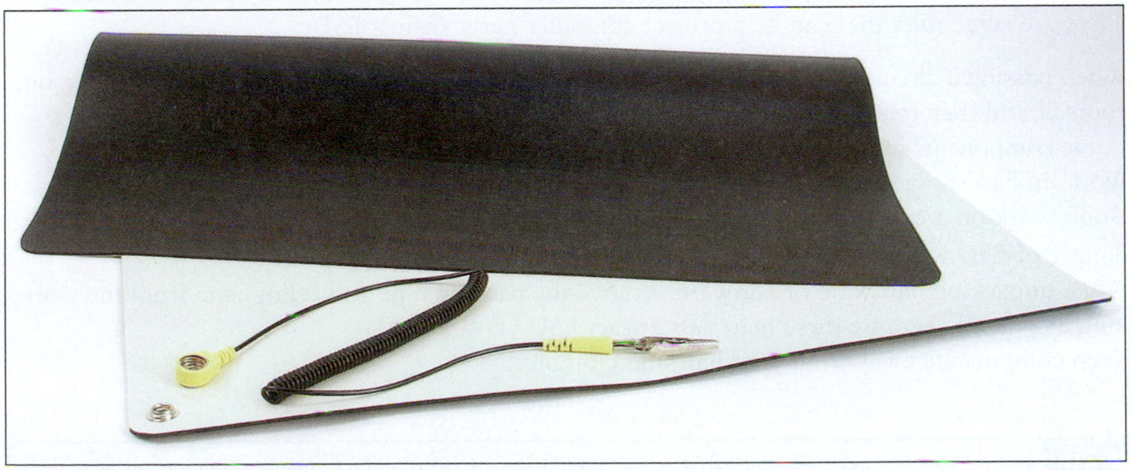

Figure A-8 An ESD mat dissipates ESD and should be connected to the ground

- ***Static shielding bags.*** New components come shipped in static shielding bags, also called antistatic bags. These bags are a type of Faraday cage, named after Michael Faraday, who built the first cage in 1836. A Faraday cage is any device that protects against an electromagnetic field. Save the bags to store other devices that are not currently installed in a computer. As you work on a computer, know that a device is not protected from ESD if you place it on top of the bag; the protection is inside the bag (see Figure A-9).

Figure A-9 An antistatic bag help protect components from ESD

> **Caution** A CRT monitor can also damage components with ESD. Don't place or store expansion cards on top of or next to a CRT monitor, which can discharge as much as 29,000 volts onto the screen.

The best way to guard against ESD is to use an ESD strap together with a ground mat. Consider an ESD strap essential equipment when working on a computer. However, if you are in a situation in which you must work without one, touch the computer case or the power supply before you touch a component in the case, which is called self-grounding. Self-grounding dissipates any charge between you and whatever you touch. Here are some rules that can help protect computer parts against ESD:

- *Rule 1:* When passing a circuit board, memory module, or other sensitive component to another person, ground yourself and then touch the other person before you pass the component.
- *Rule 2:* Leave components inside their protective bags until you are ready to use them.
- *Rule 3:* Work on hard floors, not carpet, or use antistatic spray on the carpets.
- *Rule 4:* Don't work on a computer if you or the computer have just come in from the cold because there is more danger of ESD when the atmosphere is cold and dry.
- *Rule 5:* When unpacking hardware or software, remove the packing tape and cellophane from the work area as soon as possible because these materials attract ESD.
- *Rule 6:* Keep components away from your hair and clothing.

> **A+ Exam Tip** The A+ 220-901 exam emphasizes that you should know how to protect computer equipment as you work on it, including how to protect components against damage from ESD.

Hands-On | Project A-1 Practice Handling Computer Components

Working with a partner, you'll need some computer parts and the antistatic tools you learned about in this part of the chapter. Practice touching, picking up, and passing the parts between you. As you do so, follow the rules to protect the parts against ESD. Have a third person watch as you work and point out any ways you might have exposed a part to ESD. As you work, be careful to not touch components on circuit boards or the gold fingers on the edge connector of an expansion card. When you are finished, store the parts in antistatic bags.

PHYSICALLY PROTECT YOUR EQUIPMENT FROM THE ENVIRONMENT

A+
220-902
5.2

When you protect equipment from ongoing problems with the environment, you are likely to have fewer problems later, and the less troubleshooting and repair you will have to do. Here is how you can physically protect a computer:

- ***Protect a computer against dust and other airborne particles.*** When a computer must sit in a dusty environment, around those who smoke, or where pets might leave hair, you can:
- Use a plastic keyboard cover to protect the keyboard. When the computer is turned off, cover the entire system with a protective cover or enclosure.
- Install air filters over the front or side vents of the case where air flows into the case. Put your hand over the case of a running computer to feel where the air flows in. For most systems, air flows in from the front vents or vents on the side of the case that is near the processor cooler. The air filter shown in Figure A-10 has magnets that hold the filter to the case when screw holes are not available.

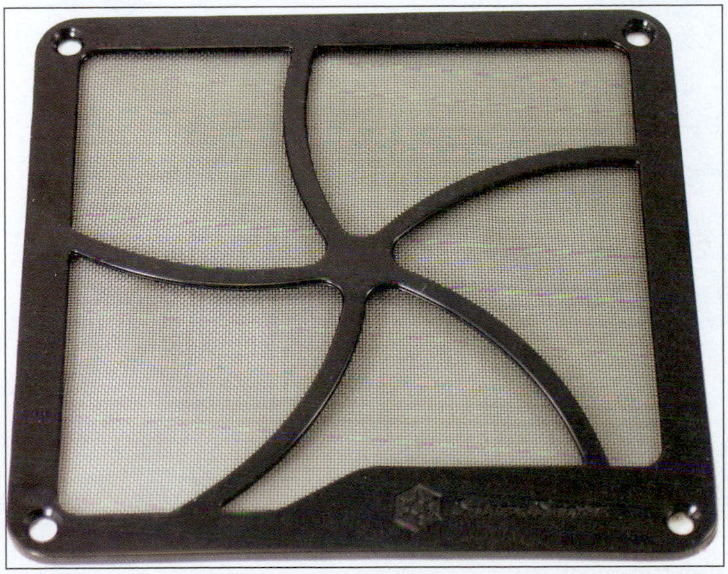

Figure A-10 This air filter is designed to fit over a case fan, power supply fan, or panel vent on the case

- Whenever you have the case cover open, be sure to use compressed air or an antistatic vacuum (see Figure A-11) to remove dust from inside the case. Figure A-12 shows a case fan that jammed because of dust and caused a system to overheat. And while you're cleaning up dust, don't forget to blow or vacuum out the keyboard.

A

Notes When working at a customer site, be sure to clean up any mess you created by blowing dust out of a computer case or keyboard.

Figure A-11 An antistatic vacuum designed to work inside sensitive electronic equipment such as computers and printers

Figure A-12 This dust-jammed case fan caused a system to overheat

- ***Allow for good ventilation inside and outside the system.*** Proper air circulation is essential to keeping a system cool. Don't block air vents on the front and rear of the computer case or on the monitor. Inside the case, make sure cables are tied up and out of the way so as to allow for airflow and not obstruct fans from turning. Put covers on expansion slot openings on the rear of the case and put faceplates over empty bays on the front of the case. Don't set a tower case directly on thick carpet because the air vent on the bottom front of the case can be blocked. If you are concerned about overheating, monitor temperatures inside and outside the case.

★ A+ Exam Tip The A+ 220-901 exam expects you to know how to keep computers and monitors well ventilated and to use protective enclosures and air filters to protect the equipment from airborne particles.

- ***High temperatures and humidity can be dangerous for hard drives.*** I once worked in a basement with PCs, and hard drives failed much too often. After we installed dehumidifiers, the hard drives became more reliable. If you suspect a problem with humidity, you can use a hygrometer to monitor the humidity in a room. High temperatures can also damage computer equipment, and you should take precautions to not allow a computer to overheat.

Notes A server room where computers stay and people generally don't stay for long hours is set to balance what is good for the equipment and to conserve energy. Low temperature and moderate humidity are best for the equipment, although no set standards exist for either. Temperatures might be set from 65 to 70 degrees F, and humidity between 30 percent and 50 percent, although some companies keep their server rooms at 80 degrees F to conserve energy. A data center where both computers and people stay is usually kept at a comfortable temperature and humidity for humans.

- ***Protect electrical equipment from power surges.*** Lightning and other electrical power surges can destroy computers and other electrical equipment. If the house or office building does not have surge protection equipment installed at the breaker box, be sure to install a protective device at each computer. The least expensive device is a power strip that is also a surge suppressor, although you might want to use a UPS for added protection.

  Lightning can also get to your equipment across network cabling coming in through an Internet connection. To protect against lightning, use a surge suppressor such as the one shown in Figure A-13 in line between the ISP device (for example, a DSL modem or cable modem) and the computer or home router to protect it from spikes across the network cables. Notice the cord on the surge suppressor, which connects it to ground.

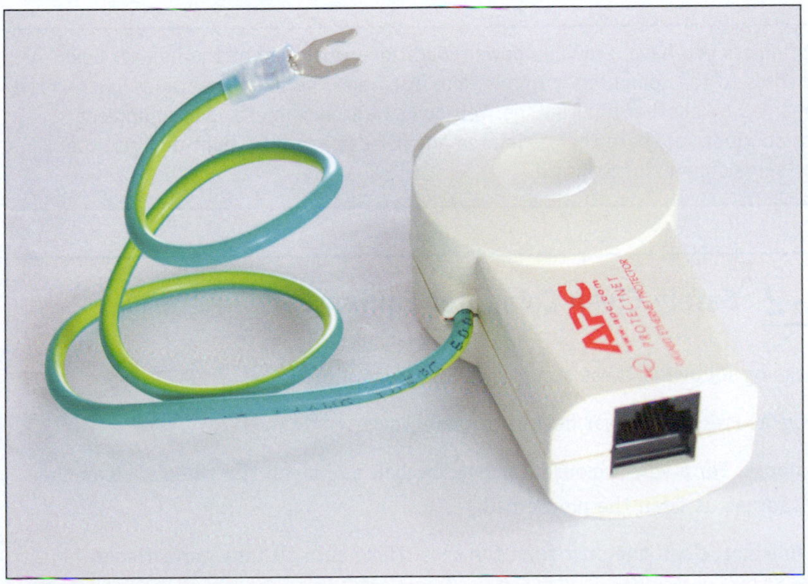

Figure A-13 Surge protector by APC for Ethernet lines

An **uninterruptible power supply (UPS)** is a device that raises the voltage when it drops during **brownouts** or **sags** (temporary voltage reductions). A UPS also does double-duty as a surge suppressor to protect the system against power surges or spikes. In addition, a UPS can serve as a battery backup to provide power for a brief time during a total blackout long enough for you to save your work and shut down the system.

A UPS is not as essential for a laptop computer as it is for a desktop because a laptop has a battery that can sustain it during a blackout.

A common UPS device is a rather heavy box that plugs into an AC outlet and provides one or more outlets for the computer and the monitor (see Figure A-14). It has an on/off switch, requires no maintenance, and is very simple to install. Use it to provide uninterruptible power to your desktop computer and monitor. It's best not to connect it to nonessential devices such as a laser printer or scanner.

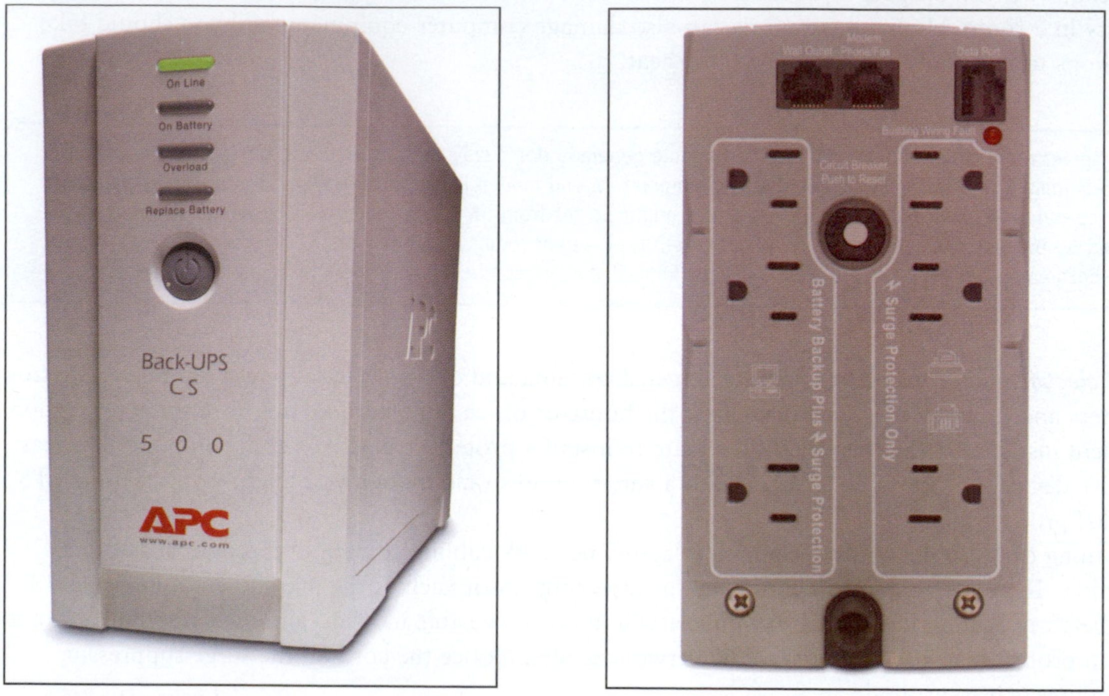

Figure A-14 Uninterruptible power supply (UPS)

> **Notes** Whenever a power outage occurs, unless you have a reliable power conditioner installed at the breaker box in your house or building, unplug all power cords to the computers, printers, monitors, and the like. Sometimes when the power returns, sudden spikes are accompanied by another brief outage. You don't want to subject your equipment to these surges. When buying a surge suppressor, look for those that guarantee against damage from lightning and that reimburse for equipment destroyed while the surge suppressor is in use.

Hands-On Project A-2 Safely Clean Computer Equipment

Practice some preventive maintenance tasks by following these steps to clean a computer:

1. Shut down the computer and unplug it. Press the power button to drain power.
2. Clean the keyboard, monitor, and mouse. For a wheel mouse, remove the ball and clean the wheels. Clean the outside of the computer case. Don't forget to clean the mouse pad.
3. Open the case and using a ground bracelet, clean the dust from the case. Make sure all fans move freely.
4. Verify the cables are out of the way of airflow. Use cable ties as necessary.
5. Check that each expansion card and memory module is securely seated in its slot.
6. Power up the system and make sure all is working.
7. Clean up around your work area. If you left dust on the floor as you blew it out of the computer case, be sure to clean it up.

PROTECTING THE ENVIRONMENT

A+
220-902
5.1, 5.2

IT support technicians need to be aware that we can do damage to the environment if we carelessly dispose of used computer equipment improperly. As a support technician, one day you're sure to face an assortment of useless equipment and consumables (see Figure A-15). Before you decide to trash it all, take a moment and ask yourself if some of the equipment can be donated or at least recycled. Think about fixing up an old computer and donating it to a needy middle school student. If you don't have the time for that, consider donating to the local computer repair class. The class can fix the computers up as a class project and donate them to young students.

Figure A-15 Keep, trash, recycle, or donate?

When disposing of any type of equipment or consumables, make sure to comply with local government environmental regulations. Table A-2 lists some items and how to dispose of them.

Part	How to Dispose
Alkaline batteries, including AAA, AA, A, C, D, and 9-volt	Dispose of these batteries in the regular trash. First check to see if there are recycling facilities in your area.
Button batteries used in digital cameras and other small equipment; battery packs used in notebooks	These batteries can contain silver oxide, mercury, lithium, or cadmium and are considered toxic waste that require special toxic waste handling. Dispose of them by returning them to the original dealer or by taking them to a recycling center. To recycle, pack them separately from other items. If you don't have a recycling center nearby, contact your county for local regulations for disposal.
Laser printer toner cartridges	Return these to the manufacturer or dealer to be recycled.
Ink-jet printer cartridges, computer cases, power supplies, and other computer parts, monitors, chemical solvents, and their containers	Check with local county or environmental officials for laws and regulations in your area for proper disposal of these items. The county might have a recycling center that will receive them. Discharge a CRT monitor before disposing of it. See the MSDS documents for chemicals to know how to dispose of them.
Storage media such as hard drives, CDs, DVDs, and BDs	Do physical damage to the device so it is not possible for sensitive data to be stolen. Then the device can be recycled or put in the trash. Your organization might be required to meet legal requirements to destroy data. If so, make sure you understand these requirements and how to comply with them.

Table A-2 Computer parts and how to dispose of them

A+ Exam Tip The A+ 220-901 exam expects you to know to follow environmental guidelines to dispose of batteries, laser printer toner, and CRT monitors, chemical solvents, and containers. If you're not certain how to dispose of a product, see its MSDS document.

Be sure a CRT monitor is discharged before you dispose of it. Most CRT monitors are designed to discharge after sitting unplugged for 60 minutes. It can be manually discharged by using a high-voltage probe with the monitor case opened. Ask a technician trained to service monitors to do this for you.

Notes Go to *www.youtube.com* and search on "discharge a CRT monitor" to see some interesting videos that demonstrate the charge inside a monitor long after the monitor is turned off and unplugged. As for proper procedures, I'm not endorsing all these videos; just watch for fun.

Hands-On Project A-3 Research Disposal Rules

Research the laws and regulations in your community concerning the disposal of batteries and old computer parts. Answer these questions regarding your community:

1. How do you properly dispose of a monitor?
2. How do you properly dispose of a battery pack used by a notebook computer?
3. How do you properly dispose of a large box of assorted computer parts, including hard drives, optical drives, computer cases, and circuit boards?

>> KEY TERMS

For explanations of key terms, see the Glossary for this text.

air filter mask
alternating current (AC)
amp
antistatic bag
antistatic wrist strap
brownout
Class C fire extinguisher
direct current (DC)
electrostatic discharge (ESD)
ESD mat
ESD strap
ground bracelet
ground mat
inverter
joule
material safety data sheet (MSDS)
ohm
rectifier
safety goggles
sag
self-grounding
static electricity
surge suppressor
transformer
trip hazard
uninterruptible power supply (UPS)
volt
watt

APPENDIX B

Entry Points for Startup Processes

This appendix contains a summary of the entry points that can affect Windows 8/7/Vista startup. The entry points include startup folders, Group Policy folders, the Scheduled Tasks folder, and registry keys.

Programs and shortcuts to programs are stored in these startup folders:

- C:\Users*username*\AppData\Roaming\Microsoft\Windows\Start\Menu\Programs\Startup
- C:\ProgramData\Microsoft\Windows\Start Menu\Programs\Startup

Startup and shutdown scripts used by Group Policy are stored in these folders:

- C:\Windows\System32\GroupPolicy\Machine\Scripts\Startup
- C:\Windows\System32\GroupPolicy\Machine\Scripts\Shutdown
- C:\Windows\System32\GroupPolicy\User\Scripts\Logon
- C:\Windows\System32\GroupPolicy\User\Scripts\Logoff

Scheduled tasks are stored in this folder:

- C:\Windows\System32\Tasks

To see a list of scheduled tasks, enter the **schtasks** command in a command prompt window. These keys cause an entry to run once and only once at startup:

- HKLM\Software\Microsoft\Windows\CurrentVersion\RunOnce
- HKLM\Software\Microsoft\Windows\CurrentVersion\RunServiceOnce
- HKLM\Software\Microsoft\Windows\CurrentVersion\RunServicesOnce
- HKCU\Software\Microsoft\Windows\CurrentVersion\RunOnce

Group Policy places entries in the following keys to affect startup:

- HKCU\Software\Microsoft\Windows\CurrentVersion\Policies\Explorer\Run
- HKLM\Software\Microsoft\Windows\CurrentVersion\Policies\Explorer\Run

Windows loads many DLL programs from the following key, which is sometimes used by malicious software. Don't delete one unless you know it's causing a problem:

- HKLM\Software\Microsoft\Windows\CurrentVersion\ShellServiceObjectDelayLoad

Entries in the keys listed next apply to all users and hold legitimate startup entries. Don't delete an entry unless you suspect it to be bad:

- HKLM\Software\Microsoft\Windows\CurrentVersion\Run
- HKCU\Software\Microsoft\Windows NT\CurrentVersion\Windows
- HKCU\Software\Microsoft\Windows NT\CurrentVersion\Windows\Run
- HKCU\Software\Microsoft\Windows\CurrentVersion\Run

These keys and their subkeys contain entries that pertain to background services that are sometimes launched at startup:

- HKLM\Software\Microsoft\Windows\CurrentVersion\RunService
- HKLM\Software\Microsoft\Windows\CurrentVersion\RunServices

The following key contains a value named BootExecute, which is normally set to autochk. It causes the system to run a type of Chkdsk program to check for hard drive integrity when it was previously shut down improperly. Sometimes another program adds itself to this value, causing a problem. For more information about this situation, see the Microsoft Knowledge Base article 151376, "How to Disable Autochk If It Stops Responding During Reboot," at *support.microsoft.com*.

- HKLM\System\CurrentControlSet\Control\Session Manager

Here is an assorted list of registry keys that have all been known to cause various problems at startup. Remember, before you delete a program entry from one of these keys, research the program file name so that you won't accidentally delete something you want to keep:

- HKCU\Software\Microsoft\Command
- HKCU\Software\Microsoft\Command Processor\AutoRun
- HKCU\Software\Microsoft\Windows\CurrentVersion\RunOnce\Setup
- HKCU\Software\Microsoft\Windows NT\CurrentVersion\Windows\load
- HKLM\Software\Microsoft\Windows NT\CurrentVersion\Windows\AppInit_DLLs
- HKLM\Software\Microsoft\Windows NT\CurrentVersion\Winlogon\System
- HKLM\Software\Microsoft\Windows NT\CurrentVersion\Winlogon\Us
- HKCR\batfile\shell\open\command
- HKCR\comfile\shell\open\command
- HKCR\exefile\shell\open\command
- HKCR\htafile\shell\open\command
- HKCR\piffile\shell\open\command
- HKCR\scrfile\shell\open\command

Finally, check out the subkeys in the following key, which apply to 32-bit programs installed in a 64-bit version of Windows:

- HKLM\Software\Wow6432Node

Other ways in which processes can be launched at startup:

- Services can be set to launch at startup. To manage services, use the Services Console (services.msc).
- Device drivers are launched at startup. For a listing of installed devices, use Device Manager (devmgmt.msc) or the System Information Utility (msinfo32.exe).

APPENDIX C
CompTIA A+ Acronyms

CompTIA provides a list of acronyms that you need to know before you sit for the A+ exams. You can download the list from the CompTIA website at *www.comptia.org*. The list is included here for your convenience. However, CompTIA occasionally updates the list, so be sure to check the CompTIA website for the latest version.

Acronym	Spelled Out
AC	alternating current
ACL	access control list
ACPI	advanced configuration power interface
ACT	activity
ADSL	asymmetrical digital subscriber line
AGP	accelerated graphics port
AHCI	Advanced host controller interface
AP	Access point
APIPA	automatic private internet protocol addressing
APM	advanced power management
ARP	address resolution protocol
ASR	automated system recovery
ATA	advanced technology attachment
ATAPI	advanced technology attachment packet interface
ATM	asynchronous transfer mode
ATX	advanced technology extended
AUP	Acceptable Use Policy
A/V	Audio Video
BIOS	basic input/output system
BNC	Bayonet-Neill-Concelman or British Naval Connector
BTX	balanced technology extended
CAPTCHA	Completely Automated Public Turing Test To Tell Computers and Humans Apart
CCFL	Cold Cathode Fluorescent Lamp
CD	compact disc
CD-ROM	compact disc-read-only memory
CD-RW	compact disc-rewritable
CDFS	compact disc file system
CFS	Central File System, Common File System, Command File System
CIFS	Common Internet File System
CMOS	complementary metal-oxide semiconductor
CNR	Communications and Networking Riser
COMx	communication port (x=port number)
CPU	central processing unit
CRT	cathode-ray tube
DAC	discretionary access control
DB-25	serial communications D-shell connector, 25 pins
DB-9	9 pin D shell connector
DC	direct current
DDOS	distributed denial of service
DDR	double data-rate
DDR RAM	double data-rate random access memory
DDR SDRAM	double data-rate synchronous dynamic random access memory

Acronym	Spelled Out
DFS	distributed file system
DHCP	dynamic host configuration protocol
DIMM	dual inline memory module
DIN	Deutsche Industrie Norm
DLT	digital linear tape
DLP	digital light processing
DMA	direct memory access
DMZ	demilitarized zone
DNS	domain name service or domain name server
DOS	denial of service
DRAM	dynamic random access memory
DRM	Digital Rights Management
DSL	digital subscriber line
DVD	digital video disc or digital versatile disc
DVD-RAM	digital video disc-random access memory
DVD-ROM	digital video disc-read only memory
DVD-R	digital video disc-recordable
DVD-RW	digital video disc-rewritable
DVI	digital visual interface
ECC	error correcting code/error checking and correction
ECP	extended capabilities port
EEPROM	electrically erasable programmable read-only memory
EFS	encrypting file system
EIDE	enhanced integrated drive electronics
EMI	electromagnetic interference
EMP	electromagnetic pulse
EPROM	erasable programmable read-only memory
EPP	enhanced parallel port
ERD	emergency repair disk
ESD	electrostatic discharge
EULA	End User License Agreement
EVGA	extended video graphics adapter/array
EVDO	evolution data optimized or evolution data only
FAT	file allocation table
FAT12	12-bit file allocation table
FAT16	16-bit file allocation table
FAT32	32-bit file allocation table
FDD	floppy disk drive
Fn	Function (referring to the function key on a laptop)
FPM	fast page-mode
FRU	field replaceable unit
FSB	Front Side Bus

Acronym	Spelled Out
FTP	file transfer protocol
FQDN	fully qualified domain name
Gb	gigabit
GB	gigabyte
GDI	graphics device interface
GHz	gigahertz
GUI	graphical user interface
GPS	global positioning system
GSM	global system for mobile communications
HAL	hardware abstraction layer
HAV	Hardware Assisted Virtualization
HCL	hardware compatibility list
HDD	hard disk drive
HDMI	high definition media interface
HPFS	high performance file system
HTML	hypertext markup language
HTPC	home theater PC
HTTP	hypertext transfer protocol
HTTPS	hypertext transfer protocol over secure sockets layer
I/O	input/output
ICMP	internet control message protocol
ICR	intelligent character recognition
IDE	integrated drive electronics
IDS	Intrusion Detection System
IEEE	Institute of Electrical and Electronics Engineers
IIS	Internet Information Services
IMAP	internet mail access protocol
IMEI	International Mobile Equipment Identity
IMSI	International Mobile Subscriber Identity
IP	internet protocol
IPCONFIG	internet protocol configuration
IPP	internet printing protocol
IPS	In-plane Switching
IPSEC	Internet Protocol Security
IR	Infrared
IrDA	Infrared Data Association
IRP	Incident Response Plan
IRQ	Interrupt Request
ISDN	Integrated Services Digital Network
ISO	International Organization for Standardization/Industry Standards Organization
ISP	Internet Service Provider
JBOD	Just a Bunch of Disks

Acronym	Spelled Out
Kb	Kilobit
KB	Kilobyte or Knowledge Base
LAN	Local Area Network
LBA	Logical Block Addressing
LC	Lucent Connector
LCD	liquid Crystal Display
LDAP	lightweight directory access protocol
LED	light emitting diode
Li-on	lithium-ion
LPD/LPR	line printer daemon / line printer remote
LPT	line printer terminal
LVD	low voltage differential
MAC	media access control / mandatory access control
MAPI	messaging application programming interface
MAU	media access unit, media attachment unit
Mb	megabit
MB	megabyte
MBR	master boot record
MBSA	Microsoft Baseline Security Analyzer
MFD	multi-function device
MFP	multi-function product
MHz	megahertz
MicroDIMM	micro dual inline memory module
MIDI	musical instrument digital interface
MIME	multipurpose internet mail extension
MIMO	Multiple Input Multiple Output
MMC	Microsoft management console
MP3	Moving Picture Experts Group Layer 3 Audio
MP4	Moving Picture Experts Group Layer 4
MPEG	Moving Picture Experts Group
MSCONFIG	Microsoft configuration
MSDS	material safety data sheet
MUI	multilingual user interface
NAC	network access control
NAS	network-attached storage
NAT	network address translation
NetBIOS	networked basic input/output system
NetBEUI	networked basic input/output system extended user interface
NFS	network file system
NIC	network interface card
NiCd	nickel cadmium
NiMH	nickel metal hydride

Acronym	Spelled Out
NLX	new low-profile extended
NNTP	network news transfer protocol
NTFS	new technology file system
NTLDR	new technology loader
NTP	Network Time Protocol
OCR	optical character recognition
OEM	original equipment manufacturer
OLED	Organic Light Emitting Diode
OS	operating system
PAN	personal area network
PATA	parallel advanced technology attachment
PC	personal computer
PCI	peripheral component interconnect
PCIe	peripheral component interconnect express
PCIX	peripheral component interconnect extended
PCL	printer control language
PCMCIA	Personal Computer Memory Card International Association
PE	Preinstallation Environment
PGA	pin grid array
PGA2	pin grid array 2
PII	Personally Identifiable Information
PIN	personal identification number
PKI	public key infrastructure
PnP	plug and play
POP3	post office protocol 3
PoS	Point of Sale
POST	power-on self test
POTS	plain old telephone service
PPP	point-to-point protocol
PPTP	point-to-point tunneling protocol
PRI	primary rate interface
PROM	programmable read-only memory
PS/2	personal system/2 connector
PSTN	public switched telephone network
PSU	power supply unit
PVC	permanent virtual circuit
PXE	preboot execution environment
QoS	quality of service
RAID	redundant array of independent (or inexpensive) discs
RAM	random access memory
RAS	remote access service
RDP	Remote Desktop Protocol

Acronym	Spelled Out
RF	radio frequency
RFI	radio frequency interference
RGB	red green blue
RIP	routing information protocol
RIS	remote installation service
RISC	reduced instruction set computer
RJ-11	registered jack function 11
RJ-45	registered jack function 45
RMA	returned materials authorization
ROM	read only memory
RTC	real-time clock
SAN	storage area network
SAS	Serial Attached SCSI
SATA	serial advanced technology attachment
SC	subscription channel
SCP	secure copy protection
SCSI	small computer system interface
SCSI ID	small computer system interface identifier
SD card	secure digital card
SDRAM	synchronous dynamic random access memory
SEC	single edge connector
SFC	system file checker
SFF	Small Form Factor
SLI	scalable link interface or system level integration or scanline interleave mode
S.M.A.R.T.	self-monitoring, analysis, and reporting technology
SMB	server message block or small to midsize business
SMTP	simple mail transfer protocol
SNMP	simple network management protocol
SoDIMM	small outline dual inline memory module
SOHO	small office/home office
SP	service pack
SPDIF	Sony-Philips digital interface format
SPGA	staggered pin grid array
SRAM	static random access memory
SSH	secure shell
SSID	service set identifier
SSL	secure sockets layer
ST	straight tip
STP	shielded twisted pair
SXGA	super extended graphics array
TB	terabyte
TCP	transmission control protocol

Acronym	Spelled Out
TCP/IP	transmission control protocol/internet protocol
TDR	time domain reflectometer
TFTP	trivial file transfer protocol
TKIP	Temporal Key Integrity Protocol
TPM	trusted platform module
UAC	user account control
UDF	user defined functions or universal disk format or universal data format
UDP	user datagram protocol
UEFI	Unified Extensible Firmware Interface
UNC	universal naming convention
UPS	uninterruptible power supply
URL	uniform resource locator
USB	universal serial bus
USMT	user state migration tool
UTP	unshielded twisted pair
UXGA	ultra extended graphics array
VESA	Video Electronics Standards Association
VFAT	virtual file allocation table
VGA	video graphics array
VM	Virtual Machine
VoIP	voice over internet protocol
VPN	virtual private network
VRAM	video random access memory
WAN	wide area network
WAP	wireless access protocol/wireless access point
WEP	wired equivalent privacy
WIFI	wireless fidelity
WINS	windows internet name service
WLAN	wireless local area network
WPA	wireless protected access
WPS	WiFi Protected Setup
WUXGA	wide ultra extended graphics array
XGA	extended graphics array
ZIF	zero-insertion-force
ZIP	zigzag inline package

GLOSSARY

100BaseT An Ethernet standard that operates at 100 Mbps and uses twisted-pair cabling up to 100 meters (328 feet). *Also called* Fast Ethernet. Variations of 100BaseT are 100BaseTX and 100BaseFX.

4-pin 12-V connector An auxiliary motherboard connector used for extra 12-V power to the processor.

8-pin 12-V connector An auxiliary motherboard connector used for extra 12-V power to the processor, providing more power than the older 4-pin auxiliary connector.

10-foot user interface Application software used on large screens to control output display menus and other clickable items in fonts large enough to read at a distance of 10 feet.

20-pin P1 connector Used by an older ATX power supply and motherboard and provided +3.3 volts, +5 volts, +12 volts, –12 volts, and an optional and rarely used –5 volts.

24-pin P1 connector Used by the ATX Version 2.2 power supply and motherboard and provides additional power for PCI Express slots.

32-bit operating system Type of operating system that processes 32 bits at a time.

64-bit operating system Type of operating system that processes 64 bits at a time.

1394a *See* FireWire 400.

1394b *See* FireWire 800.

802.11 a/b/g/n/ac The collective name for the IEEE 802.11 standards for local wireless networking, which is the technical name for Wi-Fi.

A+ Certification A certification awarded by CompTIA (the Computer Technology Industry Association) that measures an IT technician's knowledge and skills.

AC adapter A device that converts AC to DC and can use regular house current to power a laptop computer.

Accelerated Processing Unit (APU) An AMD technology that is a combination of a CPU and a graphics processor unit (GPU) in the same processor housing.

accelerometer A type of gyroscope used in mobile devices to sense the physical position of the device.

acceptable use policy (AUP) A document that explains to users what they can and cannot do on the corporate network or with company data, and the penalties for violations.

access control list (ACL) A record or list of the resources (for example, a printer, folder, or file) that a user, device, or program has access to on a corporate network, server, or workstation.

Action bar On an Android device, an area at the bottom of the screen that can contain up to five custom software buttons, called Home touch buttons. The three default buttons are back, home, and overview.

Action Center A tool in Windows 8/7 that lists errors and issues that need attention.

Active Directory A Windows Server directory database and service that is used in managing a domain to allow for a single point of administration for all shared resources on a network, including files, peripheral devices, databases, websites, users, and services.

active partition For Master Boot Record (MBR) hard drives, the primary partition on the drive that boots the OS. Windows calls the active partition the system partition.

active recovery image In Windows 8, the custom refresh image of the Windows volume that will be used when a refresh of the Windows installation is performed. *Also see* custom refresh image.

ActiveX control A small app or add-on that can be downloaded from a website along with a webpage and is executed by a browser to enhance the webpage.

adapter address *See* MAC (Media Access Control) address.

address reservation When a DHCP server assigns a static IP address to a DHCP client. For example, a network printer might require a static IP address so that computers on the network can find the printer.

ad hoc mode A peer-to-peer wireless network between computers where each wireless computer serves as its own wireless access point and is responsible for securing each connection.

administrative share The folders that are shared by default on a network domain that administrator accounts can access.

Administrative Tools A group of tools accessed through Control Panel that you can use to manage the local computer or other computers on the network.

administrator account In Windows, a user account that grants to the administrator(s) rights and privileges to all hardware and software resources, such as the right to add, delete, and change accounts and to change hardware configurations. *Compare with* standard account.

Administrators group A type of user group. When a user account is assigned to this group, the account is granted rights that are assigned to an administrator account.

Advanced Boot Options menu A Windows 7/Vista menu that appears when you press F8 when Windows starts. The menu can be used to troubleshoot problems when loading Windows.

Aero glass *See* Aero user interface.

Aero user interface The Windows 7/Vista 3D user interface that gives a glassy appearance. *Also called* Aero glass.

AES (Advanced Encryption Standard) An encryption standard used by WPA2 and is currently the strongest encryption standard used by Wi-Fi.

AFP (Apple Filing Protocol) An outdated file access protocol used by early editions of the Mac operating system by Apple and is one protocol in the suite of AppleTalk networking protocols.

AirDrop A feature of iOS whereby iPhones and iPads can transfer files between nearby devices. The devices use Bluetooth to detect nearby devices and Wi-Fi to establish connectivity and transfer files.

air filter mask A mask that filters the dust and other contaminants from the air for breathing safety. *Also called* air-purifying respirator.

Airplane mode A setting within a mobile device that disables the cellular, Wi-Fi, and Bluetooth antennas so the device cannot transmit signals.

AirPrint A technology by Apple that allows Apple computers and mobile devices to print to an AirPrint-capable printer without first installing the printer.

air-purifying respirator *See* air filter mask.

all-in-one computer A computer that has the monitor and computer case built together and uses components that are common to both a laptop and a desktop computer.

alternate IP address When configuring TCP/IP in Windows, the static IP address that Windows uses if it cannot lease an IP address from a DHCP server.

alternating current (AC) Current that cycles back and forth rather than traveling in only one direction. In the United States, the AC voltage from a standard wall outlet is normally between 110 V and 115 V. In Europe, the standard AC voltage from a wall outlet is 220 V.

A-Male connector A common type of USB connector that is flat and wide and connects an A Male USB port on a computer or USB hub.

amp (A) A measure of electrical current.

analog A continuous signal with infinite variations. *Compare with* digital, which is a series of binary values—1s and 0s.

Android An operating system used on mobile devices that is based on the Linux OS and supported by Google.

anonymous users User accounts that have not been authenticated on a remote computer.

ANSI (American National Standards Institute) A nonprofit organization dedicated to creating trade and communications standards.

answer file A text file (.bat) that contains information that Windows requires in order to do an unattended installation.

anti-malware software Utility software that can prevent infection, scan a system, and detect and remove all types of general malware, including viruses, spyware, worms, and rootkits.

antistatic bag Static shielding bags that new computer components are shipped in.

antistatic wrist strap *See* ESD strap.

antivirus software Utility software that can prevent infection, scan a system, and detect and remove viruses.

anycast address Using TCP/IP version 6, a type of IP address used by routers and identifies multiple destinations. Packets are delivered to the closest destination.

APK (Android Application Package) The format used by Android apps for distributing the app in a package of files wrapped into one file with an .apk file extension.

App Store The app on an Apple device (iPad, iPhone, or iPod touch) that can be used to download content from the iTunes Store website (*itunes.apple.com*).

Apple ID A user account that uses a valid email address and password and is associated with a credit card number that allows you to download iOS updates and patches, apps, and multimedia content.

Apple menu In OS X, the menu that appears when the user clicks the Apple icon in the upper-left corner of the screen.

AppleTalk An outdated suite of networking protocols used by early editions of the Apple Mac OS, and has been replaced by the TCP/IP suite of protocols.

application virtualization Using this virtualization, a virtual environment is created in memory for an application to virtually install itself.

Application Virtualization (App-V) Software by Microsoft used for application virtualization.

Apps Drawer An Android app that lists and manages all apps installed on the device. By default, this app's icon is in the Favorites tray on an Android screen.

apt-get A Linux and OS X command to install and remove software packages and install OS updates.

artifact Horizontally torn image on a computer screen.

ATAPI (Advanced Technology Attachment Packet Interface) An interface standard, part of the IDE/ATA standards, that allows tape drives, optical drives, and other drives to be treated like an IDE hard drive by the system.

ATA Secure Erase Standards developed by the American National Standards Institute (ANSI) that dictate how to securely erase data from solid-state devices such as a USB flash drive or SSD drive in order to protect personal privacy.

ATX (Advanced Technology Extended) The most common form factor for computer systems presently in use, originally introduced by Intel in 1995. ATX motherboards and cases make better use of space and resources than did the earlier AT form factor.

ATX12V power supply An ATX Version 2.1 power supply that provides an extra 12-V power cord with a 4-pin connector to be used by the auxiliary 4-pin power connector on motherboards used to provide extra power for processors.

audio port A port that can be used by a microphone, audio in, audio out, and stereo audio out. *Also called* a sound port.

Authenticated Users group All user accounts that have been authenticated to access the system except the Guest account. *Compare with* anonymous users.

authentication server A server responsible for authenticating users or computers to the network so they can access network resources.

autodetection A feature of UEFI/BIOS that detects a new drive and automatically selects the correct drive capacity and configuration, including the best possible standard supported by both the hard drive and the motherboard.

Automatic Private IP Address (APIPA) In TCP/IP version 4, IP address in the address range 169.254.x.y, used by a computer when it cannot successfully lease an IP address from a DHCP server.

auto-switching A function of a laptop computer AC adapter that is able to automatically switch between 110-V and 220-V AC power.

Backup and Restore The Windows 7/Vista utility used to create and update scheduled backups of user data and the system image.

Backup Operators group A type of Windows user account group. When a user account belongs to this group, it can back up and restore any files on the system regardless of its having access to these files.

ball grid array (BGA) A connection via a processor that is soldered to the motherboard, and the two are always purchased as a unit.

bandwidth In relation to analog communication, the range of frequencies that a communications channel or cable can carry. In general use, the term refers to the volume of data that can be transmitted on a bus or over a cable stated in bits per second (bps), kilobits per second (Kbps), megabits per second (Mbps), or gigabits per second (Gbps). *Also called* data throughput or line speed.

barcode reader Used to scan barcodes on products at the points of sale or when taking inventory.

base station A fixed transceiver and antenna used to create one cell within a cellular network.

Bash shell The default shell used by the terminal for many distributions of Linux.

basic disk The term Windows uses that applies to a hard drive when the drive is a stand-alone drive in the system. *Compare with* dynamic disk.

batch file A text file containing a series of OS commands. Autoexec.bat is a batch file.

bcdedit A Windows command used to manually edit the BCD (Boot Configuration Data).

BD-R Stands for BD (Blu-ray Disc) recordable.

BD-RE Stands for BD (Blu-ray Disc) rewriteable.

beamforming A technique supported by the IEEE 802.11ac Wi-Fi standard that can detect the location of connected devices and increase signal strength in that direction.

Berg power connector A type of power connector used by a power cord to provide power to a floppy disk drive.

best-effort protocol *See* connectionless protocol.

biometric authentication To authenticate to a network, computer, or other computing device by means of biometric data, such as a fingerprint or retinal data. Touch ID on an iPhone or face lock on an Android device can perform biometric authentication.

biometric device An input device that inputs biological data about a person; the data can identify a person's fingerprints, handprints, face, voice, eyes, and handwriting.

BIOS (basic input/output system) Firmware that can control much of a computer's input/output functions, such as communication with the keyboard and the monitor. *Compare with* UEFI.

BIOS setup The program in system BIOS that can change the values in CMOS RAM. *Also called* CMOS setup.

BitLocker Drive Encryption A utility in Windows 8/7/Vista that is used to lock down a hard drive by encrypting the entire Windows volume and any other volume on the drive.

BitLocker To Go A Windows utility that can encrypt data on a USB flash drive and restrict access by requiring a password.

bitmap Rows and columns of bits that collectively represent an image.

blue screen error *See* blue screen of death (BSOD).

blue screen of death (BSOD) A Windows error that occurs in kernel mode, is displayed against a blue screen, and causes the system to halt. The error might be caused by problems with devices, device drivers, or a corrupted Windows installation. *Also called* blue screen error or stop error.

Bluetooth A short-range wireless technology used to connect two devices in a small personal network.

Bluetooth PIN code A code that may be required to complete the Bluetooth connection in a pairing process.

Blu-ray Disc (BD) An optical disc technology that uses the UDF version 2.5 file system and a blue laser beam, which is shorter than any red beam used by DVD or CD discs. The shorter blue laser beam allows Blu-ray discs to store more data than a DVD.

BNC connector A connector used with thin coaxial cable. Some BNC connectors are T-shaped and called T-connectors. One end of the T connects to the NIC, and the two other ends can connect to cables or end a bus formation with a terminator.

B-Male connector A USB connector that connects a USB 1.x or 2.0 device such as a printer.

Bonjour An Apple program that is used to interface between computers and devices and share content and services between them. When iTunes is installed on a Windows computer, the installation includes Bonjour.

Boot Camp A utility in OS X that allows you to install and run Windows on a Mac computer.

Boot Configuration Data (BCD) store A small Windows database structured the same as a registry file and contains configuration information about how Windows is started. The BCD file replaces the Boot.ini file used in Windows 2000/XP.

boot loader menu A startup menu that gives the user the choice of which operating system to load, such as Windows 8 or Windows 7, when both are installed on the same system, creating a dual boot.

boot partition The hard drive partition where the Windows OS is stored. The system partition and the boot partition may be different partitions.

booting The process of starting up a computer and loading an operating system.

BootMgr In Windows 8/7/Vista, the boot manager program responsible for loading Windows.

bootrec A Windows command used to repair the BCD (Boot Configuration Data) and boot sectors.

bootsect A Windows command used to repair a dual-boot system.

botnet A network of zombies or robots. *Also see* zombie.

bridge A device that stands between two segments of a network and manages network traffic between them.

broadband A transmission technique that carries more than one type of transmission on the same medium, such as voice and DSL on a regular telephone line.

brownout Temporary reduction in voltage, which can sometimes cause data loss. *Also called* sag.

brute force attack A method to hack or discover a password by trying every single combination of characters.

buffer overflow attack Malicious software that attempts to run its code from an area of memory assigned to another program.

burn-in When a static image stays on a monitor for many hours, leaving a permanent impression of that image on the monitor.

bus The paths, or lines, on the motherboard on which data, instructions, and electrical power move from component to component.

BYOD (Bring Your Own Device) A corporate policy that allows employees or students to connect their own devices to the corporate network.

cable Internet A broadband technology that uses cable TV lines and is always connected (always up).

cable tester A tool used to test a cable to find out if it is good or to find out what type of cable it is if the cable is not labeled.

calibration The process of checking and correcting the graduations of an instrument or device such as an inkjet printer.

call tracking software A system that tracks the dates, times, and transactions of help-desk or on-site IT support calls, including the problem presented, the issues addressed, who did what, and when and how each call was resolved.

CAS Latency A method of measuring access timing to memory, which is the number of clock cycles required to write or read a column of data off a memory module. CAS stands for Column Access Strobe. *Compare with* RAS Latency.

case fan A fan inside a computer case used to draw air out of or into the case.

CAT-3 (Category 3) A rating formally used for unshielded twisted-pair (UTP) cables on a network, and is currently used for phone lines.

CAT-5 (Category 5) A rating used for unshielded twisted-pair (UTP) cables and is rated for Fast Ethernet, but is seldom used today.

CAT-5e (Category 5e) A rating used for unshielded twisted-pair (UTP) cables, rated for Fast Ethernet and Gigabit Ethernet, and is popular today.

CAT-6 (Category 6) A rating used for twisted-pair cables that has less crosstalk than CAT-5e cables. CAT-6 cables might contain a plastic cord down the center of the cable that helps to prevent crosstalk, but is less flexible and more difficult to install than CAT-5e.

CAT-6a (Category 6a) A rating used for twisted-pair cables that is thicker and faster than CAT-6 and rated for 10GBase-T (10-Gigabit Ethernet).

CAT-6e (Category 6e) An unofficial name for CAT-6a.

CAT-7 (Category 7) A rating used for twisted-pair cables that have shielding to almost completely eliminate crosstalk and improve noise reduction.

Category view Default view in Windows Control Panel that presents utilities grouped by category. *Compare with* Classic view.

cd (change directory) The Windows command to change the current default directory.

CD (compact disc) An optical disc technology that uses a red laser beam and can hold up to 700 MB of data.

CDFS (Compact Disc File System) The 32-bit file system for CD discs and some CD-R and CD-RW discs. *Also see* Universal Disk Format (UDF).

CDMA (Code Division Multiple Access) A protocol standard used by cellular WANs and cell phones for transmitting digital data over cellular networks.

CD-ROM Stands for CD-read-only memory.

CD-RW Stands for CD rewriteable.

cellular network A network that can be used when a wireless network must cover a wide area. The network is made up of cells, each controlled by a base station. *Also called* a cellular WAN.

cellular network analyzer Software and hardware that can monitor cellular networks for signal

G

strength of cell towers, wireless access points (WAPs), and repeaters, which can help technicians better position antennas in a distributed antenna system (DAS).

cellular WAN *See* cellular network.

chmod A Linux and OS X command to change modes (or permissions) for a file or directory.

chown A Linux and OS X command to change the owner of a file or directory.

central processing unit (CPU) *Also called* a microprocessor or processor. The component where almost all processing of data and instructions takes place. The CPU receives data input, processes information, and executes instructions.

Centrino A technology used by Intel whereby the processor, chipset, and wireless network adapter are all interconnected as a unit, which improves laptop performance.

Certificate of Authenticity A sticker that contains the Windows product key.

certificate of destruction Digital or paper documentation, which ensures that data has been destroyed beyond recovery.

Certification Authority (CA) An organization, such as VeriSign, that assigns digital certificates or digital signatures to individuals or organizations.

chain of custody Documentation that tracks evidence used in an investigation and includes exactly what, when, and from whom the evidence was collected, the condition of the evidence, and how the evidence was secured while in possession of a responsible party.

channel A specific radio frequency within a broader frequency.

charging In laser printing, the imaging drum is conditioned to contain a high electrical charge.

charm A shortcut that appears in the Windows 8 charms bar.

charms bar A menu that appears on the right side of any Windows 8 screen when you move your pointer to a right corner.

chassis A computer case for any type of computer.

chassis air guide (CAG) A round air duct that helps to pull and direct fresh air from outside a computer case to the cooler and processor.

child directory *See* subdirectory.

chipset A group of chips on the motherboard that controls the timing and flow of data and instructions to and from the CPU.

chkdsk (check disk) A Windows command to verify the hard drive does not have bad sectors that can corrupt the file system.

chkdsk /r A Windows command to check the hard drive for errors and repair the file system.

CIDR notation A shorthand notation (pronounced "*cider notation*") for expressing an IPv4 address and subnet mask with the IP address followed by a / slash and the number of bits in the IP address that identifies the network. For example, 15.50.35.10/20.

CIFS (Common Internet File System) A file access protocol and the cross-platform version of SMB used between Windows, Linux, Mac OS, and other operating systems. *Also called* SMB2.

Class C fire extinguisher A fire extinguisher rated to put out electrical fires.

Classic view View in Windows Control Panel that presents utilities in small or large icons and are not grouped. *Compare with* Category view.

clean boot A process of starting Windows with a basic set of drivers and startup programs that can be useful when software does not install properly.

clean install Used to install Windows on a new hard drive or to overwrite the existing operating system and applications when installing Windows on a hard drive that already has Windows installed.

client/server Two computers communicating using a local network or the Internet. One computer (the client) makes requests to the other computer (the server), which answers the request.

client-side desktop virtualization Using this virtualization, software installed on a desktop or laptop manages virtual machines used by the local user.

client-side virtualization Using this virtualization, a personal computer provides multiple virtual environments for applications.

clone In Linux and OS X, an image of the entire partition on which the OS is installed.

closed source Software owned by a vendor that requires a commercial license to install and use the software. *Also called* vendor-specific software or commercial license software.

cloud computing A service where server-side virtualization is delegated to a third-party service, and the Internet is used to connect server and client machines.

cloud printing Printing to a printer anywhere on the Internet from a personal computer or mobile device connected to the Internet.

cluster On a magnetic hard drive, one or more sectors that constitute the smallest unit of space on the drive for storing data (*also called* a file allocation unit). Files are written to a drive as groups of whole clusters.

CMOS (complementary metal-oxide semiconductor) The technology used to manufacture microchips. CMOS chips require less electricity, hold data longer after the electricity is turned off, and produce less heat than earlier technologies. The configuration or setup chip is a CMOS chip.

CMOS battery The lithium coin-cell battery on the motherboard used to power the CMOS chip that holds BIOS setup data so that the data is retained when the computer is unplugged.

CMOS RAM Memory contained on the CMOS configuration chip.

coaxial cable A cable that has a single copper wire down the middle and a braided shield around it.

cold boot *See* hard boot.

Cold Cathode Fluorescent Lamp (CCFL) An older backlighting technology that uses one or two fluorescent tubes to light a monitor panel.

commercial license As applied to software, the rights to use the software, which have been assigned to the user by the software vendor. *Also see* closed source.

community cloud Online resources and services that are shared between multiple organizations, but not available publicly.

CompactFlash (CF) card A flash memory device that allows for sizes up to 137 GB, although current sizes range up to 32 GB.

compatibility mode A group of settings that can be applied to older drivers or applications that might cause them to work using a newer version of Windows than the one the programs were designed to use.

Compatibility Support Module (CSM) A feature of UEFI that allows UEFI to be backward compatible with legacy BIOS devices and drivers.

Complete PC Backup A Vista utility that can make a backup of the entire volume on which Vista is installed and can also back up other volumes. *Compare with* system image (Windows 8/7).

Component Services (COM+) A Microsoft Management Console snap-in that can be used to register components used by installed applications.

composite video port A port used by television or by a video card that is designed to send output to a TV. A composite port is round and has only a single pin in the center of the port. *Also called* RGB port.

compressed (zipped) folder A folder with a .zip extension that contains compressed files. When files are put in the folder, they are compressed. When files are moved to a regular folder, the files are decompressed.

computer infestation *See* malicious software.

Computer Management A Windows console (compmgmt.msc) that contains several administrative tools used by support technicians to manage the local computer or other computers on the network.

computer name *See* host name.

connectionless protocol A TCP/IP protocol such as UDP that works at the OSI Transport layer and does not guarantee delivery by first connecting and checking where data is received. It might be used for broadcasting, such as streaming video or sound over the web, where guaranteed delivery is not as important as fast transmission. *Also called* a best-effort protocol. *Also see* UDP (User Datagram Protocol).

connection-oriented protocol In networking, a TCP/IP protocol that confirms a good connection has been made before transmitting data to the other end, verifies data was received, and resends it if it is not. An example of a connection-oriented protocol is TCP.

console A window that consolidates several Windows administrative tools.

contrast ratio The contrast between true black and true white on a screen.

Control Panel A window containing several small Windows utility programs called applets that are used to manage hardware, software, users, and the system.

cooler A cooling system that sits on top of a processor and consists of a fan and a heat sink.

copy The Windows command to copy a single file, group of files, or folder and its contents.

copyright The right to copy the work that belongs to the creators of the works or others to whom the creator transfers this right.

CPU *See* central processing unit (CPU).

crimper A tool used to attach a terminator or connector to the end of a cable.

crossover cable A cable used to connect two like devices such as a hub to a hub or a computer to a computer (to make the simplest network of all). A crossover cable is not rated for Gigabit Ethernet.

custom installation In the Windows setup program, the option used to overwrite the existing operating system and applications, producing a clean installation of the OS. The main advantage is that problems with the old OS are not carried forward.

custom refresh image In Windows 8, an image of the entire Windows volume, including the Windows installation. The image can be applied during a Windows 8 refresh operation.

Dashboard In OS X, a screen that contains widgets, such as a calendar, a calculator, a clock, and a weather report.

data bus Lines of the bus, a system of pathways used for communication on the motherboard, used for data.

data cartridge A full-sized cartridge that holds data and is used in a tape drive.

data loss prevention (DLP) Methods that protect corporate data from being exposed or stolen; for example, software that filters employee email to verify privacy laws are not accidentally or intentionally being violated.

data path size The number of lines on a bus that can hold data, for example, 8, 16, 32, and 64 lines, which can accommodate 8, 16, 32, and 64 bits at a time.

data source A resource on a network that includes a database and the drivers required to interface between a remote computer and the data. *Also see* Open Database Connectivity (ODBC).

Data Sources A tool in the Administrative Tools group of Control Panel that is used to allow data files to be connected to applications they normally would not use.

data throughput *See* bandwidth.

Date and Time applet Accessed through Control Panel, used to set the date and time in Windows.

DB15 port *See* VGA (Video Graphics Array) port.

DB9 port *See* serial port.

dd A Linux and OS X command to copy and convert files, directories, partitions, and entire DVDs or hard drives. You must be logged in as a superuser to use the command.

DDR *See* Double Data Rate SDRAM.

DDR2 Memory that is faster and uses less power than DDR.

DDR3 Memory that is faster and uses less power than DDR2.

DDR3L Memory that is faster and uses less power than regular DDR3.

DDR4 Memory that is faster and uses less power than DDR3.

DE15 port *See* VGA (Video Graphics Array) port.

dead pixel A pixel on an LCD monitor that is not working and can appear as a small white, black, or colored spot on the computer screen.

default gateway The gateway a computer on a network uses to access another network unless it knows to specifically use another gateway for quicker access to that network.

default printer The designated printer to which Windows prints unless another printer is selected.

default program A program associated with a file extension that is used to open the file.

defrag The Windows command that examines a magnetic hard drive for fragmented files and rewrites these files to the drive in contiguous clusters.

defragment A drive maintenance procedure that rearranges fragments or parts of files on a magnetic hard drive so each file is stored on the drive in contiguous clusters.

defragmentation tool A utility or command to rewrite a file to a disk in one contiguous chain of clusters, thus speeding up data retrieval.

degausser A machine that exposes a magnetic storage device such as a hard drive or tape drive to a strong magnetic field to completely erase the data on the storage device.

del The Windows command to delete a file or group of files. *Also called* the erase command.

deployment strategy A procedure to install Windows, device drivers, and applications on a computer, and can include the process to transfer user settings, application settings, and user data files from an old installation to the new installation.

desktop case A computer case that lies flat and sometimes serves double-duty as a monitor stand.

Destination Network Address Translation (DNAT) When a firewall using Network Address Translation (NAT) allows uninitiated communication to a computer behind the firewall through a port that is normally closed. *Also see* port forwarding.

device driver A small program stored on the hard drive and installed in Windows that tells Windows how to communicate with a specific hardware device such as a printer, network, port on the motherboard, or scanner.

Device Manager The primary Windows tool (devmgmt.msc) for managing hardware.

Devices and Printers window A window used in Windows 8/7 to manage and uninstall printers and other devices.

DHCP (Dynamic Host Configuration Protocol) A protocol used by a server to assign a dynamic IP address to a computer when it first attempts to initiate a connection to the network and requests an IP address.

DHCP client A computer or other device (such as a network printer) that requests an IP address from a DHCP server.

DHCPv6 server A DHCP server that serves up IPv6 addresses.

dictionary attack A method to discover or crack a password by trying words in a dictionary.

digital A signal consisting of a series of binary values—1s and 0s. *Compare with* analog.

digital certificate A code used to authenticate the source of a file or document or to identify and authenticate a person or organization sending data over a network. The code is assigned by a certificate authority such as VeriSign and includes a public key for encryption. Also called digital ID or digital signature.

digital rights management (DRM) Software and hardware security limitations meant to protect digital content and prevent piracy.

digitizer *See* graphics tablet.

digitizing tablet *See* graphics tablet.

DIMM (dual inline memory module) A miniature circuit board installed on a motherboard to hold memory.

dir The Windows command to list files and directories.

direct current (DC) Current that travels in only one direction (the type of electricity provided by batteries). Computer power supplies transform AC to low DC.

direct thermal printer A type of thermal printer that burns dots onto special coated paper as was done by older fax machines.

DirectX A Microsoft software development tool that software developers can use to write multimedia applications, such as games, video-editing software, and computer-aided design software.

disc image *See* ISO image.

discolored capacitor Bulging head or crusty corrosion at the base of a capacitor that might indicate a failing motherboard.

Disk Cleanup A Windows utility to delete temporary files to free up space on a drive.

disk cloning *See* drive imaging.

disk imaging *See* drive imaging.

diskpart A Windows command to manage hard drives, partitions, and volumes.

DisplayPort A port that transmits digital video and audio (not analog transmissions) and is slowly replacing VGA and DVI ports on personal computers. *Also see* Thunderbolt port.

distorted geometry Images are stretched inappropriately on a monitor.

distribution server A file server holding Windows setup files used to install Windows on computers networked to the server.

distribution share The collective files in the installation that include Windows, device drivers, and applications. The package of files is served up by a distribution server.

DMG file In Mac OS X, a disk image file similar to WIM or ISO files in Windows.

DMZ (demilitarized zone) Refers to removing firewall protection from a computer or network within an organization of protected computers and networks.

DNS (Domain Name System or Domain Name Service) A distributed pool of information (called the namespace) that keeps track of assigned host names and domain names and their corresponding IP addresses. DNS also refers to the system that allows a host to locate information in the pool and the protocol the system uses.

DNS client When Windows queries the DNS server for a name resolution, which means to find an IP address for a computer when the fully qualified domain name is known.

DNS server A Doman Name Service server that uses a DNS protocol to find an IP address for a computer when the fully qualified domain name is known. An Internet service provider is responsible for providing access to one or more DNS servers as part of the service it provides for Internet access.

dock (1) For an Android device, the area at the bottom of the Android screen where up to four apps can be pinned. (2) For a Mac computer, a bar that appears by default at the bottom of the screen and contains program icons and shortcuts to files and folders.

docking port A connector on a laptop to connect to a port replicator or docking station.

docking station A device that receives a laptop computer and provides additional secondary storage and easy connection to peripheral devices.

domain In Windows, a logical group of networked computers, such as those on a college campus, that share a centralized directory database of user account information and security for the entire domain.

domain account *See* global account.

domain name A name that identifies a network and appears before the period in a website address such as *microsoft.com*. A fully qualified domain name is sometimes loosely called a domain name. *Also see* fully qualified domain name.

Double Data Rate SDRAM (DDR SDRAM) A type of memory technology used on DIMMs that runs at twice the speed of the system clock, has one notch, and uses 184 pins. *Also called* DDR SDRAM, SDRAM II, and DDR.

double-sided A DIMM feature whereby memory chips are installed on both sides of a DIMM.

drive imaging Making an exact image of a hard drive, including partition information, boot sectors, operating system installation, and application software to replicate the hard drive on another system or recover from a hard drive crash. *Also called* disk cloning or disk imaging.

driver store The location where Windows stores a copy of the driver software when first installing a device.

DSL (Digital Subscriber Line) A telephone line that carries digital data from end to end, and is used as a type of broadband Internet access.

dual boot The ability to boot using either of two different OSs, such as Windows 8 and Windows 7. *Also called* multiboot.

dual channels A motherboard feature that improves memory performance by providing two 64-bit channels between memory and the chipset. DDR, DDR2, DDR3, and DDR4 DIMMs can use dual channels.

dual processors Two processor sockets on a server motherboard.

dual rail A power supply with a second +12-V circuit or rail used to ensure the first circuit is not overloaded.

dual ranked Double-sided DIMMs that provide two 64-bit banks. The memory controller accesses first one bank and then the other. Dual-ranked DIMMs do not perform as well as single-ranked DIMMs.

dual voltage selector switch A switch on the back of the computer case where you can switch the input voltage to the power supply to 115 V used in the United States or 220 V used in other countries.

dumb terminal *See* zero client.

dump In Linux, a collection of data that is copied to a backup media.

duplex printer A printer that is able to print on both sides of the paper.

duplexing assembly Used in a duplex printer, a duplexing assembly contains several rollers, turns the paper around, and draws it back through the print process to print on the back of the paper.

DVD (digital versatile disc or digital video disc) A technology used by optical discs that uses a red laser beam and can hold up to 17 GB of data.

DVD-ROM Stands for DVD read-only memory.

DVD-RW Stands for DVD rewriteable memory.

DVD-RW DL Stands for DVD rewriteable memory, dual layers. Dual layers almost double the storage capacity of DVD-RW discs.

DVI (Digital Video Interface) port A port that transmits digital or analog video.

DVI-A A DVI (Digital Visual Interface) video port that only transmits analog data.

DVI-D A DVI (Digital Visual Interface) video port that works only with digital monitors.

DVI-I A DVI (Digital Visual Interface) video port that supports both analog and digital monitors.

dxdiag.exe A Windows command used to display information about hardware and diagnose problems with DirectX.

dynamic disk A way to partition one or more hard drives so that the drives can work together to store data in order to increase space for data or to provide fault tolerance or improved performance. *Also see* RAID. *Compare with* basic disk.

dynamic IP address An IP address assigned by a DHCP server for the current session only, and is leased when the computer first connects to a network. When the session is terminated, the IP address is returned to the list of available addresses. *Compare with* static IP address.

dynamic RAM (DRAM) The most common type of system memory, it requires refreshing every few milliseconds.

dynamic volume A volume type used with dynamic disks by which you can create a single volume that uses space on multiple hard drives.

ECC (error-correcting code) A chipset feature on a motherboard that checks the integrity of data stored on DIMMs or RIMMs and can correct single-bit errors in a byte. More advanced ECC schemas can detect, but not correct, double-bit errors in a byte.

EFI (Extensible Firmware Interface) The original version of UEFI that was first developed by Intel.

EFI System Partition (ESP) For a GPT hard drive, the bootable partition used to boot the OS and contains the boot manager program for the OS.

electrostatic discharge (ESD) Another name for static electricity, which can damage chips and destroy motherboards, even though it might not be felt or seen with the naked eye.

elevated command prompt window A Windows command prompt window that allows commands that require administrator privileges.

email filtering To search incoming or outgoing email messages for matches kept in databases, searching for known scams and spammers to protect against social engineering.

email hoax An email message that is trying to tempt you to give out personal information or trying to scam you.

embedded MMC (eMMC) Internal storage used instead of using a solid-state drive (SSD) in inexpensive mobile devices such as cell phones, tablets, and laptops.

emergency notifications Government alerts, such as AMBER alerts, that are sent to mobile devices in an emergency.

emulator A virtual machine that emulates hardware, such as the hardware buttons on a smart phone.

Encrypted File System (EFS) A way to use a key to encode a file or folder on an NTFS volume to protect sensitive data. Because it is an integrated system service, EFS is transparent to users and applications.

End User License Agreement (EULA) A digital or printed statement of your rights to use or copy software, which you agree to when the software is installed.

enterprise license A license to use software that allows an organization to install multiple instances of the software. *Also called* site license.

entry control roster A list of people allowed into a restricted area and a log of any approved visitors that is used and maintained by security guards.

erase *See* del.

e-reader A mobile device that holds digital versions of books, newspapers, magazines, and other printed documents, which are usually downloaded to the device from the web.

escalate Assigning a problem to someone higher in the support chain of an organization. This action is normally recorded in call tracking software.

ESD mat A mat that dissipates electrostatic discharge (ESD) and is commonly used by technicians who repair and assemble computers at their workbenches or in an assembly line. *Also called* ground mat.

ESD strap A strap you wear around your wrist that is attached to the computer case, ground mat, or another ground so that electrostatic discharge (ESD) is discharged from your body before you touch sensitive components inside a computer. Also called antistatic wrist strap or ground bracelet.

Ethernet over Power (EoP) *See* powerline networking.

Ethernet port *See* network port.

Event Viewer A Windows tool (eventvwr.msc) useful for troubleshooting problems with Windows, applications, and hardware. It displays logs of significant events, such as a hardware or network failure, OS failure, OS error messages, a device or service that has failed to start, or General Protection Faults.

Everyone group In Windows, the Authenticated Users group as well as the Guest account. When you share a file or folder on the network, Windows, by default, gives access to the Everyone group.

Execute Disable Bit (EDB) A processor security feature that can work with the operating system to designate an area of memory for holding data or instructions.

executive services In Windows, a group of components running in kernel mode that interfaces between the subsystems in user mode and the HAL (hardware abstraction layer).

expand The Windows command that extracts files from compressed distribution files, which are often used to distribute files for software installation.

expansion card A circuit board inserted into a slot on the motherboard to enhance the capability of the computer.

expert system Software that uses a database of known facts and rules to simulate a human expert's reasoning and decision-making processes.

ExpressCard A PCMCIA standard for laptop I/O cards that uses the PCI Express and USB 2.0 data transfer standards. Two types of ExpressCards are ExpressCard/34 (34mm wide) and ExpressCard/54 (54mm wide). ExpressCards have been replaced by USB ports on today's laptops.

ExpressCard/34 A type of ExpressCard that is 34mm wide. An ExpressCard/34 can fit into an ExpressCard/54 slot.

ExpressCard/54 A type of ExpressCard that is 54mm wide.

ext3 The Linux file system that was the first to support journaling, which is a technique that tracks and stores changes to the hard drive and helps prevent file system corruption.

ext4 The current Linux file system, which replaced the ext3 file system. Stands for "fourth extended file system."

extended partition On an MBR hard drive, the only partition on the drive that can contain more than one logical drive. In Windows, a hard drive can have only a single extended partition. *Compare with* primary partition.

extender A device that amplifies and retransmits a wireless signal to a wider coverage area and retains the original network name.

extension magnet brush A long-handled brush made of nylon fibers that are charged with static electricity to pick up stray toner inside a laser printer.

external enclosure A housing designed to store hard drives external from the computer.

external SATA (eSATA) A standard for external drives based on SATA that uses a special external shielded SATA cable up to 2 meters long.

F connector A connector used with an RG-6 coaxial cable and is used for connections to a TV and has a single copper wire.

factory default To restore a mobile device or other computer to its state at the time of purchase. The operating system is reinstalled and all user data and settings are lost.

fanless CPU cooler A processor cooler that instead of using fans, uses heat pipes that contain a small amount of liquid that becomes vapor when heated, and the vapor draws the heat away from the processor toward the fins on the cooler. There the heat can be blown away by case fans. *Also called* passive CPU cooler.

Fast Ethernet *See* 100BaseT.

Fast Startup A Windows 8 feature to speed up startup by performing a partial hibernation at shutdown. At shutdown, Windows saves the drivers and kernel state in the Windows hibernate file, hiberfil.sys, and then reads from this file on the next cold boot.

FAT (file allocation table) A table on a hard drive, USB flash drive, or floppy disk used by the FAT file system that tracks the clusters used to contain a file.

fat client *See* thick client.

fault tolerance The degree to which a system can tolerate failures. Adding redundant components, such as disk mirroring or disk duplexing, is a way to build in fault tolerance.

Favorites tray On Android devices, the area above the Action bar that contains up to seven apps or groups of apps. These apps stay put as you move from home screen to home screen.

ferrite clamp A clamp installed on a network cable to protect against electrical interference.

fiber optic As applied to Internet access technologies, a dedicated, leased line that uses fiber-optic cable from the Internet service provider (ISP) to a residence or place of business.

fiber-optic cable Cable that transmits signals as pulses of light over glass or plastic strands inside protected tubing.

field replaceable unit (FRU) A component in a computer or device that can be replaced with a new component without sending the computer or device back to the manufacturer. Examples: power supply, DIMM, motherboard, hard disk drive.

file allocation unit *See* cluster.

file association The association between a data file and an application to open the file that is determined by the file extension.

file attributes The properties assigned to a file. Examples of file attributes are read-only and hidden status.

File Explorer The Windows 8 utility used to view and manage files and folders.

file extension A portion of the name of a file that indicates how the file is organized or formatted, the type of content in the file, and what program uses the file. In command lines, the file extension follows the file name and is separated from it by a period, for example, Msd.exe, where exe is the file extension.

File History In Windows 8, the utility that can schedule and maintain backups of data. It can also create a system image for backward compatibility with Windows 7.

file name The first part of the name assigned to a file, which does not include the file extension. In Windows, a file name can be up to 255 characters.

file recovery software Third-party software that can help recover deleted and corrupted files.

file server A computer dedicated to storing and serving up data files and folders.

file system The overall structure that an OS uses to name, store, and organize files on a disk. Examples of file systems are NTFS and FAT32. Windows is always installed on a volume that uses the NTFS file system.

Finder An app embedded in Mac OS X that functions similar to File Explorer in Windows; use it to find and access files and applications in OS X.

firewall Hardware and/or software that blocks unwanted traffic initiated from the Internet into a private network and can restrict Internet access for local computers behind the firewall.

FireWire 400 A data transmission standard used by computers and peripherals (for example, a video camera) that transmits at 400 Mbps. *Also called* 1394a.

FireWire 800 A data transmission standard used by computers and peripherals (for example, a video camera) that transmits at 800 Mbps. *Also called* 1394b.

FireWire port A port used for high-speed multimedia devices such as camcorders. *Also called* an IEEE 1394 port.

firmware Software that is permanently stored in a chip. The BIOS on a motherboard is an example of firmware.

fitness monitor A wearable computer device that can measure heart rate, count pool laps or miles jogged or biked, and a host of other activities.

fixboot A Windows 7/Vista command that repairs the boot sector of the system partition.

fixmbr A Windows 7/Vista command to repair the MBR (Master Boot Record).

flashing BIOS The process of upgrading or refreshing the programming stored on a firmware chip.

flat-panel monitor *See* LCD (liquid crystal display) monitor.

flip-chip land grid array (FCLGA) A type of socket used by processors that has blunt protruding pins on the socket that connect with lands or pads on the bottom of the processor. The chips in the processor package are flipped over so that the top of the chip makes contact with the socket.

flip-chip pin grid array (FCPGA) A type of socket used by processors that has holes aligned in rows to receive pins on the bottom of the processor. The chips in the processor are flipped over so that the top of the chip makes contact with the socket.

floppy disk drive (FDD) A drive that can hold either a 5½ inch or 3¼ inch floppy disk. *Also called* floppy drive.

floppy drive *See* floppy disk drive (FDD).

fluorescent backlighting *See* Cold Cathode Fluorescent Lamp (CCFL).

folder *See* subdirectory.

Folder Options applet Accessed through Control Panel, manages how files and folders are displayed in File Explorer or Windows Explorer.

force quit In OS X, to abruptly end an app without allowing the app to go through its close process.

force stop To abruptly end an app without allowing the app to go through its close process.

format The Windows command to prepare a hard drive volume, logical drive, or USB flash drive for use by placing tracks and sectors on its surface to store information (for example, format d:). This process erases all data on the device.

formatting *See* format.

form factor A set of specifications on the size, shape, and configuration of a computer hardware component such as a case, power supply, or motherboard.

fragmented file A file that has been written to different portions of the disk so that it is not in contiguous clusters.

front panel connector A group of wires running from the front or top of the computer case to the motherboard.

front panel header A group of pins on a motherboard that connect to wires that are connected to the front panel of the computer case.

Front Side Bus (FSB) *See* system bus.

FTP (File Transfer Protocol) A TCP/IP protocol and application that uses the Internet to transfer files between two computers.

FTP server A server using the FTP or Secure FTP protocol that downloads or uploads files to remote computers.

full duplex Communication that happens in two directions at the same time.

fully qualified domain name (FQDN) Identifies a computer and the network to which it belongs and includes the computer name and domain name. For example, *jsmith.amazon.com*. Sometimes loosely referred to as a domain name.

fuser assembly A component in laser printing that uses heat and pressure to fuse the toner to paper.

gadget A mini-app that appears on the Windows 7 desktop or Vista sidebar.

gateway Any device or computer that network traffic can use to leave one network and go to a different network.

geotracking A mobile device routinely reports its position to Apple, Google, or Microsoft at least twice a day, which makes it possible for these companies to track your device's whereabouts.

gestures In OS X, finger movements on a touch screen or the trackpad of a Mac computer.

ghost cursor A trail on the screen left behind when you move the mouse.

Gigabit Ethernet A version of Ethernet that supports rates of data transfer up to 1 gigabit per second.

gigahertz (GHz) One thousand MHz, or one billion cycles per second. *Also see* hertz and megahertz.

global account An account that is used at the domain level, created by an administrator, and stored in the SAM (security accounts manager) database on a Windows domain controller. *Also called* domain account or network ID. *Compare with* local account.

global address *See* global unicast address.

global unicast address In TCP/IP version 6, an IP address that can be routed on the Internet. *Also called* global address.

Globally Unique Identifier Partition Table (GUID or GPT) One of two methods used to organize partitions on a hard drive. A GPT partitioning system installed on a hard drive can support 128 partitions and is recommended for drives larger than 2 TB. *Compare with* Master Boot Record (MBR).

Gmail An email service provided by Google at *mail.google.com*.

Google account A user account, which is a valid email address, that is registered on the Google Play website (*play.google.com*) and is used to download content to an Android device.

Google Play The official source for Android apps, also called the Android marketplace, at *play.google.com*.

gpresult The Windows command to find out group policies that are currently applied to a system for the computer or user.

GPS (Global Positioning System) A receiver that uses the system of 24 or more satellites orbiting the Earth. The receiver locates four or more of these satellites, and from these four locations, calculates its own position in a process called triangulation.

gpupdate The Windows command to refresh local group policies as well as group policies set in Active Directory on a Windows domain.

graphical user interface (GUI) An interface that uses graphics as compared with a command-driven interface.

graphics processing unit (GPU) A processor that manipulates graphic data to form the images on a monitor screen. A GPU can be embedded on a video card, on the motherboard, or integrated within the processor.

graphics tablet An input device that can use a stylus to hand draw. It works like a pencil on the tablet and uses a USB port.

grayware A program that is potentially harmful or potentially unwanted.

grep A Linux and OS X command to search for and display a specific pattern of characters in a file or in multiple files.

ground bracelet *See* ESD strap.

ground mat *See* ESD mat.

Group Policy A console (gpedit.msc) available only in Windows professional and business editions that is used to control what users can do and how the system can be used.

GRUB (GRand Unified Bootloader) The current Linux boot loader, which can handle dual boots with another OS installed on the system. *Also see* LILO (LInux boot LOader).

GSM (Global System for Mobile Communications) An open standard for cellular networks and cell phones that uses digital communication of data and is accepted and used worldwide.

Guests group A type of user group in Windows. User accounts that belong to this group have limited rights to the system and are given a temporary profile that is deleted after the user logs off.

gyroscope A device that contains a disc that is free to move and can respond to gravity as the device is moved.

HAL (hardware abstraction layer) The low-level part of Windows, written specifically for each CPU technology, so that only the HAL must change when platform components change.

half duplex Communication between two devices whereby transmission takes place in only one direction at a time.

Handoff A technique of devices and computers made by Apple that lets you start a task on one device, such as an iPad, then pick up that task on another device, such as a Mac desktop or laptop.

hard boot Restart the computer by turning off the power or by pressing the Reset button. *Also called* a cold boot.

hard disk drive (HDD) *See* hard drive.

hard drive The main secondary storage device of a computer. Two technologies are currently used by hard drives: magnetic and solid state. *Also called* hard disk drive (HDD).

hard-link migration A method used by USMT (User State Migration Tool) that does not copy user files and settings when the source computer and destination computer are the same.

hard reset (1) For Android devices, a factory reset, which erases all data and settings and restores the device to its original factory default state. (2) For iOS devices, a forced restart similar to a full shutdown followed by a full clean boot of the device.

hardware address *See* MAC (Media Access Control) address.

hardware-assisted virtualization (HAV) A feature of a processor whereby it can provide enhanced support for hypervisor software to run virtual machines on a system. The feature must be enabled in UEFI/BIOS setup.

hardware print server A device that can connect to a USB, Bluetooth, or serial-port printer to connect the printer to the network as a network printer.

hardware RAID One of two ways to implement RAID. Hardware RAID is more reliable and better performing than software RAID, and is implemented using UEFI/BIOS on the motherboard or a RAID controller card.

HD15 port *See* VGA (Video Graphics Array) port.

HDMI (High Definition Multimedia Interface) port A digital audio and video port currently used on televisions and other home theater equipment and is often used to connect a computer to home theater equipment.

HDMI connector A connector that transmits both digital video and audio and is used on most computers and televisions.

HDMI mini connector A smaller type of HDMI connector used for connecting some devices such as a smart phone to a computer. *Also called* mini-HDMI connector.

heat sink A piece of metal, with cooling fins, that can be attached to or mounted on an integrated chip package (such as the CPU) to dissipate heat.

help The Windows command to get help about another command.

hertz (Hz) Unit of measurement for frequency, calculated in terms of vibrations, or cycles per second. For example, for 16-bit stereo sound, a frequency of 44,000 Hz is used. *Also see* megahertz and gigahertz.

hibernation A power-saving state that saves all work to the hard drive and powers down the system.

hidden share In Windows, a folder whose folder name ends with a $ symbol. When you share the folder, it does not appear in the File Explorer or Windows Explorer window of remote computers on the network.

high-level formatting A process performed by the Windows Format program (for example, FORMAT C:/S), the Windows installation program, or the Disk Management utility. The process creates the boot record, file system, and root directory on a hard drive volume or logical drive, a floppy disk, or a USB flash drive. *Also called* formatting, OS formatting, or operating system formatting. *Compare with* low-level formatting.

high-touch using a standard image A strategy to install Windows that uses a standard image for the installation. A technician must perform the installation on the local computer. *Also see* standard image.

high-touch with retail media A strategy to install Windows where all the work is done by a technician sitting at the computer using Windows setup files. The technician also installs drivers and applications after the Windows installation is finished.

HKEY_CLASSES_ROOT (HKCR) A Windows registry key that stores information to determine which application is opened when the user double-clicks a file.

HKEY_CURRENT_CONFIG (HKCC) A Windows registry key that contains information about the hardware configuration that is used by the computer at startup.

HKEY_CURRENT_USER (HKCU) A Windows registry key that contains data about the current user. The key is built when a user signs in using data kept in the HKEY_USERS key and data kept in the Ntuser.dat file of the current user.

HKEY_LOCAL_MACHINE (HKLM) An important Windows registry key that contains hardware, software, and security data. The key is built using data taken from the SAM hive, the Security hive, the Software hive, and the System hive and from data collected at startup about the hardware.

HKEY_USERS (HKU) A Windows registry key that contains data about all users and is taken from the Default hive.

homegroup In Windows, a type of peer-to-peer network where each computer shares files, folders, libraries, and printers with other computers in the homegroup. Access to the homegroup is secured using a homegroup password.

Home Theater PC (HTPC) A PC that is designed to play and possibly record music, photos, movies, and video on a television or extra-large monitor screen.

host bus *See* system bus.

host name A name that identifies a computer, printer, or other device on a network, which can be used instead of the computer's IP address to address the computer on the network. The host name together with the domain name is called the fully qualified domain name. *Also called* computer name.

Hosts file A file in the C:\Windows\System32\drivers\etc folder that contains computer names and their associated IP addresses on the local network. The file has no file extension.

hot-plugging Plugging in a device while the computer is turned on. The computer will sense the device and configure it without rebooting. In addition, the device can be unplugged without an OS error. *Also called* hot-swapping.

hotspot A small area that offers connectivity to a wireless network, such as a Wi-Fi network.

hot-swappable The ability to plug or unplugdevices without first powering down the system. USB devices are hot-swappable.

hot-swapping *See* hot-plugging.

HTPC case A case used to accommodate a home theater PC and must be small enough to fit on a shelf in an entertainment center.

HTTP (Hypertext Transfer Protocol) The TCP/IP protocol used for the World Wide Web and used by web browsers and web servers to communicate.

HTTPS (HTTP secure) The HTTP protocol working with a security protocol such as Secure Sockets Layer (SSL) or Transport Layer Security (TLS), which is better than SSL, to create a secured socket that includes data encryption.

hub A network device or box that provides a central location to connect cables and distributes incoming data packets to all other devices connected to it. *Compare with* switch.

hybrid cloud A combination of public, private, and community clouds used by the same organization. For example, a company might store data in a private cloud, but use a public cloud email service.

hybrid hard drive (H-HDD) A hard drive that uses both magnetic and solid-state drive (SSD) technologies. The bulk of storage uses the magnetic component, and a storage buffer on the drive is made of an SSD component. Windows ReadyDrive supports hybrid hard drives.

Hyper-Threading The Intel technology that allows each logical processor within the processor package to handle an individual thread in parallel with other threads being handled by other processors within the package.

Hyper Transport The AMD technology that allows each logical processor within the processor package to handle an individual thread in parallel with other threads being handled by other processors within the package.

hypervisor Software that creates and manages virtual machines on a server or on a local computer. *Also called* virtual machine manager (VMM).

IaaS (Infrastructure as a Service) A cloud computing service that provides only the hardware, which can include servers, storage devices, and networks.

iCloud A website by Apple (*www.icloud.com*) used to sync content on Apple devices in order to provide a backup of the content.

iCloud Backup A feature of an iPhone, iPad, or iPod touch whereby the device's content is backed up to the cloud at *icloud.com*.

iCloud Drive Storage space at *icloud.com* that can be synced with files stored on any Apple mobile device or any personal computer, including an OS X or Windows computer.

IDE (Integrated Drive Electronics or Integrated Device Electronics) A hard drive whose disk controller is integrated into the drive, eliminating the need for a controller cable and thus increasing speed, as well as reducing price.

IEEE 1394 port *See* FireWire port.

IEEE 802.11ac The latest Wi-Fi standard that supports up to 7 Gbps (actual speeds are currently about 1300 Mbps) and uses 5.0-GHz radio frequency and beamforming.

IEEE 802.11n A Wi-Fi standard that supports up to 600 Mbps and uses 5.0-GHz or 2.4-GHz radio frequency and supports MIMO.

ifconfig (interface configuration) A Linux and OS X command similar to the Windows ipconfig command that displays details about network interfaces and can enable and disable an interface. When affecting the interface, the command requires root privileges.

image deployment Installing a standard image on a computer.

imaging drum An electrically charged rotating drum found in laser printers.

IMAP4 (Internet Message Access Protocol, version 4) A protocol used by an email server and client that allows the client to manage email stored on the server without downloading the email. *Compare with* POP3.

IMEI (International Mobile Equipment Identity) A unique number that identifies a mobile phone or tablet device worldwide. The number can usually be found imprinted on the device or reported in the About menu of the OS.

impact paper Paper used by impact printers and comes as a box of fanfold paper or in rolls (used with receipt printers).

impact printer A type of printer that creates a printed page by using a mechanism that touches or hits the paper.

IMSI (International Mobile Subscriber Identity) A unique number that identifies a cellular subscription for a device or subscriber, along with its home country and mobile network. Some carriers store the number on a SIM card installed in the device.

Infrared (IR) An outdated wireless technology that has been mostly replaced by Bluetooth to connect personal computing devices.

infrastructure mode Wi-Fi devices connect to a Wi-Fi access point, such as a SOHO router, which is responsible for securing and managing the wireless network.

inherited permissions Permissions assigned by Windows that are attained from a parent object.

initialization files Text files that keep hardware and software configuration information, user preferences, and application settings and are used by the OS when first loaded and when needed by hardware, applications, and users.

ink cartridge A cartridge in an inkjet printer that holds the different colors of ink for the printer.

inkjet printer A type of ink dispersion printer that uses cartridges of ink. The ink is heated to a boiling point and then ejected onto the paper through tiny nozzles.

in-place upgrade A Windows installation that is launched from the Windows desktop. The installation carries forward user settings and installed applications from the old OS to the new one. A Windows OS is already in place before the installation begins.

In-Plane Switching (IPS) A class of LCD monitor that offers truer color images and better viewing angles, but is expensive and has slower response times.

interface In TCP/IP version 6, a node's attachment to a link. The attachment can be a physical attachment (for example, when using a network adapter) or a logical attachment (for example, when using a tunneling protocol). Each interface is assigned an IP address.

interface ID In TCP/IP version 6, the last 64 bits or 4 blocks of an IP address that identify the interface.

internal components The main components installed in a computer case.

Internet Options A dialog box used to manage Internet Explorer settings.

Internet Protocol version 4 (IPv4) A group of TCP/IP standards that uses IP addresses that have 32 bits.

Internet Protocol version 6 (IPv6) A group of TCP/IP standards that uses IP addresses that have 128 bits.

Internet service provider (ISP) A commercial group that provides Internet access for a monthly fee; Charter, Earthlink, and Windstream are large ISPs.

Internet telephone *See* Voice over Internet Protocol (VoIP).

intranet Any private network that uses TCP/IP protocols. A large enterprise might support an intranet that is made up of several local networks.

intrusion detection system (IDS) Software that can run on a UTM (Unified Threat Management) appliance, router, server, or workstation to monitor all network traffic and create alerts when suspicious activity happens.

intrusion prevention system (IPS) Software that can run on a UTM (Unified Threat Management) appliance, router, server, or workstation to monitor all network traffic, create alerts, and prevent the threatening traffic from burrowing into the system.

inverter An electrical device that converts DC to AC.

iOS The operating system owned and developed by Apple and used for its various mobile devices.

I/O shield A plate installed on the rear of a computer case that provides holes for I/O ports coming off the motherboard.

iPad A handheld tablet developed by Apple.

IP address A 32-bit or 128-bit address used to uniquely identify a device or interface on a network that uses TCP/IP protocols. Generally, the first numbers identify the network; the last numbers identify a host. An example of a 32-bit IP address is 206.96.103.114. An example of a 128-bit IP address is 2001:0000:B80::D3:9C5A:CC.

ipconfig (IP configuration) A Windows command that displays TCP/IP configuration information and can refresh TCP/IP assignments to a connection, including its IP address.

iPhone A smart phone developed by Apple.

iPod touch A multimedia recorder and player developed by Apple.

ISATAP In TCP/IP version 6, a tunneling protocol that has been developed for IPv6 packets to travel over an IPv4 network and stands for Intra-Site Automatic Tunnel Addressing Protocol.

ISDN (Integrated Services Digital Network) A broadband telephone line that can carry data at about five times the speed of regular telephone lines. Two channels (telephone numbers) share a single pair of wires. ISDN has been replaced by DSL.

ISO file *See* ISO image.

ISO image A file format that has an .iso file extension and holds an image of all the data, including the file system that is stored on an optical disc. ISO stands for International Organization for Standardization. *Also called* disc image or ISO file.

iTunes Store Apple website *itunes.apple.com* where apps, music, TV shows, movies, books, podcasts, and iTunes U content can be purchased and downloaded to Apple devices.

iTunes U Content at the iTunes Store website (*itunes.apple.com*) that contains lectures and even complete courses from many schools, colleges, and universities.

ITX *See* Mini-ITX.

iwconfig A Linux and OS X command similar to ifconfig, but applies only to wireless networks. Use it to display information about a wireless interface and configure a wireless adapter.

jailbreaking A process to break through the restrictions that only allow apps to an iOS device to be downloaded from the iTunes Store. Gives the user root or administrator privileges to the operating system and the entire file system and complete access to all commands and features. Note that jailbreaking voids any manufacturer warranty on the device, violates the End User License Agreement (EULA) with Apple, and might violate BYOD (Bring Your Own Device) policies in an enterprise environment.

joule A measure of work or energy. One joule of energy produces one watt of power for one second.

jumper Two small posts or metal pins that stick up side by side on the motherboard or other device and are used to hold configuration information. The jumper is considered closed if a cover is over the wires and open if the cover is missing.

kernel The portion of an OS that is responsible for interacting with the hardware.

kernel mode A Windows "privileged" processing mode that has access to hardware components.

kernel panic A Linux or OS X error from which it cannot recover, similar to a blue screen of death in Windows.

keyboard backlight A feature on some keyboards where the keys light up on the keyboard.

Keychain In OS X, a built-in password manager utility.

Key-enrollment Key (KEK) *See* Key-exchange Key (KEK).

Key-exchange Key (KEK) A Secure Boot database that holds digital signatures provided by OS manufacturers.

key fob A device, such as a type of smart card, that can fit conveniently on a key chain.

keylogger A type of spyware that tracks your keystrokes, including passwords, chat room sessions, email messages, documents, online purchases, and anything else you type on your computer. Text is logged to a text file and transmitted over the Internet without your knowledge.

keystone RJ-45 jack A jack that is used in an RJ-45 wall jack.

KVM (Keyboard, Video, and Mouse) switch A switch that allows you to use one keyboard, mouse, and monitor for multiple computers. Some KVM switches also include sound ports so that speakers and a microphone can be shared among multiple computers.

LAN (local area network) A network bound by routers that usually covers only a small area, such as one building.

land grid array (LGA) A socket that has blunt protruding pins in uniform rows on the socket that connect with lands or pads on the bottom of the processor. *Compare with* pin grid array (PGA).

laptop A portable computer that is designed for travel and mobility. Laptops use the same technology as desktop computers, with modifications for conserving voltage, taking up less space, and operating while on the move. *Also called* a notebook.

laser printer A type of printer that uses a laser beam to control how toner is placed on the page and then uses heat to fuse the toner to the page.

Last Known Good Configuration In Windows 7/Vista, registry settings and device drivers that were in effect when the computer last booted successfully. These settings are saved and can be restored during the startup process to recover from errors during the last boot. Windows 8 does not save the Last Known Good Configuration.

latency Delays in network transmissions resulting in slower network performance. Latency is measured by the round-trip time it takes for a data packet to travel from source to destination and back to source.

launcher The Android graphical user interface (GUI) that includes multiple home screens, and supports windows, panes, and 3D graphics.

Launchpad In OS X, the screen that shows all apps installed on the computer, similar to the Windows 8 Start screen.

LC (local connector) connector A fiber-optic cable connector that can be used with either single-mode or multimode fiber-optic cables and is easily terminated and smaller than an SC connector.

LCD (liquid crystal display) monitor A monitor that uses LCD technology. LCD produces an image using a liquid crystal material made of large, easily polarized molecules. *Also called* flat-panel monitor.

LED (light-emitting diode) A technology used in an LCD monitor that uses less mercury than earlier technologies.

Level 1 cache (L1 cache) Memory on the processor die used as a cache to improve processor performance.

Level 2 cache (L2 cache) Memory in the processor package but not on the processor die. The memory is used as a cache or buffer to improve processor performance. *Also see* Level 1 cache (L1 cache).

Level 3 cache (L3 cache) Cache memory further from the processor core than Level 2 cache but still in the processor package.

library In Windows 8/7, a collection of one or more folders that can be stored on different local drives or on the network.

Lightning port The connector used on newer Apple iPhones, iPods, and iPads for power and communication.

Lightweight Directory Access Protocol (LDAP) A protocol used by various client applications when the application needs to query a database.

LILO (LInux boot LOader) The outdated Linux boot loader that could handle a dual boot and has been replaced by GRUB.

line-of-sight connectivity A type of connection used by satellites that requires no obstruction from mountains, trees, and tall buildings from the satellite dish to the satellite.

line speed *See* bandwidth.

link (local link) In TCP/IP version 6, a local area network or wide area network bounded by routers. *Also called* local link.

link-local address *See* link-local unicast address.

link-local unicast address In TCP/IP version 6, an IP address used for communicating among nodes in the same link and is not allowed on the Internet. *Also called* local address *and* link-local address.

Linux An OS based on UNIX that was created by Linus Torvalds of Finland. Basic versions of this OS are open source, and all the underlying programming instructions are freely distributed.

lite-touch, high-volume deployment A strategy that uses a deployment server on the network to serve up a Windows installation after a technician starts the process at the local computer.

lithium ion Currently the most popular battery type for laptop computers that is more efficient than earlier types. Sometimes abbreviated as "Li-Ion" battery.

live CD In Linux, a CD, DVD, or flash drive that can boot up a live version of Linux, complete with Internet access and all the tools you normally have available in a hard drive installation of Linux, but without installing the OS on the hard drive.

live sign in Sign in to Windows 8 using a Microsoft account.

live tiles On the Windows 8 Start screen, some apps use live tiles, which offer continuous real-time updates.

loadstate A command used by the User State Migration Tool (USMT) to copy user settings and data temporarily stored at a safe location to a new computer. *Also see* scanstate.

local account A Windows user account that applies only to the local computer and cannot be used to access resources from other computers on the network. *Compare with* global account.

local area network (LAN) A network bound by routers or other gateway devices.

local address *See* link-local unicast address.

local bus *See* system bus.

local link *See* link.

local printer A printer connected to a computer by way of a port on the computer. *Compare with* network printer.

Local Security Policy A Windows Administrative Tools snap-in in Control Panel that can manage the group of policies in the Local Computer Policy, Computer Configuration, Windows Settings, Security Settings group of Group Policy.

local share Folders on a computer that are shared with others on the network by using a folder's Properties box. Local shares are used with a workgroup and not with a domain.

local snapshot In OS X, the temporary backups that Time Machine creates when the Mac is not connected to the backup media. When the media is later available, local snapshots are copied to the media.

Local Users and Groups For business and professional editions of Windows, a Windows utility console (lusrmgr.msc) that can be used to manage user accounts and user groups.

location data Data that a device can routinely report to a website, which can be used to locate the device on a map.

location independence A function of cloud computing whereby customers generally are not aware of where the physical devices providing cloud services are located geographically.

logical drive On an MBR hard drive, a portion or all of a hard drive extended partition that is treated by the operating system as though it were a physical drive or volume. Each logical drive is assigned a drive letter, such as drive F, and contains a file system. *Compare with* volume.

logical topology The logical way computers connect on a network.

login item In OS X, programs that are automatically launched after a user logs in. Login items are managed in the Users & Groups utility in System Preferences.

LoJack A technology by Absolute Software used to track the whereabouts of a laptop computer and, if the computer is stolen, lock down access to the computer or erase data on it. The technology is embedded in the UEFI/BIOS of many laptops.

Long Term Evolution (LTE) The latest standard used to transmit both voice and digital data over cellular networks and is expected to eventually replace CDMA and GSM.

loopback address An IP address that indicates your own computer and is used to test TCP/IP configuration on the computer.

loopback plug A device used to test a port in a computer or other device to make sure the port is working and might also test the throughput or speed of the port.

low-level formatting A process (usually performed at the factory) that electronically creates the hard drive tracks and sectors, and tests for bad spots on the disk surface. *Compare with* high-level formatting.

LPT (Line Printer Terminal) Assignments of system resources that are made to a parallel port and that are used to manage a print job. Two possible LPT configurations are referred to as LPT1: and LPT2:.

LPT port *See* parallel port.

MAC (Media Access Control) address A 48-bit (6-byte) hardware address unique to each network interface card (NIC) or onboard network controller that is assigned by the manufacturer at the factory and embedded on the device. The address is often printed on the adapter as hexadecimal numbers. An example is 00 00 0C 08 2F 35. *Also called* a physical address, an adapter address, or a hardware address.

MAC address filtering A technique used by a router or wireless access point to allow access to a private network to only certain computers or devices identified by their MAC addresses.

magnetic hard drive One of two technologies used by hard drives where data is stored as magnetic spots on disks that rotate at a high speed. *Compare with* solid-state drive (SSD).

main board *See* motherboard.

malicious software Any unwanted program that is transmitted to a computer without the user's knowledge and that is designed to do varying degrees of damage to data and software. Types of infestations include viruses, Trojan horses, worms, adware, spyware, keyloggers, browser hijackers, dialers, and downloaders. *Also called* malware or computer infestation.

malware *See* malicious software.

malware definition Information about malware that allows anti-malware software to detect and define malware. *Also called* a malware signature.

malware encyclopedia Lists of malware, including symptoms and solutions, often maintained by manufacturers of anti-malware and made available on their websites.

malware signature *See* malware definition.

MAN (metropolitan area network) A type of network that covers a large city or campus.

man-in-the-middle attack An attack that pretends to be a legitimate website, network, FTP site, or person in a chat session in order to obtain private information.

mantrap A physical security technique of using two doors on either end of a small entryway where the first door must close before the second door can open. A separate form of identification might be required for each door, such as a badge for the first door and a fingerprint scan for the second door. In addition, a security guard might monitor people as they come and go.

mapping The client computer creates and saves a shortcut, called a network drive, to a folder or drive shared by a remote computer on the network. The network drive has a drive letter associated with it, which points to the network share.

Master Boot Record (MBR) One of two methods used to organize the partition tables on a hard drive. On an MBR hard drive, the first sector on the drive is called the MBR and contains the partition table and a program BIOS uses to boot an OS from the drive. *Compare with* Globally Unique Identifier Partition Table (GUID or GPT).

master file table (MFT) The database used by the NTFS file system to track the contents of a volume or logical drive.

Material Safety Data Sheet (MSDS) A document that explains how to properly handle substances such as chemical solvents; it includes information such as physical data, toxicity, health effects, first aid, storage, disposal, and spill procedures.

md (make directory) The Windows command to create a directory.

measured service When a cloud computing vendor offers services that are metered for billing purposes or to ensure transparency between vendors and customers.

megahertz (MHz) One million Hz, or one million cycles per second. *Also see* hertz and gigahertz.

memory bank The memory a processor addresses at one time. Today's desktop and laptop processors use a memory bank that is 64 bits wide.

memory bus *See* system bus.

Memory Diagnostics A Windows utility (mdsched.exe) used to test memory.

Metro User Interface (Metro UI) *See* modern interface.

Micro-A connector A USB connector that has five pins and is smaller than the Mini-B connector. It is used on digital cameras, cell phones, and other small electronic devices.

microATX (MATX) A smaller version of the ATX form factor. MicroATX addresses some new technologies that were developed after the original introduction of ATX.

Micro-B connector A USB connector that has five pins and has a smaller height than the Mini-B connector. It is used on digital cameras, cell phones, and other small electronic devices.

microprocessor *See* central processing unit (CPU).

Microsoft account For Windows 8 and above, an email address and password that allows access to several types of online accounts, including Microsoft OneDrive, Facebook, LinkedIn, Twitter, Skype, Outlook, and others.

Microsoft Assessment and Planning (MAP) Toolkit Software that can be used by a system administrator from a network location to query hundreds of computers in a single scan to determine if a computer qualifies for a Windows upgrade.

Microsoft Exchange A server application that can handle email, contacts, and calendars and is a popular application used by large corporations for employee email, contacts, and calendars.

Microsoft Management Console (MMC) A Windows utility to build customized consoles. These consoles can be saved to a file with an .msc file extension.

Microsoft Store The official source for Windows apps at *microsoftstore.com*.

microUSB A smaller version of the regular USB connector.

MIDI (musical instrument digital interface) A set of standards that are used to represent music in digital form. A MIDI port is a 5-pin DIN port that looks like a keyboard port, only larger.

MIMO *See* multiple input/multiple output (MIMO).

Mini-B connector A USB connector that has five pins and is often used to connect small electronic devices, such as a digital camera, to a computer.

Mini-DIN-6 connector A 6-pin variation of the S-Video port and looks like a PS/2 connector used by a keyboard or mouse.

Mini DisplayPort A smaller version of DisplayPort that is used on laptops or other mobile devices.

mini-HDMI connector *See* HDMI mini connector.

Mini-ITX A smaller version of the microATX form factor. *Also called* ITX.

Mini PCI The PCI industry standard for desktop computer expansion cards, applied to a much smaller form factor for laptop expansion cards.

Mini PCI Express (Mini PCIe) A standard used for laptop internal expansion slots that follows the PCI Express standards applied to laptops.

minicartridge A tape drive cartridge that is only 3¼ x 2½ x 3/5 inches. It is small enough to allow two drives to fit into a standard 5-inch drive bay of a PC case.

miniUSB A smaller version of the regular USB connector and is smaller than microUSB.

Miracast A wireless display-mirroring technology that requires a Miracast-capable screen or dongle in order to mirror a smart phone's display to a TV, a wireless monitor, or a wireless projector.

mirrored volume The term used by Windows for the RAID 1 level that duplicates data on one drive to another drive and is used for fault tolerance. *Also see* RAID 1.

Mission Control In OS X, a utility and screen that gives an overview of all open windows and thumbnails of the Dashboard and desktops.

mobile hotspot Created by a mobile device so that other devices or computers can connect by Wi-Fi to the device and on to the Internet.

mobile payment service An app that allows you to use your smart phone or other mobile device to pay for merchandise or services at a retail checkout counter.

modem port A port used to connect dial-up phone lines to computers.

modern interface An interface that presents the Start screen to the user. *Also called* Windows 8 interface, *formerly called* Metro User Interface or Metro UI.

Molex connector A 4-pin power connector used to provide power to a PATA hard drive or optical drive.

motherboard The main board in the computer, *also called* the system board. The CPU, ROM chips, DIMMs, RIMMs, and interface cards are plugged into the motherboard.

motion controller An input device that senses the motion of your fingers and hands. *Also called* motion sensor.

motion sensor *See* motion controller.

mount point A folder that is used as a shortcut to space on another volume, which effectively increases the size of the folder to the size of the other volume. *Also see* mounted drive.

mounted drive A volume that can be accessed by way of a folder on another volume so that the folder has more available space. *Also see* mount point.

mstsc (Microsoft Terminal Services Client) A Windows command that allows you to start Remote Desktop Connection to remote in to your host computer using Remote Desktop.

MT-RJ (mechanical transfer registered jack) connector A type of connector used by fiber-optic cables and can be used with either single-mode or multimode fiber-optic cables and is more difficult to connect than the smaller LC connector.

multiboot *See* dual boot.

multicast address In TCP/IP version 6, an IP address used when packets are delivered to a group of nodes on a network.

multicasting In TCP/IP version 6, one host sends messages to multiple hosts, such as when the host transmits a video conference over the Internet.

multicore processing A processor technology whereby the processor housing contains two or more processor cores that operate at the same frequency but independently of each other.

multifactor authentication (MFA) To use more than one method to authenticate access to a computer, network, or other resource.

MultiMediaCard (MMC) A compact storage card that looks like an SD card, but the technology is different and they are not interchangeable. Generally, SD cards are faster than MMC cards.

multimeter A device used to measure the various attributes of an electrical circuit. The most common measurements are voltage, current, and resistance.

multimonitor taskbar The Windows 8 option to extend the desktop taskbar across multiple monitors. Use the taskbar properties box to adjust the taskbar.

multiple desktops A feature of Mission Control in OS X, where several desktop screens, each with its own collection of open windows, are available to the user.

multiple input/multiple output (MIMO) A feature of the IEEE 802.11n/ac standards for wireless networking whereby two or more antennas are used at both ends of transmissions to improve performance.

multiple monitor misalignment When the display is staggered across multiple monitors, making the display difficult to read. Fix the problem by adjusting the display in the Windows Screen Resolution window.

multiple monitor orientation When the display does not accurately represent the relative positions of multiple monitors. Use the Windows Screen Resolution window to move the display for each monitor so they are oriented correctly.

multiplier The factor by which the bus speed or frequency is multiplied to get the CPU clock speed.

multiprocessing Two processing units installed within a single processor and first used by the Pentium processor.

multiprocessor platform A system that contains more than one processor. The motherboard has more than one processor socket and the processors must be rated to work in this multiprocessor environment.

multitouch A touch screen on a computer or mobile device that can handle a two-finger pinch.

mutual authentication To authenticate in both directions at the same time, as both entities confirm the identity of the other.

name resolution The process of associating a character-based name with an IP address.

NAND flash memory The type of memory used in solid-state drives (SSD). NAND stands for "Not AND" and refers to the logic used when storing a 1 or 0 in the grid of rows and columns on the memory chip.

NAT (Network Address Translation) A technique that substitutes the public IP address of the router for the private IP address of computer on a private network when these computers need to communicate on the Internet. *See also* Destination Network Address Translation (DNAT).

native resolution The actual (and fixed) number of pixels built into an LCD monitor. For the clearest display, always set the resolution to the native resolution.

navigation pane In File Explorer, Windows Explorer, or the Computer window, the pane on the left side of the window where devices, drives, and folders are listed. Double-click an item to drill down into the item.

nbtstat (NetBIOS over TCP/IP Statistics) A Windows TCP/IP command that is used to display statistics about the NetBT protocol.

Near Field Communication (NFC) A wireless technology that establishes a communication link between two NFC devices (for example, two smart phones or a smart phone and an NFC tag) that are within 4 inches of each other.

neighbors In TCP/IP version 6, two or more nodes on the same link.

net localgroup A Windows TCP/IP command that adds, displays, or modifies local user groups.

net use A Windows TCP/IP command that connects or disconnects a computer from a shared resource or can display information about connections.

net user A Windows TCP/IP command used to manage user accounts.

NetBIOS A legacy suite of protocols used by Windows before TCP/IP.

NetBIOS over TCP/IP A feature of Server Message Block (SMB) protocols that allows legacy NetBIOS applications to communicate on a TCP/IP network.

netbook A low-end, inexpensive laptop with a small 9- or 10-inch screen and no optical drive that is generally used for web browsing, email, and word processing by users on the go.

NetBoot A technology that allows a Mac to boot from the network and then install OS X on the machine from a clone DMG file stored on the server.

netdom (network domain) A Windows TCP/IP command that allows administrators to manage Active Directory domains and trust relationships for Windows Server from the command prompt on the server or remotely from a Windows 8/7 workstation.

netstat (network statistics) A Windows TCP/IP command that gives statistics about TCP/IP and network activity and includes several parameters.

network adapter *See* network interface card (NIC).

Network and Sharing Center The primary Windows utility used to manage network connections.

Network Attached Storage (NAS) A device that provides multiple bays for hard drives and an Ethernet port to connect to the network. The device is likely to support RAID.

network drive map Mounting a drive to a computer, such as drive E:, that is actually hard drive space on another host computer on the network.

Network File System (NFS) A Windows component that is a distributed file system used to manage shared files on a network.

network ID *See* global account.

network interface card (NIC) An expansion card that plugs into a computer's motherboard and provides a port on the back of the card to connect a computer to a network. *Also called* a network adapter.

network multimeter A multifunctional tool that can test network connections, cables, ports, and network adapters.

Network Places Wizard *See* User Accounts.

network port A port used by a network cable to connect to the wired network. *Also called* an Ethernet port or RJ-45 port.

network printer A printer that any user on the network can access, through its own network card and connection to the network, through a connection to a stand-alone print server, or through a connection to a computer as a local printer, which is shared on the network.

network share One computer (the client) on the network appears to have a hard drive, such as drive E:, that is actually hard drive space on another host computer (the server). *Also see* mapping.

next-generation firewall (NGFW) A firewall that combines firewall software with anti-malware software and other software that protects resources on a network.

node Any device that connects to the network, such as a computer, printer, or router.

non compliant system A system that violates security best practices, such as out-of-date anti-malware software or no anti-malware software installed.

nonvolatile RAM (NVRAM) Flash memory on the motherboard that UEFI firmware uses to store device drivers and information about Secure Boot. Contents of NVRAM are not lost when the system is powered down.

North Bridge That portion of the chipset hub that connects faster I/O buses (for example, the video bus) to the system bus. *Compare with* South Bridge.

notebook *See* laptop.

Notepad A Windows text editing program.

notification area An area to the right of the Windows taskbar that holds the icons for running services; these services include the volume control and network connectivity. *Also called* the system tray or systray.

notifications Alerts and related information about apps and social media sent to mobile devices.

nslookup (namespace lookup) A TCP/IP command that lets you read information from the Internet namespace by requesting information about domain name resolutions from the DNS server's zone data.

NTFS permissions A Windows method to share a folder or file over a network and can apply to local users and network users. The folder or file must be on an NTFS volume. *Compare with* share permissions.

octet In TCP/IP version 4, each of the four numbers that are separated by periods and make up a 32-bit IP address. One octet is 8 bits.

Offline Files A Windows utility that allows users to work with files in the folder when the computer is not connected to the corporate network. When the computer is later connected, Windows syncs up the offline files and folders with those on the network.

ohm (Ω) The standard unit of measurement for electrical resistance. Resistors are rated in ohms.

OLED (organic light-emitting diode) monitor A type of monitor that uses a thin LED layer or film between two grids of electrodes and does not use backlighting.

onboard NIC A network port embedded on the motherboard.

onboard port Ports that are directly on the motherboard, such as a built-in keyboard port or onboard network port.

on-demand A service that is available to users at any time. On-demand cloud computing means the service is always available.

OneDrive Microsoft cloud service that allows users with a Microsoft account to store, sync, and share files with other people and devices.

Open Database Connectivity (ODBC) A technology that allows a client computer to create a data source so that the client can interface with a database stored on a remote (host) computer on the network. *Also see* data source.

open source Source code for an operating system or other software whereby the source code is available for free and anyone can modify and redistribute the source code.

operating system (OS) Software that controls a computer. An OS controls how system resources are used and provides a user interface, a way of managing hardware and software, and ways to work with files.

optical connector A connector used with a fiber-optic cable.

option ROM A Secure Boot driver required as the computer first boots, which is digitally signed and identified in the signature database.

Original Equipment Manufacturer (OEM) license A software license that only manufacturers or builders of personal computers can purchase to be installed only on a computer intended for sale.

OS X The latest version of the proprietary operating system only available for Macintosh computers by Apple Inc. (*apple.com*). OS X was originally based on UNIX.

OSI Model A model for understanding and developing computer-to-computer communication, it divides networking functions among seven layers: Physical, Data Link, Network, Transport, Session, Presentation, and Application.

overclocking Running a processor at a higher frequency than is recommended by the manufacturer, which can result in an unstable system, but is a popular thing to do when a computer is used for gaming.

PaaS (Platform as a Service) A cloud computing service that provides the hardware and the operating system and is responsible for updating and maintaining both.

packet A message sent over a network as a unit that contains the data and information at the beginning that identifies the type of data, where it came from, and where it's going. Also called data packet or datagram.

pagefile.sys The Windows swap file that is used to hold the virtual memory that is used to enhance physical memory installed in a system.

pairing The process of two Bluetooth devices establishing connectivity.

PAN (personal area network) A small network consisting of personal devices at close range; the devices can include smart phones, PDAs, and laptop computers.

parallel ATA (PATA) An older IDE cabling method that uses a 40-pin flat or round data cable or an 80-conductor cable and a 40-pin IDE connector. *Also see* serial ATA.

parallel port An outdated female 25-pin port on a computer that transmitted data in parallel, 8 bits at a time, and was usually used with a printer. Parallel ports have been replaced by USB ports. *Also called* an LPT1 port, LPT2 port, and LPT port.

parity An older error-checking scheme used with SIMMs in which a ninth, or "parity," bit is added. The value of the parity bit is set to either 0 or 1 to provide an even number of 1s for even parity and an odd number of 1s for odd parity.

parity error An error that occurs in parity error checking when the number of 1s in the byte is not in agreement with the expected number.

partition A division of a hard drive that can hold a volume. MBR drives can support up to four partitions on one hard drive. In Windows, GPT drives can have up to 128 partitions.

partition table A table that contains information about each partition on the drive. For MBR drives, the partition table is contained in the Master Boot Record. For GPT drives, the partition table is stored in the GPT header and a backup of the table is stored at the end of the drive.

passive CPU cooler *See* fanless CPU cooler.

patch A minor update to software that corrects an error, adds a feature, or addresses security issues. *Also called* an update. *Compare with* service pack.

patch cable *See* straight-through cable.

patch panel A device that provides multiple network ports for cables that converge in one location such as an electrical closet or server room.

path A drive and list of directories pointing to a file such as C:\Windows\System32.

PC Card A card that uses a PC Card slot on a laptop, and provides a port for peripheral devices or adds memory to the laptop. A PC Card is about the size of a credit card, but thicker.

PCI (Peripheral Component Interconnect) A bus common to personal computers that uses a 32-bit wide or a 64-bit data path. Several variations of PCI exist. On desktop systems, one or more notches on a PCI slot keep the wrong PCI cards from being inserted in the PCI slot.

PCI Express (PCIe) The latest evolution of PCI, which is not backward compatible with earlier PCI slots and cards. PCIe slots come in several sizes, including PCIe x1, PCIe x4, PCIe x8, and PCIe x16.

PCIe 6/8-pin connector A power cord connector used by high-end video cards using PCIe x16 slots to provide extra voltage to the card and can accommodate a 6-hole or 8-hole port.

PCI-X The second evolution of PCI, which is backward compatible with conventional PCI slots and cards, except 5-V PCI cards. PCI-X is focused on the server market.

PCL (Printer Control Language) A printer language developed by Hewlett-Packard that communicates to a printer how to print a page.

PCMCIA card A card used with older laptops that was one or more variations of a PC Card to add memory to a laptop or provide ports for peripheral devices. For example, modem cards, network cards for wired or wireless network, sound cards, SCSI host adapters, FireWire controllers, USB controllers, flash memory adapter, TV tuner, and hard disks.

peer-to-peer (P2P) As applied to networking, a network of computers that are all equals, or peers. Each computer has the same amount of authority, and each can act as a server to the other computers.

Performance Monitor A Microsoft Management Console snap-in that can track activity by hardware and software to measure performance.

permission propagation When Windows passes permissions from parent objects to child objects.

permissions Varying degrees of access assigned to a folder or file and given to a user account or user group. Access can include full control, write, delete, or read-only.

personal assistant *See* virtual assistant.

personal license A license to use software that gives the right to install one instance of the software.

phablet A mobile device that has the same capabilities of a smart phone or tablet and is smaller than a tablet and larger than a smart phone.

phishing Sending an email message with the intent of getting the user to reveal private information that can be used for identity theft. *Also see* spear phishing and spoofing.

physical address *See* MAC (Media Access Control) address.

physical topology The physical arrangement of connections between computers.

pickup roller A part in a printer that pushes forward a sheet of paper from the paper tray.

ping A TCP/IP command used to troubleshoot network connections. It verifies that the host can communicate with another host on the network. Stands for Packet InterNet Groper.

pin grid array (PGA) A socket that has holes aligned in uniform rows around the socket to receive the pins on the bottom of the processor. *Compare with* land grid array (LGA).

pinning To make a frequently used application more accessible, add its icon to the taskbar on the desktop.

pixel A small spot on a fine horizontal scan line. Pixels are illuminated to create an image on the monitor.

pixel pitch The distance between adjacent pixels on the screen.

plasma monitor A type of monitor that provides high contrast with better color than LCD monitors. They work by discharging xenon and neon plasma on flat glass and don't contain mercury.

platform The hardware, operating system, runtime libraries, and modules on which an application runs.

Platform Key (PK) A digital signature belonging to the motherboard or computer manufacturer. The PK authorizes turning on or off Secure Boot and updating the KEK database.

plenum The area between floors of a building.

PoE injector A device that adds power to an Ethernet cable so the cable can provide power to a device.

POP or POP3 (Post Office Protocol, version 3) The protocol that an email server and client use when the client requests the downloading of email messages. The most recent version is POP version 3. *Compare with* IMAP4.

port (1) As applied to services running on a computer, a number assigned to a process on a computer so that the process can be found by TCP/IP. *Also called* a port address or port number. (2) A physical connector, usually at the back of a computer, that allows a cable from a peripheral device, such as a printer, mouse, or modem, to be attached.

port address *See* port.

port filtering To open or close certain ports so they can or cannot be used. A firewall uses port filtering to protect a network from unwanted communication.

port forwarding A technique that allows a computer on the Internet to reach a computer on a private network using a certain port when the private network is protected by NAT and a firewall that controls the use of ports. *Also called* port mapping.

port mapping *See* port forwarding.

port number *See* port.

port triggering When a firewall opens a port because a computer behind the firewall initiates communication on another port.

POST (power-on self test) A self-diagnostic program used to perform a simple test of the CPU, RAM, and various I/O devices. The POST is performed by startup UEFI/BIOS when the computer is first turned on.

POST card A test card installed in a slot on the motherboard or plugged in to a USB port that is used to help discover and report computer errors and conflicts that occur when a computer is first turned on and before the operating system is launched. *Also called* POST diagnostic card.

POST diagnostic card *See* POST card.

PostScript A printer language developed by Adobe Systems that tells a printer how to print a page.

Power Options applet Accessed through Control Panel, manages power settings to conserve power.

Power over Ethernet (PoE) A feature that might be available on high-end wired network adapters that allows power to be transmitted over Ethernet cable to remote devices.

power supply A box inside the computer case that receives power and converts it to provide power to the motherboard and other installed devices. Power supplies provide 3.3-, 5-, and 12-V DC. *Also called* a power supply unit (PSU).

power supply tester A device that can test the output of each power cord coming from a power supply.

power supply unit (PSU) *See* power supply.

Power Users group A type of user account group. Accounts assigned to this group can read from and write to parts of the system other than their own user profile folders, install applications, and perform limited administrative tasks.

powerline networking A technique to allow Ethernet transmissions over power lines. A powerline adapter is plugged into the electrical circuit(s) at both ends and the adapters connect to the Ethernet network. Because the transmissions are not contained, encryption is required for security. *Also called* Ethernet over Power (EoP).

Preboot eXecution Environment (PXE) Programming contained in the UEFI/BIOS code on the motherboard used to start up the computer and search for a server on the network to provide a bootable operating system. *Also called* Pre-Execution Environment (PXE).

Pre-Execution Environment (PXE) *See* Preboot eXecution Environment (PXE).

presentation virtualization Using this virtualization, a remote application running on a server is controlled by a local computer.

primary partition A hard disk partition that can be used to boot the system. An MBR drive can have up to three primary partitions. In Windows, a GPT drive can have up to 128 primary partitions. *Compare with* extended partition.

principle of least privilege An approach where computer users are classified and the rights assigned are the minimum rights required to do their job.

print head The part in an inkjet or impact printer that moves across the paper, creating one line of the image with each pass.

Print Management A utility located in the Administrative Tools group in Windows 8/7/Vista professional and business editions that allows you to monitor and manage printer queues for all printers on the network.

print server Hardware or software that manages the print jobs sent to one or more printers on a network.

print spooler A queue for print jobs.

printer maintenance kit A kit purchased from a printer manufacturer that contains the parts, tools, and instructions needed to perform routine printer maintenance.

printer self-test page A test page that prints by using controls at the printer. The page allows you to eliminate a printer as a problem and usually prints tests, graphics, and information about the printer such as the printer resolution and how much memory is installed.

printui The Windows Printer User Interface command used by administrators to manage printers on the local and remote computers.

privacy filter A device that fits over a monitor screen to prevent other people from viewing the monitor from a wide angle.

private cloud Services on the Internet that an organization provides on its own servers or established virtually for a single organization's private use.

private IP address In TCP/IP version 4, an IP address that is used on a private network that is isolated from the Internet. *Compare with* public IP address.

PRL (Preferred Roaming List) A list of preferred service providers or radio frequencies your carrier wants a mobile device to use and is stored on a Removable User Identity Module (R-UIM) card installed in the device.

process A program that is running under the authority of the shell, together with the system resources assigned to it.

processor *See* central processing unit (CPU).

processor frequency The speed at which the processor operates internally. Usually expressed in GHz.

processor thermal trip error A problem when the processor overheats and the system restarts.

product activation The process that Microsoft uses to prevent software piracy. For example, once Windows 8 is activated for a particular computer, it cannot be legally installed on another computer.

Product Release Instructions (PRI) Information published by the manufacturer of an operating system that describes what to expect from a published update to the OS.

Programs and Features A window within Control Panel that lists the programs installed on a computer, where you can uninstall, change, or repair programs.

projector Used to shine a light that projects a transparent image onto a large screen and is often used in classrooms or with other large groups.

protocol A set of rules and standards that two entities use for communication. For example, TCP/IP is a suite or group of protocols that define many types of communication on a TCP/IP network.

proxy server A computer that intercepts requests that a client (for example, a browser) makes of a server (for example, a web server) and can serve up the request from a cache it maintains to improve performance or can filter requests to secure a large network.

PS/2 port A round 6-pin port used by a keyboard or mouse.

public cloud Cloud computing services provided over the Internet to the general public. Google or Yahoo! email services are examples of public cloud deployment.

public IP address In TCP/IP version 4, an IP address available to the Internet. *Compare with* private IP address.

pull automation A Windows installation that requires the local user to start the process. *Compare with* push automation.

punchdown tool A tool used to punch individual wires from a network cable into their slots to terminate the cable.

push automation An installation where a server automatically pushes the installation to a computer when a user is not likely to be sitting at the computer. *Compare with* pull automation.

PVC (polyvinyl chloride) The product used to cover Ethernet cables that is not safe to be used in a plenum because it gives off toxic fumes when burned.

quad channels Technology used by a motherboard and DIMMs that allows the memory controller to access four DIMMS at the same time. DDR3 and DDR4 DIMMs can use quad channels.

Quality of Service (QoS) A feature used by Windows and network hardware devices to improve network performance for an application that is not getting the best network performance. VoIP (Voice over IP) requires a high QoS.

quarantined computer A computer that is suspected of infection and is not allowed to use the network, is put on a different network

G

dedicated to quarantined computers, or is allowed to access only certain network resources.

quick format A format procedure, used to format a hard drive volume or other drive, that doesn't scan the volume or drive for bad sectors; use it only when a drive has been previously formatted and is in healthy condition.

Quick Launch menu The menu that appears when the Windows Start button is right-clicked or the user presses Win+X.

QuickPath Interconnect (QPI) The technology used first by the Intel X58 chipset for communication between the chipset and the processor using 16 serial lanes similar to that used by PCI Express. Replaced the 64-bit wide Front Side Bus used by previous chipsets.

radio frequency (RF) The frequency of waves generated by a radio signal, which are electromagnetic frequencies above audio and below light. For example, Wi-Fi 802.11n transmits using a radio frequency of 5 GHz and 2.4 GHz.

RAID (redundant array of inexpensive disks or redundant array of independent disks) Several methods of configuring multiple hard drives to store data to increase logical volume size and improve performance, or to ensure that if one hard drive fails, the data is still available from another hard drive.

RAID 0 Using space from two or more physical disks to increase the disk space available for a single volume. Performance improves because data is written evenly across all disks. Windows calls RAID 0 a striped volume. *Also called* striping or striped volume.

RAID 1 A type of drive imaging that duplicates data on one drive to another drive and is used for fault tolerance. Windows calls RAID 1 a mirrored volume. *Also called* mirrored volume.

RAID 1+0 *See* RAID 10.

RAID 10 A combination of RAID 1 and RAID 0 that requires at least four disks to work as an array of drives and provides the best redundancy and performance.

RAID 5 A technique that stripes data across three or more drives and uses parity checking, so that if one drive fails, the other drives can re-create the data stored on the failed drive. RAID 5 drives increase performance and provide fault tolerance. Windows calls these drives RAID-5 volumes.

RAID-5 volume The term used by Windows for RAID 5. *See* RAID 5.

RAM (random access memory) Memory modules on the motherboard containing microchips used to temporarily hold data and programs while the CPU processes both. Information in RAM is lost when the computer is turned off.

ransomware Malware that holds your computer system hostage with encryption techniques until you pay money or a time period expires when the encrypted content is destroyed.

rapid elasticity A cloud computing service that is capable of scaling up or down as a customer's need level changes.

RAS Latency A method of measuring access timing to memory, which is the number of clock cycles required to write or read a row of data off a memory module. RAS stands for Row Access Strobe. *Compare with* CAS Latency.

raw data Data sent to a printer without any formatting or processing.

RCA connector A connector used with composite and component cables that is round and has a single pin in the center.

rd (remove directory) The Windows command to delete a directory (folder) or group of directories (folders).

ReadyBoost A Windows utility that uses a flash drive or secure digital (SD) memory card to boost hard drive performance.

ReadyDrive The Windows technology that supports a hybrid hard drive.

read/write head A sealed, magnetic coil device that moves across the surface of a disk in a magnetic hard disk drive (HDD) either reading data from or writing data to the disk.

recover The Windows command that can recover a file when part of the file is corrupted.

recovery drive A Windows 8 bootable USB flash drive that can be used to recover the system when startup fails and can be created using the Recovery applet in Control Panel.

recovery image A backup of the Windows volume.

recovery partition A partition on a hard drive that contains a recovery utility and installation files.

Recovery System In OS X, a lean operating system that boots from a hidden volume on the OS X startup disk and is used to troubleshoot OS X when startup errors occur.

rectifier An electrical device that converts AC to DC. A computer power supply contains a rectifier.

Recycle Bin In Windows, location on the hard drive where deleted files are stored.

refresh A Windows 8 technique to recover from a corrupted Windows installation and can recover using a custom refresh image, a recovery partition, or the Windows setup DVD. Depending on the health of the system, user settings, data, and Windows 8 apps might be restored from backup near the end of the refresh operation.

refresh rate As applied to monitors, the number of times in one second the monitor can fill the screen with lines from top to bottom. *Also called* vertical scan rate.

registry A database that Windows uses to store hardware and software configuration information, user preferences, and setup information.

Registry Editor The Windows utility (regedit.exe) used to edit the Windows registry.

Regsvr32 A utility that is used to register component services used by an installed application.

Reliability and Performance Monitor A Vista utility (perfmon.msc) that collects, records, and displays events, called Data Collector Sets, that can help track the performance and reliability of Windows.

Reliability Monitor A Windows 8/7 utility that provides information about problems and errors that happen over time.

Remote Admin share Gives an administrator access to the Windows folder on a remote computer in a Windows domain.

remote application An application that is installed and executed on a server and is presented to a user working at a client computer.

Remote Assistance A Windows tool that allows a technician to remote in to a user's computer while the user remains signed, retains control of the session, and can see the screen. This is helpful when a technician is troubleshooting problems on a computer.

remote backup application A cloud backup service on the Internet that backs up data to the cloud and is often used for laptops, tablets, and smart phones.

Remote Desktop Connection (RDC) A Windows tool that gives a user access to a Windows desktop from anywhere on the Internet.

Remote Desktop Protocol (RDP) The Windows protocol used by Remote Desktop and Remote Assistance utilities to connect to and control a remote computer.

Remote Disc A feature of OS X that gives other computers on the network access to the Mac's optical drive.

remote network installation An automated installation where no user intervention is required.

remote printing Printing from a computer or mobile device to a printer that is not connected directly to the computer or device.

remote wipe Remotely erases all contacts, email, photos, and other data from a device to protect your privacy.

ren (rename) The Windows command to rename a file or group of files.

repair installation A reinstallation of Windows using the recovery utility and installation files stored on the recovery partition.

repeater A device that amplifies and retransmits a wireless signal to a wider coverage area and uses a new network name for the rebroadcast.

reset Restore a Window 8 installation to factory state or to the state after a clean install of Windows. The hard drive is formatted and all user data and settings are lost.

resiliency In Windows 8 Storage Spaces, the term refers to the degree the configuration can resist or recover from drive failure.

Resilient File System (ReFS) A file system that offers excellent fault tolerance and compatibility with virtualization and data redundancy in a RAID system.

resolution The number of pixels on a monitor screen that are addressable by software (example: 1024 x 768 pixels).

Resource Monitor A Windows tool that monitors the performance of the processor, memory, hard drive, and network.

G

resource pooling Cloud computing services to multiple customers that are hosted on shared physical resources and dynamically allocated to meet customer demand.

response time The time it takes to build one frame on a monitor screen.

restore point A snapshot of the Windows system, usually made before installation of new hardware or applications. Restore points are created by the System Protection utility.

REt (Resolution Enhancement technology) The term used by Hewlett-Packard to describe the way a laser printer varies the size of the dots used to create an image. This technology partly accounts for the sharp, clear image created by a laser printer.

retinal scanning As part of the authentication process, some systems use biometric data by scanning the blood vessels on the back of the eye and is considered the most reliable of all biometric data scanning.

reverse lookup To find the host name when you know a computer's IP address. The nslookup command can perform a reverse lookup.

revoked signature database (dbx) A Secure Boot database that is a blacklist of signatures for software that has been revoked and no longer trusted.

RFID badge A badge worn by an employee and used to gain entrance into a locked area of a building. A Radio Frequency Identification token transmits authentication to the system when the token gets in range of a query device.

RG-59 coaxial cable An older and thinner coaxial cable once used for cable TV.

RG-6 coaxial cable A coaxial cable used for cable TV, which replaced the older and thinner RG-59 coaxial cable.

RGB port *See* composite video port.

RIMM An older type of memory module developed by Rambus, Inc.

riser card A card that plugs into a motherboard and allows for expansion cards to be mounted parallel to the motherboard. Expansion cards are plugged into slots on the riser card.

RJ-11 *See* RJ-11 jack.

RJ-11 jack A phone line connection or port found on modems, telephones, and house phone outlets.

RJ-45 A port that looks like a large phone jack and is used by twisted-pair cable to connect to a wired network adapter or other hardware device. RJ stands for registered jack. *Also called* Ethernet port.

robocopy (robust file copy) A Windows command that is similar to and more powerful than the xcopy command, used to copy files and folders.

root account In Linux and OS X, the account that gives the user access to all the functions of the OS; the principal user account.

root certificate The original digital certificate issued by a Certification Authority.

root directory The main directory, at the top of the top-down hierarchical structure of subdirectories, created when a hard drive or disk is first formatted. In Linux, it's indicated by a forward slash. In Windows, it's indicated by a backward slash.

rooting The process of obtaining root or administrator privileges to an Android device, which then gives you complete access to the entire file system and all commands and features. Note that rooting may void any manufacturer warranty on the device and might violate BYOD (Bring Your Own Device) policies in an enterprise environment.

rootkit A type of malicious software that loads itself before the OS boot is complete and can hijack internal Windows components so that it masks information Windows provides to user-mode utilities such as File Explorer or Task Manager.

router A device that manages traffic between two or more networks and can help find the best path for traffic to get from one network to another.

RSA tokens A type of smart card that contains authentication information.

S1 state On the UEFI/BIOS power screen, one of the five S states used by ACPI power-saving mode to indicate different levels of power-savings functions. In the S1 state, the hard drive and monitor are turned off and everything else runs normally.

S2 state On the UEFI/BIOS power screen, one of the five S states used by ACPI power-saving mode to indicate different levels of power-savings functions. In S2 state, the hard drive and monitor are turned off and everything else runs normally. In addition, the processor is also turned off.

S3 state On the UEFI/BIOS power screen, one of the five S states used by ACPI power-saving mode to indicate different levels of power-savings functions. In S3 state, everything is shut down except RAM and enough of the system to respond to a wake-up. S3 is sleep mode.

S4 state On the UEFI/BIOS power screen, one of the five S states used by ACPI power-saving mode to indicate different levels of power-savings functions. In S4 state, everything in RAM is copied to a file on the hard drive and the system is shut down. When the system is turned on, the file is used to restore the system to its state before shut down. S4 is hibernation.

S5 state On the UEFI/BIOS power screen, one of the five S states used by ACPI power-saving mode to indicate different levels of power-savings functions. S5 state is the power-off state after a normal shutdown.

SaaS (Software as a Service) A cloud computing service whereby the service is responsible for the hardware, the operating systems, and the applications installed.

Safe Mode The technique of launching Windows with a minimum configuration, eliminating third-party software, and reducing Windows startup to only essential processes. The technique can sometimes launch Windows when a normal Windows startup is corrupted.

safety goggles Eye goggles worn while working in an unsafe environment such as a factory where fragments, chips, or other particles might injure eyes.

sag *See* brownout.

SATA power connector A 15-pin flat power connector that provides power to SATA drives.

SC (subscriber connector or standard connector) connector A type of snap-in connector used by fiber-optic cables and can be used with either single-mode or multimode fiber-optic cables. It is not used with the fastest fiber-optic networking.

scanstate A command used by the User State Migration Tool (USMT) to copy user settings and data from an old computer to a safe location such as a server or removable media. *Also see* loadstate.

screen orientation The layout or orientation of the screen that is either portrait or landscape.

screen resolution The number of dots or pixels on the monitor screen expressed as two numbers such as 1680 x 1050.

Screen Sharing In OS X, a utility to remotely view and control a Mac and is similar to Remote Assistance in Windows.

SCSI (Small Computer System Interface) An interface between a host adapter and the CPU that can daisy-chain as many as 7 or 15 devices on a single bus.

SDK (Software Development Kit) A group of tools that developers use to write apps. For example, Android Studio is a free SDK that is released as open source.

SDRAM II *See* Double Data Rate SDRAM.

secondary click In OS X, right-click the mouse or tap the lower-right corner of the trackpad on a Mac laptop.

secondary logon Using administrator privileges to perform an operation when you are not logged on with an account that has these privileges.

sector On a hard disk drive or SSD, the smallest unit of bytes addressable by the operating system and UEFI/BIOS. On hard disk drives, one sector usually equals 512 bytes; SSD drives might use larger sectors.

Secure Boot A UEFI feature that prevents a system from booting up with drivers or an OS that are not digitally signed and trusted by the motherboard or computer manufacturer.

Secure Digital (SD) card A type of memory card used in digital cameras, tablets, cell phones, MP3 players, digital camcorders, and other portable devices. The three standards used by SD cards are 1.x (regular SD), 2.x (SD High Capacity or SDHC), and 3.x (SD eXtended Capacity or SDXC).

Secure FTP (SFTP) A TCP/IP protocol used to transfer files from an FTP server to an FTP client using encryption.

Secure Shell (SSH) A protocol that is used to pass login information to a remote computer and control that computer over a network using encryption.

Security Center A Vista utility where you can confirm Windows Firewall, Windows Update, anti-malware settings, including that of Windows Defender, and other security settings.

security token A smart card or other device that is one factor in multifactor authentication or can serve as a replacement for a password.

self-grounding A method to safeguard against ESD that involves touching the computer case or power supply before touching a component in the computer case.

separate pad *See* separation pad.

separation pad A printer part that keeps more than one sheet of paper from moving forward.

sequential access A method of data access used by tape drives, whereby data is written or read sequentially from the beginning to the end of the tape or until the desired data is found.

serial ATA (SATA) An ATAPI interface standard for hard drives, optical drives, and other drives that uses a narrower and more reliable cable than the 80-conductor cable and is easier to configure than PATA systems. *Also see* parallel ATA.

serial port A male 9-pin or 25-pin port on a computer system used by slower I/O devices such as a mouse or modem. Data travels serially, one bit at a time, through the port. Serial ports are sometimes configured as COM1, COM2, COM3, or COM4. *Also called* DB9 port.

Server Message Block (SMB) A protocol used by Windows to share files and printers on a network.

Service Set Identifier (SSID) The name of a wireless access point and wireless network.

server-side virtualization Using this virtualization, a server provides a virtual desktop or application for users on multiple client machines.

service A program that runs in the background to support or serve Windows or an application.

service pack A collection of several patches or updates that is installed as a single update to an OS or application. *Compare with* patch.

Services console A console used by Windows to stop, start, and manage background services used by Windows and applications.

set-top box A device that makes a regular TV function as a smart TV.

setup UEFI/BIOS Used to change motherboard settings. For example, you can use it to enable or disable a device on the motherboard, change the date and time that is later passed to the OS, and select the order of boot devices for startup UEFI/BIOS to search when looking for an operating system to load.

shadow copy A copy of open files made so that open files are included in a backup.

share permissions A method to share a folder (not individual files) to remote users on the network, including assigning varying degrees of access to specific user accounts and user groups. Does not apply to local users of a computer and can be used on an NTFS or FAT volume. *Compare with* NTFS permissions.

sheet battery A secondary battery that fits on the bottom of a laptop to provide additional battery charge.

shell The portion of an OS that relates to the user and to applications.

shell prompt In Linux and OS X, the command prompt in the terminal.

shielded twisted-pair (STP) cable A cable that is made of one or more twisted pairs of wires and is surrounded by a metal shield.

Short Message Service (SMS) A technology that allows users to send a test message using a cell phone.

shoulder surfing As you work, other people secretly peek at your monitor screen to gain valuable information.

shutdown The Windows command to shut down the local computer or a remote computer.

sidebar Located on the right side of the Vista desktop and displays Vista gadgets.

side-by-side apps In Windows 8, an application or page can be snapped to the left or right side of the screen so a second page can share the screen.

signature database (db) A Secure Boot database that holds a list of digital signatures of approved operating systems, applications, and drivers that can be loaded by UEFI.

SIM (Subscriber Identity Module) card A small flash memory card that contains all the information a device needs to connect to a GSM or LTE cellular network, including a password and other authentication information needed to access the network, encryption standards used, and the services that a subscription includes.

SIMM (single inline memory module) An outdated miniature circuit board used to hold RAM. SIMMs held 8, 16, 32, or 64 MB on a single module. SIMMs have been replaced by DIMMs.

Simple Network Management Protocol (SNMP) A TCP/IP protocol used to monitor network traffic.

simple volume A type of volume used on a single hard drive. *Compare with* dynamic volume.

single channel The memory controller on a motherboard that can access only one DIMM at a time. *Compare with* dual channels and triple channels.

single-sided A DIMM that has memory chips installed on one side of the module.

single sign-on (SSO) An account that accesses multiple, independent resources, systems, or applications after signing in one time to one account. An example is a Microsoft account.

site license A license that allows a company to install multiple copies of software, or to allow multiple employees to execute the software from a file server. *Also called* enterprise license.

slack Wasted space on a hard drive caused by not using all available space at the end of a cluster.

sleep mode A power-saving state for a computer used to save power when not using the computer. *Also called* suspend mode. *Also see* S3 state.

sleep timer The number of minutes of inactivity before a computer goes into a power-saving state such as sleep mode.

small form factor (SFF) A motherboard used in low-end computers and home theater systems. Often used with an Intel Atom processor and sometimes purchased as a motherboard-processor combo unit.

S.M.A.R.T. (Self-Monitoring Analysis and Reporting Technology) A system BIOS and hard drive feature that monitors hard drive performance, disk spin-up time, temperature, distance between the head and the disk, and other mechanical activities of the drive in order to predict when the drive is likely to fail.

smart camera A digital camera that has embedded computing power to make decisions about the content of the photos or videos it records, including transmitting alerts over a wired or wireless network when it records certain content. *Also called* a vision sensor.

smart card Any small device that contains authentication information that can be keyed into a sign-in window or read by a reader to authenticate a user on a network.

smart card reader A device that can read a smart card used to authenticate a person onto a network.

smart phone A cell phone that includes abilities to send text messages, text messages with photos, videos, or other multimedia content, surf the web, manage email, play games, take photos and videos, and download and use apps.

smart TV A television that has the ability to run apps, store data, and connect to the Internet.

SMB2 *See* CIFS (Common Internet File System).

S/MIME (Secure/Multipurpose Internet Mail Extensions) A protocol that encrypts an outgoing email message and includes a digital signature and is more secure than SMTP, which does not use encryption.

SMTP (Simple Mail Transfer Protocol) A TCP/IP protocol used by email clients to send email messages to an email server and on to the recipient's email server. *Also see* POP and IMAP.

SMTP AUTH (SMTP Authentication) An improved version of SMTP and used to authenticate a user to an email server when the email client first tries to connect to the email server to send email. The protocol is based on the Simple Authentication and Security Layer (SASL) protocol.

snap-in A Windows utility that can be installed in a console window by Microsoft Management Console.

social engineering The practice of tricking people into giving out private information or allowing unsafe programs into the network or computer.

socket An established connection between a client and a server, such as the connection between a browser and web server.

SO-DIMM (small outline DIMM) A type of memory module used in laptop computers that uses DIMM technology. A DDR3 SO-DIMM has 204 pins. A DDR2 or DDR SO-DIMM has 200 pins. Older, outdated SO-DIMMs can have 72 pins or 144 pins.

soft boot To restart a computer without turning off the power, for example, in Windows 8, press Win+X, point to Shut down or sign out, and click Restart. *Also called* warm boot.

soft reset (1) For Android, to forcefully reboot the device (full shut down and cold boot) by pressing and holding the power button. (2) For iOS, to put the device in hibernation and not clear memory by pressing the Wake/sleep button.

Software Explorer A Vista tool used to control startup programs.

software piracy The act of making unauthorized copies of original software, which violates the Federal Copyright Act of 1976.

software RAID Using Windows to implement RAID. The setup is done using the Disk Management utility.

solid-state device (SSD) An electronic device with no moving parts. A storage device that uses memory chips to store data instead of spinning disks (such as those used by magnetic hard drives and CD drives). Examples of solid-state devices are USB flash drives, flash memory cards, and solid-state disks used as hard drives. Also called solid-state disk (SSD) or solid-state drive (SSD). *Compare with* magnetic hard drive.

solid-state drive (SSD) A hard drive that has no moving parts. *Also see* solid-state device (SSD).

Sound applet Accessed through Control Panel, used to select a default speaker and microphone and adjust how Windows handles sounds.

sound card An expansion card with sound ports.

sound port *See* audio port.

South Bridge That portion of the chipset hub that connects slower I/O buses (for example, a PCI bus) to the system bus. *Compare with* North Bridge.

Space In OS X, one desktop screen is called a Space. Multiple desktops or Spaces can be open and available to users.

spacer *See* standoff.

spanning A configuration of two hard drives that hold a single Windows volume to increase the size of a volume. Sometimes called JBOD (just a bunch of disks).

S/PDIF (Sony/Phillips Digital InterFace) sound port A port that connects to an external home theater audio system, providing digital audio output and the best signal quality.

spear phishing A form of phishing where an email message appears to come from a company you already do business with. *See also* phishing.

spoofing A phishing technique where you are tricked into clicking a link in an email message, which takes you to an official-looking website where you are asked to enter your user ID and password to enter the site. *See also* phishing.

spooling Placing print jobs in a print queue so that an application can be released from the printing process before printing is completed. Spooling is an acronym for simultaneous peripheral operations online.

Spotlight In OS X, the search app that can be configured to search the local computer, Wikipedia, iTunes, the Maps app, the web, and more.

spyware Malicious software that installs itself on your computer or mobile device to spy on you. It collects personal information about you that it transmits over the Internet to web-hosting sites that intend to use your personal data for harm.

staggered pin grid array (SPGA) A type of socket used by processors that has pins staggered over the socket in order to squeeze more pins into a small space.

standard account The Windows user account type that can use software and hardware and make some system changes, but cannot make changes that affect the security of the system or other users. *Compare with* administrator account.

standard image An image that includes Windows, drivers, and applications that are standard to all the computers that might use the image.

standoff Round plastic or metal pegs that separate the motherboard from the case, so that components on the back of the motherboard do not touch the case. *Also called* spacer.

Start screen Introduced in Windows 8, the Start screen contains tiles that represent lean apps, which use few system resources and are designed for social media, social networking, and the novice end user.

startup disk In OS X, the entire volume on which OS X is installed.

startup items In OS X, programs that automatically launch at startup. Apple discourages the use of startup items, which are stored in two directories: /Library/StartupItems and /System/Library/StartupItems. Normally, both directories are empty.

startup repair A Windows utility that restores many of the Windows files needed for a successful boot.

startup UEFI/BIOS Part of UEFI or BIOS firmware on the motherboard that is responsible for controlling the computer when it is first turned on. Startup UEFI/BIOS gives control over to the OS once the OS is loaded.

static electricity *See* electrostatic discharge (ESD).

static IP address A permanent IP address that is manually assigned to a computer.

static RAM (SRAM) RAM chips that retain information without the need for refreshing, as long as the computer's power is on. They are more expensive than traditional DRAM.

ST (straight tip) connector A type of connector used by fiber-optic cables and can be used with either single-mode or multimode fiber-optic cables. The connector does not support full-dupex transmissions and is not used on the fastest fiber-optic systems.

stop error *See* blue screen of death (BSOD).

storage card An adapter card used to manage hardware RAID rather than using the firmware on the motherboard.

Storage Spaces A Windows 8 utility that can create a storage pool using any number of internal or external backup drives. The utility is expected to replace Windows software RAID.

straight-through cable An Ethernet cable used to connect a computer to a switch or other network device. *Also called* a patch cable.

striped volume The term used by Windows for RAID 0. A type of dynamic volume used for two or more hard drives that writes to the disks evenly rather than filling up allotted space on one and then moving on to the next. *Compare with* spanned volume. *Also see* RAID 0.

striping *See* RAID 0.

strong password A password that is not easy to guess.

stylus A device that is included with a graphics tablet that works like a pencil on the tablet.

su A Linux and OS X command to open a new terminal shell for a different user account. Stands for "substitute user."

subdirectory A directory or folder contained in another directory or folder. *Also called* a child directory or folder.

subnet A group of local networks when several networks are tied together in a subsystem of the larger intranet. In TCP/IP version 6, one or more links that have the same 16 bits in the subnet ID of the IP address. *See* subnet ID.

subnet ID In TCP/IP version 6, the last block (16 bits) in the 64-bit prefix of an IP address. The subnet is identified using some or all of these 16 bits.

subnet mask In TCP/IP version 4, 32 bits that include a series of 1s followed by 0s. For example, 11111111.11111111.11110000.00000000, which can be written as 255.255.240.0. The 1s identify the network portion of an IP address, and the 0s identify the host portion of an IP address. The subnet mask tells Windows if a remote computer is on the same or different network.

subscription model A method of licensing software with a paid annual subscription where the software is installed on your local computer. For example, Office 365 uses a subscription model.

sudo A Linux and OS X command to execute another command as a superuser when logged in as a normal user with an account that has the right to use root commands. Stands for "substitute user to do the command."

superuser Refers to a Linux or Mac OS X user who is logged in to the root account.

surge supressor A device designed to protect against voltage spikes by blocking or grounding excessive voltage.

suspend mode *See* sleep mode.

S-Video port A 4-pin or 7-pin round video port that sends two signals over the cable, one for color and the other for brightness, and is used by some high-end TVs and video equipment.

switch A device used to connect nodes on a network in a star network topology. When it receives a packet, it uses its table of MAC addresses to decide where to send the packet.

synchronous DRAM (SDRAM) The first DIMM to run synchronized with the system clock that has two notches, and uses 168 pins.

system board *See* motherboard.

system bus The bus between the CPU and memory on the motherboard. The bus frequency in documentation is called the system speed, such as 400 MHz. *Also called* the memory bus, Front Side Bus, local bus, or host bus.

system clock A line on a bus that is dedicated to timing the activities of components connected to it. The system clock provides a continuous pulse that other devices use to time themselves.

System Configuration A Windows utility (msconfig.exe) that can identify what processes are launched at startup and can temporarily disable a process from loading.

System File Checker (SFC) A Windows utility that verifies and, if necessary, refreshes a Windows system file, replacing it with one kept in a cache of current system files.

system image The backup of the entire Windows 8/7 volume and can also include backups of other volumes. The backup is made using the Windows 8 File History or Windows 7 Backup and Restore utility.

System Information A Windows tool (msinfo32.exe) that provides details about a system, including installed hardware and software, the current system configuration, and currently running programs.

system partition The partition of the hard drive that contains the boot loader or boot manager program and the specific files required to start the Windows launch.

System Preferences In OS X, a utility to customize the OS X interface and is available on the Apple menu.

System Protection A Windows utility that automatically backs up system files and stores them in restore points on the hard drive at regular intervals and just before you install software or hardware.

system repair disc A disc you can create using Windows 7 that can be used to launch Windows RE. The disc is not available in Windows 8.

System Restore A Windows utility used to restore the system to a restore point.

system state data In Windows, files that are necessary for a successful load of the operating system.

system tray *See* notification area.

system UEFI/BIOS UEFI (Unified Extensible Firmware Interface) or BIOS (basic input/output system) firmware on the motherboard that is used to control essential devices before the OS is loaded.

System window A window that displays brief and important information about installed hardware and software and gives access to important Windows tools needed to support the system.

systray *See* notification area.

T568A Standards for wiring twisted-pair network cabling and RJ-45 connectors and have the green pair connected to pins 1 and 2 and the orange pair connected to pins 3 and 6.

T568B Standards for wiring twisted-pair network cabling and RJ-45 connectors and have the orange pair using pins 1 and 2 and the green pair connected to pins 3 and 6.

tablet A computing device with a touch screen that is larger than a smart phone and has functions similar to a smart phone.

tailgating When someone who is unauthorized follows an employee through a secured entrance to a room or building.

Task Manager A Windows utility (taskmgr.exe) that lets you view the applications and processes running on your computer as well as information about process and memory performance, network activity, and user activity.

Task Scheduler A Windows tool that can set a task or program to launch at a future time, including at startup.

taskbar A bar normally located at the bottom of the Windows desktop, displaying information about open programs and providing quick access to others.

taskkill A Windows command that uses the process PID to kill a process.

tasklist A Windows command that returns the process identifier (PID), which is a number that identifies each running process.

TCP (Transmission Control Protocol) The protocol in the TCP/IP suite of protocols that works at the OSI Transport layer and establishes a session or connection between parties and guarantees packet delivery.

TCP/IP (Transmission Control Protocol/Internet Protocol) The group or suite of protocols used for almost all networks, including the Internet. Fundamentally, TCP is responsible for error-checking transmissions, and IP is responsible for routing.

technical documentation The technical reference manuals, included with software packages and hardware, that provide directions for installation, usage, and troubleshooting. The information extends beyond that given in user manuals.

Telnet A TCP/IP protocol used by the Telnet client/server applications to allow an administrator or other user to control a computer remotely.

Teredo In TCP/IP version 6, a tunneling protocol to transmit TCP/IPv6 packets over a TCP/IPv4 network, named after the Teredo worm that bores holes in wood. Teredo IP addresses begin with 2001, and the prefix is written as 2001::/32.

terminal In Linux and OS X, the command-line interface.

tether To connect a mobile device with a cellular connection to the Internet to a computer so that the computer can access the Internet by way of the mobile device.

thermal compound A creamlike substance that is placed between the bottom of the cooler heat sink and the top of the processor to eliminate air pockets and to help to draw heat off the processor.

thermal paper Special coated paper used by thermal printers.

thermal printer A type of line printer that uses wax-based ink, which is heated by heat pins that melt the ink onto paper.

thermal transfer printer A type of thermal printer that uses a ribbon that contains wax-based ink. The heating element melts the ribbon onto special thermal paper so that it stays glued to the paper as the feeder assembly moves the paper through the printer.

thick client A regular desktop computer or laptop that is sometimes used as a client by a virtualization server. *Also called* fat client.

thin client A computer that has an operating system, but has little computing power and might only need to support a browser used to communicate with a virtualization server.

thin provisioning A technique used by Storage Spaces in Windows whereby virtual storage free space can be configured as if it has more virtual storage than the physical storage allotted to it. When the virtual storage free space is close to depletion, the administrator is prompted to install more physical storage.

third-party driver Drivers that are not included in UEFI/BIOS or Windows and must come from the manufacturer.

thread Each process that the processor is aware of; a single task that is part of a longer task or request from a program.

Thunderbolt port A port that transmits both video and data on the same port and cable. The port is shaped the same as the DisplayPort and is compatible with DisplayPort devices.

ticket An entry in a call-tracking system made by whoever receives a call for help and used to track and document actions taken. The ticket stays open until the issue is resolved.

Time Machine In OS X, a built-in backup utility that can be configured to automatically back up user-created data, applications, and system files onto an external hard drive attached either directly to the computer or through the local network.

TKIP (Temporal Key Integrity Protocol) A type of encryption protocol used by WPA to secure a wireless Wi-Fi network. *Also see* WPA (Wi-Fi Protected Access).

tone probe A two-part kit that is used to find cables in the walls of a building. *Also called* a toner probe.

toner probe *See* tone probe.

toner vacuum A vacuum cleaner designed to pick up toner used in laser printers and does not allow it to touch any conductive surface.

touch pad A common pointing device on a laptop computer.

touch screen An input device that uses a monitor or LCD panel as a backdrop for user options. Touch screens can be embedded in a monitor or LCD panel or installed as an add-on device over the monitor screen.

tower case The largest type of personal computer case. Tower cases stand vertically and can be as high as two feet tall. They have more drive bays and are a good choice for computer users who anticipate making significant upgrades.

TPM (Trusted Platform Module) A chip on a motherboard that holds an encryption key required at startup to access encrypted data on the hard drive. Windows BitLocker Encryption can use the TPM chip.

trace A wire on a circuit board that connects two components or devices.

tracert (trace route) A TCP/IP command that enables you to resolve a connectivity problem when attempting to reach a destination host such as a website.

track One of many concentric circles on the surface of a hard disk drive.

tractor feed A continuous feed within an impact printer that feeds fanfold paper through the printer rather than individual sheets, making them useful for logging ongoing events or data.

transfer belt A laser printer component that completes the transferring step in the printer.

transfer roller A soft, black roller in a laser printer that puts a positive charge on the paper. The charge pulls the toner from the drum onto the paper.

transformer An electrical device that changes the ratio of current to voltage. A computer power supply is basically a transformer and a rectifier.

trip hazard Loose cables or cords in a traffic area where people can trip over them.

triple channels When the memory controller accesses three DIMMs at the same time. DDR3 DIMMs support triple channeling.

Trojan A type of malware that tricks you into downloading and/or opening it by substituting itself for a legitimate program.

TV tuner card An adapter card that receives a TV signal and displays TV on the computer screen.

Twisted Nematic (TN) A class of LCD monitor that has fast response times to keep fast-moving images crisper, but monitors are brighter, consume more power, and have limited viewing angles.

twisted-pair cabling Cabling, such as a network cable, that uses pairs of wires twisted together to reduce crosstalk.

Type 1 hypervisor Software to manage virtual machines that is installed before any operating system is installed.

Type 2 hypervisor Software to manage virtual machines that is installed as an application in an operating system.

UDF (Universal Disk Format) A file system for optical media used by all DVD discs and some CD-R and CD-RW discs. *Also see* CDFS (Compact Disc File System).

UDP (User Datagram Protocol) A connectionless TCP/IP protocol that works at the OSI Transport layer and does not require a connection to send a packet or guarantee that the packet arrives at its destination. The protocol is commonly used for broadcasting to multiple nodes on a network or the Internet. *Compare with* TCP (Transmission Control Protocol).

UEFI CSM (Compatibility Support Module) mode Legacy BIOS in UEFI firmware.

ultra-thin client *See* zero client.

unattended installation A Windows installation that is done by storing the answers to installation questions in a text file or script that Windows calls an answer file so that the answers do not have to be typed in during the installation.

unicast address Using TCP/IP version 6, an IP address assigned to a single node on a network.

UEFI (Unified Extensible Firmware Interface) An interface between firmware on the motherboard and the operating system that improves on legacy BIOS processes for booting, handing over the boot to the OS, and loading device drivers and applications before the OS loads. UEFI also manages motherboard settings and secures the boot to ensure that no rogue operating system hijacks the system.

Unified Threat Management (UTM) A computer, security appliance, network appliance, or Internet appliance that stands between the Internet and a private network and runs firewall, anti-malware, and other software to protect the network.

uninterruptible power supply (UPS) A device that raises the voltage when it drops during brownouts.

unique local address (ULA) In TCP/IP version 6, an address used to identify a specific site within a large organization. It can work on multiple links within the same organization. The address is a hybrid between a global unicast address that works on the Internet and a link-local unicast address that works on only one link.

Universal Plug and Play (UPnP) An unsecure method a router can use to allow unfiltered communication between nodes on a private network. Hackers sometimes are able to exploit UPnP, so use with caution.

unshielded twisted-pair (UTP) cable The most popular cabling method for local networks and is the least expensive and is commonly used on LANs. The cable is made of twisted pairs of wires and is not surrounded by shielding.

Upgrade Advisor *See* Upgrade Assistant.

Upgrade Assistant Software used to find out if a system can be upgraded to Windows 8.1.

update *See* patch.

upgrade path A qualifying OS required by Microsoft in order to perform an in-place upgrade.

USB 3.0 B-Male connector A USB connector used by SuperSpeed USB 3.0 devices such as printers or scanners.

USB 3.0 Micro-B connector A small USB connector used by SuperSpeed USB 3.0 devices. The connectors are not compatible with regular Micro-B connectors.

USB (Universal Serial Bus) port A type of port designed to make installation and configuration of I/O devices easy, providing room for as many as 127 devices daisy-chained together.

USB optical drive An external optical drive that connects to a computer via a USB port.

USB to Bluetooth adapter A device that plugs into a USB port on a computer to connect to Bluetooth devices.

USB to RJ-45 dongle An adapter that plugs into a USB port and provides an RJ-45 port for a network cable to connect to a wired network.

USB to Wi-Fi dongle An adapter that plugs into a USB port and provides wireless connectivity to a Wi-Fi network.

User Account Control (UAC) dialog box A Windows security feature that displays a dialog box when an event requiring administrative privileges is about to happen.

User Accounts A Windows utility (netplwiz.exe) that can be used to change the way Windows sign-in works and to manage user accounts, including changing passwords and changing the group membership of an account. *Also called* Network Places Wizard.

user mode In Windows, a mode that provides an interface between an application and the OS, and only has access to hardware resources through the code running in kernel mode.

user profile A collection of files and settings about a user account that enables the user's personal data, desktop settings, and other operating parameters to be retained from one session to another.

user profile namespace The group of folders and subfolders in the C:\Users folder that belong to a specific user account and contain the user profile.

User State Migration Tool (USMT) A Windows utility that helps you migrate user files and preferences from one computer to another to help a user make a smooth transition from one computer to another.

Users group A type of Windows user account group. An account in this group is a standard user account, which does not have as many rights as an administrator account.

usmtutils A command used by the User State Migration Tool (USMT) that provides encryption options and hard-link management.

vendor-specific software *See* closed source.

vertical scan rate *See* refresh rate.

VGA (Video Graphics Adapter) port A 15-pin analog video port popular for many years. *Also called* DB15 port, DE15 port, or HD15 port.

VGA mode Standard VGA settings, which include a resolution of 640 x 480.

vi editor A Linux and OS X text editor that works in command mode (to enter commands) or in insert mode (to edit text).

video capture card An adapter card that captures video input and saves it to a file on the hard drive.

video memory Memory used by the video controller. The memory might be contained on a video card or be part of system memory. When part of system memory, the memory is dedicated by Windows to video.

virtual assistant A mobile device app that responds to a user's voice commands with a personable, conversational interaction to perform tasks and retrieve information. *Also called* a personal assistant.

Virtual Desktop Infrastructure (VDI) A presentation of a virtual desktop made to a client computer by a server that is serving up a virtual machine.

virtual machine (VM) Software that simulates the hardware of a physical computer, creating one or more logical machines within one physical machine.

virtual machine manager (VMM) *See* hypervisor.

virtual memory A method whereby the OS uses the hard drive as though it were RAM. *Also see* pagefile.sys.

virtual printing Printing to a file rather than directly to a printer.

virtual private network (VPN) A security technique that uses encrypted data packets between a private network and a computer somewhere on the Internet.

virtualization When one physical machine hosts multiple activities that are normally done on multiple machines.

G

virtualization server A computer that serves up virtual machines to multiple client computers and provides a virtual desktop for users on these client machines.

virtual XP mode The term used by CompTIA for Windows XP mode. *See* Windows XP mode.

virus A program that often has an incubation period, is infectious, and is intended to cause damage. A virus program might destroy data and programs.

vision sensor *See* smart camera.

Voice over LTE (VoLTE) A technology used on cellular networks for LTE to support voice communication.

VoIP (Voice over Internet Protocol) A TCP/IP protocol and an application that provides voice communication over a TCP/IP network. *Also called* Internet telephone.

volt (V) A measure of potential difference or electrical force in an electrical circuit. A computer ATX power supply usually provides five separate voltages: 112 V, 212 V, 15 V, 25 V, and 13.3 V.

volume A primary partition that has been assigned a drive letter and can be formatted with a file system such as NTFS. *Compare with* logical drive.

wait state A clock tick in which nothing happens, used to ensure that the microprocessor isn't getting ahead of slower components. A 0-wait state is preferable to a 1-wait state. Too many wait states can slow down a system.

Wake-on-LAN Configuring a computer so that it will respond to network activity when the computer is in a sleep state.

WAN (wide area network) A network or group of networks that span a large geographical area.

warm boot *See* soft boot.

watt (W) The unit of electricity used to measure power. A typical computer may use a power supply that provides 500 W.

wearable technology device A device, such as a smart watch, wristband, arm band, eyeglasses, headset, or clothing, that can perform computing tasks, including making phone calls, sending text messages, recording and transmitting data, and checking email.

wear leveling A technique used on a solid-state drive (SSD) that ensures the logical block addressing does not always address the same physical blocks in order to distribute write operations more evenly across the device.

WEP (Wired Equivalent Privacy) An encryption protocol used to secure transmissions on a Wi-Fi wireless network; however, it is no longer considered secure because the key used for encryption is static (it doesn't change).

Wi-Fi (Wireless Fidelity) The common name for standards for a local wireless network as defined by IEEE 802.11. *Also see* 802.11 a/b/g/n/ac.

Wi-Fi analyzer Hardware and/or software that monitors a Wi-Fi network to detect devices not authorized to use the network, identify attempts to hack transmissions, or detect performance and security vulnerabilities.

Wi-Fi calling On mobile devices, voice calls that use VoIP over a Wi-Fi connection to the Internet.

Wi-Fi Protected Setup (WPS) A method to make it easier for users to connect their computers to a secured wireless network when a hard-to-remember SSID and security key are used, and is considered a security risk that should be used with caution.

wildcard An * or ? character used in a command line that represents a character or group of characters in a file name or extension.

Windows 7 Windows 7 editions include Windows 7 Starter, Windows 7 Home Basic, Windows 7 Home Premium, Windows 7 Professional, Windows 7 Enterprise, and Windows 7 Ultimate. Each edition comes at a different price with different features and capabilities.

Windows 8.1 A free update or release of the Windows 8 operating system. The edition of choice for a laptop or desktop computer used in a home or small office. This edition supports homegroups, but it doesn't support joining a domain or BitLocker Encryption.

Windows 8.1 Enterprise A Windows 8 edition that allows for volume licensing in a large, corporate environment.

Windows 8.1 Pro for Students A version of Windows 8 that includes all the same features as Windows 8 Pro, but at a lower price, available only to students, faculty, and staff at eligible institutions.

Windows 8.1 Professional (Windows 8.1 Pro) A version of Windows 8 that includes additional features at a higher price. Windows 8.1 Pro supports homegroups, joining a domain, BitLocker, Client Hyper-V, Remote Desktop, and Group Policy.

Windows Assessment and Deployment Kit (ADK) The Windows ADK for Windows 8 contains a group of tools used to deploy Windows 8 in a large organization and contains the User State Migration Tool (USMT).

Windows Automated Installation Kit (AIK) The Windows AIK for Windows 7 contains a group of tools used to deploy Windows 7 in a large organization and contains the User State Migration Tool (USMT).

Windows Boot Loader One of two programs that manage the loading of Windows 8/7/Vista. The program file (winload.exe or winload.efi) is stored in C:\ Windows\System32, and it loads and starts essential Windows processes.

Windows Boot Manager (BootMgr) The Windows program that manages the initial startup of Windows. For a BIOS system, the program is bootmgr; for a UEFI system, the program is bootmgfw.efi. The program file is stored in the root of the system partition.

Windows Defender Anti-malware software embedded in Windows 8 that can detect, prevent, and clean up a system infected with viruses and other malware. Antispyware utility included in Windows 8/7/Vista.

Windows Easy Transfer A Windows tool used to transfer Windows 8/7/Vista user data and preferences to the Windows 8/7/Vista installation on another computer.

Windows Experience Index A Windows 7/Vista feature that gives a summary index designed to measure the overall performance of a system on a scale from 1.0 to 7.9.

Windows Explorer The Windows 7/Vista utility used to view and manage files and folders.

Windows Firewall A personal firewall that protects a computer from intrusion and is automatically configured when you set your network location in the Network and Sharing Center.

Windows Phone (WP) An operating system by Microsoft (*microsoft.com*) that is based on Windows and is used on various smart phones (not on tablets).

Windows pinwheel A Windows graphic that indicates the system is waiting for a response from a program or device.

Windows PowerShell A command-line interface (CLI) that processes objects, called cmdlets, which are prebuilt programs built on the .NET Framework, rather than processing text in a command line.

Windows Preinstallation Environment (Windows PE) A minimum operating system used to start the Windows installation.

Windows Pro Pack An upgrade available to Windows 8 that adds the functionality of Windows 8.1 Pro to the more basic edition.

Windows Recovery Environment (Windows RE) A lean operating system installed on the Windows 8/7/Vista setup DVD and also on the Windows 8/7 volume that can be used to troubleshoot problems when Windows refuses to start.

Windows RT A Windows 8 edition that is a lighter version, designed for tablets, netbooks, and other mobile devices.

Windows Store Access to purchase and download apps that use the Windows 8 interface.

Windows Vista Windows Vista editions include Windows Vista Starter, Windows Vista Home Basic, Windows Vista Home Premium, Windows Vista Business, Windows Vista Enterprise, and Windows Vista Ultimate. Each edition comes at a different price with different features and capabilities.

Windows XP Mode A Windows XP environment installed in Windows 8/7 that can be used to support older applications. *Also called* virtual XP mode.

Windows.old folder When using an unformatted hard drive for a clean installation, this folder is created to store the previous operating system settings and user profiles.

wireless access point (WAP) A wireless device that is used to create and manage a wireless network.

wireless LAN (WLAN) A type of LAN that does not use wires or cables to create connections, but instead transmits data over radio or infrared waves.

wireless locator A tool that can locate a Wi-Fi hotspot and tell you the strength of the RF signal.

wireless wide area network (WWAN) A wireless broadband network for computers and mobile devices that uses cellular towers for communication. *Also called* a cellular network.

wire stripper A tool used when terminating a cable. The tool cuts away the plastic jacket or coating around the wires in a cable so that a connector can be installed on the end of the cable.

workgroup In Windows, a logical group of computers and users in which administration, resources, and security are distributed throughout the network, without centralized management or security.

worm An infestation designed to copy itself repeatedly to memory, on drive space, or on a network, until little memory, disk space, or network bandwidth remains.

WPA (Wi-Fi Protected Access) A data encryption method for wireless networks that use the TKIP (Temporal Key Integrity Protocol) encryption method and the encryption keys are changed at set intervals while the wireless LAN is in use. WPA is stronger than WEP.

WPA2 (Wi-Fi Protected Access 2) A data encryption standard compliant with the IEEE 802.11i standard that uses the AES (Advanced Encryption Standard) protocol. WPA2 is currently the strongest wireless encryption standard.

x86 processor An older processor that first used the number 86 in the model number and processes 32 bits at a time.

x86-64 bit processor Hybrid processors that can process 32 bits or 64 bits.

XaaS (Anything as a Service or Everything as a Service) An open-ended cloud computing service that can provide any combination of functions depending on a customer's exact needs.

xcopy A Windows command more powerful than the copy command that is used to copy files and folders.

xD-Picture Card A type of flash memory device that has a compact design and currently holds up to 8 GB of data.

XPS Document Writer A Windows feature that creates a file with an .xps file extension. The file is similar to a .pdf file and can be viewed, edited, printed, faxed, emailed, or posted on websites.

zero client A client computer that does not have an operating system and merely provides an interface between the user and the server. *Also called* dumb terminal.

zero-day attack When a hacker discovers and exploits a security hole in software before the developer of the software can develop and provide a protective patch to close the hole.

zero-fill utility A hard drive utility that fills every sector on the drive with zeroes.

zero insertion force (ZIF) socket A socket that uses a small lever to apply even force when you install the processor into the socket.

zero-touch, high-volume deployment An installation strategy that does not require the user to start the process. Instead a server pushes the installation to a computer when a user is not likely to be sitting at it.

ZIF connector A ZIF (zero insertion force) connector uses a lever or latch to prevent force from being used on a sensitive connection.

zombie A computer that has been hacked, and the hacker is using the computer to run repetitive software in the background without the knowledge of its user. *Also see* botnet.

INDEX

3D graphics, 951
3.3-V slots, 94–95
4-pin 12-V connector, 10
4-pin auxiliary connector, 9, 12, 61
4-pin Berg connector, 10
4-pin Molex power connector, 236, 244
4-pin round video port, 2
5-V slots, 94–95
6-pin PCIe connector, 9, 10, 13, 61
7-pin round video port, 2
7-pin SATA data cable, 236
8-pin 12-V connector, 10
8-pin auxiliary connector, 9, 12, 13
8-pin PCIe connector, 9, 10, 13, 61, 97
9-Series chipsets, 91
10BaseT, 717–719
10-foot user interface, 955
15-pin analog video port, 6
15-pin SATA power connector, 236, 244
20+4-pin P1 connector, 9–10, 12–13
20-pin P1 connector, 9, 10, 11
24-pin P1 connector, 9, 12–13
32-bit architecture, 134, 327
32-bit drivers, 402
32-bit operating system, 300, 353
32-bit processors, 138
40-pin IDE cables, 16
64-bit architecture, 134, 327
64-bit drivers, 402
64-bit operating system, 300, 353
64-bit processors, 138
100BaseT, 708, 717–719
802.11 a/b/g/n/ac standards, 683–684
1394 Trade Association, 387

A

Absolute LoJack, 870
AC adapter, 18, 27, 211–213, 341
Accelerated Hub Architecture, 87
Accelerated Processing Unit (APU), 91
Accelerometer, 32, 778
Acceptable use policy (AUP), 884
Access application, 823–824
Access control list (ACL), 881
Accessories, for mobile devices, 33–34
Access to files and folders
- administrative shares, 844–846
- hidden network resources, 844–846
- mapping a network drive or printer, 842–844
- permissions, 828–830
- sharing, 830–842
- user accounts and user groups, 825–828

Acer, 67
ACL (access control list), 881
AC outlet ground tester, 36
Action bar, Android OS, 749
Action Center, 296, 302–304, 365–366, 533, 571–572, 888
Action Center, Windows Phone, 757, 795
Active Directory, 306, 807, 881
Active learning, 559–560
Active listening, 556
Active partition, 468
Active PFC, 191
Active recovery image, 463
Active volume, 486
ActiveX controls, 810, 813, 896
AC voltage, measuring, 39
Adapter address, 635
Adapter cards. *See also* Expansion cards
- installing and configuring, 400–408
- replacing expansion cards in a laptop, 405–408
- sound cards and onboard sound, 400, 404
- TV tuner and video capture cards, 400, 404–405, 955–956

Adapters, 390, 395
Address reservation, 675
Ad hoc mode network, 920
ADK Media Group, 953
ADM (Android Device Manager), 875
Administrative Events log, 514
Administrative shares, 844–846
Administrative Tools, 296, 505–506
Administrator account, 311, 384
Administrators group, 826
Adobe Illustrator by Adobe Systems, 951
Adobe Photoshop, 384
Adobe Production Premium by Adobe Systems, 953
ADSL (Asymmetric DSL), 697
Advanced Boot Options, 219–220, 597, 598–599, 610, 612
Advanced Encryption Standard (AES), 686
Advanced Intelligent Tape (AIT), 257
Advanced Micro Devices, Inc. *See* AMD processors
Advanced options screen, 606
Advanced startup mode, 603
Advanced tab, Internet Explorer, 813–814
Advanced Technology Extended (ATX). *See* ATX (Advanced Technology Extended) form factor
AdwareMedic, 1005
Aero user interface, 286, 420, 421, 535
AES (Advanced Encryption Standard), 686
AFP (Apple Filing Protocol), 650, 653
Airborne particles, 1031
AirDrop, 775–776
Air filter mask, 1028
Air filters, 1031
Air flow in computer case, 206–210
AirMagnet Spectrum ES software, 902–903
AirMagnet WiFi Analyzer by Fluke Networks, 901–902
Airplane mode, 22, 760, 782
AirPrint, 921
AIT (Advanced Intelligent Tape), 257
Alfredo Comparetti, 206
Alkaline batteries, 1035
Alligator clip, 51, 72
All-in-one computers, 18, 26–27, 67
Alternating current (AC), 1023, 1025
A-Male connector, 386
Amazon, 748
Amazon Appstore, 750, 874
Amazon Fire TV, 957
AMD chipsets, 87, 91
AMD Phenom, 445
AMD processors
- characteristics of, 141–142
- current list, 141–142
- installing in socket AM2+, 153–154
- microATX (MATX) and, 14
- processor sockets for, 86
- x86-64 bit processors, 138

AMD Radeon HD graphics processor, 955
AMD sockets, 134
AMD-V, 969
American National Standards Institute (ANSI), 16, 883
Amp, 1022
Analog, 2
Analog video ports, 412
Android Application Package (APK), 751
Android Beam, 784
Android Device Manager (ADM), 875
Android operating system/devices, 748–751
- anti-malware software, 874
- apps, 750–751
- back up and restore, 789
- battery information, 222
- Bluetooth, 784, 792
- email, configuring, 786
- failed logon restrictions, 873
- firewall, 874–875
- firmware, 791
- getting to know, 749–750
- introduction to, 748
- Linux and, 972
- locator app and remote wipe, 875
- malicious software, 898
- memory card slots, 33
- network connections, configuring, 781–785

Android operating system/devices (*continued*)
notifications, 752
PRL (Preferred Roaming List), 762
rooting, 794, 899
screen lock, 871
source code, 759
sync, 787–788
troubleshooting, 223, 790–794
updates and patches, 788–789, 874
virtual assistant, 753
Anonymous users, 828
ANSI (American National Standards Institute), 16, 883
Answer file, 375
Antec, 192
Anti-malware driver, 610
Anti-malware settings, 303
Anti-malware software. *See also* Malicious software
on Mac computers, 1005
malware symptoms, 889
mobile devices, 874, 901
multiple scans, 894
preventive maintenance, 444
remediating infected system, 892–894
in step-by-step attack plan, 887–897
System Restore and, 462
Unified Threat Management (UTM), 882
Windows Defender, 296, 303, 364, 888–889, 891, 892
Windows upgrades/installations and, 341, 342, 360
Antistatic bags, 36, 1029–1030
Antistatic vacuum, 1031–1032
Antistatic wrist strap, 1028. *See also* ESD strap
Antivirus software, 36, 341, 364, 444, 530, 874, 882, 1005. *See also* Anti-malware software; Malicious software
Anycast address, 643
Anycasting, 643
Anything as a Service or Everything as a Service (XaaS), 848
Apache, 807
APIPA (Automatic Private IP Address), 641–642, 646, 733–734
APIs, 759
APK (Android Application Package), 751
App history tab, 502
Apple, Inc., 33, 67. *See also* Apple iOS; Mac OS X operating system
Apple AirPrint, 921
Apple Care warranty, 1003
Apple Filing Protocol (AFP), 650, 653
Apple ID, 754
Apple iOS
apps, 754–755
backup procedures, 770–774, 775
Bluetooth, 762
email, configuring, 763–767
external slots, 33
factory reset, 900
failed logon restrictions, 873
getting to know, 751–753
Lightning cable, 31–32
locator app and remote wipe, 875–876
network connections, configuring, 760–763
Bluetooth connection, 762
cellular connection, 760–762
VPN connection, 763
Wi-Fi connection, 762–763
operating system overview, 751–755
overview of, 748
screen lock, 872–873
sync, back up, and restore from backup, 768–776
troubleshooting, 776–781
common problems and solutions, 778–780
tools for, 776–778
updates and patches, 874
Apple menu, 995
AppleTalk, 650
Application level of communication, 637–638
Application log, 514
Application management, 278, 497–498, 504–505
Applications. *See also* Apps for mobile devices
common port assignments, 652–653
Home Theater PC (HTPC), 955
installing, 371
priority level, 504–505
requirements of and customizing, 951
on a TCP/IP network, 648
TCP/IP protocols used by, 649–653
uninstalling, 530, 535–539
Application virtualization, 967
Application Virtualization (App-V), 967
Apps Drawer, Android OS, 749
Apps for mobile devices
Android operating system, 750–751, 787–788
Apple iOS mobile devices, 754–755
Windows Phone, 758
App Store, 754–755, 759, 874, 898, 901, 1003
App-V (Application Virtualization), 967
Apt-get command, 978
APU (Accelerated Processing Unit), 91
Arithmetic logic units (ALUs), 137
Artifacts, 428–429
A-Series chipsets, 91
A Series processors, 141
Aspect ratio, 411
Assist button, 617
Assumptions, 565
ASUS, 67
Asymmetric DSL (ADSL), 697
AT&T, 30
ATA Secure Erase, 883
Athlon 64 X2 Dual-Core processor, 87
Athlon Neo processor, 87
Athlon processors, 141, 142
Athlon X2 Dual-Core processor, 87
Atom processors, 138, 140, 141
Attitude, 546
ATX (Advanced Technology Extended) form factor
4-pin auxiliary connector, 9, 12, 61
6-pin PCIe connector, 9, 10, 13, 61
8-pin auxiliary connector, 9, 12, 13
8-pin PCIe connector, 9, 10, 13, 61, 97
20-pin P1 connector, 9, 10, 11
form factors
20+4-pin P1 connector, 9–10, 12–13
24-pin P1 connector, 9, 12–13
overview of, 81–82
power supply and, 190
ATX12V power supply, 12
Audio editing workstation, 953
Audio headers, 100
Audio ports, 3, 5, 18, 99
Audit Success events, 514
AUP (acceptable use policy), 884
Authenticated Users group, 827
Authenticating users
boot process, 591
disable Guest account, 860
for large networks, 877–879
lock workstation, 858–860
secure sign-in, 856–858
strong passwords, 860–861
TPM (Trusted Platform Module) chip, 869
Authentication server, 807
Authy, 873
AutoCAD Design Suite by Autodesk, 951
Autoconfiguration IPv4 Address, 733, 737
Autodetection, 238
Automatic Downloads, 772
Automatic Private IP Address (APIPA), 641–642, 646, 733–734
Automatic restart on system failure, 610
Automatic updates, configuring, 363–364
AutoPlay, 868
AutoRun, 868
Auto-switching, 211
AVerMedia AVerTV PVR 150 Plus TV tuner and video capture card, 405
AVG Antivirus Protection by AVG Technologies, 891
AVG Rescue CD software, 894

B

Background noise, 956
Backlighting, 409, 411
Backup and recovery plan, 454–455
Backup destination, 454
Backup Operators group, 826
Backup procedures
Android operating system, 789
Apple iOS mobile devices, 770–774, 775
custom refresh image, 462–465, 598
disaster recovery, planning for, 454–455
hardware problems and, 195–196
iTunes, 773–774
laptops and, 28
Linux, 988–990
Mac OS X operating system, 1006–1007, 1013
before opening computer case, 46
before a problem occurs, 598
registry, 524–526
troubleshooting, 563–565, 571

Windows 8 file history, 455–456
Windows Phone, 795–798
Windows system files, 460–462
Backup software, 454
Bad memory, 573
Ball grid array (BGA), 85
Bandwidth, 697
Barcode readers, 393
Base station, 20, 700
Bash shell, 973
Basic disk, 482, 485, 486
Batch files, 376, 479
Battery life, 793, 898
Battery pack, on laptops, 25, 27
BCD (Boot Configuration Data), 271, 590, 616
Bcdedit command, 615
Beamforming, 684
Beep codes, 200
Best-effort protocol, 649
BGA (ball grid array), 85
Bing, 756
Biometric authentication, 872–873
Biometric data, 879
Biometric devices, 393–394, 872–873
BIOS (basic input/output system), 37, 103. *See also* UEFI/BIOS
definition of, 330
firmware, 329–330
flashing BIOS, 117, 215
setup, 37, 103–111
accessing, 104
boot sequence, changing, 104–105
to boot to the network, 374
drive encryption and drive password protection, 109
exiting, 111
intrusion detection, 108
LoJack for laptops, 109
monitor temperature, fan speeds, and voltages, 107
motherboard, configuring, 103–111
onboard devices, configuring, 105
power-on passwords, 108–109
processor and clock speeds, 106–107
TPM chip and hard drive encryption, 110–111
using jumpers to clear BIOS settings, 118–119
view hard drive and optical drive information, 106
virtualization, support for, 109
using jumpers to clear settings, 118–119
Biostar, 14
Bitdefender Antivirus, 891
BitLocker Drive Encryption, 110–111, 296, 869–870
BitLocker To Go, 869
Bitmap, 913, 928
BlackBerry OS, 748
Blocks, 465
Block Services page, 683
Block Sites page, 682–683
Blue screen of death (BSOD), 198, 269–270, 574–575, 610, 623, 624–626
Blue system board, on laptops, 25
Bluetooth
Android operating system/devices, 784, 792
Apple iOS, 762
barcode readers, 393
data transmission speeds, 385
on laptops, 22
mobile devices, 31
no connectivity, 740
printers and, 920
tablets and, 29
troubleshooting, 779
unintended connections, 899
Bluetooth device, 20
Bluetooth PIN code, 762
Blu-ray burner, 953
Blu-ray Disc (BD) drives, 259–260, 261
B-Male connector, 386
BNC connector, 705
Bonjour Print Services for Windows, 927
Boot Camp, 1014
Boot Configuration Data (BCD), 271, 590, 616
Boot loader menu, 355–356
Boot logging, 597, 607
Boot Manager, 590
BootMgr, 468
Boot Mode, 1012
Boot partition, 468
Boot process
definition of, 588
different ways to, 588–589
power buttons and switches on computer case, 589
Windows shutdown and restart, 588–589
from recovery media, 575–576
steps to boot and start Windows, 590–597
understanding, 588–597
from a USB drive, 334
Bootrec command, 271, 615
Bootsect command, 615
Boot sector, 271
Boot sequence, changing, 104–105
Boot tab, System Configuration, 507
Botnet, 887
Box, 998
Boxed processors, 140
Bridges, 703–704
Brightness, 21, 411, 417, 427–428, 432
Brightness, of paper, 916
Bring Your Own Device (BYOD) policies, 755, 876, 902
Broadband, 697
Broadcasting, 643
Broadwell chipsets, 91, 139
Brownouts, 1033
Browser redirection, 888
Browsers, 763
Browsing history, 809
Brute force attack, 860
BSOD (blue screen of death), 198, 199, 269–270, 574–575, 610, 623, 624–626
Bubble-jet printers, 915
Buffered DIMMs, 165
Buffer overflow attack, 136
Buffers, 165
Buffer size, 238
Built-in user groups, 826–828
Burn-in, 425–426
Buses
conventional PCI, 94–95
inside processors, 137–138
introduction to, 92–94
Mini PCI, 26, 27, 97–98, 156, 405
Mini PCI Express, 26, 27, 97–98, 405–408
PCI Express (PCIe), 6, 13, 53, 80, 81, 87, 96–97, 400–402, 412, 425
PCI riser cards, 98–99
PCI-X, 96
on Pentium processors, 137
Bus lines, 11
Button batteries, 1035
BYOD (Bring Your Own Device) policies, 755, 876, 902

C

C&C (command-and-control) server, 898–899
Cable connection diagram, 51–52, 54
Cable Internet, 698–699, 736
Cable locks, 19
Cables, 15–20, 1027
Cable tester, 713, 726
Cable ties, 36
Cached print jobs, 926–927
Cache size, 238
CAD/CAM design workstation, 951–952
CAG (chassis air guide), 210
Calibrating colors, 427
Calibration, of printers, 933, 950
Call tracking software, 551–552
Camera, unauthorized use of, 899
Camtasia by TechSmith, 953
Camtasia Recorder by TechSmith, 396
Canopy Remote Backup by Atos, 876
Carbonite, 454
Car docking station, 33–34
Card service, 23
Carpenter's Level app, 32
Cartridges and replaceable parts, 932
CAs (Certification Authorities), 879, 889
Case cover, opening, 47–51
Case fans and heat sinks, 62, 187–188
CAS Latency, 166
CAT-5e, 711. *See also* Ethernet
CAT-6, 711. *See also* Ethernet
Catastrophic failure, 1028
Cat command, 978
Category view, 294–295
CCFL (Cold Cathode Fluorescent Lamp), 409
Cd (change directory) command, 473, 978
CD (compact disc) drives, 16, 57, 259–260, 261
CDFS (Compact Disc File System), 259, 468
CDMA (Code Division Multiple Access), 30, 656, 697, 760, 762

Celeron processors, 138, 140
Cell phones, 20. *See also* Mobile devices; Smart phones
Cellular network
  Apple iOS, configuring, 760–762
  laptops, 20, 22
  mobile devices, 30, 656–658
  overview of, 700
  speeds, 697
  weak signal, 778, 899
Cellular network analyzer, 902–903
Cellular WAN, 700
Central processing unit (CPU), 5. *See also* Processors
Centrino technology, 141
Certificate Manager, 889–890
Certificate of Authenticity, 360–361
Certificate of destruction, 883
Certification Authorities (CAs), 879, 889
CF (compact flash) cards, 266, 267
Chain of custody, 904
Channels, for a WLAN, 686
Channels, single, dual, triple, and quad, 161–162
Charging, laser printers, 913
Charms, 280
Charms bar, 280, 283
Chassis, 2
Chassis air guide (CAG), 210
Chat session, 822
Checklist, before installing Windows, 340–341
Child directories, 289, 473
Chip extractor, 37
Chipsets, 5, 80, 87–91, 127, 134
Chkdsk (check disk) command, 271, 476–477, 1038
Chkdsk /r command, 614, 626
Chmod command, 978, 984–985
Chown command, 978
CIDR (Classless Interdomain Routing) standards, 640
CIDR notation, 640
CIFS (Common Internet File System), 651
CLAMWIN Free Antivirus by ClamWin, 891
Class C fire extinguishers, 1025–1026
Classic view, 294–295
Clean boot, 508, 568
Cleaning, laser printers, 914
Cleaning pads and solutions, 1026–1027
Cleaning solutions/pads, 36
Clean installation, 338–339
  Windows 7, 352–354
  Windows 8.1, 350–352
Clear command, 978
Client Hyper-V, 336, 968, 970
Client/server applications
  Group Policy, 594, 822–823, 865–869, 925
  Internet Explorer, 807–814
    Advanced tab, 813–814
    Connections tab, 811–812
    General tab, 808–809
    Privacy and Content tabs, 810–811
    Programs tab, 812–813
    proxy settings, 811–812
    Security tab, 810
  network servers, 806–807
  ODBC data sources, 823–825
  Remote Assistance, 820–822
  Remote Desktop Connection (RDC), 652, 815–820
  supporting, 806–825
Client/server model, 634
Client/server networks, 305–306
Client-side desktop virtualization, 967
Client-side virtualization, 967
Clock speeds, 106–107
Clone, 988
Cloning startup disk, 1007–1008
Closed source operating systems, 759
Cloud computing, 846–847
  categories of, 847–849
  deployment models, 849–850
Cloud printing, 928–929
Cloud storage, 314
Cluster, 449
CMOS (complementary metal-oxide semiconductor), 120
CMOS battery, 26, 27, 120, 198
CMOS RAM, 120
Coaxial cable, 414, 705, 706–707
Code Division Multiple Access (CDMA), 30, 656, 697, 760, 762
Coin battery, 37, 329
Cold boot, 588
Cold Cathode Fluorescent Lamp (CCFL), 409
Color depth, 527
Colors, calibrating, 427
Column electrodes, 409
Command-and-control (C&C) server, 898–899
Command prompt window, 469–470, 597, 612–613, 977
Commercial data recovery services, 622
Commercial license, 903
Common Internet File System (CIFS), 651
Common port assignments, 652–653
Community cloud, 849
Compact Disc File System (CDFS), 259, 468
Compact flash (CF) cards, 266, 267
Compass app, 32
Compatibility
  troubleshooting, 368–370
  troubleshooting applications, 582
  UEFI CSM (Compatibility Support Module) mode, 330
  Windows 7 upgrade, 348
  Windows Compatibility Center, 328
Compatibility mode, 333
Compatibility Support Module (CSM), 112, 330
Competent support technicians, 546–550
Complete PC Backup, 465
Component Services (COM+) tool, 580–581
Component video, 415
Composite video port, 414
Compressed (zipped) folder, 292
Compressed air, 28, 36, 206, 1031
Compression, 451
CompTIA A+ acronyms, 1041–1048
Computer-aided design (CAD). *See* CAD/CAM design workstation
Computer-aided manufacturing (CAM). *See* CAD/CAM design workstation
Computer authentication, 869
Computer-illiterate customers, 555–556
Computer infestation. *See* Malicious software
Computer Management, 371, 511, 825, 845
Computer names, 646
Computer parts and tools, 1–41
  ATX form factor, 8–13
  desktop
    drives, cables, and connectors, 15–20
    expansion cards, 6
    hard drives and other drives, 6–7
    memory modules, 6
    motherboard, processor, and cooler, 5, 121–122
    overview of, 2–4
    power supply, 7–8
  desktop case, 2–17
  disposal of, 1035
  form factors, 8–15
  laptops, 17–29
    all-in-one computers, 26–27
    docking stations, 24
    expresscard slots, 22–24
    internal components, 25–26
    maintaining, 27–29
    overview of, 17–20
    special keys, buttons, and input devices, 21–22
  mobile devices
    accessories, 33–34
    connection types, 30–33
    field-replacement parts, 34
    hardware, 29–34
    maintaining, 27–29
    overview of, 29–30
    storage devices, 33
  power supply tester, 36, 38–39
  tools used by computer hardware technician, 34–40
    loopback plugs, 36, 40, 712, 725
    multimeter, 36, 39
    post diagnostic cards, 37–38, 220
Computer ribbon, 288
Computer Security Products, Inc., 880
Computrace Agent software, 109
Conditioning, laser printers, 913
Confidentiality, 554
Configuring motherboards, 103–115
  using BIOS setup, 103–111
    access BIOS setup program, 104
    change boot sequence, 104–105
    drive encryption and drive password protection, 109
    exiting, 111
    intrusion detection, 108
    LoJack technology, 109
    monitor temperature, fan speeds, and voltages, 107
    onboard devices, 105
    power-on passwords, 108–109
    processor and clock speeds, 106–107
    support for virtualization, 109
    TPM chip and hard drive encryption, 110–111
    view hard drive and optical drive information, 106
  using UEFI, 112–115

Connectionless protocol, 649
Connection-oriented protocol, 649
Connections tab, Internet Explorer, 811–812
Connection types, on mobile devices, 30–33
Connectivity. *See* Network connections
Connectors, 15–20, 190
Consoles, 296, 511, 512–513
Content filtering, 682–683
Content tab, Internet Explorer, 810–811
Continuity, measuring, 39
Contrast ratio, 411
Contrast settings, 417
Control Panel, 294–296
Conventional PCI, 94–95
Cooler, 5
Cooler Master, 192
Cooling methods and devices, 186–189
  case fans and heat sinks, 187–188
  handling, 55
  liquid cooling systems, 188–189
  processor coolers, fans, and heat sinks, 186–187
Copy command, 474–475
Copy files or folders, 293
Copyright, 903
Core dump, 988
Core i3, 80, 84, 139–140, 957
Core i5, 80, 84, 139–140, 144, 149, 300, 445, 955, 957
Core i7 processors, 80, 84, 88–89, 139–140, 953, 955
Core Max Multiplier, 106
Core processors, 138–140
Corrupted files, copy command and, 475
Cortana, 753, 756
Coworkers, troubleshooting applications and, 571–572
Cp command, 978
CPU (central processing unit), 5. *See also* Processors
CPU Fan Header, 62
CPU-Z by CPUID, 429
Creative, 404
Creative Sound Blaster Zx sound card, 953
Credibility, 548
Crimper, 715
Critical events, 514
Critical Windows settings, 444
Crossfire by AMD, 191
CrossFire technologies, 88
Cross-linked clusters, 476–477
Crossover cable, 717
CRT monitor, 1030, 1036
Crucial Technology, 169, 173–174, 239
CryptoLocker Trojan, 886, 887
Ctrl+Alt+Delete, 498–499, 856–858
Cultural differences, sensitivity to, 547–548
Culture of honor, 557
Cup for holding screws, 47–48, 72, 73
Customer complaints, 556–557
Customers, supporting
  competence and helpfulness, 546–550
  planning for good service
    active learning, 559–560
    call tracking software, 551–552
    customer decides when the work is done, 558
    difficult customers, 555–557
    escalating a problem, 558
    initial contact with customers, 552–553
    interview the customer, 553
    set and meet customer expectations, 553
    working on site, 554
    working over the phone, 554–555
    working with coworkers, 559
Custom installation, 338
Customized user groups, 828
Customizing computer systems
  audio and video editing workstation, 953
  gaming PC, 954–955
  graphics or CAD/CAM design workstation, 951–952
  home server PC, 957–958
  Home Theater PC (HTPC), 955–957
  introduction to, 950–951
  thick client and thin client, 958–959, 966
  virtualization workstation, 954
Custom log files, 515
Custom refresh image, 462–465, 598
CuteFTP by GlobalSCAPE, 651

D

DAS (distributed antenna system), 902
Dashboard, 992–993
Dashboard thumbnail, 996
Data bus, 92–93
Data cartridges, 256
Data corruption, 572
Data destruction and disposal, 882–883
Data files, managing, 613–614
Data hold switch, 39
Data Link layers, 648
Data loss prevention (DLP) software, 881
Data path size, 93
Data recovery, 196
Data sources, 823–825
Data throughput, 697
Data transmission speeds, 385
Date and Time applet, 295
DB9 port, 4
DB-15 port, 2, 413
DC (direct current), 39, 1023
DC jack, 18, 19
DC voltage, measuring, 39
Dd command, 978
DDR2, 161, 164
DDR2 SO-DIMM, 166–167
DDR3, 161, 164
DDR3 dual-channel, 171
DDR3L, 166–167
DDR3 triple-channel, 171–172
DDR4, 161, 164, 166–167
DDR memory, 420
DDR SDRAM, 160–161
DDS (Digital Data Storage), 257
DE15 port, 2
Dead pixels, 427
Debian, 972
Debugging, 607
Dedicated Video Memory, 422
Default gateway, 665
Default program, 577
Defrag command, 477–478
Defragmentation tool, 267–268, 449–450, 530
Degausser, 883
Del (delete) command, 474
Delete files or folders, 293
Dell Computer, 38, 67, 68, 192
Deluser command, 978
Demilitarized zone (DMZ), 681–682
Denial-of-service (DoS) attack, 501, 887
Dental pick, 71
Dependability, 546
Deployment strategies
  cloud computing, 849–850
  installing Windows in large enterprises, 373–375
Desktop, 2–17
  drives, cables, and connectors, 15–20
  expansion cards, 6
  hard drives and other drives, 6–7
  location of, 293
  Mac OS X operating system, 990–994
  memory modules, 6
  motherboard, processor, and cooler, 5
  motherboards, selecting, 121–122
  overview of, 2–4
  power supply, 7–8
  Windows 8, 283–285
  working inside, 46–66. *see also* Safety procedures
    opening and examining the system, 46–51
    planning and organizing, 46
    putting computer back together, 59–66
    remove expansion cards, 51–53
    removing motherboard, power supply, and drives, 54–58
Desktop case, 2
Destination Network Address Translation (DNAT), 680
Details tab, 499–500
Developing cylinder, 913
Device drivers
  definition of, 115
  installing hardware, 364–367
  installing Windows, 332–333
  needed to start Windows, 591
  for a network interface card, 666
  OS X updates, 1004
  printers, 931
  stop errors and, 625
  in System Information window, 301
  troubleshooting, 368–370
  troubleshooting I/O devices, 384
  updating speaking drivers, 435
  upgrading, 367
Device Manager
  Computer Management, 371, 511, 825, 845
  device or service fails to start, 626–627
  error messages, 366

I

Device Manager (*continued*)
  installing hardware, 366–368
  for list of installed devices, 1039
  peripheral devices and, 391
  rolling back a driver, 608
  troubleshooting, 214, 215
  troubleshooting I/O devices, 384, 422–423
  troubleshooting laptop video systems, 431
  updating drivers, 435, 444
  using to delete driver store, 218
Devices and Printers window, 921, 927, 944
Device Settings, printer properties, 929–930
Device Setup, 390
Df (disk filesystem) command, 978
DHCP (Dynamic Host Configuration Protocol) server, 638, 646, 674
DHCP client, 638
DHCPv6 server, 638, 646
Diagnostic software and tools. *See also* Utilities
  for laptops, 125
  provided by the manufacturer, 69–70
  troubleshooting hardware, 194
Dialog boxes, 293
Dial-up connections, 659–661, 697
Dial-up modems, 18, 701
Dictionary attack, 887
Differentiated Services Code Point (DSCP) value, 823
Difficult customers, 555–557
Digital, 2
Digital cameras and camcorders, 394–396
Digital certificate of destruction, 883
Digital certificates, 879, 889–890
Digital Data Storage (DDS), 257
Digital Linear Tape (DLT), 257
Digital projectors, 409–410
Digital Rights Management (DRM), 416, 904
Digital security methods and resources, 881
Digital signature, 114, 583, 763, 879
Digital subscriber line (DSL), 698–699
Digital Video Interface (DVI) port, 3, 5, 6, 413–414, 416
Digitizer, 396–397
Digitizing tablet, 396–397
Dim display, 778, 793
Dim image, 427–428
DIMM (dual inline memory module), 160–167
  amount and type that will fit on motherboard, 171–173
  buffered and registered DIMMs, 165
  CAS Latency and RAS Latency, 166
  DDR3 dual-channel, 171
  DDR3 triple-channel, 171–172
  with dual channeling, 172–173
  error checking and parity, 164–165
  installing, 175–176
  introduction to, 6, 159–161
  photo of, 5, 6, 80, 81
  single, dual, triple, and quad channels, 161–162
  single-sided and double-sided DIMMs, 163–164
  vs. SO-DIMMs, 25
  speeds, 163
DIMM slots, 6
Dir command, 471–472
Direct current (DC), 39, 1023
Directories, 288–290, 446–447, 975–977. *See also* Files and folders
Direct thermal printer, 917
DirectX, 420–421, 424, 528–529
Disaster recovery, 454–455
Disc image, 347
Discolored capacitors, 220–221
Disk Cleanup utility, 447–449
Disk Management utility, 250, 478, 511
  dynamic disks, 484–486
  hard drive troubleshooting, 486–487
  mounting a drive, 482–484
  prepare drive for first use, 481–482
  recovery partition, 617
  resize, create, and delete partitions, 480–481
  on a virtual machine, 487
Diskpart commands, 272, 482, 614–615
Disk permissions, repair, 1010
Disk Utility app, 1010–1011
Display cards. *See* Video cards
DisplayPort, 3, 18, 415–416
Display settings, 426, 429–430, 527–529
Distorted geometry, 426
Distributed antenna system (DAS), 902
Distribution server, 373
Distribution share, 374
.dll files, 579–581, 1038
DLL Library by Uniblue Systems Limited, 895
DLP (data loss prevention) software, 881
DLT (Digital Linear Tape), 257
DMG file, 1006
DMZ (demilitarized zone), 681–682
DNAT (Destination Network Address Translation), 680
DNS (Domain Name System or Domain Name Service) protocol, 647, 737
DNS client, 647
DNS server, 647, 652, 729, 731–732, 806
Dock, 990, 991
Docking ports, 24
Docking stations, 24
.docx file extension, 290
Domain account, 306
Domain controlling, 829
Domain name, 647, 680
Domain Name System or Domain Name Service (DNS) protocol, 647, 737
Domains, 305–306, 310–311
DoS (denial-of-service) attack, 501, 887
Double channel, 161–162
Double Data Rate SDRAM (DDR SDRAM, or SDRAM II, or DDR), 160–161
Double-sided DIMMs, 163–164
DRAM (dynamic RAM), 135–136, 158–159
Drive encryption, 109
Drive imaging, 373
Drive lock password protection, 109
Drive password protection, 109
Driver Rollback, 462
Drivers
  installing peripheral devices, 389–390
  for Mac OS X operating system, 1003–1005
  for optical drives, 263
  updating, 444–445
  updating motherboard drivers, 115–116
Driver signature enforcement, 610
Driver store, 218
Driver tab, Device Manager, 367
Drives. *See also* Hard drives
  in a desktop, 15–20
  handling, 46, 57
  installation order, 59
  removing from a desktop, 54–58
DRM (Digital Rights Management), 416, 904
Dropbox, 787, 847, 998
Dropped calls, 791, 899
DSCP (Differentiated Services Code Point) value, 823
DSL (digital subscriber line), 698–699
Dual boot, 338–339, 356, 986–987
Dual channeling, 172–173
Dual monitors/displays, 21, 22, 417–419, 528
Dual processors, 135
Dual rail power supply, 190
Dual ranked, 164
Dual-voltage selector switch, 7, 8, 191
Dumb terminal, 966
Dump command, 988
Duplex printer/printing, 914, 915
Dust, 206–207, 1031
DVD (digital versatile disc or digital video disc) drives, 7, 259–260, 261, 334, 953
DVI (Digital Video Interface) port, 3, 5, 6, 413–414, 416
DVI-A port, 414
DVI-D port, 413
DVI-I port, 414
Dxdiag.exe command, 420, 529
Dynamic disks, 484–486
Dynamic Host Configuration Protocol (DHCP) server, 638, 674, 806
Dynamic IP address, 638, 664–665, 943
Dynamic Link Library (DLL), 579–581, 591
Dynamic RAM (DRAM), 135–136, 158–159
Dynamic volumes, 484

E

Early launch anti-malware driver, 610
Easy Connect, 820–821
ECC (error-correcting code), 164–165
Echo command, 979
Econo Mode, 948
EDB (Execute Disable Bit), 136
Edge connector, 13
EDO (extended data out) memory, 165
EEPROM (Electronically Erasable Programmable Read-Only Memory) chips, 232

Effective permissions, 841
EFI (Extensible Firmware Interface), 112–115
EFI System Partition (ESP), 468, 486, 589, 590
EFS (Encrypted File System), 861–862
EIDE (Enhanced IDE) standard, 15
8-pin auxiliary connector, 12, 13
Elastic services and storage, 847
El Capitan, 990
Electrical fire safety, 1025–1026
Electrical noise, 1024
Electrical system
- intermittent problems, 204–205
- overheating, 206–211
- power problems with motherboard, 205
- problems with laptop power systems, 211–213
- troubleshooting, 203–213

Electricity
- measures and properties of, 1022–1025
  - AC and DC, 1023
  - hot, neutral, and ground, 1023–1025
- protecting yourself, 1025–1028
  - cleaning pads and solutions, 1026–1027
  - electrical fire safety, 1025–1026
  - lifting heavy objects, 1027
  - managing cables, 1027
  - safety goggles and air filter mask, 1028
  - working safely inside electrical devices, 1025

Electromagnetic interference (EMI), 736
Electronically Erasable Programmable Read-Only Memory (EEPROM) chips, 232
Electrostatic discharge (ESD), 35, 85, 241, 269, 1028–1031
Elevated command prompt window, 470, 947
EM64T (Extended Memory 64 Technology), 138
Email
- Android operating system, 786
- Apple iOS, 763–767
- malware symptoms and, 889
- troubleshooting Android OS, 794
- Windows Phone, 795–798

Email client, 763
Email encryption, 223
Email filtering, 881
Email hoax, 884–885
Email servers, 637, 806
Embedded broadband modem, 657–658
Embedded MMC (eMMC), 266
Embedded mobile broadband modem, 657
Emergency notifications, 752
EMI (electromagnetic interference), 736
Emulator, 970
Encrypted File System (EFS), 861–862
Encryption
- drive, 109
- email, 223
- files and folders, 861–862
- full device, 873
- hard drives, 110–111
- setting on a wireless network, 686

End User License Agreement (EULA), 755, 903
Energy Saver monitors, 425
Enhanced ATX boards, 12
Enhanced IDE (EIDE) standard, 15
Enhanced Virus Protection, 136
Enterprise license, 904
Entry control roster, 880
Environment, protecting, 1035–1036
EoP (Ethernet over Power), 708–710
Equipment, protecting, 1028–1034
- electrostatic discharge (ESD), 35, 85, 241, 269, 1028–1031
- physical protection from the environment, 1031–1034

Erase command, 474
Erase tab, Disk Utility, 1011
E-readers, 29–30
Error checking, DIMM and, 164–165
Error-checking utility, 451
Error-correcting code (ECC), 164–165
Error events, 514
Error messages
- BSOD error, 198, 199, 269–270, 574–575, 610, 623, 624–626
- Device Manager and, 366
- device or service fails to start, 626–627
- improper shutdowns, 626
- printers, 942–943
- researching, 214
- responding to, 577–583
  - .dll is missing or component is not registered, 579–581
  - application hangs, 577
  - application has never worked, 581–583
  - file association problems, 578–579
  - file fails to open, 577
  - service fails to start, 579
- stop errors, 624–626
- troubleshooting applications, 571–572
- troubleshooting hardware, 198–199
- troubleshooting Windows startup, 623–627

ESATA (external SATA), 4, 235, 237
ESATA 2.0 ports, 5, 99, 385
Escalating a problem, 558
ESD (electrostatic discharge), 35, 85, 241, 269, 1028–1031
ESD mat, 1029
ESD strap, 35–36, 50, 71, 72, 74, 122, 144, 175, 241, 400, 1028
E Series processors, 141
ESP (EFI System Partition), 468, 486, 589, 590
ESXi by VMware, 968
Ethernet
- cables and connectors, 635, 704–708, 919, 920
- port, 3, 19
- speeds, 666–667, 698
- variations of, 705

Ethernet over Power (EoP), 708–710
Ethernet wired networks, 653–656
EULA (End User License Agreement), 755, 903
Event Viewer
- Computer Management, 511
- custom log files, 515–516
- improper shutdowns, 626
- malware symptoms, 889
- optimizing Windows, 513–516
- stop errors and, 626
- troubleshooting applications, 572
- troubleshooting hardware, 215
- troubleshooting laptop video systems, 431

Everyone group, 827
Everything HelpDesk software, 551
EVGA, 192
EXecute Disable (XD), 136
Execute Disable Bit (EDB), 136
Executive services, 496, 497
ExFAT file system, 258, 264, 266, 468, 476
Exit command, 469, 979
Expand command, 475
Expansion cards, 6. *See also* Adapter cards
- in computer reassembly, 65
- conventional PCI, 94–95
- handling, 46
- installation order, 59
- installing, 124
- in laptops, 406–408
- Mini PCI and Mini PCI Express, 26, 27, 97–98, 156, 405–408
- PCI Express (PCIe), 6, 12, 13, 53, 80, 81, 87, 96–97, 400–402, 412, 425
- PCI riser cards, 98–99
- PCI-X, 96
- removing from a desktop, 51–53
- replacing in a laptop, 405–408

Expansion slots, 92–99
Expectations, customer, 553
Expert system, 567
Exposing, laser printers, 913
Express BIOS update, 117
ExpressCard/34, 23
ExpressCard/54, 23
ExpressCard slots, 22–24
Express settings, 344
ext3 file system, 981
ext4 (fourth extended file system), 981
Extended data out (EDO) memory, 165
Extended Memory 64 Technology (EM64T), 138
Extended partition, 466
Extender, 704
Extensible Firmware Interface (EFI), 112–115
Extension magnet brush, 932
External components, substitute for an internal component, 202
External customers, 550
External DVD drive, 334
External enclosures, 254–255
External SATA (eSATA), 4, 235, 237
Extractors, 36, 72
Eye strain, 411

F

F8 key, 597, 598–599
F9 key, 610
Face lock, 871

Facial recognition, 871
Factory default, 777
Factory recovery partition, 334–335
Factory reset, 791, 900
Fade-resistant ink, 916
Failed logon restrictions, 867, 873
Failed volume, 486
Fanfold paper, 917
Fanless CPU cooler, 187
Fans
- in an all-in-one computer, 26
- case fans and heat sinks, 187–188
- in laptops, 25, 156–157
- photo of, 6
- power supply and, 191
- troubleshooting power systems, 186–187

Fan speeds, monitoring, 107
Fast Ethernet, 708
Fast Startup, 588–589
FAT (file allocation table), 476–477
FAT32 file system, 258, 451, 467, 468, 476, 830
Fat client, 966
FAT file system, 258, 264, 266, 467, 830, 837
Fault tolerance, 249
Favorites tray, Android OS, 749
FCLGA (flip-chip land grid array) processor package, 85
F connector, 706–707
FCPGA (flip-chip pin grid array) package, 85
FDD (floppy disk drives), 10
Federal Copyright Act of 1976, 904
Fedora, 972
Ferrite clamp, 736
Fiber optic, 698, 700, 705, 707–708
Fiber Optic Service (FiOS), 700
Field replaceable unit (FRU), 34, 75, 214, 272, 393
File allocation table (FAT), 476–477
File allocation unit, 449
File associations, 577, 578–579
File Explorer, 258, 264, 283, 285, 287–294, 653–654, 927
File extensions, 290, 474
File History, 455
File management, 278
Filename, 290
File naming conventions, 471
File recovery software, 196
Files and folders, 465–489
- controlling access to, 825–846
  - administrative shares, 844–846
  - hidden network resources, 844–846
  - mapping a network drive or printer, 842–844
  - permissions, 828–830
  - sharing, 830–842
  - user accounts and user groups, 825–828
- copy, move, rename, or delete, 293
- creation of, 292, 293
- Disk Management utility, 480–487
  - dynamic disks, 484–486
  - hard drive troubleshooting, 486–487
  - mounting a drive, 482–484
  - prepare drive for first use, 481–482
  - resize, create, and delete partitions, 480–481
- in Linux, 975–977, 984–985
- malware symptoms and, 889
- partitions and file systems
  - commands, 469–479
  - workings of, 465–469
- partitions and file systems, workings of, 465–469
- sharing files and folders (copy), 830–842
  - share permissions, 837–838
  - troubleshooting, 838–842
  - user accounts with data access, 831–835
  - user and group information with gpresult command, 836–837
- Storage Spaces utility, 487–489
- structure of, 288–290, 446–447

File server, 806
File systems
- commands to manage files and folders, 469–479
- definition of, 329
- used by storage devices, 258–259
- workings of, 465–469
  - how partitions are used during the boot, 468–469
  - overview of, 467–468
  - partitioning systems, 289, 466–467
  - sectors and blocks, 234, 465

Final Cut Pro by Apple Computers, 953
Finder, 997
Finder window, 991
Find My iPhone/iPad, 771, 780, 875–876
Fingerprint readers, 393–394, 872
FiOS (Fiber Optic Service), 700
Fire extinguishers, 1025–1026
Fire OS, 748
FirePower Technology, 192
Firewall
- limiting Internet traffic, 678
- for mobile devices, 874–875
- scheduled maintenance, 897
- settings, 862–865
- SOHO routers, 671
- troubleshooting Internet connectivity, 737, 738
- Unified Threat Management (UTM), 882
- Windows Firewall, 296, 303, 863–865, 970

FireWire (IEEE 1394) connections, 387–388
FireWire 400 (1394a), 387–388
FireWire 800 (1394b), 387–388
FireWire cards, 400
FireWire headers, 100
FireWire port, 3
- data transmission speeds, 385
- external hard drives and, 235
- on laptops, 18
- photo of, 5, 99

Firmware
- Android operating system, 791
- BIOS, 329–330
- definition of, 37
- flashing, 445
- for Mac OS X operating system, 1003–1005
- mode, 330–332
- in printers, 931, 939–940
- of routers, 673, 678
- UEFI vs. legacy BIOS, 329–330
- updating, 444–445, 678
- of video cards, 424

Firmware chip, 37, 329
Fitness monitors, 30
Flash drive, ReadyBoost and, 533–534
Flashing UEFI/BIOS, 117–118, 215
Flashlights, 36, 72
Flash memory, 19, 232–233, 394–395
Flash pen drive. *See* USB flash drives
Flathead screwdrivers, 36, 71
Flat-panel monitor, 408
Flexguard Security System, 880
Flickering screen, 432
Flip-chip land grid array (FCLGA) processor package, 85
Flip-chip pin grid array (FCPGA) package, 85
Floppy disk drives (FDD), 10
Floppy drive connector, 9
Flowchart, troubleshooting hardware, 197
Fluorescent backlighting, 409
Folder Options, 296–297
Folder structure, 290–291
Force quit, 995
Force reset, 799
Force restart, 799
Force stop, 793
Foreign drive, 486
Format command, 614
Formatting, 258, 272, 467, 478, 486
Form factors, 8–15
- 20+4-pin P1 connector, 9–10, 12–13
- 24-pin P1 connector, 9, 12–13
- ATX form factor, 8–13
  - 4-pin auxiliary connector, 9, 12, 61
  - 6-pin PCIe connector, 9, 10, 13, 61
  - 8-pin auxiliary connector, 9, 12, 13
  - 20-pin P1 connector, 9, 10, 11
- for Home Theater PC (HTPC), 957
- microATX (MATX) form factor, 14, 80–82
- motherboards and, 80–82

Forwarded Events log, 514
FQDN (fully qualified domain name), 647, 806
Fragmented files, 267–268, 477
Frames, 702–703
Freeware utilities, 429
Frequency, 93–94, 134
Front panel connectors, 54
Front panel header, 52, 62–64
Front panel ports, 65
Front Side Bus (FSB), 87
Frozen systems, 222–223
FRU (field replaceable unit), 75, 214, 272, 393
FSB (Front Side Bus), 87
F-Secure Anti-Virus by F-Secure Corp, 891
FTP (File Transfer Protocol), 651–652, 982–984
FTP server, 671
Fujitsu/Fuji, 67, 70

Full Access to BIOS, 109
Full device encryption, 873
Full duplex, 666–667
Full retail Windows license, 326
Fully qualified domain name (FQDN), 647, 806
Function keys, 21, 22
Function switch, 39
Fuser assembly, 914, 937–938
FX processors, 141, 142

G

Gadgets, 286
Gaming PC, 954–955
Garbled characters on prints, 949
Gateway, 67, 635
GeForce GTX graphics processor, 953, 955
General tab, Internet Explorer, 808–809
Geotracking, 33, 779
Gestures, 991
GetDataBack by Runtime Software, 196, 622
Ghost by Symantec, 373
Ghost cursor, 432
Ghosted image, 949
Gigabit Ethernet, 666, 708, 711, 717–718, 958
Gigahertz (GHz), 93
Global account, 306
Global address, 644, 645
Globally Unique Identifier Partition Table (GUID or GPT) system, 466–467, 469
Global Positioning System (GPS), 22, 33, 741, 779
Global Routing Prefix, 644, 645
Global unicast address, 645
Gmail, 766–767, 786
Good service
  call tracking software, 551–552
  coworkers, working with, 559
  customer decides when the work is done, 558
  customers on site, working with, 554
  customers on the phone, working with, 554–555
  dealing with difficult customers, 555–557
  escalating a problem, 558
  initial contact with customer, 552–553
  interviewing the customer, 553
  planning for, 550–561
  set and meet customer expectations, 553
Google, 33, 748–751, 766–767, 786
Google account, 750
Google Apps Mobile Management software, 876
Google Authenticator, 873
Google Calendar, 787
Google Chrome, 749
Google Chromecast, 957
Google Cloud Platform, 848–849
Google Cloud Print, 929
Google Drive, 451, 787, 847, 998
Google Now, 753
Google Play, 750–751, 759, 787–788, 874
GoToAssist by Citrix, 555
GoToMyPC by Citrix, 819
Gpresult command, 836–837, 868
GPS (Global Positioning System), 22, 33, 741, 779
GPT (Globally Unique Identifier Partition Table) system, 271, 466–467, 469
GPU (graphics processing unit), 136, 419, 428–429
Gpupdate command, 868
GPU-Z by TechPowerUp, 429
Graphical user interface (GUI), 279, 749
Graphics, integrated, 136
Graphics adapters. *See* Video cards
Graphics cards. *See* Video cards
Graphics design workstation, 951–952
Graphics processing unit (GPU), 136, 419, 428–429
Graphics software, 527–529
Graphic tablets, 396–397
Grayware, 885
Grep command, 979
Ground bracelet, 35–36, 1028. *See also* ESD strap
Ground mat, 1029
Group Policy, 316, 594, 822–823, 865–869, 925, 1038
GRUB (GR and Unified Bootloader), 974, 986
GSM (Global System for Mobile Communication), 30
GSM (Global System for Mobile Communications), 656, 697, 760
Guest account, disabling, 860
Guests group, 826
GUI (graphical user interface), 279, 749
GUID (Globally Unique Identifier Partition Table) system, 466–467, 469
GUID Partition Table (GPT), 112, 329, 357–358, 486, 590
Gyroscope, 32, 778

H

HAL (hardware abstraction layer), 496, 497, 592, 594
Half duplex, 666–667
Handoff, 775–776
Hard boot, 588
Hard disk drive (HDD), 6, 232, 449. *See also* Hard drives
Hard drives
  all-in-one computer, 26
  BIOS setup and, 106
  cables, 16
  capacity of, 238
  cleanup, 446–453
    check for errors, 451
    defragmentation, 449–450
    directory structures, 446–447
    free up space, 451
    virtual memory paging file, 451–453
  corruption, 573
  in a desktop, 6–7
  dynamic disks, configured as, 484
  encryption of, 110–111
  external enclosures, 254–255
  handling, 57
  for high-end graphics workstations, 952
  important data on, 622–623
  installing
    in a laptop, 247–249
    in a removable bay, 245–246
    SATA drives, 239–245
    small drive in a wide bay, 246–247
  interface standards for, 235–237, 238
  introduction to, 6–7
  laptops, 25, 27, 156
  manufacturers of, 239
  moving to another system, 195–196
  photo of, 4, 7, 16
  preparing for first use, 481–482
  RAID
    dynamic disks, 484–486
    external enclosures and, 255
    for home server PC, 957
    implementing, 250–253
    setting up, 249–253
    troubleshooting, 269
    types of, 249–250
  repair and manage, 614–615
  SATA interface standards, 235–237, 247, 262
  scheduled maintenance, 450
  selecting, 238–239
  supporting, 231–272
  technologies used in, 232–234
  tracks, 465
  troubleshooting, 267–272
    with Disk Management utility, 486–487
    problems during the boot, 268–272
    slow performance, 267–268
  troubleshooting installations, 253–254
  upgrading in printers, 938–939
Hard-link migration, 375
"Hard" power button, 589
Hard reset, 777, 791
Hardware. *See also* Network hardware
  compatibility and customization, 951
  installing after a Windows installation, 364–370
  level of communication, 635
  management, 278
  mobile devices, 29–34
  on a TCP/IP network, 648
Hardware abstraction layer (HAL), 496, 497, 592, 594
Hardware address, 635
Hardware-assisted virtualization (HAV), 954, 969
Hardware problems
  back up data, 195–196
  check that hardware can support the OS, 532–533
  examine system and establish a theory, 197–201
  fix problem, verify fix, and document the outcome, 201
  interviewing the user, 195
  introduction to, 193–194
  mobile device hardware, 202–203
  troubleshooting rules, 200–201
Hardware RAID. *See* RAID (redundant array of inexpensive/independent disks)
HARDWARE subkey, 524
Hardware technician
  post diagnostic cards, 37–38, 220
  tools used by, 34–40

Hardware technician (*continued*)
loopback plugs, 36, 40, 712, 725
multimeter, 36, 39
post diagnostic cards, 37–38, 220
power supply, 38–39
Haswell chipsets, 91, 139
HAV (hardware-assisted virtualization), 954, 969
HD15 port, 2
HDD (hard disk drive), 6, 232, 449. *See also* Hard drives
HDMI (High-Definition Multimedia Interface) port, 3, 5, 18, 19, 413, 416, 955–956
HDMI mini connectors, 416
Header, 52
Header information, 638
Health (at risk) status, 486
Healthy volume, 486
Heat sinks, 186–188
introduction to, 5
on laptops, 25
in laptops, 156–157
photo of, 5, 6, 80
X58 chipset and, 89
Help command, 471
Help-desk support, 554–555
Helpful support technicians, 546–550
Hertz (Hz), 93
Hewlett Packard (HP), 67, 68, 69, 70
H-HDD (hybrid hard drive), 234
Hibernation, 298, 590
Hidden network resources, 844–846
Hidden share, 844–845
High-level formatting, 467
High-level keys, 523–524
High-touch using a standard image strategy, 373–374
High-touch with retail media strategy, 373
Hijacked home page, 888
Hiren's BootCD software, 269
Hi-Speed USB, 385, 389, 395, 535
Hives, 523–524
HKEY_CLASSES_ROOT (HKCR), 524
HKEY_CURRENT_CONFIG (HKCC), 524
HKEY_CURRENT_USER (HKCU), 524
HKEY_LOCAL_MACHINE (HKLM), 524, 525, 537, 591, 592, 594
HKEY_USERS (HKU), 524
Homegroup, 304–305
Homegroup sharing, 828–829
Home network, 307
Home page, 809
Home server PC, 957–958
Home Theater PC (HTPC), 955–957
Honesty, 548
Honeypots, 968
Honor cultures, 557
Hop, 730
Host Clock Frequency, 106
Host names, 646
Hot-plugging, 236
Hotspots, 32, 672, 700, 762
Hot-swapping, 23, 236, 330, 386, 387
How Stuff Works, Inc., 160
HTPC (Home Theater PC), 955–957
HTPC cases, 957
HTTP (Hypertext Transfer Protocol), 635, 649, 652
HTTPS (HTTP secure), 649–650, 652, 807–808
Hub architecture, 87
Hubs, 701–703
Humidity, 1033
Hybrid cloud, 850
Hybrid hard drive (H-HDD), 234
Hyper-Threading, 135
HyperTransport, 135
Hyper-V by Microsoft, 968
Hypervisors, 967–972
definition of, 336, 954
hardware requirements, 969–971
securing a virtual machine, 971–972
types 1 and 2, 968

I

IA64, 446
IaaS (Infrastructure as a Service), 848
IBUYPOWER, 955
ICCID (Integrated Circuit Card ID), 761
ICH (I/O controller hub), 87
iCloud Backup, 768–772
iCloud Drive, 768–769, 847, 998, 1000, 1006
ICMP (Internet Control Message Protocol) messages, 730
IDE (Integrated Drive Electronics), 15, 235
Identity-based access control lists, 882
IDS (intrusion detection system), 882
IEEE 802.11a/b/g/n/ac, 684
IEEE 1394, 3, 387–388
Ifconfig (interface configuration) command, 728–729, 979
Ifixit.com, 69, 202, 222
IIS (Internet Information Services), 807
I.LINK, 387
Image deployment, 374
Image drums, 936–937
Image file, and virtual printing, 928
Image processing, laser printers, 913
Image recovery process, 1013
Imaging drum, 912–913
IMAP4 (Internet Message Access Protocol, version 4), 650, 652, 763, 765–766
IMEI (International Mobile Equipment Identity), 761
Impact paper, 917
Impact printers, 917, 943
Improper shutdowns, 626
IMSI (International Mobile Subscriber Identity), 761
Information events, 514
Infrared (IR) connections, 31, 385, 388
Infrared Data Association (IrDA), 388
Infrastructure as a Service (IaaS), 848
Infrastructure mode, 920
Inherited permissions, 830
Initial contact with customers, 552–553
Initialization files, 447
Initialize Disk box, 482
Ink cartridges, 915–916, 932, 949
Inkjet printers, 914–916, 933, 943, 949, 950
In-place upgrades, 338–339, 342–346
In-Plane Switching (IPS), 409
Instances, 497
Intake fan, 210
Integrated Circuit Card ID (ICCID), 761
Integrated Drive Electronics (IDE), 15, 235
Integrated graphics, 136
Integrated Scripting Environment (ISE), 479
Integrity, 548
Intel ARK database, 140–141
Intel chipsets, 87–91
Intel Desktop Board, 163, 171
Intel DX58SO motherboard, 81
Intelligent Antivirus and Anti-malware by AVA ST Software, 891
Intel processors, 445–446
32-bit vs. 64-bit architecture, 327
characteristics of, 138–141
current list, 139–140
installing in socket LGA775, 152
installing in socket LGA1150, 144–149
installing in socket LGA1155, 150–151
installing in socket LGA1366, 151–152
photo of, 80
processor sockets for, 82–86
Intel sockets, 134
Intel Virtualization Technology, 969
Interface, 643
Interface ID, 643
Interface standards, for hard drives, 235–237, 238
Intermec Technologies, 393
Intermittent problems, in electrical system, 204–205
Internal buses, 137–138
Internal components
handling, 46
introduction to, 5–6
of a laptop, 25–26
replacing, 202
substitute an external component for, 202
Internal customers, 550
Internal memory caches, 137
International Mobile Equipment Identity (IMEI), 761
International Organization for Standardization, 347
Internet connections
for Home Theater PC (HTPC), 956
limiting traffic on network, 678–683
content filtering and parental controls, 682–683
DMZ (demilitarized zone), 681–682
port forwarding, 679–680
port triggering, 681
malware symptoms, 889
network technologies for, 696–700
cable vs. DSL, 698–699
cellular WAN, 700
fiber optic, 698, 700, 705, 707–708
satellite, 697, 699
troubleshooting, 736–737
Internet Control Message Protocol (ICMP) messages, 730
Internet Explorer, 807–814
Advanced tab, 813–814
cleanup, 896
Connections tab, 811–812

- Content tab, 810–811
- FTP, 651–652
- General tab, 808–809
- Privacy Content tab, 810–811
- Programs tab, 812–813
- proxy settings, 811–812
- Security tab, 810

Internet Information Services (IIS), 807
Internet Message Access Protocol, version 4 (IMAP4), 650, 652, 763, 765–766
Internet Options, Internet Explorer, 808
Internet Protocol version 4 (IPv4). *See* IPv4 addresses
Internet Protocol version 6 (IPv6). *See* IPv6 addresses
Internet service provider (ISP), 696
Interview the user, 563–565, 571
Intranet, 636
Intrusion detection, BIOS setup and, 108
Intrusion detection system (IDS), 882
Intrusion prevention system (IPS), 882
Invalid digital certificates, 889
Inverter, 1023
Inverter circuit boards, 409, 433–435
I/O controller hub (ICH), 87
I/O devices, 383–436
- adapter cards
  - installing and configuring, 400–408
  - replacing expansion cards in a laptop, 405–408
  - sound cards and onboard sound, 400, 404
  - TV tuner and video capture cards, 404–405, 955–956
- basic principles for supporting, 384–388
- controller board, 26
- definition of, 137
- installing, 389–399
  - barcode readers, 393
  - biometric devices, 393–394, 872–873
  - digital cameras and camcorders, 394–396
  - graphic tablets, 396–397
  - KVM switches, 399
  - MIDI devices, 397–399
  - motion controllers, 397
  - mouse or keyboard, 390–393
  - touch screens, 399
  - webcams, 396
- ports and wireless connections, 384–388
- troubleshooting, 422–436
  - Device Manager, 422–423
  - monitors and video, 424–430
  - numlock indicator light, 422
  - video system in a laptop, 431–435
- video subsystem, 408–422
  - monitor settings, 417–419
  - monitor technologies and features, 408–412
  - video cards and connectors, 412–417
  - video memory and Windows, 419–422

I/O modules, 403
IOS by Apple. *See* Apple iOS
I/O shield, 99–100, 122–123
IOS SDK (Software Development Kit), 754
IP addresses
- alternate configurations, 665
- assignment of, 638
- dynamic, 638, 664–665, 943
- dynamic vs. static, 664–665
- introduction to, 636
- overview of, 635
- printers and, 943
- public, private, and automatic private IP addresses, 641–642, 676
- settings, 645–646
- static, 638, 675–676, 681, 943
- web servers, 637
- websites, 647

iPads, 31, 222, 751–755, 872, 998
Ipconfig (IP configuration) command, 642, 645–646, 667, 728, 737
iPhones, 751–755
- iCloud Drive, 998
- iOS by Apple, 751–755
- Lightning cable, 31
- screen lock, 872
- Touch ID technology, 393
- troubleshooting, 222

iPods, 31
iPod touch, 751–755
IPS (In-Plane Switching), 409
IPS (intrusion prevention system), 882
IPv4 addresses
- alternate configurations, 665
- introduction to, 638–639
- ipconfig command, 645–646
- public, private, and automatic private IP addresses, 641–642
- for static or dynamic addressing, 664
- subnet masks, 639–641

IPv6 addresses, 638, 642–645, 665
IR (infrared) connections, 31, 385, 388
IrDA (Infrared Data Association), 388
ISATAP (Intra-Site Automatic Tunnel Addressing Protocol), 643
ISDN (Integrated Services Digital Network), 697
ISE (Integrated Scripting Environment), 479
ISO (International Organization for Standardization) image, 117, 347–348
Isolate problems, 201, 568
ISP (Internet service provider), 696
Itanium processors, 138, 327, 446
iTunes
- backup and sync, 768, 900
- content, use to back up and sync, 773–774
- Recovery mode, 777–778
- restore from backup, 775

iTunes Store app, 754–755
iTunes U, 754
ITX board, 80, 81–82. *See also* Mini-ITX motherboard
Ivy Bridge chipsets, 90, 139
Iwconfig command, 979

J

Jailbreaking, 755, 794, 899, 901
JAMMER Pro by SoundTrek, 399
Java Micro Edition (ME), 748
JBOD, 249–250
JEDEC, 160
Joule, 1022
Jump drive. *See* USB flash drives
Jumpers, 118–119, 239
JumpWin8.1, 970

K

Kaspersky Antivirus and Internet Security, 891
Kaspersky Lab, 884
Kernel mode, 497
Kernel panics, 988, 1013
Kernels, 591, 594
Keyboard backlight, 21
Keyboard bezel, 434
Keyboards, 28, 31, 390–393
Keychain, 998–999
Key drive. *See* USB flash drives
Key-exchange (or enrollment) Key (KEK), 114
Key fob, 878
Keylogger, 885–886
Keystone RJ-45 jacks, 716, 723–724
Kill command, 979
Kindle Fire, 748
Kingston Technology, 169, 173–174, 239
Knock code, 871
Knowledge base of common problems, 931
Kodi, 955
KVM (keyboard, video, and mouse) switches, 399

L

LAN (local area network), 635, 636, 696
Land grid array (LGA) socket, 84
Language, proper and polite, 547
Laptop battery, 211–213
Laptops, 17–29
- AC adapter on, 18, 27, 211–213, 341
- all-in-one computers, 26–27
- backup procedures, 28
- Bluetooth, 22
- cellular network, 20, 22
- designed for multimedia applications, 414
- displays, 410, 417
- docking stations, 24
- expansion cards, 406–408
- expresscard slots, 22–24
- installing a hard drive in, 247–249
- internal components, 25–26
- keyboard, replacing, 392–393
- LoJack, 109, 870
- maintaining, 27–29
- manufacturers, 67–70
- memory, types used in, 166–167
- memory modules, 159, 166–167, 177–179
- Mini PCI and Mini PCI Express, 97–98
- operating system, upgrading, 335, 341
- optical drive, replacing, 263–264
- overview of, 17–20
- physical security, 885
- port or slot drivers, updating, 423
- ports, 18
- power systems in, 211–213
- processor, replacing, 156–158
- speakers, 435
- special keys, buttons, and input devices, 21–22

Laptops (*continued*)
system board, replacing, 125–127
touch pad, replacing, 392–393
video system in, 431–435
external monitor, cannot connect, 431
flickering, dim, or otherwise poor video, 432
LCD panel, replacing, 433–435
touch screen unresponsive, 432
Windows, reinstalling, 616–618
Windows, upgrading, 618
wireless connectivity, 738–740
working inside
diagnostic tools provided by manufacturers, 69–70
overview of, 71–75
service manuals, 68–69
special considerations, 66–71
warranty concerns, 66–67
Large enterprise networks
authenticating users for, 877–879
deployment strategies, 373–375
Windows, installing, 372–376
Laser drum, 948
Laser printers, 912–914, 932, 933, 948–949, 950
Last Known Good Configuration, 592, 611
Latency, 697, 699
Launcher, 749
Launchpad, 991, 992
Layered protection, 856
LBA (Logical Block Addressing), 233, 234, 465
LC (local connector) connectors, 707–708
LCD (liquid crystal display) monitor, 27, 28, 408–409, 426, 433–435
LCD front bezel, 433–434
LDAP (Lightweight Directory Access Protocol), 650
Leap Motion, 397
Least invasive solutions, 568
LED (light-emitting diode), 409
Legacy BIOS firmware, 329–330
Legacy devices, 367–370
Legal issues, 549
Lenovo (formerly IBM ThinkPad), 67, 68, 70
Lenovo ThinkCentre, 26
Lenovo ThinkPad, 24
Level 1 cache (L1 cache), 135
Level 2 cache (L2 cache), 135
Level 3 cache (L3 cache), 135
LGA (land grid array) socket, 84
Library, 287
Lifting heavy objects, 1027
Light-emitting diode (LED), 409
Lightning, 1033
Lightning cable, 31, 32
Lightweight Directory Access Protocol (LDAP), 650
LILO (LInux boot LOader), 986
Limited BIOS access, 109
Linear Tape-Open (LTO), 257
Line-of-sight connectivity, 699
Link, 643
Link-local address, 644
Link-local unicast address, 644
LinkRunner Pro network multimeter, 714
LInux boot LOader (LILO), 986
Linux Mint, 972
Linux operating system, 972–990
Android operating system/devices, 972
assigning permissions to files or directories, 984–985
backups and updates, 988–990
command prompt, 977
commands, 978–981
directory and file layout, 975–977
distributions, 972
dual-boot systems and a live CD, 986–987
FTP software in Ubuntu, installing, 982–984
important directories, 977
introduction to, 972–973
as network operating system, 306
root account and user accounts, 899, 977–978
Ubuntu Desktop in a virtual machine, installing, 987
Ubuntu server on a virtual machine, installing, 974–975
vi editor, 981–984
Liquid cooling systems, 188–189, 954–955
Liquid crystal display (LCD) monitor, 27, 28, 408–409, 426, 433–435
Listening to customers, 547
Lite-touch, high-volume deployment strategy, 374–375
Lithium ion technology, 211
Live CD, 986–987
Live Parental Controls application, 682
Live sign in, 314
Live tiles, 279
Loadstate command, 376
Local account, 311, 312–314
Local address, 644
Local area network (LAN), 635, 636, 696
Local Computer Policy, 823
Local connector (LC) connectors, 707–708
Local link, 643
Local network hardware, 701–711
dial-up modems, 18, 701
Ethernet cables and connectors, 635, 704–708, 919, 920
powerline networking or Ethernet over power, 708–710
Power over Ethernet (PoE), 710
router, installing and configuring, 672–678
switches and hubs, 701–703
wireless network points and bridges, 703–704
wiring, 711–742
strategies for troubleshooting network connections, 733–742
TCP/IP utilities, 727–733
tools, 712–716
twisted-pair cable, 705–706, 717–726
Local printers, 919–920, 921–923
Local Security Authority process, 592, 594
Local security policies using group policy, 865–869
Local Security Policy snap-in, 868
Local shares, 845
Local snapshots, 1006
Local Users and Groups, 511, 828, 860
Local wired network, 19, 31–32
Local wireless network, 19, 30
Location data, 771
Location independence, 847
Location Services, 779–780
Location tracking, 899
Locator app and remote wipe, 875–876
Lock connector, 18
Lock screen, 856–858, 871
Lockups, 889
Lock workstations, 858–860
Log files, 515–516
Logical Block Addressing (LBA), 233, 234, 465
Logical drives, 466
Logical topology, 305
Login items, 1009–1010
LogMeIn, 555, 819
Logon failures, 868
Logon hours, 867
Logon Manager, 592
Logon process, 591
Logs, troubleshooting applications and, 571–572
LoJack technology, 109, 870
Long Term Evolution (LTE), 656
Loopback address, 638, 644
Loopback plugs, 36, 40, 712, 725
Loose configuration, 707
Lost clusters, 476–477
Low-level formatting, 234, 465
Low memory errors in printers, 949–950
Low-resolution video, 608
LPT port, 4
Ls command, 979
Ls –l command, 984–985
LTE (Long Term Evolution), 656, 697
LTO (Linear Tape-Open), 257

M

MAC (Media Access Control) address, 635, 636, 667, 675, 703–704
MAC address filtering, 676, 737
Mac OS X operating system, 990–1014
anti-malware software on, 1005
Boot Camp, 1014
compared to iOS, 751–752
drivers for, 1003–1005
firmware for, 1003–1005
maintaining and supporting, 1003–1011
backup and restore with Time Machine, 1006–1007, 1013
clone the startup disk, 1007–1008
drive maintenance tools, 1008–1010
repairs using Disk Utility app, 1010–1011
updates, drivers, and firmware, 1003–1005
troubleshooting startup, 1012–1013
recovery from Time Machine backup, 1013
recovery with a clone or the Internet, 1013

Repair Disk, 1012–1013
start in Safe Mode, 1012
using the Mac, 990–1003
Apple menu, 995
desktop, 990–995
Finder, 997
iCloud Drive, 998
Keychain, 998–999
kill a process, 1002–1003
multiple desktops, 996–997
sharing, 1001
Spotlight, 994, 997–998
System Preferences, 999–1000
Terminal, 1001–1002
MagicGate slot, 19
Magnetic fields, 28
Magnetic hard drive, 232, 233–234
Main board, 5
Malicious software, 885–898
categories of, 885–887
denial-of-service (DoS) attack, 501, 887
false S.M.A.R.T. alerts, 234
step-by-step attack plan, 887–897
step 1: identify malware symptoms, 888–890
step 2: quarantine infected system, 890
step 3: disable System Restore, 890–891
step 4: remediate infected system, 891–896
step 5: scheduled scans and updates, 897
step 6: enable System Protection and create restore point, 897
step 7: educate end user, 897
symptoms, 889
Malware. *See* Malicious software
Malwarebytes Anti-Malware, 891
Malware definitions, 892
Malware encyclopedias, 895
Malware signatures, 892
MAN (metropolitan area network), 696
Manage Add-ons, 813
Man command, 979
Man-in-the-middle attack, 887, 890
Mantrap, 880
Manufacturers
cases and power supplies, 192
diagnostic software, 194
diagnostic tools provided by, 69–70
hard drives, 239
laptops, 67–70
technical support, 194
MAP (Microsoft Assessment and Planning) Toolkit, 375
Mapping a network drive or printer, 842–844
Master Boot Record (MBR), 112, 329, 357–358, 466–467, 468, 481, 590
Master file table (MFT), 476–477
Material safety data sheet (MSDS), 1027
Maxel LTO Ultrium 3 data tape cartridge, 257
Maxtor, 239
Maxtor BlackArmor, 109
MBR (Master Boot Record), 112, 271, 329, 357–358, 466–467, 468, 481, 590
McAfee Total Protection, 891
Md (make directory) command, 472
Measured services, 847
Media Access Control (MAC) address, 635, 636, 667, 675, 703–704
Media Composer by Avid, 953
Megahertz (MHz), 93, 163–164
Memory, 158–167. *See also* RAM (random access memory)
in a desktop, 5, 6
determining need and how much is installed, 168–170
DIMM technologies, 160–167
EEPROM (Electronically Erasable Programmable Read-Only Memory) chips, 232
handling, 175
for high-end graphics workstations, 952, 953
installing on motherboard, 123–124
introduction to, 158–160
in laptops, 25, 159, 166–167
laptops, types of used in, 166–167
maximum supported by Windows, 327
upgrading, 167–179
amount and type currently installed, 169–170
amount and type that will fit on motherboard, 171–173
determining need and how much is installed, 167–169
installing new modules, 175–176
on a laptop, 177–179
selecting and purchasing the right modules, 173–175
upgrading in printers, 938–939
virtualization, 969
Memory bank, 163–164
Memory cache, 135
Memory cards, 264, 394–395
Memory card slot, 265–266, 394–395
Memory controller, 88
Memory Diagnostics tool, 214, 216–217, 574–576, 608, 626
Memory slots, 4
Memory Stick, 266
Memory stripe card, 879
Menu bar, Internet Explorer, 807
Metropolitan area network (MAN), 696
Metro User Interface or Metro UI, 279
MFA (multifactor authentication), 869–870, 873
MFT (master file table), 476–477
Micro-A connector, 386
MicroATX (MATX) form factor, 14, 80, 81–82, 190, 957
Micro-B connector, 386
MicroDIMMs, 159
Microphone, unauthorized use of, 899
Microphone ports, 19
Microprocessor, 5
MicroSD card, 33, 265, 267
MicroSDHC card, 395
Microsoft accounts
backup Windows Phone, 796–798
connecting to a local account or network ID, 316–317
installing Windows and, 352
using with Windows 8, 314–317
Windows 8, 311, 315
Windows 8.1, 344–346
Microsoft Assessment and Planning (MAP) Toolkit, 375
Microsoft Authenticator, 873
Microsoft Corp., 33, 67, 755–758
Microsoft Edge, 807
Microsoft Exchange, 767, 876
Microsoft Hyper-V, 109
Microsoft Management Console (MMC), 511–513
Microsoft Safety Scanner, 894
Microsoft Security Essentials, 891
Microsoft SNMP Agent application, 651
Microsoft SQL Server database, 823–824
Microsoft Store, 758
Microsoft System Center, 887
Microsystems Developments, Inc., 38
MicroUSB, 31
MIDI (musical instrument digital interface) devices, 397–399
MIDI-to-USB cable, 398
Mikkelson, Barbara, 884
Mikkelson, David, 884
MIMO (multiple input/multiple output), 684
Mini-B connector, 386
Minicartridges, 256–257
Mini-DIN -6 connector, 415
Mini-DIN port, 4
Mini DisplayPort, 415
Mini-DTX motherboard, 957
Mini-HDMI connectors, 416
Mini-ITX motherboard, 80–82, 957
Mini PCI, 26, 27, 97–98, 156, 405
Mini PCI Express (Mini PCIe), 27, 97–98, 405–408
Mini PCI Express Sierra Wireless mobile broadband Internet card, 405–406
MiniSD card, 265, 267
MiniUSB, 31
Miracast, 784
Mirrored volume, 249–250
Mission Control, 992–993, 996
Mkdir command, 979
MMC (Microsoft Management Console), 511–513
MMC (MultiMediaCard), 266
Mobile devices. *See also* Android operating system/devices; Apple iOS; Laptops; Windows Phone
accessories, 33–34
anti-malware software, 874, 901
Bluetooth, 31, 762, 784, 792
cellular network, connecting to, 30, 656–658, 760–762
connection types, 30–33
field-replacement parts, 34
hard and soft resets, 777
hardware, 29–34
maintaining, 27–29
malicious software on, 898–903
common symptoms, 898–899
tools and malware removal, 900–903

I

Mobile devices (*continued*)
  overview of, 29–30
  processor sockets, matching, 87
  security strategies, 871–877
    in corporate environments, 876–877
    device access controls, 871–873
    software security, 874–876
  storage devices, 33
  troubleshooting, 202–203, 222–224
Mobile hotspots, 32, 672, 700, 762
Mobile operating systems, 747–799
  Android, 748–751
    configuring email, 786
    configuring network connections, 781–785
    sync, update, back up, and restore from backup, 787–789
    troubleshooting, 790–794
  Apple iOS, 751–755
    configure network connections, 760–763
    configuring email, 763–767
    sync, back up, and restore from backup, 768–776
    troubleshooting, 776–781
  open source vs. closed source, 759
  Windows Phone, 755–758
    configure, sync, and troubleshoot, 794–799
    troubleshooting, 798–799
    update and restore from backup, 798
Mobile payment service, 789
Mobo, 5
Modem port, 4
Modern interface, 279–280
Molex connector, 10, 61–62
Monitors
  cannot connect to, 431
  installing dual monitors, 417–419
  settings, 417–419
  troubleshooting, 424–430
    blank screen after keyboard is left untouched, 425–426
    correcting display settings when screen is unreadable, 429–430
    indicator light/blank screen, 424–425
    poor display, 426–429
Motherboards, 79–127
  buses and expansion slots, 92–99
    conventional PCI, 94–95
    PCI Express (PCIe), 6, 12, 13, 53, 80–81, 87, 96–97, 400–402, 412, 425
    PCI riser cards, 98–99
    PCI-X, 96
  chipsets, 87–91
    AMD chipsets, 87, 91
    Intel chipsets, 87–91
  in computer reassembly, 59–60
  configuring, 103–115
    BIOS setup, 37, 103–111
    UEFI setup, 103, 112–115, 330
  in a desktop, 5
  desktop, removing from, 54–58
  documentation for, 100–102, 122, 169–170, 176, 243
  drivers, 115–116, 124
  form factors, 80–82
  handling, 46, 55
  for high-end graphics workstations, 952, 953
  installation order, 59
  installing or replacing, 122–125
  introduction to, 5
  laptops, 97–98
  laptop system board, replacing, 125–127
  maintaining, 115–120
    flashing BIOS, 117–118, 215
    flashing UEFI, 118
    replacing the CMOS battery, 120
    updating drivers, 115–116
    using jumpers to clear BIOS settings, 118–119
  memory, amount and type, 171–173
  onboard ports and connectors, 99–102
  photo of, 4
  power problems with, 205
  processor sockets, 82–87
    for AMD processors, 86
    for Intel processors, 82–86
  selecting for a desktop, 121–122
  troubleshooting, 214–221
Motion controllers, 397
Motion sensor, 397
Mounted drive, 482–484
Mount point, 482–483
Mouse, 390–393
Move files or folders, 293
Mozilla Firefox browser, 973
Mozy, 454
MSDS (material safety data sheet), 1027
MSI Computer Corporation, 412
Mstsc (Microsoft Terminal Services Client) command, 817
MT-RJ (mechanical transfer registered jack) connectors, 707–708
Multiboot, 333, 339, 354–356
Multicast address, 643
Multicasting, 643–644
Multicore processing, 135, 952
Multifactor authentication (MFA), 869–870, 873
Multifunction routers. *See* Routers
MultiMediaCard (MMC), 266
Multimeter, 36, 39, 714
Multimonitor taskbar, 528
Multiple desktops, 996–997
Multiple input/multiple output (MIMO), 684
Multiple monitors, 528
Multiplier, 137
Multiprocessing abilities, 134
Multiprocessor platform, 135
Multithreading, 134–135, 497
Musical instrument digital interface (MIDI) devices, 397–399
Mutual authentication, 877–878
Mv command, 979

N

Name resolution, 647, 806
NAND flash memory, 232
NAS (network attached storage), 254, 842
NAS ShareCenter Pro 1100, 255
NAT (Network Address Translation), 641–642
National Institute of Standards and Technology (NIST), 847
Native resolution, 411, 527
Navigation pane, 290
Nbtstat (NetBIOS over TCP/IP statistics) command, 731–732
Near Field Communication (NFC), 29, 31, 385, 784
Needle-nose pliers, 36
Nehalem chipsets, 88
Neighbors, 643
NetBIOS, 652, 731–732
NetBIOS over TCP/IP, 652
NetBIOS over TCP/IP statistics (nbtstat) command, 731–732
Netbooks, 18, 67. *See also* Laptops
NetBoot, 1013
Net commands, 731
Netdom (network domain) command, 733
.NET Framework, 479
Net localgroup command, 731
Netstat (network statistics) command, 732
Net use command, 731
Net user command, 731
Network adapters, 635–636, 666–670
Network Address Translation (NAT), 641–642
Network and Sharing Center, 308, 309, 654, 737, 838–842
Network attached storage (NAS), 254, 842
Network cable tester, 36
Network cards. *See* Network adapters
Network communications, 634–638
Network configuration, 339–340
Network connections, 633–688
  Android operating system, 781–785
  Apple iOS, 760–763
  cellular network, 20
  connecting a computer to a network, 653–670
    alternate IP address configurations, 665
    dial-up connections, 659–661, 697
    dynamic and static IP configurations, 638, 664–665, 675–676, 681, 943
    Ethernet wired or wireless Wi-Fi local network, 653–656
    network adapters, managing, 635–636, 666–670
    virtual private network (VPN), 661–664
    wireless WAN (cellular) network, 656–658
  for home server PC, 958
  local wired network, 19
  local wireless network, 19
  multifunction router for a SOHO network
    functions of a SOHO router, 670–672
    install and configure on the local network, 672–678
    limiting Internet traffic, 678–683
    wireless network, 683–688

ping (Packet InterNet Groper) command, 726–728, 737, 943–944, 979
TCP/IP and Windows networking, 634–653
identifying computers and networks, 646–648
IP addresses, assignment of, 638
IP address settings, 645–646
IPv4 addresses, 638–642
IPv6 addresses, 642–645
layers of network communication, 634–638
TCP/IP protocol layers, 648–653
troubleshooting, 733–742
GPS not functioning, 741
Internet connectivity, 736–737
no Bluetooth connectivity, 740
no connectivity or intermittent connectivity, 734–736
no wireless connectivity, 738–739
TCP/IP utilities, 737–738
Wi-Fi network not found, 739–740
Windows, 304–311
domain, 305–306
domain setup, 310–311
public and private networks, 307–308
workgroup and homegroup, 304–305
Windows 7, 309–310
Windows 8, 307–309
Windows Phone, 795
Network Connections window, 654–655
Network Discovery, 307
Network drives, mapping, 842–844
Network File System (NFS), 842
Network hardware, 695–742
local networks, 701–711
dial-up modems, 18, 701
Ethernet cables and connectors, 635, 704–708, 919, 920
powerline networking or Ethernet over power, 708–710
Power over Ethernet (PoE), 710
switches and hubs, 701–703
wireless network points and bridges, 703–704
types of networks and Internet connections, 696–700
wiring, 711–742
strategies for troubleshooting network connections, 733–742
TCP/IP utilities, 727–733
tools, 712–716
twisted-pair cable, 705–706, 717–726
Network ID, 306
Network interface card (NIC), 666
Network location, 349
Network multimeter, 714
Network Places Wizard, 857
Network port, 3, 5, 18, 99
Network printers, 919–920
installing, 921–923
mapping, 842–844
sharing, 924–927
Networks, types of, 696–700
Network screen, 308
Network security key, 655
Network security settings, 444
Network servers, 806–807
Network share, 842–844
Network wiring
setting up and troubleshooting, 711–742
TCP/IP utilities, 727–733
tools used by network technicians, 712–716
troubleshooting network connections, 733–742
GPS not functioning, 741
Internet connectivity, 736–737
no Bluetooth connectivity, 740
no connectivity or intermittent connectivity, 734–736
no wireless connectivity, 738–739
TCP/IP utilities, 737–738
Wi-Fi network not found, 739–740
twisted-pair cables and connectors, 717–726
Never Execute or No Execute (NX), 328
New Technology file system (NTFS), 258, 329, 451, 467, 476, 483, 830, 986
Next-generation firewall (NGFW), 881
NFC (Near Field Communication), 29, 31, 385, 784
NFS (Network File System), 842
NGFW (next-generation firewall), 881
NIC (network interface card), 666
Nighthawk AC1900 by NETGEAR, 671–672
NIST (National Institute of Standards and Technology), 847
NLX form factor, 81
No Access, 109
Node, 643
Non compliant systems, 887
Nonvolatile RAM (NVRAM) chip, 589
Nonvolatile storage, 298
North Bridge, 87–89, 94, 97
Notebooks. *See* Laptops
Notepad text editor, 285
Note taking, 46, 73–74, 125, 568, 569
Notification area, 284
Notification Center, 991, 993
Notifications, 749–750, 752, 757
Nozzle plate, 933
Nslookup (namespace lookup) command, 729
Ntbtlog.txt file, 607–608
NTFS (New Technology file system), 258, 329, 451, 467, 476, 483, 830, 986
NTFS permissions, 830, 832, 837–838, 839, 881
NTUSER.DAT, 446
Numlock indicator light, 422
NVRAM (nonvolatile RAM) chip, 589
NX (Never Execute or No Execute), 328

O

Octet, 638–640
ODBC (Open Database Connectivity) data sources, 823–825
OEM (Original Equipment Manufacturer), 326, 360
OEM recovery partition, 600, 616–618
OEM Windows license, 326
Off-boarding, 876
Office 365, 848
Offline disk status, 486
Offline files, 447
Offline Files utility, 447
Ohm, 1022
OLED (organic light-emitting diode) monitor, 409–410
On-boarding, 876
Onboard NIC, 666
Onboard ports and connectors, 99–102
Onboard sound, 404
On-demand service, 847
OneDrive, 311, 314–315, 451, 787, 795, 847, 998
Online backup services, 454
Online disk status, 486
Online documentation, for printers, 931
Open Database Connectivity (ODBC), 823–825
Open Handset Alliance, 748–751
Open source operating systems, 748, 759
OpenVPN, 661
Operating system level of communication, 636
Operating systems (OS), 278, 496, 759
Optical connector, 3
Optical drives
all-in-one computer, 26
BIOS setup, 106
drivers for, 263
external, 20
installing, 262–263
laptops, 18, 19, 26, 263–264
photo of, 4
standards used by, 259–262
Optimizing drives, 268
Option ROMs, 114
OptiView tablet by Fluke Networks, 901
Oracle, 748
Oracle VirtualBox, 109, 499, 954
Orientation. *See* Screen orientation
Original Equipment Manufacturer (OEM) license, 326, 360
Original USB, 385, 389
OS (operating systems), 278, 496, 759
OSI model, 648
OS X. *See* Mac OS X operating system
Outside interference, 573
Overclocking, 106, 429, 954
Overheating, 779
air circulation and, 1032
electrical system, 206–211
external enclosures, 255
impact printers, 917
improper shutdowns, 626
laptops and, 28
mobile devices, 222, 794
Overly confident customers, 556
Overwrite data, 882
Ownership of a problem, 548
Ownership of folders, 841–842

P

P1 24-pin power connector, 13, 60
P2P (peer-to-peer) network, 304–305
PaaS (Platform as a Service), 848
Packets, 702
PAE (Physical Address Extension), 328

Pagefile.sys, 451–453
Page the output, 980
Pairing process, 762
PAN (personal area network), 696
Panda Internet Security, 891
Paper jams, 942
Paper quality, 916, 948
Paper shredder, 882
Paragon ExtFS for Windows, 986
Parallel ATA (PATA) standards, 15–16, 235, 247
Parallel port, 4, 400
Parental controls, 682–683
Parent directory, 473
Parent folder, 841
Parity, 164–165, 488
Parity checking, 249–250
Parity error, 165
Parted command, 979
Partitioning systems, 289
  commands to manage files and folders, 469–479
  factory recovery partition, 334–335
  formatting, 467
  GPT (Globally Unique Identifier Partition Table) system, 271, 466–467, 469
  initializing a disk, 482
  managing in OS X, 1011
  MBR (Master Boot Record), 112, 271, 329, 357–358, 466–467, 468, 481, 590
  MBR vs. GPT, 329
  resize, create, and delete, 480–481
  size of, 339
  UEFI vs. legacy BIOS, 330
  workings of, 465–469
    during the boot, 468–469
    file systems, 467–468
    partitioning systems, 466–467
    sectors and blocks, 465
Partition table, 466
Passcode screen, 872–873
Passive CPU cooler, 187
Passwd command, 979
Passwords
  changing on a router, 673–674
  laptops and, 28
  mobile devices, 871
  strong passwords, 860–861
Password vault software, 884
PATA (Parallel ATA) standards, 15–16, 235, 247
Patch cable, 717
Patches, 300, 574
Patch management, 445–446
Patch panel, 716
Path, 290
Patience, 554–555
PC-Doctor, 70
PCI (Peripheral Component Interconnect), 11, 94–95
PCIe ×16 video card, 13
PCIe 6/8-pin connector, 10
PCIe version 1.0, 97
PCIe version 1.1, 97
PCIe version 2.0, 97
PCIe versions 3.0 and 4.0, 97
PCI expansion card, 11
PCI Express (PCIe), 12, 96–97
  chipsets and, 87
  installing adapter cards, 400–402
  photo of, 6, 13, 80, 81
  removing from a desktop, 53
  troubleshooting, 425
  video cards, 412
PCI Express Version 2, 88–89, 94–95
PCI riser cards, 98–99
PCI slots, 5, 11
PCI video card, 425
PCI-X, 96
PCMCIA (Personal Computer Memory Card International Association), 22
PC ratings, 163
PC Trial, 196
PDF files, and virtual printing, 928
Peer Name Resolution Protocol (PNRP), 820
Peer-to-peer (P2P) network, 304–305
Pentium processor, 134, 137, 138, 140
People app, 279
Performance improvement
  check that hardware can support the OS, 532–533
  clean Windows startup, 530–532
  history of problems, 533
  ReadyBoost, 533–535
  routine maintenance, 530
Performance Monitor, 511, 520–522, 533
Performance tab, 501–502
Peripheral Component Interconnect (PCI), 11, 94–95
Peripheral devices
  barcode readers, 393
  biometric devices, 393–394, 872–873
  Device Manager, 391
  digital cameras and camcorders, 394–396
  graphic tablets, 396–397
  installing, 389–399
  KVM switches, 399
  MIDI devices, 397–399
  motion controllers, 397
  mouse or keyboard, 390–393
  ports and wireless connections used by, 384–388
    FireWire (IEEE 1394) connections, 387–388
    infrared (IR) connections, 31, 385, 388
    USB connections, 385–387
  touch screens, 399, 432, 778, 793–794
  webcams, 396
Permission propagation, 830
Permissions
  advanced permissions settings, 840–841
  assigning, 828–830
  definition of, 825
  effective permissions, 841
  inherited permissions, 830
  Linux operating system, 984–985
  NTFS permissions, 830, 832, 837–838, 839, 881
  share permissions, 830, 837–838, 881
Personal area network (PAN), 696
Personal firewall, 862–863
Personal license, 904
Personal settings across devices, 314
PGA socket architecture, 84, 86
Phablets, 29
Phenom processors, 141–142
Phillips-head screwdrivers, 36, 71, 154
Phishing, 884, 885
Physical address, 635
Physical Address Extension (PAE), 328
Physical layers, 648
Physical security methods and devices, 880
Physical topology, 305
Pickup roller, 914
Pinch, 992
Ping (Packet InterNet Groper) command, 727–728, 737, 943–944, 979
Pin grid array (PGA) socket, 84, 86
Pinning to the taskbar, 284
PIN number, 871
Pixel, 408
Pixel pitch, 411
Plasma monitors, 409
Platform, 446, 847
Platform as a Service (PaaS), 848
Platform Controller Hub, 90
Platform Key (PK), 114
Play Store app, 750–751, 875
Plenum rated, 672
Plenums, 706
Plex, 955
PNRP (Peer Name Resolution Protocol), 820
PoE (Power over Ethernet), 710
Point of sale (POS), 393
Polarizer, 409
POP3 (Post Office Protocol, version 3), 650, 652, 763
Pop-up ads, 888
Pop-up Blocker, 810
Port address, 635, 637
Port assignments, 652–653
Port drivers, 423
Port forwarding, 679–680, 681
Port mapping, 679–680
Port number, 637, 647
Ports, 384–388, 637
Port scanner, 741–742
Port triggering, 681
POS (point of sale), 393
POST (power-on self test), 38, 105, 124, 592
Post Code Master card, 38
POST diagnostic cards, 37–38, 220
POST errors, 198, 200, 268–269
Post Office Protocol, version 3 (POP3), 650, 652, 763
Power button, 47
Power cords, 4
Power down system, 47
Power icon, 280
Powerline networking, 708–710
Power-on passwords, 108–109, 124
Power Options, 297–299, 426, 428, 588
Power over Ethernet (PoE), 710
PowerPoint application, 419
Power-saving states, 297–298
Power supply
  all-in-one computer, 26
  in computer reassembly, 59–60

desktop, 7–8, 54–58
installation order, 59
intermittent problems, 204–205
photo of, 4, 7
selecting, 189–193
technician tools for, 38–39
types and characteristics of, 190–191
wattage capacity, 191–192
Power supply tester, 36, 38–39
Power supply unit (PSU), 7
Power surges, 1033
Power systems, 185–224
cooling methods and devices, 186–189
case fans and heat sinks, 62, 187–188
liquid cooling systems, 188–189, 954–955
processor coolers, fans, and heat sinks, 186–187
electrical system, 203–213
intermittent problems, 204–205
overheating, 206–211
power problems with motherboard, 205
problems with laptop power systems, 211–213
hardware problems, 193–202
back up data, 195–196
examine system and establish a theory, 197–201
fix problem, verify fix, and document the outcome, 201
interviewing the user, 195
introduction to, 193–194
mobile device hardware, 202–203
mobile devices, troubleshooting, 222–224
motherboard, processor, and RAM, troubleshooting, 214–221
power supply, selecting, 189–193
Power Users group, 826
Preboot eXecution Environment or Pre-Execution Environment (PXE), 374
Preferred Roaming List (PRL), 762
Presentation virtualization, 967
Preventive maintenance
anti-malware software, 444
explaining to customers, 558
hard drive cleanup, 446–453
check for errors, 451
defragmentation, 449–450
directory structures, 446–447
Disk Cleanup utility, 447–449
free up space, 451
virtual memory paging file, 451–453
patch management, 445–446
update drivers and firmware, 444–445, 678
for Windows, 444–453
Previous generation Intel processors, 139–140
PRI (Product Release Instructions), 789
Primary partitions, 466
Principle of least privilege, 825
Printer cartridges, 1035
Printer connections, 920–921
Printer firmware print server, 924
Printer maintenance kits, 931, 934–938
Printer Properties, 929–930
Printers, 911–959
Bluetooth and, 920
cartridges and replaceable parts, 914, 915–916, 932, 949, 1035
firmware in, 931, 939–940
install, share, and manage with Windows, 365, 919–931
cloud printing, 928–929
configure features and add-on devices, 929–931
install local or network printer, 921–923
local or network, 919–920
share printer on a network, 924–927
virtual printing, 928
wired or wireless connections, 920–921
IP addresses, 943
maintenance and upgrades, 931–940
calibrating, 933, 950
cleaning, 932
firmware, 939–940
online support, 931–932
printer maintenance kits, 931, 934–938
upgrading memory or hard drive, 938–939
manufacturers, 918
mapping a network printer, 842–844
network printers, 919–920
installing, 921–923
mapping, 842–844
sharing, 924–927
security settings, 924–926
sharing with home server PC, 958
troubleshooting, 940–950
connectivity problems, 943–945
does not print, 940–947
isolate problems, 941
low memory errors, 949–950
poor print quality, 948–950
printing from Windows, 945–947
problems with printer itself, 942–943
types and features, 912–918
impact printers, 917, 943
inkjet printers, 914–916, 933, 943, 949, 950
laser printers, 912–914, 932, 933, 948–949, 950
thermal printers, 917–918
Printer self-test page, 942, 945
Printer User Interface command, 947
Print head, 915
Print Management, 517–518
Print Manager Plus by Print Manager, 928
Print quality, 948–950
Print server, 806, 924
Print spool, 945–946
Print to file, 928
Printui command, 947
Priority level of applications, 504–505
Privacy filter, 880
Privacy tab, Internet Explorer, 810–811
Private cloud, 849
Private data, 829
Private IP addresses, 641–642, 676
Private networks, 307–308
Private settings, 315
Privilege level, 582
PRL (Preferred Roaming List), 762
Process, 497
Processes tab, Task Manager, 499–500, 537
Process Library by Uniblue Systems Limited, 895
Processor architecture, 134
Processor coolers, 123–124, 140, 143, 146–148, 186–187
Processor frequency, 134
Processors
32-bit and 64-bit, 445–446
all-in-one computer, 26
BIOS setup, 106–107
desktop, 5
for high-end graphics workstations, 952, 953
for home server PC, 957
installing, 144–154
AMD processor in socket AM2+, 153–154
Intel processor in socket LGA775, 152
Intel processor in socket LGA1150, 144–149
Intel processor in socket LGA1155, 150–151
Intel processor in socket LGA1366, 151–152
on motherboard, 123–124
introduction to, 5
laptops, 25, 156–158
photo of, 4, 5, 80
selecting to match system needs, 142–143
temperature, 149
troubleshooting, 214–221
types and characteristics, 134–142
AMD processors, 141–142
how a processor works, 137–138
Intel processors, 138–141
virtualization, 969
Processor sockets, 82–87
Processor speed, 134
Processor thermal trip error, 198
Pro Client Hyper-V, 498–499
Product activation, 362
Productivity software, 283
Product keys, 340–341, 343, 349, 356–358, 362
Product Release Instructions (PRI), 789
PRO Duo slot, 394
Professional file recovery service, 196
Professionalism, 549, 559
Program files, 446, 536–537
Programs and Features window, 371
Program shortcuts, removing, 538–539
Programs tab, Internet Explorer, 812–813
Prohibited content/activity, and software, 904
Projectors, 409–410
Properties box, Device Manager, 367
Properties box, program files, 582
Protocol, 92
Protocol layers, 648–653
Protocols, 634, 648

I

Proxy server, 806, 811–812
Ps (process status) command, 979
PS/2 port, 4, 390
PS/2 to USB adapter, 390
PSU (power supply unit), 7
Public cloud, 849
Public folder, 829, 839
Public IP addresses, 641–642, 676
Public networks, 307–308
Pull automation, 375
Pulse width modulation (PWM), 186
Punchdown tool, 716
Push automation, 375
PVC (polyvinyl chloride), 706
Pwd command, 980
PXE (Preboot eXecution Environment or Pre-Execution Environment), 374

Q

Quad channel, 161–162
Quad-core processing, 138
Quality of Service (QoS), 669, 676–677, 822–823
Quarantine, 890
Quick format, 478
Quick Launch menu, 284, 287, 299
QuickPath Interconnect (QPI), 88, 106

R

Radio Frequency Identification (RFID) token, 878
Radio power levels, 687
RAID (redundant array of inexpensive/independent disks), 249–253
  dynamic disks, 484–486
  external enclosures and, 255
  for home server PC, 957
  implementing, 250–253
  setting up, 249–253
  troubleshooting, 269
  types of, 249–250
RAID Configuration Utility, 252
Rail, 190
RAM (random access memory). *See also* Memory
  introduction to, 6, 158–159
  troubleshooting, 214–221
  on video cards, 420–421
  virtual machine, 954
Rambus, Inc., 159
RAM cooler, 188
Ransomware, 886
Rapid elasticity, 847
RAS Latency, 166
RCA connector, 414
Rd (remove directory) command, 473
RDC (Remote Desktop Connection), 652, 815–820
RDP (Remote Desktop Protocol), 651
Read/write head, 233–234
ReadyBoost, 533–535
Reboot, 571
Recimg command, 463–464
Recover command, 475
Recovering backup-up items, 456–457
Recovery CD/DVD, 36
Recovery drive, 599–601, 617
Recovery media, booting from, 575–576
Recovery mode, 777–778, 791
Recovery partition, 334–335, 616–618
Recovery System, 1006–1008, 1011–1013
Rectifier, 1023
Recycle Bin, 283, 293
Red, green, and blue (RGB), 413, 414, 415
Red Hat Enterprise Linux, 972
Redirect output, 980
Refreshing a Windows 8 computer, 618–620
Refresh rate, 411, 432, 528
ReFS (Resilient File System), 467
Registered DIMMs, 165
Registering a component, 580
Registers, 137, 165
Registry, 447, 496
  cleaning, 896
  deleting entries, 537–538
  organization of, 522–524
  starting Windows, 592
  steps to restoring, 613–614
Registry Editor
  backup registry, 524–526
  deleting entries, 537
  organization of registry, 522–524
Registry keys, 523–525, 1038–1039
RegServe software, 535–539
Regsvr32 utility, 580
Reinstalling Windows
  installing over a network, 621–622
  OEM recovery partition, 616–618
  refresh a Windows 8 computer, 618–620
  reset a Windows 8 computer, 620–621
Reliability, 546
Reliability and Performance Monitor, 522
Reliability Monitor, 533, 572
Remediating infected system, 891–893
Remote Admin share, 845
Remote Assistance, 652, 820–822
Remote backup application, 876
Remote control, 956
Remote Desktop Connection (RDC), 652, 815–820
Remote Desktop Protocol (RDP), 651
Remote Desktop Services, 967
Remote Disc, 1001
Remote locks, 875–876
Remote network installation, 375
Remote printing, 920
Remote wipe, 875–876
Removable bay, 58, 245–246
Removable User Identity Module (R-UIM), 762
Ren (rename) command, 474
Rename files or folders, 293
Repair Disk, 1011, 1012–1013
Repair installation, 335
Repeater, 704
Replacement parts, 931
Reproducing a problem, 565, 571
Researching, 566
Reserved IP addresses, 638
Reset buttons, 589
Resetting a Windows 8 computer, 620–621
Resiliency, 488–489
Resilient File System (ReFS), 467
Resistance, measuring, 39
Resolution, 411, 527
Resolution Enhancement technology (REt), 913
Resource Monitor, 501–502
Resource pooling, 847
Response time, 411
Restore from backup, 775, 789, 798
Restore point, 460–461, 524, 891, 897
Restore tab, Disk Utility, 1011
REt (Resolution Enhancement technology), 913
Retention mechanism, 53
Reverse lookup, 729
Revoked signature database (dbx), 114
RFID (Radio Frequency Identification) token, 878
RG-6 coaxial cable, 706–707
RG-59 coaxial cable, 706
RGB (red, green, and blue), 413, 414, 415
Rights. *See* Privilege level
RIMM, 159–160
Riser cards, 97–98
RJ-11 connectors, 714, 715
RJ-11 jacks, 701
RJ-11 ports, 4
RJ-45 connectors, 703, 705, 706, 711, 714, 715, 717–718
RJ-45 jacks. *See* Keystone RJ-45 jacks
RJ-45 ports, 3, 653
Rm command, 980
Rmdir command, 980
Robocopy (robust file copy) command, 476, 830
Rogue antivirus software, 888
Roku, 957
Root access, 899, 900
Root account, 977–978
Root certificate, 889
Root Checker Basic, 899
Root directory, 288
Rooting, 794, 899
Rootkit, 886
Rosewill, 192
Rotating display, 18
Routers, 635
  changing the password, 673–674
  firmware of, 673, 678
  functions of, 670–672
  installing and configuring, 672–678
  MAC address filtering, 676
  Quality of Service (QoS), 676–677
  static IP addresses, 675–676
  Universal Plug and Play (UPnP), 677
  update firmware, 678
Row electrodes, 409
R-UIM (Removable User Identity Module), 762
Run box, 285, 287
Runtime Software, 196

S

SaaS (Software as a Service), 848, 967
Safari browser, 752
Safely Remove Hardware icon, 23, 264–265
Safe Mode

Android, 790
device or service fails to start, 626–627
in Mac OS X operating system, 1012
malicious software, 893–894
Ntbtlog.txt file, 607–608
printing and, 946
quarantined computer, 890, 891
troubleshooting applications, 573–574
troubleshooting Windows startup, 597
Safe Mode with Command Prompt, 609
Safe Mode with Networking, 609
Safety goggles, 1028
Safety procedures
electricity, 1025–1028
electricity, measures and properties of, 1022–1025
electrostatic discharge (ESD), 35, 85, 241, 269, 1028–1031
physical protection from the environment, 1031–1034
protecting the equipment, 1028–1034
Sags, 1033
SAM hive, 524
Samsung, 67, 239
Sandy Bridge chipsets, 90, 162
Sandy Bridge H67 chipset, 90, 139, 140
SAS (Serial Attached SCSI), 487
SATA (Serial ATA), 235, 240, 487
SATA data cables, 4, 16–17, 236, 239–240, 262
SATA drives, 9, 235, 239–245
SATA headers, 100
SATA interface standards, 235–237, 247, 262
SATA-IO (Serial ATA International Organization), 235
SATA power connector, 10, 236, 239–240, 262
SATA-style power connectors, 61–62
SATA-to-USB converter, 271
SATA-to-USB converter kit, 196, 622–623
Satellite Internet, 697, 699
Satellite TV input, 956
SC (subscriber connector or standard connector) connectors, 707–708
Scalable Linear Recording (SLR), 257
Scanstate command, 376
Scheduled maintenance, 450, 897
Scheduled tasks, 532, 1038
Screen brightness, 21, 411, 417, 427–428, 432
Screen lock, 871–873
Screen orientation, 21, 778–779
Screen Sharing, 1001
Screwdrivers, 36, 71–72, 154
Screws, 47–48, 72, 73
Scrolling, 992
SCSI interface standard, 235
SD Association, 265
SD cards, 265–266
SD card slot, 19, 394
SD eXtended Capacity or SDXC, 265–266
SD High Capacity or SDHC, 265–266, 267
SDK (Software Development Kit), 751, 754
SDLT (Super Digital Linear Tape), 257
SDRAM (synchronous DRAM), 160
SDSL (Symmetric Digital Subscriber Line), 697
Seagate Recovery Services, 196
Seagate Technology, 109, 239
Search engines, 566
Searching, for files, 291
SeaTools for DOS, 194
SeaTools for Windows, 194
Secondary click, 991
Secondary logon, 581
Second Generation Core i7, 90
Sectors, 234, 465
Secure boot, 112, 330
Secure data-destruction service, 883
Secure Digital (SD) cards, 265–266
Secure Erase utility, 883
Secure FTP (SFTP), 651
Securelist.com, 884
Secure/Multipurpose Internet Mail Extensions (S/MIME), 763
Secure Shell (SSH) protocol, 651
Secure sign-in, 856–858
Secure Sockets Layer (SSL), 649–650, 763
Security Center, 303
SECURITY hive, 524
Security key, 654, 685
Security log, 514
Security Software by Trend Micro, 891
Security strategies, 855–904
authenticate users for large networks, 877–879
data destruction and disposal, 882–883
digital security, 881
educate users, 883–885
malicious software, 885–903
categories of, 885–887
common symptoms, 898–899
step-by-step attack plan, 887–897
tools and malware removal, 900–903
mobile devices, 871–877
in corporate environments, 876–877
device access controls, 871–873
software security, 874–876
physical security, 880
printers, 924–926
shared printers, 925–927
software licensing and prohibited content/activity, 903–904
Unified Threat Management (UTM), 881–882
Windows personal computers, 856–870
authenticate users, 856–861
BitLocker Drive Encryption, 110–111, 296, 869–870
file and folder encryption, 861–862
firewall settings, 862–865
local security policies using group policy, 865–869
UEFI/BIOS to protect system, 870
Security tab, Internet Explorer, 810
Security tokens, 877–879
Self-control, 548
Self-grounding, 1030
Self-healing feature, 602
Self-Monitoring Analysis and Reporting Technology (S.M.A.R.T.), 234, 269
Sempron processors, 141, 142
Sentey, 192
Separate pad, 914
Separation pad, 914
Sequential access, 256
Serial ATA (SATA) standard, 15–16, 235. *See also* SATA data cables; SATA drives
Serial ATA International Organization (SATA-IO), 235
Serial Attached SCSI (SAS), 487
Serial cables, 920
Serial number, 67
Serial port, 4
Serial port cards, 400
Server Message Block (SMB), 650, 652–653
Server-side virtualization, 966
Service, 284
Service Control Manager, 591, 592, 594
Service Location Protocol (SLP), 653
Service manuals, 68–69
Service packs, 300, 362–364
Services, failure to start, 573, 579, 626–627
Services console, 510–511, 579, 946
Service Set Identifier (SSID), 686
Services tab, 504–505, 933
Session Manager, 591, 592, 594
Settings charm, 280, 371, 597, 602
Settings pane, 280
Set-top box, 957
Setup.exe program, 342
Setup log, 514
Setup UEFI/BIOS, 330
SFC (System File Checker), 573, 576–577, 608–609
Sfc /scannow command, 613
SFF (small form factor) board, 81
SFTP (Secure FTP), 651
Shared Folders, 511
Shared printers. *See* Network printers
Shared System Memory, 422
Share permissions, 830, 837–838, 881
Sharing files and folders, 830–842
share permissions, 837–838
troubleshooting, 838–842
user accounts with data access, 831–835
user and group information with gpresult command, 836–837
Sheet battery, 24, 212
Shell prompt, 973, 975
Shell prompt command, 988
Shielded twisted-pair (STP) cable, 705
Shortcuts, 285, 293–294
Shoulder surfing, 884
Shrink Volume, 480
Shutdown command, 478, 980
Shutdowns, improper, 626
Shutdown scripts, 868
Sidebars, 286
Side-by-side apps, 281
Sierra Wireless, 20
Signature database (db), 114
Silverstone, 192
SIM (Subscriber Identification Module) card, 30, 656, 658, 760–761
SIMMs (single inline memory modules), 159
SimpleBackupSuite, 988
Simple Network Management Protocol (SNMP), 651
Simple solutions first, 200–201, 203
Simple storage space, 488

Simple volume, 484–485
Single channel, 161–162
Single inline memory modules (SIMMs), 159
Single-sided DIMMs, 163–164
Single sign-on (SSO) account, 311, 867
Siri, 753
Site license, 904
Skylake chipsets, 91
Skype, 29
Slack, 449
Sleep mode, 297–298, 425
Sleep timers, 299
SLI by NVIDIA, 191
Slide ME, 874
Slingbox by Sling Media, 957
SLI technologies, 88
Slot drivers, 423
Slow performance, 167, 223, 267–268, 508, 533, 793, 889
SLP (Service Location Protocol), 653
SLR (Scalable Linear Recording), 257
Small form factor (SFF) board, 81
Small office or home office (SOHO), 304
Small outline DIMMs (SO-DIMMs), 25–27, 127, 156, 159–160, 166
S.M.A.R.T. (Self-Monitoring Analysis and Reporting Technology), 234, 269
Smart camera, 30
Smart card reader, 265, 877–879
Smart cards, 877–879
Smart phones, 29, 656–658. *See also* Mobile devices
Smart TV, 957
Smart watches, 30
SMB (Server Message Block), 650, 652–653
SMB2, 651
S/MIME (Secure/Multipurpose Internet Mail Extensions), 763
SMS messages, 875
SMTP (Simple Mail Transfer Protocol), 650, 652, 763
Snagit, 928
Snap-ins, 511–512, 580, 868
SNMP (Simple Network Management Protocol), 651
Snopes.com, 884
Social engineering, 883–885
Social media, 787
Sockets, 81–86, 88, 90–91, 134, 144–149, 150–154, 162, 188, 650. *See also* Processors
Socket service, 23
SO-DIMMs (small outline DIMMs), 25–27, 127, 156, 159–160, 166
Soft boot, 588
"Soft" power button, 589
Soft reset, 777, 790
Software, 36. *See also* Applications
Software, removing manually, 535–539
  delete program files, 536–537
  delete registry entries, 537–538
  remove program shortcuts, 538–539
  remove startup processes, 539
Software as a Service (SaaS), 848, 967
Software Development Kit (SDK), 751, 754
SOFTWARE hive, 524
Software licensing, 903–904
Software piracy, 904
Software RAID, 250, 484
Software Recovery Tool, 799
Software security, mobile devices, 874–876
Software Updater app, 989–990
SOHO (small office home office) routers, 304
  functions of, 670–672
  installing and configuring
    assign static IP addresses, 675–676
    changing password, 673–674
    DHCP server, 674
    improving QoS for an application, 676–677
    MAC address filtering, 676
    Universal Plug and Play, 677
    updating firmware, 678
  installing and configuring on the local network, 672–678
  limiting Internet traffic, 678–683
    content filtering and parental controls, 682–683
    DMZ (demilitarized zone), 681–682
    port forwarding, 679–680
    port triggering, 681
  setting up, 670–688
  setting up a wireless network
    channels, 686
    radio power levels, 687
    SSID, 686
    Wi-Fi Protectioned Setup (WPS), 687–688
  wireless network, setting up, 683–688
    encryption, 686
    security key, 685
Solid-state device (SSD), 33, 232–233, 264, 330, 449, 465, 883
Solid-state hybrid drive (SSHD), 234
Solid state storage, 264–267
Sony VA IO, 67
Sound applet, 296
Sound Blaster card, 404
Sound cards, 400, 404, 953
South Bridge, 81, 87–89, 94
Space, 996
Spacers, 54–55
Spanned volume, 484
Spanning, 249–250, 484
S/PDIF (Sony/Philips Digital Interface) sound port, 3, 5, 404
S/PDIF header, 100
Speaker ports, 19
Speakers, 435
Spear phishing, 885
Speckled printouts, 948
SpeedFan by Alfredo Comparetti, 107, 206, 626
Speeds, 93, 134
SPGA (staggered pin grid array) socket, 85
Spindle speed, 238
Spoofing, 885
Spotlight, 991, 994, 997–998
Sprint, 778
Spyware, 364, 885–886, 899
SRAM (static RAM), 135
SSD (solid-state device), 33, 232–233, 264, 330, 449, 465, 883
SSE2 (Streaming SIMD Extensions 2), 328
SSH (Secure Shell) protocol, 651
SSHD (solid-state hybrid drive), 234
SSH encryption, 651, 652
SSID (Service Set Identifier), 686
SSID broadcasting, 686
SSL (Secure Sockets Layer), 649–650, 763
SSO (single sign-on) account, 311, 867
ST (straight tip) connectors, 707–708
Staggered pin grid array (SPGA) socket, 85
Standard account, 311
Standard image, 373
Standby mode, 425
Standoffs, 54–55
Start screen, 279–280, 283, 284
Startup BIOS, 37
Startup disk, cloning, 1007–1008
Startup errors, 895
Startup items, 1009
Startup process, 532, 539, 1038–1039
Startup programs, 530–532
Startup repair, 219, 270, 602–604, 605–606
Startup settings, 606–610
Startup tab, Task Manager, 502–503, 530–531
Startup UEFI/BIOS, 330
Static electricity, 15, 28, 932, 1028–1031
Static IP addresses, 638, 675–676, 681, 943
Static IP configurations, 664–665
Static RAM (SRAM), 135
Static shielding bags, 1029–1030
Status indicator lights, 668
Stepper motor, 915
Stop errors, 624–626. *See also* Blue screen of death (BSOD)
Storage cards, 250–251, 400
Storage controller card, 400
Storage devices
  file systems used by, 258–259
  on mobile devices, 33
  solid state storage, 264–267
  standards used by optical drives and discs, 259–262
  supporting, 231–272
Storage media, destruction of, 883, 1035
Storage Spaces utility, 250, 487–489
STP (shielded twisted-pair) cable, 705
Straight-through cable, 717, 719–722, 726
Straight tip (ST) connectors, 707–708
Streaking, printer problem, 948
Streaming SIMD Extensions 2 (SSE2), 328
Striped volume, 249–250, 484–485
Striping, 484
Strong passwords, 860–861
Stylus, 396–397
Subdirectories, 288–289
Subkeys, 523–524, 538, 1039
Subnet ID, 645
Subnet masks, 639–641
Subnets, 636, 645
Subscriber Identification Module (SIM) card, 30, 656, 658, 760–761
Subscription model, 848
Subsystems, 496–497, 592
Su command, 980
Sudo (substitute user to do the command) command, 980, 989
SUPERAntiSpyware, 891
Super Digital Linear Tape (SDLT), 257
Superfish virus, 889–890

SuperSpeed USB, 385, 386, 389, 535
Superuser, 977
Surge suppressor, 1022, 1024, 1033
Surround sound, 957
Suspend mode, 297–298
S-Video port, 2, 413, 414, 415
Swipe, 871, 992
Switches, 671, 701–703
Symantec Endpoint Protection, 891
Symbian OS, 748
Symmetric Digital Subscriber Line (SDSL), 697
Symptoms
  of electrical system problems, 203
  of failing motherboard, processor, or memory module, 214
  of hardware problems, 198–199
  malicious software, 889
Sync
  Android operating system/devices, 787–788
  Apple iOS mobile devices, 768–776
    AirDrop and Handoff, 775–776
    iCloud Backup, 770–772
    iCloud Drive, 768–769, 847, 998, 1000, 1006
    iTunes, 768, 773–774, 900
  Windows Phone, 795–798
Synchronous DRAM (SDRAM), 160
System administrator, 977
System BIOS, 37
System board, 5, 26. *See also* Motherboards
System bus, 87
System clock, 93
System Configuration, 506–510, 579
System File Checker (SFC), 573, 576–577, 608–609
System files, 460–462, 612–616
SYSTEM hive, 524
System image, 456, 464, 597, 621
System Information window, 301–302, 449, 532–534, 1004–1005, 1039
System lockout, 780, 794
System log, 514
System partition, 468, 590, 596–597
System Preferences, in Mac OS X, 999–1000
System Protection, 460, 524, 890, 897
System Protection utility, 460, 462
System repair disc, 601
System Report, 1005
System requirements, 327–333
System Restore, 461–462, 574, 597, 612, 626, 890–891
System tray, 284
System UEFI/BIOS, 330
System Video Memory, 422
System Volume Information folder, 890
System window, 116, 138, 299–301, 310, 362
Systray, 284

T

T13 Committee, 235
T568A standard, 717–719
T568B standard, 717–722
T5688 wiring, 719–722
Tablets, 18, 29
Tailgating, 884
Tape drives, 256–258
TAR command, 988
Taskbar, 283
Taskkill command, 577
Tasklist command, 577
Task Manager, 498–505
  App history tab, 502
  Performance tab, 501–502
  priority level of applications, 504–505
  Processes and Details tabs, 499–500, 537
  Services tab, 504–505, 933
  Startup tab, 502–503, 530–531
  uninstalling applications, 537
  Users tab, 503–504
Task Scheduler, 511, 518–520, 532
TCP (Transmission Control Protocol), 649
TCP/IP (Transmission Control Protocol/ Internet Protocol), 634–635, 649–653
TCP/IP networks, 634–653
  applications and, 648
  identifying computers and networks, 646–648
  IP addresses, assignment of, 638
  IP address settings, 645–646
  IPv4 addresses, 638–642
    public, private, and automatic private IP addresses, 641–642
    subnet masks, 639–641
  IPv6 addresses, 642–645
  layers of network communication, 634–638
  protocol layers, 648–653
    used by applications, 649–653
    used by the OS, 649
  utilities for troubleshooting connectivity, 737–738
  utilities for troubleshooting wiring, 727–733
    ifconfig (interface configuration) command, 728–729
    ipconfig (IP configuration) command, 728
    nbtstat (NetBIOS over TCP/IP statistics) command, 731–732
    net commands, 731
    netdom (network domain) command, 733
    netstat (network statistics) command, 732
    nslookup (namespace lookup) command, 729
    ping (Packet InterNet Groper) command, 727–728
    tracert (trace route) command, 730
TeamViewer, 819
Technical documentation, 566
Technology Without An Interesting Name (TWAIN), 395
Telnet protocol, 650
Telnet server, 652
Temperature, 28, 107, 149
Temporary Internet Files, 809
Teredo, 643
Terminal, 973, 1001–1002
Tethering, 32, 657, 658, 700, 784–785
Text editor, 285
Theft-prevention plate, 880
Thermal compound, 143, 146–147, 209
Thermal paper, 917
Thermal printers, 917–918
Thermaltake, 192
Thermaltake multisocket cooler, 186
Thermal transfer printer, 917–918
Thick client, 958–959, 966
Thin client, 958–959, 966
ThinkPad inverter board, 433
Thin provisioning, 488
Third-party drivers, 335
Third-party file recovery software, 622
Third-party syncing apps, 787
Thread, 134–135, 497
Three-way mirroring, 488
Throughput speed, 94
Thumb drive. *See* USB flash drives
Thunderbolt cards, 400
Thunderbolt port, 3, 18
Ticket, 551
Tight configuration, 707
Time Machine, 1006–1007, 1013
Time to Live (TTL), 730
Tip boxes, 346
TKIP (Temporal Key Integrity Protocol), 686
T-Mobile, 778
TN (Twisted Nematic), 409
Todo Backup Free, 373
Toner cartridges, 935–937, 948, 1035
Toner dust, 932
Toner/tone probe, 714–715
Toner vacuum, 932
Tools tab, System Configuration, 509
Torvalds, Linus, 972
Torx screwdrivers, 36, 72
Toshiba America, 67
Total Available Graphics Memory, 422
Touch command, 980
Touch ID technology, 393, 872–873
Touch pad, 21, 392–393
Touch screens, 399, 432, 778, 793–794
Tower case, 2
TPM (Trusted Platform Module), 869–870
TPM (Trusted Platform Module) chip, 110–112
Tracert (trace route) command, 730, 737
Traces, 92–93
Tracks, 234, 465
Tractor feeds, 917
Trade known good for suspected bad, 201
Trade suspected bad for known good, 201
Trailer information, 638
Transfer belt, 914
Transferring, laser printers, 913
Transfer roller, 913, 948
Transformer, 1023
Transmission Control Protocol (TCP), 649
Transport Layer Security (TLS), 649–650
Trash Can, 991, 998, 1008–1009
Travan, 257
Trip hazard, 1027
Triple channel, 161–162
Trojans, 886, 896
Troubleshooting
  Android operating system, 790–794
  Android operating system/devices, 223, 790–794

I

Troubleshooting (*continued*)
Apple iOS mobile devices, 776–781
common problems and solutions, 778–780
tools for, 776–778
applications, error messages and, 571–572
approach problem systematically, 563
assumptions, 565
backup data, 563–565
backup procedures, 563–565, 571
Bluetooth, 779
compatibility, 368–370, 582
coworkers and, 571–572
device drivers, 368–370, 384
Device Manager, 384
Disk Management utility, 486–487
electrical system, 203–213
email on Android OS, 794
Event Viewer and, 431, 572
GPS (Global Positioning System), 741
hard drives, 267–272
with Disk Management utility, 486–487
installations, 253–254
problems during the boot, 268–272
slow performance, 267–268
hardware, diagnostic software for, 194
hardware, error messages and, 198–199
hardware, flowchart for, 197
hardware problems, rules for, 200–201
Internet connections, 736–737
introduction to, 561–563
I/O devices, 422–436
Device Manager, 422–423
monitors and video, 424–430
numlock indicator light, 422
video system in a laptop, 431–435
iPhones and iPads, 222
laptop video systems, 431
logs, 571–572
Mac OS X operating system startup, 1012–1013
mobile devices, 202–203, 222–224
monitors, 424–430
blank screen after keyboard is left untouched, 425–426
correcting display settings when screen is unreadable, 429–430
indicator light/blank screen, 424–425
poor display, 426–429
motherboards, 214–221
motherboards, processor, and RAM, 214–221
network connections, 733–742
GPS not functioning, 741
Internet connectivity, 736–737
no Bluetooth connectivity, 740
no connectivity or intermittent connectivity, 734–736
no wireless connectivity, 738–739
TCP/IP utilities, 737–738
Wi-Fi network not found, 739–740
network wiring, 711–742
GPS not functioning, 741
Internet connectivity, 736–737
no Bluetooth connectivity, 740
no connectivity or intermittent connectivity, 734–736
no wireless connectivity, 738–739
TCP/IP utilities, 737–738
Wi-Fi network not found, 739–740
PCI Express (PCIe), 425
printers, 940–950
connectivity problems, 943–945
does not print, 940–947
isolate problems, 941
low memory errors, 949–950
poor print quality, 948–950
printing from Windows, 945–947
problems with printer itself, 942–943
priorities, 564
processors, 214–221
RAID (redundant array of inexpensive disks or redundant array of independent disks), 269
RAM, 214–221
shared folders and files, 838–842
sharing files and folders, 838–842
six steps, 562–563
startup, Mac OS X operating system, 1012–1013
stay calm and do not rush, 564
step 1: interview the user and back up data, 562–565
step 2: examine system and establish a theory, 562–563, 565–567
step 3: test theory, 562–563, 567–568
step 4: plan solution and fix problem, 562–563, 568–569
step 5: verify the fix and take preventive action, 562–563, 569
step 6: document what happened, 562–563, 569
TCP/IP networks, 737–738
try simple things first, 565
user error, 564
Windows Phone, 798–799
Windows startup, error messages and, 623–627
Troubleshooting applications
application has never worked, 581–583
general steps, 571–574
step 1: interview the user and back up data, 571
step 2: error messages, the web, coworkers, and logs, 571–572
step 3: consider data or application is corrupt, 572–573
step 4: consider outside interference, 573
step 5: consider Windows problems, 573–574
memory diagnostics, 574–576
reboot, 571
specific error messages, responding to, 577–583
System File Checker (SFC), 576–577
Troubleshooting hardware
error messages, 198–199
flowchart, 725
mobile devices, 202–203
rules for, 200–201
Troubleshooting Windows startup, 587–627
boot process
different ways to boot, 588–589
steps to boot and start Windows, 590–597
UEFI/BIOS controls, 589–590
boot process, understanding, 588–597
error messages, 623–627
BSOD errors or stop errors, 624–626
device or service fails to start, 626–627
improper shutdowns, 626
hard drive, important data on, 622–623
tools for, 597–622
least invasive solutions, 602–612
before a problem occurs, 598–601
reinstalling Windows, 616–622
Windows system files and settings, 612–616
Troubleshooting wiring, utilities for TCP/IP networks, 727–733
ifconfig (interface configuration) command, 728–729
ipconfig (IP configuration) command, 728
nbtstat (NetBIOS over TCP/IP statistics) command, 731–732
net commands, 731
netdom (network domain) command, 733
netstat (network statistics) command, 732
nslookup (namespace lookup) command, 729
ping (Packet InterNet Groper) command, 727–728
tracert (trace route) command, 730
True Image by Acronis, 373
Trusted sources, 874, 881
TTL (Time to Live), 730
Turion processors, 141
TV-out connector, 6
TV tuner cards, 400, 955–956
TV tuners, 404–405
TWAIN (Technology Without An Interesting Name), 395
Tweezers, 36
Twisted Nematic (TN), 409
Twisted-pair cable, 701, 705–706, 717–726
Two-way mirroring, 488
Type 1 hypervisor, 968, 971
Type 2 hypervisor, 968

U

UAC (User Account Control) dialog box, 317–319
Ubuntu Desktop, 354, 972–973, 986, 987, 989–990
Ubuntu Server, 972–973, 974–975, 982–984, 986, 989
UDF (Universal Disk Format), 259, 468
UDP (User Datagram Protocol), 649
UEFI (Unified Extensible Firmware Interface), 103, 112–115, 330

UEFI/BIOS
adapter cards, installing, 400
controls at the beginning of the boot, 589–590
firmware, 329–330
hard drive installation, 244–245, 248
hard drive standard, 238
hardware-assisted virtualization (HAV), 954, 969
hardware RAID, 252–253
motherboard, replacing, 124
overheating, 206
peripheral devices, installing, 389
POST errors, 268–269
power buttons, 589
processors, installing, 148–149
security strategies, 880
S.M.A.R.T. (Self-Monitoring Analysis and Reporting Technology), 234
starting Windows, 589–592
troubleshooting, 215
upgrading OS, 341
Wake-on-LAN, 668–669
Windows over a network, installing, 621
UEFI CSM (Compatibility Support Module) mode, 330
UEFI Firmware Settings, 605
UEFI with BIOS, 103
Ultra-thin client, 966
Unallocated space, 486
Unassigned address, 644
Unattended installation, 375
Unicast address, 643
Unicasting, 643–644
Unified EFI Forum, 112
Unified Extensible Firmware Interface (UEFI), 37–38, 103, 112–115, 118, 330. *See also* UEFI/BIOS
Unified Threat Management (UTM), 881–882
Unintended connections, Bluetooth and, 899
Uninterruptible power supply (UPS), 212, 1033–1034
Unique local address, 644, 645
Universal Disk Format (UDF), 259, 468
Universal PCI wireless card, 95
Universal Plug and Play (UPnP), 677
University of Helsinki, 972
UNIX, 306, 972, 990
Unlock pattern, 871–872
Unshielded twisted-pair (UTP) cable, 705, 706
Updates
Android operating system, 788–789, 874
Apple iOS, 874
automatic, 363–364
Linux, 988–990
Mac OS X, 1003–1005
Upgrade Advisor, 328, 375
Upgrade Assistant, 328, 347, 375
Upgrade paths, 338
Upgrade product key, 356–358
Upgrade retail Windows license, 326
UPnP (Universal Plug and Play), 677
UPS (uninterruptible power supply), 212, 1033–1034
Upset failure, 1028
USB (Universal Serial Bus), 3
data transmission speeds, 385
external hard drives and, 235
laptops, 18
mobile devices, 33
peripheral devices, 385–387
photo of, 5, 99
printers, 920
USB 2.0 port, 19
USB 3.0 connector, 386, 387
USB 3.0 ports, 19
USB broadband modem, 657, 658
USB cards, 400
USB drive, booting from, 334
USB flash drives, 264
USB headers, 100
USB Implementers Forum, Inc, 385
USB optical drive, 20
USB smart card reader, 395
USB to Bluetooth adapter, 20
USB to PS/2 adapter, 390
USB to RJ-45 dongle, 19
USB-to-SATA converter, 196
USB to Wi-Fi dongle, 19, 20
User access Level, 109
User Account Control (UAC) dialog box, 317–319
User accounts
built-in user groups, 826–828
creating with data access, 831–835
Linux, 977–978
overview of, 825–828
privileges, 825
setting up, 371
types of, 825–826
using a Microsoft account with Windows 8, 314–317
Windows, 311–319
User Accounts utility, 857
User data, transferring, 371
User Datagram Protocol (UDP), 649
User error, 564
User groups, 825–828
User interface, 278
User interview, 195
User manuals, 69, 194
User mode, 497
User profile namespace, 446
User profiles, 446
Users, 591, 883–885, 897, 901
Users tab, 503–504
User State Migration Tool (USMT), 371, 373, 375–376
Usmtutils command, 376
Utilities
Administrative Tools, 505–506
application management, 497–498
Computer Management, 511
Disk Cleanup utility, 447–449
Disk Management utility, 250, 478, 480–487, 511
dynamic disks, 484–486
hard drive troubleshooting, 486–487
mounting a drive, 482–484
prepare drive for first use, 481–482
recovery partition, 617
resize, create, and delete partitions, 480–481
on a virtual machine, 487
Disk Utility app, 1010–1011
display settings and graphics software, 527–529
Erase tab, Disk Utility, 1011
error-checking utility, 451
Event Viewer, 513–516
freeware utilities, 429
Microsoft Management Console (MMC), 511–513
Offline Files utility, 447
Performance Monitor, 520–522
Print Management, 517–518
RAID Configuration Utility, 252
Registry Editor, 522–527
backup registry, 524–526
organization of registry, 522–524
Regsvr32 utility, 580
repairs using Disk Utility app, 1010–1011
Restore tab, Disk Utility, 1011
Secure Erase utility, 883
Services console, 510–511
shell and kernel, 496–497
Startup Repair utility, 270
Storage Spaces utility, 250, 487–489
System Configuration, 506–510
System Protection utility, 460, 462
Task Manager, 498–505
App history tab, 502
Performance tab, 501–502
priority level of applications, 504–505
Processes and Details tabs, 499–500
Services tab, 504–505
Startup tab, 502–503
Users tab, 503–504
Task Scheduler, 518–520
TCP/IP utilities, 727–733, 737–738
troubleshooting Windows startup, 597–622
least invasive solutions, 602–612
before a problem occurs, 598–601
reinstalling Windows, 616–622
Windows system files and settings, 612–616
User Accounts utility, 857
utilities for troubleshooting wiring, 727–733
ifconfig (interface configuration) command, 728–729
ipconfig (IP configuration) command, 728
nbtstat (NetBIOS over TCP/IP statistics) command, 731–732
net commands, 731
netdom (network domain) command, 733
netstat (network statistics) command, 732
nslookup (namespace lookup) command, 729
ping (Packet InterNet Groper) command, 727–728
tracert (trace route) command, 730
Utilities folder, Finder, 999
UTM (Unified Threat Management), 881–882
UTP (unshielded twisted-pair) cable, 705, 706

V

VDI (Virtual Desktop Infrastructure), 958, 966
VDSL (very-high-bit-rate DSL), 697
VeriSign, 879
Verizon, 30, 700
VGA (Video Graphics Array) port, 2, 18, 19, 413, 414, 608
VGA mode, 429
VHD (virtual hard drive), 968, 969
Vi command, 980
Video, troubleshooting, 424–430
  correcting display settings when screen is unreadable, 429–430
  poor display, 426–429
  video card installations, 424
Video capture cards, 400, 404–405, 956
Video cards
  in computer reassembly, 65
  firmware of, 424
  heat from, 188
  for high-end graphics workstations, 952
  installation problems, 424
  installing, 124
  overview of, 412–417
  power supply and, 191–192
  RAM chips in, 6
Video connectors, 412–417
Video drivers, 364, 427
Video editing workstation, 953
Video Graphics Array (VGA) port, 2, 18, 19, 413, 414, 608
Video memory, 6, 419–422
Video ports, 18, 412–413
Video subsystem, 408–422
  laptops, 431–435
  monitor settings, 417–419
  monitor technologies and features, 408–412
  video cards and connectors, 412–417
  video memory and Windows, 419–422
Vi editor (visual editor), 981–984
Viewing angle, 411
View Only BIOS access, 109
Violations of security best practices, 887
Virtual assistant, 753
VirtualBox, 336–337, 968, 970–971
VirtualBox Manager, 970
Virtual Desktop Infrastructure (VDI), 958, 966
Virtual hard drive (VHD), 968, 969
Virtualization
  BIOS support for, 109
  client-side, 967
  definition of, 966
  memory, 969
  processors, 136
  server-side, 966
  virtual machines and hypervisors, 967–972
    hardware requirements, 969–971
    securing, 971–972
    types 1 and 2, 968
Virtualization server, 958
Virtualization workstation, 954
Virtual machine (VM), 109
  Ctrl+Alt+Del, 498–499
  Disk Management utility, 487
  hypervisors and, 967–972
    hardware requirements, 969–971
    securing, 971–972
    types 1 and 2, 968
  Ubuntu Desktop, 987
  Ubuntu server, 974–975
  virtualization workstation, 954
  Windows, 335–336, 444
Virtual machine manager (VMM), 967
Virtual memory, 451
Virtual memory paging file, 451–453
Virtual PC, 336
Virtual printing, 928
Virtual private network. *See* VPN (virtual private network) connection
Virtual XP mode, 336
Virusbtn.com, 884
Virus Bulletin, Ltd, 884
Virus definitions, 364
Viruses, 214, 462, 573, 885
Vision sensors, 30
Visual processing unit (VPU), 419
Visual Studio, 970
VMM (virtual machine manager), 967
VMware Player, 336, 968
VMware Workstation or Player, 954
Voice over LTE (VoLTE), 656
VoIP voice communication, 778
Volatile storage, 298
Voltages, 107
VoLTE (Voice over LTE), 656
Volts, 1022
Volumes, 288, 329, 467
Volume setting, 21
VPN (virtual private network) connection
  Android operating system, 784–785
  Apple iOS, 763
  creating, 661–664
  digital security, 881
  firewalls, 875
  Internet Explorer, 811–812
  Unified Threat Management (UTM), 882
  virtual machine (VM), 968
VPU (visual processing unit), 419
V Series processors, 141

W

Wait state, 93
Wake-on-LAN, 668–669, 818, 843, 924
WAN (wide area network), 696
WAP (wireless access point), 671, 703–704, 711
Warm boot, 588
Warranty
  brand name computers, 204
  laptops, 66–67, 74, 156, 177, 202
  mobile devices, 202, 222
Watt, 1022
Wattage capacity, 190, 191–192
WDDM (Windows Display Driver Model), 420
Weak signal, 778, 899
Wearable technology devices, 30
Wear leveling, 233
Web-based printer utility, 934, 940
Web-based printing software, 928
Web browsers, 634, 635
Webcams, 396
Web searches, and troubleshooting, 194, 199, 571–572
Web servers, 635, 637, 652, 807
Websites, 173–175, 647
Web to Print by B2Cprint, 928
Web-to-print software, 928
Weight, of paper, 916
WEP (Wired Equivalent Privacy), 686
Western Digital, 239
Who command, 980
Wide area network (WAN), 696
Wide bay, installing a small drive in, 246–247
Wi-Fi (Wireless Fidelity), 19
  Android, 781–785, 791–792
  Apple iOS, 762–763
  data transmission speeds, 385
  hotspots, 32, 672, 700, 762
  infrastructure network, 762–763
  laptops, 22
  mobile devices, 30, 779
  network not found, 739–740
  setting up a wireless network, 683–688
    channels, 686
    encryption, 686
    radio power levels, 687
    security key, 685
    SSID, 686
    Wi-Fi Protectioned Setup (WPS), 687–688
  speeds, 698
  tablets and, 29
  unintended connections, 899
Wi-Fi ad hoc mode network, 920
Wi-Fi analyzer, 714, 901–902
Wi-Fi calling, 778
Wi-Fi Mini PCI card by MikroTik, 405–406
Wi-Fi Protected Setup (WPS), 687–688
Wi-Fi wireless local network, 653–656
Wii, 397
Wildcard characters, 471, 980
WIM (Windows Imaging File) format, 462
WiMAX technology, 697
Win32 subsystem, 496–497, 591
Windows
  blue screen of death (BSOD), 198, 269–270, 574–575, 610, 623, 624–626
  dual boot with Linux, 986
  editions of, 326
  license for, 326
  OEM, full retail, or upgrade retail license, 326
  preventive maintenance for, 444–453
  reinstalling, 616–622
    OEM recovery partition, 616–618
    over a network, 621–622
    refresh a Windows 8 computer, 618–620
  shutdown and restart, 588–589
  video memory and, 419–422
Windows, and printers, 919–931
  cloud printing, 928–929
  configure features and add-on devices, 929–931

install local or network printer, 921–923
local or network, 919–920
share printer on a network, 924–927
troubleshooting, 945–947
virtual printing, 928
wired or wireless connections, 920–921
Windows, installing, 325–376
in a large enterprise, 372–376
deployment strategies, 373–375
USMT software, 375–376
multiboot, 354–356
planning, 326–341
choices to make during installation, 339–340
choosing edition, license, and version, 326–327
choosing the type of installation, 338–339
device drivers, 332–333
final checklist, 340–341
MBR or GPT partitioning system, 329
special considerations, 333–336
system requirements, 327–333
UEFI or legacy BIOS firmware, 329–330
Windows 8 Upgrade Assistant, 328
post-installation, 360–372
activate Windows, 362
install applications, 371
install hardware, 364–370
install updates and service packs, 362–364
problems with legacy devices, 368–370
set up user accounts and transfer user data, 371
turn features on or off, 372
verify network access, 361
using an upgrade product key on a new hard drive, 356–358
Windows 7 clean install, 352–354
Windows 7 in-place upgrade, 348–349
Windows 8.1 clean install, 350–352
Windows 8.1 in-place upgrade, 342–346
Windows 8.1 upgrade from Microsoft website, 347–348
Windows, maintaining, 443–489
backup procedures, 453–465
custom refresh image, 462–465
disaster recovery, planning for, 454–455
system files, 460–462
Windows 7 Backup and Restore, 456–459
Windows 8 file history, 455–456
managing files, folders, and storage devices, 465–489
Disk Management utility, 480–487
Storage Spaces utility, 487–489
preventive maintenance, scheduling, 444–453
hard drive cleanup, 446–453
patch management, 445–446
update drivers and firmware, 444–445
routine maintenance, 530
Windows, optimizing, 495–539
improving performance, 529–535
clean Windows startup, 530–532
hardware requirements, 532–533
history of problems, 533
ReadyBoost, 533–535
routine maintenance, 530
manually removing software, 535–539
delete program files, 536–537
delete registry entries, 537–538
remove program shortcuts, 538–539
remove startup processes, 539
uninstall routine, 536
utilities and tools, 496–529
Administrative Tools, 296, 505–506
application management, 278, 497–498, 504–505
Computer Management, 371, 511, 825, 845
display settings and graphics software, 426, 429–430, 527–529
Event Viewer, 513–516
Microsoft Management Console (MMC), 511–513
Performance Monitor, 511, 520–522, 533
Print Management, 517–518
Registry Editor, 522–527
Services console, 510–511, 579, 946
shell and kernel, 496–497
System Configuration, 506–510, 579
Task Manager, 498–505
Task Scheduler, 511, 518–520, 532
Windows, security strategies, 856–870
authenticate users, 856–861
disable Guest account, 860
lock workstation, 858–860
secure sign-in, 856–858
strong passwords, 860–861
BitLocker Drive Encryption, 869–870
file and folder encryption, 861–862
firewall settings, 862–865
local security policies using group policy, 865–869
UEFI/BIOS to protect system, 870
Windows 7
Advanced Boot Options, 219–220
Aero user interface, 420, 421, 535
Backup and Restore, 456–459
clean installation, 352–354
defragmentation tool, 268
Disk Management utility, 480
editions of, 279, 326
elevated command prompt window, 470
Explorer, 287–294
familiarity with, 278
Group Policy and printers, 925
home server PC, 958
inherited permissions, 833
Last Known Good Configuration, 592, 611
mapping a network drive or printer, 843
memory needs, 167
in multiboot, 354–356
network configuration, 339–340
network connections, 309–310
network security, 307
optical drives and, 263
in-place upgrade, 348–349
processor architecture, 134
product activation, 362
recovering backup-up items, 458–459
Resource Monitor, 501
running application in Windows XP Mode, 583
setting priority for a process, 505
shutdown, 589
startup process, 595–596
startup repair, 605–606
Startup Repair utility, 270
Startup tab, 530–531
System Configuration, 509–510
system image, 464, 621
System Recovery Options, 217
system repair disc, 601
taking ownership of a folder, 841–842
Task Manager, 498, 500
upgrade paths, 338
USB devices, installing, 391
USB flash drives and, 264
vs. Windows 8, 300
Windows Defender, 364, 891
Windows Explorer, 258, 259, 264, 286, 287–294
Windows PowerShell, 479
Windows 8
clean installation, 350–352
custom refresh image, 462–465, 598
defragmentation tool, 268
desktop, 283–285
Disk Management utility, 250
dual displays, 22
editions of, 279
elevated command prompt window, 470
Fast Startup, 588–589
File Explorer, 283, 287–294
copy, move, rename, or delete files or folders, 293
creating a file, 293
creating a folder, 292
creating a shortcut, 293–294
files and directories, 288–290
file systems, 258
folder structure, 290–291
solid-state storage, 264
using, 285
file history, 455–456
home server PC, 958
memory needs, 167
modern interface, 279–280
network configuration, 339–340
network connections, 307–309
network security, 306–307
optical drives, 263
in-place upgrade, 342–346
power users of, 278
processor architecture, 134
refreshing, 618–620
resetting, 620–621
self-healing feature, 602
signing in, 281, 594
Startup Menu, 593

I

Windows 8 (*continued*)
- Startup Repair, 219, 270
- Storage Spaces utility, 250
- System Image backup, 465
- System window, 116
- Task Manager, 498–499
- tools for users and technicians, 287–304
- uninstalling applications, 371
- Upgrade Assistant, 328
- upgrade from Microsoft website, 347–348
- USB devices, installing, 391
- USB flash drives, 264
- using a Microsoft account with, 314–317
- using the interface, 281–283
- vs. Windows 7, 300
- Windows Defender, 364

Windows 8.1
- clean installation, 350–352
- editions of, 347
- free update, 279
- in multiboot, 354–356
- in-place upgrades, 342–346
- product activation, 362
- screen tips, 280
- upgrade from Microsoft website, 347–348

Windows 10, 278
Windows Assessment and Deployment Kit (ADK), 373–374, 375–376
Windows Automated Installation Kit (AIK), 373–374, 375–376
Windows Boot Loader, 590, 594
Windows Boot Manager, 592–593
Windows Compatibility Center, 328, 582
Windows data, folders for, 447
Windows Defender, 296, 303, 364, 888–889, 891, 892
Windows Display Driver Model (WDDM), 420
Windows Easy Transfer, 371
Windows Explorer, 286
- file systems, 258
- formatting with, 259
- shared printers, 927
- solid-state storage, 264
- Windows 7, 287–294

Windows features and support tools, 277–318
- interfaces, 278–287
  - Windows 7 desktop, 286–287
  - Windows 8 desktop, 283–285
  - Windows 8 modern interface, 279–280
  - Windows 8 sign in, 281–283
- network connections, 304–311
  - domain setup, 310–311
  - public and private networks, 307–308
  - Windows 7, 309–310
  - Windows 8, 307–309
  - Windows domain, 305–306
  - Windows workgroup and homegroup, 304–305
- tools for users and technicians, 287–304
  - Action Center, 302–304
  - Control Panel, 294–296
  - Folder Options, 296–297
  - Power Options, 297–298
  - System Information window, 301–302
  - System window, 299–301
- user accounts, 311–319
  - User Account Control (UAC) dialog box, 317–319
  - using a Microsoft account with Windows 8, 314–317
- Windows 8 desktop, 283–285

Windows Firewall, 296, 303, 863–865, 970
Windows Imaging File (WIM) format, 462
Windows Internet Name Service (WINS) server, 731–732
Windows kernel, 497
Windows Media Center, 955
Windows networking. *See* Network connections; TCP/IP networks
Windows.old folder, 338
Windows PE (Windows Preinstallation Environment), 374
Windows Phone, 223, 748
- apps, 758
- configuring
  - email, sync, and backup, 795–798
  - network connections, 795
- getting to know, 756–758
- malicious software, 898
- rooting, 899
- troubleshooting, 798–799
- update and restore from backup, 798
- virtual assistant, 753

Windows Phone emulator, 970
Windows pinwheel, 198
Windows PowerShell, 479
Windows Preinstallation Environment (Windows PE), 374
Windows Print Spooler service, 946
Windows Recovery Environment (Windows RE)
- command prompt window, 612–613
- commands, 470, 475, 477
- exiting, 610
- malicious software, 892
- recovery drive, 599
- registry editing, 524
- Safe Mode, 627
- self-healing feature, 602
- startup repair, 602–604
- system repair disc, 601
- Windows 7, 605–606

Windows resources on a network, 805–850
- access to files and folders
  - administrative shares, 844–846
  - hidden network resources, 844–846
  - mapping a network drive or printer, 842–844
  - permissions, 828–830
  - sharing, 830–842
  - user accounts and user groups, 825–828
- access to folders and files, controlling, 825–846
- client/server applications
  - Group Policy, 822–823
  - Internet Explorer, 807–814
  - network servers, 806–807
  - ODBC data sources, 823–825
  - Remote Assistance, 820–822
  - Remote Desktop Connection (RDC), 815–820
- cloud computing, 846–850
- network servers, 806–807
- supporting client/server applications, 806–825

Windows Server, 306
Windows shell, 496–497
Windows Startup Menu, 597, 603
Windows Store, 315
Windows Update, 303
Windows updates
- installing, 362–364
- preventive maintenance, 444, 530
- scheduled maintenance, 897
- troubleshooting applications, 573, 581
- troubleshooting hardware, 214

Windows Virtual PC, 109, 954
Windows Vista
- Aero user interface, 420, 535
- backup procedures, 465
- desktop, 286
- editions of, 326
- exFAT file system, 468
- Group Policy and printers, 925
- installation of, 348
- interfaces, 278
- network configuration, 339–340
- Reliability and Performance Monitor, 522
- Resource Monitor, 501
- Security Center, 303
- setting priority for a process, 505
- System Configuration, 510
- Task Manager, 500
- upgrade paths, 338
- upgrading, 328
- Windows Firewall, 865

Windows XP
- Power Users group, 826
- upgrade paths, 338
- on a virtual machine, 336

Windows XP Mode, 336, 583
WinPatrol by Ruiware, 532
WINS (Windows Internet Name Service) server, 731–732
Wired connections, 307–308, 697, 698
Wired Equivalent Privacy (WEP), 686
Wired printer connections, 920–921
Wireless access point (WAP), 671, 703–704, 711
Wireless adapter, 738
Wireless card, 25, 26
Wireless connections, 307–308, 384–388, 697, 738–739
Wireless keyboard, 31
Wireless LAN (WLAN), 684, 696
Wireless network points and bridges, 703–704
Wireless networks. *See* Wi-Fi (Wireless Fidelity)
Wireless printer connections, 920–921
Wireless token, 878
Wireless WAN (cellular) network, 656–658
Wireless wide area network (WWAN), 656

Wire stripper, 715
Wiring, 711–742
  setting up and troubleshooting, 711–742
  TCP/IP utilities, 727–733
  tools, 712–716
  troubleshooting network connections, 733–742
    GPS not functioning, 741
    Internet connectivity, 736–737
    no Bluetooth connectivity, 740
    no connectivity or intermittent connectivity, 734–736
    no wireless connectivity, 738–739
    TCP/IP utilities, 737–738
    Wi-Fi network not found, 739–740
  twisted-pair cable, 717–726
WLAN (wireless LAN), 684, 696
Word application, 290
Workgroup and homegroup, 304–305, 339–340, 647, 842
Workgroup sharing, 829
Work network, 307
WORM (write once and read many), 256
Worm infection, 462
Worms, 886
WPA (Wi-Fi Protected Access), 686
WPA2 (Wi-Fi Protected Access 2), 686
Wpeinit command, 614
WPS (Wi-Fi Protected Setup), 687–688
Write once and read many (WORM), 256
WWAN (wireless wide area network), 656
Wyse Zero Client, 958, 966

X

X58 chipset architecture, 88–89
X58 North Bridge, 81
x86-64 bit processors, 138
x86 processors, 137–138
XaaS (Anything as a Service or Everything as a Service), 848
XAgent malware app, 898
Xbox One, 397
Xcopy command, 475, 830
XD (eXecute Disable), 136
XD-Picture Card, 266
XenClient by Citrix, 968
XenServer by Citrix, 968
Xeon processors, 135, 138, 327, 446
Xerox Corporation, 708
XPS Document Writer, 928, 946

Y

Yosemite, 990
Youtube.com, 194

Z

Zalman, 192
Zero client, 958–959, 966
Zero-day attack, 887
Zero-fill utility, 882
Zero insertion force (ZIF) sockets, 86
Zero-touch, high-volume deployment strategy, 375
ZIF connectors, 74, 435
Zombie, 887
Zoom, 992

I